Don & Laverne
641 Remington
Fort Collins Colo
482-5439

First United Presbyterian Church
531 So College
482-6407
Fort Collins Colo

given by Mr & Mrs A.C.
Simonds on Nov. 1964

Nellie B. Simonds

The
NEW TESTAMENT
In Four Versions

The
NEW TESTAMENT
In Four Versions

KING JAMES

REVISED STANDARD

PHILLIPS MODERN ENGLISH

NEW ENGLISH BIBLE

CHRISTIANITY TODAY EDITION

First printing   1963
Second printing   1964
Third printing   1964

©

The Iversen-Ford Associates

New York, N.Y.

1963

PRINTED IN U.S.A.

LIBRARY OF CONGRESS CATALOGUE CARD NUMBER: 63-23127

CONTENTS

FOREWORD

A unique opportunity is furnished new subscribers to CHRISTIANITY TODAY by the publication of this limited edition of the New Testament in four versions. The reader has before him on facing pages parallel passages from the classic King James Version and from three modern versions or translations—the Revised Standard, Phillips Modern English, and the New English Bible.

The selection of these modern texts implies no preference on the part of CHRISTIANITY TODAY. It was made simply on the basis of current use and popularity. Evangelical scholars revising the American Standard Version had not yet completed their translation, or that effort would also have been considered.

Projected by the Staff of CHRISTIANITY TODAY as an instrument to promote the comparative reading and use of the Scriptures, this original and limited edition was produced exclusively for subscribers to the magazine. Although the project is not likely to be duplicated, the work is not intended simply as a collector's item, but for inspirational and academic use. Both as a devotional aid and as a study tool the volume provides a welcome and time-saving service.

A few years ago Thomas Nelson & Sons issued an "octapla" (as distinguished from the "tetrapla" constituted by this volume). But the texts of this publication reached *behind* the King James Version to include five earlier translations and only two subsequent versions, the American Standard and the Revised Standard, whereas this project moves *forward* from the King James Version to our own times. It should be mentioned that paragraphing of the King James Version has been added as a reader convenience; the original translation was not, of course, paragraphed in this way. The original preface or introduction to each of the included versions precedes the four texts.

CHRISTIANITY TODAY
Washington, D.C.

THE

NEW TESTAMENT

OF OUR LORD AND SAVIOUR

JESUS CHRIST

Translated out of the original Greek and with the former
translations diligently compared and revised

Set forth in 1611
And commonly known as the

KING JAMES VERSION

THE EPISTLE DEDICATORY

TO THE MOST HIGH *and* MIGHTY PRINCE JAMES *by the Grace of God*
KING OF GREAT BRITAIN, FRANCE, *and* IRELAND, DEFENDER OF THE
FAITH, &C. *The Translators of this Bible wish Grace, Mercy, and
Peace, through* JESUS CHRIST *our Lord*

Great and manifold were the blessings, most dread Sovereign, which
Almighty God, the Father of all mercies, bestowed upon us the people
of England, when first he sent Your Majesty's Royal Person to rule and
reign over us. For whereas it was the expectation of many, who
wished not well unto our Sion, that upon the setting of that bright
Occidental Star, Queen Elizabeth of most happy memory, some thick
and palpable clouds of darkness would so have overshadowed this
Land, that men should have been in doubt which way they were to
walk; and that it should hardly be known, who was to direct the unsettled State; the appearance of Your Majesty, as of the Sun in his
strength, instantly dispelled those supposed and surmised mists, and
gave unto all that were well affected exceeding cause of comfort; especially when we beheld the Government established in Your Highness,
and Your hopeful Seed, by an undoubted Title, and this also accompanied with peace and tranquillity at home and abroad.

But among all our joys, there was no one that more filled our
hearts, than the blessed continuance of the preaching of God's sacred
Word among us; which is that inestimable treasure, which excelleth
all the riches of the earth; because the fruit thereof extendeth itself,
not only to the time spent in this transitory world, but directeth and
disposeth men unto that eternal happiness which is above in heaven.

Then not to suffer this to fall to the ground, but rather to take it up,
and to continue it in that state, wherein the famous Predecessor of
Your Highness did leave it: nay, to go forward with the confidence and
resolution of a Man in maintaining the truth of Christ, and propagating
it far and near, is that which hath so bound and firmly knit the hearts
of all Your Majesty's loyal and religious people unto You, that Your
very name is precious among them: their eye doth behold You with
comfort, and they bless You in their hearts, as that sanctified Person,
who, under God, is the immediate Author of their true happiness.
And this their contentment doth not diminish or decay, but every day
increaseth and taketh strength, when they observe, that the zeal of
Your Majesty toward the house of God doth not slack or go backward, but is more and more kindled, manifesting itself abroad in the

farthest parts of Christendom, by writing in defence of the Truth, (which hath given such a blow unto that man of sin, as will not be healed,) and every day at home, by religious and learned discourse, by frequenting the house of God, by hearing the Word preached, by cherishing the Teachers thereof, by caring for the Church, as a most tender and loving nursing Father.

There are infinite arguments of this right Christian and religious affection in Your Majesty; but none is more forcible to declare it to others than the vehement and perpetuated desire of accomplishing and publishing of this work, which now with all humility we present unto Your Majesty. For when Your Highness had once out of deep judgment apprehended how convenient it was, that out of the Original Sacred Tongues, together with comparing of the labours, both in our own, and other foreign Languages, of many worthy men who went before us, there should be one more exact Translation of the Holy Scriptures into the English Tongue; Your Majesty did never desist to urge and to excite those to whom it was commended, that the work might be hastened, and that the business might be expedited in so decent a manner, as a matter of such importance might justly require.

And now at last, by the mercy of God, and the continuance of our labours, it being brought unto such a conclusion, as that we have great hopes that the Church of England shall reap good fruit thereby; we hold it our duty to offer it to Your Majesty, not only as to our King and Sovereign, but as to the principal Mover and Author of the work: humbly craving of Your most Sacred Majesty, that since things of this quality have ever been subject to the censures of illmeaning and discontented persons, it may receive approbation and patronage from so learned and judicious a Prince as Your Highness is, whose allowance and acceptance of our labours shall more honour and encourage us, than all the calumniations and hard interpretations of other men shall dismay us. So that if, on the one side, we shall be traduced by Popish Persons at home or abroad, who therefore will malign us, because we are poor instruments to make God's holy Truth to be yet more and more known unto the people, whom they desire still to keep in ignorance and darkness; or if, on the other side, we shall be maligned by selfconceited Brethren, who run their own ways, and give liking unto nothing, but what is framed by themselves, and hammered on their anvil; we may rest secure, supported within by the truth and innocency of a good conscience, having walked the ways of simplicity and integrity, as before the Lord; and sustained without by the powerful protection of Your Majesty's grace and favour, which will ever give countenance to honest and Christian endeavours against bitter censures and uncharitable imputations.

The Lord of heaven and earth bless Your Majesty with many and happy days, that, as his heavenly hand hath enriched Your Highness with many singular and extraordinary graces, so You may be the wonder of the world in this latter age for happiness and true felicity, to the honour of that great GOD, and the good of his Church, through Jesus Christ our Lord and only Saviour.

THE NEW COVENANT

COMMONLY CALLED

THE

NEW TESTAMENT

OF OUR LORD AND SAVIOR JESUS CHRIST

REVISED STANDARD VERSION

TRANSLATED FROM THE GREEK
BEING THE VERSION SET FORTH A.D. 1611
REVISED A.D. 1881 AND A.D. 1901
COMPARED WITH THE MOST ANCIENT AUTHORITIES
AND REVISED A.D. 1946

New Testament Section, Copyright 1946
By
Division of Christian Education of the National Council
of Churches of Christ in the United States of America

THOMAS NELSON & SONS
Licensee

TORONTO   NEW YORK   EDINBURGH

The text for the Revised Standard Version of the Bible
in this publication is used by permission of the Division
of Christian Education, National Council of Churches.

PREFACE

The Revised Standard Version of the New Testament is an authorized revision of the American Standard Version, published in 1901, which was a revision of the King James Version, published in 1611.

The King James Version was itself a revision rather than a new translation. The first English version of the New Testament made by translation from the Greek was that of William Tyndale, 1525; and this became the foundation for successive versions, notably those of Coverdale, 1535; the Great Bible, 1539; Geneva, 1560; and the Bishops' Bible, 1568. In 1582 a translation of the New Testament, made from the Latin Vulgate by Roman Catholic scholars, was published at Rheims. The translators of the King James Version took into account all of these preceding versions; and comparison shows that it owes something to each of them. It kept felicitous turns of phrase and apt expressions, from whatever source, which had stood the test of public usage.

As a result of the discovery of manuscripts of the New Testament more ancient than those used by translators in 1611, together with a marked development in Biblical studies, a demand for the revision of the King James Version arose in the middle of the nineteenth century. The task was undertaken, by authority of the Church of England, in 1870. The English Revised Version was published in 1881-1885; and the American Standard Version, its variant embodying the preferences of the American scholars associated in the work, was published in 1901.

Because of unhappy experience with unauthorized publications in the two decades between 1881 and 1901, which tampered with the text of the English Revised Version in the supposed interest of the American public, the American Standard Version was copyrighted, to protect the text from unauthorized changes. In 1928 this copyright was acquired by the International Council of Religious Education, and thus passed into the ownership of the churches of the United States and Canada which were associated in this Council through their boards of education and publication.

The Council appointed a Committee of scholars to have charge of the text of the American Standard Version; and in 1937 it authorized this Committee to undertake a further revision, on the ground that there is need for a version which will "embody the best results of modern scholarship as to the meaning of the Scriptures, and express this meaning in English diction which is designed for use in public and private worship and preserves those qualities which have given to the King James Version a supreme place in English literature."

Thirty-two scholars have served as members of the Committee charged with making the revision; and they have secured the review and counsel of an Advisory Board of fifty representatives of the co-operating denominations. The Committee has worked in two sections, one dealing with the Old Testament and one with the New Testament. Each section has submitted its work to the scrutiny of the members of the other section, however; and the charter of the Committee requires that all changes be agreed upon by a two-thirds vote of the total membership of the Committee. The publication of the Revised Standard Version of the Bible, containing the Old and New Testaments, was authorized by vote of the National Council of the Churches of Christ in the U.S.A. in 1951.

The King James Version of the New Testament was based upon a Greek text that was marred by mistakes, containing the accumulated errors of fourteen centuries of manuscript copying. It was essentially the Greek text of the New Testament as edited by Beza, 1589, who closely followed that published by Erasmus, 1516-1535, which was based upon a few medieval manuscripts. The earliest and best of the eight manuscripts which Erasmus consulted was from the tenth century, and he made the least use of it because it differed most from the commonly received text; Beza had access to two manuscripts of great value, dating from the fifth and sixth centuries, but he made very little use of them because they differed from the text published by Erasmus.

We now possess many more ancient manuscripts of the New Testament, and are far better equipped to seek to recover the original wording of the Greek text. The evidence for the text of the books of the New Testament is better than for any other ancient book, both in the number of extant manuscripts and in the nearness of the date of some of these manuscripts to the date when the book was originally written.

The revisers in the 1870's had most of the evidence that we now have for the Greek text, though the most ancient of all extant manuscripts of the Greek New Testament were not discovered until 1931. But they lacked the resources which discoveries within the past eighty years have afforded for understanding the vocabulary, grammar, and idioms of the Greek New Testament. An amazing body of Greek papyri has been unearthed in Egypt since the 1870's—private letters, official reports, wills, business accounts, petitions, and other such trivial, everyday recordings of the ongoing activities of human beings. In 1895 appeared the first of Adolf Deissmann's studies of these ordinary materials. He proved that many words which had hitherto been assumed to belong to what was called "Biblical Greek" were current in the spoken vernacular of the first century A.D. The New Testament was written in the Koiné, the common Greek which was spoken and understood practically everywhere throughout the Roman Empire in the early centuries of the Christian era. This development in the study of New Testament Greek has come since the work on the English Revised Version and the American Standard Version was done, and at many points sheds new light upon the meaning of the Greek text.

Another reason for revision of the King James Version is afforded by changes in English usage. The problem is presented, not so much by its archaic forms or obsolete words, as by the English words which are still in constant use but now convey different meanings from those which they had in 1611 and in the King James Version. These words were once accurate translations of the Hebrew and Greek Scriptures; but now, having changed in meaning, they have become misleading. They no longer say what the King James translators meant them to say.

The King James Version uses the word "let" in the sense of "hinder," "prevent" to mean "precede," "allow" in the sense of "approve," "communicate" for "share," "conversation" for "conduct," "comprehend" for "overcome," "ghost" for "spirit," "wealth" for "well-being," "allege" for "prove," "demand" for "ask," "take no thought" for "be not anxious," "purchase a good degree" for "gain a good standing," etc. The Greek word for "immediately" is translated in the King James Version not only by "immediately" and "straightway" but also by the terms "anon," "by and by," and "presently." There are more than three hundred such English words which are used in the King James Version in a sense substantially different from that which they now convey. It not only does the King James translators no honor, but is quite unfair to them and to the truth which they understood and expressed, to retain these words which now convey meanings they did not intend.

This preface does not undertake to set forth the lines along which the revision has proceeded. That is done in a small book entitled *An Introduction to the Revised Standard Version of the New Testament,* written by members of the New Testament Section and designed to help the general public to understand the main principles which have guided this comprehensive revision of the King James and American Standard Versions.

These principles were reaffirmed by the Committee in 1959, in connection with a study of criticisms and suggestions from various readers. As a result, a few changes have been authorized for the present and subsequent editions. Most of these are corrections of punctuation, capitalization, or footnotes. Some changes of words or phrases are made in the interest of consistency, clarity or accuracy of translation. Examples of such changes are "bread," Matthew 7.9, 1 Corinthians 10.17; "is he," Matthew 21.9 and parallels; "the Son," Matthew 27.54, Mark 15.39; "ask nothing of me," John 16.23; "for this life only," 1 Corinthians 15.19; "the husband of one wife," 1 Timothy 3.2,12; 5.9; Titus 1.6.

The Bible is more than a historical document to be preserved. And it is more than a classic of English literature to be cherished and admired. It is a record of God's dealing with men, of God's revelation of Himself and His will. It records the life and work of Him in whom the Word of God became flesh and dwelt among men. The Bible carries its full message, not to those who regard it simply as a heritage of the past or who praise its literary style, but to those who read it that they may discern and understand God's Word to men. That Word must not be disguised in phrases that are no longer clear or hidden under words that have changed or lost their meaning. It must stand forth in language that is direct and plain and meaningful to people today. It is our hope and our earnest prayer that the Revised Standard Version of the Bible may be used by God to speak to men in these momentous times, and to help them to understand and believe and obey His Word.

THE

NEW TESTAMENT

in Modern English

TRANSLATED BY J. B. PHILLIPS

I DEDICATE THIS TRANSLATION TO VERA,

MY WIFE AND FINEST CRITIC

© J. B. Phillips 1958
The Gospels © The Macmillan Company 1952, 1957
The Young Church in Action
© The Macmillan Company 1955
Letters to Young Churches
© The Macmillan Company 1947, 1957
The Book of Revelation
© The Macmillan Company 1957

Printed in the United States of America
Library of Congress catalog card number: 58-10922

TRANSLATOR'S FOREWORD

The essential principles of translation

There seem to be three necessary tests which any work of transference from one language to another must pass before it can be classed as good translation. The first is simply that it must not sound like a translation at all. If it is skillfully done, and we are not previously informed, we should be quite unaware that it *is* a translation, even though the work we are reading is far distant from us in both time and place. That is a first, and indeed fundamental test, but it is not by itself sufficient. For the translator himself may be a skillful writer, and although he may have conveyed the essential meaning, characterization and plot of the original author, he may have so strong a style of his own that he completely changes that of the original author. The example of this kind of translation which springs most readily to my mind is Fitz-Gerald's *Rubáiyát of Omar Khayyám.* I would therefore make this the second test: that a translator does his work with the least possible obtrusion of his own personality. The third and final test which a good translator should be able to pass is that of being able to produce in the hearts and minds of his readers an effect equivalent to that produced by the author upon his original readers. Of course no translator living would claim that his work successfully achieved these three ideals. But he must bear them in mind constantly as principles for his guidance.

Translation as interpretation

This seems to me to be the right place to set down a justification for my own methods. As I have frequently said, a translator is not a commentator. He is usually well aware of the different connotations which a certain passage may bear, but unless his work is to be cluttered with footnotes he is bound, after careful consideration, to set down what is the most likely meaning. Occasionally one is driven into what appears to be a paraphrase, simply because a literal translation of the original Greek would prove unintelligible. But where this has proved necessary I have always been careful to avoid giving any slant or flavor which is purely of my own making. That is why I have been rather reluctant to accept the suggestion that my translation is "interpretation"! If the word interpretation is used in a bad sense, that is, if it is meant that a work is tendentious, or that there has been a manipulation of the words of New Testament Scripture to fit some private point of view, then I would still strongly repudiate the charge!

But "interpretation" can also mean transmitting meaning from one language to another, and skilled interpreters in world affairs do not intentionally inject any meaning of their own. In this sense I gladly accept the word interpretation to describe my work. For, as I see it, the translator's function is to understand as fully and deeply as possible what the New Testament writers had to say and then, after a process of what might be called reflective digestion, to write it down in the language of the people today. And here I must say that it is essential for the interpreter to know the language of both parties. He may be a first-class scholar in New Testament Greek and know the significance of every traditional crux, and yet be abysmally ignorant of how his contemporaries outside his scholastic world are thinking and feeling.

Words and their context

After reading a large number of commentaries I have a feeling that some scholars, at least, have lived so close to the Greek Text that they have forgotten their sense of proportion. I doubt very much whether the New Testament writers were as subtle or as self-conscious as some commentators would make them appear. For the most part I am convinced that they had no idea that they were writing Holy Scripture. They would be, or indeed perhaps are, amazed to learn what meanings are sometimes read back into their simple utterances! Paul, for instance, writing in haste and urgency to some of his wayward and difficult Christians, was not tremendously concerned about dotting the i's and crossing the t's of his message. I doubt very much whether he was even concerned about being completely consistent with what he had already written. Consequently, it seems to me quite beside the point to study his writings microscopically, as it were, and deduce hidden meanings of which almost certainly he was unaware. His letters are alive, and they are moving—in both senses of that word—and their meaning can no more be appreciated by cold minute examination than can the beauty of a bird's flight be appreciated by dissection after its death. We have to take these living New Testament documents in their context, a context of supreme urgency and often of acute danger. But a word is modified very considerably by the context in which it appears, and where a translator fails to realize this, we are not far away from the result of an electronic word transmuter! The translators of the Authorized Version were certainly not unaware of this modification, even though they had an extreme reverence for the actual words of Holy Writ. Three hundred years ago they did not hesitate to translate the Greek word *ekballo* by such varying expressions as *put out, drive out, bring forth, send out, tear out, take out, leave out, cast out,* and the like, basing their decision on the context. And as a striking example of their translational freedom, in Matthew 27:44 we read that the thieves who were crucified with Jesus "cast the same in his teeth," where the Greek words mean simply, "abused him."

The translator must be flexible

I feel strongly that a translator, although he must make himself as familiar as possible with New Testament Greek usage, must steadfastly refuse to be driven by the bogey of consistency. He must be guided both by the context in which a word appears, and by the sensibilities of modern English readers. In the story of the raising of Lazarus, for example, Martha's objection to opening the grave would be natural enough to an Eastern mind. But to put into her lips the words, "by this time he's stinking," would sound to Western ears unpleasantly out of key with the rest of that moving story. Similarly, we know that the early Christians greeted one another with "an holy kiss." Yet to introduce such an expression into a modern English translation immediately reveals the gulf between the early Christians and ourselves, the very thing which I as a translator am trying to bridge. Again, it is perfectly true, if we are to translate literally, that Jesus said, "Blessed are the beggars in spirit." In an Eastern land, where the disparity between rich and poor was very great, beggars were common. But it is to my mind extremely doubtful whether the word "beggar" in our Welfare State, or indeed in most English-speaking countries, conjures up the mental image which Jesus intended to convey to his hearers. It was not the social misfit or the work-shy, spiritually speaking, but the one who was obviously and consciously in need whom Jesus described as "blessed" or "happy."

The use of insight and sympathy

Perhaps a few words about the kind of technique which I have adopted may be introduced here. I have found imaginative sympathy, not so much with words as with people, to be essential. If it is not presumptuous to say so, I attempted, as far as I could, to think myself into the heart and mind of Paul, for example, or of Mark or of John the Divine. Then I tried further to imagine myself as each of the New Testament authors writing his particular message for the people of to-day. No one could succeed in doing this superlatively well, if only because of the scantiness of our knowledge of the first century A.D. But this has been my ideal, and that is why consistency and meticulous accuracy have sometimes both been sacrificed in the attempt to transmit freshness and life across the centuries. The cross-headings which appear throughout the book are meant to make it both more readable and more intelligible; at the same time they are intended to be quite unobtrusive and can easily be ignored. But, by the use of these headings, solid and rather forbidding slabs of continuous writing (such as appear in the Greek Text) are made more assimilable to the modern reader, whose reading habits have already been "conditioned" by the comparatively recent usage of clear punctuation, intelligent paragraphing and good printer's type.

Acknowledgments

Although I have worked directly in this translation from the best available Greek Text, it would be ungracious to forget the very many people who have made the work possible. I think first of the textual critics, whose patient work gives us a text to work from which is as near as possible to that of the original writers. I am most grateful to them, as all translators must be, and I should also like to express my thanks to the numerous commentators whose works I have consulted again and again. As will be gathered from what I have said above, I have not always agreed with them, but they have informed my mind and stimulated my thoughts many times. The painstaking work of commentators, to put it at its lowest, saves the translator from being over-facile or slipshod! Again, although it would be impossible to supply a full list, I am extremely grateful to the many people—including first-rate scholars, hard-working parish priests, busy ministers, doctors, scientists, missionaries, educationists, elderly saints and lively young people—who have, over the years, written me hundreds of letters, the great majority of which were constructive and useful. Their help has been invaluable.

It has been my practice not to consult other modern translations until my own version has been finished. I do not therefore owe anything directly to any contemporary translator, much as I admire the work of Dr. J. W. C. Wand and Dr. E. V. Rieu of this country, and Dr. Edgar J. Goodspeed of the United States of America. But none of us who translates today can be unaware of the trail that was blazed for us near the beginning of this century by such pioneers as Dr. R. F. Weymouth and Dr. James Moffatt. We cannot but admit that we are in a much more favorable position because such men had the courage to break a centuries-old tradition, and translate into contemporary English.

I am particularly grateful to Dr. C. S. Lewis, to whom I sent a copy of my version of Paul's letter to Colossae when I first began the work of translating. He wrote back giving me great encouragement. And later, after many disappointments, when I eventually found a publisher in Mr. Geoffrey Bles, Dr. Lewis not only supplied the admirable title *Letters to Young Churches* but wrote an Introduction which played no small part in launching that book.

I find myself therefore indebted to all kinds of people of different nationalities and different denominations. Not the least of my gratitude is evoked by the assurance that has grown within me that here in the New Testament, at the very heart and core of our Faith, Christians are far more at one than their outward divisions would imply. From this unquestionable evidence of fundamental unity I derive not only great comfort but a great hope for the future.

Swanage, Dorset,   J. B. PHILLIPS
    1958

THE
NEW ENGLISH BIBLE
NEW TESTAMENT

A NEW ENGLISH TRANSLATION

Planned and Directed by Representatives of

THE BAPTIST UNION OF GREAT BRITAIN AND IRELAND

THE CHURCH OF ENGLAND

THE CHURCH OF SCOTLAND

THE CONGREGATIONAL UNION OF ENGLAND AND WALES

THE COUNCIL OF CHURCHES FOR WALES

THE LONDON YEARLY MEETING OF THE SOCIETY OF FRIENDS

THE METHODIST CHURCH OF GREAT BRITAIN

THE PRESBYTERIAN CHURCH OF ENGLAND

THE UNITED COUNCIL OF CHRISTIAN CHURCHES AND
RELIGIOUS COMMUNIONS IN IRELAND

THE BRITISH AND FOREIGN BIBLE SOCIETY

THE NATIONAL BIBLE SOCIETY OF SCOTLAND

©

THE DELEGATES OF THE OXFORD UNIVERSITY PRESS
AND
THE SYNDICS OF THE CAMBRIDGE UNIVERSITY PRESS
1961

OXFORD UNIVERSITY PRESS
CAMBRIDGE UNIVERSITY PRESS
1961

PREFACE

In May 1946 the General Assembly of the Church of Scotland received an overture from the Presbytery of Stirling and Dunblane recommending that a translation of the Bible be made in the language of the present day. As a result of this, delegates of the Church of England, the Church of Scotland, and the Methodist, Baptist, and Congregationalist Churches met in conference in October. They recommended that the work should be undertaken, and that a completely new translation should be made, rather than a revision, once previously contemplated, of any earlier version. In January 1947 a second conference, held like the first in the Central Hall, Westminster, included representatives of the University Presses of Oxford and Cambridge. At the request of this conference, the Churches named above appointed representatives to form the Joint Committee on the New Translation of the Bible. This Committee met for the first time in July of the same year. By January 1948, when its third meeting was held, invitations to be represented had been sent to the Presbyterian Church of England, the Society of Friends, the Churches in Wales, the Churches in Ireland, the British and Foreign Bible Society, and the National Bible Society of Scotland: these invitations were accepted.

The Bishop of Truro (Dr J. W. Hunkin) acted as Chairman from the beginning. He gave most valuable service until his death in 1950, when the Bishop of Durham (Dr A. T. P. Williams, later Bishop of Winchester) was elected to succeed him. The Reverend Dr G. S. Hendry and the Reverend Professor J. K. S. Reid, both of the Church of Scotland, have successively held the office of Secretary, to the Committee's great advantage.

The actual work of translation was entrusted by the Committee to four panels dealing respectively with the Old Testament, the Apocrypha, the New Testament, and the literary revision of the whole. Denominational considerations played no part in the appointment to membership of these panels.

Since January 1948 the Joint Committee has met regularly twice a year in the Jerusalem Chamber, Westminster Abbey, with four exceptions during 1954-1955 when the Langham Room in the precincts of the Abbey was kindly made available. At these meetings the Committee has received reports on the progress of the work from the Conveners of the four panels, and its members have had in their hands typescripts of the books so far translated and revised. They have made such comments and given such advice or decisions as they judged to be necessary, and from time to time they have met members of the panels in conference. The Committee has warmly appreciated the courteous hospitality of the Dean of Westminster and of the Trustees of the Central Hall.

Work upon the Old Testament and the Apocrypha is actively going forward. Much has been done: much remains to do. At a later time, when the whole translation has been completed, further and more particular acknowledgements will doubtless be made. But this brief preface to the translation of the New Testament must not end without an expression of the Joint Committee's thanks to all those who have given their time and knowledge to a task both long and difficult. We owe a great debt to the support and the experienced counsel of the University Presses of Oxford and Cambridge, and we acknowledge our obligation, an obligation impossible to exaggerate, to the Reverend Dr C. H. Dodd who, as Director of our enterprise, has devoted to it in full measure his scholarship, his patience, and his wisdom.

ALWYN WINTON:
Chairman of the Joint Committee

INTRODUCTION

This translation of the New Testament (to be followed in due course by the Old Testament and by the Apocrypha) was undertaken with the object of providing English readers, whether familiar with the Bible or not, with a faithful rendering of the best available Greek text into the current speech of our own time, and a rendering which should harvest the gains of recent biblical scholarship.

It is just three hundred and fifty years since King James's men put out what we have come to know as the Authorized Version. Two hundred and seventy years later the New Testament was revised. The Revised Version, which appeared in 1881, marked a new departure especially in that it abandoned the so-called Received Text, which had reigned ever since printed editions of the New Testament began, but which the advance of textual criticism had antiquated. The Revisers no longer followed (like their predecessors) the text of the majority of manuscripts, which, being for the most part of late date, had been exposed not only to the accidental corruptions of long-continued copying, but also in part to deliberate correction and 'improvement'. Instead, they followed a very small group of manuscripts, the earliest, and in their judgement the best, of those which had survived. During the eighty years which have passed since their time, textual criticism has not stood still. Manuscripts have been discovered of substantially earlier date than any which the Revisers knew. Other important sources of evidence have been either freshly discovered or made more fully available. Meanwhile the methods of textual criticism have themselves been refined and estimates of the value of manuscripts have sometimes been reconsidered. The problem of restoring a form of text as near as possible to the vanished autographs now appears less simple than it did to our predecessors. There is not at the present time any critical text which would command the same degree of general acceptance as the Revisers' text did in its day. Nor has the time come, in the judgement of competent scholars, to construct such a text, since new material constantly comes to light, and the debate continues. The present translators therefore could do no other than consider variant readings on their merits, and, having weighed the evidence for themselves, select for translation in each passage the reading which to the best of their judgement seemed most likely to represent what the author wrote. Where other readings seemed to deserve serious consideration they have been recorded in footnotes. In assessing the evidence, the translators have taken into account (a) ancient manuscripts of the New Testament in Greek, (b) manuscripts of early translations into other languages, and (c) quotations from the New Testament by early Christian writers. These three sources of evidence are collectively referred to as 'witnesses'. A large number of variants, however, are such as could make no appreciable difference to the meaning so far as it could be represented in translation, and these have been passed over in silence. The translators are well aware that their judgement is at best provisional, but they believe the text they have followed to be an improvement on that underlying the earlier translations.

So much for the text. The next step was the effort to understand the original as accurately as possible, as a preliminary to turning it into English. The Revisers of 1881 believed that a better knowledge of the Greek language made it possible to correct a number of mistranslations in the older version, though in doing so they were somewhat limited by the instruction 'to introduce as few alterations as possible . . . consistently with faithfulness'. During the past eighty years the study of the Greek language has no more stood still than has textual criticism. In particular, our knowledge of the kind of Greek used by most of the New Testament writers has been greatly enriched since 1881 by the discovery of many thousands of papyrus documents in popular or non-literary Greek of about the same period as the New Testament. It would be wrong to suggest that they lead to any far-reaching change in our understanding of the Greek of the New Testament period, but they have often made possible a better appreciation of the finer shades of idiom, which sometimes clarifies the meaning of passages in the New Testament. Its language is indeed in many respects more flexible and easy-going than the Revisers were ready to allow, and invites the translator to use a larger freedom.

Our task, however, differed in an important respect from that of the Revisers of 1881. They were instructed not only to introduce as few alterations as possible, but also 'to limit, as far as possible, the expression of such alterations to the language of the Authorized and earlier English Versions'. Today that language is even more definitely archaic, and less generally understood, than it was eighty years ago, for the rate of change in English usage has accelerated. The present translators were subject to no such limitation. The Joint Committee which promoted and controlled the enterprise decided at the outset that what was now needed was not another revision of the Authorized Version but a genuinely new translation, in which an attempt should be made consistently to use the idiom of contemporary English to convey the meaning of the Greek. The older translators, on the whole, considered that fidelity to the original demanded that they should reproduce, as far as possible, characteristic features of the language in which it was written, such as the syntactical order of words, the structure and division of sentences, and even such irregularities of grammar as were indeed natural enough to authors writing in the easy idiom of popular Hellenistic Greek, but less natural when turned into English. The present translators were enjoined to replace Greek constructions and idioms by those of contemporary English.

This meant a different theory and practice of translation, and one which laid a heavier burden on the translators. Fidelity in translation was not to mean keeping the general framework of the original intact while replacing Greek words by English words more or less equivalent. A word, indeed, in one language is seldom the exact equivalent of a word in a different language. Each word is the centre of a whole cluster of meanings and associations, and in different languages these clusters overlap but do not often coincide. The place of a word in the clause or sentence, or even in a larger unit of thought, will determine what aspect of its total meaning is in the foreground. The translator can hardly hope to convey in another language every shade of meaning that attaches to the word in the original, but if he is free to exploit a wide range of English words covering a similar area of meaning and association he may hope to carry over the meaning of the sentence as a whole. Thus we have not felt obliged (as did the Revisers of 1881) to make an effort to render the same Greek word everywhere by the same English word. We have in this respect returned to the wholesome practice of King James's men, who (as they expressly state in their preface) recognized no such obligation. We have conceived our task to be that of understanding the original as precisely as we could (using all available aids), and then saying again in our own native idiom what we believed the author to be saying in his. We have found that in practice this frequently compelled us to make decisions where the older method of translation allowed a comfortable ambiguity. In such places we have been aware that we take a risk, but we have thought it our duty to take the risk rather than remain on the fence. But in no passage of doubtful meaning does the rendering adopted represent merely the preference of any single person.

The Joint Committee appointed a panel of scholars, drawn from various British universities, whom they believed to be representative of competent biblical scholarship in this country at the present time. The procedure was for one member of the panel to be invited to submit a draft translation of a particular book or group of books. This draft was circulated in typescript to members of the panel for their consideration. They then met together and discussed the draft round a table, verse by verse, sentence by sentence. Each member brought his view about the meaning of the original to the judgement of his fellows, and discussion was continued until they reached a common mind. There are passages where no one, in the present state of our knowledge, could say with absolute certainty which of two (or even more) meanings is intended. In such cases, after careful discussion, alternative meanings have been recorded in footnotes, but only where the difference was deemed of sufficient importance. There is probably no member of the panel who has not found himself compelled to give up, perhaps with lingering regret, a cherished view about the meaning of this or that difficult or doubtful passage. But each learned much from the others, and from the discipline of working towards a common mind. In the end we accept collective responsibility for the interpretation set forth in the text of our translation.

It should be said that our intention has been to offer a translation in the strict sense, and not a paraphrase, and we have not wished to encroach on the field of the commentator. But if the best commentary is a good translation, it is also true that every intelligent translation is in a sense a paraphrase. But if paraphrase means taking the liberty of introducing into a passage something which is not there, to elucidate the meaning which is there, it can be said that we have taken this liberty only with extreme caution, and in a very few passages, where without it we could see no way to attain our aim of making the meaning as clear as it could be made. Taken as a whole, our version claims to be a translation, free, it may be, rather than literal, but a faithful translation nevertheless, so far as we could compass it.

In doing our work, we have constantly striven to follow our instructions and render the Greek, as we understood it, into the English of the present day, that is, into the natural vocabulary, constructions, and rhythms of contemporary speech. We have sought to avoid archaism, jargon, and all that is either stilted or slipshod. Since sound scholarship does not always carry with it a delicate sense of style, the Committee appointed a panel of literary advisers, to whom all the work of the translating panel has been submitted. They scrutinized it, once again, verse by verse and sentence by sentence, and took pains to secure the tone and level of language appropriate to the different kinds of writing to be found in the New Testament, whether narrative, familiar discourse, argument, rhetoric, or poetry. But always the overriding aims were accuracy and clarity. The final form of the version was reached by agreement between the two panels.

The translators are as conscious as anyone can be of the limitations and imperfections of their work. No one who has not tried it can know how impossible an art translation is. Only those who have meditated long upon the Greek original are aware of the richness and subtlety of meaning that may lie even within the most apparently simple sentence, or know the despair that attends all efforts to bring it out through the medium of a different language. Yet we may hope that we have been able to convey to our readers something at least of what the New Testament has said to us during these years of work, and trust that under the providence of Almighty God this translation may open the truth of the scriptures to many who have been hindered in their approach to it by barriers of language.

MARGINAL NUMBERS

The conventional verse divisions in the New Testament date only from 1551 and have no basis in the manuscripts. Any system of division into numbered verses is foreign to the spirit of this translation, which is intended to convey the meaning in continuous natural English rather than to correspond sentence by sentence with the Greek.

The
NEW TESTAMENT
In Four Versions

THE GOSPEL

ACCORDING TO

SAINT MATTHEW

1 The book of the generation of Jesus Christ, the son of David, the son of Abraham. 2Abraham begat Isaac; and Isaac begat Jacob; and Jacob begat Judas and his brethren; 3And Judas begat Phares and Zara of Thamar; and Phares begat Esrom; and Esrom begat Aram; 4And Aram begat Aminadab; and Aminadab begat Naasson; and Naasson begat Salmon; 5And Salmon begat Booz of Rachab; and Booz begat Obed of Ruth; and Obed begat Jesse; 6And Jesse begat David the king; and David the king begat Solomon of her *that had been the wife* of Urias; 7And Solomon begat Roboam; and Roboam begat Abia; and Abia begat Asa; 8And Asa begat Josaphat; and Josaphat begat Joram; and Joram begat Ozias; 9And Ozias begat Joatham; and Joatham begat Achaz; and Achaz begat Ezekias; 10And Ezekias begat Manasses; and Manasses begat Amon; and Amon begat Josias; 11And Josias begat Jechonias and his brethren, about the time they were carried away to Babylon: 12And after they were brought to Babylon, Jechonias begat Salathiel; and Salathiel begat Zorobabel; 13And Zorobabel begat Abiud; and Abiud begat Eliakim; and Eliakim begat Azor; 14And Azor begat Sadoc; and Sadoc begat Achim; and Achim begat Eliud; 15And Eliud begat Eleazar; and Eleazar begat Matthan; and Matthan begat Jacob; 16And Jacob begat Joseph the husband of Mary, of whom was born Jesus, who is called Christ. 17 So all the generations from Abraham to David *are* fourteen generations; and from David until the carrying away into Babylon *are* fourteen generations; and from the carrying away into Babylon unto Christ *are* fourteen generations.

18 Now the birth of Jesus Christ was on this wise: When as his mother Mary was espoused to Joseph, before they came together, she was found with child of the Holy Ghost. 19 Then Joseph her husband, being a just *man*, and not willing to make her a public example, was minded to put her away privily. 20 But while he thought on these things, behold, the angel of the Lord appeared unto him in a dream, saying, Joseph, thou son of David, fear not to take unto thee Mary thy wife: for that which is conceived in her is of the Holy Ghost. 21And she shall bring forth a son, and thou shalt call his name JESUS: for he shall save his people from their

THE GOSPEL

ACCORDING TO

MATTHEW

1 The book of the genealogy of Jesus Christ, the son of David, the son of Abraham.

2 Abraham was the father of Isaac, and Isaac the father of Jacob, and Jacob the father of Judah and his brothers, 3 and Judah the father of Perez and Zerah by Tamar, and Perez the father of Hezron, and Hezron the father of Ram,*a* 4 and Ram*a* the father of Amminadab, and Amminadab the father of Nahshon, and Nahshon the father of Salmon, 5 and Salmon the father of Boaz by Rahab, and Boaz the father of Obed by Ruth, and Obed the father of Jesse, 6 and Jesse the father of David the king.

And David was the father of Solomon by the wife of Uriah, 7 and Solomon the father of Rehoboam, and Rehoboam the father of Abijah, and Abijah the father of Asa,*b* 8 and Asa*b* the father of Jehoshaphat, and Jehoshaphat the father of Joram, and Joram the father of Uzziah, 9 and Uzziah the father of Jotham, and Jotham the father of Ahaz, and Ahaz the father of Hezekiah, 10 and Hezekiah the father of Manasseh, and Manasseh the father of Amos,*c* and Amos*c* the father of Josiah, 11 and Josiah the father of Jechoniah and his brothers, at the time of the deportation to Babylon.

12 And after the deportation to Babylon: Jechoniah was the father of Shealtiel,*d* and Shealtiel*d* the father of Zerubbabel, 13 and Zerubbabel the father of Abiud, and Abiud the father of Eliakim, and Eliakim the father of Azor, 14 and Azor the father of Zadok, and Zadok the father of Achim, and Achim the father of Eliud, 15 and Eliud the father of Eleazar, and Eleazar the father of Matthan, and Matthan the father of Jacob, 16 and Jacob the father of Joseph the husband of Mary, of whom Jesus was born, who is called Christ.

17 So all the generations from Abraham to David were fourteen generations, and from David to the deportation to Babylon fourteen generations, and from the deportation to Babylon to the Christ fourteen generations.

18 Now the birth of Jesus Christ*f* took place in this way. When his mother Mary had been betrothed to Joseph, before they came together she was found to be with child of the Holy Spirit; 19 and her husband Joseph, being a just man and unwilling to put her to shame, resolved to divorce her quietly. 20 But as he considered this, behold, an angel of the Lord appeared to him in a dream, saying, "Joseph, son of David, do not fear to take Mary your wife, for that which is conceived in her is of the Holy Spirit; 21 she will bear a son, and you shall call his name Jesus, for he will save his people from their

[a] Greek *Aram.* [b] Greek *Asaph.* [c] Other authorities read Amon. [d] Greek *Salathiel.* [f] Other ancient authorities read *of the Christ.*

THE
GOSPEL OF
MATTHEW

The ancestry of Jesus Christ   *1. 1*

This is the record of the ancestry of Jesus Christ who was the descendant of both David and Abraham:

Abraham was the father of Isaac, who was the father of Jacob, who was the father of Judah and his brothers, who was the father of Perez and Zerah (whose mother was Tamar). Perez was the father of Hezron, who was the father of Ram, who was the father of Amminadab, who was the father of Nahshon, who was the father of Salmon, who was the father of Boaz (whose mother was Rahab). Boaz was the father of Obed (whose mother was Ruth), and Obed was the father of Jesse, who was the father of King David, who was the father of Solomon (whose mother was Uriah's wife). Solomon was the father of Rehoboam, who was the father of Abijah, who was the father of Asa, who was the father of Jehoshaphat, who was the father of Joram, who was the father of Uzziah, who was the father of Jotham, who was the father of Ahaz, who was the father of Hezekiah, who was the father of Manasseh, who was the father of Amon, who was the father of Josiah, who was the father of Jechoniah and his brothers, at the time of the deportation to Babylon.

After the Babylonian exile Jechoniah was the father of Shealtiel, who was the father of Zerubbabel, who was the father of Abiud, who was the father of Eliakim, who was the father of Azor, who was the father of Sadoc, who was the father of Achim, who was the father of Eliud, who was the father of Eleazar, who was the father of Matthan, who was the father of Jacob, who was the father of Joseph who was the husband of Mary, the mother of Jesus Christ.

The genealogy of Jesus Christ may thus be traced for fourteen generations from Abraham to David, fourteen from David to the deportation to Babylon, and fourteen more from the deportation to Christ himself.

His birth in human history   *1. 18*

The birth of Jesus Christ happened like this. When Mary was engaged to Joseph, just before their marriage, she was discovered to be pregnant—by the Holy Spirit. Whereupon Joseph, her future husband, who was a good man and did not want to see her disgraced, planned to break off the engagement quietly. But while he was turning the matter over in his mind an angel of the Lord appeared to him in a dream and said, "Joseph, son of David, do not be afraid to take Mary as your wife! What she has conceived is conceived through the Holy Spirit, and she will give birth to a son, whom you will call Jesus ('the Savior') for it is he who will save his people from their sins."

THE
GOSPEL ACCORDING TO
MATTHEW

The Coming of Christ

1 A table of the descent of Jesus Christ, son of David, son of Abraham.

Abraham was the father of Isaac, Isaac of Jacob, Jacob of Judah and his brothers, Judah of Perez and Zarah (their mother was Tamar), Perez of Hezron, Hezron of Ram, Ram of Amminadab, Amminadab of Nahshon, Nahshon of Salma, Salma of Boaz (his mother was Rahab), Boaz of Obed (his mother was Ruth), Obed of Jesse; and Jesse was the father of King David.

David was the father of Solomon (his mother had been the wife of Uriah), Solomon of Rehoboam, Rehoboam of Abijah, Abijah of Asa, Asa of Jehoshaphat, Jehoshaphat of Joram, Joram of Azariah, Azariah of Jotham, Jotham of Ahaz, Ahaz of Hezekiah, Hezekiah of Manasseh, Manasseh of Amon, Amon of Josiah; and Josiah was the father of Jeconiah and his brothers at the time of the deportation to Babylon.

After the deportation Jeconiah was the father of Shealtiel, Shealtiel of Zerubbabel, Zerubbabel of Abiud, Abiud of Eliakim, Eliakim of Azor, Azor of Zadok, Zadok of Achim, Achim of Eliud, Eliud of Eleazar, Eleazar of Matthan, Matthan of Jacob, Jacob of Joseph, the husband of Mary, who gave birth to[a] Jesus called Messiah.

There were thus fourteen generations in all from Abraham to David, fourteen from David until the deportation to Babylon, and fourteen from the deportation until the Messiah.

This is the story of the birth of the Messiah. Mary his mother was betrothed to Joseph; before their marriage she found that she was with child by the Holy Spirit. Being a man of principle, and at the same time wanting to save her from exposure, Joseph desired to have the marriage contract set aside quietly. He had resolved on this, when an angel of the Lord appeared to him in a dream. 'Joseph son of David,' said the angel, 'do not be afraid to take Mary home with you as your wife. It is by the Holy Spirit that she has conceived this child. She will bear a son; and you shall give him the name Jesus (Saviour), for he will save his people from their sins.'

[a] *Some witnesses read* Joseph, to whom was betrothed Mary, a virgin, who gave birth to . . . ; *one early witness has* Joseph, and Joseph, to whom Mary, a virgin, was betrothed, was the father of . . .

K.J.V.

sins. 22 Now all this was done, that it might be fulfilled which was spoken of the Lord by the prophet, saying, 23 Behold, a virgin shall be with child, and shall bring forth a son, and they shall call his name Emmanuel, which being interpreted is, God with us. 24 Then Joseph being raised from sleep did as the angel of the Lord had bidden him, and took unto him his wife: 25And knew her not till she had brought forth her firstborn son: and he called his name JESUS.

2 Now when Jesus was born in Bethlehem of Judea in the days of Herod the king, behold, there came wise men from the east to Jerusalem, 2 Saying, Where is he that is born King of the Jews? for we have seen his star in the east, and are come to worship him. 3 When Herod the king had heard *these things,* he was troubled, and all Jerusalem with him. 4And when he had gathered all the chief priests and scribes of the people together, he demanded of them where Christ should be born. 5And they said unto him, In Bethlehem of Judea: for thus it is written by the prophet, 6And thou Bethlehem, *in* the land of Juda, art not the least among the princes of Juda: for out of thee shall come a Governor, that shall rule my people Israel. 7 Then Herod, when he had privily called the wise men, inquired of them diligently what time the star appeared. 8And he sent them to Bethlehem, and said, Go and search diligently for the young child; and when ye have found *him,* bring me word again, that I may come and worship him also. 9 When they had heard the king, they departed; and, lo, the star, which they saw in the east, went before them, till it came and stood over where the young child was. 10 When they saw the star, they rejoiced with exceeding great joy. 11 And when they were come into the house, they saw the young child with Mary his mother, and fell down, and worshipped him: and when they had opened their treasures, they presented unto him gifts; gold, and frankincense, and myrrh. 12And being warned of God in a dream that they should not return to Herod, they departed into their own country another way. 13And when they were departed, behold, the angel of the Lord appeareth to Joseph in a dream, saying, Arise, and take the young child and his mother, and flee into Egypt, and be thou there until I bring thee word: for Herod will seek the young child to destroy him. 14 When he arose, he took the young child and his mother by night, and departed into Egypt: 15And was there until the death of Herod: that it might be fulfilled which was spoken of the Lord by the prophet, saying, Out of Egypt have I called my son.
16 Then Herod, when he saw that he was

R.S.V.

sins." 22All this took place to fulfil what the Lord had spoken by the prophet:
23 "Behold, a virgin shall conceive and bear a son,
and his name shall be called Emmanuel" (which means, God with us). 24 When Joseph woke from sleep, he did as the angel of the Lord commanded him; he took his wife, 25 but knew her not until she had borne a son; and he called his name Jesus.

2 Now when Jesus was born in Bethlehem of Judea in the days of Herod the king, behold, wise men from the East came to Jerusalem, saying, 2 "Where is he who has been born king of the Jews? For we have seen his star in the East, and have come to worship him." 3 When Herod the king heard this, he was troubled, and all Jerusalem with him; 4 and assembling all the chief priests and scribes of the people, he inquired of them where the Christ was to be born. 5 They told him, "In Bethlehem of Judea; for so it is written by the prophet:
6 'And you, O Bethlehem, in the land of Judah,
are by no means least among the rulers of Judah;
for from you shall come a ruler
who will govern my people Israel.' "
7 Then Herod summoned the wise men secretly and ascertained from them what time the star appeared; 8 and he sent them to Bethlehem, saying, "Go and search diligently for the child, and when you have found him bring me word, that I too may come and worship him." 9 When they had heard the king they went their way; and lo, the star which they had seen in the East went before them, till it came to rest over the place where the child was. 10 When they saw the star, they rejoiced exceedingly with great joy; 11 and going into the house they saw the child with Mary his mother, and they fell down and worshiped him. Then, opening their treasures, they offered him gifts, gold and frankincense and myrrh. 12And being warned in a dream not to return to Herod, they departed to their own country by another way.
13 Now when they had departed, behold, an angel of the Lord appeared to Joseph in a dream and said, "Rise, take the child and his mother, and flee to Egypt, and remain there till I tell you; for Herod is about to search for the child, to destroy him." 14And he rose and took the child and his mother by night, and departed to Egypt, 15 and remained there until the death of Herod. This was to fulfil what the Lord had spoken by the prophet, "Out of Egypt have I called my son."
16 Then Herod, when he saw that he had been

PHILLIPS	N.E.B.

PHILLIPS

All this happened to fulfill what the Lord has said through the prophet—

Behold, the virgin shall be with child, and shall bring forth a son, and they shall call his name Immanuel. ("Immanuel" means "God with us.")

When Joseph woke up he did what the angel had told him. He married Mary, but had no intercourse with her until she had given birth to a son. Then he gave him the name Jesus.

Herod, suspicious of the newborn   2. 1
king, takes vindictive precautions

Jesus was born in Bethlehem, in Judaea, in the days when Herod was king of the province. Not long after his birth there arrived from the east a party of astrologers making for Jerusalem and inquiring as they went: "Where is the child born to be king of the Jews? For we saw his star in the east and we have come here to pay homage to him."

When King Herod heard about this he was deeply perturbed, as indeed were all the other people living in Jerusalem. So he summoned all the Jewish scribes and chief priests together and asked them where "Christ" should be born. Their reply was: "In Bethlehem, in Judaea, for this is what the prophet wrote about the matter—

And thou Bethlehem, land of Judah,
Art in no wise least among the princes of Judah:
For out of thee shall come forth a governor,
Which shall be shepherd of my people Israel."

Then Herod invited the wise men to meet him privately and found out from them the exact time when the star appeared. Then he sent them off to Bethlehem, saying: "When you get there, search for this little child with the utmost care. And when you have found him, come back and tell me—so that I may go and worship him too."

The wise men listened to the king and then went on their way to Bethlehem. And now the star, which they had seen in the east, went in front of them as they traveled until at last it shone immediately above the place where the little child lay. The sight of the star filled them with indescribable joy.

So they went into the house and saw the little child with his mother Mary. And they fell on their knees and worshiped him. Then they opened their treasures and presented him with gifts—gold, incense and myrrh.

Then, since they were warned in a dream not to return to Herod, they went back to their own country by a different route.

But after they had gone the angel of the Lord appeared to Joseph in a dream and said: "Get up now; take the little child and his mother and escape to Egypt. Stay there until I tell you. For Herod means to seek out the child and kill him."

So Joseph got up and, taking the child and his mother with him in the middle of the night, set off for Egypt, where he remained until Herod's death.

This again is a fulfillment of the Lord's word spoken through the prophet—

Out of Egypt did I call my son.

When Herod saw that he had been fooled by

N.E.B.

All this happened in order to fulfil what the Lord declared through the prophet: 'The virgin will conceive and bear a son, and he shall be called Emmanuel', a name which means 'God is with us'. Rising from sleep Joseph did as the angel had directed him; he took Mary home to be his wife, but had no intercourse with her until her son was born. And he named the child Jesus.

2 Jesus was born at Bethlehem in Judaea during the reign of Herod. After his birth astrologers from the east arrived in Jerusalem, asking, 'Where is the child who is born to be king of the Jews? [a] We observed the rising of his star, and we have come to pay him homage.' King Herod was greatly perturbed when he heard this; and so was the whole of Jerusalem. He called a meeting of the chief priests and lawyers of the Jewish people, and put before them the question: 'Where is it that the Messiah is to be born?' 'At Bethlehem in Judaea', they replied; and they referred him to the prophecy which reads: 'Bethlehem in the land of Judah, you are far from least in the eyes of [b] the rulers of Judah; for out of you shall come a leader to be the shepherd of my people Israel.'

Herod next called the astrologers to meet him in private, and ascertained from them the time when the star had appeared. He then sent them on to Bethlehem, and said, 'Go and make a careful inquiry for the child. When you have found him, report to me, so that I may go myself and pay him homage.'

They set out at the king's bidding; and the star which they had seen at its rising went ahead of them until it stopped above the place where the child lay. At the sight of the star they were overjoyed. Entering the house, they saw the child with Mary his mother, and bowed to the ground in homage to him; then they opened their treasures and offered him gifts: gold, frankincense, and myrrh. And being warned in a dream not to go back to Herod, they returned home another way.

After they had gone, an angel of the Lord appeared to Joseph in a dream, and said to him, 'Rise up, take the child and his mother and escape with them to Egypt, and stay there until I tell you; for Herod is going to search for the child to do away with him.' So Joseph rose from sleep, and taking mother and child by night he went away with them to Egypt, and there he stayed till Herod's death. This was to fulfil what the Lord had declared through the prophet: 'I called my son out of Egypt.'

When Herod saw how the astrologers had

[a] *Or* Where is the king of the Jews who has just been born? [b] *Or* least among.

K.J.V.

mocked of the wise men, was exceeding wroth, and sent forth, and slew all the children that were in Bethlehem, and in all the coasts thereof, from two years old and under, according to the time which he had diligently inquired of the wise men. 17 Then was fulfilled that which was spoken by Jeremy the prophet, saying, 18 In Rama was there a voice heard, lamentation, and weeping, and great mourning, Rachel weeping *for* her children, and would not be comforted, because they are not.

19 But when Herod was dead, behold, an angel of the Lord appeareth in a dream to Joseph in Egypt, 20 Saying, Arise, and take the young child and his mother, and go into the land of Israel: for they are dead which sought the young child's life. 21And he arose, and took the young child and his mother, and came into the land of Israel. 22 But when he heard that Archelaus did reign in Judea in the room of his father Herod, he was afraid to go thither: notwithstanding, being warned of God in a dream, he turned aside into the parts of Galilee: 23And he came and dwelt in a city called Nazareth: that it might be fulfilled which was spoken by the prophets, He shall be called a Nazarene.

R.S.V.

tricked by the wise men, was in a furious rage, and he sent and killed all the male children in Bethlehem and in all that region who were two years old or under, according to the time which he had ascertained from the wise men. 17 Then was fulfilled what was spoken by the prophet Jeremiah:
18 "A voice was heard in Ramah,
wailing and loud lamentation,
Rachel weeping for her children;
she refused to be consoled,
because they were no more."
19 But when Herod died, behold, an angel of the Lord appeared in a dream to Joseph in Egypt, saying, 20 "Rise, take the child and his mother, and go to the land of Israel, for those who sought the child's life are dead." 21And he rose and took the child and his mother, and went to the land of Israel. 22 But when he heard that Archelaus reigned over Judea in place of his father Herod, he was afraid to go there, and being warned in a dream he withdrew to the district of Galilee. 23And he went and dwelt in a city called Nazareth, that what was spoken by the prophets might be fulfilled, "He shall be called a Nazarene."

3 In those days came John the Baptist, preaching in the wilderness of Judea, 2And saying, Repent ye: for the kingdom of heaven is at hand. 3 For this is he that was spoken of by the prophet Esaias, saying, The voice of one crying in the wilderness, Prepare ye the way of the Lord, make his paths straight. 4And the same John had his raiment of camel's hair, and a leathern girdle about his loins; and his meat was locusts and wild honey. 5 Then went out to him Jerusalem, and all Judea, and all the region round about Jordan, 6And were baptized of him in Jordan, confessing their sins.

7 But when he saw many of the Pharisees and Sadducees come to his baptism, he said unto them, O generation of vipers, who hath warned you to flee from the wrath to come? 8 Bring forth therefore fruits meet for repentance: 9And think not to say within yourselves, We have Abraham to *our* father: for I say unto you, that God is able of these stones to raise up children unto Abraham. 10And now also the axe is laid unto the root of the trees: therefore every tree which bringeth not forth good fruit is hewn down, and cast into the fire. 11 I indeed baptize you with water unto repentance: but he that cometh after me is mightier than I, whose shoes I am not worthy to bear: he shall baptize you with the Holy Ghost, and *with* fire: 12 Whose fan *is* in his hand, and he will thoroughly purge his floor, and gather his wheat into the garner; but he will burn up the chaff with unquenchable fire.

3 In those days came John the Baptist, preaching in the wilderness of Judea, 2 "Repent, for the kingdom of heaven is at hand." 3 For this is he who was spoken of by the prophet Isaiah when he said,
"The voice of one crying in the wilderness:
Prepare the way of the Lord,
make his paths straight."
4 Now John wore a garment of camel's hair, and a leather girdle around his waist; and his food was locusts and wild honey. 5 Then went out to him Jerusalem and all Judea and all the region about the Jordan, 6 and they were baptized by him in the river Jordan, confessing their sins.

7 But when he saw many of the Pharisees and Sadducees coming for baptism, he said to them, "You brood of vipers! Who warned you to flee from the wrath to come? 8 Bear fruit that befits repentance, 9 and do not presume to say to yourselves, 'We have Abraham as our father'; for I tell you, God is able from these stones to raise up children to Abraham. 10 Even now the axe is laid to the root of the trees; every tree therefore that does not bear good fruit is cut down and thrown into the fire. 11 "I baptize you with water for repentance, but he who is coming after me is mightier than I, whose sandals I am not worthy to carry; he will baptize you with the Holy Spirit and with fire. 12 His winnowing fork is in his hand, and he will clear his threshing floor and gather his wheat into the granary, but the chaff he will burn with unquenchable fire."

PHILLIPS

the wise men, he was furiously angry. He issued orders, and killed all the male children of two years and under in Bethlehem and the surrounding district—basing his calculation on his careful questioning of the wise men.

Then Jeremiah's prophecy was fulfilled:

A voice was heard in Ramah,
Weeping and great mourning,
Rachel weeping for her children;
And she would not be comforted, because they are not.

Jesus is brought to Nazareth 2. 19

But after Herod's death an angel of the Lord again appeared to Joseph in a dream and said: "Now get up and take the infant and his mother with you and go into the land of Israel. For those who sought the child's life are dead."

So Joseph got up and took the little child and his mother with him and journeyed toward the land of Israel. But when he heard that Archelaus was now reigning as king of Judaea in the place of his father Herod, he was afraid to enter the country. Then he received warning in a dream to turn aside into the district of Galilee and came to live in a small town called Nazareth—thus fulfilling the old prophecy that he should be called a Nazarene.

The prophesied "Elijah": John the 3. 1 Baptist

In due course John the Baptist arrived, preaching in the Judaean desert: "You must change your hearts—for the kingdom of Heaven has arrived!"

This was the man whom the prophet Isaiah spoke about in the words:

The voice of one crying in the wilderness,
Make ye ready the way of the Lord,
Make his paths straight.

John wore clothes of camel's hair with a leather belt round his waist, and lived on locusts and wild honey. The people of Jerusalem and of all Judaea and the Jordan district flocked to him, and were baptized by him in the river Jordan, publicly confessing their sins.

But when he saw many Pharisees and Sadducees coming for baptism he said: "Who warned you, you serpent's brood, to escape from the wrath to come? Go and do something to show that your hearts are really changed. Don't suppose that you can say to yourselves, 'We are Abraham's children,' for I tell you that God could produce children of Abraham out of these stones!

"The ax already lies at the root of the tree, and the tree that fails to produce good fruit will be cut down and thrown into the fire. It is true that I baptize you with water as a sign of your repentance, but the one who follows me is far stronger than I am—indeed, I am not fit to carry his shoes. He will baptize you with the fire of the Holy Spirit. He comes all ready to separate the wheat from the chaff and very thoroughly will he clear his threshing floor—the wheat he will collect into the granary and the chaff he will burn with a fire that can never be put out."

N.E.B.

tricked him he fell into a passion, and gave orders for the massacre of all children in Bethlehem and its neighbourhood, of the age of two years or less, corresponding with the time he had ascertained from the astrologers. So the words spoken through Jeremiah the prophet were fulfilled: 'A voice was heard in Rama, wailing and loud laments; it was Rachel weeping for her children, and refusing all consolation, because they were no more.'

The time came that Herod died; and an angel of the Lord appeared in a dream to Joseph in Egypt and said to him, 'Rise up, take the child and his mother, and go with them to the land of Israel, for the men who threatened the child's life are dead.' So he rose, took mother and child with him, and came to the land of Israel. Hearing, however, that Archelaus had succeeded his father Herod as king of Judaea, he was afraid to go there. And being warned by a dream, he withdrew to the region of Galilee; there he settled in a town called Nazareth. This was to fulfil the words spoken through the prophets: 'He shall be called a Nazarene.'

3 About that time John the Baptist appeared as a preacher in the Judaean wilderness; his theme was: 'Repent; for the kingdom of Heaven is upon you!' It is of him that the prophet Isaiah spoke when he said, 'A voice crying aloud in the wilderness, "Prepare a way for the Lord; clear a straight path for him." '

John's clothing was a rough coat of camel's hair, with a leather belt round his waist, and his food was locusts and wild honey. They flocked to him from Jerusalem, from all Judaea, and the whole Jordan valley, and were baptized by him in the River Jordan, confessing their sins.

When he saw many of the Pharisees and Sadducees coming for baptism he said to them: 'You vipers' brood! Who warned you to escape from the coming retribution? Then prove your repentance by the fruit it bears; and do not presume to say to yourselves, "We have Abraham for our father." I tell you that God can make children for Abraham out of these stones here. Already the axe is laid to the roots of the trees; and every tree that fails to produce good fruit is cut down and thrown on the fire. I baptize you with water, for repentance; but the one who comes after me is mightier than I, and I am not fit to take off his shoes; he will baptize you with the Holy Spirit and with fire. His shovel is ready in his hand and he will winnow his threshing-floor; the wheat he will gather into his granary, but he will burn the chaff on a fire that can never go out.'

K.J.V.

13 Then cometh Jesus from Galilee to Jordan unto John, to be baptized of him. 14 But John forbade him, saying, I have need to be baptized of thee, and comest thou to me? 15And Jesus answering said unto him, Suffer *it to be so* now: for thus it becometh us to fulfil all righteousness. Then he suffered him. 16And Jesus, when he was baptized, went up straightway out of the water: and, lo, the heavens were opened unto him, and he saw the Spirit of God descending like a dove, and lighting upon him: 17And lo a voice from heaven, saying, This is my beloved Son, in whom I am well pleased.

4 Then was Jesus led up of the Spirit into the wilderness to be tempted of the devil. 2And when he had fasted forty days and forty nights, he was afterward a hungered. 3And when the tempter came to him, he said, If thou be the Son of God, command that these stones be made bread. 4 But he answered and said, It is written, Man shall not live by bread alone, but by every word that proceedeth out of the mouth of God. 5 Then the devil taketh him up into the holy city, and setteth him on a pinnacle of the temple, 6And saith unto him, If thou be the Son of God, cast thyself down: for it is written, He shall give his angels charge concerning thee: and in *their* hands they shall bear thee up, lest at any time thou dash thy foot against a stone. 7 Jesus said unto him, It is written again, Thou shalt not tempt the Lord thy God. 8Again, the devil taketh him up into an exceeding high mountain, and sheweth him all the kingdoms of the world, and the glory of them; 9And saith unto him, All these things will I give thee, if thou wilt fall down and worship me. 10 Then saith Jesus unto him, Get thee hence, Satan: for it is written, Thou shalt worship the Lord thy God, and him only shalt thou serve. 11 Then the devil leaveth him, and, behold, angels came and ministered unto him.

12 Now when Jesus had heard that John was cast into prison, he departed into Galilee; 13And leaving Nazareth, he came and dwelt in Capernaum, which is upon the sea coast, in the borders of Zabulon and Nephthalim: 14 That it might be fulfilled which was spoken by Esaias the prophet, saying, 15 The land of Zabulon, and the land of Nephthalim, *by* the way of the sea, beyond Jordan, Galilee of the Gentiles; 16 The people which sat in darkness saw great light; and to them which sat in the region and shadow of death light is sprung up.

R.S.V.

13 Then Jesus came from Galilee to the Jordan to John, to be baptized by him. 14 John would have prevented him, saying, "I need to be baptized by you, and do you come to me?" 15 But Jesus answered him, "Let it be so now; for thus it is fitting for us to fulfil all righteousness." Then he consented. 16And when Jesus was baptized, he went up immediately from the water, and behold, the heavens were opened *g* and he saw the Spirit of God descending like a dove, and alighting on him; 17 and lo, a voice from heaven, saying, "This is my beloved Son,*h* with whom I am well pleased."

4 Then Jesus was led up by the Spirit into the wilderness to be tempted by the devil. 2And he fasted forty days and forty nights, and afterward he was hungry. 3And the tempter came and said to him, "If you are the Son of God, command these stones to become loaves of bread." 4 But he answered, "It is written,
'Man shall not live by bread alone,
  but by every word that proceeds from the
    mouth of God.'"
5 Then the devil took him to the holy city, and set him on the pinnacle of the temple, 6 and said to him, "If you are the Son of God, throw yourself down; for it is written,
'He will give his angels charge of you,'
and
'On their hands they will bear you up,
  lest you strike your foot against a stone.'"
7 Jesus said to him, "Again it is written, 'You shall not tempt the Lord your God.'" 8Again, the devil took him to a very high mountain, and showed him all the kingdoms of the world and the glory of them; 9 and he said to him, "All these I will give you, if you will fall down and worship me." 10 Then Jesus said to him, "Begone, Satan! for it is written,
'You shall worship the Lord your God
  and him only shall you serve.'"
11 Then the devil left him, and behold, angels came and ministered to him.

12 Now when he heard that John had been arrested, he withdrew into Galilee; 13 and leaving Nazareth he went and dwelt in Capernaum by the sea, in the territory of Zebulun and Naphtali, 14 that what was spoken by the prophet Isaiah might be fulfilled:
15 "The land of Zebulun and the land of
    Naphtali,
  toward the sea, across the Jordan,
  Galilee of the Gentiles—
16 the people who sat in darkness
  have seen a great light,
  and for those who sat in the region and
    shadow of death light has dawned."

[g] Other ancient authorities add *to him*. [h] Or *my Son, my* (or *the*) *Beloved*.

PHILLIPS

N.E.B.

John baptizes Jesus 3. 13

Then Jesus came from Galilee to the Jordan to be baptized by John. But John tried to prevent him. "I need you to baptize *me*," he said. "Surely *you* do not come to me?" But Jesus replied, "It is right for us to meet all the Law's demands—let it be so now."

Then John agreed to his baptism. Jesus came straight out of the water afterward, and suddenly the heavens opened and he saw the Spirit of God coming down like a dove and resting upon him. And a voice came out of Heaven saying, "This is my dearly loved Son, in whom I am well pleased."

Then Jesus arrived at the Jordan from Galilee, and came to John to be baptized by him. John tried to dissuade him. 'Do you come to me?' he said; 'I need rather to be baptized by you.' Jesus replied, 'Let it be so for the present; we do well to conform in this way with all that God requires.' John then allowed him to come. After baptism Jesus came up out of the water at once, and at that moment heaven opened; he saw the Spirit of God descending like a dove to alight upon him; and a voice from heaven was heard saying, 'This is my Son, my Beloved,[a] on whom my favour rests.'

Jesus faces temptation alone in the 4. 1 desert

Then Jesus was led by the Spirit up into the desert, to be tempted by the devil. After a fast of forty days and nights he was very hungry.

"If you really are the Son of God," said the tempter, coming to him, "tell these stones to turn into loaves."

Jesus answered, "The scripture says *'Man shall not live by bread alone, but by every word that proceedeth out of the mouth of God.'"*

Then the devil took him to the holy city, and set him on the highest ledge of the Temple. "If you really are the Son of God," he said, "throw yourself down. For the scripture says—

He shall give his angels charge concerning thee:
And on their hands they shall bear thee up,
Lest haply thou dash thy foot against a stone."

"Yes," retorted Jesus, "and the scripture also says, *'Thou shalt not tempt the Lord thy God.'"*

Once again the devil took him to a very high mountain, and from there showed him all the kingdoms of the world and their magnificence. "Everything there I will give you," he said to him, "if you will fall down and worship me."

"Away with you, Satan!" replied Jesus, "the scripture says,

Thou shalt worship the Lord thy God, and him only shalt thou serve."

Then the devil let him alone, and angels came to him and took care of him.

4 Jesus was then led away by the Spirit into the wilderness, to be tempted by the devil.

For forty days and nights he fasted, and at the end of them he was famished. The tempter approached him and said, 'If you are the Son of God, tell these stones to become bread.' Jesus answered, 'Scripture says, "Man cannot live on bread alone; he lives on every word that God utters." '

The devil then took him to the Holy City and set him on the parapet of the temple. 'If you are the Son of God,' he said, 'throw yourself down; for Scripture says, "He will put his angels in charge of you, and they will support you in their arms, for fear you should strike your foot against a stone." ' Jesus answered him, 'Scripture says again, "You are not to put the Lord your God to the test." '

Once again, the devil took him to a very high mountain, and showed him all the kingdoms of the world in their glory. 'All these', he said, 'I will give you, if you will only fall down and do me homage.' But Jesus said, 'Begone, Satan; Scripture says, "You shall do homage to the Lord your God and worship him alone." '

Then the devil left him, and angels appeared and waited on him.

When he heard that John had been arrested, Jesus withdrew to Galilee; and leaving Nazareth he went and settled at Capernaum on the Sea of Galilee, in the district of Zebulun and Naphtali. This was in fulfilment of the passage in the prophet Isaiah which tells of 'the land of Zebulun, the land of Naphtali, the road by the sea, the land beyond Jordan, heathen Galilee', and says:

Jesus begins his ministry, in 4. 12 Galilee, and calls his first disciples

Now when Jesus heard that John had been arrested he went back to Galilee. He left Nazareth and came to live in Capernaum, a lake-side town in the Zebulun-Naphtali territory. In this way Isaiah's prophecy came true:

The land of Zebulun and the land of Naphtali,
Toward the sea, beyond Jordan,
Galilee of the gentiles,
The people which sat in darkness
Saw a great light,
And to them which sat in the region and shadow of death,
To them did light spring up.

'The people that lived in darkness saw a great light;
Light dawned on the dwellers in the land of death's dark shadow.'

[a] *Or* This is my only Son.

K.J.V.

17 From that time Jesus began to preach, and to say, Repent: for the kingdom of heaven is at hand.

18 And Jesus, walking by the sea of Galilee, saw two brethren, Simon called Peter, and Andrew his brother, casting a net into the sea: for they were fishers. 19And he saith unto them, Follow me, and I will make you fishers of men. 20And they straightway left *their* nets, and followed him. 21And going on from thence, he saw other two brethren, James *the son* of Zebedee, and John his brother, in a ship with Zebedee their father, mending their nets; and he called them. 22And they immediately left the ship and their father, and followed him.

23 And Jesus went about all Galilee, teaching in their synagogues, and preaching the gospel of the kingdom, and healing all manner of sickness and all manner of disease among the people. 24And his fame went throughout all Syria: and they brought unto him all sick people that were taken with divers diseases and torments, and those which were possessed with devils, and those which were lunatic, and those that had the palsy; and he healed them. 25And there followed him great multitudes of people from Galilee, and *from* Decapolis, and *from* Jerusalem, and *from* Judea, and *from* beyond Jordan.

5 And seeing the multitudes, he went up into a mountain: and when he was set, his disciples came unto him: 2And he opened his mouth, and taught them, saying, 3 Blessed *are* the poor in spirit: for theirs is the kingdom of heaven. 4 Blessed *are* they that mourn: for they shall be comforted. 5 Blessed *are* the meek: for they shall inherit the earth. 6 Blessed *are* they which do hunger and thirst after righteousness: for they shall be filled. 7 Blessed *are* the merciful: for they shall obtain mercy. 8 Blessed *are* the pure in heart: for they shall see God. 9 Blessed *are* the peacemakers: for they shall be called the children of God. 10 Blessed *are* they which are persecuted for righteousness' sake: for theirs is the kingdom of heaven. 11 Blessed are ye, when *men* shall revile you, and persecute *you,* and shall say all manner of evil against you falsely, for my sake. 12 Rejoice, and be exceeding glad: for great *is* your reward in heaven: for so persecuted they the prophets which were before you.

13 Ye are the salt of the earth: but if the salt have lost his savour, wherewith shall it be

R.S.V.

17 From that time Jesus began to preach, saying, "Repent, for the kingdom of heaven is at hand."

18 As he walked by the Sea of Galilee, he saw two brothers, Simon who is called Peter and Andrew his brother, casting a net into the sea; for they were fishermen. 19And he said to them, "Follow me, and I will make you fishers of men." 20 Immediately they left their nets and followed him. 21And going on from there he saw two other brothers, James the son of Zebedee and John his brother, in the boat with Zebedee their father, mending their nets, and he called them. 22 Immediately they left the boat and their father, and followed him.

23 And he went about all Galilee, teaching in their synagogues and preaching the gospel of the kingdom and healing every disease and every infirmity among the people. 24 So his fame spread throughout all Syria, and they brought him all the sick, those afflicted with various diseases and pains, demoniacs, epileptics, and paralytics, and he healed them. 25And great crowds followed him from Galilee and the Decapolis and Jerusalem and Judea and from beyond the Jordan.

5 Seeing the crowds, he went up on the mountain, and when he sat down his disciples came to him. 2And he opened his mouth and taught them, saying:

3 "Blessed are the poor in spirit, for theirs is the kingdom of heaven.

4 "Blessed are those who mourn, for they shall be comforted.

5 "Blessed are the meek, for they shall inherit the earth.

6 "Blessed are those who hunger and thirst for righteousness, for they shall be satisfied.

7 "Blessed are the merciful, for they shall obtain mercy.

8 "Blessed are the pure in heart, for they shall see God.

9 "Blessed are the peacemakers, for they shall be called sons of God.

10 "Blessed are those who are persecuted for righteousness' sake, for theirs is the kingdom of heaven.

11 "Blessed are you when men revile you and persecute you and utter all kinds of evil against you falsely on my account. 12 Rejoice and be glad, for your reward is great in heaven, for so men persecuted the prophets who were before you.

13 "You are the salt of the earth; but if salt has lost its taste, how shall its saltness be re-

PHILLIPS	N.E.B.

From that time Jesus began to preach and to say, "You must change your hearts—for the kingdom of Heaven has arrived."

While he was walking by the lake of Galilee he saw two brothers, Simon (Peter) and Andrew, casting their large net into the water. They were fishermen, so Jesus said to them, "Follow me and I will teach you to catch men!"

At once they left their nets and followed him. Then he went farther on and saw two more men, also brothers, James and John. They were aboard the boat with their father, Zebedee, repairing their nets, and he called them. At once they left the boat, and their father, and followed him.

Jesus teaches, preaches and heals **4. 23**

Jesus now moved about through the whole of Galilee, teaching in their synagogues and preaching the good news about the kingdom, and healing every disease and disability among the people. His reputation spread throughout Syria, and people brought to him all those who were ill, suffering from all kinds of diseases and pains—including the devil-possessed, the insane and the paralyzed. He healed them, and was followed by enormous crowds from Galilee, the Ten Towns, Jerusalem, Judaea and from beyond the river Jordan.

Jesus proclaims the new values **5. 1**
of the kingdom

When Jesus saw the vast crowds he went up the hillside, and after he had sat down his disciples came to him.

Then he began his teaching by saying to them:

"How happy are the humble-minded, for the kingdom of Heaven is theirs!

"How happy are those who know what sorrow means, for they will be given courage and comfort!

"Happy are those who claim nothing, for the whole earth will belong to them!

"Happy are those who are hungry and thirsty for goodness, for they will be fully satisfied!

"Happy are the merciful, for they will have mercy shown to them!

"Happy are the utterly sincere, for they will see God!

"Happy are those who make peace, for they will be known as sons of God!

"Happy are those who have suffered persecution for the cause of goodness, for the kingdom of Heaven is theirs!

"And what happiness will be yours when people blame you and ill-treat you and say all kinds of slanderous things against you for my sake! Be glad then, yes, be tremendously glad—for your reward in Heaven is magnificent. They persecuted the prophets before your time in exactly the same way.

"You are the earth's salt. But if the salt should become tasteless, what can make it salt again?

From that day Jesus began to proclaim the message: 'Repent; for[a] the kingdom of Heaven is upon you.'

Jesus was walking by the Sea of Galilee when he saw two brothers, Simon called Peter and his brother Andrew, casting a net into the lake; for they were fishermen. Jesus said to them, 'Come with me, and I will make you fishers of men.' They left their nets at once and followed him.

He went on, and saw another pair of brothers, James son of Zebedee and his brother John; they were in the boat with their father Zebedee, overhauling their nets. He called them, and at once they left the boat and their father, and followed him.

He went round the whole of Galilee, teaching in the synagogues, preaching the gospel of the Kingdom, and curing whatever illness or infirmity there was among the people. His fame reached the whole of Syria; and sufferers from every kind of illness, racked with pain, possessed by devils, epileptic, or paralysed, were all brought to him, and he cured them. Great crowds also followed him, from Galilee and the Ten Towns,[b] from Jerusalem and Judaea, and from Transjordan.

The Sermon on the Mount

5 When he saw the crowds he went up the hill. There he took his seat, and when his disciples had gathered round him he began to address them. And this is the teaching he gave:

'How blest are those who know that they are poor;
     the kingdom of Heaven is theirs.
How blest are the sorrowful;
     they shall find consolation.
How blest are those of a gentle spirit;
     they shall have the earth for their possession.
How blest are those who hunger and thirst to see right prevail;[c]
     they shall be satisfied.
How blest are those who show mercy;
     mercy shall be shown to them.
How blest are those whose hearts are pure;
     they shall see God.
How blest are the peacemakers;
     God shall call them his sons.
How blest are those who have suffered persecution for the cause of right;
     the kingdom of Heaven is theirs.

'How blest you are, when you suffer insults and persecution and every kind of calumny for my sake. Accept it with gladness and exultation, for you have a rich reward in heaven; in the same way they persecuted the prophets before you.

'You are salt to the world. And if salt becomes tasteless, how is its saltness to be restored? It is

[a] *Some witnesses omit* Repent; for. [b] *Greek* Decapolis. [c] *Or* to do what is right.

K.J.V.

salted? It is thenceforth good for nothing, but to be cast out, and to be trodden under foot of men. 14 Ye are the light of the world. A city that is set on a hill cannot be hid. 15 Neither do men light a candle, and put it under a bushel, but on a candlestick; and it giveth light unto all that are in the house. 16 Let your light so shine before men, that they may see your good works, and glorify your Father which is in heaven.

17 Think not that I am come to destroy the law, or the prophets: I am not come to destroy, but to fulfil. 18 For verily I say unto you, Till heaven and earth pass, one jot or one tittle shall in no wise pass from the law, till all be fulfilled. 19 Whosoever therefore shall break one of these least commandments, and shall teach men so, he shall be called the least in the kingdom of heaven: but whosoever shall do and teach *them*, the same shall be called great in the kingdom of heaven. 20 For I say unto you, That except your righteousness shall exceed *the righteousness of* the scribes and Pharisees, ye shall in no case enter into the kingdom of heaven.

21 Ye have heard that it was said by them of old time, Thou shalt not kill; and whosoever shall kill shall be in danger of the judgment: 22 But I say unto you, That whosoever is angry with his brother without a cause shall be in danger of the judgment: and whosoever shall say to his brother, Raca, shall be in danger of the council: but whosoever shall say, Thou fool, shall be in danger of hell fire. 23 Therefore if thou bring thy gift to the altar, and there rememberest that thy brother hath aught against thee; 24 Leave there thy gift before the altar, and go thy way; first be reconciled to thy brother, and then come and offer thy gift. 25 Agree with thine adversary quickly, while thou art in the way with him; lest at any time the adversary deliver thee to the judge, and the judge deliver thee to the officer, and thou be cast into prison. 26 Verily I say unto thee, Thou shalt by no means come out thence, till thou hast paid the uttermost farthing.

27 Ye have heard that it was said by them of old time, Thou shalt not commit adultery: 28 But I say unto you, That whosoever looketh on a woman to lust after her hath committed adultery with her already in his heart. 29 And if thy right eye offend thee, pluck it out, and cast *it* from thee: for it is profitable for thee that one of thy members should perish, and not *that* thy whole body should be cast into hell. 30 And if thy right hand offend thee, cut it off, and cast *it* from thee: for it is profitable for thee that one of thy members should perish, and not *that* thy whole body should be cast into hell. 31 It hath been said, Whosoever shall put away his wife, let him give her a writing of divorcement: 32 But I say unto you, That whosoever shall put away his wife, saving for the cause of fornication, causeth her to commit adultery: and whosoever shall marry her that is divorced committeth adultery.

33 Again, ye have heard that it hath been said by them of old time, Thou shalt not forswear thyself, but shalt perform unto the Lord thine oaths: 34 But I say unto you, Swear not at all;

R.S.V.

stored? It is no longer good for anything except to be thrown out and trodden under foot by men.

14 "You are the light of the world. A city set on a hill cannot be hid. 15 Nor do men light a lamp and put it under a bushel, but on a stand, and it gives light to all in the house. 16 Let your light so shine before men, that they may see your good works and give glory to your Father who is in heaven.

17 "Think not that I have come to abolish the law and the prophets; I have come not to abolish them but to fulfil them. 18 For truly, I say to you, till heaven and earth pass away, not an iota, not a dot, will pass from the law until all is accomplished. 19 Whoever then relaxes one of the least of these commandments and teaches men so, shall be called least in the kingdom of heaven; but he who does them and teaches them shall be called great in the kingdom of heaven. 20 For I tell you, unless your righteousness exceeds that of the scribes and Pharisees, you will never enter the kingdom of heaven.

21 "You have heard that it was said to the men of old, 'You shall not kill; and whoever kills shall be liable to judgment.' 22 But I say to you that every one who is angry with his brother[i] shall be liable to judgment; whoever insults[j] his brother shall be liable to the council, and whoever says, 'You fool!' shall be liable to the hell[k] of fire. 23 So if you are offering your gift at the altar, and there remember that your brother has something against you, 24 leave your gift there before the altar and go; first be reconciled to your brother, and then come and offer your gift. 25 Make friends quickly with your accuser, while you are going with him to court, lest your accuser hand you over to the judge, and the judge to the guard, and you be put in prison; 26 truly, I say to you, you will never get out till you have paid the last penny.

27 "You have heard that it was said, 'You shall not commit adultery.' 28 But I say to you that every one who looks at a woman lustfully has already committed adultery with her in his heart. 29 If your right eye causes you to sin, pluck it out and throw it away; it is better that you lose one of your members than that your whole body be thrown into hell.[k] 30 And if your right hand causes you to sin, cut it off and throw it away; it is better that you lose one of your members than that your whole body go into hell.[k]

31 "It was also said, 'Whoever divorces his wife, let him give her a certificate of divorce.' 32 But I say to you that every one who divorces his wife, except on the ground of unchastity, makes her an adulteress; and whoever marries a divorced woman commits adultery.

33 "Again you have heard that it was said to the men of old, 'You shall not swear falsely, but shall perform to the Lord what you have sworn.' 34 But I say to you, Do not swear at all, either

[i] Other ancient authorities insert *without cause.*
[j] Greek *says Raca to* (an obscure term of abuse).
[k] Greek *Gehenna.*

PHILLIPS

It is completely useless and can only be thrown out of doors and stamped underfoot.

"You are the world's light—it is impossible to hide a town built on the top of a hill. Men do not light a lamp and put it under a bucket. They put it on a lampstand, and it gives light for everybody in the house.

"Let your light shine like that in the sight of men. Let them see the good things you do and praise your Father in Heaven.

Christ's authority surpasses that 5.17 of the Law

"You must not think that I have come to abolish the Law or the Prophets; I have not come to abolish them but to complete them. Indeed, I assure you that, while Heaven and earth last, the Law will not lose a single dot or comma until its purpose is complete. This means that whoever now relaxes one of the least of these commandments and teaches men to do the same will himself be called least in the kingdom of Heaven. But whoever teaches and practices them will be called great in the kingdom of Heaven. For I tell you that your goodness must be a far better thing than the goodness of the scribes and Pharisees before you can set foot in the kingdom of Heaven at all!

"You have heard that it was said to the people in the old days, *'Thou shalt not murder,'* and anyone who does so must stand his trial. But I say to you that anyone who is angry with his brother must stand his trial; anyone who contemptuously calls his brother a fool must face the supreme court; and anyone who looks down on his brother as a lost soul is himself heading straight for the fire of destruction.

"So that if, while you are offering your gift at the altar, you should remember that your brother has something against you, you must leave your gift there before the altar and go away. Make your peace with your brother first, then come and offer your gift. Come to terms quickly with your opponent while you have the chance, or else he may hand you over to the judge and the judge in turn hand you over to the officer of the court and you will be thrown into prison. Believe me, you will never get out again till you have paid your last farthing!

"You have heard that it was said to the people in the old days, *'Thou shalt not commit adultery.'* But I say to you that every man who looks at a woman lustfully has already committed adultery with her—in his heart.

"Yes, if your right eye leads you astray pluck it out and throw it away; it is better for you to lose one of your members than that your whole body should be thrown onto the rubbish heap.

"Yes, if your right hand leads you astray cut it off and throw it away; it is better for you to lose one of your members than that your whole body should go to the rubbish heap.

"It also used to be said that whoever divorces his wife must give her a proper certificate of divorce. But I say to you that whoever divorces his wife except on the ground of unfaithfulness is making her an adulteress. And whoever marries the woman who has been divorced also commits adultery.

"Again, you have heard that the people in the old days were told—*'Thou shalt not forswear thyself, but shalt perform unto the Lord thine oaths';* but I say to you, don't use an oath at all. Don't swear by Heaven for it is

N.E.B.

now good for nothing but to be thrown away and trodden underfoot.

'You are light for all the world. A town that stands on a hill cannot be hidden. When a lamp is lit, it is not put under the meal-tub, but on the lamp-stand, where it gives light to everyone in the house. And you, like the lamp, must shed light among your fellows, so that, when they see the good you do, they may give praise to your Father in heaven.

'Do not suppose that I have come to abolish the Law and the prophets; I did not come to abolish, but to complete. I tell you this: so long as heaven and earth endure, not a letter, not a stroke, will disappear from the Law until all that must happen has happened.[a] If any man therefore sets aside even the least of the Law's demands, and teaches others to do the same, he will have the lowest place in the kingdom of Heaven, whereas anyone who keeps the Law and teaches others so will stand high in the kingdom of Heaven. I tell you, unless you show yourselves far better men than the Pharisees and the doctors of the law, you can never enter the kingdom of Heaven.

'You have learned that our forefathers were told, "Do not commit murder; anyone who commits murder must be brought to judgement." But what I tell you is this: Anyone who nurses anger against his brother[b] must be brought to judgement. If he abuses his brother he must answer for it to the court; if he sneers at him he will have to answer for it in the fires of hell.

'If, when you are bringing your gift to the altar, you suddenly remember that your brother has a grievance against you, leave your gift where it is before the altar. First go and make your peace with your brother, and only then come back and offer your gift.

'If someone sues you, come to terms with him promptly while you are both on your way to court; otherwise he may hand you over to the judge, and the judge to the constable, and you will be put in jail. I tell you, once you are there you will not be let out till you have paid the last farthing.

'You have learned that they were told, "Do not commit adultery." But what I tell you is this: If a man looks on a woman with a lustful eye, he has already committed adultery with her in his heart.

'If your right eye leads you astray, tear it out and fling it away; it is better for you to lose one part of your body than for the whole of it to be thrown into hell. And if your right hand is your undoing, cut it off and fling it away; it is better for you to lose one part of your body than for the whole of it to go to hell.

'They were told, "A man who divorces his wife must give her a note of dismissal." But what I tell you is this: If a man divorces his wife for any cause other than unchastity he involves her in adultery; and anyone who marries a woman so divorced commits adultery.

'Again, you have learned that they were told, "Do not break your oath", and, "Oaths sworn to the Lord must be kept." But what I tell you is this: You are not to swear at all—not by

[a] *Or* before all that it stands for is achieved.
[b] *Some witnesses insert* without good cause.

13

neither by heaven; for it is God's throne: 35 Nor by the earth; for it is his footstool: neither by Jerusalem; for it is the city of the great King. 36 Neither shalt thou swear by thy head, because thou canst not make one hair white or black. 37 But let your communication be, Yea, yea; Nay, nay: for whatsoever is more than these cometh of evil.

38 Ye have heard that it hath been said, An eye for an eye, and a tooth for a tooth: 39 But I say unto you, That ye resist not evil: but whosoever shall smite thee on thy right cheek, turn to him the other also. 40 And if any man will sue thee at the law, and take away thy coat, let him have *thy* cloak also. 41 And whosoever shall compel thee to go a mile, go with him twain. 42 Give to him that asketh thee, and from him that would borrow of thee turn not thou away.

43 Ye have heard that it hath been said, Thou shalt love thy neighbour, and hate thine enemy. 44 But I say unto you, Love your enemies, bless them that curse you, do good to them that hate you, and pray for them which despitefully use you, and persecute you; 45 That ye may be the children of your Father which is in heaven: for he maketh his sun to rise on the evil and on the good, and sendeth rain on the just and on the unjust. 46 For if ye love them which love you, what reward have ye? do not even the publicans the same? 47 And if ye salute your brethren only, what do ye more *than others?* do not even the publicans so? 48 Be ye therefore perfect, even as your Father which is in heaven is perfect.

by heaven, for it is the throne of God, 35 or by the earth, for it is his footstool, or by Jerusalem, for it is the city of the great King. 36 And do not swear by your head, for you cannot make one hair white or black. 37 Let what you say be simply 'Yes' or 'No'; anything more than this comes from evil.[*l*]

38 "You have heard that it was said, 'An eye for an eye and a tooth for a tooth.' 39 But I say to you, Do not resist one who is evil. But if any one strikes you on the right cheek, turn to him the other also; 40 and if any one would sue you and take your coat, let him have your cloak as well; 41 and if any one forces you to go one mile, go with him two miles. 42 Give to him who begs from you, and do not refuse him who would borrow from you.

43 "You have heard that it was said, 'You shall love your neighbor and hate your enemy.' 44 But I say to you, Love your enemies and pray for those who persecute you, 45 so that you may be sons of your Father who is in heaven; for he makes his sun rise on the evil and on the good, and sends rain on the just and on the unjust. 46 For if you love those who love you, what reward have you? Do not even the tax collectors do the same? 47 And if you salute only your brethren, what more are you doing than others? Do not even the Gentiles do the same? 48 You, therefore, must be perfect, as your heavenly Father is perfect.

6 Take heed that ye do not your alms before men, to be seen of them: otherwise ye have no reward of your Father which is in heaven. 2 Therefore when thou doest *thine* alms, do not sound a trumpet before thee, as the hypocrites do in the synagogues and in the streets, that they may have glory of men. Verily I say unto you, They have their reward. 3 But when thou doest alms, let not thy left hand know what thy right hand doeth: 4 That thine alms may be in secret: and thy Father which seeth in secret himself shall reward thee openly.

5 And when thou prayest, thou shalt not be as the hypocrites *are:* for they love to pray standing in the synagogues and in the corners of the streets, that they may be seen of men. Verily I say unto you, They have their reward. 6 But thou, when thou prayest, enter into thy closet, and when thou hast shut thy door, pray to thy Father which is in secret; and thy Father which seeth in secret shall reward thee openly. 7 But when ye pray, use not vain repetitions, as the heathen *do:* for they think that they shall be heard for their much speaking. 8 Be not ye therefore like unto them: for your Father knoweth what things ye have need of, before ye ask him. 9 After this manner therefore pray ye: Our Father which art in heaven, Hallowed be thy name. 10 Thy kingdom come. Thy will be done in earth, as *it is* in heaven. 11 Give us this day our daily

6 "Beware of practicing your piety before men in order to be seen by them; for then you will have no reward from your Father who is in heaven.

2 "Thus, when you give alms, sound no trumpet before you, as the hypocrites do in the synagogues and in the streets, that they may be praised by men. Truly, I say to you, they have their reward. 3 But when you give alms, do not let your left hand know what your right hand is doing, 4 so that your alms may be in secret; and your Father who sees in secret will reward you.

5 "And when you pray, you must not be like the hypocrites; for they love to stand and pray in the synagogues and at the street corners, that they may be seen by men. Truly, I say to you, they have their reward. 6 But when you pray, go into your room and shut the door and pray to your Father who is in secret; and your Father who sees in secret will reward you.

7 "And in praying do not heap up empty phrases as the Gentiles do; for they think that they will be heard for their many words. 8 Do not be like them, for your Father knows what you need before you ask him. 9 Pray then like this:

Our Father who art in heaven,
Hallowed be thy name.
10 Thy kingdom come,
Thy will be done,
On earth as it is in heaven.
11 Give us this day our daily bread;[*m*]

[*l*] Or *the evil one.* [*m*] Or *our bread for the morrow.*

PHILLIPS

God's throne; nor by the earth for it is his footstool; nor by Jerusalem for it is the city of the great king. No, and don't swear by your own head, for you cannot make a single hair—white or black! Whatever you have to say let your 'yes' be a plain 'yes' and your 'no' be a plain 'no'—anything more than this has a taint of evil.

"You have heard that it used to be said '*An eye for an eye and a tooth for a tooth,*' but I tell you, don't resist the man who wants to harm you. If a man hits your right cheek, turn the other one to him as well. If a man wants to sue you for your coat, let him have it and your overcoat as well. If anybody forces you to go a mile with him, do more—go two miles with him. Give to the man who asks anything from you, and don't turn away from the man who wants to borrow.

"You have heard that it used to be said '*Thou shalt love thy neighbor and hate thine enemy,*' but I tell you, Love your enemies, and pray for those who persecute you, so that you may be sons of your Heavenly Father. For he makes his sun rise upon evil men as well as good, and he sends his rain upon honest and dishonest men alike.

"For if you love only those who love you, what credit is that to you? Even tax collectors do that! And if you exchange greetings only with your own circle, are you doing anything exceptional? Even the pagans do that much. No, you are to be perfect, like your Heavenly Father.

The new life is not a matter of outward show

6. 1

"Beware of doing your good deeds conspicuously to catch men's eyes or you will miss the reward of your Heavenly Father.

"So, when you do good to other people, don't hire a trumpeter to go in front of you—like those play actors in the synagogues and streets who make sure that men admire them. Believe me, they have had all the reward they are going to get! No, when you give to charity, don't even let your left hand know what your right hand is doing, so that your giving may be secret. Your Father who knows all secrets will reward you.

"And then, when you pray, don't be like the play actors. They love to stand and pray in the synagogues and at street corners so that people may see them at it. Believe me, they have had all the reward they are going to get! But when you pray, go into your own room, shut your door and pray to your Father privately. Your Father who sees all private things will reward you. And when you pray don't rattle off long prayers like the pagans who think they will be heard because they use so many words. Don't be like them. After all, God, who is your Father, knows your needs before you ask him. Pray then like this—

Our Heavenly Father, may your name be honored;
May your kingdom come, and your will be done on earth as it is in Heaven.
Give us this day the bread we need,

N.E.B.

heaven, for it is God's throne, nor by earth, for it is his footstool, nor by Jerusalem, for it is the city of the great King, nor by your own head, because you cannot turn one hair of it white or black. Plain "Yes" or "No" is all you need to say; anything beyond that comes from the devil.

'You have learned that they were told, "An eye for an eye, and a tooth for a tooth." But what I tell you is this: Do not set yourself against the man who wrongs you. If someone slaps you on the right cheek, turn and offer him your left. If a man wants to sue you for your shirt, let him have your coat as well. If a man in authority makes you go one mile, go with him two. Give when you are asked to give; and do not turn your back on a man who wants to borrow.

'You have learned that they were told, "Love your neighbour, hate your enemy." But what I tell you is this: Love your enemies[a] and pray for your persecutors;[b] only so can you be children of your heavenly Father, who makes his sun rise on good and bad alike, and sends the rain on the honest and the dishonest. If you love only those who love you, what reward can you expect? Surely the tax-gatherers do as much as that. And if you greet only your brothers, what is there extraordinary about that? Even the heathen do as much. You must therefore be all goodness, just as your heavenly Father is all good.

6 'Be careful not to make a show of your religion before men; if you do, no reward awaits you in your Father's house in heaven.

'Thus, when you do some act of charity, do not announce it with a flourish of trumpets, as the hypocrites do in synagogue and in the streets to win admiration from men. I tell you this: they have their reward already. No; when you do some act of charity, do not let your left hand know what your right is doing; your good deed must be secret, and your Father who sees what is done in secret will reward you.[c]

'Again, when you pray, do not be like the hypocrites; they love to say their prayers standing up in synagogue and at the street-corners, for everyone to see them. I tell you this: they have their reward already. But when you pray, go into a room by yourself, shut the door, and pray to your Father who is there in the secret place; and your Father who sees what is secret will reward you.[d]

'In your prayers do not go babbling on like the heathen, who imagine that the more they say the more likely they are to be heard. Do not imitate them. Your Father knows what your needs are before you ask him.

'This is how you should pray:

"Our Father in heaven,
Thy name be hallowed;
Thy kingdom come,
Thy will be done,
On earth as in heaven.
Give us today our daily bread.[e]

[a] *Some witnesses insert* bless those who curse you, do good to those who hate you. [b] *Some witnesses insert* and those who treat you spitefully. [c] *Some witnesses add* openly. [d] *Some witnesses add* openly. [e] *Or* our bread for the morrow.

K.J.V.

bread. 12And forgive us our debts, as we forgive our debtors. 13And lead us not into temptation, but deliver us from evil: For thine is the kingdom, and the power, and the glory, for ever. Amen. 14 For if ye forgive men their trespasses, your heavenly Father will also forgive you: 15 But if ye forgive not men their trespasses, neither will your Father forgive your trespasses.

16 Moreover when ye fast, be not, as the hypocrites, of a sad countenance: for they disfigure their faces, that they may appear unto men to fast. Verily I say unto you, They have their reward. 17 But thou, when thou fastest, anoint thine head, and wash thy face; 18 That thou appear not unto men to fast, but unto thy Father which is in secret: and thy Father which seeth in secret shall reward thee openly.

19 Lay not up for yourselves treasures upon earth, where moth and rust doth corrupt, and where thieves break through and steal: 20 But lay up for yourselves treasures in heaven, where neither moth nor rust doth corrupt, and where thieves do not break through nor steal: 21 For where your treasure is, there will your heart be also. 22 The light of the body is the eye: if therefore thine eye be single, thy whole body shall be full of light. 23 But if thine eye be evil, thy whole body shall be full of darkness. If therefore the light that is in thee be darkness, how great *is* that darkness!

24 No man can serve two masters: for either he will hate the one, and love the other; or else he will hold to the one, and despise the other. Ye cannot serve God and mammon. 25 Therefore I say unto you, Take no thought for your life, what ye shall eat, or what ye shall drink; nor yet for your body, what ye shall put on. Is not the life more than meat, and the body than raiment? 26 Behold the fowls of the air: for they sow not, neither do they reap, nor gather into barns; yet your heavenly Father feedeth them. Are ye not much better than they? 27 Which of you by taking thought can add one cubit unto his stature? 28And why take ye thought for raiment? Consider the lilies of the field, how they grow; they toil not, neither do they spin: 29And yet I say unto you, That even Solomon in all his glory was not arrayed like one of these. 30 Wherefore, if God so clothe the grass of the field, which to day is, and to morrow is cast into the oven, *shall he* not much more *clothe* you, O ye of little faith? 31 Therefore take no thought, saying, What shall we eat? or, What shall we drink? or, Wherewithal shall we be clothed? 32 (For after all these things do the Gentiles seek:) for your heavenly Father knoweth that ye have need of all these things. 33 But seek ye first the kingdom of God, and his righteousness; and all these things shall be added unto you. 34 Take therefore no thought for the morrow: for the morrow shall take thought for the things of itself. Sufficient unto the day *is* the evil thereof.

R.S.V.

12 And forgive us our debts
    As we also have forgiven our debtors;
13 And lead us not into temptation,
    But deliver us from evil.[n]

14 For if you forgive men their trespasses, your heavenly Father also will forgive you; 15 but if you do not forgive men their trespasses, neither will your Father forgive your trespasses.

16 "And when you fast, do not look dismal, like the hypocrites, for they disfigure their faces that their fasting may be seen by men. Truly, I say to you, they have their reward. 17 But when you fast, anoint your head and wash your face, 18 that your fasting may not be seen by men but by your Father who is in secret; and your Father who sees in secret will reward you.

19 "Do not lay up for yourselves treasures on earth, where moth and rust[o] consume and where thieves break in and steal, 20 but lay up for yourselves treasures in heaven, where neither moth nor rust[o] consumes and where thieves do not break in and steal. 21 For where your treasure is, there will your heart be also.

22 "The eye is the lamp of the body. So, if your eye is sound, your whole body will be full of light; 23 but if your eye is not sound, your whole body will be full of darkness. If then the light in you is darkness, how great is the darkness!

24 "No one can serve two masters; for either he will hate the one and love the other, or he will be devoted to the one and despise the other. You cannot serve God and mammon.

25 "Therefore I tell you, do not be anxious about your life, what you shall eat or what you shall drink, nor about your body, what you shall put on. Is not life more than food, and the body more than clothing? 26 Look at the birds of the air: they neither sow nor reap nor gather into barns, and yet your heavenly Father feeds them. Are you not of more value than they? 27And which of you by being anxious can add one cubit to his span of life?[p] 28And why are you anxious about clothing? Consider the lilies of the field, how they grow; they neither toil nor spin; 29 yet I tell you, even Solomon in all his glory was not arrayed like one of these. 30 But if God so clothes the grass of the field, which today is alive and tomorrow is thrown into the oven, will he not much more clothe you, O men of little faith? 31 Therefore do not be anxious, saying, 'What shall we eat?' or 'What shall we drink?' or 'What shall we wear?' 32 For the Gentiles seek all these things; and your heavenly Father knows that you need them all. 33 But seek first his kingdom and his righteousness, and all these things shall be yours as well.

34 "Therefore do not be anxious about tomorrow, for tomorrow will be anxious for itself. Let the day's own trouble be sufficient for the day.

[n] Or *the evil one.* Other authorities, some ancient, add, in some form, *For thine is the kingdom and the power and the glory, for ever. Amen.* [o] Or *a worm.* [p] Or *to his stature.*

PHILLIPS

Forgive us what we owe to you, as we have also forgiven those who owe anything to us. Keep us clear of temptation, and save us from evil.

Forgiveness of fellow man is essential
6. 14

"For if you forgive other people their failures, your Heavenly Father will also forgive you. But if you will not forgive other people, neither will your Heavenly Father forgive you your failures.

"Then, when you fast, don't look like those miserable play actors! For they deliberately disfigure their faces so that people may see that they are fasting. Believe me, they have had all their reward. No, when you fast, brush your hair and wash your face so that nobody knows that you are fasting—let it be a secret between you and your Father. And your Father who knows all secrets will reward you.

Put your trust in God alone
6. 19

"Don't pile up treasures on earth, where moth and rust can spoil them and thieves can break in and steal. But keep your treasure in Heaven where there is neither moth nor rust to spoil it and nobody can break in and steal. For wherever your treasure is, you may be certain that your heart will be there too!

"The lamp of the body is the eye. If your eye is sound, your whole body will be full of light. But if your eye is evil, your whole body will be full of darkness. If all the light you have is darkness, it is dark indeed!

"No one can be loyal to two masters. He is bound to hate one and love the other, or support one and despise the other. You cannot serve God and the power of money at the same time. That is why I say to you, don't worry about living—wondering what you are going to eat or drink, or what you are going to wear. Surely life is more important than food, and the body more important than the clothes you wear. Look at the birds in the sky. They never sow nor reap nor store away in barns, and yet your Heavenly Father feeds them. Aren't you much more valuable to him than they are? Can any of you, however much he worries, make himself an inch taller? And why do you worry about clothes? Consider how the wild flowers grow. They neither work nor weave, but I tell you that even Solomon in all his glory was never arrayed like one of these! Now if God so clothes the flowers of the field, which are alive today and burned in the stove tomorrow, is he not much more likely to clothe you, you 'little-faiths'?

"So don't worry and don't keep saying, 'What shall we eat, what shall we drink or what shall we wear?' That is what pagans are always looking for; your Heavenly Father knows that you need them all. Set your heart on his kingdom and his goodness, and all these things will come to you as a matter of course.

"Don't worry at all then about tomorrow. Tomorrow can take care of itself! One day's trouble is enough for one day.

N.E.B.

Forgive us the wrong we have done,
As we have forgiven those who have wronged us.
And do not bring us to the test,
But save us from the evil one." [a]

For if you forgive others the wrongs they have done, your heavenly Father will also forgive you; but if you do not forgive others, then the wrongs you have done will not be forgiven by your Father.

'So too when you fast, do not look gloomy like the hypocrites: they make their faces unsightly so that other people may see that they are fasting. I tell you this: they have their reward already. But when you fast, anoint your head and wash your face, so that men may not see that you are fasting, but only your Father who is in the secret place; and your Father who sees what is secret will give you your reward.

'Do not store up for yourselves treasure on earth, where it grows rusty and moth-eaten, and thieves break in to steal it. Store up treasure in heaven, where there is no moth and no rust to spoil it, no thieves to break in and steal. For where your wealth is, there will your heart be also.

'The lamp of the body is the eye. If your eyes are sound, you will have light for your whole body; if the eyes are bad, your whole body will be in darkness. If then the only light you have is darkness, the darkness is doubly dark.

'No servant can be slave to two masters; for either he will hate the first and love the second, or he will be devoted to the first and think nothing of the second. You cannot serve God and Money.

'Therefore I bid you put away anxious thoughts about food and drink to keep you alive, and clothes to cover your body. Surely life is more than food, the body more than clothes. Look at the birds of the air; they do not sow and reap and store in barns, yet your heavenly Father feeds them. You are worth more than the birds! Is there a man of you who by anxious thought can add a foot to his height[b]? And why be anxious about clothes? Consider how the lilies grow in the fields; they do not work, they do not spin;[c] and yet, I tell you, even Solomon in all his splendour was not attired like one of these. But if that is how God clothes the grass in the fields, which is there today, and tomorrow is thrown on the stove, will he not all the more clothe you? How little faith you have! No, do not ask anxiously, "What are we to eat? What are we to drink? What shall we wear?" All these are things for the heathen to run after, not for you, because your heavenly Father knows that you need them all. Set your mind on God's kingdom and his justice before everything else, and all the rest will come to you as well. So do not be anxious about tomorrow; tomorrow will look after itself. Each day has troubles enough of its own.

[a] Some witnesses add For thine is the kingdom and the power and the glory, for ever. Amen. [b] Or a day to his life. [c] One witness reads Consider the lilies: they neither card nor spin, nor labour.

K.J.V.

7 Judge not, that ye be not judged. 2 For with what judgment ye judge, ye shall be judged: and with what measure ye mete, it shall be measured to you again. 3 And why beholdest thou the mote that is in thy brother's eye, but considerest not the beam that is in thine own eye? 4 Or how wilt thou say to thy brother, Let me pull out the mote out of thine eye; and, behold, a beam *is* in thine own eye? 5 Thou hypocrite, first cast out the beam out of thine own eye; and then shalt thou see clearly to cast out the mote out of thy brother's eye.

6 Give not that which is holy unto the dogs, neither cast ye your pearls before swine, lest they trample them under their feet, and turn again and rend you.

7 Ask, and it shall be given you; seek, and ye shall find; knock, and it shall be opened unto you: 8 For every one that asketh receiveth; and he that seeketh findeth; and to him that knocketh it shall be opened. 9 Or what man is there of you, whom if his son ask bread, will he give him a stone? 10 Or if he ask a fish, will he give him a serpent? 11 If ye then, being evil, know how to give good gifts unto your children, how much more shall your Father which is in heaven give good things to them that ask him? 12 Therefore all things whatsoever ye would that men should do to you, do ye even so to them: for this is the law and the prophets.

13 Enter ye in at the strait gate: for wide *is* the gate, and broad *is* the way, that leadeth to destruction, and many there be which go in thereat: 14 Because strait *is* the gate, and narrow *is* the way, which leadeth unto life, and few there be that find it.

15 Beware of false prophets, which come to you in sheep's clothing, but inwardly they are ravening wolves. 16 Ye shall know them by their fruits. Do men gather grapes of thorns, or figs of thistles? 17 Even so every good tree bringeth forth good fruit; but a corrupt tree bringeth forth evil fruit. 18 A good tree cannot bring forth evil fruit, neither *can* a corrupt tree bring forth good fruit. 19 Every tree that bringeth not forth good fruit is hewn down, and cast into the fire. 20 Wherefore by their fruits ye shall know them.

21 Not every one that saith unto me, Lord, Lord, shall enter into the kingdom of heaven; but he that doeth the will of my Father which is in heaven. 22 Many will say to me in that day, Lord, Lord, have we not prophesied in thy name? and in thy name have cast out devils? and in thy name done many wonderful works? 23 And then will I profess unto them, I never knew you: depart from me, ye that work iniquity.

24 Therefore whosoever heareth these sayings of mine, and doeth them, I will liken him unto

R.S.V.

7 "Judge not, that you be not judged. 2 For with the judgment you pronounce you will be judged, and the measure you give will be the measure you get. 3 Why do you see the speck that is in your brother's eye, but do not notice the log that is in your own eye? 4 Or how can you say to your brother, 'Let me take the speck out of your eye,' when there is the log in your own eye? 5 You hypocrite, first take the log out of your own eye, and then you will see clearly to take the speck out of your brother's eye.

6 "Do not give dogs what is holy; and do not throw your pearls before swine, lest they trample them under foot and turn to attack you.

7 "Ask, and it will be given you; seek, and you will find; knock, and it will be opened to you. 8 For every one who asks receives, and he who seeks finds, and to him who knocks it will be opened. 9 Or what man of you, if his son asks him for bread, will give him a stone? 10 Or if he asks for a fish, will give him a serpent? 11 If you then, who are evil, know how to give good gifts to your children, how much more will your Father who is in heaven give good things to those who ask him! 12 So whatever you wish that men would do to you, do so to them; for this is the law and the prophets.

13 "Enter by the narrow gate; for the gate is wide and the way is easy,*q* that leads to destruction, and those who enter by it are many. 14 For the gate is narrow and the way is hard, that leads to life, and those who find it are few.

15 "Beware of false prophets, who come to you in sheep's clothing but inwardly are ravenous wolves. 16 You will know them by their fruits. Are grapes gathered from thorns, or figs from thistles? 17 So, every sound tree bears good fruit, but the bad tree bears evil fruit. 18 A sound tree cannot bear evil fruit, nor can a bad tree bear good fruit. 19 Every tree that does not bear good fruit is cut down and thrown into the fire. 20 Thus you will know them by their fruits.

21 "Not every one who says to me, 'Lord, Lord,' shall enter the kingdom of heaven, but he who does the will of my Father who is in heaven. 22 On that day many will say to me, 'Lord, Lord, did we not prophesy in your name, and cast out demons in your name, and do many mighty works in your name?' 23 And then will I declare to them, 'I never knew you; depart from me, you evildoers.'

24 "Every one then who hears these words of mine and does them will be like a wise man who

[q] Other ancient authorities read *for the way is wide and easy.*

| PHILLIPS | N.E.B. |

The common sense behind   **7. 1**
right behavior

"Don't criticize people, and you will not be criticized. For you will be judged by the way you criticize others, and the measure you give will be the measure you receive.

"Why do you look at the speck of sawdust in your brother's eye and fail to notice the plank in your own? How can you say to your brother, 'Let me get the speck out of your eye,' when there is a plank in your own? You fraud! Take the plank out of your own eye first, and then you can see clearly enough to remove your brother's speck of dust.

"You must not give holy things to dogs, nor must you throw your pearls before pigs—or they may trample them underfoot and turn and attack you.

"Ask and it will be given to you. Search and you will find. Knock and the door will be opened for you. The one who asks will always receive; the one who is searching will always find, and the door is opened to the man who knocks.

"If any of you were asked by his son for bread would you be likely to give him a stone, or if he asks for a fish would you give him a snake? If you then, for all your evil, quite naturally give good things to your children, how much more likely is it that your Heavenly Father will give good things to those who ask him?

"Treat other people exactly as you would like to be treated by them—this is the essence of all true religion.

"Go in by the narrow gate. For the wide gate has a broad road which leads to disaster, and there are many people going that way. The narrow gate and the hard road lead out into life, and only a few are finding it.

Living, not professing, is   **7. 15**
what matters

"Be on your guard against false religious teachers, who come to you dressed up as sheep but are really greedy wolves. You can tell them by their fruit. Do you pick a bunch of grapes from a thornbush or figs from a clump of thistles? Every good tree produces good fruit, but a bad tree produces bad fruit. A good tree is incapable of producing bad fruit, and a bad tree cannot produce good fruit. The tree that fails to produce good fruit is cut down and burned. So you may know men by their fruit.

"It is not everyone who keeps saying to me 'Lord, Lord' who will enter the kingdom of Heaven, but the man who actually does my Heavenly Father's will.

"In 'that day' many will say to me, 'Lord, Lord, didn't we preach in your name, didn't we cast out devils in your name, and do many great things in your name?' Then I shall tell them plainly: 'I have never known you. Go away from me; you have worked on the side of evil!'

To follow Christ's teaching means   **7. 24**
the only real security

"Everyone then who hears these words of mine and puts them into practice is like a

---

7 'Pass no judgement, and you will not be judged. For as you judge others, so you will yourselves be judged, and whatever measure you deal out to others will be dealt back to you. Why do you look at the speck of sawdust in your brother's eye, with never a thought for the great plank in your own? Or how can you say to your brother, "Let me take the speck out of your eye", when all the time there is that plank in your own? You hypocrite! First take the plank out of your own eye, and then you will see clearly to take the speck out of your brother's.

'Do not give dogs what is holy; do not feed your pearls to pigs: they will only trample on them, and turn and tear you to pieces.

'Ask, and you will receive; seek, and you will find; knock, and the door will be opened. For everyone who asks receives, he who seeks finds, and to him who knocks, the door will be opened.

'Is there a man among you who will offer his son a stone when he asks for bread, or a snake when he asks for fish? If you, then, bad as you are, know how to give your children what is good for them, how much more will your heavenly Father give good things to those who ask him!

'Always treat others as you would like them to treat you: that is the Law and the prophets.

'Enter by the narrow gate. The gate is wide that leads to perdition, there is plenty of room on the road,[a] and many go that way; but the gate that leads to life is small and the road is narrow,[b] and those who find it are few.

'Beware of false prophets, men who come to you dressed up as sheep while underneath they are savage wolves. You will recognize them by the fruits they bear. Can grapes be picked from briars, or figs from thistles? In the same way, a good tree always yields good fruit, and a poor tree bad fruit. A good tree cannot bear bad fruit, or a poor tree good fruit. And when a tree does not yield good fruit it is cut down and burnt. That is why I say you will recognize them by their fruits.

'Not everyone who calls me "Lord, Lord" will enter the kingdom of Heaven, but only those who do the will of my heavenly Father. When that day comes, many will say to me, "Lord, Lord, did we not prophesy in your name, cast out devils in your name, and in your name perform many miracles?" Then I will tell them to their face, "I never knew you: out of my sight, you and your wicked ways!"

'What then of the man who hears these words of mine and acts upon them? He is like a man

[a] *Some witnesses read* The road that leads to perdition is wide with plenty of room. [b] *Some witnesses read* but the road that leads to life is small and narrow.

19

K.J.V.

a wise man, which built his house upon a rock:
25And the rain descended, and the floods came,
and the winds blew, and beat upon that house;
and it fell not: for it was founded upon a rock.
26And every one that heareth these sayings of
mine, and doeth them not, shall be likened unto
a foolish man, which built his house upon the
sand: 27And the rain descended, and the floods
came, and the winds blew, and beat upon that
house; and it fell: and great was the fall of it.
28And it came to pass, when Jesus had ended
these sayings, the people were astonished at his
doctrine: 29 For he taught them as *one* having
authority, and not as the scribes.

8 When he was come down from the mountain, great multitudes followed him. 2And,
behold, there came a leper and worshipped him,
saying, Lord, if thou wilt, thou canst make me
clean. 3And Jesus put forth *his* hand, and
touched him, saying, I will; be thou clean. And
immediately his leprosy was cleansed. 4And Jesus
saith unto him, See thou tell no man; but go
thy way, shew thyself to the priest, and offer the
gift that Moses commanded, for a testimony
unto them.
  5 And when Jesus was entered into Capernaum, there came unto him a centurion, beseeching him, 6And saying, Lord, my servant
lieth at home sick of the palsy, grievously tormented. 7And Jesus saith unto him, I will come
and heal him. 8 The centurion answered and
said, Lord, I am not worthy that thou shouldest
come under my roof: but speak the word only,
and my servant shall be healed. 9 For I am a
man under authority, having soldiers under me:
and I say to this *man*, Go, and he goeth; and to
another, Come, and he cometh; and to my servant, Do this, and he doeth *it*. 10 When Jesus
heard *it*, he marvelled, and said to them that followed, Verily I say unto you, I have not found
so great faith, no, not in Israel. 11And I say
unto you, That many shall come from the east
and west, and shall sit down with Abraham, and
Isaac, and Jacob, in the kingdom of heaven:
12 But the children of the kingdom shall be cast
out into outer darkness: there shall be weeping
and gnashing of teeth. 13And Jesus said unto
the centurion, Go thy way; and as thou hast
believed, *so* be it done unto thee. And his servant was healed in the selfsame hour.
  14 And when Jesus was come into Peter's
house, he saw his wife's mother laid, and sick
of a fever. 15And he touched her hand, and the
fever left her: and she arose, and ministered
unto them.
  16 When the even was come, they brought
unto him many that were possessed with devils:
and he cast out the spirits with *his* word, and
healed all that were sick: 17 That it might be
fulfilled which was spoken by Esaias the prophet,
saying, Himself took our infirmities, and bare
our sicknesses.

R.S.V.

built his house upon the rock; 25 and the rain
fell, and the floods came, and the winds blew and
beat upon that house, but it did not fall, because
it had been founded on the rock. 26And every
one who hears these words of mine and does
not do them will be like a foolish man who
built his house upon the sand; 27 and the rain
fell, and the floods came, and the winds blew
and beat against that house, and it fell; and great
was the fall of it."
  28 And when Jesus finished these sayings, the
crowds were astonished at his teaching, 29 for he
taught them as one who had authority, and not
as their scribes.

8 When he came down from the mountain,
great crowds followed him; 2 and behold, a
leper came to him and knelt before him, saying,
"Lord, if you will, you can make me clean."
3And he stretched out his hand and touched him,
saying, "I will; be clean." And immediately his
leprosy was cleansed. 4And Jesus said to him,
"See that you say nothing to any one; but go,
show yourself to the priest, and offer the gift
that Moses commanded, for a proof to the
people." *r*
  5 As he entered Capernaum, a centurion
came forward to him, beseeching him 6 and saying, "Lord, my servant is lying paralyzed at
home, in terrible distress." 7And he said to him,
"I will come and heal him." 8 But the centurion
answered him, "Lord, I am not worthy to have
you come under my roof; but only say the word,
and my servant will be healed. 9 For I am a man
under authority, with soldiers under me; and I
say to one, 'Go,' and he goes, and to another,
'Come,' and he comes, and to my slave, 'Do
this,' and he does it." 10 When Jesus heard him,
he marveled, and said to those who followed
him, "Truly, I say to you, not even*s* in Israel
have I found such faith. 11 I tell you, many will
come from east and west and sit at table with
Abraham, Isaac, and Jacob in the kingdom of
heaven, 12 while the sons of the kingdom will be
thrown into the outer darkness; there men will
weep and gnash their teeth." 13And to the centurion Jesus said, "Go; be it done for you as
you have believed." And the servant was healed
at that very moment.
  14 And when Jesus entered Peter's house, he
saw his mother-in-law lying sick with a fever;
15 he touched her hand, and the fever left her,
and she rose and served him. 16 That evening
they brought to him many who were possessed
with demons; and he cast out the spirits with a
word, and healed all who were sick. 17 This was
to fulfil what was spoken by the prophet Isaiah,
"He took our infirmities and bore our diseases."

[r] Greek *to them.* [s] Other ancient authorities read
with no one.

20

PHILLIPS

sensible man who builds his house on the rock. Down came the rain and up came the floods, while the winds blew and roared upon that house—and it did not fall because its foundations were on the rock.

"And everyone who hears these words of mine and does not follow them can be compared with a foolish man who built his house on the sand. Down came the rain and up came the floods, while the winds blew and battered that house till it collapsed, and fell with a great crash."

When Jesus had finished these words the crowd were astonished at the power behind his teaching. For his words had the ring of authority, quite unlike those of their scribes.

Jesus cures a leper and heals many other people   8. 1

Large crowds followed him when he came down from the hillside. There was a leper who came and kneeled in front of him. "Sir," he said, "if you want to, you can make me clean." Jesus stretched out his hand and placed it on the leper, saying: "Of course I want to. Be clean!" And at once the leper was clear of the leprosy.

"Mind you say nothing to anybody," Jesus told him. "Go straight off and show yourself to the priest and make the offering for your recovery that Moses prescribed, as evidence to the authorities."

Then as he was coming into Capernaum a centurion approached. "Sir," he implored him, "my servant is in bed at home paralyzed and in dreadful pain."

"I will come and heal him," said Jesus to him.

"Sir," replied the centurion, "I'm not important enough for you to come under my roof. Just give the order, please, and my servant will recover. I'm a man under authority myself, and I have soldiers under me. I can say to one man 'Go' and I know he'll go, or I can say 'Come here' to another and I know he'll come—or I can say to my slave 'Do this' and he'll always do it."

When Jesus heard this, he was astonished. "Believe me," he said to those who were following him, "I have never found faith like this, even in Israel! I tell you that many people will come from east and west and sit at my table with Abraham, Isaac and Jacob in the kingdom of Heaven. But those who should have belonged to the kingdom will be banished to the darkness outside, where there will be tears and bitter regret."

Then he said to the centurion, "Go home now, and everything will happen as you have believed it will."

And his servant was healed at that actual moment.

Then, on coming into Peter's house Jesus saw that Peter's mother-in-law had been put to bed with a high fever. He touched her hand and the fever left her. And then she got up and began to see to their needs.

When evening came they brought to him many who were possessed by evil spirits, which he expelled with a word. Indeed, he healed all who were ill. Thus was fulfilled Isaiah's prophecy—

Himself took our infirmities and bare our diseases.

N.E.B.

who had the sense to build his house on rock. The rain came down, the floods rose, the wind blew, and beat upon that house; but it did not fall, because its foundations were on rock. But what of the man who hears these words of mine and does not act upon them? He is like a man who was foolish enough to build his house on sand. The rain came down, the floods rose, the wind blew, and beat upon that house; down it fell with a great crash.'

When Jesus had finished this discourse the people were astounded at his teaching; unlike their own teachers he taught with a note of authority.

Teaching and Healing

8 After he had come down from the hill he was followed by a great crowd. And now a leper approached him, bowed low, and said, 'Sir, if only you will, you can cleanse me.' Jesus stretched out his hand, touched him, and said, 'Indeed I will; be clean again.' And his leprosy was cured immediately. Then Jesus said to him, 'Be sure you tell nobody; but go and show yourself to the priest, and make the offering laid down by Moses for your cleansing; that will certify the cure.'

When he had entered Capernaum a centurion came up to ask his help. 'Sir,' he said, 'a boy of mine lies at home paralysed and racked with pain.' Jesus said, 'I will come and cure him.'[a] But the centurion replied, 'Sir, who am I to have you under my roof? You need only say the word and the boy will be cured. I know, for I am myself under orders, with soldiers under me. I say to one, "Go", and he goes; to another, "Come here", and he comes; and to my servant, "Do this", and he does it.' Jesus heard him with astonishment, and said to the people who were following him, 'I tell you this: nowhere, even in Israel, have I found such faith.

'Many, I tell you, will come from east and west to feast with Abraham, Isaac, and Jacob in the kingdom of Heaven. But those who were born to the kingdom will be driven out into the dark, the place of wailing and grinding of teeth.'

Then Jesus said to the centurion, 'Go home now; because of your faith, so let it be.' At that moment the boy recovered.

Jesus then went to Peter's house and found Peter's mother-in-law in bed with fever. So he took her by the hand; the fever left her, and she got up and waited on him.

When evening fell, they brought to him many who were possessed by devils; and he drove the spirits out with a word and healed all who were ill, to make good the prophecy of Isaiah: 'He took away our illnesses and lifted our diseases from us.'[b]

[a] *Or* Am I to come and cure him? [b] *Or* and bore the burden of our diseases.

21

K.J.V.

18 Now when Jesus saw great multitudes about him, he gave commandment to depart unto the other side. 19And a certain scribe came, and said unto him, Master, I will follow thee whithersoever thou goest. 20And Jesus saith unto him, The foxes have holes, and the birds of the air *have* nests; but the Son of man hath not where to lay *his* head. 21And another of his disciples said unto him, Lord, suffer me first to go and bury my father. 22 But Jesus said unto him, Follow me; and let the dead bury their dead.

23 And when he was entered into a ship, his disciples followed him. 24And, behold, there arose a great tempest in the sea, insomuch that the ship was covered with the waves: but he was asleep. 25And his disciples came to *him*, and awoke him, saying, Lord, save us: we perish. 26And he saith unto them, Why are ye fearful, O ye of little faith? Then he arose, and rebuked the winds and the sea; and there was a great calm. 27 But the men marvelled, saying, What manner of man is this, that even the winds and the sea obey him!

28 And when he was come to the other side into the country of the Gergesenes, there met him two possessed with devils, coming out of the tombs, exceeding fierce, so that no man might pass by that way. 29And behold, they cried out, saying, What have we to do with thee, Jesus, thou Son of God? art thou come hither to torment us before the time? 30And there was a good way off from them a herd of many swine feeding. 31 So the devils besought him, saying, If thou cast us out, suffer us to go away into the herd of swine. 32And he said unto them, Go. And when they were come out, they went into the herd of swine: and, behold, the whole herd of swine ran violently down a steep place into the sea, and perished in the waters. 33And they that kept them fled, and went their ways into the city, and told every thing, and what was befallen to the possessed of the devils. 34And, behold, the whole city came out to meet Jesus: and when they saw him, they besought *him* that he would depart out of their coasts.

R.S.V.

18 Now when Jesus saw great crowds around him, he gave orders to go over to the other side. 19And a scribe came up and said to him, "Teacher, I will follow you wherever you go." 20And Jesus said to him, "Foxes have holes, and birds of the air have nests; but the Son of man has nowhere to lay his head." 21Another of the disciples said to him, "Lord, let me first go and bury my father." 22 But Jesus said to him, "Follow me, and leave the dead to bury their own dead."

23 And when he got into the boat, his disciples followed him. 24And behold, there arose a great storm on the sea, so that the boat was being swamped by the waves; but he was asleep. 25And they went and woke him, saying, "Save, Lord; we are perishing." 26And he said to them, "Why are you afraid, O men of little faith?" Then he rose and rebuked the winds and the sea; and there was a great calm. 27And the men marveled, saying, "What sort of man is this, that even winds and sea obey him?"

28 And when he came to the other side, to the country of the Gadarenes,[t] two demoniacs met him, coming out of the tombs, so fierce that no one could pass that way. 29And behold, they cried out, "What have you to do with us, O Son of God? Have you come here to torment us before the time?" 30 Now a herd of many swine was feeding at some distance from them. 31And the demons begged him, "If you cast us out, send us away into the herd of swine." 32And he said to them, "Go." So they came out and went into the swine; and behold, the whole herd rushed down the steep bank into the sea, and perished in the waters. 33 The herdsmen fled, and going into the city they told everything, and what had happened to the demoniacs. 34And behold, all the city came out to meet Jesus; and when they saw him, they begged him to leave their neighborhood.

9 And he entered into a ship, and passed over, and came into his own city. 2And, behold, they brought to him a man sick of the palsy, lying on a bed: and Jesus seeing their faith said unto the sick of the palsy; Son, be of good cheer; thy sins be forgiven thee. 3And, behold, certain of the scribes said within themselves, This *man* blasphemeth. 4And Jesus knowing their thoughts said, Wherefore think ye evil in your hearts? 5 For whether is easier, to say, *Thy* sins be forgiven thee; or to say, Arise, and walk?

9 And getting into a boat he crossed over and came to his own city. 2And behold, they brought to him a paralytic, lying on his bed; and when Jesus saw their faith he said to the paralytic, "Take heart, my son; your sins are forgiven." 3And behold, some of the scribes said to themselves, "This man is blaspheming." 4 But Jesus, knowing[u] their thoughts, said, "Why do you think evil in your hearts? 5 For which is easier, to say, 'Your sins are forgiven,' or to say,

[t] Other ancient authorities read *Gergesenes;* some, *Gerasenes.* [u] Other ancient authorities read *seeing.*

PHILLIPS

When Jesus had seen the great crowds around him he gave orders for departure to the other side of the lake. But before they started, one of the scribes came up to Jesus and said to him, "Master, I will follow you wherever you go."

"Foxes have earths, birds in the sky have nests, but the Son of Man has nowhere that he can call his own," replied Jesus.

Another of his disciples said, "Lord, let me first go and bury my father."

But Jesus said to him, "Follow me, and leave the dead to bury their own dead."

Jesus shows his mastery over the forces of nature   8. 23

Then he went aboard the boat, and his disciples followed him. Before long a terrific storm sprang up and the boat was awash with the waves. Jesus was sleeping soundly, and the disciples went forward and woke him up.

"Lord, save us!" they cried. "We are drowning!"

"What are you so frightened about, you little-faiths?" he replied.

Then he got to his feet and rebuked the wind and the waters and there was a great calm. The men were filled with astonishment, and kept saying, "Whatever sort of man is this—why, even the wind and the waves do what he tells them!"

When he arrived on the other side (which is the Gadarenes' country) he was met by two devil-possessed men who came out from among the tombs. They were so violent that nobody dared to use that road.

"What have you got to do with us, Jesus, you Son of God?" they screamed at him. "Have you come to torture us before the proper time?"

It happened that in the distance there was a large herd of pigs feeding. So the devils implored him, "If you throw us out, send us into the herd of pigs!"

"Then go!" said Jesus to them.

And the devils came out of the two men and went into the pigs. Then quite suddenly the whole herd rushed madly down a steep cliff into the lake and were drowned.

The swineherds took to their heels, and ran to the town. There they poured out the whole story, not forgetting what had happened to the two men who had been devil-possessed. Whereupon the whole town came out to meet Jesus, and as soon as they saw him implored him to leave their territory.

Jesus heals in his own town   9. 1

So Jesus re-embarked on the boat, crossed the lake, and came to his own town. Immediately some people arrived bringing him a paralytic lying flat on his bed. When Jesus saw the faith of those who brought him, he said to the paralytic: "Cheer up, my son! Your sins are forgiven."

At once some of the scribes thought to themselves, "This man is blaspheming." But Jesus realized what they were thinking, and said to them, "Why must you have such evil thoughts in your minds? Do you think it is easier to say to this man, 'Your sins are forgiven' or 'Get up and walk'? But to make it quite plain that the

N.E.B.

At the sight of the crowds surrounding him Jesus gave word to cross to the other shore. A doctor of the law came up, and said, 'Master, I will follow you wherever you go.' Jesus replied, 'Foxes have their holes, the birds their roosts; but the Son of Man has nowhere to lay his head.' Another man, one of his disciples, said to him, 'Lord, let me go and bury my father first.' Jesus replied, 'Follow me, and leave the dead to bury their dead.'

Jesus then got into the boat, and his disciples followed. All at once a great storm arose on the lake, till the waves were breaking right over the boat; but he went on sleeping. So they came and woke him up, crying: 'Save us, Lord; we are sinking!' 'Why are you such cowards?' he said; 'how little faith you have!' Then he stood up and rebuked the wind and the sea, and there was a dead calm. The men were astonished at what had happened, and exclaimed, 'What sort of man is this, that even the wind and the sea obey him?'

When he reached the other side, in the country of the Gadarenes, he was met by two men who came out from the tombs; they were possessed by devils, and so violent that no one dared pass that way. 'You son of God,' they shouted, 'what do you want with us? Have you come here to torment us before our time?' In the distance a large herd of pigs was feeding; and the devils begged him: 'If you drive us out, send us into that herd of pigs.' 'Begone', he said. Then they came out and went into the pigs; the whole herd rushed over the edge into the lake, and perished in the water.

The men in charge of them took to their heels, and made for the town, where they told the whole story, and what had happened to the madmen. Thereupon the whole town came out to meet Jesus; and when they saw him they begged him to leave the district and go.

9 So he got into the boat and crossed over, and came to his own town.

And now some men brought him a paralytic lying on a bed. Seeing their faith Jesus said to the man, 'Take heart, my son; your sins are forgiven.' At this some of the lawyers said to themselves, 'This is blasphemous talk.' Jesus read their thoughts, and said, 'Why do you harbour these evil thoughts? Is it easier to say, "Your sins are forgiven", or to say, "Stand up and

K.J.V.

6 But that ye may know that the Son of man hath power on earth to forgive sins, (then saith he to the sick of the palsy,) Arise, take up thy bed, and go unto thine house. 7 And he arose, and departed to his house. 8 But when the multitudes saw *it,* they marvelled, and glorified God, which had given such power unto men.

9 And as Jesus passed forth from thence, he saw a man, named Matthew, sitting at the receipt of custom: and he saith unto him, Follow me. And he arose, and followed him.

10 And it came to pass, as Jesus sat at meat in the house, behold, many publicans and sinners came and sat down with him and his disciples. 11 And when the Pharisees saw *it,* they said unto his disciples, Why eateth your master with publicans and sinners? 12 But when Jesus heard *that,* he said unto them, They that be whole need not a physician, but they that are sick. 13 But go ye and learn what *that* meaneth, I will have mercy, and not sacrifice: for I am not come to call the righteous, but sinners to repentance.

14 Then came to him the disciples of John, saying, Why do we and the Pharisees fast oft, but thy disciples fast not? 15 And Jesus said unto them, Can the children of the bridechamber mourn, as long as the bridegroom is with them? but the days will come, when the bridegroom shall be taken from them, and then shall they fast. 16 No man putteth a piece of new cloth unto an old garment; for that which is put in to fill it up taketh from the garment, and the rent is made worse. 17 Neither do men put new wine into old bottles: else the bottles break, and the wine runneth out, and the bottles perish: but they put new wine into new bottles, and both are preserved.

18 While he spake these things unto them, behold, there came a certain ruler, and worshipped him, saying, My daughter is even now dead: but come and lay thy hand upon her, and she shall live. 19 And Jesus arose, and followed him, and *so did* his disciples.

20 And, behold, a woman, which was diseased with an issue of blood twelve years, came behind *him,* and touched the hem of his garment: 21 For she said within herself, If I may but touch his garment, I shall be whole. 22 But Jesus turned

R.S.V.

'Rise and walk'? 6 But that you may know that the Son of man has authority on earth to forgive sins"—he then said to the paralytic—"Rise, take up your bed and go home." 7 And he rose and went home. 8 When the crowds saw it, they were afraid, and they glorified God, who had given such authority to men.

9 As Jesus passed on from there, he saw a man called Matthew sitting at the tax office; and he said to him, "Follow me." And he rose and followed him.

10 And as he sat at table[v] in the house, behold, many tax collectors and sinners came and sat down with Jesus and his disciples. 11 And when the Pharisees saw this, they said to his disciples, "Why does your teacher eat with tax collectors and sinners?" 12 But when he heard it, he said, "Those who are well have no need of a physician, but those who are sick. 13 Go and learn what this means, 'I desire mercy, and not sacrifice.' For I came not to call the righteous, but sinners."

14 Then the disciples of John came to him, saying, "Why do we and the Pharisees fast,[w] but your disciples do not fast?" 15 And Jesus said to them, "Can the wedding guests mourn as long as the bridegroom is with them? The days will come, when the bridegroom is taken away from them, and then they will fast. 16 And no one puts a piece of unshrunk cloth on an old garment, for the patch tears away from the garment, and a worse tear is made. 17 Neither is new wine put into old wineskins; if it is, the skins burst, and the wine is spilled, and the skins are destroyed; but new wine is put into fresh wineskins, and so both are preserved."

18 While he was thus speaking to them, behold, a ruler came in and knelt before him, saying, "My daughter has just died; but come and lay your hand on her, and she will live." 19 And Jesus rose and followed him, with his disciples. 20 And behold, a woman who had suffered from a hemorrhage for twelve years came up behind him and touched the fringe of his garment; 21 for she said to herself, "If I only touch his garment, I shall be made well." 22 Jesus turned, and seeing

[v] Greek *reclined.* [w] Other ancient authorities add *much* or *often.*

24

PHILLIPS

Son of Man has full authority on earth to forgive sins"—and here he spoke to the paralytic—"Get up, pick up your bed and go home." And the man sprang to his feet and went home. When the crowds saw what had happened they were filled with awe, and praised God for giving such power to men.

Jesus calls a "sinner" to be his disciple   9. 9

Jesus left there, and as he passed on he saw a man called Matthew sitting at his desk in the tax collector's office.

"Follow me!" he said to him—and the man got to his feet and followed him.

Later, as Jesus was in the house sitting at the dinner table, a good many tax collectors and other disreputable people came on the scene and joined him and his disciples. The Pharisees noticed this, and said to the disciples, "Why does your master have his meals with tax collectors and sinners?" But Jesus heard this and replied:

"It is not the fit and flourishing who need the doctor, but those who are ill! Suppose you go away and learn what this means: 'I desire mercy and not sacrifice.' In any case I did not come to invite the 'righteous' but the 'sinners.' "

He explains the joy and strength of the new order   9. 14

Then John's disciples approached him with the question, "Why is it that we and the Pharisees observe the fasts, but your disciples do nothing of the kind?"

"Can you expect wedding guests to mourn while they have the bridegroom with them?" replied Jesus. "The day will come when the bridegroom will be taken away from them—they will certainly fast then!

"Nobody sews a patch of unshrunken cloth onto an old coat, for the patch will pull away from the coat and the hole will be worse than ever. Nor do people put new wine into old wineskins—otherwise the skins burst, the wine is spilled and the skins are ruined. But they put new wine into new skins and both are preserved."

Jesus heals a young girl, and several others in need   9. 18

While he was saying these things to them an official came up to him and, bowing low before him, said:

"My daughter has just this moment died. Please come and lay your hand on her and she will come back to life!"

At this, Jesus got to his feet and followed him, accompanied by his disciples. And on the way a woman who had had a hemorrhage for twelve years approached him from behind and touched the edge of his cloak.

"If I can only touch his cloak," she kept saying to herself, "I shall be all right."

N.E.B.

walk"? But to convince you that the Son of Man has the right on earth to forgive sins'—he now addressed the paralytic—'stand up, take your bed, and go home.' Thereupon the man got up, and went off home. The people were filled with awe at the sight, and praised God for granting such authority to men.

As he passed on from there Jesus saw a man named Matthew at his seat in the custom-house; and he said to him, 'Follow me.' And Matthew rose and followed him.

When Jesus was at table in the house, many bad characters—tax-gatherers and others—were seated with him and his disciples. The Pharisees noticed this, and said to his disciples, 'Why is it that your master eats with tax-gatherers and sinners?' Jesus heard them and said, 'It is not the healthy that need a doctor, but the sick. Go and learn what that text means, "I require mercy, not sacrifice." I did not come to invite virtuous people, but sinners.'

Then John's disciples came to him with the question: 'Why do we and the Pharisees fast, but your disciples do not?' Jesus replied, 'Can you expect the bridegroom's friends to go mourning while the bridegroom is with them? The time will come when the bridegroom will be taken away from them; that will be the time for them to fast.

'No one sews a patch of unshrunk cloth on to an old coat; for then the patch tears away from the coat, and leaves a bigger hole. No more do you put new wine into old wine-skins; if you do, the skins burst, and then the wine runs out and the skins are spoilt. No, you put new wine into fresh skins; then both are preserved.'

Even as he spoke, there came a president of the synagogue, who bowed low before him and said, 'My daughter has just died; but come and lay your hand on her, and she will live.' Jesus rose and went with him, and so did his disciples. Then a woman who had suffered from haemorrhages for twelve years came up from behind, and touched the edge of his cloak; for she said to herself, 'If I can only touch his cloak, I shall be cured.' But Jesus turned and saw her, and

K.J.V.

him about, and when he saw her, he said, Daughter, be of good comfort; thy faith hath made thee whole. And the woman was made whole from that hour. 23 And when Jesus came into the ruler's house, and saw the minstrels and the people making a noise, 24 He said unto them, Give place: for the maid is not dead, but sleepeth. And they laughed him to scorn. 25 But when the people were put forth, he went in, and took her by the hand, and the maid arose. 26 And the fame hereof went abroad into all that land.

27 And when Jesus departed thence, two blind men followed him, crying, and saying, *Thou Son of David, have mercy on us.* 28 And when he was come into the house, the blind men came to him: and Jesus saith unto them, Believe ye that I am able to do this? They said unto him, Yea, Lord. 29 Then touched he their eyes, saying, According to your faith be it unto you. 30 And their eyes were opened; and Jesus straitly charged them, saying, See *that* no man know *it.* 31 But they, when they were departed, spread abroad his fame in all that country.

32 As they went out, behold, they brought to him a dumb man possessed with a devil. 33 And when the devil was cast out, the dumb spake: and the multitudes marvelled, saying, It was never so seen in Israel. 34 But the Pharisees said, He casteth out devils through the prince of the devils. 35 And Jesus went about all the cities and villages, teaching in their synagogues, and preaching the gospel of the kingdom, and healing every sickness and every disease among the people.

36 But when he saw the multitudes, he was moved with compassion on them, because they fainted, and were scattered abroad, as sheep having no shepherd. 37 Then saith he unto his disciples, The harvest truly *is* plenteous, but the labourers *are* few; 38 Pray ye therefore the Lord of the harvest, that he will send forth labourers into his harvest.

R.S.V.

her he said, "Take heart, daughter; your faith has made you well." And instantly the woman was made well. 23 And when Jesus came to the ruler's house, and saw the flute players, and the crowd making a tumult, 24 he said, "Depart; for the girl is not dead but sleeping." And they laughed at him. 25 But when the crowd had been put outside, he went in and took her by the hand, and the girl arose. 26 And the report of this went through all that district.

27 And as Jesus passed on from there, two blind men followed him, crying aloud, "Have mercy on us, Son of David." 28 When he entered the house, the blind men came to him; and Jesus said to them, "Do you believe that I am able to do this?" They said to him, "Yes, Lord." 29 Then he touched their eyes, saying, "According to your faith be it done to you." 30 And their eyes were opened. And Jesus sternly charged them, "See that no one knows it." 31 But they went away and spread his fame through all that district.

32 As they were going away, behold, a dumb demoniac was brought to him. 33 And when the demon had been cast out, the dumb man spoke; and the crowds marveled, saying, "Never was anything like this seen in Israel." 34 But the Pharisees said, "He casts out demons by the prince of demons."

35 And Jesus went about all the cities and villages, teaching in their synagogues and preaching the gospel of the kingdom, and healing every disease and every infirmity. 36 When he saw the crowds, he had compassion for them, because they were harassed and helpless, like sheep without a shepherd. 37 Then he said to his disciples, "The harvest is plentiful, but the laborers are few; 38 pray therefore the Lord of the harvest to send out laborers into his harvest."

10 And when he had called unto *him* his twelve disciples, he gave them power *against* unclean spirits, to cast them out, and to heal all manner of sickness and all manner of disease. 2 Now the names of the twelve apostles are these; The first, Simon, who is called Peter, and Andrew his brother; James *the son* of Zebedee, and John his brother; 3 Philip, and Bartholomew; Thomas, and Matthew the publican; James *the son* of Alpheus, and Lebbeus, whose surname was Thaddeus; 4 Simon the Canaanite, and Judas Iscariot, who also betrayed him. 5 These twelve Jesus sent forth, and commanded them, saying, Go not into the way of the Gentiles, and into *any* city of the Samaritans enter ye not: 6 But go rather to the lost sheep of the

10 And he called to him his twelve disciples and gave them authority over unclean spirits, to cast them out, and to heal every disease and every infirmity. 2 The names of the twelve apostles are these: first, Simon, who is called Peter, and Andrew his brother; James the son of Zebedee, and John his brother; 3 Philip and Bartholomew; Thomas and Matthew the tax collector; James the son of Alphaeus, and Thaddaeus;[x] 4 Simon the Cananaean, and Judas Iscariot, who betrayed him.

5 These twelve Jesus sent out, charging them, "Go nowhere among the Gentiles, and enter no town of the Samaritans, 6 but go rather to the

[x] Other ancient authorities read *Lebbaeus* or *Lebbaeus called Thaddaeus.*

PHILLIPS

N.E.B.

But Jesus turned right round and saw her. "Cheer up, my daughter," he said, "your faith has made you well!" And the woman was completely cured from that moment.

Then when Jesus came into the official's house and noticed the flute players and the noisy crowd he said, "You must all go outside; the little girl is not dead, she is fast asleep." This was met with scornful laughter. But when Jesus had forced the crowd to leave, he came right into the room, took hold of her hand, and the girl got up. And this became the talk of the whole district.

As Jesus passed on his way two blind men followed him with the cry, "Have pity on us, Son of David!" And when he had gone inside the house these two came up to him. "Do you believe I can do it?" he said to them. "Yes, Lord," they replied. Then he touched their eyes, saying, "You have believed and you will not be disappointed." Then their sight returned, but Jesus sternly warned them, "Don't let anyone know about this." Yet they went outside and spread the story throughout the whole district.

Later, when Jesus and his party were coming out, they brought to him a dumb man who was possessed by a devil. As soon as the devil had been ejected, the dumb man began to talk. The crowds were simply amazed, and said, "Nothing like this has ever been seen in Israel." But the Pharisees' comment was, "He throws out these devils because he is in league with the devil himself."

said, 'Take heart, my daughter; your faith has cured you.' And from that moment she recovered.

When Jesus arrived at the president's house and saw the flute-players and the general commotion, he said, 'Be off! The girl is not dead: she is asleep'; but they only laughed at him. But, when everyone had been turned out, he went into the room and took the girl by the hand, and she got up. This story became the talk of all the country round.

As he passed on Jesus was followed by two blind men, who cried out, 'Son of David, have pity on us!' And when he had gone indoors they came to him. Jesus asked, 'Do you believe that I have the power to do what you want?' 'Yes, sir', they said. Then he touched their eyes, and said, 'As you have believed, so let it be'; and their sight was restored. Jesus said to them sternly, 'See that no one hears about this.' But as soon as they had gone out they talked about him all over the country-side.

They were on their way out when a man was brought to him, who was dumb and possessed by a devil; the devil was cast out and the patient recovered his speech. Filled with amazement the onlookers said, 'Nothing like this has ever been seen in Israel.' [a]

So Jesus went round all the towns and villages teaching in their synagogues, announcing the good news of the Kingdom, and curing every kind of ailment and disease. The sight of the people moved him to pity: they were like sheep without a shepherd, harassed and helpless; and he said to his disciples, 'The crop is heavy, but labourers are scarce; you must therefore beg the owner to send labourers to harvest his crop.'

Jesus is touched by the people's need   9. 35

Jesus now traveled through all the towns and villages, teaching in their synagogues, proclaiming the gospel of the kingdom, and healing all kinds of illness and disability. As he looked at the vast crowds he was deeply moved with pity for them, for they were as bewildered and miserable as a flock of sheep with no shepherd.

"The harvest is great enough," he remarked to his disciples, "but the reapers are few. So you must pray to the Lord of the harvest to send men out to reap it."

Jesus sends out the twelve with divine power   10. 1

Jesus called his twelve disciples to him and gave them authority to expel evil spirits and heal all kinds of disease and infirmity. The names of the twelve apostles were:

First, Simon, called Peter, with his brother Andrew;
James and his brother John, sons of Zebedee;
Philip and Bartholomew,
Thomas, and Matthew the tax collector,
James, the son of Alphaeus, and Thaddaeus,
Simon the patriot, and Judas Iscariot, who later turned traitor.

These were the twelve whom Jesus sent out, with the instructions: "Don't turn off into any of the heathen roads, and don't go into any Samaritan town. Concentrate on the lost sheep

10 Then he called his twelve disciples to him and gave them authority to cast out unclean spirits and to cure every kind of ailment and disease.

These are the names of the twelve apostles: first Simon, also called Peter, and his brother Andrew; James son of Zebedee, and his brother John; Philip and Bartholomew, Thomas and Matthew the tax-gatherer, James son of Alphaeus, Lebbaeus,[b] Simon, a member of the Zealot party, and Judas Iscariot, the man who betrayed him.

These twelve Jesus sent out with the following instructions: 'Do not take the road to gentile lands, and do not enter any Samaritan town; but go rather to the lost sheep of the house of

[a] *Some witnesses add* (34) But the Pharisees said, 'He casts out devils by the prince of devils.' [b] *Some witnesses read* Thaddaeus.

K.J.V.

house of Israel. 7And as ye go, preach, saying, The kingdom of heaven is at hand. 8 Heal the sick, cleanse the lepers, raise the dead, cast out devils: freely ye have received, freely give. 9 Provide neither gold, nor silver, nor brass in your purses; 10 Nor scrip for *your* journey, neither two coats, neither shoes, nor yet staves: for the workman is worthy of his meat. 11And into whatsoever city or town ye shall enter, inquire who in it is worthy; and there abide till ye go thence. 12And when ye come into a house, salute it. 13And if the house be worthy, let your peace come upon it: but if it be not worthy, let your peace return to you. 14And whosoever shall not receive you, nor hear your words, when ye depart out of that house or city, shake off the dust of your feet. 15 Verily I say unto you, It shall be more tolerable for the land of Sodom and Gomorrah in the day of judgment, than for that city.

16 Behold, I send you forth as sheep in the midst of wolves: be ye therefore wise as serpents, and harmless as doves. 17 But beware of men: for they will deliver you up to the councils, and they will scourge you in their synagogues; 18And ye shall be brought before governors and kings for my sake, for a testimony against them and the Gentiles. 19 But when they deliver you up, take no thought how or what ye shall speak: for it shall be given you in that same hour what ye shall speak. 20 For it is not ye that speak, but the Spirit of your Father which speaketh in you. 21And the brother shall deliver up the brother to death, and the father the child: and the children shall rise up against *their* parents, and cause them to be put to death. 22And ye shall be hated of all *men* for my name's sake: but he that endureth to the end shall be saved. 23 But when they persecute you in this city, flee ye into another: for verily I say unto you, Ye shall not have gone over the cities of Israel, till the Son of man be come. 24 The disciple is not above *his* master, nor the servant above his lord. 25 It is enough for the disciple that he be as his master, and the servant as his lord. If they have called the master of the house Beelzebub, how much more *shall they call* them of his household? 26 Fear them not therefore: for there is nothing covered, that shall not be revealed; and hid, that shall not be known. 27 What I tell you in darkness, *that* speak ye in light: and what ye hear in the ear, *that* preach ye upon the housetops. 28And fear not them which kill the body, but are not able to kill the soul: but rather fear

R.S.V.

lost sheep of the house of Israel. 7And preach as you go, saying, 'The kingdom of heaven is at hand.' 8 Heal the sick, raise the dead, cleanse lepers, cast out demons. You received without pay, give without pay. 9 Take no gold, nor silver, nor copper in your belts, 10 no bag for your journey, nor two tunics, nor sandals, nor a staff; for the laborer deserves his food. 11And whatever town or village you enter, find out who is worthy in it, and stay with him until you depart. 12As you enter the house, salute it. 13And if the house is worthy, let your peace come upon it; but if it is not worthy, let your peace return to you. 14And if any one will not receive you or listen to your words, shake off the dust from your feet as you leave that house or town. 15 Truly, I say to you, it shall be more tolerable on the day of judgment for the land of Sodom and Gomorrah than for that town.

16 "Behold, I send you out as sheep in the midst of wolves; so be wise as serpents and innocent as doves. 17 Beware of men; for they will deliver you up to councils, and flog you in their synagogues, 18 and you will be dragged before governors and kings for my sake, to bear testimony before them and the Gentiles. 19 When they deliver you up, do not be anxious how you are to speak or what you are to say; for what you are to say will be given to you in that hour; 20 for it is not you who speak, but the Spirit of your Father speaking through you. 21 Brother will deliver up brother to death, and the father his child, and children will rise against parents and have them put to death; 22 and you will be hated by all for my name's sake. But he who endures to the end will be saved. 23 When they persecute you in one town, flee to the next; for truly, I say to you, you will not have gone through all the towns of Israel, before the Son of man comes.

24 "A disciple is not above his teacher, nor a servant[y] above his master; 25 it is enough for the disciple to be like his teacher, and the servant[y] like his master. If they have called the master of the house Beelzebul, how much more will they malign those of his household.

26 "So have no fear of them; for nothing is covered that will not be revealed, or hidden that will not be known. 27 What I tell you in the dark, utter in the light; and what you hear whispered, proclaim upon the housetops. 28And do not fear those who kill the body but cannot

[y] Or *slave.*

PHILLIPS

of the house of Israel. As you go proclaim that the kingdom of Heaven has arrived. Heal the sick, raise the dead, cure the lepers, drive out devils—give, as you have received, without any charge whatever.

"Don't take any gold or silver or even coppers to put in your purse; nor a knapsack for the journey, nor even a change of clothes, or sandals or a staff—the workman is worth his keep!

"Wherever you go, whether it is into a town or a village, find out someone who is respected, and stay with him until you leave. As you enter his house give it your blessing. If the house deserves it, the peace of your blessing will come to it. But if it doesn't, your peace will return to you.

"And if no one will welcome you or even listen to what you have to say, leave that house or town, and once outside it shake off the dust of that place from your feet. Believe me, Sodom and Gomorrah will fare better in the day of judgment than that town.

He warns them of troubles   10. 16
that lie ahead

"Here am I sending you out like sheep with wolves all round you; so be as wise as serpents and yet as harmless as doves. But be on your guard against men. For they will take you to the courts and flog you in their synagogues. You will be brought into the presence of governors and kings because of me—to give your witness to them and to the heathen.

"But when they do arrest you, never worry about how you are to speak or what you are to say. You will be told at the time what you are to say. For it will not be really you who are speaking but the Spirit of your Father speaking through you.

"Brothers are going to betray their brothers to death, and fathers their children. Children are going to betray their parents and have them executed. You yourselves will be universally hated because of my name. But the man who endures to the very end will be safe and sound.

"But when they persecute you in one town make your escape to the next. Believe me, you will not have covered the towns of Israel before the Son of Man arrives. The disciple is not superior to his teacher any more than the servant is superior to his master, for what is good enough for the teacher is good enough for the disciple as well, and the servant will not fare better than his master. If men call the master of the household the 'Prince of Evil,' what sort of names will they give to his servants? But never let them frighten you, for there is nothing covered up which is not going to be exposed nor anything private which will not be made public. The things I tell you in the dark you must say in the daylight, and the things you hear in your private ear you must proclaim from the housetops.

They should reverence God   10. 28
but have no fear of man

"Never be afraid of those who can kill the body but are powerless to kill the soul! Far

N.E.B.

Israel. And as you go proclaim the message: "The kingdom of Heaven is upon you." Heal the sick, raise the dead, cleanse lepers, cast out devils. You received without cost; give without charge.

'Provide no gold, silver, or copper to fill your purse, no pack for the road, no second coat, no shoes, no stick; the worker earns his keep.

'When you come to any town or village, look for some worthy person in it, and make your home there until you leave. Wish the house peace as you enter it, so that, if it is worthy, your peace may descend on it; if it is not worthy, your peace can come back to you. If anyone will not receive you or listen to what you say, then as you leave that house or that town shake the dust of it off your feet. I tell you this: on the day of judgement it will be more bearable for the land of Sodom and Gomorrah than for that town.

'Look, I send you out like sheep among wolves; be wary as serpents, innocent as doves.

'And be on your guard, for men will hand you over to their courts, they will flog you in the synagogues, and you will be brought before governors and kings, for my sake, to testify before them and the heathen. But when you are arrested, do not worry about what you are to say; when the time comes, the words you need will be given you; for it is not you who will be speaking: it will be the Spirit of your Father speaking in you.

'Brother will betray brother to death, and the father his child; children will turn against their parents and send them to their death. All will hate you for your allegiance to me; but the man who holds out to the end will be saved. When you are persecuted in one town, take refuge in another; I tell you this: before you have gone through all the towns of Israel the Son of Man will have come.

'A pupil does not rank above his teacher, or a servant above his master. The pupil should be content to share his teacher's lot, the servant to share his master's. If the master has been called Beelzebub, how much more his household!

'So do not be afraid of them. There is nothing covered up that will not be uncovered, nothing hidden that will not be made known. What I say to you in the dark you must repeat in broad daylight; what you hear whispered you must shout from the house-tops. Do not fear those who kill the body, but cannot kill the soul. Fear

K.J.V.

him which is able to destroy both soul and body in hell. 29Are not two sparrows sold for a farthing? and one of them shall not fall on the ground without your Father. 30 But the very hairs of your head are all numbered. 31 Fear ye not therefore, ye are of more value than many sparrows. 32 Whosoever therefore shall confess me before men, him will I confess also before my Father which is in heaven. 33 But whosoever shall deny me before men, him will I also deny before my Father which is in heaven. 34 Think not that I am come to send peace on earth: I came not to send peace, but a sword. 35 For I am come to set a man at variance against his father, and the daughter against her mother, and the daughter in law against her mother in law. 36And a man's foes *shall be* they of his own household. 37 He that loveth father or mother more than me is not worthy of me: and he that loveth son or daughter more than me is not worthy of me. 38And he that taketh not his cross, and followeth after me, is not worthy of me. 39 He that findeth his life shall lose it: and he that loseth his life for my sake shall find it.

40 He that receiveth you receiveth me; and he that receiveth me receiveth him that sent me. 41 He that receiveth a prophet in the name of a prophet shall receive a prophet's reward; and he that receiveth a righteous man in the name of a righteous man shall receive a righteous man's reward. 42And whosoever shall give to drink unto one of these little ones a cup of cold *water* only in the name of a disciple, verily I say unto you, he shall in no wise lose his reward.

R.S.V.

kill the soul; rather fear him who can destroy both soul and body in hell.[z] 29Are not two sparrows sold for a penny? And not one of them will fall to the ground without your Father's will. 30 But even the hairs of your head are all numbered. 31 Fear not, therefore; you are of more value than many sparrows. 32 So every one who acknowledges me before men, I also will acknowledge before my Father who is in heaven; 33 but whoever denies me before men, I also will deny before my Father who is in heaven. 34 "Do not think that I have come to bring peace on earth; I have not come to bring peace, but a sword. 35 For I have come to set a man against his father, and a daughter against her mother, and a daughter-in-law against her mother-in-law; 36 and a man's foes will be those of his own household. 37 He who loves father or mother more than me is not worthy of me; and he who loves son or daughter more than me is not worthy of me; 38 and he who does not take his cross and follow me is not worthy of me. 39 He who finds his life will lose it, and he who loses his life for my sake will find it.

40 "He who receives you receives me, and he who receives me receives him who sent me. 41 He who receives a prophet because he is a prophet shall receive a prophet's reward, and he who receives a righteous man because he is a righteous man shall receive a righteous man's reward. 42And whoever gives to one of these little ones even a cup of cold water because he is a disciple, truly, I say to you, he shall not lose his reward."

11 And it came to pass, when Jesus had made an end of commanding his twelve disciples, he departed thence to teach and to preach in their cities. 2 Now when John had heard in the prison the works of Christ, he sent two of his disciples, 3And said unto him, Art thou he that should come, or do we look for another? 4 Jesus answered and said unto them, Go and shew John again those things which ye do hear and see: 5 The blind receive their sight, and the lame walk, the lepers are cleansed, and the deaf hear, the dead are raised up, and the poor have the gospel preached to them. 6And blessed is *he,* whosoever shall not be offended in me.

7 And as they departed, Jesus began to say unto the multitudes concerning John, What went ye out into the wilderness to see? A reed shaken with the wind? 8 But what went ye out for to

11 And when Jesus had finished instructing his twelve disciples, he went on from there to teach and preach in their cities.

2 Now when John heard in prison about the deeds of Christ, he sent word by his disciples 3 and said to him, "Are you he who is to come, or shall we look for another?" 4And Jesus answered them, "Go and tell John what you hear and see: 5 the blind receive their sight and the lame walk, lepers are cleansed and the deaf hear, and the dead are raised up, and the poor have good news preached to them. 6And blessed is he who takes no offense at me."

7 As they went away, Jesus began to speak to the crowds concerning John: "What did you go out into the wilderness to behold? A reed shaken by the wind? 8 Why then did you go out?

[z] Greek *Gehenna.*

PHILLIPS

better to stand in awe of the one who has the power to destroy body and soul in the fires of destruction!

"Two sparrows sell for a penny, don't they? Yet not a single sparrow falls to the ground without your Father's knowledge. The very hairs of your head are all numbered. Never be afraid, then—you are far more valuable than sparrows.

"Every man who publicly acknowledges me I shall acknowledge in the presence of my Father in Heaven, but the man who disowns me before men I shall disown before my Father in Heaven.

The Prince of Peace comes   10. 34
to bring division

"Never think I have come to bring peace upon the earth. No, I have not come to bring peace but a sword! For I have come to set a man against his own father, a daughter against her own mother, and a daughter-in-law against her mother-in-law. A man's enemies will be those who live in his own house.

"Anyone who puts his love for father or mother above his love for me does not deserve to be mine, and he who loves son or daughter more than me is not worthy of me, and neither is the man who refuses to take up his cross and follow my way. The man who has found his own life will lose it, but the man who has lost it for my sake will find it.

"Whoever welcomes you, welcomes me; and whoever welcomes me is welcoming the one who sent me.

"Whoever welcomes a prophet just because he is a prophet will get a prophet's reward. And whoever welcomes a good man just because he is a good man will get a good man's reward. Believe me, anyone who gives even a drink of water to one of these little ones, just because he is my disciple, will by no means lose his reward."

When Jesus had finished giving his twelve disciples these instructions he went on from there to teach and preach in the towns in which they lived.

John inquires about Christ: 11. 2
Christ speaks about John

John the Baptist was in prison when he heard what Christ was doing, and he sent a message through his disciples asking the question, "Are you the one who was to come or are we to look for somebody else?"

Jesus gave them this reply, "Go and tell John what you see and hear—that blind men are recovering their sight, cripples are walking, lepers being healed, the deaf hearing, the dead being brought to life and the good news is being given to those in need. *And happy is the man who never loses his faith in me.*"

As John's disciples were going away, Jesus began talking to the crowd about John:

"What did you go out into the desert to look at? A reed waving in the breeze? No? Then

N.E.B.

him rather who is able to destroy both soul and body in hell.

'Are not sparrows two a penny? Yet without your Father's leave not one of them can fall to the ground. As for you, even the hairs of your head have all been counted. So have no fear; you are worth more than any number of sparrows.

'Whoever then will acknowledge me before men, I will acknowledge him before my Father in heaven; and whoever disowns me before men, I will disown him before my Father in heaven.

'You must not think that I have come to bring peace to the earth; I have not come to bring peace, but a sword. I have come to set a man against his father, a daughter against her mother, a young wife against her mother-in-law; and a man will find his enemies under his own roof.

'No man is worthy of me who cares more for father or mother than for me; no man is worthy of me who cares more for son or daughter; no man is worthy of me who does not take up his cross and walk in my footsteps. By gaining his life a man will lose it; by losing his life for my sake, he will gain it.

'To receive you is to receive me, and to receive me is to receive the One who sent me. Whoever receives a prophet as a prophet will be given a prophet's reward, and whoever receives a good man because he is a good man will be given a good man's reward. And if anyone gives so much as a cup of cold water to one of these little ones, because he is a disciple of mine, I tell you this: that man will assuredly not go unrewarded.'

11 When Jesus had finished giving his twelve disciples their instructions, he left that place and went to teach and preach in the neighbouring towns.

John, who was in prison, heard what Christ was doing, and sent his own disciples to him with this message: 'Are you the one who is to come, or are we to expect some other?' Jesus answered, 'Go and tell John what you hear and see: the blind recover their sight, the lame walk, the lepers are clean, the deaf hear, the dead are raised to life, the poor are hearing the good news—and happy is the man who does not find me a stumbling-block.'

When the messengers were on their way back, Jesus began to speak to the people about John: 'What was the spectacle that drew you to the wilderness? A reed-bed swept by the wind? No?

K.J.V.

see? A man clothed in soft raiment? behold, they that wear soft *clothing* are in kings' houses. 9 But what went ye out for to see? A prophet? yea, I say unto you, and more than a prophet. 10 For this is *he*, of whom it is written, Behold, I send my messenger before thy face, which shall prepare thy way before thee. 11 Verily I say unto you, Among them that are born of women there hath not risen a greater than John the Baptist: notwithstanding, he that is least in the kingdom of heaven is greater than he. 12And from the days of John the Baptist until now the kingdom of heaven suffereth violence, and the violent take it by force. 13 For all the prophets and the law prophesied until John. 14And if ye will receive *it*, this is Elias, which was for to come. 15 He that hath ears to hear, let him hear.

16 But whereunto shall I liken this generation? It is like unto children sitting in the markets, and calling unto their fellows, 17And saying, We have piped unto you, and ye have not danced; we have mourned unto you, and ye have not lamented. 18 For John came neither eating nor drinking, and they say, He hath a devil. 19 The Son of man came eating and drinking, and they say, Behold a man gluttonous, and a winebibber, a friend of publicans and sinners. But wisdom is justified of her children.

20 Then began he to upbraid the cities wherein most of his mighty works were done, because they repented not: 21 Woe unto thee, Chorazin! woe unto thee, Bethsaida! for if the mighty works, which were done in you, had been done in Tyre and Sidon, they would have repented long ago in sackcloth and ashes. 22 But I say unto you, It shall be more tolerable for Tyre and Sidon at the day of judgment, than for you. 23And thou, Capernaum, which art exalted unto heaven, shalt be brought down to hell: for if the mighty works, which have been done in thee, had been done in Sodom, it would have remained until this day. 24 But I say unto you, That it shall be more tolerable for the land of Sodom in the day of judgment, than for thee.

25 At that time Jesus answered and said, I thank thee, O Father, Lord of heaven and earth, because thou hast hid these things from the wise and prudent, and hast revealed them unto babes. 26 Even so, Father; for so it seemed good in thy sight. 27All things are delivered unto me of my Father: and no man knoweth the Son, but the Father; neither knoweth any man the Father, save the Son, and *he* to whomsoever the Son will reveal *him*.

28 Come unto me, all *ye* that labour and are heavy laden, and I will give you rest. 29 Take my yoke upon you, and learn of me: for I am meek and lowly in heart: and ye shall find rest unto your souls. 30 For my yoke *is* easy, and my burden is light.

R.S.V.

To see a man[a] clothed in soft raiment? Behold, those who wear soft raiment are in kings' houses. 9 Why then did you go out? To see a prophet?[b] Yes, I tell you, and more than a prophet. 10 This is he of whom it is written,

'Behold, I send my messenger before thy face, who shall prepare thy way before thee.'

11 Truly, I say to you, among those born of women there has risen no one greater than John the Baptist; yet he who is least in the kingdom of heaven is greater than he. 12 From the days of John the Baptist until now the kingdom of heaven has suffered violence,[c] and men of violence take it by force. 13 For all the prophets and the law prophesied until John; 14 and if you are willing to accept it, he is Elijah who is to come. 15 He who has ears to hear,[d] let him hear.

16 "But to what shall I compare this generation? It is like children sitting in the market places and calling to their playmates,

17 'We piped to you, and you did not dance; we wailed, and you did not mourn.'

18 For John came neither eating nor drinking, and they say, 'He has a demon'; 19 the Son of man came eating and drinking, and they say, 'Behold, a glutton and a drunkard, a friend of tax collectors and sinners!' Yet wisdom is justified by her deeds." [e]

20 Then he began to upbraid the cities where most of his mighty works had been done, because they did not repent. 21 "Woe to you, Chorazin! woe to you, Bethsaida! for if the mighty works done in you had been done in Tyre and Sidon, they would have repented long ago in sackcloth and ashes. 22 But I tell you, it shall be more tolerable on the day of judgment for Tyre and Sidon than for you. 23 And you, Capernaum, will you be exalted in heaven? You shall be brought down to Hades. For if the mighty works done in you had been done in Sodom, it would have remained until this day. 24 But I tell you that it shall be more tolerable on the day of judgment for the land of Sodom than for you."

25 At that time Jesus declared, "I thank thee, Father, Lord of heaven and earth, that thou hast hidden these things from the wise and understanding and revealed them to babes; 26 yea, Father, for such was thy gracious will.[f] 27All things have been delivered to me by my Father; and no one knows the Son except the Father, and no one knows the Father except the Son and any one to whom the Son chooses to reveal him. 28 Come to me, all who labor and are heavy laden, and I will give you rest. 29 Take my yoke upon you, and learn from me; for I am gentle and lowly in heart, and you will find rest for your souls. 30 For my yoke is easy, and my burden is light."

[a] Or *What then did you go out to see? A man . . .* [b] Other ancient authorities read *What then did you go out to see? A prophet?* [c] Or *has been coming violently.* [d] Other ancient authorities omit *to hear.* [e] Other ancient authorities read *children* (Luke 7.35). [f] Or *so it was well-pleasing before thee.*

PHILLIPS

N.E.B.

what was it you went out to see?—a man dressed in fine clothes? But the men who wear fine clothes live in the courts of kings! But what did you really go to see—a prophet? Yes, I tell you, a prophet and far more than a prophet! This is the man of whom the scripture says—

Behold, I send my messenger before thy face, Who shall prepare thy way before thee.

"Believe me, no one greater than John the Baptist has ever been born of all mankind, and yet a humble member of the kingdom of Heaven is greater than he.

"From the days of John the Baptist until now the kingdom of Heaven has been taken by storm and eager men are forcing their way into it. For the Law and all the Prophets foretold it till the time of John and—if you can believe it—John himself is the 'Elijah' who must come before the kingdom. The man who has ears to hear must use them!

"But how can I show what the people of this generation are like? They are like children sitting in the market place calling out to their friends, 'We played at weddings for you but you wouldn't dance, and we played at funerals and you wouldn't cry!' For John came in the strictest austerity and people say, 'He's crazy!' Then the Son of Man came, enjoying life, and people say, 'Look, a drunkard and a glutton—the bosom friend of the tax collector and the sinner.' Ah well, wisdom stands or falls by her own actions."

Jesus denounces apathy—and **11. 20**
thanks God that simple men
understand his message

Then Jesus began reproaching the towns where most of his miracles had taken place because their hearts were unchanged.

"Alas for you, Chorazin! Alas for you, Bethsaida! For if Tyre and Sidon had seen the demonstrations of God's power which you have seen they would have repented long ago in sackcloth and ashes. Yet I tell you this, that it will be more bearable for Tyre and Sidon in the day of judgment than for you.

"And as for you, Capernaum, are you on your way up to Heaven? I tell you you will go hurtling down among the dead! If Sodom had seen the miracles that you have seen, Sodom would be standing today. Yet I tell you now that it will be more bearable for the land of Sodom in the day of judgment than for you."

At this same time Jesus said: "O Father, Lord of Heaven and earth, I thank you for hiding these things from the clever and intelligent and for showing them to mere children. Yes, I thank you, Father, that this was your will."

Then he said: "Everything has been put in my hands by my Father, and nobody knows the Son except the Father. Nor does anyone know the Father except the Son—and the man to whom the Son chooses to reveal him.

"Come to me, all of you who are weary and overburdened, and I will give you rest! Put on my yoke and learn from me. For I am gentle and humble in heart and you will find rest for your souls. For my yoke is easy and my burden is light."

Then what did you go out to see? A man dressed in silks and satins? Surely you must look in palaces for that. But why did you go out? To see a prophet? Yes indeed, and far more than a prophet. He is the man of whom Scripture says,

"Here is my herald, whom I send on ahead of you,
And he will prepare your way before you."

I tell you this: never has there appeared on earth a mother's son greater than John the Baptist, and yet the least in the kingdom of Heaven is greater than he.

'Ever since the coming of John the Baptist the kingdom of Heaven has been subjected to violence and violent men[a] are seizing it. For all the prophets and the Law foretold things to come until John appeared, and John is the destined Elijah, if you will but accept it. If you have ears that can hear, then hear.

'How can I describe this generation? They are like the children sitting in the market-place and shouting at each other,

"We piped for you and you would not dance."
"We wept and wailed, and you would not mourn."

For John came, neither eating nor drinking, and they say, "He is possessed." The Son of Man came eating and drinking, and they say, "Look at him! a glutton and a drinker, a friend of tax-gatherers and sinners!" And yet God's wisdom is proved right by its results.'

Then he spoke of the towns in which most of his miracles had been performed, and denounced them for their impenitence. 'Alas for you, Chorazin!' he said; 'alas for you, Bethsaida! If the miracles that were performed in you had been performed in Tyre and Sidon, they would long ago have repented in sackcloth and ashes. But it will be more bearable, I tell you, for Tyre and Sidon on the day of judgement than for you. And as for you, Capernaum, will you be exalted to the skies? No, brought down to the depths! For if the miracles had been performed in Sodom which were performed in you, Sodom would be standing to this day. But it will be more bearable, I tell you, for the land of Sodom on the day of judgement than for you.'

At that time Jesus spoke these words: 'I thank thee, Father, Lord of heaven and earth, for hiding these things from the learned and wise, and revealing them to the simple. Yes, Father, such[b] was thy choice. Everything is entrusted to me by my Father; and no one knows the Son but the Father, and no one knows the Father but the Son and those to whom the Son may choose to reveal him.

'Come to me, all whose work is hard, whose load is heavy; and I will give you relief. Bend your necks to my yoke, and learn from me, for I am gentle and humble-hearted; and your souls will find relief. For my yoke is good to bear, my load is light.'

[a] *Or* has been forcing its way forward, and men of force . . . [b] *Or* Yes, I thank thee, Father, that such . . .

K.J.V.

12 At that time Jesus went on the sabbath day through the corn; and his disciples were a hungered, and began to pluck the ears of corn, and to eat. 2 But when the Pharisees saw *it,* they said unto him, Behold, thy disciples do that which is not lawful to do upon the sabbath day. 3 But he said unto them, Have ye not read what David did, when he was a hungered, and they that were with him; 4 How he entered into the house of God, and did eat the shewbread, which was not lawful for him to eat, neither for them which were with him, but only for the priests? 5 Or have ye not read in the law, how that on the sabbath days the priests in the temple profane the sabbath, and are blameless? 6 But I say unto you, That in this place is *one* greater than the temple. 7 But if ye had known what *this* meaneth, I will have mercy, and not sacrifice, ye would not have condemned the guiltless. 8 For the Son of man is Lord even of the sabbath day. 9 And when he was departed thence, he went into their synagogue:

10 And, behold, there was a man which had *his* hand withered. And they asked him, saying, Is it lawful to heal on the sabbath days? that they might accuse him. 11 And he said unto them, What man shall there be among you, that shall have one sheep, and if it fall into a pit on the sabbath day, will he not lay hold on it, and lift *it* out? 12 How much then is a man better than a sheep? Wherefore it is lawful to do well on the sabbath days. 13 Then saith he to the man, Stretch forth thine hand. And he stretched *it* forth; and it was restored whole, like as the other.

14 Then the Pharisees went out, and held a council against him, how they might destroy him. 15 But when Jesus knew *it,* he withdrew himself from thence: and great multitudes followed him, and he healed them all; 16 And charged them that they should not make him known: 17 That it might be fulfilled which was spoken by Esaias the prophet, saying, 18 Behold my servant, whom I have chosen; my beloved, in whom my soul is well pleased: I will put my Spirit upon him, and he shall shew judgment to the Gentiles. 19 He shall not strive, nor cry; neither shall any man hear his voice in the streets. 20 A bruised reed shall he not break, and smoking flax shall he not quench, till he send forth judgment unto victory. 21 And in his name shall the Gentiles trust.

22 Then was brought unto him one possessed with a devil, blind, and dumb: and he healed him, insomuch that the blind and dumb both spake and saw. 23 And all the people were amazed, and said, Is not this the Son of David?

R.S.V.

12 At that time Jesus went through the grainfields on the sabbath; his disciples were hungry, and they began to pluck ears of grain and to eat. 2 But when the Pharisees saw it, they said to him, "Look, your disciples are doing what is not lawful to do on the sabbath." 3 He said to them, "Have you not read what David did, when he was hungry, and those who were with him: 4 how he entered the house of God and ate the bread of the Presence, which it was not lawful for him to eat nor for those who were with him, but only for the priests? 5 Or have you not read in the law how on the sabbath the priests in the temple profane the sabbath, and are guiltless? 6 I tell you, something greater than the temple is here. 7 And if you had known what this means, 'I desire mercy, and not sacrifice,' you would not have condemned the guiltless. 8 For the Son of man is lord of the sabbath."

9 And he went on from there, and entered their synagogue. 10 And behold, there was a man with a withered hand. And they asked him, "Is it lawful to heal on the sabbath?" so that they might accuse him. 11 He said to them, "What man of you, if he has one sheep and it falls into a pit on the sabbath, will not lay hold of it and lift it out? 12 Of how much more value is a man than a sheep! So it is lawful to do good on the sabbath." 13 Then he said to the man, "Stretch out your hand." And the man stretched it out, and it was restored, whole like the other. 14 But the Pharisees went out and took counsel against him, how to destroy him.

15 Jesus, aware of this, withdrew from there. And many followed him, and he healed them all, 16 and ordered them not to make him known. 17 This was to fulfil what was spoken by the prophet Isaiah:

18 "Behold, my servant whom I have chosen,
    my beloved with whom my soul is well
      pleased.
I will put my Spirit upon him,
    and he shall proclaim justice to the
      Gentiles.
19 He will not wrangle or cry aloud,
    nor will any one hear his voice in the
      streets;
20 he will not break a bruised reed
    or quench a smoldering wick,
    till he brings justice to victory;
21   and in his name will the Gentiles hope."

22 Then a blind and dumb demoniac was brought to him, and he healed him, so that the dumb man spoke and saw. 23 And all the people were amazed, and said, "Can this be the Son of

Jesus rebukes the sabbatarians   **12. 1**

It happened then that Jesus passed through the cornfields on the Sabbath day. His disciples were hungry and began picking the ears of wheat and eating them. But the Pharisees saw them do it.

"There, you see," they remarked to Jesus, "your disciples are doing what the Law forbids them to do on the Sabbath."

"Haven't any of you read what David did when he and his companions were hungry?" replied Jesus, "—how he went into the house of God and ate the presentation loaves, which he and his followers were not allowed to eat since only priests can do so?

"Haven't any of you read in the Law that every Sabbath day priests in the Temple can break the Sabbath and yet remain blameless? I tell you that there is something more important than the Temple here. If you had grasped the meaning of the scripture '*I desire mercy and not sacrifice,*' you would not have been so quick to condemn the innocent! For the Son of Man is master even of the Sabbath."

Leaving there he went into their synagogue, where there happened to be a man with a shrivelled hand.

"Is it right to heal anyone on the Sabbath day?" they asked him—hoping to bring a charge against him.

"If any of you had a sheep which fell into a ditch on the Sabbath day, would he not take hold of it and pull it out?" replied Jesus. "How much more valuable is a man than a sheep? You see, it is right to do good on the Sabbath day."

Then Jesus said to the man, "Stretch out your hand!" He did stretch it out, and it was restored as sound as the other.

But the Pharisees went out and held a meeting against Jesus and discussed how they could get rid of him altogether.

Jesus retires to continue   **12. 15**
his work

But Jesus knew of this and he left the place. Large crowds followed him and he healed them all, with the strict injunction that they should not make him conspicuous by their talk, thus fulfilling Isaiah's prophecy:

Behold, my servant whom I have chosen;
My beloved in whom my soul is well pleased:
I will put my Spirit upon him,
And he shall declare judgment to the gentiles.
He shall not strive, nor cry aloud;
Neither shall anyone hear his voice in the streets.
A bruised reed shall he not break,
And smoking flax shall he not quench,
Till he send forth judgment unto victory.
And in his name shall the gentiles hope.

Then a devil-possessed man who could neither see nor speak was brought to Jesus. He healed him, so that the dumb man could both speak and see. At this the whole crowd went wild with excitement, and people kept saying, "Can this be the Son of David?"

Controversy

12 Once about that time Jesus took a walk on the Sabbath through the cornfields; and his disciples, feeling hungry, began to pluck some ears of corn and eat them. The Pharisees noticed this, and said to him, 'Look, your disciples are doing something which is forbidden on the Sabbath.' He answered, 'Have you not read what David did when he and his men were hungry? He went into the House of God and ate the consecrated loaves, though neither he nor his men had a right to eat them, but only the priests. Or have you not read in the Law that on the Sabbath the priests in the temple break the Sabbath and it is not held against them? I tell you, there is something greater than the temple here. If you had known what that text means, "I require mercy, not sacrifice", you would not have condemned the innocent. For the Son of Man is sovereign over the Sabbath.'

He went on to another place, and entered their synagogue. A man was there with a withered arm, and they asked Jesus, 'Is it permitted to heal on the Sabbath?' (Their aim was to frame a charge against him.) But he said to them, 'Suppose you had one sheep, which fell into a ditch on the Sabbath; is there one of you who would not catch hold of it and lift it out? And surely a man is worth far more than a sheep! It is therefore permitted to do good on the Sabbath.' Turning to the man he said, 'Stretch out your arm.' He stretched it out, and it was made sound again like the other. But the Pharisees, on leaving the synagogue, laid a plot to do away with him.

Jesus was aware of it and withdrew. Many followed, and he cured all who were ill; and he gave strict injunctions that they were not to make him known. This was in fulfilment of Isaiah's prophecy:

'Here is my servant, whom I have chosen,
My beloved, on whom my favour rests;
I will put my Spirit upon him,
And he will proclaim judgement among the nations.
He will not strive, he will not shout,
Nor will his voice be heard in the streets.
He will not snap off the broken reed,
Nor snuff out the smouldering wick,
Until he leads justice on to victory.
In him the nations shall place their hope.'

Then they brought him a man who was possessed; he was blind and dumb; and Jesus cured him, restoring both speech and sight. The bystanders were all amazed, and the word went

K.J.V.

24 But when the Pharisees heard *it*, they said, This *fellow* doth not cast out devils, but by Beelzebub the prince of the devils. 25And Jesus knew their thoughts, and said unto them, Every kingdom divided against itself is brought to desolation; and every city or house divided against itself shall not stand: 26And if Satan cast out Satan, he is divided against himself; how shall then his kingdom stand? 27And if I by Beelzebub cast out devils, by whom do your children cast *them* out? therefore they shall be your judges. 28 But if I cast out devils by the Spirit of God, then the kingdom of God is come unto you. 29 Or else, how can one enter into a strong man's house, and spoil his goods, except he first bind the strong man? and then he will spoil his house. 30 He that is not with me is against me; and he that gathereth not with me scattereth abroad.

31 Wherefore I say unto you, All manner of sin and blasphemy shall be forgiven unto men: but the blasphemy *against* the *Holy* Ghost shall not be forgiven unto men. 32And whosoever speaketh a word against the Son of man, it shall be forgiven him: but whosoever speaketh against the Holy Ghost, it shall not be forgiven him, neither in this world, neither in the *world* to come. 33 Either make the tree good, and his fruit good; or else make the tree corrupt, and his fruit corrupt: for the tree is known by *his* fruit. 34 O generation of vipers, how can ye, being evil, speak good things? for out of the abundance of the heart the mouth speaketh. 35A good man out of the good treasure of the heart bringeth forth good things: and an evil man out of the evil treasure bringeth forth evil things. 36 But I say unto you, That every idle word that men shall speak, they shall give account thereof in the day of judgment. 37 For by thy words thou shalt be justified, and by thy words thou shalt be condemned.

38 Then certain of the scribes and of the Pharisees answered, saying, Master, we would see a sign from thee. 39 But he answered and said unto them, An evil and adulterous generation seeketh after a sign; and there shall no sign be given to it, but the sign of the prophet Jonas: 40 For as Jonas was three days and three nights in the whale's belly; so shall the Son of man be three days and three nights in the heart of the earth. 41 The men of Nineveh shall rise in judgment with this generation, and shall condemn it: because they repented at the preaching of Jonas; and, behold, a greater than Jonas *is* here. 42 The queen of the south shall rise up in the judgment with this generation, and shall condemn it: for she came from the uttermost parts of the earth to hear the wisdom of Solomon; and, behold, a

R.S.V.

David?" 24 But when the Pharisees heard it they said, "It is only by Beelzebul, the prince of demons, that this man casts out demons." 25 Knowing their thoughts, he said to them, "Every kingdom divided against itself is laid waste, and no city or house divided against itself will stand; 26 and if Satan casts out Satan, he is divided against himself; how then will his kingdom stand? 27And if I cast out demons by Beelzebul, by whom do your sons cast them out? Therefore they shall be your judges. 28 But if it is by the Spirit of God that I cast out demons, then the kingdom of God has come upon you. 29 Or how can one enter a strong man's house and plunder his goods, unless he first binds the strong man? Then indeed he may plunder his house. 30 He who is not with me is against me, and he who does not gather with me scatters. 31 Therefore I tell you, every sin and blasphemy will be forgiven men, but the blasphemy against the Spirit will not be forgiven. 32And whoever says a word against the Son of man will be forgiven; but whoever speaks against the Holy Spirit will not be forgiven, either in this age or in the age to come.

33 "Either make the tree good, and its fruit good; or make the tree bad, and its fruit bad; for the tree is known by its fruit. 34 You brood of vipers! how can you speak good, when you are evil? For out of the abundance of the heart the mouth speaks. 35 The good man out of his good treasure brings forth good, and the evil man out of his evil treasure brings forth evil. 36 I tell you, on the day of judgment men will render account for every careless word they utter; 37 for by your words you will be justified, and by your words you will be condemned."

38 Then some of the scribes and Pharisees said to him, "Teacher, we wish to see a sign from you." 39 But he answered them, "An evil and adulterous generation seeks for a sign; but no sign shall be given to it except the sign of the prophet Jonah. 40 For as Jonah was three days and three nights in the belly of the whale, so will the Son of man be three days and three nights in the heart of the earth. 41 The men of Nineveh will arise at the judgment with this generation and condemn it; for they repented at the preaching of Jonah, and behold, something greater than Jonah is here. 42 The queen of the South will arise at the judgment with this generation and condemn it; for she came from the ends of the earth to hear the wisdom of Solomon, and behold, something greater than Solomon is here.

PHILLIPS

*The Pharisees draw an evil con- 12. 24
clusion, and Jesus rebukes them*

But the Pharisees on hearing this remark said to one another, "This man is only expelling devils because he is in league with Beelzebub, the prince of devils."

Jesus knew what they were thinking, and said to them: "Any kingdom divided against itself is bound to collapse, and no town or household divided against itself can last for long. If it is Satan who is expelling Satan, then he is divided against himself—so how do you suppose that his kingdom can continue? And if I expel devils because I am an ally of Beelzebub, what alliance do your sons make when they do the same thing? They can settle that question for you! But if I am expelling devils by the Spirit of God, *then the kingdom of God has swept over you unawares!* How do you suppose anyone could get into a strong man's house and steal his property unless he first tied up the strong man? But if he did that, he could ransack his whole house.

"The man who is not on my side is against me, and the man who does not gather with me is really scattering. That is why I tell you that men may be forgiven for every sin and blasphemy, but blasphemy against the Spirit cannot be forgiven. A man may say a word against the Son of Man and be forgiven, but whoever speaks against the Holy Spirit cannot be forgiven either in this world or in the world to come!

"You must choose between having a good tree with good fruit and a rotten tree with rotten fruit. For you can tell a tree at once by its fruit.

"You serpent's brood, how can you say anything good out of your evil hearts? For a man's words depend on what fills his heart. A good man gives out good—from the goodness stored in his heart; a bad man gives out evil—from his store of evil. I tell you that men will have to answer at the day of judgment for every careless word they utter—for it is your words that will acquit you, and your words that will condemn you!"

Jesus refuses to give a sign 12. 38

Then some of the scribes and Pharisees said, "Master, we want to see a sign from you." But Jesus told them:

"It is an evil and unfaithful generation that craves for a sign, and no sign will be given to it—except the sign of the prophet Jonah. For just as Jonah was in the belly of that great sea monster for three days and nights, so will the Son of Man be in the heart of the earth for three days and nights. The men of Nineveh will stand up with this generation in the judgment and will condemn it. For they did repent when Jonah preached to them, and you have more than Jonah's preaching with you now! The Queen of the South will stand up in the judgment with this generation and will condemn it. For she came from the ends of the earth to listen to the wisdom of Solomon, and you have more than the wisdom of Solomon with you now!

N.E.B.

round: 'Can this be the Son of David?' But when the Pharisees heard it they said, 'It is only by Beelzebub prince of devils that this man drives the devils out.'

He knew what was in their minds; so he said to them, 'Every kingdom divided against itself goes to ruin; and no town, no household, that is divided against itself can stand. And if it is Satan who casts out Satan, Satan is divided against himself; how then can his kingdom stand? And if it is by Beelzebub that I cast out devils, by whom do your own people drive them out? If this is your argument, they themselves will refute you. But if it is by the Spirit of God that I drive out the devils, then be sure the kingdom of God has already come upon you.

'Or again, how can anyone break into a strong man's house and make off with his goods unless he has first tied the strong man up before ransacking the house?

'He who is not with me is against me, and he who does not gather with me scatters.

'And so I tell you this: no sin, no slander, is beyond forgiveness for men, except slander spoken against the Spirit, and that will not be forgiven. Any man who speaks a word against the Son of Man will be forgiven; but if anyone speaks against the Holy Spirit, for him there is no forgiveness, either in this age or in the age to come.

'Either make the tree good and its fruit good, or make the tree bad and its fruit bad; you can tell a tree by its fruit. You vipers' brood! How can your words be good when you yourselves are evil? For the words that the mouth utters come from the overflowing of the heart. A good man produces good from the store of good within himself; and an evil man from evil within produces evil.

'I tell you this: there is not a thoughtless word that comes from men's lips but they will have to account for it on the day of judgement. For out of your own mouth you will be acquitted; out of your own mouth you will be condemned.'

At this some of the doctors of the law and the Pharisees said, 'Master, we should like you to show us a sign.' He answered: 'It is a wicked, godless generation that asks for a sign; and the only sign that will be given it is the sign of the prophet Jonah. Jonah was in the sea-monster's belly for three days and three nights, and in the same way the Son of Man will be three days and three nights in the bowels of the earth. At the Judgement, when this generation is on trial, the men of Nineveh will appear against it[a] and ensure its condemnation, for they repented at the preaching of Jonah; and what is here is greater than Jonah. The Queen of the South will appear at the Judgement when this generation is on trial,[b] and ensure its condemnation, for she came from the ends of the earth to hear the wisdom of Solomon; and what is here is greater than Solomon.

[a] *Or* will rise again together with it. [b] *Or* At the Judgement the Queen of the South will be raised to life together with this generation.

K.J.V.

greater than Solomon *is* here. 43 When the unclean spirit is gone out of a man, he walketh through dry places, seeking rest, and findeth none. 44 Then he saith, I will return into my house from whence I came out; and when he is come, he findeth *it* empty, swept, and garnished. 45 Then goeth he, and taketh with himself seven other spirits more wicked than himself, and they enter in and dwell there: and the last *state* of that man is worse than the first. Even so shall it be also unto this wicked generation.

46 While he yet talked to the people, behold, *his* mother and his brethren stood without, desiring to speak with him. 47 Then one said unto him, Behold, thy mother and thy brethren stand without, desiring to speak with thee. 48 But he answered and said unto him that told him, Who is my mother? and who are my brethren? 49 And he stretched forth his hand toward his disciples, and said, Behold my mother and my brethren! 50 For whosoever shall do the will of my Father which is in heaven, the same is my brother, and sister, and mother.

13 The same day went Jesus out of the house, and sat by the sea side. 2 And great multitudes were gathered together unto him, so that he went into a ship, and sat; and the whole multitude stood on the shore. 3 And he spake many things unto them in parables, saying, Behold, a sower went forth to sow; 4 And when he sowed, some *seeds* fell by the way side, and the fowls came and devoured them up: 5 Some fell upon stony places, where they had not much earth: and forthwith they sprung up, because they had no deepness of earth: 6 And when the sun was up, they were scorched; and because they had no root, they withered away. 7 And some fell among thorns; and the thorns sprung up, and choked them: 8 But other fell into good ground, and brought forth fruit, some a hundredfold, some sixtyfold, some thirtyfold. 9 Who hath ears to hear, let him hear. 10 And the disciples came, and said unto him, Why speakest thou unto them in parables? 11 He answered and said unto them, Because it is given unto you to know the mysteries of the kingdom of heaven, but to them it is not given. 12 For whosoever hath, to him shall be given, and he shall have more abundance: but whosoever hath not, from him shall be taken away even that he hath. 13 Therefore speak I to them in parables: because they seeing see not; and hearing they hear not, neither do they understand. 14 And in them is fulfilled the prophecy of Esaias, which saith, By hearing ye shall hear, and shall not understand; and seeing ye shall see, and shall not perceive: 15 For this people's heart is waxed gross, and *their* ears

R.S.V.

43 "When the unclean spirit has gone out of a man, he passes through waterless places seeking rest, but he finds none. 44 Then he says, 'I will return to my house from which I came.' And when he comes he finds it empty, swept, and put in order. 45 Then he goes and brings with him seven other spirits more evil than himself, and they enter and dwell there; and the last state of that man becomes worse than the first. So shall it be also with this evil generation."

46 While he was still speaking to the people, behold, his mother and his brothers stood outside, asking to speak to him.[g] 48 But he replied to the man who told him, "Who is my mother, and who are my brothers?" 49 And stretching out his hand toward his disciples, he said, "Here are my mother and my brothers! 50 For whoever does the will of my Father in heaven is my brother, and sister, and mother."

13 That same day Jesus went out of the house and sat beside the sea. 2 And great crowds gathered about him, so that he got into a boat and sat there; and the whole crowd stood on the beach. 3 And he told them many things in parables, saying: "A sower went out to sow. 4 And as he sowed, some seeds fell along the path, and the birds came and devoured them. 5 Other seeds fell on rocky ground, where they had not much soil, and immediately they sprang up, since they had no depth of soil, 6 but when the sun rose they were scorched; and since they had no root they withered away. 7 Other seeds fell upon thorns, and the thorns grew up and choked them. 8 Other seeds fell on good soil and brought forth grain, some a hundredfold, some sixty, some thirty. 9 He who has ears,[h] let him hear."

10 Then the disciples came and said to him, "Why do you speak to them in parables?" 11 And he answered them, "To you it has been given to know the secrets of the kingdom of heaven, but to them it has not been given. 12 For to him who has will more be given, and he will have abundance; but from him who has not, even what he has will be taken away. 13 This is why I speak to them in parables, because seeing they do not see, and hearing they do not hear, nor do they understand. 14 With them indeed is fulfilled the prophecy of Isaiah which says:

'You shall indeed hear but never understand,
    and you shall indeed see but never perceive.
15 For this people's heart has grown dull,
    and their ears are heavy of hearing,

[g] Other ancient authorities insert verse 47, *Some one told him, "Your mother and your brothers are standing outside, asking to speak to you."* [h] Other ancient authorities add here and in verse 43 *to hear.*

PHILLIPS	N.E.B.

The danger of spiritual emptiness   12. 43

"When the evil spirit goes out of a man it wanders through waterless places looking for rest and never finding it. Then it says, 'I will go back to my house from which I came.' When it arrives it finds it unoccupied, but cleaned and all in order. Then it goes and collects seven other spirits more evil than itself to keep it company, and they all go in and make themselves at home. The last state of that man is worse than the first—and that is just what will happen to this evil generation."

Jesus and his relations   12. 46

While he was still talking to the crowds, his mother and his brothers happened to be standing outside wanting to speak to him. Somebody said to him, "Look, your mother and your brothers are outside wanting to speak to you." But Jesus replied to the one who told him, "Who is my mother, and who are my brothers?" then with a gesture of his hand toward his disciples he went on: "There are my mother and brothers! For whoever does the will of my Heavenly Father is brother and sister and mother to me."

Jesus tells the parable of the seed   13. 1

It was on the same day that Jesus went out of the house and sat down by the lakeside. Such great crowds collected round him that he went aboard a small boat and sat down while all the people stood on the beach. He told them a great deal in parables, and began:
"There was once a man who went out to sow. In his sowing some of the seeds fell by the roadside and the birds swooped down and gobbled them up. Some fell on stony patches where they had very little soil. They sprang up quickly in the shallow soil, but when the sun came up they were scorched by the heat and withered away because they had no roots. Some seeds fell among thornbushes and the thorns grew up and choked the life out of them. But some fell on good soil and produced a crop—some a hundred times what had been sown, some sixty and some thirty times. The man who has ears to hear should use them!"
At this the disciples approached him and asked, "Why do you talk to them in parables?"
"Because you have been given the chance to understand the secrets of the kingdom of Heaven," replied Jesus, "but they have not. For when a man has something, more is given to him till he has plenty. But if he has nothing even his nothing will be taken away from him. This is why I speak to them in these parables; because they go through life with their eyes open, but see nothing, and with their ears open, but understand nothing of what they hear. They are the living fulfillment of Isaiah's prophecy which says:

By hearing ye shall hear, and shall in no wise understand;
And seeing ye shall see, and shall in no wise perceive:
For this people's heart is waxed gross,
And their ears are dull of hearing,

'When an unclean spirit comes out of a man it wanders over the deserts seeking a resting-place; and finding none, it says, "I will go back to the home I left." So it returns and finds the house unoccupied, swept clean, and tidy. Off it goes and collects seven other spirits more wicked than itself, and they all come in and settle down; and in the end the man's plight is worse than before. That is how it will be with this wicked generation.'
He was still speaking to the crowd when his mother and brothers appeared; they stood outside, wanting to speak to him. Someone said, 'Your mother and your brothers are here outside; they want to speak to you.' Jesus turned to the man who brought the message, and said, 'Who is my mother? Who are my brothers?'; and pointing to the disciples, he said, 'Here are my mother and my brothers. Whoever does the will of my heavenly Father is my brother, my sister, my mother.'

13 That same day Jesus went out and sat beside the lake, where so many people gathered round him that he had to get into a boat. He sat there, and all the people stood on the shore. He spoke to them in parables, at some length.
He said: 'A sower went out to sow. And as he sowed, some seed fell along the footpath; and the birds came and ate it up. Some seed fell on rocky ground, where it had little soil; it sprouted quickly because it had no depth of earth, but when the sun rose the young corn was scorched, and as it had no root it withered away. Some seed fell among thistles; and the thistles shot up, and choked the corn. And some of the seed fell into good soil, where it bore fruit, yielding a hundredfold or, it might be, sixtyfold or thirtyfold. If you have ears, then hear.'
The disciples went up to him and asked, 'Why do you speak to them in parables?' He replied, 'It has been granted to you to know the secrets of the kingdom of Heaven; but to those others it has not been granted. For the man who has will be given more, till he has enough and to spare; and the man who has not will forfeit even what he has. That is why I speak to them in parables; for they look without seeing, and listen without hearing or understanding. There is a prophecy of Isaiah which is being fulfilled for them: "You will hear and hear, but never understand; you will look and look, but never see. For this people has grown gross at heart; their ears are dull, and their eyes

K.J.V.

are dull of hearing, and their eyes they have closed; lest at any time they should see with *their* eyes, and hear with *their* ears, and should understand with *their* heart, and should be converted, and I should heal them. 16 But blessed *are* your eyes, for they see: and your ears, for they hear. 17 For verily I say unto you, That many prophets and righteous *men* have desired to see *those things* which ye see, and have not seen *them;* and to hear *those things* which ye hear, and have not heard *them.*

18 Hear ye therefore the parable of the sower. 19 When any one heareth the word of the kingdom, and understandeth *it* not, then cometh the wicked one, and catcheth away that which was sown in his heart. This is he which received seed by the way side. 20 But he that received the seed into stony places, the same is he that heareth the word, and anon with joy receiveth it; 21 Yet hath he not root in himself, but dureth for a while: for when tribulation or persecution ariseth because of the word, by and by he is offended. 22 He also that received seed among the thorns is he that heareth the word; and the care of this world, and the deceitfulness of riches, choke the word, and he becometh unfruitful. 23 But he that received seed into the good ground is he that heareth the word, and understandeth *it;* which also beareth fruit, and bringeth forth, some a hundredfold, some sixty, some thirty.

24 Another parable put he forth unto them, saying, The kingdom of heaven is likened unto a man which sowed good seed in his field: 25 But while men slept, his enemy came and sowed tares among the wheat, and went his way. 26 But when the blade was sprung up, and brought forth fruit, then appeared the tares also. 27 So the servants of the householder came and said unto him, Sir, didst not thou sow good seed in thy field? from whence then hath it tares? 28 He said unto them, An enemy hath done this. The servants said unto him, Wilt thou then that we go and gather them up? 29 But he said, Nay; lest while ye gather up the tares, ye root up also the wheat with them. 30 Let both grow together until the harvest: and in the time of harvest I will say to the reapers, Gather ye together first the tares, and bind them in bundles to burn them: but gather the wheat into my barn.

31 Another parable put he forth unto them, saying, The kingdom of heaven is like to a grain of mustard seed, which a man took, and sowed in his field: 32 Which indeed is the least of all seeds: but when it is grown, it is the greatest among herbs, and becometh a tree, so that the birds of the air come and lodge in the branches thereof.

33 Another parable spake he unto them; The kingdom of heaven is like unto leaven, which a woman took, and hid in three measures of meal,

R.S.V.

and their eyes they have closed,
lest they should perceive with their eyes,
and hear with their ears,
and understand with their heart,
and turn for me to heal them.'
16 But blessed are your eyes, for they see, and your ears, for they hear. 17 Truly, I say to you, many prophets and righteous men longed to see what you see, and did not see it, and to hear what you hear, and did not hear it.

18 "Hear then the parable of the sower. 19 When any one hears the word of the kingdom and does not understand it, the evil one comes and snatches away what is sown in his heart; this is what was sown along the path. 20 As for what was sown on rocky ground, this is he who hears the word and immediately receives it with joy; 21 yet he has no root in himself, but endures for a while, and when tribulation or persecution arises on account of the word, immediately he falls away.ⁱ 22 As for what was sown among thorns, this is he who hears the word, but the cares of the world and the delight in riches choke the word, and it proves unfruitful. 23 As for what was sown on good soil, this is he who hears the word and understands it; he indeed bears fruit, and yields, in one case a hundredfold, in another sixty, and in another thirty."

24 Another parable he put before them, saying, "The kingdom of heaven may be compared to a man who sowed good seed in his field; 25 but while men were sleeping, his enemy came and sowed weeds among the wheat, and went away. 26 So when the plants came up and bore grain, then the weeds appeared also. 27 And the servantsʲ of the householder came and said to him, 'Sir, did you not sow good seed in your field? How then has it weeds?' 28 He said to them, 'An enemy has done this.' The servantsʲ said to him, 'Then do you want us to go and gather them?' 29 But he said, 'No; lest in gathering the weeds you root up the wheat along with them. 30 Let both grow together until the harvest; and at harvest time I will tell the reapers, Gather the weeds first and bind them in bundles to be burned, but gather the wheat into my barn.' "

31 Another parable he put before them, saying, "The kingdom of heaven is like a grain of mustard seed which a man took and sowed in his field; 32 it is the smallest of all seeds, but when it has grown it is the greatest of shrubs and becomes a tree, so that the birds of the air come and make nests in its branches."

33 He told them another parable. "The kingdom of heaven is like leaven which a woman took and hid in three measures of meal, till it was all leavened."

---

[i] Or *stumbles.* [j] Or *slaves.*

PHILLIPS

And their eyes they have closed;
Lest haply they should perceive with their eyes,
And hear with their ears,
And understand with their heart,
And should turn again,
And I should heal them.

"But how fortunate you are to have eyes that see and ears that hear! Believe me, a great many prophets and good men have longed to see what you are seeing and they never saw it. Yes, and they longed to hear what you are hearing and they never heard it.

"Now listen to the parable of the sower. When a man hears the message of the kingdom and does not grasp it, the evil one comes and snatches away what was sown in his heart. This is like the seed sown by the roadside. The seed sown on the stony patches represents the man who hears the message and eagerly accepts it. But it has not taken root in him and does not last long—the moment trouble or persecution arises through the message he gives up his faith at once. The seed sown among the thorns represents the man who hears the message, and then the worries of this life and the illusions of wealth choke it to death and so it produces no 'crop' in his life. But the seed sown on good soil is the man who both hears and understands the message. His life shows a good crop, a hundred, sixty or thirty times what was sown."

Good and evil grow side by side   13. 24
in this present world

Then he put another parable before them. "The kingdom of Heaven," he said, "is like a man who sowed good seed in his field. But while his men were asleep his enemy came and sowed weeds among the wheat, and went away. When the crop came up and ripened, the weeds appeared as well. Then the owner's servants came up to him and said: 'Sir, didn't you sow good seed in your field? Where did all these weeds come from?' 'Some blackguard has done this to spite me,' he replied. 'Do you want us then to go out and pull them all up?' said the servants. 'No,' he returned, 'if you pull up the weeds now, you would pull up the wheat with them. Let them both grow together till the harvest. And at harvest-time I shall tell the reapers, 'Collect all the weeds first and tie them up in bundles ready to burn, but collect the wheat and store it in my barn.' "

The kingdom's power of growth,   13. 31
and widespread influence

Then he put another parable before them: "The kingdom of Heaven is like a tiny grain of mustard seed which a man took and sowed in his field. As a seed it is the smallest of them all, but it grows to be the biggest of all plants. It becomes a tree, big enough for birds to come and nest in its branches."

This is another of the parables he told them: "The kingdom of Heaven is like yeast, taken by a woman and put into three measures of flour until the whole lot had risen."

N.E.B.

are closed. Otherwise, their eyes might see, their ears hear, and their heart understand, and then they might turn again, and I would heal them."

'But happy are your eyes because they see, and your ears because they hear! Many prophets and saints, I tell you, desired to see what you now see, yet never saw it; to hear what you hear, yet never heard it.

'You, then, may hear the parable of the sower. When a man hears the word that tells of the Kingdom but fails to understand it, the evil one comes and carries off what has been sown in his heart. There you have the seed sown along the footpath. The seed sown on rocky ground stands for the man who, on hearing the word, accepts it at once with joy; but as it strikes no root in him he has no staying-power, and when there is trouble or persecution on account of the word he falls away at once. The seed sown among thistles represents the man who hears the word, but worldly cares and the false glamour of wealth choke it, and it proves barren. But the seed that fell into good soil is the man who hears the word and understands it, who accordingly bears fruit, and yields a hundredfold or, it may be, sixtyfold or thirtyfold.'

Here is another parable that he put before them: 'The kingdom of Heaven is like this. A man sowed his field with good seed; but while everyone was asleep his enemy came, sowed darnel among the wheat, and made off. When the corn sprouted and began to fill out, the darnel could be seen among it. The farmer's men went to their master and said, "Sir, was it not good seed that you sowed in your field? Then where has the darnel come from?" "This is an enemy's doing", he replied. "Well then," they said, "shall we go and gather the darnel?" "No," he answered; "in gathering it you might pull up the wheat at the same time. Let them both grow together till harvest; and at harvest-time I will tell the reapers, 'Gather the darnel first, and tie it in bundles for burning; then collect the wheat into my barn.' " '

And this is another parable that he put before them: 'The kingdom of Heaven is like mustard-seed, which a man took and sowed in his field. As a seed, mustard is smaller than any other; but when it has grown it is bigger than any garden-plant; it becomes a tree, big enough for the birds to come and roost among its branches.'

He told them also this parable: 'The kingdom of Heaven is like yeast, which a woman took and mixed with half a hundredweight of flour till it was all leavened.'

K.J.V.

till the whole was leavened. 34All these things spake Jesus unto the multitude in parables; and without a parable spake he not unto them: 35 That it might be fulfilled which was spoken by the prophet, saying, I will open my mouth in parables; I will utter things which have been kept secret from the foundation of the world. 36 Then Jesus sent the multitude away, and went into the house: and his disciples came unto him, saying, Declare unto us the parable of the tares of the field. 37 He answered and said unto them, He that soweth the good seed is the Son of man; 38 The field is the world; the good seed are the children of the kingdom; but the tares are the children of the wicked one; 39 The enemy that sowed them is the devil; the harvest is the end of the world; and the reapers are the angels. 40As therefore the tares are gathered and burned in the fire; so shall it be in the end of this world. 41 The Son of man shall send forth his angels, and they shall gather out of his kingdom all things that offend, and them which do iniquity; 42And shall cast them into a furnace of fire: there shall be wailing and gnashing of teeth. 43 Then shall the righteous shine forth as the sun in the kingdom of their Father. Who hath ears to hear, let him hear.

44 Again, the kingdom of heaven is like unto treasure hid in a field; the which when a man hath found, he hideth, and for joy thereof goeth and selleth all that he hath, and buyeth that field.

45 Again, the kingdom of heaven is like unto a merchantman, seeking goodly pearls: 46 Who, when he had found one pearl of great price, went and sold all that he had, and bought it.

47 Again, the kingdom of heaven is like unto a net, that was cast into the sea, and gathered of every kind: 48 Which, when it was full, they drew to shore, and sat down, and gathered the good into vessels, but cast the bad away. 49 So shall it be at the end of the world: the angels shall come forth, and sever the wicked from among the just, 50And shall cast them into the furnace of fire: there shall be wailing and gnashing of teeth. 51 Jesus saith unto them, Have ye understood all these things? They say unto him, Yea, Lord. 52 Then said he unto them, Therefore every scribe *which is* instructed unto the kingdom of heaven, is like unto a man *that is* a householder, which bringeth forth out of his treasure *things* new and old.

53 And it came to pass, *that* when Jesus had finished these parables, he departed thence. 54And when he was come into his own country, he taught them in their synagogue, insomuch

R.S.V.

34 All this Jesus said to the crowds in parables; indeed he said nothing to them without a parable. 35 This was to fulfil what was spoken by the prophet:[k]
"I will open my mouth in parables,
  I will utter what has been hidden since the foundation of the world."
36 Then he left the crowds and went into the house. And his disciples came to him, saying, "Explain to us the parable of the weeds of the field." 37 He answered, "He who sows the good seed is the Son of man; 38 the field is the world, and the good seed means the sons of the kingdom; the weeds are the sons of the evil one, 39 and the enemy who sowed them is the devil; the harvest is the close of the age, and the reapers are angels. 40 Just as the weeds are gathered and burned with fire, so will it be at the close of the age. 41 The Son of man will send his angels, and they will gather out of his kingdom all causes of sin and all evil-doers, 42 and throw them into the furnace of fire; there men will weep and gnash their teeth. 43 Then the righteous will shine like the sun in the kingdom of their Father. He who has ears, let him hear.

44 "The kingdom of heaven is like treasure hidden in a field, which a man found and covered up; then in his joy he goes and sells all that he has and buys that field.

45 "Again, the kingdom of heaven is like a merchant in search of fine pearls, 46 who, on finding one pearl of great value, went and sold all that he had and bought it.

47 "Again, the kingdom of heaven is like a net which was thrown into the sea and gathered fish of every kind; 48 when it was full, men drew it ashore and sat down and sorted the good into vessels but threw away the bad. 49 So it will be at the close of the age. The angels will come out and separate the evil from the righteous, 50 and throw them into the furnace of fire; there men will weep and gnash their teeth.

51 "Have you understood all this?" They said to him, "Yes." 52And he said to them, "Therefore every scribe who has been trained for the kingdom of heaven is like a householder who brings out of his treasure what is new and what is old."

53 And when Jesus had finished these parables, he went away from there, 54 and coming to his own country he taught them in their syna-

[k] Other ancient authorities read *the prophet Isaiah.*

PHILLIPS

All these things Jesus spoke to the crowd in parables, and he did not speak to them at all without using parables—to fulfill the prophecy:

I will open my mouth in parables;
I will utter things hidden from the foundation of the world.

Jesus again explains a parable to his disciples   13. 36

Later, he left the crowds and went indoors, where his disciples came and said, "Please explain to us the parable of the weeds in the field."

"The one who sows the good seed is the Son of Man," replied Jesus. "The field is the whole world. The good seed? That is the sons of the kingdom, while the weeds are the sons of the evil one. The blackguard who sowed them is the devil. The harvest is the end of this world. The reapers are angels.

"Just as weeds are gathered up and burned in the fire, so will it happen at the end of this world. The Son of Man will send out his angels and they will uproot from the kingdom everything that is spoiling it, and all those who live in defiance of its laws, and will throw them into the blazing furnace, where there will be tears and bitter regret. Then the good will shine out like the sun in their Father's kingdom. The man who has ears should use them!

More pictures of the kingdom of Heaven   13. 44

"Again, the kingdom of Heaven is like some treasure which has been buried in a field. A man finds it and buries it again, and goes off overjoyed to sell all his possessions to buy himself that field.

"Or again, the kingdom of Heaven is like a merchant searching for fine pearls. When he has found a single pearl of great value, he goes and sells all his possessions and buys it.

"Or the kingdom of Heaven is like a big net thrown into the sea collecting all kinds of fish. When it is full, the fishermen haul it ashore and sit down and pick out the good ones for the barrels, but they throw away the bad. That is how it will be at the end of this world. The angels will go out and pick out the wicked from among the good and throw them into the blazing furnace, where there will be tears and bitter regret.

"Have you grasped all this?"

"Yes," they replied.

"You can see, then," returned Jesus, "how every one who knows the Law and becomes a disciple of the kingdom of Heaven is like a householder who can produce from his store both the new and the old."

Jesus is not appreciated in his native town   13. 53

When Jesus had finished these parables he left the place, and came into his own country. Here he taught the people in their own synagogue, till

N.E.B.

In all this teaching to the crowds Jesus spoke in parables; in fact he never spoke to them without a parable; thus making good the prophecy of Isaiah:[a]

'I will open my mouth in parables;
I will utter things kept secret since the world was made.'

He then dismissed the people, and went into the house, where his disciples came to him and said, 'Explain to us the parable of the darnel in the field.' And this was his answer: 'The sower of the good seed is the Son of Man. The field is the world; the good seed stands for the children of the Kingdom, the darnel for the children of the evil one. The enemy who sowed the darnel is the devil. The harvest is the end of time. The reapers are angels. As the darnel, then, is gathered up and burnt, so at the end of time the Son of Man will send out his angels, who will gather out of his kingdom everything that causes offence, and all whose deeds are evil, and these will be thrown into the blazing furnace, the place of wailing and grinding of teeth. And then the righteous will shine as brightly as the sun in the kingdom of their Father. If you have ears, then hear.

'The kingdom of Heaven is like treasure lying buried in a field. The man who found it, buried it again; and for sheer joy went and sold everything he had, and bought that field.

'Here is another picture of the kingdom of Heaven. A merchant looking out for fine pearls found one of very special value; so he went and sold everything he had, and bought it.

'Again the kingdom of Heaven is like a net let down into the sea, where fish of every kind were caught in it. When it was full, it was dragged ashore. Then the men sat down and collected the good fish into pails and threw the worthless away. That is how it will be at the end of time. The angels will go forth, and they will separate the wicked from the good, and throw them into the blazing furnace, the place of wailing and grinding of teeth.

'Have you understood all this?' he asked; and they answered, 'Yes.' He said to them, 'When, therefore, a teacher of the law has become a learner in the kingdom of Heaven, he is like a householder who can produce from his store both the new and the old.'

When he had finished these parables Jesus left that place, and came to his home town, where he taught the people in their synagogue.

[a] *Some witnesses omit* of Isaiah.

K.J.V.

that they were astonished, and said, Whence hath this *man* this wisdom, and *these* mighty works? 55 Is not this the carpenter's son? is not his mother called Mary? and his brethren, James, and Joses, and Simon, and Judas? 56And his sisters, are they not all with us? Whence then hath this *man* all these things? 57And they were offended in him. But Jesus said unto them, A prophet is not without honour, save in his own country, and in his own house. 58And he did not many mighty works there because of their unbelief.

14 At that time Herod the tetrarch heard of the fame of Jesus, 2And said unto his servants, This is John the Baptist; he is risen from the dead; and therefore mighty works do shew forth themselves in him.

3 For Herod had laid hold on John, and bound him, and put *him* in prison for Herodias' sake, his brother Philip's wife. 4 For John said unto him, It is not lawful for thee to have her. 5And when he would have put him to death, he feared the multitude, because they counted him as a prophet. 6 But when Herod's birthday was kept, the daughter of Herodias danced before them, and pleased Herod. 7 Whereupon he promised with an oath to give her whatsoever she would ask. 8And she, being before instructed of her mother, said, Give me here John Baptist's head in a charger. 9And the king was sorry: nevertheless for the oath's sake, and them which sat with him at meat, he commanded *it* to be given *her*. 10And he sent, and beheaded John in the prison. 11And his head was brought in a charger, and given to the damsel: and she brought *it* to her mother. 12And his disciples came, and took up the body, and buried it, and went and told Jesus.

13 When Jesus heard *of it,* he departed thence by ship into a desert place apart: and when the people had heard *thereof,* they followed him on foot out of the cities. 14And Jesus went forth, and saw a great multitude, and was moved with compassion toward them, and he healed their sick.

15 And when it was evening, his disciples came to him, saying, This is a desert place, and the time is now past; send the multitude away, that they may go into the villages, and buy themselves victuals. 16 But Jesus said unto them, They need not depart; give ye them to eat. 17And they say unto him, We have here but five loaves, and two fishes. 18 He said, Bring them hither to me. 19And he commanded the multitude to sit down on the grass, and took the five loaves, and the two fishes, and looking up to heaven, he blessed, and brake, and gave the loaves to *his* disciples, and the disciples to the multitude. 20And they did all eat, and were filled: and they took up of the fragments that remained twelve baskets full. 21And they that had eaten were about five thousand men, beside women and children.

R.S.V.

gogue, so that they were astonished, and said, "Where did this man get this wisdom and these mighty works? 55 Is not this the carpenter's son? Is not his mother called Mary? And are not his brothers James and Joseph and Simon and Judas? 56And are not all his sisters with us? Where then did this man get all this?" 57And they took offense at him. But Jesus said to them, "A prophet is not without honor except in his own country and in his own house." 58And he did not do many mighty works there, because of their unbelief.

14 At that time Herod the tetrarch heard about the fame of Jesus; 2 and he said to his servants, "This is John the Baptist, he has been raised from the dead; that is why these powers are at work in him." 3 For Herod had seized John and bound him and put him in prison, for the sake of Herodias, his brother Philip's wife;[l] 4 because John said to him, "It is not lawful for you to have her." 5And though he wanted to put him to death, he feared the people, because they held him to be a prophet. 6 But when Herod's birthday came, the daughter of Herodias danced before the company, and pleased Herod, 7 so that he promised with an oath to give her whatever she might ask. 8 Prompted by her mother, she said, "Give me the head of John the Baptist here on a platter." 9And the king was sorry; but because of his oaths and his guests he commanded it to be given; 10 he sent and had John beheaded in the prison, 11 and his head was brought on a platter and given to the girl, and she brought it to her mother. 12And his disciples came and took the body and buried it; and they went and told Jesus.

13 Now when Jesus heard this, he withdrew from there in a boat to a lonely place apart. But when the crowds heard it, they followed him on foot from the towns. 14As he went ashore he saw a great throng; and he had compassion on them, and healed their sick. 15 When it was evening, the disciples came to him and said, "This is a lonely place, and the day is now over; send the crowds away to go into the villages and buy food for themselves." 16 Jesus said, "They need not go away; you give them something to eat." 17 They said to him, "We have only five loaves here and two fish." 18And he said, "Bring them here to me." 19 Then he ordered the crowds to sit down on the grass; and taking the five loaves and the two fish he looked up to heaven, and blessed, and broke and gave the loaves to the disciples, and the disciples gave them to the crowds. 20And they all ate and were satisfied. And they took up twelve baskets full of the broken pieces left over. 21And those who ate were about five thousand men, besides women and children.

PHILLIPS

N.E.B.

in their amazement they said: "Where does this man get this wisdom and these powers? He's only the carpenter's son. Isn't Mary his mother, and aren't James, Joseph, Simon and Judas his brothers? And aren't all his sisters living here with us? Where did he get all this?" And they were deeply offended with him.

But Jesus said to them, "No prophet goes unhonored except in his own country and in his own home!"

And he performed very few miracles there because of their lack of faith.

In amazement they asked, 'Where does he get this wisdom from, and these miraculous powers? Is he not the carpenter's son? Is not his mother called Mary, his brothers James, Joseph, Simon, and Judas? And are not all his sisters here with us? Where then has he got all this from?' So they fell foul of him, and this led him to say, 'A prophet will always be held in honour, except in his home town, and in his own family.' And he did not work many miracles there: such was their want of faith.

Herod's guilty conscience 14. 1

About this time Herod, governor of the province, heard the reports about Jesus and said to his men, "This must be John the Baptist: he has risen from the dead. That is why miraculous powers are at work in him."

For previously Herod had arrested John and had him bound and put in prison, all on account of Herodias, the wife of his brother Philip. For John had said to him, "It is not right for you to have this woman." Herod wanted to kill him for this, but he was afraid of the people, since they all thought John was a prophet. But during Herod's birthday celebrations Herodias' daughter delighted him by dancing before his guests, so much so that he swore to give her anything she liked to ask. And she, prompted by her mother, said, "I want you to give me, here and now, on a dish, the head of John the Baptist!" Herod was aghast at this, but because he had sworn in front of his guests he gave orders that she should be given what she had asked. So he sent men and had John beheaded in the prison. Then the head was carried in on a dish and presented to the young girl, who handed it to her mother. Later, John's disciples came, took his body and buried it. Then they went and told the news to Jesus. When he heard it he went away by boat to a deserted place, quite alone.

14 It was at that time that reports about Jesus reached the ears of Prince Herod. 'This is John the Baptist,' he said to his attendants; 'John has been raised to life, and that is why these miraculous powers are at work in him.'

For Herod had arrested John, put him in chains, and thrown him into prison, on account of Herodias, his brother Philip's wife; for John had told him: 'You have no right to her.' Herod would have liked to put him to death, but he was afraid of the people, in whose eyes John was a prophet. But at his birthday celebrations the daughter of Herodias danced before the guests, and Herod was so delighted that he took an oath to give her anything she cared to ask. Prompted by her mother, she said, 'Give me here on a dish the head of John the Baptist.' The king was deeply distressed when he heard it; but out of regard for his oath and for his guests, he ordered the request to be granted, and had John beheaded in prison. The head was brought in on a dish and given to the girl; and she carried it to her mother. Then John's disciples came and took away the body, and buried it; and they went and told Jesus.

Jesus feeds a tired and hungry crowd 14. 13b

Then the crowds heard of his departure and followed him out of the towns on foot. When Jesus emerged from his retreat he saw a vast crowd and was very deeply moved, and cured the sick among them. As evening fell his disciples came to him and said: "We are right in the wilds here and it is very late. Send away these crowds now, so that they can go into the villages and buy themselves food."

"There's no need for them to go away," returned Jesus. "You give them something to eat!"

"But we haven't anything here," they told him, "except five loaves and two fish." To which Jesus replied, "Bring them here to me."

He told the crowd to sit down on the grass. Then he took the five loaves and the two fish in his hands, and, looking up to Heaven, he thanked God, broke the loaves and passed them to his disciples who handed them to the crowd. Everybody ate and was satisfied. Afterward they collected twelve baskets full of the pieces which were left over. Those who ate numbered about five thousand men, apart from the women and children.

When he heard what had happened Jesus withdrew privately by boat to a lonely place; but people heard of it, and came after him in crowds by land from the towns. When he came ashore, he saw a great crowd; his heart went out to them, and he cured those of them who were sick. When it grew late the disciples came up to him and said, 'This is a lonely place, and the day has gone; send the people off to the villages to buy themselves food.' He answered, 'There is no need for them to go; give them something to eat yourselves.' 'All we have here', they said, 'is five loaves and two fishes.' 'Let me have them', he replied. So he told the people to sit down on the grass; then, taking the five loaves and the two fishes, he looked up to heaven, said the blessing, broke the loaves, and gave them to the disciples; and the disciples gave them to the people. They all ate to their hearts' content; and the scraps left over, which they picked up, were enough to fill twelve great baskets. Some five thousand men shared in this meal, to say nothing of women and children.

K.J.V.

22 And straightway Jesus constrained his disciples to get into a ship, and to go before him unto the other side, while he sent the multitudes away. 23And when he had sent the multitudes away, he went up into a mountain apart to pray: and when the evening was come, he was there alone. 24 But the ship was now in the midst of the sea, tossed with waves: for the wind was contrary. 25And in the fourth watch of the night Jesus went unto them, walking on the sea. 26And when the disciples saw him walking on the sea, they were troubled, saying, It is a spirit; and they cried out for fear. 27 But straightway Jesus spake unto them, saying, Be of good cheer; it is I; be not afraid. 28And Peter answered him and said, Lord, if it be thou, bid me come unto thee on the water. 29And he said, Come. And when Peter was come down out of the ship, he walked on the water, to go to Jesus. 30 But when he saw the wind boisterous, he was afraid; and beginning to sink, he cried, saying, Lord, save me. 31And immediately Jesus stretched forth *his* hand, and caught him, and said unto him, O thou of little faith, wherefore didst thou doubt? 32And when they were come into the ship, the wind ceased. 33 Then they that were in the ship came and worshipped him, saying, Of a truth thou art the Son of God.

34 And when they were gone over, they came into the land of Gennesaret. 35And when the men of that place had knowledge of him, they sent out into all that country round about, and brought unto him all that were diseased; 36And besought him that they might only touch the hem of his garment: and as many as touched were made perfectly whole.

15 Then came to Jesus scribes and Pharisees, which were of Jerusalem, saying, 2 Why do thy disciples transgress the tradition of the elders? for they wash not their hands when they eat bread. 3 But he answered and said unto them, Why do ye also transgress the commandment of God by your tradition? 4 For God commanded, saying, Honour thy father and mother: and, He that curseth father or mother, let him die the death. 5 But ye say, Whosoever shall say to *his* father or *his* mother, *It is* a gift, by whatsoever thou mightest be profited by me; 6And honour not his father or his mother, *he shall be free.* Thus have ye made the commandment of God of none effect by your tradition. 7 *Ye* hypocrites, well did Esaias prophesy of you, saying, 8 This people draweth nigh unto me with their mouth, and honoureth me with *their* lips; but their heart is far from me. 9 But in vain they do worship me, teaching *for* doctrines the commandments of men.

10 And he called the multitude, and said unto them, Hear, and understand: 11 Not that which goeth into the mouth defileth a man; but that which cometh out of the mouth, this defileth a man. 12 Then came his disciples, and said unto

R.S.V.

22 Then he made the disciples get into the boat and go before him to the other side, while he dismissed the crowds. 23And after he had dismissed the crowds, he went up into the hills by himself to pray. When evening came, he was there alone, 24 but the boat by this time was many furlongs distant from the land,*m* beaten by the waves; for the wind was against them. 25And in the fourth watch of the night he came to them, walking on the sea. 26 But when the disciples saw him walking on the sea, they were terrified, saying, "It is a ghost!" And they cried out for fear. 27 But immediately he spoke to them, saying, "Take heart, it is I; have no fear."

28 And Peter answered him, "Lord, if it is you, bid me come to you on the water." 29 He said, "Come." So Peter got out of the boat and walked on the water and came to Jesus; 30 but when he saw the wind,*n* he was afraid, and beginning to sink he cried out, "Lord, save me." 31 Jesus immediately reached out his hand and caught him, saying to him, "O man of little faith, why did you doubt?" 32And when they got into the boat, the wind ceased. 33And those in the boat worshiped him, saying, "Truly you are the Son of God."

34 And when they had crossed over, they came to land at Gennesaret. 35And when the men of that place recognized him, they sent round to all that region and brought to him all that were sick, 36 and besought him that they might only touch the fringe of his garment; and as many as touched it were made well.

15 Then Pharisees and scribes came to Jesus from Jerusalem and said, 2 "Why do your disciples transgress the tradition of the elders? For they do not wash their hands when they eat." 3 He answered them, "And why do you transgress the commandment of God for the sake of your tradition? 4 For God commanded, 'Honor your father and your mother,' and, 'He who speaks evil of father or mother, let him surely die.' 5 But you say, 'If any one tells his father or his mother, What you would have gained from me is given to God,*o* he need not honor his father.' 6 So, for the sake of your tradition, you have made void the word *p* of God. 7 You hypocrites! Well did Isaiah prophesy of you, when he said:

8 'This people honors me with their lips,
but their heart is far from me;

9 in vain do they worship me,
teaching as doctrines the precepts of men.'"

10 And he called the people to him and said to them, "Hear and understand: 11 not what goes into the mouth defiles a man, but what comes out of the mouth, this defiles a man." 12 Then

---

[m] Other ancient authorities read was *out on the sea.* [n] Other ancient authorities read *strong wind.* [o] Or *an offering.* [p] Other ancient authorities read *law.*

Jesus again shows his power   **14. 22**
over the forces of nature

Directly after this, Jesus insisted on his disciples' getting aboard their boat and going on ahead to the other side, while he himself sent the crowds home. And when he had sent them away he went up the hillside quite alone, to pray. When it grew late he was there by himself, while the boat was by now a long way from the shore, at the mercy of the waves, for the wind was dead against them. In the small hours Jesus went out to them, walking on the water of the lake. When the disciples caught sight of him walking on the water they were terrified. "It's a ghost!" they said, and screamed with fear.

But at once Jesus spoke to them. "It's all right! It's I myself, don't be afraid!"

"Lord, if it's really you," said Peter, "tell me to come to you on the water."

"Come on, then," replied Jesus.

Peter stepped down from the boat and did walk on the water, making for Jesus. But when he saw the fury of the wind he panicked and began to sink, calling out, "Lord save me!" At once Jesus reached out his hand and caught him, saying, "You little-faith! What made you lose your nerve like that?" Then, when they were both aboard the boat, the wind dropped. The whole crew came and kneeled down before Jesus, crying, "You are indeed the Son of God!"

When they had crossed over to the other side of the lake, they landed at Gennesaret, and when the men of that place had recognized him they sent word to the whole surrounding country and brought all the diseased to him. They implored him to let them touch just the edge of his cloak, and all those who did so were cured.

Then he made the disciples embark and go on ahead to the other side, while he sent the people away; after doing that, he went up the hill-side to pray alone. It grew late, and he was there by himself. The boat was already some furlongs from the shore,[a] battling with a head-wind and a rough sea. Between three and six in the morning he came to them, walking over the lake. When the disciples saw him walking on the lake they were so shaken that they cried out in terror: 'It is a ghost!' But at once he spoke to them: 'Take heart! It is I; do not be afraid.'

Peter called to him: 'Lord, if it is you, tell me to come to you over the water.' 'Come', said Jesus. Peter stepped down from the boat, and walked over the water towards Jesus. But when he saw the strength of the gale he was seized with fear; and beginning to sink, he cried, 'Save me, Lord.' Jesus at once reached out and caught hold of him, and said, 'Why did you hesitate? How little faith you have!' They then climbed into the boat; and the wind dropped. And the men in the boat fell at his feet, exclaiming, 'Truly you are the Son of God.'

So they finished the crossing and came to land at Gennesaret. There Jesus was recognized by the people of the place, who sent out word to all the country round. And all who were ill were brought to him, and he was begged to allow them simply to touch the edge of his cloak. And everyone who touched it was completely cured.

The dangers of tradition   **15. 1**

Then some of the scribes and Pharisees from Jerusalem came and asked Jesus, "Why do your disciples break our ancient tradition and eat their food without washing their hands properly first?"

"Tell me," replied Jesus, "why do you break God's commandment through your tradition? For God said, *'Honor thy father and thy mother,'* and *'He that speaketh evil of father or mother, let him die the death.'* But you say that if a man tells his parents, 'Whatever use I might have been to you is now given to God,' then he owes no further duty to his parents. And so your tradition empties the commandment of God of all its meaning. You hypocrites! Isaiah described you beautifully when he said:

This people honoreth me with their lips;
But their heart is far from me.
But in vain do they worship me,
Teaching as their doctrines the precepts of
    men

15 Then Jesus was approached by a group of Pharisees and lawyers from Jerusalem, with the question: 'Why do your disciples break the old-established tradition? They do not wash their hands before meals.' He answered them: 'And what of you? Why do you break God's commandment in the interest of your tradition? For God said, "Honour your father and mother", and, "The man who curses his father or mother must suffer death." But you say, "If a man says to his father or mother, 'Anything of mine which might have been used for your benefit is set apart for God', then he must not honour his father or his mother." You have made God's law null and void out of respect for your tradition. What hypocrisy! Isaiah was right when he prophesied about you: "This people pays me lip-service, but their heart is far from me; their worship of me is in vain, for they teach as doctrines the commandments of men." '

He called the crowd and said to them, 'Listen to me, and understand this: a man is not defiled by what goes into his mouth, but by what comes out of it.'

Then the disciples came to him and said, 'Do

Superficial and true cleanliness   **15. 10**

Then he called the crowd to him and said, "Listen, and understand this thoroughly! It is not what goes *into* a man's mouth that makes him common or unclean. It is what comes *out* of a man's mouth that makes him unclean."

[a] *Some witnesses read* already well out on the water.

K.J.V.

him, Knowest thou that the Pharisees were offended, after they heard this saying? 13 But he answered and said, Every plant, which my heavenly Father hath not planted, shall be rooted up. 14 Let them alone: they be blind leaders of the blind. And if the blind lead the blind, both shall fall into the ditch. 15 Then answered Peter and said unto him, Declare unto us this parable. 16And Jesus said, Are ye also yet without understanding? 17 Do not ye yet understand, that whatsoever entereth in at the mouth goeth into the belly, and is cast out into the draught? 18 But those things which proceed out of the mouth come forth from the heart; and they defile the man. 19 For out of the heart proceed evil thoughts, murders, adulteries, fornications, thefts, false witness, blasphemies: 20 These are *the things* which defile a man: but to eat with unwashen hands defileth not a man.

21 Then Jesus went thence, and departed into the coasts of Tyre and Sidon. 22And, behold, a woman of Canaan came out of the same coasts, and cried unto him, saying, Have mercy on me, O Lord, *thou* Son of David; my daughter is grievously vexed with a devil. 23 But he answered her not a word. And his disciples came and besought him, saying, Send her away; for she crieth after us. 24 But he answered and said, I am not sent but unto the lost sheep of the house of Israel. 25 Then came she and worshipped him, saying, Lord, help me. 26 But he answered and said, It is not meet to take the children's bread, and to cast *it* to dogs. 27And she said, Truth, Lord: yet the dogs eat of the crumbs which fall from their masters' table. 28 Then Jesus answered and said unto her, O woman, great *is* thy faith: be it unto thee even as thou wilt. And her daughter was made whole from that very hour. 29And Jesus departed from thence, and came nigh unto the sea of Galilee; and went up into a mountain, and sat down there. 30And great multitudes came unto him, having with them *those that were* lame, blind, dumb, maimed, and many others, and cast them down at Jesus' feet; and he healed them: 31 Insomuch that the multitude wondered, when they saw the dumb to speak, the maimed to be whole, the lame to walk, and the blind to see: and they glorified the God of Israel.

32 Then Jesus called his disciples *unto him,* and said, I have compassion on the multitude, because they continue with me now three days, and have nothing to eat: and I will not send them away fasting, lest they faint in the way. 33And his disciples say unto him, Whence should we have so much bread in the wilderness, as to fill so great a multitude? 34And Jesus saith unto them, How many loaves have ye? And they said, Seven, and a few little fishes. 35And he com-

R.S.V.

the disciples came and said to him, "Do you know that the Pharisees were offended when they heard this saying?" 13 He answered, "Every plant which my heavenly Father has not planted will be rooted up. 14 Let them alone; they are blind guides. And if a blind man leads a blind man, both will fall into a pit." 15 But Peter said to him, "Explain the parable to us." 16And he said, "Are you also still without understanding? 17 Do you not see that whatever goes into the mouth passes into the stomach, and so passes on? q 18 But what comes out of the mouth proceeds from the heart, and this defiles a man. 19 For out of the heart come evil thoughts, murder, adultery, fornication, theft, false witness, slander. 20 These are what defile a man; but to eat with unwashed hands does not defile a man."

21 And Jesus went away from there and withdrew to the district of Tyre and Sidon. 22And behold, a Canaanite woman from that region came out and cried, "Have mercy on me, O Lord, Son of David; my daughter is severely possessed by a demon." 23 But he did not answer her a word. And his disciples came and begged him, saying, "Send her away, for she is crying after us." 24 He answered, "I was sent only to the lost sheep of the house of Israel." 25 But she came and knelt before him, saying, "Lord, help me." 26And he answered, "It is not fair to take the children's bread and throw it to the dogs." 27 She said, "Yes, Lord, yet even the dogs eat the crumbs that fall from their master's table." 28 Then Jesus answered her, "O woman, great is your faith! Be it done for you as you desire." And her daughter was healed instantly.

29 And Jesus went on from there and passed along the Sea of Galilee. And he went up into the hills, and sat down there. 30And great crowds came to him, bringing with them the lame, the maimed, the blind, the dumb, and many others, and they put them at his feet, and he healed them, 31 so that the throng wondered, when they saw the dumb speaking, the maimed whole, the lame walking, and the blind seeing; and they glorified the God of Israel.

32 Then Jesus called his disciples to him and said, "I have compassion on the crowd, because they have been with me now three days, and have nothing to eat; and I am unwilling to send them away hungry, lest they faint on the way." 33And the disciples said to him, "Where are we to get bread enough in the desert to feed so great a crowd?" 34And Jesus said to them, "How many loaves have you?" They said, "Seven, and a few small fish." 35And commanding the crowd

[q] Or *is evacuated.*

PHILLIPS

Later his disciples came to him and said, "Do you know that the Pharisees are deeply offended by what you said?"

"Every plant which my Heavenly Father did not plant will be pulled up by the roots," returned Jesus. "Let them alone. They are blind guides, and when one blind man leads another blind man they will both end up in the ditch!"

"Explain this parable to us," broke in Peter.

"Are you still unable to grasp things like this?" replied Jesus. "Don't you see that whatever goes *into* the mouth passes into the stomach and then out of the body altogether? But the things that come *out* of a man's mouth come from his heart and mind, and it is they that really make a man unclean. For it is from a man's mind that evil thoughts arise—murder, adultery, lust, theft, perjury and blasphemy. These are the things which make a man unclean, not eating without washing his hands properly!"

A gentile's faith in Jesus   15. 21

Jesus then left that place and retired into the Tyre and Sidon district. There a Canaanite woman from those parts came to him crying at the top of her voice:

"Lord, have pity on me! My daughter is in a terrible state—a devil has got into her!"

Jesus made no answer, and the disciples came up to him and said, "Do send her away—she's still following us and calling out."

"I was only sent," replied Jesus, "to the lost sheep of the house of Israel."

Then the woman came and kneeled at his feet. "Lord, help me," she said.

"It is not right, you know," Jesus replied, "to take the children's food and throw it to the dogs."

"Yes, Lord, I know, but even the dogs live on the scraps that fall from their master's table!"

"You certainly don't lack faith," returned Jesus; "it shall be as you wish."

And at that moment her daughter was cured.

Jesus heals and feeds vast   15. 29
crowds of people

Jesus left there, walked along the shore of the lake of Galilee, then climbed the hill and sat down. And great crowds came to him, bringing with them people who were lame, crippled, blind, dumb and many others. They simply put them down at his feet and he healed them. The result was that the people were astonished at seeing dumb men speak, crippled men healed, lame men walking about and blind men having recovered their sight. And they praised the God of Israel.

But Jesus quietly called his disciples to him. "My heart goes out to this crowd," he said. "They've stayed with me three days now and have no more food. I don't want to send them home without anything or they will collapse on the way."

"Where could we find enough food to feed such a crowd in this deserted spot?" said the disciples.

"How many loaves have you?" asked Jesus.

"Seven, and a few small fish," they replied.

Then Jesus told the crowd to sit down com-

N.E.B.

Then the disciples came to him and said, 'Do you know that the Pharisees have taken great offence at what you have been saying?' His answer was: 'Any plant that is not of my heavenly Father's planting will be rooted up. Leave them alone; they are blind guides,[a] and if one blind man guides another they will both fall into the ditch.'

Then Peter said, 'Tell us what that parable means.' Jesus answered, 'Are you still as dull as the rest? Do you not see that whatever goes in by the mouth passes into the stomach and so is discharged into the drain? But what comes out of the mouth has its origins in the heart; and that is what defiles a man. Wicked thoughts, murder, adultery, fornication, theft, perjury, slander—these all proceed from the heart; and these are the things that defile a man; but to eat without first washing his hands, that cannot defile him.'

Jesus and His Disciples

Jesus then left that place and withdrew to the region of Tyre and Sidon. And a Canaanite woman from those parts came crying out, 'Sir! have pity on me, Son of David; my daughter is tormented by a devil.' But he said not a word in reply. His disciples came and urged him: 'Send her away; see how she comes shouting after us.' Jesus replied, 'I was sent to the lost sheep of the house of Israel, and to them alone.' But the woman came and fell at his feet and cried, 'Help me, sir.' To this Jesus replied, 'It is not right to take the children's bread and throw it to the dogs.' 'True, sir,' she answered; 'and yet the dogs eat the scraps that fall from their masters' table.' Hearing this Jesus replied, 'Woman, what faith you have! Be it as you wish!' And from that moment her daughter was restored to health.

After leaving that region Jesus took the road by the Sea of Galilee and went up to the hills. When he was seated there, crowds flocked to him, bringing with them the lame, blind, dumb, and crippled, and many other sufferers; they flung them down at his feet, and he healed them. Great was the amazement of the people when they saw the dumb speaking, the crippled strong, the lame walking, and sight restored to the blind; and they gave praise to the God of Israel.

Jesus called his disciples and said to them, 'I feel sorry for all these people; they have been with me now for three days and have nothing to eat. I do not want to send them away unfed; they might turn faint on the way.' The disciples replied, 'Where in this lonely place can we find bread enough to feed such a crowd?' 'How many loaves have you?' Jesus asked. 'Seven,' they replied; 'and there are a few small fishes.' So

[a] *Some witnesses insert* of blind men.

49

K.J.V.

manded the multitude to sit down on the ground. 36And he took the seven loaves and the fishes, and gave thanks, and brake *them*, and gave to his disciples, and the disciples to the multitude. 37And they did all eat, and were filled: and they took up of the broken *meat* that was left seven baskets full. 38And they that did eat were four thousand men, beside women and children. 39And he sent away the multitude, and took ship, and came into the coasts of Magdala.

16 The Pharisees also with the Sadducees came, and tempting desired him that he would shew them a sign from heaven. 2 He answered and said unto them, When it is evening, ye say, *It will be* fair weather: for the sky is red. 3And in the morning, *It will be* foul weather to day: for the sky is red and lowering. O *ye* hypocrites, ye can discern the face of the sky; but can ye not *discern* the signs of the times? 4A wicked and adulterous generation seeketh after a sign; and there shall no sign be given unto it, but the sign of the prophet Jonas. And he left them, and departed. 5And when his disciples were come to the other side, they had forgotten to take bread.

6 Then Jesus said unto them, Take heed and beware of the leaven of the Pharisees and of the Sadducees. 7And they reasoned among themselves, saying, *It is* because we have taken no bread. 8 *Which* when Jesus perceived, he said unto them, O ye of little faith, why reason ye among yourselves, because ye have brought no bread? 9 Do ye not yet understand, neither remember the five loaves of the five thousand, and how many baskets ye took up? 10 Neither the seven loaves of the four thousand, and how many baskets ye took up? 11 How is it that ye do not understand that I spake *it* not to you concerning bread, that ye should beware of the leaven of the Pharisees and of the Sadducees? 12 Then understood they how that he bade *them* not beware of the leaven of bread, but of the doctrine of the Pharisees and of the Sadducees.

13 When Jesus came into the coasts of Cesarea Philippi, he asked his disciples, saying, Whom do men say that I, the Son of man, am? 14And they said, Some *say that thou art* John the Baptist; some, Elias; and others, Jeremias, or one of the prophets. 15 He saith unto them, But whom say ye that I am? 16And Simon Peter answered and said, Thou art the Christ, the Son of the living God. 17And Jesus answered and said unto him, Blessed art thou, Simon Bar-jona: for flesh and blood hath not revealed *it* unto thee, but my Father which is in heaven. 18And I

R.S.V.

to sit down on the ground, 36 he took the seven loaves and the fish, and having given thanks he broke them and gave them to the disciples, and the disciples gave them to the crowds. 37And they all ate and were satisfied; and they took up seven baskets full of the broken pieces left over. 38 Those who ate were four thousand men, besides women and children. 39And sending away the crowds, he got into the boat and went to the region of Magadan.

16 And the Pharisees and Sadducees came, and to test him they asked him to show them a sign from heaven. 2 He answered them,^{r} "When it is evening, you say, 'It will be fair weather; for the sky is red.' 3And in the morning, 'It will be stormy today, for the sky is red and threatening.' You know how to interpret the appearance of the sky, but you cannot interpret the signs of the times. 4An evil and adulterous generation seeks for a sign, but no sign shall be given to it except the sign of Jonah." So he left them and departed.

5 When the disciples reached the other side, they had forgotten to bring any bread. 6 Jesus said to them, "Take heed and beware of the leaven of the Pharisees and Sadducees." 7And they discussed it among themselves, saying, "We brought no bread." 8 But Jesus, aware of this, said, "O men of little faith, why do you discuss among yourselves the fact that you have no bread? 9 Do you not yet perceive? Do you not remember the five loaves of the five thousand, and how many baskets you gathered? 10 Or the seven loaves of the four thousand, and how many baskets you gathered? 11 How is it that you fail to perceive that I did not speak about bread? Beware of the leaven of the Pharisees and Sadducees." 12 Then they understood that he did not tell them to beware of the leaven of bread, but of the teaching of the Pharisees and Sadducees.

13 Now when Jesus came into the district of Caesarea Philippi, he asked his disciples, "Who do men say that the Son of man is?" 14And they said, "Some say John the Baptist, others say Elijah, and others Jeremiah or one of the prophets." 15 He said to them, "But who do you say that I am?" 16 Simon Peter replied, "You are the Christ, the Son of the living God." 17And Jesus answered him, "Blessed are you, Simon Bar-Jona! For flesh and blood has not revealed this to you, but my Father who is in heaven. 18And I tell you, you are Peter,^{s} and on this

[r] Other ancient authorities omit the following words to the end of verse 3. [s] Greek *Petros*.

PHILLIPS

N.E.B.

fortably on the ground. And when he had taken the seven loaves and the fish into his hands, he broke them with a prayer of thanksgiving and gave them to the disciples to pass on to the people. Everybody ate and was satisfied, and they picked up seven baskets full of the pieces left over. Those who ate numbered four thousand men apart from women and children. Then Jesus sent the crowds home, boarded the boat and arrived at the district of Magadan.

he ordered the people to sit down on the ground; then he took the seven loaves and the fishes, and after giving thanks to God he broke them and gave to the disciples, and the disciples gave to the people. They all ate to their hearts' content; and the scraps left over, which they picked up, were enough to fill seven baskets. Four thousand men shared in this meal, to say nothing of women and children. He then dismissed the crowds, got into a boat, and went to the neighbourhood of Magadan.

Jesus again refuses to give a sign   16. 1

Once the Pharisees and the Sadducees arrived together to test him, and asked him to give them a sign from Heaven. But he replied, "When the evening comes you say, 'Ah, fine weather—the sky is red.' In the morning you say, 'There will be a storm today, the sky is red and threatening.' Yes, you know how to interpret the look of the sky but you have no idea how to interpret the signs of the times! A wicked and unfaithful age insists on a sign; and it will not be given any sign at all but that of the prophet Jonah." And he turned on his heel and left them.

16 The Pharisees and Sadducees came, and to test him they asked him to show them a sign from heaven. His answer was: [a] 'It is a wicked generation that asks for a sign; and the only sign that will be given it is the sign of Jonah.' So he went off and left them.

In crossing to the other side the disciples had forgotten to take bread with them. So, when Jesus said to them. 'Beware, be on your guard against the leaven of the Pharisees and Sadducees', they began to say among themselves, 'It is because we have brought no bread!' Knowing what was in their minds, Jesus said to them: 'Why do you talk about bringing no bread? Where is your faith? Do you not understand even yet? Do you not remember the five loaves for the five thousand, and how many basketfuls you picked up? Or the seven loaves for the four thousand, and how many basketfuls you picked up? How can you fail to see that I was not speaking about bread? Be on your guard, I said, against the leaven of the Pharisees and Sadducees.' Then they understood: they were to be on their guard, not against the baker's leaven of the Pharisees and Sadducees, but against their teaching.

He is misunderstood by the   16. 5
disciples

Then his disciples came to him on the other side of the lake, forgetting to bring any bread with them. "Keep your eyes open," said Jesus to them, "and be on your guard against the 'yeast' of the Pharisees and Sadducees!" But they were arguing with each other, and saying, "We forgot to bring the bread." When Jesus saw this he said to them, "Why all this argument among yourselves about not bringing any bread, you little-faiths? Don't you understand yet, or have you forgotten the five loaves and the five thousand, and how many baskets you took up afterward; or the seven loaves and the four thousand and how many baskets you took up then? I wonder why you don't yet understand that I wasn't talking about bread at all—I told you to beware of the yeast of the Pharisees and Sadducees." Then they grasped the fact that he had not told them to beware of yeast in the ordinary sense but of the teaching of the Pharisees and Sadducees.

When he came to the territory of Caesarea Philippi, Jesus asked his disciples, 'Who do men say that the Son of Man is[b]?' They answered, 'Some say John the Baptist, others Elijah, others Jeremiah, or one of the prophets.' 'And you,' he asked, 'who do you say I am?' Simon Peter answered: 'You are the Messiah, the Son of the living God.' Then Jesus said: 'Simon son of Jonah, you are favoured indeed! You did not learn that from mortal man; it was revealed to you by my heavenly Father. And I say this to

Peter's bold affirmation   16. 13

When Jesus reached the Caesarea-Philippi district he asked his disciples a question. "Who do people say the Son of Man is?"

"Well, some say John the Baptist," they told him. "Some say Elijah, others Jeremiah or one of the prophets."

"But what about you?" he said to them. "Who do you say that I am?"

Simon Peter answered, "You? You are Christ, the Son of the living God!"

"Simon, son of Jonah, you are a fortunate man indeed!" said Jesus, "for it was not your own nature but my Heavenly Father who has revealed this truth to you! Now I tell you that you

[a] Some witnesses here insert 'In the evening you say, "It will be fine weather, for the sky is red"; (3) and in the morning you say, "It will be stormy today; the sky is red and lowering." You know how to interpret the appearance of the sky; can you not interpret the signs of the times?' [b] Some witnesses read that I, the Son of Man, am.

K.J.V.

say also unto thee, That thou art Peter, and upon this rock I will build my church; and the gates of hell shall not prevail against it. 19And I will give unto thee the keys of the kingdom of heaven: and whatsoever thou shalt bind on earth shall be bound in heaven; and whatsoever thou shalt loose on earth shall be loosed in heaven. 20 Then charged he his disciples that they should tell no man that he was Jesus the Christ.

21 From that time forth began Jesus to shew unto his disciples, how that he must go unto Jerusalem, and suffer many things of the elders and chief priests and scribes, and be killed, and be raised again the third day. 22 Then Peter took him, and began to rebuke him, saying, Be it far from thee, Lord: this shall not be unto thee. 23 But he turned, and said unto Peter, Get thee behind me, Satan: thou art an offence unto me: for thou savourest not the things that be of God, but those that be of men.

24 Then said Jesus unto his disciples, If any *man* will come after me, let him deny himself, and take up his cross, and follow me. 25 For whosoever will save his life shall lose it: and whosoever will lose his life for my sake shall find it. 26 For what is a man profited, if he shall gain the whole world, and lose his own soul? or what shall a man give in exchange for his soul? 27 For the Son of man shall come in the glory of his Father with his angels; and then he shall reward every man according to his works. 28 Verily I say unto you, There be some standing here, which shall not taste of death, till they see the Son of man coming in his kingdom.

R.S.V.

rock[t] I will build my church, and the powers of death[u] shall not prevail against it. 19 I will give you the keys of the kingdom of heaven, and whatever you bind on earth shall be bound in heaven, and whatever you loose on earth shall be loosed in heaven." 20 Then he strictly charged the disciples to tell no one that he was the Christ.

21 From that time Jesus began to show his disciples that he must go to Jerusalem and suffer many things from the elders and chief priests and scribes, and be killed, and on the third day be raised. 22And Peter took him and began to rebuke him, saying, "God forbid, Lord! This shall never happen to you." 23 But he turned and said to Peter, "Get behind me, Satan! You are a hindrance[v] to me; for you are not on the side of God, but of men."

24 Then Jesus told his disciples, "If any man would come after me, let him deny himself and take up his cross and follow me. 25 For whoever would save his life will lose it, and whoever loses his life for my sake will find it. 26 For what will it profit a man, if he gains the whole world and forfeits his life? Or what shall a man give in return for his life? 27 For the Son of man is to come with his angels in the glory of his Father, and then he will repay every man for what he has done. 28 Truly, I say to you, there are some standing here who will not taste death before they see the Son of man coming in his kingdom."

17 And after six days Jesus taketh Peter, James, and John his brother, and bringeth them up into a high mountain apart, 2And was transfigured before them: and his face did shine as the sun, and his raiment was white as the light. 3And, behold, there appeared unto them Moses and Elias talking with him. 4 Then answered Peter, and said unto Jesus, Lord, it is good for us to be here: if thou wilt, let us make here three tabernacles; one for thee, and one for Moses, and one for Elias. 5 While he yet spake, behold, a bright cloud overshadowed them: and behold a voice out of the cloud, which said, This is my beloved Son, in whom I am well pleased; hear ye him. 6And when the disciples heard *it*, they fell on their face, and were sore afraid. 7And Jesus came and touched them, and said, Arise, and be not afraid. 8And when they had lifted up their eyes, they saw no man, save Jesus only. 9And as they came down from the mountain, Jesus charged them, saying, Tell the vision to no man, until the Son of man be risen again from the dead. 10And his disciples asked him,

17 And after six days Jesus took with him Peter and James and John his brother, and led them up a high mountain apart. 2And he was transfigured before them, and his face shone like the sun, and his garments became white as light. 3And behold, there appeared to them Moses and Elijah, talking with him. 4And Peter said to Jesus, "Lord, it is well that we are here; if you wish, I will make three booths here, one for you and one for Moses and one for Elijah." 5 He was still speaking, when lo, a bright cloud overshadowed them, and a voice from the cloud said, "This is my beloved Son,[w] with whom I am well pleased; listen to him." 6 When the disciples heard this, they fell on their faces, and were filled with awe. 7 But Jesus came and touched them, saying, "Rise, and have no fear." 8And when they lifted up their eyes, they saw no one but Jesus only.

9 And as they were coming down the mountain, Jesus commanded them, "Tell no one the vision, until the Son of man is raised from the dead." 10And the disciples asked him, "Then

[t] Greek *petra*. [u] Greek *the gates of Hades*. [v] Greek *stumbling block*, [w] Or *my Son, my* (or *the*) *Beloved*.

PHILLIPS

N.E.B.

are Peter the rock, and it is on this rock that I am going to found my Church, and the powers of death will never prevail against it. I will give you the keys of the kingdom of Heaven; whatever you forbid on earth will be what is forbidden in Heaven and whatever you permit on earth will be what is permitted in Heaven!" Then he impressed on his disciples that they should not tell anyone that he was Christ.

Jesus speaks about his passion,   *16. 21*
and the cost of following him

From that time onward Jesus began to explain to his disciples that he would have to go to Jerusalem, and endure much suffering from the elders, chief priests and scribes, and finally be killed; and be raised to life again on the third day.

Then Peter took him on one side and started to remonstrate with him over this. "God bless you, Master! Nothing like this must happen to you!" Then Jesus turned round and said to Peter, "Out of my way, Satan! . . . You stand right in my path, Peter, when you look at things from man's point of view and not from God's."

Then Jesus said to his disciples: "If anyone wants to follow in my footsteps he must give up all right to himself, take up his cross and follow me. For the man who wants to save his life will lose it; but the man who loses his life for my sake will find it. For what good is it for a man to gain the whole world at the price of his own soul? What could a man offer to buy back his soul once he had lost it?

"For the Son of Man will come in the glory of his Father and in the company of his angels and then he will repay every man for what he has done. Believe me, there are some standing here today who will know nothing of death till they have seen the Son of Man coming as king."

Three disciples glimpse the   *17. 1*
glory of Christ

Six days later Jesus chose Peter, James and his brother John to accompany him high up on the hillside where they were quite alone. There his whole appearance changed before their eyes, his face shining like the sun and his clothes as white as light. Then Moses and Elijah were seen talking to Jesus.

"Lord," exclaimed Peter, "it is wonderful for us to be here! If you like I could put up three shelters, one each for you and Moses and Elijah—"

But while he was still talking a bright cloud overshadowed them and a voice came out of the cloud:

"This is my dearly loved Son in whom I am well pleased. Listen to him!"

When they heard this voice the disciples fell on their faces, overcome with fear. Then Jesus came up to them and touched them.

"Get up and don't be frightened," he said. And as they raised their eyes there was no one to be seen but Jesus himself.

On their way down the hillside Jesus warned them not to tell anyone about what they had seen until after the Son of Man had risen from the dead. Then the disciples demanded, "Why is

you: You are Peter, the Rock; and on this rock I will build my church, and the forces of death shall never overpower it.[a] I will give you the keys of the kingdom of Heaven; what you forbid on earth shall be forbidden in heaven, and what you allow on earth shall be allowed in heaven.' He then gave his disciples strict orders not to tell anyone that he was the Messiah.

From that time Jesus began to make it clear to his disciples that he had to go to Jerusalem, and there to suffer much from the elders, chief priests, and lawyers; to be put to death and to be raised again on the third day. At this Peter took him by the arm and began to rebuke him: 'Heaven forbid!' he said. 'No, Lord, this shall never happen to you.' Then Jesus turned and said to Peter, 'Away with you, Satan; you are a stumbling-block to me. You think as men think, not as God thinks.'

Jesus then said to his disciples, 'If anyone wishes to be a follower of mine, he must leave self behind; he must take up his cross and come with me. Whoever cares for his own safety is lost; but if a man will let himself be lost for my sake, he will find his true self. What will a man gain by winning the whole world, at the cost of his true self? Or what can he give that will buy that self back? For the Son of Man is to come in the glory of his Father with his angels, and then he will give each man the due reward for what he has done. I tell you this: there are some standing here who will not taste death before they have seen the Son of Man coming in his kingdom.'

17 Six days later Jesus took Peter and James and John the brother of James, and led them up a high mountain where they were alone; and in their presence he was transfigured; his face shone like the sun, and his clothes became white as the light. And they saw Moses and Elijah appear, conversing with him. Then Peter spoke: 'Lord,' he said, 'how good it is that we are here! If you wish it, I will make three shelters here, one for you, one for Moses, and one for Elijah.' While he was still speaking, a bright cloud suddenly overshadowed them, and a voice called from the cloud: 'This is my Son, my Beloved,[b] on whom my favour rests; listen to him.' At the sound of the voice the disciples fell on their faces in terror. Jesus then came up to them, touched them, and said, 'Stand up; do not be afraid.' And when they raised their eyes they saw no one, but only Jesus.

On their way down the mountain Jesus enjoined them not to tell anyone of the vision until the Son of Man had been raised from the dead. The disciples put a question to him: 'Why

[a] *Or* the gates of death shall never close upon it.
[b] *Or* This is my only Son.

K.J.V.

saying, Why then say the scribes that Elias must first come? 11And Jesus answered and said unto them, Elias truly shall first come, and restore all things. 12 But I say unto you, That Elias is come already, and they knew him not, but have done unto him whatsoever they listed. Likewise shall also the Son of man suffer of them. 13 Then the disciples understood that he spake unto them of John the Baptist.

14 And when they were come to the multitude, there came to him a *certain* man, kneeling down to him, and saying, 15 Lord, have mercy on my son; for he is lunatic, and sore vexed: for ofttimes he falleth into the fire, and oft into the water. 16And I brought him to thy disciples, and they could not cure him. 17 Then Jesus answered and said, O faithless and perverse generation, how long shall I be with you? how long shall I suffer you? bring him hither to me. 18And Jesus rebuked the devil; and he departed out of him: and the child was cured from that very hour. 19 Then came the disciples to Jesus apart, and said, Why could not we cast him out? 20And Jesus said unto them, Because of your unbelief: for verily I say unto you, If ye have faith as a grain of mustard seed, ye shall say unto this mountain, Remove hence to yonder place; and it shall remove: and nothing shall be impossible unto you. 21 Howbeit this kind goeth not out but by prayer and fasting.

22 And while they abode in Galilee, Jesus said unto them, The Son of man shall be betrayed into the hands of men: 23And they shall kill him, and the third day he shall be raised again. And they were exceeding sorry.

24 And when they were come to Capernaum, they that received tribute *money* came to Peter, and said, Doth not your master pay tribute? 25 He saith, Yes. And when he was come into the house, Jesus prevented him, saying, What thinkest thou, Simon? of whom do the kings of the earth take custom or tribute? of their own children, or of strangers? 26 Peter saith unto him, Of strangers. Jesus saith unto him, Then are the children free. 27 Notwithstanding, lest we should offend them, go thou to the sea, and cast a hook, and take up the fish that first cometh up; and when thou hast opened his mouth, thou shalt find a piece of money: that take, and give unto them for me and thee.

R.S.V.

why do the scribes say that first Elijah must come?" 11 He replied, "Elijah does come, and he is to restore all things; 12 but I tell you that Elijah has already come, and they did not know him, but did to him whatever they pleased. So also the Son of man will suffer at their hands." 13 Then the disciples understood that he was speaking to them of John the Baptist.

14 And when they came to the crowd, a man came up to him and kneeling before him said, 15 "Lord, have mercy on my son, for he is an epileptic and he suffers terribly; for often he falls into the fire, and often into the water. 16And I brought him to your disciples, and they could not heal him." 17And Jesus answered, "O faithless and perverse generation, how long am I to be with you? How long am I to bear with you? Bring him here to me." 18And Jesus rebuked him, and the demon came out of him, and the boy was cured instantly. 19 Then the disciples came to Jesus privately and said, "Why could we not cast it out?" 20 He said to them, "Because of your little faith. For truly, I say to you, if you have faith as a grain of mustard seed, you will say to this mountain, 'Move hence to yonder place,' and it will move; and nothing will be impossible to you." *x*

22 As they were gathering*y* in Galilee, Jesus said to them, "The Son of man is to be delivered into the hands of men, 23 and they will kill him, and he will be raised on the third day." And they were greatly distressed.

24 When they came to Capernaum, the collectors of the half-shekel tax went up to Peter and said, "Does not your teacher pay the tax?" 25 He said, "Yes." And when he came home, Jesus spoke to him first, saying, "What do you think, Simon? From whom do kings of the earth take toll or tribute? From their sons or from others?" 26And when he said, "From others," Jesus said to him, "Then the sons are free. 27 However, not to give offense to them, go to the sea and cast a hook, and take the first fish that comes up, and when you open its mouth you will find a shekel; take that and give it to them for me and for yourself."

18 At the same time came the disciples unto Jesus, saying, Who is the greatest in the kingdom of heaven? 2And Jesus called a little

18 At that time the disciples came to Jesus, saying, "Who is the greatest in the kingdom of heaven?" 2And calling to him a child, he put

[x] Other ancient authorities insert verse 21, *"But this kind never comes out except by prayer and fasting."* [y] Other ancient authorities read *abode.*

PHILLIPS

N.E.B.

it, then, that the scribes always say Elijah must come first?"

"Yes, Elijah does come first," replied Jesus, "and begins the world's reformation. But I tell you that Elijah has come already and men did not recognize him. They did what they liked with him, and they will do the same to the Son of Man."

Then they realized that he had been referring to John the Baptist.

Jesus heals an epileptic boy   17. 14

When they returned to the crowds again a man came and kneeled in front of Jesus. "Lord, do have pity on my son," he said, "for he is a lunatic and is in a terrible state. He is always falling into the fire or into the water. I did bring him to your disciples but they couldn't cure him."

"You really are an unbelieving and difficult people," Jesus returned. "How long must I be with you, and how long must I put up with you? Bring him here to me!"

Then Jesus reprimanded the evil spirit and it went out of the boy, who was cured from that moment.

Afterward the disciples approached Jesus privately and asked, "Why weren't we able to get rid of it?"

"Because you have so little faith," replied Jesus. "I assure you that if you have as much faith as a grain of mustard seed you can say to this hill, 'Up you get and move over there!' and it will move—you will find nothing is impossible."

As they went about together in Galilee, Jesus told them: "The Son of Man is going to be handed over to the power of men, and they will kill him. And on the third day he will be raised to life again." This greatly distressed the disciples.

Jesus pays the Temple tax—   17. 24
in an unusual way!

Then when they arrived at Capernaum the Temple tax collectors came up and said to Peter, "Your master doesn't pay Temple tax, we presume?"

"Oh, yes, he does!" replied Peter. Later when he went into the house Jesus anticipated what he was going to say. "What do *you* think, Simon?" he said. "Whom do the kings of this world get their rates and taxes from—their own people or from others?"

"From others," replied Peter.

"Then the family is exempt," Jesus told him. "Yet we don't want to give offense to these people, so go down to the lake and throw in your hook. Take the first fish that bites, open his mouth and you'll find a coin. Take that and give it to them, for both of us."

Jesus commends the simplicity   18. 1
of children

It was at this time that the disciples came to Jesus with the question, "Who is really greatest in the kingdom of Heaven?" Jesus called a little

then do our teachers say that Elijah must come first?' He replied, 'Yes, Elijah will come and set everything right. But I tell you that Elijah has already come, and they failed to recognize him, and worked their will upon him; and in the same way the Son of Man is to suffer at their hands.' Then the disciples understood that he meant John the Baptist.

When they returned to the crowd, a man came up to Jesus, fell on his knees before him, and said, 'Have pity, sir, on my son: he is an epileptic and has bad fits, and he keeps falling about, often into the fire, often into water. I brought him to your disciples, but they could not cure him.' Jesus answered, 'What an unbelieving and perverse generation! How long shall I be with you? How much longer must I endure you? Bring him here to me.' Jesus then spoke sternly to the boy; the devil left him, and from that moment he was cured.

Afterwards the disciples came to Jesus and asked him privately, 'Why could not we cast it out?' He answered, 'Your faith is too weak. I tell you this: if you have faith no bigger even than a mustard-seed, you will say to this mountain, "Move from here to there!", and it will move; nothing will prove impossible for you.' [a]

They were going about together in Galilee when Jesus said to them, 'The Son of Man is to be given up into the power of men, and they will kill him; then on the third day he will be raised again.' And they were filled with grief.

On their arrival at Capernaum the collectors of the temple-tax came up to Peter and asked, 'Does your master not pay temple-tax?' 'He does', said Peter. When he went indoors Jesus forestalled him by asking, 'What do you think about this, Simon? From whom do earthly monarchs collect tax or toll? From their own citizens, or from aliens?' 'From aliens', said Peter. 'Why then,' said Jesus, 'the citizens are exempt! But as we do not want to cause difficulty for these people, go and cast a line in the lake; take the first fish that comes to the hook, open its mouth, and you will find a silver coin; take that and pay it in; it will meet the tax for us both.'

18 At that time the disciples came to Jesus and asked, 'Who is the greatest in the kingdom of Heaven?' He called a child, set him

[a] *Some witnesses add* (21) But there is no means of casting out this sort but prayer and fasting.

K.J.V.

child unto him, and set him in the midst of them, 3And said, Verily I say unto you, Except ye be converted, and become as little children, ye shall not enter into the kingdom of heaven. 4 Whosoever therefore shall humble himself as this little child, the same is greatest in the kingdom of heaven. 5And whoso shall receive one such little child in my name receiveth me. 6 But whoso shall offend one of these little ones which believe in me, it were better for him that a millstone were hanged about his neck, and *that* he were drowned in the depth of the sea.

7 Woe unto the world because of offences! for it must needs be that offences come; but woe to that man by whom the offence cometh! 8 Wherefore if thy hand or thy foot offend thee, cut them off, and cast *them* from thee: it is better for thee to enter into life halt or maimed, rather than having two hands or two feet to be cast into everlasting fire. 9And if thine eye offend thee, pluck it out, and cast *it* from thee: it is better for thee to enter into life with one eye, rather than having two eyes to be cast into hell fire. 10 Take heed that ye despise not one of these little ones; for I say unto you, That in heaven their angels do always behold the face of my Father which is in heaven. 11 For the Son of man is come to save that which was lost. 12 How think ye? if a man have a hundred sheep, and one of them be gone astray, doth he not leave the ninety and nine, and goeth into the mountains, and seeketh that which is gone astray? 13And if so be that he find it, verily I say unto you, he rejoiceth more of that *sheep,* than of the ninety and nine which went not astray. 14 Even so it is not the will of your Father which is in heaven, that one of these little ones should perish.

15 Moreover if thy brother shall trespass against thee, go and tell him his fault between thee and him alone: if he shall hear thee, thou hast gained thy brother. 16 But if he will not hear *thee, then* take with thee one or two more, that in the mouth of two or three witnesses every word may be established. 17And if he shall neglect to hear them, tell *it* unto the church: but if he neglect to hear the church, let him be unto thee as a heathen man and a publican. 18 Verily I say unto you, Whatsoever ye shall bind on earth shall be bound in heaven; and whatsoever ye shall loose on earth shall be loosed in heaven. 19Again I say unto you, That if two of you shall

R.S.V.

him in the midst of them, 3 and said, "Truly, I say to you, unless you turn and become like children, you will never enter the kingdom of heaven. 4 Whoever humbles himself like this child, he is the greatest in the kingdom of heaven.

5 "Whoever receives one such child in my name receives me; 6 but whoever causes one of these little ones who believe in me to sin,[z] it would be better for him to have a great millstone fastened round his neck and to be drowned in the depth of the sea.

7 "Woe to the world for temptations to sin! [a] For it is necessary that temptations come, but woe to the man by whom the temptation comes! 8And if your hand or your foot causes you to sin,[z] cut it off and throw it from you; it is better for you to enter life maimed or lame than with two hands or two feet to be thrown into the eternal fire. 9And if your eye causes you to sin,[z] pluck it out and throw it from you; it is better for you to enter life with one eye than with two eyes to be thrown into the hell [b] of fire.

10 "See that you do not despise one of these little ones; for I tell you that in heaven their angels always behold the face of my Father who is in heaven.[c] 12 What do you think? If a man has a hundred sheep, and one of them has gone astray, does he not leave the ninety-nine on the hills and go in search of the one that went astray? 13And if he finds it, truly, I say to you, he rejoices over it more than over the ninety-nine that never went astray. 14 So it is not the will of my[d] Father who is in heaven that one of these little ones should perish.

15 "If your brother sins against you, go and tell him his fault, between you and him alone. If he listens to you, you have gained your brother. 16 But if he does not listen, take one or two others along with you, that every word may be confirmed by the evidence of two or three witnesses. 17 If he refuses to listen to them, tell it to the church; and if he refuses to listen even to the church, let him be to you as a Gentile and a tax collector. 18 Truly, I say to you, whatever you bind on earth shall be bound in heaven, and whatever you loose on earth shall be loosed in heaven. 19Again I say to you, if two of you agree

[z] Greek *causes . . . to stumble.* [a] Greek *stumbling blocks.* [b] Greek *Gehenna.* [c] Other ancient authorities add verse 11, *For the Son of man came to save the lost.* [d] Other ancient authorities read *your.*

PHILLIPS

child to his side and set him on his feet in the middle of them all. "Believe me," he said, "unless you change your whole outlook and become like little children you will never enter the kingdom of Heaven. It is the man who can be as humble as this little child who is greatest in the kingdom of Heaven.

"Anyone who welcomes one child like this for my sake is welcoming me. But if anyone leads astray one of these little children who believe in me he would be better off thrown into the depths of the sea with a millstone hung round his neck! Alas for the world with its pitfalls! In the nature of things there must be pitfalls, yet alas for the man who is responsible for them!

The right way may mean   18. 8
costly sacrifice

"If your hand or your foot is a hindrance to your faith, cut it off and throw it away. It is a good thing to go into life maimed or crippled—rather than to have both hands and feet and be thrown onto the everlasting fire. Yes, and if your eye leads you astray, tear it out and throw it away. It is a good thing to go one-eyed into life—rather than to have both your eyes and be thrown on the fire of the rubbish heap.

"Be careful that you never despise a single one of these little ones—for I tell you that they have angels who see my Father's face continually in Heaven.

"What do you think? If a man has a hundred sheep and one wanders away from the rest, won't he leave the ninety-nine on the hillside and set out to look for the one who has wandered away? Yes, and if he should chance to find it I assure you he is more delighted over that one than he is over the ninety-nine who never wandered away. You can understand then that it is never the will of your Father in Heaven that a single one of these little ones should be lost.

Reconciliation must always   18. 15
be attempted

"But if your brother wrongs you, go and have it out with him at once—just between the two of you. If he will listen to you, you have won him back as your brother. But if he will not listen to you, take one or two others with you so that everything that is said may have the support of two or three witnesses. And if he still won't pay any attention, tell the matter to the church. And if he won't even listen to the church then he must be to you just like a pagan—or a tax collector!

The connection between earthly   18. 18
conduct and spiritual reality

"Believe me, whatever you forbid upon earth will be what is forbidden in Heaven, and whatever you permit on earth will be what is permitted in Heaven.

"And I tell you once more that if two of you

N.E.B.

in front of them, and said, 'I tell you this: unless you turn round and become like children, you will never enter the kingdom of Heaven. Let a man humble himself till he is like this child, and he will be the greatest in the kingdom of Heaven. Whoever receives one such child in my name receives me. But if a man is a cause of stumbling to one of these little ones who have faith in me, it would be better for him to have a millstone hung round his neck and be drowned in the depths of the sea. Alas for the world that such causes of stumbling arise! Come they must, but woe betide the man through whom they come!

'If your hand or your foot is your undoing, cut it off and fling it away; it is better for you to enter into life maimed or lame, than to keep two hands or two feet and be thrown into the eternal fire. If it is your eye that is your undoing, tear it out and fling it away; it is better to enter into life with one eye than to keep both eyes and be thrown into the fires of hell.

'Never despise one of these little ones; I tell you, they have their guardian angels in heaven, who look continually on the face of my heavenly Father.[a]

'What do you think? Suppose a man has a hundred sheep. If one of them strays, does he not leave the other ninety-nine on the hillside and go in search of the one that strayed? And if he should find it, I tell you this: he is more delighted over that sheep than over the ninety-nine that never strayed. In the same way, it is not your heavenly Father's will that one of these little ones should be lost.

'If your brother commits a sin,[b] go and take the matter up with him, strictly between yourselves, and if he listens to you, you have won your brother over. If he will not listen, take one or two others with you, so that all facts may be duly established on the evidence of two or three witnesses. If he refuses to listen to them, report the matter to the congregation; and if he will not listen even to the congregation, you must then treat him as you would a pagan or a tax-gatherer.

'I tell you this: whatever you forbid on earth shall be forbidden in heaven, and whatever you allow on earth shall be allowed in heaven.

'Again I tell you this: if two of you agree on

[a] *Some witnesses add* (11) *For the Son of Man came to save the lost.* [b] *Some witnesses insert against you.*

K.J.V.

agree on earth as touching any thing that they shall ask, it shall be done for them of my Father which is in heaven. 20 For where two or three are gathered together in my name, there am I in the midst of them.

21 Then came Peter to him, and said, Lord, how oft shall my brother sin against me, and I forgive him? till seven times? 22 Jesus saith unto him, I say not unto thee, Until seven times: but, Until seventy times seven.

23 Therefore is the kingdom of heaven likened unto a certain king, which would take account of his servants. 24And when he had begun to reckon, one was brought unto him, which owed him ten thousand talents. 25 But forasmuch as he had not to pay, his lord commanded him to be sold, and his wife, and children, and all that he had, and payment to be made. 26 The servant therefore fell down, and worshipped him, saying, Lord, have patience with me, and I will pay thee all. 27 Then the lord of that servant was moved with compassion, and loosed him, and forgave him the debt. 28 But the same servant went out, and found one of his fellow servants, which owed him a hundred pence: and he laid hands on him, and took *him* by the throat, saying, Pay me that thou owest. 29And his fellow servant fell down at his feet, and besought him, saying, Have patience with me, and I will pay thee all. 30And he would not: but went and cast him into prison, till he should pay the debt. 31 So when his fellow servants saw what was done, they were very sorry, and came and told unto their lord all that was done. 32 Then his lord, after that he had called him, said unto him, O thou wicked servant, I forgave thee all that debt, because thou desiredst me: 33 Shouldest not thou also have had compassion on thy fellow servant, even as I had pity on thee? 34And his lord was wroth, and delivered him to the tormentors, till he should pay all that was due unto him. 35 So likewise shall my heavenly Father do also unto you, if ye from your hearts forgive not every one his brother their trespasses.

19 And it came to pass, *that* when Jesus had finished these sayings, he departed from Galilee, and came into the coasts of Judea beyond Jordan; 2And great multitudes followed him; and he healed them there.

3 The Pharisees also came unto him, tempting him, and saying unto him, Is it lawful for a man to put away his wife for every cause? 4And he answered and said unto them, Have ye not read, that he which made *them* at the beginning made them male and female, 5And said, For this cause shall a man leave father and mother, and shall cleave to his wife: and they twain shall be one flesh? 6 Wherefore they are no more twain, but one flesh. What therefore God hath joined together, let not man put asunder. 7 They say unto

R.S.V.

on earth about anything they ask, it will be done for them by my Father in heaven. 20 For where two or three are gathered in my name, there am I in the midst of them."

21 Then Peter came up and said to him, "Lord, how often shall my brother sin against me, and I forgive him? As many as seven times?" 22 Jesus said to him, "I do not say to you seven times, but seventy times seven.*e*

23 "Therefore the kingdom of heaven may be compared to a king who wished to settle accounts with his servants. 24 When he began the reckoning, one was brought to him who owed him ten thousand talents;*f* 25 and as he could not pay, his lord ordered him to be sold, with his wife and children and all that he had, and payment to be made. 26 So the servant fell on his knees, imploring him, 'Lord, have patience with me, and I will pay you everything.' 27And out of pity for him the lord of that servant released him and forgave him the debt. 28 But that same servant, as he went out, came upon one of his fellow servants who owed him a hundred denarii;*g* and seizing him by the throat he said, 'Pay what you owe.' 29 So his fellow servant fell down and besought him, 'Have patience with me, and I will pay you.' 30 He refused and went and put him in prison till he should pay the debt. 31 When his fellow servants saw what had taken place, they were greatly distressed, and they went and reported to their lord all that had taken place. 32 Then his lord summoned him and said to him, 'You wicked servant! I forgave you all that debt because you besought me; 33 and should not you have had mercy on your fellow servant, as I had mercy on you?' 34And in anger his lord delivered him to the jailers,*h* till he should pay all his debt. 35 So also my heavenly Father will do to every one of you, if you do not forgive your brother from your heart."

19 Now when Jesus had finished these sayings, he went away from Galilee and entered the region of Judea beyond the Jordan; 2 and large crowds followed him, and he healed them there.

3 And Pharisees came up to him and tested him by asking, "Is it lawful to divorce one's wife for any cause?" 4 He answered, "Have you not read that he who made them from the beginning made them male and female, 5 and said, 'For this reason a man shall leave his father and mother and be joined to his wife, and the two shall become one'?*i* 6 So they are no longer two but one.*i* What therefore God has joined together, let no man put asunder." 7 They said to him, "Why

[e] Or *seventy-seven times.* [f] This talent was probably worth about a thousand dollars. [g] The denarius was worth about twenty cents. [h] Greek *torturers.* [i] Greek *one flesh.*

PHILLIPS

on earth agree in asking for anything it will be granted to you by my Heavenly Father. For wherever two or three people come together in my name, I am there, right among them!"

The necessity for forgiveness   18. 21

Then Peter approached him with the question, "Master, how many times can my brother wrong me and I must forgive him? Would seven times be enough?"

"No," replied Jesus, "not seven times, but seventy times seven! For the kingdom of Heaven is like a king who decided to settle his accounts with his servants. When he had started calling in his accounts, a man was brought to him who owed him millions of dollars. And when it was plain that he had no means of repaying the debt, his master gave orders for him to be sold as a slave, and his wife and children and all his possessions as well, and the money to be paid over. At this the servant fell on his knees before his master, 'Oh, be patient with me!' he cried, 'and I will pay you back every penny!' Then his master was moved with pity for him, set him free and canceled the debt.

"But when this same servant had left his master's presence, he found one of his fellow servants who owed him a few dollars. He grabbed him and seized him by the throat, crying, 'Pay up what you owe me!' At this his fellow servant fell down at his feet, and implored him, 'Oh, be patient with me, and I will pay you back!' But he refused and went out and had him put in prison until he should repay the debt.

"When the other fellow servants saw what had happened, they were horrified and went and told their master the whole incident. Then his master called him in.

" 'You wicked servant!' he said. 'Didn't I cancel all that debt when you begged me to do so? Oughtn't you to have taken pity on your fellow servant as I, your master, took pity on you?' And his master in anger handed him over to the jailers till he should repay the whole debt. This is how my Heavenly Father will treat you unless you forgive your brother from your heart."

The divine principle of marriage   19. 1

When Jesus had finished talking on these matters, he left Galilee and went on to the district of Judaea on the far side of the Jordan. Vast crowds followed him, and he cured them there.

Then the Pharisees arrived with a test question.

"Is it right," they asked, "for a man to divorce his wife on any grounds whatever?"

"Haven't you read," he answered, "that the one who created them from the beginning made them male and female and said: *'For this cause shall a man leave his father and mother, and shall cleave to his wife; and the twain shall become one flesh'?* So they are no longer two separate people but one. No man therefore must separate what God has joined together."

"Then why," they retorted, "did Moses com-

---

earth about any request you have to make, that request will be granted by my heavenly Father. For where two or three have met together in my name, I am there among them.'

Then Peter came up and asked him, 'Lord, how often am I to forgive my brother if he goes on wronging me? As many as seven times?' Jesus replied, 'I do not say seven times; I say seventy times seven.

'The kingdom of Heaven, therefore, should be thought of in this way: There was once a king who decided to settle accounts with the men who served him. At the outset there appeared before him a man whose debt ran into millions.[a] Since he had no means of paying, his master ordered him to be sold to meet the debt, with his wife, his children, and everything he had. The man fell prostrate at his master's feet. "Be patient with me," he said, "and I will pay in full"; and the master was so moved with pity that he let the man go and remitted the debt. But no sooner had the man gone out than he met a fellow-servant who owed him a few pounds;[b] and catching hold of him he gripped him by the throat and said, "Pay me what you owe." The man fell at his fellow-servant's feet, and begged him, "Be patient with me, and I will pay you"; but he refused, and had him jailed until he should pay the debt. The other servants were deeply distressed when they saw what had happened, and they went to their master and told him the whole story. He accordingly sent for the man. "You scoundrel!" he said to him; "I remitted the whole of your debt when you appealed to me; were you not bound to show your fellow-servant the same pity as I showed to you?" And so angry was the master that he condemned the man to torture until he should pay the debt in full. And that is how my heavenly Father will deal with you, unless you each forgive your brother from your hearts.'

19 When Jesus had finished this discourse he left Galilee and came into the region of Judaea across Jordan. Great crowds followed him, and he healed them there.

Some Pharisees came and tested him by asking, 'Is it lawful for a man to divorce his wife on any and every ground?'[c] He asked in return, 'Have you never read that the Creator made them from the beginning male and female?'; and he added, 'For this reason a man shall leave his father and mother, and be made one with his wife; and the two shall become one flesh. It follows that they are no longer two individuals: they are one flesh. What God has joined together, man must not separate.' 'Why then', they

[a] *Literally* who owed 10,000 talents. [b] *Literally* owed him 100 denarii. [c] *Or* Is there any ground on which it is lawful for a man to divorce his wife?

K.J.V.

him, Why did Moses then command to give a writing of divorcement, and to put her away? 8 He saith unto them, Moses because of the hardness of your hearts suffered you to put away your wives: but from the beginning it was not so. 9And I say unto you, Whosoever shall put away his wife, except *it be* for fornication, and shall marry another, committeth adultery: and whoso marrieth her which is put away doth commit adultery.

10 His disciples say unto him, If the case of the man be so with *his* wife, it is not good to marry. 11 But he said unto them, All *men* cannot receive this saying, save *they* to whom it is given. 12 For there are some eunuchs, which were so born from *their* mother's womb: and there are some eunuchs, which were made eunuchs of men: and there be eunuchs, which have made themselves eunuchs for the kingdom of heaven's sake. He that is able to receive *it*, let him receive *it*.

13 Then were there brought unto him little children, that he should put *his* hands on them, and pray: and the disciples rebuked them. 14 But Jesus said, Suffer little children, and forbid them not, to come unto me; for of such is the kingdom of heaven. 15And he laid *his* hands on them, and departed thence.

16 And, behold, one came and said unto him, Good Master, what good thing shall I do, that I may have eternal life? 17And he said unto him, Why callest thou me good? *there is* none good but one, *that is,* God: but if thou wilt enter into life, keep the commandments. 18 He saith unto him, Which? Jesus said, Thou shalt do no murder, Thou shalt not commit adultery, Thou shalt not steal, Thou shalt not bear false witness, 19 Honour thy father and *thy* mother: and, Thou shalt love thy neighbour as thyself. 20 The young man saith unto him, All these things have I kept from my youth up: what lack I yet? 21 Jesus said unto him, If thou wilt be perfect, go *and* sell that thou hast, and give to the poor, and thou shalt have treasure in heaven: and come *and* follow me. 22 But when the young man heard that saying, he went away sorrowful: for he had great possessions.

23 Then said Jesus unto his disciples, Verily I say unto you, That a rich man shall hardly enter into the kingdom of heaven. 24And again I say unto you, It is easier for a camel to go through the eye of a needle, than for a rich man to enter into the kingdom of God. 25 When his disciples heard *it*, they were exceedingly amazed, saying, Who then can be saved? 26 But Jesus beheld *them,* and said unto them, With men this is impossible; but with God all things are possible.

R.S.V.

then did Moses command one to give a certificate of divorce, and to put her away?" 8 He said to them, "For your hardness of heart Moses allowed you to divorce your wives, but from the beginning it was not so. 9And I say to you: whoever divorces his wife, except for unchastity,[j] and marries another, commits adultery." [k]

10 The disciples said to him, "If such is the case of a man with his wife, it is not expedient to marry." 11 But he said to them, "Not all men can receive this precept, but only those to whom it is given. 12 For there are eunuchs who have been so from birth, and there are eunuchs who have been made eunuchs by men, and there are eunuchs who have made themselves eunuchs for the sake of the kingdom of heaven. He who is able to receive this, let him receive it."

13 Then children were brought to him that he might lay his hands on them and pray. The disciples rebuked the people; 14 but Jesus said, "Let the children come to me, and do not hinder them; for to such belongs the kingdom of heaven." 15And he laid his hands on them and went away.

16 And behold, one came up to him, saying, "Teacher, what good deed must I do, to have eternal life?" 17And he said to him, "Why do you ask me about what is good? One there is who is good. If you would enter life, keep the commandments." 18 He said to him, "Which?" And Jesus said, "You shall not kill, You shall not commit adultery, You shall not steal, You shall not bear false witness, 19 Honor your father and mother, and, You shall love your neighbor as yourself." 20 The young man said to him, "All these I have observed; what do I still lack?" 21 Jesus said to him, "If you would be perfect, go, sell what you possess and give to the poor, and you will have treasure in heaven; and come, follow me." 22 When the young man heard this he went away sorrowful; for he had great possessions.

23 And Jesus said to his disciples, "Truly, I say to you, it will be hard for a rich man to enter the kingdom of heaven. 24Again I tell you, it is easier for a camel to go through the eye of a needle than for a rich man to enter the kingdom of God." 25 When the disciples heard this they were greatly astonished, saying, "Who then can be saved?" 26 But Jesus looked at them and said to them, "With men this is impossible, but

[j] Other ancient authorities, after *unchastity*, read *makes her commit adultery*. [k] Other ancient authorities insert *and he who marries a divorced woman commits adultery*.

PHILLIPS

mand us to give a written divorce notice and dismiss the woman?"

"It was because you knew so little of the meaning of love that Moses allowed you to divorce your wives! But that was not the original principle. I tell you that anyone who divorces his wife on any grounds except her unfaithfulness, and marries some other woman, commits adultery."

His disciples said to him, "If that is a man's position with his wife, it is not worth getting married!"

"It is not everybody who can live up to this," replied Jesus, "—only those who have a special gift. For some are incapable of marriage from birth, some are made incapable by the action of men, and some have made themselves so for the sake of the kingdom of Heaven. Let the man who can accept what I have said accept it."

Jesus welcomes children   19. 13

Then some little children were brought to him, so that he could put his hands on them and pray for them. The disciples frowned on the parents' action, but Jesus said:

"You must let little children come to me, and you must never stop them. The kingdom of Heaven belongs to little children like these!" Then he laid his hands on them and went on his way.

Jesus shows that keeping the   19. 16
commandments is not enough

Then it happened that a man came up to him and said, "Master, what good thing must I do to secure eternal life?"

"I wonder why you ask me about what is good," Jesus answered him. "Only one is good. But if you want to enter that life you must keep the commandments."

"Which ones?" he asked.

"Thou shalt do no murder, Thou shalt not commit adultery, Thou shalt not steal, Thou shalt not bear false witness, Honor thy father and thy mother, and Thou shalt love thy neighbor as thyself," replied Jesus.

"I have carefully kept all these," returned the young man. "What is still missing in my life?"

Then Jesus told him, "If you want to be perfect, go now and sell your property and give the money away to the poor—you will have riches in Heaven. Then come and follow me!"

When the young man heard that, he turned away crestfallen, for he was very wealthy.

Then Jesus remarked to his disciples: "Believe me, a rich man will find it very difficult to enter the kingdom of Heaven. Yes, I repeat, a camel could more easily squeeze through the eye of a needle than a rich man get into the kingdom of God!"

The disciples were simply amazed to hear this, and said, "Then who can possibly be saved?"

Jesus looked steadily at them and replied, "Humanly speaking it is impossible; but with God anything is possible!"

N.E.B.

objected, 'did Moses lay it down that a man might divorce his wife by note of dismissal?' He answered, 'It was because you were so unteachable that Moses gave you permission to divorce your wives; but it was not like that when all began. I tell you, if a man divorces his wife for any cause other than unchastity, and marries another, he commits adultery.' [a]

The disciples said to him, 'If that is the position with husband and wife, it is better to refrain from marriage.' To this he replied, 'That is something which not everyone can accept, but only those for whom God has appointed it. For while some are incapable of marriage because they were born so, or were made so by men, there are others who have themselves renounced marriage for the sake of the kingdom of Heaven. Let those accept it who can.'

They brought children for him to lay his hands on them with prayer. The disciples scolded them for it, but Jesus said to them, 'Let the children come to me; do not try to stop them; for the kingdom of Heaven belongs to such as these.' And he laid his hands on the children, and went his way.

And now a man came up and asked him, 'Master, what good must I do to gain eternal life?' 'Good?' said Jesus. 'Why do you ask me about that? One alone is good. But if you wish to enter into life, keep the commandments.' 'Which commandments?' he asked. Jesus answered, 'Do not murder; do not commit adultery; do not steal; do not give false evidence; honour your father and mother; and love your neighbour as yourself.' The young man answered, 'I have kept all these. Where do I still fall short?' Jesus said to him, 'If you wish to go the whole way, go, sell your possessions, and give to the poor, and then you will have riches in heaven; and come, follow me.' When the young man heard this, he went away with a heavy heart; for he was a man of great wealth.

Jesus said to his disciples, 'I tell you this: a rich man will find it hard to enter the kingdom of Heaven. I repeat, it is easier for a camel to pass through the eye of a needle than for a rich man to enter the kingdom of God.' The disciples were amazed to hear this. 'Then who can be saved?' they asked. Jesus looked them in the face, and said, 'For men this is impossible; but everything is possible for God.'

[a] *Some witnesses add* And the man who marries a woman so divorced commits adultery.

K.J.V.

27 Then answered Peter and said unto him, Behold, we have forsaken all, and followed thee; what shall we have therefore? 28And Jesus said unto them, Verily I say unto you, That ye which have followed me, in the regeneration when the Son of man shall sit in the throne of his glory, ye also shall sit upon twelve thrones, judging the twelve tribes of Israel. 29And every one that hath forsaken houses, or brethren, or sisters, or father, or mother, or wife, or children, or lands, for my name's sake, shall receive a hundredfold, and shall inherit everlasting life. 30 But many *that are* first shall be last; and the last *shall be* first.

20 For the kingdom of heaven is like unto a man *that is* a householder, which went out early in the morning to hire labourers into his vineyard. 2And when he had agreed with the labourers for a penny a day, he sent them into his vineyard. 3And he went out about the third hour, and saw others standing idle in the market-place, 4And said unto them; Go ye also into the vineyard, and whatsoever is right I will give you. And they went their way. 5Again he went out about the sixth and ninth hour, and did likewise. 6And about the eleventh hour he went out, and found others standing idle, and saith unto them, Why stand ye here all the day idle? 7 They say unto him, Because no man hath hired us. He saith unto them, Go ye also into the vineyard; and whatsoever is right, *that* shall ye receive. 8 So when even was come, the lord of the vineyard saith unto his steward, Call the labourers, and give them *their* hire, beginning from the last unto the first. 9And when they came that *were hired* about the eleventh hour, they received every man a penny. 10 But when the first came, they supposed that they should have received more; and they likewise received every man a penny. 11And when they had received *it*, they murmured against the goodman of the house, 12 Saying, These last have wrought *but* one hour, and thou hast made them equal unto us, which have borne the burden and heat of the day. 13 But he answered one of them, and said, Friend, I do thee no wrong: didst not thou agree with me for a penny? 14 Take *that* thine *is*, and go thy way: I will give unto this last, even as unto thee. 15 Is it not lawful for me to do what I will with mine own? Is thine eye evil, because I am good? 16 So the last shall be first, and the first last: for many be called, but few chosen.

17 And Jesus going up to Jerusalem took the twelve disciples apart in the way, and said unto them, 18 Behold, we go up to Jerusalem; and the Son of man shall be betrayed unto the chief priests and unto the scribes, and they shall condemn him to death, 19And shall deliver him to the Gentiles to mock, and to scourge, and to

R.S.V.

with God all things are possible." 27 Then Peter said in reply, "Lo, we have left everything and followed you. What then shall we have?" 28 Jesus said to them, "Truly, I say to you, in the new world, when the Son of man shall sit on his glorious throne, you who have followed me will also sit on twelve thrones, judging the twelve tribes of Israel. 29And every one who has left houses or brothers or sisters or father or mother or children or lands, for my name's sake, will receive a hundredfold,[l] and inherit eternal life. 30 But many that are first will be last, and the last first.

20 "For the kingdom of heaven is like a householder who went out early in the morning to hire laborers for his vineyard. 2After agreeing with the laborers for a denarius[m] a day, he sent them into his vineyard. 3And going out about the third hour he saw others standing idle in the market place; 4 and to them he said, 'You go into the vineyard too, and whatever is right I will give you.' So they went. 5 Going out again about the sixth hour and the ninth hour, he did the same. 6And about the eleventh hour he went out and found others standing; and he said to them, 'Why do you stand here idle all day?' 7 They said to him, 'Because no one has hired us.' He said to them, 'You go into the vineyard too.' 8And when evening came, the owner of the vineyard said to his steward, 'Call the laborers and pay them their wages, beginning with the last, up to the first.' 9And when those hired about the eleventh hour came, each of them received a denarius. 10 Now when the first came, they thought they would receive more; but each of them also received a denarius. 11And on receiving it they grumbled at the householder, 12 saying, 'These last worked only one hour, and you have made them equal to us who have borne the burden of the day and the scorching heat.' 13 But he replied to one of them, 'Friend, I am doing you no wrong; did you not agree with me for a denarius? 14 Take what belongs to you, and go; I choose to give to this last as I give to you. 15Am I not allowed to do what I choose with what belongs to me? Or do you begrudge my generosity?'[n] 16 So the last will be first, and the first last."

17 And as Jesus was going up to Jerusalem, he took the twelve disciples aside, and on the way he said to them, 18 "Behold, we are going up to Jerusalem; and the Son of man will be delivered to the chief priests and scribes, and they will condemn him to death, 19 and deliver him to the Gentiles to be mocked and scourged and

PHILLIPS

Jesus declares that sacrifice for   *19. 27*
the kingdom will be repaid

At this, Peter exclaimed: "Look, we have left everything and followed you. What is that going to be worth to us?"

"Believe me," said Jesus, "when I tell you that in the next world, when the Son of Man shall sit down on his glorious throne, you who have followed me will also sit on twelve thrones and become judges of the twelve tribes of Israel. Every man who has left houses or brothers or sisters or father or mother or children or land for my sake will receive it all back many times over, and will inherit eternal life. But many who are first now will be last then—and the last first!

But God's generosity may   *20. 1*
appear unfair

"For the kingdom of Heaven is like a farmer going out early in the morning to hire laborers for his vineyard. He agreed with them on a wage of a silver coin a day and sent them to work. About nine o'clock he went out and saw some others standing about in the market place with nothing to do. 'You go to the vineyard too,' he said to them, 'and I will pay you a fair wage.' And off they went. At about midday and again at about three o'clock in the afternoon he went out and did the same thing. Then about five o'clock he went out and found some others standing about. 'Why are you standing about here all day doing nothing?' he asked them. 'Because no one has employed us,' they replied. 'You go off into the vineyard as well, then,' he said.

"When evening came the owner of the vineyard said to his foreman, 'Call the laborers and pay them their wages, beginning with the last and ending with the first.' So those who were engaged at five o'clock came up and each man received a silver coin. But when the first to be employed came they reckoned they would get more, but they also received a silver coin a man. As they took their money they grumbled at the farmer and said, 'These last fellows have only put in one hour's work and you've treated them exactly the same as us who have gone through all the hard work and heat of the day!'

"But he replied to one of them: 'My friend, I'm not being unjust to you. Wasn't our agreement for a silver coin a day? Take your money and go home. It is my wish to give the latecomer as much as I give you. May I not do what I like with what belongs to me? Must you be jealous because I am generous?'

"So, many who are the last now will be first then and the first last."

Jesus' final journey to Jerusalem   *20. 17*

Then, as he was about to go up to Jerusalem, Jesus took the twelve disciples aside and spoke to them as they walked along. "Listen, we are now going up to Jerusalem, and the Son of Man will be handed over to the chief priests and the scribes—and they will condemn him to death. They will hand him over to the heathen to ridi-

N.E.B.

At this Peter said, 'Here are we who left everything to become your followers. What will there be for us?' Jesus replied, 'I tell you this: in the world that is to be, when the Son of Man is seated on his throne in heavenly splendour, you my followers will have thrones of your own, where you will sit as judges of the twelve tribes of Israel. And anyone who has left brothers or sisters, father, mother, or children, land or houses for the sake of my name will be repaid many times over, and gain eternal life. But many who are first will be last, and the last first.'

20 'The kingdom of Heaven is like this. There was once a landowner who went out early one morning to hire labourers for his vineyard; and after agreeing to pay them the usual day's wage[a] he sent them off to work. Going out three hours later he saw some more men standing idle in the market-place. "Go and join the others in the vineyard," he said, "and I will pay you a fair wage"; so off they went. At noon he went out again, and at three in the afternoon, and made the same arrangement as before. An hour before sunset he went out and found another group standing there; so he said to them, "Why are you standing about like this all day with nothing to do?" "Because no one has hired us", they replied; so he told them, "Go and join the others in the vineyard." When evening fell, the owner of the vineyard said to his steward, "Call the labourers and give them their pay, beginning with those who came last and ending with the first." Those who had started work an hour before sunset came forward, and were paid the full day's wage.[b] When it was the turn of the men who had come first, they expected something extra, but were paid the same amount as the others. As they took it, they grumbled at their employer: "These late-comers have done only one hour's work, yet you have put them on a level with us, who have sweated the whole day long in the blazing sun!" The owner turned to one of them and said, "My friend, I am not being unfair to you. You agreed on the usual wage for the day,[c] did you not? Take your pay and go home. I choose to pay the last man the same as you. Surely I am free to do what I like with my own money. Why be jealous because I am kind?" Thus will the last be first, and the first last.'

Challenge to Jerusalem

Jesus was journeying towards Jerusalem, and on the way he took the Twelve aside, and said to them, 'We are going to Jerusalem, and the Son of Man will be given up to the chief priests and the doctors of the law; they will condemn him to death and hand him over to the foreign power, to be mocked and flogged and crucified,

[a] *Literally* one denarius for the day. [b] *Literally* one denarius each. [c] *Literally* You agreed on a denarius.

K.J.V.

crucify *him:* and the third day he shall rise again.

20 Then came to him the mother of Zebedee's children with her sons, worshipping *him,* and desiring a certain thing of him. 21And he said unto her, What wilt thou? She saith unto him, Grant that these my two sons may sit, the one on thy right hand, and the other on the left, in thy kingdom. 22 But Jesus answered and said, Ye know not what ye ask. Are ye able to drink of the cup that I shall drink of, and to be baptized with the baptism that I am baptized with? They say unto him, We are able. 23And he saith unto them, Ye shall drink indeed of my cup, and be baptized with the baptism that I am baptized with: but to sit on my right hand, and on my left, is not mine to give, but *it shall be given to them* for whom it is prepared of my Father. 24And when the ten heard *it,* they were moved with indignation against the two brethren. 25 But Jesus called them *unto him,* and said, Ye know that the princes of the Gentiles exercise dominion over them, and they that are great exercise authority upon them. 26 But it shall not be so among you: but whosoever will be great among you, let him be your minister; 27And whosoever will be chief among you, let him be your servant: 28 Even as the Son of man came not to be ministered unto, but to minister, and to give his life a ransom for many. 29And as they departed from Jericho, a great multitude followed him.

30 And, behold, two blind men sitting by the way side, when they heard that Jesus passed by, cried out, saying, Have mercy on us, O Lord, *thou* Son of David. 31And the multitude rebuked them, because they should hold their peace: but they cried the more, saying, Have mercy on us, O Lord, *thou* Son of David. 32And Jesus stood still, and called them, and said, What will ye that I shall do unto you? 33 They say unto him, Lord, that our eyes may be opened. 34 So Jesus had compassion *on them,* and touched their eyes: and immediately their eyes received sight, and they followed him.

R.S.V.

crucified, and he will be raised on the third day."

20 Then the mother of the sons of Zebedee came up to him, with her sons, and kneeling before him she asked him for something. 21And he said to her, "What do you want?" She said to him, "Command that these two sons of mine may sit, one at your right hand and one at your left, in your kingdom." 22 But Jesus answered, "You do not know what you are asking. Are you able to drink the cup that I am to drink?" They said to him, "We are able." 23 He said to them, "You will drink my cup, but to sit at my right hand and at my left is not mine to grant, but it is for those for whom it has been prepared by my Father." 24And when the ten heard it, they were indignant at the two brothers. 25 But Jesus called them to him and said, "You know that the rulers of the Gentiles lord it over them, and their great men exercise authority over them. 26 It shall not be so among you; but whoever would be great among you must be your servant, 27 and whoever would be first among you must be your slave; 28 even as the Son of man came not to be served but to serve, and to give his life as a ransom for many."

29 And as they went out of Jericho, a great crowd followed him. 30 And behold, two blind men sitting by the roadside, when they heard that Jesus was passing by, cried out,[o] "Have mercy on us, Son of David!" 31 The crowd rebuked them, telling them to be silent; but they cried out the more, "Lord, have mercy on us, Son of David!" 32And Jesus stopped and called them, saying, "What do you want me to do for you?" 33 They said to him, "Lord, let our eyes be opened." 34And Jesus in pity touched their eyes, and immediately they received their sight and followed him.

21 And when they drew nigh unto Jerusalem, and were come to Bethphage, unto the mount of Olives, then sent Jesus two disciples, 2 Saying unto them, Go into the village over against you, and straightway ye shall find an ass tied, and a colt with her: loose *them,* and bring *them* unto me. 3And if any *man* say aught unto you, ye shall say, The Lord hath need of them; and straightway he will send them. 4All this was done, that it might be fulfilled which was spoken by the prophet, saying, 5 Tell ye the daughter of Sion, Behold, thy King cometh unto thee, meek, and sitting upon an ass, and a colt the foal of an ass. 6And the disciples went, and did as Jesus commanded them, 7And brought the ass, and the colt, and put on them their clothes, and they set *him* thereon. 8And a very great multitude

21 And when they drew near to Jerusalem and came to Bethphage, to the Mount of Olives, then Jesus sent two disciples, 2 saying to them, "Go into the village opposite you, and immediately you will find an ass tied, and a colt with her; untie them and bring them to me. 3 If any one says anything to you, you shall say, 'The Lord has need of them,' and he will send them immediately." 4 This took place to fulfil what was spoken by the prophet, saying,
5 "Tell the daughter of Zion,
　Behold, your king is coming to you,
　　humble, and mounted on an ass,
　　and on a colt, the foal of an ass."
6 The disciples went and did as Jesus had directed them; 7 they brought the ass and the colt, and put their garments on them, and he sat thereon. 8 Most of the crowd spread their gar-

[o] Other ancient authorities insert *Lord.*

PHILLIPS

N.E.B.

cule and flog and crucify. And on the third day he will rise again!"

At this point the mother of the sons of Zebedee arrived with her sons and knelt in front of Jesus to ask him a favor.

"What is it you want?" he asked her.

"Please say that these two sons of mine may sit one on each side of you when you are king!" she said.

"You don't know what it is you are asking," replied Jesus. "Can you two drink what I have to drink?"

"Yes, we can," they answered.

"Ah, you will indeed 'drink my drink,' " Jesus told them, "but as for sitting on either side of me, that is not for me to grant—that belongs to those for whom my Father has planned it."

When the other ten heard of this incident they were highly indignant with the two brothers.

But Jesus called them to him and said:

"You know that the rulers of the heathen lord it over them and that their great ones have absolute power? But it must not be so among you. No, whoever among you wants to be great must become the servant of you all, and if he wants to be first among you he must be your slave—just as the Son of Man has not come to be served but to serve, and to give his life to set many others free."

He restores sight to two blind men   20. 29

A great crowd followed them as they were leaving Jericho, and two blind men who were sitting by the roadside, hearing that it was Jesus who was passing by, cried out, "Have pity on us, Lord, you Son of David!" The crowd tried to hush them up, but this only made them cry out more loudly still, "Have pity on us, Lord, you Son of David!"

Jesus stood quite still and called out to them, "What do you want me to do for you?"

"Lord, let us see again!"

And Jesus, deeply moved with pity, touched their eyes. At once their sight was restored, and they followed him.

Jesus' final entry into Jerusalem   21. 1

As they approached Jerusalem and came to Bethphage and the Mount of Olives, Jesus sent two disciples ahead telling them: "Go into the village in front of you and you will at once find there an ass tethered, and a colt with her. Untie them and bring them to me. Should anyone say anything to you, you are to say, 'The Lord needs them,' and he will send them immediately."

All this happened to fulfill the prophet's saying—

Tell ye the daughter of Zion,
Behold, thy King cometh unto thee,
Meek, and riding upon an ass,
And upon a colt the foal of an ass.

So the disciples went off and followed Jesus' instructions. They brought the ass and the colt, and put their cloaks on them, and Jesus took his seat. Then most of the crowd spread their

and on the third day he will be raised to life again.'

The mother of Zebedee's sons then came before him, with her sons. She bowed low and begged a favour. 'What is it you wish?' asked Jesus. 'I want you', she said, 'to give orders that in your kingdom my two sons here may sit next to you, one at your right, and the other at your left.' Jesus turned to the brothers and said, 'You do not understand what you are asking. Can you drink the cup that I am to drink?' 'We can', they replied. Then he said to them, 'You shall indeed share my cup; but to sit at my right or left is not for me to grant; it is for those to whom it has already been assigned by my Father.'

When the other ten heard this, they were indignant with the two brothers. So Jesus called them to him and said, 'You know that in the world, rulers lord it over their subjects, and their great men make them feel the weight of authority; but it shall not be so with you. Among you, whoever wants to be great must be your servant, and whoever would be first must be the willing slave of all—like the Son of Man; he did not come to be served, but to serve, and to surrender his life as a ransom for many.'

As they were leaving Jericho he was followed by a great crowd of people. At the roadside sat two blind men. When they heard it said that Jesus was passing they shouted, 'Have pity on us, Son of David.' The people rounded on them and told them to be quiet. But they shouted all the more, 'Sir, have pity on us, have pity on us, Son of David.' Jesus stopped and called the men. 'What do you want me to do for you?' he asked. 'Sir,' they answered, 'we want our sight.' Jesus was deeply moved, and touched their eyes. At once their sight came back, and they went on after him.

21 They were now nearing Jerusalem; and when they reached Bethphage at the Mount of Olives, Jesus sent two disciples with these instructions: 'Go to the village opposite, where you will at once find a donkey tethered with her foal beside her; untie them, and bring them to me. If anyone speaks to you, say, "Our Master needs them", and he will let you take them at once.' [a] This was in fulfilment of the prophecy which says, 'Tell the daughter of Zion, "Here is your king, who comes to you in gentleness, riding on an ass, riding on the foal of a beast of burden." '

The disciples went and did as Jesus had directed, and brought the donkey and her foal; they laid their cloaks on them and Jesus mounted. Crowds of people carpeted the road with their

[a] *Or* "Our Master needs them and will send them back straight away."

K.J.V.

spread their garments in the way; others cut down branches from the trees, and strewed *them* in the way. 9And the multitudes that went before, and that followed, cried, saying, Hosanna to the Son of David: Blessed *is* he that cometh in the name of the Lord; Hosanna in the highest. 10And when he was come into Jerusalem, all the city was moved, saying, Who is this? 11And the multitude said, This is Jesus the prophet of Nazareth of Galilee.

12 And Jesus went into the temple of God, and cast out all them that sold and bought in the temple, and overthrew the tables of the money changers, and the seats of them that sold doves, 13And said unto them, It is written, My house shall be called the house of prayer; but ye have made it a den of thieves. 14And the blind and the lame came to him in the temple; and he healed them. 15And when the chief priests and scribes saw the wonderful things that he did, and the children crying in the temple, and saying, Hosanna to the Son of David; they were sore displeased, 16And said unto him, Hearest thou what these say? And Jesus saith unto them, Yea; have ye never read, Out of the mouth of babes and sucklings thou hast perfected praise?

17 And he left them, and went out of the city into Bethany; and he lodged there. 18 Now in the morning, as he returned into the city, he hungered. 19And when he saw a fig tree in the way, he came to it, and found nothing thereon, but leaves only, and said unto it, Let no fruit grow on thee henceforward for ever. And presently the fig tree withered away. 20And when the disciples saw *it*, they marvelled, saying, How soon is the fig tree withered away! 21 Jesus answered and said unto them, Verily I say unto you, If ye have faith, and doubt not, ye shall not only do this *which is done* to the fig tree, but also if ye shall say unto this mountain, Be thou removed, and be thou cast into the sea; it shall be done. 22And all things, whatsoever ye shall ask in prayer, believing, ye shall receive.

23 And when he was come into the temple, the chief priests and the elders of the people came unto him as he was teaching, and said, By what authority doest thou these things? and who gave thee this authority? 24And Jesus answered and said unto them, I also will ask you one thing, which if ye tell me, I in like wise will tell you by what authority I do these things. 25 The baptism of John, whence was it? from heaven, or of men? And they reasoned with themselves, saying, If we shall say, From heaven; he will say unto us, Why did ye not then believe him? 26 But if we shall say, Of men; we fear

R.S.V.

ments on the road, and others cut branches from the trees and spread them on the road. 9And the crowds that went before him and that followed him shouted, "Hosanna to the Son of David! Blessed is he who comes in the name of the Lord! Hosanna in the highest!" 10And when he entered Jerusalem, all the city was stirred, saying, "Who is this?" 11And the crowds said, "This is the prophet Jesus from Nazareth of Galilee."

12 And Jesus entered the temple of God [p] and drove out all who sold and bought in the temple, and he overturned the tables of the money-changers and the seats of those who sold pigeons. 13 He said to them, "It is written, 'My house shall be called a house of prayer'; but you make it a den of robbers."

14 And the blind and the lame came to him in the temple, and he healed them. 15 But when the chief priests and the scribes saw the wonderful things that he did, and the children crying out in the temple, "Hosanna to the Son of David!" they were indignant; 16 and they said to him, "Do you hear what these are saying?" And Jesus said to them, "Yes; have you never read,

'Out of the mouth of babes and sucklings
thou hast brought perfect praise'?"

17 And leaving them, he went out of the city to Bethany and lodged there.

18 In the morning, as he was returning to the city, he was hungry. 19And seeing a fig tree by the wayside he went to it, and found nothing on it but leaves only. And he said to it, "May no fruit ever come from you again!" And the fig tree withered at once. 20 When the disciples saw it they marveled, saying, "How did the fig tree wither at once?" 21And Jesus answered them, "Truly, I say to you, if you have faith and never doubt, you will not only do what has been done to the fig tree, but even if you say to this mountain, 'Be taken up and cast into the sea,' it will be done. 22And whatever you ask in prayer, you will receive, if you have faith."

23 And when he entered the temple, the chief priests and the elders of the people came up to him as he was teaching, and said, "By what authority are you doing these things, and who gave you this authority?" 24 Jesus answered them, "I also will ask you a question; and if you tell me the answer, then I also will tell you by what authority I do these things. 25 The baptism of John, whence was it? From heaven or from men?" And they argued with one another, "If we say, 'From heaven,' he will say to us, 'Why then did you not believe him?' 26 But if we say, 'From men,' we are afraid of the multitude; for

PHILLIPS

own cloaks on the road, while others cut down branches from the trees and spread them in his path. The crowds who went in front of him and the crowds who followed behind him all shouted: "God save the Son of David! Blessed is the man who comes in the name of the Lord! God save him from on high!"

And as he entered Jerusalem a shock ran through the whole city. "Who *is* this?" men cried. "This is Jesus the prophet," replied the crowd, "the man from Nazareth in Galilee!"

Then Jesus went into the Temple and drove out all the buyers and sellers there. He overturned the tables of the money-changers and the benches of those who sold doves, crying:

"It is written, *'My house shall be called a house of prayer.'* But you have turned it into a thieves' kitchen!"

And there in the Temple the blind and the lame came to him, and he healed them. But when the chief priests and the scribes saw the wonderful things he had done, and that children were shouting in the Temple the words, "God save the Son of David," they were highly indignant. "Can't you hear what these children are saying?" they asked Jesus.

"Yes," he replied, "and haven't you ever read the words, *'Out of the mouth of babes and sucklings thou hast perfected praise'?*" And he turned on his heel and went out of the city to Bethany, where he spent the night.

His strange words to the fig tree   21. 18

In the morning he came back early to the city and felt hungry. He saw a fig tree growing by the side of the road, but when he got to it he discovered there was nothing on it but leaves. "No more fruit shall ever grow on you!" he said to it, and all at once the fig tree withered away. When the disciples saw this happen they were simply amazed. "How on earth did the fig tree wither away quite suddenly like that!" they asked.

"Believe me," replied Jesus, "if you have faith and have no doubts in your heart, you will not only do this to a fig tree but even if you should say to this hill, 'Get up and throw yourself into the sea,' it will happen! Everything you ask for in prayer, if you have faith, you will receive."

Jesus meets a question   21. 23
with a counterquestion

Then when he had entered the Temple and was in the act of teaching, the chief priests and Jewish elders came up to him and said, "What authority have you for what you're doing, and who gave you that authority?"

"I am also going to ask you one question," Jesus replied to them, "and if you answer it I will tell you what authority I have for what I do. John's baptism, now, did it come from Heaven or was it purely human?"

At this they began arguing among themselves: "If we say, 'It came from Heaven,' he will say to us, 'Then why didn't you believe in him?' If on the other hand we should say, 'It was purely human'—well, frankly, we are afraid of the people—for all of them consider John was a prophet."

N.E.B.

cloaks, and some cut branches from the trees to spread in his path. Then the crowd that went ahead and the others that came behind raised the shout: 'Hosanna to the Son of David! Blessings on him who comes in the name of the Lord! Hosanna in the heavens!'

When he entered Jerusalem the whole city went wild with excitement. 'Who is this?' people asked, and the crowd replied, 'This is the prophet Jesus, from Nazareth in Galilee.'

Jesus then went into the temple and drove out all who were buying and selling in the temple precincts; he upset the tables of the money-changers and the seats of the dealers in pigeons; and said to them, 'Scripture says, "My house shall be called a house of prayer"; but you are making it a robbers' cave.'

In the temple blind men and cripples came to him, and he healed them. The chief priests and doctors of the law saw the wonderful things he did, and heard the boys in the temple shouting, 'Hosanna to the Son of David!', and they asked him indignantly, 'Do you hear what they are saying?' Jesus answered, 'I do; have you never read that text, "Thou hast made children and babes at the breast sound aloud thy praise"?' Then he left them and went out of the city to Bethany, where he spent the night.

Next morning on his way to the city he felt hungry; and seeing a fig-tree at the roadside he went up to it, but found nothing on it but leaves. He said to the tree, 'You shall never bear fruit any more!'; and the tree withered away at once. The disciples were amazed at the sight. 'How is it', they asked, 'that the tree has withered so suddenly?' Jesus answered them, 'I tell you this: if only you have faith and have no doubts, you will do what has been done to the fig-tree; and more than that, you need only say to this mountain, "Be lifted from your place and hurled into the sea", and what you say will be done. And whatever you pray for in faith you will receive.'

He entered the temple, and the chief priests and elders of the nation came to him with the question: 'By what authority are you acting like this? Who gave you this authority?' Jesus replied, 'I have a question to ask too; answer it, and I will tell you by what authority I act. The baptism of John: was it from God, or from men?' This set them arguing among themselves: 'If we say, "from God", he will say, "Then why did you not believe him?" But if we say, "from men", we are afraid of the people, for they all take

K.J.V.

the people; for all hold John as a prophet. 27And they answered Jesus, and said, We cannot tell. And he said unto them, Neither tell I you by what authority I do these things.

28 But what think ye? A *certain* man had two sons; and he came to the first, and said, Son, go work to day in my vineyard. 29 He answered and said, I will not; but afterward he repented, and went. 30And he came to the second, and said likewise. And he answered and said, I *go,* sir; and went not. 31 Whether of them twain did the will of *his* father? They say unto him, The first. Jesus saith unto them, Verily I say unto you, That the publicans and the harlots go into the kingdom of God before you. 32 For John came unto you in the way of righteousness, and ye believed him not; but the publicans and the harlots believed him: and ye, when ye had seen *it,* repented not afterward, that ye might believe him.

33 Hear another parable: There was a certain householder, which planted a vineyard, and hedged it round about, and digged a winepress in it, and built a tower, and let it out to husbandmen, and went into a far country: 34And when the time of the fruit drew near, he sent his servants to the husbandmen, that they might receive the fruits of it. 35And the husbandmen took his servants, and beat one, and killed another, and stoned another. 36Again, he sent other servants more than the first: and they did unto them likewise. 37 But last of all he sent unto them his son, saying, They will reverence my son. 38 But when the husbandmen saw the son, they said among themselves, This is the heir; come, let us kill him, and let us seize on his inheritance. 39And they caught him, and cast *him* out of the vineyard, and slew *him.* 40 When the lord therefore of the vineyard cometh, what will he do unto those husbandmen? 41 They say unto him, He will miserably destroy those wicked men, and will let out *his* vineyard unto other husbandmen, which shall render him the fruits in their seasons. 42 Jesus saith unto them, Did ye never read in the Scriptures, The stone which the builders rejected, the same is become the head of the corner: this is the Lord's doing, and it is marvellous in our eyes? 43 Therefore say I unto you, The kingdom of God shall be taken from you, and given to a nation bringing forth the fruits thereof. 44And whosoever shall fall on this stone shall be broken: but on whomsoever it shall fall, it will grind him to powder. 45And when the chief priests and Pharisees had heard his parables, they perceived that he spake of them. 46 But when they sought to lay hands on him, they feared the multitude, because they took him for a prophet.

R.S.V.

all hold that John was a prophet." 27 So they answered Jesus, "We do not know." And he said to them, "Neither will I tell you by what authority I do these things.

28 "What do you think? A man had two sons; and he went to the first and said, 'Son, go and work in the vineyard today.' 29And he answered, 'I will not'; but afterward he repented and went. 30And he went to the second and said the same; and he answered, 'I go, sir,' but did not go. 31 Which of the two did the will of his father?" They said, "The first." Jesus said to them, "Truly, I say to you, the tax collectors and the harlots go into the kingdom of God before you. 32 For John came to you in the way of righteousness, and you did not believe him, but the tax collectors and the harlots believed him; and even when you saw it, you did not afterward repent and believe him.

33 "Hear another parable. There was a householder who planted a vineyard, and set a hedge around it, and dug a wine press in it, and built a tower, and let it out to tenants, and went into another country. 34 When the season of fruit drew near, he sent his servants to the tenants, to get his fruit; 35 and the tenants took his servants and beat one, killed another, and stoned another. 36Again he sent other servants, more than the first; and they did the same to them. 37Afterward he sent his son to them, saying, 'They will respect my son.' 38 But when the tenants saw the son, they said to themselves, 'This is the heir; come, let us kill him and have his inheritance.' 39And they took him and cast him out of the vineyard, and killed him. 40 When therefore the owner of the vineyard comes, what will he do to those tenants?" 41 They said to him, "He will put those wretches to a miserable death, and let out the vineyard to other tenants who will give him the fruits in their seasons."

42 Jesus said to them, "Have you never read in the scriptures:

'The very stone which the builders rejected
has become the head of the corner;
this was the Lord's doing,
and it is marvelous in our eyes'?

43 Therefore I tell you, the kingdom of God will be taken away from you and given to a nation producing the fruits of it." *q*

45 When the chief priests and the Pharisees heard his parables, they perceived that he was speaking about them. 46 But when they tried to arrest him, they feared the multitudes, because they held him to be a prophet.

22 And Jesus answered and spake unto them again by parables, and said, 2 The kingdom of heaven is like unto a certain king, which made

22 And again Jesus spoke to them in parables, saying, 2 "The kingdom of heaven may be compared to a king who gave a marriage

[q] Other ancient authorities add verse 44, *"And he who falls on this stone will be broken to pieces; but when it falls on any one, it will crush him."*

PHILLIPS

So they answered Jesus, "We do not know." "Then I will not tell you by what authority I do these things!" returned Jesus. "But what is your opinion about this? There was a man with two sons. He went to the first and said, 'Go and work in my vineyard today, my son.' He said, 'All right, sir'—but he never went near it. Then the father approached the second son with the same request. He said, 'I won't.' But afterward he changed his mind and went. Which of these two did what their father wanted?"

"The second one," they replied.

"Yes, and I tell you that tax collectors and prostitutes are going into the kingdom of God in front of you!" retorted Jesus. "For John came to you as a saint, and you did not believe him—yet the tax collectors and the prostitutes did! And, even after seeing that, you would not change your minds and believe him.

Jesus tells a pointed story   21. 33

"Now listen to another story. There was once a man, a landowner, who planted a vineyard, fenced it round, dug out a hole for the winepress and built a watchtower. Then he let it out to farm workers and went abroad. When the vintage time approached, he sent his servants to the farm workers to receive his share of the proceeds. But they took the servants, beat up one, killed another, and drove off a third with stones. Then he sent some more servants, a larger party than the first, but they treated them in just the same way. Finally he sent his own son, thinking, 'They will respect my son.' Yet when the farm workers saw the son they said to each other, 'This fellow is the future owner. Come on, let's kill him and we shall get everything that he would have had!' So they took him, threw him out of the vineyard and killed him. Now when the owner of the vineyard returns, what will he do to those farm workers?"

"He will kill those scoundrels without mercy," they replied, "and will let the vineyard out to other tenants, who will give him the produce at the right season."

"And have you never read these words of scripture," said Jesus to them:

The stone which the builders rejected,
The same was made the head of the corner:
This was from the Lord,
And it is marvellous in our eyes?

"Here, I tell you, lies the reason why the kingdom of God is going to be taken away from you and given to a people who will produce its proper fruit."

When the chief priests and the Pharisees heard his parables they realized that he was speaking about them. They longed to get their hands on him, but they were afraid of the crowds, who regarded him as a prophet.

The kingdom is not to be   22. 1
lightly disregarded

Then Jesus began to talk to them again in parables.

"The kingdom of Heaven," he said, "is like

N.E.B.

John for a prophet.' So they answered, 'We do not know.' And Jesus said: 'Then neither will I tell you by what authority I act.

'But what do you think about this? A man had two sons. He went to the first, and said, "My boy, go and work today in the vineyard." "I will, sir", the boy replied; but he never went. The father came to the second and said the same. "I will not", he replied, but afterwards he changed his mind and went. Which of these two did as his father wished?' 'The second', they said. Then Jesus answered, 'I tell you this: tax-gatherers and prostitutes are entering the kingdom of God ahead of you. For when John came to show you the right way to live, you did not believe him, but the tax-gatherers and prostitutes did; and even when you had seen that, you did not change your minds and believe him.

'Listen to another parable. There was a landowner who planted a vineyard: he put a wall round it, hewed out a winepress, and built a watch-tower; then he let it out to vine-growers and went abroad. When the vintage season approached, he sent his servants to the tenants to collect the produce due to him. But they took his servants and thrashed one, murdered another, and stoned a third. Again, he sent other servants, this time a larger number; and they did the same to them. At last he sent to them his son. "They will respect my son", he said. But when they saw the son the tenants said to one another, "This is the heir; come on, let us kill him, and get his inheritance." And they took him, flung him out of the vineyard, and murdered him. When the owner of the vineyard comes, how do you think he will deal with those tenants?' 'He will bring those bad men to a bad end', they answered, 'and hand the vineyard over to other tenants, who will let him have his share of the crop when the season comes.' Then Jesus said to them, 'Have you never read in the scriptures: "The stone which the builders rejected has become the main corner-stone. This is the Lord's doing, and it is wonderful in our eyes"? Therefore, I tell you, the kingdom of God will be taken away from you, and given to a nation that yields the proper fruit.'[a]

When the chief priests and Pharisees heard his parables, they saw that he was referring to them; they wanted to arrest him, but they were afraid of the people, who looked on Jesus as a prophet.

22 Then Jesus spoke to them again in parables: 'The kingdom of Heaven is like this. There was a king who prepared a feast for his

[a] Some witnesses add (44) Any man who falls on this stone will be dashed to pieces; and if it falls on a man he will be crushed by it.

K.J.V.

a marriage for his son, 3And sent forth his servants to call them that were bidden to the wedding: and they would not come. 4Again, he sent forth other servants, saying, Tell them which are bidden, Behold, I have prepared my dinner: my oxen and *my* fatlings *are* killed, and all things *are* ready: come unto the marriage. 5 But they made light of *it,* and went their ways, one to his farm, another to his merchandise: 6And the remnant took his servants, and entreated *them* spitefully, and slew *them.* 7 But when the king heard *thereof,* he was wroth: and he sent forth his armies, and destroyed those murderers, and burned up their city. 8 Then saith he to his servants, The wedding is ready, but they which were bidden were not worthy. 9 Go ye therefore into the highways, and as many as ye shall find, bid to the marriage. 10 So those servants went out into the highways, and gathered together all as many as they found, both bad and good: and the wedding was furnished with guests.

11 And when the king came in to see the guests, he saw there a man which had not on a wedding garment: 12And he saith unto him, Friend, how camest thou in hither not having a wedding garment? And he was speechless. 13 Then said the king to the servants, Bind him hand and foot, and take him away, and cast *him* into outer darkness; there shall be weeping and gnashing of teeth. 14 For many are called, but few *are* chosen.

15 Then went the Pharisees, and took counsel how they might entangle him in his talk. 16And they sent out unto him their disciples with the Herodians, saying, Master, we know that thou art true, and teachest the way of God in truth, neither carest thou for any *man:* for thou regardest not the person of men. 17 Tell us therefore, What thinkest thou? Is it lawful to give tribute unto Cesar, or not? 18 But Jesus perceived their wickedness, and said, Why tempt ye me, *ye* hypocrites? 19 Shew me the tribute money. And they brought unto him a penny. 20And he saith unto them, Whose *is* this image and superscription? 21 They say unto him, Cesar's. Then saith he unto them, Render therefore unto Cesar the things which are Cesar's; and unto God the things that are God's. 22 When they had heard *these words,* they marvelled, and left him, and went their way.

23 The same day came to him the Sadducees, which say that there is no resurrection, and asked him, 24 Saying, Master, Moses said, If a man die, having no children, his brother shall marry his wife, and raise up seed unto his brother. 25 Now there were with us seven brethren: and the first, when he had married a wife, deceased, and, having no issue, left his wife unto his brother: 26 Likewise the second also, and the

R.S.V.

feast for his son, 3 and sent his servants to call those who were invited to the marriage feast; but they would not come. 4Again he sent other servants, saying, 'Tell those who are invited, Behold, I have made ready my dinner, my oxen and my fat calves are killed, and everything is ready; come to the marriage feast.' 5 But they made light of it and went off, one to his farm, another to his business, 6 while the rest seized his servants, treated them shamefully, and killed them. 7 The king was angry, and he sent his troops and destroyed those murderers and burned their city. 8 Then he said to his servants, 'The wedding is ready, but those invited were not worthy. 9 Go therefore to the thoroughfares, and invite to the marriage feast as many as you find.' 10And those servants went out into the streets and gathered all whom they found, both bad and good; so the wedding hall was filled with guests.

11 "But when the king came in to look at the guests, he saw there a man who had no wedding garment; 12 and he said to him, 'Friend, how did you get in here without a wedding garment?' And he was speechless. 13 Then the king said to the attendants, 'Bind him hand and foot, and cast him into the outer darkness; there men will weep and gnash their teeth.' 14 For many are called, but few are chosen."

15 Then the Pharisees went and took counsel how to entangle him in his talk. 16And they sent their disciples to him, along with the Herodians, saying, "Teacher, we know that you are true, and teach the way of God truthfully, and care for no man; for you do not regard the position of men. 17 Tell us, then, what you think. Is it lawful to pay taxes to Caesar, or not?" 18 But Jesus, aware of their malice, said, "Why put me to the test, you hypocrites? 19 Show me the money for the tax." And they brought him a coin.[r] 20And Jesus said to them, "Whose likeness and inscription is this?" 21 They said, "Caesar's." Then he said to them, "Render therefore to Caesar the things that are Caesar's, and to God the things that are God's." 22 When they heard it, they marveled; and they left him and went away.

23 The same day Sadducees came to him, who say that there is no resurrection; and they asked him a question, 24 saying, "Teacher, Moses said, 'If a man dies, having no children, his brother must marry the widow, and raise up children for his brother.' 25 Now there were seven brothers among us; the first married, and died, and having no children left his wife to his brother. 26 So

[r] Greek *a denarius.*

70

PHILLIPS

a king who arranged a wedding for his son. He sent his servants to summon those who had been invited to the festivities, but they refused to come. Then he tried again; he sent some more servants, saying to them: 'Tell those who have been invited, "Here is my wedding breakfast all ready, my bullocks and fat cattle have been slaughtered and everything is prepared. Come along to the festivities." ' But they took no notice of this and went off, one to his farm, and another to his business. As for the rest, they got hold of the servants, treated them disgracefully, and finally killed them. At this the king was very angry and sent his troops and killed those murderers and burned down their city. Then he said to his servants: 'The wedding feast is quite ready, but those who were invited were not good enough for it. So go off now to all the street corners and invite everyone you find there to the feast.' So the servants went out onto the streets and collected together all those whom they found, bad and good alike. And the hall became filled with guests. But when the king came in to inspect the guests, he noticed among them a man not dressed for a wedding. 'How did you come in here, my friend,' he said to him, 'without being properly dressed for the wedding?' And the man had nothing to say. Then the king said to the ushers, 'Tie him up and throw him into the darkness outside. There he can weep and regret his folly!' For many are invited but few are chosen."

A clever trap—and a   22. 15 penetrating answer

Then the Pharisees went off and discussed how they could trap him in argument. Eventually they sent their disciples with some of the Herod party to say this: "Master, we know that you are an honest man who teaches the way of God faithfully and that you are not swayed by men's opinion of you. Obviously you don't care for human approval. Now tell us— *Is it right to pay taxes to Caesar or not?"*

But Jesus, knowing their evil intention, said: "Why try this trick on me, you frauds? Show me the money you pay the tax with." They handed him a coin, and he said to them, "Whose face is this and whose name is in the inscription?"

"Caesar's," they said.

"Then give to Caesar," he replied, "what belongs to Caesar and to God what belongs to God!"

This reply staggered them and they went away and let him alone.

Jesus exposes the ignorance   22. 23 of the Sadducees

On the same day some Sadducees (who deny that there is any resurrection) approached Jesus with this question: "Master, Moses said if a man should die without any children, his brother should marry his widow and raise up a family for him. Now, we have a case of seven brothers. The first one married and died, and since he had no family he left his wife to his brother. The same thing happened with the second and

N.E.B.

son's wedding; but when he sent his servants to summon the guests he had invited, they would not come. He sent others again, telling them to say to the guests, "See now! I have prepared this feast for you. I have had my bullocks and fatted beasts slaughtered; everything is ready; come to the wedding at once." But they took no notice; one went off to his farm, another to his business, and the others seized the servants, attacked them brutally, and killed them. The king was furious; he sent troops to kill those murderers and set their town on fire. Then he said to his servants, "The wedding-feast is ready; but the guests I invited did not deserve the honour. Go out to the main thoroughfares, and invite everyone you can find to the wedding." The servants went out into the streets, and collected all they could find, good and bad alike. So the hall was packed with guests.

'When the king came in to see the company at table, he observed one man who was not dressed for a wedding. "My friend," said the king, "how do you come to be here without your wedding clothes?" He had nothing to say. The king then said to his attendants, "Bind him hand and foot; turn him out into the dark, the place of wailing and grinding of teeth." For though many are invited, few are chosen.'

Then the Pharisees went and agreed on a plan to trap him in his own words. Some of their followers were sent to him in company with men of Herod's party. They said, 'Master, you are an honest man, we know; you teach in all honesty the way of life that God requires, truckling to no man, whoever he may be. Give us your ruling on this: are we or are we not permitted to pay taxes to the Roman Emperor?' Jesus was aware of their malicious intention and said to them, 'You hypocrites! Why are you trying to catch me out? Show me the money in which the tax is paid.' They handed him a silver piece. Jesus asked, 'Whose head is this, and whose inscription?' 'Caesar's', they replied. He said to them, 'Then pay Caesar what is due to Caesar, and pay God what is due to God.' This answer took them by surprise, and they went away and left him alone.

The same day Sadducees came to him, maintaining that there is no resurrection. Their question was this: 'Master, Moses said, "If a man should die childless, his brother shall marry the widow and carry on his brother's family." Now we knew of seven brothers. The first married and died, and as he was without issue his wife was left to his brother. The same thing happened with

K.J.V.

third, unto the seventh. 27And last of all the woman died also. 28 Therefore in the resurrection, whose wife shall she be of the seven? for they all had her. 29 Jesus answered and said unto them, Ye do err, not knowing the Scriptures, nor the power of God. 30 For in the resurrection they neither marry, nor are given in marriage, but are as the angels of God in heaven. 31 But as touching the resurrection of the dead, have ye not read that which was spoken unto you by God, saying, 32 I am the God of Abraham, and the God of Isaac, and the God of Jacob? God is not the God of the dead, but of the living. 33And when the multitude heard *this,* they were astonished at his doctrine.

34 But when the Pharisees had heard that he had put the Sadducees to silence, they were gathered together. 35 Then one of them, *which was* a lawyer, asked *him a question,* tempting him, and saying, 36 Master, which *is* the great commandment in the law? 37 Jesus said unto him, Thou shalt love the Lord thy God with all thy heart, and with all thy soul, and with all thy mind. 38 This is the first and great commandment. 39And the second *is* like unto it, Thou shalt love thy neighbour as thyself. 40 On these two commandments hang all the law and the prophets.

41 While the Pharisees were gathered together, Jesus asked them, 42 Saying, What think ye of Christ? whose son is he? They say unto him, *The son* of David. 43 He saith unto them, How then doth David in spirit call him Lord, saying, 44 The Lord said unto my Lord, Sit thou on my right hand, till I make thine enemies thy footstool? 45 If David then call him Lord, how is he his son? 46And no man was able to answer him a word, neither durst any *man* from that day forth ask him any more *questions.*

R.S.V.

too the second and third, down to the seventh. 27After them all, the woman died. 28 In the resurrection, therefore, to which of the seven will she be wife? For they all had her."

29 But Jesus answered them, "You are wrong, because you know neither the scriptures nor the power of God. 30 For in the resurrection they neither marry nor are given in marriage, but are like angels⁸ in heaven. 31And as for the resurrection of the dead, have you not read what was said to you by God, 32 'I am the God of Abraham, and the God of Isaac, and the God of Jacob'? He is not God of the dead, but of the living." 33And when the crowd heard it, they were astonished at his teaching.

34 But when the Pharisees heard that he had silenced the Sadducees, they came together. 35And one of them, a lawyer, asked him a question, to test him. 36 "Teacher, which is the great commandment in the law?" 37And he said to him, "You shall love the Lord your God with all your heart, and with all your soul, and with all your mind. 38 This is the great and first commandment. 39And a second is like it, You shall love your neighbor as yourself. 40 On these two commandments depend all the law and the prophets."

41 Now while the Pharisees were gathered together, Jesus asked them a question, 42 saying, "What do you think of the Christ? Whose son is he?" They said to him, "The son of David." 43 He said to them, "How is it then that David, inspired by the Spirit,ᶠ calls him Lord, saying,
44 'The Lord said to my Lord,
　　Sit at my right hand,
　　till I put thy enemies under thy feet'?
45 If David thus calls him Lord, how is he his son?" 46And no one was able to answer him a word, nor from that day did any one dare to ask him any more questions.

23 Then spake Jesus to the multitude, and to his disciples, 2 Saying, The scribes and the Pharisees sit in Moses' seat: 3All therefore whatsoever they bid you observe, *that* observe and do; but do not ye after their works: for they say, and do not. 4 For they bind heavy burdens and grievous to be borne, and lay *them* on men's shoulders; but they *themselves* will not

23 Then said Jesus to the crowds and to his disciples, 2 "The scribes and the Pharisees sit on Moses' seat; 3 so practice and observe whatever they tell you, but not what they do; for they preach, but do not practice. 4 They bind heavy burdens, hard to bear,ᵘ and lay them on men's shoulders; but they themselves will not

[s] Other ancient authorities add *of God.* [t] Or *David in the Spirit.* [u] Other ancient authorities omit *hard to bear.*

PHILLIPS

the third, right up to the seventh. Last of all the woman herself died. Now in this 'resurrection,' whose wife will she be of these seven men—for she belonged to all of them?"

"You are very wide of the mark," replied Jesus to them, "for you are ignorant of both the scriptures and the power of God. For in the resurrection there is no such thing as marrying or being given in marriage—men live like the angels in Heaven. And as for the matter of the resurrection of the dead, haven't you ever read what was once said to you by God himself, 'I am the God of Abraham, the God of Isaac and the God of Jacob'? God is not God of the dead but of living men!" When the crowds heard this they were astounded at his teaching.

The greatest commandments   22. 34
in the Law

When the Pharisees heard that he had silenced the Sadducees they came up to him in a body, and one of them, an expert in the Law, put this test question: "Master, what are we to consider the Law's greatest commandment?"

Jesus answered him, " 'Thou shalt love the Lord thy God with all thy heart, and with all thy soul and with all thy mind.' This is the first and great commandment. And there is a second like it: 'Thou shalt love thy neighbor as thyself.' The whole of the Law and the Prophets depends on these two commandments."

Jesus puts an unanswerable   22. 41
question

Then Jesus asked the assembled Pharisees this question: "What is your opinion about Christ? Whose son is he?"

"The Son of David," they answered.

"How then," returned Jesus, "does David when inspired by the Spirit call him Lord? He says—

The Lord said unto my *Lord,*
Sit thou on my right hand,
Till I put thine enemies underneath thy feet?

If David then calls him Lord, how can he be his son?"

Nobody was able to answer this and from that day on no one dared to ask him any further questions.

He publicly warns the people   23. 1
against their religious leaders

Then Jesus addressed the crowds and his disciples. "The scribes and the Pharisees speak with the authority of Moses," he told them, "so you must do what they tell you and follow their instructions. But you must not imitate their lives! For they preach but do not practice. They pile up back-breaking burdens and lay them on other men's shoulders—yet they them-

N.E.B.

the second, and the third, and so on with all seven. Last of all the woman died. At the resurrection, then, whose wife will she be, for they had all married her?' Jesus answered: 'You are mistaken, because you know neither the scriptures nor the power of God. At the resurrection men and women do not marry, but are like angels in heaven.

'But about the resurrection of the dead, have you never read what God himself said to you: "I am the God of Abraham, the God of Isaac, and the God of Jacob"? He is not God of the dead but of the living.' The people heard what he said, and were astounded at his teaching.

Hearing that he had silenced the Sadducees, the Pharisees met together; and one of their number[a] tested him with this question: 'Master, which is the greatest commandment in the Law?' He answered, ' "Love the Lord your God with all your heart, with all your soul, with all your mind." That is the greatest commandment. It comes first. The second is like it: "Love your neighbour as yourself." Everything in the Law and the prophets hangs on these two commandments.'

Turning to the assembled Pharisees Jesus asked them, 'What is your opinion about the Messiah? Whose son is he?' 'The son of David', they replied. 'How then is it', he asked, 'that David by inspiration calls him "Lord"? For he says, "The Lord said to my Lord, 'Sit at my right hand until I put your enemies under your feet.' " If David calls him "Lord", how can he be David's son?' Not a man could say a word in reply; and from that day forward no one dared ask him another question.

23 Jesus then addressed the people and his disciples in these words: 'The doctors of the law and the Pharisees sit in the chair of Moses; therefore do what they tell you; pay attention to their words. But do not follow their practice; for they say one thing and do another. They make up heavy packs and pile them on men's shoulders, but will not raise a finger to

[a] *Some witnesses insert* a lawyer.

73

move them with one of their fingers. 5 But all their works they do for to be seen of men: they make broad their phylacteries, and enlarge the borders of their garments, 6And love the uppermost rooms at feasts, and the chief seats in the synagogues, 7And greetings in the markets, and to be called of men, Rabbi, Rabbi. 8 But be not ye called Rabbi: for one is your Master, *even* Christ; and all ye are brethren. 9And call no *man* your father upon the earth: for one is your Father, which is in heaven. 10 Neither be ye called masters: for one is your Master, *even* Christ. 11 But he that is greatest among you shall be your servant. 12And whosoever shall exalt himself shall be abased; and he that shall humble himself shall be exalted.

13 But woe unto you, scribes and Pharisees, hypocrites! for ye shut up the kingdom of heaven against men: for ye neither go in *yourselves,* neither suffer ye them that are entering to go in. 14 Woe unto you, scribes and Pharisees, hypocrites! for ye devour widows' houses, and for a pretence make long prayer: therefore ye shall receive the greater damnation. 15 Woe unto you, scribes and Pharisees, hypocrites! for ye compass sea and land to make one proselyte; and when he is made, ye make him twofold more the child of hell than yourselves. 16 Woe unto you, *ye* blind guides, which say, Whosoever shall swear by the temple, it is nothing; but whosoever shall swear by the gold of the temple, he is a debtor! 17 *Ye* fools and blind: for whether is greater, the gold, or the temple that sanctifieth the gold? 18And, Whosoever shall swear by the altar, it is nothing; but whosoever sweareth by the gift that is upon it, he is guilty. 19 *Ye* fools and blind: for whether *is* greater, the gift, or the altar that sanctifieth the gift? 20 Whoso therefore shall swear by the altar, sweareth by it, and by all things thereon. 21And whoso shall swear by the temple, sweareth by it, and by him that dwelleth therein. 22And he that shall swear by heaven, sweareth by the throne of God, and by him that sitteth thereon. 23 Woe unto you, scribes and Pharisees, hypocrites! for ye pay tithe of mint and anise and cummin, and have omitted the weightier *matters* of the law, judgment, mercy, and faith: these ought ye to have done, and not to leave the other undone. 24 *Ye* blind guides, which strain at a gnat, and swallow a camel. 25 Woe unto you, scribes and Pharisees, hypocrites! for ye make clean the outside of the cup and of the platter, but within they are full of extortion and excess. 26 *Thou* blind Pharisee, cleanse first that *which is* within the cup and platter, that the outside of them may be clean also. 27 Woe unto you, scribes and Pharisees, hypocrites! for ye are like unto whited sepulchres, which indeed appear beautiful outward, but are within full of dead *men's* bones, and of all uncleanness. 28 Even so ye also outwardly appear righteous unto men, but within ye are full of hypocrisy and iniquity. 29 Woe unto you, scribes and Pharisees, hypocrites! because ye build the tombs of the prophets, and garnish the sepulchres of the righteous, 30And say, If we had been in the days of our fathers, we would not have been partakers with them in the blood of the prophets. 31 Wherefore ye be witnesses unto yourselves, that ye are the children of them which killed the prophets. 32 Fill ye up then the measure of your fathers. 33 *Ye* serpents, *ye* generation of vipers, how can ye escape the damnation of hell?

34 Wherefore, behold, I send unto you prophets, and wise men, and scribes: and *some* of

move them with their finger. 5 They do all their deeds to be seen by men; for they make their phylacteries broad and their fringes long, 6 and they love the place of honor at feasts and the best seats in the synagogues, 7 and salutations in the market places, and being called rabbi by men. 8 But you are not to be called rabbi, for you have one teacher, and you are all brethren. 9And call no man your father on earth, for you have one Father, who is in heaven. 10 Neither be called masters, for you have one master, the Christ. 11 He who is greatest among you shall be your servant; 12 whoever exalts himself will be humbled, and whoever humbles himself will be exalted.

13 "But woe to you, scribes and Pharisees, hypocrites! because you shut the kingdom of heaven against men; for you neither enter yourselves, nor allow those who would enter to go in.[v] 15 Woe to you, scribes and Pharisees, hypocrites! for you traverse sea and land to make a single proselyte, and when he becomes a proselyte, you make him twice as much a child of hell[w] as yourselves.

16 "Woe to you, blind guides, who say, 'If any one swears by the temple, it is nothing; but if any one swears by the gold of the temple, he is bound by his oath.' 17 You blind fools! For which is greater, the gold or the temple that has made the gold sacred? 18And you say, 'If any one swears by the altar, it is nothing; but if any one swears by the gift that is on the altar, he is bound by his oath.' 19 You blind men! For which is greater, the gift or the altar that makes the gift sacred? 20 So he who swears by the altar, swears by it and by everything on it; 21 and he who swears by the temple, swears by it and by him who dwells in it; 22 and he who swears by heaven, swears by the throne of God and by him who sits upon it.

23 "Woe to you, scribes and Pharisees, hypocrites! for you tithe mint and dill and cummin, and have neglected the weightier matters of the law, justice and mercy and faith; these you ought to have done, without neglecting the others. 24 You blind guides, straining out a gnat and swallowing a camel!

25 "Woe to you, scribes and Pharisees, hypocrites! for you cleanse the outside of the cup and of the plate, but inside they are full of extortion and rapacity. 26 You blind Pharisee! first cleanse the inside of the cup and of the plate, that the outside also may be clean.

27 "Woe to you, scribes and Pharisees, hypocrites! for you are like whitewashed tombs, which outwardly appear beautiful, but within they are full of dead men's bones and all uncleanness. 28 So you also outwardly appear righteous to men, but within you are full of hypocrisy and iniquity.

29 "Woe to you, scribes and Pharisees, hypocrites! for you build the tombs of the prophets and adorn the monuments of the righteous, 30 saying, 'If we had lived in the days of our fathers, we would not have taken part with them in shedding the blood of the prophets.' 31 Thus you witness against yourselves, that you are sons of those who murdered the prophets. 32 Fill up, then, the measure of your fathers. 33 You serpents, you brood of vipers, how are you to escape being sentenced to hell?[w] 34 Therefore I send you prophets and wise men and scribes,

[v] Other authorities add here (or after verse 12) verse 14, *Woe to you, scribes and Pharisees, hypocrites! for you devour widows' houses and for a pretence you make long prayers; therefore you will receive the greater condemnation.* [w] Greek *Gehenna*

PHILLIPS

selves will not raise a finger to move them. Their whole lives are planned with an eye to effect. They increase the size of their phylacteries and lengthen the tassels of their robes; they love seats of honor at dinner parties and front places in the synagogues. They love to be greeted with respect in public places and to have men call them 'rabbi!' Don't you ever be called 'rabbi'—you have only one teacher, and all of you are brothers. And don't call any human being 'father'—for you have one Father and he is in Heaven. And you must not let people call you 'leaders'—you have only one leader, Christ! The only 'superior' among you is the one who serves the others. For every man who promotes himself will be humbled, and every man who learns to be humble will find promotion.

"But alas for you, you scribes and Pharisees, play actors that you are! You lock the doors of the kingdom of Heaven in men's faces; you will not go in yourselves neither will you allow those at the door to go inside.

"Alas for you, you scribes and Pharisees, play actors! You scour sea and land to make a single convert, and then you make him twice as ripe for destruction as you are yourselves.

"Alas for you, you blind leaders! You say, 'If anyone swears by the Temple it amounts to nothing, but if he swears by the gold of the Temple he is bound by his oath.' You blind fools, which is the more important, the gold or the Temple which sanctifies the gold? And you say, 'If anyone swears by the altar it doesn't matter, but if he swears by the gift placed on the altar he is bound by his oath.' Have you no eyes—which is more important, the gift, or the altar which sanctifies the gift? Any man who swears by the altar is swearing by the altar and whatever is offered upon it; and anyone who swears by the Temple is swearing by the Temple and by him who dwells in it; and anyone who swears by Heaven is swearing by the throne of God and by the one who sits upon that throne.

"Alas for you, scribes and Pharisees, you utter frauds! For you pay your tithe on mint and aniseed and cummin, and neglect the things which carry far more weight in the Law—justice, mercy and good faith. These are the things you should have observed—without neglecting the others. You call yourselves leaders, and yet you can't see an inch before your noses, for you filter out the mosquito and swallow the camel.

"What miserable frauds you are, you scribes and Pharisees! You clean the outside of the cup and the dish, while the inside is full of greed and self-indulgence. Can't you see, Pharisee? First wash the inside of a cup, and then you can clean the outside.

"Alas for you, you hypocritical scribes and Pharisees! You are like white-washed tombs, which look fine on the outside but inside are full of dead men's bones and all kinds of rottenness. For you appear like good men on the outside—but inside you are a mass of pretense and wickedness.

"What miserable frauds you are, you scribes and Pharisees! You build tombs for the prophets and decorate monuments for good men of the past, and then say, 'If we had lived in the times of our ancestors we should never have joined in the killing of the prophets.' Yes, 'your ancestors'—*that* shows you to be sons indeed of those who murdered the prophets. Go ahead then, and finish off what your ancestors tried to do! You serpents, you viper's brood, how do you think you are going to avoid being condemned to the rubbish heap? Listen to this: I am sending you prophets and wise and learned

N.E.B.

lift the load themselves. Whatever they do is done for show. They go about with broad phylacteries[a] and wear deep fringes on their robes; they like to have places of honour at feasts and the chief seats in synagogues, to be greeted respectfully in the street, and to be addressed as "rabbi".

'But you must not be called "rabbi"; for you have one Rabbi, and you are all brothers. Do not call any man on earth "father"; for you have one Father, and he is in heaven. Nor must you be called "teacher"; you have one Teacher, the Messiah. The greatest among you must be your servant. For whoever exalts himself will be humbled; and whoever humbles himself will be exalted.

'Alas, alas for you, lawyers and Pharisees, hypocrites that you are! You shut the door of the kingdom of Heaven in men's faces; you do not enter yourselves, and when others are entering, you stop them.[b]

'Alas for you, lawyers and Pharisees, hypocrites! You travel over sea and land to win one convert; and when you have won him you make him twice as fit for hell as you are yourselves.

'Alas for you, blind guides! You say, "If a man swears by the sanctuary, that is nothing; but if he swears by the gold in the sanctuary, he is bound by his oath." Blind fools! Which is the more important, the gold, or the sanctuary which sanctifies the gold? Or you say, "If a man swears by the altar, that is nothing; but if he swears by the offering that lies on the altar, he is bound by his oath." What blindness! Which is the more important, the offering, or the altar which sanctifies it? To swear by the altar, then, is to swear both by the altar and by whatever lies on it; to swear by the sanctuary is to swear both by the sanctuary and by him who dwells there; and to swear by heaven is to swear both by the throne of God and by him who sits upon it.

'Alas for you, lawyers and Pharisees, hypocrites! You pay tithes of mint and dill and cummin; but you have overlooked the weightier demands of the Law, justice, mercy, and good faith. It is these you should have practised, without neglecting the others. Blind guides! You strain off a midge, yet gulp down a camel!

'Alas for you, lawyers and Pharisees, hypocrites! You clean the outside of cup and dish, which you have filled inside by robbery and self-indulgence! Blind Pharisee! Clean the inside of the cup first; then the outside will be clean also.

'Alas for you, lawyers and Pharisees, hypocrites! You are like tombs covered with whitewash; they look well from outside, but inside they are full of dead men's bones and all kinds of filth. So it is with you: outside you look like honest men, but inside you are brim-full of hypocrisy and crime.

'Alas for you, lawyers and Pharisees, hypocrites! You build up the tombs of the prophets and embellish the monuments of the saints, and you say, "If we had been alive in our fathers' time, we should never have taken part with them in the murder of the prophets." So you acknowledge that you are the sons of the men who killed the prophets. Go on then, finish off what your fathers began![c]

'You snakes, you vipers' brood, how can you escape being condemned to hell? I send you therefore prophets, sages, and teachers; some of

[a] *See Deuteronomy 6. 8-9 & Exodus 13. 9.*
[b] *Some witnesses add* (14) Alas for you, lawyers and Pharisees, hypocrites! You eat up the property of widows, while you say long prayers for appearance' sake. You will receive the severest sentence.
[c] *Or* You too must come up to your fathers' standards.

K.J.V.

them ye shall kill and crucify; and *some* of
them shall ye scourge in your synagogues, and
persecute *them* from city to city: 35 That upon
you may come all the righteous blood shed
upon the earth, from the blood of righteous Abel
unto the blood of Zacharias son of Barachias,
whom ye slew between the temple and the altar.
36 Verily I say unto you, All these things shall
come upon this generation. 37 O Jerusalem, Jerusalem, *thou* that killest the prophets, and stonest
them which are sent unto thee, how often would
I have gathered thy children together, even as
a hen gathereth her chickens under *her* wings,
and ye would not! 38 Behold, your house is left
unto you desolate. 39 For I say unto you, Ye
shall not see me henceforth, till ye shall say,
Blessed *is* he that cometh in the name of the
Lord.

R.S.V.

some of whom you will kill and crucify, and
some you will scourge in your synagogues and
persecute from town to town, 35 that upon you
may come all the righteous blood shed on earth,
from the blood of innocent Abel to the blood of
Zechariah the son of Barachiah, whom you murdered between the sanctuary and the altar.
36 Truly, I say to you, all this will come upon this
generation.
37 "O Jerusalem, Jerusalem, killing the prophets and stoning those who are sent to you! How
often would I have gathered your children together as a hen gathers her brood under her
wings, and you would not! 38 Behold, your house
is forsaken and desolate.*ˣ* 39 For I tell you, you
will not see me again, until you say, 'Blessed is
he who comes in the name of the Lord.' "

24 And Jesus went out, and departed from
the temple: and his disciples came to *him*
for to shew him the buildings of the temple.
2And Jesus said unto them, See ye not all these
things? verily I say unto you, There shall not
be left here one stone upon another, that shall
not be thrown down.

3 And as he sat upon the mount of Olives,
the disciples came unto him privately, saying,
Tell us, when shall these things be? and what
shall be the sign of thy coming, and of the end
of the world? 4And Jesus answered and said
unto them, Take heed that no man deceive you.
5 For many shall come in my name, saying, I
am Christ; and shall deceive many. 6And ye shall
hear of wars and rumours of wars: see that ye
be not troubled: for all *these things* must come
to pass, but the end is not yet. 7 For nation shall
rise against nation, and kingdom against kingdom: and there shall be famines, and pestilences,
and earthquakes, in divers places. 8All these *are*
the beginning of sorrows. 9 Then shall they deliver you up to be afflicted, and shall kill you:
and ye shall be hated of all nations for my
name's sake. 10And then shall many be offended,
and shall betray one another, and shall hate one
another. 11And many false prophets shall rise,
and shall deceive many. 12And because iniquity
shall abound, the love of many shall wax cold.
13 But he that shall endure unto the end, the
same shall be saved. 14And this gospel of the
kingdom shall be preached in all the world for
a witness unto all nations; and then shall the
end come. 15 When ye therefore shall see the
abomination of desolation, spoken of by Daniel
the prophet, stand in the holy place, (whoso
readeth, let him understand,) 16 Then let them
which be in Judea flee into the mountains: 17 Let
him which is on the housetop not come down
to take any thing out of his house: 18 Neither
let him which is in the field return back to take

24 Jesus left the temple and was going away,
when his disciples came to point out to
him the buildings of the temple. 2 But he answered them, "You see all these, do you not?
Truly, I say to you, there will not be left here
one stone upon another, that will not be thrown
down."

3 As he sat on the Mount of Olives, the disciples came to him privately, saying, "Tell us,
when will this be, and what will be the sign of
your coming and of the close of the age?" 4And
Jesus answered them, "Take heed that no one
leads you astray. 5 For many will come in my
name, saying, 'I am the Christ,' and they will
lead many astray. 6And you will hear of wars
and rumors of wars; see that you are not
alarmed; for this must take place, but the end
is not yet. 7 For nation will rise against nation,
and kingdom against kingdom, and there will be
famines and earthquakes in various places: 8 all
this is but the beginning of the sufferings.
9 "Then they will deliver you up to tribulation, and put you to death; and you will be hated
by all nations for my name's sake. 10And then
many will fall away,*ʸ* and betray one another,
and hate one another. 11And many false prophets will arise and lead many astray. 12And because wickedness is multiplied, most men's love
will grow cold. 13 But he who endures to the
end will be saved. 14And this gospel of the kingdom will be preached throughout the whole
world, as a testimony to all nations; and then
the end will come.
15 "So when you see the desolating sacrilege
spoken of by the prophet Daniel, standing in
the holy place (let the reader understand),
16 then let those who are in Judea flee to the
mountains; 17 let him who is on the housetop not
go down to take what is in his house; 18 and let
him who is in the field not turn back to take his

[x] Other ancient authorities omit *and desolate.* [y]
Or *stumble.*

men; and some of these you will kill and crucify, others you will flog in your synagogues and hunt from town to town. So that on your hands is all the innocent blood spilled on this earth, from the blood of Abel the good to the blood of Zachariah, Barachiah's son, whom you murdered between the sanctuary and the altar. Yes, I tell you that all this will be laid at the doors of this generation.

Jesus mourns over Jerusalem, 23. 37 and foretells its destruction

"Oh, Jerusalem, Jerusalem! You murder the prophets and stone the messengers that are sent to you. How often have I longed to gather your children round me like a bird gathering her brood together under her wings—and you would never have it. Now all you have left is your house. I tell you that you will never see me again till the day when you cry, 'Blessed is he who comes in the name of the Lord!' "

Then Jesus went out of the Temple and was walking away when his disciples came up and drew his attention to its buildings. "You see all these?" replied Jesus. "I tell you every stone will be thrown down till there is not a single one left standing upon another."

And as he was sitting on the slope of the Mount of Olives his disciples came to him privately and said: "Tell us, when will this happen? What will be the signal for your coming and the end of this world?"

"Be careful that no one misleads you," returned Jesus, "for many men will come in my name saying, 'I am Christ,' and they will mislead many. You will hear of wars and rumors of wars—but don't be alarmed. Such things must indeed happen, but that is not the end. For one nation will rise in arms against another, and one kingdom against another, and there will be famines and earthquakes in different parts of the world. But all that is only the beginning of the birth pangs. For then comes the time when men will hand you over to persecution, and kill you. And all nations will hate you because you bear my name. Then comes the time when many will lose their faith and will betray and hate one another. Yes, and many false prophets will arise, and will mislead many people. Because of the spread of wickedness the love of most men will grow cold, though the man who holds out to the end will be saved. This good news of the kingdom will be proclaimed to men all over the world as a witness to all the nations, and then the end will come.

Jesus prophesies a future of 24. 15 suffering

"When the time comes, then, that you see the 'abomination of desolation' prophesied by Daniel 'standing in the sacred place'—the reader should note this—then is the time for those in Judaea to escape to the hills. A man on his housetop must not waste time going into his house to collect anything; a man at work in the fields must not go back home to

them you will kill and crucify, others you will flog in your synagogues and hound from city to city. And so, on you will fall the guilt of all the innocent blood spilt on the ground, from innocent Abel to Zechariah son of Berachiah, whom you murdered between the sanctuary and the altar. Believe me, this generation will bear the guilt of it all.

'O Jerusalem, Jerusalem, the city that murders the prophets and stones the messengers sent to her! How often have I longed to gather your children, as a hen gathers her brood under her wings; but you would not let me. Look, look! there is your temple, forsaken by God.[a][b] And I tell you, you shall never see me until the time when you say, "Blessings on him who comes in the name of the Lord." '

Prophecies and Warnings

24 Jesus was leaving the temple when his disciples came and pointed to the temple buildings. He answered, 'You see all these buildings? I tell you this: not one stone will be left upon another; all will be thrown down.'

When he was sitting on the Mount of Olives the disciples came to speak to him privately. 'Tell us,' they said, 'when will this happen? And what will be the signal for your coming and the end of the age?'

Jesus replied: 'Take care that no one misleads you. For many will come claiming my name and saying, "I am the Messiah"; and many will be misled by them. The time is coming when you will hear the noise of battle near at hand and the news of battles far away; see that you are not alarmed. Such things are bound to happen; but the end is still to come. For nation will make war upon nation, kingdom upon kingdom; there will be famines and earthquakes in many places. With all these things the birth-pangs of the new age begin.

'You will then be handed over for punishment and execution; and men of all nations will hate you for your allegiance to me. Many will lose their faith; they will betray one another and hate one another. Many false prophets will arise, and will mislead many; and as lawlessness spreads, men's love for one another will grow cold. But the man who holds out to the end will be saved. And this gospel of the Kingdom will be proclaimed throughout the earth as a testimony to all nations; and then the end will come.

'So when you see "the abomination of desolation", of which the prophet Daniel spoke, standing in the holy place (let the reader understand), then those who are in Judaea must take to the hills. If a man is on the roof, he must not come down to fetch his goods from the house; if in the field, he must not turn back for his coat.

[a] Or Look, your home is desolate. [b] Some witnesses add and laid waste.

K.J.V.

his clothes. 19And woe unto them that are with child, and to them that give suck in those days! 20 But pray ye that your flight be not in the winter, neither on the sabbath day: 21 For then shall be great tribulation, such as was not since the beginning of the world to this time, no, nor ever shall be. 22And except those days should be shortened, there should no flesh be saved: but for the elect's sake those days shall be shortened. 23 Then if any man shall say unto you, Lo, here *is* Christ, or there; believe *it* not. 24 For there shall arise false Christs, and false prophets, and shall shew great signs and wonders; insomuch that, if *it were* possible, they shall deceive the very elect. 25 Behold, I have told you before. 26Wherefore if they shall say unto you, Behold, he is in the desert; go not forth: behold, *he is* in the secret chambers; believe *it* not. 27 For as the lightning cometh out of the east, and shineth even unto the west; so shall also the coming of the Son of man be. 28 For wheresoever the carcass is, there will the eagles be gathered together.

29 Immediately after the tribulation of those days shall the sun be darkened, and the moon shall not give her light, and the stars shall fall from heaven, and the powers of the heavens shall be shaken: 30And then shall appear the sign of the Son of man in heaven: and then shall all the tribes of the earth mourn, and they shall see the Son of man coming in the clouds of heaven with power and great glory. 31And he shall send his angels with a great sound of a trumpet, and they shall gather together his elect from the four winds, from one end of heaven to the other. 32 Now learn a parable of the fig tree; When his branch is yet tender, and putteth forth leaves, ye know that summer *is* nigh: 33 So likewise ye, when ye shall see all these things, know that it is near, *even* at the doors. 34 Verily I say unto you, This generation shall not pass, till all these things be fulfilled. 35 Heaven and earth shall pass away, but my words shall not pass away.

36 But of that day and hour knoweth no *man*, no, not the angels of heaven, but my Father only. 37 But as the days of Noe *were,* so shall also the coming of the Son of man be. 38 For as in the days that were before the flood they were eating and drinking, marrying and giving in marriage, until the day that Noe entered into the ark, 39And knew not until the flood came, and took them all away; so shall also the coming of the Son of man be. 40 Then shall two be in the field; the one shall be taken, and the other left. 41 Two *women shall be* grinding at the mill; the one shall be taken, and the other left.

42 Watch therefore; for ye know not what hour your Lord doth come. 43 But know this, that if the goodman of the house had known in what watch the thief would come, he would have watched, and would not have suffered his house to be broken up. 44 Therefore be ye also ready: for in such an hour as ye think not the Son of man cometh. 45 Who then is a faithful and wise servant, whom his lord hath made ruler

R.S.V.

mantle. 19And alas for those who are with child and for those who give suck in those days! 20 Pray that your flight may not be in winter or on a sabbath. 21 For then there will be great tribulation, such as has not been from the beginning of the world until now, no, and never will be. 22And if those days had not been shortened, no human being would be saved; but for the sake of the elect those days will be shortened. 23 Then if any one says to you, 'Lo, here is the Christ!' or 'There he is!' do not believe it. 24 For false Christs and false prophets will arise and show great signs and wonders, so as to lead astray, if possible, even the elect. 25 Lo, I have told you beforehand. 26 So, if they say to you, 'Lo, he is in the wilderness,' do not go out; if they say, 'Lo, he is in the inner rooms,' do not believe it. 27 For as the lightning comes from the east and shines as far as the west, so will be the coming of the Son of man. 28 Wherever the body is, there the eagles[z] will be gathered together.

29 "Immediately after the tribulation of those days the sun will be darkened, and the moon will not give its light, and the stars will fall from heaven, and the powers of the heavens will be shaken; 30 then will appear the sign of the Son of man in heaven, and then all the tribes of the earth will mourn, and they will see the Son of man coming on the clouds of heaven with power and great glory; 31 and he will send out his angels with a loud trumpet call, and they will gather his elect from the four winds, from one end of heaven to the other.

32 "From the fig tree learn its lesson: as soon as its branch becomes tender and puts forth its leaves, you know that summer is near. 33 So also, when you see all these things, you know that he is near, at the very gates. 34 Truly, I say to you, this generation will not pass away till all these things take place. 35 Heaven and earth will pass away, but my words will not pass away.

36 "But of that day and hour no one knows, not even the angels of heaven, nor the Son,[a] but the Father only. 37As were the days of Noah, so will be the coming of the Son of man. 38 For as in those days before the flood they were eating and drinking, marrying and giving in marriage, until the day when Noah entered the ark, 39 and they did not know until the flood came and swept them all away, so will be the coming of the Son of man. 40 Then two men will be in the field; one is taken and one is left. 41 Two women will be grinding at the mill; one is taken and one is left. 42 Watch therefore, for you do not know on what day your Lord is coming. 43 But know this, that if the householder had known in what part of the night the thief was coming, he would have watched and would not have let his house be broken into. 44 Therefore you also must be ready; for the Son of man is coming at an hour you do not expect.

45 "Who then is the faithful and wise servant, whom his master has set over his household, to

[z] Or *vultures.* [a] Other ancient authorities omit *nor the Son.*

PHILLIPS

N.E.B.

fetch his clothes. Alas for the pregnant, alas for those with tiny babies at that time! Pray God that you may not have to make your escape in the winter or on the Sabbath day, for then there will be great misery, such as has never happened from the beginning of the world until now, and will never happen again! Yes, if those days had not been cut short no human being would survive. But for the sake of God's people those days are to be shortened.

"If anyone says to you then, 'Look, here is Christ!' or 'There he is!' don't believe it. False christs and false prophets are going to appear and will produce great signs and wonders to mislead, if it were possible, even God's own people. Listen, I am warning you. So that if people say to you, 'There he is, in the desert!' you are not to go out there. If they say, 'Here he is, in this inner room!' don't believe it. For as lightning flashes across from east to west so will the Son of Man's coming be. 'Wherever there is a dead body, there the vultures will flock.'

At the end of time the Son
of man will return

24. 29

"Immediately after the misery of those days the sun will be darkened, the moon will fail to give her light, the stars will fall from the sky, and the powers of heaven will be shaken. Then the sign of the Son of Man will appear in the sky, and all the nations of the earth will wring their hands as they see the Son of Man coming on the clouds of the sky in power and great splendor. And he will send out his angels with a loud trumpet call and they will gather together his chosen from the four winds—from one end of the heavens to the other.

"Learn what the fig tree can teach you. As soon as its branches grow full of sap and produce leaves you know that summer is near. So when you see all these things happening you may know that he is near, at your very door! Believe me, this generation will not disappear till all this has taken place. Earth and sky will pass away, but my words will never pass away! But about that actual day and time no one knows—not even the angels of Heaven, nor the Son, only the Father. For just as life went on in the days of Noah so will it be at the coming of the Son of Man. In those days before the flood people were eating, drinking, marrying and being given in marriage until the very day that Noah went into the ark, and knew nothing about the flood until it came and destroyed them all. So will it be at the coming of the Son of Man. Two men will be in the field; one is taken and one is left behind. Two women will be grinding at the hand mill; one is taken and one is left behind. You must be on the alert then, for you do not know when your master is coming. You can be sure of this, however, that if the householder had known what time of night the burglar would arrive, he would have been ready for him and would not have allowed his house to be broken into. That is why you must always be ready, for you do not know what time the Son of Man will arrive.

Alas for women with child in those days, and for those who have children at the breast! Pray that it may not be winter when you have to make your escape, or Sabbath. It will be a time of great distress, such as has never been from the beginning of the world until now, and will never be again. If that time of troubles were not cut short, no living thing could survive; but for the sake of God's chosen it will be cut short.

'Then, if anyone says to you, "Look, here is the Messiah", or, "There he is", do not believe it. Impostors will come claiming to be messiahs or prophets, and they will produce great signs and wonders to mislead even God's chosen, if such a thing were possible. See, I have forewarned you. If they tell you, "He is there in the wilderness", do not go out; or if they say, "He is there in the inner room", do not believe it. Like lightning from the east, flashing as far as the west, will be the coming of the Son of Man. 'Wherever the corpse is, there the vultures will gather.

'As soon as the distress of those days has passed, the sun will be darkened, the moon will not give her light, the stars will fall from the sky, the celestial powers will be shaken. Then will appear in heaven the sign that heralds the Son of Man. All the peoples of the world will make lamentation, and they will see the Son of Man coming on the clouds of heaven with great power and glory. With a trumpet blast he will send out his angels, and they will gather his chosen from the four winds, from the farthest bounds of heaven on every side.

'Learn a lesson from the fig-tree. When its tender shoots appear and are breaking into leaf, you know that summer is near. In the same way, when you see all these things, you may know that the end is near,[a] at the very door. I tell you this: the present generation will live to see it all. Heaven and earth will pass away; my words will never pass away.

'But about that day and hour no one knows, not even the angels in heaven, not even the Son; only the Father.

'As things were in Noah's days, so will they be when the Son of Man comes. In the days before the flood they ate and drank and married, until the day that Noah went into the ark, and they knew nothing until the flood came and swept them all away. That is how it will be when the Son of Man comes. Then there will be two men in the field; one will be taken, the other left; two women grinding at the mill; one will be taken, the other left.

'Keep awake, then; for you do not know on what day your Lord is to come. Remember, if the householder had known at what time of night the burglar was coming, he would have kept awake and not have let his house be broken into. Hold yourselves ready, therefore, because the Son of Man will come at the time you least expect him.

'Who is the trusty servant, the sensible man charged by his master to manage his household

Vigilance is essential

24. 45

"Who then is the faithful and sensible servant, whom his master put in charge of his house-

[a] Or that he is near.

K.J.V.

over his household, to give them meat in due season? 46 Blessed *is* that servant, whom his lord when he cometh shall find so doing. 47 Verily I say unto you, That he shall make him ruler over all his goods. 48 But and if that evil servant shall say in his heart, My lord delayeth his coming; 49And shall begin to smite *his* fellow servants, and to eat and drink with the drunken; 50 The lord of that servant shall come in a day when he looketh not for *him,* and in an hour that he is not aware of, 51And shall cut him asunder, and appoint *him* his portion with the hypocrites: there shall be weeping and gnashing of teeth.

25 Then shall the kingdom of heaven be likened unto ten virgins, which took their lamps, and went forth to meet the bridegroom. 2And five of them were wise, and five *were* foolish. 3 They that *were* foolish took their lamps, and took no oil with them: 4 But the wise took oil in their vessels with their lamps. 5 While the bridegroom tarried, they all slumbered and slept. 6And at midnight there was a cry made, Behold, the bridegroom cometh; go ye out to meet him. 7 Then all those virgins arose, and trimmed their lamps. 8And the foolish said unto the wise, Give us of your oil; for our lamps are gone out. 9 But the wise answered, saying, *Not so;* lest there be not enough for us and you: but go ye rather to them that sell, and buy for yourselves. 10And while they went to buy, the bridegroom came; and they that were ready went in with him to the marriage: and the door was shut. 11Afterward came also the other virgins, saying, Lord, Lord, open to us. 12 But he answered and said, Verily I say unto you, I know you not. 13 Watch therefore; for ye know neither the day nor the hour wherein the Son of man cometh.

14 For *the kingdom of heaven is* as a man travelling into a far country, *who* called his own servants, and delivered unto them his goods. 15And unto one he gave five talents, to another two, and to another one; to every man according to his several ability; and straightway took his journey. 16 Then he that had received the five talents went and traded with the same, and made *them* other five talents. 17And likewise he that *had received* two, he also gained other two. 18 But he that had received one went and digged in the earth, and hid his lord's money. 19After a long time the lord of those servants cometh, and reckoneth with them. 20And so he that had received five talents came and brought other five talents, saying, Lord, thou deliveredst unto me five talents: behold, I have gained beside them five talents more. 21 His lord said unto him, Well

R.S.V.

give them their food at the proper time? 46 Blessed is that servant whom his master when he comes will find so doing. 47 Truly, I say to you, he will set him over all his possessions. 48 But if that wicked servant says to himself, 'My master is delayed,' 49 and begins to beat his fellow servants, and eats and drinks with the drunken, 50 the master of that servant will come on a day when he does not expect him and at an hour he does not know, 51 and will punish [b] him, and put him with the hypocrites; there men will weep and gnash their teeth.

25 "Then the kingdom of heaven shall be compared to ten maidens who took their lamps and went to meet the bridegroom.[c] 2 Five of them were foolish, and five were wise. 3 For when the foolish took their lamps, they took no oil with them; 4 but the wise took flasks of oil with their lamps. 5As the bridegroom was delayed, they all slumbered and slept. 6 But at midnight there was a cry, 'Behold, the bridegroom! Come out to meet him.' 7 Then all those maidens rose and trimmed their lamps. 8And the foolish said to the wise, 'Give us some of your oil, for our lamps are going out.' 9 But the wise replied, 'Perhaps there will not be enough for us and for you; go rather to the dealers and buy for yourselves.' 10And while they went to buy, the bridegroom came, and those who were ready went in with him to the marriage feast; and the door was shut. 11Afterward the other maidens came also, saying, 'Lord, lord, open to us.' 12 But he replied, 'Truly, I say to you, I do not know you.' 13 Watch therefore, for you know neither the day nor the hour.

14 "For it will be as when a man going on a journey called his servants and entrusted to them his property; 15 to one he gave five talents,[d] to another two, to another one, to each according to his ability. Then he went away. 16 He who had received the five talents went at once and traded with them; and he made five talents more. 17 So also, he who had the two talents made two talents more. 18 But he who had received the one talent went and dug in the ground and hid his master's money. 19 Now after a long time the master of those servants came and settled accounts with them. 20And he who had received the five talents came forward, bringing five talents more, saying, 'Master, you delivered to me five talents; here I have made five talents more.' 21 His master said to him, 'Well done, good and

[b] Or *cut him in pieces.* [c] Other ancient authorities add *and the bride.* [d] This talent was probably worth about a thousand dollars.

PHILLIPS

hold to give the others their food at the proper time? Well, he is fortunate if his master finds him doing that duty on his return! Believe me, he will promote him to look after all his property. But if he should be a bad servant who says to himself, 'My master takes his time about returning,' and should begin to beat his fellow servants and eat and drink with drunkards, that servant's master will return suddenly and unexpectedly, and will punish him severely and send him off to share the penalty of the unfaithful—to his bitter sorrow and regret!

"In those days the kingdom of Heaven will be like ten bridesmaids who took their lamps and went out to meet the bridegroom. Five of them were sensible and five were foolish. The foolish ones took their lamps but did not take any oil with them. But the sensible ones brought their lamps and oil in their flasks as well. Then, as the bridegroom was a very long time, they all grew drowsy and fell asleep. But in the middle of the night there came a shout, 'Wake up, here comes the bridegroom! Out you go to meet him!' Then up got all the bridesmaids and attended to their lamps. The foolish ones said to the sensible ones, 'Please give us some of your oil—our lamps are going out!' 'Oh, no,' returned the sensible ones, 'there might not be enough for all of us. Better go to the oil shop and buy some for yourselves.' But while they had gone off to buy the oil the bridegroom arrived, and those bridesmaids who were ready went in with him for the festivities and the door was shut behind them. Later on, the rest of the bridesmaids came and said, 'Oh, please, sir, open the door for us!' But he replied, 'I tell you I don't know you!' So be on the alert—for you do not know the day or the time.

Life is hard for the fainthearted 25. 14

"It is just like a man going abroad who called his household servants together before he went and handed his property over to them to manage. He gave one five thousand dollars, another two thousand and another one thousand—according to their respective abilities. Then he went away.
"The man who had received five thousand dollars went out at once and by doing business with this sum he made another five thousand. Similarly the man with two thousand dollars made another two thousand. But the man who had received one thousand dollars went off and dug a hole in the ground and hid his master's money.
"Some years later the master of these servants arrived and went into the accounts with them. The one who had the five thousand dollars came in and brought him an additional five thousand with the words, 'You gave me five thousand dollars, sir; look, I've increased it by another five thousand.' 'Well done!' said his master, 'you're a sound, reliable servant. You've been trustworthy over a few things, now I'm going to put you in charge of much more. Come in and share your master's rejoicing.' Then the servant who had received two thousand dollars came in and said, 'You gave me two thousand dollars, sir; look, here's two thousand more that I've managed to make by it.' 'Well done!' said

N.E.B.

staff and issue their rations at the proper time? Happy that servant who is found at his task when his master comes! I tell you this: he will be put in charge of all his master's property. But if he is a bad servant and says to himself, "The master is a long time coming", and begins to bully the other servants and to eat and drink with his drunken friends, then the master will arrive on a day that servant does not expect, at a time he does not know, and will cut him in pieces. Thus he will find his place among the hypocrites, where there is wailing and grinding of teeth.

25 'When that day comes, the kingdom of Heaven will be like this. There were ten girls, who took their lamps and went out to meet the bridegroom. Five of them were foolish, and five prudent; when the foolish ones took their lamps, they took no oil with them, but the others took flasks of oil with their lamps. As the bridegroom was late in coming they all dozed off to sleep. But at midnight a cry was heard: "Here is the bridegroom! Come out to meet him." With that the girls all got up and trimmed their lamps. The foolish said to the prudent, "Our lamps are going out; give us some of your oil." "No," they said; "there will never be enough for us both. You had better go to the shop and buy some for yourselves." While they were away the bridegroom arrived; those who were ready went in with him to the wedding; and the door was shut. And then the other five came back. "Sir, sir," they cried, "open the door for us." But he answered, "I declare, I do not know you." Keep awake then; for you never know the day or the hour.

'It is like a man going abroad, who called his servants and put his capital in their hands; to one he gave five bags of gold, to another two, to another one, each according to his capacity. Then he left the country. The man who had the five bags went at once and employed them in business, and made a profit of five bags, and the man who had the two bags made two. But the man who had been given one bag of gold went off and dug a hole in the ground, and hid his master's money. A long time afterwards their master returned, and proceeded to settle accounts with them. The man who had been given the five bags of gold came and produced the five he had made: "Master," he said, "you left five bags with me; look, I have made five more." "Well done, my good and trusty servant!" said

K.J.V.

done, *thou* good and faithful servant: thou hast been faithful over a few things, I will make thee ruler over many things: enter thou into the joy of thy lord. 22 He also that had received two talents came and said, Lord, thou deliveredst unto me two talents: behold, I have gained two other talents beside them. 23 His lord said unto him, Well done, good and faithful servant; thou hast been faithful over a few things, I will make thee ruler over many things: enter thou into the joy of thy lord. 24 Then he which had received the one talent came and said, Lord, I knew thee that thou art a hard man, reaping where thou hast not sown, and gathering where thou hast not strewed: 25 And I was afraid, and went and hid thy talent in the earth: lo, *there* thou hast *that is* thine. 26 His lord answered and said unto him, *Thou* wicked and slothful servant, thou knewest that I reap where I sowed not, and gather where I have not strewed: 27 Thou oughtest therefore to have put my money to the exchangers, and *then* at my coming I should have received mine own with usury. 28 Take therefore the talent from him, and give *it* unto him which hath ten talents. 29 For unto every one that hath shall be given, and he shall have abundance: but from him that hath not shall be taken away even that which he hath. 30 And cast the unprofitable servant into outer darkness: there shall be weeping and gnashing of teeth.

31 When the Son of man shall come in his glory, and all the holy angels with him, then shall he sit upon the throne of his glory: 32 And before him shall be gathered all nations: and he shall separate them one from another, as a shepherd divideth *his* sheep from the goats: 33 And he shall set the sheep on his right hand, but the goats on the left. 34 Then shall the King say unto them on his right hand, Come, ye blessed of my Father, inherit the kingdom prepared for you from the foundation of the world: 35 For I was a hungered, and ye gave me meat: I was thirsty, and ye gave me drink: I was a stranger, and ye took me in: 36 Naked, and ye clothed me: I was sick, and ye visited me: I was in prison, and ye came unto me. 37 Then shall the righteous answer him, saying, Lord, when saw we thee a hungered, and fed *thee?* or thirsty, and gave *thee* drink? 38 When saw we thee a stranger, and took *thee* in? or naked, and clothed *thee?* 39 Or when saw we thee sick, or in prison, and came unto thee? 40 And the King shall answer and say unto them, Verily I say unto you, Inasmuch as ye have done *it* unto one of the least of these my brethren, ye have done *it* unto me. 41 Then shall he say also unto them on the left hand, Depart from me, ye cursed, into everlasting fire, prepared for the devil and his angels: 42 For I was a hungered, and ye gave me no meat: I was thirsty, and ye gave me no drink: 43 I was a stranger, and ye took me not in: naked, and ye clothed me not: sick, and in prison, and ye visited me not. 44 Then shall they also answer him, saying, Lord, when saw we thee a hungered, or athirst, or a stranger, or naked, or sick, or in prison, and did not minister unto thee? 45 Then shall he answer them, saying, Verily I say unto you, Inasmuch as ye did *it* not to one of the least of these, ye did *it* not to me. 46 And these shall go away into everlasting punishment: but the righteous into life eternal.

R.S.V.

faithful servant; you have been faithful over a little, I will set you over much; enter into the joy of your master.' 22 And he also who had the two talents came forward, saying, 'Master, you delivered to me two talents; here I have made two talents more.' 23 His master said to him, 'Well done, good and faithful servant; you have been faithful over a little, I will set you over much; enter into the joy of your master.' 24 He also who had received the one talent came forward, saying, 'Master, I knew you to be a hard man, reaping where you did not sow, and gathering where you did not winnow; 25 so I was afraid, and I went and hid your talent in the ground. Here you have what is yours.' 26 But his master answered him, 'You wicked and slothful servant! You knew that I reap where I have not sowed, and gather where I have not winnowed? 27 Then you ought to have invested my money with the bankers, and at my coming I should have received what was my own with interest. 28 So take the talent from him, and give it to him who has the ten talents. 29 For to every one who has will more be given, and he will have abundance; but from him who has not, even what he has will be taken away. 30 And cast the worthless servant into the outer darkness; there men will weep and gnash their teeth.'

31 "When the Son of man comes in his glory, and all the angels with him, then he will sit on his glorious throne. 32 Before him will be gathered all the nations, and he will separate them one from another as a shepherd separates the sheep from the goats, 33 and he will place the sheep at his right hand, but the goats at the left. 34 Then the King will say to those at his right hand, 'Come, O blessed of my Father, inherit the kingdom prepared for you from the foundation of the world; 35 for I was hungry and you gave me food, I was thirsty and you gave me drink, I was a stranger and you welcomed me, 36 I was naked and you clothed me, I was sick and you visited me, I was in prison and you came to me.' 37 Then the righteous will answer him, 'Lord, when did we see thee hungry and feed thee, or thirsty and give thee drink? 38 And when did we see thee a stranger and welcome thee, or naked and clothe thee? 39 And when did we see thee sick or in prison and visit thee?' 40 And the King will answer them, 'Truly, I say to you, as you did it to one of the least of these my brethren, you did it to me.' 41 Then he will say to those at his left hand, 'Depart from me, you cursed, into the eternal fire prepared for the devil and his angels; 42 for I was hungry and you gave me no food, I was thirsty and you gave me no drink, 43 I was a stranger and you did not welcome me, naked and you did not clothe me, sick and in prison and you did not visit me.' 44 Then they also will answer, 'Lord, when did we see thee hungry or thirsty or a stranger or naked or sick or in prison, and did not minister to thee?' 45 Then he will answer them, 'Truly, I say to you, as you did it not to one of the least of these, you did it not to me.' 46 And they will go away into eternal punishment, but the righteous into eternal life."

PHILLIPS

his master, 'you're a sound, reliable servant. You've been trustworthy over a few things, now I'm going to put you in charge of many. Come in and share your master's pleasure.'

"Then the man who had received the one thousand dollars came in and said, 'Sir, I always knew you were a hard man, reaping where you never sowed and collecting where you never laid out—so I was scared and I went off and hid your thousand dollars in the ground. Here is your money, intact.'

" 'You're a wicked, lazy servant!' his master told him. 'You say you knew that I reap where I never sowed and collect where I never laid out? Then you ought to have put my money in the bank, and when I came I should at any rate have received what belongs to me with interest. Take his thousand dollars away from him and give it to the man who now has the ten thousand!' (For the man who has something will have more given to him and will have plenty. But as for the man who has nothing, even his 'nothing' will be taken away.) 'And throw this useless servant into the darkness outside, where he can weep and wail over his stupidity.'

The final judgment   25. 31

"But when the Son of Man comes in his splendor with all his angels with him, then he will take his seat on his glorious throne. All the nations will be assembled before him and he will separate men from each other like a shepherd separating sheep from goats. He will place the sheep on his right hand and the goats on his left.

"Then the king will say to those on his right: 'Come, you who have won my Father's blessing! Take your inheritance—the kingdom reserved for you since the foundation of the world! For I was hungry and you gave me a drink. I was lonely and you made me welcome. I was naked and you clothed me. I was ill and you came and looked after me. I was in prison and you came to see me there.'

"Then the true men will answer him: 'Lord, when did we see *you* hungry and give you food? When did we see *you* thirsty and give you something to drink? When did we see *you* lonely and make you welcome, or see *you* naked and clothe you, or see *you* ill or in prison and go to see you?'

"And the king will reply, 'I assure you that whatever you did for the humblest of my brothers you did for me.'

"Then he will say to those on his left: 'Out of my presence, cursed as you are, into the eternal fire prepared for the devil and his angels! For I was hungry and you gave me nothing to eat. I was thirsty and you gave me nothing to drink. I was lonely and you never made me welcome. When I was naked you did nothing to clothe me; when I was sick and in prison you never cared about me.'

"Then they too will answer him: 'Lord, when did we ever see *you* hungry, or thirsty, or lonely, or naked, or sick, or in prison, and fail to look after you?'

"Then the king will answer them with these words, 'I assure you that whatever you failed to do to the humblest of my brothers you failed to do to me.'

"And these will go off to eternal punishment, but the true men to eternal life."

N.E.B.

the master. "You have proved trustworthy in a small way; I will now put you in charge of something big. Come and share your master's delight." The man with the two bags then came and said, "Master, you left two bags with me; look, I have made two more." "Well done, my good and trusty servant!" said the master. "You have proved trustworthy in a small way; I will now put you in charge of something big. Come and share your master's delight." Then the man who had been given one bag came and said, "Master, I knew you to be a hard man: you reap where you have not sown, you gather where you have not scattered; so I was afraid, and I went and hid your gold in the ground. Here it is—you have what belongs to you." "You lazy rascal!" said the master. "You knew that I reap where I have not sown, and gather where I have not scattered? Then you ought to have put my money on deposit, and on my return I should have got it back with interest. Take the bag of gold from him, and give it to the one with the ten bags. For the man who has will always be given more, till he has enough and to spare; and the man who has not will forfeit even what he has. Fling the useless servant out into the dark, the place of wailing and grinding of teeth!"

'When the Son of Man comes in his glory and all the angels with him, he will sit in state on his throne, with all the nations gathered before him. He will separate men into two groups, as a shepherd separates the sheep from the goats, and he will place the sheep on his right hand and the goats on his left. Then the king will say to those on his right hand, "You have my Father's blessing; come, enter and possess the kingdom that has been ready for you since the world was made. For when I was hungry, you gave me food; when thirsty, you gave me drink; when I was a stranger you took me into your home, when naked you clothed me; when I was ill you came to my help, when in prison you visited me." Then the righteous will reply, "Lord, when was it that we saw you hungry and fed you, or thirsty and gave you drink, a stranger and took you home, or naked and clothed you? When did we see you ill or in prison, and come to visit you?" And the king will answer, "I tell you this: anything you did for one of my brothers here, however humble, you did for me." Then he will say to those on his left hand, "The curse is upon you; go from my sight to the eternal fire that is ready for the devil and his angels. For when I was hungry you gave me nothing to eat, when thirsty nothing to drink; when I was a stranger you gave me no home, when naked you did not clothe me; when I was ill and in prison you did not come to my help." And they too will reply, "Lord, when was it that we saw you hungry or thirsty or a stranger or naked or ill or in prison, and did nothing for you?" And he will answer, "I tell you this: anything you did not do for one of these, however humble, you did not do for me." And they will go away to eternal punishment, but the righteous will enter eternal life.'

26 And it came to pass, when Jesus had finished all these sayings, he said unto his disciples, 2 Ye know that after two days is *the feast of* the passover, and the Son of man is betrayed to be crucified. 3 Then assembled together the chief priests, and the scribes, and the elders of the people, unto the palace of the high priest, who was called Caiaphas, 4And consulted that they might take Jesus by subtilty, and kill *him.* 5 But they said, Not on the feast *day,* lest there be an uproar among the people.

6 Now when Jesus was in Bethany, in the house of Simon the leper, 7 There came unto him a woman having an alabaster box of very precious ointment, and poured it on his head, as he sat at meat. 8 But when his disciples saw *it,* they had indignation, saying, To what purpose *is* this waste? 9 For this ointment might have been sold for much, and given to the poor. 10 When Jesus understood *it,* he said unto them, Why trouble ye the woman? for she hath wrought a good work upon me. 11 For ye have the poor always with you; but me ye have not always. 12 For in that she hath poured this ointment on my body, she did *it* for my burial. 13 Verily I say unto you, Wheresoever this gospel shall be preached in the whole world, *there* shall also this, that this woman hath done, be told for a memorial of her.

14 Then one of the twelve, called Judas Iscariot, went unto the chief priests, 15And said *unto them,* What will ye give me, and I will deliver him unto you? And they covenanted with him for thirty pieces of silver. 16And from that time he sought opportunity to betray him.

17 Now the first *day* of the *feast of* unleavened bread the disciples came to Jesus, saying unto him, Where wilt thou that we prepare for thee to eat the passover? 18And he said, Go into the city to such a man, and say unto him, The Master saith, My time is at hand; I will keep the passover at thy house with my disciples. 19And the disciples did as Jesus had appointed them; and they made ready the passover. 20 Now when the even was come, he sat down with the twelve. 21And as they did eat, he said, Verily I say unto you, that one of you shall betray me. 22And they were exceeding sorrowful, and began every one of them to say unto him, Lord, is it I? 23And he answered and said, He that dippeth *his* hand with me in the dish, the same shall betray me. 24 The Son of man goeth as it is written of him: but woe unto that man by whom the Son of man is betrayed! it had been good for that man if he had not been born. 25 Then Judas, which betrayed him, answered and said, Master, is it I? He said unto him, Thou hast said.

26 When Jesus had finished all these sayings, he said to his disciples, 2 "You know that after two days the Passover is coming, and the Son of man will be delivered up to be crucified."

3 Then the chief priests and the elders of the people gathered in the palace of the high priest, who was called Caiaphas, 4 and took counsel together in order to arrest Jesus by stealth and kill him. 5 But they said, "Not during the feast, lest there be a tumult among the people."

6 Now when Jesus was at Bethany in the house of Simon the leper, 7 a woman came up to him with an alabaster jar of very expensive ointment, and she poured it on his head, as he sat at table. 8 But when the disciples saw it, they were indignant, saying, "Why this waste? 9 For this ointment might have been sold for a large sum, and given to the poor." 10 But Jesus, aware of this, said to them, "Why do you trouble the woman? For she has done a beautiful thing to me. 11 For you always have the poor with you, but you will not always have me. 12 In pouring this ointment on my body she has done it to prepare me for burial. 13 Truly, I say to you, wherever this gospel is preached in the whole world, what she has done will be told in memory of her."

14 Then one of the twelve, who was called Judas Iscariot, went to the chief priests 15 and said, "What will you give me if I deliver him to you?" And they paid him thirty pieces of silver. 16And from that moment he sought an opportunity to betray him.

17 Now on the first day of Unleavened Bread the disciples came to Jesus, saying, "Where will you have us prepare for you to eat the passover?" 18 He said, "Go into the city to such a one, and say to him, 'The Teacher says, My time is at hand; I will keep the passover at your house with my disciples.'" 19And the disciples did as Jesus had directed them, and they prepared the passover.

20 When it was evening, he sat at table with the twelve disciples;[e] 21 and as they were eating, he said, "Truly, I say to you, one of you will betray me." 22And they were very sorrowful, and began to say to him one after another, "Is it I, Lord?" 23 He answered, "He who has dipped his hand in the dish with me will betray me. 24 The Son of man goes as it is written of him, but woe to that man by whom the Son of man is betrayed! It would have been better for that man if he had not been born." 25 Judas, who betrayed him, said, "Is it I, Master?"[f] He said to him, "You have said so."

[e] Other authorities omit *disciples.* [f] Or *Rabbi.*

PHILLIPS　　　　　　　　　　　　　**N.E.B.**

Jesus announces his coming death　26. 1

The Final Conflict

When Jesus had finished all this teaching he spoke to his disciples: "Do you realize that the Passover will begin in two days' time; and the Son of Man is going to be betrayed and crucified?"

26 When Jesus had finished this discourse he said to his disciples, 'You know that in two days' time it will be Passover, and the Son of Man is to be handed over for crucifixion.'

Then the chief priests and the elders of the nation met in the palace of the High Priest, Caiaphas; and there they conferred together on a scheme to have Jesus arrested by some trick and put to death. 'It must not be during the festival,' they said, 'or there may be rioting among the people.'

An evil plot—and an act of love　26. 3

At that very time the chief priests and elders of the people had assembled in the court of Caiaphas, the High Priest, and were discussing together how they might get hold of Jesus by some trick and kill him. But they kept saying, "It must not be during the festival or there might be a riot."

Back in Bethany, while Jesus was in the house of Simon the leper, a woman came to him with an alabaster flask of most expensive perfume, and poured it on his head as he was at table. The disciples were indignant when they saw this, and said: "What is the point of such wicked waste? Couldn't this perfume have been sold for a lot of money which could be given to the poor?" Jesus knew what they were saying and spoke to them: "Why must you make this woman feel uncomfortable? She has done a beautiful thing for me. You have the poor with you always, but you will not always have me. When she poured this perfume on my body, she was preparing it for my burial. I assure you that wherever the gospel is preached throughout the whole world, this deed of hers will also be recounted, as her memorial to me."

Jesus was at Bethany in the house of Simon the leper, when a woman came to him with a small bottle of fragrant oil, very costly; and as he sat at table she began to pour it over his head. The disciples were indignant when they saw it. 'Why this waste?' they said; 'it could have been sold for a good sum and the money given to the poor.' Jesus was aware of this, and said to them, 'Why must you make trouble for the woman? It is a fine thing she has done for me. You have the poor among you always; but you will not always have me. When she poured this oil on my body it was her way of preparing me for burial. I tell you this: wherever in all the world this gospel is proclaimed, what she has done will be told as her memorial.'

Then one of the Twelve, the man called Judas Iscariot, went to the chief priests and said, 'What will you give me to betray him to you?' They weighed him out[a] thirty silver pieces. From that moment he began to look for a good opportunity to betray him.

The betrayal is arranged　　26. 14

After this, one of the twelve, Judas Iscariot by name, approached the chief priests. "What will you give me," he said to them, "if I hand him over to you?" They settled with him for thirty silver coins, and from then on he looked for a convenient opportunity to betray Jesus.

On the first day of Unleavened Bread the disciples came to ask Jesus, 'Where would you like us to prepare for your Passover supper?' He answered, 'Go to a certain man in the city, and tell him, "The Master says, 'My appointed time is near; I am to keep Passover with my disciples at your house.'"' The disciples did as Jesus directed them and prepared for Passover.

In the evening he sat down with the twelve disciples; and during supper he said, 'I tell you this: one of you will betray me.' In great distress they exclaimed one after the other, 'Can you mean me, Lord?' He answered, 'One who has dipped his hand into this bowl with me will betray me. The Son of Man is going the way appointed for him in the scriptures; but alas for that man by whom the Son of Man is betrayed! It would be better for that man if he had never been born.' Then Judas spoke, the one who was to betray him. 'Rabbi,' he said, 'can you mean me?' Jesus replied, 'The words are yours.'[b]

The last supper　　　　　　26. 17

On the first day of unleavened bread the disciples came to Jesus with the question, "Where do you want us to make our preparations for you to eat the Passover?"

"Go into the city," Jesus replied, "to a certain man there and say to him: 'The Master says, "My time is near. I am going to keep the Passover with my disciples at your house."'" The disciples did as Jesus had instructed them and prepared the Passover. Then late in the evening he took his place at table with the twelve and during the meal he said, "I tell you plainly that one of you is going to betray me." They were deeply distressed at this and each began to say to him in turn, "Surely, Lord, I am not the one?" And his answer was: "The man who has dipped his hand into the dish with me is the man who will betray me. It is true that the Son of Man will follow the road foretold by the scriptures, but alas for the man through whom he is betrayed! It would be better for that man if he had never been born." And Judas, who actually betrayed him, said, "Master, am I the one?"

"As you say!" replied Jesus.

[a] *Or* agreed to pay him . . . [b] *Or* It is as you say.

85

K.J.V.

26 And as they were eating, Jesus took bread, and blessed *it*, and brake it, *and* gave *it* to the disciples, and said, Take, eat; this is my body. 27And he took the cup, and gave thanks, and gave *it* to them, saying, Drink ye all of it; 28 For this is my blood of the new testament, which is shed for many for the remission of sins. 29 But I say unto you, I will not drink henceforth of this fruit of the vine, until that day when I drink it new with you in my Father's kingdom. 30And when they had sung a hymn, they went out into the mount of Olives. 31 Then saith Jesus unto them, All ye shall be offended because of me this night: for it is written, I will smite the Shepherd, and the sheep of the flock shall be scattered abroad. 32 But after I am risen again, I will go before you into Galilee. 33 Peter answered and said unto him, Though all *men* shall be offended because of thee, *yet* will I never be offended. 34 Jesus said unto him, Verily I say unto thee, That this night, before the cock crow, thou shalt deny me thrice. 35 Peter said unto him, Though I should die with thee, yet will I not deny thee. Likewise also said all the disciples.

36 Then cometh Jesus with them unto a place called Gethsemane, and saith unto the disciples, Sit ye here, while I go and pray yonder. 37And he took with him Peter and the two sons of Zebedee, and began to be sorrowful and very heavy. 38 Then saith he unto them, My soul is exceeding sorrowful, even unto death: tarry ye here, and watch with me. 39And he went a little further, and fell on his face, and prayed, saying, O my Father, if it be possible, let this cup pass from me: nevertheless, not as I will, but as thou *wilt*. 40And he cometh unto the disciples, and findeth them asleep, and saith unto Peter, What, could ye not watch with me one hour? 41Watch and pray, that ye enter not into temptation: the spirit indeed *is* willing, but the flesh *is* weak. 42 He went away again the second time, and prayed, saying, O my Father, if this cup may not pass away from me, except I drink it, thy will be done. 43And he came and found them asleep again: for their eyes were heavy. 44And he left them, and went away again, and prayed the third time, saying the same words. 45 Then cometh he to his disciples, and saith unto them, Sleep on now, and take *your* rest: behold, the hour is at hand, and the Son of man is betrayed into the hands of sinners. 46 Rise, let us be going: behold, he is at hand that doth betray me.

47 And while he yet spake, lo, Judas, one of the twelve, came, and with him a great multitude with swords and staves, from the chief priests and elders of the people. 48 Now he that betrayed him gave them a sign, saying, Whomsoever I shall kiss, that same is he; hold him fast. 49And forthwith he came to Jesus, and said, Hail, Master; and kissed him. 50And Jesus said unto him, Friend, wherefore art thou come?

R.S.V.

26 Now as they were eating, Jesus took bread, and blessed, and broke it, and gave it to the disciples and said, "Take, eat; this is my body." 27And he took a cup, and when he had given thanks he gave it to them, saying, "Drink of it, all of you; 28 for this is my blood of the*ᵍ* covenant, which is poured out for many for the forgiveness of sins. 29 I tell you I shall not drink again of this fruit of the vine until that day when I drink it new with you in my Father's kingdom."

30 And when they had sung a hymn, they went out to the Mount of Olives. 31 Then Jesus said to them, "You will all fall away because of me this night; for it is written, 'I will strike the shepherd, and the sheep of the flock will be scattered.' 32 But after I am raised up, I will go before you to Galilee." 33 Peter declared to him, "Though they all fall away because of you, I will never fall away." 34 Jesus said to him, "Truly, I say to you, this very night, before the cock crows, you will deny me three times." 35 Peter said to him, "Even if I must die with you, I will not deny you." And so said all the disciples.

36 Then Jesus went with them to a place called Gethsemane, and he said to his disciples, "Sit here, while I go yonder and pray." 37And taking with him Peter and the two sons of Zebedee, he began to be sorrowful and troubled. 38 Then he said to them, "My soul is very sorrowful, even to death; remain here, and watch*ʰ* with me." 39And going a little farther he fell on his face and prayed, "My Father, if it be possible, let this cup pass from me; nevertheless, not as I will, but as thou wilt." 40And he came to the disciples and found them sleeping; and he said to Peter, "So, could you not watch*ʰ* with me one hour? 41 Watch*ʰ* and pray that you may not enter into temptation; the spirit indeed is willing, but the flesh is weak." 42Again, for the second time, he went away and prayed, "My Father, if this cannot pass unless I drink it, thy will be done." 43And again he came and found them sleeping, for their eyes were heavy. 44 So, leaving them again, he went away and prayed for the third time, saying the same words. 45 Then he came to the disciples and said to them, "Are you still sleeping and taking your rest? Behold, the hour is at hand, and the Son of man is betrayed into the hands of sinners. 46 Rise, let us be going; see, my betrayer is at hand."

47 While he was still speaking, Judas came, one of the twelve, and with him a great crowd with swords and clubs, from the chief priests and the elders of the people. 48 Now the betrayer had given them a sign, saying, "The one I shall kiss is the man; seize him." 49And he came up to Jesus at once and said, "Hail, Master!" *ᶦ* And he kissed him. 50 Jesus said to him, "Friend, why are you here?" *ʲ* Then they came up and

[g] Other ancient authorities insert *new*. [h] Or *keep awake*. [i] Or *Rabbi*. [j] Or *do that for which you have come*.

In the middle of the meal Jesus took a loaf and after blessing it he broke it into pieces and gave it to the disciples. "Take and eat this," he said, "it is my body." Then he took a cup and, after thanking God, he gave it to them with the words, "Drink this, all of you, for it is my blood, the blood of the new agreement shed to set many free from their sins. I tell you I will drink no more wine until I drink it fresh with you in my Father's kingdom." Then they sang a hymn together and went out to the Mount of Olives. There Jesus said to them, "Tonight every one of you will lose his faith in me. For the scripture says, *'I will smite the shepherd, and the sheep of the flock shall be scattered abroad.'* But after I have risen I shall go before you into Galilee!"

At this Peter exclaimed, "Even if everyone should lose his faith in you, I never will!"

"I tell you, Peter," replied Jesus, "that tonight, before the cock crows, you will disown me three times."

"Even if it means dying with you I will never disown you," said Peter. And all the disciples made the same protest.

The prayer in Gethsemane   **26. 36**

Then Jesus came with the disciples to a place called Gethsemane and said to them, "Sit down here while I go over there and pray." Then he took with him Peter and the two sons of Zebedee and began to be in terrible distress and misery. "My heart is nearly breaking," he told them, "stay here and keep watch with me." Then he walked on a little way and fell on his face and prayed, "My Father, if it is possible let this cup pass from me—yet it must not be what I want, but what you want."

Then he came back to the disciples and found them fast asleep. He spoke to Peter: "Couldn't you three keep awake with me for a single hour? Watch and pray, all of you, that you may not have to face temptation. Your spirit is willing, but human nature is weak."

Then he went away a second time and prayed, "My Father, if it is not possible for this cup to pass from me without my drinking it, then your will must be done."

And he came and found them asleep again, for they could not keep their eyes open. So he left them and went away again and prayed for the third time, using the same words as before. Then he came back to his disciples and spoke to them, "Are you still going to sleep and take your ease? In a moment you will see the Son of Man betrayed into the hands of evil men. Wake up, let us be going! Look, here comes my betrayer!"

The betrayal   **26. 47**

And while the words were still on his lips Judas, one of the twelve, appeared with a great crowd armed with swords and staves, sent by the chief priests and Jewish elders. (The traitor himself had given them a sign, "The one I kiss will be the man. Get him!")

Without any hesitation he walked up to Jesus. "Greetings, Master!" he cried, and kissed him affectionately. "Judas, my friend," replied Jesus, *"why are you here?"*

During supper Jesus took bread, and having said the blessing he broke it and gave it to the disciples with the words: 'Take this and eat; this is my body.' Then he took a cup, and having offered thanks to God he gave it to them with the words: 'Drink from it, all of you. For this is my blood, the blood of the covenant, shed for many for the forgiveness of sins. I tell you, never again shall I drink from the fruit of the vine until that day when I drink it new with you in the kingdom of my Father.'

After singing the Passover Hymn, they went out to the Mount of Olives. Then Jesus said to them, 'Tonight you will all fall from your faith on my account; for it stands written: "I will strike the shepherd down and the sheep of his flock will be scattered." But after I am raised again, I will go on before you into Galilee.' Peter replied, 'Everyone else may fall away on your account, but I never will.' Jesus said to him, 'I tell you, tonight before the cock crows you will disown me three times.' Peter said, 'Even if I must die with you, I will never disown you.' And all the disciples said the same.

Jesus then came with his disciples to a place called Gethsemane. He said to them, 'Sit here while I go over there to pray.' He took with him Peter and the two sons of Zebedee. Anguish and dismay came over him, and he said to them, 'My heart is ready to break with grief. Stop here, and stay awake with me.' He went on a little, fell on his face in prayer, and said, 'My Father, if it is possible, let this cup pass me by. Yet not as I will, but as thou wilt.'

He came to the disciples and found them asleep; and he said to Peter, 'What! Could none of you stay awake with me one hour? Stay awake, and pray that you may be spared the test. The spirit is willing, but the flesh is weak.'

He went away a second time, and prayed: 'My Father, if it is not possible for this cup to pass me by without my drinking it, thy will be done.' He came again and found them asleep, for their eyes were heavy. So he left them and went away again; and he prayed the third time, using the same words as before.

Then he came to the disciples and said to them, 'Still sleeping? Still taking your ease? The hour has come! The Son of Man is betrayed to sinful men. Up, let us go forward; the traitor is upon us.'

While he was still speaking, Judas, one of the Twelve, appeared; with him was a great crowd armed with swords and cudgels, sent by the chief priests and the elders of the nation. The traitor gave them this sign: 'The one I kiss is your man; seize him'; and stepping forward at once, he said, 'Hail, Rabbi!', and kissed him. Jesus replied, 'Friend, do what you are here to do.' [a]

[a] *Or* Friend, what are you here for?

Then came they, and laid hands on Jesus, and took him. 51And, behold, one of them which were with Jesus stretched out *his* hand, and drew his sword, and struck a servant of the high priest, and smote off his ear. 52 Then said Jesus unto him, Put up again thy sword into his place: for all they that take the sword shall perish with the sword. 53 Thinkest thou that I cannot now pray to my Father, and he shall presently give me more than twelve legions of angels? 54 But how then shall the Scriptures be fulfilled, that thus it must be? 55 In that same hour said Jesus to the multitudes, Are ye come out as against a thief with swords and staves for to take me? I sat daily with you teaching in the temple, and ye laid no hold on me. 56 But all this was done, that the Scriptures of the prophets might be fulfilled. Then all the disciples forsook him, and fled.

57 And they that had laid hold on Jesus led *him* away to Caiaphas the high priest, where the scribes and the elders were assembled. 58 But Peter followed him afar off unto the high priest's palace, and went in, and sat with the servants, to see the end. 59 Now the chief priests, and elders, and all the council, sought false witness against Jesus, to put him to death; 60 But found none: yea, though many false witnesses came, *yet* found they none. At the last came two false witnesses, 61And said, This *fellow* said, I am able to destroy the temple of God, and to build it in three days. 62And the high priest arose, and said unto him, Answerest thou nothing? what *is it which* these witness against thee? 63 But Jesus held his peace. And the high priest answered and said unto him, I adjure thee by the living God, that thou tell us whether thou be the Christ, the Son of God. 64 Jesus saith unto him, Thou hast said: nevertheless I say unto you, Hereafter shall ye see the Son of man sitting on the right hand of power, and coming in the clouds of heaven. 65 Then the high priest rent his clothes, saying, He hath spoken blasphemy; what further need have we of witnesses? behold, now ye have heard his blasphemy. 66 What think ye? They answered and said, He is guilty of death. 67 Then did they spit in his face, and buffeted him; and others smote *him* with the palms of their hands, 68 Saying, Prophesy unto us, thou Christ, Who is he that smote thee?

69 Now Peter sat without in the palace: and a damsel came unto him, saying, Thou also wast with Jesus of Galilee. 70 But he denied before *them* all, saying, I know not what thou sayest. 71And when he was gone out into the porch, another *maid* saw him, and said unto them that were there, This *fellow* was also with Jesus of Nazareth. 72And again he denied with an oath, I do not know the man. 73And after a while came unto *him* they that stood by, and said to Peter, Surely thou also art *one* of them; for thy speech bewrayeth thee. 74 Then began he to curse and to swear, *saying,* I know not the man. And immediately the cock crew. 75And Peter remem-

laid hands on Jesus and seized him. 51And behold, one of those who were with Jesus stretched out his hand and drew his sword, and struck the slave of the high priest, and cut off his ear. 52 Then Jesus said to him, "Put your sword back into its place; for all who take the sword will perish by the sword. 53 Do you think that I cannot appeal to my Father, and he will at once send me more than twelve legions of angels? 54 But how then should the scriptures be fulfilled, that it must be so?" 55 At that hour Jesus said to the crowds, "Have you come out as against a robber, with swords and clubs to capture me? Day after day I sat in the temple teaching, and you did not seize me. 56 But all this has taken place, that the scriptures of the prophets might be fulfilled." Then all the disciples forsook him and fled.

57 Then those who had seized Jesus led him to Caiaphas the high priest, where the scribes and the elders had gathered. 58 But Peter followed him at a distance, as far as the courtyard of the high priest, and going inside he sat with the guards to see the end. 59 Now the chief priests and the whole council sought false testimony against Jesus that they might put him to death, 60 but they found none, though many false witnesses came forward. At last two came forward 61 and said, "This fellow said, 'I am able to destroy the temple of God, and to build it in three days.'" 62And the high priest stood up and said, "Have you no answer to make? What is it that these men testify against you?" 63 But Jesus was silent. And the high priest said to him, "I adjure you by the living God, tell us if you are the Christ, the Son of God." 64 Jesus said to him, "You have said so. But I tell you, hereafter you will see the Son of man seated at the right hand of Power, and coming on the clouds of heaven." 65 Then the high priest tore his robes, and said, "He has uttered blasphemy. Why do we still need witnesses? You have now heard his blasphemy. 66 What is your judgment?" They answered, "He deserves death." 67 Then they spat in his face, and struck him; and some slapped him, 68 saying, "Prophesy to us, you Christ! Who is it that struck you?"

69 Now Peter was sitting outside in the courtyard. And a maid came up to him, and said, "You also were with Jesus the Galilean." 70 But he denied it before them all, saying, "I do not know what you mean." 71And when he went out to the porch, another maid saw him, and said to the bystanders, "This man was with Jesus of Nazareth." 72And again he denied it with an oath, "I do not know the man." 73After a little while the bystanders came up and said to Peter, "Certainly you are also one of them, for your accent betrays you." 74 Then he began to invoke a curse on himself and to swear, "I do not know the man." And immediately the cock crowed. 75And Peter remembered the saying of

PHILLIPS

Then the others came up, seized hold of Jesus and held him. Suddenly one of Jesus' disciples drew his sword, slashed at the High Priest's servant and cut off his ear. At this Jesus said to him: "Put your sword back into its proper place. All those who take the sword die by the sword. Do you imagine that I could not appeal to my Father, and he would at once send more than twelve legions of angels to defend me? But then how would the scriptures be fulfilled which say that all this must take place?"

And then Jesus spoke to the crowds around him: "So you've come out with your swords and staves to capture me like a bandit, have you? Day after day I set teaching in the Temple and you never laid a finger on me. But all this is happening as the prophets said it would." And at this point all the disciples deserted him and made their escape.

Jesus before the High Priest   26. 57

The men who had seized Jesus took him off to Caiaphas the High Priest in whose house the scribes and elders were assembled. Peter followed him at a safe distance right up to the High Priest's courtyard. Then he went inside and sat down with the servants and waited to see the end.

Meanwhile the chief priests and the whole council did all they could to find false evidence against Jesus to get him condemned to death. They failed completely. Even after a number of perjurers came forward they still failed. In the end two of these stood up and said, "This man said, 'I can pull down the Temple of God and rebuild it in three days.'" Then the High Priest rose to his feet and addressed Jesus: "Have you no answer? What about the evidence of these men against you?" But Jesus was silent. Then the High Priest said to him, "I command you by the living God, to tell us on your oath if you are Christ, the Son of God."

Jesus said to him: "I am. Yes, and I tell you that in the future you will see the Son of Man sitting at the right hand of power and coming on the clouds of Heaven."

At this the High Priest tore his robes and cried: "That was blasphemy! Where is the need for further witnesses? Look, you've heard the blasphemy—what's your verdict now?" And they replied, "He deserves to die."

Then they spat in his face and knocked him about, and some slapped him, crying, "Prophesy, you Christ, who was that who hit you?"

Peter disowns his master   26. 69

All this time Peter was sitting outside in the courtyard, and a maidservant came up to him and said, "Weren't you with Jesus, the man from Galilee?" But he denied it before them all, saying, "I don't know what you're talking about." Then when he had gone out into the porch, another maid caught sight of him and said to those who were there, "This man was with Jesus of Nazareth." And again he denied it with an oath—"I don't know the man!" A few minutes later those who were standing about came up to Peter and said to him, "You certainly are one of them, you know; it's obvious from your accent." At that he began to curse and swear—"I tell you I don't know the man!" Immediately the cock crew, and the words of

N.E.B.

They then came forward, seized Jesus, and held him fast.

At that moment one of those with Jesus reached for his sword and drew it, and he struck at the High Priest's servant and cut off his ear. But Jesus said to him, 'Put up your sword. All who take the sword die by the sword. Do you suppose that I cannot appeal to my Father, who would at once send to my aid more than twelve legions of angels? But how then could the scriptures be fulfilled, which say that this must be?'

At the same time Jesus spoke to the crowd. 'Do you take me for a bandit,' he said, 6 that you have come out with swords and cudgels to arrest me? Day after day I sat teaching in the temple, and you did not lay hands on me. But this has all happened to fulfil what the prophets wrote.'

Then the disciples all deserted him and ran away.

Jesus was led off under arrest to the house of Caiaphas the High Priest, where the lawyers and elders were assembled. Peter followed him at a distance till he came to the High Priest's courtyard, and going in he sat down there among the attendants, meaning to see the end of it all.

The chief priests and the whole Council tried to find some allegation against Jesus on which a death-sentence could be based; but they failed to find one, though many came forward with false evidence. Finally two men alleged that he had said, 'I can pull down the temple of God, and rebuild it in three days.' At this the High Priest rose and said to him, 'Have you no answer to the charge that these witnesses bring against you?' But Jesus kept silence. The High Priest then said, 'By the living God I charge you to tell us: Are you the Messiah, the Son of God?' Jesus replied, 'The words are yours.[a] But I tell you this: from now on, you will see the Son of Man seated at the right hand of God [b] and coming on the clouds of heaven.' At these words the High Priest tore his robes and exclaimed, 'Blasphemy! Need we call further witnesses? You have heard the blasphemy. What is your opinion?' 'He is guilty,' they answered; 'he should die.'

Then they spat in his face and beat him with their fists; and others said, as they struck him, 'Now, Messiah, if you are a prophet, tell us who hit you.'

Meanwhile Peter was sitting outside in the courtyard when a serving-maid accosted him and said, 'You were there too with Jesus the Galilean.' Peter denied it in face of them all. 'I do not know what you mean', he said. He then went out to the gateway, where another girl, seeing him, said to the people there, 'This fellow was with Jesus of Nazareth.' Once again he denied it, saying with an oath, 'I do not know the man.' Shortly afterwards the bystanders came up and said to Peter, 'Surely you are another of them; your accent gives you away!' At this he broke into curses and declared with an oath: 'I do not know the man.' At that moment the cock crew. And Peter remembered how Jesus had said,

[a] Or It is as you say. [b] Literally of the Power.

K.J.V.

bered the word of Jesus, which said unto him, Before the cock crow, thou shalt deny me thrice. And he went out, and wept bitterly.

27 When the morning was come, all the chief priests and elders of the people took counsel against Jesus to put him to death: 2And when they had bound him, they led *him* away, and delivered him to Pontius Pilate the governor. 3 Then Judas, which had betrayed him, when he saw that he was condemned, repented himself, and brought again the thirty pieces of silver to the chief priests and elders, 4 Saying, I have sinned in that I have betrayed the innocent blood. And they said, What *is that* to us? see thou *to that.* 5And he cast down the pieces of silver in the temple, and departed, and went and hanged himself. 6And the chief priests took the silver pieces, and said, It is not lawful for to put them into the treasury, because it is the price of blood. 7And they took counsel, and bought with them the potter's field, to bury strangers in. 8 Wherefore that field was called, The field of blood, unto this day. 9 Then was fulfilled that which was spoken by Jeremy the prophet, saying, And they took the thirty pieces of silver, the price of him that was valued, whom they of the children of Israel did value; 10And gave them for the potter's field, as the Lord appointed me. 11And Jesus stood before the governor: and the governor asked him, saying, Art thou the King of the Jews? And Jesus said unto him, Thou sayest. 12And when he was accused of the chief priests and elders, he answered nothing. 13 Then said Pilate unto him, Hearest thou not how many things they witness against thee? 14And he answered him to never a word; insomuch that the governor marvelled greatly. 15 Now at *that* feast the governor was wont to release unto the people a prisoner, whom they would. 16And they had then a notable prisoner, called Barabbas. 17 Therefore when they were gathered together, Pilate said unto them, Whom will ye that I release unto you? Barabbas, or Jesus which is called Christ? 18 For he knew that for envy they had delivered him. 19 When he was set down on the judgment seat, his wife sent unto him, saying, Have thou nothing to do with that just man: for I have suffered many things this day in a dream because of him. 20 But the chief priests and elders persuaded the multitude that they should ask Barabbas, and destroy Jesus. 21 The governor answered and said unto them, Whether of the twain will ye that I release unto you? They said, Barabbas. 22 Pilate saith unto them, What shall I do then with Jesus which is called Christ? *They* all say unto him, Let him be crucified. 23And the governor said, Why, what evil hath he done? But they cried out the more, saying, Let him be crucified.

R.S.V.

Jesus, "Before the cock crows, you will deny me three times." And he went out and wept bitterly.

27 When morning came, all the chief priests and the elders of the people took counsel against Jesus to put him to death; 2 and they bound him and led him away and delivered him to Pilate the governor.
3 When Judas, his betrayer, saw that he was condemned, he repented and brought back the thirty pieces of silver to the chief priests and the elders, 4 saying, "I have sinned in betraying innocent blood." They said, "What is that to us? See to it yourself." 5And throwing down the pieces of silver in the temple, he departed; and he went and hanged himself. 6 But the chief priests, taking the pieces of silver, said, "It is not lawful to put them into the treasury, since they are blood money." 7 So they took counsel, and bought with them the potter's field, to bury strangers in. 8 Therefore that field has been called the Field of Blood to this day. 9 Then was fulfilled what had been spoken by the prophet Jeremiah, saying, "And they took the thirty pieces of silver, the price of him on whom a price had been set by some of the sons of Israel, 10 and they gave them for the potter's field, as the Lord directed me."
11 Now Jesus stood before the governor; and the governor asked him, "Are you the King of the Jews?" Jesus said to him, "You have said so." 12 But when he was accused by the chief priests and elders, he made no answer. 13 Then Pilate said to him, "Do you not hear how many things they testify against you?" 14 But he gave him no answer, not even to a single charge; so that the governor wondered greatly.
15 Now at the feast the governor was accustomed to release for the crowd any one prisoner whom they wanted. 16And they had then a notorious prisoner, called Barabbas.[k] 17 So when they had gathered, Pilate said to them, "Whom do you want me to release for you, Barabbas[k] or Jesus who is called Christ?" 18 For he knew that it was out of envy that they had delivered him up. 19 Besides, while he was sitting on the judgment seat, his wife sent word to him, "Have nothing to do with that righteous man, for I have suffered much over him today in a dream." 20 Now the chief priests and the elders persuaded the people to ask for Barabbas and destroy Jesus. 21 The governor again said to them, "Which of the two do you want me to release for you?" And they said, "Barabbas." 22 Pilate said to them, "Then what shall I do with Jesus who is called Christ?" They all said, "Let him be crucified." 23And he said, "Why, what evil has he done?" But they shouted all the more, "Let him be crucified."

[k] Other ancient authorities read *Jesus Barabbas.*

PHILLIPS

Jesus came back into Peter's mind—"Before the cock crows you will disown me three times." And he went outside and wept bitterly.

When the morning came, all the chief priests and elders of the people met in council to decide how they could get Jesus executed. Then they marched him off with his hands tied, and handed him over to Pilate the governor.

The remorse of Judas   27. 3

Then Judas, who had betrayed him, saw that he was condemned and in his remorse returned the thirty silver coins to the chief priests and elders, with the words, "I was wrong—I have betrayed an innocent man to death."

"And what has that got to do with us?" they replied. "That's your affair."

And Judas flung down the silver in the Temple and went outside and hanged himself. But the chief priests picked up the money and said, "It is not legal to put this into the Temple treasury. It is, after all, blood money." So, after a further consultation, they purchased with it the Potter's Field to be a burial ground for foreigners, which is why it is called "the Field of Blood" to this day. And so the words of Jeremiah the prophet came true:

> And they took the thirty pieces of silver,
> the price of him that was priced, whom certain of the children of Israel did price; and they gave them for the potter's field, as the Lord appointed me.

Jesus before Pilate   27. 11

Meanwhile Jesus stood in front of the governor, who asked him, "Well, you—*are* you the king of the Jews?"

"Yes, I am," replied Jesus.

But while the chief priests and elders were making their accusations, he made no reply at all. So Pilate said to him, "Can you not hear the evidence they're bringing against you?" And to the governor's amazement, Jesus did not answer a single one of their accusations.

Now it was the custom at festival time for the governor to release any prisoner whom the people chose. And it happened that at this time they had a notorious prisoner called Barabbas. So when they assembled to make their usual request, Pilate said to them, "Which one do you want me to set free, Barabbas or Jesus called Christ?" For he knew very well that the latter had been handed over to him through sheer malice. And indeed while he was actually sitting on the Bench his wife sent a message to him—"Don't have anything to do with that good man! I went through agonies dreaming about him last night!" But the chief priests and elders persuaded the mob to ask for Barabbas and demand Jesus' execution. Then the governor spoke to them, "Which of these two are you asking me to release?"

"Barabbas!" they cried.

"Then what am I to do with Jesus who is called Christ?" asked Pilate.

"Have him crucified!" they all cried. At this Pilate said, "Why, what is his crime?" But their voices rose to a roar, "Have him crucified!"

N.E.B.

'Before the cock crows you will disown me three times.' He went outside, and wept bitterly.

27 When morning came, the chief priests and the elders of the nation met in conference to plan the death of Jesus. They then put him in chains and led him off, to hand him over to Pilate, the Roman Governor.

When Judas the traitor saw that Jesus had been condemned, he was seized with remorse, and returned the thirty silver pieces to the chief priests and elders. 'I have sinned,' he said; 'I have brought an innocent man to his death.' But they said, 'What is that to us? See to that yourself.' So he threw the money down in the temple and left them, and went and hanged himself.

Taking up the money, the chief priests argued: 'This cannot be put into the temple fund; it is blood-money.' So after conferring they used it to buy the Potter's Field, as a burial-place for foreigners. This explains the name 'Blood Acre', by which that field has been known ever since; and in this way fulfilment was given to the prophetic utterance of Jeremiah: 'They took[a] the thirty silver pieces, the price set on a man's head (for that was his price among the Israelites), and gave the money for the potter's field, as the Lord directed me.'

Jesus was now brought before the Governor; and as he stood there the Governor asked him, 'Are you the king of the Jews?' 'The words are yours',[b] said Jesus; and to the charges laid against him by the chief priests and elders he made no reply. Then Pilate said to him, 'Do you not hear all this evidence that is brought against you?'; but he still refused to answer one word, to the Governor's great astonishment.

At the festival season it was the Governor's custom to release one prisoner chosen by the people. There was then in custody a man of some notoriety, called Jesus[c] Bar-Abbas. When they were assembled Pilate said to them, 'Which would you like me to release to you—Jesus[c] Bar-Abbas, or Jesus called Messiah?' For he knew that it was out of spite that they had brought Jesus before him.

While Pilate was sitting in court a message came to him from his wife: 'Have nothing to do with that innocent man; I was much troubled on his account in my dreams last night.'

Meanwhile the chief priests and elders had persuaded the crowd to ask for the release of Bar-Abbas and to have Jesus put to death. So when the Governor asked, 'Which of the two do you wish me to release to you?', they said, 'Bar-Abbas.' 'Then what am I to do with Jesus called Messiah?' asked Pilate; and with one voice they answered, 'Crucify him!' 'Why, what harm has he done?' Pilate asked; but they shouted all the louder, 'Crucify him!'

[a] *Or* I took. [b] *Or* It is as you say. [c] *Some witnesses omit* Jesus.

K.J.V.

24 When Pilate saw that he could prevail nothing, but *that* rather a tumult was made, he took water, and washed *his* hands before the multitude, saying, I am innocent of the blood of this just person: see ye *to it*. 25 Then answered all the people, and said, His blood *be* on us, and on our children.

26 Then released he Barabbas unto them: and when he had scourged Jesus, he delivered *him* to be crucified. 27 Then the soldiers of the governor took Jesus into the common hall, and gathered unto him the whole band *of soldiers*. 28And they stripped him, and put on him a scarlet robe.

29 And when they had platted a crown of thorns, they put *it* upon his head, and a reed in his right hand: and they bowed the knee before him, and mocked him, saying, Hail, King of the Jews! 30And they spit upon him, and took the reed, and smote him on the head. 31And after that they had mocked him, they took the robe off from him, and put his own raiment on him, and led him away to crucify *him*. 32And as they came out, they found a man of Cyrene, Simon by name: him they compelled to bear his cross. 33And when they were come unto a place called Golgotha, that is to say, a place of a skull,

34 They gave him vinegar to drink mingled with gall: and when he had tasted *thereof*, he would not drink. 35And they crucified him, and parted his garments, casting lots: that it might be fulfilled which was spoken by the prophet, They parted my garments among them, and upon my vesture did they cast lots. 36And sitting down they watched him there; 37And set up over his head his accusation written, THIS IS JESUS THE KING OF THE JEWS. 38 Then were there two thieves crucified with him; one on the right hand, and another on the left.

39 And they that passed by reviled him, wagging their heads, 40And saying, Thou that destroyest the temple, and buildest *it* in three days, save thyself. If thou be the Son of God, come down from the cross. 41 Likewise also the chief priests mocking *him*, with the scribes and elders, said, 42 He saved others; himself he cannot save. If he be the King of Israel, let him now come down from the cross, and we will believe him. 43 He trusted in God; let him deliver him now, if he will have him: for he said, I am the Son of God. 44 The thieves also, which were crucified with him, cast the same in his teeth. 45 Now from the sixth hour there was darkness over all the land unto the ninth hour. 46And about the ninth hour Jesus cried with a loud voice, saying, Eli, Eli, lama sabachthani? that is to say, My God, my God, why hast thou forsaken me? 47 Some of them that stood there, when they heard *that*, said, This *man* calleth for Elias. 48And straightway one of them ran, and took a sponge, and filled *it* with vinegar, and put *it* on a reed, and gave him to drink. 49 The rest said, Let be, let us see whether Elias will come to save him.

50 Jesus, when he had cried again with a loud voice, yielded up the ghost. 51And, behold, the vail of the temple was rent in twain from the top to the bottom; and the earth did quake, and the rocks rent; 52And the graves were opened; and many bodies of the saints which slept arose, 53And came out of the graves after his resurrection, and went into the holy city, and appeared unto many. 54 Now when the centurion, and they that were with him, watching Jesus,

R.S.V.

24 So when Pilate saw that he was gaining nothing, but rather that a riot was beginning, he took water and washed his hands before the crowd, saying, "I am innocent of this man's blood;[l] see to it yourselves." 25And all the people answered, "His blood be on us and on our children!" 26 Then he released for them Barabbas, and having scourged Jesus, delivered him to be crucified.

27 Then the soldiers of the governor took Jesus into the praetorium, and they gathered the whole battalion before him. 28And they stripped him and put a scarlet robe upon him, 29 and plaiting a crown of thorns they put it on his head, and put a reed in his right hand. And kneeling before him they mocked him, saying, "Hail, King of the Jews!" 30And they spat upon him, and took the reed and struck him on the head. 31And when they had mocked him, they stripped him of the robe, and put his own clothes on him, and led him away to crucify him.

32 As they were marching out, they came upon a man of Cyrene, Simon by name; this man they compelled to carry his cross. 33And when they came to a place called Golgotha (which means the place of a skull), 34 they offered him wine to drink, mingled with gall; but when he tasted it, he would not drink it. 35And when they had crucified him, they divided his garments among them by casting lots; 36 then they sat down and kept watch over him there. 37And over his head they put the charge against him, which read, "This is Jesus the King of the Jews." 38 Then two robbers were crucified with him, one on the right and one on the left. 39And those who passed by derided him, wagging their heads 40 and saying, "You who would destroy the temple and build it in three days, save yourself! If you are the Son of God, come down from the cross." 41 So also the chief priests, with the scribes and elders, mocked him, saying, 42 "He saved others; he cannot save himself. He is the King of Israel; let him come down now from the cross, and we will believe in him. 43 He trusts in God; let God deliver him now, if he desires him; for he said, 'I am the Son of God.'" 44And the robbers who were crucified with him also reviled him in the same way.

45 Now from the sixth hour there was darkness over all the land [m] until the ninth hour. 46And about the ninth hour Jesus cried with a loud voice, "Eli, Eli, lama sabachthani?" that is, "My God, my God, why hast thou forsaken me?" 47And some of the bystanders hearing it said, "This man is calling Elijah." 48And one of them at once ran and took a sponge, filled it with vinegar, and put it on a reed, and gave it to him to drink. 49 But the others said, "Wait, let us see whether Elijah will come to save him." [n] 50And Jesus cried again with a loud voice and yielded up his spirit.

51 And behold, the curtain of the temple was torn in two, from top to bottom; and the earth shook, and the rocks were split; 52 the tombs also were opened, and many bodies of the saints who had fallen asleep were raised, 53 and coming out of the tombs after his resurrection they went into the holy city and appeared to many. 54 When the centurion and those who were with him, keeping watch over Jesus, saw the earth-

---

[*l*] Other authorities read *this righteous blood* or *this righteous man's blood*. [*m*] Or *earth*. [*n*] Other ancient authorities insert *And another took a spear and pierced his side, and out came water and blood.*

PHILLIPS

When Pilate realized that nothing more could be done but that there would soon be a riot, he took a bowl of water and washed his hands before the crowd, saying: "I take no responsibility for the death of this man. You must see to that yourselves." To this the whole crowd replied, "Let his blood be on us and on our children!" Whereupon Pilate released Barabbas for them, but he had Jesus flogged and handed over for crucifixion.

Then the governor's soldiers took Jesus into the governor's palace and collected the whole guard around him. There they stripped him and put a scarlet cloak upon him. They twisted some thorn twigs into a crown and put it on his head and put a stick into his right hand. They bowed low before him and jeered at him with the words, "Hail, your majesty, king of the Jews!" Then they spat on him, took the stick and hit him on the head with it. And when they had finished their fun, they stripped the cloak off again, put his own clothes upon him and led him off for crucifixion. On their way out of the city they met a man called Simon, a native of Cyrene in Africa, and they compelled him to carry Jesus' cross.

The crucifixion   27. 33

Then when they came to a place called Golgotha (which means Skull Hill) they offered him a drink of wine mixed with some bitter drug, but when he had tasted it he refused to drink. And when they had nailed him to the cross they shared out his clothes by drawing lots.

Then they sat down to keep guard over him. And over his head they put a placard with the charge against him: "THIS IS JESUS, THE KING OF THE JEWS."

Now two bandits were crucified with Jesus at the same time, one on either side of him. The passers-by nodded their heads knowingly and called out to him in mockery, "Hi, you who could pull down the Temple and build it up again in three days—why don't you save yourself? If you are the Son of God, step down from the cross!" The chief priests also joined the scribes and elders in jeering at him, saying: "He saved others, but he can't save himself! If this is the king of Israel, why doesn't he come down from the cross now, and we will believe him! He trusted in God . . . let God rescue him if he will have anything to do with him! For he said, 'I am God's son.'" Even the bandits who were crucified with him hurled abuse at him.

Then from midday until three o'clock darkness spread over the whole countryside, and then Jesus cried with a loud voice, "My God, my God, why did you forsake me?" Some of those who were standing there heard these words which Jesus spoke in Aramaic (*Eli, Eli lama sabachthani?*), and said, "This man is calling for Elijah!" And one of them ran off and fetched a sponge, soaked it in vinegar and put it on a long stick and held it up for him to drink. But the others said: "Let him alone! Let's see if Elijah will come and save him." But Jesus gave one more great cry, and died.

And the sanctuary curtain in the Temple was torn in two from top to bottom. The ground shook, rocks split and graves were opened. (A number of bodies of holy men who were asleep in death rose again. They left their graves after Jesus' resurrection and entered the holy city and appeared to many people.) When the centurion and his company who were keeping guard over

N.E.B.

Pilate could see that nothing was being gained, and a riot was starting; so he took water and washed his hands in full view of the people, saying, 'My hands are clean of this man's blood; see to that yourselves.' And with one voice the people cried, 'His blood be on us, and on our children.' He then released Bar-Abbas to them; but he had Jesus flogged, and handed him over to be crucified.

Pilate's soldiers then took Jesus into the Governor's headquarters, where they collected the whole company round him. First they stripped him and dressed him in a scarlet mantle; and plaiting a crown of thorns they placed it on his head, with a cane in his right hand. Falling on their knees before him they jeered at him: 'Hail, King of the Jews!' They spat on him, and used the cane to beat him about the head. Finally, when the mockery was over, they took off the mantle and dressed him in his own clothes.

Then they led him away to be crucified. On their way out they met a man from Cyrene, Simon by name, and pressed him into service to carry his cross.

So they came to a place called Golgotha (which means 'Place of a skull') and there they offered him a draught of wine mixed with gall; but when he had tasted it he would not drink.

After fastening him to the cross they divided his clothes among them by casting lots, and then sat down there to keep watch. Over his head was placed the inscription giving the charge: 'This is Jesus the king of the Jews.'

Two bandits were crucified with him, one on his right and the other on his left.

The passers-by hurled abuse at him: they wagged their heads and cried, 'You would pull the temple down, would you, and build it in three days? Come down from the cross and save yourself, if you are indeed the Son of God.' So too the chief priests with the lawyers and elders mocked at him: 'He saved others,' they said, 'but he cannot save himself. King of Israel, indeed! Let him come down now from the cross, and then we will believe him. Did he trust in God? Let God rescue him, if he wants him—for he said he was God's Son.' Even the bandits who were crucified with him taunted him in the same way.

Darkness fell over the whole land from midday until three in the afternoon; and about three Jesus cried aloud, '*Eli, Eli, lama sabachthani?*', which means, 'My God, my God, why hast thou forsaken me?' Some of the bystanders, on hearing this, said, 'He is calling Elijah.' One of them ran at once and fetched a sponge, which he soaked in sour wine, and held it to his lips on the end of a cane. But the others said, 'Let us see if Elijah will come to save him.'

Jesus again gave a loud cry, and breathed his last. At that moment the curtain of the temple was torn in two from top to bottom. There was an earthquake, the rocks split and the graves opened, and many of God's people arose from sleep; and coming out of their graves after his resurrection they entered the Holy City, where many saw them. And when the centurion and his men who were keeping watch over Jesus saw

K.J.V.

saw the earthquake, and those things that were done, they feared greatly, saying, Truly this was the Son of God. 55And many women were there beholding afar off, which followed Jesus from Galilee, ministering unto him: 56Among which was Mary Magdalene, and Mary the mother of James and Joses, and the mother of Zebedee's children. 57 When the even was come, there came a rich man of Arimathea, named Joseph, who also himself was Jesus' disciple: 58 He went to Pilate, and begged the body of Jesus. Then Pilate commanded the body to be delivered. 59And when Joseph had taken the body, he wrapped it in a clean linen cloth, 60And laid it in his own new tomb, which he had hewn out in the rock: and he rolled a great stone to the door of the sepulchre, and departed. 61And there was Mary Magdalene, and the other Mary, sitting over against the sepulchre.

62 Now the next day, that followed the day of the preparation, the chief priests and Pharisees came together unto Pilate, 63 Saying, Sir, we remember that that deceiver said, while he was yet alive, After three days I will rise again. 64 Command therefore that the sepulchre be made sure until the third day, lest his disciples come by night, and steal him away, and say unto the people, He is risen from the dead: so the last error shall be worse than the first. 65 Pilate said unto them, Ye have a watch: go your way, make it as sure as ye can. 66 So they went, and made the sepulchre sure, sealing the stone, and setting a watch.

R.S.V.

quake and what took place, they were filled with awe, and said, "Truly this was the Son[x] of God!"

55 There were also many women there, looking on from afar, who had followed Jesus from Galilee, ministering to him; 56 among whom were Mary Magdalene, and Mary the mother of James and Joseph, and the mother of the sons of Zebedee.

57 When it was evening, there came a rich man from Arimathea, named Joseph, who also was a disciple of Jesus. 58 He went to Pilate and asked for the body of Jesus. Then Pilate ordered it to be given to him. 59And Joseph took the body, and wrapped it in a clean linen shroud, 60 and laid it in his own new tomb, which he had hewn in the rock; and he rolled a great stone to the door of the tomb, and departed. 61 Mary Magdalene and the other Mary were there, sitting opposite the sepulchre.

62 Next day, that is, after the day of Preparation, the chief priests and the Pharisees gathered before Pilate 63 and said, "Sir, we remember how that impostor said, while he was still alive, 'After three days I will rise again.' 64 Therefore order the sepulchre to be made secure until the third day, lest his disciples go and steal him away, and tell the people, 'He has risen from the dead,' and the last fraud will be worse than the first." 65 Pilate said to them, "You have a guard[o] of soldiers; go, make it as secure as you can." [p] 66 So they went and made the sepulchre secure by sealing the stone and setting a guard.

28 In the end of the sabbath, as it began to dawn toward the first *day* of the week, came Mary Magdalene and the other Mary to see the sepulchre. 2And, behold, there was a great earthquake: for the angel of the Lord descended from heaven, and came and rolled back the stone from the door, and sat upon it. 3 His countenance was like lightning, and his raiment white as snow: 4And for fear of him the keepers did shake, and became as dead *men*. 5And the angel answered and said unto the women, Fear not ye: for I know that ye seek Jesus, which was crucified. 6 He is not here: for he is risen, as he said. Come, see the place where the Lord lay. 7And go quickly, and tell his disciples that he is risen from the dead; and, behold, he goeth before you into Galilee; there shall ye see him: lo, I have told you. 8And they departed quickly from the sepulchre with fear and great joy; and did run to bring his disciples word.

9 And as they went to tell his disciples, behold, Jesus met them, saying, All hail. And they came and held him by the feet, and worshipped him. 10 Then said Jesus unto them, Be not afraid: go tell my brethren that they go into Galilee, and there they shall see me.

11 Now when they were going, behold, some of the watch came into the city, and shewed

28 Now after the sabbath, toward the dawn of the first day of the week, Mary Magdalene and the other Mary went to see the sepulchre. 2And behold, there was a great earthquake; for an angel of the Lord descended from heaven and came and rolled back the stone, and sat upon it. 3 His appearance was like lightning, and his raiment white as snow. 4And for fear of him the guards trembled and became like dead men. 5 But the angel said to the women, "Do not be afraid; for I know that you seek Jesus who was crucified. 6 He is not here; for he has risen, as he said. Come, see the place where he[q] lay. 7 Then go quickly and tell his disciples that he has risen from the dead, and behold, he is going before you to Galilee; there you will see him. Lo, I have told you." 8 So they departed quickly from the tomb with fear and great joy, and ran to tell his disciples. 9And behold, Jesus met them and said, "Hail!" And they came up and took hold of his feet and worshiped him. 10 Then Jesus said to them, "Do not be afraid; go and tell my brethren to go to Galilee, and there they will see me."

11 While they were going, behold, some of the guard went into the city and told the chief priests

[o] Or *Take a guard.* [p] Greek *know.* [q] Other ancient authorities read *the Lord.* [x] Or *a son.*

Jesus saw the earthquake and all that was happening, they were terrified. "Indeed he *was* a son of God!" they said.

There were many women at the scene watching from a distance. They had followed Jesus from Galilee to minister to his needs. Among them were Mary of Magdala, Mary the mother of James and Joseph, and the mother of Zebedee's sons.

Jesus is buried and the tomb is guarded   27. 57

That evening Joseph, a wealthy man from Arimathaea, who was himself a disciple of Jesus, went to Pilate and asked for the body of Jesus, and Pilate gave orders for the body to be handed over to him. So Joseph took it, wrapped it in clean linen and placed it in his own new tomb which had been hewn in the rock. Then he rolled a large stone across the doorway of the tomb and went away. But Mary from Magdala and the other Mary remained there, sitting in front of the tomb.

Next day, which was the day after the preparation, the chief priests and the Pharisees went in a body to Pilate and said, "Sir, we have remembered that while this impostor was alive, he said, 'After three days I shall rise again.' Will you give the order then to have the grave closely guarded until the third day, so that there can be no chance of his disciples' coming and stealing the body and telling people that he has risen from the dead? We should then be faced with a worse fraud than the first one."

"You have a guard," Pilate told them. "Go and make it as safe as you think necessary." And they went and made the grave secure, putting a seal on the stone and leaving the soldiers on guard.

The first Lord's day: Jesus rises   28. 1

When the Sabbath was over, just as the first day of the week was dawning, Mary from Magdala and the other Mary went to look at the tomb. At that moment there was a great earthquake, for an angel of the Lord came down from Heaven, went forward and rolled back the stone, and took his seat upon it. His appearance was dazzling like lightning and his clothes were white as snow. The guards shook with terror at the sight of him and collapsed like dead men. But the angel spoke to the women: "Do not be afraid. I know that you are looking for Jesus who was crucified. He is not here—he is risen, just as he said he would. Come and look at the place where he was lying. Then go quickly and tell his disciples that he has risen from the dead. And, listen, he goes before you into Galilee! You will see him there! Now I have told you my message." Then the women went away quickly from the tomb, their hearts filled with awe and great joy, and ran to give the news to his disciples. But quite suddenly, Jesus stood before them in their path, and said, "Peace be with you!" And they went forward to meet him and, clasping his feet, worshiped him. Then Jesus said to them: "Do not be afraid. Go now and tell my brothers to go into Galilee and they shall see me there."

And while they were on their way, some of the sentries went into the city and reported to

the earthquake and all that was happening, they were filled with awe, and they said, 'Truly this man was a son of God.'

A number of women were also present, watching from a distance; they had followed Jesus from Galilee and waited on him. Among them were Mary of Magdala, Mary the mother of James and Joseph, and the mother of the sons of Zebedee.

When evening fell, there came a man of Arimathaea, Joseph by name, who was a man of means, and had himself become a disciple of Jesus. He approached Pilate, and asked for the body of Jesus; and Pilate gave orders that he should have it. Joseph took the body, wrapped it in a clean linen sheet, and laid it in his own unused tomb, which he had cut out of the rock; he then rolled a large stone against the entrance, and went away. Mary of Magdala was there, and the other Mary, sitting opposite the grave.

Next day, the morning after that Friday, the chief priests and the Pharisees came in a body to Pilate. 'Your Excellency,' they said, 'we recall how that impostor said while he was still alive, "I am to rise after three days." So will you give orders for the grave to be made secure until the third day? Otherwise his disciples may come, steal the body, and then tell the people that he has been raised from the dead; and the final deception will be worse than the first.' 'You may have your guard,' said Pilate; 'go and make it secure as best you can.' So they went and made the grave secure; they sealed the stone, and left the guard in charge.

28 The Sabbath had passed, and it was about daybreak on Sunday, when Mary of Magdala and the other Mary came to look at the grave. Suddenly there was a violent earthquake; an angel of the Lord descended from heaven; he came to the stone and rolled it away, and sat himself down on it. His face shone like lightning; his garments were white as snow. At the sight of him the guards shook with fear and lay like the dead.

The angel then addressed the women: 'You', he said, 'have nothing to fear. I know you are looking for Jesus who was crucified. He is not here; he has been raised again, as he said he would be. Come and see the place where he was laid, and then go quickly and tell his disciples: "He has been raised from the dead and is going on before you into Galilee; there you will see him." That is what I had to tell you.'

They hurried away from the tomb in awe and great joy, and ran to tell the disciples. Suddenly Jesus was there in their path. He gave them his greeting, and they came up and clasped his feet, falling prostrate before him. Then Jesus said to them, 'Do not be afraid. Go and take word to my brothers that they are to leave for Galilee. They will see me there.'

The women had started on their way when some of the guard went into the city and re-

K.J.V.

unto the chief priests all the things that were done. 12And when they were assembled with the elders, and had taken counsel, they gave large money unto the soldiers, 13 Saying, Say ye, His disciples came by night, and stole him *away* while we slept. 14And if this come to the governor's ears, we will persuade him, and secure you. 15 So they took the money, and did as they were taught: and this saying is commonly reported among the Jews until this day.

16 Then the eleven disciples went away into Galilee, into a mountain where Jesus had appointed them. 17And when they saw him, they worshipped him: but some doubted. 18And Jesus came and spake unto them, saying, All power is given unto me in heaven and in earth.

19 Go ye therefore, and teach all nations, baptizing them in the name of the Father, and of the Son, and of the Holy Ghost: 20 Teaching them to observe all things whatsoever I have commanded you: and, lo, I am with you alway, *even* unto the end of the world. Amen.

R.S.V.

all that had taken place. 12And when they had assembled with the elders and taken counsel, they gave a sum of money to the soldiers 13 and said, "Tell people, 'His disciples came by night and stole him away while we were asleep.' 14And if this comes to the governor's ears, we will satisfy him and keep you out of trouble." 15 So they took the money and did as they were directed; and this story has been spread among the Jews to this day.

16 Now the eleven disciples went to Galilee, to the mountain to which Jesus had directed them. 17And when they saw him they worshiped him; but some doubted. 18And Jesus came and said to them, "All authority in heaven and on earth has been given to me. 19 Go therefore and make disciples of all nations, baptizing them in the name of the Father and of the Son and of the Holy Spirit, 20 teaching them to observe all that I have commanded you; and lo, I am with you always, to the close of the age."

PHILLIPS

N.E.B.

the chief priests everything that had happened. They got together with the elders, and after consultation gave the soldiers a considerable sum of money and told them: "Your story must be that his disciples came after dark, and stole him away while you were asleep. If by any chance this reaches the governor's ears, we will put it right with him and see that you do not suffer for it." So they took the money and obeyed their instructions. The story was spread and is current among the Jews to this day.

Jesus gives his final commission   28. 16

But the eleven went to the hillside in Galilee where Jesus had arranged to meet them, and when they had seen him they worshiped him, though some of them were doubtful. But Jesus came and spoke these words to them: "All power in Heaven and on earth has been given to me. You, then, are to go and make disciples of all the nations and baptize them in the name of the Father and of the Son and of the Holy Spirit. Teach them to observe all that I have commanded you and, remember, I am with you always, even to the end of the world."

ported to the chief priests everything that had happened. After meeting with the elders and conferring together, the chief priests offered the soldiers a substantial bribe and told them to say, 'His disciples came by night and stole the body while we were asleep.' They added, 'If this should reach the Governor's ears, we will put matters right with him and see that you do not suffer.' So they took the money and did as they were told. This story became widely known, and is current in Jewish circles to this day.

The eleven disciples made their way to Galilee, to the mountain where Jesus had told them to meet him. When they saw him, they fell prostrate before him, though some were doubtful. Jesus then came up and spoke to them. He said: 'Full authority in heaven and on earth has been committed to me. Go forth therefore and make all nations my disciples; baptize men everywhere in the name of the Father and the Son and the Holy Spirit, and teach them to observe all that I have commanded you. And be assured, I am with you always, to the end of time.'

THE
GOSPEL ACCORDING TO
SAINT MARK

1 The beginning of the gospel of Jesus Christ, the Son of God; 2As it is written in the prophets, Behold, I send my messenger before thy face, which shall prepare thy way before thee. 3 The voice of one crying in the wilderness, Prepare ye the way of the Lord, make his paths straight. 4 John did baptize in the wilderness, and preach the baptism of repentance for the remission of sins. 5And there went out unto him all the land of Judea, and they of Jerusalem, and were all baptized of him in the river of Jordan, confessing their sins. 6And John was clothed with camel's hair, and with a girdle of a skin about his loins; and he did eat locusts and wild honey; 7And preached, saying, There cometh one mightier than I after me, the latchet of whose shoes I am not worthy to stoop down and unloose. 8 I indeed have baptized you with water: but he shall baptize you with the Holy Ghost. 9And it came to pass in those days, that Jesus came from Nazareth of Galilee, and was baptized of John in Jordan. 10And straightway coming up out of the water, he saw the heavens opened, and the Spirit like a dove descending upon him: 11And there came a voice from heaven, *saying,* Thou art my beloved Son, in whom I am well pleased. 12And immediately the Spirit driveth him into the wilderness. 13And he was there in the wilderness forty days tempted of Satan; and was with the wild beasts; and the angels ministered unto him. 14 Now after that John was put in prison, Jesus came into Galilee, preaching the gospel of the kingdom of God, 15And saying, The time is fulfilled, and the kingdom of God is at hand: repent ye, and believe the gospel. 16 Now as he walked by the sea of Galilee, he saw Simon and Andrew his brother casting a net into the sea: for they were fishers. 17And Jesus said unto them, Come ye after me, and I will make you to become fishers of men. 18And straightway they forsook their nets, and

THE
GOSPEL ACCORDING TO
MARK

1 The beginning of the gospel of Jesus Christ, the Son of God.[a]
2 As it is written in Isaiah the prophet,[b]
"Behold, I send my messenger before thy face,
who shall prepare thy way;
3 the voice of one crying in the wilderness:
Prepare the way of the Lord,
make his paths straight—"
4 John the baptizer appeared [c] in the wilderness, preaching a baptism of repentance for the forgiveness of sins. 5And there went out to him all the country of Judea, and all the people of Jerusalem; and they were baptized by him in the river Jordan, confessing their sins. 6 Now John was clothed with camel's hair, and had a leather girdle around his waist, and ate locusts and wild honey. 7And he preached, saying, "After me comes he who is mightier than I, the thong of whose sandals I am not worthy to stoop down and untie. 8 I have baptized you with water; but he will baptize you with the Holy Spirit."
9 In those days Jesus came from Nazareth of Galilee and was baptized by John in the Jordan. 10And when he came up out of the water, immediately he saw the heavens opened and the Spirit descending upon him like a dove; 11 and a voice came from heaven, "Thou art my beloved Son;[d] with thee I am well pleased."
12 The Spirit immediately drove him out into the wilderness. 13And he was in the wilderness forty days, tempted by Satan; and he was with the wild beasts; and the angels ministered to him.
14 Now after John was arrested, Jesus came into Galilee, preaching the gospel of God, 15 and saying, "The time is fulfilled, and the kingdom of God is at hand; repent, and believe in the gospel."
16 And passing along by the Sea of Galilee, he saw Simon and Andrew the brother of Simon casting a net in the sea; for they were fishermen. 17And Jesus said to them, "Follow me and I will make you become fishers of men." 18And immediately they left their nets and followed him.

[a] Other ancient authorities omit *the Son of God.*
[b] Other ancient authorities read *in the prophets.*
[c] Other ancient authorities read *John was baptizing.* [d] Or *my Son, my* (or *the*) *Beloved.*

THE
GOSPEL OF
MARK

The Gospel of Jesus Christ, the Son of God, begins with the fulfillment of this prophecy of Isaiah—

Behold, I send my messenger before thy face,
Who shall prepare thy way;
The voice of one crying in the wilderness,
Make ye ready the way of the Lord,
Make his paths straight.

For John came and began to baptize men in the desert, proclaiming baptism as the mark of a complete change of heart and of the forgiveness of sins. All the people of the Judaean countryside and everyone in Jerusalem went out to him in the desert and received his baptism in the river Jordan, publicly confessing their sins.

John himself was dressed in camel's hair, with a leather belt round his waist, and he lived on locusts and wild honey. The burden of his preaching was, "There is someone coming after me who is stronger than I—indeed I am not good enough to kneel down and undo his shoes. I have baptized you with water, but he will baptize you with the Holy Spirit."

The arrival of Jesus   1. 9

It was in those days that Jesus arrived from the Galilean village of Nazareth and was baptized by John in the Jordan. All at once, as he came up out of the water, he saw the heavens split open, and the Spirit coming down upon him like a dove. A voice came out of Heaven, saying, "You are my dearly loved Son, in whom I am well pleased!"

Then the Spirit sent him out at once into the desert, and there he remained for forty days while Satan tempted him. During this time no one was with him but wild animals, and only the angels were there to care for him.

Jesus begins to preach the gospel,   1. 14
and to call men to follow him

It was after John's arrest that Jesus came into Galilee, proclaiming the gospel of God, saying, "The time has come at last—the kingdom of God has arrived. You must change your hearts and minds and believe the good news."

As he walked along the shore of the Lake of Galilee, he saw two fishermen, Simon and his brother Andrew, casting their nets into the water.

"Come and follow me, and I will teach you to catch men!" he cried.

At once they dropped their nets, and followed him.

THE
GOSPEL ACCORDING TO
MARK

The Coming of Christ

1 Here begins the gospel of Jesus Christ the Son of God.[a]

In the prophet Isaiah it stands written: 'Here is my herald whom I send on ahead of you, and he will prepare your way. A voice crying aloud in the wilderness, "Prepare a way for the Lord; clear a straight path for him." ' And so it was that John the Baptist appeared in the wilderness proclaiming a baptism in token of repentance, for the forgiveness of sins; and they flocked to him from the whole Judaean country-side and the city of Jerusalem, and were baptized by him in the River Jordan, confessing their sins.

John was dressed in a rough coat of camel's hair, with a leather belt round his waist, and he fed on locusts and wild honey. His proclamation ran: 'After me comes one who is mightier than I. I am not fit to unfasten his shoes. I have baptized you with water; he will baptize you with the Holy Spirit.'

It happened at this time that Jesus came from Nazareth in Galilee and was baptized in the Jordan by John. At the moment when he came up out of the water, he saw the heavens torn open and the Spirit, like a dove, descending upon him. And a voice spoke from heaven: 'Thou art my Son, my Beloved;[b] on thee my favour rests.'

Thereupon the Spirit sent him away into the wilderness, and there he remained for forty days tempted by Satan. He was among the wild beasts; and the angels waited on him.

In Galilee: Success and Opposition

After John had been arrested, Jesus came into Galilee proclaiming the Gospel of God: 'The time has come; the kingdom of God is upon you; repent, and believe the Gospel.'

Jesus was walking by the shore of the Sea of Galilee when he saw Simon and his brother Andrew on the lake at work with a casting-net; for they were fishermen. Jesus said to them, 'Come with me, and I will make you fishers of men.' And at once they left their nets and followed him.

[a] Some witnesses omit the Son of God. [b] Or Thou art my only Son.

K.J.V.

followed him. 19And when he had gone a little further thence, he saw James the *son* of Zebedee, and John his brother, who also were in the ship mending their nets. 20And straightway he called them: and they left their father Zebedee in the ship with the hired servants, and went after him. 21And they went into Capernaum; and straightway on the sabbath day he entered into the synagogue, and taught. 22And they were astonished at his doctrine: for he taught them as one that had authority, and not as the scribes. 23And there was in their synagogue a man with an unclean spirit; and he cried out, 24 Saying, Let *us* alone; what have we to do with thee, thou Jesus of Nazareth? art thou come to destroy us? I know thee who thou art, the Holy One of God. 25And Jesus rebuked him, saying, Hold thy peace, and come out of him. 26And when the unclean spirit had torn him, and cried with a loud voice, he came out of him. 27And they were all amazed, insomuch that they questioned among themselves, saying, What thing is this? what new doctrine *is* this? for with authority commandeth he even the unclean spirits, and they do obey him. 28And immediately his fame spread abroad throughout all the region round about Galilee. 29And forthwith, when they were come out of the synagogue, they entered into the house of Simon and Andrew, with James and John. 30 But Simon's wife's mother lay sick of a fever; and anon they tell him of her. 31And he came and took her by the hand, and lifted her up; and immediately the fever left her, and she ministered unto them. 32And at even, when the sun did set, they brought unto him all that were diseased, and them that were possessed with devils. 33And all the city was gathered together at the door. 34And he healed many that were sick of divers diseases, and cast out many devils; and suffered not the devils to speak, because they knew him. 35And in the morning, rising up a great while before day, he went out, and departed into a solitary place, and there prayed. 36And Simon and they that were with him followed after him. 37And when they had found him, they said unto him, All *men* seek for thee. 38And he said unto them, Let us go into the next towns, that I may preach there also: for therefore came I forth. 39And he preached in their synagogues throughout all Galilee, and cast out devils. 40And there came a leper to him, beseeching him, and kneeling down to him, and saying unto him, If thou wilt, thou canst make me clean. 41And Jesus, moved with compassion, put forth *his* hand, and touched him, and saith unto him, I will; be thou clean. 42And as soon

R.S.V.

19And going on a little farther, he saw James the son of Zebedee and John his brother, who were in their boat mending the nets. 20And immediately he called them; and they left their father Zebedee in the boat with the hired servants, and followed him.

21 And they went into Capernaum; and immediately on the sabbath he entered the synagogue and taught. 22And they were astonished at his teaching, for he taught them as one who had authority, and not as the scribes. 23And immediately there was in their synagogue a man with an unclean spirit; 24 and he cried out, "What have you to do with us, Jesus of Nazareth? Have you come to destroy us? I know who you are, the Holy One of God." 25 But Jesus rebuked him, saying, "Be silent, and come out of him!" 26And the unclean spirit, convulsing him and crying with a loud voice, came out of him. 27And they were all amazed, so that they questioned among themselves, saying, "What is this? A new teaching! With authority he commands even the unclean spirits, and they obey him." 28And at once his fame spread everywhere throughout all the surrounding region of Galilee.

29 And immediately he[e] left the synagogue, and entered the house of Simon and Andrew, with James and John. 30 Now Simon's mother-in-law lay sick with a fever, and immediately they told him of her. 31And he came and took her by the hand and lifted her up, and the fever left her; and she served them.

32 That evening, at sundown, they brought to him all who were sick or possessed with demons. 33And the whole city was gathered together about the door. 34And he healed many who were sick with various diseases, and cast out many demons; and he would not permit the demons to speak, because they knew him.

35 And in the morning, a great while before day, he rose and went out to a lonely place, and there he prayed. 36And Simon and those who were with him followed him, 37and they found him and said to him, "Every one is searching for you." 38And he said to them, "Let us go on to the next towns, that I may preach there also; for that is why I came out." 39And he went throughout all Galilee, preaching in their synagogues and casting out demons.

40 And a leper came to him beseeching him, and kneeling said to him, "If you will, you can make me clean." 41 Moved with pity, he stretched out his hand and touched him, and said to him, "I will; be clean." 42And immediately the lep-

[e] Other ancient authorities read *they*.

PHILLIPS

N.E.B.

Then he went a little further along the shore and saw James the son of Zebedee, aboard a boat with his brother John, overhauling their nets. At once he called them, and they left their father Zebedee in the boat with the hired men, and went off after him.

Jesus begins healing the sick — 1. 21

They arrived at Capernaum, and on the Sabbath day Jesus walked straight into the synagogue and began teaching. They were amazed at his way of teaching, for he taught with the ring of authority—quite unlike the scribes. All at once, a man in the grip of an evil spirit appeared in the synagogue shouting out:
"What have you got to do with us, Jesus from Nazareth? Have you come to kill us? I know who you are—you're God's holy one!"
But Jesus cut him short and spoke sharply, "Hold your tongue and get out of him!"
At this the evil spirit convulsed the man, let out a loud scream and left him. Everyone present was so astounded that people kept saying to each other:
"What on earth has happened? This new teaching has authority behind it. Why, he even gives his orders to evil spirits and they obey him!"
And his reputation spread like wildfire through the whole Galilean district.
Then he got up and went straight from the synagogue to the house of Simon and Andrew, accompanied by James and John. Simon's mother-in-law was in bed with a high fever, and they lost no time in telling Jesus about her. He went up to her, took her hand and helped her to her feet. The fever left her, and she began to see to their needs.
Late that evening, after sunset, they kept bringing to him all who were sick or troubled by evil spirits. The whole population of the town gathered round the doorway. And he healed great numbers of people who were suffering from various forms of disease. In many cases he expelled evil spirits; but he would not allow them to say a word, for they knew perfectly well who he was.

He retires for private prayer — 1. 35

Then, in the early morning, while it was still dark, Jesus got up, left the house and went off to a deserted place, and there he prayed. Simon and his companions went in search of him, and when they found him, they said,
"Everyone is looking for you."
"Then we will go somewhere else, to the neighboring towns," he replied, "so that I may give my message there too—that is why I have come."
So he continued preaching in their synagogues and expelling evil spirits throughout the whole of Galilee.

Jesus cures leprosy — 1. 40

Then a leper came to Jesus, kneeled in front of him and appealed to him,
"If you want to, you can make me clean."
Jesus was filled with pity for him, and stretched out his hand and placed it on the leper, saying,
"Of course I want to—be clean!"
At once the leprosy left him and he was quite

When he had gone a little further he saw James son of Zebedee and his brother John, who were in the boat overhauling their nets. He called them; and, leaving their father Zebedee in the boat with the hired men, they went off to follow him.

They came to Capernaum, and on the Sabbath he went to synagogue and began to teach. The people were astounded at his teaching, for, unlike the doctors of the law, he taught with a note of authority. Now there was a man in the synagogue possessed by an unclean spirit. He shrieked: 'What do you want with us, Jesus of Nazareth? Have you[a] come to destroy us? I know who you are—the Holy One of God.' Jesus rebuked him: 'Be silent', he said, 'and come out of him.' And the unclean spirit threw the man into convulsions and with a loud cry left him. They were all dumbfounded and began to ask one another, 'What is this? A new kind of teaching! He speaks with authority. When he gives orders, even the unclean spirits submit.' The news spread rapidly, and he was soon spoken of all over the district of Galilee.
On leaving the synagogue they went straight to the house of Simon and Andrew; and James and John went with them. Simon's mother-in-law was ill in bed with fever. They told him about her at once. He came forward, took her by the hand, and helped her to her feet. The fever left her and she waited upon them.
That evening after sunset they brought to him all who were ill or possessed by devils; and the whole town was there, gathered at the door. He healed many who suffered from various diseases, and drove out many devils. He would not let the devils speak, because they knew who he was.
Very early next morning he got up and went out. He went away to a lonely spot and remained there in prayer. But Simon and his companions searched him out, found him, and said, 'They are all looking for you.' He answered, 'Let us move on to the country towns in the neighbourhood; I have to proclaim my message there also; that is what I came out to do.' So all through Galilee he went, preaching in the synagogues and casting out the devils.
Once he was approached by a leper, who knelt before him begging his help. 'If only you will,' said the man, 'you can cleanse me.' In warm indignation Jesus stretched out his hand,[b] touched him, and said, 'Indeed I will; be clean again.' The leprosy left him immediately, and he was

[a] *Or* You have. [b] *Some witnesses read* Jesus was sorry for him and stretched out his hand; *one witness has simply* He stretched out his hand.

K.J.V.

as he had spoken, immediately the leprosy departed from him, and he was cleansed. 43And he straitly charged him, and forthwith sent him away; 44And saith unto him, See thou say nothing to any man: but go thy way, shew thyself to the priest, and offer for thy cleansing those things which Moses commanded, for a testimony unto them. 45 But he went out, and began to publish *it* much, and to blaze abroad the matter, insomuch that Jesus could no more openly enter into the city, but was without in desert places: and they came to him from every quarter.

2 And again he entered into Capernaum after *some* days; and it was noised that he was in the house. 2And straightway many were gathered together, insomuch that there was no room to receive *them*, no, not so much as about the door: and he preached the word unto them. 3And they come unto him, bringing one sick of the palsy, which was borne of four. 4And when they could not come nigh unto him for the press, they uncovered the roof where he was: and when they had broken *it* up, they let down the bed wherein the sick of the palsy lay. 5 When Jesus saw their faith, he said unto the sick of the palsy, Son, thy sins be forgiven thee. 6 But there were certain of the scribes sitting there, and reasoning in their hearts, 7 Why doth this *man* thus speak blasphemies? who can forgive sins but God only? 8And immediately, when Jesus perceived in his spirit that they so reasoned within themselves, he said unto them, Why reason ye these things in your hearts? 9 Whether is it easier to say to the sick of the palsy, *Thy* sins be forgiven thee; or to say, Arise, and take up thy bed, and walk? 10 But that ye may know that the Son of man hath power on earth to forgive sins, (he saith to the sick of the palsy,) 11 I say unto thee, Arise, and take up thy bed, and go thy way into thine house. 12And immediately he arose, took up the bed, and went forth before them all; insomuch that they were all amazed, and glorified God, saying, We never saw it on this fashion. 13And he went forth again by the sea side; and all the multitude resorted unto him, and he taught them. 14And as he passed by, he saw Levi the *son* of Alpheus sitting at the receipt of custom, and said unto him, Follow me. And he arose and followed him. 15And it came to pass, that, as Jesus sat at meat in his house, many publicans and sinners sat also together with Jesus and his disciples: for there were many, and they followed him. 16And when the scribes and Pharisees saw him eat with publicans and sinners, they said unto his disciples, How is it that he eateth and drinketh with publicans and sinners? 17 When Jesus heard *it*, he saith unto them, They that are whole have no

R.S.V.

rosy left him, and he was made clean. 43And he sternly charged him, and sent him away at once, 44 and said to him, "See that you say nothing to any one; but go, show yourself to the priest, and offer for your cleansing what Moses commanded, for a proof to the people." [f] 45 But he went out and began to talk freely about it, and to spread the news, so that Jesus[g] could no longer openly enter a town, but was out in the country; and people came to him from every quarter.

2 And when he returned to Capernaum after some days, it was reported that he was at home. 2And many were gathered together, so that there was no longer room for them, not even about the door; and he was preaching the word to them. 3And they came, bringing to him a paralytic carried by four men. 4And when they could not get near him because of the crowd, they removed the roof above him; and when they had made an opening, they let down the pallet on which the paralytic lay. 5And when Jesus saw their faith, he said to the paralytic, "My son, your sins are forgiven." 6 Now some of the scribes were sitting there, questioning in their hearts. 7 "Why does this man speak thus? It is blasphemy! Who can forgive sins but God alone?" 8And immediately Jesus, perceiving in his spirit that they thus questioned within themselves, said to them, "Why do you question thus in your hearts? 9 Which is easier, to say to the paralytic, 'Your sins are forgiven,' or to say, 'Rise, take up your pallet and walk'? 10 But that you may know that the Son of man has authority on earth to forgive sins"—he said to the paralytic—11 "I say to you, rise, take up your pallet and go home." 12And he rose, and immediately took up the pallet and went out before them all; so that they were all amazed and glorified God, saying, "We never saw anything like this!"

13 He went out again beside the sea; and all the crowd gathered about him, and he taught them. 14And as he passed on, he saw Levi the son of Alpheus sitting at the tax office, and he said to him, "Follow me." And he rose and followed him.

15 And as he sat at table in his house, many tax collectors and sinners were sitting with Jesus and his disciples; for there were many who followed him. 16And the scribes of [h] the Pharisees, when they saw that he was eating with sinners and tax collectors, said to his disciples, "Why does he eat[i] with tax collectors and sinners?" 17And when Jesus heard it, he said to them, "Those who are well have no need of a physi-

[f] Greek *to them.* [g] Greek *he* [h] Other ancient authorities read *and.* [i] Other ancient authorities add *and drink.*

clean. Jesus sent him away there and then with the strict injunction:

"Mind you say nothing at all to anybody. Go straight off and show yourself to the priest, and make the offerings for your cleansing which Moses prescribed, as public proof of your recovery."

But he went off and began to talk a great deal about it in public, spreading his story far and wide. Consequently, it became impossible for Jesus to show his face in the towns and he had to stay outside in lonely places. Yet the people still came to him from all quarters.

Faith at Capernaum   *2. 1*

When he re-entered Capernaum some days later, a rumor spread that he was in somebody's house. Such a large crowd collected that while he was giving them his message it was impossible even to get near the doorway. Meanwhile, a group of people arrived to see him, bringing with them a paralytic whom four of them were carrying. And when they found it was impossible to get near him because of the crowd, they removed the tiles from the roof over Jesus' head and let down the paralytic's bed through the opening. And when Jesus saw their faith, he said to the man on the bed,

"My son, your sins are forgiven."

But some of the scribes were sitting there silently asking themselves:

"Why does this man talk such blasphemy? Who can possibly forgive sins but God?"

Jesus realized instantly what they were thinking, and said to them:

"Why must you argue like this in your minds? Which do you suppose is easier—to say to a paralyzed man, 'Your sins are forgiven,' or 'Get up, pick up your bed and walk'? But to prove to you that the Son of Man has full authority to forgive sins on earth, I say to you,"—and here he spoke to the paralytic—"Get up, pick up your bed and go home."

At once the man sprang to his feet, picked up his bed and walked off in full view of them all. Everyone was amazed, praised God and said,

"We have never seen anything like this before."

Then Jesus went out again by the lakeside and the whole crowd came to him, and he continued to teach them.

Jesus now calls "a sinner" to   *2. 14*
follow him

As Jesus went on his way, he saw Levi the son of Alphaeus sitting at his desk in the tax office, and he said to him,

"Follow me!"

Levi got up and followed him. Later, when Jesus was sitting at dinner in Levi's house, a large number of tax collectors and disreputable folk came in and joined him and his disciples. For there were many such people among his followers. When the scribes and Pharisees saw him eating in the company of tax collectors and outsiders, they remarked to his disciples,

"Why does he eat with tax collectors and sinners?"

When Jesus heard this, he said to them,

"It is not the fit and flourishing who need the

---

clean. Then he dismissed him with this stern warning: 'Be sure you say nothing to anybody. Go and show yourself to the priest, and make the offering laid down by Moses for your cleansing; that will certify the cure.' But the man went out and made the whole story public; he spread it far and wide, until Jesus could no longer show himself in any town, but stayed outside in the open country. Even so, people kept coming to him from all quarters.

2 When after some days he returned to Capernaum, the news went round that he was at home; and such a crowd collected that the space in front of the door was not big enough to hold them. And while he was proclaiming the message to them, a man was brought who was paralysed. Four men were carrying him, but because of the crowd they could not get him near. So they opened up the roof over the place where Jesus was, and when they had broken through they lowered the stretcher on which the paralysed man was lying. When Jesus saw their faith, he said to the paralysed man, 'My son, your sins are forgiven.'

Now there were some lawyers sitting there and they thought to themselves, 'Why does the fellow talk like that? This is blasphemy! Who but God alone can forgive sins?' Jesus knew in his own mind that this was what they were thinking, and said to them: 'Why do you harbour thoughts like these? Is it easier to say to this paralysed man, "Your sins are forgiven", or to say, "Stand up, take your bed, and walk"? But to convince you that the Son of Man has the right on earth to forgive sins'—he turned to the paralysed man —'I say to you, stand up, take your bed, and go home.' And he got up, took his stretcher at once, and went out in full view of them all, so that they were astounded and praised God. 'Never before', they said, 'have we seen the like.'

Once more he went away to the lake-side. All the crowd came to him, and he taught them there. As he went along, he saw Levi son of Alphaeus at his seat in the custom-house, and said to him, 'Follow me'; and Levi rose and followed him.

When Jesus was at table in his house, many bad characters—tax-gatherers and others—were seated with him and his disciples; for there were many who followed him. Some doctors of the law who were Pharisees noticed him eating in this bad company, and said to his disciples, 'He eats with tax-gatherers and sinners!' Jesus overheard and said to them, 'It is not the healthy that

K.J.V.

need of the physician, but they that are sick: I came not to call the righteous, but sinners to repentance. 18And the disciples of John and of the Pharisees used to fast: and they come and say unto him, Why do the disciples of John and of the Pharisees fast, but thy disciples fast not? 19And Jesus said unto them, Can the children of the bridechamber fast, while the bridegroom is with them? as long as they have the bridegroom with them, they cannot fast. 20 But the days will come, when the bridegroom shall be taken away from them, and then shall they fast in those days. 21 No man also seweth a piece of new cloth on an old garment; else the new piece that filled it up taketh away from the old, and the rent is made worse. 22And no man putteth new wine into old bottles; else the new wine doth burst the bottles, and the wine is spilled, and the bottles will be marred: but new wine must be put into new bottles. 23And it came to pass, that he went through the corn fields on the sabbath day; and his disciples began, as they went, to pluck the ears of corn. 24And the Pharisees said unto him, Behold, why do they on the sabbath day that which is not lawful? 25And he said unto them, Have ye never read what David did, when he had need, and was a hungered, he, and they that were with him? 26 How he went into the house of God in the days of Abiathar the high priest, and did eat the shewbread, which is not lawful to eat but for the priests, and gave also to them which were with him? 27And he said unto them, The sabbath was made for man, and not man for the sabbath: 28 Therefore the Son of man is Lord also of the sabbath.

R.S.V.

cian, but those who are sick; I came not to call the righteous, but sinners."
18 Now John's disciples and the Pharisees were fasting; and people came and said to him, "Why do John's disciples and the disciples of the Pharisees fast, but your disciples do not fast?" 19And Jesus said to them, "Can the wedding guests fast while the bridegroom is with them? As long as they have the bridegroom with them, they cannot fast. 20 The days will come, when the bridegroom is taken away from them, and then they will fast in that day. 21 No one sews a piece of unshrunk cloth on an old garment; if he does, the patch tears away from it, the new from the old, and a worse tear is made. 22And no one puts new wine into old wineskins; if he does, the wine will burst the skins, and the wine is lost, and so are the skins; but new wine is for fresh skins." *j*
23 One sabbath he was going through the grainfields; and as they made their way his disciples began to pluck ears of grain. 24And the Pharisees said to him, "Look, why are they doing what is not lawful on the sabbath?" 25And he said to them, "Have you never read what David did, when he was in need and was hungry, he and those who were with him: 26 how he entered the house of God, when Abiathar was high priest, and ate the bread of the Presence, which it is not lawful for any but the priests to eat, and also gave it to those who were with him?" 27And he said to them, "The sabbath was made for man, not man for the sabbath; 28 so the Son of man is lord even of the sabbath."

3 And he entered again into the synagogue; and there was a man there which had a withered hand. 2And they watched him, whether he would heal him on the sabbath day; that they might accuse him. 3And he saith unto the man which had the withered hand, Stand forth. 4And he saith unto them, Is it lawful to do good on the sabbath days, or to do evil? to save life, or to kill? But they held their peace. 5And when he had looked round about on them with anger, being grieved for the hardness of their hearts, he saith unto the man, Stretch forth thine hand. And he stretched *it* out: and his hand was restored whole as the other. 6And the Pharisees went forth, and straightway took counsel with the Herodians against him, how they might destroy him. 7 But Jesus withdrew himself with his disciples to the sea: and a great multitude from

3 Again he entered the synagogue, and a man was there who had a withered hand. 2And they watched him, to see whether he would heal him on the sabbath, so that they might accuse him. 3And he said to the man who had the withered hand, "Come here." 4And he said to them, "Is it lawful on the sabbath to do good or to do harm, to save life or to kill?" But they were silent. 5And he looked around at them with anger, grieved at their hardness of heart, and said to the man, "Stretch out your hand." He stretched it out, and his hand was restored. 6 The Pharisees went out, and immediately held counsel with the Herodians against him, how to destroy him.

7 Jesus withdrew with his disciples to the sea, and a great multitude from Galilee followed;

[*j*] Other ancient authorities omit *but new wine is for fresh skins.*

PHILLIPS

doctor, but those who are ill. I did not come to invite the 'righteous,' but the 'sinners.' "

The question of fasting   2. 18

The disciples of John and those of the Pharisees were fasting. They came and said to Jesus, "Why do those who follow John or the Pharisees keep fasts but your disciples do nothing of the kind?"

Jesus told them,

"Can you expect wedding guests to fast in the bridegroom's presence? Fasting is out of the question as long as they have the bridegroom with them. But the day will come when the bridegroom will be taken away from them—that will be the time for them to fast.

"Nobody," he continued, "sews a patch of unshrunken cloth onto an old coat. If he does, the new patch tears away from the old and the hole is worse than ever. And nobody puts new wine into old wineskins. If he does, the new wine bursts the skins, the wine is spilled and the skins are ruined. No, new wine must go into new wineskins."

Jesus rebukes the sabbatarians   2. 23

One day he happened to be going through the cornfields on the Sabbath day. And his disciples, as they made their way along, began to pick the ears of corn. The Pharisees said to him: "Look at that! Why should they do what is forbidden on the Sabbath day?"

Then he spoke to them.

"Have you never read what David did, when he and his companions were hungry? Haven't you read how he went into the house of God when Abiathar was High Priest, and ate the presentation loaves, which nobody is allowed to eat, except the priests—and gave some of the bread to his companions? The Sabbath," he continued, "was made for man's sake; man was not made for the sake of the Sabbath. That is why the Son of Man is master even of the Sabbath."

On another occasion when he went into the synagogue, there was a man there whose hand was shriveled, and they were watching Jesus closely to see whether he would heal him on the Sabbath day, so that they might bring a charge against him. Jesus said to the man with the shriveled hand,

"Stand up and come out here in front!"

Then he said to them,

"Is it right to do good on the Sabbath day, or to do harm? Is it right to save life or to kill?"

There was a dead silence. Then Jesus, deeply hurt as he sensed their inhumanity, looked round in anger at the faces surrounding him, and said to the man,

"Stretch out your hand!"

And he stretched it out, and the hand was restored as sound as the other one. The Pharisees walked straight out and discussed with Herod's party how they could have Jesus put out of the way.

Jesus' enormous popularity   3. 7

Jesus now retired to the lakeside with his disciples. A huge crowd of people followed him,

N.E.B.

need a doctor, but the sick; I did not come to invite virtuous people, but sinners.'

Once, when John's disciples and the Pharisees were keeping a fast, some people came to him and said, 'Why is it that John's disciples and the disciples of the Pharisees are fasting, but yours are not?' Jesus said to them, 'Can you expect the bridegroom's friends to fast while the bridegroom is with them? As long as they have the bridegroom with them, there can be no fasting. But the time will come when the bridegroom will be taken away from them, and on that day they will fast.

'No one sews a patch of unshrunk cloth on to an old coat; if he does, the patch tears away from it, the new from the old, and leaves a bigger hole. No one puts new wine into old wineskins; if he does, the wine will burst the skins, and then wine and skins are both lost. Fresh skins for new wine!'

One Sabbath he was going through the cornfields; and his disciples, as they went, began to pluck ears of corn. The Pharisees said to him, 'Look, why are they doing what is forbidden on the Sabbath?' He answered, 'Have you never read what David did when he and his men were hungry and had nothing to eat? He went into the House of God, in the time of Abiathar the High Priest, and ate the consecrated loaves, though no one but a priest is allowed to eat them, and even gave them to his men.'

He also said to them, 'The Sabbath was made for the sake of man and not man for the Sabbath: therefore the Son of Man is sovereign even over the Sabbath.'

3 On another occasion when he went to synagogue, there was a man in the congregation who had a withered arm; and they were watching to see whether Jesus would cure him on the Sabbath, so that they could bring a charge against him. He said to the man with the withered arm, 'Come and stand out here.' Then he turned to them: 'Is it permitted to do good or to do evil on the Sabbath, to save life or to kill?' They had nothing to say; and, looking round at them with anger and sorrow at their obstinate stupidity, he said to the man, 'Stretch out your arm.' He stretched it out and his arm was restored. But the Pharisees, on leaving the synagogue, began plotting against him with the partisans of Herod to see how they could make away with him.

Jesus went away to the lake-side with his disciples. Great numbers from Galilee, Judaea and

K.J.V.

Galilee followed him, and from Judea, 8And from Jerusalem, and from Idumea, and *from* beyond Jordan; and they about Tyre and Sidon, a great multitude, when they had heard what great things he did, came unto him. 9And he spake to his disciples, that a small ship should wait on him because of the multitude, lest they should throng him. 10 For he had healed many; insomuch that they pressed upon him for to touch him, as many as had plagues. 11And unclean spirits, when they saw him, fell down before him, and cried, saying, Thou art the Son of God. 12And he straitly charged them that they should not make him known. 13And he goeth up into a mountain, and called *unto him* whom he would: and they came unto him. 14And he ordained twelve, that they should be with him, and that he might send them forth to preach, 15And to have power to heal sicknesses, and to cast out devils: 16And Simon he surnamed Peter; 17And James the *son* of Zebedee, and John the brother of James; and he surnamed them Boanerges, which is, The sons of thunder: 18And Andrew, and Philip, and Bartholomew, and Matthew, and Thomas, and James the *son* of Alpheus, and Thaddeus, and Simon the Canaanite, 19And Judas Iscariot, which also betrayed him: and they went into a house. 20And the multitude cometh together again, so that they could not so much as eat bread. 21And when his friends heard *of it,* they went out to lay hold on him: for they said, He is beside himself.

22 And the scribes which came down from Jerusalem said, He hath Beelzebub, and by the prince of the devils casteth he out devils. 23And he called them *unto him,* and said unto them in parables, How can Satan cast out Satan? 24And if a kingdom be divided against itself, that kingdom cannot stand. 25And if a house be divided against itself, that house cannot stand. 26And if Satan rise up against himself, and be divided, he cannot stand, but hath an end. 27 No man can enter into a strong man's house, and spoil his goods, except he will first bind the strong man; and then he will spoil his house. 28 Verily I say unto you, All sins shall be forgiven unto the sons of men, and blasphemies wherewith soever they shall blaspheme: 29 But he that shall blaspheme against the Holy Ghost hath never forgiveness, but is in danger of eternal damnation: 30 Because they said, He hath an unclean spirit.

31 There came then his brethren and his mother, and, standing without, sent unto him, calling him. 32And the multitude sat about him,

R.S.V.

also from Judea 8 and Jerusalem and Idumea and from beyond the Jordan and from about Tyre and Sidon a great multitude, hearing all that he did, came to him. 9And he told his disciples to have a boat ready for him because of the crowd, lest they should crush him; 10 for he had healed many, so that all who had diseases pressed upon him to touch him. 11And whenever the unclean spirits beheld him, they fell down before him and cried out, "You are the Son of God." 12And he strictly ordered them not to make him known.

13 And he went up into the hills, and called to him those whom he desired; and they came to him. 14And he appointed twelve,[k] to be with him, and to be sent out to preach 15 and have authority to cast out demons: 16 Simon whom he surnamed Peter; 17 James the son of Zebedee and John the brother of James, whom he surnamed Boanerges, that is, sons of thunder; 18Andrew, and Philip, and Bartholomew, and Matthew, and Thomas, and James the son of Alphaeus, and Thaddaeus, and Simon the Cananaean, 19 and Judas Iscariot, who betrayed him.

Then he went home; 20 and the crowd came together again, so that they could not even eat. 21And when his friends heard it, they went out to seize him, for they said, "He is beside himself." 22And the scribes who came down from Jerusalem said, "He is possessed by Beelzebul, and by the prince of demons he casts out the demons." 23And he called them to him, and said to them in parables, "How can Satan cast out Satan? 24 If a kingdom is divided against itself, that kingdom cannot stand. 25And if a house is divided against itself, that house will not be able to stand. 26And if Satan has risen up against himself and is divided, he cannot stand, but is coming to an end. 27 But no one can enter a strong man's house and plunder his goods, unless he first binds the strong man; then indeed he may plunder his house.

28 "Truly, I say to you, all sins will be forgiven the sons of men, and whatever blasphemies they utter; 29 but whoever blasphemes against the Holy Spirit never has forgiveness, but is guilty of an eternal sin"—30 for they had said, "He has an unclean spirit."

31 And his mother and his brothers came; and standing outside they sent to him and called him. 32And a crowd was sitting about him; and

[k] Other ancient authorities add *whom also he named apostles.*

not only from Galilee, but from Judaea, Jerusalem and Idumaea, some from the district beyond the Jordan and from the neighborhood of Tyre and Sidon. This vast crowd came to him because they had heard about the sort of thing he was doing. So Jesus told his disciples to have a small boat kept in readiness for him, in case the people should crowd him too closely. For he healed so many people that all those who were in pain kept pressing forward to touch him with their hands. Evil spirits, as soon as they saw him, acknowledged his authority and screamed,

"You are the Son of God!"

But he warned them repeatedly that they must not make him known.

Jesus chooses the twelve apostles   3. 13

Later he went up onto the hillside and summoned the men whom he wanted, and they went up to him. He appointed a band of twelve to be his companions, whom he could send out to preach, with power to drive out evil spirits. These were the twelve he appointed:

Peter (which was the new name he gave Simon), James the son of Zebedee, and John his brother. (He gave them the name of Boanerges, which means the "Thunderers.") Andrew, Philip, Bartholomew, Matthew, Thomas, James the son of Alphaeus, Thaddaeus, Simon the patriot, and Judas Iscariot, who betrayed him.

Jesus exposes an absurd accusation   3. 20

Then he went indoors, but again such a crowd collected that it was impossible for them even to eat a meal. When his relatives heard of this, they set out to take charge of him, for people were saying, "He must be mad!"

The scribes who had come down from Jerusalem were saying that he was possessed by Beelzebub, and that he drove out devils because he was in league with the prince of devils. So Jesus called them to him and spoke to them in a parable—

"How can Satan be the one who drives out Satan? If a kingdom is divided against itself, then that kingdom cannot last, and if a household is divided against itself, it cannot last either. And if Satan leads a rebellion against Satan—his days are certainly numbered. No one can break into a strong man's house and steal his property, without first tying up the strong man hand and foot. But if he did that, he could ransack the whole house.

"Believe me, all men's sins can be forgiven and all their blasphemies. But there can never be any forgiveness for blasphemy against the Holy Spirit. That is an eternal sin."

He said this because they were saying, "He is in the power of an evil spirit."

The new relationships in the kingdom   3. 31

Then his mother and his brothers arrived. They stood outside the house and sent a message asking him to come out to them. There was a crowd

Jerusalem, Idumaea and Transjordan, and the neighbourhood of Tyre and Sidon, heard what he was doing and came to see him. So he told his disciples to have a boat ready for him, to save him from being crushed by the crowd. For he cured so many that sick people of all kinds came crowding in upon him to touch him. The unclean spirits too, when they saw him, would fall at his feet and cry aloud, 'You are the Son of God'; but he insisted that they should not make him known.

He then went up into the hill-country and called the men he wanted; and they went and joined him. He appointed twelve as his companions, whom he would send out to proclaim the Gospel, with a commission to drive out devils. So he appointed the Twelve: to Simon he gave the name Peter; then came the sons of Zebedee, James and his brother John, to whom he gave the name Boanerges, Sons of Thunder; then Andrew and Philip and Bartholomew and Matthew and Thomas and James the son of Alphaeus and Thaddaeus and Simon, a member of the Zealot party, and Judas Iscariot, the man who betrayed him.

He entered a house; and once more such a crowd collected round them that they had no chance to eat. When his family heard of this, they set out to take charge of him; for people were saying that he was out of his mind.[a]

The doctors of the law, too, who had come down from Jerusalem, said, 'He is possessed by Beelzebub', and, 'He drives out devils by the prince of devils.' So he called them to come forward, and spoke to them in parables: 'How can Satan drive out Satan? If a kingdom is divided against itself, that kingdom cannot stand; if a household is divided against itself, that house will never stand; and if Satan is in rebellion against himself, he is divided and cannot stand; and that is the end of him.

'On the other hand, no one can break into a strong man's house and make off with his goods unless he has first tied the strong man up; then he can ransack the house.

'I tell you this: no sin, no slander, is beyond forgiveness for men; but whoever slanders the Holy Spirit can never be forgiven; he is guilty of eternal sin.' He said this because they had declared that he was possessed by an unclean spirit.

Then his mother and his brothers arrived, and remaining outside sent in a message asking him to come out to them. A crowd was sitting round

[a] Or of him. 'He is out of his mind', they said.

K.J.V.

and they said unto him, Behold, thy mother and thy brethren without seek for thee. 33And he answered them, saying, Who is my mother, or my brethren? 34And he looked round about on them which sat about him, and said, Behold my mother and my brethren! 35 For whosoever shall do the will of God, the same is my brother, and my sister, and mother.

4 And he began again to teach by the sea side: and there was gathered unto him a great multitude, so that he entered into a ship, and sat in the sea; and the whole multitude was by the sea on the land. 2And he taught them many things by parables, and said unto them in his doctrine, 3 Hearken; Behold, there went out a sower to sow: 4And it came to pass, as he sowed, some fell by the way side, and the fowls of the air came and devoured it up. 5And some fell on stony ground, where it had not much earth; and immediately it sprang up, because it had no depth of earth: 6 But when the sun was up, it was scorched; and because it had no root, it withered away. 7And some fell among thorns, and the thorns grew up, and choked it, and it yielded no fruit. 8And other fell on good ground, and did yield fruit that sprang up and increased, and brought forth, some thirty, and some sixty, and some a hundred. 9And he said unto them, He that hath ears to hear, let him hear. 10And when he was alone, they that were about him with the twelve asked of him the parable. 11And he said unto them, Unto you it is given to know the mystery of the kingdom of God: but unto them that are without, all *these* things are done in parables: 12 That seeing they may see, and not perceive; and hearing they may hear, and not understand; lest at any time they should be converted, and *their* sins should be forgiven them. 13And he said unto them, Know ye not this parable? and how then will ye know all parables?

14 The sower soweth the word. 15And these are they by the way side, where the word is sown; but when they have heard, Satan cometh immediately, and taketh away the word that was sown in their hearts. 16And these are they likewise which are sown on stony ground; who, when they have heard the word, immediately receive it with gladness; 17And have no root in themselves, and so endure but for a time: afterward, when affliction or persecution ariseth for the word's sake, immediately they are offended. 18And these are they which are sown among thorns; such as hear the word, 19And the cares of this world, and the deceitfulness of riches, and the lusts of other things entering in, choke the word, and it becometh unfruitful. 20And these are they which are sown on good ground; such as hear the word, and receive *it,* and bring forth fruit, some thirtyfold, some sixty, and some a hundred.

R.S.V.

they said to him, "Your mother and your brothers[l] are outside, asking for you." 33And he replied, "Who are my mother and my brothers?" 34And looking around on those who sat about him, he said, "Here are my mother and my brothers! 35 Whoever does the will of God is my brother, and sister, and mother."

4 Again he began to teach beside the sea. And a very large crowd gathered about him, so that he got into a boat and sat in it on the sea; and the whole crowd was beside the sea on the land. 2And he taught them many things in parables, and in his teaching he said to them: 3 "Listen! A sower went out to sow. 4And as he sowed, some seed fell along the path, and the birds came and devoured it. 5 Other seed fell on rocky ground, where it had not much soil, and immediately it sprang up, since it had no depth of soil; 6 and when the sun rose it was scorched, and since it had no root it withered away. 7 Other seed fell among thorns and the thorns grew up and choked it, and it yielded no grain. 8And other seeds fell into good soil and brought forth grain, growing up and increasing and yielding thirtyfold and sixtyfold and a hundredfold." 9And he said, "He who has ears to hear, let him hear."

10 And when he was alone, those who were about him with the twelve asked him concerning the parables. 11And he said to them, "To you has been given the secret of the kingdom of God, but for those outside everything is in parables; 12 so that they may indeed see but not perceive, and may indeed hear but not understand; lest they should turn again, and be forgiven." 13And he said to them, "Do you not understand this parable? How then will you understand all the parables? 14 The sower sows the word. 15And these are the ones along the path, where the word is sown; when they hear, Satan immediately comes and takes away the word which is sown in them. 16And these in like manner are the ones sown upon rocky ground, who, when they hear the word, immediately receive it with joy; 17 and they have no root in themselves, but endure for a while; then, when tribulation or persecution arises on account of the word, immediately they fall away.[m] 18And others are the ones sown among thorns; they are those who hear the word, 19 but the cares of the world, and the delight in riches, and the desire for other things, enter in and choke the word, and it proves unfruitful. 20 But those that were sown upon the good soil are the ones who hear the word and accept it and bear fruit, thirtyfold and sixtyfold and a hundredfold."

PHILLIPS	N.E.B.

sitting round him when the message was brought telling him, "Your mother and your brothers are outside looking for you."

Jesus replied, "And who are really my mother and my brothers?"

And he looked round at the faces of those sitting in a circle about him.

"Look!" he said, "my mother and my brothers are here. Anyone who does the will of God is brother and sister and mother to me."

The story of the sower   4. 1

Then once again he began to teach them by the lakeside. A bigger crowd than ever collected around him so that he got into the little boat on the lake and sat down, while the crowd covered the ground right up to the water's edge. He taught them a great deal in parables, and in the course of his teaching he said:

"Listen! A man once went out to sow his seed and as he sowed, some seed fell by the roadside and the birds came and gobbled it up. Some of the seed fell among the rocks where there was not much soil, and sprang up very quickly because there was no depth of earth. But when the sun rose it was scorched, and because it had no root, it withered away. And some of the seed fell among thornbushes and the thorns grew up and choked the life out of it, and it bore no crop. And there was some seed which fell on good soil and when it grew, produced a crop which yielded thirty or sixty or even a hundred times as much as the seed."

Then he added,

"Every man who has ears should use them!"

Then when they were by themselves, his close followers and the twelve asked him about the parables, and he told them:

"The secret of the kingdom of God has been given to you. But to those who do not know the secret, everything remains in parables, so that,

seeing they may see, and not perceive;
and hearing they may hear, and not understand;
lest haply they should turn again, and it should be forgiven them."

Then he continued:

"Do you really not understand this parable? Then how are you going to understand all the other parables? The man who sows, sows the message. As for those who are by the roadside where the message is sown, as soon as they hear it Satan comes at once and takes away what has been sown in their minds. Similarly, the seed sown among the rocks represents those who hear the message without hesitation and accept it joyfully. But they have no real roots and do not last —when trouble or persecution arises because of the message, they give up their faith at once. Then there are the seeds which were sown among thornbushes. These are the people who hear the message, but the worries of this world and the false glamour of riches and all sorts of other ambitions creep in and choke the life out of what they have heard, and it produces no crop in their lives. As for the seed sown on good soil, this means the men who hear the message and accept it and do produce a crop—thirty, sixty, even a hundred times as much as they received."

and word was brought to him: 'Your mother and your brothers are outside asking for you.' He replied, 'Who is my mother? Who are my brothers?' And looking round at those who were sitting in the circle about him he said, 'Here are my mother and my brothers. Whoever does the will of God is my brother, my sister, my mother.'

4 On another occasion he began to teach by the lake-side. The crowd that gathered round him was so large that he had to get into a boat on the lake, and there he sat, with the whole crowd on the beach right down to the water's edge. And he taught them many things by parables.

As he taught he said:

'Listen! A sower went out to sow. And it happened that as he sowed, some seed fell along the footpath; and the birds came and ate it up. Some seed fell on rocky ground, where it had little soil, and it sprouted quickly because it had no depth of earth; but when the sun rose the young corn was scorched, and as it had no proper root it withered away. Some seed fell among thistles; but the thistles shot up and choked the corn, and it yielded no crop. And some of the seed fell into good soil, where it came up and grew, and bore fruit; and the yield was thirtyfold, sixtyfold, even a hundredfold.' He added, 'If you have ears to hear, then hear.'

When he was alone, the Twelve and others who were round him questioned him about the parables. He replied, 'To you the secret of the kingdom of God has been given; but to those who are outside everything comes by way of parables, so that (as Scripture says) they may look and look, but see nothing; they may hear and hear, but understand nothing; otherwise they might turn to God and be forgiven.'

So he said, 'You do not understand this parable? How then are you to understand any parable? The sower sows the word. Those along the footpath are people in whom the word is sown, but no sooner have they heard it than Satan comes and carries off the word which has been sown in them. It is the same with those who receive the seed on rocky ground; as soon as they hear the word, they accept it with joy, but it strikes no root in them; they have no staying-power; then, when there is trouble or persecution on account of the word, they fall away at once. Others again receive the seed among thistles; they hear the word, but worldly cares and the false glamour of wealth and all kinds of evil desire come in and choke the word, and it proves barren. And there are those who receive the seed in good soil; they hear the word and welcome it; and they bear fruit thirtyfold, sixtyfold, or a hundredfold.'

K.J.V.

21 And he said unto them, Is a candle brought to be put under a bushel, or under a bed? and not to be set on a candlestick? 22 For there is nothing hid, which shall not be manifested; neither was any thing kept secret, but that it should come abroad. 23 If any man have ears to hear, let him hear. 24And he said unto them, Take heed what ye hear. With what measure ye mete, it shall be measured to you; and unto you that hear shall more be given. 25 For he that hath, to him shall be given; and he that hath not, from him shall be taken even that which he hath.

26 And he said, So is the kingdom of God, as if a man should cast seed into the ground; 27And should sleep, and rise night and day, and the seed should spring and grow up, he knoweth not how. 28 For the earth bringeth forth fruit of herself; first the blade, then the ear, after that the full corn in the ear. 29 But when the fruit is brought forth, immediately he putteth in the sickle, because the harvest is come.

30 And he said, Whereunto shall we liken the kingdom of God? or with what comparison shall we compare it? 31 *It is* like a grain of mustard seed, which, when it is sown in the earth, is less than all the seeds that be in the earth: 32 But when it is sown, it groweth up, and becometh greater than all herbs, and shooteth out great branches; so that the fowls of the air may lodge under the shadow of it. 33 And with many such parables spake he the word unto them, as they were able to hear *it*. 34 But without a parable spake he not unto them: and when they were alone, he expounded all things to his disciples. 35And the same day, when the even was come, he saith unto them, Let us pass over unto the other side. 36And when they had sent away the multitude, they took him even as he was in the ship. And there were also with him other little ships. 37And there arose a great storm of wind, and the waves beat into the ship, so that it was now full. 38And he was in the hinder part of the ship, asleep on a pillow: and they awake him, and say unto him, Master, carest thou not that we perish? 39And he arose, and rebuked the wind, and said unto the sea, Peace, be still. And the wind ceased, and there was a great calm. 40And he said unto them, Why are ye so fearful? how is it that ye have no faith? 41And they feared exceedingly, and said one to another, What manner of man is this, that even the wind and the sea obey him?

R.S.V.

21 And he said to them, "Is a lamp brought in to be put under a bushel, or under a bed, and not on a stand? 22 For there is nothing hid, except to be made manifest; nor is anything secret, except to come to light. 23 If any man has ears to hear, let him hear." 24And he said to them, "Take heed what you hear; the measure you give will be the measure you get, and still more will be given you. 25 For to him who has will more be given; and from him who has not, even what he has will be taken away."

26 And he said, "The kingdom of God is as if a man should scatter seed upon the ground, 27 and should sleep and rise night and day, and the seed should sprout and grow, he knows not how. 28 The earth produces of itself, first the blade, then the ear, then the full grain in the ear. 29 But when the grain is ripe, at once he puts in the sickle, because the harvest has come."

30 And he said, "With what can we compare the kingdom of God, or what parable shall we use for it? 31 It is like a grain of mustard seed, which, when sown upon the ground, is the smallest of all the seeds on earth; 32 yet when it is sown it grows up and becomes the greatest of all shrubs, and puts forth large branches, so that the birds of the air can make nests in its shade."

33 With many such parables he spoke the word to them, as they were able to hear it; 34 he did not speak to them without a parable, but privately to his own disciples he explained everything.

35 On that day, when evening had come, he said to them, "Let us go across to the other side." 36And leaving the crowd, they took him with them, just as he was, in the boat. And other boats were with him. 37And a great storm of wind arose, and the waves beat into the boat, so that the boat was already filling. 38 But he was in the stern, asleep on the cushion; and they woke him and said to him, "Teacher, do you not care if we perish?" 39And he awoke and rebuked the wind, and said to the sea, "Peace! Be still!" And the wind ceased, and there was a great calm. 40 He said to them, "Why are you afraid? Have you no faith?" 41And they were filled with awe, and said to one another, "Who then is this, that even wind and sea obey him?"

PHILLIPS

Truth is meant to be used   *4. 21*

Then he said to them:
"Is a lamp brought into the room to be put under a bucket or underneath the bed? Surely its place is on the lampstand! There is nothing hidden which is not meant to be made perfectly plain one day, and there are no secrets which are not meant one day to be common knowledge. If a man has ears he should use them!
"Be careful how you listen," he said to them. "Whatever measure you use will be used toward you, and even more than that. For the man who has something will receive more. As for the man who has nothing, even his nothing will be taken away."

Jesus gives pictures of the   *4. 26*
kingdom's growth

Then he said:
"The kingdom of God is like a man scattering seed on the ground and then going to bed each night and getting up every morning, while the seed sprouts and grows up, though he has no idea how it happens. The earth produces a crop without any help from anyone: first a blade, then the ear of corn, then the full-grown grain in the ear. And as soon as the crop is ready, he sends his reapers in without delay, for the harvest-time has come."
Then he continued:
"What can we say the kingdom of God is like? How shall we put it in a parable? It is like a tiny grain of mustard seed which, when it is sown, is smaller than any seed that is ever sown. But after it is sown in the earth, it grows up and becomes bigger than any other plant. It shoots out great branches so that birds can come and nest in its shelter."
So he taught them his message with many parables such as their minds could take in. He did not speak to them at all without using parables, although in private he explained everything to his disciples.

Jesus shows himself master of   *4. 35*
natural forces

On the evening of that day, he said to them, "Let us cross over to the other side of the lake."
So they sent the crowd home and took him with them in the little boat in which he had been sitting, accompanied by other small craft. Then came a violent squall of wind which drove the waves aboard the boat until it was almost swamped. Jesus was in the stern asleep on the cushion. They awoke him with the words,
"Master, don't you care that we're drowning?"
And he woke up, rebuked the wind, and said to the waves,
"Hush now! Be still!"
The wind dropped and everything was very still.
"Why are you so frightened? What has happened to your faith?" he asked them.
But sheer awe swept over them, and they kept saying to one another,
"Who ever can he be?—even the wind and the waves do what he tells them!"

N.E.B.

He said to them, 'Do you bring in the lamp to put it under the meal-tub, or under the bed? Surely it is brought to be set on the lampstand? For nothing is hidden unless it is to be disclosed, and nothing put under cover unless it is to come into the open. If you have ears to hear, then hear.'
He also said, 'Take note of what you hear; the measure you give is the measure you will receive, with something more besides. For the man who has will be given more, and the man who has not will forfeit even what he has.'
He said, 'The kingdom of God is like this. A man scatters seed on the land; he goes to bed at night and gets up in the morning, and the seed sprouts and grows—how, he does not know. The ground produces a crop by itself, first the blade, then the ear, then full-grown corn in the ear; but as soon as the crop is ripe, he sets to work with the sickle, because harvest-time has come.'
He said also, 'How shall we picture the kingdom of God, or by what parable shall we describe it? It is like the mustard-seed, which is smaller than any seed in the ground at its sowing. But once sown, it springs up and grows taller than any other plant, and forms branches so large that the birds can settle in its shade.'
With many such parables he would give them his message, so far as they were able to receive it. He never spoke to them except in parables; but privately to his disciples he explained everything.

Miracles of Christ

That day, in the evening, he said to them, 'Let us cross over to the other side of the lake.' So they left the crowd and took him with them in the boat where he had been sitting; and there were other boats accompanying him. A heavy squall came on and the waves broke over the boat until it was all but swamped. Now he was in the stern asleep on a cushion; they roused him and said, 'Master, we are sinking! Do you not care?' He stood up, rebuked the wind, and said to the sea, 'Hush! Be still!' The wind dropped and there was a dead calm. He said to them, 'Why are you such cowards? Have you no faith even now?' They were awestruck and said to one another, 'Who can this be whom even the wind and the sea obey?'

5 And they came over unto the other side of the sea, into the country of the Gadarenes. 2And when he was come out of the ship, immediately there met him out of the tombs a man with an unclean spirit, 3 Who had *his* dwelling among the tombs; and no man could bind him, no, not with chains: 4 Because that he had been often bound with fetters and chains, and the chains had been plucked asunder by him, and the fetters broken in pieces: neither could any *man* tame him. 5And always, night and day, he was in the mountains, and in the tombs, crying, and cutting himself with stones. 6 But when he saw Jesus afar off, he ran and worshipped him, 7And cried with a loud voice, and said, What have I to do with thee, Jesus, *thou* Son of the most high God? I adjure thee by God, that thou torment me not. 8 (For he said unto him, Come out of the man, *thou* unclean spirit.) 9And he asked him, What *is* thy name? And he answered, saying, My name *is* Legion: for we are many. 10And he besought him much that he would not send them away out of the country. 11 Now there was there nigh unto the mountains a great herd of swine feeding. 12And all the devils besought him, saying, Send us into the swine, that we may enter into them. 13And forthwith Jesus gave them leave. And the unclean spirits went out, and entered into the swine; and the herd ran violently down a steep place into the sea, (they were about two thousand,) and were choked in the sea. 14And they that fed the swine fled, and told *it* in the city, and in the country. And they went out to see what it was that was done. 15And they come to Jesus, and see him that was possessed with the devil, and had the legion, sitting, and clothed, and in his right mind; and they were afraid. 16And they that saw *it* told them how it befell to him that was possessed with the devil, and *also* concerning the swine. 17And they began to pray him to depart out of their coasts. 18And when he was come into the ship, he that had been possessed with the devil prayed him that he might be with him. 19 Howbeit Jesus suffered him not, but saith unto him, Go home to thy friends, and tell them how great things the Lord hath done for thee, and hath had compassion on thee. 20And he departed, and began to publish in Decapolis how great things Jesus had done for him: and all *men* did marvel. 21And when Jesus was passed over again by ship unto the other side, much people gathered unto him; and he was nigh unto the sea. 22And, behold, there cometh one of the rulers of the synagogue, Jairus by name; and when he saw him, he fell at his feet, 23And besought him greatly, saying, My little daughter lieth at the point of death: *I pray thee,* come and lay thy hands on her, that she may be healed; and she shall live. 24And *Jesus* went with him; and much people followed him, and thronged him. 25And a certain woman, which had an issue of blood twelve years, 26And had suffered many things of many physicians, and had spent all that she had, and was nothing bet-

5 They came to the other side of the sea, to the country of the Gerasenes.[n] 2And when he had come out of the boat, there met him out of the tombs a man with an unclean spirit, 3 who lived among the tombs; and no one could bind him any more, even with a chain; 4 for he had often been bound with fetters and chains, but the chains he wrenched apart, and the fetters he broke in pieces; and no one had the strength to subdue him. 5 Night and day among the tombs and on the mountains he was always crying out, and bruising himself with stones. 6And when he saw Jesus from afar, he ran and worshiped him; 7 and crying out with a loud voice, he said, "What have you to do with me, Jesus, Son of the Most High God? I adjure you by God, do not torment me." 8 For he had said to him, "Come out of the man, you unclean spirit!" 9And Jesus[o] asked him, "What is your name?" He replied, "My name is Legion; for we are many." 10And he begged him eagerly not to send them out of the country. 11 Now a great herd of swine was feeding there on the hillside; 12 and they begged him, "Send us to the swine, let us enter them." 13 So he gave them leave. And the unclean spirits came out, and entered the swine; and the herd, numbering about two thousand, rushed down the steep bank into the sea, and were drowned in the sea.

14 The herdsmen fled, and told it in the city and in the country. And people came to see what it was that had happened. 15And they came to Jesus, and saw the demoniac sitting there, clothed and in his right mind, the man who had had the legion; and they were afraid. 16And those who had seen it told what had happened to the demoniac and to the swine. 17And they began to beg Jesus[p] to depart from their neighborhood. 18And as he was getting into the boat, the man who had been possessed with demons begged him that he might be with him. 19 But he refused, and said to him, "Go home to your friends, and tell them how much the Lord has done for you, and how he has had mercy on you." 20And he went away and began to proclaim in the Decapolis how much Jesus had done for him; and all men marveled.

21 And when Jesus had crossed again in the boat to the other side, a great crowd gathered about him; and he was beside the sea. 22 Then came one of the rulers of the synagogue, Jairus by name; and seeing him, he fell at his feet, 23 and besought him, saying, "My little daughter is at the point of death. Come and lay your hands on her, so that she may be made well, and live." 24And he went with him.

And a great crowd followed him and thronged about him. 25And there was a woman who had had a flow of blood for twelve years, 26 and who had suffered much under many physicians, and had spent all that she had, and was no better

Jesus meets a violent lunatic   **5. 1**

So they arrived on the other side of the lake in the country of the Gerasenes. As Jesus was getting out of the boat, a man in the grip of an evil spirit rushed out to meet him from among the tombs where he was living. It was no longer possible for any human being to restrain him even with a chain. Indeed he had frequently been secured with fetters and lengths of chain, but he had simply snapped the chains and broken the fetters in pieces. No one could do anything with him. All through the night as well as in the day-time he screamed among the tombs and on the hillside, and cut himself with stones. Now, as soon as he saw Jesus in the distance, he ran and kneeled before him, yelling at the top of his voice, "What have you got to do with me, Jesus, Son of the most high God? For God's sake, don't torture me!"

For Jesus had already said, "Come out of this man, you evil spirit!"

Then he asked him,

"What is your name?"

"My name is legion," he replied, "for there are many of us."

Then he begged and prayed him not to send "them" out of the country.

A large herd of pigs was grazing there on the hillside, and the evil spirits implored him, "Send us over to the pigs and we'll get into them!"

So Jesus allowed them to do this, and they came out of the man, and made off and went into the pigs. The whole herd of about two thou-sand stampeded down the cliff into the lake and was drowned. The swineherds took to their heels and spread their story in the city and all over the countryside. Then the people came to see what had happened. As they approached Jesus, they saw the man who had been devil-possessed sit-ting there properly clothed and perfectly sane—the same man who had been possessed by "le-gion"—and they were really frightened. Those who had seen the incident told them what had happened to the devil-possessed man and about the disaster to the pigs. Then they began to im-plore Jesus to leave their district. As he was em-barking on the small boat, the man who had been possessed begged that he might go with him. But Jesus would not allow this.

"Go home to your own people," he told him, "and tell them what the Lord has done for you, and how kind he has been to you!"

So the man went off and began to spread throughout the Ten Towns the story of what Je-sus had done for him. And they were all simply amazed.

Faith is followed by healing   **5. 21**

When Jesus had crossed again in the boat to the other side of the lake, a great crowd col-lected around him as he stood on the shore. Then came a man called Jairus, one of the syna-gogue presidents. And when he saw Jesus, he kneeled before him, pleading desperately for his help.

"My little girl is dying," he said. "Will you come and put your hands on her—then she will get better and live."

Jesus went off with him, followed by a large crowd jostling at his elbow. Among them was a woman who had had a hemorrhage for twelve years and who had gone through a great deal at the hands of many doctors, spending all her money in the process. She had derived no benefit

5 So they came to the other side of the lake, into the country of the Gerasenes. As he stepped ashore, a man possessed by an unclean spirit came up to him from among the tombs where he had his dwelling. He could no longer be controlled; even chains were useless; he had often been fettered and chained up, but he had snapped his chains and broken the fetters. No one was strong enough to master him. And so, unceasingly, night and day, he would cry aloud among the tombs and on the hill-sides and cut himself with stones. When he saw Jesus in the distance, he ran and flung himself down before him, shouting loudly, 'What do you want with me, Jesus, son of the Most High God? In God's name do not torment me.' (For Jesus was al-ready saying to him, 'Out, unclean spirit, come out of this man!') Jesus asked him, 'What is your name?' 'My name is Legion,' he said, 'there are so many of us.' And he begged hard that Jesus would not send them out of the country.

Now there happened to be a large herd of pigs feeding on the hill-side, and the spirits begged him, 'Send us among the pigs and let us go into them.' He gave them leave; and the unclean spirits came out and went into the pigs; and the herd, of about two thousand, rushed over the edge into the lake and were drowned.

The men in charge of them took to their heels and carried the news to the town and country-side; and the people came out to see what had happened. They came to Jesus and saw the mad-man who had been possessed by the legion of devils, sitting there clothed and in his right mind; and they were afraid. The spectators told them how the madman had been cured and what had happened to the pigs. Then they begged Jesus to leave the district.

As he was stepping into the boat, the man who had been possessed begged to go with him. Jesus would not allow it, but said to him, 'Go home to your own folk and tell them what the Lord in his mercy has done for you.' The man went off and spread the news in the Ten Towns[a] of all that Jesus had done for him; and they were all amazed.

As soon as Jesus had returned by boat to the other shore, a great crowd once more gathered round him. While he was by the lake-side, the president of one of the synagogues came up, Jairus by name, and, when he saw him, threw himself down at his feet and pleaded with him. 'My little daughter', he said, 'is at death's door. I beg you to come and lay your hands on her to cure her and save her life.' So Jesus went with him, accompanied by a great crowd which pressed upon him.

Among them was a woman who had suffered from haemorrhages for twelve years; and in spite of long treatment by doctors, on which she had spent all she had, there had been no im-

[a] *Greek* Decapolis.

K.J.V.

tered, but rather grew worse, 27 When she had heard of Jesus, came in the press behind, and touched his garment. 28 For she said, If I may touch but his clothes, I shall be whole. 29And straightway the fountain of her blood was dried up; and she felt in *her* body that she was healed of that plague. 30And Jesus, immediately knowing in himself that virtue had gone out of him, turned him about in the press, and said, Who touched my clothes? 31And his disciples said unto him, Thou seest the multitude thronging thee, and sayest thou, Who touched me? 32And he looked round about to see her that had done this thing. 33 But the woman fearing and trembling, knowing what was done in her, came and fell down before him, and told him all the truth. 34And he said unto her, Daughter, thy faith hath made thee whole; go in peace, and be whole of thy plague. 35 While he yet spake, there came from the ruler of the synagogue's *house certain* which said, Thy daughter is dead; why troublest thou the Master any further? 36As soon as Jesus heard the word that was spoken, he saith unto the ruler of the synagogue, Be not afraid, only believe. 37And he suffered no man to follow him, save Peter, and James, and John the brother of James. 38And he cometh to the house of the ruler of the synagogue, and seeth the tumult, and them that wept and wailed greatly. 39And when he was come in, he saith unto them, Why make ye this ado, and weep? the damsel is not dead, but sleepeth. 40And they laughed him to scorn. But when he had put them all out, he taketh the father and the mother of the damsel, and them that were with him, and entereth in where the damsel was lying. 41And he took the damsel by the hand, and said unto her, Talitha cumi; which is, being interpreted, Damsel, (I say unto thee,) arise. 42And straightway the damsel arose, and walked; for she was *of the age* of twelve years. And they were astonished with a great astonishment. 43And he charged them straitly that no man should know it; and commanded that something should be given her to eat.

R.S.V.

but rather grew worse. 27 She had heard the reports about Jesus, and came up behind him in the crowd and touched his garment. 28 For she said, "If I touch even his garments, I shall be made well." 29And immediately the hemorrhage ceased; and she felt in her body that she was healed of her disease. 30And Jesus, perceiving in himself that power had gone forth from him, immediately turned about in the crowd, and said, "Who touched my garments?" 31And his disciples said to him, "You see the crowd pressing around you, and yet you say, 'Who touched me?' " 32And he looked around to see who had done it. 33 But the woman, knowing what had been done to her, came in fear and trembling and fell down before him, and told him the whole truth. 34And he said to her, "Daughter, your faith has made you well; go in peace, and be healed of your disease."

35 While he was still speaking, there came from the ruler's house some who said, "Your daughter is dead. Why trouble the Teacher any further?" 36 But ignoring*q* what they said, Jesus said to the ruler of the synagogue, "Do not fear, only believe." 37And he allowed no one to follow him except Peter and James and John the brother of James. 38 When they came to the house of the ruler of the synagogue, he saw a tumult, and people weeping and wailing loudly. 39And when he had entered, he said to them, "Why do you make a tumult and weep? The child is not dead but sleeping." 40And they laughed at him. But he put them all outside, and took the child's father and mother and those who were with him, and went in where the child was. 41 Taking her by the hand he said to her, "Talitha cumi"; which means, "Little girl, I say to you, arise." 42And immediately the girl got up and walked; for she was twelve years old. And immediately they were overcome with amazement. 43And he strictly charged them that no one should know this, and told them to give her something to eat.

6 And he went out from thence, and came into his own country; and his disciples follow him. 2And when the sabbath day was come, he began to teach in the synagogue: and many hearing *him* were astonished, saying, From whence hath this *man* these things? and what wisdom *is* this which is given unto him, that even such mighty works are wrought by his hands? 3 Is not this the carpenter, the son of Mary, the brother of James, and Joses, and of Juda, and Simon? and are not his sisters here with us? And they were offended at him. 4 But Jesus said unto them, A prophet is not without honour, but in his own country, and among his own kin, and in his own house. 5And he could there do no mighty work, save that he laid his hands upon a few sick folk, and healed *them*. 6And he marvelled because of their unbelief.

6 He went away from there and came to his own country; and his disciples followed him. 2And on the sabbath he began to teach in the synagogue; and many who heard him were astonished, saying, "Where did this man get all this? What is the wisdom given to him? What mighty works are wrought by his hands! 3 Is not this the carpenter, the son of Mary and brother of James and Joses and Judas and Simon, and are not his sisters here with us?" And they took offense*r* at him. 4And Jesus said to them, "A prophet is not without honor, except in his own country, and among his own kin, and in his own house." 5And he could do no mighty work there, except that he laid his hands upon a few sick people and healed them. 6And he marveled because of their unbelief.

[q] Or *overhearing*. Other ancient authorities read *hearing*. [r] Or *stumbled*.

PHILLIPS

from them but, on the contrary, was getting worse. This woman had heard about Jesus and came up behind him under cover of the crowd, and touched his cloak.

"For if I can only touch his clothes," she kept saying, "I shall be all right."

The hemorrhage stopped immediately, and she knew in herself that she was cured of her trouble. At once Jesus knew intuitively that power had gone out of him, and he turned round in the middle of the crowd and said,

"Who touched my clothes?"

His disciples replied,

"You can see this crowd jostling you. How can you ask, 'Who touched me?' "

But he looked all round at their faces to see who had done so. Then the woman, scared and shaking all over because she knew that she was the one to whom this thing had happened, came and flung herself before him and told him the whole story. But he said to her,

"Daughter, it is your faith that has healed you. Go home in peace, and be free from your trouble."

While he was still speaking, messengers arrived from the synagogue president's house, saying,

"Your daughter is dead—there is no need to bother the master any further."

But when Jesus heard this, he said,

"Now, don't be afraid, just go on believing!"

Then he allowed no one to follow him except Peter and James and John, James's brother. They arrived at the president's house and Jesus noticed the hubbub and all the weeping and wailing, and as he went in, he said to the people in the house,

"Why are you making such a noise with your crying? The child is not dead; she is fast asleep."

They greeted this with a scornful laugh. But Jesus turned them all out and, taking only the father and mother and his own companions with him, went into the room where the child was. Then he took the little girl's hand and said to her in Aramaic,

"Little girl, I tell you to get up!"

At once she jumped to her feet and walked round the room, for she was twelve years old. This sight sent the others nearly out of their minds with joy. But Jesus gave them strict instructions not to let anyone know what had happened—and ordered food to be given to the little girl.

N.E.B.

provement; on the contrary, she had grown worse. She had heard what people were saying about Jesus, so she came up from behind in the crowd and touched his cloak; for she said to herself, 'If I touch even his clothes, I shall be cured.' And there and then the source of her haemorrhages dried up and she knew in herself that she was cured of her trouble. At the same time Jesus, aware that power had gone out of him, turned round in the crowd and asked, 'Who touched my clothes?' His disciples said to him, 'You see the crowd pressing upon you and yet you ask, "Who touched me?" ' Meanwhile he was looking round to see who had done it. And the woman, trembling with fear when she grasped what had happened to her, came and fell at his feet and told him the whole truth. He said to her, 'My daughter, your faith has cured you. Go in peace, free for ever from this trouble.'

While he was still speaking, a message came from the president's house, 'Your daughter is dead; why trouble the Rabbi further?' But Jesus, overhearing the message as it was delivered, said to the president of the synagogue, 'Do not be afraid; only have faith.' After this he allowed no one to accompany him except Peter and James and James's brother John. They came to the president's house, where he found a great commotion, with loud crying and wailing. So he went in and said to them, 'Why this crying and commotion? The child is not dead: she is asleep.' But they only laughed at him. After turning all the others out, he took the child's father and mother and his own companions and went in where the child was lying. Then, taking hold of her hand, he said to her, 'Talitha cum', which means, 'Get up, my child.' Immediately the girl got up and walked about—she was twelve years old. At that they were beside themselves with amazement. He gave them strict orders to let no one hear about it, and told them to give her something to eat.

The "prophet without honor"   6. 1

Then he left that district and came into his own native town, followed by his disciples. When the Sabbath day came, he began to teach in the synagogue. The congregation were astonished, and remarked:

"Where does he get all this? What is this wisdom that he has been given—and what about these marvelous things that he can do? He's only the carpenter, Mary's son, the brother of James, Joses, Judas and Simon; and his sisters are living here with us!"

And they were deeply offended with him. But Jesus said to them,

"No prophet goes unhonored—except in his native town or with his own relations or in his own home!"

And he could do nothing miraculous there apart from laying his hands on a few sick people and healing them; their lack of faith astonished him.

6 He left that place and went to his home town accompanied by his disciples. When the Sabbath came he began to teach in the synagogue; and the large congregation who heard him were amazed and said, 'Where does he get it from?', and, 'What wisdom is this that has been given him?', and, 'How does he work such miracles? Is not this the carpenter, the son of Mary,[a] the brother of James and Joseph and Judas and Simon? And are not his sisters here with us?' So they fell foul of him. Jesus said to them, 'A prophet will always be held in honour except in his home town, and among his kinsmen and family.' He could work no miracle there, except that he put his hands on a few sick people and healed them; and he was taken aback by their want of faith.

[a] *Some witnesses read* Is not this the son of the carpenter and Mary . . .

K.J.V.

And he went round about the villages, teaching.

7 And he called *unto him* the twelve, and began to send them forth by two and two; and gave them power over unclean spirits; 8And commanded them that they should take nothing for *their* journey, save a staff only; no scrip, no bread, no money in *their* purse: 9 But *be* shod with sandals; and not put on two coats. 10And he said unto them, In what place soever ye enter into a house, there abide till ye depart from that place. 11And whosoever shall not receive you, nor hear you, when ye depart thence, shake off the dust under your feet for a testimony against them. Verily I say unto you, It shall be more tolerable for Sodom and Gomorrah in the day of judgment, than for that city. 12And they went out, and preached that men should repent. 13And they cast out many devils, and anointed with oil many that were sick, and healed *them*. 14And king Herod heard *of him;* (for his name was spread abroad;) and he said, That John the Baptist was risen from the dead, and therefore mighty works do shew forth themselves in him. 15 Others said, That it is Elias. And others said, That it is a prophet, or as one of the prophets. 16 But when Herod heard *thereof,* he said, It is John, whom I beheaded: he is risen from the dead. 17 For Herod himself had sent forth and laid hold upon John, and bound him in prison for Herodias' sake, his brother Philip's wife; for he had married her. 18 For John had said unto Herod, It is not lawful for thee to have thy brother's wife. 19 Therefore Herodias had a quarrel against him, and would have killed him; but she could not: 20 For Herod feared John, knowing that he was a just man and a holy, and observed him; and when he heard him, he did many things, and heard him gladly. 21And when a convenient day was come, that Herod on his birthday made a supper to his lords, high captains, and chief *estates* of Galilee; 22And when the daughter of the said Herodias came in, and danced, and pleased Herod and them that sat with him, the king said unto the damsel, Ask of me whatsoever thou wilt, and I will give *it* thee. 23And he sware unto her, Whatsoever thou shalt ask of me, I will give *it* thee, unto the half of my kingdom. 24And she went forth, and said unto her mother, What shall I ask? And she said, The head of John the Baptist. 25And she came in straightway with haste unto the king, and asked, saying, I will that thou give me by and by in a charger the head of John the Baptist. 26And the king was exceeding sorry; *yet* for his oath's sake, and for their sakes which sat with him, he would not reject her. 27And immediately the king sent an executioner, and commanded his head to be brought: and he went and beheaded him in the prison, 28And brought his head in a charger, and gave it to the damsel: and the damsel gave it to her mother. 29And when his disciples heard *of it,* they came and took up his corpse, and laid

R.S.V.

And he went about among the villages teaching.

7 And he called to him the twelve, and began to send them out two by two, and gave them authority over the unclean spirits. 8 He charged them to take nothing for their journey except a staff; no bread, no bag, no money in their belts; 9 but to wear sandals and not put on two tunics. 10And he said to them, "Where you enter a house, stay there until you leave the place. 11And if any place will not receive you and they refuse to hear you, when you leave, shake off the dust that is on your feet for a testimony against them." 12 So they went out and preached that men should repent. 13And they cast out many demons, and anointed with oil many that were sick and healed them.

14 King Herod heard of it; for Jesus' [s] name had become known. Some[t] said, "John the baptizer has been raised from the dead; that is why these powers are at work in him." 15 But others said, "It is Elijah." And others said, "It is a prophet, like one of the prophets of old." 16 But when Herod heard of it he said, "John, whom I beheaded, has been raised." 17 For Herod had sent and seized John, and bound him in prison for the sake of Herodias, his brother Philip's wife; because he had married her. 18 For John said to Herod, "It is not lawful for you to have your brother's wife." 19And Herodias had a grudge against him, and wanted to kill him. But she could not, 20 for Herod feared John, knowing that he was a righteous and holy man, and kept him safe. When he heard him, he was much perplexed; and yet he heard him gladly. 21 But an opportunity came when Herod on his birthday gave a banquet for his courtiers and officers and the leading men of Galilee. 22 For when Herodias' daughter came in and danced, she pleased Herod and his guests; and the king said to the girl, "Ask me for whatever you wish, and I will grant it." 23And he vowed to her, "Whatever you ask me, I will give you, even half of my kingdom." 24And she went out, and said to her mother, "What shall I ask?" And she said, "The head of John the baptizer." 25And she came in immediately with haste to the king, and asked, saying, "I want you to give me at once the head of John the Baptist on a platter." 26And the king was exceedingly sorry; but because of his oaths and his guests he did not want to break his word to her. 27And immediately the king sent a soldier of the guard and gave orders to bring his head. He went and beheaded him in the prison, 28 and brought his head on a platter, and gave it to the girl; and the girl gave it to her mother. 29 When his disciples heard of it, they came and took his body, and laid it in a tomb.

[s] Greek *his.* [t] Other ancient authorities read *he.*

PHILLIPS	N.E.B.

The twelve are sent out   **6. 6b**
to preach the gospel

Then he made his way round the villages, continuing his teaching. He summoned the twelve, and began to send them out in twos, giving them power over evil spirits. He instructed them to take nothing for the road except a staff—no satchel, no bread and no money in their pockets. They were to wear sandals and not to take more than one coat. And he told them:

"Wherever you are, when you go into a house, stay there until you leave that place. And wherever people will not welcome you or listen to what you have to say, leave them and shake the dust off your feet as a protest against them!"

So they went out and preached that men should change their whole outlook. They expelled many evil spirits and anointed many sick people with oil and healed them.

Herod's guilty conscience   **6. 14**

All this came to the ears of king Herod, for Jesus' reputation was spreading, and people were saying that John the Baptist had risen from the dead, and that was why he was showing such miraculous powers. Others maintained that he was Elijah, and others that he was one of the prophets of the old days come back again. But when Herod heard of all this, he said,

"It must be John whom I beheaded, risen from the dead!"

For Herod himself had sent and arrested John and had him bound in prison, all on account of Herodias, wife of his brother Philip. He had married her, though John used to say to Herod, "It is not right for you to possess your own brother's wife." Herodias herself was furious with him for this and wanted to have him executed, but she could not do it, for Herod had a deep respect for John, knowing that he was a just and holy man, and protected him. He used to listen to him and be profoundly disturbed, and yet he enjoyed hearing him.

Then a good opportunity came, for Herod gave a birthday party for his courtiers and army commanders and for the leading people in Galilee. Herodias' daughter came in and danced, to the great delight of Herod and his guests. The king said to the girl,

"Ask me anything you like and I will give it to you!"

And he swore to her,

"I will give you whatever you ask me, up to half of my kingdom!"

And she went out and spoke to her mother, "What shall I ask for?"

And she said,

"The head of John the Baptist!"

The girl rushed back to the king's presence, and made her request.

"I want you to give me, this minute, the head of John the Baptist on a dish!" she said.

Herod was aghast, but because of his oath and the presence of his guests he did not like to refuse her. So he sent one of the palace guardsmen straightaway to bring him John's head. He went off and beheaded him in the prison, brought back his head on the dish, and gave it to the girl, who handed it to her mother. When his disciples heard what had happened, they came and took away the body and put it in a tomb.

On one of his teaching journeys round the villages he summoned the Twelve and sent them out in pairs on a mission. He gave them authority over unclean spirits, and instructed them to take nothing for the journey beyond a stick: no bread, no pack, no money in their belts. They might wear sandals, but not a second coat. 'When you are admitted to a house,' he added, 'stay there until you leave those parts. At any place where they will not receive you or listen to you, shake the dust off your feet as you leave, as a warning to them.' So they set out and called publicly for repentance. They drove out many devils, and many sick people they anointed with oil and cured.

Now King Herod heard of it, for the fame of Jesus had spread; and people were saying,[a] 'John the Baptist has been raised to life, and that is why these miraculous powers are at work in him.' Others said, 'It is Elijah.' Others again, 'He is a prophet like one of the old prophets.' But Herod, when he heard of it, said, 'This is John, whom I beheaded, raised from the dead!'

For this same Herod had sent and arrested John and put him in prison at the instance of his brother Philip's wife, Herodias, whom he had married. John had told Herod, 'You have no right to your brother's wife.' Thus Herodias nursed a grudge against him and would willingly have killed him, but she could not; for Herod went in awe of John, knowing him to be a good and holy man; so he kept him in custody. He liked to listen to him, although the listening left him greatly perplexed.

Herodias found her opportunity when Herod on his birthday gave a banquet to his chief officials and commanders and the leading men of Galilee. Her daughter came in[b] and danced, and so delighted Herod and his guests that the king said to the girl, 'Ask what you like and I will give it you.' And he swore an oath to her: 'Whatever you ask I will give you, up to half my kingdom.' She went out and said to her mother, 'What shall I ask for?' She replied, 'The head of John the Baptist.' The girl hastened back at once to the king with her request: 'I want you to give me here and now, on a dish, the head of John the Baptist.' The king was greatly distressed, but out of regard for his oath and for his guests he could not bring himself to refuse her. So the king sent a soldier of the guard with orders to bring John's head. The soldier went off and beheaded him in the prison, brought the head on a dish, and gave it to the girl; and she gave it to her mother.

When John's disciples heard the news, they came and took his body away and laid it in a tomb.

[a] *Some witnesses read* and he said . . . [b] *Or* A festive occasion came when Herod on his birthday gave . . . of Galilee. The daughter of Herodias came in . . .

K.J.V.

it in a tomb. 30And the apostles gathered themselves together unto Jesus, and told him all things, both what they had done, and what they had taught. 31And he said unto them, Come ye yourselves apart into a desert place, and rest a while: for there were many coming and going, and they had no leisure so much as to eat. 32And they departed into a desert place by ship privately. 33And the people saw them departing, and many knew him, and ran afoot thither out of all cities, and outwent them, and came together unto him. 34And Jesus, when he came out, saw much people, and was moved with compassion toward them, because they were as sheep not having a shepherd: and he began to teach them many things. 35And when the day was now far spent, his disciples came unto him, and said, This is a desert place, and now the time *is* far passed: 36 Send them away, that they may go into the country round about, and into the villages, and buy themselves bread: for they have nothing to eat. 37 He answered and said unto them, Give ye them to eat. And they say unto him, Shall we go and buy two hundred pennyworth of bread, and give them to eat? 38 He saith unto them, How many loaves have ye? go and see. And when they knew, they say, Five, and two fishes. 39And he commanded them to make all sit down by companies upon the green grass. 40And they sat down in ranks, by hundreds, and by fifties. 41And when he had taken the five loaves and the two fishes, he looked up to heaven, and blessed, and brake the loaves, and gave *them* to his disciples to set before them; and the two fishes divided he among them all. 42And they did all eat, and were filled. 43And they took up twelve baskets full of the fragments, and of the fishes. 44And they that did eat of the loaves were about five thousand men. 45And straightway he constrained his disciples to get into the ship, and to go to the other side before unto Bethsaida, while he sent away the people. 46And when he had sent them away, he departed into a mountain to pray. 47And when even was come, the ship was in the midst of the sea, and he alone on the land. 48And he saw them toiling in rowing; for the wind was contrary unto them: and about the fourth watch of the night he cometh unto them, walking upon the sea, and would have passed by them. 49 But when they saw him walking upon the sea, they supposed it had been a spirit, and cried out: 50 For they all saw him, and were troubled. And immediately he talked with them, and saith unto them, Be of good cheer: it is I; be not afraid. 51And he went up unto them into the ship; and the wind ceased: and they were sore amazed in themselves beyond measure, and wondered. 52 For they considered not *the miracle* of the

R.S.V.

30 The apostles returned to Jesus, and told him all that they had done and taught. 31And he said to them, "Come away by yourselves to a lonely place, and rest a while." For many were coming and going, and they had no leisure even to eat. 32And they went away in the boat to a lonely place by themselves. 33 Now many saw them going, and knew them, and they ran there on foot from all the towns, and got there ahead of them. 34As he landed he saw a great throng, and he had compassion on them, because they were like sheep without a shepherd; and he began to teach them many things. 35And when it grew late, his disciples came to him and said, "This is a lonely place, and the hour is now late; 36 send them away, to go into the country and villages round about and buy themselves something to eat." 37 But he answered them, "You give them something to eat." And they said to him, "Shall we go and buy two hundred denarii[u] worth of bread, and give it to them to eat?" 38And he said to them, "How many loaves have you? Go and see." And when they had found out, they said, "Five, and two fish." 39 Then he commanded them all to sit down by companies upon the green grass. 40 So they sat down in groups, by hundreds and by fifties. 41And taking the five loaves and the two fish he looked up to heaven, and blessed, and broke the loaves, and gave them to the disciples to set before the people; and he divided the two fish among them all. 42And they all ate and were satisfied. 43And they took up twelve baskets full of broken pieces and of the fish. 44And those who ate the loaves were five thousand men.

45 Immediately he made his disciples get into the boat and go before him to the other side, to Bethsaida, while he dismissed the crowd. 46And after he had taken leave of them, he went into the hills to pray. 47And when evening came, the boat was out on the sea, and he was alone on the land. 48And he saw that they were distressed in rowing, for the wind was against them. And about the fourth watch of the night he came to them, walking on the sea. He meant to pass by them, 49 but when they saw him walking on the sea they thought it was a ghost, and cried out; 50 for they all saw him, and were terrified. But immediately he spoke to them and said, "Take heart, it is I; have no fear." 51And he got into the boat with them and the wind ceased. And they were utterly astounded, 52 for they did not

---

[u] The denarius was worth about twenty cents.

The apostles return: the huge   *6. 30*
crowds make rest impossible

The apostles returned to Jesus and reported to him every detail of what they had done and taught.
"Now come along to some quiet place by yourselves, and rest for a little while," said Jesus, for there were people coming and going incessantly so that they had not even time for meals. They went off in the boat to a quiet place by themselves, but a great many saw them go and recognized them, and people from all the towns hurried around the shore on foot to forestall them. When Jesus disembarked he saw the large crowd and his heart was touched with pity for them because they seemed to him like sheep without a shepherd. And he settled down to teach them about many things. As the day wore on, his disciples came to him and said:
"We are right in the wilds here and it is getting late. Let them go now, so that they can buy themselves something to eat from the farms and villages around here."
But Jesus replied,
"You give them something to eat!"
"You mean we're to go and spend ten dollars on bread? Is that how you want us to feed them?"
"What bread have you got?" asked Jesus. "Go and have a look."
And when they had found out, they told him, "We have five loaves and two fish."

Jesus miraculously feeds five   *6. 39*
thousand people

Then Jesus directed the people to sit down in parties on the fresh grass. And they threw themselves down in groups of fifty and a hundred. Then Jesus took the five loaves and the two fish, and looking up to Heaven, thanked God, broke the loaves and gave them to the disciples to distribute to the people. And he divided the two fish among them all. Everybody ate and was satisfied. Afterward they collected twelve baskets full of pieces of bread and fish that were left over. There were five thousand men who ate the loaves.

Jesus' mastery over natural law   *6. 45*

Directly after this, Jesus made his disciples get aboard the boat and go on ahead to Bethsaida on the other side of the lake, while he himself sent the crowds home. And when he had sent them all on their way, he went off to the hillside to pray. When it grew late, the boat was in the middle of the lake, and he was by himself on land. He saw them straining at the oars, for the wind was dead against them. And in the small hours he went toward them, walking on the waters of the lake, intending to come alongside them. But when they saw him walking on the water, they thought he was a ghost, and screamed out. For they all saw him and they were absolutely terrified. But Jesus at once spoke quietly to them,
"It's all right, it is I myself; don't be afraid!"
And he climbed aboard the boat with them, and the wind dropped. But they were scared out of their wits. They had not had the sense to learn

The apostles now rejoined Jesus and reported to him all that they had done and taught. He said to them, 'Come with me, by yourselves, to some lonely place where you can rest quietly.' (For they had no leisure even to eat, so many were coming and going.) Accordingly, they set off privately by boat for a lonely place. But many saw them leave and recognized them, and came round by land, hurrying from all the towns towards the place, and arrived there first. When he came ashore, he saw a great crowd; and his heart went out to them, because they were like sheep without a shepherd; and he had much to teach them. As the day wore on, his disciples approached him and said, 'This is a lonely place and it is getting very late; send the people off to the farms and villages round about, to buy themselves something to eat.' 'Give them something to eat yourselves', he answered. They replied, 'Are we to go and spend twenty pounds[a] on bread to give them a meal?' 'How many loaves have you?' he asked; 'go and see.' They found out and told him, 'Five, and two fishes also.' He ordered them to make the people sit down in groups on the green grass, and they sat down in rows, a hundred rows of fifty each. Then, taking the five loaves and the two fishes, he looked up to heaven, said the blessing, broke the loaves, and gave them to the disciples to distribute. He also divided the two fishes among them. They all ate to their hearts' content; and twelve great basketfuls of scraps were picked up, with what was left of the fish. Those who ate the loaves numbered five thousand men.
As soon as it was over he made his disciples embark and cross to Bethsaida ahead of him, while he himself sent the people away. After taking leave of them, he went up the hill-side to pray. It grew late and the boat was already well out on the water, while he was alone on the land. Somewhere between three and six in the morning, seeing them labouring at the oars against a head-wind, he came towards them, walking on the lake. He was going to pass them by; but when they saw him walking on the lake, they thought it was a ghost, and cried out; for they all saw him and were terrified. But at once he spoke to them: 'Take heart! It is I; do not be afraid.' Then he climbed into the boat beside them, and the wind dropped. At this they were completely dumbfounded, for they had not

[a] *Literally* 200 denarii.

K.J.V.

R.S.V.

loaves; for their heart was hardened. 53And when they had passed over, they came into the land of Gennesaret, and drew to the shore. 54And when they were come out of the ship, straightway they knew him, 55And ran through that whole region round about, and began to carry about in beds those that were sick, where they heard he was. 56And whithersoever he entered, into villages, or cities, or country, they laid the sick in the streets, and besought him that they might touch if it were but the border of his garment: and as many as touched him were made whole.

understand about the loaves, but their hearts were hardened.
53 And when they had crossed over, they came to land at Gennesaret, and moored to the shore. 54And when they got out of the boat, immediately the people recognized him, 55 and ran about the whole neighborhood and began to bring sick people on their pallets to any place where they heard he was. 56And wherever he came, in villages, cities, or country, they laid the sick in the market places, and besought him that they might touch even the fringe of his garment; and as many as touched it were made well.

7 Then came together unto him the Pharisees, and certain of the scribes, which came from Jerusalem. 2And when they saw some of his disciples eat bread with defiled, that is to say, with unwashen hands, they found fault. 3 For the Pharisees, and all the Jews, except they wash *their* hands oft, eat not, holding the tradition of the elders. 4And *when they come* from the market, except they wash, they eat not. And many other things there be, which they have received to hold, *as* the washing of cups, and pots, brazen vessels, and of tables. 5 Then the Pharisees and scribes asked him, Why walk not thy disciples according to the tradition of the elders, but eat bread with unwashen hands? 6 He answered and said unto them, Well hath Esaias prophesied of you hypocrites, as it is written, This people honoureth me with *their* lips, but their heart is far from me. 7 Howbeit in vain do they worship me, teaching *for* doctrines the commandments of men. 8 For laying aside the commandment of God, ye hold the tradition of men, *as* the washing of pots and cups: and many other such like things ye do. 9And he said unto them, Full well ye reject the commandment of God, that ye may keep your own tradition. 10 For Moses said, Honour thy father and thy mother; and, Whoso curseth father or mother, let him die the death: 11 But ye say, If a man shall say to his father or mother, *It is* Corban, that is to say, a gift, by whatsoever thou mightest be profited by me; *he shall be free.* 12And ye suffer him no more to do aught for his father or his mother; 13 Making the word of God of none effect through your tradition, which ye have delivered: and many such like things do ye.
14 And when he had called all the people *unto him,* he said unto them, Hearken unto me every one *of you,* and understand: 15 There is nothing from without a man, that entering into him can defile him: but the things which come out of him, those are they that defile the man. 16 If any man have ears to hear, let him hear. 17And when he was entered into the house from the people, his disciples asked him concerning the parable. 18And he saith unto them, Are ye so without understanding also? Do ye not perceive, that whatsoever thing from without entereth into the man, *it* cannot defile him; 19 Because it entereth not into his heart, but into the belly, and goeth out into the draught, purging all meats? 20And he said, That which cometh out

7 Now when the Pharisees gathered together to him, with some of the scribes, who had come from Jerusalem, 2 they saw that some of his disciples ate with hands defiled, that is, unwashed. 3 (For the Pharisees, and all the Jews, do not eat unless they wash their hands,[v] observing the tradition of the elders; 4 and when they come from the market place, they do not eat unless they purify[w] themselves; and there are many other traditions which they observe, the washing of cups and pots and vessels of bronze.[x]) 5And the Pharisees and the scribes asked him, "Why do your disciples not live[y] according to the tradition of the elders, but eat with hands defiled?" 6And he said to them, "Well did Isaiah prophesy of you hypocrites, as it is written,

'This people honors me with their lips,
  but their heart is far from me;
7 in vain do they worship me,
  teaching as doctrines the precepts of men.'

8 You leave the commandment of God, and hold fast the tradition of men."
9 And he said to them, "You have a fine way of rejecting the commandment of God, in order to keep your tradition! 10 For Moses said, 'Honor your father and your mother'; and, 'He who speaks evil of father or mother, let him surely die'; 11 but you say, 'If a man tells his father or his mother, What you would have gained from me is Corban' (that is, given to God)[z]—12then you no longer permit him to do anything for his father or mother, 13 thus making void the word of God through your tradition which you hand on. And many such things you do."
14 And he called the people to him again, and said to them, "Hear me, all of you, and understand: 15there is nothing outside a man which by going into him can defile him; but the things which come out of a man are what defile him."[a] 17And when he had entered the house, and left the people, his disciples asked him about the parable. 18And he said to them, "Then are you also without understanding? Do you not see that whatever goes into a man from outside cannot defile him, 19 since it enters, not his heart but his stomach, and so passes on?"[b] (Thus he declared all foods clean.) 20And he said, "What comes

<hr>

[v] One Greek word is of uncertain meaning and is not translated. [w] Other ancient authorities read *baptize.* [x] Other ancient authorities add *and beds.* [y] Greek *walk.* [z] Or *an offering.* [a] Other ancient authorities add verse 16, "*If any man has ears to hear, let him hear.*" [b] Or *is evacuated.*

PHILLIPS

the lesson of the loaves. Even that miracle had not opened their eyes to see who he was.

And when they had crossed over to the other side of the lake, they landed at Gennesaret and tied up there. As soon as they came ashore, the people recognized Jesus and rushed all over the countryside and began to carry the sick around on their beds to wherever they heard that he was. Wherever he went, in villages or towns or farms, they laid down their sick right in the roadway and begged him that they might just touch the edge of his cloak. And all those who touched him were healed.

Jesus exposes the danger   **7. 1**
of man-made traditions

And now Jesus was approached by the Pharisees and some of the scribes who had come from Jerusalem. They had noticed that his disciples ate their meals with "common" hands—meaning that they had not gone through a ceremonial washing. (The Pharisees, and indeed all the Jews, will never eat unless they have washed their hands in a particular way, following a traditional rule. And they will not eat anything bought in the market until they have first performed their "sprinkling." And there are many other things which they consider important, concerned with the washing of cups, jugs and basins.) So the Pharisees and the scribes put this question to Jesus,

"Why do your disciples refuse to follow the ancient tradition, and eat their bread with 'common' hands?"

Jesus replied,

"You hypocrites, Isaiah described you beautifully when he wrote—

This people honoreth me with their lips,
But their heart is far from me.
But in vain do they worship me,
Teaching as doctrines the precepts of men.

You are so busy holding on to the traditions of men that you let go the commandment of God!"

Then he went on:

"It is wonderful to see how you can set aside the commandment of God to preserve your own tradition! For Moses said, *'Honor thy father and thy mother,'* and *'He that speaketh evil of father or mother, let him die the death.'* But you say, 'If a man says to his father or his mother, Korban—meaning, I have given God whatever duty I owed to you,' then he need not lift a finger any longer for his father or mother, so making the word of God invalid for the sake of the tradition which you hold. And this is typical of much of what you do."

Then he called the crowd close to him again, and spoke to them:

"Listen to me now, all of you, and understand this. There is nothing outside a man which can enter into him and make him 'common.' It is the things which come out of a man that make him 'common'!"

Later, when he had gone indoors away from the crowd, his disciples asked him about this parable.

"Oh, are you as dull as they are?" he said. "Can't you see that anything that goes into a man from outside cannot make him 'common' or unclean? You see, it doesn't go into his heart, but into his stomach, and passes out of the body altogether, so that all food is clean enough. But,"

N.E.B.

understood the incident of the loaves; their minds were closed.

So they finished the crossing and came to land at Gennesaret, where they made fast. When they came ashore, he was immediately recognized; and the people scoured that whole country-side and brought the sick on stretchers to any place where he was reported to be. Wherever he went, to farmsteads, villages, or towns, they laid out the sick in the market-places and begged him to let them simply touch the edge of his cloak; and all who touched him were cured.

Growing Tension

7 A group of Pharisees, with some doctors of the law who had come from Jerusalem, met him and noticed that some of his disciples were eating their food with 'defiled' hands—in other words, without washing them. (For the Pharisees and the Jews in general never eat without washing the hands,[a] in obedience to an old-established tradition; and on coming from the market-place they never eat without first washing. And there are many other points on which they have a traditional rule to maintain, for example, washing of cups and jugs and copper bowls.) Accordingly, these Pharisees and the lawyers asked him, 'Why do your disciples not conform to the ancient tradition, but eat their food with defiled hands?' He answered, 'Isaiah was right when he prophesied about you hypocrites in these words: "This people pays me lip-service, but their heart is far from me: their worship of me is in vain, for they teach as doctrines the commandments of men." You neglect the commandment of God, in order to maintain the tradition of men.'

He also said to them, 'How well you set aside the commandment of God in order to maintain[b] your tradition! Moses said, "Honour your father and your mother", and, "The man who curses his father or mother must suffer death." But you hold that if a man says to his father or mother, "Anything of mine which might have been used for your benefit is Corban" ' (meaning, set apart for God), 'he is no longer permitted to do anything for his father or mother. Thus by your own tradition, handed down among you, you make God's word null and void. And many other things that you do are just like that.'

On another occasion he called the people and said to them, 'Listen to me, all of you, and understand this: nothing that goes into a man from outside can defile him; no, it is the things that come out of him that defile a man.'[c]

When he had left the people and gone indoors, his disciples questioned him about the parable. He said to them, 'Are you as dull as the rest? Do you not see that nothing that goes from outside into a man can defile him, because it does not enter into his heart but into his stomach, and so passes out into the drain?' Thus he declared all foods clean. He went on, 'It is

[a] *Some witnesses insert* with the fist; *others insert* frequently, *or* thoroughly. [b] *Some witnesses read* establish. [c] *Some witnesses here add* (16) If you have ears to hear, then hear.

K.J.V.

of the man, that defileth the man. 21 For within, out of the heart of men, proceed evil thoughts, adulteries, fornications, murders, 22 Thefts, covetousness, wickedness, deceit, lasciviousness, an evil eye, blasphemy, pride, foolishness: 23 All these evil things come from within, and defile the man.

24 And from thence he arose, and went into the borders of Tyre and Sidon, and entered into a house, and would have no man know *it:* but he could not be hid. 25 For a *certain* woman, whose young daughter had an unclean spirit, heard of him, and came and fell at his feet: 26 The woman was a Greek, a Syrophenician by nation; and she besought him that he would cast forth the devil out of her daughter. 27 But Jesus said unto her, Let the children first be filled: for it is not meet to take the children's bread, and to cast *it* unto the dogs. 28 And she answered and said unto him, Yes, Lord: yet the dogs under the table eat of the children's crumbs. 29 And he said unto her, For this saying go thy way; the devil is gone out of thy daughter. 30 And when she was come to her house, she found the devil gone out, and her daughter laid upon the bed.

31 And again, departing from the coasts of Tyre and Sidon, he came unto the sea of Galilee, through the midst of the coasts of Decapolis. 32 And they bring unto him one that was deaf, and had an impediment in his speech; and they beseech him to put his hand upon him. 33 And he took him aside from the multitude, and put his fingers into his ears, and he spit, and touched his tongue; 34 And looking up to heaven, he sighed, and saith unto him, Ephphatha, that is, Be opened. 35 And straightway his ears were opened, and the string of his tongue was loosed, and he spake plain. 36 And he charged them that they should tell no man: but the more he charged them, so much the more a great deal they published *it;* 37 And were beyond measure astonished, saying, He hath done all things well: he maketh both the deaf to hear, and the dumb to speak.

8 In those days the multitude being very great and having nothing to eat, Jesus called his disciples *unto him,* and saith unto them, 2 I have compassion on the multitude, because they have now been with me three days, and have nothing to eat: 3 And if I send them away fasting to their own houses, they will faint by the way: for divers of them came from far. 4 And his disciples answered him, From whence can a man satisfy these *men* with bread here in the wilder-

R.S.V.

out of a man is what defiles a man. 21 For from within, out of the heart of man, come evil thoughts, fornication, theft, murder, adultery, 22 coveting, wickedness, deceit, licentiousness, envy, slander, pride, foolishness. 23 All these evil things come from within, and they defile a man."

24 And from there he arose and went away to the region of Tyre and Sidon.[c] And he entered a house, and would not have any one know it; yet he could not be hid. 25 But immediately a woman, whose little daughter was possessed by an unclean spirit, heard of him, and came and fell down at his feet. 26 Now the woman was a Greek, a Syrophoenician by birth. And she begged him to cast the demon out of her daughter. 27 And he said to her, "Let the children first be fed, for it is not right to take the children's bread and throw it to the dogs." 28 But she answered him, "Yes, Lord; yet even the dogs under the table eat the children's crumbs." 29 And he said to her, "For this saying you may go your way; the demon has left your daughter." 30 And she went home, and found the child lying in bed, and the demon gone.

31 Then he returned from the region of Tyre, and went through Sidon to the Sea of Galilee, through the region of the Decapolis. 32 And they brought to him a man who was deaf and had an impediment in his speech; and they besought him to lay his hand upon him. 33 And taking him aside from the multitude privately, he put his fingers into his ears, and he spat and touched his tongue; 34 and looking up to heaven, he sighed, and said to him, "Ephphatha," that is, "Be opened." 35 And his ears were opened, his tongue was released, and he spoke plainly. 36 And he charged them to tell no one; but the more he charged them, the more zealously they proclaimed it. 37 And they were astonished beyond measure, saying, "He has done all things well; he even makes the deaf hear and the dumb speak."

8 In those days, when again a great crowd had gathered, and they had nothing to eat, he called his disciples to him, and said to them, 2 "I have compassion on the crowd, because they have been with me now three days, and have nothing to eat; 3 and if I send them away hungry to their homes, they will faint on the way; and some of them have come a long way." 4 And his disciples answered him, "How can one feed these men with bread here in the desert?"

[c] Other ancient authorities omit *and Sidon.*

PHILLIPS

N.E.B.

he went on, "whatever comes out of a man, that is what makes a man 'common' or unclean. For it is from inside, from men's hearts and minds, that evil thoughts arise—lust, theft, murder, adultery, greed, wickedness, deceit, sensuality, envy, slander, arrogance and folly! All these evil things come from inside a man and make him unclean!"

The faith of a gentile is rewarded   7. 24

Then he got up and left that place and went off to the neighborhood of Tyre. There he went into a house and wanted no one to know where he was. But it proved impossible to remain hidden. For no sooner had he got there, than a woman who had heard about him, and who had a daughter possessed by an evil spirit, arrived and prostrated herself before him. She was a Greek, a Syrophoenician by birth, and she asked him to drive the evil spirit out of her daughter. Jesus said to her:

"You must let the children have all they want first. It is not right, you know, to take the children's food and throw it to the dogs."

But she replied,

"Yes, Lord, I know, but even the dogs under the table eat what the children leave."

"If you can answer like that," Jesus said to her, "you can go home! The evil spirit has left your daughter."

And she went back to her home and found the child lying quietly on her bed, and the evil spirit gone.

Jesus restores speech and hearing   7. 31

Once more Jesus left the neighborhood of Tyre and passed through Sidon toward the lake of Galilee, and crossed the Ten Towns territory. They brought to him a man who was deaf and unable to speak intelligibly, and they implored him to put his hand upon him. Jesus took him away from the crowd by himself. He put his fingers in the man's ears and touched his tongue with his own saliva. Then, looking up to Heaven, he gave a deep sigh and said to him in Aramaic, "Open!"

And his ears were opened and immediately whatever had tied his tongue came loose and he spoke quite plainly. Jesus gave instructions that they should tell no one about this happening, but the more he told them, the more they broadcast the news. People were absolutely amazed, and kept saying,

"How wonderfully he has done everything! He even makes the deaf hear and the dumb speak."

He again feeds the people miraculously   8. 1

About this time it happened again that a large crowd collected and had nothing to eat. Jesus called the disciples over to him and said:

"My heart goes out to this crowd; they have been with me three days now and they have no food left. If I send them off home without anything, they will collapse on the way—and some of them have come from a distance."

His disciples replied,

"Where could anyone find the food to feed them here in this deserted spot?"

what comes out of a man that defiles him. For from inside, out of a man's heart, come evil thoughts, acts of fornication, of theft, murder, adultery, ruthless greed, and malice; fraud, indecency, envy, slander, arrogance, and folly; these evil things all come from inside, and they defile the man.'

Then he left that place and went away into the territory of Tyre. He found a house to stay in, and he would have liked to remain unrecognized, but this was impossible. Almost at once a woman whose young daughter was possessed by an unclean spirit heard of him, came in, and fell at his feet. (She was a Gentile, a Phoenician of Syria by nationality.) She begged him to drive the spirit out of her daughter. He said to her, 'Let the children be satisfied first; it is not fair to take the children's bread and throw it to the dogs.' 'Sir,' she answered, 'even the dogs under the table eat the children's scraps.' He said to her, 'For saying that, you may go home content; the unclean spirit has gone out of your daughter.' And when she returned home, she found the child lying in bed; the spirit had left her.

On his return journey from Tyrian territory he went by way of Sidon to the Sea of Galilee through the territory of the Ten Towns.[a] They brought to him a man who was deaf and had an impediment in his speech, with the request that he would lay his hand on him. He took the man aside, away from the crowd, put his fingers into his ears, spat, and touched his tongue. Then, looking up to heaven, he sighed, and said to him, 'Ephphatha', which means 'Be opened.' With that his ears were opened, and at the same time the impediment was removed and he spoke plainly. Jesus forbade them to tell anyone; but the more he forbade them, the more they published it. Their astonishment knew no bounds: 'All that he does, he does well,' they said; 'he even makes the deaf hear and the dumb speak.'

8 There was another occasion about this time when a huge crowd had collected, and, as they had no food, Jesus called his disciples and said to them, 'I feel sorry for all these people; they have been with me now for three days and have nothing to eat. If I send them home unfed, they will turn faint on the way; some of them have come from a distance.' The disciples answered, 'How can anyone provide all these

[a] Greek Decapolis.

K.J.V.

ness? 5And he asked them, How many loaves have ye? And they said, Seven. 6And he commanded the people to sit down on the ground: and he took the seven loaves, and gave thanks, and brake, and gave to his disciples to set before *them;* and they did set *them* before the people. 7And they had a few small fishes: and he blessed, and commanded to set them also before *them.* 8 So they did eat, and were filled: and they took up of the broken *meat* that was left seven baskets. 9And they that had eaten were about four thousand: and he sent them away.

10 And straightway he entered into a ship with his disciples, and came into the parts of Dalmanutha. 11And the Pharisees came forth, and began to question with him, seeking of him a sign from heaven, tempting him. 12And he sighed deeply in his spirit, and saith, Why doth this generation seek after a sign? verily I say unto you, There shall no sign be given unto this generation. 13And he left them, and entering into the ship again departed to the other side.

14 Now *the disciples* had forgotten to take bread, neither had they in the ship with them more than one loaf. 15And he charged them, saying, Take heed, beware of the leaven of the Pharisees, and *of* the leaven of Herod. 16And they reasoned among themselves, saying, *It is* because we have no bread. 17And when Jesus knew *it,* he saith unto them, Why reason ye, because ye have no bread? perceive ye not yet, neither understand? have ye your heart yet hardened? 18 Having eyes, see ye not? and having ears, hear ye not? and do ye not remember? 19 When I brake the five loaves among five thousand, how many baskets full of fragments took ye up? They say unto him, Twelve. 20And when the seven among four thousand, how many baskets full of fragments took ye up? And they said, Seven. 21And he said unto them, How is it that ye do not understand?

22 And he cometh to Bethsaida; and they bring a blind man unto him, and besought him to touch him. 23And he took the blind man by the hand, and led him out of the town; and when he had spit on his eyes, and put his hands upon him, he asked him if he saw aught. 24And he looked up, and said, I see men as trees, walking. 25After that he put *his* hands again upon his eyes, and made him look up; and he was restored, and saw every man clearly. 26And he sent him away to his house, saying, Neither go into the town, nor tell *it* to any in the town.

R.S.V.

5And he asked them, "How many loaves have you?" They said, "Seven." 6And he commanded the crowd to sit down on the ground; and he took the seven loaves, and having given thanks he broke them and gave them to his disciples to set before the people; and they set them before the crowd. 7And they had a few small fish; and having blessed them, he commanded that these also should be set before them. 8And they ate, and were satisfied; and they took up the broken pieces left over, seven baskets full. 9And there were about four thousand people. 10And he sent them away; and immediately he got into the boat with his disciples, and went to the district of Dalmanutha.[d]

11 The Pharisees came and began to argue with him, seeking from him a sign from heaven, to test him. 12And he sighed deeply in his spirit, and said, "Why does this generation seek a sign? Truly, I say to you, no sign shall be given to this generation." 13And he left them, and getting into the boat again he departed to the other side.

14 Now they had forgotten to bring bread; and they had only one loaf with them in the boat. 15And he cautioned them, saying, "Take heed, beware of the leaven of the Pharisees and the leaven of Herod."[e] 16And they discussed it with one another, saying, "We have no bread." 17And being aware of it, Jesus said to them, "Why do you discuss the fact that you have no bread? Do you not yet perceive or understand? Are your hearts hardened? 18 Having eyes do you not see, and having ears do you not hear? And do you not remember? 19 When I broke the five loaves for the five thousand, how many baskets full of broken pieces did you take up?" They said to him, "Twelve." 20 "And the seven for the four thousand, how many baskets full of broken pieces did you take up?" And they said to him, "Seven." 21And he said to them, "Do you not yet understand?"

22 And they came to Bethsaida. And some people brought to him a blind man, and begged him to touch him. 23And he took the blind man by the hand, and led him out of the village; and when he had spit on his eyes and laid his hands upon him, he asked him, "Do you see anything?" 24And he looked up and said, "I see men; but they look like trees, walking." 25 Then again he laid his hands upon his eyes; and he looked intently and was restored, and saw everything clearly. 26And he sent him away to his home, saying, "Do not even enter the village."

[d] Other ancient authorities read *Magadan* or *Magdala.* [e] Other ancient authorities read *the Herodians.*

PHILLIPS

"How many loaves have you got?" Jesus asked them.

"Seven," they replied.

So Jesus told the crowd to settle themselves on the ground. Then he took the seven loaves into his hands, and with a prayer of thanksgiving broke them, and gave them to the disciples to distribute to the people; and this they did. They had a few small fish as well, and after blessing them, Jesus told the disciples to give these also to the people. They ate and they were satisfied. Moreover, they picked up seven baskets full of pieces left over. The people numbered about four thousand. Jesus sent them home, and then he boarded the boat at once with his disciples and went on to the district of Dalmanutha.

Jesus refuses to give a sign   8. 11

Now the Pharisees came out and began an argument with him, wanting a sign from Heaven. Jesus gave a deep sigh, and then said:

"What makes this generation want a sign? I can tell you this, they will certainly not be given one!"

Then he left them and got aboard the boat again, and crossed the lake.

The disciples had forgotten to take any food and had only one loaf with them in the boat. Jesus spoke seriously to them: "Keep your eyes open! Be on your guard against the 'yeast' of the Pharisees and the 'yeast' of Herod!" And this sent them into an earnest consultation among themselves because they had brought no bread. Jesus knew it and said to them:

"Why all this discussion about bringing no bread? Don't you understand or grasp what I say even yet? Are you like the people who 'having eyes, do not see, and having ears, do not hear'? Have you forgotten—when I broke five loaves for five thousand people, how many baskets full of pieces did you pick up?"

"Twelve," they replied.

"And when there were seven loaves for four thousand people, how many baskets of pieces did you pick up?"

"Seven," they said.

"And does that still mean nothing to you?" he said.

Jesus restores sight   8. 22

So they arrived at Bethsaida where a blind man was brought to him, with the earnest request that he should touch him. Jesus took the blind man's hand and led him outside the village. Then he moistened his eyes with saliva and putting his hands on him, asked,

"Can you see at all?"

The man looked up and said,

"I can see people. They look like trees—only they are walking about."

Then Jesus put his hands on his eyes once more and his sight came into focus, and he recovered and saw everything sharp and clear. And Jesus sent him off to his own house with the words,

"Don't even go into the village."

N.E.B.

people with bread in this lonely place?' 'How many loaves have you?' he asked; and they answered, 'Seven.' So he ordered the people to sit down on the ground; then he took the seven loaves, and, after giving thanks to God, he broke the bread and gave it to his disciples to distribute; and they served it out to the people. They had also a few small fishes, which he blessed and ordered them to distribute. They all ate to their hearts' content, and seven baskets were filled with the scraps that were left. The people numbered about four thousand. Then he dismissed them; and, without delay, got into the boat with his disciples and went to the district of Dalmanutha.[a]

Then the Pharisees came out and engaged him in discussion. To test him they asked him for a sign from heaven. He sighed deeply to himself and said, 'Why does this generation ask for a sign? I tell you this: no sign shall be given to this generation.' With that he left them, re-embarked, and went off to the other side of the lake.

Now they had forgotten to take bread with them; they had no more than one loaf in the boat. He began to warn them: 'Beware,' he said, 'be on your guard against the leaven of the Pharisees and the leaven of Herod.' They said among themselves, 'It is because we have no bread.' Knowing what was in their minds, he asked them, 'Why do you talk about having no bread? Have you no inkling yet? Do you still not understand? Are your minds closed? You have eyes: can you not see? You have ears: can you not hear? Have you forgotten? When I broke the five loaves among five thousand, how many basketfuls of scraps did you pick up?' 'Twelve', they said. 'And how many when I broke the seven loaves among four thousand?' They answered, 'Seven.' He said, 'Do you still not understand?'

They arrived at Bethsaida. There the people brought a blind man to Jesus and begged him to touch him. He took the blind man by the hand and led him away out of the village. Then he spat on his eyes, laid his hands upon him, and asked whether he could see anything. The man's sight began to come back, and he said, 'I see men; they look like trees, but they are walking about.' Jesus laid his hands on his eyes again; he looked hard, and now he was cured so that he saw everything clearly. Then Jesus sent him home, saying, 'Do not tell anyone in the village.'[b]

[a] Some witnesses give Magedan; others give Magdala. [b] Some witnesses read Do not go into the village.

K.J.V.

27 And Jesus went out, and his disciples, into the towns of Cesarea Philippi: and by the way he asked his disciples, saying unto them, Whom do men say that I am? 28And they answered, John the Baptist: but some *say*, Elias; and others, One of the prophets. 29And he saith unto them, But whom say ye that I am? And Peter answereth and saith unto him, Thou art the Christ. 30And he charged them that they should tell no man of him. 31And he began to teach them, that the Son of man must suffer many things, and be rejected of the elders, and *of* the chief priests, and scribes, and be killed, and after three days rise again. 32And he spake that saying openly. And Peter took him, and began to rebuke him. 33 But when he had turned about and looked on his disciples, he rebuked Peter, saying, Get thee behind me, Satan: for thou savourest not the things that be of God, but the things that be of men.

34 And when he had called the people *unto him* with his disciples also, he said unto them, Whosoever will come after me, let him deny himself, and take up his cross, and follow me. 35 For whosoever will save his life shall lose it; but whosoever shall lose his life for my sake and the gospel's, the same shall save it. 36 For what shall it profit a man, if he shall gain the whole world, and lose his own soul? 37 Or what shall a man give in exchange for his soul? 38 Whosoever therefore shall be ashamed of me and of my words, in this adulterous and sinful generation, of him also shall the Son of man be ashamed, when he cometh in the glory of his Father with the holy angels.

9 And he said unto them, Verily I say unto you, That there be some of them that stand here, which shall not taste of death, till they have seen the kingdom of God come with power.

2 And after six days Jesus taketh *with him* Peter, and James, and John, and leadeth them up into a high mountain apart by themselves: and he was transfigured before them. 3And his raiment became shining, exceeding white as snow; so as no fuller on earth can white them. 4And there appeared unto them Elias with Moses: and they were talking with Jesus. 5And Peter answered and said to Jesus, Master, it is good for us to be here: and let us make three tabernacles; one for thee, and one for Moses, and one for Elias. 6 For he wist not what to say; for they were sore afraid. 7And there was a cloud that overshadowed them: and a voice came out of the cloud, saying, This is my be-

R.S.V.

27 And Jesus went on with his disciples, to the villages of Caesarea Philippi; and on the way he asked his disciples, "Who do men say that I am?" 28And they told him, "John the Baptist; and others say, Elijah; and others one of the prophets." 29And he asked them, "But who do you say that I am?" Peter answered him, "You are the Christ." 30And he charged them to tell no one about him.

31 And he began to teach them that the Son of man must suffer many things, and be rejected by the elders and the chief priests and the scribes, and be killed, and after three days rise again. 32And he said this plainly. And Peter took him, and began to rebuke him. 33 But turning and seeing his disciples, he rebuked Peter, and said, "Get behind me, Satan! For you are not on the side of God, but of men."

34 And he called to him the multitude with his disciples, and said to them, "If any man would come after me, let him deny himself and take up his cross and follow me. 35 For whoever would save his life will lose it; and whoever loses his life for my sake and the gospel's will save it. 36 For what does it profit a man, to gain the whole world and forfeit his life? 37 For what can a man give in return for his life? 38 For whoever is ashamed of me and of my words in this adulterous and sinful generation, of him will the Son of man also be ashamed, when he comes in the glory of his Father with the holy angels.

9 And he said to them, "Truly, I say to you, there are some standing here who will not taste death before they see the kingdom of God come with power."

2 And after six days Jesus took with him Peter and James and John, and led them up a high mountain apart by themselves; and he was transfigured before them, 3 and his garments became glistening, intensely white, as no fuller on earth could bleach them. 4And there appeared to them Elijah with Moses; and they were talking to Jesus. 5And Peter said to Jesus, "Master,[f] it is well that we are here; let us make three booths, one for you and one for Moses and one for Elijah." 6 For he did not know what to say, for they were exceedingly afraid. 7And a cloud overshadowed them, and a voice came out of the

[f] Or *Rabbi.*

PHILLIPS

N.E.B.

Jesus' question: Peter's   8. 27
inspired answer

Jesus then went away with his disciples to the villages of Caesarea Philippi. On the way he asked them,
"Who are men saying that I am?"
"John the Baptist," they answered. "But others say that you are Elijah or, some say, one of the prophets."
Then he asked them,
"But what about you—who do you say that I am?"
"You are Christ!" answered Peter.
Then Jesus impressed it upon them that they must not mention this to anyone.

Jesus speaks of the future and   8. 31
of the cost of discipleship

And he began to teach them that it was inevitable that the Son of Man should go through much suffering and be utterly repudiated by the elders and chief priests and scribes, and be killed, and after three days rise again. He told them all this quite bluntly.
This made Peter draw him to one side and take him to task about what he had said. But Jesus turned and faced his disciples and rebuked Peter.
"Out of my way, Satan!" he said. "Peter, you are not looking at things from God's point of view, but from man's!"
Then he called his disciples and the people around him, and said to them:
"If anyone wants to follow in my footsteps, he must give up all right to himself, take up his cross and follow me. The man who tries to save his life will lose it; it is the man who loses his life for my sake and the gospel's who will save it. What good can it do a man to gain the whole world at the price of his own soul? What can a man offer to buy back his soul once he has lost it? If anyone is ashamed of me and my words in this unfaithful and sinful generation, the Son of Man will be ashamed of him when he comes in the Father's glory with the holy angels around him."

Jesus foretells his glory   9. 1

Then he added,
"Believe me, there are some of you standing here who will know nothing of death until you have seen the kingdom of God coming in its power!"
Six days later, Jesus took Peter and James and John with him and led them high up on a hillside where they were entirely alone. His whole appearance changed before their eyes, while his clothes became white, dazzling white—whiter than any earthly bleaching could make them. Elijah and Moses appeared to the disciples and stood there in conversation with Jesus. Peter burst out to Jesus:
"Master, it is wonderful for us to be here! Shall we put up three shelters—one for you, one for Moses and one for Elijah?"
He really did not know what to say, for they were very frightened. Then came a cloud which overshadowed them and a voice spoke out of the cloud,

Jesus and his disciples set out for the villages of Caesarea Philippi. On the way he asked his disciples, 'Who do men say I am?' They answered, 'Some say John the Baptist, others Elijah, others one of the prophets.' 'And you,' he asked, 'who do you say I am?' Peter replied: 'You are the Messiah.' Then he gave them strict orders not to tell anyone about him; and he began to teach them that the Son of Man had to undergo great sufferings, and to be rejected by the elders, chief priests, and doctors of the law; to be put to death, and to rise again three days afterwards. He spoke about it plainly. At this Peter took him by the arm and began to rebuke him. But Jesus turned round, and, looking at his disciples, rebuked Peter. 'Away with you, Satan,' he said; 'you think as men think, not as God thinks.'
Then he called the people to him, as well as his disciples, and said to them, 'Anyone who wishes to be a follower of mine must leave self behind; he must take up his cross, and come with me. Whoever cares for his own safety is lost; but if a man will let himself be lost for my sake and for the Gospel, that man is safe. What does a man gain by winning the whole world at the cost of his true self? What can he give to buy that self back? If anyone is ashamed of me and mine[a] in this wicked and godless age, the Son of Man will be ashamed of him, when he comes in the glory of his Father and of the holy angels.' [b]

9 He also said, 'I tell you this: there are some of those standing here who will not taste death before they have seen the kingdom of God already come in power.'
Six days later Jesus took Peter, James, and John with him and led them up a high mountain where they were alone; and in their presence he was transfigured; his clothes became dazzling white, with a whiteness no bleacher on earth could equal. They saw Elijah appear, and Moses with him, and there they were, conversing with Jesus. Then Peter spoke: 'Rabbi,' he said, 'how good it is that we are here! Shall we make three shelters, one for you, one for Moses, and one for Elijah?' (For he did not know what to say; they were so terrified.) Then a cloud appeared, casting its shadow over them, and out of the cloud came a voice: 'This is my Son, my

[a] *Some witnesses read* me and my words. [b] *Some witnesses read* Father with the holy angels.

K.J.V.

loved Son: hear him. 8And suddenly, when they had looked round about, they saw no man any more, save Jesus only with themselves. 9And as they came down from the mountain, he charged them that they should tell no man what things they had seen, till the Son of man were risen from the dead. 10And they kept that saying with themselves, questioning one with another what the rising from the dead should mean.

11 And they asked him, saying, Why say the scribes that Elias must first come? 12And he answered and told them, Elias verily cometh first, and restoreth all things; and how it is written of the Son of man, that he must suffer many things, and be set at nought. 13 But I say unto you, That Elias is indeed come, and they have done unto him whatsoever they listed, as it is written of him.

14 And when he came to *his* disciples, he saw a great multitude about them, and the scribes questioning with them. 15And straightway all the people, when they beheld him, were greatly amazed, and running to *him* saluted him. 16And he asked the scribes, What question ye with them? 17And one of the multitude answered and said, Master, I have brought unto thee my son, which hath a dumb spirit; 18And wheresoever he taketh him, he teareth him; and he foameth, and gnasheth with his teeth, and pineth away: and I spake to thy disciples that they should cast him out; and they could not. 19 He answereth him, and saith, O faithless generation, how long shall I be with you? how long shall I suffer you? bring him unto me. 20And they brought him unto him: and when he saw him, straightway the spirit tare him; and he fell on the ground, and wallowed foaming. 21And he asked his father, How long is it ago since this came unto him? And he said, Of a child. 22And ofttimes it hath cast him into the fire, and into the waters, to destroy him: but if thou canst do any thing, have compassion on us, and help us. 23 Jesus said unto him, If thou canst believe, all things *are* possible to him that believeth. 24And straightway the father of the child cried out, and said with tears, Lord, I believe; help thou mine unbelief. 25 When Jesus saw that the people came running together, he rebuked the foul spirit, saying unto him, *Thou* dumb and deaf spirit, I charge thee, come out of him, and enter no more into him. 26And *the spirit* cried, and rent him sore, and came out of him: and he was as one dead; insomuch that many said, He is dead. 27 But Jesus took him by the hand, and lifted him up; and he arose. 28And when he was come into the house, his disciples asked him privately, Why could not we cast him out? 29And he said unto them, This kind can come forth by nothing, but by prayer and fasting.

R.S.V.

cloud, "This is my beloved Son;[g] listen to him." 8And suddenly looking around they no longer saw any one with them but Jesus only.

9 And as they were coming down the mountain, he charged them to tell no one what they had seen, until the Son of man should have risen from the dead. 10 So they kept the matter to themselves, questioning what the rising from the dead meant. 11And they asked him, "Why do the scribes say that first Elijah must come?" 12And he said to them, "Elijah does come first to restore all things; and how is it written of the Son of man, that he should suffer many things and be treated with contempt? 13 But I tell you that Elijah has come, and they did to him whatever they pleased, as it is written of him."

14 And when they came to the disciples, they saw a great crowd about them, and scribes arguing with them. 15And immediately all the crowd, when they saw him, were greatly amazed, and ran up to him and greeted him. 16And he asked them, "What are you discussing with them?" 17And one of the crowd answered him, "Teacher, I brought my son to you, for he has a dumb spirit; 18 and wherever it seizes him, it dashes him down; and he foams and grinds his teeth and becomes rigid; and I asked your disciples to cast it out, and they were not able." 19And he answered them, "O faithless generation, how long am I to be with you? How long am I to bear with you? Bring him to me." 20And they brought the boy to him; and when the spirit saw him, immediately it convulsed the boy, and he fell on the ground and rolled about, foaming at the mouth. 21And Jesus[h] asked his father, "How long has he had this?" And he said, "From childhood. 22And it has often cast him into the fire and into the water, to destroy him; but if you can do anything, have pity on us and help us." 23And Jesus said to him, "If you can! All things are possible to him who believes." 24 Immediately the father of the child cried out[i] and said, "I believe; help my unbelief!" 25And when Jesus saw that a crowd came running together, he rebuked the unclean spirit, saying to it, "You dumb and deaf spirit, I command you, come out of him, and never enter him again." 26And after crying out and convulsing him terribly, it came out, and the boy was like a corpse; so that most of them said, "He is dead." 27 But Jesus took him by the hand and lifted him up, and he arose. 28And when he had entered the house, his disciples asked him privately, "Why could we not cast it out?" 29And he said to them, "This kind cannot be driven out by anything but prayer." [j]

---

[g] Or *my Son, my* (or *the) Beloved.* [h] Greek *he.* [i] Other ancient authorities add *with tears.* [j] Other ancient authorities add *and fasting.*

PHILLIPS

N.E.B.

"This is my dearly loved Son. Listen to him!"

Then, quite suddenly they looked all round them and saw nobody at all with them but Jesus. And as they came down the hillside, he warned them not to tell anybody what they had seen till "the Son of Man should have risen again from the dead." They treasured this remark and tried to puzzle out among themselves what "rising from the dead" could mean. Then they asked him this question,

"Why do the scribes say that Elijah must come before Christ?"

"It is quite true," he told them, "that Elijah does come first, and begins the restitution of all things. But what does the scripture say about the Son of Man? This: that he must go through much suffering and be treated with contempt! I tell you that not only has Elijah come already but they have done to him exactly what they wanted—just as the scripture says of him."

Jesus heals an epileptic boy   9. 14

Then as they rejoined the other disciples, they saw that they were surrounded by a large crowd and that some of the scribes were arguing with them. As soon as the people saw Jesus, they ran forward excitedly to welcome him.

"What is the trouble?" Jesus asked them.

A man from the crowd answered,

"Master, I brought my son to you because he has a dumb spirit. Wherever he is, it gets hold of him, throws him down on the ground and there he foams at the mouth and grinds his teeth. It's simply wearing him out. I did speak to your disciples to get them to drive it out, but they hadn't the power to do it."

Jesus answered them:

"Oh, what a faithless people you are! How long must I be with you, how long must I put up with you? Bring him here to me."

So they brought the boy to him, and as soon as the spirit saw Jesus, it convulsed the boy, who fell to the ground and writhed there, foaming at the mouth.

"How long has he been like this?" Jesus asked the father.

"Ever since he was a child," he replied. "Again and again it has thrown him into the fire or into water to finish him off. But if you can do anything, please take pity on us and help us."

"*If you can do anything!*" retorted Jesus. "Everything is possible to the man who believes."

"I do believe," the boy's father burst out. "Help me to believe more!"

When Jesus noticed that a crowd was rapidly gathering, he spoke sharply to the evil spirit, with the words,

"I command you, deaf and dumb spirit, come out of this boy, and never go into him again!"

The spirit gave a loud scream and after a dreadful convulsion left him. The boy lay there like a corpse, so that most of the bystanders said, "He is dead."

But Jesus grasped his hands and lifted him up, and then he stood on his own feet. When he had gone home, Jesus' disciples asked him privately,

"Why were we unable to drive it out?"

"Nothing can drive out this kind of thing except prayer," replied Jesus.

Beloved;[a] listen to him.' And now suddenly, when they looked around, there was nobody to be seen but Jesus alone with themselves.

On their way down the mountain, he enjoined them not to tell anyone what they had seen until the Son of Man had risen from the dead. They seized upon those words, and discussed among themselves what this 'rising from the dead' could mean. And they put a question to him: 'Why do our teachers ᴛay that Elijah must be the first to come?' He replied, 'Yes, Elijah does come first to set everything right. Yet how is it[b] that the scriptures say of the Son of Man that he is to endure great sufferings and to be treated with contempt? However, I tell you, Elijah has already come and they have worked their will upon him, as the scriptures say of him.'

When they came back to the disciples they saw a large crowd surrounding them and lawyers arguing with them. As soon as they saw Jesus the whole crowd were overcome with awe, and they ran forward to welcome him. He asked them, 'What is this argument about?' A man in the crowd spoke up: 'Master, I brought my son to you. He is possessed by a spirit which makes him speechless. Whenever it attacks him, it dashes him to the ground, and he foams at the mouth, grinds his teeth, and goes rigid. I asked your disciples to cast it out, but they failed.' Jesus answered: 'What an unbelieving and perverse generation! How long shall I be with you? How long must I endure you? Bring him to me.' So they brought the boy to him; and as soon as the spirit saw him it threw the boy into convulsions, and he fell on the ground and rolled about foaming at the mouth. Jesus asked his father, 'How long has he been like this?' 'From childhood,' he replied; 'often it has tried to make an end of him by throwing him into the fire or into water. But if it is at all possible for you, take pity upon us and help us.' 'If it is possible!' said Jesus. 'Everything is possible to one who has faith.' 'I have faith,' cried the boy's father; 'help me where faith falls short.' Jesus saw then that the crowd was closing in upon them, so he rebuked the unclean spirit. 'Deaf and dumb spirit,' he said, 'I command you, come out of him and never go back!' After crying aloud and racking him fiercely, it came out; and the boy looked like a corpse; in fact, many said, 'He is dead.' But Jesus took his hand and raised him to his feet, and he stood up.

Then Jesus went indoors, and his disciples asked him privately, 'Why could not we cast it out?' He said, 'There is no means of casting out this sort but prayer.'[c]

[a] *Or* This is my only Son. [b] *Or* Elijah, you say, comes first to set everything right: then how is it . . . [c] *Some witnesses add* and fasting.

K.J.V.

30 And they departed thence, and passed through Galilee; and he would not that any man should know *it*. 31 For he taught his disciples, and said unto them, The Son of man is delivered into the hands of men, and they shall kill him; and after that he is killed, he shall rise the third day. 32 But they understood not that saying, and were afraid to ask him.

33 And he came to Capernaum: and being in the house he asked them, What was it that ye disputed among yourselves by the way? 34 But they held their peace: for by the way they had disputed among themselves, who *should be* the greatest. 35And he sat down, and called the twelve, and saith unto them, If any man desire to be first, *the same* shall be last of all, and servant of all. 36And he took a child, and set him in the midst of them: and when he had taken him in his arms, he said unto them, 37 Whosoever shall receive one of such children in my name, receiveth me; and whosoever shall receive me, receiveth not me, but him that sent me.

38 And John answered him, saying, Master, we saw one casting out devils in thy name, and he followeth not us; and we forbade him, because he followeth not us. 39 But Jesus said, Forbid him not: for there is no man which shall do a miracle in my name, that can lightly speak evil of me. 40 For he that is not against us is on our part. 41 For whosoever shall give you a cup of water to drink in my name, because ye belong to Christ, verily I say unto you, he shall not lose his reward. 42And whosoever shall offend one of *these* little ones that believe in me, it is better for him that a millstone were hanged about his neck, and he were cast into the sea. 43And if thy hand offend thee, cut it off: it is better for thee to enter into life maimed, than having two hands to go into hell, into the fire that never shall be quenched: 44 Where their worm dieth not, and the fire is not quenched. 45And if thy foot offend thee, cut it off: it is better for thee to enter halt into life, than having two feet to be cast into hell, into the fire that never shall be quenched: 46 Where their worm dieth not, and the fire is not quenched. 47And if thine eye offend thee, pluck it out: it is better for thee to enter into the kingdom of God with one eye, than having two eyes to be cast into hell fire: 48 Where their worm dieth not, and the fire is not quenched. 49 For every one shall be salted with fire, and every sacrifice shall be salted with salt. 50 Salt *is* good: but if the salt have lost his saltness, wherewith will ye season it? Have salt in yourselves, and have peace one with another.

R.S.V.

30 They went on from there and passed through Galilee. And he would not have any one know it; 31 for he was teaching his disciples, saying to them, "The Son of man will be delivered into the hands of men, and they will kill him; and when he is killed, after three days he will rise." 32 But they did not understand the saying, and they were afraid to ask him.

33 And they came to Capernaum; and when he was in the house he asked them, "What were you discussing on the way?" 34 But they were silent; for on the way they had discussed with one another who was the greatest. 35And he sat down and called the twelve; and he said to them, "If any one would be first, he must be last of all and servant of all." 36And he took a child, and put him in the midst of them; and taking him in his arms, he said to them, 37 "Whoever receives one such child in my name receives me; and whoever receives me, receives not me but him who sent me."

38 John said to him, "Teacher, we saw a man casting out demons in your name,[k] and we forbade him, because he was not following us." 39 But Jesus said, "Do not forbid him; for no one who does a mighty work in my name will be able soon after to speak evil of me. 40 For he that is not against us is for us. 41 For truly, I say to you, whoever gives you a cup of water to drink because you bear the name of Christ, will by no means lose his reward.

42 "Whoever causes one of these little ones who believe in me to sin,[l] it would be better for him if a great millstone were hung round his neck and he were thrown into the sea. 43And if your hand causes you to sin,[l] cut it off; it is better for you to enter life maimed than with two hands to go to hell,[m] to the unquenchable fire.[n] 45And if your foot causes you to sin,[l] cut it off; it is better for you to enter life lame than with two feet to be thrown into hell.[m,n] 47And if your eye causes you to sin,[l] pluck it out; it is better for you to enter the kingdom of God with one eye than with two eyes to be thrown into hell,[m] 48 where their worm does not die, and the fire is not quenched. 49 For every one will be salted with fire.[o] 50 Salt is good; but if the salt has lost its saltness, how will you season it? Have salt in yourselves, and be at peace with one another."

[k] Other ancient authorities add *who does not follow us*. [l] Greek *stumble*. [m] Greek *Gehenna*. [n] Verses 44 and 46 (which are identical with verse 48) are omitted by the best ancient authorities. [o] Other ancient authorities add *and every sacrifice will be salted with salt*.

PHILLIPS

N.E.B.

Jesus privately warns his disciples   9. 30
of his own death

Then they left that district and went straight through Galilee. Jesus kept this journey secret, for he was teaching his disciples that the Son of Man would be betrayed into the power of men, that they would kill him and that three days after his death he would rise again. But they were completely mystified by this saying, and were afraid to question him about it.

Jesus defines the new "greatness"   9. 33

So they came to Capernaum. And when they were indoors he asked them,

"What were you discussing as we came along?"

They were silent, for on the way they had been arguing about who should be the greatest. Jesus sat down and called the twelve, and said to them,

"If any man wants to be first, he must be last and servant of all."

Then he took a little child and stood him in front of them all, and putting his arms round him, said to them:

"Anyone who welcomes one little child like this for my sake is welcoming me. And the man who welcomes me is welcoming not only me but the one who sent me!"

Then John said to him,

"Master, we saw somebody driving out evil spirits in your name, and we stopped him, for he is not one who follows us."

But Jesus replied:

"You must not stop him. No one who exerts such power in my name would readily say anything against me. For the man who is not against us is on our side. In fact, I assure you that the man who gives you a mere drink of water in my name, because you are followers of mine, will most certainly be rewarded. And I tell you too, that the man who disturbs the faith of one of the humblest of those who believe in me would be better off if he were thrown into the sea with a great millstone hung round his neck!

Entering the kingdom may mean   9. 43
painful sacrifice

"Indeed, if it is your own hand that spoils your faith, you must cut it off. It is better for you to enter life maimed than to keep both your hands and go to the rubbish heap. If your foot spoils your faith, you must cut it off. It is better for you to enter life on one foot than to keep both your feet and be thrown on to the rubbish heap. And if your eye leads you astray, pluck it out. It is better for you to go one-eyed into the kingdom of God than to keep both eyes and be thrown on to the rubbish heap, where decay never stops and the fire never goes out. For everyone will be salted with fire. Salt is a very good thing; but if it should lose its saltiness, what can you do to restore its flavor? You must have salt in yourselves, and live at peace with each other."

They now left that district and made a journey through Galilee. Jesus wished it to be kept secret; for he was teaching his disciples, and telling them, 'The Son of Man is now to be given up into the power of men, and they will kill him, and three days after being killed, he will rise again.' But they did not understand what he said, and were afraid to ask.

So they came to Capernaum; and when he was indoors, he asked them, 'What were you arguing about on the way?' They were silent, because on the way they had been discussing who was the greatest. He sat down, called the Twelve, and said to them, 'If anyone wants to be first, he must make himself last of all and servant of all.' Then he took a child, set him in front of them, and put his arm round him. 'Whoever receives one of these children in my name', he said, 'receives me; and whoever receives me, receives not me but the One who sent me.'

John said to him, 'Master, we saw a man driving out devils in your name, and as he was not one of us, we tried to stop him.' Jesus said, 'Do not stop him; no one who does a work of divine power in my name will be able in the same breath to speak evil of me. For he who is not against us is on our side. I tell you this: if anyone gives you a cup of water to drink because you are followers of the Messiah, that man assuredly will not go unrewarded.

'As for the man who leads astray one of these little ones who have faith, it would be better for him to be thrown into the sea with a millstone round his neck. If your hand is your undoing, cut it off; it is better for you to enter into life maimed than to keep both hands and go to hell and the unquenchable fire.[a] And if it is your foot that leads you astray, cut it off; it is better to enter into life a cripple than to keep both your feet and be thrown into hell.[b] And if it is your eye, tear it out; it is better to enter into the kingdom of God with one eye than to keep both eyes and be thrown into hell, where the devouring worm never dies and the fire is not quenched.

'For everyone will be salted with fire.

'Salt is a good thing; but if the salt loses its saltness, what will you season it with?

'Have salt in yourselves; and be[c] at peace with one another.'

---

[a] *Some witnesses add* (44) where the devouring worm never dies and the fire is not quenched. [b] *Some witnesses add* (46) where the devouring worm never dies and the fire is not quenched. [c] *Or* Have the salt of fellowship and be . . . ; *or* You have the salt of fellowship between you; then be . . .

K.J.V.

10 And he arose from thence, and cometh into the coasts of Judea by the farther side of Jordan: and the people resort unto him again; and, as he was wont, he taught them again.
2 And the Pharisees came to him, and asked him, Is it lawful for a man to put away *his* wife? tempting him. 3And he answered and said unto them, What did Moses command you? 4And they said, Moses suffered to write a bill of divorcement, and to put *her* away. 5And Jesus answered and said unto them, For the hardness of your heart he wrote you this precept. 6 But from the beginning of the creation God made them male and female. 7 For this cause shall a man leave his father and mother, and cleave to his wife; 8And they twain shall be one flesh: so then they are no more twain, but one flesh. 9 What therefore God hath joined together, let not man put asunder. 10And in the house his disciples asked him again of the same *matter*. 11And he saith unto them, Whosoever shall put away his wife, and marry another, committeth adultery against her. 12And if a woman shall put away her husband, and be married to another, she committeth adultery.
13 And they brought young children to him, that he should touch them; and *his* disciples rebuked those that brought *them*. 14 But when Jesus saw *it*, he was much displeased, and said unto them, Suffer the little children to come unto me, and forbid them not; for of such is the kingdom of God. 15 Verily I say unto you, Whosoever shall not receive the kingdom of God as a little child, he shall not enter therein. 16And he took them up in his arms, put *his* hands upon them, and blessed them.
17 And when he was gone forth into the way, there came one running, and kneeled to him, and asked him, Good Master, what shall I do that I may inherit eternal life? 18And Jesus said unto him, Why callest thou me good? *there is* none good but one, *that is,* God. 19 Thou knowest the commandments, Do not commit adultery, Do not kill, Do not steal, Do not bear false witness, Defraud not, Honour thy father and mother. 20And he answered and said unto him, Master, all these have I observed from my youth. 21 Then Jesus beholding him loved him, and said unto him, One thing thou lackest: go thy way, sell whatsoever thou hast, and give to the poor, and thou shalt have treasure in heaven: and come, take up the cross, and follow me. 22And he was sad at that saying, and went away grieved: for he had great possessions.
23 And Jesus looked round about, and saith unto his disciples, How hardly shall they that have riches enter into the kingdom of God! 24And the disciples were astonished at his words.

R.S.V.

10 And he left there and went to the region of Judea and beyond the Jordan, and crowds gathered to him again; and again, as his custom was, he taught them.
2 And Pharisees came up and in order to test him asked, "Is it lawful for a man to divorce his wife?" 3 He answered them, "What did Moses command you?" 4 They said, "Moses allowed a man to write a certificate of divorce, and to put her away." 5 But Jesus said to them, "For your hardness of heart he wrote you this commandment. 6 But from the beginning of creation, 'God made them male and female.' 7 'For this reason a man shall leave his father and mother and be joined to his wife,^{p} 8 and the two shall become one.' ^{q} So they are no longer two but one.^{q} 9 What therefore God has joined together, let not man put asunder."
10 And in the house the disciples asked him again about this matter. 11And he said to them, "Whoever divorces his wife and marries another, commits adultery against her; 12 and if she divorces her husband and marries another, she commits adultery."
13 And they were bringing children to him, that he might touch them; and the disciples rebuked them. 14 But when Jesus saw it he was indignant, and said to them, "Let the children come to me, do not hinder them; for to such belongs the kingdom of God. 15 Truly, I say to you, whoever does not receive the kingdom of God like a child shall not enter it." 16And he took them in his arms and blessed them, laying his hands upon them.
17 And as he was setting out on his journey, a man ran up and knelt before him, and asked him, "Good Teacher, what must I do to inherit eternal life?" 18And Jesus said to him, "Why do you call me good? No one is good but God alone. 19 You know the commandments: 'Do not kill, Do not commit adultery, Do not steal, Do not bear false witness, Do not defraud, Honor your father and mother.'" 20And he said to him, "Teacher, all these I have observed from my youth." 21And Jesus looking upon him loved him, and said to him, "You lack one thing; go, sell what you have, and give to the poor, and you will have treasure in heaven; and come, follow me." 22At that saying his countenance fell, and he went away sorrowful; for he had great possessions.
23 And Jesus looked around and said to his disciples, "How hard it will be for those who have riches to enter the kingdom of God!" 24And the disciples were amazed at his words. But

[*p*] Other ancient authorities omit *and be joined to his wife.* [*q*] Greek *one flesh.*

The divine purpose in marriage   10. 1

Then he got up and left Galilee and went off to the borders of Judaea and beyond the Jordan. Again great crowds assembled to meet him, and again, according to his custom, he taught them. Then some Pharisees arrived to ask him this test question,

"Is it right for a man to divorce his wife?"

Jesus replied by asking them,

"What has Moses commanded you to do?"

"Moses allows men to write a divorce notice and then to dismiss her," they said.

"Moses gave you that commandment," returned Jesus, "because you know so little of the meaning of love. But from the beginning of the creation, God made them male and female. *'For this cause shall a man leave his father and mother, and shall cleave to his wife; and the twain shall become one flesh.'* So that in body they are no longer two people but one. That is why man must never separate what God has joined together."

On reaching the house, his disciples questioned him again about this matter.

"Any man who divorces his wife and marries another woman," he told them, "commits adultery against his wife. And if she herself divorces her husband and marries someone else, she commits adultery."

He welcomes small children   10. 13

Then some people came to him bringing little children for him to touch. The disciples tried to discourage them. When Jesus saw this, he was indignant and told them:

"You must let little children come to me— never stop them! For the kingdom of God belongs to such as these. Indeed, I assure you that the man who does not accept the kingdom of God like a little child will never enter it."

Then he took the children in his arms and laid his hands on them and blessed them.

Jesus shows the danger of riches   10. 17

As he began to take the road again, a man came running up and fell at his feet, and asked him,

"Good master, tell me, please, what must I do to be sure of eternal life?"

"I wonder why you call me good," returned Jesus. "No one is good—only God. You know the commandments, 'Do not murder, Do not commit adultery, Do not steal, Do not bear false witness, Do not cheat, Honor thy father and mother.' "

"Master," he replied, "I have carefully kept all these since I was quite young."

Jesus looked steadily at him, and his heart warmed toward him. Then he said:

"There is one thing you still want. Go and sell everything you have, give the money away to the poor—you will have riches in Heaven. And then come back and follow me."

At these words the man's face fell and he went away in deep distress, for he was very rich. Then Jesus looked round at them all, and said to his disciples,

"How difficult it is for those who have great possessions to enter the kingdom of God!"

The disciples were staggered at these words, but Jesus continued:

---

10 On leaving those parts he came into the regions of Judaea and Transjordan; and when a crowd gathered round him once again, he followed his usual practice and taught them. The question was put to him:[a] 'Is it lawful for a man to divorce his wife?' This was to test him. He asked in return, 'What did Moses command you?' They answered, 'Moses permitted a man to divorce his wife by note of dismissal.' Jesus said to them, 'It was because you were so unteachable that he made this rule for you; but in the beginning, at the creation, God made them male and female. For this reason a man shall leave his father and mother, and be made one with his wife;[b] and the two shall become one flesh. It follows that they are no longer two individuals: they are one flesh. What God has joined together, man must not separate.'

When they were indoors again the disciples questioned him about this matter; he said to them, 'Whoever divorces his wife and marries another commits adultery against her: so too, if she divorces her husband and marries another, she commits adultery.'

They brought children for him to touch; and the disciples scolded them for it. But when Jesus saw this he was indignant, and said to them, 'Let the children come to me; do not try to stop them; for the kingdom of God belongs to such as these. I tell you, whoever does not accept the kingdom of God like a child will never enter it.' And he put his arms round them, laid his hands upon them, and blessed them.

As he was starting out on a journey, a stranger ran up, and, kneeling before him, asked, 'Good Master, what must I do to win eternal life?' Jesus said to him, 'Why do you call me good? No one is good except God alone. You know the commandments: "Do not murder; do not commit adultery; do not steal; do not give false evidence; do not defraud; honour your father and mother." ' 'But, Master,' he replied, 'I have kept all these since I was a boy.' Jesus looked straight at him; his heart warmed to him, and he said, 'One thing you lack: go, sell everything you have, and give to the poor, and you will have riches in heaven; and come, follow me.' At these words his face fell and he went away with a heavy heart; for he was a man of great wealth.

Jesus looked round at his disciples and said to them, 'How hard it will be for the wealthy to enter the kingdom of God!' They were amazed

---

[a] *Some witnesses read* The Pharisees came forward and asked him the question . . . [b] *Some witnesses omit* and be made . . . wife.

K.J.V.

But Jesus answereth again, and saith unto them, Children, how hard is it for them that trust in riches to enter into the kingdom of God! 25 It is easier for a camel to go through the eye of a needle, than for a rich man to enter into the kingdom of God. 26And they were astonished out of measure, saying among themselves, Who then can be saved? 27And Jesus looking upon them saith, With men *it is* impossible, but not with God: for with God all things are possible.

28 Then Peter began to say unto him, Lo, we have left all, and have followed thee. 29And Jesus answered and said, Verily I say unto you, There is no man that hath left house, or brethren, or sisters, or father, or mother, or wife, or children, or lands, for my sake, and the gospel's, 30 But he shall receive a hundredfold now in this time, houses, and brethren, and sisters, and mothers, and children, and lands, with persecutions; and in the world to come eternal life. 31 But many *that are* first shall be last; and the last first.

32 And they were in the way going up to Jerusalem; and Jesus went before them: and they were amazed; and as they followed, they were afraid. And he took again the twelve, and began to tell them what things should happen unto him, 33 *Saying,* Behold, we go up to Jerusalem; and the Son of man shall be delivered unto the chief priests, and unto the scribes; and they shall condemn him to death, and shall deliver him to the Gentiles: 34And they shall mock him, and shall scourge him, and shall spit upon him, and shall kill him; and the third day he shall rise again.

35 And James and John, the sons of Zebedee, come unto him, saying, Master, we would that thou shouldest do for us whatsoever we shall desire. 36And he said unto them, What would ye that I should do for you? 37 They said unto him, Grant unto us that we may sit, one on thy right hand, and the other on thy left hand, in thy glory. 38 But Jesus said unto them, Ye know not what ye ask: can ye drink of the cup that I drink of? and be baptized with the baptism that I am baptized with? 39And they said unto him, We can. And Jesus said unto them, Ye shall indeed drink of the cup that I drink of; and with the baptism that I am baptized withal shall ye be baptized: 40 But to sit on my right hand and on my left hand is not mine to give; but *it shall be given to them* for whom it is prepared. 41And when the ten heard *it,* they began to be much displeased with James and John. 42 But Jesus called them *to him,* and saith unto them, Ye know that they which are accounted to rule over the Gentiles exercise lordship over them; and their great ones exercise authority upon them. 43 But so shall it not be among you: but whosoever will be great among you, shall be your minister: 44And whosoever of you will be the chiefest, shall be servant of all. 45 For even the Son of man came not to be ministered unto,

R.S.V.

Jesus said to them again, "Children, how hard it is[r] to enter the kingdom of God! 25 It is easier for a camel to go through the eye of a needle than for a rich man to enter the kingdom of God." 26And they were exceedingly astonished, and said to him,[s] "Then who can be saved?" 27 Jesus looked at them and said, "With men it is impossible, but not with God; for all things are possible with God." 28 Peter began to say to him, "Lo, we have left everything and followed you." 29 Jesus said, "Truly, I say to you, there is no one who has left house or brothers or sisters or mother or father or children or lands, for my sake and for the gospel, 30 who will not receive a hundredfold now in this time, houses and brothers and sisters and mothers and children and lands, with persecutions, and in the age to come eternal life. 31 But many that are first will be last, and the last first."

32 And they were on the road, going up to Jerusalem, and Jesus was walking ahead of them; and they were amazed, and those who followed were afraid. And taking the twelve again, he began to tell them what was to happen to him, 33 saying, "Behold, we are going up to Jerusalem; and the Son of man will be delivered to the chief priests and the scribes, and they will condemn him to death, and deliver him to the Gentiles; 34 and they will mock him, and spit upon him, and scourge him, and kill him; and after three days he will rise."

35 And James and John, the sons of Zebedee, came forward to him, and said to him, "Teacher, we want you to do for us whatever we ask of you." 36And he said to them, "What do you want me to do for you?" 37And they said to him, "Grant us to sit, one at your right hand and one at your left, in your glory." 38 But Jesus said to them, "You do not know what you are asking. Are you able to drink the cup that I drink, or to be baptized with the baptism with which I am baptized?" 39And they said to him, "We are able." And Jesus said to them, "The cup that I drink you will drink; and with the baptism with which I am baptized, you will be baptized; 40 but to sit at my right hand or at my left is not mine to grant, but it is for those for whom it has been prepared." 41And when the ten heard it, they began to be indignant at James and John. 42And Jesus called them to him and said to them, "You know that those who are supposed to rule over the Gentiles lord it over them, and their great men exercise authority over them. 43 But it shall not be so among you; but whoever would be great among you must be your servant, 44 and whoever would be first among you must be slave of all. 45 For the Son of man also came

[r] Other ancient authorities add *for those who trust in riches.* [s] Other ancient authorities read *to one another.*

PHILLIPS

"Children, you don't know how hard it can be to get into the kingdom of Heaven. Why, a camel could more easily squeeze through the eye of a needle than a rich man get into the kingdom of God."

At this their astonishment knew no bounds, and they said to one another,

"Then who can possibly be saved?"

Jesus looked straight at them and said:

"Humanly speaking it is impossible, but not with God. Everything is possible with God."

Then Peter burst out,

"But look, we have left everything and followed you!"

"I promise you," returned Jesus, "nobody leaves home or brothers or sisters or mother or father or children or property for my sake and the gospel's without getting back a hundred times over, now in this present life, homes and brothers and sisters, mothers and children and land—though not without persecution—and in the next world eternal life. But many who are first now will then be last, and the last now will then be first."

The last journey to Jerusalem   10. 32 begins

They were now on their way going up to Jerusalem, and Jesus walked on ahead. The disciples were dismayed at this, and those who followed were afraid. Then once more he took the twelve aside and began to tell them what was going to happen to him.

"We are now going up to Jerusalem," he said, "as you can see. And the Son of Man will be betrayed into the power of the chief priests and scribes. They are going to condemn him to death and hand him over to pagans who will jeer at him and spit at him and flog him and kill him. But after three days he will rise again."

An ill-timed request   10. 35

Then Zebedee's two sons James and John approached him, saying,

"Master, we want you to grant us a special request."

"What do you want me to do for you?" answered Jesus.

"Give us permission to sit one on each side of you in the glory of your kingdom!"

"You don't know what you are asking," Jesus said to them. "Can you drink the cup I have to drink? Can you go through the baptism I have to bear?"

"Yes, we can," they replied.

Then Jesus told them,

"You will indeed drink the cup I am drinking, and you will undergo the baptism which I have to bear! But as for sitting on either side of me, that is not for me to give—such places belong to those for whom they are intended."

When the other ten heard about this, they began to be highly indignant with James and John; so Jesus called them all to him, and said:

"You know that the so-called rulers in the heathen world lord it over them, and their great men have absolute power. But it must not be so among you. No, whoever among you wants to be great must become the servant of you all, and if he wants to be first among you he must be the slave of all men! For the Son of Man

N.E.B.

that he should say this, but Jesus insisted, 'Children, how hard it is[a] to enter the kingdom of God! It is easier for a camel to pass through the eye of a needle than for a rich man to enter the kingdom of God.' They were more astonished than ever, and said to one another, 'Then who can be saved?' Jesus looked them in the face and said, 'For men it is impossible, but not for God; to God everything is possible.'

At this Peter spoke. 'We here', he said, 'have left everything to become your followers.' Jesus said, 'I tell you this: there is no one who has given up home, brothers or sisters, mother, father or children, or land, for my sake and for the Gospel, who will not receive in this age a hundred times as much—houses, brothers and sisters, mothers and children, and land—and persecutions besides; and in the age to come eternal life. But many who are first will be last and the last first.'

Challenge to Jerusalem

They were on the road, going up to Jerusalem, Jesus leading the way; and the disciples were filled with awe; while those who followed behind were afraid. He took the Twelve aside and began to tell them what was to happen to him. 'We are now going to Jerusalem,' he said; 'and the Son of Man will be given up to the chief priests and the doctors of the law; they will condemn him to death and hand him over to the foreign power. He will be mocked and spat upon, flogged and killed; and three days afterwards, he will rise again.'

James and John, the sons of Zebedee, approached him and said, 'Master, we should like you to do us a favour.' 'What is it you want me to do?' he asked. They answered, 'Grant us the right to sit in state with you, one at your right and the other at your left.' Jesus said to them, 'You do not understand what you are asking. Can you drink the cup that I drink, or be baptized with the baptism I am baptized with?' 'We can', they answered. Jesus said, 'The cup that I drink you shall drink, and the baptism I am baptized with shall be your baptism; but to sit at my right or left is not for me to grant; it is for those to whom it has already been assigned.'[b]

When the other ten heard this, they were indignant with James and John. Jesus called them to him and said, 'You know that in the world the recognized rulers lord it over their subjects, and their great men make them feel the weight of authority. That is not the way with you; among you, whoever wants to be great must be your servant, and whoever wants to be first must be the willing slave of all. For even the Son of Man did not come to be served but

[a] *Some witnesses insert* for those who trust in riches. [b] *Some witnesses add* by my Father.

K.J.V.

but to minister, and to give his life a ransom for many.

46 And they came to Jericho: and as he went out of Jericho with his disciples and a great number of people, blind Bartimeus, the son of Timeus, sat by the highway side begging. 47And when he heard that it was Jesus of Nazareth, he began to cry out, and say, Jesus, *thou* Son of David, have mercy on me. 48And many charged him that he should hold his peace: but he cried the more a great deal, *Thou* Son of David, have mercy on me. 49And Jesus stood still, and commanded him to be called. And they call the blind man, saying unto him, Be of good comfort, rise; he calleth thee. 50And he, casting away his garment, rose, and came to Jesus. 51And Jesus answered and said unto him, What wilt thou that I should do unto thee? The blind man said unto him, Lord, that I might receive my sight. 52And Jesus said unto him, Go thy way; thy faith hath made thee whole. And immediately he received his sight, and followed Jesus in the way.

11 And when they came nigh to Jerusalem, unto Bethphage and Bethany, at the mount of Olives, he sendeth forth two of his disciples, 2And saith unto them, Go your way into the village over against you: and as soon as ye be entered into it, ye shall find a colt tied, whereon never man sat; loose him, and bring *him*. 3And if any man say unto you, Why do ye this? say ye that the Lord hath need of him; and straightway he will send him hither. 4And they went their way, and found the colt tied by the door without in a place where two ways met; and they loose him. 5And certain of them that stood there said unto them, What do ye, loosing the colt? 6And they said unto them even as Jesus had commanded: and they let them go. 7And they brought the colt to Jesus, and cast their garments on him; and he sat upon him. 8And many spread their garments in the way; and others cut down branches off the trees, and strewed *them* in the way. 9And they that went before, and they that followed, cried, saying, Hosanna; Blessed *is* he that cometh in the name of the Lord: 10 Blessed *be* the kingdom of our father David, that cometh in the name of the Lord: Hosanna in the highest. 11And Jesus entered into Jerusalem, and into the temple: and when he had looked round about upon all things, and now the eventide was come, he went out unto Bethany with the twelve.

12 And on the morrow, when they were come from Bethany, he was hungry: 13And seeing a fig tree afar off having leaves, he came, if haply he might find any thing thereon: and when he came to it, he found nothing but leaves; for the time of figs was not *yet*. 14And Jesus answered and said unto it, No man eat fruit of thee hereafter for ever. And his disciples heard *it*.

15 And they come to Jerusalem: and Jesus went into the temple, and began to cast out them that sold and bought in the temple, and overthrew the tables of the money changers, and the seats of them that sold doves; 16And would not suffer that any man should carry *any* vessel

R.S.V.

not to be served but to serve, and to give his life as a ransom for many."

46 And they came to Jericho; and as he was leaving Jericho with his disciples and a great multitude, Bartimaeus, a blind beggar, the son of Timaeus, was sitting by the roadside. 47And when he heard that it was Jesus of Nazareth, he began to cry out and say, "Jesus, Son of David, have mercy on me!" 48And many rebuked him, telling him to be silent; but he cried out all the more, "Son of David, have mercy on me!" 49And Jesus stopped and said, "Call him." And they called the blind man, saying to him, "Take heart; rise, he is calling you." 50And throwing off his mantle he sprang up and came to Jesus. 51And Jesus said to him, "What do you want me to do for you?" And the blind man said to him, "Master,[*t*] let me receive my sight." 52And Jesus said to him, "Go your way; your faith has made you well." And immediately he received his sight and followed him on the way.

11 And when they drew near to Jerusalem, to Bethphage and Bethany, at the Mount of Olives, he sent two of his disciples, 2 and said to them, "Go into the village opposite you, and immediately as you enter it you will find a colt tied, on which no one has ever sat; untie it and bring it. 3 If any one says to you, 'Why are you doing this?' say, 'The Lord has need of it and will send it back here immediately.'" 4And they went away, and found a colt tied at the door out in the open street; and they untied it. 5And those who stood there said to them, "What are you doing, untying the colt?" 6And they told them what Jesus had said; and they let them go. 7And they brought the colt to Jesus, and threw their garments on it; and he sat upon it. 8And many spread their garments on the road, and others spread leafy branches which they had cut from the fields. 9And those who went before and those who followed cried out, "Hosanna! Blessed is he who comes in the name of the Lord! 10 Blessed is the kingdom of our father David that is coming! Hosanna in the highest!"

11 And he entered Jerusalem, and went into the temple; and when he had looked round at everything, as it was already late, he went out to Bethany with the twelve.

12 On the following day, when they came from Bethany, he was hungry. 13And seeing in the distance a fig tree in leaf, he went to see if he could find anything on it. When he came to it, he found nothing but leaves, for it was not the season for figs. 14And he said to it, "May no one ever eat fruit from you again." And his disciples heard it.

15 And they came to Jerusalem. And he entered the temple and began to drive out those who sold and those who bought in the temple, and he overturned the tables of the moneychangers and the seats of those who sold pigeons; 16 and he would not allow any one to carry any-

[*t*] Or *Rabbi.*

PHILLIPS

N.E.B.

himself has not come to be served but to serve, and to give his life to set many others free."

Then they came to Jericho, and as he was leaving it accompanied by his disciples and a large crowd, Bartimaeus (that is, the son of Timaeus), a blind beggar, was sitting in his usual place by the side of the road. When he heard that it was Jesus of Nazareth, he began to call out,

"Jesus, Son of David, have pity on me!"

Many of the people told him sharply to keep quiet, but he shouted all the more,

"Son of David, have pity on me!"

Jesus stood quite still and said,

"Call him here."

So they called the blind man, saying,

"It's all right now; get up, he's calling you!"

At this he threw off his coat, jumped to his feet and came to Jesus.

"What do you want me to do for you?" he asked him.

"Oh, master, let me see again!"

"Go on your way then," returned Jesus, "your faith has healed you."

And he recovered his sight at once and followed Jesus along the road.

to serve, and to surrender his life as a ransom for many.'

They came to Jericho; and as he was leaving the town, with his disciples and a large crowd, Bartimaeus son of Timaeus, a blind beggar, was seated at the roadside. Hearing that it was Jesus of Nazareth, he began to shout, 'Son of David, Jesus, have pity on me!' Many of the people rounded on him: 'Be quiet', they said; but he shouted all the more, 'Son of David, have pity on me.' Jesus stopped and said, 'Call him'; so they called the blind man and said, 'Take heart; stand up; he is calling you.' At that he threw off his cloak, sprang up, and came to Jesus. Jesus said to him, 'What do you want me to do for you?' 'Master,' the blind man answered, 'I want my sight back.' Jesus said to him, 'Go; your faith has cured you.' And at once he recovered his sight and followed him on the road.

Jesus arranges for his entry   ***11. 1***
into the city

When they were approaching Jerusalem and had come to Bethphage and Bethany on the slopes of the Mount of Olives, he sent off two of his disciples with these instructions,

"Go into the village just ahead of you and as soon as you enter it you will find a tethered colt on which no one has yet ridden. Untie it, and bring it here. If anybody asks you, 'Why are you doing this?' just say, 'The Lord needs it, and will send it back immediately.'"

So they went off and found the colt tethered by a doorway outside in the open street, and they untied it. Some of the bystanders did say, "What are you doing, untying this colt?" but they made the reply Jesus told them to make, and the men raised no objection. So they brought the colt to Jesus, threw their coats on its back, and he took his seat upon it.

Many of the people spread out their coats in his path as he rode along, and others put down straw which they had cut from the fields. The whole crowd, both those who were in front and those who were behind Jesus, shouted:

"God save him!—God bless the one who comes in the name of the Lord! God bless the coming kingdom of our father David! God save him from on high!"

Jesus entered Jerusalem and went into the Temple and looked round on all that was going on. And then, since it was already late in the day, he went out to Bethany with the twelve.

On the following day, when they had left Bethany, Jesus felt hungry. He noticed a fig tree in the distance covered with leaves, and he walked up to it to see if he could find any fruit on it. But when he got to it, he could find nothing but leaves, for it was not yet time for the figs. Then Jesus spoke to the tree,

"May nobody ever eat fruit from you!"

And the disciples heard him say it.

Then they came into Jerusalem, and Jesus went into the Temple and began to drive out those who were buying and selling there. He overturned the tables of the money-changers and the benches of the dove sellers, and he would not allow people to carry their water pots

11 They were now approaching Jerusalem, and when they reached Bethphage and Bethany, at the Mount of Olives, he sent two of his disciples with these instructions: 'Go to the village opposite, and, just as you enter, you will find tethered there a colt which no one has yet ridden. Untie it and bring it here. If anyone asks, "Why are you doing that?", say, "Our Master[a] needs it, and will send it back here without delay."' So they went off, and found the colt tethered to a door outside in the street. They were untying it when some of the bystanders asked, 'What are you doing, untying that colt?' They answered as Jesus had told them, and were then allowed to take it. So they brought the colt to Jesus and spread their cloaks on it, and he mounted. And people carpeted the road with their cloaks, while others spread brushwood which they had cut in the fields; and those who went ahead and the others who came behind shouted, 'Hosanna! Blessings on him who comes in the name of the Lord! Blessings on the coming kingdom of our father David! Hosanna in the heavens!'

He entered Jerusalem and went into the temple, where he looked at the whole scene; but, as it was now late, he went out to Bethany with the Twelve.

On the following day, after they had left Bethany, he felt hungry, and, noticing in the distance a fig-tree in leaf, he went to see if he could find anything on it. But when he came there he found nothing but leaves; for it was not the season for figs. He said to the tree, 'May no one ever again eat fruit from you!' And his disciples were listening.

So they came to Jerusalem, and he went into the temple and began driving out those who bought and sold in the temple. He upset the tables of the money-changers and the seats of the dealers in pigeons; and he would not allow anyone to use the temple court as a thoroughfare

[a] *Or* Its owner.

K.J.V.

through the temple. 17And he taught, saying unto them, Is it not written, My house shall be called of all nations the house of prayer? but ye have made it a den of thieves. 18And the scribes and chief priests heard *it*, and sought how they might destroy him: for they feared him, because all the people was astonished at his doctrine. 19And when even was come, he went out of the city.

20 And in the morning, as they passed by, they saw the fig tree dried up from the roots. 21And Peter calling to remembrance saith unto him, Master, behold, the fig tree which thou cursedst is withered away. 22And Jesus answering saith unto them, Have faith in God. 23 For verily I say unto you, That whosoever shall say unto this mountain, Be thou removed, and be thou cast into the sea; and shall not doubt in his heart, but shall believe that those things which he saith shall come to pass; he shall have whatsoever he saith. 24 Therefore I say unto you, What things soever ye desire, when ye pray, believe that ye receive *them*, and ye shall have *them*. 25And when ye stand praying, forgive, if ye have aught against any; that your Father also which is in heaven may forgive you your trespasses. 26 But if ye do not forgive, neither will your Father which is in heaven forgive your trespasses.

27 And they come again to Jerusalem: and as he was walking in the temple, there come to him the chief priests, and the scribes, and the elders, 28And say unto him, By what authority doest thou these things? and who gave thee this authority to do these things? 29And Jesus answered and said unto them, I will also ask of you one question, and answer me, and I will tell you by what authority I do these things. 30 The baptism of John, was *it* from heaven, or of men? answer me. 31And they reasoned with themselves, saying, If we shall say, From heaven; he will say, Why then did ye not believe him? 32 But if we shall say, Of men; they feared the people: for all *men* counted John, that he was a prophet indeed. 33And they answered and said unto Jesus, We cannot tell. And Jesus answering saith unto them, Neither do I tell you by what authority I do these things.

R.S.V.

thing through the temple. 17And he taught, and said to them, "Is it not written, 'My house shall be called a house of prayer for all the nations'? But you have made it a den of robbers." 18And the chief priests and the scribes heard it and sought a way to destroy him; for they feared him, because all the multitude was astonished at his teaching. 19And when evening came they[u] went out of the city.

20 As they passed by in the morning, they saw the fig tree withered away to its roots. 21And Peter remembered and said to him, "Master,[v] look! The fig tree which you cursed has withered." 22And Jesus answered them, "Have faith in God. 23 Truly, I say to you, whoever says to this mountain, 'Be taken up and cast into the sea,' and does not doubt in his heart, but believes that what he says will come to pass, it will be done for him. 24 Therefore I tell you, whatever you ask in prayer, believe that you receive it, and you will. 25And whenever you stand praying, forgive, if you have anything against any one; so that your Father also who is in heaven may forgive you your trespasses."[w]

27 And they came again to Jerusalem. And as he was walking in the temple, the chief priests and the scribes and the elders came to him, 28 and they said to him, "By what authority are you doing these things, or who gave you this authority to do them?" 29 Jesus said to them, "I will ask you a question; answer me, and I will tell you by what authority I do these things. 30 Was the baptism of John from heaven or from men? Answer me." 31And they argued with one another, "If we say, 'From heaven,' he will say, 'Why then did you not believe him?' 32 But shall we say, 'From men'?"—they were afraid of the people, for all held that John was a real prophet. 33 So they answered Jesus, "We do not know." And Jesus said to them, "Neither will I tell you by what authority I do these things."

---

12 And he began to speak unto them by parables. A *certain* man planted a vineyard, and set a hedge about *it*, and digged *a place for* the winefat, and built a tower, and let it out to husbandmen, and went into a far country. 2And at the season he sent to the husbandmen a servant, that he might receive from the husbandmen of the fruit of the vineyard. 3And they caught

12 And he began to speak to them in parables. "A man planted a vineyard, and set a hedge around it, and dug a pit for the wine press, and built a tower, and let it out to tenants, and went into another country. 2 When the time came, he sent a servant to the tenants, to get from them some of the fruit of the vineyard. 3And they took him and beat him, and sent him

[u] Other ancient authorities read *he.* [v] Or *Rabbi.* [w] Other ancient authorities add verse 26, *"But if you do not forgive, neither will your Father who is in heaven forgive your trespasses."*

PHILLIPS

through the Temple. And he taught them and said,

"Doesn't the scripture say, *'My house shall be called a house of prayer for all nations'?* But you have turned it into a thieves' kitchen!"

The chief priests and scribes heard him say this and tried to find a way of getting rid of him. But they were in fact afraid of him, for his teaching had captured the imagination of the people. And every evening he left the city.

Jesus talks of faith, prayer and forgiveness
11. 20

One morning as they were walking along, they noticed that the fig tree had withered away to the roots. Peter remembered it, and said,

"Master, look, the fig tree that you cursed is all shriveled up!"

"Have faith in God," replied Jesus to them. "I tell you that if anyone should say to this hill, 'Get up and throw yourself into the sea,' and without any doubt in his heart believe that what he says will happen, then it *will* happen! That is why I tell you, whatever you pray about and ask for, believe that you have received it and it will be yours. And whenever you stand praying, you must forgive anything that you are holding against anyone else, and your Heavenly Father will forgive you *your* sins."

Jesus' authority is directly challenged
11. 27

So they came once more to Jerusalem, and while Jesus was walking in the Temple, the chief priests, elders and scribes approached him, and asked:

"What authority have you for what you're doing? And who gave you permission to do these things?"

"I am going to ask you a question," replied Jesus, "and if you answer me I will tell you what authority I have for what I do. The baptism of John, now—did it come from Heaven or was it purely human? Tell me that."

At this they argued with one another, "If we say from Heaven, he will say, 'Then why didn't you believe in him?' but if we say it was purely human, well . . ." For they were frightened of the people, since all of them believed that John was a real prophet. So they answered Jesus,

"We do not know."

"Then I cannot tell you by what authority I do these things," returned Jesus.

Jesus tells a story, with a pointed application
12. 1

Then he began to talk to them in parables. "A man once planted a vineyard," he said, "fenced it round, dug out the hole for the winepress and built a watchtower. Then he let it out to some farm workers and went abroad. At the end of the season he sent a servant to the tenants to receive his share of the vintage. But they

for carrying goods. Then he began to teach them, and said, 'Does not Scripture say, "My house shall be called a house of prayer for all the nations"? But you have made it a robbers' cave.' The chief priests and the doctors of the law heard of this and sought some means of making away with him; for they were afraid of him, because the whole crowd was spellbound by his teaching. And when evening came he went out of the city.

Early next morning, as they passed by, they saw that the fig-tree had withered from the roots up; and Peter, recalling what had happened, said to him, 'Rabbi, look, the fig-tree which you cursed has withered.' Jesus answered them, 'Have faith in God. I tell you this: if anyone says to this mountain, "Be lifted from your place and hurled into the sea", and has no inward doubts, but believes that what he says is happening, it will be done for him. I tell you, then, whatever you ask for in prayer, believe that you have received it and it will be yours.

'And when you stand praying, if you have a grievance against anyone, forgive him, so that your Father in heaven may forgive you the wrongs you have done.' [a]

They came once more to Jerusalem. And as he was walking in the temple court the chief priests, lawyers, and elders came to him and said, 'By what authority are you acting like this? Who gave you authority to act in this way?' Jesus said to them, 'I will ask you one question; and if you give me an answer, I will tell you by what authority I act. The baptism of John: was it from God, or from men? Answer me.' This set them arguing among themselves: 'What shall we say? If we say, "from God", he will say, "Then why did you not believe him?" Shall we say, "from men"?'—but they were afraid of the people, for all held that John was in fact a prophet. So they answered Jesus, 'We do not know.' And Jesus said to them, 'Then neither will I tell you by what authority I act.'

12 He went on to speak to them in parables: 'A man planted a vineyard and put a wall round it, hewed out a winepress, and built a watch-tower; then he let it out to vine-growers and went abroad. When the vintage season came, he sent a servant to the tenants to collect from them his share of the produce. But they took

[a] *Some witnesses add* (26) But if you do not forgive others, then the wrongs you have done will not be forgiven by your Father in heaven.

K.J.V.

him, and beat him, and sent *him* away empty. 4And again he sent unto them another servant; and at him they cast stones, and wounded *him* in the head, and sent *him* away shamefully handled. 5And again he sent another; and him they killed, and many others; beating some, and killing some. 6 Having yet therefore one son, his well beloved, he sent him also last unto them, saying, They will reverence my son. 7 But those husbandmen said among themselves, This is the heir; come, let us kill him, and the inheritance shall be ours. 8And they took him, and killed *him,* and cast *him* out of the vineyard. 9 What shall therefore the lord of the vineyard do? he will come and destroy the husbandmen, and will give the vineyard unto others. 10And have ye not read this Scripture; The stone which the builders rejected is become the head of the corner: 11 This was the Lord's doing, and it is marvellous in our eyes? 12And they sought to lay hold on him, but feared the people; for they knew that he had spoken the parable against them: and they left him, and went their way.

13 And they send unto him certain of the Pharisees and of the Herodians, to catch him in *his* words. 14And when they were come, they say unto him, Master, we know that thou art true, and carest for no man; for thou regardest not the person of men, but teachest the way of God in truth: Is it lawful to give tribute to Cesar, or not? 15 Shall we give, or shall we not give? But he, knowing their hypocrisy, said unto them, Why tempt ye me? bring me a penny, that I may see *it.* 16And they brought *it.* And he saith unto them, Whose *is* this image and superscription? And they said unto him, Cesar's. 17And Jesus answering said unto them, Render to Cesar the things that are Cesar's, and to God the things that are God's. And they marvelled at him.

18 Then come unto him the Sadducees, which say there is no resurrection; and they asked him, saying, 19 Master, Moses wrote unto us, If a man's brother die, and leave *his* wife *behind him,* and leave no children, that his brother should take his wife, and raise up seed unto his brother. 20 Now there were seven brethren: and the first took a wife, and dying left no seed. 21And the second took her, and died, neither left he any seed: and the third likewise. 22And the seven had her, and left no seed: last of all the woman died also. 23 In the resurrection therefore, when they shall rise, whose wife shall she

R.S.V.

away empty-handed. 4Again he sent to them another servant, and they wounded him in the head, and treated him shamefully. 5And he sent another, and him they killed; and so with many others, some they beat and some they killed. 6 He had still one other, a beloved son; finally he sent him to them, saying, 'They will respect my son.' 7 But those tenants said to one another, 'This is the heir; come, let us kill him, and the inheritance will be ours.' 8And they took him and killed him, and cast him out of the vineyard. 9 What will the owner of the vineyard do? He will come and destroy the tenants, and give the vineyard to others. 10 Have you not read this scripture:

'The very stone which the builders rejected
  has become the head of the corner;
11 this was the Lord's doing,
  and it is marvelous in our eyes'?"

12 And they tried to arrest him, but feared the multitude, for they perceived that he had told the parable against them; so they left him and went away.

13 And they sent to him some of the Pharisees and some of the Herodians, to entrap him in his talk. 14And they came and said to him, "Teacher, we know that you are true, and care for no man; for you do not regard the position of men, but truly teach the way of God. Is it lawful to pay taxes to Caesar, or not? 15 Should we pay them, or should we not?" But knowing their hypocrisy, he said to them, "Why put me to the test? Bring me a coin,[x] and let me look at it." 16And they brought one. And he said to them, "Whose likeness and inscription is this?" They said to him, "Caesar's." 17 Jesus said to them, "Render to Caesar the things that are Caesar's, and to God the things that are God's." And they were amazed at him.

18 And Sadducees came to him, who say that there is no resurrection; and they asked him a question, saying, 19 "Teacher, Moses wrote for us that if a man's brother dies and leaves a wife, but leaves no child, the man[y] must take the wife, and raise up children for his brother. 20 There were seven brothers; the first took a wife, and when he died left no children; 21 and the second took her, and died, leaving no children; and the third likewise; 22 and the seven left no children. Last of all the woman also died. 23 In the resurrection whose wife will she be? For the seven had her as wife."

[x] Greek *a denarius.* [y] Greek *his brother.*

PHILLIPS

N.E.B.

got hold of him, knocked him about and sent him off empty-handed. The owner tried again. He sent another servant to them, but this one they knocked on the head and generally insulted. Once again he sent them another servant, but him they murdered. He sent many others and some they beat up and some they murdered. He had one man left—his own son who was very dear to him. He sent him last of all to the tenants, saying to himself, 'They will surely respect my own son.' But they said to each other, 'This fellow is the future owner—come on, let's kill him, and the property will be ours!' So they got hold of him and murdered him, and threw his body out of the vineyard. What do you suppose the owner of the vineyard is going to do? He will come and destroy the men who were working his vineyard and will hand it over to others. Have you never read this scripture—

The stone which the builders rejected,
The same was made the head of the corner;
This was from the Lord,
And it is marvelous in our eyes?"

Then they tried to get their hands on him, for they knew perfectly well that he had aimed this parable at them—but they were afraid of the people. So they left him and went away.

A test question   12. 13

Later they sent some of the Pharisees and some of the Herod party to trap him in an argument. They came up and said to him:
"Master, we know that you are an honest man and that you are not swayed by men's opinion of you. Obviously you don't care for human approval but teach the way of God with the strictest regard for truth—*is it right to pay tribute to Caesar or not: are we to pay or not to pay?*"
But Jesus saw through their hypocrisy, and said to them:
"Why try this trick on me? Bring me a coin and let me look at it."
So they brought one to him.
"Whose face is this?" asked Jesus, "and whose name is in the inscription?"
"Caesar's," they replied.
And Jesus said, "Then give to Caesar what belongs to Caesar, and to God what belongs to God!"—a reply which staggered them.

Jesus reveals the ignorance   12. 18
of the Sadducees

Then some of the Sadducees (a party which maintains that there is no resurrection) approached him, and put this question to him:
"Master, Moses instructed us that if a man's brother dies leaving a widow but no child, then the man should marry the woman and raise children for his brother. Now there were seven brothers, and the first one married and died without leaving issue. Then the second one married the widow and died leaving no issue behind him. The same thing happened with the third, and indeed the whole seven died without leaving any child behind them. Finally the woman herself died. Now in this 'resurrection,' when men rise up again, whose wife is she going to be— for she was the wife of all seven of them?"

him, thrashed him, and sent him away empty-handed. Again, he sent them another servant, whom they beat about the head and treated outrageously. So he sent another, and that one they killed; and many more besides, of whom they beat some, and killed others. He had now only one left to send, his own dear son.[a] In the end he sent him. "They will respect my son", he said. But the tenants said to one another, "This is the heir; come, let us kill him, and the property will be ours." So they seized him and killed him, and flung his body out of the vineyard. What will the owner of the vineyard do? He will come and put the tenants to death and give the vineyard to others.
'Can it be that you have never read this text: "The stone which the builders rejected has become the main corner-stone. This is the Lord's doing, and it is wonderful in our eyes"?'
Then they began to look for a way to arrest him, for they saw that the parable was aimed at them; but they were afraid of popular feeling, so they left him alone and went away.

A number of Pharisees and men of Herod's party were sent to trap him with a question. They came and said, 'Master, you are an honest man, we know, and truckle to no man, whoever he may be; you teach in all honesty the way of life that God requires. Are we or are we not permitted to pay taxes to the Roman Emperor? Shall we pay or not?' He saw how crafty their question was, and said, 'Why are you trying to catch me out? Fetch me a silver piece, and let me look at it.' They brought one, and he said to them, 'Whose head is this, and whose inscription?' 'Caesar's', they replied. Then Jesus said, 'Pay Caesar what is due to Caesar, and pay God what is due to God.' And they heard him with astonishment.
Next Sadducees came to him. (It is they who say that there is no resurrection.) Their question was this: 'Master, Moses laid it down for us that if there are brothers, and one dies leaving a wife but no child, then the next should marry the widow and carry on his brother's family. Now there were seven brothers. The first took a wife and died without issue. Then the second married her, and he too died without issue. So did the third. Eventually the seven of them died, all without issue. Finally the woman died. At the resurrection, when they come back to life, whose wife will she be, since all seven had married

[a] *Or* his only son.

141

K.J.V.

be of them? for the seven had her to wife. 24And Jesus answering said unto them, Do ye not therefore err, because ye know not the Scriptures, neither the power of God? 25 For when they shall rise from the dead, they neither marry, nor are given in marriage; but are as the angels which are in heaven. 26And as touching the dead, that they rise; have ye not read in the book of Moses, how in the bush God spake unto him, saying, I *am* the God of Abraham, and the God of Isaac, and the God of Jacob? 27 He is not the God of the dead, but the God of the living: ye therefore do greatly err.

28 And one of the scribes came, and having heard them reasoning together, and perceiving that he had answered them well, asked him, Which is the first commandment of all? 29And Jesus answered him, The first of all the commandments *is,* Hear, O Israel; The Lord our God is one Lord: 30And thou shalt love the Lord thy God with all thy heart, and with all thy soul, and with all thy mind, and with all thy strength: this *is* the first commandment. 31And the second *is* like, *namely* this, Thou shalt love thy neighbour as thyself. There is none other commandment greater than these. 32And the scribe said unto him, Well, Master, thou hast said the truth: for there is one God; and there is none other but he: 33And to love him with all the heart, and with all the understanding, and with all the soul, and with all the strength, and to love *his* neighbour as himself, is more than all whole burnt offerings and sacrifices. 34And when Jesus saw that he answered discreetly, he said unto him, Thou art not far from the kingdom of God. And no man after that durst ask him *any question.*

35 And Jesus answered and said, while he taught in the temple, How say the scribes that Christ is the son of David? 36 For David himself said by the Holy Ghost, The LORD said to my Lord, Sit thou on my right hand, till I make thine enemies thy footstool. 37 David therefore himself calleth him Lord; and whence is he *then* his son? And the common people heard him gladly.

38 And he said unto them in his doctrine, Beware of the scribes, which love to go in long clothing, and *love* salutations in the marketplaces, 39And the chief seats in the synagogues, and the uppermost rooms at feasts: 40 Which devour widows' houses, and for a pretence make long prayers: these shall receive greater damnation.

41 And Jesus sat over against the treasury, and beheld how the people cast money into the

R.S.V.

24 Jesus said to them, "Is not this why you are wrong, that you know neither the scriptures nor the power of God? 25 For when they rise from the dead, they neither marry nor are given in marriage, but are like angels in heaven. 26And as for the dead being raised, have you not read in the book of Moses, in the passage about the bush, how God said to him, 'I am the God of Abraham, and the God of Isaac, and the God of Jacob'? 27 He is not God of the dead, but of the living; you are quite wrong."

28 And one of the scribes came up and heard them disputing with one another, and seeing that he answered them well, asked him, "Which commandment is the first of all?" 29 Jesus answered, "The first is, 'Hear, O Israel: The Lord our God, the Lord is one; 30 and you shall love the Lord your God with all your heart, and with all your soul, and with all your mind, and with all your strength.' 31 The second is this, 'You shall love your neighbor as yourself.' There is no other commandment greater than these." 32And the scribe said to him, "You are right, Teacher; you have truly said that he is one, and there is no other but he; 33 and to love him with all the heart, and with all the understanding, and with all the strength, and to love one's neighbor as oneself, is much more than all whole burnt offerings and sacrifices." 34And when Jesus saw that he answered wisely, he said to him, "You are not far from the kingdom of God." And after that no one dared to ask him any question.

35 And as Jesus taught in the temple, he said, "How can the scribes say that the Christ is the son of David? 36 David himself, inspired by* the Holy Spirit, declared,

'The Lord said to my Lord,
Sit at my right hand,
till I put thy enemies under thy feet.'

37 David himself calls him Lord; so how is he his son?" And the great throng heard him gladly.

38 And in his teaching he said, "Beware of the scribes, who like to go about in long robes, and to have salutations in the market places 39 and the best seats in the synagogues and the places of honor at feasts, 40 who devour widows' houses and for a pretense make long prayers. They will receive the greater condemnation."

41 And he sat down opposite the treasury, and watched the multitude putting money into the

[z] Or *himself, in.*

PHILLIPS

Jesus replied: "Does not this show where you go wrong—and how you fail to understand both the scriptures and the power of God? When people rise from the dead they neither marry nor are they given in marriage; they live like the angels in Heaven. But as for this matter of the dead being raised, have you never read in the book of Moses, in the passage about the bush, how God spoke to him in these words, 'I am the God of Abraham and the God of Isaac and the God of Jacob'? God is not God of the dead but of living men! That is where you make your great mistake!"

The most important commandments   12. 28

Then one of the scribes approached him. He had been listening to the discussion, and noticing how well Jesus had answered them, he put this question to him,

"What are we to consider the greatest commandment of all?"

"The first and most important one is this," Jesus replied—" *Hear, O Israel: The Lord our God, the Lord is one: and thou shalt love the Lord thy God with all thy heart, and with all thy soul, and with all thy mind, and with all thy strength.'* The second is this, *'Thou shalt love thy neighbor as thyself.'* No other commandment is greater than these."

"I am well answered," replied the scribe. "You are absolutely right when you say that there is one God and no other God exists but him; and to love him with the whole of our hearts, the whole of our intelligence and the whole of our energy, and to love our neighbors as ourselves is infinitely more important than all these burnt offerings and sacrifices."

Then Jesus, noting the thoughtfulness of his reply, said to him,

"You are not far from the kingdom of God!" After this nobody felt like asking him any more questions.

Jesus criticizes the scribes' teaching and behavior   12. 35

Later, while Jesus was teaching in the Temple, he remarked,

"How can the scribes make out that Christ is David's *son,* for David himself, inspired by the Holy Spirit, said,

The Lord said unto my *Lord,*
Sit thou on my right hand,
Till I make thine enemies the footstool of thy feet.

David is himself calling Christ 'Lord'—where do they get the idea that he is his son?"

The vast crowd heard this with great delight, and Jesus continued in his teaching,

"Be on your guard against these scribes who love to walk about in long robes and to be greeted respectfully in public and to have the front seats in the synagogue and the best places at dinner parties! These are the men who grow fat on widow's property and cover up what they are doing by making lengthy prayers. They are only adding to their own punishment!"

Then Jesus sat down opposite the Temple almsbox and watched the people putting their

N.E.B.

her?' Jesus said to them, 'You are mistaken, and surely this is the reason: you do not know either the scriptures or the power of God. When they rise from the dead, men and women do not marry; they are like angels in heaven.

'Now about the resurrection of the dead, have you never read in the Book of Moses, in the story of the burning bush, how God spoke to him and said, "I am the God of Abraham, the God of Isaac, and the God of Jacob"? God is not God of the dead but of the living. You are greatly mistaken.'

Then one of the lawyers, who had been listening to these discussions and had noted how well he answered, came forward and asked him, 'Which commandment is first of all?' Jesus answered, 'The first is, "Hear, O Israel: the Lord your God is the only Lord; love the Lord your God with all your heart, with all your soul, with all your mind, and with all your strength." The second is this: "Love your neighbour as yourself." There is no other commandment greater than these.' The lawyer said to him, 'Well said, Master. You are right in saying that God is one and beside him there is no other. And to love him with all your heart, all your understanding, and all your strength, and to love your neighbour as yourself—that is far more than any burnt offerings or sacrifices.' When Jesus saw how sensibly he answered, he said to him, 'You are not far from the kingdom of God.'

After that nobody ventured to put any more questions to him; and Jesus went on to say, as he taught in the temple, 'How can the teachers of the law maintain that the Messiah is "Son of David"? David himself said, when inspired by the Holy Spirit, "The Lord said to my Lord, 'Sit at my right hand until I make your enemies your footstool.'" David himself calls him "Lord"; how can he also be David's son?'

There was a great crowd and they listened eagerly.[a] He said as he taught them, 'Beware of the doctors of the law, who love to walk up and down in long robes, receiving respectful greetings in the street; and to have the chief seats in synagogues, and places of honour at feasts. These are the men who eat up the property of widows, while they say long prayers for appearance' sake, and they will receive the severest sentence.'[b]

Once he was standing opposite the temple treasury, watching as people dropped their

[a] *Or* The mass of the people listened eagerly.
[b] *Or* As for those who eat up the property of widows, while they say long prayers for appearance' sake, they will have an even sterner judgement to face.

K.J.V.

treasury: and many that were rich cast in much. 42And there came a certain poor widow, and she threw in two mites, which make a farthing. 43And he called *unto him* his disciples, and saith unto them, Verily I say unto you, That this poor widow hath cast more in, than all they which have cast into the treasury: 44 For all *they* did cast in of their abundance; but she of her want did cast in all that she had, *even* all her living.

13 And as he went out of the temple, one of his disciples saith unto him, Master, see what manner of stones and what buildings *are here!* 2And Jesus answering said unto him, Seest thou these great buildings? there shall not be left one stone upon another, that shall not be thrown down. 3And as he sat upon the mount of Olives, over against the temple, Peter and James and John and Andrew asked him privately, 4 Tell us, when shall these things be? and what *shall be* the sign when all these things shall be fulfilled? 5And Jesus answering them began to say, Take heed lest any *man* deceive you: 6 For many shall come in my name, saying, I am *Christ;* and shall deceive many. 7And when ye shall hear of wars and rumours of wars, be ye not troubled: for *such things* must needs be; but the end *shall* not *be* yet. 8 For nation shall rise against nation, and kingdom against kingdom: and there shall be earthquakes in divers places, and there shall be famines and troubles: these *are* the beginnings of sorrows.

9 But take heed to yourselves: for they shall deliver you up to councils; and in the synagogues ye shall be beaten: and ye shall be brought before rulers and kings for my sake, for a testimony against them. 10And the gospel must first be published among all nations. 11 But when they shall lead *you,* and deliver you up, take no thought beforehand what ye shall speak, neither do ye premeditate: but whatsoever shall be given you in that hour, that speak ye: for it is not ye that speak, but the Holy Ghost. 12 Now the brother shall betray the brother to death, and the father the son; and children shall rise up against *their* parents, and shall cause them to be put to death. 13And ye shall be hated of all *men* for my name's sake: but he that shall endure unto the end, the same shall be saved.

14 But when ye shall see the abomination of desolation, spoken of by Daniel the prophet, standing where it ought not, (let him that readeth understand,) then let them that be in Judea flee to the mountains: 15And let him that is on the housetop not go down into the house, neither enter *therein,* to take any thing out of his house: 16And let him that is in the field not turn back again for to take up his garment. 17 But woe to them that are with child, and to them that give suck in those days! 18And pray ye that your flight be not in the winter. 19 For *in* those days shall be affliction, such as was not from the beginning of the creation which God created unto this time, neither shall be. 20And except that the

R.S.V.

treasury. Many rich people put in large sums. 42And a poor widow came, and put in two copper coins, which make a penny. 43 And he called his disciples to him, and said to them, "Truly, I say to you, this poor widow has put in more than all those who are contributing to the treasury. 44 For they all contributed out of their abundance; but she out of her poverty has put in everything she had, her whole living."

13 And as he came out of the temple, one of his disciples said to him, "Look, Teacher, what wonderful stones and what wonderful buildings!" 2And Jesus said to him, "Do you see these great buildings? There will not be left here one stone upon another, that will not be thrown down."

3 And as he sat on the Mount of Olives opposite the temple, Peter and James and John and Andrew asked him privately, 4 "Tell us, when will this be, and what will be the sign when these things are all to be accomplished?" 5And Jesus began to say to them, "Take heed that no one leads you astray. 6 Many will come in my name, saying, 'I am he!' and they will lead many astray. 7And when you hear of wars and rumors of wars, do not be alarmed; this must take place, but the end is not yet. 8 For nation will rise against nation, and kingdom against kingdom; there will be earthquakes in various places, there will be famines; this is but the beginning of the sufferings.

9 "But take heed to yourselves; for they will deliver you up to councils; and you will be beaten in synagogues; and you will stand before governors and kings for my sake, to bear testimony before them. 10And the gospel must first be preached to all nations. 11And when they bring you to trial and deliver you up, do not be anxious beforehand what you are to say; but say whatever is given you in that hour, for it is not you who speak, but the Holy Spirit. 12And brother will deliver up brother to death, and the father his child, and children will rise against parents and have them put to death; 13 and you will be hated by all for my name's sake. But he who endures to the end will be saved.

14 "But when you see the desolating sacrilege set up where it ought not to be (let the reader understand), then let those who are in Judea flee to the mountains; 15 let him who is on the housetop not go down, nor enter his house, to take anything away; 16 and let him who is in the field not turn back to take his mantle. 17And alas for those who are with child and for those who give suck in those days! 18 Pray that it may not happen in winter. 19 For in those days there will be such tribulation as has not been from the beginning of the creation which God created until now, and never will be. 20And if the Lord

money into it. A great many rich people put in large sums. Then a poor widow came up and dropped in two little coins, worth together about a nickel. Jesus called his disciples to his side and said to them:

"Believe me, this poor widow has put in more than all the others. For they have all put in what they can easily afford, but she in her poverty who needs so much, has given away everything, her whole living!"

money into the chest. Many rich people were giving large sums. Presently there came a poor widow who dropped in two tiny coins, together worth a farthing. He called his disciples to him. 'I tell you this,' he said: 'this widow has given more than any of the others; for those others who have given had more than enough, but she, with less than enough, has given all that she had to live on.'

Jesus prophesies the ruin of the Temple 13. 1

Then as Jesus was leaving the Temple, one of his disciples said to him,

"Look, Master, what wonderful stonework, what a size these buildings are!"

Jesus replied:

"You see these great buildings? Not a single stone will be left standing on another; every one will be thrown down!"

Then while he was sitting on the slope of the Mount of Olives facing the Temple, Peter, James, John and Andrew said to him privately:

"Tell us, when will these things happen? What sign will there be that all these things are going to be accomplished?"

So Jesus began to tell them:

"Be very careful that no one deceives you. Many are going to come in my name and say, 'I am he,' and will lead many astray. When you hear of wars and rumors of wars, don't be alarmed. Such things are bound to happen, but the end is not yet. Nation will take up arms against nation and kingdom against kingdom. There will be earthquakes in different places and terrible famines. But this is only the beginning of 'the pains.' You yourselves must keep your wits about you, for men will hand you over to their councils, and will beat you in their synagogues. You will have to stand in front of rulers and kings for my sake to bear your witness to them—for before the end comes the gospel must be proclaimed to all nations. But when they are taking you off to trial, do not worry beforehand about what you are going to say—simply say the words you are given when the time comes. For it is not really you who will speak, but the Holy Spirit.

13 As he was leaving the temple, one of his disciples exclaimed, 'Look, Master, what huge stones! What fine buildings!' Jesus said to him, 'You see these great buildings? Not one stone will be left upon another; all will be thrown down.'

When he was sitting on the Mount of Olives facing the temple he was questioned privately by Peter, James, John, and Andrew. 'Tell us,' they said, 'when will this happen? What will be the sign when the fulfilment of all this is at hand?'

Jesus began: 'Take care that no one misleads you. Many will come claiming my name, and saying, "I am he"; and many will be misled by them.

'When you hear the noise of battle near at hand and the news of battles far away, do not be alarmed. Such things are bound to happen; but the end is still to come. For nation will make war upon nation, kingdom upon kingdom; there will be earthquakes in many places; there will be famines. With these things the birth-pangs of the new age begin.

'As for you, be on your guard. You will be handed over to the courts. You will be flogged in synagogues. You will be summoned to appear before governors and kings on my account to testify in their presence. But before the end the Gospel must be proclaimed to all nations. So when you are arrested and taken away, do not worry beforehand about what you will say, but when the time comes say whatever is given you to say; for it will not be you that speak, but the Holy Spirit. Brother will betray brother to death, and the father his child; children will turn against their parents and send them to their death. All will hate you for your allegiance to me; but the man who holds out to the end will be saved.

Jesus foretells utter misery 13. 12

"A brother is going to betray his own brother to death, and a father his own child. Children will stand up against their parents and condemn them to death. There will come a time when the whole world will hate you because you are known as my followers. Yet the man who holds out to the end will be saved.

"But when you see 'the abomination of desolation' standing where it ought not (let the reader take note of this), then those who are in Judaea must fly to the hills! The man on his housetop must not go down nor go into his house to fetch anything out of it, the man in the field must not turn back to fetch his coat. Alas for the women who are pregnant at that time, and alas for those with babies at their breasts! Pray God that it may not be winter when that time comes, for there will be such utter misery in those days as has never been from the creation until now—and never will be

'But when you see "the abomination of desolation" usurping a place which is not his (let the reader understand), then those who are in Judaea must take to the hills. If a man is on the roof, he must not come down into the house to fetch anything out; if in the field, he must not turn back for his cloak. Alas for women with child in those days, and for those who have children at the breast! Pray that it may not come in winter. For those days will bring distress such as never has been until now since the beginning of the world which God created—and will never be again. If the Lord had not cut

K.J.V.

Lord had shortened those days, no flesh should be saved: but for the elect's sake, whom he hath chosen, he hath shortened the days. 21And then if any man shall say to you, Lo, here *is* Christ; or, lo, *he is* there; believe *him* not: 22 For false Christs and false prophets shall rise, and shall shew signs and wonders, to seduce, if *it were* possible, even the elect. 23 But take ye heed: behold, I have foretold you all things.

24 But in those days, after that tribulation, the sun shall be darkened, and the moon shall not give her light, 25And the stars of heaven shall fall, and the powers that are in heaven shall be shaken. 26And then shall they see the Son of man coming in the clouds with great power and glory. 27And then shall he send his angels, and shall gather together his elect from the four winds, from the uttermost part of the earth to the uttermost part of heaven. 28 Now learn a parable of the fig tree: When her branch is yet tender, and putteth forth leaves, ye know that summer is near: 29 So ye in like manner, when ye shall see these things come to pass, know that it is nigh, *even* at the doors. 30 Verily I say unto you, that this generation shall not pass, till all these things be done. 31 Heaven and earth shall pass away: but my words shall not pass away.

32 But of that day and *that* hour knoweth no man, no, not the angels which are in heaven, neither the Son, but the Father. 33 Take ye heed, watch and pray: for ye know not when the time is. 34 *For the Son of man is* as a man taking a far journey, who left his house, and gave authority to his servants, and to every man his work, and commanded the porter to watch. 35 Watch ye therefore: for ye know not when the master of the house cometh, at even, or at midnight, or at the cockcrowing, or in the morning: 36 Lest coming suddenly he find you sleeping. 37And what I say unto you I say unto all, Watch.

R.S.V.

had not shortened the days, no human being would be saved; but for the sake of the elect, whom he chose, he shortened the days. 21And then if any one says to you, 'Look, here is the Christ!' or 'Look, there he is!' do not believe it. 22 False Christs and false prophets will arise and show signs and wonders, to lead astray, if possible, the elect. 23 But take heed; I have told you all things beforehand.

24 "But in those days, after that tribulation, the sun will be darkened, and the moon will not give its light, 25 and the stars will be falling from heaven, and the powers in the heavens will be shaken. 26 And then they will see the Son of man coming in clouds with great power and glory. 27And then he will send out the angels, and gather his elect from the four winds, from the ends of the earth to the ends of heaven.

28 "From the fig tree learn its lesson: as soon as its branch becomes tender and puts forth its leaves, you know that summer is near. 29 So also, when you see these things taking place, you know that he is near, at the very gates. 30 Truly, I say to you, this generation will not pass away before all these things take place. 31 Heaven and earth will pass away, but my words will not pass away.

32 "But of that day or that hour no one knows, not even the angels in heaven, nor the Son, but only the Father. 33 Take heed, watch;[a] for you do not know when the time will come. 34 It is like a man going on a journey, when he leaves home and puts his servants in charge, each with his work, and commands the doorkeeper to be on the watch. 35 Watch therefore—for you do not know when the master of the house will come, in the evening, or at midnight, or at cockcrow, or in the morning—36 lest he come suddenly and find you asleep. 37And what I say to you I say to all: Watch."

14 After two days was *the feast of* the passover, and of unleavened bread: and the chief priests and the scribes sought how they might take him by craft, and put *him* to death. 2 But they said, Not on the feast *day,* lest there be an uproar of the people.

3 And being in Bethany, in the house of Simon the leper, as he sat at meat, there came a woman having an alabaster box of ointment of spikenard very precious; and she brake the box, and poured *it* on his head. 4And there were some that had indignation within themselves, and said, Why was this waste of the ointment made? 5 For it might have been sold for more than three hundred pence, and have been given to the poor. And they murmured against her. 6And Jesus said, Let her alone; why trouble ye her? she hath wrought a good work on me. 7 For ye have the poor with you always, and

14 It was now two days before the Passover and the feast of Unleavened Bread. And the chief priests and the scribes were seeking how to arrest him by stealth, and kill him; 2 for they said, "Not during the feast, lest there be a tumult of the people."

3 And while he was at Bethany in the house of Simon the leper, as he sat at table, a woman came with an alabaster jar of ointment of pure nard, very costly, and she broke the jar and poured it over his head. 4 But there were some who said to themselves indignantly, "Why was the ointment thus wasted? 5 For this ointment might have been sold for more than three hundred denarii,[b] and given to the poor." And they reproached her. 6 But Jesus said, "Let her alone; why do you trouble her? She has done a beautiful thing to me. 7 For you always have the poor

[a] Other ancient authorities add *and pray.* [b] The denarius was worth about twenty cents.

PHILLIPS

again. Indeed, if the Lord did not shorten those days, no human being would survive. But for the sake of the people whom he has chosen he has shortened those days.

He warns against false christs, and commands vigilance 13. 21

"If anyone tells you at that time, 'Look, here is Christ,' or 'Look, there he is,' don't believe it! For false christs and false prophets will arise and will perform signs and wonders, to deceive, if it be possible, even the men of God's choice. You must keep your eyes open! I am giving you this warning before it happens.

"But when that misery is past, the light of the sun will be darkened and the moon will not give her light; stars will be falling from the sky and the powers of heaven will rock on their foundations. Then men shall see the Son of Man coming in the clouds with great power and glory. And then shall he send out his angels to summon his chosen together from every quarter, from furthest earth to highest heaven. Let the fig tree illustrate this for you: when its branches grow tender and produce leaves, you know that summer is near. So when you see these things happening, you may know that he is near, at your very doors! I tell you that this generation will not have passed until all these things have come true. Earth and sky will pass away, but what I have told you will never pass away! But no one knows the day or the hour of this happening, not even the angels in Heaven, no, not even the Son—only the Father. Keep your eyes open, keep on the alert, for you do not know when the time will be. It is as if a man who is traveling abroad had left his house and handed it over to be managed by his servants. He has given each one his work to do and has ordered the doorkeeper to be on the lookout for his return. Just so must you keep a lookout, for you do not know when the master of the house will come—it might be late evening, or midnight, or cock-crow, or early morning—otherwise he might come unexpectedly and find you sound asleep. What I am saying to you I am saying to all; keep on the alert!"

An act of love 14. 1

In two days' time the festival of the Passover and of unleavened bread was due. Consequently, the chief priests and the scribes were trying to think of some trick by which they could get Jesus into their power and have him executed. "But it must not be during the festival," they said, "or there will be a riot."

Jesus himself was now at Bethany in the house of Simon the leper. As he was sitting at table, a woman approached him with an alabaster flask of very costly spikenard perfume. She broke the neck of the flask and poured the perfume on Jesus' head. Some of those present were highly indignant and muttered:

"What is the point of such wicked waste of perfume? It could have been sold for over thirty dollars and the money could have been given to the poor." And there was a murmur of resentment against her. But Jesus said:

"Let her alone; why must you make her feel uncomfortable? She has done a beautiful thing for me. You have the poor with you always and

N.E.B.

short that time of troubles, no living thing could survive. However, for the sake of his own, whom he has chosen, he has cut short the time.

'Then, if anyone says to you, "Look, here is the Messiah", or, "Look, there he is", do not believe it. Impostors will come claiming to be messiahs or prophets, and they will produce signs and wonders to mislead God's chosen, if such a thing were possible. But you be on your guard; I have forewarned you of it all.

'But in those days, after that distress, the sun will be darkened, the moon will not give her light; the stars will come falling from the sky, the celestial powers will be shaken. Then they will see the Son of Man coming in the clouds with great power and glory, and he will send out the angels and gather his chosen from the four winds, from the farthest bounds of earth to the farthest bounds of heaven.

'Learn a lesson from the fig-tree. When its tender shoots appear and are breaking into leaf, you know that summer is near. In the same way, when you see all this happening, you may know that the end is near,[a] at the very door. I tell you this: the present generation will live to see it all. Heaven and earth will pass away; my words will never pass away.

'But about that day or that hour no one knows, not even the angels in heaven, not even the Son; only the Father.

'Be alert, be wakeful.[b] You do not know when the moment comes. It is like a man away from home: he has left his house and put his servants in charge, each with his own work to do, and he has ordered the door-keeper to stay awake. Keep awake, then, for you do not know when the master of the house is coming. Evening or midnight, cock-crow or early dawn—if he comes suddenly, he must not find you asleep. And what I say to you, I say to everyone: Keep awake.'

The Final Conflict

14 Now the festival of Passover and Unleavened Bread was only two days off; and the chief priests and the doctors of the law were trying to devise some cunning plan to seize him and put him to death. 'It must not be during the festival,' they said, 'or we should have rioting among the people.'

Jesus was at Bethany, in the house of Simon the leper. As he sat at table, a woman came in carrying a small bottle of very costly perfume, oil of pure nard. She broke it open and poured the oil over his head. Some of those present said to one another angrily, 'Why this waste? The perfume might have been sold for thirty pounds[c] and the money given to the poor'; and they turned upon her with fury. But Jesus said, 'Let her alone. Why must you make trouble for her? It is a fine thing she has done for me. You have the poor among you always, and you

[a] Or that he is near. [b] Some witnesses add and pray. [c] Literally 300 denarii; some witnesses read more than 300 denarii.

K.J.V.

whensoever ye will ye may do them good: but me ye have not always. 8 She hath done what she could: she is come aforehand to anoint my body to the burying. 9 Verily I say unto you, Wheresoever this gospel shall be preached throughout the whole world, *this* also that she hath done shall be spoken of for a memorial of her.

10 And Judas Iscariot, one of the twelve, went unto the chief priests, to betray him unto them. 11And when they heard *it,* they were glad, and promised to give him money. And he sought how he might conveniently betray him.

12 And the first day of unleavened bread, when they killed the passover, his disciples said unto him, Where wilt thou that we go and prepare that thou mayest eat the passover? 13And he sendeth forth two of his disciples, and saith unto them, Go ye into the city, and there shall meet you a man bearing a pitcher of water: follow him. 14And wheresoever he shall go in, say ye to the goodman of the house, The Master saith, Where is the guestchamber, where I shall eat the passover with my disciples? 15And he will shew you a large upper room furnished *and* prepared: there make ready for us. 16And his disciples went forth, and came into the city, and found as he had said unto them: and they made ready the passover. 17And in the evening he cometh with the twelve. 18And as they sat and did eat, Jesus said, Verily I say unto you, One of you which eateth with me shall betray me. 19And they began to be sorrowful, and to say unto him one by one, *Is* it I? and another *said, Is* it I? 20And he answered and said unto them, *It is* one of the twelve, that dippeth with me in the dish. 21 The Son of man indeed goeth, as it is written of him: but woe to that man by whom the Son of man is betrayed! good were it for that man if he had never been born.

22 And as they did eat, Jesus took bread, and blessed, and brake *it,* and gave to them, and said, Take, eat; this is my body. 23And he took the cup, and when he had given thanks, he gave *it* to them: and they all drank of it. 24And he said unto them, This is my blood of the new testament, which is shed for many. 25 Verily I say unto you, I will drink no more of the fruit of the vine, until that day that I drink it new in the kingdom of God.

26 And when they had sung a hymn, they went out into the mount of Olives. 27And Jesus

R.S.V.

with you, and whenever you will, you can do good to them; but you will not always have me. 8 She has done what she could; she has anointed my body beforehand for burying. 9And truly, I say to you, wherever the gospel is preached in the whole world, what she has done will be told in memory of her."

10 Then Judas Iscariot, who was one of the twelve, went to the chief priests in order to betray him to them. 11And when they heard it they were glad, and promised to give him money. And he sought an opportunity to betray him.

12 And on the first day of Unleavened Bread, when they sacrificed the passover lamb, his disciples said to him, "Where will you have us go and prepare for you to eat the passover?" 13And he sent two of his disciples, and said to them, "Go into the city, and a man carrying a jar of water will meet you; follow him, 14 and wherever he enters, say to the householder, 'The Teacher says, Where is my guest room, where I am to eat the passover with my disciples?' 15And he will show you a large upper room furnished and ready; there prepare for us." 16And the disciples set out and went to the city, and found it as he had told them; and they prepared the passover.

17 And when it was evening he came with the twelve. 18And as they were at table eating, Jesus said, "Truly, I say to you, one of you will betray me, one who is eating with me." 19 They began to be sorrowful, and to say to him one after another, "Is it I?" 20 He said to them, "It is one of the twelve, one who is dipping bread in the same dish with me. 21 For the Son of man goes as it is written of him, but woe to that man by whom the Son of man is betrayed! It would have been better for that man if he had not been born."

22 And as they were eating, he took bread, and blessed, and broke it, and gave it to them, and said, "Take; this is my body." 23And he took a cup, and when he had given thanks he gave it to them, and they all drank of it. 24And he said to them, "This is my blood of the* covenant, which is poured out for many. 25 Truly, I say to you, I shall not drink again of the fruit of the vine until that day when I drink it new in the kingdom of God."

26 And when they had sung a hymn, they went out to the Mount of Olives. 27And Jesus

[c] Other ancient authorities insert *new.*

PHILLIPS	N.E.B.

you can do good to them whenever you like, but you will not always have me. She has done all she could—for she has anointed my body in preparation for burial. I assure you that wherever the gospel is preached throughout the whole world, this deed of hers will also be recounted, as her memorial to me."

Judas volunteers to betray Jesus   14. 10

Then Judas Iscariot, who was one of the twelve, went off to the chief priests to betray Jesus to them. And when they heard what he had to say, they were delighted and undertook to pay him for it. So he looked out for a convenient opportunity to betray him.

The Passover-supper prepared   14. 12

On the first day of unleavened bread, the day when the Passover was sacrificed, Jesus' disciples said,
"Where do you want us to go and make the preparations for you to eat the Passover?"
Jesus sent off two of them with these instructions:
"Go into the town and you will meet a man carrying a pitcher of water. Follow him and say to the owner of the house to which he goes, 'The master says, where is the room for me to eat the Passover with my disciples?' And he will show you a large upstairs room all ready with the furnishings that we need. That is the place where you are to make our preparations."
So the disciples set off and went into the town, found everything as he had told them, and prepared for the Passover.

The last supper together: 14. 17
the mysterious bread and wine

Late in the evening he arrived with the twelve. And while they were sitting there, right in the middle of the meal, Jesus remarked,
"Believe me, one of you is going to betray me—someone who is now having his supper with me."
This shocked and distressed them and one after another they began to say to him,
"Surely, I'm not the one?"
"It is one of the twelve," Jesus told them, "a man who is dipping his hand into the dish with me. It is true that the Son of Man will follow the road foretold by the scriptures, but alas for the man through whom he is betrayed! It would be better for that man if he had never been born."
And while they were still eating Jesus took a loaf, blessed it and broke it and gave it to them, with the words,
"Take this, it is my body."
Then he took a cup, and after thanking God, he gave it to them, and they all drank from it, and he said to them:
"This is my blood which is shed for many in the new agreement. I tell you truly I will drink no more wine until the day comes when I drink it fresh in the kingdom of God!"
Then they sang a hymn and went out to the Mount of Olives.

can help them whenever you like; but you will not always have me. She has done what lay in her power; she is beforehand with anointing my body for burial. I tell you this: wherever in all the world the Gospel is proclaimed, what she has done will be told as her memorial.'
Then Judas Iscariot, one of the Twelve, went to the chief priests to betray him to them. When they heard what he had come for, they were greatly pleased, and promised him money; and he began to look for a good opportunity to betray him.

Now on the first day of Unleavened Bread, when the Passover lambs were being slaughtered, his disciples said to him, 'Where would you like us to go and prepare for your Passover supper?' So he sent out two of his disciples with these instructions: 'Go into the city, and a man will meet you carrying a jar of water. Follow him, and when he enters a house give this message to the householder: "The Master says, 'Where is the room reserved for me to eat the Passover with my disciples?'" He will show you a large room upstairs, set out in readiness. Make the preparations for us there.' Then the disciples went off, and when they came into the city they found everything just as he had told them. So they prepared for Passover.
In the evening he came to the house with the Twelve. As they sat at supper Jesus said, 'I tell you this: one of you will betray me—one who is eating with me.' At this they were dismayed; and one by one they said to him, 'Not I, surely?' 'It is one of the Twelve', he said, 'who is dipping into the same bowl with me. The Son of Man is going the way appointed for him in the scriptures; but alas for that man by whom the Son of Man is betrayed! It would be better for that man if he had never been born.'
During supper he took bread, and having said the blessing he broke it and gave it to them, with the words: 'Take this; this is my body.' Then he took a cup, and having offered thanks to God he gave it to them; and they all drank from it. And he said, 'This is my blood of the covenant, shed for many. I tell you this: never again shall I drink from the fruit of the vine until that day when I drink it new in the kingdom of God.'
After singing the Passover Hymn, they went out to the Mount of Olives. And Jesus said, 'You

K.J.V.

saith unto them, All ye shall be offended because of me this night: for it is written, I will smite the Shepherd, and the sheep shall be scattered. 28 But after that I am risen, I will go before you into Galilee. 29 But Peter said unto him, Although all shall be offended, yet *will* not I. 30 And Jesus saith unto him, Verily I say unto thee, That this day, *even* in this night, before the cock crow twice, thou shalt deny me thrice. 31 But he spake the more vehemently, If I should die with thee, I will not deny thee in any wise. Likewise also said they all. 32 And they came to a place which was named Gethsemane: and he saith to his disciples, Sit ye here, while I shall pray. 33 And he taketh with him Peter and James and John, and began to be sore amazed, and to be very heavy; 34 And saith unto them, My soul is exceeding sorrowful unto death: tarry ye here, and watch. 35 And he went forward a little, and fell on the ground, and prayed that, if it were possible, the hour might pass from him. 36 And he said, Abba, Father, all things *are* possible unto thee; take away this cup from me: nevertheless, not what I will, but what thou wilt. 37 And he cometh, and findeth them sleeping, and saith unto Peter, Simon, sleepest thou? couldest not thou watch one hour? 38 Watch ye and pray, lest ye enter into temptation. The spirit truly *is* ready, but the flesh *is* weak. 39 And again he went away, and prayed, and spake the same words. 40 And when he returned, he found them asleep again, (for their eyes were heavy,) neither wist they what to answer him. 41 And he cometh the third time, and saith unto them, Sleep on now, and take *your* rest: it is enough, the hour is come; behold, the Son of man is betrayed into the hands of sinners. 42 Rise up, let us go; lo, he that betrayeth me is at hand.

43 And immediately, while he yet spake, cometh Judas, one of the twelve, and with him a great multitude with swords and staves, from the chief priests and the scribes and the elders. 44 And he that betrayed him had given them a token, saying, Whomsoever I shall kiss, that same is he; take him, and lead *him* away safely. 45 And as soon as he was come, he goeth straightway to him, and saith, Master, Master; and kissed him.

46 And they laid their hands on him, and

R.S.V.

said to them, "You will all fall away; for it is written, 'I will strike the shepherd, and the sheep will be scattered.' 28 But after I am raised up, I will go before you to Galilee." 29 Peter said to him, "Even though they all fall away, I will not." 30 And Jesus said to him, "Truly, I say to you, this very night, before the cock crows twice, you will deny me three times." 31 But he said vehemently, "If I must die with you, I will not deny you." And they all said the same.

32 And they went to a place which was called Gethsemane; and he said to his disciples, "Sit here, while I pray." 33 And he took with him Peter and James and John, and began to be greatly distressed and troubled. 34 And he said to them, "My soul is very sorrowful, even to death; remain here, and watch." [d] 35 And going a little farther, he fell on the ground and prayed that, if it were possible, the hour might pass from him. 36 And he said, "Abba, Father, all things are possible to thee; remove this cup from me; yet not what I will, but what thou wilt." 37 And he came and found them sleeping, and he said to Peter, "Simon, are you asleep? Could you not watch[d] one hour? 38 Watch[d] and pray that you may not enter into temptation; the spirit indeed is willing, but the flesh is weak." 39 And again he went away and prayed, saying the same words. 40 And again he came and found them sleeping, for their eyes were very heavy; and they did not know what to answer him. 41 And he came a third time, and said to them, "Are you still sleeping and taking your rest? It is enough; the hour has come; the Son of man is betrayed into the hands of sinners. 42 Rise, let us be going; see, my betrayer is at hand."

43 And immediately, while he was still speaking, Judas came, one of the twelve, and with him a crowd with swords and clubs, from the chief priests and the scribes and the elders. 44 Now the betrayer had given them a sign, saying, "The one I shall kiss is the man; seize him and lead him away safely." 45 And when he came, he went up to him at once, and said, "Master!" [e] And he kissed him. 46 And they laid hands on

---

[d] Or *keep awake.* [e] Or *Rabbi.*

PHILLIPS

"Every one of you will lose your faith in me," Jesus told them, "as the scripture says:

I will smite the shepherd,
And the sheep shall be scattered abroad.

Yet after I have risen I shall go before you into Galilee!"

Peter's bold words—   14. 29
and Jesus' reply

Then Peter said to him,
"Even if everyone should lose his faith, I never will."
"Believe me, Peter," returned Jesus, "this very night before the cock crows twice, you will disown me three times."
But Peter protested violently,
"Even if it means dying with you, I will never disown you!"
And they all made the same protest.

The last desperate prayer   14. 32
in Gethsemane

Then they arrived at a place called Gethsemane, and Jesus said to his disciples,
"Sit down here while I pray."
He took with him Peter, James and John, and began to be horror-stricken and desperately depressed.
"My heart is nearly breaking," he told them. "Stay here and keep watch for me."
Then he walked forward a little way and flung himself on the ground, praying that, if it were possible, he might not have to face the ordeal.
"Dear Father," he said, "all things are possible to you. Please—let me not have to drink this cup! Yet it is not what I want but what you want."
Then he came and found them fast asleep. He spoke to Peter:
"Are you asleep, Simon? Couldn't you manage to watch for a single hour? Watch and pray, all of you, that you may not have to face temptation. Your spirit is willing, but human nature is weak."
Then he went away again and prayed in the same words, and once more he came and found them asleep. They could not keep their eyes open and they did not know what to say for themselves. When he came back for the third time, he said:
"Are you still going to sleep and take your ease? All right—the moment has come; now you are going to see the Son of Man betrayed into the hands of evil men! Get up, let us be going! Look, here comes my betrayer!"

Judas betrays Jesus   14. 43

And indeed, while the words were still on his lips, Judas, one of the twelve, arrived with a mob armed with swords and staves, sent by the chief priests and scribes and elders. The betrayer had given them a sign; he had said: "The one I kiss will be the man. Get hold of him and you can take him away without any trouble." So he walked straight up to Jesus, cried, "Master!" and kissed him affectionately. And so they

N.E.B.

will all fall from your faith; for it stands written: "I will strike the shepherd down and the sheep will be scattered." Nevertheless, after I am raised again I will go on before you into Galilee.' Peter answered, 'Everyone else may fall away, but I will not.' Jesus said, 'I tell you this: today, this very night, before the cock crows twice, you yourself will disown me three times.' But he insisted and repeated: 'Even if I must die with you, I will never disown you.' And they all said the same.

When they reached a place called Gethsemane, he said to his disciples, 'Sit here while I pray.' And he took Peter and James and John with him. Horror and dismay came over him, and he said to them, 'My heart is ready to break with grief; stop here, and stay awake.' Then he went forward a little, threw himself on the ground, and prayed that, if it were possible, this hour might pass him by. 'Abba, Father,' he said, 'all things are possible to thee; take this cup away from me. Yet not what I will, but what thou wilt.'
He came back and found them asleep; and he said to Peter, 'Asleep, Simon? Were you not able to keep awake for one hour? Stay awake, all of you; and pray that you may be spared the test: the spirit is willing, but the flesh is weak.' Once more he went away and prayed.[a] On his return he found them asleep again, for their eyes were heavy; and they did not know how to answer him.
The third time he came and said to them, 'Still sleeping? Still taking your ease? Enough! [b] The hour has come. The Son of Man is betrayed to sinful men. Up, let us go forward! My betrayer is upon us.'
Suddenly, while he was still speaking, Judas, one of the Twelve, appeared, and with him was a crowd armed with swords and cudgels, sent by the chief priests, lawyers, and elders. Now the traitor had agreed with them upon a signal: 'The one I kiss is your man; seize him and get him safely away.' When he reached the spot, he stepped forward at once and said to Jesus, 'Rabbi', and kissed him. Then they seized him and held him fast.

[a] *Some witnesses add* using the same words.
[b] *The Greek is obscure; a possible meaning is* 'The money has been paid', 'The account is settled.'

took him. 47And one of them that stood by drew a sword, and smote a servant of the high priest, and cut off his ear. 48And Jesus answered and said unto them, Are ye come out, as against a thief, with swords and *with* staves to take me? 49 I was daily with you in the temple teaching, and ye took me not: but the Scriptures must be fulfilled. 50And they all forsook him, and fled. 51And there followed him a certain young man, having a linen cloth cast about *his* naked *body;* and the young men laid hold on him: 52And he left the linen cloth, and fled from them naked.

53 And they led Jesus away to the high priest: and with him were assembled all the chief priests and the elders and the scribes. 54And Peter followed him afar off, even into the palace of the high priest: and he sat with the servants, and warmed himself at the fire. 55And the chief priests and all the council sought for witness against Jesus to put him to death; and found none. 56 For many bare false witness against him, but their witness agreed not together. 57And there arose certain, and bare false witness against him, saying, 58 We heard him say, I will destroy this temple that is made with hands, and within three days I will build another made without hands. 59 But neither so did their witness agree together. 60And the high priest stood up in the midst, and asked Jesus, saying, Answerest thou nothing? what *is it which* these witness against thee? 61 But he held his peace, and answered nothing. Again the high priest asked him, and said unto him, Art thou the Christ, the Son of the Blessed? 62And Jesus said, I am: and ye shall see the Son of man sitting on the right hand of power, and coming in the clouds of heaven. 63 Then the high priest rent his clothes, and saith, What need we any further witnesses? 64 Ye have heard the blasphemy: what think ye? And they all condemned him to be guilty of death. 65And some began to spit on him, and to cover his face, and to buffet him, and to say unto him, Prophesy: and the servants did strike him with the palms of their hands.

66 And as Peter was beneath in the palace, there cometh one of the maids of the high priest: 67And when she saw Peter warming himself, she looked upon him, and said, And thou also wast with Jesus of Nazareth. 68 But he denied, saying, I know not, neither understand I what thou sayest. And he went out into the porch; and the cock crew. 69And a maid saw him again, and began to say to them that stood by, This is *one*

him and seized him. 47 But one of those who stood by drew his sword, and struck the slave of the high priest and cut off his ear. 48And Jesus said to them, "Have you come out as against a robber, with swords and clubs to capture me? 49 Day after day I was with you in the temple teaching, and you did not seize me. But let the scriptures be fulfilled." 50And they all forsook him, and fled.

51 And a young man followed him, with nothing but a linen cloth about his body; and they seized him, 52 but he left the linen cloth and ran away naked.

53 And they led Jesus to the high priest; and all the chief priests and the elders and the scribes were assembled. 54And Peter had followed him at a distance, right into the courtyard of the high priest; and he was sitting with the guards, and warming himself at the fire. 55 Now the chief priests and the whole council sought testimony against Jesus to put him to death; but they found none. 56 For many bore false witness against him, and their witness did not agree. 57And some stood up and bore false witness against him, saying, 58 "We heard him say, 'I will destroy this temple that is made with hands, and in three days I will build another, not made with hands.'" 59 Yet not even so did their testimony agree. 60And the high priest stood up in the midst, and asked Jesus, "Have you no answer to make? What is it that these men testify against you?" 61 But he was silent and made no answer. Again the high priest asked him, "Are you the Christ, the Son of the Blessed?" 62And Jesus said, "I am; and you will see the Son of man sitting at the right hand of Power, and coming with the clouds of heaven." 63And the high priest tore his mantle, and said, "Why do we still need witnesses? 64 You have heard his blasphemy. What is your decision?" And they all condemned him as deserving death. 65And some began to spit on him, and to cover his face, and to strike him, saying to him, "Prophesy!" And the guards received him with blows.

66 And as Peter was below in the courtyard, one of the maids of the high priest came; 67 and seeing Peter warming himself, she looked at him, and said, "You also were with the Nazarene, Jesus." 68 But he denied it, saying, "I neither know nor understand what you mean." And he went out into the gateway.*f* 69And the maid saw him, and began again to say to the bystanders,

[f] Or *fore-court*. Other ancient authorities add *and the cock crowed.*

got hold of him and held him. Somebody present drew his sword and struck at the High Priest's servant, slashing off his ear. Then Jesus spoke to them:

"So you've come out with your swords and staves to capture me like a bandit, have you? Day after day I was with you in the Temple, teaching, and you never laid a finger on me. But the scriptures must be fulfilled."

Then all the disciples deserted him and made their escape. There happened to be a young man among Jesus' followers who wore nothing but a linen shirt. They seized him, but he left the shirt in their hands and took to his heels stark naked.

Jesus before the High Priest　　14. 53

So they marched Jesus away to the High Priest in whose presence all the chief priests and elders and scribes had assembled. (Peter followed him at a safe distance, right up to the High Priest's courtyard. There he sat in the firelight with the servants, keeping himself warm.) Meanwhile, the chief priests and the whole council were trying to find some evidence against Jesus which would warrant the death penalty. But they failed completely. There were plenty of people ready to give false testimony against him, but their evidence was contradictory. Then some more perjurers stood up and said,

"We heard him say, 'I will destroy this Temple that was built by human hands and in three days I will build another made without human aid.'"

But even so their evidence conflicted. So the High Priest himself got up and took the center of the floor.

"Have you no answer to make?" he asked Jesus. "What about all this evidence against you?"

But Jesus remained silent and offered no reply. Again the High Priest asked him,

"Are you Christ, Son of the blessed one?"

And Jesus said,

"I am! Yes, you will all see the Son of Man sitting at the right hand of power, coming in the clouds of heaven."

Then the High Priest tore his robes and cried:

"Why do we still need witnesses? You heard the blasphemy; what is your opinion now?"

And their verdict was that he deserved to die. Then some of them began to spit at him. They blindfolded him and then slapped him, saying,

"Now prophesy who hit you!"

Even the servants who took him away slapped his face.

Peter, in fear, disowns his　　14. 66
master

In the meantime, while Peter was in the courtyard below, one of the High Priest's maids came and saw him warming himself. She looked closely at him, and said,

"You were with the Nazarene too—with Jesus!"

But he denied it, saying,

"I don't understand. I don't know what you're talking about."

And he walked out into the gateway, and a cock crew.

Again the maid who had noticed him began to say to the men standing there,

One of the party[a] drew his sword, and struck at the High Priest's servant, cutting off his ear. Then Jesus spoke: 'Do you take me for a bandit, that you have come out with swords and cudgels to arrest me? Day after day I was within your reach as I taught in the temple, and you did not lay hands on me. But let the scriptures be fulfilled.' Then the disciples all deserted him and ran away.

Among those following was a young man with nothing on but a linen cloth. They tried to seize him; but he slipped out of the linen cloth and ran away naked.

Then they led Jesus away to the High Priest's house, where the chief priests, elders, and doctors of the law were all assembling. Peter followed him at a distance right into the High Priest's courtyard; and there he remained, sitting among the attendants, warming himself at the fire.

The chief priests and the whole Council tried to find some evidence against Jesus to warrant a death-sentence, but failed to find any. Many gave false evidence against him, but their statements did not tally. Some stood up and gave this false evidence against him: 'We heard him say, "I will throw down this temple, made with human hands, and in three days I will build another, not made with hands."' But even on this point their evidence did not agree.

Then the High Priest stood up in his place and questioned Jesus: 'Have you no answer to the charges that these witnesses bring against you?' But he kept silence; he made no reply.

Again the High Priest questioned him: 'Are you the Messiah, the Son of the Blessed One?' Jesus said, 'I am; and you will see the Son of Man seated on the right hand of God[b] and coming with the clouds of heaven.' Then the High Priest tore his robes and said, 'Need we call further witnesses? You have heard the blasphemy. What is your opinion?' Their judgement was unanimous: that he was guilty and should be put to death.

Some began to spit on him, blindfolded him, and struck him with their fists, crying out, 'Prophesy!'[c] And the High Priest's men set upon him with blows.

Meanwhile Peter was still in the courtyard downstairs. One of the High Priest's serving-maids came by and saw him there warming himself. She looked into his face and said, 'You were there too, with this man from Nazareth, this Jesus.' But he denied it: 'I know nothing,' he said; 'I do not understand what you mean.' Then he went outside into the porch;[d] and the maid saw him there again and began to say to the

[a] Or of the bystanders. [b] Literally of the Power. [c] Some witnesses add Who hit you? as in Matthew and Luke. [d] Some witnesses insert and the cock crew.

K.J.V.

of them. 70And he denied it again. And a little after, they that stood by said again to Peter, Surely thou art *one* of them: for thou art a Galilean, and thy speech agreeth *thereto*. 71 But he began to curse and to swear, *saying*, I know not this man of whom ye speak. 72And the second time the cock crew. And Peter called to mind the word that Jesus said to him, Before the cock crow twice, thou shalt deny me thrice. And when he thought thereon, he wept.

15 And straightway in the morning the chief priests held a consultation with the elders and scribes and the whole council, and bound Jesus, and carried *him* away, and delivered *him* to Pilate. 2And Pilate asked him, Art thou the King of the Jews? And he answering said unto him, Thou sayest *it*. 3And the chief priests accused him of many things; but he answered nothing. 4And Pilate asked him again, saying, Answerest thou nothing? behold how many things they witness against thee. 5 But Jesus yet answered nothing; so that Pilate marvelled. 6 Now at *that* feast he released unto them one prisoner, whomsoever they desired. 7And there was *one* named Barabbas, *which lay* bound with them that had made insurrection with him, who had committed murder in the insurrection. 8And the multitude crying aloud began to desire *him to do* as he had ever done unto them. 9 But Pilate answered them, saying, Will ye that I release unto you the King of the Jews? 10 For he knew that the chief priests had delivered him for envy. 11 But the chief priests moved the people, that he should rather release Barabbas unto them. 12And Pilate answered and said again unto them, What will ye then that I shall do *unto him* whom ye call the King of the Jews? 13And they cried out again, Crucify him. 14 Then Pilate said unto them, Why, what evil hath he done? And they cried out the more exceedingly, Crucify him.

15 And *so* Pilate, willing to content the people, released Barabbas unto them, and delivered Jesus, when he had scourged *him*, to be crucified. 16And the soldiers led him away into the hall, called Pretorium; and they call together the whole band. 17And they clothed him with purple, and platted a crown of thorns, and put it about his *head*, 18And began to salute him, Hail, King of the Jews! 19And they smote him on the head with a reed, and did spit upon him, and bowing *their* knees worshipped him. 20And when they had mocked him, they took off the purple from him, and put his own clothes on him, and led him out to crucify him. 21And they compel one Simon a Cyrenian, who passed by, coming out of the country, the father of

R.S.V.

"This man is one of them." 70 But again he denied it. And after a little while again the bystanders said to Peter, "Certainly you are one of them; for you are a Galilean." 71 But he began to invoke a curse on himself and to swear, "I do not know this man of whom you speak." 72And immediately the cock crowed a second time. And Peter remembered how Jesus had said to him, "Before the cock crows twice, you will deny me three times." And he broke down and wept.

15 And as soon as it was morning the chief priests, with the elders and scribes, and the whole council held a consultation; and they bound Jesus and led him away and delivered him to Pilate. 2And Pilate asked him, "Are you the King of the Jews?" And he answered him, "You have said so." 3And the chief priests accused him of many things. 4And Pilate again asked him, "Have you no answer to make? See how many charges they bring against you." 5 But Jesus made no further answer, so that Pilate wondered.

6 Now at the feast he used to release for them one prisoner whom they asked. 7And among the rebels in prison, who had committed murder in the insurrection, there was a man called Barabbas. 8And the crowd came up and began to ask Pilate to do as he was wont to do for them. 9And he answered them, "Do you want me to release for you the King of the Jews?" 10 For he perceived that it was out of envy that the chief priests had delivered him up. 11 But the chief priests stirred up the crowd to have him release for them Barabbas instead. 12And Pilate again said to them, "Then what shall I do with the man whom you call the King of the Jews?" 13And they cried out again, "Crucify him." 14And Pilate said to them, "Why, what evil has he done?" But they shouted all the more, "Crucify him." 15 So Pilate, wishing to satisfy the crowd, released for them Barabbas; and having scourged Jesus, he delivered him to be crucified.

16 And the soldiers led him away inside the palace (that is, the praetorium); and they called together the whole battalion. 17And they clothed him in a purple cloak, and plaiting a crown of thorns they put it on him. 18And they began to salute him, "Hail, King of the Jews!" 19And they struck his head with a reed, and spat upon him, and they knelt down in homage to him. 20And when they had mocked him, they stripped him of the purple cloak, and put his own clothes on him. And they led him out to crucify him.

21 And they compelled a passer-by, Simon of Cyrene, who was coming in from the country, the father of Alexander and Rufus, to carry his

PHILLIPS

"This man is one of them!"

But he denied it again. A few minutes later the bystanders themselves said to Peter:

"You certainly are one of them. Why, you're a Galilean!"

But he started to curse and swear,

"I tell you I don't know the man you're talking about!"

Immediately the cock crew for the second time, and back into Peter's mind came the words of Jesus, "Before the cock crows twice, you will disown me three times."

And he broke down and wept.

Jesus before Pilate   15. 1

The moment daylight came the chief priests called together a meeting of elders, scribes and members of the whole council, bound Jesus and took him off and handed him over to Pilate. Pilate asked him straight out,

"Well, you—*are* you the king of the Jews?"

"Yes, I am," he replied.

The chief priests brought many accusations. So Pilate questioned him again,

"Have you nothing to say? Listen to all their accusations!"

But Jesus made no further answer—to Pilate's astonishment.

Now it was Pilate's custom at festival time to release a prisoner—anyone they asked for. There was in the prison at the time, with some other rioters who had committed murder in a recent outbreak, a man called Barabbas. The crowd surged forward and began to demand that Pilate should do what he usually did for them. So he spoke to them,

"Do you want me to set free the king of the Jews for you?"

For he knew perfectly well that the chief priests had handed Jesus over to him through sheer malice. But the chief priests worked upon the crowd to get them to demand Barabbas' release instead. So Pilate addressed them once more,

"Then what am I to do with the man whom you call the king of the Jews?"

They shouted back,

"Crucify him!"

But Pilate replied,

"Why, what crime has he committed?"

But their voices rose to a roar,

"Crucify him!"

And as Pilate wanted to satisfy the crowd, he set Barabbas free for them, and after having Jesus flogged handed him over to be crucified.

Then the soldiers marched him away inside the courtyard of the governor's residence and called their whole company together. They dressed Jesus in a purple robe, and twisting some thorn twigs into a crown, they put it on his head. Then they began to greet him,

"Hail, your majesty—king of the Jews!"

They hit him on the head with a stick and spat at him, and then bowed low before him on bended knee. And when they had finished their fun with him, they took off the purple cloak and dressed him again in his own clothes. Then they led him outside to crucify him. They compelled Simon, a native of Cyrene in Africa (the father of Alexander and Rufus), who was on his way from the fields at the time, to carry Jesus' cross.

N.E.B.

bystanders, 'He is one of them'; and again he denied it.

Again, a little later, the bystanders said to Peter, 'Surely you are one of them. You must be; you are a Galilean.' At this he broke out into curses, and with an oath he said, 'I do not know this man you speak of.' Then the cock crew a second time; and Peter remembered how Jesus had said to him, 'Before the cock crows twice you will disown me three times.' And he burst into tears.

15 When morning came the chief priests, having made their plan with the elders and lawyers and all the Council, put Jesus in chains; then they led him away and handed him over to Pilate. Pilate asked him, 'Are you the king of the Jews?' He replied, 'The words are yours.' [a] And the chief priests brought many charges against him. Pilate questioned him again: 'Have you nothing to say in your defence? You see how many charges they are bringing against you.' But, to Pilate's astonishment, Jesus made no further reply.

At the festival season the Governor used to release one prisoner at the people's request. As it happened, the man known as Barabbas was then in custody with the rebels who had committed murder in the rising. When the crowd appeared [b] asking for the usual favour, Pilate replied, 'Do you wish me to release for you the king of the Jews?' For he knew it was out of spite that they had brought Jesus before him. But the chief priests incited the crowd to ask him to release Barabbas rather than Jesus. Pilate spoke to them again: 'Then what shall I do with the man you call king of the Jews?' They shouted back, 'Crucify him!' 'Why, what harm has he done?' Pilate asked. They shouted all the louder, 'Crucify him!' So Pilate, in his desire to satisfy the mob, released Barabbas to them; and he had Jesus flogged and handed him over to be crucified.

Then the soldiers took him inside the courtyard (the Governor's headquarters [c]) and called together the whole company. They dressed him in purple, and having plaited a crown of thorns, placed it on his head. Then they began to salute him with, 'Hail, King of the Jews!' They beat him about the head with a cane and spat upon him, and then knelt and paid mock homage to him. When they had finished their mockery, they stripped him of the purple and dressed him in his own clothes.

Then they took him out to crucify him. A man called Simon, from Cyrene, the father of Alexander and Rufus, was passing by on his way in from the country, and they pressed him into service to carry his cross.

[a] *Or* It is as you say. [b] *Some witnesses read* shouted. [c] *Greek* praetorium.

K.J.V.

Alexander and Rufus, to bear his cross. 22And they bring him unto the place Golgotha, which is, being interpreted, The place of a skull. 23And they gave him to drink wine mingled with myrrh: but he received *it* not. 24And when they had crucified him, they parted his garments, casting lots upon them, what every man should take. 25And it was the third hour, and they crucified him. 26And the superscription of his accusation was written over, THE KING OF THE JEWS. 27And with him they crucify two thieves; the one on his right hand, and the other on his left. 28And the Scripture was fulfilled, which saith, And he was numbered with the transgressors. 29And they that passed by railed on him, wagging their heads, and saying, Ah, thou that destroyest the temple, and buildest *it* in three days, 30 Save thyself, and come down from the cross. 31 Likewise also the chief priests mocking said among themselves with the scribes, He saved others; himself he cannot save. 32 Let Christ the King of Israel descend now from the cross, that we may see and believe. And they that were crucified with him reviled him. 33And when the sixth hour was come, there was darkness over the whole land until the ninth hour. 34And at the ninth hour Jesus cried with a loud voice, saying, Eloi, Eloi, lama sabachthani? which is, being interpreted, My God, my God, why hast thou forsaken me? 35And some of them that stood by, when they heard *it,* said, Behold, he calleth Elias. 36And one ran and filled a sponge full of vinegar, and put *it* on a reed, and gave him to drink, saying, Let alone; let us see whether Elias will come to take him down. 37And Jesus cried with a loud voice, and gave up the ghost. 38And the vail of the temple was rent in twain from the top to the bottom.

39 And when the centurion, which stood over against him, saw that he so cried out, and gave up the ghost, he said, Truly this man was the Son of God. 40 There were also women looking on afar off: among whom was Mary Magdalene, and Mary the mother of James the less and of Joses, and Salome; 41 Who also, when he was in Galilee, followed him, and ministered unto him; and many other women which came up with him unto Jerusalem.

42 And now when the even was come, because it was the preparation, that is, the day before the sabbath, 43 Joseph of Arimathea, an honourable counsellor, which also waited for the kingdom of God, came, and went in boldly unto Pilate, and craved the body of Jesus. 44And Pilate marvelled if he were already dead: and calling *unto him* the centurion, he asked him whether he had been any while dead. 45And when he knew *it* of the centurion, he gave the body to Joseph. 46And he bought fine linen, and took him down, and wrapped him in the linen, and laid him in a sepulchre which was hewn out of a rock, and rolled a stone unto the door of the sepulchre. 47And Mary Magdalene and Mary *the mother* of Joses beheld where he was laid.

R.S.V.

cross. 22And they brought him to the place called Golgotha (which means the place of a skull). 23And they offered him wine mingled with myrrh; but he did not take it. 24And they crucified him, and divided his garments among them, casting lots for them, to decide what each should take. 25And it was the third hour, when they crucified him. 26And the inscription of the charge against him read, "The King of the Jews." 27And with him they crucified two robbers, one on his right and one on his left.*g* 29And those who passed by derided him, wagging their heads, and saying, "Aha! You who would destroy the temple and build it in three days, 30 save yourself, and come down from the cross!" 31 So also the chief priests mocked him to one another with the scribes, saying, "He saved others; he cannot save himself. 32 Let the Christ, the King of Israel, come down now from the cross, that we may see and believe." Those who were crucified with him also reviled him.

33 And when the sixth hour had come, there was a darkness over the whole land *h* until the ninth hour. 34And at the ninth hour Jesus cried with a loud voice, "Eloi, Eloi, lama sabachthani?" which means, "My God, my God, why hast thou forsaken me?" 35And some of the bystanders hearing it said, "Behold, he is calling Elijah." 36And one ran and, filling a sponge full of vinegar, put it on a reed and gave it to him to drink, saying, "Wait, let us see whether Elijah will come to take him down." 37And Jesus uttered a loud cry, and breathed his last. 38And the curtain of the temple was torn in two, from top to bottom. 39And when the centurion, who stood facing him, saw that he thus*i* breathed his last, he said, "Truly this man was the Son*x* of God!"

40 There were also women looking on from afar, among whom were Mary Magdalene, and Mary the mother of James the younger and of Joses, and Salome, 41 who, when he was in Galilee, followed him, and ministered to him; and also many other women who came up with him to Jerusalem.

42 And when evening had come, since it was the day of Preparation, that is, the day before the sabbath, 43 Joseph of Arimathea, a respected member of the council, who was also himself looking for the kingdom of God, took courage and went to Pilate, and asked for the body of Jesus. 44And Pilate wondered if he were already dead; and summoning the centurion, he asked him whether he was already dead.*j* 45And when he learned from the centurion that he was dead, he granted the body to Joseph. 46And he bought a linen shroud, and taking him down, wrapped him in the linen shroud, and laid him in a tomb which had been hewn out of the rock; and he rolled a stone against the door of the tomb. 47 Mary Magdalene and Mary the mother of Joses saw where he was laid.

[g] Other ancient authorities insert verse 28, *And the scripture was fulfilled which says, "He was reckoned with the transgressors."* [h] Or *earth.* [i] Other ancient authorities insert *cried out and.* [x] Or *a son.* [j] Other ancient authorities read *whether he had been some time dead.*

PHILLIPS

The crucifixion   15. 22

They took him to a place called Golgotha (which means Skull Hill) and they offered him some drugged wine, but he would not take it. Then they crucified him, and shared out his garments, drawing lots to see what each of them would get. It was about nine o'clock in the morning when they nailed him to the cross. Over his head the placard of his crime read, "THE KING OF THE JEWS." They also crucified two bandits at the same time, one on each side of him. And the passers-by jeered at him, shaking their heads in mockery, saying,

"Hi, you! You could destroy the Temple and build it up again in three days, why not come down from the cross and save yourself?"

The chief priests also made fun of him among themselves and the scribes, and said:

"He saved others, he cannot save himself. If only this Christ, the king of Israel, would come down now from the cross, we should see it and believe!"

And even the men who were crucified with him hurled abuse at him.

At midday darkness spread over the whole countryside and lasted until three o'clock in the afternoon, and at three o'clock Jesus cried out in a loud voice,

"My God, my God, why did you forsake me?"

Some of the bystanders heard these words which Jesus spoke in Aramaic (*Eloi, Eloi, lama sabachthani?*), and said,

"Listen, he's calling for Elijah!"

One man ran off and soaked a sponge in vinegar, put it on a stick, and held it up for Jesus to drink, calling out:

"Let him alone! Let's see if Elijah will come and take him down!"

But Jesus let out a great cry, and died. The curtain of the Temple sanctuary was split in two from the top to the bottom. And when the centurion who stood in front of Jesus saw how he died, he said,

"This man was certainly a son of God!"

There were some women there looking on from a distance, among them Mary of Magdala, Mary the mother of the younger James and Joses, and Salome. These were the women who used to follow Jesus as he went about in Galilee and look after him. And there were many other women there who had come up to Jerusalem with them.

The body of Jesus is reverently   15. 42
laid in a tomb

When the evening came, because it was the day of preparation, that is the day before the Sabbath, Joseph from Arimathaea, a distinguished member of the council, who was himself prepared to accept the kingdom of God, went boldly into Pilate's presence and asked for the body of Jesus. Pilate was surprised that he should be dead already and he sent for the centurion and asked whether he had been dead long. On hearing the centurion's report, he gave Joseph the body of Jesus. So Joseph brought a linen winding sheet, took Jesus down and wrapped him in it, and then put him in a tomb which had been hewn out of the solid rock, rolling a stone over the entrance to it. Mary of Magdala and Mary the mother of Joses were looking on and saw where he was laid.

N.E.B.

They brought him to the place called Golgotha, which means 'Place of a skull'. He was offered drugged wine, but he would not take it. Then they fastened him to the cross. They divided his clothes among them, casting lots to decide what each should have.

The hour of the crucifixion was nine in the morning, and the inscription giving the charge against him read, 'The king of the Jews.' Two bandits were crucified with him, one on his right and the other on his left.[a]

The passers-by hurled abuse at him: 'Aha!' they cried, wagging their heads, 'you would pull the temple down, would you, and build it in three days? Come down from the cross and save yourself!' So too the chief priests and the doctors of the law jested with one another: 'He saved others,' they said, 'but he cannot save himself. Let the Messiah, the king of Israel, come down now from the cross. If we see that, we shall believe.' Even those who were crucified with him taunted him.

At midday darkness fell over the whole land, which lasted till three in the afternoon; and at three Jesus cried aloud, *'Eli, Eli, lema sabachthani?'*, which means, 'My God, my God, why hast thou forsaken me?'[b] Some of the passers-by, on hearing this, said, 'Hark, he is calling Elijah.' A man came running with a sponge, soaked in sour wine, on the end of a cane, and held it to his lips. 'Let us see', he said, 'if Elijah is coming to take him down.' Then Jesus gave a loud cry and died. And the curtain of the temple was torn in two from top to bottom. And when the centurion who was standing opposite him saw how he died,[c] he said, 'Truly this man was a son of God.'

A number of women were also present, watching from a distance. Among them were Mary of Magdala, Mary the mother of James the younger and of Joseph, and Salome, who had all followed him and waited on him when he was in Galilee, and there were several others who had come up to Jerusalem with him.

By this time evening had come; and as it was Preparation-day (that is, the day before the Sabbath), Joseph of Arimathaea, a respected member of the Council, a man who was eagerly awaiting the kingdom of God, bravely went in to Pilate and asked for the body of Jesus. Pilate was surprised to hear that he was already dead; so he sent for the centurion and asked him whether it was long since he died. And when he heard the centurion's report, he gave Joseph leave to take the dead body. So Joseph bought a linen sheet, took him down from the cross, and wrapped him in the sheet. Then he laid him in a tomb cut out of the rock, and rolled a stone against the entrance. And Mary of Magdala and Mary the mother of Joseph were watching and saw where he was laid.

[a] *Some witnesses add* (28) Thus that text of Scripture came true which says, 'He was reckoned among criminals.' [b] *Some witnesses read* My God, my God, why hast thou shamed me? [c] *Some witnesses read* saw that he died with a cry.

157

K.J.V.   **R.S.V.**

16 And when the sabbath was past, Mary Magdalene, and Mary the *mother* of James, and Salome, had bought sweet spices, that they might come and anoint him. 2And very early in the morning, the first *day* of the week, they came unto the sepulchre at the rising of the sun. 3And they said among themselves, Who shall roll us away the stone from the door of the sepulchre? 4And when they looked, they saw that the stone was rolled away: for it was very great. 5And entering into the sepulchre, they saw a young man sitting on the right side, clothed in a long white garment; and they were affrighted. 6And he saith unto them, Be not affrighted: ye seek Jesus of Nazareth, which was crucified: he is risen; he is not here: behold the place where they laid him. 7 But go your way, tell his disciples and Peter that he goeth before you into Galilee: there shall ye see him, as he said unto you. 8And they went out quickly, and fled from the sepulchre; for they trembled and were amazed: neither said they any thing to any *man;* for they were afraid.

9 Now when *Jesus* was risen early the first *day* of the week, he appeared first to Mary Magdalene, out of whom he had cast seven devils. 10*And* she went and told them that had been with him, as they mourned and wept. 11And they, when they had heard that he was alive, and had been seen of her, believed not.

12 After that he appeared in another form unto two of them, as they walked, and went into the country. 13And they went and told *it* unto the residue: neither believed they them.

14 Afterward he appeared unto the eleven as they sat at meat, and upbraided them with their unbelief and hardness of heart, because they believed not them which had seen him after he was risen. 15And he said unto them, Go ye into all the world, and preach the gospel to every creature. 16 He that believeth and is baptized shall be saved; but he that believeth not shall be damned. 17And these signs shall follow them that believe; In my name shall they cast out devils; they shall speak with new tongues; 18 They shall take up serpents; and if they drink any deadly thing, it shall not hurt them; they shall lay hands on the sick, and they shall recover.

19 So then, after the Lord had spoken unto them, he was received up into heaven, and sat on the right hand of God. 20And they went forth, and preached every where, the Lord working with *them,* and confirming the word with signs following. Amen.

16 And when the sabbath was past, Mary Magdalene, Mary the mother of James, and Salome bought spices, so that they might go and anoint him. 2And very early on the first day of the week they went to the tomb when the sun had risen. 3And they were saying to one another, "Who will roll away the stone for us from the door of the tomb?" 4And looking up, they saw that the stone was rolled back; for it was very large. 5And entering the tomb, they saw a young man sitting on the right side, dressed in a white robe; and they were amazed. 6And he said to them, "Do not be amazed; you seek Jesus of Nazareth, who was crucified. He has risen, he is not here; see the place where they laid him. 7 But go, tell his disciples and Peter that he is going before you to Galilee; there you will see him, as he told you." 8And they went out and fled from the tomb; for trembling and astonishment had come upon them; and they said nothing to any one, for they were afraid.*ᵏ*

[k] Other texts and versions add as 16.9-20 the following passage:

9 *Now when he rose early on the first day of the week, he appeared first to Mary Magdalene, from whom he had cast out seven demons.* 10 *She went and told those who had been with him, as they mourned and wept.* 11 *But when they heard that he was alive and had been seen by her, they would not believe it.*

12 *After this he appeared in another form to two of them, as they were walking into the country.* 13 *And they went back and told the rest, but they did not believe them.*

14 *Afterward he appeared to the eleven themselves as they sat at table; and he upbraided them for their unbelief and hardness of heart, because they had not believed those who saw him after he had risen.* 15 *And he said to them, "Go into all the world and preach the gospel to the whole creation.* 16 *He who believes and is baptized will be saved; but he who does not believe will be condemned.* 17 *And these signs will accompany those who believe: in my name they will cast out demons; they will speak in new tongues;* 18 *they will pick up serpents, and if they drink any deadly thing, it will not hurt them; they will lay their hands on the sick, and they will recover."*

19 *So then the Lord Jesus, after he had spoken to them, was taken up into heaven, and sat down at the right hand of God.* 20 *And they went forth and preached everywhere, while the Lord worked with them and confirmed the message by the signs that attended it. Amen.*

Other ancient authorities add after verse 8 the following: *But they reported briefly to Peter and those with him all that they had been told. And after this, Jesus himself sent out by means of them, from east to west, the sacred and imperishable proclamation of eternal salvation.*

PHILLIPS

Early on the first Lord's day: 16. 1
the women are amazed

When the Sabbath was over, Mary of Magdala, Mary the mother of James, and Salome bought spices so that they could go and anoint him. And very early in the morning on the first day of the week, they came to the tomb, just as the sun was rising.

"Who is going to roll the stone back from the doorway of the tomb?" they asked each other.

And then as they looked closer, they saw that the stone, which was a very large one, had been rolled back. So they went into the tomb and saw a young man in a white robe sitting on the right-hand side, and they were simply astonished. But he said to them:

"There is no need to be astonished. You are looking for Jesus of Nazareth who was crucified. He has risen; he is not here. Look, here is the place where they laid him. But now go and tell his disciples, and Peter, that he will be in Galilee before you. You will see him there just as he told you."

And they got out of the tomb and ran away from it. They were trembling with excitement. They did not dare to breathe a word to anyone.

An ancient appendix 16. 9

When Jesus rose early on that first day of the week, he appeared first of all to Mary of Magdala, from whom he had driven out seven evil spirits. And she went and reported this to his sorrowing and weeping followers. They heard her say that he was alive and that she had seen him, but they did not believe it.

Later, he appeared in a different form to two of them who were out walking, as they were on their way to the country. These two came back and told the others, but they did not believe them either. Still later he appeared to the eleven themselves as they were sitting at table, and reproached them for their lack of faith and reluctance to believe those who had seen him after he had risen. Then he said to them:

"You must go out to the whole world and proclaim the gospel to every creature. He who believes it and is baptized will be saved, but he who disbelieves it will be condemned. These signs will follow those who do believe: they will drive out evil spirits in my name; they will speak with new tongues; they will pick up snakes, and if they drink anything poisonous it will do them no harm; they will lay their hands upon the sick and they will recover."

Jesus, his mission accomplished, 16. 19
returns to Heaven

After these words to them, the Lord Jesus was taken up into Heaven and was enthroned at the right hand of God. They went out and preached everywhere. The Lord worked with them, confirming their message by the signs that followed.

16 When the Sabbath was over, Mary of Magdala, Mary the mother of James, and Salome bought[a] aromatic oils intending to go and anoint him; and very early on the Sunday morning, just after sunrise, they came to the tomb. They were wondering among themselves who would roll away the stone for them from the entrance to the tomb, when they looked up and saw that the stone, huge as it was, had been rolled back already. They went into the tomb, where they saw a youth sitting on the right-hand side, wearing a white robe; and they were dumbfounded. But he said to them, 'Fear nothing; you are looking for Jesus of Nazareth, who was crucified. He has risen; he is not here; look, there is the place where they laid him. But go and give this message to his disciples and Peter: "He will go on before you into Galilee and you will see him there, as he told you." ' Then they went out and ran away from the tomb, beside themselves with terror. They said nothing to anybody, for they were afraid.[b]

And they delivered all these instructions briefly to Peter and his companions. Afterwards Jesus himself sent out by them from east to west the sacred and imperishable message of eternal salvation.[c]

When he had risen from the dead early on Sunday morning he appeared first to Mary of Magdala, from whom he had formerly cast out seven devils. She went and carried the news to his mourning and sorrowful followers, but when they were told that he was alive and that she had seen him they did not believe it.

Later he appeared in a different guise to two of them as they were walking, on their way into the country. These also went and took the news to the others, but again no one believed them.

Afterwards while the Eleven were at table he appeared to them and reproached them for their incredulity and dullness, because they had not believed those who had seen him risen from the dead. Then he said to them: 'Go forth to every part of the world, and proclaim the Good News to the whole creation. Those who believe it and receive baptism will find salvation; those who do not believe will be condemned. Faith will bring with it these miracles: believers will cast out devils in my name and speak in strange tongues; if they handle snakes or drink any deadly poison, they will come to no harm; and the sick on whom they lay their hands will recover.'

So after talking with them the Lord Jesus was taken up into heaven, and he took his seat at the right hand of God; but they went out to make their proclamation everywhere, and the Lord worked with them and confirmed their words by the miracles that followed.[d]

[a] Some witnesses omit When the Sabbath . . . Salome, reading And they went and bought . . . [b] At this point some of the most ancient witnesses bring the book to a close. [c] Some witnesses add this paragraph, which in one of them is the conclusion of the book. [d] Some witnesses give verses 9-20 either instead of, or in addition to, the paragraph And they delivered . . . eternal salvation (here printed before verse 9), and so bring the book to a close. Others insert further additional matter.

THE

GOSPEL ACCORDING TO

SAINT LUKE

THE

GOSPEL ACCORDING TO

LUKE

1 Forasmuch as many have taken in hand to set forth in order a declaration of those things which are most surely believed among us, 2 Even as they delivered them unto us, which from the beginning were eyewitnesses, and ministers of the word; 3 It seemed good to me also, having had perfect understanding of all things from the very first, to write unto thee in order, most excellent Theophilus, 4 That thou mightest know the certainty of those things, wherein thou hast been instructed.

5 There was in the days of Herod, the king of Judea, a certain priest named Zacharias, of the course of Abia: and his wife *was* of the daughters of Aaron, and her name *was* Elisabeth. 6And they were both righteous before God, walking in all the commandments and ordinances of the Lord blameless. 7And they had no child, because that Elisabeth was barren; and they both were *now* well stricken in years. 8And it came to pass, that, while he executed the priest's office before God in the order of his course, 9According to the custom of the priest's office, his lot was to burn incense when he went into the temple of the Lord. 10And the whole multitude of the people were praying without at the time of incense. 11And there appeared unto him an angel of the Lord standing on the right side of the altar of incense. 12And when Zacharias saw *him*, he was troubled, and fear fell upon him. 13 But the angel said unto him, Fear not, Zacharias: for thy prayer is heard; and thy wife Elisabeth shall bear thee a son, and thou shalt call his name John. 14And thou shalt have joy and gladness; and many shall rejoice at his birth. 15 For he shall be great in the sight of the Lord, and shall drink neither wine nor strong drink; and he shall be filled with the Holy Ghost, even from his mother's womb. 16And many of the children of Israel shall he turn to the Lord their God. 17And he shall go before him in the spirit and power of Elias, to turn the hearts of the fathers to the children, and the disobedient to the wisdom of the just; to make ready a people prepared for the Lord. 18And Zacharias said unto the angel, Whereby shall I know this? for I am an old man, and my wife well stricken in years. 19And the angel answering said unto him, I am Gabriel, that stand in the presence of God; and am sent to speak unto thee, and to shew thee these glad tidings. 20And, behold, thou shalt be dumb, and not able to speak, until the day that these things shall be performed, because thou believest not my words, which shall be fulfilled in their season. 21And the people waited for

1 Inasmuch as many have undertaken to compile a narrative of the things which have been accomplished among us, 2 just as they were delivered to us by those who from the beginning were eyewitnesses and ministers of the word, 3 it seemed good to me also, having followed all things closely*a* for some time past, to write an orderly account for you, most excellent Theophilus, 4 that you may know the truth concerning the things of which you have been informed.

5 In the days of Herod, king of Judea, there was a priest named Zechariah,*b* of the division of Abijah; and he had a wife of the daughters of Aaron, and her name was Elizabeth. 6And they were both righteous before God, walking in all the commandments and ordinances of the Lord blameless. 7 But they had no child, because Elizabeth was barren, and both were advanced in years.

8 Now while he was serving as priest before God when his division was on duty, 9 according to the custom of the priesthood, it fell to him by lot to enter the temple of the Lord and burn incense. 10And the whole multitude of the people were praying outside at the hour of incense. 11And there appeared to him an angel of the Lord standing on the right side of the altar of incense. 12And Zechariah was troubled when he saw him, and fear fell upon him. 13 But the angel said to him, "Do not be afraid, Zechariah, for your prayer is heard, and your wife Elizabeth will bear you a son, and you shall call his name John.

14 And you will have joy and gladness,
and many will rejoice at his birth;
15 for he will be great before the Lord,
and he shall drink no wine nor strong drink,
and he will be filled with the Holy Spirit,
even from his mother's womb.
16 And he will turn many of the sons of Israel
to the Lord their God,
17 and he will go before him in the spirit and
power of Elijah,
to turn the hearts of the fathers to the children,
and the disobedient to the wisdom of the just,
to make ready for the Lord a people prepared."
18And Zechariah said to the angel, "How shall I know this? For I am an old man, and my wife is advanced in years." 19And the angel answered him, "I am Gabriel, who stand in the presence of God; and I was sent to speak to you, and to bring you this good news. 20And behold, you will be silent and unable to speak until the day that these things come to pass, because you did not believe my words, which will be fulfilled in their time." 21And the people were waiting for Zecha-

[a] Or *accurately*. *[b]* Greek *Zacharias*.

160

THE
GOSPEL OF
LUKE

THE
GOSPEL ACCORDING TO
LUKE

Prefatory note   **1. 1**

Dear Theophilus,

Many people have already written an account of the events which have happened among us, basing their work on the evidence of those who we know were eyewitnesses as well as teachers of the message. I have therefore decided, since I have traced the course of these happenings carefully from the beginning, to set them down for you myself in their proper order, so that you may have reliable information about the matters in which you have already had instruction.

1 The author to Theophilus: Many writers have undertaken to draw up an account of the events that have happened among us, following the traditions handed down to us by the original eyewitnesses and servants of the Gospel. And so I in my turn, your Excellency, as one who has gone over the whole course of these events in detail, have decided to write a connected narrative for you, so as to give you authentic knowledge about the matters of which you have been informed.

A vision comes to an old   **1. 5**
priest of God

The story begins in the days when Herod was king of Judaea with a priest called Zacharias (who belonged to the Abijah section of the priesthood), whose wife Elisabeth was, like him, a descendant of Aaron. They were both truly religious people, blamelessly observing all God's commandments and requirements. They were childless through Elisabeth's infertility, and both of them were getting on in years. One day, while Zacharias was performing his priestly functions (it was the turn of his division to be on duty), it fell to him to go into the sanctuary and burn the incense. The crowded congregation outside was praying at the actual time of the incense burning, when an angel of the Lord appeared on the right side of the incense altar. When Zacharias saw him, he was terribly agitated and a sense of awe swept over him. But the angel spoke to him:

"Do not be afraid, Zacharias; your prayers have been heard. Elisabeth your wife will bear you a son, and you are to call him John. This will be joy and delight to you and many more will be glad because he is born. He will be one of God's great men; he will touch neither wine nor strong drink and he will be filled with the Holy Spirit from the moment of his birth. He will turn many of Israel's children to the Lord their God. He will go out before God in the spirit and power of Elijah—to reconcile fathers and children, and bring back the disobedient to the wisdom of good men—and he will make a people fully ready for their Lord."

But Zacharias replied to the angel:

"How can I know that this is true? I am an old man myself and my wife is getting on in years . . ."

"I am Gabriel," the angel answered. "I stand in the presence of God, and I have been sent to speak to you and tell you this good news. Because you do not believe what I have said, you shall live in silence, and you shall be unable to speak a word until the day that it happens. But be sure that everything that I have told you will come true at the proper time."

Meanwhile, the people were waiting for

The Coming of the Messiah

In the days of Herod king of Judaea there was a priest named Zechariah, of the division of the priesthood called after Abijah. His wife also was of priestly descent; her name was Elizabeth. Both of them were upright and devout, blamelessly observing all the commandments and ordinances of the Lord. But they had no children, for Elizabeth was barren, and both were well on in years.

Once, when it was the turn of his division and he was there to take part in divine service, it fell to his lot, by priestly custom, to enter the sanctuary of the Lord and offer the incense; and the whole congregation was at prayer outside. It was the hour of the incense-offering. There appeared to him an angel of the Lord, standing on the right of the altar of incense. At this sight, Zechariah was startled, and fear overcame him. But the angel said to him, 'Do not be afraid, Zechariah; your prayer has been heard: your wife Elizabeth will bear you a son, and you shall name him John. Your heart will thrill with joy and many will be glad that he was born; for he will be great in the eyes of the Lord. He shall never touch wine or strong drink. From his very birth he will be filled with the Holy Spirit; and he will bring back many Israelites to the Lord their God. He will go before him as forerunner,[a] possessed by the spirit and power of Elijah, to reconcile father and child, to convert the rebellious to the ways of the righteous, to prepare a people that shall be fit for the Lord.'

Zechariah said to the angel, 'How can I be sure of this? I am an old man and my wife is well on in years.'

The angel replied, 'I am Gabriel; I stand in attendance upon God, and I have been sent to speak to you and bring you this good news. But now listen: you will lose your powers of speech, and remain silent until the day when these things happen to you, because you have not believed me, though at their proper time my words will be proved true.'

Meanwhile the people were waiting for Zecha-

[a] *Or* In his sight he will go forth.

K.J.V.

Zacharias, and marvelled that he tarried so long in the temple. 22And when he came out, he could not speak unto them: and they perceived that he had seen a vision in the temple; for he beckoned unto them, and remained speechless. 23And it came to pass, that, as soon as the days of his ministration were accomplished, he departed to his own house. 24And after those days his wife Elisabeth conceived, and hid herself five months, saying, 25 Thus hath the Lord dealt with me in the days wherein he looked on *me*, to take away my reproach among men. 26And in the sixth month the angel Gabriel was sent from God unto a city of Galilee, named Nazareth, 27 To a virgin espoused to a man whose name was Joseph, of the house of David; and the virgin's name *was* Mary. 28And the angel came in unto her, and said, Hail, *thou that art* highly favoured, the Lord *is* with thee: blessed *art* thou among women. 29And when she saw *him*, she was troubled at his saying, and cast in her mind what manner of salutation this should be. 30And the angel said unto her, Fear not, Mary: for thou hast found favour with God. 31And, behold, thou shalt conceive in thy womb, and bring forth a son, and shalt call his name JESUS. 32 He shall be great, and shall be called the Son of the Highest; and the Lord God shall give unto him the throne of his father David: 33And he shall reign over the house of Jacob for ever; and of his kingdom there shall be no end. 34 Then said Mary unto the angel, How shall this be, seeing I know not a man? 35And the angel answered and said unto her, The Holy Ghost shall come upon thee, and the power of the Highest shall overshadow thee: therefore also that holy thing which shall be born of thee shall be called the Son of God. 36And, behold, thy cousin Elisabeth, she hath also conceived a son in her old age; and this is the sixth month with her, who was called barren. 37 For with God nothing shall be impossible. 38And Mary said, Behold the handmaid of the Lord; be it unto me according to thy word. And the angel departed from her. 39And Mary arose in those days, and went into the hill country with haste, into a city of Juda; 40And entered into the house of Zacharias, and saluted Elisabeth. 41And it came to pass, that, when Elisabeth heard the salutation of Mary, the babe leaped in her womb; and Elisabeth was filled with the Holy Ghost: 42And she spake out with a loud voice, and said, Blessed *art* thou among women, and blessed *is* the fruit of thy womb. 43And whence *is* this to me, that the mother of my Lord should come to me? 44 For, lo, as soon as the voice of thy salutation sounded in mine ears, the babe leaped in my womb for joy. 45And blessed *is* she that believed: for there shall be a performance of those things which were told her from the Lord. 46And Mary said, My soul doth magnify the Lord, 47And my spirit hath rejoiced in God my Saviour. 48 For he hath regarded the low estate of his handmaiden: for, behold, from henceforth all generations shall call me blessed. 49 For he that is mighty hath done to me great things; and holy *is* his name. 50And his mercy *is* on them that fear him from generation to generation. 51 He hath shewed strength with his arm;

R.S.V.

riah, and they wondered at his delay in the temple. 22And when he came out, he could not speak to them, and they perceived that he had seen a vision in the temple; and he made signs to them and remained dumb. 23And when his time of service was ended, he went to his home.

24 After these days his wife Elizabeth conceived, and for five months she hid herself, saying, 25 "Thus the Lord has done to me in the days when he looked on me, to take away my reproach among men."

26 In the sixth month the angel Gabriel was sent from God to a city of Galilee named Nazareth, 27 to a virgin betrothed to a man whose name was Joseph, of the house of David; and the virgin's name was Mary. 28And he came to her and said, "Hail, O favored one, the Lord is with you!" *c* 29 But she was greatly troubled at the saying, and considered in her mind what sort of greeting this might be. 30And the angel said to her, "Do not be afraid, Mary, for you have found favor with God. 31And behold, you will conceive in your womb and bear a son, and you shall call his name Jesus.

32 He will be great, and will be called the Son of the Most High;
    and the Lord God will give to him the throne of his father David,
33 and he will reign over the house of Jacob for ever;
    and of his kingdom there will be no end."

34And Mary said to the angel, "How can this be, since I have no husband?" 35And the angel said to her,

"The Holy Spirit will come upon you,
    and the power of the Most High will overshadow you;
therefore the child to be born*d* will be called holy,
    the Son of God.

36And behold, your kinswoman Elizabeth in her old age has also conceived a son; and this is the sixth month with her who was called barren. 37 For with God nothing will be impossible." 38And Mary said, "Behold, I am the handmaid of the Lord; let it be to me according to your word." And the angel departed from her.

39 In those days Mary arose and went with haste into the hill country, to a city of Judah, 40 and she entered the house of Zechariah and greeted Elizabeth. 41And when Elizabeth heard the greeting of Mary, the babe leaped in her womb; and Elizabeth was filled with the Holy Spirit 42 and she exclaimed with a loud cry, "Blessed are you among women, and blessed is the fruit of your womb! 43And why is this granted me, that the mother of my Lord should come to me? 44 For behold, when the voice of your greeting came to my ears, the babe in my womb leaped for joy. 45And blessed is she who believed that there would be*e* a fulfilment of what was spoken to her from the Lord." 46And Mary said,

"My soul magnifies the Lord,
47 and my spirit rejoices in God my Savior,
48 for he has regarded the low estate of his handmaiden.
    For behold, henceforth all generations will call me blessed;
49 for he who is mighty has done great things for me,
    and holy is his name.
50 And his mercy is on those who fear him from generation to generation.
51 He has shown strength with his arm,

[c] Other ancient authorities add *"Blessed are you among women!"* [d] Other ancient authorities add *of you.* [e] Or *believed, for there will be.*

PHILLIPS

Zacharias, wondering why he stayed so long in the sanctuary. But when he came out and was unable to speak a word to them—for although he kept making signs, not a sound came from his lips—they realized that he had seen a vision in the Temple. Later, when his days of duty were over, he went back home, and soon afterward his wife Elisabeth became pregnant and kept herself secluded for five months.

"How good the Lord is to me," she would say, "now that he has taken away the shame that I have suffered!"

A vision comes to a young woman in Nazareth
1. 26

Then, six months after Zacharias' vision, the angel Gabriel was sent from God to a Galilean town, Nazareth by name, to a young woman who was engaged to a man called Joseph (a descendant of David). The girl's name was Mary. The angel entered her room and said,

"Greetings to you, Mary. O favored one!—the Lord be with you!"

Mary was deeply perturbed at these words and wondered what such a greeting could possibly mean. But the angel said to her:

"Do not be afraid, Mary; God loves you dearly. You are going to be the mother of a son, and you will call him Jesus. He will be great and will be known as the Son of the most high. The Lord God will give him the throne of his forefather, David, and he will be king over the people of Jacob for ever. His reign shall never end."

Then Mary spoke to the angel,

"How can this be?" she said. "I am not married!"

But the angel made this reply to her:

"The Holy Spirit will come upon you, the power of the most high will overshadow you. Your child will therefore be called holy—the Son of God. Your cousin Elisabeth has also conceived a son, old as she is. Indeed, this is the sixth month for her, a woman who was called barren. For no promise of God can fail to be fulfilled."

"I belong to the Lord, body and soul," replied Mary, "let it happen as you say." And at this the angel left her.

With little delay Mary got ready and hurried off to the hillside town in Judaea where Zacharias and Elisabeth lived. She went into their house and greeted her cousin. When Elisabeth heard her greeting, the unborn child stirred inside her and she herself was filled with the Holy Spirit, and cried out:

"Blessed are you among women, and blessed is your child! What an honor it is to have the mother of my Lord come to see me! Why, as soon as your greeting reached my ears, the child within me jumped for joy! Oh, how happy is the woman who believes in God, for he does make his promises to her come true!"

Then Mary said: "My heart is overflowing with praise of my Lord; my soul is full of joy in God my Savior. For he has deigned to notice me, his humble servant, and after this, all the people who ever shall be will call me the happiest of women! The one who can do all things has done great things for me—oh, holy is his Name! Truly, his mercy rests on those who fear him in every generation. He has shown the strength of his arm, he has swept away the

N.E.B.

riah, surprised that he was staying so long inside. When he did come out he could not speak to them, and they realized that he had had a vision in the sanctuary. He stood there making signs to them, and remained dumb.

When his period of duty was completed Zechariah returned home. After this his wife Elizabeth conceived, and for five months she lived in seclusion, thinking, 'This is the Lord's doing; now at last he has deigned to take away my reproach among men.'

In the sixth month the angel Gabriel was sent from God to a town in Galilee called Nazareth, with a message for a girl betrothed to a man named Joseph, a descendant of David; the girl's name was Mary. The angel went in and said to her, 'Greetings, most favoured one! The Lord is with you.' But she was deeply troubled by what he said and wondered what this greeting might mean. Then the angel said to her, 'Do not be afraid, Mary, for God has been gracious to you; you shall conceive and bear a son, and you shall give him the name Jesus. He will be great; he will bear the title "Son of the Most High"; the Lord God will give him the throne of his ancestor David, and he will be king over Israel [a] for ever; his reign shall never end.' 'How can this be,' said Mary, 'when I have no husband?' The angel answered, 'The Holy Spirit will come upon you, and the power of the Most High will overshadow you; and for that reason the holy child to be born will be called "Son of God". [b] Moreover your kinswoman Elizabeth has herself conceived a son in her old age; and she who is reputed barren is now in her sixth month, for God's promises can never fail.' [c] 'Here am I,' said Mary; 'I am the Lord's servant; as you have spoken, so be it.' Then the angel left her.

About this time Mary set out and went straight to a town in the uplands of Judah. She went into Zechariah's house and greeted Elizabeth. And when Elizabeth heard Mary's greeting, the baby stirred in her womb. Then Elizabeth was filled with the Holy Spirit and cried aloud, 'God's blessing is on you above all women, and his blessing is on the fruit of your womb. Who am I, that the mother of my Lord should visit me? I tell you, when your greeting sounded in my ears, the baby in my womb leapt for joy. How happy is she who has had faith that the Lord's promise would be fulfilled!'

And Mary[d] said:

'Tell out, my soul, the greatness of the Lord,
rejoice, rejoice, my spirit, in God my saviour;
so tenderly has he looked upon his servant,
humble as she is.
For, from this day forth,
all generations will count me blessed,
so wonderfully has he dealt with me,
the Lord, the Mighty One.

His name is Holy;
his mercy sure from generation to generation
toward those who fear him;
the deeds his own right arm has done
disclose his might:

[a] *Literally* the house of Jacob. [b] *Or* the child to be born will be called holy, "Son of God". [c] *Some witnesses read* for with God nothing will prove impossible. [d] *So the majority of ancient witnesses; some read* Elizabeth; *the original may have had no name.*

K.J.V.

he hath scattered the proud in the imagination of their hearts. 52 He hath put down the mighty from *their* seats, and exalted them of low degree. 53 He hath filled the hungry with good things; and the rich he hath sent empty away. 54 He hath holpen his servant Israel, in remembrance of *his* mercy; 55As he spake to our fathers, to Abraham, and to his seed for ever. 56And Mary abode with her about three months, and returned to her own house. 57 Now Elisabeth's full time came that she should be delivered; and she brought forth a son. 58And her neighbours and her cousins heard how the Lord had shewed great mercy upon her; and they rejoiced with her. 59And it came to pass, that on the eighth day they came to circumcise the child; and they called him Zacharias, after the name of his father. 60And his mother answered and said, Not *so;* but he shall be called John. 61And they said unto her, There is none of thy kindred that is called by this name. 62And they made signs to his father, how he would have him called. 63And he asked for a writing table, and wrote, saying, His name is John. And they marvelled all. 64And his mouth was opened immediately, and his tongue *loosed,* and he spake, and praised God. 65And fear came on all that dwelt round about them: and all these sayings were noised abroad throughout all the hill country of Judea. 66And all they that heard *them* laid *them* up in their hearts, saying, What manner of child shall this be! And the hand of the Lord was with him. 67And his father Zacharias was filled with the Holy Ghost, and prophesied, saying, 68 Blessed *be* the Lord God of Israel; for he hath visited and redeemed his people, 69And hath raised up a horn of salvation for us in the house of his servant David; 70As he spake by the mouth of his holy prophets, which have been since the world began: 71 That we should be saved from our enemies, and from the hand of all that hate us; 72 To perform the mercy *promised* to our fathers, and to remember his holy covenant; 73 The oath which he sware to our father Abraham, 74 That he would grant unto us, that we, being delivered out of the hand of our enemies, might serve him without fear, 75 In holiness and righteousness before him, all the days of our life. 76And thou, child, shalt be called the prophet of the Highest: for thou shalt go before the face of the Lord to prepare his ways; 77 To give knowledge of salvation unto his people by the remission of their sins, 78 Through the tender mercy of our God; whereby the dayspring from on high hath visited us, 79 To give light to them that sit in darkness and *in* the shadow of death, to guide our feet into the way

R.S.V.

he has scattered the proud in the imagination of their hearts,
52 he has put down the mighty from their thrones,
and exalted those of low degree;
53 he has filled the hungry with good things,
and the rich he has sent empty away.
54 He has helped his servant Israel,
in remembrance of his mercy,
55 as he spoke to our fathers,
to Abraham and to his posterity for ever."
56And Mary remained with her about three months, and returned to her home.
57 Now the time came for Elizabeth to be delivered, and she gave birth to a son. 58And her neighbors and kinsfolk heard that the Lord had shown great mercy to her, and they rejoiced with her. 59And on the eighth day they came to circumcise the child; and they would have named him Zechariah after his father, 60 but his mother said, "Not so; he shall be called John." 61And they said to her, "None of your kindred is called by this name." 62And they made signs to his father, inquiring what he would have him called. 63And he asked for a writing tablet, and wrote, "His name is John." And they all marveled. 64And immediately his mouth was opened and his tongue loosed, and he spoke, blessing God. 65And fear came on all their neighbors. And all these things were talked about through all the hill country of Judea; 66 and all who heard them laid them up in their hearts, saying, "What then will this child be?" For the hand of the Lord was with him.
67 And his father Zechariah was filled with the Holy Spirit, and prophesied, saying,
68 "Blessed be the Lord God of Israel,
for he has visited and redeemed his people,
69 and has raised up a horn of salvation for us
in the house of his servant David,
70 as he spoke by the mouth of his holy prophets from of old,
71 that we should be saved from our enemies,
and from the hand of all who hate us;
72 to perform the mercy promised to our fathers,
and to remember his holy covenant,
73 the oath which he swore to our father Abraham, 74 to grant us
that we, being delivered from the hand of our enemies,
might serve him without fear,
75 in holiness and righteousness before him
all the days of our life.
76 And you, child, will be called the prophet of the Most High;
for you will go before the Lord to prepare his ways,
77 to give knowledge of salvation to his people
in the forgiveness of their sins,
78 through the tender mercy of our God,
when the day shall dawn upon[f] us from on high
79 to give light to those who sit in darkness and in the shadow of death,
to guide our feet into the way of peace."

[f] Or *whereby the dayspring will visit.* Other ancient authorities read *since the dayspring has visited.*

PHILLIPS

high and mighty. He has set kings down from their thrones and lifted up the humble. He has satisfied the hungry with good things and sent the rich away with empty hands. Yes, he has helped Israel, his child: he has remembered the mercy that he promised to our forefathers, to Abraham and his sons for evermore!"

The old woman's son, John, is born   1. 56

So Mary stayed with Elisabeth about three months, and then went back to her own home. Then came the time for Elisabeth's child to be born, and she gave birth to a son. Her neighbors and relations heard of the great mercy the Lord had shown her and shared her joy.

When the eighth day came, they were going to circumcise the child and call him Zacharias, after his father, but his mother said,

"Oh, no! He must be called John."

"But none of your relations is called John," they replied. And they made signs to his father to see what name he wanted the child to have. He beckoned for a writing tablet and wrote the words, "His name is John," which greatly surprised everybody. Then his power of speech suddenly came back, and his first words were to thank God. The neighbors were awestruck at this, and all these incidents were reported in the hill country of Judaea. People turned the whole matter over in their hearts, and said,

"What is this child's future going to be?" For the Lord's blessing was plainly upon him.

Then Zacharias, his father, filled with the Holy Spirit and speaking like a prophet, said:

"Blessings on the Lord, the God of Israel, because he has turned his face toward his people and has set them free! And he has raised up for us a standard of salvation in his servant David's house! Long, long ago, through the words of his holy prophets, he promised to do this for us, so that we should be safe from our enemies and secure from all who hate us. So does he continue the mercy he showed to our forefathers. So does he remember the holy agreement he made with them and the oath which he swore to our father Abraham, to make us this gift: that we should be saved from the hands of our enemies, and in his presence should serve him unafraid in holiness and righteousness all our lives.

"And you, little child, will be called the prophet of the most high, for you will go before the Lord to prepare the way for his coming. It will be for you to give his people knowledge of their salvation through the forgiveness of their sins. Because the heart of our God is full of mercy toward us, the first light of Heaven shall come to visit us—to shine on those who lie in darkness and under the shadow of death, and to guide our feet into the path of peace."

N.E.B.

the arrogant of heart and mind he has put to rout,
he has torn imperial powers from their thrones,
   but the humble have been lifted high.
The hungry he has satisfied with good things,
   the rich sent empty away.

He has ranged himself at the side of Israel his servant;
   firm in his promise to our forefathers,
he has not forgotten to show mercy to Abraham
   and his children's children, for ever.'

Mary stayed with her about three months and then returned home.

Now the time came for Elizabeth's child to be born, and she gave birth to a son. When her neighbours and relatives heard what great favour the Lord had shown her, they were as delighted as she was. Then on the eighth day they came to circumcise the child; and they were going to name him Zechariah after his father. But his mother spoke up and said, 'No! he is to be called John.' 'But', they said, 'there is nobody in your family who has that name.' They inquired of his father by signs what he would like him to be called. He asked for a writing-tablet and to the astonishment of all wrote down, 'His name is John.' Immediately his lips and tongue were freed and he began to speak, praising God. All the neighbours were struck with awe, and everywhere in the uplands of Judaea the whole story became common talk. All who heard it were deeply impressed and said, 'What will this child become?' For indeed the hand of the Lord was upon him.[a]

And Zechariah his father was filled with the Holy Spirit and uttered this prophecy:

'Praise to the God of Israel!
For he has turned to his people, saved them
   and set them free,
and has raised up a deliverer of victorious power
   from the house of his servant David.

So he promised: age after age he proclaimed
   by the lips of his holy prophets,
that he would deliver us from our enemies,
   out of the hands of all who hate us;
that he would deal mercifully with our fathers,
   calling to mind his solemn covenant.

Such was the oath he swore to our father Abraham,
   to rescue us from enemy hands,
and grant us, free from fear, to worship him
   with a holy worship, with uprightness of heart,
   in his presence, our whole life long.

And you, my child, you shall be called Prophet of the Highest,
for you will be the Lord's forerunner, to prepare his way
   and lead his people to salvation through knowledge of him,
   by the forgiveness of their sins:
for in the tender compassion of our God
   the morning sun from heaven will rise[b] upon us,
to shine on those who live in darkness, under the cloud of death,
   and to guide our feet into the way of peace.'

[a] Some witnesses read 'What will this child become, for indeed the hand of the Lord is upon him?' [b] Some witnesses read has risen.

K.J.V.

of peace. 80And the child grew, and waxed strong in spirit, and was in the deserts till the day of his shewing unto Israel.

2 And it came to pass in those days, that there went out a decree from Cesar Augustus, that all the world should be taxed. 2 (And this taxing was first made when Cyrenius was governor of Syria.) 3And all went to be taxed, every one into his own city. 4And Joseph also went up from Galilee, out of the city of Nazareth, into Judea, unto the city of David, which is called Bethlehem, (because he was of the house and lineage of David,) 5 To be taxed with Mary his espoused wife, being great with child. 6And so it was, that, while they were there, the days were accomplished that she should be delivered. 7And she brought forth her firstborn son, and wrapped him in swaddling clothes, and laid him in a manger; because there was no room for them in the inn. 8And there were in the same country shepherds abiding in the field, keeping watch over their flock by night. 9And, lo, the angel of the Lord came upon them, and the glory of the Lord shone round about them; and they were sore afraid. 10And the angel said unto them, Fear not: for, behold, I bring you good tidings of great joy, which shall be to all people. 11 For unto you is born this day in the city of David a Saviour, which is Christ the Lord. 12And this *shall be* a sign unto you; Ye shall find the babe wrapped in swaddling clothes, lying in a manger. 13And suddenly there was with the angel a multitude of the heavenly host praising God, and saying, 14 Glory to God in the highest, and on earth peace, good will toward men. 15And it came to pass, as the angels were gone away from them into heaven, the shepherds said one to another, Let us now go even unto Bethlehem, and see this thing which is come to pass, which the Lord hath made known unto us. 16And they came with haste, and found Mary and Joseph, and the babe lying in a manger. 17And when they had seen *it,* they made known abroad the saying which was told them concerning this child. 18And all they that heard *it* wondered at those things which were told them by the shepherds. 19 But Mary kept all these things, and pondered *them* in her heart. 20And the shepherds returned, glorifying and praising God for all the things that they had heard and seen, as it was told unto them. 21And when eight days were accomplished for the circumcising of the child, his name was called JESUS, which was so named of the angel be-

R.S.V.

80And the child grew and became strong in spirit, and he was in the wilderness till the day of his manifestation to Israel.

2 In those days a decree went out from Caesar Augustus that all the world should be enrolled. 2 This was the first enrollment, when Quirinius was governor of Syria. 3And all went to be enrolled, each to his own city. 4And Joseph also went up from Galilee, from the city of Nazareth, to Judea, to the city of David, which is called Bethlehem, because he was of the house and lineage of David, 5 to be enrolled with Mary, his betrothed, who was with child. 6And while they were there, the time came for her to be delivered. 7And she gave birth to her first-born son and wrapped him in swaddling cloths, and laid him in a manger, because there was no place for them in the inn.
8 And in that region there were shepherds out in the field, keeping watch over their flock by night. 9And an angel of the Lord appeared to them, and the glory of the Lord shone around them, and they were filled with fear. 10And the angel said to them, "Be not afraid; for behold, I bring you good news of a great joy which will come to all the people; 11 for to you is born this day in the city of David a Savior, who is Christ the Lord. 12And this will be a sign for you: you will find a babe wrapped in swaddling cloths and lying in a manger." 13And suddenly there was with the angel a multitude of the heavenly host praising God and saying,
14 "Glory to God in the highest,
    and on earth peace among men with whom
      he is pleased!" *g*
15 When the angels went away from them into heaven, the shepherds said to one another, "Let us go over to Bethlehem and see this thing that has happened, which the Lord has made known to us." 16And they went with haste, and found Mary and Joseph, and the babe lying in a manger. 17And when they saw it they made known the saying which had been told them concerning this child; 18 and all who heard it wondered at what the shepherds told them. 19 But Mary kept all these things, pondering them in her heart. 20And the shepherds returned, glorifying and praising God for all they had heard and seen, as it had been told them.
21 And at the end of eight days, when he was circumcised, he was called Jesus, the name given by the angel before he was conceived in the womb.

[g] Other ancient authorities read *peace, good will among men.*

The little child grew up and became strong in spirit. He lived in lonely places until the day came for him to show himself to Israel.

The census brings Mary and   2. 1
Joseph to Bethlehem

At that time a proclamation was made by Caesar Augustus that all the inhabited world should be registered. This was the first census, undertaken while Cyrenius was governor of Syria; and everybody went to the town of his birth to be registered. Joseph went up from the town of Nazareth in Galilee to David's town, Bethlehem, in Judaea, because he was a direct descendant of David, to be registered with his future wife, Mary, now in the later stages of her pregnancy. So it happened that it was while they were there in Bethlehem that she came to the end of her time. She gave birth to her first child, a son. And as there was no place for them inside the inn, she wrapped him up and laid him in a manger.

A vision comes to shepherds   2. 8
on the hillside

There were some shepherds living in the same part of the country, keeping guard throughout the night over their flock in the open fields. Suddenly an angel of the Lord stood by their side, the splendor of the Lord blazed around them, and they were terror-stricken. But the angel said to them:

"Do not be afraid! Listen, I bring you glorious news of great joy which is for all the people. This very day, in David's town, a Savior has been born for you. He is Christ, the Lord. Let this prove it to you: you will find a baby, wrapped up and lying in a manger."

And in a flash there appeared with the angel a vast host of the armies of Heaven, praising God, saying,

"Glory to God in the highest Heaven! Peace upon earth among men of goodwill!"

When the angels left them and went back into Heaven, the shepherds said to each other, "Now let us go straight to Bethlehem and see this thing which the Lord has made known to us."

So they came as fast as they could and they found Mary and Joseph—and the baby lying in the manger. And when they had seen this sight, they told everybody what had been said to them about the little child. And those who heard them were amazed at what the shepherds said. But Mary treasured all these things and turned them over in her mind. The shepherds went back to work, glorifying and praising God for everything that they had heard and seen, which had happened just as they had been told.

Mary and Joseph bring their   2. 21
newly born son to the Temple

At the end of the eight days, the time came for circumcising the child and he was called Jesus, the name given to him by the angel before his conception.

As the child grew up he became strong in spirit; he lived out in the wilds until the day when he appeared publicly before Israel.

2 In those days a decree was issued by the Emperor Augustus for a general registration throughout the Roman world. This was the first registration of its kind; it took place when Quirinius[a] was governor of Syria. For this purpose everyone made his way to his own town; and so Joseph went up to Judaea from the town of Nazareth in Galilee, to be registered at the city of David, called Bethlehem, because he was of the house of David by descent; and with him went Mary who was betrothed to him. She was pregnant, and while they were there the time came for her child to be born, and she gave birth to a son, her first-born. She wrapped him round, and laid him in a manger, because there was no room for them to lodge in the house.

Now in this same district there were shepherds out in the fields, keeping watch through the night over their flock, when suddenly there stood before them an angel of the Lord, and the splendour of the Lord shone round them. They were terror-struck, but the angel said, 'Do not be afraid; I have good news for you: there is great joy coming to the whole people. Today in the city of David a deliverer has been born to you —the Messiah, the Lord.[b] And this is your sign: you will find a baby lying all wrapped up, in a manger.' All at once there was with the angel a great company of the heavenly host, singing the praises of God:

'Glory to God in highest heaven,
And on earth his peace for men on whom his
    favour rests.' [c]

After the angels had left them and gone into heaven the shepherds said to one another, 'Come, we must go straight to Bethlehem and see this thing that has happened, which the Lord has made known to us.' So they went with all speed and found their way to Mary and Joseph; and the baby was lying in the manger. When they saw him, they recounted what they had been told about this child; and all who heard were astonished at what the shepherds said. But Mary treasured up all these things and pondered over them. Meanwhile the shepherds returned glorifying and praising God for what they had heard and seen; it had all happened as they had been told.

Eight days later the time came to circumcise him, and he was given the name Jesus, the name given by the angel before he was conceived.

[a] Or This was the first registration carried out while Quirinius . . . [b] Some witnesses read to you—the Lord's Messiah. [c] Some witnesses read And on earth his peace, his favour towards men.

K.J.V.

fore he was conceived in the womb. 22And when the days of her purification according to the law of Moses were accomplished, they brought him to Jerusalem, to present *him* to the Lord; 23 (As it is written in the law of the Lord, Every male that openeth the womb shall be called holy to the Lord;) 24And to offer a sacrifice according to that which is said in the law of the Lord, A pair of turtledoves, or two young pigeons. 25And, behold, there was a man in Jerusalem, whose name *was* Simeon; and the same man *was* just and devout, waiting for the consolation of Israel: and the Holy Ghost was upon him. 26And it was revealed unto him by the Holy Ghost, that he should not see death, before he had seen the Lord's Christ. 27And he came by the Spirit into the temple: and when the parents brought in the child Jesus, to do for him after the custom of the law, 28 Then took he him up in his arms, and blessed God, and said, 29 Lord, now lettest thou thy servant depart in peace, according to thy word: 30 For mine eyes have seen thy salvation, 31 Which thou hast prepared before the face of all people; 32A light to lighten the Gentiles, and the glory of thy people Israel. 33And Joseph and his mother marvelled at those things which were spoken of him. 34And Simeon blessed them, and said unto Mary his mother, Behold, this *child* is set for the fall and rising again of many in Israel; and for a sign which shall be spoken against; 35 (Yea, a sword shall pierce through thy own soul also;) that the thoughts of many hearts may be revealed. 36And there was one Anna, a prophetess, the daughter of Phanuel, of the tribe of Aser: she was of a great age, and had lived with a husband seven years from her virginity; 37And she *was* a widow of about fourscore and four years, which departed not from the temple, but served *God* with fastings and prayers night and day. 38And she coming in that instant gave thanks likewise unto the Lord, and spake of him to all them that looked for redemption in Jerusalem. 39And when they had performed all things according to the law of the Lord, they returned into Galilee, to their own city Nazareth. 40And the child grew, and waxed strong in spirit, filled with wisdom; and the grace of God was upon him. 41 Now his parents went to Jerusalem every year at the feast of the passover. 42And when he was twelve years old, they went up to Jerusalem after the custom of the feast. 43And when they had fulfilled the days, as they returned, the child Jesus tarried behind in Jerusalem; and Joseph and his mother knew not *of it.* 44 But they, supposing him to have been in the company, went a day's journey; and they sought him among *their* kinsfolk and acquaintance. 45And when they found him not, they turned back again to Jerusalem, seeking him. 46And it came to pass, that after three days they found him in the temple, sitting in the midst of the doctors, both hearing them, and asking them questions. 47And all that heard him were astonished at his understanding and answers. 48And when they saw him, they were amazed: and his

R.S.V.

22 And when the time came for their purification according to the law of Moses, they brought him up to Jerusalem to present him to the Lord 23 (as it is written in the law of the Lord, "Every male that opens the womb shall be called holy to the Lord") 24 and to offer a sacrifice according to what is said in the law of the Lord, "a pair of turtledoves, or two young pigeons." 25 Now there was a man in Jerusalem, whose name was Simeon, and this man was righteous and devout, looking for the consolation of Israel, and the Holy Spirit was upon him. 26And it had been revealed to him by the Holy Spirit that he should not see death before he had seen the Lord's Christ. 27And inspired by the Spirit[h] he came into the temple; and when the parents brought in the child Jesus, to do for him according to the custom of the law, 28 he took him up in his arms and blessed God and said,

29 "Lord, now lettest thou thy servant depart
    in peace,
        according to thy word;
30 for mine eyes have seen thy salvation
31 which thou hast prepared in the presence
        of all peoples,
32 a light for revelation to the Gentiles,
    and for glory to thy people Israel."

33 And his father and his mother marveled at what was said about him; 34 and Simeon blessed them and said to Mary his mother,

"Behold, this child is set for the fall and rising of many in Israel,
    and for a sign that is spoken against
35 (and a sword will pierce through your own
        soul also),
    that thoughts out of many hearts may be
        revealed."

36 And there was a prophetess, Anna, the daughter of Phanuel, of the tribe of Asher; she was of a great age, having lived with her husband seven years from her virginity, 37 and as a widow till she was eighty-four. She did not depart from the temple, worshiping with fasting and prayer night and day. 38And coming up at that very hour she gave thanks to God, and spoke of him to all who were looking for the redemption of Jerusalem.

39 And when they had performed everything according to the law of the Lord, they returned into Galilee, to their own city, Nazareth. 40And the child grew and became strong, filled with wisdom; and the favor of God was upon him.

41 Now his parents went to Jerusalem every year at the feast of the Passover. 42And when he was twelve years old, they went up according to custom; 43 and when the feast was ended, as they were returning, the boy Jesus stayed behind in Jerusalem. His parents did not know it, 44 but supposing him to be in the company they went a day's journey, and they sought him among their kinsfolk and acquaintances; 45 and when they did not find him, they returned to Jerusalem, seeking him. 46After three days they found him in the temple, sitting among the teachers, listening to them and asking them questions; 47 and all who heard him were amazed at his understanding and his answers. 48And when they saw him they were astonished; and his mother said to him,

[h] Or *in the Spirit.*

PHILLIPS

When the "purification" time, stipulated by the Law of Moses, was completed, they brought Jesus to Jerusalem to present him to the Lord. This was to fulfill a requirement of the Law—

Every male that openeth the womb shall be called holy to the Lord.

They also offered the sacrifice prescribed by the Law—

A pair of turtle doves, or two young pigeons.

In Jerusalem was a man by the name of Simeon. He was an upright man, devoted to the service of God, living in expectation of the "salvation of Israel." His heart was open to the Holy Spirit, and it had been revealed to him that he would not die before he saw the Lord's Christ. He had been led by the Spirit to go into the Temple, and when Jesus' parents brought the child in to have done to him what the Law required, he took him up in his arms, blessed God and said—
"At last, Lord, you can dismiss your servant in peace, as you promised! For with my own eyes I have seen your salvation which you have made ready for every people—a light to show truth to the gentiles and bring glory to your people Israel."
The child's father and mother were still amazed at what was said about him, when Simeon gave them his blessing. He said to Mary, the child's mother,
"This child is destined to make many fall and many rise in Israel and to set up a standard which many will attack—for he will expose the secret thoughts of many hearts. And for you . . . your very soul will be pierced by a sword."
There was also present, Anna, the daughter of Phanuel of the tribe of Asher, who was a prophetess. She was a very old woman, having had seven years' married life, and was now a widow of eighty-four. She spent her whole life in the Temple and worshiped God night and day with fastings and prayers. She came up at this very moment, praised God and spoke about Jesus to all those in Jerusalem who were expecting redemption.
When they had completed all the requirements of the Law of the Lord, they returned to Galilee, to their own town of Nazareth. The child grew up and became strong and full of wisdom. And God's blessing was upon him.

Twelve years later: the boy Jesus goes with his parents to Jerusalem   2. 41

Every year at the Passover festival, Jesus' parents used to go to Jerusalem. When he was twelve years old they went up to the city as usual for the festival. When it was over they started back home, but the boy Jesus stayed behind in Jerusalem, without his parents' knowledge. They went a day's journey assuming that he was somewhere in their company, and then they began to look for him among their relations and acquaintances. They failed to find him, however, and turned back to the city, looking for him as they went. Three days later they found him—in the Temple, sitting among the teachers, listening to them and asking them questions. All those who heard him were astonished at his powers of comprehension and at the answers that he gave. When Joseph and Mary saw him, they could hardly believe their eyes, and his mother said to him:

N.E.B.

Then, after their purification had been completed in accordance with the Law of Moses, they brought him up to Jerusalem to present him to the Lord (as prescribed in the law of the Lord: 'Every first-born male shall be deemed to belong to the Lord'), and also to make the offering as stated in the law of the Lord: 'A pair of turtle doves or two young pigeons.'
There was at that time in Jerusalem a man called Simeon. This man was upright and devout, one who watched and waited for the restoration of Israel, and the Holy Spirit was upon him. It had been disclosed to him by the Holy Spirit that he would not see death until he had seen the Lord's Messiah. Guided by the Spirit he came into the temple; and when the parents brought in the child Jesus to do for him what was customary under the Law, he took him in his arms, praised God, and said:

'This day, Master, thou givest thy servant his
    discharge in peace;
  now thy promise is fulfilled.
For I have seen with my own eyes
  the deliverance which thou hast made ready
    in full view of all the nations:
A light that will be a revelation to the
    heathen,
  and glory to thy people Israel.'

The child's father and mother were full of wonder at what was being said about him. Simeon blessed them and said to Mary his mother, 'This child is destined to be a sign which men reject; and you too shall be pierced to the heart. Many in Israel will stand or fall [a] because of him, and thus the secret thoughts of many will be laid bare.'
There was also a prophetess, Anna the daughter of Phanuel, of the tribe of Asher. She was a very old woman, who had lived seven years with her husband after she was first married, and then alone as a widow to the age of eighty-four.[b] She never left the temple, but worshipped day and night, fasting and praying. Coming up at that very moment, she returned thanks to God; and she talked about the child to all who were looking for the liberation of Jerusalem.
When they had done everything prescribed in the law of the Lord, they returned to Galilee to their own town of Nazareth. The child grew big and strong and full of wisdom; and God's favour was upon him.
Now it was the practice of his parents to go to Jerusalem every year for the Passover festival; and when he was twelve, they made the pilgrimage as usual. When the festive season was over and they started for home, the boy Jesus stayed behind in Jerusalem. His parents did not know of this; but thinking that he was with the party they journeyed on for a whole day, and only then did they begin looking for him among their friends and relations. As they could not find him they returned to Jerusalem to look for him; and after three days they found him sitting in the temple surrounded by the teachers, listening to them and putting questions; and all who heard him were amazed at his intelligence and the answers he gave. His parents were astonished to see him there, and his mother said to him,

[a] Or Many in Israel will fall and rise again . . .
[b] Or widow for another eighty-four years.

K.J.V.

mother said unto him, Son, why hast thou thus dealt with us? behold, thy father and I have sought thee sorrowing. 49And he said unto them, How is it that ye sought me? wist ye not that I must be about my Father's business? 50And they understood not the saying which he spake unto them. 51And he went down with them, and came to Nazareth, and was subject unto them: but his mother kept all these sayings in her heart. 52And Jesus increased in wisdom and stature, and in favour with God and man.

3 Now in the fifteenth year of the reign of Tiberius Cesar, Pontius Pilate being governor of Judea, and Herod being tetrarch of Galilee, and his bother Philip tetrarch of Iturea and of the region of Trachonitis, and Lysanias the tetrarch of Abilene, 2Annas and Caiaphas being the high priests, the word of God came unto John the son of Zacharias in the wilderness. 3And he came into all the country about Jordan, preaching the baptism of repentance for the remission of sins; 4As it is written in the book of the words of Esaias the prophet, saying, The voice of one crying in the wilderness, Prepare ye the way of the Lord, make his paths straight. 5 Every valley shall be filled, and every mountain and hill shall be brought low; and the crooked shall be made straight, and the rough ways *shall be* made smooth; 6And all flesh shall see the salvation of God. 7 Then said he to the multitude that came forth to be baptized of him, O generation of vipers, who hath warned you to flee from the wrath to come? 8 Bring forth therefore fruits worthy of repentance, and begin not to say within yourselves, We have Abraham to *our* father: for I say unto you, That God is able of these stones to raise up children unto Abraham. 9And now also the axe is laid unto the root of the trees: every tree therefore which bringeth not forth good fruit is hewn down, and cast into the fire. 10And the people asked him, saying, What shall we do then? 11 He answereth and saith unto them, He that hath two coats, let him impart to him that hath none; and he that hath meat, let him do likewise. 12 Then came also publicans to be baptized, and said unto him, Master, what shall we do? 13And he said unto them, Exact no more than that which is appointed you. 14And the soldiers likewise demanded of him, saying, And what shall we do? And he said unto them, Do violence to no man, neither accuse *any* falsely; and be content with your wages. 15And as the people were in expectation, and all men mused in their hearts of John, whether he were the Christ, or not; 16 John answered, saying unto *them* all, I indeed baptize you with water; but one mightier than I cometh, the latchet of whose shoes I am not worthy to unloose: he shall baptize you with the Holy Ghost and with fire: 17 Whose fan *is* in his hand, and he will thoroughly purge his floor, and will gather the wheat into his garner; but the chaff he will burn with fire unquenchable.

R.S.V.

"Son, why have you treated us so? Behold, your father and I have been looking for you anxiously." 49And he said to them, "How is it that you sought me? Did you not know that I must be in my Father's house?" 50And they did not understand the saying which he spoke to them. 51And he went down with them and came to Nazareth, and was obedient to them; and his mother kept all these things in her heart.

52 And Jesus increased in wisdom and in stature,[i] and in favor with God and man.

3 In the fifteenth year of the reign of Tiberius Caesar, Pontius Pilate being governor of Judea, and Herod being tetrarch of Galilee, and his brother Philip tetrarch of the region of Ituraea and Trachonitis, and Lysanias tetrarch of Abilene, 2 in the high-priesthood of Annas and Caiaphas, the word of God came to John the son of Zechariah in the wilderness; 3 and he went into all the region about the Jordan, preaching a baptism of repentance for the forgiveness of sins. 4As it is written in the book of the words of Isaiah the prophet,

"The voice of one crying in the wilderness:
Prepare the way of the Lord,
    make his paths straight.
5 Every valley shall be filled,
    and every mountain and hill shall be brought
      low,
and the crooked shall be made straight,
    and the rough ways shall be made smooth;
6 and all flesh shall see the salvation of God."

7 He said therefore to the multitudes that came out to be baptized by him, "You brood of vipers! Who warned you to flee from the wrath to come? 8 Bear fruits that befit repentance, and do not begin to say to yourselves, 'We have Abraham as our father'; for I tell you, God is able from these stones to raise up children to Abraham. 9 Even now the axe is laid to the root of the trees; every tree therefore that does not bear good fruit is cut down and thrown into the fire."

10 And the multitudes asked him, "What then shall we do?" 11And he answered them, "He who has two coats, let him share with him who has none; and he who has food, let him do likewise." 12 Tax collectors also came to be baptized, and said to him, "Teacher, what shall we do?" 13And he said to them, "Collect no more than is appointed you." 14 Soldiers also asked him, "And we, what shall we do?" And he said to them, "Rob no one by violence or by false accusation, and be content with your wages."

15 As the people were in expectation, and all men questioned in their hearts concerning John, whether perhaps he were the Christ, 16 John answered them all, "I baptize you with water; but he who is mightier than I is coming, the thong of whose sandals I am not worthy to untie; he will baptize you with the Holy Spirit and with fire. 17 His winnowing fork is in his hand, to clear his threshing floor, and to gather the wheat into his granary, but the chaff he will burn with unquenchable fire."

[i] Or *years*.

PHILLIPS

"Why have you treated us like this, my son? Here have your father and I been very worried, looking for you everywhere!"

And Jesus replied,

"But why were you looking for me? Did you not know that I must be in my Father's house?"

But they did not understand his reply. Then he went home with them to Nazareth and was obedient to them. And his mother treasured all these things in her heart. And as Jesus continued to grow in body and mind, he grew also in the love of God and of those who knew him.

Several years later: John prepares the way of Christ   3. 1

In the fifteenth year of the reign of the Emperor Tiberius (a year when Pontius Pilate was governor of Judaea, Herod tetrarch of Galilee, Philip, his brother, tetrarch of the territory of Ituraea and Trachonitis, and Lysanias tetrarch of Abilene, while Annas and Caiaphas were the High Priests), the word of God came to John, the son of Zacharias, while he was in the desert. He went into the whole country round about the Jordan proclaiming baptism as a mark of a complete change of heart and of the forgiveness of sins, as the book of the prophet Isaiah says—

The voice of one crying in the wilderness,
Make ye ready the way of the Lord,
Make his paths straight.
Every valley shall be filled,
And every mountain and hill shall be brought
    low:
And the crooked shall become straight,
And the rough ways smooth:
And all flesh shall see the salvation of God.

So John used to say to the crowds who came out to be baptized by him:

"Who warned you, you serpent's brood, to escape from the wrath to come? See that you do something to show that your hearts are really changed! Don't start thinking that you can say to yourselves, 'We are Abraham's children,' for I tell you that God could produce children of Abraham out of these stones! The ax already lies at the root of the tree, and the tree that fails to produce good fruit is cut down and thrown into the fire."

Then the crowds would ask him, "Then what shall we do?"

And his answer was, "The man who has two shirts must share with the man who has none, and the man who has food must do the same."

Some of the tax collectors also came to him to be baptized, and they asked him,

"Master, what are we to do?"

"You must not demand more than you are entitled to," he replied.

And the soldiers asked him, "And what are we to do?"

"Don't bully people, don't bring false charges, and be content with your pay," he replied.

The people were in a great state of expectation and were inwardly discussing whether John could possibly be Christ. But John answered them all in these words:

"It is true that I baptize you with water, but the one who follows me is stronger than I am—indeed I am not fit to undo his shoelaces—he will baptize you with the fire of the Holy Spirit. He will come all ready to separate the wheat from the chaff, and to clear the rubbish from his threshing floor. The wheat he will gather into his barn and the chaff he will burn with a fire that cannot be put out."

N.E.B.

'My son, why have you treated us like this? Your father and I have been searching for you in great anxiety.' 'What made you search?' he said. 'Did you not know that I was bound to be in my Father's house?' But they did not understand what he meant. Then he went back with them to Nazareth, and continued to be under their authority; his mother treasured up all these things in her heart. As Jesus grew up he advanced in wisdom and in favour with God and men.

3 In the fifteenth year of the Emperor Tiberius, when Pontius Pilate was governor of Judaea, when Herod was prince of Galilee, his brother Philip prince of Ituraea and Trachonitis, and Lysanias prince of Abilene, during the high-priesthood of Annas and Caiaphas, the word of God came to John son of Zechariah in the wilderness. And he went all over the Jordan valley proclaiming a baptism in token of repentance for the forgiveness of sins, as it is written in the book of the prophecies of Isaiah:

'A voice crying aloud in the wilderness,
"Prepare a way for the Lord;
Clear a straight path for him.
Every ravine shall be filled in,
And every mountain and hill levelled;
The corners shall be straightened,
And the rough ways made smooth;
And all mankind shall see God's deliverance."'

Crowds of people came out to be baptized by him, and he said to them: 'You vipers' brood! Who warned you to escape from the coming retribution? Then prove your repentance by the fruit it bears; and do not begin saying to yourselves, "We have Abraham for our father." I tell you that God can make children for Abraham out of these stones here. Already the axe is laid to the roots of the trees; and every tree that fails to produce good fruit is cut down and thrown on the fire.'

The people asked him, 'Then what are we to do?' He replied, 'The man with two shirts must share with him who has none, and anyone who has food must do the same.' Among those who came to be baptized were tax-gatherers, and they said to him, 'Master, what are we to do?' He told them, 'Exact no more than the assessment.' Soldiers on service also asked him, 'And what of us?' To them he said, 'No bullying; no blackmail; make do with your pay!'

The people were on the tiptoe of expectation, all wondering about John, whether perhaps he was the Messiah, but he spoke out and said to them all, 'I baptize you with water; but there is one to come who is mightier than I. I am not fit to unfasten his shoes. He will baptize you with the Holy Spirit and with fire. His shovel is ready in his hand, to winnow his threshing-floor and gather the wheat into his granary; but he will burn the chaff on a fire that can never go out.'

K.J.V.

18And many other things in his exhortation preached he unto the people. 19 But Herod the tetrarch, being reproved by him for Herodias his brother Philip's wife, and for all the evils which Herod had done, 20Added yet this above all, that he shut up John in prison. 21 Now when all the people were baptized, it came to pass, that Jesus also being baptized, and praying, the heaven was opened, 22And the Holy Ghost descended in a bodily shape like a dove upon him, and a voice came from heaven, which said, Thou art my beloved Son; in thee I am well pleased. 23And Jesus himself began to be about thirty years of age, being (as was supposed) the son of Joseph, which was *the son* of Heli, 24 Which was *the son* of Matthat, which was *the son* of Levi, which was *the son* of Melchi, which was *the son* of Janna, which was *the son* of Joseph, 25 Which was *the son* of Mattathias, which was *the son* of Amos, which was *the son* of Naum, which was *the son* of Esli, which was *the son* of Nagge, 26 Which was *the son* of Maath, which was *the son* of Mattathias, which was *the son* of Semei, which was *the son* of Joseph, which was *the son* of Juda, 27 Which was *the son* of Joanna, which was *the son* of Rhesa, which was *the son* of Zorobabel, which was *the son* of Salathiel, which was *the son* of Neri, 28 Which was *the son* of Melchi, which was *the son* of Addi, which was *the son* of Cosam, which was *the son* of Elmodam, which was *the son* of Er, 29 Which was *the son of* Jose, which was *the son* of Eliezer, which was *the son of* Jorim, which was *the son of* Matthat, which was *the son* of Levi, 30 Which was *the son* of Simeon, which was *the son* of Juda, which was *the son* of Joseph, which was *the son* of Jonan, which was *the son* of Eliakim, 31 Which was *the son* of Melea, which was *the son* of Menan, which was *the son* of Mattatha, which was *the son* of Nathan, which was *the son* of David, 32 Which was *the son* of Jesse, which was *the son* of Obed, which was *the son* of Booz, which was *the son* of Salmon, which was *the son* of Naasson, 33 Which was *the son* of Aminadab, which was *the son* of Aram, which was *the son of* Esrom, which was *the son* of Phares, which was *the son* of Juda, 34 Which was *the son* of Jacob, which was *the son* of Isaac, which was *the son* of Abraham, which was *the son* of Thara, which was *the son* of Nachor, 35 Which was *the son* of Saruch, which was *the son* of Ragau, which was *the son* of Phalec, which was *the son* of Heber, which was *the son* of Sala, 36 Which was *the son* of Cainan, which was *the son* of Arphaxad, which was *the son* of Sem, which was *the son* of Noe, which was *the son* of Lamech, 37 Which was *the son* of Mathusala, which was *the son* of Enoch, which was *the son* of Jared, which was *the son* of Maleleel, which was *the son* of Cainan, 38 Which was *the son* of Enos, which was *the son* of Seth, which was *the son* of Adam, which was *the son* of God.

R.S.V.

18 So, with many other exhortations, he preached good news to the people. 19 But Herod the tetrarch, who had been reproved by him for Herodias, his brother's wife, and for all the evil things that Herod had done, 20 added this to them all, that he shut up John in prison.

21 Now when all the people were baptized, and when Jesus also had been baptized and was praying, the heaven was opened, 22 and the Holy Spirit descended upon him in bodily form, as a dove, and a voice came from heaven, "Thou art my beloved Son;*j* with thee I am well pleased." *k*

23 Jesus, when he began his ministry, was about thirty years of age, being the son (as was supposed) of Joseph, the son of Heli, 24 the son of Matthat, the son of Levi, the son of Melchi, the son of Jannai, the son of Joseph, 25 the son of Mattathias, the son of Amos, the son of Nahum, the son of Esli, the son of Naggai, 26 the son of Maath, the son of Mattathias, the son of Semein, the son of Josech, the son of Joda, 27 the son of Joanan, the son of Rhesa, the son of Zerubbabel, the son of Shealtiel,*l* the son of Neri, 28 the son of Melchi, the son of Addi, the son of Cosam, the son of Elmadam, the son of Er, 29 the son of Joshua, the son of Eliezer, the son of Jorim, the son of Matthat, the son of Levi, 30 the son of Simeon, the son of Judah, the son of Joseph, the son of Jonam, the son of Eliakim, 31 the son of Melea, the son of Menna, the son of Mattatha, the son of Nathan, the son of David, 32 the son of Jesse, the son of Obed, the son of Boaz, the son of Sala, the son of Nahshon, 33 the son of Amminadab, the son of Admin, the son of Arni, the son of Hezron, the son of Perez, the son of Judah, 34 the son of Jacob, the son of Isaac, the son of Abraham, the son of Terah, the son of Nahor, 35 the son of Serug, the son of Reu, the son of Peleg, the son of Eber, the son of Shelah, 36 the son of Cainan, the son of Arphaxad, the son of Shem, the son of Noah, the son of Lamech, 37 the son of Methuselah, the son of Enoch, the son of Jared, the son of Mahalaleel, the son of Cainan, 38 the son of Enos, the son of Seth, the son of Adam, the son of God.

[*j*] Or *my Son, my* (or *the*) *Beloved*. [*k*] Other ancient authorities read *today I have begotten thee.* [*l*] Greek *Salathiel.*

PHILLIPS

These and many other things John said to the people as he exhorted them and announced the good news. But the tetrarch Herod, who had been condemned by John in the affair of Herodias, his brother's wife, as well as for the other evil things that he had done, crowned his misdeeds by putting John in prison.

Jesus is himself baptized   3. 21

When all the people had been baptized, and Jesus was praying after his own baptism, Heaven opened and the Holy Spirit came down upon him in the bodily form of a dove. Then there came a voice from Heaven, saying, "You are my dearly loved Son, in whom I am well pleased."
Jesus himself was about thirty years old at this time when he began his work.

The ancestry of Jesus   3. 23b
traced to Adam

People assumed that Jesus was the son of Joseph, who was the son of Heli, who was the son of Matthat, who was the son of Levi, who was the son of Melchi, who was the son of Jannai, who was the son of Joseph, who was the son of Mattathias, who was the son of Amos, who was the son of Nahum, who was the son of Esli, who was the son of Naggai, who was the son of Maath, who was the son of Mattathias, who was the son of Semein, who was the son of Josech, who was the son of Joda, who was the son of Joanan, who was the son of Rhesa, who was the son of Zerubbabel, who was the son of Shealtiel, who was the son of Neri, who was the son of Melchi, who was the son of Addi, who was the son of Cosam, who was the son of Elmadam, who was the son of Er, who was the son of Jesus, who was the son of Eliezer, who was the son of Jorim, who was the son of Matthat, who was the son of Levi, who was the son of Symeon, who was the son of Judas, who was the son of Joseph, who was the son of Jonam, who was the son of Eliakim, who was the son of Melea, who was the son of Menna, who was the son of Mattatha, who was the son of Nathan, who was the son of David, who was the son of Jesse, who was the son of Obed, who was the son of Boaz, who was the son of Salmon, who was the son of Nahshon, who was the son of Amminadab, who was the son of Arni, who was the son of Hezron, who was the son of Perez, who was the son of Judah, who was the son of Jacob, who was the son of Isaac, who was the son of Abraham, who was the son of Terah, who was the son of Nahor, who was the son of Serug, who was the son of Reu, who was the son of Peleg, who was the son of Eber, who was the son of Shelah, who was the son of Cainan, who was the son of Arphaxad, who was the son of Shem, who was the son of Noah, who was the son of Lamech, who was the son of Methuselah, who was the son of Enoch, who was the son of Jared, who was the son of Mahalaleel, who was the son of Cainan, who was the son of Enos, who was the son of Seth, who was the son of Adam, who was the son of God.

N.E.B.

In this and many other ways he made his appeal to the people and announced the good news. But Prince Herod, when he was rebuked by him over the affair of his brother's wife Herodias and for his other misdeeds, crowned them all by shutting John up in prison.

During a general baptism of the people, when Jesus too had been baptized and was praying, heaven opened and the Holy Spirit descended on him in bodily form like a dove; and there came a voice from heaven, 'Thou art my Son, my Beloved;[a] on thee my favour rests.'[b]
When Jesus began his work he was about thirty years old, the son, as people thought, of Joseph, son of Heli, son of Matthat, son of Levi, son of Melchi, son of Jannai, son of Joseph, son of Mattathiah, son of Amos, son of Nahum, son of Esli, son of Naggai, son of Maath, son of Mattathiah, son of Semein, son of Josech, son of Joda, son of Johanan, son of Rhesa, son of Zerubbabel, son of Shealtiel, son of Neri, son of Melchi, son of Addi, son of Cosam, son of Elmadam, son of Er, son of Joshua, son of Eliezer, son of Jorim, son of Matthat, son of Levi, son of Symeon, son of Judah, son of Joseph, son of Jonam, son of Eliakim, son of Melea, son of Menna, son of Mattatha, son of Nathan, son of David, son of Jesse, son of Obed, son of Boaz, son of Salmon, son of Nahshon, son of Amminadab,[c] son of Arni,[d] son of Hezron, son of Perez, son of Judah, son of Jacob, son of Isaac, son of Abraham, son of Terah, son of Nahor, son of Serug, son of Reu, son of Peleg, son of Eber, son of Shelah, son of Cainan, son of Arpachshad, son of Shem, son of Noah, son of Lamech, son of Methuselah, son of Enoch, son of Jared, son of Mahalaleel, son of Cainan, son of Enosh, son of Seth, son of Adam, son of God.

---

[a] *Or* Thou art my only Son. [b] *Some witnesses read* My Son art thou; this day I have begotten thee. [c] *Some witnesses add* son of Admin. [d] *Some witnesses read* Aram; *Ruth 4. 19 & 1 Chronicles 2. 9 have* Ram.

K.J.V.

4 And Jesus being full of the Holy Ghost returned from Jordan, and was led by the Spirit into the wilderness, 2 Being forty days tempted of the devil. And in those days he did eat nothing: and when they were ended, he afterward hungered. 3And the devil said unto him, If thou be the Son of God, command this stone that it be made bread. 4And Jesus answered him, saying, It is written, That man shall not live by bread alone, but by every word of God. 5And the devil, taking him up into a high mountain, shewed unto him all the kingdoms of the world in a moment of time. 6And the devil said unto him, All this power will I give thee, and the glory of them: for that is delivered unto me; and to whomsoever I will, I give it. 7 If thou therefore wilt worship me, all shall be thine. 8And Jesus answered and said unto him, Get thee behind me, Satan: for it is written, Thou shalt worship the Lord thy God, and him only shalt thou serve. 9And he brought him to Jerusalem, and set him on a pinnacle of the temple, and said unto him, If thou be the Son of God, cast thyself down from hence: 10 For it is written, He shall give his angels charge over thee, to keep thee: 11And in *their* hands they shall bear thee up, lest at any time thou dash thy foot against a stone. 12And Jesus answering said unto him, It is said, Thou shalt not tempt the Lord thy God. 13And when the devil had ended all the temptation, he departed from him for a season.

14 And Jesus returned in the power of the Spirit into Galilee: and there went out a fame of him through all the region round about. 15And he taught in their synagogues, being glorified of all.

16 And he came to Nazareth, where he had been brought up: and, as his custom was, he went into the synagogue on the sabbath day, and stood up for to read. 17And there was delivered unto him the book of the prophet Esaias. And when he had opened the book, he found the place where it was written, 18 The Spirit of the Lord *is* upon me, because he hath anointed me to preach the gospel to the poor; he hath sent me to heal the brokenhearted, to preach deliverance to the captives, and recovering of sight to the blind, to set at liberty them that are bruised, 19 To preach the acceptable year of the Lord. 20And he closed the book, and he gave *it* again to the minister, and sat down. And the eyes of all them that were in the synagogue were fastened on him. 21And he began to say unto them, This day is this Scripture fulfilled in your ears. 22And all bare him witness, and wondered at the gracious words which proceeded out of his mouth. And they said, Is not this Joseph's son? 23And he said unto them, Ye will surely say unto me this proverb, Physician, heal thy-

R.S.V.

4 And Jesus, full of the Holy Spirit, returned from the Jordan, and was led by the Spirit 2 for forty days in the wilderness, tempted by the devil. And he ate nothing in those days; and when they were ended, he was hungry. 3 The devil said to him, "If you are the Son of God, command this stone to become bread." 4And Jesus answered him, "It is written, 'Man shall not live by bread alone.' " 5And the devil took him up, and showed him all the kingdoms of the world in a moment of time, 6 and said to him, "To you I will give all this authority and their glory; for it has been delivered to me, and I give it to whom I will. 7 If you, then, will worship me, it shall all be yours." 8And Jesus answered him, "It is written,

'You shall worship the Lord your God,
  and him only shall you serve.' "

9And he took him to Jerusalem, and set him on the pinnacle of the temple, and said to him, "If you are the Son of God, throw yourself down from here; 10 for it is written,

'He will give his angels charge of you, to
  guard you,'

11 and

'On their hands they will bear you up,
  lest you strike your foot against a stone.' "

12And Jesus answered him, "It is said, 'You shall not tempt the Lord your God.' " 13And when the devil had ended every temptation, he departed from him until an opportune time.

14 And Jesus returned in the power of the Spirit into Galilee, and a report concerning him went out through all the surrounding country. 15And he taught in their synagogues, being glorified by all.

16 And he came to Nazareth, where he had been brought up; and he went to the synagogue, as his custom was, on the sabbath day. And he stood up to read; 17 and there was given to him the book of the prophet Isaiah. He opened the book and found the place where it was written,

18 "The Spirit of the Lord is upon me,
  because he has anointed me to preach good
    news to the poor.
  He has sent me to proclaim release to the
    captives
  and recovering of sight to the blind,
    to set at liberty those who are oppressed,
19 to proclaim the acceptable year of the
    Lord."

20 And he closed the book, and gave it back to the attendant, and sat down; and the eyes of all in the synagogue were fixed on him. 21And he began to say to them, "Today this scripture has been fulfilled in your hearing." 22And all spoke well of him, and wondered at the gracious words which proceeded out of his mouth; and they said, "Is not this Joseph's son?" 23And he said to them, "Doubtless you will quote to me this proverb, 'Physician, heal yourself; what we have

PHILLIPS

N.E.B.

Jesus faces temptation   *4. 1*

Jesus returned from the Jordan full of the Holy Spirit and he was led by the Spirit to spend forty days in the desert, where he was tempted by the devil. He ate nothing during that time and afterward he felt very hungry.

"If you really are the Son of God," the devil said to him, "tell this stone to turn into a loaf."

Jesus answered,

"The scripture says, *'Man shall not live by bread alone.'* "

Then the devil took him up and showed him all the kingdoms of mankind in a sudden vision, and said to him:

"I will give you all this power and magnificence, for it belongs to me and I can give it to anyone I please. It shall all be yours if you will fall down and worship me."

To this Jesus replied,

"It is written, *'Thou shalt worship the Lord thy God and him only shalt thou serve.'* "

Then the devil took him to Jerusalem and set him on the highest ledge of the Temple.

"If you really are the Son of God," he said, "throw yourself down from here, for the scripture says, *'He shall give his angels charge concerning thee, to guard thee,'* and *'On their hands they shall bear thee up, lest haply thou dash thy foot against a stone.'* "

To which Jesus replied,

"It is also said, *'Thou shalt not tempt the Lord thy God.'* "

And when the devil had exhausted every kind of temptation, he withdrew until his next opportunity.

Jesus begins his ministry   *4. 14*
in Galilee

And now Jesus returned to Galilee in the power of the Spirit, and news of him spread through all the surrounding district. He taught in their synagogues, to everyone's great admiration.

Then he came to Nazareth where he had been brought up and, according to his custom, went to the synagogue on the Sabbath day. He stood up to read the scriptures, and the book of the prophet Isaiah was handed to him. He opened the book and found the place where these words are written—

The Spirit of the Lord is upon me,
Because he anointed me to preach good tidings to the poor:
He hath sent me to proclaim release to the captives,
And recovering of sight to the blind,
To set at liberty them that are bruised,
To proclaim the acceptable year of the Lord.

Then he shut the book, handed it back to the attendant and resumed his seat. Every eye in the synagogue was fixed upon him and he began to tell them, "This very day this scripture has been fulfilled, while you have been listening to it!"

Everybody noticed what he said and was amazed at the beautiful words that came from his lips, and they kept saying,

"Isn't this Joseph's son?"

So he said to them,

"I expect you will quote this proverb to me, 'Cure yourself, doctor! Let us see you do in

4 Full of the Holy Spirit, Jesus returned from the Jordan, and for forty days was led by the Spirit up and down the wilderness and tempted by the devil.

All that time he had nothing to eat, and at the end of it he was famished. The devil said to him, 'If you are the Son of God, tell this stone to become bread.' Jesus answered, 'Scripture says, "Man cannot live on bread alone." '

Next the devil led him up and showed him in a flash all the kingdoms of the world. 'All this dominion will I give to you,' he said, 'and the glory that goes with it; for it has been put in my hands and I can give it to anyone I choose. You have only to do homage to me and it shall all be yours.' Jesus answered him, 'Scripture says, "You shall do homage to the Lord your God and worship him alone." '

The devil took him to Jerusalem and set him on the parapet of the temple. 'If you are the Son of God,' he said, 'throw yourself down; for Scripture says, "He will give his angels orders to take care of you", and again, "They will support you in their arms for fear you should strike your foot against a stone." ' Jesus answered him, 'It has been said, "You are not to test the Lord your God." '

So, having come to the end of all his temptations, the devil departed, biding his time.

In Galilee: Success and Opposition

Then Jesus, armed with the power of the Spirit, returned to Galilee; and reports about him spread through the whole country-side. He taught in their synagogues and all men sang his praises.

So he came to Nazareth, where he had been brought up, and went to synagogue on the Sabbath day as he regularly did. He stood up to read the lesson and was handed the scroll of the prophet Isaiah. He opened the scroll and found the passage which says,

'The spirit of the Lord is upon me because he has annointed me;
He has sent me to announce good news to the poor,
To proclaim release for prisoners and recovery of sight for the blind;
To let the broken victims go free,
To proclaim the year of the Lord's favour.'

He rolled up the scroll, gave it back to the attendant, and sat down; and all eyes in the synagogue were fixed on him.

He began to speak: 'Today', he said, 'in your very hearing this text has come true.' [a] There was a general stir of admiration; they were surprised that words of such grace should fall from his lips. 'Is not this Joseph's son?' they asked. Then Jesus said, 'No doubt you will quote the proverb to me, "Physician, heal yourself!", and

[a] *Or* 'Today', he said, 'this text which you have just heard has come true.'

K.J.V.

self: whatsoever we have heard done in Capernaum, do also here in thy country. 24And he said, Verily I say unto you, No prophet is accepted in his own country. 25 But I tell you of a truth, many widows were in Israel in the days of Elias, when the heaven was shut up three years and six months, when great famine was throughout all the land; 26 But unto none of them was Elias sent, save unto Sarepta, *a city* of Sidon, unto a woman *that was* a widow. 27And many lepers were in Israel in the time of Eliseus the prophet; and none of them was cleansed, saving Naaman the Syrian. 28And all they in the synagogue, when they heard these things, were filled with wrath, 29And rose up, and thrust him out of the city, and led him unto the brow of the hill whereon their city was built, that they might cast him down headlong. 30 But he, passing through the midst of them, went his way, 31And came down to Capernaum, a city of Galilee, and taught them on the sabbath days. 32And they were astonished at his doctrine: for his word was with power.

33 And in the synagogue there was a man, which had a spirit of an unclean devil, and cried out with a loud voice, 34 Saying, Let *us* alone; what have we to do with thee, *thou* Jesus of Nazareth? art thou come to destroy us? I know thee who thou art; the Holy One of God. 35And Jesus rebuked him, saying, Hold thy peace, and come out of him. And when the devil had thrown him in the midst, he came out of him, and hurt him not. 36And they were all amazed, and spake among themselves, saying, What a word *is* this! for with authority and power he commandeth the unclean spirits, and they come out. 37And the fame of him went out into every place of the country round about.

38 And he arose out of the synagogue, and entered into Simon's house. And Simon's wife's mother was taken with a great fever; and they besought him for her. 39And he stood over her, and rebuked the fever; and it left her: and immediately she arose and ministered unto them.

40 Now when the sun was setting, all they that had any sick with divers diseases brought them unto him; and he laid his hands on every one of them, and healed them. 41And devils also came out of many, crying out, and saying, Thou art Christ the Son of God. And he rebuking *them* suffered them not to speak: for they knew that he was Christ. 42And when it was day, he departed and went into a desert place: and the people sought him, and came unto him, and stayed him, that he should not depart from them. 43And he said unto them, I must preach the kingdom of God to other cities also: for therefore am I sent. 44And he preached in the synagogues of Galilee.

R.S.V.

heard you did at Capernaum, do here also in your own country.' " 24And he said, "Truly, I say to you, no prophet is acceptable in his own country. 25 But in truth, I tell you, there were many widows in Israel in the days of Elijah, when the heaven was shut up three years and six months, when there came a great famine over all the land; 26 and Elijah was sent to none of them but only to Zarephath, in the land of Sidon, to a woman who was a widow. 27And there were many lepers in Israel in the time of the prophet Elisha; and none of them was cleansed, but only Naaman the Syrian." 28 When they heard this, all in the synagogue were filled with wrath. 29And they rose up and put him out of the city, and led him to the brow of the hill on which their city was built, that they might throw him down headlong. 30 But passing through the midst of them he went away.

31 And he went down to Capernaum, a city of Galilee. And he was teaching them on the sabbath; 32 and they were astonished at his teaching, for his word was with authority. 33And in the synagogue there was a man who had the spirit of an unclean demon; and he cried out with a loud voice, 34 "Ah! *m* What have you to do with us, Jesus of Nazareth? Have you come to destroy us? I know who you are, the Holy One of God." 35 But Jesus rebuked him, saying, "Be silent, and come out of him!" And when the demon had thrown him down in the midst, he came out of him, having done him no harm. 36And they were all amazed and said to one another, "What is this word? For with authority and power he commands the unclean spirits, and they come out." 37And reports of him went out into every place in the surrounding region.

38 And he arose and left the synagogue, and entered Simon's house. Now Simon's mother-in-law was ill with a high fever, and they besought him for her. 39And he stood over her and rebuked the fever, and it left her; and immediately she rose and served them.

40 Now when the sun was setting, all those who had any that were sick with various diseases brought them to him; and he laid his hands on every one of them and healed them. 41And demons also came out of many, crying, "You are the Son of God!" But he rebuked them, and would not allow them to speak, because they knew that he was the Christ.

42 And when it was day he departed and went into a lonely place. And the people sought him and came to him, and would have kept him from leaving them; 43 but he said to them, "I must preach the good news of the kingdom of God to the other cities also; for I was sent for this purpose." 44And he was preaching in the synagogues of Judea.*n*

[*m*] Or *Let us alone.* [*n*] Other ancient authorities read *Galilee.*

PHILLIPS

your own country all that we have heard that you did in Capernaum!'" Then he added: "I assure you that no prophet is ever welcomed in his own country. I tell you the plain fact that in Elijah's time, when the heavens were shut up for three and a half years and there was a great famine through the whole country, there were plenty of widows in Israel, but Elijah was not sent to any of them. But he *was* sent to Sarepta, to a widow in the country of Sidon. In the time of Elisha the prophet, there were a great many lepers in Israel, but not one of them was healed —only Naaman, the Syrian."

But when they heard this, everyone in the synagogue was furiously angry. They sprang to their feet and drove him right out of the town, taking him to the brow of the hill on which it was built, intending to hurl him down bodily. But he walked straight through the whole crowd and went on his way.

Jesus heals in Capernaum　　　　4. 31

So he came down to Capernaum, a town in Galilee, and taught them on the Sabbath day. They were astonished at his teaching, for his words had the ring of authority.

There was a man in the synagogue under the influence of some evil spirit and he yelled at the top of his voice, "Hi! What have you got to do with us, Jesus, you Nazarene—have you come to kill us? I know who you are all right, you're God's holy one!"

Jesus cut him short and spoke sharply:

"Be quiet! Get out of him!"

And after throwing the man down in front of them, the devil did come out of him without hurting him in the slightest. At this everybody present was amazed and they kept saying to each other:

"What sort of words are these? He speaks to these evil spirits with authority and power and out they come."

And his reputation spread over the whole surrounding district.

When Jesus got up and left the synagogue he went into Simon's house. Simon's mother-in-law was suffering from a high fever, and they asked Jesus about her. He stood over her as she lay in bed, brought the fever under control and it left her. At once she got up and began to see to their needs.

Then, as the sun was setting, all those who had friends suffering from every kind of disease brought them to Jesus and he laid his hands on each one of them separately and healed them. Evil spirits came out of many of these people, shouting, "You are the Son of God!"

But he spoke sharply to them and would not allow them to say any more, for they knew perfectly well that he was Christ.

Jesus attempts to be alone—　　4. 42
in vain

At daybreak he went off to a deserted place, but the crowds tried to find him and, when they did discover him, tried to prevent him from leaving them. But he told them, "I must tell the good news of the kingdom of God to other towns as well—that is my mission."

And he continued proclaiming his message in the synagogues of Judaea.

N.E.B.

say, "We have heard of all your doings at Capernaum; do the same here in your own home town." I tell you this,' he went on: 'no prophet is recognized in his own country. There were many widows in Israel, you may be sure, in Elijah's time, when for three years and six months the skies never opened, and famine lay hard over the whole country; yet it was to none of those that Elijah was sent, but to a widow at Sarepta in the territory of Sidon. Again, in the time of the prophet Elisha there were many lepers in Israel, and not one of them was healed, but only Naaman, the Syrian.' At these words the whole congregation were infuriated. They leapt up, threw him out of the town, and took him to the brow of the hill on which it was built, meaning to hurl him over the edge. But he walked straight through them all, and went away.

Coming down to Capernaum, a town in Galilee, he taught the people on the Sabbath, and they were astounded at his teaching, for what he said had the note of authority. Now there was a man in the synagogue possessed by a devil, an unclean spirit. He shrieked at the top of his voice, 'What do you want with us, Jesus of Nazareth? Have you[a] come to destroy us? I know who you are—the Holy One of God.' Jesus rebuked him: 'Be silent', he said, 'and come out of him.' Then the devil, after throwing the man down in front of the people, left him without doing him any injury. Amazement fell on them all and they said to one another: 'What is there in this man's words? He gives orders to the unclean spirits with authority and power, and out they go.' So the news spread, and he was the talk of the whole district.

On leaving the synagogue he went to Simon's house. Simon's mother-in-law was in the grip of a high fever; and they asked him to help her. He came and stood over her and rebuked the fever. It left her, and she got up at once and waited on them.

At sunset all who had friends suffering from one disease or another brought them to him; and he laid his hands on them one by one and cured them. Devils also came out of many of them, shouting, 'You are the Son of God.' But he rebuked them and forbade them to speak, because they knew that he was the Messiah.

When day broke he went out and made his way to a lonely spot. But the people went in search of him, and when they came to where he was they pressed him not to leave them. But he said, 'I must give the good news of the kingdom of God to the other towns also, for that is what I was sent to do.' So he proclaimed the Gospel in the synagogues of Judaea.[b]

[a] *Or* You have. [b] *Or* the Jewish synagogues; *some witnesses read* the synagogues of Galilee.

5 And it came to pass, that, as the people pressed upon him to hear the word of God, he stood by the lake of Gennesaret, 2And saw two ships standing by the lake: but the fishermen were gone out of them, and were washing *their* nets. 3And he entered into one of the ships, which was Simon's, and prayed him that he would thrust out a little from the land. And he sat down, and taught the people out of the ship. 4 Now when he had left speaking, he said unto Simon, Launch out into the deep, and let down your nets for a draught. 5And Simon answering said unto him, Master, we have toiled all the night, and have taken nothing: nevertheless at thy word I will let down the net. 6And when they had this done, they inclosed a great multitude of fishes: and their net brake. 7And they beckoned unto *their* partners, which were in the other ship, that they should come and help them. And they came, and filled both the ships, so that they began to sink. 8 When Simon Peter saw *it,* he fell down at Jesus' knees, saying, Depart from me; for I am a sinful man, O Lord. 9 For he was astonished, and all that were with him, at the draught of the fishes which they had taken: 10And so *was* also James, and John, the sons of Zebedee, which were partners with Simon. And Jesus said unto Simon, Fear not; from henceforth thou shalt catch men. 11And when they had brought their ships to land, they forsook all, and followed him.

12 And it came to pass, when he was in a certain city, behold a man full of leprosy: who seeing Jesus fell on *his* face, and besought him, saying, Lord, if thou wilt, thou canst make me clean. 13And he put forth *his* hand, and touched him, saying, I will: be thou clean. And immediately the leprosy departed from him. 14And he charged him to tell no man: but go, and shew thyself to the priest, and offer for thy cleansing, according as Moses commanded, for a testimony unto them. 15 But so much the more went there a fame abroad of him: and great multitudes came together to hear, and to be healed by him of their infirmities.

16 And he withdrew himself into the wilderness, and prayed. 17And it came to pass on a certain day, as he was teaching, that there were Pharisees and doctors of the law sitting by, which were come out of every town of Galilee, and Judea, and Jerusalem: and the power of the Lord was *present* to heal them.

18 And, behold, men brought in a bed a man which was taken with a palsy: and they sought *means* to bring him in, and to lay *him* before him. 19And when they could not find by what *way* they might bring him in because of the multitude, they went upon the housetop, and let him down through the tiling with *his* couch into

5 While the people pressed upon him to hear the word of God, he was standing by the lake of Gennesaret. 2And he saw two boats by the lake; but the fishermen had gone out of them and were washing their nets. 3 Getting into one of the boats, which was Simon's, he asked him to put out a little from the land. And he sat down and taught the people from the boat. 4And when he had ceased speaking, he said to Simon, "Put out into the deep and let down your nets for a catch." 5And Simon answered, "Master, we toiled all night and took nothing! But at your word I will let down the nets." 6And when they had done this, they enclosed a great shoal of fish; and as their nets were breaking, 7 they beckoned to their partners in the other boat to come and help them. And they came and filled both the boats, so that they began to sink. 8 But when Simon Peter saw it, he fell down at Jesus' knees, saying, "Depart from me, for I am a sinful man, O Lord." 9 For he was astonished, and all that were with him, at the catch of fish which they had taken; 10 and so also were James and John, sons of Zebedee, who were partners with Simon. And Jesus said to Simon, "Do not be afraid; henceforth you will be catching men." 11And when they had brought their boats to land, they left everything and followed him.

12 While he was in one of the cities, there came a man full of leprosy; and when he saw Jesus, he fell on his face and besought him, "Lord, if you will, you can make me clean." 13And he stretched out his hand, and touched him, saying, "I will; be clean." And immediately the leprosy left him. 14And he charged him to tell no one; but "go and show yourself to the priest, and make an offering for your cleansing, as Moses commanded, for a proof to the people." *o* 15 But so much the more the report went abroad concerning him; and great multitudes gathered to hear and to be healed of their infirmities. 16 But he withdrew to the wilderness and prayed.

17 On one of those days, as he was teaching, there were Pharisees and teachers of the law sitting by, who had come from every village of Galilee and Judea and from Jerusalem; and the power of the Lord was with him to heal.*p* 18And behold, men were bringing on a bed a man who was paralyzed, and they sought to bring him in and lay him before Jesus;*q* 19 but finding no way to bring him in, because of the crowd, they went up on the roof and let him down with his bed

[*o*] Greek *to them.* [*p*] Other ancient authorities read *was present to heal them.* [*q*] Greek *him.*

PHILLIPS

N.E.B.

Simon, James and John become Jesus' followers

5. 1

One day the people were crowding closely round Jesus to hear God's message, as he stood on the shore of Lake Gennesaret. Jesus noticed two boats drawn up on the beach, for the fishermen had left them there while they were cleaning their nets. He went aboard one of the boats, which belonged to Simon, and asked him to push out a little from the shore. Then he sat down and continued his teaching of the crowds from the boat.

When he had finished speaking, he said to Simon, "Push out now into deep water and let down your nets for a catch."

Simon replied, "Master! We've worked all night and never caught a thing, but if you say so I'll let the nets down."

And when they had done this, they caught an enormous shoal of fish—so big that the nets began to tear. So they signaled to their friends in the other boat to come and help them. They came and filled both the boats to sinking point. When Simon Peter saw this, he fell on his knees before Jesus and said,

"Keep away from me, Lord, for I'm only a sinful man!"

For he and his companions (including Zebedee's sons, James and John, Simon's partners) were staggered at the haul of fish that they had made.

Jesus said to Simon: "Don't be afraid, Simon. From now on your catch will be *men*."

So they brought the boats ashore, left everything and followed him.

Jesus cures leprosy

5. 12

While he was in one of the towns, Jesus came upon a man who was a mass of leprosy. When the man saw Jesus he prostrated himself before him and begged,

"If you want to, Lord, you can make me clean."

Jesus stretched out his hand, placed it on the leper, saying:

"Certainly I want to. Be clean!"

Immediately the leprosy left him and Jesus warned him not to tell anybody, but to go and show himself to the priest and to make the offerings for his recovery that Moses prescribed, as evidence to the authorities.

Yet the news about him spread all the more, and enormous crowds collected to hear Jesus and to be healed of their diseases. But he slipped quietly away to deserted places for prayer.

Jesus cures a paralytic in soul and body

5. 17

One day while Jesus was teaching, some Pharisees and experts in the Law were sitting near him. They had come out of every village in Galilee and Judaea as well as from Jerusalem. God's power to heal people was with him. Soon some men arrived carrying a paralytic on a small bed and they kept trying to carry him in to put him down in front of Jesus. When they failed to find a way of getting him in because of the dense crowd, they went up onto the top of the house and let him down, bed and all, through the

5 One day as he stood by the Lake of Gennesaret, and the people crowded upon him to listen to the word of God, he noticed two boats lying at the water's edge; the fishermen had come ashore and were washing their nets. He got into one of the boats, which belonged to Simon, and asked him to put out a little way from the shore; then he went on teaching the crowds from his seat in the boat. When he had finished speaking, he said to Simon, 'Put out into deep water and let down your nets for a catch.' Simon answered, 'Master, we were hard at work all night and caught nothing at all; but if you say so, I will let down the nets.' They did so and made a big haul of fish; and their nets began to split. So they signalled to their partners in the other boat to come and help them. This they did, and loaded both boats to the point of sinking. When Simon saw what had happened he fell at Jesus's knees and said, 'Go, Lord, leave me, sinner that I am!' For he and all his companions were amazed at the catch they had made; so too were his partners James and John, Zebedee's sons. 'Do not be afraid,' said Jesus to Simon; 'from now on you will be catching men.' As soon as they had brought the boats to land, they left everything and followed him.

He was once in a certain town where there happened to be a man covered with leprosy; seeing Jesus, he bowed to the ground and begged his help. 'Sir,' he said, 'if only you will, you can cleanse me.' Jesus stretched out his hand, touched him, and said, 'Indeed I will; be clean again.' The leprosy left him immediately. Jesus then ordered him not to tell anybody. 'But go,' he said, 'show yourself to the priest, and make the offering laid down by Moses for your cleansing; that will certify the cure.' But the talk about him spread all the more; great crowds gathered to hear him and to be cured of their ailments. And from time to time he would withdraw to lonely places for prayer.

One day he was teaching, and Pharisees and teachers of the law were sitting round. People had come from every village of Galilee and from Judaea and Jerusalem,[a] and the power of God was with him to heal the sick. Some men appeared carrying a paralysed man on a bed. They tried to bring him in and set him down in front of Jesus, but finding no way to do so because of the crowd, they went up on to the roof and let him down through the tiling, bed and all, into

---

[a] *Some witnesses read* and Pharisees and teachers of the law, who had come from every village of Galilee and from Judaea and Jerusalem, were sitting round.

K.J.V.

the midst before Jesus. 20And when he saw their faith, he said unto him, Man, thy sins are forgiven thee. 21And the scribes and the Pharisees began to reason, saying, Who is this which speaketh blasphemies? Who can forgive sins, but God alone? 22 But when Jesus perceived their thoughts, he answering said unto them, What reason ye in your hearts? 23 Whether is easier, to say, Thy sins be forgiven thee; or to say, Rise up and walk? 24 But that ye may know that the Son of man hath power upon earth to forgive sins, (he said unto the sick of the palsy,) I say unto thee, Arise, and take up thy couch, and go into thine house. 25And immediately he rose up before them, and took up that whereon he lay, and departed to his own house, glorifying God. 26 And they were all amazed, and they glorified God, and were filled with fear, saying, We have seen strange things to day.

27 And after these things he went forth, and saw a publican, named Levi, sitting at the receipt of custom: and he said unto him, Follow me. 28And he left all, rose up, and followed him. 29And Levi made him a great feast in his own house: and there was a great company of publicans and of others that sat down with them. 30 But their scribes and Pharisees murmured against his disciples, saying, Why do ye eat and drink with publicans and sinners? 31And Jesus answering said unto them, They that are whole need not a physician; but they that are sick. 32 I came not to call the righteous, but sinners to repentance.

33 And they said unto him, Why do the disciples of John fast often, and make prayers, and likewise *the disciples* of the Pharisees; but thine eat and drink? 34And he said unto them, Can ye make the children of the bridechamber fast, while the bridegroom is with them? 35 But the days will come, when the bridegroom shall be taken away from them, and then shall they fast in those days.

36 And he spake also a parable unto them; No man putteth a piece of a new garment upon an old; if otherwise, then both the new maketh a rent, and the piece that was *taken* out of the new agreeth not with the old. 37And no man putteth new wine into old bottles; else the new wine will burst the bottles, and be spilled, and the bottles shall perish. 38 But new wine must be put into new bottles; and both are preserved. 39 No man also having drunk old *wine* straightway desireth new; for he saith, The old is better.

R.S.V.

through the tiles into the midst before Jesus. 20And when they saw their faith he said, "Man, your sins are forgiven you." 21And the scribes and the Pharisees began to question, saying, "Who is this that speaks blasphemies? Who can forgive sins but God only?" 22 When Jesus perceived their questionings, he answered them, "Why do you question in your hearts? 23 Which is easier, to say, 'Your sins are forgiven you,' or to say, 'Rise and walk'? 24 But that you may know that the Son of man has authority on earth to forgive sins"—he said to the man who was paralyzed—"I say to you, rise, take up your bed and go home." 25And immediately he rose before them, and took up that on which he lay, and went home, glorifying God. 26And amazement seized them all, and they glorified God and were filled with awe, saying, "We have seen strange things today."

27 After this he went out, and saw a tax collector, named Levi, sitting at the tax office; and he said to him, "Follow me." 28And he left everything, and rose and followed him.

29 And Levi made him a great feast in his house; and there was a large company of tax collectors and others sitting at table[r] with them. 30And the Pharisees and their scribes murmured against his disciples, saying, "Why do you eat and drink with tax collectors and sinners?" 31And Jesus answered them, "Those who are well have no need of a physician, but those who are sick; 32 I have not come to call the righteous, but sinners to repentance."

33 And they said to him, "The disciples of John fast often and offer prayers, and so do the disciples of the Pharisees, but yours eat and drink." 34And Jesus said to them, "Can you make wedding guests fast while the bridegroom is with them? 35 The days will come, when the bridegroom is taken away from them, and then they will fast in those days." 36 He told them a parable also: "No one tears a piece from a new garment and puts it upon an old garment; if he does, he will tear the new, and the piece from the new will not match the old. 37And no one puts new wine into old wineskins; if he does, the new wine will burst the skins and it will be spilled, and the skins will be destroyed. 38 But new wine must be put into fresh wineskins. 39And no one after drinking old wine desires new; for he says, 'The old is good.' "[s]

[r] Greek *reclining.* [s] Other ancient authorities read *better.*

tiles, into the middle of the crowd in front of Jesus. When Jesus saw their faith, he said to the man,

"My friend, your sins are forgiven."

The scribes and the Pharisees began to argue about this, saying: "Who is this man who talks blasphemy? Who can forgive sins? Only God can do that."

Jesus realized what was going on in their minds and spoke straight to them.

"Why must you argue like this in your minds? Which do you suppose is easier—to say, 'Your sins are forgiven' or to say, 'Get up and walk'? But to make you realize that the Son of Man has full authority on earth to forgive sins—I tell *you*," he said to the man who was paralyzed, "get up, pick up your bed and go home!"

Instantly the man sprang to his feet before their eyes, picked up the bedding on which he used to lie, and went off home, praising God. Sheer amazement gripped every man present, and they praised God and said in awed voices, "We have seen incredible things today."

Jesus calls Levi to be his disciple   5. 27

Later on, Jesus went out and looked straight at a tax collector called Levi, as he sat at his office desk.

"Follow me," he said to him.

And he got to his feet at once, left everything behind and followed him.

Then Levi gave a big reception for Jesus in his own house, and there was a great crowd of tax collectors and others at table with them. The Pharisees and their companions the scribes kept muttering indignantly about this to Jesus' disciples, saying,

"Why do you have your meals with tax collectors and sinners?"

Jesus answered them,

"It is not the healthy who need the doctor, but those who are ill. I have not come to invite the 'righteous' but the 'sinners'—to change their ways."

Jesus hints at who he is   5. 33

Then people said to him,

"Why is it that John's disciples are always fasting and praying, just like the Pharisees' disciples, but yours both eat and drink?"

Jesus answered,

"Can you expect wedding guests to fast while they have the bridegroom with them? The day will come when they will lose the bridegroom; that will be the time for them to fast!"

Then he gave them this illustration.

"Nobody tears a piece from a new coat to patch up an old one. If he does, he ruins the new one and the new piece does not match the old.

"Nobody puts new wine into old wineskins. If he does, the new wine will burst the skins—the wine will be spilled and the skins ruined. No, new wine must be put into new wineskins. Of course, nobody who has been drinking old wine will want the new at once. He is sure to say, 'The old is a good sound wine.'"

the middle of the company in front of Jesus. When Jesus saw their faith, he said, 'Man, your sins are forgiven you.'

The lawyers and the Pharisees began saying to themselves, 'Who is this fellow with his blasphemous talk? Who but God alone can forgive sins?' But Jesus knew their thoughts and answered them: 'Why do you harbour thoughts like these? Is it easier to say, "Your sins are forgiven you", or to say, "Stand up and walk"? But to convince you that the Son of Man has the right on earth to forgive sins'—he turned to the paralysed man—'I say to you, stand up, take your bed, and go home.' And at once he rose to his feet before their eyes, took up the bed he had been lying on, and went home praising God. They were all lost in amazement and praised God; filled with awe they said, 'You would never believe the things we have seen today.'

Later, when he went out, he saw a tax-gatherer, Levi by name, at his seat in the custom-house. He said to him, 'Follow me'; and he rose to his feet, left everything behind, and followed him.

Afterwards Levi held a big reception in his house for Jesus; among the guests was a large party of tax-gatherers and others. The Pharisees and the lawyers of their sect complained to his disciples: 'Why do you eat and drink?' they said, 'with tax-gatherers and sinners?' Jesus answered them: 'It is not the healthy that need a doctor, but the sick; I have not come to invite virtuous people, but to call sinners to repentance.'

Then they said to him, 'John's disciples are much given to fasting and the practice of prayer, and so are the disciples of the Pharisees; but yours eat and drink.' Jesus replied, 'Can you make the bridegroom's friends fast while the bridegroom is with them? But a time will come: the bridegroom will be taken away from them, and that will be the time for them to fast.'

He told them this parable also: 'No one tears a piece from a new cloak to patch an old one; if he does, he will have made a hole in the new cloak, and the patch from the new will not match the old. Nor does anyone put new wine into old wine-skins; if he does, the new wine will burst the skins, the wine will be wasted, and the skins ruined. Fresh skins for new wine! And no one after drinking old wine wants new; for he says, "The old wine is good." '

K.J.V.

6 And it came to pass on the second sabbath after the first, that he went through the corn fields; and his disciples plucked the ears of corn, and did eat, rubbing *them* in *their* hands. 2And certain of the Pharisees said unto them, Why do ye that which is not lawful to do on the sabbath days? 3And Jesus answering them said, Have ye not read so much as this, what David did, when himself was a hungered, and they which were with him; 4 How he went into the house of God, and did take and eat the shewbread, and gave also to them that were with him; which it is not lawful to eat but for the priests alone? 5And he said unto them, That the Son of man is Lord also of the sabbath. 6And it came to pass also on another sabbath, that he entered into the synagogue and taught: and there was a man whose right hand was withered. 7And the scribes and Pharisees watched him, whether he would heal on the sabbath day; that they might find an accusation against him. 8 But he knew their thoughts, and said to the man which had the withered hand, Rise up, and stand forth in the midst. And he arose and stood forth. 9 Then said Jesus unto them, I will ask you one thing; Is it lawful on the sabbath days to do good, or to do evil? to save life, or to destroy *it?* 10And looking round about upon them all, he said unto the man, Stretch forth thy hand. And he did so: and his hand was restored whole as the other. 11And they were filled with madness; and communed one with another what they might do to Jesus. 12And it came to pass in those days, that he went out into a mountain to pray, and continued all night in prayer to God.

13 And when it was day, he called *unto him* his disciples: and of them he chose twelve, whom also he named apostles; 14 Simon, (whom he also named Peter,) and Andrew his brother, James and John, Philip and Bartholomew, 15 Matthew and Thomas, James the *son* of Alpheus, and Simon called Zelotes, 16And Judas *the brother* of James, and Judas Iscariot, which also was the traitor.

17 And he came down with them, and stood in the plain, and the company of his disciples, and a great multitude of people out of all Judea and Jerusalem, and from the sea coast of Tyre

R.S.V.

6 On a sabbath,[t] while he was going through the grainfields, his disciples plucked and ate some ears of grain, rubbing them in their hands. 2 But some of the Pharisees said, "Why are you doing what is not lawful to do on the sabbath?" 3And Jesus answered, "Have you not read what David did when he was hungry, he and those who were with him: 4 how he entered the house of God, and took and ate the bread of the Presence, which it is not lawful for any but the priests to eat, and also gave it to those with him?" 5And he said to them, "The Son of man is lord of the sabbath."

6 On another sabbath, when he entered the synagogue and taught, a man was there whose right hand was withered. 7And the scribes and the Pharisees watched him, to see whether he would heal on the sabbath, so that they might find an accusation against him. 8 But he knew their thoughts, and he said to the man who had the withered hand, "Come and stand here." And he rose and stood there. 9And Jesus said to them, "I ask you, is it lawful on the sabbath to do good or to do harm, to save life or to destroy it?" 10And he looked around on them all, and said to him, "Stretch out your hand." And he did so, and his hand was restored. 11 But they were filled with fury and discussed with one another what they might do to Jesus.

12 In these days he went out into the hills to pray; and all night he continued in prayer to God. 13And when it was day, he called his disciples, and chose from them twelve, whom he named apostles; 14 Simon, whom he named Peter, and Andrew his brother, and James and John, and Philip, and Bartholomew, 15 and Matthew, and Thomas, and James the son of Alphaeus, and Simon who was called the Zealot, 16 and Judas the son of James, and Judas Iscariot, who became a traitor.

17 And he came down with them and stood on a level place, with a great crowd of his disciples and a great multitude of people from all Judea and Jerusalem and the seacoast of Tyre

[t] Other ancient authorities read *On the second first sabbath* (on the second sabbath after the first).

PHILLIPS

N.E.B.

Jesus speaks of the Sabbath—   6. 1

One Sabbath day, as Jesus happened to be passing through the cornfields, his disciples began picking the ears of corn, rubbing them in their hands, and eating them. Some of the Pharisees remarked,

"Why are you doing what the Law forbids men to do on the Sabbath day?"

Jesus answered them and said:

"Have you never read what David and his companions did when they were hungry? How he went into the house of God, took the presentation loaves, ate some bread himself and gave some to his companions, even though the Law does not permit anyone except the priests to eat it?"

Then he added, "The Son of Man is master even of the Sabbath."

—and provokes violent antagonism   6. 6

On another Sabbath day when he went into a synagogue to teach, there was a man there whose right hand was wasted away. The scribes and the Pharisees were watching Jesus closely to see whether he would heal on the Sabbath day, which would, of course, give them grounds for an accusation. But he knew exactly what was going on in their minds and said to the man with the wasted hand,

"Stand up and come out in front."

And he got up and stood there. Then Jesus said to them:

"I am going to ask you a question. Does the Law command us to do good on Sabbath days or do harm—to save life or destroy it?"

He looked round, meeting all their eyes, and said to the man,

"Now stretch out your hand."

He did so, and his hand was restored as sound as the other one. But they were filled with insane fury and kept discussing with one another what they could do to Jesus.

After a night of prayer Jesus   6. 12
selects the twelve

It was in those days that he went up the hillside to pray, and spent the whole night in prayer to God. When daylight came, he summoned his disciples to him and out of them he chose twelve whom he called apostles. They were—

Simon (whom he called Peter),
Andrew, his brother,
James,
John,
Philip,
Bartholomew,
Matthew,
Thomas,
James, the son of Alphaeus,
Simon, called the patriot,
Judas, the son of James, and
Judas Iscariot, who later betrayed him.

Then he came down with them and stood on a level piece of ground, surrounded by a large crowd of his disciples and a great number of people from all parts of Judaea and Jerusalem and the coastal district of Tyre and Sidon, who

6 One Sabbath he was going through the cornfields, and his disciples were plucking the ears of corn, rubbing them in their hands, and eating them. Some of the Pharisees said, 'Why are you doing what is forbidden on the Sabbath?' Jesus answered, 'So you have not read what David did when he and his men were hungry? He went into the House of God and took the consecrated loaves to eat and gave them to his men, though priests alone are allowed to eat them, and no one else.' He also said, 'The Son of Man is sovereign even over the Sabbath.'

On another Sabbath he had gone to synagogue and was teaching. There happened to be a man in the congregation whose right arm was withered; and the lawyers and the Pharisees were on the watch to see whether Jesus would cure him on the Sabbath, so that they could find a charge to bring against him. But he knew what was in their minds and said to the man with the withered arm, 'Get up and stand out here.' So he got up and stood there. Then Jesus said to them, 'I put the question to you: is it permitted to do good or to do evil on the Sabbath, to save life or to destroy it?' He looked round at them all and then said to the man, 'Stretch out your arm.' He did so, and his arm was restored. But they were beside themselves with anger, and began to discuss among themselves what they could do to Jesus.

During this time he went out one day into the hills to pray, and spent the night in prayer to God. When day broke he called his disciples to him, and from among them he chose twelve and named them Apostles: Simon, to whom he gave the name of Peter, and Andrew his brother, James and John, Philip and Bartholomew, Matthew and Thomas, James son of Alphaeus, and Simon who was called the Zealot, Judas son of James, and Judas Iscariot who turned traitor.

He came down the hill with them and took his stand on level ground. There was a large concourse of his disciples and great numbers of people from Jerusalem and Judaea and from the seaboard of Tyre and Sidon, who had come to

K.J.V.

and Sidon, which came to hear him, and to be healed of their diseases; 18And they that were vexed with unclean spirits: and they were healed. 19And the whole multitude sought to touch him: for there went virtue out of him, and healed *them* all.

20 And he lifted up his eyes on his disciples, and said, Blessed *be ye* poor: for yours is the kingdom of God. 21 Blessed *are ye* that hunger now: for ye shall be filled. Blessed *are ye* that weep now: for ye shall laugh. 22 Blessed are ye, when men shall hate you, and when they shall separate you *from their company,* and shall reproach *you,* and cast out your name as evil, for the Son of man's sake. 23 Rejoice ye in that day, and leap for joy: for, behold, your reward *is* great in heaven: for in the like manner did their fathers unto the prophets. 24 But woe unto you that are rich! for ye have received your consolation. 25 Woe unto you that are full! for ye shall hunger. Woe unto you that laugh now! for ye shall mourn and weep. 26 Woe unto you, when all men shall speak well of you! for so did their fathers to the false prophets.

27 But I say unto you which hear, Love your enemies, do good to them which hate you, 28 Bless them that curse you, and pray for them which despitefully use you. 29And unto him that smiteth thee on the *one* cheek offer also the other; and him that taketh away thy cloak forbid not *to take thy* coat also. 30 Give to every man that asketh of thee; and of him that taketh away thy goods ask *them* not again. 31And as ye would that men should do to you, do ye also to them likewise. 32 For if ye love them which love you, what thank have ye? for sinners also love those that love them. 33And if ye do good to them which do good to you, what thank have ye? for sinners also do even the same. 34And if ye lend *to them* of whom ye hope to receive, what thank have ye? for sinners also lend to sinners, to receive as much again. 35 But love ye your enemies, and do good, and lend, hoping for nothing again; and your reward shall be great, and ye shall be the children of the Highest: for he is kind unto the unthankful and *to* the evil. 36 Be ye therefore merciful, as your Father also is merciful. 37 Judge not, and ye shall not be judged: condemn not, and ye shall not be condemned: forgive, and ye shall be forgiven: 38 Give, and it shall be given unto you; good measure, pressed down, and shaken together, and running over, shall men give into your bosom. For with the same measure that ye mete withal it shall be measured to you again.

R.S.V.

and Sidon, who came to hear him and to be healed of their diseases; 18 and those who were troubled with unclean spirits were cured. 19And all the crowd sought to touch him, for power came forth from him and healed them all.

20 And he lifted up his eyes on his disciples, and said:
"Blessed are you poor, for yours is the kingdom of God.
21 "Blessed are you that hunger now, for you shall be satisfied.
"Blessed are you that weep now, for you shall laugh.
22 "Blessed are you when men hate you, and when they exclude you and revile you, and cast out your name as evil, on account of the Son of man! 23 Rejoice in that day, and leap for joy, for behold, your reward is great in heaven; for so their fathers did to the prophets.
24 "But woe to you that are rich, for you have received your consolation.
25 "Woe to you that are full now, for you shall hunger.
"Woe to you that laugh now, for you shall mourn and weep.
26 "Woe to you, when all men speak well of you, for so their fathers did to the false prophets.
27 "But I say to you that hear, Love your enemies, do good to those who hate you, 28 bless those who curse you, pray for those who abuse you. 29 To him who strikes you on the cheek, offer the other also; and from him who takes away your cloak do not withhold your coat as well. 30 Give to every one who begs from you; and of him who takes away your goods do not ask them again. 31And as you wish that men would do to you, do so to them.
32 "If you love those who love you, what credit is that to you? For even sinners love those who love them. 33And if you do good to those who do good to you, what credit is that to you? For even sinners do the same. 34And if you lend to those from whom you hope to receive, what credit is that to you? Even sinners lend to sinners, to receive as much again. 35 But love your enemies, and do good, and lend, expecting nothing in return;[v] and your reward will be great, and you will be sons of the Most High; for he is kind to the ungrateful and the selfish. 36 Be merciful, even as your Father is merciful.
37 "Judge not, and you will not be judged; condemn not, and you will not be condemned; forgive, and you will be forgiven; 38 give, and it will be given to you; good measure, pressed down, shaken together, running over, will be put into your lap. For the measure you give will be the measure you get back."

PHILLIPS

had come to hear him and to be healed of their diseases. (And even those who were troubled with evil spirits were cured.) The whole crowd were trying to touch him with their hands, for power was going out from him and he was healing them all.

Jesus declares who is happy and   **6. 20**
who is to be pitied, and defines
a new attitude toward life

Then Jesus looked steadily at his disciples and said,

"How happy are you who own nothing, for the kingdom of God is yours!

"How happy are you who are hungry now, for you will be satisfied!

"How happy are you who weep now, for you are going to laugh!

"How happy you are when men hate you and turn you out of their company; when they slander you and detest all that you stand for because you are loyal to the Son of Man. Be glad when that happens and jump for joy—your reward in Heaven is magnificent. For that is exactly how their fathers treated the prophets.

"But how miserable for you who are rich, for you have had all your comforts!

"How miserable for you who have all you want, for you are going to be hungry!

"How miserable for you who are laughing now, for you will know sorrow and tears!

"How miserable for you when everybody says nice things about you, for that is exactly how their fathers treated the false prophets.

"But I say to all of you who will listen to me: love your enemies, do good to those who hate you, bless those who curse you, and pray for those who treat you badly.

"As for the man who hits you on one cheek, offer him the other one as well! And if a man is taking away your coat, do not stop him from taking your shirt as well. Give to everyone who asks you, and when a man has taken what belongs to you, don't demand it back.

"Treat men exactly as you would like them to treat you. If you love only those who love you, what credit is that to you? Even sinners love those who love them! And if you do good only to those who do good to you, what credit is that to you? Even sinners do that. And if you lend only to those from whom you hope to get your money back, what credit is that to you? Even sinners lend to sinners and expect to get their money back. No, you are to love your *enemies* and do good and lend without hope of return. Your reward will be wonderful and you will be sons of the most high. For he is kind to the ungrateful and the wicked!

"You must be merciful, as your Father in Heaven is merciful. Don't judge other people and you will not be judged yourselves. Don't condemn and you will not be condemned. Make allowances for others and people will make allowances for you. Give and men will give to you—yes, good measure, pressed down, shaken together and running over will they pour into your lap. For whatever measure you use with other people, they will use in their dealings with you."

N.E.B.

listen to him, and to be cured of their diseases. Those who were troubled with unclean spirits were cured; and everyone in the crowd was trying to touch him, because power went out from him and cured them all.

Then turning to his disciples he began to speak:

'How blest are you who are poor; the kingdom of God is yours.

'How blest are you who now go hungry; your hunger shall be satisfied.

'How blest are you who weep now; you shall laugh.

'How blest you are when men hate you, when they outlaw you and insult you, and ban your very name as infamous, because of the Son of Man. On that day be glad and dance for joy; for assuredly you have a rich reward in heaven; in just the same way did their fathers treat the prophets.

'But alas for you who are rich; you have had your time of happiness.

'Alas for you who are well-fed now; you shall go hungry.

'Alas for you who laugh now; you shall mourn and weep.

'Alas for you when all speak well of you; just so did their fathers treat the false prophets.

'But to you who hear me I say:

'Love your enemies; do good to those who hate you; bless those who curse you; pray for those who treat you spitefully. When a man hits you on the cheek, offer him the other cheek too; when a man takes away your coat, let him have your shirt as well. Give to everyone who asks you; when a man takes what is yours, do not demand it back. Treat others as you would like them to treat you.

'If you love only those who love you, what credit is that to you? Even sinners love those who love them. Again, if you do good only to those who do good to you, what credit is that to you? Even sinners do as much. And if you lend only where you expect to be repaid, what credit is that to you? Even sinners lend to each other if they are to be repaid in full. But you must love your enemies and do good; and lend without expecting any return[a] and you will have a rich reward: you will be sons of the Most High, because he himself is kind to the ungrateful and wicked. Be compassionate as your Father is compassionate.

'Pass no judgement, and you will not be judged; do not condemn, and you will not be condemned; acquit, and you will be acquitted; give, and gifts will be given you. Good measure, pressed down, shaken together, and running over, will be poured into your lap; for whatever measure you deal out to others will be dealt to you in return.'

[a] *Or* without ever giving up hope; *some witnesses read* without giving up hope of anyone.

K.J.V.

39 And he spake a parable unto them; Can the blind lead the blind? shall they not both fall into the ditch? 40 The disciple is not above his master: but every one that is perfect shall be as his master. 41And why beholdest thou the mote that is in thy brother's eye, but perceivest not the beam that is in thine own eye? 42 Either how canst thou say to thy brother, Brother, let me pull out the mote that is in thine eye, when thou thyself beholdest not the beam that is in thine own eye? Thou hypocrite, cast out first the beam out of thine own eye, and then shalt thou see clearly to pull out the mote that is in thy brother's eye. 43 For a good tree bringeth not forth corrupt fruit; neither doth a corrupt tree bring forth good fruit. 44 For every tree is known by his own fruit. For of thorns men do not gather figs, nor of a bramble bush gather they grapes. 45A good man out of the good treasure of his heart bringeth forth that which is good; and an evil man out of the evil treasure of his heart bringeth forth that which is evil: for of the abundance of the heart his mouth speaketh.

46 And why call ye me, Lord, Lord, and do not the things which I say? 47 Whosoever cometh to me, and heareth my sayings, and doeth them, I will shew you to whom he is like: 48 He is like a man which built a house, and digged deep, and laid the foundation on a rock: and when the flood arose, the stream beat vehemently upon that house, and could not shake it; for it was founded upon a rock. 49 But he that heareth, and doeth not, is like a man that without a foundation built a house upon the earth; against which the stream did beat vehemently, and immediately it fell; and the ruin of that house was great.

R.S.V.

39 He also told them a parable: "Can a blind man lead a blind man? Will they not both fall into a pit? 40A disciple is not above his teacher, but every one when he is fully taught will be like his teacher. 41 Why do you see the speck that is in your brother's eye, but do not notice the log that is in your own eye? 42 Or how can you say to your brother, 'Brother, let me take out the speck that is in your eye,' when you yourself do not see the log that is in your own eye? You hypocrite, first take the log out of your own eye, and then you will see clearly to take out the speck that is in your brother's eye.

43 "For no good tree bears bad fruit, nor again does a bad tree bear good fruit; 44 for each tree is known by its own fruit. For figs are not gathered from thorns, nor are grapes picked from a bramble bush. 45 The good man out of the good treasure of his heart produces good, and the evil man out of his evil treasure produces evil; for out of the abundance of the heart his mouth speaks.

46 "Why do you call me 'Lord, Lord,' and not do what I tell you? 47 Every one who comes to me and hears my words and does them, I will show you what he is like: 48 he is like a man building a house, who dug deep, and laid the foundation upon rock; and when a flood arose, the stream broke against that house, and could not shake it, because it had been well built.[w] 49 But he who hears and does not do them is like a man who built a house on the ground without a foundation; against which the stream broke, and immediately it fell, and the ruin of that house was great."

7 Now when he had ended all his sayings in the audience of the people, he entered into Capernaum. 2And a certain centurion's servant, who was dear unto him, was sick, and ready to die. 3And when he heard of Jesus, he sent unto him the elders of the Jews, beseeching him that he would come and heal his servant. 4And when they came to Jesus, they besought him instantly, saying, That he was worthy for whom he should do this: 5 For he loveth our nation, and he hath built us a synagogue. 6 Then Jesus went with them. And when he was now not far from the house, the centurion sent friends to him, saying unto him, Lord, trouble not thyself; for I am not worthy that thou shouldest enter under my roof: 7 Wherefore neither thought I myself worthy to come unto thee: but say in a word, and my servant shall be healed. 8 For I also am a man set under authority, having under me soldiers, and I say unto one, Go, and he goeth; and to another, Come, and he cometh; and to my servant, Do this, and he doeth it. 9 When Jesus heard these things, he marvelled at him, and turned him about, and said unto the people that followed him, I say unto you, I have not

7 After he had ended all his sayings in the hearing of the people he entered Capernaum. 2 Now a centurion had a slave who was dear[x] to him, who was sick and at the point of death. 3 When he heard of Jesus, he sent to him elders of the Jews, asking him to come and heal his slave. 4And when they came to Jesus, they besought him earnestly, saying, "He is worthy to have you do this for him, 5 for he loves our nation, and he built us our synagogue." 6And Jesus went with them. When he was not far from the house, the centurion sent friends to him, saying to him, "Lord, do not trouble yourself, for I am not worthy to have you come under my roof; 7 therefore I did not presume to come to you. But say the word, and let my servant be healed. 8 For I am a man set under authority, with soldiers under me: and I say to one, 'Go,' and he goes; and to another, 'Come,' and he comes; and to my slave, 'Do this,' and he does it." 9 When Jesus heard this he marveled at him, and turned and said to the multitude that followed him, "I tell you, not even in Israel have

[w] Other ancient authorities read *founded upon the rock*. [x] Or *valuable*.

The need for thoroughgoing   **6. 39**
sincerity

Then he gave them an illustration—
"Can one blind man be guide to another blind man? Surely they will both fall into the ditch together. A disciple is not above his teacher, but when he is fully trained he will be like his teacher.

"Why do you look at the speck of sawdust in your brother's eye and fail to notice the plank in your own? How can you say to your brother, 'Let me take the speck out of your eye' when you cannot see the plank in your own? You fraud, take the plank out of your own eye first and then you can see clearly enough to remove your brother's speck.

"It is impossible for a good tree to produce bad fruit—as impossible as it is for a bad tree to produce good fruit. Do not men know what a tree is by its fruit? You cannot pick figs from briars, or gather a bunch of grapes from a blackberry bush! A good man produces good things from the good stored up in his heart, and a bad man produces evil things from his own stores of evil. For a man's words will always express what has been treasured in his heart.

"And what is the point of calling me, 'Lord, Lord,' without doing what I tell you to do? Let me show you what the man who comes to me, hears what I have to say, and puts it into practice, is really like. He is like a man building a house, who dug down to rock bottom and laid the foundation of his house upon it. Then when the flood came and the flood water swept down upon that house, it could not shift it because it was properly built. But the man who hears me and does nothing about it is like a man who built his house with its foundation upon soft earth. When the flood water swept down upon it, it collapsed and the whole house crashed down in ruins."

A Roman centurion's   **7. 1**
extraordinary faith in Jesus

When Jesus had finished these talks to the people, he came to Capernaum, where it happened that there was a man very seriously ill and in fact at the point of death. He was the slave of a centurion who thought very highly of him. When the centurion heard about Jesus, he sent some Jewish elders with the request that he would come and save his servant's life. When they came to Jesus, they urged him strongly to grant this request, saying that the centurion deserved to have this done for him. "He loves our nation and has built us a synagogue out of his own pocket," they said.

So Jesus went with them, but as he approached the house the centurion sent some of his personal friends with the message:

"Don't trouble yourself, sir! I'm not important enough for you to come into my house—I didn't think I was fit to come to you in person. Just give the order, please, and my servant will recover. I am used to working under orders, and I have soldiers under me. I can say to one, 'Go,' and he goes, or I can say to another, 'Come here,' and he comes; or I can say to my slave, 'Do this job,' and he does it."

These words amazed Jesus and he turned to the crowd who were following behind him, and said,

"I have never found faith like this anywhere, even in Israel!"

He also offered them a parable: 'Can one blind man be guide to another? Will they not both fall into the ditch? A pupil is not superior to his teacher; but everyone, when his training is complete, will reach his teacher's level.

'Why do you look at the speck of sawdust in your brother's eye, with never a thought for the great plank in your own? How can you say to your brother, "My dear brother, let me take the speck out of your eye", when you are blind to the plank in your own? You hypocrite! First take the plank out of your own eye, and then you will see clearly to take the speck out of your brother's.

'There is no such thing as a good tree producing worthless fruit, nor yet a worthless tree producing good fruit. For each tree is known by its own fruit: you do not gather figs from thistles, and you do not pick grapes from brambles. A good man produces good from the store of good within himself; and an evil man from evil within produces evil. For the words that the mouth utters come from the overflowing of the heart.

'Why do you keep calling me "Lord, Lord"— and never do what I tell you? Everyone who comes to me and hears what I say, and acts upon it—I will show you what he is like. He is like a man who, in building his house, dug deep and laid the foundations on rock. When the flood came, the river burst upon that house, but could not shift it, because it had been soundly built. But he who hears and does not act is like a man who built his house on the soil without foundations. As soon as the river burst upon it, the house collapsed, and fell with a great crash.'

7 When he had finished addressing the people, he went to Capernaum. A centurion there had a servant whom he valued highly; this servant was ill and near to death. Hearing about Jesus, he sent some Jewish elders with the request that he would come and save his servant's life. They approached Jesus and pressed their petition earnestly: 'He deserves this favour from you,' they said, 'for he is a friend of our nation and it is he who built us our synagogue.' Jesus went with them; but when he was not far from the house, the centurion sent friends with this message: 'Do not trouble further, sir; it is not for me to have you under my roof, and that is why I did not presume to approach you in person. But say the word and my servant will be cured. I know, for in my position I am myself under orders, with soldiers under me. I say to one, "Go", and he goes; to another, "Come here", and he comes; and to my servant, "Do this", and he does it.' When Jesus heard this, he admired the man, and, turning to the crowd that was following him, said, 'I tell you, nowhere, even in Israel, have I

K.J.V.

found so great faith, no, not in Israel. 10And they that were sent, returning to the house, found the servant whole that had been sick.

11 And it came to pass the day after, that he went into a city called Nain; and many of his disciples went with him, and much people. 12 Now when he came nigh to the gate of the city, behold, there was a dead man carried out, the only son of his mother, and she was a widow: and much people of the city was with her. 13And when the Lord saw her, he had compassion on her, and said unto her, Weep not. 14And he came and touched the bier: and they that bare *him* stood still. And he said, Young man, I say unto thee, Arise. 15And he that was dead sat up, and began to speak. And he delivered him to his mother. 16And there came a fear on all: and they glorified God, saying, That a great prophet is risen up among us; and, That God hath visited his people. 17And this rumour of him went forth throughout all Judea, and throughout all the region round about. 18And the disciples of John shewed him of all these things.

19 And John calling *unto him* two of his disciples sent *them* to Jesus, saying, Art thou he that should come? or look we for another? 20 When the men were come unto him, they said, John Baptist hath sent us unto thee, saying, Art thou he that should come? or look we for another? 21And in that same hour he cured many of *their* infirmities and plagues, and of evil spirits; and unto many *that were* blind he gave sight. 22 Then Jesus answering said unto them, Go your way, and tell John what things ye have seen and heard; how that the blind see, the lame walk, the lepers are cleansed, the deaf hear, the dead are raised, to the poor the gospel is preached. 23And blessed is *he,* whosoever shall not be offended in me.

24 And when the messengers of John were departed, he began to speak unto the people concerning John, What went ye out into the wilderness for to see? A reed shaken with the wind? 25 But what went ye out for to see? A man clothed in soft raiment? Behold, they which are gorgeously apparelled, and live delicately, are in kings' courts. 26 But what went ye out for to see? A prophet? Yea, I say unto you, and much more than a prophet. 27 This is *he,* of whom it is written, Behold, I send my messenger before thy face, which shall prepare thy way before thee.

R.S.V.

I found such faith." 10And when those who had been sent returned to the house, they found the slave well.

11 Soon afterward[y] he went to a city called Nain, and his disciples and a great crowd went with him. 12As he drew near to the gate of the city, behold, a man who had died was being carried out, the only son of his mother, and she was a widow; and a large crowd from the city was with her. 13And when the Lord saw her, he had compassion on her and said to her, "Do not weep." 14And he came and touched the bier, and the bearers stood still. And he said, "Young man, I say to you, arise." 15And the dead man sat up, and began to speak. And he gave him to his mother. 16 Fear seized them all; and they glorified God, saying, "A great prophet has arisen among us!" and "God has visited his people!" 17And this report concerning him spread through the whole of Judea and all the surrounding country.

18 The disciples of John told him of all these things. 19And John, calling to him two of his disciples, sent them to the Lord, saying, "Are you he who is to come, or shall we look for another?" 20And when the men had come to him, they said, "John the Baptist has sent us to you, saying, 'Are you he who is to come, or shall we look for another?' " 21 In that hour he cured many of diseases and plagues and evil spirits, and on many that were blind he bestowed sight. 22And he answered them, "Go and tell John what you have seen and heard: the blind receive their sight, the lame walk, lepers are cleansed, and the deaf hear, the dead are raised up, the poor have good news preached to them. 23And blessed is he who takes no offense at me."

24 When the messengers of John had gone, he began to speak to the crowds concerning John: "What did you go out into the wilderness to behold? A reed shaken by the wind? 25 What then did you go out to see? A man clothed in soft raiment? Behold, those who are gorgeously appareled and live in luxury are in kings' courts. 26 What then did you go out to see? A prophet? Yes, I tell you, and more than a prophet. 27 This is he of whom it is written,

'Behold, I send my messenger before thy face,
who shall prepare thy way before thee.'

[y] Other ancient authorities read *Next day.*

Then those who had been sent by the centurion returned to the house and found the slave perfectly well.

Jesus brings a dead youth back to life   7. 11

Not long afterward, Jesus went into a town called Nain, accompanied by his disciples and a large crowd. As they approached the city gate, it happened that some people were carrying out a dead man, the only son of his widowed mother. The usual crowd of fellow townsmen was with her. When the Lord saw her, his heart went out to her, and he said,
"Don't cry."
Then he walked up and put his hand on the bier while the bearers stood still. Then he said,
"Young man, *wake up!*"
And the dead man sat up and began to talk, and Jesus handed him to his mother. Everybody present was awestruck and they praised God, saying,
"A great prophet has arisen among us and God has turned his face toward his people."
And this report of him spread through the whole of Judaea and the surrounding countryside.

Jesus sends John a personal message   7. 18

John's disciples reported all these happenings to him. Then he summoned two of them and sent them to the Lord with this message,
"Are you the one who was to come, or are we to look for someone else?"
When the men came to Jesus, they said,
"John the Baptist has sent us to you with this message, 'Are you the one who was to come, or are we to look for someone else?'"
At that very time Jesus was healing many people of their diseases and ailments and evil spirits, and he restored sight to many who were blind. Then he answered them:
"Go and tell John what you have seen and heard. The blind are recovering their sight, cripples are walking again, lepers being healed, the deaf hearing, dead men are being brought to life again, and the good news is being given to those in need. *And happy is the man who never loses his faith in me.*"

Jesus emphasizes the greatness of John—and the greater importance of the kingdom of God   7. 24

When these messengers had gone back, Jesus began to talk to the crowd about John.
"What did you go out into the desert to look at? Was it a reed waving in the breeze? Well, *what* was it you went out to see? A man dressed in fine clothes? But the men who wear fine clothes live luxuriously in palaces. But what *did* you really go out to see? A prophet? Yes, I tell you, a prophet and far more than a prophet! This is the man of whom the scripture says,

Behold, I send my messenger before thy face,
Who shall prepare thy way before thee.

found faith like this.' And the messengers returned to the house and found the servant in good health.
Afterwards[a] Jesus went to a town called Nain, accompanied by his disciples and a large crowd. As he approached the gate of the town he met a funeral. The dead man was the only son of his widowed mother; and many of the townspeople were there with her. When the Lord saw her his heart went out to her, and he said, 'Weep no more.' With that he stepped forward and laid his hand on the bier; and the bearers halted. Then he spoke: 'Young man, rise up!' The dead man sat up and began to talk; and Jesus gave him back to his mother. Deep awe fell upon them all, and they praised God. 'A great prophet has arisen among us', they said, and again, 'God has shown his care for his people.' The story of what he had done ran through all parts of Judaea and the whole neighbourhood.
John too was informed of all this by his disciples. Summoning two of their number he sent them to the Lord with this message: 'Are you the one who is to come, or are we to expect some other?' The messengers made their way to Jesus and said, 'John the Baptist has sent us to you: he asks, "Are you the one who is to come, or are we to expect some other?"' There and then he cured many sufferers from diseases, plagues, and evil spirits; and on many blind people he bestowed sight. Then he gave them his answer: 'Go', he said, 'and tell John what you have seen and heard: how the blind recover their sight, the lame walk, the lepers are clean, the deaf hear, the dead are raised to life, the poor are hearing the good news—and happy is the man who does not find me a stumbling-block.'
After John's messengers had left, Jesus began to speak about him to the crowds: 'What was the spectacle that drew you to the wilderness? A reed-bed swept by the wind? No? Then what did you go out to see? A man dressed in silks and satins? Surely you must look in palaces for grand clothes and luxury. But what did you go out to see? A prophet? Yes indeed, and far more than a prophet. He is the man of whom Scripture says,

"Here is my herald, whom I send on ahead of you,
And he will prepare your way before you."

[a] *Some witnesses read* On the next day.

K.J.V.

28 For I say unto you, Among those that are born of women there is not a greater prophet than John the Baptist: but he that is least in the kingdom of God is greater than he. 29And all the people that heard *him,* and the publicans, justified God, being baptized with the baptism of John. 30 But the Pharisees and lawyers rejected the counsel of God against themselves, being not baptized of him.

31 And the Lord said, Whereunto then shall I liken the men of this generation? and to what are they like? 32 They are like unto children sitting in the marketplace, and calling one to another, and saying, We have piped unto you, and ye have not danced; we have mourned to you, and ye have not wept. 33 For John the Baptist came neither eating bread nor drinking wine; and ye say He hath a devil. 34 The Son of man is come eating and drinking; and ye say, Behold a gluttonous man, and a winebibber, a friend of publicans and sinners! 35 But wisdom is justified of all her children.

36 And one of the Pharisees desired him that he would eat with him. And he went into the Pharisee's house, and sat down to meat. 37And, behold, a woman in the city, which was a sinner, when she knew that *Jesus* sat at meat in the Pharisee's house, brought an alabaster box of ointment, 38And stood at his feet behind *him* weeping, and began to wash his feet with tears, and did wipe *them* with the hairs of her head, and kissed his feet, and anointed *them* with the ointment. 39 Now when the Pharisee which had bidden him saw *it,* he spake within himself, saying, This man, if he were a prophet, would have known who and what manner of woman *this is* that toucheth him; for she is a sinner. 40And Jesus answering said unto him, Simon, I have somewhat to say unto thee. And he saith, Master, say on. 41 There was a certain creditor which had two debtors: the one owed five hundred pence, and the other fifty. 42 And when they had nothing to pay, he frankly forgave them both. Tell me therefore, which of them will love him most? 43 Simon answered and said, I suppose that *he,* to whom he forgave most. And he said unto him, Thou hast rightly judged. 44And he turned to the woman, and said unto Simon, Seest thou this woman? I entered into thine house, thou gavest me no water for my feet: but she hath washed my feet with tears, and wiped *them* with the hairs of her head. 45 Thou gavest me no kiss: but this woman, since the time I came in, hath not ceased to kiss my feet. 46 My head with oil thou didst not anoint: but this woman hath anointed my feet with ointment. 47 Wherefore I say unto thee, Her sins, which are many, are forgiven; for she loved much: but to whom little is forgiven, *the same* loveth little. 48And he said unto her, Thy sins are forgiven. 49And they that sat at meat with him began to say within themselves, Who is this that forgiveth sins also? 50And he said to the woman, Thy faith hath saved thee; go in peace.

R.S.V.

28 I tell you, among those born of women none is greater than John; yet he who is least in the kingdom of God is greater than he." 29 (When they heard this all the people and the tax collectors justified God, having been baptized with the baptism of John; 30 but the Pharisees and the lawyers rejected the purpose of God for themselves, not having been baptized by him.)

31 "To what then shall I compare the men of this generation, and what are they like? 32 They are like children sitting in the market place and calling to one another,

'We piped to you, and you did not dance;
  we wailed, and you did not weep.'

33 For John the Baptist has come eating no bread and drinking no wine; and you say, 'He has a demon.' 34 The Son of man has come eating and drinking; and you say, 'Behold, a glutton and a drunkard, a friend of tax collectors and sinners!' 35 Yet wisdom is justified by all her children."

36 One of the Pharisees asked him to eat with him, and he went into the Pharisee's house, and sat at table. 37And behold, a woman of the city, who was a sinner, when she learned that he was sitting at table in the Pharisee's house, brought an alabaster flask of ointment, 38 and standing behind him at his feet, weeping, she began to wet his feet with her tears, and wiped them with the hair of her head, and kissed his feet, and anointed them with the ointment. 39 Now when the Pharisee who had invited him saw it, he said to himself, "If this man were a prophet, he would have known who and what sort of woman this is who is touching him, for she is a sinner." 40And Jesus answering said to him, "Simon, I have something to say to you." And he answered, "What is it, Teacher?" 41 "A certain creditor had two debtors; one owed five hundred denarii, and the other fifty. 42 When they could not pay, he forgave them both. Now which of them will love him more?" 43 Simon answered, "The one, I suppose, to whom he forgave more." And he said to him, "You have judged rightly." 44 Then turning toward the woman he said to Simon, "Do you see this woman? I entered your house, you gave me no water for my feet, but she has wet my feet with her tears and wiped them with her hair. 45 You gave me no kiss, but from the time I came in she has not ceased to kiss my feet. 46 You did not anoint my head with oil, but she has anointed my feet with ointment. 47 Therefore I tell you, her sins, which are many, are forgiven, for she loved much; but he who is forgiven little, loves little." 48And he said to her, "Your sins are forgiven." 49 Then those who were at table with him began to say among themselves, "Who is this, who even forgives sins?" 50And he said to the woman, "Your faith has saved you; go in peace."

PHILLIPS

Believe me, no one greater than John has ever been born, and yet a humble member of the kingdom of God is greater than he.

"All the people, yes, even the tax collectors, when they heard John, acknowledged God and were baptized by his baptism. But the Pharisees and the experts in the Law frustrated God's purpose for them, for they refused John's baptism.

"What can I say that the men of this generation are like—what sort of men are they? They are like children sitting in the market place and calling out to one another, 'We played at weddings for you, but you wouldn't dance, and we played at funerals for you, and you wouldn't cry!' For John the Baptist came in the strictest austerity and you say he is crazy. Then the Son of Man came, enjoying life, and you say, 'Look, a drunkard and a glutton, a bosom friend of the tax collector and the outsider!' Ah, well, wisdom's reputation is entirely in the hands of her children!"

Jesus contrasts unloving   **7. 36**
righteousness with loving penitence

Then one of the Pharisees asked Jesus to a meal with him. When Jesus came into the house, he took his place at the table and a woman, known in the town as a bad woman, found out that Jesus was there and brought an alabaster flask of perfume and stood behind him crying, letting her tears fall on his feet and then drying them with her hair. Then she kissed them and anointed them with the perfume. When the Pharisee who had invited him saw this, he said to himself, "If this man were really a prophet, he would know who this woman is and what sort of person is touching him. He would have realized that she is a bad woman." Then Jesus spoke to him,

"Simon, there is something I want to say to you."

"Very well, master," he returned, "say it."

"Once upon a time, there were two men in debt to the same moneylender. One owed him fifty dollars and the other five. And since they were unable to pay, he generously canceled both of their debts. Now, which one of them do you suppose will love him more?"

"Well," returned Simon, "I suppose it will be the one who has been more generously treated."

"Exactly," replied Jesus, and then turning to the woman, he said to Simon:

"You can see this woman? I came into your house but you provided no water to wash my feet. But she has washed my feet with her tears and dried them with her hair. There was no warmth in your greeting, but she, from the moment I came in, has not stopped covering my feet with kisses. You gave me no oil for my head, but she has put perfume on my feet. That is why I tell you, Simon, that her sins, many as they are, are forgiven; for she has shown me so much love. But the man who has little to be forgiven has only a little love to give."

Then he said to her,

"Your sins are forgiven."

And the men at table with him began to say to themselves,

"And who is this man, who even forgives sins?"

But Jesus said to the woman:

"It is your faith that has saved you. Go in peace."

N.E.B.

I tell you, there is not a mother's son greater than John, and yet the least in the kingdom of God is greater than he.'

When they heard him, all the people, including the tax-gatherers, praised God, for they had accepted John's baptism; but the Pharisees and lawyers, who refused his baptism, had rejected [a] God's purpose for themselves.

'How can I describe the people of this generation? What are they like? They are like children sitting in the market-place and shouting at each other,

"We piped for you and you would not dance."
"We wept and wailed, and you would not mourn."

For John the Baptist came neither eating bread nor drinking wine, and you say, "He is possessed." The Son of Man came eating and drinking, and you say, "Look at him! a glutton and a drinker, a friend of tax-gatherers and sinners!" And yet God's wisdom is proved right by all who are her children.'

One of the Pharisees invited him to dinner; he went to the Pharisee's house and took his place at table. A woman who was living an immoral life in the town had learned that Jesus was dining in the Pharisee's house and had brought oil of myrrh in a small flask. She took her place behind him, by his feet, weeping. His feet were wetted with her tears and she wiped them with her hair, kissing them and anointing them with the myrrh. When his host the Pharisee saw this he said to himself, 'If this fellow were a real prophet, he would know who this woman is that touches him, and what sort of woman she is, a sinner.' Jesus took him up and said, 'Simon, I have something to say to you.' 'Speak on, Master', said he. 'Two men were in debt to a moneylender: one owed him five hundred silver pieces, the other fifty. As neither had anything to pay with he let them both off. Now, which will love him most?' Simon replied, 'I should think the one that was let off most.' 'You are right', said Jesus. Then turning to the woman, he said to Simon, 'You see this woman? I came to your house: you provided no water for my feet; but this woman has made my feet wet with her tears and wiped them with her hair. You gave me no kiss; but she has been kissing my feet ever since I came in. You did not anoint my head with oil; but she has anointed my feet with myrrh. And so, I tell you, her great love proves that her many sins have been forgiven; where little has been forgiven, little love is shown.' Then he said to her, 'Your sins are forgiven.' The other guests began to ask themselves, 'Who is this, that he can forgive sins?' But he said to the woman, 'Your faith has saved you; go in peace.'

[a] *Or* '. . . greater than he. And all the people, including the tax-gatherers, when they heard him, accepted John's baptism and acknowledged the righteous dealing of God; but the Pharisees and lawyers, by refusing his baptism, rejected . . .'

191

K.J.V.

8 And it came to pass afterward, that he went throughout every city and village, preaching and shewing the glad tidings of the kingdom of God: and the twelve *were* with him, 2And certain women, which had been healed of evil spirits and infirmities, Mary called Magdalene, out of whom went seven devils, 3And Joanna the wife of Chuza Herod's steward, and Susanna, and many others, which ministered unto him of their substance.

4 And when much people were gathered together, and were come to him out of every city, he spake by a parable: 5A sower went out to sow his seed: and as he sowed, some fell by the way side; and it was trodden down, and the fowls of the air devoured it. 6And some fell upon a rock; and as soon as it was sprung up, it withered away, because it lacked moisture. 7And some fell among thorns; and the thorns sprang up with it, and choked it. 8And other fell on good ground, and sprang up, and bare fruit a hundredfold. And when he had said these things, he cried, He that hath ears to hear, let him hear. 9And his disciples asked him, saying, What might this parable be? 10And he said, Unto you it is given to know the mysteries of the kingdom of God: but to others in parables; that seeing they might not see, and hearing they might not understand. 11 Now the parable is this: The seed is the word of God. 12 Those by the way side are they that hear; then cometh the devil, and taketh away the word out of their hearts, lest they should believe and be saved. 13 They on the rock *are they*, which, when they hear, receive the word with joy; and these have no root, which for a while believe, and in time of temptation fall away. 14And that which fell among thorns are they, which, when they have heard, go forth, and are choked with cares and riches and pleasures of *this* life, and bring no fruit to perfection. 15 But that on the good ground are they, which in an honest and good heart, having heard the word, keep *it*, and bring forth fruit with patience.

16 No man, when he hath lighted a candle, covereth it with a vessel, or putteth *it* under a bed; but setteth *it* on a candlestick, that they which enter in may see the light. 17 For nothing is secret, that shall not be made manifest; neither *any thing* hid, that shall not be known and come abroad. 18 Take heed therefore how ye hear: for whosoever hath, to him shall be given; and whosoever hath not, from him shall be taken even that which he seemeth to have.

R.S.V.

8 Soon afterward he went on through cities and villages, preaching and bringing the good news of the kingdom of God. And the twelve were with him, 2 and also some women who had been healed of evil spirits and infirmities: Mary, called Magdalene, from whom seven demons had gone out, 3 and Joanna, the wife of Chuza, Herod's steward, and Susanna, and many others, who provided for them[z] out of their means.

4 And when a great crowd came together and people from town after town came to him, he said in a parable: 5 "A sower went out to sow his seed; and as he sowed, some fell along the path, and was trodden under foot, and the birds of the air devoured it. 6And some fell on the rock; and as it grew up, it withered away, because it had no moisture. 7And some fell among thorns; and the thorns grew with it and choked it. 8And some fell into good soil and grew, and yielded a hundredfold." As he said this, he called out, "He who has ears to hear, let him hear."

9 And when his disciples asked him what this parable meant, 10 he said, "To you it has been given to know the secrets of the kingdom of God; but for others they are in parables, so that seeing they may not see, and hearing they may not understand. 11 Now the parable is this: The seed is the word of God. 12 The ones along the path are those who have heard; then the devil comes and takes away the word from their hearts, that they may not believe and be saved. 13And the ones on the rock are those who, when they hear the word, receive it with joy; but these have no root, they believe for a while and in time of temptation fall away. 14And as for what fell among the thorns, they are those who hear, but as they go on their way they are choked by the cares and riches and pleasures of life, and their fruit does not mature. 15And as for that in the good soil, they are those who, hearing the word, hold it fast in an honest and good heart, and bring forth fruit with patience.

16 "No one after lighting a lamp covers it with a vessel, or puts it under a bed, but puts it on a stand, that those who enter may see the light. 17 For nothing is hid that shall not be made manifest, nor anything secret that shall not be known and come to light. 18 Take heed then how you hear; for to him who has will more be given, and from him who has not, even what he thinks that he has will be taken away."

---

[z] Other ancient authorities read *him*.

PHILLIPS

Not long after this incident, Jesus went through every town and village preaching and telling the people the good news of the kingdom of God. He was accompanied by the twelve and some women who had been cured of evil spirits and illnesses—Mary, known as "the woman from Magdala" (who had once been possessed by seven evil spirits), Joanna the wife of Chuza, Herod's agent; Susanna, and many others who used to look after his comfort from their own resources.

Jesus' parable of the mixed   **8. 4**
reception given to the truth

When a large crowd had collected and people were coming to him from one town after another, he spoke to them and gave them this parable:

"A sower went out to sow his seed, and while he was sowing, some of the seed fell by the roadside and was trodden down and the birds gobbled it up. Some fell on the rock, and when it sprouted it withered for lack of moisture. Some fell among thornbushes which grew up with the seeds and choked the life out of them. But some seed fell on good soil and grew and produced a crop—a hundred times what had been sown."

And when he had said this, he called out,

"Let the man who has ears to hear use them!"

Then his disciples asked him the meaning of the parable. To which Jesus replied,

"You have been given the chance to understand the secrets of the kingdom of God, but the others are given parables so that they may go through life with their eyes open and see nothing, and with their ears open, and understand nothing of what they hear.

"This is what the parable means. The seed is the message of God. The seed sown by the roadside represents those who hear the message, and then the devil comes and takes it away from their hearts so that they cannot believe it and be saved. That sown on the rock represents those who accept the message with great delight when they hear it, but have no real root. They believe for a little while but when the time of temptation comes, they lose faith. And the seed sown among the thorns represents the people who hear the message and go on their way, and with the worries and riches and pleasures of living, the life is choked out of them, and in the end they produce nothing. But the seed sown on good soil means the men who hear the message and accept it with a good and honest heart, and go on steadily producing a good crop.

Truth is not a secret to be hidden   **8. 16**
but a gift to be used

"Nobody lights a lamp and covers it with a basin or puts it under the bed. No, a man puts his lamp on a lampstand so that those who come in can see the light. For there is nothing hidden now which will not become perfectly plain and there are no secrets now which will not become as clear as daylight. So take care how you listen—more will be given to the man who has something already, but the man who has nothing will lose even what he thinks he has."

N.E.B.

8 After this he went journeying from town to town and village to village, proclaiming the good news of the kingdom of God. With him were the Twelve and a number of women who had been set free from evil spirits and infirmities: Mary, known as Mary of Magdala, from whom seven devils had come out, Joanna, the wife of Chuza a steward of Herod's, Susanna, and many others. These women provided for them out of their own resources.

People were now gathering in large numbers, and as they made their way to him from one town after another, he said in a parable: 'A sower went out to sow his seed. And as he sowed, some seed fell along the footpath, where it was trampled on, and the birds ate it up. Some seed fell on rock and, after coming up, withered for lack of moisture. Some seed fell in among thistles, and the thistles grew up with it and choked it. And some of the seed fell into good soil, and grew, and yielded a hundredfold.' As he said this he called out, 'If you have ears to hear, then hear.'

His disciples asked him what this parable meant, and he said, 'It has been granted to you to know the secrets of the kingdom of God; but the others have only parables, in order that they may look but see nothing, hear but understand nothing.

'This is what the parable means. The seed is the word of God. Those along the footpath are the men who hear it, and then the devil comes and carries off the word from their hearts for fear they should believe and be saved. The seed sown on rock stands for those who receive the word with joy when they hear it, but have no root; they are believers for a while, but in the time of testing they desert. That which fell among thistles represents those who hear, but their further growth is choked by cares and wealth and the pleasures of life, and they bring nothing to maturity. But the seed in good soil represents those who bring a good and honest heart to the hearing of the word, hold it fast, and by their perseverance yield a harvest.

'Nobody lights a lamp and then covers it with a basin or puts it under the bed. On the contrary, he puts it on a lamp-stand so that those who come in may see the light. For there is nothing hidden that will not become public, nothing under cover that will not be made known and brought into the open.

'Take care, then, how you listen; for the man who has will be given more, and the man who has not will forfeit even what he thinks he has.'

K.J.V.

19 Then came to him *his* mother and his brethren, and could not come at him for the press. 20And it was told him *by certain* which said, Thy mother and thy brethren stand without, desiring to see thee. 21And he answered and said unto them, My mother and my brethren are these which hear the word of God, and do it.

22 Now it came to pass on a certain day, that he went into a ship with his disciples: and he said unto them, Let us go over unto the other side of the lake. And they launched forth. 23 But as they sailed, he fell asleep: and there came down a storm of wind on the lake; and they were filled *with water*, and were in jeopardy. 24And they came to him, and awoke him, saying, Master, Master, we perish. Then he arose, and rebuked the wind and the raging of the water: and they ceased, and there was a calm. 25And he said unto them, Where is your faith? And they being afraid wondered, saying one to another, What manner of man is this! for he commandeth even the winds and water, and they obey him.

26 And they arrived at the country of the Gadarenes, which is over against Galilee. 27And when he went forth to land, there met him out of the city a certain man, which had devils long time, and ware no clothes, neither abode in *any* house, but in the tombs. 28 When he saw Jesus, he cried out, and fell down before him, and with a loud voice said, What have I to do with thee, Jesus, *thou* Son of God most high? I beseech thee, torment me not. 29 (For he had commanded the unclean spirit to come out of the man. For oftentimes it had caught him: and he was kept bound with chains and in fetters; and he brake the bands, and was driven of the devil into the wilderness.) 30And Jesus asked him, saying, What is thy name? And he said, Legion: because many devils were entered into him. 31And they besought him that he would not command them to go out into the deep. 32And there was there a herd of many swine feeding on the mountain: and they besought him that he would suffer them to enter into them. And he suffered them. 33 Then went the devils out of the man, and entered into the swine: and the herd ran violently down a steep place into the lake, and were choked. 34 When they that fed *them* saw what was done, they fled, and went and told *it* in the city and in the country. 35 Then they went out to see what was done; and came to Jesus, and found the man, out of whom the devils were departed, sitting at the feet of Jesus, clothed, and in his right mind: and they were afraid. 36 They also which saw *it* told them by what means he that was possessed of the devils was healed.

37 Then the whole multitude of the country

R.S.V.

19 Then his mother and his brothers came to him, but they could not reach him for the crowd. 20And he was told, "Your mother and your brothers are standing outside, desiring to see you." 21 But he said to them, "My mother and my brothers are those who hear the word of God and do it."

22 One day he got into a boat with his disciples, and he said to them, "Let us go across to the other side of the lake." So they set out, 23 and as they sailed he fell asleep. And a storm of wind came down on the lake, and they were filling with water, and were in danger. 24And they went and woke him, saying, "Master, Master, we are perishing!" And he awoke and rebuked the wind and the raging waves; and they ceased, and there was a calm. 25 He said to them, "Where is your faith?" And they were afraid, and they marveled, saying to one another, "Who then is this, that he commands even wind and water, and they obey him?"

26 Then they arrived at the country of the Gerasenes,[a] which is opposite Galilee. 27And as he stepped out on land, there met him a man from the city who had demons; for a long time he had worn no clothes, and he lived not in a house but among the tombs. 28 When he saw Jesus, he cried out and fell down before him, and said with a loud voice, "What have you to do with me, Jesus, Son of the Most High God? I beseech you, do not torment me." 29 For he had commanded the unclean spirit to come out of the man. (For many a time it had seized him; he was kept under guard, and bound with chains and fetters, but he broke the bonds and was driven by the demon into the desert.) 30 Jesus then asked him, "What is your name?" And he said, "Legion"; for many demons had entered him. 31And they begged him not to command them to depart into the abyss. 32 Now a large herd of swine was feeding there on the hillside; and they begged him to let them enter these. So he gave them leave. 33 Then the demons came out of the man and entered the swine, and the herd rushed down the steep bank into the lake and were drowned.

34 When the herdsmen saw what had happened, they fled, and told it in the city and in the country. 35 Then people went out to see what had happened, and they came to Jesus, and found the man from whom the demons had gone, sitting at the feet of Jesus, clothed and in his right mind; and they were afraid. 36And those who had seen it told them how he who had been possessed with demons was healed. 37 Then all the people of the surrounding coun-

[a] Other ancient authorities read *Gadarenes*, others *Gergesenes.*

Then his mother and his brothers arrived to see him, but could not get near him because of the crowd. So a message was passed to him,

"Your mother and your brothers are standing outside wanting to see you."

To which he replied,

"My mother and my brothers? That means those who listen to God's message and obey it."

Jesus' mastery of wind and water   8. 22

It happened on one of these days that he embarked on a boat with his disciples and said to them,

"Let us cross over to the other side of the lake."

So they set sail, and when they were under way he dropped off to sleep. Then a squall of wind swept down upon the lake and they were in grave danger of being swamped. Coming forward, they woke him up, saying,

"Master, master, we're drowning!"

Then he got up and reprimanded the wind and the stormy waters, and they died down, and everything was still. Then he said to them,

"What has happened to your faith?"

But they were frightened and bewildered and kept saying to one another:

"Who ever can this be? He gives orders even to the winds and waters and *they obey him.*"

Jesus encounters and heals a   8. 26
dangerous lunatic

They sailed on to the country of the Gerasenes which is on the opposite side of the lake to Galilee. And as Jesus disembarked, a man from the town who was possessed by evil spirits met him. He had worn no clothes for a long time and did not live inside a house, but among the tombs. When he saw Jesus, he let out a howl and fell down in front of him, yelling:

"What have you got to do with me, you Jesus, Son of the most high God? Please, please, don't torment me."

For Jesus was commanding the evil spirit to come out of the man. Again and again the evil spirit had taken control of him, and though he was bound with chains and fetters and closely watched, he would snap his bonds and go off into the desert with the devil at his heels. Then Jesus asked him,

"What is your name?"

"Legion!" he replied. For many evil spirits had gone into him, and were now begging Jesus not to order them off to the bottomless pit. It happened that there was a large herd of pigs feeding on the hillside, so they implored him to allow them to go into the pigs, and he let them go. And when the evil spirits came out of the man and went into the pigs, the whole herd rushed down the cliff into the lake and were drowned. When the swineherds saw what had happened, they took to their heels, pouring out the story to the people in the town and country-side. These people came out to see what had happened, and approached Jesus. They found the man, whom the evil spirits had left, sitting down at Jesus' feet, properly clothed and quite sane. That frightened them. Those who had seen it told the others how the man with the evil spirits had been cured. And the whole crowd of people from the district surrounding the

His mother and his brothers arrived but could not get to him for the crowd. He was told, 'Your mother and brothers are standing outside, and they want to see you.' He replied, 'My mother and my brothers—they are those who hear the word of God and act upon it.'

One day he got into a boat with his disciples and said to them, 'Let us cross over to the other side of the lake.' So they put out; and as they sailed along he went to sleep. Then a heavy squall struck the lake; they began to ship water and were in grave danger. They went to him, and roused him, crying, 'Master, Master, we are sinking!' He awoke, and rebuked the wind and the turbulent waters. The storm subsided and all was calm. 'Where is your faith?' he asked. In fear and astonishment they said to one another, 'Who can this be? He gives his orders to wind and waves, and they obey him.'

So they landed in the country of the Gergesenes,[a] which is opposite Galilee. As he stepped ashore he was met by a man from the town who was possessed by devils. For a long time he had neither worn clothes nor lived in a house, but stayed among the tombs. When he saw Jesus he cried out, and fell at his feet shouting, 'What do you want with me, Jesus, son of the Most High God? I implore you, do not torment me.'

For Jesus was already ordering the unclean spirit to come out of the man. Many a time it had seized him, and then, for safety's sake, they would secure him with chains and fetters; but each time he broke loose, and with the devil in charge made off to the solitary places.

Jesus asked him, 'What is your name?' 'Legion', he replied. This was because so many devils had taken possession of him. And they begged him not to banish them to the Abyss.

There happened to be a large herd of pigs nearby, feeding on the hill; and the spirits begged him to let them go into these pigs. He gave them leave; the devils came out of the man and went into the pigs, and the herd rushed over the edge into the lake and were drowned.

The men in charge of them saw what had happened, and, taking to their heels, they carried the news to the town and country-side; and the people came out to see for themselves. When they came to Jesus, and found the man from whom the devils had gone out sitting at his feet clothed and in his right mind, they were afraid. The spectators told them how the madman had been cured. Then the whole population of the

[a] *Some witnesses read* Gerasenes; *others read* Gadarenes.

K.J.V.

of the Gadarenes round about besought him to depart from them; for they were taken with great fear: and he went up into the ship, and returned back again. 38 Now the man, out of whom the devils were departed, besought him that he might be with him: but Jesus sent him away, saying, 39 Return to thine own house, and shew how great things God hath done unto thee. And he went his way, and published throughout the whole city how great things Jesus had done unto him. 40And it came to pass, that, when Jesus was returned, the people *gladly* received him: for they were all waiting for him.

41 And, behold, there came a man named Jairus, and he was a ruler of the synagogue; and he fell down at Jesus' feet, and besought him that he would come into his house: 42 For he had one only daughter, about twelve years of age, and she lay a dying. But as he went the people thronged him.

43 And a woman having an issue of blood twelve years, which had spent all her living upon physicians, neither could be healed of any, 44 Came behind *him,* and touched the border of his garment: and immediately her issue of blood stanched. 45And Jesus said, Who touched me? When all denied, Peter and they that were with him said, Master, the multitude throng thee and press *thee,* and sayest thou, Who touched me? 46And Jesus said, Somebody hath touched me: for I perceive that virtue is gone out of me. 47And when the woman saw that she was not hid, she came trembling, and falling down before him, she declared unto him before all the people for what cause she had touched him, and how she was healed immediately. 48And he said unto her, Daughter, be of good comfort: thy faith hath made thee whole; go in peace.

49 While he yet spake, there cometh one from the ruler of the synagogue's *house,* saying to him, Thy daughter is dead; trouble not the Master. 50 But when Jesus heard *it,* he answered him, saying, Fear not: believe only, and she shall be made whole. 51And when he came into the house, he suffered no man to go in, save Peter, and James, and John, and the father and the mother of the maiden. 52And all wept, and bewailed her: but he said, Weep not; she is not dead, but sleepeth. 53And they laughed him to scorn, knowing that she was dead. 54And he put them all out, and took her by the hand, and called, saying, Maid, arise. 55And her spirit came again, and she arose straightway: and he commanded to give her meat. 56And her parents were astonished: but he charged them that they should tell no man what was done.

R.S.V.

try of the Gerasenes[a] asked him to depart from them; for they were seized with great fear; so he got into the boat and returned. 38 The man from whom the demons had gone begged that he might be with him; but he sent him away, saying, 39 "Return to your home, and declare how much God has done for you." And he went away, proclaiming throughout the whole city how much Jesus had done for him.

40 Now when Jesus returned, the crowd welcomed him, for they were all waiting for him. 41And there came a man named Jairus, who was a ruler of the synagogue; and falling at Jesus' feet he besought him to come to his house, 42 for he had an only daughter, about twelve years of age, and she was dying.

As he went, the people pressed round him. 43And a woman who had had a flow of blood for twelve years[b] and could not be healed by any one 44 came up behind him, and touched the fringe of his garment; and immediately her flow of blood ceased. 45And Jesus said, "Who was it that touched me?" When all denied it, Peter[c] said, "Master, the multitudes surround you and press upon you!" 46 But Jesus said, "Some one touched me; for I perceive that power has gone forth from me." 47And when the woman saw that she was not hidden, she came trembling, and falling down before him declared in the presence of all the people why she had touched him, and how she had been immediately healed. 48And he said to her, "Daughter, your faith has made you well; go in peace."

49 While he was still speaking, a man from the ruler's house came and said, "Your daughter is dead; do not trouble the Teacher any more." 50 But Jesus on hearing this answered him, "Do not fear; only believe, and she shall be well." 51And when he came to the house, he permitted no one to enter with him, except Peter and John and James, and the father and mother of the child. 52And all were weeping and bewailing her; but he said, "Do not weep; for she is not dead but sleeping." 53And they laughed at him, knowing that she was dead. 54 But taking her by the hand he called, saying, "Child, arise." 55And her spirit returned, and she got up at once; and he directed that something should be given her to eat. 56And her parents were amazed; but he charged them to tell no one what had happened.

[a] Other ancient authorities read *Gadarenes,* others *Gergesenes.* [b] Other ancient authorities add *and had spent all her living upon physicians.* [c] Other ancient authorities add *and those who were with him.*

PHILLIPS

N.E.B.

Gerasenes' country begged Jesus to go away from them, for they were thoroughly frightened. Then he re-embarked on the boat and turned back. The man who had had the evil spirits kept begging to go with Jesus, but he sent him away with the words,

"Go back home and tell them all what wonderful things God has done for you."

So the man went away and told the marvelous story of what Jesus had done for him, all over the town.

On Jesus' return, the crowd welcomed him back, for they had all been looking for him.

Jesus heals in response to faith   8. 41

Then up came Jairus (who was president of the synagogue), and fell at Jesus' feet, begging him to come into his house, for his daughter, an only child about twelve years old, was dying.

But as he went, the crowds nearly suffocated him. Among them was a woman who had had a hemorrhage for twelve years and who had derived no benefit from anybody's treatment. She came up behind Jesus and touched the edge of his cloak, with the result that her hemorrhage stopped at once.

"Who was that who touched me?" said Jesus.

And when everybody denied it, Peter remonstrated,

"Master, the crowds are all round you and are pressing you on all sides. . . ."

But Jesus said,

"Somebody touched me, for I felt that power went out from me."

When the woman realized that she had not escaped notice, she came forward trembling, and fell at his feet and admitted before everybody why she had had to touch him, and how she had been instantaneously cured.

"Daughter," said Jesus, "it is your faith that has healed you—go in peace."

While he was still speaking, somebody came from the synagogue president's house to say,

"Your daughter is dead—there is no need to trouble the master any further."

But when Jesus heard this, he said to him,

"Now don't be afraid, go on believing and she will be all right."

Then when he came to the house, he would not allow anyone to go in with him except Peter, John and James, and the child's parents. All those already there were weeping and wailing over her, but he said,

"Stop crying! She is not dead, she is fast asleep."

This drew a scornful laugh from them, for they were quite certain that she had died. But he turned them all out, took the little girl's hand and called out to her,

"Wake up, my child!"

And her spirit came back and she got to her feet at once, and Jesus ordered food to be given to her. Her parents were nearly out of their minds with joy, but Jesus told them not to tell anyone what had happened.

Gergesene[a] district asked him to go, for they were in the grip of a great fear. So he got into the boat and returned. The man from whom the devils had gone out begged leave to go with him; but Jesus sent him away: 'Go back home,' he said, 'and tell them everything that God has done for you.' The man went all over the town spreading the news of what Jesus had done for him.

When Jesus returned, the people welcomed him, for they were all expecting him. Then a man appeared—Jairus was his name and he was president of the synagogue. Throwing himself down at Jesus's feet he begged him to come to his house, because he had an only daughter, about twelve years old, who was dying. And while Jesus was on his way he could hardly breathe for the crowds.

Among them was a woman who had suffered from haemorrhages for twelve years; and[b] nobody had been able to cure her. She came up from behind and touched the edge of[c] his cloak, and at once her haemorrhage stopped. Jesus said, 'Who was it that touched me?' All disclaimed it, and Peter and his companions said, 'Master, the crowds are hemming you in and pressing upon you!' But Jesus said, 'Someone did touch me, for I felt that power had gone out from me.' Then the woman, seeing that she was detected, came trembling and fell at his feet. Before all the people she explained why she had touched him and how she had been instantly cured. He said to her, 'My daughter, your faith has cured you. Go in peace.'

While he was still speaking, a man came from the president's house with the message, 'Your daughter is dead; trouble the Rabbi no further.' But Jesus heard, and interposed. 'Do not be afraid,' he said; 'only show faith and she will be well again.' On arrival at the house he allowed no one to go in with him except Peter, John, and James, and the child's father and mother. And all were weeping and lamenting for her. He said, 'Weep no more; she is not dead: she is asleep.' But they only laughed at him, well knowing that she was dead. But Jesus took hold of her hand and called her: 'Get up, my child.' Her spirit returned, she stood up immediately, and he told them to give her something to eat. Her parents were astounded; but he forbade them to tell anyone what had happened.

[a] *Some witnesses read* Gerasene; *others read* Gadarene. [b] *Some witnesses add* though she had spent all she had on doctors. [c] *Some witnesses omit* the edge of.

K.J.V.

R.S.V.

9 Then he called his twelve disciples together, and gave them power and authority over all devils, and to cure diseases. 2And he sent them to preach the kingdom of God, and to heal the sick. 3And he said unto them, Take nothing for *your* journey, neither staves, nor scrip, neither bread, neither money; neither have two coats apiece. 4And whatsoever house ye enter into, there abide, and thence depart. 5And whosoever will not receive you, when ye go out of that city, shake off the very dust from your feet for a testimony against them. 6And they departed, and went through the towns, preaching the gospel, and healing every where.

7 Now Herod the tetrarch heard of all that was done by him: and he was perplexed, because that it was said of some, that John was risen from the dead; 8And of some, that Elias had appeared; and of others, that one of the old prophets was risen again. 9And Herod said, John have I beheaded; but who is this, of whom I hear such things? And he desired to see him.

10 And the apostles, when they were returned, told him all that they had done. And he took them, and went aside privately into a desert place belonging to the city called Bethsaida. 11And the people, when they knew *it*, followed him: and he received them, and spake unto them of the kingdom of God, and healed them that had need of healing. 12And when the day began to wear away, then came the twelve, and said unto him, Send the multitude away, that they may go into the towns and country round about, and lodge, and get victuals: for we are here in a desert place. 13 But he said unto them, Give ye them to eat. And they said, We have no more but five loaves and two fishes; except we should go and buy meat for all this people. 14 For they were about five thousand men. And he said to his disciples, Make them sit down by fifties in a company. 15And they did so, and made them all sit down. 16 Then he took the five loaves and the two fishes, and looking up to heaven, he blessed them, and brake, and gave to the disciples to set before the multitude. 17And they did eat, and were all filled: and there was taken up of fragments that remained to them twelve baskets.

9 And he called the twelve together and gave them power and authority over all demons and to cure diseases, 2 and he sent them out to preach the kingdom of God and to heal. 3And he said to them, "Take nothing for your journey, no staff, nor bag, nor bread, nor money; and do not have two tunics. 4And whatever house you enter, stay there, and from there depart. 5And wherever they do not receive you, when you leave that town shake off the dust from your feet as a testimony against them." 6And they departed and went through the villages, preaching the gospel and healing everywhere.

7 Now Herod the tetrarch heard of all that was done, and he was perplexed, because it was said by some that John had been raised from the dead, 8 by some that Elijah had appeared, and by others that one of the old prophets had risen. 9 Herod said, "John I beheaded; but who is this about whom I hear such things?" And he sought to see him.

10 On their return the apostles told him what they had done. And he took them and withdrew apart to a city called Bethsaida. 11 When the crowds learned it, they followed him; and he welcomed them and spoke to them of the kingdom of God, and cured those who had need of healing. 12 Now the day began to wear away; and the twelve came and said to him, "Send the crowd away, to go into the villages and country round about, to lodge and get provisions; for we are here in a lonely place." 13 But he said to them, "You give them something to eat." They said, "We have no more than five loaves and two fish—unless we are to go and buy food for all these people." 14 For there were about five thousand men. And he said to his disciples, "Make them sit down in companies, about fifty each." 15And they did so, and made them all sit down. 16And taking the five loaves and the two fish he looked up to heaven, and blessed and broke them, and gave them to the disciples to set before the crowd. 17And all ate and were satisfied. And they took up what was left over, twelve baskets of broken pieces.

PHILLIPS	N.E.B.

Jesus commissions the twelve to preach and heal   9. 1

Then he called the twelve together and gave them power and authority over all evil spirits and the ability to heal disease. He sent them out to preach the kingdom of God and to heal the sick, with these words:

"Take nothing for your journey—neither a stick nor a purse nor food nor money, nor even extra clothes! When you come to stay at a house, remain there until you go on your way again. And where they will not welcome you, leave that town, and shake the dust off your feet as a protest against them!"

So they set out, and went from village to village preaching the gospel and healing people everywhere.

Herod's uneasy conscience after his execution of John   9. 7

All these things came to the ears of Herod the tetrarch and caused him acute anxiety, because some people were saying that John had risen from the dead, some maintaining that the prophet Elijah had appeared, and others that one of the old-time prophets had come back.

"I beheaded John," said Herod. "Who can this be that I hear all these things about?"

And he tried to find a way of seeing Jesus.

The twelve return and tell their story   9. 10

Then the apostles returned, and when they had made their report to Jesus of what they had done, he took them with him privately and retired into a town called Bethsaida.

Jesus welcomes the crowds, teaches, heals and feeds them   9. 11

But the crowds observed this and followed him. And he welcomed them and talked to them about the kingdom of God, and cured those who were in need of healing. As the day drew to its close the twelve came to him and said,

"Please dismiss the crowd now so that they can go to the villages and country round about and find some food and shelter, for we're quite in the wilds here."

"You give them something to eat!" returned Jesus.

"But we've nothing here," they replied, "except five loaves and two fish, unless you want us to go and buy food for all this crowd." (There were approximately five thousand men there.)

Then Jesus said to the disciples,

"Get them to sit down in groups of about fifty."

This they did, making them all sit down. Then he took the five loaves and the two fish and looked up to Heaven, blessed them, broke them into pieces and passed them to his disciples to serve to the crowd. Everybody ate and was satisfied. Afterward they collected twelve baskets full of broken pieces which were left over.

9 He now called the Twelve together and gave them power and authority to overcome all the devils and to cure diseases, and sent them to proclaim the kingdom of God and to heal. 'Take nothing for the journey,' he told them, 'neither stick nor pack, neither bread nor money; nor are you each to have a second coat. When you are admitted to a house, stay there, and go on from there. As for those who will not receive you, when you leave their town shake the dust off your feet as a warning to them.' So they set out and travelled from village to village, and everywhere they told the good news and healed the sick.

Now Prince Herod heard of all that was happening, and did not know what to make of it; for some were saying that John had been raised from the dead, others that Elijah had appeared, others again that one of the old prophets had come back to life. Herod said, 'As for John, I beheaded him myself; but who is this I hear such talk about?' And he was anxious to see him.

On their return the apostles told Jesus all they had done; and he took them with him and withdrew privately to a town called Bethsaida. But the crowds found out and followed him. He welcomed them, and spoke to them about the kingdom of God, and cured those who were in need of healing. When evening was drawing on, the Twelve approached him and said, 'Send these people away; then they can go into the villages and farms round about to find food and lodging; for we are in a lonely place here.' 'Give them something to eat yourselves', he replied. But they said, 'All we have is five loaves and two fishes, nothing more—unless perhaps we ourselves are to go and buy provisions for all this company.' (There were about five thousand men.) He said to his disciples, 'Make them sit down in groups of fifty or so.' They did so and got them all seated. Then, taking the five loaves and the two fishes, he looked up to heaven, said the blessing over them, broke them, and gave them to the disciples to distribute to the people. They all ate to their hearts' content; and when the scraps they left were picked up, they filled twelve great baskets.

K.J.V.

18 And it came to pass, as he was alone praying, his disciples were with him; and he asked them, saying, Whom say the people that I am? 19 They answering said, John the Baptist; but some *say,* Elias; and others *say,* that one of the old prophets is risen again. 20 He said unto them, But whom say ye that I am? Peter answering said, The Christ of God. 21And he straitly charged them, and commanded *them* to tell no man that thing; 22 Saying, The Son of man must suffer many things, and be rejected of the elders and chief priests and scribes, and be slain, and be raised the third day.

23 And he said to *them* all, If any *man* will come after me, let him deny himself, and take up his cross daily, and follow me. 24 For whosoever will save his life shall lose it: but whosoever will lose his life for my sake, the same shall save it. 25 For what is a man advantaged, if he gain the whole world, and lose himself, or be cast away? 26 For whosoever shall be ashamed of me and of my words, of him shall the Son of man be ashamed, when he shall come in his own glory, and *in his* Father's, and of the holy angels. 27 But I tell you of a truth, there be some standing here, which shall not taste of death, till they see the kingdom of God.

28 And it came to pass about an eight days after these sayings, he took Peter and John and James, and went up into a mountain to pray. 29And as he prayed, the fashion of his countenance was altered, and his raiment *was* white *and* glistering. 30And, behold, there talked with him two men, which were Moses and Elias: 31 Who appeared in glory, and spake of his decease which he should accomplish at Jerusalem. 32 But Peter and they that were with him were heavy with sleep: and when they were awake, they saw his glory, and the two men that stood with him. 33And it came to pass, as they departed from him, Peter said unto Jesus, Master, it is good for us to be here: and let us make three tabernacles; one for thee, and one for Moses, and one for Elias: not knowing what he said. 34 While he thus spake, there came a cloud, and overshadowed them: and they feared as they entered into the cloud. 35And there came a voice out of the cloud, saying, This is my beloved Son: hear him. 36And when the voice was past, Jesus was found alone. And they kept *it* close, and told no man in those days any of those things which they had seen.

R.S.V.

18 Now it happened that as he was praying alone the disciples were with him; and he asked them, "Who do the people say that I am?" 19And they answered, "John the Baptist; but others say, Elijah; and others, that one of the old prophets has risen." 20And he said to them, "But who do you say that I am?" And Peter answered, "The Christ of God." 21 But he charged and commanded them to tell this to no one, 22 saying, "The Son of man must suffer many things, and be rejected by the elders and chief priests and scribes, and be killed, and on the third day be raised."

23 And he said to all, "If any man would come after me, let him deny himself and take up his cross daily and follow me. 24 For whoever would save his life will lose it; and whoever loses his life for my sake, he will save it. 25 For what does it profit a man if he gains the whole world and loses or forfeits himself? 26 For whoever is ashamed of me and of my words, of him will the Son of man be ashamed when he comes in his glory and the glory of the Father and of the holy angels. 27 But I tell you truly, there are some standing here who will not taste death before they see the kingdom of God."

28 Now about eight days after these sayings he took with him Peter and John and James, and went up on the mountain to pray. 29And as he was praying, the appearance of his countenance was altered, and his raiment became dazzling white. 30And behold, two men talked with him, Moses and Elijah, 31 who appeared in glory and spoke of his departure, which he was to accomplish at Jerusalem. 32 Now Peter and those who were with him were heavy with sleep but kept awake, and they saw his glory and the two men who stood with him. 33And as the men were parting from him, Peter said to Jesus, "Master, it is well that we are here; let us make three booths, one for you and one for Moses and one for Elijah"—not knowing what he said. 34As he said this, a cloud came and overshadowed them; and they were afraid as they entered the cloud. 35And a voice came out of the cloud, saying, "This is my Son, my Chosen;[d] listen to him!" 36And when the voice had spoken, Jesus was found alone. And they kept silence and told no one in those days anything of what they had seen.

<hr>

[d] Other ancient authorities read *my Beloved.*

PHILLIPS

N.E.B.

Jesus asks a question and receives **9. 18**
Peter's momentous answer

Then came this incident. While Jesus was praying by himself, having only the disciples near him, he asked them this question:
"Who are the crowd saying that I am?"
"Some say that you are John the Baptist," they replied. "Others that you are Elijah, and others think that one of the old-time prophets has come to life again."
Then he said,
"And who do you say that I am?"
"God's Christ!" said Peter.

Jesus foretells his own suffering: **9. 21**
the paradox of losing life to find it

But Jesus expressly told them not to say a word to anybody, at the same time warning them of the inevitability of the Son of Man's great suffering, of his repudiation by the elders, chief priests and scribes, and of his death and of being raised to life again on the third day. Then he spoke to them all:
"If anyone wants to follow in my footsteps, he must give up all right to himself, carry his cross every day and keep close behind me. For the man who wants to save his life will lose it, but the man who loses his life for my sake will save it. For what is the use of a man gaining the whole world if he loses or forfeits his own soul? If anyone is ashamed of me and my words, the Son of Man will be ashamed of him, when he comes in his glory and the glory of the Father and the holy angels. I tell you the simple truth—there are men standing here today who will not taste death until they have seen the kingdom of God!"

Peter, John and James are allowed **9. 28**
to see the glory of Jesus

About eight days after these sayings, Jesus took Peter, James and John and went off with them to the hillside to pray. And then, while he was praying, the whole appearance of his face changed and his clothes became white and dazzling. And two men were talking with Jesus. They were Moses and Elijah—revealed in heavenly splendor, and their talk was about the way he must take and the end he must fulfill in Jerusalem. But Peter and his companions had been overcome by sleep and it was as they struggled into wakefulness that they saw the glory of Jesus and the two men standing with him. Just as they were parting from him, Peter said to Jesus:
"Master, it is wonderful for us to be here! Let us put up three shelters—one for you, one for Moses and one for Elijah." But he did not know what he was saying. While he was still talking, a cloud overshadowed them and awe swept over them as it enveloped them. A voice came out of the cloud, saying,
"This is my Son, my chosen! Listen to him!"
And while the voice was speaking, they found there was no one there at all but Jesus. The disciples were reduced to silence, and in those days never breathed a word to anyone of what they had seen.

One day when he was praying alone in the presence of his disciples, he asked them, 'Who do the people say I am?' They answered, 'Some say John the Baptist, others Elijah, others that one of the old prophets has come back to life.' 'And you,' he said, 'who do you say I am?' Peter answered, 'God's Messiah.' Then he gave them strict orders not to tell this to anyone. And he said, 'The Son of Man has to undergo great sufferings, and to be rejected by the elders, chief priests, and doctors of the law, to be put to death and to be raised again on the third day.'
And to all he said, 'If anyone wishes to be a follower of mine, he must leave self behind; day after day he must take up his cross, and come with me. Whoever cares for his own safety is lost; but if a man will let himself be lost for my sake, that man is safe. What will a man gain by winning the whole world, at the cost of his true self? For whoever is ashamed of me and mine,[a] the Son of Man will be ashamed of him, when he comes in his glory and the glory of the Father and the holy angels. And I tell you this: there are some of those standing here who will not taste death before they have seen the kingdom of God.'
About eight days after this conversation he took Peter, John, and James with him and went up into the hills to pray. And while he was praying the appearance of his face changed and his clothes became dazzling white. Suddenly there were two men talking with him; these were Moses and Elijah, who appeared in glory and spoke of his departure, the destiny he was to fulfil in Jerusalem. Meanwhile Peter and his companions had been in a deep sleep; but when they awoke, they saw his glory and the two men who stood beside him. And as these were moving away from Jesus, Peter said to him, 'Master, how good it is that we are here! Shall we make three shelters, one for you, one for Moses, and one for Elijah?'; but he spoke without knowing what he was saying. The words were still on his lips, when there came a cloud which cast a shadow over them; they were afraid as they entered the cloud, and from it came a voice: 'This is my Son, my Chosen; listen to him.' When the voice had spoken, Jesus was seen to be alone. The disciples kept silence and at that time told nobody anything of what they had seen.

[a] *Some witnesses read* me and my words.

K.J.V.

37 And it came to pass, that on the next day, when they were come down from the hill, much people met him. 38And, behold, a man of the company cried out, saying, Master, I beseech thee, look upon my son; for he is mine only child. 39And, lo, a spirit taketh him, and he suddenly crieth out; and it teareth him that he foameth again, and bruising him, hardly departeth from him. 40And I besought thy disciples to cast him out; and they could not. 41And Jesus answering said, O faithless and perverse generation, how long shall I be with you, and suffer you? Bring thy son hither. 42And as he was yet a coming, the devil threw him down, and tare *him*. And Jesus rebuked the unclean spirit, and healed the child, and delivered him again to his father.

43 And they were all amazed at the mighty power of God. But while they wondered every one at all things which Jesus did, he said unto his disciples, 44 Let these sayings sink down into your ears: for the Son of man shall be delivered into the hands of men. 45 But they understood not this saying, and it was hid from them, that they perceived it not: and they feared to ask him of that saying.

46 Then there arose a reasoning among them, which of them should be greatest. 47And Jesus, perceiving the thought of their heart, took a child, and set him by him, 48And said unto them, Whosoever shall receive this child in my name receiveth me; and whosoever shall receive me, receiveth him that sent me: for he that is least among you all, the same shall be great.

49 And John answered and said, Master, we saw one casting out devils in thy name; and we forbade him, because he followeth not with us. 50And Jesus said unto him, Forbid *him* not: for he that is not against us is for us.

51 And it came to pass, when the time was come that he should be received up, he steadfastly set his face to go to Jerusalem, 52And sent messengers before his face: and they went, and entered into a village of the Samaritans, to make ready for him. 53And they did not receive him, because his face was as though he would go to Jerusalem. 54And when his disciples James and John saw *this,* they said, Lord, wilt thou that

R.S.V.

37 On the next day, when they had come down from the mountain, a great crowd met him. 38And behold, a man from the crowd cried, "Teacher, I beg you to look upon my son, for he is my only child; 39 and behold, a spirit seizes him, and he suddenly cries out; it convulses him till he foams, and shatters him, and will hardly leave him. 40And I begged your disciples to cast it out, but they could not." 41 Jesus answered, "O faithless and perverse generation, how long am I to be with you and bear with you? Bring your son here." 42 While he was coming, the demon tore him and convulsed him. But Jesus rebuked the unclean spirit, and healed the boy, and gave him back to his father. 43And all were astonished at the majesty of God.

But while they were all marveling at everything he did, he said to his disciples, 44 "Let these words sink into your ears; for the Son of man is to be delivered into the hands of men." 45 But they did not understand this saying, and it was concealed from them, that they should not perceive it; and they were afraid to ask him about this saying.

46 And an argument arose among them as to which of them was the greatest. 47 But when Jesus perceived the thought of their hearts, he took a child and put him by his side, 48 and said to them, "Whoever receives this child in my name receives me, and whoever receives me receives him who sent me: for he who is least among you all is the one who is great."

49 John answered, "Master, we saw a man casting out demons in your name, and we forbade him, because he does not follow with us." 50 But Jesus said to him, "Do not forbid him; for he that is not against you is for you."

51 When the days drew near for him to be received up, he set his face to go to Jerusalem. 52And he sent messengers ahead of him, who went and entered a village of the Samaritans, to make ready for him; 53 but the people would not receive him, because his face was set toward Jerusalem. 54And when his disciples James and John saw it, they said, "Lord, do you want us

Jesus heals an epileptic boy   9. 37

Then on the following day, as they came down the hillside, a great crowd met him. Suddenly a man from the crowd shouted out:

"Master, please come and look at my son! He's my only child, and without any warning some spirit gets hold of him and he calls out suddenly. Then it convulses him until he foams at the mouth, and only after a fearful struggle does it go away and leave him bruised all over. I begged your disciples to get rid of it, but they couldn't."

"You really are an unbelieving and difficult people," replied Jesus. "How long must I be with you, how long must I put up with you? Bring him here to me."

But even while the boy was on his way, the spirit hurled him to the ground in a dreadful convulsion. Then Jesus reprimanded the evil spirit, healed the lad and handed him back to his father. And everybody present was amazed at this demonstration of the power of God.

The realism of Jesus in the midst   9. 43b
of enthusiasm

And while everybody was full of wonder at all the things they saw him do, Jesus was saying to the disciples,

"Store up in your minds what I tell you nowadays, for the Son of Man is going to be handed over to the power of men."

But they made no sense of this saying—something made it impossible for them to understand it, and they were afraid to ask him what he meant.

Jesus and "greatness"   9. 46

Then an argument arose among them as to who should be the greatest. But Jesus, knowing what they were arguing about, took a little child and made him stand by his side. And then he said to them:

"Anyone who accepts a little child in my name is really accepting me, and the man who accepts me is really accepting the one who sent me. It is the humblest among you all who is really the greatest."

Then John broke in,

"Master, we saw a man driving out evil spirits in your name, but we stopped him, for he is not one of us who follow you."

But Jesus told him,

"You must not stop him. The man who is not against you is on your side."

He sets off for Jerusalem to   9. 51
meet inevitable death

Now as the days before he should be taken back into Heaven were running out, he resolved to go to Jerusalem, and sent messengers in front of him. They set out and entered a Samaritan village to make preparations for him. But the people there refused to welcome him because he was obviously intending to go to Jerusalem. When the disciples James and John saw this, they said,

Next day when they came down from the hills he was met by a large crowd. All at once there was a shout from a man in the crowd: 'Master, look at my son, I implore you, my only child. From time to time a spirit seizes him, gives a sudden scream, and throws him into convulsions with foaming at the mouth, and it keeps on mauling him and will hardly let him go. I asked your disciples to cast it out, but they could not.' Jesus answered, 'What an unbelieving and perverse generation! How long shall I be with you and endure you all? Bring your son here.' But before the boy could reach him the devil dashed him to the ground and threw him into convulsions. Jesus rebuked the unclean spirit, cured the boy, and gave him back to his father. And they were all struck with awe at the majesty of God.

Amid the general wonder and admiration at all he was doing, Jesus said to his disciples, 'What I now say is for you: ponder my words. The Son of Man is going to be given up into the power of men.' But they did not understand what he said; it had been hidden from them so that they should not[a] perceive its drift; and they were afraid to ask him what it meant.

A dispute arose among them: which of them was the greatest? Jesus knew what was passing in their minds, so he took a child by the hand and stood him at his side, and said, 'Whoever receives this child in my name receives me; and whoever receives me receives the One who sent me. For the least among you all—he is the greatest.'

'Master,' said John, 'we saw a man casting out devils in your name, but as he is not one of us we tried to stop him.' Jesus said to him, 'Do not stop him, for he who is not against you is on your side.'

Journeys and Encounters

As the time approached when he was to be taken up to heaven, he set his face resolutely towards Jerusalem, and sent messengers ahead. They set out and went into a Samaritan village to make arrangements for him; but the villagers would not have him because he was making for Jerusalem. When the disciples James and John saw this they said, 'Lord, may we call down fire

[a] Or it was so obscure to them that they could not . . .

we command fire to come down from heaven, and consume them, even as Elias did? 55 But he turned, and rebuked them, and said, Ye know not what manner of spirit ye are of. 56 For the Son of man is not come to destroy men's lives, but to save *them*. And they went to another village.

57 And it came to pass, that, as they went in the way, a certain *man* said unto him, Lord, I will follow thee whithersoever thou goest. 58And Jesus said unto him, Foxes have holes, and birds of the air *have* nests; but the Son of man hath not where to lay *his* head. 59And he said unto another, Follow me. But he said, Lord, suffer me first to go and bury my father. 60 Jesus said unto him, Let the dead bury their dead: but go thou and preach the kingdom of God. 61And another also said, Lord, I will follow thee; but let me first go bid them farewell, which are at home at my house. 62And Jesus said unto him, No man, having put his hand to the plough, and looking back, is fit for the kingdom of God.

to bid fire come down from heaven and consume them?" *e* 55 But he turned and rebuked them.*f* 56And they went on to another village.

57 As they were going along the road, a man said to him, "I will follow you wherever you go." 58And Jesus said to him, "Foxes have holes, and birds of the air have nests; but the Son of man has nowhere to lay his head." 59To another he said, "Follow me." But he said, "Lord, let me first go and bury my father." 60 But he said to him, "Leave the dead to bury their own dead; but as for you, go and proclaim the kingdom of God." 61Another said, "I will follow you, Lord; but let me first say farewell to those at my home." 62 Jesus said to him, "No one who puts his hand to the plow and looks back is fit for the kingdom of God."

10 After these things the Lord appointed other seventy also, and sent them two and two before his face into every city and place, whither he himself would come. 2 Therefore said he unto them, The harvest truly *is* great, but the labourers *are* few: pray ye therefore the Lord of the harvest, that he would send forth labourers into his harvest. 3 Go your ways: behold, I send you forth as lambs among wolves. 4 Carry neither purse, nor scrip, nor shoes: and salute no man by the way. 5And into whatsoever house ye enter, first say, Peace *be* to this house. 6And if the son of peace be there, your peace shall rest upon it: if not, it shall turn to you again. 7And in the same house remain, eating and drinking such things as they give: for the labourer is worthy of his hire. Go not from house to house. 8And into whatsoever city ye enter, and they receive you, eat such things as are set before you: 9And heal the sick that are therein, and say unto them, The kingdom of God is come nigh unto you. 10 But into whatsoever city ye enter, and they receive you not, go your ways out into the streets of the same, and say, 11 Even the very dust of your city, which cleaveth on us, we do wipe off against you: notwithstanding, be ye sure of this, that the kingdom of God is come nigh unto you. 12 But I say unto you, that it shall be more tolerable in that day for Sodom, than for that city. 13 Woe unto thee, Chorazin! woe unto thee, Bethsaida! for if the mighty works had been done in Tyre and Sidon, which have been done in you, they had a great while ago repented, sitting in sackcloth and ashes. 14 But it shall be more tolerable for Tyre and Sidon at the judgment, than for you. 15And thou, Capernaum, which art exalted to heaven, shalt be thrust down to hell. 16 He that heareth you heareth me; and he that despiseth you despiseth me; and he that despiseth me despiseth him that sent me.

10 After this the Lord appointed seventy*g* others, and sent them on ahead of him, two by two, into every town and place where he himself was about to come. 2And he said to them, "The harvest is plentiful, but the laborers are few; pray therefore the Lord of the harvest to send out laborers into his harvest. 3 Go your way; behold, I send you out as lambs in the midst of wolves. 4 Carry no purse, no bag, no sandals; and salute no one on the road. 5 Whatever house you enter, first say, 'Peace be to this house!' 6And if a son of peace is there, your peace shall rest upon him; but if not, it shall return to you. 7And remain in the same house, eating and drinking what they provide, for the laborer deserves his wages; do not go from house to house. 8 Whenever you enter a town and they receive you, eat what is set before you; 9 heal the sick in it and say to them, 'The kingdom of God has come near to you.' 10 But whenever you enter a town and they do not receive you, go into its streets and say, 11 'Even the dust of your town that clings to our feet, we wipe off against you; nevertheless know this, that the kingdom of God has come near.' 12 I tell you, it shall be more tolerable on that day for Sodom than for that town.

13 "Woe to you, Chorazin! woe to you, Bethsaida! for if the mighty works done in you had been done in Tyre and Sidon, they would have repented long ago, sitting in sackcloth and ashes. 14 But it shall be more tolerable in the judgment for Tyre and Sidon than for you. 15And you, Capernaum, will you be exalted to heaven? You shall be brought down to Hades.

16 "He who hears you hears me, and he who rejects you rejects me, and he who rejects me rejects him who sent me."

[e] Other ancient authorities add *as Elijah did.* [f] Other ancient authorities add *and he said, "You do not know what manner of spirit you are of; for the Son of man came not to destroy men's lives but to save them."* [g] Other ancient authorities read *seventy-two.*

"Master, do you want us to call down fire from heaven and burn them all up?"

But Jesus turned and reproved them, and they all went on to another village.

As the little company made its way along the road, a man said to him,

"I'm going to follow you wherever you go."

And Jesus replied,

"Foxes have earths, birds have nests, but the Son of Man has nowhere that he can call his own."

But he said to another man,

"Follow me."

And he replied,

"Let me go and bury my father first."

But Jesus told him:

"Leave the dead to bury their own dead. You must come away and preach the kingdom of God."

Another man said to him,

"I am going to follow you, Lord, but first let me bid farewell to my people at home."

But Jesus told him,

"Anyone who puts his hand to the plow and then looks behind him is useless for the kingdom of God."

from heaven to burn them up[a]?' But he turned and rebuked them,[b] and they went on to another village.

As they were going along the road a man said to him, 'I will follow you wherever you go.' Jesus answered, 'Foxes have their holes, the birds their roosts; but the Son of Man has nowhere to lay his head.' To another he said, 'Follow me', but the man replied, 'Let me go and bury my father first.' Jesus said, 'Leave the dead to bury their dead; you must go and announce the kingdom of God.'

Yet another said, 'I will follow you, sir; but let me first say goodbye to my people at home.' To him Jesus said, 'No one who sets his hand to the plough and then keeps looking back[c] is fit for the kingdom of God.'

Jesus now dispatches thirty-five couples to preach and heal the sick **10. 1**

Later on, the Lord commissioned seventy other disciples, and sent them off in twos as advance parties into every town and district where he intended to go.

"There is a great harvest," he told them, "but only a few are working in it—which means you must pray to the Lord of the harvest that he will send out more reapers.

"Now go on your way. I am sending you out like lambs among wolves. Don't carry a purse or a bag or a pair of shoes, and don't stop to pass the time of day with anyone you meet on the road. When you go into a house, say first of all, 'Peace be to this household!' If there is a lover of peace there, he will accept your words of blessing, and if not, they will come back to you. Stay in the same house and eat and drink whatever they put before you—a workman deserves his wages. But don't move from one house to another.

"Whatever town you go into and the people welcome you, eat the meals they give you and heal the people who are ill there. Tell them, 'The kingdom of God is very near to you now.' But whenever you come into a town and they will not welcome you, you must go into the streets and say, 'We brush off even the dust of your town from our feet as a protest against you. But it is still true that the kingdom of God has arrived!' I assure you that it will be better for Sodom in 'that day' than for that town.

"Alas for you, Chorazin, and alas for you, Bethsaida! For if Tyre and Sidon had seen the demonstrations of God's power that you have seen, they would have repented long ago and sat in sackcloth and ashes. It will be better for Tyre and Sidon in the judgment than for you! As for you, Capernaum, are you on your way up to heaven? I tell you you will go hurtling down among the dead!"

Then he added to the seventy:

"Whoever listens to you is listening to me, and the man who has no use for you has no use for me either. And the man who has no use for me has no use for the one who sent me!"

10 After this the Lord appointed a further seventy-two[d] and sent them on ahead in pairs to every town and place he was going to visit himself. He said to them: 'The crop is heavy, but labourers are scarce; you must therefore beg the owner to send labourers to harvest his crop. Be on your way. And look, I am sending you like lambs among wolves. Carry no purse or pack, and travel barefoot. Exchange no greetings on the road. When you go into a house, let your first words be, "Peace to this house." If there is a man of peace there, your peace will rest upon him; if not, it will return and rest upon you. Stay in that one house, sharing their food and drink; for the worker earns his pay. Do not move from house to house. When you come into a town and they make you welcome, eat the food provided for you; heal the sick there, and say, "The kingdom of God has come close to you." When you enter a town and they do not make you welcome, go out into its streets and say, "The very dust of your town that clings to our feet we wipe off to your shame. Only take note of this: the kingdom of God has come close." I tell you, it will be more bearable for Sodom on the great Day than for that town.

'Alas for you, Chorazin! Alas for you, Bethsaida! If the miracles that were performed in you had been performed in Tyre and Sidon, they would have repented long ago, sitting in sackcloth and ashes. But it will be more bearable for Tyre and Sidon at the Judgement than for you. And as for you, Capernaum, will you be exalted to the skies? No, brought down to the depths!

'Whoever listens to you listens to me; whoever rejects you rejects me. And whoever rejects me rejects the One who sent me.'

[a] *Some witnesses add* as Elijah did. [b] *Some witnesses insert* 'You do not know', he said, 'to what spirit you belong; (56) for the Son of Man did not come to destroy men's lives but to save them.' [c] *Some witnesses read* No one who looks back as he sets hand to the plough . . . [d] *Some witnesses read* seventy.

K.J.V.

17 And the seventy returned again with joy, saying, Lord, even the devils are subject unto us through thy name. 18And he said unto them, I beheld Satan as lightning fall from heaven. 19 Behold, I give unto you power to tread on serpents and scorpions, and over all the power of the enemy; and nothing shall by any means hurt you. 20 Notwithstanding, in this rejoice not, that the spirits are subject unto you; but rather rejoice, because your names are written in heaven.

21 In that hour Jesus rejoiced in spirit, and said, I thank thee, O Father, Lord of heaven and earth, that thou hast hid these things from the wise and prudent, and hast revealed them unto babes: even so, Father; for so it seemed good in thy sight. 22All things are delivered to me of my Father: and no man knoweth who the Son is, but the Father; and who the Father is, but the Son, and *he* to whom the Son will reveal *him.*

23 And he turned him unto *his* disciples, and said privately, Blessed *are* the eyes which see the things that ye see: 24 For I tell you, that many prophets and kings have desired to see those things which ye see, and have not seen *them;* and to hear those things which ye hear, and have not heard *them.*

25 And, behold, a certain lawyer stood up, and tempted him, saying, Master, what shall I do to inherit eternal life? 26 He said unto him, What is written in the law? how readest thou? 27And he answering said, Thou shalt love the Lord thy God with all thy heart, and with all thy soul, and with all thy strength, and with all thy mind; and thy neighbour as thyself. 28And he said unto him, Thou hast answered right: this do, and thou shalt live. 29 But he, willing to justify himself, said unto Jesus, And who is my neighbour? 30And Jesus answering said, A certain *man* went down from Jerusalem to Jericho, and fell among thieves, which stripped him of his raiment, and wounded *him,* and departed, leaving *him* half dead. 31And by chance there came down a certain priest that way; and when he saw him, he passed by on the other side. 32And likewise a Levite, when he was at the place, came and looked *on him,* and passed by on the other side. 33 But a certain Samaritan, as he journeyed, came where he was; and when he saw him, he had compassion *on him,* 34And went to *him,* and bound up his wounds, pouring in oil and wine, and set him on his own beast, and brought him to an inn, and took care of

R.S.V.

17 The seventy[g] returned with joy, saying, "Lord, even the demons are subject to us in your name!" 18And he said to them, "I saw Satan fall like lightning from heaven. 19 Behold, I have given you authority to tread upon serpents and scorpions, and over all the power of the enemy; and nothing shall hurt you. 20 Nevertheless do not rejoice in this, that the spirits are subject to you; but rejoice that your names are written in heaven."

21 In that same hour he rejoiced in the Holy Spirit and said, "I thank thee, Father, Lord of heaven and earth, that thou hast hidden these things from the wise and understanding and revealed them to babes; yea, Father, for such was thy gracious will.[h] 22All things have been delivered to me by my Father; and no one knows who the Son is except the Father, or who the Father is except the Son and any one to whom the Son chooses to reveal him."

23 Then turning to the disciples he said privately, "Blessed are the eyes which see what you see! 24 For I tell you that many prophets and kings desired to see what you see, and did not see it, and to hear what you hear, and did not hear it."

25 And behold, a lawyer stood up to put him to the test, saying, "Teacher, what shall I do to inherit eternal life?" 26 He said to him, "What is written in the law? How do you read?" 27And he answered, "You shall love the Lord your God with all your heart, and with all your soul, and with all your strength, and with all your mind; and your neighbor as yourself." 28And he said to him, "You have answered right; do this, and you will live."

29 But he, desiring to justify himself, said to Jesus, "And who is my neighbor?" 30 Jesus replied, "A man was going down from Jerusalem to Jericho, and he fell among robbers, who stripped him and beat him, and departed, leaving him half dead. 31 Now by chance a priest was going down that road; and when he saw him he passed by on the other side. 32 So likewise a Levite, when he came to the place and saw him, passed by on the other side. 33 But a Samaritan, as he journeyed, came to where he was; and when he saw him, he had compassion, 34 and went to him and bound up his wounds, pouring on oil and wine; then he set him on his own beast and brought him to an inn, and took

[g] Other ancient authorities read *seventy-two*. [h] Or *so it was well-pleasing before thee.*

Jesus tells the returned **10. 17**
missioners not to be enthusiastic
over mere power

Later the seventy came back full of joy.
"Lord," they said, "even evil spirits obey us
when we use your name!"

"Yes," returned Jesus, "I was watching and
saw Satan fall from heaven like a flash of lightning! It is true that I have given you the power
to tread on snakes and scorpions and to overcome all the enemy's power—there is nothing at
all that can do you any harm. Yet it is not your
power over evil spirits which should give such
joy, but the fact that your names are written in
Heaven."

Jesus prays aloud to his Father **10. 21**

At that moment Jesus himself was inspired
with joy, and exclaimed:

"O Father, Lord of Heaven and earth, I thank
you for hiding these things from the clever and
intelligent and for showing them to mere children! Yes, I thank you, Father, that this was
your will." Then he went on:

"Everything has been put in my hands by my
Father; and nobody knows who the Son really
is except the Father. Nobody knows who the
Father really is except the Son—and the man to
whom the Son chooses to reveal him!"

Then he turned to his disciples and said to
them quietly:

"How fortunate you are to see what you are
seeing! I tell you that many prophets and kings
have wanted to see what you are seeing but they
never saw it, and to hear what you are hearing
but they never heard it."

Jesus shows the relevance of the **10. 25**
Law to actual living

Then one of the experts in the Law stood up
to test him and said,

"Master, what must I do to be sure of eternal
life?"

"What does the Law say and what has your
reading taught you?" said Jesus.

"The Law says, 'Thou shalt love the Lord thy
God with all thy heart and with all thy soul and
with all thy strength and with all thy mind—
and thy neighbor as thyself,'" he replied.

"Quite right," said Jesus. "Do that and you
will live."

But the man, wanting to justify himself, continued,

"But who is my 'neighbor'?"

And Jesus gave him the following reply:

"A man was once on his way down from
Jerusalem to Jericho. He fell into the hands of
bandits who stripped off his clothes, beat him
up, and left him half dead. It so happened that
a priest was going down that road, and when he
saw him he passed by on the other side. A Levite also came on the scene, and when he saw
him he too passed by on the other side. But
then a Samaritan traveler came along to the
place where the man was lying, and at the sight
of him he was touched with pity. He went across
to him and bandaged his wounds, pouring on
oil and wine. Then he put him on his own mule,
brought him to an inn and did what he could

The seventy-two[a] came back jubilant. 'In your
name, Lord,' they said, 'even the devils submit
to us.' He replied, 'I watched how Satan fell, like
lightning, out of the sky. And now you see that
I have given you the power to tread underfoot
snakes and scorpions and all the forces of the
enemy, and nothing will ever harm you.[b] Nevertheless, what you should rejoice over is not that
the spirits submit to you, but that your names
are enrolled in heaven.'

At that moment Jesus exulted in the Holy[c]
Spirit and said, 'I thank thee, Father, Lord of
heaven and earth, for hiding these things from
the learned and wise, and revealing them to the
simple. Yes, Father, such[d] was thy choice.' Then
turning to his disciples he said,[e] 'Everything is
entrusted to me by my Father; and no one
knows who the Son is but the Father, or who
the Father is but the Son, and those to whom the
Son may choose to reveal him.'

Turning to his disciples in private he said,
'Happy the eyes that see what you are seeing! I
tell you, many prophets and kings wished to see
what you now see, yet never saw it; to hear what
you hear, yet never heard it.'

On one occasion a lawyer came forward to
put this test question to him: 'Master, what
must I do to inherit eternal life?' Jesus said,
'What is written in the Law? What is your reading of it?' He replied, 'Love the Lord your God
with all your heart, with all your soul, with all
your strength, and with all your mind; and your
neighbour as yourself.' 'That is the right answer,'
said Jesus; 'do that and you will live.'

But he wanted to vindicate himself, so he said
to Jesus, 'And who is my neighbour?' Jesus replied, 'A man was on his way from Jerusalem
down to Jericho when he fell in with robbers,
who stripped him, beat him, and went off leaving
him half dead. It so happened that a priest was
going down by the same road; but when he saw
him, he went past on the other side. So too a
Levite came to the place, and when he saw him
went past on the other side. But a Samaritan
who was making the journey came upon him,
and when he saw him was moved to pity. He
went up and bandaged his wounds, bathing them
with oil and wine. Then he lifted him on to his
own beast, brought him to an inn, and looked

[a] *Some witnesses read* seventy. [b] *Or* and he will
have no way at all to harm you. [c] *Some witnesses
omit* Holy. [d] *Or* Yes, I thank thee, Father, that
such . . . [e] *Some witnesses omit* Then . . . he
said.

K.J.V.

him. 35And on the morrow when he departed, he took out two pence, and gave *them* to the host, and said unto him, Take care of him: and whatsoever thou spendest more, when I come again, I will repay thee. 36 Which now of these three, thinkest thou, was neighbour unto him that fell among the thieves? 37And he said, He that shewed mercy on him. Then said Jesus unto him, Go, and do thou likewise.

38 Now it came to pass, as they went, that he entered into a certain village: and a certain woman named Martha received him into her house. 39And she had a sister called Mary, which also sat at Jesus' feet, and heard his word. 40 But Martha was cumbered about much serving, and came to him, and said, Lord, dost thou not care that my sister hath left me to serve alone? bid her therefore that she help me. 41And Jesus answered and said unto her, Martha, Martha, thou art careful and troubled about many things: 42 But one thing is needful; and Mary hath chosen that good part, which shall not be taken away from her.

R.S.V.

care of him. 35And the next day he took out two denarii [i] and gave them to the innkeeper, saying, 'Take care of him; and whatever more you spend, I will repay you when I come back.' 36 Which of these three, do you think, proved neighbor to the man who fell among the robbers?" 37 He said, "The one who showed mercy on him." And Jesus said to him, "Go and do likewise."

38 Now as they went on their way, he entered a village; and a woman named Martha received him into her house. 39And she had a sister called Mary, who sat at the Lord's feet and listened to his teaching. 40 But Martha was distracted with much serving; and she went to him and said, "Lord, do you not care that my sister has left me to serve alone? Tell her then to help me." 41 But the Lord answered her, "Martha, Martha, you are anxious and troubled about many things; 42 one thing is needful.[j] Mary has chosen the good portion, which shall not be taken away from her."

11 And it came to pass, that, as he was praying in a certain place, when he ceased, one of his disciples said unto him, Lord, teach us to pray, as John also taught his disciples. 2And he said unto them, When ye pray, say, Our Father which art in heaven, Hallowed be thy name. Thy kingdom come. Thy will be done, as in heaven, so in earth. 3 Give us day by day our daily bread. 4And forgive us our sins; for we also forgive every one that is indebted to us. And lead us not into temptation; but deliver us from evil. 5And he said unto them, Which of you shall have a friend, and shall go unto him at midnight, and say unto him, Friend, lend me three loaves; 6 For a friend of mine in his journey is come to me, and I have nothing to set before him? 7And he from within shall answer and say, Trouble me not: the door is now shut, and my children are with me in bed; I cannot rise and give thee. 8 I say unto you, Though he will not rise and give him, because he is his friend, yet because of his importunity he will rise and give him as many as he needeth. 9And I say unto you, Ask, and it shall be given you; seek, and ye shall find; knock, and it shall be opened unto you. 10 For every one that asketh receiveth; and he that seeketh findeth; and to him that knocketh it shall be opened. 11 If a son shall ask bread of any of you that is a father,

11 He was praying in a certain place, and when he ceased, one of his disciples said to him, "Lord, teach us to pray, as John taught his disciples." 2And he said to them, "When you pray, say:

"Father, hallowed be thy name. Thy kingdom come. 3 Give us each day our daily bread;[k] 4 and forgive us our sins, for we ourselves forgive every one who is indebted to us; and lead us not into temptation."

5 And he said to them, "Which of you who has a friend will go to him at midnight and say to him, 'Friend, lend me three loaves; 6 for a friend of mine has arrived on a journey, and I have nothing to set before him'; 7 and he will answer from within, 'Do not bother me; the door is now shut, and my children are with me in bed; I cannot get up and give you anything'? 8 I tell you, though he will not get up and give him anything because he is his friend, yet because of his importunity he will rise and give him whatever he needs. 9And I tell you, Ask, and it will be given you; seek, and you will find; knock, and it will be opened to you. 10 For every one who asks receives, and he who seeks finds, and to him who knocks it will be opened. 11 What father among you, if his son asks for[i]

[i] The denarius was worth about twenty cents. [j] Other ancient authorities read *few things are needful, or only one*. [k] Or *our bread for the morrow*. [l] Other ancient authorities insert *bread, will give him a stone; or if he asks for*.

for him. Next day he took out two silver coins and gave them to the innkeeper with the words: 'Look after him, will you? I will pay you back whatever more you spend, when I come through here on my return.' Which of these three seems to you to have been a neighbor to the bandits' victim?"

"The man who gave him practical sympathy," he replied.

"Then you go and give the same," returned Jesus.

Yet emphasizes the need for quiet listening to his words   10. 38

As they continued their journey, Jesus came to a village and a woman called Martha welcomed him to her house. She had a sister by the name of Mary who settled down at the Lord's feet and was listening to what he said. But Martha was very worried about her elaborate preparations and she burst in, saying:

"Lord, don't you *mind* that my sister has left me to do everything by myself? Tell her to get up and help me!"

But the Lord answered her:

"Martha, my dear, you are worried and bothered about providing so many things. Only a few things are really needed, perhaps only one. Mary has chosen the best part and you must not tear it away from her!"

Jesus gives a model prayer   11. 1

One day it happened that Jesus was praying in a certain place, and after he had finished, one of his disciples said,

"Lord, teach us how to pray, as John used to teach his disciples."

"When you pray," returned Jesus, "you should say, 'Father, may your name be honored—may your kingdom come! Give us each day the bread we need, and forgive us our sins, for we forgive anyone who owes anything to us; and keep us clear of temptation.' "

The willingness of the Father to answer prayer   11. 5

Then he added:

"If any of you has a friend, and goes to him in the middle of the night and says, 'Lend me three loaves, my dear fellow, for a friend of mine has just arrived after a journey and I have no food to put in front of him'; and then he answers from inside the house: 'Don't bother me with your troubles. The front door is locked and my children and I have gone to bed. I simply cannot get up now and give you anything!' Yet, I tell you, that even if he won't get up and give him what he wants simply because he is his friend, yet if he persists, he will rouse himself and give him everything he needs. And so I tell you, ask and it will be given you, search and you will find, knock and the door will be opened to you. The one who asks will always receive; the one who is searching will always find, and the door is opened to the man who knocks. Some of you are fathers, and if your son asks

after him there. Next day he produced two silver pieces and gave them to the innkeeper and said, "Look after him; and if you spend any more, I will repay you on my way back." Which of these three do you think was neighbour to the man who fell into the hands of the robbers?' He answered, 'The one who showed him kindness.' Jesus said, 'Go and do as he did.'

While they were on their way Jesus came to a village where a woman named Martha made him welcome in her home. She had a sister, Mary, who seated herself at the Lord's feet and stayed there listening to his words. Now Martha was distracted by her many tasks, so she came to him and said, 'Lord, do you not care that my sister has left me to get on with the work by myself? Tell her to come and lend a hand.' But the Lord answered, 'Martha, Martha, you are fretting and fussing about so many things; but one thing is necessary.[a] The part that Mary has chosen is best; and it shall not be taken away from her.'

11 Once, in a certain place, Jesus was at prayer. When he ceased, one of his disciples said, 'Lord, teach us to pray, as John taught his disciples.' He answered, 'When you pray, say,

'Father,[b] thy name be hallowed;
Thy kingdom come.[c]
Give us each day our daily bread.[d]
And forgive us our sins,
For we too forgive all who have done us wrong.
And do not bring us to the test." '[e]

He added, 'Suppose one of you has a friend who comes to him in the middle of the night and says, "My friend, lend me three loaves, for a friend of mine on a journey has turned up at my house, and I have nothing to offer him"; and he replies from inside, "Do not bother me. The door is shut for the night; my children and I have gone to bed; and I cannot get up and give you what you want." I tell you that even if he will not provide for him out of friendship, the very shamelessness of the request will make him get up and give him all he needs. And so I say to you, ask, and you will receive; seek, and you will find; knock, and the door will be opened. For everyone who asks receives, he who seeks finds, and to him who knocks, the door will be opened.

'Is there a father among you who will offer

[a] *Some witnesses read* but few things are necessary, or rather, one alone; *others omit* you are fretting . . . necessary. [b] *Some witnesses read* Our Father in heaven. [c] *One witness reads* Thy kingdom come upon us; *some others have* Thy Holy Spirit come upon us and cleanse us; *some insert* Thy will be done, On earth as in heaven. [d] *Or* our bread for the morrow. [e] *Some witnesses add* But save us from the evil one.

K.J.V.

will he give him a stone? or if *he ask* a fish, will he for a fish give him a serpent? 12 Or if he shall ask an egg, will he offer him a scorpion? 13 If ye then, being evil, know how to give good gifts unto your children; how much more shall *your* heavenly Father give the Holy Spirit to them that ask him?

14 And he was casting out a devil, and it was dumb. And it came to pass, when the devil was gone out, the dumb spake; and the people wondered. 15 But some of them said, He casteth out devils through Beelzebub the chief of the devils. 16And others, tempting *him,* sought of him a sign from heaven. 17 But he, knowing their thoughts, said unto them, Every kingdom divided against itself is brought to desolation; and a house *divided* against a house falleth. 18 If Satan also be divided against himself, how shall his kingdom stand? because ye say that I cast out devils through Beelzebub. 19And if I by Beelzebub cast out devils, by whom do your sons cast *them* out? therefore shall they be your judges. 20 But if I with the finger of God cast out devils, no doubt the kingdom of God is come upon you. 21 When a strong man armed keepeth his palace, his goods are in peace: 22 But when a stronger than he shall come upon him, and overcome him, he taketh from him all his armour wherein he trusted, and divideth his spoils. 23 He that is not with me is against me; and he that gathereth not with me scattereth. 24 When the unclean spirit is gone out of a man, he walketh through dry places, seeking rest; and finding none, he saith, I will return unto my house whence I came out. 25And when he cometh, he findeth *it* swept and garnished. 26 Then goeth he, and taketh *to him* seven other spirits more wicked than himself; and they enter in, and dwell there: and the last *state* of that man is worse than the first.

27 And it came to pass, as he spake these things, a certain woman of the company lifted up her voice, and said unto him, Blessed *is* the womb that bare thee, and the paps which thou hast sucked. 28 But he said, Yea, rather, blessed *are* they that hear the word of God, and keep it.

R.S.V.

a fish, will instead of a fish give him a serpent; 12 or if he asks for an egg, will give him a scorpion? 13 If you then, who are evil, know how to give good gifts to your children, how much more will the heavenly Father give the Holy Spirit to those who ask him!"

14 Now he was casting out a demon that was dumb; when the demon had gone out, the dumb man spoke, and the people marveled. 15 But some of them said, "He casts out demons by Beelzebul, the prince of demons"; 16 while others, to test him, sought from him a sign from heaven. 17 But he, knowing their thoughts, said to them, "Every kingdom divided against itself is laid waste, and house falls upon house. 18And if Satan also is divided against himself, how will his kingdom stand? For you say that I cast out demons by Beelzebul. 19And if I cast out demons by Beelzebul, by whom do your sons cast them out? Therefore they shall be your judges. 20 But if it is by the finger of God that I cast out demons, then the kingdom of God has come upon you. 21 When a strong man, fully armed, guards his own palace, his goods are in peace; 22 but when one stronger than he assails him and overcomes him, he takes away his armor in which he trusted, and divides his spoil. 23 He who is not with me is against me, and he who does not gather with me scatters.

24 "When the unclean spirit has gone out of a man, he passes through waterless places seeking rest; and finding none he says, 'I will return to my house from which I came.' 25And when he comes he finds it swept and put in order. 26 Then he goes and brings seven other spirits more evil than himself, and they enter and dwell there; and the last state of that man becomes worse than the first."

27 As he said this, a woman in the crowd raised her voice and said to him, "Blessed is the womb that bore you, and the breasts that you sucked!" 28 But he said, "Blessed rather are those who hear the word of God and keep it!"

PHILLIPS

N.E.B.

you for some fish would you give him a snake instead, or if he asks you for an egg would you make him a present of a scorpion? So, if you, for all your evil, know how to give good things to your children, how much more likely is it that your Heavenly Father will give the Holy Spirit to those who ask him!"

Jesus shows the absurdity of   11. 14
"his being in league
with the devil"

Another time, Jesus was expelling an evil spirit which was preventing a man from speaking, and as soon as the evil spirit left him the dumb man found his speech, to the amazement of the crowds.

But some of them said,

"He expels these spirits because he is in league with Beelzebub, the chief of the evil spirits."

Others among them, to test him, tried to get a sign from Heaven out of him. But he knew what they were thinking, and told them:

"Any kingdom divided against itself is doomed, and a disunited household will collapse. And if Satan disagrees with Satan, how does his kingdom continue?—for I know you are saying that I expel evil spirits because I am in league with Beelzebub. But if I do expel devils because I am an ally of Beelzebub, who is your own sons' ally when they do the same thing? They can settle that question for you. But if it is by the finger of God that I am expelling evil spirits, *then the kingdom of God has swept over you unawares!*

"When a strong man armed to the teeth guards his own house, his property is in peace. But when a stronger man comes and conquers him, he removes all the arms on which he pinned his faith and divides the spoil among his friends.

"Anyone who is not with me is against me, and the man who does not gather with me is really scattering.

The danger of a spriritual   11. 24
vacuum in a man's soul

"When the evil spirit comes out of a man, it wanders through waterless places looking for rest, and when it fails to find any, it says, 'I will go back to my house from which I came.' When it arrives, it finds it cleaned and all in order. Then it goes and collects seven other spirits more evil than itself to keep it company, and they all go in and make themselves at home. The last state of that man is worse than the first."

Jesus brings sentimentality   11. 27
down to earth

And while he was still saying this, a woman in the crowd called out and said,

"Oh, what a blessing for a woman to have brought you into the world and nursed you!"

But Jesus replied,

"Yes, but a far greater blessing to hear the word of God and obey it."

his son[a] a snake when he asks for fish, or a scorpion when he asks for an egg? If you, then, bad as you are, know how to give your children what is good for them, how much more will the heavenly Father give the Holy Spirit[b] to those who ask him!'

He was driving out a devil which was dumb; and when the devil had come out, the dumb man began to speak. The people were astonished, but some of them said, 'It is by Beelzebub prince of devils that he drives the devils out.' Others, by way of a test, demanded of him a sign from heaven. But he knew what was in their minds, and said, 'Every kingdom divided against itself goes to ruin, and a divided household falls. Equally if Satan is divided against himself, how can his kingdom stand?—since, as you would have it, I drive out the devils by Beelzebub. If it is by Beelzebub that I cast out devils, by whom do your own people drive them out? If this is your argument, they themselves will refute you. But if it is by the finger of God that I drive out the devils, then be sure the kingdom of God has already come upon you.

'When a strong man fully armed is on guard over his castle his possessions are safe. But when someone stronger comes upon him and overpowers him, he carries off the arms and armour on which the man had relied and divides the plunder.

'He who is not with me is against me, and he who does not gather with me scatters.[c]

'When an unclean spirit comes out of a man it wanders over the deserts seeking a resting-place; and finding none, it says, "I will go back to the home I left." So it returns and finds the house[d] swept clean, and tidy. Off it goes and collects seven other spirits more wicked than itself, and they all come in and settle down; and in the end the man's plight is worse than before.'

While he was speaking thus, a woman in the crowd called out, 'Happy the womb that carried you and the breasts that suckled you!' He rejoined, 'No, happy are those who hear the word of God and keep it.'

---

[a] *Some witnesses insert* a stone when he asks for bread, or . . . [b] *Some witnesses read* a good gift; *some others read* good things. [c] *Some witnesses add* me. [d] *Some witnesses insert* unoccupied.

K.J.V.

29 And when the people were gathered thick together, he began to say, This is an evil generation: they seek a sign; and there shall no sign be given it, but the sign of Jonas the prophet. 30 For as Jonas was a sign unto the Ninevites, so shall also the Son of man be to this generation. 31 The queen of the south shall rise up in the judgment with the men of this generation, and condemn them: for she came from the utmost parts of the earth to hear the wisdom of Solomon; and, behold, a greater than Solomon is here. 32 The men of Nineveh shall rise up in the judgment with this generation, and shall condemn it: for they repented at the preaching of Jonas; and, behold, a greater than Jonas is here. 33 No man, when he hath lighted a candle, putteth it in a secret place, neither under a bushel, but on a candlestick, that they which come in may see the light. 34 The light of the body is the eye: therefore when thine eye is single, thy whole body also is full of light; but when thine eye is evil, thy body also is full of darkness. 35 Take heed therefore, that the light which is in thee be not darkness. 36 If thy whole body therefore be full of light, having no part dark, the whole shall be full of light, as when the bright shining of a candle doth give thee light.

37 And as he spake, a certain Pharisee besought him to dine with him: and he went in, and sat down to meat. 38And when the Pharisee saw it, he marvelled that he had not first washed before dinner. 39And the Lord said unto him, Now do ye Pharisees make clean the outside of the cup and the platter; but your inward part is full of ravening and wickedness. 40 Ye fools, did not he, that made that which is without, make that which is within also? 41 But rather give alms of such things as ye have; and, behold, all things are clean unto you. 42 But woe unto you, Pharisees! for ye tithe mint and rue and all manner of herbs, and pass over judgment and the love of God: these ought ye to have done, and not to leave the other undone. 43 Woe unto you, Pharisees! for ye love the uppermost seats in the synagogues, and greetings in the markets. 44 Woe unto you, scribes and Pharisees, hypocrites! for ye are as graves which appear not, and the men that walk over them are not aware of them.

45 Then answered one of the lawyers, and said unto him, Master, thus saying thou reproachest us also. 46And he said, Woe unto you also, ye lawyers! for ye lade men with burdens grievous to be borne, and ye yourselves touch not the burdens with one of your fingers. 47 Woe unto you! for ye build the sepulchres of the

R.S.V.

29 When the crowds were increasing, he began to say, "This generation is an evil generation; it seeks a sign, but no sign shall be given to it except the sign of Jonah. 30 For as Jonah became a sign to the men of Nineveh, so will the Son of man be to this generation. 31 The queen of the South will arise at the judgment with the men of this generation and condemn them; for she came from the ends of the earth to hear the wisdom of Solomon, and behold, something greater than Solomon is here. 32 The men of Nineveh will arise at the judgment with this generation and condemn it; for they repented at the preaching of Jonah, and behold, something greater than Jonah is here.

33 "No one after lighting a lamp puts it in a cellar or under a bushel, but on a stand, that those who enter may see the light. 34 Your eye is the lamp of your body; when your eye is sound, your whole body is full of light; but when it is not sound, your body is full of darkness. 35 Therefore be careful lest the light in you be darkness. 36 If then your whole body is full of light, having no part dark, it will be wholly bright, as when a lamp with its rays gives you light."

37 While he was speaking, a Pharisee asked him to dine with him; so he went in and sat at table. 38 The Pharisee was astonished to see that he did not first wash before dinner. 39And the Lord said to him, "Now you Pharisees cleanse the outside of the cup and of the dish, but inside you are full of extortion and wickedness. 40 You fools! Did not he who made the outside make the inside also? 41 But give for alms those things which are within; and behold, everything is clean for you.

42 "But woe to you Pharisees! for you tithe mint and rue and every herb, and neglect justice and the love of God; these you ought to have done, without neglecting the others. 43 Woe to you Pharisees! for you love the best seat in the synagogues and salutations in the market places. 44 Woe to you! for you are like graves which are not seen, and men walk over them without knowing it."

45 One of the lawyers answered him, "Teacher, in saying this you reproach us also." 46And he said, "Woe to you lawyers also! for you load men with burdens hard to bear, and you yourselves do not touch the burdens with one of your fingers. 47 Woe to you! for you build the tombs of the prophets whom your

PHILLIPS

His scathing judgment on his   **11. 29**
contemporary generation

Then as the people crowded closely around him, he continued:

"This is an evil generation! It looks for a sign and it will be given no sign except that of Jonah. Just as Jonah was a sign to the people of Nineveh, so will the Son of Man be a sign to this generation. When the judgment comes, the Queen of the South will rise up with the men of this generation and she will condemn them. For she came from the ends of the earth to listen to the wisdom of Solomon, and there is more than the wisdom of Solomon with you now! The men of Nineveh will stand up at the judgment with this generation and will condemn it. For they did repent when Jonah preached to them, and there is something more than Jonah's preaching with you now!

The need for complete sincerity   **11. 33**

"No one takes a lamp and puts it in a cupboard or under a bucket, but on a lampstand, so that those who come in can see the light. The lamp of your body is your eye. When your eye is sound, your whole body is full of light, but when your eye is evil your whole body is full of darkness. So be very careful that your light never becomes darkness. For if your whole body is full of light, with no part of it in shadow, it will all be radiant—it will be like having a bright lamp to give you light."

While he was talking, a Pharisee invited him to dinner. So he went into his house and sat down at table. The Pharisee noticed with some surprise that he did not wash before the meal. But the Lord said to him:

"You Pharisees are fond of cleaning the outside of your cups and dishes, but inside yourselves you are full of greed and wickedness! Have you no sense? Don't you realize that the one who made the outside is the maker of the inside as well? If you would only make the inside clean by doing good to others, the outside things become clean as a matter of course! But alas for you Pharisees, for you pay out your tithe of mint and rue and every little herb, and lose sight of the justice and the love of God. Yet these are the things you ought to have been concerned with—it need not mean leaving the lesser duties undone. Yes, alas for you Pharisees, who love the front seats in the synagogues and having men bow down to you in public! Alas for you, for you are like unmarked graves —men walk over your corruption without ever knowing it is there."

Jesus denounces the learned   **11. 45**
for obscuring the truth

Then one of the experts in the Law said to him,

"Master, when you say things like this, you are insulting us as well."

And he returned:

"Yes, and I do blame you experts in the Law! For you pile up back-breaking burdens for men to bear, but you yourselves will not raise a finger to lift them. Alas for you, for you build memorial tombs for the prophets—the very men whom

N.E.B.

With the crowds swarming round him he went on to say: 'This is a wicked generation. It demands a sign, and the only sign that will be given to it is the sign of Jonah. For just as Jonah was a sign to the Ninevites, so will the Son of Man be to this generation. At the Judgement, when the men of this generation are on trial, the Queen of the South will appear against[a] them and ensure their condemnation, for she came from the ends of the earth to hear the wisdom of Solomon; and what is here is greater than Solomon. The men of Nineveh will appear at the Judgement when the men of this generation are on trial, and ensure[b] their condemnation, for they repented at the preaching of Jonah; and what is here is greater than Jonah.

'No one lights a lamp and puts it in a cellar,[c] but rather on the lamp-stand so that those who enter may see the light. The lamp of your body is the eye. When your eyes are sound, you have light for your whole body; but when the eyes are bad, you are in darkness. See to it then that the light you have is not darkness. If you have light for your whole body with no trace of darkness, it will all be as bright as when a lamp flashes its rays upon you.'

When he had finished speaking, a Pharisee invited him to dinner. He came in and sat down. The Pharisee noticed with surprise that he had not begun by washing before the meal. But the Lord said to him, 'You Pharisees! You clean the outside of cup and plate; but inside you there is nothing but greed and wickedness. You fools! Did not he who made the outside make the inside too? But let what is in the cup[d] be given in charity, and all is clean.

'Alas for you Pharisees! You pay tithes of mint and rue and every garden-herb, but have no care for justice and the love of God. It is these you should have practised, without neglecting the others.[e]

'Alas for you Pharisees! You love the seats of honour in synagogues, and salutations in the market-places.

'Alas, alas, you are like unmarked graves over which men may walk without knowing it.'

In reply to this one of the lawyers said, 'Master, when you say things like this you are insulting us too.' Jesus rejoined: 'Yes, you lawyers, it is no better with you! For you load men with intolerable burdens, and will not put a single finger to the load.

'Alas, you build the tombs of the prophets

[a] *Or* will be raised to life together with . . . [b] *Or* At the Judgement the men of Nineveh will rise again together with the men of this generation and will ensure . . . [c] *Some witnesses insert* or under the meal-tub. [d] *Or* what you can afford. [e] *Some witnesses omit* It is . . . others.

213

K.J.V.

prophets, and your fathers killed them. 48 Truly ye bear witness that ye allow the deeds of your fathers: for they indeed killed them, and ye build their sepulchres. 49 Therefore also said the wisdom of God, I will send them prophets and apostles, and *some* of them they shall slay and persecute: 50 That the blood of all the prophets, which was shed from the foundation of the world, may be required of this generation; 51 From the blood of Abel unto the blood of Zacharias, which perished between the altar and the temple: verily I say unto you, It shall be required of this generation. 52 Woe unto you, lawyers! for ye have taken away the key of knowledge: ye entered not in yourselves, and them that were entering in ye hindered. 53And as he said these things unto them, the scribes and the Pharisees began to urge *him* vehemently, and to provoke him to speak of many things: 54 Laying wait for him, and seeking to catch something out of his mouth, that they might accuse him.

12 In the mean time, when there were gathered together an innumerable multitude of people, insomuch that they trode one upon another, he began to say unto his disciples first of all, Beware ye of the leaven of the Pharisees, which is hypocrisy. 2 For there is nothing covered, that shall not be revealed; neither hid, that shall not be known. 3 Therefore, whatsoever ye have spoken in darkness shall be heard in the light; and that which ye have spoken in the ear in closets shall be proclaimed upon the housetops. 4And I say unto you my friends, Be not afraid of them that kill the body, and after that have no more that they can do. 5 But I will forewarn you whom ye shall fear: Fear him, which after he hath killed hath power to cast into hell; yea, I say unto you, Fear him. 6Are not five sparrows sold for two farthings, and not one of them is forgotten before God? 7 But even the very hairs of your head are all numbered. Fear not therefore: ye are of more value than many sparrows. 8Also I say unto you, Whosoever shall confess me before men, him shall the Son of man also confess before the angels of God: 9 But he that denieth me before men shall be denied before the angels of God. 10And whosoever shall speak a word against the Son of man, it shall be forgiven him: but unto him that blasphemeth against the Holy Ghost it shall not be forgiven. 11And when they bring you unto the synagogues, and *unto* magistrates, and powers, take ye no thought how or what thing ye shall answer, or what ye shall say: 12 For the Holy Ghost shall teach you in the same hour what ye ought to say. 13 And one of the company said unto him, Master, speak to my brother, that he divide the inheritance with me. 14And he said unto him,

R.S.V.

fathers killed. 48 So you are witnesses and consent to the deeds of your fathers; for they killed them, and you build their tombs. 49 Therefore also the Wisdom of God said, 'I will send them prophets and apostles, some of whom they will kill and persecute,' 50 that the blood of all the prophets, shed from the foundation of the world, may be required of this generation, 51 from the blood of Abel to the blood of Zechariah, who perished between the altar and the sanctuary. Yes, I tell you, it shall be required of this generation. 52 Woe to you lawyers! for you have taken away the key of knowledge; you did not enter yourselves, and you hindered those who were entering."

53 As he went away from there, the scribes and the Pharisees began to press him hard, and to provoke him to speak of many things, 54 lying in wait for him, to catch at something he might say.

12 In the meantime, when so many thousands of the multitude had gathered together that they trod upon one another, he began to say to his disciples first, "Beware of the leaven of the Pharisees, which is hypocrisy. 2 Nothing is covered up that will not be revealed, or hidden that will not be known. 3 Whatever you have said in the dark shall be heard in the light, and what you have whispered in private rooms shall be proclaimed upon the housetops.

4 "I tell you, my friends, do not fear those who kill the body, and after that have no more that they can do. 5 But I will warn you whom to fear: fear him who, after he has killed, has power to cast into hell;[m] yes, I tell you, fear him! 6Are not five sparrows sold for two pennies? And not one of them is forgotten before God? 7 Why, even the hairs of your head are all numbered. Fear not; you are of more value than many sparrows.

8 "And I tell you, every one who acknowledges me before men, the Son of man also will acknowledge before the angels of God; 9 but he who denies me before men will be denied before the angels of God. 10And every one who speaks a word against the Son of man will be forgiven; but he who blasphemes against the Holy Spirit will not be forgiven. 11And when they bring you before the synagogues and the rulers and the authorities, do not be anxious how or what you are to answer or what you are to say; 12 for the Holy Spirit will teach you in that very hour what you ought to say."

13 One of the multitude said to him, "Teacher, bid my brother divide the inheritance with me." 14 But he said to him, "Man, who

[m] Greek *Gehenna*.

PHILLIPS

your fathers murdered. You show clearly enough how you approve your fathers' actions. They did the actual killing and you put up a memorial to it. That is why the wisdom of God has said, 'I will send them prophets and apostles; some they will kill and some they will persecute!' So that the blood of all the prophets shed from the foundation of the earth, from Abel to Zachariah who died between the altar and the sanctuary, shall be charged to this generation!

"Alas for you experts in the Law, for you have taken away the key of knowledge. You have never gone in yourselves and you have hindered everyone else who was at the door!"

And when he left the house, the scribes and the Pharisees began to regard him with bitter animosity and tried to draw him out on a great many subjects, waiting to pounce on some incriminating remark.

Meanwhile, the crowds had gathered in thousands, so that they were actually treading on one another's toes, and Jesus, speaking primarily to his disciples, said:

"Be on your guard against yeast—I mean the yeast of the Pharisees, which is sheer pretense. For there is nothing covered up which is not going to be exposed, nor anything private which is not going to be made public. Whatever you may say in the dark will be heard in daylight, and whatever you whisper within four walls will be shouted from the housetops.

Man need only fear God   *12. 4*

"I tell you, as friends of mine, that you need not be afraid of those who can kill the body, but afterward cannot do anything more. I will show you the only one you need to fear—the one who, after he has killed, has the power to throw you into destruction! Yes, I tell you, it is right to stand in awe of him. The market price of five sparrows is two cents, isn't it? Yet not one of them is forgotten in God's sight. Why, the very hairs of your heads are all numbered! Don't be afraid, then; you are worth more than a great many sparrows! I tell you that every man who publicly acknowledges me, I, the Son of Man, will acknowledge in the presence of the angels of God. But the man who publicly disowns me will find himself disowned before the angels of God!

"Anyone who speaks against the Son of Man will be forgiven, but there is no forgiveness for the man who speaks evil against the Holy Spirit. And when they bring you before the synagogues and magistrates and authorities, don't worry as to what defense you are going to put up or what words you are going to use. For the Holy Spirit will tell you at the time what is the right thing for you to say."

Jesus gives a warning about   *12. 13*
the love of material security

Then someone out of the crowd said to him, "Master, tell my brother to share his legacy with me."

But Jesus replied,

N.E.B.

whom your fathers murdered, and so testify that you approve of the deeds your fathers did; they committed the murders and you provide the tombs.

'This is why the Wisdom of God said, "I will send them prophets and messengers; and some of these they will persecute and kill"; so that this generation will have to answer for the blood of all the prophets shed since the foundation of the world; from the blood of Abel to the blood of Zechariah who perished between the altar and the sanctuary. I tell you, this generation will have to answer for it all.

'Alas for you lawyers! You have taken away the key of knowledge. You did not go in yourselves, and those who were on their way in, you stopped.'

After he had left the house, the lawyers and Pharisees began to assail him fiercely and to ply him with a host of questions, laying snares to catch him with his own words.

12 Meanwhile, when a crowd of many thousands had gathered, packed so close that they were treading on one another, he began to speak first to his disciples: 'Beware of the leaven of the Pharisees; I mean their hypocrisy. There is nothing covered up that will not be uncovered, nothing hidden that will not be made known. You may take it, then, that everything you have said in the dark will be heard in broad daylight, and what you have whispered behind closed doors will be shouted from the house-tops.

'To you who are my friends I say: Do not fear those who kill the body and after that have nothing more they can do. I will warn you whom to fear: fear him who, after he has killed, has authority to cast into hell. Believe me, he is the one to fear.

'Are not sparrows five for twopence? And yet not one of them is overlooked by God. More than that, even the hairs of your head have all been counted. Have no fear; you are worth more than any number of sparrows.

'I tell you this: everyone who acknowledges me before men, the Son of Man will acknowledge before the angels of God; but he who disowns me before men will be disowned before the angels of God.

'Anyone who speaks a word against the Son of Man will receive forgiveness; but for him who slanders the Holy Spirit there will be no forgiveness.

'When you are brought before synagogues and state authorities, do not begin worrying about how you will conduct your defence or what you will say. For when the time comes the Holy Spirit will instruct you what to say.'

A man in the crowd said to him, 'Master, tell my brother to divide the family property with me.' He replied, 'My good man, who set me

Man, who made me a judge or a divider over you? 15And he said unto them, Take heed, and beware of covetousness: for a man's life consisteth not in the abundance of the things which he possesseth. 16And he spake a parable unto them, saying, The ground of a certain rich man brought forth plentifully: 17And he thought within himself, saying, What shall I do, because I have no room where to bestow my fruits? 18And he said, This will I do: I will pull down my barns, and build greater; and there will I bestow all my fruits and my goods. 19And I will say to my soul, Soul, thou hast much goods laid up for many years; take thine ease, eat, drink, *and* be merry. 20 But God said unto him, *Thou* fool, this night thy soul shall be required of thee: then whose shall those things be, which thou hast provided? 21 So *is* he that layeth up treasure for himself, and is not rich toward God.

22 And he said unto his disciples, Therefore I say unto you, Take no thought for your life, what ye shall eat; neither for the body, what ye shall put on. 23 The life is more than meat, and the body *is more* than raiment. 24 Consider the ravens: for they neither sow nor reap; which neither have storehouse nor barn; and God feedeth them: how much more are ye better than the fowls? 25And which of you with taking thought can add to his stature one cubit? 26 If ye then be not able to do that thing which is least, why take ye thought for the rest? 27 Consider the lilies how they grow: they toil not, they spin not; and yet I say unto you, that Solomon in all his glory was not arrayed like one of these. 28 If then God so clothe the grass, which is to day in the field, and to morrow is cast into the oven; how much more *will he clothe* you, O ye of little faith? 29And seek not ye what ye shall eat, or what ye shall drink, neither be ye of doubtful mind. 30 For all these things do the nations of the world seek after: and your Father knoweth that ye have need of these things.

31 But rather seek ye the kingdom of God; and all these things shall be added unto you. 32 Fear not, little flock; for it is your Father's good pleasure to give you the kingdom. 33 Sell that ye have, and give alms; provide yourselves bags which wax not old, a treasure in the heavens that faileth not, where no thief approacheth, neither moth corrupteth. 34 For where your treasure is, there will your heart be also. 35 Let your loins be girded about, and *your* lights burning; 36And ye yourselves like unto men that wait for their lord, when he will return from the wedding; that, when he cometh and knocketh, they may open unto him immediately. 37 Blessed *are* those servants, whom the lord when he cometh shall find watching: verily I say unto you, that he shall gird himself, and make them to sit down to meat, and will come forth and serve them. 38And if he shall come in the second watch, or come in the third watch, and find *them* so, blessed are those servants. 39And this know, that if the goodman of the house had known what hour the thief would come, he would have

made me a judge or divider over you?" 15And he said to them, "Take heed, and beware of all covetousness; for a man's life does not consist in the abundance of his possessions." 16And he told them a parable, saying, "The land of a rich man brought forth plentifully; 17 and he thought to himself, 'What shall I do, for I have nowhere to store my crops?' 18And he said, 'I will do this: I will pull down my barns, and build larger ones; and there I will store all my grain and my goods. 19And I will say to my soul, Soul, you have ample goods laid up for many years; take your ease, eat, drink, be merry.' 20 But God said to him, 'Fool! This night your soul is required of you; and the things you have prepared, whose will they be?' 21 So is he who lays up treasure for himself, and is not rich toward God."

22 And he said to his disciples, "Therefore I tell you, do not be anxious about your life, what you shall eat, nor about your body, what you shall put on. 23 For life is more than food, and the body more than clothing. 24 Consider the ravens: they neither sow nor reap, they have neither storehouse nor barn, and yet God feeds them. Of how much more value are you than the birds! 25And which of you by being anxious can add a cubit to his span of life?[n] 26 If then you are not able to do as small a thing as that, why are you anxious about the rest? 27 Consider the lilies, how they grow; they neither toil nor spin;[o] yet I tell you, even Solomon in all his glory was not arrayed like one of these. 28 But if God so clothes the grass which is alive in the field today and tomorrow is thrown into the oven, how much more will he clothe you, O men of little faith! 29And do not seek what you are to eat and what you are to drink, nor be of anxious mind. 30 For all the nations of the world seek these things; and your Father knows that you need them. 31 Instead, seek his[p] kingdom, and these things shall be yours as well.

32 "Fear not, little flock, for it is your Father's good pleasure to give you the kingdom. 33 Sell your possessions, and give alms; provide yourselves with purses that do not grow old, with a treasure in the heavens that does not fail, where no thief approaches and no moth destroys. 34 For where your treasure is, there will your heart be also.

35 "Let your loins be girded and your lamps burning, 36 and be like men who are waiting for their master to come home from the marriage feast, so that they may open to him at once when he comes and knocks. 37 Blessed are those servants whom the master finds awake when he comes; truly, I say to you, he will gird himself and have them sit at table, and he will come and serve them. 38 If he comes in the second watch, or in the third, and finds them so, blessed are those servants! 39 But know this, that if the householder had known at what hour the thief was coming, he would have been awake

[n] Or *to his stature.* [o] Other ancient authorities read *Consider the lilies; they neither spin nor weave.* [p] Other ancient authorities read *God's.*

PHILLIPS

"My dear man, who appointed me a judge or arbitrator in your affairs?"

And then, turning to the disciples, he said to them:

"Notice that, and be on your guard against covetousness in any shape or form. For a man's real life in no way depends upon the number of his possessions."

Then he gave them a parable in these words:

"Once upon a time a rich man's farmland produced heavy crops. So he said to himself, 'What shall I do, for I have no room to store this harvest of mine?' Then he said: 'I know what I'll do. I'll pull down my barns and build bigger ones where I can store all my grain and my goods and I can say to my soul, Soul, you have plenty of good things stored up there for years to come. Relax! Eat, drink and have a good time!' But God said to him, 'You fool, this very night you will be asked for *your soul!* Then who is going to possess all that you have prepared?' That is what happens to the man who hoards things for himself and is not rich where God is concerned."

And then he added to the disciples:

"That is why I tell you; don't worry about life, wondering what you are going to eat. And stop bothering about what clothes you will need. Life is much more important than food, and the body more important than clothes. Think of the ravens. They neither sow nor reap, and they have neither store nor barn, but God feeds them. And how much more valuable do you think you are than birds? Can any of you make himself an inch taller however much he worries about it? And if you can't manage a little thing like this, why do you worry about anything else? Think of the wild flowers, and how they neither work nor weave. Yet I tell you that Solomon in all his glory was never arrayed like one of these. If God so clothes the grass, which flowers in the field today and is burned in the stove tomorrow, is he not much more likely to clothe you, you little-faiths? You must not set your heart on what you eat or drink, nor must you live in a state of anxiety. The whole heathen world is busy about getting food and drink, and your Father knows well enough that you need such things. No, set your heart on his kingdom, and your food and drink will come as a matter of course. Don't be afraid, you tiny flock! Your Father plans to give you the kingdom. Sell your possessions and give the money away. Get yourselves purses that never grow old, inexhaustible treasure in Heaven, where no thief can ever reach it, or moth ruin it. For wherever your treasure is, you may be certain that your heart will be there too!

Jesus' disciples must   **12. 35**
be on the alert

"You must be ready dressed and have your lamps alight, like men who wait to welcome their lord and master on his return from the wedding feast, so that when he comes and knocks at the door they may open it for him at once. Happy are the servants whom their lord finds on the alert when he arrives. I assure you that he will then take off his outer clothes, make them sit down to dinner, and come and wait on them. And if he should come just after midnight or in the very early morning and find them still on the alert, their happiness is assured. But be certain of this, that if the householder had known the time when the burglar would come,

N.E.B.

over you to judge or arbitrate?' [a] Then he said to the people, 'Beware! Be on your guard against greed of every kind, for even when a man has more than enough, his wealth does not give him life.' And he told them this parable: 'There was a rich man whose land yielded heavy crops. He debated with himself: "What am I to do? I have not the space to store my produce. This is what I will do," said he: "I will pull down my storehouses and build them bigger. I will collect in them all my corn and other goods, and then say to myself, 'Man, you have plenty of good things laid by, enough for many years: take life easy, eat, drink, and enjoy yourself.'" But God said to him, "You fool, this very night you must surrender your life; you have made your money —who will get it now?" That is how it is with the man who amasses wealth for himself and remains a pauper in the sight of God.[b]

'Therefore,' he said to his disciples, 'I bid you put away anxious thoughts about food to keep you alive and clothes to cover your body. Life is more than food, the body more than clothes. Think of the ravens: they neither sow nor reap; they have no storehouse or barn; yet God feeds them. You are worth far more than the birds! Is there a man among you who by anxious thought can add a foot to his height[c]? If, then, you cannot do even a very little thing, why are you anxious about the rest?

'Think of the lilies: they neither spin nor weave;[d] yet I tell you, even Solomon in all his splendour was not attired like one of these. But if that is how God clothes the grass, which is growing in the field today, and tomorrow is thrown on the stove, how much more will he clothe you! How little faith you have! And so you are not to set your mind on food and drink; you are not to worry. For all these are things for the heathen to run after; but you have a Father who knows that you need them. No, set your mind upon his kingdom, and all the rest will come to you as well.

'Have no fear, little flock; for your Father has chosen to give you the Kingdom. Sell your possessions and give in charity. Provide for yourselves purses that do not wear out, and never-failing wealth in heaven, where no thief can get near it, no moth destroy it. For where your wealth is, there will your heart be also.

'Be ready for action, with belts fastened and lamps alight. Be like men who wait for their master's return from a wedding-party, ready to let him in the moment he arrives and knocks. Happy are those servants whom the master finds on the alert when he comes. I tell you this: he will buckle his belt, seat them at table, and come and wait on them. Even if it is the middle of the night or before dawn when he comes, happy they if he finds them alert. And remember, if the householder had known what time the burglar was coming he would not have let his

[a] *Some witnesses omit* or arbitrate. [b] *Some witnesses omit* That . . . God; *others add at the end* When he said this he cried out, 'If you have ears to hear, then hear.' [c] *Or* a day to his life. [d] *Many witnesses read* they grow, they do not toil or spin.

K.J.V.

watched, and not have suffered his house to be broken through. 40 Be ye therefore ready also: for the Son of man cometh at an hour when ye think not.

41 Then Peter said unto him, Lord, speakest thou this parable unto us, or even to all? 42 And the Lord said, Who then is that faithful and wise steward, whom *his* lord shall make ruler over his household, to give *them their* portion of meat in due season? 43 Blessed *is* that servant, whom his lord when he cometh shall find so doing. 44 Of a truth I say unto you, that he will make him ruler over all that he hath. 45 But and if that servant say in his heart, My lord delayeth his coming; and shall begin to beat the menservants and maidens, and to eat and drink, and to be drunken; 46 The lord of that servant will come in a day when he looketh not for *him*, and at an hour when he is not aware, and will cut him in sunder, and will appoint him his portion with the unbelievers. 47 And that servant, which knew his lord's will, and prepared not *himself*, neither did according to his will, shall be beaten with many *stripes*. 48 But he that knew not, and did commit things worthy of stripes, shall be beaten with few *stripes*. For unto whomsoever much is given, of him shall be much required; and to whom men have committed much, of him they will ask the more.

49 I am come to send fire on the earth: and what will I, if it be already kindled? 50 But I have a baptism to be baptized with; and how am I straitened till it be accomplished! 51 Suppose ye that I am come to give peace on earth? I tell you, Nay; but rather division: 52 For from henceforth there shall be five in one house divided, three against two, and two against three. 53 The father shall be divided against the son, and the son against the father; the mother against the daughter, and the daughter against the mother; the mother in law against her daughter in law, and the daughter in law against her mother in law.

54 And he said also to the people, When ye see a cloud rise out of the west, straightway ye say, There cometh a shower; and so it is. 55 And when *ye see* the south wind blow, ye say, There will be heat; and it cometh to pass. 56 *Ye* hypocrites, ye can discern the face of the sky and of the earth; but how is it that ye do not discern this time? 57 Yea, and why even of yourselves judge ye not what is right?

58 When thou goest with thine adversary to the magistrate, *as thou art* in the way, give diligence that thou mayest be delivered from him; lest he hale thee to the judge, and the judge deliver thee to the officer, and the officer cast thee into prison. 59 I tell thee, thou shalt not depart thence, till thou hast paid the very last mite.

R.S.V.

and *q* would not have left his house to be broken into. 40 You also must be ready; for the Son of man is coming at an hour you do not expect."

41 Peter said, "Lord, are you telling this parable for us or for all?" 42 And the Lord said, "Who then is the faithful and wise steward, whom his master will set over his household, to give them their portion of food at the proper time? 43 Blessed is that servant whom his master when he comes will find so doing. 44 Truly I tell you, he will set him over all his possessions. 45 But if that servant says to himself, 'My master is delayed in coming,' and begins to beat the menservants and the maidservants, and to eat and drink and get drunk, 46 the master of that servant will come on a day when he does not expect him and at an hour he does not know, and will punish *r* him, and put him with the unfaithful. 47 And that servant who knew his master's will, but did not make ready or act according to his will, shall receive a severe beating. 48 But he who did not know, and did what deserved a beating, shall receive a light beating. Every one to whom much is given, of him will much be required; and of him to whom men commit much they will demand the more.

49 "I came to cast fire upon the earth; and would that it were already kindled! 50 I have a baptism to be baptized with; and how I am constrained until it is accomplished! 51 Do you think that I have come to give peace on earth? No, I tell you, but rather division; 52 for henceforth in one house there will be five divided, three against two and two against three; 53 they will be divided, father against son and son against father, mother against daughter and daughter against her mother, mother-in-law against her daughter-in-law and daughter-in-law against her mother-in-law."

54 He also said to the multitudes, "When you see a cloud rising in the west, you say at once, 'A shower is coming'; and so it happens. 55 And when you see the south wind blowing, you say, 'There will be scorching heat'; and it happens. 56 You hypocrites! You know how to interpret the appearance of earth and sky; but why do you not know how to interpret the present time?

57 "And why do you not judge for yourselves what is right? 58 As you go with your accuser before the magistrate, make an effort to settle with him on the way, lest he drag you to the judge, and the judge hand you over to the officer, and the officer put you in prison. 59 I tell you, you will never get out till you have paid the very last copper."

[q] Other ancient authorities omit *would have been awake and.* [r] Or *cut him in pieces.*

he would not have let his house be broken into. So you must be on the alert, for the Son of Man is coming at a time when you may not expect him."

Then Peter said to him,

"Lord, do you mean this parable for us or for everybody?"

But the Lord continued:

"Well, who will be the faithful, sensible steward whom his master will put in charge of his household to give them their supplies at the proper time? Happy is the servant if his master finds him so doing when he returns. I tell you he will promote him to look after all his property. But suppose the servant says to himself, 'My master takes his time about returning,' and then begins to beat the men and women servants and to eat and drink and get drunk, that servant's lord and master will return suddenly and unexpectedly, and he will punish him severely and send him to share the penalty of the unfaithful. The slave who knows his master's plan but does not get ready or act upon it will be severely punished, but the servant who did not know the plan, though he has done wrong, will be let off lightly. Much will be expected from the one who has been given much, and the more a man is trusted, the more people will expect of him.

"It is fire that I have come to bring upon the earth—how I could wish it were already ablaze! There is a baptism that I must undergo and how strained I am until it is over!

Jesus declares that his coming   *12. 51*
is bound to bring division

"Do you think I have come to bring peace on the earth? No, I tell you, not peace, but division! For from now on, there will be five people divided against each other in one house, three against two, and two against three. It is going to be father against son, and son against father, and mother against daughter, and daughter against mother; mother-in-law against her daughter-in-law, and daughter-in-law against mother-in-law!"

Intelligence should be used   *12. 54*
not only about the weather
but about the times in
which men live

Then he said to the crowds:

"When you see a cloud rising in the west, you say at once that it is going to rain, and so it does. And when you feel the south wind blowing, you say that it is going to be hot, and so it is. You frauds! You know how to interpret the look of the earth and the sky. Why can't you interpret the meaning of the times in which you live?

"And why can't you decide for yourselves what is right? For instance, when you are going before the magistrate with your opponent, do your best to come to terms with him while you have the chance, or he may rush you off to the judge, and the judge hand you over to the police officer, and the police officer throw you into prison. I tell you you will never get out again until you have paid your last penny."

house be broken into. Hold yourselves ready, then, because the Son of Man is coming at the time you least expect him.'

Peter said, 'Lord, do you intend this parable specially for us or is it for everyone?' The Lord said, 'Well, who is the trusty and sensible man whom his master will appoint as his steward, to manage his servants and issue their rations at the proper time? Happy that servant who is found at his task when his master comes! I tell you this: he will be put in charge of all his master's property. But if that servant says to himself, "The master is a long time coming", and begins to bully the menservants and maids, and eat and drink and get drunk; then the master will arrive on a day that servant does not expect, at a time he does not know, and will cut him in pieces. Thus he will find his place among the faithless.

'The servant who knew his master's wishes, yet made no attempt to carry them out, will be flogged severely. But one who did not know them and earned a beating will be flogged less severely. Where a man has been given much, much will be expected of him; and the more a man has had entrusted to him the more he will be required to repay.

'I have come to set fire to the earth, and how I wish it were already kindled! I have a baptism to undergo, and how hampered I am until the ordeal is over! Do you suppose I came to establish peace on earth? No indeed, I have come to bring division. For from now on, five members of a family will be divided, three against two and two against three; father against son and son against father, mother against daughter and daughter against mother, mother against son's wife and son's wife against her mother-in-law.'

He also said to the people, 'When you see cloud banking up in the west, you say at once, "It is going to rain", and rain it does. And when the wind is from the south, you say, "There will be a heat-wave", and there is. What hypocrites you are! You know how to interpret the appearance of earth and sky; how is it you cannot interpret this fateful hour?

'And why can you not judge for yourselves what is the right course? While you are going with your opponent to court, make an effort to settle with him while you are still on the way; otherwise he may drag you before the judge, and the judge hand you over to the constable, and the constable put you in jail. I tell you, you will not come out till you have paid the last farthing.'

13 There were present at that season some that told him of the Galileans, whose blood Pilate had mingled with their sacrifices. 2And Jesus answering said unto them, Suppose ye that these Galileans were sinners above all the Galileans, because they suffered such things? 3 I tell you, Nay: but, except ye repent, ye shall all likewise perish. 4 Or those eighteen, upon whom the tower in Siloam fell, and slew them, think ye that they were sinners above all men that dwelt in Jerusalem? 5 I tell you, Nay: but, except ye repent, ye shall all likewise perish.

6 He spake also this parable; A certain *man* had a fig tree planted in his vineyard; and he came and sought fruit thereon, and found none. 7 Then said he unto the dresser of his vineyard, Behold, these three years I come seeking fruit on this fig tree, and find none: cut it down; why cumbereth it the ground? 8And he answering said unto him, Lord, let it alone this year also, till I shall dig about it, and dung *it:* 9And if it bear fruit, *well:* and if not, *then* after that thou shalt cut it down.

10 And he was teaching in one of the synagogues on the sabbath. 11And, behold, there was a woman which had a spirit of infirmity eighteen years, and was bowed together, and could in no wise lift up *herself.* 12And when Jesus saw her, he called *her to him,* and said unto her, Woman, thou art loosed from thine infirmity. 13And he laid *his* hands on her: and immediately she was made straight, and glorified God. 14And the ruler of the synagogue answered with indignation, because that Jesus had healed on the sabbath day, and said unto the people, There are six days in which men ought to work: in them therefore come and be healed, and not on the sabbath day. 15 The Lord then answered him, and said, *Thou* hypocrite, doth not each one of you on the sabbath loose his ox or *his* ass from the stall, and lead *him* away to watering? 16And ought not this woman, being a daughter of Abraham, whom Satan hath bound, lo, these eighteen years, be loosed from this bond on the sabbath day? 17And when he had said these things, all his adversaries were ashamed: and all the people rejoiced for all the glorious things that were done by him.

18 Then said he, Unto what is the kingdom of God like? and whereunto shall I resemble it? 19 It is like a grain of mustard seed, which a man took, and cast into his garden; and it grew,

13 There were some present at that very time who told him of the Galileans whose blood Pilate had mingled with their sacrifices. 2And he answered them, "Do you think that these Galileans were worse sinners than all the other Galileans, because they suffered thus? 3 I tell you, No; but unless you repent you will all likewise perish. 4 Or those eighteen upon whom the tower in Siloam fell and killed them, do you think that they were worse offenders than all the others who dwelt in Jerusalem? 5 I tell you, No; but unless you repent you will all likewise perish."

6 And he told this parable: "A man had a fig tree planted in his vineyard; and he came seeking fruit on it and found none. 7And he said to the vinedresser, 'Lo, these three years I have come seeking fruit on this fig tree, and I find none. Cut it down; why should it use up the ground?' 8And he answered him, 'Let it alone, sir, this year also, till I dig about it and put on manure. 9And if it bears fruit next year, well and good; but if not, you can cut it down.'"

10 Now he was teaching in one of the synagogues on the sabbath. 11And there was a woman who had had a spirit of infirmity for eighteen years; she was bent over and could not fully straighten herself. 12And when Jesus saw her, he called her and said to her, "Woman, you are freed from your infirmity." 13And he laid his hands upon her, and immediately she was made straight, and she praised God. 14 But the ruler of the synagogue, indignant because Jesus had healed on the sabbath, said to the people, "There are six days on which work ought to be done; come on those days and be healed, and not on the sabbath day." 15 Then the Lord answered him, "You hypocrites! Does not each of you on the sabbath untie his ox or his ass from the manger, and lead it away to water it? 16And ought not this woman, a daughter of Abraham whom Satan bound for eighteen years, be loosed from this bond on the sabbath day?" 17As he said this, all his adversaries were put to shame; and all the people rejoiced at all the glorious things that were done by him.

18 He said therefore, "What is the kingdom of God like? And to what shall I compare it? 19 It is like a grain of mustard seed which a man took and sowed in his garden; and it grew

Jesus is asked about the supposed   13. 1
significance of disasters

It was just at this moment that some people came up to tell him the story of the Galileans whose blood Pilate had mixed with that of their own sacrifices. Jesus made this reply to them:

"Are you thinking that these Galileans were worse sinners than any other men of Galilee because this happened to them? I assure you that is not so. You will all die just as miserable a death unless your hearts are changed! You remember those eighteen people who were killed at Siloam when the tower collapsed upon them? Are you imagining that they were worse offenders than any of the other people who lived in Jerusalem? I assure you they were not. You will all die as tragically unless your whole outlook is changed!"

And hints at God's patience   13. 6
with the Jewish nation

Then he gave them this parable:

"Once upon a time a man had a fig tree growing in his garden, and when he came to look for the figs he found none at all. So he said to his gardener, 'Look, I have come expecting fruit on this fig tree for three years running and never found any. Better cut it down. Why should it use up valuable space!' And the gardener replied: 'Master, don't touch it this year till I have had a chance to dig round it and give it a bit of manure. Then, if it bears after that, it will be all right. But if it doesn't, then you can cut it down.' "

Jesus reduces the sabbatarians   13. 10
to silence

It happened that he was teaching in one of the synagogues on the Sabbath day. In the congregation was a woman who for eighteen years had been ill from some psychological cause; she was bent double and was quite unable to straighten herself up. When Jesus noticed her, he called her and said,

"You are set free from your illness!"

And he put his hands upon her, and at once she stood upright and praised God. But the president of the synagogue, in his annoyance at Jesus' healing on the Sabbath, announced to the congregation:

"There are six days in which men may work. Come on one of them and be healed, and not on the Sabbath day!"

But the Lord answered him, saying:

"You hypocrites, every single one of you unties his ox or his ass from the stall on the Sabbath day and leads him away to water! This woman, a daughter of Abraham, whom you all know Satan has kept bound for eighteen years—surely she should be released from such bonds on the Sabbath day!"

These words reduced his opponents to shame, but the crowd was thrilled at all the glorious things he did.

Then he went on:

"What is the kingdom of God like? What illustration can I use to make it plain to you? It is like a grain of mustard seed which a man took and dropped in his own garden. It grew

13 At that very time there were some people present who told him about the Galileans whose blood Pilate had mixed with their sacrifices. He answered them: 'Do you imagine that, because these Galileans suffered this fate, they must have been greater sinners than anyone else in Galilee? I tell you they were not; but unless you repent, you will all of you come to the same end. Or the eighteen people who were killed when the tower fell on them at Siloam—do you imagine they were more guilty than all the other people living in Jerusalem? I tell you they were not; but unless you repent, you will all of you come to the same end.'

He told them this parable: 'A man had a fig-tree growing in his vineyard; and he came looking for fruit on it, but found none. So he said to the vine-dresser, "Look here! For the last three years I have come looking for fruit on this fig-tree without finding any. Cut it down. Why should it go on using up the soil?" But he replied, "Leave it, sir, this one year while I dig round it and manure it. And if it bears next season, well and good; if not, you shall have it down." '

One Sabbath he was teaching in a synagogue, and there was a woman there possessed by a spirit that had crippled her for eighteen years. She was bent double and quite unable to stand up straight. When Jesus saw her he called her and said, 'You are rid of your trouble.' Then he laid his hands on her, and at once she straightened up and began to praise God. But the president of the synagogue, indignant with Jesus for healing on the Sabbath, intervened and said to the congregation, 'There are six working-days: come and be cured on one of them, and not on the Sabbath.' The Lord gave him his answer: 'What hypocrites you are!' he said. 'Is there a single one of you who does not loose his ox or his donkey from the manger and take it out to water on the Sabbath? And here is this woman, a daughter of Abraham, who has been kept prisoner by Satan for eighteen long years: was it wrong for her to be freed from her bonds on the Sabbath?' At these words all his opponents were covered with confusion, while the mass of the people were delighted at all the wonderful things he was doing.

'What is the kingdom of God like?' he continued. 'What shall I compare it with? It is like a mustard-seed which a man took and sowed

and waxed a great tree; and the fowls of the air lodged in the branches of it. 20And again he said, Whereunto shall I liken the kingdom of God? 21 It is like leaven, which a woman took and hid in three measures of meal, till the whole was leavened. 22And he went through the cities and villages, teaching, and journeying toward Jerusalem. 23 Then said one unto him, Lord, are there few that be saved? And he said unto them,

24 Strive to enter in at the strait gate: for many, I say unto you, will seek to enter in, and shall not be able. 25 When once the master of the house is risen up, and hath shut to the door, and ye begin to stand without, and to knock at the door, saying, Lord, Lord, open unto us; and he shall answer and say unto you, I know you not whence ye are: 26 Then shall ye begin to say, We have eaten and drunk in thy presence, and thou hast taught in our streets. 27 But he shall say, I tell you, I know you not whence ye are; depart from me, all *ye* workers of iniquity. 28 There shall be weeping and gnashing of teeth, when ye shall see Abraham, and Isaac, and Jacob, and all the prophets, in the kingdom of God, and you *yourselves* thrust out. 29And they shall come from the east, and *from* the west, and from the north, and *from* the south, and shall sit down in the kingdom of God. 30And, behold, there are last which shall be first; and there are first which shall be last.

31 The same day there came certain of the Pharisees, saying unto him, Get thee out, and depart hence; for Herod will kill thee. 32And he said unto them, Go ye, and tell that fox, Behold, I cast out devils, and I do cures to day and to morrow, and the third *day* I shall be perfected. 33 Nevertheless I must walk to day, and to morrow, and the *day* following: for it cannot be that a prophet perish out of Jerusalem. 34 O Jerusalem, Jerusalem, which killest the prophets, and stonest them that are sent unto thee; how often would I have gathered thy children together, as a hen *doth gather* her brood under *her* wings, and ye would not! 35 Behold, your house is left unto you desolate: and verily I say unto you, Ye shall not see me, until *the time* come when ye shall say, Blessed *is* he that cometh in the name of the Lord.

and became a tree, and the birds of the air made nests in its branches."

20 And again he said, "To what shall I compare the kingdom of God? 21 It is like leaven which a woman took and hid in three measures of meal, till it was all leavened."

22 He went on his way through towns and villages, teaching, and journeying toward Jerusalem. 23And some one said to him, "Lord, will those who are saved be few?" And he said to them, 24 "Strive to enter by the narrow door; for many, I tell you, will seek to enter and will not be able. 25 When once the householder has risen up and shut the door, you will begin to stand outside and to knock at the door, saying, 'Lord, open to us.' He will answer you, 'I do not know where you come from.' 26 Then you will begin to say, 'We ate and drank in your presence, and you taught in our streets.' 27 But he will say, 'I tell you, I do not know where you come from; depart from me, all you workers of iniquity!' 28 There you will weep and gnash your teeth, when you see Abraham and Isaac and Jacob and all the prophets in the kingdom of God and you yourselves thrust out. 29And men will come from east and west, and from north and south, and sit at table in the kingdom of God. 30And behold, some are last who will be first, and some are first who will be last."

31 At that very hour some Pharisees came, and said to him, "Get away from here, for Herod wants to kill you." 32And he said to them, "Go and tell that fox, 'Behold, I cast out demons and perform cures today and tomorrow, and the third day I finish my course. 33 Nevertheless I must go on my way today and tomorrow and the day following; for it cannot be that a prophet should perish away from Jerusalem.' 34 O Jerusalem, Jerusalem, killing the prophets and stoning those who are sent to you! How often would I have gathered your children together as a hen gathers her brood under her wings, and you would not! 35 Behold, your house is forsaken. And I tell you, you will not see me until you say, 'Blessed is he who comes in the name of the Lord!' "

14 And it came to pass, as he went into the house of one of the chief Pharisees to eat bread on the sabbath day, that they watched him. 2And, behold, there was a certain man be-

14 One sabbath when he went to dine at the house of a ruler who belonged to the Pharisees, they were watching him. 2And behold,

PHILLIPS

and became a tree and the birds came and nested in its branches."

Then again he said:

"What can I say the kingdom of God is like? It is like the yeast which a woman took and covered up in three measures of flour until the whole lot had risen."

The kingdom is not entered by drifting but by decision

13. 22

So he went on his way through towns and villages, teaching as he went and making his way toward Jerusalem. Someone remarked, "Lord, are only a few men to be saved?"

And Jesus told them:

"You must do your utmost to get in through the narrow door, for many, I assure you, will try to do so and will not succeed, once the master of the house has got up and shut the door. Then you may find yourselves standing outside and knocking at the door crying, 'Lord, please open the door for us.' He will reply to you, 'I don't know who you are or where you come from.' 'But . . .' you will protest, 'we have had meals with you, and you taught in our streets!' Yet he will say to you, 'I tell you I do not know where you have come from. Be off, you scoundrels!' At that time there will be tears and bitter regret—to see Abraham and Isaac and Jacob and all the prophets inside the kingdom of God, and you yourselves excluded, outside! Yes, and people will come from the east and the west, and from the north and the south, and take their seats in the kingdom of God. There are some at the back now who will be in front then, and there are some in front now who will then be far behind."

The Pharisees warn Jesus of Herod; he replies

13. 31

Just then some Pharisees arrived to tell him, "You must get right away from here, for Herod intends to kill you."

"Go and tell that fox," returned Jesus, "today and tomorrow I am expelling evil spirits and continuing my work of healing, and on the third day my work will be finished. But I must journey on today, tomorrow and the next day, for it would never do for a prophet to meet his death outside Jerusalem!

"O Jerusalem, Jerusalem, you murder the prophets and stone the messengers that are sent to you! How often have I longed to gather your children round me like a bird gathering her brood together under her wings, but you would never have it. Now, all that is left is yourselves, and your house. For I tell you that you will never see me again till the day when you cry, 'Blessed is he who comes in the name of the Lord!' "

Strict sabbatarianism is again rebuked

14. 1

One Sabbath day he went into the house of one of the leading Pharisees for a meal, and they were all watching him closely. Right in

N.E.B.

in his garden; and it grew to be a tree and the birds came to roost among its branches.'

Again he said, 'What shall I compare the kingdom of God with? It is like yeast which a woman took and mixed with half a hundred-weight of flour till it was all leavened.'

He continued his journey through towns and villages, teaching as he made his way towards Jerusalem. Someone asked him, 'Sir, are only a few to be saved?' His answer was: 'Struggle to get in through the narrow door; for I tell you that many will try to enter and not be able.

'When once the master of the house has got up and locked the door, you may stand outside and knock, and say, "Sir, let us in!", but he will only answer, "I do not know where you come from." Then you will begin to say, "We sat at table with you and you taught in our streets." But he will repeat, "I tell you, I do not know where you come from. Out of my sight, all of you, you and your wicked ways!" There will be wailing and grinding of teeth there, when you see Abraham, Isaac, and Jacob, and all the prophets, in the kingdom of God, and yourselves thrown out. From east and west people will come, from north and south, for the feast in the kingdom of God. Yes, and some who are now last will be first, and some who are first will be last.'

At that time a number of Pharisees came to him and said, 'You should leave this place and go on your way; Herod is out to kill you.' He replied, 'Go and tell that fox, "Listen: today and tomorrow I shall be casting out devils and working cures; on the third day I reach my goal." However, I must be on my way today and tomorrow and the next day, because it is unthinkable for a prophet to meet his death anywhere but in Jerusalem.

'O Jerusalem, Jerusalem, the city that murders the prophets and stones the messengers sent to her! How often have I longed to gather your children, as a hen gathers her brood under her wings; but you would not let me. Look, look! there is your temple, forsaken by God. And I tell you, you shall never see me until the time comes when you say, "Blessings on him who comes in the name of the Lord!" '

14 One Sabbath he went to have a meal in the house of a leading Pharisee; and they were watching him closely. There, in front of

K.J.V.

fore him which had the dropsy. 3And Jesus answering spake unto the lawyers and Pharisees, saying, Is it lawful to heal on the sabbath day? 4And they held their peace. And he took *him*, and healed him, and let him go; 5And answered them, saying, Which of you shall have an ass or an ox fallen into a pit, and will not straightway pull him out on the sabbath day? 6And they could not answer him again to these things.

7 And he put forth a parable to those which were bidden, when he marked how they chose out the chief rooms; saying unto them, 8 When thou art bidden of any *man* to a wedding, sit not down in the highest room; lest a more honourable man than thou be bidden of him; 9And he that bade thee and him come and say to thee, Give this man place; and thou begin with shame to take the lowest room. 10 But when thou art bidden, go and sit down in the lowest room; that when he that bade thee cometh, he may say unto thee, Friend, go up higher: then shalt thou have worship in the presence of them that sit at meat with thee. 11 For whosoever exalteth himself shall be abased; and he that humbleth himself shall be exalted.

12 Then said he also to him that bade him, When thou makest a dinner or a supper, call not thy friends, nor thy brethren, neither thy kinsmen, nor *thy* rich neighbours; lest they also bid thee again, and a recompense be made thee. 13 But when thou makest a feast, call the poor, the maimed, the lame, the blind: 14And thou shalt be blessed; for they cannot recompense thee: for thou shalt be recompensed at the resurrection of the just.

15 And when one of them that sat at meat with him heard these things, he said unto him, Blessed *is* he that shall eat bread in the kingdom of God. 16 Then said he unto him, A certain man made a great supper, and bade many: 17And sent his servant at supper time to say to them that were bidden, Come; for all things are now ready. 18And they all with one *consent* began to make excuse. The first said unto him, I have bought a piece of ground, and I must needs go and see it: I pray thee have me excused. 19And another said, I have bought five yoke of oxen, and I go to prove them: I pray thee have me excused. 20And another said, I have married a wife, and therefore I cannot come. 21 So that servant came, and shewed his lord these things. Then the master of the house being angry said to his servant, Go out quickly into the streets and lanes of the city, and bring in hither the poor, and the maimed, and the halt, and the blind. 22And the servant said, Lord, it is done as

R.S.V.

there was a man before him who had dropsy. 3And Jesus spoke to the lawyers and Pharisees, saying, "Is it lawful to heal on the sabbath, or not?" 4 But they were silent. Then he took him and healed him, and let him go. 5And he said to them, "Which of you, having an ass[s] or an ox that has fallen into a well, will not immediately pull him out on a sabbath day?" 6And they could not reply to this.

7 Now he told a parable to those who were invited, when he marked how they chose the places of honor, saying to them, 8 "When you are invited by any one to a marriage feast, do not sit down in a place of honor, lest a more eminent man than you be invited by him; 9 and he who invited you both will come and say to you, 'Give place to this man,' and then you will begin with shame to take the lowest place. 10 But when you are invited, go and sit in the lowest place, so that when your host comes he may say to you, 'Friend, go up higher'; then you will be honored in the presence of all who sit at table with you. 11 For every one who exalts himself will be humbled, and he who humbles himself will be exalted."

12 He said also to the man who had invited him, "When you give a dinner or a banquet, do not invite your friends or your brothers or your kinsmen or rich neighbors, lest they also invite you in return, and you be repaid. 13 But when you give a feast, invite the poor, the maimed, the lame, the blind, 14 and you will be blessed, because they cannot repay you. You will be repaid at the resurrection of the just."

15 When one of those who sat at table with him heard this, he said to him, "Blessed is he who shall eat bread in the kingdom of God!" 16 But he said to him, "A man once gave a great banquet, and invited many; 17 and at the time for the banquet he sent his servant to say to those who had been invited, 'Come; for all is now ready.' 18 But they all alike began to make excuses. The first said to him, 'I have bought a field, and I must go out and see it; I pray you, have me excused.' 19And another said, 'I have bought five yoke of oxen, and I go to examine them; I pray you, have me excused.' 20And another said, 'I have married a wife, and therefore I cannot come.' 21 So the servant came and reported this to his master. Then the householder in anger said to his servant, 'Go out quickly to the streets and lanes of the city, and bring in the poor and maimed and blind and lame.' 22And the servant said, 'Sir, what you com-

---

[s] Other ancient authorities read *a son*.

PHILLIPS

front of him was a man afflicted with dropsy. So Jesus spoke to the scribes and Pharisees and said,

"Well, is it right to heal on the Sabbath day or not?"

But there was no reply. So Jesus took the man and healed him and let him go. Then he said to them,

"If an ass or a cow belonging to one of you fell into a well, wouldn't you rescue him without the slightest hesitation even though it were the Sabbath?"

And this again left them quite unable to reply.

A lesson in humility   14. 7

Then he gave a little word of advice to the guests when he noticed how they were choosing the best seats.

"When you are invited to a wedding reception, don't sit down in the best seat. It might happen that a more distinguished man than you has also been invited. Then your host might say, 'I am afraid you must give up your seat for this man.' And then, with considerable embarrassment, you will have to sit in the humblest place. No, when you are invited, go and take your seat in an inconspicuous place, so that when your host comes in he may say to you, 'Come on, my dear fellow, we have a much better seat than this for you.' That is the way to be important in the eyes of all your fellow guests! For everyone who makes himself important will become insignificant, while the man who makes himself insignificant will find himself important."

Then, addressing his host, Jesus said:

"When you give a luncheon or a dinner party, don't invite your friends or your brothers or relations or wealthy neighbors, for the chances are they will invite you back, and you will be fully repaid. No, when you give a party, invite the poor, the lame, the crippled and the blind. That way lies real happiness for you. They have no means of repaying you, but you will be repaid when good men are rewarded—at the resurrection."

Then, one of the guests, hearing these remarks of Jesus, said,

"What happiness for a man to eat a meal in the kingdom of God!"

Men who are "too busy"   14. 16
for the kingdom of God

But Jesus said to him:

"Once upon a time, a man planned a big dinner party and invited a great many people. At dinnertime, he sent his servant out to tell those who were invited, 'Please come, everything is ready now.' But they all, as one man, began to make their excuses. The first one said to him: 'I have bought some land. I must go and look at it. Please excuse me.' Another one said: 'I have bought five yoke of oxen and am on my way to try them out. Please convey my apologies.' And another one said, 'I have just got married and I am sure you will understand I cannot come.' So the servant returned and reported all this to his master. The master of the house was extremely annoyed and said to his servant, 'Hurry out now into the streets and alleys of the town, and bring here the poor and· crippled and blind and lame.' Then the servant

N.E.B.

him, was a man suffering from dropsy. Jesus asked the lawyers and the Pharisees: 'Is it permitted to cure people on the Sabbath or not?' They said nothing. So he took the man, cured him, and sent him away. Then he turned to them and said, 'If one of you has a donkey[a] or an ox and it falls into a well, will he hesitate to haul it up on the Sabbath day?' To this they could find no reply.

When he noticed how the guests were trying to secure the places of honour, he spoke to them in a parable: 'When you are asked by someone to a wedding-feast, do not sit down in the place of honour. It may be that some person more distinguished than yourself has been invited; and the host will come and say to you, "Give this man your seat." Then you will look foolish as you begin to take the lowest place. No, when you receive an invitation, go and sit down in the lowest place, so that when your host comes in he will say, "Come up higher, my friend." Then all your fellow-guests will see the respect in which you are held. For everyone who exalts himself will be humbled; and whoever humbles himself will be exalted.'

Then he said to his host, 'When you give a lunch or dinner party, do not invite your friends, your brothers or other relations, or your rich neighbours; they will only ask you back again and so you will be repaid. But when you give a party, ask the poor, the crippled, the lame, and the blind; and so find happiness. For they have no means of repaying you; but you will be repaid on the day when good men rise from the dead.'

One of the company, after hearing all this, said to him, 'Happy the man who shall sit at the feast in the kingdom of God!' Jesus answered, 'A man was giving a big dinner party and had sent out many invitations. At dinnertime he sent his servant with a message for his guests, "Please come, everything is now ready." They began one and all to excuse themselves. The first said, "I have bought a piece of land, and I must go and look over it; please accept my apologies." The second said, "I have bought five yoke of oxen, and I am on my way to try them out; please accept my apologies." The next said, "I have just got married and for that reason I cannot come." When the servant came back he reported this to his master. The master of the house was angry and said to him, "Go out quickly into the streets and alleys of the town, and bring me in the poor, the crippled, the blind, and the lame." The servant said, "Sir, your or-

[a] *Some ancient witnesses read* son.

K.J.V.

thou hast commanded, and yet there is room.
23 And the lord said unto the servant, Go out
into the highways and hedges, and compel *them*
to come in, that my house may be filled. 24 For
I say unto you, That none of those men which
were bidden shall taste of my supper.

25 And there went great multitudes with him:
and he turned, and said unto them, 26 If any
man come to me, and hate not his father, and
mother, and wife, and children, and brethren,
and sisters, yea, and his own life also, he cannot be my disciple. 27 And whosoever doth not
bear his cross, and come after me, cannot be
my disciple. 28 For which of you, intending to
build a tower, sitteth not down first, and count-
eth the cost, whether he have *sufficient* to finish
it? 29 Lest haply, after he hath laid the foundation, and is not able to finish *it,* all that behold
it begin to mock him, 30 Saying, This man began
to build, and was not able to finish. 31 Or what
king, going to make war against another king,
sitteth not down first, and consulteth whether he
be able with ten thousand to meet him that
cometh against him with twenty thousand? 32 Or
else, while the other is yet a great way off, he
sendeth an ambassage, and desireth conditions
of peace. 33 So likewise, whosoever he be of you
that forsaketh not all that he hath, he cannot be
my disciple.

34 Salt *is* good: but if the salt have lost his
savour, wherewith shall it be seasoned? 35 It is
neither fit for the land, nor yet for the dunghill;
but men cast it out. He that hath ears to hear,
let him hear.

15 Then drew near unto him all the publicans
and sinners for to hear him. 2 And the Pharisees and scribes murmured, saying, This man
receiveth sinners, and eateth with them.

3 And he spake this parable unto them, saying, 4 What man of you, having a hundred sheep,
if he lose one of them, doth not leave the ninety
and nine in the wilderness, and go after that
which is lost, until he find it? 5 And when he
hath found *it,* he layeth *it* on his shoulders, rejoicing. 6 And when he cometh home, he calleth
together *his* friends and neighbours, saying unto
them, Rejoice with me; for I have found my
sheep which was lost. 7 I say unto you, that likewise joy shall be in heaven over one sinner that
repenteth, more than over ninety and nine just
persons, which need no repentance.

8 Either what woman having ten pieces of
silver, if she lose one piece, doth not light a
candle, and sweep the house, and seek diligently
till she find *it?* 9 And when she hath found *it,*
she calleth *her* friends and *her* neighbours together, saying, Rejoice with me; for I have found
the piece which I had lost. 10 Likewise, I say
unto you, there is joy in the presence of the
angels of God over one sinner that repenteth.

11 And he said, A certain man had two sons:
12 And the younger of them said to *his* father,

R.S.V.

manded has been done, and still there is room.'
23 And the master said to the servant, 'Go out
to the highways and hedges, and compel people to come in, that my house may be filled.
24 For I tell you, none of those men who were
invited shall taste my banquet.' "

25 Now great multitudes accompanied him;
and he turned and said to them, 26 "If any
one comes to me and does not hate his own
father and mother and wife and children and
brothers and sisters, yes, and even his own life,
he cannot be my disciple. 27 Whoever does
not bear his own cross and come after me, cannot be my disciple. 28 For which of you, desiring to build a tower, does not first sit down and
count the cost, whether he has enough to complete it? 29 Otherwise, when he has laid a
foundation, and is not able to finish, all who see
it begin to mock him, 30 saying, 'This man began to build, and was not able to finish.' 31 Or
what king, going to encounter another king in
war, will not sit down first and take counsel
whether he is able with ten thousand to meet
him who comes against him with twenty thousand? 32 And if not, while the other is yet a
great way off, he sends an embassy and asks
terms of peace. 33 So therefore, whoever of you
does not renounce all that he has cannot be
my disciple.

34 "Salt is good; but if salt has lost its taste,
how shall its saltness be restored? 35 It is fit
neither for the land nor for the dunghill; men
throw it away. He who has ears to hear, let
him hear."

15 Now the tax collectors and sinners were
all drawing near to hear him. 2 And the
Pharisees and the scribes murmured, saying,
"This man receives sinners and eats with them."

3 So he told them this parable: 4 "What man
of you, having a hundred sheep, if he has lost
one of them, does not leave the ninety-nine in
the wilderness, and go after the one which is
lost, until he finds it? 5 And when he has found
it, he lays it on his shoulders, rejoicing. 6 And
when he comes home, he calls together his
friends and his neighbors, saying to them, 'Rejoice with me, for I have found my sheep which
was lost.' 7 Just so, I tell you, there will be
more joy in heaven over one sinner who repents than over ninety-nine righteous persons
who need no repentance.

8 "Or what woman, having ten silver coins,[t]
if she loses one coin, does not light a lamp
and sweep the house and seek diligently until
she finds it? 9 And when she has found it, she
calls together her friends and neighbors, saying, 'Rejoice with me, for I have found the coin
which I had lost.' 10 Just so, I tell you, there is
joy before the angels of God over one sinner
who repents."

11 And he said, "There was a man who had
two sons; 12 and the younger of them said to

[t] The drachma, rendered here by *silver coin,* was
about sixteen cents.

PHILLIPS

said, 'I have done what you told me, sir, and there are still empty places.' Then the master replied: 'Now go out to the roads and hedgerows and make them come inside, so that my house may be full. For I tell you that not one of the men I invited shall have a taste of my dinner.' "

Now as Jesus proceeded on his journey, great crowds accompanied him, and he turned and spoke to them:

"If anyone comes to me without 'hating' his father and mother and wife and children and brothers and sisters, and even his own life, he cannot be a disciple of mine. The man who will not take up his cross and follow in my footsteps cannot be my disciple.

"If any of you wanted to build a tower, wouldn't he first sit down and work out the cost of it, to see if he can afford to finish it? Otherwise, when he has laid the foundation and found himself unable to complete the building, everyone who sees it will begin to jeer at him, saying, 'This is the man who started to build a tower but couldn't finish it!' Or, suppose there is a king who is going to war with another king, doesn't he sit down first and consider whether he can engage the twenty thousand of the other king with his own ten thousand? And if he decides he can't, then, while the other king is still a long way off, he sends messengers to him to ask for conditions of peace. So it is with you; only the man who says goodbye to all his possessions can be my disciple.

"Salt is a very good thing, but if salt loses its flavor, what can you use to restore it? It is no good for the ground and no good as manure. People just throw it away. Every man who has ears should use them!"

N.E.B.

ders have been carried out and there is still room." The master replied, "Go out on to the highways and along the hedgerows and make them come in; I want my house to be full. I tell you that not one of those who were invited shall taste my banquet." '

Once when great crowds were accompanying him, he turned to them and said: 'If anyone comes to me and does not hate his father and mother, wife and children, brothers and sisters, even his own life, he cannot be a disciple of mine. No one who does not carry his cross and come with me can be a disciple of mine. Would any of you think of building a tower without first sitting down and calculating the cost, to see whether he could afford to finish it? Otherwise, if he has laid its foundation and then is not able to complete it, all the onlookers will laugh at him. "There is the man", they will say, "who started to build and could not finish." Or what king will march to battle against another king, without first sitting down to consider whether with ten thousand men he can face an enemy coming to meet him with twenty thousand? If he cannot, then, long before the enemy approaches, he sends envoys, and asks for terms. So also none of you can be a disciple of mine without taking leave of all his possessions.

'Salt is a good thing; but if salt itself becomes tasteless, what will you use to season it? It is useless either on the land or on the dung-heap: it can only be thrown away. If you have ears to hear with, hear.'

Jesus speaks of the love of God   15. 1
for "the lost"

Now all the tax collectors and "outsiders" were crowding around to hear what he had to say. The Pharisees and the scribes complained of this, remarking,

"This man accepts sinners and even eats his meals with them."

So Jesus spoke to them, using this parable:

"Wouldn't any man among you who owned a hundred sheep, and lost one of them, leave the ninety-nine to themselves in the open, and go after the one which is lost until he finds it? And when he has found it, he will put it on his shoulders with great joy, and as soon as he gets home, he will call his friends and neighbors together. 'Come and celebrate with me,' he will say, 'for I have found that sheep of mine which was lost.' I tell you that it is the same in Heaven—there is more joy over one sinner whose heart is changed than over ninety-nine righteous people who have no need of repentance.

"Or if there is a woman who has ten silver coins, if she should lose one, won't she take a lamp and sweep and search the house from top to bottom until she finds it? And when she has found it, she calls her friends and neighbors together. 'Come and celebrate with me,' she says, 'for I have found that coin I lost.' I tell you, it is the same in Heaven—there is rejoicing among the angels of God over one sinner whose heart is changed."

Then he continued:

"Once there was a man who had two sons. The younger one said to his father, 'Father,

15   Another time, the tax-gatherers and other bad characters were all crowding in to listen to him; and the Pharisees and the doctors of the law began grumbling among themselves: 'This fellow', they said, 'welcomes sinners and eats with them.' He answered them with this parable: 'If one of you has a hundred sheep and loses one of them, does he not leave the ninety-nine in the open pasture and go after the missing one until he has found it? How delighted he is then! He lifts it on to his shoulders, and home he goes to call his friends and neighbours together. "Rejoice with me!" he cries. "I have found my lost sheep." In the same way, I tell you, there will be greater joy in heaven over one sinner who repents than over ninety-nine righteous people who do not need to repent.

'Or again, if a woman has ten silver pieces and loses one of them, does she not light the lamp, sweep out the house, and look in every corner till she has found it? And when she has, she calls her friends and neighbours together, and says, "Rejoice with me! I have found the piece that I lost." In the same way, I tell you, there is joy among the angels of God over one sinner who repents.'

Again he said: 'There was once a man who had two sons; and the younger said to his father,

K.J.V.

Father, give me the portion of goods that falleth *to me.* And he divided unto them *his* living. 13And not many days after the younger son gathered all together, and took his journey into a far country, and there wasted his substance with riotous living. 14And when he had spent all, there arose a mighty famine in that land; and he began to be in want. 15And he went and joined himself to a citizen of that country; and he sent him into his fields to feed swine. 16And he would fain have filled his belly with the husks that the swine did eat: and no man gave unto him. 17And when he came to himself, he said, How many hired servants of my father's have bread enough and to spare, and I perish with hunger! 18 I will arise and go to my father, and will say unto him, Father, I have sinned against heaven, and before thee, 19And am no more worthy to be called thy son: make me as one of thy hired servants. 20And he arose, and came to his father. But when he was yet a great way off, his father saw him, and had compassion, and ran, and fell on his neck, and kissed him. 21And the son said unto him, Father, I have sinned against heaven, and in thy sight, and am no more worthy to be called thy son. 22 But the father said to his servants, Bring forth the best robe, and put *it* on him; and put a ring on his hand, and shoes on *his* feet: 23And bring hither the fatted calf, and kill *it;* and let us eat, and be merry: 24 For this my son was dead, and is alive again; he was lost, and is found. And they began to be merry. 25 Now his elder son was in the field: and as he came and drew nigh to the house, he heard music and dancing. 26And he called one of the servants, and asked what these things meant. 27And he said unto him, Thy brother is come; and thy father hath killed the fatted calf, because he hath received him safe and sound. 28And he was angry, and would not go in: therefore came his father out, and entreated him. 29And he answering said to *his* father, Lo, these many years do I serve thee, neither transgressed I at any time thy commandment; and yet thou never gavest me a kid, that I might make merry with my friends: 30 But as soon as this thy son was come, which hath devoured thy living with harlots, thou hast killed for him the fatted calf. 31And he said unto him, Son, thou art ever with me, and all that I have is thine. 32 It was meet that we should make merry, and be glad: for this thy brother was dead, and is alive again; and was lost, and is found.

R.S.V.

his father, 'Father, give me the share of property that falls to me.' And he divided his living between them. 13 Not many days later, the younger son gathered all he had and took his journey into a far country, and there he squandered his property in loose living. 14And when he had spent everything, a great famine arose in that country, and he began to be in want. 15 So he went and joined himself to one of the citizens of that country, who sent him into his fields to feed swine. 16And he would gladly have fed on[u] the pods that the swine ate; and no one gave him anything. 17 But when he came to himself he said, 'How many of my father's hired servants have bread enough and to spare, but I perish here with hunger! 18 I will arise and go to my father, and I will say to him, "Father, I have sinned against heaven and before you; 19 I am no longer worthy to be called your son; treat me as one of your hired servants."' 20And he arose and came to his father. But while he was yet at a distance, his father saw him and had compassion, and ran and embraced him and kissed him. 21And the son said to him, 'Father, I have sinned against heaven and before you; I am no longer worthy to be called your son.'[v] 22 But the father said to his servants, 'Bring quickly the best robe, and put it on him; and put a ring on his hand, and shoes on his feet; 23 and bring the fatted calf and kill it, and let us eat and make merry; 24 for this my son was dead, and is alive again; he was lost, and is found.' And they began to make merry.

25 "Now his elder son was in the field; and as he came and drew near to the house, he heard music and dancing. 26And he called one of the servants and asked what this meant. 27And he said to him, 'Your brother has come, and your father has killed the fatted calf, because he has received him safe and sound.' 28 But he was angry and refused to go in. His father came out and entreated him, 29 but he answered his father, 'Lo, these many years I have served you, and I never disobeyed your command; yet you never gave me a kid, that I might make merry with my friends. 30But when this son of yours came, who has devoured your living with harlots, you killed for him the fatted calf!' 31And he said to him, 'Son, you are always with me, and all that is mine is yours. 32 It was fitting to make merry and be glad, for this your brother was dead, and is alive; he was lost, and is found.'"

16 And he said also unto his disciples, There was a certain rich man, which had a steward; and the same was accused unto him that he had wasted his goods. 2And he called him, and said unto him, How is it that I hear this of thee? give an account of thy stewardship; for thou mayest be no longer steward. 3 Then the steward said within himself, What shall I do? for my lord taketh away from me the stewardship: I

16 He also said to the disciples, "There was a rich man who had a steward, and charges were brought to him that this man was wasting his goods. 2And he called him and said to him, 'What is this that I hear about you? Turn in the account of your stewardship, for you can no longer be steward.' 3And the steward said to himself, 'What shall I do, since my master is taking the stewardship away from me? I am not strong enough to dig, and I am ashamed to

[u] Other ancient authorities read *filled his belly with.* [v] Other ancient authorities add *treat me as one of your hired servants.*

PHILLIPS

N.E.B.

give me my share of the property that will come to me.' So he divided up his property between the two of them. Before very long, the younger son collected all his belongings and went off to a foreign land, where he squandered his wealth in the wildest extravagance. And when he had run through all his money, a terrible famine arose in that country, and he began to feel the pinch. Then he went and hired himself out to one of the citizens of that country who sent him out into the fields to feed the pigs. He got to the point of longing to stuff himself with the food the pigs were eating, and not a soul gave him anything. Then he came to his senses and cried aloud, 'Why, dozens of my father's hired men have got more food than they can eat, and here am I dying of hunger! I will get up and go back to my father, and I will say to him: "Father, I have done wrong in the sight of Heaven and in your eyes. I don't deserve to be called your son any more. Please take me on as one of your hired men."' So he got up and went to his father. But while he was still some distance off, his father saw him and his heart went out to him, and he ran and fell on his neck and kissed him. But his son said: 'Father, I have done wrong in the sight of Heaven and in your eyes. I don't deserve to be called your son any more. . . .' 'Hurry!' called out his father to the servants, 'fetch the best clothes and put them on him! Put a ring on his finger and shoes on his feet, and get that calf we've fattened and kill it, and we will have a feast and a celebration! For this is my son—I thought he was dead, and he's alive again. I thought I had lost him, and he's found!' And they began to get the festivities going.

"But his elder son was out in the fields, and as he came near the house, he heard music and dancing. So he called one of the servants across to him and inquired what was the meaning of it all. 'Your brother has arrived, and your father has killed the calf we fattened because he has got him home again safe and sound,' was the reply. But he was furious and refused to go inside the house. So his father came outside and called him. Then he burst out: 'Look, how many years have I slaved for you and never disobeyed a single order of yours, and yet you have never given me so much as a young goat, so that I could give my friends a dinner! But when that son of yours arrives, who has spent all your money on prostitutes, for *him* you kill the calf we've fattened!' But the father replied: 'My dear son, you have been with me all the time and everything I have is yours. But we *had* to celebrate and show our joy. For this is your brother; I thought he was dead—and he's alive. I thought he was lost—and he is found!' "

"Father, give me my share of the property." So he divided his estate between them. A few days later the younger son turned the whole of his share into cash and left home for a distant country, where he squandered it in reckless living. He had spent it all, when a severe famine fell upon that country and he began to feel the pinch. So he went and attached himself to one of the local landowners, who sent him on to his farm to mind the pigs. He would have been glad to fill his belly with[a] the pods that the pigs were eating; and no one gave him anything. Then he came to his senses and said, "How many of my father's paid servants have more food than they can eat, and here am I, starving to death! I will set off and go to my father, and say to him, 'Father, I have sinned, against God and against you; I am no longer fit to be called your son; treat me as one of your paid servants.'" So he set out for his father's house. But while he was still a long way off his father saw him, and his heart went out to him. He ran to meet him, flung his arms round him, and kissed him. The son said, "Father, I have sinned, against God and against you; I am no longer fit to be called your son."[b] But the father said to his servants, "Quick! fetch a robe, my best one, and put it on him; put a ring on his finger and shoes on his feet. Bring the fatted calf and kill it, and let us have a feast to celebrate the day. For this son of mine was dead and has come back to life; he was lost and is found." And the festivities began.

'Now the elder son was out on the farm; and on his way back, as he approached the house, he heard music and dancing. He called one of the servants and asked what it meant. The servant told him, "Your brother has come home, and your father has killed the fatted calf because he has him back safe and sound." But he was angry and refused to go in. His father came out and pleaded with him; but he retorted, "You know how I have slaved for you all these years; I never once disobeyed your orders; and you never gave me so much as a kid, for a feast with my friends. But now that this son of yours turns up, after running through your money with his women, you kill the fatted calf for him." "My boy," said the father, "you are always with me, and everything I have is yours. How could we help celebrating this happy day? Your brother here was dead and has come back to life, was lost and is found."'

A clever rogue, and the right use of money **16. 1**

Then there is this story he told his disciples: "Once there was a rich man whose agent was reported to him to be mismanaging his property. So he summoned him and said: 'What's this that I hear about you? Give me an account of your stewardship—you're not fit to manage my household any longer.' At this the agent said to himself: 'What am I going to do now that my employer is taking away the stewardship from me? I am not strong enough to dig and I

16 He said to his disciples, 'There was a rich man who had a bailiff, and he received complaints that this man was squandering the property. So he sent for him, and said, "What is this that I hear? Produce your accounts, for you cannot be manager here any longer." The bailiff said to himself, "What am I to do now that my employer is dismissing me? I am not strong

[a] *Some witnesses read* to have his fill of . . . [b] *Some witnesses add* treat me as one of your paid servants.

K.J.V.

cannot dig; to beg I am ashamed. 4 I am resolved what to do, that, when I am put out of the stewardship, they may receive me into their houses. 5 So he called every one of his lord's debtors *unto him,* and said unto the first, How much owest thou unto my lord? 6And he said, A hundred measures of oil. And he said unto him, Take thy bill, and sit down quickly, and write fifty. 7 Then said he to another, And how much owest thou? And he said, A hundred measures of wheat. And he said unto him, Take thy bill, and write fourscore. 8And the lord commended the unjust steward, because he had done wisely: for the children of this world are in their generation wiser than the children of light. 9And I say unto you, Make to yourselves friends of the mammon of unrighteousness; that, when ye fail, they may receive you into everlasting habitations. 10 He that is faithful in that which is least is faithful also in much: and he that is unjust in the least is unjust also in much. 11 If therefore ye have not been faithful in the unrighteous mammon, who will commit to your trust the true *riches?* 12And if ye have not been faithful in that which is another man's, who shall give you that which is your own?

13 No servant can serve two masters: for either he will hate the one, and love the other; or else he will hold to the one, and despise the other. Ye cannot serve God and mammon. 14And the Pharisees also, who were covetous, heard all these things: and they derided him. 15And he said unto them, Ye are they which justify yourselves before men; but God knoweth your hearts: for that which is highly esteemed among men is abomination in the sight of God. 16 The law and the prophets *were* until John: since that time the kingdom of God is preached, and every man presseth into it. 17And it is easier for heaven and earth to pass, than one tittle of the law to fail. 18 Whosoever putteth away his wife, and marrieth another, committeth adultery: and whosoever marrieth her that is put away from *her* husband committeth adultery.

19 There was a certain rich man, which was clothed in purple and fine linen, and fared sumptuously every day: 20And there was a certain beggar named Lazarus, which was laid at his gate, full of sores, 21And desiring to be fed with the crumbs which fell from the rich man's table: moreover the dogs came and licked his sores. 22And it came to pass, that the beggar died, and was carried by the angels into Abraham's bosom: the rich man also died, and was buried; 23And in hell he lifted up his eyes, being in torments,

R.S.V.

beg. 4 I have decided what to do, so that people may receive me into their houses when I am put out of the stewardship.' 5 So, summoning his master's debtors one by one, he said to the first, 'How much do you owe my master?' 6 He said, 'A hundred measures of oil.' And he said to him, 'Take your bill, and sit down quickly and write fifty.' 7 Then he said to another, 'And how much do you owe?' He said, 'A hundred measures of wheat.' He said to him, 'Take your bill, and write eighty.' 8 The master commended the dishonest steward for his prudence; for the sons of this world *w* are wiser in their own generation than the sons of light. 9And I tell you, make friends for yourselves by means of unrighteous mammon, so that when it fails they may receive you into the eternal habitations.

10 "He who is faithful in a very little is faithful also in much; and he who is dishonest in a very little is dishonest also in much. 11 If then you have not been faithful in the unrighteous mammon, who will entrust to you the true riches? 12And if you have not been faithful in that which is another's, who will give you that which is your own? 13 No servant can serve two masters; for either he will hate the one and love the other, or he will be devoted to the one and despise the other. You cannot serve God and mammon."

14 The Pharisees, who were lovers of money, heard all this, and they scoffed at him. 15 But he said to them, "You are those who justify yourselves before men, but God knows your hearts; for what is exalted among men is an abomination in the sight of God.

16 "The law and the prophets were until John; since then the good news of the kingdom of God is preached, and every one enters it violently. 17 But it is easier for heaven and earth to pass away, than for one dot of the law to become void.

18 "Every one who divorces his wife and marries another commits adultery, and he who marries a woman divorced from her husband commits adultery.

19 "There was a rich man, who was clothed in purple and fine linen and who feasted sumptuously every day. 20And at his gate lay a poor man named Lazarus, full of sores, 21 who desired to be fed with what fell from the rich man's table; moreover the dogs came and licked his sores. 22 The poor man died and was carried by the angels to Abraham's bosom. The rich man also died and was buried; 23 and in Hades, being in torment, he lifted up his eyes,

[*w*] Greek *age.*

PHILLIPS

can't sink to begging. Ah, I know what I'll do so that when I lose my position people will welcome me into their homes!' So he sent for each one of his master's debtors. 'How much do you owe my master?' he said to the first. 'A hundred barrels of oil,' he replied. 'Here,' replied the agent, 'take your bill, sit down, hurry up and write in fifty.' Then he said to another, 'And what's the size of your debt?' 'A thousand bushels of wheat,' he replied. 'Take your bill,' said the agent, 'and write in eight hundred.' Now the master praised this rascally steward because he had been so careful for his own future. For the children of this world are considerably more shrewd in dealing with their contemporaries than the children of light. Now my advice to you is to use 'money,' tainted as it is, to make yourselves friends, so that when it comes to an end they may welcome you into eternal habitations.

"The man who is faithful in the little things will be faithful in the big things, and the man who cheats in the little things will cheat in the big things too. So that if you are not fit to be trusted to deal with the wicked wealth of this world, who will trust you with the true riches? And if you are not trustworthy with someone else's property, who will give you property of your own? No servant can serve two masters. He is bound to hate one and love the other, or give his loyalty to one and despise the other. You cannot serve God and the power of money at the same time."

Now the Pharisees, who were very fond of money, heard all this with a sneer. But he said to them:

"You are the people who advertise your goodness before men, but God knows your hearts. Remember, there are things men consider perfectly splendid which are detestable in the sight of God!

Jesus states that the kingdom   **16. 16**
of God has superseded "the
Law and the Prophets"

"The Law and the Prophets were in force until John's day. From then on the good news of the kingdom of God has been proclaimed and men are forcing their way into it.

"Yet it would be easier for Heaven and earth to disappear than for a single point of the Law to become a dead letter.

"Any man who divorces his wife and marries another woman commits adultery. And so does any man who marries the woman who was divorced from her husband.

Jesus shows the fearful   **16. 19**
consequence of social injustice

"There was once a rich man who used to dress in purple and fine linen and lead a life of daily luxury. And there was a poor man called Lazarus who was put down at his gate. He was covered with sores. He used to long to be fed with the scraps from the rich man's table. Yes, and the dogs used to come and lick his sores. Well, it happened that the poor man died, and was carried by the angels into Abraham's bosom. The rich man also died and was buried. And from among the dead he looked up and saw

N.E.B.

enough to dig, and too proud to beg. I know what I must do, to make sure that, when I have to leave, there will be people to give me house and home." He summoned his master's debtors one by one. To the first he said, "How much do you owe my master?" He replied, "A thousand gallons of olive oil." He said, "Here is your account. Sit down and make it five hundred; and be quick about it." Then he said to another, "And you, how much do you owe?" He said, "A thousand bushels of wheat", and was told, "Take your account and make it eight hundred." And the master applauded the dishonest bailiff for acting so astutely. For the worldly are more astute than the other-worldly in dealing with their own kind.

'So I say to you, use your worldly wealth to win friends for yourselves, so that when money is a thing of the past you may be received into an eternal home.

'The man who can be trusted in little things can be trusted also in great; and the man who is dishonest in little things is dishonest also in great things. If, then, you have not proved trustworthy with the wealth of this world, who will trust you with the wealth that is real? And if you have proved untrustworthy with what belongs to another, who will give you what is your own?

'No servant can be the slave of two masters; for either he will hate the first and love the second, or he will be devoted to the first and think nothing of the second. You cannot serve God and Money.'

The Pharisees, who loved money, heard all this and scoffed at him. He said to them, 'You are the people who impress your fellowmen with your righteousness; but God sees through you; for what sets itself up to be admired by men is detestable in the sight of God.

'Until John, it was the Law and the prophets: since then, there is the good news of the kingdom of God, and everyone forces his way in.

'It is easier for heaven and earth to come to an end than for one dot or stroke of the Law to lose its force.

'A man who divorces his wife and marries another commits adultery; and anyone who marries a woman divorced from her husband commits adultery.

'There was once a rich man, who dressed in purple and the finest linen, and feasted in great magnificence every day. At his gate, covered with sores, lay a poor man named Lazarus, who would have been glad to satisfy his hunger with the scraps from the rich man's table. Even the dogs used to come and lick his sores. One day the poor man died and was carried away by the angels to be with Abraham. The rich man also died and was buried, and in Hades, where

K.J.V.

and seeth Abraham afar off, and Lazarus in his bosom. 24And he cried and said, Father Abraham, have mercy on me, and send Lazarus, that he may dip the tip of his finger in water, and cool my tongue; for I am tormented in this flame. 25 But Abraham said, Son, remember that thou in thy lifetime receivedst thy good things, and likewise Lazarus evil things: but now he is comforted, and thou art tormented. 26And beside all this, between us and you there is a great gulf fixed: so that they which would pass from hence to you cannot; neither can they pass to us, that *would come* from thence. 27 Then he said, I pray thee therefore, father, that thou wouldest send him to my father's house: 28 For I have five brethren; that he may testify unto them, lest they also come into this place of torment. 29Abraham saith unto him, They have Moses and the prophets; let them hear them. 30And he said, Nay, father Abraham: but if one went unto them from the dead, they will repent. 31And he said unto him, If they hear not Moses and the prophets, neither will they be persuaded, though one rose from the dead.

17 Then said he unto the disciples, It is impossible but that offences will come: but woe *unto him*, through whom they come! 2 It were better for him that a millstone were hanged about his neck, and he cast into the sea, than that he should offend one of these little ones.

3 Take heed to yourselves: If thy brother trespass against thee, rebuke him; and if he repent, forgive him. 4And if he trespass against thee seven times in a day, and seven times in a day turn again to thee, saying, I repent; thou shalt forgive him. 5And the apostles said unto the Lord, Increase our faith. 6And the Lord said, If ye had faith as a grain of mustard seed, ye might say unto this sycamine tree, Be thou plucked up by the root, and be thou planted in the sea; and it should obey you. 7 But which of you, having a servant ploughing or feeding cattle, will say unto him by and by, when he is come from the field, Go and sit down to meat? 8And will not rather say unto him, Make ready wherewith I may sup, and gird thyself, and serve me, till I have eaten and drunken; and afterward thou shalt eat and drink? 9 Doth he thank that servant because he did the things that were commanded him? I trow not. 10 So likewise ye, when ye shall have done all those things which are commanded you, say, We are unprofitable servants: we have done that which was our duty to do.

R.S.V.

and saw Abraham far off and Lazarus in his bosom. 24And he called out, 'Father Abraham, have mercy upon me, and send Lazarus to dip the end of his finger in water and cool my tongue; for I am in anguish in this flame.' 25 But Abraham said, 'Son, remember that you in your lifetime received your good things, and Lazarus in like manner evil things; but now he is comforted here, and you are in anguish. 26And besides all this, between us and you a great chasm has been fixed, in order that those who would pass from here to you may not be able, and none may cross from there to us.' 27And he said, 'Then I beg you, father, to send him to my father's house, 28 for I have five brothers, so that he may warn them, lest they also come into this place of torment.' 29 But Abraham said, 'They have Moses and the prophets; let them hear them.' 30And he said, 'No, father Abraham; but if some one goes to them from the dead, they will repent.' 31 He said to him, 'If they do not hear Moses and the prophets, neither will they be convinced if some one should rise from the dead.' "

17 And he said to his disciples, "Temptations to sin[x] are sure to come; but woe to him by whom they come! 2 It would be better for him if a millstone were hung round his neck and he were cast into the sea, than that he should cause one of these little ones to sin.[y] 3 Take heed to yourselves; if your brother sins, rebuke him, and if he repents, forgive him; 4 and if he sins against you seven times in the day, and turns to you seven times, and says, 'I repent,' you must forgive him."

5 The apostles said to the Lord, "Increase our faith!" 6And the Lord said, "If you had faith as a grain of mustard seed, you could say to this sycamine tree, 'Be rooted up, and be planted in the sea,' and it would obey you. 7 "Will any one of you, who has a servant plowing or keeping sheep, say to him when he has come in from the field, 'Come at once and sit down at table'? 8 Will he not rather say to him, 'Prepare supper for me, and gird yourself and serve me, till I eat and drink; and afterward you shall eat and drink'? 9 Does he thank the servant because he did what was commanded? 10 So you also, when you have done all that is commanded you, say, 'We are unworthy servants; we have only done what was our duty.' "

[x] Greek *stumbling blocks.* [y] Greek *stumble.*

PHILLIPS

N.E.B.

Abraham a long way away, and Lazarus in his arms. 'Father Abraham!' he cried out, 'please pity me. Send Lazarus to dip the tip of his finger in water and cool my tongue, for I am in agony in these flames.' But Abraham replied: 'Remember, my son, that you used to have the good things in your lifetime, while Lazarus suffered the bad. Now he is being comforted here, while you are in agony. And besides this, a great chasm has been set between you and us, so that those who want to go to you from this side cannot do so, and people cannot come to us from your side.' At this he said: 'Then I beg you, father, to send him to my father's house, for I have five brothers. He could warn them about all this and prevent their coming to this place of torture.' But Abraham said, 'They have Moses and the Prophets: they can listen to them.' 'Ah no, father Abraham,' he said, 'if only someone were to go to them from the dead, they would change completely.' But Abraham told him, 'If they will not listen to Moses and the Prophets, they would not be convinced even if somebody were to rise from the dead.' "

he was in torment, he looked up; and there, far away, was Abraham with Lazarus close beside him. "Abraham, my father," he called out, "take pity on me! Send Lazarus to dip the tip of his finger in water, to cool my tongue, for I am in agony in this fire." But Abraham said, "Remember, my child, that all the good things fell to you while you were alive, and all the bad to Lazarus; now he has his consolation here and it is you who are in agony. But that is not all: there is a great chasm fixed between us; no one from our side who wants to reach you can cross it, and none may pass from your side to us." "Then, father," he replied, "will you send him to my father's house, where I have five brothers, to warn them, so that they too may not come to this place of torment?" But Abraham said, "They have Moses and the prophets; let them listen to them." "No, father Abraham," he replied, "but if someone from the dead visits them, they will repent." Abraham answered, "If they do not listen to Moses and the prophets they will pay no heed even if someone should rise from the dead." '

Jesus warns his disciples about 17. 1
spoiling the spirit of the new
kingdom

Then Jesus said to his disciples:
"It is inevitable that there should be pitfalls, but alas for the man who is responsible for them! It would be better for that man to have a millstone hung round his neck and be thrown into the sea, than that he should trip up one of these little ones. So be careful how you live. If your brother offends you, take him to task about it, and if he is sorry forgive him. Yes, if he wrongs you seven times in one day and turns to you and says, 'I am sorry' seven times, you must forgive him."
And the apostles said to the Lord,
"Give us more faith."
And he replied,
"If your faith were as big as a grain of mustard seed, you could say to this fig tree, 'Pull yourself up by the roots and plant yourself in the sea,' and it would do what you said!

17 He said to his disciples, 'Causes of stumbling are bound to arise; but woe betide the man through whom they come. It would be better for him to be thrown into the sea with a millstone round his neck than to cause one of these little ones to stumble. Keep watch on yourselves.
'If your brother wrongs you, rebuke him; and if he repents, forgive him. Even if he wrongs you seven times in a day and comes back to you seven times saying, "I am sorry", you are to forgive him.'
The apostles said to the Lord, 'Increase our faith'; and the Lord replied, 'If you had faith no bigger even than a mustard-seed, you could say to this sycamore-tree, "Be rooted up and replanted in the sea"; and it would at once obey you.
'Suppose one of you has a servant ploughing or minding sheep. When he comes back from the fields, will the master say, "Come along at once and sit down"? Will he not rather say, "Prepare my supper, buckle your belt, and then wait on me while I have my meal; you can have yours afterwards"? Is he grateful to the servant for carrying out his orders? So with you: when you have carried out all your orders, you should say, "We are servants and deserve no credit; we have only done our duty." '

Work in the kingdom must be 17. 7
taken as a matter of course

"If any of you have a servant plowing or looking after the sheep, are you likely to say to him when he comes in from the fields, 'Come straight in and sit down to your meal'? Aren't you more likely to say, 'Get my supper ready: change your coat, and wait while I eat and drink: and then, when I've finished, you can have your meal'? Do you feel particularly grateful to your servant for doing what you tell him? I don't think so. It is the same with yourselves—when you have done everything that you are told to do, you can say, 'We are not much good as servants, for we have only done what we ought to do.' "

K.J.V.

11 And it came to pass, as he went to Jerusalem, that he passed through the midst of Samaria and Galilee. 12And as he entered into a certain village, there met him ten men that were lepers, which stood afar off: 13And they lifted up *their* voices, and said, Jesus, Master, have mercy on us. 14And when he saw *them,* he said unto them, Go shew yourselves unto the priests. And it came to pass, that, as they went, they were cleansed. 15And one of them, when he saw that he was healed, turned back, and with a loud voice glorified God, 16And fell down on *his* face at his feet, giving him thanks: and he was a Samaritan. 17And Jesus answering said, Were there not ten cleansed? but where *are* the nine? 18 There are not found that returned to give glory to God, save this stranger. 19And he said unto him, Arise, go thy way: thy faith hath made thee whole.

20 And when he was demanded of the Pharisees, when the kingdom of God should come, he answered them and said, The kingdom of God cometh not with observation: 21 Neither shall they say, Lo here! or, lo there! for, behold, the kingdom of God is within you. 22And he said unto the disciples, The days will come, when ye shall desire to see one of the days of the Son of man, and ye shall not see *it.* 23And they shall say to you, See here; or, see there: go not after *them,* nor follow *them.* 24 For as the lightning, that lighteneth out of the one *part* under heaven, shineth unto the other *part* under heaven; so shall also the Son of man be in his day. 25 But first must he suffer many things, and be rejected of this generation. 26And as it was in the days of Noe, so shall it be also in the days of the Son of man. 27 They did eat, they drank, they married wives, they were given in marriage, until the day that Noe entered into the ark, and the flood came, and destroyed them all. 28 Likewise also as it was in the days of Lot; they did eat, they drank, they bought, they sold, they planted, they builded; 29 But the same day that Lot went out of Sodom it rained fire and brimstone from heaven, and destroyed *them* all. 30 Even thus shall it be in the day when the Son of man is revealed. 31 In that day, he which shall be upon the housetop, and his stuff in the house, let him not come down to take it away: and he that is in the field, let him likewise not return back. 32 Remember Lot's wife. 33 Whosoever shall seek to save his life shall lose it; and whosoever shall lose his life shall preserve it. 34 I tell you, in that night there shall be two *men* in one bed; the one shall be taken, and the other shall be left. 35 Two *women* shall be grinding together;

R.S.V.

11 On the way to Jerusalem he was passing along between Samaria and Galilee. 12And as he entered a village, he was met by ten lepers, who stood at a distance 13 and lifted up their voices and said, "Jesus, Master, have mercy on us." 14 When he saw them he said to them, "Go and show yourselves to the priests." And as they went they were cleansed. 15 Then one of them, when he saw that he was healed, turned back, praising God with a loud voice; 16 and he fell on his face at Jesus' feet, giving him thanks. Now he was a Samaritan. 17 Then said Jesus, "Were not ten cleansed? Where are the nine? 18 Was no one found to return and give praise to God except this foreigner?" 19And he said to him, "Rise and go your way; your faith has made you well."

20 Being asked by the Pharisees when the kingdom of God was coming, he answered them, "The kingdom of God is not coming with signs to be observed; 21 nor will they say, 'Lo, here it is!' or 'There!' for behold, the kingdom of God is in the midst of you." *z* 22 And he said to the disciples, "The days are coming when you will desire to see one of the days of the Son of man, and you will not see it. 23And they will say to you, 'Lo, there!' or 'Lo, here!' Do not go, do not follow them. 24 For as the lightning flashes and lights up the sky from one side to the other, so will the Son of man be in his day.*a* 25 But first he must suffer many things and be rejected by this generation. 26As it was in the days of Noah, so will it be in the days of the Son of man. 27 They ate, they drank, they married, they were given in marriage, until the day when Noah entered the ark, and the flood came and destroyed them all. 28 Likewise as it was in the days of Lot— they ate, they drank, they bought, they sold, they planted, they built, 29 but on the day when Lot went out from Sodom fire and brimstone rained from heaven and destroyed them all— 30 so will it be on the day when the Son of man is revealed. 31 On that day, let him who is on the housetop, with his goods in the house, not come down to take them away; and likewise let him who is in the field not turn back. 32 Remember Lot's wife. 33 Whoever seeks to gain his life will lose it, but whoever loses his life will preserve it. 34 I tell you, in that night there will be two men in one bed; one will be taken and the other left. 35 There will be two women grinding together; one will be taken and

[z] Or *within you.* [a] Other ancient authorities omit *in his day.*

PHILLIPS

Jesus heals ten men of leprosy: **17. 11**
only one shows his gratitude

In the course of his journey to Jerusalem,
Jesus crossed the boundary between Samaria
and Galilee, and as he was approaching a
village ten lepers met him. They kept their distance but shouted out,
"Jesus, Master, have pity on us!"
When Jesus saw them, he said,
"Go and show yourselves to the priests."
And it happened that as they went on their
way they were cured. One of their number,
when he saw that he was cured, turned round
and praised God at the top of his voice, and
then fell on his face before Jesus and thanked
him. This man was a Samaritan. And at this
Jesus remarked:
"Weren't there ten men healed? Where are the
other nine? Is nobody going to turn and praise
God for what has been done, except this
stranger?"
And he said to the man:
"Stand up now, and go on your way. It is
your faith that has made you well."

Jesus tells the Pharisees that the **17. 20**
kingdom is here and now

Later, he was asked by the Pharisees when
the kingdom of God was coming, and he gave
them this reply:
"The kingdom of God never comes by watching for it. Men cannot say, 'Look, here it is,' or
'There it is,' for the kingdom of God is inside
you."

Jesus tells his disciples **17. 22**
about the future

Then he said to the disciples:
"The time will come when you will long to
see again a single day of the Son of Man, but
you will not see it. People will say to you,
'Look, there he is,' or 'Look, here he is.' Stay
where you are and don't go off looking for him!
For the day of the Son of Man will be like
lightning flashing from one end of the sky to
the other. But before that happens, he must go
through much suffering and be utterly rejected
by this generation. In the time of the coming of
the Son of Man, life will be as it was in the days
of Noah. People ate and drank, married and
were given in marriage, right up to the day
when Noah entered the ark—and then came the
flood and destroyed them all. It will be just the
same as it was in the days of Lot. People ate
and drank, bought and sold, planted and built,
but on the day that Lot left Sodom fire and
brimstone rained from heaven, and destroyed
them all. That is how it will be on the day when
the Son of Man is revealed. When that day
comes, the man who is on the roof of his house,
with his goods inside it, must not come down to
get them. And the man out in the fields must
not turn back for anything. Remember what
happened to Lot's wife. Whoever tries to preserve his life will lose it, and the man who is
prepared to lose his life will preserve it. I tell
you, that night there will be two men in one
bed; one man will be taken and the other will be
left. Two women will be turning the grinding

N.E.B.

In the course of his journey to Jerusalem he
was travelling through the borderlands of Samaria and Galilee. As he was entering a village he
was met by ten men with leprosy. They stood
some way off and called out to him, 'Jesus,
Master, take pity on us.' When he saw them he
said, 'Go and show yourselves to the priests'; and
while they were on their way, they were made
clean. One of them, finding himself cured, turned
back praising God aloud. He threw himself
down at Jesus's feet and thanked him. And he
was a Samaritan. At this Jesus said: 'Were not
all ten cleansed? The other nine, where are they?
Could none be found to come back and give
praise to God except this foreigner?' And he
said to the man, 'Stand up and go on your way;
your faith has cured you.'

The Pharisees asked him, 'When will the kingdom of God come?' He said, 'You cannot tell by
observation when the kingdom of God comes.
There will be no saying, "Look, here it is!" or
"there it is!"; for in fact the kingdom of God
is among you.' [a]
He said to the disciples, 'The time will come
when you will long to see one of the days of
the Son of Man, but you will not see it. They
will say to you, "Look! There!" and "Look!
Here!" Do not go running off in pursuit. For
like the lightning-flash that lights up the earth
from end to end, will the Son of Man be when
his day comes. But first he must endure much
suffering and be repudiated by this generation.
'As things were in Noah's days, so will they
be in the days of the Son of Man. They ate and
drank and married, until the day that Noah went
into the ark and the flood came and made an
end of them all. As things were in Lot's days,
also: they ate and drank; they bought and sold;
they planted and built; but the day that Lot went
out from Sodom, it rained fire and sulphur from
heaven and made an end of them all—it will be
like that on the day when the Son of Man is
revealed.
'On that day the man who is on the roof and
his belongings in the house must not come down
to pick them up; he, too, who is in the fields
must not go back. Remember Lot's wife. Whoever seeks to save his life will lose it; and whoever loses it will save it, and live.
'I tell you, on that night there will be two
men in one bed: one will be taken, the other
left. There will be two women together grinding

[a] *Or* for in fact the kingdom of God is within you,
or for in fact the kingdom of God is within your
grasp, *or* for suddenly the kingdom of God will be
among you.

K.J.V.

the one shall be taken, and the other left. 36 Two *men* shall be in the field; the one shall be taken, and the other left. 37And they answered and said unto him, Where, Lord? And he said unto them, Wheresoever the body *is,* thither will the eagles be gathered together.

18 And he spake a parable unto them *to this end,* that men ought always to pray, and not to faint; 2 Saying, There was in a city a judge, which feared not God, neither regarded man: 3And there was a widow in that city; and she came unto him, saying, Avenge me of mine adversary. 4And he would not for a while: but afterward he said within himself, Though I fear not God, nor regard man; 5 Yet because this widow troubleth me, I will avenge her, lest by her continual coming she weary me. 6And the Lord said, Hear what the unjust judge saith. 7And shall not God avenge his own elect, which cry day and night unto him, though he bear long with them? 8 I tell you that he will avenge them speedily. Nevertheless, when the Son of man cometh, shall he find faith on the earth? 9And he spake this parable unto certain which trusted in themselves that they were righteous, and despised others: 10 Two men went up into the temple to pray; the one a Pharisee, and the other a publican. 11 The Pharisee stood and prayed thus with himself, God, I thank thee, that I am not as other men *are,* extortioners, unjust, adulterers, or even as this publican. 12 I fast twice in the week, I give tithes of all that I possess. 13And the publican, standing afar off, would not lift up so much as *his* eyes unto heaven, but smote upon his breast, saying, God be merciful to me a sinner. 14 I tell you, this man went down to his house justified *rather* than the other: for every one that exalteth himself shall be abased; and he that humbleth himself shall be exalted. 15And they brought unto him also infants, that he would touch them: but when *his* disciples saw *it,* they rebuked them. 16 But Jesus called them *unto him,* and said, Suffer little children to come unto me, and forbid them not: for of such is the kingdom of God. 17 Verily I say unto you, Whosoever shall not receive the kingdom of God as a little child

R.S.V.

the other left." [b] 37And they said to him, "Where, Lord?" He said to them, "Where the body is, there the eagles[c] will be gathered together."

18 And he told them a parable, to the effect that they ought always to pray and not lose heart. 2 He said, "In a certain city there was a judge who neither feared God nor regarded man; 3 and there was a widow in that city who kept coming to him and saying, 'Vindicate me against my adversary.' 4 For a while he refused; but afterward he said to himself, 'Though I neither fear God nor regard man, 5 yet because this widow bothers me, I will vindicate her, or she will wear me out by her continual coming.' " 6And the Lord said, "Hear what the unrighteous judge says. 7And will not God vindicate his elect, who cry to him day and night? Will he delay long over them? 8 I tell you, he will vindicate them speedily. Nevertheless, when the Son of man comes, will he find faith on earth?"

9 He also told this parable to some who trusted in themselves that they were righteous and despised others: 10 "Two men went up into the temple to pray, one a Pharisee and the other a tax collector. 11 The Pharisee stood and prayed thus with himself, 'God, I thank thee that I am not like other men, extortioners, unjust, adulterers, or even like this tax collector. 12 I fast twice a week, I give tithes of all that I get.' 13 But the tax collector, standing far off, would not even lift up his eyes to heaven, but beat his breast, saying, 'God, be merciful to me a sinner!' 14 I tell you, this man went down to his house justified rather than the other; for every one who exalts himself will be humbled, but he who humbles himself will be exalted."

15 Now they were bringing even infants to him that he might touch them; and when the disciples saw it, they rebuked them. 16 But Jesus called them to him, saying, "Let the children come to me, and do not hinder them; for to such belongs the kingdom of God. 17 Truly, I say to you, whoever does not receive the kingdom of God like a child shall not enter it."

[b] Other ancient authorities add verse 36, *"Two men will be in the field; one will be taken and the other left."* [c] Or *vultures.*

PHILLIPS

N.E.B.

mill together; one will be taken and the other left."

"But where, Lord?" they asked him.

" 'Wherever there is a dead body, there the vultures will flock,' " he replied.

corn: one will be taken, the other left.' [a] When they heard this they asked, 'Where, Lord?' He said, 'Where the corpse is, there the vultures will gather.'

Jesus urges his disciples to   **18. 1**
persist in prayer

Then he gave them an illustration to show that they must always pray and never lose heart.

"Once upon a time," he said, "there was a magistrate in a town who had neither fear of God nor respect for his fellow men. There was a widow in the town who kept coming to him, saying, 'Please protect me from the man who is trying to ruin me.' And for a long time he refused. But later he said to himself, 'Although I don't fear God and have no respect for men, yet this woman is such a nuisance that I shall give judgment in her favor, or else her continual visits will be the death of me!' "

Then the Lord said:

"Notice how this dishonest magistrate behaved. Do you suppose God, patient as he is, will not see justice done for his chosen, who appeal to him day and night? I assure you he will not delay in seeing justice done. Yet, when the Son of Man comes, will he find men on earth who believe in him?"

18 He spoke to them in a parable to show that they should keep on praying and never lose heart: 'There was once a judge who cared nothing for God or man, and in the same town there was a widow who constantly came before him demanding justice against her opponent. For a long time he refused; but in the end he said to himself, "True, I care nothing for God or man; but this widow is so great a nuisance that I will see her righted before she wears me out with her persistence." ' The Lord said, 'You hear what the unjust judge says; and will not God vindicate his chosen, who cry out to him day and night, while he listens patiently to them[b]? I tell you, he will vindicate them soon enough. But when the Son of Man comes, will he find faith on earth?'

Jesus tells a story against the   **18. 9**
self-righteous

Then he gave this illustration to certain people who were confident of their own goodness and looked down on others:

"Two men went up to the Temple to pray, one was a Pharisee, the other was a tax collector. The Pharisee stood and prayed like this with himself, 'O God, I do thank thee that I am not like the rest of mankind, greedy, dishonest, impure, or even like that tax collector over there. I fast twice every week; I give away a tenth part of all my income.' But the tax collector stood in a distant corner, scarcely daring to look up to Heaven, and with a gesture of despair, said, 'God, have mercy on a sinner like me.' I assure you that he was the man who went home justified in God's sight rather than the other one. For everyone who sets himself up as somebody will become a nobody, and the man who makes himself nobody will become somebody."

And here is another parable that he told. It was aimed at those who were sure of their own goodness and looked down on everyone else. 'Two men went up to the temple to pray, one a Pharisee and the other a tax-gatherer. The Pharisee stood up and prayed thus:[c] "I thank thee, O God, that I am not like the rest of men, greedy, dishonest, adulterous; or, for that matter, like this tax-gatherer. I fast twice a week; I pay tithes on all that I get." But the other kept his distance and would not even raise his eyes to heaven, but beat upon his breast, saying, "O God, have mercy on me, sinner that I am." It was this man, I tell you, and not the other, who went home acquitted of his sins. For everyone who exalts himself will be humbled; and whoever humbles himself will be exalted.'

They even brought babies for him to touch; but when the disciples saw them they scolded them for it. But Jesus called for the children and said, 'Let the little ones come to me; do not try to stop them; for the kingdom of God belongs to such as these. I tell you that whoever does not accept the kingdom of God like a child will never enter it.'

Jesus welcomes babies   **18. 15**

Then people began to bring babies to him so that he could put his hands on them. But when the disciples noticed it, they frowned on them. But Jesus called them to him, and said:

"You must let little children come to me, and you must never prevent their coming. The kingdom of Heaven belongs to little children like these. I tell you, the man who will not accept the kingdom of God like a little child will never get into it at all."

[a] *Some witnesses add* (36) two men in the fields: one will be taken, the other left. [b] *Or* delays to help them. [c] *Some witnesses read* stood up by himself and prayed thus; *others read* stood up and prayed thus privately.

K.J.V.

shall in no wise enter therein. 18And a certain ruler asked him, saying, Good Master, what shall I do to inherit eternal life? 19And Jesus said unto him, Why callest thou me good? none *is* good, save one, *that is,* God. 20 Thou knowest the commandments, Do not commit adultery, Do not kill, Do not steal, Do not bear false witness, Honour thy father and thy mother. 21And he said, All these have I kept from my youth up. 22 Now when Jesus heard these things, he said unto him, Yet lackest thou one thing: sell all that thou hast, and distribute unto the poor, and thou shalt have treasure in heaven: and come, follow me. 23And when he heard this, he was very sorrowful: for he was very rich. 24And when Jesus saw that he was very sorrowful, he said, How hardly shall they that have riches enter into the kingdom of God! 25 For it is easier for a camel to go through a needle's eye, than for a rich man to enter into the kingdom of God. 26And they that heard *it* said, Who then can be saved? 27And he said, The things which are impossible with men are possible with God. 28 Then Peter said, Lo, we have left all, and followed thee. 29And he said unto them, Verily I say unto you, There is no man that hath left house, or parents, or brethren, or wife, or children, for the kingdom of God's sake, 30 Who shall not receive manifold more in this present time, and in the world to come life everlasting.

31 Then he took *unto him* the twelve, and said unto them, Behold, we go up to Jerusalem, and all things that are written by the prophets concerning the Son of man shall be accomplished. 32 For he shall be delivered unto the Gentiles, and shall be mocked, and spitefully entreated, and spitted on: 33And they shall scourge *him,* and put him to death; and the third day he shall rise again. 34And they understood none of these things: and this saying was hid from them, neither knew they the things which were spoken.

35 And it came to pass, that as he was come nigh unto Jericho, a certain blind man sat by the way side begging: 36And hearing the multitude pass by, he asked what it meant. 37And they told him, that Jesus of Nazareth passeth by. 38And he cried, saying, Jesus, *thou* Son of David,

R.S.V.

18 And a ruler asked him, "Good Teacher, what shall I do to inherit eternal life?" 19And Jesus said to him, "Why do you call me good? No one is good but God alone. 20 You know the commandments: 'Do not commit adultery, Do not kill, Do not steal, Do not bear false witness, Honor your father and mother.'" 21And he said, "All these I have observed from my youth." 22And when Jesus heard it, he said to him, "One thing you still lack. Sell all that you have and distribute to the poor, and you will have treasure in heaven; and come, follow me." 23 But when he heard this he became sad, for he was very rich. 24 Jesus looking at him said, "How hard it is for those who have riches to enter the kingdom of God! 25 For it is easier for a camel to go through the eye of a needle than for a rich man to enter the kingdom of God." 26 Those who heard it said, "Then who can be saved?" 27 But he said, "What is impossible with men is possible with God." 28And Peter said, "Lo, we have left our homes and followed you." 29And he said to them, "Truly, I say to you, there is no man who has left house or wife or brothers or parents or children, for the sake of the kingdom of God, 30 who will not receive manifold more in this time, and in the age to come eternal life."

31 And taking the twelve, he said to them, "Behold, we are going up to Jerusalem, and everything that is written of the Son of man by the prophets will be accomplished. 32 For he will be delivered to the Gentiles, and will be mocked and shamefully treated and spit upon; 33 they will scourge him and kill him, and on the third day he will rise." 34 But they understood none of these things; this saying was hid from them, and they did not grasp what was said.

35 As he drew near to Jericho, a blind man was sitting by the roadside begging; 36 and hearing a multitude going by, he inquired what this meant. 37 They told him, "Jesus of Nazareth is passing by." 38And he cried, "Jesus, Son of

Jesus and riches   18. 18

Then one of the Jewish rulers put this question to him,

"Master, I know that you are good; tell me, please, what must I do to be sure of eternal life?"

"I wonder why you call me good?" returned Jesus. "No one is good—only the one God. You know the commandments—

"Thou shalt not commit adultery.

"Thou shalt not commit murder.

"Thou shalt not steal.

"Thou shalt not bear false witness.

"Honor thy father and thy mother."

"All these," he replied, "I have carefully kept since I was quite young."

And when Jesus heard that, he said to him:

"There is still one thing you have missed. Sell everything you possess and give the money away to the poor, and you will have riches in Heaven. Then come and follow me."

But when the man heard this, he was greatly distressed, for he was very rich.

And when Jesus saw how his face fell, he remarked:

"How difficult it is for those who have great possessions to enter the kingdom of God! A camel could squeeze through the eye of a needle more easily than a rich man could get into the kingdom of God."

Those who heard Jesus say this, exclaimed,

"Then who can possibly be saved?"

Jesus replied,

"What men find impossible is perfectly possible with God."

"Well," rejoined Peter, "we have left all that we ever had and followed you."

And Jesus told them,

"Believe me, nobody has left his home or wife, or brothers or parents or children for the sake of the kingdom of God, without receiving very much more in this present life—and eternal life in the world to come."

Jesus foretells his death and   18. 31
resurrection

Then Jesus took the twelve to one side and spoke to them:

"Listen to me. We are now going up to Jerusalem, and everything that has been written by the prophets about the Son of Man will come true. For he will be handed over to the heathen, and he is going to be jeered at and insulted and spat upon, and then they will flog him and kill him. But he will rise again on the third day."

But they did not understand any of this. His words were quite obscure to them and they had no idea of what he meant.

On the way to Jericho he heals   18. 35
a blind beggar

Then, as he was approaching Jericho, it happened that there was a blind man sitting by the roadside, begging. He heard the crowd passing and inquired what it was all about. And they told him, "Jesus the man from Nazareth is going past you." So he shouted out,

"Jesus, Son of David, have pity on me!"

A man of the ruling class put this question to him: 'Good Master, what must I do to win eternal life?' Jesus said to him, 'Why do you call me good? No one is good except God alone. You know the commandments: "Do not commit adultery; do not murder; do not steal; do not give false evidence; honour your father and mother." ' The man answered, 'I have kept all these since I was a boy.' On hearing this Jesus said, 'There is still one thing lacking: sell everything you have and distribute to the poor, and you will have riches in heaven; and come, follow me.' At these words his heart sank; for he was a very rich man. When Jesus saw it he said, 'How hard it is for the wealthy to enter the kingdom of God! It is easier for a camel to go through the eye of a needle than for a rich man to enter the kingdom of God.' Those who heard asked, 'Then who can be saved?' He answered, 'What is impossible for men is possible for God.'

Peter said, 'Here are we who gave up our belongings to become your followers.' Jesus said, 'I tell you this: there is no one who has given up home, or wife, brothers, parents, or children, for the sake of the kingdom of God, who will not be repaid many times over in this age, and in the age to come have eternal life.'

Challenge to Jerusalem

He took the Twelve aside and said, 'We are now going up to Jerusalem; and all that was written by the prophets will come true for the Son of Man. He will be handed over to the foreign power. He will be mocked, maltreated, and spat upon. They will flog him and kill him. And on the third day he will rise again.' But they understood nothing of all this; they did not grasp what he was talking about; its meaning was concealed from them.

As he approached Jericho a blind man sat at the roadside begging. Hearing a crowd going past, he asked what was happening. They told him, 'Jesus of Nazareth is passing by.' Then he shouted out, 'Jesus, Son of David, have pity on

K.J.V.

have mercy on me. 39And they which went before rebuked him, that he should hold his peace: but he cried so much the more, *Thou* Son of David, have mercy on me. 40And Jesus stood, and commanded him to be brought unto him: and when he was come near, he asked him, 41 Saying, What wilt thou that I shall do unto thee? And he said, Lord, that I may receive my sight. 42And Jesus said unto him, Receive thy sight: thy faith hath saved thee. 43And immediately he received his sight, and followed him, glorifying God: and all the people, when they saw *it,* gave praise unto God.

19 And *Jesus* entered and passed through Jericho. 2And, behold, *there was* a man named Zaccheus, which was the chief among the publicans, and he was rich. 3And he sought to see Jesus who he was; and could not for the press, because he was little of stature. 4And he ran before, and climbed up into a sycamore tree to see him; for he was to pass that *way.* 5And when Jesus came to the place, he looked up, and saw him, and said unto him, Zaccheus, make haste, and come down; for to day I must abide at thy house. 6And he made haste, and came down, and received him joyfully. 7And when they saw *it,* they all murmured, saying, That he was gone to be guest with a man that is a sinner. 8And Zaccheus stood, and said unto the Lord; Behold, Lord, the half of my goods I give to the poor; and if I have taken any thing from any man by false accusation, I restore *him* fourfold. 9And Jesus said unto him, This day is salvation come to this house, forasmuch as he also is a son of Abraham. 10 For the Son of man is come to seek and to save that which was lost. 11And as they heard these things, he added and spake a parable, because he was nigh to Jerusalem, and because they thought that the kingdom of God should immediately appear. 12 He said therefore, A certain nobleman went into a far country to receive for himself a kingdom, and to return. 13And he called his ten servants, and delivered them ten pounds, and said unto them, Occupy till I come. 14 But his citizens hated him, and sent a message after him, saying, We will not have this *man* to reign over us. 15And it came to pass, that when he was returned, having received the kingdom, then he commanded these servants to be called unto him, to whom he had given the money, that he might know how much every man had gained by trading. 16 Then came the first, saying, Lord, thy pound hath gained ten pounds. 17And he said unto him, Well, thou good servant: because thou hast been faithful in a very little, have thou authority over ten cities. 18And the second came,

R.S.V.

David, have mercy on me!" 39And those who were in front rebuked him, telling him to be silent; but he cried out all the more, "Son of David, have mercy on me!" 40And Jesus stopped, and commanded him to be brought to him; and when he came near, he asked him, 41 "What do you want me to do for you?" He said, "Lord, let me receive my sight." 42And Jesus said to him, "Receive your sight; your faith has made you well." 43And immediately he received his sight and followed him, glorifying God; and all the people, when they saw it, gave praise to God.

19 He entered Jericho and was passing through. 2And there was a man named Zacchaeus; he was a chief tax collector, and rich. 3And he sought to see who Jesus was, but he could not, on account of the crowd, because he was small of stature. 4 So he ran on ahead and climbed up into a sycamore tree to see him, for he was to pass that way. 5And when Jesus came to the place, he looked up and said to him, "Zacchaeus, make haste and come down; for I must stay at your house today." 6 So he made haste and came down, and received him joyfully. 7And when they saw it they all murmured, "He has gone in to be the guest of a man who is a sinner." 8And Zacchaeus stood and said to the Lord, "Behold, Lord, the half of my goods I give to the poor; and if I have defrauded any one of anything, I restore it fourfold." 9And Jesus said to him, "Today salvation has come to this house, since he also is a son of Abraham. 10 For the Son of man came to seek and to save the lost."

11 As they heard these things, he proceeded to tell a parable, because he was near to Jerusalem, and because they supposed that the kingdom of God was to appear immediately. 12 He said therefore, "A nobleman went into a far country to receive kingly power*d* and then return. 13 Calling ten of his servants, he gave them ten pounds,*e* and said to them, 'Trade with these till I come.' 14 But his citizens hated him and sent an embassy after him, saying, 'We do not want this man to reign over us.' 15 When he returned, having received the kingly power,*d* he commanded these servants, to whom he had given the money, to be called to him, that he might know what they had gained by trading. 16 The first came before him, saying, 'Lord, your pound has made ten pounds more.' 17And he said to him, 'Well done, good servant! Because you have been faithful in a very little, you shall have authority over ten cities.' 18And

[d] Greek *a kingdom.* [e] The mina, rendered here by *pound,* was equal to about twenty dollars.

Those who were in front tried to hush his cries. But that made him call out all the more, "Son of David, have pity on me!"

So Jesus stood quite still and ordered the man to be brought to him. And when he was quite close, he said to him,

"What do you want me to do for you?"

"Lord, make me see again," he cried.

"You can see again! Your faith has cured you," returned Jesus.

And his sight was restored at once, and he followed Jesus, praising God. All the people who saw it thanked God too.

The chief tax collector is converted to faith in Jesus

19. 1

Then he went into Jericho and was making his way through it. And here we find a wealthy man called Zacchaeus, a chief collector of taxes, wanting to see what sort of person Jesus was. But the crowd prevented him from doing so, for he was very short. So he ran ahead and climbed up into a sycamore tree to get a view of Jesus as he was heading that way. When Jesus reached the spot, he looked up and saw the man and said:

"Zacchaeus, hurry up and come down. I must be your guest today."

So Zacchaeus hurriedly climbed down and gladly welcomed him. But the bystanders muttered their disapproval, saying,

"Now he has gone to stay with a real sinner."

But Zacchaeus himself stopped and said to the Lord:

"Look, sir, I will give half my property to the poor. And if I have swindled anybody out of anything I will pay him back four times as much."

Jesus said to him:

"Salvation has come to this house today! Zacchaeus is a descendant of Abraham, and it was the lost that the Son of Man came to seek —and to save."

Life requires courage, and is hard on those who dare not use their gifts

19. 11

Then as the crowd still listened attentively, Jesus went on to give them this parable. For the fact that he was nearing Jerusalem made them imagine that the kingdom of God was on the point of appearing.

"Once upon a time a man of good family went abroad to accept a kingdom and then return. He summoned ten of his servants and gave them each ten dollars, with the words, 'Use this money to trade with until I come back.' But the citizens detested him and they sent a delegation after him, to say, 'We will not have this man to be our king.' Then later, when he had received his kingdom, he returned and gave orders for the servants to whom he had given the money to be called to him, so that he could find out what profit they had made. The first came into his presence, and said, 'Sire, your ten dollars have made a hundred dollars more.' 'Splendid, my good fellow,' he said, 'since you have proved trustworthy over this small amount, I am going to put you in charge of ten towns.' The second came in and said, 'Sire, your

me.' The people in front told him sharply to hold his tongue; but he called out all the more, 'Son of David, have pity on me.' Jesus stopped and ordered the man to be brought to him. When he came up he asked him, 'What do you want me to do for you?' 'Sir, I want my sight back', he answered. Jesus said to him, 'Have back your sight; your faith has cured you.' He recovered his sight instantly; and he followed Jesus, praising God. And all the people gave praise to God for what they had seen.

19 Entering Jericho he made his way through the city. There was a man there named Zacchaeus; he was superintendent of taxes and very rich. He was eager to see what Jesus looked like; but, being a little man, he could not see him for the crowd. So he ran on ahead and climbed a sycamore-tree in order to see him, for he was to pass that way. When Jesus came to the place, he looked up and said, 'Zacchaeus, be quick and come down; I must come and stay with you today.' He climbed down as fast as he could and welcomed him gladly. At this there was a general murmur of disapproval. 'He has gone in', they said, 'to be the guest of a sinner.' But Zacchaeus stood there and said to the Lord, 'Here and now, sir, I give half my possessions to charity; and if I have cheated anyone, I am ready to repay him four times over.' Jesus said to him, 'Salvation has come to this house today! —for this man too is a son of Abraham, and the Son of Man has come to seek and save what is lost.'

While they were listening to this, he went on to tell them a parable, because he was now close to Jerusalem and they thought the reign of God might dawn at any moment. He said, 'A man of noble birth went on a long journey abroad, to be appointed king and then return. But first he called ten of his servants and gave them a pound each, saying, "Trade with this while I am away." His fellow-citizens hated him, and they sent a delegation on his heels to say, "We do not want this man as our king." However, back he came as king, and sent for the servants to whom he had given the money, to see what profit each had made. The first came and said, "Your pound, sir, has made ten more." "Well done," he replied; "you are a good servant. You have shown yourself trustworthy in a very small matter, and you shall have charge of ten cities." The second came and said, "Your pound, sir,

K.J.V.

saying, Lord, thy pound hath gained five pounds. 19And he said likewise to him, Be thou also over five cities. 20And another came, saying, Lord, behold, *here is* thy pound, which I have kept laid up in a napkin: 21 For I feared thee, because thou art an austere man: thou takest up that thou layedst not down, and reapest that thou didst not sow. 22And he saith unto him, Out of thine own mouth will I judge thee, *thou* wicked servant. Thou knewest that I was an austere man, taking up that I laid not down, and reaping that I did not sow: 23 Wherefore then gavest not thou my money into the bank, that at my coming I might have required mine own with usury? 24And he said unto them that stood by, Take from him the pound, and give *it* to him that hath ten pounds. 25 (And they said unto him, Lord, he hath ten pounds.) 26 For I say unto you, That unto every one which hath shall be given; and from him that hath not, even that he hath shall be taken away from him. 27 But those mine enemies, which would not that I should reign over them, bring hither, and slay *them* before me.

28 And when he had thus spoken, he went before, ascending up to Jerusalem. 29And it came to pass, when he was come nigh to Bethphage and Bethany, at the mount called *the mount* of Olives, he sent two of his disciples, 30 Saying, Go ye into the village over against *you;* in the which at your entering ye shall find a colt tied, whereon yet never man sat: loose him, and bring *him hither.* 31And if any man ask you, Why do ye loose *him?* thus shall ye say unto him, Because the Lord hath need of him. 32And they that were sent went their way, and found even as he had said unto them. 33And as they were loosing the colt, the owners thereof said unto them, Why loose ye the colt? 34And they said, The Lord hath need of him. 35And they brought him to Jesus: and they cast their garments upon the colt, and they set Jesus thereon. 36And as he went, they spread their clothes in the way. 37And when he was come nigh, even now at the descent of the mount of Olives, the whole multitude of the disciples began to rejoice and praise God with a loud voice for all the mighty works that they had seen; 38 Saying, Blessed *be* the King that cometh in the name of the Lord: peace in heaven, and glory in the highest. 39And some of the Pharisees from among the multitude said unto him, Master, rebuke thy disciples. 40And he answered and said unto them, I tell you that, if these should hold their peace, the stones would immediately cry out.

41 And when he was come near, he beheld the city, and wept over it, 42 Saying, If thou hadst known, even thou, at least in this thy day, the things *which belong* unto thy peace! but now they are hid from thine eyes. 43 For the days shall come upon thee, that thine enemies shall cast a trench about thee, and compass thee

R.S.V.

the second came, saying, 'Lord, your pound has made five pounds.' 19And he said to him, 'And you are to be over five cities.' 20 Then another came, saying, 'Lord, here is your pound, which I kept laid away in a napkin; 21 for I was afraid of you, because you are a severe man; you take up what you did not lay down, and reap what you did not sow.' 22 He said to him, 'I will condemn you out of your own mouth, you wicked servant! You knew that I was a severe man, taking up what I did not lay down and reaping what I did not sow? 23 Why then did you not put my money into the bank, and at my coming I should have collected it with interest?' 24And he said to those who stood by, 'Take the pound from him, and give it to him who has the ten pounds.' 25 (And they said to him, 'Lord, he has ten pounds!') 26 'I tell you, that to every one who has will more be given; but from him who has not, even what he has will be taken away. 27 But as for these enemies of mine, who did not want me to reign over them, bring them here and slay them before me.' "

28 And when he had said this, he went on ahead, going up to Jerusalem. 29 When he drew near to Bethphage and Bethany, at the mount that is called Olivet, he sent two of the disciples, 30 saying, "Go into the village opposite, where on entering you will find a colt tied, on which no one has ever yet sat; untie it and bring it here. 31 If any one asks you, 'Why are you untying it?' you shall say this, 'The Lord has need of it.' " 32 So those who were sent went away and found it as he had told them. 33And as they were untying the colt, its owners said to them, "Why are you untying the colt?" 34And they said, "The Lord has need of it." 35And they brought it to Jesus, and throwing their garments on the colt they set Jesus upon it. 36And as he rode along, they spread their garments on the road. 37As he was now drawing near, at the descent of the Mount of Olives, the whole multitude of the disciples began to rejoice and praise God with a loud voice for all the mighty works that they had seen, 38 saying, "Blessed is the King who comes in the name of the Lord! Peace in heaven and glory in the highest!" 39 And some of the Pharisees in the multitude said to him, "Teacher, rebuke your disciples." 40 He answered, "I tell you, if these were silent, the very stones would cry out."

41 And when he drew near and saw the city he wept over it, 42 saying, "Would that even today you knew the things that make for peace! But now they are hid from your eyes. 43 For the days shall come upon you, when your enemies will cast up a bank about you and surround you,

PHILLIPS

ten dollars have made fifty dollars.' And he said to him, 'Good, you're appointed governor of five towns.' When the last came, he said, 'Sire, here are your ten dollars, which I have been keeping wrapped up in a handkerchief. I have been scared—I know you're a hard man, getting something for nothing and reaping where you never sowed.' To which he replied: 'You scoundrel, your own words condemn you! You knew perfectly well, did you, that I am a hard man who gets something for nothing and reaps where he never sowed? Then why didn't you put my money into the bank, and then when I returned I could have had it back with interest?' Then he said to those who were standing by, 'Take away his ten dollars and give it to the fellow who has a hundred.'

" 'But, sire, he has a hundred dollars already,' they said to him. 'Yes,' he replied, 'and I tell you that the man who has something will get more given to him. But as for the man who has nothing, even his "nothing" will be taken away. And as for these enemies of mine who objected to my being their king, bring them here and execute them in my presence.' "

After these words, Jesus walked on ahead of them on his way to Jerusalem.

Jesus arranges his own entrance   19. 29
into Jerusalem

Then as he was approaching Bethphage and Bethany, near the hill called the Mount of Olives, he sent off two of his disciples, telling them:

"Go into the village just ahead of you, and there you will find a colt tied on which no one has ever yet ridden. Untie it and bring it here. And if anybody asks you, 'Why are you untying it?' just say, 'The Lord needs it.' "

So the messengers went off and found things just as he had told them. In fact, as they were untying the colt, the owners did say, "Why are you untying it?" and they replied, "The Lord needs it." So they brought it to Jesus and, throwing their cloaks upon it, mounted Jesus on its back. Then as he rode along, people spread out their coats in the roadway. And as he approached the city, where the road slopes down from the Mount of Olives, the whole crowd of his disciples joyfully shouted praises to God for all the marvelous things that they had seen him do.

"God bless the king who comes in the name of the Lord!" they cried. "There is peace in Heaven and glory on high!"

There were some Pharisees in the crowd who said to Jesus,

"Master, restrain your disciples!"

To which he replied,

"I tell you that if they kept quiet, the very stones in the road would burst out cheering!"

The sight of the city   19. 41
moves him to tears

And as he came still nearer to the city, he caught sight of it and wept over it, saying:

"Ah, if you only knew, even at this eleventh hour, on what your peace depends—but you cannot see it. The time is coming when your enemies will encircle you with ramparts, surrounding you and hemming you in on every side.

N.E.B.

has made five more"; and he also was told, "You too, take charge of five cities." The third came and said, "Here is your pound, sir; I kept it put away in a handkerchief. I was afraid of you, because you are a hard man: you draw out what you never put in and reap what you did not sow." "You rascal!" he replied; "I will judge you by your own words. You knew, did you, that I am a hard man, that I draw out what I never put in, and reap what I did not sow? Then why did you not put my money on deposit, and I could have claimed it with interest when I came back?" Turning to his attendants he said, "Take the pound from him and give it to the man with ten." "But, sir," they replied, "he has ten already." "I tell you," he went on, "the man who has will always be given more; but the man who has not will forfeit even what he has. But as for those enemies of mine who did not want me for their king, bring them here and slaughter them in my presence." '

With that Jesus went forward and began the ascent to Jerusalem. As he approached Bethphage and Bethany at the hill called Olivet, he sent two of the disciples with these instructions: 'Go to the village opposite; as you enter it you will find tethered there a colt which no one has yet ridden. Untie it and bring it here. If anyone asks why you are untying it, say, "Our Master needs it." ' The two went on their errand and found it as he had told them; and while they were untying the colt, its owners asked, 'Why are you untying that colt?' They answered, 'The Master needs it.' So they brought the colt to Jesus.

Then they threw their cloaks on the colt, for Jesus to mount, and they carpeted the road with them as he went on his way. And now, as he approached the descent from the Mount of Olives, the whole company of his disciples in their joy began to sing aloud the praises of God for all the things they had seen:

'Blessings on him who comes as king in the name of the Lord!
Peace in heaven, glory in highest heaven!'

Some Pharisees who were in the crowd said to him, 'Master, reprimand your disciples.' He answered, 'I tell you, if my disciples keep silence the stones will shout aloud.'

When he came in sight of the city, he wept over it and said, 'If only you had known, on this great day, the way that leads to peace! But no; it is hidden from your sight. For a time will come upon you, when your enemies will set up siege-works against you; they will encircle you

243

K.J.V.

round, and keep thee in on every side, 44And shall lay thee even with the ground, and thy children within thee; and they shall not leave in thee one stone upon another; because thou knewest not the time of thy visitation. 45And he went into the temple, and began to cast out them that sold therein, and them that bought; 46 Saying unto them, It is written, My house is the house of prayer; but ye have made it a den of thieves. 47And he taught daily in the temple. But the chief priests and the scribes and the chief of the people sought to destroy him, 48And could not find what they might do: for all the people were very attentive to hear him.

20 And it came to pass, *that* on one of those days, as he taught the people in the temple, and preached the gospel, the chief priests and the scribes came upon *him* with the elders, 2And spake unto him, saying, Tell us, by what authority doest thou these things? or who is he that gave thee this authority? 3And he answered and said unto them, I will also ask you one thing; and answer me: 4 The baptism of John, was it from heaven, or of men? 5And they reasoned with themselves, saying, If we shall say, From heaven; he will say, Why then believed ye him not? 6 But and if ye say, Of men; all the people will stone us: for they be persuaded that John was a prophet. 7And they answered, that they could not tell whence *it was.* 8And Jesus said unto them, Neither tell I you by what authority I do these things. 9 Then began he to speak to the people this parable; A certain man planted a vineyard, and let it forth to husbandmen, and went into a far country for a long time. 10And at the season he sent a servant to the husbandmen, that they should give him of the fruit of the vineyard: but the husbandmen beat him, and sent *him* away empty. 11And again he sent another servant: and they beat him also, and entreated *him* shamefully, and sent *him* away empty. 12And again he sent a third: and they wounded him also, and cast *him* out. 13 Then said the lord of the vineyard, What shall I do? I will send my beloved son: it may be they will reverence *him* when they see him. 14 But when the husbandmen saw him, they reasoned among themselves, saying, This is the heir: come, let us kill him, that the inheritance may be ours. 15 So they cast him out of the vineyard, and killed *him.* What therefore shall the lord of the vineyard do unto them? 16 He shall come and destroy these husbandmen, and shall give the vineyard to others. And when they heard *it,*

R.S.V.

and hem you in on every side, 44 and dash you to the ground, you and your children within you, and they will not leave one stone upon another in you; because you did not know the time of your visitation."

45 And he entered the temple and began to drive out those who sold, 46 saying to them, "It is written, 'My house shall be a house of prayer'; but you have made it a den of robbers."

47 And he was teaching daily in the temple. The chief priests and the scribes and the principal men of the people sought to destroy him; 48 but they did not find anything they could do, for all the people hung upon his words.

20 One day, as he was teaching the people in the temple and preaching the gospel, the chief priests and the scribes with the elders came up 2 and said to him, "Tell us by what authority you do these things, or who it is that gave you this authority." 3 He answered them, "I also will ask you a question; now tell me, 4 Was the baptism of John from heaven or from men?" 5And they discussed it with one another, saying, "If we say, 'From heaven,' he will say, 'Why did you not believe him?' 6 But if we say, 'From men,' all the people will stone us; for they are convinced that John was a prophet." 7 So they answered that they did not know whence it was. 8 And Jesus said to them, "Neither will I tell you by what authority I do these things."

9 And he began to tell the people this parable: "A man planted a vineyard, and let it out to tenants, and went into another country for a long while. 10 When the time came, he sent a servant to the tenants, that they should give him some of the fruit of the vineyard; but the tenants beat him, and sent him away empty-handed. 11And he sent another servant; him also they beat and treated shamefully, and sent him away empty-handed. 12And he sent yet a third; this one they wounded and cast out. 13 Then the owner of the vineyard said, 'What shall I do? I will send my beloved son; it may be they will respect him.' 14 But when the tenants saw him, they said to themselves, 'This is the heir; let us kill him, that the inheritance may be ours.' 15And they cast him out of the vineyard and killed him. What then will the owner of the vineyard do to them? 16 He will come and destroy those tenants, and give the vineyard to others." When they heard this, they said, "God forbid!"

PHILLIPS

And they will hurl you and all your children to the ground—yes, they will not leave you one stone standing upon another—all because you did not know when God Himself was visiting you!"

Then he went into the Temple, and proceeded to throw out the traders there.

"It is written," he told them, " *'My house shall be a house of prayer,'* but you have turned it into a thieves' kitchen!"

Jesus teaches daily in the Temple 19. 47

Then day after day he was teaching inside the Temple. The chief priests, the scribes and the national leaders were all the time trying to get rid of him, but they could not find any way to do it since all the people hung upon his words.

Then one day as he was teaching the people in the Temple, and preaching the gospel to them, the chief priests, the scribes and elders confronted him in a body and asked him this direct question,

"Tell us by whose authority you act as you do—who gave you such authority?"

"I have a question for you, too," replied Jesus. "John's baptism, now—tell me, did it come from Heaven or was it purely human?"

At this they began arguing with one another, saying:

"If we say, 'from Heaven,' he will say to us, 'Then why didn't you believe in him?' but if we say it was purely human, this mob will stone us to death, for they are convinced that John was a prophet." So they replied that they did not know where it came from.

"Then," returned Jesus, "neither will I tell you by what authority I do what I am doing."

He tells the people   20. 9
a pointed story

Then he turned to the people and told them this parable:

"There was once a man who planted a vineyard, let it out to farm workers, and went abroad for some time. Then, when the season arrived, he sent a servant to the farm workers so that they could give him the proceeds of the vineyard. But the farm workers beat him up and sent him back empty-handed. So he sent another servant, and they beat him up as well, manhandling him disgracefully, and sent him back empty-handed. Then he sent a third servant, but after wounding him severely they threw him out. Then the owner of the vineyard said, 'What shall I do now? I will send them my son who is so dear to me. Perhaps they will respect *him.*' But when the farm workers saw him, they talked the matter over with one another and said, 'This man is the heir—come on, let's kill him, and we shall get everything that he would have had!' And they threw him outside the vineyard and killed him. What then do you suppose the owner will do to them? He will come and destroy the men who were working his property, and hand it over to others."

When they heard this, they said, "God forbid!"

N.E.B.

and hem you in at every point; they will bring you to the ground, you and your children within your walls, and not leave you one stone standing on another, because you did not recognize God's moment when it came.'

Then he went into the temple and began driving out the traders, with these words: 'Scripture says, "My house shall be a house of prayer"; but you have made it a robbers' cave.'

Day by day he taught in the temple. And the chief priests and lawyers were bent on making an end of him, with the support of the leading citizens, but found they were helpless, because the people all hung upon his words.

20 One day, as he was teaching the people in the temple and telling them the good news, the priests and lawyers, and the elders with them, came upon him and accosted him. 'Tell us', they said, 'by what authority you are acting like this; who gave you this authority?' He answered them, 'I have a question to ask you too: tell me, was the baptism of John from God or from men?' This set them arguing among themselves: 'If we say, "from God", he will say, "Why did you not believe him?" And if we say, "from men", the people will all stone us, for they are convinced that John was a prophet.' So they replied that they could not tell. And Jesus said to them, 'Neither will I tell you by what authority I act.'

He went on to tell the people this parable: 'A man planted a vineyard, let it out to vine-growers, and went abroad for a long time. When the season came, he sent a servant to the tenants to collect from them his share of the produce; but the tenants thrashed him and sent him away empty-handed. He tried again and sent a second servant; but he also was thrashed, outrageously treated, and sent away empty-handed. He tried once more with a third; this one too they wounded and flung out. Then the owner of the vineyard said, "What am I to do? I will send my own dear son;[a] perhaps they will respect him." But when the tenants saw him they talked it over together. "This is the heir," they said; "let us kill him so that the property may come to us." So they flung him out of the vineyard and killed him. What then will the owner of the vineyard do to them? He will come and put these tenants to death and let the vineyard to others.'

When they heard this, they said, 'God forbid!'

[a] *Or* my only son.

245

K.J.V.

they said, God forbid. 17And he beheld them, and said, What is this then that is written, The stone which the builders rejected, the same is become the head of the corner? 18 Whosoever shall fall upon that stone shall be broken; but on whomsoever it shall fall, it will grind him to powder.

19 And the chief priests and the scribes the same hour sought to lay hands on him; and they feared the people: for they perceived that he had spoken this parable against them. 20And they watched *him*, and sent forth spies, which should feign themselves just men, that they might take hold of his words, that so they might deliver him unto the power and authority of the governor. 21And they asked him, saying, Master, we know that thou sayest and teachest rightly, neither acceptest thou the person *of any,* but teachest the way of God truly: 22 Is it lawful for us to give tribute unto Cesar, or no? 23 But he perceived their craftiness, and said unto them, Why tempt ye me? 24 Shew me a penny. Whose image and superscription hath it? They answered and said, Cesar's. 25And he said unto them, Render therefore unto Cesar the things which be Cesar's, and unto God the things which be God's. 26And they could not take hold of his words before the people: and they marvelled at his answer, and held their peace.

27 Then came to *him* certain of the Sadducees, which deny that there is any resurrection; and they asked him, 28 Saying, Master, Moses wrote unto us, If any man's brother die, having a wife, and he die without children, that his brother should take his wife, and raise up seed unto his brother. 29 There were therefore seven brethren: and the first took a wife, and died without children. 30And the second took her to wife, and he died childless. 31And the third took her; and in like manner the seven also: and they left no children, and died. 32 Last of all the woman died also. 33 Therefore in the resurrection whose wife of them is she? for seven had her to wife. 34And Jesus answering said unto them, The children of this world marry, and are given in marriage: 35 But they which shall be accounted worthy to obtain that world, and the resurrection from the dead, neither marry, nor are given in marriage: 36 Neither can they die any more: for they are equal unto the angels; and are the children of God, being the children of the resurrection. 37 Now that the dead are raised, even Moses shewed at the bush, when he calleth the Lord the God of Abraham, and the God of Isaac, and the God of Jacob. 38 For he is not a God of the dead, but of the living: for all live unto him.

39 Then certain of the scribes answering said, Master, thou hast well said. 40And after that

R.S.V.

17 But he looked at them and said, "What then is this that is written:

'The very stone which the builders rejected
has become the head of the corner'?
18 Every one who falls on that stone will be broken to pieces; but when it falls on any one it will crush him."

19 The scribes and the chief priests tried to lay hands on him at that very hour, but they feared the people; for they perceived that he had told this parable against them. 20 So they watched him, and sent spies, who pretended to be sincere, that they might take hold of what he said, so as to deliver him up to the authority and jurisdiction of the governor. 21 They asked him, "Teacher, we know that you speak and teach rightly, and show no partiality, but truly teach the way of God. 22 Is it lawful for us to give tribute to Caesar, or not?" 23 But he perceived their craftiness, and said to them, 24 "Show me a coin.[f] Whose likeness and inscription has it?" They said, "Caesar's." 25 He said to them, "Then render to Caesar the things that are Caesar's, and to God the things that are God's." 26And they were not able in the presence of the people to catch him by what he said; but marveling at his answer they were silent.

27 There came to him some Sadducees, those who say that there is no resurrection, 28 and they asked him a question, saying, "Teacher, Moses wrote for us that if a man's brother dies, having a wife but no children, the man[g] must take the wife and raise up children for his brother. 29 Now there were seven brothers; the first took a wife, and died without children; 30 and the second 31 and the third took her, and likewise all seven left no children and died. 32 Afterward the woman also died. 33 In the resurrection, therefore, whose wife will the woman be? For the seven had her as wife."

34 And Jesus said to them, "The sons of this age marry and are given in marriage; 35 but those who are accounted worthy to attain to that age and to the resurrection from the dead neither marry nor are given in marriage, 36 for they cannot die any more, because they are equal to angels and are sons of God, being sons of the resurrection. 37 But that the dead are raised, even Moses showed, in the passage about the bush, where he calls the Lord the God of Abraham and the God of Isaac and the God of Jacob. 38 Now he is not God of the dead, but of the living; for all live to him." 39And some of the scribes answered, "Teacher, you have spoken well." 40 For they no longer dared to ask him any question.

[f] Greek denarius. [g] Greek his brother.

PHILLIPS	N.E.B.

PHILLIPS

But he looked them straight in the eyes and said,

"Then what is the meaning of this scripture—

The stone which the builders rejected,
The same was made the head of the corner?

The man who falls on that stone will be broken, and the man on whom it falls will be crushed to powder."

The authorities resort to trickery   20. 19

The scribes and chief priests longed to get their hands on him at that moment, but they were afraid of the people. They knew well enough that his parable referred to them. They watched him, however, and sent some spies into the crowd, pretending that they were honest men, to fasten on something that he might say which could be used to hand him over to the authority and power of the governor.

These men asked him:

"Master, we know that what you say and teach is right, and that you teach the way of God truly without fear or favor. Now, *is it right for us to pay taxes to Caesar or not?*"

But Jesus saw through their cunning and said to them:

"Show me one of the coins. Whose face is this, and whose name is in the inscription?"

"Caesar's," they said.

"Then give to Caesar," he replied, "what belongs to Caesar, and to God what belongs to God."

So his reply gave them no sort of handle that they could use against him publicly. And in fact they were so taken aback by his answer that they had nothing more to say.

Jesus exposes the ignorance   20. 27
of the Sadducees

Then up came some of the Sadducees (who deny that there is any resurrection) and they asked him:

"Master, Moses told us in the scripture, 'If a man's brother should die without any children, he should marry the widow and raise up a family for his brother.' Now, there were once seven brothers. The first got married and died childless, and the second and the third married the woman, and in fact all the seven married her and died without leaving any children. Lastly, the woman herself died. Now, in this 'resurrection' whose wife is she of these seven men, for she belonged to all of them?"

"People in this world," Jesus replied, "marry and are given in marriage. But those who are considered worthy of reaching that world, which means rising from the dead, neither marry nor are they given in marriage. They cannot die any more but live like the angels; for being children of the resurrection, they are the sons of God. But that the dead are raised, even Moses showed to be true in the story of the bush, when he calls the Lord the God of Abraham, the God of Isaac and the God of Jacob. For God is not God of the dead, but of the living. For all men are alive to him."

To this some of the scribes replied,

"Master, that was a good answer."

And indeed nobody had the courage to ask

N.E.B.

But he looked straight at them and said, 'Then what does this text of Scripture mean: "The stone which the builders rejected has become the main corner-stone"? Any man who falls on that stone will be dashed to pieces; and if it falls on a man he will be crushed by it.'

The lawyers and chief priests wanted to lay hands on him there and then, for they saw that this parable was aimed at them; but they were afraid of the people. So they watched their opportunity and sent secret agents in the guise of honest men, to seize upon some word of his as a pretext for handing him over to the authority and jurisdiction of the Governor. They put a question to him: 'Master,' they said, 'we know that what you speak and teach is sound; you pay deference to no one, but teach in all honesty the way of life that God requires. Are we or are we not permitted to pay taxes to the Roman Emperor?' He saw through their trick and said, 'Show me a silver piece. Whose head does it bear, and whose inscription?' 'Caesar's,' they replied. 'Very well then,' he said, 'pay Caesar what is due to Caesar, and pay God what is due to God.' Thus their attempt to catch him out in public failed, and, astonished by his reply, they fell silent.

Then some Sadducees came forward. They are the people who deny that there is a resurrection. Their question was this: 'Master, Moses laid it down for us that if there are brothers, and one dies leaving a wife but no child, then the next should marry the widow and carry on his brother's family. Now, there were seven brothers: the first took a wife and died childless; then the second married her, then the third. In this way the seven of them died leaving no children. Afterwards the woman also died. At the resurrection whose wife is she to be, since all seven had married her?' Jesus said to them, 'The men and women of this world marry; but those who have been judged worthy of a place in the other world and of the resurrection from the dead, do not marry, for they are not subject to death any longer. They are like angels; they are sons of God, because they share in the resurrection. That the dead are raised to life again is shown by Moses himself in the story of the burning bush, when he calls the Lord, "the God of Abraham, Isaac, and Jacob". God is not God of the dead but of the living; for him all are[a] alive.'

At this some of the lawyers said, 'Well spoken, Master.' For there was no further question that they ventured to put to him.

[a] *Or* they are all.

K.J.V.

they durst not ask him any *question at all*. 41And he said unto them, How say they that Christ is David's son? 42And David himself saith in the book of Psalms, The LORD said unto my Lord, Sit thou on my right hand, 43 Till I make thine enemies thy footstool. 44 David therefore calleth him Lord, how is he then his son?

45 Then in the audience of all the people he said unto his disciples, 46 Beware of the scribes, which desire to walk in long robes, and love greetings in the markets, and the highest seats in the synagogues, and the chief rooms at feasts; 47 Which devour widows' houses, and for a shew make long prayers: the same shall receive greater damnation.

21 And he looked up, and saw the rich men casting their gifts into the treasury. 2And he saw also a certain poor widow casting in thither two mites. 3And he said, Of a truth I say unto you, that this poor widow hath cast in more than they all: 4 For all these have of their abundance cast in unto the offerings of God: but she of her penury hath cast in all the living that she had.

5 And as some spake of the temple, how it was adorned with goodly stones and gifts, he said, 6*As for* these things which ye behold, the days will come, in the which there shall not be left one stone upon another, that shall not be thrown down. 7And they asked him, saying, Master, but when shall these things be? and what sign *will there be* when these things shall come to pass? 8And he said, Take heed that ye be not deceived: for many shall come in my name, saying, I am *Christ;* and the time draweth near: go ye not therefore after them. 9 But when ye shall hear of wars and commotions, be not terrified: for these things must first come to pass; but the end *is* not by and by. 10 Then said he unto them, Nation shall rise against nation, and kingdom against kingdom: 11And great earthquakes shall be in divers places, and fam-

R.S.V.

41 But he said to them, "How can they say that the Christ is David's son? 42 For David himself says in the Book of Psalms,

'The Lord said to my Lord,
   Sit at my right hand,
43 till I make thy enemies a stool for thy feet.'
44 David thus calls him Lord; so how is he his son?"

45 And in the hearing of all the people he said to his disciples, 46 "Beware of the scribes, who like to go about in long robes, and love salutations in the market places and the best seats in the synagogues and the places of honor at feasts, 47 who devour widows' houses and for a pretense make long prayers. They will receive the greater condemnation."

21 He looked up and saw the rich putting their gifts into the treasury; 2 and he saw a poor widow put in two copper coins. 3And he said, "Truly I tell you, this poor widow has put in more than all of them; 4 for they all contributed out of their abundance, but she out of her poverty put in all the living that she had."

5 And as some spoke of the temple, how it was adorned with noble stones and offerings, he said, 6 "As for these things which you see, the days will come when there shall not be left here one stone upon another that will not be thrown down." 7And they asked him, "Teacher, when will this be, and what will be the sign when this is about to take place?" 8And he said, "Take heed that you are not led astray; for many will come in my name, saying, 'I am he!' and, 'The time is at hand!' Do not go after them. 9And when you hear of wars and tumults, do not be terrified; for this must first take place, but the end will not be at once."

10 Then he said to them, "Nation will rise against nation, and kingdom against kingdom; 11 there will be great earthquakes, and in vari-

PHILLIPS

N.E.B.

him any more questions. But Jesus went on to say,

"How can they say that Christ is David's *son?* For David himself says in the book of psalms—

The Lord said unto my *Lord,*
Sit thou on my right hand,
Till I make thine enemies the footstool of thy feet.

David is plainly calling him 'Lord.' How then can he be his *son?*"

He said to them, 'How can they say that the Messiah is son of David? For David himself says in the Book of Psalms: "The Lord said to my Lord, 'Sit at my right hand until I make your enemies your footstool.' " Thus David calls him "Lord"; how then can he be David's son?'

In the hearing of all the people Jesus said to his disciples: 'Beware of the lawyers who love to walk up and down in long robes, and have a great liking for respectful greetings in the street, the chief seats in our synagogues, and places of honour at feasts. These are the men who eat up the property of widows, while they say long prayers for appearance' sake; and they will receive the severest sentence.'

Jesus warns his disciples against religious pretentiousness 20. 45

Then while everybody was listening, Jesus remarked to his disciples:

"Be on your guard against the scribes, who enjoy walking round in long robes and love having men bow to them in public, getting front seats in the synagogue, and the best places at dinner parties—while all the time they are battening on widows' property and covering it up with long prayers. These men are only heading for deeper damnation."

Then he looked up and saw the rich people dropping their gifts into the treasury, and he noticed a poor widow drop in two coppers, and he commented,

"I assure you that this poor widow has put in more than all of them, for they have all put in what they can easily spare, but she in her poverty has given away her whole living."

21 He looked up and saw the rich people dropping their gifts into the chest of the temple treasury; and he noticed a poor widow putting in two tiny coins. 'I tell you this,' he said: 'this poor widow has given more than any of them; for those others who have given had more than enough, but she, with less than enough, has given all she had to live on.'

Jesus foretells the destruction of the Temple 21. 5

Then when some of them were talking about the Temple and pointing out the beauty of its lovely stonework and the various ornaments that people had given, he said,

"Yes, you can gaze on all this today, but the time is coming when not a single stone will be left upon another, without being thrown down."

So they asked him,

"Master, when will this happen, and what sign will there be that these things are going to take place?"

"Be careful that you are not deceived," he replied. "There will be many coming in my name, saying 'I am he' and 'The time is very near now.' Never follow men like that. And when you hear about wars and disturbances, don't be alarmed. These things must indeed happen first, but the end will not come immediately."

Some people were talking about the temple and the fine stones and votive offerings with which it was adorned. He said, 'These things which you are gazing at—the time will come when not one stone of them will be left upon another: all will be thrown down.' 'Master,' they asked, 'when will it all come about? What will be the sign when it is due to happen?'

He said, 'Take care that you are not misled. For many will come claiming my name and saying, "I am he", and, "The Day is upon us." Do not follow them. And when you hear of wars and insurrections, do not fall into a panic. These things are bound to happen first; but the end does not follow immediately. Nation will make war upon nation, kingdom upon kingdom; there will be great earthquakes, and famines and

And prophesies world-wide suffering 21. 10

Then he continued:

"Nation will rise up against nation, and kingdom against kingdom; there will be great earthquakes and famines and plagues in this

K.J.V.

ines, and pestilences; and fearful sights and great signs shall there be from heaven. 12 But before all these, they shall lay their hands on you, and persecute *you*, delivering *you* up to the synagogues, and into prisons, being brought before kings and rulers for my name's sake. 13 And it shall turn to you for a testimony. 14 Settle *it* therefore in your hearts, not to meditate before what ye shall answer: 15 For I will give you a mouth and wisdom, which all your adversaries shall not be able to gainsay nor resist. 16 And ye shall be betrayed both by parents, and brethren, and kinsfolks, and friends; and *some* of you shall they cause to be put to death. 17 And ye shall be hated of all *men* for my name's sake. 18 But there shall not a hair of your head perish. 19 In your patience possess ye your souls. 20 And when ye shall see Jerusalem compassed with armies, then know that the desolation thereof is nigh. 21 Then let them which are in Judea flee to the mountains; and let them which are in the midst of it depart out; and let not them that are in the countries enter thereinto. 22 For these be the days of vengeance, that all things which are written may be fulfilled. 23 But woe unto them that are with child, and to them that give suck, in those days! for there shall be great distress in the land, and wrath upon this people. 24 And they shall fall by the edge of the sword, and shall be led away captive into all nations: and Jerusalem shall be trodden down of the Gentiles, until the times of the Gentiles be fulfilled.

25 And there shall be signs in the sun, and in the moon, and in the stars; and upon the earth distress of nations, with perplexity; the sea and the waves roaring; 26 Men's hearts failing them for fear, and for looking after those things which are coming on the earth: for the powers of heaven shall be shaken. 27 And then shall they see the Son of man coming in a cloud with power and great glory. 28 And when these things begin to come to pass, then look up, and lift up your heads; for your redemption draweth nigh. 29 And he spake to them a parable; Behold the fig tree, and all the trees; 30 When they now shoot forth, ye see and know of your own selves that summer is now nigh at hand. 31 So likewise ye, when ye see these things come to pass, know ye that the kingdom of God is nigh at hand. 32 Verily I say unto you, This generation shall not pass away, till all be fulfilled. 33 Heaven and earth shall pass away; but my words shall not pass away.

34 And take heed to yourselves, lest at any time your hearts be overcharged with surfeiting, and drunkenness, and cares of this life, and *so* that day come upon you unawares. 35 For as a snare shall it come on all them that dwell on the face of the whole earth. 36 Watch ye therefore, and pray always, that ye may be accounted worthy to escape all these things that shall come to pass, and to stand before the Son of man. 37 And in the daytime he was teaching in the temple; and at night he went out, and abode in the mount that is called *the mount* of Olives. 38 And all the people came early in the morning to him in the temple, for to hear him.

R.S.V.

ous places famines and pestilences; and there will be terrors and great signs from heaven. 12 But before all this they will lay their hands on you and persecute you, delivering you up to the synagogues and prisons, and you will be brought before kings and governors for my name's sake. 13 This will be a time for you to bear testimony. 14 Settle it therefore in your minds, not to meditate beforehand how to answer; 15 for I will give you a mouth and wisdom, which none of your adversaries will be able to withstand or contradict. 16 You will be delivered up even by parents and brothers and kinsmen and friends, and some of you they will put to death; 17 you will be hated by all for my name's sake. 18 But not a hair of your head will perish. 19 By your endurance you will gain your lives.

20 "But when you see Jerusalem surrounded by armies, then know that its desolation has come near. 21 Then let those who are in Judea flee to the mountains, and let those who are inside the city depart, and let not those who are out in the country enter it; 22 for these are days of vengeance, to fulfil all that is written. 23 Alas for those who are with child and for those who give suck in those days! For great distress shall be upon the earth and wrath upon this people; 24 they will fall by the edge of the sword, and be led captive among all nations; and Jerusalem will be trodden down by the Gentiles, until the times of the Gentiles are fulfilled.

25 "And there will be signs in sun and moon and stars, and upon the earth distress of nations in perplexity at the roaring of the sea and the waves, 26 men fainting with fear and with foreboding of what is coming on the world; for the powers of the heavens will be shaken. 27 And then they will see the Son of man coming in a cloud with power and great glory. 28 Now when these things begin to take place, look up and raise your heads, because your redemption is drawing near."

29 And he told them a parable: "Look at the fig tree, and all the trees; 30 as soon as they come out in leaf, you see for yourselves and know that the summer is already near. 31 So also, when you see these things taking place, you know that the kingdom of God is near. 32 Truly, I say to you, this generation will not pass away till all has taken place. 33 Heaven and earth will pass away, but my words will not pass away.

34 "But take heed to yourselves lest your hearts be weighed down with dissipation and drunkenness and cares of this life, and that day come upon you suddenly like a snare; 35 for it will come upon all who dwell upon the face of the whole earth. 36 But watch at all times, praying that you may have strength to escape all these things that will take place, and to stand before the Son of man."

37 And every day he was teaching in the temple, but at night he went out and lodged on the mount called Olivet. 38 And early in the morning all the people came to him in the temple to hear him.

PHILLIPS

N.E.B.

place or that. There will be dreadful sights, and great signs from heaven. But before all this happens, men will arrest you and persecute you, handing you over to synagogue or prison, or bringing you before kings and governors, for my name's sake. This will be your chance to witness for me. So make up your minds not to think out your defense beforehand. I will give you such eloquence and wisdom that none of your opponents will be able to resist or contradict it. But you will be betrayed, even by parents and brothers and kinsfolk and friends, and there will be some of you who will be killed and you will be hated everywhere for my name's sake. Yet, not a hair of your head will perish. Hold on, and you will win your souls!

"But when you see Jerusalem surrounded by armed forces, then you will know that the time of her devastation has arrived. Then is the time for those who are in Judaea to fly to the hills. And those who are in the city itself must get out of it, and those who are already in the country must not try to get into the city. For these are the days of vengeance, when all that the scriptures have said will come true. Alas for those who are pregnant and those who have tiny babies in those days! For there will be bitter misery in the land and great anger against this people. They will die by the sword. They will be taken off as prisoners into all nations. Jerusalem will be trampled underfoot by the heathen until the heathen's day is over. There will be signs in the sun and moon and stars, and on the earth there will be dismay among the nations and bewilderment at the roar of the surging sea. Men's courage will fail completely as they realize what is threatening the world, for the very powers of heaven will be shaken. Then men will see the Son of Man coming in a cloud with great power and splendor! But when these things begin to happen, look up, hold your heads high, for you will soon be free."

Vigilance is essential   21. 29

Then he gave them a parable.

"Look at a fig tree, or indeed any tree, when it begins to burst its buds, and you realize without anybody telling you that summer is nearly here. So, when you see these things happening, you can be equally sure that the kingdom of God has nearly come. Believe me, this generation will not disappear until all this has taken place. Earth and heaven will pass away, but my words will never pass away.

"Be on your guard—see to it that your minds are never clouded by dissipation or drunkenness or the worries of this life, or else that day may catch you like the springing of a trap—for it will come upon every inhabitant of the whole earth.

"You must be vigilant at all times, praying that you may be strong enough to come safely through all that is going to happen, and stand in the presence of the Son of Man."

And every day he went on teaching in the Temple, and every evening he went off and spent the night on the hill which is called the Mount of Olives. And the people used to come early in the morning to listen to him in the Temple.

plagues in many places; in the sky terrors and great portents.

'But before all this happens they will set upon you and persecute you. You will be brought before synagogues and put in prison; you will be haled before kings and governors for your allegiance to me. This will be your opportunity to testify; so make up your minds not to prepare your defence beforehand, because I myself will give you power of utterance and a wisdom which no opponent will be able to resist or refute. Even your parents and brothers, your relations and friends, will betray you. Some of you will be put to death; and you will be hated by all for your allegiance to me. But not a hair of your head shall be lost. By standing firm you will win true life for yourselves.

'But when you see Jerusalem encircled by armies, then you may be sure that her destruction is near. Then those who are in Judaea must take to the hills; those who are in the city itself must leave it, and those who are out in the country must not enter; because this is the time of retribution, when all that stands written is to be fulfilled. Alas for women who are with child in those days, or have children at the breast! For there will be great distress in the land and a terrible judgement upon this people. They will fall at the sword's point; they will be carried captive into all countries; and Jerusalem will be trampled down by foreigners until their day has run its course.

'Portents will appear in sun, moon, and stars. On earth nations will stand helpless, not knowing which way to turn from the roar and surge of the sea; men will faint with terror at the thought of all that is coming upon the world; for the celestial powers will be shaken. And then they will see the Son of Man coming on a cloud with great power and glory. When all this begins to happen, stand upright and hold your heads high, because your liberation is near.'

He told them this parable: 'Look at the fig-tree, or any other tree. As soon as it buds, you can see for yourselves that summer is near. In the same way when you see all this happening, you may be sure that the kingdom of God is near.

'I tell you this: the present generation will live to see it all. Heaven and earth will pass away; my words will never pass away.

'Keep a watch on yourselves; do not let your minds be dulled by dissipation and drunkenness and worldly cares so that the great Day closes upon you suddenly like a trap; for that day will come on all men, wherever they are, the whole world over. Be on the alert, praying at all times for strength to pass safely through all these imminent troubles and to stand in the presence of the Son of Man.'

His days were given to teaching in the temple; and then he would leave the city and spend the night on the hill called Olivet. And in the early morning the people flocked to listen to him in the temple.[a]

[a] *Some witnesses here insert the passage printed on p. 295.*

22 Now the feast of unleavened bread drew nigh, which is called the passover. 2And the chief priests and scribes sought how they might kill him; for they feared the people.

3 Then entered Satan into Judas surnamed Iscariot, being of the number of the twelve. 4And he went his way, and communed with the chief priests and captains, how he might betray him unto them. 5And they were glad, and covenanted to give him money. 6And he promised, and sought opportunity to betray him unto them in the absence of the multitude.

7 Then came the day of unleavened bread, when the passover must be killed. 8And he sent Peter and John, saying, Go and prepare us the passover, that we may eat. 9And they said unto him, Where wilt thou that we prepare? 10And he said unto them, Behold, when ye are entered into the city, there shall a man meet you, bearing a pitcher of water; follow him into the house where he entereth in. 11And ye shall say unto the goodman of the house, The Master saith unto thee, Where is the guestchamber, where I shall eat the passover with my disciples? 12And he shall shew you a large upper room furnished: there make ready. 13And they went, and found as he had said unto them: and they made ready the passover. 14And when the hour was come, he sat down, and the twelve apostles with him. 15And he said unto them, With desire I have desired to eat this passover with you before I suffer: 16 For I say unto you, I will not any more eat thereof, until it be fulfilled in the kingdom of God. 17And he took the cup, and gave thanks, and said, Take this, and divide *it* among yourselves: 18 For I say unto you, I will not drink of the fruit of the vine, until the kingdom of God shall come.

19 And he took bread, and gave thanks, and brake *it,* and gave unto them, saying, This is my body which is given for you: this do in remembrance of me. 20 Likewise also the cup after supper, saying, This cup *is* the new testament in my blood, which is shed for you.

21 But, behold, the hand of him that betrayeth me *is* with me on the table. 22And truly the Son of man goeth, as it was determined: but woe

22 Now the feast of Unleavened Bread drew near, which is called the Passover. 2And the chief priests and the scribes were seeking how to put him to death; for they feared the people.

3 Then Satan entered into Judas called Iscariot, who was of the number of the twelve; 4 he went away and conferred with the chief priests and captains how he might betray him to them. 5And they were glad, and engaged to give him money. 6 So he agreed, and sought an opportunity to betray him to them in the absence of the multitude.

7 Then came the day of Unleavened Bread, on which the passover lamb had to be sacrificed. 8 So Jesus[h] sent Peter and John, saying, "Go and prepare the passover for us, that we may eat it." 9 They said to him, "Where will you have us prepare it?" 10 He said to them, "Behold, when you have entered the city, a man carrying a jar of water will meet you; follow him into the house which he enters, 11 and tell the householder, 'The Teacher says to you, Where is the guest room, where I am to eat the passover with my disciples?' 12And he will show you a large upper room furnished; there make ready." 13And they went, and found it as he had told them; and they prepared the passover.

14 And when the hour came, he sat at table, and the apostles with him. 15And he said to them, "I have earnestly desired to eat this passover with you before I suffer; 16 for I tell you I shall not eat it[i] until it is fulfilled in the kingdom of God." 17And he took a cup, and when he had given thanks he said, "Take this, and divide it among yourselves; 18 for I tell you that from now on I shall not drink of the fruit of the vine until the kingdom of God comes." 19And he took bread, and when he had given thanks he broke it and gave it to them, saying, "This is my body.[j] 21 But behold the hand of him who betrays me is with me on the table. 22 For the Son of man goes as it has been determined; but woe to that man by whom he is betrayed!"

[h] Greek *he.* [i] Other ancient authorities read *never eat it again.* [j] Other ancient authorities add *which is given for you. Do this in remembrance of me.* 20*And likewise the cup after supper, saying, "This cup which is poured out for you is the new covenant in my blood."*

PHILLIPS

Judas Iscariot becomes the   **22. 1**
tool of the authorities

Now as the feast of unleavened bread, called the Passover, was approaching, fear of the people made the chief priests and scribes try desperately to find a way of getting rid of Jesus. Then a diabolical plan came into the mind of Judas Iscariot, who was one of the twelve. He went and discussed with the chief priests and officers a method of getting Jesus into their hands. They were delighted and arranged to pay him for it. He agreed, and began to look for a suitable opportunity for betrayal when there was no crowd present.

Jesus makes arrangements for his   **22. 7**
last Passover with his disciples

Then the day of unleavened bread arrived, on which the Passover lamb had to be sacrificed, and Jesus sent off Peter and John with the words, "Go and make all the preparations for us to eat the Passover."

"Where would you like us to do this?" they asked.

And he replied:

"Listen, just as you're going into the city a man carrying a jug of water will meet you. Follow him to the house he is making for. Then say to the owner of the house, 'The master has this message for you—which is the room where my disciples and I may eat the Passover?' And he will take you upstairs and show you a large room furnished for our needs. Make all the preparations there."

So they went off and found everything exactly as he had told them it would be, and they made the Passover preparations.

Then, when the time came, he took his seat at table with the apostles, and spoke to them:

"With all my heart I have longed to eat this Passover with you before the time comes for me to suffer. Believe me, I shall not eat the Passover again until all that it means is fulfilled in the Kingdom of God."

Then taking a cup from them, he thanked God and said,

"Take this and share it amongst yourselves, for I tell you that I shall drink no more wine until the kingdom of God comes."

The mysterious words which   **22. 19**
were remembered later

Then he took a loaf and, after thanking God, he broke it and gave it to them, with these words,

"This is my body which is given for you: do this in remembrance of me."

So too, he gave them a cup after supper with the words:

"This cup is the new agreement made in my own blood which is shed for you. Yet the hand of the man who is betraying me lies with mine at this moment on the table. The Son of Man goes on his appointed way: yet alas for the man by whom he is betrayed!"

N.E.B.

The Final Conflict

22 Now the festival of Unleavened Bread, known as Passover, was approaching, and the chief priests and the doctors of the law were trying to devise some means of doing away with him; for they were afraid of the people.

Then Satan entered into Judas Iscariot, who was one of the Twelve; and Judas went to the chief priests and officers of the temple police to discuss ways and means of putting Jesus into their power. They were greatly pleased and undertook to pay him a sum of money. He agreed, and began to look out for an opportunity to betray him to them without collecting a crowd.

Then came the day of Unleavened Bread, on which the Passover victim had to be slaughtered, and Jesus sent Peter and John with these instructions: 'Go and prepare for our Passover supper.' 'Where would you like us to make the preparations?' they asked. He replied, 'As soon as you set foot in the city a man will meet you carrying a jar of water. Follow him into the house that he enters and give this message to the householder: "The Master says, 'Where is the room in which I may eat the Passover with my disciples?' " He will show you a large room upstairs all set out: make the preparations there.' They went and found everything as he had said. So they prepared for Passover.

When the time came he took his place at table, and the apostles with him; and he said to them, 'How I have longed[a] to eat this Passover with you before my death! For I tell you, never again shall I[b] eat it until the time when it finds its fulfilment in the kingdom of God.'

Then he took a cup, and after giving thanks he said, 'Take this and share it among yourselves; for I tell you, from this moment I shall drink from the fruit of the vine no more until the time when the kingdom of God comes.' And he took bread, gave thanks, and broke it; and he gave it to them, with the words: 'This is my body.'[c]

'But mark this—my betrayer is here, his hand with mine on the table. For the Son of Man is going his appointed way; but alas for that man

---

[a] *Or* said to them, 'I longed . . .' [b] *Some witnesses read* For I tell you, I shall not . . . [c] *Some witnesses add, in whole or in part, and with various arrangements, the following:* 'which is given for you; do this as a memorial of me.' (20) *In the same way he took the cup after supper, and said,* 'This cup, poured out for you, is the new covenant sealed by my blood.'

K.J.V.

unto that man by whom he is betrayed! 23And they began to inquire among themselves, which of them it was that should do this thing.

24 And there was also a strife among them, which of them should be accounted the greatest. 25And he said unto them, The kings of the Gentiles exercise lordship over them; and they that exercise authority upon them are called benefactors. 26 But ye *shall* not *be* so: but he that is greatest among you, let him be as the younger; and he that is chief, as he that doth serve. 27 For whether *is* greater, he that sitteth at meat, or he that serveth? *is* not he that sitteth at meat? but I am among you as he that serveth. 28 Ye are they which have continued with me in my temptations. 29And I appoint unto you a kingdom, as my Father hath appointed unto me; 30 That ye may eat and drink at my table in my kingdom, and sit on thrones judging the twelve tribes of Israel.

31 And the Lord said, Simon, Simon, behold, Satan hath desired *to have* you, that he may sift *you* as wheat: 32 But I have prayed for thee, that thy faith fail not: and when thou art converted, strengthen thy brethren. 33And he said unto him, Lord, I am ready to go with thee, both into prison, and to death. 34And he said, I tell thee, Peter, the cock shall not crow this day, before that thou shalt thrice deny that thou knowest me. 35And he said unto them, When I sent you without purse, and scrip, and shoes, lacked ye any thing? And they said, Nothing. 36 Then said he unto them, But now, he that hath a purse, let him take *it,* and likewise *his* scrip: and he that hath no sword, let him sell his garment, and buy one. 37 For I say unto you, that this that is written must yet be accomplished in me, And he was reckoned among the transgressors: for the things concerning me have an end. 38And they said, Lord, behold, here *are* two swords. And he said unto them, It is enough.

39 And he came out, and went, as he was wont, to the mount of Olives; and his disciples also followed him. 40And when he was at the place, he said unto them, Pray that ye enter not into temptation. 41And he was withdrawn from them about a stone's cast, and kneeled down, and prayed, 42 Saying, Father, if thou be willing, remove this cup from me: nevertheless, not my will, but thine, be done. 43And there appeared an angel unto him from heaven, strengthening him. 44And being in an agony he prayed more

R.S.V.

23 And they began to question one another, which of them it was that would do this.

24 A dispute also arose among them, which of them was to be regarded as the greatest. 25And he said to them, "The kings of the Gentiles exercise lordship over them; and those in authority over them are called benefactors. 26 But not so with you; rather let the greatest among you become as the youngest, and the leader as one who serves. 27 For which is the greater, one who sits at table, or one who serves? Is it not the one who sits at table? But I am among you as one who serves.

28 "You are those who have continued with me in my trials; 29 as my Father appointed a kingdom for me, so do I appoint for you 30 that you may eat and drink at my table in my kingdom, and sit on thrones judging the twelve tribes of Israel.

31 "Simon, Simon, behold, Satan demanded to have you,[k] that he might sift you[k] like wheat, 32 but I have prayed for you that your faith may not fail; and when you have turned again, strengthen your brethren." 33And he said to him, "Lord, I am ready to go with you to prison and to death." 34 He said, "I tell you, Peter, the cock will not crow this day, until you three times deny that you know me."

35 And he said to them, "When I sent you out with no purse or bag or sandals, did you lack anything?" They said, "Nothing." 36 He said to them, "But now, let him who has a purse take it, and likewise a bag. And let him who has no sword sell his mantle and buy one. 37 For I tell you that this scripture must be fulfilled in me, 'And he was reckoned with transgressors'; for what is written about me has its fulfilment." 38And they said, "Look, Lord, here are two swords." And he said to them, "It is enough."

39 And he came out, and went, as was his custom, to the Mount of Olives; and the disciples followed him. 40And when he came to the place he said to them, "Pray that you may not enter into temptation." 41And he withdrew from them about a stone's throw, and knelt down and prayed, 42 "Father, if thou art willing, remove this cup from me; nevertheless not my will, but thine, be done." 43And there appeared to him an angel from heaven, strengthening him. 44And being in an agony he prayed more earnestly; and

[k] The Greek word for *you* here is plural; in verse 32 it is singular.

Jesus again teaches humility   22. 23

And at this they began to debate among themselves as to which of them would do this thing.

And then a dispute arose among them as to who should be considered the most important.

But Jesus said to them:

"Among the heathen it is their kings who lord it over them, and their rulers are given the title of 'benefactors.' But it must not be so with you! *Your* greatest man must become like a junior and your leader must be a servant. Who is the greater, the man who sits down to dinner or the man who serves him? Obviously, the man who sits down to dinner—yet *I* am the one who is the servant among you. But you are the men who have stood by me in all that I have gone through, and as surely as my Father has given me my kingdom, so I give you the right to eat and drink at my table in that kingdom. Yes, you will sit on thrones and rule the twelve tribes of Israel!

The personal warning to Simon   22. 31

"Oh, Simon, Simon, do you know that Satan has asked to have you all to sift like wheat?—But I have prayed for *you* that you may not lose your faith. Yes, when you have turned back to me, you must strengthen these brothers of yours."

Peter said to him,

"Lord, I am ready to go to prison, or even to die with you!"

"I tell you, Peter," returned Jesus, "before the cock crows today you will deny three times that you know me!"

Jesus tells his disciples that the   22. 35
crisis has arrived

Then he continued to them all,

"That time when I sent you out without any purse or wallet or shoes—did you find you needed anything?"

"No, not a thing," they replied.

"But now," Jesus continued, "if you have a purse or wallet, take it with you, and if you have no sword, sell your coat and buy one! for I tell you that this scripture must be fulfilled in me—

And he was reckoned with transgressors.

So comes the end of what they wrote about me."

Then the disciples said,

"Lord, look, here are two swords."

And Jesus returned,

"That is enough."

Then he went out of the city and up onto the Mount of Olives, as he had often done before, with the disciples following him. And when he reached his usual place, he said to them,

"Pray that you may not have to face temptation!"

Then he went off by himself, about a stone's throw away, and falling on his knees, prayed in these words—

"Father, if you are willing, take this cup away from me—but it is not my will, but yours, that must be done."

And an angel from Heaven appeared, strengthening him. He was in agony and prayed even

by whom he is betrayed!' At this they began to ask among themselves which of them it could possibly be who was to do this thing.

Then a jealous dispute broke out: who among them should rank highest? But he said, 'In the world, kings lord it over their subjects; and those in authority are called their country's "Benefactors". Not so with you: on the contrary, the highest among you must bear himself like the youngest, the chief of you like a servant. For who is greater—the one who sits at table or the servant who waits on him? Surely the one who sits at table. Yet here am I among you like a servant.

'You are the men who have stood firmly by me in my times of trial; and now I vest in you the kingship which my Father vested in me; you shall eat and drink at my table in my kingdom and sit[a] on thrones as judges of the twelve tribes of Israel.

'Simon, Simon, take heed: Satan has been given leave to sift all of you like wheat; but for you I have prayed that your faith may not fail; and when you have come to yourself, you must lend strength to your brothers.' 'Lord,' he replied, 'I am ready to go with you to prison and death.' Jesus said, 'I tell you, Peter, the cock will not crow tonight until you have three times over denied that you know me.'

He said to them, 'When I sent you out barefoot without purse or pack, were you ever short of anything?' 'No,' they answered. 'It is different now,' he said; 'whoever has a purse had better take it with him, and his pack too; and if he has no sword, let him sell his cloak to buy one. For Scripture says, "And he was counted among the outlaws", and these words, I tell you, must find fulfilment in me; indeed, all that is written of me is being fulfilled.' 'Look, Lord,' they said, 'we have two swords here.' 'Enough, enough!' he replied.

Then he went out and made his way as usual to the Mount of Olives, accompanied by the disciples. When he reached the place he said to them, 'Pray that you may be spared the hour of testing.' He himself withdrew from them about a stone's throw, knelt down, and began to pray: 'Father, if it be thy will, take this cup away from me. Yet not my will but thine be done.'

And now there appeared to him an angel from heaven bringing him strength, and in anguish of

---

[a] *Or* trial; and as my Father gave me the right to reign, so I give you the right to eat and to drink . . . and to sit . . .

K.J.V.

earnestly: and his sweat was as it were great drops of blood falling down to the ground. 45And when he rose up from prayer, and was come to his disciples, he found them sleeping for sorrow, 46And said unto them, Why sleep ye? rise and pray, lest ye enter into temptation.

47 And while he yet spake, behold a multitude, and he that was called Judas, one of the twelve, went before them, and drew near unto Jesus to kiss him. 48 But Jesus said unto him, Judas, betrayest thou the Son of man with a kiss? 49 When they which were about him saw what would follow, they said unto him, Lord, shall we smite with the sword?

50 And one of them smote the servant of the high priest, and cut off his right ear. 51And Jesus answered and said, Suffer ye thus far. And he touched his ear, and healed him. 52 Then Jesus said unto the chief priests, and captains of the temple, and the elders, which were come to him, Be ye come out, as against a thief, with swords and staves? 53 When I was daily with you in the temple, ye stretched forth no hands against me: but this is your hour, and the power of darkness.

54 Then took they him, and led *him,* and brought him into the high priest's house. And Peter followed afar off. 55And when they had kindled a fire in the midst of the hall, and were set down together, Peter sat down among them. 56 But a certain maid beheld him as he sat by the fire, and earnestly looked upon him, and said, This man was also with him. 57And he denied him, saying, Woman, I know him not. 58And after a little while another saw him, and said, Thou art also of them. And Peter said, Man, I am not. 59And about the space of one hour after another confidently affirmed, saying, Of a truth this *fellow* also was with him; for he is a Galilean. 60And Peter said, Man, I know not what thou sayest. And immediately, while he yet spake, the cock crew. 61And the Lord turned, and looked upon Peter. And Peter remembered the word of the Lord, how he had said unto him, Before the cock crow, thou shalt deny me thrice. 62And Peter went out, and wept bitterly.

63 And the men that held Jesus mocked him, and smote *him.* 64And when they had blindfolded him, they struck him on the face, and asked him, saying, Prophesy, who is it that smote thee? 65And many other things blasphemously spake they against him.

R.S.V.

his sweat became like great drops of blood falling down upon the ground.[l] 45And when he rose from prayer, he came to the disciples and found them sleeping for sorrow, 46 and he said to them, "Why do you sleep? Rise and pray that you may not enter into temptation."

47 While he was still speaking, there came a crowd, and the man called Judas, one of the twelve, was leading them. He drew near to Jesus to kiss him; 48 but Jesus said to him, "Judas, would you betray the Son of man with a kiss?" 49And when those who were about him saw what would follow, they said, "Lord, shall we strike with the sword?" 50And one of them struck the slave of the high priest and cut off his right ear. 51 But Jesus said, "No more of this!" And he touched his ear and healed him. 52 Then Jesus said to the chief priests and captains of the temple and elders, who had come out against him, "Have you come out as against a robber, with swords and clubs? 53 When I was with you day after day in the temple, you did not lay hands on me. But this is your hour, and the power of darkness."

54 Then they seized him and led him away, bringing him into the high priest's house. Peter followed at a distance; 55 and when they had kindled a fire in the middle of the courtyard and sat down together, Peter sat among them. 56 Then a maid, seeing him as he sat in the light and gazing at him, said, "This man also was with him." 57 But he denied it, saying, "Woman, I do not know him." 58And a little later some one else saw him and said, "You also are one of them." But Peter said, "Man, I am not." 59And after an interval of about an hour still another insisted, saying, "Certainly this man also was with him; for he is a Galilean." 60 But Peter said, "Man, I do not know what you are saying." And immediately, while he was still speaking, the cock crowed. 61And the Lord turned and looked at Peter. And Peter remembered the word of the Lord, how he had said to him, "Before the cock crows today, you will deny me three times." 62And he went out and wept bitterly.

63 Now the men who were holding Jesus mocked him and beat him; 64 they also blindfolded him and asked him, "Prophesy! Who is it that struck you?" 65And they spoke many other words against him, reviling him.

[*l*] Other ancient authorities omit verses 43 and 44.

| **PHILLIPS** | **N.E.B.** |

more intensely so that his sweat was like great drops of blood falling to the ground. Then he got to his feet from his prayer and walking back to the disciples, he found them sleeping through sheer grief.

"Why are you sleeping?" he said to them. "You must get up and go on praying that you may not have to face temptation."

The mob arrives and   22. 47
Judas betrays

While he was still speaking a crowd of people arrived, led by the man called Judas, one of the twelve. He stepped up to Jesus to kiss him.

"Judas, would you betray the Son of Man with a kiss?" said Jesus to him.

And the disciples, seeing what was going to happen, cried,

"Lord, shall we use our swords?"

And one of them did slash at the High Priest's servant, cutting off his right ear. But Jesus retorted,

"That will do!"

And he touched his ear and healed him. Then he spoke to the chief priests, Temple officers and elders who were there to arrest him:

"So you have come out with your swords and staves as if I were a bandit. Day after day I was with you in the Temple and you never laid a finger on me—but this is your hour and the power of darkness is yours!"

Jesus is arrested: Peter follows   22. 54
but denies his master three times

Then they arrested him and marched him off to the High Priest's house. Peter followed at a distance, and sat down among some people who had lighted a fire in the middle of the courtyard and were sitting round it. A maidservant saw him sitting there in the firelight, peered into his face and said,

"This man was with him too."

But he denied it and said,

"I don't know him, girl!"

A few minutes later someone else noticed Peter, and said,

"You're one of these men too."

But Peter said,

"Man, I am not!"

Then about an hour later someone else insisted,

"I am convinced this fellow was with him. Why, he is a Galilean!"

"Man," returned Peter, "I don't know what you're talking about."

And immediately, while he was still speaking, the cock crew. The Lord turned his head and looked straight at Peter, into whose mind flashed the words that the Lord had said to him . . . "You will disown me three times before the cock crows today." And he went outside and wept bitterly.

Then the men who held Jesus made a great game of knocking him about. And they blindfolded him and asked him,

"Now, prophet, guess who hit you that time!"

And that was only the beginning of the way they insulted him.

spirit he prayed the more urgently; and his sweat was like clots of blood falling to the ground.[a]

When he rose from prayer and came to the disciples he found them asleep, worn out by grief. 'Why are you sleeping?' he said. 'Rise and pray that you may be spared the test.'

While he was still speaking a crowd appeared with the man called Judas, one of the Twelve, at their head. He came up to Jesus to kiss him; but Jesus said, 'Judas, would you betray the Son of Man with a kiss?'

When his followers saw what was coming, they said, 'Lord, shall we use our swords?' And one of them struck at the High Priest's servant, cutting off his right ear. But Jesus answered, 'Let them have their way.' Then he touched the man's ear and healed him.[b]

Turning to the chief priests, the officers of the temple police, and the elders, who had come to seize him, he said, 'Do you take me for a bandit, that you have come out with swords and cudgels to arrest me? Day after day, when I was in the temple with you, you kept your hands off me. But this is your moment—the hour when darkness reigns.'

Then they arrested him and led him away. They brought him to the High Priest's house, and Peter followed at a distance. They lit a fire in the middle of the courtyard and sat round it, and Peter sat among them. A serving-maid who saw him sitting in the firelight stared at him and said, 'This man was with him too.' But he denied it: 'Woman,' he said, 'I do not know him.' A little later someone else noticed him and said, 'You also are one of them.' But Peter said to him, 'No, I am not.' About an hour passed and another spoke more strongly still: 'Of course this fellow was with him. He must have been; he is a Galilean.' But Peter said, 'Man, I do not know what you are talking about.' At that moment, while he was still speaking, a cock crew; and the Lord turned and looked straight at Peter. And Peter remembered the Lord's words, 'Tonight before the cock crows you will disown me three times.'[c]

The men who were guarding Jesus mocked at him. They beat him, they blindfolded him, and they kept asking him, 'Now, prophet, who hit you? Tell us that.' And so they went on heaping insults upon him.

[a] *Some witnesses omit* And now . . . ground. [b] *Or* 'Let me do as much as this', and touching the man's ear, he healed him. [c] *Some witnesses add* (62) He went outside, and wept bitterly, *as in Matthew 26. 75.*

K.J.V.

66 And as soon as it was day, the elders of the people and the chief priests and the scribes came together, and led him into their council, saying, 67 Art thou the Christ? tell us. And he said unto them, If I tell you, ye will not believe: 68 And if I also ask *you,* ye will not answer me, nor let *me* go. 69 Hereafter shall the Son of man sit on the right hand of the power of God. 70 Then said they all, Art thou then the Son of God? And he said unto them, Ye say that I am. 71 And they said, What need we any further witness? for we ourselves have heard of his own mouth.

23 And the whole multitude of them arose, and led him unto Pilate. 2 And they began to accuse him, saying, We found this *fellow* perverting the nation, and forbidding to give tribute to Cesar, saying that he himself is Christ a king. 3 And Pilate asked him, saying, Art thou the King of the Jews? And he answered him and said, Thou sayest *it.* 4 Then said Pilate to the chief priests and *to* the people, I find no fault in this man. 5 And they were the more fierce, saying, He stirreth up the people, teaching throughout all Jewry, beginning from Galilee to this place. 6 When Pilate heard of Galilee, he asked whether the man were a Galilean. 7 And as soon as he knew that he belonged unto Herod's jurisdiction, he sent him to Herod, who himself also was at Jerusalem at that time.

8 And when Herod saw Jesus, he was exceeding glad: for he was desirous to see him of a long *season,* because he had heard many things of him; and he hoped to have seen some miracle done by him. 9 Then he questioned with him in many words; but he answered him nothing. 10 And the chief priests and scribes stood and vehemently accused him. 11 And Herod with his men of war set him at nought, and mocked *him,* and arrayed him in a gorgeous robe, and sent him again to Pilate.

12 And the same day Pilate and Herod were made friends together; for before they were at enmity between themselves.

13 And Pilate, when he had called together the chief priests and the rulers and the people, 14 Said unto them, Ye have brought this man unto me, as one that perverteth the people: and, behold, I, having examined *him* before you, have found no fault in this man touching those things whereof ye accuse him: 15 No, nor yet Herod: for I sent you to him; and, lo, nothing worthy of

R.S.V.

66 When day came, the assembly of the elders of the people gathered together, both chief priests and scribes; and they led him away to their council, and they said, 67 "If you are the Christ, tell us." But he said to them, "If I tell you, you will not believe; 68 and if I ask you, you will not answer. 69 But from now on the Son of man shall be seated at the right hand of the power of God." 70 And they all said, "Are you the Son of God, then?" And he said to them, "You say that I am." 71 And they said, "What further testimony do we need? We have heard it ourselves from his own lips."

23 Then the whole company of them arose, and brought him before Pilate. 2 And they began to accuse him, saying, "We found this man perverting our nation, and forbidding us to give tribute to Caesar, and saying that he himself is Christ a king." 3 And Pilate asked him, "Are you the King of the Jews?" And he answered him, "You have said so." 4 And Pilate said to the chief priests and the multitudes, "I find no crime in this man." 5 But they were urgent, saying, "He stirs up the people, teaching throughout all Judea, from Galilee even to this place."

6 When Pilate heard this, he asked whether the man was a Galilean. 7 And when he learned that he belonged to Herod's jurisdiction, he sent him over to Herod, who was himself in Jerusalem at that time. 8 When Herod saw Jesus, he was very glad, for he had long desired to see him, because he had heard about him, and he was hoping to see some sign done by him. 9 So he questioned him at some length; but he made no answer. 10 The chief priests and the scribes stood by, vehemently accusing him. 11 And Herod with his soldiers treated him with contempt and mocked him; then, arraying him in gorgeous apparel, he sent him back to Pilate. 12 And Herod and Pilate became friends with each other that very day, for before this they had been at enmity with each other.

13 Pilate then called together the chief priests and the rulers and the people, 14 and said to them, "You brought me this man as one who was perverting the people; and after examining him before you, behold, I did not find this man guilty of any of your charges against him; 15 neither did Herod, for he sent him back to us. Behold, nothing deserving death has been

PHILLIPS

In the early morning Jesus is   22. 66
formally interrogated

Then when daylight came, the assembly of the elders of the people, which included both chief priests and scribes, met and marched him off to their own council. There they asked him,

"If you really are Christ, tell us!"

"If I tell you, you will never believe me, and if I ask you a question, you will not answer me. But from now on the Son of Man will take his seat at the right hand of almighty God."

Then they all said,

"So you are the Son of God then?"

"You are right; I am," Jesus told them.

Then they said,

"Why do we need to call any more witnesses, for we ourselves have heard this thing from his own lips?"

Jesus is taken before   23. 1
Pilate and Herod

Then they rose up in a body and took him off to Pilate, and began their accusation in these words,

"Here is this man whom we have found corrupting our people, and telling them that it is wrong to pay taxes to Caesar, claiming that he himself is Christ, a king."

But Pilate addressed his question to Jesus,

"Are you the king of the Jews?"

"Yes, I am," he replied.

Then Pilate spoke to the chief priests and the crowd,

"I find nothing criminal about this man."

But they pressed their charge, saying:

"He's a troublemaker among the people. He teaches through the whole of Judaea, all the way from Galilee to this place."

When Pilate heard this, he inquired whether the man were a Galilean, and when he discovered that he came under Herod's jurisdiction, he passed him on to Herod who happened to be in Jerusalem at that time. When Herod saw Jesus, he was delighted, for he had been wanting to see him for a long time. He had heard a lot about Jesus and was hoping to see him perform a miracle. He questioned him very thoroughly, but Jesus gave him absolutely no reply, though the chief priests and scribes stood there making the most violent accusations. So Herod joined his own soldiers in scoffing and jeering at Jesus. Finally, they dressed him up in a gorgeous cloak, and sent him back to Pilate. On that day Herod and Pilate became firm friends, though previously they had been at daggers drawn.

Pilate declares Jesus' innocence   23. 13

Then Pilate summoned the chief priests, the officials and the people, and addressed them in these words:

"You have brought this man to me as a mischief-maker among the people, and I want you all to realize that, after examining him in your presence, I have found nothing criminal about him, in spite of all your accusations. And neither has Herod, for he has sent him back to us. Obviously, then, he has done nothing to de-

N.E.B.

When day broke, the elders of the nation, chief priests, and doctors of the law assembled, and he was brought before their Council. 'Tell us,' they said, 'are you the Messiah?' 'If I tell you,' he replied, 'you will not believe me; and if I ask questions, you will not answer. But from now on, the Son of Man will be seated at the right hand of Almighty God.' *a* 'You are the Son of God, then?' they all said, and he replied, 'It is you who say I am.' *b* They said, 'Need we call further witnesses? We have heard it ourselves from his own lips.'

23 With that the whole assembly rose, and they brought him before Pilate. They opened the case against him by saying, 'We found this man subverting our nation, opposing the payment of taxes to Caesar, and claiming to be Messiah, a king.' *c* Pilate asked him, 'Are you the king of the Jews?' He replied, 'The words are yours.' *d* Pilate then said to the chief priests and the crowd, 'I find no case for this man to answer.' But they insisted: 'His teaching is causing disaffection among the people all through Judaea. It started from Galilee and has spread as far as this city.'

When Pilate heard this, he asked if the man was a Galilean, and on learning that he belonged to Herod's jurisdiction he remitted the case to him, for Herod was also in Jerusalem at that time. When Herod saw Jesus he was greatly pleased; having heard about him, he had long been wanting to see him, and had been hoping to see some miracle performed by him. He questioned him at some length without getting any reply; but the chief priests and lawyers appeared and pressed the case against him vigorously. Then Herod and his troops treated him with contempt and ridicule, and sent him back to Pilate dressed in a gorgeous robe. That same day Herod and Pilate became friends: till then there had been a standing feud between them.

Pilate now called together the chief priests, councillors, and people, and said to them, 'You brought this man before me on a charge of subversion. But, as you see, I have myself examined him in your presence and found nothing in him to support your charges. No more did Herod, for he has referred him back to us. Clearly he has

[a] *Literally* of the Power of God. [b] *Or* You are right, for I am. [c] *Or* to be an anointed king. [d] *Or* It is as you say.

K.J.V.

death is done unto him. 16 I will therefore chastise him, and release *him*. 17 (For of necessity he must release one unto them at the feast.) 18 And they cried out all at once, saying, Away with this *man*, and release unto us Barabbas: 19 (Who for a certain sedition made in the city, and for murder, was cast into prison.) 20 Pilate therefore, willing to release Jesus, spake again to them. 21 But they cried, saying, Crucify *him*, crucify him. 22 And he said unto them the third time, Why, what evil hath he done? I have found no cause of death in him: I will therefore chastise him, and let *him* go. 23 And they were instant with loud voices, requiring that he might be crucified: and the voices of them and of the chief priests prevailed. 24 And Pilate gave sentence that it should be as they required. 25 And he released unto them him that for sedition and murder was cast into prison, whom they had desired; but he delivered Jesus to their will. 26 And as they led him away, they laid hold upon one Simon, a Cyrenian, coming out of the country, and on him they laid the cross, that he might bear *it* after Jesus.

27 And there followed him a great company of people, and of women, which also bewailed and lamented him. 28 But Jesus turning unto them said, Daughters of Jerusalem, weep not for me, but weep for yourselves, and for your children. 29 For, behold, the days are coming, in the which they shall say, Blessed *are* the barren, and the wombs that never bare, and the paps which never gave suck. 30 Then shall they begin to say to the mountains, Fall on us; and to the hills, Cover us. 31 For if they do these things in a green tree, what shall be done in the dry? 32 And there were also two others, malefactors, led with him to be put to death. 33 And when they were come to the place, which is called Calvary, there they crucified him, and the malefactors, one on the right hand, and the other on the left.

34 Then said Jesus, Father, forgive them; for they know not what they do. And they parted his raiment, and cast lots. 35 And the people stood beholding. And the rulers also with them derided *him*, saying, He saved others; let him save himself, if he be Christ, the chosen of God. 36 And the soldiers also mocked him, coming to him, and offering him vinegar, 37 And saying, If thou be the King of the Jews, save thyself. 38 And a superscription also was written over him in letters of Greek, and Latin, and Hebrew, THIS IS THE KING OF THE JEWS.

39 And one of the malefactors which were hanged railed on him, saying, If thou be Christ,

R.S.V.

done by him; 16 I will therefore chastise him and release him." *m*

18 But they all cried out together, "Away with this man, and release to us Barabbas"— 19 a man who had been thrown into prison for an insurrection started in the city, and for murder. 20 Pilate addressed them once more, desiring to release Jesus; 21 but they shouted out, "Crucify, crucify him!" 22 A third time he said to them, "Why, what crime has he done? I have found in him no crime deserving death; I will therefore chastise him and release him." 23 But they were urgent, demanding with loud cries that he should be crucified. And their voices prevailed. 24 So Pilate gave sentence that their demand should be granted. 25 He released the man who had been thrown into prison for insurrection and murder, whom they asked for; but Jesus he delivered up to their will.

26 And as they led him away, they seized one Simon of Cyrene, who was coming in from the country, and laid on him the cross, to carry it behind Jesus. 27 And there followed him a great multitude of the people, and of women who bewailed and lamented him. 28 But Jesus turning to them said, "Daughters of Jerusalem, do not weep for me, but weep for yourselves and for your children. 29 For behold, the days are coming when they will say, 'Blessed are the barren, and the wombs that never bore, and the breasts that never gave suck!' 30 Then they will begin to say to the mountains, 'Fall on us'; and to the hills, 'Cover us.' 31 For if they do this when the wood is green, what will happen when it is dry?"

32 Two others also, who were criminals, were led away to be put to death with him. 33 And when they came to the place which is called The Skull, there they crucified him, and the criminals, one on the right and one on the left. 34 And Jesus said, "Father, forgive them; for they know not what they do." *n* And they cast lots to divide his garments. 35 And the people stood by, watching; but the rulers scoffed at him, saying, "He saved others; let him save himself, if he is the Christ of God, his Chosen One!" 36 The soldiers also mocked him, coming up and offering him vinegar, 37 and saying, "If you are the King of the Jews, save yourself!" 38 There was also an inscription over him, *o* "This is the King of the Jews."

39 One of the criminals who were hanged railed at him, saying, "Are you not the Christ?

---

[m] Here, or after verse 19, other ancient authorities add verse 17, *Now he was obliged to release one man to them at the festival.* [n] Other ancient authorities omit the sentence *And Jesus . . . what they do.* [o] Other ancient authorities add *in letters of Greek and Latin and Hebrew.*

PHILLIPS

N.E.B.

serve the death penalty. I propose, therefore, to teach him a sharp lesson and let him go."

But they all yelled as one man:

"Take this man away! We want Barabbas set free!"

(Barabbas was a man who had been put in prison for causing a riot in the city and for murder.) But Pilate wanted to set Jesus free and he called out to them again, but they shouted back at him,

"Crucify, crucify him!"

Then he spoke to them, for the third time:

"What is his crime, then? I have found nothing in him that deserves execution; I am going to teach him his lesson and let him go."

But they shouted him down, yelling their demand that he should be crucified.

Their shouting won the day, and Pilate pronounced the official decision that their request should be granted. He released the man for whom they asked, the man who had been imprisoned for rioting and murder, and surrendered Jesus to their demands.

And as they were marching him away, they caught hold of Simon, a native of Cyrene in Africa, who was on his way home from the fields, and put the cross on his back for him to carry behind Jesus.

On the way to the cross   **23. 27**

A huge crowd of people followed him, including women who wrung their hands and wept for him. But Jesus turned to them and said:

"Women of Jerusalem, do not shed your tears for me, but for yourselves and for your children! For the days are coming when men will say, 'Lucky are the women who are childless—the bodies which have never borne, and the breasts which have never given nourishment.' Then men will begin to say to the mountains, 'Fall upon us!' and will say to the hills, 'Cover us up!' For if this is what men do when the wood is green, what will they do when it is seasoned?"

Jesus is crucified   **23. 32**
with two criminals

Two criminals were also led out with him for execution, and when they came to the place called The Skull, they crucified him with the criminals, one on either side of him. But Jesus himself was saying.

"Father, forgive them; they do not know what they are doing."

Then they shared out his clothes by casting lots.

The people stood and stared while their rulers continued to scoff, saying, "He saved other people, let's see him save himself, if he is really God's Christ—his chosen!"

The soldiers also mocked him by coming up and presenting sour wine to him, saying,

"If you are the king of the Jews, why not save yourself?" for there was a placard over his head which read, "THIS IS THE KING OF THE JEWS."

One of the criminals hanging there covered him with abuse, and said,

"Aren't you Christ? Why don't you save yourself—and us?"

done nothing to deserve death. I therefore propose to let him off with a flogging.' But[a] there was a general outcry, 'Away with him! Give us Barabbas.' (This man had been put in prison for a rising that had taken place in the city, and for murder.) Pilate addressed them again, in his desire to release Jesus, but they shouted back, 'Crucify him, crucify him!' For the third time he spoke to them: 'Why, what wrong has he done? I have not found him guilty of any capital offence. I will therefore let him off with a flogging.' But they insisted on their demand, shouting that Jesus should be crucified. Their shouts prevailed and Pilate decided that they should have their way. He released the man they asked for, the man who had been put in prison for insurrection and murder, and gave Jesus up to their will.

As they led him away to execution they seized upon a man called Simon, from Cyrene, on his way in from the country, put the cross on his back, and made him walk behind Jesus carrying it.

Great numbers of people followed, many women among them, who mourned and lamented over him. Jesus turned to them and said, 'Daughters of Jerusalem, do not weep for me; no, weep for yourselves and your children. For the days are surely coming when they will say, "Happy are the barren, the wombs that never bore a child, the breasts that never fed one." Then they will start saying to the mountains, "Fall on us", and to the hills, "Cover us." For if these things are done when the wood is green, what will happen when it is dry?'

There were two others with him, criminals who were being led away to execution; and when they reached the place called The Skull, they crucified him there, and the criminals with him, one on his right and the other on his left. Jesus said, 'Father, forgive them; they do not know what they are doing.'[b]

They divided his clothes among them by casting lots. The people stood looking on, and their rulers jeered at him: 'He saved others: now let him save himself, if this is God's Anointed, his Chosen.' The soldiers joined in the mockery and came forward offering him their sour wine. 'If you are the king of the Jews,' they said, 'save yourself.' There was an inscription above his head which ran: 'This is the king of the Jews.'

One of the criminals who hung there with him taunted him: 'Are not you the Messiah? Save

---

[a] *Some witnesses read* (17) At festival time he was obliged to release one person for them; (18) and now . . . [b] *Some witnesses omit* Jesus said, 'Father . . . doing.'

K.J.V.

save thyself and us. 40 But the other answering rebuked him, saying, Dost not thou fear God, seeing thou art in the same condemnation? 41And we indeed justly; for we receive the due reward of our deeds: but this man hath done nothing amiss. 42And he said unto Jesus, Lord, remember me when thou comest into thy kingdom. 43And Jesus said unto him, Verily I say unto thee, To day shalt thou be with me in paradise. 44And it was about the sixth hour, and there was a darkness over all the earth until the ninth hour. 45And the sun was darkened, and the vail of the temple was rent in the midst.

46 And when Jesus had cried with a loud voice, he said, Father, into thy hands I commend my spirit: and having said thus, he gave up the ghost. 47 Now when the centurion saw what was done, he glorified God, saying, Certainly this was a righteous man. 48And all the people that came together to that sight, beholding the things which were done, smote their breasts, and returned. 49And all his acquaintance, and the women that followed him from Galilee, stood afar off, beholding these things.

50 And, behold, *there was* a man named Joseph, a counsellor; *and he was* a good man, and a just: 51 (The same had not consented to the counsel and deed of them:) *he was* of Arimathea, a city of the Jews; who also himself waited for the kingdom of God. 52 This *man* went unto Pilate, and begged the body of Jesus. 53And he took it down, and wrapped it in linen, and laid it in a sepulchre that was hewn in stone, wherein never man before was laid. 54And that day was the preparation, and the sabbath drew on. 55And the women also, which came with him from Galilee, followed after, and beheld the sepulchre, and how his body was laid. 56And they returned, and prepared spices and ointments; and rested the sabbath day according to the commandment.

R.S.V.

Save yourself and us!" 40 But the other rebuked him, saying, "Do you not fear God, since you are under the same sentence of condemnation? 41And we indeed justly; for we are receiving the due reward of our deeds; but this man has done nothing wrong." 42And he said, "Jesus, remember me when you come in your kingly power." [p] 43And he said to him, "Truly, I say to you, today you will be with me in Paradise."

44 It was now about the sixth hour, and there was darkness over the whole land [q] until the ninth hour, 45 while the sun's light failed; [r] and the curtain of the temple was torn in two. 46 Then Jesus, crying with a loud voice, said, "Father, into thy hands I commit my spirit!" And having said this he breathed his last. 47Now when the centurion saw what had taken place, he praised God, and said, "Certainly this man was innocent!" 48And all the multitudes who assembled to see the sight, when they saw what had taken place, returned home beating their breasts. 49And all his acquaintances and the women who had followed him from Galilee stood at a distance and saw these things.

50 Now there was a man named Joseph from the Jewish town of Arimathea. He was a member of the council, a good and righteous man, 51 who had not consented to their purpose and deed, and he was looking for the kingdom of God. 52 This man went to Pilate and asked for the body of Jesus. 53 Then he took it down and wrapped it in a linen shroud, and laid him in a rock-hewn tomb, where no one had ever yet been laid. 54 It was the day of Preparation, and the sabbath was beginning. [s] 55 The women who had come with him from Galilee followed, and saw the tomb, and how his body was laid; 56 then they returned, and prepared spices and ointments.

On the sabbath they rested according to the commandment.

24 Now upon the first *day* of the week, very early in the morning, they came unto the sepulchre, bringing the spices which they had prepared, and certain *others* with them. 2And they found the stone rolled away from the sepulchre. 3And they entered in, and found not the body of the Lord Jesus. 4And it came to pass, as they were much perplexed thereabout, behold, two men stood by them in shining gar-

24 But on the first day of the week, at early dawn, they went to the tomb, taking the spices which they had prepared. 2And they found the stone rolled away from the tomb, 3 but when they went in they did not find the body. [t] 4 While they were perplexed about this, behold, two men stood by them in dazzling ap-

[p] Greek *kingdom.* [q] Or *earth.* [r] Or *the sun was eclipsed.* Other ancient authorities read *the sun was darkened.* [s] Greek *was dawning.* [t] Other ancient authorities add *of the Lord Jesus.*

PHILLIPS

But the other one checked him with the words:

"Aren't you afraid of God even when you're getting the same punishment as he is? And it's fair enough for us, for we've only got what we deserve, but this man never did anything wrong in his life."

Then he said,

"Jesus, remember me when you come into your kingdom."

And Jesus answered,

"I tell you truly, this very day you will be with me in paradise."

The darkness, and   23. 44
the death of Jesus

It was now about midday, but darkness came over the whole countryside until three in the afternoon, for there was an eclipse of the sun. The veil in the Temple sanctuary was split in two. Then Jesus gave a great cry and said,

"Father, I commend my spirit into your hands."

And with these words, he died.

When the centurion saw what had happened, he exclaimed reverently,

"That was indeed a good man!"

And the whole crowd who had collected for the spectacle, when they saw what had happened, went home in deep distress. And those who had known him, as well as the women who had followed him from Galilee, remained standing at a distance and saw all this happen.

Joseph from Arimathaea lays   23. 50
the body of Jesus in a tomb

Now there was a man called Joseph, a member of the Jewish council. He was a good and just man, and had neither agreed with their plan nor voted for their decision. He came from the Jewish City of Arimathaea and was awaiting the kingdom of God. He went to Pilate and asked for Jesus' body. He took it down and wrapped it in linen and placed it in a rock-hewn tomb which had not been used before.

It was now the day of the preparation and the Sabbath was beginning to dawn, so the women who had accompanied Jesus from Galilee followed Joseph, noted the tomb and the position of the body, and then went home to prepare spices and perfumes. On the Sabbath they rested, in obedience to the commandment.

The first day of the week: 24. 1
the empty tomb

But at the first signs of dawn on the first day of the week, they went to the tomb, taking with them the aromatic spices they had prepared. They discovered that the stone had been rolled away from the tomb, but on going inside, the body of the Lord Jesus was not to be found. While they were still puzzling over this, two men suddenly stood at their elbow, dressed in

N.E.B.

yourself, and us.' But the other answered sharply, 'Have you no fear of God? You are under the same sentence as he. For us it is plain justice; we are paying the price for our misdeeds; but this man has done nothing wrong.' And he said, 'Jesus, remember me when you come to your throne.' [a] He answered, 'I tell you this: today you shall be with me in Paradise.'

By now it was about midday and there came a darkness over the whole land, which lasted until three in the afternoon; the sun was in eclipse. And the curtain of the temple was torn in two. Then Jesus gave a loud cry and said, 'Father, into thy hands I commit my spirit'; and with these words he died. The centurion saw it all, and gave praise to God. 'Beyond all doubt', he said, 'this man was innocent.'

The crowd who had assembled for the spectacle, when they saw what had happened, went home beating their breasts.

His friends had all been standing at a distance; the women who had accompanied him from Galilee stood with them and watched it all.

Now there was a man called Joseph, a member of the Council, a good, upright man, who had dissented from their policy and the action they had taken. He came from the Jewish town of Arimathaea, and he was one who looked forward to the kingdom of God. This man now approached Pilate and asked for the body of Jesus. Taking it down from the cross, he wrapped it in a linen sheet, and laid it in a tomb cut out of the rock, in which no one had been laid before. It was Friday, and the Sabbath was about to begin.

The women who had accompanied him from Galilee followed; they took note of the tomb and observed how his body was laid. Then they went home and prepared spices and perfumes; and on the Sabbath they rested in obedience to the commandment.

24 But on the Sunday morning very early they came to the tomb bringing the spices they had prepared. Finding that the stone had been rolled away from the tomb, they went inside; but the body was not to be found. While they stood utterly at a loss, all of a sudden two men in dazzling garments were at their side.

[a] *Some witnesses read* come in royal power.

K.J.V.

ments: 5And as they were afraid, and bowed down *their* faces to the earth, they said unto them, Why seek ye the living among the dead? 6 He is not here, but is risen: remember how he spake unto you when he was yet in Galilee, 7 Saying, The Son of man must be delivered into the hands of sinful men, and be crucified, and the third day rise again. 8And they remembered his words, 9And returned from the sepulchre, and told all these things unto the eleven, and to all the rest. 10 It was Mary Magdalene, and Joanna, and Mary *the mother* of James, and other *women that were* with them, which told these things unto the apostles. 11And their words seemed to them as idle tales, and they believed them not. 12 Then arose Peter, and ran unto the sepulchre; and stooping down, he beheld the linen clothes laid by themselves, and departed, wondering in himself at that which was come to pass.

13 And, behold, two of them went that same day to a village called Emmaus, which was from Jerusalem *about* threescore furlongs. 14And they talked together of all these things which had happened. 15And it came to pass, that, while they communed *together* and reasoned, Jesus himself drew near, and went with them. 16 But their eyes were holden that they should not know him. 17And he said unto them, What manner of communications *are* these that ye have one to another, as ye walk, and are sad? 18And the one of them, whose name was Cleopas, answering said unto him, Art thou only a stranger in Jerusalem, and hast not known the things which are come to pass there in these days? 19And he said unto them, What things? And they said unto him, Concerning Jesus of Nazareth, which was a prophet mighty in deed and word before God and all the people: 20And how the chief priests and our rulers delivered him to be condemned to death, and have crucified him. 21 But we trusted that it had been he which should have redeemed Israel: and beside all this, to day is the third day since these things were done. 22 Yea, and certain women also of our company made us astonished, which were early at the sepulchre; 23And when they found not his body, they came, saying, that they had also seen a vision of angels, which said that he was alive. 24And certain of them which were with us went to the sepulchre, and found *it* even so as the women had said: but him they saw not. 25 Then he said unto them, O fools, and slow of heart to believe all that the prophets have spoken: 26 Ought not Christ to have suffered these things, and to enter into his glory? 27And beginning at Moses and all the prophets, he expounded unto them in all the Scriptures the things concerning himself. 28And they drew nigh unto the village, whither they went: and he made as though he would have gone further. 29 But they constrained him, saying, Abide with us; for it is toward evening, and the day is far spent. And he went in to tarry with them. 30And it came to pass, as he sat at meat with them, he took bread, and blessed *it*, and brake, and gave

R.S.V.

parel; 5 and as they were frightened and bowed their faces to the ground, the men said to them, "Why do you seek the living among the dead? *u* 6 Remember how he told you, while he was still in Galilee, 7 that the Son of man must be delivered into the hands of sinful men, and be crucified, and on the third day rise." 8And they remembered his words, 9 and returning from the tomb they told all this to the eleven and to all the rest. 10 Now it was Mary Magdalene and Joanna and Mary the mother of James and the other women with them who told this to the apostles; 11 but these words seemed to them an idle tale, and they did not believe them.*v*

13 That very day two of them were going to a village named Emmaus, about seven miles*w* from Jerusalem, 14 and talking with each other about all these things that had happened. 15 While they were talking and discussing together, Jesus himself drew near and went with them. 16 But their eyes were kept from recognizing him. 17And he said to them, "What is this conversation which you are holding with each other as you walk?" And they stood still, looking sad. 18 Then one of them, named Cleopas, answered him, "Are you the only visitor to Jerusalem who does not know the things that have happened there in these days?" 19And he said to them, "What things?" And they said to him, "Concerning Jesus of Nazareth, who was a prophet mighty in deed and word before God and all the people, 20 and how our chief priests and rulers delivered him up to be condemned to death, and crucified him. 21 But we had hoped that he was the one to redeem Israel. Yes, and besides all this, it is now the third day since this happened. 22 Moreover, some women of our company amazed us. They were at the tomb early in the morning 23 and did not find his body; and they came back saying that they had even seen a vision of angels, who said that he was alive. 24 Some of those who were with us went to the tomb, and found it just as the women had said; but him they did not see." 25And he said to them, "O foolish men, and slow of heart to believe all that the prophets have spoken! 26 Was it not necessary that the Christ should suffer these things and enter into his glory?" 27And beginning with Moses and all the prophets, he interpreted to them in all the scriptures the things concerning himself.

28 So they drew near to the village to which they were going. He appeared to be going further, 29 but they constrained him, saying, "Stay with us, for it is toward evening and the day is now far spent." So he went in to stay with them. 30 When he was at table with them, he took the bread and blessed, and broke it, and

[u] Other ancient authorities add *He is not here, but has risen*. [v] Other ancient authorities add verse 12, *But Peter rose and ran to the tomb; stooping and looking in, he saw the linen cloths by themselves; and he went home wondering at what had happened*. [w] Greek *sixty stadia;* other ancient authorities read *a hundred and sixty stadia*.

PHILLIPS

dazzling light. The women were terribly frightened, and turned their eyes away and looked at the ground. But the two men spoke to them,

"Why do you look for the living among the dead? He is not here: he has risen! Remember that he said to you, while he was still in Galilee —that the Son of Man must be betrayed into the hands of sinful men, and must be crucified, and must rise again on the third day."

Then they did remember what he had said, and they turned their backs on the tomb and went and told all this to the eleven and the others who were with them.

It was Mary of Magdala, Joanna, Mary, the mother of James, and their companions who made this report to the apostles. But it struck them as sheer imagination, and they did not believe the women. Only Peter got up and ran to the tomb. He stooped down and saw the linen clothes lying there all by themselves, and he went home wondering what had happened.

The walk to Emmaus   24. 13

Then on the same day we find two of them going off to Emmaus, a village about seven miles from Jerusalem. As they went they were deep in conversation about everything that had happened. While they were absorbed in their serious talk and discussion, Jesus himself approached and walked along with them, but something prevented them from recognizing him. Then he spoke to them,

"What is all this discussion that you are having on your walk?"

They stopped, their faces drawn with misery, and the one called Cleopas replied,

"You must be the only stranger in Jerusalem who hasn't heard all the things that have happened there recently!"

"What things?" asked Jesus.

"Oh, all about Jesus, from Nazareth. There was a man—a prophet strong in what he did and what he said, in God's eyes as well as the people's. Haven't you heard how our chief priests and rulers handed him over for execution, and had him crucified? But we were hoping he was the one who was to come and set Israel free. . . .

"Yes, and as if that were not enough, it's getting on for three days since all this happened; and some of our womenfolk have disturbed us profoundly. For they went to the tomb at dawn, and then when they couldn't find his body they said that they had had a vision of angels who said that he was alive. Some of our people went straight off to the tomb and found things just as the women had described them—but they didn't see *him!*"

Then he himself spoke to them:

"Aren't you failing to understand, and slow to believe in all that the prophets have said? Was it not inevitable that Christ should suffer like that and so find his glory?"

Then, beginning with Moses and all the prophets, he explained to them everything in the scriptures that referred to himself.

They were by now approaching the village to which they were going. He gave the impression that he meant to go on further, but they stopped him with the words,

"Do stay with us. It is nearly evening and soon the day will be over."

So he went indoors to stay with them. Then it happened! While he was sitting at table with them he took the loaf, gave thanks, broke it and

N.E.B.

They were terrified, and stood with eyes cast down, but the men said, 'Why search among the dead for one who lives? [a] Remember what he told you while he was still in Galilee, about the Son of Man: how he must be given up into the power of sinful men and be crucified, and must rise again on the third day.' Then they recalled his words, and, returning from the tomb, they reported all this to the Eleven and all the others.

The women were Mary of Magdala, Joanna, and Mary the mother[b] of James, and they, with the other women, told the apostles. But the story appeared to them to be nonsense, and they would not believe them.[c]

That same day two of them were on their way to a village called Emmaus, which lay about seven miles from Jerusalem, and they were talking together about all these happenings. As they talked and discussed it with one another, Jesus himself came up and walked along with them; but something held their eyes from seeing who it was. He asked them, 'What is it you are debating as you walk?' They halted, their faces full of gloom, and one, called Cleopas, answered, 'Are you the only person staying in Jerusalem not to know[d] what has happened there in the last few days?' 'What do you mean?' he said. 'All this about Jesus of Nazareth,' they replied, 'a prophet powerful in speech and action before God and the whole people; how our chief priests and rulers handed him over to be sentenced to death, and crucified him. But we had been hoping that he was the man to liberate Israel. What is more, this is the third day since it happened, and now some women of our company have astounded us: they went early to the tomb, but failed to find his body, and returned with a story that they had seen a vision of angels who told them he was alive. So some of our people went to the tomb and found things just as the women had said; but him they did not see.'

'How dull you are!' he answered. 'How slow to believe all that the prophets said! Was not the Messiah bound to suffer thus before entering upon his glory?' Then he began with Moses and all the prophets, and explained to them the passages which referred to himself in every part of the scriptures.

By this time they had reached the village to which they were going, and he made as if to continue his journey, but they pressed him: 'Stay with us, for evening draws on, and the day is almost over.' So he went in to stay with them. And when he had sat down with them at table, he took bread and said the blessing; he broke

[a] *Some witnesses insert* He is not here: he has risen. [b] *Or* wife, *or* daughter. [c] *Some witnesses add* (12) Peter, however, got up and ran to the tomb, and, peering in, saw the wrappings and nothing more; and he went home amazed at what had happened. [d] *Or* Have you been staying by yourself in Jerusalem, that you do not know . . .

K.J.V.

to them. 31And their eyes were opened, and they knew him; and he vanished out of their sight. 32And they said one to another, Did not our heart burn within us, while he talked with us by the way, and while he opened to us the Scriptures? 33And they rose up the same hour, and returned to Jerusalem, and found the eleven gathered together, and them that were with them, 34 Saying, The Lord is risen indeed, and hath appeared to Simon. 35And they told what things *were done* in the way, and how he was known of them in breaking of bread.

36 And as they thus spake, Jesus himself stood in the midst of them, and saith unto them, Peace *be* unto you. 37 But they were terrified and affrighted, and supposed that they had seen a spirit. 38And he said unto them, Why are ye troubled? and why do thoughts arise in your hearts? 39 Behold my hands and my feet, that it is I myself: handle me, and see; for a spirit hath not flesh and bones, as ye see me have. 40And when he had thus spoken, he shewed them *his* hands and *his* feet. 41And while they yet believed not for joy, and wondered, he said unto them, Have ye here any meat? 42And they gave him a piece of a broiled fish, and of a honeycomb. 43And he took *it*, and did eat before them. 44And he said unto them, These *are* the words which I spake unto you, while I was yet with you, that all things must be fulfilled, which were written in the law of Moses, and *in* the prophets, and *in* the psalms, concerning me. 45 Then opened he their understanding, that they might understand the Scriptures, 46And said unto them, Thus it is written, and thus it behooved Christ to suffer, and to rise from the dead the third day: 47And that repentance and remission of sins should be preached in his name among all nations, beginning at Jerusalem. 48And ye are witnesses of these things.

49 And, behold, I send the promise of my Father upon you: but tarry ye in the city of Jerusalem, until ye be endued with power from on high.

50 And he led them out as far as to Bethany, and he lifted up his hands, and blessed them. 51And it came to pass, while he blessed them, he was parted from them, and carried up into heaven. 52And they worshipped him, and returned to Jerusalem with great joy: 53And were continually in the temple, praising and blessing God. Amen.

R.S.V.

gave it to them. 31And their eyes were opened and they recognized him; and he vanished out of their sight. 32 They said to each other, "Did not our hearts burn within us while he talked to us on the road, while he opened to us the scriptures?" 33And they rose that same hour and returned to Jerusalem; and they found the eleven gathered together and those who were with them, 34 who said, "The Lord has risen indeed, and has appeared to Simon!" 35 Then they told what had happened on the road, and how he was known to them in the breaking of the bread.

36 As they were saying this, Jesus himself stood among them.* 37 But they were startled and frightened, and supposed that they saw a spirit. 38And he said to them, "Why are you troubled, and why do questionings rise in your hearts? 39 See my hands and my feet, that it is I myself; handle me, and see; for a spirit has not flesh and bones as you see that I have." * 41And while they still disbelieved for joy, and wondered, he said to them, "Have you anything here to eat?" 42 They gave him a piece of broiled fish, 43 and he took it and ate before them.

44 Then he said to them, "These are my words which I spoke to you, while I was still with you, that everything written about me in the law of Moses and the prophets and the psalms must be fulfilled." 45 Then he opened their minds to understand the scriptures, 46 and said to them, "Thus it is written, that the Christ should suffer and on the third day rise from the dead, 47 and that repentance and forgiveness of sins should be preached in his name to all nations,* beginning from Jerusalem. 48 You are witnesses of these things. 49And behold, I send the promise of my Father upon you; but stay in the city, until you are clothed with power from on high."

50 Then he led them out as far as Bethany, and lifting up his hands he blessed them. 51 While he blessed them, he parted from them.* 52And they* returned to Jerusalem with great joy, 53 and were continually in the temple blessing God.

[x] Other ancient authorities add *and said to them, 'Peace to you!'* [y] Other ancient authorities add verse 40, *And when he had said this, he showed them his hands and his feet.* [z] Or *nations. Beginning from Jerusalem you are witnesses.* [a] Other ancient authorities add *and was carried up into heaven.* [b] Other ancient authorities add *worshiped him, and*

PHILLIPS

passed it to them. Their eyes opened wide and they knew him! But he vanished from their sight. Then they said to each other,

"Weren't our hearts glowing while he was with us on the road, and when he made the scriptures so plain to us?"

And they got to their feet without delay and turned back to Jerusalem. There they found the eleven and their friends all together, full of the news—

"The Lord is really risen—he has appeared to Simon now!"

Then they told the story of their walk, and how they recognized him when he broke the loaf.

Jesus suddenly appears to the disciples   24. 36

And while they were still talking about these things, Jesus himself stood among them and said,

"Peace be to you all!"

But they shrank back in terror, for they thought they were seeing a ghost.

"Why are you so worried?" said Jesus, "and why do doubts arise in your minds? Look at my hands and my feet—it is really I myself! Feel me and see; ghosts have no flesh or bones as you can see that I have."

But while they still could not believe it through sheer joy, and were quite bewildered, Jesus said to them,

"Have you anything here to eat?"

They gave him a piece of broiled fish and part of a honeycomb, which he took and ate before their eyes. Then he said,

"Here and now are fulfilled the words that I told you when I was with you: that everything written about me in the Law of Moses and in the prophets and psalms must come true."

Then he opened their minds so that they could understand the scriptures, and added:

"That is how it was written, and that is why it was inevitable that Christ should suffer, and rise from the dead on the third day. So must the change of heart which leads to the forgiveness of sins be proclaimed in his name to all nations, beginning at Jerusalem.

Jesus commissions them with the new message   24. 48

"You are eyewitnesses of these things. Now I hand over to you the command of my Father. Stay in the city, then, until you are clothed with power from on high."

Then he led them outside as far as Bethany, where he blessed them with uplifted hands. While he was in the act of blessing them he was parted from them and was carried up to Heaven. They worshiped him, and turned back to Jerusalem with great joy, and spent their days in the Temple, praising and blessing God.

N.E.B.

the bread, and offered it to them. Then their eyes were opened, and they recognized him; and he vanished from their sight. They said to one another, 'Did we not feel our hearts on fire as he talked with us on the road and explained the scriptures to us?'

Without a moment's delay they set out and returned to Jerusalem. There they found that the Eleven and the rest of the company had assembled, and were saying, 'It is true: the Lord has risen; he has appeared to Simon.' Then they gave their account of the events of their journey and told how he had been recognized by them at the breaking of the bread.

As they were talking about all this, there he was, standing among them.[a] Startled and terrified, they thought they were seeing a ghost. But he said, 'Why are you so perturbed? Why do questionings arise in your minds? Look at my hands and feet. It is I myself. Touch me and see; no ghost has flesh and bones as you can see that I have.'[b] They were still unconvinced, still wondering, for it seemed too good to be true. So he asked them, 'Have you anything here to eat?' They offered him a piece of fish they had cooked, which he took and ate before their eyes.

And he said to them, 'This is what I meant by saying, while I was still with you, that everything written about me in the Law of Moses and in the prophets and psalms was bound to be fulfilled.' Then he opened their minds to understand the scriptures. 'This', he said, 'is what is written: that the Messiah is to suffer death and to rise from the dead on the third day, and that in his name repentance bringing the forgiveness of sins is to be proclaimed to all nations. Begin from Jerusalem: it is you who are the witnesses to all this. And mark this: I am sending upon you my Father's promised gift; so stay here in this city until you are armed with the power from above.'

Then he led them out as far as Bethany, and blessed them with uplifted hands; and in the act of blessing he parted from them.[c] And they[d] returned to Jerusalem with great joy, and spent all their time in the temple praising God.

[a] *Some witnesses insert* And he said to them, 'Peace be with you!' [b] *Some witnesses insert* (40) After saying this he showed them his hands and feet. [c] *Some witnesses add* and was carried up into heaven. [d] *Some witnesses insert* worshipped him and . . .

THE GOSPEL

ACCORDING TO

SAINT JOHN

THE GOSPEL

ACCORDING TO

JOHN

1 In the beginning was the Word, and the Word was with God, and the Word was God. 2 The same was in the beginning with God. 3 All things were made by him; and without him was not any thing made that was made. 4 In him was life; and the life was the light of men. 5 And the light shineth in darkness; and the darkness comprehended it not.

6 There was a man sent from God, whose name was John. 7 The same came for a witness, to bear witness of the Light, that all men through him might believe. 8 He was not that Light, but was sent to bear witness of that Light. 9 That was the true Light, which lighteth every man that cometh into the world. 10 He was in the world, and the world was made by him, and the world knew him not. 11 He came unto his own, and his own received him not. 12 But as many as received him, to them gave he power to become the sons of God, even to them that believe on his name: 13 Which were born, not of blood, nor of the will of the flesh, nor of the will of man, but of God. 14 And the Word was made flesh, and dwelt among us, (and we beheld his glory, the glory as of the only begotten of the Father,) full of grace and truth.

15 John bare witness of him, and cried, saying, This was he of whom I spake, He that cometh after me is preferred before me; for he was before me. 16 And of his fulness have all we received, and grace for grace. 17 For the law was given by Moses, but grace and truth came by Jesus Christ. 18 No man hath seen God at any time; the only begotten Son, which is in the bosom of the Father, he hath declared him.

19 And this is the record of John, when the Jews sent priests and Levites from Jerusalem to ask him, Who art thou? 20 And he confessed, and denied not; but confessed, I am not the Christ. 21 And they asked him, What then? Art thou Elias? And he saith, I am not. Art thou that Prophet? And he answered, No. 22 Then said they unto him, Who art thou? that we may give an answer to them that sent us. What sayest

1 In the beginning was the Word, and the Word was with God, and the Word was God. 2 He was in the beginning with God; 3 all things were made through him, and without him was not anything made that was made. 4 In him was life,[a] and the life was the light of men. 5 The light shines in the darkness, and the darkness has not overcome it.

6 There was a man sent from God, whose name was John. 7 He came for testimony, to bear witness to the light, that all might believe through him. 8 He was not the light, but came to bear witness to the light.

9 The true light that enlightens every man was coming into the world. 10 He was in the world, and the world was made through him, yet the world knew him not. 11 He came to his own home, and his own people received him not. 12 But to all who received him, who believed in his name, he gave power to become children of God; 13 who were born, not of blood nor of the will of the flesh nor of the will of man, but of God.

14 And the Word became flesh and dwelt among us, full of grace and truth; we have beheld his glory, glory as of the only Son from the Father. 15 (John bore witness to him, and cried, "This was he of whom I said, 'He who comes after me ranks before me, for he was before me.'") 16 And from his fulness have we all received, grace upon grace. 17 For the law was given through Moses; grace and truth came through Jesus Christ. 18 No one has ever seen God; the only Son,[b] who is in the bosom of the Father, he has made him known.

19 And this is the testimony of John, when the Jews sent priests and Levites from Jerusalem to ask him, "Who are you?" 20 He confessed, he did not deny, but confessed, "I am not the Christ." 21 And they asked him, "What then? Are you Elijah?" He said, "I am not." "Are you the prophet?" And he answered, "No." 22 They said to him then, "Who are you? Let us have an answer for those who sent us. What do

THE GOSPEL
OF
JOHN

THE GOSPEL
ACCORDING TO
JOHN

Prologue   **1. 1**

At the beginning God expressed himself. That personal expression, that word, was with God and was God, and he existed with God from the beginning. All creation took place through him, and none took place without him. In him appeared life and this life was the light of mankind. The light still shines in the darkness, and the darkness has never put it out.

The gospel's beginning on earth   **1. 6**

A man called John was sent by God as a witness to the light, so that any man who heard his testimony might believe in the light. This man was not himself the light: he was sent simply as a personal witness to that light. That was the true light which shines upon every man as he comes into the world. He came into the world—the world he had created—and the world failed to recognize him. He came into his own creation, and his own people would not accept him. Yet wherever men did accept him he gave them the power to become sons of God. These were the men who truly believed in him, and their birth depended not on the course of nature nor on any impulse or plan of man, but on God.

So the word of God became a human being and lived among us. We saw his splendor (the splendor as of a father's only son), full of grace and truth. And it was about him that John stood up and testified, exclaiming: "Here is the one I was speaking about when I said that although he would come after me he would always be in front of me; for he existed before I was born!" Indeed, every one of us has shared in his riches—there is a grace in our lives because of his grace. For while the Law was given by Moses, love and truth came through Jesus Christ. It is true that no one has ever seen God at any time. Yet the divine and only Son, who lives in the closest intimacy with the Father, has made him known.

John's witness   **1. 19**

This then is the testimony of John, when the Jews sent priests and Levites to ask him who he was. He admitted with complete candor, "I am not Christ."

So they asked him, "Who are you then? Are you Elijah?"

"No, I am not," he replied.

"Are you the Prophet?"

"No," he replied.

"Well, then," they asked again, "who are you? We want to give an answer to the people who sent us. What would you call yourself?"

The Coming of Christ

1 When all things began, the Word already
was.[a] The Word dwelt with God, and what God was, the Word was. The Word, then, was with God at the beginning, and through him all things came to be; no single thing was created without him. All that came to be was alive with his life,[b] and that life was the light of men. The light shines on in the dark, and the darkness has never quenched it.

There appeared a man named John, sent from God; he came as a witness to testify to the light, that all might become believers through him. He was not himself the light; he came to bear witness to the light. The real light which enlightens every man was even then coming into the world.[c]

He was in the world;[d] but the world, though it owed its being to him, did not recognize him. He entered his own realm, and his own would not receive him. But to all who did receive him, to those who have yielded him their allegiance, he gave the right to become children of God, not born of any human stock, or by the fleshly desire of a human father, but the offspring of God himself. So the Word became flesh; he came to dwell among us, and we saw his glory, such glory as befits the Father's only Son, full of grace and truth.

Here is John's testimony to him: he cried aloud, 'This is the man I meant when I said, "He comes after me, but takes rank before me"; for before I was born, he already was.'

Out of his full store we have all received grace upon grace; for while the Law was given through Moses, grace and truth came through Jesus Christ. No one has ever seen God; but God's only Son, he who is nearest to the Father's heart, he has made him known.[e]

This is the testimony which John gave when the Jews of Jerusalem sent a deputation of priests and Levites to ask him who he was. He confessed without reserve and avowed, 'I am not the Messiah.' 'What then? Are you Elijah?' 'No', he replied. 'Are you the prophet we await?' He answered 'No.' 'Then who are you?' they asked. 'We must give an answer to those who sent us. What account do you give of yourself?' He an-

[a] *Or* The Word was at the creation. [b] *Or* no single created thing came into being without him. There was life in him . . . [c] *Or* The light was in being, light absolute, enlightening every man born into the world. [d] *Or* The Word, then, was in the world. [e] *Some witnesses read* but the only one, the one nearest to the Father's heart, has made him known; *others read* but the only one, himself God, the nearest to the Father's heart, has made him known.

K.J.V.

thou of thyself? 23 He said, I *am* the voice of one crying in the wilderness, Make straight the way of the Lord, as said the prophet Esaias. 24And they which were sent were of the Pharisees. 25And they asked him, and said unto him, Why baptizest thou then, if thou be not that Christ, nor Elias, neither that Prophet? 26 John answered them, saying, I baptize with water: but there standeth one among you, whom ye know not; 27 He it is, who coming after me is preferred before me, whose shoe's latchet I am not worthy to unloose. 28 These things were done in Bethabara beyond Jordan, where John was baptizing.

29 The next day John seeth Jesus coming unto him, and saith, Behold the Lamb of God, which taketh away the sin of the world! 30 This is he of whom I said, After me cometh a man which is preferred before me; for he was before me. 31And I knew him not: but that he should be made manifest to Israel, therefore am I come baptizing with water. 32And John bare record, saying, I saw the Spirit descending from heaven like a dove, and it abode upon him. 33And I knew him not: but he that sent me to baptize with water, the same said unto me, Upon whom thou shalt see the Spirit descending, and remaining on him, the same is he which baptizeth with the Holy Ghost. 34And I saw, and bare record that this is the Son of God.

35 Again the next day after, John stood, and two of his disciples; 36And looking upon Jesus as he walked, he saith, Behold the Lamb of God! 37And the two disciples heard him speak, and they followed Jesus. 38 Then Jesus turned, and saw them following, and saith unto them, What seek ye? They said unto him, Rabbi, (which is to say, being interpreted, Master,) where dwellest thou? 39 He saith unto them, Come and see. They came and saw where he dwelt, and abode with him that day: for it was about the tenth hour. 40 One of the two which heard John *speak*, and followed him, was Andrew, Simon Peter's brother. 41 He first findeth his own brother Simon, and saith unto him, We have found the Messias, which is, being interpreted, the Christ. 42And he brought him to Jesus. And when Jesus beheld him, he said, Thou art Simon the son of Jona: thou shalt be called Cephas, which is by interpretation, A stone.

43 The day following Jesus would go forth into Galilee, and findeth Philip, and saith unto him, Follow me. 44 Now Philip was of Bethsaida, the city of Andrew and Peter. 45 Philip findeth Nathanael, and saith unto him, We have found him, of whom Moses in the law, and the prophets, did write, Jesus of Nazareth, the son of Joseph. 46And Nathanael said unto him, Can there any good thing come out of Nazareth? Philip saith unto him, Come and see. 47 Jesus saw Nathanael coming to him, and saith of him, Behold an Israelite indeed, in whom is no guile! 48 Nathanael saith unto him, Whence knowest thou me? Jesus answered and said unto him, Be-

R.S.V.

you say about yourself?" 23 He said, "I am the voice of one crying in the wilderness, 'Make straight the way of the Lord,' as the prophet Isaiah said."

24 Now they had been sent from the Pharisees. 25 They asked him, "Then why are you baptizing, if you are neither the Christ, nor Elijah, nor the prophet?" 26 John answered them, "I baptize with water; but among you stands one whom you do not know, 27 even he who comes after me, the thong of whose sandal I am not worthy to untie." 28 This took place in Bethany beyond the Jordan, where John was baptizing.

29 The next day he saw Jesus coming toward him, and said, "Behold, the Lamb of God, who takes away the sin of the world! 30 This is he of whom I said, 'After me comes a man who ranks before me, for he was before me.' 31 I myself did not know him; but for this I came baptizing with water, that he might be revealed to Israel." 32And John bore witness, "I saw the Spirit descend as a dove from heaven, and it remained on him. 33 I myself did not know him; but he who sent me to baptize with water said to me, 'He on whom you see the Spirit descend and remain, this is he who baptizes with the Holy Spirit.' 34And I have seen and have borne witness that this is the Son of God."

35 The next day again John was standing with two of his disciples; 36 and he looked at Jesus as he walked, and said, "Behold, the Lamb of God!" 37 The two disciples heard him say this, and they followed Jesus. 38 Jesus turned, and saw them following, and said to them, "What do you seek?" And they said to him, "Rabbi" (which means Teacher), "where are you staying?" 39 He said to them, "Come and see." They came and saw where he was staying; and they stayed with him that day, for it was about the tenth hour. 40 One of the two who heard John speak, and followed him, was Andrew, Simon Peter's brother. 41 He first found his brother Simon, and said to him, "We have found the Messiah" (which means Christ). 42 He brought him to Jesus. Jesus looked at him, and said, "So you are Simon the son of John? You shall be called Cephas" (which means Peter[c]).

43 The next day Jesus decided to go to Galilee. And he found Philip and said to him, "Follow me." 44 Now Philip was from Bethsaida, the city of Andrew and Peter. 45 Philip found Nathanael, and said to him, "We have found him of whom Moses in the law and also the prophets wrote, Jesus of Nazareth, the son of Joseph." 46 Nathanael said to him, "Can anything good come out of Nazareth?" Philip said to him, "Come and see." 47 Jesus saw Nathanael coming to him, and said of him, "Behold, an Israelite indeed, in whom is no guile!" 48 Nathanael said to him, "How do you know me?" Jesus answered

---

[c] From the word for *rock* in Aramaic and Greek, respectively.

PHILLIPS

"I am a voice shouting in the desert, *'Make straight the way of the Lord!'* as Isaiah the prophet said."

Now some of the Pharisees had been sent to John, and they questioned him, "What is the reason, then, for your baptizing people if you are not Christ and not Elijah and not the Prophet?"

To which John returned, "I do baptize—with water. But somewhere among you stands a man you do not know. He comes after me, it is true, but I am not fit to undo his shoes!" (All this happened in the Bethany on the far side of the Jordan where the baptisms of John took place.)

On the following day, John saw Jesus coming toward him and said, "Look, there is the lamb of God who will take away the sin of the world! This is the man I meant when I said 'A man comes after me who is always in front of me, for he existed before I was born!' It is true I have not known him, yet it was to make him known to the people of Israel that I came and baptized people with water."

Then John gave this testimony: "I have seen the Spirit come down like a dove from Heaven and rest upon him. Indeed, it is true that I did not recognize him by myself, but he who sent me to baptize with water told me this: 'The one on whom you will see the Spirit coming down and resting is the man who baptizes with the Holy Spirit!' Now I have seen this happen and I declare publicly before you all that he is the Son of God!"

Men begin to follow Jesus   *1. 35*

On the following day John was again standing with two of his disciples. He looked straight at Jesus as he walked along and said, "There is the lamb of God!" The two disciples heard what he said and followed Jesus. Then Jesus turned round and when he saw them following him, spoke to them. "What do you want?" he said.

"Master, where are you staying?" they replied.

"Come and see," returned Jesus.

So they went and saw where he was staying and remained with him the rest of that day. (It was then about four o'clock in the afternoon.) One of the two men who had heard what John said and had followed Jesus was Andrew, Simon Peter's brother. He went straight off and found his own brother, Simon, and told him, "We have found the Messiah!" (meaning, of course, Christ). And he brought him to Jesus.

Jesus looked steadily at him and said: "You are Simon, the son of John. From now on your name is Cephas" (that is, Peter, meaning "a rock").

The following day Jesus decided to go into Galilee. He found Philip and said to him, "Follow me!" Philip was a man from Bethsaida, the town that Andrew and Peter came from. Now Philip found Nathanael and told him. "We have discovered the man whom Moses wrote about in the Law and about whom the Prophets wrote too. He is Jesus, the son of Joseph, and comes from Nazareth."

"Can anything good come out of Nazareth?" retorted Nathanael.

"You come and see," replied Philip.

Jesus saw Nathanael coming toward him and remarked, "Now here is a true man of Israel; there is no deceit in him!"

"How can you know me?" returned Nathanael.

N.E.B.

swered in the words of the prophet Isaiah: 'I am a voice crying aloud in the wilderness, "Make the Lord's highway straight." '

Some Pharisees who were in the deputation asked him, 'If you are not the Messiah, nor Elijah, nor the prophet, why then are you baptizing?' 'I baptize in water,' John replied, 'but among you, though you do not know him, stands the one who is to come after me. I am not good enough to unfasten his shoes.' This took place at Bethany beyond Jordan, where John was baptizing.

The next day he saw Jesus coming towards him. 'Look,' he said, 'there is the Lamb of God; it is he who takes away the sin of the world. This is he of whom I spoke when I said, "After me a man is coming who takes rank before me"; for before I was born, he already was. I myself did not know who he was; but the very reason why I came, baptizing in water, was that he might be revealed to Israel.'

John testified further: 'I saw the Spirit coming down from heaven like a dove and resting upon him. I did not know him, but he who sent me to baptize in water told me, "When you see the Spirit coming down upon someone and resting upon him you will know that this is he who is to baptize in Holy Spirit." I saw it myself, and I have borne witness. This is God's Chosen One.' [a]

The next day again John was standing with two of his disciples when Jesus passed by. John looked towards him and said, 'There is the Lamb of God.' The two disciples heard him say this, and followed Jesus. When he turned and saw them following him, he asked, 'What are you looking for?' They said, 'Rabbi' (which means a teacher), 'where are you staying?' 'Come and see', he replied. So they went and saw where he was staying, and spent the rest of the day with him. It was then about four in the afternoon.

One of the two who followed Jesus after hearing what John said was Andrew, Simon Peter's brother. The first thing he did was to find [b] his brother Simon. He said to him, 'We have found the Messiah' (which is the Hebrew for 'Christ'). He brought Simon to Jesus, who looked him in the face, and said, 'You are Simon, son of John. You shall be called Cephas' (that is, Peter, the Rock).

The next day Jesus decided to leave for Galilee. He met Philip, who, like Andrew and Peter, came from Bethsaida, and said to him, 'Follow me.' Philip went to find Nathanael, and told him, 'We have met the man spoken of by Moses in the Law, and by the prophets: it is Jesus son of Joseph, from Nazareth.' 'Nazareth!' Nathanael exclaimed; 'can anything good come from Nazareth?' Philip said, 'Come and see.' When Jesus saw Nathanael coming, he said, 'Here is an Israelite worthy of the name; there is nothing false in him.' Nathanael asked him, 'How do you come to know me?' Jesus replied, 'I saw you

[a] *Some witnesses read* This is the Son of God.
[b] *Some witnesses read* In the morning he found . . .

K.J.V.

fore that Philip called thee, when thou wast under the fig tree, I saw thee. 49 Nathanael answered and saith unto him, Rabbi, thou art the Son of God; thou art the King of Israel. 50 Jesus answered and said unto him, Because I said unto thee, I saw thee under the fig tree, believest thou? thou shalt see greater things than these. 51And he saith unto him, Verily, verily, I say unto you, Hereafter ye shall see heaven open, and the angels of God ascending and descending upon the Son of man.

2 And the third day there was a marriage in Cana of Galilee; and the mother of Jesus was there: 2And both Jesus was called, and his disciples, to the marriage. 3And when they wanted wine, the mother of Jesus saith unto him, They have no wine. 4 Jesus saith unto her, Woman, what have I to do with thee? mine hour is not yet come. 5 His mother saith unto the servants, Whatsoever he saith unto you, do it. 6And there were set there six waterpots of stone, after the manner of the purifying of the Jews, containing two or three firkins apiece. 7 Jesus saith unto them, Fill the waterpots with water. And they filled them up to the brim. 8And he saith unto them, Draw out now, and bear unto the governor of the feast. And they bare it. 9 When the ruler of the feast had tasted the water that was made wine, and knew not whence it was, (but the servants which drew the water knew,) the governor of the feast called the bridegroom, 10And saith unto him, Every man at the beginning doth set forth good wine; and when men have well drunk, then that which is worse: but thou hast kept the good wine until now. 11 This beginning of miracles did Jesus in Cana of Galilee, and manifested forth his glory; and his disciples believed on him.

12 After this he went down to Capernaum, he, and his mother, and his brethren, and his disciples; and they continued there not many days.

13 And the Jews' passover was at hand, and Jesus went up to Jerusalem, 14And found in the temple those that sold oxen and sheep and doves, and the changers of money sitting: 15And when he had made a scourge of small cords, he drove them all out of the temple, and the sheep, and the oxen; and poured out the changers' money, and overthrew the tables; 16And said unto them that sold doves, Take these things hence; make not my Father's house a house of merchandise. 17And his disciples remembered that it was written, The zeal of thine house hath eaten me up.

18 Then answered the Jews and said unto him, What sign shewest thou unto us, seeing that thou doest these things? 19 Jesus answered and said unto them, Destroy this temple, and in three days I will raise it up. 20 Then said the Jews, Forty and six years was this temple in building,

R.S.V.

him, "Before Philip called you, when you were under the fig tree, I saw you." 49 Nathanael answered him, "Rabbi, you are the Son of God! You are the King of Israel!" 50 Jesus answered him, "Because I said to you, I saw you under the fig tree, do you believe? You shall see greater things than these." 51And he said to him, "Truly, truly, I say to you, you will see heaven opened, and the angels of God ascending and descending upon the Son of man."

2 On the third day there was a marriage at Cana in Galilee, and the mother of Jesus was there; 2 Jesus also was invited to the marriage, with his disciples. 3 When the wine failed, the mother of Jesus said to him, "They have no wine." 4And Jesus said to her, "O woman, what have you to do with me? My hour has not yet come." 5 His mother said to the servants, "Do whatever he tells you." 6 Now six stone jars were standing there, for the Jewish rites of purification, each holding twenty or thirty gallons. 7 Jesus said to them, "Fill the jars with water." And they filled them up to the brim. 8 He said to them, "Now draw some out, and take it to the steward of the feast." So they took it. 9 When the steward of the feast tasted the water now become wine, and did not know where it came from (though the servants who had drawn the water knew), the steward of the feast called the bridegroom 10 and said to him, "Every man serves the good wine first; and when men have drunk freely, then the poor wine; but you have kept the good wine until now." 11 This, the first of his signs, Jesus did at Cana in Galilee, and manifested his glory; and his disciples believed in him.

12 After this he went down to Capernaum, with his mother and his brothers and his disciples; and there they stayed for a few days.

13 The Passover of the Jews was at hand, and Jesus went up to Jerusalem. 14 In the temple he found those who were selling oxen and sheep and pigeons, and the money-changers at their business. 15And making a whip of cords, he drove them all, with the sheep and oxen, out of the temple; and he poured out the coins of the money-changers and overturned their tables. 16 And he told those who sold the pigeons, "Take these things away; you shall not make my Father's house a house of trade." 17 His disciples remembered that it was written, "Zeal for thy house will consume me." 18 The Jews then said to him, "What sign have you to show us for doing this?" 19 Jesus answered them, "Destroy this temple, and in three days I will raise it up." 20 The Jews then said, "It has taken forty-six years to build this temple, and will

PHILLIPS

"When you were underneath that fig tree," replied Jesus, "before Philip called you, I saw you."

At which Nathanael exclaimed, "Master, you are the Son of God, you are the king of Israel!"

"Do you believe in me," replied Jesus, "because I said I had seen you underneath that fig tree? You are going to see something greater than that! Believe me," he added, "I tell you all that you will see Heaven wide open and God's angels ascending and descending around the Son of Man!"

The Son of God and a village wedding   2. 1

Two days later there was a wedding in the Galilean village of Cana. Jesus' mother was there and he and his disciples were invited to the festivities. Then it happened that the supply of wine gave out, and Jesus' mother told him, "They have no more wine."

"Is that your concern, or mine?" replied Jesus. "My time has not come yet."

So his mother said to the servants, "Mind you do whatever he tells you."

In the room six very large stone water jars stood on the floor (actually for the Jewish ceremonial cleansing), each holding about twenty gallons. Jesus gave instructions for these jars to be filled with water, and the servants filled them to the brim. Then he said to them, "Now draw some out and take it to the master of ceremonies," which they did. When this man tasted the water, which had now become wine, without knowing where it came from (though naturally the servants who had drawn the water knew), he called out to the bridegroom and said to him, "Everybody I know puts his good wine on first and then when men have had plenty to drink, he brings out the poor stuff. But you have kept back your good wine till now!" Jesus gave this, the first of his signs, at Cana in Galilee. He demonstrated his power and his disciples believed in him.

Jesus in the Temple   2. 12

After this incident, Jesus, accompanied by his mother, his brothers and his disciples, went down to Capernaum and stayed there a few days. The Jewish Passover was approaching and Jesus made the journey up to Jerusalem. In the Temple he discovered cattle and sheep dealers and pigeon sellers, as well as money-changers sitting at their tables. So he made a rough whip out of rope and drove the whole lot of them, sheep and cattle as well, out of the Temple. He sent the coins of the money-changers flying and turned their tables upside down. Then he said to the pigeon dealers, "Take those things out of here. Don't you dare turn my Father's house into a market!" His disciples remembered the scripture—

The zeal of thine house shall eat me up.

As a result of this, the Jews said to him, "What sign can you give us to justify what you are doing?"

"Destroy this temple," Jesus retorted, "and I will rebuild it in three days!"

To which the Jews replied, "This Temple took

N.E.B.

under the fig-tree before Philip spoke to you.' 'Rabbi,' said Nathanael, 'you are the Son of God; you are king of Israel.' Jesus answered, 'Is this the ground of your faith, that I told you I saw you under the fig-tree? You shall see greater things than that.' Then he added, 'In truth, in very truth I tell you all, you shall see heaven wide open, and God's angels ascending and descending upon the Son of Man.'

Christ the Giver of Life

2 On the third day there was a wedding at Cana-in-Galilee. The mother of Jesus was there, and Jesus and his disciples were guests also. The wine gave out, so Jesus's mother said to him, 'They have no wine left.' He answered, 'Your concern, mother, is not mine. My hour has not yet come.' His mother said to the servants, 'Do whatever he tells you.' There were six stone water-jars standing near, of the kind used for Jewish rites of purification; each held from twenty to thirty gallons. Jesus said to the servants, 'Fill the jars with water', and they filled them to the brim. 'Now draw some off', he ordered, 'and take it to the steward of the feast'; and they did so. The steward tasted the water now turned into wine, not knowing its source; though the servants who had drawn the water knew. He hailed the bridegroom and said, 'Everyone serves the best wine first, and waits until the guests have drunk freely before serving the poorer sort; but you have kept the best wine till now.'

This deed at Cana-in-Galilee is the first of the signs by which Jesus revealed his glory and led his disciples to believe in him.

After this he went down to Capernaum in company with his mother, his brothers, and his disciples, but they did not stay there long. As it was near the time of the Jewish Passover, Jesus went up to Jerusalem. There he found in the temple the dealers in cattle, sheep, and pigeons, and the money-changers seated at their tables. Jesus made a whip of cords and drove them all out of the temple, sheep, cattle, and all. He upset the tables of the money-changers, scattering their coins. Then he turned on the dealers in pigeons: 'Take them out,' he said; 'you must not turn my Father's house into a market.' His disciples recalled the words of Scripture, 'Zeal for thy house shall destroy me.' The Jews challenged Jesus: 'What sign', they asked, 'can you show as authority for your action?' 'Destroy this temple,' Jesus replied, 'and in three days I will raise it again.' They said, 'It has taken forty-six years to build this temple. Are you going to raise it again

K.J.V.

and wilt thou rear it up in three days? 21 But he spake of the temple of his body. 22 When therefore he was risen from the dead, his disciples remembered that he had said this unto them; and they believed the Scripture, and the word which Jesus had said.

23 Now when he was in Jerusalem at the passover, in the feast *day,* many believed in his name, when they saw the miracles which he did. 24 But Jesus did not commit himself unto them, because he knew all *men,* 25And needed not that any should testify of man: for he knew what was in man.

3 There was a man of the Pharisees, named Nicodemus, a ruler of the Jews: 2 The same came to Jesus by night, and said unto him, Rabbi, we know that thou art a teacher come from God: for no man can do these miracles that thou doest, except God be with him. 3 Jesus answered and said unto him, Verily, verily, I say unto thee, Except a man be born again, he cannot see the kingdom of God. 4 Nicodemus saith unto him, How can a man be born when he is old? can he enter the second time into his mother's womb, and be born? 5 Jesus answered, Verily, verily, I say unto thee, Except a man be born of water and *of* the Spirit, he cannot enter into the kingdom of God. 6 That which is born of the flesh is flesh; and that which is born of the Spirit is spirit. 7 Marvel not that I said unto thee, Ye must be born again. 8 The wind bloweth where it listeth, and thou hearest the sound thereof, but canst not tell whence it cometh, and whither it goeth: so is every one that is born of the Spirit. 9 Nicodemus answered and said unto him, How can these things be? 10 Jesus answered and said unto him, Art thou a master of Israel, and knowest not these things? 11 Verily, verily, I say unto thee, We speak that we do know, and testify that we have seen; and ye receive not our witness. 12 If I have told you earthly things, and ye believe not, how shall ye believe, if I tell you *of* heavenly things? 13And no man hath ascended up to heaven, but he that came down from heaven, *even* the Son of man which is in heaven.

14 And as Moses lifted up the serpent in the wilderness, even so must the Son of man be lifted up: 15 That whosoever believeth in him should not perish, but have eternal life.

16 For God so loved the world, that he gave his only begotten Son, that whosoever believeth in him should not perish, but have everlasting life. 17 For God sent not his Son into the world to condemn the world; but that the world through him might be saved.

18 He that believeth on him is not condemned: but he that believeth not is condemned already, because he hath not believed in the name of the only begotten Son of God. 19And this is the condemnation, that light is come into the world, and men loved darkness rather than light, because their deeds were evil. 20 For every one that doeth evil hateth the light, neither cometh to the light, lest his deeds should be reproved. 21 But he that doeth truth cometh to the light, that his deeds may be made manifest, that they are wrought in God.

R.S.V.

you raise it up in three days?" 21 But he spoke of the temple of his body. 22 When therefore he was raised from the dead, his disciples remembered that he had said this; and they believed the scripture and the word which Jesus had spoken.

23 Now when he was in Jerusalem at the Passover feast, many believed in his name when they saw the signs which he did; 24 but Jesus did not trust himself to them, 25 because he knew all men and needed no one to bear witness of man; for he himself knew what was in man.

3 Now there was a man of the Pharisees, named Nicodemus, a ruler of the Jews. 2 This man came to Jesus^d by night and said to him, "Rabbi, we know that you are a teacher come from God; for no one can do these signs that you do, unless God is with him." 3 Jesus answered him, "Truly, truly, I say to you, unless one is born anew,^e he cannot see the kingdom of God." 4 Nicodemus said to him, "How can a man be born when he is old? Can he enter a second time into his mother's womb and be born?" 5 Jesus answered, "Truly, truly, I say to you, unless one is born of water and the Spirit, he cannot enter the kingdom of God. 6 That which is born of the flesh is flesh, and that which is born of the Spirit is spirit.^f 7 Do not marvel that I said to you, 'You must be born anew.' ^e 8 The wind ^f blows where it wills, and you hear the sound of it, but you do not know whence it comes or whither it goes; so it is with every one who is born of the Spirit." 9 Nicodemus said to him, "How can this be?" 10 Jesus answered him, "Are you a teacher of Israel, and yet you do not understand this? 11 Truly, truly, I say to you, we speak of what we know, and bear witness to what we have seen; but you do not receive our testimony. 12 If I have told you earthly things and you do not believe, how can you believe if I tell you heavenly things? 13 No one has ascended into heaven but he who descended from heaven, the Son of man.^g 14And as Moses lifted up the serpent in the wilderness, so must the Son of man be lifted up, 15 that whoever believes in him may have eternal life." ^h

16 For God so loved the world that he gave his only Son, that whoever believes in him should not perish but have eternal life. 17 For God sent the Son into the world, not to condemn the world, but that the world might be saved through him. 18 He who believes in him is not condemned; he who does not believe is condemned already, because he has not believed in the name of the only Son of God. 19And this is the judgment, that the light has come into the world, and men loved darkness rather than light, because their deeds were evil. 20 For every one who does evil hates the light, and does not come to the light, lest his deeds should be exposed. 21 But he who does what is true comes to the light, that it may be clearly seen that his deeds have been wrought in God.

[d] Greek *him.* [e] Or *from above.* [f] The same Greek word means both *wind* and *spirit.* [g] Other ancient authorities add *who is in heaven.* [h] Some interpreters hold that the quotation continues through verse 21.

PHILLIPS

forty-six years to build, and are you going to rebuild it in three days?"

He was, in fact, speaking about the temple of his own body, and when he was raised from the dead the disciples remembered what he had said to them and that made them believe both the scripture and what Jesus had said.

While he was in Jerusalem at Passover time, during the festivities, many believed in him as they saw the signs that he gave. But Jesus, on his side, did not trust himself to them—for he knew them all. He did not need anyone to tell him what people were like: he understood human nature.

N.E.B.

in three days?' But the temple he was speaking of was his body. After his resurrection his disciples recalled what he had said, and they believed the Scripture and the words that Jesus had spoken.

While he was in Jerusalem for Passover many gave their allegiance to him when they saw the signs that he performed. But Jesus for his part would not trust himself to them. He knew men so well, all of them, that he needed no evidence from others about a man, for he himself could tell what was in a man.

Jesus and a religious leader   3. 1

One night Nicodemus, a leading Jew and a Pharisee, came to see Jesus.

"Master," he began, "we realize that you are a teacher who has come from God. Obviously no one could show the signs that you show unless God were with him."

"Believe me," returned Jesus, "a man cannot even see the kingdom of God without being born again."

"And how can a man who's getting old possibly be born?" replied Nicodemus. "How can he go back into his mother's womb and be born a second time?"

"I assure you," said Jesus, "that unless a man is born from water and from spirit he cannot enter the kingdom of God. Flesh gives birth to flesh and spirit gives birth to spirit: you must not be surprised that I told you that all of you must be born again. The wind blows where it likes, you can hear the sound of it but you have no idea where it comes from and where it goes. Nor can you tell how a man is born by the wind of the Spirit."

"How on earth can things like this happen?" replied Nicodemus.

"So you are a teacher of Israel," said Jesus, "and you do not recognize such things? I assure you that we are talking about something we really know and we are witnessing to something we have actually observed, yet men like you will not accept our evidence. Yet if I have spoken to you about things which happen on this earth and you will not believe me, what chance is there that you will believe me if I tell you about what happens in Heaven? No one has ever been up to Heaven except the Son of Man who came down from Heaven. The Son of Man must be lifted above the heads of men—as Moses lifted up that serpent in the desert—so that any man who believes in him may have eternal life. For God loved the world so much that he gave his only Son so that everyone who believes in him should not be lost, but should have eternal life. You must understand that God has not sent his Son into the world to pass sentence upon it, but to save it—through him. Any man who believes in him is not judged at all. It is the one who will not believe who stands already condemned, because he will not believe in the character of God's only Son. This *is* the judgment—that light has entered the world and men have preferred darkness to light because their deeds are evil. Anybody who does wrong hates the light and keeps away from it, for fear his deeds may be exposed. But anybody who is living by the truth will come to the light to make it plain that all he has done has been done through God."

3   There was one of the Pharisees named Nicodemus, a member of the Jewish Council, who came to Jesus by night. 'Rabbi,' he said, 'we know that you are a teacher sent by God; no one could perform these signs of yours unless God were with him.' Jesus answered, 'In truth, in very truth I tell you, unless a man has been born over again he cannot see the kingdom of God.' 'But how is it possible', said Nicodemus, 'for a man to be born when he is old? Can he enter his mother's womb a second time and be born?' Jesus answered, 'In truth I tell you, no one can enter the kingdom of God without being born from water and spirit. Flesh can give birth only to flesh; it is spirit that gives birth to spirit. You ought not to be astonished, then, when I tell you that you must be born over again. The wind *a* blows where it wills; you hear the sound of it, but you do not know where it comes from, or where it is going. So with everyone who is born from spirit*a*.'

Nicodemus replied, 'How is this possible?' 'What!' said Jesus. 'Is this famous teacher of Israel ignorant of such things? In very truth I tell you, we speak of what we know, and testify to what we have seen, and yet you all reject our testimony. If you disbelieve me when I talk to you about things on earth, how are you to believe if I should talk about the things of heaven?

'No one ever went up into heaven except the one who came down from heaven, the Son of Man whose home is in heaven.*b* This Son of Man must be lifted up as the serpent was lifted up by Moses in the wilderness, so that everyone who has faith in him may in him possess eternal life.

'God loved the world so much that he gave his only Son, that everyone who has faith in him may not die but have eternal life. It was not to judge the world that God sent his Son into the world, but that through him the world might be saved.

'The man who puts his faith in him does not come under judgement; but the unbeliever has already been judged in that he has not given his allegiance to God's only Son. Here lies the test: the light has come into the world, but men preferred darkness to light because their deeds were evil. Bad men all hate the light and avoid it, for fear their practices should be shown up. The honest man comes to the light so that it may be clearly seen that God is in all he does.'

---

[a] *A single Greek word with both meanings.* [b] *Some witnesses omit* whose home is in heaven.

K.J.V.

22 After these things came Jesus and his disciples into the land of Judea; and there he tarried with them, and baptized.
23 And John also was baptizing in Enon near to Salim, because there was much water there: and they came, and were baptized. 24 For John was not yet cast into prison.
25 Then there arose a question between *some* of John's disciples and the Jews about purifying. 26And they came unto John, and said unto him, Rabbi, he that was with thee beyond Jordan, to whom thou barest witness, behold, the same baptizeth, and all *men* come to him. 27 John answered and said, A man can receive nothing, except it be given him from heaven. 28 Ye yourselves bear me witness, that I said, I am not the Christ, but that I am sent before him. 29 He that hath the bride is the bridegroom: but the friend of the bridegroom, which standeth and heareth him, rejoiceth greatly because of the bridegroom's voice: this my joy therefore is fulfilled. 30 He must increase, but I *must* decrease. 31 He that cometh from above is above all: he that is of the earth is earthly, and speaketh of the earth: he that cometh from heaven is above all. 32And what he hath seen and heard, that he testifieth; and no man receiveth his testimony. 33 He that hath received his testimony hath set to his seal that God is true. 34 For he whom God hath sent speaketh the words of God: for God giveth not the Spirit by measure *unto him*. 35 The Father loveth the Son, and hath given all things into his hand. 36 He that believeth on the son hath everlasting life: and he that believeth not the Son shall not see life; but the wrath of God abideth on him.

4 When therefore the Lord knew how the Pharisees had heard that Jesus made and baptized more disciples than John, 2 (Though Jesus himself baptized not, but his disciples,) 3 He left Judea, and departed again into Galilee. 4And he must needs go through Samaria. 5 Then cometh he to a city of Samaria, which is called Sychar, near to the parcel of ground that Jacob gave to his son Joseph. 6 Now Jacob's well was there. Jesus therefore, being wearied with *his* journey, sat thus on the well: *and* it was about the sixth hour. 7 There cometh a woman of Samaria to draw water: Jesus saith unto her, Give me to drink. 8 (For his disciples were gone away unto the city to buy meat.) 9 Then saith the woman of Samaria unto him, How is it that thou, being a Jew, askest drink of me, which am a woman of Samaria? for the Jews have no dealings with the Samaritans. 10 Jesus answered and said unto her, If thou knewest the gift of God, and who it is that saith to thee, Give me to drink; thou wouldest have asked of him, and he would have given thee living water. 11 The woman saith unto him, Sir, thou hast nothing to draw with, and the well is deep: from whence then hast thou that living water? 12Art thou greater than our father Jacob, which gave us the well, and drank thereof himself, and his chil-

R.S.V.

22 After this Jesus and his disciples went into the land of Judea; there he remained with them and baptized. 23 John also was baptizing at Aenon near Salim, because there was much water there; and people came and were baptized. 24 For John had not yet been put in prison.
25 Now a discussion arose between John's disciples and a Jew over purifying. 26And they came to John, and said to him, "Rabbi, he who was with you beyond the Jordan, to whom you bore witness, here he is, baptizing, and all are going to him." 27 John answered, "No one can receive anything except what is given him from heaven. 28 You yourselves bear me witness, that I said, I am not the Christ, but I have been sent before him. 29 He who has the bride is the bridegroom; the friend of the bridegroom, who stands and hears him, rejoices greatly at the bridegroom's voice; therefore this joy of mine is now full. 30 He must increase, but I must decrease." [i]
31 He who comes from above is above all; he who is of the earth belongs to the earth, and of the earth he speaks; he who comes from heaven is above all. 32 He bears witness to what he has seen and heard, yet no one receives his testimony; 33 he who receives his testimony sets his seal to this, that God is true. 34 For he whom God has sent utters the words of God, for it is not by measure that he gives the Spirit; 35 the Father loves the Son, and has given all things into his hand. 36 He who believes in the Son has eternal life; he who does not obey the Son shall not see life, but the wrath of God rests upon him.

4 Now when the Lord knew that the Pharisees had heard that Jesus was making and baptizing more disciples than John 2 (although Jesus himself did not baptize, but only his disciples), 3 he left Judea and departed again to Galilee. 4 He had to pass through Samaria. 5 So he came to a city of Samaria, called Sychar, near the field that Jacob gave to his son Joseph. 6 Jacob's well was there, and so Jesus, wearied as he was with his journey, sat down beside the well. It was about the sixth hour.
7 There came a woman of Samaria to draw water. Jesus said to her, "Give me a drink." 8 For his disciples had gone away into the city to buy food. 9 The Samaritan woman said to him, "How is it that you, a Jew, ask a drink of me, a woman of Samaria?" For Jews have no dealings with Samaritans. 10 Jesus answered her, "If you knew the gift of God, and who it is that is saying to you, 'Give me a drink,' you would have asked him, and he would have given you living water." 11 The woman said to him, "Sir, you have nothing to draw with, and the well is deep; where do you get that living water? 12Are you greater than our father Jacob, who gave us the well, and drank from it himself, and his sons,

[i] Some interpreters hold that the quotation continues through verse 36.

276

PHILLIPS

N.E.B.

Jesus and John again
3. 22

After this Jesus went into the country of Judaea with his disciples and stayed there with them while the work of baptism was being carried on. John, too, was in Aenon near Salim, baptizing people because there were plenty of water in that district and they were still coming to him for baptism. (John, of course, had not yet been put in prison.)

This led to a question arising between John's disciples and one of the Jews about the whole matter of being cleansed. They approached John and said to him, "Master, look, the man who was with you on the other side of the Jordan, the one you testified to, is now baptizing and everybody is coming to him!"

"A man can receive nothing at all," replied John, "unless it is given him from Heaven. You yourselves can witness that I said, 'I am not Christ but I have been sent as his forerunner.' It is the bridegroom who possesses the bride, yet the bridegroom's friend who merely stands and listens to him can be overjoyed to hear the bridegroom's voice. That is why my happiness is now complete. He must grow greater and greater and I less and less.

"The one who comes from above is naturally above everybody. The one who arises from the earth belongs to the earth and speaks from the earth. The one who comes from Heaven is above all others and he bears witness to what he has seen and heard—yet no one is accepting his testimony. Yet if a man does accept it, he is acknowledging the fact that God is true. For the one whom God sent speaks the authentic words of God—and there can be no measuring of the Spirit given to *him!* The Father loves the Son and has put everything into his hand. The man who believes in the Son has eternal life. The man who refuses to believe in the Son will not see life; he lives under the anger of God."

After this, Jesus went into Judaea with his disciples, stayed there with them, and baptized. John too was baptizing at Aenon, near to Salim, because water was plentiful in that region; and people were constantly coming for baptism. This was before John's imprisonment.

Some of John's disciples had fallen into a dispute with Jews about purification; so they came to him and said, 'Rabbi, there was a man with you on the other side of the Jordan, to whom you bore your witness. Here he is, baptizing, and crowds are flocking to him.' John's answer was: 'A man can have only what God gives him. You yourselves can testify that I said, "I am not the Messiah; I have been sent as his forerunner." It is the bridegroom to whom the bride belongs. The bridegroom's friend, who stands by and listens to him, is overjoyed at hearing the bridegroom's voice. This joy, this perfect joy, is now mine. As he grows greater, I must grow less.'

He who comes from above is above all others; he who is from the earth belongs to the earth and uses earthly speech. He who comes from heaven[a] bears witness to what he has seen and heard, yet no one accepts his witness. To accept his witness is to attest that God speaks true; for he whom God sent utters the words of God, so measureless is God's gift of the Spirit. The Father loves the Son and has entrusted him with all authority. He who puts his faith in the Son has hold of eternal life, but he who disobeys the Son shall not see that life; God's wrath rests upon him.

Jesus meets a Samaritan woman
4. 1

Now, when the Lord found that the Pharisees had heard that "Jesus is making and baptizing more disciples than John"—although, in fact, it was not Jesus who did the baptizing but his disciples—he left Judaea and went off again to Galilee, which meant his passing through Samaria. There he came to a little town called Sychar, which is near the historic plot of land that Jacob gave to his son, Joseph, and "Jacob's Spring" was there. Jesus, tired with the journey, sat down beside it, just as he was. The time was about midday. Presently, a Samaritan woman arrived to draw some water.

"Please give me a drink," Jesus said to her, for his disciples had gone away to the town to buy food. The Samaritan woman said to him, "How can you, a Jew, ask for a drink from me, a woman of Samaria?" (For Jews have no dealings with Samaritans.)

"If you knew what God can give," Jesus replied, "and if you knew who it is that said to you, 'Give me a drink,' I think you would have asked him, and he would have given you living water!"

"Sir," said the woman, "you have nothing to draw water with and this well is deep—where can you get your living water? Are you a greater man than our ancestor, Jacob, who gave us this well, and drank here himself with his family, and his cattle?"

4 A report now reached the Pharisees: 'Jesus is winning and baptizing more disciples than John'; although, in fact, it was only the disciples who were baptizing and not Jesus himself. When Jesus learned this, he left Judaea and set out once more for Galilee. He had to pass through Samaria, and on his way came to a Samaritan town called Sychar, near the plot of ground which Jacob gave to his son Joseph and the spring called Jacob's well. It was about noon, and Jesus, tired after his journey, sat down by the well.

The disciples had gone away to the town to buy food. Meanwhile a Samaritan woman came to draw water. Jesus said to her, 'Give me a drink.' The Samaritan woman said, 'What! You, a Jew, ask a drink of me, a Samaritan woman?' (Jews and Samaritans, it should be noted, do not use vessels in common.[b]) Jesus answered her, 'If only you knew what God gives, and who it is that is asking you for a drink, you would have asked him and he would have given you living water.' 'Sir,' the woman said, 'you have no bucket and this well is deep. How can you give me "living water"? Are you a greater man than Jacob our ancestor, who gave us the well, and drank from it himself, he and his sons, and his cattle

[a] *Some witnesses insert* is above all and . . . [b] *Or* Jews, it should be noted, are not on familiar terms with Samaritans; *some witnesses omit these words.*

K.J.V.

dren, and his cattle? 13 Jesus answered and said unto her, Whosoever drinketh of this water shall thirst again: 14 But whosoever drinketh of the water that I shall give him shall never thirst; but the water that I shall give him shall be in him a well of water springing up into everlasting life. 15 The woman saith unto him, Sir, give me this water, that I thirst not, neither come hither to draw. 16 Jesus saith unto her, Go, call thy husband, and come hither. 17 The woman answered and said, I have no husband. Jesus said unto her, Thou hast well said, I have no husband: 18 For thou hast had five husbands; and he whom thou now hast is not thy husband: in that saidst thou truly. 19 The woman saith unto him, Sir, I perceive that thou art a prophet. 20 Our fathers worshipped in this mountain; and ye say, that in Jerusalem is the place where men ought to worship. 21 Jesus saith unto her, Woman, believe me, the hour cometh, when ye shall neither in this mountain, nor yet at Jerusalem, worship the Father. 22 Ye worship ye know not what: we know what we worship; for salvation is of the Jews. 23 But the hour cometh, and now is, when the true worshippers shall worship the Father in spirit and in truth: for the Father seeketh such to worship him. 24 God *is* a Spirit: and they that worship him must worship *him* in spirit and in truth. 25 The woman saith unto him, I know that Messias cometh, which is called Christ: when he is come, he will tell us all things. 26 Jesus saith unto her, I that speak unto thee am *he*.

27 And upon this came his disciples, and marvelled that he talked with the woman: yet no man said, What seekest thou? or, Why talkest thou with her? 28 The woman then left her waterpot, and went her way into the city, and saith to the men, 29 Come, see a man, which told me all things that ever I did: is not this the Christ? 30 Then they went out of the city, and came unto him.

31 In the mean while his disciples prayed him, saying, Master, eat. 32 But he said unto them, I have meat to eat that ye know not of. 33 Therefore said the disciples one to another, Hath any man brought him *aught* to eat? 34 Jesus saith unto them, My meat is to do the will of him that sent me, and to finish his work. 35 Say not ye, There are yet four months, and *then* cometh harvest? behold, I say unto you, Lift up your eyes, and look on the fields; for they are white already to harvest. 36And he that reapeth receiveth wages, and gathereth fruit unto life eternal: that both he that soweth and he that reapeth may rejoice together. 37And herein is that saying true, One soweth, and another reapeth. 38 I sent you to reap that whereon ye bestowed no labour: other men laboured, and ye are entered into their labours.

39 And many of the Samaritans of that city believed on him for the saying of the woman, which testified, He told me all that ever I did. 40 So when the Samaritans were come unto him, they besought him that he would tarry with them: and he abode there two days. 41And many more believed because of his own word; 42And said unto the woman, Now we believe, not be-

R.S.V.

and his cattle?" 13 Jesus said to her, "Every one who drinks of this water will thirst again, 14 but whoever drinks of the water that I shall give him will never thirst; the water that I shall give him will become in him a spring of water welling up to eternal life." 15 The woman said to him, "Sir, give me this water, that I may not thirst, nor come here to draw."

16 Jesus said to her, "Go, call your husband, and come here." 17 The woman answered him, "I have no husband." Jesus said to her, "You are right in saying, 'I have no husband'; 18 for you have had five husbands, and he whom you now have is not your husband; this you said truly." 19 The woman said to him, "Sir, I perceive that you are a prophet. 20 Our fathers worshiped on this mountain; and you say that in Jerusalem is the place where men ought to worship." 21 Jesus said to her, "Woman, believe me, the hour is coming when neither on this mountain nor in Jerusalem will you worship the Father. 22 You worship what you do not know; we worship what we know, for salvation is from the Jews. 23 But the hour is coming, and now is, when the true worshipers will worship the Father in spirit and truth, for such the Father seeks to worship him. 24 God is spirit, and those who worship him must worship in spirit and truth." 25 The woman said to him, "I know that Messiah is coming (he who is called Christ); when he comes, he will show us all things." 26 Jesus said to her, "I who speak to you am he."

27 Just then his disciples came. They marveled that he was talking with a woman, but none said, "What do you wish?" or, "Why are you talking with her?" 28 So the woman left her water jar, and went away into the city, and said to the people, 29 "Come, see a man who told me all that I ever did. Can this be the Christ?" 30 They went out of the city and were coming to him.

31 Meanwhile the disciples besought him, saying, "Rabbi, eat." 32 But he said to them, "I have food to eat of which you do not know." 33 So the disciples said to one another, "Has any one brought him food?" 34 Jesus said to them, "My food is to do the will of him who sent me, and to accomplish his work. 35 Do you not say, 'There are yet four months, then comes the harvest'? I tell you, lift up your eyes, and see how the fields are already white for harvest. 36 He who reaps receives wages, and gathers fruit for eternal life, so that sower and reaper may rejoice together. 37 For here the saying holds true, 'One sows and another reaps.' 38 I sent you to reap that for which you did not labor; others have labored, and you have entered into their labor."

39 Many Samaritans from that city believed in him because of the woman's testimony, "He told me all that I ever did." 40 So when the Samaritans came to him, they asked him to stay with them; and he stayed there two days. 41And many more believed because of his word. 42 They said to the woman, "It is no longer be-

PHILLIPS

Jesus said to her, "Everyone who drinks this water will be thirsty again. But whoever drinks the water I will give him will never be thirsty again. For my gift will become a spring in the man himself, welling up into eternal life."

The woman said, "Sir, give me this water, so that I may stop being thirsty—and not have to come here to draw water any more!"

"Go and call your husband and then come back here," said Jesus to her.

"I haven't got a husband!" the woman answered.

"You are quite right in saying, 'I haven't got a husband,'" replied Jesus, "for you have had five husbands and the man you have now is not your husband at all. Yes, you spoke the simple truth when you said that."

"Sir," said the woman again, "I can see that you are a prophet! Now our ancestors worshiped on this hillside, but you Jews say that Jerusalem is the place where men ought to worship—"

"Believe me," returned Jesus, "the time is coming when worshiping the Father will not be a matter of 'on this hillside' or 'in Jerusalem.' Nowadays you are worshiping with your eyes shut. We Jews are worshiping with our eyes open, for the salvation of mankind is to come from our race. Yet the time is coming, yes, and has already come, when true worshipers will worship the Father in spirit and in reality. Indeed, the Father looks for men who will worship him like that. God is Spirit, and those who worship him can only worship in spirit and in reality."

"Of course I know that Messiah is coming," returned the woman, "you know, the one who is called Christ. When he comes he will make everything plain to us."

"I am Christ, speaking to you now," said Jesus.

At this point his disciples arrived, and were very surprised to find him talking to a woman, but none of them asked, "What do you want?" or "What are you talking to her about?" So the woman left her water pot behind and went into the town and began to say to the people, "Come out and see the man who told me everything I've ever done! Can this be 'Christ'?" So they left the town and started to come to Jesus.

Meanwhile the disciples were begging him, "Master, do eat something."

To which Jesus replied, "I have food to eat that you know nothing about."

This, of course, made the disciples ask each other, "Do you think anyone has brought him any food?"

Jesus said to them: "My food is doing the will of him who sent me and finishing the work he has given me. Don't you say, 'Four months more and then comes the harvest'? But I tell you to open your eyes and look at the fields—they are gleaming white, all ready for the harvest! The reaper is already being rewarded and getting in a harvest for eternal life, so that both sower and reaper may be glad together. For in this harvest the old saying comes true, 'One man sows and another reaps.' I have sent you to reap a harvest for which you never labored; other men have worked hard and you have reaped the result of their labors."

Many of the Samaritans who came out of that town believed in him through the woman's testimony—"He told me everything I've ever done." And when they arrived they begged him to stay with them. He did stay there two days, and far more believed in him because of what he himself said. As they told the woman: "We don't believe any longer now because of what

N.E.B.

too?' Jesus said, 'Everyone who drinks this water will be thirsty again, but whoever drinks the water that I shall give him will never suffer thirst any more. The water that I shall give him will be an inner spring always welling up for eternal life.' 'Sir,' said the woman, 'give me that water, and then I shall not be thirsty, nor have to come all this way to draw.'

Jesus replied, 'Go home, call your husband and come back.' She answered, 'I have no husband.' 'You are right', said Jesus, 'in saying that you have no husband, for, although you have had five husbands, the man with whom you are now living is not your husband; you told me the truth there.' 'Sir,' she replied, 'I can see that you are a prophet. Our fathers worshipped on this mountain, but you Jews say that the temple where God should be worshipped is in Jerusalem.' 'Believe me,' said Jesus, 'the time is coming when you will worship the Father neither on this mountain, nor in Jerusalem. You Samaritans worship without knowing what you worship, while we worship what we know. It is from the Jews that salvation comes. But the time approaches, indeed it is already here, when those who are real worshippers will worship the Father in spirit and in truth. Such are the worshippers whom the Father wants. God is spirit, and those who worship him must worship in spirit and in truth.' The woman answered, 'I know that Messiah' (that is Christ) 'is coming. When he comes he will tell us everything.' Jesus said, 'I am he, I who am speaking to you now.'

At that moment his disciples returned, and were astonished to find him talking with a woman; but none of them said, 'What do you want?' or, 'Why are you talking with her?' The woman put down her water-jar and went away to the town, where she said to the people, 'Come and see a man who has told me everything I ever did. Could this be the Messiah?' They came out of the town and made their way towards him.

Meanwhile the disciples were urging him, 'Rabbi, have something to eat.' But he said, 'I have food to eat of which you know nothing.' At this the disciples said to one another, 'Can someone have brought him food?' But Jesus said, 'It is meat and drink for me to do the will of him who sent me until I have finished his work.

'Do you not say, "Four months more and then comes harvest"? But look, I tell you, look round on the fields; they are already white, ripe for harvest. The reaper is drawing his pay and gathering a crop for eternal life, so that sower and reaper may rejoice together. That is how the saying comes true: "One sows, and another reaps." I sent you to reap a crop for which you have not toiled. Others toiled and you have come in for the harvest of their toil.'

Many Samaritans of that town came to believe in him because of the woman's testimony: 'He told me everything I ever did.' So when these Samaritans had come to him they pressed him to stay with them; and he stayed there two days. Many more became believers because of what they heard from his own lips. They told the woman, 'It is no longer because of what you

K.J.V.

cause of thy saying: for we have heard *him* ourselves, and know that this is indeed the Christ, the Saviour of the world.

43 Now after two days he departed thence, and went into Galilee. 44 For Jesus himself testified, that a prophet hath no honour in his own country. 45 Then when he was come into Galilee, the Galileans received him, having seen all the things that he did at Jerusalem at the feast: for they also went unto the feast. 46 So Jesus came again into Cana of Galilee, where he made the water wine. And there was a certain nobleman, whose son was sick at Capernaum. 47 When he heard that Jesus was come out of Judea into Galilee, he went unto him, and besought him that he would come down, and heal his son: for he was at the point of death. 48 Then said Jesus unto him, Except ye see signs and wonders, ye will not believe. 49 The nobleman saith unto him, Sir, come down ere my child die. 50 Jesus saith unto him, Go thy way; thy son liveth. And the man believed the word that Jesus had spoken unto him, and he went his way. 51And as he was now going down, his servants met him, and told *him*, saying, Thy son liveth. 52 Then inquired he of them the hour when he began to amend. And they said unto him, Yesterday at the seventh hour the fever left him. 53 So the father knew that *it was* at the same hour, in the which Jesus said unto him, Thy son liveth: and himself believed, and his whole house. 54 This *is* again the second miracle *that* Jesus did, when he was come out of Judea into Galilee.

5 After this there was a feast of the Jews; and Jesus went up to Jerusalem. 2 Now there is at Jerusalem by the sheep *market* a pool, which is called in the Hebrew tongue Bethesda, having five porches. 3 In these lay a great multitude of impotent folk, of blind, halt, withered, waiting for the moving of the water. 4 For an angel went down at a certain season into the pool, and troubled the water: whosoever then first after the troubling of the water stepped in was made whole of whatsoever disease he had. 5And a certain man was there, which had an infirmity thirty and eight years. 6 When Jesus saw him lie, and knew that he had been now a long time *in that case,* he saith unto him, Wilt thou be made whole? 7 The impotent man answered him, Sir, I have no man, when the water is troubled, to put me into the pool: but while I am coming, another steppeth down before me. 8 Jesus saith unto him, Rise, take up thy bed, and walk. 9And immediately the man was made whole, and took up his bed, and walked: and on the same day was the sabbath.

10 The Jews therefore said unto him that was cured, It is the sabbath day: it is not lawful for thee to carry *thy* bed. 11 He answered them, He that made me whole, the same said unto me,

R.S.V.

cause of your words that we believe, for we have heard for ourselves, and we know that this is indeed the Savior of the world."

43 After the two days he departed to Galilee. 44 For Jesus himself testified that a prophet has no honor in his own country. 45 So when he came to Galilee, the Galileans welcomed him, having seen all that he had done in Jerusalem at the feast, for they too had gone to the feast.

46 So he came again to Cana in Galilee, where he had made the water wine. And at Capernaum there was an official whose son was ill. 47 When he heard that Jesus had come from Judea to Galilee, he went and begged him to come down and heal his son, for he was at the point of death. 48 Jesus therefore said to him, "Unless you see signs and wonders you will not believe." 49 The official said to him, "Sir, come down before my child dies." 50 Jesus said to him, "Go; your son will live." The man believed the word that Jesus spoke to him and went his way. 51As he was going down, his servants met him and told him that his son was living. 52 So he asked them the hour when he began to mend, and they said to him, "Yesterday at the seventh hour the fever left him." 53 The father knew that was the hour when Jesus had said to him, "Your son will live"; and he himself believed, and all his household. 54 This was now the second sign that Jesus did when he had come from Judea to Galilee.

5 After this there was a feast of the Jews, and Jesus went up to Jerusalem.

2 Now there is in Jerusalem by the Sheep Gate a pool, in Hebrew called Bethzatha,[j] which has five porticoes. 3 In these lay a multitude of invalids, blind, lame, paralyzed.[k] 5 One man was there, who had been ill for thirty-eight years. 6 When Jesus saw him and knew that he had been lying there a long time, he said to him, "Do you want to be healed?" 7 The sick man answered him, "Sir, I have no man to put me into the pool when the water is troubled, and while I am going another steps down before me." 8 Jesus said to him, "Rise, take up your pallet, and walk." 9And at once the man was healed, and he took up his pallet and walked.

Now that day was the sabbath. 10 So the Jews said to the man who was cured, "It is the sabbath, it is not lawful for you to carry your pallet." 11 But he answered them, "The man who healed me said to me, 'Take up your pallet,

[j] Other ancient authorities read *Bethesda,* others *Bethsaida.* [k] Other ancient authorities insert, wholly or in part, *waiting for the moving of the water;* 4 *for an angel of the Lord went down at certain seasons into the pool, and troubled the water: whoever stepped in first after the troubling of the water was healed of whatever disease he had.*

PHILLIPS	N.E.B.

you said. We have heard him with our own ears. We know now that this must be the man who will save the world!"

Jesus, in Cana again, heals in response to faith   4. 43

After the two days were over, Jesus left and went away to Galilee. (For Jesus himself testified that a prophet enjoys no honor in his own country.) And on his arrival the people received him with open arms. For they had seen all that he had done in Jerusalem during the festival, since they had themselves been present. So Jesus came again to Cana in Galilee, the place where he made the water into wine. At Capernaum there was an official whose son was very ill. When he heard that Jesus had left Judaea and had arrived in Galilee, he went off to see him and begged him to come down and heal his son, who was by this time at the point of death.

Jesus said to him, "I suppose you will never believe unless you see signs and wonders!"

"Sir," returned the official, "please come down before my boy dies!"

"You can go home," returned Jesus, "your son is alive and well."

And the man believed what Jesus had said to him and went on his way.

On the journey back his servants met him with the report, "Your son is alive and well." So he asked them at what time he had begun to recover, and they replied, "The fever left him yesterday at one o'clock in the afternoon." Then the father knew that this must have happened at the very moment when Jesus had said to him, "Your son is alive and well." And he and his whole household believed in Jesus. This, then, was the second sign that Jesus gave on his return from Judaea to Galilee.

Jesus heals in Jerusalem   5. 1

Some time later came one of the Jewish feast days and Jesus went up to Jerusalem. There is in Jerusalem near the sheep gate a pool surrounded by five arches, which has the Hebrew name of Bethzatha. Under these arches a great many sick people were in the habit of lying; some of them were blind, some lame, and some had withered limbs. (They used to wait there for the "moving of the water," for at certain times an angel used to come down into the pool and disturb the water, and then the first person who stepped into the water after the disturbance would be healed of whatever he was suffering from.) One particular man had been there ill for thirty-eight years. When Jesus saw him lying there on his back—knowing that he had been like that for a long time, he said to him, "Do you want to get well again?"

"Sir," replied the sick man, "I just haven't got anybody to put me into the pool when the water is all stirred up. While I'm trying to get there somebody else gets down into it first."

"Get up," said Jesus, "pick up your bed and walk!"

At once the man recovered, picked up his bed and walked.

This happened on a Sabbath day, which made the Jews keep on telling the man who had been healed, "It's the Sabbath, you know; it's not right for you to carry your bed."

"The man who made me well," he replied, "was the one who told me, 'Pick up your bed and walk.'"

said that we believe, for we have heard him ourselves; and we know that this is in truth the Saviour of the world.'

When the two days were over he set out for Galilee; for Jesus himself declared that a prophet is without honour in his own country. On his arrival in Galilee the Galileans gave him a welcome, because they had seen all that he did at the festival in Jerusalem; they had been at the festival themselves.

Once again he visited Cana-in-Galilee, where he had turned the water into wine. An officer in the royal service was there, whose son was lying ill at Capernaum. When he heard that Jesus had come from Judaea into Galilee, he came to him and begged him to go down and cure his son, who was at the point of death. Jesus said to him, 'Will none of you ever believe without seeing signs and portents?' The officer pleaded with him, 'Sir, come down before my boy dies.' Then Jesus said, 'Return home; your son will live.' The man believed what Jesus said and started for home. When he was on his way down his servants met him with the news, 'Your boy is going to live.' So he asked them what time it was when he got better. They said, 'Yesterday at one in the afternoon the fever left him.' The father noted that this was the exact time when Jesus had said to him, 'Your son will live', and he and all his household became believers.

This was now the second sign which Jesus performed after coming down from Judaea into Galilee.

5 Later on Jesus went up to Jerusalem for one of the Jewish festivals.[a] Now at the Sheep-Pool in Jerusalem there is a place with five colonnades. Its name in the language of the Jews is Bethesda. In these colonnades there lay a crowd of sick people, blind, lame, and paralysed.[b] Among them was a man who had been crippled for thirty-eight years. When Jesus saw him lying there and was aware that he had been ill a long time, he asked him, 'Do you want to recover?' 'Sir,' he replied, 'I have no one to put me in the pool when the water is disturbed, but while I am moving, someone else is in the pool before me.' Jesus answered, 'Rise to your feet, take up your bed and walk.' The man recovered instantly, took up his stretcher, and began to walk.

That day was a Sabbath. So the Jews said to the man who had been cured, 'It is the Sabbath. You are not allowed to carry your bed on the Sabbath.' He answered, 'The man who cured me said, "Take up your bed and walk."'

---

[a] Some witnesses read for the Jewish festival. [b] Some witnesses add waiting for the disturbance of the water; some further insert (4) for from time to time an angel came down into the pool and stirred up the water. The first to plunge in after this disturbance recovered from whatever disease had afflicted him.

K.J.V.

Take up thy bed, and walk. 12 Then asked they him, What man is that which said unto thee, Take up thy bed, and walk? 13And he that was healed wist not who it was: for Jesus had conveyed himself away, a multitude being in *that* place. 14Afterward Jesus findeth him in the temple, and said unto him, Behold, thou art made whole: sin no more, lest a worse thing come unto thee. 15 The man departed, and told the Jews that it was Jesus, which had made him whole. 16And therefore did the Jews persecute Jesus, and sought to slay him, because he had done these things on the sabbath day.

17 But Jesus answered them, My Father worketh hitherto, and I work. 18 Therefore the Jews sought the more to kill him, because he not only had broken the sabbath, but said also that God was his Father, making himself equal with God. 19 Then answered Jesus and said unto them, Verily, verily, I say unto you, The Son can do nothing of himself, but what he seeth the Father do: for what things soever he doeth, these also doeth the Son likewise. 20 For the Father loveth the Son, and sheweth him all things that himself doeth: and he will shew him greater works than these, that ye may marvel. 21 For as the Father raiseth up the dead, and quickeneth *them;* even so the Son quickeneth whom he will. 22 For the Father judgeth no man, but hath committed all judgment unto the Son: 23 That all *men* should honour the Son, even as they honour the Father. He that honoureth not the Son honoureth not the Father which hath sent him. 24 Verily, verily, I say unto you, He that heareth my word, and believeth on him that sent me, hath everlasting life, and shall not come into condemnation; but is passed from death unto life. 25 Verily, verily, I say unto you, The hour is coming, and now is, when the dead shall hear the voice of the Son of God: and they that hear shall live. 26 For as the Father hath life in himself; so hath he given to the Son to have life in himself; 27And hath given him authority to execute judgment also, because he is the Son of man. 28 Marvel not at this: for the hour is coming, in the which all that are in the graves shall hear his voice, 29And shall come forth; they that have done good, unto the resurrection of life; and they that have done evil, unto the resurrection of damnation. 30 I can of mine own self do nothing: as I hear, I judge: and my judgment is just; because I seek not mine own will, but the will of the Father which hath sent me. 31 If I bear witness of myself, my witness is not true.

32 There is another that beareth witness of me; and I know that the witness which he witnesseth of me is true. 33 Ye sent unto John, and he bare witness unto the truth. 34 But I receive not testimony from man: but these things I say, that ye might be saved. 35 He was a burning and a shining light: and ye were willing for a season to rejoice in his light.

36 But I have greater witness than *that* of

R.S.V.

and walk.' " 12 They asked him, "Who is the man who said to you, 'Take up your pallet, and walk'?" 13 Now the man who had been healed did not know who it was, for Jesus had withdrawn, as there was a crowd in the place. 14Afterward, Jesus found him in the temple, and said to him, "See, you are well! Sin no more, that nothing worse befall you." 15 The man went away and told the Jews that it was Jesus who had healed him. 16And this was why the Jews persecuted Jesus, because he did this on the sabbath. 17 But Jesus answered them, "My Father is working still, and I am working." 18 This was why the Jews sought all the more to kill him, because he not only broke the sabbath but also called God his Father, making himself equal with God.

19 Jesus said to them, "Truly, truly, I say to you, the Son can do nothing of his own accord, but only what he sees the Father doing; for whatever he does, that the Son does likewise. 20 For the Father loves the Son, and shows him all that he himself is doing; and greater works than these will he show him, that you may marvel. 21 For as the Father raises the dead and gives them life, so also the Son gives life to whom he will. 22 The Father judges no one, but has given all judgment to the Son, 23 that all may honor the Son, even as they honor the Father. He who does not honor the Son does not honor the Father who sent him. 24 Truly, truly, I say to you, he who hears my word and believes him who sent me has eternal life; he does not come into judgment, but has passed from death to life.

25 "Truly, truly, I say to you, the hour is coming, and now is, when the dead will hear the voice of the Son of God, and those who hear will live. 26 For as the Father has life in himself, so he has granted the Son also to have life in himself, 27 and has given him authority to execute judgment, because he is the Son of man. 28 Do not marvel at this; for the hour is coming when all who are in the tombs will hear his voice 29 and come forth, those who have done good, to the resurrection of life, and those who have done evil, to the resurrection of judgment.

30 "I can do nothing on my own authority; as I hear, I judge; and my judgment is just, because I seek not my own will but the will of him who sent me. 31 If I bear witness to myself, my testimony is not true; 32 there is another who bears witness to me, and I know that the testimony which he bears to me is true. 33 You sent to John, and he has borne witness to the truth. 34 Not that the testimony which I receive is from man; but I say this that you may be saved. 35 He was a burning and shining lamp, and you were willing to rejoice for a while in his light. 36 But the testimony which I have is greater than

PHILLIPS

Then they asked him, "And who is the man who told you to do that?"

But the one who had been healed had no idea who it was, for Jesus had slipped away in the dense crowd. Later Jesus found him in the Temple and said to him, "Look: you are a fit man now. Do not sin again or something worse might happen to you!"

Then the man went off and informed the Jews that the one who had made him well was Jesus. It was because Jesus did such things on the Sabbath day that the Jews persecuted him. But Jesus' answer to them was this, "My Father is still at work and therefore I work as well."

This remark made the Jews all the more determined to kill him, because not only did he break the Sabbath but he referred to God as his own Father, so putting himself on equal terms with God.

Jesus makes his tremendous claim 5. 19

Jesus said to them: "I assure you that the Son can do nothing of his own accord, but what he sees the Father doing. What the Son does is always modeled on what the Father does, for the Father loves the Son and shows him everything that he does himself. Yes, and he will show him even greater things than these to fill you with wonder. For just as the Father raises the dead and makes them live, so does the Son give life to any man he chooses. The Father is no man's judge: he has put judgment entirely into the Son's hands so that all men may honor the Son equally with the Father. The man who does not honor the Son does not honor the Father who sent him. I solemnly assure you that the man who hears what I have to say and believes in the one who has sent me has eternal life. He does not have to face judgment; he has already passed from death into life. Yes, I assure you that a time is coming, in fact has already come, when the dead will hear the voice of the Son of God and when they have heard it they will live! For just as the Father has life in himself, so by the Father's gift the Son also has life in himself. And he has given him authority to judge because he is Son of Man. No, do not be surprised—the time is coming when all those who are dead and buried will hear his voice and out they will come—those who have done right will rise again to life, but those who have done wrong will rise to face judgment!

"By myself I can do nothing. As I hear, I judge, and my judgment is true because I do not live to please myself but to do the will of the Father who sent me. You may say that I am bearing witness about myself, that therefore what I say about myself has no value, but I would remind you that there is one who witnesses about me and I know that his witness about me is absolutely true. You sent to John, and he testified to the truth. Not that it is man's testimony that I accept—I only tell you this to help you to be saved. John certainly was a lamp that burned and shone, and for a time you were willing to enjoy the light that he gave. But I have a higher testimony than John's. The work

N.E.B.

They asked him, 'Who is the man who told you to take up your bed and walk?' But the cripple who had been cured did not know; for the place was crowded and Jesus had slipped away. A little later Jesus found him in the temple and said to him, 'Now that you are well again, leave your sinful ways, or you may suffer something worse.' The man went away and told the Jews that it was Jesus who had cured him.

It was works of this kind done on the Sabbath that stirred the Jews to persecute Jesus. He defended himself by saying, 'My Father has never yet ceased his work, and I am working too.' This made the Jews still more determined to kill him, because he was not only breaking the Sabbath, but, by calling God his own Father, he claimed equality with God.

To this charge Jesus replied, 'In truth, in very truth I tell you, the Son can do nothing by himself; he does only what he sees the Father doing: what the Father does, the Son does. For the Father loves the Son and shows him all his works, and will show greater yet, to fill you with wonder. As the Father raises the dead and gives them life, so the Son gives life to men, as he determines. And again, the Father does not judge anyone, but has given full jurisdiction to the Son; it is his will that all should pay the same honour to the Son as to the Father. To deny honour to the Son is to deny it to the Father who sent him.

'In very truth, anyone who gives heed to what I say and puts his trust in him who sent me has hold of eternal life, and does not come up for judgement, but has already passed from death to life. In truth, in very truth I tell you, a time is coming, indeed it is already here, when the dead shall hear the voice of the Son of God, and all who hear shall come to life. For as the Father has life-giving power in himself, so has the Son, by the Father's gift.

'As Son of Man, he has also been given the right to pass judgement. Do not wonder at this, because the time is coming when all who are in the grave shall hear his voice and move forth: those who have done right will rise to life; those who have done wrong will rise to hear their doom. I cannot act by myself; I judge as I am bidden, and my verdict is just, because my aim is not my own will, but the will of him who sent me.

'If I testify on my own behalf, that testimony does not hold good. There is another who bears witness for me, and I know that his testimony holds. Your messengers have been to John; you have his testimony to the truth. Not that I rely on human testimony, but I remind you of it for your own salvation. John was a lamp, burning brightly, and for a time you were ready to exult in his light. But I rely on a testimony higher

K.J.V.

John: for the works which the Father hath given me to finish, the same works that I do, bear witness of me, that the Father hath sent me. 37And the Father himself, which hath sent me, hath borne witness of me. Ye have neither heard his voice at any time, nor seen his shape. 38And ye have not his word abiding in you: for whom he hath sent, him ye believe not.

39 Search the Scriptures; for in them ye think ye have eternal life: and they are they which testify of me. 40And ye will not come to me, that ye might have life. 41 I receive not honour from men. 42 But I know you, that ye have not the love of God in you. 43 I am come in my Father's name, and ye receive me not: if another shall come in his own name, him ye will receive. 44 How can ye believe, which receive honour one of another, and seek not the honour that *cometh* from God only? 45 Do not think that I will accuse you to the Father: there is *one* that accuseth you, *even* Moses, in whom ye trust. 46 For had ye believed Moses, ye would have believed me: for he wrote of me. 47 But if ye believe not his writings, how shall ye believe my words?

6 After these things Jesus went over the sea of Galilee, which is *the sea* of Tiberias. 2And a great multitude followed him, because they saw his miracles which he did on them that were diseased. 3And Jesus went up into a mountain, and there he sat with his disciples. 4And the passover, a feast of the Jews, was nigh.

5 When Jesus then lifted up *his* eyes, and saw a great company come unto him, he saith unto Philip, Whence shall we buy bread, that these may eat? 6And this he said to prove him: for he himself knew what he would do. 7 Philip answered him, Two hundred pennyworth of bread is not sufficient for them, that every one of them may take a little. 8 One of his disciples, Andrew, Simon Peter's brother, saith unto him, 9 There is a lad here, which hath five barley loaves, and two small fishes: but what are they among so many? 10And Jesus said, Make the men sit down. Now there was much grass in the place. So the men sat down, in number about five thousand. 11And Jesus took the loaves; and when he had given thanks, he distributed to the disciples, and the disciples to them that were set down; and likewise of the fishes as much as they would. 12 When they were filled, he said unto his disciples, Gather up the fragments that remain, that nothing be lost. 13 Therefore they gathered *them* together, and filled twelve baskets with the fragments of the five barley loaves, which remained over and above unto them that had eaten. 14 Then those men, when they had seen the miracle that Jesus did, said, This is of a truth that Prophet that should come into the world.

15 When Jesus therefore perceived that they would come and take him by force, to make him a king, he departed again into a mountain himself alone. 16And when even was *now* come, his disciples went down unto the sea, 17And entered into a ship, and went over the sea toward Capernaum. And it was now dark, and Jesus was not come to them. 18And the sea arose by reason of a great wind that blew. 19 So when they had

R.S.V.

that of John; for the works which the Father has granted me to accomplish, these very works which I am doing, bear me witness that the Father has sent me. 37And the Father who sent me has himself borne witness to me. His voice you have never heard, his form you have never seen; 38 and you do not have his word abiding in you, for you do not believe him whom he has sent. 39 You search the scriptures, because you think that in them you have eternal life; and it is they that bear witness to me; 40 yet you refuse to come to me that you may have life. 41 I do not receive glory from men. 42 But I know that you have not the love of God within you. 43 I have come in my Father's name, and you do not receive me; if another comes in his own name, him you will receive. 44 How can you believe, who receive glory from one another and do not seek the glory that comes from the only God? 45 Do not think that I shall accuse you to the Father; it is Moses who accuses you, on whom you set your hope. 46 If you believed Moses, you would believe me, for he wrote of me. 47 But if you do not believe his writings, how will you believe my words?"

6 After this Jesus went to the other side of the Sea of Galilee, which is the Sea of Tiberias. 2And a multitude followed him, because they saw the signs which he did on those who were diseased. 3 Jesus went up into the hills, and there sat down with his disciples. 4 Now the Passover, the feast of the Jews, was at hand. 5 Lifting up his eyes, then, and seeing that a multitude was coming to him, Jesus said to Philip, "How are we to buy bread, so that these people may eat?" 6 This he said to test him, for he himself knew what he would do. 7 Philip answered him, "Two hundred denarii[1] would not buy enough bread for each of them to get a little." 8 One of his disciples, Andrew, Simon Peter's brother, said to him, 9 "There is a lad here who has five barley loaves and two fish; but what are they among so many?" 10 Jesus said, "Make the people sit down." Now there was much grass in the place; so the men sat down, in number about five thousand. 11 Jesus then took the loaves, and when he had given thanks, he distributed them to those who were seated; so also the fish, as much as they wanted. 12And when they had eaten their fill, he told his disciples, "Gather up the fragments left over, that nothing may be lost." 13 So they gathered them up and filled twelve baskets with fragments from the five barley loaves, left by those who had eaten. 14 When the people saw the sign which he had done, they said, "This is indeed the prophet who is to come into the world!"

15 Perceiving then that they were about to come and take him by force to make him king, Jesus withdrew again to the hills by himself.

16 When evening came, his disciples went down to the sea, 17 got into a boat, and started across the sea to Capernaum. It was now dark, and Jesus had not yet come to them. 18 The sea rose because a strong wind was blowing. 19 When they had rowed about three or four

[1] The denarius was worth about twenty cents.

| PHILLIPS | N.E.B. |

that the Father gave me to complete, yes, these very actions which I do are my witness that the Father has sent me. This is how the Father who sent me has given his own personal testimony to me.

"Now you have never at any time heard what he says or seen what he is like. Nor do you really believe his word in your hearts, for you refuse to believe the man whom he has sent. You pore over the scriptures, for you imagine that you will find eternal life in them. And all the time they give their testimony to me! But you are not willing to come to me to have real life! Men's approval or disapproval means nothing to me, but I can tell that you have none of the love of God in your hearts. I have come in the name of my Father and you will not accept me. Yet if another man comes simply in his own name, you will accept him. How on earth can you believe while you are for ever looking for one another's approval and not for the glory that comes from the one God? There is no need for you to think that I have come to accuse you before the Father. You already have an accuser—Moses, in whom you put all your confidence! For if you really believed Moses, you would be bound to believe me; for it was about me that he wrote. But if you do not believe what he wrote, how can you believe what I say?"

than John's. There is enough to testify that the Father has sent me, in the works my Father gave me to do and to finish—the very works I have in hand. This testimony to me was given by the Father who sent me, although you never heard his voice, or saw his form. But his word has found no home in you, for you do not believe the one whom he sent. You study the scriptures diligently, supposing that in having them you have eternal life; yet, although their testimony points to me, you refuse to come to me for that life.

'I do not look to men for honour. But with you it is different, as I know well, for you have no love for God in you. I have come accredited by my Father, and you have no welcome for me; if another comes self-accredited you will welcome him. How can you have faith so long as you receive honour from one another, and care nothing for the honour that comes from him who alone is God? Do not imagine that I shall be your accuser at God's tribunal. Your accuser is Moses, the very Moses on whom you have set your hope. If you believed Moses you would believe what I tell you, for it was about me that he wrote. But if you do not believe what he wrote, how are you to believe what I say?'

Jesus shows his power over material things
6. 1

After this, Jesus crossed the Lake of Galilee (or Tiberias), and a great crowd followed him because they had seen the signs which he gave in his dealings with the sick. But Jesus went up the hillside and sat down there with his disciples. The Passover, the Jewish festival, was near. So Jesus, raising his eyes and seeing a great crowd on their way toward him, said to Philip, "Where can we buy food for these people to eat?" (He said this to test Philip, for he himself knew what he was going to do.)

"Ten dollars' worth of bread would not be enough for them," Philip replied, "even if they had only a little each."

Then Andrew, Simon Peter's brother, another disciple, put in, "There is a boy here who has five small barley loaves and a couple of fish, but what's the good of that for such a crowd?"

Then Jesus said, "Get the people to sit down."

There was plenty of grass there, and the men, some five thousand of them, sat down. Then Jesus took the loaves, gave thanks for them and distributed them to the people sitting on the grass, and he distributed the fish in the same way, giving them as much as they wanted. When they had eaten enough, Jesus said to his disciples, "Collect the pieces that are left over so that nothing is wasted."

So they did as he suggested and filled twelve baskets with the broken pieces of the five barley loaves, which were left over after the people had eaten! When the men saw this sign of Jesus' power, they kept saying, "This certainly is the Prophet who was to come into the world!"

Then Jesus, realizing that they were going to carry him off and make him their king, retired once more to the hillside quite alone.

In the evening his disciples went down to the lake, embarked on the boat and made their way across the lake to Capernaum. Darkness had already fallen and Jesus had not returned to them. A strong wind sprang up and the water grew very rough. When they had rowed about three

6 Some time later Jesus withdrew to the farther shore of the Sea of Galilee (or Tiberias), and a large crowd of people followed who had seen the signs he performed in healing the sick. Then Jesus went up the hill-side and sat down with his disciples. It was near the time of Passover, the great Jewish festival. Raising his eyes and seeing a large crowd coming towards him, Jesus said to Philip, 'Where are we to buy bread to feed these people?' This he said to test him; Jesus himself knew what he meant to do. Philip replied, 'Twenty pounds[a] would not buy enough bread for every one of them to have a little.' One of his disciples, Andrew, the brother of Simon Peter, said to him, 'There is a boy here who has five barley loaves and two fishes; but what is that among so many?' Jesus said, 'Make the people sit down.' There was plenty of grass there, so the men sat down, about five thousand of them. Then Jesus took the loaves, gave thanks, and distributed them to the people as they sat there. He did the same with the fishes, and they had as much as they wanted. When everyone had had enough, he said to his disciples, 'Collect the pieces left over, so that nothing may be lost.' This they did, and filled twelve baskets with the pieces left uneaten of the five barley loaves.

When the people saw the sign Jesus had performed, the word went round, 'Surely this must be the prophet that was to come into the world.' Jesus, aware that they meant to come and seize him to proclaim him king, withdrew again to the hills by himself.

At nightfall his disciples went down to the sea, got into their boat, and pushed off to cross the water to Capernaum. Darkness had already fallen, and Jesus had not yet joined them. By now a strong wind was blowing and the sea grew rough. When they had rowed about three or

[a] *Literally* 200 denarii.

K.J.V.

rowed about five and twenty or thirty furlongs, they see Jesus walking on the sea, and drawing nigh unto the ship: and they were afraid. 20 But he saith unto them, It is I; be not afraid. 21 Then they willingly received him into the ship: and immediately the ship was at the land whither they went.

22 The day following, when the people, which stood on the other side of the sea, saw that there was none other boat there, save that one whereinto his disciples were entered, and that Jesus went not with his disciples into the boat, but *that* his disciples were gone away alone; 23 Howbeit there came other boats from Tiberias nigh unto the place where they did eat bread, after that the Lord had given thanks: 24 When the people therefore saw that Jesus was not there, neither his disciples, they also took shipping, and came to Capernaum, seeking for Jesus. 25And when they had found him on the other side of the sea, they said unto him, Rabbi, when camest thou hither? 26 Jesus answered them and said, Verily, verily, I say unto you, Ye seek me, not because ye saw the miracles, but because ye did eat of the loaves, and were filled. 27 Labour not for the meat which perisheth, but for that meat which endureth unto everlasting life, which the Son of man shall give unto you: for him hath God the Father sealed. 28 Then said they unto him, What shall we do, that we might work the works of God? 29 Jesus answered and said unto them, This is the work of God, that ye believe on him whom he hath sent. 30 They said therefore unto him, What sign shewest thou then, that we may see, and believe thee? what dost thou work? 31 Our fathers did eat manna in the desert; as it is written, He gave them bread from heaven to eat. 32 Then Jesus said unto them, Verily, verily, I say unto you, Moses gave you not that bread from heaven; but my Father giveth you the true bread from heaven. 33 For the bread of God is he which cometh down from heaven, and giveth life unto the world. 34 Then said they unto him, Lord, evermore give us this bread. 35And Jesus said unto them, I am the bread of life: he that cometh to me shall never hunger; and he that believeth on me shall never thirst. 36 But I said unto you, That ye also have seen me, and believe not. 37All that the Father giveth me shall come to me; and him that cometh to me I will in no wise cast out. 38 For I came down from heaven, not to do mine own will, but the will of him that sent me. 39And this is the Father's will which hath sent me, that of all which he hath given me I should lose nothing, but should raise it up again at the last day. 40And this is the will of him that sent me, that every one which seeth the Son, and believeth on him, may have everlasting life: and I will raise him up at the last day. 41 The Jews then murmured at him, because he said, I am the bread which came down from heaven. 42And they said, Is not this Jesus, the son of Joseph, whose father and mother we know? how is it then that he saith, I came down from heaven? 43 Jesus therefore answered and said unto them, Murmur not among yourselves. 44 No man can come to me, except the Father which hath sent me draw him:

R.S.V.

miles,[m] they saw Jesus walking on the sea and drawing near to the boat. They were frightened, 20 but he said to them, "It is I; do not be afraid." 21 Then they were glad to take him into the boat, and immediately the boat was at the land to which they were going.

22 On the next day the people who remained on the other side of the sea saw that there had been only one boat there, and that Jesus had not entered the boat with his disciples, but that his disciples had gone away alone. 23 However, boats from Tiberias came near the place where they ate the bread after the Lord had given thanks. 24 So when the people saw that Jesus was not there, nor his disciples, they themselves got into the boats and went to Capernaum, seeking Jesus.

25 When they found him on the other side of the sea, they said to him, "Rabbi, when did you come here?" 26 Jesus answered them, "Truly, truly, I say to you, you seek me, not because you saw signs, but because you ate your fill of the loaves. 27 Do not labor for the food which perishes, but for the food which endures to eternal life, which the Son of man will give to you; for on him has God the Father set his seal." 28 Then they said to him, "What must we do, to be doing the works of God?" 29 Jesus answered them, "This is the work of God, that you believe in him whom he has sent." 30 So they said to him, "Then what sign do you do, that we may see, and believe you? What work do you perform? 31 Our fathers ate the manna in the wilderness; as it is written, 'He gave them bread from heaven to eat.'" 32 Jesus then said to them, "Truly, truly, I say to you, it was not Moses who gave you the bread from heaven; my Father gives you the true bread from heaven. 33 For the bread of God is that which comes down from heaven, and gives life to the world." 34 They said to him, "Lord, give us this bread always."

35 Jesus said to them, "I am the bread of life; he who comes to me shall not hunger, and he who believes in me shall never thirst. 36 But I said to you that you have seen me and yet do not believe. 37 All that the Father gives me will come to me; and him who comes to me I will not cast out. 38 For I have come down from heaven, not to do my own will, but the will of him who sent me; 39 and this is the will of him who sent me, that I should lose nothing of all that he has given me, but raise it up at the last day. 40 For this is the will of my Father, that every one who sees the Son and believes in him should have eternal life; and I will raise him up at the last day."

41 The Jews then murmured at him, because he said, "I am the bread which came down from heaven." 42 They said, "Is not this Jesus, the son of Joseph, whose father and mother we know? How does he now say, 'I have come down from heaven'?" 43 Jesus answered them, "Do not murmur among yourselves. 44 No one can come to me unless the Father who sent me draws him; and I will raise him up at the

[m] Greek *twenty-five or thirty stadia.*

or four miles, they saw Jesus walking on the water and coming toward the boat, and they were terrified. But he spoke to them, "Don't be afraid: it is I myself."

So they gladly took him aboard, and at once the boat reached the shore they were making for.

Jesus teaches about the true bread 6. 22

The following day, the crowd, who had remained on the other side of the lake, noticed that only the one boat had been there, and that Jesus had not embarked on it with his disciples, but that they had in fact gone off by themselves. Some other small boats from Tiberias had landed quite near the place where they had eaten the food and the Lord had given thanks. When the crowd realized that neither Jesus nor the disciples were there any longer, they themselves got into the boats and went off to Capernaum to look for Jesus. When they had found him on the other side of the lake, they said to him, "Master, when did you come here?"

"Believe me," replied Jesus, "you are looking for me now not because you saw my signs but because you ate that food and had all you wanted. You should not work for the food which does not last but for that food which lasts on into eternal life. This is the food the Son of Man will give you, and he is the one who bears the stamp of God the Father."

This made them ask him, "What must we do to carry out the work of God?"

"The work of God for you," replied Jesus, "is to believe in the one whom he has sent to you."

Then they asked him, "Then what sign can you give us that will make us believe in you? What work are you doing? Our forefathers ate manna in the desert just as the scripture says,

He gave them bread out of Heaven to eat."

To which Jesus replied, "Yes, but what matters is not that Moses *gave you* bread from Heaven but that my Father *is giving you* the true bread from Heaven. For the bread of God which comes down from Heaven gives life to the world."

This made them say to him, "Lord, please give us this bread, always!"

Then Jesus said to them: "I myself am the bread of life. The man who comes to me will never be hungry and the man who believes in me will never again be thirsty. Yet I have told you that you have seen me and do not believe. Everything that my Father gives me will come to me and I will never refuse anyone who comes to me. For I have come down from Heaven, not to do what I want, but to do the will of him who sent me. The will of him who sent me is that I should not lose anything of what he has given me, but should raise it up when the last day comes. And this is the will of the one who sent me, that everyone who sees the Son and trusts him should have eternal life, and I will raise him up when the last day comes."

At this, the Jews began grumbling at him because he said, "I am the bread which came down from Heaven," remarking, "Is not this Jesus, the son of Joseph, whose parents we know? How can he say that 'I have come down from Heaven'?"

So Jesus answered them: "Do not grumble among yourselves. Nobody comes to me unless he is drawn to me by the Father who sent me,

four miles they saw Jesus walking on the sea and approaching the boat. They were terrified, but he called out, 'It is I; do not be afraid.' Then they were ready to take him aboard, and immediately the boat reached the land they were making for.

Next morning the crowd was standing on the opposite shore. They had seen only one boat there, and Jesus, they knew, had not embarked with his disciples, who had gone away without him. Boats from Tiberias, however, came ashore[a] near the place where the people had eaten the bread over which the Lord gave thanks.[b] When the people saw that neither Jesus nor his disciples were any longer there, they themselves went aboard these boats and made for Capernaum in search of Jesus. They found him on the other side. 'Rabbi,' they said, 'when did you come here?' Jesus replied, 'In very truth I know that you have come looking for me because your hunger was satisfied with the loaves you ate, not because you saw signs. You must work, not for this perishable food, but for the food that lasts, the food of eternal life.

'This food the Son of Man will give you, for he it is upon whom the Father has set the seal of his authority.' 'Then what must we do', they asked him, 'if we are to work as God would have us work?' Jesus replied, 'This is the work that God requires: believe in the one whom he has sent.'

They said, 'What sign can you give us to see, so that we may believe you? What is the work you do? Our ancestors had manna to eat in the desert; as Scripture says, "He gave them bread from heaven to eat." ' Jesus answered, 'I tell you this: the truth is, not that Moses gave you the bread from heaven, but that my Father gives you the real bread from heaven. The bread that God gives comes down[c] from heaven and brings life to the world.' They said to him, 'Sir, give us this bread now and always.' Jesus said to them, 'I am the bread of life. Whoever comes to me shall never be hungry, and whoever believes in me shall never be thirsty. But you, as I said, do not believe although you have seen.[d] All that the Father gives me will come to me, and the man who comes to me I will never turn away. I have come down from heaven, not to do my own will, but the will of him who sent me. It is his will that I should not lose even one of all that he has given me, but raise them all up on the last day. For it is my Father's will that everyone who looks upon the Son and puts his faith in him shall possess eternal life; and I will raise him up on the last day.'

At this the Jews began to murmur disapprovingly because he said, 'I am the bread which came down from heaven.' They said, 'Surely this is Jesus son of Joseph; we know his father and mother. How can he now say, "I have come down from heaven"?' Jesus answered, 'Stop murmuring among yourselves. No man can come to me unless he is drawn by the Father who sent me; and I will raise him up on the last day.

[a] *Some witnesses read* Other boats from Tiberias came ashore . . . [b] *Some witnesses omit* over which . . . thanks. [c] *Or* is he who comes down . . . [d] *Some witnesses add* me.

K.J.V.

and I will raise him up at the last day. 45 It is written in the prophets, And they shall be all taught of God. Every man therefore that hath heard, and hath learned of the Father, cometh unto me. 46 Not that any man hath seen the Father, save he which is of God, he hath seen the Father. 47 Verily, verily, I say unto you, He that believeth on me hath everlasting life. 48 I am that bread of life. 49 Your fathers did eat manna in the wilderness, and are dead. 50 This is the bread which cometh down from heaven, that a man may eat thereof, and not die. 51 I am the living bread which came down from heaven: if any man eat of this bread, he shall live for ever: and the bread that I will give is my flesh, which I will give for the life of the world. 52 The Jews therefore strove among themselves, saying, How can this man give us *his* flesh to eat? 53 Then Jesus said unto them, Verily, verily, I say unto you, Except ye eat the flesh of the Son of man, and drink his blood, ye have no life in you. 54 Whoso eateth my flesh, and drinketh my blood, hath eternal life; and I will raise him up at the last day. 55 For my flesh is meat indeed, and my blood is drink indeed. 56 He that eateth my flesh, and drinketh my blood, dwelleth in me, and I in him. 57 As the living Father hath sent me, and I live by the Father; so he that eateth me, even he shall live by me. 58 This is that bread which came down from heaven: not as your fathers did eat manna, and are dead: he that eateth of this bread shall live for ever. 59 These things said he in the synagogue, as he taught in Capernaum. 60 Many therefore of his disciples, when they had heard *this*, said, This is a hard saying; who can hear it? 61 When Jesus knew in himself that his disciples murmured at it, he said unto them, Doth this offend you? 62 *What* and if ye shall see the Son of man ascend up where he was before? 63 It is the Spirit that quickeneth; the flesh profiteth nothing: the words that I speak unto you, *they* are spirit, and *they* are life. 64 But there are some of you that believe not. For Jesus knew from the beginning who they were that believed not, and who should betray him. 65 And he said, Therefore said I unto you, that no man can come unto me, except it were given unto him of my Father.

66 From that *time* many of his disciples went back, and walked no more with him. 67 Then said Jesus unto the twelve, Will ye also go away? 68 Then Simon Peter answered him, Lord, to whom shall we go? thou hast the words of eternal life. 69 And we believe and are sure that thou art that Christ, the Son of the living God. 70 Jesus answered them, Have not I chosen you twelve, and one of you is a devil? 71 He spake of Judas Iscariot *the son* of Simon: for he it was that should betray him, being one of the twelve.

R.S.V.

last day. 45 It is written in the prophets, 'And they shall all be taught by God.' Every one who has heard and learned from the Father comes to me. 46 Not that any one has seen the Father except him who is from God; he has seen the Father. 47 Truly, truly, I say to you, he who believes has eternal life. 48 I am the bread of life. 49 Your fathers ate the manna in the wilderness, and they died. 50 This is the bread which comes down from heaven, that a man may eat of it and not die. 51 I am the living bread which came down from heaven; if any one eats of this bread, he will live for ever; and the bread which I shall give for the life of the world is my flesh."

52 The Jews then disputed among themselves, saying, "How can this man give us his flesh to eat?" 53 So Jesus said to them, "Truly, truly, I say to you, unless you eat the flesh of the Son of man and drink his blood, you have no life in you; 54 he who eats my flesh and drinks my blood has eternal life, and I will raise him up at the last day. 55 For my flesh is food indeed, and my blood is drink indeed. 56 He who eats my flesh and drinks my blood abides in me, and I in him. 57 As the living Father sent me, and I live because of the Father, so he who eats me will live because of me. 58 This is the bread which came down from heaven, not such as the fathers ate and died; he who eats this bread will live for ever." 59 This he said in the synagogue, as he taught at Capernaum.

60 Many of his disciples, when they heard it, said, "This is a hard saying; who can listen to it?" 61 But Jesus, knowing in himself that his disciples murmured at it, said to them, "Do you take offense at this? 62 Then what if you were to see the Son of man ascending where he was before? 63 It is the spirit that gives life, the flesh is of no avail; the words that I have spoken to you are spirit and life. 64 But there are some of you that do not believe." For Jesus knew from the first who those were that did not believe, and who it was that should betray him. 65 And he said, "This is why I told you that no one can come to me unless it is granted him by the Father."

66 After this many of his disciples drew back and no longer went about with him. 67 Jesus said to the twelve, "Will you also go away?" 68 Simon Peter answered him, "Lord, to whom shall we go? You have the words of eternal life; 69 and we have believed, and have come to know, that you are the Holy One of God." 70 Jesus answered them, "Did I not choose you, the twelve, and one of you is a devil?" 71 He spoke of Judas the son of Simon Iscariot, for he, one of the twelve, was to betray him.

7 After these things Jesus walked in Galilee: for he would not walk in Jewry, because the

7 After this Jesus went about in Galilee; he would not go about in Judea, because the

PHILLIPS

and I will raise him up when the last day comes. In the Prophets it is written—

And they shall all be taught of God,

and this means that everybody who has heard the Father's voice and learned from him will come to me. Not that anyone has ever seen the Father except the one who comes from God— he has seen the Father. I assure you that the man who trusts in him has eternal life already. I myself am the bread of life. Your forefathers ate manna in the desert, *and they died.* This is bread that comes down from Heaven, so that a man may eat it and not die. I myself am the living bread which came down from Heaven, and if anyone eats this bread he will live for ever. The bread which I will give is my body and I shall give it for the life of the world."

This led to a fierce argument among the Jews, some of them saying, "How can this man give us his body to eat?"

So Jesus said to them: "Unless you do eat the body of the Son of Man and drink his blood, you are not really living at all. The man who eats my flesh and drinks my blood has eternal life and I will raise him up when the last day comes. For my body is real food and my blood is real drink. The man who eats my body and drinks my blood shares my life and I share his. Just as the living Father sent me and I am alive because of the Father, so the man who lives on me will live because of me. *This* is the bread which came down from Heaven! It is not like the manna which your forefathers used to eat, *and died.* The man who eats this bread will live for ever."

Jesus said all these things while teaching in the synagogue at Capernaum. Many of his disciples heard him say these things, and commented, "This is hard teaching indeed; who could accept that?"

Then Jesus, knowing intuitively that his disciples were complaining about what he had just said, went on: "Is this too much for you? Then what would happen if you were to see the Son of Man going up to the place where he was before? It is the Spirit which gives life. The flesh will not help you. The things which I have told you are spiritual and are life. But some of you will not believe me."

For Jesus knew from the beginning which of his followers did not trust him and who was the man who would betray him. Then he added, "This is why I said to you, 'No one can come to me unless my Father puts it into his heart to come.' "

As a consequence of this, many of his disciples withdrew and no longer followed him. So Jesus said to the twelve, "And are you too wanting to go away?"

"Lord," answered Simon Peter, "who else should we go to? Your words have the ring of eternal life! And we believe and are convinced that you are the holy one of God."

Jesus replied, "Did I not choose you twelve— and one of you has the devil in his heart?"

He was speaking of Judas, the son of Simon Iscariot, one of the twelve, who was planning to betray him.

N.E.B.

It is written in the prophets: "And they shall all be taught by God." Everyone who has listened to the Father and learned from him comes to me.

'I do not mean that anyone has seen the Father. He who has come from God has seen the Father, and he alone. In truth, in very truth I tell you, the believer possesses eternal life. I am the bread of life. Your forefathers ate the manna in the desert and they are dead. I am speaking of the bread that comes down from heaven, which a man may eat, and never die. I am that living bread which has come down from heaven: if anyone eats this bread he shall live for ever. Moreover, the bread which I will give is my own flesh; I give it for the life of the world.'

This led to a fierce dispute among the Jews. 'How can this man give us his flesh to eat?' they said. Jesus replied, 'In truth, in very truth I tell you, unless you eat the flesh of the Son of Man and drink his blood you can have no life in you. Whoever eats my flesh and drinks my blood possesses eternal life, and I will raise him up on the last day. My flesh is real food; my blood is real drink. Whoever eats my flesh and drinks my blood dwells continually in me and I dwell in him. As the living Father sent me, and I live because of the Father, so he who eats me shall live because of me. This is the bread which came down from heaven; and it is not like the bread which our fathers ate: they are dead, but whoever eats this bread shall live for ever.'

This was spoken in synagogue when Jesus was teaching in Capernaum. Many of his disciples on hearing it exclaimed, 'This is more than we can stomach! Why listen to such words?' Jesus was aware that his disciples were murmuring about it and asked them, 'Does this shock you? What if you see the Son of Man ascending to the place where he was before? The spirit alone gives life; the flesh is of no avail; the words which I have spoken to you are both spirit and life. And yet there are some of you who have no faith.' For Jesus knew all along who were without faith and who was to betray him. So he said, 'This is why I told you that no one can come to me unless it has been granted to him by the Father.'

From that time on, many of his disciples withdrew and no longer went about with him. So Jesus asked the Twelve, 'Do you also want to leave me?' Simon Peter answered him, 'Lord, to whom shall we go? Your words are words of eternal life. We have faith, and we know that you are the Holy One of God.' Jesus answered, 'Have I not chosen you, all twelve? Yet one of you is a devil.' He meant Judas, son of Simon Iscariot. He it was who would betray him, and he was one of the Twelve.

Jesus delays his arrival   **7. 1**
at the festival

The Great Controversy

After this, Jesus moved about in Galilee but decided not to do so in Judaea since the Jews

7 Afterwards Jesus went about in Galilee. He wished to avoid Judaea because the Jews

K.J.V.

Jews sought to kill him. 2 Now the Jews' feast of tabernacles was at hand. 3 His brethren therefore said unto him, Depart hence, and go into Judea, that thy disciples also may see the works that thou doest. 4 For *there is* no man *that* doeth any thing in secret, and he himself seeketh to be known openly. If thou do these things, shew thyself to the world. 5 For neither did his brethren believe in him. 6 Then Jesus said unto them, My time is not yet come: but your time is always ready. 7 The world cannot hate you; but me it hateth, because I testify of it, that the works thereof are evil. 8 Go ye up unto this feast: I go not up yet unto this feast; for my time is not yet full come. 9 When he had said these words unto them, he abode *still* in Galilee.

10 But when his brethren were gone up, then went he also up unto the feast, not openly, but as it were in secret. 11 Then the Jews sought him at the feast, and said, Where is he? 12And there was much murmuring among the people concerning him: for some said, He is a good man: others said, Nay; but he deceiveth the people. 13 Howbeit no man spake openly of him for fear of the Jews.

14 Now about the midst of the feast Jesus went up into the temple, and taught. 15And the Jews marvelled, saying, How knoweth this man letters, having never learned? 16 Jesus answered them, and said, My doctrine is not mine, but his that sent me. 17 If any man will do his will, he shall know of the doctrine, whether it be of God, or *whether* I speak of myself. 18 He that speaketh of himself seeketh his own glory: but he that seeketh his glory that sent him, the same is true, and no unrighteousness is in him. 19 Did not Moses give you the law, and *yet* none of you keepeth the law? Why go ye about to kill me? 20 The people answered and said, Thou hast a devil: who goeth about to kill thee? 21 Jesus answered and said unto them, I have done one work, and ye all marvel. 22 Moses therefore gave unto you circumcision; (not because it is of Moses, but of the fathers;) and ye on the sabbath day circumcise a man. 23 If a man on the sabbath day receive circumcision, that the law of Moses should not be broken; are ye angry at me, because I have made a man every whit whole on the sabbath day? 24 Judge not according to the appearance, but judge righteous judgment. 25 Then said some of them of Jerusalem, Is not this he, whom they seek to kill? 26 But, lo, he speaketh boldly, and they say nothing unto him. Do the rulers know indeed that this is the very Christ? 27 Howbeit we know this man whence he is: but when Christ cometh, no man

R.S.V.

Jews[n] sought to kill him. 2 Now the Jews' feast of Tabernacles was at hand. 3 So his brothers said to him, "Leave here and go to Judea, that your disciples may see the works you are doing. 4 For no man works in secret if he seeks to be known openly. If you do these things, show yourself to the world." 5 For even his brothers did not believe in him. 6 Jesus said to them, "My time has not yet come, but your time is always here. 7 The world cannot hate you, but it hates me because I testify of it that its works are evil. 8 Go to the feast yourselves; I am not[o] going up to this feast, for my time has not yet fully come." 9 So saying, he remained in Galilee.

10 But after his brothers had gone up to the feast, then he also went up, not publicly but in private. 11 The Jews were looking for him at the feast, and saying, "Where is he?" 12And there was much muttering about him among the people. While some said, "He is a good man," others said, "No, he is leading the people astray." 13 Yet for fear of the Jews no one spoke openly of him.

14 About the middle of the feast Jesus went up into the temple and taught. 15 The Jews marveled at it, saying, "How is it that this man has learning,[p] when he has never studied?" 16 So Jesus answered them, "My teaching is not mine, but his who sent me; 17 if any man's will is to do his will, he shall know whether the teaching is from God or whether I am speaking on my own authority. 18 He who speaks on his own authority seeks his own glory; but he who seeks the glory of him who sent him is true, and in him there is no falsehood. 19 Did not Moses give you the law? Yet none of you keeps the law. Why do you seek to kill me?" 20 The people answered, "You have a demon! Who is seeking to kill you?" 21 Jesus answered them, "I did one deed, and you all marvel at it. 22 Moses gave you circumcision (not that it is from Moses, but from the fathers), and you circumcise a man upon the sabbath. 23 If on the sabbath a man receives circumcision, so that the law of Moses may not be broken, are you angry with me because on the sabbath I made a man's whole body well? 24 Do not judge by appearances, but judge with right judgment."

25 Some of the people of Jerusalem therefore said, "Is not this the man whom they seek to kill? 26And here he is, speaking openly, and they say nothing to him! Can it be that the authorities really know that this is the Christ? 27 Yet we know where this man comes from; and when the Christ appears, no one will know

[n] Or *Judeans.* [o] Other ancient authorities add *yet.* [p] Or *this man knows his letters.*

PHILLIPS

were planning to take his life. A Jewish festival, "The feast of the tabernacles," was approaching, and his brothers said to him, "You ought to leave here and go to Judaea so that your disciples can see what you are doing, for nobody works in secret if he wants to be known publicly. If you are going to do things like this, let the world see what you are doing." For not even his brothers had any faith in him. Jesus replied by saying: "It is not yet the right time for me, but any time is right for you. You see, it is impossible for you to arouse the world's hatred, but I provoke hatred because I show the world how evil its deeds really are. No, you go up to the festival; I shall not go up now, for it is not yet time for me to go." And after these remarks he remained where he was in Galilee.

Later, after his brothers had gone up to the festival, he went up himself, not openly but as though he did not want to be seen. Consequently, the Jews kept looking for him at the festival and asking, "Where is that man?" And there was an undercurrent of discussion about him among the crowds. Some would say, "He is a good man," others maintained that he was not, but that he was "misleading the people." Nobody, however, spoke openly about him for fear of the Jews.

Jesus openly declares his authority   7. 14

But at the very height of the festival, Jesus went up to the Temple and began teaching. The Jews were amazed and remarked, "How does this man know all this—he has never been taught?"

Jesus replied to them: "My teaching is not really mine but comes from the one who sent me. If anyone wants to do God's will, he will know whether my teaching is from God or whether I merely speak on my own authority. A man who speaks on his own authority has an eye for his own reputation. But the man who is considering the glory of God who sent him is a true man. There can be no dishonesty about him.

"Did not Moses give you the Law? Yet not a single one of you obeys the Law. Why are you trying to kill me?"

The crowd answered: "You must be mad! Who is trying to kill you?"

Jesus answered them: "I have done one thing and you are all amazed at it. Moses gave you circumcision (not that it came from Moses originally but from your forefathers), and you will circumcise a man even on the Sabbath. If a man receives the cutting of circumcision on the Sabbath to avoid breaking the Law of Moses, why should you be angry with me because I have made a man's body perfectly whole on the Sabbath? You must not judge by the appearance of things but by the reality!"

Some of the people of Jerusalem, hearing him talk like this, were saying: "Isn't this the man whom they are trying to kill? It's amazing—he talks quite openly and they haven't a word to say to him. Surely our rulers haven't decided that this really is Christ! But then, we know this man and where he comes from—when Christ comes, no one will know where he comes from."

N.E.B.

were looking for a chance to kill him. As the Jewish Feast of Tabernacles was close at hand, his brothers said to him, 'You should leave this district and go into Judaea, so that your disciples there may see the great things you are doing. Surely no one can hope to be in the public eye if he works in seclusion. If you really are doing such things as these, show yourself to the world.' For even his brothers were not believers in him. Jesus said to them, 'The right time for me has not yet come, but any time is right for you. The world cannot hate you; but it hates me for exposing the wickedness of its ways. Go to the festival yourselves. I am not*a* going up to this festival because the right time for me has not yet come.' With this answer he stayed behind in Galilee.

Later, when his brothers had gone to the festival, he went up himself, not publicly, but almost in secret. The Jews were looking for him at the festival and asking, 'Where is he?', and there was much whispering about him in the crowds. 'He is a good man', said some. 'No,' said others, 'he is leading the people astray.' However, no one talked about him openly, for fear of the Jews.

When the festival was already half over, Jesus went up to the temple and began to teach. The Jews were astonished: 'How is it', they said, 'that this untrained man has such learning?' Jesus replied, 'The teaching that I give is not my own; it is the teaching of him who sent me. Whoever has the will to do the will of God shall know whether my teaching comes from him or is merely my own. Anyone whose teaching is merely his own, aims at honour for himself. But if a man aims at the honour of him who sent him he is sincere, and there is nothing false in him.

'Did not Moses give you the Law? Yet you all break it. Why are you trying to kill me?' The crowd answered, 'You are possessed! Who wants to kill you?' Jesus replied, 'Once only have I done work on the Sabbath, and you are all taken aback. But consider: Moses gave you the law of circumcision (not that it originated with Moses but with the patriarchs) and you circumcise on the Sabbath. Well then, if a child is circumcised on the Sabbath to avoid breaking the Law of Moses, why are you indignant with me for giving health on the Sabbath to the whole of a man's body? Do not judge superficially, but be just in your judgements.'

At this some of the people of Jerusalem began to say, 'Is not this the man they want to put to death? And here he is, speaking openly, and they have not a word to say to him. Can it be that our rulers have actually decided that this is the Messiah? And yet we know where this man comes from, but when the Messiah appears

[a] *Some witnesses read* not yet.

K.J.V.

knoweth whence he is. 28 Then cried Jesus in the temple as he taught, saying, Ye both know me, and ye know whence I am: and I am not come of myself, but he that sent me is true, whom ye know not. 29 But I know him; for I am from him, and he hath sent me. 30 Then they sought to take him: but no man laid hands on him, because his hour was not yet come. 31 And many of the people believed on him, and said, When Christ cometh, will he do more miracles than these which this *man* hath done?

32 The Pharisees heard that the people murmured such things concerning him; and the Pharisees and the chief priests sent officers to take him. 33 Then said Jesus unto them, Yet a little while am I with you, and *then* I go unto him that sent me. 34 Ye shall seek me, and shall not find *me:* and where I am, *thither* ye cannot come. 35 Then said the Jews among themselves, Whither will he go, that we shall not find him? will he go unto the dispersed among the Gentiles, and teach the Gentiles? 36 What *manner of* saying is this that he said, Ye shall seek me, and shall not find *me:* and where I am, *thither* ye cannot come? 37 In the last day, that great *day* of the feast, Jesus stood and cried, saying, If any man thirst, let him come unto me, and drink. 38 He that believeth on me, as the Scripture hath said, out of his belly shall flow rivers of living water. 39 (But this spake he of the Spirit, which they that believe on him should receive: for the Holy Ghost was not yet *given;* because that Jesus was not yet glorified.)

40 Many of the people therefore, when they heard this saying, said, Of a truth this is the Prophet. 41 Others said, This is the Christ. But some said, Shall Christ come out of Galilee? 42 Hath not the Scripture said, That Christ cometh of the seed of David, and out of the town of Bethlehem, where David was? 43 So there was a division among the people because of him. 44 And some of them would have taken him; but no man laid hands on him.

45 Then came the officers to the chief priests and Pharisees; and they said unto them, Why have ye not brought him? 46 The officers answered, Never man spake like this man. 47 Then answered them the Pharisees, Are ye also deceived? 48 Have any of the rulers or of the Pharisees believed on him? 49 But this people who knoweth not the law are cursed. 50 Nicodemus saith unto them, (he that came to Jesus by night, being one of them,) 51 Doth our law judge *any* man, before it hear him, and know what he doeth? 52 They answered and said unto him, Art thou also of Galilee? Search, and look: for out of Galilee ariseth no prophet.

R.S.V.

where he comes from." 28 So Jesus proclaimed, as he taught in the temple, "You know me, and you know where I come from? But I have not come of my own accord; he who sent me is true, and him you do not know. 29 I know him, for I come from him, and he sent me." 30 So they sought to arrest him; but no one laid hands on him, because his hour had not yet come. 31 Yet many of the people believed in him; they said, "When the Christ appears, will he do more signs than this man has done?"

32 The Pharisees heard the crowd thus muttering about him, and the chief priests and Pharisees sent officers to arrest him. 33 Jesus then said, "I shall be with you a little longer, and then I go to him who sent me; 34 you will seek me and you will not find me; where I am you cannot come." 35 The Jews said to one another, "Where does this man intend to go that we shall not find him? Does he intend to go to the Dispersion among the Greeks and teach the Greeks? 36 What does he mean by saying, 'You will seek me and you will not find me,' and, 'Where I am you cannot come'?"

37 On the last day of the feast, the great day, Jesus stood up and proclaimed, "If any one thirst, let him come to me and drink. 38 He who believes in me, as[q] the scripture has said, 'Out of his heart shall flow rivers of living water.'" 39 Now this he said about the Spirit, which those who believed in him were to receive; for as yet the Spirit had not been given, because Jesus was not yet glorified.

40 When they heard these words, some of the people said, "This is really the prophet." 41 Others said, "This is the Christ." But some said, "Is the Christ to come from Galilee? 42 Has not the scripture said that the Christ is descended from David, and comes from Bethlehem, the village where David was?" 43 So there was a division among the people over him. 44 Some of them wanted to arrest him, but no one laid hands on him.

45 The officers then went back to the chief priests and Pharisees, who said to them, "Why did you not bring him?" 46 The officers answered, "No man ever spoke like this man!" 47 The Pharisees answered them, "Are you led astray, you also? 48 Have any of the authorities or of the Pharisees believed in him? 49 But this crowd, who do not know the law, are accursed." 50 Nicodemus, who had gone to him before, and who was one of them, said to them, 51 "Does our law judge a man without first giving him a hearing and learning what he does?" 52 They replied, "Are you from Galilee too? Search and you will see that no prophet is to rise from Galilee." r

[q] Or *let him come to me, and let him who believes in me drink. As.* [r] Other ancient authorities add 7.53-8.11 either here or at the end of this Gospel or after Luke 21.38, with variations of the text.

Jesus makes more unique claims   7. 28

Then Jesus, in the middle of his teaching, called out in the Temple: "So you know me and know where I have come from? But I have not come of my own accord; I am sent by one who is true and you do not know him! I do know him, because I come from him and he has sent me here."

Then they attempted to arrest him, but actually no one laid a finger on him because the right moment had not yet come. Many of the crowd believed in him and kept on saying, "When Christ comes, is he going to show greater signs than this man?"

The Pharisees heard the crowd whispering these things about him, and they and the chief priests sent officers to arrest him. Then Jesus said: "I shall be with you only a little while longer and then I am going to him who sent me. You will look for me then but you will never find me. You cannot come where I shall be."

This made the Jews say to one another: "Where is he going to hide himself so that we cannot find him? Surely he's not going to our refugees among the Greeks to teach Greeks? What does he mean when he says, 'You will look for me and you will never find me' and 'You cannot come where I shall be'?"

Then, on the last day, the climax of the festival, Jesus stood up and cried out: "If any man is thirsty, he can come to me and drink! The man who believes in me, as the scripture said, will have rivers of living water flowing from his inmost heart." (Here he was speaking about the Spirit which those who believe in him would receive. The Holy Spirit had not yet been given because Jesus had not yet been glorified.) When they heard these words, some of the people were saying, "This really is the Prophet." Others said, "This is Christ!" But some said: "And does Christ come from Galilee? Don't the scriptures say that Christ will be descended from David, and will come from Bethlehem, the village where David lived?"

So the people were in two minds about him—some of them wanted to arrest him, but so far no one laid any hands on him.

Then the officers returned to the Pharisees and chief priests, who said to them, "Why haven't you brought him?"

"No man ever spoke like that!" they replied.

"Has he pulled the wool over your eyes, too?" retorted the Pharisees. "Have any of the authorities or any of the Pharisees believed in him? But this crowd, who know nothing about the Law, is damned anyway!"

One of their number, Nicodemus (the one who had previously been to see Jesus), remarked to them, "But surely our Law does not condemn the accused without hearing what he has to say, and finding out what he has done?"

"Are you a Galilean, too?" they answered him. "Look where you will—you won't find that any prophet comes out of Galilee!"

no one is to know where he comes from.' Thereupon Jesus cried aloud as he taught in the temple, 'No doubt you know me; no doubt you know where I come from.[a] Yet I have not come of my own accord. I was sent by the One who truly is, and him you do not know. I know him because I come from him and he it is who sent me.' At this they tried to seize him, but no one laid a hand on him because his appointed hour had not yet come. Yet among the people many believed in him. 'When the Messiah comes,' they said, 'is it likely that he will perform more signs than this man?'

The Pharisees overheard these mutterings of the people about him, so the chief priests and the Pharisees sent temple police to arrest him. Then Jesus said, 'For a little longer I shall be with you; then I am going away to him who sent me. You will look for me, but you will not find me. Where I am, you cannot come.' So the Jews said to one another, 'Where does he intend to go, that we should not be able to find him? Will he go to the Dispersion among the Greeks, and teach the Greeks? What did he mean by saying, "You will look for me, but you will not find me. Where I am, you cannot come"?'[b]

On the last and greatest day of the festival Jesus stood and cried aloud, 'If anyone is thirsty let him come to me; whoever believes in me, let him drink.' As Scripture says, 'Streams of living water shall flow out from within him.'[c] He was speaking of the Spirit which believers in him would receive later; for the Spirit had not yet been given, because Jesus had not yet been glorified.

On hearing this some of the people said, 'This must certainly be the expected prophet.' Others said, 'This is the Messiah.' Others again, 'Surely the Messiah is not to come from Galilee? Does not Scripture say that the Messiah is to be of the family of David, from David's village of Bethlehem?' Thus he caused a split among the people. Some were for seizing him, but no one laid hands on him.

The temple police came back to the chief priests and Pharisees, who asked, 'Why have you not brought him?' 'No man,' they answered, 'ever spoke as this man speaks.' The Pharisees retorted, 'Have you too been misled? Is there a single one of our rulers who has believed in him, or of the Pharisees? As for this rabble, which cares nothing for the Law, a curse is on them.' Then one of their number, Nicodemus (the man who had once visited Jesus), intervened. 'Does our law', he asked them, 'permit us to pass judgement on a man unless we have first given him a hearing and learned the facts?' 'Are you a Galilean too?' they retorted. 'Study the scriptures and you will find that prophets do not come from Galilee.'[d]

---

[a] Or Do you know me? And do you know where I come from? [b] Some witnesses here insert the passage printed on p. 295. [c] Or 'If any man is thirsty let him come to me and drink. He who believes in me, as Scripture says, streams of living water shall flow out from within him.' [d] Some witnesses here insert the passage 7. 53-8. 11, which is printed on p. 295.

K.J.V.

R.S.V.

53 And every man went unto his own house.

8 Jesus went unto the mount of Olives. 2And early in the morning he came again into the temple, and all the people came unto him; and he sat down, and taught them. 3And the scribes and Pharisees brought unto him a woman taken in adultery; and when they had set her in the midst, 4 They say unto him, Master, this woman was taken in adultery, in the very act. 5 Now Moses in the law commanded us, that such should be stoned: but what sayest thou? 6 This they said, tempting him, that they might have to accuse him. But Jesus stooped down, and with *his* finger wrote on the ground, *as though he heard them not.* 7 So when they continued asking him, he lifted up himself, and said unto them, He that is without sin among you, let him first cast a stone at her. 8And again he stooped down, and wrote on the ground. 9And they which heard *it,* being convicted by *their own* conscience, went out one by one, beginning at the eldest, *even* unto the last: and Jesus was left alone, and the woman standing in the midst. 10 When Jesus had lifted up himself, and saw none but the woman, he said unto her, Woman, where are those thine accusers? hath no man condemned thee? 11 She said, No man, Lord. And Jesus said unto her, Neither do I condemn thee: go, and sin no more.
12 Then spake Jesus again unto them, saying, I am the light of the world: he that followeth me shall not walk in darkness, but shall have the light of life. 13 The Pharisees therefore said unto him, Thou bearest record of thyself; thy record is not true. 14 Jesus answered and said unto them, Though I bear record of myself, *yet* my record is true: for I know whence I came, and whither I go; but ye cannot tell whence I come, and whither I go. 15 Ye judge after the flesh; I judge no man. 16And yet if I judge, my judgment is true: for I am not alone, but I and the Father that sent me. 17 It is also written in your law, that the testimony of two men is true. 18 I am one that bear witness of myself, and the Father that sent me beareth witness of me. 19 Then said they unto him, Where is thy Father? Jesus answered, Ye neither know me, nor my Father: if ye had known me, ye should have known my Father also. 20 These words spake Jesus in the treasury, as he taught in the temple: and no man laid hands on him; for his hour was not yet come. 21 Then said Jesus again unto them, I go my way, and ye shall seek me, and shall die in your sins: whither I go, ye cannot

8 *53 They went each to his own house,* * 1 *but Jesus went to the Mount of Olives.* 2 *Early in the morning he came again to the temple; all the people came to him, and he sat down and taught them.* 3 *The scribes and the Pharisees brought a woman who had been caught in adultery, and placing her in the midst* 4 *they said to him, "Teacher, this woman has been caught in the act of adultery.* 5 *Now in the law Moses commanded us to stone such. What do you say about her?"* 6 *This they said to test him, that they might have some charge to bring against him. Jesus bent down and wrote with his finger on the ground.* 7 *And as they continued to ask him, he stood up and said to them, "Let him who is without sin among you be the first to throw a stone at her."* 8 *And once more he bent down and wrote with his finger on the ground.* 9 *But when they heard it, they went away, one by one, beginning with the eldest, and Jesus was left alone with the woman standing before him.* 10 *Jesus looked up and said to her, "Woman, where are they? Has no one condemned you?"* 11 *She said, "No one, Lord." And Jesus said, "Neither do I condemn you; go, and do not sin again."* 12Again Jesus spoke to them, saying, "I am the light of the world; he who follows me will not walk in darkness, but will have the light of life." 13 The Pharisees then said to him, "You are bearing witness to yourself; your testimony is not true." 14 Jesus answered, "Even if I do bear witness to myself, my testimony is true, for I know whence I have come and whither I am going, but you do not know whence I come or whither I am going. 15 You judge according to the flesh, I judge no one. 16 Yet even if I do judge, my judgment is true, for it is not I alone that judge, but I and he[s] who sent me. 17 In your law it is written that the testimony of two men is true; 18 I bear witness to myself, and the Father who sent me bears witness to me." 19 They said to him therefore, "Where is your Father?" Jesus answered, "You know neither me nor my Father; if you knew me, you would know my Father also." 20 These words he spoke in the treasury, as he taught in the temple; but no one arrested him, because his hour had not yet come.
21 Again he said to them, "I go away, and you will seek me and die in your sin; where I

---

* Other ancient authorities add 7.53-8.11 either here or at the end of this Gospel or after Luke 21.38, with variations of the text.

[s] Other ancient authorities read *the Father.*

So they broke up their meeting and went home, while Jesus went off to the Mount of Olives.

Jesus deflates the rigorists 8. 2

Early next morning he returned to the Temple and the entire crowd came to him. So he sat down and began to teach them. But the scribes and Pharisees brought in to him a woman who had been caught in adultery. They made her stand in front, and then said to him, "Now, master, this woman has been caught in adultery, in the very act. According to the Law, Moses commanded us to stone such women to death. Now, what do you say about her?"

They said this to test him, so that they might have some good grounds for an accusation. But Jesus stooped down and began to write with his finger in the dust on the ground. But as they persisted in their questioning, he straightened himself up and said to them, "Let the one among you who has never sinned throw the first stone at her." Then he stooped down again and continued writing with his finger on the ground. And when they heard what he said, they were convicted by their own consciences and went out, one by one, beginning with the eldest until they had all gone.

Jesus was left alone, with the woman still standing where they had put her. So he stood up and said to her, "Where are they all—did no one condemn you?"

And she said, "No one, sir."

"Neither do I condemn you," said Jesus to her. "Go home and do not sin again."

Jesus' bold claims—about 8. 12
himself—and his Father

Later, Jesus spoke to the people again and said: "I am the light of the world. The man who follows me will never walk in the dark but will live his life in the light."

This made the Pharisees say to him, "You are testifying to yourself—your evidence is not valid."

Jesus answered: "Even if I am testifying to myself, my evidence is valid, for I know where I have come from and I know where I am going. But as for you, you have no idea where I come from or where I am going. You are judging by human standards, but I am not judging anyone. Yet, if I should judge, my decision would be just, for I am not alone—the Father who sent me is with me. In your Law, it is stated that the witness of two persons is valid. I am one testifying to myself and the second witness to me is the Father who sent me."

"And where is this father of yours?" they replied.

"You do not know my Father," returned Jesus, "any more than you know me: if you had known me you would have known him."

Jesus made these statements while he was teaching in the Temple treasury. Yet no one arrested him, for his time had not yet come.

Later, Jesus spoke to them again and said: "I am going away and you will try to find me, but you will die in your sins. You cannot come where I am going."

An Incident in the Temple*

8 *And they went each to his home, and Jesus to the Mount of Olives. At daybreak he appeared again in the temple, and all the people gathered round him. He had taken his seat and was engaged in teaching them when the doctors of the law and the Pharisees brought in a woman detected in adultery. Making her stand out in the middle they said to him, 'Master, this woman was caught in the very act of adultery. In the Law Moses has laid down that such women are to be stoned. What do you say about it?' They put the question as a test, hoping to frame a charge against him. Jesus bent down and wrote with his finger on the ground. When they continued to press their question he sat up straight and said, 'That one of you who is faultless shall throw the first stone.' Then once again he bent down and wrote on the ground. When they heard what he said, one by one they went away,*ᵃ* the eldest first; and Jesus was left alone, with the woman still standing there. Jesus again sat up and *ᵇ* said to the woman, 'Where are they? Has no one condemned you?' 'No one, sir,' she said. Jesus replied, 'No more do I. You may go; do not sin again.'*

Once again Jesus addressed the people: 'I am the light of the world. No follower of mine shall wander in the dark; he shall have the light of life.' The Pharisees said to him, 'You are witness in your own cause; your testimony is not valid.' Jesus replied, 'My testimony is valid, even though I do bear witness about myself; because I know where I come from, and where I am going. You do not know either where I come from or where I am going. You judge by worldly standards. I pass judgement on no man, but if I do judge, my judgement is valid because it is not I alone who judge, but I and he who sent me. In your own law it is written that the testimony of two witnesses is valid. Here am I, a witness in my own cause, and my other witness is the Father who sent me.' They asked, 'Where is your father?' Jesus replied, 'You know neither me nor my Father; if you knew me you would know my Father as well.'

These words were spoken by Jesus in the treasury as he taught in the temple. Yet no one arrested him, because his hour had not yet come.

Again he said to them, 'I am going away. You will look for me, but you will die in your sin;

---

* This passage, which in the most widely received editions of the New Testament is printed in the text of John, 7. 53-8. 11, has no fixed place in our ancient witnesses. Some of them do not contain it at all. Some place it after Luke 21. 38, others after John 7. 36, or 7. 52, or 21. 24.

[a] Some witnesses insert convicted by their conscience. [b] Some witnesses insert seeing no one but the woman.

K.J.V.

come. 22 Then said the Jews, Will he kill himself? because he saith, Whither I go, ye cannot come. 23 And he said unto them, Ye are from beneath; I am from above: ye are of this world; I am not of this world. 24 I said therefore unto you, that ye shall die in your sins: for if ye believe not that I am *he,* ye shall die in your sins. 25 Then said they unto him, Who art thou? And Jesus saith unto them, Even *the same* that I said unto you from the beginning. 26 I have many things to say and to judge of you: but he that sent me is true; and I speak to the world those things which I have heard of him. 27 They understood not that he spake to them of the Father. 28 Then said Jesus unto them, When ye have lifted up the Son of man, then shall ye know that I am *he,* and *that* I do nothing of myself; but as my Father hath taught me, I speak these things. 29 And he that sent me is with me: the Father hath not left me alone; for I do always those things that please him. 30 As he spake these words, many believed on him. 31 Then said Jesus to those Jews which believed on him, If ye continue in my word, *then* are ye my disciples indeed; 32 And ye shall know the truth, and the truth shall make you free.

33 They answered him, We be Abraham's seed, and were never in bondage to any man: how sayest thou, Ye shall be made free? 34 Jesus answered them, Verily, verily, I say unto you, Whosoever committeth sin is the servant of sin. 35 And the servant abideth not in the house for ever: *but* the Son abideth ever. 36 If the Son therefore shall make you free, ye shall be free indeed. 37 I know that ye are Abraham's seed; but ye seek to kill me, because my word hath no place in you. 38 I speak that which I have seen with my Father: and ye do that which ye have seen with your father. 39 They answered and said unto him, Abraham is our father. Jesus saith unto them, If ye were Abraham's children, ye would do the works of Abraham. 40 But now ye seek to kill me, a man that hath told you the truth, which I have heard of God: this did not Abraham. 41 Ye do the deeds of your father. Then said they to him, We be not born of fornication; we have one Father, *even* God. 42 Jesus said unto them, If God were your Father, ye would love me: for I proceeded forth and came from God; neither came I of myself, but he sent me. 43 Why do ye not understand my speech? *even* because ye cannot hear my word. 44 Ye are of *your* father the devil, and the lusts of your father ye will do: he was a murderer from the beginning, and abode not in the truth, because there is no truth in him. When he speaketh a lie, he speaketh of his own: for he is a liar, and the father of it. 45 And because I tell *you* the truth, ye believe me not. 46 Which of you convinceth me of sin? And if I say the truth, why do ye not believe me? 47 He that is of God heareth God's words: ye therefore hear *them* not, because ye are not

R.S.V.

am going, you cannot come." 22 Then said the Jews, "Will he kill himself, since he says, 'Where I am going, you cannot come'?" 23 He said to them, "You are from below, I am from above; you are of this world, I am not of this world. 24 I told you that you would die in your sins, for you will die in your sins unless you believe that I am he." 25 They said to him, "Who are you?" Jesus said to them, "Even what I have told you from the beginning.[t] 26 I have much to say about you and much to judge; but he who sent me is true, and I declare to the world what I have heard from him." 27 They did not understand that he spoke to them of the Father. 28 So Jesus said, "When you have lifted up the Son of man, then you will know that I am he, and that I do nothing on my own authority but speak thus as the Father taught me. 29 And he who sent me is with me; he has not left me alone, for I always do what is pleasing to him." 30 As he spoke thus, many believed in him.

31 Jesus then said to the Jews who had believed in him, "If you continue in my word, you are truly my disciples, 32 and you will know the truth, and the truth will make you free." 33 They answered him, "We are descendants of Abraham, and have never been in bondage to any one. How is it that you say, 'You will be made free'?"

34 Jesus answered them, "Truly, truly, I say to you, every one who commits sin is a slave to sin. 35 The slave does not continue in the house for ever; the son continues for ever. 36 So if the Son makes you free, you will be free indeed. 37 I know that you are descendants of Abraham; yet you seek to kill me, because my word finds no place in you. 38 I speak of what I have seen with my Father, and you do what you have heard from your father."

39 They answered him, "Abraham is our father." Jesus said to them, "If you were Abraham's children, you would do what Abraham did, 40 but now you seek to kill me, a man who has told you the truth which I heard from God; this is not what Abraham did. 41 You do what your father did." They said to him, "We were not born of fornication; we have one Father, even God." 42 Jesus said to them, "If God were your Father, you would love me, for I proceeded and came forth from God; I came not of my own accord, but he sent me. 43 Why do you not understand what I say? It is because you cannot bear to hear my word. 44 You are of your father the devil, and your will is to do your father's desires. He was a murderer from the beginning, and has nothing to do with the truth, because there is no truth in him. When he lies, he speaks according to his own nature, for he is a liar and the father of lies. 45 But, because I tell the truth, you do not believe me. 46 Which of you convicts me of sin? If I tell the truth, why do you not believe me? 47 He who is of God hears the words of God; the reason why you do not hear them is that you are not of God."

---

[t] Or *Why do I talk to you at all?*

PHILLIPS

This made the Jews say: "Is he going to kill himself, then? Is *that* why he says, 'You cannot come where I am going'?"

"The difference between us," Jesus said to them, "is that you come from below and I am from above. You belong to this world but I do not. That is why I told you you will die in your sins. For unless you believe that I am who I am, you will die in your sins."

Then they said, *"Who are you?"*

"I am what I have told you I was from the beginning," replied Jesus. "There is much in you that I could speak about and condemn. But he who sent me is true, and I am only speaking to this world what I myself have heard from him."

They did not realize that he was talking to them about the Father. So Jesus resumed: "When you have lifted up the Son of Man, then you will realize that I am who I say I am, and that I do nothing on my own authority but speak simply as my Father has taught me. The one who sent me is with me now: the Father has never left me alone, for I always do what pleases him." And even while he said these words, many people believed in him.

Jesus speaks of personal freedom 8. 31

So Jesus said to the Jews who believed in him: "If you are faithful to what I have said, you are truly my disciples. And you will know the truth and the truth will set you free!"

"But we are descendants of Abraham," they replied, "and we have never in our lives been any man's slaves. How can you say to us, 'You will be set free'?"

Jesus returned: "Believe me when I tell you that every man who commits sin is a slave. For a slave is no permanent part of a household, but a son is. If the Son, then, sets you free, you are really free! I know that you are descended from Abraham, but some of you are looking for a way to kill me because you can't bear my words. I am telling you what I have seen in the presence of my Father, and you are doing what you have seen in the presence of your father."

"Our father is Abraham!" they retorted.

"If you were the children of Abraham, you would do the sort of things Abraham did. But in fact, at this moment, you are looking for a way to kill me, simply because I am a man who has told you the truth that I have heard from God. Abraham would never have done that. No, you are doing your father's work."

"We are not illegitimate!" they retorted. "We have one Father—God."

"If God were really your Father," replied Jesus, "you would have loved me. For I came from God; and I am here. I did not come of my own accord—he sent me, and I am here. Why do you not understand my words? It is because you cannot hear what I am saying. Your father is the devil, and what you are wanting to do is what your father longs to do. He always was a murderer, and has never dealt with the truth, since the truth will have nothing to do with him. Whenever he tells a lie, he speaks in character, for he is a liar and the father of lies. And it is because I speak the truth that you will not believe me. Which of you can prove me guilty of sin? If I am speaking the truth, why is it that you do not believe me? The man who is born of God can hear the words of God, and the reason why you cannot hear the words of God is simply this, that you are not the sons of God."

N.E.B.

where I am going you cannot come.' The Jews then said, 'Perhaps he will kill himself: is that what he means when he says, "Where I am going you cannot come"?' So Jesus continued, 'You belong to this world below, I to the world above. Your home is in this world, mine is not. That is why I told you that you would die in your sins. If you do not believe that I am what I am, you will die in your sins.' They asked him, 'Who are you?' Jesus answered, 'Why should I speak to you at all?[a] I have much to say about you—and in judgement. But he who sent me speaks the truth, and what I heard from him I report to the world.'

They did not understand that he was speaking to them about the Father. So Jesus said to them, 'When you have lifted up the Son of Man you will know that I am what I am. I do nothing on my own authority, but in all that I say, I have been taught by my Father. He who sent me is present with me, and has not left me alone; for I always do what is acceptable to him.' As he said this, many put their faith in him.

Turning to the Jews who had believed him, Jesus said, 'If you dwell within the revelation I have brought, you are indeed my disciples; you shall know the truth, and the truth will set you free.' They replied, 'We are Abraham's descendants; we have never been in slavery to any man. What do you mean by saying, "You will become free men"?' 'In very truth I tell you', said Jesus, 'that everyone who commits sin is a slave. The slave has no permanent standing in the household, but the son belongs to it for ever. If then the Son sets you free, you will indeed be free.

'I know that you are descended from Abraham, but you are bent on killing me because my teaching makes no headway with you. I am revealing in words what I saw in my Father's presence; and you are revealing in action what you learned from your father.' They retorted, 'Abraham is our father.' 'If you were Abraham's children', Jesus replied, 'you would do as Abraham did.[b] As it is, you are bent on killing me, a man who told you the truth, as I heard it from God. That is not how Abraham acted. You are doing your own father's work.'

They said, 'We are not base-born; God is our father, and God alone.' Jesus said, 'If God were your father, you would love me, for God is the source of my being, and from him I come. I have not come of my own accord; he sent me. Why do you not understand my language? It is because my revelation is beyond your grasp.

'Your father is the devil and you choose to carry out your father's desires. He was a murderer from the beginning, and is not rooted in the truth; there is no truth in him. When he tells a lie he is speaking his own language, for he is a liar and the father of lies. But I speak the truth and therefore you do not believe me. Which of you can prove me in the wrong?[c] If what I say is true, why do you not believe me? He who has God for his father listens to the words of God. You are not God's children; that is why you do not listen.'

[a] *Or* What I have told you all along. [b] *Some witnesses read* 'If you are Abraham's children', Jesus replied, 'do as Abraham did.' [c] *Or* Which of you convicts me of sin?

K.J.V.

of God. 48 Then answered the Jews, and said unto him, Say we not well that thou art a Samaritan, and hast a devil? 49 Jesus answered, I have not a devil; but I honour my Father, and ye do dishonour me. 50 And I seek not mine own glory: there is one that seeketh and judgeth. 51 Verily, verily, I say unto you, If a man keep my saying, he shall never see death. 52 Then said the Jews unto him, Now we know that thou hast a devil. Abraham is dead, and the prophets; and thou sayest, If a man keep my saying, he shall never taste of death. 53 Art thou greater than our father Abraham, which is dead? and the prophets are dead: whom makest thou thyself? 54 Jesus answered, If I honour myself, my honour is nothing: it is my Father that honoureth me; of whom ye say, that he is your God: 55 Yet ye have not known him; but I know him: and if I should say, I know him not, I shall be a liar like unto you: but I know him, and keep his saying. 56 Your father Abraham rejoiced to see my day: and he saw it, and was glad. 57 Then said the Jews unto him, Thou art not yet fifty years old, and hast thou seen Abraham? 58 Jesus said unto them, Verily, verily, I say unto you, Before Abraham was, I am. 59 Then took they up stones to cast at him: but Jesus hid himself, and went out of the temple, going through the midst of them, and so passed by.

R.S.V.

48 The Jews answered him, "Are we not right in saying that you are a Samaritan and have a demon?" 49 Jesus answered, "I have not a demon; but I honor my Father, and you dishonor me. 50 Yet I do not seek my own glory; there is One who seeks it and he will be the judge. 51 Truly, truly, I say to you, if any one keeps my word, he will never see death." 52 The Jews said to him, "Now we know that you have a demon. Abraham died, as did the prophets; and you say, 'If any one keeps my word, he will never taste death.' 53 Are you greater than our father Abraham, who died? And the prophets died! Who do you claim to be?" 54 Jesus answered, "If I glorify myself, my glory is nothing; it is my Father who glorifies me, of whom you say that he is your God. 55 But you have not known him; I know him. If I said, I do not know him, I should be a liar like you; but I do know him and I keep his word. 56 Your father Abraham rejoiced that he was to see my day; he saw it and was glad." 57 The Jews then said to him, "You are not yet fifty years old, and have you seen Abraham?" [u] 58 Jesus said to them, "Truly, truly, I say to you, before Abraham was, I am." 59 So they took up stones to throw at him; but Jesus hid himself, and went out of the temple.

9 And as *Jesus* passed by, he saw a man which was blind from *his* birth. 2 And his disciples asked him, saying, Master, who did sin, this man, or his parents, that he was born blind? 3 Jesus answered, Neither hath this man sinned, nor his parents: but that the works of God should be made manifest in him. 4 I must work the works of him that sent me, while it is day: the night cometh, when no man can work. 5 As long as I am in the world, I am the light of the world. 6 When he had thus spoken, he spat on the ground, and made clay of the spittle, and he anointed the eyes of the blind man with the clay, 7 And said unto him, Go, wash in the pool of Siloam, (which is by interpretation, Sent.) He went his way therefore, and washed, and came seeing.

8 The neighbours therefore, and they which before had seen him that he was blind, said, Is not this he that sat and begged? 9 Some said, This is he: others *said*, He is like him: *but* he said, I am *he*. 10 Therefore said they unto him, How were thine eyes opened? 11 He answered and said, A man that is called Jesus made clay, and anointed mine eyes, and said unto me, Go to the pool of Siloam, and wash: and I went and washed, and I received sight. 12 Then said they unto him, Where is he? He said, I know not.

13 They brought to the Pharisees him that aforetime was blind. 14 And it was the sabbath day when Jesus made the clay, and opened his eyes. 15 Then again the Pharisees also asked him how he had received his sight. He said unto them, He put clay upon mine eyes, and I washed,

9 As he passed by, he saw a man blind from his birth. 2 And his disciples asked him, "Rabbi, who sinned, this man or his parents, that he was born blind?" 3 Jesus answered, "It was not that this man sinned, or his parents, but that the works of God might be made manifest in him. 4 We must work the works of him who sent me, while it is day; night comes, when no one can work. 5 As long as I am in the world, I am the light of the world." 6 As he said this, he spat on the ground and made clay of the spittle and anointed the man's eyes with the clay, 7 saying to him, "Go, wash in the pool of Siloam" (which means Sent). So he went and washed and came back seeing. 8 The neighbors and those who had seen him before as a beggar, said, "Is not this the man who used to sit and beg?" 9 Some said, "It is he"; others said, "No, but he is like him." He said, "I am the man." 10 They said to him, "Then how were your eyes opened?" 11 He answered, "The man called Jesus made clay and anointed my eyes and said to me, 'Go to Siloam and wash'; so I went and washed and received my sight." 12 They said to him, "Where is he?" He said, "I do not know."

13 They brought to the Pharisees the man who had formerly been blind. 14 Now it was a sabbath day when Jesus made the clay and opened his eyes. 15 The Pharisees again asked him how he had received his sight. And he said to them, "He put clay on my eyes, and I washed, and I

[u] Other ancient authorities read *has Abraham seen you?*

PHILLIPS

"How right we are," retorted the Jews, "in calling you a Samaritan, and mad at that!"

"No," replied Jesus, "I am not mad. I am honoring my Father, and you are trying to dishonor me. But I am not concerned with my own glory: there is one whose concern it is, and he is the true judge. Believe me when I tell you that if anybody accepts my words, he will never see death at all."

"Now we know that you're mad," replied the Jews. "Why, Abraham died and the prophets, too, and yet you say, 'If a man accepts my words, he will never experience death!' Are you greater than our father, Abraham? He died, and so did the prophets—who are you making yourself out to be?"

"If I were trying to glorify myself," returned Jesus, "such glory would be worthless. But it is my Father who glorifies me, the very one who you say is your God—though you have never known him. But I know him, and if I said I did not know him, I should be as much a liar as you are! But I do know him and I am faithful to what he says. As for your father, Abraham, his great joy was that he would see my coming. Now he has seen it and he is overjoyed."

"Look," said the Jews to him, "you are not fifty yet—and has Abraham seen you?"

"I tell you in solemn truth," returned Jesus, "before there was an Abraham, I AM!"

At this, they picked up stones to hurl at him, but Jesus disappeared and made his way out of the Temple.

Jesus and blindness, physical　　**9. 1**
and spiritual

Later, as Jesus walked along he saw a man who had been blind from birth.

"Master, whose sin caused this man's blindness," asked the disciples, "his own or his parents'?"

"He was not born blind because of his own sin or that of his parents," returned Jesus, "but to show the power of God at work in him. We must carry on the work of him who sent me while the daylight lasts. Night is coming, when no one can work. I am the world's light as long as I am in it."

Having said this, he spat on the ground and made a sort of clay with the saliva. This he applied to the man's eyes and said, "Go and wash in the pool of Siloam." (Siloam means "one who has been sent.") So the man went off and washed and came home with his sight restored.

His neighbors and the people who had often seen him before as a beggar remarked, "Isn't this the man who used to sit and beg?"

"Yes, that's the one," said some.

Others said, "No, but he's very like him."

But he himself said, "I'm the man, all right!"

"Then how was your blindness cured?" they asked.

"The man called Jesus made some clay and smeared it on my eyes," he replied, "and then he said, 'Go to Siloam and wash.' So off I went and washed—and that's how I got my sight!"

"Where is he now?" they asked.

"I don't know," he returned.

So they brought the man who had once been blind before the Pharisees. (It should be noted that Jesus made the clay and restored his sight on a Sabbath day.) The Pharisees asked the question all over again as to how he had become able to see.

N.E.B.

The Jews answered, 'Are we not right in saying that you are a Samaritan, and that you are possessed?' 'I am not possessed,' said Jesus; 'the truth is that I am honouring my Father, but you dishonour me. I do not care about my own glory; there is one who does care, and he is judge. In very truth I tell you, if anyone obeys my teaching he shall never know what it is to die.'

The Jews said, 'Now we are certain that you are possessed. Abraham is dead; the prophets are dead; and yet you say, "If anyone obeys my teaching he shall not know what it is to die." Are you greater than our father Abraham, who is dead? The prophets are dead too. What do you claim to be?'

Jesus replied, 'If I glorify myself, that glory of mine is worthless. It is the Father who glorifies me, he of whom you say, "He is our God", though you do not know him. But I know him; if I said that I did not know him I should be a liar like you. But in truth I know him and obey his word.

'Your father Abraham was overjoyed to see my day; he saw it and was glad.' The Jews protested, 'You are not yet fifty years old. How can you have seen Abraham?' [a] Jesus said, 'In very truth I tell you, before Abraham was born, I am.'

They picked up stones to throw at him, but Jesus was not to be seen; and he left the temple. [b]

9 As he went on his way Jesus saw a man blind from his birth. His disciples put the question, 'Rabbi, who sinned, this man or his parents? Why was he born blind?' 'It is not that this man or his parents sinned,' Jesus answered; 'he was born blind that God's power might be displayed in curing him. While daylight lasts we [c] must carry on the work of him who sent me; night comes, when no one can work. While I am in the world I am the light of the world.'

With these words he spat on the ground and made a paste with the spittle; he spread it on the man's eyes, and said to him, 'Go and wash in the pool of Siloam.' (The name means 'sent'.) The man went away and washed, and when he returned he could see.

His neighbours and those who were accustomed to see him begging said, 'Is not this the man who used to sit and beg?' Others said, 'Yes, this is the man.' Others again said, 'No, but it is someone like him.' The man himself said, 'I am the man.' They asked him, 'How were your eyes opened?' He replied, 'The man called Jesus made a paste and smeared my eyes with it, and told me to go to Siloam and wash. I went and washed, and gained my sight.' 'Where is he?' they asked. He answered, 'I do not know.'

The man who had been blind was brought before the Pharisees. As it was a Sabbath day when Jesus made the paste and opened his eyes, the Pharisees now asked him by what means he had gained his sight. The man told them, 'He spread a paste on my eyes; then I washed, and now I

[a] *Some witnesses read* How can Abraham have seen you? [b] *Or the division may be made after the words* was not to be seen; *the paragraph following would then begin* Then Jesus left the temple, and as he went . . . [c] *Some witnesses read* I.

299

K.J.V.

and do see. 16 Therefore said some of the Pharisees, This man is not of God, because he keepeth not the sabbath day. Others said, How can a man that is a sinner do such miracles? And there was a division among them. 17 They say unto the blind man again, What sayest thou of him, that he hath opened thine eyes? He said, He is a prophet. 18 But the Jews did not believe concerning him, that he had been blind, and received his sight, until they called the parents of him that had received his sight. 19 And they asked them, saying, Is this your son, who ye say was born blind? how then doth he now see? 20 His parents answered them and said, We know that this is our son, and that he was born blind: 21 But by what means he now seeth, we know not; or who hath opened his eyes, we know not: he is of age; ask him: he shall speak for himself. 22 These *words* spake his parents, because they feared the Jews: for the Jews had agreed already, that if any man did confess that he was Christ, he should be put out of the synagogue. 23 Therefore said his parents, He is of age; ask him. 24 Then again called they the man that was blind, and said unto him, Give God the praise: we know that this man is a sinner. 25 He answered and said, Whether he be a sinner *or no,* I know not: one thing I know, that, whereas I was blind, now I see. 26 Then said they to him again, What did he to thee? how opened he thine eyes? 27 He answered them, I have told you already, and ye did not hear: wherefore would ye hear *it* again? will ye also be his disciples? 28 Then they reviled him, and said, Thou art his disciple; but we are Moses' disciples. 29 We know that God spake unto Moses: *as for* this *fellow,* we know not from whence he is. 30 The man answered and said unto them, Why herein is a marvellous thing, that ye know not from whence he is, and *yet* he hath opened mine eyes. 31 Now we know that God heareth not sinners: but if any man be a worshipper of God, and doeth his will, him he heareth. 32 Since the world began was it not heard that any man opened the eyes of one that was born blind. 33 If this man were not of God, he could do nothing. 34 They answered and said unto him, Thou wast altogether born in sins, and dost thou teach us? And they cast him out. 35 Jesus heard that they had cast him out; and when he had found him, he said unto him, Dost thou believe on the Son of God? 36 He answered and said, Who is he, Lord, that I might believe on him? 37 And Jesus said unto him, Thou hast both seen him, and it is he that talketh with thee. 38 And he said, Lord, I believe. And he worshipped him.

39 And Jesus said, For judgment I am come into this world, that they which see not might see; and that they which see might be made blind. 40 And *some* of the Pharisees which were with him heard these words, and said unto him, Are we blind also? 41 Jesus said unto them, If ye were blind, ye should have no sin: but now ye say, We see; therefore your sin remaineth.

R.S.V.

see." 16 Some of the Pharisees said, "This man is not from God, for he does not keep the sabbath." But others said, "How can a man who is a sinner do such signs?" There was a division among them. 17 So they again said to the blind man, "What do you say about him, since he has opened your eyes?" He said, "He is a prophet."

18 The Jews did not believe that he had been blind and had received his sight, until they called the parents of the man who had received his sight, 19 and asked them, "Is this your son, who you say was born blind? How then does he now see?" 20 His parents answered, "We know that this is our son, and that he was born blind; 21 but how he now sees we do not know, nor do we know who opened his eyes. Ask him; he is of age, he will speak for himself." 22 His parents said this because they feared the Jews, for the Jews had already agreed that if any one should confess him to be Christ, he was to be put out of the synagogue. 23 Therefore his parents said, "He is of age, ask him."

24 So for the second time they called the man who had been blind, and said to him, "Give God the praise; we know that this man is a sinner." 25 He answered, "Whether he is a sinner, I do not know; one thing I know, that though I was blind, now I see." 26 They said to him, "What did he do to you? How did he open your eyes?" 27 He answered them, "I have told you already, and you would not listen. Why do you want to hear it again? Do you too want to become his disciples?" 28 And they reviled him, saying, "You are his disciple, but we are disciples of Moses. 29 We know that God has spoken to Moses, but as for this man, we do not know where he comes from." 30 The man answered, "Why, this is a marvel! You do not know where he comes from, and yet he opened my eyes. 31 We know that God does not listen to sinners, but if any one is a worshiper of God and does his will, God listens to him. 32 Never since the world began has it been heard that any one opened the eyes of a man born blind. 33 If this man were not from God, he could do nothing." 34 They answered him, "You were born in utter sin, and would you teach us?" And they cast him out.

35 Jesus heard that they had cast him out, and having found him he said, "Do you believe in the Son of man?" [v] 36 He answered, "And who is he, sir, that I may believe in him?" 37 Jesus said to him, "You have seen him, and it is he who speaks to you." 38 He said, "Lord, I believe"; and he worshiped him. 39 Jesus said, "For judgment I came into this world, that those who do not see may see, and that those who see may become blind." 40 Some of the Pharisees near him heard this, and they said to him, "Are we also blind?" 41 Jesus said to them, "If you were blind, you would have no guilt; but now that you say, 'We see,' your guilt remains.

[v] Other ancient authorities read *the Son of God.*

PHILLIPS

"He put clay on my eyes; I washed it off; now I can see—that's all," he replied.

Some of the Pharisees commented, "This man cannot be from God since he does not observe the Sabbath."

"But how can a sinner give such wonderful signs as these?" others demurred. And they were in two minds about him. Finally, they asked the blind man again: "And what do *you* say about him? You're the one whose sight was restored."

"I believe he is a prophet," he replied.

The Jews did not really believe that the man had been blind and then had become able to see, until they had summoned his parents and asked them: "Is this your son who you say was born blind? How does it happen that he can now see?"

"We know that this is our son, and we know that he was born blind," returned his parents, "but how he can see now, or who made him able to see, we have no idea. Why don't you ask him? He is a grown-up man; he can speak for himself."

His parents said this because they were afraid of the Jews who had already agreed that anybody who admitted that Christ had done this thing should be excommunicated. It was this fear which made his parents say, "Ask him, he is a grown-up man."

So, once again they summoned the man who had been born blind and said to him: "You should give God the glory for what has happened to you. We know that this man is a sinner."

"Whether he is a sinner or not, I couldn't tell, but one thing I am sure of," the man replied, "I used to be blind; now I can see!"

"But what did he *do* to you—how did he make you see?" they continued.

"I've told you before," he replied. "Weren't you listening? Why do you want to hear it all over again? Are you wanting to be his disciples too?"

At this, they turned on him furiously.

"You're the one who is his disciple! We are disciples of Moses. We know that God spoke to Moses, but as for this man, we don't even know where he came from."

"Now here's the extraordinary thing," he retorted, "you don't know where he came from and yet he gave me the gift of sight. Everybody knows that God does not listen to sinners. It is the man who has a proper respect for God and does what God wants him to do—he's the one God listens to. Why, since the world began, nobody's ever heard of a man who was born blind being given his sight. If this man did not come from God, he couldn't do such a thing!"

"You misbegotten wretch!" they flung back at him. "Are you trying to teach *us?*" And they threw him out.

Jesus heard that they had expelled him and when he had found him, he said, "Do you believe in the Son of Man?"

"And who is he, sir?" the man replied. "Tell me, so that I can believe in him."

"You have seen him," replied Jesus. "It is the one who is talking to you now."

"Lord, I do believe," he said, and worshiped him.

Then Jesus said, "My coming into this world is itself a judgment—those who cannot see have their eyes opened and those who think they can see become blind."

Some of the Pharisees near him overheard this and said, "So we're blind, too, are we?"

"If you were blind," returned Jesus, "nobody could blame you but, as you insist 'We can see,' your guilt remains."

N.E.B.

can see.' Some of the Pharisees said, 'This fellow is no man of God; he does not keep the Sabbath.' Others said, 'How could such signs come from a sinful man?' So they took different sides.

Then they continued to question him: 'What have you to say about him? It was your eyes he opened.' He answered, 'He is a prophet.' The Jews would not believe that the man had been blind and had gained his sight, until they had summoned his parents and questioned them: 'Is this man your son? Do you say that he was born blind? How is it that he can see now?' The parents replied, 'We know that he is our son, and that he was born blind. But how it is that he can now see, or who opened his eyes, we do not know. Ask him; he is of age; he will speak for himself.' His parents gave this answer because they were afraid of the Jews; for the Jewish authorities had already agreed that anyone who acknowledged Jesus as Messiah should be banned from the synagogue. That is why the parents said, 'He is of age; ask him.'

So for the second time they summoned the man who had been blind, and said, 'Speak the truth before God. We know that this fellow is a sinner.' 'Whether or not he is a sinner, I do not know,' the man replied. 'All I know is this: once I was blind, now I can see.' 'What did he do to you?' they asked. 'How did he open your eyes?' 'I have told you already,' he retorted, 'but you took no notice. Why do you want to hear it again? Do you also want to become his disciples?' Then they became abusive. 'You are that man's disciple,' they said, 'but we are disciples of Moses. We know that God spoke to Moses, but as for this fellow, we do not know where he comes from.'

The man replied, 'What an extraordinary thing! Here is a man who has opened my eyes, yet you do not know where he comes from! It is common knowledge that God does not listen to sinners; he listens to anyone who is devout and obeys his will. To open the eyes of a man born blind—it is unheard of since time began. If that man had not come from God he could have done nothing.' 'Who are you to give us lessons,' they retorted, 'born and bred in sin as you are?' Then they expelled him from the synagogue.

Jesus heard that they had expelled him. When he found him he asked, 'Have you faith in the Son of Man[a]?' The man answered, 'Tell me who he is, sir, that I should put my faith in him.' 'You have seen him,' said Jesus; 'indeed, it is he who is speaking to you.' 'Lord, I believe', he said, and bowed before him.

Jesus said, 'It is for judgement that I have come into this world—to give sight to the sightless and to make blind those who see.' Some Pharisees in his company asked, 'Do you mean that we are blind?' 'If you were blind,' said Jesus, 'you would not be guilty, but because you say "We see", your guilt remains.'

[a] *Some witnesses read* Son of God.

K.J.V.

10 Verily, verily, I say unto you, He that entereth not by the door into the sheepfold, but climbeth up some other way, the same is a thief and a robber. 2 But he that entereth in by the door is the shepherd of the sheep. 3 To him the porter openeth; and the sheep hear his voice: and he calleth his own sheep by name, and leadeth them out. 4And when he putteth forth his own sheep, he goeth before them, and the sheep follow him: for they know his voice. 5And a stranger will they not follow, but will flee from him; for they know not the voice of strangers. 6 This parable spake Jesus unto them; but they understood not what things they were which he spake unto them. 7 Then said Jesus unto them again, Verily, verily, I say unto you, I am the door of the sheep. 8All that ever came before me are thieves and robbers: but the sheep did not hear them. 9 I am the door: by me if any man enter in, he shall be saved, and shall go in and out, and find pasture. 10 The thief cometh not, but for to steal, and to kill, and to destroy: I am come that they might have life, and that they might have *it* more abundantly. 11 I am the good shepherd: the good shepherd giveth his life for the sheep. 12 But he that is a hireling, and not the shepherd, whose own sheep are not, seeth the wolf coming, and leaveth the sheep, and fleeth; and the wolf catcheth them, and scattereth the sheep. 13 The hireling fleeth, because he is a hireling, and careth not for the sheep. 14 I am the good shepherd, and know my *sheep*, and am known of mine. 15As the Father knoweth me, even so know I the Father: and I lay down my life for the sheep. 16And other sheep I have, which are not of this fold: them also I must bring, and they shall hear my voice; and there shall be one fold, *and* one shepherd. 17 Therefore doth my Father love me, because I lay down my life, that I might take it again. 18 No man taketh it from me, but I lay it down of myself. I have power to lay it down, and I have power to take it again. This commandment have I received of my Father.

19 There was a division therefore again among the Jews for these sayings. 20And many of them said, He hath a devil, and is mad; why hear ye him? 21 Others said, These are not the words of him that hath a devil. Can a devil open the eyes of the blind?

22 And it was at Jerusalem the feast of the dedication, and it was winter. 23And Jesus walked in the temple in Solomon's porch. 24 Then came the Jews round about him, and said unto him, How long dost thou make us to doubt? If thou be the Christ, tell us plainly. 25 Jesus answered them, I told you, and ye believed not: the works that I do in my Father's name, they bear witness of me. 26But ye believe not, because ye are not of my sheep, as I said unto you. 27 My sheep hear my voice, and I know them, and they follow me: 28And I give unto them eternal life; and they shall never perish, neither shall any *man* pluck them out of my hand. 29 My

R.S.V.

10 "Truly, truly, I say to you, he who does not enter the sheepfold by the door but climbs in by another way, that man is a thief and a robber; 2 but he who enters by the door is the shepherd of the sheep. 3 To him the gatekeeper opens; the sheep hear his voice, and he calls his own sheep by name and leads them out. 4 When he has brought out all his own, he goes before them, and the sheep follow him, for they know his voice. 5 A stranger they will not follow, but they will flee from him, for they do not know the voice of strangers." 6 This figure Jesus used with them, but they did not understand what he was saying to them.

7 So Jesus again said to them, "Truly, truly, I say to you, I am the door of the sheep. 8All who came before me are thieves and robbers; but the sheep did not heed them. 9 I am the door; if any one enters by me, he will be saved, and will go in and out and find pasture. 10 The thief comes only to steal and kill and destroy; I came that they may have life, and have it abundantly. 11 I am the good shepherd. The good shepherd lays down his life for the sheep. 12 He who is a hireling and not a shepherd, whose own the sheep are not, sees the wolf coming and leaves the sheep and flees; and the wolf snatches them and scatters them. 13 He flees because he is a hireling and cares nothing for the sheep. 14 I am the good shepherd; I know my own and my own know me, 15 as the Father knows me and I know the Father; and I lay down my life for the sheep. 16And I have other sheep, that are not of this fold; I must bring them also, and they will heed my voice. So there shall be one flock, one shepherd. 17 For this reason the Father loves me, because I lay down my life, that I may take it again. 18 No one takes it from me, but I lay it down of my own accord. I have power to lay it down, and I have power to take it again; this charge I have received from my Father."

19 There was again a division among the Jews because of these words. 20 Many of them said, "He has a demon, and he is mad; why listen to him?" 21 Others said, "These are not the sayings of one who has a demon. Can a demon open the eyes of the blind?"

22 It was the feast of the Dedication at Jerusalem; 23 it was winter, and Jesus was walking in the temple, in the portico of Solomon. 24 So the Jews gathered round him and said to him, "How long will you keep us in suspense? If you are the Christ, tell us plainly." 25 Jesus answered them, "I told you, and you do not believe. The works that I do in my Father's name, they bear witness to me; 26 but you do not believe, because you do not belong to my sheep. 27 My sheep hear my voice, and I know them, and they follow me; 28 and I give them eternal life, and they shall never perish, and no one shall snatch them out of my hand. 29 My Father,

Jesus declares himself the true   **10. 1**
shepherd of men

Then Jesus said: "Believe me when I tell you that anyone who does not enter the sheepfold through the door, but climbs in by some other way, is a thief and a rogue. It is the shepherd of the flock who goes in by the door. It is to him the doorkeeper opens the door and it is his voice that the sheep recognize. He calls his own sheep by name and leads them out of the fold, and when he has driven all his own flock outside, he goes in front of them himself, and the sheep follow him because they know his voice. They will never follow a stranger—indeed, they will run away from him, for they do not recognize strange voices."

Jesus gave them this illustration, but they did not grasp the point of what he was saying to them. So Jesus said to them once more: "I do assure you that I myself am the door for the sheep. All who have gone before me are like thieves and rogues, but the sheep did not listen to them. I am the door. If a man goes in through me, he will be safe and sound; he can come in and out and find his food. The thief comes with the sole intention of stealing and killing and destroying, but I came to bring them life, and far more life than before. I am the good shepherd. The good shepherd will give his life for the sake of his sheep. But the hired man, who is not the shepherd, and does not own the sheep, will see the wolf coming, desert the sheep and run away. And the wolf will attack the flock and send them flying. The hired man runs away because he is only a hired man and has no interest in the sheep. I am the good shepherd, and I know those that are mine and my sheep know me, just as the Father knows me and I know the Father. And I am giving my life for the sake of the sheep.

"And I have other sheep who do not belong to this fold. I must lead these also, and they will hear my voice. So there will be one flock and one shepherd. This is the reason why the Father loves me—that I lay down my life, and I lay it down to take it up again! No one is taking it from me, but I lay it down of my own free will. I have the power to lay it down and I have the power to take it up again. This is an order that I have received from my Father."

Jesus plainly declares who he is   **10. 19**

Once again, the Jews were in two minds about him because of these words, many of them remarking: "The devil's in him and he's insane. Why do you listen to him?"

But others were saying, "This is not the sort of thing a devil-possessed man would say! Can a devil make a blind man see?"

Then came the dedication festival at Jerusalem. It was wintertime and Jesus was walking about inside the Temple in Solomon's cloisters. So the Jews closed in on him and said: "How much longer are you going to keep us in suspense? If you really are Christ, tell us so straight out!"

"I have told you," replied Jesus, "and you do not believe it. What I have done in my Father's name is sufficient to prove my claim, but you do not believe because you are not my sheep. My sheep recognize my voice and I know who they are. They follow me and I give them eternal life. They will never die and no one can snatch them out of my hand. My Father, who has given

10 'In truth I tell you, in very truth, the man who does not enter the sheepfold by the door, but climbs in some other way, is nothing but a thief or a robber. The man who enters by the door is the shepherd in charge of the sheep. The door-keeper admits him, and the sheep hear his voice; he calls his own sheep by name, and leads them out. When he has brought them all out, he goes ahead and the sheep follow, because they know his voice. They will not follow a stranger; they will run away from him, because they do not recognize the voice of strangers.'

This was a parable that Jesus told them, but they did not understand what he meant by it.

So Jesus spoke again: 'In truth, in very truth I tell you, I am the door of the sheepfold. The sheep paid no heed to any who came before me, for these were all thieves and robbers. I am the door; anyone who comes into the fold through me shall be safe. He shall go in and out and shall find pasturage.

'The thief comes only to steal, to kill, to destroy; I have come that men may have life, and may have it in all its fullness. I am the good shepherd; the good shepherd lays down his life for the sheep. The hireling, when he sees the wolf coming, abandons the sheep and runs away, because he is no shepherd and the sheep are not his. Then the wolf harries the flock and scatters the sheep. The man runs away because he is a hireling and cares nothing for the sheep.

'I am the good shepherd; I know my own sheep and my sheep know me—as the Father knows me and I know the Father—and I lay down my life for the sheep. But there are other sheep of mine, not belonging to this fold, whom I must bring in; and they too will listen to my voice. There will then be one flock, one shepherd. The Father loves me because I lay down my life, to receive it back again. No one has robbed me of it; I am laying it down of my own free will. I have the right to lay it down, and I have the right to receive it back again; this charge I have received from my Father.'

These words once again caused a split among the Jews. Many of them said, 'He is possessed, he is raving. Why listen to him?' Others said, 'No one possessed by an evil spirit could speak like this. Could an evil spirit open blind men's eyes?'

It was winter, and the festival of the Dedication was being held in Jerusalem. Jesus was walking in the temple precincts, in Solomon's Cloister. The Jews gathered round him and asked: 'How long must you keep us in suspense? If you are the Messiah say so plainly.' 'I have told you,' said Jesus, 'but you do not believe. My deeds done in my Father's name are my credentials, but because you are not sheep of my flock you do not believe. My own sheep listen to my voice; I know them and they follow me. I give them eternal life and they shall never perish; no one shall snatch them from my care. My Father who has given them to me is

K.J.V.

Father, which gave *them* me, is greater than all; and no *man* is able to pluck *them* out of my Father's hand. 30 I and *my* Father are one. 31 Then the Jews took up stones again to stone him. 32 Jesus answered them, Many good works have I shewed you from my Father; for which of those works do ye stone me? 33 The Jews answered him, saying, For a good work we stone thee not; but for blasphemy; and because that thou, being a man, makest thyself God. 34 Jesus answered them, Is it not written in your law, I said, Ye are gods? 35 If he called them gods, unto whom the word of God came, and the Scripture cannot be broken; 36 Say ye of him, whom the Father hath sanctified, and sent into the world, Thou blasphemest; because I said, I am the Son of God? 37 If I do not the works of my Father, believe me not. 38 But if I do, though ye believe not me, believe the works; that ye may know, and believe, that the Father *is* in me, and I in him. 39 Therefore they sought again to take him; but he escaped out of their hand, 40 And went away again beyond Jordan into the place where John at first baptized; and there he abode. 41 And many resorted unto him, and said, John did no miracle: but all things that John spake of this man were true. 42 And many believed on him there.

11 Now a certain *man* was sick, *named* Lazarus, of Bethany, the town of Mary and her sister Martha. 2 (It was *that* Mary which anointed the Lord with ointment, and wiped his feet with her hair, whose brother Lazarus was sick.) 3 Therefore his sisters sent unto him, saying, Lord, behold, he whom thou lovest is sick. 4 When Jesus heard *that*, he said, This sickness is not unto death, but for the glory of God, that the Son of God might be glorified thereby. 5 Now Jesus loved Martha, and her sister, and Lazarus. 6 When he had heard therefore that he was sick, he abode two days still in the same place where he was. 7 Then after that saith he to *his* disciples, Let us go into Judea again. 8 *His* disciples say unto him, Master, the Jews of late sought to stone thee; and goest thou thither again? 9 Jesus answered, Are there not twelve hours in the day? If any man walk in the day, he stumbleth not, because he seeth the light of this world. 10 But if a man walk in the night, he stumbleth, because there is no light in him. 11 These things said he: and after that he saith unto them, Our friend Lazarus sleepeth; but I go, that I may awake him out of sleep. 12 Then said his disciples, Lord, if he sleep, he shall do well. 13 Howbeit Jesus spake of his death: but they thought that he had spoken of taking of rest in sleep. 14 Then said Jesus unto them plainly, Lazarus is dead. 15 And I am glad for your sakes that I was not there, to the intent ye may believe; nevertheless let us go unto him. 16 Then said Thomas, which is called Didymus, unto his fellow disciples, Let us also go, that we may die

R.S.V.

who has given them to me,[w] is greater than all, and no one is able to snatch them out of the Father's hand. 30 I and the Father are one." 31 The Jews took up stones again to stone him. 32 Jesus answered them, "I have shown you many good works from the Father; for which of these do you stone me?" 33 The Jews answered him, "We stone you for no good work but for blasphemy; because you, being a man, make yourself God." 34 Jesus answered them, "Is it not written in your law, 'I said, you are gods'? 35 If he called them gods to whom the word of God came (and scripture cannot be broken), 36 do you say of him whom the Father consecrated and sent into the world, 'You are blaspheming,' because I said, 'I am the Son of God'? 37 If I am not doing the works of my Father, then do not believe me; 38 but if I do them, even though you do not believe me, believe the works, that you may know and understand that the Father is in me and I am in the Father." 39 Again they tried to arrest him, but he escaped from their hands.

40 He went away again across the Jordan to the place where John at first baptized, and there he remained. 41 And many came to him; and they said, "John did no sign, but everything that John said about this man was true." 42 And many believed in him there.

11 Now a certain man was ill, Lazarus of Bethany, the village of Mary and her sister Martha. 2 It was Mary who anointed the Lord with ointment and wiped his feet with her hair, whose brother Lazarus was ill. 3 So the sisters sent to him, saying, "Lord, he whom you love is ill." 4 But when Jesus heard it he said, "This illness is not unto death; it is for the glory of God, so that the Son of God may be glorified by means of it." 5 Now Jesus loved Martha and her sister and Lazarus. 6 So when he heard that he was ill, he stayed two days longer in the place where he was. 7 Then after this he said to the disciples, "Let us go into Judea again." 8 The disciples said to him, "Rabbi, the Jews were but now seeking to stone you, and you are going there again?" 9 Jesus answered, "Are there not twelve hours in the day? If any one walks in the day, he does not stumble, because he sees the light of this world. 10 But if any one walks in the night, he stumbles, because the light is not in him." 11 Thus he spoke, and then he said to them, "Our friend Lazarus has fallen asleep, but I go to awake him out of sleep." 12 The disciples said to him, "Lord, if he has fallen asleep, he will recover." 13 Now Jesus had spoken of his death, but they thought that he meant taking rest in sleep. 14 Then Jesus told them plainly, "Lazarus is dead; 15 and for your sake I am glad that I was not there, so that you may believe. But let us go to him." 16 Thomas, called the Twin, said to his fellow disciples, "Let us also go, that we may die with him."

[w] Other ancient authorities read *What my Father has given to me.*

PHILLIPS

them to me, is greater than all. And no one can tear anything out of the Father's hand. I and the Father are one."

Again the Jews reached for stones to stone him to death but Jesus answered them, "I have shown you many good things from the Father—for which of these do you intend to stone me?"

"We're not going to stone you for any good things," replied the Jews, "but for blasphemy: because you, who are only a man, are making yourself out to be God."

"Is it not written in your own Law," replied Jesus, " 'I have said ye are gods'? And if he called those men 'gods' to whom the word of God came (and the scripture cannot be broken), can you say to the one whom the Father has consecrated and sent into the world, 'You are blaspheming' because I said, 'I am the Son of God'? If I fail to do what my Father does, then do not believe me. But if I do, even though you have no faith in me personally, then believe in the things that I do. Then you may come to know and realize that the Father is in me and I am in the Father."

And again they tried to arrest him, but he moved out of their reach.

Then Jesus went off again across the Jordan to the place where John had first baptized and there he stayed. A great many people came to him, and said, "John never gave us any sign but all that he said about this man was true."

And in that place many believed in him.

Jesus shows his power over death 11. 1

Now there was a man by the name of Lazarus who became seriously ill. He lived in Bethany, the village where Mary and her sister Martha lived. (Lazarus was the brother of the Mary who poured perfume upon the Lord and wiped his feet with her hair.) So the sisters sent word to Jesus: "Lord, your friend is very ill."

When Jesus received the message, he said, "This illness is not meant to end in death; it is going to bring glory to God—for it will show the glory of the Son of God."

Now Jesus loved Martha and her sister and Lazarus. So when he heard of Lazarus' illness he stayed where he was two days longer. Only then did he say to the disciples, "Let us go back into Judaea."

"Master!" returned the disciples, "only a few days ago, the Jews were trying to stone you to death—are you going there again?"

"There are twelve hours of daylight every day, are there not?" replied Jesus. "If a man walks in the daytime, he does not stumble, for he has the daylight to see by. But if he walks at night he stumbles, because he cannot see where he is going."

Jesus spoke these words; then after a pause he said to them, "Our friend Lazarus has fallen asleep, but I am going to wake him up."

At this, his disciples said, "Lord, if he has fallen asleep, he will be all right."

Actually Jesus had spoken about his death, but they thought that he was speaking of falling into natural sleep. This made Jesus tell them quite plainly: "Lazarus has died, and I am glad that I was not there—for your sakes, that you may learn to believe. And now, let us go to him."

Thomas (known as the twin) then said to his fellow disciples, "Come on, then, let us all go and die with him!"

N.E.B.

greater than all, and no one can snatch them[a] out of the Father's care. My Father and I are one.'

Once again the Jews picked up stones to stone him. At this Jesus said to them, 'I have set before you many good deeds, done by my Father's power; for which of these would you stone me?' The Jews replied, 'We are not going to stone you for any good deed, but for your blasphemy. You, a mere man, claim to be a god.' Jesus answered, 'Is it not written in your own Law, "I said: You are gods"? Those are called gods to whom the word of God was delivered—and Scripture cannot be set aside. Then why do you charge me with blasphemy because I, consecrated and sent into the world by the Father, said, "I am God's son"?

'If I am not acting as my Father would, do not believe me. But if I am, accept the evidence of my deeds, even if you do not believe me, so that you may recognize and know that the Father is in me, and I in the Father.'

This provoked them to one more attempt to seize him. But he escaped from their clutches.

Victory over Death

Jesus withdrew again across the Jordan, to the place where John had been baptizing earlier. There he stayed, while crowds came to him. They said, 'John gave us no miraculous sign, but all that he said about this man was true.' Many came to believe in him there.

11 There was a man named Lazarus who had fallen ill. His home was at Bethany, the village of Mary and her sister Martha. (This Mary, whose brother Lazarus had fallen ill, was the woman who anointed the Lord with ointment and wiped his feet with her hair.) The sisters sent a message to him: 'Sir, you should know that your friend lies ill.' When Jesus heard this he said, 'This sickness will not end in death; it has come for the glory of God, to bring glory to the Son of God.' And therefore, though he loved Martha and her sister and Lazarus, after hearing of his illness Jesus waited for two days in the place where he was.

After this, he said to his disciples, 'Let us go back to Judaea.' 'Rabbi,' his disciples said, 'it is not long since the Jews there were wanting to stone you. Are you going there again?' Jesus replied, 'Are there not twelve hours of daylight? Anyone can walk in day-time without stumbling, because he sees the light of this world. But if he walks after nightfall he stumbles, because the light fails him.'

After saying this he added, 'Our friend Lazarus has fallen asleep, but I shall go and wake him.' The disciples said, 'Master, if he has fallen asleep he will recover.' Jesus, however, had been speaking of his death, but they thought that he meant natural sleep. Then Jesus spoke out plainly: 'Lazarus is dead. I am glad not to have been there; it will be for your good and for the good of your faith. But let us go to him.' Thomas, called 'the Twin', said to his fellow-disciples, 'Let us also go, that we may die with him.'

[a] *Some witnesses read* My Father is greater than all, and that which he has given me no one can snatch . . . ; *others read* That which my Father has given me is greater than all, and no one can snatch it . . .

K.J.V.

with him. 17 Then when Jesus came, he found that he had *lain* in the grave four days already. 18 Now Bethany was nigh unto Jerusalem, about fifteen furlongs off: 19And many of the Jews came to Martha and Mary, to comfort them concerning their brother. 20 Then Martha, as soon as she heard that Jesus was coming, went and met him: but Mary sat *still* in the house. 21 Then said Martha unto Jesus, Lord, if thou hadst been here, my brother had not died. 22 But I know, that even now, whatsoever thou wilt ask of God, God will give *it* thee. 23 Jesus saith unto her, Thy brother shall rise again. 24 Martha saith unto him, I know that he shall rise again in the resurrection at the last day. 25 Jesus said unto her, I am the resurrection, and the life: he that believeth in me, though he were dead, yet shall he live: 26And whosoever liveth and believeth in me shall never die. Believest thou this? 27 She saith unto him, Yea, Lord: I believe that thou art the Christ, the Son of God, which should come into the world. 28And when she had so said, she went her way, and called Mary her sister secretly, saying, The Master is come, and calleth for thee. 29As soon as she heard *that,* she arose quickly, and came unto him. 30 Now Jesus was not yet come into the town, but was in that place where Martha met him. 31 The Jews then which were with her in the house, and comforted her, when they saw Mary, that she rose up hastily and went out, followed her, saying, She goeth unto the grave to weep there. 32 Then when Mary was come where Jesus was, and saw him, she fell down at his feet, saying unto him, Lord, if thou hadst been here, my brother had not died. 33 When Jesus therefore saw her weeping, and the Jews also weeping which came with her, he groaned in the spirit, and was troubled, 34And said, Where have ye laid him? They say unto him, Lord, come and see. 35 Jesus wept. 36 Then said the Jews, Behold how he loved him! 37And some of them said, Could not this man, which opened the eyes of the blind, have caused that even this man should not have died? 38 Jesus therefore again groaning in himself cometh to the grave. It was a cave, and a stone lay upon it. 39 Jesus said, Take ye away the stone. Martha, the sister of him that was dead, saith unto him, Lord, by this time he stinketh: for he hath been *dead* four days. 40 Jesus saith unto her, Said I not unto thee, that, if thou wouldest believe, thou shouldest see the glory of God? 41 Then they took away the stone *from the place* where the dead was laid. And Jesus lifted up *his* eyes, and said, Father, I thank thee that thou hast heard me. 42And I knew that thou hearest me always: but because of the people which stand by I said *it,* that they may believe that thou hast sent me. 43And when he thus had spoken, he cried with a loud voice, Lazarus, come forth. 44And he that was dead came forth, bound hand and foot with graveclothes; and his face was bound about with a napkin. Jesus saith unto them, Loose him, and

R.S.V.

17 Now when Jesus came, he found that Lazarus[x] had already been in the tomb four days. 18 Bethany was near Jerusalem, about two miles[y] off, 19 and many of the Jews had come to Martha and Mary to console them concerning their brother. 20 When Martha heard that Jesus was coming, she went and met him, while Mary sat in the house. 21 Martha said to Jesus, "Lord, if you had been here, my brother would not have died. 22And even now I know that whatever you ask from God, God will give you." 23 Jesus said to her, "Your brother will rise again." 24 Martha said to him, "I know that he will rise again in the resurrection at the last day." 25 Jesus said to her, "I am the resurrection and the life;[z] he who believes in me, though he die, yet shall he live, 26 and whoever lives and believes in me shall never die. Do you believe this?" 27 She said to him, "Yes, Lord; I believe that you are the Christ, the Son of God, he who is coming into the world."

28 When she had said this, she went and called her sister Mary, saying quietly, "The Teacher is here and is calling for you." 29And when she heard it, she rose quickly and went to him. 30 Now Jesus had not yet come to the village, but was still in the place where Martha had met him. 31 When the Jews who were with her in the house, consoling her, saw Mary rise quickly and go out, they followed her, supposing that she was going to the tomb to weep there. 32 Then Mary, when she came where Jesus was and saw him, fell at his feet, saying to him, "Lord, if you had been here, my brother would not have died." 33 When Jesus saw her weeping, and the Jews who came with her also weeping, he was deeply moved in spirit and troubled; 34 and he said, "Where have you laid him?" They said to him, "Lord, come and see." 35 Jesus wept. 36 So the Jews said, "See how he loved him!" 37 But some of them said, "Could not he who opened the eyes of the blind man have kept this man from dying?"

38 Then Jesus, deeply moved again, came to the tomb; it was a cave, and a stone lay upon it. 39 Jesus said, "Take away the stone." Martha, the sister of the dead man, said to him, "Lord, by this time there will be an odor, for he has been dead four days." 40 Jesus said to her, "Did I not tell you that if you would believe you would see the glory of God?" 41 So they took away the stone. And Jesus lifted up his eyes and said, "Father, I thank thee that thou hast heard me. 42 I knew that thou hearest me always, but I have said this on account of the people standing by, that they may believe that thou didst send me." 43 When he had said this, he cried with a loud voice, "Lazarus, come out." 44 The dead man came out, his hands and feet bound with bandages, and his face wrapped with a cloth. Jesus said to them, "Unbind him, and let him go."

PHILLIPS

When Jesus arrived, he found that Lazarus had already been in the grave four days. Now Bethany is quite near Jerusalem, rather less than two miles away, and a good many of the Jews had come out to see Martha and Mary to offer them sympathy over their brother's death. When Martha heard that Jesus was on his way, she went out and met him, while Mary stayed in the house.

"If only you had been here, Lord," said Martha, "my brother would never have died. And I know that, even now, God will give you whatever you ask from him."

"Your brother will rise again," Jesus replied to her.

"I know," said Martha, "that he will rise again in the resurrection at the last day."

"I myself am the resurrection and the life," Jesus told her. "The man who believes in me will live even though he dies, and anyone who is alive and believes in me will never die at all. Can you believe that?"

"Yes, Lord," replied Martha. "I do believe that you are Christ, the Son of God, the one who was to come into the world." Saying this she went away and called Mary her sister, whispering, "The master's here and is asking for you." When Mary heard this she sprang to her feet and went to him. Now Jesus had not yet arrived at the village itself, but was still where Martha had met him. So when the Jews who had been condoling with Mary in the house saw her get up quickly and go out, they followed her, imagining that she was going to the grave to weep there.

When Mary met Jesus, she looked at him and then fell down at his feet. "If only you had been here, Lord," she said, "my brother would never have died."

When Jesus saw Mary weep and noticed the tears of the Jews who came with her, he was deeply moved and visibly distressed.

"Where have you put him?" he asked.

"Lord, come and see," they replied, and at this Jesus himself wept.

"Look how much he loved him!" remarked the Jews, though some of them asked, "Could he not have kept this man from dying if he could open that blind man's eyes?"

Jesus was again deeply moved at these words, and went on to the grave. It was a cave, and a stone lay in front of it.

"Take away the stone," said Jesus.

"But, Lord," said Martha, the dead man's sister, "he has been dead four days. By this time he will be decaying. . . ."

"Did I not tell you," replied Jesus, "that if you believed, you would see the wonder of what God can do?"

Then they took the stone away, and Jesus raised his eyes and said, "Father, I thank you that you have heard me. I know that you always hear me, but I have said this for the sake of these people standing here so that they may believe that you have sent me."

And when he had said this, he called out in a loud voice, "Lazarus, come out!"

And the dead man came out, his hands and feet bound with graveclothes and his face muffled with a handkerchief.

"Now unbind him," Jesus told them, "and let him go home."

N.E.B.

On his arrival Jesus found that Lazarus had already been four days in the tomb. Bethany was just under two miles from Jerusalem, and many of the people had come from the city to Martha and Mary to condole with them on their brother's death. As soon as she heard that Jesus was on his way, Martha went to meet him, while Mary stayed at home.

Martha said to Jesus, 'If you had been here, sir, my brother would not have died. Even now I know that whatever you ask of God, God will grant you.' Jesus said, 'Your brother will rise again.' 'I know that he will rise again', said Martha, 'at the resurrection on the last day.' Jesus said, 'I am the resurrection and I am life.[a] If a man has faith in me, even though he die, he shall come to life; and no one who is alive and has faith shall ever die. Do you believe this?' 'Lord, I do,' she answered; 'I now believe that you are the Messiah, the Son of God who was to come into the world.'

With these words she went to call her sister Mary, and taking her aside, she said, 'The Master is here; he is asking for you.' When Mary heard this she rose up quickly and went to him. Jesus had not yet reached the village, but was still at the place where Martha left him. The Jews who were in the house condoling with Mary, when they saw her start up and leave the house, went after her, for they supposed that she was going to the tomb to weep there.

So Mary came to the place where Jesus was. As soon as she caught sight of him she fell at his feet and said, 'O sir, if you had only been here my brother would not have died.' When Jesus saw her weeping and the Jews her companions weeping, he sighed heavily and was deeply moved. 'Where have you laid him?' he asked. They replied, 'Come and see, sir.' Jesus wept. The Jews said, 'How dearly he must have loved him!' But some of them said, 'Could not this man, who opened the blind man's eyes, have done something to keep Lazarus from dying?'

Jesus again sighed deeply; then he went over to the tomb. It was a cave, with a stone placed against it. Jesus said, 'Take away the stone.' Martha, the dead man's sister, said to him, 'Sir, by now there will be a stench; he has been there four days.' Jesus said, 'Did I not tell you that if you have faith you will see the glory of God?' So they removed the stone.

Then Jesus looked upwards and said, 'Father, I thank thee: thou hast heard me. I knew already that thou always hearest me, but I spoke for the sake of the people standing round, that they might believe that thou didst send me.'

Then he raised his voice in a great cry: 'Lazarus, come forth.' The dead man came out, his hands and feet swathed in linen bands, his face wrapped in a cloth. Jesus said, 'Loose him; let him go.'

[a] *Some witnesses omit* and I am life.

K.J.V.

let him go. 45 Then many of the Jews which came to Mary, and had seen the things which Jesus did, believed on him. 46 But some of them went their ways to the Pharisees, and told them what things Jesus had done.

47 Then gathered the chief priests and the Pharisees a council, and said, What do we? for this man doeth many miracles. 48 If we let him thus alone, all *men* will believe on him; and the Romans shall come and take away both our place and nation. 49And one of them, *named* Caiaphas, being the high priest that same year, said unto them, Ye know nothing at all, 50 Nor consider that it is expedient for us, that one man should die for the people, and that the whole nation perish not. 51And this spake he not of himself: but being high priest that year, he prophesied that Jesus should die for that nation; 52And not for that nation only, but that also he should gather together in one the children of God that were scattered abroad. 53 Then from that day forth they took counsel together for to put him to death. 54 Jesus therefore walked no more openly among the Jews; but went thence unto a country near to the wilderness, into a city called Ephraim, and there continued with his disciples.

55 And the Jews' passover was nigh at hand: and many went out of the country up to Jerusalem before the passover, to purify themselves. 56 Then sought they for Jesus, and spake among themselves, as they stood in the temple, What think ye, that he will not come to the feast? 57 Now both the chief priests and the Pharisees had given a commandment, that, if any man knew where he were, he should shew *it*, that they might take him.

12 Then Jesus six days before the passover came to Bethany, where Lazarus was which had been dead, whom he raised from the dead. 2 There they made him a supper; and Martha served: but Lazarus was one of them that sat at the table with him. 3 Then took Mary a pound of ointment of spikenard, very costly, and anointed the feet of Jesus, and wiped his feet with her hair: and the house was filled with the odour of the ointment. 4 Then saith one of his disciples, Judas Iscariot, Simon's *son*, which should betray him, 5 Why was not this ointment sold for three hundred pence, and given to the poor? 6 This he said, not that he cared for the poor; but because he was a thief, and had the bag, and bare what was put therein. 7 Then said Jesus, Let her alone: against the day of my burying hath she kept this. 8 For the poor always ye have with you; but me ye have not always. 9 Much people of the Jews therefore knew that he was there: and they came not for Jesus' sake only, but that they might see Lazarus also, whom he had raised from the dead.

10 But the chief priests consulted that they

R.S.V.

45 Many of the Jews therefore, who had come with Mary and had seen what he did, believed in him; 46 but some of them went to the Pharisees and told them what Jesus had done. 47 So the chief priests and the Pharisees gathered the council, and said, "What are we to do? For this man performs many signs. 48 If we let him go on thus, every one will believe in him, and the Romans will come and destroy both our holy place[a] and our nation." 49 But one of them, Caiaphas, who was high priest that year, said to them, "You know nothing at all; 50 you do not understand that it is expedient for you that one man should die for the people, and that the whole nation should not perish." 51 He did not say this of his own accord, but being high priest that year he prophesied that Jesus should die for the nation, 52 and not for the nation only, but to gather into one the children of God who are scattered abroad. 53 So from that day on they took counsel how to put him to death.

54 Jesus therefore no longer went about openly among the Jews, but went from there to the country near the wilderness, to a town called Ephraim; and there he stayed with the disciples.

55 Now the Passover of the Jews was at hand, and many went up from the country to Jerusalem before the Passover, to purify themselves. 56 They were looking for Jesus and saying to one another as they stood in the temple, "What do you think? That he will not come to the feast?" 57 Now the chief priests and the Pharisees had given orders that if any one knew where he was, he should let them know, so that they might arrest him.

12 Six days before the Passover, Jesus came to Bethany, where Lazarus was, whom Jesus had raised from the dead. 2 There they made him a supper; Martha served, and Lazarus was one of those at table with him. 3 Mary took a pound of costly ointment of pure nard and anointed the feet of Jesus and wiped his feet with her hair; and the house was filled with the fragrance of the ointment. 4 But Judas Iscariot, one of his disciples (he who was to betray him), said, 5 "Why was this ointment not sold for three hundred denarii[b] and given to the poor?" 6 This he said, not that he cared for the poor but because he was a thief, and as he had the money box he used to take what was put into it. 7 Jesus said, "Let her alone, let her keep it for the day of my burial. 8 The poor you always have with you, but you do not always have me."

9 When the great crowd of the Jews learned that he was there, they came, not only on account of Jesus but also to see Lazarus, whom he had raised from the dead. 10 So the chief priests planned to put Lazarus also to death,

[a] Greek *our place*. [b] The denarius was worth about twenty cents.

PHILLIPS	N.E.B.

Jesus' miracle leads to deadly   **11. 45**
hostility

After this many of the Jews who had accompanied Mary and observed what Jesus did believed in him. But some of them went off to the Pharisees and told them what Jesus had done. Consequently, the Pharisees and chief priests summoned the council and said: "What can we do? This man obviously shows many remarkable signs. If we let him go on doing this sort of thing we shall have everybody believing in him. Then we shall have the Romans coming and that will be the end of our holy place and our very existence as a nation!"

But one of them, Caiaphas, who was High Priest that year, addressed the meeting: "You plainly don't understand what is involved here. You do not realize that it would be a good thing for us if one man should die for the sake of the people—instead of the whole nation being destroyed." (He did not make this remark on his own initiative but, since he was High Priest that year, he was in fact inspired to say that Jesus was going to die for the nation's sake—and in fact not for that nation only, but to bring together into one family all the children of God scattered throughout the world.) From that day, then, they planned to kill him. As a consequence Jesus made no further public appearance among the Jews but went away to the countryside on the edge of the desert, and stayed with his disciples in a town called Ephraim. The Jewish Passover was approaching, and many people went up from the country to Jerusalem before the actual Passover, to go through a ceremonial cleansing. They were looking for Jesus there and kept saying to one another as they stood in the Temple, "What do you think? Surely he won't come to the festival?"

It should be understood that the chief priests and the Pharisees had issued an order that anyone who knew of Jesus' whereabouts should tell them, so that they could arrest him.

An act of love as the end   **12. 1**
approaches

Six days before the Passover, Jesus came to Bethany, the village of Lazarus whom he had raised from the dead. They gave a supper for him there, and Martha waited on the party while Lazarus took his place at table with Jesus. Then Mary took a whole pound of very expensive perfume and anointed Jesus' feet and then wiped them with her hair. The entire house was filled with the fragrance of the perfume. But one of his disciples, Judas Iscariot (the man who was going to betray Jesus), burst out: "Why on earth wasn't this perfume sold? It's worth thirty dollars, which could have been given to the poor!"

He said this, not because he cared about the poor, but because he was dishonest, and when he was in charge of the purse used to help himself from the contents.

But Jesus replied to this outburst: "Let her alone, let her keep this for the day of my burial. You have the poor with you always—you will not always have me!"

The large crowd of Jews discovered that he was there and came to the scene—not only because of Jesus but to catch sight of Lazarus, the man whom he had raised from the dead. Then the chief priests planned to kill Lazarus as well,

Now many of the Jews who had come to visit Mary and had seen what Jesus did, put their faith in him. But some of them went off to the Pharisees and reported what he had done. Thereupon the chief priests and the Pharisees convened a meeting of the Council. 'What action are we taking?' they said. 'This man is performing many signs. If we leave him alone like this the whole populace will believe in him. Then the Romans will come and sweep away our temple and our nation.' But one of them, Caiaphas, who was High Priest that year, said, 'You know nothing whatever; you do not use your judgement; it is more to your interest that one man should die for the people, than that the whole nation should be destroyed.' He did not say this of his own accord, but as the High Priest in office that year, he was prophesying that Jesus would die for the nation—die not for the nation alone but to gather together the scattered children of God. So from that day on they plotted his death.

Accordingly Jesus no longer went about publicly in Judaea, but left that region for the country bordering on the desert, and came to a town called Ephraim, where he stayed with his disciples.

The Jewish Passover was now at hand, and many people went up from the country to Jerusalem to purify themselves before the festival. They looked out for Jesus, and as they stood in the temple they asked one another, 'What do you think? Perhaps he is not coming to the festival.' Now the chief priests and the Pharisees had given orders that anyone who knew where he was should give information, so that they might arrest him.

12 Six days before the Passover festival Jesus came to Bethany, where Lazarus lived whom he had raised from the dead. There a supper was given in his honour, at which Martha served, and Lazarus sat among the guests with Jesus. Then Mary brought a pound of very costly perfume, oil of pure nard, and anointed the feet of Jesus and wiped them with her hair, till the house was filled with the fragrance. At this, Judas Iscariot, a disciple of his—the one who was to betray him—said, 'Why was this perfume not sold for thirty pounds[a] and given to the poor?' He said this, not out of any care for the poor, but because he was a thief; he used to pilfer the money put into the common purse, which was in his charge. 'Leave her alone', said Jesus. 'Let her keep it till the day when she prepares for my burial; for you have the poor among you always, but you will not always have me.'[b]

A great number of the Jews heard that he was there, and came not only to see Jesus but also Lazarus whom he had raised from the dead. The chief priests then resolved to do away with

[a] *Literally* for 300 denarii. [b] *Some witnesses omit* for you have . . . have me.

K.J.V.

might put Lazarus also to death; 11 Because that by reason of him many of the Jews went away, and believed on Jesus.

12 On the next day much people that were come to the feast, when they heard that Jesus was coming to Jerusalem, 13 Took branches of palm trees, and went forth to meet him, and cried, Hosanna: blessed *is* the King of Israel that cometh in the name of the Lord. 14And Jesus, when he had found a young ass, sat thereon; as it is written, 15 Fear not, daughter of Sion: behold, thy King cometh, sitting on an ass's colt. 16 These things understood not his disciples at the first: but when Jesus was glorified, then remembered they that these things were written of him, and *that* they had done these things unto him. 17 The people therefore that was with him when he called Lazarus out of his grave, and raised him from the dead, bare record. 18 For this cause the people also met him, for that they heard that he had done this miracle. 19 The Pharisees therefore said among themselves, Perceive ye how ye prevail nothing? behold, the world is gone after him.

20 And there were certain Greeks among them that came up to worship at the feast: 21 The same came therefore to Philip, which was of Bethsaida of Galilee, and desired him, saying, Sir, we would see Jesus. 22 Philip cometh and telleth Andrew: and again Andrew and Philip tell Jesus.

23 And Jesus answered them, saying, The hour is come, that the Son of man should be glorified. 24 Verily, verily, I say unto you, Except a corn of wheat fall into the ground and die, it abideth alone: but if it die, it bringeth forth much fruit. 25 He that loveth his life shall lose it; and he that hateth his life in this world shall keep it unto life eternal. 26 If any man serve me, let him follow me; and where I am, there shall also my servant be: if any man serve me, him will *my* Father honour. 27 Now is my soul troubled; and what shall I say? Father, save me from this hour: but for this cause came I unto this hour. 28 Father, glorify thy name. Then came there a voice from heaven, *saying,* I have both glorified *it,* and will glorify *it* again. 29 The people therefore that stood by, and heard *it,* said that it thundered: others said, An angel spake to him. 30 Jesus answered and said, This voice came not because of me, but for your sakes. 31 Now is the judgment of this world: now shall the prince of this world be cast out. 32And I, if I be lifted up from the earth, will draw all *men* unto me. 33 This he said, *signifying* what death he should die. 34 The people answered him, We have heard out of the law that Christ abideth for ever: and how sayest thou, The Son of man must be lifted up? who is this Son of man? 35 Then Jesus said unto them, Yet a little while is the light with you. Walk while ye have the light, lest darkness come upon you:

R.S.V.

11 because on account of him many of the Jews were going away and believing in Jesus.

12 The next day a great crowd who had come to the feast heard that Jesus was coming to Jerusalem. 13 So they took branches of palm trees and went out to meet him, crying, "Hosanna! Blessed is he who comes in the name of the Lord, even the King of Israel!" 14And Jesus found a young ass and sat upon it; as it is written,

15 "Fear not, daughter of Zion;
behold, your king is coming,
sitting on an ass's colt!"

16 His disciples did not understand this at first; but when Jesus was glorified, then they remembered that this had been written of him and had been done to him. 17 The crowd that had been with him when he called Lazarus out of the tomb and raised him from the dead bore witness. 18 The reason why the crowd went to meet him was that they heard he had done this sign. 19 The Pharisees then said to one another, "You see that you can do nothing; look, the world has gone after him."

20 Now among those who went up to worship at the feast were some Greeks. 21 So these came to Philip, who was from Bethsaida in Galilee, and said to him, "Sir, we wish to see Jesus." 22 Philip went and told Andrew; Andrew went with Philip and they told Jesus. 23And Jesus answered them, "The hour has come for the Son of man to be glorified. 24 Truly, truly, I say to you, unless a grain of wheat falls into the earth and dies, it remains alone; but if it dies, it bears much fruit. 25 He who loves his life loses it, and he who hates his life in this world will keep it for eternal life. 26 If any one serves me, he must follow me; and where I am, there shall my servant be also; if any one serves me, the Father will honor him.

27 "Now is my soul troubled. And what shall I say? 'Father, save me from this hour'? No, for this purpose I have come to this hour. 28 Father, glorify thy name." Then a voice came from heaven, "I have glorified it, and I will glorify it again." 29 The crowd standing by heard it and said that it had thundered. Others said, "An angel has spoken to him." 30 Jesus answered, "This voice has come for your sake, not for mine. 31 Now is the judgment of this world, now shall the ruler of this world be cast out; 32 and I, when I am lifted up from the earth, will draw all men to myself." 33 He said this to show by what death he was to die. 34 The crowd answered him, "We have heard from the law that the Christ remains for ever. How can you say that the Son of man must be lifted up? Who is this Son of man?" 35 Jesus said to them, "The light is with you for a little longer. Walk while you have the light, lest the darkness overtake you; he who walks

PHILLIPS

because he was the reason for many of the Jews' going away and putting their faith in Jesus.

Jesus experiences a   **12. 12**
temporary triumph

The next day, the great crowd who had come to the festival heard that Jesus was coming into Jerusalem, and went out to meet him with palm branches in their hands, shouting, "God save him! God bless the man who comes in the name of the Lord, God bless the king of Israel!"

For Jesus had found a young ass and was seated upon it, just as the scripture foretold—

Fear not, daughter of Zion: behold, thy king cometh, sitting on an ass's colt.

(The disciples did not realize the significance of what was happening at the time, but when Jesus was glorified, then they recollected that these things had been written about him and that they had carried them out for him.)

The people who had been with him, when he had summoned Lazarus from the grave and raised him from the dead, were continually talking about him. This accounts for the crowd who went out to meet him, for they had heard that he had given this sign. Seeing all this, the Pharisees remarked to one another, "You see? —There's nothing one can do! The whole world is running after him."

Among those who had come up to worship at the festival were some Greeks. They approached Philip (whose home town was Bethsaida in Galilee) with the request, "Sir, we want to see Jesus."

Philip went and told Andrew, and Andrew went with Philip and told Jesus.

Jesus told them: "The time has come for the Son of Man to be glorified. I tell you truly that unless a grain of wheat falls into the earth and dies, it remains a single grain of wheat; but if it dies, it brings a good harvest. The man who loves his own life will destroy it, and the man who hates his life in this world will preserve it for eternal life. If a man wants to enter my service, he must follow my way; and where I am, my servant will also be. And my Father will honor every man who enters my service.

"Now comes my hour of heartbreak, and what can I say, 'Father, save me from this hour'? No, it was for this very purpose that I came to this hour. 'Father, honor your own name!' "

At this there came a voice from Heaven, "I have honored it and I will honor it again!"

When the crowd of bystanders heard this, they said it thundered, but some of them said, "An angel spoke to him."

Then Jesus said: "That voice came for your sake, not for mine. Now is the time for the judgment of this world to begin, and now will the spirit that rules this world be driven out. As for me, if I am lifted up from the earth, I will draw all men to myself." (He said this to show the kind of death he was going to die.)

Then the crowd said: "We have heard from the Law that Christ lives for ever. How can you say that the Son of Man must be 'lifted up'? Who is this Son of Man?"

At this, Jesus said to them: "You have the light with you only a little while longer. Go on while the light is good, before the darkness comes down upon you. For the man who walks

N.E.B.

Lazarus as well, since on his account many Jews were going over to Jesus and putting their faith in him.

The next day the great body of pilgrims who had come to the festival, hearing that Jesus was on the way to Jerusalem, took palm branches and went out to meet him, shouting, 'Hosanna! Blessings on him who comes in the name of the Lord! God bless the king of Israel!' Jesus found a donkey and mounted it, in accordance with the text of Scripture: 'Fear no more, daughter of Zion; see, your king is coming, mounted on an ass's colt.'

At the time his disciples did not understand this, but after Jesus had been glorified they remembered that this had been written about him, and that this had happened to him. The people who were present when he called Lazarus out of the tomb and raised him from the dead told what they had seen and heard. That is why the crowd went to meet him; they had heard of this sign that he had performed. The Pharisees said to one another, 'You see you are doing no good at all; why, all the world has gone after him.'

Among those who went up to worship at the festival were some Greeks. They came to Philip, who was from Bethsaida in Galilee, and said to him, 'Sir, we should like to see Jesus.' So Philip went and told Andrew, and the two of them went to tell Jesus. Then Jesus replied: 'The hour has come for the Son of Man to be glorified. In truth, in very truth I tell you, a grain of wheat remains a solitary grain unless it falls into the ground and dies; but if it dies, it bears a rich harvest. The man who loves himself is lost, but he who hates himself in this world will be kept safe for eternal life. If anyone serves me, he must follow me; where I am, my servant will be. Whoever serves me will be honoured by my Father.

'Now my soul is in turmoil, and what am I to say? Father, save me from this hour.[a] No, it was for this that I came to this hour. Father, glorify thy name.' A voice sounded from heaven: 'I have glorified it, and I will glorify it again.' The crowd standing by said it was thunder, while others said, 'An angel has spoken to him.' Jesus replied, 'This voice spoke for your sake, not mine. Now is the hour of judgement for this world; now shall the Prince of this world be driven out. And I shall draw all men to myself, when I am lifted up from the earth.' This he said to indicate the kind of death he was to die.

The people answered, 'Our Law teaches us that the Messiah continues for ever. What do you mean by saying that the Son of Man must be lifted up? What Son of Man is this?' Jesus answered them: 'The light is among you still, but not for long. Go on your way while you have the light, so that darkness may not overtake you. He who journeys in the dark does not know

[a] *Or* . . . turmoil. Shall I say, "Father, save me from this hour"?

K.J.V.

for he that walketh in darkness knoweth not whither he goeth. 36 While ye have light, believe in the light, that ye may be the children of light. These things spake Jesus, and departed, and did hide himself from them.

37 But though he had done so many miracles before them, yet they believed not on him: 38 That the saying of Esaias the prophet might be fulfilled, which he spake, Lord, who hath believed our report? and to whom hath the arm of the Lord been revealed? 39 Therefore they could not believe, because that Esaias said again, 40 He hath blinded their eyes, and hardened their heart; that they should not see with *their* eyes, nor understand with *their* heart, and be converted, and I should heal them. 41 These things said Esaias, when he saw his glory, and spake of him.

42 Nevertheless among the chief rulers also many believed on him; but because of the Pharisees they did not confess *him,* lest they should be put out of the synagogue: 43 For they loved the praise of men more than the praise of God.

44 Jesus cried and said, He that believeth on me, believeth not on me, but on him that sent me. 45And he that seeth me seeth him that sent me. 46 I am come a light into the world, that whosoever believeth on me should not abide in darkness. 47And if any man hear my words, and believe not, I judge him not: for I came not to judge the world, but to save the world. 48 He that rejecteth me, and receiveth not my words, hath one that judgeth him: the word that I have spoken, the same shall judge him in the last day. 49 For I have not spoken of myself; but the Father which sent me, he gave me a commandment, what I should say, and what I should speak. 50And I know that his commandment is life everlasting: whatsoever I speak therefore, even as the Father said unto me, so I speak.

R.S.V.

in the darkness does not know where he goes. 36 While you have the light, believe in the light, that you may become sons of light."

When Jesus had said this, he departed and hid himself from them. 37 Though he had done so many signs before them, yet they did not believe in him; 38 it was that the word spoken by the prophet Isaiah might be fulfilled:

"Lord, who has believed our report,
and to whom has the arm of the Lord been revealed?"

39 Therefore they could not believe. For Isaiah again said,

40 "He has blinded their eyes and hardened their heart,
lest they should see with their eyes and perceive with their heart,
and turn for me to heal them."

41 Isaiah said this because he saw his glory and spoke of him. 42 Nevertheless many even of the authorities believed in him, but for fear of the Pharisees they did not confess it, lest they should be put out of the synagogue: 43 for they loved the praise of men more than the praise of God.

44 And Jesus cried out and said, "He who believes in me, believes not in me but in him who sent me. 45And he who sees me sees him who sent me. 46 I have come as light into the world, that whoever believes in me may not remain in darkness. 47 If any one hears my sayings and does not keep them, I do not judge him; for I did not come to judge the world but to save the world. 48 He who rejects me and does not receive my sayings has a judge; the word that I have spoken will be his judge on the last day. 49 For I have not spoken on my own authority; the Father who sent me has himself given me commandment what to say and what to speak. 50And I know that his commandment is eternal life. What I say, therefore, I say as the Father has bidden me."

13 Now before the feast of the passover, when Jesus knew that his hour was come that he should depart out of this world unto the Father, having loved his own which were in the world, he loved them unto the end. 2And supper being ended, the devil having now put into the heart of Judas Iscariot, Simon's *son,* to betray him; 3 Jesus knowing that the Father had given all things into his hands, and that he was come from God, and went to God; 4 He riseth from supper, and laid aside his garments; and took a towel, and girded himself. 5After that he poureth water into a basin, and began to wash the disciples' feet, and to wipe *them* with the towel wherewith he was girded. 6 Then cometh he to Simon Peter: and Peter saith unto him, Lord, dost thou wash my feet? 7 Jesus answered and said unto him, What I do thou knowest not now; but thou shalt know hereafter. 8 Peter saith unto him, Thou shalt never wash my feet. Jesus answered him, If I wash thee not, thou hast no part with me. 9 Simon Peter saith unto him, Lord, not my feet only, but also *my* hands and *my*

13 Now before the feast of the Passover, when Jesus knew that his hour had come to depart out of this world to the Father, having loved his own who were in the world, he loved them to the end. 2And during supper, when the devil had already put it into the heart of Judas Iscariot, Simon's son, to betray him, 3 Jesus, knowing that the Father had given all things into his hands, and that he had come from God and was going to God, 4 rose from supper, laid aside his garments, and girded himself with a towel. 5 Then he poured water into a basin, and began to wash the disciples' feet, and to wipe them with the towel with which he was girded. 6 He came to Simon Peter; and Peter said to him, "Lord, do you wash my feet?" 7 Jesus answered him, "What I am doing you do not know now, but afterward you will understand." 8 Peter said to him, "You shall never wash my feet." Jesus answered him, "If I do not wash you, you have no part in me." 9 Simon Peter said to him, "Lord, not my feet only but also

PHILLIPS

in the dark has no idea where he is going. You must believe in the light while you have the light, that you may become the sons of light."

Jesus said all these things, and then went away, out of their sight. But though he had given so many signs, yet they did not believe in him, so that the prophecy of Isaiah was fulfilled, when he said,

Lord, who hath believed our report?
And to whom hath the arm of the Lord been revealed?

Thus, they could not believe, for Isaiah said again—

He hath blinded their eyes, and he hardened their heart:
Lest they should see with their eyes, and perceive with their heart,
And should turn,
And I should heal them.

Isaiah said these things because he saw the glory of Christ, and spoke about him. Nevertheless, many even of the authorities did believe in him. But they would not admit it for fear of the Pharisees, in case they should be excommunicated. They were more concerned to have the approval of men than to have the approval of God.

But later, Jesus cried aloud: "Every man who believes in me is believing in the one who sent me: and every man who sees me is seeing the one who sent me. I have come into the world as light, so that no one who believes in me need remain in the dark. Yet, if anyone hears my sayings and does not keep them, I do not judge him—for I did not come to judge the world but to save it. Every man who rejects me and will not accept my sayings has a judge—at the last day, the very words that I have spoken will be his judge. For I have not spoken on my own authority: the Father who sent me has commanded me what to say and what to speak. And I know that what he commands means eternal life. All that I say I speak only in accordance with what the Father has told me."

N.E.B.

where he is going. While you have the light, trust to the light, that you may become men of light.' After these words Jesus went away from them into hiding.

In spite of the many signs which Jesus had performed in their presence they would not believe in him, for the prophet Isaiah's utterance had to be fulfilled: 'Lord, who has believed what we reported, and to whom has the Lord's power been revealed?' So it was that they could not believe, for there is another saying of Isaiah's: 'He has blinded their eyes and dulled their minds, lest they should see with their eyes, and perceive with their minds, and turn to me to heal them.' Isaiah said this because[a] he saw his glory and spoke about him.

For all that, even among those in authority a number believed in him, but would not acknowledge him on account of the Pharisees, for fear of being banned from the synagogue. For they valued their reputation with men rather than the honour which comes from God.

So Jesus cried aloud: 'When a man believes in me, he believes in him who sent me rather than in me; seeing me, he sees him who sent me. I have come into the world as light, so that no one who has faith in me should remain in darkness. But if anyone hears my words and pays no regard to them, I am not his judge; I have not come to judge the world, but to save the world. There is a judge for the man who rejects me and does not accept my words; the word that I spoke will be his judge on the last day. I do not speak on my own authority, but the Father who sent me has himself commanded me what to say and how to speak. I know that his commands are eternal life. What the Father has said to me, therefore —that is what I speak.'

Jesus teaches his disciples humility   **13. 1**

Before the festival of the Passover began, Jesus realized that the time had come for him to leave this world and return to the Father. He had loved those who were his own in this world and he loved them to the end. By suppertime, the devil had already put the thought of betraying Jesus into the mind of Judas Iscariot, Simon's son. Jesus, with the full knowledge that the Father had put everything into his hands and that he had come from God and was going to God, rose from the supper table, took off his outer clothes, picked up a towel and fastened it round his waist. Then he poured water into the basin and began to wash the disciples' feet and to dry them with the towel around his waist.

So he came to Simon Peter, who said to him, "Lord, are you going to wash my feet?"

"You do not realize now what I am doing," replied Jesus, "but later on you will understand."

Then Peter said to him, "You must never wash my feet!"

"Unless you let me wash you, Peter," replied Jesus, "you cannot share my lot."

"Then," returned Simon Peter, "please—not

Farewell Discourses

13 It was before the Passover festival. Jesus knew that his hour had come and he must leave this world and go to the Father. He had always loved his own who were in the world, and now he was to show the full extent of his love.

The devil had already put it into the mind of Judas son of Simon Iscariot to betray him. During supper, Jesus, well aware that the Father had entrusted everything to him, and that he had come from God and was going back to God, rose from table, laid aside his garments, and taking a towel, tied it round him. Then he poured water into a basin, and began to wash his disciples' feet and to wipe them with the towel.

When it was Simon Peter's turn, Peter said to him, 'You, Lord, washing my feet?' Jesus replied, 'You do not understand now what I am doing, but one day you will.' Peter said, 'I will never let you wash my feet.' 'If I do not wash you,' Jesus replied, 'you are not in fellowship with me.' 'Then, Lord,' said Simon Peter, 'not

[a] *Some witnesses read* when.

K.J.V.

head. 10 Jesus saith to him, He that is washed needeth not save to wash *his* feet, but is clean every whit: and ye are clean, but not all. 11 For he knew who should betray him; therefore said he, Ye are not all clean. 12 So after he had washed their feet, and had taken his garments, and was set down again, he said unto them, Know ye what I have done to you? 13 Ye call me Master and Lord: and ye say well; for *so* I am. 14 If I then, *your* Lord and Master, have washed your feet; ye also ought to wash one another's feet. 15 For I have given you an example, that ye should do as I have done to you. 16 Verily, verily, I say unto you, The servant is not greater than his lord; neither he that is sent greater than he that sent him. 17 If ye know these things, happy are ye if ye do them.

18 I speak not of you all: I know whom I have chosen: but that the Scripture may be fulfilled, He that eateth bread with me hath lifted up his heel against me. 19 Now I tell you before it come, that, when it is come to pass, ye may believe that I am *he*. 20 Verily, verily, I say unto you, He that receiveth whomsoever I send receiveth me; and he that receiveth me receiveth him that sent me. 21 When Jesus had thus said, he was troubled in spirit, and testified, and said, Verily, verily, I say unto you, that one of you shall betray me. 22 Then the disciples looked one on another, doubting of whom he spake. 23 Now there was leaning on Jesus' bosom one of his disciples, whom Jesus loved. 24 Simon Peter therefore beckoned to him, that he should ask who it should be of whom he spake. 25 He then lying on Jesus' breast saith unto him, Lord, who is it? 26 Jesus answered, He it is, to whom I shall give a sop, when I have dipped *it*. And when he had dipped the sop, he gave *it* to Judas Iscariot, *the son* of Simon. 27 And after the sop Satan entered into him. Then said Jesus unto him, That thou doest, do quickly. 28 Now no man at the table knew for what intent he spake this unto him. 29 For some *of them* thought, because Judas had the bag, that Jesus had said unto him, Buy *those things* that we have need of against the feast; or, that he should give something to the poor. 30 He then, having received the sop, went immediately out; and it was night.

31 Therefore, when he was gone out, Jesus said, Now is the Son of man glorified, and God is glorified in him. 32 If God be glorified in him, God shall also glorify him in himself, and shall straightway glorify him. 33 Little children, yet a little while I am with you. Ye shall seek me; and as I said unto the Jews, Whither I go, ye cannot come; so now I say to you. 34 A new commandment I give unto you, That ye love one

R.S.V.

my hands and my head!" 10 Jesus said to him, "He who has bathed does not need to wash, except for his feet,*e* but he is clean all over; and you are clean, but not all of you." 11 For he knew who was to betray him; that was why he said, "You are not all clean."

12 When he had washed their feet, and taken his garments, and resumed his place, he said to them, "Do you know what I have done to you? 13 You call me Teacher and Lord; and you are right, for so I am. 14 If I then, your Lord and Teacher, have washed your feet, you also ought to wash one another's feet. 15 For I have given you an example, that you also should do as I have done to you. 16 Truly, truly, I say to you, a servant*d* is not greater than his master; nor is he who is sent greater than he who sent him. 17 If you know these things, blessed are you if you do them. 18 I am not speaking of you all; I know whom I have chosen; it is that the scripture may be fulfilled, 'He who ate my bread has lifted his heel against me.' 19 I tell you this now, before it takes place, that when it does take place you may believe that I am he. 20 Truly, truly, I say to you, he who receives any one whom I send receives me; and he who receives me receives him who sent me."

21 When Jesus had thus spoken, he was troubled in spirit, and testified, "Truly, truly, I say to you, one of you will betray me." 22 The disciples looked at one another, uncertain of whom he spoke. 23 One of his disciples, whom Jesus loved, was lying close to the breast of Jesus; 24 so Simon Peter beckoned to him and said, "Tell us who it is of whom he speaks." 25 So lying thus, close to the breast of Jesus, he said to him, "Lord, who is it?" 26 Jesus answered, "It is he to whom I shall give this morsel when I have dipped it." So when he had dipped the morsel, he gave it to Judas, the son of Simon Iscariot. 27 Then after the morsel, Satan entered into him. Jesus said to him, "What you are going to do, do quickly." 28 Now no one at the table knew why he said this to him. 29 Some thought that, because Judas had the money box, Jesus was telling him, "Buy what we need for the feast"; or, that he should give something to the poor. 30 So, after receiving the morsel, he immediately went out; and it was night.

31 When he had gone out, Jesus said, "Now is the Son of man glorified, and in him God is glorified; 32 if God is glorified in him, God will also glorify him in himself, and glorify him at once. 33 Little children, yet a little while I am with you. You will seek me; and as I said to the Jews so now I say to you, 'Where I am going you cannot come.' 34 A new commandment I give to you, that you love one another; even as I have loved you, that you also love one

[c] Other ancient authorities omit *except for his feet*. [d] Or *slave*.

314

PHILLIPS

just my feet but my hands and my face as well!"

"The man who has bathed," returned Jesus, "only needs to wash his feet to be clean all over. And you are clean—though not all of you."

(For Jesus knew his betrayer and that is why he said, "though not all of you.")

When Jesus had washed their feet and put on his clothes, he sat down again and spoke to them, "Do you realize what I have just done to you? You call me 'teacher' and 'Lord' and you are quite right, for I am your teacher and your Lord. But if I, your teacher and Lord, have washed your feet, you must be ready to wash one another's feet. I have given you this as an example so that you may do as I have done. Believe me, the servant is not greater than his master and the messenger is not greater than the man who sent him. Once you have realized these things, you will find your happiness in doing them.

Jesus foretells his betrayal   13. 18

"I am not speaking about all of you—I know the men I have chosen. But let this scripture be fulfilled—

He that eateth my bread lifted up his heel against me.

From now onward, I shall tell you about things before they happen, so that when they do happen you may believe that I am the one I claim to be. I tell you truly that anyone who accepts my messenger will be accepting me, and anyone who accepts me will be accepting the one who sent me."

After Jesus had said this, he was clearly in anguish of soul, and he added solemnly, "I tell you plainly, one of you is going to betray me."

At this the disciples stared at one another, completely mystified as to whom he could mean. And it happened that one of them, whom Jesus loved, was sitting very close to him. So Simon Peter nodded to this man and said, "Tell us whom he means."

He simply leaned forward on Jesus' shoulder, and asked, "Lord, who is it?"

And Jesus answered, "It is the one I am going to give this piece of bread to, after I have dipped it in the dish."

Then he took a piece of bread, dipped it in the dish and gave it to Simon's son, Judas Iscariot. After he had taken the piece of bread, Satan entered his heart. Then Jesus said to him, "Be quick about your business!"

No one else at table knew what he meant in telling him this. Indeed, some of them thought that, since Judas had charge of the purse, Jesus was telling him to buy what they needed for the festival, or that he should give something to the poor. So Judas took the piece of bread and went out quickly—into the night.

When he had gone, Jesus spoke: "Now comes the glory of the Son of Man, and the glory of God in him! If God is glorified through him then God will glorify the Son of Man—and that without delay. Oh, my children, I am with you such a short time! You will look for me, and I have to tell you as I told the Jews, 'Where I am going, you cannot follow.' Now I am giving you a new command—love one another. Just as I have loved you, you must love one another.

N.E.B.

my feet only; wash my hands and head as well!'

Jesus said, 'A man who has bathed needs no further washing;[a] he is altogether clean; and you are clean, though not every one of you.' He added the words 'not every one of you' because he knew who was going to betray him.

After washing their feet and taking his garments again, he sat down. 'Do you understand', he asked, 'what I have done for you? You call me "Master" and "Lord", and rightly so, for that is what I am. Then if I, your Lord and Master, have washed your feet, you also ought to wash one another's feet. I have set you an example: you are to do as I have done for you. In very truth I tell you, a servant is not greater than his master, nor a messenger than the one who sent him. If you know this, happy are you if you act upon it.

'I am not speaking about all of you; I know whom I have chosen. But there is a text of Scripture to be fulfilled: "He who eats bread with me has turned against me." [b] I tell you this now, before the event, that when it happens you may believe that I am what I am. In very truth I tell you, he who receives any messenger of mine receives me; receiving me, he receives the One who sent me.'

After saying this, Jesus exclaimed in deep agitation of spirit, 'In truth, in very truth I tell you, one of you is going to betray me.' The disciples looked at one another in bewilderment: whom could he be speaking of? One of them, the disciple he loved, was reclining close beside Jesus. So Simon Peter nodded to him and said, 'Ask who it is he means.' That disciple, as he reclined, leaned back close to Jesus and asked, 'Lord, who is it?' Jesus replied, 'It is the man to whom I give this piece of bread when I have dipped it in the dish.' Then, after dipping it in the dish, he took it out and gave it to Judas son of Simon Iscariot. As soon as Judas had received it Satan entered him. Jesus said to him, 'Do quickly what you have to do.' No one at the table understood what he meant by this. Some supposed that, as Judas was in charge of the common purse, Jesus was telling him to buy what was needed for the festival, or to make some gift to the poor. Judas, then, received the bread and went out. It was night.

When he had gone out Jesus said, 'Now the Son of Man is glorified, and in him God is glorified. If God is glorified in him,[c] God will also glorify him in himself; and he will glorify him now. My children, for a little longer I am with you; then you will look for me, and, as I told the Jews, I tell you now, where I am going you cannot come. I give you a new commandment: love one another; as I have loved you, so you are to love one another. If there is this love

[a] Some witnesses read needs only to wash his feet. [b] Literally has lifted his heel against me. [c] Some witnesses omit If God . . . in him.

K.J.V.

another; as I have loved you, that ye also love one another. 35 By this shall all *men* know that ye are my disciples, if ye have love one to another.

36 Simon Peter said unto him, Lord, whither goest thou? Jesus answered him, Whither I go, thou canst not follow me now; but thou shalt follow me afterwards. 37 Peter said unto him, Lord, why cannot I follow thee now? I will lay down my life for thy sake. 38 Jesus answered him, Wilt thou lay down thy life for my sake? Verily, verily, I say unto thee, The cock shall not crow, till thou hast denied me thrice.

14 Let not your heart be troubled: ye believe in God, believe also in me. 2 In my Father's house are many mansions: if *it were* not *so*, I would have told you. I go to prepare a place for you. 3 And if I go and prepare a place for you, I will come again, and receive you unto myself; that where I am, *there* ye may be also. 4 And whither I go ye know, and the way ye know. 5 Thomas saith unto him, Lord, we know not whither thou goest; and how can we know the way? 6 Jesus saith unto him, I am the way, the truth, and the life: no man cometh unto the Father, but by me. 7 If ye had known me, ye should have known my Father also: and from henceforth ye know him, and have seen him. 8 Philip saith unto him, Lord, shew us the Father, and it sufficeth us. 9 Jesus saith unto him, Have I been so long time with you, and yet hast thou not known me, Philip? he that hath seen me hath seen the Father; and how sayest thou *then*, Shew us the Father? 10 Believest thou not that I am in the Father, and the Father in me? the words that I speak unto you I speak not of myself: but the Father that dwelleth in me, he doeth the works. 11 Believe me that I *am* in the Father, and the Father in me: or else believe me for the very works' sake. 12 Verily, verily, I say unto you, He that believeth on me, the works that I do shall he do also; and greater *works* than these shall he do; because I go unto my Father. 13 And whatsoever ye shall ask in my name, that will I do, that the Father may be glorified in the Son. 14 If ye shall ask any thing in my name, I will do *it*.

15 If ye love me, keep my commandments. 16 And I will pray the Father, and he shall give you another Comforter, that he may abide with you for ever; 17 *Even* the Spirit of truth; whom the world cannot receive, because it seeth him

R.S.V.

another. 35 By this all men will know that you are my disciples, if you have love for one another."

36 Simon Peter said to him, "Lord, where are you going?" Jesus answered, "Where I am going you cannot follow me now; but you shall follow afterward." 37 Peter said to him, "Lord, why cannot I follow you now? I will lay down my life for you." 38 Jesus answered, "Will you lay down your life for me? Truly, truly, I say to you, the cock will not crow, till you have denied me three times.

14 "Let not your hearts be troubled; believe[e] in God, believe also in me. 2 In my Father's house are many rooms; if it were not so, would I have told you that I go to prepare a place for you? 3 And when I go and prepare a place for you, I will come again and will take you to myself, that where I am you may be also. 4 And you know the way where I am going." [f] 5 Thomas said to him, "Lord, we do not know where you are going; how can we know the way?" 6 Jesus said to him, "I am the way, and the truth, and the life; no one comes to the Father, but by me. 7 If you had known me, you would have known my Father also; henceforth you know him and have seen him."

8 Philip said to him, "Lord, show us the Father, and we shall be satisfied." 9 Jesus said to him, "Have I been with you so long, and yet you do not know me, Philip? He who has seen me has seen the Father; how can you say, 'Show us the Father'? 10 Do you not believe that I am in the Father and the Father in me? The words that I say to you I do not speak on my own authority; but the Father who dwells in me does his works. 11 Believe me that I am in the Father and the Father in me; or else believe me for the sake of the works themselves.

12 "Truly, truly, I say to you, he who believes in me will also do the works that I do; and greater works than these will he do, because I go to the Father. 13 Whatever you ask in my name, I will do it, that the Father may be glorified in the Son; 14 if you ask[g] anything in my name, I will do it.

15 "If you love me, you will keep my commandments. 16 And I will pray the Father, and he will give you another Counselor, to be with you for ever, 17 even the Spirit of truth, whom the world cannot receive, because it neither sees

[e] Or *you believe*. [f] Other ancient authorities read *where I am going you know, and the way you know.* [g] Other ancient authorities add *me*.

PHILLIPS

This is how all men will know that you are my disciples, because you have such love for one another."

Simon Peter said to him, "Lord, where are you going?"

"I am going," replied Jesus, "where you cannot follow me now, though you will follow me later."

"Lord, why can't I follow you now?" said Peter. "I would lay down my life for you!"

"Would you lay down your life for me?" replied Jesus. "Believe me, you will disown me three times before the cock crows!

Jesus reveals spiritual truths 14. 1

"You must not let yourselves be distressed—you must hold on to your faith in God and to your faith in me. There are many rooms in my Father's House. If there were not, should I have told you that I am going away to prepare a place for you? It is true that I am going away to prepare a place for you, but it is just as true that I am coming again to welcome you into my own home, so that you may be where I am. You know where I am going and you know the road I am going to take."

"Lord," Thomas remonstrated, "we do not know where you're going, and how can we know what road you're going to take?"

"I myself am the road," replied Jesus, "and the truth and the life. No one approaches the Father except through me. If you had known who I am, you would have known my Father. From now on, you do know him and you have seen him."

Jesus explains his relationship 14. 8
with the Father

Then Philip said to him, "Show us the Father, Lord, and we shall be satisfied."

"Have I been such a long time with you," returned Jesus, "without your really knowing me, Philip? The man who has seen me has seen the Father. How can you say, 'Show us the Father'? Do you not believe that I am in the Father and the Father is in me? The very words I say to you are not my own. It is the Father who lives in me who carries out his work through me. Do you believe me when I say that I am in the Father and the Father is in me? But if you cannot, then believe me because of what you see me do. I assure you that the man who believes in me will do the same things that I have done, yes, and he will do even greater things than these, for I am going away to the Father. Whatever you ask the Father in my name, I will do—that the Son may bring glory to the Father. And if you ask me anything in my name, I will grant it.

Jesus promises the Spirit 14. 15

"If you really love me, you will keep the commandments I have given you and I shall ask the Father to give you someone else to stand by you, to be with you always. I mean the Spirit of truth, whom the world cannot accept, for it can neither see nor recognize that Spirit.

N.E.B.

among you, then all will know that you are my disciples.'

Simon Peter said to him, 'Lord, where are you going?' Jesus replied, 'Where I am going you cannot follow me now, but one day you will.' Peter said, 'Lord, why cannot I follow you now? I will lay down my life for you.' Jesus answered, 'Will you indeed lay down your life for me? I tell you in very truth, before the cock crows you will have denied me three times.

14 'Set your troubled hearts at rest. Trust in God always; trust also in me. There are many dwelling-places in my Father's house; if it were not so I should have told you; for I am going there on purpose to prepare a place for you.[a] And if I go and prepare a place for you, I shall come again and receive you to myself, so that where I am you may be also; and my way there is known to you.'[b] Thomas said, 'Lord, we do not know where you are going, so how can we know the way?' Jesus replied, 'I am the way; I am the truth and I am life; no one comes to the Father except by me.

'If you knew me you would know my Father too.[c] From now on you do know him; you have seen him.' Philip said to him, 'Lord, show us the Father and we ask no more.' Jesus answered, 'Have I been all this time with you, Philip, and you still do not know me? Anyone who has seen me has seen the Father. Then how can you say, "Show us the Father"? Do you not believe that I am in the Father, and the Father in me? I am not myself the source of the words I speak to you: it is the Father who dwells in me doing his own work. Believe me when I say that I am in the Father and the Father in me; or else accept the evidence of the deeds themselves. In truth, in very truth I tell you, he who has faith in me will do what I am doing; and he will do greater things still because I am going to the Father. Indeed anything you ask in my name I will do, so that the Father may be glorified in the Son. If you ask[d] anything in my name I will do it.

'If you love me you will obey my commands; and I will ask the Father, and he will give you another to be your Advocate, who will be with you for ever—the Spirit of truth. The world cannot receive him, because the world neither sees

[a] *Or if it were not so, should I have told you that I am going to prepare a place for you?* [b] *Some witnesses read* also. You know where I am going and you know the way. [c] *Some witnesses read* If you know me you will know my Father too. [d] *Some witnesses insert* me.

K.J.V.

not, neither knoweth him: but ye know him; for he dwelleth with you, and shall be in you. 18 I will not leave you comfortless: I will come to you. 19 Yet a little while, and the world seeth me no more; but ye see me: because I live, ye shall live also. 20 At that day ye shall know that I *am* in my Father, and ye in me, and I in you. 21 He that hath my commandments, and keepeth them, he it is that loveth me: and he that loveth me shall be loved of my Father, and I will love him, and will manifest myself to him. 22 Judas saith unto him, not Iscariot, Lord, how is it that thou wilt manifest thyself unto us, and not unto the world? 23 Jesus answered and said unto him, If a man love me, he will keep my words: and my Father will love him, and we will come unto him, and make our abode with him. 24 He that loveth me not keepeth not my sayings: and the word which ye hear is not mine, but the Father's which sent me. 25 These things have I spoken unto you, being *yet* present with you. 26 But the Comforter, *which is* the Holy Ghost, whom the Father will send in my name, he shall teach you all things, and bring all things to your remembrance, whatsoever I have said unto you. 27 Peace I leave with you, my peace I give unto you: not as the world giveth, give I unto you. Let not your heart be troubled, neither let it be afraid. 28 Ye have heard how I said unto you, I go away, and come *again* unto you. If ye loved me, ye would rejoice, because I said, I go unto the Father: for my Father is greater than I. 29And now I have told you before it come to pass, that, when it is come to pass, ye might believe. 30 Hereafter I will not talk much with you: for the prince of this world cometh, and hath nothing in me. 31 But that the world may know that I love the Father; and as the Father gave me commandment, even so I do. Arise, let us go hence.

R.S.V.

him nor knows him; you know him, for he dwells with you, and will be in you. 18 "I will not leave you desolate; I will come to you. 19 Yet a little while, and the world will see me no more, but you will see me; because I live, you will live also. 20 In that day you will know that I am in my Father, and you in me, and I in you. 21 He who has my commandments and keeps them, he it is who loves me; and he who loves me will be loved by my Father, and I will love him and manifest myself to him." 22 Judas (not Iscariot) said to him, "Lord, how is it that you will manifest yourself to us, and not to the world?" 23 Jesus answered him, "If a man loves me, he will keep my word, and my Father will love him, and we will come to him and make our home with him. 24 He who does not love me does not keep my words; and the word which you hear is not mine but the Father's who sent me. 25 "These things I have spoken to you, while I am still with you. 26 But the Counselor, the Holy Spirit, whom the Father will send in my name, he will teach you all things, and bring to your remembrance all that I have said to you. 27 Peace I leave with you; my peace I give to you; not as the world gives do I give to you. Let not your hearts be troubled, neither let them be afraid. 28 You heard me say to you, 'I go away, and I will come to you.' If you loved me, you would have rejoiced, because I go to the Father; for the Father is greater than I. 29And now I have told you before it takes place, so that when it does take place, you may believe. 30 I will no longer talk much with you, for the ruler of this world is coming. He has no power over me; 31 but I do as the Father has commanded me, so that the world may know that I love the Father. Rise, let us go hence.

15 I am the true vine, and my Father is the husbandman. 2 Every branch in me that beareth not fruit he taketh away: and every *branch* that beareth fruit, he purgeth it, that it may bring forth more fruit. 3 Now ye are clean through the word which I have spoken unto you. 4 Abide in me, and I in you. As the branch cannot bear fruit of itself, except it abide in the vine; no more can ye, except ye abide in me. 5 I am the vine, ye *are* the branches. He that abideth in me, and I in him, the same bringeth forth much fruit; for without me ye can do nothing. 6 If a man abide not in me, he is cast forth as a branch, and is withered; and men gather them, and cast *them* into the fire, and they are burned. 7 If ye abide in me, and my words abide in you, ye shall ask what ye will, and it shall be done unto you. 8 Herein is my Father glorified, that ye bear much fruit; so shall ye be my disciples. 9As the Father hath loved me, so have I loved you: continue ye in my love. 10 If ye keep my commandments, ye shall

15 "I am the true vine, and my Father is the vinedresser. 2 Every branch of mine that bears no fruit, he takes away, and every branch that does bear fruit he prunes, that it may bear more fruit. 3 You are already made clean by the word which I have spoken to you. 4Abide in me, and I in you. As the branch cannot bear fruit by itself, unless it abides in the vine, neither can you, unless you abide in me. 5 I am the vine, you are the branches. He who abides in me, and I in him, he it is that bears much fruit, for apart from me you can do nothing. 6 If a man does not abide in me, he is cast forth as a branch and withers; and the branches are gathered, thrown into the fire and burned. 7 If you abide in me, and my words abide in you, ask whatever you will, and it shall be done for you. 8 By this my Father is glorified, that you bear much fruit, and so prove to be my disciples. 9As the Father has loved me, so have I loved you; abide in my love. 10 If you keep my commandments, you will abide in my love, just as I have kept my Father's command-

PHILLIPS

But you recognize him, for he is with you now and will be in your hearts. I am not going to leave you alone in the world—I am coming to you. In a very little while, the world will see me no more but you will see me, because I am really alive and you will be alive too. When that day comes, you will realize that I am in my Father, that you are in me, and I am in you.

"Every man who knows my commandments and obeys them is the man who really loves me, and every man who really loves me will himself be loved by my Father, and I too will love him and make myself known to him."

Then Judas (not Iscariot) said, "Lord, how is it that you are going to make yourself known to us but not to the world?"

And to this Jesus replied: "When a man loves me, he follows my teaching. Then my Father will love him, and we will come to that man and make our home within him. The man who does not really love me will not follow my teaching. Indeed, what you are hearing from me now is not really my saying, but comes from the Father who sent me.

"I have said all this while I am still with you. But the one who is coming to stand by you, the Holy Spirit whom the Father will send in my name, will be your teacher and will bring to your minds all that I have said to you.

"I leave behind with you—peace; I give you my own peace and my gift is nothing like the peace of this world. You must not be distressed and you must not be daunted. You have heard me say, 'I am going away and I am coming back to you.' If you really loved me, you would be glad because I am going to my Father, for my Father is greater than I. And I have told you of it now, before it happens, so that when it does happen your faith in me will not be shaken. I shall not be able to talk much longer to you, for the spirit that rules this world is coming very close. He has no hold over me, but I go on my way to show the world that I love the Father and do what he sent me to do. . . . Get up now! Let us leave this place.

N.E.B.

nor knows him; but you know him, because he dwells with you and is[a] in you. I will not leave you bereft; I am coming back to you. In a little while the world will see me no longer, but you will see me; because I live, you too will live; then you will know that I am in my Father, and you in me and I in you. The man who has received my commands and obeys them—he it is who loves me; and he who loves me will be loved by my Father; and I will love him and disclose myself to him.'

Judas asked him—the other Judas, not Iscariot—'Lord, what can have happened, that you mean to disclose yourself to us alone and not to the world?' Jesus replied, 'Anyone who loves me will heed what I say; then my Father will love him, and we will come to him and make our dwelling with him; but he who does not love me does not heed what I say. And the word you hear is not mine: it is the word of the Father who sent me. I have told you all this while I am still here with you; but your Advocate, the Holy Spirit whom the Father will send in my name, will teach you everything, and will call to mind all that I have told you.

'Peace is my parting gift to you, my own peace, such as the world cannot give. Set your troubled hearts at rest, and banish your fears. You heard me say, "I am going away, and coming back to you." If you loved me you would have been glad to hear that I was going to the Father; for the Father is greater than I. I have told you now, beforehand, so that when it happens you may have faith.

'I shall not talk much longer with you, for the Prince of this world approaches. He has no rights over me; but the world must be shown that I love the Father, and do exactly as he commands; so up, let us go forward![b]

Jesus teaches union with himself **15. 1**

"I am the real vine; my Father is the vine-dresser. He removes any of my branches which are not bearing fruit and he prunes every branch that does bear fruit to increase its yield. Now, you have already been pruned by my words. You must go on growing in me and I will grow in you. For just as the branch cannot bear any fruit unless it shares the life of the vine, so you can produce nothing unless you go on growing in me. I am the vine itself; you are the branches. It is the man who shares my life and whose life I share who proves fruitful. For the plain fact is that apart from me you can do nothing at all. The man who does not share my life is like a branch that is broken off and withers away. He becomes just like the dry sticks that men pick up and use for firewood. But if you live your life in me, and my words live in your hearts, you can ask for whatever you like and it will come true for you. This is how my Father will be glorified—in your becoming fruitful and being my disciples.

"I have loved you just as the Father has loved me. You must go on living in my love. If you keep my commandments you will live in my love just as I have kept my Father's command-

15 'I am the real vine, and my Father is the gardener. Every barren branch of mine he cuts away; and every fruiting branch he cleans, to make it more fruitful still. You have already been cleansed by the word that I spoke to you. Dwell in me, as I in you. No branch can bear fruit by itself, but only if it remains united with the vine; no more can you bear fruit, unless you remain united with me.

'I am the vine, and you the branches. He who dwells in me, as I dwell in him, bears much fruit; for apart from me you can do nothing. He who does not dwell in me is thrown away like a withered branch. The withered branches are heaped together, thrown on the fire, and burnt.

'If you dwell in me, and my words dwell in you, ask what you will, and you shall have it. This is my Father's glory, that you may bear fruit in plenty and so be my disciples.[c] As the Father has loved me, so I have loved you. Dwell in my love. If you heed my commands,

[a] *Some witnesses read* shall be. [b] *Or* for the Prince of this world is coming, though he has nothing in common with me. But he is coming so that the world may recognize that I love the Father, and do exactly as he commands. Up, and let us go forward to meet him! [c] *Or* that you may bear fruit in plenty. Thus you will be my disciples.

K.J.V.

abide in my love; even as I have kept my Father's commandments, and abide in his love. 11 These things have I spoken unto you, that my joy might remain in you, and *that* your joy might be full. 12 This is my commandment, That ye love one another, as I have loved you. 13 Greater love hath no man than this, that a man lay down his life for his friends. 14 Ye are my friends, if ye do whatsoever I command you. 15 Henceforth I call you not servants; for the servant knoweth not what his lord doeth: but I have called you friends; for all things that I have heard of my Father I have made known unto you. 16 Ye have not chosen me, but I have chosen you, and ordained you, that ye should go and bring forth fruit, and *that* your fruit should remain; that whatsoever ye shall ask of the Father in my name, he may give it you. 17 These things I command you, that ye love one another. 18 If the world hate you, ye know that it hated me before *it hated* you. 19 If ye were of the world, the world would love his own; but because ye are not of the world, but I have chosen you out of the world, therefore the world hateth you. 20 Remember the word that I said unto you, The servant is not greater than his lord. If they have persecuted me, they will also persecute you; if they have kept my saying, they will keep yours also. 21 But all these things will they do unto you for my name's sake, because they know not him that sent me. 22 If I had not come and spoken unto them, they had not had sin: but now they have no cloak for their sin. 23 He that hateth me hateth my Father also. 24 If I had not done among them the works which none other man did, they had not had sin: but now have they both seen and hated both me and my Father. 25 But *this cometh to pass,* that the word might be fulfilled that is written in their law, They hated me without a cause. 26 But when the Comforter is come, whom I will send unto you from the Father, *even* the Spirit of truth, which proceedeth from the Father, he shall testify of me: 27 And ye also shall bear witness, because ye have been with me from the beginning.

R.S.V.

ments and abide in his love. 11 These things I have spoken to you, that my joy may be in you, and that your joy may be full. 12 "This is my commandment, that you love one another as I have loved you. 13 Greater love has no man than this, that a man lay down his life for his friends. 14 You are my friends if you do what I command you. 15 No longer do I call you servants,[h] for the servant[i] does not know what his master is doing; but I have called you friends, for all that I have heard from my Father I have made known to you. 16 You did not choose me, but I chose you and appointed you that you should go and bear fruit and that your fruit should abide; so that whatever you ask the Father in my name, he may give it to you. 17 This I command you, to love one another. 18 "If the world hates you, know that it has hated me before it hated you. 19 If you were of the world, the world would love its own; but because you are not of the world, but I chose you out of the world, therefore the world hates you. 20 Remember the word that I said to you, 'A servant[i] is not greater than his master.' If they persecuted me, they will persecute you; if they kept my word, they will keep yours also. 21 But all this they will do to you on my account, because they do not know him who sent me. 22 If I had not come and spoken to them, they would not have sin; but now they have no excuse for their sin. 23 He who hates me hates my Father also. 24 If I had not done among them the works which no one else did, they would not have sin; but now they have seen and hated both me and my Father. 25 It is to fulfil the word that is written in their law, 'They hated me without a cause.' 26 But when the Counselor comes, whom I shall send to you from the Father, even the Spirit of truth, who proceeds from the Father, he will bear witness to me; 27 and you also are witnesses, because you have been with me from the beginning.

16 These things have I spoken unto you, that ye should not be offended. 2 They shall put you out of the synagogues: yea, the time cometh, that whosoever killeth you will think that he doeth God service. 3 And these things will they do unto you, because they have not known the Father, nor me. 4 But these things have I told you, that when the time shall come, ye may remember that I told you of them. And these things I said not unto you at the beginning, because I was with you. 5 But now I go my way to him that sent me; and none of you

16 "I have said all this to you to keep you from falling away. 2 They will put you out of the synagogues; indeed, the hour is coming when whoever kills you will think he is offering service to God. 3 And they will do this because they have not known the Father, nor me. 4 But I have said these things to you, that when their hour comes you may remember that I told you of them.

"I did not say these things to you from the beginning, because I was with you. 5 But now I am going to him who sent me; yet none of

ments and live in his love. I have told you this so that you can share my joy, and that your happiness may be complete. This is my commandment: that you love one another as I have loved you. There is no greater love than this— that a man should lay down his life for his friends. You are my friends if you do what I tell you to do. I shall not call you servants any longer, for a servant does not share his master's confidence. No, I call you friends, now, because I have told you everything that I have heard from the Father.

"It is not that you have chosen me; but it is I who have chosen you. I have appointed you to go and bear fruit that will be lasting; so that whatever you ask the Father in my name, he will give it to you.

Jesus speaks of the   **15. 17**
world's hatred

"This I command you, love one another! If the world hates you, you know that it hated me first. If you belonged to the world, the world would love its own. But because you do not belong to the world and I have chosen you out of it, the world will hate you. Do you remember what I said to you, 'The servant is not greater than his master'? If they have persecuted me, they will persecute you as well, but if they have followed my teaching, they will also follow yours. They will do all these things to you as my disciples because they do not know the one who sent me. If I had not come and spoken to them, they would not have been guilty of sin, but now they have no excuse for their sin. The man who hates me, hates my Father as well. If I had not done among them things that no other man has ever done, they would not have been guilty of sin, but as it is they have seen and they have hated both me and my Father. Yet this only fulfills what is written in their Law—

They hated me without a cause.

But when the helper comes, that is, the Spirit of truth, who comes from the Father and whom I myself will send to you from the Father, he will speak plainly about me. And you yourselves will also speak plainly about me, for you have been with me from the first.

Jesus speaks of the future   **16. 1**
without his bodily presence

"I am telling you this now so that your faith in me may not be shaken. They will excommunicate you from their synagogues. Yes, the time is coming when a man who kills you will think he is thereby serving God! They will act like this because they have never had any true knowledge of the Father or of me, but I have told you all this so that when the time comes for it to happen you may remember that I told you about it. I have not spoken like this to you before, because I have been with you; but now the time has come for me to go away to the one who sent me. None of you asks me, 'Where are

you will dwell in my love, as I have heeded my Father's commands and dwell in his love.

'I have spoken thus to you, so that my joy may be in you, and your joy complete.[a] This is my commandment: love one another, as I have loved you. There is no greater love than this, that a man should lay down his life for his friends. You are my friends, if you do what I command you. I call you servants no longer; a servant does not know what his master is about. I have called you friends, because I have disclosed to you everything that I heard from my Father. You did not choose me: I chose you. I appointed you to go on and bear fruit, fruit that shall last; so that the Father may give you all that you ask in my name. This is my commandment to you: love one another.

'If the world hates you, it hated me first, as you know well.[b] If you belonged to the world, the world would love its own; but because you do not belong to the world, because I have chosen you out of the world, for that reason the world hates you. Remember what I said: "A servant is not greater than his master." As they persecuted me, they will persecute you; they will follow your teaching as little as they have followed mine. It is on my account that they will treat you thus, because they do not know the One who sent me.

'If I had not come and spoken to them, they would not have been guilty of sin; but now they have no excuse for their sin: he who hates me, hates my Father. If I had not worked among them and accomplished what no other man has done, they would not have been guilty of sin; but now they have both seen and hated both me and my Father.[c] However, this text in their Law had to come true:[d] "They hated me without reason."

'But when your Advocate has come, whom I will send you from the Father—the Spirit of truth that issues from the Father—he will bear witness to me. And you also are my witnesses, because you have been with me from the first.

16 'I have told you all this to guard you against the breakdown of your faith. They will ban you from the synagogue; indeed, the time is coming when anyone who kills you will suppose that he is performing a religious duty. They will do these things because they do not know either the Father or me. I have told you all this so that when the time comes for it to happen you may remember my warning. I did not tell you this at first, because then I was with you; but now I am going away to him who sent me. None of you asks me "Where are you go-

[a] *Or* so that I may have joy in you and your joy may be complete. [b] *Or* bear in mind that it hated me first. [c] *Or* but now they have indeed seen my work and yet have hated both me and my Father. [d] *Or* let this text in their Law come true.

K.J.V.

asketh me, Whither goest thou? 6 But because I have said these things unto you, sorrow hath filled your heart. 7 Nevertheless I tell you the truth; It is expedient for you that I go away: for if I go not away, the Comforter will not come unto you; but if I depart, I will send him unto you. 8And when he is come, he will reprove the world of sin, and of righteousness, and of judgment: 9 Of sin, because they believe not on me; 10 Of righteousness, because I go to my Father, and ye see me no more; 11 Of judgment, because the prince of this world is judged. 12 I have yet many things to say unto you, but ye cannot bear them now. 13 Howbeit when he, the Spirit of truth, is come, he will guide you into all truth: for he shall not speak of himself; but whatsoever he shall hear, *that* shall he speak: and he will shew you things to come. 14 He shall glorify me: for he shall receive of mine, and shall shew *it* unto you. 15All things that the Father hath are mine: therefore said I, that he shall take of mine, and shall shew *it* unto you. 16A little while, and ye shall not see me: and again, a little while, and ye shall see me, because I go to the Father. 17 Then said *some* of his disciples among themselves, What is this that he saith unto us, A little while, and ye shall not see me: and again, a little while, and ye shall see me: and, Because I go to the Father? 18 They said therefore, What is this that he saith, A little while? we cannot tell what he saith. 19 Now Jesus knew that they were desirous to ask him, and said unto them, Do ye inquire among yourselves of that I said, A little while, and ye shall not see me: and again, a little while, and ye shall see me? 20 Verily, verily, I say unto you, That ye shall weep and lament, but the world shall rejoice; and ye shall be sorrowful, but your sorrow shall be turned into joy. 21 A woman when she is in travail hath sorrow, because her hour is come: but as soon as she is delivered of the child, she remembereth no more the anguish, for joy that a man is born into the world. 22And ye now therefore have sorrow: but I will see you again, and your heart shall rejoice, and your joy no man taketh from you. 23And in that day ye shall ask me nothing. Verily, verily, I say unto you, Whatsoever ye shall ask the Father in my name, he will give *it* you. 24 Hitherto have ye asked nothing in my name: ask, and ye shall receive, that your joy may be full. 25 These things have I spoken unto you in proverbs: but the time cometh, when I shall no more speak unto you in proverbs, but I shall shew you plainly of the Father. 26At that day ye shall ask in my name: and I say not unto you, that I will pray the Father for you: 27 For the Father himself loveth you, because ye have loved me, and have

R.S.V.

you asks me, 'Where are you going?' 6 But because I have said these things to you, sorrow has filled your hearts. 7 Nevertheless I tell you the truth: it is to your advantage that I go away, for if I do not go away, the Counselor will not come to you; but if I go, I will send him to you. 8And when he comes, he will convince the world of sin and of righteousness and of judgment: 9 of sin, because they do not believe in me; 10 of righteousness, because I go to the Father, and you will see me no more; 11 of judgment, because the ruler of this world is judged. 12 "I have yet many things to say to you, but you cannot bear them now. 13 When the Spirit of truth comes, he will guide you into all the truth; for he will not speak on his own authority, but whatever he hears he will speak, and he will declare to you the things that are to come. 14 He will glorify me, for he will take what is mine and declare it to you. 15All that the Father has is mine; therefore I said that he will take what is mine and declare it to you. 16 "A little while, and you will see me no more; again a little while, and you will see me." 17 Some of his disciples said to one another, "What is this that he says to us, 'A little while, and you will not see me, and again a little while, and you will see me'; and, 'because I go to the Father'?" 18 They said, "What does he mean by 'a little while'? We do not know what he means." 19 Jesus knew that they wanted to ask him; so he said to them, "Is this what you are asking yourselves, what I meant by saying, 'A little while, and you will not see me, and again a little while, and you will see me'? 20 Truly, truly, I say to you, you will weep and lament, but the world will rejoice; you will be sorrowful, but your sorrow will turn into joy. 21 When a woman is in travail she has sorrow, because her hour has come; but when she is delivered of the child, she no longer remembers the anguish, for joy that a child *j* is born into the world. 22 So you have sorrow now, but I will see you again and your hearts will rejoice, and no one will take your joy from you. 23 In that day you will ask nothing of me. Truly, truly, I say to you, if you ask anything of the Father, he will give it to you in my name. 24 Hitherto you have asked nothing in my name; ask, and you will receive, that your joy may be full. 25 "I have said this to you in figures; the hour is coming when I shall no longer speak to you in figures but tell you plainly of the Father. 26 In that day you will ask in my name; and I do not say to you that I shall pray the Father for you; 27 for the Father himself loves you, because you have loved me and have believed that I came

[*j*] Greek *a human being.*

322

you going?' That is because you are so distressed at what I have told you. Yet I am telling you the simple truth when I assure you that it is a good thing for you that I should go away. For if I did not go away, the divine helper would not come to you. But if I go, then I will send him to you. When he comes, he will convince the world of the meaning of sin, of true goodness and of judgment. He will expose their sin because they do not believe in me; he will reveal true goodness for I am going away to the Father and you will see me no longer; and he will show them the meaning of judgment, for the spirit which rules this world will have been judged.

"I have much more to tell you but you cannot bear it now. Yet when that one I have spoken to you about comes—the Spirit of truth—he will guide you into everything that is true. For he will not be speaking of his own accord but exactly as he hears, and he will inform you about what is to come. He will bring glory to me, for he will draw on my truth and reveal it to you. Whatever the Father possesses is also mine; that is why I tell you that he will draw on my truth and will show it to you.

The disciples are puzzled: *16. 16*
 Jesus explains

"In a little while you will not see me any longer, and again, in a little while you will see me."

At this some of his disciples remarked to each other, "What is this that he tells us now, 'A little while and you will not see me, and again, in a little while you will see me' and 'for I am going away to the Father'? What is this 'little while' that he talks about?" they were saying. "We simply do not know what he means!"

Jesus knew that they wanted to ask him what he meant, so he said to them: "Are you trying to find out from each other what I meant when I said, 'In a little while you will not see me, and again, in a little while you will see me'? I tell you truly that you are going to be both sad and sorry while the world is glad. Yes, you will be deeply distressed, but your pain will turn into joy. When a woman gives birth to a child, she certainly knows pain when her time comes. Yet as soon as she has given birth to the child, she no longer remembers her agony for joy that a man has been born into the world. Now you are going through pain, but I shall see you again and your hearts will thrill with joy—the joy that no one can take away from you—and on that day you will not ask me any questions.

"I assure you that whatever you ask the Father he will give you in my name. Up to now you have asked nothing in my name; ask now, and you will receive, that your joy may be overflowing.

Jesus speaks further   *16. 25*
 of the future

"I have been speaking to you in parables— but the time is coming to give up parables and tell you plainly about the Father. When that time comes, you will make your requests to him in my name, for I need make no promise to plead to the Father for you, for the Father himself loves you, because you have loved me and

ing?" Yet you are plunged into grief because of what I have told you. Nevertheless I tell you the truth: it is for your good that I am leaving you. If I do not go, your Advocate will not come, whereas if I go, I will send him to you. When he comes, he will confute the world, and show where wrong and right and judgement lie. He will convict them of wrong, by their refusal to believe in me; he will convince them that right is on my side, by showing that I go to the Father when I pass from your sight; and he will convince them of divine judgement, by showing that the Prince of this world stands condemned.

'There is still much that I could say to you, but the burden would be too great for you now. However, when he comes who is the Spirit of truth, he will guide you into all the truth; for he will not speak on his own authority, but will tell only what he hears; and he will make known to you the things that are coming. He will glorify me, for everything that he makes known to you he will draw from what is mine. All that the Father has is mine, and that is why I said, "Everything that he makes known to you he will draw from what is mine."

'A little while, and you see me no more; again a little while, and you will see me.' Some of his disciples said to one another, 'What does he mean by this: "A little while, and you will not see me, and again a little while, and you will see me", and by this: "Because I am going to my Father"?' So they asked, 'What is this "little while" that he speaks of? We do not know what he means.'

Jesus knew that they were wanting to question him, and said, 'Are you discussing what I said: "A little while, and you will not see me, and again a little while, and you will see me"? In very truth I tell you, you will weep and mourn, but the world will be glad. But though you will be plunged in grief, your grief will be turned to joy. A woman in labour is in pain because her time has come; but when the child is born she forgets the anguish in her joy that a man has been born into the world. So it is with you: for the moment you are sad at heart; but I shall see you again, and then you will be joyful, and no one shall rob you of your joy. When that day comes you will ask nothing of me. In very truth I tell you, if you ask the Father for anything in my name, he will give it you.[a] So far you have asked nothing in my name. Ask and you will receive, that your joy may be complete.

'Till now I have been using figures of speech; a time is coming when I shall no longer use figures, but tell you of the Father in plain words. When that day comes you will make your request in my name, and I do not say that I shall pray to the Father for you, for the Father loves you himself, because you have loved me and

---

[a] *Some witnesses read* if you ask the Father for anything, he will give it you in my name.

K.J.V.

believed that I came out from God. 28 I came forth from the Father, and am come into the world: again, I leave the world, and go to the Father. 29 His disciples said unto him, Lo, now speakest thou plainly, and speakest no proverb. 30 Now are we sure that thou knowest all things, and needest not that any man should ask thee: by this we believe that thou camest forth from God. 31 Jesus answered them, Do ye now believe? 32 Behold, the hour cometh, yea, is now come, that ye shall be scattered, every man to his own, and shall leave me alone: and yet I am not alone, because the Father is with me. 33 These things I have spoken unto you, that in me ye might have peace. In the world ye shall have tribulation: but be of good cheer; I have overcome the world.

17 These words spake Jesus, and lifted up his eyes to heaven, and said, Father, the hour is come; glorify thy Son, that thy Son also may glorify thee: 2As thou hast given him power over all flesh, that he should give eternal life to as many as thou hast given him. 3And this is life eternal, that they might know thee the only true God, and Jesus Christ, whom thou hast sent. 4 I have glorified thee on the earth: I have finished the work which thou gavest me to do. 5And now, O Father, glorify thou me with thine own self with the glory which I had with thee before the world was. 6 I have manifested thy name unto the men which thou gavest me out of the world: thine they were, and thou gavest them me; and they have kept thy word. 7 Now they have known that all things whatsoever thou hast given me are of thee. 8 For I have given unto them the words which thou gavest me; and they have received *them*, and have known surely that I came out from thee, and they have believed that thou didst send me. 9 I pray for them: I pray not for the world, but for them which thou hast given me; for they are thine. 10And all mine are thine, and thine are mine; and I am glorified in them. 11And now I am no more in the world, but these are in the world, and I come to thee. Holy Father, keep through thine own name those whom thou hast given me, that they may be one, as we *are*. 12 While I was with them in the world, I kept them in thy name: those that thou gavest me I have kept, and none of them is lost, but the son of perdition; that the Scripture might be fulfilled. 13And now come I to thee; and these things I speak in the world, that they might have my joy fulfilled in themselves. 14 I have given them thy word; and the world hath hated them, because they are not of the world, even as I am not of the world. 15 I pray not that thou shouldest take them out of the world, but that thou shouldest keep them from the evil. 16 They are not of the world, even as I am not of the world. 17 Sanctify them through thy truth: thy word is truth. 18As thou hast sent me into the world, even so have I also sent them into the world. 19And for their sakes I sanctify my-

R.S.V.

from the Father. 28 I came from the Father and have come into the world; again, I am leaving the world and going to the Father."
29 His disciples said, "Ah, now you are speaking plainly, not in any figure! 30 Now we know that you know all things, and need none to question you; by this we believe that you came from God." 31 Jesus answered them, "Do you now believe? 32 The hour is coming, indeed it has come, when you will be scattered, every man to his home, and will leave me alone; yet I am not alone, for the Father is with me. 33 I have said this to you, that in me you may have peace. In the world you have tribulation; but be of good cheer, I have overcome the world."

17 When Jesus had spoken these words, he lifted up his eyes to heaven and said, "Father, the hour has come; glorify thy Son that the Son may glorify thee, 2 since thou hast given him power over all flesh, to give eternal life to all whom thou hast given him. 3And this is eternal life, that they know thee the only true God, and Jesus Christ whom thou hast sent. 4 I glorified thee on earth, having accomplished the work which thou gavest me to do; 5 and now, Father, glorify thou me in thy own presence with the glory which I had with thee before the world was made.
6 "I have manifested thy name to the men whom thou gavest me out of the world; thine they were, and thou gavest them to me, and they have kept thy word. 7 Now they know that everything that thou hast given me is from thee; 8 for I have given them the words which thou gavest me, and they have received them and know in truth that I came from thee; and they have believed that thou didst send me. 9 I am praying for them; I am not praying for the world but for those whom thou hast given me, for they are thine; 10 all mine are thine, and thine are mine, and I am glorified in them. 11And now I am no more in the world, but they are in the world, and I am coming to thee. Holy Father, keep them in thy name, which thou hast given me, that they may be one, even as we are one. 12 While I was with them, I kept them in thy name, which thou hast given me; I have guarded them, and none of them is lost but the son of perdition, that the scripture might be fulfilled. 13 But now I am coming to thee; and these things I speak in the world, that they may have my joy fulfilled in themselves. 14 I have given them thy word; and the world has hated them because they are not of the world, even as I am not of the world. 15 I do not pray that thou shouldst take them out of the world, but that thou shouldst keep them from the evil one.[k] 16 They are not of the world, even as I am not of the world. 17 Sanctify them in the truth; thy word is truth. 18As thou didst send me into the world, so I have sent them into the world. 19And

[k] Or *from evil.*

PHILLIPS

have believed that I came from God. Yes, I did come from the Father and I came into the world. Now I leave the world behind and return to the Father."

"Now you are speaking plainly," cried the disciples, "and are not using parables. Now we know that everything is known to you—no more questions are needed. This makes us sure that you did come from God."

"So you believe in me now?" replied Jesus. "The time is coming, indeed, it has already come, when you will be scattered, every one of you going home and leaving me alone. Yet I am not really alone, for the Father is with me. I have told you all this so that you may find your peace in me. You will find trouble in the world—but, never lose heart, I have conquered the world!"

N.E.B.

believed that I came from God. I came from the Father and have come into the world. Now I am leaving the world again and going to the Father.' His disciples said, 'Why, this is plain speaking; this is no figure of speech. We are certain now that you know everything, and do not need to be questioned; because of this we believe that you have come from God.'

Jesus answered, 'Do you now believe? Look,[a] the hour is coming, has indeed already come, when you are all to be scattered, each to his home, leaving me alone. Yet I am not alone, because the Father is with me. I have told you all this so that in me you may find peace. In the world you will have trouble. But courage! The victory is mine; I have conquered the world.'

*Jesus' prayer for his disciples—   17. 1
present and future*

When Jesus had said these words, he raised his eyes to Heaven and said: "Father, the hour has come. Glorify your Son now so that he may bring glory to you, for you have given him authority over all men to give eternal life to all that you have given to him. And this is eternal life, to know you, the only true God, and him whom you have sent—Jesus Christ.

"I have brought you honor upon earth, I have completed the task which you gave me to do. Now, Father, honor me in your own presence with the glory that I knew with you before the world was made. I have shown your self to the men whom you gave me from the world. They were your men and you gave them to me, and they have accepted your word. Now they realize that all that you have given me comes from you—and that every message that you gave me I have given them. They have accepted it all and have come to know in their hearts that I did come from you—they are convinced that you sent me.

"I am praying to you for them: I am not praying for the world but for the men whom you gave me, for they are yours—everything that is mine is yours and yours mine—and they have done me honor. Now I am no longer in the world, but they are in the world and I am returning to you. Holy Father, keep the men you gave me by your power that they may be one, as we are one. As long as I was with them, I kept them by the power that you gave me; I guarded them, and not one of them was destroyed, except the son of destruction—that the scripture might come true.

"And now I come to you and I say these things in the world that these men may find my joy completed in themselves. I have given them your word, and the world has hated them, for they are no more sons of the world than I am. I am not praying that you will take them out of the world but that you will keep them from the evil one. They are no more the sons of the world than I am—make them holy by the truth for your word is the truth. I have sent them to the world just as you sent me to the world and

17 After these words Jesus looked up to heaven and said:

'Father, the hour has come. Glorify thy Son, that the Son may glorify thee. For thou hast made him sovereign over all mankind, to give eternal life to all whom thou hast given him. This is eternal life: to know thee who alone art truly God, and Jesus Christ whom thou hast sent.

'I have glorified thee on earth by completing the work which thou gavest me to do; and now, Father, glorify me in thine own presence with the glory which I had with thee before the world began.

'I have made thy name known to the men whom thou didst give me out of the world. They were thine, thou gavest them to me, and they have obeyed thy command. Now they know that all thy gifts have come to me from thee; for I have taught them all that I learned from thee, and they have received it: they know with certainty that I came from thee; they have had faith to believe that thou didst send me.

'I pray for them; I am not praying for the world but for those whom thou hast given me, because they belong to thee. All that is mine is thine, and what is thine is mine; and through them has my glory shone.

'I am to stay no longer in the world, but they are still in the world, and I am on my way to thee. Holy Father, protect by the power of thy name those whom thou hast given me,[b] that they may be one, as we are one. When I was with them, I protected by the power of thy name those whom thou hast given me,[c] and kept them safe. Not one of them is lost except the man who must be lost, for Scripture has to be fulfilled.

'And now I am coming to thee; but while I am still in the world I speak these words, so that they may have my joy within them in full measure. I have delivered thy word to them, and the world hates them because they are strangers in the world, as I am. I pray thee, not to take them out of the world, but to keep them from the evil one. They are strangers in the world, as I am. Consecrate them by the truth;[d] thy word is truth. As thou hast sent me into the world, I have sent them into the world, and for

[a] Or At the moment you believe; but look . . .
[b] Or protect them by the power of thy name which thou hast given me, or keep in loyalty to thee those whom thou hast given me. [c] Or protected them by the power of thy name which thou hast given me, or kept in loyalty to thee those whom thou hast given me. [d] Or in truth.

K.J.V.

self, that they also might be sanctified through the truth. 20 Neither pray I for these alone, but for them also which shall believe on me through their word; 21 That they all may be one; as thou, Father, *art* in me, and I in thee, that they also may be one in us: that the world may believe that thou hast sent me. 22And the glory which thou gavest me I have given them; that they may be one, even as we are one: 23 I in them, and thou in me, that they may be made perfect in one; and that the world may know that thou hast sent me, and hast loved them, as thou hast loved me. 24 Father, I will that they also, whom thou hast given me, be with me where I am; that they may behold my glory, which thou hast given me: for thou lovedst me before the foundation of the world. 25 O righteous Father, the world hath not known thee: but I have known thee, and these have known that thou hast sent me. 26And I have declared unto them thy name, and will declare *it;* that the love wherewith thou hast loved me may be in them, and I in them.

18 When Jesus had spoken these words, he went forth with his disciples over the brook Cedron, where was a garden, into the which he entered, and his disciples. 2And Judas also, which betrayed him, knew the place: for Jesus ofttimes resorted thither with his disciples. 3 Judas then, having received a band *of men* and officers from the chief priests and Pharisees, cometh thither with lanterns and torches and weapons. 4 Jesus therefore, knowing all things that should come upon him, went forth, and said unto them, Whom seek ye? 5 They answered him, Jesus of Nazareth. Jesus saith unto them, I am *he.* And Judas also, which betrayed him, stood with them. 6As soon then as he had said unto them, I am *he,* they went backward, and fell to the ground. 7 Then asked he them again, Whom seek ye? And they said, Jesus of Nazareth. 8 Jesus answered, I have told you that I am *he:* if therefore ye seek me, let these go their way: 9 That the saying might be fulfilled, which he spake, Of them which thou gavest me have I lost none. 10 Then Simon Peter having a sword drew it, and smote the high priest's servant, and cut off his right ear. The servant's name was Malchus. 11 Then said Jesus unto Peter, Put up thy sword into the sheath: the cup which my Father hath given me, shall I not drink it? 12 Then the band and the captain and officers of the Jews took Jesus, and bound him, 13And led him away to Annas first; for he was father in law to Caiaphas, which was the high priest that same year. 14 Now Caiaphas was he, which gave counsel to the Jews, that it was expedient that one man should die for the people.

15 And Simon Peter followed Jesus, and *so did* another disciple: that disciple was known unto the high priest, and went in with Jesus into the palace of the high priest. 16 But Peter stood at the door without. Then went out that other

R.S.V.

for their sake I consecrate myself, that they also may be consecrated in truth.

20 "I do not pray for these only, but also for those who believe in me through their word, 21 that they may all be one; even as thou, Father, art in me, and I in thee, that they also may be in us, so that the world may believe that thou hast sent me. 22 The glory which thou hast given me I have given to them, that they may be one even as we are one, 23 I in them and thou in me, that they may become perfectly one, so that the world may know that thou hast sent me and hast loved them even as thou hast loved me. 24 Father, I desire that they also, whom thou hast given me, may be with me where I am, to behold my glory which thou hast given me in thy love for me before the foundation of the world. 25 O righteous Father, the world has not known thee, but I have known thee; and these know that thou hast sent me. 26 I made known to them thy name, and I will make it known, that the love with which thou hast loved me may be in them, and I in them."

18 When Jesus had spoken these words, he went forth with his disciples across the Kidron valley, where there was a garden, which he and his disciples entered. 2 Now Judas, who betrayed him, also knew the place; for Jesus often met there with his disciples. 3 So Judas, procuring a band of soldiers and some officers from the chief priests and the Pharisees, went there with lanterns and torches and weapons. 4 Then Jesus, knowing all that was to befall him, came forward and said to them, "Whom do you seek?" 5 They answered him, "Jesus of Nazareth." Jesus said to them, "I am he." Judas, who betrayed him, was standing with them. 6 When he said to them, "I am he," they drew back and fell to the ground. 7Again he asked them, "Whom do you seek?" And they said, "Jesus of Nazareth." 8 Jesus answered, "I told you that I am he; so, if you seek me, let these men go." 9 This was to fulfil the word which he had spoken, "Of those whom thou gavest me I lost not one." 10 Then Simon Peter, having a sword, drew it and struck the high priest's slave and cut off his right ear. The slave's name was Malchus. 11 Jesus said to Peter, "Put your sword into its sheath; shall I not drink the cup which the Father has given me?"

12 So the band of soldiers and their captain and the officers of the Jews seized Jesus and bound him. 13 First they led him to Annas; for he was the father-in-law of Caiaphas, who was high priest that year. 14 It was Caiaphas who had given counsel to the Jews that it was expedient that one man should die for the people.

15 Simon Peter followed Jesus, and so did another disciple. As this disciple was known to the high priest, he entered the court of the high priest along with Jesus, 16 while Peter stood outside at the door. So the other disciple, who

PHILLIPS

I consecrate myself for their sakes that they may be made holy by the truth.

"I am not praying only for these men but for all those who will believe in me through their message, that they may all be one. Just as you, Father, live in me and I live in you, I am asking that they may live in us, that the world may believe that you did send me. I have given them the honor that you gave me, that they may be one, as we are one—I in them and you in me, that they may grow complete into one, so that the world may realize that you sent me and have loved them as you loved me. Father, I want those whom you have given me to be with me where I am; I want them to see that glory which you have made mine—for you loved me before the world began. Father of goodness and truth, the world has not known you, but I have known you and these men now know that you have sent me. I have made your self known to them and I will continue to do so that the love which you have had for me may be in their hearts—and that I may be there also."

Jesus is arrested in the garden   18. 1

When Jesus had spoken these words, he went out with his disciples across the Cedron valley to a place where there was a garden, and they went into it together. Judas who betrayed him knew the place, for Jesus often met his disciples there. So Judas fetched the guard and the officers which the chief priests and Pharisees had provided for him, and came to the place with torches and lanterns and weapons. Jesus, fully realizing all that was going to happen to him, went forward and said to them, "Who are you looking for?"

"Jesus of Nazareth," they answered.

"I am the man," said Jesus. (Judas who was betraying him was standing there with the others.)

When he said to them, "I am the man," they retreated and fell to the ground. So Jesus asked them again, "Who are you looking for?"

And again they said, "Jesus of Nazareth."

"I have told you that I am the man," replied Jesus. "If I am the man you are looking for, let these others go." (Thus fulfilling his previous words, "I have not lost one of those whom you gave me.")

At this, Simon Peter, who had a sword, drew it and slashed at the High Priest's servant, cutting off his right ear. (The servant's name was Malchus.) But Jesus said to Peter, "Put your sword back into its sheath. Am I not to drink the cup the Father has given me?"

Peter follows Jesus,   18. 12
only to deny him

Then the guard, with their captain and the Jewish officers, took hold of Jesus and tied his hands together, and led him off to Annas first, for he was father-in-law to Caiaphas, who was High Priest that year. Caiaphas was the man who advised the Jews, "that it would be a good thing that one man should die for the sake of the people." Behind Jesus followed Simon Peter, and one other disciple who was known personally to the High Priest. He went in with Jesus into the High Priest's courtyard, but Peter was left standing at the door outside. So this

N.E.B.

their sake I now consecrate myself, that they too may be consecrated by the truth.[a]

'But it is not for these alone that I pray, but for those also who through their words put their faith in me; may they all be one: as thou, Father, art in me, and I in thee, so also may they be in us, that the world may believe that thou didst send me. The glory which thou gavest me I have given to them, that they may be one, as we are one; I in them and thou in me, may they be perfectly one. Then the world will learn that thou didst send me, that thou didst love them as thou didst me.

'Father, I desire that these men, who are thy gift to me, may be with me where I am, so that they may look upon my glory, which thou hast given me because thou didst love me before the world began. O righteous Father, although the world does not know thee, I know thee, and these men know that thou didst send me. I made thy name known to them, and will make it known, so that the love thou hadst for me may be in them, and I may be in them.'

The Final Conflict

18 After these words, Jesus went out with his disciples, and crossed the Kedron ravine. There was a garden there, and he and his disciples went into it. The place was known to Judas, his betrayer, because Jesus had often met there with his disciples. So Judas took a detachment of soldiers, and police provided by the chief priests and the Pharisees, equipped with lanterns, torches, and weapons, and made his way to the garden. Jesus, knowing all that was coming upon him, went out to them and asked, 'Who is it you want?' 'Jesus of Nazareth', they answered. Jesus said, 'I am he.' And there stood Judas the traitor with them. When he said, 'I am he', they drew back and fell to the ground. Again Jesus asked, 'Who is it you want?' 'Jesus of Nazareth', they answered. Then Jesus said, 'I have told you that I am he. If I am the man you want, let these others go.' (This was to make good his words, 'I have not lost one of those whom thou gavest me.') Thereupon Simon Peter drew the sword he was wearing and struck at the High Priest's servant, cutting off his right ear. (The servant's name was Malchus.) Jesus said to Peter, 'Sheathe your sword. This is the cup my Father has given me; shall I not drink it?'

The troops with their commander, and the Jewish police, now arrested Jesus and secured him. They took him first to Annas.[b] Annas was father-in-law of Caiaphas, the High Priest for that year[b]—the same Caiaphas who had advised the Jews that it would be to their interest if one man died for the whole people. Jesus was followed by Simon Peter and another disciple. This disciple, who was acquainted with the High Priest, went with Jesus into the High Priest's courtyard, but Peter halted at the door outside. So the other disciple, the High Priest's acquaintance, went out again and spoke to the woman at the door, and brought Peter in. The maid on

[a] Or in truth. [b] See note on verse 24.

K.J.V.

disciple, which was known unto the high priest, and spake unto her that kept the door, and brought in Peter. 17 Then saith the damsel that kept the door unto Peter, Art not thou also *one* of this man's disciples? He saith, I am not. 18And the servants and officers stood there, who had made a fire of coals, for it was cold; and they warmed themselves: and Peter stood with them, and warmed himself.

19 The high priest then asked Jesus of his disciples, and of his doctrine. 20 Jesus answered him, I spake openly to the world; I ever taught in the synagogue, and in the temple, whither the Jews always resort; and in secret have I said nothing. 21 Why askest thou me? ask them which heard me, what I have said unto them: behold, they know what I said. 22And when he had thus spoken, one of the officers which stood by struck Jesus with the palm of his hand, saying, Answerest thou the high priest so? 23 Jesus answered him, If I have spoken evil, bear witness of the evil: but if well, why smitest thou me? 24 Now Annas had sent him bound unto Caiaphas the high priest. 25And Simon Peter stood and warmed himself. They said therefore unto him, Art not thou also *one* of his disciples? He denied *it*, and said, I am not. 26 One of the servants of the high priest, being *his* kinsman whose ear Peter cut off, saith, Did not I see thee in the garden with him? 27 Peter then denied again; and immediately the cock crew.

28 Then led they Jesus from Caiaphas unto the hall of judgment: and it was early; and they themselves went not into the judgment hall, lest they should be defiled; but that they might eat the passover. 29 Pilate then went out unto them, and said, What accusation bring ye against this man? 30 They answered and said unto him, If he were not a malefactor, we would not have delivered him up unto thee. 31 Then said Pilate unto them, Take ye him, and judge him according to your law. The Jews therefore said unto him, It is not lawful for us to put any man to death: 32 That the saying of Jesus might be fulfilled, which he spake, signifying what death he should die. 33 Then Pilate entered into the judgment hall again, and called Jesus, and said unto him, Art thou the King of the Jews? 34 Jesus answered him, Sayest thou this thing of thyself, or did others tell it thee of me? 35 Pilate answered, Am I a Jew? Thine own nation and the chief priests have delivered thee unto me:

R.S.V.

was known to the high priest, went out and spoke to the maid who kept the door, and brought Peter in. 17 The maid who kept the door said to Peter, "Are not you also one of this man's disciples?" He said, "I am not." 18 Now the servants*i* and officers had made a charcoal fire, because it was cold, and they were standing and warming themselves; Peter also was with them, standing and warming himself.

19 The high priest then questioned Jesus about his disciples and his teaching. 20 Jesus answered him, "I have spoken openly to the world; I have always taught in synagogues and in the temple, where all Jews come together; I have said nothing secretly. 21 Why do you ask me? Ask those who have heard me, what I said to them; they know what I said." 22 When he had said this, one of the officers standing by struck Jesus with his hand, saying, "Is that how you answer the high priest?" 23 Jesus answered him, "If I have spoken wrongly, bear witness to the wrong; but if I have spoken rightly, why do you strike me?" 24Annas then sent him bound to Caiaphas the high priest.

25 Now Simon Peter was standing and warming himself. They said to him, "Are not you also one of his disciples?" He denied it and said, "I am not." 26 One of the servants*i* of the high priest, a kinsman of the man whose ear Peter had cut off, asked, "Did I not see you in the garden with him?" 27 Peter again denied it; and at once the cock crowed.

28 Then they led Jesus from the house of Caiaphas to the praetorium. It was early. They themselves did not enter the praetorium, so that they might not be defiled, but might eat the passover. 29 So Pilate went out to them and said, "What accusation do you bring against this man?" 30 They answered him, "If this man were not an evildoer, we would not have handed him over." 31 Pilate said to them, "Take him yourselves and judge him by your own law." The Jews said to him, "It is not lawful for us to put any man to death." 32 This was to fulfil the word which Jesus had spoken to show by what death he was to die.

33 Pilate entered the praetorium again and called Jesus, and said to him, "Are you the King of the Jews?" 34 Jesus answered, "Do you say this of your own accord, or did others say it to you about me?" 35 Pilate answered, "Am I a Jew? Your own nation and the chief priests have handed you over to me; what have you done?"

[l] Or *slaves*.

PHILLIPS

N.E.B.

other disciple, who was acquainted with the High Priest, went out and spoke to the doorkeeper, and brought Peter inside. The young woman at the door remarked to Peter, "Are you one of this man's disciples, too?"

"No, I am not," retorted Peter.

In the courtyard, the servants and officers stood around a charcoal fire which they had made, for it was cold. They were warming themselves, and Peter stood there with them, keeping himself warm.

Meanwhile the High Priest interrogated Jesus about his disciples and about his own teaching.

"I have always spoken quite openly to the world," replied Jesus. "I have always taught in the synagogue or in the Temple where all Jews meet together, and I have said nothing in secret. Why do you question me? Why not question those who have heard me about what I said to them? Obviously they are the ones who know what I actually said."

As he said this, one of those present, an officer, slapped Jesus with his open hand, remarking, "Is that the way for you to answer the High Priest?"

"If I have said anything wrong," Jesus said to him, "you must give evidence about it, but if what I said was true why do you strike me?"

Then Annas sent him, with his hands still tied, to the High Priest, Caiaphas.

Peter's denial   18. 25

In the meantime Simon Peter was still standing, keeping himself warm. Some of them said to him, "Surely you too are one of his disciples, aren't you?"

And he denied it and said, "No, I am not."

Then one of the High Priest's servants, a relation of the man whose ear Peter had cut off, remarked, "Didn't I see you in the garden with him?"

And again Peter denied it. And immediately the cock crew.

Jesus is taken before the   18. 28
Roman authority

Then they led Jesus from Caiaphas' presence into the palace. It was now early morning and the Jews themselves did not go into the palace, for fear that they would be contaminated and would not be able to eat the Passover. So Pilate walked out to them and said, "What is the charge that you are bringing against this man?"

"If he were not an evildoer, we should not have handed him over to you," they replied.

To which Pilate retorted, "Then take him yourselves and judge him according to your law."

"We are not allowed to put a man to death," replied the Jews (thus fulfilling Christ's prophecy of the method of his own death).

So Pilate went back into the palace and called Jesus to him. "Are you the king of the Jews?" he asked.

"Are you asking this of your own accord," replied Jesus, "or have other people spoken to you about me?"

"Do you think *I* am a Jew?" replied Pilate. "It's your people and your chief priests who handed you over to me. What have you done, anyway?"

duty at the door said to Peter, 'Are you another of this man's disciples?' 'I am not', he said. The servants and the police had made a charcoal fire, because it was cold, and were standing round it warming themselves. And Peter too was standing with them, sharing the warmth.

The High Priest questioned Jesus about his disciples and about what he taught. Jesus replied, 'I have spoken openly to all the world; I have always taught in synagogue and in the temple, where all Jews congregate; I have said nothing in secret. Why question me? Ask my hearers what I told them; they know what I said.' When he said this, one of the police struck him on the face, exclaiming, 'Is that the way to answer the High Priest?' Jesus replied, 'If I spoke amiss, state it in evidence; if I spoke well, why strike me?'

So Annas sent him bound to Caiaphas the High Priest.[a]

Meanwhile Peter stood warming himself. The others asked, 'Are you another of his disciples?' But he denied it: 'I am not', he said. One of the High Priest's servants, a relation of the man whose ear Peter had cut off, insisted, 'Did I not see you with him in the garden?' Peter denied again; and just then a cock crew.

From Caiaphas Jesus was led into the Governor's headquarters. It was now early morning, and the Jews themselves stayed outside the headquarters to avoid defilement, so that they could eat the Passover meal.[b] So Pilate went out to them and asked, 'What charge do you bring against this man?' 'If he were not a criminal,' they replied, 'we should not have brought him before you.' Pilate said, 'Take him away and try him by your own law.' The Jews answered, 'We are not allowed to put any man to death.' Thus they ensured the fulfilment of the words by which Jesus had indicated the manner of his death.

Pilate then went back into his headquarters and summoned Jesus. 'Are you the king of the Jews?' he asked.[c] Jesus said, 'Is that your own idea, or have others suggested it to you?' 'What! am I a Jew?' said Pilate. 'Your own nation and their chief priests have brought you before me.

[a] *Some witnesses give this verse after* first to Annas *in verse 13; others at the end of verse 13*. [b] *Or* could share in the offerings of the Passover season. [c] *Or* 'You are king of the Jews, I take it', he said.

K.J.V.

what hast thou done? 36 Jesus answered, My kingdom is not of this world: if my kingdom were of this world, then would my servants fight, that I should not be delivered to the Jews: but now is my kingdom not from hence. 37 Pilate therefore said unto him, Art thou a king then? Jesus answered, Thou sayest that I am a king. To this end was I born, and for this cause came I into the world, that I should bear witness unto the truth. Every one that is of the truth heareth my voice. 38 Pilate saith unto him, What is truth? And when he had said this, he went out again unto the Jews, and saith unto them, I find in him no fault *at all*. 39 But ye have a custom, that I should release unto you one at the passover: will ye therefore that I release unto you the King of the Jews? 40 Then cried they all again, saying, Not this man, but Barabbas. Now Barabbas was a robber.

19 Then Pilate therefore took Jesus, and scourged *him*. 2And the soldiers platted a crown of thorns, and put *it* on his head, and they put on him a purple robe, 3And said, Hail, King of the Jews! and they smote him with their hands. 4 Pilate therefore went forth again, and saith unto them, Behold, I bring him forth to you, that ye may know that I find no fault in him. 5 Then came Jesus forth, wearing the crown of thorns, and the purple robe. And *Pilate* saith unto them, Behold the man! 6 When the chief priests therefore and officers saw him, they cried out, saying, Crucify *him*, crucify *him*. Pilate saith unto them, Take ye him, and crucify *him:* for I find no fault in him. 7 The Jews answered him, We have a law, and by our law he ought to die, because he made himself the Son of God.

8 When Pilate therefore heard that saying, he was the more afraid; 9And went again into the judgment hall, and saith unto Jesus, Whence art thou? But Jesus gave him no answer. 10 Then saith Pilate unto him, Speakest thou not unto me? knowest thou not that I have power to crucify thee, and have power to release thee? 11 Jesus answered, Thou couldest have no power *at all* against me, except it were given thee from above: therefore he that delivered me unto thee hath the greater sin. 12And from thenceforth Pilate sought to release him: but the Jews cried out, saying, If thou let this man go, thou art not Cesar's friend: whosoever maketh himself a king speaketh against Cesar.

13 When Pilate therefore heard that saying, he brought Jesus forth, and sat down in the judgment seat in a place that is called the Pavement, but in the Hebrew, Gabbatha. 14And it was the preparation of the passover, and about the sixth hour: and he saith unto the Jews, Behold your King! 15 But they cried out, Away with *him*, away with *him*, crucify him. Pilate saith unto them, Shall I crucify your King? The chief priests answered, We have no king but Cesar. 16 Then delivered he him therefore unto them to be crucified. And they took Jesus, and

R.S.V.

36 Jesus answered, "My kingship is not of this world; if my kingship were of this world, my servants would fight, that I might not be handed over to the Jews; but my kingship is not from the world." 37 Pilate said to him, "So you are a king?" Jesus answered, "You say that I am a king. For this I was born, and for this I have come into the world, to bear witness to the truth. Every one who is of the truth hears my voice." 38 Pilate said to him, "What is truth?"

After he had said this, he went out to the Jews again, and told them, "I find no crime in him. 39 But you have a custom that I should release one man for you at the Passover; will you have me release for you the King of the Jews?" 40 They cried out again, "Not this man, but Barabbas!" Now Barabbas was a robber.

19 Then Pilate took Jesus and scourged him. 2And the soldiers plaited a crown of thorns, and put it on his head, and arrayed him in a purple robe; 3 they came up to him, saying, "Hail, King of the Jews!" and struck him with their hands. 4 Pilate went out again, and said to them, "Behold, I am bringing him out to you, that you may know that I find no crime in him." 5 So Jesus came out, wearing the crown of thorns and the purple robe. Pilate said to them, "Here is the man!" 6 When the chief priests and the officers saw him, they cried out, "Crucify him, crucify him!" Pilate said to them, "Take him yourselves and crucify him, for I find no crime in him." 7 The Jews answered him, "We have a law, and by that law he ought to die, because he has made himself the Son of God." 8 When Pilate heard these words, he was the more afraid; 9 he entered the praetorium again and said to Jesus, "Where are you from?" But Jesus gave no answer. 10 Pilate therefore said to him, "You will not speak to me? Do you not know that I have power to release you, and power to crucify you?" 11 Jesus answered him, "You would have no power over me unless it had been given you from above; therefore he who delivered me to you has the greater sin."

12 Upon this Pilate sought to release him, but the Jews cried out, "If you release this man, you are not Caesar's friend; every one who makes himself a king sets himself against Caesar." 13 When Pilate heard these words, he brought Jesus out and sat down on the judgment seat at a place called The Pavement, and in Hebrew, Gabbatha. 14 Now it was the day of Preparation of the Passover; it was about the sixth hour. He said to the Jews, "Here is your King!" 15 They cried out, "Away with him, away with him, crucify him!" Pilate said to them, "Shall I crucify your King?" The chief priests answered, "We have no king but Caesar." 16 Then he handed him over to them to be crucified.

PHILLIPS

"My kingdom is not founded in this world—if it were, my servants would have fought to prevent my being handed over to the Jews. But in fact my kingdom is not founded on all this!"

"So you are a king, are you?" returned Pilate.

"Indeed I am a king," Jesus replied; "the reason for my birth and the reason for my coming into the world is to witness to the truth. Every man who loves truth recognizes my voice."

To which Pilate retorted, "What is 'truth'?" and went straight out again to the Jews and said:

"I find nothing criminal about him at all. But I have an arrangement with you to set one prisoner free at Passover time. Do you wish me then to set free for you the 'king of the Jews'?"

At this, they shouted out again, "No, not this man, but Barabbas!"

Barabbas was a bandit.

N.E.B.

What have you done?' Jesus replied, 'My kingdom does not belong to this world. If it did, my followers would be fighting to save me from arrest by the Jews. My kingly authority comes from elsewhere.' 'You are a king, then?' said Pilate. Jesus answered, ' "King" is your word. My task is to bear witness to the truth. For this was I born; for this I came into the world, and all who are not deaf to truth listen to my voice.' Pilate said, 'What is truth?', and with those words went out again to the Jews. 'For my part,' he said, 'I find no case against him. But you have a custom that I release one prisoner for you at Passover. Would you like me to release the king of the Jews?' Again the clamour rose: 'Not him; we want Barabbas!' (Barabbas was a bandit.)

Pilate's vain efforts to save Jesus   19. 1

Then Pilate took Jesus and had him flogged, and the soldiers twisted thorn twigs into a crown and put it on his head, threw a purple robe around him and kept coming into his presence, saying, "Hail, king of the Jews!" And then they slapped him with their open hands.

Then Pilate went outside again and said to them, "Look, I bring him out before you here, to show that I find nothing criminal about him at all."

And at this Jesus came outside too, wearing the thorn crown and the purple robe.

"Look," said Pilate, "here's the man!"

The sight of him made the chief priests and Jewish officials shout at the top of their voices, "Crucify! Crucify!"

"You take him and crucify him," retorted Pilate. "He's no criminal as far as I can see!"

The Jews answered him, "We have a Law, and according to that Law, he must die, for he made himself out to be Son of God!"

When Pilate heard them say this, he became much more uneasy, and returned to the palace again and spoke to Jesus, "Where *do* you come from?"

But Jesus gave him no reply. So Pilate said to him: "Won't you speak to me? Don't you realize that I have the power to set you free, and I have the power to have you crucified?"

"You have no power at all against me," replied Jesus, "except what was given to you from above. And for that reason the one who handed me over to you is even more guilty than you are."

From that moment Pilate tried hard to set him free, but the Jews were shouting: "If you set this man free, you are no friend of Caesar! Anyone who makes himself out to be a king is anti-Caesar!"

When Pilate heard this, he led Jesus outside and sat down upon the Judgment seat in the place called the Pavement (in Hebrew, Gabbatha). It was the preparation day of the Passover and it was now getting on toward midday. Pilate now said to the Jews, "Look, here's your king!"

At which they yelled, "Take him away, take him away, crucify him!"

"Am I to crucify your king?" Pilate asked them.

"Caesar is our king and no one else," replied the chief priests. And at this Pilate handed Jesus over to them for crucifixion.

19 Pilate now took Jesus and had him flogged; and the soldiers plaited a crown of thorns and placed it on his head, and robed him in a purple cloak. Then time after time they came up to him, crying, 'Hail, King of the Jews!', and struck him on the face.

Once more Pilate came out and said to the Jews, 'Here he is; I am bringing him out to let you know that I find no case against him'; and Jesus came out, wearing the crown of thorns and the purple cloak. 'Behold the Man!' said Pilate. The chief priests and their henchmen saw him and shouted, 'Crucify! crucify!' 'Take him and crucify him yourselves,' said Pilate; 'for my part I find no case against him.' The Jews answered, 'We have a law; and by that law he ought to die, because he has claimed to be Son of God.'

When Pilate heard that, he was more afraid than ever, and going back into his headquarters he asked Jesus, 'Where have you come from?' But Jesus gave him no answer. 'Do you refuse to speak to me?' said Pilate. 'Surely you know that I have authority to release you, and I have authority to crucify you?' 'You would have no authority at all over me', Jesus replied, 'if it had not been granted you from above; and therefore the deeper guilt lies with the man who handed me over to you.'

From that moment Pilate tried hard to release him; but the Jews kept shouting, 'If you let this man go, you are no friend to Caesar; any man who claims to be a king is defying Caesar.' When Pilate heard what they were saying, he brought Jesus out and took his seat on the tribunal at the place known as 'The Pavement' ('Gabbatha' in the language of the Jews). It was the eve of Passover,[a] about noon. Pilate said to the Jews, 'Here is your king.' They shouted, 'Away with him! Away with him! Crucify him!' 'Crucify your king?' said Pilate. 'We have no king but Caesar', the Jews replied. Then at last, to satisfy them, he handed Jesus over to be crucified.

[a] *Or* It was Friday in Passover.

K.J.V.

led *him* away. 17And he bearing his cross went forth into a place called *the place* of a skull, which is called in the Hebrew Golgotha: 18 Where they crucified him, and two others with him, on either side one, and Jesus in the midst.

19 And Pilate wrote a title, and put *it* on the cross. And the writing was, JESUS OF NAZARETH THE KING OF THE JEWS. 20 This title then read many of the Jews; for the place where Jesus was crucified was nigh to the city: and it was written in Hebrew, *and* Greek, *and* Latin. 21 Then said the chief priests of the Jews to Pilate, Write not, The King of the Jews; but that he said, I am King of the Jews. 22 Pilate answered, What I have written I have written.

23 Then the soldiers, when they had crucified Jesus, took his garments, and made four parts, to every soldier a part; and also *his* coat: now the coat was without seam, woven from the top throughout. 24 They said therefore among themselves, Let us not rend it, but cast lots for it, whose it shall be: that the Scripture might be fulfilled, which saith, They parted my raiment among them, and for my vesture they did cast lots. These things therefore the soldiers did.

25 Now there stood by the cross of Jesus his mother, and his mother's sister, Mary the *wife* of Cleophas, and Mary Magdalene. 26 When Jesus therefore saw his mother, and the disciple standing by, whom he loved, he saith unto his mother, Woman, behold thy son! 27 Then saith he to the disciple, Behold thy mother! And from that hour that disciple took her unto his own *home.*

28 After this, Jesus knowing that all things were now accomplished, that the Scripture might be fulfilled, saith, I thirst. 29 Now there was set a vessel full of vinegar: and they filled a sponge with vinegar, and put *it* upon hyssop, and put *it* to his mouth. 30 When Jesus therefore had received the vinegar, he said, It is finished: and he bowed his head, and gave up the ghost. 31 The Jews therefore, because it was the preparation, that the bodies should not remain upon the cross on the sabbath day, (for that sabbath day was a high day,) besought Pilate that their legs might be broken, and *that* they might be taken away. 32 Then came the soldiers, and brake the legs of the first, and of the other which was crucified with him. 33 But when they came to Jesus, and saw that he was dead already, they brake not his legs: 34 But one of the soldiers with a spear pierced his side, and forthwith came there out blood and water. 35And he that saw *it* bare record, and his record is true; and he knoweth that he saith true, that ye might believe. 36 For these things were done, that the Scripture should be fulfilled, A bone of him shall not be broken.

R.S.V.

17 So they took Jesus, and he went out, bearing his own cross, to the place called the place of a skull, which is called in Hebrew Golgotha. 18 There they crucified him, and with him two others, one on either side, and Jesus between them. 19 Pilate also wrote a title and put it on the cross; it read, "Jesus of Nazareth, the King of the Jews." 20 Many of the Jews read this title, for the place where Jesus was crucified was near the city; and it was written in Hebrew, in Latin, and in Greek. 21 The chief priests of the Jews then said to Pilate, "Do not write, 'The King of the Jews,' but, 'This man said, I am King of the Jews.'" 22 Pilate answered, "What I have written I have written."

23 When the soldiers had crucified Jesus they took his garments and made four parts, one for each soldier; also his tunic. But the tunic was without seam, woven from top to bottom; 24 so they said to one another, "Let us not tear it, but cast lots for it to see whose it shall be." This was to fulfil the scripture,

"They parted my garments among them,
and for my clothing they cast lots."

25 So the soldiers did this. But standing by the cross of Jesus were his mother, and his mother's sister, Mary the wife of Clopas, and Mary Magdalene. 26 When Jesus saw his mother, and the disciple whom he loved standing near, he said to his mother, "Woman, behold, your son!" 27 Then he said to the disciple, "Behold, your mother!" And from that hour the disciple took her to his own home.

28 After this Jesus, knowing that all was now finished, said (to fulfil the scripture), "I thirst." 29A bowl full of vinegar stood there; so they put a sponge full of the vinegar on hyssop and held it to his mouth. 30 When Jesus had received the vinegar, he said, "It is finished"; and he bowed his head and gave up his spirit. 31 Since it was the day of Preparation, in order to prevent the bodies from remaining on the cross on the sabbath (for that sabbath was a high day), the Jews asked Pilate that their legs might be broken, and that they might be taken away. 32 So the soldiers came and broke the legs of the first, and of the other who had been crucified with him; 33 but when they came to Jesus and saw that he was already dead, they did not break his legs. 34 But one of the soldiers pierced his side with a spear, and at once there came out blood and water. 35 He who saw it has borne witness—his testimony is true, and he knows that he tells the truth—that you also may believe. 36 For these things took place that the scripture might be fulfilled, "Not a bone of him

| PHILLIPS | N.E.B. |

PHILLIPS

The crucifixion   19. 17

So they took Jesus and he went out carrying the cross himself, to a place called Skull Hill (in Hebrew, Golgotha). There they crucified him, and two others, one on either side of him with Jesus in the middle. Pilate had a placard written out and put on the cross, reading, "JESUS OF NAZARETH, THE KING OF THE JEWS." This placard was read by many of the Jews because the place where Jesus was crucified was quite near Jerusalem, and it was written in Hebrew as well as in Latin and Greek. So the chief priests said to Pilate, "You should not write 'The King of the Jews,' but 'This man said, I am King of the Jews.'"

To which Pilate retorted, "Indeed? What I have written, I have written."

When the soldiers had crucified Jesus, they divided his clothes between them, taking a quarter-share each. There remained his shirt, which was seamless—woven in one piece from the top to the bottom. So they said to each other, "Don't let us tear it; let's draw lots and see who gets it."

This happened to fulfill the scripture which says—

They parted my garments among them,
And upon my vesture did they cast lots.

Jesus provides for his mother   19. 25
from the cross

While the soldiers were doing this, Jesus' mother was standing near the cross with her sister, and with them Mary, the wife of Clopas, and Mary of Magdala. Jesus saw his mother and the disciple whom he loved standing by her side, and said to her, "Look, there is your son!" And then he said to the disciple, "And there is your mother!"

And from that time the disciple took Mary into his own home.

After this, Jesus realizing that everything was now completed, said (fulfilling the saying of scripture), "I am thirsty."

There was a bowl of sour wine standing there. So they soaked a sponge in the wine, put it on a spear, and pushed it up toward his mouth. When Jesus had taken it, he cried, "It is finished!" His head fell forward, and he died.

The body of Jesus is removed   19. 31

As it was the day of preparation for the Passover, the Jews wanted to avoid the bodies being left on the crosses over the Sabbath (for that was a particularly important Sabbath), and they requested Pilate to have the men's legs broken and the bodies removed. So the soldiers went and broke the legs of the first man and of the other who was crucified with Jesus. But when they came to him, they saw that he was dead already and they did not break his legs. But one of the soldiers pierced his side with a spear, and at once there was an outrush of blood and water. And the man who saw this is our witness: his evidence is true. (He is certain that he is speaking the truth, so that you may believe as well.) For this happened to fulfill the scripture,

A bone of him shall not be broken.

N.E.B.

Jesus was now taken in charge and, carrying his own cross, went out to the Place of the Skull, as it is called (or, in the Jews' language, 'Golgotha'), where they crucified him, and with him two others, one on the right, one on the left, and Jesus between them.

And Pilate wrote an inscription to be fastened to the cross; it read, 'Jesus of Nazareth King of the Jews.' This inscription was read by many Jews, because the place where Jesus was crucified was not far from the city, and the inscription was in Hebrew, Latin, and Greek. Then the Jewish chief priests said to Pilate, 'You should not write "King of the Jews"; write, "He claimed to be king of the Jews."' Pilate replied, 'What I have written, I have written.'

The soldiers, having crucified Jesus, took possession of his clothes, and divided them into four parts, one for each soldier, leaving out the tunic. The tunic was seamless, woven in one piece throughout; so they said to one another, 'We must not tear this; let us toss for it'; and thus the text of Scripture came true: 'They shared my garments among them, and cast lots for my clothing.'

That is what the soldiers did. But meanwhile near the cross where Jesus hung stood his mother, with her sister, Mary wife of Clopas, and Mary of Magdala. Jesus saw his mother, with the disciple whom he loved standing beside her. He said to her, 'Mother, there is your son'; and to the disciple, 'There is your mother'; and from that moment the disciple took her into his home.

After that, Jesus, aware that all had now come to its appointed end, said in fulfilment of Scripture, 'I thirst.' A jar stood there full of sour wine; so they soaked a sponge with the wine, fixed it on a javelin,[a] and held it up to his lips. Having received the wine, he said, 'It is accomplished!' He bowed his head and gave up his spirit.[b]

Because it was the eve of Passover,[c] the Jews were anxious that the bodies should not remain on the cross for the coming Sabbath, since that Sabbath was a day of great solemnity; so they requested Pilate to have the legs broken and the bodies taken down. The soldiers accordingly came to the first of his fellow-victims and to the second, and broke their legs; but when they came to Jesus, they found that he was already dead, so they did not break his legs. But one of the soldiers stabbed his side with a lance, and at once there was a flow of blood and water. This is vouched for by an eyewitness, whose evidence is to be trusted. He knows that he speaks the truth, so that you too may believe; for this happened in fulfilment of the text of Scripture: 'No bone of his shall be broken.'

[a] So one witness; the others read on marjoram.
[b] Or breathed out his life. [c] Or Because it was Friday in Passover . . .

K.J.V.

37And again another Scripture saith, They shall look on him whom they pierced.

38 And after this Joseph of Arimathea, being a disciple of Jesus, but secretly for fear of the Jews, besought Pilate that he might take away the body of Jesus: and Pilate gave *him* leave. He came therefore, and took the body of Jesus. 39And there came also Nicodemus, (which at the first came to Jesus by night,) and brought a mixture of myrrh and aloes, about a hundred pound *weight.* 40 Then took they the body of Jesus, and wound it in linen clothes with the spices, as the manner of the Jews is to bury. 41 Now in the place where he was crucified there was a garden; and in the garden a new sepulchre, wherein was never man yet laid. 42 There laid they Jesus therefore because of the Jews' preparation *day;* for the sepulchre was nigh at hand.

20 The first *day* of the week cometh Mary Magdalene early, when it was yet dark, unto the sepulchre, and seeth the stone taken away from the sepulchre. 2 Then she runneth, and cometh to Simon Peter, and to the other disciple, whom Jesus loved, and saith unto them, They have taken away the Lord out of the sepulchre, and we know not where they have laid him. 3 Peter therefore went forth, and that other disciple, and came to the sepulchre. 4 So they ran both together: and the other disciple did outrun Peter, and came first to the sepulchre. 5And he stooping down, *and looking in,* saw the linen clothes lying; yet went he not in. 6 Then cometh Simon Peter following him, and went into the sepulchre, and seeth the linen clothes lie, 7And the napkin, that was about his head, not lying with the linen clothes, but wrapped together in a place by itself. 8 Then went in also that other disciple, which came first to the sepulchre, and he saw, and believed. 9 For as yet they knew not the Scripture, that he must rise again from the dead. 10 Then the disciples went away again unto their own home.

11 But Mary stood without at the sepulchre weeping: and as she wept, she stooped down, *and looked* into the sepulchre, 12And seeth two angels in white sitting, the one at the head, and the other at the feet, where the body of Jesus had lain. 13And they say unto her, Woman, why weepest thou? She saith unto them, Because they have taken away my Lord, and I know not where they have laid him. 14And when she had thus said, she turned herself back, and saw Jesus standing, and knew not that it was Jesus. 15 Jesus saith unto her, Woman, why weepest thou? whom seekest thou? She, supposing him to be the gardener, saith unto him, Sir, if thou have borne him hence, tell me where thou hast laid him, and I will take him away. 16 Jesus saith unto her, Mary. She turned herself, and saith unto him, Rabboni: which is to say, Master. 17 Jesus saith unto her, Touch me not; for I am not yet ascended to my Father: but go to my brethren, and say unto them, I ascend unto my Father, and your Father; and *to* my God, and your God.

R.S.V.

shall be broken." 37And again another scripture says, "They shall look on him whom they have pierced."

38 After this Joseph of Arimathea, who was a disciple of Jesus, but secretly, for fear of the Jews, asked Pilate that he might take away the body of Jesus, and Pilate gave him leave. So he came and took away his body. 39 Nicodemus also, who had at first come to him by night, came bringing a mixture of myrrh and aloes, about a hundred pounds' weight. 40 They took the body of Jesus, and bound it in linen cloths with the spices, as is the burial custom of the Jews. 41 Now in the place where he was crucified there was a garden, and in the garden a new tomb where no one had ever been laid. 42 So because of the Jewish day of Preparation, as the tomb was close at hand, they laid Jesus there.

20 Now on the first day of the week Mary Magdalene came to the tomb early, while it was still dark, and saw that the stone had been taken away from the tomb. 2 So she ran, and went to Simon Peter and the other disciple, the one whom Jesus loved, and said to them, "They have taken the Lord out of the tomb, and we do not know where they have laid him." 3 Peter then came out with the other disciple, and they went toward the tomb. 4 They both ran, but the other disciple outran Peter and reached the tomb first; 5 and stooping to look in, he saw the linen cloths lying there, but he did not go in. 6 Then Simon Peter came, following him, and went into the tomb; he saw the linen cloths lying, 7 and the napkin, which had been on his head, not lying with the linen cloths but rolled up in a place by itself. 8 Then the other disciple, who reached the tomb first, also went in, and he saw and believed; 9 for as yet they did not know the scripture, that he must rise from the dead. 10 Then the disciples went back to their homes.

11 But Mary stood weeping outside the tomb, and as she wept she stooped to look into the tomb; 12 and she saw two angels in white, sitting where the body of Jesus had lain, one at the head and one at the feet. 13 They said to her, "Woman, why are you weeping?" She said to them, "Because they have taken away my Lord, and I do not know where they have laid him." 14 Saying this, she turned round and saw Jesus standing, but she did not know that it was Jesus. 15 Jesus said to her, "Woman, why are you weeping? Whom do you seek?" Supposing him to be the gardener, she said to him, "Sir, if you have carried him away, tell me where you have laid him, and I will take him away." 16 Jesus said to her, "Mary." She turned and said to him in Hebrew, "Rabboni!" (which means Teacher). 17 Jesus said to her, "Do not hold me, for I have not yet ascended to the Father; but go to my brethren and say to them, I am ascending to my Father and your Father,

PHILLIPS

And again another scripture says—

They shall look on him whom they pierced.

After it was all over, Joseph (who came from Arimathaea and was a disciple of Jesus, though secretly for fear of the Jews), requested Pilate that he might take away Jesus' body, and Pilate gave him permission. So he came and took his body down. Nicodemus also, the man who had come to him at the beginning by night, arrived bringing a mixture of myrrh and aloes, weighing about a hundred pounds. So they took his body and wound it round with linen strips with the spices, according to the Jewish custom of preparing a body for burial. In the place where he was crucified, there was a garden containing a new tomb in which nobody had yet been laid. Because it was the preparation day and because the tomb was conveniently near, they laid Jesus in this tomb.

The first day of the week: 20. 1
the risen Lord

But on the first day of the week, Mary of Magdala arrived at the tomb, very early in the morning, while it was still dark, and noticed that the stone had been taken away from the tomb. At this she ran, found Simon Peter and the other disciple whom Jesus loved, and told them, "They have taken the Lord out of the tomb and we don't know where they have put him."

Peter and the other disciple set off at once for the tomb, the two of them running together. The other disciple ran faster than Peter and was the first to arrive at the tomb. He stooped and looked inside and noticed the linen cloths lying there but did not go in himself. Hard on his heels came Simon Peter and went straight into the tomb. He noticed that the linen cloths were lying there, and that the handkerchief, which had been round Jesus' head, was not lying with the linen cloths but was rolled up by itself, a little way apart. Then the other disciple, who was the first to arrive at the tomb, came inside as well, saw what had happened and believed. (They did not yet understand the scripture which said that he must rise from the dead.) So the disciples went back again to their homes.

But Mary stood just outside the tomb, and she was crying. And as she cried, she looked into the tomb and saw two angels in white who sat, one at the head and the other at the foot of the place where the body of Jesus had lain. The angels spoke to her. "Why are you crying?" they asked.

"Because they have taken away my Lord, and I don't know where they have put him!" she said.

Then she turned and noticed Jesus standing there, without realizing that it was Jesus. "Why are you crying?" said Jesus to her. "Who are you looking for?"

She, supposing that he was the gardener, said, "Oh, sir, if you have carried him away, please tell me where you have put him and I will take him away."

Jesus said to her, "Mary!"

At this she turned right round and said to him, in Hebrew, "Master!"

"No!" said Jesus, "do not hold me now. I have not yet gone up to the Father. Go and tell my brothers that I am going up to my Father, and your Father, to my God and your God."

N.E.B.

And another text says, 'They shall look on him whom they pierced.'

After that, Pilate was approached by Joseph of Arimathaea, a disciple of Jesus, but a secret disciple for fear of the Jews, who[a] asked to be allowed to remove the body of Jesus. Pilate gave the permission; so Joseph came and took the body away. He was joined by Nicodemus (the man who had first visited Jesus by night), who brought with him a mixture of myrrh and aloes, more than half a hundredweight. They took the body of Jesus and wrapped it, with the spices, in strips of linen cloth according to Jewish burial-customs. Now at the place where he had been crucified there was a garden, and in the garden a new tomb, not yet used for burial. There, because the tomb was near at hand and it was the eve of the Jewish Sabbath, they laid Jesus.

20 Early on the Sunday morning, while it was still dark, Mary of Magdala came to the tomb. She saw that the stone had been moved away from the entrance, and ran to Simon Peter and the other disciple, the one whom Jesus loved. 'They have taken the Lord out of his tomb,' she cried, 'and we do not know where they have laid him.' So Peter and the other set out and made their way to the tomb. They were running side by side, but the other disciple outran Peter and reached the tomb first. He peered in and saw the linen wrappings lying there, but did not enter. Then Simon Peter came up, following him, and he went into the tomb. He saw the linen wrappings lying, and the napkin which had been over his head, not lying with the wrappings but rolled together in a place by itself. Then the disciple who had reached the tomb first went in too, and he saw and believed; until then they had not understood the scriptures, which showed that he must rise from the dead.

So the disciples went home again; but Mary stood at the tomb outside, weeping. As she wept, she peered into the tomb; and she saw two angels in white sitting there, one at the head, and one at the feet, where the body of Jesus had lain. They said to her, 'Why are you weeping?' She answered, 'They have taken my Lord away, and I do not know where they have laid him.' With these words she turned round and saw Jesus standing there, but did not recognize him. Jesus said to her, 'Why are you weeping? Who is it you are looking for?' Thinking it was the gardener, she said, 'If it is you, sir, who removed him, tell me where you have laid him, and I will take him away.' Jesus said, 'Mary!' She turned to him and said, 'Rabbuni!' (which is Hebrew for 'My Master'). Jesus said, 'Do not cling to me,[b] for I have not yet ascended to the Father. But go to my brothers, and tell them that I am now ascending[c] to my Father

---

[a] Or of Arimathaea. He was a disciple of Jesus, but had gone into hiding for fear of the Jews. He now . . . [b] Or Touch me no more. [c] Or I am going to ascend . . .

K.J.V.

18 Mary Magdalene came and told the disciples that she had seen the Lord, and *that* he had spoken these things unto her.

19 Then the same day at evening, being the first *day* of the week, when the doors were shut where the disciples were assembled for fear of the Jews, came Jesus and stood in the midst, and saith unto them, Peace *be* unto you. 20And when he had so said, he shewed unto them *his* hands and his side. Then were the disciples glad, when they saw the Lord. 21 Then said Jesus to them again, Peace *be* unto you: as *my* Father hath sent me, even so send I you. 22And when he had said this, he breathed on *them*, and saith unto them, Receive ye the Holy Ghost: 23 Whosoever sins ye remit, they are remitted unto them; *and* whosoever *sins* ye retain, they are retained.

24 But Thomas, one of the twelve, called Didymus, was not with them when Jesus came. 25 The other disciples therefore said unto him, We have seen the Lord. But he said unto them, Except I shall see in his hands the print of the nails, and put my finger into the print of the nails, and thrust my hand into his side, I will not believe.

26 And after eight days again his disciples were within, and Thomas with them: *then* came Jesus, the doors being shut, and stood in the midst, and said, Peace *be* unto you. 27 Then saith he to Thomas, Reach hither thy finger, and behold my hands; and reach hither thy hand, and thrust *it* into my side; and be not faithless, but believing. 28 And Thomas answered and said unto him, My Lord and my God. 29 Jesus saith unto him, Thomas, because thou hast seen me, thou hast believed: blessed *are* they that have not seen, and *yet* have believed.

30 And many other signs truly did Jesus in the presence of his disciples, which are not written in this book: 31 But these are written, that ye might believe that Jesus is the Christ, the Son of God; and that believing ye might have life through his name.

R.S.V.

to my God and your God." 18 Mary Magdalene went and said to the disciples, "I have seen the Lord"; and she told them that he had said these things to her.

19 On the evening of that day, the first day of the week, the doors being shut where the disciples were, for fear of the Jews, Jesus came and stood among them and said to them, "Peace be with you." 20 When he had said this, he showed them his hands and his side. Then the disciples were glad when they saw the Lord. 21 Jesus said to them again, "Peace be with you. As the Father has sent me, even so I send you." 22And when he had said this, he breathed on them, and said to them, "Receive the Holy Spirit. 23 If you forgive the sins of any, they are forgiven; if you retain the sins of any, they are retained."

24 Now Thomas, one of the twelve, called the Twin, was not with them when Jesus came. 25 So the other disciples told him, "We have seen the Lord." But he said to them, "Unless I see in his hands the print of the nails, and place my finger in the mark of the nails, and place my hand in his side, I will not believe."

26 Eight days later, his disciples were again in the house, and Thomas was with them. The doors were shut, but Jesus came and stood among them, and said, "Peace be with you." 27 Then he said to Thomas, "Put your finger here, and see my hands; and put out your hand, and place it in my side; do not be faithless, but believing." 28 Thomas answered him, "My Lord and my God!" 29 Jesus said to him, "Have you believed because you have seen me? Blessed are those who have not seen and yet believe."

30 Now Jesus did many other signs in the presence of the disciples, which are not written in this book; 31 but these are written that you may believe that Jesus is the Christ, the Son of God, and that believing you may have life in his name.

21 After these things Jesus shewed himself again to the disciples at the sea of Tiberias; and on this wise shewed he *himself*. 2 There were together Simon Peter, and Thomas called Didymus, and Nathanael of Cana in Galilee, and the *sons* of Zebedee, and two other of his disciples. 3 Simon Peter saith unto them, I go a fishing. They say unto him, We also go with thee. They went forth, and entered into a ship immediately; and that night they caught nothing. 4 But when the morning was now come, Jesus stood on the shore; but the disciples knew not that it was Jesus. 5 Then Jesus saith unto them, Children, have ye any meat? They answered him, No. 6 And he said unto them, Cast the net on the right side of the ship, and ye shall find. They cast therefore, and now they were not able to draw it for the multitude of fishes. 7 Therefore that disciple whom Jesus loved saith unto Peter, It is the Lord. Now when Simon Peter heard that it was the Lord, he girt *his* fisher's coat *unto him,* (for he was naked,) and did cast him-

21 After this Jesus revealed himself again to the disciples by the Sea of Tiberias; and he revealed himself in this way. 2 Simon Peter, Thomas called the Twin, Nathanael of Cana in Galilee, the sons of Zebedee, and two others of his disciples were together. 3 Simon Peter said to them, "I am going fishing." They said to him, "We will go with you." They went out and got into the boat; but that night they caught nothing. 4 Just as day was breaking, Jesus stood on the beach; yet the disciples did not know that it was Jesus. 5 Jesus said to them, "Children, have you any fish?" They answered him, "No." 6 He said to them, "Cast the net on the right side of the boat, and you will find some." So they cast it, and now they were not able to haul it in, for the quantity of fish. 7 That disciple whom Jesus loved said to Peter, "It is the Lord!" When Simon Peter heard that it was the Lord, he put on his clothes, for he was stripped for work, and

And Mary of Magdala went off to the disciples, with the news, "I have seen the Lord!" and she told them what he had said to her.

In the evening of that first day of the week, the disciples had met together with the doors locked for fear of the Jews. Jesus came and stood right in the middle of them and said, "Peace be with you!"

Then he showed them his hands and his side, and when they saw the Lord the disciples were overjoyed.

Jesus said to them again: "Yes, peace be with you! Just as the Father sent me, so I am going to send you."

And then he breathed upon them and said, "Receive holy spirit.* If you forgive any men's sins, they are forgiven, and if you hold them unforgiven, they are unforgiven."

The risen Jesus and Thomas 20. 24

But one of the twelve, Thomas (called the twin), was not with them when Jesus came. The other disciples kept on telling him, "We have seen the Lord," but he replied, "Unless I see in his own hands the mark of the nails, and put my finger where the nails were, and put my hand into his side, I will never believe!"

Just over a week later, the disciples were indoors again and Thomas was with them. The doors were shut, but Jesus came and stood in the middle of them and said, "Peace be with you!"

Then he said to Thomas, "Put your finger here—look, here are my hands. Take your hand and put it in my side. You must not doubt, but believe."

"My Lord and my God!" cried Thomas.

"Is it because you have seen me that you believe?" Jesus said to him. "Happy are those who have never seen me and yet have believed!"

Jesus gave a great many other signs in the presence of his disciples which are not recorded in this book. But these have been written so that you may believe that Jesus is Christ, the Son of God, and that in that faith you may have life as his disciples.

The risen Jesus and Peter 21. 1

Later on, Jesus showed himself again to his disciples on the shore of Lake Tiberias, and he did it in this way. Simon Peter, Thomas (called the twin), Nathanael from Cana of Galilee, the sons of Zebedee and two other disciples were together, when Simon Peter said,

"I'm going fishing."

"All right," they replied, "we'll go with you."

So they went out and got into the boat and during the night caught nothing at all. But just as dawn began to break, Jesus stood there on the beach, although the disciples had no idea that it was Jesus.

"Have you caught anything, lads?" Jesus called out to them.

"No," they replied.

"Throw the net on the right side of the boat," said Jesus, "and you'll have a catch."

So they threw out the net and found that they were now not strong enough to pull it in because it was so full of fish! At this, the disciple that Jesus loved said to Peter, "It is the Lord!"

Hearing this, Peter slipped on his clothes, for

and your Father, my God and your God.' Mary of Magdala went to the disciples with her news: 'I have seen the Lord!' she said, and gave them his message.

Late that Sunday evening, when the disciples were together behind locked doors, for fear of the Jews, Jesus came and stood among them. 'Peace be with you!' he said, and then showed them his hands and his side. So when the disciples saw the Lord, they were filled with joy. Jesus repeated, 'Peace be with you!', and then said, 'As the Father sent me, so I send you.' He then breathed on them, saying, 'Receive the Holy Spirit! If you forgive any man's sins, they stand forgiven; if you pronounce them unforgiven, unforgiven they remain.'

One of the Twelve, Thomas, that is 'the Twin', was not with the rest when Jesus came. So the disciples told him, 'We have seen the Lord.' He said, 'Unless I see the mark of the nails on his hands, unless I put my finger into the place where the nails were, and my hand into his side, I will not believe it.'

A week later his disciples were again in the room, and Thomas was with them. Although the doors were locked, Jesus came and stood among them, saying, 'Peace be with you!' Then he said to Thomas, 'Reach your finger here: see my hands; reach your hand here and put it into my side; be unbelieving no longer, but believe.' Thomas said, 'My Lord and my God!' Jesus said, 'Because you have seen me you have found faith. Happy are they who never saw me and yet have found faith.'

There were indeed many other signs that Jesus performed in the presence of his disciples, which are not recorded in this book. Those here written have been recorded in order that you may hold the faith[a] that Jesus is the Christ, the Son of God, and that through this faith you may possess eternal life by his name.

21 Some time later, Jesus showed himself to his disciples once again, by the Sea of Tiberias; and in this way. Simon Peter and Thomas 'the Twin' were together with Nathanael of Cana-in-Galilee. The sons of Zebedee and two other disciples were also there. Simon Peter said, 'I am going out fishing.' 'We will go with you', said the others. So they started and got into the boat. But that night they caught nothing.

Morning came, and there stood Jesus on the beach, but the disciples did not know that it was Jesus. He called out to them, 'Friends, have you caught anything?' They answered 'No.' He said, 'Shoot the net to starboard, and you will make a catch.' They did so, and found they could not haul the net aboard, there were so many fish in it. Then the disciple whom Jesus loved said to Peter, 'It is the Lord!' When Simon Peter heard that, he wrapped his coat about him (for he had

---

* Lit., "receive holy spirit." Historically the Holy Spirit was not given until Pentecost.

[a] *Some witnesses read* that you may come to believe . . .

K.J.V.

self into the sea. 8And the other disciples came in a little ship, (for they were not far from land, but as it were two hundred cubits,) dragging the net with fishes. 9As soon then as they were come to land, they saw a fire of coals there, and fish laid thereon, and bread. 10 Jesus saith unto them, Bring of the fish which ye have now caught. 11 Simon Peter went up, and drew the net to land full of great fishes, a hundred and fifty and three: and for all there were so many, yet was not the net broken. 12 Jesus saith unto them, Come and dine. And none of the disciples durst ask him, Who art thou? knowing that it was the Lord. 13 Jesus then cometh, and taketh bread, and giveth them, and fish likewise. 14 This is now the third time that Jesus shewed himself to his disciples, after that he was risen from the dead.

15 So when they had dined, Jesus saith to Simon Peter, Simon, *son* of Jonas, lovest thou me more than these? He saith unto him, Yea, Lord; thou knowest that I love thee. He saith unto him, Feed my lambs. 16 He saith to him again the second time, Simon, *son* of Jonas, lovest thou me? He saith unto him, Yea, Lord; thou knowest that I love thee. He saith unto him, Feed my sheep. 17 He saith unto him the third time, Simon, *son* of Jonas, lovest thou me? Peter was grieved because he said unto him the third time, Lovest thou me? And he said unto him, Lord, thou knowest all things; thou knowest that I love thee. Jesus saith unto him, Feed my sheep. 18 Verily, verily, I say unto thee, When thou wast young, thou girdedst thyself, and walkedst whither thou wouldest: but when thou shalt be old, thou shalt stretch forth thy hands, and another shall gird thee, and carry *thee* whither thou wouldest not. 19 This spake he, signifying by what death he should glorify God. And when he had spoken this, he saith unto him, Follow me. 20 Then Peter, turning about, seeth the disciple whom Jesus loved following; which also leaned on his breast at supper, and said, Lord, which is he that betrayeth thee? 21 Peter seeing him saith to Jesus, Lord, and what *shall* this man *do?* 22 Jesus saith unto him, If I will that he tarry till I come, what *is that* to thee? follow thou me. 23 Then went this saying abroad among the brethren, that that disciple should not die: yet Jesus said not unto him, He shall not die; but, If I will that he tarry till I come, what *is that* to thee? 24 This is the disciple which testifieth of these things, and wrote these things: and we know that his testimony is true. 25And there are also many other things which Jesus did, the which, if they should be written every one, I suppose that even the world itself could not contain the books that should be written. Amen.

R.S.V.

sprang into the sea. 8 But the other disciples came in the boat, dragging the net full of fish, for they were not far from the land, but about a hundred yards[m] off.

9 When they got out on land, they saw a charcoal fire there, with fish lying on it, and bread. 10 Jesus said to them, "Bring some of the fish that you have just caught." 11 So Simon Peter went aboard and hauled the net ashore, full of large fish, a hundred and fifty-three of them; and although there were so many, the net was not torn. 12 Jesus said to them, "Come and have breakfast." Now none of the disciples dared ask him, "Who are you?" They knew it was the Lord. 13 Jesus came and took the bread and gave it to them, and so with the fish. 14 This was now the third time that Jesus was revealed to the disciples after he was raised from the dead.

15 When they had finished breakfast, Jesus said to Simon Peter, "Simon, son of John, do you love me more than these?" He said to him, "Yes, Lord; you know that I love you." He said to him, "Feed my lambs." 16A second time he said to him, "Simon, son of John, do you love me?" He said to him, "Yes, Lord; you know that I love you." He said to him, "Tend my sheep." 17 He said to him the third time, "Simon, son of John, do you love me?" Peter was grieved because he said to him the third time, "Do you love me?" And he said to him, "Lord, you know everything; you know that I love you." Jesus said to him, "Feed my sheep. 18 Truly, truly, I say to you, when you were young, you girded yourself and walked where you would; but when you are old, you will stretch out your hands, and another will gird you and carry you where you do not wish to go." 19 (This he said to show by what death he was to glorify God.) And after this he said to him, "Follow me."

20 Peter turned and saw following them the disciple whom Jesus loved, who had lain close to his breast at the supper and had said, "Lord, who is it that is going to betray you?" 21 When Peter saw him, he said to Jesus, "Lord, what about this man?" 22 Jesus said to him, "If it is my will that he remain until I come, what is that to you? Follow me!" 23 The saying spread abroad among the brethren that this disciple was not to die; yet Jesus did not say to him that he was not to die, but, "If it is my will that he remain until I come, what is that to you?"

24 This is the disciple who is bearing witness to these things, and who has written these things; and we know that his testimony is true.

25 But there are also many other things which Jesus did; were every one of them to be written, I suppose that the world itself could not contain the books that would be written.

[m] Greek *two hundred cubits.*

PHILLIPS

he had been naked, and plunged into the sea. The other disciples followed in the boat, for they were only about a hundred yards from the shore, dragging in the net full of fish. When they had landed, they saw that a charcoal fire was burning, with a fish placed on it, and some bread. Jesus said to them, "Bring me some of the fish you've just caught."

So Simon Peter got into the boat and hauled the net ashore full of large fish, one hundred and fifty-three altogether. But in spite of the large number the net was not torn.

Then Jesus said to them, "Come and have your breakfast."

None of the disciples dared to ask him who he was; they knew it was the Lord.

Jesus went and took the bread and gave it to them and gave them all fish as well. This is already the third time that Jesus showed himself to his disciples after his resurrection from the dead.

When they had finished breakfast Jesus said to Simon Peter, "Simon, son of John, do you love me more than these others?"

"Yes, Lord," he replied, "you know that I am your friend."

"Then feed my lambs," returned Jesus. Then he said for the second time,

"Simon, son of John, do you love me?"

"Yes, Lord," returned Peter. "You know that I am your friend."

"Then care for my sheep," replied Jesus. Then for the third time, Jesus spoke to him and said, "Simon, son of John, *are* you my friend?"

Peter was deeply hurt because Jesus' third question to him was "Are you my friend?" and he said: "Lord, you know everything. You know that I am your friend!"

"Then feed my sheep," Jesus said to him. "I tell you truly, Peter, that when you were younger, you used to dress yourself and go where you liked, but when you are an old man, you are going to stretch out your hands and someone else will dress you and take you where you do not want to go."

(He said this to show the kind of death by which Peter was going to honor God.)

Then Jesus said to him, "You must follow me."

Then Peter turned round and noticed the disciple whom Jesus loved following behind them. (He was the one who had his head on Jesus' shoulder at supper and had asked, "Lord, who is the one who is going to betray you?") So he said, "Yes, Lord, but what about him?"

"If it is my wish," returned Jesus, "for him to stay until I come, is that your business, Peter? You must follow me."

This gave rise to the saying among the brothers that this disciple would not die. Yet, of course, Jesus did not say, "He will not die," but simply, "If it is my wish for him to stay until I come, is that your business?"

N.E.B.

stripped) and plunged into the sea. The rest of them came on in the boat, towing the net full of fish; for they were not far from land, only about a hundred yards.

When they came ashore, they saw a charcoal fire there, with fish laid on it, and some bread. Jesus said, 'Bring some of your catch.' Simon Peter went aboard and dragged the net to land, full of big fish, a hundred and fifty-three of them; and yet, many as they were, the net was not torn. Jesus said, 'Come and have breakfast.' None of the disciples dared to ask 'Who are you?' They knew it was the Lord. Jesus now came up, took the bread, and gave it to them, and the fish in the same way.

This makes the third time that Jesus appeared to his disciples after his resurrection from the dead.

After breakfast, Jesus said to Simon Peter, 'Simon son of John, do you love me more than all else[a]?' 'Yes, Lord,' he answered, 'you know that I love you.'[b] 'Then feed my lambs', he said. A second time he asked, 'Simon son of John, do you love me?' 'Yes, Lord, you know I love you.'[b] 'Then tend my sheep.' A third time he said, 'Simon son of John, do you love me[c]?' Peter was hurt that he asked him a third time, 'Do you love me?'[d] 'Lord,' he said, 'you know everything; you know I love you.'[b] Jesus said, 'Feed my sheep.

'And further, I tell you this in very truth: when you were young you fastened your belt about you and walked where you chose; but when you are old you will stretch out your arms, and a stranger will bind you fast, and carry you where you have no wish to go.' He said this to indicate the manner of death by which Peter was to glorify God. Then he added, 'Follow me.'

Peter looked round, and saw the disciple whom Jesus loved following—the one who at supper had leaned back close to him to ask the question, 'Lord, who is it that will betray you?' When he caught sight of him, Peter asked, 'Lord, what will happen to him?' Jesus said, 'If it should be my will that he wait until I come, what is it to you? Follow me.'

That saying of Jesus became current in the brotherhood, and was taken to mean that that disciple would not die. But in fact Jesus did not say that he would not die; he only said, 'If it should be my will that he wait until I come, what is it to you?'

It is this same disciple who attests what has here been written. It is in fact he who wrote it, and we know that his testimony is true.

There is much else that Jesus did. If it were all to be recorded in detail, I suppose the whole world would not hold the books that would be written.

All the above was written   **21. 24**
by an eyewitness

Now it is this same disciple who is hereby giving his testimony to these things and has written them down. We know that his witness is reliable. Of course, there are many other things which Jesus did, and I suppose that if each one were written down in detail, there would not be room in the whole world for all the books that would have to be written.

[a] *Or* more than they do. [b] *Or* that I am your friend. [c] *Or* are you my friend. [d] *Or* that at the third asking he should have said, 'Are you my friend?'

THE ACTS OF THE

APOSTLES

THE ACTS OF THE

APOSTLES

1 The former treatise have I made, O Theophilus, of all that Jesus began both to do and teach, 2 Until the day in which he was taken up, after that he through the Holy Ghost had given commandments unto the apostles whom he had chosen: 3 To whom also he shewed himself alive after his passion by many infallible proofs, being seen of them forty days, and speaking of the things pertaining to the kingdom of God: 4And, being assembled together with *them*, commanded them that they should not depart from Jerusalem, but wait for the promise of the Father, which, *saith he,* ye have heard of me. 5 For John truly baptized with water; but ye shall be baptized with the Holy Ghost not many days hence. 6 When they therefore were come together, they asked of him, saying, Lord, wilt thou at this time restore again the kingdom to Israel? 7And he said unto them, It is not for you to know the times or the seasons, which the Father hath put in his own power. 8 But ye shall receive power, after that the Holy Ghost is come upon you: and ye shall be witnesses unto me both in Jerusalem, and in all Judea, and in Samaria, and unto the uttermost part of the earth. 9And when he had spoken these things, while they beheld, he was taken up; and a cloud received him out of their sight. 10And while they looked steadfastly toward heaven as he went up, behold, two men stood by them in white apparel; 11 Which also said, Ye men of Galilee, why stand ye gazing up into heaven? this same Jesus, which is taken up from you into heaven, shall so come in like manner as ye have seen him go into heaven. 12 Then returned they unto Jerusalem from the mount called Olivet, which is from Jerusalem a sabbath day's journey. 13And when they were come in, they went up into an upper room, where abode both Peter, and James, and John, and Andrew, Philip, and Thomas, Bartholomew, and Matthew, James *the son* of Alpheus, and Simon Zelotes, and Judas *the brother* of James. 14 These all continued with one accord in prayer and supplication, with the women, and Mary the mother of Jesus, and with his brethren.

1 In the first book, O Theophilus, I have dealt with all that Jesus began to do and teach, 2 until the day when he was taken up, after he had given commandment through the Holy Spirit to the apostles whom he had chosen. 3 To them he presented himself alive after his passion by many proofs, appearing to them during forty days, and speaking of the kingdom of God. 4And while staying*a* with them he charged them not to depart from Jerusalem, but to wait for the promise of the Father, which, he said, "you heard from me, 5 for John baptized with water, but before many days you shall be baptized with the Holy Spirit."

6 So when they had come together, they asked him, "Lord, will you at this time restore the kingdom to Israel?" 7 He said to them, "It is not for you to know times or seasons which the Father has fixed by his own authority. 8 But you shall receive power when the Holy Spirit has come upon you; and you shall be my witnesses in Jerusalem and in all Judea and Samaria and to the end of the earth." 9And when he had said this, as they were looking on, he was lifted up, and a cloud took him out of their sight. 10And while they were gazing into heaven as he went, behold, two men stood by them in white robes, 11 and said, "Men of Galilee, why do you stand looking into heaven? This Jesus, who was taken up from you into heaven, will come in the same way as you saw him go into heaven."

12 Then they returned to Jerusalem from the mount called Olivet, which is near Jerusalem, a sabbath day's journey away; 13 and when they had entered, they went up to the upper room, where they were staying, Peter and John and James and Andrew, Philip and Thomas, Bartholomew and Matthew, James the son of Alphaeus and Simon the Zealot and Judas the son of James. 14All these with one accord devoted themselves to prayer, together with the women and Mary the mother of Jesus, and with his brothers.

[a] Or *eating.*

340

THE ACTS OF THE

APOSTLES

Introduction

1. 1

My dear Theophilus,

In my first book I gave you some account of all that Jesus began to do and teach until the time of his ascension. Before he ascended he gave his instructions, through the Holy Spirit, to the special messengers of his choice. For after his suffering he showed himself alive to them in many convincing ways, and appeared to them repeatedly over a period of forty days talking with them about the affairs of the kingdom of God.

Jesus' parting words before his ascension

1. 4

On one occasion, while he was eating a meal with them, he emphasized that they were not to leave Jerusalem, but to wait for the Father's promise.

"You have already heard me speak about this," he said, "for John used to baptize with water, but before many days are passed you will be baptized with the Holy Spirit."

This naturally brought them all together, and they asked him,

"Lord, is this the time when you are going to restore the kingdom to Israel?"

To this he replied,

"You cannot know times and dates which have been fixed by the Father's sole authority. But you are to be given power when the Holy Spirit has come to you. You will be witnesses to me, not only in Jerusalem, not only throughout Judaea, not only in Samaria, but to the very ends of the earth!"

When he had said these words he was lifted up before their eyes till a cloud hid him from their sight. While they were still gazing up into the sky as he went, suddenly two men dressed in white stood beside them and said,

"Men of Galilee, why are you standing here looking up into the sky? This very Jesus who has been taken up from you into Heaven will come back in just the same way as you have seen him go."

At this they returned to Jerusalem from the Mount of Olives which is near the city, only a Sabbath day's journey away. On entering Jerusalem they went straight to the upstairs room where they had been staying. There were Peter, John, James, Andrew, Philip, Thomas, Bartholomew, Matthew, James the son of Alphaeus, Simon the patriot, and Judas the son of James. By common consent all these men, together with the women who had followed Jesus, Mary his mother, as well as his brothers, devoted themselves to prayer.

ACTS OF THE

APOSTLES

The Beginnings of the Church

1 In the first part of my work, Theophilus, I wrote of all that Jesus did and taught from the beginning until the day when, after giving instructions through the Holy Spirit to the apostles whom he had chosen, he was taken up to heaven. He showed himself to these men after his death, and gave ample proof that he was alive: over a period of forty days he appeared to them and taught them about the kingdom of God. While he was in their company he told them not to leave Jerusalem. 'You must wait', he said, 'for the promise made by my Father, about which you have heard me speak: John, as you know, baptized with water, but you will be baptized with the Holy Spirit, and within the next few days.'

So, when they were all together, they asked him, 'Lord, is this the time when you are to establish once again the sovereignty of Israel?' He answered, 'It is not for you to know about dates or times, which the Father has set within his own control. But you will receive power when the Holy Spirit comes upon you; and you will bear witness for me in Jerusalem, and all over Judaea and Samaria, and away to the ends of the earth.'

When he had said this, as they watched, he was lifted up, and a cloud removed him from their sight. As he was going, and as they were gazing intently into the sky, all at once there stood beside them two men in white who said, 'Men of Galilee, why stand there looking up into the sky? This Jesus, who has been taken away from you up to heaven, will come in the same way as you have seen him go.'

Then they returned to Jerusalem from the hill called Olivet, which is near Jerusalem, no farther than a Sabbath day's journey. Entering the city they went to the room upstairs where they were lodging: Peter and John and James and Andrew, Philip and Thomas, Bartholomew and Matthew, James son of Alphaeus and Simon the Zealot, and Judas son of James. All these were constantly at prayer together, and with them a group of women, including Mary the mother of Jesus, and his brothers.

K.J.V.

15 And in those days Peter stood up in the midst of the disciples, and said, (the number of names together were about a hundred and twenty,) 16 Men *and* brethren, this Scripture must needs have been fulfilled, which the Holy Ghost by the mouth of David spake before concerning Judas, which was guide to them that took Jesus. 17 For he was numbered with us, and had obtained part of this ministry. 18 Now this man purchased a field with the reward of iniquity; and falling headlong, he burst asunder in the midst, and all his bowels gushed out. 19And it was known unto all the dwellers at Jerusalem; insomuch as that field is called, in their proper tongue, Aceldama, that is to say, The field of blood. 20 For it is written in the book of Psalms, Let his habitation be desolate, and let no man dwell therein: and, His bishoprick let another take. 21 Wherefore of these men which have companied with us all the time that the Lord Jesus went in and out among us, 22 Beginning from the baptism of John, unto that same day that he was taken up from us, must one be ordained to be a witness with us of his resurrection. 23 And they appointed two, Joseph called Barsabas, who was surnamed Justus, and Matthias. 24And they prayed, and said, Thou, Lord, which knowest the hearts of all *men*, shew whether of these two thou hast chosen, 25 That he may take part of this ministry and apostleship, from which Judas by transgression fell, that he might go to his own place. 26And they gave forth their lots; and the lot fell upon Matthias; and he was numbered with the eleven apostles.

R.S.V.

15 In those days Peter stood up among the brethren (the company of persons was in all about a hundred and twenty), and said, 16 "Brethren, the scripture had to be fulfilled, which the Holy Spirit spoke beforehand by the mouth of David, concerning Judas who was guide to those who arrested Jesus. 17 For he was numbered among us, and was allotted his share in this ministry. 18 (Now this man bought a field with the reward of his wickedness; and falling headlong[b] he burst open in the middle and all his bowels gushed out. 19And it became known to all the inhabitants of Jerusalem, so that the field was called in their language Akeldama, that is, Field of Blood.) 20 For it is written in the book of Psalms,

'Let his habitation become desolate,
  and let there be no one to live in it';
and
'His office let another take.'

21 So one of the men who have accompanied us during all the time that the Lord Jesus went in and out among us, 22 beginning from the baptism of John until the day when he was taken up from us—one of these men must become with us a witness to his resurrection." 23And they put forward two, Joseph called Barsabbas, who was surnamed Justus, and Matthias. 24And they prayed and said, "Lord, who knowest the hearts of all men, show which one of these two thou hast chosen 25 to take the place in this ministry and apostleship from which Judas turned aside, to go to his own place." 26And they cast lots for them, and the lot fell on Matthias; and he was enrolled with the eleven apostles.

2 And when the day of Pentecost was fully come, they were all with one accord in one place. 2And suddenly there came a sound from heaven as of a rushing mighty wind, and it filled all the house where they were sitting. 3And there appeared unto them cloven tongues like as of fire, and it sat upon each of them. 4And they were all filled with the Holy Ghost, and began to speak with other tongues, as the Spirit gave them utterance. 5And there were dwelling at Jerusalem Jews, devout men, out of every nation under heaven. 6 Now when this was noised abroad, the multitude came together, and were confounded, because that every man heard them speak in his own language. 7And they were all amazed and marvelled, saying one to another, Behold, are not all these which speak Galileans? 8And how hear we every man in our own tongue, wherein we were born? 9 Parthians, and Medes,

2 When the day of Pentecost had come, they were all together in one place. 2And suddenly a sound came from heaven like the rush of a mighty wind, and it filled all the house where they were sitting. 3And there appeared to them tongues as of fire, distributed and resting on each one of them. 4And they were all filled with the Holy Spirit and began to speak in other tongues, as the Spirit gave them utterance. 5 Now there were dwelling in Jerusalem Jews, devout men from every nation under heaven. 6And at this sound the multitude came together, and they were bewildered, because each one heard them speaking in his own language. 7And they were amazed and wondered, saying, "Are not all these who are speaking Galileans? 8And how is it that we hear, each of us in his own native language? 9 Parthians and Medes and

[b] Or *swelling up.*

342

PHILLIPS

N.E.B.

Judas' place is filled   1. 15

It was during this period that Peter stood up among the brothers—there were about a hundred and twenty present at the time—and said,

"My brothers, the prophecy of scripture given through the Holy Spirit by the lips of David concerning Judas was bound to come true. He was the man who acted as guide to those who arrested Jesus, though he was one of our number and he had a share in this ministry of ours."

(This man had bought a piece of land with the proceeds of his infamy, but his body swelled up and his intestines burst. This fact became well known to all the residents of Jerusalem so that the piece of land came to be called in their language Akeldama, which means "the field of blood.")

"Now it is written in the book of psalms of such a man:

Let his habitation be made desolate,
And let no man dwell therein:

and

His office let another take.

"It becomes necessary then that whoever joins us must be someone who has been in our company during the whole time that the Lord Jesus lived his life with us, from the beginning when John baptized him until the day when He was taken up from us. This man must be an eye-witness with us to the resurrection of Jesus."

Two men were put forward, Joseph called Barsabas who was also called Justus, and Matthias. Then they prayed,

"Thou, Lord, who knowest the hearts of all men, show us which of these two thou hast chosen to accept that apostle's ministry which Judas forfeited to go where he belonged."

Then they drew lots for these men, and the lot fell to Matthias, and thereafter he was considered equally an apostle with the eleven.

The first Pentecost   2. 1
for the young Church

Then when the actual day of Pentecost came they were all assembled together. Suddenly there was a sound from heaven like the rushing of a violent wind, and it filled the whole house where they were seated. Before their eyes appeared tongues like flames, which separated off and settled above the head of each one of them. They were all filled with the Holy Spirit and began to speak in different languages as the Spirit gave them power to proclaim his message.

The Church's first impact   2. 5
on devout Jews

Now there were staying in Jerusalem Jews of deep faith from every nation of the world. When they heard this sound a crowd quickly collected and were completely bewildered because each one of them heard these men speaking in his own language. They were absolutely amazed and said in their astonishment,

"Listen, surely all these speakers are Galileans? Then how does it happen that every single one of us can hear the particular language he has known from a child? There are Parthians, Medes and Elamites; there are men whose

It was during this time that Peter stood up before the assembled brotherhood, about one hundred and twenty in all, and said: 'My friends, the prophecy in Scripture was bound to come true, which the Holy Spirit, through the mouth of David, uttered about Judas who acted as guide to those who arrested Jesus. For he was one of our number and had his place in this ministry.' (This Judas, be it noted, after buying a plot of land with the price of his villainy, fell forward on the ground, and burst open, so that his entrails poured out. This became known to everyone in Jerusalem, and they named the property in their own language Akeldama, which means 'Blood Acre'.) 'The text I have in mind', Peter continued, 'is in the Book of Psalms: "Let his homestead fall desolate; let there be none to inhabit it"; and again, "Let another take over his charge." Therefore one of those who bore us company all the while we had the Lord Jesus with us, coming and going, from John's ministry of baptism until the day when he was taken up from us—one of those must now join us as a witness to his resurrection.'

Two names were put forward: Joseph, who was known as Barsabbas, and bore the added name of Justus; and Matthias. Then they prayed and said, 'Thou, Lord, who knowest the hearts of all men, declare which of these two thou hast chosen to receive this office of ministry and apostleship which Judas abandoned to go where he belonged.' They drew lots and the lot fell on Matthias, who was then assigned a place among the twelve apostles.[a]

2 While the day of Pentecost was running its course they were all together in one place, when suddenly there came from the sky a noise like that of a strong driving wind, which filled the whole house where they were sitting. And there appeared to them tongues like flames of fire, dispersed among them and resting on each one. And they were all filled with the Holy Spirit and began to talk in other tongues, as the Spirit gave them power of utterance.

Now there were living in Jerusalem devout Jews[b] drawn from every nation under heaven; and at this sound the crowd gathered, all bewildered because each one heard the apostles talking in his own language. They were amazed and in their astonishment exclaimed, 'Why, they are all Galileans, are they not, these men who are speaking? How is it then that we hear them, each of us in his own native language? Parthians, Medes, Elamites; inhabitants of Mesopotamia, of

[a] Some witnesses read was then appointed a colleague of the eleven apostles. [b] Some witnesses read devout men.

343

K.J.V.

and Elamites, and the dwellers in Mesopotamia, and in Judea, and Cappadocia, in Pontus, and Asia, 10 Phrygia, and Pamphylia, in Egypt, and in the parts of Libya about Cyrene, and strangers of Rome, Jews and proselytes, 11 Cretes and Arabians, we do hear them speak in our tongues the wonderful works of God. 12And they were all amazed, and were in doubt, saying one to another, What meaneth this? 13 Others mocking said, These men are full of new wine.

14 But Peter, standing up with the eleven, lifted up his voice, and said unto them, Ye men of Judea, and all *ye* that dwell at Jerusalem, be this known unto you, and hearken to my words: 15 For these are not drunken, as ye suppose, seeing it is *but* the third hour of the day. 16 But this is that which was spoken by the prophet Joel; 17And it shall come to pass in the last days, saith God, I will pour out of my Spirit upon all flesh: and your sons and your daughters shall prophesy, and your young men shall see visions, and your old men shall dream dreams: 18And on my servants and on my handmaidens I will pour out in those days of my Spirit; and they shall prophesy: 19And I will shew wonders in heaven above, and signs in the earth beneath; blood, and fire, and vapour of smoke: 20 The sun shall be turned into darkness, and the moon into blood, before that great and notable day of the Lord come: 21And it shall come to pass, *that* whosoever shall call on the name of the Lord shall be saved. 22 Ye men of Israel, hear these words; Jesus of Nazareth, a man approved of God among you by miracles and wonders and signs, which God did by him in the midst of you, as ye yourselves also know: 23 Him, being delivered by the determinate counsel and foreknowledge of God, ye have taken, and by wicked hands have crucified and slain: 24 Whom God hath raised up, having loosed the pains of death: because it was not possible that he should be holden of it. 25 For David speaketh concerning him, I foresaw the Lord always before my face; for he is on my right hand, that I should not be moved: 26 Therefore did my heart rejoice, and my tongue was glad; moreover also my flesh shall rest in hope: 27 Because thou wilt not leave my soul in hell, neither wilt thou suffer thine Holy One to see corruption. 28 Thou hast made known to me the ways of life; thou shalt make

R.S.V.

Elamites and residents of Mesopotamia, Judea and Cappadocia, Pontus and Asia, 10 Phrygia and Pamphylia, Egypt and the parts of Libya belonging to Cyrene, and visitors from Rome, both Jews and proselytes, 11 Cretans and Arabians, we hear them telling in our own tongues the mighty works of God." 12And all were amazed and perplexed, saying to one another, "What does this mean?" 13 But others mocking said, "They are filled with new wine."

14 But Peter, standing with the eleven, lifted up his voice and addressed them, "Men of Judea and all who dwell in Jerusalem, let this be known to you, and give ear to my words. 15 For these men are not drunk, as you suppose, since it is only the third hour of the day; 16 but this is what was spoken by the prophet Joel:

17 'And in the last days it shall be, God declares,
that I will pour out my Spirit upon all flesh,
and your sons and your daughters shall prophesy,
and your young men shall see visions,
and your old men shall dream dreams;
18 yea, and on my menservants and my maidservants in those days
I will pour out my Spirit; and they shall prophesy.
19 And I will show wonders in the heaven above
and signs on the earth beneath,
blood, and fire, and vapor of smoke;
20 the sun shall be turned into darkness
and the moon into blood,
before the day of the Lord comes,
the great and manifest day.
21 And it shall be that whoever calls on the name of the Lord shall be saved.'

22 "Men of Israel, hear these words: Jesus of Nazareth, a man attested to you by God with mighty works and wonders and signs which God did through him in your midst, as you yourselves know—23 this Jesus, delivered up according to the definite plan and foreknowledge of God, you crucified and killed by the hands of lawless men. 24 But God raised him up, having loosed the pangs of death, because it was not possible for him to be held by it. 25 For David says concerning him,

'I saw the Lord always before me,
for he is at my right hand that I may not be shaken;
26 therefore my heart was glad, and my tongue rejoiced;
moreover my flesh will dwell in hope.
27 For thou wilt not abandon my soul to Hades,
nor let thy Holy One see corruption.
28 Thou hast made known to me the ways of life;
thou wilt make me full of gladness with thy presence.'

PHILLIPS

homes are in Mesopotamia, in Judaea and Cappadocia, Pontus, Asia, Phrygia, Pamphylia, Egypt, and the parts of Africa near Cyrene, as well as visitors from Rome! There are Jews and proselytes, men from Crete and men from Arabia, yet we can all hear these men speaking of the magnificence of God in our native language."

Everyone was utterly amazed and did not know what to make of it. Indeed they kept saying to each other,

"What on earth can this mean?"

But there were others who laughed mockingly and said,

"These fellows have drunk too much new wine!"

Peter explains the fulfillment of God's promise   2. 14

Then Peter, with the eleven standing by him, raised his voice and addressed them:

"Fellow Jews, and all who are living now in Jerusalem, listen carefully to what I say while I explain to you what has happened! These men are not drunk as you suppose—it is after all only nine o'clock in the morning of this great feast day. No, this is something which was predicted by the prophet Joel,

And it shall be in the last days, saith God,
I will pour forth of my Spirit upon all flesh:
And your sons and your daughters shall
    prophesy,
And your young men shall see visions,
And your old men shall dream dreams:
Yea and on my servants and on my hand-
    maidens in those days
Will I pour forth of my Spirit; and they shall
    prophesy.
And I will shew wonders in the heaven above,
And signs on the earth beneath;
Blood, and fire, and vapor of smoke:
The sun shall be turned into darkness,
And the moon into blood,
Before the day of the Lord come,
That great and notable day:
And it shall be, that whosoever shall call on
    the name of the Lord shall be saved.

"Men of Israel, I beg of you to listen to my words. Jesus of Nazareth was a man proved to you by God himself through the works of power, the miracles and the signs which God showed through him here amongst you—as you very well know. This man, who was put into your power by the predetermined plan and foreknowledge of God, you nailed up and murdered, and you used for your purpose men without the Law! But God would not allow the bitter pains of death to touch him. He raised him to life again—and indeed there was nothing by which death could hold such a man. When David speaks about him he says,

I beheld the Lord always before my face;
For he is on my right hand, that I should not
    be moved:
Therefore my heart was glad, and my tongue
    rejoiced;
Moreover my flesh also shall dwell in hope:
Because thou wilt not leave my soul in Hades,
Neither wilt thou give thy holy one to see cor-
    ruption.
Thou madest known unto me the ways of life;
Thou shalt make me full of gladness with thy
    countenance.

N.E.B.

Judaea and Cappadocia, of Pontus and Asia, of Phrygia and Pamphylia, of Egypt and the districts of Libya around Cyrene; visitors from Rome, both Jews and proselytes, Cretans and Arabs, we hear them telling in our own tongues the great things God has done.' And they were all amazed and perplexed, saying to one another, 'What can this mean?' Others said contemptuously, 'They have been drinking!'

But Peter stood up with the Eleven, raised his voice, and addressed them: 'Fellow Jews, and all you who live in Jerusalem, mark this and give me a hearing. These men are not drunk, as you imagine; for it is only nine in the morning. No, this is what the prophet spoke of: "God says, 'This will happen in the last days: I will pour out upon everyone a portion of my spirit; and your sons and daughters shall prophesy; your young men shall see visions, and your old men shall dream dreams. Yes, I will endue even my slaves, both men and women, with a portion of my spirit, and they shall prophesy. And I will show portents in the sky above, and signs on the earth below—blood and fire and drifting smoke. The sun shall be turned to darkness, and the moon to blood, before that great, resplendent day, the day of the Lord, shall come. And then, everyone who invokes the name of the Lord shall be saved.' "

'Men of Israel, listen to me: I speak of Jesus of Nazareth, a man singled out by God and made known to you through miracles, portents, and signs, which God worked among you through him, as you well know. When he had been given up to you, by the deliberate will and plan of God, you used heathen men to crucify and kill him. But God raised him to life again, setting him free from the pangs of death,[a] because it could not be that death should keep him in its grip.

'For David says of him:

"I foresaw that the presence of the Lord would
    be with me always,
For he is at my right hand so that I may not
    be shaken;
Therefore my heart was glad and my tongue
    spoke my joy;
Moreover, my flesh shall dwell in hope,
For thou wilt not abandon my soul to Hades,
Nor let thy loyal servant suffer corruption.
Thou hast shown me the ways of life,
Thou wilt fill me with gladness by thy pres-
    ence."

[a] *Some witnesses read* of Hades.

K.J.V.

me full of joy with thy countenance. 29 Men *and* brethren, let me freely speak unto you of the patriarch David, that he is both dead and buried, and his sepulchre is with us unto this day. 30 Therefore being a prophet, and knowing that God had sworn with an oath to him, that of the fruit of his loins, according to the flesh, he would raise up Christ to sit on his throne; 31 He, seeing this before, spake of the resurrection of Christ, that his soul was not left in hell, neither his flesh did see corruption. 32 This Jesus hath God raised up, whereof we all are witnesses. 33 Therefore being by the right hand of God exalted, and having received of the Father the promise of the Holy Ghost, he hath shed forth this, which ye now see and hear. 34 For David is not ascended into the heavens: but he saith himself, The Lord said unto my Lord, Sit thou on my right hand, 35 Until I make thy foes thy footstool. 36 Therefore let all the house of Israel know assuredly, that God hath made that same Jesus, whom ye have crucified, both Lord and Christ.

37 Now when they heard *this*, they were pricked in their heart, and said unto Peter and to the rest of the apostles, Men *and* brethren, what shall we do? 38 Then Peter said unto them, Repent, and be baptized every one of you in the name of Jesus Christ for the remission of sins, and ye shall receive the gift of the Holy Ghost. 39 For the promise is unto you, and to your children, and to all that are afar off, *even* as many as the Lord our God shall call. 40And with many other words did he testify and exhort, saying, Save yourselves from this untoward generation. 41 Then they that gladly received his word were baptized: and the same day there were added *unto them* about three thousand souls. 42And they continued steadfastly in the apostles' doctrine and fellowship, and in breaking of bread, and in prayers. 43And fear came upon every soul: and many wonders and signs were done by the apostles. 44And all that believed were together, and had all things common; 45And sold their possessions and goods, and parted them to all *men,* as every man had need. 46And they, continuing daily with one accord in the temple, and breaking bread from house to house, did eat their meat with gladness and singleness of heart, 47 Praising God, and having favour with all the people. And the Lord added to the church daily such as should be saved.

R.S.V.

29 "Brethren, I may say to you confidently of the patriarch David that he both died and was buried, and his tomb is with us to this day. 30 Being therefore a prophet, and knowing that God had sworn with an oath to him that he would set one of his descendants upon his throne, 31 he foresaw and spoke of the resurrection of the Christ, that he was not abandoned to Hades, nor did his flesh see corruption. 32 This Jesus God raised up, and of that we all are witnesses. 33 Being therefore exalted at the right hand of God, and having received from the Father the promise of the Holy Spirit, he has poured out this which you see and hear. 34 For David did not ascend into the heavens; but he himself says,

'The Lord said to my Lord, Sit at my right hand,

35 till I make thy enemies a stool for thy feet.' 36 Let all the house of Israel therefore know assuredly that God has made him both Lord and Christ, this Jesus whom you crucified."

37 Now when they heard this they were cut to the heart, and said to Peter and the rest of the apostles, "Brethren, what shall we do?" 38And Peter said to them, "Repent, and be baptized every one of you in the name of Jesus Christ for the forgiveness of your sins; and you shall receive the gift of the Holy Spirit. 39 For the promise is to you and to your children and to all that are far off, every one whom the Lord our God calls to him." 40And he testified with many other words and exhorted them, saying, "Save yourselves from this crooked generation." 41 So those who received his word were baptized, and there were added that day about three thousand souls. 42And they devoted themselves to the apostles' teaching and fellowship, to the breaking of bread and the prayers.

43 And fear came upon every soul; and many wonders and signs were done through the apostles. 44And all who believed were together and had all things in common; 45 and they sold their possessions and goods and distributed them to all, as any had need. 46And day by day, attending the temple together and breaking bread in their homes, they partook of food with glad and generous hearts, 47 praising God and having favor with all the people. And the Lord added to their number day by day those who were being saved.

PHILLIPS

"Men and brother Jews, I can surely speak freely to you about the patriarch David. There is no doubt that he died and was buried, and his grave is here among us to this day. But while he was alive he was a prophet. He knew that God had given him a most solemn promise that he would place one of his descendants upon his throne. He foresaw the resurrection of Christ, and it is this of which he is speaking. Christ was not deserted in death and his body was never destroyed. *Christ is the man Jesus, whom God raised up—a fact of which all of us are eyewitnesses!* He has been raised to the right hand of God; he has received from the Father and poured out upon us the promised Holy Spirit—*that* is what you now see and hear! David never ascended to Heaven, but he certainly said,

The Lord said unto my *Lord,*
Sit thou on my right hand,
Till I make thine enemies the footstool of thy feet.

"Now therefore the whole nation of Israel must know beyond the shadow of a doubt that this Jesus, whom you crucified, God has declared to be both Lord and Christ."

The reaction to Peter's speech   2. 37

When they heard this they were cut to the quick, and they cried to Peter and the other apostles,
"Men and fellow Jews, what shall we do now?"
Peter told them,
"You must repent and every one of you must be baptized in the name of Jesus Christ, so that you may have your sins forgiven and receive the gift of the Holy Spirit. For this great promise is for you and your children—yes, and for all who are far away, for as many as the Lord our God shall call to himself!"
Peter said much more than this as he gave his testimony and implored them, saying,
"Save yourselves from this perverted generation!"

The first large-scale conversion   2. 41

Then those who welcomed his message were baptized, and on that day alone about three thousand souls were added to the number of disciples. They continued steadily learning the teaching of the apostles, and joined in their fellowship, in the breaking of bread, and in prayer.
Everyone felt a deep sense of awe while many miracles and signs took place through the apostles. All the believers shared everything in common; they sold their possessions and goods and divided the proceeds among the fellowship according to individual need. Day after day they met by common consent in the Temple; they broke bread together in their homes, sharing meals with simple joy. They praised God continually and all the people respected them. Every day the Lord added to their number those who were finding salvation.

N.E.B.

'Let me tell you plainly, my friends, that the patriarch David died and was buried, and his tomb is here to this very day. It is clear therefore that he spoke as a prophet who knew that God had sworn to him that one of his own direct descendants should sit on his throne; and when he said he was not abandoned to Hades, and his flesh never suffered corruption, he spoke with foreknowledge of the resurrection of the Messiah. The Jesus we speak of has been raised by God, as we can all bear witness. Exalted thus with[a] God's right hand, he received the Holy Spirit from the Father, as was promised, and all that you now see and hear flows from him. For it was not David who went up to heaven; his own words are: "The Lord said to my Lord, 'Sit at my right hand until I make your enemies your footstool.' " Let all Israel then accept as certain that God has made this Jesus, whom you crucified, both Lord and Messiah.'

When they heard this they were cut to the heart, and said to Peter and the apostles,[b] 'Friends, what are we to do?' 'Repent,' said Peter, 'repent and be baptized, every one of you, in the name of Jesus the Messiah for the forgiveness of your sins; and you will receive the gift of the Holy Spirit. For the promise is to you, and to your children, and to all who are far away, everyone whom the Lord our God may call.'

In these and many other words he pressed his case and pleaded with them: 'Save yourselves', he said, 'from this crooked age.' Then those who accepted his word were baptized, and some three thousand were added to their number that day.

They met constantly to hear the apostles teach, and to share the common life, to break bread, and to pray. A sense of awe was everywhere, and many marvels and signs were brought about through the apostles. All whose faith had drawn them together held everything in common:[c] they would sell their property and possessions and make a general distribution as the need of each required. With one mind they kept up their daily attendance at the temple, and, breaking bread in private houses, shared their meals with unaffected joy, as they praised God and enjoyed the favour of the whole people. And day by day the Lord added to their number those whom he was saving.

[a] *Or* at. [b] *Some witnesses read* the rest of the apostles. [c] *Or* All who had become believers held everything together in common.

347

3 Now Peter and John went up together into the temple at the hour of prayer, *being* the ninth *hour*. 2And a certain man lame from his mother's womb was carried, whom they laid daily at the gate of the temple which is called Beautiful, to ask alms of them that entered into the temple; 3 Who, seeing Peter and John about to go into the temple, asked an alms. 4And Peter, fastening his eyes upon him with John, said, Look on us. 5And he gave heed unto them, expecting to receive something of them. 6 Then Peter said, Silver and gold have I none; but such as I have give I thee: In the name of Jesus Christ of Nazareth rise up and walk. 7And he took him by the right hand, and lifted *him* up: and immediately his feet and ankle bones received strength. 8And he leaping up stood, and walked, and entered with them into the temple, walking and leaping, and praising God. 9And all the people saw him walking and praising God: 10And they knew that it was he which sat for alms at the Beautiful gate of the temple: and they were filled with wonder and amazement at that which had happened unto him. 11And as the lame man which was healed held Peter and John, all the people ran together unto them in the porch that is called Solomon's, greatly wondering.

12 And when Peter saw *it*, he answered unto the people, Ye men of Israel, why marvel ye at this? or why look ye so earnestly on us, as though by our own power or holiness we had made this man to walk? 13 The God of Abraham, and of Isaac, and of Jacob, the God of our fathers, hath glorified his Son Jesus; whom ye delivered up, and denied him in the presence of Pilate, when he was determined to let *him* go. 14 But ye denied the Holy One and the Just, and desired a murderer to be granted unto you; 15And killed the Prince of life, whom God hath raised from the dead; whereof we are witnesses. 16And his name, through faith in his name, hath made this man strong, whom ye see and know: yea, the faith which is by him hath given him this perfect soundness in the presence of you all. 17And now, brethren, I wot that through ignorance ye did *it*, as *did* also your rulers. 18 But those things, which God before had shewed by the mouth of all his prophets, that Christ should suffer, he hath so fulfilled.

19 Repent ye therefore, and be converted, that your sins may be blotted out, when the times of refreshing shall come from the presence of the Lord; 20And he shall send Jesus Christ, which before was preached unto you: 21 Whom the heaven must receive until the times of restitution of all things, which God hath spoken by the mouth of all his holy prophets since the world began. 22 For Moses truly said unto the fathers, A Prophet shall the Lord your God raise up unto you of your brethren, like unto me; him shall ye hear in all things whatsoever he shall say unto you. 23And it shall come to pass, *that* every soul,

3 Now Peter and John were going up to the temple at the hour of prayer, the ninth hour. 2And a man lame from birth was being carried, whom they laid daily at that gate of the temple which is called Beautiful to ask alms of those who entered the temple. 3 Seeing Peter and John about to go into the temple, he asked for alms. 4And Peter directed his gaze at him, with John, and said, "Look at us." 5And he fixed his attention upon them, expecting to receive something from them. 6 But Peter said, "I have no silver and gold, but I give you what I have; in the name of Jesus Christ of Nazareth, walk." 7And he took him by the right hand and raised him up; and immediately his feet and ankles were made strong. 8And leaping up he stood and walked and entered the temple with them, walking and leaping and praising God. 9And all the people saw him walking and praising God, 10 and recognized him as the one who sat for alms at the Beautiful Gate of the temple; and they were filled with wonder and amazement at what had happened to him.

11 While he clung to Peter and John, all the people ran together to them in the portico called Solomon's, astounded. 12And when Peter saw it he addressed the people, "Men of Israel, why do you wonder at this, or why do you stare at us, as though by our own power or piety we had made him walk? 13 The God of Abraham and of Isaac and of Jacob, the God of our fathers, glorified his servant[c] Jesus, whom you delivered up and denied in the presence of Pilate, when he had decided to release him. 14 But you denied the Holy and Righteous One, and asked for a murderer to be granted to you, 15 and killed the Author of life, whom God raised from the dead. To this we are witnesses. 16And his name, by faith in his name, has made this man strong whom you see and know; and the faith which is through Jesus[d] has given the man this perfect health in the presence of you all.

17 "And now, brethren, I know that you acted in ignorance, as did also your rulers. 18 But what God foretold by the mouth of all the prophets, that his Christ should suffer, he thus fulfilled. 19 Repent therefore, and turn again, that your sins may be blotted out, that times of refreshing may come from the presence of the Lord, 20 and that he may send the Christ appointed for you, Jesus, 21 whom heaven must receive until the time for establishing all that God spoke by the mouth of his holy prophets from of old. 22 Moses said, 'The Lord God will raise up for you a prophet from your brethren as he raised me up. You shall listen to him in whatever he tells you. 23And it shall be that

[c] Or *child.* [d] Greek *him.*

PHILLIPS   N.E.B.

A public miracle and its explanation   3. 1

One afternoon Peter and John were on their way to the Temple for the three o'clock hour of prayer. A man who had been lame from birth was being carried along in the crowd, for it was the daily practice to put him down at what was known as the Beautiful Gate of the Temple, so that he could beg from the people as they went in. As this man saw Peter and John just about to enter he asked them to give him something. Peter looked intently at the man and so did John. Then Peter said,

"Look straight at us!"

The man looked at them expectantly, hoping that they would give him something.

"If you are expecting silver or gold," Peter said to him, "I have neither, but what I have I will certainly give you. In the name of Jesus Christ of Nazareth, *walk!*"

Then he took him by the right hand and helped him up. At once his feet and ankle bones were strengthened, and he positively jumped to his feet, stood, and then walked. Then he went with them into the Temple, where he walked about, leaping and praising God. Everyone noticed him as he walked and praised God and recognized him as the same beggar who used to sit at the Beautiful Gate, and they were all overcome with wonder and sheer astonishment at what had happened to him. Then while the man himself still clung to Peter and John all the people in their excitement ran together and crowded round them in Solomon's Porch. When Peter saw this he spoke to the crowd.

"Men of Israel, why are you so surprised at this, and why are you staring at us as though we had made this man walk through some power or piety of our own? It is the God of Abraham and Isaac and Jacob, the God of our fathers, who has done this thing to honor his servant Jesus—the man whom you betrayed and denied in the presence of Pilate, even when he had decided to let him go. But you disowned the holy and righteous one, and begged to be granted instead a man who was a murderer! You killed the prince of life, but God raised him from the dead—a fact of which we are eyewitnesses. It is the name of this same Jesus, it is faith in that name, which has cured this man whom you see and recognize. Yes, it was faith in Christ which gave this man perfect health and strength in full view of you all.

Peter explains ancient prophecy   3. 17

"Now of course I know, my brothers, that you had no idea what you were doing any more than your leaders had. But God had foretold through all his prophets that his Christ must suffer and this was how his words came true. Now you must repent and turn to God so that your sins may be wiped out, that time after time your souls may know the refreshment that comes from the presence of God. Then he will send you Jesus, your long-heralded Christ, although for the time he must remain in Heaven until that universal restoration of which God spoke in ancient times through all his holy prophets. For Moses said,

A prophet shall the Lord God raise up unto you from among your brethren, like unto me; to him shall ye hearken in all things whatsoever he shall speak unto you. And it shall be

3 One day at three in the afternoon, the hour of prayer, Peter and John were on their way up to the temple. Now a man who had been a cripple from birth used to be carried there and laid every day by the gate of the temple called 'Beautiful Gate', to beg from people as they went in. When he saw Peter and John on their way into the temple he asked for charity. But Peter fixed his eyes on him, as John did also, and said, 'Look at us.' Expecting a gift from them, the man was all attention. And Peter said, 'I have no silver or gold; but what I have I give you: in the name of Jesus Christ of Nazareth, walk.' Then he grasped him by the right hand and pulled him up; and at once his feet and ankles grew strong; he sprang up, stood on his feet, and started to walk. He entered the temple with them, leaping and praising God as he went. Everyone saw him walking and praising God, and when they recognized him as the man who used to sit begging at Beautiful Gate, they were filled with wonder and amazement at what had happened to him.

And as he was clutching Peter and John all the people came running in astonishment towards them in Solomon's Cloister, as it is called. Peter saw them coming and met them with these words: 'Men of Israel, why be surprised at this? Why stare at us as if we had made this man walk by some power or godliness of our own? The God of Abraham, Isaac and Jacob, the God of our fathers, has given the highest honour to his servant Jesus, whom you committed for trial and repudiated in Pilate's court—repudiated the one who was holy and righteous when Pilate had decided to release him. You begged as a favour the release of a murderer, and killed him who has led the way to life. But God raised him from the dead; of that we are witnesses. And the name of Jesus, by awakening faith, has strengthened this man, whom you see and know, and this faith has made him completely well, as you can all see for yourselves.

'And now, my friends, I know quite well that you acted in ignorance, and so did your rulers; but this is how God fulfilled what he had foretold in the utterances of all the prophets: that his Messiah should suffer. Repent then and turn to God, so that your sins may be wiped out. Then the Lord may grant you a time of recovery and send you the Messiah he has already appointed, that is, Jesus. He must be received into heaven until the time of universal restoration comes, of which God spoke by his holy prophets.[a] Moses said, "The Lord God will raise up a prophet for you from among yourselves as he raised me;[b] you shall listen to everything he says to you, and anyone who refuses to listen to that

[a] *Some witnesses add* from the beginning of the world. [b] *Or* like me.

K.J.V.

which will not hear that Prophet, shall be destroyed from among the people. 24 Yea, and all the prophets from Samuel and those that follow after, as many as have spoken, have likewise foretold of these days. 25 Ye are the children of the prophets, and of the covenant which God made with our fathers, saying unto Abraham, And in thy seed shall all the kindreds of the earth be blessed. 26 Unto you first God, having raised up his Son Jesus, sent him to bless you, in turning away every one of you from his iniquities.

4 And as they spake unto the people, the priests, and the captain of the temple, and the Sadducees, came upon them, 2 Being grieved that they taught the people, and preached through Jesus the resurrection from the dead. 3 And they laid hands on them, and put *them* in hold unto the next day: for it was now eventide. 4 Howbeit many of them which heard the word believed; and the number of the men was about five thousand.

5 And it came to pass on the morrow that their rulers, and elders, and scribes, 6 And Annas the high priest, and Caiaphas, and John, and Alexander, and as many as were of the kindred of the high priest, were gathered together at Jerusalem. 7 And when they had set them in the midst, they asked, By what power, or by what name, have ye done this? 8 Then Peter, filled with the Holy Ghost, said unto them, Ye rulers of the people, and elders of Israel, 9 If we this day be examined of the good deed done to the impotent man, by what means he is made whole; 10 Be it known unto you all, and to all the people of Israel, that by the name of Jesus Christ of Nazareth, whom ye crucified, whom God raised from the dead, *even* by him doth this man stand here before you whole. 11 This is the stone which was set at nought of you builders, which is become the head of the corner. 12 Neither is there salvation in any other: for there is none other name under heaven given among men, whereby we must be saved.

13 Now when they saw the boldness of Peter and John, and perceived that they were unlearned and ignorant men, they marvelled; and they took knowledge of them, that they had been with Jesus. 14 And beholding the man which was healed standing with them, they could say nothing against it. 15 But when they had commanded them to go aside out of the council, they con-

R.S.V.

every soul that does not listen to that prophet shall be destroyed from the people.' 24 And all the prophets who have spoken, from Samuel and those who came afterward, also proclaimed these days. 25 You are the sons of the prophets and of the covenant which God gave to your fathers, saying to Abraham, 'And in your posterity shall all the families of the earth be blessed.' 26 God, having raised up his servant,*c* sent him to you first, to bless you in turning every one of you from your wickedness."

4 And as they were speaking to the people, the priests and the captain of the temple and the Sadducees came upon them, 2 annoyed because they were teaching the people and proclaiming in Jesus the resurrection from the dead. 3 And they arrested them and put them in custody until the morrow, for it was already evening. 4 But many of those who heard the word believed; and the number of the men came to about five thousand.

5 On the morrow their rulers and elders and scribes were gathered together in Jerusalem, 6 with Annas the high priest and Caiaphas and John and Alexander, and all who were of the high-priestly family. 7 And when they had set them in the midst, they inquired, "By what power or by what name did you do this?" 8 Then Peter, filled with the Holy Spirit, said to them, "Rulers of the people and elders, 9 if we are being examined today concerning a good deed done to a cripple, by what means this man has been healed, 10 be it known to you all, and to all the people of Israel, that by the name of Jesus Christ of Nazareth, whom you crucified, whom God raised from the dead, by him this man is standing before you well. 11 This is the stone which was rejected by you builders, but which has become the head of the corner. 12 And there is salvation in no one else, for there is no other name under heaven given among men by which we must be saved."

13 Now when they saw the boldness of Peter and John, and perceived that they were uneducated, common men, they wondered; and they recognized that they had been with Jesus. 14 But seeing the man that had been healed standing beside them, they had nothing to say in opposition. 15 But when they had commanded them to go aside out of the council, they con-

[c] Or *child.*

PHILLIPS

that every soul, which shall not hearken to that prophet, shall be utterly destroyed from among the people.

Indeed, all the prophets from Samuel onwards who have spoken at all have foretold these days. You are the sons of the prophets and heirs of the agreement which God made with our fathers when he said to Abraham, 'Through your children shall all the families of the earth be blessed.' It was to you first that God sent his servant after he had raised him up to bring you great blessing by turning every one of you away from his evil ways."

The first clash with Jewish   4. 1
authorities

While they were still talking to the people the priests, the captain of the temple guard and the Sadducees moved toward them, thoroughly incensed that they should be teaching the people and should assure them that the resurrection of the dead had been proved through the rising of Jesus. So they arrested them and, since it was now evening, kept them in custody until the next day. Nevertheless, many of those who had heard what they said believed, and the number of men alone rose to about five thousand.

Peter's boldness at formal   4. 5
questioning

Next day the leading members of the council, the elders and scribes met in Jerusalem with Annas the High Priest, Caiaphas, John, Alexander, and the whole of the High Priest's family. They had the apostles brought in to stand before them and they asked them formally,

"By what power and in whose name have you done this thing?"

At this Peter, filled with the Holy Spirit, spoke to them,

"Leaders of the people and elders, if we are being called in question today over the matter of a kindness done to a helpless man and as to how he was healed, it is high time that all of you and the whole people of Israel knew that it was done in the name of Jesus Christ of Nazareth! He is the one whom you crucified but whom God raised from the dead, and it is by his power that this man at our side stands in your presence perfectly well. He is the 'stone which you builders rejected, which has now become the head of the corner.' In no one else can salvation be found. For in all the world no other name has been given to men but this, and it is by this name that we must be saved!"

The embarrassment of the   4. 13
authorities

When they saw the complete assurance of Peter and John, who were obviously uneducated and untrained men, they were staggered. They recognized them as men who had been with Jesus, yet since they could see the man who had been cured standing beside them, they could find no effective reply. All they could do was to order them out of the Sanhedrin and hold a conference among themselves.

N.E.B.

prophet must be extirpated from Israel." And so said all the prophets, from Samuel onwards; with one voice they all predicted this present time.

'You are the heirs of the prophets; you are within the covenant which God made with your fathers, when he said to Abraham, "And in your offspring all the families on earth shall find blessing." When God raised up his Servant, he sent him to you first, to bring you blessing by turning every one of you from your wicked ways.'

4 They were still addressing the people when the chief [a] priests came upon them, together with the Controller of the Temple and the Sadducees, exasperated at their teaching the people and proclaiming the resurrection from the dead —the resurrection of Jesus. They were arrested and put in prison for the night, as it was already evening. But many of those who had heard the message became believers. The number of men now reached about five thousand.

Next day the Jewish rulers, elders, and doctors of the law met in Jerusalem. There were present Annas the High Priest, Caiaphas, Jonathan,[b] Alexander, and all who were of the high-priestly family. They brought the apostles before the court and began the examination. 'By what power', they asked, 'or by what name have such men as you done this?' Then Peter, filled with the Holy Spirit, answered, 'Rulers of the people and elders, if the question put to us today is about help given to a sick man, and we are asked by what means he was cured, here is the answer, for all of you and for all the people of Israel: it was by the name of Jesus Christ of Nazareth, whom you crucified, whom God raised from the dead; it is by his name[c] that this man stands here before you fit and well. This Jesus is the stone rejected by the builders which has become the keystone—and you are the builders. There is no salvation in anyone else at all,[d] for there is no other name under heaven granted to men, by which we may receive salvation.'

Now as they observed the boldness of Peter and John, and noted that they were untrained laymen, they began to wonder, then recognized them as former companions of Jesus. And when they saw the man who had been cured standing with them, they had nothing to say in reply. So they ordered them to leave the court, and then

---

[a] *Some witnesses omit* chief. [b] *Some witnesses read* John. [c] *Some witnesses insert* and no other. [d] *Some witnesses omit* There is no . . . at all.

K.J.V.

ferred among themselves, 16 Saying, What shall we do to these men? for that indeed a notable miracle hath been done by them *is* manifest to all them that dwell in Jerusalem; and we cannot deny *it*. 17 But that it spread no further among the people, let us straitly threaten them, that they speak henceforth to no man in this name. 18And they called them, and commanded them not to speak at all nor teach in the name of Jesus. 19 But Peter and John answered and said unto them, Whether it be right in the sight of God to hearken unto you more than unto God, judge ye. 20 For we cannot but speak the things which we have seen and heard. 21 So when they had further threatened them, they let them go, finding nothing how they might punish them, because of the people: for all *men* glorified God for that which was done. 22 For the man was above forty years old, on whom this miracle of healing was shewed.

23 And being let go, they went to their own company, and reported all that the chief priests and elders had said unto them. 24And when they heard that, they lifted up their voice to God with one accord, and said, Lord, thou *art* God, which hast made heaven, and earth, and the sea, and all that in them is; 25 Who by the mouth of thy servant David hast said, Why did the heathen rage, and the people imagine vain things? 26 The kings of the earth stood up, and the rulers were gathered together against the Lord, and against his Christ. 27 For of a truth against thy holy child Jesus, whom thou hast anointed, both Herod, and Pontius Pilate, with the Gentiles, and the people of Israel, were gathered together, 28 For to do whatsoever thy hand and thy counsel determined before to be done. 29And now, Lord, behold their threatenings: and grant unto thy servants, that with all boldness they may speak thy word, 30 By stretching forth thine hand to heal; and that signs and wonders may be done by the name of thy holy child Jesus.

31 And when they had prayed, the place was shaken where they were assembled together; and they were all filled with the Holy Ghost, and they spake the word of God with boldness. 32And the multitude of them that believed were of one heart and of one soul: neither said any *of them* that aught of the things which he possessed was his own; but they had all things common. 33And with great power gave the apostles witness of the resurrection of the Lord Jesus: and great grace was upon them all. 34 Neither was there any among them that lacked: for as many as were possessors of lands or houses sold them, and brought the prices of the things that

R.S.V.

ferred with one another, 16 saying, "What shall we do with these men? For that a notable sign has been performed through them is manifest to all the inhabitants of Jerusalem, and we cannot deny it. 17 But in order that it may spread no further among the people, let us warn them to speak no more to any one in this name." 18 So they called them and charged them not to speak or teach at all in the name of Jesus. 19 But Peter and John answered them, "Whether it is right in the sight of God to listen to you rather than to God, you must judge; 20 for we cannot but speak of what we have seen and heard." 21And when they had further threatened them, they let them go, finding no way to punish them, because of the people; for all men praised God for what had happened. 22 For the man on whom this sign of healing was performed was more than forty years old.

23 When they were released they went to their friends and reported what the chief priests and the elders had said to them. 24And when they heard it, they lifted their voices together to God and said, "Sovereign Lord, who didst make the heaven and the earth and the sea and everything in them, 25 who by the mouth of our father David, thy servant,*ᵉ* didst say by the Holy Spirit,

'Why did the Gentiles rage,
  and the peoples imagine vain things?
26 The kings of the earth set themselves in array,
  and the rulers were gathered together,
  against the Lord and against his Anointed'—*ᵉ*

27 for truly in this city there were gathered together against thy holy servant*ᵉ* Jesus, whom thou didst anoint, both Herod and Pontius Pilate, with the Gentiles and the peoples of Israel, 28 to do whatever thy hand and thy plan had predestined to take place. 29And now, Lord, look upon their threats, and grant to thy servants*ᶠ* to speak thy word with all boldness, 30 while thou stretchest out thy hand to heal, and signs and wonders are performed through the name of thy holy servant*ᵉ* Jesus." 31And when they had prayed, the place in which they were gathered together was shaken; and they were all filled with the Holy Spirit and spoke the word of God with boldness.

32 Now the company of those who believed were of one heart and soul, and no one said that any of the things which he possessed was his own, but they had everything in common. 33And with great power the apostles gave their testimony to the resurrection of the Lord Jesus, and great grace was upon them all. 34 There was not a needy person among them, for as many as were possessors of lands or houses sold them, and brought the proceeds of what was sold

[c] Or *child.* [e] Or *Christ.* [f] Or *slaves.*

352

PHILLIPS

"What are we going to do with these men?" they said to each other. "It is evident to everyone living in Jerusalem that an extraordinary miracle has taken place through them, and that is something we cannot deny. Nevertheless, to prevent such a thing spreading further among the people, let us warn them that if they say anything more to anyone in his name it will be at their peril."

So they called them in and ordered them bluntly not to speak or teach a single further word about the name of Jesus. But Peter and John gave them this reply:

"Whether it is right in the eyes of God for us to listen to what you say rather than to what he says, you must decide; for we cannot help speaking about what we have actually seen and heard!"

After further threats they let them go. They could not think of any way of punishing them because of the attitude of the people. Everybody was thanking God for what had happened—that this miracle of healing had taken place in a man who was more than forty years old.

The united prayer of the young Church—   4. 23

After their release the apostles went back to their friends and reported to them what the chief priests and elders had said to them. When they heard it they raised their voices to God in united prayer and said,

"Almighty Lord, thou art the one who hast made the heaven and the earth, the sea and all that is in them. It was thou who didst speak by the Holy Spirit through the lips of our forefather David thy servant in the words:

Why did the gentiles rage,
And the peoples imagine vain things?
The kings of the earth set themselves in array,
And the rulers were gathered together,
Against the Lord, and against his anointed:

For indeed in this city the rulers have gathered together against thy holy servant, Jesus, thine anointed—yes, Herod and Pontius Pilate, the gentiles and the peoples of Israel have gathered together to carry out what thine hand and will had planned to happen. And now, O Lord, observe their threats and give thy servants courage to speak thy word fearlessly, while thou dost stretch out thine hand to heal, and cause signs and wonders to be performed in the name of thy holy servant Jesus."

When they had prayed their meeting-place was shaken; they were all filled with the Holy Spirit and spoke the Word of God fearlessly.

—and their close fellowship   4. 32

Among the large number who had become believers there was complete agreement of heart and soul. Not one of them claimed any of his possessions as his own but everything was common property to all. The apostles continued to give their witness to the resurrection of the Lord Jesus with great force, and a wonderful spirit of generosity pervaded the whole fellowship. Indeed, there was not a single person in need among them, for those who owned land or property would sell it and bring the proceeds of the

N.E.B.

discussed the matter among themselves. 'What are we to do with these men?' they said; 'for it is common knowledge in Jerusalem that a notable miracle has come about through them; and we cannot deny it. But to stop this from spreading further among the people, we had better caution them never again to speak to anyone in this name.' They then called them in and ordered them to refrain from all public speaking and teaching in the name of Jesus.

But Peter and John said to them in reply: 'Is it right in God's eyes for us to obey you rather than God? Judge for yourselves. We cannot possibly give up speaking of things we have seen and heard.'

The court repeated the caution and discharged them. They could not see how they were to punish them, because the people were all giving glory to God for what had happened. The man upon whom this miracle of healing had been performed was over forty years old.

As soon as they were discharged they went back to their friends and told them everything that the chief priests and elders had said. When they heard it, they raised their voices as one man and called upon God:

'Sovereign Lord, maker of heaven and earth and sea and of everything in them, who by the Holy Spirit,[a] through the mouth of David thy servant, didst say,

"Why did the Gentiles rage and the peoples lay their plots in vain?
The kings of the earth took their stand and the rulers made common cause
Against the Lord and against his Messiah."

They did indeed make common cause in this very city against thy holy servant Jesus whom thou didst anoint as Messiah. Herod and Pontius Pilate conspired with the Gentiles and peoples of Israel to do all the things which, under thy hand and by thy decree, were foreordained. And now, O Lord, mark their threats, and enable thy servants to speak thy word with all boldness. Stretch out thy hand to heal and cause signs and wonders to be done through the name of thy holy servant Jesus.'

When they had ended their prayer, the building where they were assembled rocked, and all were filled with the Holy Spirit and spoke the word of God with boldness.

The whole body of believers was united in heart and soul. Not a man of them claimed any of his possessions as his own, but everything was held in common, while the apostles bore witness with great power to the resurrection of the Lord Jesus. They were all held in high esteem; for they had never a needy person among them, because all who had property in land or houses sold it,

[a] Some witnesses omit by the Holy Spirit.

K.J.V.

were sold, 35And laid *them* down at the apostles' feet: and distribution was made unto every man according as he had need. 36And Joses, who by the apostles was surnamed Barnabas, (which is, being interpreted, The son of consolation,) a Levite, *and* of the country of Cyprus, 37 Having land, sold *it*, and brought the money, and laid *it* at the apostles' feet.

5 But a certain man named Ananias, with Sapphira his wife, sold a possession, 2And kept back *part* of the price, his wife also being privy *to it*, and brought a certain part, and laid *it* at the apostles' feet. 3 But Peter said, Ananias, why hath Satan filled thine heart to lie to the Holy Ghost, and to keep back *part* of the price of the land? 4 While it remained, was it not thine own? and after it was sold, was it not in thine own power? why hast thou conceived this thing in thine heart? thou hast not lied unto men, but unto God. 5And Ananias hearing these words fell down, and gave up the ghost: and great fear came on all them that heard these things. 6And the young men arose, wound him up, and carried *him* out, and buried *him*. 7And it was about the space of three hours after, when his wife, not knowing what was done, came in. 8And Peter answered unto her, Tell me whether ye sold the land for so much? And she said, Yea, for so much. 9 Then Peter said unto her, How is it that ye have agreed together to tempt the Spirit of the Lord? behold, the feet of them which have buried thy husband *are* at the door, and shall carry thee out. 10 Then fell she down straightway at his feet, and yielded up the ghost: and the young men came in, and found her dead, and, carrying *her* forth, buried *her* by her husband. 11And great fear came upon all the church, and upon as many as heard these things.

12 And by the hands of the apostles were many signs and wonders wrought among the people; (and they were all with one accord in Solomon's porch. 13And of the rest durst no man join himself to them: but the people magnified them. 14And believers were the more added to the Lord, multitudes both of men and women;) 15 Insomuch that they brought forth the sick into the streets, and laid *them* on beds and couches,

R.S.V.

35 and laid it at the apostles' feet; and distribution was made to each as any had need. 36 Thus Joseph who was surnamed by the apostles Barnabas (which means, Son of encouragement), a Levite, a native of Cyprus, 37 sold a field which belonged to him, and brought the money and laid it at the apostles' feet.

5 But a man named Ananias with his wife Sapphira sold a piece of property, 2 and with his wife's knowledge he kept back some of the proceeds, and brought only a part and laid it at the apostles' feet. 3 But Peter said, "Ananias, why has Satan filled your heart to lie to the Holy Spirit and to keep back part of the proceeds of the land? 4 While it remained unsold, did it not remain your own? And after it was sold, was it not at your disposal? How is it that you have contrived this deed in your heart? You have not lied to men but to God." 5 When Ananias heard these words, he fell down and died. And great fear came upon all who heard of it. 6 The young men rose and wrapped him up and carried him out and buried him.

7 After an interval of about three hours his wife came in, not knowing what had happened. 8And Peter said to her, "Tell me whether you sold the land for so much." And she said, "Yes, for so much." 9 But Peter said to her, "How is it that you have agreed together to tempt the Spirit of the Lord? Hark, the feet of those that have buried your husband are at the door, and they will carry you out." 10 Immediately she fell down at his feet and died. When the young men came in they found her dead, and they carried her out and buried her beside her husband. 11And great fear came upon the whole church, and upon all who heard of these things.

12 Now many signs and wonders were done among the people by the hands of the apostles. And they were all together in Solomon's Portico. 13 None of the rest dared join them, but the people held them in high honor. 14And more than ever believers were added to the Lord, multitudes both of men and women, 15 so that they even carried out the sick into the streets, and laid them on beds and pallets, that as Peter

sales and place it at the apostles' feet. They distributed to each one according to his need.

Generosity and covetousness   4. 36

It was at this time that Barnabas (the name, meaning son of comfort, given by the apostles to Joseph, a Levite from Cyprus) sold his farm and put the proceeds at the apostles' disposal.

But there was a man named Ananias who, with his wife Sapphira, had sold a piece of property but, with her full knowledge, reserved part of the price for himself. He brought the remainder to put at the apostles' disposal. But Peter said to him,

"Ananias, why has Satan so filled your mind that you could cheat the Holy Spirit and keep back for yourself part of the price of the land? Before the land was sold it was yours, and after the sale the disposal of the price you received was entirely in your hands, wasn't it? Then whatever made you think of such a thing as this? You have not lied to men, but to God!"

As soon as Ananias heard these words he collapsed and died. All who were within earshot were appalled at this incident. The young men got to their feet and after wrapping up his body carried him out and buried him.

About three hours later it happened that his wife came in not knowing what had taken place. Peter spoke directly to her,

"Tell me, did you sell your land for so much?"

"Yes," she replied, "that was it."

Then Peter said to her,

"How could you two have agreed to put the Spirit of the Lord to such a test? Listen, you can hear the footsteps of the men who have just buried your husband coming back through the door, and they will carry you out as well!"

Immediately she collapsed at Peter's feet and died. When the young men came into the room they found her a dead woman, and they carried her out and buried her by the side of her husband. At this happening a deep sense of awe swept over the whole Church and indeed over all those who heard about it.

The young Church takes its   5. 12b
stand in the Temple—

By common consent they all used to meet now in Solomon's Porch. But as far as the others were concerned no one dared to associate with them, even though their general popularity was very great. Yet more and more believers in the Lord joined them, both men and women in really large numbers.

—and miraculous power   5. 15
radiates from it

Many signs and wonders were now happening among the people through the apostles' ministry. In consequence people would bring out their sick into the streets and lay them down on stretchers or beds, so that as Peter came by at

brought the proceeds of the sale, and laid the money at the feet of the apostles; it was then distributed to any who stood in need.

For instance, Joseph, surnamed by the apostles Barnabas (which means 'Son of Exhortation'), a Levite, by birth a Cypriot, owned an estate, which he sold; he brought the money, and laid it at the apostles' feet.

5 But there was another man, called Ananias, with his wife Sapphira, who sold a property. With the full knowledge of his wife he kept back part of the purchase-money, and part he brought and laid at the apostles' feet. But Peter said, 'Ananias, how was it that Satan so possessed your mind that you lied to the Holy Spirit, and kept back part of the price of the land? While it remained, did it not remain yours? When it was turned into money, was it not still at your own disposal? What made you think of doing this thing? You have lied not to men but to God.' When Ananias heard these words he dropped dead; and all the others who heard were awestruck. The younger men rose and covered his body, then carried him out and buried him.

About three hours passed, and then his wife came in, unaware of what had happened. Peter turned to her and said, 'Tell me, were you paid such and such a price for the land?' 'Yes,' she said, 'that was the price.' Then Peter said, 'Why did you both conspire to put the Spirit of the Lord to the test? Hark! there at the door are the footsteps of those who buried your husband; and they will carry you away.' And suddenly she dropped dead at his feet. When the young men came in, they found her dead; and they carried her out and buried her beside her husband. And a great awe fell upon the whole church, and upon all who heard of these events; and many remarkable and wonderful things took place among the people at the hands of the apostles.

They used to meet by common consent in Solomon's Cloister, no one from outside their number venturing to join with them. But people in general spoke highly of them,[a] and more than that, numbers of men and women were added to their ranks as believers in the Lord.[b] In the end the sick were actually carried out into the streets and laid there on beds and stretchers, so that

[a] Or . . . Cloister. Although others did not venture to join them, the common people spoke highly of them. [b] Or and an ever-increasing number of believers, both men and women, were added to the Lord.

K.J.V.

that at the least the shadow of Peter passing by might overshadow some of them. 16 There came also a multitude *out* of the cities round about unto Jerusalem, bringing sick folks, and them which were vexed with unclean spirits: and they were healed every one.

17 Then the high priest rose up, and all they that were with him, (which is the sect of the Sadducees,) and were filled with indignation, 18And laid their hands on the apostles, and put them in the common prison. 19 But the angel of the Lord by night opened the prison doors, and brought them forth, and said, 20 Go, stand and speak in the temple to the people all the words of this life. 21And when they heard *that,* they entered into the temple early in the morning, and taught. But the high priest came, and they that were with him, and called the council together, and all the senate of the children of Israel, and sent to the prison to have them brought. 22 But when the officers came, and found them not in the prison, they returned, and told, 23 Saying, The prison truly found we shut with all safety, and the keepers standing without before the doors: but when we had opened, we found no man within. 24 Now when the high priest and the captain of the temple and the chief priests heard these things, they doubted of them whereunto this would grow. 25 Then came one and told them, saying, Behold, the men whom ye put in prison are standing in the temple, and teaching the people. 26 Then went the captain with the officers, and brought them without violence: for they feared the people, lest they should have been stoned. 27And when they had brought them, they set *them* before the council: and the high priest asked them, 28 Saying, Did not we straitly command you that ye should not teach in this name? and, behold, ye have filled Jerusalem with your doctrine, and intend to bring this man's blood upon us.

29 Then Peter and the *other* apostles answered and said, We ought to obey God rather than men. 30 The God of our fathers raised up Jesus, whom ye slew and hanged on a tree. 31 Him hath God exalted with his right hand *to be* a Prince and a Saviour, for to give repentance to Israel, and forgiveness of sins. 32And we are his witnesses of these things; and *so is* also the Holy Ghost, whom God hath given to them that obey him.

33 When they heard *that,* they were cut *to the heart,* and took counsel to slay them. 34 Then stood there up one in the council, a Pharisee,

R.S.V.

came by at least his shadow might fall on some of them. 16 The people also gathered from the towns around Jerusalem, bringing the sick and those afflicted with unclean spirits, and they were all healed.

17 But the high priest rose up and all who were with him, that is, the party of the Sadducees, and filled with jealousy 18 they arrested the apostles and put them in the common prison. 19 But at night an angel of the Lord opened the prison doors and brought them out and said, 20 "Go and stand in the temple and speak to the people all the words of this Life." 21And when they heard this, they entered the temple at daybreak and taught.

Now the high priest came and those who were with him and called together the council and all the senate of Israel, and sent to the prison to have them brought. 22 But when the officers came, they did not find them in the prison, and they returned and reported, 23 "We found the prison securely locked and the sentries standing at the doors, but when we opened it we found no one inside." 24 Now when the captain of the temple and the chief priests heard these words, they were much perplexed about them, wondering what this would come to. 25And some one came and told them, "The men whom you put in prison are standing in the temple and teaching the people." 26 Then the captain with the officers went and brought them, but without violence, for they were afraid of being stoned by the people.

27 And when they had brought them, they set them before the council. And the high priest questioned them, 28 saying, "We strictly charged you not to teach in this name, yet here you have filled Jerusalem with your teaching and you intend to bring this man's blood upon us." 29 But Peter and the apostles answered, "We must obey God rather than men. 30 The God of our fathers raised Jesus whom you killed by hanging him on a tree. 31 God exalted him at his right hand as Leader and Savior, to give repentance to Israel and forgiveness of sins. 32And we are witnesses to these things, and so is the Holy Spirit whom God has given to those who obey him."

33 When they heard this they were enraged and wanted to kill them. 34 But a Pharisee in the council named Gamaliel, a teacher of the

least his shadow might fall upon some of them. In addition a large crowd collected from the cities round about Jerusalem, bringing with them their sick and all those who were suffering from evil spirits. And they were all cured.

Furious opposition reduced to   *5. 17*
impotence

All this roused the High Priest and his allies the Sadducean party, and in a fury of jealousy they had the apostles arrested and put into the common jail. But during the night an angel of the Lord opened the prison doors and led them out, saying,

"Go and stand and speak in the Temple. Tell the people all about this new life!"

After receiving these instructions they entered the Temple about daybreak, and began to teach. When the High Priest arrived he and his supporters summoned the Sanhedrin and indeed the whole senate of the people of Israel. Then he sent to the jail to have the apostles brought in. But when the officers arrived at the prison they could not find them there. They came back and reported,

"We found the prison securely locked and the guards standing on duty at the doors, but when we opened up we found no one inside."

When the captain of the Temple guard and the chief priests heard this report they were completely mystified at the apostles' disappearance and wondered what further developments there would be. However, someone arrived and reported to them,

"Why, the men you put in jail are standing in the Temple teaching the people!"

Then the captain went out with his men and fetched them. They dared not use any violence, however, for the people might have stoned them. So they brought them in and made them stand before the Sanhedrin. The High Priest called for an explanation.

"We gave you the strictest possible orders," he said to them, "not to give any teaching in this name. And look what has happened—you have filled Jerusalem with your teaching, and what is more you are determined to fasten the guilt of that man's death upon us!"

The apostles speak the   *5. 29*
unpalatable truth

Then Peter and the apostles answered him,

"It is our duty to obey the orders of God rather than the orders of men. It was the God of our fathers who raised up Jesus, whom you murdered by hanging him on a cross of wood. God has raised this man to his own right hand as prince and savior, to bring repentance and the forgiveness of sins to Israel. What is more, we are witnesses to these matters, and so is the Holy Spirit which God gives to those who obey his commands."

Calm counsel temporarily prevails *5. 33*

When the members of the council heard these words they were so furious that they wanted to kill them. But one man stood up in the assem-

even the shadow of Peter might fall on one or another as he passed by; and the people from the towns round Jerusalem flocked in, bringing those who were ill or harassed by unclean spirits, and all of them were cured.

Then the High Priest and his colleagues, the Sadducean party as it then was, were goaded into action by jealousy. They proceeded to arrest the apostles, and put them in official custody. But an angel of the Lord opened the prison doors during the night, brought them out, and said, 'Go, take your place in the temple and speak to the people, and tell them about this new life and all it means.' Accordingly they entered the temple at daybreak and went on with their teaching.

When the High Priest arrived with his colleagues they summoned the 'Sanhedrin', that is, the full senate of the Israelite nation, and sent to the jail to fetch the prisoners. But the police who went to the prison failed to find them there, so they returned and reported, 'We found the jail securely locked at every point, with the warders at their posts by the doors, but when we opened them we found no one inside.' When they heard this, the Controller of the Temple and the chief priests were wondering what could have become of them,[a] and then a man arrived with the report, 'Look! the men you put in prison are there in the temple teaching the people.' At that the Controller went off with the police and fetched them, but without using force for fear of being stoned by the people.

So they brought them and stood them before the Council; and the High Priest began his examination. 'We expressly ordered you', he said, 'to desist from teaching in that name; and what has happened? You have filled Jerusalem with your teaching, and you are trying to make us responsible for that man's death.' Peter replied for himself and the apostles: 'We must obey God rather than men. The God of our fathers raised up Jesus whom you had done to death[b] by hanging him on a gibbet. He it is whom God has exalted with his own right hand[c] as leader and saviour, to grant Israel repentance and forgiveness of sins. And we are witnesses to all this, and so is the Holy Spirit given by God to those who are obedient to him.'

This touched them on the raw, and they wanted to put them to death. But a member of the Council rose to his feet, a Pharisee called

[a] *Or* wondering about them, what this could possibly mean. [b] *Or* . . . Jesus, and you did him to death . . . [c] *Or* at his right hand.

K.J.V.

named Gamaliel, a doctor of the law, had in reputation among all the people, and commanded to put the apostles forth a little space; 35And said unto them, Ye men of Israel, take heed to yourselves what ye intend to do as touching these men. 36 For before these days rose up Theudas, boasting himself to be somebody; to whom a number of men, about four hundred, joined themselves: who was slain; and all, as many as obeyed him, were scattered, and brought to nought. 37After this man rose up Judas of Galilee in the days of the taxing, and drew away much people after him: he also perished; and all, *even* as many as obeyed him, were dispersed. 38And now I say unto you, Refrain from these men, and let them alone: for if this counsel or this work be of men, it will come to nought: 39 But if it be of God, ye cannot overthrow it; lest haply ye be found even to fight against God. 40And to him they agreed: and when they had called the apostles, and beaten *them,* they commanded that they should not speak in the name of Jesus, and let them go.

41 And they departed from the presence of the council, rejoicing that they were counted worthy to suffer shame for his name. 42And daily in the temple, and in every house, they ceased not to teach and preach Jesus Christ.

6 And in those days, when the number of the disciples was multiplied, there arose a murmuring of the Grecians against the Hebrews, because their widows were neglected in the daily ministration. 2 Then the twelve called the multitude of the disciples *unto them,* and said, It is not reason that we should leave the word of God, and serve tables. 3 Wherefore, brethren, look ye out among you seven men of honest report, full of the Holy Ghost and wisdom, whom we may appoint over this business. 4 But we will give ourselves continually to prayer, and to the ministry of the word.

5 And the saying pleased the whole multitude: and they chose Stephen, a man full of faith and of the Holy Ghost, and Philip, and Prochorus, and Nicanor, and Timon, and Parmenas, and Nicolas a proselyte of Antioch; 6 Whom they set before the apostles: and when they had prayed, they laid *their* hands on them. 7And the word of God increased; and the number of the disciples multiplied in Jerusalem greatly; and a great company of the priests were obedient to the faith. 8And Stephen, full of faith and power, did great wonders and miracles among the people.

9 Then there arose certain of the synagogue, which is called *the synagogue* of the Libertines, and Cyrenians, and Alexandrians, and of them

R.S.V.

law, held in honor by all the people, stood up and ordered the men to be put outside for a while. 35And he said to them, "Men of Israel, take care what you do with these men. 36 For before these days Theudas arose, giving himself out to be somebody, and a number of men, about four hundred, joined him; but he was slain and all who followed him were dispersed and came to nothing. 37After him Judas the Galilean arose in the days of the census and drew away some of the people after him; he also perished, and all who followed him were scattered. 38 So in the present case I tell you, keep away from these men and let them alone; for if this plan or this undertaking is of men, it will fail; 39 but if it is of God, you will not be able to overthrow them. You might even be found opposing God!"

40 So they took his advice, and when they had called in the apostles, they beat them and charged them not to speak in the name of Jesus, and let them go. 41 Then they left the presence of the council, rejoicing that they were counted worthy to suffer dishonor for the name. 42And every day in the temple and at home they did not cease teaching and preaching Jesus as the Christ.

6 Now in these days when the disciples were increasing in number, the Hellenists murmured against the Hebrews because their widows were neglected in the daily distribution. 2And the twelve summoned the body of the disciples and said, "It is not right that we should give up preaching the word of God to serve tables. 3 Therefore, brethren, pick out from among you seven men of good repute, full of the Spirit and of wisdom, whom we may appoint to this duty. 4 But we will devote ourselves to prayer and to the ministry of the word." 5And what they said pleased the whole multitude, and they chose Stephen, a man full of faith and of the Holy Spirit, and Philip, and Prochorus, and Nicanor, and Timon, and Parmenas, and Nicolaus, a proselyte of Antioch. 6 These they set before the apostles, and they prayed and laid their hands upon them.

7 And the word of God increased; and the number of the disciples multiplied greatly in Jerusalem, and a great many of the priests were obedient to the faith.

8 And Stephen, full of grace and power, did great wonders and signs among the people. 9 Then some of those who belonged to the synagogue of the Freedmen (as it was called), and of the Cyrenians, and of the Alexandrians, and

PHILLIPS

bly, a Pharisee by the name of Gamaliel, a teacher of the Law who was held in great respect by the people, and gave orders for the apostles to be taken outside for a few minutes. Then he addressed the assembly:

"Men of Israel, be very careful of what action you intend to take against these men! Remember that some time ago a man called Theudas made himself conspicuous by claiming to be someone or other, and he had a following of four hundred men. He was killed, all his followers were dispersed, and the movement came to nothing. Then later, in the days of the census, that man Judas from Galilee appeared and enticed many of the people to follow him. But he too died and his whole following melted away. My advice to you now therefore is to let these men alone; leave them to themselves. For if this teaching or movement is merely human it will collapse of its own accord. But if it should be from God you cannot defeat them, and you might actually find yourselves to be fighting against God!"

They accepted his advice and called in the apostles. They had them beaten and after commanding them not to speak in the name of Jesus they let them go. So the apostles went out from the presence of the Sanhedrin full of joy that they had been considered worthy to bear humiliation for the sake of the name. Then day after day in the Temple and in people's houses they continued to teach unceasingly and to proclaim the good news of Jesus Christ.

The first deacons are chosen   6. 1

About this time, when the number of disciples was continually increasing, the Greeks complained that in the daily distribution of food the Hebrew widows were being given preferential treatment. The twelve summoned the whole body of the disciples together, and said,

"It is not right that we should have to neglect preaching the Word of God in order to look after the accounts. You, our brothers, must look round and pick out from your number seven men of good reputation who are both practical and spiritually-minded and we will put them in charge of this matter. Then we shall devote ourselves wholeheartedly to prayer and the ministry of the Word."

This brief speech met with unanimous approval and they chose Stephen, a man full of faith and the Holy Spirit, Philip, Prochorus, Nicanor, Timon, Parmenas, and Nicolas of Antioch who had previously been a convert to the Jewish faith. They brought these men before the apostles, and they, after prayer, laid their hands upon them.

So the Word of God gained more and more ground. The number of disciples in Jerusalem very greatly increased, while a considerable proportion of the priesthood accepted the faith.

The attack on the new deacon,   6. 8
Stephen

Stephen, full of grace and spiritual power, continued to perform miracles and remarkable signs among the people. However, members of a Jewish synagogue known as the Libertines, together with some from the synagogues of Cyrene and Alexandria, as well as some men from

N.E.B.

Gamaliel, a teacher of the law held in high regard by all the people. He moved that the men be put outside for a while. Then he said, 'Men of Israel, be cautious in deciding what to do with these men. Some time ago Theudas came forward, claiming to be somebody, and a number of men, about four hundred, joined him. But he was killed and his whole following was broken up and disappeared. After him came Judas the Galilean at the time of the census; he induced some people to revolt under his leadership, but he too perished and his whole following was scattered. And so now: keep clear of these men, I tell you; leave them alone. For if this idea of theirs or its execution is of human origin, it will collapse; but if it is from God, you will never be able to put them down, and you risk finding yourselves at war with God.'

They took his advice. They sent for the apostles and had them flogged; then they ordered them to give up speaking in the name of Jesus, and discharged them. So the apostles went out from the Council rejoicing that they had been found worthy to suffer indignity for the sake of the Name. And every day they went steadily on with their teaching in the temple and in private houses, telling the good news of Jesus the Messiah.[a]

The Church Moves Outwards

6 During this period, when disciples were growing in number, there was disagreement between those of them who spoke Greek[b] and those who spoke the language of the Jews.[c] The former party complained that their widows were being overlooked in the daily distribution. So the Twelve called the whole body of disciples together and said, 'It would be a grave mistake for us to neglect the word of God in order to wait at table. Therefore, friends, look out seven men of good reputation from your number, men full of the Spirit and of wisdom, and we will appoint them to deal with these matters, while we devote ourselves to prayer and to the ministry of the Word.' This proposal proved acceptable to the whole body. They elected Stephen, a man full of faith and of the Holy Spirit, Philip, Prochorus, Nicanor, Timon, Parmenas, and Nicolas of Antioch, a former convert to Judaism. These they presented to the apostles, who prayed and laid their hands on them.

The word of God now spread more and more widely; the number of disciples in Jerusalem went on increasing rapidly, and very many of the priests adhered to the Faith.

Stephen, who was full of grace and power, began to work great miracles and signs among the people. But some members of the synagogue

---

[a] Or the good news that the Messiah was Jesus.
[b] Literally the Hellenists. [c] Literally the Hebrews.

K.J.V.

of Cilicia and of Asia, disputing with Stephen. 10And they were not able to resist the wisdom and the spirit by which he spake. 11 Then they suborned men, which said, We have heard him speak blasphemous words against Moses, and *against* God. 12And they stirred up the people, and the elders, and the scribes, and came upon *him*, and caught him, and brought *him* to the council, 13And set up false witnesses, which said, This man ceaseth not to speak blasphemous words against this holy place, and the law: 14 For we have heard him say, that this Jesus of Nazareth shall destroy this place, and shall change the customs which Moses delivered us. 15And all that sat in the council, looking steadfastly on him, saw his face as it had been the face of an angel.

7 Then said the high priest, Are these things so? 2And he said, Men, brethren, and fathers, hearken; The God of glory appeared unto our father Abraham, when he was in Mesopotamia, before he dwelt in Charran, 3And said unto him, Get thee out of thy country, and from thy kindred, and come into the land which I shall shew thee. 4 Then came he out of the land of the Chaldeans, and dwelt in Charran: and from thence, when his father was dead, he removed him into this land, wherein ye now dwell. 5And he gave him none inheritance in it, no, not *so much as* to set his foot on: yet he promised that he would give it to him for a possession, and to his seed after him, when *as yet* he had no child. 6And God spake on this wise, That his seed should sojourn in a strange land; and that they should bring them into bondage, and entreat *them* evil four hundred years. 7And the nation to whom they shall be in bondage will I judge, said God: and after that shall they come forth, and serve me in this place. 8And he gave him the covenant of circumcision: and so *Abraham* begat Isaac, and circumcised him the eighth day; and Isaac *begat* Jacob; and Jacob *begat* the twelve patriarchs. 9And the patriarchs, moved with envy, sold Joseph into Egypt: but God was with him, 10And delivered him out of all his afflictions, and gave him favour and wisdom in the sight of Pharaoh king of Egypt; and he made him governor over Egypt and all his house. 11 Now there came a dearth over all the land of Egypt and Chanaan, and great affliction: and our fathers found no sustenance. 12 But when Jacob heard that there was corn in Egypt, he sent out our fathers first. 13And at the second *time* Joseph was made known to his brethren; and Joseph's kindred was made known unto

R.S.V.

of those from Cilicia and Asia, arose and disputed with Stephen. 10 But they could not withstand the wisdom and the Spirit with which he spoke. 11 Then they secretly instigated men, who said, "We have heard him speak blasphemous words against Moses and God." 12And they stirred up the people and the elders and the scribes, and they came upon him and seized him and brought him before the council, 13 and set up false witnesses who said, "This man never ceases to speak words against this holy place and the law; 14 for we have heard him say that this Jesus of Nazareth will destroy this place, and will change the customs which Moses delivered to us." 15And gazing at him, all who sat in the council saw that his face was like the face of an angel.

7 And the high priest said, "Is this so?" 2And Stephen said:

"Brethren and fathers, hear me. The God of glory appeared to our father Abraham, when he was in Mesopotamia, before he lived in Haran, 3 and said to him, 'Depart from your land and from your kindred and go into the land which I will show you.' 4 Then he departed from the land of the Chaldeans, and lived in Haran. And after his father died, God removed him from there into this land in which you are now living; 5 yet he gave him no inheritance in it, not even a foot's length, but promised to give it to him in possession and to his posterity after him, though he had no child. 6And God spoke to this effect, that his posterity would be aliens in a land belonging to others, who would enslave them and ill-treat them four hundred years. 7 'But I will judge the nation which they serve,' said God, 'and after that they shall come out and worship me in this place.' 8And he gave him the covenant of circumcision. And so Abraham became the father of Isaac, and circumcised him on the eighth day; and Isaac became the father of Jacob, and Jacob of the twelve patriarchs.

9 "And the patriarchs, jealous of Joseph, sold him into Egypt; but God was with him, 10 and rescued him out of all his afflictions, and gave him favor and wisdom before Pharaoh, king of Egypt, who made him governor over Egypt and over all his household. 11 Now there came a famine throughout all Egypt and Canaan, and great affliction, and our fathers could find no food. 12 But when Jacob heard that there was grain in Egypt, he sent forth our fathers the first time. 13And at the second visit Joseph made himself known to his brothers, and Joseph's fam-

PHILLIPS

Cilicia and Asia, tried debating with Stephen, but found themselves quite unable to stand up against either his practical wisdom or the spiritual force with which he spoke. In desperation they bribed men to allege, "We have heard this man making blasphemous statements against Moses and against God." At the same time they worked upon the feelings of the people, the elders and the scribes. Then they suddenly confronted Stephen, seized him and marched him off before the Sanhedrin. There they brought forward false witnesses to say, "This man's speeches are one long attack against this holy place and the Law. We have heard him say that Jesus of Nazareth will destroy this place and change the customs which Moses handed down to us." All who sat there in the Sanhedrin looked intently at Stephen, and as they looked his face appeared to them like the face of an angel.

N.E.B.

called the Synagogue of Freedmen, comprising Cyrenians and Alexandrians and people from Cilicia and Asia, came forward and argued with Stephen, but could not hold their own against the inspired wisdom with which he spoke. They then put up men who alleged that they had heard him make blasphemous statements against Moses and against God. They stirred up the people and the elders and doctors of the law, set upon him and seized him, and brought him before the Council. They produced false witnesses who said, 'This man is for ever saying things against this holy place and against the Law. For we have heard him say that Jesus of Nazareth will destroy this place and alter the customs handed down to us by Moses.' And all who were sitting in the Council fixed their eyes on him, and his face appeared to them like the face of an angel.

Stephen makes his defense from Israel's history: The time of Abraham   *7. 1*

Then the High Priest said,
"Is this statement true?"
And Stephen answered,
"My brothers and my fathers, listen to me. Our glorious God appeared to our forefather Abraham while he was in Mesopotamia before he ever came to live in Haran, and said to him, *'Get thee out of thy land and from thy kindred, and come into a land which I shall shew thee.'* That was how he came to leave the land of the Chaldeans and settle in Haran. And it was from there after his father's death that God moved him into this very land where you are living today. Yet God gave him no part of it as an inheritance, not a foot that he could call his own, and yet promised that it should eventually belong to him and his descendants—even though at the time he had no descendant at all. And this is the way in which God spoke to him: he told him that his descendants should live as strangers in a foreign land where they would become slaves and be ill treated for four hundred years, *'And the nation to which they shall be in bondage will I judge, said God; and after that shall they come forth, and serve me in this place.'*
"Further, he gave him the agreement of circumcision, so that when Abraham became the father of Isaac he circumcised him on the eighth day.

Stephen's defense: the patriarchs   *7. 8b*

"Isaac became the father of Jacob, and Jacob the father of the twelve patriarchs. Then the patriarchs in their jealousy of Joseph sold him as a slave into Egypt. But God was with him and saved him from all his troubles and gave him favor and wisdom in the eyes of Pharaoh the king of Egypt. Pharaoh made him governor of Egypt and put him in charge of his own entire household.
"Then came the famine over all the land of Egypt and Canaan which caused great suffering, and our forefathers could find no food. But when Jacob heard that there was corn in Egypt he sent our forefathers out of their own country for the first time. It was on their second visit that Joseph was recognized by his brothers, and

7 Then the High Priest asked, 'Is this so?' And he said, 'My brothers, fathers of this nation, listen to me. The God of glory appeared to Abraham our ancestor while he was in Mesopotamia, before he had settled in Harran, and said: "Leave your country and your kinsfolk and come away to a land that I will show you." Thereupon he left the land of the Chaldaeans and settled in Harran. From there, after his father's death, God led him to migrate to this land where you now live. He gave him nothing in it to call his own, not one yard; but promised to give it in possession to him and his descendants after him, though he was then childless. God spoke in these terms: "Abraham's descendants shall live as aliens in a foreign land, held in slavery and oppression for four hundred years. And I will pass judgement", said God, "on the nation whose slaves they are; and after that they shall come out free, and worship me in this place." He then gave him the covenant of circumcision, and so, after Isaac was born, he circumcised him on the eighth day; and Isaac begot Jacob, and Jacob the twelve patriarchs.
'The patriarchs out of jealousy sold Joseph into slavery in Egypt, but God was with him and rescued him from all his troubles. He also gave him a presence and powers of mind which so commended him to Pharaoh king of Egypt, that he appointed him chief administrator for Egypt and the whole of the royal household.
'But famine struck the whole of Egypt and Canaan, and caused great hardship; and our ancestors could find nothing to eat. But Jacob heard that there was food in Egypt and sent our fathers there. This was their first visit. On the second visit Joseph was recognized by his broth-

K.J.V.

Pharaoh. 14 Then sent Joseph, and called his father Jacob to *him,* and all his kindred, three-score and fifteen souls. 15 So Jacob went down into Egypt, and died, he, and our fathers, 16And were carried over into Sychem, and laid in the sepulchre that Abraham bought for a sum of money of the sons of Emmor, *the father* of Sychem. 17 But when the time of the promise drew nigh, which God had sworn to Abraham, the people grew and multiplied in Egypt, 18 Till another king arose, which knew not Joseph. 19 The same dealt subtilly with our kindred, and evil entreated our fathers, so that they cast out their young children, to the end they might not live. 20 In which time Moses was born, and was exceeding fair, and nourished up in his father's house three months: 21And when he was cast out, Pharaoh's daughter took him up, and nourished him for her own son. 22And Moses was learned in all the wisdom of the Egyptians, and was mighty in words and in deeds. 23And when he was full forty years old, it came into his heart to visit his brethren the children of Israel. 24And seeing one *of them* suffer wrong, he defended *him,* and avenged him that was oppressed, and smote the Egyptian: 25 For he supposed his brethren would have understood how that God by his hand would deliver them; but they understood not. 26And the next day he shewed himself unto them as they strove, and would have set them at one again, saying, Sirs, ye are brethren; why do ye wrong one to another? 27 But he that did his neighbour wrong thrust him away, saying, Who made thee a ruler and a judge over us? 28 Wilt thou kill me, as thou didst the Egyptian yesterday? 29 Then fled Moses at this saying, and was a stranger in the land of Madian, where he begat two sons. 30And when forty years were expired, there appeared to him in the wilderness of mount Sina an angel of the Lord in a flame of fire in a bush. 31 When Moses saw *it,* he wondered at the sight: and as he drew near to behold *it,* the voice of the Lord came unto him, 32 *Saying,* I *am* the God of thy fathers, the God of Abraham, and the God of Isaac, and the God of Jacob. Then Moses trembled, and durst not behold. 33 Then said the Lord to him, Put off thy shoes from thy feet: for the place where thou standest is holy ground. 34 I have seen, I have seen the affliction of my

R.S.V.

ily became known to Pharaoh. 14And Joseph sent and called to him Jacob his father and all his kindred, seventy-five souls; 15 and Jacob went down into Egypt. And he died, himself and our fathers, 16 and they were carried back to Shechem and laid in the tomb that Abraham had bought for a sum of silver from the sons of Hamor in Shechem.

17 "But as the time of the promise drew near, which God had granted to Abraham, the people grew and multiplied in Egypt 18 till there arose over Egypt another king who had not known Joseph. 19 He dealt craftily with our race and forced our fathers to expose their infants, that they might not be kept alive. 20At this time Moses was born, and was beautiful before God. And he was brought up for three months in his father's house; 21 and when he was exposed, Pharaoh's daughter adopted him and brought him up as her own son. 22And Moses was instructed in all the wisdom of the Egyptians, and he was mighty in his words and deeds.

23 "When he was forty years old, it came into his heart to visit his brethren, the sons of Israel. 24And seeing one of them being wronged, he defended the oppressed man and avenged him by striking the Egyptian. 25 He supposed that his brethren understood that God was giving them deliverance by his hand, but they did not understand. 26And on the following day he appeared to them as they were quarreling and would have reconciled them, saying, 'Men, you are brethren, why do you wrong each other?' 27 But the man who was wronging his neighbor thrust him aside, saying, 'Who made you a ruler and a judge over us? 28 Do you want to kill me as you killed the Egyptian yesterday?' 29At this retort Moses fled, and became an exile in the land of Midian, where he became the father of two sons.

30 "Now when forty years had passed, an angel appeared to him in the wilderness of Mount Sinai, in a flame of fire in a bush. 31 When Moses saw it he wondered at the sight; and as he drew near to look, the voice of the Lord came, 32 'I am the God of your fathers, the God of Abraham and of Isaac and of Jacob.' And Moses trembled and did not dare to look. 33And the Lord said to him, 'Take off the shoes from your feet, for the place where you are standing is holy ground. 34 I have surely seen the

his ancestry became plain to Pharaoh. Then Joseph sent and invited to come and live with him his father and all his kinsmen, seventy-five people in all. So Jacob came down to Egypt and both he and our fathers ended their days there. After their death they were carried back into Shechem and laid in the tomb which Abraham had bought with silver from the sons of Hamor, in Shechem.

"But as the time drew near for the fulfillment of the promise which God had made to Abraham, our people grew more and more numerous in Egypt. Finally another king came to the Egyptian throne who knew nothing of Joseph. This man cleverly victimized our race. He treated our forefathers abominably, forcing them to expose their infant children so that the race should die out.

Stephen's defense: God's providence and Moses
7. 20

"It was at this very time that Moses was born. He was a child of remarkable beauty, and for three months he was brought up in his father's house, and then when the time came for him to be abandoned Pharaoh's daughter adopted him and brought him up as her own son. So Moses was trained in all the wisdom of the Egyptians, and became not only an excellent speaker but a man of action as well.

Moses' first abortive attempt at rescue
7. 23

"Now when he was turned forty the thought came into his mind that he should go and visit his own brothers, the sons of Israel. He saw one of them being unjustly treated, went to the rescue and paid rough justice for the man who had been ill treated by striking down the Egyptian. He fully imagined that his brothers would understand that God was using him to rescue them. But they did not understand. Indeed, on the very next day he came upon two of them who were quarreling and urged them to make peace, saying, 'Men, you are brothers. What good can come from your injuring each other?' But the man who was wronging his neighbor pushed Moses aside, saying, 'Who made you a ruler and judge over us? Do you want to kill me as you killed that Egyptian yesterday?' At that retort Moses fled and lived as an exile in the land of Midian, where he became the father of two sons.

Moses hears the voice of God
7. 30

"It was forty years later in the desert of Mount Sinai that an angel appeared to him in the flames of a burning bush, and the sight filled Moses with wonder. As he approached to look at it more closely the voice of the Lord spoke to him, saying, 'I am the God of thy fathers, the God of Abraham, and the God of Isaac, and the God of Jacob.' Then Moses trembled and was afraid to look any more. But the Lord spoke to him and said, *'Loose the shoes from thy feet: for the place whereon thou standest is holy ground. I have surely seen the affliction of my*

ers, and his family connexions were disclosed to Pharaoh. So Joseph sent an invitation to his father Jacob and all his relatives, seventy-five persons altogether; and Jacob went down into Egypt. There he ended his days, as also our forefathers did. Their remains were later removed to Shechem and buried in the tomb which Abraham had bought and paid for from the clan of Emmor at Shechem.

'Now as the time approached for God to fulfil the promise he had made to Abraham, our nation in Egypt grew and increased in numbers. At length another king, who knew nothing of Joseph, ascended the throne of Egypt. He made a crafty attack on our race, and cruelly forced our ancestors to expose their children so that they should not survive. At this time Moses was born. He was a fine child, and pleasing to God. For three months he was nursed in his father's house, and when he was exposed, Pharaoh's daughter herself adopted him and brought him up as her own son. So Moses was trained in all the wisdom of the Egyptians, a powerful speaker and a man of action.

'He was approaching the age of forty, when it occurred to him to look into the conditions of his fellow-countrymen the Israelites. He saw one of them being ill-treated, so he went to his aid, and avenged the victim by striking down the Egyptian. He thought his fellow-countrymen would understand that God was offering them deliverance through him, but they did not understand. The next day he came upon two of them fighting, and tried to bring them to make up their quarrel. "My men," he said, "you are brothers; why are you ill-treating one another?" But the man who was at fault pushed him away. "Who set you up as a ruler and judge over us?" he said. "Are you going to kill me like the Egyptian you killed yesterday?" At this Moses fled the country and settled in Midianite territory. There two sons were born to him.

'After forty years had passed, an angel appeared to him in the flame of a burning bush in the desert near Mount Sinai. Moses was amazed at the sight. But as he approached to look closely, the voice of the Lord was heard: "I am the God of your fathers, the God of Abraham, Isaac, and Jacob." Moses was terrified and dared not look. Then the Lord said to him, "Take off your shoes; the place where you are standing is holy ground. I have indeed seen how my people are oppressed

K.J.V.

people which is in Egypt, and I have heard their groaning, and am come down to deliver them. And now come, I will send thee into Egypt. 35 This Moses whom they refused, saying, Who made thee a ruler and a judge? the same did God send *to be* a ruler and a deliverer by the hand of the angel which appeared to him in the bush. 36 He brought them out, after that he had shewed wonders and signs in the land of Egypt, and in the Red sea, and in the wilderness forty years.

37 This is that Moses, which said unto the children of Israel, A Prophet shall the Lord your God raise up unto you of your brethren, like unto me; him shall ye hear. 38 This is he, that was in the church in the wilderness with the angel which spake to him in the mount Sina, and *with* our fathers: who received the lively oracles to give unto us: 39 To whom our fathers would not obey, but thrust *him* from them, and in their hearts turned back again into Egypt, 40 Saying unto Aaron, Make us gods to go before us: for *as for* this Moses, which brought us out of the land of Egypt, we wot not what is become of him. 41 And they made a calf in those days, and offered sacrifice unto the idol, and rejoiced in the works of their own hands. 42 Then God turned, and gave them up to worship the host of heaven; as it is written in the book of the prophets, O ye house of Israel, have ye offered to me slain beasts and sacrifices *by the space of* forty years in the wilderness? 43 Yea, ye took up the tabernacle of Moloch, and the star of your god Remphan, figures which ye made to worship them: and I will carry you away beyond Babylon. 44 Our fathers had the tabernacle of witness in the wilderness, as he had appointed, speaking unto Moses, that he should make it according to the fashion that he had seen. 45 Which also our fathers that came after brought in with Jesus into the possession of the Gentiles, whom God drave out before the face of our fathers, unto the days of David; 46 Who found favour before God, and desired to find a tabernacle for the God of Jacob. 47 But Solomon built him a house. 48 Howbeit the Most High dwelleth not in temples made with hands; as saith the prophet, 49 Heaven *is* my throne, and earth *is* my footstool: what house will ye build me? saith the Lord: or what *is* the place of my rest? 50 Hath not my hand made all these things?

51 Ye stiffnecked and uncircumcised in heart and ears, ye do always resist the Holy Ghost:

R.S.V.

ill-treatment of my people that are in Egypt and heard their groaning, and I have come down to deliver them. And now come, I will send you to Egypt.'

35 "This Moses whom they refused, saying, 'Who made you a ruler and a judge?' God sent as both ruler and deliverer by the hand of the angel that appeared to him in the bush. 36 He led them out, having performed wonders and signs in Egypt and at the Red Sea, and in the wilderness for forty years. 37 This is the Moses who said to the Israelites, 'God will raise up for you a prophet from your brethren as he raised me up.' 38 This is he who was in the congregation in the wilderness with the angel who spoke to him at Mount Sinai, and with our fathers; and he received living oracles to give to us. 39 Our fathers refused to obey him, but thrust him aside, and in their hearts they turned to Egypt, 40 saying to Aaron, 'Make for us gods to go before us; as for this Moses who led us out from the land of Egypt, we do not know what has become of him.' 41 And they made a calf in those days, and offered a sacrifice to the idol and rejoiced in the works of their hands. 42 But God turned and gave them over to worship the host of heaven, as it is written in the book of the prophets:

'Did you offer to me slain beasts and sacrifices,
forty years in the wilderness, O house of Israel?
43 And you took up the tent of Moloch,
and the star of the god Rephan,
the figures which you made to worship;
and I will remove you beyond Babylon.'

44 "Our fathers had the tent of witness in the wilderness, even as he who spoke to Moses directed him to make it, according to the pattern that he had seen. 45 Our fathers in turn brought it in with Joshua when they dispossessed the nations which God thrust out before our fathers. So it was until the days of David, 46 who found favor in the sight of God and asked leave to find a habitation for the God of Jacob. 47 But it was Solomon who built a house for him. 48 Yet the Most High does not dwell in houses made with hands; as the prophet says,

49 'Heaven is my throne,
and earth my footstool.
What house will you build for me, says the Lord,
or what is the place of my rest?
50 Did not my hand make all these things?'

51 "You stiff-necked people, uncircumcised in heart and ears, you always resist the Holy

PHILLIPS

people which is in Egypt, and have heard their groaning, and I am come down to deliver them: and now come, I will send thee into Egypt.'

But Israel rejects Moses   7. 35

"So this same Moses whom they had rejected in the words, 'Who appointed you a ruler and judge?' God sent to be both ruler and deliverer with the help of the angel who had appeared to him in the bush. This is the man who showed wonders and signs in Egypt and in the Red Sea, the man who led them out of Egypt and was their leader in the desert for forty years. He was Moses, the man who said to the sons of Israel, *'A prophet shall God raise up unto you from among your brethren, like unto me.'* In that church in the desert this was the man who was the mediator between the angel who used to talk with him on Mount Sinai and our fathers. This was the man who received words, living words, which were to be given to you; and this was the man to whom our forefathers turned a deaf ear! They disregarded him, and in their hearts hankered after Egypt. They said to Aaron, 'Make us gods to go before us. For as for this Moses who led us out of Egypt, we do not know what has become of him.' In those days they even made a calf, and offered sacrifices to their idol. They rejoiced in the work of their own hands. So God turned away from them and left them to worship the Host of Heaven, as it is written in the book of the prophets,

Did ye offer unto me slain beasts and sacrifices
Forty years in the wilderness, O house of Israel?
And ye took up the tabernacle of Moloch,
And the star of the god Rephan,
The figures which ye made to worship them:
And I will carry you away beyond Babylon.

God's privileges to Israel   7. 44

"There in the desert our forefathers possessed the Tabernacle of witness made according to the pattern which Moses saw when God instructed him to build it. This Tabernacle was handed down to our forefathers, and they brought it here when the Gentiles were defeated under Joshua, for God drove them out as our ancestors advanced. Here it stayed until the time of David. David won the approval of God and prayed that he might find a habitation for the God of Jacob, even though it was not he but Solomon who actually built a house for him. Yet of course the most high does not live in man-made houses. As the prophet says,

The heaven is my throne,
And the earth the footstool of my feet:
What manner of house will ye build me? saith the Lord:
Or what is the place of my rest?
Did not my hand make all these things?

Yet Israel is blind and disobedient   7. 51

"You obstinate people, heathen in your thinking, heathen in the way you are listening to me now! It is always the same—you never fail to

in Egypt and have heard their groans; and I have come down to rescue them. Up, then; let me send you to Egypt."

'This Moses, whom they had rejected with the words, "Who made you ruler and judge?"—this very man was commissioned as ruler and liberator by God himself, speaking through the angel who appeared to him in the bush. It was Moses who led them out, working miracles and signs in Egypt, at the Red Sea, and for forty years in the desert. It was he again who said to the Israelites, "God will raise up a prophet for you from among yourselves as he raised me." [a] He it was who, when they were assembled there in the desert, conversed with the angel who spoke to him on Mount Sinai, and with our forefathers; he received the living utterances of God, to pass on to us.

'But our forefathers would not accept his leadership. They thrust him aside. They wished themselves back in Egypt, and said to Aaron, "Make us gods to go before us. As for that Moses, who brought us out of Egypt, we do not know what has become of him." That was when they made the bull-calf, and offered sacrifice to the idol, and held a feast in honour of the thing their hands had made. But God turned away from them and gave them over to the worship of the hosts of heaven, as it stands written in the book of the prophets: "Did you bring me victims and offerings those forty years in the desert, you house of Israel? No, you carried aloft the shrine of Moloch and the star of the god Rephan, the images which you had made for your adoration. I will banish you beyond Babylon."

'Our forefathers had the Tent of the Testimony in the desert, as God commanded when he told Moses to make it after the pattern which he had seen. Our fathers of the next generation, with Joshua, brought it with them when they dispossessed the nations whom God drove out before them, and there it was until the time of David. David found favour with God and asked to be allowed to provide a dwelling-place for the God of Jacob;[b] but it was Solomon who built him a house. However, the Most High does not live in houses made by men: as the prophet says, "Heaven is my throne and earth my footstool. What kind of house will you build for me, says the Lord; where is my resting-place? Are not all these things of my own making?"

'How stubborn you are, heathen still at heart and deaf to the truth! You always fight against

[a] *Or* like me. [b] *Some witnesses read* for the house of Jacob.

K.J.V.

as your fathers *did*, so *do* ye. 52 Which of the prophets have not your fathers persecuted? and they have slain them which shewed before of the coming of the Just One; of whom ye have been now the betrayers and murderers: 53 Who have received the law by the disposition of angels, and have not kept *it*.

54 When they heard these things, they were cut to the heart, and they gnashed on him with *their* teeth. 55 But he, being full of the Holy Ghost, looked up steadfastly into heaven, and saw the glory of God, and Jesus standing on the right hand of God, 56And said, Behold, I see the heavens opened, and the Son of man standing on the right hand of God. 57 Then they cried out with a loud voice, and stopped their ears, and ran upon him with one accord, 58And cast *him* out of the city, and stoned *him:* and the witnesses laid down their clothes at a young man's feet, whose name was Saul. 59And they stoned Stephen, calling upon *God*, and saying, Lord Jesus, receive my spirit. 60And he kneeled down, and cried with a loud voice, Lord, lay not this sin to their charge. And when he had said this, he fell asleep.

8 And Saul was consenting unto his death. And at that time there was a great persecution against the church which was at Jerusalem; and they were all scattered abroad throughout the regions of Judea and Samaria, except the apostles. 2And devout men carried Stephen *to his burial,* and made great lamentation over him. 3As for Saul, he made havoc of the church, entering into every house, and haling men and women committed *them* to prison. 4 Therefore they that were scattered abroad went every where preaching the word. 5 Then Philip went down to the city of Samaria, and preached Christ unto them. 6And the people with one accord gave heed unto those things which Philip spake, hearing and seeing the miracles which he did. 7 For unclean spirits, crying with loud voice, came out of many that were possessed *with them:* and many taken with palsies, and that were lame, were healed. 8And there was great joy in that city. 9 But there was a certain man, called Simon, which beforetime in the same city used sorcery,

R.S.V.

Spirit. As your fathers did, so do you. 52 Which of the prophets did not your fathers persecute? And they killed those who announced beforehand the coming of the Righteous One, whom you have now betrayed and murdered, 53 you who received the law as delivered by angels and did not keep it."

54 Now when they heard these things they were enraged, and they ground their teeth against him. 55 But he, full of the Holy Spirit, gazed into heaven and saw the glory of God, and Jesus standing at the right hand of God; 56 and he said, "Behold, I see the heavens opened, and the Son of man standing at the right hand of God." 57 But they cried out with a loud voice and stopped their ears and rushed together upon him. 58 Then they cast him out of the city and stoned him; and the witnesses laid down their garments at the feet of a young man named Saul. 59And as they were stoning Stephen, he prayed, "Lord Jesus, receive my spirit." 60And he knelt down and cried with a loud voice, "Lord, do not hold this sin against them." And when he had said this, he fell asleep.

8 And Saul was consenting to his death. And on that day a great persecution arose against the church in Jerusalem; and they were all scattered throughout the region of Judea and Samaria, except the apostles. 2 Devout men buried Stephen, and made great lamentation over him. 3 But Saul laid waste the church, and entering house after house, he dragged off men and women and committed them to prison.

4 Now those who were scattered went about preaching the word. 5 Philip went down to a city of Samaria, and proclaimed to them the Christ. 6And the multitudes with one accord gave heed to what was said by Philip, when they heard him and saw the signs which he did. 7 For unclean spirits came out of many who were possessed, crying with a loud voice; and many who were paralyzed or lame were healed. 8 So there was much joy in that city.

9 But there was a man named Simon who had previously practiced magic in the city and

PHILLIPS

N.E.B.

resist the Holy Spirit! Just as your fathers did, so are you doing now. Can you name a single prophet whom your fathers did not persecute? They killed the men who long ago foretold the coming of the just one, and now in our own day you have become his betrayers and his murderers. You are the men who have received the Law of God miraculously, by the hand of angels, *and you are the men who have disobeyed it!*"

The truth arouses murderous fury   7. 54

These words stung them to fury and they ground their teeth at him in rage. Stephen, filled through all his being with the Holy Spirit, looked steadily up into Heaven. He saw the glory of God, and Jesus himself standing at his right hand.

"Look!" he exclaimed, "the heavens are opened and I can see the Son of Man standing at God's right hand!"

At this they put their fingers in their ears. Yelling with fury, as one man they made a rush at him and hustled him out of the city and stoned him. The witnesses* of the execution flung their clothes at the feet of a young man by the name of Saul.

So they stoned Stephen while he called upon God, and said,

"Jesus, Lord, receive my spirit!"

Then, on his knees, he cried in ringing tones, "Lord, forgive them for this sin."

And with these words he fell into the sleep of death, while Saul gave silent assent to his execution.

Widespread persecution follows   8. 1b
Stephen's death

On that very day a great storm of persecution burst upon the Church in Jerusalem. All Church members except the apostles were scattered over the countryside of Judaea and Samaria. While reverent men buried Stephen and mourned deeply over him, Saul harassed the Church bitterly. He would go from house to house, drag out both men and women and have them committed to prison. Those who were dispersed by this action went throughout the country, preaching the good news of the message as they went. Philip, for instance, went down to the city of Samaria and preached Christ to the people there. His words met with a ready and sympathetic response from the large crowds who listened to him and saw the miracles which he performed. With loud cries evil spirits came out of those who had been possessed by them; and many paralyzed and lame people were cured. As a result there was great rejoicing in that city.

A magician believes in Christ   8. 9

But there was a man named Simon in the city who had been practicing magic for some time

the Holy Spirit. Like fathers, like sons. Was there ever a prophet whom your fathers did not persecute? They killed those who foretold the coming of the Righteous One; and now you have betrayed him and murdered him, you who received the Law as God's angels gave it to you, and yet have not kept it.'

This touched them on the raw and they ground their teeth with fury. But Stephen, filled with the Holy Spirit, and gazing intently up to heaven, saw the glory of God, and Jesus standing at God's right hand. 'Look,' he said, 'there is a rift in the sky; I can see the Son of Man standing at God's right hand!' At this they gave a great shout and stopped their ears. Then they made one rush at him and, flinging him out of the city, set about stoning him. The witnesses laid their coats at the feet of a young man named Saul. So they stoned Stephen, and as they did so, he called out, 'Lord Jesus, receive my spirit.' Then he fell on his knees and cried aloud, 'Lord, do not hold this sin against them', and with that he died.

8 And Saul was among those who approved of his murder.

This was the beginning of a time of violent persecution for the church in Jerusalem; and all except the apostles were scattered over the country districts of Judaea and Samaria. Stephen was given burial by certain devout men, who made a great lamentation for him. Saul, meanwhile, was harrying the church; he entered house after house, seizing men and women, and sending them to prison.

As for those who had been scattered, they went through the country preaching the Word. Philip came down to a city in Samaria and began proclaiming the Messiah to them. The crowds, to a man, listened eagerly to what Philip said, when they heard him and saw the miracles that he performed. For in many cases of possession the unclean spirits came out with a great outcry; and many paralysed and crippled folk were cured; and there was great joy in that city.

A man named Simon had been in the city for some time, and had swept the Samaritans off

---

* In Jewish Law the "witnesses" were also the executioners.

K.J.V.

and bewitched the people of Samaria, giving out that himself was some great one: 10 To whom they all gave heed, from the least to the greatest, saying, This man is the great power of God. 11And to him they had regard, because that of long time he had bewitched them with sorceries. 12 But when they believed Philip preaching the things concerning the kingdom of God, and the name of Jesus Christ, they were baptized, both men and women. 13 Then Simon himself believed also: and when he was baptized, he continued with Philip, and wondered, beholding the miracles and signs which were done. 14 Now when the apostles which were at Jerusalem heard that Samaria had received the word of God, they sent unto them Peter and John: 15 Who, when they were come down, prayed for them, that they might receive the Holy Ghost: 16 (For as yet he was fallen upon none of them: only they were baptized in the name of the Lord Jesus.) 17 Then laid they *their* hands on them, and they received the Holy Ghost. 18And when Simon saw that through laying on of the apostles' hands the Holy Ghost was given, he offered them money, 19 Saying, Give me also this power, that on whomsoever I lay hands, he may receive the Holy Ghost. 20 But Peter said unto him, Thy money perish with thee, because thou hast thought that the gift of God may be purchased with money. 21 Thou hast neither part nor lot in this matter: for thy heart is not right in the sight of God. 22 Repent therefore of this thy wickedness, and pray God, if perhaps the thought of thine heart may be forgiven thee. 23 For I perceive that thou art in the gall of bitterness, and *in* the bond of iniquity. 24 Then answered Simon, and said, Pray ye to the Lord for me, that none of these things which ye have spoken come upon me. 25And they, when they had testified and preached the word of the Lord, returned to Jerusalem, and preached the gospel in many villages of the Samaritans. 26And the angel of the Lord spake unto Philip, saying, Arise, and go toward the south, unto the way that goeth down from Jerusalem unto Gaza, which is desert. 27And he arose and went: and, behold, a man of Ethiopia, a eunuch of great authority under

R.S.V.

amazed the nation of Samaria, saying that he himself was somebody great. 10 They all gave heed to him, from the least to the greatest, saying, "This man is that power of God which is called Great." 11And they gave heed to him, because for a long time he had amazed them with his magic. 12 But when they believed Philip as he preached good news about the kingdom of God and the name of Jesus Christ, they were baptized, both men and women. 13 Even Simon himself believed, and after being baptized he continued with Philip. And seeing signs and great miracles performed, he was amazed. 14 Now when the apostles at Jerusalem heard that Samaria had received the word of God, they sent to them Peter and John, 15 who came down and prayed for them that they might receive the Holy Spirit; 16 for it had not yet fallen on any of them, but they had only been baptized in the name of the Lord Jesus. 17 Then they laid their hands on them and they received the Holy Spirit. 18 Now when Simon saw that the Spirit was given through the laying on of the apostles' hands, he offered them money, 19 saying, "Give me also this power, that any one on whom I lay my hands may receive the Holy Spirit." 20 But Peter said to him, "Your silver perish with you, because you thought you could obtain the gift of God with money! 21 You have neither part nor lot in this matter, for your heart is not right before God. 22 Repent therefore of this wickedness of yours, and pray to the Lord that, if possible, the intent of your heart may be forgiven you. 23 For I see that you are in the gall of bitterness and in the bond of iniquity." 24And Simon answered, "Pray for me to the Lord, that nothing of what you have said may come upon me."

25 Now when they had testified and spoken the word of the Lord, they returned to Jerusalem, preaching the gospel to many villages of the Samaritans.

26 But an angel of the Lord said to Philip, "Rise and go toward the south*g* to the road that goes down from Jerusalem to Gaza." This is a desert road. 27And he rose and went. And behold, an Ethiopian, a eunuch, a minister of

[g] Or *at noon.*

PHILLIPS

and mystifying the people of Samaria. He pretended that he was somebody great and everyone from the lowest to the highest was fascinated by him. Indeed, they used to say, "This man must be that great power of God." He had influenced them for a long time, astounding them by his magical practices. But when they had come to believe Philip as he proclaimed to them the good news of the kingdom of God and of the name of Jesus Christ, men and women alike were baptized. Even Simon himself became a believer and after his baptism attached himself closely to Philip. As he saw the signs and remarkable demonstrations of power which took place, he lived in a state of constant wonder.

God confirms Samaria's acceptance of the gospel
8. 14

When the apostles in Jerusalem heard that Samaria had accepted the Word of God, they sent Peter and John down to them. When these two had arrived they prayed for the Samaritans that they might receive the Holy Spirit for as yet he had not fallen upon any of them. They were living simply as men and women who had been baptized in the name of the Lord Jesus. So then and there they laid their hands on them and they received the Holy Spirit.

Simon's monstrous suggestion is sternly rebuked
8. 18

When Simon saw how the Spirit was given through the apostles' laying their hands upon people he offered them money with the words,

"Give me this power too, so that if I were to put my hands on anyone he could receive the Holy Spirit."

But Peter said to him,

"To hell with you and your money!* How dare you think you could buy the gift of God? You can have no share or place in this ministry, for your heart is not honest before God. All you can do now is to repent of this wickedness of yours and pray earnestly to God that the evil intention of your heart may be forgiven. For I can see inside you, and I see a man bitter with jealousy and bound with his own sin!"

To this Simon answered,

"Please pray to the Lord for me that none of these things that you have spoken about may come upon me!"

When Peter and John had given their clear witness and spoken the Word of the Lord, they returned to Jerusalem, preaching the good news to many Samaritan villages as they went.

Philip is given a unique opportunity
8. 26

But an angel of the Lord said to Philip,

"Get up and go south down the road which runs from Jerusalem to Gaza, out in the desert."

Philip arose and began his journey. At this very moment an Ethiopian eunuch, a minister

* These words are exactly what the Greek means. It is a pity that their real meaning is obscured by modern slang usage.

N.E.B.

their feet with his magical arts, claiming to be someone great. All of them, high and low, listened eagerly to him. 'This man', they said, 'is that power of God which is called "The Great Power".' They listened because they had for so long been carried away by his magic. But when they came to believe Philip with his good news about the kingdom of God and the name of Jesus Christ, they were baptized, men and women alike. Even Simon himself believed, and was baptized, and thereupon was constantly in Philip's company. He was carried away when he saw the powerful signs and miracles that were taking place.

The apostles in Jerusalem now heard that Samaria had accepted the word of God. They sent off Peter and John, who went down there and prayed for the converts, asking that they might receive the Holy Spirit. For until then the Spirit had not come upon any of them. They had been baptized into the name of the Lord Jesus, that and nothing more. So Peter and John laid their hands on them and they received the Holy Spirit.

When Simon saw that the Spirit was bestowed through the laying on of the apostles' hands, he offered them money and said, 'Give me the same power too, so that when I lay my hands on anyone, he will receive the Holy Spirit.' 'You and your money,' said Peter sternly, 'may you come to a bad end, for thinking God's gift is for sale! You have no part nor lot in this, for you are dishonest with God. Repent of this wickedness and pray the Lord to forgive you for imagining such a thing. I can see that you are doomed to taste the bitter fruit and wear the fetters of sin.' [a] Simon answered, 'Pray to the Lord for me yourselves and ask that none of the things you have spoken of may fall upon me.'

And so, after giving their testimony and speaking the word of the Lord, they took the road back to Jerusalem, bringing the good news to many Samaritan villages on the way.

Then the angel of the Lord said to Philip, 'Start out and go south to the road that leads down from Jerusalem to Gaza.' (This is the desert road.) So he set out and was on his way when he caught sight of an Ethiopian. This man was a eunuch, a high official of the Kandake, or

[a] *Literally* you are for gall of bitterness and a fetter of unrighteousness.

K.J.V.

Candace queen of the Ethiopians, who had the charge of all her treasure, and had come to Jerusalem for to worship, 28 Was returning, and sitting in his chariot read Esaias the prophet. 29 Then the Spirit said unto Philip, Go near, and join thyself to this chariot. 30And Philip ran thither to *him*, and heard him read the prophet Esaias, and said, Understandest thou what thou readest? 31And he said, How can I, except some man should guide me? And he desired Philip that he would come up and sit with him. 32 The place of the Scripture which he read was this, He was led as a sheep to the slaughter; and like a lamb dumb before his shearer, so opened he not his mouth: 33 In his humiliation his judgment was taken away: and who shall declare his generation? for his life is taken from the earth. 34And the eunuch answered Philip, and said, I pray thee, of whom speaketh the prophet this? of himself, or of some other man? 35 Then Philip opened his mouth, and began at the same Scripture, and preached unto him Jesus. 36And as they went on *their* way, they came unto a certain water: and the eunuch said, See, *here is* water; what doth hinder me to be baptized? 37And Philip said, If thou believest with all thine heart, thou mayest. And he answered and said, I believe that Jesus Christ is the Son of God. 38And he commanded the chariot to stand still: and they went down both into the water, both Philip and the eunuch; and he baptized him. 39And when they were come up out of the water, the Spirit of the Lord caught away Philip, that the eunuch saw him no more: and he went on his way rejoicing. 40 But Philip was found at Azotus: and passing through he preached in all the cities, till he came to Cesarea.

R.S.V.

Candace the queen of the Ethiopians, in charge of all her treasure, had come to Jerusalem to worship 28 and was returning; seated in his chariot, he was reading the prophet Isaiah. 29And the Spirit said to Philip, "Go up and join this chariot." 30 So Philip ran to him, and heard him reading Isaiah the prophet, and asked, "Do you understand what you are reading?" 31And he said, "How can I, unless some one guides me?" And he invited Philip to come up and sit with him. 32 Now the passage of the scripture which he was reading was this:

"As a sheep led to the slaughter
  or a lamb before its shearer is dumb,
  so he opens not his mouth.
33 In his humiliation justice was denied him.
  Who can describe his generation?
  For his life is taken up from the earth."

34And the eunuch said to Philip, "About whom, pray, does the prophet say this, about himself or about some one else?" 35 Then Philip opened his mouth, and beginning with this scripture he told him the good news of Jesus. 36And as they went along the road they came to some water, and the eunuch said, "See, here is water! What is to prevent my being baptized?" [h] 38And he commanded the chariot to stop, and they both went down into the water, Philip and the eunuch, and he baptized him. 39And when they came up out of the water, the Spirit of the Lord caught up Philip; and the eunuch saw him no more, and went on his way rejoicing. 40 But Philip was found at Azotus, and passing on he preached the gospel to all the towns till he came to Caesarea.

9 And Saul, yet breathing out threatenings and slaughter against the disciples of the Lord, went unto the high priest, 2And desired of him letters to Damascus to the synagogues, that if he found any of this way, whether they were men or women, he might bring them bound unto Jerusalem. 3And as he journeyed, he came near Damascus: and suddenly there shined round about him a light from heaven: 4And he fell to the earth, and heard a voice saying unto him, Saul, Saul, why persecutest thou me? 5And he said, Who art thou, Lord? And the Lord said, I am Jesus whom thou persecutest: *it is* hard for thee to kick against the pricks. 6And he trembling and astonished said, Lord, what wilt thou have me to do? And the Lord *said* unto him, Arise, and go into the city, and it shall be told thee what thou must do. 7And the men which journeyed with him stood speechless, hearing a voice, but seeing no man. 8And Saul arose from the earth; and when his eyes were opened, he saw no man: but they led him by the hand, and brought *him* into Damascus. 9And he was three days without sight, and neither did eat nor drink.

9 But Saul, still breathing threats and murder against the disciples of the Lord, went to the high priest 2 and asked him for letters to the synagogues at Damascus, so that if he found any belonging to the Way, men or women, he might bring them bound to Jerusalem. 3 Now as he journeyed he approached Damascus, and suddenly a light from heaven flashed about him. 4And he fell to the ground and heard a voice saying to him, "Saul, Saul, why do you persecute me?" 5And he said, "Who are you, Lord?" And he said, "I am Jesus, whom you are persecuting; 6 but rise and enter the city, and you will be told what you are to do." 7 The men who were traveling with him stood speechless, hearing the voice but seeing no one. 8 Saul arose from the ground; and when his eyes were opened, he could see nothing; so they led him by the hand and brought him into Damascus. 9And for three days he was without sight, and neither ate nor drank.

[h] Other ancient authorities add all or most of verse 37, *And Philip said, "If you believe with all your heart, you may." And he replied, "I believe that Jesus Christ is the Son of God."*

and in fact the treasurer to Candace, queen of the Ethiopians, was on his way home after coming to Jerusalem to worship. He was sitting in his carriage reading the prophet Isaiah. The Spirit said to Philip,

"Approach this carriage, and keep close to it."

Then as Philip ran forward he heard the man reading the prophet Isaiah, and he said,

"Do you understand what you are reading?"

And he replied,

"How can I unless I have someone to guide me?"

And he invited Philip to get up and sit by his side. The passage of scripture he was reading was this:

He was led as a sheep to the slaughter;
And as a lamb before his shearer is dumb,
So he openeth not his mouth:
In his humiliation his judgment was taken
  away?
His generation who shall declare?
For his life is taken from the earth.

The eunuch turned to Philip and said,

"Tell me, I beg you, about whom is the prophet saying this—is he speaking about himself or about someone else?"

Then Philip began, and using this scripture as a starting point, he told the eunuch the good news about Jesus. As they proceeded along the road they came to some water, and the eunuch said,

"Look, here is some water; is there any reason why I should not be baptized now?"

And he gave orders for the carriage to stop. Then both of them went down to the water and Philip baptized the eunuch. When they came up out of the water the Spirit of the Lord took Philip away suddenly and the eunuch saw no more of him, but proceeded on his journey with a heart full of joy. Philip found himself at Azotus and as he passed through the countryside he went on telling the good news in all the cities until he came to Caesarea.

Queen, of Ethiopia, in charge of all her treasure. He had been to Jerusalem on a pilgrimage and was now on his way home, sitting in his carriage and reading aloud the prophet Isaiah. The Spirit said to Philip, 'Go and join the carriage.' When Philip ran up he heard him reading the prophet Isaiah and said, 'Do you understand what you are reading?' He said, 'How can I understand unless someone will give me the clue?' So he asked Philip to get in and sit beside him.

The passage he was reading was this: 'He was led like a sheep to be slaughtered; and like a lamb that is dumb before the shearer, he does not open his mouth. He has been humiliated and has no redress. Who will be able to speak of his posterity? For his life is cut off and he is gone from the earth.'

'Now', said the eunuch to Philip, 'tell me, please, who it is that the prophet is speaking about here: himself or someone else?' Then Philip began. Starting from this passage, he told him the good news of Jesus. As they were going along the road, they came to some water. 'Look,' said the eunuch, 'here is water: what is there to prevent my being baptized?';[a] and he ordered the carriage to stop. Then they both went down into the water, Philip and the eunuch; and he baptized him. When they came up out of the water the Spirit snatched Philip away, and the eunuch saw no more of him, but went on his way well content. Philip appeared at Azotus, and toured the country, preaching in all the towns till he reached Caesarea.

The crisis for Saul   9. 1

But Saul, still breathing murderous threats against the disciples of the Lord, went to the High Priest and begged him for letters to the synagogues in Damascus, so that if he should find there any followers of the Way, whether men or women, he could bring them back to Jerusalem as prisoners.

But on his journey, as he neared Damascus, a light from Heaven suddenly blazed around him, and he fell to the ground. Then he heard a voice speaking to him,

"Saul, Saul, why are you persecuting me?"

"Who are you, Lord?" he asked.

"I am Jesus whom you are persecuting," was the reply. "But now stand up and go into the city and there you will be told what you must do."

His companions on the journey stood there speechless, for they had heard the voice but could see no one. Saul got up from the ground, but when he opened his eyes he could see nothing. So they took him by the hand and led him into Damascus. There he remained sightless for three days, and during that time he had nothing either to eat or drink.

9 Meanwhile Saul was still breathing murderous threats against the disciples of the Lord. He went to the High Priest and applied for letters to the synagogues at Damascus authorizing him to arrest anyone he found, men or women, who followed the new way, and bring them to Jerusalem. While he was still on the road and nearing Damascus, suddenly a light flashed from the sky all around him. He fell to the ground and heard a voice saying, 'Saul, Saul, why do you persecute me?' 'Tell me, Lord,' he said, 'who you are.' The voice answered, 'I am Jesus, whom you are persecuting. But get up and go into the city, and you will be told what you have to do.' Meanwhile the men who were travelling with him stood speechless; they heard the voice but could see no one. Saul got up from the ground, but when he opened his eyes he could not see; so they led him by the hand and brought him into Damascus. He was blind for three days, and took no food or drink.

[a] Some witnesses insert (37) Philip said, 'If you whole-heartedly believe, it is permitted.' He replied, 'I believe that Jesus Christ is the Son of God.'

K.J.V.

10 And there was a certain disciple at Damascus, named Ananias; and to him said the Lord in a vision, Ananias. And he said, Behold, I *am here,* Lord. 11And the Lord *said* unto him, Arise, and go into the street which is called Straight, and inquire in the house of Judas for *one* called Saul, of Tarsus: for, behold, he prayeth, 12And hath seen in a vision a man named Ananias coming in, and putting *his* hand on him, that he might receive his sight. 13 Then Ananias answered, Lord, I have heard by many of this man, how much evil he hath done to thy saints at Jerusalem: 14And here he hath authority from the chief priests to bind all that call on thy name. 15 But the Lord said unto him, Go thy way: for he is a chosen vessel unto me, to bear my name before the Gentiles, and kings, and the children of Israel: 16 For I will shew him how great things he must suffer for my name's sake. 17And Ananias went his way, and entered into the house; and putting his hands on him said, Brother Saul, the Lord, *even* Jesus, that appeared unto thee in the way as thou camest, hath sent me, that thou mightest receive thy sight, and be filled with the Holy Ghost. 18And immediately there fell from his eyes as it had been scales: and he received sight forthwith, and arose, and was baptized. 19And when he had received meat, he was strengthened. Then was Saul certain days with the disciples which were at Damascus. 20And straightway he preached Christ in the synagogues, that he is the Son of God. 21 But all that heard *him* were amazed, and said; Is not this he that destroyed them which called on this name in Jerusalem, and came hither for that intent, that he might bring them bound unto the chief priests? 22 But Saul increased the more in strength, and confounded the Jews which dwelt at Damascus, proving that this is very Christ.

23 And after that many days were fulfilled, the Jews took counsel to kill him: 24 But their laying wait was known of Saul. And they watched the gates day and night to kill him. 25 Then the disciples took him by night, and let

R.S.V.

10 Now there was a disciple at Damascus named Ananias. The Lord said to him in a vision, "Ananias." And he said, "Here I am, Lord." 11And the Lord said to him, "Rise and go to the street called Straight, and inquire in the house of Judas for a man of Tarsus named Saul; for behold, he is praying, 12 and he has seen a man named Ananias come in and lay his hands on him so that he might regain his sight." 13 But Ananias answered, "Lord, I have heard from many about this man, how much evil he has done to thy saints at Jerusalem; 14 and here he has authority from the chief priests to bind all who call upon thy name." 15 But the Lord said to him, "Go, for he is a chosen instrument of mine to carry my name before the Gentiles and kings and the sons of Israel; 16 for I will show him how much he must suffer for the sake of my name." 17 So Ananias departed and entered the house. And laying his hands on him he said, "Brother Saul, the Lord Jesus, who appeared to you on the road by which you came, has sent me that you may regain your sight and be filled with the Holy Spirit." 18And immediately something like scales fell from his eyes and he regained his sight. Then he rose and was baptized, 19 and took food and was strengthened.

For several days he was with the disciples at Damascus. 20And in the synagogues immediately he proclaimed Jesus, saying, "He is the Son of God." 21And all who heard him were amazed, and said, "Is not this the man who made havoc in Jerusalem of those who called on this name? And he has come here for this purpose, to bring them bound before the chief priests." 22 But Saul increased all the more in strength, and confounded the Jews who lived in Damascus by proving that Jesus was the Christ.

23 When many days had passed, the Jews plotted to kill him, 24 but their plot became known to Saul. They were watching the gates day and night, to kill him; 25 but his disciples took him by night and let him down over the wall, lowering him in a basket.

God's preparation for the   **9. 10**
converted Saul

Now in Damascus there was a disciple by the name of Ananias. The Lord spoke to this man in a dream, calling him by his name.

"I am here, Lord," he replied.

Then the Lord said to him,

"Get up and go down to the street called Straight and inquire at the house of Judas for a man named Saul from Tarsus. At this moment he is praying and he sees in his mind's eye a man by the name of Ananias coming into the house, and placing his hands upon him to restore his sight."

But Ananias replied,

"Lord, I have heard on all hands about this man and how much harm he has done to your holy people in Jerusalem! Why even now he holds powers from the chief priests to arrest all who call upon your name."

But the Lord said to him,

"Go on your way, for this man is my chosen instrument to bear my name before the gentiles and their kings, as well as to the sons of Israel. Indeed, I myself will show him what he must suffer for the sake of my name."

Then Ananias set out and went to the house, and there he laid his hands upon Saul, and said,

"Saul, brother, the Lord has sent me—Jesus who appeared to you on your journey here—so that you may recover your sight and be filled with the Holy Spirit."

Immediately something like scales fell from Saul's eyes, and he could see again. He got to his feet and was baptized. Then he took some food and regained his strength.

Saul's conversion astounds   **9. 19b**
the disciples

Saul stayed with the disciples in Damascus for some time. Without delay he proclaimed Jesus in the synagogues declaring that he is the Son of God. All his hearers were staggered and kept saying,

"Isn't this the man who so bitterly persecuted those who called on the name in Jerusalem, and came down here with the sole object of taking back all such people as prisoners before the chief priests?"

But Saul went on from strength to strength, reducing to confusion the Jews who lived at Damascus by proving beyond doubt that this man is Christ.

The long revenge on the   **9. 23**
"renegade" begins

After some time the Jews made a plot to kill Saul, but news of this came to his ears. Although in their murderous scheme the Jews watched the gates day and night for him, Saul's disciples took him one night and let him down through an opening in the wall by lowering him in a basket.

There was a disciple in Damascus named Ananias. He had a vision in which he heard the voice of the Lord: 'Ananias!' 'Here I am, Lord', he answered. The Lord said to him, 'Go at once to Straight Street, to the house of Judas, and ask for a man from Tarsus named Saul. You will find him at prayer; he has had a vision of a man named Ananias coming in and laying his hands on him to restore his sight.' Ananias answered, 'Lord, I have often heard about this man and all the harm he has done to thy people in Jerusalem. And here he is with authority from the chief priests to arrest all who invoke thy name.' But the Lord said to him, 'You must go, for this man is my chosen instrument to bring my name before the nations and their kings, and before the people of Israel. I myself will show him all that he must go through for my name's sake.'

So Ananias went. He entered the house, laid his hands on him and said, 'Saul, my brother, the Lord Jesus, who appeared to you on your way here, has sent me to you so that you may recover your sight, and be filled with the Holy Spirit.' And immediately it seemed that scales fell from his eyes, and he regained his sight. Thereupon he was baptized, and afterwards he took food and his strength returned.

He stayed some time with the disciples in Damascus. Soon he was proclaiming Jesus publicly in the synagogues: 'This', he said, 'is the Son of God.' All who heard were astounded. 'Is not this the man', they said, 'who was in Jerusalem trying to destroy those who invoke this name? Did he not come here for the sole purpose of arresting them and taking them to the chief priests?' But Saul grew more and more forceful, and silenced the Jews of Damascus with his cogent proofs that Jesus was the Messiah.

As the days mounted up, the Jews hatched a plot against his life; but their plans became known to Saul. They kept watch on the city gates day and night so that they might murder him; but his converts took him one night and let him down by the wall, lowering him in a basket.

him down by the wall in a basket. 26And when Saul was come to Jerusalem he assayed to join himself to the disciples: but they were all afraid of him, and believed not that he was a disciple. 27 But Barnabas took him, and brought *him* to the apostles, and declared unto them how he had seen the Lord in the way, and that he had spoken to him, and how he had preached boldly at Damascus in the name of Jesus. 28And he was with them coming in and going out at Jerusalem. 29And he spake boldly in the name of the Lord Jesus, and disputed against the Grecians: but they went about to slay him. 30 *Which* when the brethren knew, they brought him down to Cesarea, and sent him forth to Tarsus. 31 Then had the churches rest throughout all Judea and Galilee and Samaria, and were edified; and walking in the fear of the Lord, and in the comfort of the Holy Ghost, were multiplied.

32 And it came to pass, as Peter passed throughout all *quarters,* he came down also to the saints which dwelt at Lydda. 33And there he found a certain man named Eneas, which had kept his bed eight years, and was sick of the palsy. 34And Peter said unto him, Eneas, Jesus Christ maketh thee whole: arise, and make thy bed. And he arose immediately. 35And all that dwelt at Lydda and Saron saw him, and turned to the Lord.

36 Now there was at Joppa a certain disciple named Tabitha, which by interpretation is called Dorcas: this woman was full of good works and almsdeeds which she did. 37And it came to pass in those days, that she was sick, and died: whom when they had washed, they laid *her* in an upper chamber. 38And forasmuch as Lydda was nigh to Joppa, and the disciples had heard that Peter was there, they sent unto him two men, desiring *him* that he would not delay to come to them. 39 Then Peter arose and went with them. When he was come, they brought him into the upper chamber: and all the widows stood by him weeping, and shewing the coats and garments which Dorcas made, while she was with them. 40 But Peter put them all forth, and kneeled down, and prayed; and turning *him* to the body said, Tabitha, arise. And she opened her eyes: and when she saw Peter, she sat up. 41And he gave her *his* hand, and lifted her up; and when he had called the saints and widows, he presented

26 And when he had come to Jerusalem he attempted to join the disciples; and they were all afraid of him, for they did not believe that he was a disciple. 27 But Barnabas took him, and brought him to the apostles, and declared to them how on the road he had seen the Lord, who spoke to him, and how at Damascus he had preached boldly in the name of Jesus. 28 So he went in and out among them at Jerusalem, 29 preaching boldly in the name of the Lord. And he spoke and disputed against the Hellenists; but they were seeking to kill him. 30And when the brethren knew it, they brought him down to Caesarea, and sent him off to Tarsus. 31 So the church throughout all Judea and Galilee and Samaria had peace and was built up; and walking in the fear of the Lord and in the comfort of the Holy Spirit it was multiplied.

32 Now as Peter went here and there among them all, he came down also to the saints that lived at Lydda. 33 There he found a man named Aeneas, who had been bedridden for eight years and was paralyzed. 34And Peter said to him, "Aeneas, Jesus Christ heals you; rise and make your bed." And immediately he rose. 35And all the residents of Lydda and Sharon saw him, and they turned to the Lord.

36 Now there was at Joppa a disciple named Tabitha, which means Dorcas or Gazelle. She was full of good works and acts of charity. 37 In those days she fell sick and died; and when they had washed her, they laid her in an upper room. 38 Since Lydda was near Joppa, the disciples, hearing that Peter was there, sent two men to him entreating him, "Please come to us without delay." 39 So Peter rose and went with them. And when he had come, they took him to the upper room. All the widows stood beside him weeping, and showing coats and garments which Dorcas made while she was with them. 40 But Peter put them all outside and knelt down and prayed; then turning to the body he said, "Tabitha, rise." And she opened her eyes, and when she saw Peter she sat up. 41And he gave her his hand and lifted her up. Then calling the

PHILLIPS

N.E.B.

At Jerusalem Saul is suspect: **9. 26**
Barnabas conciliates

When Saul reached Jerusalem he tried to join the disciples. But they were all afraid of him, finding it impossible to believe that he was a disciple. Barnabas, however, took him by the hand and introduced him to the apostles, and explained to them how he had seen the Lord on his journey, and how the Lord had spoken to him. He further explained how Saul had spoken in Damascus with the utmost boldness in the name of Jesus. After that Saul joined with them in all their activities in Jerusalem, preaching fearlessly in the name of the Lord. He used to talk and argue with the Greek-speaking Jews, but they made several attempts on his life. When the brothers realized this they took him down to Caesarea and sent him off to Tarsus.

A time of peace   **9. 31**

The whole Church throughout Judaea, Galilee and Samaria now enjoyed a period of peace. It became established and as it went forward in reverence for the Lord and in the strengthening presence of the Holy Spirit, continued to grow in numbers.

Peter heals at Lydda   **9. 32**

Now it happened that Peter, in the course of traveling about among them all, came down to God's people living at Lydda. There he found a man called Aeneas who had been bedridden for eight years through paralysis. Peter said to him,
"Aeneas, Jesus Christ heals you! Get up and make your bed."
He got to his feet at once. And all those who lived in Lydda and Sharon saw him and turned to the Lord.

—and again at Joppa   **9. 36**

Then there was a woman in Joppa, a disciple called Tabitha, whose name in Greek was Dorcas (meaning Gazelle). She was a woman whose whole life was full of good and kindly actions, but in those days she became seriously ill and died. So when they had washed her body they laid her in an upper room. Now Lydda is quite near Joppa, and when the disciples heard that Peter was in Lydda, they sent two men to him and begged him,
"Please come to us without delay."
Peter got up and went back with them, and when he arrived in Joppa they took him to the room upstairs. All the widows stood around him with tears in their eyes, holding out for him to see the dresses and cloaks which Dorcas used to make for them while she was with them. But Peter put them all outside the room and knelt down and prayed. Then he turned to the body and said,
"Tabitha, get up!"
She opened her eyes, and as soon as she saw Peter she sat up. He took her by the hand, helped her to her feet, and then called out to the believers and widows and presented her to

When he reached Jerusalem he tried to join the body of disciples there; but they were all afraid of him, because they did not believe that he was really a convert. Barnabas, however, took him by the hand and introduced him to the apostles. He described to them how Saul had seen the Lord on his journey, and heard his voice, and how he had spoken out boldly in the name of Jesus at Damascus. Saul now stayed with them, moving about freely in Jerusalem. He spoke out boldly and openly in the name of the Lord, talking and debating with the Greek-speaking Jews.[a] But they planned to murder him, and when the brethren learned of this they escorted him to Caesarea and saw him off to Tarsus.

Meanwhile the church, throughout Judaea, Galilee, and Samaria, was left in peace to build up its strength. In the fear of the Lord, upheld by the Holy Spirit, it held on its way and grew in numbers.

Peter was making a general tour, in the course of which he went down to visit God's people at Lydda. There he found a man named Aeneas who had been bed-ridden with paralysis for eight years. Peter said to him, 'Aeneas, Jesus Christ cures you; get up and make your bed', and immediately he stood up. All who lived in Lydda and Sharon saw him; and they turned to the Lord.

In Joppa there was a disciple named Tabitha (in Greek, Dorcas, meaning a gazelle), who filled her days with acts of kindness and charity. At that time she fell ill and died; and they washed her body and laid it in a room upstairs. As Lydda was near Joppa, the disciples, who had heard that Peter was there, sent two men to him with the urgent request, 'Please come over to us without delay.' Peter thereupon went off with them. When he arrived they took him upstairs to the room, where all the widows came and stood round him in tears, showing him the shirts and coats that Dorcas used to make while she was with them. Peter sent them all outside, and knelt down and prayed. Then, turning towards the body, he said, 'Tabitha, arise.' She opened her eyes, saw Peter, and sat up. He gave her his hand and helped her to her feet. Then he called the members of the congregation and the widows

[a] *Literally* the Hellenists.

375

K.J.V.

her alive. 42And it was known throughout all Joppa; and many believed in the Lord. 43And it came to pass, that he tarried many days in Joppa with one Simon a tanner.

10 There was a certain man in Cesarea called Cornelius, a centurion of the band called the Italian *band,* 2A devout *man,* and one that feared God with all his house, which gave much alms to the people, and prayed to God always. 3 He saw in a vision evidently, about the ninth hour of the day, an angel of God coming in to him, and saying unto him, Cornelius. 4And when he looked on him, he was afraid, and said, What is it, Lord? And he said unto him, Thy prayers and thine alms are come up for a memorial before God. 5And now send men to Joppa, and call for *one* Simon, whose surname is Peter: 6 He lodgeth with one Simon a tanner, whose house is by the sea side: he shall tell thee what thou oughtest to do. 7And when the angel which spake unto Cornelius was departed, he called two of his household servants, and a devout soldier of them that waited on him continually; 8And when he had declared all *these* things unto them, he sent them to Joppa.

9 On the morrow, as they went on their journey, and drew nigh unto the city, Peter went up upon the housetop to pray about the sixth hour: 10And he became very hungry, and would have eaten: but while they made ready, he fell into a trance, 11And saw heaven opened, and a certain vessel descending unto him, as it had been a great sheet knit at the four corners, and let down to the earth: 12 Wherein were all manner of fourfooted beasts of the earth, and wild beasts, and creeping things, and fowls of the air. 13And there came a voice to him, Rise, Peter; kill, and eat. 14 But Peter said, Not so, Lord; for I have never eaten any thing that is common or unclean. 15And the voice *spake* unto him again the second time, What God hath cleansed, *that* call not thou common. 16 This was done thrice: and the vessel was received up again into heaven. 17 Now while Peter doubted in himself what this vision which he had seen should mean, behold, the men which were sent from Cornelius had made inquiry for Simon's house, and stood before the gate, 18And called, and asked whether Simon, which was surnamed Peter, were lodged there.

19 While Peter thought on the vision, the Spirit said unto him, Behold, three men seek thee. 20Arise therefore, and get thee down, and go with them, doubting nothing: for I have sent

R.S.V.

saints and widows he presented her alive. 42And it became known throughout all Joppa, and many believed in the Lord. 43And he stayed in Joppa for many days with one Simon, a tanner.

10 At Caesarea there was a man named Cornelius, a centurion of what was known as the Italian Cohort, 2 a devout man who feared God with all his household, gave alms liberally to the people, and prayed constantly to God. 3About the ninth hour of the day he saw clearly in a vision an angel of God coming in and saying to him, "Cornelius." 4And he stared at him in terror, and said, "What is it, Lord?" And he said to him, "Your prayers and your alms have ascended as a memorial before God. 5And now send men to Joppa, and bring one Simon who is called Peter; 6 he is lodging with Simon, a tanner, whose house is by the seaside." 7 When the angel who spoke to him had departed, he called two of his servants and a devout soldier from among those that waited on him, 8 and having related everything to them, he sent them to Joppa.

9 The next day, as they were on their journey and coming near the city, Peter went up on the housetop to pray, about the sixth hour. 10And he became hungry and desired something to eat; but while they were preparing it, he fell into a trance 11 and saw the heaven opened, and something descending, like a great sheet, let down by four corners upon the earth. 12 In it were all kinds of animals and reptiles and birds of the air. 13And there came a voice to him, "Rise, Peter; kill and eat." 14 But Peter said, "No, Lord; for I have never eaten anything that is common or unclean." 15And the voice came to him again a second time, "What God has cleansed, you must not call common." 16 This happened three times, and the thing was taken up at once to heaven.

17 Now while Peter was inwardly perplexed as to what the vision which he had seen might mean, behold, the men that were sent by Cornelius, having made inquiry for Simon's house, stood before the gate 18 and called out to ask whether Simon who was called Peter was lodging there. 19And while Peter was pondering the vision, the Spirit said to him, "Behold, three men are looking for you. 20 Rise and go down, and accompany them without hesitation; for I

them alive. This became known throughout the whole of Joppa and many believed in the Lord. Peter himself remained there for some time, staying with a tanner called Simon.

God speaks to a good-living   **10. 1**
gentile

There was a man in Caesarea by the name of Cornelius, a centurion in what was called the Italian regiment. He was a deeply religious man who reverenced God, as did all his household. He made many charitable gifts to the people and was a real man of prayer. About three o'clock one afternoon he saw perfectly clearly in a dream an angel of God coming into his room, approaching him, and saying,
"Cornelius!"
He stared at the angel in terror, and said,
"What is it, Lord?"
The angel replied,
"Your prayers and your deeds of charity have gone up to Heaven and are remembered before God. Now send men to Joppa for a man called Simon, who is also known as Peter. He is staying as a guest with another Simon, a tanner, whose house is down by the sea."
When the angel who had spoken to him had gone, Cornelius called out for two of his house servants and a devout soldier, who was one of his personal attendants. He told them the whole story and then sent them off to Joppa.

Peter's startling vision   **10. 9**

Next day, while these men were still on their journey and approaching the city, Peter went up about midday on to the flat roof of the house to pray. He became very hungry and longed for something to eat. But while the meal was being prepared he fell into a trance and saw the heavens open and something like a great sheet descending upon the earth, let down by its four corners. In it were all kinds of animals, reptiles and birds. Then came a voice which said to him,
"Get up, Peter, kill and eat!"
But Peter said,
"Never, Lord! For not once in all my life have I ever eaten anything common or unclean."
Then the voice spoke to him a second time,
"You must not call what God has cleansed common."
This happened three times, and then the thing was gone, taken back into heaven.

The meaning of the vision   **10. 17**
becomes apparent

While Peter was still puzzling about the meaning of the vision which he had just seen, the men sent by Cornelius had arrived asking for the house of Simon. They were in fact standing at the very doorway of the house calling out to inquire if Simon, surnamed Peter, were lodging there. Peter was still thinking deeply about the vision when the Spirit said to him,
"Three men are here looking for you. Get up and go downstairs. Go with them without any misgiving, for I myself have sent them."

and showed her to them alive. The news spread all over Joppa, and many came to believe in the Lord. Peter stayed on in Joppa for some time with one Simon, a tanner.

10 At Caesarea there was a man named Cornelius, a centurion in the Italian Cohort, as it was called. He was a religious man, and he and his whole family joined in the worship of God. He gave generously to help the Jewish people, and was regular in his prayers to God. One day about three in the afternoon he had a vision in which he clearly saw an angel of God, who came into his room and said, 'Cornelius!' He stared at him in terror. 'What is it, my lord?' he asked. The angel said, 'Your prayers and acts of charity have gone up to heaven to speak for you before God. And now send to Joppa for a man named Simon, also called Peter: he is lodging with another Simon, a tanner, whose house is by the sea.' So when the angel who was speaking to him had gone, he summoned two of his servants and a military orderly who was a religious man, told them the whole story, and sent them to Joppa.

Next day, while they were still on their way and approaching the city, about noon Peter went up on the roof to pray. He grew hungry and wanted something to eat. While they were getting it ready, he fell into a trance. He saw a rift in the sky, and a thing coming down that looked like a great sheet of sail-cloth. It was slung by the four corners, and was being lowered to the ground. In it he saw creatures of every kind, whatever walks or crawls or flies. Then there was a voice which said to him, 'Up, Peter, kill and eat.' But Peter said, 'No, Lord, no: I have never eaten anything profane or unclean.' The voice came again a second time: 'It is not for you to call profane what God counts clean.' This happened three times; and then the thing was taken up again into the sky.

While Peter was still puzzling over the meaning of the vision he had seen, the messengers of Cornelius had been asking the way to Simon's house, and now arrived at the entrance. They called out and asked if Simon Peter was lodging there. But Peter was thinking over the vision, when the Spirit said to him, 'Some[a] men are here looking for you; make haste and go downstairs. You may go with them without any mis-

[a] *One witness reads* Two; *others read* Three.

K.J.V.

them. 21 Then Peter went down to the men which were sent unto him from Cornelius; and said, Behold, I am he whom ye seek: what *is* the cause wherefore ye are come? 22And they said, Cornelius the centurion, a just man, and one that feareth God, and of good report among all the nation of the Jews, was warned from God by a holy angel to send for thee into his house, and to hear words of thee. 23 Then called he them in, and lodged *them*. And on the morrow Peter went away with them, and certain brethren from Joppa accompanied him. 24And the morrow after they entered into Cesarea. And Cornelius waited for them, and had called together his kinsmen and near friends. 25And as Peter was coming in, Cornelius met him, and fell down at his feet, and worshipped *him*. 26 But Peter took him up, saying, Stand up; I myself also am a man. 27And as he talked with him, he went in, and found many that were come together. 28And he said unto them, Ye know how that it is an unlawful thing for a man that is a Jew to keep company, or come unto one of another nation; but God hath shewed me that I should not call any man common or unclean. 29 Therefore came I *unto you* without gainsaying, as soon as I was sent for: I ask therefore for what intent ye have sent for me? 30And Cornelius said, Four days ago I was fasting until this hour; and at the ninth hour I prayed in my house, and, behold, a man stood before me in bright clothing, 31And said, Cornelius, thy prayer is heard, and thine alms are had in remembrance in the sight of God. 32 Send therefore to Joppa, and call hither Simon, whose surname is Peter; he is lodged in the house of *one* Simon a tanner by the sea side: who, when he cometh, shall speak unto thee. 33 Immediately therefore I sent to thee; and thou hast well done that thou art come. Now therefore are we all here present before God, to hear all things that are commanded thee of God.

34 Then Peter opened *his* mouth, and said, Of a truth I perceive that God is no respecter of persons: 35 But in every nation he that feareth him, and worketh righteousness, is accepted with him. 36 The word which *God* sent unto the children of Israel, preaching peace by Jesus Christ: (he is Lord of all:) 37 That word, *I say,* ye know, which was published throughout all Judea, and began from Galilee, after the baptism which John preached; 38 How God anointed Jesus of Nazareth with the Holy Ghost and with power: who went about doing good, and healing all that were oppressed of the devil; for God was with him. 39And we are witnesses of all things which he did both in the land of the Jews,

R.S.V.

have sent them." 21And Peter went down to the men and said, "I am the one you are looking for; what is the reason for your coming?" 22And they said, "Cornelius, a centurion, an upright and God-fearing man, who is well spoken of by the whole Jewish nation, was directed by a holy angel to send for you to come to his house, and to hear what you have to say." 23 So he called them in to be his guests.

The next day he rose and went off with them, and some of the brethren from Joppa accompanied him. 24And on the following day they entered Caesarea. Cornelius was expecting them and had called together his kinsmen and close friends. 25 When Peter entered, Cornelius met him and fell down at his feet and worshiped him. 26 But Peter lifted him up, saying, "Stand up; I too am a man." 27And as he talked with him, he went in and found many persons gathered; 28 and he said to them, "You yourselves know how unlawful it is for a Jew to associate with or to visit any one of another nation; but God has shown me that I should not call any man common or unclean. 29 So when I was sent for, I came without objection. I ask then why you sent for me."

30 And Cornelius said, "Four days ago, about this hour, I was keeping the ninth hour of prayer in my house; and behold, a man stood before me in bright apparel, 31 saying, 'Cornelius, your prayer has been heard and your alms have been remembered before God. 32 Send therefore to Joppa and ask for Simon who is called Peter; he is lodging in the house of Simon, a tanner, by the seaside.' 33 So I sent to you at once, and you have been kind enough to come. Now therefore we are all here present in the sight of God, to hear all that you have been commanded by the Lord."

34 And Peter opened his mouth and said: "Truly I perceive that God shows no partiality, 35 but in every nation any one who fears him and does what is right is acceptable to him. 36 You know the word which he sent to Israel, preaching good news of peace by Jesus Christ (he is Lord of all), 37 the word which was proclaimed throughout all Judea, beginning from Galilee after the baptism which John preached: 38 how God anointed Jesus of Nazareth with the Holy Spirit and with power; how he went about doing good and healing all that were oppressed by the devil, for God was with him. 39And we are witnesses to all that he did both in the country of the Jews and in Jerusalem.

PHILLIPS

So Peter went down to the men and said,
"I am the man you are looking for; what
brings you here?"

They replied,

"Cornelius the centurion, a good-living and
God-fearing man, whose character can be
vouched for by the whole Jewish people, was
commanded by a holy angel to send for you to
come to his house, and to listen to your message."

Then Peter invited them in and entertained
them.

Peter, obeying the Spirit,   *10. 23b*
disobeys Jewish Law

On the next day he got up and set out with
them, accompanied by some of the brothers
from Joppa, arriving at Caesarea on the day
after that. Cornelius was expecting them and had
invited together all his relations and intimate
friends. As Peter entered the house Cornelius
met him by falling on his knees before him and
worshiping him. But Peter roused him with the
words,

"Stand up, I am a human being too!"

Then Peter went right into the house in deep
conversation with Cornelius and found that a
large number of people had assembled. Then he
spoke to them,

"You all know that it is forbidden for a man
who is a Jew to associate with, or even visit, a
man of another nation. But God has shown me
plainly that no man must be called 'common' or
'unclean.' That is why I came here when I was
sent for without raising any objection. Now I
want to know what made you send for me."

Then Cornelius replied,

"Three days ago, about this time, I was observing the afternoon hour of prayer in my
house, when suddenly a man in shining clothes
stood before me and said, 'Cornelius, your
prayer has been heard and your charitable gifts
have been remembered before God. Now you
must send to Joppa and invite here a man called
Simon whose surname is Peter. He is staying in
the house of a tanner by the name of Simon,
down by the sea.' So I sent to you without delay
and you have been most kind in coming. Now
we are all here in the presence of God to listen
to everything that the Lord has commanded you
to say."

Peter's momentous discovery   *10. 34*

Then Peter began to speak,

"In solemn truth I can see now that God is no
respecter of persons, but that in every nation
the man who reverences him and does what is
right is acceptable to him! He has sent his message to the sons of Israel by giving us the good
news of peace through Jesus Christ—he is the
Lord of us all. You must know the story of
Jesus of Nazareth—why, it has spread through
the whole of Judaea, beginning from Galilee
after the baptism that John proclaimed. You
must have heard how God anointed him with
the power of the Holy Spirit, of how he went
about doing good and healing all who suffered
from the devil's power—because God was with
him. Now we are eyewitnesses of everything that
he did, both in the Judaean country and in

N.E.B.

giving, for it was I who sent them.' Peter came
down to the men and said, 'You are looking for
me? Here I am. What brings you here?' 'We are
from the centurion Cornelius,' they replied, 'a
good and religious man, acknowledged as such
by the whole Jewish nation. He was directed by a
holy angel to send for you to his house and to
listen to what you have to say.' So Peter asked
them in and gave them a night's lodging. Next
day he set out with them, accompanied by some
members of the congregation at Joppa.

The day after that, he arrived at Caesarea.
Cornelius was expecting them and had called together his relatives and close friends. When
Peter arrived, Cornelius came to meet him, and
bowed to the ground in deep reverence. But Peter
raised him to his feet and said, 'Stand up; I am
a man like anyone else.' Still talking with him
he went in and found a large gathering. He said
to them, 'I need not tell you that a Jew is forbidden by his religion to visit or associate with
a man of another race; yet God has shown me
clearly that I must not call any man profane or
unclean. That is why I came here without demur
when you sent for me. May I ask what was your
reason for sending?'

Cornelius said, 'Four days ago, just about this
time, I was in the house here saying the afternoon prayers, when suddenly a man in shining
robes stood before me. He said: "Cornelius,
your prayer has been heard and your acts of
charity remembered before God. Send to Joppa,
then, to Simon Peter, and ask him to come. He
is lodging in the house of Simon the tanner, by
the sea." So I sent to you there and then; it was
kind of you to come. And now we are all met
here before God, to hear all that the Lord has
ordered you to say.'

Peter began: 'I now see how true it is that
God has no favourites, but that in every nation
the man who is godfearing and does what is
right is acceptable to him. He sent his word to
the Israelites and gave the good news of peace
through Jesus Christ, who is Lord of all. I need
not tell you what happened lately all over the
land of the Jews, starting from Galilee after the
baptism proclaimed by John. You know about
Jesus of Nazareth, how God anointed him with
the Holy Spirit and with power. He went about
doing good and healing all who were oppressed
by the devil, for God was with him. And we can
bear witness to all that he did in the Jewish

K.J.V.

and in Jerusalem; whom they slew and hanged on a tree: 40 Him God raised up the third day, and shewed him openly; 41 Not to all the people, but unto witnesses chosen before of God, *even* to us, who did eat and drink with him after he rose from the dead. 42And he commanded us to preach unto the people, and to testify that it is he which was ordained of God *to be* the Judge of quick and dead. 43 To him give all the prophets witness, that through his name whosoever believeth in him shall receive remission of sins.

44 While Peter yet spake these words, the Holy Ghost fell on all them which heard the word. 45And they of the circumcision which believed were astonished, as many as came with Peter, because that on the Gentiles also was poured out the gift of the Holy Ghost. 46 For they heard them speak with tongues, and magnify God. Then answered Peter, 47 Can any man forbid water, that these should not be baptized, which have received the Holy Ghost as well as we? 48And he commanded them to be baptized in the name of the Lord. Then prayed they him to tarry certain days.

R.S.V.

They put him to death by hanging him on a tree; 40 but God raised him on the third day and made him manifest; 41 not to all the people but to us who were chosen by God as witnesses, who ate and drank with him after he rose from the dead. 42And he commanded us to preach to the people, and to testify that he is the one ordained by God to be judge of the living and the dead. 43 To him all the prophets bear witness that every one who believes in him receives forgiveness of sins through his name."

44 While Peter was still saying this, the Holy Spirit fell on all who heard the word. 45And the believers from among the circumcised who came with Peter were amazed, because the gift of the Holy Spirit had been poured out even on the Gentiles. 46 For they heard them speaking in tongues and extolling God. Then Peter declared, 47 "Can any one forbid water for baptizing these people who have received the Holy Spirit just as we have?" 48And he commanded them to be baptized in the name of Jesus Christ. Then they asked him to remain for some days.

11 And the apostles and brethren that were in Judea heard that the Gentiles had also received the word of God. 2And when Peter was come up to Jerusalem, they that were of the circumcision contended with him, 3 Saying, Thou wentest in to men uncircumcised, and didst eat with them. 4 But Peter rehearsed *the matter* from the beginning, and expounded *it* by order unto them, saying, 5 I was in the city of Joppa praying: and in a trance I saw a vision, A certain vessel descend, as it had been a great sheet, let down from heaven by four corners; and it came even to me: 6 Upon the which when I had fastened mine eyes, I considered, and saw fourfooted beasts of the earth, and wild beasts, and creeping things, and fowls of the air. 7And I heard a voice saying unto me, Arise, Peter; slay and eat. 8 But I said, Not so, Lord: for nothing common or unclean hath at any time entered into my mouth. 9 But the voice answered me again from heaven, What God hath cleansed, *that* call not thou common. 10And this was done three times: and all were drawn up again into heaven. 11And, behold, immediately there were three men already come unto the house where I was, sent from Cesarea unto me. 12And the Spirit bade me go with them, nothing doubting. Moreover these six brethren accompanied me, and we entered into the man's house: 13And he shewed us how he had seen an angel in his house, which stood and said unto him, Send men to Joppa, and call for Simon, whose surname is

11 Now the apostles and the brethren who were in Judea heard that the Gentiles also had received the word of God. 2 So when Peter went up to Jerusalem, the circumcision party criticized him, 3 saying, "Why did you go to uncircumcised men and eat with them?" 4 But Peter began and explained to them in order: 5 "I was in the city of Joppa praying; and in a trance I saw a vision, something descending, like a great sheet, let down from heaven by four corners; and it came down to me. 6 Looking at it closely I observed animals and beasts of prey and reptiles and birds of the air. 7And I heard a voice saying to me, 'Rise, Peter; kill and eat.' 8 But I said, 'No, Lord; for nothing common or unclean has ever entered my mouth.' 9 But the voice answered a second time from heaven, 'What God has cleansed you must not call common.' 10 This happened three times, and all was drawn up again into heaven. 11At that very moment three men arrived at the house in which we were, sent to me from Caesarea. 12And the Spirit told me to go with them, making no distinction. These six brethren also accompanied me, and we entered the man's house. 13And he told us how he had seen the angel standing in his house and saying, 'Send to Joppa and

PHILLIPS

Jerusalem itself, and yet they murdered him by hanging him on a cross. But on the third day God raised that same Jesus and let him be clearly seen, not indeed by the whole people, but by witnesses whom God had previously chosen. We are those witnesses, we who ate and drank with him after he had risen from the dead! Moreover, we are the men whom he commanded to preach to the people and bear fearless witness to the fact that he is the one appointed by God to be the judge of both the living and the dead. It is to him that all the prophets bear witness, that every man who believes in him may receive forgiveness of sins through his name."

The Holy Spirit confirms   10. 44
Peter's action

While Peter was still speaking these words the Holy Spirit fell upon all who were listening to his message. The Jewish believers who had come with Peter were absolutely amazed that the gift of the Holy Spirit was being poured out on gentiles also; for they heard them speaking in foreign tongues and glorifying God.

Then Peter exclaimed,

"Could anyone refuse water or object to these men being baptized—men who have received the Holy Spirit just as we did ourselves?"

And he gave orders for them to be baptized in the name of Jesus Christ. Afterwards they asked him to stay with them for some days.

The Church's disquiet   11. 1
at Peter's action

Now the apostles and the brothers who were in Judaea heard that the gentiles also had received God's message. So when Peter next visited Jerusalem the circumcision party were full of criticism, saying to him, "You actually went in and shared a meal with uncircumcised men!"

Peter's explanation   11. 4

But Peter began to explain how the situation had actually arisen.

"I was in the city of Joppa praying," he said, "and while completely unconscious of my surroundings I saw a vision—something like a great sheet coming down toward me, let down from heaven by its four corners. It came right down to me and when I looked at it closely I saw animals and wild beasts, reptiles and birds. Then I heard a voice say to me, 'Get up, Peter, kill and eat.' But I said, 'Never, Lord, for nothing common or unclean has ever passed my lips.' But the voice from Heaven spoke a second time and said, 'You must not call what God has cleansed common!' This happened three times, and then the whole thing was drawn up again into heaven. The extraordinary thing is that at that very moment three men arrived at the house where we were staying, sent to me personally from Caesarea. The Spirit told me to go with these men without any misgiving. And these six of our brothers accompanied me and we went into the man's house. He told us how he had seen the angel standing in his house, saying, 'Send to Joppa and bring Simon, surnamed

N.E.B.

country-side and in Jerusalem. He was put to death by hanging on a gibbet; but God raised him to life on the third day, and allowed him to appear, not to the whole people, but to witnesses whom God had chosen in advance—to us, who ate and drank with him after he rose from the dead. He commanded us to proclaim him to the people, and affirm that he is the one who has been designated by God as judge of the living and the dead. It is to him that all the prophets testify, declaring that everyone who trusts in him receives forgiveness of sins through his name.'

Peter was still speaking when the Holy Spirit came upon all who were listening to the message. The believers who had come with Peter, men of Jewish birth, were astonished that the gift of the Holy Spirit should have been poured out even on Gentiles. For they could hear them speaking in tongues of ecstasy and acclaiming the greatness of God. Then Peter spoke: 'Is anyone prepared to withhold the water for baptism from these persons, who have received the Holy Spirit just as we did ourselves?' Then he ordered them to be baptized in the name of Jesus Christ. After that they asked him to stay on with them for a time.

11 News came to the apostles and the members of the church in Judaea that Gentiles too had accepted the word of God; and when Peter came up to Jerusalem those who were of Jewish birth raised the question with him. 'You have been visiting men who are uncircumcised,' they said, 'and sitting at table with them!' Peter began by laying before them the facts as they had happened.

'I was in the city of Joppa', he said, 'at prayer; and while in a trance I had a vision: a thing was coming down that looked like a great sheet of sail-cloth, slung by the four corners and lowered from the sky till it reached me. I looked intently to make out what was in it and I saw four-footed creatures of the earth, wild beasts, and things that crawl or fly. Then I heard a voice saying to me, "Up, Peter, kill and eat." But I said, "No, Lord, no: nothing profane or unclean has ever entered my mouth." A voice from heaven answered a second time, "It is not for you to call profane what God counts clean." This happened three times, and then they were all drawn up again into the sky. At that moment three men, who had been sent to me from Caesarea, arrived at the house where I was[a] staying; and the Spirit told me to go with them.[b] My six companions here came with me and we went into the man's house. He told us how he had seen an angel standing in his house who said, "Send to

[a] *Some witnesses read* we were. [b] *Some witnesses add* making no distinctions; *others add* without any misgiving, *as in 10. 20.*

381

K.J.V.

Peter; 14 Who shall tell thee words, whereby thou and all thy house shall be saved. 15And as I began to speak, the Holy Ghost fell on them, as on us at the beginning. 16 Then remembered I the word of the Lord, how that he said, John indeed baptized with water; but ye shall be baptized with the Holy Ghost. 17 Forasmuch then as God gave them the like gift as *he did* unto us, who believed on the Lord Jesus Christ, what was I, that I could withstand God? 18 When they heard these things, they held their peace, and glorified God, saying, Then hath God also to the Gentiles granted repentance unto life.

19 Now they which were scattered abroad upon the persecution that arose about Stephen travelled as far as Phenice, and Cyprus, and Antioch, preaching the word to none but unto the Jews only. 20And some of them were men of Cyprus and Cyrene, which, when they were come to Antioch, spake unto the Grecians, preaching the Lord Jesus. 21And the hand of the Lord was with them: and a great number believed, and turned unto the Lord.

22 Then tidings of these things came unto the ears of the church which was in Jerusalem: and they sent forth Barnabas, that he should go as far as Antioch. 23 Who, when he came, and had seen the grace of God, was glad, and exhorted them all, that with purpose of heart they would cleave unto the Lord. 24 For he was a good man, and full of the Holy Ghost and of faith: and much people was added unto the Lord. 25 Then departed Barnabas to Tarsus, for to seek Saul: 26And when he had found him, he brought him unto Antioch. And it came to pass, that a whole year they assembled themselves with the church, and taught much people. And the disciples were called Christians first in Antioch.

27 And in these days came prophets from Jerusalem unto Antioch. 28And there stood up one of them named Agabus, and signified by the Spirit that there should be great dearth throughout all the world: which came to pass in the days of Claudius Cesar. 29 Then the disciples, every man according to his ability, determined to send relief unto the brethren which dwelt in Judea: 30 Which also they did, and sent it to the elders by the hands of Barnabas and Saul.

R.S.V.

bring Simon called Peter; 14 he will declare to you a message by which you will be saved, you and all your household.' 15As I began to speak, the Holy Spirit fell on them just as on us at the beginning. 16And I remembered the word of the Lord, how he said, 'John baptized with water, but you shall be baptized with the Holy Spirit.' 17 If then God gave the same gift to them as he gave to us when we believed in the Lord Jesus Christ, who was I that I could withstand God?" 18 When they heard this they were silenced. And they glorified God, saying, "Then to the Gentiles also God has granted repentance unto life."

19 Now those who were scattered because of the persecution that arose over Stephen traveled as far as Phoenicia and Cyprus and Antioch, speaking the word to none except Jews. 20 But there were some of them, men of Cyprus and Cyrene, who on coming to Antioch spoke to the Greeks[i] also, preaching the Lord Jesus. 21And the hand of the Lord was with them, and a great number that believed turned to the Lord. 22 News of this came to the ears of the church in Jerusalem, and they sent Barnabas to Antioch. 23 When he came and saw the grace of God, he was glad; and he exhorted them all to remain faithful to the Lord with steadfast purpose; 24 for he was a good man, full of the Holy Spirit and of faith. And a large company was added to the Lord. 25 So Barnabas went to Tarsus to look for Saul; 26 and when he had found him, he brought him to Antioch. For a whole year they met with[j] the church, and taught a large company of people; and in Antioch the disciples were for the first time called Christians.

27 Now in these days prophets came down from Jerusalem to Antioch. 28And one of them named Agabus stood up and foretold by the spirit that there would be a great famine over all the world; and this took place in the days of Claudius. 29And the disciples determined, every one according to his ability, to send relief to the brethren who lived in Judea; 30 and they did so, sending it to the elders by the hand of Barnabas and Saul.

[i] Other ancient authorities read *Hellenists.* [j] Or *were guests of.*

PHILLIPS

Peter. He will give you a message which will save both you and your whole household.' While I was beginning to tell them this message the Holy Spirit fell upon them just as on us at the beginning. There came into my mind the words of our Lord when he said, 'John indeed baptized with water, but you will be baptized with the Holy Spirit.' If then God gave them exactly the same gift as he gave to us when we believed on the Lord Jesus Christ, who was I to think that I could hinder the working of God?"

The flexibility of the young Church   11. 18

When they heard this they had no further objection to raise. And they praised God, saying,
"Then obviously God has given to the gentiles as well the gift of repentance which leads to life."

Persecution has spread the gospel   11. 19

Now those who had been dispersed by the persecution which arose over Stephen traveled as far as Phoenicia, Cyprus and Antioch, giving the message as they went to Jews only. However, among their number were natives of Cyprus and Cyrene, and these men, on their arrival at Antioch, proclaimed their message to the Greeks as well, telling them the good news of the Lord Jesus. The hand of the Lord was with them, and a great number believed and turned to the Lord. News of these things came to the ears of the church in Jerusalem and they sent Barnabas to Antioch. When he arrived and saw this working of God's grace, he was delighted. He urged them all to be resolute in their faithfulness to the Lord, for he was a good man, full of the Holy Spirit and of faith. So it happened that a considerable number of people became followers of the Lord.

Believers are called "Christians" for the first time   11. 25

Then Barnabas went to Tarsus to find Saul. When he found him he brought him up to Antioch. Then for a whole year they met together with the church and taught a large crowd. It was in Antioch that the disciples were first given the name of "Christians."

The young Church and famine relief   11. 27

During this period some prophets came down from Jerusalem to Antioch. One of them by the name of Agabus stood up and foretold by the Spirit that there was to be a great famine throughout the world. (This actually happened in the days of Claudius.) The disciples determined to send relief to the brothers in Judaea, each contributing as he was able. This they did, sending their contribution to the elders there personally through Barnabas and Saul.

N.E.B.

Joppa for Simon also called Peter. He will speak words that will bring salvation to you and all your household." Hardly had I begun speaking, when the Holy Spirit came upon them, just as upon us at the beginning. Then I recalled what the Lord had said: "John baptized with water, but you will be baptized with the Holy Spirit." God gave them no less a gift than he gave us when we put our trust in the Lord Jesus Christ; then how could I possibly stand in God's way?'

When they heard this their doubts were silenced. They gave praise to God and said, 'This means that God has granted life-giving repentance to the Gentiles also.'

Meanwhile those who had been scattered after the persecution that arose over Stephen made their way to Phoenicia, Cyprus, and Antioch, bringing the message to Jews only and to no others. But there were some natives of Cyprus and Cyrene among them, and these, when they arrived at Antioch, began to speak to pagans as well, telling them the good news of the Lord Jesus. The power of the Lord was with them, and a great many became believers, and turned to the Lord.

The news reached the ears of the church in Jerusalem; and they sent Barnabas to Antioch. When he arrived and saw the divine grace at work, he rejoiced, and encouraged them all to hold fast to the Lord with resolute hearts; for he was a good man, full of the Holy Spirit and of faith. And large numbers were won over to the Lord.

He then went off to Tarsus to look for Saul; and when he had found him, he brought him to Antioch. For a whole year the two of them lived in fellowship with the congregation there, and gave instruction to large numbers. It was in Antioch that the disciples first got the name of Christians.

During this period some prophets came down from Jerusalem to Antioch. One of them, Agabus by name, was inspired to stand up and predict a severe and world-wide famine, which in fact occurred in the reign of Claudius. So the disciples agreed to make a contribution, each according to his means, for the relief of their fellow-Christians in Judaea. This they did, and sent it off in the charge of Barnabas and Saul to the elders.

12 Now about that time Herod the king stretched forth *his* hands to vex certain of the church. 2And he killed James the brother of John with the sword. 3And because he saw it pleased the Jews, he proceeded further to take Peter also. (Then were the days of unleavened bread.) 4And when he had apprehended him, he put *him* in prison, and delivered *him* to four quaternions of soldiers to keep him; intending after Easter to bring him forth to the people. 5 Peter therefore was kept in prison: but prayer was made without ceasing of the church unto God for him. 6And when Herod would have brought him forth, the same night Peter was sleeping between two soldiers, bound with two chains: and the keepers before the door kept the prison. 7And, behold, the angel of the Lord came upon *him*, and a light shined in the prison: and he smote Peter on the side, and raised him up, saying, Arise up quickly. And his chains fell off from *his* hands. 8And the angel said unto him, Gird thyself, and bind on thy sandals: and so he did. And he saith unto him, Cast thy garment about thee, and follow me. 9And he went out, and followed him; and wist not that it was true which was done by the angel; but thought he saw a vision. 10 When they were past the first and the second ward, they came unto the iron gate that leadeth unto the city; which opened to them of his own accord: and they went out, and passed on through one street; and forthwith the angel departed from him. 11And when Peter was come to himself, he said, Now I know of a surety, that the Lord hath sent his angel, and hath delivered me out of the hand of Herod, and *from* all the expectation of the people of the Jews. 12And when he had considered *the thing*, he came to the house of Mary the mother of John, whose surname was Mark; where many were gathered together praying. 13And as Peter knocked at the door of the gate, a damsel came to hearken, named Rhoda. 14And when she knew Peter's voice, she opened not the gate for gladness, but ran in, and told how Peter stood before the gate. 15And they said unto her, Thou art mad. But she constantly affirmed that it was even so. Then said they, It is his angel. 16 But Peter continued knocking: and when they had opened *the door*, and saw him, they were astonished. 17 But he, beckoning unto them with the hand to hold their peace, declared unto them how the Lord had brought him out of the prison. And he said, Go shew these things unto James, and to the brethren. And he departed, and went into another place. 18 Now as soon as it was day, there was no small stir among the soldiers, what was become of Peter. 19And when Herod had sought for him, and found him not, he examined the keepers, and commanded that *they*

12 About that time Herod the king laid violent hands upon some who belonged to the church. 2 He killed James the brother of John with the sword; 3 and when he saw that it pleased the Jews, he proceeded to arrest Peter also. This was during the days of Unleavened Bread. 4And when he had seized him, he put him in prison, and delivered him to four squads of soldiers to guard him, intending after the Passover to bring him out to the people. 5 So Peter was kept in prison; but earnest prayer for him was made to God by the church. 6 The very night when Herod was about to bring him out, Peter was sleeping between two soldiers, bound with two chains, and sentries before the door were guarding the prison; 7 and behold, an angel of the Lord appeared, and a light shone in the cell; and he struck Peter on the side and woke him, saying, "Get up quickly." And the chains fell off his hands. 8And the angel said to him, "Dress yourself and put on your sandals." And he did so. And he said to him, "Wrap your mantle around you and follow me." 9And he went out and followed him; he did not know that what was done by the angel was real, but thought he was seeing a vision. 10 When they had passed the first and second guard, they came to the iron gate leading into the city. It opened to them of its own accord, and they went out and passed on through one street; and immediately the angel left him. 11And Peter came to himself, and said, "Now I am sure that the Lord has sent his angel and rescued me from the hand of Herod and from all that the Jewish people were expecting." 12 When he realized this, he went to the house of Mary, the mother of John whose other name was Mark, where many were gathered together and were praying. 13And when he knocked at the door of the gateway, a maid named Rhoda came to answer. 14 Recognizing Peter's voice, in her joy she did not open the gate but ran in and told that Peter was standing at the gate. 15 They said to her, "You are mad." But she insisted that it was so. They said, "It is his angel!" 16 But Peter continued knocking; and when they opened, they saw him and were amazed. 17 But motioning to them with his hand to be silent, he described to them how the Lord had brought him out of the prison. And he said, "Tell this to James and to the brethren." Then he departed and went to another place. 18 Now when day came, there was no small stir among the soldiers over what had become of Peter. 19And when Herod had sought for him and could not find him, he examined the sentries and ordered that they should be put to

Herod kills James and imprisons Peter 12. 1

It was at this time that King Herod laid violent hands on some of the church members. James, John's brother, he executed with the sword, and when he found this action pleased the Jews he went on to arrest Peter as well. It was during the days of unleavened bread that he actually made the arrest. He put Peter in prison with no less than four platoons of soldiers to guard him, intending to bring him out to the people after the Passover. So Peter was closely guarded in the prison, while the church prayed to God earnestly on his behalf.

Peter's miraculous rescue 12. 6

On the very night that Herod was planning to bring him out, Peter was asleep between two soldiers, chained with double chains, while guards maintained a strict watch in the doorway of the prison. Suddenly an angel of the Lord appeared, and light shone in the cell. He tapped Peter on the side and woke him up, saying, "Get up quickly." His chains fell away from his hands and the angel said to him, "Fasten your belt and put on your sandals." And he did so. Then the angel continued, "Wrap your cloak round you and follow me." So Peter followed him out, not knowing whether what the angel was doing were real—indeed he felt he must be taking part in a vision. So they passed right through the first and second guard-points and came to the iron gate that led out into the city. This opened for them of its own accord, and they went out and had passed along one street when the angel suddenly vanished from Peter's sight. Then Peter came to himself and said aloud, "Now I know for certain that the Lord has sent his angel to rescue me from the power of Herod and from all that the Jewish people are expecting." As the truth broke upon him he went to the house of Mary, the mother of John surnamed Mark, where many were gathered together in prayer. As he knocked upon the door a young maid called Rhoda came to answer it, but on recognizing Peter's voice failed to open the door from sheer joy. Instead she ran inside and reported that Peter was standing on the doorstep. At this they said to her,

"You must be mad!"

But she insisted that it was true. Then they said,

"Then it is his angel."

But Peter continued to stand there knocking on the door, and when they opened it and recognized him they were simply amazed. Peter, however, made a gesture to them to stop talking while he explained to them how the Lord had brought him out of prison. Then he said,

"Go and tell James and the other brothers what has happened."

After this he left them and went on to another place.

Peter's escape infuriates Herod 12. 18

But when morning came there was a great commotion among the soldiers as to what could have happened to Peter. When Herod had had a search put out for him without success, he cross-examined the guards and then ordered

---

12 It was about this time that King Herod attacked certain members of the church. He beheaded James, the brother of John, and then, when he saw that the Jews approved, proceeded to arrest Peter also. This happened during the festival of Unleavened Bread. Having secured him, he put him in prison under a military guard, four squads of four men each, meaning to produce him in public after Passover. So Peter was kept in prison under constant watch, while the church kept praying fervently for him to God.

On the very night before Herod had planned to bring him forward, Peter was asleep between two soldiers, secured by two chains, while outside the doors sentries kept guard over the prison. All at once an angel of the Lord stood there, and the cell was ablaze with light. He tapped Peter on the shoulder and woke him. 'Quick! Get up', he said, and the chains fell away from his wrists. The angel then said to him, 'Do up your belt and put your shoes on.' He did so. 'Now wrap your cloak round you and follow me.' He followed him out, with no idea that the angel's intervention was real: he thought it was just a vision. But they passed the first guard-post, then the second, and reached the iron gate leading out into the city, which opened for them of its own accord. And so they came out and walked the length of one street; and the angel left him.

Then Peter came to himself. 'Now I know it is true,' he said; 'the Lord has sent his angel and rescued me from Herod's clutches and from all that the Jewish people were expecting.' When he realized how things stood, he made for the house of Mary, the mother of John Mark, where a large company was at prayer. He knocked at the outer door and a maid called Rhoda came to answer it. She recognized Peter's voice and was so overjoyed that instead of opening the door she ran in and announced that Peter was standing outside. 'You are crazy', they told her; but she insisted that it was so. Then they said, 'It must be his guardian angel.'

Meanwhile Peter went on knocking, and when they opened the door and saw him, they were astounded. With a movement of the hand he signed to them to keep quiet, and told them how the Lord had brought him out of prison. 'Report this to James and the members of the church', he said. Then he left the house and went off elsewhere.

When morning came, there was consternation among the soldiers: what could have become of Peter? Herod made close search, but failed to

K.J.V.

should be put to death. And he went down from Judea to Cesarea, and *there* abode.

20 And Herod was highly displeased with them of Tyre and Sidon: but they came with one accord to him, and, having made Blastus the king's chamberlain their friend, desired peace; because their country was nourished by the king's *country*. 21And upon a set day Herod, arrayed in royal apparel, sat upon his throne, and made an oration unto them. 22And the people gave a shout, *saying, It is* the voice of a god, and not of a man. 23And immediately the angel of the Lord smote him, because he gave not God the glory: and he was eaten of worms, and gave up the ghost.

24 But the word of God grew and multiplied. 25And Barnabas and Saul returned from Jerusalem, when they had fulfilled *their* ministry, and took with them John, whose surname was Mark.

R.S.V.

death. Then he went down from Judea to Caesarea, and remained there.

20 Now Herod was angry with the people of Tyre and Sidon; and they came to him in a body, and having persuaded Blastus, the king's chamberlain, they asked for peace, because their country depended on the king's country for food. 21 On an appointed day Herod put on his royal robes, took his seat upon the throne, and made an oration to them. 22And the people shouted, "The voice of a god, and not of man!" 23 Immediately an angel of the Lord smote him, because he did not give God the glory; and he was eaten by worms and died.

24 But the word of God grew and multiplied. 25 And Barnabas and Saul returned from[k] Jerusalem when they had fulfilled their mission, bringing with them John whose other name was Mark.

13 Now there were in the church that was at Antioch certain prophets and teachers; as Barnabas, and Simeon that was called Niger, and Lucius of Cyrene, and Manaen, which had been brought up with Herod the tetrarch, and Saul. 2As they ministered to the Lord, and fasted, the Holy Ghost said, Separate me Barnabas and Saul for the work whereunto I have called them. 3And when they had fasted and prayed, and laid *their* hands on them, they sent *them* away.

4 So they, being sent forth by the Holy Ghost, departed unto Seleucia; and from thence they sailed to Cyprus. 5And when they were at Salamis, they preached the word of God in the synagogues of the Jews: and they had also John to *their* minister. 6And when they had gone through the isle unto Paphos, they found a certain sorcerer, a false prophet, a Jew, whose name *was* Bar-jesus: 7 Which was with the deputy of the country, Sergius Paulus, a prudent man; who called for Barnabas and Saul, and desired to hear the word of God. 8 But Elymas the sorcerer (for so is his name by interpretation) withstood them, seeking to turn away the deputy from the faith. 9 Then Saul, (who also *is called* Paul,) filled with the Holy Ghost, set his eyes on him, 10And said, O full of all subtilty and all mischief, *thou* child of the devil, *thou* enemy of all righteousness, wilt thou not cease to pervert the right ways of the Lord? 11And now, behold, the hand of the Lord *is* upon thee, and thou shalt be blind, not seeing the sun for a season. And immediately there fell on him a mist and a darkness; and he went about seeking some to lead him by the hand. 12 Then the deputy, when

13 Now in the church at Antioch there were prophets and teachers, Barnabas, Symeon who was called Niger, Lucius of Cyrene, Manaen a member of the court of Herod the tetrarch, and Saul. 2 While they were worshiping the Lord and fasting, the Holy Spirit said, "Set apart for me Barnabas and Saul for the work to which I have called them." 3 Then after fasting and praying they laid their hands on them and sent them off.

4 So, being sent out by the Holy Spirit, they went down to Seleucia; and from there they sailed to Cyprus. 5 When they arrived at Salamis, they proclaimed the word of God in the synagogues of the Jews. And they had John to assist them. 6 When they had gone through the whole island as far as Paphos, they came upon a certain magician, a Jewish false prophet, named Bar-Jesus. 7 He was with the proconsul, Sergius Paulus, a man of intelligence, who summoned Barnabas and Saul and sought to hear the word of God. 8 But Elymas the magician (for that is the meaning of his name) withstood them, seeking to turn away the proconsul from the faith. 9 But Saul, who is also called Paul, filled with the Holy Spirit, looked intently at him 10 and said, "You son of the devil, you enemy of all righteousness, full of all deceit and villainy, will you not stop making crooked the straight paths of the Lord? 11And now, behold, the hand of the Lord is upon you, and you shall be blind and unable to see the sun for a time." Immediately mist and darkness fell upon him and he went about seeking people to lead him by the hand. 12 Then the proconsul believed, when he

[k] Other ancient authorities read *to.*

their execution. Then he left Judaea and went down to Caesarea and stayed there.

But Herod dies a terrible death   12. 20

Now Herod was very angry with the people of Tyre and Sidon. They approached him in a body and after winning over Blastus the king's chamberlain, they begged him for peace. They were forced to do this because their country's food supply was dependent on the king's dominions. So on an appointed day Herod put on his royal robes, took his seat on the public throne and made a speech to them. At this the people kept shouting, "This is a god speaking, not a mere man!" Immediately an angel of the Lord struck him down because he did not give God the glory. And in fearful internal agony he died.

The message continues to spread   12. 24

But the Word of the Lord continued to gain ground and increase its influence. Barnabas and Saul returned from Jerusalem when they had completed their mission there, bringing with them John whose surname was Mark.

Saul and Barnabas are called to a   13. 1 special task

Now there were in the church at Antioch both prophets and teachers—Barnabas, for example, Simeon surnamed Niger, Lucius the Cyrenian, Manaen the foster brother of the governor Herod, and Saul. While they were worshiping the Lord and fasting, the Holy Spirit spoke to them, saying,

"Set Barnabas and Saul apart for me for a task to which I have called them."

At this, after further fasting and prayer, they laid their hands on them and set them free for this work. So these two, sent at the Holy Spirit's command, went down to Seleucia and from there they sailed off to Cyprus. On their arrival at Salamis they began to proclaim God's message in the Jewish synagogues, having John as their assistant. As they made their way through the island as far as Paphos they came across a man named Bar-Jesus, a Jew who was both a false prophet and a magician. This man was attached to Sergius Paulus, the proconsul, who was himself a man of intelligence. He sent for Barnabas and Saul as he was anxious to hear God's message. But Elymas the magician (for that is the translation of his name) opposed them, doing his best to dissuade the proconsul from accepting the faith. Then Saul (who is also called Paul), filled with the Holy Spirit, eyed him closely and said,

"You son of the devil, you enemy of all true goodness, you monster of trickery and evil, is it not high time you gave up trying to pervert the truth of the Lord? Now listen, the Lord himself will touch you, for some time you will not see the light of the sun—you will be blind!"

Immediately a mist and then an utter blackness came over his eyes, and he went round trying to find someone to lead him by the hand. When the proconsul saw what had happened he

The Church Breaks Barriers

13 There were at Antioch, in the congregation there, certain prophets and teachers: Barnabas, Simeon called Niger, Lucius of Cyrene, Manaen, who had been at the court of Prince Herod, and Saul. While they were keeping a fast and offering worship to the Lord, the Holy Spirit said, 'Set Barnabas and Saul apart for me, to do the work to which I have called them.' Then, after further fasting and prayer, they laid their hands on them and let them go.

So these two, sent out on their mission by the Holy Spirit, came down to Seleucia, and from there sailed to Cyprus. Arriving at Salamis, they declared the word of God in the Jewish synagogues. They had John with them as their assistant. They went through the whole island as far as Paphos, and there they came upon a sorcerer, a Jew who posed as a prophet, Bar-Jesus by name. He was in the retinue of the Governor, Sergius Paulus, an intelligent man, who had sent for Barnabas and Saul and wanted to hear the word of God. This Elymas the sorcerer (so his name may be translated) opposed them, trying to turn the Governor away from the Faith. But Saul, also known as Paul, filled with the Holy Spirit, looked him in the face and said, 'You utter impostor and charlatan! You son of the devil, enemy of all goodness, will you never stop falsifying the straight ways of the Lord? Look now, the hand of the Lord strikes: you shall be blind, and for a time you shall not see the sunlight.' Instantly mist and darkness came over him and he groped about for someone to lead him by the hand. When the Governor saw

find him, so he interrogated the guards and ordered their execution.

Afterwards he left Judaea to reside for a time at Caesarea. He had for some time been furiously angry with the people of Tyre and Sidon, who now by common agreement presented themselves at his court. There they won over Blastus the royal chamberlain, and sued for peace, because their country drew its supplies from the king's territory. So, on an appointed day, attired in his royal robes and seated on the rostrum, Herod harangued them; and the populace shouted back, 'It is a god speaking, not a man!' Instantly an angel of the Lord struck him down, because he had usurped the honour due to God; he was eaten up with worms and died.

Meanwhile the word of God continued to grow and spread.

Barnabas and Saul, their task fulfilled, returned from Jerusalem,[a] taking John Mark with them.

[a] Some witnesses read their task fulfilled, returned to Jerusalem; or, as it might be rendered, their task at Jerusalem fulfilled, returned.

K.J.V.

he saw what was done, believed, being astonished at the doctrine of the Lord. 13 Now when Paul and his company loosed from Paphos, they came to Perga in Pamphylia: and John departing from them returned to Jerusalem.
14 But when they departed from Perga, they came to Antioch in Pisidia, and went into the synagogue on the sabbath day, and sat down. 15And after the reading of the law and the prophets, the rulers of the synagogue sent unto them, saying, *Ye* men *and* brethren, if ye have any word of exhortation for the people, say on. 16 Then Paul stood up, and beckoning with *his* hand said, Men of Israel, and ye that fear God, give audience. 17 The God of this people of Israel chose our fathers, and exalted the people when they dwelt as strangers in the land of Egypt, and with a high arm brought he them out of it. 18And about the time of forty years suffered he their manners in the wilderness. 19And when he had destroyed seven nations in the land of Chanaan, he divided their land to them by lot. 20And after that he gave *unto them* judges about the space of four hundred and fifty years, until Samuel the prophet. 21And afterward they desired a king: and God gave unto them Saul the son of Cis, a man of the tribe of Benjamin, by the space of forty years. 22And when he had removed him, he raised up unto them David to be their king; to whom also he gave testimony, and said, I have found David the *son* of Jesse, a man after mine own heart, which shall fulfil all my will. 23 Of this man's seed hath God, according to *his* promise, raised unto Israel a Saviour, Jesus: 24 When John had first preached before his coming the baptism of repentance to all the people of Israel. 25And as John fulfilled his course, he said, Whom think ye that I am? I am not *he.* But, behold, there cometh one after me, whose shoes of *his* feet I am not worthy to loose. 26 Men *and* brethren, children of the stock of Abraham, and whosoever among you feareth God, to you is the word of this salvation sent. 27 For they that dwell at Jerusalem, and their rulers, because they knew him not, nor yet the voices of the prophets which are read every sabbath day, they have fulfilled *them* in condemning *him.* 28And though they found no cause of death *in him,* yet desired they Pilate that he should be slain. 29And when they had fulfilled all that was written of him, they took *him* down from the tree, and laid *him* in a sepulchre. 30 But God raised him from the dead: 31And he was seen many days of them which came up with him from Galilee to Jerusalem, who are his

R.S.V.

saw what had occurred, for he was astonished at the teaching of the Lord.
13 Now Paul and his company set sail from Paphos, and came to Perga in Pamphylia. And John left them and returned to Jerusalem; 14 but they passed on from Perga and came to Antioch of Pisidia. And on the sabbath day they went into the synagogue and sat down. 15After the reading of the law and the prophets, the rulers of the synagogue sent to them, saying, "Brethren, if you have any word of exhortation for the people, say it." 16 So Paul stood up, and motioning with his hand said:
"Men of Israel, and you that fear God, listen. 17 The God of this people Israel chose our fathers and made the people great during their stay in the land of Egypt, and with uplifted arm he led them out of it. 18And for about forty years he bore with[m] them in the wilderness. 19And when he had destroyed seven nations in the land of Canaan, he gave them their land as an inheritance, for about four hundred and fifty years. 20And after that he gave them judges until Samuel the prophet. 21 Then they asked for a king; and God gave them Saul the son of Kish, a man of the tribe of Benjamin, for forty years. 22And when he had removed him, he raised up David to be their king; of whom he testified and said, 'I have found in David the son of Jesse a man after my heart, who will do all my will.' 23 Of this man's posterity God has brought to Israel a Savior, Jesus, as he promised. 24 Before his coming John had preached a baptism of repentance to all the people of Israel. 25And as John was finishing his course, he said, 'What do you suppose that I am? I am not he. No, but after me one is coming, the sandals of whose feet I am not worthy to untie.'
26 "Brethren, sons of the family of Abraham, and those among you that fear God, to us has been sent the message of this salvation. 27 For those who live in Jerusalem and their rulers, because they did not recognize him nor understand the utterances of the prophets which are read every sabbath, fulfilled these by condemning him. 28 Though they could charge him with nothing deserving death, yet they asked Pilate to have him killed. 29And when they had fulfilled all that was written of him, they took him down from the tree, and laid him in a tomb. 30 But God raised him from the dead; 31 and for many days he appeared to those who came up with him from Galilee to Jerusalem,

[m] Other ancient authorities read *cared for* (Deut. 1.31).

believed, for he was shaken to the core at the Lord's teaching.

Saul (now Paul) comes to   13. 13
Antioch in Pisidia

Then Paul and his companions set sail from Paphos and went to Perga in Pamphylia. There John left them and turned back to Jerusalem, but they continued their journey through Perga to the Antioch in Pisidia. They went to the synagogue on the Sabbath day and took their seats. After the reading of the Law and Prophets, the leaders of the synagogue sent to them with a message,
"Men and brothers, if you have any message of encouragement for the people, by all means speak."

Paul shows the Jews where   13. 16
their history leads

So Paul stood up, and motioning with his hand, began:
"Men of Israel and all of you who fear God, listen to me. The God of this people Israel chose our fathers and prospered the people even while they were exiles in the land of Egypt. Then he lifted up his arm and led them out of that land. Yes, and he bore with them for forty years in the desert. He destroyed seven nations in the land of Canaan before he gave them that land as their inheritance for some four hundred and fifty years. After that he gave them judges until the time of the prophet Samuel. Then when they begged for a king God gave them Saul the son of Kish, a man of the tribe of Benjamin, to be their king for forty years. After he had deposed him he raised David to the throne, a man of whom God himself bore testimony in the words, *I have found David, the son of Jesse, a man after my own heart, who shall do all my will.* From the descendants of this man, according to his promise, God has brought Jesus to Israel to be their savior. John came before him to prepare his way preaching the baptism of repentance for all the people of Israel. Indeed, as John reached the end of his time he said these words: 'What do you think I am? I am not he. But know this, someone comes after me whose shoelace I am not fit to untie!'

Now the message is urgent and   13. 26
contemporary

"Men and brothers, sons of the race of Abraham, and all among you who fear God, it is to us that this message of salvation has now been sent! For the people of Jerusalem and their rulers refused to recognize him and to understand the voice of the prophets which are read every Sabbath day—even though in condemning him they fulfilled these very prophecies! For though they found no cause for putting him to death, they begged Pilate to have him executed. And when they had completed everything that was written about him, they took him down from the cross and laid him in a tomb. But God raised him from the dead. For many days he was seen by those who had come up from Galilee to

what had happened he became a believer, deeply impressed by what he learned about the Lord.

Leaving Paphos, Paul and his companions went by sea to Perga in Pamphylia; John, however, left them and returned to Jerusalem. From Perga they continued their journey as far as Pisidian Antioch. On the Sabbath they went to synagogue and took their seats; and after the readings from the Law and the prophets, the officials of the synagogue sent this message to them: 'Friends, if you have anything to say to the people by way of exhortation, let us hear it.' Paul rose, made a gesture with his hand, and began:

'Men of Israel and you who worship our God, listen to me! The God of this people of Israel chose our fathers. When they were still living as aliens in Egypt he made them into a nation and brought them out of that country with arm outstretched. For some forty years he bore with their conduct[a] in the desert. Then in the Canaanite country he overthrew seven nations, whose lands he gave them to be their heritage for some four hundred and fifty years, and afterwards appointed judges for them until the time of the prophet Samuel.

'Then they asked for a king and God gave them Saul the son of Kish, a man of the tribe of Benjamin, who reigned for forty years. Then he removed him and set up David as their king, giving him his approval in these words: "I have found David son of Jesse to be a man after my own heart, who will carry out all my purposes." This is the man from whose posterity God, as he promised, has brought Israel a saviour, Jesus. John made ready for his coming by proclaiming baptism as a token of repentance to the whole people of Israel. And when John was nearing the end of his course, he said, "I am not what you think I am. No, after me comes one whose shoes I am not fit to unfasten."

'My brothers, you who come of the stock of Abraham, and others among you who revere our God, we are the people to whom the message of this salvation has been sent. The people of Jerusalem and their rulers did not recognize him, or understand the words of the prophets which are read Sabbath by Sabbath; indeed they fulfilled them by condemning him. Though they failed to find grounds for the sentence of death, they asked Pilate to have him executed. And when they had carried out all that the scriptures said about him, they took him down from the gibbet and laid him in a tomb. But God raised him from the dead; and there was a period of many days during which he appeared to those who had come up with him from Galilee to Jerusalem.

[a] *Some witnesses read* he sustained them.

K.J.V.

witnesses unto the people. 32And we declare unto you glad tidings, how that the promise which was made unto the fathers, 33 God hath fulfilled the same unto us their children, in that he hath raised up Jesus again; as it is also written in the second psalm, Thou art my Son, this day have I begotten thee. 34And as concerning that he raised him up from the dead, *now* no more to return to corruption, he said on this wise, I will give you the sure mercies of David. 35 Wherefore he saith also in another *psalm*, Thou shalt not suffer thine Holy One to see corruption. 36 For David, after he had served his own generation by the will of God, fell on sleep, and was laid unto his fathers, and saw corruption: 37 But he, whom God raised again, saw no corruption.

38 Be it known unto you therefore, men *and* brethren, that through this man is preached unto you the forgiveness of sins: 39And by him all that believe are justified from all things, from which ye could not be justified by the law of Moses. 40 Beware therefore, lest that come upon you, which is spoken of in the prophets; 41 Behold, ye despisers, and wonder, and perish: for I work a work in your days, a work which ye shall in no wise believe, though a man declare it unto you. 42And when the Jews were gone out of the synagogue, the Gentiles besought that these words might be preached to them the next sabbath. 43 Now when the congregation was broken up, many of the Jews and religious proselytes followed Paul and Barnabas; who, speaking to them, persuaded them to continue in the grace of God.

44 And the next sabbath day came almost the whole city together to hear the word of God. 45 But when the Jews saw the multitudes, they were filled with envy, and spake against those things which were spoken by Paul, contradicting and blaspheming. 46 Then Paul and Barnabas waxed bold, and said, It was necessary that the word of God should first have been spoken to you: but seeing ye put it from you, and judge yourselves unworthy of everlasting life, lo, we turn to the Gentiles. 47 For so hath the Lord commanded us, *saying*, I have set thee to be a light of the Gentiles, that thou shouldest be for salvation unto the ends of the earth. 48And when the Gentiles heard this, they were glad, and glorified the word of the Lord: and as many as were ordained to eternal life believed. 49And the word of the Lord was published throughout all the region. 50 But the Jews stirred up the devout and honourable women, and the chief men of the city, and raised persecution against Paul and Barnabas, and expelled them out of their coasts. 51 But they shook off the dust of their feet

R.S.V.

who are now his witnesses to the people. 32And we bring you the good news that what God promised to the fathers, 33 this he has fulfilled to us their children by raising Jesus; as also it is written in the second psalm,

'Thou art my Son,
    today I have begotten thee.'

34And as for the fact that he raised him from the dead, no more to return to corruption, he spoke in this way,

'I will give you the holy and sure blessings of
    David.'

35 Therefore he says also in another psalm,

'Thou wilt not let thy Holy One see corruption.'

36 For David, after he had served the counsel of God in his own generation, fell asleep, and was laid with his fathers, and saw corruption; 37 but he whom God raised up saw no corruption. 38 Let it be known to you therefore, brethren, that through this man forgiveness of sins is proclaimed to you, 39 and by him every one that believes is freed from everything from which you could not be freed by the law of Moses. 40 Beware, therefore, lest there come upon you what is said in the prophets:

41 'Behold, you scoffers, and wonder, and
    perish;
for I do a deed in your days,
    a deed you will never believe, if one de-
    clares it to you.' "

42 As they went out, the people begged that these things might be told them the next sabbath. 43And when the meeting of the synagogue broke up, many Jews and devout converts to Judaism followed Paul and Barnabas, who spoke to them and urged them to continue in the grace of God.

44 The next sabbath almost the whole city gathered together to hear the word of God. 45 But when the Jews saw the multitudes, they were filled with jealousy, and contradicted what was spoken by Paul, and reviled him. 46And Paul and Barnabas spoke out boldly, saying, "It was necessary that the word of God should be spoken first to you. Since you thrust it from you, and judge yourselves unworthy of eternal life, behold, we turn to the Gentiles. 47 For so the Lord has commanded us, saying,

'I have set you to be a light for the Gentiles,
    that you may bring salvation to the uttermost
    parts of the earth.' "

48 And when the Gentiles heard this, they were glad and glorified the word of God; and as many as were ordained to eternal life believed. 49And the word of the Lord spread throughout all the region. 50 But the Jews incited the devout women of high standing and the leading men of the city, and stirred up persecution against Paul and Barnabas, and drove them out of their district. 51 But they shook off

PHILLIPS

Jerusalem with him, and these men are now his witnesses to the people. And as for us we tell you the good news that the promise made to our forefathers has come true—that, in raising up Jesus, God has fulfilled it for us their children. This is endorsed in the second psalm: 'Thou art my son, this day have I begotten thee.' And as for the fact of God's raising him from the dead, never to return to corruption, he has spoken in these words: 'I will give you the sure mercies of David.' And then going further he says in another psalm: 'Thou shalt not suffer thine holy one to see corruption.' For David, remember, after he had served God's purpose in his own generation fell asleep and was laid with his ancestors. He did in fact 'see corruption,' but this man whom God raised never saw corruption! It is therefore imperative, men and brothers, that every one of you should realize that forgiveness of sins is proclaimed to you through this man. And through faith in him a man is absolved from all those things from which the Law of Moses could never set him free. Take care then that this saying of the prophets should never apply to you:

Behold, ye despisers, and wonder, and perish;
For I work a work in your days,
A work which ye shall in no wise believe, if one declare it unto you."

Paul succeeds in arousing   13. 42
deep interest—

As they were going out the people kept on asking them to say all this again on the following Sabbath. After the meeting of the synagogue broke up, many of the Jews and devout proselytes followed Paul and Barnabas who spoke personally to them and urged them to put their trust in the grace of God.

—but a week later he meets   13. 44
bitter opposition

On the next Sabbath almost the entire population of the city assembled to hear the message of God, but when the Jews saw the crowds they were filled with jealousy and contradicted what Paul was saying, covering him with abuse. At this Paul and Barnabas did not mince their words but said,
"We felt it our duty to speak the message of God to you first, but since you spurn it and evidently do not think yourselves fit for eternal life, watch us now as we turn to the gentiles! Indeed the Lord has commanded us to do so in the words:

I have set thee for a light of the gentiles,
That thou shouldest be for salvation unto the uttermost part of the earth."

When the gentiles heard this they were delighted and thanked God for his message. All those who were destined for eternal life believed, and the Word of the Lord spread over the whole country. But the Jews worked upon the feelings of religious and respectable women and some of the leading citizens, and succeeded in starting a persecution against Paul and Barnabas, and expelled them from the district. But they on their part simply shook off the dust from

N.E.B.

'They are now his witnesses before our nation; and we are here to give you the good news that God, who made the promise to the fathers, has fulfilled it for the children[a] by raising Jesus from the dead, as indeed it stands written, in the second [b] Psalm: "You are my son; this day have I begotten you." Again, that he raised him from the dead, never again to revert to corruption, he declares in these words: "I will give you the blessings promised to David, holy and sure." This is borne out by another passage: "Thou wilt not let thy loyal servant suffer corruption." As for David, when he had served the purpose of God in his own generation, he died, and was gathered to his fathers, and suffered corruption; but the one whom God raised up did not suffer corruption; and you must understand, my brothers, that it is through him that forgiveness of sins is now being proclaimed to you. It is through him that everyone who has faith is acquitted of everything for which there was no acquittal under the Law of Moses. Beware, then, lest you bring down upon yourselves the doom proclaimed by the prophets: "See this, you scoffers, wonder, and begone; for I am doing a deed in your days, a deed which you will never believe when you are told of it." '

As they were leaving the synagogue they were asked to come again and speak on these subjects next Sabbath; and after the congregation had dispersed, many Jews and gentile worshippers went along with Paul and Barnabas, who spoke to them and urged them to hold fast to the grace of God.

On the following Sabbath almost the whole city gathered to hear the word of God. When the Jews saw the crowds, they were filled with jealous resentment, and contradicted what Paul and Barnabas said, with violent abuse. But Paul and Barnabas were outspoken in their reply. 'It was necessary', they said, 'that the word of God should be declared to you first. But since you reject it and thus condemn yourselves as unworthy of eternal life, we now turn to the Gentiles. For these are our instructions from the Lord: "I have appointed you to be a light for the Gentiles, and a means of salvation to earth's farthest bounds." ' When the Gentiles heard this, they were overjoyed and thankfully acclaimed the word of the Lord, and those who were marked out for eternal life became believers. So the word of the Lord spread far and wide through the region. But the Jews stirred up feeling among the women of standing who were worshippers, and among the leading men of the city; a persecution was started against Paul and Barnabas, and they were expelled from the district. So they

[a] *Some witnesses read* our children; *others read* us their children. [b] *Some witnesses read* first.

K.J.V.

against them, and came unto Iconium. 52And the disciples were filled with joy, and with the Holy Ghost.

14 And it came to pass in Iconium, that they went both together into the synagogue of the Jews, and so spake, that a great multitude both of the Jews and also of the Greeks believed. 2 But the unbelieving Jews stirred up the Gentiles, and made their minds evil affected against the brethren. 3 Long time therefore abode they speaking boldly in the Lord, which gave testimony unto the word of his grace, and granted signs and wonders to be done by their hands. 4 But the multitude of the city was divided: and part held with the Jews, and part with the apostles. 5And when there was an assault made both of the Gentiles, and also of the Jews with their rulers, to use *them* despitefully, and to stone them, 6 They were ware of *it*, and fled unto Lystra and Derbe, cities of Lycaonia, and unto the region that lieth round about: 7And there they preached the gospel.

8 And there sat a certain man at Lystra, impotent in his feet, being a cripple from his mother's womb, who never had walked: 9 The same heard Paul speak: who steadfastly beholding him, and perceiving that he had faith to be healed, 10 Said with a loud voice, Stand upright on thy feet. And he leaped and walked. 11And when the people saw what Paul had done, they lifted up their voices, saying in the speech of Lycaonia, The gods are come down to us in the likeness of men. 12And they called Barnabas, Jupiter; and Paul, Mercurius, because he was the chief speaker. 13 Then the priest of Jupiter, which was before their city, brought oxen and garlands unto the gates, and would have done sacrifice with the people. 14 *Which* when the apostles, Barnabas and Paul, heard *of*, they rent their clothes, and ran in among the people, crying out, 15And saying, Sirs, why do ye these things? We also are men of like passions with you, and preach unto you that ye should turn from these vanities unto the living God, which made heaven, and earth, and the sea, and all things that are therein: 16 Who in times past suffered all nations to walk in their own ways. 17 Nevertheless he left not himself without witness, in that he did good, and gave us rain from heaven, and fruitful seasons, filling our hearts with food and gladness. 18And with these sayings scarce restrained they the people, that they had not done sacrifice unto them.

R.S.V.

the dust from their feet against them, and went to Iconium. 52 And the disciples were filled with joy and with the Holy Spirit.

14 Now at Iconium they entered together into the Jewish synagogue, and so spoke that a great company believed, both of Jews and of Greeks. 2 But the unbelieving Jews stirred up the Gentiles and poisoned their minds against the brethren. 3 So they remained for a long time, speaking boldly for the Lord, who bore witness to the word of his grace, granting signs and wonders to be done by their hands. 4 But the people of the city were divided; some sided with the Jews, and some with the apostles. 5 When an attempt was made by both Gentiles and Jews, with their rulers, to molest them and to stone them, 6 they learned of it and fled to Lystra and Derbe, cities of Lycaonia, and to the surrounding country; 7 and there they preached the gospel.

8 Now at Lystra there was a man sitting, who could not use his feet; he was a cripple from birth, who had never walked. 9 He listened to Paul speaking; and Paul, looking intently at him and seeing that he had faith to be made well, 10 said in a loud voice, "Stand upright on your feet." And he sprang up and walked. 11And when the crowds saw what Paul had done, they lifted up their voices, saying in Lycaonian, "The gods have come down to us in the likeness of men!" 12 Barnabas they called Zeus, and Paul, because he was the chief speaker, they called Hermes. 13And the priest of Zeus, whose temple was in front of the city, brought oxen and garlands to the gates and wanted to offer sacrifice with the people. 14 But when the apostles Barnabas and Paul heard of it, they tore their garments and rushed out among the multitude, crying, 15 "Men, why are you doing this? We also are men, of like nature with you, and bring you good news, that you should turn from these vain things to a living God who made the heaven and the earth and the sea and all that is in them. 16 In past generations he allowed all the nations to walk in their own ways; 17 yet he did not leave himself without witness, for he did good and gave you from heaven rains and fruitful seasons, satisfying your hearts with food and gladness." 18 With these words they scarcely restrained the people from offering sacrifice to them.

their feet in protest and went on to Iconium. And the disciples continued to be full of joy and the Holy Spirit.

shook the dust off their feet in protest against them and went to Iconium. And the converts were filled with joy and with the Holy Spirit.

Jewish behavior repeats itself   14. 1

Much the same thing happened at Iconium. On their arrival they went to the Jewish synagogue and spoke with such conviction that a very large number of both Jews and Greeks believed. But the unbelieving Jews stirred up the feelings of the gentiles and poisoned their minds against the brothers. So they remained there for a long time and spoke fearlessly for the Lord, who made it plain that they were proclaiming the Word of his grace, by allowing them to perform signs and miracles. But the great mass of the people of the city were divided in their opinions, some taking the side of the Jews, and some that of the apostles. But when a hostile movement arose from both gentiles and Jews in collaboration with the authorities to insult and stone them, they got to know about it, fled to the Lycaonian cities of Lystra and Derbe, and the surrounding countryside—and from there they continued to proclaim the gospel.

A miracle in a completely   14. 8
pagan city

Now it happened one day at Lystra that a man was sitting who had no power in his feet. He had in fact been lame from birth and had never been able to walk. He was listening to Paul as he spoke, and Paul, looking him straight in the eye and seeing that he had the faith to be made well, said in a loud voice,
"Stand straight up on your feet!"
And he sprang to his feet and walked. When the crowd saw what Paul had done they shouted in the Lycaonian language,
"The gods have come down to us in human form!"
They began to call Barnabas Jupiter, and Paul Mercury, since he was the chief speaker. What is more, the high priests of Jupiter whose temple was at the gateway of the city, brought garlanded oxen to the gates and wanted to offer sacrifice with the people. But when the apostles, Barnabas and Paul, heard of their intention they tore their clothes and rushed into the crowd, crying at the top of their voices,
"Men, men, why are you doing these things? We are only human beings with feelings just like yours! We are here to tell you good news— that you should turn from these meaningless things to the living God! He is the one who made heaven and earth, the sea and all that is in them. In generations gone by he allowed all nations to go on in their own ways—not that he left men without evidence of himself. For he had shown kindnesses to you; he has sent you rain from heaven and fruitful seasons, giving you food and happiness to your hearts' content."
Yet even with these words they only just succeeded in restraining the crowd from making sacrifices to them.

14 At Iconium similarly they went[a] into the Jewish synagogue and spoke to such purpose that a large body both of Jews and Greeks became believers. But the unconverted Jews stirred up the Gentiles and poisoned their minds against the Christians. For some time Paul and Barnabas stayed on and spoke boldly and openly in reliance on the Lord; and he confirmed the message of his grace by causing signs and miracles to be worked at their hands. The mass of the townspeople were divided, some siding with the Jews, others with the apostles. But when a move was made by Gentiles and Jews together, with the connivance of the city authorities, to maltreat them and stone them, they got wind of it and made their escape to the Lycaonian cities of Lystra and Derbe and the surrounding country, where they continued to spread the good news.

At Lystra sat a crippled man, lame from birth, who had never walked in his life. This man listened while Paul was speaking. Paul looked him in the face and saw that he had the faith to be cured, so he said to him in a loud voice, 'Stand up straight on your feet'; and he sprang up and started to walk. When the crowds saw what Paul had done, they shouted, in their native Lycaonian, 'The gods have come down to us in human form.' And they called Barnabas Jupiter, and Paul they called Mercury, because he was the spokesman. And the priest of Jupiter, whose temple was just outside the city, brought oxen and garlands to the gates, and he and all the people were about to offer sacrifice.

But when the apostles Barnabas and Paul heard of it, they tore their clothes and rushed into the crowd shouting, 'Men, what is this that you are doing? We are only human beings, no less mortal than you. The good news we bring tells you to turn from these follies to the living God, who made heaven and earth and sea and everything in them. In past ages he allowed all nations to go their own way; and yet he has not left you without some clue to his nature, in the kindness he shows: he sends you rain from heaven and crops in their seasons, and gives you food and good cheer in plenty.'

With these words they barely managed to prevent the crowd from offering sacrifice to them.

K.J.V.

19 And there came thither *certain* Jews from Antioch and Iconium, who persuaded the people, and, having stoned Paul, drew *him* out of the city, supposing he had been dead. 20 Howbeit, as the disciples stood round about him, he rose up, and came into the city: and the next day he departed with Barnabas to Derbe. 21And when they had preached the gospel to that city, and had taught many, they returned again to Lystra, and *to* Iconium, and Antioch, 22 Confirming the souls of the disciples, *and* exhorting them to continue in the faith, and that we must through much tribulation enter into the kingdom of God. 23And when they had ordained them elders in every church, and had prayed with fasting, they commended them to the Lord, on whom they believed. 24And after they had passed throughout Pisidia, they came to Pamphylia. 25And when they had preached the word in Perga, they went down into Attalia: 26And thence sailed to Antioch, from whence they had been recommended to the grace of God for the work which they fulfilled. 27And when they were come, and had gathered the church together, they rehearsed all that God had done with them, and how he had opened the door of faith unto the Gentiles. 28And there they abode long time with the disciples.

15 And certain men which came down from Judea taught the brethren, *and said,* Except ye be circumcised after the manner of Moses, ye cannot be saved. 2 When therefore Paul and Barnabas had no small dissension and disputation with them, they determined that Paul and Barnabas, and certain other of them, should go up to Jerusalem unto the apostles and elders about this question. 3And being brought on their way by the church, they passed through Phenice and Samaria, declaring the conversion of the Gentiles: and they caused great joy unto all the brethren. 4And when they were come to Jerusalem, they were received of the church, and *of* the apostles and elders, and they declared all things that God had done with them. 5 But there rose up certain of the sect of the Pharisees which believed, saying, That it was needful to circumcise them, and to command *them* to keep the law of Moses. 6 And the apostles and elders came together for to consider of this matter. 7And when there had been much disputing, Peter rose up, and said unto them, Men *and* brethren, ye know how that a good while ago God made choice among us, that the Gentiles by my mouth should hear the word of the gospel, and believe. 8And God, which knoweth the hearts, bare them witness, giving them the Holy Ghost, even as *he did* unto us; 9And put no difference between us and them, purifying their hearts by faith.

R.S.V.

19 But Jews came there from Antioch and Iconium; and having persuaded the people, they stoned Paul and dragged him out of the city, supposing that he was dead. 20 But when the disciples gathered about him, he rose up and entered the city; and on the next day he went on with Barnabas to Derbe. 21 When they had preached the gospel to that city and had made many disciples, they returned to Lystra and to Iconium and to Antioch, 22 strengthening the souls of the disciples, exhorting them to continue in the faith, and saying that through many tribulations we must enter the kingdom of God. 23And when they had appointed elders for them in every church, with prayer and fasting, they committed them to the Lord in whom they believed. 24 Then they passed through Pisidia, and came to Pamphylia. 25And when they had spoken the word in Perga, they went down to Attalia; 26 and from there they sailed to Antioch, where they had been commended to the grace of God for the work which they had fulfilled. 27And when they arrived, they gathered the church together and declared all that God had done with them, and how he had opened a door of faith to the Gentiles. 28And they remained no little time with the disciples.

15 But some men came down from Judea and were teaching the brethren, "Unless you are circumcised according to the custom of Moses, you cannot be saved." 2And when Paul and Barnabas had no small dissension and debate with them, Paul and Barnabas and some of the others were appointed to go up to Jerusalem to the apostles and the elders about this question. 3 So, being sent on their way by the church, they passed through both Phoenicia and Samaria, reporting the conversion of the Gentiles, and they gave great joy to all the brethren. 4 When they came to Jerusalem, they were welcomed by the church and the apostles and the elders, and they declared all that God had done with them. 5 But some believers who belonged to the party of the Pharisees rose up, and said, "It is necessary to circumcise them, and to charge them to keep the law of Moses." 6 The apostles and the elders were gathered together to consider this matter. 7And after there had been much debate, Peter rose and said to them, "Brethren, you know that in the early days God made choice among you, that by my mouth the Gentiles should hear the word of the gospel and believe. 8And God who knows the heart bore witness to them, giving them the Holy Spirit just as he did to us; 9 and he made no distinction between us and them, but cleansed their hearts

PHILLIPS

N.E.B.

Paul is dogged by his Jewish enemies — 14. 19

Then some Jews arrived from Antioch and Iconium and after turning the minds of the people against Paul they stoned him and dragged him out of the city thinking he was dead. But while the disciples were gathered in a circle round him, Paul got up and walked back into the city. And the very next day he went out with Barnabas to Derbe, and when they had preached the gospel to that city and made many disciples, they turned back to Lystra, Iconium and Antioch. They put fresh heart into the disciples there, urging them to stand firm in the faith, and reminding them that it is *"through many tribulations that we must enter into the kingdom of God."* They appointed elders for them in each church, and with prayer and fasting commended these men to the Lord in whom they had believed. Then they crossed Pisidia and arrived in Pamphylia. They proclaimed their message in Perga and then went down to Attalia. From there they sailed back to Antioch (in Syria) where they had first been commended to the grace of God for the task which they had now completed. When they arrived there they called the church together and reported to them how greatly God had worked with them and how he had opened the door of faith for the gentiles. And here at Antioch they spent a considerable time with the disciples.

Then Jews from Antioch and Iconium came on the scene and won over the crowds. They stoned Paul, and dragged him out of the city, thinking him dead. The converts formed a ring round him, and he got to his feet and went into the city. Next day he left with Barnabas for Derbe.

After bringing the good news to that town, where they gained many converts, they returned to Lystra, then to Iconium, and then to Antioch, heartening the converts and encouraging them to be true to their religion. They warned them that to enter the kingdom of God we must pass through many hardships. They also appointed elders for them in each congregation, and with prayer and fasting committed them to the Lord in whom they had put their faith.

Then they passed through Pisidia and came into Pamphylia. When they had given the message at Perga, they went down to Attalia, and from there set sail for Antioch, where they had originally been commended to the grace of God for the task which they had now completed. When they arrived and had called the congregation together, they reported all that God had helped them to do, and how he had thrown open the gates of faith to the Gentiles. And they stayed for some time with the disciples there.

The opposition from reactionaries — 15. 1

Then some men came down from Judaea and began to teach the brothers, saying, "unless you are circumcised according to the custom of Moses you cannot be saved." Naturally this caused a serious upset among them and much earnest discussion followed with Paul and Barnabas. Finally it was agreed that Paul and Barnabas should go up to Jerusalem with some of their own people to confer with the apostles and elders about the whole question.

The church sent them off on their journey and as they went through Phoenicia and Samaria they told the story of the conversion of the gentiles and all the brothers were overjoyed to hear about it. On their arrival at Jerusalem they were welcomed by the church, by the apostles and elders, and they reported how greatly God had worked with them. But some members of the Pharisees' party who had become believers stood up and declared that it was absolutely essential that these men be told that they must be circumcised and observe the Law of Moses.

15 Now certain persons who had come down from Judaea began to teach the brotherhood that those who were not circumcised in accordance with Mosaic practice could not be saved. That brought them into fierce dissension and controversy with Paul and Barnabas. And so it was arranged that these two and some others from Antioch should go up to Jerusalem to see the apostles and elders about this question.

They were sent on their way by the congregation, and travelled through Phoenicia and Samaria, telling the full story of the conversion of the Gentiles. The news caused great rejoicing among all the Christians there.

When they reached Jerusalem they were welcomed by the church and the apostles and elders, and reported all that God had helped them to do. Then some of the Pharisaic party who had become believers came forward and said, 'They must be circumcised and told to keep the Law of Moses.'

Peter declares that God is doing something new — 15. 6

The apostles and elders met to consider this matter. After an exhaustive inquiry Peter stood up and addressed them in these words:

"Men and brothers, you know that from the earliest days God chose me as the one from whose lips the gentiles should hear the Word and should believe it. Moreover, God who knows men's inmost thoughts had plainly shown that this is so, for when he had cleansed their hearts through their faith he gave the Holy

The apostles and elders held a meeting to look into this matter; and, after a long debate, Peter rose and addressed them. 'My friends,' he said, 'in the early days, as you yourselves know, God made his choice among you and ordained that from my lips the Gentiles should hear and believe the message of the Gospel. And God, who can read men's minds, showed his approval of them by giving the Holy Spirit to them, as he did to us. He made no difference between them and us; for he purified their hearts by faith.

K.J.V.

10 Now therefore why tempt ye God, to put a yoke upon the neck of the disciples, which neither our fathers nor we were able to bear? 11 But we believe that through the grace of the Lord Jesus Christ we shall be saved, even as they.

12 Then all the multitude kept silence, and gave audience to Barnabas and Paul, declaring what miracles and wonders God had wrought among the Gentiles by them.

13 And after they had held their peace, James answered, saying, Men *and* brethren, hearken unto me: 14 Simeon hath declared how God at the first did visit the Gentiles, to take out of them a people for his name. 15 And to this agree the words of the prophets; as it is written, 16 After this I will return, and will build again the tabernacle of David, which is fallen down; and I will build again the ruins thereof, and I will set it up: 17 That the residue of men might seek after the Lord, and all the Gentiles, upon whom my name is called, saith the Lord, who doeth all these things. 18 Known unto God are all his works from the beginning of the world. 19 Wherefore my sentence is, that we trouble not them, which from among the Gentiles are turned to God: 20 But that we write unto them, that they abstain from pollutions of idols, and *from* fornication, and *from* things strangled, and *from* blood. 21 For Moses of old time hath in every city them that preach him, being read in the synagogues every sabbath day. 22 Then pleased it the apostles and elders, with the whole church, to send chosen men of their own company to Antioch with Paul and Barnabas; *namely,* Judas surnamed Barsabas, and Silas, chief men among the brethren: 23 And they wrote *letters* by them after this manner; The apostles and elders and brethren *send* greeting unto the brethren which are of the Gentiles in Antioch and Syria and Cilicia: 24 Forasmuch as we have heard, that certain which went out from us have troubled you with words, subverting your souls, saying, Ye *must* be circumcised, and keep the law; to whom we gave no *such* commandment: 25 It seemed good unto us, being assembled with one accord, to send chosen men unto you with our beloved Barnabas and Paul, 26 Men that have hazarded their lives for the name of our Lord Jesus Christ. 27 We have sent therefore Judas and Silas, who shall also tell *you* the same things by mouth. 28 For it seemed good to the Holy Ghost, and to us, to lay upon you no greater burden than these necessary things; 29 That ye abstain from meats of-

R.S.V.

by faith. 10 Now therefore why do you make trial of God by putting a yoke upon the neck of the disciples which neither our fathers nor we have been able to bear? 11 But we believe that we shall be saved through the grace of the Lord Jesus, just as they will."

12 And all the assembly kept silence; and they listened to Barnabas and Paul as they related what signs and wonders God had done through them among the Gentiles. 13 After they finished speaking, James replied, "Brethren, listen to me. 14 Symeon has related how God first visited the Gentiles, to take out of them a people for his name. 15 And with this the words of the prophets agree, as it is written,

16 'After this I will return,
    and I will rebuild the dwelling of David,
        which has fallen;
    I will rebuild its ruins,
        and I will set it up,
17 that the rest of men may seek the Lord,
    and all the Gentiles who are called by my
        name,
18 says the Lord, who has made these things
    known from of old.'

19 Therefore my judgment is that we should not trouble those of the Gentiles who turn to God, 20 but should write to them to abstain from the pollutions of idols and from unchastity and from what is strangled [n] and from blood. 21 For from early generations Moses has had in every city those who preach him, for he is read every sabbath in the synagogues."

22 Then it seemed good to the apostles and the elders, with the whole church, to choose men from among them and send them to Antioch with Paul and Barnabas. They sent Judas called Barsabbas, and Silas, leading men among the brethren, 23 with the following letter: "The brethren, both the apostles and the elders, to the brethren who are of the Gentiles in Antioch and Syria and Cilicia, greeting. 24 Since we have heard that some persons from us have troubled you with words, unsettling your minds, although we gave them no instructions, 25 it has seemed good to us in assembly to choose men and send them to you with our beloved Barnabas and Paul, 26 men who have risked their lives for the sake of our Lord Jesus Christ. 27 We have therefore sent Judas and Silas, who themselves will tell you the same things by word of mouth. 28 For it has seemed good to the Holy Spirit and to us to lay upon you no greater burden than these necessary things: 29 that you abstain from

[n] Other early authorities omit *and from what is strangled.*

Spirit to the gentiles exactly as he did to us. Why then must you now strain the patience of God by trying to put on the shoulders of these disciples a burden which neither our fathers nor we were able to bear? Surely the fact is that it is by the grace of the Lord Jesus that we are saved by faith, just as they are!"

These words produced absolute silence, and they listened to Barnabas and Paul while they gave a detailed account of the signs and wonders which God had worked through them among the gentiles.

James expresses the feeling 15. 13
of the meeting

Silence again followed their words and then James made this reply:

"Men and brothers, listen to me. Symeon has shown how in the first place God chose a people from among the nations who should bear his name. This is in full agreement with what the prophets wrote, as in this scripture:

After these things I will return,
And I will build again the tabernacle of David, which is fallen;
And I will build again the ruins thereof,
And I will set it up:
That the residue of men may seek after the Lord,
And all the gentiles, upon whom my name is called,
Saith the Lord who maketh these things known from the beginning of the world.

"I am firmly of the opinion that we should not put any additional obstacles before any gentiles who are turning toward God. Instead, I think we should write to them telling them to avoid anything polluted by idols, sexual immorality, eating the meat of strangled animals, or tasting blood. For after all, for many generations now Moses has had his preachers in every city and has been read aloud in the synagogues every Sabbath day."

The Church's deputation: the 15. 22
message to gentile Christians

Then the apostles, the elders and the whole Church agreed to choose representatives and send them to Antioch with Paul and Barnabas. Their names were Judas, surnamed Barsabas, and Silas, both leading men of the brotherhood. They carried with them a letter bearing this message: "The apostles and elders who are your brothers send their greetings to the brothers who are gentiles in Antioch, Syria and Cilicia. Since we have heard that some of our number have caused you deep distress and have unsettled your minds by giving you a message which certainly did not originate from us, we are unanimously agreed to send you chosen representatives with our well loved Barnabas and Paul—men who have risked their lives for the name of our Lord Jesus Christ. So we have sent you Judas and Silas who will give you the same message personally by word of mouth. For it has seemed right to the Holy Spirit and to us to lay no further burden upon you except what is absolutely essential, namely, that you avoid what has been sacrificed to idols, tasting blood,

Then why do you now provoke God by laying on the shoulders of these converts a yoke which neither we nor our fathers were able to bear? No, we believe that it is by the grace of the Lord Jesus that we are saved, and so are they.'

At that the whole company fell silent and listened to Barnabas and Paul as they told of all the signs and miracles that God had worked among the Gentiles through them.

When they had finished speaking, James summed up: 'My friends,' he said, 'listen to me. Simeon has told how it first happened that God took notice of the Gentiles, to choose from among them a people to bear his name; and this agrees with the words of the prophets, as Scripture has it:

"Thereafter I will return and rebuild the fallen house of David;
Even from its ruins I will rebuild it, and set it up again,
That they may seek the Lord—all the rest of mankind,
And the Gentiles, whom I have claimed for my own.
Thus says the Lord, whose work it is,
Made known long ago."

'My judgement therefore is that we should impose no irksome restrictions on those of the Gentiles who are turning to God, but instruct them by letter to abstain from things polluted by contact with idols, from fornication, from anything that has been strangled, and from blood.[a] Moses, after all, has never lacked spokesmen in every town for generations past; he is read in the synagogues Sabbath by Sabbath.'

Then the apostles and elders, with the agreement of the whole church, resolved to choose representatives and send them to Antioch with Paul and Barnabas. They chose two leading men in the community, Judas Barsabbas and Silas, and gave them this letter to deliver:

'We, the apostles and elders, send greetings as brothers to our brothers of gentile origin in Antioch, Syria, and Cilicia. Forasmuch as we have heard that some of our number, without any instructions from us, have[b] disturbed you with their talk and unsettled your minds, we have resolved unanimously to send to you our chosen representatives with our well-beloved Barnabas and Paul, who have devoted themselves to the cause of our Lord Jesus Christ. We are therefore sending Judas and Silas, who will themselves confirm this by word of mouth. It is the decision of the Holy Spirit, and our decision, to lay no further burden upon you beyond these essentials: you are to abstain from meat that has been offered to idols, from blood, from anything

[a] *Some witnesses omit* from fornication; *others omit* from anything that has been strangled; *some add* (*after* blood) *and to refrain from doing to others what they would not like done to themselves.*
[b] *Some witnesses read* have gone out and . . .

K.J.V.

fered to idols, and from blood, and from things strangled, and from fornication: from which if ye keep yourselves, ye shall do well. Fare ye well. 30 So when they were dismissed, they came to Antioch: and when they had gathered the multitude together, they delivered the epistle: 31 *Which* when they had read, they rejoiced for the consolation. 32And Judas and Silas, being prophets also themselves, exhorted the brethren with many words, and confirmed *them*. 33And after they had tarried *there* a space, they were let go in peace from the brethren unto the apostles. 34 Notwithstanding it pleased Silas to abide there still. 35 Paul also and Barnabas continued in Antioch, teaching and preaching the word of the Lord, with many others also.

36 And some days after, Paul said unto Barnabas, Let us go again and visit our brethren in every city where we have preached the word of the Lord, *and see* how they do. 37And Barnabas determined to take with them John, whose surname was Mark. 38 But Paul thought not good to take him with them, who departed from them from Pamphylia, and went not with them to the work. 39And the contention was so sharp between them, that they departed asunder one from the other: and so Barnabas took Mark, and sailed unto Cyprus; 40And Paul chose Silas, and departed, being recommended by the brethren unto the grace of God. 41And he went through Syria and Cilicia, confirming the churches.

R.S.V.

what has been sacrificed to idols and from blood and from what is strangled [n] and from unchastity. If you keep yourselves from these, you will do well. Farewell."

30 So when they were sent off, they went down to Antioch; and having gathered the congregation together, they delivered the letter. 31And when they read it, they rejoiced at the exhortation. 32And Judas and Silas, who were themselves prophets, exhorted the brethren with many words and strengthened them. 33And after they had spent some time, they were sent off in peace by the brethren to those who had sent them.[o] 35 But Paul and Barnabas remained in Antioch, teaching and preaching the word of the Lord, with many others also.

36 And after some days Paul said to Barnabas, "Come, let us return and visit the brethren in every city where we proclaimed the word of the Lord, and see how they are." 37And Barnabas wanted to take with them John called Mark. 38 But Paul thought best not to take with them one who had withdrawn from them in Pamphylia, and had not gone with them to the work. 39And there arose a sharp contention, so that they separated from each other; Barnabas took Mark with him and sailed away to Cyprus, 40 but Paul chose Silas and departed, being commended by the brethren to the grace of the Lord. 41And he went through Syria and Cilicia, strengthening the churches.

16 Then came he to Derbe and Lystra: and, behold, a certain disciple was there, named Timotheus, the son of a certain woman, which was a Jewess, and believed; but his father *was* a Greek: 2 Which was well reported of by the brethren that were at Lystra and Iconium. 3 Him would Paul have to go forth with him; and took and circumcised him because of the Jews which were in those quarters: for they knew all that his father was a Greek. 4And as they went through the cities, they delivered them the decrees for to keep, that were ordained of the apostles and elders which were at Jerusalem. 5And so were the churches established in the faith, and increased in number daily. 6 Now when they had gone throughout Phrygia and the

16 And he came also to Derbe and to Lystra. A disciple was there, named Timothy, the son of a Jewish woman who was a believer; but his father was a Greek. 2 He was well spoken of by the brethren at Lystra and Iconium. 3 Paul wanted Timothy to accompany him; and he took him and circumcised him because of the Jews that were in those places, for they all knew that his father was a Greek. 4As they went on their way through the cities, they delivered to them for observance the decisions which had been reached by the apostles and elders who were at Jerusalem. 5 So the churches were strengthened in the faith, and they increased in numbers daily.

6 And they went through the region of Phrygia and Galatia, having been forbidden by

[n] Other early authorities omit *and from what is strangled*. [o] Other ancient authorities insert verse 34, *But it seemed good to Silas to remain there.*

PHILLIPS

eating the meat of what has been strangled, and sexual immorality. Keep yourselves clear of these things and you will make good progress. Farewell."

The message is received   15. 30
with delight

So this party, sent off by the Church, went down to Antioch and after gathering the congregation together, handed over the letter to them. And they, when they read it, were delighted with the encouragement it gave them. Judas and Silas were themselves both inspired preachers and greatly encouraged and strengthened the brothers by many talks to them. Then, after spending some time there, the brothers sent them back in peace to those who had commissioned them. Paul and Barnabas however stayed on in Antioch teaching and preaching the gospel of the Word of the Lord in company with many others.

Paul and Barnabas flatly   15. 36
disagree but the work prospers

Some days later Paul spoke to Barnabas, "Now let us go back and visit the brothers in every city where we have proclaimed the Word of the Lord to see how they are."
Barnabas wanted to take John, surnamed Mark, as their companion. But Paul disapproved of taking with them a man who had deserted them in Pamphylia and was not prepared to go on with them in their work. There was a sharp clash of opinion, so much so that they went their separate ways, Barnabas taking Mark and sailing to Cyprus, while Paul chose Silas and set out on his journey, commended to the grace of the Lord by the brothers as he did so. He traveled through Syria and Cilicia and strengthened the churches.

Paul chooses Timothy as   16. 1
companion

He also went to Derbe and Lystra. At Lystra there was a disciple by the name of Timothy whose mother was a Jewish Christian, though his father was a Greek. Timothy was held in high regard by the brothers at Lystra and Iconium, and Paul wanted to take him on as his companion. Everybody knew that his father was a Greek, and Paul therefore had him circumcised because of the attitude of the Jews in these places. As they went on their way through the cities they passed on to them for their observance the decisions which had been reached by the apostles and elders in Jerusalem. Consequently the churches grew stronger and stronger in the faith and their numbers increased daily.

Paul and Silas find their journey   16. 6
divinely directed

They made their way through Phrygia and Galatia, but the Holy Spirit prevented them

N.E.B.

that has been strangled,[a] and from fornication.[b] If you keep yourselves free from these things you will be doing right. Farewell.'
So they were sent off on their journey and travelled down to Antioch, where they called the congregation together, and delivered the letter. When it was read, they all rejoiced at the encouragement it brought. Judas and Silas, who were prophets themselves, said much to encourage and strengthen the members, and, after spending some time there, were dismissed with the good wishes of the brethren, to return to those who had sent them.[c] But Paul and Barnabas stayed on at Antioch, and there, along with many others, they taught and preached the word of the Lord.

Paul Leads the Advance

After a while Paul said to Barnabas, 'Ought we not to go back now to see how our brothers are faring in the various towns where we proclaimed the word of the Lord?' Barnabas wanted to take John Mark with them; but Paul judged that the man who had deserted them in Pamphylia and had not gone on to share in their work was not the man to take with them now. The dispute was so sharp that they parted company. Barnabas took Mark with him and sailed for Cyprus, while Paul chose Silas. He started on his journey, commended by the brothers to the grace of the Lord, and travelled through Syria and Cilicia bringing new strength to the congregations.

16 He went on to Derbe and to Lystra, and there he found a disciple named Timothy, the son of a Jewish Christian mother and a Greek father. He was well spoken of by the Christians at Lystra and Iconium, and Paul wanted to have him in his company when he left the place. So he took him and circumcised him, out of consideration for the Jews who lived in those parts; for they all knew that his father was a Greek. As they made their way from town to town they handed on the decisions taken by the apostles and elders in Jerusalem and enjoined their observance. And so, day by day, the congregations grew stronger in faith and increased in numbers.
They travelled through the Phrygian and Galatian region,[d] because they were prevented by the

[a] Some witnesses omit from anything that has been strangled. [b] Some witnesses omit and from fornication; and some add and refrain from doing to others what you would not like done to yourselves. [c] Some witnesses add (34) But Silas decided to remain there. [d] Or through Phrygia and the Galatian region.

K.J.V.

region of Galatia, and were forbidden of the Holy Ghost to preach the word in Asia, 7After they were come to Mysia, they assayed to go into Bithynia: but the Spirit suffered them not. 8And they passing by Mysia came down to Troas. 9And a vision appeared to Paul in the night; There stood a man of Macedonia, and prayed him, saying, Come over into Macedonia, and help us. 10And after he had seen the vision, immediately we endeavoured to go into Macedonia, assuredly gathering that the Lord had called us for to preach the gospel unto them. 11 Therefore loosing from Troas, we came with a straight course to Samothracia, and the next *day* to Neapolis; 12And from thence to Philippi, which is the chief city of that part of Macedonia, *and* a colony: and we were in that city abiding certain days. 13And on the sabbath we went out of the city by a river side, where prayer was wont to be made; and we sat down, and spake unto the women which resorted *thither*.

14 And a certain woman named Lydia, a seller of purple, of the city of Thyatira, which worshipped God, heard *us:* whose heart the Lord opened, that she attended unto the things which were spoken of Paul. 15And when she was baptized, and her household, she besought *us,* saying, If ye have judged me to be faithful to the Lord, come into my house, and abide *there.* And she constrained us.

16 And it came to pass, as we went to prayer, a certain damsel possessed with a spirit of divination met us, which brought her masters much gain by soothsaying: 17 The same followed Paul and us, and cried, saying, These men are the servants of the most high God, which shew unto us the way of salvation. 18 And this did she many days. But Paul, being grieved, turned and said to the spirit, I command thee in the name of Jesus Christ to come out of her. And he came out the same hour.

19 And when her masters saw that the hope of their gains was gone, they caught Paul and Silas, and drew *them* into the marketplace unto the rulers, 20And brought them to the magistrates, saying, These men, being Jews, do exceedingly trouble our city, 21And teach customs, which are not lawful for us to receive, neither to observe, being Romans. 22And the multitude rose up together against them; and the magistrates rent off their clothes, and commanded to beat *them.* 23And when they had laid many stripes upon them, they cast *them* into prison, charging the jailer to keep them safely: 24 Who, having received such a charge, thrust them into the inner prison, and made their feet fast in the stocks.

R.S.V.

the Holy Spirit to speak the word in Asia. 7And when they had come opposite Mysia, they attempted to go into Bithynia, but the Spirit of Jesus did not allow them; 8 so, passing by Mysia, they went down to Troas. 9And a vision appeared to Paul in the night: a man of Macedonia was standing beseeching him and saying, "Come over to Macedonia and help us." 10And when he had seen the vision, immediately we sought to go on into Macedonia, concluding that God had called us to preach the gospel to them.

11 Setting sail therefore from Troas, we made a direct voyage to Samothrace, and the following day to Neapolis, 12 and from there to Philippi, which is the leading city of the district[a] of Macedonia, and a Roman colony. We remained in this city some days; 13 and on the sabbath day we went outside the gate to the riverside, where we supposed there was a place of prayer; and we sat down and spoke to the women who had come together. 14 One who heard us was a woman named Lydia, from the city of Thyatira, a seller of purple goods, who was a worshiper of God. The Lord opened her heart to give heed to what was said by Paul. 15And when she was baptized, with her household, she besought us, saying, "If you have judged me to be faithful to the Lord, come to my house and stay." And she prevailed upon us.

16 As we were going to the place of prayer, we were met by a slave girl who had a spirit of divination and brought her owners much gain by soothsaying. 17 She followed Paul and us, crying, "These men are servants of the Most High God, who proclaim to you the way of salvation." 18And this she did for many days. But Paul was annoyed, and turned and said to the spirit, "I charge you in the name of Jesus Christ to come out of her." And it came out that very hour.

19 But when her owners saw that their hope of gain was gone, they seized Paul and Silas and dragged them into the market place before the rulers; 20 and when they had brought them to the magistrates they said, "These men are Jews and they are disturbing our city. 21 They advocate customs which it is not lawful for us Romans to accept or practice." 22 The crowd joined in attacking them; and the magistrates tore the garments off them and gave orders to beat them with rods. 23 And when they had inflicted many blows upon them, they threw them into prison, charging the jailer to keep them safely. 24 Having received this charge, he put them into the inner prison and fastened their feet in the stocks.

[x] The Greek text is uncertain.

PHILLIPS

from speaking God's message in Asia. When they came to Mysia they tried to enter Bithynia, but again the Spirit of Jesus would not allow them. So they passed by Mysia and came down to Troas, where one night Paul had a vision of a Macedonian man standing and appealing to him in the words: "Come over to Macedonia and help us!" As soon as Paul had seen this vision we made every effort to get on to Macedonia, convinced that God had called us to give them the good news.

The gospel comes to Europe: 16. 11 a businesswoman is converted

So we set sail from Troas and ran a straight course to Samothrace, and on the following day to Neapolis. From there we went to Philippi, a Roman garrison town and the chief city in that part of Macedonia. We spent some days in Philippi and on the Sabbath day we went out of the city gate to the riverside, where we supposed there was a place for prayer. There we sat down and spoke to the women who had assembled. One of our hearers was a woman named Lydia. (She came from Thyatira and was a dealer in purple-dyed cloth.) She was already a believer in God, and he opened her heart to accept Paul's words. When she and her household had been baptized she appealed to us, saying,

"If you are satisfied that I am a true believer in the Lord, then come down to my house and stay there."

And she insisted on our doing so.

Conflict with evil spirits 16. 16 and evil men

One day while we were going to the place of prayer we were met by a young girl who had a spirit of clairvoyance and brought her owners a good deal of profit by foretelling the future. She would follow Paul and the rest of us, crying out, "These men are servants of the most high God, and they are telling you the way of salvation." She continued this behavior for many days, and then Paul, in a burst of irritation, turned round and spoke to the spirit in her,

"I command you in the name of Jesus Christ to come out of her!"

And it came out immediately. But when the girl's owners saw that their hope of making money out of her had disappeared, they seized Paul and Silas and dragged them before the authorities in the market square. There they brought them before the chief magistrates and said,

"These men are Jews and are causing a great disturbance in our city. They are proclaiming customs which it is illegal for us as Roman citizens to accept or practice."

At this the crowd joined in the attack, and the magistrates had them stripped and ordered them to be beaten with rods. Then, after giving them a severe beating, they threw them into prison, instructing the jailer to keep them safe. On receiving such strict orders, he hustled them into the inner jail and fastened their feet securely in the stocks.

N.E.B.

Holy Spirit from delivering the message in the province of Asia; and when they approached the Mysian border they tried to enter Bithynia; but the Spirit of Jesus would not allow them, so they skirted [a] Mysia and reached the coast at Troas. During the night a vision came to Paul: a Macedonian stood there appealing to him and saying, 'Come across to Macedonia and help us.' After he had seen this vision we at once set about getting a passage to Macedonia, concluding that God had called us to bring them the good news.

So we sailed from Troas and made a straight run to Samothrace, the next day to Neapolis, and from there to Philippi, a city of the first rank in that district of Macedonia, and a Roman colony. Here we stayed for some days, and on the Sabbath day we went outside the city gate by the river-side, where we thought there would be a place of prayer,[b] and sat down and talked to the women who had gathered there. One of them named Lydia, a dealer in purple fabric from the city of Thyatira, who was a worshipper of God, was listening, and the Lord opened her heart to respond to what Paul said. She was baptized, and her household with her, and then she said to us, 'If you have judged me to be a believer in the Lord, I beg you to come and stay in my house.' And she insisted on our going.

Once, when we were on our way to the place of prayer, we met a slave-girl who was possessed by an oracular spirit and brought large profits to her owners by telling fortunes. She followed Paul and the rest of us, shouting, 'These men are servants of the Supreme God, and are declaring to you a way of salvation.' She did this day after day, until Paul could bear it no longer. Rounding on the spirit he said, 'I command you in the name of Jesus Christ to come out of her', and it went out there and then.

When the girl's owners saw that their hope of gain had gone, they seized Paul and Silas and dragged them to the city authorities in the main square; and bringing them before the magistrates, they said, 'These men are causing a disturbance in our city; they are Jews; they are advocating customs which it is illegal for us Romans to adopt and follow.' The mob joined in the attack; and the magistrates tore off the prisoners' clothes and ordered them to be flogged. After giving them a severe beating they flung them into prison and ordered the jailer to keep them under close guard. In view of these orders, he put them in the inner prison and secured their feet in the stocks.

[a] *Possibly* traversed. [b] *Some witnesses read* where there was a recognized place of prayer.

K.J.V.

25 And at midnight Paul and Silas prayed, and sang praises unto God: and the prisoners heard them. 26And suddenly there was a great earthquake, so that the foundations of the prison were shaken: and immediately all the doors were opened, and every one's bands were loosed. 27And the keeper of the prison awaking out of his sleep, and seeing the prison doors open, he drew out his sword, and would have killed himself, supposing that the prisoners had been fled. 28 But Paul cried with a loud voice, saying, Do thyself no harm: for we are all here. 29 Then he called for a light, and sprang in, and came trembling, and fell down before Paul and Silas, 30And brought them out, and said, Sirs, what must I do to be saved? 31And they said, Believe on the Lord Jesus Christ, and thou shalt be saved, and thy house. 32And they spake unto him the word of the Lord, and to all that were in his house. 33And he took them the same hour of the night, and washed *their* stripes; and was baptized, he and all his, straightway. 34And when he had brought them into his house, he set meat before them, and rejoiced, believing in God with all his house. 35And when it was day, the magistrates sent serjeants, saying, Let those men go. 36And the keeper of the prison told this saying to Paul, The magistrates have sent to let you go: now therefore depart, and go in peace. 37 But Paul said unto them, They have beaten us openly uncondemned, being Romans, and have cast *us* into prison; and now do they thrust us out privily? nay verily; but let them come themselves and fetch us out. 38And the serjeants told these words unto the magistrates: and they feared, when they heard that they were Romans. 39And they came and besought them, and brought *them* out, and desired *them* to depart out of the city. 40And they went out of the prison, and entered into *the house of* Lydia: and when they had seen the brethren, they comforted them, and departed.

17 Now when they had passed through Amphipolis and Apollonia, they came to Thessalonica, where was a synagogue of the Jews: 2And Paul, as his manner was, went in unto them, and three sabbath days reasoned with them out of the Scriptures, 3 Opening and alleging, that Christ must needs have suffered, and

R.S.V.

25 But about midnight Paul and Silas were praying and singing hymns to God, and the prisoners were listening to them, 26 and suddenly there was a great earthquake, so that the foundations of the prison were shaken; and immediately all the doors were opened and every one's fetters were unfastened. 27 When the jailer woke and saw that the prison doors were open, he drew his sword and was about to kill himself, supposing that the prisoners had escaped. 28 But Paul cried with a loud voice, "Do not harm yourself, for we are all here." 29And he called for lights and rushed in, and, trembling with fear he fell down before Paul and Silas, 30 and brought them out and said, "Men, what must I do to be saved?" 31And they said, "Believe in the Lord Jesus, and you will be saved, you and your household." 32And they spoke the word of the Lord to him and to all that were in his house. 33And he took them the same hour of the night, and washed their wounds, and he was baptized at once, with all his family. 34 Then he brought them up into his house, and set food before them; and he rejoiced with all his household that he had believed in God.

35 But when it was day, the magistrates sent the police, saying, "Let those men go." 36And the jailer reported the words to Paul, saying, "The magistrates have sent to let you go; now therefore come out and go in peace." 37 But Paul said to them, "They have beaten us publicly, uncondemned, men who are Roman citizens, and have thrown us into prison; and do they now cast us out secretly? No! let them come themselves and take us out." 38 The police reported these words to the magistrates, and they were afraid when they heard that they were Roman citizens; 39 so they came and apologized to them. And they took them out and asked them to leave the city. 40 So they went out of the prison, and visited Lydia; and when they had seen the brethren, they exhorted them and departed.

17 Now when they had passed through Amphipolis and Apollonia, they came to Thessalonica, where there was a synagogue of the Jews. 2And Paul went in, as was his custom, and for three weeks[p] he argued with them from the scriptures, 3 explaining and proving that it was necessary for the Christ to suffer and to rise

[p] Or *sabbaths*.

402

PHILLIPS

The midnight deliverance: 16. 25
the jailer becomes a Christian

But about midnight Paul and Silas were praying and singing hymns to God while the other
prisoners were listening to them. Suddenly there
was a great earthquake, big enough to shake the
foundations of the prison. Immediately all the
doors flew open and everyone's chains were unfastened. When the jailer woke and saw that the
doors of the prison had been opened he drew
his sword and was on the point of killing himself, for he imagined that all the prisoners had
escaped. But Paul called out to him at the top
of his voice,
"Don't hurt yourself—we are all here!"
Then the jailer called for lights, rushed in, and
trembling all over, fell at the feet of Paul and
Silas. He led them outside, and said,
"Sirs, what must I do to be saved?"
And they replied,
"Believe in the Lord Jesus and then you will
be saved, you and your household."
Then they told him and all the members of
his household the message of God. There and
then in the middle of the night he took them
aside and washed their wounds, and he himself
and all his family were baptized without delay.
Then he took them into his house and offered
them food, he and his whole household overjoyed at finding faith in God.

Paul, in a strong position,   16. 35
makes the authorities apologize

When morning came, the magistrates sent
their constables with the message, "Let those
men go." The jailer reported this message to
Paul, saying,
"The magistrates have sent to have you released. So now you can leave this place and go
on your way in peace."
But Paul said to the constables,
"They beat us publicly without any kind of
trial; they threw us into prison despite the fact
that we are Roman citizens. And now do they
want to get rid of us in this underhand way? Oh
no, let them come and take us out themselves!"
The constables reported this to the magistrates, who were thoroughly alarmed when they
heard that they were Romans. So they came in
person and apologized to them, and after taking
them outside the prison, requested them to leave
the city. But on leaving the prison Paul and
Silas went to Lydia's house, and when they had
seen the brothers and given them fresh courage,
they took their leave.

Bitter opposition at   17. 1
Thessalonica—

Next they journeyed through Amphipolis and
Apollonia and arrived at Thessalonica. Here
there was a synagogue of the Jews which Paul
entered, following his usual custom. On three
Sabbath days he argued with them from the
scriptures, explaining and quoting passages to
prove the necessity for the death of Christ and
his rising again from the dead. "This Jesus whom

N.E.B.

About midnight Paul and Silas, at their prayers, were singing praises to God, and the other
prisoners were listening, when suddenly there
was such a violent earthquake that the foundations of the jail were shaken; all the doors burst
open and all the prisoners found their fetters
unfastened. The jailer woke up to see the prison
doors wide open, and assuming that the prisoners had escaped, drew his sword intending to
kill himself. But Paul shouted, 'Do yourself no
harm; we are all here.' The jailer called for
lights, rushed in and threw himself down before
Paul and Silas, trembling with fear. He then
escorted them out and said, 'Masters, what must
I do to be saved?' They said, 'Put your trust in
the Lord Jesus, and you will be saved, you and
your household.' Then they spoke the word of
the Lord*a* to him and to everyone in his house.
At that late hour of the night he took them and
washed their wounds; and immediately afterwards he and his whole family were baptized.
He brought them into his house, set out a meal,
and rejoiced with his whole household in his
new-found faith in God.
When daylight came the magistrates sent their
officers with instructions to release the men. The
jailer reported the message to Paul: 'The magistrates have sent word that you are to be released.
So now you may go free, and blessings on your
journey.'*b* But Paul said to the officers: 'They
gave us a public flogging, though we are Roman
citizens and have not been found guilty; they
threw us into prison, and are they now to
smuggle us out privately? No indeed! Let them
come in person and escort us out.' The officers
reported his words. The magistrates were
alarmed to hear that they were Roman citizens,
and came and apologized to them. Then they
escorted them out and requested them to go
away from the city. On leaving the prison, they
went to Lydia's house, where they met their
fellow-Christians, and spoke words of encouragement to them; then they departed.

17 They now travelled by way of Amphipolis and Apollonia and came to Thessalonica, where there was a Jewish synagogue.
Following his usual practice Paul went to their
meetings; and for the next three Sabbaths he
argued with them, quoting texts of Scripture
which he expounded and applied to show that
the Messiah had to suffer and rise from the

[a] *Some witnesses read* of God. [b] *Some witnesses*
read . . . *free and take your journey.*

risen again from the dead; and that this Jesus, whom I preach unto you, is Christ. 4And some of them believed, and consorted with Paul and Silas; and of the devout Greeks a great multitude, and of the chief women not a few.

5 But the Jews which believed not, moved with envy, took unto them certain lewd fellows of the baser sort, and gathered a company, and set all the city on an uproar, and assaulted the house of Jason, and sought to bring them out to the people. 6And when they found them not, they drew Jason and certain brethren unto the rulers of the city, crying, These that have turned the world upside down are come hither also; 7 Whom Jason hath received: and these all do contrary to the decrees of Cesar, saying that there is another king, *one* Jesus. 8And they troubled the people and the rulers of the city, when they heard these things. 9And when they had taken security of Jason, and of the others, they let them go.

10 And the brethren immediately sent away Paul and Silas by night unto Berea: who coming *thither* went into the synagogue of the Jews. 11 These were more noble than those in Thessalonica, in that they received the word with all readiness of mind, and searched the Scriptures daily, whether those things were so. 12 Therefore many of them believed; also of honourable women which were Greeks, and of men, not a few. 13 But when the Jews of Thessalonica had knowledge that the word of God was preached of Paul at Berea, they came thither also, and stirred up the people. 14And then immediately the brethren sent away Paul to go as it were to the sea: but Silas and Timotheus abode there still. 15And they that conducted Paul brought him unto Athens: and receiving a commandment unto Silas and Timotheus for to come to him with all speed, they departed.

16 Now while Paul waited for them at Athens, his spirit was stirred in him, when he saw the city wholly given to idolatry. 17 Therefore disputed he in the synagogue with the Jews, and with the devout persons, and in the market daily with them that met with him. 18 Then certain philosophers of the Epicureans, and of the Stoics, encountered him. And some said, What will this babbler say? other some, He seemeth to be a setter forth of strange gods: because he preached unto them Jesus, and the resurrection. 19And they took him, and brought him unto Areopagus, saying, May we know what this new doctrine, whereof thou speakest, *is?* 20 For thou bringest certain strange things to our ears: we

from the dead, and saying, "This Jesus, whom I proclaim to you, is the Christ." 4And some of them were persuaded, and joined Paul and Silas; as did a great many of the devout Greeks and not a few of the leading women. 5 But the Jews were jealous, and taking some wicked fellows of the rabble, they gathered a crowd, set the city in an uproar, and attacked the house of Jason, seeking to bring them out to the people. 6And when they could not find them, they dragged Jason and some of the brethren before the city authorities, crying, "These men who have turned the world upside down have come here also, 7 and Jason has received them; and they are all acting against the decrees of Caesar, saying that there is another king, Jesus." 8And the people and the city authorities were disturbed when they heard this. 9And when they had taken security from Jason and the rest, they let them go.

10 The brethren immediately sent Paul and Silas away by night to Beroea; and when they arrived they went into the Jewish synagogue. 11 Now these Jews were more noble than those in Thessalonica, for they received the word with all eagerness, examining the scriptures daily to see if these things were so. 12 Many of them therefore believed, with not a few Greek women of high standing as well as men. 13 But when the Jews of Thessalonica learned that the word of God was proclaimed by Paul at Beroea also, they came there too, stirring up and inciting the crowds. 14 Then the brethren immediately sent Paul off on his way to the sea, but Silas and Timothy remained there. 15 Those who conducted Paul brought him as far as Athens; and receiving a command for Silas and Timothy to come to him as soon as possible, they departed.

16 Now while Paul was waiting for them at Athens, his spirit was provoked within him as he saw that the city was full of idols. 17 So he argued in the synagogue with the Jews and the devout persons, and in the market place every day with those who chanced to be there. 18 Some also of the Epicurean and Stoic philosophers met him. And some said, "What would this babbler say?" Others said, "He seems to be a preacher of foreign divinities"—because he preached Jesus and the resurrection. 19And they took hold of him and brought him to the Areopagus, saying, "May we know what this new teaching is which you present? 20 For you bring some strange things to our ears; we wish to

I am proclaiming to you," he concluded, "is God's Christ!" Some of them were convinced and threw in their lot with Paul and Silas, and they were joined by a great many believing Greeks and a considerable number of influential women. But the Jews, in a fury of jealousy, got hold of some of the unprincipled loungers of the market place, gathered a crowd together and set the city in an uproar. Then they attacked Jason's house in an attempt to bring Paul and Silas out before the people. When they could not find them they hustled Jason and some of the brothers before the civic authorities, shouting, "These are the men who have turned the world upside down and have now come here, and Jason has taken them into his house. What is more, all these men act against the decrees of Caesar, saying that there is another king called Jesus!" By these words the Jews succeeded in alarming both the people and the authorities, and they only released Jason and the others after binding them over to keep the peace.

—followed by encouragement 17. 10 at Beroea

Without delay the brothers dispatched Paul and Silas off to Beroea that night. On their arrival there they went to the Jewish synagogue. The Jews proved more generous-minded than those in Thessalonica, for they accepted the message most eagerly and studied the scriptures every day to see if what they were now being told were true. Many of them became believers, as did a number of Greek women of social standing and quite a number of men. But when the Jews at Thessalonica found out that God's message had been proclaimed by Paul at Beroea as well, they came there too to cause trouble and spread alarm among the people. The brothers at Beroea then sent Paul off at once to make his way to the seacoast, but Silas and Timothy remained there. The men who accompanied Paul took him as far as Athens and returned with instructions for Silas and Timothy to rejoin Paul as soon as possible.

Paul is irritated by the idols 17. 16 of Athens

Paul had some days to wait at Athens for Silas and Timothy to arrive, and while he was there his soul was exasperated beyond endurance at the sight of a city so completely idolatrous. He felt compelled to discuss the matter with the Jews in the synagogue as well as with God-fearing gentiles, and he even argued daily in the open market place with the passers-by. While he was speaking there some Epicurean and Stoic philosophers came across him, and some of them remarked,

"What is this cock sparrow trying to say?"

Others said,

"He seems to be trying to proclaim some more gods to us, and outlandish ones at that!"

For Paul was actually proclaiming "Jesus" and "the resurrection." So they got hold of him and conducted him to their council, the Areopagus. There they asked him,

"May we know what this new teaching of yours really is? You talk of matters which sound strange to our ears, and we should like to know

dead. 'And this Jesus,' he said, 'whom I am proclaiming to you, is the Messiah.' Some of them were convinced and joined Paul and Silas; so did a great number of godfearing Greeks and a good many influential women.[a]

But the Jews in their jealousy recruited some low fellows from the dregs of the populace, roused the rabble, and had the city in an uproar. They mobbed Jason's house, with the intention of bringing Paul and Silas before the town assembly. Failing to find them, they dragged Jason himself and some members of the congregation before the magistrates, shouting, 'The men who have made trouble all over the world have now come here; and Jason has harboured them. They all flout the Emperor's laws, and assert that there is a rival king, Jesus.' These words caused a great commotion in the mob, which affected the magistrates also. They bound over Jason and the others, and let them go.

As soon as darkness fell, the members of the congregation sent Paul and Silas off to Beroea. On arrival, they made their way to the synagogue. The Jews here were more liberal-minded than those at Thessalonica: they received the message with great eagerness, studying the scriptures every day to see whether it was as they said. Many of them therefore became believers, and so did a fair number of Greeks, women of standing as well as men. But when the Thessalonian Jews learned that the word of God had now been proclaimed by Paul in Beroea, they came on there to stir up trouble and rouse the rabble. Thereupon the members of the congregation sent Paul off at once to go down to the coast, while Silas and Timothy both stayed behind. Paul's escort brought him as far as Athens, and came away with instructions for Silas and Timothy to rejoin him with all speed.

Now while Paul was waiting for them at Athens he was exasperated to see how the city was full of idols. So he argued in the synagogue with the Jews and gentile worshippers, and also in the city square every day with casual passers-by. And some of the Epicurean and Stoic philosophers joined issue with him. Some said, 'What can this charlatan be trying to say?'; others, 'He would appear to be a propagandist for foreign deities'—this because he was preaching about Jesus and Resurrection. So they took him and brought him before the Court of Areopagus[b] and said, 'May we know what this new doctrine is that you propound? You are introducing ideas that sound strange to us, and we

---

[a] *Some witnesses read* a good many wives of leading men. [b] *Or* brought him to Mars' Hill.

K.J.V.

would know therefore what these things mean.
21 (For all the Athenians, and strangers which
were there, spent their time in nothing else, but
either to tell or to hear some new thing.)
22 Then Paul stood in the midst of Mars' hill,
and said, *Ye* men of Athens, I perceive that in
all things ye are too superstitious. 23 For as I
passed by, and beheld your devotions, I found
an altar with this inscription, TO THE UN-
KNOWN GOD. Whom therefore ye ignorantly
worship, him declare I unto you. 24 God that
made the world and all things therein, seeing
that he is Lord of heaven and earth, dwelleth
not in temples made with hands; 25 Neither is
worshipped with men's hands, as though he
needed any thing, seeing he giveth to all life,
and breath, and all things; 26And hath made of
one blood all nations of men for to dwell on all
the face of the earth, and hath determined the
times before appointed, and the bounds of their
habitation; 27 That they should seek the Lord,
if haply they might feel after him, and find him,
though he be not far from every one of us:
28 For in him we live, and move, and have our
being; as certain also of your own poets have
said, For we are also his offspring. 29 Forasmuch then as we are the offspring of God, we
ought not to think that the Godhead is like unto
gold, or silver, or stone, graven by art and man's
device. 30And the times of this ignorance God
winked at; but now commandeth all men every
where to repent: 31 Because he hath appointed
a day, in the which he will judge the world in
righteousness by *that* man whom he hath ordained; *whereof* he hath given assurance unto
all *men,* in that he hath raised him from the
dead.
32 And when they heard of the resurrection
of the dead, some mocked: and others said, We
will hear thee again of this *matter.* 33 So Paul
departed from among them. 34 Howbeit certain
men clave unto him, and believed: among the
which *was* Dionysius the Areopagite, and a
woman named Damaris, and others with them.

18 After these things Paul departed from
Athens, and came to Corinth; 2And found
a certain Jew named Aquila, born in Pontus,
lately come from Italy, with his wife Priscilla,
(because that Claudius had commanded all Jews
to depart from Rome,) and came unto them.
3And because he was of the same craft, he abode
with them, and wrought: (for by their occupation they were tentmakers.) 4And he reasoned
in the synagogue every sabbath, and persuaded
the Jews and the Greeks. 5And when Silas and

R.S.V.

know therefore what these things mean." 21 Now
all the Athenians and the foreigners who lived
there spent their time in nothing except telling
or hearing something new.
22 So Paul, standing in the middle of the
Areopagus, said: "Men of Athens, I perceive
that in every way you are very religious. 23 For
as I passed along and observed the objects of
your worship, I found also an altar with this
inscription, 'To an unknown god.' What therefore you worship as unknown, this I proclaim
to you. 24 The God who made the world and
everything in it, being Lord of heaven and earth,
does not live in shrines made by man, 25 nor is
he served by human hands, as though he needed
anything, since he himself gives to all men life
and breath and everything. 26And he made from
one every nation of men to live on all the face
of the earth, having determined allotted periods
and the boundaries of their habitation, 27 that
they should seek God, in the hope that they
might feel after him and find him. Yet he is not
far from each one of us, 28 for
'In him we live and move and have our
being';
as even some of your poets have said,
'For we are indeed his offspring.'
29 Being then God's offspring, we ought not to
think that the Deity is like gold, or silver, or
stone, a representation by the art and imagination of man. 30 The times of ignorance God
overlooked, but now he commands all men
everywhere to repent, 31 because he has fixed a
day on which he will judge the world in righteousness by a man whom he has appointed, and
of this he has given assurance to all men by
raising him from the dead."
32 Now when they heard of the resurrection
of the dead, some mocked; but others said,
"We will hear you again about this." 33 So Paul
went out from among them. 34 But some men
joined him and believed, among them Dionysius the Areopagite and a woman named Damaris and others with them.

18 After this he left Athens and went to
Corinth. 2And he found a Jew named
Aquila, a native of Pontus, lately come from
Italy with his wife Priscilla, because Claudius
had commanded all the Jews to leave Rome. And
he went to see them; 3 and because he was of the
same trade he stayed with them, and they
worked, for by trade they were tentmakers.
4And he argued in the synagogue every sabbath,
and persuaded Jews and Greeks.
5 When Silas and Timothy arrived from

what they mean." (For all the Athenians, and even foreign visitors to Athens, had an obsession for any novelty and would spend their whole time talking about or listening to anything new.)

Paul's speech to the "gentlemen   17. 22 of Athens"

So Paul got to his feet in the middle of their council, and began,

"Gentlemen of Athens, my own eyes tell me that you are in all respects an extremely religious people. For as I made my way here and looked at your shrines I particularly noticed one altar on which were inscribed the words, TO GOD THE UNKNOWN. It is this God whom you are worshiping in ignorance that I am here to proclaim to you! God who made the world and all that is in it, being Lord of both Heaven and earth, does not live in temples made by human hands, nor is he ministered to by human hands, as though he had need of anything—seeing that he is the one who gives to all men life and breath and everything else. From one forefather he has created every race of men to live over the face of the whole earth. He has determined the times of their existence and the limits of their habitation, so that they might search for God, in the hope that they might feel for him and find him— yes, even though he is not far from any one of us. Indeed, it is in him that we live and move and have our being. Some of your own poets have endorsed this in the words, 'For we are indeed his children.' If then we are the children of God, we ought not to imagine God in terms of gold or silver or stone, contrived by human art or imagination. Now while it is true that God has overlooked the days of ignorance he now commands all men everywhere to repent. For he has fixed a day on which he will judge the whole world in justice by the standard of a man whom he has appointed. That this is so he has guaranteed to all men by raising this man from the dead."

But when his audience heard Paul talk about the resurrection from the dead some of them laughed outright, but others said,

"We should like to hear you speak again on this subject."

So with this mixed reception Paul retired from their assembly. Yet some did in fact join him and accept the faith, including Dionysius a member of the Areopagus, a woman by the name of Damaris, and some others as well.

At Corinth Paul is yet again   18. 1 rejected by the Jews

Before long Paul left Athens and went on to Corinth where he found a Jew called Aquila, a native of Pontus. This man had recently come from Italy with his wife Priscilla, because Claudius had issued a decree that all Jews should leave Rome. He went to see them in their house and because they practiced the same trade as himself he stayed with them. They all worked together, for their trade was tent-making. Every Sabbath Paul used to speak in the synagogue trying to persuade both Jews and Greeks. By the time Silas and Timothy arrived from

should like to know what they mean.' (Now the Athenians in general and the foreigners there had no time for anything but talking or hearing about the latest novelty.)

Then Paul stood up before the Court of Areopagus[a] and said: 'Men of Athens, I see that in everything that concerns religion you are uncommonly scrupulous. For as I was going round looking at the objects of your worship, I noticed among other things an altar bearing the inscription "To an Unknown God". What you worship but do not know—this is what I now proclaim.

'The God who created the world and everything in it, and who is Lord of heaven and earth, does not live in shrines made by men. It is not because he lacks anything that he accepts service at men's hands, for he is himself the universal giver of life and breath and all else. He created every race of men of one stock, to inhabit the whole earth's surface. He fixed the epochs of their history[b] and the limits of their territory. They were to seek God, and, it might be, touch and find him; though indeed he is not far from each one of us, for in him we live and move, in him we exist; as some of your own poets[c] have said, "We are also his offspring." As God's offspring, then, we ought not to suppose that the deity is like an image in gold or silver or stone, shaped by human craftsmanship and design. As for the times of ignorance, God has overlooked them; but now he commands mankind, all men everywhere, to repent, because he has fixed the day on which he will have the world judged, and justly judged, by a man of his choosing; of this he has given assurance to all by raising him from the dead.'

When they heard about the raising of the dead, some scoffed; and others said, 'We will hear you on this subject some other time.' And so Paul left the assembly. However, some men joined him and became believers, including Dionysius, a member of the Court of Areopagus; also a woman named Damaris, and others besides.

18 After this he left Athens and went to Corinth. There he fell in with a Jew named Aquila, a native of Pontus, and his wife Priscilla; he had recently arrived from Italy because Claudius had issued an edict that all Jews should leave Rome. Paul approached them and, because he was of the same trade, he made his home with them, and they carried on business together; they were tent-makers. He also held discussions in the synagogue Sabbath by Sabbath, trying to convince both Jews and pagans.

Then Silas and Timothy came down from

[a] Or in the middle of Mars' Hill. [b] Or fixed the ordered seasons . . . [c] Some witnesses read some among you.

K.J.V.

Timotheus were come from Macedonia, Paul was pressed in the spirit, and testified to the Jews *that* Jesus *was* Christ. 6And when they opposed themselves, and blasphemed, he shook *his* raiment, and said unto them, Your blood *be* upon your own heads; I *am* clean: from henceforth I will go unto the Gentiles.

7 And he departed thence, and entered into a certain *man's* house, named Justus, *one* that worshipped God, whose house joined hard to the synagogue. 8And Crispus, the chief ruler of the synagogue, believed on the Lord with all his house; and many of the Corinthians hearing believed, and were baptized. 9 Then spake the Lord to Paul in the night by a vision, Be not afraid, but speak, and hold not thy peace: 10 For I am with thee, and no man shall set on thee to hurt thee: for I have much people in this city. 11And he continued *there* a year and six months, teaching the word of God among them.

12 And when Gallio was the deputy of Achaia, the Jews made insurrection with one accord against Paul, and brought him to the judgment seat, 13 Saying, This *fellow* persuadeth men to worship God contrary to the law. 14And when Paul was now about to open *his* mouth, Gallio said unto the Jews, If it were a matter of wrong or wicked lewdness, O *ye* Jews, reason would that I should bear with you: 15 But if it be a question of words and names, and *of* your law, look ye *to it;* for I will be no judge of such *matters.* 16And he drave them from the judgment seat. 17 Then all the Greeks took Sosthenes, the chief ruler of the synagogue, and beat *him* before the judgment seat. And Gallio cared for none of those things.

18 And Paul *after this* tarried *there* yet a good while, and then took his leave of the brethren, and sailed thence into Syria, and with him Priscilla and Aquila; having shorn *his* head in Cenchrea: for he had a vow. 19And he came to Ephesus, and left them there: but he himself entered into the synagogue, and reasoned with the Jews. 20 When they desired *him* to tarry longer time with them, he consented not; 21 But bade them farewell, saying, I must by all means keep this feast that cometh in Jerusalem: but I will return again unto you, if God will. And he sailed from Ephesus. 22And when he had landed at Cesarea, and gone up, and saluted the church, he went down to Antioch. 23And after he had spent some time *there,* he departed, and went over *all* the country of Galatia and Phrygia in order, strengthening all the disciples.

R.S.V.

Macedonia, Paul was occupied with preaching, testifying to the Jews that the Christ was Jesus. 6And when they opposed and reviled him, he shook out his garments and said to them, "Your blood be upon your heads! I am innocent. From now on I will go to the Gentiles." 7And he left there and went to the house of a man named Titius[q] Justus, a worshiper of God; his house was next door to the synagogue. 8 Crispus, the ruler of the synagogue, believed in the Lord, together with all his household; and many of the Corinthians hearing Paul believed and were baptized. 9And the Lord said to Paul one night in a vision, "Do not be afraid, but speak and do not be silent; 10 for I am with you, and no man shall attack you to harm you; for I have many people in this city." 11And he stayed a year and six months, teaching the word of God among them.

12 But when Gallio was proconsul of Achaia, the Jews made a united attack upon Paul and brought him before the tribunal, 13 saying, "This man is persuading men to worship God contrary to the law." 14 But when Paul was about to open his mouth, Gallio said to the Jews, "If it were a matter of wrongdoing or vicious crime, I should have reason to bear with you, O Jews; 15 but since it is a matter of questions about words and names and your own law, see to it yourselves; I refuse to be a judge of these things." 16And he drove them from the tribunal. 17And they all seized Sosthenes, the ruler of the synagogue, and beat him in front of the tribunal. But Gallio paid no attention to this.

18 After this Paul stayed many days longer, and then took leave of the brethren and sailed for Syria, and with him Priscilla and Aquila. At Cenchreae he cut his hair, for he had a vow. 19And they came to Ephesus, and he left them there; but he himself went into the synagogue and argued with the Jews. 20 When they asked him to stay for a longer period, he declined; 21 but on taking leave of them he said, "I will return to you if God wills," and he set sail from Ephesus.

22 When he had landed at Caesarea, he went up and greeted the church, and then went down to Antioch. 23After spending some time there he departed and went from place to place through the region of Galatia and Phrygia, strengthening all the disciples.

---

[q] Other early authorities read *Titus*.

Macedonia Paul was completely absorbed in preaching the message, showing the Jews as clearly as he could that Jesus is Christ. However, when they turned against him and abused him he shook his garments at them, and said,

"Your blood be on your own heads! From now on I go with a perfectly clear conscience to the gentiles."

Then he left them and went to the house of a man called Titius Justus, a man who reverenced God and whose house was next door to the synagogue. Crispus, the leader of the synagogue, became a believer in the Lord, with all his household, and many of the Corinthians who heard the message believed and were baptized. Then one night the Lord spoke to Paul in a vision,

"Do not be afraid, but go on speaking and let no one silence you, for I myself am with you and no man shall lift a finger to harm you. There are many in this city who belong to me."

So Paul settled down there for eighteen months and taught them God's message.

Paul's enemies fail to impress the governor   18. 12

Then, while Gallio was governor of Achaia, the Jews banded together to attack Paul, and took him to court, saying,

"This man is perverting men's minds to make them worship God in a way that is contrary to the Law."

Paul was all ready to speak, but before he could utter a word Gallio said to the Jews,

"Listen, Jews! If this were a matter of some crime or wrongdoing I might reasonably be expected to put up with you. But since it is a question which concerns a word and names and your own Law, you must attend to it yourselves. I flatly refuse to be judge in these matters."

And he had them ejected from the court. Then they got hold of Sosthenes, the synagogue leader, and beat him in front of the courthouse. But Gallio remained completely unmoved.

Paul returns, and reports to Jerusalem and Antioch   18. 18

Paul stayed for some time after this incident and then took leave of the brothers and sailed for Syria, taking Priscilla and Aquila with him. At Cenchrea he had his hair cut short, for he had taken a solemn vow. They all arrived at Ephesus and there Paul left Aquila and Priscilla, but he himself went into the synagogue and debated with the Jews. When they asked him to stay longer he refused, bidding them farewell with the words, "If it is God's will I will come back to you again." Then he set sail from Ephesus and went down to Caesarea. Here he disembarked and after paying his respects to the church in Jerusalem, he went down to Antioch. He spent some time there before he left and proceeded to visit systematically throughout Galatia and Phrygia, putting new heart into all the disciples as he went.

Macedonia, and Paul devoted himself entirely to preaching, affirming before the Jews that the Messiah was Jesus. But when they opposed him and resorted to abuse, he shook out the skirts of his cloak and said to them, 'Your blood be on your own heads! My conscience is clear; now I shall go to the Gentiles.' With that he left, and went to the house of a worshipper of God named Titius Justus, who lived next door to the synagogue. Crispus, who held office in the synagogue, now became a believer in the Lord, with all his household; and a number of Corinthians listened and believed, and were baptized. One night in a vision the Lord said to Paul, 'Have no fear: go on with your preaching and do not be silenced, for I am with you and no one shall attempt to do you harm;[a] and there are many in this city who are my people.' So he settled down for eighteen months, teaching the word of God among them.

But when Gallio was proconsul of Achaia, the Jews set upon Paul in a body and brought him into court. 'This man', they said, 'is inducing people to worship God in ways that are against the law.' Paul was just about to speak when Gallio said to them, 'If it had been a question of crime or grave misdemeanour, I should, of course, have given you Jews a patient hearing, but if it is some bickering about words and names and your Jewish law, you may see to it yourselves; I have no mind to be a judge of these matters.' And he had them ejected from the court. Then there was a general attack on Sosthenes, who held office in the synagogue, and they gave him a beating in full view of the bench. But all this left Gallio quite unconcerned.

Paul stayed on for some time, and then took leave of the brotherhood and set sail for Syria, accompanied by Priscilla and Aquila. At Cenchreae he had his hair cut off, because he was under a vow. When they reached Ephesus he parted from them and went himself into the synagogue, where he held a discussion with the Jews. He was asked to stay longer, but declined and set out from Ephesus, saying, as he took leave of them, 'I shall come back to you if it is God's will.' On landing at Caesarea, he went up and paid his respects to the church, and then went down to Antioch. After spending some time there, he set out again and made a journey through the Galatian country and on through Phrygia, bringing new strength to all the converts.

[a] Or and you will not be harmed by anyone's attacks.

| K.J.V. | R.S.V. |

24 And a certain Jew named Apollos, born at Alexandria, an eloquent man, *and* mighty in the Scriptures, came to Ephesus. 25 This man was instructed in the way of the Lord; and being fervent in the spirit, he spake and taught diligently the things of the Lord, knowing only the baptism of John. 26And he began to speak boldly in the synagogue: whom when Aquila and Priscilla had heard, they took him unto *them,* and expounded unto him the way of God more perfectly. 27And when he was disposed to pass into Achaia, the brethren wrote, exhorting the disciples to receive him: who, when he was come, helped them much which had believed through grace: 28 For he mightily convinced the Jews, *and that* publicly, shewing by the Scriptures that Jesus was Christ.

24 Now a Jew named Apollos, a native of Alexandria, came to Ephesus. He was an eloquent man, well versed in the scriptures. 25 He had been instructed in the way of the Lord; and being fervent in spirit, he spoke and taught accurately the things concerning Jesus, though he knew only the baptism of John. 26 He began to speak boldly in the synagogue; but when Priscilla and Aquila heard him, they took him and expounded to him the way of God more accurately. 27And when he wished to cross to Achaia, the brethren encouraged him, and wrote to the disciples to receive him. When he arrived, he greatly helped those who through grace had believed, 28 for he powerfully confuted the Jews in public, showing by the scriptures that the Christ was Jesus.

19 And it came to pass, that, while Apollos was at Corinth, Paul having passed through the upper coasts came to Ephesus: and finding certain disciples, 2 He said unto them, Have ye received the Holy Ghost since ye believed? And they said unto him, We have not so much as heard whether there be any Holy Ghost. 3And he said unto them, Unto what then were ye baptized? And they said, Unto John's baptism. 4 Then said Paul, John verily baptized with the baptism of repentance, saying unto the people, that they should believe on him which should come after him, that is, on Christ Jesus. 5 When they heard *this,* they were baptized in the name of the Lord Jesus. 6And when Paul had laid *his* hands upon them, the Holy Ghost came on them; and they spake with tongues, and prophesied. 7And all the men were about twelve. 8And he went into the synagogue, and spake boldly for the space of three months, disputing and persuading the things concerning the kingdom of God. 9 But when divers were hardened, and believed not, but spake evil of that way before the multitude, he departed from them, and separated the disciples, disputing daily in the school of one Tyrannus. 10And this continued by the space of two years; so that all they which dwelt in Asia heard the word of the Lord Jesus, both Jews and Greeks. 11And God wrought special miracles by the hands of Paul: 12 So that from his body were brought unto the sick handkerchiefs or aprons, and the diseases departed from them, and the evil spirits went out of them.

19 While Apollos was at Corinth, Paul passed through the upper country and came to Ephesus. There he found some disciples. 2And he said to them, "Did you receive the Holy Spirit when you believed?" And they said, "No, we have never even heard that there is a Holy Spirit." 3And he said, "Into what then were you baptized?" They said, "Into John's baptism." 4And Paul said, "John baptized with the baptism of repentance, telling the people to believe in the one who was to come after him, that is, Jesus." 5 On hearing this, they were baptized in the name of the Lord Jesus. 6And when Paul had laid his hands upon them, the Holy Spirit came on them; and they spoke with tongues and prophesied. 7 There were about twelve of them in all.

8 And he entered the synagogue and for three months spoke boldly, arguing and pleading about the kingdom of God; 9 but when some were stubborn and disbelieved, speaking evil of the Way before the congregation, he withdrew from them, taking the disciples with him, and argued daily in the hall of Tyrannus.[r] 10 This continued for two years, so that all the residents of Asia heard the word of the Lord, both Jews and Greeks.

11 And God did extraordinary miracles by the hands of Paul, 12 so that handkerchiefs or aprons were carried away from his body to the sick, and diseases left them and the evil spirits

[r] Other ancient authorities add *from the fifth hour to the tenth.*

410

PHILLIPS

Apollos speaks powerfully at   *18. 24*
Ephesus and Corinth

Now a Jew called Apollos, a native of Alexandria and a gifted speaker, well versed in the scriptures, arrived at Ephesus. He had been instructed in the way of the Lord, and he spoke with burning zeal, teaching the facts about Jesus faithfully even though he knew only the baptism of John. This man began to speak with great boldness in the synagogue. But when Priscilla and Aquila heard him they took him aside and explained the way of God to him more accurately. Then as he wanted to cross into Achaia, the brothers gave him every encouragement and wrote a letter to the disciples there, asking them to make him welcome. On his arrival he proved a source of great strength to those who had believed through grace, for by his powerful arguments he publicly refuted the Jews, quoting from the scriptures to prove that Jesus is Christ.

Ephesus has its own Pentecost   *19. 1*

While Apollos was in Corinth Paul journeyed through the upper parts of the country and arrived at Ephesus. There he discovered some disciples, and he asked them,

"Did you receive the Holy Spirit when you believed?"

"No," they replied, "we have never even heard that there is a Holy Spirit."

"Well then, how were you baptized?" asked Paul.

"We were baptized with John's baptism," they replied.

"John's baptism was a baptism to show a change of heart," Paul explained, "but he always told the people that they must believe in the one who should come after him, that is, in Jesus."

When these men heard this they were baptized in the name of the Lord Jesus, and then, when Paul had laid his hands on them, the Holy Spirit came upon them and they began to speak with tongues and the inspiration of prophets. (There were about twelve of them in all.)

Paul's two-year ministry   *19. 8*
at Ephesus

Then Paul made his way into the synagogue there and for three months he spoke with the utmost confidence, using both argument and persuasion as he talked of the kingdom of God. But when some of them hardened in their attitude toward the message and refused to believe it and, what is more, spoke offensively about the Way in public, Paul left them, and withdrew his disciples, and held daily discussions in the lecture hall of Tyrannus. He continued this practice for two years, so that all who lived in Asia, both Greeks and Jews, could hear the Lord's message. God gave most unusual demonstrations of power through Paul's hands, so much so that people took to the sick any handkerchiefs or clothing which had been in contact with his body, and they were cured of their diseases and their evil spirits left them.

N.E.B.

Now there arrived at Ephesus a Jew named Apollos, an Alexandrian by birth, an eloquent man,[a] powerful in his use of the scriptures. He had been instructed in the way of the Lord and was full of spiritual fervour; and in his discourses he taught accurately the facts about Jesus,[b] though he knew only John's baptism. He now began to speak boldly in the synagogue, where Priscilla and Aquila heard him; they took him in hand and expounded the new way[c] to him in greater detail. Finding that he wished to go across to Achaia, the brotherhood gave him their support, and wrote to the congregation there to make him welcome. From the time of his arrival, he was very helpful to those who had by God's grace become believers; for he was indefatigable in confuting the Jews, demonstrating publicly from the scriptures that the Messiah is Jesus.

19 While Apollos was at Corinth, Paul travelled through the inland regions till he came to Ephesus. There he found a number of converts, to whom he said, 'Did you receive the Holy Spirit when you became believers?' 'No,' they replied, 'we have not even heard that there is a Holy Spirit.' He said, 'Then what baptism were you given?' 'John's baptism', they answered. Paul then said, 'The baptism that John gave was a baptism in token of repentance, and he told the people to put their trust in one who was to come after him, that is, in Jesus.' On hearing this they were baptized into the name of the Lord Jesus; and when Paul had laid his hands on them, the Holy Spirit came upon them and they spoke in tongues of ecstasy and prophesied. Altogether they were about a dozen men.

During the next three months he attended the synagogue and, using argument and persuasion, spoke boldly and freely about the kingdom of God. But when some proved obdurate and would not believe, speaking evil of the new way before the whole congregation, he left them, withdrew his converts, and continued to hold discussions daily in the lecture-hall of Tyrannus. This went on for two years, with the result that the whole population of the province of Asia, both Jews and pagans, heard the word of the Lord. And through Paul God worked miracles of an unusual kind: when handkerchiefs and scarves which had been in contact with his skin were carried to the sick, they were rid of their diseases and the evil spirits came out of them.

[a] *Or* a learned man. [b] *Some witnesses read* about the Lord. [c] *Some witnesses read* the way of God.

K.J.V.

13 Then certain of the vagabond Jews, exorcists, took upon them to call over them which had evil spirits the name of the Lord Jesus, saying, We adjure you by Jesus whom Paul preacheth. 14And there were seven sons of *one* Sceva, a Jew, *and* chief of the priests, which did so. 15And the evil spirit answered and said, Jesus I know, and Paul I know; but who are ye? 16And the man in whom the evil spirit was leaped on them, and overcame them, and prevailed against them, so that they fled out of that house naked and wounded. 17And this was known to all the Jews and Greeks also dwelling at Ephesus; and fear fell on them all, and the name of the Lord Jesus was magnified. 18And many that believed came, and confessed, and shewed their deeds. 19 Many of them also which used curious arts brought their books together, and burned them before all *men:* and they counted the price of them, and found *it* fifty thousand *pieces* of silver. 20 So mightily grew the word of God and prevailed.

21 After these things were ended, Paul purposed in the spirit, when he had passed through Macedonia and Achaia, to go to Jerusalem, saying, After I have been there, I must also see Rome. 22 So he sent into Macedonia two of them that ministered unto him, Timotheus and Erastus; but he himself stayed in Asia for a season. 23And the same time there arose no small stir about that way. 24 For a certain *man* named Demetrius, a silversmith, which made silver shrines for Diana, brought no small gain unto the craftsmen; 25 Whom he called together with the workmen of like occupation, and said, Sirs, ye know that by this craft we have our wealth. 26 Moreover ye see and hear, that not alone at Ephesus, but almost throughout all Asia, this Paul hath persuaded and turned away much people, saying that they be no gods, which are made with hands: 27 So that not only this our craft is in danger to be set at nought; but also that the temple of the great goddess Diana should be despised, and her magnificence should be destroyed, whom all Asia and the world worshippeth. 28And when they heard *these sayings,* they were full of wrath, and cried out, saying, Great *is* Diana of the Ephesians. 29And the whole city was filled with confusion: and having caught Gaius and Aristarchus, men of Macedonia, Paul's companions in travel, they rushed with one accord into the theatre. 30And when Paul would have entered in unto the people, the

R.S.V.

came out of them. 13 Then some of the itinerant Jewish exorcists undertook to pronounce the name of the Lord Jesus over those who had evil spirits, saying, "I adjure you by the Jesus whom Paul preaches." 14 Seven sons of a Jewish high priest named Sceva were doing this. 15 But the evil spirit answered them, "Jesus I know, and Paul I know; but who are you?" 16And the man in whom the evil spirit was leaped on them, mastered all of them, and overpowered them, so that they fled out of that house naked and wounded. 17And this became known to all residents of Ephesus, both Jews and Greeks; and fear fell upon them all; and the name of the Lord Jesus was extolled. 18 Many also of those who were now believers came, confessing and divulging their practices. 19And a number of those who practiced magic arts brought their books together and burned them in the sight of all; and they counted the value of them and found it came to fifty thousand pieces of silver. 20 So the word of the Lord grew and prevailed mightily.

21 Now after these events Paul resolved in the Spirit to pass through Macedonia and Achaia and go to Jerusalem, saying, "After I have been there, I must also see Rome." 22And having sent into Macedonia two of his helpers, Timothy and Erastus, he himself stayed in Asia for a while. 23 About that time there arose no little stir concerning the Way. 24 For a man named Demetrius, a silversmith, who made silver shrines of Artemis, brought no little business to the craftsmen. 25 These he gathered together, with the workmen of like occupation, and said, "Men, you know that from this business we have our wealth. 26And you see and hear that not only at Ephesus but almost throughout all Asia this Paul has persuaded and turned away a considerable company of people, saying that gods made with hands are not gods. 27And there is danger not only that this trade of ours may come into disrepute but also that the temple of the great goddess Artemis may count for nothing, and that she may even be deposed from her magnificence, she whom all Asia and the world worship."

28 When they heard this they were enraged, and cried out, "Great is Artemis of the Ephesians!" 29 So the city was filled with the confusion; and they rushed together into the theater, dragging with them Gaius and Aristarchus, Macedonians who were Paul's companions in travel. 30 Paul wished to go in among the crowd, but

PHILLIPS

N.E.B.

*The violence of evil and
the power of "the name"* 19. 13

But there were some itinerant Jewish exorcists who attempted to invoke the name of the Lord Jesus when dealing with those who had evil spirits. They would say, "I command you in the name of Jesus whom Paul preaches." Seven brothers, sons of a chief priest called Sceva, were engaged in this practice on one occasion, when the evil spirit answered, "Jesus I know, and I am acquainted with Paul, but who on earth are you?" And the man in whom the evil spirit was living sprang at them and over-powered them all with such violence that they rushed out of that house wounded, with their clothes torn off their backs. This incident be-came known to all the Jews and Greeks who were living in Ephesus, and a great sense of awe came over them all, while the name of the Lord Jesus became highly respected. Many of those who had professed their faith began openly to admit their former practices. A number of those who had previously practiced magic collected their books and burned them publicly. (They estimated the value of these books and found it to be no less than ten thousand dollars.) In this way the Word of the Lord continued to grow irresistibly in power and influence.

Paul speaks of his plans 19. 21

After these events Paul set his heart on going to Jerusalem by way of Macedonia and Achaia, remarking,

"After I have been there I must see Rome as well."

Then he dispatched to Macedonia two of his assistants, Timothy and Erastus, while he him-self stayed for a while in Asia.

The silversmiths' riot at Ephesus 19. 23

Now it happened about this time that a great commotion arose concerning the Way. A man by the name of Demetrius, a silversmith who made silver shrines for Diana, provided con-siderable business for his craftsmen. He gath-ered these men together with workers in similar trades, and spoke to them,

"Men," he said, "you all realize how our pros-perity depends on this particular work. If you use your eyes and ears you also know that not only in Ephesus but practically throughout Asia this man Paul has succeeded in changing the minds of a great number of people by telling them that gods made by human hands are not gods at all. Now the danger is not only that this trade of ours might fall into disrepute, but also that the temple of the great goddess Diana herself might come to be lightly regarded. There is a further danger, that her actual majesty might be degraded, she whom the whole of Asia, and indeed the whole world, worships!"

When they heard this they were furiously angry, and shouted,

"Great is Diana of the Ephesians!"

Soon the whole city was in an uproar, and on a common impulse the people rushed into the theater dragging with them Gaius and Aris-tarchus, two Macedonians who were Paul's trav-eling companions. Paul himself wanted to go in among the crowd, but the disciples would not

But some strolling Jewish exorcists tried their hand at using the name of the Lord Jesus on those possessed by evil spirits; they would say, 'I adjure you by Jesus whom Paul proclaims.' There were seven sons of Sceva, a Jewish chief priest, who were using this method, when the evil spirit answered back and said, 'Jesus I ac-knowledge, and I know about Paul, but who are you?' And the man with the evil spirit flew at them, overpowered them all, and handled them with such violence that they ran out of the house stripped and battered. This became known to everybody in Ephesus, whether Jew or pagan; they were all awestruck, and the name of the Lord Jesus gained in honour. Moreover many of those who had become believers came and openly confessed that they had been using magi-cal spells. And a good many of those who for-merly practised magic collected their books and burnt them publicly. The total value was reck-oned up and it came to fifty thousand pieces of silver. In such ways the word of the Lord showed its power, spreading more and more widely and effectively.

When things had reached this stage, Paul made up his mind [a] to visit Macedonia and Achaia and then go on to Jerusalem; and he said, 'After I have been there, I must see Rome also.' So he sent two of his assistants, Timothy and Erastus, to Macedonia, while he himself stayed some time longer in the province of Asia.

Now about that time, the Christian movement gave rise to a serious disturbance. There was a man named Demetrius, a silversmith who made silver shrines of Diana and provided a great deal of employment for the craftsmen. He called a meeting of these men and the workers in al-lied trades, and addressed them. 'Men,' he said, 'you know that our high standard of living de-pends on this industry. And you see and hear how this fellow Paul with his propaganda has perverted crowds of people, not only at Ephesus but also in practically the whole of the province of Asia. He is telling them that gods made by human hands are not gods at all. There is danger for us here; it is not only that our line of business will be discredited, but also that the sanctuary of the great goddess Diana will cease to command respect; and then it will not be long before she who is worshipped by all Asia and the civilized world is brought down from her divine pre-eminence.'

When they heard this they were roused to fury and shouted, 'Great is Diana of the Ephesians!' The whole city was in confusion; they seized Paul's travelling-companions, the Macedonians Gaius and Aristarchus, and made a concerted rush with them into the theatre. Paul wanted to appear before the assembly but

[a] *Or* Paul, led by the Spirit, resolved . . .

disciples suffered him not. 31And certain of the chief of Asia, which were his friends, sent unto him, desiring *him* that he would not adventure himself into the theatre. 32 Some therefore cried one thing, and some another: for the assembly was confused; and the more part knew not wherefore they were come together. 33And they drew Alexander out of the multitude, the Jews putting him forward. And Alexander beckoned with the hand, and would have made his defence unto the people. 34 But when they knew that he was a Jew, all with one voice about the space of two hours cried out, Great *is* Diana of the Ephesians. 35And when the townclerk had appeased the people, he said, *Ye* men of Ephesus, what man is there that knoweth not how that the city of the Ephesians is a worshipper of the great goddess Diana, and of the *image* which fell down from Jupiter? 36 Seeing then that these things cannot be spoken against, ye ought to be quiet, and to do nothing rashly. 37 For ye have brought hither these men, which are neither robbers of churches, nor yet blasphemers of your goddess. 38 Wherefore if Demetrius, and the craftsmen which are with him, have a matter against any man, the law is open, and there are deputies: let them implead one another. 39 But if ye inquire any thing concerning other matters, it shall be determined in a lawful assembly. 40 For we are in danger to be called in question for this day's uproar, there being no cause whereby we may give an account of this concourse. 41And when he had thus spoken, he dismissed the assembly.

the disciples would not let him; 31 some of the Asiarchs also, who were friends of his, sent to him and begged him not to venture into the theater. 32 Now some cried one thing, some another; for the assembly was in confusion, and most of them did not know why they had come together. 33 Some of the crowd prompted Alexander, whom the Jews had put forward. And Alexander motioned with his hand, wishing to make a defense to the people. 34 But when they recognized that he was a Jew, for about two hours they all with one voice cried out, "Great is Artemis of the Ephesians!" 35And when the town clerk had quieted the crowd, he said, "Men of Ephesus, what man is there who does not know that the city of the Ephesians is temple keeper of the great Artemis, and of the sacred stone that fell from the sky? *s* 36 Seeing then that these things cannot be contradicted, you ought to be quiet and do nothing rash. 37 For you have brought these men here who are neither sacrilegious nor blasphemers of our goddess. 38 If therefore Demetrius and the craftsmen with him have a complaint against any one, the courts are open, and there are proconsuls; let them bring charges against one another. 39 But if you seek anything further,*t* it shall be settled in the regular assembly. 40 For we are in danger of being charged with rioting today, there being no cause that we can give to justify this commotion." 41And when he had said this, he dismissed the assembly.

20 And after the uproar was ceased, Paul called unto *him* the disciples, and embraced *them,* and departed for to go into Macedonia. 2And when he had gone over those parts, and had given them much exhortation, he came into Greece, 3And *there* abode three months. And when the Jews laid wait for him, as he was about to sail into Syria, he purposed to return through Macedonia. 4And there accompanied him into Asia Sopater of Berea; and of the Thessalonians, Aristarchus and Secundus; and Gaius of Derbe, and Timotheus; and of Asia, Tychicus and Trophimus. 5 These going before tarried for us at Troas. 6And we sailed away from Philippi after the days of unleavened bread, and came unto them to Troas in five days; where we abode seven days. 7And upon the first *day* of the week, when the disciples came together to break bread, Paul preached unto them, ready to depart on

20 After the uproar ceased, Paul sent for the disciples and having exhorted them took leave of them and departed for Macedonia. 2 When he had gone through these parts and had given them much encouragement, he came to Greece. 3 There he spent three months, and when a plot was made against him by the Jews as he was about to set sail for Syria, he determined to return through Macedonia. 4 Sopater of Beroea, the son of Pyrrhus, accompanied him; and of the Thessalonians, Aristarchus and Secundus; and Gaius of Derbe, and Timothy; and the Asians, Tychicus and Trophimus. 5 These went on and were waiting for us at Troas, 6 but we sailed away from Philippi after the days of Unleavened Bread, and in five days we came to them at Troas, where we stayed for seven days.

7 On the first day of the week, when we were gathered together to break bread, Paul talked with them, intending to depart on the morrow;

[s] The meaning of the Greek is uncertain. [t] Other ancient authorities read *about other matters.*

PHILLIPS

allow him. Moreover, some high-ranking officials who were Paul's friends sent to him begging him not to risk himself in the theater. Meanwhile some were shouting one thing and some another, and the whole assembly was at sixes and sevens, for most of them had no idea why they had come together at all. A man called Alexander whom the Jews put forward was pushed into the forefront of the crowd, and there, after making a gesture with his hand, he tried to make a speech of defense to the people. But as soon as they realized that he was a Jew they shouted as one man for about two hours, "Great is Diana of the Ephesians!"

Public authority intervenes   19. 35

But when the town clerk had finally quietened the crowd, he said,

"Gentlemen of Ephesus, who in the world could be ignorant of the fact that our city of Ephesus is temple guardian of the great Diana and of the image which fell down from Jupiter himself? These are undeniable facts and it is your plain duty to remain calm and do nothing which you might afterwards regret. For you have brought these men forward, though they are neither plunderers of the temple, nor have they uttered any blasphemy against our goddess. If Demetrius and his fellow craftsmen have a charge to bring against anyone, well, the courts are open and there are magistrates; let them take legal action. But if you require anything beyond that then it must be resolved in the regular assembly. For all of us are in danger of being charged with rioting over today's events —particularly as we have no real excuse to offer for this commotion."

And with these words he dismissed the assembly.

Paul departs on his second   20. 1
journey to Europe

After this disturbance had died down, Paul sent for the disciples and after speaking encouragingly said good-bye to them, and went on his way to Macedonia. As he made his journey through these districts he spoke many heartening words to the people and then went on to Greece, where he stayed for three months. Then when he was on the point of setting sail for Syria the Jews made a further plot against him and he decided to make his way back through Macedonia. His companions on the journey were Sopater a Beroean, the son of Pyrrhus; two Thessalonians, Aristarchus and Secundus; Gaius from Derbe, Timothy, and two Asians, Tychicus and Trophimus. This party proceeded to Troas to await us there, while we sailed from Philippi after the days of unleavened bread, and joined them five days later at Troas, where we spent a week.

Paul's enthusiasm leads to   20. 7
an accident

On the first day of the week, when we were assembled for the breaking of bread, Paul, since he intended to leave on the following day, be-

N.E.B.

the other Christians would not let him. Even some of the dignitaries of the province, who were friendly towards him, sent and urged him not to venture into the theatre. Meanwhile some were shouting one thing, some another; for the assembly was in confusion and most of them did not know what they had all come for. But some of the crowd explained the trouble to Alexander, whom the Jews had pushed to the front, and he, motioning for silence, attempted to make a defence before the assembly. But when they recognized that he was a Jew, a single cry arose from them all: for about two hours they kept on shouting, 'Great is Diana of the Ephesians!'

The town clerk, however, quieted the crowd. 'Men of Ephesus,' he said, 'all the world knows that our city of Ephesus is temple-warden of the great Diana and of that symbol of her which fell from heaven. Since these facts are beyond dispute, your proper course is to keep quiet and do nothing rash. These men whom you have brought here as culprits have committed no sacrilege and uttered no blasphemy against our goddess. If therefore Demetrius and his craftsmen have a case against anyone, assizes are held and there are such people as proconsuls; let the parties bring their charges and countercharges. If, on the other hand, you have some further question to raise, it will be dealt with in the statutory assembly. We certainly run the risk of being charged with riot for this day's work. There is no justification for it, and if the issue is raised we shall be unable to give any explanation of this uproar.' With that he dismissed the assembly.

20 When the disturbance had ceased, Paul sent for the disciples and, after encouraging them, said good-bye and set out on his journey to Macedonia. He travelled through those parts of the country, often speaking words of encouragement to the Christians there, and so came into Greece. When he had spent three months there and was on the point of embarking for Syria, a plot was laid against him by the Jews, so he decided to return by way of Macedonia. He was accompanied by Sopater son of Pyrrhus, from Beroea, the Thessalonians Aristarchus and Secundus, Gaius the Doberian[a] and Timothy, and the Asians Tychicus and Trophimus. These went ahead and waited for us at Troas; we ourselves set sail from Philippi after the Passover season,[b] and in five days reached them at Troas, where we spent a week.

On the Saturday night, in our assembly for the breaking of bread, Paul, who was to leave

[a] Some witnesses read the Derbaean. [b] Literally after the days of Unleavened Bread.

K.J.V.

the morrow; and continued his speech until midnight. 8And there were many lights in the upper chamber, where they were gathered together. 9And there sat in a window a certain young man named Eutychus, being fallen into a deep sleep: and as Paul was long preaching, he sunk down with sleep, and fell down from the third loft, and was taken up dead. 10And Paul went down, and fell on him, and embracing *him* said, Trouble not yourselves; for his life is in him. 11 When he therefore was come up again, and had broken bread, and eaten, and talked a long while, even till break of day, so he departed. 12And they brought the young man alive, and were not a little comforted.

13 And we went before to ship, and sailed unto Assos, there intending to take in Paul: for so had he appointed, minding himself to go afoot. 14And when he met with us at Assos, we took him in, and came to Mitylene. 15And we sailed thence, and came the next *day* over against Chios; and the next *day* we arrived at Samos, and tarried at Trogyllium; and the next *day* we came to Miletus. 16 For Paul had determined to sail by Ephesus, because he would not spend the time in Asia: for he hasted, if it were possible for him, to be at Jerusalem the day of Pentecost.

17 And from Miletus he sent to Ephesus, and called the elders of the church. 18And when they were come to him, he said unto them, Ye know, from the first day that I came into Asia, after what manner I have been with you at all seasons, 19 Serving the Lord with all humility of mind, and with many tears, and temptations, which befell me by the lying in wait of the Jews: 20And how I kept back nothing that was profitable *unto you,* but have shewed you, and have taught you publicly, and from house to house, 21 Testifying both to the Jews, and also to the Greeks, repentance toward God, and faith toward our Lord Jesus Christ. 22And now, behold, I go bound in the spirit unto Jerusalem, not knowing the things that shall befall me there: 23 Save that the Holy Ghost witnesseth in every city, saying that bonds and afflictions abide me. 24 But none of these things move me, neither count I my life dear unto myself, so that I might finish my course with joy, and the ministry, which I have received of the Lord Jesus, to testify the gospel of the grace of God. 25And now, behold, I know that ye all among whom I have gone preaching the kingdom of God, shall see my face no more. 26 Wherefore I take you to record this day, that I *am* pure from the blood of all *men.* 27 For I have not shunned to declare unto you all the counsel of God.

28 Take heed therefore unto yourselves, and to all the flock, over the which the Holy Ghost hath made you overseers, to feed the church of God, which he hath purchased with his own blood. 29 For I know this, that after my departing shall grievous wolves enter in among you,

R.S.V.

and he prolonged his speech until midnight. 8 There were many lights in the upper chamber where we were gathered. 9And a young man named Eutychus was sitting in the window. He sank into a deep sleep as Paul talked still longer; and being overcome by sleep, he fell down from the third story and was taken up dead. 10 But Paul went down and bent over him, and embracing him said, "Do not be alarmed, for his life is in him." 11And when Paul had gone up and had broken bread and eaten, he conversed with them a long while, until daybreak, and so departed. 12And they took the lad away alive, and were not a little comforted.

13 But going ahead to the ship, we set sail for Assos, intending to take Paul aboard there; for so he had arranged, intending himself to go by land. 14And when he met us at Assos, we took him on board and came to Mitylene. 15And sailing from there we came the following day opposite Chios; the next day we touched at Samos; and *u* the day after that we came to Miletus. 16 For Paul had decided to sail past Ephesus, so that he might not have to spend time in Asia; for he was hastening to be at Jerusalem, if possible, on the day of Pentecost.

17 And from Miletus he sent to Ephesus and called to him the elders of the church. 18And when they came to him, he said to them:

"You yourselves know how I lived among you all the time from the first day that I set foot in Asia, 19 serving the Lord with all humility and with tears and with trials which befell me through the plots of the Jews; 20 how I did not shrink from declaring to you anything that was profitable, and teaching you in public and from house to house, 21 testifying both to Jews and to Greeks of repentance to God and of faith in our Lord Jesus Christ. 22And now, behold, I am going to Jerusalem, bound in the Spirit, not knowing what shall befall me there; 23 except that the Holy Spirit testifies to me in every city that imprisonment and afflictions await me. 24 But I do not account my life of any value nor as precious to myself, if only I may accomplish my course and the ministry which I received from the Lord Jesus, to testify to the gospel of the grace of God. 25And now, behold, I know that all you among whom I have gone about preaching the kingdom will see my face no more. 26 Therefore I testify to you this day that I am innocent of the blood of all of you, 27 for I did not shrink from declaring to you the whole counsel of God. 28 Take heed to yourselves and to all the flock, in which the Holy Spirit has made you guardians, to feed the church of the Lord *v* which he obtained with his own blood.*w* 29 I know that after my departure fierce wolves will come in among you, not sparing the flock;

[u] Other ancient authorities add *after remaining at Trogyllium.* [v] Other ancient authorities read *of God.* [w] Or *with the blood of his Own.*

gan to speak to them and prolonged his address until almost midnight. There were a great many lamps burning in the upper room where we met, and a young man called Eutychus who was sitting on the window sill fell fast asleep as Paul's address became longer and longer. Finally, completely overcome by sleep, he fell to the ground from the third story and was picked up as dead. But Paul went down, bent over him and holding him gently in his arms, said,

"Don't be alarmed; he is still alive."

Then he went upstairs again and, when he had broken bread and eaten, continued a long earnest talk with them until daybreak, and so finally departed. As for the boy, they took him home alive, feeling immeasurably relieved.

We sail to Miletus   20. 13

Meanwhile we had gone aboard the ship and sailed on ahead for Assos, intending to pick up Paul there, for that was the arrangement he had made, since he himself had planned to go overland. When he met us on our arrival at Assos we took him aboard and went on to Mitylene. We sailed from there and arrived off the coast of Chios the next day. On the day following we crossed to Samos, and the day after that we reached Miletus. For Paul had decided to sail past Ephesus with the idea of spending as little time as possible in Asia. He hoped, if it should prove possible, to reach Jerusalem in time for the day of Pentecost.

Paul's moving farewell message   20. 17
to the elders of Ephesus

At Miletus he sent to Ephesus to summon the elders of the church. On their arrival he addressed them in these words:

"I am sure you know how I have lived among you ever since I first set foot in Asia. You know how I have served the Lord most humbly and what tears I have shed over the trials that have come to me through the plots of the Jews. You know I have never shrunk from telling you anything that was for your good, nor from teaching you in public or in your own homes. On the contrary I have most emphatically urged upon both Jews and Greeks repentance towards God and faith in our Lord Jesus. And now here I am, compelled by the Spirit to go to Jerusalem. I do not know what may happen to me there, except that the Holy Spirit warns me that imprisonment and persecution await me in every city that I visit. But frankly I do not consider my own life valuable to me so long as I can finish my course and complete the ministry which the Lord Jesus has given me in declaring the good news of the grace of God. Now I know well enough that not one of you among whom I have moved as I preached the kingdom of God will ever see my face again. That is why I must tell you solemnly today that my conscience is clear as far as any of you is concerned, for I have never shrunk from declaring to you the complete will of God. Now be on your guard for yourselves and for every flock of which the Holy Spirit has made you guardians—you are to be shepherds to the Church of God, which he won at the cost of his own blood. I know that after my departure savage wolves will come in among you without mercy for the flock. Yes,

next day, addressed them, and went on speaking until midnight. Now there were many lamps in the upper room where we were assembled; and a youth named Eutychus, who was sitting on the window-ledge, grew more and more sleepy as Paul went on talking. At last he was completely overcome by sleep, fell from the third floor to the ground, and was picked up for dead. Paul went down, threw himself upon him, seizing him in his arms, and said to him, 'Stop this commotion: there is still life in him.' He then went upstairs, broke bread and ate, and after much conversation, which lasted until dawn, he departed. And they took the boy away alive and were immensely comforted.

We went ahead to the ship and sailed for Assos, where we were to take Paul aboard. He had made this arrangement, as he was going to travel by road. When he met us at Assos, we took him aboard and went on to Mitylene. Next day we sailed from there and arrived opposite Chios, and on the second day we made Samos. On the following day[a] we reached Miletus. For Paul had decided to pass by Ephesus and so avoid having to spend time in the province of Asia; he was eager to be in Jerusalem, if he possibly could, on the day of Pentecost. He did, however, send from Miletus to Ephesus and summon the elders of the congregation; and when they joined him, he spoke as follows:

'You know how, from the day that I first set foot in the province of Asia, for the whole time that I was with you, I served the Lord in all humility amid the sorrows and trials that came upon me through the machinations of the Jews. You know that I kept back nothing that was for your good: I delivered the message to you; I taught you, in public and in your homes; with Jews and pagans alike I insisted on repentance before God and trust in our Lord Jesus. And now, as you see, I am on my way to Jerusalem, under the constraint of the Spirit.[b] Of what will befall me there I know nothing, except that in city after city the Holy Spirit assures me that imprisonment and hardships await me. For myself, I set no store by life; I only want to finish the race, and complete the task which the Lord Jesus assigned to me, of bearing my testimony to the gospel of God's grace.

'One word more: I have gone about among you proclaiming the Kingdom, but now I know that none of you will see my face again. That being so, I here and now declare that no man's fate can be laid at my door; for I have kept back nothing; I have disclosed to you the whole purpose of God. Keep watch over yourselves and over all the flock of which the Holy Spirit has given you charge, as shepherds of the church of the Lord,[c] which he won for himself by his own blood.[d] I know that when I am gone, savage wolves will come in among you and will

[a] *Some witnesses read* . . . Samos, and, after stopping at Trogyllium, on the following day . . . [b] *Or* under an inner compulsion. [c] *Some witnesses read* of God. [d] *Or* by the blood of his Own.

K.J.V.

not sparing the flock. 30 Also of your own selves shall men arise, speaking perverse things, to draw away disciples after them. 31 Therefore watch, and remember, that by the space of three years I ceased not to warn every one night and day with tears. 32And now, brethren, I commend you to God, and to the word of his grace, which is able to build you up, and to give you an inheritance among all them which are sanctified. 33 I have coveted no man's silver, or gold, or apparel. 34 Yea, ye yourselves know, that these hands have ministered unto my necessities, and to them that were with me. 35 I have shewed you all things, how that so labouring ye ought to support the weak, and to remember the words of the Lord Jesus, how he said, It is more blessed to give than to receive.

36 And when he had thus spoken, he kneeled down, and prayed with them all. 37And they all wept sore, and fell on Paul's neck, and kissed him, 38 Sorrowing most of all for the words which he spake, that they should see his face no more. And they accompanied him unto the ship.

21 And it came to pass, that after we were gotten from them, and had launched, we came with a straight course unto Coos, and the *day* following unto Rhodes, and from thence unto Patara: 2And finding a ship sailing over unto Phenicia, we went aboard, and set forth. 3 Now when we had discovered Cyprus, we left it on the left hand, and sailed into Syria, and landed at Tyre: for there the ship was to unlade her burden. 4And finding disciples, we tarried there seven days: who said to Paul through the Spirit, that he should not go up to Jerusalem. 5And when we had accomplished those days, we departed and went our way; and they all brought us on our way, with wives and children, till *we were* out of the city: and we kneeled down on the shore, and prayed. 6And when we had taken our leave one of another, we took ship; and they returned home again. 7And when we had finished *our* course from Tyre, we came to Ptolemais, and saluted the brethren, and abode with them one day. 8And the next *day* we that were of Paul's company departed, and came unto Cesarea; and we entered into the house of Philip the evangelist, which was *one* of the seven; and abode with him. 9And the same man had four daughters, virgins, which did prophesy. 10And as we tarried *there* many days, there came down from Judea a certain prophet, named Agabus. 11And when he was come unto us, he took Paul's girdle, and bound his own hands and feet, and said, Thus saith the Holy Ghost, So shall the Jews at Jerusalem bind the man that owneth this girdle, and shall deliver *him* into the hands of the Gentiles. 12And when we heard these things, both we, and they of that place, besought him not to go up to Jerusalem. 13 Then Paul answered, What mean ye to weep and to break mine heart? for I am ready not to be bound only, but also to die at Jerusalem for

R.S.V.

30 and from among your own selves will arise men speaking perverse things, to draw away the disciples after them. 31 Therefore be alert, remembering that for three years I did not cease night or day to admonish every one with tears. 32And now I commend you to God and to the word of his grace, which is able to build you up and to give you the inheritance among all those who are sanctified. 33 I coveted no one's silver or gold or apparel. 34 You yourselves know that these hands ministered to my necessities, and to those who were with me. 35 In all things I have shown you that by so toiling one must help the weak, remembering the words of the Lord Jesus, how he said, 'It is more blessed to give than to receive.' "

36 And when he had spoken thus, he knelt down and prayed with them all. 37And they all wept and embraced Paul and kissed him, 38 sorrowing most of all because of the word he had spoken, that they should see his face no more. And they brought him to the ship.

21 And when we had parted from them and set sail, we came by a straight course to Cos, and the next day to Rhodes, and from there to Patara.*ˣ* 2And having found a ship crossing to Phoenicia, we went aboard, and set sail. 3 When we had come in sight of Cyprus, leaving it on the left we sailed to Syria, and landed at Tyre; for there the ship was to unload its cargo. 4And having sought out the disciples, we stayed there for seven days. Through the Spirit they told Paul not to go on to Jerusalem. 5And when our days there were ended, we departed and went on our journey; and they all, with wives and children, brought us on our way till we were outside the city; and kneeling down on the beach we prayed and bade one another farewell. 6 Then we went on board the ship, and they returned home.

7 When we had finished the voyage from Tyre, we arrived at Ptolemais; and we greeted the brethren and stayed with them for one day. 8 On the morrow we departed and came to Caesarea; and we entered the house of Philip the evangelist, who was one of the seven, and stayed with him. 9And he had four unmarried daughters, who prophesied. 10 While we were staying for some days, a prophet named Agabus came down from Judea. 11And coming to us he took Paul's girdle and bound his own feet and hands, and said, "Thus says the Holy Spirit, 'So shall the Jews at Jerusalem bind the man who owns this girdle and deliver him into the hands of the Gentiles.' " 12 When we heard this, we and the people there begged him not to go up to Jerusalem. 13 Then Paul answered, "What are you doing, weeping and breaking my heart? For I am ready not only to be imprisoned but even to die at Jerusalem for the name of the

PHILLIPS

and even from among you men will arise speaking perversions of the truth, trying to draw away the disciples and make them followers of themselves. This is why I tell you to keep on the alert, remembering that for three years I never failed night and day to warn every one of you, even with tears in my eyes. Now I commend you to the Lord and to the message of his grace which can build you up and give you your place among all those who are consecrated to God. I have never coveted anybody's gold or silver or clothing. You know well enough that these hands of mine have provided for my own needs and for those of my companions. In everything I have shown you that by such hard work we must help the weak and must remember the words of the Lord Jesus when he said, 'To give is happier than to receive.' "

With these words he knelt down with them all and prayed. All of them were in tears, and throwing their arms round Paul's neck they kissed him affectionately. What saddened them most of all was his saying that they would never see his face again. And they went with him down to the ship.

The brothers at Tyre warn Paul   21. 1
not to go to Jerusalem

When he had finally said farewell to them we set sail, running a straight course to Cos, and the next day we went to Rhodes and from there to Patara. Here we found a ship bound for Phoenicia, and we went aboard her and set sail. After sighting Cyprus and leaving it on our left we sailed for Syria and put in at Tyre, since that was where the ship was to discharge her cargo. We sought out the disciples there and stayed with them for a week. They felt led by the Spirit again and again to warn Paul not to go up to Jerusalem. But when our time was up we left them and continued our journey. They all came out to see us off, bringing their wives and children with them, accompanying us till we were outside the city. Then kneeling down on the beach we prayed and said good-bye to each other. Then we went aboard the ship, while the disciples went back home. We sailed away from Tyre and arrived at Ptolemais. We greeted the brothers there and stayed with them for just one day. On the following day we left and proceeded to Caesarea and there we went to stay at the house of Philip the evangelist, one of the seven deacons. He had four unmarried daughters, all of whom spoke by the Spirit of God. During our stay there of several days a prophet by the name of Agabus came down from Judaea. When he came to see us he took Paul's girdle and used it to tie his own hands and feet together, saying, "The Holy Spirit says this: the man to whom this girdle belongs will be bound like this by the Jews in Jerusalem and handed over to the gentiles!"

We all warn Paul, but he is   21. 12
immovable

When we heard him say this, we and the people there begged Paul not to go up to Jerusalem. Then Paul answered us,

"What do you mean by unnerving me with all your tears? I am perfectly prepared not only to be bound but to die in Jerusalem for the sake of the name of the Lord Jesus."

N.E.B.

not spare the flock. Even from your own body there will be men coming forward who will distort the truth to induce the disciples to break away and follow them. So be on the alert; remember how for three years, night and day, I never ceased to counsel each of you, and how I wept over you.

'And now I commend you to God and to his gracious word, which has power to build you up and give you your heritage among all who are dedicated to him. I have not wanted anyone's money or clothes for myself; you all know that these hands of mine earned enough for the needs of me and my companions. I showed you that it is our duty to help the weak in this way, by hard work, and that we should keep in mind the words of the Lord Jesus, who himself said, "Happiness lies more in giving than in receiving." '

As he finished speaking, he knelt down with them all and prayed. Then there were loud cries of sorrow from them all, as they folded Paul in their arms and kissed him. What distressed them most was his saying that they would never see his face again. So they escorted him to his ship.

21 When we had parted from them and set sail, we made a straight run and came to Cos; next day to Rhodes, and thence to Patara.[a] There we found a ship bound for Phoenicia, so we went aboard and sailed in her. We came in sight of Cyprus, and leaving it on our port beam, we continued our voyage to Syria, and put in at Tyre, for there the ship was to unload her cargo. We went and found the disciples and stayed there a week; and they, warned by the Spirit, urged Paul to abandon his visit to Jerusalem. But when our time ashore was ended, we left and continued our journey; and they and their wives and children all escorted us out of the city. We knelt down on the beach and prayed, then bade each other good-bye; we went aboard, and they returned home.

We made the passage from Tyre and reached Ptolemais, where we greeted the brotherhood and spent one day with them. Next day we left and came to Caesarea. We went to the home of Philip the evangelist, who was one of the Seven, and stayed with him. He had four unmarried daughters, who possessed the gift of prophecy. When we had been there several days, a prophet named Agabus arrived from Judaea. He came to us, took Paul's belt, bound his own feet and hands with it, and said, 'These are the words of the Holy Spirit: Thus will the Jews in Jerusalem bind the man to whom this belt belongs, and hand him over to the Gentiles.' When we heard this, we and the local people begged and implored Paul to abandon his visit to Jerusalem. Then Paul gave his answer: 'Why all these tears? Why are you trying to weaken my resolution? For my part I am ready not merely to be bound but even to die for the name of the Lord Jesus.'

[a] *Some witnesses add* and **Myra.**

419

K.J.V.

the name of the Lord Jesus. 14And when he would not be persuaded, we ceased, saying, The will of the Lord be done. 15And after those days we took up our carriages, and went up to Jerusalem. 16 There went with us also *certain* of the disciples of Cesarea, and brought with them one Mnason of Cyprus, an old disciple, with whom we should lodge. 17And when we were come to Jerusalem, the brethren received us gladly. 18And the *day* following Paul went in with us unto James; and all the elders were present. 19And when he had saluted them, he declared particularly what things God had wrought among the Gentiles by his ministry. 20And when they heard *it,* they glorified the Lord, and said unto him, Thou seest, brother, how many thousands of Jews there are which believe; and they are all zealous of the law: 21And they are informed of thee, that thou teachest all the Jews which are among the Gentiles to forsake Moses, saying that they ought not to circumcise *their* children, neither to walk after the customs. 22 What is it therefore? the multitude must needs come together: for they will hear that thou art come. 23 Do therefore this that we say to thee: We have four men which have a vow on them; 24 Them take, and purify thyself with them, and be at charges with them, that they may shave *their* heads: and all may know that those things, whereof they were informed concerning thee, are nothing; but *that* thou thyself also walkest orderly, and keepest the law. 25As touching the Gentiles which believe, we have written *and* concluded that they observe no such thing, save only that they keep themselves from *things* offered to idols, and from blood, and from strangled, and from fornication. 26 Then Paul took the men, and the next day purifying himself with them entered into the temple, to signify the accomplishment of the days of purification, until that an offering should be offered for every one of them. 27And when the seven days were almost ended, the Jews which were of Asia, when they saw him in the temple, stirred up all the people, and laid hands on him, 28 Crying out, Men of Israel, help: This is the man, that teacheth all *men* every where against the people, and the law, and this place: and further brought Greeks also into the temple, and hath polluted this holy place. 29 (For they had seen before with him in the city Trophimus an Ephesian, whom they supposed that Paul had brought into the temple.) 30And all the city was moved, and the people ran together: and they took Paul, and drew him out of the temple: and forthwith the doors were shut. 31And as they went about to kill him, tidings came unto the chief captain

R.S.V.

Lord Jesus." 14And when he would not be persuaded, we ceased and said, "The will of the Lord be done."

15 After these days we made ready and went up to Jerusalem. 16And some of the disciples from Caesarea went with us, bringing us to the house of Mnason of Cyprus, an early disciple, with whom we should lodge.

17 When we had come to Jerusalem, the brethren received us gladly. 18 On the following day Paul went in with us to James; and all the elders were present. 19After greeting them, he related one by one the things that God had done among the Gentiles through his ministry. 20And when they heard it, they glorified God. And they said to him, "You see, brother, how many thousands there are among the Jews of those who have believed; they are all zealous for the law, 21 and they have been told about you that you teach all the Jews who are among the Gentiles to forsake Moses, telling them not to circumcise their children or observe the customs. 22 What then is to be done? They will certainly hear that you have come. 23 Do therefore what we tell you. We have four men who are under a vow; 24 take these men and purify yourself along with them and pay their expenses, so that they may shave their heads. Thus all will know that there is nothing in what they have been told about you but that you yourself live in observance of the law. 25 But as for the Gentiles who have believed, we have sent a letter with our judgment that they should abstain from what has been sacrificed to idols and from blood and from what is strangled *y* and from unchastity." 26 Then Paul took the men, and the next day he purified himself with them and went into the temple, to give notice when the days of purification would be fulfilled and the offering presented for every one of them.

27 When the seven days were almost completed, the Jews from Asia, who had seen him in the temple, stirred up all the crowd, and laid hands on him, 28 crying out, "Men of Israel, help! This is the man who is teaching men everywhere against the people and the law and this place; moreover he also brought Greeks into the temple, and he has defiled this holy place." 29 For they had previously seen Trophimus the Ephesian with him in the city, and they supposed that Paul had brought him into the temple. 30 Then all the city was aroused, and the people ran together; they seized Paul and dragged him out of the temple, and at once the gates were shut. 31And as they were trying to kill him, word came to the tribune of the cohort

[y] Other early authorities omit *and from what is strangled.*

PHILLIPS

Since he could not be dissuaded all we could do was to say, "May the Lord's will be done," and hold our tongues.

Paul is warmly welcomed at first   21. 15

After this we made our preparations and went up to Jerusalem. Some of the disciples from Caesarea accompanied us and they brought us to the house of Mnason, a native of Cyprus and one of the earliest disciples, with whom we were going to stay. On our arrival at Jerusalem the brothers gave us a very warm welcome. On the following day Paul went with us to visit James, and all the elders were present. When he had greeted them he gave them a detailed account of all that God had done among the gentiles through his ministry, and they, on hearing this account, glorified God. Then they said to him, "You know, brother, how many thousands there are among the Jews who have become believers, and that every one of these is a staunch upholder of the Law. They have been told about you—that you teach all Jews who live among the gentiles to disregard the Law of Moses, and tell them not to circumcise their children nor observe the old customs. What will happen now, for they are simply bound to hear that you have arrived? Now why not follow this suggestion of ours? We have four men here under a vow. Suppose you join them and be purified with them, pay their expenses so that they may have their hair cut short, and then everyone will know there is no truth in the stories about you, but that you yourself observe the Law. As for those gentiles who have believed, we have sent them a letter with our decision that they should abstain from what has been offered to idols, from blood and from what has been strangled, and from sexual immorality."

But his enemies attempt to   21. 26
murder him

So Paul joined the four men and on the following day, after being purified with them, went into the Temple to give notice of the time when the period of purification would be finished and an offering would be made on behalf of each one of them. The seven days were almost over when the Jews from Asia caught sight of Paul in the Temple. They stirred up the whole crowd and seized him, shouting, "Men of Israel, help! This is the man who is teaching everybody everywhere to despise our people, our Law and this place. Why, he has even brought Greeks into the Temple and he has defiled this holy place!" For they had previously seen Trophimus the Ephesian with Paul in the city and they had concluded that Paul had brought him into the Temple. The whole city was stirred by this speech and a mob collected who seized Paul and dragged him outside the Temple, and the doors were slammed behind him.

Paul is rescued by Roman   21. 31
soldiers

They were trying to kill him when a report reached the ears of the colonel of the regiment

N.E.B.

So, as he would not be persuaded, we gave up and said, 'The Lord's will be done.'

At the end of our stay we packed our baggage and took the road up to Jerusalem. Some of the disciples from Caesarea came along with us, bringing a certain Mnason of Cyprus, a Christian from the early days, with whom we were to lodge. So we reached Jerusalem, where the brotherhood welcomed us gladly.

Next day Paul paid a visit to James; we were with him, and all the elders attended. He greeted them, and then described in detail all that God had done among the Gentiles through his ministry. When they heard this, they gave praise to God. Then they said to Paul: 'You see, brother, how many thousands of converts we have among the Jews, all of them staunch upholders of the Law. Now they have been given certain information about you: it is said that you teach all the Jews in the gentile world to turn their backs on Moses, telling them to give up circumcising their children and following our way of life. What is the position, then? They are sure to hear that you have arrived. You must therefore do as we tell you. We have four men here who are under a vow; take them with you and go through the ritual of purification with them, paying their expenses, after which they may shave their heads. Then everyone will know that there is nothing in the stories they were told about you, but that you are a practising Jew and keep the Law yourself. As for the gentile converts, we sent them our decision that they must abstain from meat that has been offered to idols, from blood, from anything that has been strangled,[a] and from fornication.' So Paul took the four men, and next day, after going through the ritual of purification with them, he went into the temple to give notice of the date when the period of purification would end and the offering be made for each one of them.

From Jerusalem to Rome

But just before the period of seven days was up, the Jews from the province of Asia saw him in the temple. They stirred up the whole crowd, and seized him, shouting, 'Men of Israel, help, help! This is the fellow who spreads his doctrine all over the world, attacking our people, our law, and this sanctuary. On top of all this he has brought Greeks into the temple and profaned this holy place.' For they had previously seen Trophimus the Ephesian with him in the city, and assumed that Paul had brought him into the temple.

The whole city was in a turmoil, and people came running from all directions. They seized Paul and dragged him out of the temple; and at once the doors were shut. While they were clamouring for his death, a report reached the officer commanding the cohort, that all Jerusa-

[a] Some witnesses omit from anything that has been strangled.

K.J.V.

of the band, that all Jerusalem was in an uproar: 32 Who immediately took soldiers and centurions, and ran down unto them: and when they saw the chief captain and the soldiers, they left beating of Paul. 33 Then the chief captain came near, and took him, and commanded *him* to be bound with two chains; and demanded who he was, and what he had done. 34And some cried one thing, some another, among the multitude: and when he could not know the certainty for the tumult, he commanded him to be carried into the castle. 35And when he came upon the stairs, so it was, that he was borne of the soldiers for the violence of the people. 36 For the multitude of the people followed after, crying, Away with him. 37And as Paul was to be led into the castle, he said unto the chief captain, May I speak unto thee? Who said, Canst thou speak Greek? 38Art not thou that Egyptian, which before these days madest an uproar, and leddest out into the wilderness four thousand men that were murderers? 39 But Paul said, I am a man *which am* a Jew of Tarsus, *a city* in Cilicia, a citizen of no mean city: and, I beseech thee, suffer me to speak unto the people. 40And when he had given him license, Paul stood on the stairs, and beckoned with the hand unto the people. And when there was made a great silence, he spake unto *them* in the Hebrew tongue, saying,

22 Men, brethren, and fathers, hear ye my defence *which I make* now unto you. 2 (And when they heard that he spake in the Hebrew tongue to them, they kept the more silence: and he saith,) 3 I am verily a man *which am* a Jew, born in Tarsus, *a city* in Cilicia, yet brought up in this city at the feet of Gamaliel, *and* taught according to the perfect manner of the law of the fathers, and was zealous toward God, as ye all are this day. 4And I persecuted this way unto the death, binding and delivering into prisons both men and women. 5As also the high priest doth bear me witness, and all the estate of the elders: from whom also I received letters unto the brethren, and went to Damascus, to bring them which were there bound unto Jerusalem, for to be punished. 6And it came to pass, that, as I made my journey, and was come nigh unto Damascus about noon, suddenly there shone from heaven a great light round about me. 7And I fell unto the ground, and heard a voice saying unto me, Saul, Saul, why persecutest thou me? 8And I answered, Who art thou, Lord? And he said unto me, I am Jesus of Nazareth, whom thou persecutest. 9And they that were with me saw indeed the light, and were afraid; but they heard not the voice of him that spake to me. 10And I said, What shall I do, Lord? And the Lord said unto me, Arise, and go into Damascus; and there it shall be told thee of all things which are appointed for thee to do. 11And when I could not see for the glory of that light, being led by the hand of them that were with me, I came into Damascus. 12And one Ananias, a devout man according to the law, having a good report of all the Jews which dwelt *there,* 13 Came unto me, and stood, and said unto me, Brother Saul, receive thy sight. And the same hour I looked up upon him. 14And he said, The God of our fathers hath chosen thee, that thou shouldest know his will, and see that Just One, and

R.S.V.

that all Jerusalem was in confusion. 32 He at once took soldiers and centurions, and ran down to them; and when they saw the tribune and the soldiers, they stopped beating Paul. 33 Then the tribune came up and arrested him, and ordered him to be bound with two chains. He inquired who he was and what he had done. 34 Some in the crowd shouted one thing, some another; and as he could not learn the facts because of the uproar, he ordered him to be brought into the barracks. 35And when he came to the steps, he was actually carried by the soldiers because of the violence of the crowd; 36 for the mob of the people followed, crying, "Away with him!"

37 As Paul was about to be brought into the barracks, he said to the tribune, "May I say something to you?" And he said, "Do you know Greek? 38Are you not the Egyptian, then, who recently stirred up a revolt and led the four thousand men of the Assassins out into the wilderness?" 39 Paul replied, "I am a Jew, from Tarsus in Cilicia, a citizen of no mean city; I beg you, let me speak to the people." 40And when he had given him leave, Paul, standing on the steps, motioned with his hand to the people; and when there was a great hush, he spoke to them in the Hebrew language, saying:

22 "Brethren and fathers, hear the defense which I now make before you." 2 And when they heard that he addressed them in the Hebrew language, they were the more quiet. And he said: 3 "I am a Jew, born at Tarsus in Cilicia, but brought up in this city at the feet of Gamaliel, educated according to the strict manner of the law of our fathers, being zealous for God as you all are this day. 4 I persecuted this Way to the death, binding and delivering to prison both men and women, 5 as the high priest and the whole council of elders bear me witness. From them I received letters to the brethren, and I journeyed to Damascus to take those also who were there and bring them in bonds to Jerusalem to be punished.

6 "As I made my journey and drew near to Damascus, about noon a great light from heaven suddenly shone about me. 7And I fell to the ground and heard a voice saying to me, 'Saul, Saul, why do you persecute me?' 8And I answered, 'Who are you, Lord?' And he said to me, 'I am Jesus of Nazareth whom you are persecuting.' 9 Now those who were with me saw the light but did not hear the voice of the one who was speaking to me. 10And I said, 'What shall I do, Lord?' And the Lord said to me, 'Rise, and go into Damascus, and there you will be told all that is appointed for you to do.' 11And when I could not see because of the brightness of that light, I was led by the hand by those who were with me, and came into Damascus.

12 "And one Ananias, a devout man according to the law, well spoken of by all the Jews who lived there, 13 came to me, and standing by me said to me, 'Brother Saul, receive your sight.' And in that very hour I received my sight and saw him. 14And he said, 'The God of our fathers appointed you to know his will, to see the Just One and to hear a voice from his

PHILLIPS

that the whole of Jerusalem was in an uproar. Without a moment's delay he took soldiers and centurions and ran down to them. When they saw the colonel and the soldiers they stopped beating Paul. The colonel came up to Paul and arrested him and ordered him to be bound with two chains. Then he inquired who the man was and what he had been doing. Some of the crowd shouted one thing and some another, and since he could not be certain of the facts because of the shouting that was going on, the colonel ordered him to be brought to the barracks. When Paul got to the steps he was actually carried by the soldiers because of the violence of the mob. For the mass of the people followed, shouting, "Kill him!" Just as they were going to take him into the barracks Paul asked the colonel,

"May I say something to you?"

"So you know Greek, do you?" the colonel replied. "Aren't you that Egyptian who not long ago raised a riot and led those four thousand assassins into the desert?"

"I am a Jew," replied Paul. "I am a man of Tarsus, a citizen of that not insignificant city. I ask you to let me speak to the people."

Paul attempts to   *21. 40; 22. 1*
defend himself

On being given permission Paul stood on the steps and made a gesture with his hand to the people. There was a deep hush as he began to speak to them in Hebrew.

"My brothers and my fathers, listen to what I have to say in my own defense."

As soon as they heard him addressing them in Hebrew the silence became intense.

"I myself am a Jew," Paul went on. "I was born in Tarsus in Cilicia, but I was brought up here in this city, I received my training at the feet of Gamaliel, and I was schooled in the strictest observance of our fathers' Law. I was as much on fire with zeal for God as you all are today. I am also the man who persecuted this Way to the death, arresting both men and women and throwing them into prison, as the High Priest and the whole council can readily testify. Indeed, it was after receiving letters from them to their brothers in Damascus that I was on my way to that city, intending to arrest any followers of the Way I could find there and bring them back to Jerusalem for punishment. Then this happened to me. As I was on my journey and getting near to Damascus, about midday a great light from Heaven suddenly blazed around me. I fell to the ground, and I heard a voice saying to me, 'Saul, Saul, why are you persecuting me?' I replied, 'Who are you, Lord?' He said to me, 'I am Jesus of Nazareth whom you are persecuting.' My companions naturally saw the light, but they did not hear the voice of the one who was talking to me. 'What am I to do, Lord?' I asked. And the Lord told me, 'Get up and go to Damascus and there you will be told of all that has been determined for you to do.' I was blinded by the brightness of that light and my companions had to take me by the hand as we went on to Damascus. There, there was a man called Ananias, a reverent observer of the Law and a man highly respected by all the Jews who lived there. He came to visit me and as he stood by my side said, 'Saul, brother, you may see again!' At once I regained my sight and looked up at him. 'The God of our fathers,' he went on, 'has chosen you to know

N.E.B.

lem was in an uproar. He immediately took a force of soldiers with their centurions and came down on the rioters at the double. As soon as they saw the commandant and his troops, they stopped beating Paul. The commandant stepped forward, arrested him, and ordered him to be shackled with two chains; he then asked who the man was and what he had been doing. Some in the crowd shouted one thing, some another. As he could not get at the truth because of the hubbub, he ordered him to be taken into barracks. When Paul reached the steps, he had to be carried by the soldiers because of the violence of the mob. For the whole crowd were at their heels yelling, 'Kill him!'

Just before Paul was taken into the barracks he said to the commandant, 'May I say something to you?' The commandant said, 'So you speak Greek, do you? Then you are not the Egyptian who started a revolt some time ago and led a force of four thousand terrorists out into the wilds?' Paul replied, 'I am a Jew, a Tarsian from Cilicia, a citizen of no mean city. I ask your permission to speak to the people.' When permission had been given, Paul stood on the steps and with a gesture called for the attention of the people. As soon as quiet was restored, he addressed them in the Jewish language:

22 'Brothers and fathers, give me a hearing while I make my defence before you.' When they heard him speaking to them in their own language, they listened the more quietly. 'I am a true-born Jew,' he said, 'a native of Tarsus in Cilicia. I was brought up in this city, and as a pupil of Gamaliel I was thoroughly trained in every point of our ancestral law. I have always been ardent in God's service, as you all are today. And so I began to persecute this movement to the death, arresting its followers, men and women alike, and putting them in chains. For this I have as witnesses the High Priest and the whole Council of Elders. I was given letters from them to our fellow-Jews at Damascus, and had started out to bring the Christians there to Jerusalem as prisoners for punishment; and this is what happened. I was on the road and nearing Damascus, when suddenly about midday a great light flashed from the sky all around me, and I fell to the ground. Then I heard a voice saying to me, "Saul, Saul, why do you persecute me?" I answered, "Tell me, Lord, who you are." "I am Jesus of Nazareth," he said, "whom you are persecuting." My companions saw the light, but did not hear the voice that spoke to me. "What shall I do, Lord?" I said, and the Lord replied, "Get up and continue your journey to Damascus; there you will be told of all the tasks that are laid upon you." As I had been blinded by the brilliance of that light, my companions led me by the hand, and so I came to Damascus.

'There, a man called Ananias, a devout observer of the Law and well spoken of by all the Jews of that place, came and stood beside me and said, "Saul, my brother, recover your sight." Instantly I recovered my sight and saw him. He went on: "The God of our fathers appointed you to know his will and to see the Righteous

K.J.V.

shouldest hear the voice of his mouth. 15 For thou shalt be his witness unto all men of what thou hast seen and heard. 16And now why tarriest thou? arise, and be baptized, and wash away thy sins, calling on the name of the Lord. 17And it came to pass, that, when I was come again to Jerusalem, even while I prayed in the temple, I was in a trance; 18And saw him saying unto me, Make haste, and get thee quickly out of Jerusalem: for they will not receive thy testimony concerning me. 19And I said, Lord, they know that I imprisoned and beat in every synagogue them that believed on thee: 20And when the blood of thy martyr Stephen was shed, I also was standing by, and consenting unto his death, and kept the raiment of them that slew him. 21And he said unto me, Depart: for I will send thee far hence unto the Gentiles. 22And they gave him audience unto this word, and *then* lifted up their voices, and said, Away with such a *fellow* from the earth: for it is not fit that he should live. 23And as they cried out, and cast off *their* clothes, and threw dust into the air, 24 The chief captain commanded him to be brought into the castle, and bade that he should be examined by scourging; that he might know wherefore they cried so against him. 25And as they bound him with thongs, Paul said unto the centurion that stood by, Is it lawful for you to scourge a man that is a Roman, and uncondemned? 26 When the centurion heard *that*, he went and told the chief captain, saying, Take heed what thou doest; for this man is a Roman. 27 Then the chief captain came, and said unto him, Tell me, art thou a Roman? He said, Yea. 28And the chief captain answered, With a great sum obtained I this freedom. And Paul said, But I was *free* born. 29 Then straightway they departed from him which should have examined him: and the chief captain also was afraid, after he knew that he was a Roman, and because he had bound him. 30 On the morrow, because he would have known the certainty wherefore he was accused of the Jews, he loosed him from *his* bands, and commanded the chief priests and all their council to appear, and brought Paul down, and set him before them.

R.S.V.

mouth; 15 for you will be a witness for him to all men of what you have seen and heard. 16And now why do you wait? Rise and be baptized, and wash away your sins, calling on his name.' 17 "When I had returned to Jerusalem and was praying in the temple, I fell into a trance 18 and saw him saying to me, 'Make haste and get quickly out of Jerusalem, because they will not accept your testimony about me.' 19And I said, 'Lord, they themselves know that in every synagogue I imprisoned and beat those who believed in thee. 20And when the blood of Stephen thy witness was shed, I also was standing by and approving, and keeping the garments of those who killed him.' 21And he said to me, 'Depart; for I will send you far away to the Gentiles.' "

22 Up to this word they listened to him; then they lifted up their voices and said, "Away with such a fellow from the earth! For he ought not to live." 23And as they cried out and waved their garments and threw dust into the air, 24 the tribune commanded him to be brought into the barracks, and ordered him to be examined by scourging, to find out why they shouted thus against him. 25 But when they had tied him up with the thongs, Paul said to the centurion who was standing by, "Is it lawful for you to scourge a man who is a Roman citizen, and uncondemned?" 26 When the centurion heard that, he went to the tribune and said to him, "What are you about to do? For this man is a Roman citizen." 27 So the tribune came and said to him, "Tell me, are you a Roman citizen?" And he said, "Yes." 28 The tribune answered, "I bought this citizenship for a large sum." Paul said, "But I was born a citizen." 29 So those who were about to examine him withdrew from him instantly; and the tribune also was afraid, for he realized that Paul was a Roman citizen and that he had bound him.

30 But on the morrow, desiring to know the real reason why the Jews accused him, he unbound him, and commanded the chief priests and all the council to meet, and he brought Paul down and set him before them.

PHILLIPS

his will, to see the righteous one, to hear words from his own lips, so that you may become his witness before all men of what you have seen and heard. And now what are you waiting for? Get up and be baptized! Be clean from your sins as you call on his name.'

Paul claims that God sent him to the gentiles   22. 17

"Then it happened that after my return to Jerusalem, while I was at prayer in the Temple, unconscious of everything else, I saw him and he said to me, 'Make haste and leave Jerusalem at once, for they will not accept your testimony about me.' And I said, 'But, Lord, they know how I have been through all the synagogues imprisoning and beating all those who believe in you. They know also that when the blood of your martyr Stephen was shed I stood by, giving my approval—why, I was even holding in my arms the outer garments of those who killed him.' But he said to me, 'Go, for I will send you far away to the gentiles.'"

The consequence of Paul's speech   22. 22

They had listened to him until he said this, but now they raised a great shout,
"Kill him, and rid the earth of such a man! He is not fit to live!"
As they were yelling and ripping their clothes and hurling dust into the air, the colonel gave orders to bring Paul into the barracks and directed that he should be examined by scourging, so that he might discover the reason for such an uproar against him. But when they had strapped him up, Paul spoke to the centurion standing by,
"Is it legal for you to flog a man who is a Roman citizen, and untried at that?"
On hearing this the centurion went in to the colonel and reported to him, saying,
"Do you realize what you were about to do? This man is a Roman citizen!"
Then the colonel himself came up to Paul and said,
"Tell me, are you a Roman citizen?"
And he said,
"Yes."
Whereupon the colonel replied,
"It cost me a good deal to get my citizenship."
"Ah," replied Paul, "but I was born a citizen."
Then those who had been about to examine him left hurriedly, while even the colonel himself was alarmed at discovering that Paul was a Roman and that he had had him bound.

Roman fair-mindedness   22. 30

Next day the colonel, determined to get to the bottom of Paul's accusation by the Jews, released him and ordered the assembly of the chief priests and the whole Sanhedrin. Then he took Paul down and placed him in front of them.

N.E.B.

One and to hear his very voice, because you are to be his witness before the world, and testify to what you have seen and heard. And now why delay? Be baptized at once, with invocation of his name, and wash away your sins."

'After my return to Jerusalem, I was praying in the temple when I fell into a trance and saw him there, speaking to me. "Make haste", he said, "and leave Jerusalem without delay, for they will not accept your testimony about me." "Lord," I said, "they know that I imprisoned those who believe in thee, and flogged them in every synagogue; and when the blood of Stephen thy witness was shed I stood by, approving, and I looked after the clothes of those who killed him." But he said to me, "Go, for I am sending you far away to the Gentiles."'

Up to this point they had given him a hearing; but now they began shouting, 'Down with him! A scoundrel like that is better dead!' And as they were yelling and waving their cloaks and flinging dust in the air, the commandant ordered him to be brought into the barracks and gave instructions to examine him by flogging, and find out what reason there was for such an outcry against him. But when they tied him up for the lash,[a] Paul said to the centurion who was standing there, 'Can you legally flog a man who is a Roman citizen, and moreover has not been found guilty?' When the centurion heard this, he went and reported it to the commandant. 'What do you mean to do?' he said. 'This man is a Roman citizen.' The commandant came to Paul. 'Tell me, are you a Roman citizen?' he asked. 'Yes', said he. The commandant rejoined, 'It cost me a large sum to acquire this citizenship.' Paul said, 'But it was mine by birth.' Then those who were about to examine him withdrew hastily, and the commandant himself was alarmed when he realized that Paul was a Roman citizen and that he had put him in irons.

The following day, wishing to be quite sure what charge the Jews were bringing against Paul, he released him and ordered the chief priests and the entire Council to assemble. He then took Paul down and stood him before them.

[a] *Or* tied him up with thongs.

23 And Paul, earnestly beholding the council, said, Men *and* brethren, I have lived in all good conscience before God until this day. 2And the high priest Ananias commanded them that stood by him to smite him on the mouth. 3 Then said Paul unto him, God shall smite thee, *thou* whited wall: for sittest thou to judge me after the law, and commandest me to be smitten contrary to the law? 4And they that stood by said, Revilest thou God's high priest? 5 Then said Paul, I wist not, brethren, that he was the high priest: for it is written, Thou shalt not speak evil of the ruler of thy people. 6 But when Paul perceived that the one part were Sadducees, and the other Pharisees, he cried out in the council, Men *and* brethren, I am a Pharisee, the son of a Pharisee: of the hope and resurrection of the dead I am called in question. 7And when he had so said, there arose a dissension between the Pharisees and the Sadducees: and the multitude was divided. 8 For the Sadducees say that there is no resurrection, neither angel, nor spirit: but the Pharisees confess both. 9And there arose a great cry: and the scribes *that were* of the Pharisees' part arose, and strove, saying, We find no evil in this man: but if a spirit or an angel hath spoken to him, let us not fight against God. 10And when there arose a great dissension, the chief captain, fearing lest Paul should have been pulled in pieces of them, commanded the soldiers to go down, and to take him by force from among them, and to bring *him* into the castle. 11And the night following the Lord stood by him, and said, Be of good cheer, Paul: for as thou hast testified of me in Jerusalem, so must thou bear witness also at Rome. 12And when it was day, certain of the Jews banded together, and bound themselves under a curse, saying that they would neither eat nor drink till they had killed Paul. 13And they were more than forty which had made this conspiracy. 14And they came to the chief priests and elders, and said, We have bound ourselves under a great curse, that we will eat nothing until we have slain Paul. 15 Now therefore ye with the council signify to the chief captain that he bring him down unto you to morrow, as though ye would inquire something more perfectly concerning him: and we, or ever

23 And Paul, looking intently at the council, said, "Brethren, I have lived before God in all good conscience up to this day." 2And the high priest Ananias commanded those who stood by him to strike him on the mouth. 3 Then Paul said to him, "God shall strike you, you whitewashed wall! Are you sitting to judge me according to the law, and yet contrary to the law you order me to be struck?" 4 Those who stood by said, "Would you revile God's high priest?" 5And Paul said, "I did not know, brethren, that he was the high priest; for it is written, 'You shall not speak evil of a ruler of your people.'" 6 But when Paul perceived that one part were Sadducees and the other Pharisees, he cried out in the council, "Brethren, I am a Pharisee, a son of Pharisees; with respect to the hope and the resurrection of the dead I am on trial." 7And when he had said this, a dissension arose between the Pharisees and the Sadducees; and the assembly was divided. 8 For the Sadducees say that there is no resurrection, nor angel, nor spirit; but the Pharisees acknowledge them all. 9 Then a great clamor arose; and some of the scribes of the Pharisees' party stood up and contended, "We find nothing wrong in this man. What if a spirit or an angel spoke to him?" 10And when the dissension became violent, the tribune, afraid that Paul would be torn in pieces by them, commanded the soldiers to go down and take him by force from among them and bring him into the barracks.

11 The following night the Lord stood by him and said, "Take courage, for as you have testified about me at Jerusalem, so you must bear witness also at Rome."

12 When it was day, the Jews made a plot and bound themselves by an oath neither to eat nor drink till they had killed Paul. 13 There were more than forty who made this conspiracy. 14And they went to the chief priests and elders, and said, "We have strictly bound ourselves by an oath to taste no food till we have killed Paul. 15 You therefore, along with the council, give notice now to the tribune to bring him down to you, as though you were going to determine his case more exactly. And we are ready to kill him before he comes near."

PHILLIPS

N.E.B.

Paul again attempts defense 23. 1

Paul looked steadily at the Sanhedrin and spoke to them,

"Men and brothers, I have lived my life with a perfectly clear conscience before God up to the present day—" Then Ananias the High Priest ordered those who were standing near to strike him on the mouth. At this Paul said to him,

"God will strike you, you whitewashed wall! How dare you sit there judging me by the Law and give orders for me to be struck, which is clean contrary to the Law?"

Those who stood by said,

"Do you mean to insult God's High Priest?" But Paul said,

"My brothers, I did not know that he was the High Priest, for it is written:

Thou shalt not speak evil of a ruler of thy people."

Paul seizes his opportunity 23. 6

Then Paul, realizing that part of the council were Sadducees and the other part Pharisees, raised his voice and said to them,

"I am a Pharisee, the son of Pharisees. It is for my hope in the resurrection of the dead that I am on trial!"

At these words an immediate tension arose between the Pharisees and the Sadducees, and the meeting was divided. For the Sadducees claim that there is no resurrection and that there is neither angel nor spirit, while the Pharisees believe in all three. A great uproar ensued and some of the scribes of the Pharisees' party jumped to their feet and protested violently,

"We find nothing wrong with this man! Suppose some angel or spirit has really spoken to him?"

As the tension mounted the colonel began to fear that Paul would be torn to pieces between them. He therefore ordered his soldiers to come down and rescue him from them and bring him back to the barracks.

God's direct encouragement to Paul 23. 11

That night the Lord stood by Paul, and said, "Take heart! For as you have witnessed boldly for me in Jerusalem so you must give your witness for me in Rome."

Paul's acute danger 23. 12

Early in the morning the Jews made a conspiracy and bound themselves by a solemn oath that they would neither eat nor drink until they had killed Paul. Over forty of them were involved in this plot, and they approached the chief priests and elders and said,

"We have bound ourselves by a solemn oath to let nothing pass our lips until we have killed Paul. Now you and the council must make it plain to the colonel that you want him to bring Paul down to you, suggesting that you want to examine his case more closely. We shall be standing by ready to kill him before he gets here."

23 Paul fixed his eyes on the Council and said, 'My brothers, I have lived all my life, and still live today, with a perfectly clear conscience before God.' At this the High Priest Ananias ordered his attendants to strike him on the mouth. Paul retorted, 'God will strike you, you whitewashed wall! You sit there to judge me in accordance with the Law; and then in defiance of the Law you order me to be struck!' The attendants said, 'Would you insult God's High Priest?' 'My brothers,' said Paul, 'I had no idea that he was High Priest; Scripture, I know, says: "You must not abuse the ruler of your people." '

Now Paul was well aware that one section of them were Sadducees and the other Pharisees, so he called out in the Council, 'My brothers, I am a Pharisee, a Pharisee born and bred; and the true issue in this trial is our hope of the resurrection of the dead.' At these words the Pharisees and Sadducees fell out among themselves, and the assembly was divided. (The Sadducees deny that there is any resurrection, or angel, or spirit, but the Pharisees accept them.) So a great uproar broke out; and some of the doctors of the law belonging to the Pharisaic party openly took sides and declared, 'We can find no fault with this man; perhaps an angel or spirit has spoken to him.' The dissension was mounting, and the commandant was afraid that Paul would be torn in pieces, so he ordered the troops to go down, pull him out of the crowd, and bring him into the barracks.

The following night the Lord appeared to him and said, 'Keep up your courage; you have affirmed the truth about me in Jerusalem, and you must do the same in Rome.'

When day broke, the Jews banded together and took an oath not to eat or drink until they had killed Paul. There were more than forty in this conspiracy. They came to the chief priests and elders and said, 'We have bound ourselves by a solemn oath not to taste food until we have killed Paul. It is now for you, acting with the Council, to apply to the commandant to bring him down to you, on the pretext of a closer investigation of his case; and we have arranged to do away with him before he arrives.'

K.J.V.

he come near, are ready to kill him. 16And when Paul's sister's son heard of their lying in wait, he went and entered into the castle, and told Paul. 17 Then Paul called one of the centurions unto *him*, and said, Bring this young man unto the chief captain: for he hath a certain thing to tell him. 18 So he took him, and brought *him* to the chief captain, and said, Paul the prisoner called me unto *him*, and prayed me to bring this young man unto thee, who hath something to say unto thee. 19 Then the chief captain took him by the hand, and went *with him* aside privately, and asked *him*, What is that thou hast to tell me? 20And he said, The Jews have agreed to desire thee that thou wouldest bring down Paul to morrow into the council, as though they would inquire somewhat of him more perfectly. 21 But do not thou yield unto them: for there lie in wait for him of them more than forty men, which have bound themselves with an oath, that they will neither eat nor drink till they have killed him: and now are they ready, looking for a promise from thee. 22 So the chief captain *then* let the young man depart, and charged *him, See thou* tell no man that thou hast shewed these things to me. 23And he called unto *him* two centurions, saying, Make ready two hundred soldiers to go to Cesarea, and horsemen threescore and ten, and spearmen two hundred, at the third hour of the night; 24And provide *them* beasts, that they may set Paul on, and bring *him* safe unto Felix the governor. 25And he wrote a letter after this manner: 26 Claudius Lysias unto the most excellent governor Felix *sendeth* greeting. 27 This man was taken of the Jews, and should have been killed of them: then came I with an army, and rescued him, having understood that he was a Roman. 28And when I would have known the cause wherefore they accused him, I brought him forth into their council: 29 Whom I perceived to be accused of questions of their law, but to have nothing laid to his charge worthy of death or of bonds. 30And when it was told me how that the Jews laid wait for the man, I sent straightway to thee, and gave commandment to his accusers also to say before thee what *they had* against him. Farewell. 31 Then the soldiers, as it was commanded them, took Paul, and brought *him* by night to Antipatris. 32 On the morrow they left the horsemen to go with him, and returned to the castle: 33 Who, when they came to Cesarea, and delivered the epistle to the governor, presented

R.S.V.

16 Now the son of Paul's sister heard of their ambush; so he went and entered the barracks and told Paul. 17And Paul called one of the centurions and said, "Bring this young man to the tribune; for he has something to tell him." 18 So he took him and brought him to the tribune and said, "Paul the prisoner called me and asked me to bring this young man to you, as he has something to say to you." 19 The tribune took him by the hand, and going aside asked him privately, "What is it that you have to tell me?" 20And he said, "The Jews have agreed to ask you to bring Paul down to the council tomorrow, as though they were going to inquire somewhat more closely about him. 21 But do not yield to them; for more than forty of their men lie in ambush for him, having bound themselves by an oath neither to eat nor drink till they have killed him; and now they are ready, waiting for the promise from you." 22 So the tribune dismissed the young man, charging him, "Tell no one that you have informed me of this."

23 Then he called two of the centurions and said, "At the third hour of the night get ready two hundred soldiers with seventy horsemen and two hundred spearmen to go as far as Caesarea. 24Also provide mounts for Paul to ride, and bring him safely to Felix the governor." 25And he wrote a letter to this effect:

26 "Claudius Lysias to his Excellency the governor Felix, greeting. 27 This man was seized by the Jews, and was about to be killed by them, when I came upon them with the soldiers and rescued him, having learned that he was a Roman citizen. 28And desiring to know the charge on which they accused him, I brought him down to their council. 29 I found that he was accused about questions of their law, but charged with nothing deserving death or imprisonment. 30And when it was disclosed to me that there would be a plot against the man, I sent him to you at once, ordering his accusers also to state before you what they have against him."

31 So the soldiers, according to their instructions, took Paul and brought him by night to Antipatris. 32And on the morrow they returned to the barracks, leaving the horsemen to go on with him. 33 When they came to Caesarea and delivered the letter to the governor, they pre-

Leakage of information leads   23. 16
to Paul's protection

However, Paul's nephew got wind of this plot and he came and found his way into the barracks and told Paul about it. Paul called one of the centurions and said,

"Take this young man to the colonel for he has something to report to him."

So the centurion took him and brought him into the colonel's presence, and said,

"The prisoner Paul called me and requested that this young man should be brought to you as he has something to say to you."

The colonel took his hand and drew him aside (where they could not be overheard), and asked,

"What have you got to tell me?"

And he replied,

"The Jews have agreed to ask you to bring Paul down to the Sanhedrin tomorrow as though they were going to inquire more carefully into his case. But I beg you not to let them persuade you. For more than forty of them are waiting for him—they have sworn a solemn oath that they will neither eat nor drink until they have killed him. They are all ready at this moment—all they want now is for you to give the order."

At this the colonel dismissed the young man with the caution,

"Don't let a soul know that you have given me this information."

Then he summoned two of his centurions, and said,

"Get two hundred men ready to proceed to Caesarea, with seventy horsemen and two hundred spearmen, by nine o'clock tonight." (Mounts were also to be provided to carry Paul safely to Felix the governor.)

The Roman view of Paul's   23. 25
position

He further wrote a letter to Felix of which this is a copy:

"Claudius Lysias sends greeting to his excellency the governor Felix,

"This man had been seized by the Jews and was on the point of being murdered by them when I arrived with my troops and rescued him, since I had discovered that he was a Roman citizen. Wishing to find out what the accusation was that they were making against him, I had him brought down to their Sanhedrin. There I discovered he was being accused over questions of their law, and that there was no charge against him which deserved either death or imprisonment. Now however, that I have received private information of a plot against his life, I have sent him to you without delay. At the same time I have notified his accusers that they must make their charges against him in your presence."

Paul is taken into protective   23. 31
custody

The soldiers, acting on their orders, took Paul and, riding through that night, brought him down to Antipatris. Next day they returned to the barracks, leaving the horsemen to accompany him further. They went into Caesarea and after delivering the letter to the governor, they

But the son of Paul's sister heard of the ambush; he went to the barracks, obtained entry, and reported it to Paul. Paul called one of the centurions and said, 'Take this young man to the commandant; he has something to report.' The centurion took him and brought him to the commandant. 'The prisoner Paul', he said, 'sent for me and asked me to bring this young man to you; he has something to tell you.' The commandant took him by the arm, drew him aside, and asked him, 'What is it you have to report?' He said, 'The Jews have made a plan among themselves and will request you to bring Paul down to the Council tomorrow, on the pretext of obtaining more precise information about him. Do not listen to them; for a party more than forty strong are lying in wait for him. They have sworn not to eat or drink until they have done away with him; they are now ready, and wait only for your consent.' So the commandant dismissed the young man, with orders not to let anyone know that he had given him this information.

Then he called a couple of his centurions and issued these orders: 'Get ready two hundred infantry to proceed to Caesarea, together with seventy cavalrymen and two hundred light-armed troops;[a] parade three hours after sunset. Provide also mounts for Paul so that he may ride through under safe escort to Felix the Governor.' And he wrote a letter to this effect:

'Claudius Lysias to His Excellency the Governor Felix. Your Excellency: This man was seized by the Jews and was on the point of being murdered when I intervened with the troops and removed him, because I discovered that he was a Roman citizen. As I wished to ascertain the charge on which they were accusing him, I took him down to their Council. I found that the accusation had to do with controversial matters in their law, but there was no charge against him meriting death or imprisonment. However, I have now been informed of an attempt to be made on the man's life, so I am sending him to you at once, and have also instructed his accusers to state their case against him before you.'[b]

Acting on their orders, the infantry took Paul and brought him by night to Antipatris. Next day they returned to their barracks, leaving the cavalry to escort him the rest of the way. The cavalry entered Caesarea, delivered the letter

---

[a] *Or* two hundred spearmen (*the meaning of the Greek word is uncertain*). [b] *Some witnesses read* '. . . before you. Farewell.'

K.J.V.

Paul also before him. 34And when the governor had read *the letter,* he asked of what province he was. And when he understood that *he was* of Cilicia; 35 I will hear thee, said he, when thine accusers are also come. And he commanded him to be kept in Herod's judgment hall.

24 And after five days Ananias the high priest descended with the elders, and *with* a certain orator *named* Tertullus, who informed the governor against Paul. 2And when he was called forth, Tertullus began to accuse *him,* saying, Seeing that by thee we enjoy great quietness, and that very worthy deeds are done unto this nation by thy providence, 3 We accept *it* always, and in all places, most noble Felix, with all thankfulness. 4 Notwithstanding, that I be not further tedious unto thee, I pray thee that thou wouldest hear us of thy clemency a few words. 5 For we have found this man *a* pestilent *fellow,* and a mover of sedition among all the Jews throughout the world, and a ringleader of the sect of the Nazarenes: 6 Who hath gone about to profane the temple: whom we took, and would have judged according to our law. 7 But the chief captain Lysias came *upon us,* and with great violence took *him* away out of our hands, 8 Commanding his accusers to come unto thee: by examining of whom thyself mayest take knowledge of all these things, whereof we accuse him. 9And the Jews also assented, saying that these things were so. 10 Then Paul, after that the governor had beckoned unto him to speak, answered, Forasmuch as I know that thou hast been of many years a judge unto this nation, I do the more cheerfully answer for myself: 11 Because that thou mayest understand, that there are yet but twelve days since I went up to Jerusalem for to worship. 12And they neither found me in the temple disputing with any man, neither raising up the people, neither in the synagogues, nor in the city: 13 Neither can they prove the things whereof they now accuse me. 14 But this I confess unto thee, that after the way which they call heresy, so worship I the God of my fathers, believing all things which are written in the law and in the prophets: 15And have hope toward God, which they themselves also allow, that there shall be a resurrection of the dead, both of the just and unjust. 16And herein do I exercise myself, to have always a conscience void of offence toward God, and *toward* men. 17 Now after many years I came to bring alms to my nation, and offerings. 18 Whereupon certain Jews from Asia found me purified in the temple, neither with multitude,

R.S.V.

sented Paul also before him. 34 On reading the letter, he asked to what province he belonged. When he learned that he was from Cilicia 35 he said, "I will hear you when your accusers arrive." And he commanded him to be guarded in Herod's praetorium.

24 And after five days the high priest Ananias came down with some elders and a spokesman, one Tertullus. They laid before the governor their case against Paul; 2 and when he was called, Tertullus began to accuse him, saying:
"Since through you we enjoy much peace, and since by your provision, most excellent Felix, reforms are introduced on behalf of this nation, 3 in every way and everywhere we accept this with all gratitude. 4 But, to detain you no further, I beg you in your kindness to hear us briefly. 5 For we have found this man a pestilent fellow, an agitator among all the Jews throughout the world, and a ringleader of the sect of the Nazarenes. 6 He even tried to profane the temple, but we seized him.*z* 8 By examining him yourself you will be able to learn from him about everything of which we accuse him."
9 The Jews also joined in the charge, affirming that all this was so.
10 And when the governor had motioned to him to speak, Paul replied:
"Realizing that for many years you have been judge over this nation, I cheerfully make my defense. 11 As you may ascertain, it is not more than twelve days since I went up to worship at Jerusalem; 12 and they did not find me disputing with any one or stirring up a crowd, either in the temple or in the synagogues, or in the city. 13 Neither can they prove to you what they now bring up against me. 14 But this I admit to you, that according to the Way, which they call a sect, I worship the God of our fathers, believing everything laid down by the law or written in the prophets, 15 having a hope in God which these themselves accept, that there will be a resurrection of both the just and the unjust. 16 So I always take pains to have a clear conscience toward God and toward men. 17 Now after some years I came to bring to my nation alms and offerings. 18 As I was doing this, they found me purified in the temple, without any crowd or

[z] Other ancient authorities add *and we would have judged him according to our law.* 7 *But the chief captain Lysias came and with great violence took him out of our hands,* 8 *commanding his accusers to come before you.*

handed Paul over to him. When the governor
had read the letter he asked Paul what province
he came from, and on learning that he came
from Cilicia, he said,

"I will hear your case as soon as your accusers
arrive."

Then he ordered him to be kept under guard
in Herod's palace.

to the Governor, and handed Paul over to him.
He read the letter, asked him what province he
was from, and learned that he was from Cilicia.
'I will hear your case', he said, 'when your
accusers arrive.' He then ordered him to be held
in custody at his headquarters in Herod's palace.

The "professional" puts the case   24. 1
against Paul

Five days later Ananias the High Priest came
down himself with some of the elders and a
lawyer by the name of Tertullus. They presented
their case against Paul before the governor, and
when Paul had been summoned, Tertullus began
the prosecution in these words:

"We owe it to you personally, your excellency,
that we enjoy lasting peace, and we know that
it is due to your foresight that the nation enjoys
improved conditions of living. At all times, and
indeed everywhere, we acknowledge these things
with the deepest gratitude. However—for I must
not detain you too long—I beg you to give us
a brief hearing with your customary kindness.
The simple fact is that we have found this man
a pestilential disturber of the peace among the
Jews all over the world. He is a ringleader of
the Nazareth sect, and he was on the point of
desecrating the Temple when we overcame him.
But you yourself will soon discover from the
man himself all the facts about which we are
accusing him."

24 Five days later the High Priest Ananias
came down, accompanied by some of the
elders and an advocate named Tertullus, and
they laid an information against Paul before the
Governor. When the prisoner was called, Tertullus opened the case.

'Your Excellency,' he said, 'we owe it to you
that we enjoy unbroken peace. It is due to your
provident care that, in all kinds of ways and
in all sorts of places, improvements are being
made for the good of this province. We welcome
this, sir, most gratefully. And now, not to take
up too much of your time, I crave your indulgence for a brief statement of our case. We have
found this man to be a perfect pest, a fomenter
of discord among the Jews all over the world,
a ringleader of the sect of the Nazarenes. He
even made an attempt to profane the temple;
and then we arrested him.[a] If you will examine
him yourself you can ascertain from him the
truth of all the charges we bring.' The Jews supported the attack, alleging that the facts were as
he stated.

Then the Governor motioned to Paul to speak,
and he began his reply: 'Knowing as I do that
for many years you have administered justice in
this province, I make my defence with confidence. You can ascertain the facts for yourself.
It is not more than twelve days since I went up
to Jerusalem on a pilgrimage. They did not find
me arguing with anyone, or collecting a crowd,
either in the temple or in the synagogues or up
and down the city; and they cannot make good
the charges they bring against me. But this much
I will admit: I am a follower of the new way
(the "sect" they speak of), and it is in that
manner that I worship the God of our fathers;
for I believe all that is written in the Law and the
prophets, and in reliance on God I hold the
hope, which my accusers too accept, that there
is to be a resurrection of good and wicked alike.
Accordingly I, no less than they, train myself
to keep at all times a clear conscience before
God and man.

'After an absence of several years I came to
bring charitable gifts to my nation and to offer
sacrifices. They found me in the temple ritually
purified and engaged in this service. I had no

Paul is given the chance   24. 9
to defend himself

While Tertullus was speaking the Jews kept
joining in, asserting that these were the facts.
Then Paul, at a nod from the governor, made
his reply:

"I am well aware that you have been governor
of this nation for many years, and I can therefore make my defense with every confidence.
You can easily verify the fact that it is not more
than twelve days ago that I went up to worship
at Jerusalem. I was never found either arguing
with anyone in the Temple or gathering a crowd,
either in the synagogues or in the open air.
These men are quite unable to prove the charges
they are now making against me. I will freely
admit to you, however, that I do worship the
God of our fathers according to the Way which
they call a heresy, although in fact I believe in
the scriptural authority of both the Law and
the Prophets. I have the same hope in God
which they themselves hold, that there is to be
a resurrection of both good men and bad. With
this hope before me I do my utmost to live my
whole life with a clear conscience before God
and man.

Paul has nothing to hide   24. 17

"It was in fact after several years' absence
from Jerusalem that I came back to make charitable gifts to my own nation and to make my
offerings. It was in the middle of these duties
that they found me, a man purified in the Tem-

[a] *Some witnesses insert* It was our intention to
try him under our law; (7) but Lysias the commandant intervened and took him by force out of
our hands, (8) ordering his accusers to come before you.

K.J.V.

nor with tumult. 19 Who ought to have been here before thee, and object, if they had aught against me. 20 Or else let these same *here* say, if they have found any evil doing in me, while I stood before the council, 21 Except it be for this one voice, that I cried standing among them, Touching the resurrection of the dead I am called in question by you this day. 22And when Felix heard these things, having more perfect knowledge of *that* way, he deferred them, and said, When Lysias the chief captain shall come down, I will know the uttermost of your matter. 23And he commanded a centurion to keep Paul, and to let *him* have liberty, and that he should forbid none of his acquaintance to minister or come unto him. 24And after certain days, when Felix came with his wife Drusilla, which was a Jewess, he sent for Paul, and heard him concerning the faith in Christ. 25And as he reasoned of righteousness, temperance, and judgment to come, Felix trembled, and answered, Go thy way for this time; when I have a convenient season, I will call for thee. 26 He hoped also that money should have been given him of Paul, that he might loose him: wherefore he sent for him the oftener, and communed with him. 27 But after two years Porcius Festus came into Felix' room: and Felix, willing to shew the Jews a pleasure, left Paul bound.

R.S.V.

tumult. But some Jews from Asia—19 they ought to be here before you and to make an accusation, if they have anything against me. 20 Or else let these men themselves say what wrongdoing they found when I stood before the council, 21 except this one thing which I cried out while standing among them, 'With respect to the resurrection of the dead I am on trial before you this day.' "

22 But Felix, having a rather accurate knowledge of the Way, put them off, saying, "When Lysias the tribune comes down, I will decide your case." 23 Then he gave orders to the centurion that he should be kept in custody but should have some liberty, and that none of his friends should be prevented from attending to his needs.

24 After some days Felix came with his wife Drusilla, who was a Jewess; and he sent for Paul and heard him speak upon faith in Christ Jesus. 25And as he argued about justice and self-control and future judgment, Felix was alarmed and said, "Go away for the present; when I have an opportunity I will summon you." 26At the same time he hoped that money would be given him by Paul. So he sent for him often and conversed with him. 27 But when two years had elapsed, Felix was succeeded by Porcius Festus; and desiring to do the Jews a favor, Felix left Paul in prison.

25 Now when Festus was come into the province, after three days he ascended from Cesarea to Jerusalem. 2 Then the high priest and the chief of the Jews informed him against Paul, and besought him, 3And desired favour against him, that he would send for him to Jerusalem, laying wait in the way to kill him. 4 But Festus answered, that Paul should be kept at Cesarea, and that he himself would depart shortly *thither*. 5 Let them therefore, said he, which among you are able, go down with *me*, and accuse this man, if there be any wickedness in him. 6And when he had tarried among them more than ten days, he went down unto Cesarea; and the next day sitting on the judgment seat commanded Paul to be brought. 7And when he was come, the Jews which came down from Jerusalem stood round about, and laid many and grievous complaints against Paul, which they could not prove.

25 Now when Festus had come into his province, after three days he went up to Jerusalem from Caesarea. 2And the chief priests and the principal men of the Jews informed him against Paul; and they urged him, 3 asking as a favor to have the man sent to Jerusalem, planning an ambush to kill him on the way. 4 Festus replied that Paul was being kept at Caesarea, and that he himself intended to go there shortly. 5 "So," said he, "let the men of authority among you go down with me, and if there is anything wrong about the man, let them accuse him." 6 When he had stayed among them not more than eight or ten days, he went down to Caesarea; and the next day he took his seat on the tribunal and ordered Paul to be brought. 7And when he had come, the Jews who had gone down from Jerusalem stood about him, bringing against him many serious charges which they

PHILLIPS

ple. There was no mob and there was no disturbance until these Jews from Asia came, who should in my opinion have come before you and made their accusation, if they had anything against me. Or else, let these men themselves speak out now and say what crime they found me guilty of when I stood before the Sanhedrin—unless it was that one sentence that I shouted as I stood among them. All I said was this, 'It is about the resurrection of the dead that I am on trial before you this day.'"

Felix defers decision   24. 22

Then Felix, who was better acquainted with the Way than most people, adjourned the case and said,
"As soon as Colonel Lysias arrives I will give you my decision."
Then he gave orders to the centurion to keep Paul in custody, but to grant him reasonable liberty and allow any of his personal friends to look after his needs.

Felix plays for safety—and   24. 24
hopes for personal gain

Some days later Felix arrived with his wife Drusilla, herself a Jewess, and sent for Paul, and heard what he had to say about faith in Christ Jesus. But while Paul was talking about goodness, self-control and the judgment that is to come, Felix became alarmed, and said,
"You may go for the present. When I find a convenient moment I will send for you again."
At the same time he nursed a secret hope that Paul would pay him money—which is why Paul was frequently summoned to come and talk with him. However, when two full years had passed, Felix was succeeded by Porcius Festus and, as he wanted to remain in favor with the Jews, he left Paul still a prisoner.

Felix's successor begins his   25. 1
duties with vigor—

Three days after Festus had taken over his province he went up from Caesarea to Jerusalem. The chief priests and elders of the Jews informed him of the case against Paul and begged him as a special favor to have Paul sent to Jerusalem. They themselves had already made a plot to kill him on the way. But Festus replied that Paul was in custody in Caesarea, and that he himself was going there shortly.
"What you must do," he told them, "is to provide some competent men of your own to go down with me and if there is anything wrong with the man they can present their charges against him."
Festus spent not more than eight or ten days among them at Jerusalem and then went down to Caesarea. On the day after his arrival he took his seat on the bench and ordered Paul to be brought in. As soon as he arrived the Jews from Jerusalem stood up on all sides of him, bringing forward many serious accusations which they were quite unable to substantiate. Paul, in his defense, maintained,

N.E.B.

crowd with me, and there was no disturbance. But some Jews from the province of Asia were there, and if they had any charge against me it is they who ought to have been in court to state it. Failing that, it is for these persons here present to say what crime they discovered when I was brought before the Council, apart from this one open assertion which I made as I stood there: "The true issue in my trial before you today is the resurrection of the dead." '
Then Felix, who happened to be well informed about the Christian movement, adjourned the hearing. 'When Lysias the commanding officer comes down', he said, 'I will go into your case.' He gave orders to the centurion to keep Paul under open arrest and not to prevent any of his friends from making themselves useful to him.
Some days later Felix came with his wife Drusilla, who was a Jewess, and sending for Paul he let him talk to him about faith in Christ Jesus. But when the discourse turned to questions of morals, self-control, and the coming judgement, Felix became alarmed and exclaimed, 'That will do for the present; when I find it convenient I will send for you again.' At the same time he had hopes of a bribe from Paul; and for this reason he sent for him very often and talked with him. When two years had passed, Felix was succeeded by Porcius Festus. Wishing to curry favour with the Jews, Felix left Paul in custody.

25   Three days after taking up his appointment Festus went up from Caesarea to Jerusalem, where the chief priests and the Jewish leaders brought before him the case against Paul. They asked Festus to favour them against him, and pressed for him to be brought up to Jerusalem, for they were planning an ambush to kill him on the way. Festus, however, replied, 'Paul is in safe custody at Caesarea, and I shall be leaving Jerusalem shortly myself; so let your leading men come down with me, and if there is anything wrong, let them prosecute him.'
After spending eight or ten days at most in Jerusalem, he went down to Caesarea, and next day he took his seat in court and ordered Paul to be brought up. When he appeared, the Jews who had come down from Jerusalem stood round bringing many grave charges, which they

K.J.V.

8 While he answered for himself, Neither against the law of the Jews, neither against the temple, nor yet against Cesar, have I offended any thing at all. 9 But Festus, willing to do the Jews a pleasure, answered Paul, and said, Wilt thou go up to Jerusalem, and there be judged of these things before me? 10 Then said Paul, I stand at Cesar's judgment seat, where I ought to be judged: to the Jews have I done no wrong, as thou very well knowest. 11 For if I be an offender, or have committed any thing worthy of death, I refuse not to die: but if there be none of these things whereof these accuse me, no man may deliver me unto them. I appeal unto Cesar. 12 Then Festus, when he had conferred with the council, answered, Hast thou appealed unto Cesar? unto Cesar shalt thou go. 13 And after certain days king Agrippa and Bernice came unto Cesarea to salute Festus. 14 And when they had been there many days, Festus declared Paul's cause unto the king, saying, There is a certain man left in bonds by Felix: 15 About whom, when I was at Jerusalem, the chief priests and the elders of the Jews informed *me,* desiring *to have* judgment against him. 16 To whom I answered, It is not the manner of the Romans to deliver any man to die, before that he which is accused have the accusers face to face, and have license to answer for himself concerning the crime laid against him. 17 Therefore, when they were come hither, without any delay on the morrow I sat on the judgment seat, and commanded the man to be brought forth. 18 Against whom when the accusers stood up, they brought none accusation of such things as I supposed: 19 But had certain questions against him of their own superstition, and of one Jesus, which was dead, whom Paul affirmed to be alive. 20 And because I doubted of such manner of questions, I asked *him* whether he would go to Jerusalem, and there be judged of these matters. 21 But when Paul had appealed to be reserved unto the hearing of Augustus, I commanded him to be kept till I might send him to Cesar. 22 Then Agrippa said unto Festus, I would also hear the man myself. To morrow, said he, thou shalt

R.S.V.

could not prove. 8 Paul said in his defense, "Neither against the law of the Jews, nor against the temple, nor against Caesar have I offended at all." 9 But Festus, wishing to do the Jews a favor, said to Paul, "Do you wish to go up to Jerusalem, and there be tried on these charges before me?" 10 But Paul said, "I am standing before Caesar's tribunal, where I ought to be tried; to the Jews I have done no wrong, as you know very well. 11 If then I am a wrongdoer, and have committed anything for which I deserve to die, I do not seek to escape death; but if there is nothing in their charges against me, no one can give me up to them. I appeal to Caesar." 12 Then Festus, when he had conferred with his council, answered, "You have appealed to Caesar; to Caesar you shall go."

13 Now when some days had passed, Agrippa the king and Bernice arrived at Caesarea to welcome Festus. 14 And as they stayed there many days, Festus laid Paul's case before the king, saying, "There is a man left prisoner by Felix; 15 and when I was at Jerusalem, the chief priests and the elders of the Jews gave information about him, asking for sentence against him. 16 I answered them that it was not the custom of the Romans to give up any one before the accused met the accusers face to face, and had opportunity to make his defense concerning the charge laid against him. 17 When therefore they came together here, I made no delay, but on the next day took my seat on the tribunal and ordered the man to be brought in. 18 When the accusers stood up, they brought no charge in his case of such evils as I supposed; 19 but they had certain points of dispute with him about their own superstition and about one Jesus, who was dead, but whom Paul asserted to be alive. 20 Being at a loss how to investigate these questions, I asked whether he wished to go to Jerusalem and be tried there regarding them. 21 But when Paul had appealed to be kept in custody for the decision of the emperor, I commanded him to be held until I could send him to Caesar." 22 And Agrippa said to Festus, "I should like to hear the man myself." "Tomorrow," said he, "you shall hear him."

"I have committed no offense in any way against the Jewish Law, or against the Temple or against Caesar."

—but is afraid of antagonizing the Jews 25. 9

But Festus, wishing to gain the goodwill of the Jews, spoke direct to Paul,

"Are you prepared to go up to Jerusalem and stand your trial over these matters in my presence there?"

But Paul replied,

"I am standing in Caesar's court and that is where I should be judged. I have done the Jews no harm, as you very well know. It comes to this: if I were a criminal and had committed some crime which deserved the death penalty, I should not try to evade sentence of death. But as in fact there is no truth in the accusations these men have made, I am not prepared to be used as a means of gaining their favor—*I appeal to Caesar!*"

Then Festus, after a conference with his advisers, replied to Paul,

"You have appealed to Caesar—then to Caesar you shall go!"

Festus outlines Paul's case to Agrippa 25. 13

Some days later king Agrippa and Bernice arrived at Caesarea on a state visit to Festus. They prolonged their stay for some days, and this gave Festus an opportunity of laying Paul's case before the king.

"I have a man here," he said, "who was left a prisoner by Felix. When I was in Jerusalem the chief priests and Jewish elders made allegations against him and demanded his conviction! I told them that the Romans were not in the habit of giving anybody up to please anyone, until the accused had had the chance of facing his accusers personally and been given the opportunity of defending himself on the charges made against him. Since these Jews came back here with me, I wasted no time but on the very next day I took my seat on the bench and ordered the man to be brought in. But when his accusers got up to speak they did not charge him with any such crimes as I had anticipated. Their differences with him were about their own religion and concerning a certain Jesus who had died, but whom Paul claimed to be still alive. I did not feel qualified to investigate such matters and so I asked the man if he were willing to go to Jerusalem and stand his trial over these matters there. But when he appealed to have his case reserved for the decision of the emperor himself, I ordered him to be kept in custody until such time as I could send him to Caesar."

Then Agrippa said to Festus,

"I have been wanting to hear this man myself."

"Then you shall hear him tomorrow," replied Festus.

were unable to prove. Paul's plea was: 'I have committed no offence, either against the Jewish law, or against the temple, or against the Emperor.' Festus, anxious to ingratiate himself with the Jews, turned to Paul and asked, 'Are you willing to go up to Jerusalem and stand trial on these charges before me there?' But Paul said, 'I am now standing before the Emperor's tribunal, and that is where I must be tried. Against the Jews I have committed no offence, as you very well know. If I am guilty of any capital crime, I do not ask to escape the death penalty; but if there is no substance in the charges which these men bring against me, it is not open to anyone to hand me over as a sop to them. I appeal to Caesar!' Then Festus, after conferring with his advisers, replied, 'You have appealed to Caesar: to Caesar you shall go.'

After an interval of some days King Agrippa and Bernice arrived at Caesarea on a courtesy visit to Festus. They spent several days there, and during this time Festus laid Paul's case before the king. 'We have a man', he said, 'left in custody by Felix; and when I was in Jerusalem the chief priests and elders of the Jews laid an information against him, demanding his condemnation. I answered them, "It is not Roman practice to hand over any accused man before he is confronted with his accusers and given an opportunity of answering the charge." So when they had come here with me I lost no time; the very next day I took my seat in court and ordered the man to be brought up. But when his accusers rose to speak, they brought none of the charges I was expecting; they merely had certain points of disagreement with him about their peculiar religion, and about someone called Jesus, a dead man whom Paul alleged to be alive. Finding myself out of my depth in such discussions, I asked if he was willing to go to Jerusalem and stand his trial there on these issues. But Paul appealed to be remanded in custody for His Imperial Majesty's decision, and I ordered him to be detained until I could send him to the Emperor.' Agrippa said to Festus, 'I should rather like to hear the man myself.' 'Tomorrow', he answered, 'you shall hear him.'

K.J.V.

hear him. 23And on the morrow, when Agrippa was come, and Bernice, with great pomp, and was entered into the place of hearing, with the chief captains, and principal men of the city, at Festus' commandment Paul was brought forth. 24And Festus said, King Agrippa, and all men which are here present with us, ye see this man, about whom all the multitude of the Jews have dealt with me, both at Jerusalem, and *also* here, crying that he ought not to live any longer. 25 But when I found that he had committed nothing worthy of death, and that he himself hath appealed to Augustus, I have determined to send him. 26 Of whom I have no certain thing to write unto my lord. Wherefore I have brought him forth before you, and specially before thee, O king Agrippa, that, after examination had, I might have somewhat to write. 27 For it seemeth to me unreasonable to send a prisoner, and not withal to signify the crimes *laid* against him.

26 Then Agrippa said unto Paul, Thou art permitted to speak for thyself. Then Paul stretched forth the hand, and answered for himself: 2 I think myself happy, king Agrippa, because I shall answer for myself this day before thee touching all the things whereof I am accused of the Jews: 3 Especially *because I know* thee to be expert in all customs and questions which are among the Jews: wherefore I beseech thee to hear me patiently. 4 My manner of life from my youth, which was at the first among mine own nation at Jerusalem, know all the Jews; 5 Which knew me from the beginning, if they would testify, that after the most straitest sect of our religion I lived a Pharisee. 6And now I stand and am judged for the hope of the promise made of God unto our fathers: 7 Unto which *promise* our twelve tribes, instantly serving *God* day and night, hope to come. For which hope's sake, king Agrippa, I am accused of the Jews. 8 Why should it be thought a thing incredible with you, that God should raise the dead? 9 I verily thought with myself, that I ought to do many things contrary to the name of Jesus of Nazareth. 10 Which thing I also did in Jerusalem: and many of the saints did I shut up in prison, having received authority from the chief priests; and when they were put to death, I gave my voice against *them*. 11And I punished them oft in every synagogue, and compelled *them* to blaspheme; and being exceedingly mad against them, I persecuted *them* even unto strange cities. 12 Whereupon as I went to Damascus with authority and commission from the chief priests, 13At midday, O king, I saw in the way a light from heaven, above the brightness of the sun, shining round about me and them which journeyed with me. 14And when we were all fallen to the earth, I heard a voice speaking unto me,

R.S.V.

23 So on the morrow Agrippa and Bernice came with great pomp, and they entered the audience hall with the military tribunes and the prominent men of the city. Then by command of Festus Paul was brought in. 24And Festus said, "King Agrippa and all who are present with us, you see this man about whom the whole Jewish people petitioned me, both at Jerusalem and here, shouting that he ought not to live any longer. 25 But I found that he had done nothing deserving death; and as he himself appealed to the emperor, I decided to send him. 26 But I have nothing definite to write to my lord about him. Therefore I have brought him before you, and, especially before you, King Agrippa, that, after we have examined him, I may have something to write. 27 For it seems to me unreasonable, in sending a prisoner, not to indicate the charges against him."

26 Agrippa said to Paul, "You have permission to speak for yourself." Then Paul stretched out his hand and made his defense: 2 "I think myself fortunate that it is before you, King Agrippa, I am to make my defense today against all the accusations of the Jews, 3 because you are especially familiar with all customs and controversies of the Jews; therefore I beg you to listen to me patiently. 4 "My manner of life from my youth, spent from the beginning among my own nation and at Jerusalem, is known by all the Jews. 5 They have known for a long time, if they are willing to testify, that according to the strictest party of our religion I have lived as a Pharisee. 6And now I stand here on trial for hope in the promise made by God to our fathers, 7 to which our twelve tribes hope to attain, as they earnestly worship night and day. And for this hope I am accused by Jews, O king! 8 Why is it thought incredible by any of you that God raises the dead? 9 "I myself was convinced that I ought to do many things in opposing the name of Jesus of Nazareth. 10And I did so in Jerusalem; I not only shut up many of the saints in prison, by authority from the chief priests, but when they were put to death I cast my vote against them. 11And I punished them often in all the synagogues and tried to make them blaspheme; and in raging fury against them, I persecuted them even to foreign cities. 12 "Thus I journeyed to Damascus with the authority and commission of the chief priests. 13At midday, O king, I saw on the way a light from heaven, brighter than the sun, shining round me and those who journeyed with me. 14And when we had all fallen to the ground, I heard a voice saying to me in the Hebrew

PHILLIPS	N.E.B.

Festus formally explains the   **25. 23**
difficulty of Paul's case

When the next day came, Agrippa and Bernice proceeded to the audience chamber with great pomp and ceremony, with an escort of military officers and prominent townsmen. Festus ordered Paul to be brought in and then he spoke:

"King Agrippa and all of you who are present, you see here the man about whom the whole Jewish people both at Jerusalem and in this city have petitioned me. They din it into my ears that he ought not to live any longer, but I for my part discovered nothing that he has done which deserves the death penalty. And since he has appealed to Caesar, I have decided to send him to Rome. Frankly, I have nothing specific to write to the emperor about him, and I have therefore brought him forward before you all, and especially before you, King Agrippa, so that from your examination of him there may emerge some charge which I may put in writing. For it seems ridiculous to me to send a prisoner before the emperor without indicating the charges against him."

Then Agrippa said to Paul, "You have our permission to speak for yourself."

Paul repeats his story   **26. 1b**
on a state occasion

So Paul, with that characteristic gesture of the hand, began his defense:

"King Agrippa, in answering all the charges that the Jews have made against me, I must say how fortunate I consider myself to be in making my defense before you personally today. For I know that you are thoroughly familiar with all the customs and disputes that exist among the Jews. I therefore ask you to listen to me patiently.

"The fact that I lived from my youth upwards among my own people in Jerusalem is well known to all Jews. They have known all the time, and could witness to the fact if they wished, that I lived as a Pharisee according to the strictest sect of our religion. Even today I stand here on trial because of a hope that I hold in a promise that God made to our forefathers—a promise for which our twelve tribes serve God zealously day and night, hoping to see it fulfilled. It is about this hope, your majesty, that I am being accused by Jews! Why does it seem incredible to you all that God should raise the dead? I once thought it my duty to oppose with the utmost vigor the name of Jesus of Nazareth. Yes, that is what I did in Jerusalem, and I had many of God's people imprisoned on the authority of the chief priests, and when they were on trial for their lives I gave my vote against them. Many and many a time in all the synagogues I had them punished and I used to try and force them to deny their Lord. I was mad with fury against them, and I hounded them to distant cities. Once, your majesty, on my way to Damascus on this business, armed with the full authority and commission of the chief priests, at midday I saw a light from Heaven, far brighter than the sun, blazing about me and my fellow travelers. We all fell to the ground and I heard a voice saying to me

So next day Agrippa and Bernice came in full state and entered the audience-chamber accompanied by high-ranking officers and prominent citizens; and on the orders of Festus Paul was brought up. Then Festus said, 'King Agrippa, and all you gentlemen here present with us, you see this man: the whole body of the Jews approached me both in Jerusalem and here, loudly insisting that he had no right to remain alive. But it was clear to me that he had committed no capital crime, and when he himself appealed to His Imperial Majesty, I decided to send him. But I have nothing definite about him to put in writing for our Sovereign. Accordingly I have brought him up before you all and particularly before you, King Agrippa, so that as a result of this preliminary inquiry I may have something to report. There is no sense, it seems to me, in sending on a prisoner without indicating the charges against him.'

26 Agrippa said to Paul, 'You have our permission to speak for yourself.' Then Paul stretched out his hand and began his defence:

'I consider myself fortunate, King Agrippa, that it is before you that I am to make my defence today upon all the charges brought against me by the Jews, particularly as you are expert in all Jewish matters, both our customs and our disputes. And therefore I beg you to give me a patient hearing.

'My life from my youth up, the life I led from the beginning among my people and in Jerusalem, is familiar to all Jews. Indeed they have known me long enough and could testify, if they only would, that I belonged to the strictest group in our religion: I lived as a Pharisee. And it is for a hope kindled by God's promise to our forefathers that I stand in the dock today. Our twelve tribes hope to see the fulfilment of that promise, worshipping with intense devotion day and night; and for this very hope I am impeached, and impeached by Jews, Your Majesty. Why is it considered incredible among you that God should raise dead men to life?

'I myself once thought it my duty to work actively against the name of Jesus of Nazareth; and I did so in Jerusalem. It was I who imprisoned many of God's people by authority obtained from the chief priests; and when they were condemned to death, my vote was cast against them. In all the synagogues I tried by repeated punishment to make them renounce their faith; indeed my fury rose to such a pitch that I extended my persecution to foreign cities.

'On one such occasion I was travelling to Damascus with authority and commission from the chief priests; and as I was on my way, Your Majesty, in the middle of the day I saw a light from the sky, more brilliant than the sun, shining all around me and my travelling-companions. We all fell to the ground, and then I heard a voice saying to me in the Jewish language, "Saul,

K.J.V.

and saying in the Hebrew tongue, Saul, Saul, why persecutest thou me? *it is* hard for thee to kick against the pricks. 15And I said, Who art thou, Lord? And he said, I am Jesus whom thou persecutest. 16 But rise, and stand upon thy feet: for I have appeared unto thee for this purpose, to make thee a minister and a witness both of these things which thou hast seen, and of those things in the which I will appear unto thee; 17 Delivering thee from the people, and *from* the Gentiles, unto whom now I send thee, 18 To open their eyes, *and* to turn *them* from darkness to light, and *from* the power of Satan unto God, that they may receive forgiveness of sins, and inheritance among them which are sanctified by faith that is in me. 19 Whereupon, O king Agrippa, I was not disobedient unto the heavenly vision: 20 But shewed first unto them of Damascus, and at Jerusalem, and throughout all the coasts of Judea, and *then* to the Gentiles, that they should repent and turn to God, and do works meet for repentance. 21 For these causes the Jews caught me in the temple, and went about to kill *me.* 22 Having therefore obtained help of God, I continue unto this day, witnessing both to small and great, saying none other things than those which the prophets and Moses did say should come: 23 That Christ should suffer, *and* that he should be the first that should rise from the dead, and should shew light unto the people, and to the Gentiles. 24And as he thus spake for himself, Festus said with a loud voice, Paul, thou art beside thyself; much learning doth make thee mad. 25 But he said, I am not mad, most noble Festus; but speak forth the words of truth and soberness. 26 For the king knoweth of these things, before whom also I speak freely: for I am persuaded that none of these things are hidden from him; for this thing was not done in a corner. 27 King Agrippa, believest thou the prophets? I know that thou believest. 28 Then Agrippa said unto Paul, Almost thou persuadest me to be a Christian. 29And Paul said, I would to God, that not only thou, but also all that hear me this day, were both almost, and altogether such as I am, except these bonds. 30And when he had thus spoken, the king rose up, and the governor, and Bernice, and they that sat with them: 31And when they were gone aside, they talked between themselves, saying, This man doeth nothing worthy of death or of bonds. 32 Then said Agrippa unto Festus, This man might have been set at liberty, if he had not appealed unto Cesar.

R.S.V.

language, 'Saul, Saul, why do you persecute me? It hurts you to kick against the goads.' 15And I said, 'Who are you, Lord?' And the Lord said, 'I am Jesus whom you are persecuting. 16 But rise and stand upon your feet; for I have appeared to you for this purpose, to appoint you to serve and bear witness to the things in which you have seen me and to those in which I will appear to you, 17 delivering you from the people and from the Gentiles—to whom I send you 18 to open their eyes, that they may turn from darkness to light and from the power of Satan to God, that they may receive forgiveness of sins and a place among those who are sanctified by faith in me.'
19 "Wherefore, O King Agrippa, I was not disobedient to the heavenly vision, 20 but declared first to those at Damascus, then at Jerusalem and throughout all the country of Judea, and also to the Gentiles, that they should repent and turn to God and perform deeds worthy of their repentance. 21 For this reason the Jews seized me in the temple and tried to kill me. 22 To this day I have had the help that comes from God, and so I stand here testifying both to small and great, saying nothing but what the prophets and Moses said would come to pass: 23 that the Christ must suffer, and that, by being the first to rise from the dead, he would proclaim light both to the people and to the Gentiles."
24 And as he thus made his defense, Festus said with a loud voice, "Paul, you are mad; your great learning is turning you mad." 25 But Paul said, "I am not mad, most excellent Festus, but I am speaking the sober truth. 26 For the king knows about these things, and to him I speak freely; for I am persuaded that none of these things has escaped his notice, for this was not done in a corner. 27 King Agrippa, do you believe the prophets? I know that you believe." 28And Agrippa said to Paul, "In a short time you think to make me a Christian!" 29And Paul said, "Whether short or long, I would to God that not only you but also all who hear me this day might become such as I am—except for these chains."
30 Then the king rose, and the governor and Bernice and those who were sitting with them; 31 and when they had withdrawn, they said to one another, "This man is doing nothing to deserve death or imprisonment." 32And Agrippa said to Festus, "This man could have been set free if he had not appealed to Caesar."

438

PHILLIPS

in Hebrew, 'Saul, Saul, why are you persecuting me? It is not easy for you to kick against your own conscience.' 'Who are you, Lord?' I said. And the Lord said to me, 'I am Jesus whom you are persecuting. Now get up and stand on your feet for I have shown myself to you for a reason—you are chosen to be my servant and a witness of what you have seen of me today, and of other visions of myself which I will give you. I will keep you safe both from your own people and from the gentiles to whom I now send you. I send you to open their eyes, to turn them from darkness to light, from the power of Satan to God himself, so that they may know forgiveness of their sins and take their place with all those who are made holy by their faith in me.' After that, King Agrippa, I could not disobey the heavenly vision. But both in Damascus and in Jerusalem, through the whole of Judaea, and to the gentiles, I preached that men should repent and turn to God and live lives to prove their change of heart. This is why the Jews seized me in the Temple and tried to kill me. To this day I have received help from God himself, and I stand here as a witness to high and low, adding nothing to what the prophets and Moses foretold should take place, that is, that Christ should suffer, that he should be the first to rise from the dead, and so proclaim the message of light both to our people and to the gentiles!"

Festus concludes that Paul's enthusiasm is insanity   26. 24

While he was thus defending himself Festus burst out,
"You are raving, Paul! All your learning has driven you mad!"
But Paul replied,
"I am not mad, your excellency. I speak nothing but the sober truth. The king knows of these matters, and I can speak freely before him. I cannot believe that any of these matters has escaped his notice, for it has been no hole-and-corner business. King Agrippa, do you believe the prophets? But I know that you believe them."
"Much more of this, Paul," returned Agrippa, "and you will be making me a Christian!"
"Ah," replied Paul, "whether it means 'much more' or 'only a little,' I would to God that you and all who can hear me this day might stand where I stand—but without these chains!"

The Roman officials consider Paul innocent   26. 30

Then the king rose to his feet and so did the governor and Bernice and those sitting with them, and when they had retired from the assembly they discussed the matter among themselves and agreed, "This man is doing nothing to deserve either death or imprisonment."
Agrippa remarked to Festus,
"He might easily have been discharged if he had not appealed to Caesar."

N.E.B.

Saul, why do you persecute me? It is hard for you, this kicking against the goad." I said, "Tell me, Lord, who you are"; and the Lord replied, "I am Jesus, whom you are persecuting. But now, rise to your feet and stand upright. I have appeared to you for a purpose: to appoint you my servant and witness, to testify both to what you have seen and to what you shall yet see of me. I will rescue you from this people and from the Gentiles to whom I am sending you. I send you to open their eyes and turn them from darkness to light, from the dominion of Satan to God, so that, by trust in me, they may obtain forgiveness of sins, and a place with those whom God has made his own."
'And so, King Agrippa, I did not disobey the heavenly vision. I turned first to the inhabitants of Damascus, and then to Jerusalem and all the country of Judaea, and to the Gentiles, and sounded the call to repent and turn to God, and to prove their repentance by deeds. That is why the Jews seized me in the temple and tried to do away with me. But I had God's help, and so to this very day I stand and testify to great and small alike. I assert nothing beyond what was foretold by the prophets and by Moses: that the Messiah must suffer, and that he, the first to rise from the dead, would announce the dawn to Israel and to the Gentiles.'
While Paul was thus making his defence, Festus shouted at the top of his voice, 'Paul, you are raving; too much study is driving you mad.' 'I am not mad, Your Excellency,' said Paul; 'what I am saying is sober truth. The king is well versed in these matters, and to him I can speak freely. I do not believe that he can be unaware of any of these facts, for this has been no hole-and-corner business. King Agrippa, do you believe the prophets? I know you do.' Agrippa said to Paul, 'You think it will not take much to win me over and make a Christian of me.' 'Much or little,' said Paul, 'I wish to God that not only you, but all those also who are listening to me today, might become what I am, apart from these chains.'
With that the king rose, and with him the Governor, Bernice, and the rest of the company, and after they had withdrawn they talked it over. 'This man', they said, 'is doing nothing that deserves death or imprisonment.' Agrippa said to Festus, 'The fellow could have been discharged, if he had not appealed to the Emperor.'

K.J.V.

27 And when it was determined that we should sail into Italy, they delivered Paul and certain other prisoners unto *one* named Julius, a centurion of Augustus' band. 2And entering into a ship of Adramyttium, we launched, meaning to sail by the coasts of Asia; *one* Aristarchus, a Macedonian of Thessalonica, being with us. 3And the next *day* we touched at Sidon. And Julius courteously entreated Paul, and gave *him* liberty to go unto his friends to refresh himself. 4And when we had launched from thence, we sailed under Cyprus, because the winds were contrary. 5And when we had sailed over the sea of Cilicia and Pamphylia, we came to Myra, *a city* of Lycia. 6And there the centurion found a ship of Alexandria sailing into Italy; and he put us therein. 7And when we had sailed slowly many days, and scarce were come over against Cnidus, the wind not suffering us, we sailed under Crete, over against Salmone; 8And, hardly passing it, came unto a place which is called the Fair Havens; nigh whereunto was the city *of* Lasea. 9 Now when much time was spent, and when sailing was now dangerous, because the fast was now already past, Paul admonished *them,* 10And said unto them, Sirs, I perceive that this voyage will be with hurt and much damage, not only of the lading and ship, but also of our lives. 11 Nevertheless the centurion believed the master and the owner of the ship, more than those things which were spoken by Paul. 12And because the haven was not commodious to winter in, the more part advised to depart thence also, if by any means they might attain to Phenice, *and there* to winter; *which is* a haven of Crete, and lieth toward the southwest and northwest. 13And when the south wind blew softly, supposing that they had obtained *their* purpose, loosing *thence,* they sailed close by Crete. 14 But not long after there arose against it a tempestuous wind, called Euroclydon. 15And when the ship was caught, and could not bear up into the wind, we let *her* drive. 16And running under a certain island which is called Clauda, we had much work to come by the boat: 17 Which when they had taken up, they used helps, undergirding the ship; and, fearing lest they should fall into the quicksands, strake sail, and so were driven. 18And we being exceedingly tossed with a tempest, the next *day* they lightened the ship; 19And the third *day* we cast out with our own hands the tackling of the ship. 20And when neither sun nor stars in many days appeared, and no small tempest lay on *us,* all hope that we should be saved was then taken away. 21 But after long abstinence, Paul stood forth in the midst of them, and said, Sirs, ye should have hearkened unto me, and not have loosed from

R.S.V.

27 And when it was decided that we should sail for Italy, they delivered Paul and some other prisoners to a centurion of the Augustan Cohort, named Julius. 2And embarking in a ship of Adramyttium, which was about to sail to the ports along the coast of Asia, we put to sea, accompanied by Aristarchus, a Macedonian from Thessalonica. 3 The next day we put in at Sidon; and Julius treated Paul kindly, and gave him leave to go to his friends and be cared for. 4And putting to sea from there we sailed under the lee of Cyprus, because the winds were against us. 5And when we had sailed across the sea which is off Cilicia and Pamphylia, we came to Myra in Lycia. 6 There the centurion found a ship of Alexandria sailing for Italy, and put us on board. 7 We sailed slowly for a number of days, and arrived with difficulty off Cnidus, and as the wind did not allow us to go on, we sailed under the lee of Crete off Salmone. 8 Coasting along it with difficulty, we came to a place called Fair Havens, near which was the city of Lasea.

9 As much time had been lost, and the voyage was already dangerous because the fast had already gone by, Paul advised them, 10 saying, "Sirs, I perceive that the voyage will be with injury and much loss, not only of the cargo and the ship, but also of our lives." 11 But the centurion paid more attention to the captain and to the owner of the ship than to what Paul said. 12And because the harbor was not suitable to winter in, the majority advised to put to sea from there, on the chance that somehow they could reach Phoenix, a harbor of Crete, looking northeast and southeast,*a* and winter there.

13 And when the south wind blew gently, supposing that they had obtained their purpose, they weighed anchor and sailed along Crete, close inshore. 14 But soon a tempestuous wind, called the northeaster, struck down from the land; 15 and when the ship was caught and could not face the wind, we gave way to it and were driven. 16And running under the lee of a small island called Cauda,*b* we managed with difficulty to secure the boat; 17 after hoisting it up, they took measures*c* to undergird the ship; then, fearing that they should run on the Syrtis, they lowered the gear, and so were driven. 18As we were violently storm-tossed, they began next day to throw the cargo overboard; 19 and the third day they cast out with their own hands the tackle of the ship. 20And when neither sun nor stars appeared for many a day, and no small tempest lay on us, all hope of our being saved was at last abandoned.

21 As they had been long without food, Paul then came forward among them and said, "Men, you should have listened to me, and should not

[a] Or *southwest and northwest.* [b] Other ancient authorities read *Clauda.* [c] Greek *helps.*

The last journey begins   **27. 1**

As soon as it was decided that we should sail away to Italy, Paul and some other prisoners were turned over to a centurion named Julius, of the emperor's own regiment. We embarked on a ship hailing from Adramyttium, bound for the Asian ports, and set sail. Among our company was Aristarchus, a Macedonian from Thessalonica. On the following day we put in at Sidon, where Julius treated Paul most considerately by allowing him to visit his friends and accept their hospitality. From Sidon we put to sea again and sailed to leeward of Cyprus, since the wind was against us. Then, when we had crossed the gulf that lies off the coasts of Cilicia and Pamphylia, we arrived at Myra in Lycia. There the centurion found an Alexandrian ship bound for Italy and put us aboard her. For several days we beat slowly up to windward and only just succeeded in arriving off Cnidus. Then, since the wind was still blowing against us, we sailed under the lee of Crete, and rounded Cape Salmone. Coasting along with difficulty we came to a place called Fair Havens, near which is the city of Lasea. We had by now lost a great deal of time and sailing had already become dangerous as it was so late in the year.

Paul's warning is disregarded   **27. 9b**

So Paul warned them, and said,
"Men, I can see that this voyage is likely to result in damage and considerable loss—not only to ship and cargo, but even of our own lives as well."
But Julius paid more attention to the helmsman and the captain than to Paul's words of warning. Moreover, since the harbor is unsuitable for a ship to winter in, the majority were in favor of setting sail again in the hope of reaching Phoenix and wintering there. Phoenix is a harbor in Crete, facing southwest and northwest. So, when a moderate breeze sprang up, thinking they had obtained just what they wanted, they weighed anchor and coasted along, hugging the shores of Crete. But before long a terrific gale, which they called a northeaster, swept down upon us from the land. The ship was caught by it and since she could not be brought up into the wind we had to let her fall off and run before it. Then, running under the lee of a small island called Clauda, we managed with some difficulty to secure the ship's boat. After hoisting it aboard they used cables to brace the ship. To add to the difficulties they were afraid all the time of drifting on to the Syrtis banks, so they shortened sail and lay to, drifting. The next day, as we were still at the mercy of the violent storm, they began to throw cargo overboard. On the third day with their own hands they threw the ship's tackle over the side. Then, when for many days there was no glimpse of sun or stars and we were still in the grip of the gale, all hope of our being saved was given up.

Paul's practical courage   **27. 21**
and faith

Nobody had eaten for some time, when Paul came forward among the men and said,
"Men, you should have listened to me and

27 When it was decided that we should sail for Italy, Paul and some other prisoners were handed over to a centurion named Julius, of the Augustan Cohort. We embarked in a ship of Adramyttium, bound for ports in the province of Asia, and put out to sea. In our party was Aristarchus, a Macedonian from Thessalonica. Next day we landed at Sidon; and Julius very considerately allowed Paul to go to his friends to be cared for. Leaving Sidon we sailed under the lee of Cyprus because of the head-winds, then across the open sea off the coast of Cilicia and Pamphylia, and so reached Myra in Lycia.

There the centurion found an Alexandrian vessel bound for Italy and put us aboard. For a good many days we made little headway, and we were hard put to it to reach Cnidus. Then, as the wind continued against us, off Salmone we began to sail under the lee of Crete, and, hugging the coast, struggled on to a place called Fair Havens, not far from the town of Lasea.

By now much time had been lost, the Fast was already over, and it was risky to go on with the voyage. Paul therefore gave them this advice: 'I can see, gentlemen,' he said, 'that this voyage will be disastrous: it will mean grave loss, loss not only of ship and cargo but also of life.' But the centurion paid more attention to the captain and to the owner of the ship than to what Paul said; and as the harbour was unsuitable for wintering, the majority were in favour of putting out to sea, hoping, if they could get so far, to winter at Phoenix, a Cretan harbour exposed south-west and north-west. So when a southerly breeze sprang up, they thought that their purpose was as good as achieved, and, weighing anchor, they sailed along the coast of Crete hugging the land. But before very long a fierce wind, the 'North-easter' as they call it, tore down from the landward side. It caught the ship and, as it was impossible to keep head to wind, we had to give way and run before it. We ran under the lee of a small island called Cauda, and with a struggle managed to get the ship's boat under control. When they had hoisted it aboard, they made use of tackle and undergirded the ship. Then, because they were afraid of running on to the shallows of Syrtis, they lowered the mainsail and let her drive. Next day, as we were making very heavy weather, they began to lighten the ship; and on the third day they jettisoned the ship's gear with their own hands. For days on end there was no sign of either sun or stars, a great storm was raging, and our last hopes of coming through alive began to fade.

When they had gone for a long time without food, Paul stood up among them and said, 'You should have taken my advice, gentlemen, not to

Crete, and to have gained this harm and loss. 22And now I exhort you to be of good cheer: for there shall be no loss of *any man's* life among you, but of the ship. 23 For there stood by me this night the angel of God, whose I am, and whom I serve, 24 Saying, Fear not, Paul; thou must be brought before Cesar: and, lo, God hath given thee all them that sail with thee. 25 Wherefore, sirs, be of good cheer: for I believe God, that it shall be even as it was told me. 26 Howbeit we must be cast upon a certain island. 27 But when the fourteenth night was come, as we were driven up and down in Adria, about midnight the shipmen deemed that they drew near to some country; 28And sounded, and found *it* twenty fathoms: and when they had gone a little further, they sounded again, and found *it* fifteen fathoms. 29 Then fearing lest we should have fallen upon rocks, they cast four anchors out of the stern, and wished for the day. 30And as the shipmen were about to flee out of the ship, when they had let down the boat into the sea, under colour as though they would have cast anchors out of the fore-ship, 31 Paul said to the centurion and to the soldiers, Except these abide in the ship, ye cannot be saved. 32 Then the soldiers cut off the ropes of the boat, and let her fall off. 33And while the day was coming on, Paul besought *them* all to take meat, saying, This day is the fourteenth day that ye have tarried and continued fasting, having taken nothing. 34 Wherefore I pray you to take *some* meat; for this is for your health: for there shall not a hair fall from the head of any of you. 35And when he had thus spoken, he took bread, and gave thanks to God in presence of them all; and when he had broken *it,* he began to eat. 36 Then were they all of good cheer, and they also took *some* meat. 37And we were in all in the ship two hundred threescore and sixteen souls. 38And when they had eaten enough, they lightened the ship, and cast out the wheat into the sea. 39And when it was day, they knew not the land: but they discovered a certain creek with a shore, into the which they were minded, if it were possible, to thrust in the ship. 40And when they had taken up the anchors, they committed *themselves* unto the sea, and loosed the rudder bands, and hoised up the mainsail to the wind, and made toward shore. 41And falling into a place where two seas met, they ran the ship aground; and the forepart stuck fast, and remained unmoveable, but the hinder part was broken with the violence of the waves. 42And the soldiers' counsel was to kill the prisoners, lest any of them should swim out, and escape. 43 But the

have set sail from Crete and incurred this injury and loss. 22 I now bid you take heart; for there will be no loss of life among you, but only of the ship. 23 For this very night there stood by me an angel of the God to whom I belong and whom I worship, 24 and he said, 'Do not be afraid, Paul; you must stand before Caesar; and lo, God has granted you all those who sail with you.' 25 So take heart, men, for I have faith in God that it will be exactly as I have been told. 26 But we shall have to run on some island."

27 When the fourteenth night had come, as we were drifting across the sea of Adria, about midnight the sailors suspected that they were nearing land. 28 So they sounded and found twenty fathoms; a little farther on they sounded again and found fifteen fathoms. 29And fearing that we might run on the rocks, they let out four anchors from the stern, and prayed for day to come. 30And as the sailors were seeking to escape from the ship, and had lowered the boat into the sea, under pretense of laying out anchors from the bow, 31 Paul said to the centurion and the soldiers, "Unless these men stay in the ship, you cannot be saved." 32 Then the soldiers cut away the ropes of the boat, and let it go.

33 As day was about to dawn, Paul urged them all to take some food, saying, "Today is the fourteenth day that you have continued in suspense and without food, having taken nothing. 34 Therefore I urge you to take some food; it will give you strength, since not a hair is to perish from the head of any of you." 35And when he had said this, he took bread, and giving thanks to God in the presence of all he broke it and began to eat. 36 Then they all were encouraged and ate some food themselves. 37 (We were in all two hundred and seventy-six[d] persons in the ship.) 38And when they had eaten enough, they lightened the ship, throwing out the wheat into the sea.

39 Now when it was day, they did not recognize the land, but they noticed a bay with a beach, on which they planned if possible to bring the ship ashore. 40 So they cast off the anchors and left them in the sea, at the same time loosening the ropes that tied the rudders; then hoisting the foresail to the wind they made for the beach. 41 But striking a shoal[e] they ran the vessel aground; the bow stuck and remained immovable, and the stern was broken up by the surf. 42 The soldiers' plan was to kill the prisoners, lest any should swim away and escape; 43 but the centurion, wishing to save Paul, kept

[d] Other ancient authorities read *seventy-six* or *about seventy-six.* [e] Greek *place of two seas.*

PHILLIPS

not set sail from Crete and suffered this damage and loss. However, now I beg you to keep up your spirits for no one's life is going to be lost, though we shall lose the ship. I know this because last night, the angel of God to whom I belong, and whom I serve, stood by me and said, 'Have no fear, Paul! You must stand before Caesar. And God, as a mark of his favor toward you, has granted you the lives of those who are sailing with you.' Take courage then, men, for I believe God, and I am certain that everything will happen exactly as I have been told. But we shall have to run the ship ashore on some island."

At last we near land　　　　　**27. 27**

On the fourteenth night of the storm, as we were drifting in the Adriatic, about midnight the sailors sensed that we were nearing land. Indeed, when they sounded they found twenty fathoms, and then after sailing on only a little way they sounded again and found fifteen. So, for fear that we might be hurled on the rocks, they threw out four anchors from the stern and prayed for daylight. The sailors wanted to desert the ship and they got as far as letting a boat down into the sea, pretending that they were going to run out anchors from the bow. But Paul said to the centurion and the soldiers,

"Unless these men stay aboard the ship there is no hope of your being saved."

At this the soldiers cut the ropes of the boat and let her fall away.

Paul's sturdy common sense　　　**27. 33**

Then while everyone waited for the day to break Paul urged them to take some food, saying,

"For two weeks now you've had no food— you haven't had a bite while you've been on watch. Now take some food, I beg you—you need it for your own well-being, for not a hair of anyone's head will be lost."

When he had said this he took some bread and, after thanking God before them all, he broke it and began to eat. This raised everybody's spirits and they began to take food themselves. There were about two hundred and seventy-six of us all told aboard that ship. When they had eaten enough they lightened the ship by throwing the grain over the side.

Land at last—but we lose　　　**27. 39**
the ship

When daylight came no one recognized the land. But they made out a bay with a sandy shore where they planned to beach the ship if they could. So they cut away the anchors and left them in the sea, and at the same time cut the ropes which held the steering oars. They then hoisted the foresail to catch the wind and made for the beach. But they struck a shoal and the ship ran aground. The bow stuck fast, while the stern began to break up under the strain. The soldiers' plan had been to kill the prisoners in case any of them should try to swim to shore and escape. But the centurion, in his desire to

N.E.B.

sail from Crete; then you would have avoided this damage and loss. But now I urge you not to lose heart; not a single life will be lost, only the ship. For last night there stood by me an angel of the God whose I am and whom I worship. "Do not be afraid, Paul," he said; "it is ordained that you shall appear before the Emperor; and, be assured, God has granted you the lives of all who are sailing with you." So keep up your courage: I trust in God that it will turn out as I have been told; though we have to be cast ashore on some island.'

The fourteenth night came and we were still drifting in the Sea of Adria. In the middle of the night the sailors felt that land was getting nearer. They sounded and found twenty fathoms. Sounding again after a short interval they found fifteen fathoms; and fearing that we might be cast ashore on a rugged coast they dropped four anchors from the stern and prayed for daylight to come. The sailors tried to abandon ship; they had already lowered the ship's boat, pretending they were going to lay out anchors from the bows, when Paul said to the centurion and the soldiers, 'Unless these men stay on board you can none of you come off safely.' So the soldiers cut the ropes of the boat and let her drop away.

Shortly before daybreak Paul urged them all to take some food. 'For the last fourteen days', he said, 'you have lived in suspense and gone hungry; you have eaten nothing whatever. So I beg you to have something to eat; your lives depend on it. Remember, not a hair of your heads will be lost.' With these words, he took bread, gave thanks to God in front of them all, broke it, and began eating. Then they all plucked up courage, and took food themselves. There were on board two hundred and seventy-six of us in all. When they had eaten as much as they wanted they lightened the ship by dumping the corn in the sea.

When day broke they could not recognize the land, but they noticed a bay with a sandy beach, on which they planned, if possible, to run the ship ashore. So they slipped the anchors and let them go; at the same time they loosened the lashings of the steering-paddles, set the foresail to the wind, and let her drive to the beach. But they found themselves caught between cross-currents and ran the ship aground, so that the bow stuck fast and remained immovable, while the stern was being pounded to pieces by the breakers. The soldiers thought they had better kill the prisoners for fear that any should swim away and escape; but the centurion wanted to

K.J.V.

centurion, willing to save Paul, kept them from *their* purpose; and commanded that they which could swim should cast *themselves* first *into the sea,* and get to land: 44And the rest, some on boards, and some on *broken pieces* of the ship. And so it came to pass, that they escaped all safe to land.

28 And when they were escaped, then they knew that the island was called Melita. 2And the barbarous people shewed us no little kindness: for they kindled a fire, and received us every one, because of the present rain, and because of the cold. 3And when Paul had gathered a bundle of sticks, and laid *them* on the fire, there came a viper out of the heat, and fastened on his hand. 4And when the barbarians saw the *venomous* beast hang on his hand, they said among themselves, No doubt this man is a murderer, whom, though he hath escaped the sea, yet vengeance suffereth not to live. 5And he shook off the beast into the fire, and felt no harm. 6Howbeit they looked when he should have swollen, or fallen down dead suddenly: but after they had looked a great while, and saw no harm come to him, they changed their minds, and said that he was a god. 7 In the same quarters were possessions of the chief man of the island, whose name was Publius; who received us, and lodged us three days courteously. 8And it came to pass, that the father of Publius lay sick of a fever and of a bloody flux: to whom Paul entered in, and prayed, and laid his hands on him, and healed him. 9 So when this was done, others also, which had diseases in the island, came, and were healed: 10 Who also honoured us with many honours; and when we departed, they laded *us* with such things as were necessary. 11And after three months we departed in a ship of Alexandria, which had wintered in the isle, whose sign was Castor and Pollux. 12And landing at Syracuse, we tarried *there* three days. 13And from thence we fetched a compass, and came to Rhegium: and after one day the south wind blew, and we came the next day to Puteoli: 14 Where we found brethren, and were desired to tarry with them seven days: and so we went toward Rome. 15And from thence, when the brethren heard of us, they came to meet us as far as Appii Forum, and the Three Taverns; whom when Paul saw, he

R.S.V.

them from carrying out their purpose. He ordered those who could swim to throw themselves overboard first and make for the land, 44 and the rest on planks or on pieces of the ship. And so it was that all escaped to land.

28 After we had escaped, we then learned that the island was called Malta. 2And the natives showed us unusual kindness, for they kindled a fire and welcomed us all, because it had begun to rain and was cold. 3 Paul had gathered a bundle of sticks and put them on the fire, when a viper came out because of the heat and fastened on his hand. 4 When the natives saw the creature hanging from his hand, they said to one another, "No doubt this man is a murderer. Though he has escaped from the sea, justice has not allowed him to live." 5 He, however, shook off the creature into the fire and suffered no harm. 6 They waited, expecting him to swell up or suddenly fall down dead; but when they had waited a long time and saw no misfortune come to him, they changed their minds and said that he was a god. 7 Now in the neighborhood of that place were lands belonging to the chief man of the island, named Publius, who received us and entertained us hospitably for three days. 8 It happened that the father of Publius lay sick with fever and dysentery; and Paul visited him and prayed, and putting his hands on him healed him. 9And when this had taken place, the rest of the people on the island who had diseases also came and were cured. 10 They presented many gifts to us;*f* and when we sailed, they put on board whatever we needed. 11 After three months we set sail in a ship which had wintered in the island, a ship of Alexandria, with the Twin Brothers as figurehead. 12 Putting in at Syracuse, we stayed there for three days. 13And from there we made a circuit and arrived at Rhegium; and after one day a south wind sprang up, and on the second day we came to Puteoli. 14 There we found brethren, and were invited to stay with them for seven days. And so we came to Rome. 15And the brethren there, when they heard of us, came as far as the Forum of Appius and Three Taverns to meet us. On seeing them Paul thanked

[*f*] Or *honored us with many honors.*

444

PHILLIPS

N.E.B.

save Paul, put a stop to this, and gave orders that all those who could swim should jump overboard first and get to land, while the rest should follow, some on planks and others on the wreckage of the ship. So it came true that everyone reached the shore in safety.

bring Paul safely through and prevented them from carrying out their plan. He gave orders that those who could swim should jump overboard first and get to land; the rest were to follow, some on planks, some on parts of the ship. And thus it was that all came safely to land.

A small incident establishes   28. 1
Paul's reputation

After our escape we discovered that the island was called Melita. The natives treated us with uncommon kindness. Because of the driving rain and the cold they lit a fire and made us all welcome. Then when Paul had collected a large bundle of sticks and was about to put it on the fire, a viper driven out by the heat fastened itself on his hand. When the natives saw the creature hanging from his hand they said to each other, "This man is obviously a murderer. He has escaped from the sea but justice will not let him live." But Paul shook off the viper into the fire without suffering any ill effect. Naturally they expected him to swell up or suddenly fall down dead, but after waiting a long time and seeing nothing untoward happen to him, they changed their minds and kept saying that he was a god.

Paul's acts of healing: the   28. 7
islanders' gratitude

In that part of the island were estates belonging to the governor, whose name was Publius. This man welcomed us and entertained us most kindly for three days. Now it happened that Publius' father was lying ill with fever and dysentery. Paul visited him and after prayer laid his hands on him and healed him. After that all the other sick people on the island came forward and were cured. Consequently they loaded us with presents, and when the time came for us to sail they provided us with everything we needed.

Spring returns and we resume   28. 11
our journey

It was no less than three months later that we set sail in an Alexandrian ship which had wintered in the island, a ship that had the heavenly twins as her figurehead. We put in at Syracuse and stayed there three days, and from there we tacked round to Rhegium. A day later the south wind sprang up and we sailed to Puteoli, reaching it in only two days. There we found some of the brothers and they begged us to stay a week with them, and so we finally came to Rome.

A Christian welcome awaits us   28. 15
in the capital

The brothers there had heard about us and came out from the city to meet us, as far as the Market of Appius and the Three Taverns. When Paul saw them he thanked God and his spirits

28 Once we had made our way to safety we identified the island as Malta. The rough islanders treated us with uncommon kindness: because it was cold and had started to rain, they lit a bonfire and made us all welcome. Paul had got together an armful of sticks and put them on the fire, when a viper, driven out by the heat, fastened on his hand. The islanders, seeing the snake hanging on to his hand, said to one another, 'The man must be a murderer; he may have escaped from the sea, but divine justice has not let him live.' Paul, however, shook off the snake into the fire and was none the worse. They still expected that any moment he would swell up or drop down dead, but after waiting a long time without seeing anything extraordinary happen to him, they changed their minds and now said, 'He is a god.'

In the neighbourhood of that place there were lands belonging to the chief magistrate of the island, whose name was Publius. He took us in and entertained us hospitably for three days. It so happened that this man's father was in bed suffering from recurrent bouts of fever and dysentery. Paul visited him and, after prayer, laid his hands upon him and healed him; whereupon the other sick people on the island came also and were cured. They honoured us with many marks of respect, and when we were leaving they put on board provision for our needs.

Three months had passed when we set sail in a ship which had wintered in the island; she was the *Castor and Pollux* of Alexandria. We put in at Syracuse and spent three days there; then we sailed round and arrived at Rhegium. After one day a south wind sprang up and we reached Puteoli in two days. There we found fellow-Christians and were invited to stay a week with them. And so to Rome. The Christians there had had news of us and came out to meet us as far as Appii Forum and Tres Tabernae, and when Paul saw them, he gave thanks to God and took courage.

K.J.V.

thanked God, and took courage. 16And when we came to Rome, the centurion delivered the prisoners to the captain of the guard: but Paul was suffered to dwell by himself with a soldier that kept him. 17And it came to pass, that after three days Paul called the chief of the Jews together: and when they were come together, he said unto them, Men *and* brethren, though I have committed nothing against the people, or customs of our fathers, yet was I delivered prisoner from Jerusalem into the hands of the Romans: 18 Who, when they had examined me, would have let *me* go, because there was no cause of death in me. 19 But when the Jews spake against *it*, I was constrained to appeal unto Cesar; not that I had aught to accuse my nation of. 20 For this cause therefore have I called for you, to see *you*, and to speak with *you:* because that for the hope of Israel I am bound with this chain. 21And they said unto him, We neither received letters out of Judea concerning thee, neither any of the brethren that came shewed or spake any harm of thee. 22 But we desire to hear of thee what thou thinkest: for as concerning this sect, we know that every where it is spoken against. 23And when they had appointed him a day, there came many to him into *his* lodging; to whom he expounded and testified the kingdom of God, persuading them concerning Jesus, both out of the law of Moses, and *out of* the prophets, from morning till evening. 24And some believed the things which were spoken, and some believed not. 25And when they agreed not among themselves, they departed, after that Paul had spoken one word, Well spake the Holy Ghost by Esaias the prophet unto our fathers, 26 Saying, Go unto this people, and say, Hearing ye shall hear, and shall not understand; and seeing ye shall see, and not perceive: 27 For the heart of this people is waxed gross, and their ears are dull of hearing, and their eyes have they closed; lest they should see with *their* eyes, and hear with *their* ears, and understand with *their* heart, and should be converted, and I should heal them. 28 Be it known therefore unto you, that the salvation of God is sent unto the Gentiles, and *that* they will hear it. 29And when he had said these words, the Jews departed, and had great

R.S.V.

God and took courage. 16And when we came into Rome, Paul was allowed to stay by himself, with the soldier that guarded him.

17 After three days he called together the local leaders of the Jews; and when they had gathered, he said to them, "Brethren, though I had done nothing against the people or the customs of our fathers, yet I was delivered prisoner from Jerusalem into the hands of the Romans. 18 When they had examined me, they wished to set me at liberty, because there was no reason for the death penalty in my case. 19 But when the Jews objected, I was compelled to appeal to Caesar—though I had no charge to bring against my nation. 20 For this reason therefore I have asked to see you and speak with you, since it is because of the hope of Israel that I am bound with this chain." 21And they said to him, "We have received no letters from Judea about you, and none of the brethren coming here has reported or spoken any evil about you. 22 But we desire to hear from you what your views are; for with regard to this sect we know that everywhere it is spoken against."

23 When they had appointed a day for him, they came to him at his lodging in great numbers. And he expounded the matter to them from morning till evening, testifying to the kingdom of God and trying to convince them about Jesus both from the law of Moses and from the prophets. 24And some were convinced by what he said, while others disbelieved. 25 So, as they disagreed among themselves, they departed, after Paul had made one statement: "The Holy Spirit was right in saying to your fathers through Isaiah the prophet:

26 'Go to this people, and say,
You shall indeed hear but never understand,
and you shall indeed see but never perceive.
27 For this people's heart has grown dull,
and their ears are heavy of hearing,
and their eyes they have closed;
lest they should perceive with their eyes,
and hear with their ears,
and understand with their heart,
and turn for me to heal them.'

28 Let it be known to you then that this salvation of God has been sent to the Gentiles; they will listen." *g*

[g] Other ancient authorities add verse 29, *And when he had said these words, the Jews departed, holding much dispute among themselves.*

PHILLIPS

N.E.B.

rose. When we reached Rome Paul was given permission to live alone with the soldier who was guarding him.

Paul explains himself frankly   **28. 17**
to the Jews in Rome

Three days later Paul invited the leading Jews to meet him, and when they arrived he spoke to them,

"Men and brothers, although I have done nothing against our people or the customs of our forefathers, I was handed over to the Romans as a prisoner in Jerusalem. They examined me and were prepared to release me, since they found me guilty of nothing deserving the death penalty. But the attacks of the Jews there forced me to appeal to Caesar—not that I had any charge to make against my own nation. But it is because of this accusation of the Jews that I have asked to see you and talk matters over with you. In actual fact it is on account of the hope of Israel that I am here in chains."

But they replied,

"We have received no letters about you from Judaea, nor have any of the brothers who have arrived here said anything, officially or unofficially, against you. We want to hear you state your views, although as far as this sect is concerned we do know that serious objections have been raised to it everywhere."

Paul's earnest and prolonged   **28. 23**
effort to win his own people
for Christ

When they had arranged a day for him they came to his lodging in great numbers. From morning till evening he explained the kingdom of God to them, giving his personal testimony, trying to persuade them about Jesus from the Law of Moses and the Prophets. As a result several of them were won over by his words, but others would not believe. When they could not reach any agreement among themselves and began to go away, Paul added as a parting shot, "How rightly did the Holy Spirit speak to your forefathers through the prophet Isaiah when he said,

Go thou unto this people, and say,
By hearing ye shall hear, and shall in no wise
    understand;
And seeing ye shall see, and shall in no wise
    perceive:
For this people's heart is waxed gross,
And their ears are dull of hearing,
And their eyes they have closed;
Lest haply they should perceive with their
    eyes,
And hear with their ears,
And understand with their heart,
And should turn again,
And I should heal them.

"Let it be plainly understood then that this salvation of our God has been sent to the gentiles, and they at least will listen to it!"

When we entered Rome Paul was allowed to lodge by himself with a soldier in charge of him. Three days later he called together the local Jewish leaders; and when they were assembled, he said to them: 'My brothers, I, who never did anything against our people or the customs of our forefathers, am here as a prisoner; I was handed over to the Romans at Jerusalem. They examined me and would have liked to release me because there was no capital charge against me; but the Jews objected, and I had no option but to appeal to the Emperor; not that I had any accusation to bring against my own people. That is why I have asked to see you and talk to you, because it is for the sake of the hope of Israel that I am in chains, as you see.' They replied, 'We have had no communication from Judaea, nor has any countryman of ours arrived with any report or gossip to your discredit. We should like to hear from you what your views are; all we know about this sect is that no one has a good word to say for it.'

So they fixed a day, and came in large numbers as his guests. He dealt at length with the whole matter; he spoke urgently of the kingdom of God and sought to convince them about Jesus by appealing to the Law of Moses and the prophets. This went on from dawn to dusk. Some were won over by his arguments; others remained sceptical. Without reaching any agreement among themselves they began to disperse, but not before Paul had said one thing more: 'How well the Holy Spirit spoke to your fathers through the prophet Isaiah when he said, "Go to this people and say: You will hear and hear, but never understand; you will look and look, but never see. For this people has grown gross at heart; their ears are dull, and their eyes are closed. Otherwise, their eyes might see, their ears hear, and their heart understand, and then they might turn again, and I would heal them." Therefore take notice that this salvation of God has been sent to the Gentiles: the Gentiles will listen.' [a]

---

[a] *Some witnesses add* (29) After he had spoken, the Jews went away, arguing vigorously among themselves.

K.J.V.

reasoning among themselves. 30And Paul dwelt two whole years in his own hired house, and received all that came in unto him, 31 Preaching the kingdom of God, and teaching those things which concern the Lord Jesus Christ, with all confidence, no man forbidding him.

R.S.V.

30 And he lived there two whole years at his own expense,ʰ and welcomed all who came to him, 31 preaching the kingdom of God and teaching about the Lord Jesus Christ quite openly and unhindered.

[h] Or in his own hired dwelling.

PHILLIPS

N.E.B.

The last glimpse of Paul . . .   28. 30

So Paul stayed for two full years in his own rented apartment welcoming all who came to see him. He proclaimed to them all the kingdom of God and gave them the teaching of the Lord Jesus Christ with the utmost freedom and without hindrance from anyone.

He stayed there two full years at his own expense, with a welcome for all who came to him, proclaiming the kingdom of God and teaching the facts about the Lord Jesus Christ quite openly and without hindrance.

K.J.V.

THE EPISTLE OF
PAUL THE APOSTLE
TO THE
ROMANS

R.S.V.

THE
LETTER OF PAUL TO THE
ROMANS

1 Paul, a servant of Jesus Christ, called *to be* an apostle, separated unto the gospel of God, 2 (Which he had promised afore by his prophets in the holy Scriptures,) 3 Concerning his Son Jesus Christ our Lord, which was made of the seed of David according to the flesh; 4And declared *to be* the Son of God with power, according to the Spirit of holiness, by the resurrection from the dead: 5 By whom we have received grace and apostleship, for obedience to the faith among all nations, for his name: 6Among whom are ye also the called of Jesus Christ: 7 To all that be in Rome, beloved of God, called *to be* saints: Grace to you, and peace, from God our Father and the Lord Jesus Christ. 8 First, I thank my God through Jesus Christ for you all, that your faith is spoken of throughout the whole world. 9 For God is my witness, whom I serve with my spirit in the gospel of his Son, that without ceasing I make mention of you always in my prayers; 10 Making request, if by any means now at length I might have a prosperous journey by the will of God to come unto you. 11 For I long to see you, that I may impart unto you some spiritual gift, to the end ye may be established; 12 That is, that I may be comforted together with you by the mutual faith both of you and me. 13 Now I would not have you ignorant, brethren, that oftentimes I purposed to come unto you, (but was let hitherto,) that I might have some fruit among you also, even as among other Gentiles. 14 I am debtor both to the Greeks, and to the Barbarians; both to the wise, and to the unwise. 15 So, as much as in me is, I am ready to preach the gospel to you that are at Rome also. 16 For I am not ashamed of the gospel of Christ: for it is the power of God unto salvation to every one that believeth; to the Jew first, and also to the Greek. 17 For therein is the righteousness of God revealed from faith to faith: as it is written, The just shall live by faith. 18 For the wrath of God is revealed from heaven against all ungodliness and

1 Paul, a servant[a] of Jesus Christ, called to be an apostle, set apart for the gospel of God 2 which he promised beforehand through his prophets in the holy scriptures, 3 the gospel concerning his Son, who was descended from David according to the flesh 4 and designated Son of God in power according to the Spirit of holiness by his resurrection from the dead, Jesus Christ our Lord, 5 through whom we have received grace and apostleship to bring about the obedience of faith for the sake of his name among all the nations, 6 including yourselves who are called to belong to Jesus Christ; 7 To all God's beloved in Rome, who are called to be saints:

Grace to you and peace from God our Father and the Lord Jesus Christ.

8 First, I thank my God through Jesus Christ for all of you, because your faith is proclaimed in all the world. 9 For God is my witness, whom I serve with my spirit in the gospel of his Son, that without ceasing I mention you always in my prayers, 10 asking that somehow by God's will I may now at last succeed in coming to you. 11 For I long to see you, that I may impart to you some spiritual gift to strengthen you, 12 that is, that we may be mutually encouraged by each other's faith, both yours and mine. 13 I want you to know, brethren, that I have often intended to come to you (but thus far have been prevented), in order that I may reap some harvest among you as well as among the rest of the Gentiles. 14 I am under obligation both to Greeks and to barbarians, both to the wise and to the foolish: 15 so I am eager to preach the gospel to you also who are in Rome.

16 For I am not ashamed of the gospel: it is the power of God for salvation to every one who has faith, to the Jew first and also to the Greek. 17 For in it the righteousness of God is revealed through faith for faith; as it is written, "He who through faith is righteous shall live."[b]

18 For the wrath of God is revealed from heaven against all ungodliness and wickedness

---

[a] Or *slave.* [b] Or *The righteous shall live by faith.*

450

PHILLIPS

THE LETTER TO
THE CHRISTIANS AT
ROME

THE
LETTER OF PAUL TO THE
ROMANS

The Gospel according to Paul

This letter comes to you from Paul, a servant of Jesus Christ, called as a messenger and appointed for the service of that gospel of God which was long ago promised by the prophets in the holy scriptures.

The gospel is centered in God's Son, a descendant of David by human genealogy and patently marked out as the Son of God by the power of that Spirit of holiness which raised him to life again from the dead. He is our Lord, Jesus Christ, from whom we received grace and our commission in his name to forward obedience to the faith in all nations. And of this great number you at Rome are also called to belong to him.

To you all then, loved of God and called to be Christ's men and women, grace and peace from God the Father and from the Lord Jesus Christ.

A personal message   1. 8

I must begin by telling you how I thank God through Jesus Christ for you all, since the news of your faith has become known everywhere. Before God, whom I serve with my spirit in the gospel of his Son, I assure you that you are always in my prayers. I am constantly asking him that he will somehow make it possible for me now, at long last, to come to Rome. I am longing to see you: I want to bring you some spiritual strength, and that will mean that I shall be strengthened by you, each of us helped by the other's faith.

Then I should like you to know, my brothers, that I have long intended to come to you (but something has always prevented me), for I should like to see some results among you, as I have among other gentiles. I feel myself under a sort of universal obligation, I owe something to all men, from cultured Greek to ignorant savage. That is why I want, as far as my ability will carry me, to preach the gospel to you who live in Rome as well. For I am not ashamed of the gospel. I see it as the very power of God working for the salvation of everyone who believes it, both Jew and Greek. I see in it God's plan for imparting righteousness to men, a process begun and continued by their faith. For, as the scripture says:

The righteous shall live by faith.

The righteousness of God and   1. 18
the sin of man

Now the holy anger of God is disclosed from Heaven against the godlessness and evil of those

1 From Paul, servant of Christ Jesus, apostle by God's call, set apart for the service of the Gospel.

This gospel God announced beforehand in sacred scriptures through his prophets. It is about his Son: on the human level he was born of David's stock, but on the level of the spirit— the Holy Spirit—he was declared Son of God by a mighty act in that he rose from the dead:[a] it is about Jesus Christ our Lord. Through him I received the privilege of a commission in his name to lead to faith and obedience men in all nations, yourselves among them, you who have heard the call and belong to Jesus Christ.

I send greetings to all of you in Rome whom God loves and has called to be his dedicated people. Grace and peace to you from God our Father and the Lord Jesus Christ.

Let me begin by thanking my God, through Jesus Christ, for you all, because all over the world they are telling the story of your faith. God is my witness, the God to whom I offer the humble service of my spirit by preaching the gospel of his Son: God knows how continually I make mention of you in my prayers, and am always asking that by his will I may, somehow or other, succeed at long last in coming to visit you. For I long to see you; I want to bring you some spiritual gift to make you strong; or rather, I want to be among you to receive encouragement myself through the influence of your faith on me as of mine on you.

But I should like you to know,[b] my brothers, that I have often planned to come, though so far without success, in the hope of achieving something among you, as I have in other parts of the world. I am under obligation to Greek and non-Greek, to learned and simple; hence my eagerness to declare the Gospel to you in Rome as well as to others. For I am not ashamed of the Gospel. It is the saving power of God for everyone who has faith—the Jew first, but the Greek also—because here is revealed God's way of righting wrong, a way that starts from faith and ends in faith;[c] as Scripture says, 'he shall gain life who is justified through faith'.

For we see divine retribution revealed from heaven and falling upon all the godless wicked-

[a] Or declared Son of God with full powers from the time when he rose from the dead. [b] Some witnesses read I believe you know. [c] Or . . . wrong. It is based on faith and addressed to faith.

K.J.V.

unrighteousness of men, who hold the truth in unrighteousness; 19 Because that which may be known of God is manifest in them; for God hath shewed *it* unto them. 20 For the invisible things of him from the creation of the world are clearly seen, being understood by the things that are made, *even* his eternal power and God-head; so that they are without excuse: 21 Because that, when they knew God, they glorified *him* not as God, neither were thankful; but became vain in their imaginations, and their foolish heart was darkened. 22 Professing themselves to be wise, they became fools, 23 And changed the glory of the uncorruptible God into an image made like to corruptible man, and to birds, and fourfooted beasts, and creeping things. 24 Wherefore God also gave them up to uncleanness, through the lusts of their own hearts, to dishonour their own bodies between themselves: 25 Who changed the truth of God into a lie, and worshipped and served the creature more than the Creator, who is blessed for ever. Amen. 26 For this cause God gave them up unto vile affections: for even their women did change the natural use into that which is against nature: 27 And likewise also the men, leaving the natural use of the woman, burned in their lust one toward another; men with men working that which is unseemly, and receiving in themselves that recompense of their error which was meet. 28 And even as they did not like to retain God in *their* knowledge, God gave them over to a reprobate mind, to do those things which are not convenient; 29 Being filled with all unrighteousness, fornication, wickedness, covetousness, maliciousness; full of envy, murder, debate, deceit, malignity; whisperers, 30 Backbiters, haters of God, despiteful, proud, boasters, inventors of evil things, disobedient to parents, 31 Without understanding, covenant-breakers, without natural affection, implacable, unmerciful: 32 Who, knowing the judgment of God, that they which commit such things are worthy of death, not only do the same, but have pleasure in them that do them.

R.S.V.

of men who by their wickedness suppress the truth. 19 For what can be known about God is plain to them, because God has shown it to them. 20 Ever since the creation of the world his invisible nature, namely, his eternal power and deity, has been clearly perceived in the things that have been made. So they are without excuse; 21 for although they knew God they did not honor him as God or give thanks to him, but they became futile in their thinking and their senseless minds were darkened. 22 Claiming to be wise, they became fools, 23 and exchanged the glory of the immortal God for images resembling mortal man or birds or animals or reptiles.

24 Therefore God gave them up in the lusts of their hearts to impurity, to the dishonoring of their bodies among themselves, 25 because they exchanged the truth about God for a lie and worshiped and served the creature rather than the Creator, who is blessed for ever! Amen.

26 For this reason God gave them up to dishonorable passions. Their women exchanged natural relations for unnatural, 27 and the men likewise gave up natural relations with women and were consumed with passion for one another, men committing shameless acts with men and receiving in their own persons the due penalty for their error.

28 And since they did not see fit to acknowledge God, God gave them up to a base mind and to improper conduct. 29 They were filled with all manner of wickedness, evil, covetousness, malice. Full of envy, murder, strife, deceit, malignity, they are gossips, 30 slanderers, haters of God, insolent, haughty, boastful, inventors of evil, disobedient to parents, 31 foolish, faithless, heartless, ruthless. 32 Though they know God's decree that those who do such things deserve to die, they not only do them but approve those who practice them.

2 Therefore thou art inexcusable, O man, whosoever thou art that judgest: for wherein thou judgest another, thou condemnest thyself; for thou that judgest doest the same

2 Therefore you have no excuse, O man, whoever you are, when you judge another; for in passing judgment upon him you condemn yourself, because you, the judge, are doing the

men who render truth dumb and inoperative by their wickedness. It is not that they do not know the truth about God: indeed he has made it quite plain to them. For since the beginning of the world the invisible attributes of God, for example, his eternal power and divinity, have been plainly discernible through things which he has made and which are commonly seen and known, thus leaving these men without a rag of excuse. They knew all the time that there is a God, yet they refused to acknowledge him as such, or to thank him for what he is or does. Thus they became fatuous in their argumentations, and plunged their silly minds still further into the dark. Behind a façade of "wisdom" they became just fools, fools who would exchange the glory of the immortal God for an imitation image of a mortal man, or of creatures that run or fly or crawl. They gave up God: and therefore God gave them up—to be the playthings of their own foul desires in dishonoring their own bodies.

The fearful consequence of   *1. 25*
deliberate atheism

These men deliberately forfeited the truth of God and accepted a lie, paying homage and giving service to the creature instead of to the Creator, who alone is worthy to be worshiped for ever and ever, amen. God therefore handed them over to disgraceful passions. Their women exchanged the normal practices of sexual intercourse for something which is abnormal and unnatural. Similarly the men, turning from natural intercourse with women, were swept into lustful passions for one another. Men with men performed these shameful horrors, receiving, of course, in their own personalities the consequences of sexual perversity.

Moreover, since they considered themselves too high and mighty to acknowledge God, he allowed them to become the slaves of their degenerate minds, and to perform unmentionable deeds. They became filled with wickedness, rottenness, greed and malice; their minds became steeped in envy, murder, quarrelsomeness, deceitfulness and spite. They became whisperers-behind-doors, stabbers-in-the-back, God-haters; they overflowed with insolent pride and boastfulness, and their minds teemed with diabolical invention. They scoffed at duty to parents; they mocked at learning, recognized no obligations of honor, lost all natural affection, and had no use for mercy. More than this—being well aware of God's pronouncement that all who do these things deserve to die, they not only continued their own practices, but did not hesitate to give their thorough approval to others who did the same.

ness of men. In their wickedness they are stifling the truth. For all that may be known of God by men lies plain before their eyes; indeed God himself has disclosed it to them. His invisible attributes, that is to say his everlasting power and deity, have been visible, ever since the world began, to the eye of reason, in the things he has made. There is therefore no possible defence for their conduct; knowing God, they have refused to honour him as God, or to render him thanks. Hence all their thinking has ended in futility, and their misguided minds are plunged in darkness. They boast of their wisdom, but they have made fools of themselves, exchanging the splendour of immortal God for an image shaped like mortal man, even for images like birds, beasts, and creeping things.

For this reason God has given them up to the vileness of their own desires, and the consequent degradation of their bodies, because they have bartered away the true God for a false one,[a] and have offered reverence and worship to created things instead of to the Creator, who is blessed for ever; amen.

In consequence, I say, God has given them up to shameful passions. Their women have exchanged natural intercourse for unnatural, and their men in turn, giving up natural relations with women, burn with lust for one another; males behave indecently with males, and are paid in their own persons the fitting wage of such perversion.

Thus, because they have not seen fit to acknowledge God, he has given them up to their own depraved reason. This leads them to break all rules of conduct. They are filled with every kind of injustice, mischief, rapacity, and malice; they are one mass of envy, murder, rivalry, treachery, and malevolence; whisperers and scandal-mongers, hateful to God, insolent, arrogant, and boastful; they invent new kinds of mischief, they show no loyalty to parents, no conscience, no fidelity to their plighted word; they are without natural affection and without pity. They know well enough the just decree of God, that those who behave like this deserve to die, and yet they do it; not only so, they actually applaud such practices.

Yet we cannot judge them, for we   *2. 1*
also are sinners: God is the only judge

Now if you feel inclined to set yourself up as a judge of those who sin, let me assure you, whoever you are, that you are in no position to do so. For at whatever point you condemn others you automatically condemn yourself, since you, the judge, commit the same sins. God's judgment, we know, is utterly impartial in its action against such evildoers. What makes

2 You therefore have no defence—you who sit in judgement, whoever you may be—for in judging your fellow-man you condemn yourself, since you, the judge, are equally guilty.

[a] *Or* the truth of God for the lie.

K.J.V.

things. 2 But we are sure that the judgment of God is according to truth against them which commit such things. 3 And thinkest thou this, O man, that judgest them which do such things, and doest the same, that thou shalt escape the judgment of God? 4 Or despisest thou the riches of his goodness and forbearance and long suffering; not knowing that the goodness of God leadeth thee to repentance? 5 But, after thy hardness and impenitent heart, treasurest up unto thyself wrath against the day of wrath and revelation of the righteous judgment of God; 6 Who will render to every man according to his deeds: 7 To them who by patient continuance in well doing seek for glory and honour and immortality, eternal life: 8 But unto them that are contentious, and do not obey the truth, but obey unrighteousness, indignation and wrath, 9 Tribulation and anguish, upon every soul of man that doeth evil; of the Jew first, and also of the Gentile; 10 But glory, honour, and peace, to every man that worketh good; to the Jew first, and also to the Gentile: 11 For there is no respect of persons with God. 12 For as many as have sinned without law shall also perish without law; and as many as have sinned in the law shall be judged by the law; 13 (For not the hearers of the law *are* just before God, but the doers of the law shall be justified. 14 For when the Gentiles, which have not the law, do by nature the things contained in the law, these, having not the law, are a law unto themselves: 15 Which shew the work of the law written in their hearts, their conscience also bearing witness, and *their* thoughts the mean while accusing or else excusing one another;) 16 In the day when God shall judge the secrets of men by Jesus Christ according to my gospel. 17 Behold, thou art called a Jew, and restest in the law, and makest thy boast of God, 18 And knowest *his* will, and approvest the things that are more excellent, being instructed out of the law; 19 And art confident that thou thyself art a guide of the blind, a light of them which are in darkness, 20 An instructor of the foolish, a teacher of babes, which hast the form of knowledge and of the truth in the law. 21 Thou therefore which teachest another, teachest thou not thyself? thou that preachest a man should not steal, dost thou steal? 22 Thou that sayest a man should not commit adultery, dost thou commit adultery? thou that abhorrest idols, dost thou commit sacrilege? 23 Thou that makest thy boast of the

R.S.V.

very same things. 2 We know that the judgment of God rightly falls upon those who do such things. 3 Do you suppose, O man, that when you judge those who do such things and yet do them yourself, you will escape the judgment of God? 4 Or do you presume upon the riches of his kindness and forbearance and patience? Do you not know that God's kindness is meant to lead you to repentance? 5 But by your hard and impenitent heart you are storing up wrath for yourself on the day of wrath when God's righteous judgment will be revealed. 6 For he will render to every man according to his works: 7 to those who by patience in well-doing seek for glory and honor and immortality, he will give eternal life; 8 but for those who are factious and do not obey the truth, but obey wickedness, there will be wrath and fury. 9 There will be tribulation and distress for every human being who does evil, the Jew first and also the Greek, 10 but glory and honor and peace for every one who does good, the Jew first and also the Greek. 11 For God shows no partiality.

12 All who have sinned without the law will also perish without the law, and all who have sinned under the law will be judged by the law. 13 For it is not the hearers of the law who are righteous before God, but the doers of the law who will be justified. 14 When Gentiles who have not the law do by nature what the law requires, they are a law to themselves, even though they do not have the law. 15 They show that what the law requires is written on their hearts, while their conscience also bears witness and their conflicting thoughts accuse or perhaps excuse them 16 on that day when, according to my gospel, God judges the secrets of men by Christ Jesus.

17 But if you call yourself a Jew and rely upon the law and boast of your relation to God 18 and know his will and approve what is excellent, because you are instructed in the law, 19 and if you are sure that you are a guide to the blind, a light to those who are in darkness, 20 a corrector of the foolish, a teacher of children, having in the law the embodiment of knowledge and truth—21 you then who teach others, will you not teach yourself? While you preach against stealing, do you steal? 22 You who say that one must not commit adultery, do you commit adultery? You who abhor idols, do you rob temples? 23 You who boast in the law,

PHILLIPS

you think that you, who so readily judge the sins of others, can consider yourself beyond the judgment of God? Are you, perhaps, misinterpreting God's generosity and patient mercy toward you as weakness on his part? Don't you realize that God's kindness is meant to lead you to repentance? Or are you by your obstinate refusal to repent simply storing up for yourself an experience of the wrath of God in the day when, in his holy anger against evil, he shows his hand in righteous judgment?

There is no doubt at all that he will "render to every man according to his works," and that means eternal life to those who, in patiently doing good, aim at the unseen (but real) glory and honor of the eternal world. It also means anger and wrath for those who rebel against God's plan of life, and refuse to obey his rules, and who, in so doing, make themselves the very servants of evil. Yes, it means bitter pain and a fearful undoing for every human soul who works on the side of evil, for the Jew first and then the Greek. But, let me repeat, there is glory and honor and peace for every worker on the side of good, for the Jew first and then the Greek. For there is no preferential treatment with God.

God's judgment is absolutely just   2. 12

All who have sinned without knowledge of the Law will die without reference to the Law; and all who have sinned knowing the Law shall be judged according to the Law. It is not familiarity with the Law that justifies a man in the sight of God, but obedience to it.

When the gentiles, who have no knowledge of the Law, act in accordance with it by the light of nature, they show that they have a law in themselves, for they demonstrate the effect of a law operating in their own hearts. Their own consciences endorse the existence of such a law, for there is something which condemns or excuses their actions.

We may be sure that all this will be taken into account in the day of true judgment, when God will judge men's secret lives by Christ Jesus, as my gospel plainly states.

You Jews are privileged—do you   2. 17
live up to your privileges?

Now you, my reader, who bear the name of Jew, take your stand upon the Law, and are, so to speak, proud of your God. You know his plan, and are able through your knowledge of the Law truly to appreciate moral values. You can, therefore, confidently look upon yourself as a guide to those who do not know the way, and as a light to those who are groping in the dark. You can instruct those who have no spiritual wisdom: you can teach those who, spiritually speaking, are only just out of the cradle. You have a certain grasp of the basis of true knowledge. You have without doubt very great advantages. But, prepared as you are to instruct others, do you ever teach yourself anything? You preach against stealing, for example, but are you sure of your own honesty? You denounce the practice of adultery, but are you sure of your own purity? You loathe idolatry, but *how honest are you toward the property of heathen temples?* Everyone knows

N.E.B.

It is admitted that God's judgement is rightly passed upon all who commit such crimes as these; and do you imagine—you who pass judgement on the guilty while committing the same crimes yourself—do you imagine that you, any more than they, will escape the judgement of God? Or do you think lightly of his wealth of kindness, of tolerance, and of patience, without recognizing that God's kindness is meant to lead you to a change of heart? In the rigid obstinacy of your heart you are laying up for yourself a store of retribution for the day of retribution, when God's just judgement will be revealed, and he will pay every man for what he has done. To those who pursue glory, honour, and immortality by steady persistence in well-doing, he will give eternal life; but for those who are governed by selfish ambition, who refuse obedience to the truth and take the wrong for their guide, there will be the fury of retribution. There will be grinding misery for every human being who is an evil-doer, for the Jew first and for the Greek also; and for every well-doer there will be glory, honour, and peace, for the Jew first and also for the Greek.

For God has no favourites: those who have sinned outside the pale of the Law of Moses will perish outside its pale, and all who have sinned under that law will be judged by the law. It is not by hearing the law, but by doing it, that men will be justified before God. When Gentiles who do not possess the law carry out its precepts by the light of nature, then, although they have no law, they are their own law, for they display the effect of the law inscribed on their hearts. Their conscience is called as witness, and their own thoughts argue the case on either side, against them or even for them, on the day when God judges the secrets of human hearts through Christ Jesus. So my gospel declares.

But as for you—you may bear the name of Jew; you rely upon the law and are proud of your God; you know his will; you are aware of moral distinctions because you receive instruction from the law; you are confident that you are the one to guide the blind, to enlighten the benighted, to train the stupid, and to teach the immature, because in the law you see the very shape of knowledge and truth. You, then, who teach your fellow-man, do you fail to teach yourself? You proclaim, 'Do not steal'; but are you yourself a thief? You say, 'Do not commit adultery'; but are you an adulterer? You abominate false gods; but do you rob their shrines?

K.J.V.

law, through breaking the law dishonourest thou God? 24 For the name of God is blasphemed among the Gentiles through you, as it is written. 25 For circumcision verily profiteth, if thou keep the law: but if thou be a breaker of the law, thy circumcision is made uncircumcision. 26 Therefore, if the uncircumcision keep the righteousness of the law, shall not his uncircumcision be counted for circumcision? 27And shall not uncircumcision which is by nature, if it fulfil the law, judge thee, who by the letter and circumcision dost transgress the law? 28 For he is not a Jew, which is one outwardly; neither *is that* circumcision, which is outward in the flesh: 29 But he *is* a Jew, which is one inwardly; and circumcision *is that* of the heart, in the spirit, *and* not in the letter; whose praise *is* not of men, but of God.

3 What advantage then hath the Jew? or what profit *is there* of circumcision? 2 Much every way: chiefly, because that unto them were committed the oracles of God. 3 For what if some did not believe? shall their unbelief make the faith of God without effect? 4 God forbid: yea, let God be true, but every man a liar; as it is written, That thou mightest be justified in thy sayings, and mightest overcome when thou art judged. 5 But if our unrighteousness commend the righteousness of God, what shall we say? *Is* God unrighteous who taketh vengeance? (I speak as a man) 6 God forbid: for then how shall God judge the world? 7 For if the truth of God hath more abounded through my lie unto his glory; why yet am I also judged as a sinner? 8And not *rather,* (as we be slanderously reported, and as some affirm that we say,) Let us do evil, that good may come? whose damnation is just. 9 What then? are we better *than they?* No, in no wise: for we have before proved both Jews and Gentiles, that they are all under sin; 10As it is written, There is none righteous, no, not one: 11 There is none that understandeth, there is none that seeketh after God.

R.S.V.

do you dishonor God by breaking the law? 24 For, as it is written, "The name of God is blasphemed among the Gentiles because of you." 25 Circumcision indeed is of value if you obey the law; but if you break the law, your circumcision becomes uncircumcision. 26 So, if a man who is uncircumcised keeps the precepts of the law, will not his uncircumcision be regarded as circumcision? 27 Then those who are physically uncircumcised but keep the law will condemn you who have the written code and circumcision but break the law. 28 For he is not a real Jew who is one outwardly, nor is true circumcision something external and physical. 29 He is a Jew who is one inwardly, and real circumcision is a matter of the heart, spiritual and not literal. His praise is not from men but from God.

3 Then what advantage has the Jew? Or what is the value of circumcision? 2 Much in every way. To begin with, the Jews are entrusted with the oracles of God. 3 What if some were unfaithful? Does their faithlessness nullify the faithfulness of God? 4 By no means! Let God be true though every man be false, as it is written,

"That thou mayest be justified in thy words, and prevail when thou art judged."

5 But if our wickedness serves to show the justice of God, what shall we say? That God is unjust to inflict wrath on us? (I speak in a human way.) 6 By no means! For then how could God judge the world? 7 But if through my falsehood God's truthfulness abounds to his glory, why am I still being condemned as a sinner? 8And why not do evil that good may come?—as some people slanderously charge us with saying. Their condemnation is just.

9 What then? Are we Jews any better off? *c* No, not at all; for I *d* have already charged that all men, both Jews and Greeks, are under the power of sin, 10 as it is written:

"None is righteous, no, not one;
11 no one understands, no one seeks for God.

---

[c] Or *at any disadvantage?* [d] Greek *we.*

| PHILLIPS | N.E.B. |

how proud you are of the Law, but that means a proportionate dishonor to God when men know that you break it! Don't you know that the very name of God is cursed among the gentiles because of the behavior of Jews? There is, you know, a verse of scripture to that effect.

Being a true "Jew" is an inward not an outward matter   2. 25

That most intimate sign of belonging to God that we call circumcision does indeed mean something if you keep the Law. But if you flout the Law you are to all intents and purposes uncircumcising yourself! Conversely, if an uncircumcised man keep the Law's commandments, does he not thereby "circumcise" himself? Moreover, is it not plain to you that those who are physically uncircumcised, and yet keep the Law, are a continual judgment upon you who, for all your circumcision and knowledge of the Law, break it?

I have come to the conclusion that a true Jew is not the man who is merely a Jew outwardly, and real circumcision is not just a matter of the body. The true Jew is one who belongs to God in heart, a man whose circumcision is not just an outward physical affair but is a God-made sign upon the heart and soul, and results in a life lived not for the approval of man, but for the approval of God.

Jews are privileged, but even they have failed   3. 1

Is there any advantage then in being one of the chosen people? Does circumcision mean anything? Yes, of course, a great deal in every way. You have only to think of one thing to begin with—it was the Jews to whom God's messages were entrusted. Some of them were undoubtedly faithless, but what then? Can you imagine that their faithlessness could disturb the faithfulness of God? Of course not! Let us think of God as true, even if every living man be proved a liar. Remember the scripture?

That thou mightest be justified in thy words, And mightest prevail when thou comest into judgment.

But if our wickedness advertises the goodness of God, do we feel that God is being unfair to punish us in return? (I'm using a human tit-for-tat argument.) Not a bit of it! What sort of person would God be then to judge the world? It is like saying that if my lying throws into sharp relief the truth of God and, so to speak, enhances his reputation, then why should he repay me by judging me a sinner? Similarly, why not do evil that good may be, by contrast, all the more conspicuous and valuable? (As a matter of fact, I am reported as urging this very thing, by some slanderously and others quite seriously! But, of course, such an argument is quite properly condemned.)

Are we Jews then a march ahead of other men? By no means. For I have shown above that all men from Jews to Greeks are under the condemnation of sin. The scriptures endorse this fact plainly enough.

There is none righteous, no, not one.
There is none that understandeth,
There is none that seeketh after God;

While you take pride in the law, you dishonour God by breaking it. For, as Scripture says, 'Because of you the name of God is dishonoured among the Gentiles.'

Circumcision has value, provided you keep the law; but if you break the law, then your circumcision is as if it had never been. Equally, if an uncircumcised man keeps the precepts of the law, will he not count as circumcised? He may be uncircumcised in his natural state, but by fulfilling the law he will pass judgement on you who break it, for all your written code and your circumcision. The true Jew is not he who is such in externals, neither is the true circumcision the external mark in the flesh. The true Jew is he who is such inwardly, and the true circumcision is of the heart, directed not by written precepts but by the Spirit; such a man receives his commendation not from men but from God.

3 Then what advantage has the Jew? What is the value of circumcision? Great, in every way. In the first place, the Jews were entrusted with the oracles of God. What if some of them were unfaithful? Will their faithlessness cancel the faithfulness of God? Certainly not! God must be true though every man living were a liar; for we read in Scripture, 'When thou speakest thou shalt be vindicated, and win the verdict when thou art on trial.'

Another question: if our injustice serves to bring out God's justice, what are we to say? Is it unjust of God (I speak of him in human terms) to bring retribution upon us? Certainly not! If God were unjust, how could he judge the world?

Again, if the truth of God brings him all the greater honour because of my falsehood, why should I any longer be condemned as a sinner? Why not indeed 'do evil that good may come', as some libellously report me as saying? To condemn such men as these is surely no injustice.

What then? Are we Jews any better off? [a] No, not at all! [b] For we have already formulated the charge that Jews and Greeks alike are all under the power of sin. This has scriptural warrant:

'There is no just man, not one;
No one who understands, no one who seeks God.

---

[a] Or Are we Jews any worse off? [b] Or Not in all respects.

K.J.V.

12 They are all gone out of the way, they are together become unprofitable; there is none that doeth good, no, not one. 13 Their throat *is* an open sepulchre; with their tongues they have used deceit; the poison of asps *is* under their lips: 14 Whose mouth *is* full of cursing and bitterness: 15 Their feet *are* swift to shed blood: 16 Destruction and misery *are* in their ways: 17 And the way of peace have they not known: 18 There is no fear of God before their eyes. 19 Now we know that what things soever the law saith, it saith to them who are under the law: that every mouth may be stopped, and all the world may become guilty before God. 20 Therefore by the deeds of the law there shall no flesh be justified in his sight: for by the law *is* the knowledge of sin. 21 But now the righteousness of God without the law is manifested, being witnessed by the law and the prophets; 22 Even the righteousness of God *which is* by faith of Jesus Christ unto all and upon all them that believe; for there is no difference: 23 For all have sinned, and come short of the glory of God; 24 Being justified freely by his grace through the redemption that is in Christ Jesus: 25 Whom God hath set forth *to be* a propitiation through faith in his blood, to declare his righteousness for the remission of sins that are past, through the forbearance of God; 26 To declare, *I say*, at this time his righteousness: that he might be just, and the justifier of him which believeth in Jesus. 27 Where *is* boasting then? It is excluded. By what law? of works? Nay; but by the law of faith. 28 Therefore we conclude that a man is justified by faith without the deeds of the law. 29 *Is he* the God of the Jews only? *is he* not also of the Gentiles? Yes, of the Gentiles also: 30 Seeing *it is* one God, which shall justify the circumcision by faith, and uncircumcision through faith. 31 Do we then make void the law through faith? God forbid: yea, we establish the law.

R.S.V.

12 All have turned aside, together they have
　　gone wrong;
　　no one does good, not even one."
13 "Their throat is an open grave,
　　they use their tongues to deceive."
"The venom of asps is under their lips."
14 "Their mouth is full of curses and bitter-
　　ness."
15 "Their feet are swift to shed blood,
16 in their paths are ruin and misery,
　　17 and the way of peace they do not know."
18 "There is no fear of God before their eyes."
19 Now we know that whatever the law says it speaks to those who are under the law, so that every mouth may be stopped, and the whole world may be held accountable to God. 20 For no human being will be justified in his sight by works of the law, since through the law comes knowledge of sin.

21 But now the righteousness of God has been manifested apart from law, although the law and the prophets bear witness to it, 22 the righteousness of God through faith in Jesus Christ for all who believe. For there is no distinction; 23 since all have sinned and fall short of the glory of God, 24 they are justified by his grace as a gift, through the redemption which is in Christ Jesus, 25 whom God put forward as an expiation by his blood, to be received by faith. This was to show God's righteousness, because in his divine forbearance he had passed over former sins; 26 it was to prove at the present time that he himself is righteous and that he justifies him who has faith in Jesus.

27 Then what becomes of our boasting? It is excluded. On what principle? On the principle of works? No, but on the principle of faith. 28 For we hold that a man is justified by faith apart from works of law. 29 Or is God the God of Jews only? Is he not the God of Gentiles also? Yes, of Gentiles also, 30 since God is one; and he will justify the circumcised on the ground of their faith and the uncircumcised through their faith. 31 Do we then overthrow the law by this faith? By no means! On the contrary, we uphold the law.

4 What shall we say then that Abraham our father, as pertaining to the flesh, hath found? 2 For if Abraham were justified by works, he

4 What then shall we say about[e] Abraham, our forefather according to the flesh? 2 For

[e] Other ancient authorities read *was gained by*.

PHILLIPS

They have all turned aside; they are together
　become unprofitable;
There is none that doeth good, no, not so
　much as one:
Their throat is an open sepulcher;
With their tongues they have used deceit;
The poison of asps is under their lips:
Whose mouth is full of cursing and bitterness:
Their feet are swift to shed blood;
Destruction and misery are in their ways:
And the way of peace have they not known;
There is no fear of God before their eyes.

We know what the message of the Law is, to
those who live under it—that every excuse may
die on the lips of him who makes it and no
living man may think himself beyond the judgment of God. 'No man can justify himself before God' by a perfect performance of the Law's
demands—indeed it is the straightedge of the
Law that shows us how crooked we are.

God's new plan—righteousness　　3. 21
by faith, not through the Law

But now we are seeing the righteousness of
God declared quite apart from the Law (though
amply testified to by both Law and Prophets)—
it is a righteousness imparted to, and operating
in, all who have faith in Jesus Christ. (For there
is no distinction to be made anywhere: everyone
has sinned; everyone falls short of the beauty of
God's plan.) Under this divine "system" a man
who has faith is now freely acquitted in the eyes
of God by his generous dealing in the redemptive
act of Christ Jesus. God has appointed him as
the means of propitiation, a propitiation accomplished by the shedding of his blood, to be
received and made effective in ourselves by
faith. God has done this to demonstrate his
righteousness both by the wiping out of the
sins of the past (the time when he withheld his
hand), and by showing in the present time that
he is a just God and that he justifies every man
who has faith in Jesus Christ.

Faith, not pride of achievement　　3. 27

What happens now to human pride of achievement? There is no more room for it. Why, because failure to keep the Law has killed it?
Not at all, but because the whole matter is now
on a different plane—believing instead of
achieving. We see now that a man is justified
before God by the fact of his faith in God's appointed Savior and not by what he has managed
to achieve under the Law.

And God is God of both Jews and gentiles;
let us be quite clear about that! The one God
is ready to justify the circumcised by faith and
the uncircumcised by faith also.

Are we then undermining the Law by this
insistence on faith? Not a bit of it! We put the
Law in its proper place.

Let us go back and consider our　　4. 1
father Abraham

Now how does all this affect the position of
our ancestor Abraham? Well, if justification

N.E.B.

All have swerved aside, all alike have become
　debased;
There is no one to show kindness; no, not one.

Their throat is an open grave,
They use their tongues for treachery,
Adders' venom is on their lips,
And their mouth is full of bitter curses.

Their feet hasten to shed blood,
Ruin and misery lie along their paths,
They are strangers to the high-road of peace,
And reverence for God does not enter their
　thoughts.'

Now all the words of the law are addressed, as
we know, to those who are within the pale of
the law, so that no one may have anything to
say in self-defence, but the whole world may be
exposed to the judgement of God. For (again
from Scripture) 'no human being can be justified in the sight of God' for having kept the law:
law brings only the consciousness of sin.

But now, quite independently of law, God's
justice has been brought to light. The Law and
the prophets both bear witness to it: it is God's
way of righting wrong, effective through faith in
Christ for all who have such faith—all, without
distinction. For all alike have sinned, and are
deprived of the divine splendour, and all are
justified by God's free grace alone, through his
act of liberation in the person of Christ Jesus.
For God designed him to be the means of ex-
piating sin by his sacrificial death, effective
through faith. God meant by this to demonstrate
his justice, because in his forbearance he had
overlooked the sins of the past—to demonstrate
his justice now in the present, showing that he
is both himself just and justifies any man who
puts his faith in Jesus.

What room then is left for human pride? It
is excluded. And on what principle? The keeping
of the law would not exclude it, but faith does.
For our argument is that a man is justified by
faith quite apart from success in keeping the law.

Do you suppose God is the God of the Jews
alone? Is he not the God of Gentiles also? Certainly, of Gentiles also, if it be true that God is
one. And he will therefore justify both the circumcised in virtue of their faith, and the uncircumcised through their faith. Does this mean
that we are using faith to undermine law? By no
means: we are placing law itself on a firmer
footing.

4 What, then, are we to say about Abraham,
　our ancestor in the natural line? If Abraham

K.J.V.

hath *whereof* to glory; but not before God. 3 For what saith the Scripture? Abraham believed God, and it was counted unto him for righteousness. 4 Now to him that worketh is the reward not reckoned of grace, but of debt. 5 But to him that worketh not, but believeth on him that justifieth the ungodly, his faith is counted for righteousness. 6 Even as David also describeth the blessedness of the man, unto whom God imputeth righteousness without works, 7 *Saying*, Blessed *are* they whose iniquities are forgiven, and whose sins are covered. 8 Blessed *is* the man to whom the Lord will not impute sin. 9 *Cometh* this blessedness then upon the circumcision *only,* or upon the uncircumcision also? for we say that faith was reckoned to Abraham for righteousness. 10 How was it then reckoned? when he was in circumcision, or in uncircumcision? Not in circumcision, but in uncircumcision. 11And he received the sign of circumcision, a seal of the righteousness of the faith which *he had yet* being uncircumcised: that he might be the father of all them that believe, though they be not circumcised; that righteousness might be imputed unto them also: 12And the father of circumcision to them who are not of the circumcision only, but who also walk in the steps of that faith of our father Abraham, which *he had* being yet uncircumcised. 13 For the promise, that he should be the heir of the world, *was* not to Abraham, or to his seed, through the law, but through the righteousness of faith. 14 For if they which are of the law *be* heirs, faith is made void, and the promise made of none effect: 15 Because the law worketh wrath: for where no law is, *there is* no transgression. 16 Therefore *it is* of faith, that *it might be* by grace; to the end the promise might be sure to all the seed; not to that only which is of the law, but to that also which is of the faith of Abraham; who is the father of us all, 17 (As it is written, I have made thee a father of many

R.S.V.

if Abraham was justified by works, he has something to boast about, but not before God. 3 For what does the scripture say? "Abraham believed God, and it was reckoned to him as righteousness." 4 Now to one who works, his wages are not reckoned as a gift but as his due. 5 And to one who does not work but trusts him who justifies the ungodly, his faith is reckoned as righteousness. 6 So also David pronounces a blessing upon the man to whom God reckons righteousness apart from works:

7 "Blessed are those whose iniquities are forgiven, and whose sins are covered;

8 blessed is the man against whom the Lord will not reckon his sin."

9 Is this blessing pronounced only upon the circumcised, or also upon the uncircumcised? We say that faith was reckoned to Abraham as righteousness. 10 How then was it reckoned to him? Was it before or after he had been circumcised? It was not after, but before he was circumcised. 11 He received circumcision as a sign or seal of the righteousness which he had by faith while he was still uncircumcised. The purpose was to make him the father of all who believe without being circumcised and who thus have righteousness reckoned to them, 12 and likewise the father of the circumcised who are not merely circumcised but also follow the example of the faith which our father Abraham had before he was circumcised.

13 The promise to Abraham and his descendants, that they should inherit the world, did not come through the law but through the righteousness of faith. 14 If it is the adherents of the law who are to be the heirs, faith is null and the promise is void. 15 For the law brings wrath, but where there is no law there is no transgression.

16 That is why it depends on faith, in order that the promise may rest on grace and be guaranteed to all his descendants—not only to the adherents of the law but also to those who share the faith of Abraham, for he is the father of us all, 17 as it is written, "I have made you

PHILLIPS

were by achievement he could quite fairly be proud of what he achieved—but not, I am sure, proud before God. For what does the scripture say about him?

And Abraham believed God, and it was reckoned unto him for righteousness.

Now if a man *works,* his wages are not counted as a gift but as a fair reward. But if a man, irrespective of his work, has faith in him who justifies the sinful, then that man's *faith* is counted as righteousness, and that is the gift of God. This is the happy state of the man whom God accounts righteous, apart from his achievements, as David expresses it:

Blessed are they whose iniquities are forgiven
And whose sins are covered.
Blessed is the man to whom the Lord will not reckon sin.

It is a matter of faith, not   *4. 9*
 circumcision

Now the question, an important one, arises: is this happiness for the circumcised only, or for the uncircumcised as well?

Note this carefully. We began by saying that Abraham's faith was counted unto him for righteousness. When this happened, was he a circumcised man? He was not; he was still uncircumcised. It was *afterward* that the sign of circumcision was given to him, as a seal upon that righteousness which God was accounting to him *as yet an uncircumcised man!* God's purpose here is twofold. First, that Abraham might be the spiritual father of all who since that time, despite their uncircumcision, show the faith that is counted as righteousness. Then, secondly, that he might be the circumcised father of all those who are not only circumcised, but are living by the same sort of faith which he himself had before he was circumcised.

The promise, from the beginning,   *4. 13*
 was made to faith

The ancient promise made to Abraham and his descendants, that they should eventually possess the world, was given not because of any achievements made through obedience to the Law, but because of the righteousness which had its root in faith. For if, after all, they who pin their faith to keeping the Law were to inherit God's world, it would make nonsense of faith in God himself, and destroy the whole point of the promise.

For we have already noted that the Law can produce no promise, only the threat of wrath to come. And, indeed, if there were no Law the question of sin would not arise.

The whole thing, then, is a matter of faith on man's part and generosity on God's. He gives the security of his own promise to all men who can be called "children of Abraham," that is, both those who have lived in faith by the Law, and those who have exhibited a faith like that of Abraham. To whichever group we belong, Abraham is in a real sense our father, as the scripture says:

A father of many nations have I made thee.

N.E.B.

was justified by anything he had done, then he has a ground for pride. But he has no such ground before God; for what does Scripture say? 'Abraham put his faith in God, and that faith was counted to him as righteousness.' Now if a man does a piece of work, his wages are not 'counted' as a favour; they are paid as debt. But if without any work to his credit he simply puts his faith in him who acquits the guilty, then his faith is indeed 'counted as righteousness'. In the same sense David speaks of the happiness of the man whom God 'counts' as just, apart from any specific acts of justice: 'Happy are they', he says, 'whose lawless deeds are forgiven, whose sins are buried away; happy is the man whose sins the Lord does not count against him.' Is this happiness confined to the circumcised, or is it for the uncircumcised also? Consider: we say, 'Abraham's faith was counted as righteousness'; in what circumstances was it so counted? Was he circumcised at the time, or not? He was not yet circumcised, but uncircumcised; and he later received the symbolic rite of circumcision as the hall-mark of the righteousness which faith had given him when he was still uncircumcised. Consequently, he is the father of all who have faith when uncircumcised, so that righteousness is 'counted' to them; and at the same time he is the father of such of the circumcised as do not rely upon their circumcision alone, but also walk in the footprints of the faith which our father Abraham had while he was yet uncircumcised.

For it was not through law that Abraham, or his posterity, was given the promise that the world should be his inheritance, but through the righteousness that came from faith. For if those who hold by the law, and they alone, are heirs, then faith is empty and the promise goes for nothing, because law can bring only retribution; but where there is no law there can be no breach of law. The promise was made on the ground of faith, in order that it might be a matter of sheer grace, and that it might be valid for all Abraham's posterity, not only for those who hold by the law, but for those also who have the faith of Abraham. For he is the father of us all, as Scripture says: 'I have appointed you to be fa-

K.J.V.

nations,) before him whom he believed, *even* God, who quickeneth the dead, and calleth those things which be not as though they were: 18 Who against hope believed in hope, that he might become the father of many nations, according to that which was spoken, So shall thy seed be. 19And being not weak in faith, he considered not his own body now dead, when he was about a hundred years old, neither yet the deadness of Sarah's womb: 20 He staggered not at the promise of God through unbelief; but was strong in faith, giving glory to God; 21And being fully persuaded, that what he had promised, he was able also to perform. 22And therefore it was imputed to him for righteousness. 23 Now it was not written for his sake alone, that it was imputed to him; 24 But for us also, to whom it shall be imputed, if we believe on him that raised up Jesus our Lord from the dead; 25 Who was delivered for our offences, and was raised again for our justification.

5 Therefore being justified by faith, we have peace with God through our Lord Jesus Christ: 2 By whom also we have access by faith into this grace wherein we stand, and rejoice in hope of the glory of God. 3And not only *so,* but we glory in tribulations also; knowing that tribulation worketh patience; 4And patience, experience; and experience, hope: 5And hope maketh not ashamed; because the love of God is shed abroad in our hearts by the Holy Ghost which is given unto us. 6 For when we were yet without strength, in due time Christ died for the ungodly. 7 For scarcely for a righteous man will one die: yet peradventure for a good man some would even dare to die. 8 But God commendeth his love toward us, in that, while we were yet sinners, Christ died for us. 9 Much more then, being now justified by his blood, we shall be saved from wrath through him. 10 For if, when we were enemies, we were reconciled to God by the death of his Son; much more, being reconciled, we shall be saved by his life. 11And not only *so,* but we also joy in God through our Lord Jesus Christ, by whom we have now re-

R.S.V.

the father of many nations"—in the presence of the God in whom he believed, who gives life to the dead and calls into existence the things that do not exist. 18 In hope he believed against hope, that he should become the father of many nations; as he had been told, "So shall your descendants be." 19 He did not weaken in faith when he considered his own body, which was as good as dead because he was about a hundred years old, or when he considered the barrenness of Sarah's womb. 20 No distrust made him waver concerning the promise of God, but he grew strong in his faith as he gave glory to God, 21 fully convinced that God was able to do what he had promised. 22 That is why his faith was "reckoned to him as righteousness." 23 But the words, "it was reckoned to him," were written not for his sake alone, 24 but for ours also. It will be reckoned to us who believe in him that raised from the dead Jesus our Lord, 25 who was put to death for our trespasses and raised for our justification.

5 Therefore, since we are justified by faith, we[f] have peace with God through our Lord Jesus Christ. 2 Through him we have obtained access[g] to this grace in which we stand, and we[h] rejoice in our hope of sharing the glory of God. 3 More than that, we[h] rejoice in our sufferings, knowing that suffering produces endurance, 4 and endurance produces character, and character produces hope, 5 and hope does not disappoint us, because God's love has been poured into our hearts through the Holy Spirit which has been given to us.

6 While we were yet helpless, at the right time Christ died for the ungodly. 7 Why, one will hardly die for a righteous man—though perhaps for a good man one will dare even to die. 8 But God shows his love for us in that while we were yet sinners Christ died for us. 9 Since, therefore, we are now justified by his blood, much more shall we be saved by him from the wrath of God. 10 For if while we were enemies we were reconciled to God by the death of his Son, much more, now that we are reconciled, shall we be saved by his life. 11 Not only so, but we also rejoice in God through our Lord Jesus Christ, through whom we have now received our reconciliation.

[f] Other ancient authorities read *let us.* [g] Other ancient authorities add *by faith.* [h] Or *let us.*

PHILLIPS

This faith is valid because of the existence of God himself, who can make the dead live, and speak his word to those who are yet unborn.

Abraham was a shining example   4. 18
of faith

Abraham, when hope was dead within him, went on hoping in faith, believing that he would become "the father of many nations." He relied on the word of God which definitely referred to "thy seed." With undaunted faith he looked at the facts—his own impotence (he was practically a hundred years old at the time) and his wife Sarah's apparent barrenness. Yet he refused to allow any distrust of a definite pronouncement of God to make him waver. He drew strength from his faith, and, while giving the glory to God, remained absolutely convinced that God was able to implement his own promise. This was the "faith" which was 'counted unto him for righteousness.'

Now this counting of faith for righteousness was not recorded simply for Abraham's credit, but as a divine principle which should apply to us as well. Faith is to be reckoned as righteousness to us also, who believe in him who raised from the dead Jesus our Lord, who was delivered to death for our sins and raised again to secure our justification.

Faith means the certainty of God's   5. 1
love, now and hereafter

Since then it is by faith that we are justified, let us grasp the fact that we *have* peace with God through our Lord Jesus Christ. Through him we have confidently entered into this new relationship of grace, and here we take our stand, in happy certainty of the glorious things he has for us in the future.

This doesn't mean, of course, that we have only a hope of future joys—we can be full of joy here and now even in our trials and troubles. Taken in the right spirit these very things will give us patient endurance; this in turn will develop a mature character, and a character of this sort produces a steady hope, a hope that will never disappoint us. Already we have some experience of the love of God flooding through our hearts by the Holy Spirit given to us. And we can see that it was while we were powerless to help ourselves that Christ died for sinful men. In human experience it is a rare thing for one man to give his life for another, even if the latter be a good man, though there have been a few who have had the courage to do it. Yet the proof of God's amazing love is this: that it was *while we were sinners* that Christ died for us. Moreover if he did that for us while we were sinners, now that we are men justified by the shedding of his blood, what reason have we to fear the wrath of God? If, while we were his enemies, Christ reconciled us to God by *dying for us,* surely now that we are reconciled we may be perfectly certain of our salvation through his *living in us.* Nor, I am sure, is this a matter of bare salvation—we may hold our heads high in the light of God's love because of the reconciliation which Christ has made.

N.E.B.

ther of many nations.' This promise, then, was valid before God, the God in whom he put his faith, the God who makes the dead live and summons things that are not yet in existence as if they already were. When hope seemed hopeless, his faith was such that he became 'father of many nations', in agreement with the words which had been spoken to him: 'Thus shall your posterity be.' Without any weakening of faith he contemplated his own body, as good as dead (for he was about a hundred years old), and the deadness of Sarah's womb, and never doubted God's promise, but, strong in faith, gave honour to God, in the firm conviction of his power to do what he had promised. And that is why Abraham's faith was 'counted to him as righteousness'.

Those words were written, not for Abraham's sake alone, but for our sake too: it is to be 'counted' in the same way to us who have faith in the God who raised Jesus our Lord from the dead; for he was delivered to death for our misdeeds, and raised to life to justify us.[a]

5 Therefore, now that we have been justified through faith, let us continue at peace[b] with God through our Lord Jesus Christ, through whom we have been allowed to enter the sphere of God's grace, where we now stand. Let us exult[c] in the hope of the divine splendour that is to be ours. More than this: let us even exult[d] in our present sufferings, because we know that suffering trains us to endure, and endurance brings proof that we have stood the test, and this proof is the ground of hope. Such a hope is no mockery, because God's love has flooded our inmost heart through the Holy Spirit he has given us.

For at the very time when we were still powerless, then Christ died for the wicked. Even for a just man one of us would hardly die, though perhaps for a good man one might actually brave death; but Christ died for us while we were yet sinners, and that is God's own proof of his love towards us. And so, since we have now been justified by Christ's sacrificial death, we shall all the more certainly be saved through him from final retribution. For if, when we were God's enemies, we were reconciled to him through the death of his Son, much more, now that we are reconciled, shall we be saved by his life. But that is not all: we also exult in God through our Lord Jesus, through whom we have now been granted reconciliation.

[a] *Or* raised to life because we were now justified.
[b] *Some witnesses read* we are at peace. [c] *Or* We exult. [d] *Or* we even exult.

K.J.V.

ceived the atonement. 12 Wherefore, as by one man sin entered into the world, and death by sin; and so death passed upon all men, for that all have sinned: 13 (For until the law sin was in the world: but sin is not imputed when there is no law. 14 Nevertheless death reigned from Adam to Moses, even over them that had not sinned after the similitude of Adam's transgression, who is the figure of him that was to come. 15 But not as the offence, so also *is* the free gift: for if through the offence of one many be dead, much more the grace of God, and the gift by grace, *which is* by one man, Jesus Christ, hath abounded unto many. 16 And not as *it was* by one that sinned, *so is* the gift: for the judgment *was* by one to condemnation, but the free gift *is* of many offences unto justification. 17 For if by one man's offence death reigned by one; much more they which receive abundance of grace and of the gift of righteousness shall reign in life by one, Jesus Christ.) 18 Therefore, as by the offence of one *judgment came* upon all men to condemnation; even so by the righteousness of one *the free gift came* upon all men unto justification of life. 19 For as by one man's disobedience many were made sinners, so by the obedience of one shall many be made righteous. 20 Moreover the law entered, that the offence might abound. But where sin abounded, grace did much more abound: 21 That as sin hath reigned unto death, even so might grace reign through righteousness unto eternal life by Jesus Christ our Lord.

R.S.V.

12 Therefore as sin came into the world through one man and death through sin, and so death spread to all men because all men sinned—13 sin indeed was in the world before the law was given, but sin is not counted where there is no law. 14 Yet death reigned from Adam to Moses, even over those whose sins were not like the transgression of Adam, who was a type of the one who was to come. 15 But the free gift is not like the trespass. For if many died through one man's trespass, much more have the grace of God and the free gift in the grace of that one man Jesus Christ abounded for many. 16 And the free gift is not like the effect of that one man's sin. For the judgment following one trespass brought condemnation, but the free gift following many trespasses brings justification. 17 If, because of one man's trespass, death reigned through that one man, much more will those who receive the abundance of grace and the free gift of righteousness reign in life through the one man Jesus Christ. 18 Then as one man's trespass led to condemnation for all men, so one man's act of righteousness leads to acquittal and life for all men. 19 For as by one man's disobedience many were made sinners, so by one man's obedience many will be made righteous. 20 Law came in, to increase the trespass; but where sin increased, grace abounded all the more, 21 so that, as sin reigned in death, grace also might reign through righteousness to eternal life through Jesus Christ our Lord.

6 What shall we say then? Shall we continue in sin, that grace may abound? 2 God forbid. How shall we, that are dead to sin, live any longer therein? 3 Know ye not, that so many of us as were baptized into Jesus Christ were

6 What shall we say then? Are we to continue in sin that grace may abound? 2 By no means! How can we who died to sin still live in it? 3 Do you not know that all of us who have been baptized into Christ Jesus were baptized

PHILLIPS

N.E.B.

A brief résumé—the consequence **5. 12**
of sin and the gift of God

This, then, is what has happened. Sin made its entry into the world through one man, and through sin, death. The entail of sin and death passed on to the whole human race, and no one could break it for no one was himself free from sin.

Sin, you see, was in the world long before the Law, though I suppose, technically speaking, it was not "sin" where there was no law to define it. Nevertheless death, the complement of sin, held sway over mankind from Adam to Moses, even over those whose sin was quite unlike Adam's.

Adam, the first man, corresponds in some degree to the man who was to come. But the gift of God through Christ is a very different matter from the "account rendered" through the sin of Adam. For while as a result of one man's sin death by natural consequence became the common lot of men, it was by the generosity of God, the free giving of the grace of the one man Jesus Christ, that the love of God overflowed for the benefit of all men.

Nor is the effect of God's gift the same as the effect of that one man's sin. For in the one case one man's sin brought its inevitable judgment, and the result was condemnation. But, in the other, countless men's sins are met with the free gift of grace, and the result is justification before God.

For if one man's offense meant that men should be slaves to death all their lives, it is a far greater thing that through another man, Jesus Christ, men by their acceptance of his more than sufficient grace and righteousness should live all their lives like kings!

We see, then, that as one act of sin exposed the whole race of men to God's judgment and condemnation, so one act of perfect righteousness presents all men freely acquitted in the sight of God. One man's disobedience placed all men under the threat of condemnation, but one man's obedience has the power to present all men righteous before God.

Grace is a bigger thing **5. 20**
than the Law

Now we find that the Law keeps slipping into the picture to point the vast extent of sin. Yet, though sin is shown to be wide and deep, thank God his grace is wider and deeper still! The whole outlook changes—sin used to be the master of men and in the end handed them over to death: now grace is the ruling factor, with righteousness as its purpose and its end the bringing of men to the eternal Life of God through Jesus Christ our Lord.

Righteousness by faith, **6. 1**
in practice

Now what is our response to be? Shall we sin to our heart's content and see how far we can exploit the grace of God? What a ghastly thought! We, who have died to sin—how could we live in sin a moment longer? Have you forgotten that all of us who were baptized into Jesus Christ were, by that very action, sharing

Mark what follows. It was through one man that sin entered the world, and through sin death, and thus death pervaded the whole human race, inasmuch as all men have sinned. For sin was already in the world before there was law, though in the absence of law no reckoning is kept of sin. But death held sway from Adam to Moses, even over those who had not sinned as Adam did, by disobeying a direct command—and Adam foreshadows the Man who was to come.

But God's act of grace is out of all proportion to Adam's wrongdoing. For if the wrongdoing of that one man brought death upon so many, its effect is vastly exceeded by the grace of God and the gift that came to so many by the grace of the one man, Jesus Christ. And again, the gift of God is not to be compared in its effect with that one man's sin; for the judicial action, following upon the one offence, issued in a verdict of condemnation, but the act of grace, following upon so many misdeeds, issued in a verdict of acquittal. For if by the wrongdoing of that one man death established its reign, through a single sinner, much more shall those who receive in far greater measure God's grace, and his gift of righteousness, live and reign through the one man, Jesus Christ.

It follows, then, that as the issue of one misdeed was condemnation for all men, so the issue of one just act is acquittal and life for all men. For as through the disobedience of the one man the many were made sinners, so through the obedience of the one man the many will be made righteous.

Law intruded into this process to multiply lawbreaking. But where sin was thus multiplied, grace immeasurably exceeded it, in order that, as sin established its reign by way of death, so God's grace might establish its reign in righteousness, and issue in eternal life through Jesus Christ our Lord.

6 What are we to say, then? Shall we persist in sin, so that there may be all the more grace? No, no! We died to sin: how can we live in it any longer? Have you forgotten that when we were baptized into union with Christ Jesus we

K.J.V.

baptized into his death? 4 Therefore we are buried with him by baptism into death: that like as Christ was raised up from the dead by the glory of the Father, even so we also should walk in newness of life. 5 For if we have been planted together in the likeness of his death, we shall be also *in the likeness* of *his* resurrection: 6 Knowing this, that our old man is crucified with *him*, that the body of sin might be destroyed, that henceforth we should not serve sin. 7 For he that is dead is freed from sin. 8 Now if we be dead with Christ, we believe that we shall also live with him: 9 Knowing that Christ being raised from the dead dieth no more; death hath no more dominion over him. 10 For in that he died, he died unto sin once: but in that he liveth, he liveth unto God. 11 Likewise reckon ye also yourselves to be dead indeed unto sin, but alive unto God through Jesus Christ our Lord. 12 Let not sin therefore reign in your mortal body, that ye should obey it in the lusts thereof. 13 Neither yield ye your members *as* instruments of unrighteousness unto sin: but yield yourselves unto God, as those that are alive from the dead, and your members *as* instruments of righteousness unto God. 14 For sin shall not have dominion over you: for ye are not under the law, but under grace. 15 What then? shall we sin, because we are not under the law, but under grace? God forbid. 16 Know ye not, that to whom ye yield yourselves servants to obey, his servants ye are to whom ye obey; whether of sin unto death, or of obedience unto righteousness? 17 But God be thanked, that ye were the servants of sin, but ye have obeyed from the heart that form of doctrine which was delivered you. 18 Being then made free from sin, ye became the servants of righteousness. 19 I speak after the manner of men because of the infirmity of your flesh: for as ye have yielded your members servants to uncleanness and to iniquity unto iniquity; even so now yield your members servants to righteousness unto holiness. 20 For when ye were the servants of sin, ye were free from righteousness. 21 What fruit had ye then in those things whereof ye are now ashamed? for the end of those things *is* death. 22 But now being made free from sin, and become servants to God, ye have your fruit unto holiness, and the end everlasting life. 23 For the wages of sin *is* death; but the gift of God *is* eternal life through Jesus Christ our Lord.

R.S.V.

into his death? 4 We were buried therefore with him by baptism into death, so that as Christ was raised from the dead by the glory of the Father, we too might walk in newness of life.

5 For if we have been united with him in a death like his, we shall certainly be united with him in a resurrection like his. 6 We know that our old self was crucified with him so that the sinful body might be destroyed, and we might no longer be enslaved to sin. 7 For he who has died is freed from sin. 8 But if we have died with Christ, we believe that we shall also live with him. 9 For we know that Christ being raised from the dead will never die again; death no longer has dominion over him. 10 The death he died he died to sin, once for all, but the life he lives he lives to God. 11 So you also must consider yourselves dead to sin and alive to God in Christ Jesus.

12 Let not sin therefore reign in your mortal bodies, to make you obey their passions. 13 Do not yield your members to sin as instruments of wickedness, but yield yourselves to God as men who have been brought from death to life, and your members to God as instruments of righteousness. 14 For sin will have no dominion over you, since you are not under law but under grace.

15 What then? Are we to sin because we are not under law but under grace? By no means! 16 Do you not know that if you yield yourselves to any one as obedient slaves, you are slaves of the one whom you obey, either of sin, which leads to death, or of obedience, which leads to righteousness? 17 But thanks be to God, that you who were once slaves of sin have become obedient from the heart to the standard of teaching to which you were committed, 18 and, having been set free from sin, have become slaves of righteousness. 19 I am speaking in human terms, because of your natural limitations. For just as you once yielded your members to impurity and to greater and greater iniquity, so now yield your members to righteousness for sanctification.

20 When you were slaves of sin, you were free in regard to righteousness. 21 But then what return did you get from the things of which you are now ashamed? The end of those things is death. 22 But now that you have been set free from sin and have become slaves of God, the return you get is sanctification and its end, eternal life. 23 For the wages of sin is death, but the free gift of God is eternal life in Christ Jesus our Lord.

7 Know ye not, brethren, (for I speak to them that know the law,) how that the law hath dominion over a man as long as he liveth? 2 For the woman which hath a husband is bound by the law to *her* husband so long as he liveth; but if the husband be dead, she is loosed from

7 Do you not know, brethren—for I am speaking to those who know the law—that the law is binding on a person only during his life? 2 Thus a married woman is bound by law to her husband as long as he lives; but if her husband dies she is discharged from the law

PHILLIPS

in his death? We were dead and buried with him in baptism, so that just as he was raised from the dead by that splendid revelation of the Father's power so we too might rise to life on a new plane altogether. If we have, as it were, shared his death, let us rise and live our new lives with him! Let us never forget that our old selves died with him on the cross that the tyranny of sin over us might be broken—for a dead man can safely be said to be immune to the power of sin. And if we were dead men with him we can believe that we shall also be men newly alive with him. We can be sure that the risen Christ never dies again—death's power to touch him is finished. He died, because of sin, once: he lives for God for ever. In the same way look upon yourselves as dead to the appeal and power of sin but alive and sensitive to the call of God through Jesus Christ our Lord.

Do not, then, allow sin to establish any power over your mortal bodies in making you give way to your lusts. Nor hand over your organs to be, as it were, weapons of evil for the devil's purposes. But, like men rescued from certain death, put yourselves in God's hands as weapons of good for his own purposes. For sin is not meant to be your master—you are no longer living under the Law, but under grace.

The new service completely   6. 15
ousts the old

Now, what shall we do? Shall we go on sinning because we have no Law to condemn us any more, but are living under grace? Never! Just think what it would mean. You *belong* to the power which you choose to obey, whether you choose sin, whose reward is death, or God, obedience to whom means the reward of righteousness. Thank God that you, who were at one time the servants of sin, honestly responded to the impact of Christ's teaching when you came under its influence. Then, released from the service of sin, you entered the service of righteousness. (I use an everyday illustration because human nature grasps truth more readily that way.) In the past you voluntarily gave your bodies to the service of vice and wickedness—for the purpose of becoming wicked. So, now, give yourselves to the service of righteousness—for the purpose of becoming really good. For when you were employed by sin you owed no duty to righteousness. Yet what sort of harvest did you reap from those things that today you blush to remember? In the long run those things mean one thing only—death.

But now that you are employed by God, you owe no duty to sin, and you reap the fruit of being made righteous, while at the end of the road there is life for evermore.

Sin *pays* its servants: the wage is death. But God *gives* to those who serve him: his free gift is eternal life through Christ Jesus our Lord.

How to be free from the Law   7. 1

You know very well, my brothers (for I am speaking to those well acquainted with the subject), that the Law can only exercise authority over a man so long as he is alive. A married woman, for example, is bound by law to her husband so long as he is alive. But if he dies,

N.E.B.

were baptized into his death? By baptism we were buried with him, and lay dead, in order that, as Christ was raised from the dead in the splendour of the Father, so also we might set our feet upon the new path of life.

For if we have become incorporate with him in a death like his, we shall also be one with him in a resurrection like his. We know that the man we once were has been crucified with Christ, for the destruction of the sinful self, so that we may no longer be the slaves of sin, since a dead man is no longer answerable for his sin. But if we thus died with Christ, we believe that we shall also come to life with him. We know that Christ, once raised from the dead, is never to die again: he is no longer under the dominion of death. For in dying as he died, he died to sin, once for all, and in living as he lives, he lives to God. In the same way you must regard yourselves as dead to sin and alive to God, in union with Christ Jesus.

So sin must no longer reign in your mortal body, exacting obedience to the body's desires. You must no longer put its several parts at sin's disposal, as implements for doing wrong. No: put yourselves at the disposal of God, as dead men raised to life; yield your bodies to him as implements for doing right; for sin shall no longer be your master, because you are no longer under law, but under the grace of God.

What then? Are we to sin, because we are not under law but under grace? Of course not. You know well enough that if you put yourselves at the disposal of a master, to obey him, you are slaves of the master whom you obey; and this is true whether you serve sin, with death as its result; or obedience, with righteousness as its result. But God be thanked, you, who once were slaves of sin, have yielded whole-hearted obedience to the pattern of teaching to which you were made subject,[a] and, emancipated from sin, have become slaves of righteousness (to use words that suit your human weakness)—I mean, as you once yielded your bodies to the service of impurity and lawlessness, making for moral anarchy, so now you must yield them to the service of righteousness, making for a holy life.

When you were slaves of sin, you were free from the control of righteousness; and what was the gain? Nothing but what now makes you ashamed, for the end of that is death. But now, freed from the commands of sin, and bound to the service of God, your gains are such as make for holiness, and the end is eternal life. For sin pays a wage, and the wage is death, but God gives freely, and his gift is eternal life, in union with Christ Jesus our Lord.

7 You cannot be unaware, my friends—I am speaking to those who have some knowledge of law—that a person is subject to the law so long as he is alive, and no longer. For example, a married woman is by law bound to her husband while he lives; but if her husband dies, she

[a] *Or* which was handed on to you.

K.J.V.

the law of *her* husband. 3 So then if, while *her* husband liveth, she be married to another man, she shall be called an adulteress: but if her husband be dead, she is free from that law; so that she is no adulteress, though she be married to another man. 4 Wherefore, my brethren, ye also are become dead to the law by the body of Christ; that ye should be married to another, *even* to him who is raised from the dead, that we should bring forth fruit unto God. 5 For when we were in the flesh, the motions of sins, which were by the law, did work in our members to bring forth fruit unto death. 6 But now we are delivered from the law, that being dead wherein we were held; that we should serve in newness of spirit, and not *in* the oldness of the letter. 7 What shall we say then? *Is* the law sin? God forbid. Nay, I had not known sin, but by the law: for I had not known lust, except the law had said, Thou shalt not covet. 8 But sin, taking occasion by the commandment, wrought in me all manner of concupiscence. For without the law sin *was* dead. 9 For I was alive without the law once: but when the commandment came, sin revived, and I died. 10And the commandment, which *was ordained* to life, I found *to be* unto death. 11 For sin, taking occasion by the commandment, deceived me, and by it slew *me*. 12 Wherefore the law *is* holy, and the commandment holy, and just, and good. 13 Was then that which is good made death unto me? God forbid. But sin, that it might appear sin, working death in me by that which is good; that sin by the commandment might become exceeding sinful. 14 For we know that the law is spiritual: but I am carnal, sold under sin. 15 For that which I do, I allow not: for what I would, that do I not; but what I hate, that do I. 16 If then I do that which I would not, I consent unto the law that *it is* good. 17 Now then it is no more I that do it, but sin that dwelleth in me. 18 For I know that in me (that is, in my flesh,) dwelleth no good thing: for to will is present with me; but *how* to perform that which is good

R.S.V.

concerning the husband. 3Accordingly, she will be called an adulteress if she lives with another man while her husband is alive. But if her husband dies she is free from that law, and if she marries another man she is not an adulteress.

4 Likewise, my brethren, you have died to the law through the body of Christ, so that you may belong to another, to him who has been raised from the dead in order that we may bear fruit for God. 5 While we were living in the flesh, our sinful passions, aroused by the law, were at work in our members to bear fruit for death. 6 But now we are discharged from the law, dead to that which held us captive, so that we serve not under the old written code but in the new life of the Spirit.

7 What then shall we say? That the law is sin? By no means! Yet, if it had not been for the law, I should not have known sin. I should not have known what it is to covet if the law had not said, "You shall not covet." 8 But sin, finding opportunity in the commandment, wrought in me all kinds of covetousness. Apart from the law sin lies dead. 9 I was once alive apart from the law, but when the commandment came, sin revived and I died; 10 the very commandment which promised life proved to be death to me. 11 For sin, finding opportunity in the commandment, deceived me and by it killed me. 12 So the law is holy, and the commandment is holy and just and good.

13 Did that which is good, then, bring death to me? By no means! It was sin, working death in me through what is good, in order that sin might be shown to be sin, and through the commandment might become sinful beyond measure. 14 We know that the law is spiritual; but I am carnal, sold under sin. 15 I do not understand my own actions. For I do not do what I want, but I do the very thing I hate. 16 Now if I do what I do not want, I agree that the law is good. 17 So then it is no longer I that do it, but sin which dwells within me. 18 For I know that nothing good dwells within me, that is, in my flesh. I can will what is right, but I cannot do it.

PHILLIPS

then his legal claim over her disappears. This means that, if she should give herself to another man while her husband is alive, she incurs the stigma of adultery. But if, after her husband's death, she does exactly the same thing, no one could call her an adulteress, for the legal hold over her has been dissolved by her husband's death.

There is, I think, a fair analogy here. The death of Christ on the cross has made you "dead" to the claims of the Law, and you are free to give yourselves in marriage, so to speak, to another, the one who was raised from the dead, that you may be productive for God.

While we were "in the flesh" the Law stimulated our sinful passions and so worked in our nature that we became productive—for death! But now that we stand clear of the Law, the claims which existed are dissolved by our "death," and we are free to serve God not in the old obedience to the letter of the Law, but in a new way, in the Spirit.

Sin and the Law   7. 7

It now begins to look as if sin and the Law were very much the same thing. Can this be a fact? Of course it cannot. But it must in fairness be admitted that I should never have had sin brought home to me but for the Law. For example, I should never have felt guilty of the sin of coveting if I had not heard the Law saying "Thou shalt not covet." But the sin in me, finding in the commandment an opportunity to express itself, stimulated all my covetous desires. For sin, in the absence of the Law, has no chance to function technically as "sin." As long, then, as I was without the Law I was, spiritually speaking, alive. But when the commandment arrived, sin sprang to life and I "died." The commandment, which was meant to be a direction to life, I found was a sentence to death. The commandment gave sin an opportunity, and without my realizing what was happening, it "killed" me.

The Law is itself good   7. 12

It can scarcely be doubted that in reality the Law itself is holy, and the commandment is holy, fair and good. Can it be that something that is intrinsically good could mean death to me? No, what happened was this. Sin, at the touch of the Law, was forced to expose itself as sin, and *that* meant death for me. The contact of the Law showed the sinful nature of sin.

But it cannot make men good   7. 14

After all, the Law itself is really concerned with the spiritual—it is I who am carnal, and have sold my soul to sin. In practice, what happens? My own behavior baffles me. For I find myself not doing what I really want to do but doing what I really loathe. Yet surely if I do things that I really don't want to do, I am admitting that I really agree with the Law. But it cannot be said that "I" am doing them at all —it must be sin that has made its home in my nature. (And indeed, I know from experience that the carnal side of my being can scarcely be called the home of good!) I often find that

N.E.B.

is discharged from the obligations of the marriage-law. If, therefore, in her husband's lifetime she consorts with another man, she will incur the charge of adultery; but if her husband dies she is free of the law, and she does not commit adultery by consorting with another man. So you, my friends, have died to the law by becoming identified with the body of Christ, and accordingly you have found another husband in him who rose from the dead, so that we may bear fruit for God. While we lived on the level of our lower nature, the sinful passions evoked by the law worked in our bodies, to bear fruit for death. But now, having died to that which held us bound, we are discharged from the law, to serve God in a new way, the way of the spirit, in contrast to the old way, the way of a written code.

What follows? Is the law identical with sin? Of course not. But except through law I should never have become acquainted with sin. For example, I should never have known what it was to covet, if the law had not said, 'Thou shalt not covet.' Through that commandment sin found its opportunity, and produced in me all kinds of wrong desires. In the absence of law, sin is a dead thing. There was a time when, in the absence of law, I was fully alive; but when the commandment came, sin sprang to life and I died. The commandment which should have led to life proved in my experience to lead to death, because sin found its opportunity in the commandment, seduced me, and through the commandment killed me.

Therefore the law is in itself holy, and the commandment is holy and just and good. Are we to say then that this good thing was the death of me? By no means. It was sin that killed me, and thereby sin exposed its true character: it used a good thing to bring about my death, and so, through the commandment, sin became more sinful than ever.

We know that the law is spiritual; but I am not: I am unspiritual, the purchased slave of sin. I do not even acknowledge my own actions as mine, for what I do is not what I want to do, but what I detest. But if what I do is against my will, it means that I agree with the law and hold it to be admirable. But as things are, it is no longer I who perform the action, but sin that lodges in me. For I know that nothing good lodges in me—in my unspiritual nature, I mean —for though the will to do good is there, the

K.J.V.

I find not. 19 For the good that I would, I do not: but the evil which I would not, that I do. 20 Now if I do that I would not, it is no more I that do it, but sin that dwelleth in me. 21 I find then a law, that, when I would do good, evil is present with me. 22 For I delight in the law of God after the inward man: 23 But I see another law in my members, warring against the law of my mind, and bringing me into captivity to the law of sin which is in my members. 24 O wretched man that I am! who shall deliver me from the body of this death? 25 I thank God through Jesus Christ our Lord. So then with the mind I myself serve the law of God; but with the flesh the law of sin.

8 *There is* therefore now no condemnation to them which are in Christ Jesus, who walk not after the flesh, but after the Spirit. 2 For the law of the Spirit of life in Christ Jesus hath made me free from the law of sin and death. 3 For what the law could not do, in that it was weak through the flesh, God sending his own Son in the likeness of sinful flesh, and for sin, condemned sin in the flesh: 4 That the righteousness of the law might be fulfilled in us, who walk not after the flesh, but after the Spirit. 5 For they that are after the flesh do mind the things of the flesh; but they that are after the Spirit, the things of the Spirit. 6 For to be carnally minded *is* death; but to be spiritually minded *is* life and peace. 7 Because the carnal mind *is* enmity against God: for it is not subject to the law of God, neither indeed can be. 8 So then they that are in the flesh cannot please God. 9 But ye are not in the flesh, but in the Spirit, if so be that the Spirit of God dwell in you. Now if any man have not the Spirit of Christ, he is none of his. 10 And if Christ *be* in you, the body *is* dead because of sin; but the Spirit *is* life because of righteousness. 11 But if the Spirit of him that raised up Jesus from the dead dwell in you, he that raised up Christ from the dead shall also quicken your mortal bodies by his Spirit that dwelleth in you. 12 Therefore, brethren, we are debtors, not to the flesh, to live after the flesh. 13 For if ye live after the flesh, ye shall die: but if ye through the Spirit do mortify the deeds of the body, ye shall live.

R.S.V.

19 For I do not do the good I want, but the evil I do not want is what I do. 20 Now if I do what I do not want, it is no longer I that do it, but sin which dwells within me.

21 So I find it to be a law that when I want to do right, evil lies close at hand. 22 For I delight in the law of God, in my inmost self, 23 but I see in my members another law at war with the law of my mind and making me captive to the law of sin which dwells in my members. 24 Wretched man that I am! Who will deliver me from this body of death? 25 Thanks be to God through Jesus Christ our Lord! So then, I of myself serve the law of God with my mind, but with my flesh I serve the law of sin.

8 There is therefore now no condemnation for those who are in Christ Jesus. 2 For the law of the Spirit of life in Christ Jesus has set me free from the law of sin and death. 3 For God has done what the law, weakened by the flesh, could not do: sending his own Son in the likeness of sinful flesh and for sin,[i] he condemned sin in the flesh, 4 in order that the just requirement of the law might be fulfilled in us, who walk not according to the flesh but according to the Spirit. 5 For those who live according to the flesh set their minds on the things of the flesh, but those who live according to the Spirit set their minds on the things of the Spirit. 6 To set the mind on the flesh is death, but to set the mind on the Spirit is life and peace. 7 For the mind that is set on the flesh is hostile to God; it does not submit to God's law, indeed it cannot; 8 and those who are in the flesh cannot please God.

9 But you are not in the flesh, you are in the Spirit, if the Spirit of God really dwells in you. Any one who does not have the Spirit of Christ does not belong to him. 10 But if Christ is in you, although your bodies are dead because of sin, your spirits are alive because of righteousness. 11 If the Spirit of him who raised Jesus from the dead dwells in you, he who raised Christ Jesus from the dead will give life to your mortal bodies also through his Spirit which dwells in you.

12 So then, brethren, we are debtors, not to the flesh, to live according to the flesh—13 for if you live according to the flesh you will die, but if by the Spirit you put to death the deeds

[i] Or *and as a sin offering.*

470

PHILLIPS

I have the will to do good, but not the power. That is, I don't accomplish the good I set out to do, and the evil I don't really want to do I find I am always doing. Yet if I do things that I don't really want to do then it is not, I repeat, "I" who do them, but the sin which has made its home within me. When I come up against the Law I want to do good, but in practice I do evil. My conscious mind wholeheartedly endorses the Law, yet I observe an entirely different principle at work in my nature. This is in continual conflict with my conscious attitude, and makes me an unwilling prisoner to the law of sin and death. In my mind I am God's willing servant, but in my own nature I am bound fast, as I say, to the law of sin and death. It is an agonizing situation, and who on earth can set me free from the clutches of my own sinful nature? I thank God there *is* a way out through Jesus Christ our Lord.

The way out—new life in Christ **8. 1**

No condemnation now hangs over the head of those who are "in" Christ Jesus. For the new spiritual principle of life "in" Christ Jesus lifts me out of the old vicious circle of sin and death.
The Law never succeeded in producing righteousness—the failure was always the weakness of human nature. But God has met this by sending his own Son Jesus Christ to live in that human nature which causes the trouble. And, *while Christ was actually taking upon himself the sins of men, God condemned that sinful nature.* So that we are able to meet the Law's requirements, so long as we are living no longer by the dictates of our sinful nature, but in obedience to the promptings of the Spirit. The carnal attitude sees no further than natural things. But the spiritual attitude reaches out after the things of the spirit. The former attitude means, bluntly, death: the latter means life and inward peace. And this is only to be expected, for the carnal attitude is inevitably opposed to the purpose of God, and neither can nor will follow his laws for living. Men who hold this attitude cannot possibly please God.

What the presence of Christ **8. 9**
within means

But you are not carnal but spiritual if the Spirit of God finds a home within you. You cannot, indeed, be a Christian at all unless you have something of his spirit in you. Now if Christ does live within you his presence means that your sinful nature is dead, but your spirit becomes alive because of the righteousness he brings with him. I said that our nature is "dead" in the presence of Christ, and so it is, because of its sin. Nevertheless once the Spirit of him who raised Christ Jesus from the dead lives within you he will, by the same Spirit, bring to your whole being new strength and vitality.
So then, my brothers, you can see that we have no particular reason to feel grateful to our sensual nature, or to live life on the level of the instincts. Indeed that way of living leads to certain spiritual death. But if on the other hand you cut the nerve of your instinctive actions by obeying the Spirit, you are on the way to real living.

N.E.B.

deed is not. The good which I want to do, I fail to do; but what I do is the wrong which is against my will; and if what I do is against my will, clearly it is no longer I who am the agent, but sin that has its lodging in me.
I discover this principle, then: that when I want to do the right, only the wrong is within my reach. In my inmost self I delight in the law of God, but I perceive that there is in my bodily members a different law, fighting against the law that my reason approves and making me a prisoner under the law[a] that is in my members, the law of sin. Miserable creature that I am, who is there to rescue me out of this body doomed to death[b]? God alone, through Jesus Christ our Lord! Thanks be to God! In a word then, I myself, subject to God's law as a rational being, am yet,[c] in my unspiritual nature, a slave to the law of sin.

8 The conclusion of the matter is this: there is no condemnation for those who are united with Christ Jesus, because in Christ Jesus the life-giving law of the Spirit has set you free from the law of sin and death. What the law could never do, because our lower nature robbed it of all potency, God has done: by sending his own Son in a form like that of our own sinful nature, and as a sacrifice for sin,[d] he has passed judgement against sin within that very nature, so that the commandment of the law may find fulfilment in us, whose conduct, no longer under the control of our lower nature, is directed by the Spirit.
Those who live on the level of our lower nature have their outlook formed by it, and that spells death; but those who live on the level of the spirit have the spiritual outlook, and that is life and peace. For the outlook of the lower nature is enmity with God; it is not subject to the law of God; indeed it cannot be: those who live on such a level cannot possibly please God.
But that is not how you live. You are on the spiritual level, if only God's Spirit dwells within you; and if a man does not possess the Spirit of Christ, he is no Christian. But if Christ is dwelling within you, then although the body is a dead thing because you sinned, yet the spirit is life itself because you have been justified.[e] Moreover, if the Spirit of him who raised Jesus from the dead dwells within you, then the God who raised Christ Jesus from the dead will also give new life to your mortal bodies through his indwelling Spirit.
It follows, my friends, that our lower nature has no claim upon us; we are not obliged to live on that level. If you do so, you must die. But if by the Spirit you put to death all the base pursuits of the body, then you will live.

[a] *Or* by means of the law. [b] *Or* out of the body doomed to this death. [c] *Or* Thus, left to myself, while subject . . . rational being, I am yet . . . [d] *Or* and to deal with sin. [e] *Or* so that you may live rightly.

K.J.V.

14 For as many as are led by the Spirit of God, they are the sons of God. 15 For ye have not received the spirit of bondage again to fear; but ye have received the Spirit of adoption, whereby we cry, Abba, Father. 16 The Spirit itself beareth witness with our spirit, that we are the children of God: 17And if children, then heirs; heirs of God, and joint heirs with Christ; if so be that we suffer with *him,* that we may be also glorified together. 18 For I reckon that the sufferings of this present time *are* not worthy *to be compared* with the glory which shall be revealed in us. 19 For the earnest expectation of the creature waiteth for the manifestation of the sons of God. 20 For the creature was made subject to vanity, not willingly, but by reason of him who hath subjected *the same* in hope; 21 Because the creature itself also shall be delivered from the bondage of corruption into the glorious liberty of the children of God. 22 For we know that the whole creation groaneth and travaileth in pain together until now. 23And not only *they,* but ourselves also, which have the firstfruits of the Spirit, even we ourselves groan within ourselves, waiting for the adoption, *to wit,* the redemption of our body. 24 For we are saved by hope: but hope that is seen is not hope: for what a man seeth, why doth he yet hope for? 25 But if we hope for that we see not, *then* do we with patience wait for *it.* 26 Likewise the Spirit also helpeth our infirmities: for we know not what we should pray for as we ought: but the Spirit itself maketh intercession for us with groanings which cannot be uttered. 27And he that searcheth the hearts knoweth what *is* the mind of the Spirit, because he maketh intercession for the saints according to *the will of* God. 28And we know that all things work together for good to them that love God, to them who are the called according to *his* purpose. 29 For whom he did foreknow, he also did predestinate *to be* conformed to the image of his Son, that he might be the firstborn among many brethren. 30 Moreover, whom he did predestinate, them he also called: and whom he called, them he also justified: and whom he justified, them he also glori-

R.S.V.

of the body you will live. 14 For all who are led by the Spirit of God are sons of God. 15 For you did not receive the spirit of slavery to fall back into fear, but you have received the spirit of sonship. When we cry, "Abba! Father!" 16 it is the Spirit himself bearing witness with our spirit that we are children of God, 17 and if children, then heirs, heirs of God and fellow heirs with Christ, provided we suffer with him in order that we may also be glorified with him.

18 I consider that the sufferings of this present time are not worth comparing with the glory that is to be revealed to us. 19 For the creation waits with eager longing for the revealing of the sons of God; 20 for the creation was subjected to futility, not of its own will but by the will of him who subjected it in hope; 21 because the creation itself will be set free from its bondage to decay and obtain the glorious liberty of the children of God. 22 We know that the whole creation has been groaning in travail together until now; 23 and not only the creation, but we ourselves, who have the first fruits of the Spirit, groan inwardly as we wait for adoption as sons, the redemption of our bodies. 24 For in this hope we were saved. Now hope that is seen is not hope. For who hopes for what he sees? 25 But if we hope for what we do not see, we wait for it with patience.

26 Likewise the Spirit helps us in our weakness; for we do not know how to pray as we ought, but the Spirit himself intercedes for us with sighs too deep for words. 27And he who searches the hearts of men knows what is the mind of the Spirit, because[j] the Spirit intercedes for the saints according to the will of God.

28 We know that in everything God works for good [k] with those who love him,[l] who are called according to his purpose. 29 For those whom he foreknew he also predestined to be conformed to the image of his Son, in order that he might be the first-born among many brethren. 30And those whom he predestined he also called; and those whom he called he also justified; and those whom he justified he also glorified.

[j] Or *that.* [k] Other ancient authorities read *in everything he works for good,* or *everything works for good.* [l] Greek *God.*

Christis is within—follow the lead **8. 14**
of his Spirit

All who follow the leading of God's Spirit
are God's own sons. Nor are you meant to re-
lapse into the old slavish attitude of fear—you
have been adopted into the very family circle
of God and you can say with a full heart,
"Father, my Father." The Spirit himself endorses our inward conviction that we really are
the children of God. Think what that means. If
we are his children we share his treasures, and
all that Christ claims as his will belong to all of
us as well! Yes, if we share in his sufferings we
shall certainly share in his glory.

Present distress is temporary **8. 18**
and negligible

In my opinion whatever we may have to go
through now is less than nothing compared with
the magnificent future God has planned for us.
The whole creation is on tiptoe to see the wonderful sight of the sons of God coming into
their own. The world of creation cannot as yet
see reality, not because it chooses to be blind,
but because in God's purpose it has been so
limited—yet it has been given hope. And the
hope is that in the end the whole of created
life will be rescued from the tyranny of change
and decay, and have its share in that magnificent liberty which can only belong to the children of God!
It is plain to anyone with eyes to see that at
the present time all created life groans in a sort
of universal travail. And it is plain, too, that we
who have a foretaste of the Spirit are in a state
of painful tension, while we wait for that redemption of our bodies which will mean that at
last we have realized our full sonship in him. We
were saved by this hope, but in our moments of
impatience let us remember that hope always
means waiting for something that we do not
yet possess. But if we hope for something we
cannot see, then we must settle down to wait for
it in patience.

This is not mere theory—the **8. 26**
Spirit helps us to find it true

The Spirit of God not only maintains this
hope within us, but helps us in our present limitations. For example, we do not know how to
pray worthily as sons of God, but his Spirit
within us is actually praying for us in those
agonizing longings which never find words.
And God who knows the heart's secrets understands, of course, the Spirit's intention as he
prays for those who love God.
Moreover we know that to those who love
God, who are called according to his plan, everything that happens fits into a pattern for good.
God, in his foreknowledge, chose them to bear
the family likeness of his Son, that he might be
the eldest of a family of many brothers. He
chose them long ago; when the time came he
called them, he made them righteous in his
sight and then lifted them to the splendor of life
as his own sons.

For all who are moved by the Spirit of God
are sons of God. The Spirit you have received
is not a spirit of slavery leading you back into
a life of fear, but a Spirit that makes us sons,
enabling us to cry 'Abba! Father!' In that cry
the Spirit of God joins with our spirit in testifying that we are God's children; and if children,
then heirs. We are God's heirs and Christ's fel-
low-heirs, if we share his sufferings now in
order to share his splendour hereafter.
For I reckon that the sufferings we now endure bear no comparison with the splendour, as
yet unrevealed, which is in store for us. For the
created universe waits with eager expectation
for God's sons to be revealed. It was made the
victim of frustration, not by its own choice, but
because of him who made it so;[a] yet always
there was hope, because[b] the universe itself is to
be freed from the shackles of mortality and
enter upon the liberty and splendour of the
children of God. Up to the present, we know, the
whole created universe groans in all its parts as
if in the pangs of childbirth. Not only so, but
even we, to whom the Spirit is given as firstfruits
of the harvest to come, are groaning inwardly
while we wait for God to make us his sons and[c]
set our whole body free. For we have been
saved, though only in hope. Now to see is no
longer to hope: why should a man endure and
wait[d] for what he already sees? But if we hope
for something we do not yet see, then, in waiting
for it, we show our endurance.
In the same way the Spirit comes to the aid of
our weakness. We do not even know how we
ought to pray,[e] but through our inarticulate
groans the Spirit himself is pleading for us, and
God who searches our inmost being knows what
the Spirit means, because he pleads for God's
own people in God's own way; and in everything, as we know, he co-operates for good with
those who love God[f] and are called according
to his purpose. For God knew his own before
ever they were, and also ordained that they
should be shaped to the likeness of his Son,
that he might be the eldest among a large family of brothers; and it is these, so fore-ordained,
whom he has also called. And those whom he
called he has justified, and to those whom he
justified he has also given his splendour.

[a] *Or* because God subjected it. [b] *Or* with the
hope that . . . [c] *Some witnesses omit* make us
his sons and. [d] *Some witnesses read* why should
a man hope . . . [e] *Or* what it is right to pray for.
[f] *Or* and, as we know, all things work together for
good for those who love God; *some witnesses read*
and we know God himself co-operates for good with
those who love God.

K.J.V.

fied. 31 What shall we then say to these things? If God *be* for us, who *can be* against us? 32 He that spared not his own Son, but delivered him up for us all, how shall he not with him also freely give us all things? 33 Who shall lay any thing to the charge of God's elect? *It is* God that justifieth. 34 Who *is* he that condemneth? *It is* Christ that died, yea rather, that is risen again, who is even at the right hand of God, who also maketh intercession for us. 35 Who shall separate us from the love of Christ? *shall* tribulation, or distress, or persecution, or famine, or nakedness, or peril, or sword? 36As it is written, For thy sake we are killed all the day long; we are accounted as sheep for the slaughter. 37 Nay, in all these things we are more than conquerors through him that loved us. 38 For I am persuaded, that neither death, nor life, nor angels, nor principalities, nor powers, nor things present, nor things to come, 39 Nor height, nor depth, nor any other creature, shall be able to separate us from the love of God, which is in Christ Jesus our Lord.

9 I say the truth in Christ, I lie not, my conscience also bearing me witness in the Holy Ghost, 2 That I have great heaviness and continual sorrow in my heart. 3 For I could wish that myself were accursed from Christ for my brethren, my kinsmen according to the flesh: 4 Who are Israelites; to whom *pertaineth* the adoption, and the glory, and the covenants, and the giving of the law, and the service *of God,* and the promises; 5 Whose *are* the fathers, and of whom as concerning the flesh Christ *came,* who is over all, God blessed for ever. Amen. 6 Not as though the word of God hath taken none effect. For they *are* not all Israel, which are of Israel: 7 Neither, because they are the seed of Abraham, *are they* all children: but, In

R.S.V.

31 What then shall we say to this? If God is for us, who is against us? 32 He who did not spare his own Son but gave him up for us all, will he not also give us all things with him? 33 Who shall bring any charge against God's elect? It is God who justifies; 34 who is to condemn? Is it Christ Jesus, who died, yes, who was raised from the dead, who is at the right hand of God, who indeed intercedes for us? *m* 35 Who shall separate us from the love of Christ? Shall tribulation, or distress, or persecution, or famine, or nakedness, or peril, or sword? 36As it is written,

"For thy sake we are being killed all the day long;

we are regarded as sheep to be slaughtered." 37 No, in all these things we are more than conquerors through him who loved us. 38 For I am sure that neither death, nor life, nor angels, nor principalities, nor things present, nor things to come, nor powers, 39 nor height, nor depth, nor anything else in all creation, will be able to separate us from the love of God in Christ Jesus our Lord.

9 I am speaking the truth in Christ, I am not lying; my conscience bears me witness in the Holy Spirit, 2 that I have great sorrow and unceasing anguish in my heart. 3 For I could wish that I myself were accursed and cut off from Christ for the sake of my brethren, my kinsmen by race. 4 They are Israelites, and to them belong the sonship, the glory, the covenants, the giving of the law, the worship, and the promises; 5 to them belong the patriarchs, and of their race, according to the flesh, is the Christ. God who is over all be blessed for ever.*n* Amen.

6 But it is not as though the word of God had failed. For not all who are descended from Israel belong to Israel, 7 and not all are children of Abraham because they are his descendants; but "Through Isaac shall your descendants

[*m*] Or *It is Christ Jesus . . . for us.* [*n*] Or *Christ, who is God over all, blessed for ever.*

PHILLIPS

We hold, in Christ, an   *8. 31*
impregnable position

In face of all this, what is there left to say? If
God is for us, who can be against us? He who
did not hesitate to spare his own Son but gave
him up for us all—can we not trust such a God
to give us, with him, everything else that we can
need?

Who would dare to accuse us, whom God has
chosen? The judge himself has declared us free
from sin. Who is in a position to condemn?
Only Christ, and Christ died for us, Christ rose
for us, Christ reigns in power for us, Christ
prays for us!

Who can separate us from the love of Christ?
Can trouble, pain or persecution? Can lack of
clothes and food, danger to life and limb, the
threat of force of arms? Indeed some of us
know the truth of that ancient text:

For thy sake we are killed all the day long;
We were accounted as sheep for the slaughter.

No, in all these things we win an overwhelming victory through him who has proved
his love for us.

I have become absolutely convinced that
neither death nor life, neither messenger of
Heaven nor monarch of earth, neither what
happens today nor what may happen tomorrow,
neither a power from on high nor a power from
below, nor anything else in God's whole world
has any power to separate us from the love of
God in Christ Jesus our Lord!

The fly in the ointment—the   *9. 1*
infidelity of my own race

Before Christ and my own conscience in the
Holy Spirit I assure you that I am speaking the
plain truth when I say that there is something
that makes me feel very depressed, like a pain
that never leaves me. It is the condition of my
brothers and fellow Israelites, and I have actually reached the pitch of wishing myself cut off
from Christ if it meant that they could be won
for God.

Just think what the Israelites have had given
to them. The privilege of being adopted as sons
of God, the experience of seeing something of
the glory of God, the receiving of the agreements made with God, the gift of the Law, true
ways of worship, God's own promises—all these
are theirs. The patriarchs are theirs, and so too,
as far as human descent goes, is Christ himself,
Christ who is God over all, blessed for ever.

God's purpose is not utterly   *9. 6*
defeated by this infidelity

Now this does not mean that God's word to
Israel has failed. For you cannot count all
"Israelites" as the true Israel of God. Nor can
all Abraham's descendants be considered truly
children of Abraham. The promise was that "in
Isaac shall thy children be called." That means
that it is not the natural descendants who automatically inherit the promise, but, on the contrary, that the children of the promise (that is,
the sons of God) are to be considered truly
Abraham's children. For it was a promise when

N.E.B.

With all this in mind, what are we to say? If
God is on our side, who is against us? He did
not spare his own Son, but surrendered him for
us all; and with this gift how can he fail to
lavish upon us all he has to give? Who will be
the accuser of God's chosen ones? It is God
who pronounces acquittal: then who can condemn? It is Christ—Christ who died, and, more
than that, was raised from the dead—who is at
God's right hand, and indeed pleads our cause.[a]
Then what can separate us from the love of
Christ? Can affliction or hardship? Can persecution, hunger, nakedness, peril, or the sword? 'We
are being done to death for thy sake all day
long,' as Scripture says; 'we have been treated
like sheep for slaughter'—and yet, in spite of all,
overwhelming victory is ours through him who
loved us. For I am convinced that there is nothing in death or life, in the realm of spirits or
superhuman powers, in the world as it is or the
world as it shall be, in the forces of the universe,
in heights or depths—nothing in all creation that
can separate us from the love of God in Christ
Jesus our Lord.

The Purpose of God in History

9 I am speaking the truth as a Christian, and
my own conscience, enlightened by the Holy
Spirit, assures me it is no lie: in my heart there
is great grief and unceasing sorrow. For I could
even pray to be outcast from Christ myself for
the sake of my brothers, my natural kinsfolk.
They are Israelites: they were made God's sons;
theirs is the splendour of the divine presence,
theirs the covenants, the law, the temple worship,
and the promises. Theirs are the patriarchs, and
from them, in natural descent, sprang the Messiah.[b] May God, supreme above all, be blessed
for ever![c] Amen.

It is impossible that the word of God should
have proved false. For not all descendants of
Israel are truly Israel, nor, because they are
Abraham's offspring, are they all his true chil-

[a] *Or* Who will be the accuser of God's chosen
ones? Will it be God himself? No, he it is who pronounces acquittal. Who will be the judge to condemn? Will it be Christ—he who died, and, more
than that, . . . right hand? No, he it is who pleads
our cause. [b] *Greek* Christ. [c] *Or* sprang the
Messiah, supreme above all, God blessed for ever;
or sprang the Messiah, who is supreme above all.
Blessed be God for ever!

K.J.V.

Isaac shall thy seed be called. 8 That is, They which are the children of the flesh, these *are* not the children of God: but the children of the promise are counted for the seed. 9 For this *is* the word of promise, At this time will I come, and Sarah shall have a son. 10And not only *this;* but when Rebecca also had conceived by one, *even* by our father Isaac, 11 (For *the children* being not yet born, neither having done any good or evil, that the purpose of God according to election might stand, not of works, but of him that calleth;) 12 It was said unto her, The elder shall serve the younger. 13 As it is written, Jacob have I loved, but Esau have I hated. 14 What shall we say then? *Is there* unrighteousness with God? God forbid. 15 For he saith to Moses, I will have mercy on whom I will have mercy, and I will have compassion on whom I will have compassion. 16 So then *it is* not of him that willeth, nor of him that runneth, but of God that sheweth mercy. 17 For the Scripture saith unto Pharaoh, Even for this same purpose have I raised thee up, that I might shew my power in thee, and that my name might be declared throughout all the earth. 18 Therefore hath he mercy on whom he will *have mercy,* and whom he will he hardeneth. 19 Thou wilt say then unto me, Why doth he yet find fault? For who hath resisted his will? 20 Nay but, O man, who art thou that repliest against God? Shall the thing formed say to him that formed *it,* Why hast thou made me thus? 21 Hath not the potter power over the clay, of the same lump to make one vessel unto honour, and another unto dishonour? 22 *What* if God, willing to shew *his* wrath, and to make his power known, endured with much longsuffering the vessels of wrath fitted to destruction: 23And that he might make known the riches of his glory on the vessels of mercy, which he had afore prepared unto glory, 24 Even us, whom he hath called, not of the Jews only, but also of the Gentiles? 25As he saith also in Osee, I will call them my people, which were not my people; and her beloved, which was not beloved. 26And it shall come to pass, *that* in the place where it was said unto them, Ye *are* not my people; there shall they be called the children of the living God. 27 Esaias also crieth concerning

R.S.V.

be named." 8 This means that it is not the children of the flesh who are the children of God, but the children of the promise are reckoned as decendants. 9 For this is what the promise said, "About this time I will return and Sarah shall have a son." 10And not only so, but also when Rebecca had conceived children by one man, our forefather Isaac, 11 though they were not yet born and had done nothing either good or bad, in order that God's purpose of election might continue, not because of works but because of his call, 12 she was told, "The elder will serve the younger." 13As it is written, "Jacob I loved, but Esau I hated."

14 What shall we say then? Is there injustice on God's part? By no means! 15 For he says to Moses, "I will have mercy on whom I have mercy, and I will have compassion on whom I have compassion." 16 So it depends not upon man's will or exertion, but upon God's mercy. 17 For the scripture says to Pharaoh, "I have raised you up for the very purpose of showing my power in you, so that my name may be proclaimed in all the earth." 18 So then he has mercy upon whomever he wills, and he hardens the heart of whomever he wills.

19 You will say to me then, "Why does he still find fault? For who can resist his will?" 20 But who are you, a man, to answer back to God? Will what is molded say to its molder, "Why have you made me thus?" 21 Has the potter no right over the clay, to make out of the same lump one vessel for beauty and another for menial use? 22 What if God, desiring to show his wrath and to make known his power, has endured with much patience the vessels of wrath made for destruction, 23 in order to make known the riches of his glory for the vessels of mercy, which he has prepared beforehand for glory, 24 even us whom he has called, not from the Jews only but also from the Gentiles? 25As indeed he says in Hosea,

"Those who were not my people
I will call 'my people,'
and her who was not beloved
I will call 'my beloved.'"
26 "And in the very place where it was said to
them, 'You are not my people,'
they will be called 'sons of the living
God.'"
27 And Isaiah cries out concerning Israel:

PHILLIPS

God said: "About this time I will come and Sarah shall have a son." (Everybody, remember, thought it quite impossible for Sarah to have a child.) And then, again, a word of promise came to Rebecca, at the time when she was pregnant with two children by the one man, Isaac our forefather. It came before the children were born or had done anything good or bad, plainly showing that God's act of choice has nothing to do with achievements, good or bad, but is entirely a matter of his will. The promise was:

The elder shall serve the younger.

And we get a later endorsement of this divine choice in the words:

Jacob I loved, but Esau I hated.

We must not jump to conclusions 9. 14 about God

Now do we conclude that God is monstrously unfair? Never! God said long ago to Moses:

I will have mercy on whom I have mercy, and I will have compassion on whom I have compassion.

It is obviously not a question of human will or human effort, but of divine mercy. The scripture says to Pharaoh:

For this very purpose did I raise thee up, that I might show in thee my power, and that my name might be published abroad in all the earth.

It seems plain, then, that God chooses on whom he will have mercy, and whom he will harden in their sin.

Of course I can almost hear your retort: "If this is so, and God's will is irresistible, why does God blame men for what they do?" But the question really is this: "Who are you, a man, to make any such reply to God?" When a craftsman makes anything he doesn't expect it to turn round and say, "Why did you make me like this?" The potter, for instance, is always assumed to have complete control over the clay, making with one part of the lump a lovely vase, and with another a pipe for sewage. Can we not assume that God has the same control over human clay? May it not be that God, though he must sooner or later expose his wrath against sin and show his controlling hand, has yet most patiently endured the presence in his world of things that cry out to be destroyed? Can we not see, in this, his purpose in demonstrating the boundless resources of his glory upon those whom he considers fit to receive his mercy, and whom he long ago planned to raise to glorious life? And by these chosen people I mean you and me, whom he has called out from both Jews and gentiles. He says in Hosea:

I will call that my people, which was not my people;
And her beloved, which was not beloved.
And it shall be, that in the place where it was said unto them, Ye are not my people,
There shall they be called sons of the living God.

And Isaiah, speaking about Israel, proclaims:

N.E.B.

dren;[a] but, in the words of Scripture, 'Through the line of Isaac your posterity shall be traced.'[b] That is to say, it is not those born in the course of nature who are children of God; it is the children born through God's promise who are reckoned as Abraham's descendants. For the promise runs: 'At the time fixed I will come, and Sarah shall have a son.'

But that is not all, for Rebekah's children had one and the same father, our ancestor Isaac; and yet, in order that God's selective purpose might stand, based not upon men's deeds but upon the call of God, she was told, even before they were born, when they had as yet done nothing, good or ill, 'The elder shall be servant to the younger'; and that accords with the text of Scripture, 'Jacob I loved and Esau I hated.'

What shall we say to that? Is God to be charged with injustice? By no means. For he says to Moses, 'Where I show mercy, I will show mercy, and where I pity, I will pity.' Thus it does not depend on man's will or effort, but on God's mercy. For Scripture says to Pharaoh, 'I have raised you up for this very purpose, to exhibit my power in my dealings with you, and to spread my fame over all the world.' Thus he not only shows mercy as he chooses, but also makes men stubborn as he chooses.

You will say, 'Then why does God blame a man? For who can resist his will?' Who are you, sir, to answer God back? Can the pot speak to the potter and say, 'Why did you make me like this?'? Surely the potter can do what he likes with the clay. Is he not free to make out of the same lump two vessels, one to be treasured, the other for common use?

But what if God, desiring to exhibit[c] his retribution at work and to make his power known, tolerated very patiently those vessels which were objects of retribution due for destruction, and did so in order to make known the full wealth of his splendour upon vessels which were objects of mercy, and which from the first had been prepared for this splendour?

Such vessels are we, whom he has called from among Gentiles as well as Jews, as it says in the Book of Hosea: 'Those who were not my people I will call My People, and the unloved nation I will call my Beloved. For in the very place where they were told "you are no people of mine", they shall be called Sons of the living God.' But Isaiah makes this proclamation about

[a] Or all children of God. [b] Or God's call shall be for your descendants in the line of Isaac. [c] Or although he had the will to exhibit . . .

Israel, Though the number of the children of Israel be as the sand of the sea, a remnant shall be saved: 28 For he will finish the work, and cut *it* short in righteousness: because a short work will the Lord make upon the earth. 29 And as Esaias said before, Except the Lord of Sabaoth had left us a seed, we had been as Sodoma, and been made like unto Gomorrah. 30 What shall we say then? That the Gentiles, which followed not after righteousness, have attained to righteousness, even the righteousness which is of faith. 31 But Israel, which followed after the law of righteousness, hath not attained to the law of righteousness. 32 Wherefore? Because *they sought it* not by faith, but as it were by the works of the law. For they stumbled at that stumblingstone; 33 As it is written, Behold, I lay in Sion a stumblingstone and rock of offence: and whosoever believeth on him shall not be ashamed.

"Though the number of the sons of Israel be as the sand of the sea, only a remnant of them will be saved; 28 for the Lord will execute his sentence upon the earth with vigor and dispatch." 29 And as Isaiah predicted,

"If the Lord of hosts had not left us children,
we would have fared like Sodom and been
made like Gomorrah."

30 What shall we say, then? That Gentiles who did not pursue righteousness have attained it, that is, righteousness through faith; 31 but that Israel who pursued the righteousness which is based on law did not succeed in fulfilling that law. 32 Why? Because they did not pursue it through faith, but as if it were based on works. They have stumbled over the stumbling stone, 33 as it is written,

"Behold, I am laying in Zion a stone that will
make men stumble,
a rock that will make them fall;
and he who believes in him will not be put to
shame."

10 Brethren, my heart's desire and prayer to God for Israel is, that they might be saved. 2 For I bear them record that they have a zeal of God, but not according to knowledge. 3 For they, being ignorant of God's righteousness, and going about to establish their own righteousness, have not submitted themselves unto the righteousness of God. 4 For Christ *is* the end of the law for righteousness to every one that believeth. 5 For Moses describeth the righteousness which is of the law, That the man which doeth those things shall live by them. 6 But the righteousness which is of faith speaketh on this wise, Say not in thine heart, Who shall ascend into heaven? (that is, to bring Christ down *from above:*) 7 Or, Who shall descend into the deep? (that is, to bring up Christ again from the dead.) 8 But what saith it? The word is nigh thee, *even* in thy mouth, and in thy heart: that is, the word of faith, which we preach; 9 That if thou shalt confess with thy mouth the Lord Jesus, and shalt believe in thine heart that God hath raised him from the dead, thou shalt be saved. 10 For with the heart man believeth unto righteousness; and with the mouth confession is made unto salvation. 11 For the Scripture saith, Whosoever believeth on him shall not be ashamed. 12 For there is no difference between the Jew and the Greek: for the same Lord over all is rich unto all that call upon him. 13 For whosoever shall call upon the name of the Lord

10 Brethren, my heart's desire and prayer to God for them is that they may be saved. 2 I bear them witness that they have a zeal for God, but it is not enlightened. 3 For, being ignorant of the righteousness that comes from God, and seeking to establish their own, they did not submit to God's righteousness. 4 For Christ is the end of the law, that every one who has faith may be justified.

5 Moses writes that the man who practices the righteousness which is based on the law shall live by it. 6 But the righteousness based on faith says, Do not say in your heart, "Who will ascend into heaven?" (that is, to bring Christ down) 7 or "Who will descend into the abyss?" (that is, to bring Christ up from the dead). 8 But what does it say? The word is near you, on your lips and in your heart (that is, the word of faith which we preach); 9 because, if you confess with your lips that Jesus is Lord and believe in your heart that God raised him from the dead, you will be saved. 10 For man believes with his heart and so is justified, and he confesses with his lips and so is saved. 11 The scripture says, "No one who believes in him will be put to shame." 12 For there is no distinction between Jew and Greek; the same Lord is Lord of all and bestows his riches upon all who call upon him. 13 For, "every one who calls upon the name of the Lord will be saved."

PHILLIPS

If the number of the children of Israel be as the sand of the sea, it is the remnant that shall be saved:
For the Lord will execute his word upon the earth, finishing it and cutting it short.

And previously, Isaiah said:

Except the Lord of Sabaoth had left us a seed,
We had become as Sodom, and had been made like unto Gomorrah.

At present the gentiles have gone further than the Jews   9. 30

Now, how far have we got? That the gentiles who never had the Law's standard of righteousness to guide them, have attained righteousness, righteousness-by-faith. But Israel, following the Law of righteousness, failed to reach the goal of righteousness. And why? Because their minds were fixed on what they achieved instead of on what they believed. They tripped over that very stone the scripture mentions:

Behold, I lay in Zion a stone of stumbling and a rock of offense:
And he that believeth on him shall not be put to shame.

How Israel has missed the way   10. 1

My brothers, from the bottom of my heart I long and pray to God that Israel may be saved! I know from experience what a passion for God they have; but, alas, it is not a passion based on knowledge. They do not know God's righteousness, and all the time they are going about trying to prove their own righteousness they have the wrong attitude to receive his. For Christ means the end of the struggle for righteousness-by-the-Law for everyone who believes in him.
Moses writes of righteousness-by-the-Law when he says that the man who perfectly obeys the Law shall find life in it. But righteousness-by-faith says something like this:
"You need not say in your heart, 'Who could go up to Heaven to bring Christ down to us, or who could descend into the depths to bring him up from the dead?' For the secret is very near you, in *your own heart*, in *your own mouth!*" It is the secret of faith, which is the burden of our preaching, and it says, in effect, "If you openly admit by *your own mouth* that Jesus Christ is the Lord, and if you believe in *your own heart* that God raised him from the dead, you will be saved." For it is believing *in the heart* that makes a man righteous before God, and it is stating his belief by *his own mouth* that confirms his salvation. And the scripture says: "Whosoever believes in him shall not be disappointed." And that "whosoever" means anyone, without distinction between Jew or Greek. For all have the same Lord, whose boundless resources are available to all who turn to him in faith. For:

Whosoever shall call upon the name of the Lord shall be saved.

N.E.B.

Israel: 'Though the Israelites be countless as the sands of the sea, it is but a remnant that shall be saved; for the Lord's sentence on the land will be summary and final'; as also he said previously, 'If the Lord of Hosts had not left us the mere germ of a nation, we should have become like Sodom, and no better than Gomorrah.'
Then what are we to say? That Gentiles, who made no effort after righteousness, nevertheless achieved it, a righteousness based on faith; whereas Israel made great efforts after a law of righteousness, but never attained to it. Why was this? Because their efforts were not based on faith, but (as they supposed) on deeds. They stumbled over the 'stumbling-stone' mentioned in Scripture: 'Here I lay in Zion a stumbling-stone and a rock to trip them up; but he who has faith in him will not be put to shame.'

10 Brothers, my deepest desire and my prayer to God is for their salvation. To their zeal for God I can testify; but it is an ill-informed zeal. For they ignore God's way of righteousness, and try to set up their own, and therefore they have not submitted themselves to God's righteousness. For Christ ends the law and brings righteousness for everyone who has faith.[a]
Of legal righteousness Moses writes, 'The man who does this shall gain life by it.' But the righteousness that comes by faith says, 'Do not say to yourself, "Who can go up to heaven?" ' (that is to bring Christ down), 'or, "Who can go down to the abyss?" ' (to bring Christ up from the dead). But what does it say? 'The word is near you: it is upon your lips and in your heart.' This means the word of faith which we proclaim. If on your lips is the confession, 'Jesus is Lord', and in your heart the faith that God raised him from the dead, then you will find salvation. For the faith that leads to righteousness is in the heart, and the confession that leads to salvation is upon the lips.
Scripture says, 'Everyone who has faith in him will be saved from shame'—everyone: there is no distinction between Jew and Greek, because the same Lord is Lord of all, and is rich enough for the need of all who invoke him. For everyone, as it says again—'everyone who in-

---

[a] *Or* Christ is the end of the law as a way to righteousness for everyone who has faith.

K.J.V.

shall be saved. 14 How then shall they call on him in whom they have not believed? and how shall they believe in him of whom they have not heard? and how shall they hear without a preacher? 15And how shall they preach, except they be sent? as it is written, How beautiful are the feet of them that preach the gospel of peace, and bring glad tidings of good things! 16 But they have not all obeyed the gospel. For Esaias saith, Lord, who hath believed our report? 17 So then faith *cometh* by hearing, and hearing by the word of God. 18 But I say, Have they not heard? Yes verily, their sound went into all the earth, and their words unto the ends of the world. 19 But I say, Did not Israel know? First Moses saith, I will provoke you to jealousy by *them that are* no people, *and* by a foolish nation I will anger you. 20 But Esaias is very bold, and saith, I was found of them that sought me not; I was made manifest unto them that asked not after me. 21 But to Israel he saith, All day long I have stretched forth my hands unto a disobedient and gainsaying people.

R.S.V.

14 But how are men to call upon him in whom they have not believed? And how are they to believe in him of whom they have never heard? And how are they to hear without a preacher? 15And how can men preach unless they are sent? As it is written, "How beautiful are the feet of those who preach good news!" 16 But they have not all heeded the gospel; for Isaiah says, "Lord, who has believed what he has heard from us?" 17 So faith comes from what is heard, and what is heard comes by the preaching of Christ.

18 But I ask, have they not heard? Indeed they have; for

"Their voice has gone out to all the earth,
　and their words to the ends of the world."

19Again I ask, did Israel not understand? First Moses says,

"I will make you jealous of those who are not a nation;
　with a foolish nation I will make you angry."

20 Then Isaiah is so bold as to say,

"I have been found by those who did not seek me;
　I have shown myself to those who did not ask for me."

21 But of Israel he says, "All day long I have held out my hands to a disobedient and contrary people."

11 I say then, Hath God cast away his people? God forbid. For I also am an Israelite, of the seed of Abraham, *of* the tribe of Benjamin. 2 God hath not cast away his people which he foreknew. Wot ye not what the Scripture saith of Elias? how he maketh intercession to God against Israel, saying, 3 Lord, they have killed thy prophets, and digged down thine altars; and I am left alone, and they seek my life. 4 But what saith the answer of God unto him? I have reserved to myself seven thousand men, who have not bowed the knee to *the image of* Baal. 5 Even so then at this present time also there is a remnant according to the election of grace. 6And if by grace, then *is it* no more of

11 I ask, then, has God rejected his people? By no means! I myself am an Israelite, a descendant of Abraham, a member of the tribe of Benjamin. 2 God has not rejected his people whom he foreknew. Do you not know what the scripture says of Elijah, how he pleads with God against Israel? 3 "Lord, they have killed thy prophets, they have demolished thy altars, and I alone am left, and they seek my life." 4 But what is God's reply to him? "I have kept for myself seven thousand men who have not bowed the knee to Baal." 5 So too at the present time there is a remnant, chosen by grace. 6 But

Can we offer the excuse of   *10. 14*
ignorance on Israel's behalf?

Now how can they call on one in whom they
have never believed? How can they believe in
one of whom they have never heard? And how
can they hear unless someone proclaims him?
And who will go to tell them unless he is sent?
As the scripture puts it:

How beautiful are the feet of them that bring
    glad tidings of good things!

Yet all who have heard have not responded
to the gospel. Isaiah asks, you remember,

Lord, who hath believed our report?

(Belief, you see, can only come from hearing
the message, and the message is the word of
Christ.)
But when I ask myself: "Did they never
hear?" I have to answer that they *have* heard,
for

Their sound went out into all the earth,
And their words unto the ends of the world.

Then I say to myself: "Did Israel not know?"
And my answer must be that they did. For
Moses says:

I will provoke you to jealousy with that which
    is no nation,
With a nation void of understanding will I
    anger you.

And Isaiah, more daring still, puts these words
into the mouth of God:

I was found of them that sought me not.
I became manifest unto them that asked not
    of me.

And then, speaking of Israel:

All the day long did I spread out my hands
    unto a disobedient and gainsaying people.

Israel's failure—yet remember   *11. 1*
the faithful few

This leads naturally to the question, "Has
God then totally repudiated his people?" Certainly not! I myself, for one, am an Israelite, a
descendant of Abraham and of the tribe of
Benjamin. It is unthinkable that God should
have repudiated his own people, the people
whose destiny he himself appointed. Don't you
remember what the scripture says in the story
of Elijah? How he pleaded with God on Israel's
behalf:

Lord, they have killed thy prophets
They have digged down thine altars:
And I am left alone, and they seek my life.

And do you remember God's reply?

I have left for myself seven thousand men
Who have not bowed the knee to Baal.

In just the same way, there is at the present
time a minority, chosen by the grace of God.
And if it is a matter of the grace of God, it

vokes the name of the Lord will be saved'. How
could they invoke one in whom they had no
faith? And how could they have faith in one
they had never heard of? And how hear without
someone to spread the news? And how could
anyone spread the news without a commission
to do so? And that is what Scripture affirms:
'How welcome are the feet of the messengers of
good news!'
But not all have responded to the good news.
For Isaiah says, 'Lord, who has believed our
message?' We conclude that faith is awakened by
the message, and the message that awakens it
comes through the word of Christ.
But, I ask, can it be that they never heard it?
Of course they did: 'Their voice has sounded all
over the earth, and their words to the bounds of
the inhabited world.' But, I ask again, can it be
that Israel failed to recognize the message? In
reply, I first cite Moses, who says, 'I will use a
nation that is no nation to stir your envy, and
a foolish nation to rouse your anger.' But Isaiah
is still more daring: 'I was found', he says, 'by
those who were not looking for me; I was clearly
shown to those who never asked about me';
while to Israel he says, 'All day long I have
stretched out my hands to an unruly and recalci-
trant people.'

11 I ask then, has God rejected his people? I
    cannot believe it! I am an Israelite myself,
of the stock of Abraham, of the tribe of Benjamin. No! God has not rejected the people which
he acknowledged of old as his own. You know
(do you not?) what Scripture says in the story
of Elijah—how Elijah pleads with God against
Israel: 'Lord, they have killed thy prophets, they
have overthrown thine altars, and I alone am left,
and they are seeking my life.' But what does the
oracle say to him? 'I have left myself seven
thousand men who have not done homage to
Baal.' In just the same way at the present time a
'remnant' has come into being, selected by the
grace of God. But if it is by grace, then it does

K.J.V.

works: otherwise grace is no more grace. But if *it be* of works, then is it no more grace: otherwise work is no more work. 7 What then? Israel hath not obtained that which he seeketh for; but the election hath obtained it, and the rest were blinded 8 (According as it is written, God hath given them the spirit of slumber, eyes that they should not see, and ears that they should not hear;) unto this day. 9And David saith, Let their table be made a snare, and a trap, and a stumblingblock, and a recompense unto them: 10 Let their eyes be darkened, that they may not see, and bow down their back alway. 11 I say then, Have they stumbled that they should fall? God forbid: but *rather* through their fall salvation *is come* unto the Gentiles, for to provoke them to jealousy. 12 Now if the fall of them *be* the riches of the world, and the diminishing of them the riches of the Gentiles; how much more their fulness? 13 For I speak to you Gentiles, inasmuch as I am the apostle of the Gentiles, I magnify mine office: 14 If by any means I may provoke to emulation *them which are* my flesh, and might save some of them. 15 For if the casting away of them *be* the reconciling of the world, what *shall* the receiving *of them be*, but life from the dead? 16 For if the firstfruit *be* holy, the lump *is* also *holy:* and if the root *be* holy, so *are* the branches. 17 And if some of the branches be broken off, and thou, being a wild olive tree, wert graffed in among them, and with them partakest of the root and fatness of the olive tree; 18 Boast not against the branches. But if thou boast, thou bearest not the root, but the root thee. 19 Thou wilt say then, The branches were broken off, that I might be graffed in. 20 Well; because of unbelief they were broken off, and thou standest by faith. Be not highminded, but fear: 21 For if God spared not the natural branches, *take heed* lest he also spare not thee. 22 Behold therefore the goodness and severity of God: on them which fell, severity; but toward thee, goodness, if thou

R.S.V.

if it is by grace, it is no longer on the basis of works; otherwise grace would no longer be grace.

7 What then? Israel failed to obtain what it sought. The elect obtained it, but the rest were hardened, 8 as it is written,

"God gave them a spirit of stupor,
  eyes that should not see and ears that should
    not hear,
  down to this very day."
9And David says,
  "Let their feast become a snare and a trap,
    a pitfall and a retribution for them;
  10 let their eyes be darkened so that they
    cannot see,
    and bend their backs for ever."

11 So I ask, have they stumbled so as to fall? By no means! But through their trespass salvation has come to the Gentiles, so as to make Israel jealous. 12 Now if their trespass means riches for the world, and if their failure means riches for the Gentiles, how much more will their full inclusion mean!

13 Now I am speaking to you Gentiles. Inasmuch then as I am an apostle to the Gentiles, I magnify my ministry 14 in order to make my fellow Jews jealous, and thus save some of them. 15 For if their rejection means the reconciliation of the world, what will their acceptance mean but life from the dead? 16 If the dough offered as first fruits is holy, so is the whole lump; and if the root is holy, so are the branches.

17 But if some of the branches were broken off, and you, a wild olive shoot, were grafted in their place to share the richness[o] of the olive tree, 18 do not boast over the branches. If you do boast, remember it is not you that support the root, but the root that supports you. 19 You will say, "Branches were broken off so that I might be grafted in." 20 That is true. They were broken off because of their unbelief, but you stand fast only through faith. So do not become proud, but stand in awe. 21 For if God did not spare the natural branches, neither will he spare you. 22 Note then the kindness and the severity of God: severity toward those who have fallen, but God's kindness to you, provided you con-

[o] Other ancient authorities read *rich root.*

PHILLIPS

N.E.B.

cannot be a question of their actions especially deserving God's favor, for that would make grace meaningless.

What conclusion do we reach now? That Israel did not, on the whole, obtain the object of his striving, but a chosen few "got there," while the remainder became more and more insensitive to the righteousness of God. This is borne out by the scripture:

God gave them a spirit of stupor,
Eyes that they should not see,
And ears that they should not hear,
Unto this very day.

And David says of them:

Let their table be made a snare, and a trap,
And a stumbling block, and a recompense unto them:
Let their eyes be darkened, that they may not see,
And bow Thou down their back alway.

In the providence of God   11. 11
disaster has been turned
to good account

Now I ask myself, "Was this fall of theirs an utter disaster?" It was not! For through their failure the benefit of salvation has passed to the gentiles, with the result that Israel is made to see and feel what it has missed. For if their failure has so enriched the world, and their defection proved such a benefit to the gentiles, think what tremendous advantages their fulfilling of God's plan could mean!

Now a word to you who are gentiles. I should like you to know that I make as much as I can of my ministry as "God's messenger to the gentiles" so as to make my kinsfolk jealous and thus save some of them. For if their exclusion from the pale of salvation has meant the reconciliation of the rest of mankind to God, what would their inclusion mean? It would be nothing less than life from the dead! If the flour is consecrated to God so is the whole loaf, and if the roots of a tree are dedicated to God every branch will belong to him also.

A word of warning   11. 17

But if some of the branches of the tree have been broken off, while you, like shoots of wild olive, have been grafted in, and share like a natural branch the rich nourishment of the root, don't let yourself feel superior to those former branches. (If you feel inclined that way, remind yourself that you do not support the root; the root supports you.) You may make the natural retort, "But the branches were broken off to make room for my grafting!" It wasn't quite like that. They lost their position because they failed to believe; you only maintain yours because you do believe. The situation does not call for conceit but for a certain wholesome fear. If God removed the natural branches for a good reason, take care that you don't give him the same reason for removing you. You must try to appreciate both the kindness and the strict justice of God. Those who fell experienced his justice, while you are experiencing his kindness, and will continue to do so as long as you do not

not rest on deeds done, or grace would cease to be grace.

What follows? What Israel sought, Israel has not achieved, but the selected few have achieved it. The rest were made blind to the truth, exactly as it stands written: 'God brought upon them a numbness of spirit; he gave them blind eyes and deaf ears, and so it is still.' Similarly David says:

'May their table be a snare and a trap,
Both stumbling-block and retribution!
May their eyes be darkened so that they do not see!
Bow down their back forever!'

I now ask, did their failure mean complete downfall? Far from it! Because they offended, salvation has come to the Gentiles, to stir Israel to emulation. But if their offence means the enrichment of the world, and if their falling-off means the enrichment of the Gentiles, how much more their coming to full strength!

But I have something to say to you Gentiles. I am a missionary to the Gentiles, and as such I give all honour to that ministry when I try to stir emulation in the men of my own race, and so to save some of them. For if their rejection has meant the reconciliation of the world, what will their acceptance mean? Nothing less than life from the dead! If the first portion of dough is consecrated, so is the whole lump. If the root is consecrated, so are the branches. But if some of the branches have been lopped off, and you, a wild olive, have been grafted in among them, and have come to share the same root and sap as the olive, do not make yourself superior to the branches. If you do so, remember that it is not you who sustain the root: the root sustains you.

You will say, 'Branches were lopped off so that I might be grafted in.' Very well: they were lopped off for lack of faith, and by faith you hold your place. Put away your pride, and be on your guard; for if God did not spare the native branches, no more will he spare you. Observe the kindness and the severity of God—severity to those who fell away, divine kindness to you, if

K.J.V.

continue in *his* goodness: otherwise thou also shalt be cut off. 23And they also, if they abide not still in unbelief, shall be graffed in: for God is able to graff them in again. 24 For if thou wert cut out of the olive tree which is wild by nature, and wert graffed contrary to nature into a good olive tree; how much more shall these, which be the natural *branches,* be graffed into their own olive tree? 25 For I would not, brethren, that ye should be ignorant of this mystery, lest ye should be wise in your own conceits, that blindness in part is happened to Israel, until the fulness of the Gentiles be come in. 26And so all Israel shall be saved: as it is written, There shall come out of Sion the Deliverer, and shall turn away ungodliness from Jacob: 27 For this *is* my covenant unto them, when I shall take away their sins. 28As concerning the gospel, *they are* enemies for your sakes: but as touching the election, *they are* beloved for the fathers' sakes. 29 For the gifts and calling of God *are* without repentance. 30 For as ye in times past have not believed God, yet have now obtained mercy through their unbelief: 31 Even so have these also now not believed, that through your mercy they also may obtain mercy. 32 For God hath concluded them all in unbelief, that he might have mercy upon all. 33 O the depth of the riches both of the wisdom and knowledge of God! how unsearchable *are* his judgments, and his ways past finding out! 34 For who hath known the mind of the Lord? or who hath been his counsellor? 35 Or who hath first given to him, and it shall be recompensed unto him again? 36 For of him, and through him, and to him, *are* all things: to whom *be* glory for ever. Amen.

R.S.V.

tinue in his kindness; otherwise you too will be cut off. 23And even the others, if they do not persist in their unbelief, will be grafted in, for God has the power to graft them in again. 24 For if you have been cut from what is by nature a wild olive tree, and grafted, contrary to nature, into a cultivated olive tree, how much more will these natural branches be grafted back into their own olive tree.

25 Lest you be wise in your own conceits, I want you to understand this mystery, brethren: a hardening has come upon part of Israel, until the full number of the Gentiles come in, 26 and so all Israel will be saved; as it is written,

"The Deliverer will come from Zion,
    he will banish ungodliness from Jacob";
27 "and this will be my covenant with them
    when I take away their sins."

28As regards the gospel they are enemies of God, for your sake; but as regards election they are beloved for the sake of their forefathers. 29 For the gifts and the call of God are irrevocable. 30 Just as you were once disobedient to God but now have received mercy because of their disobedience, 31 so they have now been disobedient in order that by the mercy shown to you they also may*p* receive mercy. 32 For God has consigned all men to disobedience, that he may have mercy upon all.

33 O the depth of the riches and wisdom and knowledge of God! How unsearchable are his judgments and how inscrutable his ways!
34 "For who has known the mind of the Lord,
    or who has been his counselor?"
35 "Or who has given a gift to him
    that he might be repaid?"
36 For from him and through him and to him are all things. To him be glory for ever. Amen.

12 I beseech you therefore, brethren, by the mercies of God, that ye present your bodies a living sacrifice, holy, acceptable unto God, *which is* your reasonable service. 2And be not conformed to this world: but be ye transformed

12 I appeal to you therefore, brethren, by the mercies of God, to present your bodies as a living sacrifice, holy and acceptable to God, which is your spiritual worship. 2 Do not be conformed to this world *q* but be transformed

abuse that kindness. Otherwise you too will be cut off from the tree. And as for the fallen branches, unless they are obstinate in their unbelief, they will be grafted in again. Such a restoration is by no means beyond the power of God. And, in any case, if you who were, so to speak, cuttings from a wild olive, were grafted in, is it not a far simpler matter for the natural branches to be grafted back into the parent stem?

God still has a plan for Israel   11. 25

Now I don't want you, my brothers, to start imagining things, and I must therefore share with you my knowledge of God's secret plan. It is this, that the partial insensibility which has come to Israel is only to last until the full number of the gentiles has been called in. Once this has happened, all Israel will be saved, as the scripture says:

There shall come out of Zion the deliverer;
He shall turn away ungodliness from Jacob:
And this is my covenant unto them,
When I shall take away their sins.

As far as the gospel goes, they are at present God's enemies—which is to your advantage. But as far as God's purpose in choosing is concerned, they are still beloved for their fathers' sakes. For once they are made, God does not withdraw his gifts or his calling.

The whole scheme looks   11. 30
topsy-turvy, until we see the
amazing wisdom of God!

Just as in the past you were disobedient to God but have found that mercy which might have been theirs but for their disobedience, so they, who at the present moment are disobedient, will eventually share the mercy which has been extended to you. God has all men penned together in the prison of disobedience, that he may have mercy upon them all. Frankly, I stand amazed at the unfathomable complexity of God's wisdom and God's knowledge. How could man ever understand his reasons for action, or explain his methods of working? For:

Who hath known the mind of the Lord?
Or who hath been his counselor?
Or who hath first given to him, and it shall be
   recompensed unto him again?
For of him, and through him, and unto him,
   are all things.
To him be the glory for ever, amen.

We have seen God's mercy and   12. 1
wisdom: how shall we respond?

With eyes wide open to the mercies of God, I beg you, my brothers, as an act of intelligent worship, to give him your bodies, as a living sacrifice, consecrated to him and acceptable by him. Don't let the world around you squeeze you into its own mold, but let God remold your

only you remain within its scope; otherwise you too will be cut off, whereas they, if they do not continue faithless, will be grafted in; for it is in God's power to graft them in again. For if you were cut from your native wild olive and against all nature grafted into the cultivated olive, how much more readily will they, the natural olive-branches, be grafted into their native stock!

For there is a deep truth here, my brothers, of which I want you to take account, so that you may not be complacent about your own discernment: this partial blindness has come upon Israel only until the Gentiles have been admitted in full strength; when that has happened, the whole of Israel will be saved, in agreement with the text of Scripture:

'From Zion shall come the Deliverer;
He shall remove wickedness from Jacob.
And this is the covenant I will grant them,
When I take away their sins.'

In the spreading of the Gospel they are treated as God's enemies for your sake; but God's choice stands, and they are his friends for the sake of the patriarchs. For the gracious gifts of God and his calling are irrevocable. Just as formerly you were disobedient to God, but now have received mercy in the time of their disobedience, so now, when you receive mercy, they have proved disobedient, but only in order that they too may receive mercy. For in making all mankind prisoners to disobedience, God's purpose was to show mercy to all mankind.

O depth of wealth, wisdom, and knowledge in God! How unsearchable his judgements, how untraceable his ways! Who knows the mind of the Lord? Who has been his counsellor? Who has ever made a gift to him, to receive a gift in return? Source, Guide, and Goal of all that is—to him be glory for ever! Amen.

Christian Behaviour

12 Therefore, my brothers, I implore you by God's mercy to offer your very selves to him: a living sacrifice, dedicated and fit for his acceptance, the worship offered by mind and heart.[a] Adapt yourselves no longer to the pattern of this present world, but let your minds be re-

[a] *Or . . .* acceptance, for such is the worship which you, as rational creatures, should offer.

K.J.V.

by the renewing of your mind, that ye may prove what *is* that good, and acceptable, and perfect will of God. 3 For I say, through the grace given unto me, to every man that is among you, not to think *of himself* more highly than he ought to think; but to think soberly, according as God hath dealt to every man the measure of faith. 4 For as we have many members in one body, and all members have not the same office: 5 So we, *being* many, are one body in Christ, and every one members one of another. 6 Having then gifts differing according to the grace that is given to us, whether prophecy, *let us prophesy* according to the proportion of faith; 7 Or ministry, *let us wait* on *our* ministering; or he that teacheth, on teaching; 8 Or he that exhorteth, on exhortation: he that giveth, *let him do it* with simplicity; he that ruleth, with diligence; he that sheweth mercy, with cheerfulness. 9 *Let* love be without dissimulation. Abhor that which is evil; cleave to that which is good. 10 *Be* kindly affectioned one to another with brotherly love; in honour preferring one another; 11 Not slothful in business; fervent in spirit; serving the Lord; 12 Rejoicing in hope; patient in tribulation; continuing instant in prayer; 13 Distributing to the necessity of saints; given to hospitality. 14 Bless them which persecute you: bless, and curse not. 15 Rejoice with them that do rejoice, and weep with them that weep. 16 *Be* of the same mind one toward another. Mind not high things, but condescend to men of low estate. Be not wise in your own conceits. 17 Recompense to no man evil for evil. Provide things honest in the sight of all men. 18 If it be possible, as much as lieth in you, live peaceably with all men. 19 Dearly beloved, avenge not yourselves, but *rather* give place unto wrath: for it is written, Vengeance *is* mine; I will repay, saith the Lord. 20 Therefore if thine enemy hunger, feed him; if he thirst, give him drink: for in so doing thou shalt heap coals of fire on his head. 21 Be not overcome of evil, but overcome evil with good.

R.S.V.

by the renewal of your mind, that you may prove what is the will of God, what is good and acceptable and perfect.[r]

3 For by the grace given to me I bid every one among you not to think of himself more highly than he ought to think, but to think with sober judgment, each according to the measure of faith which God has assigned him. 4 For as in one body we have many members, and all the members do not have the same function, 5 so we, though many, are one body in Christ, and individually members one of another. 6 Having gifts that differ according to the grace given to us, let us use them: if prophecy, in proportion to our faith; 7 if service, in our serving; he who teaches, in his teaching; 8 he who exhorts, in his exhortation; he who contributes, in liberality; he who gives aid, with zeal; he who does acts of mercy, with cheerfulness.

9 Let love be genuine; hate what is evil, hold fast to what is good; 10 love one another with brotherly affection; outdo one another in showing honor. 11 Never flag in zeal, be aglow with the Spirit, serve the Lord. 12 Rejoice in your hope, be patient in tribulation, be constant in prayer. 13 Contribute to the needs of the saints, practice hospitality.

14 Bless those who persecute you; bless and do not curse them. 15 Rejoice with those who rejoice, weep with those who weep. 16 Live in harmony with one another; do not be haughty, but associate with the lowly;[s] never be conceited. 17 Repay no one evil for evil, but take thought for what is noble in the sight of all. 18 If possible, so far as it depends upon you, live peaceably with all. 19 Beloved, never avenge yourselves, but leave it[t] to the wrath of God; for it is written, "Vengeance is mine, I will repay, says the Lord." 20 No, "if your enemy is hungry, feed him; if he is thirsty, give him drink; for by so doing you will heap burning coals upon his head." 21 Do not be overcome by evil, but overcome evil with good.

[r] Or *what is the good and acceptable and perfect will of God.* [s] Or *give yourselves to humble tasks.* [t] Greek *give place.*

minds from within, so that you may prove in practice that the plan of God for you is good, meets all his demands and moves toward the goal of true maturity.

As your spiritual teacher I give this piece of advice to each one of you. Don't cherish exaggerated ideas of yourself or your importance, but try to have a sane estimate of your capabilities by the light of the faith that God has given to you all. For just as you have many members in one physical body and those members differ in their functions, so we, though many in number, compose one body in Christ and are all members of one another. Through the grace of God we have different gifts. If our gift is preaching, let us preach to the limit of our vision. If it is serving others let us concentrate on our service; if it is teaching let us give all we have to our teaching; and if our gift be the stimulating of the faith of others let us set ourselves to it. Let the man who is called to give, give freely; let the man who wields authority think of his responsibility; and let the man who feels sympathy for his fellows act cheerfully.

Let us have real Christian   *12. 9*
behavior

Let us have no imitation Christian love. Let us have a genuine break with evil and a real devotion to good. Let us have real warm affection for one another as between brothers, and a willingness to let the other man have the credit. Let us not allow slackness to spoil our work and let us keep the fires of the spirit burning, as we do our work for the Lord. Base your happiness on your hope in Christ. When trials come endure them patiently; steadfastly maintain the habit of prayer. Give freely to fellow Christians in want, never grudging a meal or a bed to those who need them. And as for those who try to make your life a misery, bless them. Don't curse, bless. Share the happiness of those who are happy, and the sorrow of those who are sad. Live in harmony with one another. Don't become snobbish but take a real interest in ordinary people. Don't become set in your own opinions. Don't pay back a bad turn by a bad turn, to *anyone*. See that your public behavior is above criticism. As far as your responsibility goes, live at peace with everyone. Never take vengeance into your own hands, my dear friends: stand back and let God punish if he will. For it is written:

Vengeance belongeth unto me: I will recompense.

And these are God's words:

If thine enemy hunger, feed him;
If he thirst, give him to drink:
For in so doing thou shalt heap coals of fire upon his head.

Don't allow yourself to be overpowered by evil. Take the offensive—overpower evil with good!

made and your whole nature thus transformed. Then you will be able to discern the will of God, and to know what is good, acceptable, and perfect.

In virtue of the gift that God in his grace has given me I say to everyone among you: do not be conceited or think too highly of yourself; but think your way to a sober estimate based on the measure of faith that God has dealt to each of you. For just as in a single human body there are many limbs and organs, all with different functions, so all of us, united with Christ, form one body, serving individually as limbs and organs to one another.

The gifts we possess differ as they are allotted to us by God's grace, and must be exercised accordingly: the gift of inspired utterance, for example, in proportion to a man's faith; or the gift of administration, in administration. A teacher should employ his gift in teaching, and one who has the gift of stirring speech should use it to stir his hearers. If you give to charity, give with all your heart; if you are a leader, exert yourself to lead; if you are helping others in distress, do it cheerfully.

Love in all sincerity, loathing evil and clinging to the good. Let love for our brotherhood breed warmth of mutual affection. Give pride of place to one another in esteem.

With unflagging energy, in ardour of spirit, serve the Lord.[a]

Let hope keep you joyful; in trouble stand firm; persist in prayer.

Contribute to the needs of God's people, and practise hospitality.

Call down blessings on your persecutors—blessings, not curses.

With the joyful be joyful, and mourn with the mourners.

Have equal regard for one another. Do not be haughty, but go about with humble folk. Do not keep thinking how wise you are.

Never pay back evil for evil. Let your aims be such as all men count honourable. If possible, so far as it lies with you, live at peace with all men. My dear friends, do not seek revenge, but leave a place for divine retribution; for there is a text which reads, 'Justice is mine, says the Lord, I will repay.' But there is another text: 'If your enemy is hungry, feed him; if he is thirsty, give him a drink; by doing this you will heap live coals on his head.' Do not let evil conquer you, but use good to defeat evil.

[a] *Some witnesses read* meet the demands of the hour.

13 Let every soul be subject unto the higher powers. For there is no power but of God: the powers that be are ordained of God. 2 Whosoever therefore resisteth the power, resisteth the ordinance of God: and they that resist shall receive to themselves damnation. 3 For rulers are not a terror to good works, but to the evil. Wilt thou then not be afraid of the power? do that which is good, and thou shalt have praise of the same: 4 For he is the minister of God to thee for good. But if thou do that which is evil, be afraid; for he beareth not the sword in vain: for he is the minister of God, a revenger to *execute* wrath upon him that doeth evil. 5 Wherefore *ye* must needs be subject, not only for wrath, but also for conscience' sake. 6 For, for this cause pay ye tribute also: for they are God's ministers, attending continually upon this very thing. 7 Render therefore to all their dues: tribute to whom tribute *is due;* custom to whom custom; fear to whom fear; honour to whom honour. 8 Owe no man any thing, but to love one another: for he that loveth another hath fulfilled the law. 9 For this, Thou shalt not commit adultery, Thou shalt not kill, Thou shalt not steal, Thou shalt not bear false witness, Thou shalt not covet; and if *there be* any other commandment, it is briefly comprehended in this saying, namely, Thou shalt love thy neighbour as thyself. 10 Love worketh no ill to his neighbour: therefore love *is* the fulfilling of the law. 11And that, knowing the time, that now *it is* high time to awake out of sleep: for now *is* our salvation nearer than when we believed. 12 The night is far spent, the day is at hand: let us therefore cast off the works of darkness, and let us put on the armour of light. 13 Let us walk honestly, as in the day; not in rioting and drunkenness, not in chambering and wantonness, not in strife and envying: 14 But put ye on the Lord Jesus Christ, and make not provision for the flesh, to *fulfil* the lusts *thereof.*

13 Let every person be subject to the governing authorities. For there is no authority except from God, and those that exist have been instituted by God. 2 Therefore he who resists the authorities resists what God has appointed, and those who resist will incur judgment. 3 For rulers are not a terror to good conduct, but to bad. Would you have no fear of him who is in authority? Then do what is good, and you will receive his approval, 4 for he is God's servant for your good. But if you do wrong, be afraid, for he does not bear the sword in vain; he is the servant of God to execute his wrath on the wrongdoer. 5 Therefore one must be subject, not only to avoid God's wrath but also for the sake of conscience. 6 For the same reason you also pay taxes, for the authorities are ministers of God, attending to this very thing. 7 Pay all of them their dues, taxes to whom taxes are due, revenue to whom revenue is due, respect to whom respect is due, honor to whom honor is due.

8 Owe no one anything, except to love one another; for he who loves his neighbor has fulfilled the law. 9 The commandments, "You shall not commit adultery, You shall not kill, You shall not steal, You shall not covet," and any other commandment, are summed up in this sentence, "You shall love your neighbor as yourself." 10 Love does no wrong to a neighbor; therefore love is the fulfilling of the law.

11 Besides this you know what hour it is, how it is full time now for you to wake from sleep. For salvation is nearer to us now than when we first believed; 12 the night is far gone, the day is at hand. Let us then cast off the works of darkness and put on the armor of light; 13 let us conduct ourselves becomingly as in the day, not in reveling and drunkenness, not in debauchery and licentiousness, not in quarreling and jealousy. 14 But put on the Lord Jesus Christ, and make no provision for the flesh, to gratify its desires.

14 Him that is weak in the faith receive ye, *but* not to doubtful disputations. 2 For one believeth that he may eat all things: another, who is weak, eateth herbs. 3 Let not him that eateth despise him that eateth not; and let not

14 As for the man who is weak in faith, welcome him, but not for disputes over opinions. 2 One believes he may eat anything, while the weak man eats only vegetables. 3 Let not him who eats despise him who abstains, and let

PHILLIPS

The Christian and the civil law   13. 1

Every Christian ought to obey the civil authorities, for all legitimate authority is derived from God's authority, and the existing authority is appointed under God. To oppose authority then is to oppose God, and such opposition is bound to be punished.

The honest citizen has no need to fear the keepers of law and order, but the dishonest man will always be nervous of them. If you want to avoid this anxiety just lead a law-abiding life, and all that can come your way is a word of approval. The officer is God's servant for your protection. But if you are leading a wicked life you have reason to be alarmed. The "power of the law" which is vested in every legitimate officer is no empty phrase. He is, in fact, divinely appointed to inflict God's punishment upon evil-doers.

You should, therefore, obey the authorities, not simply because it is the safest, but because it is the right thing to do. It is right, too, for you to pay taxes, for the civil authorities are appointed by God for the good purposes of public order and well-being. Give everyone his legitimate due, whether it be rates, or taxes, or reverence, or respect!

To love others is the   13. 8
highest conduct

Keep out of debt altogether, except that perpetual debt of love which we owe one another. The man who loves his neighbor has obeyed the whole Law in regard to his neighbor. For the commandments, "Thou shalt not commit adultery," "Thou shalt not kill," "Thou shalt not steal," "Thou shalt not covet" and all other commandments are summed up in this one saying: "Thou shalt love thy neighbor as thyself." Love hurts nobody: therefore love is the answer to the Law's commands.

Wake up and live!   13. 11

Why all this stress on behavior? Because, as I think you have realized, the present time is of the highest importance—it is time to wake up to reality. Every day brings God's salvation nearer.

The night is nearly over; the day has almost dawned. Let us therefore fling away the things that men do in the dark; let us arm ourselves for the fight of the day! Let us live cleanly, as in the daylight, not in the "delights" of getting drunk or playing with sex, nor yet in quarreling or jealousies. Let us be Christ's men from head to foot, and give no chances to the flesh to have its fling.

Don't criticize one another's   14. 1
convictions

Welcome a man whose faith is weak, but not with the idea of arguing over his scruples. One man believes that he may eat anything; another man, without this strong conviction, is a vegetarian. The meat eater should not despise the vegetarian, nor should the vegetarian condemn

N.E.B.

13 Every person must submit to the supreme authorities. There is no authority but by act of God, and the existing authorities are instituted by him; consequently anyone who rebels against authority is resisting a divine institution, and those who so resist have themselves to thank for the punishment they will receive. For government, a terror to crime, has no terrors for good behaviour. You wish to have no fear of the authorities? Then continue to do right and you will have their approval, for they are God's agents working for your good. But if you are doing wrong, then you will have cause to fear them; it is not for nothing that they hold the power of the sword, for they are God's agents of punishment, for retribution on the offender. That is why you are obliged to submit. It is an obligation imposed not merely by fear of retribution but by conscience. That is also why you pay taxes. The authorities are in God's service and to these duties they devote their energies.

Discharge your obligations to all men; pay tax and toll, reverence and respect, to those to whom they are due. Leave no claim outstanding against you, except that of mutual love. He who loves his neighbour has satisfied every claim of the law. For the commandments, 'Thou shalt not commit adultery, thou shalt not kill, thou shalt not steal, thou shalt not covet', and any other commandment there may be, are all summed up in the one rule, 'Love your neighbour as yourself.' Love cannot wrong a neighbour; therefore the whole law is summed up in love.[a]

In all this, remember how critical the moment is. It is time for you to wake out of sleep, for deliverance is nearer to us now than it was when first we believed. It is far on in the night; day is near. Let us therefore throw off the deeds of darkness and put on our armour as soldiers of the light. Let us behave with decency as befits the day: no revelling or drunkenness, no debauchery or vice, no quarrels or jealousies! Let Christ Jesus himself be the armour that you wear; give no more thought to satisfying the bodily appetites.

14 If a man is weak in his faith you must accept him without attempting to settle doubtful points. For instance, one man will have faith enough to eat all kinds of food, while a weaker man eats only vegetables. The man who eats must not hold in contempt the man who does

[a] *Or* the whole law is fulfilled by love.

K.J.V.

him which eateth not judge him that eateth: for God hath received him. 4 Who art thou that judgest another man's servant? to his own master he standeth or falleth; yea, he shall be holden up: for God is able to make him stand. 5 One man esteemeth one day above another: another esteemeth every day *alike.* Let every man be fully persuaded in his own mind. 6 He that regardeth the day, regardeth *it* unto the Lord; and he that regardeth not the day, to the Lord he doth not regard *it.* He that eateth, eateth to the Lord, for he giveth God thanks; and he that eateth not, to the Lord he eateth not, and giveth God thanks. 7 For none of us liveth to himself, and no man dieth to himself. 8 For whether we live, we live unto the Lord; and whether we die, we die unto the Lord: whether we live therefore, or die, we are the Lord's. 9 For to this end Christ both died, and rose, and revived, that he might be Lord both of the dead and living. 10 But why dost thou judge thy brother? or why dost thou set at nought thy brother? for we shall all stand before the judgment seat of Christ. 11 For it is written, *As* I live, saith the Lord, every knee shall bow to me, and every tongue shall confess to God. 12 So then every one of us shall give account of himself to God. 13 Let us not therefore judge one another any more: but judge this rather, that no man put a stumblingblock or an occasion to fall in *his* brother's way. 14 I know, and am persuaded by the Lord Jesus, that *there is* nothing unclean of itself: but to him that esteemeth any thing to be unclean, to him *it is* unclean. 15 But if thy brother be grieved with *thy* meat, now walkest thou not charitably. Destroy not him with thy meat, for whom Christ died. 16 Let not then your good be evil spoken of: 17 For the kingdom of God is not meat and drink; but righteousness, and peace, and joy in the Holy Ghost. 18 For he that in these things serveth Christ *is* acceptable to God, and approved of men. 19 Let us therefore follow after the things which make for peace, and things wherewith one may edify another. 20 For meat destroy not the work of God. All things indeed *are* pure; but *it is* evil for that man who eateth with offence. 21 *It is* good neither to eat flesh, nor to drink wine, nor *any thing* whereby thy brother stumbleth, or is offended, or is made

R.S.V.

not him who abstains pass judgment on him who eats; for God has welcomed him. 4 Who are you to pass judgment on the servant of another? It is before his own master that he stands or falls. And he will be upheld, for the Master is able to make him stand.

5 One man esteems one day as better than another, while another man esteems all days alike. Let every one be fully convinced in his own mind. 6 He who observes the day, observes it in honor of the Lord. He also who eats, eats in honor of the Lord, since he gives thanks to God; while he who abstains, abstains in honor of the Lord and gives thanks to God. 7 None of us lives to himself, and none of us dies to himself. 8 If we live, we live to the Lord, and if we die, we die to the Lord; so then, whether we live or whether we die, we are the Lord's. 9 For to this end Christ died and lived again, that he might be Lord both of the dead and of the living.

10 Why do you pass judgment on your brother? Or you, why do you despise your brother? For we shall all stand before the judgment seat of God; 11 for it is written,

"As I live, says the Lord, every knee shall
　　bow to me,
　and every tongue shall give praise" to God."
12 So each of us shall give account of himself to God.

13 Then let us no more pass judgment on one another, but rather decide never to put a stumbling block or hindrance in the way of a brother. 14 I know and am persuaded in the Lord Jesus that nothing is unclean in itself; but it is unclean for any one who thinks it unclean. 15 If your brother is being injured by what you eat, you are no longer walking in love. Do not let what you eat cause the ruin of one for whom Christ died. 16 So do not let what is good to you be spoken of as evil. 17 For the kingdom of God does not mean food and drink but righteousness and peace and joy in the Holy Spirit; 18 he who thus serves Christ is acceptable to God and approved by men. 19 Let us then pursue what makes for peace and for mutual upbuilding. 20 Do not, for the sake of food, destroy the work of God. Everything is indeed clean, but it is wrong for any one to make others fall by what he eats; 21 it is right not to eat meat or drink wine or do anything that makes your brother

PHILLIPS

the meat eater—they should reflect that God has accepted them both. After all, who are you to criticize the servant of somebody else, especially when that somebody else is God? It is to his own master that he gives, or fails to give, satisfactory service. And don't doubt that satisfaction, for God is well able to transform men into servants who are satisfactory.

People are different—make   14. 5
allowances

Again, one man thinks some days of more importance than others. Another man considers them all alike. Let every one be definite in his own convictions. If a man specially observes one particular day, he does so "to the Lord." The man who eats, eats "to the Lord," for he thanks God for the food. The man who fasts also does it "to the Lord," for he thanks God for the benefits of fasting. The truth is that we neither live nor die as self-contained units. At every turn life links us to the Lord, and when we die we come face to face with him. In life or death we are in the hands of the Lord. Christ lived and died that he might be the Lord in both life and death.

Why, then, criticize your brother's actions, why try to make him look small? We shall all be judged one day, not by one another's standards or even our own, but by the judgment of God. It is written:

As I live, saith the Lord, to me every knee shall bow,
And every tongue shall confess to God.

It is to God alone that we have to answer for our actions.

This should be our attitude   14. 13

Let us therefore stop turning critical eyes on one another. If we must be critical, let us be critical of our own conduct and see that we do nothing to make a brother stumble or fall.

I am convinced, and I say this as in the presence of the Lord Christ, that nothing is intrinsically unholy. But none the less it is unholy to the man who thinks it is. If your habit of unrestricted diet seriously upsets your brother, you are no longer living in love toward him. And surely you wouldn't let food mean ruin to a man for whom Christ died. You mustn't let something that is all right for you look like an evil practice to somebody else. After all, the kingdom of Heaven is not a matter of whether you get what you like to eat and drink, but of righteousness and peace and joy in the Holy Spirit. If you put these things first in serving Christ you will please God and are not likely to offend men. So let us concentrate on the things which make for harmony, and on the growth of one another's character. Surely we shouldn't wish to undo God's work for the sake of a plate of meat!

I freely admit that all food is, in itself, harmless, but it can be harmful to the man who eats it with a guilty conscience. We should be willing to be both vegetarians and teetotalers if by doing otherwise we should impede a brother's

N.E.B.

not, and he who does not eat must not pass judgement on the one who does; for God has accepted him. Who are you to pass judgement on someone else's servant? Whether he stands or falls is his own Master's business; and stand he will, because his Master has power to enable him to stand.

Again, this man regards one day more highly than another, while that man regards all days alike. On such a point everyone should have reached conviction in his own mind. He who respects the day has the Lord in mind in doing so, and he who eats meat has the Lord in mind when he eats, since he gives thanks to God; and he who abstains has the Lord in mind no less, since he too gives thanks to God.

For no one of us lives, and equally no one of us dies, for himself alone. If we live, we live for the Lord; and if we die, we die for the Lord. Whether therefore we live or die, we belong to the Lord. This is why Christ died and came to life again, to establish his lordship over dead and living. You, sir, why do you pass judgement on your brother? And you, sir, why do you hold your brother in contempt? We shall all stand before God's tribunal. For Scripture says, 'As I live, says the Lord, to me every knee shall bow and every tongue acknowledge God.' So, you see, each of us will have to answer for himself.

Let us therefore cease judging one another, but rather make this simple judgement: that no obstacle or stumbling-block be placed in a brother's way. I am absolutely convinced, as a Christian, that nothing is impure in itself; only, if a man considers a particular thing impure, then to him it is impure. If your brother is outraged by what you eat, then your conduct is no longer guided by love. Do not by your eating bring disaster to a man for whom Christ died! What for you is a good thing must not become an occasion for slanderous talk; for the kingdom of God is not eating and drinking, but justice, peace, and joy, inspired by the Holy Spirit. He who thus shows himself a servant of Christ is acceptable to God and approved by men.

Let us then pursue the things that make for peace and build up the common life. Do not ruin the work of God for the sake of food. Everything is pure in itself, but anything is bad for the man who by his eating causes another to fall. It is a fine thing to abstain from eating meat or drinking wine, or doing anything which causes

K.J.V.

weak. 22 Hast thou faith? have *it* to thyself before God. Happy *is* he that condemneth not himself in that thing which he alloweth. 23And he that doubteth is damned if he eat, because *he eateth* not of faith: for whatsoever *is* not of faith is sin.

15 We then that are strong ought to bear the infirmities of the weak, and not to please ourselves. 2 Let every one of us please *his* neighbour for *his* good to edification. 3 For even Christ pleased not himself; but, as it is written, The reproaches of them that reproached thee fell on me. 4 For whatsoever things were written aforetime were written for our learning, that we through patience and comfort of the Scriptures might have hope. 5 Now the God of patience and consolation grant you to be likeminded one toward another according to Christ Jesus: 6 That ye may with one mind *and* one mouth glorify God, even the Father of our Lord Jesus Christ. 7 Wherefore receive ye one another, as Christ also received us, to the glory of God. 8 Now I say that Jesus Christ was a minister of the circumcision for the truth of God, to confirm the promises *made* unto the fathers: 9And that the Gentiles might glorify God for *his* mercy; as it is written, For this cause I will confess to thee among the Gentiles, and sing unto thy name. 10And again he saith, Rejoice, ye Gentiles, with his people. 11And again, Praise the Lord, all ye Gentiles; and laud him, all ye people. 12 And again, Esaias saith, There shall be a root of Jesse, and he that shall rise to reign over the Gentiles; in him shall the Gentiles trust. 13 Now the God of hope fill you with all joy and peace in believing, that ye may abound in hope, through the power of the Holy Ghost. 14And I myself also am persuaded of you, my brethren, that ye also are full of good-

R.S.V.

stumble.ᵛ 22 The faith that you have, keep between yourself and God; happy is he who has no reason to judge himself for what he approves. 23 But he who has doubts is condemned, if he eats, because he does not act from faith; for whatever does not proceed from faith is sin.ʷ

15 We who are strong ought to bear with the failings of the weak, and not to please ourselves; 2 let each of us please his neighbor for his good, to edify him. 3 For Christ did not please himself; but, as it is written, "The reproaches of those who reproached thee fell on me." 4 For whatever was written in former days was written for our instruction, that by steadfastness and by the encouragement of the scriptures we might have hope. 5 May the God of steadfastness and encouragement grant you to live in such harmony with one another, in accord with Christ Jesus, 6 that together you may with one voice glorify the God and Father of our Lord Jesus Christ.

7 Welcome one another, therefore, as Christ has welcomed you, for the glory of God. 8 For I tell you that Christ became a servant to the circumcised to show God's truthfulness, in order to confirm the promises given to the patriarchs, 9 and in order that the Gentiles might glorify God for his mercy. As it is written,

"Therefore I will praise thee among the
    Gentiles,
  and sing to thy name";
10 and again it is said,
  "Rejoice, O Gentiles, with his people";
11 and again,
  "Praise the Lord, all Gentiles,
  and let all the peoples praise him";
12 and further Isaiah says,
  "The root of Jesse shall come,
  he who rises to rule the Gentiles;
  in him shall the Gentiles hope."

13 May the God of hope fill you with all joy and peace in believing, so that by the power of the Holy Spirit you may abound in hope.

14 I myself am satisfied about you, my brethren, that you yourselves are full of goodness,

[v] Other ancient authorities add *or be upset or be weakened.* [w] Other authorities, some ancient, insert here Ch. 16.25-27.

progress in the faith. Your personal convictions are a matter of faith between yourself and God, and you are happy if you have no qualms about what you allow yourself to eat. Yet if a man eats meat with an uneasy conscience about it, you may be sure he is wrong to do so. For his action does not spring from his faith, and when we act apart from our faith we sin.

Christian behavior to one another   15. 1

We who have strong faith ought to shoulder the burden of the doubts and qualms of others and not just to go our own sweet way. Our actions should mean the good of others—should help them to build up their characters. For even Christ did not choose his own pleasure, but as it is written:

The reproaches of them that reproached thee fell upon me.

For all those words which were written long ago are meant to teach us today; that when we read in the scriptures of the endurance of men and of all the help that God gave them in those days, we may be encouraged to go on hoping in our own time. May the God who inspires men to endure, and gives them a Father's care, give you a mind united toward one another because of your common loyalty to Jesus Christ. And then, as one man, you will sing from the heart the praises of God the Father of our Lord Jesus Christ. So open your hearts to one another as Christ has opened his heart to you, and God will be glorified.

A reminder—Christ the universal   15. 8
savior

Christ was made a servant of the Jews to prove God's trustworthiness, since he personally implemented the promises made long ago to the fathers, and also that the gentiles might bring glory to God for his mercy to them. It is written:

Therefore will I give praise unto thee among the gentiles
And sing unto thy name.

And again:

Rejoice, ye gentiles, with his people.

And yet again:

Praise the Lord, all ye gentiles;
And let all the peoples praise him.

And then Isaiah says:

There shall be the root of Jesse,
And he that ariseth to rule over the gentiles:
On him shall the gentiles hope.

May the God of hope fill *you* with joy and peace in your faith, that by the power of the Holy Spirit, your whole life and outlook may be radiant with hope.

What I have tried to do   15. 14

For myself I feel certain that you, my brothers, have real Christian character and experience,

your brother's downfall. If you have a clear conviction, apply it to yourself in the sight of God. Happy is the man who can make his decision with a clear conscience! [a] But a man who has doubts is guilty if he eats, because his action does not arise from his conviction, and anything which does not arise from conviction is sin.[b]

15 Those of us who have a robust conscience must accept as our own burden the tender scruples of weaker men, and not consider ourselves. Each of us must consider his neighbour and think what is for his good and will build up the common life. For Christ too did not consider himself, but might have said, in the words of Scripture, 'The reproaches of those who reproached thee fell upon me.' For all the ancient scriptures were written for our own instruction, in order that through the encouragement they give us we may maintain our hope with fortitude. And may God, the source of all fortitude and all encouragement, grant that you may agree with one another after the manner of Christ Jesus, so that with one mind and one voice you may praise the God and Father of our Lord Jesus Christ.

In a word, accept one another as Christ accepted us, to the glory of God. I mean that Christ became a servant of the Jewish people to maintain the truth of God by making good his promises to the patriarchs, and at the same time to give the Gentiles cause to glorify God for his mercy. As Scripture says, 'Therefore I will praise thee among the Gentiles and sing hymns to thy name'; and again, 'Gentiles, make merry together with his own people'; and yet again, 'All Gentiles, praise the Lord; let all peoples praise him.' Once again, Isaiah says, 'There shall be the Root of Jesse, the one raised up to govern the Gentiles; on him the Gentiles shall set their hope.' And may the God of hope fill you with all joy and peace by your faith in him, until, by the power of the Holy Spirit, you overflow with hope.

My friends, I have no doubt in my own mind that you yourselves are quite full of goodness

[a] *Or* who does not bring judgement upon himself by what he approves! [b] *See p. 499, note c.*

K.J.V.

ness, filled with all knowledge, able also to admonish one another. 15 Nevertheless, brethren, I have written the more boldly unto you in some sort, as putting you in mind, because of the grace that is given to me of God, 16 That I should be the minister of Jesus Christ to the Gentiles, ministering the gospel of God, that the offering up of the Gentiles might be acceptable, being sanctified by the Holy Ghost. 17 I have therefore whereof I may glory through Jesus Christ in those things which pertain to God. 18 For I will not dare to speak of any of those things which Christ hath not wrought by me, to make the Gentiles obedient, by word and deed, 19 Through mighty signs and wonders, by the power of the Spirit of God; so that from Jerusalem, and round about unto Illyricum, I have fully preached the gospel of Christ. 20 Yea, so have I strived to preach the gospel, not where Christ was named, lest I should build upon another man's foundation: 21 But as it is written, To whom he was not spoken of, they shall see: and they that have not heard shall understand. 22 For which cause also I have been much hindered from coming to you. 23 But now having no more place in these parts, and having a great desire these many years to come unto you; 24 Whensoever I take my journey into Spain, I will come to you: for I trust to see you in my journey, and to be brought on my way thitherward by you, if first I be somewhat filled with your *company*. 25 But now I go unto Jerusalem to minister unto the saints. 26 For it hath pleased them of Macedonia and Achaia to make a certain contribution for the poor saints which are at Jerusalem. 27 It hath pleased them verily; and their debtors they are. For if the Gentiles have been made partakers of their spiritual things, their duty is also to minister unto them in carnal things. 28 When therefore I have performed this, and have sealed to them this fruit, I will come by you into Spain. 29 And I am sure that, when I come unto you, I shall come in the fullness of the blessing of the gospel of Christ. 30 Now I beseech you, brethren, for the Lord Jesus Christ's sake, and for the love of the Spirit, that ye strive together with me in *your* prayers to God for me; 31 That I may be delivered from them that do not believe in Judea; and that my service which *I have* for Jerusalem may be accepted of the saints; 32 That I may come unto you with joy by the will of God, and may with you be refreshed. 33 Now the God of peace *be* with you all Amen.

R.S.V.

filled with all knowledge, and able to instruct one another. 15 But on some points I have written to you very boldly by way of reminder, because of the grace given me by God 16 to be a minister of Christ Jesus to the Gentiles in the priestly service of the gospel of God, so that the offering of the Gentiles may be acceptable, sanctified by the Holy Spirit. 17 In Christ Jesus, then, I have reason to be proud of my work for God. 18 For I will not venture to speak of anything except what Christ has wrought through me to win obedience from the Gentiles, by word and deed, 19 by the power of signs and wonders, by the power of the Holy Spirit, so that from Jerusalem and as far round as Illyricum I have fully preached the gospel of Christ, 20 thus making it my ambition to preach the gospel, not where Christ has already been named, lest I build on another man's foundation, 21 but as it is written,

"They shall see who have never been told of him,
　and they shall understand who have never heard of him."

22 This is the reason why I have so often been hindered from coming to you. 23 But now, since I no longer have any room for work in these regions, and since I have longed for many years to come to you, 24 I hope to see you in passing as I go to Spain, and to be sped on my journey there by you, once I have enjoyed your company for a little. 25 At present, however, I am going to Jerusalem with aid for the saints. 26 For Macedonia and Achaia have been pleased to make some contribution for the poor among the saints at Jerusalem; 27 they were pleased to do it, and indeed they are in debt to them, for if the Gentiles have come to share in their spiritual blessings, they ought also to be of service to them in material blessings. 28 When therefore I have completed this, and have delivered to them what has been raised,* I shall go on by way of you to Spain; 29 and I know that when I come to you I shall come in the fulness of the blessing[y] of Christ.

30 I appeal to you, brethren, by our Lord Jesus Christ and by the love of the Spirit, to strive together with me in your prayers to God on my behalf, 31 that I may be delivered from the unbelievers in Judea, and that my service for Jerusalem may be acceptable to the saints, 32 so that by God's will I may come to you with joy and be refreshed in your company. 33 The God of peace be with you all. Amen.

[x] Greek *sealed to them this fruit*. [y] Other ancient authorities insert *of the gospel*.

494

PHILLIPS

and that you are capable of keeping one another on the right road. Nevertheless I have written to you with a certain frankness, to refresh your minds with truths that you already know, by virtue of my commission as minister of Christ Jesus to the gentiles in the service of the gospel of God. For my constant endeavor is to present the gentiles to God as an offering which he can accept, because they are sanctified by the Holy Spirit. And I think I have something to be proud of (through Christ, of course) in my work for God. I am not competent to speak of the work Christ has done through others, but I do know that through me he has secured the obedience of gentiles in word and deed, working by sign and miracle and all the power of the Holy Spirit. I have fully preached the gospel from Jerusalem and the surrounding country as far as Illyricum. My constant ambition has been to preach the gospel where the name of Christ was previously unknown, and to avoid as far as possible building on another man's foundation, so that:

They shall see, to whom no tiding of him came,
And they who have not heard shall understand.

My future plans   15. 22

Perhaps this will explain why I have so frequently been prevented from coming to see you. But now, since my work in these places no longer needs my presence, and since for many years I have had a great desire to see you, I hope to visit you on my way to Spain. I hope also that you will speed me on my journey, after I have had the satisfaction of seeing you all. At the moment my next call is to Jerusalem, to look after the welfare of the Christians there. The churches in Macedonia and Achaia, you see, have thought it a good thing to make a contribution toward the poor Christians in Jerusalem. They have thought it a good thing to make this gesture and yet, really, they received "a good thing" from them first! For if the gentiles have had a share in the Jews' spiritual "good things" it is only fair that they should look after the Jews as far as the good things of this world are concerned.
When I have completed this task, then, and turned their gesture into a good deed done, I shall come to you en route for Spain. I feel sure that in this long-looked-for visit I shall bring with me the full blessing of Christ.
Now, my brothers, I am going to ask you, for the sake of our Lord Jesus Christ and for the love we bear one another in the Spirit, to stand behind me in earnest prayer to God on my behalf—that I may not fall into the hands of the unbelievers in Judaea, and that the Jerusalem Christians may receive the gift I am taking to them in the spirit in which it was made. Then I shall come to you, in the purpose of God, with a happy heart, and may even enjoy with you a little holiday.
The God of peace be with you all amen.

N.E.B.

and equipped with knowledge of every kind, well able to give advice to one another; nevertheless I have written to refresh your memory, and written somewhat boldly at times, in virtue of the gift I have from God. His grace has made me a minister of Christ Jesus to the Gentiles; my priestly service is the preaching of the gospel of God, and it falls to me to offer the Gentiles to him as[a] an acceptable sacrifice, consecrated by the Holy Spirit.
Thus in the fellowship of Christ Jesus I have ground for pride in the service of God. I will venture to speak of those things alone in which I have been Christ's instrument to bring the Gentiles into his allegiance, by word and deed, by the force of miraculous signs and by the power of the Holy Spirit. As a result I have completed the preaching of the gospel of Christ from Jerusalem as far round as Illyricum. It is my ambition to bring the gospel to places where the very name of Christ has not been heard, for I do not want to build on another man's foundation; but, as Scripture says,

'They who had no news of him shall see,
And they who never heard of him shall understand.'

That is why I have been prevented all this time from coming to you. But now I have no further scope in these parts, and I have been longing for many years to visit you on my way to Spain; for I hope to see you as I travel through, and to be sent there with your support after having enjoyed your company for a while. But at the moment I am on my way to Jerusalem, on an errand to God's people there. For Macedonia and Achaia have resolved to raise a common fund for the benefit of the poor among God's people at Jerusalem. They have resolved to do so, and indeed they are under an obligation to them. For if the Jewish Christians shared their spiritual treasures with the Gentiles, the Gentiles have a clear duty to contribute to their material needs. So when I have finished this business and delivered the proceeds under my own seal, I shall set out for Spain by way of your city, and I am sure that when I arrive I shall come to you with a full measure of the blessing of Christ.
I implore you by our Lord Jesus Christ and by the love that the Spirit inspires, be my allies in the fight; pray to God for me that I may be saved from unbelievers in Judaea and that my errand to Jerusalem may find acceptance with God's people, so that by his will I may come to you in a happy frame of mind and enjoy a time of rest with you. The God of peace be with you all. Amen.[b]

---

[a] *Or* . . . of God, so that the worship which the Gentiles offer may be . . . [b] *See p. 499, note c.*

16 I commend unto you Phebe our sister, which is a servant of the church which is at Cenchrea: 2 That ye receive her in the Lord, as becometh saints, and that ye assist her in whatsoever business she hath need of you: for she hath been a succourer of many, and of myself also. 3 Greet Priscilla and Aquila, my helpers in Christ Jesus: 4 Who have for my life laid down their own necks: unto whom not only I give thanks, but also all the churches of the Gentiles. 5 Likewise *greet* the church that is in their house. Salute my well beloved Epenetus, who is the firstfruits of Achaia unto Christ. 6 Greet Mary, who bestowed much labour on us. 7 Salute Andronicus and Junia, my kinsmen, and my fellow prisoners, who are of note among the apostles, who also were in Christ before me. 8 Greet Amplias, my beloved in the Lord. 9 Salute Urbane, our helper in Christ, and Stachys my beloved. 10 Salute Apelles approved in Christ. Salute them which are of Aristobulus' *household.* 11 Salute Herodion my kinsman. Greet them that be of the *household* of Narcissus, which are in the Lord. 12 Salute Tryphena and Tryphosa, who labour in the Lord. Salute the beloved Persis, which laboured much in the Lord. 13 Salute Rufus chosen in the Lord, and his mother and mine. 14 Salute Asyncritus, Phlegon, Hermas, Patrobas, Hermes, and the brethren which are with them. 15 Salute Philologus, and Julia, Nereus, and his sister, and Olympas, and all the saints which are with them. 16 Salute one another with a holy kiss. The churches of Christ salute you. 17 Now I beseech you, brethren, mark them which cause divisions and offences contrary to the doctrine which ye have learned; and avoid them. 18 For they that are such serve not our Lord Jesus Christ, but their own belly; and by good words and fair speeches deceive the hearts of the simple. 19 For your obedience is come abroad unto all *men.* I am glad therefore on your behalf: but yet I would have you wise unto that which is good, and simple concerning evil. 20 And the God of peace shall bruise Satan under your feet shortly. The grace of our Lord Jesus Christ *be* with you. Amen. 21 Timotheus my workfellow, and Lucius, and Jason, and Sosipater, my kinsmen, salute you. 22 I Tertius, who wrote *this* epistle, salute you in the Lord. 23 Gaius mine host, and of the whole church, saluteth you. Erastus the chamberlain of the city saluteth you, and Quartus a brother. 24 The grace of our Lord Jesus Christ *be* with you all. Amen. 25 Now to him that is of power to stablish you according to my gospel, and the preaching of Jesus Christ,

16 I commend to you our sister Phoebe, a deaconess of the church at Cenchreae, 2 that you may receive her in the Lord as befits the saints, and help her in whatever she may require from you, for she has been a helper of many and of myself as well. 3 Greet Prisca and Aquila, my fellow workers in Christ Jesus, 4 who risked their necks for my life, to whom not only I but also all the churches of the Gentiles give thanks; 5 greet also the church in their house. Greet my beloved Epaenetus, who was the first convert in Asia for Christ. 6 Greet Mary, who has worked hard among you. 7 Greet Andronicus and Junias, my kinsmen and my fellow prisoners; they are men of note among the apostles, and they were in Christ before me. 8 Greet Ampliatus, my beloved in the Lord. 9 Greet Urbanus, our fellow worker in Christ, and my beloved Stachys. 10 Greet Apelles, who is approved in Christ. Greet those who belong to the family of Aristobulus. 11 Greet my kinsman Herodion. Greet those in the Lord who belong to the family of Narcissus. 12 Greet those workers in the Lord, Tryphaena and Tryphosa. Greet the beloved Persis, who has worked hard in the Lord. 13 Greet Rufus, eminent in the Lord, also his mother and mine. 14 Greet Asyncritus, Phlegon, Hermes, Patrobas, Hermas, and the brethren who are with them. 15 Greet Philologus, Julia, Nereus and his sister, and Olympas, and all the saints who are with them. 16 Greet one another with a holy kiss. All the churches of Christ greet you.

17 I appeal to you, brethren, to take note of those who create dissensions and difficulties, in opposition to the doctrine which you have been taught; avoid them. 18 For such persons do not serve our Lord Christ, but their own appetites,[z] and by fair and flattering words they deceive the hearts of the simple-minded. 19 For while your obedience is known to all, so that I rejoice over you, I would have you wise as to what is good and guileless as to what is evil; 20 then the God of peace will soon crush Satan under your feet. The grace of our Lord Jesus Christ be with you.[a]

21 Timothy, my fellow worker, greets you; so do Lucius and Jason and Sosipater, my kinsmen.

22 I Tertius, the writer of this letter, greet you in the Lord.

23 Gaius, who is host to me and to the whole church, greets you. Erastus, the city treasurer, and our brother Quartus, greet you.[b]

25 Now to him who is able to strengthen you according to my gospel and the preaching of

[z] Greek *their own belly* (Phil. 3.19). [a] Other ancient authorities omit this sentence. [b] Other ancient authorities insert verse 24, *The grace of our Lord Jesus Christ be with you all. Amen.*

Personal greetings and messages   16. 1

I want this letter to introduce to you Phoebe, our sister, a deaconess of the church at Cenchreae. Please give her a Christian welcome, and any assistance with her work that she may need. She has herself been of great assistance to many, not excluding myself.

Shake hands for me with Prisca and Aquila. They have not only worked with me for Christ Jesus, but they have risked their necks to save my life. Not only I, but all the gentile churches, owe them a great debt. Give my love to the little church that meets in their house.

Shake the hand of dear Epaenetus, Achaia's first man to be won for Christ, and of course greet Mary who has worked so hard for you. A handshake too for Andronicus and Junias my kinsmen and fellow prisoners; they are outstanding men among the messengers and were Christians before I was.

Another warm greeting for Ampliatus, dear Christian that he is, and also for Urbanus, who has worked with me, and dear old Stachys, too.

More greetings from me, please, to:

Apelles, the man who has proved his faith;

The household of Aristobulus;

Herodion, my kinsman;

Narcissus' household, who are Christians.

Remember me to Tryphena and Tryphosa, who work so hard for the Lord, and to my dear Persis who has also done great work for him.

Shake the hand of Rufus for me—that splendid Christian—and greet his mother, who has been mother to me too. Greetings to Asyncritus, Phlegon, Hermes, Patrobas, Hermas and their Christian group: also to Philologus and Julia, Nereus and his sister, and Olympas and the Christians who are with them.

Give one another a hearty handshake all round for my sake. The greetings of all the churches I am in touch with come to you with this letter.

A final warning   16. 17

And now I implore you, my brothers, to keep a watchful eye on those who cause trouble and make difficulties among you, in plain opposition to the teaching you have been given, and steer clear of them. Such men do not really serve our Lord Christ at all but are utterly self-centered. Yet with their plausible and attractive arguments they deceive those who are too simplehearted to see through them.

Your loyalty to the principles of the gospel is known everywhere, and that gives me great joy. I want to see you experts in good, and not even beginners in evil. It will not be long before the God of peace will crush Satan under your feet. May the grace of our Lord Jesus Christ be with you.

Timothy, who works with me, sends his greetings, and so do Lucius and Jason and Sosipater my fellow countrymen. (Paul has just told me that I, Tertius, who have been taking down this epistle from his dictation, may send you my Christian greetings too.) Gaius, my host (and the host as a matter of fact of the whole church here), sends you his greetings. Erastus, our town clerk, and Quartus, another Christian brother, send greetings too.

Now to him who is able to set you on your feet as his own sons—according to my gospel, according to the preaching of Jesus Christ himself, and in accordance with the disclosing of

I commend to you Phoebe, a fellow-Christian who holds office in the congregation at Cenchreae. Give her, in the fellowship of Christ, a welcome worthy of God's people, and stand by her in any business in which she may need your help, for she has herself been a good friend to many, including myself.

Give my greetings to Prisca and Aquila, my fellow-workers in Christ. They risked their necks to save my life, and not I alone but all the gentile congregations are grateful to them. Greet also the congregation at their house.

Give my greetings to my dear friend Epaenetus, the first convert to Christ in Asia, and to Mary, who toiled hard for you. Greet Andronicus and Junias[a] my fellow-countrymen and comrades in captivity. They are eminent among the apostles, and they were Christians before I was.

Greetings to Ampliatus, my dear friend in the fellowship of the Lord, to Urban my comrade in Christ, and to my dear Stachys. My greetings to Apelles, well proved in Christ's service, to the household of Aristobulus, and my countryman Herodion, and to those of the household of Narcissus who are in the Lord's fellowship. Greet Tryphaena and Tryphosa, who toil in the Lord's service, and dear Persis who has toiled in his service so long. Give my greetings to Rufus, an outstanding follower of the Lord, and to his mother, whom I call mother too. Greet Asyncritus, Phlegon, Hermes, Patrobas, Hermas, and all friends in their company. Greet Philologus and Julia,[b] Nereus and his sister, and Olympas, and all God's people associated with them.

Greet one another with the kiss of peace. All Christ's congregations send you their greetings.

I implore you, my friends, keep your eye on those who stir up quarrels and lead others astray, contrary to the teaching you received. Avoid them, for such people are servants not of Christ our Lord but of their own appetites, and they seduce the minds of innocent people with smooth and specious words. The fame of your obedience has spread everywhere. This makes me happy about you; yet I should wish you to be experts in goodness but simpletons in evil; and the God of peace will soon crush Satan beneath your feet. The grace of our Lord Jesus be with you![c]

Greetings to you from my colleague Timothy, and from Lucius, Jason, and Sosipater my fellow-countrymen. (I Tertius, who took this letter down, add my Christian greetings.) Greetings also from Gaius, my host and host of the whole congregation, and from Erastus, treasurer of this city, and our brother Quartus.[d]

To him who has power to make your standing sure, according to the Gospel I brought you and the proclamation of Jesus Christ, according

[a] Or Junia; some ancient witnesses read Julia, or Julias. [b] Or Julias; some witnesses read Junia, or Junias. [c] The words The grace . . . with you are omitted at this point in some witnesses; in some, these or similar words are given as verse 24, and in some others after verse 27 (see note on verse 23). [d] Some witnesses add (24) The grace of our Lord Jesus Christ be with you all!

K.J.V.

according to the revelation of the mystery, which was kept secret since the world began, 26 But now is made manifest, and by the Scriptures of the prophets, according to the commandment of the everlasting God, made known to all nations for the obedience of faith: 27 To God only wise, *be* glory through Jesus Christ for ever. Amen.

Written to the Romans from Corinthus, *and* *sent* by Phebe servant of the church at Cenchrea.

R.S.V.

Jesus Christ, according to the revelation of the mystery which was kept secret for long ages 26 but is now disclosed and through the prophetic writings is made known to all nations, according to the command of the eternal God, to bring about the obedience of faith—27 to the only wise God be glory for evermore through Jesus Christ! Amen.

PHILLIPS

that secret purpose which, after long ages of silence, has now been made known (in full agreement with the writings of the prophets long ago), by the command of the everlasting God to all the gentiles, that they might turn to him in the obedience of faith—to him, I say, the only God who is wise, be glory for ever through Jesus Christ, amen!

PAUL

N.E.B.

to the revelation of that divine secret kept in silence for long ages but now disclosed, and through prophetic scriptures by eternal God's command made known to all nations, to bring them to faith and obedience—to God who alone is wise, through Jesus Christ,[a] be glory for endless ages! Amen.[b] [c]

[a] *Some witnesses insert* to whom. [b] *Here some witnesses add* The grace of our Lord Jesus Christ be with you! [c] *Some witnesses place verses 25-27 at the end of chapter 14, one other places them at the end of chapter 15, and others omit them altogether.*

THE FIRST EPISTLE OF
PAUL THE APOSTLE
TO THE
CORINTHIANS

THE FIRST
LETTER OF PAUL TO THE
CORINTHIANS

1 Paul, called *to be* an apostle of Jesus Christ through the will of God, and Sosthenes *our* brother, 2 Unto the church of God which is at Corinth, to them that are sanctified in Christ Jesus, called *to be* saints, with all that in every place call upon the name of Jesus Christ our Lord, both theirs and ours: 3 Grace *be* unto you, and peace, from God our Father, and *from* the Lord Jesus Christ. 4 I thank my God always on your behalf, for the grace of God which is given you by Jesus Christ; 5 That in every thing ye are enriched by him, in all utterance, and *in* all knowledge; 6 Even as the testimony of Christ was confirmed in you: 7 So that ye come behind in no gift; waiting for the coming of our Lord Jesus Christ: 8 Who shall also confirm you unto the end, *that ye may be* blameless in the day of our Lord Jesus Christ. 9 God *is* faithful, by whom ye were called unto the fellowship of his Son Jesus Christ our Lord. 10 Now I beseech you, brethren, by the name of our Lord Jesus Christ, that ye all speak the same thing, and *that* there be no divisions among you; but *that* ye be perfectly joined together in the same mind and in the same judgment. 11 For it hath been declared unto me of you, my brethren, by them *which are of the house* of Chloe, that there are contentions among you. 12 Now this I say, that every one of you saith, I am of Paul; and I of Apollos; and I of Cephas; and I of Christ. 13 Is Christ divided? was Paul crucified for you? or were ye baptized in the name of Paul? 14 I thank God that I baptized none of you, but Crispus and Gaius; 15 Lest any should say that I had baptized in mine own name. 16And I baptized also the household of Stephanas: besides, I know not whether I baptized any other. 17 For Christ sent me not to baptize, but to preach the

1 Paul, called by the will of God to be an apostle of Christ Jesus, and our brother Sosthenes,
2 To the church of God which is at Corinth, to those sanctified in Christ Jesus, called to be saints together with all those who in every place call on the name of our Lord Jesus Christ, both their Lord and ours:
3 Grace to you and peace from God our Father and the Lord Jesus Christ.

4 I give thanks to God [a] always for you because of the grace of God which was given you in Christ Jesus, 5 that in every way you were enriched in him with all speech and all knowledge—6 even as the testimony to Christ was confirmed among you—7 so that you are not lacking in any spiritual gift, as you wait for the revealing of our Lord Jesus Christ; 8 who will sustain you to the end, guiltless in the day of our Lord Jesus Christ. 9 God is faithful, by whom you were called into the fellowship of his Son, Jesus Christ our Lord.
10 I appeal to you, brethren, by the name of our Lord Jesus Christ, that all of you agree and that there be no dissensions among you, but that you be united in the same mind and the same judgment. 11 For it has been reported to me by Chloe's people that there is quarreling among you, my brethren. 12 What I mean is that each one of you says, "I belong to Paul," or "I belong to Apollos," or "I belong to Cephas," or "I belong to Christ." 13 Is Christ divided? Was Paul crucified for you? Or were you baptized in the name of Paul? 14 I am thankful [b] that I baptized none of you except Crispus and Gaius; 15 lest any one should say that you were baptized in my name. 16 (I did baptize also the household of Stephanas. Beyond that, I do not know whether I baptized any one else.) 17 For Christ did not send me to baptize but to preach the gospel, and not with

[a] Other ancient authorities read *my God.* [b] Other ancient authorities read *I thank God.*

THE FIRST LETTER TO THE CHRISTIANS AT

CORINTH

Paul, commissioned by the will of God as a messenger of Christ Jesus, and Sosthenes, a Christian brother, to the church of God at Corinth—to those whom Christ Jesus has made holy, who are called to be God's men and women, to all true believers in Jesus Christ, their Lord and ours—grace and peace be to you from God the Father and the Lord, Jesus Christ!

I am thankful for your faith   *1. 4*

I am always thankful to God for what the gift of his grace in Christ Jesus has meant to you—how, as the Christian message has become established among you, he has enriched your whole lives, from the words on your lips to the understanding in your hearts. And you have been eager to receive his gifts during this time of waiting for his final appearance. He will keep you steadfast in the faith to the end, so that when his day comes you need fear no condemnation. God is utterly dependable, and it is he who has called you into fellowship with his Son Jesus Christ, our Lord.

But I am anxious over your   *1. 10* *"divisions"*

Now I do beg you, my brothers, by all that our Lord Jesus Christ means to you, to speak with one voice, and not allow yourselves to be split up into parties. All together you should be achieving a unity in thought and judgment. For I know, from what some of Chloe's people have told me, that you are each making different claims—"I am one of Paul's men," says one; "I am one of Apollos'," says another; or "I am one of Cephas'"; while someone else says, "I owe my faith to Christ alone."

Do consider how serious   *1. 13* *these divisions are!*

What *are* you saying? Is there more than one Christ? Was it Paul who died on the cross for you? Were you baptized in the name of Paul? It makes me thankful that I didn't actually baptize any of you (except Crispus and Gaius), or perhaps someone would be saying I did it in my own name. (Oh, yes, I did baptize Stephanas' family, but I can't remember anyone else.) For Christ did not send me to see how many I could baptize, but to proclaim the gospel. And I have not done this by the persuasiveness of clever

THE FIRST LETTER OF PAUL TO THE

CORINTHIANS

Unity and Order in the Church

1 From Paul, apostle of Jesus Christ at God's call and by God's will, together with our colleague Sosthenes, to the congregation of God's people at Corinth, dedicated to him in Christ Jesus, claimed by him as his own, along with all men everywhere who invoke the name of our Lord Jesus Christ—their Lord as well as ours.

Grace and peace to you from God our Father and the Lord Jesus Christ.

I am always thanking God for you. I thank him for his grace given to you in Christ Jesus. I thank him for all the enrichment that has come to you in Christ. You possess full knowledge and you can give full expression to it, because in you the evidence for the truth of Christ has found confirmation. There is indeed no single gift you lack, while you wait expectantly for our Lord Jesus Christ to reveal himself. He will keep you firm to the end, without reproach on the Day of our Lord Jesus. It is God himself who called you to share in the life of his Son Jesus Christ our Lord; and God keeps faith.

I appeal to you, my brothers, in the name of our Lord Jesus Christ: agree among yourselves, and avoid divisions; be firmly joined in unity of mind and thought. I have been told, my brothers, by Chloe's people that there are quarrels among you. What I mean is this: each of you is saying, 'I am Paul's man', or 'I am for Apollos'; 'I follow Cephas', or 'I am Christ's.' Surely Christ has not been divided among you! Was it Paul who was crucified for you? Was it in the name of Paul that you were baptized? Thank God, I never baptized one of you—except Crispus and Gaius. So no one can say you were baptized in my name.—Yes, I did baptize the household of Stephanas; I cannot think of anyone else. Christ did not send me to baptize, but to proclaim the Gospel; and to do it without relying on the

K.J.V.

gospel: not with wisdom of words, lest the cross of Christ should be made of none effect. 18 For the preaching of the cross is to them that perish, foolishness; but unto us which are saved, it is the power of God. 19 For it is written, I will destroy the wisdom of the wise, and will bring to nothing the understanding of the prudent. 20 Where *is* the wise? where *is* the scribe? where *is* the disputer of this world? hath not God made foolish the wisdom of this world? 21 For after that in the wisdom of God the world by wisdom knew not God, it pleased God by the foolishness of preaching to save them that believe. 22 For the Jews require a sign, and the Greeks seek after wisdom: 23 But we preach Christ crucified, unto the Jews a stumblingblock, and unto the Greeks foolishness; 24 But unto them which are called, both Jews and Greeks, Christ the power of God, and the wisdom of God. 25 Because the foolishness of God is wiser than men; and the weakness of God is stronger than men. 26 For ye see your calling, brethren, how that not many wise men after the flesh, not many mighty, not many noble, *are called:* 27 But God hath chosen the foolish things of the world to confound the wise; and God hath chosen the weak things of the world to confound the things which are mighty; 28 And base things of the world, and things which are despised, hath God chosen, *yea,* and things which are not, to bring to nought things that are: 29 That no flesh should glory in his presence. 30 But of him are ye in Christ Jesus, who of God is made unto us wisdom, and righteousness, and sanctification, and redemption: 31 That, according as it is written, He that glorieth, let him glory in the Lord.

R.S.V.

eloquent wisdom, lest the cross of Christ be emptied of its power.

18 For the word of the cross is folly to those who are perishing, but to us who are being saved it is the power of God. 19 For it is written,

"I will destroy the wisdom of the wise,
    and the cleverness of the clever I will thwart."

20 Where is the wise man? Where is the scribe? Where is the debater of this age? Has not God made foolish the wisdom of the world? 21 For since, in the wisdom of God, the world did not know God through wisdom, it pleased God through the folly of what we preach to save those who believe. 22 For Jews demand signs and Greeks seek wisdom, 23 but we preach Christ crucified, a stumbling block to Jews and folly to Gentiles, 24 but to those who are called, both Jews and Greeks, Christ the power of God and the wisdom of God. 25 For the foolishness of God is wiser than men, and the weakness of God is stronger than men.

26 For consider your call, brethren; not many of you were wise according to worldly standards, not many were powerful, not many were of noble birth; 27 but God chose what is foolish in the world to shame the wise, God chose what is weak in the world to shame the strong, 28 God chose what is low and despised in the world, even things that are not, to bring to nothing things that are, 29 so that no human being might boast in the presence of God. 30 He is the source of your life in Christ Jesus, whom God made our wisdom, our righteousness and sanctification and redemption; 31 therefore, as it is written, "Let him who boasts, boast of the Lord."

2 And I, brethren, when I came to you, came not with excellency of speech or of wisdom, declaring unto you the testimony of God. 2 For I determined not to know any thing among you, save Jesus Christ, and him crucified. 3 And I was with you in weakness, and in fear, and in much trembling. 4 And my speech and my preaching *was* not with enticing words of man's wisdom, but in demonstration of the Spirit and of power:

2 When I came to you, brethren, I did not come proclaiming to you the testimony[c] of God in lofty words or wisdom. 2 For I decided to know nothing among you except Jesus Christ and him crucified. 3 And I was with you in weakness and in much fear and trembling; 4 and my speech and my message were not in plausible words of wisdom, but in demonstration of the

[c] Other ancient authorities read *mystery* (or *secret*).

PHILLIPS

N.E.B.

words, for I have no desire to rob the cross of its power. The preaching of the cross is, I know, nonsense to those who are involved in this dying world, but to us who are being saved from that death it is nothing less than the power of God.

The cross shows that God's   *1. 19*
wisdom is not man's wisdom
by any means

It is written:

I will destroy the wisdom of the wise,
And the prudence of the prudent will I reject.

For consider, what have the philosopher, the writer and the critic of this world to show for all their wisdom? Has not God made the wisdom of this world look foolish? For it was after the world in its wisdom had failed to know God, that he in his wisdom chose to save all who would believe by the "simplemindedness" of the gospel message. For the Jews ask for miraculous proofs and the Greeks an intellectual panacea, but all we preach is Christ crucified—a stumbling block to the Jews and sheer nonsense to the gentiles, but for those who are called, whether Jews or Greeks, Christ the power of God and the wisdom of God. And this is really only natural, for God's "foolishness" is wiser than men, and his "weakness" is stronger than men.

Nor are God's values the   *1. 26*
same as man's

For look at your own calling as Christians, my brothers. You don't see among you many of the wise (according to this world's judgment) nor many of the ruling class, nor many from the noblest families. But God has chosen what the world calls foolish to shame the wise; he has chosen what the world calls weak to shame the strong. He has chosen things of little strength and small repute, yes and even things which have no real existence to explode the pretensions of the things that are—that no man may boast in the presence of God. Yet from this same God you have received your standing in Jesus Christ, and he has become for us the true wisdom, a matter, in practice, of being made righteous and holy, in fact, of being redeemed. And this makes us see the truth of the scripture:

He that glorieth, let him glory in the Lord.

I came to you in God's strength,   *2. 1*
not my own

In the same way, my brothers, when I came to proclaim to you God's secret purpose, I did not come equipped with any brilliance of speech or intellect. You may as well know now that it was my secret determination to concentrate entirely on Jesus Christ himself and the fact of his death upon the cross. As a matter of fact, in myself I was feeling far from strong; I was nervous and rather shaky. What I said and preached had none of the attractiveness of the clever mind, but it was a demonstration of the power

language of worldly wisdom, so that the fact of Christ on his cross might have its full weight.

This doctrine of the cross is sheer folly to those on their way to ruin, but to us who are on the way to salvation it is the power of God. Scripture says, 'I will destroy the wisdom of the wise, and bring to nothing the cleverness of the clever.' Where is your wise man now, your man of learning, or your subtle debater—limited, all of them, to this passing age? God has made the wisdom of this world look foolish. As God in his wisdom ordained, the world failed to find him by its wisdom, and he chose to save those who have faith by the folly of the Gospel. Jews call for miracles, Greeks look for wisdom; but we proclaim Christ—yes, Christ nailed to the cross; and though this is a stumbling-block to Jews and folly to Greeks, yet to those who have heard his call, Jews and Greeks alike, he is the power of God and the wisdom of God.

Divine folly is wiser than the wisdom of man, and divine weakness stronger than man's strength. My brothers, think what sort of people you are, whom God has called. Few of you are men of wisdom, by any human standard; few are powerful or highly born. Yet, to shame the wise, God has chosen what the world counts folly, and to shame what is strong, God has chosen what the world counts weakness. He has chosen things low and contemptible, mere nothings, to overthrow the existing order. And so there is no place for human pride in the presence of God. You are in Christ Jesus by God's act, for God has made him our wisdom; he is our righteousness; in him we are consecrated and set free. And so (in the words of Scripture), 'If a man is proud, let him be proud of the Lord.'

2 As for me, brothers, when I came to you, I declared the attested truth of God *a* without display of fine words or wisdom. I resolved that while I was with you I would think of nothing but Jesus Christ—Christ nailed to the cross. I came before you weak, as I was then, nervous and shaking with fear. The word I spoke, the gospel I proclaimed, did not sway you with subtle arguments; it carried conviction by spirit-

[a] *Some witnesses read* I declared God's secret purpose . . .

K.J.V.

5 That your faith should not stand in the wisdom of men, but in the power of God. 6 Howbeit we speak wisdom among them that are perfect: yet not the wisdom of this world, nor of the princes of this world, that come to nought: 7 But we speak the wisdom of God in a mystery, *even* the hidden *wisdom*, which God ordained before the world unto our glory; 8 Which none of the princes of this world knew: for had they known *it*, they would not have crucified the Lord of glory. 9 But as it is written, Eye hath not seen, nor ear heard, neither have entered into the heart of man, the things which God hath prepared for them that love him. 10 But God hath revealed *them* unto us by his Spirit: for the Spirit searcheth all things, yea, the deep things of God. 11 For what man knoweth the things of a man, save the spirit of man which is in him? even so the things of God knoweth no man, but the Spirit of God. 12 Now we have received, not the spirit of the world, but the Spirit which is of God; that we might know the things that are freely given to us of God. 13 Which things also we speak, not in the words which man's wisdom teacheth, but which the Holy Ghost teacheth; comparing spiritual things with spiritual. 14 But the natural man receiveth not the things of the Spirit of God: for they are foolishness unto him: neither can he know *them*, because they are spiritually discerned. 15 But he that is spiritual judgeth all things, yet he himself is judged of no man. 16 For who hath known the mind of the Lord, that he may instruct him? But we have the mind of Christ.

3 And I, brethren, could not speak unto you as unto spiritual, but as unto carnal, *even* as unto babes in Christ. 2 I have fed you with milk, and not with meat: for hitherto ye were not able *to bear it,* neither yet now are ye able. 3 For ye are yet carnal: for whereas *there is*

R.S.V.

Spirit and power, 5 that your faith might not rest in the wisdom of men but in the power of God.

6 Yet among the mature we do impart wisdom, although it is not a wisdom of this age or of the rulers of this age, who are doomed to pass away. 7 But we impart a secret and hidden wisdom of God, which God decreed before the ages for our glorification. 8 None of the rulers of this age understood this; for if they had, they would not have crucified the Lord of glory. 9 But, as it is written,

"What no eye has seen, nor ear heard,
    nor the heart of man conceived,
    what God has prepared for those who love
        him,"

10 God has revealed to us through the Spirit. For the Spirit searches everything, even the depths of God. 11 For what person knows a man's thoughts except the spirit of the man which is in him? So also no one comprehends the thoughts of God except the Spirit of God. 12 Now we have received not the spirit of the world, but the Spirit which is from God, that we might understand the gifts bestowed on us by God. 13 And we impart this in words not taught by human wisdom but taught by the Spirit, interpreting spiritual truths to those who possess the Spirit.[d]

14 The unspiritual [e] man does not receive the gifts of the Spirit of God, for they are folly to him, and he is not able to understand them because they are spiritually discerned. 15 The spiritual man judges all things, but is himself to be judged by no one. 16 "For who has known the mind of the Lord so as to instruct him?" But we have the mind of Christ.

3 But I, brethren, could not address you as spiritual men, but as men of the flesh, as babes in Christ. 2 I fed you with milk, not solid food; for you were not ready for it; and even yet you are not ready, 3 for you are still of the flesh. For while there is jealousy and

[d] Or *interpreting spiritual truths in spiritual language; or comparing spiritual things with spiritual.*
[e] Or *natural.*

of the Spirit! Plainly God's purpose was that your faith should rest not upon man's cleverness but upon the power of God.

There is, of course, a real wisdom,   *2. 6*
which God allows us to share
with him

We do, of course, speak "wisdom" among those who are spiritually mature, but it is not what is called wisdom by this world, nor by the powers-that-be, who soon will be only the powers that have been. The wisdom we speak of is that mysterious secret wisdom of God which he planned before the Creation for our glory today. None of the powers of this world have known this wisdom—if they had they would never have crucified the Lord of glory! But, as it is written:

Things which eye saw not, and ear heard not,
And which entered not into the heart of man,
Whatsoever things God prepared for them that
love him.

But God has, through the Spirit, let us share his secret. For nothing is hidden from the Spirit, not even the deep wisdom of God. For who could really understand a man's inmost thoughts except the spirit of the man himself? How much less could anyone understand the thoughts of God except the very Spirit of God? And the marvelous thing is this, that we now receive not the spirit of the world but the Spirit of God himself, so that we can actually understand something of God's generosity toward us.

This wisdom is only understood   *2. 13*
by the spiritual

It is these things that we talk about, not using the expressions of the human intellect but those which the Holy Spirit teaches us, explaining spiritual things to those who are spiritual.
But the unspiritual man simply cannot accept the matters which the Spirit deals with—they just don't make sense to him, for, after all, you must be spiritual to see spiritual things. The spiritual man, on the other hand, has an insight into the meaning of everything, though his insight may baffle the man of the world. This is because the former is sharing in God's wisdom, and

Who hath known the mind of the Lord,
That he should instruct him?

Incredible as it may sound, we who are spiritual have the very thoughts of Christ!

But I cannot yet call you spiritual   *3. 1*

I, my brothers, was unable to talk to you as spiritual men: I had to talk to you as unspiritual, as yet babies in the Christian life. And my practice has been to feed you, as it were, with "milk" and not with "meat." You were unable to digest "meat" in those days, and I don't believe you can do it now. For you are still unspiritual: all

ual power, so that your faith might be built not upon human wisdom but upon the power of God.
And yet I do speak words of wisdom to those who are ripe for it, not a wisdom belonging to this passing age, nor to any of its governing powers, which are declining to their end; I speak God's hidden wisdom, his secret purpose framed from the very beginning to bring us to our full glory. The powers that rule the world have never known it; if they had, they would not have crucified the Lord of glory. But, in the words of Scripture, 'Things beyond our seeing, things beyond our hearing, things beyond our imagining, all prepared by God for those who love him', these it is that God has revealed to us through the Spirit.
For the Spirit explores everything, even the depths of God's own nature. Among men, who knows what a man is but the man's own spirit within him? In the same way, only the Spirit of God knows what God is. This is the Spirit that we have received from God, and not the spirit of the world, so that we may know all that God of his own grace gives us; and, because we are interpreting spiritual truths to those who have the Spirit, we speak of these gifts of God in words found for us not by our human wisdom but by the Spirit. A man who is unspiritual refuses what belongs to the Spirit of God; it is folly to him; he cannot grasp it, because it needs to be judged in the light of the Spirit. A man gifted with the Spirit can judge the worth of everything, but is not himself subject to judgement by his fellow-men. For (in the words of Scripture) 'who knows the mind of the Lord? Who can advise him?' We, however, possess the mind of Christ.

3 For my part, my brothers, I could not speak to you as I should speak to people who have the Spirit. I had to deal with you on the merely natural plane, as infants in Christ. And so I gave you milk to drink, instead of solid food, for which you were not yet ready. Indeed, you are still not ready for it, for you are still on the

K.J.V.

among you envying, and strife, and divisions, are ye not carnal, and walk as men? 4 For while one saith, I am of Paul; and another, I *am* of Apollos; are ye not carnal? 5 Who then is Paul, and who *is* Apollos, but ministers by whom ye believed, even as the Lord gave to every man? 6 I have planted, Apollos watered; but God gave the increase. 7 So then neither is he that planteth any thing, neither he that watereth; but God that giveth the increase. 8 Now he that planteth and he that watereth are one: and every man shall receive his own reward according to his own labour. 9 For we are labourers together with God: ye are God's husbandry, *ye are* God's building. 10According to the grace of God which is given unto me, as a wise masterbuilder, I have laid the foundation, and another buildeth thereon. But let every man take heed how he buildeth thereupon. 11 For other foundation can no man lay than that is laid, which is Jesus Christ. 12 Now if any man build upon this foundation gold, silver, precious stones, wood, hay, stubble; 13 Every man's work shall be made manifest: for the day shall declare it, because it shall be revealed by fire; and the fire shall try every man's work of what sort it is. 14 If any man's work abide which he hath built thereupon, he shall receive a reward. 15 If any man's work shall be burned, he shall suffer loss: but he himself shall be saved; yet so as by fire. 16 Know ye not that ye are the temple of God, and *that* the Spirit of God dwelleth in you? 17 If any man defile the temple of God, him shall God destroy; for the temple of God is holy, which *temple* ye are. 18 Let no man deceive himself. If any man among you seemeth to be wise in this world, let him become a fool, that he may be wise. 19 For the wisdom of this world is foolishness with God: for it is written, He taketh the wise in their own craftiness. 20And again, The Lord knoweth the thoughts of the wise, that they are vain. 21 Therefore let no man glory in men: for all things are yours; 22 Whether Paul, or Apollos, or Cephas, or the world, or life, or death, or things present, or things to come; all are yours; 23And ye are Christ's; and Christ *is* God's.

R.S.V.

strife among you, are you not of the flesh, and behaving like ordinary men? 4 For when one says, "I belong to Paul," and another, "I belong to Apollos," are you not merely men?

5 What then is Apollos? What is Paul? Servants through whom you believed, as the Lord assigned to each. 6 I planted, Apollos watered, but God gave the growth. 7 So neither he who plants nor he who waters is anything, but only God who gives the growth. 8 He who plants and he who waters are equal, and each shall receive his wages according to his labor. 9 For we are fellow workers for God;[f] you are God's field, God's building.

10 According to the commission of God given to me, like a skilled master builder I laid a foundation, and another man is building upon it. Let each man take care how he builds upon it. 11 For no other foundation can any one lay than that which is laid, which is Jesus Christ. 12 Now if any one builds on the foundation with gold, silver, precious stones, wood, hay, stubble —13 each man's work will become manifest; for the Day will disclose it, because it will be revealed with fire, and the fire will test what sort of work each one has done. 14 If the work which any man has built on the foundation survives, he will receive a reward. 15 If any man's work is burned up, he will suffer loss, though he himself will be saved, but only as through fire.

16 Do you not know that you are God's temple and that God's Spirit dwells in you? 17 If any one destroys God's temple, God will destroy him. For God's temple is holy, and that temple you are.

18 Let no one deceive himself. If any one among you thinks that he is wise in this age, let him become a fool that he may become wise. 19 For the wisdom of this world is folly with God. For it is written, "He catches the wise in their craftiness," 20 and again, "The Lord knows that the thoughts of the wise are futile." 21 So let no one boast of men. For all things are yours, 22 whether Paul or Apollos or Cephas or the world or life or death or the present or the future, all are yours; 23 and you are Christ's; and Christ is God's.

[f] Greek *God's fellow workers.*

PHILLIPS

the time that there is jealousy and squabbling among you you show that you are—you are living just like men of the world. While one of you says, "I am one of Paul's converts," and another says, "I am one of Apollos'," are you not plainly unspiritual?

After all, who is Paul? Who is Apollos? No more than servants through whom you came to believe as the Lord gave each man his opportunity. I may have done the planting and Apollos the watering, but it was God who made the seed grow! The planter and the waterer are nothing compared with him who gives life to the seed. Planter and waterer are alike insignificant, though each shall be rewarded according to his particular work.

We work on God's foundation   3. 9

In this work, we work with God, and that means that you are a field under God's cultivation, or, if you like, a house being built to his plan. I, like a master-builder who knows his job, by the grace God has given me, lay the foundation; someone else builds upon it. I say only this, let the builder be careful how he builds! The foundation is laid already, and no one can lay another, for it is Jesus Christ himself. But any man who builds on the foundation using as his material gold, silver, precious stones, wood, hay or stubble, must know that each man's work will one day be shown for what it is. The day will show it plainly enough, for the day will arise in a blaze of fire, and that fire will prove the nature of each man's work. If the work that a man has built upon the foundation will stand this test, he will be rewarded. But if a man's work be destroyed under the test, he loses it all. He personally will be safe, though rather like a man rescued from a fire.

Make no mistake: you are   3. 16
God's holy building

Don't you realize that you yourselves are the temple of God, and that God's Spirit lives in you? God will destroy anyone who defiles his temple, for his temple is holy—*and that is exactly what you are!*

Let no one be under any illusion over this. If any man among you thinks himself one of the world's clever ones, let him discard his cleverness that he may learn to be truly wise. For this world's cleverness is stupidity to God. It is written:

He that taketh the wise in their craftiness.

And again:

The Lord knoweth the reasonings of the wise, that they are vain.

So let no one boast of men. Everything belongs to you! Paul, Apollos or Cephas; the world, life, death, the present or the future, everything is yours! For you belong to Christ, and Christ belongs to God!

N.E.B.

merely natural plane. Can you not see that while there is jealousy and strife among you, you are living on the purely human level of your lower nature? When one says, 'I am Paul's man', and another, 'I am for Apollos', are you not all too human?

After all, what is Apollos? What is Paul? We are simply God's agents in bringing you to the faith. Each of us performed the task which the Lord allotted to him: I planted the seed, and Apollos watered it; but God made it grow. Thus it is not the gardeners with their planting and watering who count, but God, who makes it grow. Whether they plant or water, they work as a team,[a] though each will get his own pay for his own labour. We are God's fellow-workers;[b] and you are God's garden.

Or again, you are God's building. I am like a skilled master-builder who by God's grace laid the foundation, and someone else is putting up the building. Let each take care how he builds. There can be no other foundation beyond that which is already laid; I mean Jesus Christ himself. If anyone builds on that foundation with gold, silver, and fine stone, or with wood, hay, and straw, the work that each man does will at last be brought to light; the day of judgement will expose it. For that day dawns in fire, and the fire will test the worth of each man's work. If a man's building stands, he will be rewarded; if it burns, he will have to bear the loss; and yet he will escape with his life, as one might from a fire. Surely you know that you are God's temple, where the Spirit of God dwells. Anyone who destroys God's temple will himself be destroyed[c] by God, because the temple of God is holy; and that temple you are.

Make no mistake about this: if there is anyone among you who fancies himself wise—wise, I mean, by the standards of this passing age—he must become a fool to gain true wisdom. For the wisdom of this world is folly in God's sight. Scripture says, 'He traps the wise in their own cunning', and again, 'The Lord knows that the arguments of the wise are futile.' So never make mere men a cause for pride. For though everything belongs to you—Paul, Apollos, and Cephas, the world, life, and death, the present and the future, all of them belong to you—yet you belong to Christ, and Christ to God.

---

[a] *Or* Whether they plant or water, it is all the same. [b] *Or* We are fellow-workers in God's service. [c] *Some witnesses read* is himself destroyed.

4 Let a man so account of us, as of the ministers of Christ, and stewards of the mysteries of God. 2 Moreover it is required in stewards, that a man be found faithful. 3 But with me it is a very small thing that I should be judged of you, or of man's judgment: yea, I judge not mine own self. 4 For I know nothing by myself; yet am I not hereby justified: but he that judgeth me is the Lord. 5 Therefore judge nothing before the time, until the Lord come, who both will bring to light the hidden things of darkness, and will make manifest the counsels of the hearts: and then shall every man have praise of God. 6And these things, brethren, I have in a figure transferred to myself and *to* Apollos for your sakes; that ye might learn in us not to think *of men* above that which is written, that no one of you be puffed up for one against another. 7 For who maketh thee to differ *from another?* and what hast thou that thou didst not receive? now if thou didst receive *it,* why dost thou glory, as if thou hadst not received *it?* 8 Now ye are full, now ye are rich, ye have reigned as kings without us: and I would to God ye did reign, that we also might reign with you. 9 For I think that God hath set forth us the apostles last, as it were appointed to death: for we are made a spectacle unto the world, and to angels, and to men. 10 We *are* fools for Christ's sake, but ye *are* wise in Christ; we *are* weak, but ye *are* strong; ye *are* honourable, but we *are* despised. 11 Even unto this present hour we both hunger, and thirst, and are naked, and are buffeted, and have no certain dwellingplace; 12And labour, working with our own hands: being reviled, we bless; being persecuted, we suffer it: 13 Being defamed, we entreat: we are made as the filth of the world, *and are* the offscouring of all things unto this day. 14 I write not these things to shame you, but as my beloved sons I warn *you.* 15 For though ye have ten thousand instructors in Christ, yet *have ye* not many fathers: for in

4 This is how one should regard us, as servants of Christ and stewards of the mysteries of God. 2 Moreover it is required of stewards that they be found trustworthy. 3 But with me it is a very small thing that I should be judged by you or by any human court. I do not even judge myself. 4 I am not aware of anything against myself, but I am not thereby acquitted. It is the Lord who judges me. 5 Therefore do not pronounce judgment before the time, before the Lord comes, who will bring to light the things now hidden in darkness and will disclose the purposes of the heart. Then every man will receive his commendation from God.

6 I have applied all this to myself and Apollos for your benefit, brethren, that you may learn by us to live according to scripture, that none of you may be puffed up in favor of one against another. 7 For who sees anything different in you? What have you that you did not receive? If then you received it, why do you boast as if it were not a gift?

8 Already you are filled! Already you have become rich! Without us you have become kings! And would that you did reign, so that we might share the rule with you! 9 For I think that God has exhibited us apostles as last of all, like men sentenced to death; because we have become a spectacle to the world, to angels and to men. 10 We are fools for Christ's sake, but you are wise in Christ. We are weak, but you are strong. You are held in honor, but we in disrepute. 11 To the present hour we hunger and thirst, we are ill-clad and buffeted and homeless, 12 and we labor, working with our own hands. When reviled, we bless; when persecuted, we endure; 13 when slandered, we try to conciliate; we have become, and are now, as the refuse of the world, the offscouring of all things.

14 I do not write this to make you ashamed, but to admonish you as my beloved children. 15 For though you have countless guides in Christ, you do not have many fathers. For I

PHILLIPS

N.E.B.

Trust us, but make no hasty judgments
4. 1

You should look upon us as ministers of Christ, as trustees of the secrets of God. And it is a prime requisite in a trustee that he should prove worthy of his trust. But, as a matter of fact, it matters very little to me what you, or any man, thinks of me—I don't even value my opinion of myself. For I might be quite ignorant of any fault in myself—but that doesn't justify me before God. My only true judge is the Lord.

The moral of this is that we should make no hasty or premature judgments. When the Lord comes he will bring into the light of day all that at present is hidden in darkness, and he will expose the secret motives of men's hearts. Then shall God himself give each man his share of praise.

Having your favorite teacher is not only silly but wrong
4. 6

I have used myself and Apollos above as an illustration, so that you might learn from what I have said about us not to assess man above his value in God's sight, and may thus avoid the friction that comes from exalting one teacher against another. For who makes you different from somebody else, and what have you got that was not given to you? And if anything has been given to you, why boast of it as if it were something you had achieved yourself?

Think sometimes of what your happiness has cost us!
4. 8

Oh, I know you are rich and flourishing! You've been living like kings, haven't you, while we've been away? I would to God you were really kings in God's sight so that we might reign with you!

I sometimes think that God means us, the messengers, to appear last in the procession of mankind, like the men who are to die in the arena. For indeed we are made a public spectacle before the angels of Heaven and the eyes of men. We are looked upon as fools, for Christ's sake, but you are wise in the Christian faith. We are considered weak, but you have become strong: you have found honor, we little but contempt. Up to this very hour we are hungry and thirsty, ill-clad, knocked about and practically homeless. We still have to work for our living by manual labor. Men curse us, but we return a blessing: they make our lives miserable, but we take it patiently. They ruin our reputations, but we go on trying to win them for God. We are the world's rubbish, the scum of the earth, yes, up to this very day.

A personal plea
4. 14

I don't write these things merely to make you feel uncomfortable, but that you may realize facts, as my dear children. After all, you may have ten thousand teachers in the Christian faith, but you cannot have many fathers! For in Christ

4 We must be regarded as Christ's underlings and as stewards of the secrets of God. Well then, stewards are expected to show themselves trustworthy. For my part, if I am called to account by you or by any human court of judgement, it does not matter to me in the least. Why, I do not even pass judgement on myself, for I have nothing on my conscience; but that does not mean I stand acquitted. My judge is the Lord. So pass no premature judgement; wait until the Lord comes. For he will bring to light what darkness hides, and disclose men's inward motives; then will be the time for each to receive from God such praise as he deserves.

Into this general picture, my friends, I have brought Apollos and myself on your account, so that you may take our case as an example, and learn to 'keep within the rules', as they say, and may not be inflated with pride as you patronize one and flout the other. Who makes you, my friend, so important? What do you possess that was not given you? If then you really received it all as a gift, why take the credit to yourself?

All of you, no doubt, have everything you could desire. You have come into your fortune already. You have come into your kingdom—and left us out. How I wish you had indeed won your kingdom; then you might share it with us! For it seems to me God has made us apostles the most abject of mankind. We are like men condemned to death in the arena, a spectacle to the whole universe—angels as well as men. We are fools for Christ's sake, while you are such sensible Christians. We are weak; you are so powerful. We are in disgrace; you are honoured. To this day we go hungry and thirsty and in rags; we are roughly handled; we wander from place to place; we wear ourselves out working with our own hands. They curse us, and we bless; they persecute us, and we submit to it; they slander us, and we humbly make our appeal. We are treated as the scum of the earth, the dregs of humanity, to this very day.

I am not writing thus to shame you, but to bring you to reason; for you are my dear children. You may have ten thousand tutors in Christ, but you have only one father. For in

K.J.V.

Christ Jesus I have begotten you through the gospel. 16 Wherefore I beseech you, be ye followers of me. 17 For this cause have I sent unto you Timotheus, who is my beloved son, and faithful in the Lord, who shall bring you into remembrance of my ways which be in Christ, as I teach every where in every church. 18 Now some are puffed up, as though I would not come to you. 19 But I will come to you shortly, if the Lord will, and will know, not the speech of them which are puffed up, but the power. 20 For the kingdom of God *is* not in word, but in power. 21 What will ye? shall I come unto you with a rod, or in love, and *in* the spirit of meekness?

5 It is reported commonly *that there is* fornication among you, and such fornication as is not so much as named among the Gentiles, that one should have his father's wife. 2And ye are puffed up, and have not rather mourned, that he that hath done this deed might be taken away from among you. 3 For I verily, as absent in body, but present in spirit, have judged already, as though I were present, *concerning* him that hath so done this deed, 4 In the name of our Lord Jesus Christ, when ye are gathered together, and my spirit, with the power of our Lord Jesus Christ, 5 To deliver such a one unto Satan for the destruction of the flesh, that the spirit may be saved in the day of the Lord Jesus. 6 Your glorying *is* not good. Know ye not that a little leaven leaveneth the whole lump? 7 Purge out therefore the old leaven, that ye may be a new lump, as ye are unleavened. For even Christ our passover is sacrificed for us: 8 Therefore let us keep the feast, not with old leaven, neither with the leaven of malice and wickedness; but with the unleavened *bread* of sincerity and truth. 9 I wrote unto you in an epistle not to company with fornicators: 10 Yet not altogether with the fornicators of this world, or with the covetous, or extortioners, or with idolaters; for then must ye needs go out of the world. 11 But now I have written unto you not to keep company, if any man that is called a brother be a fornicator, or covetous, or an idolater, or a railer, or a drunkard, or an extortioner; with such a one no not to eat. 12 For what have I to do to judge them also that are without? do not ye judge them that are within? 13 But them that are without God judgeth. Therefore put away from among yourselves that wicked person.

6 Dare any of you, having a matter against another, go to law before the unjust, and not before the saints? 2 Do ye not know that the

R.S.V.

became your father in Christ Jesus through the gospel. 16 I urge you, then, be imitators of me. 17 Therefore I sent *g* to you Timothy, my beloved and faithful child in the Lord, to remind you of my ways in Christ, as I teach them everywhere in every church. 18 Some are arrogant, as though I were not coming to you. 19 But I will come to you soon, if the Lord wills, and I will find out not the talk of these arrogant people but their power. 20 For the kingdom of God does not consist in talk but in power. 21 What do you wish? Shall I come to you with a rod, or with love in a spirit of gentleness?

5 It is actually reported that there is immorality among you, and of a kind that is not found even among pagans; for a man is living with his father's wife. 2And you are arrogant! Ought you not rather to mourn? Let him who has done this be removed from among you.

3 For though absent in body I am present in spirit, and as if present, I have already pronounced judgment 4 in the name of the Lord Jesus on the man who has done such a thing. When you are assembled, with the power of our Lord Jesus, 5 you are to deliver this man to Satan for the destruction of the flesh, that his spirit may be saved in the day of the Lord Jesus.ʰ

6 Your boasting is not good. Do you not know that a little leaven leavens the whole lump? 7 Cleanse out the old leaven that you may be a new lump, as you really are unleavened. For Christ, our paschal lamb, has been sacrificed. 8 Let us, therefore, celebrate the festival, not with the old leaven, the leaven of malice and evil, but with the unleavened bread of sincerity and truth.

9 I wrote to you in my letter not to associate with immoral men; 10 not at all meaning the immoral of this world, or the greedy and robbers, or idolaters, since then you would need to go out of the world. 11 But rather I wroteⁱ to you not to associate with any one who bears the name of brother if he is guilty of immorality or greed, or is an idolater, reviler, drunkard, or robber—not even to eat with such a one. 12 For what have I to do with judging outsiders? Is it not those inside the church whom you are to judge? 13 God judges those outside. "Drive out the wicked person from among you."

6 When one of you has a grievance against a brother, does he dare go to law before the unrighteous instead of the saints? 2 Do you not

[g] Or *am sending.* [h] Other ancient authorities omit *Jesus.* [i] Or *now I write.*

PHILLIPS

N.E.B.

Jesus I am your spiritual father through the gospel; that is why I implore you to follow the footsteps of me your father. I have sent Timothy to you to help you in this. For he himself is my much-loved and faithful son in the Lord, and he will remind you of those ways of living in Christ which I teach in every church to which I go.

Some of you have apparently grown conceited enough to think that I should not visit you. But please God it will not be long before I do come to you in person. Then I shall be able to see what power, apart from their words, these pretentious ones among you really possess. For the kingdom of God is not a matter of a spate of words but of the power of Christian living.

Now it's up to you to choose! Shall I come to you ready to chastise you, or in love and gentleness?

Christ Jesus you are my offspring, and mine alone, through the preaching of the Gospel. I appeal to you therefore to follow my example. That is the very reason why I have sent Timothy, who is a dear son to me and a most trustworthy Christian; he will remind you of the way of life in Christ which I follow, and which I teach everywhere in all our congregations. There are certain persons who are filled with self-importance because they think I am not coming to Corinth. I shall come very soon, if the Lord will; and then I shall take the measure of these self-important people, not by what they say, but by what power is in them. The kingdom of God is not a matter of talk, but of power. Choose, then: am I to come to you with a rod in my hand, or in love and a gentle spirit?

A horrible sin and a stern remedy 5. 1

It is actually reported that there is sexual immorality among you, and immorality of a kind that even pagans condemn—a man has apparently taken his father's wife! Are you still proud of your church? Shouldn't you be overwhelmed with sorrow and shame? The man who has done such a thing should certainly be expelled from your fellowship!

I know I am not with you physically but I am with you in spirit, and I assure you as solemnly as if I were actually present before your assembly that I have already pronounced judgment in the name of the Lord Jesus on the man who has done this thing, and I do this with full divine authority. My judgment is this: that the man should be left to the mercy of Satan so that while his body will experience the destructive powers of sin his spirit may yet be saved in the day of the Lord Jesus.

Your pride in your church is lamentably out of place. Don't you know how a little yeast can permeate the whole lump? Clear out every bit of the old yeast that you may be new unleavened bread! We Christians have had a Passover Lamb sacrificed for us—none other than Christ himself! So let us "keep the feast" with no trace of the yeast of the old life, nor the yeast of vice and wickedness, but with the unleavened bread of unadulterated truth!

In my previous letter I said, "Don't mix with the immoral." I didn't mean, of course, that you were to have no contact at all with the immoral of this world, nor with any cheats or thieves or idolaters—for that would mean going out of the world altogether! But in this letter I tell you not to associate with any professing Christian who is known to be an impure man or a swindler, an idolater, a man with a foul tongue, a drunkard or a thief. My instruction is: "Don't even eat with such a man." Those outside the church it is not my business to judge. But surely it is your business to judge those who are inside the church—God alone can judge those who are outside. It is your plain duty to expel from your church this wicked man!

I actually hear reports of sexual immorality **5** among you, immorality such as even pagans do not tolerate: the union of a man with his father's wife. And you can still be proud of yourselves! You ought to have gone into mourning; a man who has done such a deed should have been rooted out of your company. For my part, though I am absent in body, I am present in spirit, and my judgement upon the man who did this thing is already given, as if I were indeed present: you all being assembled in the name of our Lord Jesus, and I with you in spirit, with the power of our Lord Jesus over us, this man is to be consigned to Satan for the destruction of the body, so that his spirit may be saved on the Day of the Lord.

Your self-satisfaction ill becomes you. Have you never heard the saying, 'A little leaven leavens all the dough'? The old leaven of corruption is working among you. Purge it out, and then you will be bread of a new baking, as it were unleavened Passover bread. For indeed our Passover has begun; the sacrifice is offered—Christ himself! So we who observe the festival must not use the old leaven, the leaven of corruption and wickedness, but only the unleavened bread which is sincerity and truth.

In my letter I wrote that you must have nothing to do with loose livers. I was not, of course, referring to pagans who lead loose lives or are grabbers and swindlers or idolaters. To avoid them you would have to get right out of the world. I now write that you must have nothing to do with any so-called Christian who leads a loose life, or is grasping, or idolatrous, a slanderer, a drunkard, or a swindler. You should not even eat with any such person. What business of mine is it to judge outsiders? God is their judge. You are judges within the fellowship. Root out the evil-doer from your community.

Don't go to law in pagan courts 6. 1

When any of you has a grievance against another, aren't you ashamed to bring the matter to be settled before a pagan court instead of before the church? Don't you know that Chris-

If one of your number has a dispute with **6** another, has he the face to take it to pagan law-courts instead of to the community of God's people? It is God's people who are to judge the

K.J.V.

saints shall judge the world? and if the world shall be judged by you, are ye unworthy to judge the smallest matters? 3 Know ye not that we shall judge angels? how much more things that pertain to this life? 4 If then ye have judgments of things pertaining to this life, set them to judge who are least esteemed in the church. 5 I speak to your shame. Is it so, that there is not a wise man among you? no, not one that shall be able to judge between his brethren? 6 But brother goeth to law with brother, and that before the unbelievers. 7 Now therefore there is utterly a fault among you, because ye go to law one with another. Why do ye not rather take wrong? Why do ye not rather *suffer yourselves to* be defrauded? 8 Nay, ye do wrong, and defraud, and that *your* brethren. 9 Know ye not that the unrighteous shall not inherit the kingdom of God? Be not deceived: neither fornicators, nor idolaters, nor adulterers, nor effeminate, nor abusers of themselves with mankind, 10 Nor thieves, nor covetous, nor drunkards, nor revilers, nor extortioners, shall inherit the kingdom of God. 11 And such were some of you: but ye are washed, but ye are sanctified, but ye are justified in the name of the Lord Jesus, and by the Spirit of our God. 12 All things are lawful unto me, but all things are not expedient: all things are lawful for me, but I will not be brought under the power of any. 13 Meats for the belly, and the belly for meats: but God shall destroy both it and them. Now the body *is* not for fornication, but for the Lord; and the Lord for the body. 14 And God hath both raised up the Lord, and will also raise up us by his own power. 15 Know ye not that your bodies are the members of Christ? shall I then take the members of Christ, and make *them* the members of a harlot? God forbid. 16 What! know ye not that he which is joined to a harlot is one body? for two, saith he, shall be one flesh. 17 But he that is joined unto the Lord is one spirit. 18 Flee fornication. Every sin that a man doeth is without the body; but he that committeth fornication sinneth against his own body. 19 What! know ye not that your body is the temple of the Holy Ghost *which is* in you, which ye have of God, and ye are not your own? 20 For ye are bought with a price: therefore glorify God in your body, and in your spirit, which are God's.

R.S.V.

know that the saints will judge the world? And if the world is to be judged by you, are you incompetent to try trivial cases? 3 Do you not know that we are to judge angels? How much more, matters pertaining to this life! 4 If then you have such cases, why do you lay them before those who are least esteemed by the church? 5 I say this to your shame. Can it be that there is no man among you wise enough to decide between members of the brotherhood, 6 but brother goes to law against brother, and that before unbelievers?

7 To have lawsuits at all with one another is defeat for you. Why not rather suffer wrong? Why not rather be defrauded? 8 But you yourselves wrong and defraud, and that even your own brethren.

9 Do you not know that the unrighteous will not inherit the kingdom of God? Do not be deceived; neither the immoral, nor idolaters, nor adulterers, nor homosexuals,*j* 10 nor thieves, nor the greedy, nor drunkards, nor revilers, nor robbers will inherit the kingdom of God. 11 And such were some of you. But you were washed, you were sanctified, you were justified in the name of the Lord Jesus Christ and in the Spirit of our God.

12 "All things are lawful for me," but not all things are helpful. "All things are lawful for me," but I will not be enslaved by anything. 13 "Food is meant for the stomach and the stomach for food"—and God will destroy both one and the other. The body is not meant for immorality, but for the Lord, and the Lord for the body. 14 And God raised the Lord and will also raise us up by his power. 15 Do you not know that your bodies are members of Christ? Shall I therefore take the members of Christ and make them members of a prostitute? Never! 16 Do you not know that he who joins himself to a prostitute becomes one body with her? For, as it is written, "The two shall become one."*k* 17 But he who is united to the Lord becomes one spirit with him. 18 Shun immorality. Every other sin which a man commits is outside the body; but the immoral man sins against his own body. 19 Do you not know that your body is a temple of the Holy Spirit within you, which you have from God? You are not your own; 20 you were bought with a price. So glorify God in your body.

[*j*] Two Greek words are rendered by this expression. [*k*] Greek *one flesh.*

PHILLIPS

tians will one day judge the world? And if you are to judge the world do you consider yourselves incapable of settling such infinitely smaller matters? Don't you also know that we shall judge the very angels themselves—how much more then matters of this world only! In any case, if you find you have to judge matters of this world, why choose as judges those who count for nothing in the church? I say this deliberately to rouse your sense of shame. Are you really unable to find among your number one man with enough sense to decide a dispute between one and another of you, or must one brother resort to the law against another and that before those who have no faith in Christ? It is surely obvious that something must be seriously wrong in your church for you to be having lawsuits at all. Why not *let* yourself be wronged or cheated? For when you go to law against your brother you yourself do him wrong, for you cheat him of Christian love and forgiveness.

Have you forgotten that the kingdom of God will never belong to the wicked? Don't be under any illusion—neither the impure, the idolater or the adulterer; neither the effeminate, the pervert or the thief; neither the swindler, the drunkard, the foul-mouthed or the rapacious shall have any share in the kingdom of God. *And such men, remember, were some of you!* But you have cleansed yourselves from all that; you have been made whole in spirit; you have been justified in the name of the Lord Jesus and in the very Spirit of our God.

Christian liberty does not mean moral license   6. 12

As a Christian I *may* do anything, but that does not mean that everything is good for me to do. I may do everything, but I must not be the slave of anything. Food was meant for the stomach and the stomach for food; but God has no permanent purpose for either. But you cannot say that our physical body was made for sexual promiscuity; it was made for God, and God is the answer to our deepest longings. The God who raised the Lord from the dead will also raise us mortal men by his power. Have you realized the almost incredible fact that your bodies are integral parts of Christ himself? Am I then to take parts of Christ and join them to a prostitute? Never! Don't you realize that when a man joins himself to a prostitute he makes with her a physical unity? For, God says, "the two shall be one flesh." On the other hand the man who joins himself to the Lord is one with him in spirit.

Avoid sexual looseness like the plague! Every other sin that a man commits is done outside his own body, but this is an offense against his own body. Have you forgotten that your body is the temple of the Holy Spirit, who lives in you, and is God's gift to you, and that you are not the owner of your own body? You have been bought, and at what a price! Therefore bring glory to God in your body.

N.E.B.

world; surely you know that. And if the world is to come before you for judgement, are you incompetent to deal with these trifling cases? Are you not aware that we are to judge angels? How much more, mere matters of business! If therefore you have such business disputes, how can you entrust jurisdiction to outsiders, men who count for nothing in our community? I write this to shame you. Can it be that there is not a single wise man among you able to give a decision in a brother-Christian's cause? Must brother go to law with brother—and before unbelievers? Indeed, you already fall below your standard in going to law with one another at all. Why not rather suffer injury? Why not rather let yourself be robbed? So far from this, you actually injure and rob—injure and rob your brothers! Surely you know that the unjust will never come into possession of the kingdom of God. Make no mistake: no fornicator or idolater, none who are guilty either of adultery or of homosexual perversion, no thieves or grabbers or drunkards or slanderers or swindlers, will possess the kingdom of God. Such were some of you. But you have been through the purifying waters; you have been dedicated to God and justified through the name of the Lord Jesus and the Spirit of our God.

'I am free to do anything', you say. Yes, but not everything is for my good. No doubt I am free to do anything, but I for one will not let anything make free with me. 'Food is for the belly and the belly for food', you say. True; and one day God will put an end to both. But it is not true that the body is for lust; it is for the Lord—and the Lord for the body. God not only raised our Lord from the dead; he will also raise us by his power. Do you not know that your bodies are limbs and organs of Christ? Shall I then take from Christ his bodily parts and make them over to a harlot? Never! You surely know that anyone who links himself with a harlot becomes physically one with her (for Scripture says, 'The pair shall become one flesh'); but he who links himself with Christ is one with him, spiritually. Shun fornication. Every other sin that a man can commit is outside the body; but the fornicator sins against his own body. Do you not know that your body is a shrine of the indwelling Holy Spirit, and the Spirit is God's gift to you? You do not belong to yourselves; you were bought at a price. Then honour God in your body.

7 Now concerning the things whereof ye wrote unto me: *It is* good for a man not to touch a woman. 2 Nevertheless, *to avoid* fornication, let every man have his own wife, and let every woman have her own husband. 3 Let the husband render unto the wife due benevolence: and likewise also the wife unto the husband. 4 The wife hath not power of her own body, but the husband: and likewise also the husband hath not power of his own body, but the wife. 5 Defraud ye not one the other, except *it be* with consent for a time, that ye may give yourselves to fasting and prayer; and come together again, that Satan tempt you not for your incontinency. 6 But I speak this by permission, *and* not of commandment. 7 For I would that all men were even as I myself. But every man hath his proper gift of God, one after this manner, and another after that. 8 I say therefore to the unmarried and widows, It is good for them if they abide even as I. 9 But if they cannot contain, let them marry: for it is better to marry than to burn. 10 And unto the married I command, *yet* not I, but the Lord, Let not the wife depart from *her* husband: 11 But and if she depart, let her remain unmarried, or be reconciled to *her* husband: and let not the husband put away *his* wife. 12 But to the rest speak I, not the Lord: If any brother hath a wife that believeth not, and she be pleased to dwell with him, let him not put her away. 13 And the woman which hath a husband that believeth not, and if he be pleased to dwell with her, let her not leave him. 14 For the unbelieving husband is sanctified by the wife, and the unbelieving wife is sanctified by the husband: else were your children unclean; but now are they holy. 15 But if the unbelieving depart, let him depart. A brother or a sister is not under bondage in such *cases:* but God hath called us to peace. 16 For what knowest thou, O wife, whether thou shalt save *thy* husband? or how knowest thou, O man, whether thou shalt save *thy* wife? 17 But as God hath distributed to every man, as the Lord hath called every one, so let him walk. And so ordain I in all churches. 18 Is any man called being circumcised? let him not become uncircumcised. Is any called in uncircumcision? let him not be circumcised. 19 Circumcision is nothing, and uncircum-

7 Now concerning the matters about which you wrote. It is well for a man not to touch a woman. 2 But because of the temptation to immorality, each man should have his own wife and each woman her own husband. 3 The husband should give to his wife her conjugal rights, and likewise the wife to her husband. 4 For the wife does not rule over her own body, but the husband does; likewise the husband does not rule over his own body, but the wife does. 5 Do not refuse one another except perhaps by agreement for a season, that you may devote yourselves to prayer; but then come together again, lest Satan tempt you through lack of self-control. 6 I say this by way of concession, not of command. 7 I wish that all were as I myself am. But each has his own special gift from God, one of one kind and one of another.

8 To the unmarried and the widows I say that it is well for them to remain single as I do. 9 But if they cannot exercise self-control, they should marry. For it is better to marry than to be aflame with passion.

10 To the married I give charge, not I but the Lord, that the wife should not separate from her husband 11 (but if she does, let her remain single or else be reconciled to her husband)—and that the husband should not divorce his wife.

12 To the rest I say, not the Lord, that if any brother has a wife who is an unbeliever, and she consents to live with him, he should not divorce her. 13 If any woman has a husband who is an unbeliever, and he consents to live with her, she should not divorce him. 14 For the unbelieving husband is consecrated through his wife, and the unbelieving wife is consecrated through her husband. Otherwise, your children would be unclean, but as it is they are holy. 15 But if the unbelieving partner desires to separate, let it be so; in such a case the brother or sister is not bound. For God has called us[1] to peace. 16 Wife, how do you know whether you will save your husband? Husband, how do you know whether you will save your wife?

17 Only, let every one lead the life which the Lord has assigned to him, and in which God has called him. This is my rule in all the churches. 18 Was any one at the time of his call already circumcised? Let him not seek to remove the marks of circumcision. Was any one at the time of his call uncircumcised? Let him not seek circumcision. 19 For neither circumcision counts

PHILLIPS

N.E.B.

The question of marriage   **7. 1**
in present circumstances

The Christian in a Pagan Society

Now let me deal with the questions raised in your letter.

It is a good principle for a man to have no physical contact with women. Nevertheless, because casual liaisons are so prevalent, let every man have his own wife and every woman her own husband. The husband should give his wife what is due to her as his wife, and the wife should be as fair to her husband. The wife has no longer full rights over her own person, but shares them with her husband. In the same way the husband shares his personal rights with his wife. Do not cheat each other of normal sexual intercourse, unless of course you both decide to abstain temporarily to make special opportunity for fasting and prayer. But afterward you should resume relations as before, or you will expose yourselves to the obvious temptation of the devil.

I give the advice above more as a concession than as a command. I wish that all men were like myself, but I realize that everyone has his own particular gift from God, some one thing and some another. Yet to those who are unmarried or widowed I say definitely that it is a good thing to remain unattached, as I am. But if they find they have not the gift of self-control in such matters, by all means let them get married. I think it is far better for them to be married than to be tortured by unsatisfied desire.

To those who are already married my command, or rather, the Lord's command, is that the wife should not leave her husband. But if she is separated from him she should either remain unattached or else be reconciled to her husband. A husband is not, in similar circumstances, to divorce his wife.

Advice over marriage between   **7. 12**
Christian and pagan

To other people my advice (though this is not a divine command) is this. For a brother who has a non-Christian wife who is willing to live with him he should not divorce her. A wife in a similar position should not divorce her husband. For the unbelieving husband is, in a sense, consecrated by being joined to the person of his wife; the unbelieving wife is similarly "consecrated" by the Christian brother she has married. If this were not so then your children would bear the stains of paganism, whereas they are actually consecrated to God.

But if the unbelieving partner decides to separate, then let there be a separation. The Christian partner need not consider himself bound in such cases. Yet God has called us to live in peace, and after all how can you, who are a wife, know whether you will be able to save your husband or not? And the same applies to you who are a husband.

I merely add to the above that each man should live his life with the gifts that God has given him and in the condition in which God has called him. This is the rule I lay down in all the churches.

For example, if a man was circumcised when God called him he should not attempt to remove the signs of his circumcision. If on the other hand he was uncircumcised he should not become circumcised. Being circumcised or not being circumcised, what do they matter?

7 And now for the matters you wrote about. It is a good thing for a man to have nothing to do with women;[a] but because there is so much immorality, let each man have his own wife and each woman her own husband. The husband must give the wife what is due to her, and the wife equally must give the husband his due. The wife cannot claim her body as her own; it is her husband's. Equally, the husband cannot claim his body as his own; it is his wife's. Do not deny yourselves to one another, except when you agree upon a temporary abstinence in order to devote yourselves to prayer; afterwards you may come together again; otherwise, for lack of self-control, you may be tempted by Satan.

All this I say by way of concession, not command. I should like you all to be as I am myself; but everyone has the gift God has granted him, one this gift and another that.

To the unmarried and to widows I say this: it is a good thing if they stay as I am myself; but if they cannot control themselves, they should marry. Better be married than burn with vain desire.

To the married I give this ruling, which is not mine but the Lord's: a wife must not separate herself from her husband; if she does, she must either remain unmarried or be reconciled to her husband; and the husband must not divorce his wife.

To the rest I say this, as my own word, not as the Lord's: if a Christian has a heathen wife, and she is willing to live with him, he must not divorce her; and a woman who has a heathen husband willing to live with her must not divorce her husband. For the heathen husband now belongs to God through his Christian wife, and the heathen wife through her Christian husband. Otherwise your children would not belong to God, whereas in fact they do. If on the other hand the heathen partner wishes for a separation, let him have it. In such cases the Christian husband or wife is under no compulsion; but God's call is a call to live in peace. Think of it: as a wife you may be your husband's salvation; as a husband you may be your wife's salvation.

However that may be, each one must order his life according to the gift the Lord has granted him and his condition when God called him. That is what I teach in all our congregations. Was a man called with the marks of circumcision on him? Let him not remove them. Was he uncircumcised when he was called? Let him not be circumcised. Circumcision or uncircumcision is neither here nor there; what

[a] *Or* You say, 'It is a good thing . . . women'; . . .

515

K.J.V.

cision is nothing, but the keeping of the commandments of God. 20 Let every man abide in the same calling wherein he was called. 21Art thou called *being* a servant? care not for it: but if thou mayest be made free, use *it* rather. 22 For he that is called in the Lord, *being* a servant, is the Lord's freeman: likewise also he that is called, *being* free, is Christ's servant. 23 Ye are bought with a price; be not ye the servants of men. 24 Brethren, let every man, wherein he is called, therein abide with God. 25 Now concerning virgins I have no commandment of the Lord: yet I give my judgment, as one that hath obtained mercy of the Lord to be faithful. 26 I suppose therefore that this is good for the present distress, *I say,* that *it is* good for a man so to be. 27Art thou bound unto a wife? seek not to be loosed. Art thou loosed from a wife? seek not a wife. 28 But and if thou marry, thou hast not sinned; and if a virgin marry, she hath not sinned. Nevertheless such shall have trouble in the flesh: but I spare you. 29 But this I say, brethren, the time *is* short: it remaineth, that both they that have wives be as though they had none; 30And they that weep, as though they wept not; and they that rejoice, as though they rejoiced not; and they that buy, as though they possessed not; 31And they that use this world, as not abusing *it:* for the fashion of this world passeth away. 32 But I would have you without carefulness. He that is unmarried careth for the things that belong to the Lord, how he may please the Lord: 33 But he that is married careth for the things that are of the world, how he may please *his* wife. 34 There is difference *also* between a wife and a virgin. The unmarried woman careth for the things of the Lord, that she may be holy both in body and in spirit: but she that is married careth for the things of the world, how she may please *her* husband. 35And this I speak for your own profit; not that I may cast a snare upon you, but for that which is comely, and that ye may attend upon the Lord without distraction. 36 But if any man think that he behaveth himself uncomely toward his virgin, if she pass the flower of *her* age, and need so require, let him do what he will, he sinneth not: let them marry. 37 Nevertheless he that standeth steadfast in his heart, having no necessity, but hath power over his own will, and hath so de-

R.S.V.

for anything nor uncircumcision, but keeping the commandments of God. 20 Every one should remain in the state in which he was called. 21 Were you a slave when called? Never mind. But if you can gain your freedom, avail yourself of the opportunity.[x] 22 For he who was called in the Lord as a slave is a freedman of the Lord. Likewise he who was free when called is a slave of Christ. 23 You were bought with a price; do not become slaves of men. 24 So, brethren, in whatever state each was called, there let him remain with God.

25 Now concerning the unmarried, I have no command of the Lord, but I give my opinion as one who by the Lord's mercy is trustworthy. 26 I think that in view of the impending[m] distress it is well for a person to remain as he is. 27Are you bound to a wife? Do not seek to be free. Are you free from a wife? Do not seek marriage. 28 But if you marry, you do not sin, and if a girl marries she does not sin. Yet those who marry will have worldly troubles, and I would spare you that. 29 I mean, brethren, the appointed time has grown very short; from now on, let those who have wives live as though they had none, 30 and those who mourn as though they were not mourning, and those who rejoice as though they were not rejoicing, and those who buy as though they had no goods, 31 and those who deal with the world as though they had no dealings with it. For the form of this world is passing away.

32 I want you to be free from anxieties. The unmarried man is anxious about the affairs of the Lord, how to please the Lord; 33 but the married man is anxious about worldly affairs, how to please his wife, 34 and his interests are divided. And the unmarried woman or girl is anxious about the affairs of the Lord, how to be holy in body and spirit; but the married woman is anxious about worldly affairs, how to please her husband. 35 I say this for your own benefit, not to lay any restraint upon you, but to promote good order and to secure your undivided devotion to the Lord.

36 If any one thinks that he is not behaving properly toward his betrothed, if his passions are strong, and it has to be, let him do as he wishes: let them marry—it is no sin. 37 But whoever is firmly established in his heart, being under no necessity but having his desire under

[x] Or *make use of your present condition instead.*
[m] Or *present.*

PHILLIPS

The great thing is to obey the orders of God. Everyone should stick to the calling in which he heard the call of God. Were you a slave when you heard the call? Don't let that worry you, though if you find the opportunity to become free you had better take it. But a slave who is called to life in Christ is set free in the eyes of the Lord. And a man who was free when God called him becomes a slave—to Christ himself! You have been redeemed, at tremendous cost; don't therefore sell yourselves as slaves to men! My brothers, let every one of us continue to live his life with God in the state in which he was when he was called.

In present circumstances it is really better not to marry

7. 25

Now as far as young unmarried women are concerned, I must confess that I have no direct commands from the Lord. Nevertheless, I give you my considered opinion as of one who is, I think, to be trusted after all his experience of God's mercy.

My opinion is this, that amid all the difficulties of the present time you would do best to remain just as you are. Are you married? Well, don't try to be separated. Are you unattached? Then don't try to get married. But if you, a man, should marry, don't think that you have done anything sinful. And the same applies to a young woman. Yet I do believe that those who take this step are bound to find the married state an extra burden in these critical days, and I should like you to be as unencumbered as possible. All our futures are so foreshortened, indeed, that those who have wives should live, so to speak, as though they had none! There is no time to indulge in sorrow, no time for enjoying our joys; those who buy have no time to enjoy their possessions, and indeed their every contact with the world must be as light as possible, for the present scheme of things is rapidly passing away. That is why I should like you to be as free from worldly entanglements as possible. The unmarried man is free to concern himself with the Lord's affairs, and how he may please him. But the married man is sure to be concerned also with matters of this world, that he may please his wife—his interests are divided. You find the same difference in the case of the unmarried and the married woman. The unmarried concerns herself with the Lord's affairs, and her aim in life is to make herself holy, in body and in spirit. But the married woman must concern herself with the things of this world, and her aim will be to please her husband.

I tell you these things to help you; I am not putting difficulties in your path but setting before you an ideal, so that your service of God may be as far as possible free from worldly distractions.

But marriage is not wrong

7. 36

But if any man feels he is not behaving honorably toward the woman he loves, especially as she is beginning to lose her first youth and the emotional strain is considerable, let him do what his heart tells him to do—let them be married; there is no sin in that. Yet for the man of steadfast purpose who is able to bear the strain and has his own desires well under con-

N.E.B.

matters is to keep God's commands. Every man should remain in the condition in which he was called. Were you a slave when you were called? Do not let that trouble you; but if a chance of liberty should come, take it.[a] For the man who as a slave received the call to be a Christian is the Lord's freedman, and, equally, the free man who received the call is a slave in the service of Christ. You were bought at a price; do not become slaves of men. Thus each one, my friends, is to remain before God in the condition in which he received his call.

On the question of celibacy, I have no instructions from the Lord, but I give my judgement as one who by God's mercy is fit to be trusted.

It is my opinion, then, that in a time of stress like the present this is the best way for a man to live—it is best for a man to be as he is. Are you bound in marriage? Do not seek a dissolution. Has your marriage been dissolved? Do not seek a wife. If, however, you do marry, there is nothing wrong in it; and if a virgin marries, she has done no wrong. But those who marry will have pain and grief in this bodily life, and my aim is to spare you.

What I mean, my friends, is this. The time we live in will not last long. While it lasts, married men should be as if they had no wives; mourners should be as if they had nothing to grieve them, the joyful as if they did not rejoice; buyers must not count on keeping what they buy, nor those who use the world's wealth on using it to the full. For the whole frame of this world is passing away.

I want you to be free from anxious care. The unmarried man cares for the Lord's business; his aim is to please the Lord. But the married man cares for worldly things; his aim is to please his wife; and he has a divided mind. The unmarried or celibate woman cares[b] for the Lord's business; her aim is to be dedicated to him in body as in spirit; but the married woman cares for worldly things; her aim is to please her husband.

In saying this I have no wish to keep you on a tight rein. I am thinking simply of your own good, of what is seemly, and of your freedom to wait upon the Lord without distraction.

But if a man has a partner in celibacy[c] and feels that he is not behaving properly towards her, if, that is, his instincts are too strong for him,[d] and something must be done, he may do as he pleases; there is nothing wrong in it; let them marry.[e] But if a man is steadfast in his purpose, being under no compulsion, and has

[a] Or but even if a chance of liberty should come, choose rather to make good use of your servitude. [b] Some witnesses read . . . his wife. And there is a difference between the wife and the virgin. The unmarried woman cares . . . [c] Or a virgin daughter (or ward). [d] Or if she is ripe for marriage. [e] Or let the girl and her lover marry.

K.J.V.

creed in his heart that he will keep his virgin,
doeth well. 38 So then he that giveth *her* in marriage doeth well; but he that giveth *her* not in
marriage doeth better. 39 The wife is bound by
the law as long as her husband liveth; but if her
husband be dead, she is at liberty to be married
to whom she will; only in the Lord. 40 But she
is happier if she so abide, after my judgment:
and I think also that I have the Spirit of God.

8 Now as touching things offered unto idols,
we know that we all have knowledge. Knowledge puffeth up, but charity edifieth. 2And if
any man think that he knoweth any thing, he
knoweth nothing yet as he ought to know. 3 But
if any man love God, the same is known of him.
4As concerning therefore the eating of those
things that are offered in sacrifice unto idols,
we know that an idol *is* nothing in the world,
and that *there is* none other God but one. 5 For
though there be that are called gods, whether
in heaven or in earth, (as there be gods many,
and lords many,) 6 But to us *there is but* one
God, the Father, of whom *are* all things, and
we in him; and one Lord Jesus Christ, by whom
are all things, and we by him. 7 Howbeit *there
is* not in every man that knowledge: for some
with conscience of the idol unto this hour eat
it as a thing offered unto an idol; and their conscience being weak is defiled. 8 But meat commendeth us not to God: for neither, if we eat,
are we the better; neither, if we eat not, are we
the worse. 9 But take heed lest by any means
this liberty of yours become a stumblingblock
to them that are weak. 10 For if any man see
thee which hast knowledge sit at meat in the
idol's temple, shall not the conscience of him
which is weak be emboldened to eat those things
which are offered to idols; 11And through thy
knowledge shall the weak brother perish, for
whom Christ died? 12 But when ye sin so against
the brethren, and wound their weak conscience,
ye sin against Christ. 13 Wherefore, if meat make
my brother to offend, I will eat no flesh while
the world standeth, lest I make my brother to
offend.

9 Am I not an apostle? am I not free? have I
not seen Jesus Christ our Lord? are not ye
my work in the Lord? 2 If I be not an apostle

R.S.V.

control, and has determined this in his heart, to
keep her as his betrothed, he will do well. 38 So
that he who marries his betrothed does well; and
he who refrains from marriage will do better.

39 A wife is bound to her husband as long
as he lives. If the husband dies, she is free to
be married to whom she wishes, only in the
Lord. 40 But in my judgment she is happier if
she remains as she is. And I think that I have
the Spirit of God.

8 Now concerning food offered to idols: we
know that "all of us possess knowledge."
"Knowledge" puffs up, but love builds up.
2 If any one imagines that he knows something,
he does not yet know as he ought to know.
3 But if one loves God, one is known by him.
4 Hence, as to the eating of food offered to
idols, we know that "an idol has no real existence," and that "there is no God but one." 5 For
although there may be so-called gods in heaven
or on earth—as indeed there are many "gods"
and many "lords"—6 yet for us there is one
God, the Father, from whom are all things and
for whom we exist, and one Lord, Jesus Christ,
through whom are all things and through whom
we exist.

7 However, not all possess this knowledge.
But some, through being hitherto accustomed to
idols, eat food as really offered to an idol; and
their conscience, being weak, is defiled. 8 Food
will not commend us to God. We are no worse
off if we do not eat, and no better off if we do.
9 Only take care lest this liberty of yours somehow become a stumbling block to the weak.
10 For if any one sees you, a man of knowledge,
at table in an idol's temple, might he not be
encouraged, if his conscience is weak, to eat
food offered to idols? 11And so by your knowledge this weak man is destroyed, the brother
for whom Christ died. 12 Thus, sinning against
your brethren and wounding their conscience
when it is weak, you sin against Christ. 13 Therefore, if food is a cause of my brother's falling,
I will never eat meat, lest I cause my brother to
fall.

9 Am I not free? Am I not an apostle? Have
I not seen Jesus our Lord? Are not you my
workmanship in the Lord? 2 If to others I am

trol, if he decides not to marry the young woman, he too will be doing the right thing. Both of them are right, one in marrying and the other in refraining from marriage, but the latter has chosen the better of two right courses.

A woman is bound to her husband while he is alive, but if he dies she is free to marry whom she likes—but let her be guided by the Lord. In my opinion she would be happier to remain as she is, unmarried. And I think I am here expressing not only my opinion, but the will of the Spirit as well.

A practical problem: shall we be guided by superior knowledge or love? 8. 1

Now to deal with the matter of meat which has been sacrificed to idols. It is easy to think that we "know" over problems like this, but we should remember that while knowledge may make a man look big, it is only love that can make him grow to his full stature. For whatever a man may know, he still has a lot to learn; but if he loves God, he is opening his whole life to the Spirit of God.

In this matter, then, of eating meat which has been offered to idols, knowledge tells us that no idol has any real existence, and that there is no God but one. For though there are so-called gods both in heaven and in earth, gods and lords galore in fact, to us there is only one God, the Father, from whom everything comes, and for whom we live. And there is one Lord Jesus Christ, by whom everything exists, and by whom we ourselves are alive. But this knowledge of ours is not shared by all men. For some, who until now have been used to idols, eat the meat as meat really sacrificed to a god, and their delicate conscience is thereby injured. Now our acceptance by God is not a matter of meat. If we eat it, that does not make us better men, nor are we the worse if we do not eat it. You must be careful that your freedom to eat meat does not in any way hinder anyone whose faith is not as robust as yours. For suppose you with your knowledge of God should be observed eating meat in an idol's temple, are you not encouraging the man with a delicate conscience to do the same? Surely you would not want your superior knowledge to bring spiritual disaster to a weaker brother for whom Christ died? And when you sin like this and damage the weak consciences of your brethren you really sin against Christ. This makes me determined that, if there is any possibility of meat injuring my brother, I will have none of it as long as I live, for fear I might do him harm.

A word of personal defense to my critics 9. 1

Is there any doubt that I am a genuine messenger, any doubt that I am a free man? Have I not seen Jesus our Lord with my own eyes? Are not you yourselves samples of my work for the Lord? Even if other people should refuse

complete control of his own choice; and if he has decided in his own mind to preserve his partner[a] in her virginity, he will do well. Thus, he who marries his partner[b] does well, and he who does not will do better.

A wife is bound to her husband as long as he lives. But if the husband die, she is free to marry whom she will, provided the marriage is within the Lord's fellowship. But she is better off as she is; that is my opinion, and I believe that I too have the Spirit of God.

8 Now about food consecrated to heathen deities.

Of course we all 'have knowledge', as you say. This 'knowledge' breeds conceit; it is love that builds. If anyone fancies that he knows, he knows nothing yet, in the true sense of knowing. But if a man loves,[c] he is acknowledged by God.[d]

Well then, about eating this consecrated food: of course, as you say, 'a false god has no existence in the real world. There is no god but one.' For indeed, if there be so-called gods, whether in heaven or on earth—as indeed there are many 'gods' and many 'lords'—yet for us there is one God, the Father, from whom all being comes, towards whom we move; and there is one Lord, Jesus Christ, through whom all things came to be, and we through him.

But not everyone knows this. There are some who have been so accustomed to idolatry[e] that even now they eat this food with a sense of its heathen consecration, and their conscience, being weak, is polluted by the eating. Certainly food will not bring us into God's presence: if we do not eat, we are none the worse, and if we eat, we are none the better. But be careful that this liberty of yours does not become a pitfall for the weak. If a weak character sees you sitting down to a meal in a heathen temple—you, who 'have knowledge'—will not his conscience be emboldened to eat food consecrated to the heathen deity? This 'knowledge' of yours is utter disaster to the weak, the brother for whom Christ died. In thus sinning against your brothers and wounding their conscience,[f] you sin against Christ. And therefore, if food be the downfall of my brother, I will never eat meat any more, for I will not be the cause of my brother's downfall.

9 Am I not a free man? Am I not an apostle? Did I not see Jesus our Lord? Are not you my own handiwork, in the Lord? If others do

[a] *Or* his daughter. [b] *Or* gives his daughter in marriage. [c] *Some witnesses read* loves God. [d] *Or* he is recognized. [e] *Some witnesses read* in whom the consciousness of the false god is so persistent . . . [f] *Some witnesses insert* weak as it is.

K.J.V.

unto others, yet doubtless I am to you: for the seal of mine apostleship are ye in the Lord. 3 Mine answer to them that do examine me is this: 4 Have we not power to eat and to drink? 5 Have we not power to lead about a sister, a wife, as well as other apostles, and *as* the brethren of the Lord, and Cephas? 6 Or I only and Barnabas, have not we power to forbear working? 7 Who goeth a warfare any time at his own charges? who planteth a vineyard, and eateth not of the fruit thereof? or who feedeth a flock, and eateth not of the milk of the flock? 8 Say I these things as a man? or saith not the law the same also? 9 For it is written in the law of Moses, Thou shalt not muzzle the mouth of the ox that treadeth out the corn. Doth God take care for oxen? 10 Or saith he *it* altogether for our sakes? For our sakes, no doubt, *this* is written: that he that plougheth should plough in hope; and that he that thresheth in hope should be partaker of his hope. 11 If we have sown unto you spiritual things, *is it* a great thing if we shall reap your carnal things? 12 If others be partakers of *this* power over you, *are* not we rather? Nevertheless we have not used this power; but suffer all things, lest we should hinder the gospel of Christ. 13 Do ye not know that they which minister about holy things live *of the things* of the temple? and they which wait at the altar are partakers with the altar? 14 Even so hath the Lord ordained that they which preach the gospel should live of the gospel. 15 But I have used none of these things: neither have I written these things, that it should be so done unto me: for *it were* better for me to die, than that any man should make my glorying void. 16 For though I preach the gospel, I have nothing to glory of: for necessity is laid upon me; yea, woe is unto me, if I preach not the gospel! 17 For if I do this thing willingly, I have a reward: but if against my will, a dispensation *of the gospel* is committed unto me. 18 What is my reward then? *Verily* that, when I preach the gos-

R.S.V.

not an apostle, at least I am to you; for you are the seal of my apostleship in the Lord. 3 This is my defense to those who would examine me. 4 Do we not have the right to our food and drink? 5 Do we not have the right to be accompanied by a wife,[n] as the other apostles and the brothers of the Lord and Cephas? 6 Or is it only Barnabas and I who have no right to refrain from working for a living? 7 Who serves as a soldier at his own expense? Who plants a vineyard without eating any of its fruit? Who tends a flock without getting some of the milk? 8 Do I say this on human authority? Does not the law say the same? 9 For it is written in the law of Moses, "You shall not muzzle an ox when it is treading out the grain." Is it for oxen that God is concerned? 10 Does he not speak entirely for our sake? It was written for our sake, because the plowman should plow in hope and the thresher thresh in hope of a share in the crop. 11 If we have sown spiritual good among you, is it too much if we reap your material benefits? 12 If others share this rightful claim upon you, do not we still more?

Nevertheless, we have not made use of this right, but we endure anything rather than put an obstacle in the way of the gospel of Christ. 13 Do you not know that those who are employed in the temple service get their food from the temple, and those who serve at the altar share in the sacrificial offerings? 14 In the same way, the Lord commanded that those who proclaim the gospel should get their living by the gospel.

15 But I have made no use of any of these rights, nor am I writing this to secure any such provision. For I would rather die than have any one deprive me of my ground for boasting. 16 For if I preach the gospel, that gives me no ground for boasting. For necessity is laid upon me. Woe to me if I do not preach the gospel! 17 For if I do this of my own will, I have a reward; but if not of my own will, I am entrusted with a commission. 18 What then is my reward? Just this: that in my preaching I may

---

[n] Greek *a sister as wife.*

to recognize my divine commission, yet to you at any rate I shall always be a true messenger, for you are a living proof of God's call to me. This is my real ground of defense to those who cross-examine me.

Aren't we allowed to eat and drink? May we not travel with a Christian wife like the other messengers, like other Christian brothers, and like Cephas? Are Barnabas and I the only ones not allowed to leave their ordinary work to give time to the ministry?

Even a preacher of the gospel has some rights! 9. 7

Just think for a moment. Does any soldier ever go to war at his own expense? Does any man plant a vineyard and have no share in its fruits? Does the shepherd who tends the flock never taste the milk? This is, I know, an argument from everyday life, but it is a principle endorsed by the Law. For is it not written in the Law of Moses:

Thou shalt not muzzle the ox when he treadeth out the corn?

Now does this imply merely God's care for oxen, or does it include his care for us too? Surely we are included! You might even say that the words were written for us. For both the plowman as he plows and the thresher as he threshes should have some hope of an ultimate share in the harvest. If we have sown for you the seed of spiritual things, need you be greatly perturbed because we reap some of your material things? And if there are others with the right to have these things from you, have not we an even greater right? Yet we have never exercised this right and have put up with all sorts of things, so that we might not hinder the spread of the gospel.

I am entitled to a reward, yet I have not taken it 9. 13

Are you ignorant of the fact that those who minister sacred things take part of the sacred food of the Temple for their own use, and those who attend the altar have their share of what is placed on the altar? On the same principle the Lord has ordered that those who proclaim the gospel should receive their livelihood from those who accept the gospel.

But I have never used any of these privileges, nor am I writing now to suggest that I should be given them. Indeed I would rather die than have anyone make this boast of mine an empty one!

My reward is to make the gospel free to all men 9. 16

For I take no special pride in the fact that I preach the gospel. I feel compelled to do so; I should be utterly miserable if I failed to preach it. If I do this work because I choose to do so then I am entitled to a reward. But if it is no choice of mine, but a sacred responsibility put upon me, what can I expect in the way of re-

not accept me as an apostle, you at least are bound to do so, for you are yourselves the very seal of my apostolate, in the Lord.

To those who put me in the dock this is my answer: Have I no right to eat and drink? Have I no right to take a Christian wife about with me, like the rest of the apostles and the Lord's brothers, and Cephas? Or are Barnabas and I alone bound to work for our living? Did you ever hear of a man serving in the army at his own expense? or planting a vineyard without eating the fruit of it? or tending a flock without using its milk? Do not suppose I rely on these human analogies; in the Law of Moses we read, 'A threshing ox shall not be muzzled.' Do you suppose God's concern is with oxen? Or is the reference clearly to ourselves? Of course it refers to us, in the sense that the ploughman should plough and the thresher thresh in the hope of getting some of the produce. If we have sown a spiritual crop for you, is it too much to expect from you a material harvest? If you allow others these rights, have not we a stronger claim?

But I have availed myself of no such right. On the contrary, I put up with all that comes my way rather than offer any hindrance to the gospel of Christ. You know (do you not?) that those who perform the temple service eat the temple offerings, and those who wait upon the altar claim their share of the sacrifice. In the same way the Lord gave instructions that those who preach the Gospel should earn their living by the Gospel. But I have never taken advantage of any such right, nor do I intend to claim it in this letter. I had rather die! No one shall make my boast an empty boast. Even if I preach the Gospel, I can claim no credit for it; I cannot help myself; it would be misery to me not to preach. If I did it of my own choice, I should be earning my pay; but since I do it apart from my own choice, I am simply discharging a trust.[a] Then what is my pay? The satisfaction of

[a] Or If I do it willingly I am earning my pay; if I did it unwillingly I should still have a trust laid upon me.

K.J.V.

pel, I may make the gospel of Christ without charge, that I abuse not my power in the gospel. 19 For though I be free from all *men*, yet have I made myself servant unto all, that I might gain the more. 20And unto the Jews I became as a Jew, that I might gain the Jews; to them that are under the law, as under the law, that I might gain them that are under the law; 21 To them that are without law, as without law, (being not without law to God, but under the law to Christ,) that I might gain them that are without law. 22 To the weak became I as weak, that I might gain the weak: I am made all things to all *men*, that I might by all means save some. 23And this I do for the gospel's sake, that I might be partaker thereof with *you*. 24 Know ye not that they which run in a race run all, but one receiveth the prize? So run, that ye may obtain. 25And every man that striveth for the mastery is temperate in all things. Now they *do it* to obtain a corruptible crown; but we an incorruptible. 26 I therefore so run, not as uncertainly; so fight I, not as one that beateth the air: 27 But I keep under my body, and bring *it* into subjection: lest that by any means, when I have preached to others, I myself should be a castaway.

R.S.V.

make the gospel free of charge, not making full use of my right in the gospel.

19 For though I am free from all men, I have made myself a slave to all, that I might win the more. 20 To the Jews I became as a Jew, in order to win Jews; to those under the law I became as one under the law—though not being myself under the law—that I might win those under the law. 21 To those outside the law I became as one outside the law—not being without law toward God but under the law of Christ—that I might win those outside the law. 22 To the weak I became weak, that I might win the weak. I have become all things to all men, that I might by all means save some. 23 I do it all for the sake of the gospel, that I may share in its blessings.

24 Do you not know that in a race all the runners compete, but only one receives the prize? So run that you may obtain it. 25 Every athlete exercises self-control in all things. They do it to receive a perishable wreath, but we an imperishable. 26 Well, I do not run aimlessly, I do not box as one beating the air; 27 but I pommel my body and subdue it, lest after preaching to others I myself should be disqualified.

10 Moreover, brethren, I would not that ye should be ignorant, how that all our fathers were under the cloud, and all passed through the sea; 2And were all baptized unto Moses in the cloud and in the sea; 3And did all eat the same spiritual meat; 4And did all drink the same spiritual drink; for they drank of that spiritual Rock that followed them: and that Rock was Christ. 5 But with many of them God was not well pleased: for they were overthrown in the wilderness. 6 Now these things were our examples, to the intent we should not lust after evil things, as they also lusted. 7 Neither be ye idolaters, as *were* some of them; as it is written, The people sat down to eat and drink, and rose up to play. 8 Neither let us commit fornication, as some of them committed, and fell in one day three and twenty thousand. 9 Neither let us tempt Christ, as some of them also tempted, and were destroyed of serpents. 10 Neither murmur ye, as some of them also murmured, and were destroyed of the destroyer. 11 Now all these things happened unto them for ensamples: and they are written for our admonition, upon whom

10 I want you to know, brethren, that our fathers were all under the cloud, and all passed through the sea, 2 and all were baptized into Moses in the cloud and in the sea, 3 and all ate the same supernatural [o] food 4 and all drank the same supernatural [o] drink. For they drank from the supernatural [o] Rock which followed them, and the Rock was Christ. 5 Nevertheless with most of them God was not pleased; for they were overthrown in the wilderness.

6 Now these things are warnings for us, not to desire evil as they did. 7 Do not be idolaters as some of them were; as it is written, "The people sat down to eat and drink and rose up to dance." 8 We must not indulge in immorality as some of them did and twenty-three thousand fell in a single day. 9 We must not put the Lord [p] to the test, as some of them did and were destroyed by serpents; 10 nor grumble, as some of them did and were destroyed by the Destroyer. 11 Now these things happened to them as a warning, but they were written down for our instruction, upon whom the end of

[o] Greek *spiritual*. [p] Other ancient authorities read *Christ*.

PHILLIPS

ward? This, that when I preach the gospel, I can make it absolutely free of charge, and need not claim what is my rightful due as a preacher. For though I am no man's slave, yet I have made myself everyone's slave, that I might win more men to Christ. To the Jews I was a Jew that I might win the Jews. To those who were under the Law I put myself in the position of being under the Law (although in fact I stand free of it), that I might win those who are under the Law. To those who had no Law I myself became like a man without the Law (even though in fact I cannot be a lawless man for I am bound by the law of Christ), so that I might win the men who have no Law. To the weak I became a weak man, that I might win the weak. I have, in short, been all things to all sorts of men that by every possible means I might win some to God. I do all this for the sake of the gospel; I want to play my part in it properly.

To preach the gospel faithfully   9. 24
is my set purpose

Do you remember how, on a racing-track, every competitor runs, but only one wins the prize? Well, you ought to run with your minds fixed on winning the prize! Every competitor in athletic events goes into serious training. Athletes will take tremendous pains—for a fading crown of leaves. But our contest is for an eternal crown that will never fade.

I run the race then with determination. I am no shadowboxer; I really fight! I am my body's sternest master, for fear that when I have preached to others I should myself be disqualified.

Spiritual experience does not   10. 1
guarantee infallibility

For I should like to remind you, my brothers, that our ancestors all had the experience of being guided by the cloud in the desert and of crossing the sea dry-shod. They were all, so to speak, "baptized" into Moses by these experiences. They all shared the same spiritual food and drank the same spiritual drink (for they drank from the spiritual rock which followed them, and that rock was Christ). Yet in spite of all these wonderful experiences many of them failed to please God, and left their bones in the desert. Now in these events our ancestors stand as examples to us, warning us not to crave after evil things as they did. Nor are you to worship false gods as they did. The scripture says,

The people sat down to eat and drink, and rose up to play.

Neither should we give way to sexual immorality as did some of them, for we read that twenty-three thousand fell in a single day! Nor should we dare to exploit the goodness of God as some of them did, and fell victims to poisonous snakes. Nor yet must you curse the lot that God has appointed to you as they did, and met their end at the hand of the angel of death.

Now these things which happened to our ancestors are illustrations of the way in which God works, and they were written down to be a warning to us who are the heirs of the ages which have gone before us.

N.E.B.

preaching the Gospel without expense to anyone; in other words, of waiving the rights which my preaching gives me.

I am a free man and own no master; but I have made myself every man's servant, to win over as many as possible. To Jews I became like a Jew, to win Jews; as they are subject to the Law of Moses, I put myself under that law to win them although I am not myself subject to it. To win Gentiles, who are outside the Law, I made myself like one of them, although I am not in truth outside God's law, being under the law of Christ. To the weak I became weak, to win the weak. Indeed, I have become everything in turn to men of every sort, so that in one way or another I may save some. All this I do for the sake of the Gospel, to bear my part in proclaiming it.

You know (do you not?) that at the sports all the runners run the race, though only one wins the prize. Like them, run to win! But every athlete goes into strict training. They do it to win a fading wreath; we, a wreath that never fades. For my part, I run with a clear goal before me; I am like a boxer who does not beat the air; I bruise my own body and make it know its master, for fear that after preaching to others I should find myself rejected.

10 You should understand, my brothers, that our ancestors were all under the pillar of cloud, and all of them passed through the Red Sea; and so they all received baptism into the fellowship of Moses in cloud and sea. They all ate the same supernatural food, and all drank the same supernatural drink; I mean, they all drank from the supernatural rock that accompanied their travels—and that rock was Christ. And yet, most of them were not accepted by God, for the desert was strewn with their corpses.

These events happened as symbols to warn us not to set our desires on evil things, as they did. Do not be idolaters, like some of them; as Scripture has it, 'the people sat down to feast and stood up to play'. Let us not commit fornication, as some of them did—and twenty-three thousand died in one day. Let us not put the power of the Lord [a] to the test, as some of them did—and were destroyed by serpents. Do not grumble against God, as some of them did—and were destroyed by the Destroyer.

All these things that happened to them were symbolic, and were recorded for our benefit as a warning. For upon us the fulfilment of the

[a] Some witnesses read of Christ.

K.J.V.

the ends of the world are come. 12 Wherefore let him that thinketh he standeth take heed lest he fall. 13 There hath no temptation taken you but such as is common to man: but God *is* faithful, who will not suffer you to be tempted above that ye are able; but will with the temptation also make a way to escape, that ye may be able to bear *it.* 14 Wherefore, my dearly beloved, flee from idolatry. 15 I speak as to wise men; judge ye what I say. 16 The cup of blessing which we bless, is it not the communion of the blood of Christ? The bread which we break, is it not the communion of the body of Christ? 17 For we *being* many are one bread, *and* one body: for we are all partakers of that one bread. 18 Behold Israel after the flesh: are not they which eat of the sacrifices partakers of the altar? 19 What say I then? that the idol is any thing, or that which is offered in sacrifice to idols is any thing? 20 But *I say,* that the things which the Gentiles sacrifice, they sacrifice to devils, and not to God: and I would not that ye should have fellowship with devils. 21 Ye cannot drink the cup of the Lord, and the cup of devils: ye cannot be partakers of the Lord's table, and of the table of devils. 22 Do we provoke the Lord to jealousy? are we stronger than he? 23 All things are lawful for me, but all things are not expedient: all things are lawful for me, but all things edify not. 24 Let no man seek his own, but every man another's *wealth.* 25 Whatsoever is sold in the shambles, *that* eat, asking no question for conscience' sake: 26 For the earth *is* the Lord's, and the fulness thereof. 27 If any of them that believe not bid you *to a feast,* and ye be disposed to go; whatsoever is set before you, eat, asking no question for conscience' sake. 28 But if any man say unto you, This is offered in sacrifice unto idols, eat not for his sake that shewed it, and for conscience' sake: for the earth *is* the Lord's, and the fulness thereof: 29 Conscience, I say, not thine own, but of the other: for why is my liberty judged of another *man's* conscience? 30 For if I by grace be a partaker, why am I evil spoken of for that for which I give thanks? 31 Whether therefore ye eat, or drink, or whatsoever ye do, do all to the glory of God. 32 Give none offence, neither to the Jews, nor to the Gentiles, nor to the church

R.S.V.

the ages has come. 12 Therefore let any one who thinks that he stands take heed lest he fall. 13 No temptation has overtaken you that is not common to man. God is faithful, and he will not let you be tempted beyond your strength, but with the temptation will also provide the way of escape, that you may be able to endure it. 14 Therefore, my beloved, shun the worship of idols. 15 I speak as to sensible men; judge for yourselves what I say. 16 The cup of blessing which we bless, is it not a participation*q* in the blood of Christ? The bread which we break, is it not a participation*q* in the body of Christ? 17 Because there is one bread, we who are many are one body, for we all partake of the one bread. 18 Consider the practice of Israel; are not those who eat the sacrifices partners in the altar? 19 What do I imply then? That food offered to idols is anything, or that an idol is anything? 20 No, I imply that what pagans sacrifice they offer to demons and not to God. I do not want you to be partners with demons. 21 You cannot drink the cup of the Lord and the cup of demons. You cannot partake of the table of the Lord and the table of demons. 22 Shall we provoke the Lord to jealousy? Are we stronger than he? 23 "All things are lawful," but not all things are helpful. "All things are lawful," but not all things build up. 24 Let no one seek his own good, but the good of his neighbor. 25 Eat whatever is sold in the meat market without raising any question on the ground of conscience. 26 For "the earth is the Lord's, and everything in it." 27 If one of the unbelievers invites you to dinner and you are disposed to go, eat whatever is set before you without raising any question on the ground of conscience. 28 (But if some one says to you, "This has been offered in sacrifice," then out of consideration for the man who informed you, and for conscience' sake—29 I mean his conscience, not yours—do not eat it.) For why should my liberty be determined by another man's scruples? 30 If I partake with thankfulness, why am I denounced because of that for which I give thanks? 31 So, whether you eat or drink, or whatever you do, do all to the glory of God. 32 Give no offense to Jews or to Greeks or to the church of

[q] Or *communion.*

524

PHILLIPS

So let the man who feels sure of his standing today be careful that he does not fall tomorrow.

God still governs human   *10. 13*
experience

No temptation has come your way that is too hard for flesh and blood to bear. But God can be trusted not to allow you to suffer any temptation beyond your powers of endurance. He will see to it that every temptation has a way out, so that it will never be impossible for you to bear it.

We have great spiritual   *10. 14*
privileges: let us live up to them

The lesson we must learn, my brothers, is at all costs to avoid worshiping a false god. I am speaking to you as intelligent men: think over what I am saying.

The cup of blessing which we bless, is it not a very sharing in the blood of Christ? When we break the bread do we not actually share in the body of Christ? The very fact that we all share one bread makes us all one body. Look at the Jews of our own day. Isn't there a fellowship between all those who eat the altar sacrifices?

Now am I implying that a false god really exists, or that sacrifices made to any god have some value? Not at all! I say emphatically that gentile sacrifices are made to evil spiritual powers and not to God at all. I don't want you to have any fellowship with such powers. You cannot drink both the cup of the Lord and the cup of devils. You cannot be a guest at the Lord's table and at the table of devils. Are we trying to arouse the wrath of God? Have we forgotten how completely we are in his hands?

The Christian's guiding principle   *10. 23*
is love, not knowledge

As I have said before, the Christian position is this: I may do anything, but everything is not useful. Yes, I may do anything, but everything is not constructive. Let no man, then, set his own advantage as his objective, but rather the good of his neighbor.

You should eat whatever is sold in the meat market without asking any of the questions of an overscrupulous conscience. The whole earth and all that is in it belongs to the Lord.

If a pagan asks you to dinner and you want to go, feel free to eat whatever is set before you, without asking any questions through conscientious scruples. But if your host should say straight out, "This meat has been offered to an idol," then don't eat it, for his sake—I mean for the sake of conscience, not yours but his.

Now why should my freedom to eat be at the mercy of someone else's conscience? Or why should an evil be said of me when I have eaten meat with thankfulness, and have thanked God for it? Because, whatever you do, eating or drinking or anything else, everything should be done to bring glory to God.

Do nothing that might make men stumble, whether they are Jews or Greeks or members of the Church of God. I myself try to adapt my-

N.E.B.

ages has come. If you feel sure that you are standing firm, beware! You may fall. So far you have faced no trial beyond what man can bear. God keeps faith, and he will not allow you to be tested above your powers, but when the test comes he will at the same time provide a way out, by enabling you to sustain it.

So then, dear friends, shun idolatry. I speak to you as men of sense. Form your own judgement on what I say. When we bless 'the cup of blessing', is it not a means of sharing in the blood of Christ? When we break the bread, is it not a means of sharing in the body of Christ? Because there is one loaf, we, many as we are, are one body;[a] for it is one loaf of which we all partake.

Look at the Jewish people. Are not those who partake in the sacrificial meal sharers in the altar? What do I imply by this? that an idol is anything but an idol? or food offered to it anything more than food? No: but the sacrifices the heathen offer are offered (in the words of Scripture) 'to demons and to that which is not God'; and I will not have you become partners with demons. You cannot drink the cup of the Lord and the cup of demons. You cannot partake of the Lord's table and the table of demons. Can we defy the Lord? Are we stronger than he?

'We are free to do anything', you say. Yes, but is everything good for us? 'We are free to do anything', but does everything help the building of the community? Each of you must regard, not his own interests, but the other man's.

You may eat anything sold in the meat-market without raising questions of conscience; for the earth is the Lord's and everything in it.

If an unbeliever invites you to a meal and you care to go, eat whatever is put before you, without raising questions of conscience. But if somebody says to you, 'This food has been offered in sacrifice', then, out of consideration for him, and for conscience' sake, do not eat it—not your conscience, I mean, but the other man's.

'What?' you say, 'is my freedom to be called in question by another man's conscience? If I partake with thankfulness, why am I blamed for eating food over which I have said grace?' Well, whether you eat or drink, or whatever you are doing, do all for the honour of God: give no offence to Jews, or Greeks, or to the church of

---

[a] *Or* For we, many as we are, are one loaf, one body.

525

K.J.V.

of God: 33 Even as I please all *men* in all *things,* not seeking mine own profit, but the *profit* of many, that they may be saved.

11 Be ye followers of me, even as I also *am* of Christ. 2 Now I praise you, brethren, that ye remember me in all things, and keep the ordinances, as I delivered *them* to you. 3 But I would have you know, that the head of every man is Christ; and the head of the woman *is* the man; and the head of Christ *is* God. 4 Every man praying or prophesying, having *his* head covered, dishonoureth his head. 5 But every woman that prayeth or prophesieth with *her* head uncovered dishonoureth her head: for that is even all one as if she were shaven. 6 For if the woman be not covered, let her also be shorn: but if it be a shame for a woman to be shorn or shaven, let her be covered. 7 For a man indeed ought not to cover *his* head, forasmuch as he is the image and glory of God: but the woman is the glory of the man. 8 For the man is not of the woman; but the woman of the man. 9 Neither was the man created for the woman; but the woman for the man. 10 For this cause ought the woman to have power on *her* head because of the angels. 11 Nevertheless neither is the man without the woman, neither the woman without the man, in the Lord. 12 For as the woman *is* of the man, even so *is* the man also by the woman; but all things of God. 13 Judge in yourselves: is it comely that a woman pray unto God uncovered? 14 Doth not even nature itself teach you, that, if a man have long hair, it is a shame unto him? 15 But if a woman have long hair, it is a glory to her: for *her* hair is given her for a covering. 16 But if any man seem to be contentious, we have no such custom, neither the churches of God. 17 Now in this that I declare *unto you* I praise *you* not, that ye come together not for the better, but for the worse. 18 For first of all, when ye come together in the church, I hear that there be divisions among you; and I partly believe it. 19 For there must be also heresies among you, that they which are approved may be made manifest among you. 20 When ye come together therefore into one place, *this* is not to eat the Lord's supper. 21 For in eating every one taketh before *other* his own supper: and one is hungry, and another is drunken. 22 What! have ye not houses to eat and to drink in? or despise ye the church of God, and shame them that have not? What shall I say to you? shall I praise you in this? I praise

R.S.V.

God, 33 just as I try to please all men in everything I do, not seeking my own advantage, but that of many, that they may be saved.

11 Be imitators of me, as I am of Christ.

2 I commend you because you remember me in everything and maintain the traditions even as I have delivered them to you. 3 But I want you to understand that the head of every man is Christ, the head of a woman is her husband, and the head of Christ is God. 4 Any man who prays or prophesies with his head covered dishonors his head, 5 but any woman who prays or prophesies with her head unveiled dishonors her head—it is the same as if her head were shaven. 6 For if a woman will not veil herself, then she should cut off her hair; but if it is disgraceful for a woman to be shorn or shaven, let her wear a veil. 7 For a man ought not to cover his head, since he is the image and glory of God; but woman is the glory of man. 8 (For man was not made from woman, but woman from man. 9 Neither was man created for woman, but woman for man.) 10 That is why a woman ought to have a veil [r] on her head, because of the angels. 11 (Nevertheless, in the Lord woman is not independent of man nor man of woman; 12 for as woman was made from man, so man is now born of woman. And all things are from God.) 13 Judge for yourselves; is it proper for a woman to pray to God with her head uncovered? 14 Does not nature itself teach you that for a man to wear long hair is degrading to him, 15 but if a woman has long hair, it is her pride? For her hair is given to her for a covering. 16 If any one is disposed to be contentious, we recognize no other practice, nor do the churches of God.

17 But in the following instructions I do not commend you, because when you come together it is not for the better but for the worse. 18 For, in the first place, when you assemble as a church, I hear that there are divisions among you; and I partly believe it, 19 for there must be factions among you in order that those who are genuine among you may be recognized. 20 When you meet together, it is not the Lord's supper that you eat. 21 For in eating, each one goes ahead with his own meal, and one is hungry and another is drunk. 22 What! Do you not have houses to eat and drink in? Or do you despise the church of God and humiliate those who have nothing? What shall I say to you? Shall I commend you in this? No, I will not.

[r] Greek *authority* (the veil being a symbol of this).

PHILLIPS

self to all men without considering my own advantage but *their* advantage, that if possible they may be saved.

Copy me, my brothers, as I copy Christ himself.

The reasons that lie behind   *11. 2* some of the traditions

I must give you credit for remembering what I taught you and adhering to the traditions I passed on to you. But I want you to know that Christ is the head of every individual man, just as a man is the "head" of the woman and God is the head of Christ. If a man prays or preaches with his head covered, he is dishonoring his own head. But in the case of a woman, if she prays or preaches with her head uncovered it is just as much a disgrace as if she had had it closely shaved. For if a woman does not cover her head she might just as well have her hair cropped. And if to be cropped or closely shaven is a sign of disgrace to women (as it is with many peoples), then that is all the more reason for her to cover her head. A man ought not to cover his head, for he represents the very person and glory of God, while the woman reflects the person and glory of the man. For man does not exist because woman exists, but vice versa. Man was not created originally for the sake of woman, but woman was created for the sake of man. For this reason a woman ought to bear on her head an outward sign of man's authority for all the angels to see.

Of course, in the sight of God neither "man" nor "woman" has any separate existence. For if woman was made originally for man, no man is now born except by a woman, and both man and woman, like everything else, owe their existence to God. But use your own judgment: Do you think it right and proper for a woman to pray to God bareheaded? Isn't there a natural principle here, that makes us feel that long hair is disgraceful to a man, but of glorious beauty to a woman? We feel this because the long hair is the cover provided by nature for the woman's head. But if anyone wants to be argumentative about it, I can only say that we and the churches of God generally hold this ruling on the matter.

I must mention serious faults   *11. 17* in your church

But in giving you the following rules, I cannot commend your conduct, for it seems that your church meetings do you more harm than good! For first, when you meet for worship I hear that you split up into small groups, and I think there must be truth in what I hear. For there must be cliques among you or your favorite leaders would not be so conspicuous. It follows, then, that when you are assembled in one place you do not eat the *Lord's* supper. For everyone tries to grab his food before anyone else, with the result that one goes hungry and another has too much to drink! Haven't you houses of your own to have your meals in, or are you making a convenience of the church of God and causing acute embarrassment to those who have no other home?

Am I to commend this sort of conduct? Most certainly not!

N.E.B.

God. For my part I always try to meet everyone half-way, regarding not my own good but the good of the many, so that they may be saved.

11 Follow my example as I follow Christ's.

I commend you for always keeping me in mind, and maintaining the tradition I handed on to you. But I wish you to understand that, while every man has Christ for his Head, woman's head is man,[a] as Christ's Head is God. A man who keeps his head covered when he prays or prophesies brings shame on his head; a woman, on the contrary, brings shame on her head if she prays or prophesies bare-headed: it is as bad as if her head were shaved. If a woman is not to wear a veil she might as well have her hair cut off; but if it is a disgrace for her to be cropped and shaved, then she should wear a veil. A man has no need to cover his head, because man is the image of God, and the mirror of his glory, whereas woman reflects the glory of man.[b] For man did not originally spring from woman, but woman was made out of man; and man was not created for woman's sake, but woman for the sake of man; and therefore it is woman's duty to have a sign of authority[c] on her head, out of regard for the angels.[d] And yet, in Christ's fellowship woman is as essential to man as man to woman. If woman was made out of man, it is through woman that man now comes to be; and God is the source of all.

Judge for yourselves: is it fitting for a woman to pray to God bare-headed? Does not Nature herself teach you that while flowing locks disgrace a man, they are a woman's glory? For her locks were given for covering.

However, if you insist on arguing, let me tell you, there is no such custom among us, or in any of the congregations of God's people.

In giving you these injunctions I must mention a practice which I cannot commend: your meetings tend to do more harm than good. To begin with, I am told that when you meet as a congregation you fall into sharply divided groups; and I believe there is some truth in it (for dissensions are necessary if only to show which of your members are sound). The result is that when you meet as a congregation, it is impossible for you to eat the Lord's Supper, because each of you is in such a hurry to eat his own, and while one goes hungry another has too much to drink. Have you no homes of your own to eat and drink in? Or are you so contemptuous of the church of God that you shame its poorer members? What am I to say? Can I commend you? On this point, certainly not!

[a] *Or* a woman's head is her husband. [b] *Or* a woman reflects her husband's glory. [c] *Some witnesses read* to have a veil. [d] *Or* and therefore a woman should keep her dignity on her head, for fear of the angels.

K.J.V.

you not. 23 For I have received of the Lord that which also I delivered unto you, That the Lord Jesus, the *same* night in which he was betrayed, took bread: 24And when he had given thanks, he brake *it*, and said, Take, eat; this is my body, which is broken for you: this do in remembrance of me. 25After the same manner also *he took* the cup, when he had supped, saying, This cup is the new testament in my blood: this do ye, as oft as ye drink *it*, in remembrance of me. 26 For as often as ye eat this bread, and drink this cup, ye do shew the Lord's death till he come. 27 Wherefore whosoever shall eat this bread, and drink *this* cup of the Lord, unworthily, shall be guilty of the body and blood of the Lord. 28 But let a man examine himself, and so let him eat of *that* bread, and drink of *that* cup. 29 For he that eateth and drinketh unworthily, eateth and drinketh damnation to himself, not discerning the Lord's body. 30 For this cause many *are* weak and sickly among you, and many sleep. 31 For if we would judge ourselves, we should not be judged. 32 But when we are judged, we are chastened of the Lord, that we should not be condemned with the world. 33 Wherefore, my brethren, when ye come together to eat, tarry one for another. 34And if any man hunger, let him eat at home; that ye come not together unto condemnation. And the rest will I set in order when I come.

R.S.V.

23 For I received from the Lord what I also delivered to you, that the Lord Jesus on the night when he was betrayed took bread, 24 and when he had given thanks, he broke it, and said, "This is my body which is for*s* you. Do this in remembrance of me." 25 In the same way also the cup, after supper, saying, "This cup is the new covenant in my blood. Do this, as often as you drink it, in remembrance of me." 26 For as often as you eat this bread and drink the cup, you proclaim the Lord's death until he comes. 27 Whoever, therefore, eats the bread or drinks the cup of the Lord in an unworthy manner will be guilty of profaning the body and blood of the Lord. 28 Let a man examine himself, and so eat of the bread and drink of the cup. 29 For any one who eats and drinks without discerning the body eats and drinks judgment upon himself. 30 That is why many of you are weak and ill, and some have died.*f* 31 But if we judged ourselves truly, we should not be judged. 32 But when we are judged by the Lord, we are chastened *u* so that we may not be condemned along with the world.

33 So then, my brethren, when you come together to eat, wait for one another—34 if any one is hungry, let him eat at home—lest you come together to be condemned. About the other things I will give directions when I come.

12 Now concerning spiritual *gifts*, brethren, I would not have you ignorant. 2 Ye know that ye were Gentiles, carried away unto these dumb idols, even as ye were led. 3 Wherefore I give you to understand, that no man speaking by the Spirit of God calleth Jesus accursed: and *that* no man can say that Jesus is the Lord, but by the Holy Ghost. 4 Now there are diversities of gifts, but the same Spirit. 5And there are differences of administrations, but the same Lord. 6And there are diversities of operations, but it is the same God which worketh all in all. 7 But the manifestation of the Spirit is given to every man to profit withal. 8 For to one is given by

12 Now concerning spiritual gifts, brethren, I do not want you to be uninformed. 2 You know that when you were heathen, you were led astray to dumb idols, however you may have been moved. 3 Therefore I want you to understand that no one speaking by the Spirit of God ever says "Jesus be cursed!" and no one can say "Jesus is Lord" except by the Holy Spirit.

4 Now there are varieties of gifts, but the same Spirit; 5 and there are varieties of service, but the same Lord; 6 and there are varieties of working, but it is the same God who inspires them all in every one. 7 To each is given the manifestation of the Spirit for the common good. 8 To one is given through the Spirit the ut-

[*s*] Other ancient authorities read *broken for*. [*t*] Greek *have fallen asleep* (as in 15.6,20) [*u*] Or *when we are judged we are being chastened by the Lord*.

PHILLIPS

To partake of the Lord's Supper **11. 23**
is a supremely serious thing

The teaching I gave you was given me personally by the Lord himself, and it was this: the Lord Jesus, in the same night in which he was betrayed, took bread, and when he had given thanks he broke it and said, "Take, eat, this is my body which is being broken for you. Do this in remembrance of me." Similarly, when supper was ended, he took the cup saying, "This cup is the new agreement in my blood: do this, whenever you drink it, in remembrance of me."

This can only mean that whenever you eat this bread or drink of this cup, you are proclaiming that the Lord has died for you, and you will do that until he comes again. So that, whoever eats the bread or drinks the cup of the Lord without proper reverence is sinning against the body and blood of the Lord.

No, a man should thoroughly examine himself, and only then should he eat the bread or drink of the cup. He that eats and drinks carelessly is eating and drinking a judgment on himself, for he is blind to the presence of the Lord's body.

Careless communion means **11. 30**
spiritual weakness: let us
take due care

It is this careless participation which is the reason for the many feeble and sickly Christians in your church, and the explanation of the fact that many of you are spiritually asleep.

If we were closely to examine ourselves beforehand, we should avoid the judgment of God. But when God does judge us, he disciplines us as his own sons, that we may not be involved in the general condemnation of the world.

Now, my brothers, when you come together to eat this bread, wait your proper turn. If a man is really hungry let him satisfy his appetite at home. Don't let your communions be God's judgments upon you!

The other matters I will settle in person, when I come.

The Holy Spirit inspires men's **12. 1**
faith and imparts spiritual gifts

Now I want to give you some further information in some spiritual matters. You have not forgotten that you were gentiles, following dumb idols just as your impulses led you. Now I want you to understand, as Christians, that no one speaking by the Spirit of God could call Jesus accursed, and no one could say that he is the Lord, except by the Holy Spirit.

Men have different gifts, but it is the same Spirit who gives them. There are different ways of serving God, but it is the same Lord who is served. God works through different men in different ways, but it is the same God who achieves his purposes through them all. Each man is given his gift by the Spirit that he may use it for the common good.

One man's gift by the Spirit is to speak with

N.E.B.

For the tradition which I handed on to you came to me from the Lord himself: that the Lord Jesus, on the night of his arrest, took bread and, after giving thanks to God, broke it and said: 'This is my body, which is for you; do this as a memorial of me.' In the same way, he took the cup after supper, and said: 'This cup is the new covenant sealed by my blood. Whenever you drink it, do this as a memorial of me.' For every time you eat this bread and drink the cup, you proclaim the death of the Lord, until he comes.

It follows that anyone who eats the bread or drinks the cup of the Lord unworthily will be guilty of desecrating the body and blood of the Lord. A man must test himself before eating his share of the bread and drinking from the cup. For he who eats and drinks eats and drinks judgement on himself if he does not discern the Body. That is why many of you are feeble and sick, and a number have died. But if we examined ourselves, we should not thus fall under judgement. When, however, we do fall under the Lord's judgement, he is disciplining us, to save us from being condemned with the rest of the world.

Therefore, my brothers, when you meet for a meal, wait for one another. If you are hungry, eat at home, so that in meeting together you may not fall under judgement. The other matters I will arrange when I come.

Spiritual Gifts

12 About gifts of the Spirit, there are some things of which I do not wish you to remain ignorant.

You know how, in the days when you were still pagan, you were swept off to those dumb heathen gods, however you happened to be led.[a] For this reason I must impress upon you that no one who says 'A curse on Jesus!' can be speaking under the influence of the Spirit of God. And no one can say 'Jesus is Lord!' except under the influence of the Holy Spirit.

There are varieties of gifts, but the same Spirit. There are varieties of service, but the same Lord. There are many forms of work, but all of them, in all men, are the work of the same God. In each of us the Spirit is manifested in one particular way, for some useful purpose. One man, through the Spirit, has the gift of wise

[a] *Or* . . . pagan, you would be seized by some power which drove you to those dumb heathen gods.

K.J.V.

the Spirit the word of wisdom; to another the word of knowledge by the same Spirit; 9 To another faith by the same Spirit; to another the gifts of healing by the same Spirit; 10 To another the working of miracles; to another prophecy; to another discerning of spirits; to another *divers* kinds of tongues; to another the interpretation of tongues: 11 But all these worketh that one and the selfsame Spirit, dividing to every man severally as he will. 12 For as the body is one, and hath many members, and all the members of that one body, being many, are one body: so also *is* Christ. 13 For by one Spirit are we all baptized into one body, whether *we be* Jews or Gentiles, whether *we be* bond or free; and have been all made to drink into one Spirit. 14 For the body is not one member, but many. 15 If the foot shall say, Because I am not the hand, I am not of the body; is it therefore not of the body? 16And if the ear shall say, Because I am not the eye, I am not of the body; is it therefore not of the body? 17 If the whole body *were* an eye, where *were* the hearing? If the whole *were* hearing, where *were* the smelling? 18 But now hath God set the members every one of them in the body, as it hath pleased him. 19And if they were all one member, where *were* the body? 20 But now *are they* many members, yet but one body. 21And the eye cannot say unto the hand, I have no need of thee: nor again the head to the feet, I have no need of you. 22 Nay, much more those members of the body, which seem to be more feeble, are necessary: 23And those *members* of the body, which we think to be less honourable, upon these we bestow more abundant honour; and our uncomely *parts* have more abundant comeliness. 24 For our comely *parts* have no need: but God hath tempered the body together, having given more abundant honour to that *part* which lacked: 25 That there should be no schism in the body; but *that* the members should have the same care one for another. 26And whether one member suffer, all the members suffer with it; or one member be honoured, all the members rejoice with it. 27 Now ye are the body of Christ, and members in particular. 28And God hath set some in the church, first apostles, secondarily prophets, thirdly teachers, after that miracles, then gifts of healings, helps, governments, diversities of tongues. 29*Are* all apostles? *are* all prophets? *are* all teachers? *are* all workers of miracles? 30 Have all the gifts of healing? do all speak with tongues? do all interpret? 31 But covet earnestly the best gifts: and yet shew I unto you a more excellent way.

R.S.V.

terance of wisdom, and to another the utterance of knowledge according to the same Spirit, 9 to another faith by the same Spirit, to another gifts of healing by the one Spirit, 10 to another the working of miracles, to another prophecy, to another the ability to distinguish between spirits, to another various kinds of tongues, to another the interpretation of tongues. 11All these are inspired by one and the same Spirit, who apportions to each one individually as he wills.

12 For just as the body is one and has many members, and all the members of the body, though many, are one body, so it is with Christ. 13 For by one Spirit we were all baptized into one body—Jews or Greeks, slaves or free—and all were made to drink of one Spirit.

14 For the body does not consist of one member but of many. 15 If the foot should say, "Because I am not a hand, I do not belong to the body," that would not make it any less a part of the body. 16And if the ear should say, "Because I am not an eye, I do not belong to the body," that would not make it any less a part of the body. 17 If the whole body were an eye, where would be the hearing? If the whole body were an ear, where would be the sense of smell? 18 But as it is, God arranged the organs in the body, each one of them, as he chose. 19 If all were a single organ, where would the body be? 20As it is, there are many parts, yet one body. 21 The eye cannot say to the hand, "I have no need of you," nor again the head to the feet, "I have no need of you." 22 On the contrary, the parts of the body which seem to be weaker are indispensable, 23 and those parts of the body which we think less honorable we invest with the greater honor, and our unpresentable parts are treated with greater modesty, 24 which our more presentable parts do not require. But God has so adjusted the body, giving the greater honor to the inferior part, 25 that there may be no discord in the body, but that the members may have the same care for one another. 26 If one member suffers, all suffer together; if one member is honored, all rejoice together.

27 Now you are the body of Christ and individually members of it. 28And God has appointed in the church first apostles, second prophets, third teachers, then workers of miracles, then healers, helpers, administrators, speakers in various kinds of tongues. 29 Are all apostles? Are all prophets? Are all teachers? Do all work miracles? 30 Do all possess gifts of healing? Do all speak with tongues? Do all interpret? 31 But earnestly desire the higher gifts.

And I will show you a still more excellent way.

PHILLIPS

wisdom, another's to speak with knowledge. The same Spirit gives to another man faith, to another the ability to heal, to another the power to do great deeds. The same Spirit gives to another man the gift of preaching the word of God, to another the ability to discriminate in spiritual matters, to another speech in different tongues and to yet another the power to interpret the tongues. Behind all these gifts is the operation of the same Spirit, who distributes to each individual man, as he wills.

The human body is an example   12. 12
of an organic unity

As the human body, which has many parts, is a unity, and those parts, despite their multiplicity, constitute one single body, so it is with Christ. For we were all baptized by the Spirit into one body, whether we were Jews, Greeks, slaves or free men, and we have all had experience of the same Spirit.

Now the body is not one member but many. If the foot should say, "Because I am not a hand I don't belong to the body," does that alter the fact that the foot *is* a part of the body? Or if the ear should say, "Because I am not an eye I don't belong to the body," does that mean that the ear really is not part of the body? After all, if the body were all one eye, for example, where would be the sense of hearing? Or if it were all one ear, where would be the sense of smell? But God has arranged all the parts in the one body, according to his design. For if everything were concentrated in one part, how could there be a body at all? The fact is there are many parts, but only one body. So that the eye cannot say to the hand, "I don't need you!" nor, again, can the head say to the feet, "I don't need you!" On the contrary, those parts of the body which have no obvious function are the more essential to health; and to those parts of the body which seem to us to be less deserving of notice we have to allow the highest honor of function. The parts which do not look beautiful have a deeper beauty in the work they do, while the parts which look beautiful may not be at all essential to life! But God has harmonized the whole body by giving importance of function to the parts which lack apparent importance, that the body should work together as a whole with all the members in sympathetic relationship with one another. So it happens that if one member suffers all the other members suffer with it, and if one member is honored all the members share a common joy.

Now you are together the body of Christ, and individually you are members of him. And in his Church God has appointed first some to be his messengers, secondly, some to be preachers of power; thirdly, teachers. After them he has appointed workers of spiritual power, men with the gift of healing, helpers, organizers and those with the gift of speaking in "tongues."

As we look at the body of Christ do we find all are his messengers, all are preachers, or all teachers? Do we find all wielders of spiritual power, all able to heal, all able to speak with tongues, or all able to interpret the tongues? No, we find God's distribution of gifts is on the same principles of harmony that he has shown in the human body.

You should set your hearts on the best spiritual gifts, but I shall show you a way which surpasses them all.

N.E.B.

speech, while another, by the power of the same Spirit, can put the deepest knowledge into words. Another, by the same Spirit, is granted faith; another, by the one Spirit, gifts of healing, and another miraculous powers; another has the gift of prophecy, and another ability to distinguish true spirits from false; yet another has the gift of ecstatic utterance of different kinds, and another the ability to interpret it. But all these gifts are the work of one and the same Spirit, distributing them separately to each individual at will.

For Christ is like a single body with its many limbs and organs, which, many as they are, together make up one body. For indeed we were all brought into one body by baptism, in the one Spirit, whether we are Jews or Greeks, whether slaves or free men, and that one Holy Spirit was poured out for all of us to drink.

A body is not one single organ, but many. Suppose the foot should say, 'Because I am not a hand, I do not belong to the body', it does belong to the body none the less. Suppose the ear were to say, 'Because I am not an eye, I do not belong to the body', it does still belong to the body. If the body were all eye, how could it hear? If the body were all ear, how could it smell? But, in fact, God appointed each limb and organ to its own place in the body, as he chose. If the whole were one single organ, there would not be a body at all; in fact, however, there are many different organs, but one body. The eye cannot say to the hand, 'I do not need you'; nor the head to the feet, 'I do not need you.' Quite the contrary: those organs of the body which seem to be more frail than others are indispensable, and those parts of the body which we regard as less honourable are treated with special honour. To our unseemly parts is given a more than ordinary seemliness, whereas our seemly parts need no adorning. But God has combined the various parts of the body, giving special honour to the humbler parts, so that there might be no sense of division in the body, but that all its organs might feel the same concern for one another. If one organ suffers, they all suffer together. If one flourishes, they all rejoice together.

Now you are Christ's body, and each of you a limb or organ of it. Within our community God has appointed, in the first place apostles, in the second place prophets, thirdly teachers; then miracle-workers, then those who have gifts of healing, or ability to help others or power to guide them, or the gift of ecstatic utterance of various kinds. Are all apostles? all prophets? all teachers? Do all work miracles? Have all gifts of healing? Do all speak in tongues of ecstasy? Can all interpret them? The higher gifts are those you should aim at.

And now I will show you the best way of all.

13 Though I speak with the tongues of men and of angels, and have not charity, I am become *as* sounding brass, or a tinkling cymbal. 2And though I have *the gift of* prophecy, and understand all mysteries, and all knowledge; and though I have all faith, so that I could remove mountains, and have not charity, I am nothing. 3And though I bestow all my goods to feed *the poor,* and though I give my body to be burned, and have not charity, it profiteth me nothing. 4 Charity suffereth long, *and* is kind; charity envieth not; charity vaunteth not itself, is not puffed up, 5 Doth not behave itself unseemly, seeketh not her own, is not easily provoked, thinketh no evil; 6 Rejoiceth not in iniquity, but rejoiceth in the truth; 7 Beareth all things, believeth all things, hopeth all things, endureth all things. 8 Charity never faileth: but whether *there be* prophecies, they shall fail; whether *there be* tongues, they shall cease; whether *there be* knowledge, it shall vanish away. 9 For we know in part, and we prophesy in part. 10 But when that which is perfect is come, then that which is in part shall be done away. 11 When I was a child, I spake as a child, I understood as a child, I thought as a child: but when I became a man, I put away childish things. 12 For now we see through a glass, darkly; but then face to face: now I know in part; but then shall I know even as also I am known. 13And now abideth faith, hope, charity, these three; but the greatest of these *is* charity.

13 If I speak in the tongues of men and of angels, but have not love, I am a noisy gong or a clanging cymbal. 2And if I have prophetic powers, and understand all mysteries and all knowledge, and if I have all faith, so as to remove mountains, but have not love, I am nothing. 3 If I give away all I have, and if I deliver my body to be burned,[v] but have not love, I gain nothing.

4 Love is patient and kind; love is not jealous or boastful; 5 it is not arrogant or rude. Love does not insist on its own way; it is not irritable or resentful; 6 it does not rejoice at wrong, but rejoices in the right. 7 Love bears all things, believes all things, hopes all things, endures all things.

8 Love never ends; as for prophecies, they will pass away; as for tongues, they will cease; as for knowledge, it will pass away. 9 For our knowledge is imperfect and our prophecy is imperfect; 10 but when the perfect comes, the imperfect will pass away. 11 When I was a child, I spoke like a child, I thought like a child, I reasoned like a child; when I became a man, I gave up childish ways. 12 For now we see in a mirror dimly, but then face to face. Now I know in part; then I shall understand fully, even as I have been fully understood. 13 So faith, hope, love abide, these three; but the greatest of these is love.

14 Follow after charity, and desire spiritual *gifts,* but rather that ye may prophesy. 2 For he that speaketh in an *unknown* tongue speaketh not unto men, but unto God: for no man understandeth *him;* howbeit in the spirit he speaketh mysteries. 3 But he that prophesieth speaketh unto men *to* edification, and exhortation, and comfort. 4 He that speaketh in an *unknown* tongue edifieth himself; but he that prophesieth edifieth the church. 5 I would that ye all spake with tongues, but rather that ye

14 Make love your aim, and earnestly desire the spiritual gifts, especially that you may prophesy. 2 For one who speaks in a tongue speaks not to men but to God; for no one understands him, but he utters mysteries in the Spirit. 3 On the other hand, he who prophesies speaks to men for their upbuilding and encouragement and consolation. 4 He who speaks in a tongue edifies himself, but he who prophesies edifies the church. 5 Now I want you all to speak in tongues, but even more to prophesy. He who

[v] Other ancient authorities read *body that I may glory.*

Christian love—the highest and best gift   13. 1

If I speak with the eloquence of men and of angels, but have no love, I become no more than blaring brass or crashing cymbal. If I have the gift of foretelling the future and hold in my mind not only all human knowledge but the very secrets of God, and if I also have that absolute faith which can move mountains, but have no love, I amount to nothing at all. If I dispose of all that I possess, yes, even if I give my own body to be burned, but have no love, I achieve precisely nothing.

This love of which I speak is slow to lose patience—it looks for a way of being constructive. It is not possessive: it is neither anxious to impress nor does it cherish inflated ideas of its own importance.

Love has good manners and does not pursue selfish advantage. It is not touchy. It does not keep account of evil or gloat over the wickedness of other people. On the contrary, it is glad with all good men when truth prevails.

Love knows no limit to its endurance, no end to its trust, no fading of its hope; it can outlast anything. It is, in fact, the one thing that still stands when all else has fallen.

All gifts except love will be superseded one day   13. 9

For if there are prophecies they will be fulfilled and done with, if there are "tongues" the need for them will disappear, if there is knowledge it will be swallowed up in truth. For our knowledge is always incomplete and our prophecy is always incomplete, and when the complete comes, that is the end of the incomplete.

When I was a little child I talked and felt and thought like a little child. Now that I am a man my childish speech and feeling and thought have no further significance for me.

At present we are men looking at puzzling reflections in a mirror. The time will come when we shall see reality whole and face to face! At present all I know is a little fraction of the truth, but the time will come when I shall know it as fully as God now knows me!

In this life we have three great lasting qualities—faith, hope and love. But the greatest of them is love.

"Tongues" are not the greatest gift   14. 1

Follow, then, the way of love, while you set your heart on the gifts of the Spirit. The highest gift you can wish for is to be able to speak the messages of God. The man who speaks in a "tongue" addresses not men (for no one understands a word he says) but God: and only in his spirit is he speaking spiritual secrets. But he who preaches the word of God is using his speech for the building up of the faith of one man, the encouragement of another or the consolation of another. The speaker in a "tongue" builds up his own soul, but the preacher builds up the Church of God.

I should indeed like you all to speak with "tongues," but I would much rather that you all preached the word of God. For the preacher of

13 I may speak in tongues of men or of angels, but if I am without love, I am a sounding gong or a clanging cymbal. I may have the gift of prophecy, and know every hidden truth; I may have faith strong enough to move mountains; but if I have no love, I am nothing. I may dole out all I possess, or even give my body to be burnt,[a] but if I have no love, I am none the better.

Love is patient; love is kind and envies no one. Love is never boastful, nor conceited, nor rude; never selfish, not quick to take offence. Love keeps no score of wrongs; does not gloat over other men's sins, but delights in the truth. There is nothing love cannot face; there is no limit to its faith, its hope, and its endurance.

Love will never come to an end. Are there prophets? their work will be over. Are there tongues of ecstasy? they will cease. Is there knowledge? it will vanish away; for our knowledge and our prophecy alike are partial, and the partial vanishes when wholeness comes. When I was a child, my speech, my outlook, and my thoughts were all childish. When I grew up, I had finished with childish things. Now we see only puzzling reflections in a mirror, but then we shall see face to face. My knowledge now is partial; then it will be whole, like God's knowledge of me. In a word, there are three things that last for ever: faith, hope, and love; but the greatest of them all is love.

14 Put love first; but there are other gifts of the Spirit at which you should aim also, and above all prophecy. When a man is using the language of ecstasy he is talking with God, not with men, for no man understands him; he is no doubt inspired, but he speaks mysteries. On the other hand, when a man prophesies, he is talking to men, and his words have power to build; they stimulate and they encourage. The language of ecstasy is good for the speaker himself, but it is prophecy that builds up a Christian community. I should be pleased for you all to use the tongues of ecstasy, but better pleased for you

[a] *Some witnesses read* even seek glory by self-sacrifice.

K.J.V.

prophesied: for greater *is* he that prophesieth than he that speaketh with tongues, except he interpret, that the church may receive edifying. 6 Now, brethren, if I come unto you speaking with tongues, what shall I profit you, except I shall speak to you either by revelation, or by knowledge, or by prophesying, or by doctrine? 7 And even things without life giving sound, whether pipe or harp, except they give a distinction in the sounds, how shall it be known what is piped or harped? 8 For if the trumpet give an uncertain sound, who shall prepare himself to the battle? 9 So likewise ye, except ye utter by the tongue words easy to be understood, how shall it be known what is spoken? for ye shall speak into the air. 10 There are, it may be, so many kinds of voices in the world, and none of them *is* without signification. 11 Therefore if I know not the meaning of the voice, I shall be unto him that speaketh a barbarian, and he that speaketh *shall be* a barbarian unto me. 12 Even so ye, forasmuch as ye are zealous of spiritual *gifts,* seek that ye may excel to the edifying of the church. 13 Wherefore let him that speaketh in an *unknown* tongue pray that he may interpret. 14 For if I pray in an *unknown* tongue, my spirit prayeth, but my understanding is unfruitful. 15 What is it then? I will pray with the spirit, and I will pray with the understanding also: I will sing with the spirit, and I will sing with the understanding also. 16 Else, when thou shalt bless with the spirit, how shall he that occupieth the room of the unlearned say Amen at thy giving of thanks, seeing he understandeth not what thou sayest? 17 For thou verily givest thanks well, but the other is not edified. 18 I thank my God, I speak with tongues more than ye all: 19 Yet in the church I had rather speak five words with my understanding, that *by my voice* I might teach others also, than ten thousand words in an *unknown* tongue. 20 Brethren, be not children in understanding: howbeit in malice be ye children, but in understanding be men. 21 In the law it is written, With *men of* other tongues and other lips will I speak unto this people; and yet for all that will they not hear me, saith the Lord. 22 Wherefore tongues are for a sign, not to them that believe, but to them that believe not: but prophesying *serveth* not for them that believe not, but for them

R.S.V.

prophesies is greater than he who speaks in tongues, unless some one interprets, so that the church may be edified. 6 Now, brethren, if I come to you speaking in tongues, how shall I benefit you unless I bring you some revelation or knowledge or prophecy or teaching? 7 If even lifeless instruments, such as the flute or the harp, do not give distinct notes, how will any one know what is played? 8 And if the bugle gives an indistinct sound, who will get ready for battle? 9 So with yourselves; if you in a tongue utter speech that is not intelligible, how will any one know what is said? For you will be speaking into the air. 10 There are doubtless many different languages in the world, and none is without meaning; 11 but if I do not know the meaning of the language, I shall be a foreigner to the speaker and the speaker a foreigner to me. 12 So with yourselves; since you are eager for manifestations of the Spirit, strive to excel in building up the church. 13 Therefore, he who speaks in a tongue should pray for the power to interpret. 14 For if I pray in a tongue, my spirit prays but my mind is unfruitful. 15 What am I to do? I will pray with the spirit and I will pray with the mind also; I will sing with the spirit and I will sing with the mind also. 16 Otherwise, if you bless[w] with the spirit, how can any one in the position of an outsider[x] say the "Amen" to your thanksgiving when he does not know what you are saying? 17 For you may give thanks well enough, but the other man is not edified. 18 I thank God that I speak in tongues more than you all; 19 nevertheless, in church I would rather speak five words with my mind, in order to instruct others, than ten thousand words in a tongue. 20 Brethren, do not be children in your thinking; be babes in evil, but in thinking be mature. 21 In the law it is written, "By men of strange tongues and by the lips of foreigners will I speak to this people, and even then they will not listen to me, says the Lord." 22 Thus, tongues are a sign not for believers but for unbelievers, while prophecy is not for unbelievers

[w] That is, *give thanks to God.* [x] Or *him that is without gifts.*

PHILLIPS

the word does a greater work than the speaker with "tongues," unless of course the latter interprets his words for the benefit of the Church.

Unless "tongues" are interpreted 14. 6 do they help the Church?

For suppose I came to you, my brothers, speaking with "tongues," what good could I do you unless I could give you some revelation of truth, some knowledge in spiritual things, some message from God, or some teaching about the Christian life?

Even in the case of inanimate objects which are capable of making sound, such as a flute or harp, if the sounds all sound alike, who can tell what tune is being played? Unless the bugle note is clear who will be called to arms? So, in your case, unless you make intelligible sounds with your "tongue" how can anyone know what you are talking about? You might just as well be addressing an empty room!

There are in the world a great variety of spoken sounds and each has a distinct meaning. But if the sounds of the speaker's voice mean nothing to me I am a foreigner to him, and he is a foreigner to me.

So, with yourselves, since you are so eager to possess spiritual gifts, concentrate your ambition upon receiving those which make for the real growth of your church. And that means if one of your number speaks with a "tongue," he should pray that he may be able to interpret what he says.

If I pray in a "tongue" my spirit is praying but my mind is inactive. I am therefore determined to pray with my spirit *and* my mind, and if I sing I will sing with both spirit and mind. Otherwise, if you are blessing God with your spirit, how can those who are ungifted say amen to your thanksgiving, since they do not know what you are talking about? You may be thanking God splendidly, but it doesn't help the other man at all. I thank God that I have a greater gift of "tongues" than any of you, yet when I am in church I would rather speak five words with my mind (which might teach something to other people) than ten thousand words in a "tongue" which nobody understands.

You must use your minds in this 14. 20 matter of "tongues"

My brothers, don't be like excitable children but use your intelligence! By all means be innocent as babes as far as evil is concerned, but where your minds are concerned be full-grown men! In the Law it is written:

By men of strange tongues and by the lips of strangers will I speak unto this people: and not even thus will they hear me, saith the Lord.

That means that "tongues" are a sign of God's power, not for those who are unbelievers but to those who already believe.* Preaching the word

* This is the sole instance of the translator's departing from the accepted text. He felt bound to conclude, from the sense of the next three verses, that we have here either a slip of the pen on the part of Paul, or, more probably, a copyist's error.

N.E.B.

to prophesy. The prophet is worth more than the man of ecstatic speech—unless indeed he can explain its meaning, and so help to build up the community. Suppose, my friends, that when I come to you I use ecstatic language: what good shall I do you, unless what I say contains something by way of revelation, or enlightenment, or prophecy, or instruction?

Even with inanimate things that produce sounds—a flute, say, or a lyre—unless their notes mark definite intervals, how can you tell what tune is being played? Or again, if the trumpet-call is not clear, who will prepare for battle? In the same way if your ecstatic utterance yields no precise meaning, how can anyone tell what you are saying? You will be talking into the air. How many different kinds of sound there are, or may be, in the world! Nothing is altogether soundless. Well then, if I do not know the meaning of the sound the speaker makes, his words will be gibberish to me, and mine to him. You are, I know, eager for gifts of the Spirit; then aspire above all to excel in those which build up the church.

I say, then, that the man who falls into ecstatic utterance should pray for the ability to interpret. If I use such language in my prayer, the Spirit in me prays, but my intellect lies fallow. What then? I will pray as I am inspired to pray, but I will also pray intelligently. I will sing hymns as I am inspired to sing, but I will sing intelligently too. Suppose you are praising God in the language of inspiration: how will the plain man who is present be able to say 'Amen' to your thanksgiving, when he does not know what you are saying? Your prayer of thanksgiving may be all that could be desired, but it is no help to the other man. Thank God, I am more gifted in ecstatic utterance than any of you,[a] but in the congregation I would rather speak five intelligible words, for the benefit of others as well as myself, than thousands of words in the language of ecstasy.

Do not be childish, my friends. Be as innocent of evil as babes, but at least be grown-up in your thinking. We read in the Law: 'I will speak to this nation through men of strange tongues, and by the lips of foreigners; and even so they will not heed me, says the Lord.' Clearly then these 'strange tongues' are not intended as a sign for believers, but for unbelievers, whereas prophecy is designed not for unbelievers but for those who

[a] *Or* . . . man. I say the thanksgiving; I use ecstatic speech more than any of you.

K.J.V.

which believe. 23 If therefore the whole church be come together into one place, and all speak with tongues, and there come in *those that are* unlearned, or unbelievers, will they not say that ye are mad? 24 But if all prophesy, and there come in one that believeth not, or *one* unlearned, he is convinced of all, he is judged of all: 25And thus are the secrets of his heart made manifest; and so falling down on *his* face he will worship God, and report that God is in you of a truth. 26 How is it then, brethren? when ye come together, every one of you hath a psalm, hath a doctrine, hath a tongue, hath a revelation, hath an interpretation. Let all things be done unto edifying. 27 If any man speak in an *unknown* tongue, *let it be* by two, or at the most *by* three, and *that* by course; and let one interpret. 28 But if there be no interpreter, let him keep silence in the church; and let him speak to himself, and to God. 29 Let the prophets speak two or three, and let the other judge. 30 If *any thing* be revealed to another that sitteth by, let the first hold his peace. 31 For ye may all prophesy one by one, that all may learn, and all may be comforted. 32And the spirits of the prophets are subject to the prophets. 33 For God is not *the author* of confusion, but of peace, as in all churches of the saints. 34 Let your women keep silence in the churches: for it is not permitted unto them to speak; but *they are commanded* to be under obedience, as also saith the law. 35And if they will learn any thing, let them ask their husbands at home: for it is a shame for women to speak in the church. 36 What! came the word of God out from you? or came it unto you only? 37 If any man think himself to be a prophet, or spiritual, let him acknowledge that the things that I write unto you are the commandments of the Lord. 38 But if any man be ignorant, let him be ignorant. 39 Wherefore, brethren, covet to prophesy, and forbid not to speak with tongues. 40 Let all things be done decently and in order.

R.S.V.

but for believers. 23 If, therefore, the whole church assembles and all speak in tongues, and outsiders or unbelievers enter, will they not say that you are mad? 24 But if all prophesy, and an unbeliever or outsider enters, he is convicted by all, he is called to account by all, 25 the secrets of his heart are disclosed; and so, falling on his face, he will worship God and declare that God is really among you. 26 What then, brethren? When you come together, each one has a hymn, a lesson, a revelation, a tongue, or an interpretation. Let all things be done for edification. 27 If any speak in a tongue, let there be only two or at most three, and each in turn; and let one interpret. 28 But if there is no one to interpret, let each of them keep silence in church and speak to himself and to God. 29 Let two or three prophets speak, and let the others weigh what is said. 30 If a revelation is made to another sitting by, let the first be silent. 31 For you can all prophesy one by one, so that all may learn and all be encouraged; 32 and the spirits of prophets are subject to prophets. 33 For God is not a God of confusion but of peace.

As in all the churches of the saints, 34 the women should keep silence in the churches. For they are not permitted to speak, but should be subordinate, as even the law says. 35 If there is anything they desire to know, let them ask their husbands at home. For it is shameful for a woman to speak in church. 36 What! Did the word of God originate with you, or are you the only ones it has reached?

37 If any one thinks that he is a prophet, or spiritual, he should acknowledge that what I am writing to you is a command of the Lord. 38 If any one does not recognize this, he is not recognized. 39 So, my brethren, earnestly desire to prophesy, and do not forbid speaking in tongues; 40 but all things should be done decently and in order.

PHILLIPS

of God, on the other hand, is a sign of God's power to those who do not believe rather than to believers. So that, if at a full church meeting you are all speaking with "tongues" and men come in who are both uninstructed and without faith, will they not say that you are insane? But if you are preaching God's word and such a man should come into your meeting, he is convicted and challenged by your united speaking of the truth. His secrets are exposed and he will fall on his knees acknowledging God and saying that God is truly among you!

Some practical regulations for   14. 26
the exercise of spiritual gifts

Well, then, my brothers, whenever you meet let everyone be ready to contribute a psalm, a piece of teaching, a spiritual truth, or a "tongue" with an interpreter. Everything should be done to make your church strong in the faith.

If the question of speaking with a "tongue" arises, confine the speaking to two or three at the most and have someone to interpret what is said. If you have no interpreter then let the speaker with a "tongue" keep silent in the church and speak only to himself and God. Don't have more than two or three preachers either, while the others think over what has been said. But should a message of truth come to one who is seated, then the original speaker should stop talking. For in this way you can all have opportunity to give a message, one after the other, and everyone will learn something and everyone will have his faith stimulated. The spirit of a true preacher is under that preacher's control, for God is not a God of disorder but of harmony, as is plain in all the churches.

The speaking of women in   14. 34
church is forbidden

Let women be silent in church; they are not to be allowed to speak. They must submit to this regulation, as the Law itself instructs. If they have questions to ask they must ask their husbands at home, for there is something indecorous about a woman's speaking in church.

You must accept the rules   14. 36
I have given by authority

Do I see you questioning my instructions? Are you beginning to imagine that the word of God originated in your church, or that you have a monopoly of God's truth? If any of your number think himself a true preacher and a spiritually-minded man, let him recognize that what I have written is by divine command! As for those who don't know it, well, we must just leave them in ignorance.

In conclusion then, my brothers, set your heart on preaching the word of God, while not forbidding the use of "tongues." Let everything be done decently and in order.

N.E.B.

hold the faith. So if the whole congregation is assembled and all are using the 'strange tongues' of ecstasy, and some uninstructed persons or unbelievers should enter, will they not think you are mad? But if all are uttering prophecies, the visitor, when he enters, hears from everyone something that searches his conscience and brings conviction, and the secrets of his heart are laid bare. So he will fall down and worship God, crying, 'God is certainly among you!'

To sum up, my friends: when you meet for worship, each of you contributes a hymn, some instruction, a revelation, an ecstatic utterance, or the interpretation of such an utterance. All of these must aim at one thing: to build up the church. If it is a matter of ecstatic utterance, only two should speak, or at most three, one at a time, and someone must interpret. If there is no interpreter, the speaker had better not address the meeting at all, but speak to himself and to God. Of the prophets, two or three may speak, while the rest exercise their judgement upon what is said. If someone else, sitting in his place, receives a revelation, let the first speaker stop. You can all prophesy, one at a time, so that the whole congregation may receive instruction and encouragement. It is for prophets to control prophetic inspiration, for the God who inspires them is not a God of disorder but of peace.

As in all congregations of God's people, women[a] should not address the meeting. They have no licence to speak, but should keep their place as the law directs. If there is something they want to know, they can ask their own husbands at home. It is a shocking thing that a woman should address the congregation.

Did the word of God originate with you? Or are you the only people to whom it came? If anyone claims to be inspired or a prophet, let him recognize that what I write has the Lord's authority. If he does not recognize this, he himself should not be recognized.[b]

In short, my friends, be eager to prophesy; do not forbid ecstatic utterance; but let all be done decently and in order.

[a] *Or* of peace, as in all communities of God's people. Women . . . [b] *Some witnesses read* If he does not acknowledge this, he is not acknowledged (by God).

15 Moreover, brethren, I declare unto you the gospel which I preached unto you, which also ye have received, and wherein ye stand; 2 By which also ye are saved, if ye keep in memory what I preached unto you, unless ye have believed in vain. 3 For I delivered unto you first of all that which I also received, how that Christ died for our sins according to the Scriptures; 4And that he was buried, and that he rose again the third day according to the Scriptures: 5And that he was seen of Cephas, then of the twelve: 6After that, he was seen of above five hundred brethren at once; of whom the greater part remain unto this present, but some are fallen asleep. 7After that, he was seen of James; then of all the apostles. 8And last of all he was seen of me also, as of one born out of due time. 9 For I am the least of the apostles, that am not meet to be called an apostle, because I persecuted the church of God. 10 But by the grace of God I am what I am: and his grace which *was bestowed* upon me was not in vain; but I laboured more abundantly than they all: yet not I, but the grace of God which was with me. 11 Therefore whether *it were* I or they, so we preach, and so ye believed. 12 Now if Christ be preached that he rose from the dead, how say some among you that there is no resurrection of the dead? 13 But if there be no resurrection of the dead, then is Christ not risen: 14And if Christ be not risen, then *is* our preaching vain, and your faith *is* also vain. 15 Yea, and we are found false witnesses of God; because we have testified of God that he raised up Christ: whom he raised not up, if so be that the dead rise not. 16 For if the dead rise not, then is not Christ raised: 17And if Christ be not raised, your faith *is* vain; ye are yet in your sins. 18 Then they also which are fallen asleep in Christ are perished. 19 If in this life only we have hope in Christ, we are of all men most miserable. 20 But now is Christ risen from the dead, *and* become the firstfruits of them that slept. 21 For since by man *came* death, by man *came* also the resurrection of the dead. 22 For as in Adam all die, even so in Christ shall all be made alive. 23 But every man in his own order: Christ the firstfruits; afterward they that are

15 Now I would remind you, brethren, in what terms I preached to you the gospel, which you received, in which you stand, 2 by which you are saved, if you hold it fast—unless you believed in vain.

3 For I delivered to you as of first importance what I also received, that Christ died for our sins in accordance with the scriptures, 4 that he was buried, that he was raised on the third day in accordance with the scriptures, 5 and that he appeared to Cephas, then to the twelve. 6 Then he appeared to more than five hundred brethren at one time, most of whom are still alive, though some have fallen asleep. 7 Then he appeared to James, then to all the apostles. 8 Last of all, as to one untimely born, he appeared also to me. 9 For I am the least of the apostles, unfit to be called an apostle, because I persecuted the church of God. 10 But by the grace of God I am what I am, and his grace toward me was not in vain. On the contrary, I worked harder than any of them, though it was not I, but the grace of God which is with me. 11 Whether then it was I or they, so we preach and so you believed.

12 Now if Christ is preached as raised from the dead, how can some of you say that there is no resurrection of the dead? 13 But if there is no resurrection of the dead, then Christ has not been raised; 14 if Christ has not been raised, then our preaching is in vain and your faith is in vain. 15 We are even found to be misrepresenting God, because we testified of God that he raised Christ, whom he did not raise if it is true that the dead are not raised. 16 For if the dead are not raised, then Christ has not been raised. 17 If Christ has not been raised, your faith is futile and you are still in your sins. 18 Then those also who have fallen asleep in Christ have perished. 19 If for this life only we have hoped in Christ, we are of all men most to be pitied.

20 But in fact Christ has been raised from the dead, the first fruits of those who have fallen asleep. 21 For as by a man came death, by a man has come also the resurrection of the dead. 22 For as in Adam all die, so also in Christ shall all be made alive. 23 But each in his own order: Christ the first fruits, then at his coming those

PHILLIPS

A reminder of the gospel message: **15. 1**
the resurrection is an integral
part of our faith

Now, my brothers, I want to speak about the gospel which I have previously preached to you, which you accepted, in which you are at present standing, and by which, if you remain faithful to the message I gave you, your salvation is being worked out—unless, of course, your faith had no meaning behind it at all.

For I passed on to you—as among the first to hear it, the message I had myself received—that Christ died for our sins, as the scriptures said he would; that he was buried and rose again on the third day, again as the scriptures foretold. He was seen by Cephas, then by the twelve, and subsequently he was seen simultaneously by over five hundred Christians, of whom the majority are still alive, though some have since died. He was then seen by James, then by all the messengers. And last of all, as if to one born abnormally late, he appeared to me! I am the least of the messengers, and indeed I do not deserve that title at all, because I persecuted the Church of God. But what I am now I am by the grace of God. The grace he gave me has not proved a barren gift. I have worked harder than any of the others—and yet it was not I but this same grace of God within me. In any event, whoever has done the work, whether I or they, this has been the message and this has been the foundation of your faith.

If the resurrection is the heart of   **15. 12**
the gospel how can any Christian
deny life after death?

Now if the rising of Christ from the dead is the very heart of our message, how can some of you deny that there is any resurrection? For if there is no such thing as the resurrection of the dead, then Christ was never raised. And if Christ was not raised then neither our preaching nor your faith has any meaning at all. Further it would mean that we are lying in our witness for God, for we have given our solemn testimony that he did raise up Christ—and that is utterly false if it should be true that the dead do not, in fact, rise again! For if the dead do not rise neither did Christ rise, and if Christ did not rise your faith is futile and your sins have never been forgiven. Moreover those who have died believing in Christ are utterly dead and gone. Truly, if our hope in Christ were limited to this life only we should, of all mankind, be the most to be pitied!

But Christianity rests on a fact   **15. 20**
—Christ did rise

But the glorious fact is that Christ *did* rise from the dead: he has become the very first to rise of all who sleep the sleep of death. As death entered the world through a man, so has rising from the dead come to us through a man! As members of a sinful race all men die; as members of the Christ of God all men shall be raised to life, each in his proper order, with Christ the very first and after him all who belong to him when he comes.

N.E.B.

Life After Death

15 And now, my brothers, I must remind you of the gospel that I preached to you; the gospel which you received, on which you have taken your stand, and which is now bringing you salvation. Do you still hold fast the Gospel as I preached it to you? If not, your conversion was in vain.[a]

First and foremost, I handed on to you the facts which had been imparted to me: that Christ died for our sins, in accordance with the scriptures; that he was buried; that he was raised to life on the third day, according to the scriptures; and that he appeared to Cephas, and afterwards to the Twelve. Then he appeared to over five hundred of our brothers at once, most of whom are still alive, though some have died. Then he appeared to James, and afterwards to all the apostles.

In the end he appeared even to me; though this birth of mine was monstrous, for I had persecuted the church of God and am therefore inferior to all other apostles—indeed not fit to be called an apostle. However, by God's grace I am what I am, nor has his grace been given to me in vain; on the contrary, in my labours I have outdone them all—not I, indeed, but the grace of God working with me. But what matter, I or they? This is what we all proclaim, and this is what you believed.

Now if this is what we proclaim, that Christ was raised from the dead, how can some of you say there is no resurrection of the dead? If there be no resurrection, then Christ was not raised; and if Christ was not raised, then our gospel is null and void, and so is your faith; and we turn out to be lying witnesses for God, because we bore witness that he raised Christ to life, whereas, if the dead are not raised, he did not raise him. For if the dead are not raised, it follows that Christ was not raised; and if Christ was not raised, your faith has nothing in it and you are still in your old state of sin. It follows also that those who have died within Christ's fellowship are utterly lost. If it is for this life only that Christ has given us hope,[b] we of all men are most to be pitied.

But the truth is, Christ was raised to life—the firstfruits of the harvest of the dead. For since it was a man who brought death into the world, a man also brought resurrection of the dead. As in Adam all men die, so in Christ all will be brought to life; but each in his own proper place: Christ the firstfruits, and afterwards, at

[a] *Or* Do you remember the terms in which I preached the Gospel to you?—for I assume you did not accept it thoughtlessly. [b] *Or* If it is only an uncertain hope that our life in Christ has given us . . .

K.J.V.

Christ's at his coming. 24 Then *cometh* the end, when he shall have delivered up the kingdom to God, even the Father; when he shall have put down all rule, and all authority and power. 25 For he must reign, till he hath put all enemies under his feet. 26 The last enemy *that* shall be destroyed *is* death. 27 For he hath put all things under his feet. But when he saith, All things are put under *him, it is* manifest that he is excepted, which did put all things under him. 28 And when all things shall be subdued unto him, then shall the Son also himself be subject unto him that put all things under him, that God may be all in all. 29 Else what shall they do which are baptized for the dead, if the dead rise not at all? why are they then baptized for the dead? 30 And why stand we in jeopardy every hour? 31 I protest by your rejoicing which I have in Christ Jesus our Lord, I die daily. 32 If after the manner of men I have fought with beasts at Ephesus, what advantageth it me, if the dead rise not? let us eat and drink; for to morrow we die. 33 Be not deceived: evil communications corrupt good manners. 34 Awake to righteousness, and sin not; for some have not the knowledge of God: I speak *this* to your shame. 35 But some *man* will say, How are the dead raised up? and with what body do they come? 36 *Thou* fool, that which thou sowest is not quickened, except it die: 37 And that which thou sowest, thou sowest not that body that shall be, but bare grain, it may chance of wheat, or of some other *grain:* 38 But God giveth it a body as it hath pleased him, and to every seed his own body. 39 All flesh *is* not the same flesh: but *there is* one *kind of* flesh of men, another flesh of beasts, another of fishes, *and* another of birds. 40 *There are* also celestial bodies, and bodies terrestrial: but the glory of the celestial *is* one, and the *glory* of the terrestrial *is* another. 41 *There is* one glory of the sun, and another glory of the moon, and another glory of the stars; for *one*

R.S.V.

who belong to Christ. 24 Then comes the end, when he delivers the kingdom to God the Father after destroying every rule and every authority and power. 25 For he must reign until he has put all his enemies under his feet. 26 The last enemy to be destroyed is death. 27 "For God *z* has put all things in subjection under his feet." But when it says, "All things are put in subjection under him," it is plain that he is excepted who put all things under him. 28 When all things are subjected to him, then the Son himself will also be subjected to him who put all things under him, that God may be everything to every one.

29 Otherwise, what do people mean by being baptized on behalf of the dead? If the dead are not raised at all, why are people baptized on their behalf? 30 Why am I in peril every hour? 31 I protest, brethren, by my pride in you which I have in Christ Jesus our Lord, I die every day! 32 What do I gain if, humanly speaking, I fought with beasts at Ephesus? If the dead are not raised, "Let us eat and drink, for tomorrow we die." 33 Do not be deceived: "Bad company ruins good morals." 34 Come to your right mind, and sin no more. For some have no knowledge of God. I say this to your shame.

35 But some one will ask, "How are the dead raised? With what kind of body do they come?" 36 You foolish man! What you sow does not come to life unless it dies. 37 And what you sow is not the body which is to be, but a bare kernel, perhaps of wheat or of some other grain. 38 But God gives it a body as he has chosen, and to each kind of seed its own body. 39 For not all flesh is alike, but there is one kind for men, another for animals, another for birds, and another for fish. 40 There are celestial bodies and there are terrestrial bodies; but the glory of the celestial is one, and the glory of the terrestrial is another. 41 There is one glory of the sun, and another glory of the moon, and another glory of the stars; for star differs from star in glory.

[z] Greek *he.*

PHILLIPS

Then, and not till then, comes the end when Christ, having abolished all other rule, authority and power, hands over the kingdom to God the Father. Christ's reign will and must continue until every enemy has been conquered. The last enemy of all to be destroyed is death itself. The scripture says:

He hath put all things in subjection under his feet.

But in the term "all things" it is quite obvious that God, who brings them all under subjection to Christ, is himself excepted. Nevertheless, when everything created has been made obedient to God, then shall the Son acknowledge himself subject to God the Father, who gave the Son power over all things. Thus, in the end, shall God be wholly and absolutely God.

To refuse to believe in the   15. 29
resurrection is both foolish
and wicked

Further, you should consider this, that if there is to be no resurrection what is the point of some of you being baptized for the dead by proxy? Why should you be baptized for *dead bodies?* And why should I live a life of such hourly danger? I assure you, by the certainty of Jesus Christ that we possess, that I face death every day of my life! And if, to use the popular expression, I have "fought with wild beasts" here in Ephesus, what is the good of an ordeal like that if there is no life after this one? Let us rather eat, drink and be merry, for tomorrow we die!

Don't let yourselves be deceived. Talking about things that are not true is bound to be reflected in practical conduct. Come back to your senses, and don't dabble in sinful doubts. Remember that there are men who have plenty to say but have no knowledge of God. You should be ashamed that I have to write like this at all!

Parallels in nature help us to   15. 35
grasp the truths of the
resurrection

But perhaps someone will ask: "How is the resurrection achieved? With what sort of body do the dead arrive?" Now that is talking without using your minds! In your own experience you know that a seed does not germinate without itself "dying." When you sow a seed you do not sow the "body" that will eventually be produced, but bare grain, of wheat, for example, or one of the other seeds. God gives the seed a "body" according to his laws—a different "body" to each kind of seed.

Then again, even in this world, all flesh is not identical. There is a difference in the flesh of human beings, animals, fish and birds. There are bodies which exist in this world, and bodies which exist in the heavens. These bodies are not, as it were, in competition; the splendor of an earthly body is quite a different thing from the splendor of a heavenly body. The sun, the moon and the stars all have their own particular splendor, while among the stars themselves there are different kinds of splendor.

N.E.B.

his coming, those who belong to Christ. Then comes the end, when he delivers up the kingdom to God the Father, after abolishing every kind of domination, authority, and power. For he is destined to reign until God has put all enemies under his feet; and the last enemy to be abolished is death.[a] Scripture says, 'He has put all things in subjection under his feet.' But in saying 'all things', it clearly means to exclude God who subordinates them; and when all things are thus subject to him, then the Son himself will also be made subordinate to God who made all things subject to him, and thus God will be all in all.

Again, there are those who receive baptism on behalf of the dead. Why should they do this? If the dead are not raised to life at all, what do they mean by being baptized on their behalf?

And we ourselves—why do we face these dangers hour by hour? Every day I die: I swear it by my pride in you, my brothers—for in Christ Jesus our Lord I am proud of you. If, as the saying is, I 'fought wild beasts' at Ephesus, what have I gained by it?[b] If the dead are never raised to life, 'let us eat and drink, for tomorrow we die'.

Make no mistake: 'Bad company is the ruin of a good character.' Come back to a sober and upright life and leave your sinful ways. There are some who know nothing of God; to your shame I say it.

But, you may ask, how are the dead raised? In what kind of body? A senseless question! The seed you sow does not come to life unless it has first died; and what you sow is not the body that shall be, but a naked grain, perhaps of wheat, or of some other kind; and God clothes it with the body of his choice, each seed with its own particular body. All flesh is not the same flesh: there is flesh of men, flesh of beasts, of birds, and of fishes—all different. There are heavenly bodies and earthly bodies; and the splendour of the heavenly bodies is one thing, the splendour of the earthly, another. The sun has a splendour of its own, the moon another splendour, and the stars another, for star differs from star in brightness. So it is with the resurrec-

[a] *Or* Then at the end, when . . . power (for he . . . feet), the last enemy, death, will be abolished.
[b] *Or* If, as men do, I had fought wild beasts at Ephesus, what good would it be to me? *or* If I had been in no better case than one fighting beasts in the arena at Ephesus, what good would it be to me?

K.J.V.

star differeth from *another* star in glory. 42 So also *is* the resurrection of the dead. It is sown in corruption, it is raised in incorruption: 43 It is sown in dishonour, it is raised in glory: it is sown in weakness, it is raised in power: 44 It is sown a natural body, it is raised a spiritual body. There is a natural body, and there is a spiritual body. 45And so it is written, The first man Adam was made a living soul; the last Adam was made a quickening spirit. 46 Howbeit that *was* not first which is spiritual, but that which is natural; and afterward that which is spiritual. 47 The first man *is* of the earth, earthy: the second man *is* the Lord from heaven. 48As *is* the earthy, such *are* they also that are earthy: and as *is* the heavenly, such *are* they also that are heavenly. 49And as we have borne the image of the earthy, we shall also bear the image of the heavenly. 50 Now this I say, brethren, that flesh and blood cannot inherit the kingdom of God; neither doth corruption inherit incorruption. 51 Behold, I shew you a mystery; We shall not all sleep, but we shall all be changed, 52 In a moment, in the twinkling of an eye, at the last trump: for the trumpet shall sound, and the dead shall be raised incorruptible, and we shall be changed. 53 For this corruptible must put on incorruption, and this mortal *must* put on immortality. 54 So when this corruptible shall have put on incorruption, and this mortal shall have put on immortality, then shall be brought to pass the saying that is written, Death is swallowed up in victory. 55 O death, where *is* thy sting? O grave, where *is* thy victory? 56 The sting of death *is* sin; and the strength of sin *is* the law. 57 But thanks *be* to God, which giveth us the victory through our Lord Jesus Christ. 58 Therefore, my beloved brethren, be ye steadfast, unmoveable, always abounding in the work of the Lord, forasmuch as ye know that your labour is not in vain in the Lord.

R.S.V.

42 So is it with the resurrection of the dead. What is sown is perishable, what is raised is imperishable. 43 It is sown in dishonor, it is raised in glory. It is sown in weakness, it is raised in power. 44 It is sown a physical body, it is raised a spiritual body. If there is a physical body, there is also a spiritual body. 45 Thus it is written, "The first man Adam became a living being"; the last Adam became a life-giving spirit. 46 But it is not the spiritual which is first but the physical, and then the spiritual. 47 The first man was from the earth, a man of dust; the second man is from heaven. 48As was the man of dust, so are those who are of the dust; and as is the man of heaven, so are those who are of heaven. 49 Just as we have borne the image of the man of dust, we shall *a* also bear the image of the man of heaven. 50 I tell you this, brethren: flesh and blood cannot inherit the kingdom of God, nor does the perishable inherit the imperishable.

51 Lo! I tell you a mystery. We shall not all sleep, but we shall all be changed, 52 in a moment, in the twinkling of an eye, at the last trumpet. For the trumpet will sound, and the dead will be raised imperishable, and we shall be changed. 53 For this perishable nature must put on the imperishable, and this mortal nature must put on immortality. 54 When the perishable puts on the imperishable, and the mortal puts on immortality, then shall come to pass the saying that is written:

"Death is swallowed up in victory."
55 "O death, where is thy victory?
    O death, where is thy sting?"
56 The sting of death is sin, and the power of sin is the law. 57 But thanks be to God, who gives the victory through our Lord Jesus Christ.

58 Therefore, my beloved brethren, be steadfast, immovable, always abounding in the work of the Lord, knowing that in the Lord your labor is not in vain.

16 Now concerning the collection for the saints, as I have given order to the churches of Galatia, even so do ye. 2 Upon the first *day* of the week let every one of you lay by him in store, as *God* hath prospered him, that there be no gatherings when I come. 3And when I come, whomsoever ye shall approve by *your* letters, them will I send to bring your liberality unto Jerusalem. 4And if it be meet that I go also,

16 Now concerning the contribution for the saints: as I directed the churches of Galatia, so you also are to do. 2 On the first day of every week, each of you is to put something aside and store it up, as he may prosper, so that contributions need not be made when I come. 3And when I arrive, I will send those whom you accredit by letter to carry your gift to Jerusalem. 4 If it seems advisable that I should go also, they will accompany me.

[a] Other ancient authorities read *let us.*

PHILLIPS

There are illustrations here of the raising of the dead. The body is "sown" in corruption; it is raised beyond the reach of corruption. It is "sown" in dishonor; it is raised in splendor. It is sown in weakness; it is raised in power. It is sown a natural body; it is raised a spiritual body. As there is a natural body so will there be a spiritual body.

It is written, moreover, that,

The first man Adam became a living soul.

So the last Adam is a life-giving Spirit. But we should notice that the order is "natural" first and then "spiritual." The first man came out of the earth, a material creature. The second man came from Heaven and was the Lord himself. For the life of this world men are made like the material man; but for the life that is to come they are made like the one from Heaven. So that just as we have been made like the material pattern, so we shall be made like the Heavenly pattern. For I assure you, my brothers, it is utterly impossible for flesh and blood to possess the kingdom of God. The transitory could never possess the everlasting.

The dead and the living will be fitted for immortality   15. 51

Listen, and I shall tell you a secret. We shall not all die, but suddenly, in the twinkling of an eye, every one of us will be changed as the trumpet sounds! The trumpet will sound and the dead shall be raised beyond the reach of corruption, and we who are still alive shall suddenly be utterly changed. For this perishable nature of ours must be wrapped in imperishability; these bodies which are mortal must be wrapped in immortality. So when the perishable is lost in the imperishable, the mortal lost in the immortal, this saying will come true:

Death is swallowed up in victory.

For where now, O death, is your power to hurt us? Where now, O grave, is the victory you hoped to win? It is sin which gives death its sting, and it is the Law which gives sin its strength. All thanks to God, then, who gives us the victory over these things through our Lord Jesus Christ!

And so, brothers of mine, stand firm! Let nothing move you as you busy yourselves in the Lord's work. Be sure that nothing you do for him is ever lost or ever wasted.

The matter of the fund: my own immediate plans   16. 1

Now as far as the fund for Christians in need is concerned, I should like you to follow the same rule as I gave to the Galatian church.

On the first day of the week let everyone put so much by him, according to his financial prosperity, so that there will be no need for collections when I come. Then, on my arrival, I shall send whomever you approve to take your gift, with my recommendation to Jerusalem. If it seems right for me to go as well, we shall

N.E.B.

tion of the dead. What is sown in the earth as a perishable thing is raised imperishable. Sown in humiliation, it is raised in glory; sown in weakness, it is raised in power; sown as an animal body, it is raised as a spiritual body.

If there is such a thing as an animal body, there is also a spiritual body. It is in this sense that Scripture says, 'The first man, Adam, became an animate being', whereas the last Adam has become a life-giving spirit. Observe, the spiritual does not come first; the animal body comes first, and then the spiritual. The first man was made 'of the dust of the earth': the second man is from heaven. The man made of dust is the pattern of all men of dust, and the heavenly man is the pattern of all the heavenly. As we have worn the likeness of the man made of dust, so we shall wear the likeness of the heavenly man.

What I mean, my brothers, is this: flesh and blood can never possess the kingdom of God, and the perishable cannot possess immortality. Listen! I will unfold a mystery: we shall not all die, but we shall all be changed in a flash, in the twinkling of an eye, at the last trumpet-call. For the trumpet will sound, and the dead will rise immortal, and we shall be changed. This perishable being must be clothed with the imperishable, and what is mortal must be clothed with immortality. And when[a] our mortality has been clothed with immortality, then the saying of Scripture will come true: 'Death is swallowed up; victory is won!' 'O Death, where is your victory? O Death, where is your sting?' The sting of death is sin, and sin gains its power from the law; but, God be praised, he gives us the victory through our Lord Jesus Christ.

Therefore, my beloved brothers, stand firm and immovable, and work for the Lord always, work without limit, since you know that in the Lord your labour cannot be lost.

Christian Giving

16 And now about the collection in aid of God's people: you should follow my directions to our congregations in Galatia. Every Sunday each of you is to put aside and keep by him a sum in proportion to his gains, so that there may be no collecting when I come. When I arrive, I will give letters of introduction to persons approved by you, and send them to carry your gift to Jerusalem. If it should se m worth while for me to go as well, they shal' with me.

[a] *Some witnesses insert* our perishable natu been clothed with the imperishable, and . .

K.J.V.

they shall go with me. 5 Now I will come unto you, when I shall pass through Macedonia: for I do pass through Macedonia. 6 And it may be that I will abide, yea, and winter with you, that ye may bring me on my journey whithersoever I go. 7 For I will not see you now by the way; but I trust to tarry a while with you, if the Lord permit. 8 But I will tarry at Ephesus until Pentecost. 9 For a great door and effectual is opened unto me, and *there are* many adversaries. 10 Now if Timotheus come, see that he may be with you without fear: for he worketh the work of the Lord, as I also *do*. 11 Let no man therefore despise him: but conduct him forth in peace, that he may come unto me: for I look for him with the brethren. 12 As touching *our* brother Apollos, I greatly desired him to come unto you with the brethren: but his will was not at all to come at this time; but he will come when he shall have convenient time. 13 Watch ye, stand fast in the faith, quit you like men, be strong. 14 Let all your things be done with charity. 15 I beseech you, brethren, (ye know the house of Stephanas, that it is the firstfruits of Achaia, and *that* they have addicted themselves to the ministry of the saints,) 16 That ye submit yourselves unto such, and to every one that helpeth with *us*, and laboureth. 17 I am glad of the coming of Stephanas and Fortunatus and Achaicus: for that which was lacking on your part they have supplied. 18 For they have refreshed my spirit and yours: therefore acknowledge ye them that are such. 19 The churches of Asia salute you. Aquila and Priscilla salute you much in the Lord, with the church that is in their house. 20 All the brethren greet you. Greet ye one another with a holy kiss. 21 The salutation of *me* Paul with mine own hand. 22 If any man love not the Lord Jesus Christ, let him be Anathema, Maran atha. 23 The grace of our Lord Jesus Christ *be* with you. 24 My love *be* with you all in Christ Jesus. Amen.

The first *epistle* to the Corinthians was written from Philippi by Stephanas, and Fortunatus, and Achaicus, and Timotheus.

R.S.V.

5 I will visit you after passing through Macedonia, for I intend to pass through Macedonia, 6 and perhaps I will stay with you or even spend the winter, so that you may speed me on my journey, wherever I go. 7 For I do not want to see you now just in passing; I hope to spend some time with you, if the Lord permits. 8 But I will stay in Ephesus until Pentecost, 9 for a wide door for effective work has opened to me, and there are many adversaries.

10 When Timothy comes, see that you put him at ease among you, for he is doing the work of the Lord, as I am. 11 So let no one despise him. Speed him on his way in peace, that he may return to me; for I am expecting him with the brethren.

12 As for our brother Apollos, I strongly urged him to visit you with the other brethren, but it was not at all his will *b* to come now. He will come when he has opportunity.

13 Be watchful, stand firm in your faith, be courageous, be strong. 14 Let all that you do be done in love.

15 Now, brethren, you know that the household of Stephanas were the first converts in Achaia, and they have devoted themselves to the service of the saints; 16 I urge you to be subject to such men and to every fellow worker and laborer. 17 I rejoice at the coming of Stephanas and Fortunatus and Achaicus, because they have made up for your absence; 18 for they refreshed my spirit as well as yours. Give recognition to such men.

19 The churches of Asia send greetings. Aquila and Prisca, together with the church in their house, send you hearty greetings in the Lord. 20 All the brethren send greetings. Greet one another with a holy kiss.

21 I, Paul, write this greeting with my own hand. 22 If any one has no love for the Lord, let him be accursed. Our Lord, come! *c* 23 The grace of the Lord Jesus be with you. 24 My love be with you all in Christ Jesus. Amen.

[b] Or *God's will for him.* [c] Greek *Maranatha.*

PHILLIPS

make up a party together. I shall come to you after my intended journey through Macedonia and I may stay with you a while or even spend the winter with you. Then you can see me on my way—wherever it is that I go next. I don't wish to see you now, for it would merely be in passing, and I hope to spend some time with you, if it is the Lord's will. I shall stay here in Ephesus until the feast of Pentecost, for there is a great opportunity of doing useful work, and there are many people against me.

News of Timothy and Apollos   16. 10

If Timothy comes to you, put him at his ease. He is as genuine a worker for the Lord as I am, and there is therefore no reason to look down on him. Send him on his way in peace, for I am expecting him to come to me here with the other Christian brothers. As for our brother Apollos, I pressed him strongly to go to you with the rest, but it was definitely not God's will for him to do so then. However, he will come to you as soon as an opportunity occurs.

A little sermon in a nutshell!   16. 13

Be on your guard, stand firm in the faith, live like men, be strong! Let everything that you do be done in love.

A request, and final greetings   16. 15

You remember the household of Stephanas, the first men of Achaia to be won for Christ? Well, they have made up their minds to devote their lives to looking after Christian brothers. I do beg you to recognize them as Christ's ministers, and to extend your recognition to all their helpers and workers.

I am very glad that Stephanas, Fortunatus and Achaicus have arrived. They have made up for my not seeing you. They are a tonic to me and to you. You should appreciate having men like that!

Greetings from the churches of Asia. Aquila and Prisca send you their warmest Christian greetings and so does the church that meets in their house. All the Christians here send greetings. I should like you to shake hands all round as a sign of Christian love.

Here is my own greeting, written by me, Paul. If any man does not love the Lord, let him be accursed; may the Lord soon come!

The grace of the Lord Jesus be with you and my love be with you all in Christ Jesus.

PAUL

N.E.B.

I shall come to Corinth after passing through Macedonia—for I am travelling by way of Macedonia—and I may stay with you, perhaps even for the whole winter, and then you can help me on my way wherever I go next. I do not want this to be a flying visit; I hope to spend some time with you, if the Lord permits. But I shall remain at Ephesus until Whitsuntide, for a great opportunity has opened for effective work, and there is much opposition.

If Timothy comes, see that you put him at his ease; for it is the Lord's work that he is engaged upon, as I am myself; so no one must slight him. Send him happily on his way to join me, since I am waiting for him with our friends. As for our friend Apollos, I urged him strongly to go to Corinth with the others, but he was quite determined not to go[a] at present; he will go when opportunity offers.

Be alert; stand firm in the faith; be valiant and strong. Let all you do be done in love.

I have a request to make of you, my brothers. You know that the Stephanas family were the first converts in Achaia, and have laid themselves out to serve God's people. I wish you to give their due position to such persons, and indeed to everyone who labours hard at our common task. It is a great pleasure to me that Stephanas, Fortunatus, and Achaicus have arrived, because they have done what you had no chance to do; they have relieved my mind—and no doubt yours too. Such men deserve recognition.

Greetings from the congregations in Asia. Many greetings in the Lord from Aquila and Prisca and the congregation at their house. Greetings from all the brothers. Greet one another with the kiss of peace.

This greeting is in my own hand—PAUL.

If anyone does not love the Lord, let him be outcast.
Marana tha—Come, O Lord!
The grace of the Lord Jesus Christ be with you.
My love to you all in Christ Jesus. Amen.

---

[a] *Or* but it was by no means the will of God that he should go . . .

THE SECOND EPISTLE OF
PAUL THE APOSTLE
TO THE
CORINTHIANS

THE SECOND
LETTER OF PAUL TO THE
CORINTHIANS

1 Paul, an apostle of Jesus Christ by the will of God, and Timothy *our* brother, unto the church of God which is at Corinth, with all the saints which are in all Achaia: 2 Grace *be* to you, and peace, from God our Father, and *from* the Lord Jesus Christ. 3 Blessed *be* God, even the Father of our Lord Jesus Christ, the Father of mercies, and the God of all comfort; 4 Who comforteth us in all our tribulation, that we may be able to comfort them which are in any trouble, by the comfort wherewith we ourselves are comforted of God. 5 For as the sufferings of Christ abound in us, so our consolation also aboundeth by Christ. 6And whether we be afflicted, *it is* for your consolation and salvation, which is effectual in the enduring of the same sufferings which we also suffer: or whether we be comforted, *it is* for your consolation and salvation. 7And our hope of you *is* steadfast, knowing, that as ye are partakers of the sufferings, so *shall ye be* also of the consolation. 8 For we would not, brethren, have you ignorant of our trouble which came to us in Asia, that we were pressed out of measure, above strength, insomuch that we despaired even of life: 9 But we had the sentence of death in ourselves, that we should not trust in ourselves, but in God which raiseth the dead: 10 Who delivered us from so great a death, and doth deliver: in whom we trust that he will yet deliver *us;* 11 Ye also helping together by prayer for us, that for the gift *bestowed* upon us by the means of many persons thanks may be given by many on our behalf. 12 For our rejoicing is this, the testimony of our conscience, that in simplicity and

1 Paul, an apostle of Christ Jesus by the will of God, and Timothy our brother.
To the church of God which is at Corinth, with all the saints who are in the whole of Achaia:
2 Grace to you and peace from God our Father and the Lord Jesus Christ.

3 Blessed be the God and Father of our Lord Jesus Christ, the Father of mercies and God of all comfort, 4 who comforts us in all our affliction, so that we may be able to comfort those who are in any affliction, with the comfort with which we ourselves are comforted by God. 5 For as we share abundantly in Christ's sufferings, so through Christ we share abundantly in comfort too.[a] 6 If we are afflicted, it is for your comfort and salvation; and if we are comforted, it is for your comfort, which you experience when you patiently endure the same sufferings that we suffer. 7 Our hope for you is unshaken; for we know that as you share in our sufferings, you will also share in our comfort.
8 For we do not want you to be ignorant, brethren, of the affliction we experienced in Asia; for we were so utterly, unbearably crushed that we despaired of life itself. 9 Why, we felt that we had received the sentence of death; but that was to make us rely not on ourselves but on God who raises the dead; 10 he delivered us from so deadly a peril, and he will deliver us; on him we have set our hope that he will deliver us again. 11 You also must help us by prayer, so that many will give thanks on our behalf for the blessing granted us in answer to many prayers.
12 For our boast is this, the testimony of our conscience that we have behaved in the world,

---

[a] Or, *For as the sufferings of Christ abound for us, so also our comfort abounds through Christ.*

THE SECOND LETTER TO THE CHRISTIANS AT

CORINTH

This letter comes to you from Paul, God's messenger for Christ Jesus by the will of God, and from brother Timothy, and is addressed to the church of God in Corinth and all Christians throughout Achaia.

May grace and peace come to you from God our Father and from the Lord Jesus Christ.

God's encouragements are adequate 1. 3 for all life's troubles

Thank God, the Father of our Lord Jesus Christ, that he is our Father and the source of all mercy and comfort. For he gives us comfort in our trials so that we in turn may be able to give the same sort of strong sympathy to others in theirs. Indeed, experience shows that the more we share Christ's suffering, the more we are able to give of his encouragement. This means that if we experience trouble we can pass on to you comfort and spiritual help; for if we ourselves have been comforted we know how to encourage you to endure patiently the same sort of troubles that we have ourselves endured. We are quite confident that if you have to suffer troubles as we have done, then, like us, you will find the comfort and encouragement of God.

Man's extremity is God's   1. 8 opportunity

We should like you, our brothers, to know something of what we went through in Asia. At that time we were completely overwhelmed; the burden was more than we could bear; in fact we told ourselves that this was the end. Yet we believe now that we had this experience of coming to the end of our tether that we might learn to trust, not in ourselves, but in God who can raise the dead. It was God who preserved us from imminent death, and it is he who still preserves us. Further, we trust him to keep us safe in the future, and here you can join in and help by praying for us, so that the good that is done to us in answer to many prayers will mean eventually that many will thank God for our preservation.

Our dealings with you have   1. 12 always been straightforward

Now it is a matter of pride to us—endorsed by our conscience—that our activities in this

THE SECOND LETTER OF PAUL TO THE

CORINTHIANS

Personal Religion and the Ministry

1 From Paul, apostle of Christ Jesus by God's will, and our colleague Timothy, to the congregation of God's people at Corinth, together with all who are dedicated to him throughout the whole of Achaia.

Grace and peace to you from God our Father and the Lord Jesus Christ.

Praise be to the God and Father of our Lord Jesus Christ, the all-merciful Father, the God whose consolation never fails us! He comforts us in all our troubles, so that we in turn may be able to comfort others in any trouble of theirs and to share with them the consolation we ourselves receive from God. As Christ's cup of suffering overflows, and we suffer with him, so also through Christ our consolation overflows. If distress be our lot, it is the price we pay for your salvation; if our lot be consolation, it is to help us to bring you comfort, and strength to face with fortitude the same sufferings we now endure. And our hope for you is firmly grounded;[a] for we know that if you have part in the suffering, you have part also in the divine consolation.

In saying this, we should like you to know, dear friends, how serious was the trouble that came upon us in the province of Asia. The burden of it was far too heavy for us to bear, so heavy that we even despaired of life. Indeed, we felt in our hearts that we had received a death-sentence. This was meant to teach us not to place reliance on ourselves, but on God who raises the dead. From such mortal peril God delivered us; and he will deliver us again,[b] he on whom our hope is fixed. Yes, he will continue to deliver us, if you will co-operate by praying for us. Then, with so many people praying for our deliverance, there will be many to give thanks on our behalf for the gracious favour God has shown towards us.

There is one thing we are proud of: our conscience assures us that in our dealings with our

[a] *Some witnesses give these clauses* If distress . . . firmly grounded *in different sequence.* [b] *Some witnesses read* and he still delivers us.

547

K.J.V.

godly sincerity, not with fleshly wisdom, but by the grace of God, we have had our conversation in the world, and more abundantly to youward. 13 For we write none other things unto you, than what ye read or acknowledge; and I trust ye shall acknowledge even to the end; 14 As also ye have acknowledged us in part, that we are your rejoicing, even as ye also *are* ours in the day of the Lord Jesus. 15And in this confidence I was minded to come unto you before, that ye might have a second benefit; 16And to pass by you into Macedonia, and to come again out of Macedonia unto you, and of you to be brought on my way toward Judea. 17 When I therefore was thus minded, did I use lightness? or the things that I purpose, do I purpose according to the flesh, that with me there should be yea, yea, and nay, nay? 18 But as God *is* true, our word toward you was not yea and nay. 19 For the Son of God, Jesus Christ, who was preached among you by us, *even* by me and Silvanus and Timotheus, was not yea and nay, but in him was yea. 20 For all the promises of God in him *are* yea, and in him Amen, unto the glory of God by us. 21 Now he which stablisheth us with you in Christ, and hath anointed us, *is* God; 22 Who hath also sealed us, and given the earnest of the Spirit in our hearts. 23 Moreover I call God for a record upon my soul, that to spare you I came not as yet unto Corinth. 24 Not for that we have dominion over your faith, but are helpers of your joy: for by faith ye stand.

R.S.V.

and still more toward you, with holiness and godly sincerity, not by earthly wisdom but by the grace of God. 13 For we write you nothing but what you can read and understand; I hope you will understand fully, 14 as you have understood in part, that you can be proud of us as we can be of you, on the day of the Lord Jesus.

15 Because I was sure of this, I wanted to come to you first, so that you might have a double pleasure;[b] 16 I wanted to visit you on my way to Macedonia, and to come back to you from Macedonia and have you send me on my way to Judea. 17 Was I vacillating when I wanted to do this? Do I make my plans like a worldly man, ready to say Yes and No at once? 18As surely as God is faithful, our word to you has not been Yes and No. 19 For the Son of God, Jesus Christ, whom we preached among you, Silvanus and Timothy and I, was not Yes and No; but in him it is always Yes. 20 For all the promises of God find their Yes in him. That is why we utter the Amen through him, to the glory of God. 21 But it is God who establishes us with you in Christ, and has commissioned us; 22 he has put his seal upon us and given us his Spirit in our hearts as a guarantee.

23 But I call God to witness against me—it was to spare you that I refrained from coming to Corinth. 24 Not that we lord it over your faith; we work with you for your joy, for you stand firm in your faith.

2 But I determined this with myself, that I would not come again to you in heaviness. 2 For if I make you sorry, who is he then that maketh me glad, but the same which is made sorry by me? 3And I wrote this same unto you, lest, when I came, I should have sorrow from them of whom I ought to rejoice; having confidence in you all, that my joy is *the joy* of you all. 4 For out of much affliction and anguish of heart I wrote unto you with many tears; not that ye should be grieved, but that ye might know the love which I have more abundantly unto you. 5 But if any have caused grief, he hath not grieved me, but in part: that I may not over-

2 For I made up my mind not to make you another painful visit. 2 For if I cause you pain, who is there to make me glad but the one whom I have pained? 3And I wrote as I did, so that when I came I might not be pained by those who should have made me rejoice, for I felt sure of all of you, that my joy would be the joy of you all. 4 For I wrote you out of much affliction and anguish of heart and with many tears, not to cause you pain but to let you know the abundant love that I have for you.

5 But if any one has caused pain, he has caused it not to me, but in some measure—not

[b] Other ancient authorities read *favor*.

world, particularly our dealings with you, have been absolutely aboveboard and sincere before God. They have not been marked by any worldly wisdom, but by the grace of God. Our letters to you have no double meaning—they mean just what you understand them to mean when you read them. I hope you will always understand these letters, as I believe some of you have understood me, and realize that you can be as honestly proud of us as we shall be of you on the day of the Lord Jesus.

Change of plan does not necessarily mean fickleness of heart

1. 15

Trusting you, and believing that you trusted us, our original plan was to pay you a visit first, and give you a double "treat." We meant to come here to Macedonia after first visiting you, and then to visit you again on leaving here. You could thus have helped us on our way toward Judaea. Because we had to change this plan, does it mean that we are fickle? Do you think I plan with my tongue in my cheek, saying "yes" and meaning "no"? We solemnly assure you that as certainly as God is faithful so we have never given you a message meaning "yes" and "no." Jesus Christ, the Son of God, whom Silvanus, Timothy and I have preached to you, is himself no doubtful quantity, he is the divine "Yes." Every promise of God finds its affirmative in him, and through him can be said the final amen, to the glory of God. We owe our position in Christ to this God of positive promise: it is he who has consecrated us to this special work, he who has given us the living guarantee of the Spirit in our hearts. Are we then the men to say one thing and mean another?

I have never wanted to hurt you

1. 23

No, I declare before God that it was to avoid hurting you that I did not come to Corinth. We are not trying to dominate you and your faith— your faith is firm enough—but we can work with you to increase your joy.

And I made up my mind that I would not pay you another painful visit. For what point is there in my depressing the very people who can give me such joy? The real purpose of my previous letter was in fact to save myself from being saddened by those whom I might reasonably expect to bring me joy. I have such confidence in you that my joy depends on all of you! I wrote to you in deep distress and out of a most unhappy heart (I don't mind telling you I shed tears over that letter), not, believe me, to cause you pain, but to show you how deep is my care for your welfare.

A word of explanation

2. 5

There was a reason for my stern words; this is my advice now. If the behavior of a certain person has caused distress, it does not mean so

fellow-men, and above all in our dealings with you, our conduct has been governed by a devout and godly sincerity,[a] by the grace of God and not by worldly wisdom. There is nothing in our letters to you but what you can read for yourselves, and understand too. Partial as your present knowledge of us is, you will I hope come to understand fully that you have as much reason to be proud of us, as we of you, on the Day of our Lord Jesus.

It was because I felt so confident about all this that I had intended to come first of all to you[b] and give you the benefit of a double visit: I meant to visit you on my way to Macedonia, and after leaving Macedonia, to return to you, and you would then send me on my way to Judaea. That was my intention; did I lightly change my mind?[c] Or do I, when I frame my plans, frame them as a worldly man might, so that it should rest with me to say 'yes' and 'yes', or 'no' and 'no'? As God is true, the language in which we address you is not an ambiguous blend of Yes and No. The Son of God, Christ Jesus, proclaimed among you by us (by Silvanus and Timothy, I mean, as well as myself), was never a blend of Yes and No. With him it was, and is, Yes. He is the Yes pronounced upon God's promises, every one of them. That is why, when we give glory to God, it is through Christ Jesus that we say 'Amen'. And if you and we belong to Christ, guaranteed as his and anointed, it is all God's doing; it is God also who has set his seal upon us, and as a pledge of what is to come has given the Spirit to dwell in our hearts.

I appeal to God to witness what I am going to say; I stake my life upon it: it was out of consideration for you that I did not after all come to Corinth. Do not think we are dictating the terms of your faith; your hold on the faith is secure enough. We are working with you for your own happiness.

2 So I made up my mind that my next visit to you must not be another painful one. If I cause pain to you, who is left to cheer me up, except you, whom I have offended? This is precisely the point I made in my letter: I did not want, I said, to come and be made miserable by the very people who ought to have made me happy; and I had sufficient confidence in you all to know that for me to be happy is for all of you to be happy. That letter I sent you came out of great distress and anxiety; how many tears I shed as I wrote it! But I never meant to cause you pain; I wanted you rather to know the love, the more than ordinary love, that I have for you.

Any injury that has been done, has not been done to me; to some extent, not to labour the

[a] *Some witnesses read* by sincere and godly singleness of mind. [b] *Or* had originally intended to come to you . . . [c] *Or* In forming this intention, did I act irresponsibly?

K.J.V.

charge you all. 6 Sufficient to such a man *is* this punishment, which *was inflicted* of many. 7 So that contrariwise ye *ought* rather to forgive *him,* and comfort *him,* lest perhaps such a one should be swallowed up with overmuch sorrow. 8 Wherefore I beseech you that ye would confirm *your* love toward him. 9 For to this end also did I write, that I might know the proof of you, whether ye be obedient in all things. 10 To whom ye forgive any thing, I *forgive* also: for if I forgave any thing, to whom I forgave *it,* for your sakes *forgave I it* in the person of Christ; 11 Lest Satan should get an advantage of us: for we are not ignorant of his devices. 12 Furthermore, when I came to Troas to *preach* Christ's gospel, and a door was opened unto me of the Lord, 13 I had no rest in my spirit, because I found not Titus my brother; but taking my leave of them, I went from thence into Macedonia. 14 Now thanks *be* unto God, which always causeth us to triumph in Christ, and maketh manifest the savour of his knowledge by us in every place. 15 For we are unto God a sweet savour of Christ, in them that are saved, and in them that perish: 16 To the one *we are* the savour of death unto death; and to the other the savour of life unto life. And who *is* sufficient for these things? 17 For we are not as many, which corrupt the word of God: but as of sincerity, but as of God, in the sight of God speak we in Christ.

R.S.V.

to put it too severely—to you all. 6 For such a one this punishment by the majority is enough; 7 so you should rather turn to forgive and comfort him, or he may be overwhelmed by excessive sorrow. 8 So I beg you to reaffirm your love for him. 9 For this is why I wrote, that I might test you and know whether you are obedient in everything. 10 Any one whom you forgive, I also forgive. What I have forgiven, if I have forgiven anything, has been for your sake in the presence of Christ, 11 to keep Satan from gaining the advantage over us; for we are not ignorant of his designs.

12 When I came to Troas to preach the gospel of Christ, a door was opened for me in the Lord; 13 but my mind could not rest because I did not find my brother Titus there. So I took leave of them and went on to Macedonia.

14 But thanks be to God, who in Christ always leads us in triumph, and through us spreads the fragrance of the knowledge of him everywhere. 15 For we are the aroma of Christ to God among those who are being saved and among those who are perishing, 16 to one a fragrance from death to death, to the other a fragrance from life to life. Who is sufficient for these things? 17 For we are not, like so many, peddlers of God's word; but as men of sincerity, as commissioned by God, in the sight of God we speak in Christ.

3 Do we begin again to commend ourselves? or need we, as some *others,* epistles of commendation to you, or *letters* of commendation from you? 2 Ye are our epistle written in our hearts, known and read of all men: 3 *Forasmuch as ye are* manifestly declared to be the epistle of Christ ministered by us, written not with ink, but with the Spirit of the living God; not in tables of stone, but in fleshly tables of the heart. 4 And such trust have we through Christ to God-ward: 5 Not that we are sufficient of ourselves to think any thing as of ourselves; but our sufficiency *is* of God; 6 Who also hath made us able ministers of the new testament; not of the letter, but of the spirit: for the letter killeth, but the spirit giveth life. 7 But if the ministration of death, written *and* engraven in stones,

3 Are we beginning to commend ourselves again? Or do we need, as some do, letters of recommendation to you, or from you? 2 You yourselves are our letter of recommendation, written on your*°* hearts, to be known and read by all men; 3 and you show that you are a letter from Christ delivered by us, written not with ink but with the Spirit of the living God, not on tablets of stone but on tablets of human hearts.

4 Such is the confidence that we have through Christ toward God. 5 Not that we are sufficient of ourselves to claim anything as coming from us; our sufficiency is from God, 6 who has qualified us to be ministers of a new covenant, not in a written code but in the Spirit; for the written code kills, but the Spirit gives life.

7 Now if the dispensation of death, carved in letters on stone, came with such splendor that

[c] Other ancient authorities read *our.*

much that he has injured me, but that to some extent (I do not wish to exaggerate) he has injured all of you. But now I think that the punishment you have inflicted on him has been sufficient. Now is the time to offer him forgiveness and comfort, for it is possible for a man in his position to be completely overwhelmed by remorse. I ask you to show him plainly now that you love him. My previous letter was something of a test—I wanted to make sure that you would follow my orders implicitly. If you will forgive a certain person, rest assured that I forgive him too. Insofar as I had anything personally to forgive, I do forgive him, as before Christ. We don't want Satan to win any victory here, and well we know his methods!

And a further confidence　　　2. 12

Well, when I came to Troas to preach the gospel of Christ, although there was an obvious God-given opportunity, I must confess I was on edge the whole time because there was no sign of brother Titus. So I said goodbye and went from there to Macedonia. Thanks be to God who leads us, wherever we are, on Christ's triumphant way and makes our knowledge of him spread throughout the world like a lovely perfume! We Christians have the unmistakable "scent" of Christ, discernible alike to those who are being saved and to those who are heading for death. To the latter it seems like the deathly smell of doom; to the former it has the refreshing fragrance of life itself.

Who could think himself adequate for a responsibility like this? Only the man who refuses to join that large class which traffics in the Word of God—the man who speaks, as we do, in the name of God, under the eyes of God, as Christ's chosen minister.

You yourselves are the proof　　3. 1
of our ministry

Is this going to be more self-advertisement in your eyes? Do we need, as some apparently do, to exchange testimonials before we can be friends? You yourselves are our testimonial, written in our hearts and yet open for anyone to inspect and read. You are an open letter about Christ which we ourselves have written, not with pen and ink but with the Spirit of the living God. Our message has been engraved, not in stone but in living men and women.

We dare to say such things because of the confidence we have in God through Christ. Not that we are in any way confident of our own resources—our ability comes from God. It is he who makes us competent administrators of the new agreement, and we deal not in the letter but in the Spirit. The letter of the Law leads to the death of the soul; the Spirit of God alone can give life to the soul.

The splendor of our ministry　　3. 7
outshines that of Moses

The administration of the Law which was engraved in stone (and which led in fact to spiritual death) was so magnificent that the Israelites

point, it has been done to you all. The penalty on which the general meeting has agreed has met the offence well enough. Something very different is called for now: you must forgive the offender and put heart into him; the man's sorrow must not be made so severe as to overwhelm him. I urge you therefore to assure him of your love for him by a formal act. I wrote, I may say, to see how you stood the test, whether you fully accepted my authority. But anyone who has your forgiveness has mine too; and when I speak of forgiving (so far as there is anything for me to forgive), I mean that as the representative of Christ I have forgiven him for your sake.[a] For Satan must not be allowed to get the better of us; we know his wiles all too well.

Then when I came to Troas, where I was to preach the gospel of Christ, and where an opening awaited me for the Lord's work, I still found no relief of mind, for my colleague Titus was not there to meet me; so I took leave of the people there and went off to Macedonia. But thanks be to God, who continually leads us about, captives in Christ's triumphal procession, and everywhere uses us to reveal and spread abroad the fragrance of the knowledge of himself! We are indeed the incense offered by Christ to God, both for those who are on the way to salvation, and for those who are on the way to perdition: to the latter it is a deadly fume that kills, to the former a vital fragrance that brings life. Who is equal to such a calling? At least we do not go hawking the word of God about, as so many do; when we declare the word we do it in sincerity, as from God and in God's sight, as members of Christ.

3 Are we beginning all over again to produce our credentials? Do we, like some people, need letters of introduction to you, or from you? No, you are all the letter we need, a letter written on our heart; any man can see it for what it is and read it for himself. And as for you, it is plain that you are a letter that has come from Christ, given to us to deliver: a letter written not with ink but with the Spirit of the living God, written not on stone tablets but on the pages of the human heart.

It is in full reliance upon God, through Christ, that we make such claims. There is no question of our being qualified in ourselves: we cannot claim anything as our own. Such qualification as we have comes from God; it is he who has qualified us to dispense his new covenant—a covenant expressed not in a written document, but in a spiritual bond; for the written law condemns to death, but the Spirit gives life.

The law, then, engraved letter by letter upon stone, dispensed death, and yet it was inaugurated with divine splendour. That splendour, though it was soon to fade, made the face of Moses so

[a] *Or* that I have forgiven him for your sake, in the presence of Christ.

551

K.J.V.

was glorious, so that the children of Israel could not steadfastly behold the face of Moses for the glory of his countenance; which *glory* was to be done away; 8 How shall not the ministration of the spirit be rather glorious? 9 For if the ministration of condemnation *be* glory, much more doth the ministration of righteousness exceed in glory. 10 For even that which was made glorious had no glory in this respect, by reason of the glory that excelleth. 11 For if that which is done away *was* glorious, much more that which remaineth *is* glorious. 12 Seeing then that we have such hope, we use great plainness of speech: 13And not as Moses, *which* put a vail over his face, that the children of Israel could not steadfastly look to the end of that which is abolished: 14 But their minds were blinded: for until this day remaineth the same vail untaken away in the reading of the old testament; which *vail* is done away in Christ. 15 But even unto this day, when Moses is read, the vail is upon their heart. 16 Nevertheless, when it shall turn to the Lord, the vail shall be taken away. 17 Now the Lord is that Spirit: and where the Spirit of the Lord *is,* there *is* liberty. 18 But we all, with open face beholding as in a glass the glory of the Lord, are changed into the same image from glory to glory, *even* as by the Spirit of the Lord.

R.S.V.

the Israelites could not look at Moses' face because of its brightness, fading as this was, 8 will not the dispensation of the Spirit be attended with greater splendor? 9 For if there was splendor in the dispensation of condemnation, the dispensation of righteousness must far exceed it in splendor. 10 Indeed, in this case, what once had splendor has come to have no splendor at all, because of the splendor that surpasses it. 11 For if what faded away came with splendor, what is permanent must have much more splendor.

12 Since we have such a hope, we are very bold, 13 not like Moses, who put a veil over his face so that the Israelites might not see the end of the fading splendor. 14 But their minds were hardened; for to this day, when they read the old covenant, that same veil remains unlifted, because only through Christ is it taken away. 15 Yes, to this day whenever Moses is read a veil lies over their minds; 16 but when a man turns to the Lord the veil is removed. 17 Now the Lord is the Spirit, and where the Spirit of the Lord is, there is freedom. 18And we all, with unveiled face, beholding[d] the glory of the Lord, are being changed into his likeness from one degree of glory to another; for this comes from the Lord who is the Spirit.

4 Therefore, seeing we have this ministry, as we have received mercy, we faint not; 2 But have renounced the hidden things of dishonesty, not walking in craftiness, nor handling the word of God deceitfully; but, by manifestation of the truth, commending ourselves to every man's conscience in the sight of God. 3 But if our gospel be hid, it is hid to them that are lost: 4 In whom the god of this world hath blinded the minds of them which believe not, lest the light of the glorious gospel of Christ, who is the image of God, should shine unto them. 5 For we preach not ourselves, but Christ Jesus the Lord; and ourselves your servants for Jesus' sake. 6 For God, who commanded the light to shine out of darkness, hath shined in our hearts, to *give* the light of the knowledge of the glory of God in the face of Jesus Christ. 7 But we have this treasure in earthen vessels, that the excellency of the

4 Therefore, having this ministry by the mercy of God,[e] we do not lose heart. 2 We have renounced disgraceful, underhanded ways; we refuse to practice cunning or to tamper with God's word, but by the open statement of the truth we would commend ourselves to every man's conscience in the sight of God. 3And even if our gospel is veiled, it is veiled only to those who are perishing. 4 In their case the god of this world has blinded the minds of the unbelievers, to keep them from seeing the light of the gospel of the glory of Christ, who is the likeness of God. 5 For what we preach is not ourselves, but Jesus Christ as Lord, with ourselves as your servants[f] for Jesus' sake. 6 For it is the God who said, "Let light shine out of darkness," who has shone in our hearts to give the light of the knowledge of the glory of God in the face of Christ.

7 But we have this treasure in earthen vessels, to show that the transcendent power belongs to

[d] Or *reflecting.* [e] Greek *as we have received mercy.* [f] Or *slaves.*

were unable to look unflinchingly at Moses' face, for it was alight with heavenly splendor. Now if the old administration held such heavenly, even though transitory, splendor, can we not see what a much more glorious thing is the new administration of the Spirit of Life? If to administer a system which is to end in condemning men was a splendid task, how infinitely more splendid is it to administer a system which ends in making men good! And while it is true that the former temporary glory has been completely eclipsed by the latter, we do well to remember that it is eclipsed simply because the present permanent plan is such a very much more glorious thing than the old.

Our ministry is an open and　3. 12
splendid thing

With this hope in our hearts we are quite frank and open in our ministry. We are not like Moses, who veiled his face to prevent the Israelites from seeing its fading glory. But it was their minds really which were blinded, for even today when the old agreement is read to them there is still a veil over their minds—though the veil has actually been lifted by Christ. Yes, alas, even to this day there is still a veil over their hearts when the writings of Moses are read. Yet if they "turned to the Lord" the veil would disappear. For the Lord to whom they could turn is the Spirit of the new agreement, and wherever the Spirit of the Lord is, men's souls are set free.

But all of us who are Christians have no veils on our faces, but reflect like mirrors the glory of the Lord. We are transfigured in ever-increasing splendor into his own image, and the transformation comes from the Lord who is the Spirit.

Ours is a straightforward ministry　4. 1
bringing light into darkness

This is the ministry which God in his mercy has given us, and nothing can daunt us. We use no hocus-pocus, no clever tricks, no dishonest manipulation of the Word of God. We speak the plain truth and so commend ourselves to every man's conscience in the sight of God. If our gospel is "veiled," the veil must be in the minds of those who are spiritually dying. The spirit of this world has blinded the minds of those who do not believe, and prevents the light of the glorious gospel of Christ, the image of God, from shining on them. For it is Christ Jesus as Lord whom we preach, not ourselves; we are your servants for Jesus' sake. God, who first ordered light to shine in darkness, has flooded our hearts with his light. We now can enlighten men only because we can give them knowledge of the glory of God, as we see it in the face of Jesus Christ.

We experience death—we give life,　4. 7
by the power of God

This priceless treasure we hold, so to speak, in a common earthenware jar—to show that the splendid power of it belongs to God and not to

bright that the Israelites could not gaze steadily at him. But if so, must not even greater splendour rest upon the divine dispensation of the Spirit? If splendour accompanied the dispensation under which we are condemned, how much richer in splendour must that one be under which we are acquitted! Indeed, the splendour that once was is now no splendour at all; it is outshone by a splendour greater still. For if that which was soon to fade had its moment of splendour, how much greater is the splendour of that which endures!

With such a hope as this we speak out boldly; it is not for us to do as Moses did: he put a veil over his face to keep the Israelites from gazing on that fading splendour until it was gone. But in any case their minds had been made insensitive, for that same veil is there to this very day when the lesson is read from the old covenant; and it is never lifted, because only in Christ is the old covenant abrogated. But to this very day, every time the Law of Moses is read, a veil lies over the minds of the hearers. However, as Scripture says of Moses, 'whenever he turns to the Lord the veil is removed'.[a] Now the Lord of whom this passage speaks is the Spirit; and where the Spirit of the Lord is, there is liberty. And because for us there is no veil over the face, we all reflect as in a mirror the splendour of the Lord; thus we are transfigured into his likeness, from splendour to splendour; such is the influence of the Lord who is Spirit.

4 Seeing then that we have been entrusted with this commission, which we owe entirely to God's mercy, we never lose heart. We have renounced the deeds that men hide for very shame; we neither practise cunning nor distort the word of God; only by declaring the truth openly do we recommend ourselves, and then it is to the common conscience of our fellow-men and in the sight of God. And if indeed our gospel be found veiled, the only people who find it so are those on the way to perdition. Their unbelieving minds are so blinded by the god of this passing age, that the gospel of the glory of Christ, who is the very image of God, cannot dawn upon them and bring them light. It is not ourselves that we proclaim; we proclaim Christ Jesus as Lord, and ourselves as your servants, for Jesus' sake. For the same God who said, 'Out of darkness let light shine', has caused his light to shine within us, to give the light of revelation —the revelation of the glory of God in the face of Jesus Christ.

We are no better than pots of earthenware to contain this treasure, and this proves that such

[a] *Or* as Scripture says, when one turns to the Lord the veil is removed.

K.J.V.

power may be of God, and not of us. 8 *We are* troubled on every side, yet not distressed; *we are* perplexed, but not in despair; 9 Persecuted, but not forsaken; cast down, but not destroyed; 10Always bearing about in the body the dying of the Lord Jesus, that the life also of Jesus might be made manifest in our body. 11 For we which live are alway delivered unto death for Jesus' sake, that the life also of Jesus might be made manifest in our mortal flesh. 12 So then death worketh in us, but life in you. 13 We having the same spirit of faith, according as it is written, I believed, and therefore have I spoken; we also believe, and therefore speak; 14 Knowing that he which raised up the Lord Jesus shall raise up us also by Jesus, and shall present *us* with you. 15 For all things *are* for your sakes, that the abundant grace might through the thanksgiving of many redound to the glory of God. 16 For which cause we faint not; but though our outward man perish, yet the inward *man* is renewed day by day. 17 For our light affliction, which is but for a moment, worketh for us a far more exceeding *and* eternal weight of glory; 18 While we look not at the things which are seen, but at the things which are not seen: for the things which are seen *are* temporal; but the things which are not seen *are* eternal.

5 For we know that, if our earthly house of *this* tabernacle were dissolved, we have a building of God, a house not made with hands, eternal in the heavens. 2 For in this we groan, earnestly desiring to be clothed upon with our house which is from heaven: 3 If so be that being clothed we shall not be found naked. 4 For we that are in *this* tabernacle do groan, being burdened: not for that we would be unclothed, but clothed upon, that mortality might be swallowed up of life. 5 Now he that hath wrought us for the selfsame thing *is* God, who also hath given unto us the earnest of the Spirit. 6 Therefore *we are* always confident, knowing that, whilst we are at home in the body, we are absent from the Lord: 7 (For we walk by faith, not by sight:) 8 We are confident, *I say,* and willing rather to be absent from the body, and to be present with the Lord. 9 Wherefore we labour, that, whether present or absent, we may be accepted of him. 10 For we must all appear before

R.S.V.

God and not to us. 8 We are afflicted in every way, but not crushed; perplexed, but not driven to despair; 9 persecuted, but not forsaken; struck down, but not destroyed; 10 always carrying in the body the death of Jesus, so that the life of Jesus may also be manifested in our bodies. 11 For while we live we are always being given up to death for Jesus' sake, so that the life of Jesus may be manifested in our mortal flesh. 12 So death is at work in us, but life in you.

13 Since we have the same spirit of faith as he had who wrote, "I believed, and so I spoke," we too believe, and so we speak, 14 knowing that he who raised the Lord Jesus will raise us also with Jesus and bring us with you into his presence. 15 For it is all for your sake, so that as grace extends to more and more people it may increase thanksgiving, to the glory of God.

16 So we do not lose heart. Though our outer nature is wasting away, our inner nature is being renewed every day. 17 For this slight momentary affliction is preparing for us an eternal weight of glory beyond all comparison, 18 because we look not to the things that are seen but to the things that are unseen; for the things that are seen are transient, but the things that are unseen are eternal.

5 For we know that if the earthly tent we live in is destroyed, we have a building from God, a house not made with hands, eternal in the heavens. 2 Here indeed we groan, and long to put on our heavenly dwelling, 3 so that by putting it on we may not be found naked. 4 For while we are still in this tent, we sigh with anxiety; not that we would be unclothed, but that we would be further clothed, so that what is mortal may be swallowed up by life. 5 He who has prepared us for this very thing is God, who has given us the Spirit as a guarantee.

6 So we are always of good courage; we know that while we are at home in the body we are away from the Lord, 7 for we walk by faith, not by sight. 8 We are of good courage, and we would rather be away from the body and at home with the Lord. 9 So whether we are at home or away, we make it our aim to please him. 10 For we must all appear before the judg-

PHILLIPS

N.E.B.

us. We are handicapped on all sides, but we are never frustrated; we are puzzled, but never in despair. We are persecuted, but we never have to stand it alone: we may be knocked down but we are never knocked out! Every day we experience something of the death of Jesus, so that we may also know the power of the life of Jesus in these bodies of ours. Yes, we who are living are always being exposed to death for Jesus' sake, so that the life of Jesus may be plainly seen in our mortal lives. We are always facing death, but this means that you know more and more of life. Our faith is like that mentioned in the scripture:

I believed and therefore did I speak.

For we too speak because we believe, and we know for certain that he who raised the Lord Jesus from death shall also raise us with Jesus. We shall all stand together before him.

We live a transitory life with our   4. 15
eyes on the life eternal

We wish you could see how all this is working out for your benefit, and how the more grace God gives, the more thanksgiving will redound to his glory. This is the reason that we never collapse. The outward man does indeed suffer wear and tear, but every day the inward man receives fresh strength. These little troubles (which are really so transitory) are winning for us a permanent, glorious and solid reward out of all proportion to our pain. For we are looking all the time not at the visible things but at the invisible. The visible things are transitory: it is the invisible things that are really permanent.

We know, for instance, that if our earthly dwelling were taken down, like a tent, we have a permanent house in Heaven, made, not by man, but by God. In this present frame we sigh with deep longing for the heavenly house, for we do not want to face utter nakedness when death destroys our present dwelling—these bodies of ours. As long as we are clothed in this temporary dwelling we have a painful longing, not because we want just to get rid of these "clothes" but because we want to know the full cover of the permanent house that will be ours. We want our transitory life to be absorbed into the life that is eternal.

Death can have no terrors, for it   5. 5
means being with God

Now the power that has planned this experience for us is God, and he has given us his Spirit as a guarantee of its truth. This makes us confident, whatever happens. We realize that being "at home" in the body means that to some extent we are "away" from the Lord, for we have to live by trusting him without seeing him. We are so sure of this that we would really rather be "away" from the body and be "at home" with the Lord.

It is our aim, therefore, to please him, whether we are "at home" or "away." For every one of

transcendent power does not come from us, but is God's alone. Hard-pressed on every side, we are never hemmed in; bewildered, we are never at our wits' end; hunted, we are never abandoned to our fate; struck down, we are not left to die. Wherever we go we carry death with us in our body, the death that Jesus died, that in this body also life may reveal itself, the life that Jesus lives. For continually, while still alive, we are being surrendered into the hands of death, for Jesus' sake, so that the life of Jesus also may be revealed in this mortal body of ours. Thus death is at work in us, and life in you.

But Scripture says, 'I believed, and therefore I spoke out', and we too, in the same spirit of faith, believe and therefore speak out; for we know that he who raised the Lord Jesus to life will with Jesus raise us too, and bring us to his presence, and you with us. Indeed, it is for your sake that all things are ordered, so that, as the abounding grace of God is shared by more and more, the greater may be the chorus of thanksgiving that ascends to the glory of God.

No wonder we do not lose heart! Though our outward humanity is in decay, yet day by day we are inwardly renewed. Our troubles are slight and short-lived; and their outcome an eternal glory which outweighs them far. Meanwhile our eyes are fixed, not on the things that are seen, but on the things that are unseen: for what is seen passes away; what is unseen is eternal.

5 For we know that if the earthly frame that houses us today should be demolished, we possess a building which God has provided—a house not made by human hands, eternal, and in heaven. In this present body we do indeed groan; we yearn to have our heavenly habitation put on over this one—in the hope that, being thus clothed, we shall not find ourselves naked. We groan indeed, we who are enclosed within this earthly frame; we are oppressed because we do not want to have the old body stripped off. Rather our desire is to have the new body put on over it, so that our mortal part may be absorbed into life immortal. God himself has shaped us for this very end; and as a pledge of it he has given us the Spirit.

Therefore we never cease to be confident. We know that so long as we are at home in the body we are exiles from the Lord; faith is our guide, we do not see him.[a] We are confident, I repeat, and would rather leave our home in the body and go to live with the Lord. We therefore make it our ambition, wherever we are, here or there, to be acceptable to him. For we must all have

[a] Or faith is our guide and not the things we see.

K.J.V.

the judgment seat of Christ; that every one may receive the things *done* in his *body,* according to that he hath done, whether *it be* good or bad. 11 Knowing therefore the terror of the Lord, we persuade men; but we are made manifest unto God; and I trust also are made manifest in your consciences. 12 For we commend not ourselves again unto you, but give you occasion to glory on our behalf, that ye may have somewhat to *answer* them which glory in appearance, and not in heart. 13 For whether we be beside ourselves, *it is* to God: or whether we be sober, *it is* for your cause. 14 For the love of Christ constraineth us; because we thus judge, that if one died for all, then were all dead: 15 And *that* he died for all, that they which live should not henceforth live unto themselves, but unto him which died for them, and rose again. 16 Wherefore henceforth know we no man after the flesh: yea, though we have known Christ after the flesh, yet now henceforth know we *him* no more. 17 Therefore if any man *be* in Christ, *he is* a new creature: old things are passed away; behold, all things are become new. 18 And all things *are* of God, who hath reconciled us to himself by Jesus Christ, and hath given to us the ministry of reconciliation; 19 To wit, that God was in Christ, reconciling the world unto himself, not imputing their trespasses unto them; and hath committed unto us the word of reconciliation. 20 Now then we are ambassadors for Christ, as though God did beseech *you* by us: we pray *you* in Christ's stead, be ye reconciled to God. 21 For he hath made him *to be* sin for us, who knew no sin; that we might be made the righteousness of God in him.

6 We then, *as* workers together *with him,* beseech *you* also that ye receive not the grace of God in vain. 2 (For he saith, I have heard thee in a time accepted, and in the day of salvation have I succoured thee: behold, now *is* the accepted time; behold, now *is* the day of salvation.) 3 Giving no offence in any thing, that the ministry be not blamed: 4 But in all *things* approving ourselves as the ministers of God, in much patience, in afflictions, in necessities, in distresses, 5 In stripes, in imprisonments, in tumults, in labours, in watchings, in fastings; 6 By pureness, by knowledge, by longsuffering, by kindness, by the Holy Ghost, by love unfeigned,

R.S.V.

ment seat of Christ, so that each one may receive good or evil, according to what he has done in the body. 11 Therefore, knowing the fear of the Lord, we persuade men; but what we are is known to God, and I hope it is known also to your conscience. 12 We are not commending ourselves to you again but giving you cause to be proud of us, so that you may be able to answer those who pride themselves on a man's position and not on his heart. 13 For if we are beside ourselves, it is for God; if we are in our right mind, it is for you. 14 For the love of Christ controls us, because we are convinced that one has died for all; therefore all have died. 15 And he died for all, that those who live might live no longer for themselves but for him who for their sake died and was raised.

16 From now on, therefore, we regard no one from a human point of view; even though we once regarded Christ from a human point of view, we regard him thus no longer. 17 Therefore, if any one is in Christ, he is a new creation;*ᵍ* the old has passed away, behold, the new has come. 18 All this is from God, who through Christ reconciled us to himself and gave us the ministry of reconciliation; 19 that is, God was in Christ reconciling*ʰ* the world to himself, not counting their trespasses against them, and entrusting to us the message of reconciliation. 20 So we are ambassadors for Christ, God making his appeal through us. We beseech you on behalf of Christ, be reconciled to God. 21 For our sake he made him to be sin who knew no sin, so that in him we might become the righteousness of God.

6 Working together with him, then, we entreat you not to accept the grace of God in vain. 2 For he says,
"At the acceptable time I have listened to you,
    and helped you on the day of salvation."
Behold, now is the acceptable time; behold, now is the day of salvation. 3 We put no obstacle in any one's way, so that no fault may be found with our ministry, 4 but as servants of God we commend ourselves in every way: through great endurance, in afflictions, hardships, calamities, 5 beatings, imprisonments, tumults, labors, watching, hunger; 6 by purity, knowledge, forbearance, kindness, the Holy Spirit, genuine love,

[*g*] Or *creature.* [*h*] Or *in Christ God was reconciling.*

PHILLIPS

us will have to stand without pretense before Christ our judge, and we shall be rewarded for what we did when we lived in our bodies, whether it was good or bad.

Our ministry is based on solemn convictions   5. 11

All our persuading of men, then, is with this solemn fear of God in our minds. What we are is utterly plain to God—and I hope to your consciences as well. (No, we are not recommending ourselves to you again, but we can give you grounds for legitimate pride in us—if that is what you need to meet those who are so proud of the outward rather than the inward qualification.) If we are "mad" it is for God's glory; if we are perfectly sane it is for your benefit. At any rate there has been no selfish motive. The very spring of our actions is the love of Christ. We look at it like this: if one died for all men then, in a sense, they all died, and his purpose in dying for them is that their lives should now be no longer lived for themselves but for him who died and rose again for them. This means that our knowledge of men can no longer be based on their outward lives (indeed, even though we knew Christ as a man we do not know him like that any longer). For if a man is in Christ he becomes a new person altogether—the past is finished and gone, everything has become fresh and new. All this is God's doing, for he has reconciled us to himself through Jesus Christ; and he has made us agents of the reconciliation. God was in Christ personally reconciling the world to himself—not counting their sins against them—and has commissioned us with the message of reconciliation. We are now Christ's ambassadors, as though God were appealing direct to you through us. As his personal representative we say, "Make your peace with God." For God caused Christ, who himself knew nothing of sin, actually to *be* sin for our sakes, so that in Christ we might be made good with the goodness of God.

The hard but glorious life of God's ministers   6.1

As cooperators with God himself we beg you, then, not to fail to use the grace of God. For God's word is:

At an acceptable time I hearkened unto thee,
And in a day of salvation did I succor thee.

Now *is* the "acceptable time," and this very day *is* the "day of salvation."
As far as we are concerned we do not wish to stand in anyone's way, nor do we wish to bring discredit on the ministry God has given us. Indeed we want to prove ourselves genuine ministers of God whatever we have to go through —patient endurance of troubles or even disasters, being flogged or imprisoned; being mobbed, having to work like slaves, having to go without food or sleep. All this we want to meet with sincerity, with insight and patience; by sheer

N.E.B.

our lives laid open before the tribunal of Christ, where each must receive what is due to him for his conduct in the body, good or bad.

With this fear of the Lord before our eyes we address our appeal to men. To God our lives lie open, as I hope they also lie open to you in your heart of hearts. This is not another attempt to recommend ourselves to you: we are rather giving you a chance to show yourselves proud of us; then you will have something to say to those whose pride is all in outward show and not in inward worth. It may be we are beside ourselves, but it is for God; if we are in our right mind, it is for you. For the love of Christ leaves us no choice, when once we have reached the conclusion that one man died for all and therefore all mankind has died. His purpose in dying for all was that men, while still in life, should cease to live for themselves, and should live for him who for their sake died and was raised to life. With us therefore worldly standards have ceased to count in our estimate of any man; even if once they counted in our understanding of Christ, they do so now no longer. When anyone is united to Christ, there is a new world;[a] the old order has gone, and a new order has already begun.[b]
From first to last this has been the work of God. He has reconciled us men to himself through Christ, and he has enlisted us in this service of reconciliation. What I mean is, that God was in Christ reconciling the world to himself,[c] no longer holding men's misdeeds against them, and that he has entrusted us with the message of reconciliation. We come therefore as Christ's ambassadors. It is as if God were appealing to you through us: in Christ's name, we implore you, be reconciled to God! Christ was innocent of sin, and yet for our sake God made him one with the sinfulness of men,[d] so that in him we might be made one with the goodness of God himself.

6 Sharing in God's work, we urge this appeal upon you: you have received the grace of God; do not let it go for nothing. God's own words are:

'In the hour of my favour I gave heed to you; On the day of deliverance I came to your aid.'

The hour of favour has now come; now, I say, has the day of deliverance dawned.
In order that our service may not be brought into discredit, we avoid giving offence in anything. As God's servants, we try to recommend ourselves in all circumstances by our steadfast endurance: in hardships and dire straits; flogged, imprisoned, mobbed; overworked, sleepless, starving. We recommend ourselves by the innocence of our behaviour, our grasp of truth, our pa-

[a] *Or* a new act of creation. [b] *Or* when anyone is united to Christ he is a new creature: his old life is over; a new life has already begun. [c] *Or* God was reconciling the world to himself by Christ. [d] *Or* and yet God made him a sin-offering for us.

K.J.V.

7 By the word of truth, by the power of God, by the armour of righteousness on the right hand and on the left, 8 By honour and dishonour, by evil report and good report: as deceivers, and *yet* true; 9 As unknown, and *yet* well known; as dying, and, behold, we live; as chastened, and not killed; 10 As sorrowful, yet alway rejoicing; as poor, yet making many rich; as having nothing, and *yet* possessing all things. 11 O *ye* Corinthians, our mouth is open unto you, our heart is enlarged. 12 Ye are not straitened in us, but ye are straitened in your own bowels. 13 Now for a recompense in the same, (I speak as unto *my* children,) be ye also enlarged. 14 Be ye not unequally yoked together with unbelievers: for what fellowship hath righteousness with unrighteousness? and what communion hath light with darkness? 15 And what concord hath Christ with Belial? or what part hath he that believeth with an infidel? 16 And what agreement hath the temple of God with idols? for ye are the temple of the living God; as God hath said, I will dwell in them, and walk in *them;* and I will be their God, and they shall be my people. 17 Wherefore come out from among them, and be ye separate, saith the Lord, and touch not the unclean *thing;* and I will receive you, 18 And will be a Father unto you, and ye shall be my sons and daughters, saith the Lord Almighty.

R.S.V.

7 truthful speech, and the power of God; with the weapons of righteousness for the right hand and for the left; 8 in honor and dishonor, in ill repute and good repute. We are treated as impostors, and yet are true; 9 as unknown, and yet well known; as dying, and behold we live; as punished, and yet not killed; 10 as sorrowful, yet always rejoicing; as poor, yet making many rich; as having nothing, and yet possessing everything.

11 Our mouth is open to you, Corinthians; our heart is wide. 12 You are not restricted by us, but you are restricted in your own affections. 13 In return—I speak as to children—widen your hearts also.

14 Do not be mismated with unbelievers. For what partnership have righteousness and iniquity? Or what fellowship has light with darkness? 15 What accord has Christ with Belial? [i] Or what has a believer in common with an unbeliever? 16 What agreement has the temple of God with idols? For we are the temple of the living God; as God said,

"I will live in them and move among them,
and I will be their God,
and they shall be my people.
17 Therefore come out from them,
and be separate from them, says the Lord,
and touch nothing unclean;
then I will welcome you,
18 and I will be a father to you,
and you shall be my sons and daughters,
says the Lord Almighty."

7 Having therefore these promises, dearly beloved, let us cleanse ourselves from all filthiness of the flesh and spirit, perfecting holiness in the fear of God. 2 Receive us; we have wronged no man, we have corrupted no man, we have defrauded no man. 3 I speak not *this* to condemn *you:* for I have said before, that ye are in our hearts to die and live with *you.*

7 Since we have these promises, beloved, let us cleanse ourselves from every defilement of body and spirit, and make holiness perfect in the fear of God.

2 Open your hearts to us; we have wronged no one, we have corrupted no one, we have taken advantage of no one. 3 I do not say this to condemn you, for I said before that you are in our hearts, to die together and to live to-

[i] Greek *Beliar.*

kindness and the Holy Spirit; with genuine love, speaking the plain truth, and living by the power of God. Our sole defense, our only weapon, is a life of integrity, whether we meet honor or dishonor, praise or blame. Called "impostors" we must be true, called "nobodies" we must be in the public eye. Never far from death, yet here we are alive, always "going through it" yet never "going under." We know sorrow, yet our joy is inextinguishable. We have "nothing to bless ourselves with," yet we bless many others with true riches. We are penniless, and yet in reality we have everything worth having.

We have used utter frankness. 6. 11
Won't you do the same?

Oh, our dear friends in Corinth, we are hiding nothing from you and our hearts are absolutely open to you. Any stiffness between us must be on your side, for we assure you there is none on ours. Do reward me (I talk to you as though you were my own children) with the same complete candor!

We must warn you against 6. 14
entanglement with pagans

Don't link up with unbelievers and try to work with them. What common interest can there be between goodness and evil? How can light and darkness share life together? How can there be harmony between Christ and the devil? What can a believer have in common with an unbeliever? What common ground can idols hold with the temple of God? For we, remember, are ourselves living temples of the living God, as God has said:

I will dwell in them and walk in them:
And I will be their God, and they shall be my
people.

Wherefore

Come ye out from among them and be ye
separate, saith the Lord,
And touch no unclean thing;
And I will receive you,
And will be to you a Father,
And ye shall be to me sons and daughters,
Saith the Lord Almighty.

With these promises ringing in our ears, dear friends, let us keep clear of anything that smirches body or soul. Let us prove our reverence for God by consecrating ourselves to him completely.

Does "that letter" still rankle? 7. 2
Hear my explanation

Do make room in your hearts again for us! Not one of you has ever been wronged or ruined or cheated by us. I don't say this to condemn your attitude, but simply because, as I said before, whether we live or die you live in our

tience and kindliness; by gifts of the Holy Spirit, by sincere love, by declaring the truth, by the power of God. We wield the weapons of righteousness in right hand and left. Honour and dishonour, praise and blame, are alike our lot: we are the impostors who speak the truth, the unknown men whom all men know; dying we still live on; disciplined by suffering, we are not done to death; in our sorrows we have always cause for joy; poor ourselves, we bring wealth to many; penniless, we own the world.

Men of Corinth, we have spoken very frankly to you; we have opened our heart wide to you all. On our part there is no constraint; any constraint there may be is in yourselves. In fair exchange then (may a father speak so to his children?) open wide your hearts to us.

Problems of Church Life
and Discipline

Do not unite yourselves with unbelievers; they are no fit mates for you. What has righteousness to do with wickedness? Can light consort with darkness? Can Christ agree with Belial, or a believer join hands with an unbeliever? Can there be a compact between the temple of God and the idols of the heathen? And the temple of the living God is what we are. God's own words are: 'I will live and move about among them; I will be their God, and they shall be my people.' And therefore, 'come away and leave them, separate yourselves, says the Lord; do not touch what is unclean. Then I will accept you, says the Lord, the Ruler of all being; I will be a father to you, and you shall be my sons and daughters.'

7 Such are the promises that have been made to us, dear friends. Let us therefore cleanse ourselves from all that can defile flesh or spirit, and in the fear of God complete our consecration.

Do make a place for us in your hearts! We have wronged no one, ruined no one, taken advantage of no one. I do not want to blame you. Why, as I have told you before, the place you have in our heart is such that, come death, come life, we meet it together. I am perfectly frank

K.J.V.

4 Great *is* my boldness of speech toward you, great *is* my glorying of you: I am filled with comfort, I am exceeding joyful in all our tribulation. 5 For, when we were come into Macedonia, our flesh had no rest, but we were troubled on every side; without *were* fightings, within *were* fears. 6 Nevertheless God, that comforteth those that are cast down, comforted us by the coming of Titus; 7And not by his coming only, but by the consolation wherewith he was comforted in you, when he told us your earnest desire, your mourning, your fervent mind toward me; so that I rejoiced the more. 8 For though I made you sorry with a letter, I do not repent, though I did repent: for I perceive that the same epistle hath made you sorry, though *it were* but for a season. 9 Now I rejoice, not that ye were made sorry, but that ye sorrowed to repentance: for ye were made sorry after a godly manner, that ye might receive damage by us in nothing. 10 For godly sorrow worketh repentance to salvation not to be repented of: but the sorrow of the world worketh death. 11 For behold this selfsame thing, that ye sorrowed after a godly sort, what carefulness it wrought in you, yea, *what* clearing of yourselves, yea, *what* indignation, yea, *what* fear, yea, *what* vehement desire, yea, *what* zeal, yea, *what* revenge! In all *things* ye have approved yourselves to be clear in this matter. 12 Wherefore, though I wrote unto you, *I did it* not for his cause that had done the wrong, nor for his cause that suffered wrong, but that our care for you in the sight of God might appear unto you. 13 Therefore we were comforted in your comfort: yea, and exceedingly the more joyed we for the joy of Titus, because his spirit was refreshed by you all. 14 For if I have boasted any thing to him of you, I am not ashamed; but as we spake all things to you in truth, even so our boasting, which *I made* before Titus, is found a truth. 15And his inward affection is more abundant toward you, whilst he remembereth the obedience of you all, how with fear and trembling ye received him. 16 I rejoice therefore that I have confidence in you in all *things*.

R.S.V.

gether. 4 I have great confidence in you; I have great pride in you; I am filled with comfort. With all our affliction, I am overjoyed.

5 For even when we came into Macedonia, our bodies had no rest but we were afflicted at every turn—fighting without and fear within. 6 But God, who comforts the downcast, comforted us by the coming of Titus, 7 and not only by his coming but also by the comfort with which he was comforted in you, as he told us of your longing, your mourning, your zeal for me, so that I rejoiced still more. 8 For even if I made you sorry with my letter, I do not regret it (though I did regret it), for I see that that letter grieved you, though only for a while. 9 As it is, I rejoice, not because you were grieved, but because you were grieved into repenting; for you felt a godly grief, so that you suffered no loss through us. 10 For godly grief produces a repentance that leads to salvation and brings no regret, but worldly grief produces death. 11 For see what earnestness this godly grief has produced in you, what eagerness to clear yourselves, what indignation, what alarm, what longing, what zeal, what punishment! At every point you have proved yourselves guiltless in the matter. 12 So although I wrote to you, it was not on account of the one who did the wrong, nor on account of the one who suffered the wrong, but in order that your zeal for us might be revealed to you in the sight of God. 13 Therefore we are comforted.

And besides our own comfort we rejoiced still more at the joy of Titus, because his mind has been set at rest by you all. 14 For if I have expressed to him some pride in you, I was not put to shame; but just as everything we said to you was true, so our boasting before Titus has proved true. 15And his heart goes out all the more to you, as he remembers the obedience of you all, and the fear and trembling with which you received him. 16 I rejoice, because I have perfect confidence in you.

8 Moreover, brethren, we do you to wit of the grace of God bestowed on the churches of Macedonia; 2 How that in a great trial of affliction, the abundance of their joy and their deep poverty abounded unto the riches of their liberality. 3 For to *their* power, I bear record, yea, and beyond *their* power *they were* willing of themselves; 4 Praying us with much entreaty that we would receive the gift, and *take upon us* the fellowship of the ministering to the saints. 5And *this they did,* not as we hoped, but first gave their own selves to the Lord, and unto us

8 We want you to know, brethren, about the grace of God which has been shown in the churches of Macedonia, 2 for in a severe test of affliction, their abundance of joy and their extreme poverty have overflowed in a wealth of liberality on their part. 3 For they gave according to their means, as I can testify, and beyond their means, of their own free will, 4 begging us earnestly for the favor of taking part in the relief of the saints—5 and this, not as we expected, but first they gave themselves to the Lord

PHILLIPS

hearts. To your face I talk to you with utter frankness; behind your back I talk about you with deepest pride. Whatever troubles I have gone through, the thought of you has filled me with comfort and deep happiness.

For even when we arrived in Macedonia we had a wretched time with trouble all round us—wrangling outside and anxiety within. Not but what God, who cheers the depressed, gave us the comfort of the arrival of Titus. And it wasn't merely his coming that cheered us, but the comfort you had given him, for he could tell us of your eagerness to help, your deep sympathy and keen interest on my behalf. All that made me doubly glad to see him. For although my letter had hurt you I don't regret it now (as I did, I must confess, at one time). I can see that the letter did upset you, though only for a time, and now I am glad I sent it, not because I want to hurt you but because it made you grieve for things that were wrong. In other words, the result was to make you sorry as God would have had you sorry, and not merely to make you offended by what we said. The sorrow which God uses means a change of heart and leads to salvation—it is the world's sorrow that is such a deadly thing. You can look back now and see how the hand of God was in that sorrow. Look how seriously it made you think, how eager it made you to prove your innocence, how indignant it made you and, in some cases, how afraid! Look how it made you long for my presence, how it stirred up your keenness for the faith, how ready it made you to punish the offender! Yes, that letter cleared the air for you as nothing else would have done.

Now I did not write that letter really for the sake of the man who sinned, or even for the sake of the one who was sinned against, but to let you see for yourselves, in the sight of God, how deeply you really do care for us. That is why we now feel so deeply comforted, and our sense of joy was greatly enhanced by the satisfaction that your attitude had obviously given Titus. You see, I had told him of my pride in you, and you have not let me down. I have always spoken the truth *to* you, and this proves that my proud words *about* you were true as well. Titus himself has a much greater love for you, now that he has seen for himself the obedience you gave him, and the respect and reverence with which you treated him. I am profoundly glad to have my confidence in you so fully proved.

N.E.B.

with you. I have great pride in you. In all our many troubles my cup is full of consolation, and overflows with joy.

Even when we reached Macedonia there was still no relief for this poor body of ours: instead, there was trouble at every turn, quarrels all round us, forebodings in our heart. But God, who brings comfort to the downcast, has comforted us by the arrival of Titus, and not merely by his arrival, but by his being so greatly comforted about you. He has told us how you long for me, how sorry you are, and how eager to take my side; and that has made me happier still.

Even if I did wound you by the letter I sent, I do not now regret it. I may have been sorry for it when I saw that the letter had caused you pain, even if only for a time; but now I am happy, not that your feelings were wounded but that the wound led to a change of heart. You bore the smart as God would have you bear it, and so you are no losers by what we did. For the wound which is borne in God's way brings a change of heart too salutary to regret; but the hurt which is borne in the world's way brings death. You bore your hurt in God's way, and see what its results have been! It made you take the matter seriously and vindicate yourselves. How angered you were, how apprehensive! How your longing for me awoke, yes, and your devotion and your eagerness to see justice done! At every point you have cleared yourselves of blame in this trouble. And so, although I did send you that letter, it was not the offender or his victim that most concerned me. My aim in writing was to help to make plain to you, in the sight of God, how truly you are devoted to us. That is why we have been so encouraged.

But besides being encouraged ourselves we have also been delighted beyond everything by seeing how happy Titus is: you have all helped to set his mind completely at rest. Anything I may have said to him to show my pride in you has been justified. Every word we ever addressed to you bore the mark of truth; and the same holds of the proud boast we made in the presence of Titus: that also has proved true. His heart warms all the more to you as he recalls how ready you all were to do what he asked, meeting him as you did in fear and trembling. How happy I am now to have complete confidence in you!

The Macedonian churches have   **8. 1**
given magnificently: will you
not do so too?

Now, my brothers, we must tell you about the grace that God has given to the Macedonian churches. Somehow, in most difficult circumstances, their joy and the fact of being down to their last penny themselves, produced a magnificent concern for other people. I can guarantee that they were willing to give to the limit of their means, yes and beyond their means, without the slightest urging from me or anyone else. In fact they simply begged us to accept their gifts and so let them share the honor of supporting their brothers in Christ. Nor was their gift, as I must confess I had expected, a mere cash payment. Instead they made a complete dedication of themselves first to the Lord and then to us, as God's appointed ministers.

8 We must tell you, friends, about the grace of generosity which God has imparted to[a] our congregations in Macedonia. The troubles they have been through have tried them hard, yet in all this they have been so exuberantly happy that from the depths of their poverty they have shown themselves lavishly open-handed. Going to the limit of their resources, as I can testify, and even beyond that limit, they begged us most insistently, and on their own initiative, to be allowed to share in this generous service to their fellow-Christians. And their giving surpassed our expectations; for they gave their very selves, offering them in the first instance to

[a] *Or* how gracious God has been to . . .

K.J.V.

by the will of God. 6 Insomuch that we desired Titus, that as he had begun, so he would also finish in you the same grace also. 7 Therefore, as ye abound in every *thing, in* faith, and utterance, and knowledge, and *in* all diligence, and *in* your love to us, *see* that ye abound in this grace also. 8 I speak not by commandment, but by occasion of the forwardness of others, and to prove the sincerity of your love. 9 For ye know the grace of our Lord Jesus Christ, that, though he was rich, yet for your sakes he became poor, that ye through his poverty might be rich. 10And herein I give *my* advice: for this is expedient for you, who have begun before, not only to do, but also to be forward a year ago. 11 Now therefore perform the doing *of it;* that as *there was* a readiness to will, so *there may be* a performance also out of that which ye have. 12 For if there be first a willing mind, *it is* accepted according to that a man hath, *and* not according to that he hath not. 13 For *I mean* not that other men be eased, and ye burdened: 14 But by an equality, *that* now at this time your abundance *may be a supply* for their want, that their abundance also may be *a supply* for your want; that there may be equality: 15As it is written, He that *had gathered* much had nothing over; and he that *had gathered* little had no lack. 16 But thanks *be* to God, which put the same earnest care into the heart of Titus for you. 17 For indeed he accepted the exhortation; but being more forward, of his own accord he went unto you. 18And we have sent with him the brother, whose praise *is* in the gospel throughout all the churches; 19And not *that* only, but who was also chosen of the churches to travel with us with this grace, which is administered by us to the glory of the same Lord, and *declaration of* your ready mind: 20Avoiding this, that no man should blame us in this abundance which is administered by us: 21 Providing for honest things, not only in the sight of the Lord, but also in the sight of men. 22And we have sent with them our brother, whom we have oftentimes proved diligent in many things, but now much more diligent, upon the great confidence which *I have* in you. 23 Whether *any do inquire* of Titus, *he is* my partner and fellow helper concerning you: or our brethren *be inquired of, they are* the messengers of the churches, *and* the glory of Christ. 24 Wherefore shew ye to them, and before the churches, the proof of your love, and of our boasting on your behalf.

R.S.V.

and to us by the will of God. 6 Accordingly we have urged Titus that as he had already made a beginning, he should also complete among you this gracious work. 7 Now as you excel in everything—in faith, in utterance, in knowledge, in all earnestness, and in your love for us—see that you excel in this gracious work also.

8 I say this not as a command, but to prove by the earnestness of others that your love also is genuine. 9 For you know the grace of our Lord Jesus Christ, that though he was rich, yet for your sake he became poor, so that by his poverty you might become rich. 10And in this matter I give my advice: it is best for you now to complete what a year ago you began not only to do but to desire, 11 so that your readiness in desiring it may be matched by your completing it out of what you have. 12 For if the readiness is there, it is acceptable according to what a man has, not according to what he has not. 13 I do not mean that others should be eased and you burdened, 14 but that as a matter of equality your abundance at the present time should supply their want, so that their abundance may supply your want, that there may be equality. 15As it is written, "He who gathered much had nothing over, and he who gathered little had no lack."

16 But thanks be to God who puts the same earnest care for you into the heart of Titus. 17 For he not only accepted our appeal, but being himself very earnest he is going to you of his own accord. 18 With him we are sending the brother who is famous among all the churches for his preaching of the gospel; 19 and not only that, but he has been appointed by the churches to travel with us in this gracious work which we are carrying on, for the glory of the Lord and to show our good will. 20 We intend that no one should blame us about this liberal gift which we are administering, 21 for we aim at what is honorable not only in the Lord's sight but also in the sight of men. 22And with them we are sending our brother whom we have often tested and found earnest in many matters, but who is now more earnest than ever because of his great confidence in you. 23As for Titus, he is my partner and fellow worker in your service; and as for our brethren, they are messengers[j] of the churches, the glory of Christ. 24 So give proof, before the churches, of your love and of our boasting about you to these men.

[j] Greek *apostles.*

562

PHILLIPS

Now this has made us ask Titus, who has already done so much among you, to complete his task by arranging for you too to share in this work of generosity. Already you are well to the fore in every good quality—you have faith, you can express that faith in words; you have knowledge, enthusiasm and your love for us. Could you not add generosity to your virtues? I don't want you to read this as an order. It is only my suggestion, prompted by what I have seen in others of eagerness to help, and here is a way to prove the reality of your love. Do you remember the generosity of Jesus Christ, the Lord of us all? He was rich beyond our telling, yet he became poor for your sakes so that his poverty might make you rich.

I merely suggest that you finish   8. 10
your original generous gesture

Here is my opinion in the matter. I think it would be a good thing for you, who were the first a year ago to think of helping, as well as the first to give, to carry through what you then intended to do. Finish it, then, as well as you can, and show that you can complete what you set out to do with as much efficiency as you showed readiness to begin. After all, the important thing is to be willing to give as much as we can—that is what God accepts, and no one is asked to give what he has not got. Of course, I don't mean that others should be relieved to an extent that leaves you in distress. It is a matter of share and share alike. At present your plenty should supply their need, and then at some future date their plenty may supply your need. In that way we share with each other, as the scripture says:

He that gathered much had nothing over,
And he that gathered little had no lack.

Titus is bringing you this letter   8. 16
personally

Thank God Titus feels the same deep concern for you as we do! He accepts the suggestion outlined above, and in his enthusiasm comes to you personally at his own request. We are sending with him that brother whose services to the gospel are universally praised in the churches. He has been unanimously chosen to travel with us in this work of administering the gifts of others. It is a task that brings glory to God and demonstrates also the willingness of us Christians to help each other. Naturally we want to avoid the slightest breath of criticism in the distribution of their gifts, and to be absolutely aboveboard not only in the sight of God but in the eyes of men.

With these two we are also sending our brother, of whose keenness we have ample proof and whose interest is especially aroused on this occasion as he has such confidence in you. As for Titus, he is our colleague and partner in your affairs, and both the brothers are official messengers of the churches and shining examples of their faith. So do let them, and all the churches, see how genuine is your love, and justify all the nice things we have said about you!

N.E.B.

the Lord, but also, under God, to us. The upshot is that we have asked Titus, who began it all, to visit you and bring this work of generosity also to completion. You are so rich in everything— in faith, speech, knowledge, and zeal of every kind, as well as in the loving regard you have for us[a]—surely you should show yourselves equally lavish in this generous service! This is not meant as an order; by telling you how keen others are I am putting your love to the test. For you know how generous our Lord Jesus Christ has been: he was rich, yet for your sake he became poor, so that through his poverty you might become rich.

Here is my considered opinion on the matter. What I ask you to do is in your own interests. You made a good beginning last year both in the work you did and in your willingness to undertake it. Now I want you to go on and finish it: be as eager to complete the scheme as you were to adopt it, and give according to your means. Provided there is an eager desire to give, God accepts what a man has; he does not ask for what he has not. There is no question of relieving others at the cost of hardship to yourselves; it is a question of equality. At the moment your surplus meets their need, but one day your need may be met from their surplus. The aim is equality; as Scripture has it, 'The man who got much had no more than enough, and the man who got little did not go short.'

I thank God that he has made Titus as keen on your behalf as we are! For Titus not only welcomed our request; he is so eager that by his own desire he is now leaving to come to you. With him we are sending one of our company whose reputation is high among our congregations everywhere for his services to the Gospel. Moreover they have duly appointed him to travel with us and help in this beneficent work, by which we do honour to the Lord himself and show our own eagerness to serve. We want to guard against any criticism of our handling of this generous gift; for our aims are entirely honourable, not only in the Lord's eyes, but also in the eyes of men.

With these men we are sending another of our company whose enthusiasm we have had many opportunities of testing, and who is now all the more earnest because of the great confidence he has in you. If there is any question about Titus, he is my partner and my associate in dealings with you; as for the others, they are delegates of our congregations, an honour to Christ.[b] Then give them clear expression of your love and justify our pride in you; justify it to them, and through them to the congregations.

---

[a] *Some witnesses read* the love we have for you, *or* the love which we have kindled in your hearts.
[b] *Or* they are . . . congregations; they reflect Christ.

K.J.V.

R.S.V.

9 For as touching the ministering to the saints, it is superfluous for me to write to you: 2 For I know the forwardness of your mind, for which I boast of you to them of Macedonia, that Achaia was ready a year ago; and your zeal hath provoked very many. 3 Yet have I sent the brethren, lest our boasting of you should be in vain in this behalf; that, as I said, ye may be ready: 4 Lest haply if they of Macedonia come with me, and find you unprepared, we (that we say not, ye) should be ashamed in this same confident boasting. 5 Therefore I thought it necessary to exhort the brethren, that they would go before unto you, and make up beforehand your bounty, whereof ye had notice before, that the same might be ready, as *a matter of* bounty, and not as *of* covetousness. 6 But this *I say,* He which soweth sparingly shall reap also sparingly; and he which soweth bountifully shall reap also bountifully. 7 Every man according as he purposeth in his heart, *so let him give;* not grudgingly, or of necessity: for God loveth a cheerful giver. 8And God *is* able to make all grace abound toward you; that ye, always having all sufficiency in all *things,* may abound to every good work: 9 (As it is written, He hath dispersed abroad; he hath given to the poor: his righteousness remaineth for ever. 10 Now he that ministereth seed to the sower both minister bread for *your* food, and multiply your seed sown, and increase the fruits of your righteousness:) 11 Being enriched in every thing to all bountifulness, which causeth through us thanksgiving to God. 12 For the administration of this service not only supplieth the want of the saints, but is abundant also by many thanksgivings unto God; 13 While by the experiment of this ministration they glorify God for your professed subjection unto the gospel of Christ, and for *your* liberal distribution unto them, and unto all *men;* 14And by their prayer for you, which long after you for the exceeding grace of God in you. 15 Thanks *be* unto God for his unspeakable gift.

9 Now it is superfluous for me to write to you about the offering for the saints, 2 for I know your readiness, of which I boast about you to the people of Macedonia, saying that Achaia has been ready since last year; and your zeal has stirred up most of them. 3 But I am sending the brethren so that our boasting about you may not prove vain in this case, so that you may be ready, as I said you would be; 4 lest if some Macedonians come with me and find that you are not ready, we be humiliated—to say nothing of you—for being so confident. 5 So I thought it necessary to urge the brethren to go on to you before me, and arrange in advance for this gift you have promised, so that it may be ready not as an exaction but as a willing gift.

6 The point is this: he who sows sparingly will also reap sparingly, and he who sows bountifully will also reap bountifully. 7 Each one must do as he has made up his mind, not reluctantly or under compulsion, for God loves a cheerful giver. 8And God is able to provide you with every blessing in abundance, so that you may always have enough of everything and may provide in abundance for every good work. 9As it is written,

"He scatters abroad, he gives to the poor;
    his righteousness[k] endures for ever."

10 He who supplies seed to the sower and bread for food will supply and multiply your resources[l] and increase the harvest of your righteousness.[k] 11 You will be enriched in every way for great generosity, which through us will produce thanksgiving to God; 12 for the rendering of this service not only supplies the wants of the saints but also overflows in many thanksgivings to God. 13 Under the test of this service, you[m] will glorify God by your obedience in acknowledging the gospel of Christ, and by the generosity of your contribution for them and for all others; 14 while they long for you and pray for you, because of the surpassing grace of God in you. 15 Thanks be to God for his inexpressible gift!

10 Now I Paul myself beseech you by the meekness and gentleness of Christ, who in presence *am* base among you, but being absent am bold toward you: 2 But I beseech *you,* that

10 I, Paul, myself entreat you, by the meekness and gentleness of Christ—I who am humble when face to face with you, but bold to you when I am away!—2 I beg of you that

[k] Or *benevolence.* [l] Greek *sowing.* [m] Or *they.*

PHILLIPS   **N.E.B.**

A word in confidence about 9. 1
this gift of yours

Of course I know it is really quite superfluous for me to be writing to you about this matter of giving to fellow Christians, for I know how willing you are. Indeed I have told the Macedonians with some pride that "Achaia was ready to undertake this service twelve months ago." Your enthusiasm has consequently been a stimulus to many of them. I am, however, sending the brothers just to make sure that our pride in you is not unjustified. For, between ourselves, it would never do if some of the Macedonians were to accompany me on my visit to you and find you unprepared for this act of generosity! We (not to speak of you) should be horribly ashamed, just because we had been so proud and confident of you. This is my reason, then, for urging the brothers to visit you before I come myself, so that they can get your promised gift ready in good time. But, having let you into my confidence, I should like it to be a spontaneous gift, and not money squeezed out of you by what I have said. All I shall say is that poor sowing means a poor harvest, and generous sowing means a generous harvest.

Giving does not only help 9. 7
the one who receives

Let everyone give as his heart tells him, neither grudgingly nor under compulsion, for God loves the man who gives cheerfully. After all, God can give you everything that you need, so that you may always have sufficient both for yourselves and for giving away to other people. As the scripture says:

He hath scattered abroad, he hath given to the poor;
His righteousness abideth for ever.

He who gives the seed to the sower and turns that seed into bread to eat will give you the seed of generosity to sow and, for harvest, the satisfying bread of good deeds done. The more you are enriched by God, the more scope will there be for generous giving, and your gifts, administered through us, will mean that many will thank God. For your giving does not end in meeting the wants of your fellow Christians. It also results in an overflowing tide of thanksgiving to God. Moreover, your very giving proves the reality of your faith, and that means that men thank God that you practice the gospel that you profess to believe in, as well as for the actual gifts you make to them and to others. And yet further, men will pray for you and feel drawn to you because you have obviously received a generous measure of the grace of God.

Thank God, then, for his indescribable generosity to you!

We are not merely human agents 10. 1
but God-appointed ministers

Now I am going to appeal to you personally, by the gentleness and sympathy of Christ himself. Yes, I, Paul, the one who is "humble enough in our presence but outspoken when away from us," am begging you to make it un-

9 About the provision of aid for God's people, it is superfluous for me to write to you. I know how eager you are to help; I speak of it with pride to the Macedonians: I tell them that Achaia had everything ready last year; and most of them have been fired by your zeal. My purpose in sending these friends is to ensure that what we have said about you in this matter should not prove to be an empty boast. By that I mean, I want you to be prepared, as I told them you were; for if I bring with me men from Macedonia and they find you are not prepared, what a disgrace it will be to us, let alone to you, after all the confidence we have shown! I have accordingly thought it necessary to ask these friends to go on ahead to Corinth, to see that your promised bounty is in order before I come; it will then be awaiting me as a bounty indeed, and not as an extortion.

Remember: sparse sowing, sparse reaping; sow bountifully, and you will reap bountifully. Each person should give as he has decided for himself; there should be no reluctance, no sense of compulsion; God loves a cheerful giver. And it is in God's power to provide you richly with every good gift; thus you will have ample means in yourselves to meet each and every situation, with enough and to spare for every good cause. Scripture says of such a man: 'He has lavished his gifts on the needy, his benevolence stands fast for ever.' Now he who provides seed for sowing and bread for food will provide the seed for you to sow; he will multiply it and swell the harvest of your benevolence, and you will always be rich enough to be generous. Through our action such generosity will issue in thanksgiving to God, for as a piece of willing service this is not only a contribution towards the needs of God's people; more than that, it overflows in a flood of thanksgiving to God. For through the proof which this affords, many will give honour to God when they see how humbly you obey him and how faithfully you confess the gospel of Christ; and will thank him for your liberal contribution to their need and to the general good. And as they join in prayer on your behalf, their hearts will go out to you because of the richness of the grace which God has imparted to you. Thanks be to God for his gift beyond words!

Trials of a Christian Missionary

10 But I, Paul, appeal to you by the gentleness and magnanimity of Christ—I, so feeble (you say) when I am face to face with you, so brave when I am away. Spare me, I beg you, the

K.J.V.

I may not be bold when I am present with that confidence, wherewith I think to be bold against some, which think of us as if we walked according to the flesh. 3 For though we walk in the flesh, we do not war after the flesh: 4 (For the weapons of our warfare *are* not carnal, but mighty through God to the pulling down of strong holds;) 5 Casting down imaginations, and every high thing that exalteth itself against the knowledge of God, and bringing into captivity every thought to the obedience of Christ; 6And having in a readiness to revenge all disobedience, when your obedience is fulfilled. 7 Do ye look on things after the outward appearance? If any man trust to himself that he is Christ's, let him of himself think this again, that, as he *is* Christ's, even so *are* we Christ's. 8 For though I should boast somewhat more of our authority, which the Lord hath given us for edification, and not for your destruction, I should not be ashamed: 9 That I may not seem as if I would terrify you by letters. 10 For *his* letters, say they, *are* weighty and powerful; but *his* bodily presence *is* weak, and *his* speech contemptible. 11 Let such a one think this, that, such as we are in word by letters when we are absent, such *will we* be also in deed when we are present. 12 For we dare not make ourselves of the number, or compare ourselves with some that commend themselves: but they, measuring themselves by themselves, and comparing themselves among themselves, are not wise. 13 But we will not boast of things without *our* measure, but according to the measure of the rule which God hath distributed to us, a measure to reach even unto you. 14 For we stretch not ourselves beyond *our measure*, as though we reached not unto you; for we are come as far as to you also in *preaching* the gospel of Christ: 15 Not boasting of things without *our* measure, *that is,* of other men's labours; but having hope, when your faith is increased, that we shall be enlarged by you according to our rule abundantly, 16 To preach the gospel in the *regions* beyond you, *and* not to boast in another man's line of things made ready to our hand. 17 But he that glorieth, let him glory in the Lord. 18 For not he that commendeth himself is approved, but whom the Lord commendeth.

R.S.V.

when I am present I may not have to show boldness with such confidence as I count on showing against some who suspect us of acting in worldly fashion. 3 For though we live in the world we are not carrying on a worldly war, 4 for the weapons of our warfare are not worldly but have divine power to destroy strongholds. 5 We destroy arguments and every proud obstacle to the knowledge of God, and take every thought captive to obey Christ, 6 being ready to punish every disobedience, when your obedience is complete.

7 Look at what is before your eyes. If any one is confident that he is Christ's, let him remind himself that as he is Christ's, so are we. 8 For even if I boast a little too much of our authority, which the Lord gave for building you up and not for destroying you, I shall not be put to shame. 9 I would not seem to be frightening you with letters. 10 For they say, "His letters are weighty and strong, but his bodily presence is weak, and his speech of no account." 11 Let such people understand that what we say by letter when absent, we do when present. 12 Not that we venture to class or compare ourselves with some of those who commend themselves. But when they measure themselves by one another, and compare themselves with one another, they are without understanding.

13 But we will not boast beyond limit, but will keep to the limits God has apportioned us, to reach even to you. 14 For we are not overextending ourselves, as though we did not reach you; we were the first to come all the way to you with the gospel of Christ. 15 We do not boast beyond limit, in other men's labors; but our hope is that as your faith increases, our field among you may be greatly enlarged, 16 so that we may preach the gospel in lands beyond you, without boasting of work already done in another's field. 17 "Let him who boasts, boast of the Lord." 18 For it is not the man who commends himself that is accepted, but the man whom the Lord commends.

necessary for me to be outspoken and stern in your presence. For I am afraid otherwise that I shall have to do some plain speaking to those of you who will persist in reckoning that our activities are on the purely human level. The truth is that, although of course we lead normal human lives, the battle we are fighting is on the spiritual level. The very weapons we use are not those of human warfare but powerful in God's warfare for the destruction of the enemy's strongholds. Our battle is to bring down every deceptive fantasy and every imposing defense that men erect against the true knowledge of God. We even fight to capture every thought until it acknowledges the authority of Christ. Once we are sure of your obedience, we shall not shrink from dealing with those who refuse to obey.

I really am a Christian,   10. 7
you know!

Do look at things which stare you in the face! So-and-So considers himself to belong to Christ. All right; but let him reflect that we belong to Christ every bit as much as he. You may think that I have boasted unduly of my authority (which the Lord gave me, remember, to build you up, not to break you down), but I don't think I have done anything to be ashamed of. Yet I don't want you to think of me merely as the man who writes you terrifying letters. I know my critics say, "His letters are impressive and moving but his actual presence is feeble and his speaking beneath contempt." Let them realize that we can be just as "impressive and moving" in person as they say we are in our letters.

God's appointment means more   10. 12
than self-recommendation

Of course, we shouldn't dare include ourselves in the same class as those who write their own testimonials, or even to compare ourselves with them! All they are doing, of course, is to measure themselves by their own standards or by comparisons within their own circle, and that doesn't make for accurate estimation, you may be sure. No, we shall not make any wild claims, but simply judge ourselves by that line of duty which God has marked out for us, and that line includes our work on your behalf. We do not exceed our duty when we embrace your interests, for it was our preaching of the gospel which brought us into contact with you. Our pride is not in matters beyond our proper sphere nor in the labors of other men. No, our hope is that your growing faith will mean the expansion of our sphere of action, so that before long we shall be preaching the gospel in districts beyond you, instead of being proud of work that has already been done in someone else's province.

But,

He that glorieth let him glory in the Lord.

It is not self-commendation that matters; it is winning the approval of God.

necessity of such bravery when I come, for I reckon I could put on as bold a face as you please against those who charge us with moral weakness. Weak men we may be, but it is not as such that we fight our battles. The weapons we wield are not merely human,[a] but divinely potent to demolish strongholds; we demolish sophistries and all that rears its proud head against the knowledge of God; we compel every human thought to surrender in obedience to Christ; and we are prepared to punish all rebellion when once you have put yourselves in our hands.

Look facts in the face.[b] Someone is convinced, is he, that he belongs to Christ? Let him think again, and reflect that we belong to Christ as much as he does. Indeed, if I am somewhat overboastful about our authority—an authority given by the Lord to build you up, not pull you down —I shall make my boast good. So you must not think of me as one who scares you by the letters he writes. 'His letters', so it is said, 'are weighty and powerful; but when he appears he has no presence, and as a speaker he is beneath contempt.' People who talk in that way should reckon with this: when I come, my actions will show the same man as my letters showed in my absence.

We should not dare to class ourselves or compare ourselves with any of those who put forward their own claims. What fools they are to measure themselves by themselves, to find in themselves their own standard of comparison![c] With us there will be no attempt to boast beyond our proper sphere; and our sphere is determined by the limit God laid down for us, which permitted us to come as far as Corinth. We are not overstretching our commission, as we should be if it did not extend to you, for we were the first to reach Corinth in preaching the gospel of Christ. And we do not boast of work done where others have laboured, work beyond our proper sphere. Our hope is rather that, as your faith grows, we may attain a position among you greater than ever before, but still within the limits of our sphere. Then we can carry the Gospel to lands that lie beyond you, never priding ourselves on work already done in another man's sphere. If a man must boast, let him boast of the Lord. Not the man who recommends himself, but the man whom the Lord recommends—he and he alone is to be accepted.

[a] Or charge us with worldly standards. We live, no doubt, in the world; but it is not on that level that we fight our battles. The weapons we wield are not those of the world . . . [b] Or You are looking only at what catches the eye. [c] Some witnesses read On the contrary we measure ourselves by ourselves, by our own standard of comparison.

K.J.V.

11 Would to God ye could bear with me a little in *my* folly: and indeed bear with me. 2 For I am jealous over you with godly jealousy: for I have espoused you to one husband, that I may present *you as* a chaste virgin to Christ. 3 But I fear, lest by any means, as the serpent beguiled Eve through his subtilty, so your minds should be corrupted from the simplicity that is in Christ. 4 For if he that cometh preacheth another Jesus, whom we have not preached, or *if* ye receive another spirit, which ye have not received, or another gospel, which ye have not accepted, ye might well bear with *him*. 5 For I suppose I was not a whit behind the very chiefest apostles. 6 But though *I be* rude in speech, yet not in knowledge; but we have been thoroughly made manifest among you in all things. 7 Have I committed an offence in abasing myself that ye might be exalted, because I have preached to you the gospel of God freely? 8 I robbed other churches, taking wages *of them*, to do you service. 9 And when I was present with you, and wanted, I was chargeable to no man: for that which was lacking to me the brethren which came from Macedonia supplied: and in all *things* I have kept myself from being burdensome unto you, and *so* will I keep *myself*. 10 As the truth of Christ is in me, no man shall stop me of this boasting in the regions of Achaia. 11 Wherefore? because I love you not? God knoweth. 12 But what I do, that I will do, that I may cut off occasion from them which desire occasion; that wherein they glory, they may be found even as we. 13 For such *are* false apostles, deceitful workers, transforming themselves into the apostles of Christ. 14 And no marvel; for Satan himself is transformed into an angel of light. 15 Therefore *it is* no great thing if his ministers also be transformed as the ministers of righteousness; whose end shall be according to their works. 16 I say again, Let no man think me a fool; if otherwise, yet as a fool receive me, that I may boast myself a little. 17 That which I speak, I speak *it* not after the Lord, but as it were foolishly, in this confidence of boasting. 18 Seeing that many glory after the flesh, I will glory also. 19 For ye suffer fools gladly, seeing ye *yourselves* are wise. 20 For ye suffer, if a man bring you into bondage, if a man devour *you*, if a man take *of you*, if a man exalt himself, if a man smite you on the face. 21 I speak as concerning reproach, as though we had been weak. Howbeit, whereinsoever any is bold, (I speak foolishly,) I am bold also. 22 Are they Hebrews? so *am* I. Are they Israelites? so *am* I. Are they

R.S.V.

11 I wish you would bear with me in a little foolishness. Do bear with me! 2 I feel a divine jealousy for you, for I betrothed you to Christ to present you as a pure bride to her one husband. 3 But I am afraid that as the serpent deceived Eve by his cunning, your thoughts will be led astray from a sincere and pure devotion to Christ. 4 For if some one comes and preaches another Jesus than the one we preached, or if you receive a different spirit from the one you received, or if you accept a different gospel from the one you accepted, you submit to it readily enough. 5 I think that I am not in the least inferior to these superlative apostles. 6 Even if I am unskilled in speaking, I am not in knowledge; in every way we have made this plain to you in all things.

7 Did I commit a sin in abasing myself so that you might be exalted, because I preached God's gospel without cost to you? 8 I robbed other churches by accepting support from them in order to serve you. 9 And when I was with you and was in want, I did not burden any one, for my needs were supplied by the brethren who came from Macedonia. So I refrained and will refrain from burdening you in any way. 10 As the truth of Christ is in me, this boast of mine shall not be silenced in the regions of Achaia. 11 And why? Because I do not love you? God knows I do!

12 And what I do I will continue to do, in order to undermine the claim of those who would like to claim that in their boasted mission they work on the same terms as we do. 13 For such men are false apostles, deceitful workmen, disguising themselves as apostles of Christ. 14 And no wonder, for even Satan disguises himself as an angel of light. 15 So it is not strange if his servants also disguise themselves as servants of righteousness. Their end will correspond to their deeds.

16 I repeat, let no one think me foolish; but even if you do, accept me as a fool, so that I too may boast a little. 17 (What I am saying I say not with the Lord's authority but as a fool, in this boastful confidence; 18 since many boast of worldly things, I too will boast.) 19 For you gladly bear with fools, being wise yourselves! 20 For you bear it if a man makes slaves of you, or preys upon you, or takes advantage of you, or puts on airs, or strikes you in the face. 21 To my shame, I must say, we were too weak for that!

But whatever any one dares to boast of—I am speaking as a fool—I also dare to boast of that. 22 Are they Hebrews? So am I. Are they Israelites? So am I. Are they descendants of

Why do you so readily accept the 11. 1 false and reject the true?

I wish you could put up with a little of my foolishness—please try! My jealousy over you is the right sort of jealousy, for in my eyes you are like a fresh, unspoiled girl whom I am presenting as fiancée to your true husband, Christ himself. I am afraid that your minds may be seduced from a singlehearted devotion to him by the same subtle means that the serpent used toward Eve. For apparently you cheerfully accept a man who comes to you preaching a different Jesus from the one we told you about, and you readily receive a spirit and a gospel quite different from the ones you originally accepted. Yet I cannot believe I am in the least inferior to these extraspecial messengers of yours. Perhaps I am not a polished speaker, but I do know what I am talking about, and both what I am and what I say is pretty familiar to you. Perhaps I made a mistake in cheapening myself (though I did it to help you) by preaching the gospel without a fee. As a matter of fact I was only able to do this by "robbing" other churches, for it was what they paid me that made it possible to minister to you free of charge. Even when I was with you and very hard up, I did not bother any of you. It was the brothers who came from Macedonia who brought me all that I needed. Yes, I kept myself from being a burden to you then, and so I intend to do in the future. By the truth of Christ within me, no one shall stop my being proud of this independence through all Achaia!

Does this mean that I do not love you? God knows it doesn't, but I am determined to maintain this boast, so as to cut the ground from under the feet of those who profess to be God's messengers on the same terms as I am. *God's* messengers? They are counterfeits of the real thing, dishonest practitioners, "God's messengers" only by their own appointment. Nor do their tactics surprise me when I consider how Satan himself masquerades as an angel of light. It is only to be expected that his agents shall have the appearance of ministers of righteousness—but they will get their deserts one day.

If you like self-commendations, 11. 16 listen to mine!

Once more, let me advise you not to look upon me as a fool. Yet if you do, then listen to what this "fool" has to boast about.

I am not now speaking as the Lord commands me but as a fool who must be "in on" this business of boasting. Since all the others are so proud of themselves, let me do a little boasting as well. From your heights of superior wisdom I am sure you can smile tolerantly on a fool. Oh, you're tolerant, all right! You don't mind, do you, if a man takes away your liberty, spends your money, takes advantage of you, puts on airs or even smacks your face? I am almost ashamed to say that I never did brave strong things like that to you. Yet in whatever particular they enjoy such confidence I (speaking as a fool, remember) have just as much confidence.

Are they Hebrews? So am I.

Are they Israelites? So am I.

Are they descendants of Abraham? So am I.

Are they ministers of Christ? I have more claim to this title than they. This is a silly game but look at this list:

11 I wish you would bear with me in a little of my folly; please do bear with me. I am jealous for you, with a divine jealousy; for I betrothed you to Christ, thinking to present you as a chaste virgin to her true and only husband. But as the serpent in his cunning seduced Eve, I am afraid that your thoughts may be corrupted and you may lose your[a] single-hearted devotion to Christ. For if someone comes who proclaims another Jesus, not the Jesus whom we proclaimed, or if you then receive a spirit different from the Spirit already given to you, or a gospel different from the gospel you have already accepted, you manage to put up with that well enough. Have I in any way come short of those superlative apostles? I think not. I may be no speaker, but knowledge I have; at all times we have made known to you the full truth.

Or was this my offence, that I made no charge for preaching the gospel of God, lowering myself to help in raising you? It is true that I took toll of other congregations, accepting[b] support from them to serve you. Then, while I was with you, if I ran short I sponged on no one; anything I needed was fully met by our friends who came from Macedonia; I made it a rule, as I always shall, never to be a burden to you. As surely as the truth of Christ is in me, I will preserve my pride in this matter throughout Achaia, and nothing shall stop me. Why? Is it that I do not love you? God knows I do.

And I shall go on doing as I am doing now, to cut the ground from under those who would seize any chance to put their vaunted apostleship on the same level as ours. Such men are sham-apostles, crooked in all their practices, masquerading as apostles of Christ. There is nothing surprising about that; Satan himself masquerades as an angel of light. It is therefore a simple thing for his agents to masquerade as agents of good. But they will meet the end their deeds deserve.

I repeat: let no one take me for a fool; but if you must, then give me the privilege of a fool, and let me have my little boast like others. I am not speaking here as a Christian, but like a fool, if it comes to bragging. So many people brag of their earthly distinctions that I shall do so too. How gladly you bear with fools, being yourselves so wise! If a man tyrannizes over you, exploits you, gets you in his clutches, puts on airs, and hits you in the face, you put up with it. And we, you say, have been weak! I admit the reproach.

But if there is to be bravado (and here I speak as a fool), I can indulge in it too. Are they Hebrews? So am I. Israelites? So am I. Abraham's descendants? So am I. Are they servants

[a] *Some witnesses insert* purity and . . . [b] *Or* Did I take toll of other congregations by accepting . . . ?

K.J.V.

the seed of Abraham? so *am* I. 23 Are they ministers of Christ? (I speak as a fool,) I *am* more; in labours more abundant, in stripes above measure, in prisons more frequent, in deaths oft. 24 Of the Jews five times received I forty *stripes* save one. 25 Thrice was I beaten with rods, once was I stoned, thrice I suffered shipwreck, a night and a day I have been in the deep; 26 *In* journeyings often, *in* perils of waters, *in* perils of robbers, *in* perils by *mine own* countrymen, *in* perils by the heathen, *in* perils in the city, *in* perils in the wilderness, *in* perils in the sea, *in* perils among false brethren; 27 In weariness and painfulness, in watchings often, in hunger and thirst, in fastings often, in cold and nakedness. 28 Beside those things that are without, that which cometh upon me daily, the care of all the churches. 29 Who is weak, and I am not weak? who is offended, and I burn not? 30 If I must needs glory, I will glory of the things which concern mine infirmities. 31 The God and Father of our Lord Jesus Christ, which is blessed for evermore, knoweth that I lie not. 32 In Damascus the governor under Aretas the king kept the city of the Damascenes with a garrison, desirous to apprehend me: 33 And through a window in a basket was I let down by the wall, and escaped his hands.

12 It is not expedient for me doubtless to glory. I will come to visions and revelations of the Lord. 2 I knew a man in Christ above fourteen years ago, (whether in the body, I cannot tell; or whether out of the body, I cannot tell: God knoweth;) such a one caught up to the third heaven. 3 And I knew such a man, (whether in the body, or out of the body, I cannot tell: God knoweth;) 4 How that he was caught up into paradise, and heard unspeakable words, which it is not lawful for a man to utter. 5 Of such a one will I glory: yet of myself I will not glory, but in mine infirmities. 6 For though I would desire to glory, I shall not be a fool; for I will say the truth: but *now* I forbear, lest any man should think of me above that which he seeth me *to be*, or *that* he heareth of me. 7 And lest I should be exalted above measure through the abundance of the revelations, there was given to me a thorn in the flesh, the messenger of Satan to buffet me, lest I should be exalted above measure. 8 For this thing I besought the Lord thrice, that it might depart from me. 9 And he said unto me, My grace is sufficient for thee: for my strength is made perfect in weakness. Most gladly therefore will I rather glory in my infirmities, that the power of Christ may rest upon me. 10 Therefore I take pleasure in infirmities, in reproaches, in necessities, in persecutions, in distresses for Christ's sake: for when I

R.S.V.

Abraham? So am I. 23 Are they servants of Christ? I am a better one—I am talking like a madman—with far greater labors, far more imprisonments, with countless beatings, and often near death. 24 Five times I have received at the hands of the Jews the forty lashes less one. 25 Three times I have been beaten with rods; once I was stoned. Three times I have been shipwrecked; a night and a day I have been adrift at sea; 26 on frequent journeys, in danger from rivers, danger from robbers, danger from my own people, danger from Gentiles, danger in the city, danger in the wilderness, danger at sea, danger from false brethren; 27 in toil and hardship, through many a sleepless night, in hunger and thirst, often without food, in cold and exposure. 28 And, apart from other things, there is the daily pressure upon me of my anxiety for all the churches. 29 Who is weak, and I am not weak? Who is made to fall, and I am not indignant?

30 If I must boast, I will boast of the things that show my weakness. 31 The God and Father of the Lord Jesus, he who is blessed for ever, knows that I do not lie. 32 At Damascus, the governor under King Aretas guarded the city of Damascus in order to seize me, 33 but I was let down in a basket through a window in the wall, and escaped his hands.

12 I must boast; there is nothing to be gained by it, but I will go on to visions and revelations of the Lord. 2 I know a man in Christ who fourteen years ago was caught up to the third heaven—whether in the body or out of the body I do not know, God knows. 3 And I know that this man was caught up into Paradise—whether in the body or out of the body I do not know, God knows—4 and he heard things that cannot be told, which man may not utter. 5 On behalf of this man I will boast, but on my own behalf I will not boast, except of my weaknesses. 6 Though if I wish to boast, I shall not be a fool, for I shall be speaking the truth. But I refrain from it, so that no one may think more of me than he sees in me or hears from me. 7 And to keep me from being too elated by the abundance of revelations, a thorn was given me in the flesh, a messenger of Satan, to harass me, to keep me from being too elated. 8 Three times I besought the Lord about this, that it should leave me; 9 but he said to me, "My grace is sufficient for you, for my power is made perfect in weakness." I will all the more gladly boast of my weaknesses, that the power of Christ may rest upon me. 10 For the sake of Christ, then, I am content with weaknesses, insults, hardships, persecutions, and calamities; for when I am weak, then I am strong.

570

PHILLIPS

I have worked harder than any of them.
I have served more prison sentences!
I have been beaten times without number.
I have faced death again and again.
I have been beaten the regulation thirty-nine stripes by the Jews five times.
I have been beaten with rods three times.
I have been stoned once.
I have been shipwrecked three times.
I have been twenty-four hours in the open sea.
In my travels I have been in constant danger from rivers and floods, from bandits, from my own countrymen, and from pagans. I have faced danger in city streets, danger in the desert, danger on the high seas, danger among false Christians. I have known exhaustion, pain, long vigils, hunger and thirst, doing without meals, cold and lack of clothing.

Apart from all external trials I have the daily burden of responsibility for all the churches. Do you think anyone is weak without my feeling his weakness? Does anyone have his faith upset without my longing to restore him?

Oh, if I am going to boast, let me boast of the things which have shown up my weakness! The God and Father of the Lord Jesus, he who is blessed for ever, knows that I speak the simple truth.

In Damascus, the town governor, acting by king Aretas' order, had men out to arrest me. I escaped by climbing through a window and being let down the wall in a basket. That's the sort of dignified exit I can boast about.

I have real grounds for "boasting," 12. 1 but I shall only hint at them

No, I don't think it's really a good thing for me to boast at all, but I shall just mention visions and revelations of the Lord himself. I know a man in Christ who, fourteen years ago, had the experience of being caught up into the third Heaven. I don't know whether it was an actual physical experience; only God knows that. All I know is that this man was caught up into paradise. (I repeat, I do not know whether this was a physical happening or not; God alone knows.) This man heard words that cannot, and indeed must not, be translated into human speech. I am honestly proud of an experience like that, but I have made up my mind not to boast of anything personal, except of what may be called my weaknesses. If I should want to boast I should certainly be no fool to be proud of my experiences, and I should be speaking nothing but the sober truth. Yet I am not going to do so, for I don't want anyone to think more highly of me than his experience of me and what he hears of me should warrant. So tremendous, however, were the revelations that God gave me that, in order to prevent my becoming absurdly conceited, I was given a physical handicap—one of Satan's angels—to harass me and effectually stop any conceit. Three times I begged the Lord for it to leave me, but his reply has been, "My grace is enough for you: for where there is weakness, my power is shown the more completely." Therefore, I have cheerfully made up my mind to be proud of my weaknesses, because they mean a deeper experience of the power of Christ. I can even enjoy weaknesses, suffering, privations, persecutions and difficulties for Christ's sake. For my very weakness makes me strong in him.

N.E.B.

of Christ? I am mad to speak like this, but I can outdo them. More overworked than they, scourged more severely, more often imprisoned, many a time face to face with death. Five times the Jews have given me the thirty-nine strokes; three times I have been beaten with rods; once I was stoned; three times I have been shipwrecked, and for twenty-four hours I was adrift on the open sea. I have been constantly on the road; I have met dangers from rivers, dangers from robbers, dangers from my fellow-countrymen, dangers from foreigners, dangers in towns, dangers in the country, dangers at sea, dangers from false friends. I have toiled and drudged, I have often gone without sleep; hungry and thirsty, I have often gone fasting; and I have suffered from cold and exposure.

Apart from these external things,[a] there is the responsibility that weighs on me every day, my anxious concern for all our congregations. If anyone is weak, do I not share his weakness? If anyone is made to stumble, does my heart not blaze with indignation? If boasting there must be, I will boast of the things that show up my weakness. The God and Father of the Lord Jesus (blessed be his name for ever!) knows that what I say is true. When I was in Damascus, the commissioner of King Aretas kept the city under observation so as to have me arrested; and I was let down in a basket, through a window in the wall, and so escaped his clutches.

12 I am obliged to boast. It does no good; but I shall go on to tell of visions and revelations granted by the Lord. I know a Christian man who fourteen years ago (whether in the body or out of it, I do not know—God knows) was caught up as far as the third heaven. And I know that this same man (whether in the body or out of it, I do not know—God knows) was caught up into paradise, and heard words so secret that human lips may not repeat them. About such a man as that I am ready to boast; but I will not boast on my own account, except of my weaknesses. If I should choose to boast, it would not be the boast of a fool, for I should be speaking the truth. But I refrain, because I should not like anyone to form an estimate of me which goes beyond the evidence of his own eyes and ears. And so, to keep me from being unduly elated by the magnificence of such revelations, I was given[b] a sharp pain in my body[c] which came as Satan's messenger to bruise me; this was to save me from being unduly elated. Three times I begged the Lord to rid me of it, but his answer was: 'My grace is all you need; power comes to its full strength in weakness.' I shall therefore prefer to find my joy and pride in the very things that are my weakness; and then the power of Christ will come and rest upon me. Hence I am well content, for Christ's sake, with weakness, contempt, persecution, hardship, and frustration; for when I am weak, then I am strong.

[a] Or Apart from things which I omit. [b] Some witnesses read . . . ears, and because of the magnificence of the revelations themselves. Therefore to keep me from being unduly elated I was given . . . [c] Or a painful wound to my pride (literally a stake, or thorn, for the flesh).

K.J.V.

am weak, then am I strong. 11 I am become a fool in glorying; ye have compelled me: for I ought to have been commended of you: for in nothing am I behind the very chiefest apostles, though I be nothing. 12 Truly the signs of an apostle were wrought among you in all patience, in signs, and wonders, and mighty deeds. 13 For what is it wherein ye were inferior to other churches, except it be that I myself was not burdensome to you? forgive me this wrong. 14 Behold, the third time I am ready to come to you; and I will not be burdensome to you: for I seek not yours, but you: for the children ought not to lay up for the parents, but the parents for the children. 15And I will very gladly spend and be spent for you; though the more abundantly I love you, the less I be loved. 16 But be it so, I did not burden you: nevertheless, being crafty, I caught you with guile. 17 Did I make a gain of you by any of them whom I sent unto you? 18 I desired Titus, and with him I sent a brother. Did Titus make a gain of you? walked we not in the same spirit? walked we not in the same steps? 19Again, think ye that we excuse ourselves unto you? we speak before God in Christ: but we do all things, dearly beloved, for your edifying. 20 For I fear, lest, when I come, I shall not find you such as I would, and that I shall be found unto you such as ye would not: lest there be debates, envyings, wraths, strifes, backbitings, whisperings, swellings, tumults: 21And lest, when I come again, my God will humble me among you, and that I shall bewail many which have sinned already, and have not repented of the uncleanness and fornication and lasciviousness which they have committed.

R.S.V.

11 I have been a fool! You forced me to it, for I ought to have been commended by you. For I am not at all inferior to these superlative apostles, even though I am nothing. 12 The signs of a true apostle were performed among you in all patience, with signs and wonders and mighty works. 13 For in what were you less favored than the rest of the churches, except that I myself did not burden you? Forgive me this wrong!

14 Here for the third time I am ready to come to you. And I will not be a burden, for I seek not what is yours but you; for children ought not to lay up for their parents, but parents for their children. 15 I will most gladly spend and be spent for your souls. If I love you the more, am I to be loved the less? 16 But granting that I myself did not burden you, I was crafty, you say, and got the better of you by guile. 17 Did I take advantage of you through any of those whom I sent to you? 18 I urged Titus to go, and sent the brother with him. Did Titus take advantage of you? Did we not act in the same spirit? Did we not take the same steps?

19 Have you been thinking all along that we have been defending ourselves before you? It is in the sight of God that we have been speaking in Christ, and all for your upbuilding, beloved. 20 For I fear that perhaps I may come and find you not what I wish, and that you may find me not what you wish; that perhaps there may be quarreling, jealousy, anger, selfishness, slander, gossip, conceit, and disorder. 21 I fear that when I come again my God may humble me before you, and I may have to mourn over many of those who sinned before and have not repented of the impurity, immorality, and licentiousness which they have practiced.

13 This is the third time I am coming to you. In the mouth of two or three witnesses shall every word be established. 2 I told you before, and foretell you, as if I were present,

13 This is the third time I am coming to you. Any charge must be sustained by the evidence of two or three witnesses. 2 I warned those who sinned before and all the others, and I

PHILLIPS

N.E.B.

This boasting is silly, but you   **12. 11**
made it necessary

I have made a fool of myself in this "boasting" business, but you forced me to do it. If only you had had a better opinion of me it would have been quite unnecessary. For I am not really in the least inferior, nobody as I am, to these extraspecial messengers. You have had an exhaustive demonstration of the power God gives to a genuine messenger of his in the miracles, signs and works of spiritual power that you saw with your own eyes. What makes you feel so inferior to other churches? Is it because I have not allowed you to support me financially? My humblest apologies for this great wrong!

What can be your grounds for   **12. 14**
suspicion of me?

Now I am all ready to visit you for the third time, and I am still not going to be a burden to you. It is you I want—not your money. Children don't have to put by their savings for their parents; parents do that for their children. Consequently I will most gladly spend and be spent for your good, even though it means that the more I love you, the less you love me.

"All right then," I hear you say, "we agree that he himself had none of our money." But are you thinking that I nevertheless was rogue enough to catch you by some trick? Just think. Did I make any profit out of the messengers I sent you? I asked Titus to go, and sent the brother with him. You don't think Titus made anything out of you, do you? Yet didn't I act in the same spirit as he, and take the same line as he did?

Remember what I really am,   **12. 19**
and whose authority I have

Are you thinking all this time that I am trying to justify myself in your eyes? Actually I am speaking in Christ before God himself, and my only reason for so doing is to help you in your spiritual life.

For I must confess that I am afraid that when I come I shall not perhaps find you as I should like to find you, and that you will not find me coming quite as you would like me to come. I am afraid of finding arguments, jealousy, ill-feeling, divided loyalties, slander, whispering, pride and disharmony. When I come, will God make me feel ashamed of you as I stand among you? Shall I have to grieve over many who have sinned already and are not yet sorry for the impurity, the immorality and the lustfulness of which they are guilty?

This third time I am really coming to you in person. Remember the ancient Law: "In the mouth of two or three witnesses shall every word be established." My previous warning, given on my second visit, still stands and, though absent,

I am being very foolish, but it was you who drove me to it; my credentials should have come from you. In no respect did I fall short of these superlative apostles, even if I am a nobody. The marks of a true apostle were there, in the work I did among you, which called for such constant fortitude, and was attended by signs, marvels, and miracles. Is there anything in which you were treated worse than the other congregations—except this, that I never sponged upon you? How unfair of me! I crave forgiveness.

Here am I preparing to pay you a third visit; and I am not going to sponge upon you. It is you I want, not your money; parents should make provision for their children, not children for their parents. As for me, I will gladly spend what I have for you—yes, and spend myself to the limit. If I love you overmuch, am I to be loved the less? But, granted that I did not prove a burden to you, still I was unscrupulous enough, you say, to use a trick to catch you. Who, of the men I have sent to you, was used by me to defraud you? I begged Titus to visit you, and I sent our friend with him. Did Titus defraud you? Have we not both been guided by the same Spirit, and followed the same course?

Perhaps you think that all this time we have been addressing our defence to you. No; we are speaking in God's sight, and as Christian men. Our whole aim, my own dear people, is to build you up. I fear that when I come I may perhaps find you different from what I wish you to be, and that you may find me also different from what you wish. I fear I may find quarrelling and jealousy, angry tempers and personal rivalries, backbiting and gossip, arrogance and general disorder. I am afraid that, when I come again, my God may humiliate me in your presence, that I may have tears to shed over many of those who have sinned in the past and have not repented of their unclean lives, their fornication and sensuality.

13 This will be my third visit to you; and all facts must be established by the evidence of two or three witnesses. To those who have sinned in the past, and to everyone else, I repeat

K.J.V.

the second time; and being absent now I write to them which heretofore have sinned, and to all other, that, if I come again, I will not spare: 3 Since ye seek a proof of Christ speaking in me, which to you-ward is not weak, but is mighty in you. 4 For though he was crucified through weakness, yet he liveth by the power of God. For we also are weak in him, but we shall live with him by the power of God toward you. 5 Examine yourselves, whether ye be in the faith; prove your own selves. Know ye not your own selves, how that Jesus Christ is in you, except ye be reprobates? 6 But I trust that ye shall know that we are not reprobates. 7 Now I pray to God that ye do no evil; not that we should appear approved, but that ye should do that which is honest, though we be as reprobates. 8 For we can do nothing against the truth, but for the truth. 9 For we are glad, when we are weak, and ye are strong: and this also we wish, *even* your perfection. 10 Therefore I write these things being absent, lest being present I should use sharpness, according to the power which the Lord hath given me to edification, and not to destruction. 11 Finally, brethren, farewell. Be perfect, be of good comfort, be of one mind, live in peace; and the God of love and peace shall be with you. 12 Greet one another with a holy kiss. 13 All the saints salute you. 14 The grace of the Lord Jesus Christ, and the love of God, and the communion of the Holy Ghost, *be* with you all. Amen.

The second *epistle* to the Corinthians was written from Philippi, *a city* of Macedonia, by Titus and Lucas.

R.S.V.

warn them now while absent, as I did when present on my second visit, that if I come again I will not spare them—3 since you desire proof that Christ is speaking in me. He is not weak in dealing with you, but is powerful in you. 4 For he was crucified in weakness, but lives by the power of God. For we are weak in him, but in dealing with you we shall live with him by the power of God.

5 Examine yourselves, to see whether you are holding to your faith. Test yourselves. Do you not realize that Jesus Christ is in you?—unless indeed you fail to meet the test! 6 I hope you will find out that we have not failed. 7 But we pray God that you may not do wrong—not that we may appear to have met the test, but that you may do what is right, though we may seem to have failed. 8 For we cannot do anything against the truth, but only for the truth. 9 For we are glad when we are weak and you are strong. What we pray for is your improvement. 10 I write this while I am away from you, in order that when I come I may not have to be severe in my use of the authority which the Lord has given me for building up and not for tearing down.

11 Finally, brethren, farewell. Mend your ways, heed my appeal, agree with one another, live in peace, and the God of love and peace will be with you. 12 Greet one another with a holy kiss. 13 All the saints greet you.

14 The grace of the Lord Jesus Christ and the love of God and the fellowship of [n] the Holy Spirit be with you all.

[n] Or *and participation in.*

I repeat it now as though I were present—my coming will *not* mean leniency for those who had sinned before that visit and those who have sinned since. It will in fact be a proof that I speak by the power of Christ. The Christ you have to deal with is not a weak person outside you, but a tremendous power inside you. He was "weak" enough to be crucified, yes, but he lives now by the power of God. I am weak as he was weak, but I am strong enough to deal with you for I share his life by the power of God.

Why not test yourselves instead of me?

13. 5

You should be looking at yourselves to make sure that you are really Christ's. It is yourselves that you should be testing, not me. You ought to know by this time that Christ is in you, unless you are not real Christians at all. And when you have applied your test, I am confident that you will soon find that I myself am a genuine Christian. I pray God that you may find the right answer to your test, not because I have any need of your approval, but because I earnestly want you to find the right answer, even if that should make me no real Christian. For, after all, we can make no progress against the truth; we can only work for the truth.

We are glad to be weak if it means that you are strong. Our ambition for you is true Christian maturity. Hence the tone of this letter, so that when I do come I shall not be obliged to use that power of severity which God has given me—though even that is not meant to break you down but to build you up.

Finally, farewell

13. 11

Finally, then, my brothers, cheer up! Straighten yourselves out, comfort yourselves, agree with one another and live at peace. So shall the God of love and peace be ever with you.

A handshake all round, please! All the Christians here send greeting.

The grace of the Lord Jesus Christ, the love of God and the fellowship that is ours in the Holy Spirit be with you all!

PAUL

the warning I gave before; I gave it in person on my second visit, and I give it now in absence. It is that when I come this time, I will show no leniency. Then you will have the proof you seek of the Christ who speaks through me, the Christ who, far from being weak with you, makes his power felt among you. True, he died on the cross in weakness, but he lives by the power of God; and we who share his weakness shall by the power of God live with him in your service.

Examine yourselves: are you living the life of faith? Put yourselves to the test. Surely you recognize that Jesus Christ is among you?—unless of course you prove unequal to the test. I hope you will come to see that we are not unequal to it. Our prayer to God is that we may not have to hurt you; we are not concerned to be vindicated ourselves; we want you to do what is right, even if we should seem to be discredited. For we have no power to act against the truth, but only for it. We are well content to be weak at any time if only you are strong. Indeed, my whole prayer is that all may be put right with you. My purpose in writing this letter before I come, is to spare myself, when I come, any sharp exercise of authority—authority which the Lord gave me for building up and not for pulling down.

And now, my friends, farewell. Mend your ways; take our appeal to heart; agree with one another; live in peace; and the God of love and peace will be with you. Greet one another with the kiss of peace. All God's people send you greetings.

The grace of the Lord Jesus Christ, and the love of God, and fellowship in the Holy Spirit, be with you all.

K.J.V.

THE EPISTLE OF
PAUL THE APOSTLE
TO THE
GALATIANS

R.S.V.

THE
LETTER OF PAUL TO THE
GALATIANS

1 Paul, an apostle, (not of men, neither by man, but by Jesus Christ, and God the Father, who raised him from the dead;) 2And all the brethren which are with me, unto the churches of Galatia: 3 Grace *be* to you, and peace, from God the Father, and *from* our Lord Jesus Christ, 4 Who gave himself for our sins, that he might deliver us from this present evil world, according to the will of God and our Father: 5 To whom *be* glory for ever and ever. Amen. 6 I marvel that ye are so soon removed from him that called you into the grace of Christ unto another gospel: 7 Which is not another; but there be some that trouble you, and would pervert the gospel of Christ. 8 But though we, or an angel from heaven, preach any other gospel unto you than that which we have preached unto you, let him be accursed. 9As we said before, so say I now again, If any *man* preach any other gospel unto you than that ye have received, let him be accursed. 10 For do I now persuade men, or God? or do I seek to please men? for if I yet pleased men, I should not be the servant of Christ. 11 But I certify you, brethren, that the gospel which was preached of me is not after man. 12 For I neither received it of man, neither was I taught *it*, but by the revelation of Jesus Christ. 13 For ye have heard of my conversation in time past in the Jews' religion, how that beyond measure I persecuted the church of God, and wasted it: 14And profited in the Jews' religion above many my equals in mine own nation, being more exceedingly zealous of the traditions of my fathers. 15 But when it pleased God, who separated me from my mother's womb, and called *me* by his grace, 16 To reveal his Son in me, that I might preach him among the heathen; immediately I conferred not with flesh and blood: 17 Neither went I up to Jerusalem to them which were apostles before me; but I went into Arabia, and returned again unto Damascus. 18 Then after three years I went

1 Paul an apostle—not from men nor through man, but through Jesus Christ and God the Father, who raised him from the dead—2 and all the brethren who are with me,

To the churches of Galatia:

3 Grace to you and peace from God the Father and our Lord Jesus Christ, 4 who gave himself for our sins to deliver us from the present evil age, according to the will of our God and Father; 5 to whom be the glory for ever and ever. Amen.

6 I am astonished that you are so quickly deserting him who called you in the grace of Christ and turning to a different gospel—7 not that there is another gospel, but there are some who trouble you and want to pervert the gospel of Christ. 8 But even if we, or an angel from heaven, should preach to you a gospel contrary to that which we preached to you, let him be accursed. 9As we have said before, so now I say again, If any one is preaching to you a gospel contrary to that which you received, let him be accursed.

10 Am I now seeking the favor of men, or of God? Or am I trying to please men? If I were still pleasing men, I should not be a servant[a] of Christ.

11 For I would have you know, brethren, that the gospel which was preached by me is not man's[b] gospel. 12 For I did not receive it from man, nor was I taught it, but it came through a revelation of Jesus Christ. 13 For you have heard of my former life in Judaism, how I persecuted the church of God violently and tried to destroy it; 14 and I advanced in Judaism beyond many of my own age among my people, so extremely zealous was I for the traditions of my fathers. 15 But when he who had set me apart before I was born, and had called me through his grace, 16 was pleased to reveal his Son to[c] me, in order that I might preach him among the Gentiles, I did not confer with flesh and blood, 17 nor did I go up to Jerusalem to those who were apostles before me, but I went away into Arabia; and again I returned to Damascus.

18 Then after three years I went up to Jerusa-

[a] Or *slave*. [b] Greek *according to man*. [c] Greek *in*.

THE LETTER TO
THE CHRISTIANS IN
GALATIA

THE
LETTER OF PAUL TO THE
GALATIANS

Faith and Freedom

I, Paul, who am appointed and commissioned a messenger not by man but by Jesus Christ and God the Father (who raised him from the dead), I and all the brothers with me send the churches in Galatia greeting. Grace and peace to you from God the Father and from our Lord Jesus Christ, who according to the will of our God and Father gave himself for our sins and thereby rescued us from the present evil world order. To him be glory for ever and ever!

1 From Paul, an apostle, not by human appointment or human commission, but by commission from Jesus Christ and from God the Father who raised him from the dead. I and the group of friends now with me send greetings to the Christian congregations of Galatia.

Grace and peace to you from God the Father and our Lord Jesus Christ,*[a]* who sacrificed himself for our sins, to rescue us out of this present age of wickedness, as our God and Father willed: to whom be glory for ever and ever. Amen.

The gospel is God's truth: men 1. 6
must not dare to pervert it

I am amazed that you have so quickly transferred your allegiance from him who called you in the grace of Christ to another "gospel"! Not, of course, that it is or ever could be another gospel, but there are obviously men who are upsetting your faith with a travesty of the gospel of Christ. Yet I say that if I, or an angel from Heaven, were to preach to you any other gospel than the one you have heard, may he be damned! You have heard me say it before, and now I put it down in black and white—may anybody who preaches any other gospel than the one you have already heard be a damned soul! (Does that make you think now that I am serving man's interests or God's? If I were trying to win human approval I should never be Christ's servant.)

I am astonished to find you turning so quickly away from him who called you by grace,*[b]* and following a different gospel. Not that it is in fact another gospel; only there are persons who unsettle your minds by trying to distort the gospel of Christ. But if anyone, if we ourselves or an angel from heaven, should preach a gospel at variance with the gospel we preached to you, he shall be held outcast. I now repeat what I have said before: if anyone preaches a gospel at variance with the gospel which you received, let him be outcast!

Does my language now sound as if I were canvassing for men's support? Whose support do I want but God's alone? Do you think I am currying favour with men? If I still sought men's favour, I should be no servant of Christ.

I must make it clear to you, my friends, that the gospel you heard me preach is no human invention. I did not take it over from any man; no man taught it me; I received it through a revelation of Jesus Christ.

The gospel was given to me by 1. 11
Christ himself, and not by any
human agency, as my story
will show

The gospel I preach to you is no human invention. No man gave it to me, no man taught it to me; it came to me as a direct revelation from Jesus Christ. For you have heard of my past career in the Jewish religion, how I persecuted the Church of God with fanatical zeal and, in fact, did my best to destroy it. I was ahead of most of my contemporaries in the Jewish religion, and had a greater enthusiasm for the old traditions. But when the time came for God (who had chosen me from the moment of my birth, and then called me by his grace) to reveal his Son within me so that I might proclaim him to the non-Jewish world, I did not, as might have been expected, talk over the matter with any human being. I did not even go to Jerusalem to meet those who were God's messengers before me—no, I went away to Arabia and later came back to Damascus. It was not until three years later that I went up to Jerusalem to see

You have heard what my manner of life was when I was still a practising Jew: how savagely I persecuted the church of God, and tried to destroy it; and how in the practice of our national religion I was outstripping many of my Jewish contemporaries in my boundless devotion to the traditions of my ancestors. But then in his good pleasure God, who had set me apart from birth and called me through his grace, chose to reveal his Son to me and through me, in order that I might proclaim him among the Gentiles. When that happened, without consulting any human being, without going up to Jerusalem to see those who were apostles before me, I went off at once to Arabia, and afterwards returned to Damascus.

Three years later I did go up to Jerusalem to

[a] Some witnesses read God our Father and the Lord Jesus Christ. *[b] Some witnesses read* from Christ who called you by grace, *or from* him who called you by grace of Christ.

up to Jerusalem to see Peter, and abode with him fifteen days. 19 But other of the apostles saw I none, save James the Lord's brother. 20 Now the things which I write unto you, behold, before God, I lie not. 21Afterwards I came into the regions of Syria and Cilicia; 22And was unknown by face unto the churches of Judea which were in Christ: 23 But they had heard only, That he which persecuted us in times past now preacheth the faith which once he destroyed. 24And they glorified God in me.

lem to visit Cephas, and remained with him fifteen days. 19 But I saw none of the other apostles except James the Lord's brother. 20 (In what I am writing to you, before God, I do not lie!) 21 Then I went into the regions of Syria and Cilicia. 22And I was still not known by sight to the churches of Christ in Judea; 23 they only heard it said, "He who once persecuted us is now preaching the faith he once tried to destroy." 24And they glorified God because of me.

2 Then fourteen years after I went up again to Jerusalem with Barnabas, and took Titus with *me* also. 2And I went up by revelation, and communicated unto them that gospel which I preach among the Gentiles, but privately to them which were of reputation, lest by any means I should run, or had run, in vain. 3 But neither Titus, who was with me, being a Greek, was compelled to be circumcised: 4And that because of false brethren unawares brought in, who came in privily to spy out our liberty which we have in Christ Jesus, that they might bring us into bondage: 5 To whom we gave place by subjection, no, not for an hour; that the truth of the gospel might continue with you. 6 But of those who seemed to be somewhat, whatsoever they were, it maketh no matter to me: God accepteth no man's person: for they who seemed *to be somewhat* in conference added nothing to me: 7 But contrariwise, when they saw that the gospel of the uncircumcision was committed unto me, as *the gospel* of the circumcision *was* unto Peter; 8 (For he that wrought effectually in Peter to the apostleship of the circumcision, the same was mighty in me toward the Gentiles;) 9And when James, Cephas, and John, who seemed to be pillars, perceived the grace that was given unto me, they gave to me and Barnabas the right hands of fellowship; that we *should go* unto the heathen, and they unto the circumcision. 10 Only *they would* that we should remember the poor; the same which I also was forward to do. 11 But when Peter was come to Antioch, I withstood him to the face, because he was to be blamed. 12 For before that certain came from James, he did eat with the Gentiles: but when they were come, he withdrew and separated himself, fearing them which were of the circumcision. 13And the other Jews dissembled likewise with him; insomuch that Barnabas also was carried away with their dissimulation. 14 But when I saw that they walked not uprightly

2 Then after fourteen years I went up again to Jerusalem with Barnabas, taking Titus along with me. 2 I went up by revelation; and I laid before them (but privately before those who were of repute) the gospel which I preach among the Gentiles, lest somehow I should be running or had run in vain. 3 But even Titus, who was with me, was not compelled to be circumcised, though he was a Greek. 4 But because of false brethren secretly brought in, who slipped in to spy out our freedom which we have in Christ Jesus, that they might bring us into bondage— 5 to them we did not yield submission even for a moment, that the truth of the gospel might be preserved for you. 6And from those who were reputed to be something (what they were makes no difference to me; God shows no partiality) —those, I say, who were of repute added nothing to me; 7 but on the contrary, when they saw that I had been entrusted with the gospel to the uncircumcised, just as Peter had been entrusted with the gospel to the circumcised 8 (for he who worked through Peter for the mission to the circumcised worked through me also for the Gentiles), 9 and when they perceived the grace that was given to me, James and Cephas and John, who were reputed to be pillars, gave to me and Barnabas the right hand of fellowship, that we should go to the Gentiles and they to the circumcised; 10 only they would have us remember the poor, which very thing I was eager to do.

11 But when Cephas came to Antioch I opposed him to his face, because he stood condemned. 12 For before certain men came from James, he ate with the Gentiles; but when they came he drew back and separated himself, fearing the circumcision party. 13And with him the rest of the Jews acted insincerely, so that even Barnabas was carried away by their insincerity. 14 But when I saw that they were not straight-

Cephas, and I only stayed with him just over a fortnight. I did not meet any of the other messengers, except James, the Lord's brother.

All this that I am telling you is, I assure you before God, the plain truth. Later, I visited districts in Syria and Cilicia, but I was still personally unknown to the churches of Judaea. All they knew of me, in fact, was the saying: "The man who used to persecute us is now preaching the faith he once tried to destroy." And they thanked God for what had happened to me.

Years later I met church leaders in Jerusalem: no criticism of my gospel was made 2. 1

Fourteen years later, I went up to Jerusalem again, this time with Barnabas, and we took Titus with us. My visit on this occasion was by divine command, and I gave a full exposition of the gospel which I preach among the gentiles. I did this first in private conference with the church leaders, to make sure that what I had done and proposed doing was acceptable to them. Not one of them intimated that Titus, because he was a Greek, ought to be circumcised. In fact, the suggestion would never have arisen but for the presence of some pseudo-Christians, who wormed their way into our meeting to spy on the liberty we enjoy in Christ Jesus, and then attempted to tie us up with rules and regulations. We did not give those men an inch, for the truth of the gospel for you and all gentiles was at stake. And as far as the leaders of the conference were concerned (I neither know nor care what their exact position was: God is not impressed with a man's office), they had nothing to add to my gospel. In fact they recognized that the gospel for the uncircumcised was as much my commission as the gospel for the circumcised was Peter's. For the God who had done such great work in Peter's ministry for the Jews was plainly doing the same in my ministry for the gentiles. When, therefore, James, Cephas and John (who were the recognized "pillars" of the church there) saw how God had given me his grace, they held out to Barnabas and me the right hand of fellowship, in full agreement that our mission was to the gentiles and theirs to the Jews. The only suggestion they made was that we should not forget the poor—and with this I was, of course, only too ready to agree.

I had once to defend the truth of the gospel even against a Church leader 2. 11

Later, however, when Cephas came to Antioch I had to oppose him publicly, for he was then plainly in the wrong. It happened like this. Until the arrival of some of James' companions, he, Peter, was in the habit of eating his meals with the gentiles. After they came, however, he withdrew and ate separately from the gentiles—out of sheer fear of what the Jews might think. The other Jewish Christians carried out a similar piece of deception, and the force of their bad example was so great that even Barnabas was affected by it. But when I saw that this behavior

get to know Cephas. I stayed with him for a fortnight, without seeing any other of the apostles, except[a] James the Lord's brother. What I write is plain truth; before God I am not lying.

Next I went to the regions of Syria and Cilicia, and remained unknown by sight[b] to Christ's congregations in Judaea. They only heard it said, 'Our former persecutor is preaching the good news of the faith which once he tried to destroy'; and they praised God for me.

2 Next, fourteen years later, I went again[c] to Jerusalem with Barnabas, taking Titus with us. I went up because it had been revealed by God that I should do so. I laid before them—but at a private interview with the men of repute—the gospel which I am accustomed to preach to the Gentiles, to make sure that the race I had run, and was running, should not be run in vain. Yet even my companion Titus, Greek though he is, was not compelled to be circumcised. That course was urged only as a concession to certain[d] sham-Christians, interlopers who had stolen in to spy upon the liberty we enjoy in the fellowship of Christ Jesus. These men wanted to bring us into bondage, but not for one moment did I yield to their dictation; I was determined that the full truth of the Gospel should be maintained for you.[e]

But as for the men of high reputation (not that their importance matters to me: God does not recognize these personal distinctions)—these men of repute, I say, did not prolong the consultation,[f] but on the contrary acknowledged that I had been entrusted with the Gospel for Gentiles as surely as Peter had been entrusted with the Gospel for Jews. For God whose action made Peter an apostle to the Jews, also made me an apostle to the Gentiles.

Recognizing, then, the favour thus bestowed upon me, those reputed pillars of our society, James, Cephas, and John, accepted Barnabas and myself as partners, and shook hands upon it, agreeing that we should go to the Gentiles while they went to the Jews. All they asked was that we should keep their poor in mind, which was the very thing I made[g] it my business to do.

But when Cephas came to Antioch, I opposed him to his face, because he was clearly in the wrong. For until certain persons[h] came from James he was taking his meals with gentile Christians; but when they[i] came he drew back and began to hold aloof, because he was afraid of the advocates of circumcision. The other Jewish Christians showed the same lack of principle; even Barnabas was carried away and played false like the rest. But when I saw that their conduct

[a] Or but only. [b] Or unknown personally. [c] Some witnesses omit again. [d] Or The question was later raised because of certain . . . [e] Or, following the reading of some witnesses, Yet even . . . is, was under no absolute compulsion to be circumcised, but for the sake of certain . . . of Christ Jesus, with the intention of bringing us into bondage, I yielded to their demand for the moment, to ensure that gospel truth should not be prevented from reaching you. [f] Or gave me no further instructions. [g] Or had made, or have made. [h] Some witnesses read a certain person. [i] Some witnesses read he.

K.J.V.

according to the truth of the gospel, I said unto Peter before *them* all, If thou, being a Jew, livest after the manner of Gentiles, and not as do the Jews, why compellest thou the Gentiles to live as do the Jews? 15 We *who are* Jews by nature, and not sinners of the Gentiles, 16 Knowing that a man is not justified by the works of the law, but by the faith of Jesus Christ, even we have believed in Jesus Christ, that we might be justified by the faith of Christ, and not by the works of the law: for by the works of the law shall no flesh be justified. 17 But if, while we seek to be justified by Christ, we ourselves also are found sinners, *is* therefore Christ the minister of sin? God forbid. 18 For if I build again the things which I destroyed, I make myself a transgressor. 19 For I through the law am dead to the law, that I might live unto God. 20 I am crucified with Christ: nevertheless I live; yet not I, but Christ liveth in me: and the life which I now live in the flesh I live by the faith of the Son of God, who loved me, and gave himself for me. 21 I do not frustrate the grace of God: for if righteousness *come* by the law, then Christ is dead in vain.

3 O foolish Galatians, who hath bewitched you, that ye should not obey the truth, before whose eyes Jesus Christ hath been evidently set forth, crucified among you? 2 This only would I learn of you, Received ye the Spirit by the works of the law, or by the hearing of faith? 3 Are ye so foolish? having begun in the Spirit, are ye now made perfect by the flesh? 4 Have ye suffered so many things in vain? if *it be* yet in vain. 5 He therefore that ministereth to you the Spirit, and worketh miracles among you, *doeth he it* by the works of the law, or by the hearing of faith? 6 Even as Abraham believed God, and it was accounted to him for righteousness. 7 Know ye therefore that they which are of faith, the same are the children of Abraham. 8 And the Scripture, foreseeing that God would justify the heathen through faith, preached before the gospel unto Abraham, *saying,* In thee shall all nations be blessed. 9 So then they which be of faith are blessed with faithful Abraham. 10 For as many as are of the works of the law are under the curse: for it is written, Cursed *is* every one that continueth not in all things which are written in the book of the law to do them.

R.S.V.

forward about the truth of the gospel, I said to Cephas before them all, "If you, though a Jew, live like a Gentile and not like a Jew, how can you compel the Gentiles to live like Jews?" 15 We ourselves, who are Jews by birth and not Gentile sinners, 16 yet who know that a man is not justified [d] by works of the law but through faith in Jesus Christ, even we have believed in Christ Jesus, in order to be justified by faith in Christ, and not by works of the law, because by works of the law shall no one be justified. 17 But if, in our endeavor to be justified in Christ, we ourselves were found to be sinners, is Christ then an agent of sin? Certainly not! 18 But if I build up again those things which I tore down, then I prove myself a transgressor. 19 For I through the law died to the law, that I might live to God. 20 I have been crucified with Christ; it is no longer I who live, but Christ who lives in me; and the life I now live in the flesh I live by faith in the Son of God, who loved me and gave himself for me. 21 I do not nullify the grace of God; for if justification [e] were through the law, then Christ died to no purpose.

3 O foolish Galatians! Who has bewitched you, before whose eyes Jesus Christ was publicly portrayed as crucified? 2 Let me ask you only this: Did you receive the Spirit by works of the law, or by hearing with faith? 3 Are you so foolish? Having begun with the Spirit, are you now ending with the flesh? 4 Did you experience so many things in vain?—if it really is in vain. 5 Does he who supplies the Spirit to you and works miracles among you do so by works of the law, or by hearing with faith?

6 Thus Abraham "believed God, and it was reckoned to him as righteousness." 7 So you see that it is men of faith who are the sons of Abraham. 8 And the scripture, foreseeing that God would justify the Gentiles by faith, preached the gospel beforehand to Abraham, saying, "In you shall all the nations be blessed." 9 So then, those who are men of faith are blessed with Abraham who had faith.

10 For all who rely on works of the law are under a curse; for it is written, "Cursed be every one who does not abide by all things written in

[d] Or *reckoned righteous;* and so elsewhere. [e] Or *righteousness.*

PHILLIPS

N.E.B.

was a contradiction of the truth of the gospel, I said to Cephas so that everyone could hear, "If you, who are a Jew, do not live like a Jew but like a gentile, why on earth do you try to make gentiles live like Jews?" And then I went on to explain that we, who are Jews by birth and not gentile sinners, know that a man is justified not by performing what the Law commands but by faith in Jesus Christ. We ourselves are justified by our faith and not by our obedience to the Law, for we have recognized that no one can achieve justification by doing the "works of the Law." Now if, as we seek the real truth about justification, we find we are as much sinners as the gentiles, does that mean that Christ makes us sinners? Of course not! But if I attempt to build again the whole structure of justification by the Law then I do, in earnest, make myself a sinner. For under the Law I "died," and now I am dead to the Law's demands so that I may live for God. As far as the Law is concerned I may consider that I died on the cross with Christ. And my present life is not that of the old "I," but the living Christ within me. The bodily life I now live, I live believing in the Son of God, who loved me and sacrificed himself for me. Consequently I refuse to stultify the grace of God by reverting to the Law. For if righteousness were possible under the Law then Christ died for nothing!

did not square with[a] the truth of the Gospel, I said to Cephas, before the whole congregation, 'If you, a Jew born and bred, live like a Gentile, and not like a Jew, how can you insist that Gentiles must live like Jews?'

We ourselves are Jews by birth, not Gentiles and sinners. But we know that no man is ever justified by doing what the law demands, but only through faith in Christ Jesus; so we too have put our faith in Jesus Christ, in order that we might be justified through this faith, and not through deeds dictated by law; for by such deeds, Scripture says, no mortal man shall be justified.

If now, in seeking to be justified in Christ, we ourselves no less than the Gentiles turn out to be sinners against the law[b] does that mean that Christ is an abettor of sin? No, never! No, if I start building up again a system which I have pulled down, then it is that I show myself up as a transgressor of the law. For through the law I died to law—to live for God. I have been crucified with Christ: the life I now live is not my life, but the life which Christ lives in me; and my present bodily life is lived by faith in the Son of God, who loved me and sacrificed himself for me. I will not nullify the grace of God; if righteousness comes by law, then Christ died for nothing.

What has happened to   *3. 1*
your life of faith?

O you dear idiots of Galatia, who saw Jesus Christ the crucified so plainly, who has been casting a spell over you? I shall ask you one simple question: Did you receive the Spirit by trying to keep the Law or by believing the message of the gospel? Surely you can't be so idiotic as to think that a man begins his spiritual life in the Spirit and then completes it by reverting to outward observances? Has all your painful experience brought you nowhere? I simply cannot believe it of you! Does God, who gives you his Spirit and works miracles among you, do these things because you have obeyed the Law or because you have believed the gospel? Ask yourselves that.

3 You stupid Galatians! You must have been bewitched—you before whose eyes Jesus Christ was openly displayed upon his cross! Answer me one question: did you receive the Spirit by keeping the law or by believing the gospel message[c]? Can it be that you are so stupid? You started with the spiritual; do you now look to the material to make you perfect? Have all your great experiences been in vain—if vain indeed they should be? I ask then: when God gives you the Spirit and works miracles among you, why is this? Is it because you keep the law, or is it because you have faith in the gospel message? Look at Abraham: he put his faith in God, and that faith was counted to him as righteousness.

You may take it, then, that it is the men of faith who are Abraham's sons. And Scripture, foreseeing that God would justify the Gentiles through faith, declared the Gospel to Abraham beforehand: 'In you all nations shall find blessing.' Thus it is the men of faith who share the blessing with faithful Abraham.

On the other hand those who rely on obedience to the law are under a curse; for Scripture says, 'Cursed are all who do not persevere in doing everything that is written in the Book

The futility of trying to be justified   *3. 6*
by the Law: the promises to men
of faith

You can go right back to Abraham to see the principle of faith in God. He, we are told, "believed God and it was counted unto him for righteousness." Can you not see, then, that all those who "believe God" are the real "sons of Abraham"? The scripture, foreseeing that God would justify the gentiles "by faith," really proclaimed the gospel centuries ago in the words spoken to Abraham, "In thee shall all nations be blessed." All men of faith share the blessing of Abraham who "believed God."

Everyone, however, who is involved in trying to keep the Law's demands falls under a curse, for it is written:

Cursed is everyone which continueth not
In *all things* which are written in the book of
   the Law,
To do them.

[a] *Or* I saw that they were not making progress towards . . . [b] *Or* no less than the Gentiles have accepted the position of sinners against the law. [c] *Or* or by the message of faith, *or* or by hearing and believing.

K.J.V.

11 But that no man is justified by the law in the sight of God, *it is* evident: for, The just shall live by faith. 12And the law is not of faith: but, The man that doeth them shall live in them. 13 Christ hath redeemed us from the curse of the law, being made a curse for us: for it is written, Cursed *is* every one that hangeth on a tree: 14 That the blessing of Abraham might come on the Gentiles through Jesus Christ; that we might receive the promise of the Spirit through faith. 15 Brethren, I speak after the manner of men; Though *it be* but a man's covenant, yet *if it be* confirmed, no man disannulleth, or addeth thereto. 16 Now to Abraham and his seed were the promises made. He saith not, And to seeds, as of many; but as of one, And to thy seed, which is Christ. 17And this I say, *that* the covenant, that was confirmed before of God in Christ, the law, which was four hundred and thirty years after, cannot disannul, that it should make the promise of none effect. 18 For if the inheritance *be* of the law, *it is* no more of promise: but God gave *it* to Abraham by promise. 19 Wherefore then *serveth* the law? It was added because of transgressions, till the seed should come to whom the promise was made; *and it was* ordained by angels in the hand of a mediator. 20 Now a mediator is not *a mediator* of one, but God is one. 21 *Is* the law then against the promises of God? God forbid: for if there had been a law given which could have given life, verily righteousness should have been by the law. 22 But the Scripture hath concluded all under sin, that the promise by faith of Jesus Christ might be given to them that believe. 23 But before faith came, we were kept under the law, shut up unto the faith which should afterwards be revealed. 24 Wherefore the law

R.S.V.

the book of the law, and do them." 11 Now it is evident that no man is justified before God by the law; for "He who through faith is righteous shall live";[f] 12 but the law does not rest on faith, for "He who does them shall live by them." 13 Christ redeemed us from the curse of the law, having become a curse for us—for it is written, "Cursed be every one who hangs on a tree"—14 that in Christ Jesus the blessing of Abraham might come upon the Gentiles, that we might receive the promise of the Spirit through faith.

15 To give a human example, brethren: no one annuls even a man's will,[g] or adds to it, once it has been ratified. 16 Now the promises were made to Abraham and to his offspring. It does not say, "And to offsprings," referring to many; but, referring to one, "And to your offspring," which is Christ. 17 This is what I mean: the law, which came four hundred and thirty years afterward, does not annul a covenant previously ratified by God, so as to make the promise void. 18 For if the inheritance is by the law, it is no longer by promise; but God gave it to Abraham by a promise.

19 Why then the law? It was added because of transgressions, till the offspring should come to whom the promise had been made; and it was ordained by angels through an intermediary. 20 Now an intermediary implies more than one; but God is one.

21 Is the law then against the promises of God? Certainly not; for if a law had been given which could make alive, then righteousness would indeed be by the law. 22 But the scripture consigned all things to sin, that what was promised to faith in Jesus Christ might be given to those who believe.

23 Now before faith came, we were confined under the law, kept under restraint until faith should be revealed. 24 So that the law was our

---

[f] Or *the righteous shall live by faith.* [g] Or *covenant* (as in verse 17).

PHILLIPS

It is made still plainer that no one is justified in God's sight by obeying the Law, for:

The righteous shall live by *faith*.

And the Law is not a matter of faith at all but of doing, as, for example, in the scripture:

He that *doeth* them shall live in them.

Now Christ has redeemed us from the curse of the Law's condemnation, by himself becoming a curse for us when he was crucified. For the scripture is plain:

Cursed is everyone that hangeth on a tree.

God's purpose is therefore plain: that the blessing promised to Abraham might reach the gentiles through Christ Jesus, and the promise of the Spirit might become ours by faith.

The Law cannot interfere with the original promise   3. 15

Let me give you an everyday illustration, my brothers. Once a contract has been properly drawn up and signed, it is honored by both parties, and can neither be disregarded nor modified by a third party.

Now the promises were made to Abraham and his seed. (Note in passing that the scripture says not "seeds" but uses the singular "seed," meaning Christ.) I say then that the Law, which came into existence four hundred and thirty years later, cannot render null and void the original "contract" which God had made, and thus rob the promise of its value. For if the receiving of the promised blessing were now made to depend on the Law, that would amount to a cancellation of the original "contract" which God made with Abraham as a promise.

Where then lies the point of the Law? It was an addition made to underline the existence and extent of sin until the arrival of the "seed" to whom the promise referred. The Law was inaugurated in the presence of angels and by the hand of a human intermediary. The very fact that there was an intermediary is enough to show that this was not the fulfilling of the promise. For the promise of God needs neither angelic witness nor human intermediary but depends on him alone.

Is the Law then to be looked upon as a contradiction of the promise? Certainly not, for if there could have been a law which gave men spiritual life then that law would have produced righteousness (which would have been, of course, in full harmony with the purpose of the promise). But, as things are, the scripture has all men "imprisoned" for their sins, because they are found guilty by the Law, that to men in such condition the promise might come to release all who believe in Jesus Christ.

By faith we are rescued from the Law and become sons of God   3. 23

Before the coming of faith we were all imprisoned under the power of the Law, with our only hope of deliverance the faith that was to be shown to us. Or, to change the metaphor, the Law was like a strict governess in charge of us

N.E.B.

of the Law.' It is evident that no one is ever justified before God in terms of law; because we read, 'he shall gain life who is justified through faith'. Now law is not at all a matter of having faith: we read, 'he who does this shall gain life by what he does'.

Christ bought us freedom from the curse of the law by becoming for our sake an accursed thing; for Scripture says, 'Cursed is everyone who is hanged on a tree.' And the purpose of it all was that the blessing of Abraham should in Jesus Christ be extended to the Gentiles, so that we might receive the promised Spirit through faith.

My brothers, let me give you an illustration. Even in ordinary life, when a man's will and testament has been duly executed, no one else can set it aside or add a codicil. Now the promises were pronounced to Abraham and to his 'issue'. It does not say 'issues' in the plural, but in the singular, 'and to your issue'; and the 'issue' intended is Christ. What I am saying is this: a testament, or covenant, had already been validated by God; it cannot be invalidated, and its promises rendered ineffective, by a law made four hundred and thirty years later. If the inheritance is by legal right, then it is not by promise; but it was by promise that God bestowed it as a free gift on Abraham.

Then what of the law? It was added to make wrongdoing a legal offence.[a] It was a temporary measure pending the arrival of the 'issue' to whom the promise was made. It was promulgated through angels, and there was an intermediary; but an intermediary is not needed for one party acting alone, and God is one.

Does the law, then, contradict the promises? No, never! If a law had been given which had power to bestow life, then indeed righteousness would have come from keeping the law. But Scripture has declared the whole world to be prisoners in subjection to sin, so that faith in Jesus Christ may be the ground on which the promised blessing is given, and given to those who have such faith.

Before this faith came, we were close prisoners in the custody of law, pending the revelation of faith. Thus the law was a kind of tutor in charge

[a] *Or* added because of offences.

K.J.V.

was our schoolmaster *to bring us* unto Christ, that we might be justified by faith. 25 But after that faith is come, we are no longer under a schoolmaster. 26 For ye are all the children of God by faith in Christ Jesus. 27 For as many of you as have been baptized into Christ have put on Christ. 28 There is neither Jew nor Greek, there is neither bond nor free, there is neither male nor female: for ye are all one in Christ Jesus. 29 And if ye *be* Christ's, then are ye Abraham's seed, and heirs according to the promise.

4 Now I say, *That* the heir, as long as he is a child, differeth nothing from a servant, though he be lord of all; 2 But is under tutors and governors until the time appointed of the father. 3 Even so we, when we were children, were in bondage under the elements of the world: 4 But when the fulness of the time was come, God sent forth his Son, made of a woman, made under the law, 5 To redeem them that were under the law, that we might receive the adoption of sons. 6 And because ye are sons, God hath sent forth the Spirit of his Son into your hearts, crying, Abba, Father. 7 Wherefore thou art no more a servant, but a son; and if a son, then an heir of God through Christ. 8 Howbeit then, when ye knew not God, ye did service unto them which by nature are no gods. 9 But now, after that ye have known God, or rather are known of God, how turn ye again to the weak and beggarly elements, whereunto ye desire again to be in bondage? 10 Ye observe days, and months, and times, and years. 11 I am afraid of you, lest I have bestowed upon you labour in vain. 12 Brethren, I beseech you, be as I *am;* for I *am* as ye *are:* ye have not injured me at all. 13 Ye know how through infirmity of the flesh I preached the gospel unto you at the first. 14 And my temptation which was in my flesh ye despised not, nor rejected; but received me as an angel of God, *even* as Christ Jesus. 15 Where is then the blessedness ye spake of? for I bear you record, that, if *it had been* possible, ye would have plucked out your own eyes, and have given them to me. 16 Am I therefore become your enemy, because I tell you the truth? 17 They zealously affect you, *but* not well; yea, they would exclude you, that ye might affect them. 18 But *it is* good to be zealously affected

R.S.V.

custodian until Christ came, that we might be justified by faith. 25 But now that faith has come, we are no longer under a custodian; 26 for in Christ Jesus you are all sons of God, through faith. 27 For as many of you as were baptized into Christ have put on Christ. 28 There is neither Jew nor Greek, there is neither slave nor free, there is neither male nor female; for you are all one in Christ Jesus. 29 And if you are Christ's, then you are Abraham's offspring, heirs according to promise.

4 I mean that the heir, as long as he is a child, is no better than a slave, though he is the owner of all the estate; 2 but he is under guardians and trustees until the date set by the father. 3 So with us; when we were children, we were slaves to the elemental spirits of the universe. 4 But when the time had fully come, God sent forth his Son, born of woman, born under the law, 5 to redeem those who were under the law, so that we might receive adoption as sons. 6 And because you are sons, God has sent the Spirit of his Son into our hearts, crying, "Abba! Father!" 7 So through God you are no longer a slave but a son, and if a son then an heir.

8 Formerly, when you did not know God, you were in bondage to beings that by nature are no gods; 9 but now that you have come to know God, or rather to be known by God, how can you turn back again to the weak and beggarly elemental spirits, whose slaves you want to be once more? 10 You observe days, and months, and seasons, and years! 11 I am afraid I have labored over you in vain.

12 Brethren, I beseech you, become as I am, for I also have become as you are. You did me no wrong; 13 you know it was because of a bodily ailment that I preached the gospel to you at first; 14 and though my condition was a trial to you, you did not scorn or despise me, but received me as an angel of God, as Christ Jesus. 15 What has become of the satisfaction you felt? For I bear you witness that, if possible, you would have plucked out your eyes and given them to me. 16 Have I then become your enemy by telling you the truth? [h] 17 They make much of you, but for no good purpose; they want to shut you out, that you may make much of them. 18 For a good purpose it is always good to be

[h] Or *by dealing truly with you.*

PHILLIPS

N.E.B.

until we went to the school of Christ and learned to be justified by faith in him. Once we had that faith we were completely free from the governess's authority. For now that you have faith in Christ Jesus you are all sons of God. All of you who were baptized "into" Christ have put on the family likeness of Christ. Gone is the distinction between Jew and Greek, slave and free man, male and female—you are all one in Christ Jesus! And if you belong to Christ, you are true descendants of Abraham, you are true heirs of his promise.

But you must realize that so long as an heir is a child, though he is destined to be master of everything, he is, in practice, no different from a servant. He has to obey a guardian or trustee until the time which his father has chosen for him to receive his inheritance. So is it with us: while we were "children" we lived under the authority of basic moral principles. But when the proper time came God sent his son, born of a human mother and born under the jurisdiction of the Law, that he might redeem those who were under the authority of the Law and lead us into becoming, by adoption, true sons of God. It is because you really are his sons that God has sent the Spirit of his Son into our hearts to cry "Father, dear Father." You, my brother, are not a servant any longer; through God you are a *son*. And, if you are a son, then you are certainly an heir.

Consider your own progress: do   *4. 8*
you want to go backward?

At one time when you had no knowledge of God, you were under the authority of gods who had no real existence. But now that you have come to know God, or rather, are known by him, how can you revert to dead and sterile principles and consent to be under their power all over again? Your religion is beginning to be a matter of observing certain days or months or seasons or years. Frankly, you stagger me, you make me wonder if all my efforts over you have been wasted!

I appeal to you by our past   *4. 12*
friendship, don't be misled

I do beg you to follow me here, my brothers. I am a man like yourselves, and I have nothing against you personally. You know how handicapped I was by illness when I first preached the gospel to you. You didn't shrink from me or let yourselves be revolted by the disease which was such a trial to you. No, you welcomed me as though I were an angel of God, or even as though I were Christ Jesus himself! What has happened to that fine spirit of yours? I guarantee that in those days you would, if you could, have plucked out your eyes and given them to me. Have I now become your enemy because I continue to tell you the truth? Oh, I know how keen these men are to win you over, but can't you see that it is for their own ends? They would like to see you and me separated altogether, and have your zeal all to themselves. Don't think I'm jealous—it is a grand thing that men should be

of us until Christ should come,[a] when we should be justified through faith; and now that faith has come, the tutor's charge is at an end.

For through faith you are all sons of God in union with Christ Jesus. Baptized into union with him, you have all put on Christ as a garment. There is no such thing as Jew and Greek, slave and freeman, male and female; for you are all one person in Christ Jesus. But if you thus belong to Christ, you are the 'issue' of Abraham, and so heirs by promise.

4 This is what I mean: so long as the heir is a minor, he is no better off than a slave, even though the whole estate is his; he is under guardians and trustees until the date fixed by his father. And so it was with us. During our minority we were slaves to the elemental spirits of the universe,[b] but when the term was completed, God sent his own Son, born of a woman, born under the law, to purchase freedom for the subjects of the law, in order that we might attain the status of sons.

To prove that you are sons, God has sent into our hearts the Spirit of his Son, crying 'Abba! Father!' You are therefore no longer a slave but a son, and if a son, then also by God's own act an heir.

Formerly, when you did not acknowledge God, you were the slaves of beings which in their nature are no gods.[c] But now that you do acknowledge God—or rather, now that he has acknowledged you—how can you turn back to the mean and beggarly spirits of the elements?[d] Why do you propose to enter their service all over again? You keep special days and months and seasons and years. You make me fear that all the pains I spent on you may prove to be labour lost.

Put yourselves in my place, my brothers, I beg you, for I have put myself in yours. It is not that you did me any wrong. As you know, it was bodily illness that originally[e] led to my bringing you the Gospel, and you resisted any temptation to show scorn or disgust at the state of my poor body,[f] you welcomed me as if I were an angel of God, as you might have welcomed Christ Jesus himself. Have you forgotten how happy you thought yourselves in having me with you? I can say this for you: you would have torn out your very eyes, and given them to me, had that been possible! And have I now made myself your enemy by being honest with you?

The persons I have referred to are envious of you, but not with an honest envy:[g] what they really want is to bar the door to you so that you may come to envy[h] them. It is always a fine thing to deserve an honest envy[i]—always, and not

[a] *Or* a kind of tutor to conduct us to Christ. [b] *Or* the elements of the natural world, *or* elementary ideas belonging to this world. [c] *Or* were slaves to 'gods' which in reality do not exist. [d] *See note on* 4. 3. [e] *Or* formerly, *or* on the first of my two visits. [f] *Or* you showed neither scorn nor disgust at the trial my poor body was enduring. [g] *Or* paying court to you, but not with honest intentions. [h] *Or* pay court to. [i] *Or* to be honourably wooed.

K.J.V.

always in *a* good *thing,* and not only when I am present with you. 19 My little children, of whom I travail in birth again until Christ be formed in you, 20 I desire to be present with you now, and to change my voice; for I stand in doubt of you. 21 Tell me, ye that desire to be under the law, do ye not hear the law? 22 For it is written, that Abraham had two sons, the one by a bondmaid, the other by a free woman. 23 But he *who was* of the bondwoman was born after the flesh; but he of the free woman *was* by promise. 24 Which things are an allegory: for these are the two covenants; the one from the mount Sinai, which gendereth to bondage, which is Agar. 25 For this Agar is mount Sinai in Arabia, and answereth to Jerusalem which now is, and is in bondage with her children. 26 But Jerusalem which is above is free, which is the mother of us all. 27 For it is written, Rejoice, thou barren that bearest not; break forth and cry, thou that travailest not: for the desolate hath many more children than she which hath a husband. 28 Now we, brethren, as Isaac was, are the children of promise. 29 But as then he that was born after the flesh persecuted him *that was born* after the Spirit, even so *it is* now. 30 Nevertheless what saith the Scripture? Cast out the bondwoman and her son: for the son of the bondwoman shall not be heir with the son of the free woman. 31 So then, brethren, we are not children of the bondwoman, but of the free.

R.S.V.

made much of, and not only when I am present with you. 19 My little children, with whom I am again in travail until Christ be formed in you! 20 I could wish to be present with you now and to change my tone, for I am perplexed about you.

21 Tell me, you who desire to be under law, do you not hear the law? 22 For it is written that Abraham had two sons, one by a slave and one by a free woman. 23 But the son of the slave was born according to the flesh, the son of the free woman through promise. 24 Now this is an allegory: these women are two covenants. One is from Mount Sinai, bearing children for slavery; she is Hagar. 25 Now Hagar is Mount Sinai in Arabia;[i] she corresponds to the present Jerusalem, for she is in slavery with her children. 26 But the Jerusalem above is free, and she is our mother. 27 For it is written,

"Rejoice, O barren one that dost not bear;
  break forth and shout, thou who art not in travail;
for the desolate hath more children
  than she who hath a husband."

28 Now we,[j] brethren, like Isaac, are children of promise. 29 But as at that time he who was born according to the flesh persecuted him who was born according to the Spirit, so it is now. 30 But what does the scripture say? "Cast out the slave and her son; for the son of the slave shall not inherit with the son of the free woman." 31 So, brethren, we are not children of the slave but of the free woman.

---

5 Stand fast therefore in the liberty wherewith Christ hath made us free, and be not entangled again with the yoke of bondage. 2 Behold, I Paul say unto you, that if ye be circumcised, Christ shall profit you nothing. 3 For I testify again to every man that is circumcised, that he is a debtor to do the whole law. 4 Christ is become of no effect unto you, whosoever of you are justified by the law; ye are fallen from grace. 5 For we through the Spirit wait for the hope of righteousness by faith. 6 For in Jesus Christ neither circumcision availeth any thing, nor uncircumcision; but faith which worketh by

5 For freedom Christ has set us free; stand fast therefore, and do not submit again to a yoke of slavery.

2 Now I, Paul, say to you that if you receive circumcision, Christ will be of no advantage to you. 3 I testify again to every man who receives circumcision that he is bound to keep the whole law. 4 You are severed from Christ, you who would be justified by the law; you have fallen away from grace. 5 For through the Spirit, by faith, we wait for the hope of righteousness. 6 For in Christ Jesus neither circumcision nor uncircumcision is of any avail, but faith working

[i] Other ancient authorities read *For Sinai is a mountain in Arabia.* [j] Other ancient authorities read *you.*

PHILLIPS

keen to win you, whether I'm there or not, provided it is for the truth. Oh, my dear children, I feel the pangs of childbirth all over again till Christ be formed within you, and how I long to be with you now! Perhaps I could then alter my tone to suit your mood. As it is, I honestly don't know how to deal with you.

Let us see what the Law itself has to say   4. 21

Now tell me, you who want to be under the Law, have you heard what the Law says? It is written that Abraham had two sons, one by the slave and the other by the free woman. The child of the slave was born in the ordinary course of nature, but the child of the free woman was born in accordance with God's promise. This can be regarded as an allegory. Here are the two agreements represented by the two women: the one from Mount Sinai bearing children into slavery, typified by Hagar (Mount Sinai being in Arabia, the land of the descendants of Ishmael, Hagar's son), and corresponding to present-day Jerusalem—for the Jews are still, spiritually speaking, "slaves." But the free woman typifies the heavenly Jerusalem, which is the mother of us all, and is spiritually "free." It is written:

Rejoice, thou barren that bearest not;
Break forth and cry, thou that travailest not:
For more are the children of the desolate
Than of her which hath the husband.

Now we, my brothers, are like Isaac, for we are children born "by promise." But just as in those far-off days the natural son persecuted the "spiritual" son, so it is today. Yet what is the scriptural instruction?

Cast out the handmaid and her son:
For the son of the handmaid shall not inherit
With the son of the free woman.

So then, my brothers, we are not to look upon ourselves as the sons of the slave woman but of the free, not sons of slavery under the Law but sons of freedom under grace.

Do not lose your freedom by giving in to those who urge circumcision   5. 1

Plant your feet firmly therefore within the freedom that Christ has won for us, and do not let yourselves be caught again in the shackles of slavery. Listen! I, Paul, say this to you as solemnly as I can: if you consent to be circumcised then Christ will be of no use to you at all. I will say it again: every man who consents to be circumcised is bound to obey all the rest of the Law! If you try to be justified by the Law you automatically cut yourself off from the power of Christ; you put yourself outside the range of his grace. For it is *by faith* that we await in his Spirit the righteousness we hope to see. In Christ Jesus there is no validity in either circumcision or uncircumcision; it is a matter of faith, faith which expresses itself in love.

N.E.B.

only when I am present with you, dear children. For my children you are, and I am in travail with you over again until you take the shape of Christ. I wish I could be with you now; then I could modify my tone;[a] as it is, I am at my wits' end about you.

Tell me now, you who are so anxious to be under law, will you not listen to what the Law says? It is written there that Abraham had two sons, one by his slave and the other by his free-born wife. The slave-woman's son was born in the course of nature, the free woman's through God's promise. This is an allegory. The two women stand for two covenants. The one bearing children into slavery is the covenant that comes from Mount Sinai: that is Hagar. Sinai is a mountain in Arabia and it represents the Jerusalem of today, for she and her children are in slavery. But the heavenly Jerusalem is the free woman; she is our mother. For Scripture says, 'Rejoice, O barren woman who never bore child; break into a shout of joy, you who never knew a mother's pangs; for the deserted wife shall have more children than she who lives with the husband.'

And you, my brothers, like Isaac, are children of God's promise. But just as in those days the natural-born son persecuted the spiritual son, so it is today. But what does Scripture say? 'Drive out the slave-woman and her son, for the son of the slave shall not share the inheritance with the free woman's son.' You see, then, my brothers, we are no slave-woman's children; our mother is the free woman.

5 Christ set us free, to be free men.[b] Stand firm, then, and refuse to be tied to the yoke of slavery again.

Mark my words: I, Paul, say to you that if you receive circumcision Christ will do you no good at all. Once again, you can take it from me that every man who receives circumcision is under obligation to keep the entire law. When you seek to be justified by way of law, your relation with Christ is completely severed: you have fallen out of the domain of God's grace. For to us, our hope of attaining that righteousness which we eagerly await is the work of the Spirit through faith. If we are in union with Christ Jesus circumcision makes no difference at all, nor does the want of it; the only thing that counts is faith active in love.[c]

[a] *Or* now, and could exchange words with you. [b] *Or* What Christ has done is to set us free. [c] *Or* inspired by love.

K.J.V.

love. 7 Ye did run well; who did hinder you that ye should not obey the truth? 8 This persuasion *cometh* not of him that calleth you. 9A little leaven leaveneth the whole lump. 10 I have confidence in you through the Lord, that ye will be none otherwise minded: but he that troubleth you shall bear his judgment, whosoever he be. 11And I, brethren, if I yet preach circumcision, why do I yet suffer persecution? then is the offence of the cross ceased. 12 I would they were even cut off which trouble you. 13 For, brethren, ye have been called unto liberty; only *use* not liberty for an occasion to the flesh, but by love serve one another. 14 For all the law is fulfilled in one word, *even* in this; Thou shalt love thy neighbour as thyself. 15 But if ye bite and devour one another, take heed that ye be not consumed one of another. 16 *This* I say then, Walk in the Spirit, and ye shall not fulfil the lust of the flesh. 17 For the flesh lusteth against the Spirit, and the Spirit against the flesh: and these are contrary the one to the other; so that ye cannot do the things that ye would. 18 But if ye be led of the Spirit, ye are not under the law. 19 Now the works of the flesh are manifest, which are *these,* Adultery, fornication, uncleanness, lasciviousness, 20 Idolatry, witchcraft, hatred, variance, emulations, wrath, strife, seditions, heresies, 21 Envyings, murders, drunkenness, revellings, and such like: of the which I tell you before, as I have also told *you* in time past, that they which do such things shall not inherit the kingdom of God. 22 But the fruit of the Spirit is love, joy, peace, longsuffering, gentleness, goodness, faith, 23 Meekness, temperance: against such there is no law. 24And they that are Christ's have crucified the flesh with the affections and lusts. 25 If we live in the Spirit, let us also walk in the Spirit. 26 Let us not be desirous of vainglory, provoking one another, envying one another.

6 Brethren, if a man be overtaken in a fault, ye which are spiritual, restore such a one in the spirit of meekness; considering thyself, lest thou also be tempted. 2 Bear ye one another's burdens, and so fulfil the law of Christ. 3 For if a man think himself to be something, when he

R.S.V.

through love. 7 You were running well; who hindered you from obeying the truth? 8 This persuasion is not from him who called you. 9A little leaven leavens the whole lump. 10 I have confidence in the Lord that you will take no other view than mine; and he who is troubling you will bear his judgment, whoever he is. 11 But if I, brethren, still preach circumcision, why am I still persecuted? In that case the stumbling block of the cross has been removed. 12 I wish those who unsettle you would mutilate themselves!

13 For you were called to freedom, brethren; only do not use your freedom as an opportunity for the flesh, but through love be servants of one another. 14 For the whole law is fulfilled in one word, "You shall love your neighbor as yourself." 15 But if you bite and devour one another take heed that you are not consumed by one another.

16 But I say, walk by the Spirit, and do not gratify the desires of the flesh. 17 For the desires of the flesh are against the Spirit, and the desires of the Spirit are against the flesh; for these are opposed to each other, to prevent you from doing what you would. 18 But if you are led by the Spirit you are not under the law. 19 Now the works of the flesh are plain: immorality, impurity, licentiousness, 20 idolatry, sorcery, enmity, strife, jealousy, anger, selfishness, dissension, party spirit, 21 envy,[k] drunkenness, carousing, and the like. I warn you, as I warned you before, that those who do such things shall not inherit the kingdom of God. 22 But the fruit of the Spirit is love, joy, peace, patience, kindness, goodness, faithfulness, 23 gentleness, self-control; against such there is no law. 24And those who belong to Christ Jesus have crucified the flesh with its passions and desires.

25 If we live by the Spirit, let us also walk by the Spirit. 26 Let us have no self-conceit, no provoking of one another, no envy of one another.

6 Brethren, if a man is overtaken in any trespass, you who are spiritual should restore him in a spirit of gentleness. Look to yourself, lest you too be tempted. 2 Bear one another's burdens, and so fulfil the law of Christ. 3 For if any one thinks he is something, when he is

[k] Other ancient authorities add *murder.*

PHILLIPS

You were making splendid progress; who put you off the course you had set for the truth? That sort of "persuasion" does not come from the one who is calling you. Alas, it takes only a little leaven to affect the whole lump! I feel confident in the Lord that you will not take any fatal step. But whoever it is who is worrying you will have a serious charge to answer one day.

And as for me, my brothers, if I were still advocating circumcision (as some apparently allege!), why am I still suffering persecution? I suppose if I would only recommend this little rite all the hostility which the preaching of the cross provokes would disappear! I wish those who are so eager to cut your bodies would cut themselves off from you altogether!

It is to freedom that you have been called, my brothers. Only be careful that freedom does not become mere opportunity for your lower nature. You should be free to serve one another in love. For after all, the whole Law toward others is summed up by this one command, "Thou shalt love thy neighbor as thyself."

But if freedom means merely that you are free to attack and tear one another to pieces, be careful that it doesn't mean that between you, you destroy your fellowship altogether!

The way to live in freedom is by the Spirit   5. 16

Here is my advice. Live your whole life in the Spirit and you will not satisfy the desires of your lower nature. For the whole energy of the lower nature is set against the Spirit, while the whole power of the Spirit is contrary to the lower nature. Here is the conflict, and that is why you are not free to do what you want to do. But if you follow the leading of the Spirit, you stand clear of the Law.

The activities of the lower nature are obvious. Here is a list: sexual immorality, impurity of mind, sensuality, worship of false gods, witchcraft, hatred, quarreling, jealousy, bad temper, rivalry, factions, party spirit, envy, drunkenness, orgies and things like that. I solemnly assure you, as I did before, that those who indulge in such things will never inherit God's kingdom. The Spirit, however, produces in human life fruits such as these: love, joy, peace, patience, kindness, generosity, fidelity, tolerance and self-control—and no law exists against any of them.

Those who belong to Christ Jesus have crucified their old nature with all that it loved and lusted for. If our lives are centered in the Spirit, let us be guided by the Spirit. Let us not be ambitious for our own reputations, for that only means making one another jealous.

Some practical wisdom   6. 1

Even if a man should be detected in some sin, my brothers, the spiritual ones among you should quietly set him back on the right path, not with any feeling of superiority but being yourselves on guard against temptation. Carry one another's burdens and so live out the law of Christ.

If a man thinks he is "somebody," he is deceiving himself, for that very thought proves

N.E.B.

You were running well; who was it hindered you from following the truth? Whatever persuasion he used, it did not come from God who is calling you; 'a little leaven', remember, 'leavens all the dough'. United with you in the Lord, I am confident that you will not take the wrong view; but the man who is unsettling your minds, whoever he may be, must bear God's judgement. And I, my friends, if I am still advocating circumcision, why is it I am still persecuted? In that case, my preaching of the cross is a stumbling-block no more. As for these agitators, they had better go the whole way and make eunuchs of themselves!

You, my friends, were called to be free men; only do not turn your freedom into licence for your lower nature, but be servants to one another in love. For the whole law can be summed up in a single commandment: 'Love your neighbour as yourself.' But if you go on fighting one another, tooth and nail, all you can expect is mutual destruction.

I mean this: if you are guided by the Spirit you will not fulfil the desires of your lower nature. That nature sets its desires against the Spirit, while the Spirit fights against it. They are in conflict with one another so that what you will to do you cannot do. But if you are led by the Spirit, you are not under law.

Anyone can see the kind of behaviour that belongs to the lower nature: fornication, impurity, and indecency; idolatry and sorcery; quarrels, a contentious temper, envy, fits of rage, selfish ambitions, dissensions, party intrigues, and jealousies; drinking bouts, orgies, and the like. I warn you, as I warned you before, that those who behave in such ways will never inherit the kingdom of God.

But the harvest of the Spirit is love, joy, peace, patience, kindness, goodness, fidelity, gentleness, and self-control. There is no law dealing with such things as these. And those who belong to Christ Jesus have crucified the lower nature with its passions and desires. If the Spirit is the source of our life, let the Spirit also direct our course.

We must not be conceited, challenging one another to rivalry, jealous of one another.

6 If a man should do something wrong, my brothers, on a sudden impulse,[a] you who are endowed with the Spirit must set him right again very gently. Look to yourself, each one of you: you may be tempted too. Help one another to carry these heavy loads, and in this way you will fulfil the law of Christ.

For if a man imagines himself to be somebody, when he is nothing, he is deluding him-

[a] *Or* If a man is caught doing something wrong, my brothers, . . .

K.J.V.

is nothing, he deceiveth himself. 4 But let every man prove his own work, and then shall he have rejoicing in himself alone, and not in another. 5 For every man shall bear his own burden. 6 Let him that is taught in the word communicate unto him that teacheth in all good things. 7 Be not deceived; God is not mocked: for whatsoever a man soweth, that shall he also reap. 8 For he that soweth to his flesh shall of the flesh reap corruption; but he that soweth to the Spirit shall of the Spirit reap life everlasting. 9And let us not be weary in well doing: for in due season we shall reap, if we faint not. 10As we have therefore opportunity, let us do good unto all *men,* especially unto them who are of the household of faith. 11Ye see how large a letter I have written unto you with mine own hand. 12As many as desire to make a fair shew in the flesh, they constrain you to be circumcised; only lest they should suffer persecution for the cross of Christ. 13 For neither they themselves who are circumcised keep the law; but desire to have you circumcised, that they may glory in your flesh. 14 But God forbid that I should glory, save in the cross of our Lord Jesus Christ, by whom the world is crucified unto me, and I unto the world. 15 For in Christ Jesus neither circumcision availeth any thing, nor uncircumcision, but a new creature. 16And as many as walk according to this rule, peace *be* on them, and mercy, and upon the Israel of God. 17 From henceforth let no man trouble me: for I bear in my body the marks of the Lord Jesus. 18 Brethren, the grace of our Lord Jesus Christ *be* with your spirit. Amen.

Unto the Galatians written from Rome.

R.S.V.

nothing, he deceives himself. 4 But let each one test his own work, and then his reason to boast will be in himself alone and not in his neighbor. 5 For each man will have to bear his own load. 6 Let him who is taught the word share all good things with him who teaches.

7 Do not be deceived; God is not mocked, for whatever a man sows, that he will also reap. 8 For he who sows to his own flesh will from the flesh reap corruption; but he who sows to the Spirit will from the Spirit reap eternal life. 9And let us not grow weary in well-doing, for in due season we shall reap, if we do not lose heart. 10 So then, as we have opportunity, let us do good to all men, and especially to those who are of the household of faith.

11 See with what large letters I am writing to you with my own hand. 12 It is those who want to make a good showing in the flesh that would compel you to be circumcised, and only in order that they may not be persecuted for the cross of Christ. 13 For even those who receive circumcision do not themselves keep the law, but they desire to have you circumcised that they may glory in your flesh. 14 But far be it from me to glory except in the cross of our Lord Jesus Christ, by which[1] the world has been crucified to me, and I to the world. 15 For neither circumcision counts for anything, nor uncircumcision, but a new creation. 16 Peace and mercy be upon all who walk by this rule, upon the Israel of God.

17 Henceforth let no man trouble me; for I bear on my body the marks of Jesus.

18 The grace of our Lord Jesus Christ be with your spirit, brethren. Amen.

[1] Or *through whom.*

PHILLIPS

that he is nobody. Let every man learn to assess properly the value of his own work and he can then be glad when he has done something worth doing without depending on the approval of others. For every man must "shoulder his own pack."

The man under Christian instruction should be willing to contribute toward the livelihood of his teacher.

The inevitability of life's harvest   6. 7

Don't be under any illusion: you cannot make a fool of God! A man's harvest in life will depend entirely on what he sows. If he sows for his own lower nature his harvest will be the decay and death of his own nature. But if he sows for the Spirit he will reap the harvest of everlasting life by the Spirit. Let us not grow tired of doing good, for, unless we throw in our hand, the ultimate harvest is assured. Let us then do good to all men as opportunity offers, especially to those who belong to the Christian household.

A final appeal, in my own   6. 11
handwriting

Look at these huge letters* I am making in writing these words to you with my own hand! These men who are always urging you to be circumcised—what are they after? They want to present a pleasing front to the world and they want to avoid being persecuted for the cross of Christ. For even those who have been circumcised do not themselves keep the Law. But they want you circumcised so that they may be able to boast about your submission to their ruling. Yet God forbid that I should boast about anything or anybody except the cross of our Lord Jesus Christ, which means that the world is a dead thing to me and I am a dead man to the world! For in Christ it is not circumcision or uncircumcision that counts, but the power of new birth. To all who live by this principle, to the true Israel of God, may there be peace and mercy!

Let no one interfere with me after this. I carry on my scarred body the marks of Jesus.

The grace of our Lord Jesus Christ, my brothers, be with your spirit.

                       PAUL

N.E.B.

self. Each man should examine his own conduct for himself; then he can measure his achievement by comparing himself with himself and not with anyone else. For everyone has his own proper burden to bear.

When anyone is under instruction in the faith, he should give his teacher a share of all good things he has.

Make no mistake about this: God is not to be fooled; a man reaps what he sows. If he sows seed in the field of his lower nature, he will reap from it a harvest of corruption, but if he sows in the field of the Spirit, the Spirit will bring him a harvest of eternal life. So let us never tire of doing good, for if we do not slacken our efforts we shall in due time reap our harvest. Therefore, as opportunity offers, let us work for the good of all, especially members of the household of the faith.

You see these big letters? I am now writing to you in my own hand. It is all those who want to make a fair outward and bodily show who are trying to force circumcision upon you; their sole object is to escape persecution for the cross of Christ. For even those who do receive circumcision are not thoroughgoing observers of the law: they only want you to be circumcised in order to boast of your having submitted to that outward rite. But God forbid that I should boast of anything but the cross of our Lord Jesus Christ, through which[a] the world is crucified to me and I to the world! Circumcision is nothing; uncircumcision is nothing; the only thing that counts is new creation! Whoever they are who take this principle for their guide, peace and mercy be upon them, and upon the whole Israel of God!

In future let no one make trouble for me, for I bear the marks of Jesus branded on my body.

The grace of our Lord Jesus Christ be with your spirit, my brothers. Amen.

---

* According to centuries-old Eastern usage, this could easily mean, "Note how heavily I have pressed upon the pen in writing this." Thus it could be translated, "Notice how heavily I underline these words to you."

[a] Or whom.

K.J.V.

THE EPISTLE OF
PAUL THE APOSTLE
TO THE
EPHESIANS

R.S.V.

THE
LETTER OF PAUL TO THE
EPHESIANS

1 Paul, an apostle of Jesus Christ by the will of God, to the saints which are at Ephesus, and to the faithful in Christ Jesus: 2 Grace *be* to you, and peace, from God our Father, and *from* the Lord Jesus Christ. 3 Blessed *be* the God and Father of our Lord Jesus Christ, who hath blessed us with all spiritual blessings in heavenly *places* in Christ: 4According as he hath chosen us in him before the foundation of the world, that we should be holy and without blame before him in love: 5 Having predestinated us unto the adoption of children by Jesus Christ to himself, according to the good pleasure of his will, 6 To the praise of the glory of his grace, wherein he hath made us accepted in the beloved: 7 In whom we have redemption through his blood, the forgiveness of sins, according to the riches of his grace; 8 Wherein he hath abounded toward us in all wisdom and prudence; 9 Having made known unto us the mystery of his will, according to his good pleasure which he hath purposed in himself: 10 That in the dispensation of the fulness of times he might gather together in one all things in Christ, both which are in heaven, and which are on earth; *even* in him: 11 In whom also we have obtained an inheritance, being predestinated according to the purpose of him who worketh all things after the counsel of his own will: 12 That we should be to the praise of his glory, who first trusted in Christ. 13 In whom ye also *trusted,* after that ye heard the word of truth, the gospel of your salvation: in whom also, after that ye believed, ye were sealed with that Holy Spirit of promise, 14 Which is the earnest of our inheritance until the redemption of the purchased possession, unto the praise of his glory. 15 Wherefore I also, after I heard of your faith in the Lord Jesus, and love unto all the saints, 16 Cease not to give thanks for you, making mention of you in my prayers; 17 That the God of our Lord Jesus Christ, the Father of glory, may give unto you the spirit of wisdom and revelation in the knowl-

1 Paul, an apostle of Christ Jesus by the will of God, To the saints who are also faithful *a* in Christ Jesus:
2 Grace to you and peace from God our Father and the Lord Jesus Christ.

3 Blessed be the God and Father of our Lord Jesus Christ, who has blessed us in Christ with every spiritual blessing in the heavenly places, 4 even as he chose us in him before the foundation of the world, that we should be holy and blameless before him. 5 He destined us in love*b* to be his sons through Jesus Christ, according to the purpose of his will, 6 to the praise of his glorious grace which he freely bestowed on us in the Beloved. 7 In him we have redemption through his blood, the forgiveness of our trespasses, according to the riches of his grace 8 which he lavished upon us. 9 For he has made known to us in all wisdom and insight the mystery of his will, according to his purpose which he set forth in Christ 10 as a plan for the fulness of time, to unite all things in him, things in heaven and things on earth.
11 In him, according to the purpose of him who accomplishes all things according to the counsel of his will, 12 we who first hoped in Christ have been destined and appointed to live for the praise of his glory. 13 In him you also, who have heard the word of truth, the gospel of your salvation, and have believed in him, were sealed with the promised Holy Spirit, 14 which is the guarantee of our inheritance until we acquire possession of it, to the praise of his glory.
15 For this reason, because I have heard of your faith in the Lord Jesus and your love*c* toward all the saints, 16 I do not cease to give thanks for you, remembering you in my prayers, 17 that the God of our Lord Jesus Christ, the Father of glory, may give you a spirit of wisdom and of revelation in the knowledge of him,

[a] Other ancient authorities read *who are at Ephesus and faithful.* [b] Or *before him in love, having destined us.* [c] Other ancient authorities omit *your love.*

PHILLIPS

THE LETTER
TO THE CHRISTIANS AT
EPHESUS
(AND IN OTHER PLACES)

Paul, messenger of Christ Jesus by God's will, to
all faithful Christians at Ephesus (and other
places where this letter is read): grace and peace
be to you from God our Father and the Lord
Jesus Christ.

Praise God for what he has done   *1. 3*
for us Christians!

Praise be to the God and Father of our Lord
Jesus Christ for giving us through Christ every
possible spiritual benefit as citizens of Heaven!
For consider what he has done—before the
foundation of the world he chose us to become,
in Christ, his holy and blameless children living
within his constant care. He planned, in his purpose of love, that we should be adopted as his
own children through Jesus Christ—that we
might learn to praise that glorious generosity of
his which has made us welcome in the everlasting
love he bears toward the Beloved. It is through
him, at the cost of his own blood, that we are
redeemed, freely forgiven through that full and
generous grace which has overflowed into our
lives and opened our eyes to the truth. For God
has allowed us to know the secret of his plan,
and it is this: he purposes in his sovereign will
that all human history shall be consummated in
Christ, that everything that exists in Heaven or
earth shall find its perfection and fulfillment in
him. And here is the staggering thing—that in all
which will one day belong to him we have been
promised a share (since we were long ago destined for this by the one who achieves his purposes by his sovereign will), so that we, as the
first to put our confidence in Christ, may bring
praise to his glory! And you too trusted him,
when you had heard the message of truth, the
gospel of your salvation. And after you gave
your confidence to him you were, so to speak,
stamped with the promised Holy Spirit as a guarantee of purchase, until the day when God completes the redemption of what he has paid for
as His own; and that will again be to the praise
of his glory.

I thank God for you,   *1. 15*
and pray for you

Since, then, I heard of this faith of yours in
the Lord Jesus and the practical way in which
you are expressing it toward fellow Christians, I
thank God continually for you and I never give
up praying for you; and this is my prayer. That
God, the God of our Lord Jesus Christ and the
all-glorious Father, will give you spiritual wisdom and the insight to know more of him: that

N.E.B.

THE
LETTER OF PAUL TO THE
EPHESIANS

The Glory of Christ in the Church

1 From Paul, apostle of Christ Jesus, commissioned by the will of God, to God's people at
Ephesus,[a] believers incorporate in Christ Jesus.
    Grace to you and peace from God our Father
and the Lord Jesus Christ.
    Praise be to the God and Father of our Lord
Jesus Christ, who has bestowed on us in Christ
every spiritual blessing in the heavenly realms.
In Christ he chose us before the world was
founded, to be dedicated, to be without blemish in his sight, to be full of love; and he[b] destined us—such was his will and pleasure—to be
accepted as his sons through Jesus Christ, that
the glory of his gracious gift, so graciously bestowed on us in his Beloved, might redound to
his praise. For in Christ our release is secured
and our sins are forgiven through the shedding
of his blood. Therein lies the richness of God's
free grace lavished upon us, imparting full wisdom and insight. He has made known to us his
hidden purpose—such was his will and pleasure
determined beforehand in Christ—to be put into
effect when the time was ripe: namely, that the
universe, all in heaven and on earth, might be
brought into a unity in Christ.
    In Christ indeed we have been given our share
in the heritage, as was decreed in his design
whose purpose is everywhere at work. For it was
his will that we, who were the first to set our
hope on Christ,[c] should cause his glory to be
praised. And you too, when you had heard the
message of the truth, the good news of your salvation, and had believed it, became incorporate
in Christ and received the seal of the promised
Holy Spirit; and that Spirit is the pledge that
we shall enter upon our heritage, when God has
redeemed what is his own, to his praise and
glory.
    Because of all this, now that I have heard of
the faith you have in the Lord Jesus and of the
love you bear towards all God's people, I never
cease to give thanks for you when I mention you
in my prayers. I pray that the God of our Lord
Jesus Christ, the all-glorious Father, may give
you the spiritual powers of wisdom and vision,

---

[a] *Some witnesses omit* at Ephesus. [b] *Or . . .*
sight. In his love he . . . [c] *Or who already en-*
joyed the hope of Christ, *or* whose expectation and
hope are in Christ.

593

K.J.V.

R.S.V.

edge of him: 18 The eyes of your understanding being enlightened; that ye may know what is the hope of his calling, and what the riches of the glory of his inheritance in the saints, 19And what *is* the exceeding greatness of his power to us-ward who believe, according to the working of his mighty power, 20 Which he wrought in Christ, when he raised him from the dead, and set *him* at his own right hand in the heavenly *places,* 21 Far above all principality, and power, and might, and dominion, and every name that is named, not only in this world, but also in that which is to come: 22And hath put all *things* under his feet, and gave him *to be* the head over all *things* to the church, 23 Which is his body, the fulness of him that filleth all in all.

18 having the eyes of your hearts enlightened, that you may know what is the hope to which he has called you, what are the riches of his glorious inheritance in the saints, 19 and what is the immeasurable greatness of his power in us who believe, according to the working of his great might 20 which he accomplished in Christ when he raised him from the dead and made him sit at his right hand in the heavenly places, 21 far above all rule and authority and power and dominion, and above every name that is named, not only in this age but also in that which is to come; 22 and he has put all things under his feet and has made him the head over all things for the church, 23 which is his body, the fulness of him who fills all in all.

2 And you *hath he quickened,* who were dead in trespasses and sins; 2 Wherein in time past ye walked according to the course of this world, according to the prince of the power of the air, the spirit that now worketh in the children of disobedience: 3Among whom also we all had our conversation in times past in the lusts of our flesh, fulfilling the desires of the flesh and of the mind; and were by nature the children of wrath, even as others. 4 But God, who is rich in mercy, for his great love wherewith he loved us, 5 Even when we were dead in sins, hath quickened us together with Christ, (by grace ye are saved;) 6And hath raised *us* up together, and made *us* sit together in heavenly *places* in Christ Jesus: 7 That in the ages to come he might shew the exceeding riches of his grace, in *his* kindness toward us, through Christ Jesus. 8 For by grace are ye saved through faith; and that not of yourselves: *it is* the gift of God: 9 Not of works, lest any man should boast. 10 For we are his workmanship, created in Christ Jesus unto good works, which God hath before ordained that we should walk in them. 11 Wherefore remember, that ye *being* in time past Gentiles in the flesh, who are called Uncircumcision by that which is called the Circumcision in the flesh made by hands; 12 That at that time ye were without Christ, being aliens from the commonwealth of Israel, and strangers from the covenants of promise, having no hope, and without God in the world: 13 But now, in Christ Jesus, ye who sometime were far off are made nigh by the blood of Christ. 14 For he is our peace, who hath made both one, and hath broken down the middle wall of partition *between us;* 15 Having abolished in his flesh the enmity, *even* the law of commandments *contained* in ordinances; for to make in himself of twain one new man, *so* making peace; 16And that he might reconcile both unto God in one body by the cross, having slain

2 And you he made alive, when you were dead through the trespasses and sins 2 in which you once walked, following the course of this world, following the prince of the power of the air, the spirit that is now at work in the sons of disobedience. 3Among these we all once lived in the passions of our flesh, following the desires of body and mind, and so we were by nature children of wrath, like the rest of mankind. 4 But God, who is rich in mercy, out of the great love with which he loved us, 5 even when we were dead through our trespasses, made us alive together with Christ (by grace you have been saved), 6 and raised us up with him, and made us sit with him in the heavenly places in Christ Jesus, 7 that in the coming ages he might show the immeasurable riches of his grace in kindness toward us in Christ Jesus. 8 For by grace you have been saved through faith; and this is not your own doing, it is the gift of God—9 not because of works, lest any man should boast. 10 For we are his workmanship, created in Christ Jesus for good works, which God prepared beforehand, that we should walk in them. 11 Therefore remember that at one time you Gentiles in the flesh, called the uncircumcision by what is called the circumcision, which is made in the flesh by hands—12 remember that you were at that time separated from Christ, alienated from the commonwealth of Israel, and strangers to the covenants of promise, having no hope and without God in the world. 13 But now in Christ Jesus you who once were far off have been brought near in the blood of Christ. 14 For he is our peace, who has made us both one, and has broken down the dividing wall of hostility, 15 by abolishing in his flesh the law of commandments and ordinances, that he might create in himself one new man in place of the two, so making peace, 16 and might reconcile us both to God in one body through the cross,

you may receive that inner illumination of the spirit which will make you realize how great is the hope to which he is calling you—the magnificence and splendor of the inheritance promised to Christians—and how tremendous is the power available to us who believe in God. That power is the same divine energy which was demonstrated in Christ when he raised him from the dead and gave him the place of supreme honor in Heaven—a place that is infinitely superior to any conceivable command, authority, power or control, and which carries with it a name far beyond any name that could ever be used in this world or the world to come.

God has placed everything under the power of Christ and has set him up as head of everything for the Church. For the Church is his body, and in that body lives fully the one who fills the whole wide universe.

by which there comes the knowledge of him. I pray that your inward eyes may be illumined, so that you may know what is the hope to which he calls you, what the wealth and glory of the share he offers you among his people in their heritage, and how vast the resources of his power open to us who trust in him. They are measured by his strength and the might which he exerted in Christ when he raised him from the dead, when he enthroned him at his right hand in the heavenly realms, far above all government and authority, all power and dominion, and any title of sovereignty that can be named, not only in this age but in the age to come. He put everything in subjection beneath his feet, and appointed him as supreme head to the church, which is his body and as such holds within it the fullness of him who himself receives the entire fullness of God.[a]

We were all dead: God gave us life through Christ   2. 1

To you, who were spiritually dead all the time that you drifted along on the stream of this world's ideas of living, and obeyed its unseen ruler (who is still operating in those who do not respond to the truth of God), to you Christ has given life! We all lived like that in the past, and followed the impulses and imaginations of our evil nature, being in fact under the wrath of God by nature, like everyone else. But even though we were dead in our sins God, who is rich in mercy, because of the great love he had for us, gave us life together with Christ—it is, remember, by grace and not by achievement that you are saved—and has lifted us right out of the old life to take our place with him in Christ Jesus in the Heavens. Thus he shows for all time the tremendous generosity of the grace and kindness he has expressed toward us in Christ Jesus. It was nothing you could or did achieve—it was God's gift of grace which saved you. No one can pride himself upon earning the love of God. The fact is that what we are we owe to the hand of God upon us. For we are his workmanship, created in Christ Jesus to do those good deeds which God planned for us to do.

2 Time was when you were dead in your sins and wickedness, when you followed the evil ways of this present age, when you obeyed the commander of the spiritual powers of the air, the spirit now at work among God's rebel subjects. We too were of their number: we all lived our lives in sensuality, and obeyed the promptings of our own instincts and notions. In our natural condition we, like the rest, lay under the dreadful judgement of God. But God, rich in mercy, for the great love he bore us, brought us to life with Christ even when we were dead in our sins; it is by his grace you are saved. And in union with Christ Jesus he raised us up and enthroned us with him in the heavenly realms, so that he might display in the ages to come how immense are the resources of his grace, and how great his kindness to us in Christ Jesus. For it is by his grace you are saved, through trusting him; it is not your own doing. It is God's gift, not a reward for work done. There is nothing for anyone to boast of. For we are God's handiwork, created in Christ Jesus to devote ourselves to the good deeds for which God has designed us.

You were gentiles: we were Jews. God has made us fellow Christians   2. 11

Do not lose sight of the fact that you were born "gentiles," known by those whose bodies were circumcised as "the uncircumcised." You were without Christ; you were utter strangers to God's chosen community, Israel; and you had no knowledge of, or right to, the promised agreements. You had nothing to look forward to and no God to whom you could turn. But now, through the blood of Christ, you who were once outside the pale are with us inside the circle of God's love in Christ Jesus. For Christ is our living peace. He has made a unity of the conflicting elements of Jew and gentile by breaking down the barrier which lay between us. By his sacrifice he removed the hostility of the Law, with all its commandments and rules, and made in himself out of the two, Jew and Gentile, one new man, thus producing peace. For he reconciled both to God by the sacrifice of one body on

Remember then your former condition: you, Gentiles as you are outwardly,[b] you, 'the uncircumcised' so called by those who are called 'the circumcised' (but only with reference to an outward rite)—you were at that time separate from Christ, strangers to the community of Israel, outside God's covenants and the promise that goes with them. Your world was a world without hope and without God. But now in union with Christ Jesus you who once were far off have been brought near through the shedding of Christ's blood. For he is himself our peace. Gentiles and Jews, he has made the two one, and in his own body of flesh and blood has broken down the enmity which stood like a dividing wall between them; for he annulled the law with its rules and regulations, so as to create out of the two a single new humanity in himself, thereby making peace. This was his purpose, to reconcile the two in a single body

[a] Or as supreme head to the church, which is his body and as such holds within it the fullness of him who fills the universe in all its parts; or as supreme head to the church which is his body, and to be all that he himself is who fills the universe in all its parts. [b] Or by birth.

K.J.V.

the enmity thereby: 17And came and preached peace to you which were afar off, and to them that were nigh. 18 For through him we both have access by one Spirit unto the Father. 19 Now therefore ye are no more strangers and foreigners, but fellow citizens with the saints, and of the household of God; 20And are built upon the foundation of the apostles and prophets, Jesus Christ himself being the chief corner *stone;* 21 In whom all the building fitly framed together groweth unto a holy temple in the Lord: 22 In whom ye also are builded together for a habitation of God through the Spirit.

3 For this cause I Paul, the prisoner of Jesus Christ for you Gentiles, 2 If ye have heard of the dispensation of the grace of God which is given me to you-ward: 3 How that by revelation he made known unto me the mystery; (as I wrote afore in few words; 4 Whereby, when ye read, ye may understand my knowledge in the mystery of Christ,) 5 Which in other ages was not made known unto the sons of men, as it is now revealed unto his holy apostles and prophets by the Spirit; 6 That the Gentiles should be fellow heirs, and of the same body, and partakers of his promise in Christ by the gospel: 7 Whereof I was made a minister, according to the gift of the grace of God given unto me by the effectual working of his power. 8 Unto me, who am less than the least of all saints, is this grace given, that I should preach among the Gentiles the unsearchable riches of Christ; 9And to make all *men* see what *is* the fellowship of the mystery, which from the beginning of the world hath been hid in God, who created all things by Jesus Christ: 10 To the intent that now unto the principalities and powers in heavenly *places* might be known by the church the manifold wisdom of God, 11According to the eternal purpose which he purposed in Christ Jesus our Lord: 12 In whom we have boldness and access with confidence by the faith of him. 13 Wherefore I desire that ye faint not at my tribulations for you, which is your glory. 14 For this cause I bow my knees unto the Father of our Lord Jesus Christ, 15 Of whom the whole family in heaven and earth is named, 16 That he would grant you, according to the riches of his glory, to be strengthened with might by his Spirit in the inner man; 17 That Christ may dwell in your hearts by faith; that ye, being rooted and grounded in love, 18 May be able to comprehend with all saints what *is* the breadth, and length, and depth, and height; 19And to know the love of Christ, which passeth knowledge, that ye might be filled with all the fulness of God.

R.S.V.

thereby bringing the hostility to an end. 17And he came and preached peace to you who were far off and peace to those who were near; 18 for through him we both have access in one Spirit to the Father. 19 So then you are no longer strangers and sojourners, but you are fellow citizens with the saints and members of the household of God, 20 built upon the foundation of the apostles and prophets, Christ Jesus himself being the cornerstone, 21 in whom the whole structure is joined together and grows into a holy temple in the Lord; 22 in whom you also are built into it for a dwelling place of God in the Spirit.

3 For this reason I, Paul, a prisoner for Christ Jesus on behalf of you Gentiles—2 assuming that you have heard of the stewardship of God's grace that was given to me for you, 3 how the mystery was made known to me by revelation, as I have written briefly. 4 When you read this you can perceive my insight into the mystery of Christ, 5 which was not made known to the sons of men in other generations as it has now been revealed to his holy apostles and prophets by the Spirit; 6 that is, how the Gentiles are fellow heirs, members of the same body, and partakers of the promise in Christ Jesus through the gospel.

7 Of this gospel I was made a minister according to the gift of God's grace which was given me by the working of his power. 8 To me, though I am the very least of all the saints, this grace was given, to preach to the Gentiles the unsearchable riches of Christ, 9 and to make all men see what is the plan of the mystery hidden for ages in[d] God who created all things; 10 that through the church the manifold wisdom of God might now be made known to the principalities and powers in the heavenly places. 11 This was according to the eternal purpose which he has realized in Christ Jesus our Lord, 12 in whom we have boldness and confidence of access through our faith in him. 13 So I ask you not to[e] lose heart over what I am suffering for you, which is your glory.

14 For this reason I bow my knees before the Father, 15 from whom every family in heaven and on earth is named, 16 that according to the riches of his glory he may grant you to be strengthened with might through his Spirit in the inner man, 17 and that Christ may dwell in your hearts through faith; that you, being rooted and grounded in love, 18 may have power to comprehend with all the saints what is the breadth and length and height and depth, 19 and to know the love of Christ which surpasses knowledge, that you may be filled with all the fulness of God.

[d] Or *by.* [e] Or *I ask that I may not.*

PHILLIPS

the cross, and by this act made utterly irrelevant the antagonism between them. Then he came and told both you who were far from God and us who were near that the war was over. And it is through him that both of us now can approach the Father in the one Spirit.

So you are no longer outsiders or aliens, but fellow citizens with every other Christian—you belong now to the household of God. Firmly beneath you is the foundation, God's messengers and prophets, the actual foundation-stone being Christ Jesus himself. In him each separate piece of building, properly fitting into its neighbor, grows together into a temple consecrated to the Lord. You are all part of this building in which God himself lives by his Spirit.

God has made me minister to you gentiles 3. 1

It is in this great cause that I, Paul, have become a prisoner of Christ Jesus for you gentiles. For you must have heard how God gave me grace to become your minister, and how he allowed me to understand his secret by giving me a direct revelation. (What I have written briefly of this above will explain to you my knowledge of the mystery of Christ.) This secret was hidden to past generations of mankind, but it has now, by the Spirit, been made plain to God's consecrated messengers and prophets. It is simply this: that the gentiles, who were previously excluded from God's agreements, are to be equal heirs with his chosen people, equal members and equal partners in God's promise given by Christ through the gospel. And I was made a minister of that gospel by the grace he gave me, and by the power with which he equipped me. Yes, to me, less than the least of all Christians, has God given this grace, to enable me to proclaim to the gentiles the incalculable riches of Christ, and to make plain to all men the meaning of that divine secret which he who created everything has kept hidden from the creation until now. The purpose is that all the angelic powers should now see the complex wisdom of God's plan being worked out through the Church, in conformity to that timeless purpose which he centered in Christ Jesus, our Lord. It is in the same Jesus, because we have faith in him, that we dare, even with confidence, to approach God. In view of these tremendous issues, I beg you not to lose heart because I am now suffering for my part in bringing you the gospel. Indeed, you should be honored.

I pray that you may know God's power in practice 3. 14

When I think of the greatness of this great plan I fall on my knees before the Father (from whom all fatherhood, earthly or heavenly, derives its name), and I pray that out of the glorious richness of his resources he will enable you to know the strength of the Spirit's inner reinforcement—that Christ may actually live in your hearts by your faith. And I pray that you, firmly fixed in love yourselves, may be able to grasp (with all Christians) how wide and deep and long and high is the love of Christ—and to know for yourselves that love so far beyond our comprehension. May you be filled through all your being with God himself!

N.E.B.

to God through the cross, on which he killed the enmity.[a]

So he came and proclaimed the good news: peace to you who were far off, and peace to those who were near by; for through him we both alike have access to the Father in the one Spirit. Thus you are no longer aliens in a foreign land, but fellow-citizens with God's people, members of God's household. You are built upon the foundation laid by the apostles and prophets, and Christ Jesus himself is the foundation-stone.[b] In him the whole building[c] is bonded together and grows into a holy temple in the Lord. In him you too are being built with all the rest into a spiritual dwelling for God.

3 With this in mind I make my prayer, I, Paul, who in the cause of you Gentiles am now the prisoner of Christ Jesus—for surely you have heard how God has assigned the gift of his grace to me for your benefit. It was by a revelation that his secret was made known to me. I have already written a brief account of this, and by reading it you may perceive that I understand the secret of Christ. In former generations this was not disclosed to the human race; but now it has been revealed by inspiration to his dedicated apostles and prophets, that through the Gospel the Gentiles are joint heirs with the Jews, part of the same body, sharers together in the promise made in Christ Jesus. Such is the gospel of which I was made a minister, by God's gift, bestowed unmerited on me in the working of his power. To me, who am less than the least of all God's people, he has granted of his grace the privilege of proclaiming to the Gentiles the good news of the unfathomable riches of Christ, and of bringing to light how this hidden purpose was to be put into effect. It was hidden for long ages in God the creator of the universe, in order that now, through the church, the wisdom of God in all its varied forms might be made known to the rulers and authorities in the realms of heaven. This is in accord with his age-long purpose, which he achieved in Christ Jesus our Lord. In him we have access to God with freedom, in the confidence born of trust in him. I beg you, then, not to lose heart over my sufferings for you: indeed, they are your glory.

With this in mind, then, I kneel in prayer to the Father, from whom every family[d] in heaven and on earth takes its name, that out of the treasures of his glory he may grant you strength and power through his Spirit in your inner being, that through faith Christ may dwell in your hearts in love. With deep roots and firm foundations, may you be strong to grasp, with all God's people, what is the breadth and length and height and depth of the love of Christ, and to know it, though it is beyond knowledge. So may you attain to fullness of being, the fullness of God himself.[e]

[a] Or . . . cross. Thus in his own person he put the enmity to death. [b] Or built upon the foundation of the apostles and prophets, and Christ Jesus himself is the keystone. [c] Or every structure. [d] Or his whole family. [e] Or the fullness which God requires.

K.J.V.

20 Now unto him that is able to do exceeding abundantly above all that we ask or think, according to the power that worketh in us, 21 Unto him *be* glory in the church by Christ Jesus throughout all ages, world without end. Amen.

4 I therefore, the prisoner of the Lord, beseech you that ye walk worthy of the vocation wherewith ye are called, 2 With all lowliness and meekness, with longsuffering, forbearing one another in love; 3 Endeavouring to keep the unity of the Spirit in the bond of peace. 4 *There is* one body, and one Spirit, even as ye are called in one hope of your calling; 5 One Lord, one faith, one baptism, 6 One God and Father of all, who *is* above all, and through all, and in you all. 7 But unto every one of us is given grace according to the measure of the gift of Christ. 8 Wherefore he saith, When he ascended up on high, he led captivity captive, and gave gifts unto men. 9 (Now that he ascended, what is it but that he also descended first into the lower parts of the earth? 10 He that descended is the same also that ascended up far above all heavens, that he might fill all things.) 11 And he gave some, apostles; and some, prophets; and some, evangelists; and some, pastors and teachers; 12 For the perfecting of the saints, for the work of the ministry, for the edifying of the body of Christ: 13 Till we all come in the unity of the faith, and of the knowledge of the Son of God, unto a perfect man, unto the measure of the stature of the fulness of Christ: 14 That we *henceforth* be no more children, tossed to and fro, and carried about with every wind of doctrine, by the sleight of men, *and* cunning craftiness, whereby they lie in wait to deceive; 15 But speaking the truth in love, may grow up into him in all things, which is the head, *even* Christ: 16 From whom the whole body fitly joined together and compacted by that which every joint supplieth, according to the effectual working in the measure of every part, maketh increase of the body unto the edifying of itself in love.

R.S.V.

20 Now to him who by the power at work within us is able to do far more abundantly than all that we ask or think, 21 to him be glory in the church and in Christ Jesus to all generations, for ever and ever. Amen.

4 I therefore, a prisoner for the Lord, beg you to lead a life worthy of the calling to which you have been called, 2 with all lowliness and meekness, with patience, forbearing one another in love, 3 eager to maintain the unity of the Spirit in the bond of peace. 4 There is one body and one Spirit, just as you were called to the one hope that belongs to your call, 5 one Lord, one faith, one baptism, 6 one God and Father of us all, who is above all and through all and in all. 7 But grace was given to each of us according to the measure of Christ's gift. 8 Therefore it is said,

"When he ascended on high he led a host of captives,
and he gave gifts to men."

9 (In saying, "He ascended," what does it mean but that he had also descended into the lower parts of the earth? 10 He who descended is he who also ascended far above all the heavens, that he might fill all things.) 11 And his gifts were that some should be apostles, some prophets, some evangelists, some pastors and teachers, 12 for the equipment of the saints, for the work of ministry, for building up the body of Christ, 13 until we all attain to the unity of the faith and of the knowledge of the Son of God, to mature manhood, to the measure of the stature of the fulness of Christ; 14 so that we may no longer be children, tossed to and fro and carried about with every wind of doctrine, by the cunning of men, by their craftiness in deceitful wiles. 15 Rather, speaking the truth in love, we are to grow up in every way into him who is the head, into Christ, 16 from whom the whole body, joined and knit together by every joint with which it is supplied, when each part is working properly, makes bodily growth and upbuilds itself in love.

PHILLIPS	N.E.B.

Now to him who by his power within us is able to do infinitely more than we ever dare to ask or imagine—to him be glory in the Church and in Christ Jesus for ever and ever, amen!

Now to him who is able to do immeasurably more than all we can ask or conceive, by the power which is at work among us, to him be glory in the church and in Christ Jesus from generation to generation evermore! Amen.

Christians should be at one, as God is one   4. 1

As God's prisoner, then, I beg you to live lives worthy of your high calling. Accept life with humility and patience, making allowances for one another because you love one another. Make it your aim to be at one in the Spirit, and you will inevitably be at peace with one another. You all belong to one body, of which there is one Spirit, just as you all experienced one calling to one hope. There is one Lord, one faith, one baptism, one God, one Father of us all, who is the one over all, the one working through all and the one living in all.

4 I entreat you, then—I, a prisoner for the Lord's sake: as God has called you, live up to your calling. Be humble always and gentle, and patient too. Be forbearing with one another and charitable. Spare no effort to make fast with bonds of peace the unity which the Spirit gives. There is one body and one Spirit, as there is also one hope held out in God's call to you; one Lord, one faith, one baptism; one God and Father of all, who is over all and through all and in all.

But each of us has been given his gift, his due portion of Christ's bounty. Therefore Scripture says:

God's gifts vary, but it is the same God who gives   4. 7

Naturally there are different gifts and functions; individually grace is given to us in different ways out of the rich diversity of Christ's giving. As the scripture says:

When he ascended on high, he led captivity captive,
And gave gifts unto men.

(Note the implication here—to say that Christ "ascended" means that he must previously have "descended," that is, from the height of Heaven to the depth of this world. The one who made this descent is identically the same person as he who has now ascended high above the very Heavens—that the whole universe from lowest to highest might know his presence.)

His "gifts unto men" were varied. Some he made his messengers, some prophets, some preachers of the gospel; to some he gave the power to guide and teach his people. His gifts were made that Christians might be properly equipped for their service, that the whole body might be built up until the time comes when, in the unity of common faith and common knowledge of the Son of God, we arrive at real maturity—that measure of development which is meant by "the fullness of Christ."

'He ascended into the heights
With captives in his train;
He gave gifts to men.'

Now, the word 'ascended' implies that he also descended to the lowest level, down to the very earth.[a] He who descended is no other than he who ascended far above all heavens, so that he might fill the universe. And these were his gifts: some to be apostles, some prophets, some evangelists, some pastors and teachers, to equip God's people for work in his service, to the building up of the body of Christ. So shall we all at last attain to the unity inherent in our faith and our knowledge of the Son of God—to mature manhood, measured by nothing less than the full stature of Christ. We are no longer to be children, tossed by the waves and whirled about by every fresh gust of teaching, dupes of crafty rogues and their deceitful schemes. No, let us speak the truth in love; so shall we fully grow up into Christ. He is the head, and on him the whole body depends. Bonded and knit together by every constituent joint, the whole frame grows through the due activity of each part, and builds itself up in love.

True maturity means growing up "into" Christ   4. 14

We are not meant to remain as children at the mercy of every chance wind of teaching and the jockeying of men who are expert in the crafty presentation of lies. But we are meant to hold firmly to the truth in love, and to grow up in every way into Christ, the head. For it is from the head that the whole body, as a harmonious structure knit together by the joints with which it is provided, grows by the proper functioning of individual parts to its full maturity in love.

[a] *Or* descended to the regions beneath the earth.

K.J.V.

17 This I say therefore, and testify in the Lord, that ye henceforth walk not as other Gentiles walk, in the vanity of their mind, 18 Having the understanding darkened, being alienated from the life of God through the ignorance that is in them, because of the blindness of their heart: 19 Who being past feeling have given themselves over unto lasciviousness, to work all uncleanness with greediness. 20 But ye have not so learned Christ; 21 If so be that ye have heard him, and have been taught by him, as the truth is in Jesus: 22 That ye put off concerning the former conversation the old man, which is corrupt according to the deceitful lusts; 23And be renewed in the spirit of your mind; 24And that ye put on the new man, which after God is created in righteousness and true holiness. 25 Wherefore putting away lying, speak every man truth with his neighbour: for we are members one of another. 26 Be ye angry, and sin not: let not the sun go down upon your wrath: 27 Neither give place to the devil. 28 Let him that stole steal no more: but rather let him labour, working with *his* hands the thing which is good, that he may have to give to him that needeth. 29 Let no corrupt communication proceed out of your mouth, but that which is good to the use of edifying, that it may minister grace unto the hearers. 30And grieve not the Holy Spirit of God, whereby ye are sealed unto the day of redemption. 31 Let all bitterness, and wrath, and anger, and clamour, and evil speaking, be put away from you, with all malice: 32And be ye kind one to another, tenderhearted, forgiving one another, even as God for Christ's sake hath forgiven you.

5 Be ye therefore followers of God, as dear children; 2And walk in love, as Christ also hath loved us, and hath given himself for us an offering and a sacrifice to God for a sweet-smelling savour. 3 But fornication, and all uncleanness, or covetousness, let it not be once named among you, as becometh saints; 4 Neither filthiness, nor foolish talking, nor jesting, which are not convenient: but rather giving of thanks. 5 For this ye know, that no whoremonger, nor unclean person, nor covetous man, who is an idolater, hath any inheritance in the kingdom of Christ and of God. 6 Let no man deceive you with vain words: for because of these things cometh the wrath of God upon the children of

R.S.V.

17 Now this I affirm and testify in the Lord, that you must no longer live as the Gentiles do, in the futility of their minds; 18 they are darkened in their understanding, alienated from the life of God because of the ignorance that is in them, due to their hardness of heart; 19 they have become callous and have given themselves up to licentiousness, greedy to practice every kind of uncleanness. 20 You did not so learn Christ!—21 assuming that you have heard about him and were taught in him, as the truth is in Jesus. 22 Put off your old nature which belongs to your former manner of life and is corrupt through deceitful lusts, 23 and be renewed in the spirit of your minds, 24 and put on the new nature, created after the likeness of God in true righteousness and holiness.

25 Therefore, putting away falsehood, let every one speak the truth with his neighbor, for we are members one of another. 26 Be angry but do not sin; do not let the sun go down on your anger, 27 and give no opportunity to the devil. 28 Let the thief no longer steal, but rather let him labor, doing honest work with his hands, so that he may be able to give to those in need. 29 Let no evil talk come out of your mouths, but only such as is good for edifying, as fits the occasion, that it may impart grace to those who hear. 30And do not grieve the Holy Spirit of God, in whom you were sealed for the day of redemption. 31 Let all bitterness and wrath and anger and clamor and slander be put away from you, with all malice, 32 and be kind to one another, tenderhearted, forgiving one another, as God in Christ forgave you.

5 Therefore be imitators of God, as beloved children. 2And walk in love, as Christ loved us and gave himself up for us, a fragrant offering and sacrifice to God. 3 But immorality and all impurity or covetousness must not even be named among you, as is fitting among saints. 4 Let there be no filthiness, nor silly talk, nor levity, which are not fitting; but instead let there be thanksgiving. 5 Be sure of this, that no immoral or impure man, or one who is covetous (that is, an idolater), has any inheritance in the kingdom of Christ and of God. 6 Let no one deceive you with empty words, for it is because of these things that the wrath of God comes upon the sons of disobedi-

*Have no more to do with the   4. 17
old life! Learn the new*

This is my instruction, then, which I gave you
from the Lord. Do not live any longer as the
gentiles live. For they live blindfold in a world
of illusion, and are cut off from the life of God
through ignorance and insensitiveness. They have
stifled their consciences and then surrendered
themselves to sensuality, practicing any form of
impurity which lust can suggest. But you have
learned nothing like that from Christ, if you
have really heard his voice and understood the
truth that Jesus has taught you. No, what you
learned was to fling off the dirty clothes of the
old way of living, which were rotted through
and through with lust's illusions, and, with yourselves mentally and spiritually remade, to put on
the clean fresh clothes of the new life which
was made by God's design for righteousness and
the holiness which is no illusion.

Finish, then, with lying, and tell your neighbor
the truth. For we are not separate units but intimately related to one another in Christ. If you
are angry, be sure that it is not out of wounded
pride or bad temper. Never go to bed angry—
don't give the devil that sort of foothold.

The new life means positive good   4. 28

If you used to be a thief you must not only
give up stealing, but you must learn to make an
honest living, so that you may be able to give
to those in need.

Let there be no more foul language, but good
words instead—words suitable for the occasion,
which God can use to help other people. Never
hurt the Holy Spirit. He is, remember, the personal pledge of your eventual full redemption.

Let there be no more resentment, no more
anger or temper, no more violent self-assertive-
ness, no more slander and no more malicious
remarks. Be kind to one another; be understanding. Be as ready to forgive others as God
for Christ's sake has forgiven you.

As children copy their fathers you, as God's
children, are to copy him. Live your lives in
love—the same sort of love which Christ gives
us and which he perfectly expressed when he
gave himself up for us in sacrifice to God. But
as for sexual immorality in all its forms, and
the itch to get your hands on what belongs to
other people—don't even talk about such things;
they are no fit subjects for Christians to talk
about. The keynote of your conversation should
not be nastiness or silliness or flippancy, but a
sense of all that we owe to God.

*Evil is as utterly different from   5. 5
good as light from darkness*

For of this much you can be quite certain:
that neither the immoral nor the dirty-minded
nor the covetous man (which latter is, in effect,
worshiping a false god) has any inheritance in
the kingdom of Christ and of God. Don't let
anyone fool you on this point, however plausible
his argument. It is these very things which bring
down the wrath of God upon the disobedient.

This then is my word to you, and I urge it
upon you in the Lord's name. Give up living like
pagans with their good-for-nothing notions. Their
wits are beclouded, they are strangers to the
life that is in God, because ignorance prevails
among them and their minds have grown hard
as stone. Dead to all feeling, they have abandoned themselves to vice, and stop at nothing
to satisfy their foul desires. But that is not how
you learned Christ. For were you not told of
him, were you not as Christians taught the truth
as it is in Jesus?—that, leaving your former way
of life, you must lay aside that old human nature
which, deluded by its lusts, is sinking towards
death. You must be made new in mind and
spirit, and put on the new nature of God's creat-
ing, which shows itself in the just and devout life
called for by the truth.

Then throw off falsehood; speak the truth to
each other, for all of us are the parts of one
body.

If you are angry, do not let anger lead you
into sin; do not let sunset find you still nursing
it; leave no loop-hole for the devil.

The thief must give up stealing, and instead
work hard and honestly with his own hands, so
that he may have something to share with the
needy.

No bad language must pass your lips, but only
what is good and helpful to the occasion, so that
it brings a blessing to those who hear it. And do
not grieve the Holy Spirit of God, for that Spirit
is the seal with which you were marked for the
day of our final liberation. Have done with spite
and passion, all angry shouting and cursing, and
bad feeling of every kind.

Be generous to one another, tender-hearted,
forgiving one another as God in Christ forgave
you.

5 In a word, as God's dear children, try to be
like him, and live in love as Christ loved you,
and gave himself up on your behalf as an offering and sacrifice whose fragrance is pleasing to
God.

Fornication and indecency of any kind, or
ruthless greed, must not be so much as mentioned among you, as befits the people of God.
No coarse, stupid, or flippant talk; these things
are out of place; you should rather be thanking
God. For be very sure of this: no one given
to fornication or indecency, or the greed which
makes an idol of gain, has any share in the kingdom of Christ and of God.

Let no one deceive you with shallow arguments; it is for all these things that God's dreadful judgement is coming upon his rebel subjects.

K.J.V.

disobedience. 7 Be not ye therefore partakers with them. 8 For ye were sometime darkness, but now *are ye* light in the Lord: walk as children of light; 9 (For the fruit of the Spirit *is* in all goodness and righteousness and truth;) 10 Proving what is acceptable unto the Lord. 11And have no fellowship with the unfruitful works of darkness, but rather reprove *them*. 12 For it is a shame even to speak of those things which are done of them in secret. 13 But all things that are reproved are made manifest by the light: for whatsoever doth make manifest is light. 14 Wherefore he saith, Awake thou that sleepest, and arise from the dead, and Christ shall give thee light. 15 See then that ye walk circumspectly, not as fools, but as wise, 16 Redeeming the time, because the days are evil. 17 Wherefore be ye not unwise, but understanding what the will of the Lord *is*. 18And be not drunk with wine, wherein is excess; but be filled with the Spirit; 19 Speaking to yourselves in psalms and hymns and spiritual songs, singing and making melody in your heart to the Lord; 20 Giving thanks always for all things unto God and the Father in the name of our Lord Jesus Christ; 21 Submitting yourselves one to another in the fear of God. 22 Wives, submit yourselves unto your own husbands, as unto the Lord. 23 For the husband is the head of the wife, even as Christ is the head of the church: and he is the Saviour of the body. 24 Therefore as the church is subject unto Christ, so *let* the wives *be* to their own husbands in every thing. 25 Husbands, love your wives, even as Christ also loved the church, and gave himself for it; 26 That he might sanctify and cleanse it with the washing of water by the word, 27 That he might present it to himself a glorious church, not having spot, or wrinkle, or any such thing; but that it should be holy and without blemish. 28 So ought men to love their wives as their own bodies. He that loveth his wife loveth himself. 29 For no man ever yet hated his own flesh; but nourisheth and cherisheth it, even as the Lord the church: 30 For we are members of his body, of his flesh, and of his bones. 31 For this cause shall a man leave his father and mother, and shall be joined unto his wife, and they two shall be one flesh.

R.S.V.

ence. 7 Therefore do not associate with them, 8 for once you were darkness, but now you are light in the Lord; walk as children of light 9 (for the fruit of light is found in all that is good and right and true), 10 and try to learn what is pleasing to the Lord. 11 Take no part in the unfruitful works of darkness, but instead expose them. 12 For it is a shame even to speak of the things that they do in secret; 13 but when anything is exposed by the light it becomes visible, for anything that becomes visible is light. 14 Therefore it is said,

"Awake, O sleeper, and arise from the dead, and Christ shall give you light."

15 Look carefully then how you walk, not as unwise men but as wise, 16 making the most of the time, because the days are evil. 17 Therefore do not be foolish, but understand what the will of the Lord is. 18And do not get drunk with wine, for that is debauchery; but be filled with the Spirit, 19 addressing one another in psalms and hymns and spiritual songs, singing and making melody to the Lord with all your heart, 20 always and for everything giving thanks in the name of our Lord Jesus Christ to God the Father.

21 Be subject to one another out of reverence for Christ. 22 Wives, be subject to your husbands, as to the Lord. 23 For the husband is the head of the wife as Christ is the head of the church, his body, and is himself its Savior. 24As the church is subject to Christ, so let wives also be subject in everything to their husbands. 25 Husbands, love your wives, as Christ loved the church and gave himself up for her, 26 that he might sanctify her, having cleansed her by the washing of water with the word, 27 that he might present the church to himself in splendor, without spot or wrinkle or any such thing, that she might be holy and without blemish. 28 Even so husbands should love their wives as their own bodies. He who loves his wife loves himself. 29 For no man ever hates his own flesh, but nourishes and cherishes it, as Christ does the church, 30 because we are members of his body. 31 "For this reason a man shall leave his father and mother and be joined to his wife, and the

PHILLIPS

Have nothing to do with men like that—once you were "darkness" but now you are "light." Live then as children of the light. The light produces in men quite the opposite of sins like these—everything that is wholesome and good and true. Let your lives be living proofs of the things which please God. Steer clear of the activities of darkness; let your lives show by contrast how dreary and futile these things are. (You know the sort of things I mean—to detail their secret doings is really too shameful.) For light is capable of "showing up" everything for what it really is. It is even possible (after all, it happened with you!) for light to turn the thing it shines upon into light also. Thus God speaks through the scriptures:

Awake thou that sleepest, and arise from the dead,
And Christ shall shine upon thee.

You know the truth—let your life show it!

5. 15

Live life, then, with a due sense of responsibility, not as men who do not know the meaning and purpose of life but as *those who do*. Make the best use of your time, despite all the difficulties of these days. Don't be vague, but firmly grasp what you know to be the will of the Lord. Don't get your stimulus from wine (for there is always the danger of excessive drinking), but let the Spirit stimulate your souls. Express your joy in singing among yourselves psalms and hymns and spiritual songs, making music in your hearts for the ears of the Lord! Thank God at all times for everything, in the name of our Lord Jesus Christ. And "fit in with" one another, because of your common reverence for Christ.

Christ and the Church the pattern relationship for husband and wife

5. 22

You wives must learn to adapt yourselves to your husbands, as you submit yourselves to the Lord, for the husband is the "head" of the wife in the same way that Christ is head of the Church and savior of his body. The willing subjection of the Church to Christ should be reproduced in the submission of wives to their husbands. But, remember, this means that the husband must give his wife the same sort of love that Christ gave to the Church, when he sacrificed himself for her. Christ gave himself to make her holy, having cleansed her through the baptism of his Word—to make her an altogether glorious Church in his eyes. She is to be free from spots, wrinkles or any other disfigurements—a Church holy and perfect.

Men ought to give their wives the love they naturally have for their own bodies. The love a man gives his wife is the extending of his love for himself to enfold her. Nobody ever hates or neglects his own body; he feeds it and looks after it. And that is what Christ does for his body, the Church. And we are all members of that body.

For this cause shall a man leave his father and mother,
And shall cleave to his wife; and the twain shall become one flesh.

N.E.B.

Have no part or lot with them. For though you were once all darkness, now as Christians you are light. Live like men who are at home in daylight, for where light is, there all goodness springs up, all justice and truth. Make sure what would have the Lord's approval; take no part in the barren deeds of darkness, but show them up for what they are. The things they do in secret it would be shameful even to mention. But everything, when once the light has shown it up, is illumined, and everything thus illumined is all light. And so the hymn says:

'Awake, sleeper,
Rise from the dead,
And Christ will shine upon you.'

Be most careful then how you conduct yourselves: like sensible men, not like simpletons. Use the present opportunity to the full, for these are evil days. So do not be fools, but try to understand what the will of the Lord is. Do not give way to drunkenness and the dissipation that goes with it, but let the Holy Spirit fill you: speak to one another in psalms, hymns, and [a] songs; sing and make music in your hearts to the Lord; and in the name of our Lord Jesus Christ give thanks every day for everything to our God and Father.

Be subject to one another out of reverence for Christ.

Wives, be subject to your husbands as to the Lord; for the man is the head of the woman, just as Christ also is the head of the church. Christ is, indeed, the Saviour of the body; but just as the church is subject to Christ, so must women be to their husbands in everything.

Husbands, love your wives, as Christ also loved the church and gave himself up for it, to consecrate it, cleansing it by water and word, so that he might present the church to himself all glorious, with no stain or wrinkle or anything of the sort, but holy and without blemish. In the same way men also are bound to love their wives, as they love their own bodies. In loving his wife a man loves himself. For no one ever hated his own body: on the contrary, he provides and cares for it; and that is how Christ treats the church, because it is his body, of which we are living parts. Thus it is that (in the words of Scripture) 'a man shall leave his father and mother and shall be joined to his wife, and the

[a] *Some witnesses insert* spiritual, *as in Colossians 3. 16.*

K.J.V.

32 This is a great mystery: but I speak concerning Christ and the church. 33 Nevertheless, let every one of you in particular so love his wife even as himself; and the wife *see* that she reverence *her* husband.

6 Children, obey your parents in the Lord: for this is right. 2 Honour thy father and mother; which is the first commandment with promise; 3 That it may be well with thee, and thou mayest live long on the earth. 4And, ye fathers, provoke not your children to wrath: but bring them up in the nurture and admonition of the Lord. 5 Servants, be obedient to them that are *your* masters according to the flesh, with fear and trembling, in singleness of your heart, as unto Christ; 6 Not with eyeservice, as menpleasers; but as the servants of Christ, doing the will of God from the heart; 7 With good will doing service, as to the Lord, and not to men: 8 Knowing that whatsoever good thing any man doeth, the same shall he receive of the Lord, whether *he be* bond or free. 9And, ye masters, do the same things unto them, forbearing threatening: knowing that your Master also is in heaven; neither is there respect of persons with him. 10 Finally, my brethren, be strong in the Lord, and in the power of his might. 11 Put on the whole armour of God, that ye may be able to stand against the wiles of the devil. 12 For we wrestle not against flesh and blood, but against principalities, against powers, against the rulers of the darkness of this world, against spiritual wickedness in high *places.* 13 Wherefore take unto you the whole armour of God, that ye may be able to withstand in the evil day, and having done all, to stand. 14 Stand therefore, having your loins girt about with truth, and having on the breastplate of righteousness; 15And your feet shod with the preparation of the gospel of peace; 16Above all, taking the shield of faith, wherewith ye shall be able to quench all the fiery darts of the wicked. 17And take the helmet of salvation, and the sword of the Spirit, which is the word of God: 18 Praying always with all prayer and supplication in the Spirit, and watching thereunto with all perseverance and supplication for all saints; 19And for me, that utterance may be given unto me, that I may open my mouth boldly, to make known the mystery of the gospel, 20 For which I am an ambassador in bonds; that therein I may speak boldly, as I ought to speak. 21 But that ye also may know my affairs, *and* how I do, Tychicus, a beloved brother and faithful minister in the Lord,

R.S.V.

two shall become one." 32 This is a great mystery, and I take it to mean Christ and the church; 33 however, let each one of you love his wife as himself, and let the wife see that she respects her husband.

6 Children, obey your parents in the Lord, for this is right. 2 "Honor your father and mother" (this is the first commandment with a promise), 3 "that it may be well with you and that you may live long on the earth." 4 Fathers, do not provoke your children to anger, but bring them up in the discipline and instruction of the Lord.

5 Slaves, be obedient to those who are your earthly masters, with fear and trembling, in singleness of heart, as to Christ; 6 not in the way of eye-service, as men-pleasers, but as servants*f* of Christ, doing the will of God from the heart, 7 rendering service with a good will as to the Lord and not to men, 8 knowing that whatever good any one does, he will receive the same again from the Lord, whether he is a slave or free. 9 Masters, do the same to them, and forbear threatening, knowing that he who is both their Master and yours is in heaven, and that there is no partiality with him.

10 Finally, be strong in the Lord and in the strength of his might. 11 Put on the whole armor of God, that you may be able to stand against the wiles of the devil. 12 For we are not contending against flesh and blood, but against the principalities, against the powers, against the world rulers of this present darkness, against the spiritual hosts of wickedness in the heavenly places. 13 Therefore take the whole armor of God, that you may be able to withstand in the evil day, and having done all, to stand. 14 Stand therefore, having girded your loins with truth, and having put on the breastplate of righteousness, 15 and having shod your feet with the equipment of the gospel of peace; 16 above all taking the shield of faith, with which you can quench all the flaming darts of the evil one. 17And take the helmet of salvation, and the sword of the Spirit, which is the word of God. 18 Pray at all times in the Spirit, with all prayer and supplication. To that end keep alert with all perseverance, making supplication for all the saints, 19 and also for me, that utterance may be given me in opening my mouth boldly to proclaim the mystery of the gospel, 20 for which I am an ambassador in chains; that I may declare it boldly, as I ought to speak.

21 Now that you also may know how I am and what I am doing, Tychicus the beloved brother and faithful minister in the Lord will tell

[*f*] Or *slaves.*

PHILLIPS

The marriage relationship is doubtless a great mystery, but I am speaking of something deeper still—the marriage of Christ and his Church.

In practice what I have said amounts to this: let every one of you who is a husband love his wife as he loves himself, and let the wife reverence her husband.

Children and parents: 6. 1
servants and masters

Children, the right thing for you to do is to obey your parents as those whom the Lord has set over you. The first commandment to contain a promise was:

Honor thy father and thy mother
That it may be well with thee, and that thou mayest live long on the earth.

Fathers, don't overcorrect your children or make it difficult for them to obey the commandment. Bring them up with Christian teaching in Christian discipline.

Slaves, obey your human masters sincerely with a proper sense of respect and responsibility, as service rendered to Christ himself; not with the idea of currying favor with men, but as the servants of Christ conscientiously doing what you believe to be the will of God for you. You may be sure that God will reward a man for good work, irrespectively of whether the man be slave or free. And as for you employers, be as conscientious and responsible toward those who serve you as you expect them to be toward you, neither misusing the power over others that has been put in your hands, nor forgetting that you are responsible yourselves to a Heavenly employer who makes no distinction between master and man.

Be forewarned and forearmed in   6. 10
your spiritual conflict

In conclusion, be strong—not in yourselves but in the Lord, in the power of his boundless resource. Put on God's complete armor so that you can successfully resist all the devil's methods of attack. For our fight is not against any physical enemy: it is against organizations and powers that are spiritual. We are up against the unseen power that controls this dark world, and spiritual agents from the very headquarters of evil. Therefore you must wear the whole armor of God that you may be able to resist evil in its day of power, and that even when you have fought to a standstill you may still stand your ground. Take your stand then with truth as your belt, righteousness your breastplate, the gospel of peace firmly on your feet, salvation as your helmet and in your hand the sword of the Spirit, the Word of God. Above all be sure you take faith as your shield, for it can quench every burning missile the enemy hurls at you. Pray at all times with every kind of spiritual prayer, keeping alert and persistent as you pray for all Christ's men and women. And pray for me, too, that I may be able to speak freely here to make known the secret of that gospel for which I am, so to speak, an ambassador in chains. Pray that I may speak out about it as is my plain and obvious duty.

Tychicus, beloved brother and faithful Chris-

N.E.B.

two shall become a single body'. It is a great truth that is hidden here. I for my part refer it to Christ and to the church, but it applies also individually: each of you must love his wife as his very self; and the woman must see to it that she pays her husband all respect.

6 Children, obey your parents, for it is right that you should. 'Honour your father and mother' is the first commandment with a promise attached, in the words: 'that it may be well with you and that you may live long in the land'.

You fathers, again, must not goad your children to resentment, but give them the instruction, and the correction, which belong to a Christian upbringing.

Slaves, obey your earthly masters with fear and trembling, single-mindedly, as serving Christ. Do not offer merely the outward show of service, to curry favour with men, but, as slaves of Christ, do whole-heartedly the will of God. Give the cheerful service of those who serve the Lord, not men. For you know that whatever good each man may do, slave or free, will be repaid him by the Lord.

You masters, also, must do the same by them. Give up using threats; remember you both have the same Master in heaven, and he has no favourites.

Finally then, find your strength in the Lord, in his mighty power. Put on all the armour which God provides, so that you may be able to stand firm against the devices of the devil. For our fight is not against human foes, but against cosmic powers, against the authorities and potentates of this dark world, against the superhuman forces of evil in the heavens. Therefore, take up God's armour; then you will be able to stand your ground when things are at their worst, to complete every task and still to stand. Stand firm, I say. Buckle on the belt of truth; for coat of mail put on integrity; let the shoes on your feet be the gospel of peace, to give you firm footing; and, with all these, take up the great shield of faith, with which you will be able to quench all the flaming arrows of the evil one. Take salvation for helmet; for sword, take that which the Spirit gives you—the words that come from God. Give yourselves wholly to prayer and entreaty; pray on every occasion in the power of the Spirit. To this end keep watch and persevere, always interceding for all God's people; and pray for me, that I may be granted the right words when I open my mouth, and may boldly and freely make known his hidden purpose, for which I am an ambassador—in chains. Pray that I may speak of it boldly, as it is my duty to speak.

You will want to know about my affairs, and how I am; Tychicus will give you all the news. He is our dear brother and trustworthy helper in

K.J.V.

shall make known to you all things: 22 Whom I have sent unto you for the same purpose, that ye might know our affairs, and *that* he might comfort your hearts. 23 Peace *be* to the brethren, and love with faith, from God the Father and the Lord Jesus Christ. 24 Grace *be* with all them that love our Lord Jesus Christ in sincerity. Amen.

Written from Rome unto the Ephesians by Tychicus.

R.S.V.

you everything. 22 I have sent him to you for this very purpose, that you may know how we are, and that he may encourage your hearts.

23 Peace be to the brethren, and love with faith, from God the Father and the Lord Jesus Christ. 24 Grace be with all who love our Lord Jesus Christ with love undying.

PHILLIPS

tian minister, will tell you personally what I am doing and how I am getting on. I am sending him to you bringing this letter for that purpose, so that you will know exactly how we are and may take fresh heart.

Peace be to all Christian brothers, and love with faith from God the Father and the Lord Jesus Christ!

Grace be with all those who love our Lord Jesus Christ with unfailing love.

PAUL

N.E.B.

the Lord's work. I am sending him to you on purpose to let you know all about us, and to put fresh heart into you.

Peace to the brotherhood and love, with faith, from God the Father and the Lord Jesus Christ. God's grace be with all who love our Lord Jesus Christ, grace and immortality.[a]

[a] Or who love . . . Christ with love imperishable.

K.J.V.

THE EPISTLE OF
PAUL THE APOSTLE
TO THE
PHILIPPIANS

1 Paul and Timotheus, the servants of Jesus Christ, to all the saints in Christ Jesus which are at Philippi, with the bishops and deacons: 2 Grace *be* unto you, and peace, from God our Father and *from* the Lord Jesus Christ. 3 I thank my God upon every remembrance of you, 4 Always in every prayer of mine for you all making request with joy, 5 For your fellowship in the gospel from the first day until now; 6 Being confident of this very thing, that he which hath begun a good work in you will perform *it* until the day of Jesus Christ: 7 Even as it is meet for me to think this of you all, because I have you in my heart; inasmuch as both in my bonds, and in the defence and confirmation of the gospel, ye all are partakers of my grace. 8 For God is my record, how greatly I long after you all in the bowels of Jesus Christ. 9 And this I pray, that your love may abound yet more and more in knowledge and *in* all judgment; 10 That ye may approve things that are excellent; that ye may be sincere and without offence till the day of Christ; 11 Being filled with the fruits of righteousness, which are by Jesus Christ, unto the glory and praise of God. 12 But I would ye should understand, brethren, that the things *which happened* unto me have fallen out rather unto the furtherance of the gospel; 13 So that my bonds in Christ are manifest in all the palace, and in all other *places;* 14 And many of the brethren in the Lord, waxing confident by my bonds, are much more bold to speak the word without fear. 15 Some indeed preach Christ even of envy and strife; and some also of good will: 16 The one preach Christ of contention, not sincerely, supposing to add affliction to my bonds: 17 But the other of love, knowing that I am set for the defence of the gospel. 18 What then? notwithstanding, every way, whether in pretence, or

R.S.V.

THE
LETTER OF PAUL TO THE
PHILIPPIANS

1 Paul and Timothy, servants[a] of Christ Jesus, To all the saints in Christ Jesus who are at Philippi, with the bishops[b] and deacons: 2 Grace to you and peace from God our Father and the Lord Jesus Christ.

3 I thank my God in all my remembrance of you, 4 always in every prayer of mine for you all making my prayer with joy, 5 thankful for your partnership in the gospel from the first day until now. 6 And I am sure that he who began a good work in you will bring it to completion at the day of Jesus Christ. 7 It is right for me to feel thus about you all, because I hold you in my heart, for you are all partakers with me of grace, both in my imprisonment and in the defense and confirmation of the gospel. 8 For God is my witness, how I yearn for you all with the affection of Christ Jesus. 9 And it is my prayer that your love may abound more and more, with knowledge and all discernment, 10 so that you may approve what is excellent, and may be pure and blameless for the day of Christ, 11 filled with the fruits of righteousness which come through Jesus Christ, to the glory and praise of God.

12 I want you to know, brethren, that what has happened to me has really served to advance the gospel, 13 so that it has become known throughout the whole praetorian guard[c] and to all the rest that my imprisonment is for Christ; 14 and most of the brethren have been made confident in the Lord because of my imprisonment, and are much more bold to speak the word of God without fear.

15 Some indeed preach Christ from envy and rivalry, but others from good will. 16 The latter do it out of love, knowing that I am put here for the defense of the gospel; 17 the former proclaim Christ out of partisanship, not sincerely but thinking to afflict me in my imprisonment. 18 What then? Only that in every way, whether

[a] Or *slaves.* [b] Or *overseers.* [c] Greek *in the whole praetorium.*

PHILLIPS	N.E.B.

THE LETTER
TO THE CHRISTIANS AT
PHILIPPI

THE
LETTER OF PAUL TO THE
PHILIPPIANS

The Apostle and His Friends

Paul and Timothy, servants of Jesus Christ, to the bishops, deacons and all true Christians at Philippi, grace and peace from God our Father and Jesus Christ the Lord!

1 From Paul and Timothy, servants of Christ Jesus, to all those of God's people, incorporate in Christ Jesus, who live at Philippi, including their bishops and deacons.

Grace to you and peace from God our Father and the Lord Jesus Christ.

*I have the most pleasant memories 1. 3
of you all*

I thank my God for you Christians at Philippi whenever I think of you. My constant prayers for you are a real joy, for they bring back to my mind how we have worked together for the gospel from the earliest days until now. I feel sure that the one who has begun his good work in you will go on developing it until the day of Jesus Christ.

It is only natural that I should feel like this about you all—you are very dear to me. For during the time I was in prison as well as when I was out defending and demonstrating the power of the gospel we shared together the grace of God. God knows how much I long, with the deepest Christian love and affection, for your companionship. My prayer for you is that you may have still more love—a love that is full of knowledge and wise insight. I want you to be able always to recognize the highest and the best, and to live sincere and blameless lives until the day of Christ. I want to see your lives full of true goodness, produced by the power that Jesus Christ gives you to the praise and glory of God.

I thank my God whenever I think of you; and when I pray for you all, my prayers are always joyful, because of the part you have taken in the work of the Gospel from the first day until now. Of one thing I am certain: the One who started the good work in you will bring it to completion by the Day of Christ Jesus. It is indeed only right that I should feel like this about you all, because you hold me in such affection, and because, whether I lie in prison or appear in the dock to vouch for the truth of the Gospel, you all share in the privilege that is mine.[a] God knows how I long for you all, with the deep yearning of Christ Jesus himself. And this is my prayer, that your love may grow ever richer and richer in knowledge and insight of every kind, and may thus bring you the gift of true discrimination.[b] Then on the Day of Christ you will be flawless and without blame, reaping the full harvest of righteousness that comes through Jesus Christ, to the glory and praise of God.

Friends, I want you to understand that the work of the Gospel has been helped on, rather than hindered, by this business of mine. My imprisonment in Christ's cause has become common knowledge to all at headquarters[c] here, and indeed among the public at large; and it has given confidence to most of our fellow-Christians to speak the word of God fearlessly and with extraordinary courage.

*My imprisonment has turned out 1. 12
to be no bad thing*

Now, concerning myself, I want you to know, my brothers, that what has happened to me has, in effect, turned out to the advantage of the gospel. For, first of all, my imprisonment means a personal witness for Christ before the palace guards, not to mention others who come and go. Then, it means that most of our brothers, somehow taking fresh heart in the Lord from the very fact that I am a prisoner for Christ's sake, have shown far more courage in boldly proclaiming the Word of God. I know that some are preaching Christ out of jealousy, in order to annoy me, but some are preaching him in good faith. These latter are preaching out of their love for me. For they know that God has set me here in prison to defend our right to preach the gospel. The motive of the former is questionable—they preach in a partisan spirit, hoping to make my chains even more galling than they would otherwise be. But what does it matter? However they may look at it, the fact remains

Some, indeed, proclaim Christ in a jealous and quarrelsome spirit; others proclaim him in true goodwill, and these are moved by love for me; they know that it is to defend the Gospel that I am where I am. But the others, moved by personal rivalry, present Christ from mixed motives, meaning to stir up fresh trouble for me as I lie in prison.[d] What does it matter? One way or

[a] *Or* I am justified in taking this view about you all, because I hold you in closest union, as those who, when I lie . . . of the Gospel, all share in the privilege that is mine. [b] *Or* may teach you by experience what things are most worth while. [c] *Or* to all the imperial guard, *or* to all at the Residency (*Greek* Praetorium). [d] *Or* meaning to make use of my imprisonment to stir up fresh trouble.

K.J.V.

in truth, Christ is preached; and I therein do rejoice, yea, and will rejoice. 19 For I know that this shall turn to my salvation through your prayer, and the supply of the Spirit of Jesus Christ, 20According to my earnest expectation and *my* hope, that in nothing I shall be ashamed, but *that* with all boldness, as always, *so* now also Christ shall be magnified in my body, whether *it be* by life, or by death. 21 For to me to live *is* Christ, and to die *is* gain. 22 But if I live in the flesh, this *is* the fruit of my labour: yet what I shall choose I wot not. 23 For I am in a strait betwixt two, having a desire to depart, and to be with Christ; which is far better: 24 Nevertheless to abide in the flesh *is* more needful for you. 25And having this confidence, I know that I shall abide and continue with you all for your furtherance and joy of faith; 26 That your rejoicing may be more abundant in Jesus Christ for me by my coming to you again. 27 Only let your conversation be as it becometh the gospel of Christ: that whether I come and see you, or else be absent, I may hear of your affairs, that ye stand fast in one spirit, with one mind striving together for the faith of the gospel; 28And in nothing terrified by your adversaries: which is to them an evident token of perdition, but to you of salvation, and that of God. 29 For unto you it is given in the behalf of Christ, not only to believe on him, but also to suffer for his sake; 30 Having the same conflict which ye saw in me, and now hear *to be* in me.

R.S.V.

in pretense or in truth, Christ is proclaimed; and in that I rejoice.

19 Yes, and I shall rejoice. For I know that through your prayers and the help of the Spirit of Jesus Christ this will turn out for my deliverance, 20 as it is my eager expectation and hope that I shall not be at all ashamed, but that with full courage now as always Christ will be honored in my body, whether by life or by death. 21 For to me to live is Christ, and to die is gain. 22 If it is to be life in the flesh, that means fruitful labor for me. Yet which I shall choose I cannot tell. 23 I am hard pressed between the two. My desire is to depart and be with Christ, for that is far better. 24 But to remain in the flesh is more necessary on your account. 25 Convinced of this, I know that I shall remain and continue with you all, for your progress and joy in the faith, 26 so that in me you may have ample cause to glory in Christ Jesus, because of my coming to you again.

27 Only let your manner of life be worthy of the gospel of Christ, so that whether I come and see you or am absent, I may hear of you that you stand firm in one spirit, with one mind striving side by side for the faith of the gospel, 28 and not frightened in anything by your opponents. This is a clear omen to them of their destruction, but of your salvation, and that from God. 29 For it has been granted to you that for the sake of Christ you should not only believe in him but also suffer for his sake, 30 engaged in the same conflict which you saw and now hear to be mine.

2 If *there be* therefore any consolation in Christ, if any comfort of love, if any fellowship of the Spirit, if any bowels and mercies, 2 Fulfil ye my joy, that ye be likeminded, having the same love, *being* of one accord, of one mind. 3 *Let* nothing *be done* through strife or vainglory; but in lowliness of mind let each esteem other better than themselves. 4 Look not every man on his own things, but every man also on the things of others. 5 Let this mind be in you, which was also in Christ Jesus: 6 Who, being in the form of God, thought it not robbery to be equal with God: 7 But made himself of no reputation, and took upon him the form of a servant, and was made in the likeness of men: 8And being found in fashion as a man, he humbled him-

2 So if there is any encouragement in Christ, any incentive of love, any participation in the Spirit, any affection and sympathy, 2 complete my joy by being of the same mind, having the same love, being in full accord and of one mind. 3 Do nothing from selfishness or conceit, but in humility count others better than yourselves. 4 Let each of you look not only to his own interests, but also to the interests of others. 5 Have this mind among yourselves, which you have in Christ Jesus, 6 who, though he was in the form of God, did not count equality with God a thing to be grasped, 7 but emptied himself, taking the form of a servant,*d* being born in the likeness of men. 8And being found in human form he humbled himself and became

[d] Or *slave*.

PHILLIPS

N.E.B.

that Christ *is* being preached, whether sincerely or not, and that fact makes me very happy. Yes, and I shall go on being very happy, for I know that what is happening will be for the good of my own soul, thanks to your prayers and the resources of the Spirit of Jesus Christ. It all accords with my own earnest wishes and hopes, which are that I should never be in any way ashamed, but that now, as always, I should honor Christ with the utmost boldness by the way I live, whether that means I am to face death or to go on living. For living to me means simply "Christ," and if I die I should merely gain more of him. I realize, of course, that the work which I have started may make it necessary for me to go on living in this world. I should find it very hard to make a choice. I am torn in two directions—on the one hand I long to leave this world and live with Christ, and that is obviously the best thing for me. Yet, on the other hand, it is probably more necessary for you that I should stay here on earth. That is why I feel pretty well convinced that I shall not leave this world yet, but shall be able to stand by you, to help you forward in Christian living and to find increasing joy in your faith. So you can look forward to making much of me as your minister in Christ when I come to see you again!

But whatever happens, make sure that your everyday life is worthy of the gospel of Christ. So that whether I do come and see you, or merely hear about you from a distance, I may know that you are standing fast in a united spirit, battling with a single mind for the faith of the gospel and not caring two straws for your enemies. The very fact that they are your enemies is plain proof that they are lost to God, while the fact that you have such men as enemies is plain proof that you yourselves are being saved by God. You are given, in this battle, the privilege not merely of believing in Christ but also of suffering for his sake. It is now your turn to take part in that battle you once saw me engaged in, and which, in point of fact, I am still fighting.

Above all things be loving, humble, united
2. 1

Now if your experience of Christ's encouragement and love means anything to you, if you have known something of the fellowship of his Spirit, and all that it means in kindness and deep sympathy, do make my best hopes for you come true! Live together in harmony, live together in love, as though you had only one mind and one spirit between you. Never act from motives of rivalry or personal vanity, but in humility think more of one another than you do of yourselves. None of you should think only of his own affairs, but each should learn to see things from other people's point of view.

Let Christ be your example of humility
2. 5

Let Christ Jesus be your example as to what your attitude should be. For he, who had always been God by nature, did not cling to his prerogatives as God's equal, but stripped himself of all privilege by consenting to be a slave by nature and being born as mortal man. And, having become man, he humbled himself by living a life

another, in pretence or in sincerity, Christ is set forth, and for that I rejoice.

Yes, and rejoice I will, knowing well that the issue of it all will be my deliverance, because you are praying for me and the Spirit of Jesus Christ is given me for support.[a] For, as I passionately hope, I shall have no cause to be ashamed, but shall speak so boldly that now as always the greatness of Christ will shine out clearly in my person, whether through my life or through my death. For to me life is Christ, and death gain; but what if my living on in the body may serve some good purpose? Which then am I to choose? I cannot tell. I am torn two ways: what I should like is to depart and be with Christ; that is better by far; but for your sake there is greater need for me to stay on in the body. This indeed I know for certain: I shall stay, and stand by you all to help you forward and to add joy to your faith, so that when I am with you again, your pride in me may be unbounded in Christ Jesus.

Only, let your conduct be worthy of the gospel of Christ, so that whether I come and see you for myself or hear about you from a distance, I may know that you are standing firm, one in spirit, one in mind, contending as one man for the gospel faith, meeting your opponents without so much as a tremor. This is a sure sign to them that their doom is sealed, but a sign of your salvation, and one afforded by God himself; for you have been granted the privilege not only of believing in Christ but also of suffering for him. You and I are engaged in the same contest; you saw me in it once, and, as you hear, I am in it still.

2

If then our common life in Christ yields anything to stir the heart, any loving consolation, any sharing of the Spirit, any warmth of affection or compassion, fill up my cup of happiness by thinking and feeling alike, with the same love for one another, the same turn of mind, and a common care for unity. Rivalry and personal vanity should have no place among you, but you should humbly reckon others better than yourselves. You must look to each other's interest and not merely to your own.

Let your bearing towards one another arise out of your life in Christ Jesus.[b] For the divine nature was his from the first; yet he did not think to snatch at equality with God,[c] but made himself nothing, assuming the nature of a slave. Bearing the human likeness, revealed in human shape, he humbled himself, and in obedience

[a] *Or* supplies me with all I need. [b] *Or* Have that bearing towards one another which was also found in Christ Jesus. [c] *Or* yet he did not prize his equality with God.

K.J.V.

self, and became obedient unto death, even the death of the cross. 9 Wherefore God also hath highly exalted him, and given him a name which is above every name: 10 That at the name of Jesus every knee should bow, of *things* in heaven, and *things* in earth, and *things* under the earth; 11And *that* every tongue should confess that Jesus Christ *is* Lord, to the glory of God the Father. 12 Wherefore, my beloved, as ye have always obeyed, not as in my presence only, but now much more in my absence, work out your own salvation with fear and trembling: 13 For it is God which worketh in you both to will and to do of *his* good pleasure. 14 Do all things without murmurings and disputings: 15 That ye may be blameless and harmless, the sons of God, without rebuke, in the midst of a crooked and perverse nation, among whom ye shine as lights in the world; 16 Holding forth the word of life; that I may rejoice in the day of Christ, that I have not run in vain, neither laboured in vain. 17 Yea, and if I be offered upon the sacrifice and service of your faith, I joy, and rejoice with you all. 18 For the same cause also do ye joy, and rejoice with me. 19 But I trust in the Lord Jesus to send Timotheus shortly unto you, that I also may be of good comfort, when I know your state. 20 For I have no man likeminded, who will naturally care for your state. 21 For all seek their own, not the things which are Jesus Christ's. 22 But ye know the proof of him, that, as a son with the father, he hath served with me in the gospel. 23 Him therefore I hope to send presently, so soon as I shall see how it will go with me. 24 But I trust in the Lord that I also myself shall come shortly. 25 Yet I supposed it necessary to send to you Epaphroditus, my brother, and companion in labour, and fellow soldier, but your messenger, and he that ministered to my wants. 26 For he longed after you all, and was full of heaviness, because that ye had heard that he had been sick. 27 For indeed he was sick nigh unto death: but God had mercy on him; and not on him only, but on me also, lest I should have sorrow upon sorrow. 28 I sent him therefore the more carefully, that, when ye see him again, ye may rejoice, and that I may be the less sorrowful. 29 Receive him therefore in the Lord with all gladness; and hold such in reputation: 30 Because for the work of Christ he was nigh unto death, not regarding his life, to supply your lack of service toward me.

R.S.V.

obedient unto death, even death on a cross. 9 Therefore God has highly exalted him and bestowed on him the name which is above every name, 10 that at the name of Jesus every knee should bow, in heaven and on earth and under the earth, 11 and every tongue confess that Jesus Christ is Lord, to the glory of God the Father.

12 Therefore, my beloved, as you have always obeyed, so now, not only as in my presence but much more in my absence, work out your own salvation with fear and trembling; 13 for God is at work in you, both to will and to work for his good pleasure.

14 Do all things without grumbling or questioning, 15 that you may be blameless and innocent, children of God without blemish in the midst of a crooked and perverse generation, among whom you shine as lights in the world, 16 holding fast the word of life, so that in the day of Christ I may be proud that I did not run in vain or labor in vain. 17 Even if I am to be poured as a libation upon the sacrificial offering of your faith, I am glad and rejoice with you all. 18 Likewise you also should be glad and rejoice with me.

19 I hope in the Lord Jesus to send Timothy to you soon, so that I may be cheered by news of you. 20 I have no one like him, who will be genuinely anxious for your welfare. 21 They all look after their own interests, not those of Jesus Christ. 22 But Timothy's worth you know, how as a son with a father he has served with me in the gospel. 23 I hope therefore to send him just as soon as I see how it will go with me; 24 and I trust in the Lord that shortly I myself shall come also.

25 I have thought it necessary to send to you Epaphroditus my brother and fellow worker and fellow soldier, and your messenger and minister to my need, 26 for he has been longing for you all, and has been distressed because you heard that he was ill. 27 Indeed he was ill, near to death. But God had mercy on him, and not only on him but on me also, lest I should have sorrow upon sorrow. 28 I am the more eager to send him, therefore, that you may rejoice at seeing him again, and that I may be less anxious. 29 So receive him in the Lord with all joy; and honor such men, 30 for he nearly died for the work of Christ, risking his life to complete your service to me.

PHILLIPS

of utter obedience, even to the extent of dying, *and the death he died was the death of a common criminal.* That is why God has now lifted him so high, and has given him the name beyond all names, so that at the name of Jesus "every knee shall bow," whether in Heaven or earth or under the earth. And that is why, in the end, "every tongue shall confess" that Jesus Christ is the Lord, to the glory of God the Father.

God is himself at work within you   2. 12

So then, my dearest friends, as you have always followed my advice—and that not only when I was present to give it—so now that I am far away be keener than ever to work out the salvation that God has given you with a proper sense of awe and responsibility. For it is God who is at work within you, giving you the will and the power to achieve his purpose.

Do all you have to do without grumbling or arguing, so that you may be God's children, blameless, sincere and wholesome, living in a warped and diseased world, and shining there like lights in a dark place. For you hold in your hands the very word of life. Thus can you give me something to be proud of in the day of Christ, for I shall know then that I did not spend my energy in vain. Yes, and if it should happen that my lifeblood is, so to speak, poured out upon the sacrifice and offering which your faith means to God, then I can still be very happy, and I can share my happiness with you all. I should like to feel that you could be glad about this too, and could share with me the happiness I speak of.

I am sending Epaphroditus with this letter, and Timothy later   2. 19

But I hope in the Lord Jesus that it will not be long before I can send Timothy to you, and then I shall be cheered by a firsthand account of you and your doings. I have nobody else with a genuine interest in your well-being. All the others seem to be wrapped up in their own affairs and do not really care for the business of Jesus Christ. But you know how Timothy has proved his worth, working with me for the gospel like a son with his father. I hope to send him to you as soon as I can tell how things will work out for me, but God gives me some hope that it will not be long before I am able to come myself as well. I have considered it desirable, however, to send you Epaphroditus. He has been to me brother, fellow worker and comrade-in-arms, as well as being the messenger you sent to see to my wants. He has been homesick for you, and was worried because he knew that you had heard that he was ill. Indeed he was ill, very dangerously ill, but God had mercy on him —and incidentally on me as well, so that I did not have the sorrow of losing him to add to my sufferings. I am particularly anxious, therefore, to send him to you so that when you see him again you may be glad, and to know of your joy will lighten my own sorrows. Welcome him in the Lord with great joy! You should hold men like him in highest honor, for his loyalty to Christ brought him very near death—he risked his life to do for me in person what distance prevented you all from doing.

N.E.B.

accepted even death—death on a cross. Therefore God raised him to the heights and bestowed on him the name above all names, that at the name of Jesus every knee should bow—in heaven, on earth, and in the depths—and every tongue confess, 'Jesus Christ is Lord', to the glory of God the Father.

So you too, my friends, must be obedient, as always; even more, now that I am away, than when I was with you. You must work out your own salvation in fear and trembling; for it is God who works in you, inspiring both the will and the deed, for his own chosen purpose.

Do all you have to do without complaint or wrangling. Show yourselves guileless and above reproach, faultless children of God in a warped and crooked generation, in which you shine[a] like stars in a dark world[b] and proffer the word of life.[c] Thus you will be my pride on the Day of Christ, proof that I did not run my race in vain, or work in vain. But if my life-blood is to crown that sacrifice which is the offering up of your faith, I am glad of it, and I share my gladness with you all. Rejoice, you no less than I, and let us share our joy.

I hope (under the Lord Jesus) to send Timothy to you soon; it will cheer me to hear news of you. There is no one else here who sees things as I do, and takes[d] a genuine interest in your concerns; they are all bent on their own ends, not on the cause of Christ Jesus. But Timothy's record is known to you: you know that he has been at my side in the service of the Gospel like a son working under his father. Timothy, then, I hope to send as soon as ever I can see how things are going with me; and I am confident, under the Lord, that I shall myself be coming before long.

I feel also I must send our brother Epaphroditus, my fellow-worker and comrade, whom you commissioned to minister to my needs. He has been missing all of you sadly, and has been distressed that you heard he was ill. (He was indeed dangerously ill, but God was merciful to him, and merciful no less to me, to spare me sorrow upon sorrow.) For this reason I am all the more eager to send him, to give you the happiness of seeing him again, and to relieve my sorrow. Welcome him then in the fellowship of the Lord with whole-hearted delight. You should honor men like him; in Christ's cause he came near to death, risking his life to render me the service you could not give.

[a] Or . . . generation. Shine out among them . . .
[b] Or in the firmament. [c] Or as the very principle of its life. [d] Or no one else here like him, who takes . . .

K.J.V.

3 Finally, my brethren, rejoice in the Lord. To write the same things to you, to me indeed *is* not grievous, but for you *it is* safe. 2 Beware of dogs, beware of evil workers, beware of the concision. 3 For we are the circumcision, which worship God in the spirit, and rejoice in Christ Jesus, and have no confidence in the flesh. 4 Though I might also have confidence in the flesh. If any other man thinketh that he hath whereof he might trust in the flesh, I more: 5 Circumcised the eighth day, of the stock of Israel, *of* the tribe of Benjamin, a Hebrew of the Hebrews; as touching the law, a Pharisee; 6 Concerning zeal, persecuting the church; touching the righteousness which is in the law, blameless. 7 But what things were gain to me, those I counted loss for Christ. 8 Yea doubtless, and I count all things *but* loss for the excellency of the knowledge of Christ Jesus my Lord: for whom I have suffered the loss of all things, and do count them *but* dung, that I may win Christ, 9And be found in him, not having mine own righteousness, which is of the law, but that which is through the faith of Christ, the righteousness which is of God by faith: 10 That I may know him, and the power of his resurrection, and the fellowship of his sufferings, being made conformable unto his death; 11 If by any means I might attain unto the resurrection of the dead. 12 Not as though I had already attained, either were already perfect: but I follow after, if that I may apprehend that for which also I am apprehended of Christ Jesus. 13 Brethren, I count not myself to have apprehended: but *this* one thing *I do,* forgetting those things which are behind, and reaching forth unto those things which are before, 14 I press toward the mark for the prize of the high calling of God in Christ Jesus. 15 Let us therefore, as many as be perfect, be thus minded: and if in any thing ye be otherwise minded, God shall reveal even this unto you. 16 Nevertheless, whereto we have already attained, let us walk by the same rule, let us mind

R.S.V.

3 Finally, my brethren, rejoice in the Lord. To write the same things to you is not irksome to me, and is safe for you. 2 Look out for the dogs, look out for the evil-workers, look out for those who mutilate the flesh. 3 For we are the true circumcision, who worship God in spirit,*e* and glory in Christ Jesus, and put no confidence in the flesh. 4 Though I myself have reason for confidence in the flesh also. If any other man thinks he has reason for confidence in the flesh, I have more: 5 circumcised on the eighth day, of the people of Israel, of the tribe of Benjamin, a Hebrew born of Hebrews; as to the law a Pharisee, 6 as to zeal a persecutor of the church, as to righteousness under the law blameless. 7 But whatever gain I had, I counted as loss for the sake of Christ. 8 Indeed I count everything as loss because of the surpassing worth of knowing Christ Jesus my Lord. For his sake I have suffered the loss of all things, and count them as refuse, in order that I may gain Christ 9 and be found in him, not having a righteousness of my own, based on law, but that which is through faith in Christ, the righteousness from God that depends on faith; 10 that I may know him and the power of his resurrection, and may share his sufferings, becoming like him in his death, 11 that if possible I may attain the resurrection from the dead. 12 Not that I have already obtained this or am already perfect; but I press on to make it my own, because Christ Jesus has made me his own. 13 Brethren, I do not consider that I have made it my own; but one thing I do, forgetting what lies behind and straining forward to what lies ahead, 14 I press on toward the goal for the prize of the upward call of God in Christ Jesus. 15 Let those of us who are mature be thus minded; and if in anything you are otherwise minded, God will reveal that also to you. 16 Only let us hold true to what we have attained.

[e] Other ancient authorities read *worship by the Spirit of God.*

PHILLIPS

In conclusion, my brothers, delight yourselves in the Lord! It doesn't bore me to repeat a piece of advice like this, and if you follow it you will find it a great safeguard to your souls.

The "circumcision" party are the 3. 2 enemies of your faith and freedom

Be on your guard against these curs, these wicked workmen, these would-be mutilators of your bodies! We are, remember, truly circumcised when we worship God by the Spirit, when we find our joy in Jesus Christ and put no confidence in what we are in the flesh.

I was even more of a Jew than 3. 4 these Jews, yet knowing Christ has changed my whole life

If it were right to have such confidence, I could certainly have it, and if any of these men thinks he has grounds for such confidence I can assure him I have more. I was born from the people of Israel; I was circumcised on the eighth day; I was a member of the tribe of Benjamin; I was in fact a full-blooded Jew. As far as keeping the Law is concerned I was a Pharisee, and you can judge my enthusiasm for the Jewish faith by my active persecution of the Church. As far as the Law's righteousness is concerned, I don't think anyone could have found fault with me. Yet every advantage that I had gained I considered lost for Christ's sake. Yes, and I look upon everything as loss compared with the overwhelming gain of knowing Christ Jesus my Lord. For his sake I did in actual fact suffer the loss of everything, but I considered it useless rubbish compared with being able to win Christ. For now my place is in him, and I am not dependent upon any of the self-achieved righteousness of the Law. God has given me that genuine righteousness which comes from faith in Christ. How changed are my ambitions! Now I long to know Christ and the power shown by his resurrection: now I long to share his sufferings, even to die as he died, so that I may perhaps attain, as he did, the resurrection from the dead. Yet, my brothers, I do not consider myself to have "arrived," spiritually, nor do I consider myself already perfect. But I keep going on, grasping ever more firmly that purpose for which Christ Jesus grasped me. My brothers, I do not consider myself to have fully grasped it even now. But I do concentrate on this: I leave the past behind and with hands outstretched to whatever lies ahead I go straight for the goal—my reward the honor of my high calling by God in Christ Jesus.

My ambition is the true goal of 3. 15 the spiritually adult: make it yours too

All of us who are spiritually adult should set ourselves this sort of ambition, and if at present you cannot see this, yet you will find that this is the attitude which God is leading you to adopt. It is important that we go forward in the light of such truth as we have ourselves attained to.

N.E.B.

3 And now, friends, farewell; I wish you joy in the Lord.

To repeat what I have written to you before is no trouble to me, and it is a safeguard for you. Beware of those dogs and their malpractices. Beware of those who insist on mutilation— 'circumcision' I will not call it; we are the circumcised, we whose worship is spiritual,[a] whose pride is in Christ Jesus, and who put no confidence in anything external. Not that I am without grounds myself even for confidence of that kind. If anyone thinks he has grounds to base his claims on externals, I could make a stronger case for myself: circumcised on my eighth day, Israelite by race, of the tribe of Benjamin, a Hebrew born and bred;[b] in my attitude to the law, a Pharisee; in pious zeal, a persecutor of the church; in legal rectitude, faultless. But all such assets I have written off because of Christ. I would say more: I count everything sheer loss, because all is far outweighed by the gain of knowing Christ Jesus my Lord, for whose sake I did in fact lose everything. I count it so much garbage,[c] for the sake of gaining Christ and finding myself incorporate in him, with no righteousness of my own, no legal rectitude, but the righteousness which comes[d] from faith in Christ, given by God in response to faith. All I care for is to know Christ, to experience the power of his resurrection, and to share his sufferings, in growing conformity with his death, if only I may finally arrive at the resurrection from the dead. It is not to be thought that I have already achieved all this. I have not yet reached perfection, but I press on, hoping to take hold of that for which Christ once took hold of me. My friends, I do not reckon myself to have got hold of it yet. All I can say is this: forgetting what is behind me, and reaching out for that which lies ahead, I press towards the goal to win the prize which is God's call to the life above, in Christ Jesus.

Let us then keep to this way of thinking, those of us who are mature. If there is any point on which you think differently, this also God will make plain to you. Only let our conduct be consistent with the level we have already reached.

[a] *Some witnesses read* who worship God in the spirit; *others read* who worship by the Spirit of God. [b] *Or* a Hebrew-speaking Jew of a Hebrew-speaking family. [c] *Or* dung. [d] *Or* and in him finding that, though I have no righteousness of my own, no legal rectitude, I have the righteousness which comes . . .

K.J.V.

the same thing. 17 Brethren, be followers together of me, and mark them which walk so as ye have us for an ensample. 18 (For many walk, of whom I have told you often, and now tell you even weeping, *that they are* the enemies of the cross of Christ: 19 Whose end *is* destruction, whose God *is their* belly, and *whose* glory *is* in their shame, who mind earthly things.) 20 For our conversation is in heaven; from whence also we look for the Saviour, the Lord Jesus Christ: 21 Who shall change our vile body, that it may be fashioned like unto his glorious body, according to the working whereby he is able even to subdue all things unto himself.

4 Therefore, my brethren dearly beloved and longed for, my joy and crown, so stand fast in the Lord, *my* dearly beloved. 2 I beseech Euodias, and beseech Syntyche, that they be of the same mind in the Lord. 3 And I entreat thee also, true yokefellow, help those women which laboured with me in the gospel, with Clement also, and *with* other my fellow labourers, whose names *are* in the book of life. 4 Rejoice in the Lord always: *and* again I say, Rejoice. 5 Let your moderation be known unto all men. The Lord *is* at hand. 6 Be careful for nothing; but in every thing by prayer and supplication with thanksgiving let your requests be made known unto God. 7 And the peace of God, which passeth all understanding, shall keep your hearts and minds through Christ Jesus. 8 Finally, brethren, whatsoever things are true, whatsoever things *are* honest, whatsoever things *are* just, whatsoever things *are* pure, whatsoever things *are* lovely, whatsoever things *are* of good report; if *there be* any virtue, and if *there be* any praise, think on these things. 9 Those things, which ye have both learned, and received, and heard, and seen in me, do: and the God of peace shall be with you. 10 But I rejoiced in the Lord greatly, that now at the last your care of me hath flourished again; wherein ye were also careful, but ye lacked opportunity. 11 Not that I speak in respect of want: for I have learned, in whatsoever state I am, *therewith* to be content. 12 I know both how to be abased, and I know how to abound: every where and in all things I am instructed both to be full and to be hungry, both to abound and to suffer need. 13 I can do all things through Christ which strengtheneth me. 14 Notwithstanding, ye have well done, that ye did communicate with my affliction. 15 Now ye Philippians know also, that in the beginning of the gospel, when I departed from Macedonia, no church communicated with me as concerning giving and

R.S.V.

17 Brethren, join in imitating me, and mark those who so live as you have an example in us. 18 For many, of whom I have often told you and now tell you even with tears, live as enemies of the cross of Christ. 19 Their end is destruction, their god is the belly, and they glory in their shame, with minds set on earthly things. 20 But our commonwealth is in heaven, and from it we await a Savior, the Lord Jesus Christ, 21 who will change our lowly body to be like his glorious body, by the power which enables him even to subject all things to himself.

4 Therefore, my brethren, whom I love and long for, my joy and crown, stand firm thus in the Lord, my beloved.
2 I entreat Euodia and I entreat Syntyche to agree in the Lord. 3 And I ask you also, true yokefellow, help these women, for they have labored side by side with me in the gospel together with Clement and the rest of my fellow workers, whose names are in the book of life.
4 Rejoice in the Lord always; again I will say, Rejoice. 5 Let all men know your forbearance. The Lord is at hand. 6 Have no anxiety about anything, but in everything by prayer and supplication with thanksgiving let your requests be made known to God. 7 And the peace of God, which passes all understanding, will keep your hearts and your minds in Christ Jesus.

8 Finally, brethren, whatever is true, whatever is honorable, whatever is just, whatever is pure, whatever is lovely, whatever is gracious, if there is any excellence, if there is anything worthy of praise, think about these things. 9 What you have learned and received and heard and seen in me, do; and the God of peace will be with you.
10 I rejoice in the Lord greatly that now at length you have revived your concern for me; you were indeed concerned for me, but you had no opportunity. 11 Not that I complain of want; for I have learned, in whatever state I am, to be content. 12 I know how to be abased, and I know how to abound; in any and all circumstances I have learned the secret of facing plenty and hunger, abundance and want. 13 I can do all things in him who strengthens me.
14 Yet it was kind of you to share my trouble. 15 And you Philippians yourselves know that in the beginning of the gospel, when I left Macedonia, no church entered into partnership with me in giving and receiving except you only;

PHILLIPS

Let me be your example here, my brothers: let my example be the standard by which you can tell who are the genuine Christians among those about you. For there are many, of whom I have told you before and tell you again now, even with tears, that they are the enemies of the cross of Christ. These men are heading for utter destruction—their god is their own appetite; their pride is in what they should be ashamed of; and this world is the limit of their horizon. But we are citizens of Heaven; our outlook goes beyond this world to the hopeful expectation of the savior who will come from Heaven, the Lord Jesus Christ. He will change these wretched bodies of ours so that they resemble his own glorious body, by that power of his which makes him the master of everything that is.

So, my brothers whom I love and long for, my joy and my crown, do stand firmly in the Lord, and remember how much I love you.

Be united, be joyful, be at peace   *4. 2*

Euodias and Syntyche, I beg you by name to make up your differences as Christians should! And you, my true fellow worker, I ask you to help these women. They both worked hard with me for the gospel, as did Clement and all my other fellow workers whose names are in the book of life.

Delight yourselves in the Lord; yes, find your joy in him at all times. Have a reputation for gentleness, and never forget the nearness of your Lord.

Don't worry over anything whatever; tell God every detail of your needs in earnest and thankful prayer, and the peace of God, which transcends human understanding, will keep constant guard over your hearts and minds as they rest in Christ Jesus.

Here is a last piece of advice. If you believe in goodness and if you value the approval of God, fix your minds on whatever is true and honorable and just and pure and lovely and praiseworthy. Model your conduct on what you have learned from me, on what I have told you and shown you, and you will find that the God of peace will be with you.

The memory of your generosity   *4. 10*
is an abiding joy to me

It has been a great joy to me that after all this time you have shown such interest in my welfare. I don't mean that you had forgotten me, but up till now you had no opportunity of expressing your concern. Nor do I mean that I have been in actual need, for I have learned to be content, whatever the circumstances may be. I know now how to live when things are difficult and I know how to live when things are prosperous. In general and in particular I have learned the secret of facing either plenty or poverty. I am ready for anything through the strength of the one who lives within me. Nevertheless I am not disparaging the way in which you were willing to share my troubles. You Philippians will remember that in the early days of the gospel when I left Macedonia, you were the only church who shared with me the fellow-

N.E.B.

Agree together, my friends, to follow my example. You have us for a model; watch those whose way of life conforms to it. For, as I have often told you, and now tell you with tears in my eyes, there are many whose way of life makes them enemies of the cross of Christ. They are heading for destruction, appetite is their god, and they glory in their shame. Their minds are set on earthly things. We, by contrast, are citizens of heaven, and from heaven we expect our deliverer to come, the Lord Jesus Christ. He will transfigure the body belonging to our humble state, and give it a form like that of his own resplendent body, by the very power which enables him to make all things subject to himself.

4 Therefore, my friends, beloved friends whom I long for, my joy, my crown, stand thus firm in the Lord, my beloved!

I beg Euodia, and I beg Syntyche, to agree together in the Lord's fellowship. Yes, and you too, my loyal comrade, I ask you to help these women, who shared my struggles in the cause of the Gospel, with Clement and my other fellow-workers, whose[a] names are in the book of life.

Farewell; I wish you all joy in the Lord. I will say it again: all joy be yours.

Let your magnanimity be manifest to all.

The Lord is near; have no anxiety, but in everything make your requests known to God in prayer and petition with thanksgiving. Then the peace of God, which is beyond our utmost understanding,[b] will keep guard over your hearts and your thoughts, in Christ Jesus.

And now, my friends, all that is true, all that is noble, all that is just and pure, all that is lovable and gracious,[c] whatever is excellent and admirable—fill all your thoughts with these things.

The lessons I taught you, the tradition I have passed on, all that you heard me say or saw me do, put into practice; and the God of peace will be with you.

It is a great joy to me, in the Lord, that after so long your care for me has now blossomed afresh. You did care about me before for that matter; it was opportunity that you lacked. Not that I am alluding to want, for I have learned to find resources in myself whatever my circumstances. I know what it is to be brought low, and I know what it is to have plenty. I have been very thoroughly initiated into the human lot with all its ups and downs—fullness and hunger, plenty and want. I have strength for anything through him who gives me power. But it was kind of you to share the burden of my troubles.

As you know yourselves, Philippians, in the early days of my mission, when I set out from Macedonia, you were the only congregation that

[a] *Some witnesses read* my fellow-workers, and the others whose . . . [b] *Or* of far more worth than human reasoning. [c] *Or* of good repute.

K.J.V.

receiving, but ye only. 16 For even in Thessalonica ye sent once and again unto my necessity. 17 Not because I desire a gift: but I desire fruit that may abound to your account. 18 But I have all, and abound: I am full, having received of Epaphroditus the things *which were sent* from you, an odour of a sweet smell, a sacrifice acceptable, well pleasing to God. 19 But my God shall supply all your need according to his riches in glory by Christ Jesus. 20 Now unto God and our Father *be* glory for ever and ever. Amen. 21 Salute every saint in Christ Jesus. The brethren which are with me greet you. 22 All the saints salute you, chiefly they that are of Cesar's household. 23 The grace of our Lord Jesus Christ *be* with you all. Amen.

It was written to the Philippians from Rome by Epaphroditus.

R.S.V.

16 for even in Thessalonica you sent me help[f] once and again. 17 Not that I seek the gift; but I seek the fruit which increases to your credit. 18 I have received full payment, and more; I am filled, having received from Epaphroditus the gifts you sent, a fragrant offering, a sacrifice acceptable and pleasing to God. 19 And my God will supply every need of yours according to his riches in glory in Christ Jesus. 20 To our God and Father be glory for ever and ever. Amen.

21 Greet every saint in Christ Jesus. The brethren who are with me greet you. 22 All the saints greet you, especially those of Caesar's household.

23 The grace of the Lord Jesus Christ be with your spirit.

[f] Other ancient authorities read *money for my needs.*

PHILLIPS

ship of giving and receiving. Even in Thessalonica you twice sent me help when I was in need. It isn't the value of the gift that I am keen on; it is the reward that will come to you because of these gifts that you have made.

Now I have everything I want—in fact I am rich. Yes, I am quite content, thanks to your gifts received through Epaphroditus. Your generosity is like a lovely fragrance, a sacrifice that pleases the very heart of God. My God will supply all that you need from his glorious resources in Christ Jesus. And may glory be to our God and our Father for ever and ever, amen!

Farewell messages   *4. 21*

Greetings to every true Christian, from me and all the brothers here with me. All the Christians here would like to send their best wishes, particularly those who belong to the Emperor's household.

The grace of the Lord Jesus Christ be with your spirit.

                                         PAUL

N.E.B.

were my partners in payments and receipts; for even at Thessalonica you contributed to my needs, not once but twice over. Do not think I set my heart upon the gift; all I care for is the profit accruing to you. However, here I give you my receipt for everything—for more than everything; I am paid in full, now that I have received from Epaphroditus what you sent. It is a fragrant offering, an acceptable sacrifice, pleasing to God. And my God will supply all your wants out of the magnificence of his riches in Christ Jesus. To our God and Father be glory for endless ages! Amen.

Give my greetings, in the fellowship of Christ, to each one of God's people. The brothers who are now with me send their greetings to you, and so do all God's people here, particularly those who belong to the imperial establishment.

The grace of our Lord Jesus Christ be with your spirit.

K.J.V.

THE EPISTLE OF

PAUL THE APOSTLE

TO THE

COLOSSIANS

1 Paul, an apostle of Jesus Christ by the will of God, and Timotheus *our* brother, 2 To the saints and faithful brethren in Christ which are at Colosse: Grace *be* unto you, and peace, from God our Father and the Lord Jesus Christ. 3 We give thanks to God and the Father of our Lord Jesus Christ, praying always for you, 4 Since we heard of your faith in Christ Jesus, and of the love *which ye have* to all the saints, 5 For the hope which is laid up for you in heaven, whereof ye heard before in the word of the truth of the gospel; 6 Which is come unto you, as *it is* in all the world; and bringeth forth fruit, as *it doth* also in you, since the day ye heard *of it,* and knew the grace of God in truth: 7As ye also learned of Epaphras our dear fellow servant, who is for you a faithful minister of Christ; 8 Who also declared unto us your love in the Spirit. 9 For this cause we also, since the day we heard *it,* do not cease to pray for you, and to desire that ye might be filled with the knowledge of his will in all wisdom and spiritual understanding; 10 That ye might walk worthy of the Lord unto all pleasing, being fruitful in every good work, and increasing in the knowledge of God; 11 Strengthened with all might, according to his glorious power, unto all patience and longsuffering with joyfulness; 12 Giving thanks unto the Father, which hath made us meet to be partakers of the inheritance of the saints in light: 13 Who hath delivered us from the power of darkness, and hath translated *us* into the kingdom of his dear Son: 14 In whom we have redemption through his blood, *even* the forgive-

R.S.V.

THE

LETTER OF PAUL TO THE

COLOSSIANS

1 Paul, an apostle of Christ Jesus by the will of God, and Timothy our brother,
2 To the saints and faithful brethren in Christ at Colossae:
Grace to you and peace from God our Father.

3 We always thank God, the Father of our Lord Jesus Christ, when we pray for you, 4 because we have heard of your faith in Christ Jesus and of the love which you have for all the saints, 5 because of the hope laid up for you in heaven. Of this you have heard before in the word of the truth, the gospel 6 which has come to you, as indeed in the whole world it is bearing fruit and growing—so among yourselves, from the day you heard and understood the grace of God in truth, 7 as you learned it from Epaphras our beloved fellow servant. He is a faithful minister of Christ on our[a] behalf 8 and has made known to us your love in the Spirit.
9 And so, from the day we heard of it, we have not ceased to pray for you, asking that you may be filled with the knowledge of his will in all spiritual wisdom and understanding, 10 to lead a life worthy of the Lord, fully pleasing to him, bearing fruit in every good work and increasing in the knowledge of God. 11 May you be strengthened with all power, according to his glorious might, for all endurance and patience with joy, 12 giving thanks to the Father, who has qualified us[b] to share in the inheritance of the saints in light. 13 He has delivered us from the dominion of darkness and transferred us to the kingdom of his beloved Son, 14 in whom we have redemption, the forgiveness of sins.

[a] Other ancient authorities read *your.* [b] Other ancient authorities read *you.*

THE LETTER
TO THE CHRISTIANS AT
COLOSSAE

Paul, a messenger of Christ Jesus by God's will, and our brother Timothy send this greeting to all faithful Christians at Colossae: grace and peace be to you from God our Father!

We thank God for you and pray   1. 3
constantly for you

I want you to know by this letter that we here are constantly praying for you, and whenever we do we thank God the Father of our Lord Jesus Christ because you believe in Christ Jesus and because you are showing true Christian love toward other Christians. We know that you are showing these qualities because you have grasped the hope reserved for you in Heaven—that hope which first became yours when the truth was brought to you. It is, of course, part of the gospel itself, which has reached you as it spreads all over the world. Wherever that gospel goes, it produces Christian character, and develops it, as it has done in your own case from the time you first heard and realized the truth of God's grace.

You learned these things, we understand, from Epaphras, who is in the same service as we are. He is a most well-loved minister of Christ, and has your well-being very much at heart. As a matter of fact, it was from him that we heard about your growth in Christian love, so you will understand that since we heard about you we have never missed you in our prayers. We are asking God that you may see things, as it were, from his point of view by being given spiritual insight and understanding. We also pray that your outward lives, which men see, may bring credit to your master's name, and that you may bring joy to his heart by bearing genuine Christian fruit, and that your knowledge of God may grow yet deeper.

We pray for you to have real   1. 11
Christian experience

As you live this new life, we pray that you will be strengthened from God's boundless resources, so that you will find yourselves able to pass through an experience and endure it with joy. You will even be able to thank God in the midst of pain and distress because you are privileged to share the lot of those who are living in the light. For we must never forget that he rescued us from the power of darkness, and reestablished us in the kingdom of his beloved Son. For it is by his Son alone that we have been redeemed and have had our sins forgiven.

THE
LETTER OF PAUL TO THE
COLOSSIANS

The Centre of Christian Belief

1 From Paul, apostle of Christ Jesus commissioned by the will of God, and our colleague Timothy, to God's people at Colossae, brothers in the faith, incorporate in Christ.

Grace to you and peace from God our Father.

In all our prayers to God, the Father of our Lord Jesus Christ, we thank him for you, because we have heard of the faith you hold in Christ Jesus, and the love you bear towards all God's people. Both spring from the hope stored up for you in heaven—that hope of which you learned when the message of the true Gospel first came to you. In the same way it is coming to men the whole world over; everywhere it is growing and bearing fruit as it does among you, and has done since the day when you heard of the graciousness of God and recognized it for what in truth it is. You were taught this by Epaphras, our dear fellow-servant, a trusted worker for Christ on our[a] behalf, and it is he who has brought us the news of your God-given love.[b]

For this reason, ever since the day we heard of it, we have not ceased to pray for you. We ask God that you may receive from him all wisdom and spiritual understanding for full insight into his will, so that your manner of life may be worthy of the Lord and entirely pleasing to him. We pray that you may bear fruit in active goodness of every kind, and grow in the knowledge of God. May he strengthen you, in his glorious might, with ample power to meet whatever comes with fortitude, patience, and joy; and to give thanks[c] to the Father who has made you fit to share the heritage of God's people in the realm of light.

He rescued us from the domain of darkness and brought us away into the kingdom of his dear Son, in whom our release is secured and

[a] *Some witnesses read* your. [b] *Or* your love within the fellowship of the Spirit. [c] *Or* with fortitude and patience, and to give joyful thanks . . .

K.J.V.

ness of sins: 15 Who is the image of the invisible God, the firstborn of every creature: 16 For by him were all things created, that are in heaven, and that are in earth, visible and invisible, whether *they be* thrones, or dominions, or principalities, or powers: all things were created by him, and for him: 17And he is before all things, and by him all things consist: 18And he is the head of the body, the church: who is the beginning, the firstborn from the dead; that in all things he might have the preeminence. 19 For it pleased *the Father* that in him should all fulness dwell; 20And, having made peace through the blood of his cross, by him to reconcile all things unto himself; by him, *I say,* whether *they be* things in earth, or things in heaven. 21And you, that were sometime alienated and enemies in *your* mind by wicked works, yet now hath he reconciled 22 In the body of his flesh through death, to present you holy and unblameable and unreproveable in his sight: 23 If ye continue in the faith grounded and settled, and *be* not moved away from the hope of the gospel, which ye have heard, *and* which was preached to every creature which is under heaven; whereof I Paul am made a minister; 24 Who now rejoice in my sufferings for you, and fill up that which is behind of the afflictions of Christ in my flesh for his body's sake, which is the church: 25 Whereof I am made a minister, according to the dispensation of God which is given to me for you, to fulfil the word of God; 26 *Even* the mystery which hath been hid from ages and from generations, but now is made manifest to his saints: 27 To whom God would make known what *is* the riches of the glory of this mystery among the Gentiles; which is Christ in you, the hope of glory: 28 Whom we preach, warning every man, and teaching every man in all wisdom; that we may present every man perfect in Christ Jesus: 29 Whereunto I also labour, striving according to his working, which worketh in me mightily.

R.S.V.

15 He is the image of the invisible God, the first-born of all creation; 16 for in him all things were created, in heaven and on earth, visible and invisible, whether thrones or dominions or principalities or authorities—all things were created through him and for him. 17 He is before all things, and in him all things hold together. 18 He is the head of the body, the church; he is the beginning, the first-born from the dead, that in everything he might be pre-eminent. 19 For in him all the fulness of God was pleased to dwell, 20 and through him to reconcile to himself all things, whether on earth or in heaven, making peace by the blood of his cross.

21 And you, who once were estranged and hostile in mind, doing evil deeds, 22 he has now reconciled in his body of flesh by his death, in order to present you holy and blameless and irreproachable before him, 23 provided that you continue in the faith, stable and steadfast, not shifting from the hope of the gospel which you heard, which has been preached to every creature under heaven, and of which I, Paul, became a minister.

24 Now I rejoice in my sufferings for your sake, and in my flesh I complete what is lacking in Christ's afflictions for the sake of his body, that is, the church, 25 of which I became a minister according to the divine office which was given to me for you, to make the word of God fully known, 26 the mystery hidden for ages and generations° but now made manifest to his saints. 27 To them God chose to make known how great among the Gentiles are the riches of the glory of this mystery, which is Christ in you, the hope of glory. 28 Him we proclaim, warning every man and teaching every man in all wisdom, that we may present every man mature in Christ. 29 For this I toil, striving with all the energy which he mightily inspires within me.

[c] Or *from angels and men.*

PHILLIPS	N.E.B.

PHILLIPS

Who Christ is, and what he has done
1. 15

Now Christ is the visible expression of the invisible God. He existed before creation began, for it was through him that everything was made, whether spiritual or material, seen or unseen. Through him, and for him, also, were created power and dominion, ownership and authority. In fact, every single thing was created through, and for, him. He is both the first principle and the upholding principle of the whole scheme of creation. And now he is the head of the body which is the Church. Life from nothing began through him, and life from the dead began through him, and he is, therefore, justly called the Lord of all. It was in him that the full nature of God chose to live, and through him God planned to reconcile in his own person, as it were, everything on earth and everything in Heaven by virtue of the sacrifice of the cross.

And you yourselves, who were strangers to God, and, in fact, through the evil things you had done, his spiritual enemies, he has now reconciled through the death of his body on the cross, so that he might welcome you to his presence clean and pure, without blame or reproach. This reconciliation assumes, of course, that you maintain a firm position in the faith, and do not allow yourselves to be shifted away from the hope of the gospel, which you have heard, and which, indeed, the whole world is now having an opportunity of hearing.

My divine commission
1. 23b

I myself have been made a minister of the same gospel, and though it is true at this moment that I am suffering on behalf of you who have heard the gospel, yet I am far from sorry about it. Indeed, I am glad, because it gives me a chance to complete in my own sufferings something of the untold pains which Christ suffers on behalf of his body, the Church. For I am a minister of the Church by divine commission, a commission granted to me for your benefit and for a special purpose: that I might fully declare God's Word—that sacred mystery which up till now has been hidden in every age and every generation, but which is now as clear as daylight to those who love God. They are those to whom God has planned to give a vision of the full wonder and splendor of his secret plan for the nations. And the secret is simply this: Christ *in you!* Yes, Christ *in you* bringing with him the hope of all the glorious things to come.

To preach and teach Christ is everything to us
1. 28

So, naturally, we proclaim Christ! We warn everyone we meet, and we teach everyone we can, all that we know about him, so that, if possible, we may bring every man up to his full maturity in Christ Jesus. This is what I am working at all the time, with all the strength that God gives me.

N.E.B.

our sins forgiven. He is the image of the invisible God; his is the primacy over[a] all created things. In him everything in heaven and on earth was created, not only things visible but also the invisible orders of thrones, sovereignties, authorities, and powers: the whole universe has been created through him and for him. And he exists before everything, and all things are held together in him. He is, moreover, the head of the body, the church. He is its origin, the first to return from the dead, to be in all things alone supreme. For in him the complete being of God, by God's own choice, came to dwell. Through him God chose to reconcile the whole universe to himself, making peace through the shedding of his blood upon the cross—to reconcile all things, whether on earth or in heaven, through him alone.

Formerly you were yourselves estranged from God; you were his enemies in heart and mind, and your deeds were evil. But now by Christ's death in his body of flesh and blood God has reconciled you to himself, so that he may present you before himself as dedicated men, without blemish and innocent in his sight. Only you must continue in your faith, firm on your foundations, never to be dislodged from the hope offered in the gospel which you heard. This is the gospel which has been proclaimed in the whole creation under heaven; and I, Paul, have become its minister.

It is now my happiness to suffer for you. This is my way of helping to complete, in my poor human flesh, the full tale of Christ's afflictions still to be endured, for the sake of his body which is the church. I became its servant by virtue of the task assigned to me by God for your benefit: to deliver his message in full; to announce the secret hidden for long ages and through many generations, but now disclosed to God's people, to whom it was his will to make it known—to make known how rich and glorious it is among all nations. The secret is this: Christ in[b] you, the hope of a glory to come.

He it is whom we proclaim. We admonish everyone without distinction, we instruct everyone in all the ways of wisdom, so as to present each one of you as a mature member of Christ's body. To this end I am toiling strenuously with all the energy and power of Christ at work in me.

[a] *Or* image of the invisible God, born before . . .
[b] *Or* among.

K.J.V.

2 For I would that ye knew what great conflict I have for you, and *for* them at Laodicea, and *for* as many as have not seen my face in the flesh; 2 That their hearts might be comforted, being knit together in love, and unto all riches of the full assurance of understanding, to the acknowledgment of the mystery of God, and of the Father, and of Christ; 3 In whom are hid all the treasures of wisdom and knowledge. 4And this I say, lest any man should beguile you with enticing words. 5 For though I be absent in the flesh, yet am I with you in the spirit, joying and beholding your order, and the steadfastness of your faith in Christ. 6As ye have therefore received Christ Jesus the Lord, *so* walk ye in him: 7 Rooted and built up in him, and stablished in the faith, as ye have been taught, abounding therein with thanksgiving. 8 Beware lest any man spoil you through philosophy and vain deceit, after the tradition of men, after the rudiments of the world, and not after Christ. 9 For in him dwelleth all the fulness of the Godhead bodily. 10And ye are complete in him, which is the head of all principality and power: 11 In whom also ye are circumcised with the circumcision made without hands, in putting off the body of the sins of the flesh by the circumcision of Christ: 12 Buried with him in baptism, wherein also ye are risen with *him* through the faith of the operation of God, who hath raised him from the dead. 13And you, being dead in your sins and the uncircumcision of your flesh, hath he quickened together with him, having forgiven you all trespasses; 14 Blotting out the handwriting of ordinances that was against us, which was contrary to us, and took it out of the way, nailing it to his cross; 15*And* having spoiled principalities and powers, he made a shew of them openly, triumphing over them in it. 16 Let no man therefore judge you in meat, or in drink, or in

R.S.V.

2 For I want you to know how greatly I strive for you, and for those at Laodicea, and for all who have not seen my face, 2 that their hearts may be encouraged as they are knit together in love, to have all the riches of assured understanding and the knowledge of God's mystery, of Christ, 3 in whom are hid all the treasures of wisdom and knowledge. 4 I say this in order that no one may delude you with beguiling speech. 5 For though I am absent in body, yet I am with you in spirit, rejoicing to see your good order and the firmness of your faith in Christ.

6 As therefore you received Christ Jesus the Lord, so live in him, 7 rooted and built up in him and established in the faith, just as you were taught, abounding in thanksgiving.

8 See to it that no one makes a prey of you by philosophy and empty deceit, according to human tradition, according to the elemental spirits of the universe, and not according to Christ. 9 For in him the whole fulness of deity dwells bodily, 10 and you have come to fulness of life in him, who is the head of all rule and authority. 11 In him also you were circumcised with a circumcision made without hands, by putting off the body of flesh in the circumcision of Christ; 12 and you were buried with him in baptism, in which you were also raised with him through faith in the working of God, who raised him from the dead. 13And you, who were dead in trespasses and the uncircumcision of your flesh, God made alive together with him, having forgiven us all our trespasses, 14 having canceled the bond which stood against us with its legal demands; this he set aside, nailing it to the cross. 15 He disarmed the principalities and powers and made a public example of them, triumphing over them in him.[d]

16 Therefore let no one pass judgment on you in questions of food and drink or with re-

---

[d] Or *in it* (that is, the cross).

PHILLIPS

I wish you could understand how deep is my anxiety for you, and for those at Laodicea, and for all who have never met me. How I long that you may be encouraged, and find out more and more how strong are the bonds of Christian love. How I long for you to grow more certain in your knowledge and more sure in your grasp of God himself. May your spiritual experience become richer as you see more and more fully God's great secret, Christ himself! For it is *in him,* and in him alone, that men will find all the treasures of wisdom and knowledge.

Let me warn you against   2. 4
"intellectuals"

I write like this to prevent you from being led astray by someone or other's attractive arguments. For though I am a long way away from you in body, in spirit I am by your side, watching like a proud father the solid steadfastness of your faith in Christ. Just as you received Christ Jesus the Lord, so go on living in him—in simple faith. Grow out of him as a plant grows out of the soil it is planted in, becoming more and more sure of the faith as you were taught it, and your lives will overflow with joy and thankfulness.

Be careful that nobody spoils your faith through intellectualism or high-sounding nonsense. Such stuff is at best founded on men's ideas of the nature of the world, and disregards Christ! Yet it is in him that God gives a full and complete expression of himself (within the physical limits that he set himself in Christ). Moreover, your own completeness is only realized in him, who is the authority over all authorities, and the supreme power over all powers.

The old Law can't condemn   2. 11
you now

In Christ you were circumcised, not by any physical act, but by being set free from the sins of the flesh by virtue of Christ's circumcision. You, so to speak, shared in that, just as in baptism you shared in his death, and in him are sharing the miracle of rising again to new life— and all this because you have faith in the tremendous power of God, who raised Christ from the dead. You, who were spiritually dead because of your sins and your uncircumcision (that is, the fact that you were outside the Law), God has now made to share in the very life of Christ! He has forgiven you all our sins: Christ has utterly wiped out the damning evidence of broken laws and commandments which always hung over our heads, and has completely annulled it by nailing it over his own head on the cross. And then, having drawn the sting of all the powers ranged against us, he exposed them, shattered, empty and defeated, in his final glorious triumphant act!

It is the spiritual, not the material,   2. 16
attitude which matters

In view of these tremendous facts, don't let anyone worry you by criticizing what you eat

N.E.B.

2 For I want you to know how strenuous are my exertions for you and the Laodiceans and all who have never set eyes on me. I want them to continue in good heart and in the unity of love, and to come to the full wealth of conviction which understanding brings, and grasp God's secret. That secret is Christ himself; in him lie hidden all God's treasures of wisdom and knowledge. I tell you this to save you from being talked *ᵃ* into error by specious arguments. For though absent in body, I am with you in spirit, and rejoice to see your orderly array and the firm front which your faith in Christ presents.

Therefore, since Jesus was delivered to you as Christ and Lord, live your lives in union with him. Be rooted in him; be built in him; be consolidated in the faith you were taught;*ᵇ* let your hearts overflow with thankfulness. Be on your guard; do not let your minds be captured by hollow and delusive speculations, based on traditions of man-made teaching and centred on the elemental spirits*ᶜ* of the world and not on Christ.

For it is in Christ that the complete being of the Godhead dwells embodied,*ᵈ* and in him you have been brought to completion. Every power and authority in the universe is subject to him as Head. In him also you were circumcised, not in a physical sense, but by being divested of the lower nature; this is Christ's way of circumcision. For in baptism*ᵉ* you were buried with him, in baptism also you were raised to life with him through your faith in the active power of God who raised him from the dead. And although you were dead because of your sins and because you were morally uncircumcised, he has made you alive with Christ. For he has forgiven us all our sins; he has cancelled the bond which pledged us to the decrees of the law. It stood against us, but he has set it aside, nailing it to the cross. On that cross he discarded the cosmic powers and authorities like a garment; he made a public spectacle of them and led them*ᶠ* as captives in his triumphal procession.

Allow no one therefore to take you to task about what you eat or drink, or over the observ-

---

[a] *Or* What I mean is this: no one must talk you . . . [b] *Or* by your faith, as you were taught. [c] *Or* rudimentary notions. [d] *Or* corporately. [e] *Or* . . . nature, in the very circumcision of Christ himself; for in baptism . . . [f] *Or* he stripped himself of his physical body, and thereby boldly made a spectacle of the cosmic powers and authorities, and led them . . . ; *or* he despoiled the cosmic powers and authorities, and boldly made a spectacle of them, leading them . . .

K.J.V.

respect of a holyday, or of the new moon, or of the sabbath *days:* 17 Which are a shadow of things to come; but the body *is* of Christ. 18 Let no man beguile you of your reward in a voluntary humility and worshipping of angels, intruding into those things which he hath not seen, vainly puffed up by his fleshly mind, 19And not holding the Head, from which all the body by joints and bands having nourishment ministered, and knit together, increaseth with the increase of God. 20 Wherefore if ye be dead with Christ from the rudiments of the world, why, as though living in the world, are ye subject to ordinances, 21 (Touch not; taste not; handle not; 22 Which all are to perish with the using;) after the commandments and doctrines of men? 23 Which things have indeed a shew of wisdom in willworship, and humility, and neglecting of the body; not in any honour to the satisfying of the flesh.

3 If ye then be risen with Christ, seek those things which are above, where Christ sitteth on the right hand of God. 2 Set your affection on things above, not on things on the earth. 3 For ye are dead, and your life is hid with Christ in God. 4 When Christ, *who is* our life, shall appear, then shall ye also appear with him in glory. 5 Mortify therefore your members which are upon the earth; fornication, uncleanness, inordinate affection, evil concupiscence, and covetousness, which is idolatry: 6 For which things' sake the wrath of God cometh on the children of disobedience: 7 In the which ye also walked sometime, when ye lived in them. 8 But now ye also put off all these; anger, wrath, malice, blasphemy, filthy communication out of your mouth. 9 Lie not one to another, seeing that ye have put off the old man with his deeds; 10And have put on the new *man,* which is renewed in knowledge after the image of him that created him: 11 Where there is neither Greek nor Jew, circumcision nor uncircumcision, Barbarian, Scythian, bond *nor* free: but Christ *is* all, and in all. 12 Put on therefore, as the elect of God, holy and beloved, bowels of mercies, kindness, humbleness of mind, meekness, longsuffering; 13 Forbearing one another, and forgiving one another, if any

R.S.V.

gard to a festival or a new moon or a sabbath. 17 These are only a shadow of what is to come; but the substance belongs to Christ. 18 Let no one disqualify you, insisting on self-abasement and worship of angels, taking his stand on visions, puffed up without reason by his sensuous mind, 19 and not holding fast to the Head, from whom the whole body, nourished and knit together through its joints and ligaments, grows with a growth that is from God.
20 If with Christ you died to the elemental spirits of the universe, why do you live as if you still belonged to the world? Why do you submit to regulations, 21 "Do not handle, Do not taste, Do not touch" 22 (referring to things which all perish as they are used), according to human precepts and doctrines? 23 These have indeed an appearance of wisdom in promoting rigor of devotion and self-abasement and severity to the body, but they are of no value in checking the indulgence of the flesh.*

3 If then you have been raised with Christ, seek the things that are above, where Christ is, seated at the right hand of God. 2 Set your minds on things that are above, not on things that are on earth. 3 For you have died, and your life is hid with Christ in God. 4 When Christ who is our life appears, then you also will appear with him in glory.
5 Put to death therefore what is earthly in you: immorality, impurity, passion, evil desire, and covetousness, which is idolatry. 6 On account of these the wrath of God is coming.ᶠ 7 In these you once walked, when you lived in them. 8 But now put them all away: anger, wrath, malice, slander, and foul talk from your mouth. 9 Do not lie to one another, seeing that you have put off the old nature with its practices 10 and have put on the new nature, which is being renewed in knowledge after the image of its creator. 11 Here there cannot be Greek and Jew, circumcised and uncircumcised, barbarian, Scythian, slave, free man, but Christ is all, and in all.
12 Put on then, as God's chosen ones, holy and beloved, compassion, kindness, lowliness, meekness, and patience, 13 forbearing one another and, if one has a complaint against an-

[e] Or *are of no value, serving only to indulge the flesh.* [f] Other ancient authorities add *upon the sons of disobedience.*

or drink, or what holy days you ought to observe, or bothering you over new moons or Sabbaths. All these things have at most only a symbolical value: the solid fact is Christ. Nor let any man cheat you of your joy in Christ by persuading you to make yourselves "humble" and fall down and worship angels. Such a man, inflated by an unspiritual imagination, is pushing his way into matters he knows nothing about, and in his cleverness forgetting the head. It is from the head alone that the body, by natural channels, is nourished and built up and grows according to God's laws of growth.

So if, through your faith in Christ, you are dead to the principles of this world's life, why, as if you were still part and parcel of this worldwide system, do you take the slightest notice of these purely human prohibitions—"Don't touch this," "Don't taste that" and "Don't handle the other"? "This," "that" and "the other" will all pass away after use! I know that these regulations look wise with their self-inspired efforts at worship, their policy of self-humbling, and their studied neglect of the body. But in actual practice they do honor, not to God, but to man's own pride.

ance of festival, new moon, or sabbath. These are no more than a shadow of what was to come; the solid reality is Christ's. You are not to be disqualified by the decision of people who go in for self-mortification and angel-worship, and try to enter into some vision of their own. Such people, bursting with the futile conceit of worldly minds, lose hold upon the Head; yet it is from the Head that the whole body, with all its joints and ligaments, receives its supplies, and thus knit together grows according to God's design.

Did you not die with Christ and pass beyond reach of the elemental spirits[a] of the world? Then why behave as though you were still living the life of the world? Why let people dictate to you: 'Do not handle this, do not taste that, do not touch the other'—all of them things that must perish as soon as they are used? That is to follow merely human injunctions and teaching. True, it has an air of wisdom, with its forced piety, its self-mortification, and its severity to the body; but it is of no use at all in combating sensuality.

*Live a new life by the power
of the risen Christ* **3. 1**

If you are then "risen" with Christ, reach out for the highest gifts of Heaven, where Christ reigns in power. Give your heart to the heavenly things, not to the passing things of earth. For, as far as this world is concerned, you are already dead, and your true life is a hidden one in God, through Christ. One day, Christ, the secret center of our lives, will show himself openly, and you will all share in that magnificent dénouement.

In so far, then, as you have to live upon this earth, consider yourselves dead to worldly contacts: have nothing to do with sexual immorality, dirty-mindedness, uncontrolled passion, evil desire, and the lust for other people's goods, which last, remember, is as serious a sin as idolatry. It is because of these very things that the holy anger of God falls upon those who refuse to obey him. And never forget that you had your part in those dreadful things when you lived that old life.

But now, put all these things behind you. No more evil temper or furious rage: no more evil thoughts or words about others, no more evil thoughts or words about God, and no more filthy conversation. Don't tell one another lies any more, for you have finished with the old man and all he did and have begun life as the new man, who is out to learn what he ought to be, according to the plan of God. In this new man of God's design there is no distinction between Greek and Hebrew, Jew or gentile, foreigner or savage, slave or free man. Christ is all that matters, for Christ lives in them all.

3 Were you not raised to life with Christ? Then aspire to the realm above, where Christ is, seated at the right hand of God, and let your thoughts dwell on that higher realm, not on this earthly life. I repeat, you died; and now your life lies hidden with Christ in God. When Christ, who is our life, is manifested, then you too will be manifested with him in glory.

Then put to death those parts of you which belong to the earth—fornication, indecency, lust, foul cravings, and the ruthless greed which is nothing less than idolatry. Because of these, God's dreadful judgement is impending; and in the life you once lived these are the ways you yourselves followed. But now you yourselves must lay aside all anger, passion, malice, cursing, filthy talk—have done with them! Stop lying to one another, now that you have discarded the old nature with its deeds and have put on the new nature, which is being constantly renewed in the image of its Creator and brought to know God. There is no question here of Greek and Jew, circumcised and uncircumcised, barbarian, Scythian, freeman, slave; but Christ is all, and is in all.

Then put on the garments that suit God's chosen people, his own, his beloved: compassion, kindness, humility, gentleness, patience. Be forbearing with one another, and forgiving, where any of you has cause for complaint: you must

The expression of the new life (i) **3. 12**

As, therefore, God's picked representatives of the new humanity, purified and beloved of God himself, be merciful in action, kindly in heart, humble in mind. Accept life, and be most patient and tolerant with one another, always ready to forgive if you have a difference with anyone.

[a] *Or* rudimentary notions.

K.J.V.

man have a quarrel against any: even as Christ forgave you, so also *do* ye. 14And above all these things *put on* charity, which is the bond of perfectness. 15And let the peace of God rule in your hearts, to the which also ye are called in one body; and be ye thankful. 16 Let the word of Christ dwell in you richly in all wisdom; teaching and admonishing one another in psalms and hymns and spiritual songs, singing with grace in your hearts to the Lord. 17And whatsoever ye do in word or deed, *do* all in the name of the Lord Jesus, giving thanks to God and the Father by him. 18 Wives, submit yourselves unto your own husbands, as it is fit in the Lord. 19 Husbands, love *your* wives, and be not bitter against them. 20 Children, obey *your* parents in all things: for this is well pleasing unto the Lord. 21 Fathers, provoke not your children *to anger*, lest they be discouraged. 22 Servants, obey in all things *your* masters according to the flesh; not with eyeservice, as menpleasers; but in singleness of heart, fearing God: 23And whatsoever ye do, do *it* heartily, as to the Lord, and not unto men; 24 Knowing that of the Lord ye shall receive the reward of the inheritance: for ye serve the Lord Christ. 25 But he that doeth wrong shall receive for the wrong which he hath done: and there is no respect of persons.

4 Masters, give unto *your* servants that which is just and equal; knowing that ye also have a Master in heaven. 2 Continue in prayer, and watch in the same with thanksgiving; 3 Withal praying also for us, that God would open unto us a door of utterance, to speak the mystery of Christ, for which I am also in bonds: 4 That I may make it manifest, as I ought to speak. 5 Walk in wisdom toward them that are without, redeeming the time. 6 Let your speech *be* always with grace, seasoned with salt, that ye may know how ye ought to answer every man. 7All my state shall Tychicus declare unto you, *who is* a beloved brother, and a faithful minister and fellow servant in the Lord: 8 Whom I have sent unto

R.S.V.

other, forgiving each other; as the Lord has forgiven you, so you also must forgive. 14And above all these put on love, which binds everything together in perfect harmony. 15And let the peace of Christ rule in your hearts, to which indeed you were called in the one body. And be thankful. 16 Let the word of Christ dwell in you richly, as you teach and admonish one another in all wisdom, and as you sing psalms and hymns and spiritual songs with thankfulness in your hearts to God. 17And whatever you do, in word or deed, do everything in the name of the Lord Jesus, giving thanks to God the Father through him.

18 Wives, be subject to your husbands, as is fitting in the Lord. 19 Husbands, love your wives, and do not be harsh with them. 20 Children, obey your parents in everything, for this pleases the Lord. 21 Fathers, do not provoke your children, lest they become discouraged. 22 Slaves, obey in everything those who are your earthly masters, not with eyeservice, as men-pleasers, but in singleness of heart, fearing the Lord. 23 Whatever your task, work heartily, as serving the Lord and not men, 24 knowing that from the Lord you will receive the inheritance as your reward; you are serving the Lord Christ. 25 For the wrongdoer will be paid back for the wrong he has done, and there is no partiality.

4 Masters, treat your slaves justly and fairly, knowing that you also have a Master in heaven.
2 Continue steadfastly in prayer, being watchful in it with thanksgiving; 3 and pray for us also, that God may open to us a door for the word, to declare the mystery of Christ, on account of which I am in prison, 4 that I may make it clear, as I ought to speak.
5 Conduct yourselves wisely toward outsiders, making the most of the time. 6 Let your speech always be gracious, seasoned with salt, so that you may know how you ought to answer every one.

7 Tychicus will tell you all about my affairs; he is a beloved brother and faithful minister and fellow servant in the Lord. 8 I have sent him

PHILLIPS

Forgive as freely as the Lord has forgiven you. And, above everything else, be truly loving, for love is the golden chain of all the virtues. Let the peace of Christ rule in your hearts, remembering that as members of the one body you are called to live in harmony, and never forget to be thankful for what God has done for you.

Let Christ's teaching live in your hearts, making you rich in the true wisdom. Teach and help one another along the right road with your psalms and hymns and Christian songs, singing God's praises with joyful hearts. And whatever work you may have to do, do everything in the name of the Lord Jesus, thanking God the Father through him.

The expression of the new life (ii)   3. 18

Wives, adapt yourselves to your husbands, that your marriage may be a Christian unity. Husbands, be sure you give your wives much love and sympathy; don't let bitterness or resentment spoil your marriage. As for you children, your duty is to obey your parents, for at your age this is one of the best things you can do to show your love for the Lord. Fathers, don't overcorrect your children, or they will grow up feeling inferior and frustrated. Slaves, your job is to obey your masters, not with the idea of currying favor, but as a sincere expression of your devotion to the Lord. Whatever you do, put your whole heart and soul into it, as into work done for the Lord, and not merely for men—knowing that your real reward, a heavenly one, will come from the Lord, since you are actually employed by the Lord Christ, and not just by your earthly master.

But the wicked man will be punished for his misdeeds, and naturally no distinction will be made between master and man. Remember, then, you employers, that your responsibility is to be fair and just toward those whom you employ, never forgetting that you yourselves have a heavenly employer.

Some simple, practical advice   4. 2

Always maintain the habit of prayer: be both alert and thankful as you pray. Include us in your prayers, please, that God may open for us a door for the entrance of the gospel. Pray that we may talk freely of the mystery of Christ (for which talking I am at present in chains), and that I may make that mystery plain to men, which I know is my duty.

Be wise in your behavior toward non-Christians, and make the best possible use of your time. Speak pleasantly to them, but never sentimentally, and learn how to give a proper answer to every questioner.

Greetings and farewell   4. 7

Tychicus (a well loved brother, a faithful minister and a fellow servant of the Lord) will tell you all about my present circumstances. This is partly why I am sending him to you. The other

N.E.B.

forgive as the Lord forgave you. To crown all, there must be love, to bind all together and complete the whole. Let Christ's peace be arbiter in your hearts: to this peace you were called as members of a single body. And be filled with gratitude. Let the message of Christ dwell among you in all its richness. Instruct and admonish each other with the utmost wisdom. Sing thankfully in your hearts to God,[a] with psalms and hymns and spiritual songs. Whatever you are doing, whether you speak or act, do everything in the name of the Lord Jesus, giving thanks to God the Father through him.

Wives, be subject to your husbands: that is your Christian duty. Husbands, love your wives and do not be harsh with them. Children, obey your parents in everything, for that is pleasing to God and is the Christian way. Fathers, do not exasperate your children, for fear they grow disheartened. Slaves, give entire obedience to your earthly masters, not merely with an outward show of service, to curry favour with men, but with single-mindedness, out of reverence for the Lord. Whatever you are doing, put your whole heart into it, as if you were doing it for the Lord and not for men, knowing that there is a Master who will give you your heritage as a reward for your service. Christ is the Master whose slaves you must be. Dishonesty will be requited, and he has no favourites.

4 Masters, be just and fair to your slaves, knowing that you too have a Master in heaven.

Persevere in prayer, with mind awake and thankful heart; and include a prayer for us, that God may give us an opening for preaching, to tell the secret of Christ; that indeed is why I am now in prison. Pray that I may make the secret plain, as it is my duty to do.

Behave wisely towards those outside your own number; use the present opportunity to the full. Let your conversation be always gracious, and never insipid; study how best to talk with each person you meet.

You will hear all about my affairs from Tychicus, our dear brother and trustworthy helper and fellow-servant in the Lord's work. I

[a] Some witnesses read the Lord.

K.J.V.

you for the same purpose, that he might know your estate, and comfort your hearts; 9 With Onesimus, a faithful and beloved brother, who is *one* of you. They shall make known unto you all things which *are done* here. 10Aristarchus my fellow prisoner saluteth you, and Marcus, sister's son to Barnabas, (touching whom ye received commandments: if he come unto you, receive him;) 11And Jesus, which is called Justus, who are of the circumcision. These only *are my* fellow workers unto the kingdom of God, which have been a comfort unto me. 12 Epaphras, who is *one* of you, a servant of Christ, saluteth you, always labouring fervently for you in prayers, that ye may stand perfect and complete in all the will of God. 13 For I bear him record, that he hath a great zeal for you, and them *that are* in Laodicea, and them in Hierapolis. 14 Luke, the beloved physician, and Demas, greet you. 15 Salute the brethren which are in Laodicea, and Nymphas, and the church which is in his house. 16And when this epistle is read among you, cause that it be read also in the church of the Laodiceans; and that ye likewise read the *epistle* from Laodicea. 17And say to Archippus, Take heed to the ministry which thou hast received in the Lord, that thou fulfil it. 18 The salutation by the hand of me Paul. Remember my bonds. Grace *be* with you. Amen.

Written from Rome to the Colossians by Tychicus and Onesimus.

R.S.V.

to you for this very purpose, that you may know how we are and that he may encourage your hearts, 9 and with him Onesimus, the faithful and beloved brother, who is one of yourselves. They will tell you of everything that has taken place here.

10 Aristarchus my fellow prisoner greets you, and Mark the cousin of Barnabas (concerning whom you have received instructions—if he comes to you, receive him), 11 and Jesus who is called Justus. These are the only men of the circumcision among my fellow workers for the kingdom of God, and they have been a comfort to me. 12 Epaphras, who is one of yourselves, a servant*g* of Christ Jesus, greets you, always remembering you earnestly in his prayers, that you may stand mature and fully assured in all the will of God. 13 For I bear him witness that he has worked hard for you and for those in Laodicea and in Hierapolis. 14 Luke the beloved physician and Demas greet you. 15 Give my greetings to the brethren at Laodicea, and to Nympha and the church in her house. 16And when this letter has been read among you, have it read also in the church of the Laodiceans; and see that you read also the letter from Laodicea. 17And say to Archippus, "See that you fulfil the ministry which you have received in the Lord."

18 I, Paul, write this greeting with my own hand. Remember my fetters. Grace be with you.

[g] Or *slave*.

reasons are that you may find out how we are all getting on, and that he may put new heart into you. With him is Onesimus, one of your own congregation (well loved and faithful, too). Between them they will tell you of conditions and activities here.

Aristarchus, who is also in prison here, sends greetings, and so does Barnabas' cousin, Mark. I believe I told you before about him; if he comes to you, make him welcome. Jesus Justus is here too. Only these few fellow Jews are working with me for the kingdom, but what a help they have been!

Epaphras, another member of your church, and a real servant of Christ Jesus, sends his greeting. He works hard for you even here, for he prays constantly and earnestly for you, that you may become mature Christians, and may fulfill God's will for you. From my own observation I can tell you that he has a real passion for your welfare, and for that of the churches at Laodicea and Hierapolis.

Luke, our beloved doctor, and Demas send their best wishes. My own greetings to the Christians in Laodicea, and to Nymphas and the congregation who meet in her house.

When you have had this letter read in your church, see that the Laodiceans have it read in their church too; and see that you read the letter I have written to them.

A brief message to Archippus: God ordained you to your work—see that you don't fail him!

My personal greeting to you written by myself.

Don't forget I'm in prison. Grace be with you.

PAUL

am sending him to you on purpose to let you know all about us and to put fresh heart into you. With him comes Onesimus, our trustworthy and dear brother, who is one of yourselves. They will tell you all the news here.

Aristarchus, Christ's captive like myself, sends his greetings; so does Mark, the cousin of Barnabas (you have had instructions about him; if he comes, make him welcome), and Jesus Justus. Of the Jewish Christians, these are the only ones who work with me for the kingdom of God, and they have been a great comfort to me. Greetings from Epaphras, servant of Christ, who is one of yourselves. He prays hard for you all the time, that you may stand fast, ripe in conviction[a] and wholly devoted to doing God's will. For I can vouch for him, that he works tirelessly for you and the people at Laodicea and Hierapolis. Greetings to you from our dear friend Luke, the doctor, and from Demas. Give our greetings to the brothers at Laodicea, and Nympha[b] and the congregation at her[c] house. And when this letter is read among you, see that it is also read to the congregation at Laodicea, and that you in return read the one from Laodicea. This special word to Archippus: 'Attend to the duty entrusted to you in the Lord's service, and discharge it to the full.'

This greeting is in my own hand—PAUL. Remember I am in prison. God's grace be with you.

[a] *Or* stand fast, mature and complete . . . [b] *Or* Nymphas. [c] *Some witnesses read* his.

K.J.V.

THE FIRST EPISTLE
OF PAUL THE APOSTLE
TO THE
THESSALONIANS

1 Paul, and Silvanus, and Timotheus, unto the church of the Thessalonians *which is* in God the Father, and *in* the Lord Jesus Christ: Grace *be* unto you, and peace, from God our Father, and the Lord Jesus Christ. 2 We give thanks to God always for you all, making mention of you in our prayers; 3 Remembering without ceasing your work of faith, and labour of love, and patience of hope in our Lord Jesus Christ, in the sight of God and our Father; 4 Knowing, brethren beloved, your election of God. 5 For our gospel came not unto you in word only, but also in power, and in the Holy Ghost, and in much assurance; as ye know what manner of men we were among you for your sake. 6And ye became followers of us, and of the Lord, having received the word in much affliction, with joy of the Holy Ghost: 7 So that ye were ensamples to all that believe in Macedonia and Achaia. 8 For from you sounded out the word of the Lord not only in Macedonia and Achaia, but also in every place your faith to God-ward is spread abroad; so that we need not to speak any thing. 9 For they themselves shew of us what manner of entering in we had unto you, and how ye turned to God from idols to serve the living and true God; 10And to wait for his Son from heaven, whom he raised from the dead, *even* Jesus, which delivered us from the wrath to come.

2 For yourselves, brethren, know our entrance in unto you, that it was not in vain: 2 But even after that we had suffered before, and were shamefully entreated, as ye know, at Philippi, we were bold in our God to speak unto you the gospel of God with much contention. 3 For our exhortation *was* not of deceit, nor of uncleanness, nor in guile: 4 But as we were allowed of God to be put in trust with the gospel, even so we speak; not as pleasing men, but God, which trieth our hearts. 5 For neither at any time used

R.S.V.

THE FIRST
LETTER OF PAUL TO THE
THESSALONIANS

1 Paul, Silvanus, and Timothy,
To the church of the Thessalonians in God the Father and the Lord Jesus Christ:
Grace to you and peace.

2 We give thanks to God always for you all, constantly mentioning you in our prayers, 3 remembering before our God and Father your work of faith and labor of love and steadfastness of hope in our Lord Jesus Christ. 4 For we know, brethren beloved by God, that he has chosen you; 5 for our gospel came to you not only in word, but also in power and in the Holy Spirit and with full conviction. You know what kind of men we proved to be among you for your sake. 6And you became imitators of us and of the Lord, for you received the word in much affliction, with joy inspired by the Holy Spirit; 7 so that you became an example to all the believers in Macedonia and in Achaia. 8 For not only has the word of the Lord sounded forth from you in Macedonia and Achaia, but your faith in God has gone forth everywhere, so that we need not say anything. 9 For they themselves report concerning us what a welcome we had among you, and how you turned to God from idols, to serve a living and true God, 10 and to wait for his Son from heaven, whom he raised from the dead, Jesus who delivers us from the wrath to come.

2 For you yourselves know, brethren, that our visit to you was not in vain; 2 but though we had already suffered and been shamefully treated at Philippi, as you know, we had courage in our God to declare to you the gospel of God in the face of great opposition. 3 For our appeal does not spring from error or uncleanness, nor is it made with guile; 4 but just as we have been approved by God to be entrusted with the gospel, so we speak, not to please men, but to please God who tests our hearts. 5 For we

632

THE FIRST LETTER TO THE CHRISTIANS IN

THESSALONICA

THE FIRST LETTER OF PAUL TO THE

THESSALONIANS

Hope and Discipline

To the church of the Thessalonians, founded on God the Father and the Lord Jesus Christ, grace and peace from Paul, Silvanus and Timothy.

Your faith cheers us and   *1. 2*
encourages many others

We are always thankful as we pray for you all, for we never forget that your faith has meant solid achievement, your love has meant hard work, and the hope that you have in our Lord Jesus Christ means sheer dogged endurance in the life that you live before God, the Father of us all.

We know that God not only loves you but has selected you for a special purpose. For we remember how our gospel came to you not as mere words, but as a message with power behind it—the effectual power, in fact, of the Holy Spirit. You know how we lived among you. You remember how you set yourselves to copy us, and through us, the Lord himself. You remember how, although accepting the message meant bitter persecution, yet you experienced the joy of the Holy Spirit. You thus became examples to all who believe in Macedonia and Achaia. You have become a sort of sounding board from which the Word of the Lord has rung out, not only in Macedonia and Achaia but everywhere that the story of your faith in God has become known. We find we don't have to tell people about it. They tell *us* the story of our coming to you: how you turned from idols to serve the true living God, and how your whole lives now look forward to the coming of his Son from Heaven—the Son Jesus, whom God raised from the dead, and who personally delivered us from the judgment which hung over our heads.

The spirit of our visit to you   *2. 1*
is well known to you all

My brothers, you know from your own experience that our visit to you was no failure. We had, as you also know, been treated abominably at Philippi, and we came on to you only because God gave us courage. We came to tell you the gospel, whatever the opposition might be.

Our message to you is true, our motives are pure, our conduct is absolutely aboveboard. We speak under the solemn sense of being entrusted by God with the gospel. We do not aim to please men, but to please God who knows us through and through. No one could ever say,

1 From Paul, Silvanus, and Timothy to the congregation of Thessalonians who belong to God the Father and the Lord Jesus Christ. Grace to you and peace.

We always thank God for you all, and mention you in our prayers continually. We call to mind, before our God and Father, how your faith has shown itself in action, your love in labour, and your hope of our Lord Jesus Christ in fortitude. We are certain, brothers beloved by God, that he has chosen you and that[a] when we brought you the Gospel, we brought it not in mere words but in the power of the Holy Spirit, and with strong conviction, as you know well. That is the kind of men we were at Thessalonica, and it was for your sake.

And you, in your turn, followed the example set by us and by the Lord; the welcome you gave the message meant grave suffering for you, yet you rejoiced in the Holy Spirit; thus you have become a model for all believers in Macedonia and in Achaia. From Thessalonica the word of the Lord rang out; and not in Macedonia and Achaia alone, but everywhere your faith in God has reached men's ears. No words of ours are needed, for they themselves spread the news of our visit to you and its effect: how you turned from idols, to be servants of the living and true God, and to wait expectantly for the appearance from heaven of his Son Jesus, whom he raised from the dead, Jesus our deliverer from the terrors of judgement to come.

2 You know for yourselves, brothers, that our visit to you was not fruitless. Far from it; after all the injury and outrage which to your knowledge we had suffered at Philippi, we declared the gospel of God to you frankly and fearlessly, by the help of our God. A hard struggle it was. Indeed, the appeal we make never springs from error or base motive; there is no attempt to deceive; but God has approved us as fit to be entrusted with the Gospel, and on those terms we speak. We do not curry favour with men; we seek only the favour of God, who is continually testing our hearts. Our words

[a] *Or* . . . chosen you, because . . .

633

K.J.V.

we flattering words, as ye know, nor a cloak of covetousness; God *is* witness: 6 Nor of men sought we glory, neither of you, nor *yet* of others, when we might have been burdensome, as the apostles of Christ. 7 But we were gentle among you, even as a nurse cherisheth her children: 8 So being affectionately desirous of you, we were willing to have imparted unto you, not the gospel of God only, but also our own souls, because ye were dear unto us. 9 For ye remember, brethren, our labour and travail: for labouring night and day, because we would not be chargeable unto any of you, we preached unto you the gospel of God. 10 Ye *are* witnesses, and God *also,* how holily and justly and unblameably we behaved ourselves among you that believe: 11As ye know how we exhorted and comforted and charged every one of you, as a father *doth* his children, 12 That ye would walk worthy of God, who hath called you unto his kingdom and glory. 13 For this cause also thank we God without ceasing, because, when ye received the word of God which ye heard of us, ye received *it* not *as* the word of men, but, as it is in truth, the word of God, which effectually worketh also in you that believe. 14 For ye, brethren, became followers of the churches of God which in Judea are in Christ Jesus: for ye also have suffered like things of your own countrymen, even as they *have* of the Jews: 15 Who both killed the Lord Jesus, and their own prophets, and have persecuted us; and they please not God, and are contrary to all men: 16 Forbidding us to speak to the Gentiles that they might be saved, to fill up their sins always: for the wrath is come upon them to the uttermost. 17 But we, brethren, being taken from you for a short time in presence, not in heart, endeavoured the more abundantly to see your face with great desire. 18 Wherefore we would have come unto you, even I Paul, once and again; but Satan hindered us. 19 For what *is* our hope, or joy, or crown of rejoicing? *Are* not even ye in the presence of our Lord Jesus Christ at his coming? 20 For ye are our glory and joy.

R.S.V.

never used either words of flattery, as you know, or a cloak for greed, as God is witness; 6 nor did we seek glory from men, whether from you or from others, though we might have made demands as apostles of Christ. 7 But we were gentle *a* among you, like a nurse taking care of her children. 8 So, being affectionately desirous of you, we were ready to share with you not only the gospel of God but also our own selves, because you had become very dear to us.

9 For you remember our labor and toil, brethren; we worked night and day, that we might not burden any of you, while we preached to you the gospel of God. 10 You are witnesses, and God also, how holy and righteous and blameless was our behavior to you believers; 11 for you know how, like a father with his children, we exhorted each one of you and encouraged you and charged you 12 to lead a life worthy of God, who calls you into his own kingdom and glory.

13 And we also thank God constantly for this, that when you received the word of God which you heard from us, you accepted it not as the word of men but as what it really is, the word of God, which is at work in you believers. 14 For you, brethren, became imitators of the churches of God in Christ Jesus which are in Judea; for you suffered the same things from your own countrymen as they did from the Jews, 15 who killed both the Lord Jesus and the prophets, and drove us out, and displease God and oppose all men 16 by hindering us from speaking to the Gentiles that they may be saved —so as always to fill up the measure of their sins. But God's wrath has come upon them at last! *b*

17 But since we were bereft of you, brethren, for a short time, in person not in heart, we endeavored the more eagerly and with great desire to see you face to face; 18 because we wanted to come to you—I, Paul, again and again —but Satan hindered us. 19 For what is our hope or joy or crown of boasting before our Lord Jesus at his coming? Is it not you? 20 For you are our glory and joy.

[a] Other ancient authorities read *babes.* [b] Or *completely,* or *for ever.*

634

PHILLIPS

as again you know, that we used flattery to conceal greedy motives, and God himself is witness to our honesty. We made no attempt to win honor from men, either from you or from anybody else, though I suppose as Christ's own messengers we might have done so. Our attitude among you was one of tenderness, rather like that of a devoted nurse among her babies. Because we loved you, it was a joy to us to give you not only the gospel of God but our very hearts—so dear did you become to us. Our struggles and hard work, my brothers, must be still fresh in your minds. Day and night we worked so that our preaching of the gospel to you might not cost you a penny. You are witnesses, as is God himself, that our life among you believers was honest, straightforward and above criticism. You will remember how we dealt with each one of you personally, like a father with his own children, stimulating your faith and courage and giving you instruction. Our only object was to help you to live lives worthy of the God who has called you to share the splendor of his own kingdom.

And so we are continually thankful that when you heard us preach the Word of God you accepted it, not as a mere human message, but as it really is, God's Word, a power in the lives of you who believe.

You have experienced persecution 2. 14 like your Jewish brothers

For you, my brothers, fell into line with the churches of God which have come into being through Christ Jesus in Judaea. For when you suffered at the hands of your fellow countrymen you were sharing the experience of the Judaean Christian churches, who suffered persecution by the Jews. It was the Jews who killed their own prophets, the Jews who killed the Lord Jesus, and the Jews who drove out us, his messengers. Their present attitude is in opposition to both God and man. They refused to let us speak to those who were not Jews, to tell them the news of salvation. Alas, I fear they are completing the full tale of their sins, and the wrath of God is over their heads.

Absence has indeed made our 2. 17 hearts grow fonder

Since we have been physically separated from you, my brothers (though never for a moment separated in heart), we have longed all the more to see you face to face. Yes, I, Paul, have longed to come and see you more than once—but somehow Satan prevented our coming.

For who could take your place as our hope and joy and pride when Jesus comes? Who but you, as you will stand before him at his coming? Yes, you are indeed our pride and our joy!

N.E.B.

have never been flattering words, as you have cause to know; nor, as God is our witness, have they ever been a cloak for greed. We have never sought honour from men, from you or from anyone else, although as Christ's own envoys we might have made our weight felt; but we were as gentle with you as a nurse caring fondly for her children. With such yearning love we chose to impart to you not only the gospel of God but our very selves, so dear had you become to us. Remember, brothers, how we toiled and drudged. We worked for a living night and day, rather than be a burden to anyone, while we proclaimed before you the good news of God.

We call you to witness, yes and God himself, how devout and just and blameless was our behaviour towards you who are believers. As you well know, we dealt with you one by one, as a father deals with his children, appealing to you by encouragement, as well as by solemn injunctions, to live lives worthy of the God who calls you into his kingdom and glory.

This is why we thank God continually, because when we handed on God's message, you received it, not as the word of men, but as what it truly is, the very word of God at[a] work in you who hold the faith. You have fared like the congregations in Judaea, God's people in Christ Jesus. You have been treated by your countrymen as they are treated by the Jews, who killed the Lord Jesus and the prophets[b] and drove us out, the Jews who are heedless of God's will and enemies of their fellow-men, hindering us from speaking to the Gentiles to lead them to salvation. All this time they have been making up the full measure of their guilt, and now retribution has overtaken them for good and all.[c]

My friends, when for a short spell you were lost to us—lost to sight, not to our hearts—we were exceedingly anxious to see you again. So we did propose to come to Thessalonica—I, Paul, more than once—but Satan thwarted us. For after all, what hope or joy or crown of pride is there for us, what indeed but you, when we stand before our Lord Jesus at his coming? It is you who are indeed our glory and our joy.

---

[a] Or word of God who is at . . . [b] Some witnesses read their own prophets. [c] Or now at last retribution has overtaken them.

K.J.V.

3 Wherefore when we could no longer forbear, we thought it good to be left at Athens alone; 2And sent Timotheus, our brother, and minister of God, and our fellow labourer in the gospel of Christ, to establish you, and to comfort you concerning your faith: 3 That no man should be moved by these afflictions: for yourselves know that we are appointed thereunto. 4 For verily, when we were with you, we told you before that we should suffer tribulation; even as it came to pass, and ye know. 5 For this cause, when I could no longer forbear, I sent to know your faith, lest by some means the tempter have tempted you, and our labour be in vain. 6 But now when Timotheus came from you unto us, and brought us good tidings of your faith and charity, and that ye have good remembrance of us always, desiring greatly to see us, as we also to see you: 7 Therefore, brethren, we were comforted over you in all our affliction and distress by your faith: 8 For now we live, if ye stand fast in the Lord. 9 For what thanks can we render to God again for you, for all the joy wherewith we joy for your sakes before our God; 10 Night and day praying exceedingly that we might see your face, and might perfect that which is lacking in your faith? 11 Now God himself and our Father, and our Lord Jesus Christ, direct our way unto you. 12And the Lord make you to increase and abound in love one toward another, and toward all *men*, even as we *do* toward you: 13 To the end he may stablish your hearts unblameable in holiness before God, even our Father, at the coming of our Lord Jesus Christ with all his saints.

R.S.V.

3 Therefore when we could bear it no longer, we were willing to be left behind at Athens alone, 2 and we sent Timothy, our brother and God's servant in the gospel of Christ, to establish you in your faith and to exhort you, 3 that no one be moved by these afflictions. You yourselves know that this is to be our lot. 4 For when we were with you, we told you beforehand that we were to suffer affliction; just as it has come to pass, and as you know. 5 For this reason, when I could bear it no longer, I sent that I might know your faith, for fear that somehow the tempter had tempted you and that our labor would be in vain.

6 But now that Timothy has come to us from you, and has brought us the good news of your faith and love and reported that you always remember us kindly and long to see us, as we long to see you—7 for this reason, brethren, in all our distress and affliction we have been comforted about you through your faith; 8 for now we live, if you stand fast in the Lord. 9 For what thanksgiving can we render to God for you, for all the joy which we feel for your sake before our God, 10 praying earnestly night and day that we may see you face to face and supply what is lacking in your faith?

11 Now may our God and Father himself, and our Lord Jesus, direct our way to you; 12 and may the Lord make you increase and abound in love to one another and to all men, as we do to you, 13 so that he may establish your hearts unblamable in holiness before our God and Father, at the coming of our Lord Jesus with all his saints.

4 Furthermore then we beseech you, brethren, and exhort *you* by the Lord Jesus, that as ye have received of us how ye ought to walk and to please God, *so* ye would abound more and more. 2 For ye know what commandments we gave you by the Lord Jesus. 3 For this is the will of God, *even* your sanctification, that ye should abstain from fornication; 4 That every one of you should know how to possess his vessel in sanctification and honour; 5 Not in the lust of concupiscence, even as the Gentiles which know not God: 6 That no *man* go beyond and defraud his brother in *any* matter: because that the Lord *is* the avenger of all such, as we also have forewarned you and testified. 7 For God hath not called us unto uncleanness, but unto

4 Finally, brethren, we beseech and exhort you in the Lord Jesus, that as you learned from us how you ought to live and to please God, just as you are doing, you do so more and more. 2 For you know what instructions we gave you through the Lord Jesus. 3 For this is the will of God, your sanctification: that you abstain from immorality; 4 that each one of you know how to take a wife for himself in holiness and honor, 5 not in the passion of lust like heathen who do not know God; 6 that no man transgress, and wrong his brother in this matter,[c] because the Lord is an avenger in all these things, as we solemnly forewarned you. 7 For God has not called us for uncleanness, but in

[c] Or *defraud his brother in business.*

PHILLIPS

And so at length, when the separation became intolerable, we thought the best plan was for me to stay at Athens alone, while Timothy, our brother and fellow worker in the gospel of Christ, was sent to strengthen and encourage you in your faith. We did not want any of you to lose heart at the troubles you were going through, but to realize that we Christians must expect such things. Actually we did warn you what to expect, when we were with you, and our words have come true, as you know. You will understand that, when the suspense became unbearable, I sent someone to find out how your faith was standing the strain, and to make sure that the tempter's activities had not destroyed our work.

The good news about you   3. 6
is a tonic to us

But now that Timothy has just come straight from you to us—with a glowing account of your faith and love, and definite news that you cherish happy memories of us and long to see us as much as we to see you—how these things have cheered us in all the miseries and troubles we ourselves are going through! To know that you are standing fast in the Lord is indeed a breath of life to us. How can we thank our God enough for all the joy you give us as we serve him, praying earnestly day and night to see you again face to face, and to complete whatever is imperfect in your faith?

This is our prayer for you   3. 11

So may God our Father himself and our Lord Jesus guide our steps to you. May the Lord give you the same increasing and overflowing love for one another and toward all men as we have toward you. May he establish you, holy and blameless in heart and soul, before God, the Father of us all, when our Lord Jesus comes with all who belong to him.

Purity, love and hard work   4. 1
are good rules for life

To sum up, my brothers, we beg and pray you by the Lord Jesus, that you continue to learn more and more of the life that pleases God, the sort of life we told you about before. You will remember the instructions we gave you then in the name of the Lord Jesus. God's plan is to make you holy, and that entails first of all a clean cut with sexual immorality. Every one of you should learn to control his body, keeping it pure and treating it with respect, and never regarding it as an instrument for self-gratification, as do pagans with no knowledge of God. You cannot break this rule without in some way cheating your fellow men. And you must remember that God will punish all who do offend in this matter, and we have warned you how we have seen this work out in our experience of life. The calling of God is not to impurity but to

N.E.B.

3 So when we could bear it no longer, we decided to remain alone at Athens, and sent Timothy, our brother and God's fellow-worker[a] in the service of the gospel of Christ, to encourage you to stand firm for the faith and, under all these hardships, not to be shaken;[b] for you know that this is our appointed lot. When we were with you we warned you that we were bound to suffer hardship; and so it has turned out, as you know. And thus it was that when I could bear it no longer, I sent to find out about your faith, fearing that the tempter might have tempted you and my labour might be lost.

But now Timothy has just arrived from Thessalonica, bringing good news of your faith and love. He tells us that you always think kindly of us, and are as anxious to see us as we are to see you. And so in all our difficulties and hardships your faith reassures us about you. It is the breath of life to us that you stand firm in the Lord. What thanks can we return to God for you? What thanks for all the joy you have brought us, making us rejoice before our God while we pray most earnestly night and day to be allowed to see you again and to mend your faith where it falls short?

May our God and Father himself, and our Lord Jesus, bring us direct to you; and may the Lord make your love mount and overflow towards one another and towards all, as our love does towards you. May he make your hearts firm, so that you may stand before our God and Father holy and faultless when our Lord Jesus comes with all those who are his own.

4 And now, my friends, we have one thing to beg and pray of you, by our fellowship with the Lord Jesus. We passed on to you the tradition of the way we must live to please God; you are indeed already following it, but we beg you to do so yet more thoroughly.

For you know what orders we gave you, in the name of the Lord Jesus. This is the will of God, that you should be holy: you must abstain from fornication; each one of you must learn to gain mastery over his body, to hallow and honour it, not giving way to lust like the pagans who are ignorant of God; and no man must do his brother wrong in this matter,[c] or invade his rights, because, as we told you before with all emphasis, the Lord punishes all such offences. For God called us to holiness, not to impurity.

[a] Or and fellow-worker for God; one witness has simply and fellow-worker. [b] Or beguiled away. [c] Or must overreach his brother in his business (or in lawsuits).

K.J.V.

holiness. 8 He therefore that despiseth, despiseth not man, but God, who hath also given unto us his Holy Spirit. 9 But as touching brotherly love ye need not that I write unto you: for ye yourselves are taught of God to love one another. 10And indeed ye do it toward all the brethren which are in all Macedonia: but we beseech you, brethren, that ye increase more and more; 11And that ye study to be quiet, and to do your own business, and to work with your own hands, as we commanded you; 12 That ye may walk honestly toward them that are without, and *that* ye may have lack of nothing. 13 But I would not have you to be ignorant, brethren, concerning them which are asleep, that ye sorrow not, even as others which have no hope. 14 For if we believe that Jesus died and rose again, even so them also which sleep in Jesus will God bring with him. 15 For this we say unto you by the word of the Lord, that we which are alive *and* remain unto the coming of the Lord shall not prevent them which are asleep. 16 For the Lord himself shall descend from heaven with a shout, with the voice of the archangel, and with the trump of God: and the dead in Christ shall rise first: 17 Then we which are alive *and* remain shall be caught up together with them in the clouds, to meet the Lord in the air: and so shall we ever be with the Lord. 18 Wherefore comfort one another with these words.

R.S.V.

holiness. 8 Therefore whoever disregards this, disregards not man but God, who gives his Holy Spirit to you.

9 But concerning love of the brethren you have no need to have any one write to you, for you yourselves have been taught by God to love one another; 10 and indeed you do love all the brethren throughout Macedonia. But we exhort you, brethren, to do so more and more, 11 to aspire to live quietly, to mind your own affairs, and to work with your hands, as we charged you; 12 so that you may command the respect of outsiders, and be dependent on nobody.

13 But we would not have you ignorant, brethren, concerning those who are asleep, that you may not grieve as others do who have no hope. 14 For since we believe that Jesus died and rose again, even so, through Jesus, God will bring with him those who have fallen asleep. 15 For this we declare to you by the word of the Lord, that we who are alive, who are left until the coming of the Lord, shall not precede those who have fallen asleep. 16 For the Lord himself will descend from heaven with a cry of command, with the archangel's call, and with the sound of the trumpet of God. And the dead in Christ will rise first; 17 then we who are alive, who are left, shall be caught up together with them in the clouds to meet the Lord in the air; and so we shall always be with the Lord. 18 Therefore comfort one another with these words.

5 But of the times and the seasons, brethren, ye have no need that I write unto you. 2 For yourselves know perfectly that the day of the Lord so cometh as a thief in the night. 3 For when they shall say, Peace and safety; then sudden destruction cometh upon them, as travail upon a woman with child; and they shall not escape. 4 But ye, brethren, are not in darkness, that that day should overtake you as a thief. 5 Ye are all the children of light, and the children of the day: we are not of the night, nor of darkness. 6 Therefore let us not sleep, as *do* others; but let us watch and be sober. 7 For they that sleep sleep in the night; and they that be drunken are drunken in the night. 8 But let us, who are of the day, be sober, putting on the breastplate of faith and love; and for a helmet, the hope of salvation. 9 For God hath not appointed us to wrath, but to obtain salvation by our Lord Jesus Christ, 10 Who died for us, that, whether we wake or sleep, we should live together with him. 11 Wherefore comfort yourselves together, and edify one another, even as

5 But as to the times and the seasons, brethren, you have no need to have anything written to you. 2 For you yourselves know well that the day of the Lord will come like a thief in the night. 3 When people say, "There is peace and security," then sudden destruction will come upon them as travail comes upon a woman with child, and there will be no escape. 4 But you are not in darkness, brethren, for that day to surprise you like a thief. 5 For you are all sons of light and sons of the day; we are not of the night or of darkness. 6 So then let us not sleep, as others do, but let us keep awake and be sober. 7 For those who sleep sleep at night, and those who get drunk are drunk at night. 8 But, since we belong to the day, let us be sober, and put on the breastplate of faith and love, and for a helmet the hope of salvation. 9 For God has not destined us for wrath, but to obtain salvation through our Lord Jesus Christ, 10 who died for us so that whether we wake or sleep we might live with him. 11 Therefore encourage one another and build one another up, just as you are doing.

PHILLIPS

N.E.B.

the most thorough purity, and anyone who makes light of the matter is not making light of a man's ruling but of God's command. It is not for nothing that the Spirit God gives us is called the *Holy* Spirit.

Next, as regards brotherly love, you don't need any written instructions. God himself is teaching you to love one another, and you are already extending your love to all the Macedonians. Yet we urge you to have more and more of this love, and to make it your ambition to have no ambition! Be busy with your own affairs and do your work yourselves. The result will be a reputation for honesty in the world outside and an honorable independence.

God's message regarding those who have died   **4. 13**

Now we don't want you, my brothers, to be in any doubt about those who "fall asleep" in death, or to grieve over them like men who have no hope. After all, if we believe that Jesus died and rose again from death, then we can believe that God will just as surely bring with Jesus all who are "asleep" in him. Here we have a definite message from the Lord. It is that those who are still living when he comes will not in any way precede those who have previously fallen asleep. One word of command, one shout from the archangel, one blast from the trumpet of God and the Lord himself will come down from Heaven! Those who have died in Christ will be the first to rise, and then we who are still living on the earth will be swept up with them into the clouds to meet the Lord in the air. And after that we shall be with him for ever. So by all means use this message to encourage one another.

We must keep awake for his sudden coming   **5. 1**

But as far as times and seasons go, my brothers, you don't need written instructions. You are well aware that the day of the Lord will come as unexpectedly as a burglary to a householder. When men are saying, "Peace and security," catastrophe will sweep down upon them as suddenly and inescapably as birth pangs to a pregnant woman.

But because you, my brothers, are not living in darkness the day cannot take you completely by surprise. After all, burglary only takes place at night! You are all sons of light, sons of the day, and none of us belongs to darkness or to the night. Let us then never fall into the sleep that stupefies the rest of the world: let us keep awake, with our wits about us. Night is the time for sleep and the time when men get drunk, but we men of the daylight should be alert, with faith and love as our breastplate and the hope of our salvation as our helmet. For God did not choose us to condemn us, but that we might secure his salvation through Jesus Christ our Lord. He died for us, so that whether we are "awake" or "asleep" we share his life. So go on cheering and strengthening one another with thoughts like these, as I have no doubt you have been doing.

Anyone therefore who flouts these rules is flouting, not man, but God who bestows upon you his Holy Spirit.

About love for our brotherhood you need no words of mine, for you are yourselves taught by God to love one another, and you are in fact practising this rule of love towards all your fellow-Christians throughout Macedonia. Yet we appeal to you, brothers, to do better still. Let it be your ambition to keep calm and look after your own business, and to work with your hands, as we ordered you, so that you may command the respect of those outside your own number, and at the same time may never be in want.

We want you not to remain in ignorance, brothers, about those who sleep in death; you should not grieve like the rest of men, who have no hope. We believe that Jesus died and rose again; and so it will be for those who died as Christians; God will bring them to life with Jesus.[a]

For this we tell you as the Lord's word: we who are left alive until the Lord comes shall not forestall those who have died; because at the word of command, at the sound of the archangel's voice and God's trumpet-call, the Lord himself will descend from heaven; first the Christian dead will rise, then we who are left alive shall join them, caught up in clouds to meet the Lord in the air. Thus we shall always be with the Lord. Console one another, then, with these words.

5 About dates and times, my friends, we need not write to you, for you know perfectly well that the Day of the Lord comes like a thief in the night. While they are talking of peace and security, all at once calamity is upon them, sudden as the pangs that come upon a woman with child; and there will be no escape. But you, my friends, are not in the dark, that the day should overtake you like a thief.[b] You are all children of light, children of day. We do not belong to night or darkness, and we must not sleep like the rest, but keep awake and sober. Sleepers sleep at night, and drunkards are drunk at night, but we, who belong to daylight, must keep sober, armed with faith and love for breastplate, and the hope of salvation for helmet. For God has not destined us to the terrors of judgement, but to the full attainment of salvation through our Lord Jesus Christ. He died for us so that we, awake or asleep, might live in company with him. Therefore hearten one another, fortify one another—as indeed you do.

[a] *Or* will bring them in company with Jesus.
[b] *Some witnesses read* thieves.

K.J.V.

also ye do. 12And we beseech you, brethren, to know them which labour among you, and are over you in the Lord, and admonish you; 13And to esteem them very highly in love for their work's sake. *And* be at peace among yourselves. 14 Now we exhort you, brethren, warn them that are unruly, comfort the feebleminded, support the weak, be patient toward all *men.* 15 See that none render evil for evil unto any *man;* but ever follow that which is good, both among yourselves, and to all *men.* 16 Rejoice evermore. 17 Pray without ceasing. 18 In every thing give thanks: for this is the will of God in Christ Jesus concerning you. 19 Quench not the Spirit. 20 Despise not prophesyings. 21 Prove all things; hold fast that which is good. 22Abstain from all appearance of evil. 23And the very God of peace sanctify you wholly; and *I pray God* your whole spirit and soul and body be preserved blameless unto the coming of our Lord Jesus Christ. 24 Faithful *is* he that calleth you, who also will do *it.* 25 Brethren, pray for us. 26 Greet all the brethren with a holy kiss. 27 I charge you by the Lord, that this epistle be read unto all the holy brethren. 28 The grace of our Lord Jesus Christ *be* with you. Amen.

The first *epistle* unto the Thessalonians was written from Athens.

R.S.V.

12 But we beseech you, brethren, to respect those who labor among you and are over you in the Lord and admonish you, 13 and to esteem them very highly in love because of their work. Be at peace among yourselves. 14And we exhort you, brethren, admonish the idle, encourage the fainthearted, help the weak, be patient with them all. 15 See that none of you repays evil for evil, but always seek to do good to one another and to all. 16 Rejoice always, 17 pray constantly, 18 give thanks in all circumstances; for this is the will of God in Christ Jesus for you. 19 Do not quench the Spirit, 20 do not despise prophesying, 21 but test everything; hold fast what is good, 22 abstain from every form of evil.

23 May the God of peace himself sanctify you wholly; and may your spirit and soul and body be kept sound and blameless at the coming of our Lord Jesus Christ. 24 He who calls you is faithful, and he will do it.

25 Brethren, pray for us.

26 Greet all the brethren with a holy kiss.

27 I adjure you by the Lord that this letter be read to all the brethren.

28 The grace of our Lord Jesus Christ be with you.

PHILLIPS

Reverence your ministers: regulate   **5. 12**
the conduct of church members

We ask you too, my brothers, to get to know those who work so hard among you. They are your spiritual leaders to keep you on the right path. Because of this high task of theirs, hold them in highest honor.

Live together in peace, and our instruction to this end is to reprimand the unruly, encourage the timid, help the weak and be very patient with all men. Be sure that no one repays a bad turn by a bad turn; good should be your objective always, among yourselves and in the world at large.

Be happy in your faith at all times. Never stop praying. Be thankful, whatever the circumstances may be.

If you follow this advice you will be working out the will of God expressed to you in Christ Jesus.

Final advice and farewell   **5. 19**

Never damp the fire of the Spirit, and never despise what is spoken in the name of the Lord. By all means use your judgment, and hold on to whatever is really good. Steer clear of evil in any form.

May the God of peace make you holy through and through. May you be kept in soul and mind and body in spotless integrity until the coming of our Lord Jesus Christ. He who calls you is utterly faithful and he will finish what he has set out to do.

Pray for us, my brothers. Give a handshake all round among the brotherhood. God's command, which I give you now, is that this letter should be read to all the brothers.

The grace of our Lord Jesus Christ be with you all.

PAUL

N.E.B.

We beg you, brothers, to acknowledge those who are working so hard among you, and in the Lord's fellowship are your leaders and counsellors. Hold them in the highest possible esteem and affection for the work they do.

You must live at peace among yourselves. And we would urge you, brothers, to admonish the careless, encourage the faint-hearted, support the weak, and to be very patient with them all.

See to it that no one pays back wrong for wrong, but always aim at doing the best you can for each other and for all men.

Be always joyful; pray continually; give thanks whatever happens; for this is what God in Christ wills for you.

Do not stifle inspiration, and do not despise prophetic utterances, but bring them all to the test and then keep what is good in them and avoid the bad of whatever kind.[a]

May God himself, the God of peace, make you holy in every part, and keep you sound in spirit, soul, and body, without fault when our Lord Jesus Christ comes. He who calls you is to be trusted; he will do it.

Brothers, pray for us also.

Greet all our brothers with the kiss of peace.

I adjure you by the Lord to have this letter read to the whole brotherhood.

The grace of our Lord Jesus Christ be with you!

[a] *Or* . . . utterances. Put everything to the test; keep hold of what is good and avoid every kind of evil.

THE SECOND

OF PAUL THE APOSTLE

TO THE

THESSALONIANS

THE SECOND

LETTER OF PAUL TO THE

THESSALONIANS

1 Paul, and Silvanus, and Timotheus, unto the church of the Thessalonians in God our Father and the Lord Jesus Christ: 2 Grace unto you, and peace, from God our Father and the Lord Jesus Christ. 3 We are bound to thank God always for you, brethren, as it is meet, because that your faith groweth exceedingly, and the charity of every one of you all toward each other aboundeth; 4 So that we ourselves glory in you in the churches of God, for your patience and faith in all your persecutions and tribulations that ye endure: 5 *Which is* a manifest token of the righteous judgment of God, that ye may be counted worthy of the kingdom of God, for which ye also suffer: 6 Seeing *it is* a righteous thing with God to recompense tribulation to them that trouble you; 7 And to you who are troubled rest with us, when the Lord Jesus shall be revealed from heaven with his mighty angels, 8 In flaming fire taking vengeance on them that know not God, and that obey not the gospel of our Lord Jesus Christ: 9 Who shall be punished with everlasting destruction from the presence of the Lord, and from the glory of his power; 10 When he shall come to be glorified in his saints, and to be admired in all them that believe (because our testimony among you was believed) in that day. 11 Wherefore also we pray always for you, that our God would count you worthy of *this* calling, and fulfil all the good pleasure of *his* goodness, and the work of faith with power: 12 That the name of our Lord Jesus Christ may be glorified in you, and ye in him, according to the grace of our God and the Lord Jesus Christ.

1 Paul, Silvanus, and Timothy,
To the church of the Thessalonians in God our Father and the Lord Jesus Christ:
2 Grace to you and peace from God the Father and the Lord Jesus Christ.

3 We are bound to give thanks to God always for you, brethren, as is fitting, because your faith is growing abundantly, and the love of every one of you for one another is increasing. 4 Therefore we ourselves boast of you in the churches of God for your steadfastness and faith in all your persecutions and in the afflictions which you are enduring.
5 This is evidence of the righteous judgment of God, that you may be made worthy of the kingdom of God, for which you are suffering— 6 since indeed God deems it just to repay with affliction those who afflict you, 7 and to grant rest with us to you who are afflicted, when the Lord Jesus is revealed from heaven with his mighty angels in flaming fire, 8 inflicting vengeance upon those who do not know God and upon those who do not obey the gospel of our Lord Jesus. 9 They shall suffer the punishment of eternal destruction and exclusion from the presence of the Lord and from the glory of his might, 10 when he comes on that day to be glorified in his saints, and to be marveled at in all who have believed, because our testimony to you was believed. 11 To this end we always pray for you, that our God may make you worthy of his call, and may fulfil every good resolve and work of faith by his power, 12 so that the name of our Lord Jesus may be glorified in you, and you in him, according to the grace of our God and the Lord Jesus Christ.

THE SECOND LETTER TO THE CHRISTIANS IN

THESSALONICA

To the church of the Thessalonians, founded on God our Father and Jesus Christ the Lord, from Paul, Silvanus and Timothy; grace to you and peace from God the Father and the Lord Jesus Christ!

Your sufferings are a guarantee   1. 3 of great joy one day

My brothers, nowadays I thank God for you not only in common fairness but as a moral obligation! Your faith has made such strides, and (without any individual exceptions) your love toward one another has reached such proportions that we actually boast about you in the churches of God, because you have shown such endurance and faith in all the trials and persecutions you have gone through, and in all the afflictions you are now enduring.

These qualities show how justly the judgment of God works out in your case. Without doubt he intends to use your suffering to make you worthy of his kingdom, yet his justice will one day repay trouble to those who have troubled you, and peace to all of us who, like you, have suffered. This judgment will issue eventually in the final dénouement of the personal coming of the Lord Jesus from Heaven with the angels of his power. It will bring full justice in dazzling flame upon those who have refused to know God or to obey the gospel of our Lord Jesus. Their punishment will be eternal exclusion from the radiance of the face of the Lord, and the glorious majesty of his power. But to those whom he has made holy his coming will mean splendor unimaginable. It will be a breath-taking wonder to all who believe—including you, for you have believed the message that we have given you.

In view of this great prospect, we pray for you constantly, that God will think you worthy of this calling, and that he will effect in you all that his goodness desires to do, and that your faith makes possible. We pray that the name of our Lord Jesus may become more glorious through you, and that you may share something of his glory—all through the grace of our God and the Lord Jesus Christ.

THE SECOND LETTER OF PAUL TO THE

THESSALONIANS

Hope and Discipline

1 From Paul, Silvanus, and Timothy to the congregation of Thessalonians who belong to God our Father and the Lord Jesus Christ.

Grace to you and peace from God the Father and the Lord Jesus Christ.

Our thanks are always due to God for you, brothers. It is right that we should thank him, because your faith increases mightily, and the love you have, each for all and all for each, grows ever greater. Indeed we boast about you ourselves among the congregations of God's people, because your faith remains so steadfast under all your persecutions, and all the troubles you endure. See how this brings out the justice of God's judgement. It will prove you worthy of the kingdom of God, for which indeed you are suffering.

It is surely just that God should balance the account by sending trouble to those who trouble you, and relief to you who are troubled, and to us as well, when our Lord Jesus Christ is revealed from heaven with his mighty angels in blazing fire. Then he will do justice upon those who refuse to acknowledge God and upon those who will not obey[a] the gospel of our Lord Jesus. They will suffer the punishment of eternal ruin, cut off from the presence of the Lord and the splendour of his might, when on that great Day he comes to be glorified among his own and adored among all believers; for you did indeed believe the testimony we brought you.

With this in mind we pray for you always, that our God may count you worthy of his calling, and mightily bring to fulfilment every good purpose and every act inspired by faith, so that the name of our Lord Jesus may be glorified in you, and you in him, according to the grace of our God and the Lord Jesus Christ.

[a] *Or* justice upon those who refuse . . . and will not obey . . .

2 Now we beseech you, brethren, by the coming of our Lord Jesus Christ, and *by* our gathering together unto him, 2 That ye be not soon shaken in mind, or be troubled, neither by spirit, nor by word, nor by letter as from us, as that the day of Christ is at hand. 3 Let no man deceive you by any means: for *that day shall not come,* except there come a falling away first, and that man of sin be revealed, the son of perdition; 4 Who opposeth and exalteth himself above all that is called God, or that is worshipped; so that he as God sitteth in the temple of God, shewing himself that he is God. 5 Remember ye not, that, when I was yet with you, I told you these things? 6And now ye know what withholdeth that he might be revealed in his time. 7 For the mystery of iniquity doth already work: only he who now letteth *will let,* until he be taken out of the way. 8And then shall that Wicked be revealed, whom the Lord shall consume with the spirit of his mouth, and shall destroy with the brightness of his coming: 9 *Even him,* whose coming is after the working of Satan with all power and signs and lying wonders, 10And with all deceivableness of unrighteousness in them that perish; because they received not the love of the truth, that they might be saved. 11And for this cause God shall send them strong delusion, that they should believe a lie: 12 That they all might be damned who believed not the truth, but had pleasure in unrighteousness. 13 But we are bound to give thanks always to God for you, brethren beloved of the Lord, because God hath from the beginning chosen you to salvation through sanctification of the Spirit and belief of the truth: 14 Whereunto he called you by our gospel, to the obtaining of the glory of our Lord Jesus Christ. 15 Therefore, brethren, stand fast, and hold the traditions which ye have been taught, whether by word, or our epistle. 16 Now our Lord Jesus Christ himself, and God, even our Father, which hath loved us, and hath given *us* everlasting consolation and good hope through grace, 17 Comfort your hearts, and stablish you in every good word and work.

2 Now concerning the coming of our Lord Jesus Christ and our assembling to meet him, we beg you, brethren, 2 not to be quickly shaken in mind or excited, either by spirit or by word, or by letter purporting to be from us, to the effect that the day of the Lord has come. 3 Let no one deceive you in any way; for that day will not come, unless the rebellion comes first, and the man of lawlessness[a] is revealed, the son of perdition, 4 who opposes and exalts himself against every so-called god or object of worship, so that he takes his seat in the temple of God, proclaiming himself to be God. 5 Do you not remember that when I was still with you I told you this? 6And you know what is restraining him now so that he may be revealed in his time. 7 For the mystery of lawlessness is already at work; only he who now restrains it will do so until he is out of the way. 8And then the lawless one will be revealed, and the Lord Jesus will slay him with the breath of his mouth and destroy him by his appearing and his coming. 9 The coming of the lawless one by the activity of Satan will be with all power and with pretended signs and wonders, 10 and with all wicked deception for those who are to perish, because they refused to love the truth and so be saved. 11 Therefore God sends upon them a strong delusion, to make them believe what is false, 12 so that all may be condemned who did not believe the truth but had pleasure in unrighteousness.

13 But we are bound to give thanks to God always for you, brethren beloved by the Lord, because God chose you from the beginning[b] to be saved, through sanctification by the Spirit[c] and belief in the truth. 14 To this he called you through our gospel, so that you may obtain the glory of our Lord Jesus Christ. 15 So then, brethren, stand firm and hold to the traditions which you were taught by us, either by word of mouth or by letter.

16 Now may our Lord Jesus Christ himself, and God our Father, who loved us and gave us eternal comfort and good hope through grace, 17 comfort your hearts and establish them in every good work and word.

3 Finally, brethren, pray for us, that the word of the Lord may have *free* course, and be glorified, even as *it is* with you: 2And that we may be delivered from unreasonable and wicked

3 Finally, brethren, pray for us, that the word of the Lord may speed on and triumph, as it did among you, 2 and that we may be delivered from wicked and evil men; for not all

[a] Other ancient authorities read *sin.* [b] Other ancient authorities read *as the first converts.* [c] Or *of spirit.*

Before Christ's coming there will be certain signs

2. 1

Now we do implore you, by the very certainty of the coming of our Lord Jesus Christ, and of our meeting him together, to keep your heads and not be thrown off your balance by any prediction or message or letter purporting to come from us, and saying that the day of the Lord has already come. Don't let anyone deceive you by any means whatsoever. That day will not come before there arises a definite rejection of God and the appearance of the lawless man. He is the product of all that leads to death, and he sets himself up in opposition to every religion. He himself takes his seat in the temple of God, to show that he really claims to be God.

I expect you remember now how I talked about this when I was with you. You will probably also remember how I used to talk about a "restraining power" which would operate until the time should come for the emergence of this man. Evil is already insidiously at work, but its activities are restricted until what I have called the "restraining power" is removed. When that happens the lawless man will be plainly seen—though the truth of the Lord Jesus spells his doom, and the radiance of the coming of the Lord Jesus will be his utter destruction. The lawless man is produced by the spirit of evil and armed with all the force, wonders and signs that falsehood can devise. To those involved in this dying world he will come with evil's undiluted power to deceive, for they have refused to love the truth which could have saved them. God sends upon them, therefore, the full force of evil's delusion, so that they put their faith in an utter fraud and meet the inevitable judgment of all who have refused to believe the truth and who have made evil their playfellow.

You, thank God, belong to those who believe the truth

2. 13

But we can thank God continually for you, brothers, whom the Lord loves. He has chosen you from the beginning to save you, to make you holy by the work of his Spirit and your own belief in the truth. It was his call that you followed when we preached the gospel to you, and he has set before you the prospect of sharing the glory of our Lord Jesus Christ. So stand firm, and hold on! Be loyal to the teachings we passed on to you, whether by word of mouth or in our writings.

May our Lord Jesus Christ and God our Father (who has loved us and given us unending encouragement and unfailing hope by his grace) inspire you with courage and confidence in every good thing you say or do.

We ask your prayers for God's work here

3. 1

Finally, my brothers, do pray for us here. Pray that the Lord's message may go forward unhindered and may bring him glory, as it has done with you. Pray, too, that we may not be

2 And now, brothers, about the coming of our Lord Jesus Christ and his gathering of us to himself: I beg you, do not suddenly lose your heads or alarm yourselves, whether at some oracular utterance, or pronouncement, or some letter purporting to come from us, alleging that the Day of the Lord is already here. Let no one deceive you in any way whatever. That day cannot come before the final rebellion against God, when wickedness will be revealed in human form, the man doomed to perdition. He is the Enemy. He rises in his pride against every god, so called, every object of men's worship, and even takes his seat in the temple of God claiming to be a god himself.

You cannot but remember that I told you this while I was still with you; you must now be aware of the restraining hand which ensures that he shall be revealed only at the proper time. For already the secret power of wickedness is at work, secret only for the present until the Restrainer disappears from the scene. And then he will be revealed, that wicked man whom the Lord Jesus will destroy with the breath of his mouth, and annihilate by the radiance of his coming. But the coming of that wicked man is the work of Satan. It will be attended by all the powerful signs and miracles of the Lie, and all the deception that sinfulness can impose on those doomed to destruction. Destroyed they shall be, because they did not open their minds to love of the truth, so as to find salvation. Therefore God puts them under a delusion, which works upon them to believe the lie, so that they may all be brought to judgement, all who do not believe the truth but make sinfulness their deliberate choice.

But we are bound to thank God for you, brothers beloved by the Lord, because from the beginning of time God chose you[a] to find salvation in the Spirit that consecrates you, and in the truth that you believe. It was for this that he called you through the gospel we brought, so that you might possess for your own the splendour of our Lord Jesus Christ.

Stand firm, then, brothers, and hold fast to the traditions which you have learned from us by word or by letter. And may our Lord Jesus Christ himself and God our Father, who has shown us such love, and in his grace has given us such unfailing encouragement and such bright hopes, still encourage and fortify you in every good deed and word!

3 And now, brothers, pray for us, that the word of the Lord may have everywhere the swift and glorious course that it has had among you, and that we may be rescued from wrong-

[a] *Some witnesses read* because God chose you as his firstfruits . . .

K.J.V.

men: for all *men* have not faith. 3 But the Lord is faithful, who shall stablish you, and keep *you* from evil. 4And we have confidence in the Lord touching you, that ye both do and will do the things which we command you. 5And the Lord direct your hearts into the love of God, and into the patient waiting for Christ. 6 Now we command you, brethren, in the name of our Lord Jesus Christ, that ye withdraw yourselves from every brother that walketh disorderly, and not after the tradition which he received of us. 7 For yourselves know how ye ought to follow us: for we behaved not ourselves disorderly among you; 8 Neither did we eat any man's bread for nought; but wrought with labour and travail night and day, that we might not be chargeable to any of you: 9 Not because we have not power, but to make ourselves an ensample unto you to follow us. 10 For even when we were with you, this we commanded you, that if any would not work, neither should he eat. 11 For we hear that there are some which walk among you disorderly, working not at all, but are busybodies. 12 Now them that are such we command and exhort by our Lord Jesus Christ, that with quietness they work, and eat their own bread. 13 But ye, brethren, be not weary in well doing. 14And if any man obey not our word by this epistle, note that man, and have no company with him, that he may be ashamed. 15 Yet count *him* not as an enemy, but admonish *him* as a brother. 16 Now the Lord of peace himself give you peace always by all means. The Lord *be* with you all. 17 The salutation of Paul with mine own hand, which is the token in every epistle: so I write. 18 The grace of our Lord Jesus Christ *be* with you all. Amen.

The second *epistle* to the Thessalonians was written from Athens.

R.S.V.

have faith. 3 But the Lord is faithful; he will strengthen you and guard you from evil.[d] 4And we have confidence in the Lord about you, that you are doing and will do the things which we command. 5 May the Lord direct your hearts to the love of God and to the steadfastness of Christ.

6 Now we command you, brethren, in the name of our Lord Jesus Christ, that you keep away from any brother who is living in idleness and not in accord with the tradition that you received from us. 7 For you yourselves know how you ought to imitate us; we were not idle when we were with you, 8 we did not eat any one's bread without paying, but with toil and labor we worked night and day, that we might not burden any of you. 9 It was not because we have not that right, but to give you in our conduct an example to imitate. 10 For even when we were with you, we gave you this command: If any one will not work, let him not eat. 11 For we hear that some of you are living in idleness, mere busybodies, not doing any work. 12 Now such persons we command and exhort in the Lord Jesus Christ to do their work in quietness and to earn their own living. 13 Brethren, do not be weary in well-doing.

14 If any one refuses to obey what we say in this letter, note that man, and have nothing to do with him, that he may be ashamed. 15 Do not look on him as an enemy, but warn him as a brother.

16 Now may the Lord of peace himself give you peace at all times in all ways. The Lord be with you all.

17 I, Paul, write this greeting with my own hand. This is the mark in every letter of mine; it is the way I write. 18 The grace of our Lord Jesus Christ be with you all.

---

[d] Or *the evil one.*

646

PHILLIPS

embroiled with bigoted and wicked men; for all men, alas, have not faith. Yet the Lord is utterly to be depended upon by all who have faith in him, and he will give you stability and protection against all that is evil. It is he who makes us feel confident about you, that you are acting and will act in accordance with our commands. May the Lord guide your hearts into ever deeper understanding of his love and of the patient suffering of Christ.

Remember our example: everyone 3. 6 *should do his fair share of work*

One further order we must give you in the name of our Lord Jesus Christ: don't associate with the brother whose life is undisciplined, and who despises the teaching we gave you. You know well that we ourselves are your examples here, and that our lives among you were never undisciplined. We did not eat anyone's food without paying for it. In fact we toiled and labored night and day to avoid being the slightest expense to any of you. This was not because we had no right to ask our necessities of you, but because we wanted to set you an example. When we were actually with you we gave you this principle to work on: "If a man will not work, he shall not eat." Now we hear that you have some among you living quite undisciplined lives, never doing a stroke of work, and busy only in other people's affairs. Our order to such men, indeed our appeal by the Lord Jesus Christ, is to settle down to work and eat the food they have earned themselves.

And the rest of you—don't get tired of honest work! If anyone refuses to obey the command given above, mark that man; do not associate with him until he is ashamed of himself. I don't mean, of course, treat him as an enemy, but reprimand him as a brother.

My blessing on you all! 3. 16

Now may the Lord of peace personally give you his peace at all times and in all ways. The Lord be with you all.

This is the farewell message of PAUL, written in my own writing—my "mark" on all my letters. This is how I write.

The grace of our Lord Jesus Christ be with you all.

N.E.B.

headed and wicked men; for it is not all who have faith. But the Lord is to be trusted, and he will fortify you and guard you from the evil one. We feel perfect confidence about you, in the Lord, that you are doing and will continue to do what we order. May the Lord direct your hearts towards God's love and the steadfastness of Christ!

These are our orders to you, brothers, in the name of our Lord Jesus Christ: hold aloof from every Christian brother who falls into idle habits, and does not follow the tradition you received from us. You know yourselves how you ought to copy our example: we were no idlers among you; we did not accept board and lodging from anyone without paying for it; we toiled and drudged, we worked for a living night and day, rather than be a burden to any of you—not because we have not the right to maintenance, but to set an example for you to imitate. For even during our stay with you we laid down the rule: the man who will not work shall not eat. We mention this because we hear that some of your number are idling their time away, minding everybody's business but their own. To all such we give these orders, and we appeal to them in the name of the Lord Jesus Christ to work quietly for their living.

My friends, never tire of doing right. If anyone disobeys our instructions given by letter, mark him well, and have no dealings with him until he is ashamed of himself. I do not mean treat him as an enemy, but give him friendly advice, as one of the family. May the Lord of peace himself give you peace at all times and in all ways.[a] The Lord be with you all.

The greeting is in my own hand, signed with my name, PAUL; this authenticates all my letters; this is how I write. The grace[b] of our Lord Jesus Christ be with you all.

[a] *Some witnesses read* at all times, wherever you may be. [b] *Or* . . . letters. My message is this: the grace . . .

K.J.V.

THE FIRST EPISTLE

OF PAUL THE APOSTLE

TO

TIMOTHY

R.S.V.

THE FIRST

LETTER OF PAUL TO

TIMOTHY

1 Paul, an apostle of Jesus Christ by the commandment of God our Saviour, and Lord Jesus Christ, *which is* our hope; 2 Unto Timothy, *my* own son in the faith: Grace, mercy, *and* peace, from God our Father, and Jesus Christ our Lord. 3As I besought thee to abide still at Ephesus, when I went into Macedonia, that thou mightest charge some that they teach no other doctrine, 4 Neither give heed to fables and endless genealogies, which minister questions, rather than godly edifying which is in faith: *so do.* 5 Now the end of the commandment is charity out of a pure heart, and *of* a good conscience, and *of* faith unfeigned: 6 From which some having swerved have turned aside unto vain jangling; 7 Desiring to be teachers of the law; understanding neither what they say, nor whereof they affirm. 8 But we know that the law *is* good, if a man use it lawfully; 9 Knowing this, that the law is not made for a righteous man, but for the lawless and disobedient, for the ungodly and for sinners, for unholy and profane, for murderers of fathers and murderers of mothers, for manslayers, 10 For whoremongers, for them that defile themselves with mankind, for menstealers, for liars, for perjured persons, and if there be any other thing that is contrary to sound doctrine; 11According to the glorious gospel of the blessed God, which was committed to my trust. 12And I thank Christ Jesus our Lord, who hath enabled me, for that he counted me faithful, putting me into the ministry; 13 Who was before a blasphemer, and a persecutor, and injurious: but I obtained mercy, because I did *it* ignorantly in unbelief. 14And the grace of our Lord was exceeding abundant with faith and love which is in Christ Jesus. 15 This *is* a faithful saying, and worthy of all acceptation, that Christ Jesus came into the world to save sinners; of whom I am chief. 16 Howbeit for this cause I

1 Paul, an apostle of Christ Jesus by command of God our Savior and of Christ Jesus our hope,
2 To Timothy, my true child in the faith:
Grace, mercy, and peace from God the Father and Christ Jesus our Lord.

3 As I urged you when I was going to Macedonia, remain at Ephesus that you may charge certain persons not to teach any different doctrine, 4 nor to occupy themselves with myths and endless genealogies which promote speculations rather than the divine training[a] that is in faith; 5 whereas the aim of our charge is love that issues from a pure heart and a good conscience and sincere faith. 6 Certain persons by swerving from these have wandered away into vain discussion, 7 desiring to be teachers of the law, without understanding either what they are saying or the things about which they make assertions.
8 Now we know that the law is good, if any one uses it lawfully, 9 understanding this, that the law is not laid down for the just but for the lawless and disobedient, for the ungodly and sinners, for the unholy and profane, for murderers of fathers and murderers of mothers, for manslayers, 10 immoral persons, sodomites, kidnapers, liars, perjurers, and whatever else is contrary to sound doctrine, 11 in accordance with the glorious gospel of the blessed God with which I have been entrusted.
12 I thank him who has given me strength for this, Christ Jesus our Lord, because he judged me faithful by appointing me to his service, 13 though I formerly blasphemed and persecuted and insulted him; but I received mercy because I had acted ignorantly in unbelief, 14 and the grace of our Lord overflowed for me with the faith and love that are in Christ Jesus. 15 The saying is sure and worthy of full acceptance, that Christ Jesus came into the world to save sinners. And I am the foremost of sinners; 16 but I received mercy for this reason, that in

[a] Or *stewardship*, or *order.*

THE FIRST LETTER TO

TIMOTHY

Paul, Jesus Christ's messenger by command of
God our savior and Christ Jesus our hope, to
Timothy my true son in the faith: grace, mercy
and peace be to you from God the Father and
Christ Jesus our Lord.

A reminder   *1. 3*

I am repeating in this letter the advice I gave
you just before I went to Macedonia and urged
you to stay at Ephesus. I wanted you to do this
so that you could order certain persons to stop
inventing new doctrines and to leave hoary old
myths and interminable genealogies alone. Such
things lead men to speculation rather than to
ordered living which results from faith in God.
The ultimate aim of the Christian ministry, after
all, is to produce the love which springs from
a pure heart, a good conscience and a genuine
faith. Some seem to have forgotten this and to
have lost themselves in endless words. They want
a reputation as teachers of the Law, yet they
fail to realize the meaning of their own words,
still less of the subject they are so dogmatic
about. We know, of course, that the Law is
good in itself and has a legitimate function. Yet
we also know that the Law is not really meant
for the good man, but for the man who has
neither principles nor self-control, for the man
who is really wicked, who has neither scruples
nor reverence. Yes, the Law is directed against
the sort of people who attack their own parents,
who kill their fellows, who are sexually uncontrolled or perverted, or who traffic in the bodies
of others. It is against liars and perjurers—in
fact it is against any and every action which
contradicts the wholesome teaching of the glorious gospel which our blessed God has given and
entrusted to me.

My debt to Jesus Christ   *1. 12*

I am deeply grateful to Christ Jesus our Lord
(to whom I owe all that I have accomplished)
for trusting me enough to appoint me his minister, despite the fact that I had previously blasphemed his name, persecuted his Church and
insulted him. I believe he was merciful to me
because what I did was done in the ignorance of
a man without faith. Our Lord poured out his
grace upon me, giving me tremendous faith in,
and love for, himself. This statement is completely reliable and should be universally accepted:—*Christ Jesus entered the world to rescue
sinners.* I realize that I was the worst of them
all, and that because of this very fact God was
particularly merciful to me. It was a kind of

THE FIRST

LETTER OF PAUL TO

TIMOTHY

Church Order

1 From Paul, apostle of Christ Jesus by command of God our Saviour and Christ Jesus
our hope, to Timothy his true-born son in the
faith.
Grace, mercy, and peace to you from God the
Father and Christ Jesus our Lord.
When I was starting for Macedonia, I urged
you to stay on at Ephesus. You were to command certain persons to give up teaching er-
roneous doctrines and studying those interminable myths and genealogies, which issue in mere
speculation and cannot make known God's plan
for us, which works through faith.[a]
The aim and object of this command is the
love which springs from a clean heart, from a
good conscience, and from faith that is genuine.
Through falling short of these, some people have
gone astray into a wilderness of words. They set
out to be teachers of the moral law, without understanding either the words they use or the
subjects about which they are so dogmatic.
We all know that the law is an excellent thing,
provided we treat it as law, recognizing that it
is not aimed at good citizens, but at the lawless
and unruly, the impious and sinful, the irreligious
and worldly; at parricides and matricides, murderers and fornicators, perverts, kidnappers, liars,
perjurers—in fact all whose behaviour flouts the
wholesome teaching which conforms with the
gospel entrusted to me, the gospel which tells of
the glory of God in his eternal felicity.
I thank him who has made me equal to the
task, Christ Jesus our Lord; I thank him for
judging me worthy of this trust and appointing
me to his service—although in the past I had
met him with abuse and persecution and outrage.
But because I acted ignorantly in unbelief I was
dealt with mercifully; the grace of our Lord was
lavished upon me, with the faith and love which
are ours in Christ Jesus.
Here are words you may trust, words that
merit full acceptance: 'Christ Jesus came into
the world to save sinners'; and among them I
stand first. But I was mercifully dealt with for

[a] *Or* cannot promote the faithful discharge of
God's stewardship.

649

K.J.V.

obtained mercy, that in me first Jesus Christ might shew forth all longsuffering, for a pattern to them which should hereafter believe on him to life everlasting. 17 Now unto the King eternal, immortal, invisible, the only wise God, *be* honour and glory for ever and ever. Amen. 18 This charge I commit unto thee, son Timothy, according to the prophecies which went before on thee, that thou by them mightest war a good warfare; 19 Holding faith, and a good conscience; which some having put away, concerning faith have made shipwreck: 20 Of whom is Hymeneus and Alexander; whom I have delivered unto Satan, that they may learn not to blaspheme.

2 I exhort therefore, that, first of all, supplications, prayers, intercessions, *and* giving of thanks, be made for all men; 2 For kings, and *for* all that are in authority; that we may lead a quiet and peaceable life in all godliness and honesty. 3 For this *is* good and acceptable in the sight of God our Saviour; 4 Who will have all men to be saved, and to come unto the knowledge of the truth. 5 For *there is* one God, and one mediator between God and men, the man Christ Jesus; 6 Who gave himself a ransom for all, to be testified in due time. 7 Whereunto I am ordained a preacher, and an apostle, (I speak the truth in Christ, *and* lie not,) a teacher of the Gentiles in faith and verity. 8 I will therefore that men pray every where, lifting up holy hands, without wrath and doubting. 9 In like manner also, that women adorn themselves in modest apparel, with shamefacedness and sobriety; not with braided hair, or gold, or pearls, or costly array; 10 But (which becometh women professing godliness) with good works. 11 Let the woman learn in silence with all subjection. 12 But I suffer not a woman to teach, nor to usurp authority over the man, but to be in silence. 13 For Adam was first formed, then Eve. 14And Adam was not deceived, but the woman being deceived was in the transgression. 15 Notwithstanding she shall be saved in childbearing, if they continue in faith and charity and holiness with sobriety.

R.S.V.

me, as the foremost, Jesus Christ might display his perfect patience for an example to those who were to believe in him for eternal life. 17 To the King of ages, immortal, invisible, the only God, be honor and glory for ever and ever.[b] Amen.

18 This charge I commit to you, Timothy, my son, in accordance with the prophetic utterances which pointed to you, that inspired by them you may wage the good warfare, 19 holding faith and a good conscience. By rejecting conscience, certain persons have made shipwreck of their faith, 20 among them Hymenaeus and Alexander, whom I have delivered to Satan that they may learn not to blaspheme.

2 First of all, then, I urge that supplications, prayers, intercessions, and thanksgivings be made for all men, 2 for kings and all who are in high positions, that we may lead a quiet and peaceable life, godly and respectful in every way. 3 This is good, and it is acceptable in the sight of God our Savior, 4 who desires all men to be saved and to come to the knowledge of the truth. 5 For there is one God, and there is one mediator between God and men, the man Christ Jesus, 6 who gave himself as a ransom for all, the testimony to which was borne at the proper time. 7 For this I was appointed a preacher and apostle (I am telling the truth, I am not lying), a teacher of the Gentiles in faith and truth.

8 I desire then that in every place the men should pray, lifting holy hands without anger or quarreling; 9 also that women should adorn themselves modestly and sensibly in seemly apparel, not with braided hair or gold or pearls or costly attire 10 but by good deeds, as befits women who profess religion. 11 Let a woman learn in silence with all submissiveness. 12 I permit no woman to teach or to have authority over men; she is to keep silent. 13 For Adam was formed first, then Eve; 14 and Adam was not deceived, but the woman was deceived and became a transgressor. 15 Yet woman will be saved through bearing children,[c] if she continues[d] in faith and love and holiness, with modesty.

demonstration of the extent of Christ's patience toward the worst of men, to serve as an example to all who in the future should trust him for eternal life.

So to the king of all the ages, the immortal, invisible, and only God, be honor and glory for ever and ever, amen!

My personal charge to you   1. 18

Timothy my son, I give you the following charge. (And may I say, before I give it to you, that it is in full accord with those prophecies made at your ordination, which sent you out to battle for the right armed only with your faith and a clear conscience. Some, alas, have laid these simple weapons contemptuously aside and, as far as their faith is concerned, have run their ships on the rocks. Hymenaeus and Alexander are men of this sort, and as a matter of fact I had to expel them from the Church to teach them not to blaspheme.) Here then is my charge:

First, supplications, prayers, intercessions and thanksgivings should be made on behalf of all men: for kings and rulers in positions of responsibility, so that our common life may be lived in peace and quiet, with a proper sense of God and of our responsibility to him for what we do with our lives. In the sight of God our savior this is undoubtedly the right thing to pray for; for his purpose is that all men should be saved and come to realize the truth. And that is, that there is only one God, and only one intermediary between God and men, the Man Jesus Christ. He gave himself as a ransom for us all—an act of redemption which happened once, but which stands for all time as a witness to what he is. I was appointed proclaimer and messenger of this great act of his, to teach (incredible as it may sound) the gentile world to believe and know the truth.

My views on men and women   2. 8
in the church

Therefore, I want the men to pray in all the churches with sincerity, without resentment or doubt in their minds. The women should be dressed quietly, and their demeanor should be modest and serious. The adornment of a Christian woman is not a matter of an elaborate coiffure, expensive clothes or valuable jewelry, but the living of a good life. A woman should learn quietly and humbly. Personally, I don't allow women to teach, nor do I ever put them in positions of authority over men—I believe their role is to be receptive. (My reasons are that man was created before woman. Further, it was Eve and not Adam who was first deceived and fell into sin. Nevertheless I believe that women will come safely through childbirth if they maintain a life of faith, love, holiness and gravity.)

this very purpose, that Jesus Christ might find in me the first occasion for displaying all his patience, and that I might be typical of all who were in future to have faith in him and gain eternal life. Now to the King of all worlds, immortal, invisible, the only God, be honour and glory for ever and ever! Amen.

This charge, son Timothy, I lay upon you, following that prophetic utterance which first pointed you out to me. So fight gallantly, armed with faith and a good conscience. It was through spurning conscience that certain persons made shipwreck of their faith, among them Hymenaeus and Alexander, whom I consigned to Satan, in the hope that through this discipline they might learn not to be blasphemous.

2 First of all, then, I urge that petitions, prayers, intercessions, and thanksgivings be offered for all men; for sovereigns and all in high office, that we may lead a tranquil and quiet life in full observance of religion and high standards of morality. Such prayer is right, and approved by God our Saviour, whose will it is that all men should find salvation and come to know the truth. For there is one God, and also one mediator between God and men, Christ Jesus, himself man, who sacrificed himself to win freedom for all mankind, so providing, at the fitting time, proof of the divine purpose; of this I was appointed herald and apostle (this is no lie, but the truth), to instruct the nations in the true faith.

It is my desire, therefore, that everywhere prayers be said by the men of the congregation, who shall lift up their hands with a pure intention, excluding angry or quarrelsome thoughts. Women again must dress in becoming manner, modestly and soberly, not with elaborate hairstyles, not decked out with gold or pearls, or expensive clothes, but with good deeds, as befits women who claim to be religious. A woman must be a learner, listening quietly and with due submission. I do not permit a woman to be a teacher, nor must woman domineer over man; she should be quiet. For Adam was created first, and Eve afterwards; and it was not Adam who was deceived; it was the woman who, yielding to deception, fell into sin. Yet she will be saved through motherhood[a]—if only women continue in faith,[b] love, and holiness, with a sober mind.

[a] *Or* saved through the Birth of the Child, *or* brought safely through childbirth. [b] *Or* if only husband and wife continue in mutual fidelity . . .

K.J.V.

3 This *is* a true saying, If a man desire the office of a bishop, he desireth a good work. 2A bishop then must be blameless, the husband of one wife, vigilant, sober, of good behaviour, given to hospitality, apt to teach; 3 Not given to wine, no striker, not greedy of filthy lucre; but patient, not a brawler, not covetous; 4 One that ruleth well his own house, having his children in subjection with all gravity; 5 (For if a man know not how to rule his own house, how shall he take care of the church of God?) 6 Not a novice, lest being lifted up with pride he fall into the condemnation of the devil. 7 Moreover he must have a good report of them which are without; lest he fall into reproach and the snare of the devil. 8 Likewise *must* the deacons *be* grave, not double-tongued, not given to much wine, not greedy of filthy lucre; 9 Holding the mystery of the faith in a pure conscience. 10And let these also first be proved; then let them use the office of a deacon, being *found* blameless. 11 Even so *must their* wives *be* grave, not slanderers, sober, faithful in all things. 12 Let the deacons be the husbands of one wife, ruling their children and their own houses well. 13 For they that have used the office of a deacon well purchase to themselves a good degree, and great boldness in the faith which is in Christ Jesus. 14 These things write I unto thee, hoping to come unto thee shortly: 15 But if I tarry long, that thou mayest know how thou oughtest to behave thyself in the house of God, which is the church of the living God, the pillar and ground of the truth. 16And without controversy great is the mystery of godliness: God was manifest in the flesh, justified in the Spirit, seen of angels, preached unto the Gentiles, believed on in the world, received up into glory.

R.S.V.

3 The saying is sure: If any one aspires to the office of bishop, he desires a noble task. 2 Now a bishop must be above reproach, the husband of one wife, temperate, sensible, dignified, hospitable, an apt teacher, 3 no drunkard, not violent but gentle, not quarrelsome, and no lover of money. 4 He must manage his own household well, keeping his children submissive and respectful in every way; 5 for if a man does not know how to manage his own household, how can he care for God's church? 6 He must not be a recent convert, or he may be puffed up with conceit and fall into the condemnation of the devil;*f* 7 moreover he must be well thought of by outsiders, or he may fall into reproach and the snare of the devil.*f*
8 Deacons likewise must be serious, not double-tongued, not addicted to much wine, not greedy for gain; 9 they must hold the mystery of the faith with a clear conscience. 10And let them also be tested first; then if they prove themselves blameless let them serve as deacons. 11 The women likewise must be serious, no slanderers, but temperate, faithful in all things. 12 Let deacons be the husband of one wife, and let them manage their children and their households well; 13 for those who serve well as deacons gain a good standing for themselves and also great confidence in the faith which is in Christ Jesus.
14 I hope to come to you soon, but I am writing these instructions to you so that, 15 if I am delayed, you may know how one ought to behave in the household of God, which is the church of the living God, the pillar and bulwark of the truth. 16 Great indeed, we confess, is the mystery of our religion:
He*h* was manifested in the flesh,
　vindicated *i* in the Spirit,
　　seen by angels,
　preached among the nations,
　believed on in the world,
　　taken up in glory.

[f] Or *slanderer.* [h] Greek *Who;* other ancient authorities read *God;* others, *Which.* [i] Or *justified.*

PHILLIPS

N.E.B.

The sort of men to bear office: 3. 1
bishops

It is quite true to say that a man who sets his heart on holding office has laudable ambition. Well, for the office of a bishop a man must be of blameless reputation, he must be married to one wife only, and be a man of self-control and discretion. He must be a man of disciplined life; he must be hospitable and have the gift of teaching. He must be neither intemperate nor violent, but gentle. He must not be a controversialist nor must he be fond of money-grabbing. He must have proper authority in his own household, and be able to control and command the respect of his children. (For if a man cannot rule in his own house how can he look after the Church of God?) He must not be a beginner in the faith, for fear of his becoming conceited and sharing the devil's downfall. He should, in addition to the above qualifications, have a good reputation with the outside world, in case his good name is attacked and he is caught by the devil that way.

Deacons 3. 8

Deacons, similarly, should be men of serious outlook and sincere conviction. They too should be temperate and not greedy for money. They should hold the mystery of the faith with complete sincerity.

Let them serve a period of probation first, and only serve as deacons if they prove satisfactory. Their wives should share their serious outlook, and must be women of discretion and self-control—women who can be trusted. Deacons should be men with only one wife, able to control their children and manage their own households properly. Those who do well as deacons earn for themselves a certain legitimate standing, as well as gaining confidence and freedom in the Christian faith.

The tremendous responsibility 3. 14
of being God's minister

At the moment of writing I hope to be with you soon, but if there should be any considerable delay then what I have written will show you the sort of character men of God's household ought to have. It is, remember, the Church of the living God, the pillar and the foundation of the truth. No one would deny that this religion of ours is a tremendous mystery, resting as it does on the one who showed himself as a human being, and met, as such, every demand of the Spirit in the sight of the angels. He has been proclaimed among the nations, believed in throughout the world, and received back into the glory of Heaven.

3 There is a popular saying:[a] 'To aspire to leadership is an honourable ambition.' Our leader, therefore, or bishop, must be above reproach, faithful to his one wife,[b] sober, temperate, courteous, hospitable, and a good teacher; he must not be given to drink, or a brawler, but of a forbearing disposition, avoiding quarrels, and no lover of money. He must be one who manages his own household well and wins obedience from his children, and a man of the highest principles. If a man does not know how to control his own family, how can he look after a congregation of God's people? He must not be a convert newly baptized, for fear the sin of conceit should bring upon him a judgement contrived by the devil.[c] He must moreover have a good reputation with the non-Christian public, so that he may not be exposed to scandal and get caught in the devil's snare.

Deacons, likewise, must be men of high principle, not indulging in double talk, given neither to excessive drinking nor to money-grabbing. They must be men who combine a clear conscience with a firm hold on the deep truths of our faith. No less than bishops, they must first undergo a scrutiny, and if there is no mark against them, they may serve. Their wives,[d] equally, must be women of high principle, who will not talk scandal, sober and trustworthy in every way. A deacon must be faithful to his one wife,[b] and good at managing his children and his own household. For deacons with a good record of service may claim a high standing and the right to speak openly on matters of the Christian faith.

I am hoping to come to you before long, but I write this in case I am delayed, to let you know how men ought to conduct themselves in God's household, that is, the church of the living God, the pillar and bulwark of the truth. And great beyond all question is the mystery of our religion:

'He who was manifested in the body,
   vindicated in the spirit,
      seen by angels;
who was proclaimed among the nations,
   believed in throughout the world,
      glorified in high heaven.'

[a] Some witnesses read Here are words you may trust, which some interpreters attach to the end of the preceding paragraph. [b] Or married to one wife, or married only once. [c] Or the judgement once passed on the devil. [d] Or . . . serve. Deaconesses . . .

K.J.V.

4 Now the Spirit speaketh expressly, that in the latter times some shall depart from the faith, giving heed to seducing spirits, and doctrines of devils; 2 Speaking lies in hypocrisy; having their conscience seared with a hot iron; 3 Forbidding to marry, *and commanding* to abstain from meats, which God hath created to be received with thanksgiving of them which believe and know the truth. 4 For every creature of God *is* good, and nothing to be refused, if it be received with thanksgiving: 5 For it is sanctified by the word of God and prayer. 6 If thou put the brethren in remembrance of these things, thou shalt be a good minister of Jesus Christ, nourished up in the words of faith and of good doctrine, whereunto thou hast attained. 7 But refuse profane and old wives' fables, and exercise thyself *rather* unto godliness. 8 For bodily exercise profiteth little: but godliness is profitable unto all things, having promise of the life that now is, and of that which is to come. 9 This *is* a faithful saying, and worthy of all acceptation. 10 For therefore we both labour and suffer reproach, because we trust in the living God, who is the Saviour of all men, specially of those that believe. 11 These things command and teach. 12 Let no man despise thy youth; but be thou an example of the believers, in word, in conversation, in charity, in spirit, in faith, in purity. 13 Till I come, give attendance to reading, to exhortation, to doctrine. 14 Neglect not the gift that is in thee, which was given thee by prophecy, with the laying on of the hands of the presbytery. 15 Meditate upon these things; give thyself wholly to them; that thy profiting may appear to all. 16 Take heed unto thyself, and unto the doctrine; continue in them: for in doing this thou shalt both save thyself, and them that hear thee.

5 Rebuke not an elder, but entreat *him* as a father; *and* the younger men as brethren; 2 The elder women as mothers; the younger as sisters, with all purity. 3 Honour widows that are widows indeed. 4 But if any widow have children

R.S.V.

4 Now the Spirit expressly says that in later times some will depart from the faith by giving heed to deceitful spirits and doctrines of demons, 2 through the pretensions of liars whose consciences are seared, 3 who forbid marriage and enjoin abstinence from foods which God created to be received with thanksgiving by those who believe and know the truth. 4 For everything created by God is good, and nothing is to be rejected if it is received with thanksgiving; 5 for then it is consecrated by the word of God and prayer.

6 If you put these instructions before the brethren, you will be a good minister of Christ Jesus, nourished on the words of the faith and of the good doctrine which you have followed. 7 Have nothing to do with godless and silly myths. Train yourself in godliness; 8 for while bodily training is of some value, godliness is of value in every way, as it holds promise for the present life and also for the life to come. 9 The saying is sure and worthy of full acceptance. 10 For to this end we toil and strive,[j] because we have our hope set on the living God, who is the Savior of all men, especially of those who believe.

11 Command and teach these things. 12 Let no one despise your youth, but set the believers an example in speech and conduct, in love, in faith, in purity. 13 Till I come, attend to the public reading of scripture, to preaching, to teaching. 14 Do not neglect the gift you have, which was given you by prophetic utterance when the elders laid their hands upon you. 15 Practice these duties, devote yourself to them, so that all may see your progress. 16 Take heed to yourself and to your teaching; hold to that, for by so doing you will save both yourself and your hearers.

5 Do not rebuke an older man but exhort him as you would a father; treat younger men like brothers, 2 older women like mothers, younger women like sisters, in all purity.

3 Honor widows who are real widows. 4 If a widow has children or grandchildren, let them

[j] Other ancient authorities read *suffer reproach*.

Beware of false teachers: warn your people

4. 1

God's Spirit specifically tells us that in later days there will be men who abandon the true faith and allow themselves to be spiritually seduced by teachings of demons, teachings given by men who are lying hypocrites, whose consciences are as dead as seared flesh. These men forbid marriage and command abstinence from foods—good things which, in fact, God intends to be thankfully enjoyed by those who believe in him and know the truth. Everything God made is good, and is meant to be gratefully used, not despised. (The holiness or otherwise of a certain food, for instance, depends not on its nature but on whether it is eaten thankfully or not.) It is consecrated by the Word of God and by prayer.

You will be doing your duty as Christ's minister if you remind your church members of these things, and you will show yourself as one who owes his strength to the truth of the faith he has absorbed and the sound teaching he has followed. But steer clear of all these stupid Godless fictions.

Take time and trouble to keep yourself spiritually fit. Bodily fitness has a certain value, but spiritual fitness is essential, both for this present life and for the life to come. There is no doubt about this at all, and Christians should remember it. It is because we realize the paramount importance of the spiritual that we labor and struggle. We place our whole confidence in the living God, the savior of all men, and particularly of those who believe in him. These convictions should be the basis of your instruction and teaching.

A little personal advice

4. 12

Don't let people look down on you because you are young; see that they look up to you because you are an example to them in your speech and behavior, in your love and faith and sincerity. Concentrate until my arrival on your reading and on your preaching and teaching. Do not neglect the gift that was given to you in the proclaiming of God's Word when the assembled elders laid their hands on you. Give your whole attention, all your energies, to these things, so that your progress is plain for all to see. Keep a critical eye both upon your own life and on the teaching you give, and if you continue to follow the line I have indicated you will not only save your own soul but the souls of your hearers as well.

Don't reprimand a senior member of your church; appeal to him as a father. Treat the young men as brothers, and the older women as mothers. Treat the younger women as sisters, and no more.

How to deal with widows in the church

5. 3

You should treat with great consideration widows who are really alone in the world. But remember that if a widow has children or grandchildren it is primarily their duty to show the

4 The Spirit says expressly that in after times some will desert from the faith and give their minds to subversive doctrines inspired by devils, through the specious falsehoods of men whose own conscience is branded with the devil's sign. They forbid marriage and inculcate abstinence from certain foods, though God created them to be enjoyed with thanksgiving by believers who have inward knowledge of the truth. For everything that God created is good, and nothing is to be rejected when it is taken with thanksgiving, since it is hallowed by God's own word and by prayer.

By offering such advice as this to the brotherhood you will prove a good servant of Christ Jesus, bred in the precepts of our faith and of the sound instruction which you have followed. Have nothing to do with those godless myths, fit only for old women. Keep yourself in training for the practice of religion. The training of the body does bring limited benefit, but the benefits of religion are without limit, since it holds promise not only for this life but for the life to come. Here are words you may trust, words that merit full acceptance: 'With this before us we labour and struggle,[a] because[b] we have set our hope on the living God, who is the Saviour of all men'—the Saviour, above all, of believers.

Pass on these orders and these teachings. Let no one slight you because you are young, but make yourself an example to believers in speech and behaviour, in love, fidelity, and purity. Until I arrive devote your attention to the public reading of the scriptures, to exhortation, and to teaching. Do not neglect the spiritual endowment you possess, which was given you, under the guidance of prophecy, through the laying on of the hands of the elders as a body.[c]

Make these matters your business and your absorbing interest, so that your progress may be plain to all. Persevere in them, keeping close watch on yourself and your teaching; by doing so you will further the salvation of yourself and your hearers.

5 Never be harsh with an elder; appeal to him as if he were your father. Treat the younger men as brothers, the older women as mothers, and the younger as your sisters, in all purity.

The status of widow is to be granted only to widows who are such in the full sense. But if a widow has children or grandchildren, then they

[a] *Some witnesses read* suffer reproach. [b] *Or* since 'It holds promise . . . to come.' These are words . . . acceptance. For this is the aim of all our labour and struggle, since . . . [c] *Or* through your ordination as an elder.

K.J.V.

or nephews, let them learn first to shew piety at home, and to requite their parents: for that is good and acceptable before God. 5 Now she that is a widow indeed, and desolate, trusteth in God, and continueth in supplications and prayers night and day. 6 But she that liveth in pleasure is dead while she liveth. 7 And these things give in charge, that they may be blameless. 8 But if any provide not for his own, and specially for those of his own house, he hath denied the faith, and is worse than an infidel. 9 Let not a widow be taken into the number under threescore years old, having been the wife of one man, 10 Well reported of for good works; if she have brought up children, if she have lodged strangers, if she have washed the saints' feet, if she have relieved the afflicted, if she have diligently followed every good work. 11 But the younger widows refuse: for when they have begun to wax wanton against Christ, they will marry; 12 Having damnation, because they have cast off their first faith. 13 And withal they learn *to be* idle, wandering about from house to house; and not only idle, but tattlers also and busybodies, speaking things which they ought not. 14 I will therefore that the younger women marry, bear children, guide the house, give none occasion to the adversary to speak reproachfully. 15 For some are already turned aside after Satan. 16 If any man or woman that believeth have widows, let them relieve them, and let not the church be charged; that it may relieve them that are widows indeed. 17 Let the elders that rule well be counted worthy of double honour, especially they who labour in the word and doctrine. 18 For the Scripture saith, Thou shalt not muzzle the ox that treadeth out the corn. And, The labourer *is* worthy of his reward. 19 Against an elder receive not an accusation, but before two or three witnesses. 20 Them that sin rebuke before all, that others also may fear. 21 I charge *thee* before God, and the Lord Jesus Christ, and the elect angels, that thou observe these things without preferring one before another, doing nothing by partiality. 22 Lay hands suddenly on no man, neither be partaker of other men's sins: keep thyself pure. 23 Drink no longer water, but

R.S.V.

first learn their religious duty to their own family and make some return to their parents; for this is acceptable in the sight of God. 5 She who is a real widow, and is left all alone, has set her hope on God and continues in supplications and prayers night and day; 6 whereas she who is self-indulgent is dead even while she lives. 7 Command this, so that they may be without reproach. 8 If any one does not provide for his relatives, and especially for his own family, he has disowned the faith and is worse than an unbeliever.

9 Let a widow be enrolled if she is not less than sixty years of age, having been the wife of one husband; 10 and she must be well attested for her good deeds, as one who has brought up children, shown hospitality, washed the feet of the saints, relieved the afflicted, and devoted herself to doing good in every way. 11 But refuse to enrol younger widows; for when they grow wanton against Christ they desire to marry, 12 and so they incur condemnation for having violated their first pledge. 13 Besides that, they learn to be idlers, gadding about from house to house, and not only idlers but gossips and busybodies, saying what they should not. 14 So I would have younger widows marry, bear children, rule their households, and give the enemy no occasion to revile us. 15 For some have already strayed after Satan. 16 If any believing woman[1] has relatives who are widows, let her assist them; let the church not be burdened, so that it may assist those who are real widows.

17 Let the elders who rule well be considered worthy of double honor, especially those who labor in preaching and teaching; 18 for the scripture says, "You shall not muzzle an ox when it is treading out the grain," and, "The laborer deserves his wages." 19 Never admit any charge against an elder except on the evidence of two or three witnesses. 20 As for those who persist in sin, rebuke them in the presence of all, so that the rest may stand in fear. 21 In the presence of God and of Christ Jesus and of the elect angels I charge you to keep these rules without favor, doing nothing from partiality. 22 Do not be hasty in the laying on of hands, nor participate in another man's sins; keep yourself pure.

23 No longer drink only water, but use a

[1] Other ancient authorities read *man or woman;* others, simply *man.*

PHILLIPS

genuineness of their religion in their own homes by repaying their parents for what has been done for them, and God readily accepts such service.

But the widow who is really alone and desolate can only hope in God, and she will pray to him day and night. The widow who plunges into all the pleasure that the world can give her is killing her own soul.

You should therefore make the following rules for the widows, to avoid abuses:

1. You should make it clear that for a man to refuse to look after his own relations, especially those actually living in his house, is a denial of the faith he professes. He is far worse than a man who makes no profession.

2. Widows for your church list should be at least sixty years of age, should have had only one husband and have a well founded reputation for having lived a good life. Some such questions as these should be asked:—has she brought up her children well, has she been hospitable to strangers, has she been willing to serve fellow Christians in menial ways, has she relieved those in distress, has she, in a word, conscientiously done all the good she can?

3. Don't put the younger widows on your list. My experience is that when their natural desires grow stronger than their spiritual devotion to Christ they want to marry again, thus proving themselves unfaithful to their loyalty. Moreover, they get into habits of slackness by being so much in and out of other people's houses. In fact they easily become worse than lazy, and degenerate into gossips and busybodies with dangerous tongues.

4. My advice is that the younger widows should, normally, marry again, bear children and run their own households. They should certainly not be the means of lowering the reputation of the church, although some, alas, have already played into the enemy's hands.

5. As a general rule it should be taken for granted that any Christian, man or woman, who has a widow in the family should do everything possible for her, and not allow her to become the church's responsibility. The church will then be free to look after those widows who are alone in the world.

You and your elders   5. 17

Elders with a gift of leadership should be considered worthy of respect, and of adequate salary, particularly if they work hard at their preaching and teaching. Remember the scriptural principle:

Thou shalt not muzzle the ox when he treadeth out the corn,

and

The laborer is worthy of his hire.

Take no notice of charges brought against an elder unless they can be substantiated by proper witnesses. If sin is actually proved, then the offenders should be publicly rebuked as a salutary warning to others.

Timothy, I solemnly charge you in the sight of God and Christ Jesus and the holy angels to follow these orders with the strictest impartiality and to have no favorites.

Never be in a hurry to ordain a man, or you may be making yourself responsible for his sins. Be careful that your own life is pure. (By the

N.E.B.

should learn as their first duty to show loyalty to the family and to repay what they owe to their parents and grandparents; for this God approves. A widow, however, in the full sense, one who is alone in the world, has all her hope set on God, and regularly attends the meetings for prayer and worship night and day. But a widow given over to self-indulgence is as good as dead. Add these orders to the rest, so that the widows may be above reproach. But if anyone does not make provision for his relations, and especially for members of his own household, he has denied the faith and is worse than an unbeliever.

A widow should not be put on the roll under sixty years of age. She must have been faithful in marriage to one man, and must produce evidence of good deeds performed, showing whether she has had the care of children, or given hospitality, or washed the feet of God's people, or supported those in distress—in short, whether she has taken every opportunity of doing good.

Younger widows may not be placed on the roll. For when their passions draw them away from Christ, they hanker after marriage and stand condemned for breaking their troth with him. Moreover, in going round from house to house they learn to be idle, and worse than idle, gossips and busybodies, speaking of things better left unspoken. It is my wish, therefore, that young widows shall marry again, have children, and preside over a home; then they will give no opponent occasion for slander. For there have in fact been widows who have taken the wrong turning and gone to the devil.

If a Christian man or woman has widows in the family, he must support them himself;[a] the congregation must be relieved of the burden, so that it may be free to support those who are widows in the full sense of the term.

Elders who do well as leaders should be reckoned worthy of a double stipend, in particular those who labour at preaching and teaching. For Scripture says, 'A threshing ox shall not be muzzled'; and besides, 'the workman earns his pay'.

Do not entertain a charge against an elder unless it is supported by two or three witnesses. Those who commit sins you must expose publicly, to put fear into the others. Before God and Christ Jesus and the angels who are his chosen, I solemnly charge you, maintain these rules, and never pre-judge the issue, but act with strict impartiality. Do not be over-hasty in laying on hands in ordination,[b] or you may find yourself responsible for other people's misdeeds; keep your own hands clean.

Stop drinking nothing but water; take a little

[a] *Some witnesses read* If a Christian woman has widows in her family, she must support them herself. [b] *Or* in restoring an offender by the laying on of hands.

K.J.V.

use a little wine for thy stomach's sake and thine often infirmities. 24 Some men's sins are open beforehand, going before to judgment; and some *men* they follow after. 25 Likewise also the good works *of some* are manifest beforehand; and they that are otherwise cannot be hid.

6 Let as many servants as are under the yoke count their own masters worthy of all honour, that the name of God and *his* doctrine be not blasphemed. 2And they that have believing masters, let them not despise *them,* because they are brethren; but rather do *them* service, because they are faithful and beloved, partakers of the benefit. These things teach and exhort. 3 If any man teach otherwise, and consent not to wholesome words, *even* the words of our Lord Jesus Christ, and to the doctrine which is according to godliness; 4 He is proud, knowing nothing, but doting about questions and strifes of words, whereof cometh envy, strife, railings, evil surmisings, 5 Perverse disputings of men of corrupt minds, and destitute of the truth, supposing that gain is godliness: from such withdraw thyself. 6 But godliness with contentment is great gain. 7 For we brought nothing into *this* world, *and it is* certain we can carry nothing out. 8And having food and raiment, let us be therewith content. 9 But they that will be rich fall into temptation and a snare, and *into* many foolish and hurtful lusts, which drown men in destruction and perdition. 10 For the love of money is the root of all evil: which while some coveted after, they have erred from the faith, and pierced themselves through with many sorrows. 11 But thou, O man of God, flee these things; and follow after righteousness, godliness, faith, love, patience, meekness. 12 Fight the good fight of faith, lay hold on eternal life, whereunto thou art also called, and hast professed a good profession before many witnesses. 13 I give thee charge in the sight of God, who quickeneth all things, and *before* Christ Jesus, who before Pon-

R.S.V.

little wine for the sake of your stomach and your frequent ailments.
24 The sins of some men are conspicuous, pointing to judgment, but the sins of others appear later. 25 So also good deeds are conspicuous; and even when they are not, they cannot remain hidden.

6 Let all who are under the yoke of slavery regard their masters as worthy of all honor, so that the name of God and the teaching may not be defamed. 2 Those who have believing masters must not be disrespectful on the ground that they are brethren; rather they must serve all the better since those who benefit by their service are believers and beloved.
Teach and urge these duties. 3 If any one teaches otherwise and does not agree with the sound words of our Lord Jesus Christ and the teaching which accords with godliness, 4 he is puffed up with conceit, he knows nothing; he has a morbid craving for controversy and for disputes about words, which produce envy, dissension, slander, base suspicions, 5 and wrangling among men who are depraved in mind and bereft of the truth, imagining that godliness is a means of gain. 6 There is great gain in godliness with contentment; 7 for we brought nothing into the world, and *m* we cannot take anything out of the world; 8 but if we have food and clothing, with these we shall be content. 9 But those who desire to be rich fall into temptation, into a snare, into many senseless and hurtful desires that plunge men into ruin and destruction. 10 For the love of money is the root of all evils; it is through this craving that some have wandered away from the faith and pierced their hearts with many pangs.
11 But as for you, man of God, shun all this; aim at righteousness, godliness, faith, love, steadfastness, gentleness. 12 Fight the good fight of the faith; take hold of the eternal life to which you were called when you made the good confession in the presence of many witnesses. 13 In the presence of God who gives life to all things, and of Christ Jesus who in his testimony before Pontius Pilate made the good confession,

[m] Other ancient authorities insert *it is certain that.*

way, I should advise you to drink wine in moderation, instead of water. It will do your stomach good and help you to get over your frequent spells of illness.) Remember that some men's sins are obvious, and are equally obviously bringing them to judgment. The sins of other men are not apparent, but are dogging them, nevertheless, under the surface. Similarly some virtues are plain to see, while others, though not at all conspicuous, will eventually make themselves felt.

wine for your digestion, for your frequent ailments.

While there are people whose offences are so obvious that they run before them into court, there are others whose offences have not yet overtaken them. Similarly, good deeds are obvious, or even if they are not, they cannot be concealed for ever.

The behavior of slaves in the church
6. 1

Christian slaves should treat their masters with respect, and avoid causing dishonor to the name of God and our teaching. If they have Christian masters they should not despise them because they work for brothers in the faith. Indeed they should serve them all the better because they are thereby benefiting those who have the same faith and love as themselves.

6 All who wear the yoke of slavery must count their own masters worthy of all respect, so that the name of God and the Christian teaching are not brought into disrepute. If the masters are believers, the slaves must not respect them any less for being their Christian brothers. Quite the contrary; they must be all the better servants because those who receive the benefit of their service are one with them in faith and love.

The dangers of false doctrine and the love of money
6. 3

This is the sort of thing you should teach, and if anyone tries to teach some doctrinal novelty which is not compatible with sound teaching (which we base on Christ's own words and which leads to Christ-like living), then he is a conceited idiot! His mind is a morbid jumble of disputation and argument, things which lead to nothing but jealousy, quarreling, insults and malicious innuendoes—continual wrangling, in fact, among men of warped minds who have lost their real hold on the truth but hope to make some profit out of the Christian religion. There is a real profit, of course, but it comes only to those who live contentedly as God would have them live. We brought absolutely nothing with us when we entered this world and we can be sure we shall take absolutely nothing with us when we leave it. Surely then, as far as physical things are concerned, it is sufficient for us to keep our bodies fed and clothed. For men who set their hearts on being wealthy expose themselves to temptation. They fall into one of the world's traps, and lay themselves open to all sorts of silly and wicked desires, which are quite capable of utterly ruining and destroying their souls. For loving money leads to all kinds of evil, and some men in the struggle to be rich have lost their faith and caused themselves untold agonies of mind.

This is what you are to teach and preach. If anyone is teaching otherwise, and will not give his mind to wholesome precepts—I mean those of our Lord Jesus Christ—and to good religious teaching, I call him a pompous ignoramus. He is morbidly keen on mere verbal questions and quibbles, which give rise to jealousy, quarrelling, slander, base suspicions, and endless wrangles: all typical of men who have let their reasoning powers become atrophied and have lost grip of the truth. They think religion should yield dividends; and of course religion does yield high dividends, but only to the man whose resources are within him. We brought nothing into the world, because when we leave it we cannot take anything with us either, but if we have food and covering we may rest content. Those who want to be rich fall into temptations and snares and many foolish harmful desires which plunge men into ruin and perdition. The love of money is the root of all evil things, and there are some who in reaching for it have wandered from the faith and spiked themselves on many thorny griefs.

But you, man of God, must shun all this, and pursue justice, piety, fidelity, love, fortitude, and gentleness. Run the great race of faith and take hold of eternal life. For to this you were called; and you confessed your faith nobly before many witnesses. Now in the presence of God, who gives life to all things, and of Jesus Christ, who himself made the same noble confession and gave his testimony to it before Pontius Pilate, I

Maintain a fearless witness until the last day
6. 11

But you, the man of God, keep clear of such things. Set your heart not on riches, but on goodness, Christ-likeness, faith, love, patience and humility. Fight the worthwhile battle of the faith, keep your grip on that life eternal to which you have been called, and to which you boldly professed your loyalty before many witnesses. I charge you in the sight of God who gives us life, and Jesus Christ who fearlessly witnessed to the truth before Pontius Pilate, to keep your com-

K.J.V.

tius Pilate witnessed a good confession; 14 That thou keep *this* commandment without spot, unrebukeable, until the appearing of our Lord Jesus Christ: 15 Which in his times he shall shew, *who is* the blessed and only Potentate, the King of kings, and Lord of lords; 16 Who only hath immortality, dwelling in the light which no man can approach unto; whom no man hath seen, nor can see: to whom *be* honour and power everlasting. Amen. 17 Charge them that are rich in this world, that they be not highminded, nor trust in uncertain riches, but in the living God, who giveth us richly all things to enjoy; 18 That they do good, that they be rich in good works, ready to distribute, willing to communicate; 19 Laying up in store for themselves a good foundation against the time to come, that they may lay hold on eternal life. 20 O Timothy, keep that which is committed to thy trust, avoiding profane *and* vain babblings, and oppositions of science falsely so called: 21 Which some professing have erred concerning the faith. Grace *be* with thee. Amen.

The first to Timothy was written from Laodicea, which is the chiefest city of Phrygia Pacatiana.

R.S.V.

14 I charge you to keep the commandment unstained and free from reproach until the appearing of our Lord Jesus Christ; 15 and this will be made manifest at the proper time by the blessed and only Sovereign, the King of kings and Lord of lords, 16 who alone has immortality and dwells in unapproachable light, whom no man has ever seen or can see. To him be honor and eternal dominion. Amen.

17 As for the rich in this world, charge them not to be haughty, nor to set their hopes on uncertain riches but on God who richly furnishes us with everything to enjoy. 18 They are to do good, to be rich in good deeds, liberal and generous, 19 thus laying up for themselves a good foundation for the future, so that they may take hold of the life which is life indeed.

20 O Timothy, guard what has been entrusted to you. Avoid the godless chatter and contradictions of what is falsely called knowledge, 21 for by professing it some have missed the mark as regards the faith.

Grace be with you.

mission clean and above reproach until the final coming of Christ. This will be, in his own time, the final dénouement of God, who is the blessed controller of all things, the king over all kings and the master of all masters, the only source of immortality, the one who lives in unapproachable light, the one whom no mortal eye has ever seen or ever can see. To him be acknowledged all honor and power for ever, amen!

Have a word for the rich   6. 17

Tell those who are rich in this present world not to be contemptuous of others, and not to rest the weight of their confidence on the transitory power of wealth but on the living God, who generously gives us everything for our enjoyment. Tell them to do good, to be rich in kindly actions, to be ready to give to others and to sympathize with those in distress. Their security should be invested in the life to come, so that they may be sure of holding a share in the life which is permanent.

My final appeal   6. 20

O Timothy, guard most carefully your divine commission. Avoid the Godless mixture of contradictory notions which is falsely known as "knowledge"—some have followed it *and lost their faith.*

Grace be with you.

                                        PAUL

charge you to obey your orders irreproachably and without fault until our Lord Jesus Christ appears. That appearance God will bring to pass in his own good time—God who in eternal felicity alone holds sway. He is King of kings and Lord of lords; he alone possesses immortality, dwelling in unapproachable light. No man has ever seen or ever can see him. To him be honour and might for ever! Amen.

Instruct those who are rich in this world's goods not to be proud, and not to fix their hopes on so uncertain a thing as money, but upon God, who endows us richly with all things to enjoy. Tell them to hoard a wealth of noble actions by doing good, to be ready to give away and to share, and so acquire a treasure which will form a good foundation for the future. Thus they will grasp the life which is life indeed.

Timothy, keep safe that which has been entrusted to you. Turn a deaf ear to empty and worldly chatter, and the contradictions of so-called 'knowledge', for many who lay claim to it have shot far wide of the faith.

Grace be with you all!

THE SECOND EPISTLE

OF PAUL THE APOSTLE

TO

TIMOTHY

THE SECOND

LETTER OF PAUL TO

TIMOTHY

1 Paul, an apostle of Jesus Christ by the will of God, according to the promise of life which is in Christ Jesus, 2 To Timothy, *my* dearly beloved son: Grace, mercy, *and* peace, from God the Father and Christ Jesus our Lord. 3 I thank God, whom I serve from *my* fore-fathers with pure conscience, that without ceasing I have remembrance of thee in my prayers night and day; 4 Greatly desiring to see thee, being mindful of thy tears, that I may be filled with joy; 5 When I call to remembrance the unfeigned faith that is in thee, which dwelt first in thy grandmother Lois, and thy mother Eunice; and I am persuaded that in thee also. 6 Wherefore I put thee in remembrance, that thou stir up the gift of God, which is in thee by the putting on of my hands. 7 For God hath not given us the spirit of fear; but of power, and of love, and of a sound mind. 8 Be not thou therefore ashamed of the testimony of our Lord, nor of me his prisoner: but be thou partaker of the afflictions of the gospel according to the power of God; 9 Who hath saved us, and called *us* with a holy calling, not according to our works, but according to his own purpose and grace, which was given us in Christ Jesus before the world began; 10 But is now made manifest by the appearing of our Saviour Jesus Christ, who hath abolished death, and hath brought life and immortality to light through the gospel: 11 Whereunto I am appointed a preacher, and an apostle, and a teacher of the Gentiles. 12 For the which cause I also suffer these things: nevertheless I am not ashamed; for I know whom I have believed, and am persuaded that he is able to keep that which I have committed unto him against that day. 13 Hold fast the form of sound words, which thou hast heard of me, in faith and love which is in Christ Jesus. 14 That good thing which was committed unto thee keep by the Holy Ghost which dwelleth in us. 15 This thou knowest, that all they which are in Asia be turned away from me; of whom are Phygellus and Hermogenes. 16 The Lord give mercy unto

1 Paul, an apostle of Christ Jesus by the will of God according to the promise of the life which is in Christ Jesus,
2 To Timothy, my beloved child:
Grace, mercy, and peace from God the Father and Christ Jesus our Lord.

3 I thank God whom I serve with a clear conscience, as did my fathers, when I remember you constantly in my prayers. 4 As I remember your tears, I long night and day to see you, that I may be filled with joy. 5 I am reminded of your sincere faith, a faith that dwelt first in your grandmother Lois and your mother Eunice and now, I am sure, dwells in you. 6 Hence I remind you to rekindle the gift of God that is within you through the laying on of my hands; 7 for God did not give us a spirit of timidity but a spirit of power and love and self-control.
8 Do not be ashamed then of testifying to our Lord, nor of me his prisoner, but take your share of suffering for the gospel in the power of God, 9 who saved us and called us with a holy calling, not in virtue of our works but in virtue of his own purpose and the grace which he gave us in Christ Jesus ages ago, 10 and now has manifested through the appearing of our Savior Christ Jesus, who abolished death and brought life and immortality to light through the gospel. 11 For this gospel I was appointed a preacher and apostle and teacher, 12 and therefore I suffer as I do. But I am not ashamed, for I know whom I have believed, and I am sure that he is able to guard until that Day what has been entrusted to me.[a] 13 Follow the pattern of the sound words which you have heard from me, in the faith and love which are in Christ Jesus; 14 guard the truth that has been entrusted to you by the Holy Spirit who dwells within us.
15 You are aware that all who are in Asia turned away from me, and among them Phygelus and Hermogenes. 16 May the Lord grant mercy

---

[a] Or *what I have entrusted to him.*

THE SECOND
LETTER TO
TIMOTHY

THE SECOND
LETTER OF PAUL TO
TIMOTHY

Character of a Christian Minister

Paul, messenger by God's appointment in the promised life of Christ Jesus, to Timothy, my own dearly loved son: grace, mercy and peace be to you from God the Father and Christ Jesus, our Lord.

I thank God for your faith: *1. 3*
guard it well

I thank the God of my forefathers, whom I serve with a clear conscience, as I remember you constantly in my prayers. Every day and every night I have been longing to see you, for I can't forget how moved you were when I left you, and to have you with me again would be the greatest possible joy. I often think of that genuine faith of yours—a faith that first appeared in your grandmother Lois, then in Eunice your mother, and is now, I am convinced, in you as well. Because of this faith, I now remind you to stir up that inner fire which God gave you at your ordination through my hands. For God has not given us a spirit of fear, but a spirit of power and love and a sound mind. So never be ashamed of bearing witness to our Lord, nor of me, his prisoner. Accept, as I do, all the hardship that faithfulness to the gospel entails in the strength that God gives you. For he has rescued us from all that is really evil and called us to a life of holiness—not because of any of our achievements but for his own purpose. Before time began he planned to give us in Christ Jesus the grace to achieve this purpose, but it is only since our savior Christ Jesus has been revealed that the method has become apparent. For Christ has completely abolished death, and has now, through the gospel, opened to us men the shining possibilities of the life that is eternal. It is this gospel that I am commissioned to proclaim; it is of this gospel that I am appointed both messenger and teacher, and it is for this gospel that I am now suffering these things. Yet I am not in the least ashamed. For I know the one in whom I have placed my confidence, and I am perfectly certain that the work he has committed to me is safe in his hands until that day.

So keep my words in your mind as the pattern of sound teaching, given to you in the faith and love of Christ Jesus. Take the greatest care of the good things which were entrusted to you by the Holy Spirit who lives within us.

1   From Paul, apostle of Jesus Christ by the will of God, whose promise of life is fulfilled in Christ Jesus, to Timothy his dear son.

Grace, mercy, and peace to you from God the Father and our Lord Jesus Christ.

I thank God—whom I, like my forefathers, worship with a pure intention—when I mention you in my prayers; this I do constantly night and day. And when I remember the tears you shed, I long to see you again to make my happiness complete. I am reminded of the sincerity of your faith, a faith which was alive in Lois your grandmother and Eunice your mother before you, and which, I am confident, lives in you also. That is why I now remind you to stir into flame the gift of God which is within you through the laying on of my hands. For the spirit that God gave us is no craven spirit, but one to inspire strength, love, and self-discipline. So never be ashamed of your testimony to our Lord, nor of me his prisoner, but take your share of suffering for the sake of the Gospel, in the strength that comes from God. It is he who brought us salvation and called us to a dedicated life, not for any merit of ours but of his own purpose and his own grace, which was granted to us in Christ Jesus from all eternity, but has now at length been brought fully into view by the appearance on earth of our Saviour Jesus Christ. For he has broken the power of death and brought life and immortality to light through the Gospel.

Of this Gospel I, by his appointment, am herald, apostle, and teacher. That is the reason for my present plight; but I am not ashamed of it, because I know who it is in whom[a] I have trusted, and am confident of his power to keep safe what he has put into my charge,[b] until the great Day. Keep before you an outline of the sound teaching which[c] you heard from me, living by the faith and love which are ours in Christ Jesus. Guard the treasure put into our charge, with the help of the Holy Spirit dwelling within us.

As you know, everyone in the province of Asia deserted me, including Phygelus and Hermogenes. But may the Lord's mercy rest on the

Deserters—and a friend   *1. 15*

You will know, I expect, that all those who are in Asia have turned against me, Phygelus and Hermogenes among them. But may the Lord

[a] *Or* I know the one whom . . . [b] *Or* what I have put into his charge. [c] *Or* Keep before you as a model of sound teaching that which . . .

K.J.V.

the house of Onesiphorus; for he oft refreshed me, and was not ashamed of my chain: 17 But, when he was in Rome, he sought me out very diligently, and found *me*. 18 The Lord grant unto him that he may find mercy of the Lord in that day: and in how many things he ministered unto me at Ephesus, thou knowest very well.

2 Thou therefore, my son, be strong in the grace that is in Christ Jesus. 2And the things that thou hast heard of me among many witnesses, the same commit thou to faithful men, who shall be able to teach others also. 3 Thou therefore endure hardness, as a good soldier of Jesus Christ. 4 No man that warreth entangleth himself with the affairs of *this* life; that he may please him who hath chosen him to be a soldier. 5And if a man also strive for masteries, *yet* is he not crowned, except he strive lawfully. 6 The husbandman that laboureth must be first partaker of the fruits. 7 Consider what I say; and the Lord give thee understanding in all things. 8 Remember that Jesus Christ of the seed of David was raised from the dead, according to my gospel: 9 Wherein I suffer trouble, as an evil doer, *even* unto bonds; but the word of God is not bound. 10 Therefore I endure all things for the elect's sake, that they may also obtain the salvation which is in Christ Jesus with eternal glory. 11 *It is* a faithful saying: For if we be dead with *him,* we shall also live with *him:* 12 If we suffer, we shall also reign with *him:* if we deny *him,* he also will deny us: 13 If we believe not, *yet* he abideth faithful: he cannot deny himself. 14 Of these things put *them* in remembrance, charging *them* before the Lord that they strive not about words to no profit, *but* to the subverting of the hearers. 15 Study to shew thyself approved unto God, a workman that needeth not to be ashamed, rightly dividing the word of truth. 16 But shun profane *and* vain babblings: for they will increase unto more ungodliness. 17And their word will eat as doth a canker: of whom is Hymeneus and Philetus; 18 Who concerning the truth have erred, saying that the resurrection is past already; and overthrow the faith of some. 19 Nevertheless the foundation of God standeth sure, having this seal, The Lord knoweth them that are his. And, Let every one that nameth the name of Christ depart from iniquity. 20 But in a great house there are not only vessels of gold and of silver, but also of wood and of earth; and some to honour, and some to dishonour. 21 If a man therefore purge himself from these, he shall be

R.S.V.

to the household of Onesiphorus, for he often refreshed me; he was not ashamed of my chains, 17 but when he arrived in Rome he searched for me eagerly and found me—18 may the Lord grant him to find mercy from the Lord on that Day—and you well know all the service he rendered at Ephesus.

2 You then, my son, be strong in the grace that is in Christ Jesus, 2 and what you have heard from me before many witnesses entrust to faithful men who will be able to teach others also. 3 Take your share of suffering as a good soldier of Christ Jesus. 4 No soldier on service gets entangled in civilian pursuits, since his aim is to satisfy the one who enlisted him. 5 An athlete is not crowned unless he competes according to the rules. 6 It is the hard-working farmer who ought to have the first share of the crops. 7 Think over what I say, for the Lord will grant you understanding in everything.

8 Remember Jesus Christ, risen from the dead, descended from David, as preached in my gospel, 9 the gospel for which I am suffering and wearing fetters like a criminal. But the word of God is not fettered. 10 Therefore I endure everything for the sake of the elect, that they also may obtain the salvation which in Christ Jesus goes with eternal glory. 11 The saying is sure:

If we have died with him, we shall also live with him;

12 if we endure, we shall also reign with him; if we deny him, he also will deny us;

13 if we are faithless, he remains faithful—for he cannot deny himself.

14 Remind them of this, and charge them before the Lord [b] to avoid disputing about words, which does no good, but only ruins the hearers. 15 Do your best to present yourself to God as one approved, a workman who has no need to be ashamed, rightly handling the word of truth. 16Avoid such godless chatter, for it will lead people into more and more ungodliness, 17 and their talk will eat its way like gangrene. Among them are Hymenaeus and Philetus, 18 who have swerved from the truth by holding that the resurrection is past already. They are upsetting the faith of some. 19 But God's firm foundation stands, bearing this seal: "The Lord knows those who are his," and "Let every one who names the name of the Lord depart from iniquity."

20 In a great house there are not only vessels of gold and silver but also of wood and earthenware, and some for noble use, some for ignoble. 21 If any one purifies himself from what is

[b] Other ancient authorities read *God.*

PHILLIPS

have mercy on the household of Onesiphorus. Many times did that man put fresh heart into me, and he was not in the least ashamed of my being a prisoner in chains. Indeed, when he was in Rome he went to a great deal of trouble to find me—may the Lord grant he finds his mercy in that day!—and you well know in how many ways he helped me at Ephesus as well.

N.E.B.

house of Onesiphorus! He has often relieved me in my troubles. He was not ashamed to visit a prisoner, but took pains to search me out when he came to Rome, and found me. I pray that the Lord may grant him to find mercy from the Lord on the great Day. The many services he rendered at Ephesus you know better than I could tell you.

Above all things be faithful   2. 1

So, my son, be strong in the grace that Christ Jesus gives. Everything that you have heard me teach in public you should in turn entrust to reliable men, who will be able to pass it on to others.

Put up with your share of hardship as a loyal soldier in Christ's army. Remember: 1. That no soldier on active service gets himself entangled in business, or he will not please his commanding officer. 2. A man who enters an athletic contest wins no prize unless he keeps the rules laid down. 3. Only the man who works on the land has the right to the first share of its produce. Consider these three illustrations of mine and the Lord will help you to understand all that I mean.

Remember always, as the center of everything, Jesus Christ, a descendant of David, yet raised by God from the dead according to my Gospel. For preaching this I am having to endure being chained in prison as if I were some sort of criminal. But they cannot chain the Word of God, and I can endure all these things for the sake of those whom God is calling, so that they too may receive the salvation of Christ Jesus, and its complement of glory after the world of time. I rely on this saying: *If we died with him we shall also live with him: if we suffer we shall also reign with him. If we deny him he will also deny us: yet if we are faithless he always remains faithful. He cannot deny his own nature.*

Hold fast to the true: 2. 14
avoid dangerous error

Remind your people of things like this, and tell them as before God not to fight wordy battles, which help no one and may undermine the faith of those who hear them.

For yourself, concentrate on winning God's approval, on being a workman with nothing to be ashamed of, and who knows how to use the word of truth to the best advantage. But steer clear of these un-Christian babblings, which in practice lead further and further away from Christian living. For their teachings are as dangerous as blood poisoning to the body, and spread like sepsis from a wound. Hymenaeus and Philetus are responsible for this sort of thing, and they are men who are palpable traitors to the truth, for they say that the resurrection has already occurred and, of course, badly upset some people's faith.

God's solid foundation still stands, however, with this double inscription: *The Lord knows those who belong to him,* and *Let every true Christian have no dealings with evil.*

In any big household there are naturally not only gold and silver vessels but wooden and earthenware ones as well. Some are used for the highest purposes and some for the lowest. If a man keeps himself clean from the contami-

2 Now therefore, my son, take strength from the grace of God which is ours in Christ Jesus. You heard my teaching in the presence of many witnesses; put that teaching into the charge of men you can trust, such men as will be competent to teach others.

Take your share of hardship, like a good soldier of Christ Jesus. A soldier on active service will not let himself be involved in civilian affairs; he must be wholly at his commanding officer's disposal. Again, no athlete can win a prize unless he has kept the rules. The farmer who gives his labour has first claim on the crop. Reflect on what I say, for the Lord will help you to full understanding.

Remember Jesus Christ, risen from the dead, born of David's line. This is the theme of my gospel, in whose service I am exposed to hardship, even to the point of being shut up like a common criminal; but the word of God is not shut up. And I endure it all for the sake of God's chosen ones, with this end in view, that they too may attain the glorious and eternal salvation which is in Christ Jesus.

Here are words you may trust:

'If we died with him, we shall live with him;
If we endure, we shall reign with him.
If we deny him, he will deny us.
If we are faithless, he keeps faith,
For he cannot deny himself.'

Go on reminding people of this, and adjure them before God to stop disputing about mere words; it does no good, and is the ruin of those who listen. Try hard to show yourself worthy of God's approval, as a labourer who need not be ashamed, driving a straight furrow, in your proclamation of the truth. Avoid empty and worldly chatter; those who indulge in it will stray further and further into godless courses, and the infection of their teaching will spread like a gangrene. Such are Hymenaeus and Philetus; they have shot wide of the truth in saying that our resurrection has already taken place, and are upsetting people's faith. But God has laid a foundation, and it stands firm, with this inscription: 'The Lord knows his own', and, 'Everyone who takes the Lord's name upon his lips must forsake wickedness.' Now in any great house there are not only utensils of gold and silver, but also others of wood or earthenware; the former are valued, the latter held cheap. To be among those which are valued and dedicated, a thing of use to the Master of the house, a man must cleanse

K.J.V.

a vessel unto honour, sanctified, and meet for the master's use, *and* prepared unto every good work. 22 Flee also youthful lusts: but follow righteousness, faith, charity, peace, with them that call on the Lord out of a pure heart. 23 But foolish and unlearned questions avoid, knowing that they do gender strifes. 24And the servant of the Lord must not strive; but be gentle unto all *men*, apt to teach, patient; 25 In meekness instructing those that oppose themselves; if God peradventure will give them repentance to the acknowledging of the truth; 26And *that* they may recover themselves out of the snare of the devil, who are taken captive by him at his will.

3 This know also, that in the last days perilous times shall come. 2 For men shall be lovers of their own selves, covetous, boasters, proud, blasphemers, disobedient to parents, unthankful, unholy, 3 Without natural affection, trucebreakers, false accusers, incontinent, fierce, despisers of those that are good, 4 Traitors, heady, highminded, lovers of pleasures more than lovers of God; 5 Having a form of godliness, but denying the power thereof: from such turn away. 6 For of this sort are they which creep into houses, and lead captive silly women laden with sins, led away with divers lusts, 7 Ever learning, and never able to come to the knowledge of the truth. 8 Now as Jannes and Jambres withstood Moses, so do these also resist the truth: men of corrupt minds, reprobate concerning the faith. 9 But they shall proceed no further: for their folly shall be manifest unto all *men*, as theirs also was. 10 But thou hast fully known my doctrine, manner of life, purpose, faith, longsuffering, charity, patience, 11 Persecutions, afflictions, which came unto me at Antioch, at Iconium, at Lystra; what persecutions I endured: but out of *them* all the Lord delivered me. 12 Yea, and all that will live godly in Christ Jesus shall suffer persecution. 13 But evil men and seducers shall wax worse and worse, deceiving, and being deceived. 14 But continue thou in the things which thou hast learned and hast

R.S.V.

ignoble, then he will be a vessel for noble use, consecrated and useful to the master of the house, ready for any good work. 22 So shun youthful passions and aim at righteousness, faith, love, and peace, along with those who call upon the Lord from a pure heart. 23 Have nothing to do with stupid, senseless controversies; you know that they breed quarrels. 24And the Lord's servant must not be quarrelsome but kindly to every one, an apt teacher, forbearing, 25 correcting his opponents with gentleness. God may perhaps grant that they will repent and come to know the truth, 26 and they may escape from the snare of the devil, after being captured by him to do his will.*

3 But understand this, that in the last days there will come times of stress. 2 For men will be lovers of self, lovers of money, proud, arrogant, abusive, disobedient to their parents, ungrateful, unholy, 3 inhuman, implacable, slanderers, profligates, fierce, haters of good, 4 treacherous, reckless, swollen with conceit, lovers of pleasure rather than lovers of God, 5 holding the form of religion but denying the power of it. Avoid such people. 6 For among them are those who make their way into households and capture weak women, burdened with sins and swayed by various impulses, 7 who will listen to anybody and can never arrive at a knowledge of the truth. 8As Jannes and Jambres opposed Moses, so these men also oppose the truth, men of corrupt mind and counterfeit faith; 9 but they will not get very far, for their folly will be plain to all, as was that of those two men.

10 Now you have observed my teaching, my conduct, my aim in life, my faith, my patience, my love, my steadfastness, 11 my persecutions, my sufferings, what befell me at Antioch, at Iconium, and at Lystra, what persecutions I endured; yet from them all the Lord rescued me. 12 Indeed all who desire to live a godly life in Christ Jesus will be persecuted, 13 while evil men and impostors will go on from bad to worse, deceivers and deceived. 14 But as for you, continue in what you have learned and have firmly

[c] Or *by him, to do his* (that is, God's) *will.*

PHILLIPS

nations of evil he will be a vessel used for honorable purposes, clean and serviceable for the use of the master of the household, all ready, in fact, for any good purpose.

Be positively good—and patient   2. 22

Turn your back on the turbulent desires of youth and give your positive attention to goodness, faith, love and peace in company with all those who approach God in sincerity. But have nothing to do with silly and ill-informed controversies which lead inevitably, as you know, to strife. And the Lord's servant must not be a man of strife: he must be kind to all, ready and able to teach: he must have patience and the ability gently to correct those who oppose his message. He must always bear in mind the possibility that God will give them a different outlook, and that they may come to know the truth. They may come to their senses and be rescued from the snare of the devil by the servant of the Lord and set to work for God's purposes.

A warning of what to expect   3. 1

But you must realize that in the last days the times will be full of danger. Men will become utterly self-centered, greedy for money, full of big words. They will be proud and contemptuous, without any regard for what their parents taught them. They will be utterly lacking in gratitude, purity and normal human affections. They will be men of unscrupulous speech and have no control of themselves. They will be passionate and unprincipled, treacherous, self-willed and conceited, loving all the time what gives them pleasure instead of loving God. They will maintain a façade of "religion," but their conduct will deny its validity. You must keep clear of people like this.

From their number come those creatures who worm their way into people's houses, and find easy prey in silly women with an exaggerated sense of sin and morbid cravings—who are always learning and yet never able to grasp the truth. These men are as much enemies to the truth as Jannes and Jambres were to Moses. Their minds are distorted, and they are traitors to the faith. But in the long run they won't get very far. Their folly will become as obvious to everybody as did that of Moses' opponents.

Your knowledge of the truth   3. 10
should be your safeguard

But you, Timothy, have known intimately both what I have taught and how I have lived. My purpose and my faith are no secrets to you. You saw my endurance and love and patience as I met all those persecutions and difficulties at Antioch, Iconium and Lystra. And you know how the Lord brought me safely through them all. Persecution is inevitable for those who are determined to live really Christian lives, while wicked and deceitful men will go from bad to worse, deluding others and deluding themselves. Yet you must go on steadily in those things that you have learned and which you know are

N.E.B.

himself from all those evil things;[a] then he will be fit for any honourable purpose.

Turn from the wayward impulses of youth, and pursue justice, integrity, love, and peace with all who invoke the Lord in singleness of mind. Have nothing to do with foolish and ignorant speculations. You know they breed quarrels, and the servant of the Lord must not be quarrelsome, but kindly towards all. He should be a good teacher, tolerant, and gentle when discipline is needed for the refractory. The Lord may grant them a change of heart and show them the truth, and thus they may come to their senses and escape from the devil's snare, in which they have been caught and held at his will.[b]

3 You must face the fact: the final age of this world is to be a time of troubles. Men will love nothing but money and self; they will be arrogant, boastful, and abusive; with no respect for parents, no gratitude, no piety, no natural affection; they will be implacable in their hatreds, scandal-mongers, intemperate and fierce, strangers to all goodness, traitors, adventurers, swollen with self-importance. They will be men who put pleasure in the place of God, men who preserve the outward form of religion, but are a standing denial of its reality. Keep clear of men like these. They are the sort that insinuate themselves into private houses and there get miserable women into their clutches, women burdened with a sinful past, and led on by all kinds of desires, who are always wanting to be taught, but are incapable of reaching a knowledge of the truth. As Jannes and Jambres defied Moses, so these men defy the truth; they have lost the power to reason, and they cannot pass the tests of faith. But their successes will be short-lived, for, like those opponents of Moses, they will come to be recognized by everyone for the fools they are.

But you, my son, have followed, step by step, my teaching and my manner of life, my resolution, my faith, patience, and spirit of love, and my fortitude under persecutions and sufferings—all that I went through at Antioch, at Iconium, at Lystra, all the persecutions I endured; and the Lord rescued me out of them all. Yes, persecution will come to all who want to live a godly life as Christians, whereas wicked men and charlatans will make progress from bad to worse, deceiving and deceived. But for your part, stand by the truths you have learned and are

[a] Or must separate himself from these persons.
[b] Or escape from the devil's snare, caught now by God and made subject to his will.

K.J.V.

been assured of, knowing of whom thou hast learned *them;* 15And that from a child thou hast known the holy Scriptures, which are able to make thee wise unto salvation through faith which is in Christ Jesus. 16 All Scripture is given by inspiration of God, and *is* profitable for doctrine, for reproof, for correction, for instruction in righteousness: 17 That the man of God may be perfect, thoroughly furnished unto all good works.

4 I charge *thee* therefore before God, and the Lord Jesus Christ, who shall judge the quick and the dead at his appearing and his kingdom; 2 Preach the word; be instant in season, out of season; reprove, rebuke, exhort with all long-suffering and doctrine. 3 For the time will come when they will not endure sound doctrine; but after their own lusts shall they heap to themselves teachers, having itching ears; 4And they shall turn away *their* ears from the truth, and shall be turned unto fables. 5 But watch thou in all things, endure afflictions, do the work of an evangelist, make full proof of thy ministry. 6 For I am now ready to be offered, and the time of my departure is at hand. 7 I have fought a good fight, I have finished *my* course, I have kept the faith: 8 Henceforth there is laid up for me a crown of righteousness, which the Lord, the righteous judge, shall give me at that day: and not to me only, but unto all them also that love his appearing. 9 Do thy diligence to come shortly unto me: 10 For Demas hath forsaken me, having loved this present world, and is departed unto Thessalonica; Crescens to Galatia, Titus unto Dalmatia. 11 Only Luke is with me. Take Mark, and bring him with thee: for he is profitable to me for the ministry. 12And Tychicus have I sent to Ephesus. 13 The cloak that I left at Troas with Carpus, when thou comest, bring *with thee,* and the books, *but* especially the parchments. 14Alexander the coppersmith did me much evil: the Lord reward him according to his works: 15 Of whom be thou ware also; for he hath greatly withstood our words. 16At my first answer no man stood with me, but all *men* forsook me: *I pray God* that it may not be laid to their charge. 17 Notwithstanding the Lord stood with me, and strengthened me; that by me the preaching might be fully known, and *that* all the Gentiles might hear: and I was delivered out of the mouth of the lion. 18And the

R.S.V.

believed, knowing from whom you learned it 15 and how from childhood you have been acquainted with the sacred writings which are able to instruct you for salvation through faith in Christ Jesus. 16All scripture is inspired by God and *d* profitable for teaching, for reproof, for correction, and for training in righteousness, 17 that the man of God may be complete, equipped for every good work.

4 I charge you in the presence of God and of Christ Jesus who is to judge the living and the dead, and by his appearing and his kingdom: 2 preach the word, be urgent in season and out of season, convince, rebuke, and exhort, be unfailing in patience and in teaching. 3 For the time is coming when people will not endure sound teaching, but having itching ears they will accumulate for themselves teachers to suit their own likings, 4 and will turn away from listening to the truth and wander into myths. 5As for you, always be steady, endure suffering, do the work of an evangelist, fulfil your ministry.

6 For I am already on the point of being sacrificed; the time of my departure has come. 7 I have fought the good fight, I have finished the race, I have kept the faith. 8 Henceforth there is laid up for me the crown of righteousness, which the Lord, the righteous judge, will award to me on that Day, and not only to me but also to all who have loved his appearing.

9 Do your best to come to me soon. 10 For Demas, in love with this present world, has deserted me and gone to Thessalonica; Crescens has gone to Galatia,*e* Titus to Dalmatia. 11 Luke alone is with me. Get Mark and bring him with you; for he is very useful in serving me. 12 Tychicus I have sent to Ephesus. 13 When you come, bring the cloak that I left with Carpus at Troas, also the books, and above all the parchments. 14Alexander the coppersmith did me great harm; the Lord will requite him for his deeds. 15 Beware of him yourself, for he strongly opposed our message. 16At my first defense no one took my part; all deserted me. May it not be charged against them! 17 But the Lord stood by me and gave me strength to proclaim the word fully, that all the Gentiles might hear it. So I was rescued from the lion's mouth. 18 The Lord will

[d] Or *Every scripture inspired by God is also.*
[e] Other ancient authorities read *Gaul.*

PHILLIPS

N.E.B.

true. Remember from what sort of people your knowledge has come, and how from early childhood your mind has been familiar with the holy scriptures, which can open the mind to the salvation which comes through believing in Christ Jesus. All scripture is inspired by God and is useful for teaching the faith and correcting error, for resetting the direction of a man's life and training him in good living. The scriptures are the comprehensive equipment of the man of God, and fit him fully for all branches of his work.

assured of. Remember from whom you learned them; remember that from early childhood you have been familiar with the sacred writings which have power to make you wise and lead you to salvation through faith in Christ Jesus. Every inspired scripture has its use for teaching the truth and refuting error, or for reformation of manners and discipline in right living, so that the man who belongs to God may be efficient and equipped for good work of every kind.

My time is nearly over: ***4. 1***
you must carry on

I solemnly charge you, Timothy, in the presence of God and of Christ Jesus who will judge the living and the dead, by his appearing and his kingdom, to preach the Word of God. Never lose your sense of urgency, in season or out of season. Prove, correct, and encourage, using the utmost patience in your teaching. For the time is coming when men will not tolerate wholesome teaching. They will want something to tickle their own fancies, and they will collect teachers who will pander to their own desires. They will no longer listen to the truth, but will wander off after man-made fictions.

For yourself, stand fast in all that you are doing, meeting whatever suffering this may involve. Go on steadily preaching the gospel and carry out to the full the commission that God gave you.

As for me, I feel that the last drops of my life are being poured out for God. The time for my departure has arrived. The glorious fight that God gave me I have fought, the course that I was set I have finished, and I have kept the faith. The future for me holds the crown of righteousness which God, the true judge, will give to me in that day—and not, of course, only to me but to all those who have loved what they have seen of him.

Personal messages   ***4. 9***

Do your best to come to me as soon as you can. Demas, loving this present world, I fear, has left me and gone to Thessalonica. Crescens has gone to Galatia, and Titus is away in Dalmatia. Only Luke is with me now.

When you come, pick up Mark and bring him with you. I can certainly find a job for him here. (I had to send Tychicus off to Ephesus.) And please bring with you the cloak I left with Carpus at Troas, and the books, especially the manuscripts. Alexander the coppersmith did me a great deal of harm—the Lord will reward him for what he did—and I should be very careful of him if I were you. He has been an obstinate opponent of our teaching.

The first time I had to defend myself no one was on my side—they all deserted me, God forgive them! Yet the Lord himself stood by me and gave me the strength to proclaim the message clearly and fully, so that the gentiles could hear it, and I was rescued "from the lion's mouth." I am sure the Lord will rescue me from every

4 Before God, and before Christ Jesus who is to judge men living and dead, I adjure you by his coming appearance and his reign, proclaim the message, press it home on all occasions,[a] convenient or inconvenient, use argument, reproof, and appeal, with all the patience that the work of teaching requires. For the time will come when they will not stand wholesome teaching, but will follow their own fancy and gather a crowd of teachers to tickle their ears. They will stop their ears to the truth and turn to mythology. But you yourself must keep calm and sane at all times; face hardship, work to spread the Gospel, and do all the duties of your calling.

As for me, already my life is being poured out on the altar, and the hour for my departure is upon me. I have run the great race, I have finished the course, I have kept faith. And now the prize awaits me, the garland of righteousness which the Lord, the all-just Judge, will award me on that great Day; and it is not for me alone, but for all who have set their hearts on his coming appearance.

Do your best to join me soon; for Demas has deserted me because his heart was set on this world; he has gone to Thessalonica, Crescens to Galatia,[b] Titus to Dalmatia; I have no one with me but Luke. Pick up Mark and bring him with you, for I find him a useful assistant. Tychicus I have sent to Ephesus. When you come, bring the cloak I left with Carpus at Troas, and the books, above all my notebooks.

Alexander the copper-smith did me a great deal of harm. Retribution will fall upon him from the Lord. You had better be on your guard against him too, for he violently opposed everything I said. At the first hearing of my case no one came into court to support me; they all left me in the lurch; I pray that it may not be held against them. But the Lord stood by me and lent me strength, so that I might be his instrument in making the full proclamation of the Gospel for the whole pagan world to hear; and thus I was rescued out of the lion's jaws. And the Lord will

---

[a] *Or* be on duty at all times. [b] *Or* Gaul; *some witnesses read* Gallia.

K.J.V.

Lord shall deliver me from every evil work, and will preserve *me* unto his heavenly kingdom: to whom *be* glory for ever and ever. Amen. 19 Salute Prisca and Aquila, and the household of Onesiphorus. 20 Erastus abode at Corinth: but Trophimus have I left at Miletum sick. 21 Do thy diligence to come before winter. Eubulus greeteth thee, and Pudens, and Linus, and Claudia, and all the brethren. 22 The Lord Jesus Christ *be* with thy spirit. Grace *be* with you. Amen.

The second *epistle* unto Timotheus, ordained the first bishop of the church of the Ephesians, was written from Rome, when Paul was brought before Nero the second time.

R.S.V.

rescue me from every evil and save me for his heavenly kingdom. To him be the glory for ever and ever. Amen.

19 Greet Prisca and Aquila, and the house hold of Onesiphorus. 20 Erastus remained at Corinth; Trophimus I left ill at Miletus. 21 Do your best to come before winter. Eubulus sends greetings to you, as do Pudens and Linus and Claudia and all the brethren.

22 The Lord be with your spirit. Grace be with you.

PHILLIPS

evil plot, and will keep me safe until I reach
his heavenly kingdom. Glory be to him for ever
and ever, amen!

Closing greetings   *4. 19*

Give my love to Prisca and Aquila and Onesiphorus and his family. Erastus is still staying
on at Corinth, and Trophimus I had to leave
sick at Miletus.

Do your best to get here before the winter.
Eubulus, Pudens, Linus, Claudia and all here
send their greetings to you. The Lord be with
your spirit. Grace be with you.

PAUL

N.E.B.

rescue me from every attempt to do me harm,
and keep me safe until his heavenly reign begins.[a] Glory to him for ever and ever! Amen.

Greetings to Prisca and Aquila, and the household of Onesiphorus.

Erastus stayed behind at Corinth, and I left
Trophimus ill at Miletus. Do try to get here before winter.

Greetings from Eubulus, Pudens, Linus, and
Claudia, and from all the brotherhood here.

The Lord be with your spirit. Grace be with
you all!

[a] *Or* from all that evil can do, and bring me safely
into his heavenly kingdom.

K.J.V.

THE
EPISTLE OF PAUL
TO
TITUS

1 Paul, a servant of God, and an apostle of Jesus Christ, according to the faith of God's elect, and the acknowledging of the truth which is after godliness; 2 In hope of eternal life, which God, that cannot lie, promised before the world began; 3 But hath in due times manifested his word through preaching, which is committed unto me according to the commandment of God our Saviour; 4 To Titus, *mine* own son after the common faith: Grace, mercy, *and* peace, from God the Father and the Lord Jesus Christ our Saviour. 5 For this cause left I thee in Crete, that thou shouldest set in order the things that are wanting, and ordain elders in every city, as I had appointed thee: 6 If any be blameless, the husband of one wife, having faithful children not accused of riot or unruly. 7 For a bishop must be blameless, as the steward of God; not selfwilled, not soon angry, not given to wine, no striker, not given to filthy lucre; 8 But a lover of hospitality, a lover of good men, sober, just, holy, temperate; 9 Holding fast the faithful word as he hath been taught, that he may be able by sound doctrine both to exhort and to convince the gainsayers. 10 For there are many unruly and vain talkers and deceivers, specially they of the circumcision; 11 Whose mouths must be stopped, who subvert whole houses, teaching things which they ought not, for filthy lucre's sake. 12 One of themselves, *even* a prophet of their own, said, The Cretians *are* always liars, evil beasts, slow bellies. 13 This witness is true. Wherefore rebuke them sharply, that they may be sound in the faith; 14 Not giving heed to Jewish fables, and commandments of men, that turn from the truth. 15 Unto the pure all things *are* pure: but unto them that are defiled and unbe-

R.S.V.

THE
LETTER OF PAUL TO
TITUS

1 Paul, a servant[a] of God and an apostle of Jesus Christ, to further the faith of God's elect and their knowledge of the truth which accords with godliness, 2 in hope of eternal life which God, who never lies, promised ages ago 3 and at the proper time manifested in his word through the preaching with which I have been entrusted by command of God our Savior;

4 To Titus, my true child in a common faith:

Grace and peace from God the Father and Christ Jesus our Savior.

5 This is why I left you in Crete, that you might amend what was defective, and appoint elders in every town as I directed you, 6 if any man is blameless, the husband of one wife, and his children are believers and not open to the charge of being profligate or insubordinate. 7 For a bishop, as God's steward, must be blameless; he must not be arrogant or quick-tempered or a drunkard or violent or greedy for gain, 8 but hospitable, a lover of goodness, master of himself, upright, holy, and self-controlled; 9 he must hold firm to the sure word as taught, so that he may be able to give instruction in sound doctrine and also to confute those who contradict it. 10 For there are many insubordinate men, empty talkers and deceivers, especially the circumcision party; 11 they must be silenced, since they are upsetting whole families by teaching for base gain what they have no right to teach. 12 One of themselves, a prophet of their own, said, "Cretans are always liars, evil beasts, lazy gluttons." 13 This testimony is true. Therefore rebuke them sharply, that they may be sound in the faith, 14 instead of giving heed to Jewish myths or to commands of men who reject the truth. 15 To the pure all things are pure, but to the corrupt and unbelieving nothing is pure;

[a] Or *slave.*

THE LETTER TO

TITUS

Paul, a servant of God and messenger of Jesus Christ in the faith God gives to his chosen, in the knowledge of the truth that comes from a God-fearing life, and in the hope of the everlasting life which God, who cannot lie, promised before the beginning of time—(at the right moment he made his Word known in the declaration which has been entrusted to me by his command)—to Titus, my true son in our common faith, be grace, mercy and peace from God the Father and the Lord Jesus Christ our savior.

Men who are appointed to the   *1. 5*
ministry must be of the
highest character

I left you in Crete to set right matters which needed attention, and gave you instructions to appoint elders in every city. They were to be men of unquestioned integrity with only one wife, and with children brought up as Christians and not likely to be accused of loose living or lawbreaking. To exercise spiritual oversight a man must be of unimpeachable virtue, for he is God's agent in the affairs of his household. He must not be aggressive or hot-tempered or overfond of wine; nor must he be violent or greedy for financial gain. On the contrary, he must be hospitable, a genuine lover of what is good, a man who is discreet, fair-minded, holy and self-controlled: a man who takes his stand on the orthodox faith, so that he can by sound teaching both stimulate faith and confute opposition.

Be on your guard against   *1. 10*
counterfeit Christians

For there are many, especially among the Jews, who will not recognize authority, who talk nonsense and yet in so doing have managed to deceive men's minds. They must be silenced, for they upset the faith of whole households, teaching what they have no business to teach for the sake of what they can get. One of them, yes, one of their prophets, has said: "Men of Crete are always liars, evil and beastly, lazy and greedy." There is truth in this testimonial of theirs! Don't hesitate to reprimand them sharply, for you want them to be sound and healthy Christians, with a proper contempt for Jewish fairy tales and orders issued by men who have forsaken the path of truth. Everything is wholesome to those who are themselves wholesome. But nothing is wholesome to those who are themselves unwholesome and who have no

THE

LETTER OF PAUL TO

TITUS

Training for the Christian Life

1 From Paul, servant of God and apostle of Jesus Christ, marked as such by faith and knowledge and hope—the faith of God's chosen people, knowledge of the truth as our religion has it, and the hope of eternal life.[a] Yes, it is eternal life that God, who cannot lie, promised long ages ago, and now in his own good time he has openly declared himself in the proclamation which was entrusted to me by ordinance of God our Saviour.

To Titus, my true-born son in the faith which we share, grace and peace from God our Father and Christ Jesus our Saviour.

My intention in leaving you behind in Crete was that you should set in order what was left over, and in particular should institute elders in each town. In doing so, observe the tests I prescribed: is he a man of unimpeachable character, faithful to his one wife,[b] the father of children who are believers, who are under no imputation of loose living, and are not out of control? For as God's steward a bishop must be a man of unimpeachable character. He must not be overbearing or short-tempered; he must be no drinker, no brawler, no money-grubber, but hospitable, right-minded, temperate, just, devout, and self-controlled. He must adhere to the true doctrine, so that he may be well able both to move his hearers with wholesome teaching and to confute objectors.

There are all too many, especially among Jewish converts, who are out of all control; they talk wildly and lead men's minds astray. Such men must be curbed, because they are ruining whole families by teaching things they should not, and all for sordid gain. It was a Cretan prophet, one of their own countrymen, who said, 'Cretans were always liars, vicious brutes, lazy gluttons'—and he told the truth! All the more reason why you should pull them up sharply, so that they may come to a sane belief, instead of lending their ears to Jewish myths and commandments of merely human origin, the work of men who turn their backs upon the truth.

To the pure all things are pure; but nothing is pure to the tainted minds of disbelievers, tainted

---

[a] *Or* apostle of Jesus Christ, to bring God's chosen people to faith and to a knowledge of the truth as our religion has it, with its hope for eternal life.
[b] *See note on 1 Timothy 3. 2.*

K.J.V.

lieving *is* nothing pure; but even their mind and conscience is defiled. 16 They profess that they know God; but in works they deny *him*, being abominable, and disobedient, and unto every good work reprobate.

2 But speak thou the things which become sound doctrine: 2 That the aged men be sober, grave, temperate, sound in faith, in charity, in patience. 3 The aged women likewise, that *they be* in behaviour as becometh holiness, not false accusers, not given to much wine, teachers of good things; 4 That they may teach the young women to be sober, to love their husbands, to love their children, 5 *To be* discreet, chaste, keepers at home, good, obedient to their own husbands, that the word of God be not blasphemed. 6 Young men likewise exhort to be soberminded. 7 In all things shewing thyself a pattern of good works: in doctrine *shewing* uncorruptness, gravity, sincerity, 8 Sound speech, that cannot be condemned; that he that is of the contrary part may be ashamed, having no evil thing to say of you. 9 *Exhort* servants to be obedient unto their own masters, *and* to please *them* well in all things; not answering again; 10 Not purloining, but shewing all good fidelity; that they may adorn the doctrine of God our Saviour in all things. 11 For the grace of God that bringeth salvation hath appeared to all men, 12 Teaching us that, denying ungodliness and worldly lusts, we should live soberly, righteously, and godly, in this present world; 13 Looking for that blessed hope, and the glorious appearing of the great God and our Saviour Jesus Christ; 14 Who gave himself for us, that he might redeem us from all iniquity, and purify unto himself a peculiar people, zealous of good works. 15 These things speak, and exhort, and rebuke with all authority. Let no man despise thee.

3 Put them in mind to be subject to principalities and powers, to obey magistrates, to be ready to every good work, 2 To speak evil of no man, to be no brawlers, *but* gentle, shew-

R.S.V.

their very minds and consciences are corrupted. 16 They profess to know God, but they deny him by their deeds; they are detestable, disobedient, unfit for any good deed.

2 But as for you, teach what befits sound doctrine. 2 Bid the older men be temperate, serious, sensible, sound in faith, in love, and in steadfastness. 3 Bid the older women likewise to be reverent in behavior, not to be slanderers or slaves to drink; they are to teach what is good, 4 and so train the young women to love their husbands and children, 5 to be sensible, chaste, domestic, kind, and submissive to their husbands, that the word of God may not be discredited. 6 Likewise urge the younger men to control themselves. 7 Show yourself in all respects a model of good deeds, and in your teaching show integrity, gravity, 8 and sound speech that cannot be censured, so that an opponent may be put to shame, having nothing evil to say of us. 9 Bid slaves to be submissive to their masters and to give satisfaction in every respect; they are not to be refractory, 10 nor to pilfer, but to show entire and true fidelity, so that in everything they may adorn the doctrine of God our Savior.

11 For the grace of God has appeared for the salvation of all men, 12 training us to renounce irreligion and worldly passions, and to live sober, upright, and godly lives in this world, 13 awaiting our blessed hope, the appearing of the glory of our great God and Savior[c] Jesus Christ, 14 who gave himself for us to redeem us from all iniquity and to purify for himself a people of his own who are zealous for good deeds.

15 Declare these things; exhort and reprove with all authority. Let no one disregard you.

3 Remind them to be submissive to rulers and authorities, to be obedient, to be ready for any honest work, 2 to speak evil of no one, to avoid quarreling, to be gentle, and to show

[c] Or *of the great God and our Savior.*

PHILLIPS

N.E.B.

faith in God—their very minds and consciences are diseased. They profess to know God, but their actual behavior denies their profession, for they are obviously vile and rebellious and when it comes to doing any real good they are palpable frauds.

Good character should follow good teaching   2. 1

Now you must tell them the sort of character which should spring from sound teaching. The old men should be temperate, serious, wise—spiritually healthy through their faith and love and patience. Similarly the old women should be reverent in their behavior, should not make unfounded complaints and should not be overfond of wine. They should be examples of the good life, so that the younger women may learn to love their husbands and their children, to be sensible and chaste, home lovers, kindhearted and willing to adapt themselves to their husbands—a good advertisement for the Christian faith. The young men, too, you should urge to take life seriously, letting your own life stand as a pattern of good living. In all your teaching show the strictest regard for truth, and show that you appreciate the seriousness of the matters you are dealing with. Your speech should be unaffected and logical, so that your opponent may feel ashamed at finding nothing in which to pick holes.

The duty of slaves—and of us all   2. 9

Slaves should be told that it is their duty as Christians to obey their masters and to give them satisfactory service in every way. They are not to "answer back" or to be light-fingered, but they are to show themselves utterly trustworthy, a living testimonial to the teaching of God our savior. For the grace of God, which can save every man, has now become known, and it teaches us to have no more to do with Godlessness or the desires of this world but to live, here and now, responsible, honorable and God-fearing lives. And while we live this life we hope and wait for the glorious dénouement of the great God and of Jesus Christ our savior. For he gave himself for us, that he might rescue us from all our evil ways and make for himself a people of his own, clean and pure, with our hearts set upon living a life that is good. Tell men of these things, Titus. Urge them to action, using a reprimand where necessary with all the authority of God's minister—and as such let no one treat you with contempt.

Instructions for the Christians of Crete   3. 1

Remind your people to recognize the power of those who rule and bear authority. They must obey the laws of the state and be prepared to render whatever good service they can. They are not to speak evil of any man; they must not be argumentative but gentle, showing themselves

alike in reason and conscience. They profess to acknowledge God, but deny him by their actions. Their detestable obstinacy disqualifies them for any good work.

2 For your own part, what you say must be in keeping with wholesome doctrine. Let the older men know that they should be sober, high-principled, and temperate, sound in faith, in love, and in endurance. The older women, similarly, should be reverent in their bearing, not scandal-mongers or slaves to strong drink; they must set a high standard, and school the younger women to be loving wives and mothers, temperate, chaste, and kind, busy at home, respecting the authority of their own husbands. Thus the Gospel will not be brought into disrepute.

Urge the younger men, similarly, to be temperate in all things, and set them a good example yourself. In your teaching, you must show integrity and high principle, and use wholesome speech to which none can take exception. This will shame any opponent, when he finds not a word to say to our discredit.

Tell slaves to respect their masters' authority in everything, and to comply with their demands without answering back; not to pilfer, but to show themselves strictly honest and trustworthy; for in all such ways they will add lustre to the doctrine of God our Saviour.

For the grace of God has dawned upon the world with healing for all mankind; and by it we are disciplined to renounce godless ways and worldly desires, and to live a life of temperance, honesty, and godliness in the present age, looking forward to the happy fulfilment of our hopes when the splendour of our great God and Saviour[a] Christ Jesus will appear. He it is who sacrificed himself for us, to set us free from all wickedness and to make us a pure people marked out for his own, eager to do good.

These, then, are your themes; urge them and argue them. And speak with authority: let no one slight you.

3 Remind them to be submissive to the government and the authorities, to obey them, and to be ready for any honourable form of work;[b] to slander no one, not to pick quarrels, to show forbearance and a consistently gentle disposition towards all men.

[a] Or of the great God and our Saviour . . . [b] Or ready always to do good.

K.J.V.

ing all meekness unto all men. 3 For we ourselves also were sometime foolish, disobedient, deceived, serving divers lusts and pleasures, living in malice and envy, hateful, *and* hating one another. 4 But after that the kindness and love of God our Saviour toward man appeared, 5 Not by works of righteousness which we have done, but according to his mercy he saved us, by the washing of regeneration, and renewing of the Holy Ghost; 6 Which he shed on us abundantly through Jesus Christ our Saviour; 7 That being justified by his grace, we should be made heirs according to the hope of eternal life. 8 *This is* a faithful saying, and these things I will that thou affirm constantly, that they which have believed in God might be careful to maintain good works. These things are good and profitable unto men. 9 But avoid foolish questions, and genealogies, and contentions, and strivings about the law; for they are unprofitable and vain. 10 A man that is a heretic, after the first and second admonition, reject; 11 Knowing that he that is such is subverted, and sinneth, being condemned of himself. 12 When I shall send Artemas unto thee, or Tychicus, be diligent to come unto me to Nicopolis: for I have determined there to winter. 13 Bring Zenas the lawyer and Apollos on their journey diligently, that nothing be wanting unto them. 14 And let ours also learn to maintain good works for necessary uses, that they be not unfruitful. 15 All that are with me salute thee. Greet them that love us in the faith. Grace *be* with you all. Amen.

It was written to Titus, ordained the first bishop of the church of the Cretians, from Nicopolis of Macedonia.

R.S.V.

perfect courtesy toward all men. 3 For we ourselves were once foolish, disobedient, led astray, slaves to various passions and pleasures, passing our days in malice and envy, hated by men and hating one another; 4 but when the goodness and loving kindness of God our Savior appeared, 5 he saved us, not because of deeds done by us in righteousness, but in virtue of his own mercy, by the washing of regeneration and renewal in the Holy Spirit, 6 which he poured out upon us richly through Jesus Christ our Savior, 7 so that we might be justified by his grace and become heirs in hope of eternal life. 8 The saying is sure.

I desire you to insist on these things, so that those who have believed in God may be careful to apply themselves to good deeds;[d] these are excellent and profitable to men. 9 But avoid stupid controversies, genealogies, dissensions, and quarrels over the law, for they are unprofitable and futile. 10 As for a man who is factious, after admonishing him once or twice, have nothing more to do with him, 11 knowing that such a person is perverted and sinful; he is self-condemned.

12 When I send Artemas or Tychicus to you, do your best to come to me at Nicopolis, for I have decided to spend the winter there. 13 Do your best to speed Zenas the lawyer and Apollos on their way; see that they lack nothing. 14 And let our people learn to apply themselves to good deeds,[d] so as to help cases of urgent need, and not to be unfruitful.

15 All who are with me send greetings to you. Greet those who love us in the faith. Grace be with you all.

[d] Or *enter honorable occupations.*

PHILLIPS

agreeable to everybody. For we ourselves have known what it is to be ignorant, disobedient and deceived, the slaves of various desires and pleasant feelings, while our lives were spent in malice and jealousy—we were hateful and we hated one another. But when the kindness of God our savior and his love toward man appeared, he saved us in his mercy—not by virtue of any moral achievements of ours, but by the cleansing power of a new birth and the moral renewal of the Holy Spirit, which he gave us so generously through Jesus Christ our Savior. The result is that we are acquitted by his grace, and can look forward to inheriting life for evermore. This is solid truth: I want you to speak about these matters with absolute certainty, so that those who have believed in God may concentrate upon a life of goodness.

Subjects like this are always good and useful, but mind you steer clear of stupid arguments, genealogies, controversies and quarrels over the Law. They settle nothing and lead nowhere. If a man is still argumentative after the second warning you should reject him. You can be sure that he has a moral twist, and he knows it.

Final messages   *3. 12*

As soon as I send Artemas to you (or perhaps it will be Tychicus), do your best to come to me at Nicopolis, for I have made up my mind to spend the winter there. See that Zenas the lawyer and Apollos have what they require and give them a good send-off. And our people should learn to earn what they require by leading an honest life and so be self-supporting.

All those here with me send you greetings. Please give our greetings to all who love us in the faith. Grace be with you all.

                                        PAUL

N.E.B.

For at one time we ourselves in our folly and obstinacy were all astray. We were slaves to passions and pleasures of every kind. Our days were passed in malice and envy; we were odious ourselves and we hated one another. But when the kindness and generosity of God our Saviour dawned upon the world, then, not for any good deeds of our own, but because he was merciful, he saved us through the water of rebirth and the renewing power of[a] the Holy Spirit. For he sent down the Spirit upon us plentifully through Jesus Christ our Saviour, so that, justified by his grace, we might in hope become heirs to eternal life. These are words you may trust.

Such are the points I should wish you to insist on. Those who have come to believe in God should see that they engage in honourable occupations, which are not only honourable in themselves, but also useful to their fellow-men.[b] But steer clear of foolish speculations, genealogies, quarrels, and controversies over the Law; they are unprofitable and pointless.

A heretic should be warned once, and once again; after that, have done with him, recognizing that a man of that sort has a distorted mind and stands self-condemned in his sin.

When I send Artemas to you, or Tychicus, make haste to join me at Nicopolis, for that is where I have determined to spend the winter. Do your utmost to help Zenas the lawyer and Apollos on their travels, and see that they are not short of anything. And our own people must be taught to engage in honest employment to produce the necessities of life; they must not be unproductive.

All who are with me send you greetings. My greetings to those who are our friends in truth.[c] Grace be with you all!

[a] *Or* the water of rebirth and of renewal by . . .
[b] *Or* should make it their business to practise virtue. These precepts are good in themselves and useful to society. [c] *Or* our friends in the faith.

K.J.V.	R.S.V.

THE

EPISTLE OF PAUL

TO

PHILEMON

THE

LETTER OF PAUL TO

PHILEMON

Paul, a prisoner of Jesus Christ, and Timothy *our* brother, unto Philemon our dearly beloved, and fellow labourer, 2And to *our* beloved Apphia, and Archippus our fellow soldier, and to the church in thy house: 3 Grace to you, and peace, from God our Father and the Lord Jesus Christ. 4 I thank my God, making mention of thee always in my prayers, 5 Hearing of thy love and faith, which thou hast toward the Lord Jesus, and toward all saints; 6 That the communication of thy faith may become effectual by the acknowledging of every good thing which is in you in Christ Jesus. 7 For we have great joy and consolation in thy love, because the bowels of the saints are refreshed by thee, brother. 8 Wherefore, though I might be much bold in Christ to enjoin thee that which is convenient, 9 Yet for love's sake I rather beseech *thee,* being such a one as Paul the aged, and now also a prisoner of Jesus Christ. 10 I beseech thee for my son Onesimus, whom I have begotten in my bonds: 11 Which in time past was to thee unprofitable, but now profitable to thee and to me: 12 Whom I have sent again: thou therefore receive him, that is, mine own bowels: 13 Whom I would have retained with me, that in thy stead he might have ministered unto me in the bonds of the gospel: 14 But without thy mind would I do nothing; that thy benefit should not be as it were of necessity, but willingly. 15 For perhaps he therefore departed for a season, that thou shouldest receive him for ever; 16 Not now as a servant, but above a servant, a brother beloved, specially to me, but how much more unto thee, both in the flesh, and in the Lord? 17 If thou count me therefore a partner, receive him as myself. 18 If he hath wronged thee, or oweth *thee* aught, put that on mine account; 19 I Paul have written *it* with mine own hand, I will repay *it:* albeit I do not say to thee how thou owest unto me even thine own self besides. 20 Yea, brother, let me have joy of thee in the Lord: refresh my bowels in the Lord. 21 Having confidence in thy obedience I wrote unto thee, knowing that thou wilt also do more than I say. 22 But withal prepare me also a lodging: for I trust that through your prayers I

1 Paul, a prisoner for Christ Jesus, and Timothy our brother,
To Philemon our beloved fellow worker 2 and Apphia our sister and Archippus our fellow soldier, and the church in your house:
3 Grace to you and peace from God our Father and the Lord Jesus Christ.

4 I thank my God always when I remember you in my prayers, 5 because I hear of your love and of the faith which you have toward the Lord Jesus and all the saints, 6 and I pray that the sharing of your faith may promote the knowledge of all the good that is ours in Christ. 7 For I have derived much joy and comfort from your love, my brother, because the hearts of the saints have been refreshed through you.

8 Accordingly, though I am bold enough in Christ to command you to do what is required, 9 yet for love's sake I prefer to appeal to you— I, Paul, an ambassador[a] and now a prisoner also for Christ Jesus—10 I appeal to you for my child, Onesimus, whose father I have become in my imprisonment. 11 (Formerly he was useless to you, but now he is indeed useful[b] to you and to me.) 12 I am sending him back to you, sending my very heart. 13 I would have been glad to keep him with me, in order that he might serve me on your behalf during my imprisonment for the gospel; 14 but I preferred to do nothing without your consent in order that your goodness might not be by compulsion but of your own free will. 15 Perhaps this is why he was parted from you for a while, that you might have him back for ever, 16 no longer as a slave but more than a slave, as a beloved brother, especially to me but how much more to you, both in the flesh and in the Lord. 17 So if you consider me your partner, receive him as you would receive me. 18 If he has wronged you at all, or owes you anything, charge that to my account. 19 I, Paul, write this with my own hand, I will repay it— to say nothing of your owing me even your own self. 20 Yes, brother, I want some benefit from you in the Lord. Refresh my heart in Christ. 21 Confident of your obedience, I write to you, knowing that you will do even more than I say. 22 At the same time, prepare a guest room for me, for I am hoping through your prayers to be granted to you.

[a] Or *an old man.* [b] The name Onesimus means *useful* or (compare verse 20) *beneficial.*

THE LETTER TO
PHILEMON

THE
LETTER OF PAUL TO
PHILEMON

A Runaway Slave

Paul, a prisoner for the sake of Jesus Christ, and brother Timothy to Philemon our much-loved fellow worker, Apphia our sister and Archippus who is with us in the fight; to the church that meets in your house—grace and peace be to you from God our Father and from the Lord Jesus Christ.

From Paul, a prisoner of Christ Jesus, and our colleague Timothy, to Philemon our dear friend and fellow-worker, and Apphia our sister, and Archippus our comrade-in-arms, and the congregation at your house.

Grace to you and peace from God our Father and the Lord Jesus Christ.

I thank my God always when I mention you in my prayers, for I hear of your love and faith towards the Lord Jesus and towards all God's people. My prayer is that your fellowship with us in our common faith may deepen the understanding of all the blessings that our union with Christ brings us.[a] For I am delighted and encouraged by your love: through you, my brother, God's people have been much refreshed.

Accordingly, although in Christ I might make bold to point out your duty, yet, because of that same love, I would rather appeal to you. Yes, I, Paul, ambassador as I am of Christ Jesus—and now his prisoner—appeal to you about my child, whose father I have become in this prison. I mean Onesimus, once so little use to you, but now useful indeed, both to you and to me. I am sending him back to you, and in doing so I am sending a part of myself. I should have liked to keep him with me, to look after me as you would wish, here in prison for the Gospel. But I would rather do nothing without your consent, so that your kindness may be a matter not of compulsion, but of your own free will. For perhaps this is why you lost him for a time, that you might have him back for good, no longer as a slave, but as more than a slave—as a dear brother, very dear indeed to me and how much dearer to you, both as man and as Christian.

If, then, you count me partner in the faith, welcome him as you would welcome me. And if he has done you any wrong or is in your debt, put that down to my account. Here is my signature, PAUL; I undertake to repay—not to mention that you owe your very self to me as well. Now brother, as a Christian, be generous with me, and relieve my anxiety; we are both in Christ!

I write to you confident that you will meet my wishes; I know that you will in fact do better than I ask. And one thing more: have a room ready for me, for I hope that, in answer to your prayers, God will grant me to you.

A personal appeal   4

I always thank God for you, Philemon, in my constant prayers for you all, for I have heard how you love and trust both the Lord Jesus himself and those who believe in him. And I pray that those who share your faith may also share your knowledge of all the good things that believing in Christ Jesus can mean to us. It is your love, my brother, that gives us such comfort and happiness, for it cheers the hearts of your fellow Christians. And although I could rely on my authority in Christ and dare to *order* you to do what I consider right, I am not doing that. No, I am appealing to that love of yours, a simple personal appeal from Paul the old man, in prison for Jesus Christ's sake. I am appealing for my child. Yes, I have become a father though I have been under lock and key, and the child's name is—Onesimus! Oh, I know you have found him pretty useless in the past but he is going to be useful now, to both of us. I am sending him back to you: *will you receive him as my son, part of me?* I should have dearly loved to have kept him with me: he could have done what you would have done—looked after me here in prison for the gospel's sake. But I would do nothing without consulting you first, for if you have a favor to give me, let it be spontaneous and not forced from you by circumstances!

It occurs to me that there has been a purpose in your losing him. You lost him, a slave, for a time; now you are having him back for good, not merely as a slave, but as a brother Christian. He is already especially loved by me—how much more will you be able to love him, both as a man and as a fellow Christian! You and I have so much in common, haven't we? Then do welcome him as you would welcome me. If you feel he has wronged or cheated you put it down to my account. I've written this with my own hand: I, Paul, hereby promise to repay you. (Of course I'm not stressing the fact that you might be said to owe me your very soul!) Now do grant me this favor, my brother—such an act of love will do my old heart good. As I send you this letter I know you'll do what I ask—I believe, in fact, you'll do more.

Will you do something else? Get the guest room ready for *me,* for I have great hopes that through your prayers I myself will be returned to you as well!

[a] *Or* that bring us to Christ.

K.J.V.

shall be given unto you. 23 There salute thee Epaphras, my fellow prisoner in Christ Jesus; 24 Marcus, Aristarchus, Demas, Lucas, my fellow labourers. 25 The grace of our Lord Jesus Christ *be* with your spirit. Amen.

Written from Rome to Philemon, by Onesimus a servant.

R.S.V.

23 Epaphras, my fellow prisoner in Christ Jesus, sends greetings to you, 24 and so do Mark, Aristarchus, Demas, and Luke, my fellow workers.

25 The grace of the Lord Jesus Christ be with your spirit.

PHILLIPS	N.E.B.
Epaphras, here in prison with me, sends his greetings: so do Mark, Aristarchus, Demas and Luke, all fellow workers for God. The grace of our Lord Jesus Christ be with your spirit, amen. <div align="center">PAUL</div>	Epaphras, Christ's captive like myself, sends you greetings. So do Mark, Aristarchus, Demas, and Luke, my fellow-workers. The grace of the Lord Jesus Christ be with your spirit!

THE EPISTLE

OF PAUL THE APOSTLE

TO THE   THE LETTER TO THE

HEBREWS   HEBREWS

1 God, **who** at sundry times and in divers manners spake in time past unto the fathers by the prophets, 2 Hath in these last days spoken unto us by *his* Son, whom he hath appointed heir of all things, by whom also he made the worlds; 3 Who being the brightness of *his* glory, and the express image of his person, and upholding all things by the word of his power, when he had by himself purged our sins, sat down on the right hand of the Majesty on high; 4 Being made so much better than the angels, as he hath by inheritance obtained a more excellent name than they. 5 For unto which of the angels said he at any time, Thou art my Son, this day have I begotten thee? And again, I will be to him a Father, and he shall be to me a Son? 6 And again, when he bringeth in the firstbegotten into the world, he saith, And let all the angels of God worship him. 7 And of the angels he saith, Who maketh his angels spirits, and his ministers a flame of fire. 8 But unto the Son *he saith,* Thy throne, O God, *is* for ever and ever: a sceptre of righteousness *is* the sceptre of thy kingdom. 9 Thou hast loved righteousness, and hated iniquity; therefore God, *even* thy God, hath anointed thee with the oil of gladness above thy fellows. 10 And, Thou, Lord, in the beginning hast laid the foundation of the earth; and the heavens are the works of thine hands. 11 They shall perish, but thou remainest: and they all

1 In many and various ways God spoke of old to our fathers by the prophets; 2 but in these last days he has spoken to us by a Son, whom he appointed the heir of all things, through whom also he created the world. 3 He reflects the glory of God and bears the very stamp of his nature, upholding the universe by his word of power. When he had made purification for sins, he sat down at the right hand of the Majesty on high, 4 having become as much superior to angels as the name he has obtained is more excellent than theirs.

5 For to what angel did God ever say,
"Thou art my Son,
today I have begotten thee"?
Or again,
"I will be to him a father,
and he shall be to me a son"?
6 And again, when he brings the first-born into the world, he says,
"Let all God's angels worship him."
7 Of the angels he says,
"Who makes his angels winds,
and his servants flames of fire."
8 But of the Son he says,
"Thy throne, O God,[a] is for ever and ever,
the righteous scepter is the scepter of thy[b]
kingdom.
9 Thou hast loved righteousnes and hated
lawlessness;
therefore God, thy God, has anointed thee
with the oil of gladness beyond thy comrades."
10 And,
"Thou, Lord, didst found the earth in the
beginning,
and the heavens are the work of thy
hands;
11 they will perish, but thou remainest;
they will all grow old like a garment,

[a] Or *God is thy throne.* [b] Other ancient authorities read *his.*

THE LETTER TO

JEWISH CHRISTIANS

(THE LETTER TO THE HEBREWS)

God, who gave to our forefathers many different glimpses of the truth in the words of the prophets, has now, at the end of the present age, given us the truth in the Son. Through the Son God made the whole universe, and to the Son he has ordained that all creation shall ultimately belong. This Son, radiance of the glory of God, flawless expression of the nature of God, himself the upholding principle of all that is, effected in person the reconciliation between God and man and then took his seat at the right hand of the majesty on high—thus proving himself, by the more glorious name that he has won, far greater than all the angels of God.

Scripture endorses this superiority 1. 5

For to which of the angels did he ever say such words as these:

Thou art my Son,
This day have I begotten thee?

Or, again:

I will be to him a Father,
And he shall be to me a Son?

Further, when he brings his first-born into this world of men, he says:

Let all the angels of God worship him.

This is what he says of the angels:

Who maketh his angels winds
And his ministers a flame of fire.

But when he speaks of the Son, he says:

Thy throne, O *God,* is for ever and ever;
And the scepter of uprightness is the scepter
   of thy kingdom.
Thou hast loved righteousness and hated iniquity;
Therefore God, thy God, hath anointed thee
With the oil of gladness above thy fellows.

He also says:

Thou, *Lord,* in the beginning hast laid the
   foundation of the earth,
And the heavens are the work of thy hands:
They shall perish, but thou continuest:
And they all shall wax old as doth a garment;

A LETTER TO

HEBREWS

Christ Divine and Human

1 When in former times God spoke to our forefathers, he spoke in fragmentary and varied fashion through the prophets. But in this the final age he has spoken to us in the Son whom he has made heir to the whole universe, and through whom he created all orders of existence: the Son who is the effulgence of God's splendour and the stamp of God's very being, and sustains[a] the universe by his word of power. When he had brought about the purgation of sins, he took his seat at the right hand of Majesty on high, raised as far above the angels, as the title he has inherited is superior to theirs.

For God never said to any angel, 'Thou art my Son; today I have begotten thee', or again, 'I will be father to him, and he shall be my son.' Again, when he presents the first-born to the world, he says, 'Let all the angels of God pay him homage.' Of the angels he says,

'He who makes his angels winds,
   And his ministers a fiery flame';

but of the Son,   •

'Thy throne, O God, is for ever and ever,
   And the sceptre[b] of justice is the sceptre of his
      kingdom.
Thou hast loved right and hated wrong;
Therefore, O God, thy God [c] has set thee above
      thy fellows,
By anointing with the oil of exultation.'

And again,

'By thee, Lord, were earth's foundations laid of
      old,
And the heavens are the work of thy hands.
They shall pass away, but thou endurest;
Like clothes they shall all grow old;

[a] *Or* bears along. [b] *Or* God is thy throne for ever and ever, And thy sceptre . . . [c] *Or* Therefore God who is thy God . . .

683

K.J.V.

shall wax old as doth a garment; 12And as a vesture shalt thou fold them up, and they shall be changed: but thou art the same, and thy years shall not fail. 13 But to which of the angels said he at any time, Sit on my right hand, until I make thine enemies thy footstool? 14Are they not all ministering spirits, sent forth to minister for them who shall be heirs of salvation?

2 Therefore we ought to give the more earnest heed to the things which we have heard, lest at any time we should let *them* slip. 2 For if the word spoken by angels was steadfast, and every transgression and disobedience received a just recompense of reward; 3 How shall we escape, if we neglect so great salvation; which at the first began to be spoken by the Lord, and was confirmed unto us by them that heard *him;* 4 God also bearing *them* witness, both with signs and wonders, and with divers miracles, and gifts of the Holy Ghost, according to his own will? 5 For unto the angels hath he not put in subjection the world to come, whereof we speak. 6 But one in a certain place testified, saying, What is man, that thou art mindful of him? or the son of man, that thou visitest him? 7 Thou madest him a little lower than the angels; thou crownedst him with glory and honour, and didst set him over the works of thy hands: 8 Thou hast put all things in subjection under his feet. For in that he put all in subjection under him, he left nothing *that is* not put under him. But now we see not yet all things put under him. 9 But we see Jesus, who was made a little lower than the angels for the suffering of death, crowned with glory and honour; that he by the grace of God should taste death for every man. 10 For it became him, for whom *are* all things, and by whom *are* all things, in bringing many sons unto glory, to make the captain of their salvation perfect through sufferings. 11 For both he that sanctifieth and they who are sanctified *are* all of one: for which cause he is not ashamed to call them brethren, 12 Saying, I will declare

R.S.V.

12 like a mantle thou wilt roll them up,
   and they will be changed.[c]
But thou art the same,
   and thy years will never end."
13 But to what angel has he ever said,
"Sit at my right hand,
   till I make thy enemies
   a stool for thy feet"?
14Are they not all ministering spirits sent forth to serve, for the sake of those who are to obtain salvation?

2 Therefore we must pay the closer attention to what we have heard, lest we drift away from it. 2 For if the message declared by angels was valid and every transgression or disobedience received a just retribution, 3 how shall we escape if we neglect such a great salvation? It was declared at first by the Lord, and it was attested to us by those who heard him, 4 while God also bore witness by signs and wonders and various miracles and by gifts of the Holy Spirit distributed according to his own will.
5 For it was not to angels that God subjected the world to come, of which we are speaking. 6 It has been testified somewhere,
"What is man that thou art mindful of him,
   or the son of man, that thou carest for him?
7 Thou didst make him for a little while lower
   than the angels,
   thou hast crowned him with glory and honor,[d]
8 putting everything in subjection under his
   feet."
Now in putting everything in subjection to him, he left nothing outside his control. As it is, we do not yet see everything in subjection to him. 9 But we see Jesus, who for a little while was made lower than the angels, crowned with glory and honor because of the suffering of death, so that by the grace of God he might taste death for every one. 10 For it was fitting that he, for whom and by whom all things exist, in bringing many sons to glory, should make the pioneer of their salvation perfect through suffering. 11 For he who sanctifies and those who are sanctified have all one origin. That is why he is not ashamed to call them brethren,12 saying,
"I will proclaim thy name to my brethren,

[c] Other ancient authorities add *like a garment.*
[d] Other ancient authorities insert *and didst set him over the works of thy hands.*

PHILLIPS

And as a mantle shalt thou roll them up,
As a garment, and they shall be changed:
But thou art the same,
And thy years shall not fail.

But does he ever say this of any of the angels:

Sit thou on my right hand,
Till I make thine enemies the footstool of thy
  feet?

Surely the angels are no more than spirits in the service of God, commissioned to serve the heirs of God's salvation.

The angels had authority in past   2. 1
ages: today the Son is the
authority

We ought, therefore, to pay the greatest attention to the truth that we have heard and not allow ourselves to drift away from it. For if the message given through angels proved authentic, so that defiance of it and disobedience to it received appropriate retribution, how shall we escape if we refuse to pay proper attention to the salvation which is offered us today? For this salvation came first through the words of the Lord himself: it was confirmed for our hearing by men who had heard him speak, and God moreover has plainly endorsed their witness by signs and miracles, by all kinds of spiritual power, and by gifts of the Holy Spirit, distributed according to his will.

For though in past ages God did grant authority to angels, yet he did not put the future world of men under their control, and it is this world that we are now talking about.

But someone has said:

What is man, that thou art mindful of him?
Or the son of man, that thou visitest him?
Thou madest him a little lower than the angels;
Thou crownedst him with glory and honor,
And didst set him over the works of thy
  hands:
Thou didst put all things in subjection under
  his feet.

Notice that the writer puts "all things" under the sovereignty of man: he left nothing outside his control. But we do not yet see "all things" under his control.

Christ became man, not angel,   2. 9
to save mankind

What we actually see is Jesus, after being made temporarily inferior to the angels (and so subject to pain and death), in order that he should, by God's grace, taste death for every man, now crowned with glory and honor. It was right and proper that in bringing many sons to glory, God (from whom and by whom everything exists) should make the leader of their salvation a perfect leader through the fact that he suffered. For the one who makes men holy and the men who are made holy share a common humanity. So that he is not ashamed to call them his brothers, for he says:

I will declare thy name unto my brethren,

N.E.B.

Thou shalt fold them up like a cloak;
Yes, they shall be changed like any garment.
But thou art the same, and thy years shall have
  no end.'

To which of the angels has he ever said, 'Sit at my right hand until I make thy enemies thy footstool'? What are they all but ministrant spirits, sent out to serve, for the sake of those who are to inherit salvation?

2 Thus we are bound to pay all the more heed to what we have been told, for fear of drifting from our course. For if the word spoken through angels had such force that any transgression or disobedience met with due retribution, what escape can there be for us if we ignore a deliverance so great? For this deliverance was first announced through the lips of the Lord himself; those who heard him confirmed it to us, and God added his testimony by signs, by miracles, by manifold works of power, and by distributing the gifts of the Holy Spirit at his own will.

For it is not to angels that he has subjected the world to come, which is our theme. But there is somewhere a solemn assurance which runs:

'What is man, that thou rememberest him,
Or the son of man, that thou hast regard to
  him?
Thou didst make him for a short while lower
  than the angels;
Thou didst crown him with glory and honour;
Thou didst put all things in subjection beneath
  his feet.'

For in subjecting all things to him, he left nothing that is not subject. But in fact we do not yet see all things in subjection to man. In Jesus, however, we do see one who[a] for a short while was made lower than the angels, crowned now with glory and honour because he suffered death, so that, by God's gracious will, in tasting death he should stand[b] for us all.

It was clearly fitting that God for whom and through whom all things exist should, in bringing many sons to glory, make the leader who delivers them perfect through sufferings. For a consecrating priest and those whom he consecrates are all of one stock; and that is why the Son does not shrink from calling men his brothers, when he says, 'I will proclaim thy name to my

[a] *Or* in subjection to him. But we see Jesus, who
. . . [b] *Some witnesses read* so that apart from
God he should taste death . . .

K.J.V.

thy name unto my brethren, in the midst of the church will I sing praise unto thee. 13And again, I will put my trust in him. And again, Behold I and the children which God hath given me. 14 Forasmuch then as the children are partakers of flesh and blood, he also himself likewise took part of the same; that through death he might destroy him that had the power of death, that is, the devil; 15And deliver them, who through fear of death were all their lifetime subject to bondage. 16 For verily he took not on *him the nature of* angels; but he took on *him* the seed of Abraham. 17 Wherefore in all things it behooved him to be made like unto *his* brethren, that he might be a merciful and faithful high priest in things *pertaining* to God, to make reconciliation for the sins of the people. 18 For in that he himself hath suffered being tempted, he is able to succour them that are tempted.

R.S.V.

in the midst of the congregation I will praise thee."
13And again,
"I will put my trust in him."
And again,
"Here am I, and the children God has given me."
14 Since therefore the children share in flesh and blood, he himself likewise partook of the same nature, that through death he might destroy him who has the power of death, that is, the devil, 15 and deliver all those who through fear of death were subject to lifelong bondage. 16 For surely it is not with angels that he is concerned but with the descendants of Abraham. 17 Therefore he had to be made like his brethren in every respect, so that he might become a merciful and faithful high priest in the service of God, to make expiation for the sins of the people. 18 For because he himself has suffered and been tempted, he is able to help those who are tempted.

3 Wherefore, holy brethren, partakers of the heavenly calling, consider the Apostle and High Priest of our profession, Christ Jesus; 2 Who was faithful to him that appointed him, as also Moses *was faithful* in all his house. 3 For this *man* was counted worthy of more glory than Moses, inasmuch as he who hath builded the house hath more honour than the house. 4 For every house is builded by some *man;* but he that built all things *is* God. 5And Moses verily *was* faithful in all his house as a servant, for a testimony of those things which were to be spoken after; 6 But Christ as a son over his own house; whose house are we, if we hold fast the confidence and the rejoicing of the hope firm unto the end. 7 Wherefore as the Holy Ghost saith, To day if ye will hear his voice, 8 Harden not your hearts, as in the provocation, in the day of temptation in the wilderness: 9 When your fathers tempted me, proved me, and saw my works forty years. 10 Wherefore I was grieved with that generation, and said, They do always err in *their* heart; and they have not known my ways. 11 So I sware in my wrath, They shall not enter

3 Therefore, holy brethren, who share in a heavenly call, consider Jesus, the apostle and high priest of our confession. 2 He was faithful to him who appointed him, just as Moses also was faithful in[e] God's house. 3 Yet Jesus has been counted worthy of as much more glory than Moses as the builder of a house has more honor than the house. 4 (For every house is built by some one, but the builder of all things is God.) 5 Now Moses was faithful in all God's house as a servant, to testify to the things that were to be spoken later, 6 but Christ was faithful over God's[f] house as a son. And we are his house if we hold fast our confidence and pride in our hope.[g]
7 Therefore, as the Holy Spirit says,
"Today, when you hear his voice,
8 do not harden your hearts as in the rebellion,
on the day of testing in the wilderness,
9 where your fathers put me to the test
and saw my works for forty years.
10 Therefore I was provoked with that generation,
and said, 'They always go astray in their hearts;
they have not known my ways.'
11 As I swore in my wrath,
'They shall never enter my rest.' "

[e] Other ancient authorities insert *all.* [f] Greek *his.* [g] Other ancient authorities insert *firm to the end.*

686

In the midst of the congregation will I sing thy praise.

And again, speaking as a man, he says:

I will put my trust in him.

And, one more instance, in these words:

Behold, I and the children which God hath given me. . . .

Since, then, "the children" have a common physical nature as human beings, he also became a human being, so that by going through death as a man he might destroy him who had the power of death, that is, the devil; and might also set free those who lived their whole lives a prey to the fear of death. It is plain that for this purpose he did not become an angel; he became a *man,* in actual fact a descendant of Abraham. It was imperative that he should be made like his brothers in every respect, if he were to become a High Priest both compassionate and faithful in the things of God, and at the same time able to make atonement for the sins of the people. For by virtue of his own suffering under temptation he is able to help those who are exposed to temptation.

brothers; in full assembly I will sing thy praise'; and again, 'I will keep my trust fixed on him'; and again, 'Here am I, and the children whom God has given me.' The children of a family share the same flesh and blood; and so he too shared ours, so that through death he might break the power of him who had death at his command, that is, the devil; and might liberate those who, through fear of death, had all their lifetime been in servitude. It is not angels, mark you, that he takes to himself, but the sons of Abraham. And therefore he had to be made like these brothers of his in every way, so that he might be merciful and faithful as their high priest before God, to expiate the sins of the people. For since he himself has passed through the test of suffering, he is able to help those who are meeting their test now.

Moses was a faithful servant: **3. 1**
Christ a faithful Son

So then, my brothers in holiness who share the highest of all callings, I want you to think of Jesus the messenger and High Priest of the faith we hold. See him as faithful to the charge God gave him, and compare him with Moses who also faithfully discharged his duty in the household of God. For this man has been considered worthy of greater honor than Moses, just as the builder of a house may be truly said to have more honor than the house itself. Every house is built by someone, but the builder of everything is God himself. Moses was certainly faithful in all his duties in God's household, but he was faithful as a servant and his work was only a foreshadowing of the truth that would be known later. But Christ was faithful as a son in the household of his own Father. And we are members of this household if we maintain our trust and joyful hope steadfast to the end.

3   Therefore, brothers in the family of God, who share a heavenly calling, think of the Apostle and High Priest of the religion we profess,[a] who was faithful to God who appointed him. Moses also was faithful in God's household; and Jesus, of whom I speak, has been deemed worthy of greater honour than Moses, as the founder of a house enjoys more honour than his household. For every house has its founder; and the founder of all is God. Moses, then, was faithful as a servitor in God's whole household; his task was to bear witness to the words that God would speak; but Christ is faithful as a son, set over his household. And we are that household of his, if only we are fearless and keep our hope high.

'Today', therefore, as the Holy Spirit says—

Let us be on our guard that   **3. 7**
unbelief does not creep in

We ought to take note of these words which the Holy Spirit says:

Today if ye shall hear his voice,
Harden not your hearts, as in the provocation,
Like as in the day of the temptation in the wilderness,
Wherewith your fathers tempted me by proving me,
And saw my works forty years.
Wherefore I was displeased with this generation,
And said, they do always err in their heart:
But they did not know my ways;
As I sware in my wrath,
They shall not enter into my rest.

'Today if you hear his voice,
Do not grow stubborn as in those days of rebellion,
At that time of testing in the desert,
Where your forefathers tried me and tested me,
And saw[b] the things I did for forty years.
And so, I was indignant with that generation
And I said, Their hearts are for ever astray;
They would not discern my ways;
As I vowed in my anger, they shall never enter my rest.'

[a] *Or* of him whom we confess as God's Envoy and High Priest. [b] *Or* Though they saw . . .

K.J.V.

into my rest. 12 Take heed, brethren, lest there be in any of you an evil heart of unbelief, in departing from the living God. 13 But exhort one another daily, while it is called To day; lest any of you be hardened through the deceitfulness of sin. 14 For we are made partakers of Christ, if we hold the beginning of our confidence steadfast unto the end; 15 While it is said, To day if ye will hear his voice, harden not your hearts, as in the provocation. 16 For some, when they had heard, did provoke: howbeit not all that came out of Egypt by Moses. 17 But with whom was he grieved forty years? *was it* not with them that had sinned, whose carcasses fell in the wilderness? 18 And to whom sware he that they should not enter into his rest, but to them that believed not? 19 So we see that they could not enter in because of unbelief.

4 Let us therefore fear, lest, a promise being left *us* of entering into his rest, any of you should seem to come short of it. 2 For unto us was the gospel preached, as well as unto them: but the word preached did not profit them, not being mixed with faith in them that heard *it*. 3 For we which have believed do enter into rest, as he said, As I have sworn in my wrath, if they shall enter into my rest: although the works were finished from the foundation of the world. 4 For he spake in a certain place of the seventh *day* on this wise, And God did rest the seventh day from all his works. 5 And in this *place* again, If they shall enter into my rest. 6 Seeing therefore it remaineth that some must enter therein, and they to whom it was first preached entered not in because of unbelief: 7 Again, he limiteth a certain day, saying in David, To day, after so long a time; as it is said, To day if ye will hear his voice, harden not your hearts. 8 For if Jesus had given them rest, then would he not afterward have spoken of another day. 9 There remaineth therefore a rest to the people of God. 10 For he that is entered into his rest, he also hath ceased from his own works, as God *did* from his. 11 Let us labour therefore to enter into that rest, lest any man fall after the same

R.S.V.

12 Take care, brethren, lest there be in any of you an evil, unbelieving heart, leading you to fall away from the living God. 13 But exhort one another every day, as long as it is called "today," that none of you may be hardened by the deceitfulness of sin. 14 For we share in Christ, if only we hold our first confidence firm to the end, 15 while it is said,

"Today, when you hear his voice,
　do not harden your hearts as in the rebellion."

16 Who were they that heard and yet were rebellious? Was it not all those who left Egypt under the leadership of Moses? 17 And with whom was he provoked forty years? Was it not with those who sinned, whose bodies fell in the wilderness? 18 And to whom did he swear that they should never enter his rest, but to those who were disobedient? 19 So we see that they were unable to enter because of unbelief.

4 Therefore, while the promise of entering his rest remains, let us fear lest any of you be judged to have failed to reach it. 2 For good news came to us just as to them; but the message which they heard did not benefit them, because it did not meet with faith in the hearers.[h] 3 For we who have believed enter that rest, as he has said,

"As I swore in my wrath,
　'They shall never enter my rest,'"
although his works were finished from the foundation of the world. 4 For he has somewhere spoken of the seventh day in this way, "And God rested on the seventh day from all his works." 5 And again in this place he said,
"They shall never enter my rest."
6 Since therefore it remains for some to enter it, and those who formerly received the good news failed to enter because of disobedience, 7 again he sets a certain day, "Today," saying through David so long afterward, in the words already quoted,

"Today, when you hear his voice,
　do not harden your hearts."
8 For if Joshua had given them rest, God[i] would not speak later of another day. 9 So then, there remains a sabbath rest for the people of God; 10 for whoever enters God's rest also ceases from his labors as God did from his.

11 Let us therefore strive to enter that rest, that no one fall by the same sort of disobedience.

---

[h] Other manuscripts read *they were not united in faith with the hearers.* [i] Greek *he.*

PHILLIPS

You should therefore be most careful, my brothers, that there should not be in any of you that wickedness of heart which refuses to trust, and deserts the cause of the living God. Help one another to stand firm in the faith every day, while it is still called "today," and beware that none of you becomes deaf and blind to God through the delusive glamour of sin. For we continue to share in all that Christ has for us so long as we steadily maintain until the end the trust with which we began. These words are still being said for our ears to hear:

Today if ye shall hear his voice,
Harden not your hearts, as in the provocation.

For who was it who heard the Word of God and yet provoked his indignation? Was it not all who were rescued from slavery in Egypt under the leadership of Moses? And who was it with whom God was displeased for forty long years? Was it not those who, after all their hearing of God's Word, fell into sin, and left their bones in the desert? And to whom did God swear that they should never enter into his rest? Was it not these very men who refused to trust him?

Yes, it is all too plain that it was refusal to trust God that prevented those men from entering his rest.

Men failed in the past to find God's rest: Let us not fail! 4. 1

Now since the same promise of rest is offered to us today, let us be continually on our guard that none of us even looks like failing to attain it. For we too have had a gospel preached to us, as those men had. Yet the message proclaimed to them did them no good, because they only heard and did not believe as well. It is only as a result of our faith and trust that we experience that rest. For he said:

As I sware in my wrath,
They shall not enter into my rest:

not because the rest was not prepared—it had been ready since the work of creation was completed, as he says elsewhere in the scriptures, speaking of the seventh day of creation,

And God rested on the seventh day from all his works.

In the passage above he says, "They shall not enter into my rest." It is clear that some were intended to experience this rest and, since the previous hearers of the message failed to attain to it because they would not believe God, he proclaims a further opportunity when he says through David, many years later, "today," just as he had said "today" before.

Today if ye shall hear his voice,
Harden not your hearts.

For if Joshua had given them the rest, we should not find God saying, at a much later date, "today." There still exists, therefore, a full and complete rest for the people of God. And he who experiences his rest is resting from his own work as fully as God from his.

Let us then be eager to know this rest for ourselves, and let us beware that no one misses it through falling into the same kind of unbelief

N.E.B.

See to it, brothers, that no one among you has the wicked, faithless heart of a deserter from the living God; but day by day, while that word 'Today' still sounds in your ears, encourage one another, so that no one of you is made stubborn by the wiles of sin. For we have become Christ's partners[a] if only we keep our original confidence firm to the end.

When Scripture says, 'Today if you hear his voice, do not grow stubborn as in those days of rebellion', who, I ask, were those who heard and rebelled? All those, surely, whom Moses had led out of Egypt? And with whom was God indignant for forty years? With those, surely, who had sinned, whose bodies lay where they fell in the desert? And to whom did he vow that they should not enter his rest, if not to those who had refused to believe? We perceive that it was unbelief which prevented their entering.

4 Therefore we must have before us the fear that while the promise of entering his rest remains open, one or another among you should be found to have missed his chance. For indeed we have heard the good news, as they did. But in them the message they heard did no good, because they brought no admixture of faith to the hearing of it. It is we, we who have become believers, who enter the rest referred to in the words, 'As I vowed in my anger, they shall never enter my rest.' Yet God's work has been finished ever since the world was created; for does not Scripture somewhere speak thus of the seventh day: 'God rested from his work on the seventh day'?—and once again in the passage above we read, 'They shall never enter my rest.' The fact remains that someone must enter it, and since those who first heard the good news failed to enter through unbelief, God fixes another day. Speaking through the lips of David after many long years, he uses the words already quoted: 'Today if you hear his voice, do not grow stubborn.' If Joshua had given them rest, God would not thus have spoken of another day after that. Therefore, a sabbath rest still awaits the people of God; for anyone who enters God's rest, rests from his own work as God did from his. Let us then make every effort to enter that rest, so that no one may fall by following this evil example of unbelief.

[a] Or have been given a share in Christ.

K.J.V.

example of unbelief. 12 For the word of God *is* quick, and powerful, and sharper than any two-edged sword, piercing even to the dividing asunder of soul and spirit, and of the joints and marrow, and *is* a discerner of the thoughts and intents of the heart. 13 Neither is there any creature that is not manifest in his sight: but all things *are* naked and opened unto the eyes of him with whom we have to do. 14 Seeing then that we have a great high priest, that is passed into the heavens, Jesus the Son of God, let us hold fast *our* profession. 15 For we have not a high priest which cannot be touched with the feeling of our infirmities; but was in all points tempted like as *we are, yet* without sin. 16 Let us therefore come boldly unto the throne of grace, that we may obtain mercy, and find grace to help in time of need.

5 For every high priest taken from among men is ordained for men in things *pertaining* to God, that he may offer both gifts and sacrifices for sins: 2 Who can have compassion on the ignorant, and on them that are out of the way; for that he himself also is compassed with infirmity. 3 And by reason hereof he ought, as for the people, so also for himself, to offer for sins. 4 And no man taketh this honour unto himself, but he that is called of God, as *was* Aaron. 5 So also Christ glorified not himself to be made a high priest; but he that said unto him, Thou art my Son, to day have I begotten thee. 6 As he saith also in another *place,* Thou *art* a priest for ever after the order of Melchisedec. 7 Who in the days of his flesh, when he had offered up prayers and supplications with strong crying and tears unto him that was able to save him from death, and was heard in that he feared; 8 Though he were a Son, yet learned he obedience by the things which he suffered; 9 And being made perfect, he became the author of eternal salvation unto all them that obey him; 10 Called of God a high priest after the order of Mel-

R.S.V.

12 For the word of God is living and active, sharper than any two-edged sword, piercing to the division of soul and spirit, of joints and marrow, and discerning the thoughts and intentions of the heart. 13 And before him no creature is hidden, but all are open and laid bare to the eyes of him with whom we have to do.

14 Since then we have a great high priest who has passed through the heavens, Jesus, the Son of God, let us hold fast our confession. 15 For we have not a high priest who is unable to sympathize with our weaknesses, but one who in every respect has been tempted as we are, yet without sinning. 16 Let us then with confidence draw near to the throne of grace, that we may receive mercy and find grace to help in time of need.

5 For every high priest chosen from among men is appointed to act on behalf of men in relation to God, to offer gifts and sacrifices for sins. 2 He can deal gently with the ignorant and wayward, since he himself is beset with weakness. 3 Because of this he is bound to offer sacrifice for his own sins as well as for those of the people. 4 And one does not take the honor upon himself, but he is called by God, just as Aaron was.

5 So also Christ did not exalt himself to be made a high priest, but was appointed by him who said to him,

"Thou art my Son,
　　today I have begotten thee";
6 as he says also in another place,
"Thou art a priest for ever,
　　after the order of Melchizedek."

7 In the days of his flesh, Jesus[j] offered up prayers and supplications, with loud cries and tears, to him who was able to save him from death, and he was heard for his godly fear. 8 Although he was a Son, he learned obedience through what he suffered; 9 and being made perfect he became the source of eternal salvation to all who obey him, 10 being designated by God a high priest after the order of Melchizedek.

[j] Greek *he.*

PHILLIPS

as those we have mentioned. For the Word that God speaks is alive and active: it cuts more keenly than any two-edged sword: it strikes through to the place where soul and spirit meet, to the innermost intimacies of a man's being: it exposes the very thoughts and motives of a man's heart. No creature has any cover from the sight of God; everything lies naked and exposed before the eyes of him with whom we have to do.

For our help and comfort—Jesus 4. 14 the great High Priest

Seeing that we have a great High Priest who has entered the inmost Heaven, Jesus the Son of God, let us hold firmly to our faith. For we have no superhuman High Priest to whom our weaknesses are unintelligible—he himself has shared fully in all our experience of temptation, except that he never sinned.

Let us therefore approach the throne of grace with fullest confidence, that we may receive mercy for our failures and grace to help in the hour of need.

A High Priest must be duly 5. 1 qualified and divinely appointed

Note that when a man is chosen as High Priest he is appointed on men's behalf as their representative in the things of God—he offers gifts to God and makes the necessary sacrifices for sins on behalf of his fellow men. He must be able to deal sympathetically with the ignorant and foolish because he realizes that he is himself prone to human weakness. This naturally means that the offering which he makes for sin is made on his own personal behalf as well as on behalf of those whom he represents.

Note also that nobody chooses for himself the honor of being a High Priest, but he is called by God to the work, as was Aaron, the first High Priest in ancient times.

Thus we see that the Christ did not choose for himself the glory of being High Priest, but he was honored by the one who said:

Thou art my Son,
This day have I begotten thee.

And he says in another passage:

Thou art a priest for ever
After the order of Melchizedek.

Christ, the perfect High Priest, 5. 7 was the perfect Son

Christ, in the days when he was a man on earth, appealed to the one who could save him from death in desperate prayer and the agony of tears. His prayers were heard; he was freed from his shrinking from death but, Son though he was, he had to prove the meaning of obedience through all that he suffered. Then, when he had been proved the perfect Son, he became the source of eternal salvation to all who should obey him, being now designated by God himself as High Priest "after the order of Melchizedek."

N.E.B.

For the word of God is alive and active. It cuts more keenly than any two-edged sword, piercing as far as the place where life and spirit, joints and marrow, divide. It sifts the purposes and thoughts of the heart. There is nothing in creation that can hide from him; everything lies naked and exposed to the eyes of the One with whom we have to reckon.

Since therefore we have a great high priest who has passed through the heavens, Jesus the Son of God, let us hold fast to the religion we profess. For ours is not a high priest unable to sympathize with our weaknesses, but one who, because of his likeness to us, has been tested every way,[a] only without sin. Let us therefore boldly approach the throne of our gracious God, where we may receive mercy and in his grace find timely help.

The Shadow and the Real

5 For every high priest is taken from among men and appointed their representative before God, to offer gifts and sacrifices for sins. He is able to bear patiently with the ignorant and erring, since he too is beset by weakness; and because of this he is bound to make sin-offerings for himself no less than for the people. And nobody arrogates the honour to himself: he is called by God, as indeed Aaron was. So it is with Christ; he did not confer upon himself the glory of becoming high priest: it was granted by God, who said to him, 'Thou art my Son; today I have begotten thee'; as also in another place he says, 'Thou art a priest for ever, in the succession of Melchizedek.' In the days of his earthly life he offered up prayers and petitions, with loud cries and tears, to God who was able to deliver him from the grave. Because of his humble submission his prayer was heard: son though he was, he learned obedience in the school of suffering, and, once perfected, became the source of eternal salvation for all who obey him, named by God high priest in the succession of Melchizedek.

[a] Or who has been tested every way, as we are.

K.J.V.	R.S.V.

chisedec. 11 Of whom we have many things to say, and hard to be uttered, seeing ye are dull of hearing. 12 For when for the time ye ought to be teachers, ye have need that one teach you again which *be* the first principles of the oracles of God; and are become such as have need of milk, and not of strong meat. 13 For every one that useth milk *is* unskilful in the word of righteousness: for he is a babe. 14 But strong meat belongeth to them that are of full age, *even* those who by reason of use have their senses exercised to discern both good and evil.

11 About this we have much to say which is hard to explain, since you have become dull of hearing. 12 For though by this time you ought to be teachers, you need some one to teach you again the first principles of God's word. You need milk, not solid food; 13 for every one who lives on milk is unskilled in the word of righteousness, for he is a child. 14 But solid food is for the mature, for those who have their faculties trained by practice to distinguish good from evil.

6 Therefore leaving the principles of the doctrine of Christ, let us go on unto perfection; not laying again the foundation of repentance from dead works, and of faith toward God, 2 Of the doctrine of baptisms, and of laying on of hands, and of resurrection of the dead, and of eternal judgment. 3 And this will we do, if God permit. 4 For *it is* impossible for those who were once enlightened, and have tasted of the heavenly gift, and were made partakers of the Holy Ghost, 5 And have tasted the good word of God, and the powers of the world to come, 6 If they shall fall away, to renew them again unto repentance; seeing they crucify to themselves the Son of God afresh, and put *him* to an open shame. 7 For the earth which drinketh in the rain that cometh oft upon it, and bringeth forth herbs meet for them by whom it is dressed, receiveth blessing from God: 8 But that which beareth thorns and briers *is* rejected, and *is* nigh unto cursing; whose end *is* to be burned. 9 But, beloved, we are persuaded better things of you, and things that accompany salvation, though we thus speak. 10 For God *is* not unrighteous to forget your work and labour of love, which ye have shewed toward his name, in that ye have ministered to the saints, and do minister. 11 And we desire that every one of you do shew the same diligence to the full assurance of hope unto the

6 Therefore let us leave the elementary doctrines of Christ and go on to maturity, not laying again a foundation of repentance from dead works and of faith toward God, 2 with instruction[k] about ablutions, the laying on of hands, the resurrection of the dead, and eternal judgment. 3 And this we will do if God permits.[l] 4 For it is impossible to restore again to repentance those who have once been enlightened, who have tasted the heavenly gift, and have become partakers of the Holy Spirit, 5 and have tasted the goodness of the word of God and the powers of the age to come, 6 if they then commit apostasy, since they crucify the Son of God on their own account and hold him up to contempt. 7 For land which has drunk the rain that often falls upon it, and brings forth vegetation useful to those for whose sake it is cultivated, receives a blessing from God. 8 But if it bears thorns and thistles, it is worthless and near to being cursed; its end is to be burned.

9 Though we speak thus, yet in your case, beloved, we feel sure of better things that belong to salvation. 10 For God is not so unjust as to overlook your work and the love which you showed for his sake in serving the saints, as you still do. 11 And we desire each one of you to show the same earnestness in realizing the full

[k] Other ancient manuscripts read *of instruction.*
[l] Other ancient manuscripts read *let us do this if God permits.*

There is much food for thought   **5. 11**
here—but only for the
mature Christian

There is a great deal that we should like to
say about this high priesthood, but it is not easy
to explain to you since you seem so slow to
grasp spiritual truth. At a time when you should
be teaching others, you need teachers yourselves
to repeat to you the ABC of God's revelation to
men. You have become people who need a milk
diet and cannot face solid food! For anyone who
continues to live on "milk" is obviously immature—he simply has not grown up. "Solid food"
is only for the adult, that is, for the man who
has developed by experience his power to discriminate between what is good and what is bad
for him.

Can we not leave spiritual   **6. 1**
babyhood behind—and go on
to maturity?

Let us leave behind the elementary teaching
about Christ and go forward to adult understanding. Let us not lay over and over again the
foundation truths—repentance from the deeds
which led to death, believing in God, baptism
and laying on of hands, belief in the life to
come and the final judgment. No, if God allows,
let us go on.

Going back to the foundations   **6. 4**
will not help those who have
deliberately turned away from
God

When you find men who have been enlightened, who have experienced salvation and received the Holy Spirit, who have known the
wholesome nourishment of the Word of God
and touched the spiritual resources of the eternal
world and who then fall away, it proves impossible to make them repent as they did at first. For
they are recrucifying the Son of God in their
own souls, and by their conduct exposing him to
shame and contempt. Ground which absorbs
the rain that is constantly falling upon it and
produces plants which are useful to those who
cultivate it is ground which has the blessing of
God. But ground which produces nothing but
thorns and thistles is of no value and is bound
sooner or later to be condemned—the only thing
to do is to burn it clean.

We want you to make God's   **6. 9**
promises real through your
faith, hope and patience

But although we give these words of warning
we feel sure that you, whom we love, are capable of better things and will enjoy the full experience of salvation. God is not unfair: He will
not lose sight of all that you have done nor of
the loving labor which you have shown for his
sake in looking after fellow Christians (as you
are still doing). It is our earnest wish that every
one of you should show a similar keenness in

About Melchizedek we have much to say,
much that is difficult to explain, now that you
have grown so dull of hearing. For indeed,
though by this time you ought to be teachers,
you need someone to teach you the ABC of
God's oracles over again; it has come to this,
that you need milk instead of solid food. Anyone
who lives on milk, being an infant, does not
know[a] what is right. But grown men can take
solid food; their perceptions are trained by long
use to discriminate between good and evil.

6   Let us then stop discussing the rudiments
of Christianity. We ought not to be laying
over again the foundations of faith in God and
of repentance from the deadness of our former
ways, by instruction[b] about cleansing rites and
the laying-on-of-hands, about the resurrection of
the dead and eternal judgement. Instead, let us
advance towards maturity; and so we shall, if
God permits.

For when men have once been enlightened,
when they have had a taste of the heavenly gift
and a share in the Holy Spirit, when they have
experienced the goodness of God's word and the
spiritual energies of the age to come, and after
all this have fallen away, it is impossible to
bring them again to repentance; for with their
own hands they are crucifying[c] the Son of God
and making mock of his death. When the earth
drinks in the rain that falls upon it from time
to time, and yields a useful crop to those for
whom it is cultivated, it is receiving its share of
blessing from God; but if it bears thorns and
thistles, it is worthless and God's curse hangs
over it; the end of that is burning. But although
we speak as we do, we are convinced that you,
my friends, are in the better case, and this makes
for your salvation. For God would not be so
unjust as to forget all that you did for love of
his name, when you rendered service to his people, as you still do. But we long for every one
of you to show the same eager concern, until

[a] *Or* is incompetent to speak of . . . [b] *Or* laying the foundations over again: repentance from the
deadness of our former ways and faith in God, instruction . . . [c] *Or* crucifying again.

K.J.V.

end: 12 That ye be not slothful, but followers of them who through faith and patience inherit the promises. 13 For when God made promise to Abraham, because he could swear by no greater, he sware by himself, 14 Saying, Surely blessing I will bless thee, and multiplying I will multiply thee. 15And so, after he had patiently endured, he obtained the promise. 16 For men verily swear by the greater: and an oath for confirmation *is* to them an end of all strife. 17 Wherein God, willing more abundantly to shew unto the heirs of promise the immutability of his counsel, confirmed *it* by an oath: 18 That by two immutable things, in which *it was* impossible for God to lie, we might have a strong consolation, who have fled for refuge to lay hold upon the hope set before us: 19 Which *hope* we have as an anchor of the soul, both sure and steadfast, and which entereth into that within the vail; 20 Whither the forerunner is for us entered, *even* Jesus, made a high priest for ever after the order of Melchisedec.

7 For this Melchisedec, king of Salem, priest of the most high God, who met Abraham returning from the slaughter of the kings, and blessed him; 2 To whom also Abraham gave a tenth part of all; first being by interpretation King of righteousness, and after that also King of Salem, which is, King of peace; 3 Without father, without mother, without descent, having neither beginning of days, nor end of life; but made like unto the Son of God; abideth a priest continually. 4 Now consider how great this man *was,* unto whom even the patriarch Abraham gave the tenth of the spoils. 5And verily they that are of the sons of Levi, who receive the office of the priesthood, have a commandment to take tithes of the people according to the law, that is, of their brethren, though they come out of the loins of Abraham: 6 But he whose descent is not counted from them received tithes of Abraham, and blessed him that had the promises. 7And without all contradiction the less is blessed of the better. 8And here men that die receive tithes; but there he *receiveth them,* of whom it is witnessed that he liveth. 9And as I may so say, Levi also, who receiveth tithes, paid tithes in Abraham. 10 For he was yet in the loins of his

R.S.V.

assurance of hope until the end, 12 so that you may not be sluggish, but imitators of those who through faith and patience inherit the promises.

13 For when God made a promise to Abraham, since he had no one greater by whom to swear, he swore by himself, 14 saying, "Surely I will bless you and multiply you." 15And thus Abraham,[m] having patiently endured, obtained the promise. 16 Men indeed swear by a greater than themselves, and in all their disputes an oath is final for confirmation. 17 So when God desired to show more convincingly to the heirs of the promise the unchangeable character of his purpose, he interposed with an oath, 18 so that through two unchangeable things, in which it is impossible that God should prove false, we who have fled for refuge might have strong encouragement to seize the hope set before us. 19 We have this as a sure and steadfast anchor of the soul, a hope that enters into the inner shrine behind the curtain, 20 where Jesus has gone as a forerunner on our behalf, having become a high priest for ever after the order of Melchizedek.

7 For this Melchizedek, king of Salem, priest of the Most High God, met Abraham returning from the slaughter of the kings and blessed him; 2 and to him Abraham apportioned a tenth part of everything. He is first, by translation of his name, king of righteousness, and then he is also king of Salem, that is, king of peace. 3 He is without father or mother or genealogy, and has neither beginning of days nor end of life, but resembling the Son of God he continues a priest for ever.

4 See how great he is! Abraham the patriarch gave him a tithe of the spoils. 5And those descendants of Levi who receive the priestly office have a commandment in the law to take tithes from the people, that is, from their brethren, though these also are descended from Abraham. 6 But this man who has not their genealogy received tithes from Abraham and blessed him who had the promises. 7 It is beyond dispute that the inferior is blessed by the superior. 8 Here tithes are received by mortal men; there, by one of whom it is testified that he lives. 9 One might even say that Levi himself, who receives tithes, paid tithes through Abraham, 10 for he was still in the loins of his ancestor when Melchizedek met him.

PHILLIPS

fully grasping the hope that is within you until the end. We do not want any of you to grow slack, but to follow the example of those who through sheer patient faith came to possess the promises.

When God made his promise to Abraham he swore by himself, for there was no one greater by whom he could swear, and he said:

Surely blessing I will bless thee
And multiplying I will multiply thee.

And then Abraham, after patient endurance, found the promise true.

Among men it is customary to swear by something greater than themselves. And if a statement is confirmed by an oath, that is the end of all quibbling. So in this matter, God, wishing to show beyond doubt that his plan was unchangeable, confirmed it with an oath. So that by two utterly immutable things, the word of God and the oath of God, who cannot lie, we who are refugees from this dying world might have a source of strength, and might grasp the hope that he holds out to us. This hope we hold as the utterly reliable anchor for our souls, fixed in the innermost shrine of Heaven, where Jesus has already entered on our behalf, having become, as we have seen, "High Priest for ever after the order of Melchizedek."

The mysterious Melchizedek: his superiority to Abraham and the Levites
7. 1

Now this Melchizedek was, we know, king of Salem and priest of God most high. He met Abraham when the latter was returning from the defeat of the kings, and blessed him. Abraham gave him a tribute of a tenth part of all the spoils of battle.

(Melchizedek means "king of righteousness," and his other title is "king of peace" [for Salem means peace]. He had no father or mother and no family tree. He was not born nor did he die, but, being like the Son of God, is a perpetual priest.)

Now notice the greatness of this man. Even Abraham the patriarch pays him a tribute of a tenth part of the spoils. Further, we know that, according to the Law, the descendants of Levi who accept the office of priest have the right to demand a "tenth" from the people, that is, from their brothers, despite the fact that the latter are descendants of Abraham. But here we have one who is quite independent of Levitic ancestry taking a "tenth" from Abraham, and giving a blessing to Abraham, the holder of God's promises! And no one can deny that the receiver of a blessing is inferior to the one who gives it. Again, in the one case it is mortal men who receive the "tenths," and in the other it is one who, we are assured, is alive. One might say that even Levi, the proper receiver of "tenths," has paid his tenth to this man, for in a sense he already existed in the body of his father Abraham when Melchizedek met him.

N.E.B.

your hope is finally realized. We want you not to become lazy, but to imitate those who, through faith and patience, are inheriting the promises.

When God made his promise to Abraham, he swore by himself, because he had no one greater to swear by: 'I vow that I will bless you abundantly and multiply your descendants.' Thus it was that Abraham, after patient waiting, attained the promise. Men swear by a greater than themselves, and the oath provides a confirmation to end all dispute; and so God, desiring to show even more clearly to the heirs of his promise how unchanging was his purpose, guaranteed it by oath. Here, then, are two irrevocable acts in which God could not possibly play us false, to give powerful encouragement to us, who have claimed his protection by grasping[a] the hope set before us. That hope we hold. It is like an anchor for our lives, an anchor safe and sure. It enters in through the veil, where Jesus has entered on our behalf as forerunner, having become a high priest for ever in the succession of Melchizedek.

7 This Melchizedek, king of Salem, priest of God Most High, met Abraham returning from the rout of the kings and blessed him; and Abraham gave him a tithe of everything as his portion. His name, in the first place, means 'king of righteousness'; next he is king of Salem, that is, 'king of peace'. He has no father, no mother, no lineage; his years have no beginning, his life no end. He is like the Son of God: he remains a priest for all time.

Consider now how great he must be for Abraham the patriarch to give him a tithe of the finest of the spoil. The descendants of Levi who take the priestly office are commanded by the Law to tithe the people, that is, their kinsmen, although they too are descendants of Abraham. But Melchizedek, though he does not trace his descent from them, has tithed Abraham himself, and given his blessing to the man who received the promises; and beyond all dispute the lesser is always blessed by the greater. Again, in the one instance tithes are received by men who must die; but in the other, by one whom Scripture affirms to be alive. It might even be said that Levi, who receives tithes, has himself been tithed through Abraham; for he was still in his ancestor's loins when Melchizedek met him.

[a] Or to give to us, who have claimed his protection, a powerful incentive to grasp . . .

K.J.V.

father, when Melchisedec met him. 11 If therefore perfection were by the Levitical priesthood, (for under it the people received the law,) what further need *was there* that another priest should rise after the order of Melchisedec, and not be called after the order of Aaron? 12 For the priesthood being changed, there is made of necessity a change also of the law. 13 For he of whom these things are spoken pertaineth to another tribe, of which no man gave attendance at the altar. 14 For *it is* evident that our Lord sprang out of Juda; of which tribe Moses spake nothing concerning priesthood. 15And it is yet far more evident: for that after the similitude of Melchisedec there ariseth another priest, 16 Who is made, not after the law of a carnal commandment, but after the power of an endless life. 17 For he testifieth, Thou *art* a priest for ever after the order of Melchisedec. 18 For there is verily a disannulling of the commandment going before for the weakness and unprofitableness thereof. 19 For the law made nothing perfect, but the bringing in of a better hope *did;* by the which we draw nigh unto God. 20And inasmuch as not without an oath *he was made priest:* 21 (For those priests were made without an oath; but this with an oath by him that said unto him, The Lord sware and will not repent, Thou *art* a priest for ever after the order of Melchisedec:) 22 By so much was Jesus made a surety of a better testament. 23And they truly were many priests, because they were not suffered to continue by reason of death: 24 But this *man,* because he continueth ever, hath an unchangeable priesthood. 25 Wherefore he is able also to save them to the uttermost that come unto God by him, seeing he ever liveth to make intercession for them. 26 For such a high priest became us, *who is* holy, harmless, undefiled, separate from sinners, and made higher than the heavens; 27 Who needeth not daily, as those high priests, to offer up sacrifice, first for his own sins, and then for the people's: for this he did once, when

R.S.V.

11 Now if perfection had been attainable through the Levitical priesthood (for under it the people received the law), what further need would there have been for another priest to arise after the order of Melchizedek, rather than one named after the order of Aaron? 12 For when there is a change in the priesthood, there is necessarily a change in the law as well. 13 For the one of whom these things are spoken belonged to another tribe, from which no one has ever served at the altar. 14 For it is evident that our Lord was descended from Judah, and in connection with that tribe Moses said nothing about priests.

15 This becomes even more evident when another priest arises in the likeness of Melchizedek, 16 who has become a priest, not according to a legal requirement concerning bodily descent but by the power of an indestructible life. 17 For it is witnessed of him,

"Thou art a priest for ever,
after the order of Melchizedek."

18 On the one hand, a former commandment is set aside because of its weakness and uselessness 19 (for the law made nothing perfect); on the other hand, a better hope is introduced, through which we draw near to God.

20 And it was not without an oath. 21 Those who formerly became priests took their office without an oath, but this one was addressed with an oath,

"The Lord has sworn
and will not change his mind,
'Thou art a priest for ever.' "

22 This makes Jesus the surety of a better covenant.

23 The former priests were many in number, because they were prevented by death from continuing in office; 24 but he holds his priesthood permanently, because he continues for ever. 25 Consequently he is able for all time to save those who draw near to God through him, since he always lives to make intercession for them.

26 For it was fitting that we should have such a high priest, holy, blameless, unstained, separated from sinners, exalted above the heavens. 27 He has no need, like those high priests, to offer sacrifices daily, first for his own sins and then for those of the people; he did this once for

PHILLIPS

The revival of the Melchizedek   **7. 11**
priesthood means that the
Levitical priesthood is
superseded

We may go further. If it be possible to bring
men to spiritual maturity through the Levitical
priestly system (for that is the system under
which the people were given the Law), why does
the necessity arise for another priest to make his
appearance *after the order of Melchizedek*, instead of following the normal priestly calling of
Aaron? For if there is a transference of priestly
powers, there will necessarily follow an altera-
tion of the Law regarding priesthood. He who
is described as our High Priest belongs to another tribe, no member of which had ever attended the altar! For it is a matter of history
that our Lord was a descendant of Judah, and
Moses made no mention of priesthood in connection with that tribe.

How fundamental is this change becomes all
the more apparent when we see this other priest
appearing according to the Melchizedek pattern,
and deriving his priesthood not by virtue of a
command imposed from outside, but from the
power of indestructible life within. For the witness to him, as we have seen, is:

Thou art a priest for ever
After the order of Melchizedek.

Quite plainly, then, there is a definite cancellation of the previous commandment because of
its ineffectiveness and uselessness—the Law was
incapable of bringing anyone to real maturity—
followed by the introduction of a better hope,
through which we approach our God.

The High Priesthood of Christ   **7. 20**
rests upon the oath of God

This means a "better" hope for us because
Jesus has become our priest by the oath of God.
Other men have been priests without any sworn
guarantee, but Jesus has the oath of him that
said of him:

The Lord sware and will not repent himself,
Thou art a priest for ever.

And he is, by virtue of this fact, himself the
living guarantee of a "better" agreement. Human High Priests have always been changing, for
death made a permanent appointment impossible. But Christ, because he lives for ever, possesses a priesthood that needs no successor. This
means that he can save fully and completely
those who approach God through him, for he is
always living to intercede on their behalf.

Christ the perfect High Priest,   **7. 26**
who meets our need

Here is the High Priest we need. A Man who
is holy, faultless, unstained, beyond the very
reach of sin and lifted above the very Heavens.
There is no need for him, like the High Priests
we know, to offer up daily sacrifices, first for
his own sins and then for the people's. He made
one sacrifice, once for all, when he offered up
himself.

N.E.B.

Now if perfection had been attainable through
the Levitical priesthood (for it is on this basis
that the people were given the Law), what further need would there have been to speak of
another priest arising, in the succession of Melchizedek, instead of the succession of Aaron?
For a change of priesthood must mean a change
of law. And the One here spoken of belongs to
a different tribe, no member of which has ever
had anything to do with the altar. For it is very
evident that our Lord is sprung from Judah, a
tribe to which Moses made no reference in
speaking of priests.

The argument becomes still clearer, if the
new priest who arises is one like Melchizedek,
owing his priesthood not to a system of earthbound rules but to the power of a life that cannot be destroyed. For here is the testimony:
'Thou art a priest for ever, in the succession of
Melchizedek.' The earlier rules are cancelled as
impotent and useless, since the Law brought
nothing to perfection; and a better hope is introduced, through which we draw near to God.

How great a difference it makes that an oath
was sworn! There was no oath sworn when those
others were made priests; but for this priest an
oath was sworn, as Scripture says of him: 'The
Lord has sworn and will not go back on his
word, "Thou art a priest for ever." ' How far
superior must the covenant also be of which
Jesus is the guarantor! Those other priests are
appointed in numerous succession, because they
are prevented by death from continuing in office;
but the priesthood which Jesus holds is perpetual,
because he remains for ever. That is why he is
also able to save absolutely those who approach
God through him; he is always living to plead on
their behalf.

Such a high priest does indeed fit our condition—devout, guileless, undefiled, separated from
sinners, raised high above the heavens. He has no
need to offer sacrifices daily, as the high priests
do, first for his own sins and then for those of
the people; for this he did once and for all when

K.J.V.

he offered up himself. 28 For the law maketh men high priests which have infirmity; but the word of the oath, which was since the law, *maketh* the Son, who is consecrated for evermore.

8 Now of the things which we have spoken *this is* the sum: We have such a high priest, who is set on the right hand of the throne of the Majesty in the heavens; 2A minister of the sanctuary, and of the true tabernacle, which the Lord pitched, and not man. 3 For every high priest is ordained to offer gifts and sacrifices: wherefore *it is* of necessity that this man have somewhat also to offer. 4 For if he were on earth, he should not be a priest, seeing that there are priests that offer gifts according to the law: 5 Who serve unto the example and shadow of heavenly things, as Moses was admonished of God when he was about to make the tabernacle: for, See, saith he, *that* thou make all things according to the pattern shewed to thee in the mount. 6 But now hath he obtained a more excellent ministry, by how much also he is the mediator of a better covenant, which was established upon better promises. 7 For if that first *covenant* had been faultless, then should no place have been sought for the second. 8 For finding fault with them, he saith, Behold, the days come, saith the Lord, when I will make a new covenant with the house of Israel and with the house of Judah: 9 Not according to the covenant that I made with their fathers, in the day when I took them by the hand to lead them out of the land of Egypt; because they continued not in my covenant, and I regarded them not, saith the Lord. 10 For this *is* the covenant that I will make with the house of Israel after those days, saith the Lord; I will put my laws into their mind, and write them in their hearts: and I will be to them a God, and they shall be to me a people: 11And they shall not teach every man his neighbour, and every man his brother, saying, Know the Lord: for all shall know me, from the least to the greatest. 12 For I will be merciful to their unrighteousness, and their sins and their iniquities will I remember no more. 13 In that he saith, A new *covenant,* he hath made the first old. Now that which decayeth and waxeth old *is* ready to vanish away.

R.S.V.

all when he offered up himself. 28 Indeed, the law appoints men in their weakness as high priests, but the word of the oath, which came later than the law, appoints a Son who has been made perfect for ever.

8 Now the point in what we are saying is this: we have such a high priest, one who is seated at the right hand of the throne of the Majesty in heaven, 2 a minister in the sanctuary and the true tent [n] which is set up not by man but by the Lord. 3 For every high priest is appointed to offer gifts and sacrifices; hence it is necessary for this priest also to have something to offer. 4 Now if he were on earth, he would not be a priest at all, since there are priests who offer gifts according to the law. 5 They serve a copy and shadow of the heavenly sanctuary; for when Moses was about to erect the tent, [n] he was instructed by God, saying, "See that you make everything according to the pattern which was shown you on the mountain." 6 But as it is, Christ [o] has obtained a ministry which is as much more excellent than the old as the covenant he mediates is better, since it is enacted on better promises. 7 For if that first covenant had been faultless, there would have been no occasion for a second.

8 For he finds fault with them when he says:
"The days will come, says the Lord,
  when I will establish a new covenant with
    the house of Israel
  and with the house of Judah;
9 not like the covenant that I made with
    their fathers
  on the day when I took them by the hand
  to lead them out of the land of Egypt;
  for they did not continue in my covenant,
  and so I paid no heed to them, says the
    Lord.
10 This is the covenant that I will make with
    the house of Israel
  after those days, says the Lord:
  I will put my laws into their minds,
  and write them on their hearts,
  and I will be their God,
  and they shall be my people.
11 And they shall not teach every one his
    fellow
  or every one his brother, saying, 'Know
    the Lord,'
  for all shall know me,
  from the least of them to the greatest.
12 For I will be merciful toward their iniquities,
  and I will remember their sins no more."
13 In speaking of a new covenant he treats the first as obsolete. And what is becoming obsolete and growing old is ready to vanish away.

---

[n] Or *tabernacle.* [o] Greek *he.*

PHILLIPS

N.E.B.

The Law makes for its High Priests men of human weakness. But the word of the oath, which came after the Law, makes for High Priest the Son, who is perfect for ever!

he offered up himself. The high priests made by the Law are men in all their frailty; but the priest appointed by the words of the oath which supersedes the Law is the Son, made perfect now for ever.

Christ our High Priest in Heaven 8. 1 is High Priest of a new agreement

Now to sum up—we have an ideal High Priest such as has been described above. He has taken his seat on the right hand of the heavenly majesty. He is the minister of the sanctuary and of the real tabernacle—that is, the one which the Lord has set up and not man. Every High Priest is appointed to offer gifts and make sacrifices. It follows, therefore, that in these holy places this man has something that he is offering.

Now if he were still living on earth he would not be a priest at all, for there are already priests offering the gifts prescribed by the Law. These men are serving what is only a pattern or reproduction of things that exist in Heaven. (Moses, you will remember, when he was going to construct the tabernacle, was cautioned by God in these words:

See that thou make all things
According to the pattern that was showed thee
in the mount.)

But Christ has been given a far higher ministry for he mediates a higher agreement, which in turn rests upon higher promises. If the first agreement had proved satisfactory there would have been no need for the second.

Actually, however, God does show himself dissatisfied, for he says to those under the first agreement:

Behold, the days come, saith the Lord,
That I will make a new covenant with the house of Israel and with the house of Judah;
Not according to the covenant that I made with their fathers
In the day that I took them by the hand to lead them forth out of the land of Egypt;
For they continued not in my covenant,
And I regarded them not, saith the Lord.
For this is the covenant that I will make with the house of Israel
After those days, saith the Lord;
I will put my laws into their mind,
And on their heart also will I write them:
And I will be to them a God,
And they shall be to me a people:
And they shall not teach every man his fellow citizen,
And every man his brother, saying, Know the Lord:
For all shall know me,
From the least to the greatest of them:
For I will be merciful to their iniquities,
And their sins will I remember no more.

The mere fact that God speaks of a new covenant or agreement makes the old one out of date. And when a thing grows weak and out of date it is obviously soon going to be dispensed with altogether.

8 Now this is my main point: just such a high priest we have, and he has taken his seat at the right hand of the throne of Majesty in the heavens, a ministrant in the real sanctuary, the tent pitched by the Lord and not by man. Every high priest is appointed to offer gifts and sacrifices: hence, this one too must have[a] something to offer. Now if he had been on earth, he would not even have been a priest, since there are already priests who offer the gifts which the Law prescribes, though they minister in a sanctuary which is only a copy and shadow of the heavenly. This is implied when Moses, about to erect the tent, is instructed by God: 'See to it that you make everything according to the pattern shown you on the mountain.' But in fact the ministry which has fallen to Jesus is as far superior to theirs as are the covenant he mediates and the promises upon which it is legally secured.

Had that first covenant been faultless, there would have been no need to look for a second in its place. But God, finding fault with them, says, 'The days are coming, says the Lord, when I will conclude a new covenant with the house of Israel and the house of Judah. It will not be like the covenant I made with their forefathers when I took them by the hand to lead them out of Egypt; because they did not abide by the terms of that covenant, and I abandoned them, says the Lord. For the covenant I will make with the house of Israel after those days, says the Lord, is this: I will set my laws in their understanding and write them on their hearts; and I will be their God, and they shall be my people. And they shall not teach one another, saying to brother and fellow-citizen,[b] "Know the Lord!" For all of them shall know me, from small to great; I will be merciful to their wicked deeds, and their sins I will remember no more at all.' By speaking of a new covenant, he has pronounced the first one old; and anything that is growing old and ageing will shortly disappear.

9 Then verily the first *covenant* had also ordinances of divine service, and a worldly
sanctuary. 2 For there was a tabernacle made;
the first, wherein *was* the candlestick, and the
table, and the shewbread; which is called the
sanctuary. 3And after the second vail, the tabernacle which is called the holiest of all; 4 Which
had the golden censer, and the ark of the covenant overlaid round about with gold, wherein
was the golden pot that had manna, and Aaron's
rod that budded, and the tables of the covenant;
5And over it the cherubim of glory shadowing
the mercy seat; of which we cannot now speak
particularly. 6 Now when these things were thus
ordained, the priests went always into the first
tabernacle, accomplishing the service *of God.*
7 But into the second *went* the high priest alone
once every year, not without blood, which he
offered for himself, and *for* the errors of the
people: 8 The Holy Ghost this signifying, that
the way into the holiest of all was not yet made
manifest, while as the first tabernacle was yet
standing: 9 Which *was* a figure for the time then
present, in which were offered both gifts and
sacrifices, that could not make him that did the
service perfect, as pertaining to the conscience;
10 *Which stood* only in meats and drinks, and
divers washings, and carnal ordinances, imposed
on them until the time of reformation. 11 But
Christ being come a high priest of good things
to come, by a greater and more perfect tabernacle, not made with hands, that is to say, not
of this building; 12 Neither by the blood of
goats and calves, but by his own blood he entered in once into the holy place, having obtained eternal redemption *for us.* 13 For if the
blood of bulls and of goats, and the ashes of a
heifer sprinkling the unclean, sanctifieth to the
purifying of the flesh; 14 How much more shall
the blood of Christ, who through the eternal
Spirit offered himself without spot to God, purge
your conscience from dead works to serve the
living God? 15And for this cause he is the
mediator of the new testament, that by means of
death, for the redemption of the transgressions
that were under the first testament, they which
are called might receive the promise of eternal
inheritance. 16 For where a testament *is,* there
must also of necessity be the death of the testator.
17 For a testament *is* of force after men are

9 Now even the first covenant had regulations for worship and an earthly sanctuary.
2 For a tent[p] was prepared, the outer one, in
which were the lampstand and the table and the
bread of the Presence;[q] it is called the Holy
Place. 3 Behind the second curtain stood a tent[p]
called the Holy of Holies, 4 having the golden
altar of incense and the ark of the covenant
covered on all sides with gold, which contained
a golden urn holding the manna, and Aaron's
rod that budded, and the tables of the covenant;
5 above it were the cherubim of glory overshadowing the mercy seat. Of these things we
cannot now speak in detail.
6 These preparations having thus been made,
the priests go continually into the outer tent,[p]
performing their ritual duties; 7 but into the
second only the high priest goes, and he but
once a year, and not without taking blood which
he offers for himself and for the errors of the
people. 8 By this the Holy Spirit indicates that
the way into the sanctuary is not yet opened
as long as the outer tent[p] is still standing
9 (which is symbolic for the present age). According to this arrangement, gifts and sacrifices
are offered which cannot perfect the conscience
of the worshiper, 10 but deal only with food and
drink and various ablutions, regulations for the
body imposed until the time of reformation.
11 But when Christ appeared as a high priest
of the good things that have come,[r] then
through the greater and more perfect tent[p] (not
made with hands, that is, not of this creation)
12 he entered once for all into the Holy Place,
taking[s] not the blood of goats and calves but
his own blood, thus securing an eternal redemption. 13 For if the sprinkling of defiled persons
with the blood of goats and bulls and with the
ashes of a heifer sanctifies for the purification of
the flesh, 14 how much more shall the blood
of Christ, who through the eternal Spirit offered
himself without blemish to God, purify your[t]
conscience from dead works to serve the living
God.
15 Therefore he is the mediator of a new
covenant, so that those who are called may receive the promised eternal inheritance, since a
death has occurred which redeems them from
the transgressions under the first covenant.[u]
16 For where a will[u] is involved, the death of the
one who made it must be established. 17 For a
will[u] takes effect only at death, since it is not

[p] Or *tabernacle.* [q] Greek *the presentation of the
loaves.* [r] Other manuscripts read *good things to
come.* [s] Greek *through.* [t] Other manuscripts read
our. [u] The Greek word here used means both
covenant and *will.*

PHILLIPS　　　　　　　　　　　　**N.E.B.**

The sanctuary under the old agreement
9. 1

Now the first agreement had certain rules for the service of God, and it had a sanctuary, a holy place in this world for the eternal God. A tent was erected: in the outer compartment were placed the lamp standard, the table and the sacred loaves. Inside, beyond the curtain, was the inner tent called the holy of holies, in which were the golden incense altar and the gold-covered ark of the agreement, containing the golden jar of manna, Aaron's budding staff and the stone tablets inscribed with the words of the actual agreement. Above these things were fixed representations of the cherubim of glory, casting their shadow over the ark's covering, known as the mercy seat. (All this is full of meaning but we cannot enter now into a detailed explanation.)

Under this arrangement the outer tent was habitually used by the priests in the regular discharge of their religious duties. But the inner tent was entered once a year only, by the High Priest, alone, bearing a sacrifice of shed blood to be offered for his own sins and those of the people.

The old arrangements stood as symbols until Christ, the truth, came
9. 8

By these things the Holy Spirit means us to understand that the way to the holy of holies was not yet open, that is, so long as the first tent and all that it stands for still exist. For in this outer tent we see a picture of the present time, in which both gifts and sacrifices are offered and yet are incapable of cleansing the soul of the worshiper. The ceremonies are concerned with food and drink, various washings and rules for bodily conduct, and were only intended to be valid until the time when Christ should establish the truth. For now Christ has come among us, the High Priest of the good things which were to come, and has passed through a greater and more perfect tent which no human hand had made (for it was no part of this world of ours). It was not with goats' or calves' blood but with his own blood that he entered once for all into the holy of holies, having won for us men eternal reconciliation with God. And if the blood of bulls and goats and the ashes of a burnt heifer were, when sprinkled on the unholy, sufficient to make the body pure, then how much more will the blood of Christ himself, who in his eternal spirit offered himself to God as the perfect sacrifice, purify our souls from the deeds of death, that we may serve the living God!

The death of Christ gives him power to administer the new agreement
9. 15

Christ is consequently the administrator of an entirely new agreement, having the power, by virtue of his death, to redeem transgressions committed under the first agreement: to enable those who obey God's call to enjoy the promises of the eternal inheritance. For, as in the case of a will, the agreement is only valid after death. While

9 The first covenant indeed had its ordinances of divine service and its sanctuary, but a material sanctuary. For a tent was prepared—the first tent—in which was the lamp-stand, and the table with the bread of the Presence; this is called the Holy Place. Beyond the second curtain was the tent called the Most Holy Place. Here was a golden altar of incense, and the ark of the covenant plated all over with gold, in which were a golden jar containing the manna, and Aaron's staff which once budded, and the tablets of the covenant; and above it the cherubim of God's glory, overshadowing the place of expiation. On these we cannot now enlarge.

Under this arrangement, the priests are always entering the first tent in the discharge of their duties; but the second is entered only once a year, and by the high priest alone, and even then he must take with him the blood which he offers on his own behalf and for the people's sins of ignorance. By this the Holy Spirit signifies that so long as the earlier tent still stands, the way into the sanctuary remains unrevealed. (All this is symbolic, pointing to the present time.) The offerings and sacrifices there prescribed cannot give the worshipper inward perfection. It is only a matter of food and drink and various rites of cleansing—outward ordinances in force until the time of reformation.

But now Christ has come, high priest of good things already in being.[a] The tent of his priesthood is a greater and more perfect one, not made by men's hands, that is, not belonging to this created world; the blood of his sacrifice is his own blood, not the blood of goats and calves; and thus he has entered the sanctuary once and for all and secured an eternal deliverance. For if the blood of goats and bulls and the sprinkled ashes of a heifer have power to hallow those who have been defiled and restore their external purity, how much greater is the power of the blood of Christ; he offered himself without blemish to God, a spiritual and eternal sacrifice; and his blood will cleanse our conscience from the deadness of our former ways and fit us for the service of the living God.

And therefore he is the mediator of a new covenant, or testament, under which, now that there has been a death to bring deliverance from sins committed under the former covenant, those whom God has called may receive the promise of the eternal inheritance. For where there is a testament it is necessary for the death of the testator to be established. A testament is operative only after a death: it cannot possibly have

[a] *Some witnesses read* good things which were (*or* are) to be.

K.J.V.

dead: otherwise it is of no strength at all while the testator liveth. 18 Whereupon neither the first *testament* was dedicated without blood. 19 For when Moses had spoken every precept to all the people according to the law, he took the blood of calves and of goats, with water, and scarlet wool, and hyssop, and sprinkled both the book and all the people, 20 Saying, This *is* the blood of the testament which God hath enjoined unto you. 21 Moreover he sprinkled likewise with blood both the tabernacle, and all the vessels of the ministry. 22 And almost all things are by the law purged with blood; and without shedding of blood is no remission. 23 *It was* therefore necessary that the patterns of things in the heavens should be purified with these; but the heavenly things themselves with better sacrifices than these. 24 For Christ is not entered into the holy places made with hands, *which are* the figures of the true; but into heaven itself, now to appear in the presence of God for us: 25 Nor yet that he should offer himself often, as the high priest entereth into the holy place every year with blood of others; 26 For then must he often have suffered since the foundation of the world: but now once in the end of the world hath he appeared to put away sin by the sacrifice of himself. 27 And as it is appointed unto men once to die, but after this the judgment: 28 So Christ was once offered to bear the sins of many; and unto them that look for him shall he appear the second time without sin unto salvation.

R.S.V.

in force as long as the one who made it is alive. 18 Hence even the first covenant was not ratified without blood. 19 For when every commandment of the law had been declared by Moses to all the people, he took the blood of calves and goats, with water and scarlet wool and hyssop, and sprinkled both the book itself and all the people, 20 saying, "This is the blood of the covenant which God commanded you." 21 And in the same way he sprinkled with the blood both the tent[p] and all the vessels used in worship. 22 Indeed, under the law almost everything is purified with blood, and without the shedding of blood there is no forgiveness of sins.

23 Thus it was necessary for the copies of the heavenly things to be purified with these rites, but the heavenly things themselves with better sacrifices than these. 24 For Christ has entered, not into a sanctuary made with hands, a copy of the true one, but into heaven itself, now to appear in the presence of God on our behalf. 25 Nor was it to offer himself repeatedly, as the high priest enters the Holy Place yearly with blood not his own; 26 for then he would have had to suffer repeatedly since the foundation of the world. But as it is, he has appeared once for all at the end of the age to put away sin by the sacrifice of himself. 27 And just as it is appointed for men to die once, and after that comes judgment, 28 so Christ, having been offered once to bear the sins of many, will appear a second time, not to deal with sin but to save those who are eagerly waiting for him.

10 For the law having a shadow of good things to come, *and* not the very image of the things, can never with those sacrifices, which they offered year by year continually, make the comers thereunto perfect. 2 For then would they not have ceased to be offered? because that the worshippers once purged should have had no more conscience of sins. 3 But in those *sacrifices there is* a remembrance again *made* of sins every year. 4 For *it is* not possible that the blood of bulls and of goats should take away sins. 5 Wherefore, when he cometh into the world, he saith, Sacrifice and offering thou wouldest not,

10 For since the law has but a shadow of the good things to come instead of the true form of these realities, it can never, by the same sacrifices which are continually offered year after year, make perfect those who draw near. 2 Otherwise, would they not have ceased to be offered? If the worshipers had once been cleansed, they would no longer have any consciousness of sin. 3 But in these sacrifices there is a reminder of sin year after year. 4 For it is impossible that the blood of bulls and goats should take away sins.

5 Consequently, when Christ[v] came into the world, he said,
"Sacrifices and offerings thou hast not desired,
but a body hast thou prepared for me;

[p] Or *tabernacle*. [v] Greek *he.*

the testator lives, a will has no legal power. And indeed we find that even the first agreement of God's will was not put into force without the shedding of blood. For when Moses had told the people every command of the Law he took calves' and goats' blood with water and scarlet wool, and sprinkled both the book and all the people with a sprig of hyssop, saying: "This is the blood of the agreement God makes with you." Moses also sprinkled with blood the tent itself and all the sacred vessels. And you will find that in the Law almost all cleansing is made by means of blood—as the common saying has it: "No shedding of blood, no remission of sin."

Christ has achieved the real appearance before God for us   9. 23

It was necessary for the earthly reproductions of heavenly realities to be purified by such methods, but the actual heavenly things could only be made pure in God's sight by higher sacrifices than these. Christ did not therefore enter into any holy places made by human hands (however truly these may represent heavenly realities), but he entered Heaven itself to make his appearance before God as High Priest on our behalf. There is no intention that he should offer himself regularly, like the High Priest entering the holy of holies every year with the blood of another creature. For that would mean that he would have to suffer death every time he entered Heaven from the beginning of the world! No, the fact is that now, at this point in time, the end of the present age, he has appeared once for all to abolish sin by the sacrifice of himself. And just as surely as it is appointed for all men to die once, and after that pass to their judgment, so is it certain that Christ was offered once to bear the sins of many and after that, to those who look for him, he will appear a second time, not this time to deal with sin, but to bring to full salvation those who eagerly await him.

Sacrifices under the Law were "typical," not final   10. 1

The Law possessed only a dim outline of the benefits Christ would bring, and did not actually reproduce them. Consequently it was incapable of perfecting the souls of those who offered their regular annual sacrifices. For if it had, surely the sacrifices would have been discontinued—on the grounds that the worshipers, having been really cleansed, would have had no further consciousness of sin. In practice, however, the sacrifices amounted to an annual reminder of sins; for the blood of bulls and goats cannot really remove the guilt of sin.

Christ, however, makes the old order obsolete and makes the perfect sacrifice   10. 5

Therefore, when Christ enters the world, he says:

Sacrifice and offering thou wouldest not,
But a body didst thou prepare for me;

force while the testator is alive. Thus we find that the former covenant itself was not inaugurated without blood. For when, as the Law directed, Moses had recited all the commandments to the people, he took the blood of the calves, with water, scarlet wool, and marjoram, and sprinkled the law-book itself and all the people, saying, 'This is the blood of the covenant which God has enjoined upon you.' In the same way he also sprinkled the tent and all the vessels of divine service with blood. Indeed, according to the Law, it might almost be said, everything is cleansed by blood and without the shedding of blood there is no forgiveness.

If, then, these sacrifices cleanse the copies of heavenly things, those heavenly things themselves require better sacrifices to cleanse them. For Christ has entered, not that sanctuary made by men's hands which is only a symbol of the reality, but heaven itself, to appear now before God on our behalf. Nor is he there to offer himself again and again, as the high priest enters the sanctuary year by year with blood not his own. If that were so, he would have had to suffer many times since the world was made. But as it is, he has appeared once and for all at the climax of history to abolish sin by the sacrifice of himself. And as it is the lot of men to die once, and after death comes judgement, so Christ was offered once to bear the burden of men's sins,[a] and will appear a second time, sin done away, to bring salvation to those who are watching for him.

10 For the Law contains but a shadow, and no true image,[b] of the good things which were to come; it provides for the same sacrifices year after year, and with these it can never bring the worshippers to perfection for all time.[c] If it could, these sacrifices would surely have ceased to be offered, because the worshippers, cleansed once for all, would no longer have any sense of sin. But instead, in these sacrifices year after year sins are brought to mind, because sins can never be removed by the blood of bulls and goats.

That is why, at his coming into the world, he says:

'Sacrifice and offering thou didst not desire,
But thou hast prepared a body for me.

[a] Or to remove men's sins. [b] Some witnesses read a shadow and likeness . . . [c] Or bring to perfection the worshippers who come continually.

K.J.V.

but a body hast thou prepared me: 6 In burnt offerings and *sacrifices* for sin thou hast had no pleasure. 7 Then said I, Lo, I come (in the volume of the book it is written of me) to do thy will, O God. 8 Above when he said, Sacrifice and offering and burnt offerings and *offering* for sin thou wouldest not, neither hadst pleasure *therein;* which are offered by the law; 9 Then said he, Lo, I come to do thy will, O God. He taketh away the first, that he may establish the second. 10 By the which will we are sanctified through the offering of the body of Jesus Christ once *for all.* 11 And every priest standeth daily ministering and offering oftentimes the same sacrifices, which can never take away sins: 12 But this man, after he had offered one sacrifice for sins for ever, sat down on the right hand of God; 13 From henceforth expecting till his enemies be made his footstool. 14 For by one offering he hath perfected for ever them that are sanctified. 15 *Whereof* the Holy Ghost also is a witness to us: for after that he had said before, 16 This *is* the covenant that I will make with them after those days, saith the Lord; I will put my laws into their hearts, and in their minds will I write them; 17 And their sins and iniquities will I remember no more. 18 Now where remission of these *is, there is* no more offering for sin. 19 Having therefore, brethren, boldness to enter into the holiest by the blood of Jesus, 20 By a new and living way, which he hath consecrated for us, through the vail, that is to say, his flesh; 21 And *having* a high priest over the house of God; 22 Let us draw near with a true heart in full assurance of faith, having our hearts sprinkled from an evil conscience, and our bodies washed with pure water. 23 Let us hold fast the profession of *our* faith without wavering; for he *is* faithful that promised; 24 And let us consider one another to provoke unto love and to good works: 25 Not forsaking the assembling of ourselves together, as the manner of some *is;* but exhorting *one another:* and so much the more, as ye see the day approaching. 26 For if we sin wilfully after that we have received the knowledge of the truth, there remaineth no more sacrifice for sins, 27 But a certain fearful looking for of judgment and fiery indignation, which

R.S.V.

6 in burnt offerings and sin offerings thou hast taken no pleasure.
7 Then I said, 'Lo, I have come to do thy will, O God,'
as it is written of me in the roll of the book.''
8 When he said above, "Thou hast neither desired nor taken pleasure in sacrifices and offerings and burnt offerings and sin offerings" (these are offered according to the law), 9 then he added, "Lo, I have come to do thy will." He abolishes the first in order to establish the second. 10 And by that will we have been sanctified through the offering of the body of Jesus Christ once for all.

11 And every priest stands daily at his service, offering repeatedly the same sacrifices, which can never take away sins. 12 But when Christ[w] had offered for all time a single sacrifice for sins, he sat down at the right hand of God, 13 then to wait until his enemies should be made a stool for his feet. 14 For by a single offering he has perfected for all time those who are sanctified. 15 And the Holy Spirit also bears witness to us; for after saying,
16 "This is the covenant that I will make with them
after those days, says the Lord:
I will put my laws on their hearts,
and write them on their minds,"
17 then he adds,
"I will remember their sins and their misdeeds no more."
18 Where there is forgiveness of these, there is no longer any offering for sin.

19 Therefore, brethren, since we have confidence to enter the sanctuary by the blood of Jesus, 20 by the new and living way which he opened for us through the curtain, that is, through his flesh, 21 and since we have a great priest over the house of God, 22 let us draw near with a true heart in full assurance of faith, with our hearts sprinkled clean from an evil conscience and our bodies washed with pure water. 23 Let us hold fast the confession of our hope without wavering, for he who promised is faithful; 24 and let us consider how to stir up one another to love and good works, 25 not neglecting to meet together, as is the habit of some, but encouraging one another, and all the more as you see the Day drawing near.

26 For if we sin deliberately after receiving the knowledge of the truth, there no longer remains a sacrifice for sins, 27 but a fearful prospect of judgment, and a fury of fire which

[w] Greek *this one.*

704

PHILLIPS

In whole burnt offerings and sacrifices for sin
thou hadst no pleasure:
Then said I, Lo, I am come
(In the roll of the book it is written of me)
To do thy will, O God.

After saying that God has "no pleasure in
sacrifice, offering and burnt offering" (which are
made according to the Law), Christ then says,
"Lo, I am come to do thy will." That means that
he is dispensing with the old order of sacrifices,
and establishing a new order of obedience to
the will of God, and in that will we have been
made holy by the single unique offering of the
body of Jesus Christ.
Every human priest stands day by day performing his religious duties and offering time
after time the same sacrifices—which can never
actually remove sins. But this man, after offering
one sacrifice for sins for ever, took his seat at
God's right hand, from that time offering no
more sacrifice, but waiting until "his enemies are
made his footstool." For by virtue of that one
offering he has perfected for all time every one
whom he makes holy. The Holy Spirit himself
endorses this truth for us, when he says, first:

This is the covenant that I will make with
them
After those days, saith the Lord;
I will put my laws on their heart,
And upon their mind also will I write them.

And then, he adds:

And their sins and their iniquities will I remember no more.

Where God grants remission of sin there can be
no question of making further atonement.

Through Christ we can   10. 19
confidently approach God

So, by virtue of the blood of Jesus, you and I,
my brothers, may now have confidence to enter
the holy of holies by a fresh and living Way,
which he has opened up for us by himself passing through the curtain, that is, his own human
nature. Further, since we have a great High
Priest set over the household of God, let us draw
near with true hearts and fullest confidence,
knowing that our inmost souls have been purified
by the sprinkling of his blood just as our bodies
are cleansed by the washing of clean water. In
this confidence let us hold on to the hope that we
profess without the slightest hesitation—for he
is utterly dependable—and let us think of one
another and how we can encourage one another
to love and do good deeds. And let us not hold
aloof from our church meetings, as some do.
Let us do all we can to help one another's faith,
and this the more earnestly as we see the final
day drawing ever nearer.

A warning: let us not abuse   10. 26
the great sacrifice

Now if we sin deliberately after we have
known and accepted the truth, there can be no
further sacrifice for sin for us but only a terrifying expectation of judgment and the fire of

N.E.B.

Whole-offerings and sin-offerings thou didst not
delight in.
Then I said, "Here am I: as it is written of me
in the scroll,
I have come, O God, to do thy will." '

First he says, 'Sacrifices and offerings, whole-offerings and sin-offerings, thou didst not desire
nor delight in'—although the Law prescribes
them—and then he says, 'I have come to do
thy will.' He thus annuls the former to establish
the latter. And it is by the will of God that we
have been consecrated, through the offering of
the body of Jesus Christ once and for all.
Every priest stands performing his service daily
and offering time after time the same sacrifices,
which can never remove sins. But Christ offered
for all time one sacrifice for sins, and took his
seat at the right hand of God, where he waits
henceforth until his enemies are made his footstool. For by one offering he has perfected for
all time those who are thus consecrated. Here
we have also the testimony of the Holy Spirit:
he first says, 'This is the covenant which I will
make with them after those days, says the Lord:
I will set my laws in their hearts and write them
on their understanding'; then he adds, 'and their
sins and wicked deeds I will remember no more
at all.' And where these have been forgiven, there
is no longer any offering for sin.

So now, my friends, the blood of Jesus makes
us free to enter boldly into the sanctuary by the
new, living way which he has opened for us
through the curtain, the way of his flesh.[a] We
have, moreover, a great priest set over the household of God; so let us make our approach in
sincerity of heart and full assurance of faith, our
guilty hearts sprinkled clean, our bodies washed
with pure water. Let us be firm and unswerving
in the confession of our hope, for the Giver of
the promise may be trusted. We ought to see how
each of us may best arouse others to love and
active goodness, not staying away from our meetings, as some do, but rather encouraging one
another, all the more because you see the Day
drawing near.
For if we persist in sin after receiving the
knowledge of the truth, no sacrifice for sins remains: only a terrifying expectation of judgement
and a fierce fire which will consume God's ene-

[a] *Or* through the curtain of his flesh.

K.J.V.

shall devour the adversaries. 28 He that despised Moses' law died without mercy under two or three witnesses: 29 Of how much sorer punishment, suppose ye, shall he be thought worthy, who hath trodden under foot the Son of God, and hath counted the blood of the covenant, wherewith he was sanctified, an unholy thing, and hath done despite unto the Spirit of grace? 30 For we know him that hath said, Vengeance *belongeth* unto me, I will recompense, saith the Lord. And again, The Lord shall judge his people. 31 *It is* a fearful thing to fall into the hands of the living God. 32 But call to remembrance the former days, in which, after ye were illuminated, ye endured a great fight of afflictions; 33 Partly, whilst ye were made a gazingstock both by reproaches and afflictions; and partly, whilst ye became companions of them that were so used. 34 For ye had compassion of me in my bonds, and took joyfully the spoiling of your goods, knowing in yourselves that ye have in heaven a better and an enduring substance. 35 Cast not away therefore your confidence, which hath great recompense of reward. 36 For ye have need of patience, that, after ye have done the will of God, ye might receive the promise. 37 For yet a little while, and he that shall come will come, and will not tarry. 38 Now the just shall live by faith: but if *any man* draw back, my soul shall have no pleasure in him. 39 But we are not of them who draw back unto perdition; but of them that believe to the saving of the soul.

R.S.V.

will consume the adversaries. 28 A man who has violated the law of Moses dies without mercy at the testimony of two or three witnesses. 29 How much worse punishment do you think will be deserved by the man who has spurned the Son of God, and profaned the blood of the covenant by which he was sanctified, and outraged the Spirit of grace? 30 For we know him who said, "Vengeance is mine, I will repay." And again, "The Lord will judge his people." 31 It is a fearful thing to fall into the hands of the living God.

32 But recall the former days when, after you were enlightened, you endured a hard struggle with sufferings, 33 sometimes being publicly exposed to abuse and affliction, and sometimes being partners with those so treated. 34 For you had compassion on the prisoners, and you joyfully accepted the plundering of your property, since you knew that you yourselves had a better possession and an abiding one. 35 Therefore do not throw away your confidence, which has a great reward. 36 For you have need of endurance, so that you may do the will of God and receive what is promised.

37 "For yet a little while,
　　and the coming one shall come and shall
　　not tarry;
38 but my righteous one shall live by faith,
　　and if he shrinks back,
　　my soul has no pleasure in him."
39 But we are not of those who shrink back and are destroyed, but of those who have faith and keep their souls.

11 Now faith is the substance of things hoped for, the evidence of things not seen. 2 For by it the elders obtained a good report. 3 Through faith we understand that the worlds were framed by the word of God, so that things which are seen were not made of things which do appear. 4 By faith Abel offered unto God a more excellent sacrifice than Cain, by which he obtained witness that he was righteous, God testifying of his gifts: and by it he being dead yet

11 Now faith is the assurance of things hoped for, the conviction of things not seen. 2 For by it the men of old received divine approval. 3 By faith we understand that the world was created by the word of God, so that what is seen was made out of things which do not appear. 4 By faith Abel offered to God a more acceptable sacrifice than Cain, through which he received approval as righteous, God bearing witness by accepting his gift; he died, but through

PHILLIPS

God's indignation, which will one day consume all that sets itself against him. The man who showed contempt for Moses' Law died without hope of appeal on the evidence of two or three of his fellows. How much more dreadful a punishment will he be thought to deserve who has poured scorn on the Son of God, treated like dirt the blood of the agreement which had once made him holy, and insulted the very Spirit of grace? For we know the one who said:

Vengeance belongeth unto me, I will recompense.

And, again:

The Lord shall judge his people.

Truly it is a terrible thing for a man who has done this to fall into the hands of the living God!

Recollect your former faith,   10. 32 and stand firm today!

You must never forget those past days when you had received the light and went through such a great and painful struggle. It was partly because everyone's eye was on you as you endured harsh words and hard experiences, partly because you threw in your lot with those who suffered much the same. You sympathized with those who were put in prison and you were cheerful when your own goods were confiscated, for you knew that you had a much more solid and lasting treasure in Heaven. Don't throw away your trust now—it carries with it a rich reward in the world to come. Patient endurance is what you need if, after doing God's will, you are to receive what he has promised.

For yet a very little while,
He that cometh shall come, and shall not tarry.
But my righteous one shall live by faith;
And if he shrink back, my soul hath no pleasure in him.

Surely we are not going to be men who cower back and are lost, but men who maintain their faith until the salvation of their souls is complete!

Now faith means putting our full confidence in the things we hope for; it means being certain of things we cannot see. It was this kind of faith that won their reputation for the saints of old. And it is after all only by faith that our minds accept as fact that the whole scheme of time and space was created by God's command—that the world which we can see has come into being through principles which are invisible.

Faith is the distinctive mark of   11. 4 the saints of the old agreement

ABEL

It was because of his faith that Abel made a better sacrifice to God than Cain, and he had evidence that God looked upon him as a righteous man, whose gifts he could accept. And

N.E.B.

mies. If a man disregards the Law of Moses, he is put to death without pity on the evidence of two or three witnesses. Think how much more severe a penalty that man will deserve who has trampled under foot the Son of God, profaned the blood of the covenant by which he was consecrated, and affronted God's gracious Spirit! For we know who it is that has said, 'Justice is mine: I will repay'; and again, 'The Lord will judge his people.' It is a terrible thing to fall into the hands of the living God.

Remember the days gone by, when, newly enlightened, you met the challenge of great sufferings and held firm. Some of you were abused and tormented to make a public show, while others stood loyally by those who were so treated. For indeed you shared the sufferings of the prisoners, and you cheerfully accepted the seizure of your possessions, knowing that you possessed something better and more lasting. Do not then throw away your confidence, for it carries a great reward. You need endurance, if you are to do God's will and win what he has promised. For 'soon, very soon' (in the words of Scripture), 'he who is to come will come; he will not delay; and by faith my righteous servant shall find life; but if a man shrinks back, I take no pleasure in him.' But we are not among those who shrink back and are lost; we have the faith to make life our own.

A Call to Faith

11 And what is faith? Faith gives substance[a] to our hopes, and makes us certain of realities we do not see.

It is for their faith that the men of old stand on record.

By faith we perceive that the universe was fashioned by the word of God, so that the visible came forth from the invisible.

By faith Abel offered a sacrifice greater than Cain's, and through faith his goodness was attested, for his offerings had God's approval; and through faith he continued to speak after his death.

[a] Or assurance.

K.J.V.

speaketh. 5 By faith Enoch was translated that he should not see death; and was not found, because God had translated him: for before his translation he had this testimony, that he pleased God. 6 But without faith *it is* impossible to please *him:* for he that cometh to God must believe that he is, and *that* he is a rewarder of them that diligently seek him. 7 By faith Noah, being warned of God of things not seen as yet, moved with fear, prepared an ark to the saving of his house; by the which he condemned the world, and became heir of the righteousness which is by faith. 8 By faith Abraham, when he was called to go out into a place which he should after receive for an inheritance, obeyed; and he went out, not knowing whither he went. 9 By faith he sojourned in the land of promise, as *in* a strange country, dwelling in tabernacles with Isaac and Jacob, the heirs with him of the same promise: 10 For he looked for a city which hath foundations, whose builder and maker *is* God. 11 Through faith also Sarah herself received strength to conceive seed, and was delivered of a child when she was past age, because she judged him faithful who had promised. 12 Therefore sprang there even of one, and him as good as dead, *so many* as the stars of the sky in multitude, and as the sand which is by the sea shore innumerable. 13 These all died in faith, not having received the promises, but having seen them afar off, and were persuaded of *them,* and embraced *them,* and confessed that they were strangers and pilgrims on the earth. 14 For they that say such things declare plainly that they seek a country. 15 And truly, if they had been mindful of that *country* from whence they came out, they might have had opportunity to have returned. 16 But now they desire a better *country,* that is, a heavenly: wherefore God is not ashamed to be called their God: for he hath prepared for them a city. 17 By faith Abraham, when he was tried, offered up Isaac: and he that

R.S.V.

his faith he is still speaking. 5 By faith Enoch was taken up so that he should not see death; and he was not found, because God had taken him. Now before he was taken he was attested as having pleased God. 6 And without faith it is impossible to please him. For whoever would draw near to God must believe that he exists and that he rewards those who seek him. 7 By faith Noah, being warned by God concerning events as yet unseen, took heed and constructed an ark for the saving of his household; by this he condemned the world and became an heir of the righteousness which comes by faith.

8 By faith Abraham obeyed when he was called to go out to a place which he was to receive as an inheritance; and he went out, not knowing where he was to go. 9 By faith he sojourned in the land of promise, as in a foreign land, living in tents with Isaac and Jacob, heirs with him of the same promise. 10 For he looked forward to the city which has foundations, whose builder and maker is God. 11 By faith Sarah herself received power to conceive, even when she was past the age, since she considered him faithful who had promised. 12 Therefore from one man, and him as good as dead, were born descendants as many as the stars of heaven and as the innumerable grains of sand by the seashore.

13 These all died in faith, not having received what was promised, but having seen it and greeted it from afar, and having acknowledged that they were strangers and exiles on the earth. 14 For people who speak thus make it clear that they are seeking a homeland. 15 If they had been thinking of that land from which they had gone out, they would have had opportunity to return. 16 But as it is, they desire a better country, that is, a heavenly one. Therefore God is not ashamed to be called their God, for he has prepared for them a city.

17 By faith Abraham, when he was tested, offered up Isaac, and he who had received the

PHILLIPS

though Cain killed him, yet by his faith he still speaks to us today.

ENOCH

It was because of his faith that Enoch was promoted to the eternal world without experiencing death. He disappeared from this world because God promoted him, and before that happened his reputation was that "he pleased God." And without faith it is impossible to please him. The man who approaches God must have faith in two things, first that God exists and secondly that it is worth a man's while to try to find God.

NOAH

It was through his faith that Noah, on receiving God's warning of impending disaster, reverently constructed an ark to save his household. This action of faith condemned the unbelief of the rest of the world, and won for Noah the righteousness before God which follows such a faith.

ABRAHAM

It was by faith that Abraham obeyed the summons to go out to a place which he would eventually possess, and he set out in complete ignorance of his destination. It was faith that kept him journeying like a foreigner through the land of promise, with no more home than the tents which he shared with Isaac and Jacob, co-heirs with him of the promise. For Abraham's eyes were looking forward to that city with solid foundations of which God himself is both architect and builder.

SARAH

It was by faith that even Sarah gained the physical vitality to become a mother despite her great age, and she gave birth to a child when far beyond the normal years of childbearing. She could do this because she believed that the one who had given the promise was utterly trustworthy. So it happened that from one man, who as a potential father was already considered dead, there arose a race "as numerous as the stars," as "countless as the sands of the seashore."

N.E.B.

By faith Enoch was carried away to another life without passing through death; he was not to be found, because God had taken him. For it is the testimony of Scripture that before he was taken he had pleased God, and without faith it is impossible to please him; for anyone who comes to God must believe that he exists and that he rewards those who search for him.

By faith Noah, divinely warned about the unseen future, took good heed and built an ark to save his household. Through his faith he put the whole world in the wrong, and made good his own claim to the righteousness which comes of faith.

By faith Abraham obeyed the call to go out to a land destined for himself and his heirs, and left home without knowing where he was to go. By faith he settled as an alien in the land promised him, living in tents, as did Isaac and Jacob, who were heirs to the same promise. For he was looking forward to the city with firm foundations, whose architect and builder is God.

By faith even Sarah herself received strength to conceive, though she was past the age, because she judged that he who had promised would keep faith; and therefore from one man, and one as good as dead, there sprang descendants numerous as the stars or as the countless grains of sand on the sea-shore.

All these persons died in faith. They were not yet in possession of the things promised, but had seen them far ahead and hailed them, and confessed themselves no more than strangers or passing travellers on earth. Those who use such language show plainly that they are looking for a country of their own. If their hearts had been in the country they had left, they could have found opportunity to return. Instead, we find them longing for a better country—I mean, the heavenly one. That is why God is not ashamed to be called their God; for he has a city ready for them.

By faith Abraham, when the test came, offered up Isaac: he had received the promises, and yet he was on the point of offering his only son, of

---

All the heroes of faith looked forward to their true country   11. 13

All these whom we have mentioned maintained their faith but died without actually receiving God's promises, though they had seen them in the distance, had hailed them as true and were quite convinced of their reality. They freely admitted that they lived on this earth as exiles and foreigners. Men who say that mean, of course, that their eyes are fixed upon their true homeland. If they had meant the particular country they had left behind, they had ample opportunity to return. No, the fact is that they longed for a better country altogether, nothing less than a heavenly one. And because of this faith of theirs, God is not ashamed to be called their God, for in sober truth he has prepared for them a city.

Abraham's faith once more   11. 17

It was by faith that Abraham, when put to the test, offered Isaac for sacrifice. Yes, the man

K.J.V.

had received the promises offered up his only begotten *son,* 18 Of whom it was said, That in Isaac shall thy seed be called: 19Accounting that God *was* able to raise *him* up, even from the dead; from whence also he received him in a figure. 20 By faith Isaac blessed Jacob and Esau concerning things to come. 21 By faith Jacob, when he was a dying, blessed both the sons of Joseph; and worshipped, *leaning* upon the top of his staff. 22 By faith Joseph, when he died, made mention of the departing of the children of Israel; and gave commandment concerning his bones. 23 By faith Moses, when he was born, was hid three months of his parents, because they saw *he was* a proper child; and they were not afraid of the king's commandment. 24 By faith Moses, when he was come to years, refused to be called the son of Pharaoh's daughter; 25 Choosing rather to suffer affliction with the people of God, than to enjoy the pleasures of sin for a season; 26 Esteeming the reproach of Christ greater riches than the treasures in Egypt: for he had respect unto the recompense of the reward. 27 By faith he forsook Egypt, not fearing the wrath of the king: for he endured, as seeing him who is invisible. 28 Through faith he kept the passover, and the sprinkling of blood, lest he that destroyed the firstborn should touch them. 29 By faith they passed through the Red sea as by dry *land:* which the Egyptians assaying to do were drowned. 30 By faith the walls of Jericho fell down, after they were compassed about seven days. 31 By faith the harlot Rahab perished not with them that believed not, when she had received the spies with peace. 32And what shall I more say? for the time would fail me to tell of Gideon, and *of* Barak, and *of* Samson, and *of* Jephthah; *of* David also, and Samuel, and *of* the prophets: 33 Who through faith subdued kingdoms, wrought righteousness, obtained promises, stopped the mouths of lions, 34 Quenched the violence of fire, escaped the edge of the sword, out of weakness were made

R.S.V.

promises was ready to offer up his only son, 18 of whom it was said, "Through Isaac shall your descendants be named." 19 He considered that God was able to raise men even from the dead; hence, figuratively speaking, he did receive him back. 20 By faith Isaac invoked future blessings on Jacob and Esau. 21 By faith Jacob, when dying, blessed each of the sons of Joseph, bowing in worship over the head of his staff. 22 By faith Joseph, at the end of his life, made mention of the exodus of the Israelites and gave directions concerning his burial.*ˣ* 23 By faith Moses, when he was born, was hid for three months by his parents, because they saw that the child was beautiful; and they were not afraid of the king's edict. 24 By faith Moses, when he was grown up, refused to be called the son of Pharaoh's daughter, 25 choosing rather to share ill-treatment with the people of God than to enjoy the fleeting pleasures of sin. 26 He considered abuse suffered for the Christ greater wealth than the treasures of Egypt, for he looked to the reward. 27 By faith he left Egypt, not being afraid of the anger of the king; for he endured as seeing him who is invisible. 28 By faith he kept the Passover and sprinkled the blood, so that the Destroyer of the first-born might not touch them. 29 By faith the people crossed the Red Sea as if on dry land; but the Egyptians, when they attempted to do the same, were drowned. 30 By faith the walls of Jericho fell down after they had been encircled for seven days. 31 By faith Rahab the harlot did not perish with those who were disobedient, because she had given friendly welcome to the spies. 32 And what more shall I say? For time would fail me to tell of Gideon, Barak, Samson, Jephthah, of David and Samuel and the prophets—33 who through faith conquered kingdoms, enforced justice, received promises, stopped the mouths of lions, 34 quenched raging fire, escaped the edge of the sword, won strength out of weak-

[x] Greek *bones.*

PHILLIPS

who had heard God's promises was prepared to offer up his only son of whom it had been said, "In Isaac shall thy seed be called." He believed that God could raise his son up, even if he were dead. And he did, in a manner of speaking, receive him back from death.

The faith of Isaac, Jacob and Joseph

11. 20

It was by faith that Isaac gave Jacob and Esau his blessing, for his words dealt with what should happen in the future. It was by faith that the dying Jacob blessed each of Joseph's sons as he bowed in prayer over his staff. It was by faith that Joseph on his deathbed spoke of the exodus of the Israelites, and gave confident orders about the disposal of his own mortal remains.

Moses

11. 23

It was by faith that Moses was hidden by his parents for three months after his birth, for they saw that he was a beautiful child and refused to be daunted by the king's decree. It was also by faith that Moses himself when grown up refused to be called the son of Pharaoh's daughter. He preferred sharing the burden of God's people to enjoying the temporary advantages of alliance with a sinful nation. He considered the "reproach of Christ" more precious than all the wealth of Egypt, for he looked steadily at the ultimate, not the immediate, reward.

By faith he left Egypt; he defied the king's anger with the strength that came from obedience to the invisible king.

By faith Moses kept the first Passover and made the blood sprinkling, so that the angel of death which killed the first-born should not touch his people.

By faith the people walked through the Red Sea as though it were dry land; and the Egyptians who tried to do the same thing were drowned.

Rahab

11. 30

It was by faith that the walls of Jericho collapsed, for the people had obeyed God's command to encircle them for seven days.

It was because of her faith that Rahab the prostitute did not share the fate of the disobedient, for she welcomed the Israelites sent out to reconnoitre.

The Old Testament is full of examples of faith

11. 32

And what other examples shall I give? There is simply not time to continue by telling the stories of Gideon, Barak, Samson and Jephtha; of David, Samuel and the prophets. Through their faith these men conquered kingdoms, ruled in justice and proved the truth of God's promises. They shut the mouths of lions, they quenched the furious blaze of fire, they escaped from death itself. From being weaklings they

N.E.B.

whom he had been told, 'Through the line of Isaac your posterity shall be traced.' For he reckoned that God had power even to raise from the dead—and from the dead, he did, in a sense, receive him back.

By faith Isaac blessed Jacob and Esau and spoke of things to come. By faith Jacob, as he was dying, blessed each of Joseph's sons, and worshipped God, leaning on the top of his staff. By faith Joseph, at the end of his life, spoke of the departure of Israel from Egypt, and instructed them what to do with his bones.

By faith, when Moses was born, his parents hid him for three months, because they saw what a fine child he was; they were not afraid of the king's edict. By faith Moses, when he grew up, refused to be called the son of Pharaoh's daughter, preferring to suffer hardship with the people of God rather than enjoy the transient pleasures of sin. He considered the stigma that rests on God's Anointed greater wealth than the treasures of Egypt, for his eyes were fixed upon the coming day of recompense. By faith he left Egypt, and not because he feared the king's anger; for he was resolute, as one who saw the invisible God.

By faith he celebrated the Passover and sprinkled the blood, so that the destroying angel might not touch the first-born of Israel. By faith they crossed the Red Sea as though it were dry land, whereas the Egyptians, when they attempted the crossing, were drowned.

By faith the walls of Jericho fell down after they had been encircled on seven successive days. By faith the prostitute Rahab escaped the doom of the unbelievers, because she had given the spies a kindly welcome.

Need I say more? Time is too short for me to tell the stories of Gideon, Barak, Samson, and Jephthah, of David and Samuel and the prophets. Through faith they overthrew kingdoms, established justice, saw God's promises fulfilled. They muzzled ravening lions, quenched the fury of fire, escaped death by the sword. Their weakness

K.J.V.

strong, waxed valiant in fight, turned to flight the armies of the aliens. 35 Women received their dead raised to life again: and others were tortured, not accepting deliverance; that they might obtain a better resurrection: 36And others had trial of *cruel* mockings and scourgings, yea, moreover of bonds and imprisonment: 37 They were stoned, they were sawn asunder, were tempted, were slain with the sword: they wandered about in sheepskins and goatskins; being destitute, afflicted, tormented; 38 Of whom the world was not worthy: they wandered in deserts, and *in* mountains, and *in* dens and caves of the earth. 39And these all, having obtained a good report through faith, received not the promise: 40 God having provided some better thing for us, that they without us should not be made perfect.

12 Wherefore, seeing we also are compassed about with so great a cloud of witnesses, let us lay aside every weight, and the sin which doth so easily beset *us,* and let us run with patience the race that is set before us, 2 Looking unto Jesus the author and finisher of *our* faith; who for the joy that was set before him endured the cross, despising the shame, and is set down at the right hand of the throne of God. 3 For consider him that endured such contradiction of sinners against himself, lest ye be wearied and faint in your minds. 4 Ye have not yet resisted unto blood, striving against sin. 5And ye have forgotten the exhortation which speaketh unto you as unto children, My son, despise not thou the chastening of the Lord, nor faint when thou art rebuked of him: 6 For whom the Lord loveth he chasteneth, and scourgeth every son whom he receiveth. 7 If ye endure chastening, God dealeth with you as with sons; for what son is he whom the father chasteneth not? 8 But if ye be without chastisement, whereof all are partakers, then are ye bastards, and not sons. 9 Furthermore, we have had fathers of our flesh which corrected *us,* and we gave *them* reverence: shall we not much rather be in subjection unto the Father of spirits, and live? 10 For they verily for a few days chastened *us* after their own pleasure; but he for *our* profit, that *we* might be partakers of his holiness. 11 Now no chastening for the present seemeth to be joyous, but grievous: nevertheless, afterward it yieldeth the peaceable

R.S.V.

ness, became mighty in war, put foreign armies to flight. 35 Women received their dead by resurrection. Some were tortured, refusing to accept release, that they might rise again to a better life. 36 Others suffered mocking and scourging, and even chains and imprisonment. 37 They were stoned, they were sawn in two,[y] they were killed with the sword; they went about in skins of sheep and goats, destitute, afflicted, ill-treated—38 of whom the world was not worthy—wandering over deserts and mountains, and in dens and caves of the earth. 39 And all these, though well attested by their faith, did not receive what was promised, 40 since God had foreseen something better for us, that apart from us they should not be made perfect.

12 Therefore, since we are surrounded by so great a cloud of witnesses, let us also lay aside every weight, and sin which clings so closely, and let us run with perseverance the race that is set before us, 2 looking to Jesus the pioneer and perfecter of our faith, who for the joy that was set before him endured the cross, despising the shame, and is seated at the right hand of the throne of God.

3 Consider him who endured from sinners such hostility against himself, so that you may not grow weary or faint-hearted. 4 In your struggle against sin you have not yet resisted to the point of shedding your blood. 5And have you forgotten the exhortation which addresses you as sons?—

"My son, do not regard lightly the discipline of the Lord,
　　nor lose courage when you are punished by him.
6 For the Lord disciplines him whom he loves,
　　and chastises every son whom he receives."
7 It is for discipline that you have to endure. God is treating you as sons; for what son is there whom his father does not discipline? 8 If you are left without discipline, in which all have participated, then you are illegitimate children and not sons. 9 Besides this, we have had earthly fathers to discipline us and we respected them. Shall we not much more be subject to the Father of spirits and live? 10 For they disciplined us for a short time at their pleasure, but he disciplines us for our good, that we may share his holiness. 11 For the moment all discipline seems painful rather than pleasant; later it yields

---

[y] Other manuscripts add *they were tempted.*

PHILLIPS

became strong men and mighty warriors; they routed whole armies of foreigners. Women received their dead raised to life again, while others were tortured and refused to be ransomed, because they wanted to deserve a more honorable resurrection in the world to come. Others were exposed to the test of public mockery and flogging, and to the torture of being left bound in prison. They were killed by stoning, by being sawn in two; they were tempted by specious promises of release and then were killed with the sword. Many became refugees with nothing but sheepskins or goatskins to cover them. They lost everything and yet were spurned and ill-treated by a world that was too evil to see their worth. They lived as vagrants in the desert, on the mountains, or in caves or holes in the ground.

All these won a glowing testimony to their faith, but they did not then and there receive the fulfillment of the promise. God had something better planned for our day, and it was not his plan that they should reach perfection without us.

We should consider these examples and Christ the perfect example   12. 1

Surrounded then as we are by these serried ranks of witnesses, let us strip off everything that hinders us, as well as the sin which dogs our feet, and let us run the race that we have to run with patience, our eyes fixed on Jesus the source and the goal of our faith. For he himself endured a cross and thought nothing of its shame because of the joy he knew would follow his suffering; and he is now seated at the right hand of God's throne. Think constantly of him enduring all that sinful men could say against him, and you will not lose your purpose or your courage.

Look upon suffering as heavenly discipline   12. 4

After all, your fight against sin has not yet meant the shedding of blood, and you have perhaps lost sight of that piece of advice which reminds you of your sonship in God:

My son, regard not lightly the chastening of
   the Lord,
Nor faint when thou art reproved of him;
For whom the Lord loveth he chasteneth,
And scourgeth every son whom he receiveth.

Bear what you have to bear as "chastening"— as God's dealing with you as sons. No true son ever grows up uncorrected by his father. For if you had no experience of the correction which all sons have to bear you might well doubt the legitimacy of your sonship. After all, when we were children we had fathers who corrected us, and we respected them for it. Can we not much more readily submit to the discipline of the Father of men's souls, and learn how to live?

For our fathers used to correct us according to their own ideas during the brief days of childhood. But God corrects us all our days for our own benefit, to teach us his holiness. Now obviously no "chastening" seems pleasant at the

N.E.B.

was turned to strength, they grew powerful in war, they put foreign armies to rout. Women received back their dead raised to life. Others were tortured to death, disdaining release, to win a better resurrection. Others, again, had to face jeers and flogging, even fetters and prison bars. They were stoned,[a] they were sawn in two, they were put to the sword, they went about dressed in skins of sheep or goats, in poverty, distress, and misery. They were too good for this world. They were refugees in deserts and on the hills, hiding in caves and holes in the ground. These also, one and all, are commemorated for their faith; and yet they did not enter upon the promised inheritance, because, with us in mind, God had made a better plan, that only in company with us should they reach their perfection.

12 And what of ourselves? With all these witnesses to faith around us like a cloud, we must throw off every encumbrance, every sin to which we cling,[b] and run with resolution the race for which we are entered, our eyes fixed on Jesus, on whom faith depends from start to finish: Jesus who, for the sake of the joy that lay ahead of him,[c] endured the cross, making light of its disgrace, and has taken his seat at the right hand of the throne of God.

Think of him who submitted to such opposition from sinners: that will help you not to lose heart and grow faint. In your struggle against sin, you have not yet resisted to the point of shedding your blood. You have forgotten the text of Scripture which addresses you as sons and appeals to you in these words:

'My son, do not think lightly of the Lord's discipline,
Nor lose heart when he corrects you;
For the Lord disciplines those whom he loves;
He lays the rod on every son whom he acknowledges.'

You must endure it as discipline: God is treating you as sons. Can anyone be a son, who is not disciplined by his father? If you escape the discipline in which all sons share, you must be bastards and no true sons. Again, we paid due respect to the earthly fathers who disciplined us; should we not submit even more readily to our spiritual Father, and so attain life? They disciplined us for this short life according to their lights; but he does so for our true welfare, so that we may share his holiness. Discipline, no doubt, is never pleasant; at the time it seems

[a] *Some witnesses insert* they were put to the question. [b] *Or* every clinging sin; *one witness reads* the sin which all too readily distracts us. [c] *Or* who, in place of the joy that was open to him, . . .

K.J.V.

fruit of righteousness unto them which are exercised thereby. 12 Wherefore lift up the hands which hang down, and the feeble knees; 13And make straight paths for your feet, lest that which is lame be turned out of the way; but let it rather be healed. 14 Follow peace with all *men*, and holiness, without which no man shall see the Lord: 15 Looking diligently lest any man fail of the grace of God; lest any root of bitterness springing up trouble *you*, and thereby many be defiled; 16 Lest there *be* any fornicator, or profane person, as Esau, who for one morsel of meat sold his birthright. 17 For ye know how that afterward, when he would have inherited the blessing, he was rejected: for he found no place of repentance, though he sought it carefully with tears. 18 For ye are not come unto the mount that might be touched, and that burned with fire, nor unto blackness, and darkness, and tempest, 19And the sound of a trumpet, and the voice of words; which *voice* they that heard entreated that the word should not be spoken to them any more: 20 (For they could not endure that which was commanded, And if so much as a beast touch the mountain, it shall be stoned, or thrust through with a dart: 21And so terrible was the sight, *that* Moses said, I exceedingly fear and quake:) 22 But ye are come unto mount Sion, and unto the city of the living God, the heavenly Jerusalem, and to an innumerable company of angels, 23 To the general assembly and church of the firstborn, which are written in heaven, and to God the Judge of all, and to the spirits of just men made perfect, 24And to Jesus the mediator of the new covenant, and to the blood of sprinkling, that speaketh better things than *that of* Abel. 25 See that ye refuse not him that speaketh: for if they escaped not who refused him that spake on earth, much more *shall not* we *escape*, if we turn away from him that *speaketh* from heaven: 26 Whose voice then shook the earth: but now he hath promised, saying, Yet once more I shake not the earth only, but also heaven. 27And this *word*, Yet once more, signifieth the removing of those things that are shaken, as of things that are made, that those things which cannot be shaken may remain. 28 Wherefore we receiving a kingdom

R.S.V.

the peaceful fruit of righteousness to those who have been trained by it. 12 Therefore lift your drooping hands and strengthen your weak knees, 13 and make straight paths for your feet, so that what is lame may not be put out of joint but rather be healed. 14 Strive for peace with all men, and for the holiness without which no one will see the Lord. 15 See to it that no one fail to obtain the grace of God; that no "root of bitterness" spring up and cause trouble, and by it the many become defiled; 16 that no one be immoral or irreligious like Esau, who sold his birthright for a single meal. 17 For you know that afterward, when he desired to inherit the blessing, he was rejected, for he found no chance to repent, though he sought it with tears. 18 For you have not come to what may be touched, a blazing fire, and darkness, and gloom, and a tempest, 19 and the sound of a trumpet, and a voice whose words made the hearers entreat that no further messages be spoken to them. 20 For they could not endure the order that was given, "If even a beast touches the mountain, it shall be stoned." 21 Indeed, so terrifying was the sight that Moses said, "I tremble with fear." 22 But you have come to Mount Zion and to the city of the living God, the heavenly Jerusalem, and to innumerable angels in festal gathering, 23 and to the assembly[z] of the first-born who are enrolled in heaven, and to a judge who is God of all, and to the spirits of just men made perfect, 24 and to Jesus, the mediator of a new covenant, and to the sprinkled blood that speaks more graciously than the blood of Abel. 25 See that you do not refuse him who is speaking. For if they did not escape when they refused him who warned them on earth, much less shall we escape if we reject him who warns from heaven. 26 His voice then shook the earth; but now he has promised, "Yet once more I will shake not only the earth but also the heaven." 27 This phrase, "Yet once more," indicates the removal of what is shaken, as of what has been made, in order that what cannot be shaken may remain. 28 Therefore let us be grate-

[z] Or *angels, and to the festal gathering and assembly.*

PHILLIPS	N.E.B.

time: it is in fact most unpleasant. Yet when it is all over we can see that it has quietly produced the fruit of real goodness in the characters of those who have accepted it in the right spirit. So tighten your loosening grip and steady your wavering hand. Don't wander away from the path but forge steadily onward. On the right path the limping foot recovers strength and does not collapse.

In times of testing be especially 12. 14 on your guard against certain sins

Let it be your ambition to live at peace with all men and to achieve holiness "without which no man shall see the Lord." Be careful that none of you fails to respond to the grace which God gives, for if he does there can very easily spring up in him a bitter spirit which is not only bad in itself but can also poison the lives of many others. Be careful, too, that none of you falls into impurity or loses his reverence for the things of God and then, like Esau, is ready to sell his birthright to satisfy the momentary hunger of his body. Remember how afterward, when he wanted to have the blessing which was his birthright, he was refused. He never afterward found the way of repentance, though he sought it desperately and with tears.

Your experience is not that 12. 18 of the old agreement but of the new

You have not had to approach things which your senses could experience as they did in the old days—flaming fire, black darkness, rushing wind and out of it a trumpet blast, a voice speaking human words. So terrible was that voice that those who heard it begged and prayed that it might stop speaking, for what it had already commanded was more than they could bear—that "if even a beast touch this mountain it must be stoned." So fearful was the spectacle that Moses cried out, "I am terrified and tremble at this sight!"

No, you have been allowed to approach the true Mount Zion, the City of the living God, the heavenly Jerusalem. You have drawn near to the countless angelic army, the festal assembly of Heaven and the Church of the first-born whose names are written above. You have drawn near to God, the judge of all, to the souls of good men made perfect, and to Jesus, mediator of a new agreement, to the cleansing of blood which tells a better story than the age-old sacrifice of Abel.

So be sure you do not refuse to hear the voice of God! For if they who refused to hear those who spoke to them on earth did not escape, how little chance of escape is there for us if we refuse to hear the one who speaks from Heaven. Then his voice shook the earth, but now he promises:

Yet once more will I make to tremble
Not the earth only, but also the heaven.

This means that in this final "shaking" all that is impermanent will be removed, that is, everything that is merely "made," and only the unshakable things will remain. Since then we

painful, but in the end it yields for those who have been trained by it the peaceful harvest of an honest life. Come, then, stiffen your drooping arms and shaking knees, and keep your steps from wavering. Then the disabled limb will not be put out of joint, but regain its former powers.

Aim at peace with all men, and a holy life, for without that no one will see the Lord. See to it that there is no one among you who forfeits the grace of God, no bitter, noxious weed growing up to poison the whole, no immoral person, no one worldly-minded like Esau. He sold his birthright for a single meal, and you know that although he wanted afterwards to claim the blessing, he was rejected; for he found no way open for second thoughts, although he strove, to the point of tears, to find one.

Remember where you stand: not before the palpable, blazing fire of Sinai, with the darkness, gloom, and whirlwind, the trumpet-blast and the oracular voice, which they heard, and begged to hear no more; for they could not bear the command, 'If even an animal touches the mountain, it must be stoned.' So appalling was the sight, that Moses said, 'I shudder with fear.'

No, you stand before Mount Zion and the city of the living God, heavenly Jerusalem, before myriads of angels, the full concourse and assembly of the first-born citizens of heaven, and God the judge of all, and the spirits of good men made perfect, and Jesus the mediator of a new covenant, whose sprinkled blood has better things to tell than the blood of Abel. See that you do not refuse to hear the voice that speaks. Those who refused to hear the oracle speaking on earth found no escape; still less shall we escape if we refuse to hear the One who speaks from heaven. Then indeed his voice shook the earth, but now he has promised, 'Yet once again I will shake not earth alone, but the heavens also.' The words 'once again'—and only once—imply that the shaking of these created things means their removal, and then what is not shaken will remain. The kingdom we are given

K.J.V.

which cannot be moved, let us have grace, whereby we may serve God acceptably with reverence and godly fear: 29 For our God *is* a consuming fire.

13 Let brotherly love continue. 2 Be not forgetful to entertain strangers: for thereby some have entertained angels unawares. 3 Remember them that are in bonds, as bound with them; *and* them which suffer adversity, as being yourselves also in the body. 4 Marriage *is* honourable in all, and the bed undefiled: but whoremongers and adulterers God will judge. 5 *Let your* conversation *be* without covetousness; *and be* content with such things as ye have: for he hath said, I will never leave thee, nor forsake thee. 6 So that we may boldly say, The Lord *is* my helper, and I will not fear what man shall do unto me. 7 Remember them which have the rule over you, who have spoken unto you the word of God: whose faith follow, considering the end of *their* conversation. 8 Jesus Christ the same yesterday, and to day, and for ever. 9 Be not carried about with divers and strange doctrines: for *it is* a good thing that the heart be established with grace; not with meats, which have not profited them that have been occupied therein. 10 We have an altar, whereof they have no right to eat which serve the tabernacle. 11 For the bodies of those beasts, whose blood is brought into the sanctuary by the high priest for sin, are burned without the camp. 12 Wherefore Jesus also, that he might sanctify the people with his own blood, suffered without the gate. 13 Let us go forth therefore unto him without the camp, bearing his reproach. 14 For here have we no continuing city, but we seek one to come. 15 By him therefore let us offer the sacrifice of praise to God continually, that is, the fruit of *our* lips, giving thanks to his name. 16 But to do good and to communicate forget not: for with such sacrifices God is well pleased. 17 Obey them that have the rule over you, and submit yourselves: for they watch for your souls, as they that must give account, that they may do it with joy, and not with grief: for that *is* unprofit-

R.S.V.

ful for receiving a kingdom that cannot be shaken, and thus let us offer to God acceptable worship, with reverence and awe; 29 for our God is a consuming fire.

13 Let brotherly love continue. 2 Do not neglect to show hospitality to strangers, for thereby some have entertained angels unawares. 3 Remember those who are in prison, as though in prison with them; and those who are ill-treated, since you also are in the body. 4 Let marriage be held in honor among all, and let the marriage bed be undefiled; for God will judge the immoral and adulterous. 5 Keep your life free from love of money, and be content with what you have; for he has said, "I will never fail you nor forsake you." 6 Hence we can confidently say,

"The Lord is my helper,
  I will not be afraid;
  what can man do to me?"

7 Remember your leaders, those who spoke to you the word of God; consider the outcome of their life, and imitate their faith. 8 Jesus Christ is the same yesterday and today and for ever. 9 Do not be led away by diverse and strange teachings; for it is well that the heart be strengthened by grace, not by foods, which have not benefited their adherents. 10 We have an altar from which those who serve the tent[a] have no right to eat. 11 For the bodies of those animals whose blood is brought into the sanctuary by the high priest as a sacrifice for sin are burned outside the camp. 12 So Jesus also suffered outside the gate in order to sanctify the people through his own blood. 13 Therefore let us go forth to him outside the camp, bearing abuse for him. 14 For here we have no lasting city, but we seek the city which is to come. 15 Through him then let us continually offer up a sacrifice of praise to God, that is, the fruit of lips that acknowledge his name. 16 Do not neglect to do good and to share what you have, for such sacrifices are pleasing to God.

17 Obey your leaders and submit to them; for they are keeping watch over your souls, as men who will have to give account. Let them do this joyfully, and not sadly, for that would be of no advantage to you.

[a] Or *tabernacle.*

have been given a kingdom that is "unshakable," let us serve God with thankfulness in the ways which please him, but always with reverence and holy fear. For it is perfectly true that our God is a burning fire.

is unshakable; let us therefore give thanks to God, and so worship him as he would be worshipped, with reverence and awe; for our God is a devouring fire.

Some practical instructions for Christian living 13. 1

Never let your brotherly love fail, nor refuse to extend your hospitality to strangers—sometimes men have entertained angels unawares. Think constantly of those in prison as if you were prisoners at their side. Think too of all who suffer as if you shared their pain.

Both honorable marriage and chastity should be respected by all of you. God himself will judge those who traffic in the bodies of others or defile the relationship of marriage. Keep your lives free from the lust for money: be content with what you have.

God has said:

I will in no wise fail thee,
Neither will I in any wise forsake thee.

We, therefore, can confidently say:

The Lord is my helper; I will not fear:
What shall man do unto me?

Be loyal to your leaders and, above all, to Christ 13. 7

Never forget your leaders, who first spoke to you the Word of God. Remember how they lived, and imitate their faith.

Jesus Christ is always the same, yesterday, to-day and for ever. Do not be swept off your feet by various peculiar teachings. Spiritual stability depends on the grace of God, and not on rules of diet—which after all have not spiritually benefited those who have made a specialty of that kind of thing. We have an Altar from which those who still serve the tabernacle have no right to eat.

When the blood of animals was presented as a sin offering by the High Priest in the sanctuary, their bodies were burned outside the precincts of the camp. That is why Jesus, when he sanctified men by the shedding of his own blood, suffered and died outside the city gates. Let us go out to him, then, beyond the boundaries of the camp, proudly bearing his "disgrace." For we have no permanent city here on earth; we are looking for one in the world to come. Our constant sacrifice to God should be the praise of lips that give thanks to his name. Yet we should not forget to do good and to share our good things with others, for these too are the sort of sacrifices God will accept.

Obey your rulers and recognize their authority. They are like men standing guard over your spiritual good, and they have great responsibility. Try to make their work a pleasure and not a burden—by so doing you will help not only them but yourselves.

13 Never cease to love your fellow-Christians. Remember to show hospitality. There are some who, by so doing, have entertained angels without knowing it.

Remember those in prison as if you were there with them; and those who are being maltreated, for you like them are still in the world.

Marriage is honourable; let us all keep it so, and the marriage-bond inviolate; for God's judgement will fall on fornicators and adulterers.

Do not live for money; be content with what you have; for God himself has said, 'I will never leave you or desert you'; and so we can take courage and say, 'The Lord is my helper, I will not fear; what can man do to me?'

Remember your leaders, those who first spoke God's message to you; and reflecting upon the outcome of their life and work, follow the example of their faith.

Jesus Christ is the same yesterday, today, and for ever. So do not be swept off your course by all sorts of outlandish teachings; it is good that our souls should gain their strength from the grace of God, and not from scruples about what we eat, which have never done any good to those who were governed by them.

Our altar is one from which[a] the priests of the sacred tent have no right to eat. As you know, those animals whose blood is brought as a sin-offering by the high priest into the sanctuary, have their bodies burnt outside the camp, and therefore Jesus also suffered outside the gate, to consecrate the people by his own blood. Let us then go to him outside the camp, bearing the stigma that he bore. For here we have no permanent home, but we are seekers after the city which is to come. Through Jesus, then, let us continually offer up to God the sacrifice of praise, that is, the tribute of lips which acknowledge his name, and never forget to show kindness and to share what you have with others; for such are the sacrifices which God approves.

Obey your leaders and defer to them; for they are tireless in their concern for you, as men who must render an account. Let it be a happy task for them, and not pain and grief, for that would bring you no advantage.

[a] *Or* one like that from which . . .

K.J.V.

able for you. 18 Pray for us: for we trust we have a good conscience, in all things willing to live honestly. 19 But I beseech *you* the rather to do this, that I may be restored to you the sooner. 20 Now the God of peace, that brought again from the dead our Lord Jesus, that great Shepherd of the sheep, through the blood of the everlasting covenant, 21 Make you perfect in every good work to do his will, working in you that which is well pleasing in his sight, through Jesus Christ; to whom *be* glory for ever and ever. Amen. 22And I beseech you, brethren, suffer the word of exhortation: for I have written a letter unto you in few words. 23 Know ye that *our* brother Timothy is set at liberty; with whom, if he come shortly, I will see you. 24 Salute all them that have the rule over you, and all the saints. They of Italy salute you. 25 Grace *be* with you all. Amen.

Written to the Hebrews from Italy by Timothy.

R.S.V.

18 Pray for us, for we are sure that we have a clear conscience, desiring to act honorably in all things. 19 I urge you the more earnestly to do this in order that I may be restored to you the sooner.
20 Now may the God of peace who brought again from the dead our Lord Jesus, the great shepherd of the sheep, by the blood of the eternal covenant, 21 equip you with everything good that you may do his will, working in you[b] that which is pleasing in his sight, through Jesus Christ; to whom be glory for ever and ever. Amen.

22 I appeal to you, brethren, bear with my word of exhortation, for I have written to you briefly. 23 You should understand that our brother Timothy has been released, with whom I shall see you if he comes soon. 24 Greet all your leaders and all the saints. Those who come from Italy send you greetings. 25 Grace be with all of you. Amen.

[b] Other ancient authorities read *us*.

PHILLIPS

Personal: our blessing   *13. 18*
and our greetings

Pray for us. Our conscience is clear before God, and our great desire is to lead a life that is completely honest. Please pray earnestly, that I may be restored to you the sooner.

Now the God of peace, who brought back from the dead that great shepherd of the sheep, our Lord Jesus, by the blood of the everlasting agreement, equip you thoroughly for the doing of his will! May he effect in you everything that pleases him through Jesus Christ, to whom be glory for ever and ever.

All I have said, my brothers, I ask you to accept as though it were an appeal in person, although I have compressed it into a short letter.

You will be glad to know that brother Timothy is now at liberty. If he comes here soon, he and I will perhaps visit you together.

Greetings to all your leaders and all your church members. The Christians of Italy send their greeting.

Grace be with you all.

N.E.B.

Pray for us; for we are convinced that our conscience is clear; our one desire is always to do what is right. All the more earnestly I ask for your prayers, that I may be restored to you the sooner.

May the God of peace, who brought up from the dead our Lord Jesus, the great Shepherd of the sheep, by the blood of the eternal covenant, make you perfect in all goodness so that you may do his will, and may he make of us what he would have us be through Jesus Christ, to whom be glory for ever and ever! Amen.

I beg you, brothers, bear with this exhortation; for it is after all a short letter. I have news for you: our friend Timothy has been released; and if he comes in time he will be with me when I see you.

Greet all your leaders and all God's people. Greetings to you from our Italian friends.

God's grace be with you all!

K.J.V.

THE

GENERAL EPISTLE

OF

JAMES

R.S.V.

THE LETTER OF

JAMES

1 James, a servant of God and of the Lord Jesus Christ, to the twelve tribes which are scattered abroad, greeting. 2 My brethren, count it all joy when ye fall into divers temptations; 3 Knowing *this,* that the trying of your faith worketh patience. 4 But let patience have *her* perfect work, that ye may be perfect and entire, wanting nothing. 5 If any of you lack wisdom, let him ask of God, that giveth to all *men* liberally, and upbraideth not; and it shall be given him. 6 But let him ask in faith, nothing wavering: for he that wavereth is like a wave of the sea driven with the wind and tossed. 7 For let not that man think that he shall receive any thing of the Lord. 8 A doubleminded man *is* unstable in all his ways. 9 Let the brother of low degree rejoice in that he is exalted: 10 But the rich, in that he is made low: because as the flower of the grass he shall pass away. 11 For the sun is no sooner risen with a burning heat, but it withereth the grass, and the flower thereof falleth, and the grace of the fashion of it perisheth: so also shall the rich man fade away in his ways. 12 Blessed *is* the man that endureth temptation: for when he is tried, he shall receive the crown of life, which the Lord hath promised

1 James, a servant of God and of the Lord Jesus Christ,
To the twelve tribes in the Dispersion:
Greeting.

2 Count it all joy, my brethren, when you meet various trials, 3 for you know that the testing of your faith produces steadfastness. 4 And let steadfastness have its full effect, that you may be perfect and complete, lacking in nothing.
5 If any of you lacks wisdom, let him ask God, who gives to all men generously and without reproaching, and it will be given him. 6 But let him ask in faith, with no doubting, for he who doubts is like a wave of the sea that is driven and tossed by the wind. 7,8 For that person must not suppose that a double-minded man, unstable in all his ways, will receive anything from the Lord.
9 If the lowly brother boast in his exaltation, 10 and the rich in his humiliation, because like the flower of the grass he will pass away. 11 For the sun rises with its scorching heat and withers the grass; its flower falls, and its beauty perishes. So will the rich man fade away in the midst of his pursuits.
12 Blessed is the man who endures trial, for when he has stood the test he will receive the crown of life which God has promised to those

PHILLIPS	N.E.B.

THE LETTER OF

JAMES

James, a servant of God and of the Lord Jesus Christ, sends greeting to the twelve dispersed tribes.

The Christian can even   *1. 2*
 welcome trouble

When all kinds of trials and temptations crowd into your lives, my brothers, don't resent them as intruders, but welcome them as friends! Realize that they come to test your faith and to produce in you the quality of endurance. But let the process go on until that endurance is fully developed, and you will find you have become men of mature character with the right sort of independence. And if, in the process, any of you does not know how to meet any particular problem he has only to ask God—who gives generously to all men without making them feel foolish or guilty—and he may be quite sure that the necessary wisdom will be given him. But he must ask in sincere faith without secret doubts as to whether he really wants God's help or not. The man who trusts God, but with inward reservations, is like a wave of the sea, carried forward by the wind one moment and driven back the next. That sort of man cannot hope to receive anything from the Lord, and the life of a man of divided loyalty will reveal instability at every turn.

Rich and poor can be glad—   *1. 9*
 for different reasons!

The brother who is poor may be glad because God has called him to the true riches. The rich may be glad that God has shown him his spiritual poverty. For the rich man, as such, will wither away as surely as summer flowers. One day the sunrise brings a scorching wind; the grass withers at once and so do all the flowers—all that lovely sight is destroyed. Just as surely will the rich man and all his extravagant ways fall into the blight of decay.

No temptation comes from God,   *1. 12*
 only highest good

The man who patiently endures the temptations and trials that come to him is the truly happy man. For once his testing is complete he will receive the crown of life which the Lord has promised to all who love him.

A LETTER OF

JAMES

Practical Religion

1 From James, a servant of God and the Lord Jesus Christ.

Greetings to the Twelve Tribes dispersed throughout the world.

My brothers, whenever you have to face trials of many kinds, count yourselves supremely happy, in the knowledge that such testing of your faith breeds fortitude, and if you give fortitude full play you will go on to complete a balanced character that will fall short in nothing. If any of you falls short in wisdom, he should ask God for it and it will be given him, for God is a generous giver who neither refuses nor reproaches anyone. But he must ask in faith, without a doubt in his mind; for the doubter is like a heaving sea ruffled by the wind. A man of that kind must not expect the Lord to give him anything; he is double-minded, and never can keep[a] a steady course.

The brother in humble circumstances may well be proud that God lifts him up; and the wealthy brother must find his pride in being brought low. For the rich man will disappear like the flower of the field; once the sun is up with its scorching heat the flower withers, its petals fall, and what was lovely to look at is lost for ever. So shall the rich man wither away as he goes about his business.

Happy the man who remains steadfast under trial, for having passed that test he will receive for his prize the gift of life promised to those who love God. No one under trial or temptation

---

[a] *Or* anything; a double-minded man never keeps . . .

K.J.V.

to them that love him. 13 Let no man say when he is tempted, I am tempted of God: for God cannot be tempted with evil, neither tempteth he any man: 14 But every man is tempted, when he is drawn away of his own lust, and enticed. 15 Then when lust hath conceived, it bringeth forth sin; and sin, when it is finished, bringeth forth death. 16 Do not err, my beloved brethren. 17 Every good gift and every perfect gift is from above, and cometh down from the Father of lights, with whom is no variableness, neither shadow of turning. 18 Of his own will begat he us with the word of truth, that we should be a kind of firstfruits of his creatures. 19 Wherefore, my beloved brethren, let every man be swift to hear, slow to speak, slow to wrath: 20 For the wrath of man worketh not the righteousness of God. 21 Wherefore lay apart all filthiness and superfluity of naughtiness, and receive with meekness the engrafted word, which is able to save your souls. 22 But be ye doers of the word, and not hearers only, deceiving your own selves. 23 For if any be a hearer of the word, and not a doer, he is like unto a man beholding his natural face in a glass: 24 For he beholdeth himself, and goeth his way, and straightway forgetteth what manner of man he was. 25 But whoso looketh into the perfect law of liberty, and continueth *therein,* he being not a forgetful hearer, but a doer of the work, this man shall be blessed in his deed. 26 If any man among you seem to be religious, and bridleth not his tongue, but deceiveth his own heart, this man's religion *is* vain. 27 Pure religion and undefiled before God and the Father is this, To visit the fatherless and widows in their affliction, *and* to keep himself unspotted from the world.

R.S.V.

who love him. 13 Let no one say when he is tempted, "I am tempted by God"; for God cannot be tempted with evil and he himself tempts no one; 14 but each person is tempted when he is lured and enticed by his own desire. 15 Then desire when it has conceived gives birth to sin; and sin when it is full-grown brings forth death.

16 Do not be deceived, my beloved brethren. 17 Every good endowment and every perfect gift is from above, coming down from the Father of lights with whom there is no variation or shadow due to change.[a] 18 Of his own will he brought us forth by the word of truth that we should be a kind of first fruits of his creatures.

19 Know this, my beloved brethren. Let every man be quick to hear, slow to speak, slow to anger, 20 for the anger of man does not work the righteousness of God. 21 Therefore put away all filthiness and rank growth of wickedness and receive with meekness the implanted word, which is able to save your souls.

22 But be doers of the word, and not hearers only, deceiving yourselves. 23 For if any one is a hearer of the word and not a doer, he is like a man who observes his natural face in a mirror; 24 for he observes himself and goes away and at once forgets what he was like. 25 But he who looks into the perfect law, the law of liberty, and perseveres, being no hearer that forgets but a doer that acts, he shall be blessed in his doing.

26 If any one thinks he is religious, and does not bridle his tongue but deceives his heart, this man's religion is vain. 27 Religion that is pure and undefiled before God and the Father is this: to visit orphans and widows in their affliction, and to keep oneself unstained from the world.

2 My brethren, have not the faith of our Lord Jesus Christ, *the Lord* of glory, with respect of persons. 2 For if there come unto your assembly a man with a gold ring, in goodly apparel, and there come in also a poor man in vile raiment; 3 And ye have respect to him that weareth the gay clothing, and say unto him, Sit thou here in a good place; and say to the poor, Stand thou there, or sit here under my footstool: 4 Are ye not then partial in yourselves, and are become judges of evil thoughts? 5 Hearken, my beloved brethren, Hath not God chosen the poor of this

2 My brethren, show no partiality as you hold the faith of our Lord Jesus Christ, the Lord of glory. 2 For if a man with gold rings and in fine clothing comes into your assembly, and a poor man in shabby clothing also comes in, 3 and you pay attention to the one who wears the fine clothing and say, "Have a seat here, please," while you say to the poor man, "Stand there," or, "Sit at my feet," 4 have you not made distinctions among yourselves, and become judges with evil thoughts? 5 Listen, my beloved brethren. Has not God chosen those who are

[a] Other ancient authorities read *variation due to a shadow of turning.*

PHILLIPS

A man must not say when he is tempted, "God is tempting me." For God cannot be tempted by evil, and does not himself tempt anyone. No, a man's temptation is due to the pull of his own inward desires, which can be enormously attractive. His own desire takes hold of him, and that produces sin. And sin in the long run means death—make no mistake about that, brothers of mine! But every good endowment that we possess and every complete gift that we have received must come from above, from the Father of all lights, with whom there is never the slightest variation or shadow of inconsistency. By his own wish he made us his own sons through the Word of truth, that we might be, so to speak, the first specimens of his new creation.

Hear God's Word and put it into practice: that is real religion
1. 19

In view of what he has made us then, dear brothers, let every man be quick to listen but slow to use his tongue, and slow to lose his temper. For man's temper is never the means of achieving God's true goodness.

Have done, then, with impurity and every other evil which touches the lives of others, and humbly accept the message that God has sown in your hearts, and which can save your souls. Don't, I beg you, only hear the message, but put it into practice; otherwise you are merely deluding yourselves. The man who simply hears and does nothing about it is like a man catching the reflection of his own face in a mirror. He sees himself, it is true, but he goes on with whatever he was doing without the slightest recollection of what sort of person he saw in the mirror. But the man who looks into the perfect mirror of God's law, the law of liberty, and makes a habit of so doing, is not the man who sees and forgets. He puts that law into practice and he wins true happiness.

If anyone appears to be "religious" but cannot control his tongue, he deceives himself and we may be sure that his religion is useless. Religion that is pure and genuine in the sight of God the Father will show itself by such things as visiting orphans and widows in their distress and keeping oneself uncontaminated by the world.

Avoid snobbery: keep the royal law
2. 1

Don't ever attempt, my brothers, to combine snobbery with faith in our glorious Lord Jesus Christ! Suppose one man comes into your meeting well dressed and with a gold ring on his finger, and another man, obviously poor, arrives in shabby clothes. If you pay special attention to the well dressed man by saying, "Please sit here—it's an excellent seat," and say to the poor man, "You stand over there, please, or if you must sit, sit on the floor," doesn't that prove that you are making class distinctions in your mind, and setting yourselves up to assess a man's quality?—a very bad thing. For do notice, my brothers, that God chose poor men, whose only wealth was their faith, and made

N.E.B.

should say, 'I am being tempted by God'; for God is untouched by evil,[a] and does not himself tempt anyone. Temptation arises when a man is enticed and lured away by his own lust; then lust conceives, and gives birth to sin; and sin full-grown breeds death.

Do not deceive yourselves, my friends. All good giving and[b] every perfect gift comes from above, from the Father of the lights of heaven. With him there is no variation, no play of passing shadows.[c] Of his set purpose, by declaring the truth, he gave us birth to be a kind of firstfruits of his creatures.

Of that you may be certain, my friends. But each of you must be quick to listen, slow to speak, and slow to be angry. For a man's anger cannot promote the justice of God. Away then with all that is sordid, and the malice that hurries to excess, and quietly accept the message planted in your hearts, which can bring you salvation.

Only be sure that you act on the message and do not merely listen; for that would be to mislead yourselves. A man who listens to the message but never acts upon it is like one who looks in a mirror at the face nature gave him. He glances at himself and goes away, and at once forgets what he looked like. But the man who looks closely into the perfect law, the law that makes us free, and who lives in its company, does not forget what he hears, but acts upon it; and that is the man who by acting will find happiness.

A man may think he is religious, but if he has no control over his tongue, he is deceiving himself; that man's religion is futile. The kind of religion which is without stain or fault in the sight of God our Father is this: to go to the help of orphans and widows in their distress and keep oneself untarnished by the world.

2 My brothers, believing as you do in our Lord Jesus Christ, who reigns in glory, you must never show snobbery. For instance, two visitors may enter your place of worship, one a well-dressed man with gold rings, and the other a poor man in shabby clothes. Suppose you pay special attention to the well-dressed man and say to him, 'Please take this seat', while to the poor man you say, 'You can stand; or you may sit here[d] on the floor by my footstool', do you not see that you are inconsistent and judge by false standards?

Listen, my friends. Has not God chosen those who are poor in the eyes of the world to be

[a] *Or* God cannot be tempted by evil. [b] *Or* All giving is good, and . . . [c] *Some witnesses read* no variation, or shadow caused by change. [d] *Some witnesses read* Stand where you are or sit here . . . ; *others read* Stand where you are or sit . . .

K.J.V.

world rich in faith, and heirs of the kingdom which he hath promised to them that love him? 6 But ye have despised the poor. Do not rich men oppress you, and draw you before the judgment seats? 7 Do not they blaspheme that worthy name by the which ye are called? 8 If ye fulfil the royal law according to the Scripture, Thou shalt love thy neighbour as thyself, ye do well: 9 But if ye have respect to persons, ye commit sin, and are convinced of the law as transgressors. 10 For whosoever shall keep the whole law, and yet offend in one *point*, he is guilty of all. 11 For he that said, Do not commit adultery, said also, Do not kill. Now if thou commit no adultery, yet if thou kill, thou art become a transgressor of the law. 12 So speak ye, and so do, as they that shall be judged by the law of liberty. 13 For he shall have judgment without mercy, that hath shewed no mercy; and mercy rejoiceth against judgment. 14 What *doth it* profit, my brethren, though a man say he hath faith, and have not works? can faith save him? 15 If a brother or sister be naked, and destitute of daily food, 16 And one of you say unto them, Depart in peace, be *ye* warmed and filled; notwithstanding ye give them not those things which are needful to the body; what *doth it* profit? 17 Even so faith, if it hath not works, is dead, being alone. 18 Yea, a man may say, Thou hast faith, and I have works: shew me thy faith without thy works, and I will shew thee my faith by my works. 19 Thou believest that there is one God; thou doest well: the devils also believe, and tremble. 20 But wilt thou know, O vain man, that faith without works is dead? 21 Was not Abraham our father justified by works, when he had offered Isaac his son upon the altar? 22 Seest thou how faith wrought with his works, and by works was faith made perfect? 23 And the Scripture was fulfilled which saith, Abraham believed God, and it was imputed unto him for righteousness: and he was called the Friend of God. 24 Ye see then how that by works a man is justified, and not by faith only. 25 Likewise also was not Rahab the harlot justified by works, when she had received the messengers, and had sent *them* out another way? 26 For as the body without the spirit is dead, so faith without works is dead also.

R.S.V.

poor in the world to be rich in faith and heirs of the kingdom which he has promised to those who love him? 6 But you have dishonored the poor man. Is it not the rich who oppress you, is it not they who drag you into court? 7 Is it not they who blaspheme that honorable name by which you are called?

8 If you really fulfil the royal law, according to the scripture, "You shall love your neighbor as yourself," you do well. 9 But if you show partiality, you commit sin, and are convicted by the law as transgressors. 10 For whoever keeps the whole law but fails in one point has become guilty of all of it. 11 For he who said, "Do not commit adultery," said also, "Do not kill." If you do not commit adultery but do kill, you have become a transgressor of the law. 12 So speak and so act as those who are to be judged under the law of liberty. 13 For judgment is without mercy to one who has shown no mercy; yet mercy triumphs over judgment.

14 What does it profit, my brethren, if a man says he has faith but has not works? Can his faith save him? 15 If a brother or sister is ill-clad and in lack of daily food, 16 and one of you says to them, "Go in peace, be warmed and filled," without giving them the things needed for the body, what does it profit? 17 So faith by itself, if it has no works, is dead.

18 But some one will say, "You have faith and I have works." Show me your faith apart from your works, and I by my works will show you my faith. 19 You believe that God is one; you do well. Even the demons believe—and shudder. 20 Do you want to be shown, you foolish fellow, that faith apart from works is barren? 21 Was not Abraham our father justified by works, when he offered his son Isaac upon the altar? 22 You see that faith was active along with his works, and faith was completed by works, 23 and the scripture was fulfilled which says, "Abraham believed God, and it was reckoned to him as righteousness"; and he was called the friend of God. 24 You see that a man is justified by works and not by faith alone. 25 And in the same way was not also Rahab the harlot justified by works when she received the messengers and sent them out another way? 26 For as the body apart from the spirit is dead, so faith apart from works is dead.

them heirs to the kingdom promised to those who love him. And if you behave as I have suggested, it is the poor man that you are insulting. Look around you. Isn't it the rich who are always trying to "boss" you? Isn't it the rich who drag you into litigation? Isn't it usually the rich who blaspheme the glorious name by which you are known?

If you obey the royal law, expressed by the scripture, "Thou shalt love thy neighbor as thyself," all is well. But once you allow any invidious distinctions to creep in, you are sinning; you have broken God's Law. Remember that a man who keeps the whole Law but for a single exception is none the less a law-breaker. The one who said, "Thou shalt not commit adultery," also said, "Thou shalt do no murder." If you were to keep clear of adultery but were to murder a man you would have become a breaker of God's whole Law.

Anyway, you should speak and act as men who will be judged by the law of freedom. The man who makes no allowances for others will find none made for him. It is still true that "mercy smiles in the face of judgment."

The relation between faith and action   2. 14

Now what use is it, my brothers, for a man to say he "has faith" if his actions do not correspond with it? Could that sort of faith save anyone's soul? If a fellow man or woman has no clothes to wear and nothing to eat, and one of you say, "Good luck to you, I hope you'll keep warm and find enough to eat," and yet give them nothing to meet their physical needs, what on earth is the good of that? Yet that is exactly what a bare faith without a corresponding life is like—useless and dead. If we only "have faith" man could easily challenge us by saying: "You say that you have faith and I have merely good actions. Well, all you can do is to show me a faith without corresponding actions, but I can show you by my actions that I have faith as well."

To the man who thinks that faith by itself is enough I feel inclined to say, "So you believe that there is one God? That's fine. So do all the devils in hell, and shudder in terror!" For, my dear shortsighted man, can't you see far enough to realize that faith without the right actions is dead and useless? Think of Abraham, our ancestor. Wasn't it his action which really justified him in God's sight when his faith led him to offer his son Isaac on the altar? Can't you see that his faith and his actions were, so to speak, partners—that his faith was implemented by his deed? That is what the scripture means when it says:

And Abraham believed God,
And it was reckoned unto him for righteousness;
And he was called the friend of God.

A man is justified before God by what he does as well as by what he believes. Rahab, who was a prostitute and a foreigner, has been quoted as an example of faith, yet surely it was her action that pleased God, when she welcomed Joshua's reconnoitering party and sent them safely back by a different route.

Yes, faith without action is as dead as a body without a soul.

rich in faith and to inherit the kingdom he has promised to those who love him? And yet you have insulted the poor man. Moreover, are not the rich your oppressors? Is it not they who drag you into court and pour contempt on the honoured name by which God has claimed you?

If, however, you are observing the sovereign law laid down in Scripture, 'Love your neighbour as yourself', that is excellent. But if you show snobbery, you are committing a sin and you stand convicted by that law as transgressors. For if a man keeps the whole law apart from one single point, he is guilty of breaking all of it. For the One who said, 'Thou shalt not commit adultery', said also, 'Thou shalt not commit murder.' You may not be an adulterer, but if you commit murder you are a law-breaker all the same. Always speak and act as men who are to be judged under a law of freedom. In that judgement there will be no mercy for the man who has shown no mercy. Mercy triumphs over judgement.

My brothers, what use is it for a man to say he has faith when he does nothing to show it? Can that faith save him? Suppose a brother or a sister is in rags with not enough food for the day, and one of you says, 'Good luck to you, keep yourselves warm, and have plenty to eat', but does nothing to supply their bodily needs, what is the good of that? So with faith; if it does not lead to action, it is in itself a lifeless thing.

But someone may object: 'Here is one who claims to have faith and another who points to his deeds.' To which I reply: 'Prove to me that this faith you speak of is real though not accompanied by deeds, and by my deeds I will prove to you my faith.' You have faith enough to believe that there is one God. Excellent! The devils have faith like that, and it makes them tremble. But can you not see, you quibbler, that faith divorced from deeds is barren? Was it not by his action, in offering his son Isaac upon the altar, that our father Abraham was justified? Surely you can see that faith was at work in his actions, and that by these actions the integrity of his faith was fully proved. Here was fulfilment of the words of Scripture: 'Abraham put his faith in God, and that faith was counted to him as righteousness'; and elsewhere he is called 'God's friend'. You see then that a man is justified by deeds and not by faith in itself. The same is true of the prostitute Rahab also. Was not she justified by her action in welcoming the messengers into her house and sending them away by a different route? As the body is dead when there is no breath left in it, so faith divorced from deeds is lifeless as a corpse.

3 My brethren, be not many masters, knowing that we shall receive the greater condemnation. 2 For in many things we offend all. If any man offend not in word, the same *is* a perfect man, *and* able also to bridle the whole body. 3 Behold, we put bits in the horses' mouths, that they may obey us; and we turn about their whole body. 4 Behold also the ships, which though *they be* so great, and *are* driven of fierce winds, yet are they turned about with a very small helm, whithersoever the governor listeth. 5 Even so the tongue is a little member, and boasteth great things. Behold, how great a matter a little fire kindleth! 6And the tongue *is* a fire, a world of iniquity: so is the tongue among our members, that it defileth the whole body, and setteth on fire the course of nature; and it is set on fire of hell. 7 For every kind of beasts, and of birds, and of serpents, and of things in the sea, is tamed, and hath been tamed of mankind: 8 But the tongue can no man tame; *it is* an unruly evil, full of deadly poison. 9 Therewith bless we God, even the Father; and therewith curse we men, which are made after the similitude of God. 10 Out of the same mouth proceedeth blessing and cursing. My brethren, these things ought not so to be. 11 Doth a fountain send forth at the same place sweet *water* and bitter? 12 Can the fig tree, my brethren, bear olive berries? either a vine, figs? so *can* no fountain both yield salt water and fresh. 13 Who *is* a wise man and endued with knowledge among you? let him shew out of a good conversation his works with meekness of wisdom. 14 But if ye have bitter envying and strife in your hearts, glory not, and lie not against the truth. 15 This wisdom descendeth not from above, but *is* earthly, sensual, devilish. 16 For where envying and strife *is*, there *is* confusion and every evil work. 17 But the wisdom that is from above is first pure, then peaceable, gentle, *and* easy to be entreated, full of mercy and good fruits, without partiality, and without hypocrisy. 18And the fruit of righteousness is sown in peace of them that make peace.

3 Let not many of you become teachers, my brethren, for you know that we who teach shall be judged with greater strictness. 2 For we all make many mistakes, and if any one makes no mistakes in what he says he is a perfect man, able to bridle the whole body also. 3 If we put bits into the mouths of horses that they may obey us, we guide their whole bodies. 4 Look at the ships also; though they are so great and are driven by strong winds, they are guided by a very small rudder wherever the will of the pilot directs. 5 So the tongue is a little member and boasts of great things. How great a forest is set ablaze by a small fire! 6 And the tongue is a fire. The tongue is an unrighteous world among our members, staining the whole body, setting on fire the cycle of nature,[b] and set on fire by hell.[c] 7 For every kind of beast and bird, of reptile and sea creature, can be tamed and has been tamed by humankind, 8 but no human being can tame the tongue—a restless evil, full of deadly poison. 9 With it we bless the Lord and Father, and with it we curse men, who are made in the likeness of God. 10 From the same mouth come blessing and cursing. My brethren, this ought not to be so. 11 Does a spring pour forth from the same opening fresh water and brackish? 12 Can a fig tree, my brethren, yield olives, or a grapevine figs? No more can salt water yield fresh.

13 Who is wise and understanding among you? By his good life let him show his works in the meekness of wisdom. 14 But if you have bitter jealousy and selfish ambition in your hearts, do not boast and be false to the truth. 15 This wisdom is not such as comes down from above, but is earthly, unspiritual, devilish. 16 For where jealousy and selfish ambition exist, there will be disorder and every vile practice. 17 But the wisdom from above is first pure, then peaceable, gentle, open to reason, full of mercy and good fruits, without uncertainty or insincerity. 18And the harvest of righteousness is sown in peace by those who make peace.

---

[b] Or *wheel of birth.* [c] Greek *Gehenna.*

726

*The responsibility of a 3. 1
teacher's position*

Don't aim at adding to the number of teachers, my brothers, I beg you! Remember that we who are teachers will be judged by a much higher standard.

The danger of the tongue 3. 2

We all make mistakes in all kinds of ways, but the man who can claim that he never says the wrong thing can consider himself perfect, for if he can control his tongue he can control every other part of his personality! Men control the movements of a large animal like the horse with a tiny bit placed in its mouth. Ships too, for all their size and the momentum they have with a strong wind behind them, are controlled by a very small rudder according to the course chosen by the helmsman. The human tongue is physically small, but what tremendous effects it can boast of! A whole forest can be set ablaze by a tiny spark of fire, and the tongue is as dangerous as any fire, with vast potentialities for evil. It can poison the whole body; it can make the whole of life a blazing hell.

Beasts, birds, reptiles and all kinds of sea creatures can be, and in fact are, tamed by man, but no one can tame the human tongue. It is an evil always liable to break out, and the poison it spreads is deadly. We use the tongue to bless our Father, God, and we use the same tongue to curse our fellow men, who are all created in God's likeness. Blessing and curses come out of the same mouth—surely, my brothers, this is the sort of thing that never ought to happen! Have you ever known a spring give sweet and bitter water simultaneously? Have you ever seen a fig tree with a crop of olives, or seen figs growing on a vine? It is just as impossible for a spring to give fresh and salt water at the same time.

*Real, spiritual, wisdom means 3. 13
humility, not rivalry*

Are there some wise and understanding men among you? Then your lives will be an example of the humility that is born of true wisdom. But if your heart is full of rivalry and bitter jealousy, then do not boast of your wisdom—don't deny the truth that you must recognize in your inmost heart. You may acquire a certain superficial wisdom, but it does not come from God— it comes from this world, from your own lower nature, even from the devil. For wherever you find jealousy and rivalry you also find disharmony and all other kinds of evil. The wisdom that comes from God is first utterly pure, then peace-loving, gentle, approachable, full of tolerant thoughts and kindly actions, with no breath of favoritism or hint of hypocrisy. And the wise are peacemakers who go on quietly sowing for a harvest of righteousness—in other people and in themselves.

3 My brothers, not many of you should become teachers, for you may be certain that we who teach shall ourselves be judged with greater strictness. All of us often go wrong; the man who never says a wrong thing is a perfect character, able to bridle his whole being. If we put bits into horses' mouths to make them obey our will, we can direct their whole body. Or think of ships: large they may be, yet even when driven by strong gales they can be directed by a tiny rudder on whatever course the helmsman chooses. So with the tongue. It is a small member but it can make huge claims.[a]

What a huge stack of timber[b] can be set ablaze by the tiniest spark! And the tongue is in effect a fire. It represents among our members the world with all its wickedness; it pollutes our whole being; it keeps the wheel of our existence red-hot, and its flames are fed by hell. Beasts and birds of every kind, creatures that crawl on the ground or swim in the sea, can be subdued and have been subdued by mankind; but no man can subdue the tongue. It is an intractable evil, charged with deadly venom. We use it to sing the praises of our Lord and Father, and we use it to invoke curses upon our fellow-men who are made in God's likeness. Out of the same mouth come praises and curses. My brothers, this should not be so. Does a fountain gush with both fresh and brackish water from the same opening? Can a fig-tree, my brothers, yield olives, or a vine figs? No more does salt water yield fresh.

Who among you is wise or clever? Let his right conduct give practical proof of it, with the modesty that comes of wisdom. But if you are harbouring bitter jealousy and selfish ambition in your hearts, consider whether your claims are not false, and a defiance of the truth. This is not the wisdom that comes from above; it is earthbound, sensual, demonic. For with jealousy and ambition come disorder and evil of every kind. But the wisdom from above is in the first place pure; and then peace-loving, considerate, and open to reason; it is straightforward and sincere, rich in mercy and in the kindly deeds that are its fruit. True justice is the harvest reaped by peacemakers from seeds sown in a spirit of peace.

[a] *Or* it is a great boaster. [b] *Or* What a huge forest . . .

4 From whence *come* wars and fightings among you? *come they* not hence, *even* of your lusts that war in your members? 2 Ye lust, and have not: ye kill, and desire to have, and cannot obtain: ye fight and war, yet ye have not, because ye ask not. 3 Ye ask, and receive not, because ye ask amiss, that ye may consume *it* upon your lusts. 4 Ye adulterers and adulteresses, know ye not that the friendship of the world is enmity with God? whosoever therefore will be a friend of the world is the enemy of God. 5 Do ye think that the Scripture saith in vain, The spirit that dwelleth in us lusteth to envy? 6 But he giveth more grace. Wherefore he saith, God resisteth the proud, but giveth grace unto the humble. 7 Submit yourselves therefore to God. Resist the devil, and he will flee from you. 8 Draw nigh to God, and he will draw nigh to you. Cleanse *your* hands, *ye* sinners; and purify *your* hearts, *ye* doubleminded. 9 Be afflicted, and mourn, and weep: let your laughter be turned to mourning, and *your* joy to heaviness. 10 Humble yourselves in the sight of the Lord, and he shall lift you up. 11 Speak not evil one of another, brethren. He that speaketh evil of *his* brother, and judgeth his brother, speaketh evil of the law, and judgeth the law: but if thou judge the law, thou art not a doer of the law, but a judge. 12 There is one lawgiver, who is able to save and to destroy: who art thou that judgest another? 13 Go to now, ye that say, To day or to morrow we will go into such a city, and continue there a year, and buy and sell, and get gain: 14 Whereas ye know not what *shall be* on the morrow. For what *is* your life? It is even a vapour, that appeareth for a little time, and then vanisheth away. 15 For that ye *ought* to say, If

4 What causes wars, and what causes fightings among you? Is it not your passions that are at war in your members? 2 You desire and do not have; so you kill. And you covet[d] and cannot obtain; so you fight and wage war. You do not have, because you do not ask. 3 You ask and do not receive, because you ask wrongly, to spend it on your passions. 4 Unfaithful creatures! Do you not know that friendship with the world is enmity with God? Therefore whoever wishes to be a friend of the world makes himself an enemy of God. 5 Or do you suppose it is in vain that the scripture says, "He yearns jealously over the spirit which he has made to dwell in us"? 6 But he gives more grace; therefore it says, "God opposes the proud, but gives grace to the humble." 7 Submit yourselves therefore to God. Resist the devil and he will flee from you. 8 Draw near to God and he will draw near to you. Cleanse your hands, you sinners, and purify your hearts, you men of double mind. 9 Be wretched and mourn and weep. Let your laughter be turned to mourning and your joy to dejection. 10 Humble yourselves before the Lord and he will exalt you.

11 Do not speak evil against one another, brethren. He that speaks evil against a brother or judges his brother, speaks evil against the law and judges the law. But if you judge the law, you are not a doer of the law but a judge. 12 There is one lawgiver and judge, he who is able to save and to destroy. But who are you that you judge your neighbor?

13 Come now, you who say, "Today or tomorrow we will go into such and such a town and spend a year there and trade and get gain"; 14 whereas you do not know about tomorrow. What is your life? For you are a mist that appears for a little time and then vanishes. 15 In-

[d] Or *you kill and you covet.*

PHILLIPS

N.E.B.

Your jealousies spring from love   4. 1
of what the world can give

But what about the feuds and struggles that exist among you—where do you suppose they come from? Can't you see that they arise from conflicting passions within yourselves? You crave for something and don't get it; you are murderously jealous of what others have got and which you can't possess yourselves; you struggle and fight with one another. You don't get what you want because you don't ask God for it. And when you do ask he doesn't give it to you, for you ask in quite the wrong spirit—you want only to satisfy your own desires.

You are like unfaithful wives, flirting with the glamour of this world, and never realizing that to be the world's lover means becoming the enemy of God! Anyone who deliberately chooses to be the world's friend is thereby making himself God's enemy. Do you think what the scriptures have to say about this is a mere formality? Or do you imagine that this spirit of passionate jealousy is the Spirit he has caused to live in us? No, he gives us grace potent enough to meet this and every other evil spirit, if we are humble enough to receive it. That is why he says:

God resisteth the proud,
But giveth grace to the humble.

You should be humble, not proud   4. 7

Be humble then before God. But resist the devil and you'll find he'll run away from you. Come close to God and he will come close to you. Realize that you have sinned, and get your hands clean again. Realize that you have been disloyal, and get your hearts made true once more. As you come close to God you should be deeply sorry, you should be grieved, you should even be in tears. Your laughter will have to become mourning, your high spirits will have to become heartfelt dejection. You will have to feel very small in the sight of God before he will set you on your feet once more.

It is for God to judge, not for us   4. 11

Never pull one another to pieces, my brothers. If you do you are judging your brother and setting yourself up in the place of God's Law; you have become in fact a critic of the Law. Yet if you start to criticize the Law instead of obeying it you are setting yourself up as judge, and there is only one judge, the one who gave the Law, to whom belongs absolute power of life and death. How can you then be so silly as to imagine that you are your neighbor's judge?

It is still true that man proposes,   4. 13
but God disposes

Just a moment, now, you who say: "We are going to such-and-such a city today or tomorrow. We shall stay there a year doing business and make a profit"! How do you know what will happen even tomorrow? What, after all, is your life? It is like a puff of smoke visible for a little while and then dissolving into thin air. Your re-

4 What causes conflicts and quarrels among you? Do they not spring from the aggressiveness of your bodily desires? You want something which you cannot have, and so you are bent on murder; you are envious, and cannot attain your ambition, and so you quarrel and fight. You do not get what you want, because you do not pray for it. Or, if you do, your requests are not granted because you pray from wrong motives, to spend what you get on your pleasures. You false, unfaithful creatures! Have you never learned that love of the world is enmity to God? Whoever chooses to be the world's friend makes himself God's enemy. Or do you suppose that Scripture has no meaning when it says that the spirit which God implanted in man turns towards envious desires? And yet the grace he gives is stronger. Thus Scripture says, 'God opposes the arrogant and gives grace to the humble.' Be submissive then to God. Stand up to the devil and he will turn and run. Come close to God, and he will come close to you. Sinners, make your hands clean; you who are doubleminded, see that your motives are pure. Be sorrowful, mourn and weep. Turn your laughter into mourning and your gaiety into gloom. Humble yourselves before God and he will lift you high.

Brothers, you must never disparage one another. He who disparages a brother or passes judgement on his brother disparages the law and judges the law. But if you judge the law, you are not keeping it but sitting in judgement upon it. There is only one lawgiver and judge, the One who is able to save life and destroy it. So who are you to judge your neighbour?

A word with you, you who say, 'Today or tomorrow we will go off to such and such a town and spend a year there trading and making money.' Yet you have no idea what tomorrow will bring. Your life, what is it? You are no more than a mist, seen for a little while and then dispersing. What you ought to say is: 'If

K.J.V.

the Lord will, we shall live, and do this, or that. 16 But now ye rejoice in your boastings: all such rejoicing is evil. 17 Therefore to him that knoweth to do good, and doeth *it* not, to him it is sin.

5 Go to now, *ye* rich men, weep and howl for your miseries that shall come upon *you.* 2 Your riches are corrupted, and your garments are motheaten. 3 Your gold and silver is cankered; and the rust of them shall be a witness against you, and shall eat your flesh as it were fire. Ye have heaped treasure together for the last days. 4 Behold, the hire of the labourers who have reaped down your fields, which is of you kept back by fraud, crieth: and the cries of them which have reaped are entered into the ears of the Lord of Sabaoth. 5 Ye have lived in pleasure on the earth, and been wanton; ye have nourished your hearts, as in a day of slaughter. 6 Ye have condemned *and* killed the just; *and* he doth not resist you. 7 Be patient therefore, brethren, unto the coming of the Lord. Behold, the husbandman waiteth for the precious fruit of the earth, and hath long patience for it, until he receive the early and latter rain. 8 Be ye also patient; stablish your hearts: for the coming of the Lord draweth nigh. 9 Grudge not one against another, brethren, lest ye be condemned: behold, the judge standeth before the door. 10 Take, my brethren, the prophets, who have spoken in the name of the Lord, for an example of suffering affliction, and of patience. 11 Behold, we count them happy which endure. Ye have heard of the patience of Job, and have seen the end of the Lord; that the Lord is very pitiful, and of tender mercy. 12 But above all things, my brethren, swear not, neither by heaven, neither by the earth, neither by any other oath: but let your yea be yea; and *your* nay, nay; lest ye

R.S.V.

stead you ought to say, "If the Lord wills, we shall live and we shall do this or that." 16As it is, you boast in your arrogance. All such boasting is evil. 17 Whoever knows what is right to do and fails to do it, for him it is sin.

5 Come now, you rich, weep and howl for the miseries that are coming upon you. 2 Your riches have rotted and your garments are moth-eaten. 3 Your gold and silver have rusted, and their rust will be evidence against you and will eat your flesh like fire. You have laid up treasure[e] for the last days. 4 Behold, the wages of the laborers who mowed your fields, which you kept back by fraud, cry out; and the cries of the harvesters have reached the ears of the Lord of hosts. 5 You have lived on the earth in luxury and in pleasure; you have fattened your hearts in a day of slaughter. 6 You have condemned, you have killed the righteous man; he does not resist you.

7 Be patient, therefore, brethren, until the coming of the Lord. Behold, the farmer waits for the precious fruit of the earth, being patient over it until it receives the early and the late rain. 8 You also be patient. Establish your hearts, for the coming of the Lord is at hand. 9 Do not grumble, brethren, against one another, that you may not be judged; behold, the Judge is standing at the doors. 10As an example of suffering and patience, brethren, take the prophets who spoke in the name of the Lord. 11 Behold, we call those happy who were steadfast. You have heard of the steadfastness of Job, and you have seen the purpose of the Lord, how the Lord is compassionate and merciful.

12 But above all, my brethren, do not swear, either by heaven or by earth or with any other oath, but let your yes be yes and your no be no, that you may not fall under condemnation.

[e] Or *will eat your flesh, since you have stored up fire.*

PHILLIPS

N.E.B.

marks should be prefaced with, "If it is the Lord's will, we shall still be alive and shall do so-and-so." As it is, you get a certain pride in yourself in planning your future with such confidence. That sort of pride is all wrong.

No doubt you agree with the above in theory. Well, remember that if a man knows what is right and fails to do it, his failure is a real sin.

it be the Lord's will, we shall live to do this or that.' But instead, you boast and brag, and all such boasting is wrong. Well then, the man who knows the good he ought to do and does not do it is a sinner.

Riches are going to prove a   **5. 1**
liability, not an asset, to the selfish

And now, you plutocrats, is the time for you to weep and moan because of the miseries in store for you! Your richest goods are ruined; your hoard of clothes is moth-eaten; your gold and silver are tarnished. Yes, their very tarnish will be the evidence of your wicked hoarding and you will shrink from them as if they were red-hot. You have made a fine pile in these last days, haven't you? But look, here is the pay of the reaper you hired and whom you cheated, and it is shouting out against you! And the cries of the other laborers you swindled are heard by the Lord of Hosts himself. Yes, you have had a magnificent time on this earth, and have indulged yourselves to the full. You have picked out just what you wanted like soldiers looting after battle. You have condemned and ruined innocent men in your career, and they have been powerless to stop you.

5 Next a word to you who have great possessions. Weep and wail over the miserable fate descending on you. Your riches have rotted; your fine clothes are moth-eaten; your silver and gold have rusted away, and their very rust will be evidence against you and consume your flesh like fire. You have piled up wealth in an age that is near its close. The wages you never paid to the men who mowed your fields are loud against you, and the outcry of the reapers has reached the ears of the Lord of Hosts. You have lived on earth in wanton luxury, fattening yourselves like cattle—and the day for slaughter has come. You have condemned the innocent and murdered him; he offers no resistance.

Be patient, my brothers, until the Lord comes. The farmer looking for the precious crop his land may yield can only wait in patience, until the winter and spring rains have fallen. You too must be patient and stout-hearted, for the coming of the Lord is near. My brothers, do not blame your troubles on one another, or you will fall under judgement; and there stands the Judge, at the door. If you want a pattern of patience under ill-treatment, take the prophets who spoke in the name of the Lord; remember: 'We count those happy who stood firm.' You have all heard how Job stood firm, and you have seen how the Lord treated him in the end. For the Lord is full of pity and compassion.

Ultimate justice will surely come: **5. 7**
be patient meanwhile

But be patient, my brothers, as you wait for the Lord to come. Look at the farmer quietly awaiting his precious harvest. See how he has to possess his soul in patience till the land has had the early and late rains. So must you be patient, resting your hearts on the ultimate certainty. The Lord's coming is very near.

Don't make complaints against one another in the meantime, my brothers—you may be the one at fault yourself. The judge himself is already at the door.

For our example of the patient endurance of suffering we can take the prophets who have spoken in the Lord's name. Remember that it is usually those who have patiently endured to whom we accord the word "blessed." You have heard of Job's patient endurance and how God dealt with him in the end, and therefore you have seen that the Lord is merciful and full of understanding pity for us men.

Above all things, my brothers, do not use oaths, whether 'by heaven' or 'by earth' or by anything else. When you say yes or no, let it be plain 'Yes' or 'No', for fear that you expose yourselves to judgement.

Don't emphasize with oaths: **5. 12**
speak the plain truth

It is of the highest importance, my brothers, that your speech should be free from oaths (whether they are "by" Heaven or earth or anything else). Your yes should be a plain yes, and your no a plain no, and then you cannot go wrong in the matter.

K.J.V.

fall into condemnation. 13 Is any among you afflicted? let him pray. Is any merry? let him sing psalms. 14 Is any sick among you? let him call for the elders of the church; and let them pray over him, anointing him with oil in the name of the Lord: 15And the prayer of faith shall save the sick, and the Lord shall raise him up; and if he have committed sins, they shall be forgiven him. 16 Confess *your* faults one to another, and pray one for another, that ye may be healed. The effectual fervent prayer of a righteous man availeth much. 17 Elias was a man subject to like passions as we are, and he prayed earnestly that it might not rain: and it rained not on the earth by the space of three years and six months. 18And he prayed again, and the heaven gave rain, and the earth brought forth her fruit. 19 Brethren, if any of you do err from the truth, and one convert him; 20 Let him know, that he which converteth the sinner from the error of his way shall save a soul from death, and shall hide a multitude of sins.

R.S.V.

13 Is any one among you suffering? Let him pray. Is any cheerful? Let him sing praise. 14 Is any among you sick? Let him call for the elders of the church, and let them pray over him, anointing him with oil in the name of the Lord; 15 and the prayer of faith will save the sick man, and the Lord will raise him up; and if he has committed sins, he will be forgiven. 16 Therefore confess your sins to one another, and pray for one another, that you may be healed. The prayer of a righteous man has great power in its effects. 17 Elijah was a man of like nature with ourselves and he prayed fervently that it might not rain, and for three years and six months it did not rain on the earth. 18 Then he prayed again and the heaven gave rain, and the earth brought forth its fruit.

19 My brethren, if any one among you wanders from the truth and some one brings him back, 20 let him know that whoever brings back a sinner from the error of his way will save his soul from death and will cover a multitude of sins.

PHILLIPS	N.E.B.

PHILLIPS

Prayer is a great weapon   5. 13

If any of you is in trouble let him pray. If anyone is flourishing let him sing praises to God. If anyone is ill he should send for the church elders. They should pray over him, anointing him with oil in the Lord's name. Believing prayer will save the sick man; the Lord will restore him and any sins that he has committed will be forgiven. You should get into the habit of admitting your sins to one another, and praying for one another, so that if sickness comes to you you may be healed.

Tremendous power is made available through a good man's earnest prayer. Do you remember Elijah? He was a man like us but he prayed earnestly that it should not rain. In fact, not a drop fell on the land for three and a half years. Then he prayed again; the heavens gave the rain and the earth sprouted with vegetation as usual.

A concluding hint   5. 19

My brothers, if any of you should wander away from the truth and another should turn him back on the right path, then the latter may be sure that in turning a man back from his wandering course he has rescued a soul from death, and his loving action will "cover a multitude of sins."

JAMES

N.E.B.

Is anyone among you in trouble? He should turn to prayer. Is anyone in good heart? He should sing praises. Is one of you ill? He should send for the elders of the congregation to pray over him and anoint him with oil in the name of the Lord. The prayer offered in faith will save the sick man, the Lord will raise him from his bed, and any sins he may have committed will be forgiven. Therefore confess your sins to one another, and pray for one another, and then you will be healed. A good man's prayer is powerful and effective. Elijah was a man with human frailties like our own; and when he prayed earnestly that there should be no rain, not a drop fell on the land for three years and a half; then he prayed again, and down came the rain and the land bore crops once more.

My brothers, if one of your number should stray from the truth and another succeed in bringing him back, be sure of this: any man who brings a sinner back from his crooked ways will be rescuing his soul from death and cancelling innumerable sins.

THE FIRST

EPISTLE GENERAL

OF

PETER

THE

FIRST LETTER OF

PETER

1 Peter, an apostle of Jesus Christ, to the strangers scattered throughout Pontus, Galatia, Cappadocia, Asia, and Bithynia, 2 Elect according to the foreknowledge of God the Father, through sanctification of the Spirit, unto obedience and sprinkling of the blood of Jesus Christ: Grace unto you, and peace, be multiplied. 3 Blessed *be* the God and Father of our Lord Jesus Christ, which according to his abundant mercy hath begotten us again unto a lively hope by the resurrection of Jesus Christ from the dead, 4 To an inheritance incorruptible, and undefiled, and that fadeth not away, reserved in heaven for you, 5 Who are kept by the power of God through faith unto salvation ready to be revealed in the last time. 6 Wherein ye greatly rejoice, though now for a season, if need be, ye are in heaviness through manifold temptations: 7 That the trial of your faith, being much more precious than of gold that perisheth, though it be tried with fire, might be found unto praise and honour and glory at the appearing of Jesus Christ: 8 Whom having not seen, ye love; in whom, though now ye see *him* not, yet believing, ye rejoice with joy unspeakable and full of glory: 9 Receiving the end of your faith, *even* the salvation of *your* souls. 10 Of which salvation the prophets have inquired and searched diligently, who prophesied of the grace *that should come* unto you: 11 Searching what, or what manner of time the Spirit of Christ which was in them did signify, when it testified beforehand the sufferings of Christ, and the glory that should follow. 12 Unto whom it was revealed, that not unto themselves, but unto us they did minister the things, which are now reported unto you by them that have preached the gospel unto you with the Holy Ghost sent down from heaven; which things the angels desire to look

1 Peter, an apostle of Jesus Christ,
1 To the exiles of the Dispersion in Pontus, Galatia, Cappadocia, Asia, and Bithynia, 2 chosen and destined by God the Father and sanctified by the Spirit for obedience to Jesus Christ and for sprinkling with his blood:
May grace and peace be multiplied to you.

3 Blessed be the God and Father of our Lord Jesus Christ! By his great mercy we have been born anew to a living hope through the resurrection of Jesus Christ from the dead, 4 and to an inheritance which is imperishable, undefiled, and unfading, kept in heaven for you, 5 who by God's power are guarded through faith for a salvation ready to be revealed in the last time. 6 In this you rejoice,*a* though now for a little while you may have to suffer various trials, 7 so that the genuineness of your faith, more precious than gold which though perishable is tested by fire, may redound to praise and glory and honor at the revelation of Jesus Christ. 8 Without having seen*b* him you*c* love him; though you do not now see him you*c* believe in him and rejoice with unutterable and exalted joy. 9 As the outcome of your faith you obtain the salvation of your souls.

10 The prophets who prophesied of the grace that was to be yours searched and inquired about this salvation; 11 they inquired what person or time was indicated by the Spirit of Christ within them when predicting the sufferings of Christ and the subsequent glory. 12 It was revealed to them that they were serving not themselves but you, in the things which have now been announced to you by those who preached the good news to you through the Holy Spirit sent from heaven, things into which angels long to look.

[*a*] Or *Rejoice in this.* [*b*] Other ancient authorities read *known.* [*c*] Or omit *you.*

THE
FIRST LETTER OF
PETER

THE
FIRST LETTER OF
PETER

The Calling of a Christian

Peter, a messenger of Jesus Christ, sends this letter to the exiles of the dispersed tribes (in Pontus, Galatia, Cappadocia, Asia and Bithynia), whom God the Father knew and chose long ago to be made holy by his Spirit, that they might obey Jesus Christ and be cleansed by his blood: may you know more and more of God's grace and peace.

Your faith is being tested,   *1. 3*
but your future is magnificent

Thank God, the God and Father of our Lord Jesus Christ, that in his great mercy we men have been born again into a life full of hope, through Christ's rising again from the dead! You can now hope for a perfect inheritance beyond the reach of change and decay, "reserved" in Heaven for you. And in the meantime you are guarded by the power of God operating through your faith, till you enter fully into the salvation which is all ready for the dénouement of the last day. This means tremendous joy to you, I know, even though at present you are temporarily harassed by all kinds of trials and temptations. This is no accident—it happens to prove your faith, which is infinitely more valuable than gold, and gold, as you know, even though it is ultimately perishable, must be purified by fire. This proving of your faith is planned to result in praise and honor and glory in the day when Jesus Christ reveals himself. And though you have never seen him, yet I know that you love him. At present you trust him without being able to see him, and even now he brings you a joy that words cannot express and which has in it a hint of the glories of Heaven; and all the time you are receiving the result of your faith in him—the salvation of your own souls. The prophets of old did their utmost to discover and obtain this salvation. They did not find it, but they prophesied of this grace that has now come to you. They tried hard to discover to what time and to what sort of circumstances the Spirit of Christ working in them was referring. For he foretold the sufferings of Christ and the glories that should follow them. It was then made clear to them that they were dealing with matters not meant for themselves, but for you. It is these very matters which have been made plain to you by those who preached the gospel to you by the Holy Spirit sent from Heaven—and these are facts to command the interest of the very angels!

1 From Peter, apostle of Jesus Christ, to those of God's scattered people who lodge for a while in Pontus, Galatia, Cappadocia, Asia, and Bithynia—chosen of old in the purpose of God the Father, hallowed to his service by the Spirit, and consecrated with the sprinkled blood of Jesus Christ.

Grace and peace to you in fullest measure.

Praise be to the God and Father of our Lord Jesus Christ, who in his mercy gave us new birth into a living hope by the resurrection of Jesus Christ from the dead! The inheritance to which we are born is one that nothing can destroy or spoil or wither. It is kept for you in heaven, and you, because you put your faith in God, are under the protection of his power until salvation comes—the salvation which is even now in readiness and will be revealed at the end of time.

This is cause for great joy, even though you smart for a little while, if need be, under trials of many kinds. Even gold passes through the assayer's fire, and more precious than perishable gold is faith which has stood the test. These trials come so that your faith may prove itself worthy of all praise, glory, and honour when Jesus Christ is revealed.

You have not seen him, yet you love him; and trusting in him now without seeing him, you are transported with a joy too great for words, while you reap the harvest of your faith, that is, salvation for your souls. This salvation was the theme which the prophets pondered and explored, those who prophesied about the grace of God awaiting you. They tried to find out what was the time,[a] and what the circumstances, to which the spirit of Christ in them pointed, foretelling the sufferings in store for Christ and the splendours to follow; and it was disclosed to them that the matter they treated of was not for their time but for yours. And now it has been openly announced to you through preachers who brought you the Gospel in the power of the Holy Spirit sent from heaven. These are things that angels long to see into.

---

[a] *Or* who was the person . . .

K.J.V.

into. 13 Wherefore gird up the loins of your mind, be sober, and hope to the end for the grace that is to be brought unto you at the revelation of Jesus Christ; 14As obedient children, not fashioning yourselves according to the former lusts in your ignorance: 15 But as he which hath called you is holy, so be ye holy in all manner of conversation; 16 Because it is written, Be ye holy; for I am holy. 17And if ye call on the Father, who without respect of persons judgeth according to every man's work, pass the time of your sojourning *here* in fear: 18 Forasmuch as ye know that ye were not redeemed with corruptible things, *as* silver and gold, from your vain conversation *received* by tradition from your fathers; 19 But with the precious blood of Christ, as of a lamb without blemish and without spot: 20 Who verily was foreordained before the foundation of the world, but was manifest in these last times for you, 21 Who by him do believe in God, that raised him up from the dead, and gave him glory; that your faith and hope might be in God. 22 Seeing ye have purified your souls in obeying the truth through the Spirit unto unfeigned love of the brethren, *see that ye* love one another with a pure heart fervently: 23 Being born again, not of corruptible seed, but of incorruptible, by the word of God, which liveth and abideth for ever. 24 For all flesh *is* as grass, and all the glory of man as the flower of grass. The grass withereth, and the flower thereof falleth away: 25 But the word of the Lord endureth for ever. And this is the word which by the gospel is preached unto you.

R.S.V.

13 Therefore gird up your minds, be sober, set your hope fully upon the grace that is coming to you at the revelation of Jesus Christ. 14As obedient children, do not be conformed to the passions of your former ignorance, 15 but as he who called you is holy, be holy yourselves in all your conduct; 16 since it is written, "You shall be holy, for I am holy." 17And if you invoke as Father him who judges each one impartially according to his deeds, conduct yourselves with fear throughout the time of your exile. 18 You know that you were ransomed from the futile ways inherited from your fathers, not with perishable things such as silver or gold, 19 but with the precious blood of Christ, like that of a lamb without blemish or spot. 20 He was destined before the foundation of the world but was made manifest at the end of the times for your sake. 21 Through him you have confidence in God, who raised him from the dead and gave him glory, so that your faith and hope are in God.[d]

22 Having purified your souls by your obedience to the truth for a sincere love of the brethren, love one another earnestly from the heart. 23 You have been born anew, not of perishable seed but of imperishable, through the living and abiding word of God; 24 for

"All flesh is like grass
and all its glory like the flower of grass.
The grass withers, and the flower falls,
25 but the word of the Lord abides for ever."
That word is the good news which was preached to you.

2 Wherefore laying aside all malice, and all guile, and hypocrisies, and envies, and all evil speakings, 2As newborn babes, desire the sincere milk of the word, that ye may grow thereby: 3 If so be ye have tasted that the Lord *is* gracious. 4 To whom coming, *as unto* a living stone, disallowed indeed of men, but chosen of God, *and* precious, 5 Ye also, as lively stones, are built up a spiritual house, a holy priesthood, to offer up spiritual sacrifices, acceptable to God by Jesus Christ. 6 Wherefore also it is contained

2 So put away all malice and all guile and insincerity and envy and all slander. 2 Like newborn babes, long for the pure spiritual milk, that by it you may grow up to salvation; 3 for you have tasted the kindness of the Lord.

4 Come to him, to that living stone, rejected by men but in God's sight chosen and precious; 5 and like living stones be yourselves built into a spiritual house, to be a holy priesthood, to offer spiritual sacrifices acceptable to God through Jesus Christ. 6 For it stands in scripture:

[d] Or *so that your faith is hope in God.*

PHILLIPS

Consider soberly what God   *1. 13*
has done for you

So brace up your minds, and, as men who know what they are doing, rest the full weight of your hopes on the grace that will be yours when Jesus Christ reveals himself. Live as obedient children before God. Don't let your character be molded by the desires of your ignorant days, but be holy in every department of your lives, for the one who has called you is himself holy. The scripture says:

Ye shall be holy; for I am holy.

If you pray to a Father who judges men by their actions without the slightest favoritism, then you should spend the time of your stay here on earth with reverent fear. For you must realize all the time that you have been "ransomed" from the futile way of living passed on to you by your fathers' traditions, not with some money payment of transient value, but by the costly shedding of blood. The price was in fact the lifeblood of Christ, the unblemished and unstained lamb of sacrifice. It is true that God chose him to fulfill his part before the world was founded, but it was for your benefit that he was revealed in these last days—for you who found your faith in God through Christ. And God raised him from the dead and gave him unimaginable splendor, so that all your faith and hope might be centered in God.

Let your life match your   *1. 22*
high calling

Now that you have, by obeying the truth, made your souls clean enough for a genuine love of your fellows, see that you do love one another, fervently and from the heart. For you are sons of God now; the live, permanent Word of the living God has given you his own indestructible heredity. It is true that:

All flesh is as grass,
And all the glory thereof as the flower of
    grass.
The grass withereth, and the flower falleth:
But the word of the Lord abideth for ever.

The Word referred to, as far as you are concerned, is the message of the gospel that was preached to you.

Have done, then, with all evil and deceit, all pretense and jealousy and slander. You are babies, newborn in God's family, and you should be crying out for unadulterated spiritual milk to make you grow up to salvation! And so you will, if you have already tasted the goodness of the Lord.

To change the metaphor, you come to him, as living stones to the immensely valuable living stone (which men rejected but God chose), to be built up into a spiritual House of God, in which you, like holy priests, can offer those spiritual sacrifices which are acceptable to God by Jesus Christ. There is a passage to this effect in scripture, and it runs like this:

N.E.B.

You must therefore be like men stripped for action, perfectly self-controlled. Fix your hopes on the gift of grace which is to be yours when Jesus Christ is revealed. As obedient children, do not let your characters be shaped any longer by the desires you cherished in your days of ignorance. The One who called you is holy; like him, be holy in all your behaviour, because Scripture says, 'You shall be holy, for I am holy.'

If you say 'our Father' to the One who judges every man impartially on the record of his deeds, you must stand in awe of him while you live out your time on earth. Well you know that it was no perishable stuff, like gold or silver, that bought your freedom from the empty folly of your traditional ways. The price was paid in precious blood, as it were of a lamb without mark or blemish—the blood of Christ. He was predestined before the foundation of the world, and in this last period of time he was made manifest for your sake. Through him you have come to trust in God who raised him from the dead and gave him glory, and so your faith and hope are fixed on God.

Now that by obedience to the truth you have purified your souls until you feel sincere affection towards your brother Christians, love one another whole-heartedly with all your strength. You have been born anew, not of mortal parentage but of immortal, through the living and enduring word of God.[a] For (as Scripture says)

'All mortals are like grass;
All their splendour like the flower of the field;
The grass withers, the flower falls;
But the word of the Lord endures for evermore.'

And this 'word' is the word of the Gospel preached to you.

2 Then away with all malice and deceit, away with all pretence and jealousy and recrimination of every kind! Like the new-born infants you are, you must crave for pure milk (spiritual milk, I mean), so that you may thrive upon it to your souls' health. Surely you have tasted that the Lord is good.

So come to him, our living Stone—the stone rejected by men but choice and precious in the sight of God. Come, and let yourselves be built, as living stones, into a spiritual temple; become a holy priesthood,[b] to offer spiritual sacrifices acceptable to God through Jesus Christ. For it stands written:

[a] *Or* through the word of the living and enduring God. [b] *Or* a spiritual temple for the holy work of priesthood.

K.J.V.

in the Scripture, Behold, I lay in Sion a chief corner stone, elect, precious: and he that believeth on him shall not be confounded. 7 Unto you therefore which believe *he is* precious: but unto them which be disobedient, the stone which the builders disallowed, the same is made the head of the corner, 8And a stone of stumbling, and a rock of offence, *even to them* which stumble at the word, being disobedient: whereunto also they were appointed. 9 But ye *are* a chosen generation, a royal priesthood, a holy nation, a peculiar people; that ye should shew forth the praises of him who hath called you out of darkness into his marvellous light: 10 Which in time past *were* not a people, but *are* now the people of God: which had not obtained mercy, but now have obtained mercy. 11 Dearly beloved, I beseech *you* as strangers and pilgrims, abstain from fleshly lusts, which war against the soul; 12 Having your conversation honest among the Gentiles: that, whereas they speak against you as evil doers, they may by *your* good works, which they shall behold, glorify God in the day of visitation. 13 Submit yourselves to every ordinance of man for the Lord's sake: whether it be to the king, as supreme; 14 Or unto governors, as unto them that are sent by him for the punishment of evil doers, and for the praise of them that do well. 15 For so is the will of God, that with well doing ye may put to silence the ignorance of foolish men: 16As free, and not using *your* liberty for a cloak of maliciousness, but as the servants of God. 17 Honour all *men.* Love the brotherhood. Fear God. Honour the king. 18 Servants, *be* subject to *your* masters with all fear; not only to the good and gentle, but also to the froward. 19 For this *is* thankworthy, if a man for conscience toward God endure grief, suffering wrongfully. 20 For what glory *is it,* if, when ye be buffeted for your faults, ye shall take it patiently? but if, when ye do well, and suffer *for it,* ye take it patiently, this *is* acceptable with God. 21 For even hereunto were ye called: because Christ also suffered for us, leaving us an example, that ye should follow his steps: 22 Who did no sin, neither was guile found in his mouth: 23 Who, when he was reviled, reviled not again;

R.S.V.

"Behold, I am laying in Zion a stone, a cornerstone chosen and precious,
and he who believes in him will not be put to shame."
7 To you therefore who believe, he is precious, but for those who do not believe,
"The very stone which the builders rejected has become the head of the corner,"
8 and
"A stone that will make men stumble, a rock that will make them fall";
for they stumble because they disobey the word, as they were destined to do.
9 But you are a chosen race, a royal priesthood, a holy nation, God's own people,[e] that you may declare the wonderful deeds of him who called you out of darkness into his marvelous light. 10 Once you were no people but now you are God's people; once you had not received mercy but now you have received mercy.

11 Beloved, I beseech you as aliens and exiles to abstain from the passions of the flesh that wage war against your soul. 12 Maintain good conduct among the Gentiles, so that in case they speak against you as wrongdoers, they may see your good deeds and glorify God on the day of visitation.
13 Be subject for the Lord's sake to every human institution,[f] whether it be to the emperor as supreme, 14 or to governors as sent by him to punish those who do wrong and to praise those who do right. 15 For it is God's will that by doing right you should put to silence the ignorance of foolish men. 16 Live as free men, yet without using your freedom as a pretext for evil; but live as servants of God. 17 Honor all men. Love the brotherhood. Fear God. Honor the emperor.
18 Servants, be submissive to your masters with all respect, not only to the kind and gentle but also to the overbearing. 19 For one is approved if, mindful of God, he endures pain while suffering unjustly. 20 For what credit is it, if when you do wrong and are beaten for it you take it patiently? But if when you do right and suffer for it you take it patiently, you have God's approval. 21 For to this you have been called, because Christ also suffered for you, leaving you an example, that you should follow in his steps. 22 He committed no sin; no guile was found on his lips. 23 When he was reviled,

PHILLIPS

Behold I lay in Zion a chief cornerstone, elect, precious:
And he that believeth on him shall not be put to shame.

It is to you who believe in him that he is "precious," but to those who disobey God it is true that

The stone which the builders rejected,
The same was made the head of the corner.

And he is, to them,

A stone of stumbling and a rock of offense.

Yes, they stumble at the Word of God for in their hearts they are unwilling to obey it—which makes stumbling a foregone conclusion. But you are God's "chosen generation," his "royal priesthood," his "holy nation," his "peculiar people" —all the old titles of God's people now belong to you. It is for you now to demonstrate the goodness of him who has called you out of darkness into his amazing light. In the past you were not "a people" at all: now you are the people of God. In the past you had no experience of his mercy, but now it is intimately yours.

Your behavior to the outside world   2. 11

I beg you, as those whom I love, who live in this world as strangers and "temporary residents," to keep clear of the desires of your lower natures, for they are always at war with your souls. Your conduct among the surrounding peoples in your different countries should always be good and right, so that although they may in the usual way slander you as evildoers, yet when disasters come they may glorify God when they see how well you conduct yourselves.

Obey every man-made authority for the Lord's sake—whether it is the emperor, as the supreme ruler, or the governors whom he has appointed to punish evildoers and reward those who do good service. It is the will of God that you may thus silence the ill-informed criticisms of the foolish. As free men you should never use your freedom as an excuse for doing something that is wrong, for you are at all times the servants of God. You should have respect for everyone; you should love our brotherhood, fear God and honor the emperor.

A word to household servants   2. 18

You who are servants should submit to your masters with proper respect—not only to the good and kind, but also to the difficult. A man does something valuable when he endures pain, as in the sight of God, though he knows he is suffering unjustly. After all, it is no credit to you if you are patient in bearing a punishment which you have richly deserved! But if you do your duty and are punished for it and can still accept it patiently, you are doing something worthwhile in God's sight. Indeed this is your calling. For Christ suffered for you and left you a personal example, and wants you to follow in his steps. He was guilty of no sin nor of the slightest prevarication. Yet when he was insulted he offered no insult in return. When he suffered he

N.E.B.

'I lay in Zion a choice corner-stone of great worth.
The man who has faith in it will not be put to shame.'

The great worth of which it speaks is for you who have faith. For those who have no faith, the stone which the builders rejected has become not only the corner-stone,[a] but also 'a stone to trip over, a rock to stumble against'. They stumble when they disbelieve the Word. Such was their appointed lot!

But you are a chosen race, a royal priesthood, a dedicated nation, and a people claimed by God for his own, to proclaim the triumphs of him who has called you out of darkness into his marvellous light. You are now the people of God, who once were not his people; outside his mercy once, you have now received his mercy.

Dear friends, I beg you, as aliens in a foreign land, to abstain from the lusts of the flesh which are at war with the soul. Let all your behaviour be such as even pagans can recognize as good, and then, whereas they malign you as criminals now, they will come to see for themselves that you live good lives, and will give glory to God on the day when he comes to hold assize.

Submit yourselves to every human institution for the sake of the Lord, whether to the sovereign as supreme, or to the governor as his deputy for the punishment of criminals and the commendation of those who do right. For it is the will of God that by your good conduct you should put ignorance and stupidity to silence.

Live as free men; not however as though your freedom were there to provide a screen for wrongdoing, but as slaves in God's service. Give due honour to everyone: love to the brotherhood, reverence to God, honour to the sovereign.

Servants, accept the authority of your masters with all due submission, not only when they are kind and considerate, but even when they are perverse. For it is a fine[b] thing if a man endure the pain of undeserved suffering because God is in his thoughts. What credit is there in fortitude when you have done wrong and are beaten for it? But when you have behaved well and suffer for it, your fortitude is a fine thing[c] in the sight of God. To that you were called, because Christ suffered[d] on your behalf, and thereby left you an example; it is for you to follow in his steps. He committed no sin, he was convicted of no falsehood; when he was abused he did not retort with abuse, when he suffered he uttered no

[a] Or the apex of the building. [b] Or creditable.
[c] Or is creditable. [d] Some witnesses read died.

K.J.V.

when he suffered, he threatened not; but committed *himself* to him that judgeth righteously: 24 Who his own self bare our sins in his own body on the tree, that we, being dead to sins, should live unto righteousness: by whose stripes ye were healed. 25 For ye were as sheep going astray; but are now returned unto the Shepherd and Bishop of your souls.

3 Likewise, ye wives, *be* in subjection to your own husbands; that, if any obey not the word, they also may without the word be won by the conversation of the wives; 2 While they behold your chaste conversation *coupled* with fear. 3 Whose adorning, let it not be that outward *adorning* of plaiting the hair, and of wearing of gold, or of putting on of apparel; 4 But *let it be* the hidden man of the heart, in that which is not corruptible, *even the ornament* of a meek and quiet spirit, which is in the sight of God of great price. 5 For after this manner in the old time the holy women also, who trusted in God, adorned themselves, being in subjection unto their own husbands: 6 Even as Sarah obeyed Abraham, calling him lord: whose daughters ye are, as long as ye do well, and are not afraid with any amazement. 7 Likewise, ye husbands, dwell with *them* according to knowledge, giving honour unto the wife, as unto the weaker vessel, and as being heirs together of the grace of life; that your prayers be not hindered. 8 Finally, *be* ye all of one mind, having compassion one of another; love as brethren, *be* pitiful, *be* courteous: 9 Not rendering evil for evil, or railing for railing: but contrariwise blessing; knowing that ye are thereunto called, that ye should inherit a blessing. 10 For he that will love life, and see good days, let him refrain his tongue from evil, and his lips that they speak no guile: 11 Let him eschew evil, and do good; let him seek peace, and ensue it. 12 For the eyes of the Lord *are* over the righteous, and his ears *are open* unto their prayers: but the face of the Lord *is* against them that do evil. 13 And who *is* he that will harm you, if ye be followers of that which is good? 14 But and if ye suffer for righteousness' sake, happy *are ye:* and be not afraid of their terror, neither be troubled; 15 But sanctify the Lord God in your hearts: and *be* ready

R.S.V.

he did not revile in return; when he suffered, he did not threaten; but he trusted to him who judges justly. 24 He himself bore our sins in his body on the tree,[g] that we might die to sin and live to righteousness. By his wounds you have been healed. 25 For you were straying like sheep, but have now returned to the Shepherd and Guardian of your souls.

3 Likewise you wives, be submissive to your husbands, so that some, though they do not obey the word, may be won without a word by the behavior of their wives, 2 when they see your reverent and chaste behavior. 3 Let not yours be the outward adorning with braiding of hair, decoration of gold, and wearing of robes, 4 but let it be the hidden person of the heart with the imperishable jewel of a gentle and quiet spirit, which in God's sight is very precious. 5 So once the holy women who hoped in God used to adorn themselves and were submissive to their husbands, 6 as Sarah obeyed Abraham, calling him lord. And you are now her children if you do right and let nothing terrify you.

7 Likewise you husbands, live considerately with your wives, bestowing honor on the woman as the weaker sex, since you are joint heirs of the grace of life, in order that your prayers may not be hindered.

8 Finally, all of you, have unity of spirit, sympathy, love of the brethren, a tender heart and a humble mind. 9 Do not return evil for evil or reviling for reviling; but on the contrary bless, for to this you have been called, that you may obtain a blessing.
10 For
　　"He that would love life
　　　and see good days,
　　let him keep his tongue from evil
　　　and his lips from speaking guile;
　11 let him turn away from evil and do right;
　　　let him seek peace and pursue it.
　12 For the eyes of the Lord are upon the
　　　righteous,
　　and his ears are open to their prayer.
　　But the face of the Lord is against those
　　　that do evil."

13 Now who is there to harm you if you are zealous for what is right? 14 But even if you do suffer for righteousness' sake, you will be blessed. Have no fear of them, nor be troubled, 15 but in your hearts reverence Christ as Lord. Always be prepared to make a defense to any

---

[g] Or *carried up . . . to the tree.*

made no threats of revenge. He simply committed his cause to the one who judges fairly. And he personally bore our sins in his own body on the cross, so that we might be dead to sin and be alive to all that is good. It was the suffering that he bore which has healed you. You had wandered away like so many sheep, but now you have returned to the shepherd and guardian of your souls.

A word to married Christians *3. 1*

In the same spirit you married women should adapt yourselves to your husbands, so that even if they do not obey the Word of God they may be won to God without any word being spoken, simply by seeing the pure and reverent behavior of you, their wives. Your beauty should not be dependent on an elaborate coiffure, or on the wearing of jewelry or fine clothes, but on the inner personality—the unfading loveliness of a calm and gentle spirit, a thing very precious in the eyes of God. This was the secret of the beauty of the holy women of ancient times who trusted in God and were submissive to their husbands. Sarah, you will remember, obeyed Abraham and called him her lord. And you have become, as it were, her true descendants today as long as you too live good lives and do not give way to hysterical fears.

Similarly, you husbands should try to understand the wives you live with, honoring them as physically weaker yet equally heirs with you of the grace of life. If you don't do this, you will find it impossible to pray properly.

Be good to one another— *3. 8*
and to all men

To sum up, you should all be of one mind living like brothers with true love and sympathy for one another, generous and courteous at all times. Never pay back a bad turn with a bad turn or an insult with another insult, but on the contrary pay back with good. For this is your calling—to do good and one day to inherit all the goodness of God. For

He that would love life,
And see good days,
Let him refrain his tongue from evil,
And his lips that they speak no guile:
And let him turn away from evil, and do good;
Let him seek peace and pursue it.
For the eyes of the Lord are upon the righteous,
And his ears unto their supplication:
But the face of the Lord is against them that do evil.

Do good, even if you suffer for it *3. 13*

After all, who in the ordinary way is likely to injure you for being enthusiastic for good? And if it should happen that you suffer "for righteousness' sake," that is a privilege. You need neither fear their threats nor worry about them; simply concentrate on being completely devoted to Christ in your hearts. Be ready at any time to

threats, but committed his cause to the One who judges justly. In his own person he carried our sins to[a] the gallows, so that we might cease to live for sin and begin to live for righteousness. By his wounds you have been healed. You were straying like sheep, but now you have turned towards the Shepherd and Guardian of your souls.

3 In the same way you women must accept the authority of your husbands, so that if there are any of them who disbelieve the Gospel they may be won over, without a word being said, by observing the chaste and reverent behaviour of their wives. Your beauty should reside, not in outward adornment—the braiding of the hair, or jewellery, or dress—but in the inmost centre of your being, with its imperishable ornament, a gentle, quiet spirit, which is of high value in the sight of God. Thus it was among God's people in days of old: the women who fixed their hopes on him adorned themselves by submission to their husbands. Such was Sarah, who obeyed Abraham and called him 'my master'. Her children you have now become, if you do good and show no fear.

In the same way, you husbands must conduct your married life with understanding: pay honour to the woman's body, not only because it is weaker, but also because you share together in the grace of God which gives you life. Then your prayers will not be hindered.

To sum up: be one in thought and feeling, all of you; be full of brotherly affection, kindly and humble-minded. Do not repay wrong with wrong, or abuse with abuse; on the contrary, retaliate with blessing, for a blessing is the inheritance to which you yourselves have been called.

'Whoever loves life and would see good days
Must restrain his tongue from evil
And his lips from deceit;
Must turn from wrong and do good,
Seek peace and pursue it.
For the Lord's eyes are turned towards the righteous,
His ears are open to their prayers;
But the Lord's face is set against wrong-doers.'

Who is going to do you wrong if you are devoted to what is good? And yet if you should suffer for your virtues, you may count yourselves happy. Have no fear of them:[b] do not be perturbed, but hold the Lord Christ in reverence in your hearts.[c] Be always ready with your defence

[a] Or on. [b] Or Do not fear what they fear. [c] Or hold Christ in reverence in your hearts, as Lord.

K.J.V.

always to *give* an answer to every man that asketh you a reason of the hope that is in you, with meekness and fear: 16 Having a good conscience; that, whereas they speak evil of you, as of evil doers, they may be ashamed that falsely accuse your good conversation in Christ. 17 For *it is* better, if the will of God be so, that ye suffer for well doing, than for evil doing. 18 For Christ also hath once suffered for sins, the just for the unjust, that he might bring us to God, being put to death in the flesh, but quickened by the Spirit: 19 By which also he went and preached unto the spirits in prison; 20 Which sometime were disobedient, when once the longsuffering of God waited in the days of Noah, while the ark was a preparing, wherein few, that is, eight souls were saved by water. 21 The like figure whereunto *even* baptism doth also now save us, (not the putting away of the filth of the flesh, but the answer of a good conscience toward God,) by the resurrection of Jesus Christ: 22 Who is gone into heaven, and is on the right hand of God; angels and authorities and powers being made subject unto him.

4 Forasmuch then as Christ hath suffered for us in the flesh, arm yourselves likewise with the same mind: for he that hath suffered in the flesh hath ceased from sin; 2 That he no longer should live the rest of *his* time in the flesh to the lusts of men, but to the will of God. 3 For the time past of *our* life may suffice us to have wrought the will of the Gentiles, when we walked in lasciviousness, lusts, excess of wine, revellings, banquetings, and abominable idolatries: 4 Wherein they think it strange that ye run not with *them* to the same excess of riot, speaking evil of *you:* 5 Who shall give account to him that is ready to judge the quick and the dead. 6 For, for this cause was the gospel preached also to them that are dead; that they might be judged according to men in the flesh, but live according to God in the spirit. 7 But the end of all things is at hand: be ye therefore sober, and watch unto prayer. 8 And above all things have fervent charity among yourselves: for charity shall cover the multitude of sins. 9 Use hospitality one to another without grudging. 10 As every man hath received the gift, *even so* minister the same one to another, as good stewards of the manifold grace of God. 11 If any man speak, *let him speak* as the oracles of God; if any man minister, *let him do it* as of the ability which God giveth; that God in all things may be glorified through Jesus Christ: to whom be praise

R.S.V.

one who calls you to account for the hope that is in you, yet do it with gentleness and reverence; 16 and keep your conscience clear, so that, when you are abused, those who revile your good behavior in Christ may be put to shame. 17 For it is better to suffer for doing right, if that should be God's will, than for doing wrong. 18 For Christ also died *[h]* for sins once for all, the righteous for the unrighteous, that he might bring us to God, being put to death in the flesh but made alive in the spirit; 19 in which he went and preached to the spirits in prison, 20 who formerly did not obey, when God's patience waited in the days of Noah, during the building of the ark, in which a few, that is, eight persons, were saved through water. 21 Baptism, which corresponds to this, now saves you, not as a removal of dirt from the body but as an appeal to God for a clear conscience, through the resurrection of Jesus Christ, 22 who has gone into heaven and is at the right hand of God, with angels, authorities, and powers subject to him.

4 Since therefore Christ suffered in the flesh,*[i]* arm yourselves with the same thought, for whoever has suffered in the flesh has ceased from sin, 2 so as to live for the rest of the time in the flesh no longer by human passions but by the will of God. 3 Let the time that is past suffice for doing what the Gentiles like to do, living in licentiousness, passions, drunkenness, revels, carousing, and lawless idolatry. 4 They are surprised that you do not now join them in the same wild profligacy, and they abuse you; 5 but they will give account to him who is ready to judge the living and the dead. 6 For this is why the gospel was preached even to the dead, that though judged in the flesh like men, they might live in the spirit like God.

7 The end of all things is at hand; therefore keep sane and sober for your prayers. 8 Above all hold unfailing your love for one another, since love covers a multitude of sins. 9 Practice hospitality ungrudgingly to one another. 10 As each has received a gift, employ it for one another, as good stewards of God's varied grace: 11 whoever speaks, as one who utters oracles of God; whoever renders service, as one who renders it by the strength which God supplies; in order that in everything God may be glorified through Jesus Christ. To him belong glory and dominion for ever and ever. Amen.

[h] Other ancient authorities read *suffered.* [i] Other ancient authorities add *for us;* some *for you.*

give a quiet and reverent answer to any man who wants a reason for the hope that you have within you. Make sure that your conscience is perfectly clear, so that if men should speak slanderously of you as rogues they may come to feel ashamed of themselves for libeling your good Christian behavior.

If it is the will of God that you should suffer it is really better to suffer unjustly than because you have deserved it. Remember that Christ the just suffered for us the unjust, to bring us to God. That meant the death of his body, but he came to life again in the spirit. It was in the spirit that he went and preached to the imprisoned souls of those who had been disobedient in the days of Noah—the days of God's great patience during the period of the building of the ark, in which eventually only eight souls were saved in the flood. And I cannot help pointing out what a perfect illustration this is of the way you have been admitted to the safety of the Christian "ark" by baptism, which means, of course, far more than the mere washing of a dirty body: it means the ability to face God with a clear conscience. For there is in every true baptism the virtue of Christ's rising from the dead. And he has now entered Heaven and is at God's right hand, with all angels, authorities and powers subservient to him.

whenever you are called to account for the hope that is in you, but make that defence with modesty and respect. Keep your conscience clear, so that when you are abused, those who malign your Christian conduct may be put to shame. It is better to suffer for well-doing, if such should be the will of God, than for doing wrong. For Christ also died *a* for our sins*b* once and for all. He, the just, suffered for the unjust, to bring us to God.

In the body he was put to death; in the spirit he was brought to life. And in the spirit he went and made his proclamation to the imprisoned spirits. They had refused obedience long ago, while God waited patiently in the days of Noah and the building of the ark, and in the ark a few persons, eight in all, were brought to safety through the water. This water prefigured the water of baptism through which you are now brought to safety. Baptism is not the washing away of bodily pollution, but the appeal made to God by a good conscience; and it brings salvation through the resurrection of Jesus Christ, who entered heaven after receiving the submission of angelic authorities and powers, and is now at the right hand of God.

Following Christ will mean pain   4. 1

Since Christ had to suffer physically for you, you must fortify yourselves with the same inner attitude that he must have had. You must realize that to be dead to sin inevitably means pain, and you should not therefore spend the rest of your time here on earth indulging your physical nature, but in doing the will of God. Our past life may have been good enough for pagan purposes, though it meant sensuality, lust, drunkenness, orgies, carousals and worshiping forbidden gods. Indeed your former companions may think it very queer that you will no longer join with them in their riotous excesses, and accordingly say all sorts of unpleasant things about you. Don't worry: they are the ones who will have to explain their behavior before the one who is prepared to judge all men, whether living or dead. (For that is why the dead also had the gospel preached to them—that it might judge the lives they lived as men and give them also the opportunity to share the eternal life of God in the spirit.)

4 Remembering that Christ endured bodily suffering, you must arm yourselves with a temper of mind like his. When a man has thus endured bodily suffering he has finished with sin, and for the rest of his days on earth he may live, not for the things that men desire, but for what God wills. You had time enough in the past to do all the things that men want to do in the pagan world. Then you lived in licence and debauchery, drunkenness, riot, and tippling, and the forbidden worship of idols. Now, when you no longer plunge with them into all this reckless dissipation, they cannot understand it, and they vilify you accordingly; but they shall answer for it to him who stands ready to pass judgement on the living and the dead. Why was the Gospel preached to those who are dead? In order that, although in the body they received the sentence common to men, they might in the spirit be alive with the life of God.

Your attitude in these last days   4. 7

We are near the end of all things now, and you should therefore be calm, self-controlled men of prayer. Above everything else be sure that you have real deep love for one another, remembering how love can "cover a multitude of sins." Be hospitable to one another without secretly wishing you hadn't got to be! Serve one another with the particular gifts God has given each of you, as faithful dispensers of the magnificently varied grace of God. If any of you is a preacher then he should preach his message as from God. And in whatever way a man serves the Church he should do it recognizing the fact that God gives him his ability, so that God may be glorified in everything through Jesus Christ. To him belong glory and power for ever, amen!

The end of all things is upon us, so you must lead an ordered and sober life, given to prayer. Above all, keep your love for one another at full strength, because love cancels innumerable sins. Be hospitable to one another without complaining. Whatever gift each of you may have received, use it in service to one another, like good stewards dispensing the grace of God in its varied forms. Are you a speaker? Speak as if you uttered oracles of God. Do you give service? Give it as in the strength which God supplies. In all things so act that the glory may be God's through Jesus Christ; to him belong glory and power for ever and ever. Amen.

[a] *Some witnesses read* suffered. [b] *Some witnesses read* for sins; *others read* for us.

K.J.V.

and dominion for ever and ever. Amen. 12 Beloved, think it not strange concerning the fiery trial which is to try you, as though some strange thing happened unto you: 13 But rejoice, inasmuch as ye are partakers of Christ's sufferings; that, when his glory shall be revealed, ye may be glad also with exceeding joy. 14 If ye be reproached for the name of Christ, happy *are ye;* for the Spirit of glory and of God resteth upon you: on their part he is evil spoken of, but on your part he is glorified. 15 But let none of you suffer as a murderer, or *as* a thief, or *as* an evil doer, or as a busybody in other men's matters. 16 Yet if *any man suffer* as a Christian, let him not be ashamed; but let him glorify God on this behalf. 17 For the time *is come* that judgment must begin at the house of God: and if *it* first *begin* at us, what shall the end *be* of them that obey not the gospel of God? 18 And if the righteous scarcely be saved, where shall the ungodly and the sinner appear? 19 Wherefore, let them that suffer according to the will of God commit the keeping of their souls *to him* in well doing, as unto a faithful Creator.

5 The elders which are among you I exhort, who am also an elder, and a witness of the sufferings of Christ, and also a partaker of the glory that shall be revealed: 2 Feed the flock of God which is among you, taking the oversight *thereof,* not by constraint, but willingly; not for filthy lucre, but of a ready mind; 3 Neither as being lords over *God's* heritage, but being ensamples to the flock. 4 And when the chief Shepherd shall appear, ye shall receive a crown of glory that fadeth not away. 5 Likewise, ye younger, submit yourselves unto the elder. Yea, all *of you* be subject one to another, and be clothed with humility: for God resisteth the proud, and giveth grace to the humble. 6 Humble yourselves therefore under the mighty hand of God, that he may exalt you in due time: 7 Casting all your care upon him; for he careth for you. 8 Be sober, be vigilant; because your adversary the devil, as a roaring lion, walketh about, seeking whom he may devour: 9 Whom resist steadfast in the faith, knowing that the same afflictions are accomplished in your breth-

R.S.V.

12 Beloved, do not be surprised at the fiery ordeal which comes upon you to prove you, as though something strange were happening to you. 13 But rejoice in so far as you share Christ's sufferings, that you may also rejoice and be glad when his glory is revealed. 14 If you are reproached for the name of Christ, you are blessed, because the spirit of glory[j] and of God rests upon you. 15 But let none of you suffer as a murderer, or a thief, or a wrongdoer, or a mischief-maker; 16 yet if one suffers as a Christian, let him not be ashamed, but under that name let him glorify God. 17 For the time has come for judgment to begin with the household of God; and if it begins with us, what will be the end of those who do not obey the gospel of God? 18 And

"If the righteous man is scarcely saved,
   where will the impious and sinner appear?"
19 Therefore let those who suffer according to God's will do right and entrust their souls to a faithful Creator.

5 So I exhort the elders among you, as a fellow elder and a witness of the sufferings of Christ as well as a partaker in the glory that is to be revealed. 2 Tend the flock of God that is your charge,[k] not by constraint but willingly,[l] not for shameful gain but eagerly, 3 not as domineering over those in your charge but being examples to the flock. 4 And when the chief Shepherd is manifested you will obtain the unfading crown of glory. 5 Likewise you that are younger be subject to the elders. Clothe yourselves, all of you, with humility toward one another, for "God opposes the proud, but gives grace to the humble." 6 Humble yourselves therefore under the mighty hand of God, that in due time he may exalt you. 7 Cast all your anxieties on him, for he cares about you. 8 Be sober, be watchful. Your adversary the devil prowls around like a roaring lion, seeking some one to devour. 9 Resist him, firm in your faith, knowing that the same experience of suffering is required of your

[j] Other ancient authorities insert *and of power.*
[k] Other ancient authorities add *exercising the oversight.* [l] Other ancient authorities add *as God would have you.*

PHILLIPS

N.E.B.

Your attitude to persecution   *4. 12*

And now, dear friends of mine, I beg you not to be unduly alarmed at the fiery ordeals which come to test your faith, as though this were some abnormal experience. You should be glad, because it means that you are called to share Christ's sufferings. One day, when he shows himself in full splendor to men, you will be filled with the most tremendous joy. If you are reproached for being Christ's followers, that is a great privilege, for you can be sure that God's Spirit of glory is resting upon you. But take care that none of your number suffers as a murderer or a thief, a rogue or a spy! If he suffers as a Christian he has nothing to be ashamed of and may glorify God in Christ's name.

The time has evidently arrived for God's judgment to begin, and it is beginning at his own House. And if it starts with us, what is it going to mean to those who refuse to obey the gospel of God? If even the good man is only just saved, what will be the fate of the wicked and the sinner? And if it is true that we are living in a time of judgment, then those who suffer according to God's will can only commit their souls to their faithful creator, and go on doing all the good they can.

My dear friends, do not be bewildered by the fiery ordeal that is upon you, as though it were something extraordinary. It gives you a share in Christ's sufferings, and that is cause for joy; and when his glory is revealed, your joy will be triumphant. If Christ's name is flung in your teeth as an insult, count yourselves happy, because then that glorious Spirit which is the Spirit of God is resting upon you. If you suffer, it must not be for murder, theft, or sorcery,[a] nor for infringing the rights of others. But if anyone suffers as a Christian, he should feel it no disgrace, but confess that name to the honour of God.

The time has come for the judgement to begin; it is beginning with God's own household. And if it is starting with you, how will it end for those who refuse to obey the gospel of God? And if it is hard enough for the righteous to be saved, what will become of the impious and sinful? So even those who suffer, if it be according to God's will, should commit their souls to him—by doing good; their Maker will not fail them.

A word to your leaders   *5. 1*

Now may I who am myself an elder say a word to you my fellow elders? I speak as one who actually saw Christ suffer, and as one who will share with you the glories that are to be unfolded to us. I urge you then to see that your "flock of God" is properly fed and cared for. Accept the responsibility of looking after them willingly and not because you feel you can't get out of it, doing your work not for what you can make, but because you are really concerned for their well-being. You should aim not at being "little tin gods" but as examples of Christian living in the eyes of the flock committed to your charge. And then, when the chief shepherd reveals himself, you will receive that crown of glory which cannot fade.

5 And now I appeal to the elders of your community, as a fellow-elder and a witness of Christ's sufferings, and also a partaker in the splendour that is to be revealed. Tend that flock of God whose shepherds you are, and do it, not under compulsion, but of your own free will, as God would have it; not for gain but out of sheer devotion; not tyrannizing over those who are allotted to your care, but setting an example to the flock. And then, when the Head Shepherd appears, you will receive for your own the unfading garland of glory.

In the same way you younger men must be subordinate to your elders. Indeed, all of you should wrap yourselves in the garment of humility towards each other, because God sets his face against the arrogant but favours the humble. Humble yourselves then under God's mighty hand, and he will lift you up in due time. Cast all your cares on him, for you are his charge.

Learn to be humble and to trust   *5. 5*

You younger members must also submit to the elders. Indeed all of you should defer to one another and wear the "overall" of humility in serving each other. God is always against the proud, but he is always ready to give grace to the humble. So, humble yourselves under God's strong hand, and in his own good time he will lift you up. You can throw the whole weight of your anxieties upon him, for you are his personal concern.

Awake! be on the alert! Your enemy the devil, like a roaring lion, prowls round looking for someone to devour. Stand up to him, firm in faith, and remember that your brother Christians are going through the same kinds of suffering

Resist the devil: you are   *5. 8*
in God's hands

Be self-controlled and vigilant always, for your enemy the devil is always about, prowling like a lion roaring for its prey. Resist him, standing firm in your faith, and remember that the strain is the same for all your fellow Christians in other

[a] *Or* other crime.

K.J.V.

ren that are in the world. 10 But the God of all grace, who hath called us unto his eternal glory by Christ Jesus, after that ye have suffered a while, make you perfect, stablish, strengthen, settle *you.* 11 To him *be* glory and dominion for ever and ever. Amen. 12 By Silvanus, a faithful brother unto you, as I suppose, I have written briefly, exhorting, and testifying that this is the true grace of God wherein ye stand. 13 The *church that is* at Babylon, elected together with *you,* saluteth you; and *so doth* Marcus my son. 14 Greet ye one another with a kiss of charity. Peace *be* with you all that are in Christ Jesus. Amen.

R.S.V.

brotherhood throughout the world. 10And after you have suffered a little while, the God of all grace, who has called you to his eternal glory in Christ, will himself restore, establish, and strengthen[m] you. 11 To him be the dominion for ever and ever. Amen.

12 By Silvanus, a faithful brother as I regard him, I have written briefly to you, exhorting and declaring that this is the true grace of God; stand fast in it. 13 She who is at Babylon, who is likewise chosen, sends you greetings; and so does my son Mark. 14 Greet one another with the kiss of love.

Peace to all of you that are in Christ.

[m] Other ancient authorities read *restore, establish, strengthen and settle.*

PHILLIPS

parts of the world. And after you have borne these sufferings a very little while, the God of all grace, who has called you to share his eternal splendor through Christ, will himself make you whole and secure and strong. All power is his for ever and ever, amen!

Final greetings   5. 12

I am sending this short letter by Silvanus, whom I know to be a faithful brother, to stimulate your faith and assure you that the above words represent the true grace of God. See that you stand fast in that grace!

Your sister-church here in "Babylon" sends you greetings, and so does my son Mark. Give one another a handshake all round as a sign of love.

Peace be to all true Christians.

                                                    PETER

N.E.B.

while they are in the world. And the God of all grace, who called you into his eternal glory in Christ, will himself, after your brief suffering, restore, establish, and strengthen you on a firm foundation. He holds dominion for ever and ever. Amen.

I write you this brief appeal through Silvanus, our trusty brother as I hold him, adding my testimony that this is the true grace of God. In this stand fast.

Greetings from her who dwells in Babylon, chosen by God like you, and from my son Mark. Greet one another with the kiss of love.

Peace to you all who belong to Christ!

K.J.V.

THE SECOND
EPISTLE GENERAL
OF
PETER

1 Simon Peter, a servant and an apostle of Jesus Christ, to them that have obtained like precious faith with us through the righteousness of God and our Saviour Jesus Christ: 2 Grace and peace be multiplied unto you through the knowledge of God, and of Jesus our Lord, 3 According as his divine power hath given unto us all things that *pertain* unto life and godliness, through the knowledge of him that hath called us to glory and virtue: 4 Whereby are given unto us exceeding great and precious promises; that by these ye might be partakers of the divine nature, having escaped the corruption that is in the world through lust. 5 And besides this, giving all diligence, add to your faith virtue; and to virtue, knowledge; 6 And to knowledge, temperance; and to temperance, patience; and to patience, godliness; 7 And to godliness, brotherly kindness; and to brotherly kindness, charity. 8 For if these things be in you, and abound, they make *you that ye shall* neither *be* barren nor unfruitful in the knowledge of our Lord Jesus Christ. 9 But he that lacketh these things is blind, and cannot see afar off, and hath forgotten that he was purged from his old sins. 10 Wherefore the rather, brethren, give diligence to make your calling and election sure: for if ye do these things, ye shall never fall: 11 For so an entrance shall be ministered unto you abundantly into the everlasting kingdom of our Lord and Saviour Jesus Christ. 12 Wherefore I will not be negligent to put you always in remembrance of these things, though ye know *them,* and be established in the present truth. 13 Yea, I think it meet, as long as I am in this tabernacle, to stir you up by putting *you* in remembrance; 14 Knowing that shortly I must put off *this* my tabernacle, even as our Lord Jesus Christ hath shewed me. 15 Moreover I will endeavour that ye may be able after my decease to have these things al-

R.S.V.

THE
SECOND LETTER OF
PETER

1 Simon Peter, a servant and apostle of Jesus Christ,
To those who have obtained a faith of equal standing with ours in the righteousness of our God and Savior Jesus Christ:[a]
2 May grace and peace be multiplied to you in the knowledge of God and of Jesus our Lord.

3 His divine power has granted to us all things that pertain to life and godliness, through the knowledge of him who called us to[b] his own glory and excellence, 4 by which he has granted to us his precious and very great promises, that through these you may escape from the corruption that is in the world because of passion, and become partakers of the divine nature. 5 For this very reason make every effort to supplement your faith with virtue, and virtue with knowledge, 6 and knowledge with self-control, and self-control with steadfastness, and steadfastness with godliness, 7 and godliness with brotherly affection, and brotherly affection with love. 8 For if these things are yours and abound, they keep you from being ineffective or unfruitful in the knowledge of our Lord Jesus Christ. 9 For whoever lacks these things is blind and shortsighted and has forgotten that he was cleansed from his old sins. 10 Therefore, brethren, be the more zealous to confirm your call and election, for if you do this you will never fall; 11 so there will be richly provided for you an entrance into the eternal kingdom of our Lord and Savior Jesus Christ.
12 Therefore I intend always to remind you of these things, though you know them and are established in the truth that you have. 13 I think it right, as long as I am in this body,[c] to arouse you by way of reminder, 14 since I know that the putting off of my body[c] will be soon, as our Lord Jesus Christ showed me. 15 And I will see to it that after my departure you may be able at any time to recall these things.

[a] Or *of our God and the Savior Jesus Christ.*
[b] Or *by.* [c] Greek *tent.*

THE
SECOND LETTER OF
PETER

THE
SECOND LETTER OF
PETER

The Remedy for Doubt

Simon Peter, a servant and messenger of Jesus Christ, sends this letter to those who have been given a faith as valuable as ours in the righteousness of our God, and Savior Jesus Christ. May you know more and more of grace and peace as your knowledge of God and Jesus our Lord grows deeper.

God has done his part: *1. 3*
see that you do yours

He has by his own action given us everything that is necessary for living the truly good life, in allowing us to know the one who has called us to him, through his own glorious goodness. It is through him that God's greatest and most precious promises have become available to us men, making it possible for you to escape the inevitable disintegration that lust produces in the world and to share God's essential nature. For this very reason you must do your utmost from your side, and see that your faith carries with it real goodness of life. Your goodness must be accompanied by knowledge, your knowledge by self-control, your self-control by the ability to endure. Your endurance too must always be accompanied by devotion to God; that in turn must have in it the quality of brotherliness, and your brotherliness must lead on to Christian love. If you have these qualities existing and growing in you then it means that knowing our Lord Jesus Christ has not made your lives either complacent or unproductive. The man whose life fails to exhibit these qualities is shortsighted—he can no longer see the reason why he was cleansed from his former sins.

Set your minds, then, on endorsing by your conduct the fact that God has called and chosen you. If you go along the lines I have indicated above, there is no reason why you should stumble, and if you have lived the sort of life I have recommended God will open wide to you the gates of the eternal kingdom of our Lord and savior Jesus Christ.

Truth will bear repetition   *1. 12*

I shall not fail to remind you of things like this although you know them and are already established in the truth. I consider it my duty, as long as I live in the temporary dwelling of this body, to stimulate you by these reminders. I know that I shall have to leave this body at very short notice, as our Lord Jesus Christ made clear to me. Consequently I shall make the most of every opportunity, so that after I am gone you will remember these things.

From Simeon Peter, servant and apostle of Jesus Christ, to those who through the justice of our God and Saviour Jesus Christ share our faith and enjoy equal privilege with ourselves.

Grace and peace be yours in fullest measure, through the knowledge of God and Jesus our Lord.

His divine power has bestowed on us everything that makes for life and true religion, enabling us to know the One who called us by his own splendour and might. Through this might and splendour he has given us his promises, great beyond all price, and through them you may escape the corruption with which lust has infected the world, and come to share in the very being of God.

With all this in view, you should try your hardest to supplement your faith with virtue, virtue with knowledge, knowledge with self-control, self-control with fortitude, fortitude with piety, piety with brotherly kindness, and brotherly kindness with love.

These are gifts which, if you possess and foster them, will keep you from being either useless or barren in the knowledge of our Lord Jesus Christ. The man who lacks them is short-sighted and blind; he has forgotten how he was cleansed from his former sins. All the more then, my friends, exert yourselves to clinch God's choice and calling of you. If you behave so, you will never come to grief. Thus you will be afforded full and free admission into the eternal kingdom of our Lord and Saviour Jesus Christ.

And so I will not hesitate to remind you of this again and again, although you know it and are well grounded in the truth that has already reached you. Yet I think it right to keep refreshing your memory so long as I still lodge in this body. I know that very soon I must leave it; indeed our Lord Jesus Christ has told me so.[a] But I will see to it that after I am gone you will have means of remembering these things at all times.

---

[a] *Or* I must leave it, as our Lord Jesus Christ told me.

K.J.V.

ways in remembrance. 16 For we have not followed cunningly devised fables, when we made known unto you the power and coming of our Lord Jesus Christ, but were eyewitnesses of his majesty. 17 For he received from God the Father honour and glory, when there came such a voice to him from the excellent glory, This is my beloved Son, in whom I am well pleased. 18And this voice which came from heaven we heard, when we were with him in the holy mount. 19 We have also a more sure word of prophecy; whereunto ye do well that ye take heed, as unto a light that shineth in a dark place, until the day dawn, and the daystar arise in your hearts: 20 Knowing this first, that no prophecy of the Scripture is of any private interpretation. 21 For the prophecy came not in old time by the will of man: but holy men of God spake *as they were* moved by the Holy Ghost.

2 But there were false prophets also among the people, even as there shall be false teachers among you, who privily shall bring in damnable heresies, even denying the Lord that bought them, and bring upon themselves swift destruction. 2And many shall follow their pernicious ways; by reason of whom the way of truth shall be evil spoken of. 3And through covetousness shall they with feigned words make merchandise of you: whose judgment now of a long time lingereth not, and their damnation slumbereth not. 4 For if God spared not the angels that sinned, but cast *them* down to hell, and delivered *them* into chains of darkness, to be reserved unto judgment; 5And spared not the old world, but saved Noah the eighth *person*, a preacher of righteousness, bringing in the flood upon the world of the ungodly; 6And turning the cities of Sodom and Gomorrah into ashes condemned *them* with an overthrow, making *them* an ensample unto those that after should live ungodly; 7And delivered just Lot, vexed with the filthy conversation of the wicked: 8 (For that righteous man dwelling among them, in seeing and hearing, vexed *his* righteous soul from day to day with *their* unlawful deeds:) 9 The Lord knoweth how to deliver the godly out of temptation, and to reserve the unjust unto the day of judgment to be punished: 10 But chiefly them that walk after the flesh in the lust of uncleanness, and despise government. Presumptuous *are they*, selfwilled, they are not afraid to speak evil of dignities. 11 Whereas angels, which are greater in power and might, bring not railing accusation against them before the Lord.

R.S.V.

16 For we did not follow cleverly devised myths when we made known to you the power and coming of our Lord Jesus Christ, but we were eyewitnesses of his majesty. 17 For when he received honor and glory from God the Father and the voice was borne to him by the Majestic Glory, "This is my beloved Son,*d* with whom I am well pleased," 18 we heard this voice borne from heaven, for we were with him on the holy mountain. 19And we have the prophetic word made more sure. You will do well to pay attention to this as to a lamp shining in a dark place, until the day dawns and the morning star rises in your hearts. 20 First of all you must understand this, that no prophecy of scripture is a matter of one's own interpretation, 21 because no prophecy ever came by the impulse of man, but men moved by the Holy Spirit spoke from God.*e*

2 But false prophets also arose among the people, just as there will be false teachers among you, who will secretly bring in destructive heresies, even denying the Master who bought them, bringing upon themselves swift destruction. 2And many will follow their licentiousness, and because of them the way of truth will be reviled. 3And in their greed they will exploit you with false words; from of old their condemnation has not been idle, and their destruction has not been asleep.
4 For if God did not spare the angels when they sinned, but cast them into hell *f* and committed them to pits of nether gloom to be kept until the judgment; 5 if he did not spare the ancient world, but preserved Noah, a herald of righteousness, with seven other persons, when he brought a flood upon the world of the ungodly; 6 if by turning the cities of Sodom and Gomorrah to ashes he condemned them to extinction and made them an example to those who were to be ungodly; 7 and if he rescued righteous Lot, greatly distressed by the licentiousness of the wicked 8 (for by what that righteous man saw and heard as he lived among them, he was vexed in his righteous soul day after day with their lawless deeds), 9 then the Lord knows how to rescue the godly from trial, and to keep the unrighteous under punishment until the day of judgment, 10 and especially those who indulge in the lust of defiling passion and despise authority.
Bold and wilful, they are not afraid to revile the glorious ones, 11 whereas angels, though greater in might and power, do not pronounce a reviling judgment upon them before the Lord.

[d] Or *my Son, my* (or *the) Beloved.* [e] Other authorities read *moved by the Holy Spirit holy men of God spoke.* [f] Greek *Tartarus.*

PHILLIPS

We were not following a cleverly written-up story when we told you about the power and coming of the Lord Jesus Christ—we actually saw his majesty with our own eyes. He received honor and glory from God the Father himself when that voice said to him, out of the sublime glory of Heaven, "This is my beloved Son, in whom I am well pleased." We actually heard that voice speaking from Heaven while we were with him on the sacred mountain. The word of prophecy was fulfilled in our hearing! You should give that word your closest attention, for it shines like a lamp amidst all the dirt and darkness of the world, until the day dawns, and the morning star rises in your hearts.

False prophets will flourish, *1. 20*
but only for a time

But you must understand this at the outset, that no prophecy of scripture arose from an individual's interpretation of the truth. No prophecy came because a man wanted it to: men of God spoke because they were inspired by the Holy

Spirit. But even in those days there were false prophets, just as there will be false teachers among you today. They will be men who will subtly introduce dangerous heresies. They will thereby deny the Lord who redeemed them, and it will not be long before they bring on themselves their own downfall. Many will follow their pernicious teaching and thereby bring discredit on the way of truth. In their lust to make converts these men will try to exploit you too with their bogus arguments. But judgment has been for some time hard on their heels and their downfall is inevitable. For if God did not spare angels who sinned against him, but banished them to the dark imprisonment of hell till judgment day: if he did not spare the ancient world but saved only Noah (the solitary voice that cried out for righteousness) and his seven companions when he brought the flood upon the world in its wickedness; and if God reduced the entire cities of Sodom and Gomorrah to ashes (when he sentenced them to destruction as a fearful example to those who wanted to live in defiance of his laws), and yet saved Lot the righteous man, in acute mental distress at the filthy lives of the godless—Lot, remember, was a good man suffering spiritual agonies day after day at what he saw and heard of their lawlessness—then you may be absolutely certain that the Lord knows how to rescue a good man surrounded by temptation, and how to reserve his punishment for the wicked until his day comes.

Let me show you what these men *2. 10*
are really like

His judgment is chiefly reserved for those who have indulged all the foulness of their lower natures, and have nothing but contempt for authority. These men are arrogant and presumptuous—they think nothing of scoffing at the glories of the unseen world. Yet even angels, who are their superiors in strength and power, do not bring insulting criticisms of such things before the Lord.

N.E.B.

It was not on tales artfully spun that we relied when we told you of the power of our Lord Jesus Christ and his coming; we saw him with our own eyes in majesty, when at the hands of God the Father he was invested with honour and glory, and there came to him from the sublime Presence a voice which said: 'This is my Son, my Beloved,[a] on whom my favour rests.' This voice from heaven we ourselves heard; when it came, we were with him on the sacred mountain.

All this only confirms for us the message of the prophets,[b] to which you will do well to attend, because it is like a lamp shining in a murky place, until the day breaks and the morning star rises to illuminate your minds.

But first note this: no one can interpret any prophecy of Scripture by himself. For it was not through any human whim that men prophesied of old; men they were, but, impelled by the Holy Spirit, they spoke the words of God.

2 But Israel had false prophets as well as true; and you likewise will have false teachers among you. They will import disastrous heresies, disowning the very Master who bought them, and bringing swift disaster on their own heads. They will gain many adherents to their dissolute practices, through whom the true way will be brought into disrepute. In their greed for money they will trade on your credulity with sheer fabrications.

But the judgement long decreed for them has not been idle; perdition waits for them with unsleeping eyes. God did not spare the angels who sinned, but consigned them to the dark pits of hell,[c] where they are reserved for judgement. He did not spare the world of old (except for Noah, preacher of righteousness, whom he preserved with seven others), but brought the deluge upon that world of godless men. The cities of Sodom and Gomorrah God burned to ashes, and condemned them to total destruction, making them an object-lesson for godless men in future days. But he rescued Lot, who was a good man, shocked by the dissolute habits of the lawless society in which he lived; day after day every sight, every sound, of their evil courses tortured that good man's heart. Thus the Lord is well able to rescue the godly out of trials, and to reserve the wicked under punishment until the day of judgement.

Above all he will punish those who follow their abominable lusts. They flout authority; reckless and headstrong, they are not afraid to insult celestial beings, whereas angels, for all their superior strength and might, employ no insults in seeking judgement against them before the Lord.

[a] *Or* This is my only Son. [b] *Or* And in the message of the prophets we have something still more certain. [c] *Some witnesses read* consigned them to darkness and chains in hell.

K.J.V.

12 But these, as natural brute beasts made to be taken and destroyed, speak evil of the things that they understand not; and shall utterly perish in their own corruption; 13 And shall receive the reward of unrighteousness, *as* they that count it pleasure to riot in the daytime. Spots *they are* and blemishes, sporting themselves with their own deceivings while they feast with you; 14 Having eyes full of adultery, and that cannot cease from sin; beguiling unstable souls: a heart they have exercised with covetous practices; cursed children: 15 Which have forsaken the right way, and are gone astray, following the way of Balaam *the son* of Bosor, who loved the wages of unrighteousness; 16 But was rebuked for his iniquity: the dumb ass speaking with man's voice forbade the madness of the prophet. 17 These are wells without water, clouds that are carried with a tempest; to whom the mist of darkness is reserved for ever. 18 For when they speak great swelling *words* of vanity, they allure through the lusts of the flesh, *through much* wantonness, those that were clean escaped from them who live in error. 19 While they promise them liberty, they themselves are the servants of corruption: for of whom a man is overcome, of the same is he brought in bondage. 20 For if after they have escaped the pollutions of the world through the knowledge of the Lord and Saviour Jesus Christ, they are again entangled therein, and overcome, the latter end is worse with them than the beginning. 21 For it had been better for them not to have known the way of righteousness, than, after they have known *it*, to turn from the holy commandment delivered unto them. 22 But it is happened unto them according to the true proverb, The dog *is* turned to his own vomit again; and, The sow that was washed to her wallowing in the mire.

3 This second epistle, beloved, I now write unto you; in *both* which I stir up your pure minds by way of remembrance: 2 That ye may be mindful of the words which were spoken before by the holy prophets, and of the commandment of us the apostles of the Lord and Saviour: 3 Knowing this first, that there shall come in the last days scoffers, walking after their own lusts, 4 And saying, Where is the promise of his coming? for since the fathers fell asleep, all things continue as *they were* from the beginning of the creation. 5 For this they willingly are ignorant of, that by the word of God the heavens were of old, and the earth standing out of the water and in the water: 6 Whereby the world that then was, being overflowed with water, perished: 7 But the heavens and the earth, which are now, by the same word are kept in store, reserved unto fire against the day of judgment and perdition of ungodly men. 8 But, beloved, be not ignorant of this one thing, that one day *is* with the Lord as a thousand

R.S.V.

12 But these, like irrational animals, creatures of instinct, born to be caught and killed, reviling in matters of which they are ignorant, will be destroyed in the same destruction with them, 13 suffering wrong for their wrongdoing. They count it pleasure to revel in the daytime. They are blots and blemishes, reveling in their dissipation,*g* carousing with you. 14 They have eyes full of adultery, insatiable for sin. They entice unsteady souls. They have hearts trained in greed. Accursed children! 15 Forsaking the right way they have gone astray; they have followed the way of Balaam, the son of Beor, who loved gain from wrongdoing, 16 but was rebuked for his own transgression; a dumb ass spoke with human voice and restrained the prophet's madness. 17 These are waterless springs and mists driven by a storm; for them the nether gloom of darkness has been reserved. 18 For, uttering loud boasts of folly, they entice with licentious passions of the flesh men who have barely escaped from those who live in error. 19 They promise them freedom, but they themselves are slaves of corruption; for whatever overcomes a man, to that he is enslaved. 20 For if, after they have escaped the defilements of the world through the knowledge of our Lord and Savior Jesus Christ, they are again entangled in them and overpowered, the last state has become worse for them than the first. 21 For it would have been better for them never to have known the way of righteousness than after knowing it to turn back from the holy commandment delivered to them. 22 It has happened to them according to the true proverb, The dog turns back to his own vomit, and the sow is washed only to wallow in the mire.

3 This is now the second letter that I have written to you, beloved, and in both of them I have aroused your sincere mind by way of reminder; 2 that you should remember the predictions of the holy prophets and the commandment of the Lord and Savior through your apostles. 3 First of all you must understand this, that scoffers will come in the last days with scoffing, following their own passions 4 and saying, "Where is the promise of his coming? For ever since the fathers fell asleep, all things have continued as they were from the beginning of creation." 5 They deliberately ignore this fact, that by the word of God heavens existed long ago, and an earth formed out of water and by means of water, 6 through which the world that then existed was deluged with water and perished. 7 But by the same word the heavens and earth that now exist have been stored up for fire, being kept until the day of judgment and destruction of ungodly men.

8 But do not ignore this one fact, beloved, that with the Lord one day is as a thousand

[g] Other ancient authorities read *love feasts.*

PHILLIPS

But these men, with no more sense than the unreasoning brute beasts which are born to be caught and killed, scoff at things outside their own experience, and will most certainly be destroyed in their own corruption. Their wickedness has earned them an evil end and they will be paid in full.

These are the men who delight in daylight self-indulgence; they are foul spots and blots, playing their tricks at your very dinner tables. Their eyes cannot look at a woman without lust; they captivate the unstable ones, and their technique of getting what they want is, through long practice, highly developed. They are born under a curse, for they have abandoned the right road and wandered off to follow the old trail of Balaam, son of Beor, the man who had no objection to wickedness as long as he was paid for it. But he, you remember, was sharply reprimanded for his wickedness—by a donkey, of all things, speaking with a human voice to check the prophet's wicked infatuation!

These men are like wells without a drop of water in them, like the changing shapes of whirling storm clouds, and their fate will be the black night of utter darkness. With their high-sounding nonsense they use the sensual pull of the lower passions to attract those who were just on the point of cutting loose from their companions in misconduct. They promise them liberty. Liberty!—when they themselves are bound hand and foot to utter depravity. For a man is the slave of whatever masters him. If men have escaped from the world's contaminations through knowing our Lord and savior Jesus Christ, and then become entangled and defeated all over again, their last position is far worse than their first. It would be better for them not to have known the way of goodness at all, rather than after knowing it to turn their backs on the sacred commandments given to them. Alas, for them, the old proverbs have come true about the "dog returning to his vomit," and "the sow that had been washed going back to wallow in the muck."

God delays the last day, in his mercy
3. 1

This is the second letter I have written to you, dear friends of mine, and in both of them I have tried to stimulate you, as men with minds uncontaminated by error, by simply reminding you of what you really know already. For I want you to remember the words spoken of old by the holy prophets as well as the commands of our Lord and savior, given to you through his messengers.

First of all you must realize that in the last days mockers will undoubtedly come—men whose only guide in life is what they want for themselves—and they will say: "What has happened to his promised coming? Since the first Christians fell asleep, everything remains exactly as it was since the beginning of creation!" They are deliberately shutting their eyes to a fact that they know very well, that there were, by God's command, heavens in the old days and an earth formed out of the water and surrounded by water. It was by water that the world of those days was deluged and destroyed, but the present heavens and earth are, also by God's command, being carefully kept and maintained for the fire of the day of judgment and the destruction of wicked men.

But you should never lose sight of this fact, dear friends, that time is not the same with the

N.E.B.

These men are like brute beasts, born in the course of nature to be caught and killed. They pour abuse upon things they do not understand; like the beasts they will perish, suffering hurt for the hurt they have inflicted. To carouse in broad daylight is their idea of pleasure; while they sit with you at table they are an ugly blot on your company, because they revel in their own deceptions.[a]

They have eyes for nothing but women, eyes never at rest from sin. They lure the unstable to their ruin; past masters in mercenary greed, God's curse is on them! They have abandoned the straight road and lost their way. They have followed in the steps of Balaam son of Beor, who consented to take pay for doing wrong, but was sharply rebuked for his offence when the dumb beast spoke with a human voice and put a stop to the prophet's madness.

These men are springs that give no water, mists driven by a storm; the place reserved for them is blackest darkness. They utter big, empty words, and make of sensual lusts and debauchery a bait to catch those who have barely begun to escape from their heathen environment. They promise them freedom, but are themselves slaves of corruption; for a man is the slave of whatever has mastered him. They had once escaped the world's defilements through the knowledge of our Lord and Saviour Jesus Christ; yet if they have entangled themselves in these all over again, and are mastered by them, their plight in the end is worse than before. How much better never to have known the right way, than, having known it, to turn back and abandon the sacred commandments delivered to them! For them the proverb has proved true: 'The dog returns to its own vomit', and, 'The sow after a wash rolls in the mud again.'

3 This is now my second letter to you, my friends. In both of them I have been recalling to you what you already know, to rouse you to honest thought. Remember the predictions made by God's own prophets, and the commands given by the Lord and Saviour through your apostles.

Note this first: in the last days there will come men who scoff at religion and live self-indulgent lives, and they will say: 'Where now is the promise of his coming? Our fathers have been laid to their rest, but still everything continues exactly as it has always been since the world began.'

In taking this view they lose sight of the fact[b] that there were heavens and earth long ago, created by God's word out of water and with water; and by water that first world was destroyed, the water of the deluge. And the present heavens and earth, again by God's word, have been kept in store for burning; they are being reserved until the day of judgement when the godless will be destroyed.

And here is one point, my friends, which you must not lose sight of: with the Lord one day

[a] *Or* in their mock love-feasts; *some witnesses read* in their love-feasts. [b] *Or* They choose to overlook the fact . . .

K.J.V.

years, and a thousand years as one day. 9 The Lord is not slack concerning his promise, as some men count slackness; but is longsuffering to us-ward, not willing that any should perish, but that all should come to repentance. 10 But the day of the Lord will come as a thief in the night; in the which the heavens shall pass away with a great noise, and the elements shall melt with fervent heat, the earth also and the works that are therein shall be burned up. 11 *Seeing* then *that* all these things shall be dissolved, what manner *of persons* ought ye to be in *all* holy conversation and godliness, 12 Looking for and hasting unto the coming of the day of God, wherein the heavens being on fire shall be dissolved, and the elements shall melt with fervent heat? 13 Nevertheless we, according to his promise, look for new heavens and a new earth, wherein dwelleth righteousness. 14 Wherefore, beloved, seeing that ye look for such things, be diligent that ye may be found of him in peace, without spot, and blameless. 15And account *that* the longsuffering of our Lord *is* salvation; even as our beloved brother Paul also according to the wisdom given unto him hath written unto you; 16As also in all *his* epistles, speaking in them of these things; in which are some things hard to be understood, which they that are unlearned and unstable wrest, as *they do* also the other Scriptures, unto their own destruction. 17 Ye therefore, beloved, seeing ye know *these things* before, beware lest ye also, being led away with the error of the wicked, fall from your own steadfastness. 18 But grow in grace, and *in* the knowledge of our Lord and Saviour Jesus Christ. To him *be* glory both now and for ever. Amen.

R.S.V.

years, and a thousand years as one day. 9 The Lord is not slow about his promise as some count slowness, but is forbearing toward you,[h] not wishing that any should perish, but that all should reach repentance. 10 But the day of the Lord will come like a thief, and then the heavens will pass away with a loud noise, and the elements will be dissolved with fire, and the earth and the works that are upon it will be burned up.

11 Since all these things are thus to be dissolved, what sort of persons ought you to be in lives of holiness and godliness, 12 waiting for and hastening[i] the coming of the day of God, because of which the heavens will be kindled and dissolved, and the elements will melt with fire! 13 But according to his promise we wait for new heavens and a new earth in which righteousness dwells.

14 Therefore, beloved, since you wait for these, be zealous to be found by him without spot or blemish, and at peace. 15And count the forbearance of our Lord as salvation. So also our beloved brother Paul wrote to you according to the wisdom given him, 16 speaking of this as he does in all his letters. There are some things in them hard to understand, which the ignorant and unstable twist to their own destruction, as they do the other scriptures. 17 You therefore, beloved, knowing this beforehand, beware lest you be carried away with the error of lawless men and lose your own stability. 18 But grow in the grace and knowledge of our Lord and Savior Jesus Christ. To him be the glory both now and to the day of eternity. Amen.

PHILLIPS

Lord as it is with us—to him a day may be a thousand years, and a thousand years only a day. It is not that he is dilatory about keeping his own promise as some men seem to think; the fact is that he is very patient toward you. He has no wish that any man should be destroyed: he wishes that all men should come to repent. Yet it remains true that the day of the Lord will come as suddenly and unexpectedly as a thief. In that day the heavens will disappear in a terrific tearing blast; the very elements will disintegrate in heat and the earth and all that is in it will be burned up to nothing.

Never lose sight　　　　*3. 11*
of the eternal world

In view of the fact that all of these things are to be dissolved, what sort of people ought you to be? Surely men of good and holy character, who live expecting and earnestly longing for the coming of the day of God. True, this day will mean that the heavens will disappear in fire and the elements disintegrate in fearful heat, but our hopes are set not on these but on the new heavens and the new earth which he has promised us, and in which nothing but good shall live.

Because, my dear friends, you have a hope like this before you, I urge you to make certain that such a day would find you at peace with God and man, clean and blameless in his sight. Meanwhile, consider that God's patience is meant to be man's salvation, as our dear brother Paul pointed out in his letter to you, written out of the wisdom God gave him. In that letter, as indeed in all his letters, he referred to these matters. There are, of course, some things in his letters which are difficult to understand, and which, unhappily, ill-informed and unbalanced people distort (as they do the other scriptures), and bring disaster on their own heads.

But you, my friends whom I love, are forewarned, and should therefore be very careful not to be carried away by the errors of wicked men and so lose your proper foothold. On the contrary, you should grow in grace and in your knowledge of our Lord and savior Jesus Christ— to him be glory now and until the dawning of the day of eternity!

N.E.B.

is like a thousand years and a thousand years like one day. It is not that the Lord is slow in fulfilling his promise, as some suppose, but that he is very patient with you, because it is not his will for any to be lost, but for all to come to repentance.

But the Day of the Lord will come; it will come, unexpected as a thief. On that day the heavens will disappear with a great rushing sound, the elements will disintegrate in flames, and the earth with all that is in it will be laid bare.[a]

Since the whole universe is to break up in this way, think what sort of people you ought to be, what devout and dedicated lives you should live! Look eagerly for the coming of the Day of God and work to hasten it on; that day will set the heavens ablaze until they fall apart, and will melt the elements in flames. But we have his promise, and look forward to new heavens and a new earth, the home of justice.

With this to look forward to, do your utmost to be found at peace with him, unblemished and above reproach in his sight. Bear in mind that our Lord's patience with us is our salvation, as Paul, our friend and brother, said when he wrote to you with his inspired wisdom. And so he does in all his other letters, wherever he speaks of this subject, though they contain some obscure passages, which the ignorant and unstable misinterpret to their own ruin, as they do the other scripture.[b]

But you, my friends, are forewarned. Take care, then, not to let these unprincipled men seduce you with their errors; do not lose your own safe foothold. But grow in the grace and in the knowledge of our Lord and Saviour Jesus Christ.[c] To him be glory now and for all eternity!

[a] *Some witnesses read* will be burnt up. [b] *Or* his other writings. [c] *Or* But grow up, by the grace of our Lord and Saviour Jesus Christ, and by knowing him.

K.J.V.

THE FIRST
EPISTLE GENERAL
OF
JOHN

1 That which was from the beginning, which we have heard, which we have seen with our eyes, which we have looked upon, and our hands have handled, of the Word of life; 2 (For the life was manifested, and we have seen *it,* and bear witness, and shew unto you that eternal life, which was with the Father, and was manifested unto us;) 3 That which we have seen and heard declare we unto you, that ye also may have fellowship with us: and truly our fellowship *is* with the Father, and with his Son Jesus Christ. 4And these things write we unto you, that your joy may be full. 5 This then is the message which we have heard of him, and declare unto you, that God is light, and in him is no darkness at all. 6 If we say that we have fellowship with him, and walk in darkness, we lie, and do not the truth: 7 But if we walk in the light, as he is in the light, we have fellowship one with another, and the blood of Jesus Christ his Son cleanseth us from all sin. 8 If we say that we have no sin, we deceive ourselves, and the truth is not in us. 9 If we confess our sins, he is faithful and just to forgive us *our* sins, and to cleanse us from all unrighteousness. 10 If we say that we have not sinned, we make him a liar, and his word is not in us.

2 My little children, these things write I unto you, that ye sin not. And if any man sin, we have an advocate with the Father, Jesus Christ the righteous: 2And he is the propitiation for our sins: and not for ours only, but also for *the sins of* the whole world. 3And hereby we do know that we know him, if we keep his commandments. 4 He that saith, I know him, and keepeth not his commandments, is a liar, and the truth is not in him. 5 But whoso keepeth his

R.S.V.

THE
FIRST LETTER OF
JOHN

1 That which was from the beginning, which we have heard, which we have seen with our eyes, which we have looked upon and touched with our hands, concerning the word of life— 2 the life was made manifest, and we saw it, and testify to it, and proclaim to you the eternal life which was with the Father and was made manifest to us—3 that which we have seen and heard we proclaim also to you, so that you may have fellowship with us; and our fellowship is with the Father and with his Son Jesus Christ. 4And we are writing this that our[a] joy may be complete.

5 This is the message we have heard from him and proclaim to you, that God is light and in him is no darkness at all. 6 If we say we have fellowship with him while we walk in darkness, we lie and do not live according to the truth; 7 but if we walk in the light, as he is in the light, we have fellowship with one another, and the blood of Jesus his Son cleanses us from all sin. 8 If we say we have no sin, we deceive ourselves, and the truth is not in us. 9 If we confess our sins, he is faithful and just, and will forgive our sins and cleanse us from all unrighteousness. 10 If we say we have not sinned, we make him a liar, and his word is not in us.

2 My little children, I am writing this to you so that you may not sin; but if any one does sin, we have an advocate with the Father, Jesus Christ the righteous; 2 and he is the expiation for our sins, and not for ours only but also for the sins of the whole world. 3And by this we may be sure that we know him, if we keep his commandments. 4 He who says "I know him" but disobeys his commandments is a liar, and the truth is not in him; 5 but whoever

[a] Other ancient authorities read *your.*

THE
FIRST LETTER OF
JOHN

We are writing to you about something which has always existed yet which we ourselves actually saw and heard: something which we had opportunity to observe closely and even to hold in our hands, and yet, as we know now, was something of the very Word of life himself! For it was *life* which appeared before us: we saw it, we are eyewitnesses of it, and are now writing to you about it. It was the very life of all ages, the life that has always existed with the Father, which actually became visible in person to us mortal men. We repeat, we really saw and heard what we are now writing to you about. We want you to be with us in this—in this fellowship with the Father, and Jesus Christ his Son. We must write and tell you about it, because the more that fellowship extends, the greater the joy it brings to us who are already in it.

Experience of living "in the light" 1. 5

Here, then, is the message which we heard from him: GOD IS LIGHT, and no shadow of darkness can exist in him. Consequently, if we were to say that we enjoyed fellowship with him and still went on living in darkness, we should be both telling and living a lie. But if we really are living in the same light in which he eternally exists, then we have true fellowship with each other, and the blood which his Son shed for us keeps us clean from all sin. If we refuse to admit that we are sinners, then we live in a world of illusion and truth becomes a stranger to us. But if we freely admit that we have sinned, we find God utterly reliable and straightforward—he forgives our sins and makes us thoroughly clean from all that is evil. For if we take up the attitude "we have not sinned," we flatly deny God's diagnosis of our condition and cut ourselves off from what he has to say to us.

Love and obedience are essentials 2. 1
for living in the light

I write these things to you (may I call you "my children"—for that's how I think of you), to help you to avoid sin. But if a man should sin, remember that our advocate before the Father is Jesus Christ the righteous, the one who made personal atonement for our sins (and for those of the rest of the world as well). It is only when we obey God's laws that we can be quite sure that we really know him. The man who claims to know God but does not obey his laws is not only a liar but lives in self-delusion. In practice, the more a man learns to obey God's

THE
FIRST LETTER OF
JOHN

Recall to Fundamentals

1 It was there from the beginning; we have heard it; we have seen it with our own eyes; we looked upon it, and felt it with our own hands; and it is of this we tell. Our theme is the word of life. This life was made visible; we have seen it and bear our testimony; we here declare to you the eternal life which dwelt with the Father and was made visible to us. What we have seen and heard we declare to you, so that you and we together may share in a common life, that life which we share with the Father and his Son Jesus Christ. And we write this in order that the joy of us all may be complete.

Here is the message we heard from him and pass on to you: that God is light, and in him there is no darkness at all. If we claim to be sharing in his life while we walk in the dark, our words and our lives are a lie; but if we walk in the light as he himself is in the light, then we share together a common life, and we are being cleansed from every sin by the blood of Jesus his Son.

If we claim to be sinless, we are self-deceived and strangers to the truth. If we confess our sins, he is just, and may be trusted to forgive our sins and cleanse us from every kind of wrong; but if we say we have committed no sin, we make him out to be a liar, and then his word has no place in us.

2 My children, in writing thus to you my purpose is that you should not commit sin. But snould anyone commit a sin, we have one to plead our cause[a] with the Father, Jesus Christ, and he is just. He is himself the remedy for the defilement of our sins, not our sins only but the sins of all the world.

Here is the test by which we can make sure that we know him: do we keep his commands? The man who says, 'I know him', while he disobeys his commands, is a liar and a stranger to the truth; but in the man who is obedient to his

[a] *Literally* we have an advocate . . .

K.J.V.

word, in him verily is the love of God perfected: hereby know we that we are in him. 6 He that saith he abideth in him ought himself also so to walk, even as he walked. 7 Brethren, I write no new commandment unto you, but an old commandment which ye had from the beginning. The old commandment is the word which ye have heard from the beginning. 8Again, a new commandment I write unto you, which thing is true in him and in you: because the darkness is past, and the true light now shineth. 9 He that saith he is in the light, and hateth his brother, is in darkness even until now. 10 He that loveth his brother abideth in the light, and there is none occasion of stumbling in him. 11 But he that hateth his brother is in darkness, and walketh in darkness, and knoweth not whither he goeth, because that darkness hath blinded his eyes. 12 I write unto you, little children, because your sins are forgiven you for his name's sake. 13 I write unto you, fathers, because ye have known him *that is* from the beginning. I write unto you, young men, because ye have overcome the wicked one. I write unto you, little children, because ye have known the Father. 14 I have written unto you, fathers, because ye have known him *that is* from the beginning. I have written unto you, young men, because ye are strong, and the word of God abideth in you, and ye have overcome the wicked one. 15 Love not the world, neither the things *that are* in the world. If any man love the world, the love of the Father is not in him. 16 For all that *is* in the world, the lust of the flesh, and the lust of the eyes, and the pride of life, is not of the Father, but is of the world. 17And the world passeth away, and the lust thereof: but he that doeth the will of God abideth for ever. 18 Little children, it is the last time: and as ye have heard that antichrist shall come, even now are there many antichrists; whereby we know that it is the last time. 19 They went out from us, but they were not of us; for if they had been of us, they would *no doubt* have continued with us: but *they went out*, that they might be made manifest that they were not all

R.S.V.

keeps his word, in him truly love for God is perfected. By this we may be sure that we are in him: 6 he who says he abides in him ought to walk in the same way in which he walked.

7 Beloved, I am writing you no new commandment, but an old commandment which you had from the beginning; the old commandment is the word which you have heard. 8 Yet I am writing you a new commandment, which is true in him and in you, because[b] the darkness is passing away and the true light is already shining. 9 He who says he is in the light and hates his brother is in the darkness still. 10 He who loves his brother abides in the light, and in it [c] there is no cause for stumbling. 11 But he who hates his brother is in the darkness and walks in the darkness, and does not know where he is going, because the darkness has blinded his eyes.

12 I am writing to you, little children, because your sins are forgiven for his sake. 13 I am writing to you, fathers, because you know him who is from the beginning. I am writing to you, young men, because you have overcome the evil one. I write to you, children, because you know the Father. 14 I write to you, fathers, because you know him who is from the beginning. I write to you, young men, because you are strong, and the word of God abides in you, and you have overcome the evil one.

15 Do not love the world or the things in the world. If any one loves the world, love for the Father is not in him. 16 For all that is in the world, the lust of the flesh and the lust of the eyes and the pride of life, is not of the Father but is of the world. 17 And the world passes away, and the lust of it; but he who does the will of God abides for ever.

18 Children, it is the last hour; and as you have heard that antichrist is coming, so now many antichrists have come; therefore we know that it is the last hour. 19 They went out from us, but they were not of us; for if they had been of us, they would have continued with us; but they went out, that it might be plain that they

[b] Or *that*. [c] Or *him*.

PHILLIPS

laws, the more truly and fully does he express his love for him. Obedience is the test of whether we really live "in God" or not. The life of a man who professes to be living in God must bear the stamp of Christ.

I am not really writing to tell you of any new command, brothers of mine. It is the old, original command which you had at the beginning; it is the old message which you have heard before. And yet as I give it to you again I know that it is true—in your life as it was in his. For the darkness is beginning to lift and the true light is now shining in the world. Anyone who claims to be "in the light" and hates his brother is, in fact, still in complete darkness. The man who loves his brother lives and moves in the light, and has no reason to stumble. But the man who hates his brother is shut off from the light and gropes his way in the dark without seeing where he is going. To move in the dark is to move blindfold.

As I write I visualize you, my children   2. 12

I write this letter to you all, as my dear children, because your sins are forgiven for his name's sake. I write to you who are now fathers, because you have known him who has always existed. And to you vigorous young men I am writing because you have been strong in defeating the evil one. Yes, I have written these lines to you all, dear children, because you know the Father; to you fathers because of your experience of the one who has always existed, and to you young men because you have all the vigor of youth, because you have a hold on God's truth and because you have defeated the evil one.

See "the world" for what it is   2. 15

Never give your hearts to this world or to any of the things in it. A man cannot love the Father and love the world at the same time. For the whole world system, based as it is on men's primitive desires, their greedy ambitions and the glamour of all that they think splendid, is not derived from the Father at all, but from the world itself. The world and all its passionate desires will one day disappear. But the man who is following God's will is part of the permanent and cannot die.

Little antichrists are abroad already   2. 18

Even now, dear children, we are getting near the end of things. You have heard, I expect, the prophecy about the coming of antichrist. Believe me, there are antichrists about already, which confirms my belief that we are near the end. These men went out from our company, it is true, but they never really belonged to it. If they had really belonged to us they would have stayed. In fact, their going proves beyond doubt that men like that were not "our men" at all.

N.E.B.

word, the divine love has indeed come to its perfection.

Here is the test by which we can make sure that we are in him: whoever claims to be dwelling in him, binds himself to live as Christ himself lived. Dear friends, I give you no new command. It is the old command which you always had before you; the old command is the message which you heard at the beginning. And yet again it is a new command that I am giving you—new in the sense that the darkness is passing and the real light already shines. Christ has made this true, and it is true in your own experience.

A man may say, 'I am in the light'; but if he hates his brother, he is still in the dark. Only the man who loves his brother dwells in light: there is nothing to make him stumble. But one who hates his brother is in darkness; he walks in the dark and has no idea where he is going, because the darkness has made him blind.

I write to you, my children, because your sins have been forgiven for his sake.[a]

I write to you, fathers, because you know him who is and has been from the beginning.[b]

I write to you, young men, because you have mastered the evil one.

To you, children, I have written because you know the Father.

To you, fathers, I have written because you know him who is and has been from the beginning.[b]

To you, young men, I have written because you are strong; God's word is in you, and you have mastered the evil one.

Do not set your hearts on the godless world or anything in it. Anyone who loves the world is a stranger to the Father's love. Everything the world affords, all that panders to the appetites, or entices the eyes, all the glamour of its life, springs not from the Father but from the godless world. And that world is passing away with all its allurements, but he who does God's will stands for evermore.

My children, this is the last hour! You were told that Antichrist was to come, and now many antichrists have appeared; which proves to us that this is indeed the last hour. They went out from our company, but never really belonged to us; if they had, they would have stayed with us. They went out, so that it might be clear that not all in our company truly belong to it.[c]

[a] *Or* forgiven, since you bear his name. [b] *Or* him whom we have known from the beginning. [c] *Or* that none of them truly belong to us.

K.J.V.

of us. 20 But ye have an unction from the Holy One, and ye know all things. 21 I have not written unto you because ye know not the truth, but because ye know it, and that no lie is of the truth. 22 Who is a liar but he that denieth that Jesus is the Christ? He is antichrist, that denieth the Father and the Son. 23 Whosoever denieth the Son, the same hath not the Father: [*but*] *he that acknowledgeth the Son hath the Father also.* 24 Let that therefore abide in you, which ye have heard from the beginning. If that which ye have heard from the beginning shall remain in you, ye also shall continue in the Son, and in the Father. 25And this is the promise that he hath promised us, *even* eternal life. 26 These things have I written unto you concerning them that seduce you. 27 But the anointing which ye have received of him abideth in you, and ye need not that any man teach you: but as the same anointing teacheth you of all things, and is truth, and is no lie, and even as it hath taught you, ye shall abide in him. 28And now, little children, abide in him; that, when he shall appear, we may have confidence, and not be ashamed before him at his coming. 29 If ye know that he is righteous, ye know that every one that doeth righteousness is born of him.

R.S.V.

all are not of us. 20 But you have been anointed by the Holy One, and you all know.[d] 21 I write to you, not because you do not know the truth, but because you know it, and know that no lie is of the truth. 22 Who is the liar but he who denies that Jesus is the Christ? This is the antichrist, he who denies the Father and the Son. 23 No one who denies the Son has the Father. He who confesses the Son has the Father also. 24 Let what you heard from the beginning abide in you. If what you heard from the beginning abides in you, then you will abide in the Son and in the Father. 25And this is what he has promised us,[e] eternal life.

26 I write this to you about those who would deceive you; 27 but the anointing which you received from him abides in you, and you have no need that any one should teach you; as his anointing teaches you about everything, and is true, and is no lie, just as it has taught you, abide in him.

28 And now, little children, abide in him, so that when he appears we may have confidence and not shrink from him in shame at his coming. 29 If you know that he is righteous, you may be sure that every one who does right is born of him.

3 Behold, what manner of love the Father hath bestowed upon us, that we should be called the sons of God: therefore the world knoweth us not, because it knew him not. 2 Beloved, now are we the sons of God, and it doth not yet appear what we shall be: but we know that, when he shall appear, we shall be like him; for we shall see him as he is. 3And every man that hath this hope in him purifieth himself, even as he is pure. 4 Whosoever committeth sin transgresseth also the law: for sin is the transgression of the law. 5And ye know that he was manifested to take away our sins; and in him is no sin. 6 Whosoever abideth in him sinneth not:

3 See what love the Father has given us, that we should be called children of God; and so we are. The reason why the world does not know us is that it did not know him. 2 Beloved, we are God's children now; it does not yet appear what we shall be, but we know that when he appears we shall be like him, for we shall see him as he is. 3And every one who thus hopes in him purifies himself as he is pure.

4 Every one who commits sin is guilty of lawlessness; sin is lawlessness. 5 You know that he appeared to take away sins, and in him there is no sin. 6 No one who abides in him sins; no

---

[d] Other ancient authorities read *you know everything.* [e] Other ancient authorities read *you.*

Be on your guard   **2. 20, 21**
against error

God has given you all a certain amount of spiritual insight, and indeed I have not written this warning as if I were writing to men who don't know what error is. I write because your eyes are clear enough to discern a lie when you come across it. And what, I ask you, is the crowning lie? Surely the denial that Jesus is God's anointed one, his Christ. I say, therefore, that any man who refuses to acknowledge the Father and the Son is an antichrist. The man who will not recognize the Son cannot possibly know the Father; yet the man who believes in the Son will find that he knows the Father as well.

For yourselves I beg you to stick to the original teaching. If you do, you will be living in fellowship with both the Father and the Son. And that means sharing his own life for ever, as he has promised.

It is true that I felt I had to write the above about men who would dearly love to lead you astray. Yet I know that the touch of his Spirit never leaves you, and you don't really need a human teacher. You know that his Spirit teaches you about all things, always telling you the truth and never telling you a lie. So, as he had taught you, live continually in him. Yes, now, little children, remember to live continually in him. So that if he were suddenly to reveal himself we should still know exactly where we stand, and should not have to shrink away from his presence.

What it means to be sons of God   **2. 29**

You all know that God is really good. You may be just as sure that the man who leads a really good life is a true child of God.

Consider the incredible love that the Father has shown us in allowing us to be called "children of God"—and that is not just what we are called, but what we *are*. Our heredity on the Godward side is no mere figure of speech—which explains why the world will no more recognize us than it recognized Christ.

Oh, dear children of mine (forgive the affection of an old man!), have you realized it? Here and now we *are* God's children. We don't know what we shall become in the future. We only know that, if reality were to break through, we should reflect his likeness, for we should see him as he really is!

Everyone who has at heart a hope like that keeps himself pure, for he knows how pure Christ is.

Conduct will show who is   **3. 4**
a man's spiritual father

Everyone who commits sin breaks God's law, for that is what sin is, by definition—a breaking of God's law. You know, moreover, that Christ became man for the purpose of removing sin, and that he himself was quite free from sin. The man who lives "in Christ" does not habitually sin. The regular sinner has never seen

You, no less than they, are among the initiated;[a] this is the gift of the Holy One, and by it you all have knowledge.[b] It is not because you are ignorant of the truth that I have written to you, but because you know it, and because lies, one and all, are alien to the truth.

Who is the liar? Who but he that denies that Jesus is the Christ? He is Antichrist, for he denies both the Father and the Son: to deny the Son is to be without the Father; to acknowledge the Son is to have the Father too. You therefore must keep in your hearts that which you heard at the beginning; if what you heard then still dwells in you, you will yourselves dwell in the Son and also in the Father. And this is the promise that he himself gave us, the promise of eternal life.

So much for those who would mislead you. But as for you, the initiation[c] which you received from him stays with you; you need no other teacher, but learn all you need to know from his initiation, which is real and no illusion. As he taught you, then, dwell in him.

Even now, my children, dwell in him, so that when he appears we may be confident and unashamed before him at his coming. If you know that he is righteous, you must recognize that every man who does right is his child.

3 How great is the love that the Father has shown to us! We were called God's children, and such we are;[d] and the reason why the godless world does not recognize us is that it has not known him. Here and now, dear friends, we are God's children; what we shall be has not yet been disclosed, but we know that when it is disclosed[e] we shall be like him,[f] because we shall see him as he is. Everyone who has this hope before him purifies himself, as Christ is pure.

To commit sin is to break God's law: sin, in fact, is lawlessness. Christ appeared, as you know, to do away with sins, and there is no sin in him. No man therefore who dwells in him is

[a] *Literally* have an anointing (*Greek* chrism).
[b] *Some witnesses read* you have all knowledge.
[c] *Literally* the anointing. [d] *Or* We are called children of God! Not only called, we really are his children. [e] *Or* when he appears. [f] *Or* we are God's children, though he has not yet appeared; what we shall be we know, for when he does appear we shall be like him.

K.J.V.

whosoever sinneth hath not seen him, neither known him. 7 Little children, let no man deceive you: he that doeth righteousness is righteous, even as he is righteous. 8 He that committeth sin is of the devil; for the devil sinneth from the beginning. For this purpose the Son of God was manifested, that he might destroy the works of the devil. 9 Whosoever is born of God doth not commit sin; for his seed remaineth in him: and he cannot sin, because he is born of God. 10 In this the children of God are manifest, and the children of the devil: whosoever doeth not righteousness is not of God, neither he that loveth not his brother. 11 For this is the message that ye heard from the beginning, that we should love one another. 12 Not as Cain, who was of that wicked one, and slew his brother. And wherefore slew he him? Because his own works were evil, and his brother's righteous. 13 Marvel not, my brethren, if the world hate you. 14 We know that we have passed from death unto life, because we love the brethren. He that loveth not his brother abideth in death. 15 Whosoever hateth his brother is a murderer: and ye know that no murderer hath eternal life abiding in him. 16 Hereby perceive we the love of God, because he laid down his life for us: and we ought to lay down our lives for the brethren. 17 But whoso hath this world's good, and seeth his brother have need, and shutteth up his bowels of compassion from him, how dwelleth the love of God in him? 18 My little children, let us not love in word, neither in tongue; but in deed and in truth. 19 And hereby we know that we are of the truth, and shall assure our hearts before him. 20 For if our heart condemn us, God is greater than our heart, and knoweth all things. 21 Beloved, if our heart condemn us not, then have we confidence toward God. 22 And whatsoever we ask, we receive of him, because we keep his commandments, and do those things that are pleasing in his sight. 23 And this is his commandment, That we should believe on the name of his Son Jesus Christ, and love one another, as he gave us commandment. 24 And he that keepeth his commandments dwelleth in him, and he in him. And hereby we know that he abideth in us, by the Spirit which he hath given us.

R.S.V.

one who sins has either seen him or known him. 7 Little children, let no one deceive you. He who does right is righteous, as he is righteous. 8 He who commits sin is of the devil; for the devil has sinned from the beginning. The reason the Son of God appeared was to destroy the works of the devil. 9 No one born of God commits sin; for God's[f] nature abides in him, and he cannot sin because he is[g] born of God. 10 By this it may be seen who are the children of God, and who are the children of the devil: whoever does not do right is not of God, nor he who does not love his brother.

11 For this is the message which you have heard from the beginning, that we should love one another, 12 and not be like Cain who was of the evil one and murdered his brother. And why did he murder him? Because his own deeds were evil and his brother's righteous. 13 Do not wonder, brethren, that the world hates you. 14 We know that we have passed out of death into life, because we love the brethren. He who does not love remains in death. 15 Any one who hates his brother is a murderer, and you know that no murderer has eternal life abiding in him. 16 By this we know love, that he laid down his life for us; and we ought to lay down our lives for the brethren. 17 But if any one has the world's goods and sees his brother in need, yet closes his heart against him, how does God's love abide in him? 18 Little children, let us not love in word or speech but in deed and in truth.

19 By this we shall know that we are of the truth, and reassure our hearts before him 20 whenever our hearts condemn us; for God is greater than our hearts, and he knows everything. 21 Beloved, if our hearts do not condemn us, we have confidence before God; 22 and we receive from him whatever we ask, because we keep his commandments and do what pleases him. 23 And this is his commandment, that we should believe in the name of his Son Jesus Christ and love one another, just as he has commanded us. 24 All who keep his commandments abide in him, and he in them. And by this we know that he abides in us, by the Spirit which he has given us.

[f] Greek his. [g] Or for the offspring of God abide in him, and they cannot sin because they are.

or known him. You, my children, are younger than I am, and I don't want you to be taken in by any clever talk just here. The man who lives a consistently good life is a good man, as surely as God is good. But the man whose life is habitually sinful is spiritually a son of the devil, for the devil is behind all sin, as he always has been. Now the Son of God came to earth with the express purpose of liquidating the devil's activities. The man who is really God's son does not practice sin, for God's nature is in him, for good, and such a heredity is incapable of sin.

Here we have a clear indication as to who are the children of God and who are the children of the Devil. The man who does not lead a good life is no son of God, nor is the man who fails to love his brother. For the original command, as you know, is that we should love one another. We are none of us to have the spirit of Cain, who was a son of the devil and murdered his brother. Have you realized his motive? It was just because he realized the goodness of his brother's life and the rottenness of his own. Don't be surprised, therefore, if the world hates you.

Love and life are interconnected 3. 14

We know that we have crossed the frontier from death to life because we do love our brothers. The man without love for his brother is living in death already. The man who actively hates his brother is a potential murderer, and you will readily see that the eternal life of God cannot live in the heart of a murderer.

We know and to some extent realize the love of God for us because Christ expressed it in laying down his life for us. We must in turn express our love by laying down our lives for those who are our brothers. But as for the well-to-do man who sees his brother in want but shuts his eyes—and his heart—how could anyone believe that the love of God lives in him? My children, let us love not merely in theory or in words—let us love in sincerity and in practice!

Living in love means confidence 3. 19
in God

If we live like this, we shall know that we are children of the truth and can reassure ourselves in the sight of God, even if our own hearts make us feel guilty. For God is infinitely greater than our hearts, and he knows everything. And if, dear friends of mine, when we realize this our hearts no longer accuse us, we may have the utmost confidence in God's presence. We receive whatever we ask for, because we are obeying his orders and following his plans. His orders are that we should put our trust in the name of his Son, Jesus Christ, and love one another—as we used to hear him say in person.

The man who does obey God's commands lives in God and God lives in him, and the guarantee of his presence within us is the Spirit he has given us.

a sinner; the sinner has not seen him and does not know him.

My children, do not be misled: it is the man who does right who is righteous, as God is righteous; the man who sins is a child of the devil, for the devil has been a sinner from the first; and the Son of God appeared for the very purpose of undoing the devil's work.

A child of God does not commit sin, because the divine seed remains in him; he cannot be a sinner, because he is God's child. That is the distinction between the children of God and the children of the devil: no one who does not do right is God's child, nor is anyone who does not love his brother. For the message you have heard from the beginning is this: that we should love one another; unlike Cain, who was a child of the evil one and murdered his brother. And why did he murder him? Because his own actions were wrong, and his brother's were right.

My brothers, do not be surprised if the world hates you. We for our part have crossed over from death to life; this we know, because we love our brothers. The man who does not love is still in the realm of death, for everyone who hates his brother is a murderer, and no murderer, as you know, has eternal life within him. It is by this that we know what love is: that Christ laid down his life for us. And we in our turn are bound to lay down our lives for our brothers. But if a man has enough to live on, and yet when he sees his brother in need shuts up his heart against him, how can it be said that the divine love[a] dwells in him?

My children, love must not be a matter of words or talk; it must be genuine, and show itself in action. This is how we may know that we belong to the realm of truth, and convince ourselves in his sight that even if our conscience condemns us, God is greater than our conscience[b] and knows all.

Dear friends, if our conscience does not condemn us, then we can approach God with confidence, and obtain from him whatever we ask, because we are keeping his commands and doing what he approves. This is his command: to give our allegiance to his Son Jesus Christ and love one another as he commanded. When we keep his commands we dwell in him and he dwells in us. And this is how we can make sure that he dwells within us: we know it from the Spirit he has given us.

[a] Or that love for God . . . [b] Or and reassure ourselves in his sight in matters where our conscience condemns us, because God is greater than our conscience . . . ; or and yet we shall do well to convince ourselves that if even our own conscience condemns us, still more will God who is greater than conscience . . .

4 Beloved, believe not every spirit, but try the spirits whether they are of God: because many false prophets are gone out into the world. 2 Hereby know ye the Spirit of God: Every spirit that confesseth that Jesus Christ is come in the flesh is of God: 3And every spirit that confesseth not that Jesus Christ is come in the flesh is not of God: and this is that *spirit* of antichrist, whereof ye have heard that it should come; and even now already is it in the world. 4 Ye are of God, little children, and have overcome them: because greater is he that is in you, than he that is in the world. 5 They are of the world: therefore speak they of the world, and the world heareth them. 6 We are of God: he that knoweth God heareth us; he that is not of God heareth not us. Hereby know we the spirit of truth, and the spirit of error. 7 Beloved, let us love one another: for love is of God; and every one that loveth is born of God, and knoweth God. 8 He that loveth not, knoweth not God; for God is love. 9 In this was manifested the love of God toward us, because that God sent his only begotten Son into the world, that we might live through him. 10 Herein is love, not that we loved God, but that he loved us, and sent his Son *to be* the propitiation for our sins. 11 Beloved, if God so loved us, we ought also to love one another. 12 No man hath seen God at any time. If we love one another, God dwelleth in us, and his love is perfected in us. 13 Hereby know we that we dwell in him, and he in us, because he hath given us of his Spirit. 14And we have seen and do testify that the Father sent the Son *to be* the Saviour of the world. 15 Whosoever shall confess that Jesus is the Son of God, God dwelleth in him, and he in God. 16And we have known and believed the love that God hath to us. God is love; and he that dwelleth in love dwelleth in God, and God in him. 17 Herein is our love made perfect, that we may have boldness in the day of judgment: because as he is, so are we in this world. 18 There is no fear in love; but perfect love casteth out fear: because fear hath torment. He that feareth is not made perfect in love. 19 We love him, because he first loved us. 20 If a man say, I love God, and hateth his brother, he is a liar: for he

4 Beloved, do not believe every spirit, but test the spirits to see whether they are of God; for many false prophets have gone out into the world. 2 By this you know the Spirit of God: every spirit which confesses that Jesus Christ has come in the flesh is of God, 3 and every spirit which does not confess Jesus is not of God. This is the spirit of antichrist, of which you heard that it was coming, and now it is in the world already. 4 Little children, you are of God, and have overcome them; for he who is in you is greater than he who is in the world. 5 They are of the world, therefore what they say is of the world, and the world listens to them. 6 We are of God. Whoever knows God listens to us, and he who is not of God does not listen to us. By this we know the spirit of truth and the spirit of error.

7 Beloved, let us love one another; for love is of God, and he who loves is born of God and knows God. 8 He who does not love does not know God; for God is love. 9 In this the love of God was made manifest among us, that God sent his only Son into the world, so that we might live through him. 10 In this is love, not that we loved God but that he loved us and sent his Son to be the expiation for our sins. 11 Beloved, if God so loved us, we also ought to love one another. 12 No man has ever seen God; if we love one another, God abides in us and his love is perfected in us.

13 By this we know that we abide in him and he in us, because he has given us of his own Spirit. 14 And we have seen and testify that the Father has sent his Son as the Savior of the world. 15 Whoever confesses that Jesus is the Son of God, God abides in him, and he in God. 16 So we know and believe the love God has for us. God is love, and he who abides in love abides in God, and God abides in him. 17 In this is love perfected with us, that we may have confidence for the day of judgment, because as he is so are we in this world. 18 There is no fear in love, but perfect love casts out fear. For fear has to do with punishment, and he who fears is not perfected in love. 19 We love, because he first loved us. 20 If any one says, "I love God," and hates his brother, he is a liar;

PHILLIPS

I repeat my warning   **4. 1**
against false teaching

Don't trust every spirit, dear friends of mine, but test them to discover whether they come from God or not. For the world is full of false prophets. You can test them in this simple way: every spirit that acknowledges the fact that Jesus Christ actually became man, comes from God, but the spirit which denies this fact does not come from God. The latter comes from the antichrist, which you were warned would come and which is already in the world.

You, my children, who belong to God have already defeated this spirit, because the one who lives in you is far stronger than the antichrist in the world. The agents of the antichrist are children of the world; they speak the world's language and the world, of course, pays attention to what they say. We are God's children and only the man who knows God hears our message; what we say means nothing to the man who is not himself a child of God. This gives us a ready means of distinguishing the true from the false.

Let us love: God has shown us   **4. 7**
love at its highest

To you whom I love I say, let us go on loving one another, for love comes from God. Every man who truly loves is God's son and has some knowledge of him. But the man who does not love cannot know him at all, for God is love.

To us, the greatest demonstration of God's love for us has been his sending his only Son into the world to give us life through him. We see real love, not in the fact that we loved God, but that he loved us and sent his Son to make personal atonement for our sins. If God loved us as much as that, surely we, in our turn, should love one another!

It is true that no human being has ever had a direct vision of God. Yet if we love one another God does actually live within us, and his love grows in us toward perfection. And, as I wrote above, the guarantee of our living in him and his living in us is the share of his own Spirit which he gives us.

Knowing Christ means more love   **4. 14**
and confidence, less and less fear

We ourselves are eyewitnesses able and willing to testify to the fact that the Father did send the Son to save the world. Everyone who acknowledges that Jesus is the Son of God finds that God lives in him, and he lives in God. So have we come to know and trust the love God has for us. God *is* love, and the man whose life is lived in love does, in fact, live in God, and God does, in fact, live in him. So our love for him grows more and more, filling us with complete confidence for the day when he shall judge all men—for we realize that our life in this world is actually his life lived in us. Love contains no fear—indeed fully developed love expels every particle of fear, for fear always contains some of the torture of feeling guilty. This means that the man who lives in fear has not yet had his love perfected.

Yes, we love him because he first loved us. If

N.E.B.

4 But do not trust any and every spirit, my friends; test the spirits, to see whether they are from God, for among those who have gone out into the world there are many prophets falsely inspired. This is how we may recognize the Spirit of God: every spirit which acknowledges that Jesus Christ has come in the flesh is from God, and every spirit which does not thus acknowledge Jesus is not from God. This is what is meant by 'Antichrist';[a] you have been told that he was to come, and here he is, in the world already!

But you, my children, are of God's family, and you have the mastery over these false prophets, because he who inspires you is greater than he who inspires the godless world. They are of that world, and so therefore is their teaching; that is why the world listens to them. But we belong to God, and a man who knows God listens to us, while he who does not belong to God refuses us a hearing. That is how we distinguish the spirit of truth from the spirit of error.

Dear friends, let us love one another, because love is from God. Everyone who loves is a child of God and knows God, but the unloving know nothing of God. For God is love; and his love was disclosed to us in this, that he sent his only Son into the world to bring us life. The love I speak of is not our love for God, but the love he showed to us in sending his Son as the remedy for the defilement of our sins. If God thus loved us, dear friends, we in turn are bound to love one another. Though God has never been seen by any man, God himself dwells in us if we love one another; his love is brought to perfection within us.

Here is the proof that we dwell in him and he dwells in us: he has imparted his Spirit to us. Moreover, we have seen for ourselves, and we attest, that the Father sent the Son to be the saviour of the world, and if a man acknowledges that Jesus is the Son of God, God dwells in him and he dwells in God. Thus we have come to know and believe the love which God has for us.

God is love; he who dwells in love is dwelling in God, and God in him. This is for us the perfection of love, to have confidence on the day of judgement, and this we can have, because even in this world we are as he is. There is no room for fear in love; perfect love banishes fear. For fear brings with it the pains of judgement, and anyone who is afraid has not attained to love in its perfection. We love because he loved us first. But if a man says, 'I love God', while hating his brother, he is a liar. If he does not love the

---

[a] *Or* This is the spirit of Antichrist.

K.J.V.

that loveth not his brother whom he hath seen, how can he love God whom he hath not seen? 21 And this commandment have we from him, That he who loveth God love his brother also.

5 Whosoever believeth that Jesus is the Christ is born of God: and every one that loveth him that begat loveth him also that is begotten of him. 2 By this we know that we love the children of God, when we love God, and keep his commandments. 3 For this is the love of God, that we keep his commandments: and his commandments are not grievous. 4 For whatsoever is born of God overcometh the world: and this is the victory that overcometh the world, *even* our faith. 5 Who is he that overcometh the world, but he that believeth that Jesus is the Son of God? 6 This is he that came by water and blood, *even* Jesus Christ; not by water only, but by water and blood. And it is the Spirit that beareth witness, because the Spirit is truth. 7 For there are three that bear record in heaven, the Father, the Word, and the Holy Ghost: and these three are one. 8 And there are three that bear witness in earth, the spirit, and the water, and the blood: and these three agree in one. 9 If we receive the witness of men, the witness of God is greater: for this is the witness of God which he hath testified of his Son. 10 He that believeth on the Son of God hath the witness in himself: he that believeth not God hath made him a liar; because he believeth not the record that God gave of his Son. 11 And this is the record, that God hath given to us eternal life, and this life is in his Son. 12 He that hath the Son hath life; *and* he that hath not the Son of God hath not life. 13 These things have I written unto you that believe on the name of the Son of God; that ye may know that ye have eternal life, and that ye may believe on the name of the Son of God. 14 And this is the confidence that we have in him, that, if we ask any thing according to his will, he heareth us: 15 And if we know that he hear us, whatsoever we ask, we know that we have the petitions that we desired of him. 16 If any man see his brother sin a sin *which is* not unto death, he shall ask, and he shall give him life for them that sin not unto death. There is a sin unto death: I do not say that he shall pray for it. 17 All unrighteousness is sin: and there is a sin not unto death.

R.S.V.

for he who does not love his brother whom he has seen, cannot [h] love God whom he has not seen. 21 And this commandment we have from him, that he who loves God should love his brother also.

5 Every one who believes that Jesus is the Christ is a child of God, and every one who loves the parent loves the child. 2 By this we know that we love the children of God, when we love God and obey his commandments. 3 For this is the love of God, that we keep his commandments. And his commandments are not burdensome. 4 For whatever is born of God overcomes the world; and this is the victory that overcomes the world, our faith. 5 Who is it that overcomes the world but he who believes that Jesus is the Son of God?

6 This is he who came by water and blood, Jesus Christ, not with the water only but with the water and the blood. 7 And the Spirit is the witness, because the Spirit is the truth. 8 There are three witnesses, the Spirit, the water, and the blood; and these three agree. 9 If we receive the testimony of men, the testimony of God is greater; for this is the testimony of God that he has borne witness to his Son. 10 He who believes in the Son of God has the testimony in himself. He who does not believe God has made him a liar, because he has not believed in the testimony that God has borne to his Son. 11 And this is the testimony, that God gave us eternal life, and this life is in his Son. 12 He who has the Son has life; he who has not the Son of God has not life.

13 I write this to you who believe in the name of the Son of God, that you may know that you have eternal life. 14 And this is the confidence which we have in him, that if we ask anything according to his will he hears us. 15 And if we know that he hears us in whatever we ask, we know that we have obtained the requests made of him. 16 If any one sees his brother committing what is not a mortal sin, he will ask, and God [i] will give him life for those whose sin is not mortal. There is sin which is mortal; I do not say that one is to pray for that. 17 All wrongdoing is sin, but there is sin which is not mortal.

[h] Other ancient authorities read *how can he.*
[i] Greek *he.*

PHILLIPS

N.E.B.

a man says, "I love God" and hates his brother, he is a liar. For if he does not love the brother before his eyes how can he love the one beyond his sight? And in any case it is his explicit command that the one who loves God must love his brother too.

brother whom he has seen, it cannot be that he loves God whom he has not seen. And indeed this command comes to us from Christ himself: that he who loves God must also love his brother.

Only real faith in Christ as God's Son can make a man confident, obedient and loving

5. 1

Everyone who really believes that Jesus is the Christ proves himself one of God's family. The man who loves the Father cannot help loving the Father's own Son.

The test of the genuineness of our love for God's family lies in this question—do we love God himself and do we obey his commands? For loving God means obeying his commands, and these commands of his are not burdensome, for God's "heredity" within us will always conquer the world outside us. In fact, this faith of ours is the only way in which the world has been conquered. For who could ever be said to conquer the world, in the true sense, except the man who really believes that Jesus is God's Son? Jesus Christ himself is the one who came by water and by blood—not by water only, but by the water and the blood. The Spirit bears witness to this, for the Spirit is the truth. The witness therefore is a triple one—the Spirit in our own hearts, the signs of the water of baptism and the blood of atonement—and they all say the same thing. If we are prepared to accept human testimony, God's own testimony concerning his own Son is surely infinitely more valuable. The man who really believes in the Son of God will find God's testimony in his own heart. The man who will not believe God is making him out to be a liar, because he is deliberately refusing to accept the testimony that God has given concerning his own Son. This is, that God has given men eternal life and this real life is to be found only on his Son. It follows naturally that any man who has genuine contact with Christ has this life; and if he has not, then he does not possess this life at all.

I have written like this to you who already believe in the name of God's Son so that you may be quite sure that, here and now, you possess eternal life. We have such confidence in him that we are certain that he hears every request that is made in accord with his own plan. And since we know that he invariably gives his attention to our prayers, whatever they are about, we can be quite sure that our prayers will be answered.

5 Everyone who believes that Jesus is the Christ is a child of God, and to love the parent means to love his child; it follows that when we love God and obey his commands we love his children too. For to love God is to keep his commands; and they are not burdensome, because every child of God is victor over the godless world. The victory that defeats the world is our faith, for who is victor over the world but he who believes that Jesus is the Son of God?

This is he who came with water and blood: Jesus Christ. He came, not by water alone, but by water and blood; and there is the Spirit to bear witness, because the Spirit is truth. For there are three witnesses, the Spirit, the water, and the blood, and these three are in agreement. We accept human testimony, but surely divine testimony is stronger, and this threefold testimony is indeed that of God himself, the witness he has borne to his Son. He who believes in the Son of God has this testimony in his own heart, but he who disbelieves God, makes him out to be a liar, by refusing to accept God's own witness to his Son. The witness is this: that God has given us eternal life, and that this life is found in his Son. He who possesses the Son has life indeed; he who does not possess the Son of God has not that life.

This letter is to assure you that you have eternal life. It is addressed to those who give their allegiance to the Son of God.

We can approach God with confidence for this reason: if we make requests which accord with his will he listens to us; and if we know that our requests are heard, we know also that the things we ask for are ours.

If a man sees his brother committing a sin which is not a deadly sin, he should pray to God for him, and he will grant him life—that is, when men are not guilty of deadly sin. There is such a thing as deadly sin, and I do not suggest that he should pray about that; but although all wrongdoing is sin, not all sin is deadly sin.

Help each other to live without sin

5. 16

If any of you should see his brother committing a sin (I don't mean deliberately turning his back on God and embracing evil), he should pray to God for him and secure fresh life for the sinner. It is possible to commit sin that is a deliberate embracing of evil and that leads to spiritual death—that is not the sort of sin I have in mind when I recommend prayer for the sinner. Every failure to obey God's laws is sin, of course, but there is sin that does not preclude repentance and forgiveness.

K.J.V.

18 We know that whosoever is born of God sinneth not; but he that is begotten of God keepeth himself, and that wicked one toucheth him not. 19*And* we know that we are of God, and the whole world lieth in wickedness. 20And we know that the Son of God is come, and hath given us an understanding, that we may know him that is true; and we are in him that is true, *even* in his Son Jesus Christ. This is the true God, and eternal life. 21 Little children, keep yourselves from idols. Amen.

R.S.V.

18 We know that any one born of God does not sin, but He who was born of God keeps him, and the evil one does not touch him.

19 We know that we are of God, and the whole world is in the power of the evil one.

20 And we know that the Son of God has come and has given us understanding, to know him who is true; and we are in him who is true, in his Son Jesus Christ. This is the true God and eternal life. 21 Little children, keep yourselves from idols.

PHILLIPS

Our certain knowledge   *5. 18*

We know that the true child of God does not sin; he is in the charge of God's own Son and the evil one must keep his distance.

We know that we ourselves are children of God, and we also know that the world around us is under the power of the evil one. We know too that the Son of God has actually come to this world, and has shown us the way to know the one who is true. We know that our real life is in the true one, and in his Son Jesus Christ. This is the real God and this is real, eternal life.

But be on your guard, my dear children, against every false god!

JOHN

N.E.B.

We know that no child of God is a sinner; it is the Son of God who keeps him safe, and the evil one cannot touch him.

We know that we are of God's family, while the whole godless world lies in the power of the evil one.

We know that the Son of God has come and given us understanding to know him who is real; indeed we are in him who is real, since we are in his Son Jesus Christ. This is the true God, this is eternal life. My children, be on the watch against false gods.

K.J.V.

THE

SECOND EPISTLE

OF

JOHN

The elder unto the elect lady and her children, whom I love in the truth; and not I only, but also all they that have known the truth; 2 For the truth's sake, which dwelleth in us, and shall be with us for ever. 3 Grace be with you, mercy, *and* peace, from God the Father, and from the Lord Jesus Christ, the Son of the Father, in truth and love. 4 I rejoiced greatly that I found of thy children walking in truth, as we have received a commandment from the Father. 5 And now I beseech thee, lady, not as though I wrote a new commandment unto thee, but that which we had from the beginning, that we love one another. 6 And this is love, that we walk after his commandments. This is the commandment, That, as ye have heard from the beginning, ye should walk in it. 7 For many deceivers are entered into the world, who confess not that Jesus Christ is come in the flesh. This is a deceiver and an antichrist. 8 Look to yourselves, that we lose not those things which we have wrought, but that we receive a full reward. 9 Whosoever transgresseth, and abideth not in the doctrine of Christ, hath not God. He that abideth in the doctrine of Christ, he hath both the Father and the Son. 10 If there come any unto you, and bring not this doctrine, receive him not into *your* house, neither bid him God speed: 11 For he that biddeth him God speed is partaker of his evil deeds. 12 Having many things to write unto you, I would not *write* with paper and ink: but I trust to come unto you, and speak face to face, that our joy may be full. 13 The children of thy elect sister greet thee. Amen.

R.S.V.

THE

SECOND LETTER OF

JOHN

1 The elder to the elect lady and her children, whom I love in the truth, and not only I but also all who know the truth, 2 because of the truth which abides in us and will be with us for ever:

3 Grace, mercy, and peace will be with us, from God the Father and from Jesus Christ the Father's Son, in truth and love.

4 I rejoiced greatly to find some of your children following the truth, just as we have been commanded by the Father. 5 And now I beg you, lady, not as though I were writing you a new commandment, but the one we have had from the beginning, that we love one another. 6 And this is love, that we follow his commandments; this is the commandment, as you have heard from the beginning, that you follow love. 7 For many deceivers have gone out into the world, men who will not acknowledge the coming of Jesus Christ in the flesh; such a one is the deceiver and the antichrist. 8 Look to yourselves, that you may not lose what you[a] have worked for, but may win a full reward. 9 Any one who goes ahead and does not abide in the doctrine of Christ does not have God; he who abides in the doctrine has both the Father and the Son. 10 If any one comes to you and does not bring this doctrine, do not receive him into the house or give him any greeting; 11 for he who greets him shares his wicked work.

12 Though I have much to write to you, I would rather not use paper and ink, but I hope to come to see you and talk with you face to face, so that our joy may be complete.
13 The children of your elect sister greet you.

[a] Other ancient authorities read *we*.

THE
SECOND LETTER OF
JOHN

THE
SECOND LETTER OF
JOHN

Truth and Love

This letter comes from the Elder to a certain Christian lady and her children, held in the highest affection not only by me but by all who know the truth. For that truth's sake (which even now we know and which will be our companion for ever) I wish you, in all love and sincerity, grace, mercy and peace from God the Father and the Lord Jesus Christ, the Father's Son.

The elder to the Lady chosen by God, and her children, whom I love in truth—and not I alone but all who know the truth—for the sake of the truth that dwells among us and will be with us for ever.

Grace, mercy, and peace shall be with us from God the Father and from Jesus Christ the Son of the Father, in truth and love.

I was delighted to find that some of your children are living by the truth, as we were commanded by the Father. And now I have a request to make of you. Do not think I am giving a new command; I am recalling the one we have had before us from the beginning: let us love one another. And love means following the commands of God. This is the command which was given you from the beginning, to be your rule of life.

Many deceivers have gone out into the world, who do not acknowledge Jesus Christ as coming in the flesh. These are the persons described as the Antichrist, the arch-deceiver. Beware of them, so that you may not lose all that we worked for, but receive your reward in full.

Anyone who runs ahead too far, and does not stand by the doctrine of the Christ, is without God; he who stands by that doctrine possesses both the Father and the Son. If anyone comes to you who does not bring this doctrine, do not welcome him into your house or give him a greeting; for anyone who gives him a greeting is an accomplice in his wicked deeds.

I have much to write to you, but I do not care to put it down in black and white. But I hope to visit you and talk with you face to face, so that our joy may be complete. The children of your Sister, chosen by God, send their greetings.

Let us love, but have no dealings with lies   4

I was overjoyed to find some of your children living the life of truth, as the Father himself instructed us. I beg you now, dear lady, not as though I were issuing any new order but simply reminding you of the original one, to see that we continue to love one another. Real love means obeying the Father's orders, and you have known from the beginning that you must live in obedience to him. For the world is becoming full of impostors—men who will not admit that Jesus Christ really became man. Now this is the very spirit of deceit and is antichrist. Take care of yourselves; don't throw away all the labor that has been spent on you, but persevere till God gives you your reward.

Have nothing to do with false teachers   9

The man who is so "advanced" that he is not content with what Christ taught has in fact no God. The man who bases his life on Christ's teaching, however, has both the Father and the Son as his God. If any teacher comes to you who is disloyal to what Christ taught, don't have him inside your house. Don't even wish him "Godspeed," unless you want to share in the evil that he is doing.

Personal   12

I have a lot that I could write to you, but somehow I find it hard to put down on paper. I hope to come and see you personally, and we shall have a heart-to-heart talk together—and how we shall enjoy that! Your sister's children send their love.

                                   JOHN

THE
THIRD EPISTLE
OF
JOHN

THE
THIRD LETTER OF
JOHN

The elder unto the well beloved Gaius, whom I love in the truth. 2 Beloved, I wish above all things that thou mayest prosper and be in health, even as thy soul prospereth. 3 For I rejoiced greatly, when the brethren came and testified of the truth that is in thee, even as thou walkest in the truth. 4 I have no greater joy than to hear that my children walk in truth. 5 Beloved, thou doest faithfully whatsoever thou doest to the brethren, and to strangers; 6 Which have borne witness of thy charity before the church: whom if thou bring forward on their journey after a godly sort, thou shalt do well: 7 Because that for his name's sake they went forth, taking nothing of the Gentiles. 8 We therefore ought to receive such, that we might be fellow helpers to the truth. 9 I wrote unto the church: but Diotrephes, who loveth to have the preeminence among them, receiveth us not. 10 Wherefore, if I come, I will remember his deeds which he doeth, prating against us with malicious words: and not content therewith, neither doth he himself receive the brethren, and forbiddeth them that would, and casteth *them* out of the church. 11 Beloved, follow not that which is evil, but that which is good. He that doeth good is of God: but he that doeth evil

1 The elder to the beloved Gaius, whom I love in the truth.
2 Beloved, I pray that all may go well with you and that you may be in health; I know that it is well with your soul. 3 For I greatly rejoiced when some of the brethren arrived and testified to the truth of your life, as indeed you do follow the truth. 4 No greater joy can I have than this, to hear that my children follow the truth.
5 Beloved, it is a loyal thing you do when you render any service to the brethren, especially to strangers, 6 who have testified to your love before the church. You will do well to send them on their journey as befits God's service. 7 For they have set out for his sake and have accepted nothing from the heathen. 8 So we ought to support such men, that we may be fellow workers in the truth.
9 I have written something to the church; but Diotrephes, who likes to put himself first, does not acknowledge my authority. 10 So if I come, I will bring up what he is doing, prating against me with evil words. And not content with that, he refuses himself to welcome the brethren, and also stops those who want to welcome them and puts them out of the church.
11 Beloved, do not imitate evil but imitate good. He who does good is of God; he who does

THE
THIRD LETTER OF
JOHN

THE
THIRD LETTER OF
JOHN

Trouble in the Church

The Elder sends this personal letter to his very dear friend Gaius with love in the truth.

I thank God for you and pray for you 2

My heartfelt prayer for you, my very dear friend, is that you may be as healthy and prosperous in every way as you are in soul. I was delighted when the brothers arrived and spoke so highly of the sincerity of your life—obviously you are living in the truth. Nothing brings me greater joy nowadays than hearing that "my children" are living "in the truth."

Your actions have been just right 5

You are doing a fine faithful piece of work, dear friend, in looking after the brothers who come your way, especially when you have never seen them before. They have testified to your love before the church. It is a fine thing to help them on their way—it shows you realize the importance of what they are doing. They set out on this work, as you know, for the sake of "the name" and they accept no help from non-Christians. We ought to give such men a real welcome and prove that we too are cooperating with the truth.

I know about Diotrephes 9

I did write a letter to the church, but Diotrephes, who wants to be head of everything, does not recognize us! If I do come to you, I shall not forget his actions nor the slanderous things he has said against us. And it doesn't stop there, alas, for although he wants to be leader he refuses the duty of welcoming the brothers himself, and stops those who would like to do so—he even excommunicates them!

A little piece of advice: and 11
I shall soon be seeing you personally

Never let evil be your example, dear friend of mine, but always good. The man who does good is God's man, but the man who does evil does not know God at all.

The elder to dear Gaius, whom I love in truth.

My dear Gaius, I pray that you may enjoy good health, and that all may go well with you, as I know it goes well with your soul. I was delighted when friends came and told me how true you have been; indeed you are true in your whole life. Nothing gives me greater joy than to hear that my children are living by the truth.

My dear friend, you show a fine loyalty in everything that you do for these our fellow-Christians, strangers though they are to you. They have spoken of your kindness before the congregation here. Please help them on their journey in a manner worthy of the God we serve. It was on Christ's work that they went out; and they would accept nothing from pagans. We are bound to support such men, and so play our part in spreading the truth.

I sent a letter to the congregation, but Diotrephes, their would-be leader, will have nothing to do with us. If I come, I will bring up the things he is doing. He lays baseless and spiteful charges against us; not satisfied with that, he refuses to receive our friends, and he interferes with those who would do so, and tries to expel them from the congregation.

My dear friend, do not imitate bad examples, but good ones. The well-doer is a child of God; the evil-doer has never seen God.

K.J.V.

hath not seen God. 12 Demetrius hath good report of all *men,* and of the truth itself: yea, and we *also* bear record; and ye know that our record is true. 13 I had many things to write, but I will not with ink and pen write unto thee: 14 But I trust I shall shortly see thee, and we shall speak face to face. Peace *be* to thee. *Our* friends salute thee. Greet the friends by name.

R.S.V.

evil has not seen God. 12 Demetrius has testimony from every one, and from the truth itself; I testify to him too, and you know my testimony is true.

13 I had much to write to you, but I would rather not write with pen and ink; 14 I hope to see you soon, and we will talk together face to face.

15 Peace be to you. The friends greet you. Greet the friends, every one of them.

PHILLIPS

Everyone has a good word to say for Demetrius, and the very truth speaks well of him. He has our warm recommendation also, and you know you can trust what we say about anyone.

There is a great deal I want to say to you but I can't put it down in black and white. I hope to see you before long, and we will have a heart-to-heart talk. Peace be with you. All our friends here send love: please give ours personally to all our friends at your end.

JOHN

N.E.B.

Demetrius gets a good testimonial from everybody—yes, and from the truth itself. I add my testimony, and you know that my testimony is true.

I have much to write to you, but I do not care to set it down with pen and ink. I hope to see you very soon, and we will talk face to face. Peace be with you. Our friends send their greetings. Greet our friends individually.

THE
GENERAL EPISTLE
OF
JUDE

THE LETTER OF
JUDE

Jude, the servant of Jesus Christ, and brother of James, to them that are sanctified by God the Father, and preserved in Jesus Christ, *and* called: 2 Mercy unto you, and peace, and love, be multiplied. 3 Beloved, when I gave all diligence to write unto you of the common salvation, it was needful for me to write unto you, and exhort *you* that ye should earnestly contend for the faith which was once delivered unto the saints. 4 For there are certain men crept in unawares, who were before of old ordained to this condemnation, ungodly men, turning the grace of our God into lasciviousness, and denying the only Lord God, and our Lord Jesus Christ. 5 I will therefore put you in remembrance, though ye once knew this, how that the Lord, having saved the people out of the land of Egypt, afterward destroyed them that believed not. 6 And the angels which kept not their first estate, but left their own habitation, he hath reserved in everlasting chains under darkness unto the judgment of the great day. 7 Even as Sodom and Gomorrah, and the cities about them in like manner, giving themselves over to fornication, and going after strange flesh, are set forth for an example, suffering the vengeance of eternal fire. 8 Likewise also these *filthy* dreamers defile the flesh, despise dominion, and speak evil of dignities. 9 Yet Michael the archangel, when contending with the devil he disputed about the body of Moses, durst not bring against him a railing accusation, but said, The Lord rebuke thee. 10 But these speak evil of those things which they know not: but what they know naturally, as brute beasts, in those things they corrupt themselves. 11 Woe unto them! for they have gone in the way of Cain, and ran greedily after the error of Balaam for reward, and per-

Jude, a servant of Jesus Christ and brother of James,
To those who are called, beloved in God the Father and kept for Jesus Christ:
2 May mercy, peace, and love be multiplied to you.

3 Beloved, being very eager to write to you of our common salvation, I found it necessary to write appealing to you to contend for the faith which was once for all delivered to the saints. 4 For admission has been secretly gained by some who long ago were designated for this condemnation, ungodly persons who pervert the grace of our God into licentiousness and deny our only Master and Lord, Jesus Christ.[a]

5 Now I desire to remind you, though you were once for all fully informed, that he[b] who saved a people out of the land of Egypt, afterward destroyed those who did not believe. 6 And the angels that did not keep their own position but left their proper dwelling have been kept by him in eternal chains in the nether gloom until the judgment of the great day; 7 just as Sodom and Gomorrah and the surrounding cities, which likewise acted immorally and indulged in unnatural lust, serve as an example by undergoing a punishment of eternal fire.

8 Yet in like manner these men in their dreamings defile the flesh, reject authority, and revile the glorious ones.[c] 9 But when the archangel Michael, contending with the devil, disputed about the body of Moses, he did not presume to pronounce a reviling judgment upon him, but said, "The Lord rebuke you." 10 But these men revile whatever they do not understand, and by those things that they know by instinct as irrational animals do, they are destroyed. 11 Woe to them! For they walk in the way of Cain, and abandon themselves for the sake of gain to Balaam's error, and perish in

[a] Or *the only Master and our Lord Jesus Christ.*
[b] Ancient authorities read *Jesus* or *the Lord* or *God.* [c] Greek *glories.*

THE LETTER OF

JUDE

Jude, a servant of Jesus Christ and brother of James, to those who have obeyed the call, who are loved by God the Father and kept in the faith by Jesus Christ—may you ever experience more and more of mercy, peace and love!

The reason for this letter 3

I fully intended, dear friends, to write to you about our common salvation, but I feel compelled to make my letter to you an earnest appeal to put up a real fight for the faith which has been once for all committed to those who belong to Christ. For there are men who have surreptitiously entered the Church but who have for a long time been heading straight for the condemnation I shall plainly give them. They have no real reverence for God, and they abuse his grace as an opportunity for immorality. They will not recognize the only master, Jesus Christ our Lord.

Past history warns us that 5
the unfaithful have mingled
with the faithful

I want to remind you of something that you really know already: that although the Lord saved all the people from the land of Egypt, yet afterward he brought to their downfall those who would not trust him. And the very angels who failed in their high duties and abandoned their proper sphere have been deprived by God of both light and liberty until the judgment of the great day. Sodom and Gomorrah and the adjacent cities who, in the same way as these men today, gave themselves up to sexual immorality and perversion, stand in their punishment as a permanent warning of the fire of judgment. Yet these men are defiling their bodies by their filthy fantasies in just the same way; they show utter contempt for authority and make a jest of the heavenly glories. But I would remind you that even the archangel Michael when he was contending with the devil in the dispute over the body of Moses did not dare to condemn him with mockery. He simply said, the Lord rebuke you!

These fellows, however, are ready to mock at anything that is beyond their immediate knowledge, while in the things that they know by instinct like unreasoning beasts they have become utterly depraved. I say, Woe to them! For they have taken the road of Cain; for what they could get they have rushed into the same error as Balaam; they have destroyed themselves by rebelling against God as did Korah long ago.

A LETTER OF

JUDE

The Danger of False Belief

From Jude, servant of Jesus Christ and brother of James, to those whom God has called, who live in the love of God the Father and in the safe keeping of Jesus Christ.

Mercy, peace, and love be yours in fullest measure.

My friends, I was fully engaged in writing to you about our salvation—which is yours no less than ours—when it became urgently necessary to write at once and appeal to you to join the struggle in defence of the faith, the faith which God entrusted to his people once and for all. It is in danger from certain persons who have wormed their way in, the very men whom Scripture long ago marked down for the doom they have incurred. They are the enemies of religion; they pervert the free favour of our God into licentiousness, disowning Jesus Christ, our only Master and Lord.[a]

You already know it all, but let me remind you how the Lord,[b] having once delivered the people of Israel out of Egypt, next time destroyed those who were guilty of unbelief. Remember too the angels, how some of them were not content to keep the dominion given to them but abandoned their proper home; and God has reserved them for judgement on the great Day, bound beneath the darkness in everlasting chains. Remember Sodom and Gomorrah and the neighbouring towns; like the angels, they committed fornication and followed unnatural lusts; and they paid the penalty in eternal fire, an example for all to see.

So too with these men today. Their dreams lead them to defile the body, to flout authority, and to insult celestial beings. In contrast, when the archangel Michael was in debate with the devil, disputing the possession of Moses's body, he did not presume to condemn him in insulting words,[c] but said, 'May the Lord rebuke you!'

But these men pour abuse upon things they do not understand; the things they do understand, by instinct like brute beasts, prove their undoing. Alas for them! They have gone the way of Cain; they have plunged into Balaam's error for pay; they have rebelled like Korah, and they share his doom.

[a] Or disowning our one and only Master, and Jesus Christ our Lord. [b] Some witnesses read Jesus (which might be understood as Joshua). [c] Or to charge him with blasphemy.

K.J.V.

ished in the gainsaying of Core. 12 These are spots in your feasts of charity, when they feast with you, feeding themselves without fear: clouds *they are* without water, carried about of winds; trees whose fruit withereth, without fruit, twice dead, plucked up by the roots; 13 Raging waves of the sea, foaming out their own shame; wandering stars, to whom is reserved the blackness of darkness for ever. 14And Enoch also, the seventh from Adam, prophesied of these, saying, Behold, the Lord cometh with ten thousands of his saints, 15 To execute judgment upon all, and to convince all that are ungodly among them of all their ungodly deeds which they have ungodly committed, and of all their hard *speeches* which ungodly sinners have spoken against him. 16 These are murmurers, complainers, walking after their own lusts; and their mouth speaketh great swelling *words,* having men's persons in admiration because of advantage. 17 But, beloved, remember ye the words which were spoken before of the apostles of our Lord Jesus Christ; 18 How that they told you there should be mockers in the last time, who should walk after their own ungodly lusts. 19 These be they who separate themselves, sensual, having not the Spirit. 20 But ye, beloved, building up yourselves on your most holy faith, praying in the Holy Ghost, 21 Keep yourselves in the love of God, looking for the mercy of our Lord Jesus Christ unto eternal life. 22And of some have compassion, making a difference: 23And others save with fear, pulling *them* out of the fire; hating even the garment spotted by the flesh. 24 Now unto him that is able to keep you from falling, and to present *you* faultless before the presence of his glory with exceeding joy, 25 To the only wise God our Saviour, *be* glory and majesty, dominion and power, both now and ever. Amen.

R.S.V.

Korah's rebellion. 12 These are blemishes[d] on your love feasts, as they boldly carouse together, looking after themselves; waterless clouds, carried along by winds; fruitless trees in late autumn, twice dead, uprooted; 13 wild waves of the sea, casting up the foam of their own shame; wandering stars for whom the nether gloom of darkness has been reserved for ever.

14 It was of these also that Enoch in the seventh generation from Adam prophesied, saying, "Behold, the Lord came with his holy myriads, 15 to execute judgment on all, and to convict all the ungodly of all their deeds of ungodliness which they have committed in such an ungodly way, and of all the harsh things which ungodly sinners have spoken against him." 16 These are grumblers, malcontents, following their own passions, loud-mouthed boasters, flattering people to gain advantage.

17 But you must remember, beloved, the predictions of the apostles of our Lord Jesus Christ; 18 they said to you, "In the last time there will be scoffers, following their own ungodly passions." 19 It is these who set up divisions, worldly people, devoid of the Spirit. 20 But you, beloved, build yourselves up on your most holy faith; pray in the Holy Spirit; 21 keep yourselves in the love of God; wait for the mercy of our Lord Jesus Christ unto eternal life. 22And convince some, who doubt; 23 save some, by snatching them out of the fire; on some have mercy with fear, hating even the garment spotted by the flesh.[e]

24 Now to him who is able to keep you from falling and to present you without blemish before the presence of his glory with rejoicing, 25 to the only God, our Savior through Jesus Christ our Lord, be glory, majesty, dominion, and authority, before all time and now and for ever. Amen.

---

[d] Or *reefs.* [e] The Greek text in this sentence is uncertain at several points.

PHILLIPS	N.E.B.

PHILLIPS

Be on your guard against **12**
these wicked men

These men are a menace to the good fellowship of your feasts, for they eat in your company without a qualm yet they care for no one but themselves. They are like clouds driven up by the wind, but they bring no rain. They are like trees with the leaves of autumn but without a single fruit—they are doubly dead, for they have no roots either. They are like raging waves of the sea producing only the spume of their own shameful deeds. They are like stars which follow no orbit, and their proper place is the everlasting blackness of the regions beyond the light. It was of men like these that Enoch (seventh descendant from Adam) prophesied when he said:

Behold, the Lord came with ten thousands of his holy ones, to execute judgment upon all, and to convict all the ungodly of all their works of ungodliness which they have ungodly wrought, and of all the hard things which ungodly sinners have spoken against him.

These are the men who complain and curse their fate while trying all the time to mold life according to their own desires. They "talk big" but will pay men great respect if it is to their own advantage.

Forewarned is forearmed **17**

Now do remember, dear friends, the words that the messengers of Jesus Christ gave us beforehand when they said, "There will come in the last days mockers who live according to their own godless desires." These are the men who split communities, for they are led by human emotions and never by the Spirit of God.

Look after your own faith: **20**
save whom you can

But you, dear friends of mine, build yourselves up on the foundation of your most holy faith and by praying through the Holy Spirit keep yourselves within the love of God. Wait patiently for the mercy of our Lord Jesus Christ which will bring you to the life eternal. For some of these men you can feel pity and you can treat them differently. Others you must try to save by fear, snatching them as it were out of the fire while hating the very garments their deeds have befouled.

Ascription **24**

Now to him who is able to keep you from falling and to present you before his glory without fault and with unspeakable joy, to the only God, our savior, be glory and majesty, power and authority, through Jesus Christ our Lord, before time was, now, and in all ages to come, amen.

JUDE

N.E.B.

These men are a blot on your love-feasts, where they eat and drink without reverence. They are shepherds who take care only of themselves. They are clouds carried away by the wind without giving rain, trees that in season bear no fruit, dead twice over and pulled up by the roots. They are fierce waves of the sea, foaming shameful deeds; they are stars that have wandered from their course, and the place for ever reserved for them is blackest darkness.

It was to them that Enoch, the seventh in descent from Adam, directed his prophecy when he said: 'I saw the Lord come with his myriads of angels, to bring all men to judgement and to convict all the godless of all the godless deeds they had committed, and of all the defiant words which godless sinners had spoken against him.'

They are a set of grumblers and malcontents. They follow their lusts. Big words come rolling from their lips, and they court favour to gain their ends. But you, my friends, should remember the predictions made by the apostles of our Lord Jesus Christ. This was the warning they gave you: 'In the final age there will be men who pour scorn on religion, and follow their own godless lusts.'

These men draw a line between spiritual and unspiritual persons, although they are themselves*a* wholly unspiritual. But you, my friends, must fortify yourselves in your most sacred faith. Continue to pray in the power of the Holy Spirit. Keep yourselves in the love of God, and look forward to the day when our Lord Jesus Christ in his mercy will give eternal life.

There are some doubting souls who need your pity;*b* snatch them from the flames and save them.*c* There are others for whom your pity must be mixed with fear; hate the very clothing that is contaminated with sensuality.

Now to the One who can keep you from falling and set you in the presence of his glory, jubilant and above reproach, to the only God our Saviour, be glory and majesty, might and authority, through Jesus Christ our Lord, before all time, now, and for evermore. Amen.

[a] *Or* These men create divisions; they are . . .
[b] *Some witnesses read* There are some who raise disputes; these you should refute. [c] *So one witness; the rest read* some you should snatch from the flames and save.

THE REVELATION OF

St. JOHN the Divine

THE REVELATION TO

JOHN

1 The Revelation of Jesus Christ, which God gave unto him, to shew unto his servants things which must shortly come to pass; and he sent and signified it by his angel unto his servant John: 2 Who bare record of the word of God, and of the testimony of Jesus Christ, and of all things that he saw. 3 Blessed is he that readeth, and they that hear the words of this prophecy, and keep those things which are written therein: for the time is at hand.

4 John to the seven churches which are in Asia: Grace be unto you, and peace, from him which is, and which was, and which is to come; and from the seven Spirits which are before his throne; 5And from Jesus Christ, who is the faithful witness, and the first-begotten of the dead, and the prince of the kings of the earth. Unto him that loved us, and washed us from our sins in his own blood, 6And hath made us kings and priests unto God and his Father; to him be glory and dominion for ever and ever. Amen. 7 Behold, he cometh with clouds; and every eye shall see him, and they also which pierced him: and all kindreds of the earth shall wail because of him. Even so, Amen. 8 I am Alpha and Omega, the beginning and the ending, saith the Lord, which is, and which was, and which is to come, the Almighty. 9 I John, who also am your brother, and companion in tribulation, and in the kingdom and patience of Jesus Christ, was in the isle that is called Patmos, for the word of God, and for the testimony of Jesus Christ. 10 I was in the Spirit on the Lord's day, and heard behind me a great voice, as of a trumpet, 11 Saying, I am Alpha and Omega, the first and the last: and, What thou seest, write in a book, and send it unto the seven churches which are in Asia; unto Ephesus, and unto Smyrna, and unto Pergamos, and unto Thyatira, and unto Sardis, and unto Philadelphia, and unto Laodicea. 12And I turned to see the voice that spake with me. And being turned, I saw seven golden candlesticks; 13And in the midst of the seven candlesticks one like unto the Son of man, clothed with a garment down to the foot, and girt about the paps with a golden girdle. 14 His head and his hairs were white like wool, as white as snow; and his eyes were as a flame of fire; 15And his feet like unto fine brass, as if they burned in a furnace; and his voice as

1 The revelation of Jesus Christ, which God gave him to show to his servants what must soon take place; and he made it known by sending his angel to his servant John, 2 who bore witness to the word of God and to the testimony of Jesus Christ, even to all that he saw. 3 Blessed is he who reads aloud the words of the prophecy, and blessed are those who hear, and who keep what is written therein; for the time is near.

4 John to the seven churches that are in Asia: Grace to you and peace from him who is and who was and who is to come, and from the seven spirits who are before his throne, 5 and from Jesus Christ the faithful witness, the firstborn of the dead, and the ruler of kings on earth. To him who loves us and has freed us from our sins by his blood 6 and made us a kingdom, priests to his God and Father, to him be glory and dominion for ever and ever. Amen. 7 Behold, he is coming with the clouds, and every eye will see him, every one who pierced him; and all tribes of the earth will wail on account of him. Even so. Amen. 8 "I am the Alpha and the Omega," says the Lord God, who is and who was and who is to come, the Almighty.

9 I John, your brother, who share with you in Jesus the tribulation and the kingdom and the patient endurance, was on the island called Patmos on account of the word of God and the testimony of Jesus. 10 I was in the Spirit on the Lord's day, and I heard behind me a loud voice like a trumpet 11 saying, "Write what you see in a book and send it to the seven churches, to Ephesus and to Smyrna and to Pergamum and to Thyatira and to Sardis and to Philadelphia and to Laodicea."

12 Then I turned to see the voice that was speaking to me, and on turning I saw seven golden lampstands, 13 and in the midst of the lampstands one like a son of man, clothed with a long robe and with a golden girdle round his breast; 14 his head and his hair were white as white wool, white as snow; his eyes were like a flame of fire, 15 his feet were like burnished bronze, refined as in a furnace, and his voice was

THE REVELATION OF

JOHN

THE REVELATION OF

JOHN

Concerning this book   *1. 1*

This is a Revelation from Jesus Christ, which God gave him so that he might show his servants what must very soon take place. He made it known by sending his angel to his servant John, who is the witness of all that he saw—the message of God, and the testimony of Jesus Christ.

Happy is the man who reads this prophecy and happy are those who hear it read and pay attention to its message; for the time is near.

John's greeting and ascription   *1. 4*

John, to the seven Churches in Asia:
Grace and peace be to you from him who is and who was and who is coming, from the seven Spirits before his throne, and from Jesus Christ the faithful witness, firstborn of the dead, and ruler of kings upon earth. To him who loves us and has set us free from our sins through his own blood, who has made us a kingdom of priests to his God and Father, to him be glory and power for timeless ages, amen!

See, he is coming in the clouds and every eye shall see him, even those who pierced him, and his coming will mean bitter sorrow to every tribe upon the earth. So let it be!

"I am Alpha and Omega," says the Lord God, "who is and who was and who is coming, the Almighty."

The message to the   *1. 9*
seven Churches

I, John, who am your brother and your companion in the distress, the kingdom and the faithful endurance to which Jesus calls us, was on the island called Patmos because I had spoken God's message and borne witness to Jesus. On the Lord's day I knew myself inspired by the Spirit, and I heard from behind me a voice loud as a trumpet call, saying,

"Write down in a book what you see, and send it to the seven Churches—to Ephesus, Smyrna, Pergamum, Thyatira, Sardis, Philadelphia and Laodicea!"

I turned to see whose voice it was that was speaking to me, and when I had turned I saw seven golden lampstands, and among these lampstands I saw someone like a Son of Man. He was dressed in a long robe with a golden girdle around his breast; his head and his hair were white as snow-white wool, his eyes blazed like fire, and his feet shone as the finest bronze glows in the furnace. His voice had the sound of a

1 This is the revelation given by God to Jesus Christ. It was given to him so that he might show his servants what must shortly happen. He made it known by sending his angel to his servant John, who, in telling all that he saw, has borne witness to the word of God and to the testimony of Jesus Christ.[a]

Happy is the man who reads, and happy those who listen to the words of this prophecy and heed what is written in it. For the hour of fulfilment is near.

A Message from Christ
to the Churches

John to the seven churches in the province of Asia.

Grace be to you and peace, from him who is and who was and who is to come, from the seven spirits before his throne, and from Jesus Christ, the faithful witness, the first-born from the dead and ruler of the kings of the earth.

To him who loves us and freed us from our sins with his life's blood, who made of us a royal house, to serve as the priests of his God and Father—to him be glory and dominion for ever and ever! Amen.

Behold, he is coming with the clouds! Every eye shall see him, and among them those who pierced him; and all the peoples of the world shall lament in remorse. So it shall be. Amen.

'I am the Alpha and the Omega', says the Lord God, who is and who was and who is to come, the sovereign Lord of all.

I, John, your brother, who share with you in the suffering and the sovereignty and the endurance which is ours in Jesus—I was on the island called Patmos because I had preached God's word and borne my testimony to Jesus. It was on the Lord's day, and I was caught up by the Spirit; and behind me I heard a loud voice, like the sound of a trumpet, which said to me, 'Write down what you see on a scroll and send it to the seven churches: to Ephesus, Smyrna, Pergamum, Thyatira, Sardis, Philadelphia, and Laodicea.' I turned to see whose voice it was that spoke to me; and when I turned I saw seven standing lamps of gold, and among the lamps one like a son of man, robed down to his feet, with a golden girdle round his breast. The hair of his head was white as snow-white wool, and his eyes flamed like fire; his feet gleamed like burnished brass refined in a furnace, and his voice was like

[a] *Or* has borne his testimony to the word of God and to Jesus Christ.

K.J.V.

the sound of many waters. 16And he had in his right hand seven stars: and out of his mouth went a sharp twoedged sword: and his countenance *was* as the sun shineth in his strength. 17And when I saw him, I fell at his feet as dead. And he laid his right hand upon me, saying unto me, Fear not; I am the first and the last: 18 I *am* he that liveth, and was dead; and, behold, I am alive for evermore, Amen; and have the keys of hell and of death. 19 Write the things which thou hast seen, and the things which are, and the things which shall be hereafter; 20 The mystery of the seven stars which thou sawest in my right hand, and the seven golden candlesticks. The seven stars are the angels of the seven churches: and the seven candlesticks which thou sawest are the seven churches.

2 Unto the angel of the church of Ephesus write; These things saith he that holdeth the seven stars in his right hand, who walketh in the midst of the seven golden candlesticks; 2 I know thy works, and thy labour, and thy patience, and how thou canst not bear them which are evil: and thou hast tried them which say they are apostles, and are not, and hast found them liars: 3And hast borne, and hast patience, and for my name's sake hast laboured, and hast not fainted. 4 Nevertheless I have *somewhat* against thee, because thou hast left thy first love. 5 Remember therefore from whence thou art fallen, and repent, and do the first works; or else I will come unto thee quickly, and will remove thy candlestick out of his place, except thou repent. 6 But this thou hast, that thou hatest the deeds of the Nicolaitans, which I also hate. 7 He that hath an ear, let him hear what the Spirit saith unto the churches; To him that overcometh will I give to eat of the tree of life, which is in the midst of the paradise of God. 8And unto the angel of the church in Smyrna write; These things saith the first and the last, which was dead, and is alive; 9 I know thy works, and tribulation, and poverty, (but thou art rich) and I *know* the blasphemy of them which say they are Jews, and are not, but *are* the synagogue of Satan. 10 Fear none of those things which thou shalt suffer: behold, the devil shall cast *some* of you into prison, that ye may be tried; and ye shall have tribulation ten days: be thou faithful unto death, and I will give thee a crown of life. 11 He that hath an ear, let him hear what the Spirit saith unto the churches; He that overcometh shall not be hurt of the second

R.S.V.

like the sound of many waters; 16 in his right hand he held seven stars, from his mouth issued a sharp two-edged sword, and his face was like the sun shining in full strength. 17 When I saw him, I fell at his feet as though dead. But he laid his right hand upon me, saying, "Fear not, I am the first and the last, 18 and the living one; I died, and behold I am alive for evermore, and I have the keys of Death and Hades. 19 Now write what you see, what is and what is to take place hereafter. 20As for the mystery of the seven stars which you saw in my right hand, and the seven golden lampstands, the seven stars are the angels of the seven churches and the seven lampstands are the seven churches.

2 "To the angel of the church in Ephesus write: 'The words of him who holds the seven stars in his right hand, who walks among the seven golden lampstands.

2 "'I know your works, your toil and your patient endurance, and how you cannot bear evil men but have tested those who call themselves apostles but are not, and found them to be false; 3 I know you are enduring patiently and bearing up for my name's sake, and you have not grown weary. 4 But I have this against you, that you have abandoned the love you had at first. 5 Remember then from what you have fallen, repent and do the works you did at first. If not, I will come to you and remove your lampstand from its place, unless you repent. 6 Yet this you have, you hate the works of the Nicolaitans, which I also hate. 7 He who has an ear, let him hear what the Spirit says to the churches. To him who conquers I will grant to eat of the tree of life, which is in the paradise of God.'

8 "And to the angel of the church in Smyrna write: 'The words of the first and the last, who died and came to life.

9 "'I know your tribulation and your poverty (but you are rich) and the slander of those who say that they are Jews and are not, but are a synagogue of Satan. 10 Do not fear what you are about to suffer. Behold, the devil is about to throw some of you into prison, that you may be tested, and for ten days you will have tribulation. Be faithful unto death, and I will give you the crown of life. 11 He who has an ear, let him hear what the Spirit says to the churches. He who conquers shall not be hurt by the second death.'

great waterfall, and I saw that in his right hand he held seven stars. A sharp two-edged sword came out of his mouth, and his face was ablaze like the sun at its height.

When my eyes took in this sight I fell at his feet like a dead man. And then he placed his right hand upon me and said:

"Do not be afraid. I am the first and the last, the living one. I am he who was dead, and now you see me alive for timeless ages! I hold in my hand the keys of death and the grave. Therefore, write down what you have seen, both the things which are now, and the things which are to be hereafter. The secret meaning of the seven stars which you saw in my right hand, and of the seven golden lampstands is this: The seven stars are the angels of the seven Churches and the seven lampstands are the Churches themselves.

(1) *To the loveless Church* 2. 1

"Write this to the angel of the Church in Ephesus:

"These words are spoken by the one who holds the seven stars safe in his right hand, and who walks among the seven golden lampstands. I know what you have done; I know how hard you have worked and what you have endured. I know that you will not tolerate wicked men, that you have put to the test self-styled 'apostles,' who are nothing of the sort, and have found them to be liars. I know your powers of endurance—how you have suffered for the sake of my name and have not grown weary. But I hold this against you, that you do not love as you did at first. Remember then how far you have fallen. Repent and live as you lived at first. Otherwise, if your heart remains unchanged, I shall come to you and remove your lampstand from its place.

"Yet you have this to your credit, that you hate the practices of the Nicolaitans, which I myself detest. Let every listener hear what the Spirit says to the Churches:

"To the victorious I will give the right to eat from the tree of life which grows in the paradise of God.

(2) *To the persecuted Church* 2. 8

"Write this to the angel of the Church in Smyrna:

"These words are spoken by the first and the last, who died and came to life again. I know of your tribulation and of your poverty—though in fact you are rich! I know how you are slandered by those who call themselves Jews, but in fact are no Jews but a synagogue of Satan. Have no fear of what you will suffer. I tell you now that the devil is going to cast some of your number into prison where your faith will be tested and your distress will last for ten days. Be faithful in the face of death and I will give you the crown of life. Let every listener hear what the Spirit says to the Churches:

"The victorious cannot suffer the slightest hurt from the second death.

the sound of rushing waters. In his right hand he held seven stars, and out of his mouth came a sharp two-edged sword; and his face shone like the sun in full strength.

When I saw him, I fell at his feet as though dead. But he laid his right hand upon me and said, 'Do not be afraid. I am the first and the last, and I am the living one; for I was dead and now I am alive for evermore, and I hold the keys of death and Hades. Write down therefore what you have seen, what is now, and what will be hereafter.

'Here is the secret meaning of the seven stars which you saw in my right hand, and of the seven lamps of gold: the seven stars are the angels of the seven churches, and the seven lamps are the seven churches.

2 'To the angel of the church at Ephesus write:

' "These are the words of the One who holds the seven stars in his right hand and walks among the seven lamps of gold: I know all your ways, your toil and your fortitude. I know you cannot endure evil men; you have put to the proof those who claim to be apostles but are not, and have found them false. Fortitude you have; you have borne up in my cause and never flagged. But I have this against you: you have lost your early love. Think from what a height you have fallen; repent, and do as you once did. Otherwise, if you do not repent, I shall come to you and remove your lamp from its place. Yet you have this in your favour: you hate the practices of the Nicolaitans, as I do. Hear, you who have ears to hear, what the Spirit says to the churches! To him who is victorious I will give the right to eat from the tree of life that stands in the Garden of God." '

'To the angel of the church at Smyrna write:

' "These are the words of the First and the Last, who was dead and came to life again: I know how hard pressed you are, and poor—and yet you are rich; I know how you are slandered by those who claim to be Jews but are not—they are Satan's synagogue. Do not be afraid of the suffering to come. The Devil will throw some of you into prison, to put you to the test; and for ten days you will suffer cruelly. Only be faithful till death, and I will give you the crown of life. Hear, you who have ears to hear, what the Spirit says to the churches! He who is victorious cannot be harmed by the second death." '

K.J.V.

death. 12And to the angel of the church in Pergamos write; These things saith he which hath the sharp sword with two edges; 13 I know thy works, and where thou dwellest, *even* where Satan's seat *is:* and thou holdest fast my name, and hast not denied my faith, even in those days wherein Antipas *was* my faithful martyr, who was slain among you, where Satan dwelleth. 14 But I have a few things against thee, because thou hast there them that hold the doctrine of Balaam, who taught Balak to cast a stumblingblock before the children of Israel, to eat things sacrificed unto idols, and to commit fornication. 15 So hast thou also them that hold the doctrine of the Nicolaitans, which thing I hate. 16 Repent; or else I will come unto thee quickly, and will fight against them with the sword of my mouth. 17 He that hath an ear, let him hear what the Spirit saith unto the churches; To him that overcometh will I give to eat of the hidden manna, and will give him a white stone, and in the stone a new name written, which no man knoweth saving he that receiveth *it.* 18And unto the angel of the church in Thyatira write; These things saith the Son of God, who hath his eyes like unto a flame of fire, and his feet *are* like fine brass; 19 I know thy works, and charity, and service, and faith, and thy patience, and thy works; and the last *to be* more than the first. 20 Notwithstanding I have a few things against thee, because thou sufferest that woman Jezebel, which calleth herself a prophetess, to teach and to seduce my servants to commit fornication, and to eat things sacrificed unto idols. 21And I gave her space to repent of her fornication; and she repented not. 22 Behold, I will cast her into a bed, and them that commit adultery with her into great tribulation, except they repent of their deeds. 23And I will kill her children with death; and all the churches shall know that I am he which searcheth the reins and hearts: and I will give unto every one of you according to your works. 24 But unto you I say, and unto the rest in Thyatira, as many as have not this doctrine, and which have not known the depths of Satan, as they speak; I will put upon you none other burden. 25 But that which ye have *already,* hold fast till I come. 26And he that overcometh, and keepeth my works unto the end, to him will I give power over the nations: 27And he shall rule them with a rod of iron; as the vessels of a potter shall they be broken to shivers: even as I received of my Father. 28And I will give him the morning star. 29 He that hath an ear, let him hear what the Spirit saith unto the churches.

R.S.V.

12 "And to the angel of the church in Pergamum write: 'The words of him who has the sharp two-edged sword.

13 " 'I know where you dwell, where Satan's throne is; you hold fast my name and you did not deny my faith even in the days of Antipas my witness, my faithful one, who was killed among you, where Satan dwells. 14 But I have a few things against you: you have some there who hold the teaching of Balaam, who taught Balak to put a stumbling block before the sons of Israel, that they might eat food sacrificed to idols and practice immorality. 15 So you also have some who hold the teaching of the Nicolaitans. 16 Repent then. If not, I will come to you soon and war against them with the sword of my mouth. 17 He who has an ear, let him hear what the Spirit says to the churches. To him who conquers I will give some of the hidden manna, and I will give him a white stone, with a new name written on the stone which no one knows except him who receives it.'

18 "And to the angel of the church in Thyatira write: 'The words of the Son of God, who has eyes like a flame of fire, and whose feet are like burnished bronze.

19 " 'I know your works, your love and faith and service and patient endurance, and that your latter works exceed the first. 20 But I have this against you, that you tolerate the woman Jezebel, who calls herself a prophetess and is teaching and beguiling my servants to practice immorality and to eat food sacrificed to idols. 21 I gave her time to repent, but she refuses to repent of her immorality. 22 Behold, I will throw her on a sickbed, and those who commit adultery with her I will throw into great tribulation, unless they repent of her doings; 23 and I will strike her children dead. And all the churches shall know that I am he who searches mind and heart, and I will give to each of you as your works deserve. 24 But to the rest of you in Thyatira, who do not hold this teaching, who have not learned what some call the deep things of Satan, to you I say, I do not lay upon you any other burden; 25 only hold fast what you have, until I come. 26 He who conquers and who keeps my works until the end, I will give him power over the nations, 27 and he shall rule them with a rod of iron, as when earthen pots are broken in pieces, even as I myself have received power from my Father; 28 and I will give him the morning star. 29 He who has an ear, let him hear what the Spirit says to the churches.'

3 And unto the angel of the church in Sardis write; These things saith he that hath the seven Spirits of God, and the seven stars; I know thy works, that thou hast a name that

3 "And to the angel of the church in Sardis write: 'The words of him who has the seven spirits of God and the seven stars.

" 'I know your works; you have the name of

(3) To the over-tolerant Church   2. 12

"Write this to the angel of the Church in Pergamum:

"These words are spoken by him who has the sharp two-edged sword. I know where you live— where Satan sits enthroned. I know that you hold fast to my name and that you never denied your faith in me even in the days when Antipas, my faithful witness, was martyred before your eyes in the very house of Satan.

"Yet I have a few things against you—some of your number cling to the teaching of Balaam, the man who taught Balak how to entice the children of Israel into eating meat sacrificed to idols and into sexual immorality. I have also against you the fact that among your number are some who hold just as closely to the teaching of the Nicolaitans. Repent, then, or else I shall come to you quickly and make war upon them with the sword of my mouth. Let the listener hear what the Spirit says to the Churches:

"I will give the victorious some of the hidden manna, and I will also give him a white stone with a new name written upon it which no man knows except the man who receives it.

(4) To the compromising Church 2. 18

"Write this to the angel of the Church in Thyatira:

"These are the words of the Son of God whose eyes blaze like fire and whose feet shine like the finest bronze:

"I know what you have done. I know of your love and your loyalty, your service and your endurance. Moreover, I know that you are doing more than you did at first. But I have this against you, that you tolerate that woman Jezebel who calls herself a prophetess, but who by her teaching deceives my servants into sexual immorality and eating idols'-meat. I have given her time to repent but she has shown no desire to repent of her immorality. See, now, how I throw her into bed and her lovers with her, and I will send them terrible suffering unless they repent of what she has done. As for her children, I shall strike them dead. Then all the Churches will know that I am the one who searches men's hearts and minds, and that I will reward each one of you according to your deeds.

"But for the rest of you at Thyatira, who do not hold this teaching, and have not learned what they call 'the deep things of Satan,' I will lay no further burden upon you, except that you hold on to what you have until I come!

"To the one who is victorious, who carries out my work to the end, I will give authority over the nations, just as I myself have received authority from my Father, and I will give him the morning star. He shall 'shepherd them with a rod of iron'; he shall 'dash them in pieces like a potter's vessel.' Let the listener hear what the Spirit says to the Churches.

(5) To the sleeping Church   3. 1

"Write this to the angel of the Church in Sardis:

"These are the words of him who holds in his hand the seven Spirits of God and the seven stars:

"I know what you have done, that you have a

'To the angel of the church at Pergamum write:

' "These are the words of the One who has the sharp two-edged sword: I know where you live; it is the place where Satan has his throne. And yet you are holding fast to my cause. You did not deny your faith in me even at the time when Antipas, my faithful witness, was killed in your city, the home of Satan. But I have a few matters to bring against you: you have in Pergamum some that hold to the teaching of Balaam, who taught Balak to put temptation in the way of the Israelites. He encouraged them to eat food sacrificed to idols and to commit fornication, and in the same way you also have some who hold the doctrine of the Nicolaitans. So repent! If you do not, I shall come to you soon and make war upon them with the sword that comes out of my mouth. Hear, you who have ears to hear, what the Spirit says to the churches! To him who is victorious I will give some of the hidden manna; I will give him also a white stone, and on the stone will be written a new name, known to none but him that receives it."

'To the angel of the church at Thyatira write:

' "These are the words of the Son of God, whose eyes flame like fire and whose feet gleam like burnished brass: I know all your ways, your love and faithfulness, your good service and your fortitude; and of late you have done even better than at first. Yet I have this against you: you tolerate that Jezebel, the woman who claims to be a prophetess, who by her teaching lures my servants into fornication and into eating food sacrificed to idols. I have given her time to repent, but she refuses to repent of her fornication. So I will throw her on to a bed of pain,[a] and plunge her lovers into terrible suffering, unless they forswear what she is doing; and her children I will strike dead. This will teach all the churches that I am the searcher of men's hearts and thoughts, and that I will reward each one of you according to his deeds. And now I speak to you others in Thyatira, who do not accept this teaching and have had no experience of what they like to call the deep secrets of Satan; on you I will impose no further burden. Only hold fast to what you have, until I come. To him who is victorious, to him who perseveres in doing my will to the end, I will give authority over the nations—that same authority which I received from my Father—and he shall rule them with an iron rod, smashing them to bits like earthenware; and I will give him also the morning star. Hear, you who have ears to hear, what the Spirit says to the churches!"

3 'To the angel of the church at Sardis write: ' "These are the words of the One who holds the seven spirits of God, the seven stars: I know all your ways; that though you have a

[a] *One witness reads* into a furnace.

K.J.V.

thou livest, and art dead. 2 Be watchful, and strengthen the things which remain, that are ready to die: for I have not found thy works perfect before God. 3 Remember therefore how thou hast received and heard, and hold fast, and repent. If therefore thou shalt not watch, I will come on thee as a thief, and thou shalt not know what hour I will come upon thee. 4 Thou hast a few names even in Sardis which have not defiled their garments; and they shall walk with me in white: for they are worthy. 5 He that overcometh, the same shall be clothed in white raiment; and I will not blot out his name out of the book of life, but I will confess his name before my Father, and before his angels. 6 He that hath an ear, let him hear what the Spirit saith unto the churches. 7And to the angel of the church in Philadelphia write; These things saith he that is holy, he that is true, he that hath the key of David, he that openeth, and no man shutteth; and shutteth, and no man openeth; 8 I know thy works: behold, I have set before thee an open door, and no man can shut it: for thou hast a little strength, and hast kept my word, and hast not denied my name. 9 Behold, I will make them of the synagogue of Satan, which say they are Jews, and are not, but do lie; behold, I will make them to come and worship before thy feet, and to know that I have loved thee. 10 Because thou hast kept the word of my patience, I also will keep thee from the hour of temptation, which shall come upon all the world, to try them that dwell upon the earth. 11 Behold, I come quickly: hold that fast which thou hast, that no man take thy crown. 12 Him that overcometh will I make a pillar in the temple of my God, and he shall go no more out: and I will write upon him the name of my God, and the name of the city of my God, *which is* new Jerusalem, which cometh down out of heaven from my God: and *I will write upon him* my new name. 13 He that hath an ear, let him hear what the Spirit saith unto the churches. 14And unto the angel of the church of the Laodiceans write; These things saith the Amen, the faithful and true witness, the beginning of the creation of God; 15 I know thy works, that thou art neither cold nor hot: I would thou wert cold or hot. 16 So then because thou art lukewarm, and neither cold nor hot, I will spew thee out of my mouth. 17 Because thou sayest, I am rich, and increased with goods, and have need of nothing; and knowest not that thou art wretched, and miserable, and poor, and blind, and naked: 18 I counsel thee to buy of me gold tried in the fire, that thou mayest be rich; and white raiment, that thou mayest be clothed, and *that* the shame of thy nakedness do not appear; and anoint thine eyes with eyesalve, that thou mayest see. 19As many as I love, I rebuke and chasten: be zealous therefore, and repent. 20 Be-

R.S.V.

being alive, and you are dead. 2Awake, and strengthen what remains and is on the point of death, for I have not found your works perfect in the sight of my God. 3 Remember then what you received and heard; keep that, and repent. If you will not awake, I will come like a thief, and you will not know at what hour I will come upon you. 4 Yet you have still a few names in Sardis, people who have not soiled their garments; and they shall walk with me in white, for they are worthy. 5 He who conquers shall be clad thus in white garments, and I will not blot his name out of the book of life; I will confess his name before my Father and before his angels. 6 He who has an ear, let him hear what the Spirit says to the churches.'

7 "And to the angel of the church in Philadelphia write: 'The words of the holy one, the true one, who has the key of David, who opens and no one shall shut, who shuts and no one opens.

8 " 'I know your works. Behold, I have set before you an open door, which no one is able to shut; I know that you have but little power, and yet you have kept my word and have not denied my name. 9 Behold, I will make those of the synagogue of Satan who say that they are Jews and are not, but lie—behold, I will make them come and bow down before your feet, and learn that I have loved you. 10 Because you have kept my word of patient endurance, I will keep you from the hour of trial which is coming on the whole world, to try those who dwell upon the earth. 11 I am coming soon; hold fast what you have, so that no one may seize your crown. 12 He who conquers, I will make him a pillar in the temple of my God; never shall he go out of it, and I will write on him the name of my God, and the name of the city of my God, the new Jerusalem which comes down from my God out of heaven, and my own new name. 13 He who has an ear, let him hear what the Spirit says to the churches.'

14 "And to the angel of the church in Laodicea write: 'The words of the Amen, the faithful and true witness, the beginning of God's creation.

15 " 'I know your works: you are neither cold nor hot. Would that you were cold or hot! 16 So, because you are lukewarm, and neither cold nor hot, I will spew you out of my mouth. 17 For you say, I am rich, I have prospered, and I need nothing; not knowing that you are wretched, pitiable, poor, blind, and naked. 18 Therefore I counsel you to buy from me gold refined by fire, that you may be rich, and white garments to clothe you and to keep the shame of your nakedness from being seen, and salve to anoint your eyes, that you may see. 19 Those whom I love, I reprove and chasten; so be zealous and repent. 20 Behold, I stand at the door

reputation for being alive, but that in fact you are dead. Now wake up! Strengthen what you still have before it dies! For I have not found any of your deeds complete in the sight of my God. Remember then what you were given and what you were taught. Hold to those things and repent. If you refuse to wake up, then I will come to you like a thief, and you will have no idea of the hour of my coming.

"Yet you still have a few names in Sardis of people who have not soiled their garments. They shall walk with me in white, for they have deserved to do so. The victorious shall wear such white garments, and never will I erase his name from the book of life. Indeed, I will speak his name openly in the presence of my Father and of his angels. Let the listener hear what the Spirit says to the Churches.

(6) *To the Church*   3. 7
with opportunity

"Then write this to the angel of the Church in Philadelphia:

"These are the words of the holy one and the true, who holds the key of David, who opens and no man shall shut, and who shuts and no man shall open. I know what you have done. See, I have given you a door flung wide open, which no man can close! For you have some little power and have been faithful to my message and have not denied my name. See how I deal with those of Satan's synagogue, who claim to be Jews, yet are no Jews but liars! Watch how I make them come and bow down before your feet and acknowledge that I have loved you. Because you have obeyed my call to patient endurance I will keep you safe from the hour of trial which is to come upon the whole world, to test all who live upon the earth. I am coming soon; hold fast to what you have—let no one deprive you of your crown. As for the victorious, I will make him a pillar in the Temple of my God, and he will never leave it. I will write upon him the name of my God, and the name of the city of my God, the new Jerusalem which comes down out of Heaven from my God. And I will write upon him my own new name. Let the listener hear what the Spirit says to the Churches.

(7) *To the complacent Church*   3. 14

"Then write this to the angel of the Church in Laodicea:

"These are the words of the Amen, the faithful and true witness, the beginning of God's creation:

"I know what you have done, and that you are neither cold nor hot. I could wish that you were either cold or hot! But since you are lukewarm and neither hot nor cold, I intend to spit you out of my mouth! While you say, 'I am rich, I have prospered, and there is nothing that I need,' you have no eyes to see that you are wretched, pitiable, poverty-stricken, blind and naked. My advice to you is to buy from me that gold which is purified in the furnace so that you may be rich, and white garments to wear so that you may hide the shame of your nakedness, and salve to put on your eyes to make you see. All those whom I love I correct and discipline. Therefore, shake off your complacency and repent. See, I stand knocking at the door. If any-

name for being alive, you are dead. Wake up, and put some strength into what is left, which must otherwise die! For I have not found any work of yours completed in the eyes of my God. So remember the teaching you received; observe it, and repent. If you do not wake up, I shall come upon you like a thief, and you will not know the moment of my coming. Yet you have a few persons in Sardis who have not polluted their clothing. They shall walk with me in white, for so they deserve. He who is victorious shall thus be robed all in white; his name I will never strike off the roll of the living, for in the presence of my Father and his angels I will acknowledge him as mine. Hear, you who have ears to hear, what the Spirit says to the churches!"

'To the angel of the church at Philadelphia write:

' "These are the words of the holy one, the true one, who holds the key of David; when he opens none may shut, when he shuts none may open: I know all your ways; and look, I have set before you an open door, which no one can shut. Your strength, I know, is small, yet you have observed my commands and have not disowned my name. So this is what I will do: I will make those of Satan's synagogue, who claim to be Jews but are lying frauds, come and fall down at your feet; and they shall know that you are my beloved people. Because you have kept my command and stood fast, I will also keep you from the ordeal that is to fall upon the whole world and test its inhabitants. I am coming soon; hold fast what you have, and let no one rob you of your crown. He who is victorious—I will make him a pillar in the temple of my God; he shall never leave it. And I will write the name of my God upon him, and the name of the city of my God, that new Jerusalem which is coming down out of heaven from my God, and my own new name. Hear, you who have ears to hear, what the Spirit says to the churches!'

'To the angel of the church at Laodicea write:

' "These are the words of the Amen, the faithful and true witness, the prime source of all God's creation: I know all your ways; you are neither hot nor cold. How I wish you were either hot or cold! But because you are lukewarm, neither hot nor cold, I will spit you out of my mouth. You say, 'How rich I am! And how well I have done! I have everything I want in the world.' In fact, though you do not know it, you are the most pitiful wretch, poor, blind, and naked. So I advise you to buy from me gold refined in the fire, to make you truly rich, and white clothes to put on to hide the shame of your nakedness, and ointment for your eyes so that you may see. All whom I love I reprove and discipline. Be on your mettle therefore and repent. Here I stand knocking at the door; if any-

K.J.V.

hold, I stand at the door, and knock: if any man hear my voice, and open the door, I will come in to him, and will sup with him, and he with me. 21 To him that overcometh will I grant to sit with me in my throne, even as I also overcame, and am set down with my Father in his throne. 22 He that hath an ear, let him hear what the Spirit saith unto the churches.

4 After this I looked, and, behold, a door *was* opened in heaven: and the first voice which I heard *was* as it were of a trumpet talking with me; which said, Come up hither, and I will shew thee things which must be hereafter. 2And immediately I was in the Spirit: and, behold, a throne was set in heaven, and *one* sat on the throne. 3And he that sat was to look upon like a jasper and a sardine stone: and *there was* a rainbow round about the throne, in sight like unto an emerald. 4And round about the throne *were* four and twenty seats: and upon the seats I saw four and twenty elders sitting, clothed in white raiment; and they had on their heads crowns of gold. 5And out of the throne proceeded lightnings and thunderings and voices: and *there were* seven lamps of fire burning before the throne, which are the seven Spirits of God. 6And before the throne *there was* a sea of glass like unto crystal: and in the midst of the throne, and round about the throne, *were* four beasts full of eyes before and behind. 7And the first beast *was* like a lion, and the second beast like a calf, and the third beast had a face as a man, and the fourth beast *was* like a flying eagle. 8And the four beasts had each of them six wings about *him;* and *they were* full of eyes within: and they rest not day and night, saying, Holy, holy, holy, Lord God Almighty, which was, and is, and is to come. 9And when those beasts give glory and honour and thanks to him that sat on the throne, who liveth for ever and ever, 10 The four and twenty elders fall down before him that sat on the throne, and worship him that liveth for ever and ever, and cast their crowns before the throne, saying, 11 Thou art worthy, O Lord, to receive glory and honour and power: for thou hast created all things, and for thy pleasure they are and were created.

5 And I saw in the right hand of him that sat on the throne a book written within and on the back side, sealed with seven seals. 2And I saw a strong angel proclaiming with a loud voice, Who is worthy to open the book, and to loose the seals thereof? 3And no man in heaven, nor in earth, neither under the earth, was able to open the book, neither to look thereon. 4And I wept much, because no man was found worthy to open and to read the book, neither to look

R.S.V.

and knock; if any one hears my voice and opens the door, I will come in to him and eat with him, and he with me. 21 He who conquers, I will grant him to sit with me on my throne, as I myself conquered and sat down with my Father on his throne. 22 He who has an ear, let him hear what the Spirit says to the churches.' "

4 After this I looked, and lo, in heaven an open door! And the first voice, which I had heard speaking to me like a trumpet, said, "Come up hither, and I will show you what must take place after this." 2At once I was in the Spirit, and lo, a throne stood in heaven, with one seated on the throne! 3And he who sat there appeared like jasper and carnelian, and round the throne was a rainbow that looked like an emerald. 4 Round the throne were twenty-four thrones, and seated on the thrones were twenty-four elders, clad in white garments, with golden crowns upon their heads. 5 From the throne issue flashes of lightning, and voices and peals of thunder, and before the throne burn seven torches of fire, which are the seven spirits of God; 6 and before the throne there is as it were a sea of glass, like crystal.

And round the throne, on each side of the throne, are four living creatures, full of eyes in front and behind: 7 the first living creature like a lion, the second living creature like an ox, the third living creature with the face of a man, and the fourth living creature like a flying eagle. 8And the four living creatures, each of them with six wings, are full of eyes all round and within, and day and night they never cease to sing,

"Holy, holy, holy, is the Lord God Almighty,
  who was and is and is to come!"

9And whenever the living creatures give glory and honor and thanks to him who is seated on the throne, who lives for ever and ever, 10 the twenty-four elders fall down before him who is seated on the throne and worship him who lives for ever and ever; they cast their crowns before the throne, singing,

11 "Worthy art thou, our Lord and God,
  to receive glory and honor and power,
  for thou didst create all things,
  and by thy will they existed and were created."

5 And I saw in the right hand of him who was seated on the throne a scroll written within and on the back, sealed with seven seals; 2 and I saw a strong angel proclaiming with a loud voice, "Who is worthy to open the scroll and break its seals?" 3And no one in heaven or on earth or under the earth was able to open the scroll or to look into it, 4 and I wept much that no one was found worthy to open the

one listens to my voice and opens the door, I will go into his house and dine with him, and he with me. As for the victorious, I will give him the honor of sitting beside me on my throne, just as I myself have won the victory and have taken my seat beside my Father on his throne. Let the listener hear what the Spirit says to the Churches."

one hears my voice and opens the door, I will come in and sit down to supper with him and he with me. To him who is victorious I will grant a place on my throne, as I myself was victorious and sat down with my Father on his throne. Hear, you who have ears to hear, what the Spirit says to the churches!" '

The vision of Heaven 4. 1

Later I looked again, and before my eyes a door stood open in Heaven, and in my ears was the voice with the ring of a trumpet, which I had heard at first, speaking to me and saying, "Come up here, and I will show you what must happen in the future."

Immediately I knew myself to be inspired by the Spirit, and in my vision I saw that a throne had been set up in Heaven, and there was someone seated upon the throne. His appearance blazed like diamond and topaz, and all around the throne shone a halo like an emerald rainbow. In a circle around the throne there were twenty-four thrones and seated upon them twenty-four elders dressed in white with golden crowns upon their heads. From the central throne come flashes of lightning, noises and peals of thunder. Seven lamps are burning before the throne, and they are the seven Spirits of God. In front of the throne there appears a sea of glass as clear as crystal. On each side, encircling the throne, are four living creatures covered with eyes in front and behind. The first living creature is like a lion, the second is like a calf, the third has a face like a man, and the fourth living creature appears like an eagle in flight. These four creatures have each of them six wings and are covered with eyes, all around them, and even within them. Day and night they never cease to say,

"Holy, holy, holy is the Lord God, the Almighty, who was and who is and who is coming."

The ceaseless worship of Heaven 4. 9

And whenever the living creatures give glory and honor and thanksgiving to the one who sits upon the throne, who lives for timeless ages, the twenty-four elders prostrate themselves before him who is seated upon the throne and worship the one who lives for timeless ages. They cast their crowns before the throne and say,

"Thou art worthy, O Lord our God, to receive glory and honor and power, for thou didst create all things; by thy will they existed and were created."

The sealed book of future events 5. 1

Then I noticed in the right hand of the one seated upon the throne a book filled with writing both inside and on its back, and it was sealed with seven seals. And I saw a mighty angel who called out in a loud voice,

"Who is fit to open the book and break its seals?"

And no one in Heaven or upon earth or under the earth was able to open the book, or even to look at it. I began to weep bitterly because no one could be found fit to open the book, or even

The Opening of the Sealed Book

4 After this I looked, and there before my eyes was a door opened in heaven; and the voice that I had first heard speaking to me like a trumpet said, 'Come up here, and I will show you what must happen hereafter.' At once I was caught up by the Spirit. There in heaven stood a throne, and on the throne sat one whose appearance was like the gleam of jasper and cornelian; and round the throne was a rainbow, bright as an emerald. In a circle about this throne were twenty-four other thrones, and on them sat twenty-four elders, robed in white and wearing crowns of gold. From the throne went out flashes of lightning and peals of thunder. Burning before the throne were seven flaming torches, the seven spirits of God, and in front of it stretched what seemed a sea of glass, like a sheet of ice.

In the centre, round the throne itself, were four living creatures, covered with eyes, in front and behind. The first creature was like a lion, the second like an ox, the third had a human face, the fourth was like an eagle in flight. The four living creatures, each of them with six wings, had eyes all over, inside and out; and by day and by night without a pause they sang:

'Holy, holy, holy is God the sovereign Lord of all, who was, and is, and is to come!'

As often as the living creatures give glory and honour and thanks to the One who sits on the throne, who lives for ever and ever, the twenty-four elders fall down before the One who sits on the throne and worship him who lives for ever and ever; and as they lay their crowns before the throne they cry:

'Thou art worthy, O Lord our God, to receive glory and honour and power, because thou didst create all things; by thy will they were created, and have their being!'

5 Then I saw in the right hand of the One who sat on the throne a scroll, with writing inside and out, and it was sealed up with seven seals. And I saw a mighty angel proclaiming in a loud voice, 'Who is worthy to open the scroll and to break its seals?' There was no one in heaven or on earth or under the earth able to open the scroll or to look inside it. I was in tears because no one was found who was worthy

thereon. 5And one of the elders saith unto me, Weep not: behold, the Lion of the tribe of Juda, the Root of David, hath prevailed to open the book, and to loose the seven seals thereof. 6And I beheld, and, lo, in the midst of the throne and of the four beasts, and in the midst of the elders, stood a Lamb, as it had been slain, having seven horns and seven eyes, which are the seven Spirits of God sent forth into all the earth. 7And he came and took the book out of the right hand of him that sat upon the throne. 8And when he had taken the book, the four beasts and four *and* twenty elders fell down before the Lamb, having every one of them harps, and golden vials full of odours, which are the prayers of saints. 9And they sung a new song, saying, Thou art worthy to take the book, and to open the seals thereof: for thou wast slain, and hast redeemed us to God by thy blood out of every kindred, and tongue, and people, and nation; 10And hast made us unto our God kings and priests: and we shall reign on the earth. 11And I beheld, and I heard the voice of many angels round about the throne, and the beasts, and the elders: and the number of them was ten thousand times ten thousand, and thousands of thousands; 12 Saying with a loud voice, Worthy is the Lamb that was slain to receive power, and riches, and wisdom, and strength, and honour, and glory, and blessing. 13And every creature which is in heaven, and on the earth, and under the earth, and such as are in the sea, and all that are in them, heard I saying, Blessing, and honour, and glory, and power, *be* unto him that sitteth upon the throne, and unto the Lamb for ever and ever. 14And the four beasts said, Amen. And the four *and* twenty elders fell down and worshipped him that liveth for ever and ever.

scroll or to look into it. 5 Then one of the elders said to me, "Weep not; lo, the Lion of the tribe of Judah, the Root of David, has conquered, so that he can open the scroll and its seven seals."

6 And between the throne and the four living creatures and among the elders, I saw a Lamb standing, as though it had been slain, with seven horns and with seven eyes, which are the seven spirits of God sent out into all the earth; 7 and he went and took the scroll from the right hand of him who was seated on the throne. 8And when he had taken the scroll, the four living creatures and the twenty-four elders fell down before the Lamb, each holding a harp, and with golden bowls full of incense, which are the prayers of the saints; 9 and they sang a new song, saying,

"Worthy art thou to take the scroll and to
　　open its seals,
for thou wast slain and by thy blood didst
　　ransom men for God
from every tribe and tongue and people
　　and nation,
10 and hast made them a kingdom and priests
　　to our God,
and they shall reign on earth."

11 Then I looked, and I heard around the throne and the living creatures and the elders the voice of many angels, numbering myriads of myriads and thousands of thousands, 12 saying with a loud voice, "Worthy is the Lamb who was slain, to receive power and wealth and wisdom and might and honor and glory and blessing!" 13And I heard every creature in heaven and on earth and under the earth and in the sea, and all therein, saying, "To him who sits upon the throne and to the Lamb be blessing and honor and glory and might for ever and ever!" 14And the four living creatures said, "Amen!" and the elders fell down and worshiped.

6 And I saw when the Lamb opened one of the seals, and I heard, as it were the noise of thunder, one of the four beasts saying, Come and see. 2And I saw, and behold a white horse: and he that sat on him had a bow; and a crown was given unto him: and he went forth con-

6 Now I saw when the Lamb opened one of the seven seals, and I heard one of the four living creatures say, as with a voice of thunder, "Come!" 2And I saw, and behold, a white horse, and its rider had a bow; and a crown was given to him, and he went out conquering and to conquer.

PHILLIPS

to look at it, when one of the elders said to me: "Do not weep. See, the lion from the tribe of Judah, the root of David, has won the victory and is able to open the book and break its seven seals."

Then, standing in the very center of the throne and of the four living creatures and of the elders, I saw a Lamb that seemed to have been slaughtered. He had seven horns and seven eyes, which are the seven Spirits of God and are sent out into every corner of the earth. Then he came and took the book from the right hand of him who was seated upon the throne.

The new hymn of the created and   5. 8
of the redeemed

When he had taken the book, the four living creatures and the twenty-four elders prostrated themselves before the Lamb. Each of them had a harp, and they had golden bowls full of incense, which are the prayers of the saints. They sang a new song and these are the words they sang:

"Worthy art thou to take the book and break its seals, for thou hast been slain and by thy blood hast purchased for God men from every tribe, and tongue, and people, and nation! Thou hast made them a kingdom of priests for our God, and they shall reign as kings upon the earth."

The hymn of the whole company   5. 11
of Heaven

Then in my vision I heard the voices of many angels encircling the throne, the living creatures and the elders. There were myriads of myriads and thousands of thousands, crying in a great voice,

"Worthy is the Lamb who was slain, to receive power and riches and wisdom, and strength and honor and glory and blessing!"

Then I heard the voice of everything created in Heaven, upon earth, under the earth and upon the sea, and all that are in them saying,

"Blessing and honor and glory and power be given to him who sits upon the throne, and to the Lamb, for timeless ages!"

The four living creatures said, "Amen," while the elders fell down and worshiped.

N.E.B.

to open the scroll or to look inside it. But one of the elders said to me: 'Do not weep; for the Lion from the tribe of Judah, the Root of David, has won the right to open the scroll and break its seven seals.'

Then I saw standing in the very middle of the throne, inside the circle of living creatures and the circle of elders,[a] a Lamb with the marks of slaughter upon him. He had seven horns and seven eyes, the eyes which are the seven spirits of God sent out over all the world. And the Lamb went up and took the scroll from the right hand of the One who sat on the throne. When he took it, the four living creatures and the twenty-four elders fell down before the Lamb. Each of the elders had a harp, and they held golden bowls full of incense, the prayers of God's people, and they were singing a new song:

'Thou art worthy to take the scroll and to break its seals, for thou wast slain and by thy blood didst purchase for God men of every tribe and language, people and nation; thou hast made of them a royal house, to serve our God as priests; and they shall reign upon earth.'

Then as I looked I heard the voices of countless angels. These were all round the throne and the living creatures and the elders. Myriads upon myriads there were, thousands upon thousands, and they cried aloud:

'Worthy is the Lamb, the Lamb that was slain, to receive all power and wealth, wisdom and might, honour and glory and praise!'

Then I heard every created thing in heaven and on earth and under the earth and in the sea, all that is in them, crying:

'Praise and honour, glory and might, to him who sits on the throne and to the Lamb for ever and ever!'

And the four living creatures said, 'Amen', and the elders fell down and worshipped.

THE LAMB BREAKS
THE SEALS

The first rider: conquest   6. 1

Then I watched while the Lamb broke one of the seven seals, and I heard one of the four living creatures say in a voice of thunder, "Come out!"

I looked, and before my eyes was a white horse. Its rider carried a bow, and he was given a crown. He rode out conquering and bent on conquest.

6 Then I watched as the Lamb broke the first of the seven seals; and I heard one of the four living creatures say in a voice like thunder, 'Come!' And there before my eyes was a white horse, and its rider held a bow. He was given a crown, and he rode forth, conquering and to conquer.

[a] Or standing between the throne, with the four living creatures, and the elders . . .

K.J.V.

quering, and to conquer. 3And when he had opened the second seal, I heard the second beast say, Come and see. 4And there went out another horse *that was* red: and *power* was given to him that sat thereon to take peace from the earth, and that they should kill one another: and there was given unto him a great sword. 5And when he had opened the third seal, I heard the third beast say, Come and see. And I beheld, and lo a black horse; and he that sat on him had a pair of balances in his hand. 6And I heard a voice in the midst of the four beasts say, A measure of wheat for a penny, and three measures of barley for a penny; and *see* thou hurt not the oil and the wine. 7And when he had opened the fourth seal, I heard the voice of the fourth beast say, Come and see. 8And I looked, and behold a pale horse: and his name that sat on him was Death, and Hell followed with him. And power was given unto them over the fourth part of the earth, to kill with sword, and with hunger, and with death, and with the beasts of the earth. 9And when he had opened the fifth seal, I saw under the altar the souls of them that were slain for the word of God, and for the testimony which they held: 10And they cried with a loud voice, saying, How long, O Lord, holy and true, dost thou not judge and avenge our blood on them that dwell on the earth? 11And white robes were given unto every one of them; and it was said unto them, that they should rest yet for a little season, until their fellow servants also and their brethren, that should be killed as they *were*, should be fulfilled. 12And I beheld when he had opened the sixth seal, and, lo, there was a great earthquake; and the sun became black as sackcloth of hair, and the moon became as blood. 13And the stars of heaven fell unto the earth, even as a fig tree casteth her untimely figs, when she is shaken of a mighty wind. 14And the heaven departed as a scroll when it is rolled together; and every mountain and island were moved out of their places. 15And the kings of the earth, and the great men, and the rich men, and the chief captains, and the mighty men, and every bond man, and every free man, hid themselves in the dens and in the rocks of the mountains; 16And said to the mountains and rocks, Fall on us, and hide us from the face of him that sitteth on the throne, and from the wrath of the Lamb: 17For the great day of his wrath is come; and who shall be able to stand?

R.S.V.

3 When he opened the second seal, I heard the second living creature say, "Come!" 4And out came another horse, bright red; its rider was permitted to take peace from the earth, so that men should slay one another; and he was given a great sword.

5 When he opened the third seal, I heard the third living creature say, "Come!" And I saw, and behold, a black horse, and its rider had a balance in his hand; 6 and I heard what seemed to be a voice in the midst of the four living creatures saying, "A quart of wheat for a denarius,[a] and three quarts of barley for a denarius;[a] but do not harm oil and wine!"

7 When he opened the fourth seal, I heard the voice of the fourth living creature say, "Come!" 8And I saw, and behold, a pale horse, and its rider's name was Death, and Hades followed him; and they were given power over a fourth of the earth, to kill with sword and with famine and with pestilence and by wild beasts of the earth.

9 When he opened the fifth seal, I saw under the altar the souls of those who had been slain for the word of God and for the witness they had borne; 10 they cried out with a loud voice, "O sovereign Lord, holy and true, how long before thou wilt judge and avenge our blood on those who dwell upon the earth?" 11 Then they were each given a white robe and told to rest a little longer, until the number of their fellow servants and their brethren should be complete, who were to be killed as they themselves had been.

12 When he opened the sixth seal, I looked, and behold, there was a great earthquake; and the sun became black as sackcloth, the full moon became like blood, 13 and the stars of the sky fell to the earth as the fig tree sheds its winter fruit when shaken by a gale; 14 the sky vanished like a scroll that is rolled up, and every mountain and island was removed from its place. 15 Then the kings of the earth and the great men and the generals and the rich and the strong, and every one, slave and free, hid in the caves and among the rocks of the mountains, 16 calling to the mountains and rocks, "Fall on us and hide us from the face of him who is seated on the throne, and from the wrath of the Lamb; 17 for the great day of their wrath has come, and who can stand before it?"

---

[a] The denarius was worth about twenty cents.

The second rider: war   *6. 3*

Then, when the Lamb broke the second seal, I heard the second living creature cry,
"Come out!"
And another horse came forth, red in color. Its rider was given power to deprive the earth of peace, so that men should kill one another. A huge sword was put into his hand.

The third rider: famine   *6. 5*

When the Lamb broke the third seal, I heard the third living creature say,
"Come out!"
I looked again and there before my eyes was a black horse. Its rider had a pair of scales in his hand, and I heard a voice which seemed to come from the four living creatures, saying,
"A quart of wheat for a quarter, and three quarts of barley for a quarter—but no tampering with the oil or the wine!"

The fourth rider: death   *6. 7*

Then, when he broke the fourth seal I heard the voice of the fourth living creature cry,
"Come out!"
Again I looked, and there appeared a horse sickly green in color. The name of its rider was death, and the grave followed close behind him. A quarter of the earth was put into their power, to kill with the sword, by famine, by violence, and through the wild beasts of the earth.

The cry of the martyrs in Heaven *6. 9*

When the Lamb broke the fifth seal, I could see, beneath the altar, the souls of those who had been killed for the sake of the Word of God and because of the faithfulness of their witness. They cried out in a loud voice, saying,
"How long shall it be, O Lord of all, holy and true, before Thou shalt judge and avenge our blood upon the inhabitants of the earth?"
Then each of them was given a white robe, and they were told to be patient a little longer, until the number of their fellow servants and of their brethren, who were to die as they had died, should be complete.

The awe-full wrath of God   *6. 12*

Then I watched while he broke the sixth seal. There was a tremendous earthquake, the sun turned dark like coarse black cloth, and the full moon was red as blood. The stars of the sky fell upon the earth, just as a fig tree sheds unripe figs when shaken in a gale. The sky vanished as though it were a scroll being rolled up, and every mountain and island was jolted out of its place. Then the kings of the earth, and the great men, the captains, the wealthy, the powerful, and every man, whether slave or free, hid themselves in caves and among mountain rocks. They called out to the mountains and the rocks:
"Fall down upon us and hide us from the face of him who sits upon the throne, and from the wrath of the Lamb! For the great day of their wrath has come, and who can stand against it?"

When the Lamb broke the second seal, I heard the second creature say, 'Come!' And out came another horse, all red. To its rider was given power to take peace from the earth and make men slaughter one another; and he was given a great sword.

When he broke the third seal, I heard the third creature say, 'Come!' And there, as I looked, was a black horse; and its rider held in his hand a pair of scales. And I heard what sounded like a voice from the midst of the living creatures, which said, 'A whole day's wage for a quart of flour, a whole day's wage for three quarts of barley-meal! But spare the olive and the vine.'

When he broke the fourth seal, I heard the voice of the fourth creature say, 'Come!' And there, as I looked, was another horse, sickly pale; and its rider's name was Death, and Hades came close behind. To him was given power over a quarter of the earth, with the right to kill by sword and by famine, by pestilence and wild beasts.

When he broke the fifth seal, I saw underneath [a] the altar the souls of those who had been slaughtered for God's word and for the testimony they bore. They gave a great cry: 'How long, sovereign Lord, holy and true, must it be before thou wilt vindicate us and avenge our blood on the inhabitants of the earth?' Each of them was given a white robe; and they were told to rest a little while longer, until the tally should be complete of all their brothers in Christ's service who were to be killed as they had been.

Then I watched as he broke the sixth seal. And there was a violent earthquake; the sun turned black as a funeral pall and the moon all red as blood; the stars in the sky fell to the earth, like figs shaken down by a gale; the sky vanished, as a scroll is rolled up, and every mountain and island was moved from its place. Then the kings of the earth, magnates and marshals, the rich and the powerful, and all men, slave or free, hid themselves in caves and mountain crags; and they called out to the mountains and the crags, 'Fall on us and hide us from the face of the One who sits on the throne and from the vengeance of the Lamb.' For the great day of their vengeance has come, and who will be able to stand?

[a] *Or* at the foot of . . .

K.J.V.

R.S.V.

7 And after these things I saw four angels standing on the four corners of the earth, holding the four winds of the earth, that the wind should not blow on the earth, nor on the sea, nor on any tree. 2And I saw another angel ascending from the east, having the seal of the living God: and he cried with a loud voice to the four angels, to whom it was given to hurt the earth and the sea, 3 Saying, Hurt not the earth, neither the sea, nor the trees, till we have sealed the servants of our God in their foreheads. 4And I heard the number of them which were sealed: *and there were* sealed a hundred *and* forty *and* four thousand of all the tribes of the children of Israel. 5 Of the tribe of Juda *were* sealed twelve thousand. Of the tribe of Reuben *were* sealed twelve thousand. Of the tribe of Gad *were* sealed twelve thousand. 6 Of the tribe of Aser *were* sealed twelve thousand. Of the tribe of Nephthalim *were* sealed twelve thousand. Of the tribe of Manasses *were* sealed twelve thousand. 7 Of the tribe of Simeon *were* sealed twelve thousand. Of the tribe of Levi *were* sealed twelve thousand. Of the tribe of Issachar *were* sealed twelve thousand. 8 Of the tribe of Zabulon *were* sealed twelve thousand. Of the tribe of Joseph *were* sealed twelve thousand. Of the tribe of Benjamin *were* sealed twelve thousand. 9After this I beheld, and, lo, a great multitude, which no man could number, of all nations, and kindreds, and people, and tongues, stood before the throne, and before the Lamb, clothed with white robes, and palms in their hands; 10And cried with a loud voice, saying, Salvation to our God which sitteth upon the throne, and unto the Lamb. 11And all the angels stood round about the throne, and *about* the elders and the four beasts, and fell before the throne on their faces, and worshipped God, 12 Saying, Amen: Blessing, and glory, and wisdom, and thanksgiving, and honour, and power, and might, *be* unto our God for ever and ever. Amen. 13And one of the elders answered, saying unto me, What are these which are arrayed in white robes? and whence came they? 14And I said unto him, Sir, thou knowest. And he said to me, These are they which came out of great tribulation, and have washed their robes, and made them white in the blood of the Lamb. 15 Therefore are they before the throne of God, and serve him day and night in his temple: and he that sitteth on the throne shall dwell among them. 16 They shall hunger no more, neither thirst any more; neither shall the sun light on them, nor any heat. 17 For the Lamb which is in the midst of the throne shall feed them, and shall lead them unto living fountains of waters: and God shall wipe away all tears from their eyes.

7 After this I saw four angels standing at the four corners of the earth, holding back the four winds of the earth, that no wind might blow on earth or sea or against any tree. 2 Then I saw another angel ascend from the rising of the sun, with the seal of the living God, and he called with a loud voice to the four angels who had been given power to harm earth and sea, 3 saying, "Do not harm the earth or the sea or the trees, till we have sealed the servants of our God upon their foreheads." 4And I heard the number of the sealed, a hundred and forty-four thousand sealed, out of every tribe of the sons of Israel, 5 twelve thousand sealed out of the tribe of Judah, twelve thousand of the tribe of Reuben, twelve thousand of the tribe of Gad, 6 twelve thousand of the tribe of Asher, twelve thousand of the tribe of Naphtali, twelve thousand of the tribe of Manasseh, 7 twelve thousand of the tribe of Simeon, twelve thousand of the tribe of Levi, twelve thousand of the tribe of Issachar, 8 twelve thousand of the tribe of Zebulun, twelve thousand of the tribe of Joseph, twelve thousand sealed out of the tribe of Benjamin.

9 After this I looked, and behold, a great multitude which no man could number, from every nation, from all tribes and peoples and tongues, standing before the throne and before the Lamb, clothed in white robes, with palm branches in their hands, 10 and crying out with a loud voice, "Salvation belongs to our God who sits upon the throne, and to the Lamb!" 11And all the angels stood round the throne and round the elders and the four living creatures, and they fell on their faces before the throne and worshiped God, 12 saying, "Amen! Blessing and glory and wisdom and thanksgiving and honor and power and might be to our God for ever and ever! Amen."

13 Then one of the elders addressed me, saying, "Who are these, clothed in white robes, and whence have they come?" 14 I said to him, "Sir, you know." And he said to me, "These are they who have come out of the great tribulation; they have washed their robes and made them white in the blood of the Lamb.

15 Therefore are they before the throne of God,
and serve him day and night within his temple;
and he who sits upon the throne will shelter them with his presence.
16 They shall hunger no more, neither thirst any more;
the sun shall not strike them, nor any scorching heat.
17 For the Lamb in the midst of the throne will be their shepherd,
and he will guide them to springs of living water;
and God will wipe away every tear from their eyes."

PHILLIPS	N.E.B.

Judgment stayed for the sealing 7. 1
of God's people

Later I saw four angels standing at the four corners of the earth holding in check the four winds of the earth that none should blow upon the earth or upon the sea or upon any tree. Then I saw another angel ascending out of the east, holding the seal of the living God. He cried out in a loud voice to the four angels who had the power to harm the earth and the sea:

"Do no harm to the earth, nor to the sea, nor to the trees until we have sealed the servants of our God upon their foreheads."

I heard the number of those who were thus sealed and it was 144,000, from every tribe of the sons of Israel. Twelve thousand were sealed from the tribe of Judah; twelve thousand from the tribe of Reuben; twelve thousand from the tribe of Gad; twelve thousand from the tribe of Asher; twelve thousand from the tribe of Naphtali; twelve thousand from the tribe of Manasseh; twelve thousand from the tribe of Simeon; twelve thousand from the tribe of Levi; twelve thousand from the tribe of Issachar; twelve thousand from the tribe of Zebulun; twelve thousand from the tribe of Joseph; and twelve thousand were sealed from the tribe of Benjamin.

The countless host 7. 9
of the redeemed

When this was done I looked again, and before my eyes appeared a vast crowd beyond man's power to number. They came from every nation and tribe and people and language, and they stood before the throne and the Lamb, dressed in white robes with palm branches in their hands. With a great voice they shouted these words:

"Salvation belongs to our God who sits upon the throne and to the Lamb!"

Then all the angels stood encircling the throne, the elders and the four living creatures, and prostrated themselves with heads bowed before the throne and worshiped God saying,

"Amen! Blessing and glory and wisdom and thanksgiving and honor and power and strength be given to our God for timeless ages!"

The countless host explained 7. 13

Then one of the elders addressed me and asked,

"These who are dressed in white robes—who are they, and where do they come from?"

"You know, my Lord," I answered him.

Then he told me:

"These are those who have come through the great oppression; they have washed their robes and made them white in the blood of the Lamb. That is why they now have their place before the throne of God, and serve him day and night in his temple. He who sits upon the throne will be their shelter. They will never again know hunger or thirst. The sun shall never beat upon them, neither shall there be any scorching heat, for the Lamb who is in the center of the throne will be their shepherd and will lead them to springs of living water. And God will wipe away every tear from their eyes."

7 After this I saw four angels stationed at the four corners of the earth, holding back the four winds so that no wind should blow on sea or land or on any tree. Then I saw another angel rising out of the east, carrying the seal of the living God; and he called aloud to the four angels who had been given the power to ravage land and sea: 'Do no damage to sea or land or trees until we have set the seal of our God upon the foreheads of his servants.' And I heard the number of those who had received the seal. From all the tribes of Israel there were a hundred and forty-four thousand: twelve thousand from the tribe of Judah, twelve thousand from the tribe of Reuben, twelve thousand from the tribe of Gad, twelve thousand from the tribe of Asher, twelve thousand from the tribe of Naphtali, twelve thousand from the tribe of Manasseh, twelve thousand from the tribe of Simeon, twelve thousand from the tribe of Levi, twelve thousand from the tribe of Issachar, twelve thousand from the tribe of Zebulun, twelve thousand from the tribe of Joseph, and twelve thousand from the tribe of Benjamin.

After this I looked and saw a vast throng, which no one could count, from every nation, of all tribes, peoples, and languages, standing in front of the throne and before the Lamb. They were robed in white and had palms in their hands, and they shouted together:

'Victory to our God who sits on the throne, and to the Lamb!'

And all the angels stood round the throne and the elders and the four living creatures, and they fell on their faces before the throne and worshipped God, crying:

'Amen! Praise and glory and wisdom, thanksgiving and honour, power and might, be to our God for ever and ever! Amen.'

Then one of the elders turned to me and said, 'These men that are robed in white—who are they and from where do they come?' But I answered, 'My lord, you know, not I.' Then he said to me, 'These are the men who have passed through the great ordeal; they have washed their robes and made them white in the blood of the Lamb. That is why they stand before the throne of God and minister to him day and night in his temple; and he who sits on the throne will dwell with them. They shall never again feel hunger or thirst, the sun shall not beat on them nor any scorching heat, because the Lamb who is at the heart of the throne will be their shepherd and will guide them to the springs of the water of life; and God will wipe all tears from their eyes.'

K.J.V.

R.S.V.

8 And when he had opened the seventh seal, there was silence in heaven about the space of half an hour. 2And I saw the seven angels which stood before God; and to them were given seven trumpets. 3And another angel came and stood at the altar, having a golden censer; and there was given unto him much incense, that he should offer *it* with the prayers of all saints upon the golden altar which was before the throne. 4And the smoke of the incense, *which came* with the prayers of the saints, ascended up before God out of the angel's hand. 5And the angel took the censer, and filled it with fire of the altar, and cast *it* into the earth: and there were voices, and thunderings, and lightnings, and an earthquake. 6And the seven angels which had the seven trumpets prepared themselves to sound. 7 The first angel sounded, and there followed hail and fire mingled with blood, and they were cast upon the earth: and the third part of trees was burnt up, and all green grass was burnt up. 8And the second angel sounded, and as it were a great mountain burning with fire was cast into the sea: and the third part of the sea became blood; 9And the third part of the creatures which were in the sea, and had life, died; and the third part of the ships were destroyed. 10And the third angel sounded, and there fell a great star from heaven, burning as it were a lamp, and it fell upon the third part of the rivers, and upon the fountains of waters; 11And the name of the star is called Wormwood: and the third part of the waters became wormwood; and many men died of the waters, because they were made bitter. 12And the fourth angel sounded, and the third part of the sun was smitten, and the third part of the moon, and the third part of the stars; so as the third part of them was darkened, and the day shone not for a third part of it, and the night

8 When the Lamb opened the seventh seal, there was silence in heaven for about half an hour. 2 Then I saw the seven angels who stand before God, and seven trumpets were given to them. 3And another angel came and stood at the altar with a golden censer; and he was given much incense to mingle with the prayers of all the saints upon the golden altar before the throne; 4 and the smoke of the incense rose with the prayers of the saints from the hand of the angel before God. 5 Then the angel took the censer and filled it with fire from the altar and threw it on the earth; and there were peals of thunder, loud noises, flashes of lightning, and an earthquake.

6 Now the seven angels who had the seven trumpets made ready to blow them.

7 The first angel blew his trumpet, and there followed hail and fire, mixed with blood, which fell on the earth; and a third of the earth was burnt up, and a third of the trees were burnt up, and all green grass was burnt up.

8 The second angel blew his trumpet, and something like a great mountain, burning with fire, was thrown into the sea; 9 and a third of the sea became blood, a third of the living creatures in the sea died, and a third of the ships were destroyed.

10 The third angel blew his trumpet, and a great star fell from heaven, blazing like a torch, and it fell on a third of the rivers and on the fountains of water. 11 The name of the star is Wormwood. A third of the waters became wormwood, and many died of the water, because it was made bitter.

12 The fourth angel blew his trumpet, and a third of the sun was struck, and a third of the moon, and a third of the stars, so that a third of their light was darkened; a third of the day was kept from shining, and likewise a third of the night.

The seventh seal: complete silence 8. 1

Then, when he had broken the seventh seal, there was utter silence in Heaven for what seemed to me half an hour.

The vision of the seven trumpeters 8. 2

Then I saw the seven angels who stand in the presence of God, and seven trumpets were put into their hands.

Then another angel came and stood by the altar holding a golden censer. He was given a great quantity of incense to add to the prayers of all the saints, to be laid upon the golden altar before the throne. And the smoke of the incense rose up before God from the angel's hand, mingled with the prayers of the saints. Then the angel took the censer, filled it with fire from the altar, and hurled it upon the earth. And at that there were thunderings and noises, flashes of lightning and an earthquake.

Then the seven angels who were holding the seven trumpets prepared to blow them.

The first trumpet: hail and fire 8. 7

The first angel blew his trumpet. Hail and fire mingled with blood appeared, and were hurled upon the earth. One-third of the earth was burned up, one-third of all the trees was burned up, and every blade of green grass was burned up.

The second trumpet: 8. 8
the blazing mountain

The second angel blew his trumpet, and something like a vast mountain blazing with fire was thrown into the sea. A third part of the sea turned into blood, a third of all live creatures in the sea died, and a third part of all shipping was destroyed.

The third trumpet: 8. 10
the poisonous star

Then the third angel blew his trumpet and there fell from the sky a huge star blazing like a torch. It fell upon a third of the rivers and springs of water. The name of the star is said to be Apsinthus (Wormwood). A third of all the waters turned into wormwood, and many people died because the waters had become so bitter.

The fourth trumpet: 8. 12
light from the sky diminishes

The fourth angel blew his trumpet, and a third part of the sun, a third part of the moon and a third of the stars were struck. A third part of the light of each of them was darkened, so that light by day and light by night were both diminished by a third part.

8 Now when the Lamb broke the seventh seal, there was silence in heaven for what seemed half an hour. Then I looked, and the seven angels that stand in the presence of God were given seven trumpets.

Then another angel came and stood at the altar, holding a golden censer; and he was given a great quantity of incense to offer with the prayers of all God's people upon the golden altar in front of the throne. And from the angel's hand the smoke of the incense went up before God with the prayers of his people. Then the angel took the censer, filled it from the altar fire, and threw it down upon the earth; and there were peals of thunder, lightning, and an earthquake.

The Powers of Darkness Conquered

Then the seven angels that held the seven trumpets prepared to blow them.

The first blew his trumpet; and there came hail and fire mingled with blood, and this was hurled upon the earth. A third of the earth was burnt, a third of the trees were burnt, all the green grass was burnt.

The second angel blew his trumpet; and what looked like a great blazing mountain was hurled into the sea. A third of the sea was turned to blood, a third of the living creatures in it died, and a third of the ships on it foundered.

The third angel blew his trumpet; and a great star shot from the sky, flaming like a torch; and it fell on a third of the rivers and springs. The name of the star was Wormwood; and a third of the water turned to wormwood, and men in great numbers died of the water because it had been poisoned.

The fourth angel blew his trumpet; and a third part of the sun was struck, a third of the moon, and a third of the stars, so that the third part went dark and a third of the light of the day failed, and of the night.

K.J.V.

likewise. 13And I beheld, and heard an angel flying through the midst of heaven, saying with a loud voice, Woe, woe, woe, to the inhabiters of the earth by reason of the other voices of the trumpet of the three angels, which are yet to sound!

9 And the fifth angel sounded, and I saw a star fall from heaven unto the earth: and to him was given the key of the bottomless pit. 2And he opened the bottomless pit; and there arose a smoke out of the pit, as the smoke of a great furnace; and the sun and the air were darkened by reason of the smoke of the pit. 3And there came out of the smoke locusts upon the earth: and unto them was given power, as the scorpions of the earth have power. 4And it was commanded them that they should not hurt the grass of the earth, neither any green thing, neither any tree; but only those men which have not the seal of God in their foreheads. 5And to them it was given that they should not kill them, but that they should be tormented five months: and their torment *was* as the torment of a scorpion, when he striketh a man. 6And in those days shall men seek death, and shall not find it; and shall desire to die, and death shall flee from them. 7And the shapes of the locusts *were* like unto horses prepared unto battle; and on their heads *were* as it were crowns like gold, and their faces *were* as the faces of men. 8And they had hair as the hair of women, and their teeth were as *the teeth* of lions. 9And they had breastplates, as it were breastplates of iron; and the sound of their wings *was* as the sound of chariots of many horses running to battle. 10And they had tails like unto scorpions, and there were stings in their tails: and their power *was* to hurt men five months. 11And they had a king over them, *which is* the angel of the bottomless pit, whose name in the Hebrew tongue *is* Abaddon, but in the Greek tongue hath *his* name Apollyon. 12 One woe is past; *and,* behold, there come two woes more hereafter. 13And the sixth angel sounded, and I heard a voice from the four horns of the golden altar which is before God, 14 Saying to the sixth angel which had the trumpet, Loose the four angels which are bound in the great river Euphrates. 15And the four angels were loosed, which were prepared for an hour, and a day, and a month, and a year, for to slay the third part of men. 16And the number of the army of the horsemen *were* two hundred thousand thousand: and I heard the number of them. 17And thus I saw the horses in the vision, and them that sat on them, having breastplates of fire, and of jacinth, and brimstone: and the heads of the horses *were* as the heads of lions; and out of their mouths issued fire and smoke and brimstone. 18 By these three was the third part of men killed, by the fire, and by the smoke, and by the brimstone, which issued out of their mouths. 19 For their power is in their mouth, and in their tails: for their tails *were* like unto serpents, and had heads, and with them they do

R.S.V.

13 Then I looked, and I heard an eagle crying with a loud voice, as it flew in midheaven, "Woe, woe, woe to those who dwell on the earth, at the blasts of the other trumpets which the three angels are about to blow!"

9 And the fifth angel blew his trumpet, and I saw a star fallen from heaven to earth, and he was given the key of the shaft of the bottomless pit; 2 he opened the shaft of the bottomless pit, and from the shaft rose smoke like the smoke of a great furnace, and the sun and the air were darkened with the smoke from the shaft. 3 Then from the smoke came locusts on the earth, and they were given power like the power of scorpions of the earth; 4 they were told not to harm the grass of the earth or any green growth or any tree, but only those of mankind who have not the seal of God upon their foreheads; 5 they were allowed to torture them for five months, but not to kill them, and their torture was like the torture of a scorpion, when it stings a man. 6And in those days men will seek death and will not find it; they will long to die, and death will fly from them.

7 In appearance the locusts were like horses arrayed for battle; on their heads were what looked like crowns of gold; their faces were like human faces, 8 their hair like women's hair, and their teeth like lions' teeth; 9 they had scales like iron breastplates, and the noise of their wings was like the noise of many chariots with horses rushing into battle. 10 They have tails like scorpions, and stings, and their power of hurting men for five months lies in their tails. 11 They have as king over them the angel of the bottomless pit; his name in Hebrew is Abaddon, and in Greek he is called Apollyon.[b]

12 The first woe has passed; behold, two woes are still to come.

13 Then the sixth angel blew his trumpet, and I heard a voice from the four horns of the golden altar before God, 14 saying to the sixth angel who had the trumpet, "Release the four angels who are bound at the great river Euphrates." 15 So the four angels were released, who had been held ready for the hour, the day, the month, and the year, to kill a third of mankind. 16 The number of the troops of cavalry was twice ten thousand times ten thousand; I heard their number. 17And this was how I saw the horses in my vision: the riders wore breastplates the color of fire and of sapphire[c] and of sulphur, and the heads of the horses were like lions' heads, and fire and smoke and sulphur issued from their mouths. 18 By these three plagues a third of mankind was killed, by the fire and smoke and sulphur issuing from their mouths. 19 For the power of the horses is in their mouths and in their tails; their tails are like serpents, with heads, and by means of them they wound.

[b] Or *Destroyer.* [c] Greek *hyacinth.*

798

The cry of pity from midheaven 8. 13

Then in my vision I saw a solitary eagle flying in midheaven, crying in a loud voice, "Alas, alas, alas for the inhabitants of the earth, for there are three more trumpet blasts which the three angels shall sound!"

Then I looked, and I heard an eagle calling with a loud cry as it flew in mid-heaven: 'Woe, woe, woe to the inhabitants of the earth when the trumpets sound which the three last angels must now blow!'

*The fifth trumpet: 9. 1
the fathomless pit*

The fifth angel blew his trumpet. I saw a star that had fallen down from Heaven to earth, and he was given the key to the fathomless pit. Then he opened the pit, and smoke like the smoke of a vast furnace rose out of it, so that the light of the sun and the air itself grew dark from the smoke of the pit.

Then out of the smoke emerged locusts to descend upon the earth. They were given powers like those of earthly scorpions. They had orders to do no harm to any grass, green thing or tree upon the earth, but to injure only those human beings who did not bear the seal of God upon their foreheads. They were given no power to kill men, but only to torture them for five months. The torture they could inflict was like the pain of a scorpion's sting.

In those days men will seek death but they will never find it; they will long to die but death will elude them. These locusts looked to me in my vision like horses prepared for battle. On their heads were what appeared to be crowns like gold; their faces were like human faces, and they had long hair like women. Their teeth were like lions' teeth, their breasts were like iron breastplates, and the noise of their wings was like the noise of a host of chariots and horses charging into battle. They have tails and stings like scorpions, and it is in their tails that they possess the power to injure men for five months. They have as their king the angel of the pit, whose name in Hebrew is Abaddon and in Greek Apollyon (meaning the destroyer).

The first disaster is now past, but I see two more approaching.

9 Then the fifth angel blew his trumpet; and I saw a star that had fallen to the earth, and the star was given the key of the shaft of the abyss. With this he opened the shaft of the abyss; and from the shaft smoke rose like smoke from a great furnace, and the sun and the air were darkened by the smoke from the shaft. Then over the earth, out of the smoke, came locusts, and they were given the powers that earthly scorpions have. They were told to do no injury to the grass or to any plant or tree, but only to those men who had not received the seal of God on their foreheads. These they were allowed to torment for five months, with torment like a scorpion's sting; but they were not to kill them. During that time these men will seek death, but they will not find it; they will long to die, but death will elude them.

In appearance the locusts were like horses equipped for battle. On their heads were what looked like golden crowns; their faces were like human faces and their hair like women's hair; they had teeth like lions' teeth, and wore breast-plates like iron; the sound of their wings was like the noise of horses and chariots rushing to battle; they had tails like scorpions, with stings in them, and in their tails lay their power to plague mankind for five months. They had for their king the angel of the abyss, whose name, in Hebrew, is Abaddon, and in Greek, Apollyon, or the Destroyer.

The first woe has now passed. But there are still two more to come.

*The sixth trumpet: 9. 13
the destroying angels*

Then the sixth angel blew his trumpet, and I heard a solitary voice speaking from the four corners of the golden altar that stands in the presence of God. And it said to the sixth angel who held the trumpet, "Release the four angels who are bound at the great river Euphrates!"

Then these four angels who had been held ready for the hour, the day, the month and the year, were set free to kill a third part of all mankind. The number of their horsemen was two hundred million—I heard what their number was. In my vision I saw these horses and their riders, and their breastplates were fiery-red, blue and yellow. The horses' heads looked to me like the heads of lions, and out of their mouths poured fire and smoke and sulfur. A third of all mankind died from the fearful effects of these three, the fire, the smoke and the sulfur which pour out of their mouths. For the power of these horses lies in their mouths and in their tails. Indeed their tails are like serpents with heads, and with these they inflict injury.

The sixth angel then blew his trumpet; and I heard a voice coming from between the horns of the golden altar that stood in the presence of God. It said to the sixth angel, who held the trumpet: 'Release the four angels held bound at the great river Euphrates!' So the four angels were let loose, to kill a third of mankind. They had been held ready for this moment, for this very year and month, day and hour. And their squadrons of cavalry, whose count I heard, numbered two hundred million.

This was how I saw the horses and their riders in my vision: They wore breastplates, fiery red, blue, and sulphur-yellow; the horses had heads like lions' heads, and out of their mouths came fire, smoke, and sulphur. By these three plagues, that is, by the fire, the smoke, and the sulphur that came from their mouths, a third of mankind was killed. The power of the horses lay in their mouths, and in their tails also; for their tails were like snakes, with heads, and with them too they dealt injuries.

hurt. 20And the rest of the men which were not killed by these plagues yet repented not of the works of their hands, that they should not worship devils, and idols of gold, and silver, and brass, and stone, and of wood; which neither can see, nor hear, nor walk: 21 Neither repented they of their murders, nor of their sorceries, nor of their fornication, nor of their thefts.

10 And I saw another mighty angel come down from heaven, clothed with a cloud: and a rainbow *was* upon his head, and his face *was* as it were the sun, and his feet as pillars of fire: 2And he had in his hand a little book open: and he set his right foot upon the sea, and *his* left *foot* on the earth, 3And cried with a loud voice, as *when* a lion roareth: and when he had cried, seven thunders uttered their voices. 4And when the seven thunders had uttered their voices, I was about to write: and I heard a voice from heaven saying unto me, Seal up those things which the seven thunders uttered, and write them not. 5And the angel which I saw stand upon the sea and upon the earth lifted up his hand to heaven, 6And sware by him that liveth for ever and ever, who created heaven, and the things that therein are, and the earth, and the things that therein are, and the sea, and the things which are therein, that there should be time no longer: 7 But in the days of the voice of the seventh angel, when he shall begin to sound, the mystery of God should be finished, as he hath declared to his servants the prophets. 8And the voice which I heard from heaven spake unto me again, and said, Go *and* take the little book which is open in the hand of the angel which standeth upon the sea and upon the earth. 9And I went unto the angel, and said unto him, Give me the little book. And he said unto me, Take *it,* and eat it up; and it shall make thy belly bitter, but it shall be in thy mouth sweet as honey. 10And I took the little book out of the angel's hand, and ate it up; and it was in my mouth sweet as honey: and as soon as I had eaten it, my belly was bitter. 11And he said unto me, Thou must prophesy again before many peoples, and nations, and tongues, and kings.

11 And there was given me a reed like unto a rod: and the angel stood, saying, Rise, and measure the temple of God, and the altar, and them that worship therein. 2 But the court which is without the temple leave out, and measure it not; for it is given unto the Gentiles: and the holy city shall they tread under foot forty *and* two months. 3And I will give *power* unto my two witnesses, and they shall prophesy a thousand two hundred *and* threescore days, clothed

20 The rest of mankind, who were not killed by these plagues, did not repent of the works of their hands nor give up worshiping demons and idols of gold and silver and bronze and stone and wood, which cannot either see or hear or walk; 21 nor did they repent of their murders or their sorceries or their immorality or their thefts.

10 Then I saw another mighty angel coming down from heaven, wrapped in a cloud, with a rainbow over his head, and his face was like the sun, and his legs like pillars of fire. 2 He had a little scroll open in his hand. And he set his right foot on the sea, and his left foot on the land, 3 and called out with a loud voice, like a lion roaring; when he called out, the seven thunders sounded. 4And when the seven thunders had sounded, I was about to write, but I heard a voice from heaven saying, "Seal up what the seven thunders have said, and do not write it down." 5And the angel whom I saw standing on sea and land lifted up his right hand to heaven 6 and swore by him who lives for ever and ever, who created heaven and what is in it, the earth and what is in it, and the sea and what is in it, that there should be no more delay, 7 but that in the days of the trumpet call to be sounded by the seventh angel, the mystery of God, as he announced to his servants the prophets, should be fulfilled.

8 Then the voice which I had heard from heaven spoke to me again, saying, "Go, take the scroll which is open in the hand of the angel who is standing on the sea and on the land." 9 So I went to the angel and told him to give me the little scroll; and he said to me, "Take it and eat; it will be bitter to your stomach, but sweet as honey in your mouth." 10And I took the little scroll from the hand of the angel and ate it; it was sweet as honey in my mouth, but when I had eaten it my stomach was made bitter. 11And I was told, "You must again prophesy about many peoples and nations and tongues and kings."

11 Then I was given a measuring rod like a staff, and I was told: "Rise and measure the temple of God and the altar and those who worship there, 2 but do not measure the court outside the temple; leave that out, for it is given over to the nations, and they will trample over the holy city for forty-two months. 3And I will grant my two witnesses power to prophesy for one thousand two hundred and sixty days, clothed in sackcloth."

PHILLIPS	N.E.B.

The rest of mankind, who did not die in this fearful destruction, neither repented of the works of their own hands nor ceased to worship evil powers and idols of gold, silver, brass, stone, or wood, which can neither see nor hear nor move. Neither did they repent of their murders, their sorceries, their sexual sins, nor of their thieving.

The rest of mankind who survived these plagues still did not abjure the gods their hands had fashioned, nor cease their worship of devils and of idols made from gold, silver, bronze, stone, and wood, which cannot see or hear or walk. Nor did they repent of their murders, their sorcery, their fornication, or their robberies.

The angel with the little book 10. 1

Then I saw another mighty angel descending from Heaven. He was clothed in a cloud, and there was a rainbow around his head. His face blazed like the sun, his legs like pillars of fire, and he had a little book lying open in his hand. He planted his right foot on the sea and his left foot on the land, and then shouted with a loud voice like the roar of a lion. And when he shouted the seven thunders lifted their voices. When the seven thunders had rolled I was on the point of writing but I heard a voice from Heaven, saying,

"Seal up what the seven thunders said, but do not write it down!"

Then the angel whom I had seen bestriding the sea and the land raised his right hand to Heaven and swore by the living one of the timeless ages, who created Heaven, earth and sea and all that is in them:

"There shall be no more delay! In the days which shall soon be announced by the trumpet blast of the seventh angel the mysterious purpose of God shall be completed, as he assured his servants the prophets."

Then the voice which I had heard from Heaven was again in my ears, saying,

"Go and take the little book which lies open in the hand of the angel whose feet are planted on both sea and land."

So I went off toward the angel, asking him to give me the little book.

"Take it," he said to me, "and eat it up. It will be bitter to your stomach, but sweet as honey in your mouth."

Then I took the little book from the angel's hand and swallowed it. It was as sweet as honey to the taste but when I had eaten it up it was bitter to my stomach.

10 Then I saw another mighty angel coming down from heaven. He was wrapped in cloud, with the rainbow round his head; his face shone like the sun and his legs were like pillars of fire. In his hand he held a little scroll unrolled. His right foot he planted on the sea, and his left on the land. Then he gave a great shout, like the roar of a lion; and when he shouted, the seven thunders spoke. I was about to write down what the seven thunders had said; but I heard a voice from heaven saying, 'Seal up what the seven thunders have said; do not write it down.' Then the angel that I saw standing on the sea and the land raised his right hand to heaven and swore by him who lives for ever and ever, who created heaven and earth and the sea and everything in them: 'There shall be no more delay; but when the time comes for the seventh angel to sound his trumpet, the hidden purpose of God will have been fulfilled, as he promised to his servants the prophets.'

Then the voice which I heard from heaven was speaking to me again, and it said, 'Go and take the open scroll in the hand of the angel that stands on the sea and the land.' So I went to the angel and asked him to give me the little scroll. He said to me, 'Take it, and eat it. It will turn your stomach sour, although in your mouth it will taste sweet as honey.' So I took the little scroll from the angel's hand and ate it, and in my mouth it did taste sweet as honey; but when I swallowed it my stomach turned sour.

Then they said to me, 'Once again you must utter prophecies over peoples and nations and languages and many kings.'

John is instructed to prophesy 10. 11

Then they said to me, "It is again your duty to prophesy about many peoples, nations, lan-

guages and kings." And I was given a measuring rod like a staff, and I was told: "Get up and measure the Temple of God, and the altar, and count those who worship there. But leave out of your measurement the courtyard outside the Temple—do not measure that at all. For it has been given over to the nations, and they will trample over the holy city for forty-two months.

11 I was given a long cane, a kind of measuring-rod, and told: 'Now go and measure the temple of God, the altar, and the number of the worshippers. But have nothing to do with the outer court of the temple; do not measure that; for it has been given over to the Gentiles, and they will trample the Holy City underfoot for forty-two months. And I have two witnesses, whom I will appoint to prophesy, dressed in sackcloth, all through those twelve hundred and

God's two witnesses 11. 3

"And I will give authority to my two witnesses to proclaim the message, clothed in sackcloth for twelve hundred and sixty days."

K.J.V.

in sackcloth. 4 These are the two olive trees, and the two candlesticks standing before the God of the earth. 5And if any man will hurt them, fire proceedeth out of their mouth, and devoureth their enemies: and if any man will hurt them, he must in this manner be killed. 6 These have power to shut heaven, that it rain not in the days of their prophecy: and have power over waters to turn them to blood, and to smite the earth with all plagues, as often as they will. 7And when they shall have finished their testimony, the beast that ascendeth out of the bottomless pit shall make war against them, and shall overcome them, and kill them. 8And their dead bodies *shall lie* in the street of the great city, which spiritually is called Sodom and Egypt, where also our Lord was crucified. 9And they of the people and kindreds and tongues and nations shall see their dead bodies three days and a half, and shall not suffer their dead bodies to be put in graves. 10And they that dwell upon the earth shall rejoice over them, and make merry, and shall send gifts one to another; because these two prophets tormented them that dwelt on the earth. 11And after three days and a half the Spirit of life from God entered into them, and they stood upon their feet; and great fear fell upon them which saw them. 12And they heard a great voice from heaven saying unto them, Come up hither. And they ascended up to heaven in a cloud; and their enemies beheld them. 13And the same hour was there a great earthquake, and the tenth part of the city fell, and in the earthquake were slain of men seven thousand: and the remnant were affrighted, and gave glory to the God of heaven. 14 The second woe is past; *and,* behold, the third woe cometh quickly. 15And the seventh angel sounded; and there were great voices in heaven, saying, The kingdoms of this world are become *the kingdoms* of our Lord, and of his Christ; and he shall reign for ever and ever. 16And the four and twenty elders, which sat before God on their seats, fell upon their faces, and worshipped God, 17 Saying, We give thee thanks, O Lord God Almighty, which art, and wast, and art to come; because thou hast taken to thee thy great power, and hast reigned. 18And the nations were angry, and thy wrath is come, and the time of the dead, that they should be judged, and that thou shouldest give reward unto thy servants the

R.S.V.

4 These are the two olive trees and the two lampstands which stand before the Lord of the earth. 5And if any one would harm them, fire pours from their mouth and consumes their foes; if any one would harm them, thus he is doomed to be killed. 6 They have power to shut the sky, that no rain may fall during the days of their prophesying, and they have power over the waters to turn them into blood, and to smite the earth with every plague, as often as they desire. 7And when they have finished their testimony, the beast that ascends from the bottomless pit will make war upon them and conquer them and kill them, 8 and their dead bodies will lie in the street of the great city which is allegorically[d] called Sodom and Egypt, where their Lord was crucified. 9 For three days and a half men from the peoples and tribes and tongues and nations gaze at their dead bodies and refuse to let them be placed in a tomb, 10 and those who dwell on the earth will rejoice over them and make merry and exchange presents, because these two prophets had been a torment to those who dwell on the earth. 11 But after the three and a half days a breath of life from God entered them, and they stood up on their feet, and great fear fell on those who saw them. 12 Then they heard a loud voice from heaven saying to them, "Come up hither!" And in the sight of their foes they went up to heaven in a cloud. 13And at that hour there was a great earthquake, and a tenth of the city fell; seven thousand people were killed in the earthquake, and the rest were terrified and gave glory to the God of heaven.

14 The second woe has passed; behold, the third woe is soon to come.

15 Then the seventh angel blew his trumpet, and there were loud voices in heaven, saying, "The kingdom of the world has become the kingdom of our Lord and of his Christ, and he shall reign for ever and ever." 16And the twenty-four elders who sit on their thrones before God fell on their faces and worshiped God, 17 saying,

"We give thanks to thee, Lord God Almighty, who art and who wast,
    that thou hast taken thy great power
        and begun to reign.
18 The nations raged, but thy wrath came,
    and the time for the dead to be judged,
    for rewarding thy servants, the prophets
        and saints,

---

[d] Greek *spiritually*.

These are the two olive trees and the two lampstands which stand before the Lord of the earth. If anyone tries to harm them, fire issues from their mouths and consumes their enemies. Indeed, if anyone should try to hurt them, this is the way in which he will certainly meet his death. These witnesses have power to shut up the sky and stop any rain from falling during the time of their preaching. Moreover, they have power to turn the waters into blood, and to strike the earth with any plague as often as they wish.

The emergence of the animal   11. 7

Then, when their work of witness is complete, the animal will come up out of the pit and go to war with them. It will conquer and kill them, and their bodies will lie in the street of the great city, which is called by those with spiritual understanding, "Sodom" and "Egypt" —the very place where their Lord himself was crucified. For three and a half days men from all peoples and tribes and languages and nations will gaze upon their bodies and will not allow them to be buried. The inhabitants of the earth will gloat over them and will hold celebrations and send one another presents, because these two prophets had brought such misery to the inhabitants of the earth.

The resurrection and ascension   11. 11
of the two witnesses

But after three and a half days the Spirit of life from God entered them and they stood upright on their feet. This struck terror into the hearts of those who were watching them, and they heard a tremendous voice speaking to these two from Heaven, saying,
"Come up here!"
And they went up to Heaven in a cloud in full view of their enemies. And at that moment there was a great earthquake, and a tenth part of the city fell in ruins and seven thousand people were known to have been killed in the earthquake. The rest were terrified, and acknowledged the glory of the God of Heaven.

The seventh trumpet: 11. 14
(i) the worship of Heaven

The second disaster is now past, and I see the third disaster following hard upon the heels of the second. The seventh angel blew his trumpet. There arose loud voices in Heaven and they were saying,
"The kingship of the world now belongs to our Lord and to his Christ, and he shall be king for timeless ages!"
Then the twenty-four elders, who sit upon their thrones in the presence of God, prostrated themselves and, with bowed heads, worshipped God, saying:
"We thank thee, O Lord who art God the Almighty, who art and who wast, that thou hast assumed thy great power and hast become king. The nations were full of fury, but now thy wrath has come and with it the time for the dead to be judged and for reward to be given to thy

sixty days.' These are the two olive-trees and the two lamps that stand in the presence of the Lord of the earth. If anyone seeks to do them harm, fire pours from their mouths and consumes their enemies; and thus shall the man die who seeks to do them harm. These two have the power to shut up the sky, so that no rain may fall during the time of their prophesying; and they have the power to turn water to blood and to strike the earth at will with every kind of plague. But when they have completed their testimony, the beast that comes up from the abyss will wage war upon them and will defeat and kill them. Their corpses will lie in the street of the great city, whose name in allegory is Sodom, or Egypt, where also their Lord was crucified. For three days and a half men from every people and tribe, of every language and nation, gaze upon their corpses and refuse them burial. All men on earth gloat over them, make merry, and exchange presents; for these two prophets were a torment to the whole earth. But at the end of the three days and a half the breath of life from God came into them; and they stood up on their feet to the terror of all who saw it. Then a loud voice was heard speaking to them from heaven, which said, 'Come up here!' And they went up to heaven in a cloud, in full view of their enemies. At that same moment there was a violent earthquake, and a tenth of the city fell. Seven thousand people were killed in the earthquake; the rest in terror did homage to the God of heaven.

The second woe has now passed. But the third is soon to come.

Then the seventh angel blew his trumpet; and voices were heard in heaven shouting:

'The sovereignty of the world has passed to our Lord and his Christ, and he shall reign for ever and ever!'

And the twenty-four elders, seated on their thrones before God, fell on their faces and worshipped God, saying:

'We give thee thanks, O Lord God, sovereign over all, who art and who wast, because thou hast taken thy great power into thy hands and entered upon thy reign. The nations raged, but thy day of retribution has come. Now is the time for the dead to be judged; now is the time for recompense to thy servants the prophets, to thy dedicated people, and all who

prophets, and to the saints, and them that fear thy name, small and great; and shouldest destroy them which destroy the earth. 19And the temple of God was opened in heaven, and there was seen in his temple the ark of his testament: and there were lightnings, and voices, and thunderings, and an earthquake, and great hail.

12 And there appeared a great wonder in heaven; a woman clothed with the sun, and the moon under her feet, and upon her head a crown of twelve stars: 2And she being with child cried, travailing in birth, and pained to be delivered. 3And there appeared another wonder in heaven; and behold a great red dragon, having seven heads and ten horns, and seven crowns upon his heads. 4And his tail drew the third part of the stars of heaven, and did cast them to the earth: and the dragon stood before the woman which was ready to be delivered, for to devour her child as soon as it was born. 5And she brought forth a man child, who was to rule all nations with a rod of iron: and her child was caught up unto God, and *to* his throne. 6And the woman fled into the wilderness, where she hath a place prepared of God, that they should feed her there a thousand two hundred *and* threescore days. 7And there was war in heaven: Michael and his angels fought against the dragon; and the dragon fought and his angels, 8And prevailed not; neither was their place found any more in heaven. 9And the great dragon was cast out, that old serpent, called the Devil, and Satan, which deceiveth the whole world: he was cast out into the earth, and his angels were cast out with him. 10And I heard a loud voice saying in heaven, Now is come salvation, and strength, and the kingdom of our God, and the power of his Christ: for the accuser of our brethren is cast down, which accused them before our God day and night. 11And they overcame him by the blood of the Lamb, and by the word of their testimony; and they loved not their lives unto the death. 12Therefore rejoice,

and those who fear thy name, both small and great,
and for destroying the destroyers of the earth."
19 Then God's temple in heaven was opened, and the ark of his covenant was seen within his temple; and there were flashes of lightning, loud noises, peals of thunder, an earthquake, and heavy hail.

12 And a great portent appeared in heaven, a woman clothed with the sun, with the moon under her feet, and on her head a crown of twelve stars; 2 she was with child and she cried out in her pangs of birth, in anguish for delivery. 3And another portent appeared in heaven; behold, a great red dragon, with seven heads and ten horns, and seven diadems upon his heads. 4 His tail swept down a third of the stars of heaven, and cast them to the earth. And the dragon stood before the woman who was about to bear a child, that he might devour her child when she brought it forth; 5 she brought forth a male child, one who is to rule all the nations with a rod of iron, but her child was caught up to God and to his throne, 6 and the woman fled into the wilderness, where she has a place prepared by God, in which to be nourished for one thousand two hundred and sixty days.
7 Now war arose in heaven, Michael and his angels fighting against the dragon; and the dragon and his angels fought, 8 but they were defeated and there was no longer any place for them in heaven. 9And the great dragon was thrown down, that ancient serpent, who is called the Devil and Satan, the deceiver of the whole world—he was thrown down to the earth, and his angels were thrown down with him. 10And I heard a loud voice in heaven, saying, "Now the salvation and the power and the kingdom of our God and the authority of his Christ have come, for the accuser of our brethren has been thrown down, who accuses them day and night before our God. 11And they have conquered him by the blood of the Lamb and by the word of their testimony, for they loved not their lives even unto death. 12 Rejoice then, O heaven and

servants, the prophets and the saints, and all who fear thy name, both small and great. Now is the time for destroying the destroyers of the earth!"

Then the Temple of God in Heaven was thrown open and the ark of his agreement within his Temple could be clearly seen. Accompanying this sight were flashes of lightning, loud noises, peals of thunder, an earthquake and a violent storm of hail.

The seventh trumpet: 12. 1
(ii) the sign of the woman

Then a huge sign became visible in the sky— the figure of a woman clothed with the sun, with the moon under her feet and a crown of twelve stars upon her head. She was pregnant, and cried out in her labor and in the pains of bringing forth her child.

The seventh trumpet: 12. 3
(iii) the dragon, the enemy
of the woman

Then another sign became visible in the sky, and I saw that it was a huge red dragon with seven heads and ten horns, with a diadem upon each of his heads. His tail swept down a third of the stars in the sky and hurled them upon the earth. The dragon took his place in front of the woman who was about to give birth to a child, so that as soon as she did so he might devour it. She gave birth to a male child who is to shepherd all the nations "with a rod of iron." Her child was snatched up to God and to his throne, while the woman fled into the desert where she has a place prepared for her by God's command. There they will take care of her for twelve hundred and sixty days.

War in Heaven   12. 7

Then war broke out in Heaven. Michael and his angels battled with the dragon. The dragon and his angels fought back, but they did not prevail and they were expelled from Heaven. So the huge dragon, the serpent of ancient times, who is called the devil and Satan, the deceiver of the whole world, was hurled down upon the earth, and his angels were hurled down with him.

The victory of Heaven   12. 10
proclaimed

Then I heard a great voice in Heaven cry: "Now the salvation of the power and kingdom of our God, and the authority of his Christ, have come! For the accuser of our brethren has been thrown down from his place, where he stood before our God accusing them day and night. Now they have conquered him through the blood of the Lamb, and through the Word to which they bore witness. They did not cherish life even in the face of death!
"Therefore, rejoice, O Heavens, and all you

honour thy name, both great and small, the time to destroy those who destroy the earth.'

Then God's temple in heaven was laid open, and within the temple was seen the ark of his covenant. There came flashes of lightning and peals of thunder, an earthquake, and a storm of hail.

12 Next appeared a great portent in heaven, a woman robed with the sun, beneath her feet the moon, and on her head a crown of twelve stars. She was pregnant, and in the anguish of her labour she cried out to be delivered. Then a second portent appeared in heaven: a great red dragon with seven heads and ten horns; on his heads were seven diadems, and with his tail he swept down a third of the stars in the sky and flung them to the earth. The dragon stood in front of the woman who was about to give birth, so that when her child was born he might devour it. She gave birth to a male child, who is destined to rule all nations with an iron rod. But her child was snatched up to God and his throne; and the woman herself fled into the wilds, where she had a place prepared for her by God, there to be sustained for twelve hundred and sixty days.

Then war broke out in heaven. Michael and his angels waged war upon the dragon. The dragon and his angels fought, but they had not the strength to win, and no foothold was left them in heaven. So the great dragon was thrown down, that serpent of old that led the whole world astray, whose name is Satan, or the Devil —thrown down to the earth, and his angels with him.

Then I heard a voice in heaven proclaiming aloud: 'This is the hour of victory for our God, the hour of his sovereignty and power, when his Christ comes to his rightful rule! For the accuser of our brothers is overthrown, who day and night accused them before our God. By the sacrifice of the Lamb they have conquered him, and by the testimony which they uttered;[a] for they did not hold their lives too dear to lay them down. Rejoice then, you heavens and you that

[a] Or the word of God to which they bore witness.

K.J.V.

ye heavens, and ye that dwell in them. Woe to the inhabiters of the earth and of the sea! for the devil is come down unto you, having great wrath, because he knoweth that he hath but a short time. 13And when the dragon saw that he was cast unto the earth, he persecuted the woman which brought forth the man *child*. 14And to the woman were given two wings of a great eagle, that she might fly into the wilderness, into her place, where she is nourished for a time, and times, and half a time, from the face of the serpent. 15And the serpent cast out of his mouth water as a flood after the woman, that he might cause her to be carried away of the flood. 16And the earth helped the woman; and the earth opened her mouth, and swallowed up the flood which the dragon cast out of his mouth. 17And the dragon was wroth with the woman, and went to make war with the remnant of her seed, which keep the commandments of God, and have the testimony of Jesus Christ.

13 And I stood upon the sand of the sea, and saw a beast rise up out of the sea, having seven heads and ten horns, and upon his horns ten crowns, and upon his heads the name of blasphemy. 2And the beast which I saw was like unto a leopard, and his feet were as *the feet* of a bear, and his mouth as the mouth of a lion: and the dragon gave him his power, and his seat, and great authority. 3And I saw one of his heads as it were wounded to death; and his deadly wound was healed: and all the world wondered after the beast. 4And they worshipped the dragon which gave power unto the beast: and they worshipped the beast, saying, Who *is* like unto the beast? who is able to make war with him? 5And there was given unto him a mouth speaking great things and blasphemies; and power was given unto him to continue forty *and* two months. 6And he opened his mouth in blasphemy against God, to blaspheme his name, and his tabernacle, and them that dwell in heaven. 7And it was given unto him to make war with the saints, and to overcome them: and power was given him over all kindreds, and tongues, and nations. 8And all that dwell upon the earth shall worship him, whose names are not written in the book of life of the Lamb slain from the foundation of the world. 9If any man have an ear, let him hear. 10 He that leadeth into captivity shall go into captivity: he that killeth with the sword must be killed with the sword. Here is the patience and the faith of the

R.S.V.

you that dwell therein! But woe to you, O earth and sea, for the devil has come down to you in great wrath, because he knows that his time is short!"
13 And when the dragon saw that he had been thrown down to the earth, he pursued the woman who had borne the male child. 14 But the woman was given the two wings of the great eagle that she might fly from the serpent into the wilderness, to the place where she is to be nourished for a time, and times, and half a time. 15 The serpent poured water like a river out of his mouth after the woman, to sweep her away with the flood. 16 But the earth came to the help of the woman, and the earth opened its mouth and swallowed the river which the dragon had poured from his mouth. 17 Then the dragon was angry with the woman, and went off to make war on the rest of her offspring, on those who keep the commandments of God and bear testimony to Jesus. And he stood *e* on the sand of the sea.

13 And I saw a beast rising out of the sea, with ten horns and seven heads, with ten diadems upon its horns and a blasphemous name upon its heads. 2And the beast that I saw was like a leopard, its feet were like a bear's, and its mouth was like a lion's mouth. And to it the dragon gave his power and his throne and great authority. 3 One of its heads seemed to have a mortal wound, but its mortal wound was healed, and the whole earth followed the beast with wonder. 4 Men worshiped the dragon, for he had given his authority to the beast, and they worshiped the beast, saying, "Who is like the beast, and who can fight against it?"
5 And the beast was given a mouth uttering haughty and blasphemous words, and it was allowed to exercise authority for forty-two months; 6 it opened its mouth to utter blasphemies against God, blaspheming his name and his dwelling, that is, those who dwell in heaven. 7Also it was allowed to make war on the saints and to conquer them.*f* And authority was given it over every tribe and people and tongue and nation, 8 and all who dwell on earth will worship it, every one whose name has not been written before the foundation of the world in the book of life of the Lamb that was slain. 9 If any one has an ear, let him hear:
10 If any one is to be taken captive,
　　to captivity he goes;
　if any one slays with the sword,
　　with the sword must he be slain.
Here is a call for the endurance and faith of the saints.

[e] Other ancient authorities read *And I stood*, connecting the sentence with 13.1 [f] Other ancient authorities omit this sentence.

PHILLIPS	N.E.B.

PHILLIPS

who live in the Heavens! But alas for the earth and the sea, for the devil has come down to you in great fury, knowing that his time is short!"

The dragon's enmity   **12. 13**
against the woman

And when the dragon saw that he had been cast down upon the earth, he began to pursue the woman who had given birth to the male child. But she was given two great eagle's wings so that she could fly to her place in the desert, where she is kept safe from the serpent for a time and times and half a time. Then the serpent ejected water from his mouth, streaming like a river in pursuit of the woman, to drown her in its flood. But the earth came to the woman's rescue, opened its mouth and swallowed up the river which the dragon had emitted from his mouth. Then the dragon raged with fury against the woman and went off to make war against the rest of her children—those who keep the commandments of God and bear their witness to Jesus.

The animal from the sea   **13. 1**

Then, as I stood on the sand of the seashore, there rose out of the sea before my eyes an animal with seven heads and ten horns. There were diadems upon its horns and blasphemous names upon its heads. The animal which I saw had the appearance of a leopard, though it had the feet of a bear and a mouth like the mouth of a lion. Then the dragon gave it his own power and throne and great authority. One of its heads appeared to have been wounded to death but the mortal wound had healed.

The whole earth followed the animal with wonder, and they worshiped the dragon because he had given authority to the animal. Then they worshiped the animal, too, saying:

"Who is like the animal? Who could make war against it?"

It was allowed to speak monstrous blasphemies and to exert its authority for forty-two months.

So it poured out blasphemies against God, blaspheming his name and his dwelling-place and those who live in Heaven. Moreover, it was permitted to make war upon the saints and to conquer them; the authority given to it extended over every tribe and people and language and nation. All the inhabitants of the earth will worship it—all those whose names have not been written in the book of life which belongs to the Lamb slain from the foundation of the world.

Parenthetical: a word   **13. 9**
to the reader

Let the listener hear this:
If any man is destined for captivity he will go into captivity. If any man kills with the sword he must himself be killed with the sword. Amid all this stands the endurance and faith of the saints.

N.E.B.

dwell in them! But woe to you, earth and sea, for the Devil has come down to you in great fury, knowing that his time is short!'

When the dragon found that he had been thrown down to the earth, he went in pursuit of the woman who had given birth to the male child. But the woman was given two great eagle's wings, to fly to the place in the wilds where for three years and a half she was to be sustained, out of reach of the serpent. From his mouth the serpent spewed a flood of water after the woman to sweep her away with its spate. But the earth came to her rescue and opened its mouth and swallowed the river which the dragon spewed from his mouth. At this the dragon grew furious with the woman, and went off to wage war on the rest of her offspring, that is, on those who keep God's commandments and maintain their testimony to Jesus.

13 He took his stand on the sea-shore.
Then[a] out of the sea I saw a beast rising. It had ten horns and seven heads. On its horns were ten diadems, and on each head a blasphemous name. The beast I saw was like a leopard, but its feet were like a bear's and its mouth like a lion's mouth. The dragon conferred upon it his power and rule, and great authority. One of its heads appeared to have received a death-blow; but the mortal wound was healed. The whole world went after the beast in wondering admiration. Men worshipped the dragon because he had conferred his authority upon the beast; they worshipped the beast also, and chanted, 'Who is like the Beast? Who can fight against it?'

The beast was allowed to mouth bombast and blasphemy, and was given the right to reign for forty-two months. It opened its mouth in blasphemy against God, reviling his name and his heavenly dwelling.[b] It was also allowed to wage war on God's people and to defeat them, and was granted[c] authority over every tribe and people, language and nation. All on earth will worship it, except those whose names the Lamb that was slain keeps in his roll of the living, written there since the world was made.

Hear, you who have ears to hear! Whoever is meant for prison, to prison he goes. Whoever takes the sword to kill, by the sword he is bound to be killed. Here the fortitude and faithfulness of God's people have their place.

[a] *Some witnesses read* . . . testimony to Jesus. Then I stood by the sea-shore and . . . [b] *Some witnesses read* reviling his name and his dwelling-place, that is, those that live in heaven. [c] *Some witnesses read* It was granted . . . (*omitting the words* was also . . . them, and).

K.J.V.

saints. 11And I beheld another beast coming up out of the earth; and he had two horns like a lamb, and he spake as a dragon. 12And he exerciseth all the power of the first beast before him, and causeth the earth and them which dwell therein to worship the first beast, whose deadly wound was healed. 13And he doeth great wonders, so that he maketh fire come down from heaven on the earth in the sight of men, 14And deceiveth them that dwell on the earth by *the means of* those miracles which he had power to do in the sight of the beast; saying to them that dwell on the earth, that they should make an image to the beast, which had the wound by a sword, and did live. 15And he had power to give life unto the image of the beast, that the image of the beast should both speak, and cause that as many as would not worship the image of the beast should be killed. 16And he causeth all, both small and great, rich and poor, free and bond, to receive a mark in their right hand, or in their foreheads: 17And that no man might buy or sell, save he that had the mark, or the name of the beast, or the number of his name. 18Here is wisdom. Let him that hath understanding count the number of the beast: for it is the number of a man; and his number *is* Six hundred threescore *and* six.

14 And I looked, and, lo, a Lamb stood on the mount Sion, and with him a hundred forty *and* four thousand, having his Father's name written in their foreheads. 2And I heard a voice from heaven, as the voice of many waters, and as the voice of a great thunder: and I heard the voice of harpers harping with their harps: 3And they sung as it were a new song before the throne, and before the four beasts, and the elders: and no man could learn that song but the hundred *and* forty *and* four thousand, which were redeemed from the earth. 4 These are they which were not defiled with women; for they are virgins. These are they which follow the Lamb whithersoever he goeth. These were redeemed from among men, *being* the firstfruits unto God and to the Lamb. 5And in their mouth was found no guile: for they are without fault before the throne of God. 6And I saw another angel fly in the midst of heaven, having the everlasting gospel to preach unto them that dwell on the earth, and to every nation, and kindred, and tongue, and people, 7 Saying with a loud voice, Fear God, and give glory to him; for the hour of his judgment is come: and worship him that made heaven, and earth, and the sea, and the fountains of waters. 8And there followed another angel, saying, Baby-

R.S.V.

11 Then I saw another beast which rose out of the earth; it had two horns like a lamb and it spoke like a dragon. 12 It exercises all the authority of the first beast in its presence, and makes the earth and its inhabitants worship the first beast, whose mortal wound was healed. 13 It works great signs, even making fire come down from heaven to earth in the sight of men; 14 and by the signs which it is allowed to work in the presence of the beast, it deceives those who dwell on earth, bidding them make an image for the beast which was wounded by the sword and yet lived; 15 and it was allowed to give breath to the image of the beast so that the image of the beast should even speak, and to cause those who would not worship the image of the beast to be slain. 16Also it causes all, both small and great, both rich and poor, both free and slave, to be marked on the right hand or the forehead, 17 so that no one can buy or sell unless he has the mark, that is, the name of the beast or the number of its name. 18 This calls for wisdom: let him who has understanding reckon the number of the beast, for it is a human number, its number is six hundred and sixty-six.*g*

14 Then I looked, and lo, on Mount Zion stood the Lamb, and with him a hundred and forty-four thousand who had his name and his Father's name written on their foreheads. 2And I heard a voice from heaven like the sound of many waters and like the sound of loud thunder; the voice I heard was like the sound of harpers playing on their harps, 3 and they sing a new song before the throne and before the four living creatures and before the elders. No one could learn that song except the hundred and forty-four thousand who had been redeemed from the earth. 4 It is these who have not defiled themselves with women, for they are chaste;*h* it is these who follow the Lamb wherever he goes; these have been redeemed from mankind as first fruits for God and the Lamb, 5 and in their mouth no lie was found, for they are spotless.

6 Then I saw another angel flying in midheaven, with an eternal gospel to proclaim to those who dwell on earth, to every nation and tribe and tongue and people; 7 and he said with a loud voice, "Fear God and give him glory, for the hour of his judgment has come; and worship him who made heaven and earth, the sea and the fountains of water."

8 Another angel, a second, followed, saying,

---

[g] Other ancient authorities read *six hundred and sixteen.* [h] Greek *virgins.*

The animal from the earth 13. 11

Then I saw another animal rising out of the earth, and it had two horns like a lamb but it spoke in the voice of a dragon. It uses the full authority of the first animal in its presence. It compels the earth and all its inhabitants to worship the first animal—the one with the mortal wound which had healed. It performs great signs: before men's eyes it makes fire fall down from heaven to earth. It deceives the inhabitants of the earth by the signs which it is allowed to perform in the presence of the animal, and it tells them to make a statue in honor of the animal which received the sword thrust and yet survived. Further, it was allowed to give the breath of life to the statue of the animal so that the statue could speak and condemn to death all those who do not worship its statue. Then it compels all, small and great, rich and poor, free men and slaves, to receive a mark on their right hands or on their foreheads. The purpose of this is that no one should be able to buy or sell unless he bears the mark of the name of the animal or the number of its name. Understanding is needed here: let every thinking man calculate the number of the animal. It is the number of a man, and its number is six hundred and sixty-six.

Then I saw another beast, which came up out of the earth; it had two horns like a lamb's, but spoke like a dragon. It wielded all the authority of the first beast in its presence, and made the earth and its inhabitants worship this first beast, whose mortal wound had been healed. It worked great miracles, even making fire come down from heaven to earth before men's eyes. By the miracles it was allowed to perform in the presence of the beast it deluded the inhabitants of the earth, and made them erect an image in honour of the beast that had been wounded by the sword and yet lived. It was allowed to give breath to the image of the beast, so that it could speak, and could cause all who would not worship the image to be put to death. Moreover, it caused everyone, great and small, rich and poor, slave and free, to be branded with a mark on his right hand or forehead, and no one was allowed to buy or sell unless he bore this beast's mark, either name or number. (Here is the key; and anyone who has intelligence may work out the number of the beast. The number represents a man's name, and the numerical value of its letters is six hundred and sixty-six.)

The vision of the Lamb 14. 1
and the first of the redeemed

Visions of the End

Then I looked again and before my eyes the Lamb was standing on Mount Sion, and with him were a hundred and forty-four thousand who had his name and his Father's name written upon their foreheads. Then I heard a sound coming from Heaven like the roar of a great waterfall and the heavy rolling of thunder. Yet the sound which I heard was also like the music of harpists sweeping their strings. And now they are singing a new song of praise before the throne, and before the four living creatures and the elders. No one could learn that song except the one hundred and forty-four thousand who had been redeemed from the earth. These are the men who have never defiled themselves with women, for they are celibate. These are the men who follow the Lamb wherever he may go; these men have been redeemed from among mankind as first fruits to God and to the Lamb. They have never been guilty of any falsehood; they are beyond reproach.

14 Then I looked, and on Mount Zion stood the Lamb, and with him were a hundred and forty-four thousand who had his name and the name of his Father written on their foreheads. I heard a sound from heaven like the noise of rushing water and the deep roar of thunder; it was the sound of harpers playing on their harps. There before the throne, and the four living creatures and the elders, they were singing a new song. That song no one could learn except the hundred and forty-four thousand, who alone from the whole world had been ransomed. These are men who did not defile themselves with women, for they have kept themselves chaste, and they follow the Lamb wherever he goes. They have been ransomed as the firstfruits of humanity for God and the Lamb. No lie was found in their lips; they are faultless.

Then I saw an angel flying in mid-heaven, with an eternal gospel to proclaim to those on earth, to every nation and tribe, language and people. He cried in a loud voice, 'Fear God and pay him homage; for the hour of his judgement has come! Worship him who made heaven and earth, the sea and the water-springs!'

Then another angel, a second, followed, and

The angel with the gospel 14. 6

Then I saw another angel flying in midheaven, holding the everlasting gospel to proclaim to the inhabitants of the earth—to every nation and tribe and language and people. He was crying in a loud voice:

"Reverence God, and give glory to him; for the hour of his judgment has come! Worship him who made Heaven and earth, the sea and the springs of water."

The angel of doom 14. 8

Then another, a second angel, followed him crying:

K.J.V.

lon is fallen, is fallen, that great city, because she made all nations drink of the wine of the wrath of her fornication. 9And the third angel followed them, saying with a loud voice, If any man worship the beast and his image, and receive *his* mark in his forehead, or in his hand, 10 The same shall drink of the wine of the wrath of God, which is poured out without mixture into the cup of his indignation; and he shall be tormented with fire and brimstone in the presence of the holy angels, and in the presence of the Lamb: 11And the smoke of their torment ascendeth up for ever and ever: and they have no rest day nor night, who worship the beast and his image, and whosoever receiveth the mark of his name. 12 Here is the patience of the saints: here *are* they that keep the commandments of God, and the faith of Jesus. 13And I heard a voice from heaven saying unto me, Write, Blessed *are* the dead which die in the Lord from henceforth: Yea, saith the Spirit, that they may rest from their labours; and their works do follow them. 14And I looked, and behold a white cloud, and upon the cloud *one* sat like unto the Son of man, having on his head a golden crown, and in his hand a sharp sickle. 15And another angel came out of the temple, crying with a loud voice to him that sat on the cloud, Thrust in thy sickle, and reap: for the time is come for thee to reap; for the harvest of the earth is ripe. 16And he that sat on the cloud thrust in his sickle on the earth; and the earth was reaped. 17And another angel came out of the temple which is in heaven, he also having a sharp sickle. 18And another angel came out from the altar, which had power over fire; and cried with a loud cry to him that had the sharp sickle, saying, Thrust in thy sharp sickle, and gather the clusters of the vine of the earth; for her grapes are fully ripe. 19And the angel thrust in his sickle into the earth, and gathered the vine of the earth, and cast *it* into the great winepress of the wrath of God. 20And the winepress was trodden without the city, and blood came out of the winepress, even unto the horse bridles, by the space of a thousand *and* six hundred furlongs.

R.S.V.

"Fallen, fallen is Babylon the great, she who made all nations drink the wine of her impure passion."

9 And another angel, a third, followed them, saying with a loud voice, "If any one worships the beast and its image, and receives a mark on his forehead or on his hand, 10 he also shall drink the wine of God's wrath, poured unmixed into the cup of his anger, and he shall be tormented with fire and brimstone in the presence of the holy angels and in the presence of the Lamb. 11And the smoke of their torment goes up for ever and ever; and they have no rest, day or night, these worshipers of the beast and its image, and whoever receives the mark of its name."

12 Here is a call for the endurance of the saints, those who keep the commandments of God and the faith of Jesus.

13 And I heard a voice from heaven saying, "Write this: Blessed are the dead who die in the Lord henceforth." "Blessed indeed," says the Spirit, "that they may rest from their labors, for their deeds follow them!"

14 Then I looked, and lo, a white cloud, and seated on the cloud one like a son of man, with a golden crown on his head, and a sharp sickle in his hand. 15And another angel came out of the temple, calling with a loud voice to him who sat upon the cloud, "Put in your sickle, and reap, for the hour to reap has come, for the harvest of the earth is fully ripe." 16 So he who sat upon the cloud swung his sickle on the earth, and the earth was reaped.

17 And another angel came out of the temple in heaven, and he too had a sharp sickle. 18 Then another angel came out from the altar, the angel who has power over fire, and he called with a loud voice to him who had the sharp sickle, "Put in your sickle, and gather the clusters of the vine of the earth, for its grapes are ripe." 19 So the angel swung his sickle on the earth and gathered the vintage of the earth, and threw it into the great wine press of the wrath of God; 20 and the wine press was trodden outside the city, and blood flowed from the wine press, as high as a horse's bridle, for one thousand six hundred stadia.[i]

[i] About two hundred miles.

PHILLIPS

"Fallen, fallen is Babylon the great! She who made all nations drink the wine of her passionate unfaithfulness!"

The angel of judgment   14. 9

Then a third angel followed these two, crying in a loud voice:

"If any man worships the animal and its statue and bears its mark upon his forehead or upon his hand, then that man shall drink the wine of God's passion, poured undiluted into the cup of his wrath. He shall be tortured by fire and sulfur in the presence of the holy angels and of the Lamb. The smoke of such men's torture ascends for timeless ages, and there is no respite from it day or night. Such are the worshipers of the animal and its statue, and among their number are all who bear the mark of its name."

The call to stand fast   14. 12

In all this stands the endurance of the saints—those who keep the commandments of God and their faith in Jesus.

The security of the saints   14. 13

Then I heard a voice from Heaven, saying,
"Write this! From henceforth happy are the dead who die in the Lord!"
"Happy indeed," says the Spirit, "for they rest from their labors and their deeds go with them!"

The harvest of God's wrath   14. 14

Once again I looked, and a white cloud appeared before me with someone sitting upon the cloud with the appearance of a man. He had a golden crown on his head, and held a sharp sickle in his hand. Then another angel came out from the Temple, calling in a loud voice to the one sitting on the cloud,
"Thrust in your sickle and reap, for the time of reaping has come and the harvest of the earth is fully ripe!"
Then the one sitting upon the cloud swung his sickle upon the earth, and the reaping of the earth was done.
Then another angel came out from the Temple in Heaven, and he also had a sharp sickle. Yet another angel came out from the altar where he has command over the fire, and called out in a loud voice to the angel with the sharp sickle,
"Thrust in your sharp sickle and harvest the clusters from the vineyard of the earth, for the grapes are fully ripe!"
Then the angel swung his sickle upon the earth and gathered the harvest of the earth's vineyard, and threw it into the great winepress of the wrath of God. The grapes were trodden outside the city, and out of the winepress flowed blood for two hundred miles in a stream as high as the horses' bridles.

N.E.B.

he cried, 'Fallen, fallen is Babylon the great, she who has made all nations drink the fierce wine of [a] her fornication!'

Yet a third angel followed, crying out loud, 'Whoever worships the beast and its image and receives its mark on his forehead or hand, he shall drink the wine of God's wrath, poured undiluted into the cup of his vengeance. He shall be tormented in sulphurous flames before the holy angels and before the Lamb. The smoke of their torment will rise for ever and ever, and there will be no respite day or night for those who worship the beast and its image or receive the mark of its name.' Here the fortitude of God's people has its place—in keeping God's commands and remaining loyal to Jesus.

Moreover, I heard a voice from heaven, saying, 'Write this: "Happy are the dead who die in the faith of Christ! Henceforth",[b] says the Spirit,[c] "they may rest from their labours; for they take with them the record of their deeds." '

Then as I looked there appeared a white cloud, and on the cloud sat one like a son of man. He had on his head a crown of gold and in his hand a sharp sickle. Another angel came out of the temple and called in a loud voice to him who sat on the cloud: 'Stretch out your sickle and reap; for harvest-time has come, and earth's crop is over-ripe.' So he who sat on the cloud put his sickle to the earth and its harvest was reaped.

Then another angel came out of the heavenly temple, and he also had a sharp sickle. Then from the altar came yet another, the angel who has authority over fire, and he shouted to the one with the sharp sickle: 'Stretch out your sickle, and gather in earth's grape-harvest, for its clusters are ripe.' So the angel put his sickle to the earth and gathered in its grapes, and threw them into the great winepress of God's wrath. The winepress was trodden outside the city, and for two hundred miles around blood flowed from the press to the height of the horses' bridles.

[a] Or drink the wine of God's wrath upon . . .
[b] Or Assuredly. [c] Some witnesses read ". . . the dead who henceforth die in the faith of Christ!" "Yes," says the Spirit . . .

K.J.V.

15 And I saw another sign in heaven, great and marvellous, seven angels having the seven last plagues; for in them is filled up the wrath of God. 2And I saw as it were a sea of glass mingled with fire: and them that had gotten the victory over the beast, and over his image, and over his mark, *and* over the number of his name, stand on the sea of glass, having the harps of God. 3And they sing the song of Moses the servant of God, and the song of the Lamb, saying, Great and marvellous *are* thy works, Lord God Almighty; just and true *are* thy ways, thou King of saints. 4 Who shall not fear thee, O Lord, and glorify thy name? for *thou* only *art* holy: for all nations shall come and worship before thee; for thy judgments are made manifest. 5And after that I looked, and, behold, the temple of the tabernacle of the testimony in heaven was opened: 6And the seven angels came out of the temple, having the seven plagues, clothed in pure and white linen, and having their breasts girded with golden girdles. 7And one of the four beasts gave unto the seven angels seven golden vials full of the wrath of God, who liveth for ever and ever. 8And the temple was filled with smoke from the glory of God, and from his power; and no man was able to enter into the temple, till the seven plagues of the seven angels were fulfilled.

R.S.V.

15 Then I saw another portent in heaven, great and wonderful, seven angels with seven plagues, which are the last, for with them the wrath of God is ended.

2 And I saw what appeared to be a sea of glass mingled with fire, and those who had conquered the beast and its image and the number of its name, standing beside the sea of glass with harps of God in their hands. 3And they sing the song of Moses, the servant of God, and the song of the Lamb, saying,

"Great and wonderful are thy deeds,
  O Lord God the Almighty!
Just and true are thy ways,
  O King of the ages! *j*
  4 Who shall not fear and glorify thy name, O
    Lord?
For thou alone art holy.
All nations shall come and worship thee,
  for thy judgments have been revealed."

5 After this I looked, and the temple of the tent of witness in heaven was opened, 6 and out of the temple came the seven angels with the seven plagues, robed in pure bright linen, and their breasts girded with golden girdles. 7And one of the four living creatures gave the seven angels seven golden bowls full of the wrath of God who lives for ever and ever; 8 and the temple was filled with smoke from the glory of God and from his power, and no one could enter the temple until the seven plagues of the seven angels were ended.

16 And I heard a great voice out of the temple saying to the seven angels, Go your ways, and pour out the vials of the wrath of God upon the earth. 2And the first went, and poured out his vial upon the earth; and there fell a noisome and grievous sore upon the men which had the mark of the beast, and *upon* them which worshipped his image. 3And the second angel poured out his vial upon the sea; and it became as the blood of a dead *man:* and

16 Then I heard a loud voice from the temple telling the seven angels, "Go and pour out on the earth the seven bowls of the wrath of God."

2 So the first angel went and poured his bowl on the earth, and foul and evil sores came upon the men who bore the mark of the beast and worshiped its image.

3 The second angel poured his bowl into the sea, and it became like the blood of a dead man, and every living thing died that was in the sea.

[*j*] Other ancient authorities read *the nations.*

PHILLIPS

N.E.B.

The seven last plagues prepared 15. 1

Then I saw another sign in Heaven, vast and awe-inspiring: seven angels are holding the seven last plagues, and with these the wrath of God is brought to an end.

The hymn of the redeemed 15. 2

And I saw what appeared to be a sea of glass shot through with fire, and upon this glassy sea were standing those who had emerged victorious from the fight with the animal, its statue, and the number which denotes its name. In their hands they hold harps which God has given them, and they are singing the song of Moses the servant of God, and the song of the Lamb, and these are the words they sing:
"Great and wonderful are thy works, O Lord God, the Almighty! Just and true are thy ways, thou king of the nations! Who should not reverence thee, O Lord, and glorify thy name? For thou alone art holy; therefore all nations shall come and worship before thee, for thy just judgments have been made plain!"

The angels leave the Temple 15. 5
of God—

Later in my vision I saw the Temple of the tabernacle of testimony in Heaven wide open, and out of the Temple came forth the seven angels who hold the seven plagues. They were dressed in spotless shining linen, and they were girded round their breasts with golden girdles.
Then one of the four living creatures gave to the seven angels seven golden bowls filled with the wrath of God who lives for timeless ages. The Temple was filled with smoke from the glory and power of God, and no one could enter the Temple until the seven plagues of the seven angels were past and over.

—and are ordered to pour out 16. 1
the bowls of his wrath

Then I heard a loud voice from the Temple saying to the seven angels,
"Go and pour out upon the earth the seven bowls of the wrath of God!"

The first bowl: ulcers 16. 2

The first angel went off and emptied his bowl upon the earth. Whereupon loathsome and malignant ulcers attacked all those who bore the mark of the animal and worshiped its statue.

The second bowl: 16. 3
death in the sea

The second angel emptied his bowl into the sea, which turned into a fluid like the blood of a corpse, and every living thing in it died.

15 Then I saw another great and astonishing portent in heaven: seven angels with seven plagues, the last plagues of all, for with them the wrath of God is consummated.
I saw what seemed a sea of glass shot with fire, and beside the sea of glass, holding the harps which God had given them, were those who had won the victory over the beast and its image and the number of its name.
They were singing the song of Moses, the servant of God, and the song of the Lamb, as they chanted:

'Great and marvellous are thy deeds, O Lord God, sovereign over all; just and true are thy ways, thou king of the ages.[a] Who shall not revere thee, Lord, and do homage to thy name? For thou alone art holy. All nations shall come and worship in thy presence, for thy just dealings stand revealed.'

After this, as I looked, the sanctuary of the heavenly Tent of Testimony was thrown open, and out of it came the seven angels with the seven plagues. They were robed in fine linen, clean and shining, and had golden girdles round their breasts. Then one of the four living creatures gave the seven angels seven golden bowls full of the wrath of God who lives for ever and ever; and the sanctuary was filled with smoke from the glory of God and his power, so that no one could enter it until the seven plagues of the seven angels were completed.

16 Then from the sanctuary I heard a loud voice, and it said to the seven angels, 'Go and pour out the seven bowls of God's wrath on the earth.'
So the first angel went and poured his bowl on the earth; and foul malignant sores appeared on those men that wore the mark of the beast and worshipped its image.
The second angel poured his bowl on the sea, and it turned to blood like the blood from a corpse; and every living thing in the sea died.

[a] Some witnesses read king of the nations.

K.J.V.

every living soul died in the sea. 4And the third angel poured out his vial upon the rivers and fountains of waters; and they became blood. 5And I heard the angel of the waters say, Thou art righteous, O Lord, which art, and wast, and shalt be, because thou hast judged thus. 6 For they have shed the blood of saints and prophets, and thou hast given them blood to drink; for they are worthy. 7And I heard another out of the altar say, Even so, Lord God Almighty, true and righteous *are* thy judgments. 8And the fourth angel poured out his vial upon the sun; and power was given unto him to scorch men with fire. 9And men were scorched with great heat, and blasphemed the name of God, which hath power over these plagues: and they repented not to give him glory. 10And the fifth angel poured out his vial upon the seat of the beast; and his kingdom was full of darkness; and they gnawed their tongues for pain, 11And blasphemed the God of heaven because of their pains and their sores, and repented not of their deeds. 12And the sixth angel poured out his vial upon the great river Euphrates; and the water thereof was dried up, that the way of the kings of the east might be prepared. 13And I saw three unclean spirits like frogs *come* out of the mouth of the dragon, and out of the mouth of the beast, and out of the mouth of the false prophet. 14 For they are the spirits of devils, working miracles, *which* go forth unto the kings of the earth and of the whole world, to gather them to the battle of that great day of God Almighty. 15 Behold, I come as a thief. Blessed *is* he that watcheth, and keepeth his garments, lest he walk naked, and they see his shame. 16And he gathered them together into a place called in the Hebrew tongue Armageddon. 17And the seventh angel poured out his vial into the air; and there came a great voice out of the temple of heaven, from the throne, saying, It is done.

R.S.V.

4 The third angel poured his bowl into the rivers and the fountains of water, and they became blood. 5And I heard the angel of water say,

"Just art thou in these thy judgments,
thou who art and wast, O Holy One.
6 For men have shed the blood of saints and prophets,
and thou hast given them blood to drink.
It is their due!"
7And I heard the altar cry,
"Yea, Lord God the Almighty,
true and just are thy judgments!"

8 The fourth angel poured his bowl on the sun, and it was allowed to scorch men with fire; 9 men were scorched by the fierce heat, and they cursed the name of God who had power over these plagues, and they did not repent and give him glory.

10 The fifth angel poured his bowl on the throne of the beast, and its kingdom was in darkness; men gnawed their tongues in anguish 11 and cursed the God of heaven for their pain and sores, and did not repent of their deeds.

12 The sixth angel poured his bowl on the great river Euphrates, and its water was dried up, to prepare the way for the kings from the east. 13And I saw, issuing from the mouth of the dragon and from the mouth of the beast and from the mouth of the false prophet, three foul spirits like frogs; 14 for they are demonic spirits, performing signs, who go abroad to the kings of the whole world, to assemble them for battle on the great day of God the Almighty. 15 ("Lo, I am coming like a thief! Blessed is he who is awake, keeping his garments that he may not go naked and be seen exposed!") 16And they assembled them at the place which is called in Hebrew Armageddon.

17 The seventh angel poured his bowl into the air, and a great voice came out of the tem-

The third bowl: 16. 4
water becomes blood

Then the third angel emptied his bowl into the rivers and springs of water, and they turned into blood. And I heard the angel of the waters say:
"Just art thou in these thy judgments, thou who art and wast the holy one! For they have spilled the blood of saints and prophets, and now thou hast given them blood to drink. They have what they deserve."
And I heard the altar say,
"Yes, O Lord, God Almighty, thy judgments are true and right."

The fourth bowl: scorching heat 16. 8

The fourth angel emptied his bowl over the sun, and the sun was given power to scorch men in its fiery blaze. Then men were terribly burned in the heat, and they blasphemed the name of God who has control over these afflictions; but they neither repented nor gave him glory.

The fifth bowl: 16. 10
the plague of darkness

Then the fifth angel emptied his bowl upon the throne of the animal. Its kingdom was plunged into darkness; men gnawed their tongues in agony, cursed the God of Heaven for their pain and their ulcers, but refused to repent of what they had done.

The sixth bowl: 16. 12
the great river dried up

Then the sixth angel emptied his bowl upon the great river Euphrates. The waters of that river were dried up to prepare a road for the kings from the east. And then I noticed three foul spirits, looking like frogs, emerging from the mouths of the dragon, the animal, and the false prophet. They are diabolical spirits performing wonders and they set out to muster all the kings of the world for battle on the great day of God, the Almighty.
So they brought them together to the place called, in Hebrew, Armageddon.

The words in the background 16. 15

"See, I am coming like a thief! Happy is the man who stays awake and keeps his clothes at his side, so that he will not have to walk naked and men see his shame."

The seventh bowl: 16. 17
devastation from the air

The seventh angel emptied his bowl into the air. A loud voice came out of the Temple, from the throne, saying,

The third angel poured his bowl on the rivers and springs, and they turned to blood. Then I heard the angel of the waters say, 'Just art thou in these thy judgements, thou Holy One who art and wast; for they shed the blood of thy people and of thy prophets, and thou hast given them blood to drink. They have their deserts!' And I heard the altar cry, 'Yes, Lord God, sovereign over all, true and just are thy judgements!'

The fourth angel poured his bowl on the sun; and it was allowed to burn men with its flames. They were fearfully burned; but they only cursed the name of God who had the power to inflict such plagues, and they refused to repent or do him homage.

The fifth angel poured his bowl on the throne of the beast; and its kingdom was plunged in darkness. Men gnawed their tongues in agony, but they only cursed the God of heaven for their pains and sores, and would not repent of what they had done.

The sixth angel poured his bowl on the great river Euphrates; and its water was dried up, to prepare the way for the kings from the east.

Then I saw coming from the mouth of the dragon, the mouth of the beast, and the mouth of the false prophet, three foul spirits like frogs. These spirits were devils, with power to work miracles. They were sent out to muster all the kings of the world for the great day of battle of God the sovereign Lord. ('That is the day when I come like a thief! Happy the man who stays awake and keeps on his clothes, so that he will not have to go naked and ashamed for all to see!') So they assembled the kings at the place called in Hebrew Armageddon.

Then the seventh angel poured his bowl on the air; and out of the sanctuary came a loud voice from the throne, which said, 'It is over!'

/

18And there were voices, and thunders, and lightnings; and there was a great earthquake, such as was not since men were upon the earth, so mighty an earthquake, *and* so great. 19And the great city was divided into three parts, and the cities of the nations fell: and great Babylon came in remembrance before God, to give unto her the cup of the wine of the fierceness of his wrath. 20And every island fled away, and the mountains were not found. 21And there fell upon men a great hail out of heaven, *every stone* about the weight of a talent: and men blasphemed God because of the plague of the hail; for the plague thereof was exceeding great.

ple, from the throne, saying, "It is done!" 18And there were flashes of lightning, loud noises, peals of thunder, and a great earthquake such as had never been since men were on the earth, so great was that earthquake. 19 The great city was split into three parts, and the cities of the nations fell, and God remembered great Babylon, to make her drain the cup of the fury of his wrath. 20And every island fled away, and no mountains were to be found; 21 and great hailstones, heavy as a hundredweight, dropped on men from heaven, till men cursed God for the plague of the hail, so fearful was that plague.

17 And there came one of the seven angels which had the seven vials, and talked with me, saying unto me, Come hither; I will shew unto thee the judgment of the great whore that sitteth upon many waters; 2 With whom the kings of the earth have committed fornication, and the inhabitants of the earth have been made drunk with the wine of her fornication. 3 So he carried me away in the spirit into the wilderness: and I saw a woman sit upon a scarlet coloured beast, full of names of blasphemy, having seven heads and ten horns. 4And the woman was arrayed in purple and scarlet colour, and decked with gold and precious stones and pearls, having a golden cup in her hand full of abominations and filthiness of her fornication: 5And upon her forehead *was* a name written, MYSTERY, BABYLON THE GREAT, THE MOTHER OF HARLOTS AND ABOMINATIONS OF THE EARTH. 6And I saw the woman drunken with the blood of the saints, and with the blood of the martyrs of Jesus: and when I saw her, I wondered with great admiration. 7And the angel said unto me, Wherefore didst thou marvel? I will tell thee the mystery of the woman, and of the beast that carrieth her, which hath the seven heads and ten horns. 8 The beast that thou sawest was, and is not; and shall ascend out of the bottomless pit, and go into perdition: and they that dwell on the earth shall wonder, whose names were not written in the book of life from the foundation of the world, when they behold the beast that was, and is not, and yet is. 9And here *is* the mind which hath wisdom. The seven heads are seven mountains, on which the woman sitteth. 10And there are seven kings: five are fallen, and one is, *and* the other is not yet come; and when he cometh, he must continue a short space. 11And the beast that was, and is not, even he is the eighth, and is of the seven, and goeth into perdition. 12And the ten horns which thou sawest are ten kings, which have received no

17 Then one of the seven angels who had the seven bowls came and said to me, "Come, I will show you the judgment of the great harlot who is seated upon many waters, 2 with whom the kings of the earth have committed fornication, and with the wine of whose fornication the dwellers on earth have become drunk." 3And he carried me away in the Spirit into a wilderness, and I saw a woman sitting on a scarlet beast which was full of blasphemous names, and it had seven heads and ten horns. 4 The woman was arrayed in purple and scarlet, and bedecked with gold and jewels and pearls, holding in her hand a golden cup full of abominations and the impurities of her fornication; 5 and on her forehead was written a name of mystery: "Babylon the great, mother of harlots and of earth's abominations." 6And I saw the woman, drunk with the blood of the saints and the blood of the martyrs of Jesus.

When I saw her I marveled greatly. 7 But the angel said to me, "Why marvel? I will tell you the mystery of the woman, and of the beast with seven heads and ten horns that carries her. 8 The beast that you saw was, and is not, and is to ascend from the bottomless pit and go to perdition; and the dwellers on earth whose names have not been written in the book of life from the foundation of the world, will marvel to behold the beast, because it was and is not and is to come. 9 This calls for a mind with wisdom: the seven heads are seven hills on which the woman is seated; 10 they are also seven kings, five of whom have fallen, one is, the other has not yet come, and when he comes he must remain only a little while. 11As for the beast that was and is not, it is an eighth but it belongs to the seven, and it goes to perdition. 12And the ten horns that you saw are ten kings who have not yet received royal power, but they

PHILLIPS

N.E.B.

"The end has come!"

Then followed flashes of lightning, noises and peals of thunder. There was a terrific earthquake, the like of which no man has ever seen since mankind began to live upon the earth—so great and tremendous was this earthquake. The great city was split into three parts, and the cities of all the nations fell in ruins. And God called to mind Babylon the great and made her drink the cup of the wine of his furious wrath. Every island fled and the mountains vanished. Great hailstones like heavy weights fell from the sky, and men blasphemed God for the curse of the hail, for it fell upon them with savage and fearful blows.

The judgment of the evil woman announced   17. 1

Then came one of the seven angels who held the seven bowls, and said to me:

"Come, and I will show you the judgment passed upon the great harlot who is seated upon many waters. It is with her that the kings of the earth have debauched themselves and the inhabitants of the earth have become drunk on the wine of her filthiness."

The gorgeous mother of evil   17. 3

Then he carried me away in spirit into the desert. There I saw a woman riding upon a scarlet animal, covered with blasphemous titles and having seven heads and ten horns. The woman herself was dressed in purple and scarlet, glittering with gold, jewels and pearls. In her hand she held a golden cup full of the earth's filthiness and her own foul impurity. On her forehead is written a name with a secret meaning—BABYLON THE GREAT, MOTHER OF ALL HARLOTS AND OF THE EARTH'S ABOMINATIONS.

The vision explained   17. 6

Then I noticed that the woman was drunk with the blood of the saints and of the martyrs for Jesus. As I watched her, I was filled with utter amazement, but the angel said to me:

"Why are you amazed? I will explain to you the mystery of the woman and of the animal with seven heads and ten horns which carries her. The animal, which you saw, once lived but now is no more—it will come up out of the pit only to meet with destruction. The inhabitants of the earth, whose names have not been written in the book of life from the foundation of the world, will be utterly astonished when they see that the animal was, and is not, and yet is to come. (Here we need a mind with understanding.)

"The seven heads are seven hills on which the woman takes her seat. There are also seven kings; five have been dethroned, one reigns, and the other has not yet appeared—when he comes he must remain only for a short time. As for the animal which once lived but now lives no longer, it is an eighth king which belongs to the seven, but it goes to utter destruction. The ten horns which you saw are ten kings who have not yet received their power to reign, but they will re-

And there followed flashes of lightning and peals of thunder, and a violent earthquake, like none before it in human history, so violent it was. The great city was split in three; the cities of the world fell in ruin; and God did not forget Babylon the great, but made her drink the cup which was filled with the fierce wine of his vengeance. Every island vanished; there was not a mountain to be seen. Huge hailstones, weighing perhaps a hundredweight, fell on men from the sky; and they cursed God for the plague of hail, because that plague was so severe.

17 Then one of the seven angels that held the seven bowls came and spoke to me and said, 'Come, and I will show you the judgement on the great whore, enthroned above the ocean. The kings of the earth have committed fornication with her, and on the wine of her fornication men all over the world have made themselves drunk.' In the Spirit he carried me away into the wilds, and there I saw a woman mounted on a scarlet beast which was covered with blasphemous names and had seven heads and ten horns. The woman was clothed in purple and scarlet and bedizened with gold and jewels and pearls. In her hand she held a gold cup, full of obscenities and the foulness of her fornication; and written on her forehead was a name with a secret meaning: 'Babylon the great, the mother of whores and of every obscenity on earth.' The woman, I saw, was drunk with the blood of God's people and with the blood of those who had borne their testimony to Jesus.

As I looked at her I was greatly astonished. But the angel said to me, 'Why are you so astonished? I will tell you the secret of the woman and of the beast she rides, with the seven heads and the ten horns. The beast you have seen is he who once was alive, and is alive no longer, but has yet to ascend out of the abyss before going to perdition. Those on earth whose names have not been inscribed in the roll of the living ever since the world was made will all be astonished to see the beast; for he once was alive, and is alive no longer, and has still to appear.

'But here is the clue for those who can interpret it. The seven heads are seven hills on which the woman sits. They represent also seven kings,[a] of whom five have already fallen, one is now reigning, and the other has yet to come; and when he does come he is only to last for a little while. As for the beast that once was alive and is alive no longer, he is an eighth—and yet he is one of the seven, and he is going to perdition. The ten horns you saw are ten kings who have not yet begun to reign, but who for one hour are

[a] Or emperors.

K.J.V.

kingdom as yet; but receive power as kings one hour with the beast. 13 These have one mind, and shall give their power and strength unto the beast. 14 These shall make war with the Lamb, and the Lamb shall overcome them: for he is Lord of lords, and King of kings: and they that are with him *are* called, and chosen, and faithful. 15And he saith unto me, The waters which thou sawest, where the whore sitteth, are peoples, and multitudes, and nations, and tongues. 16And the ten horns which thou sawest upon the beast, these shall hate the whore, and shall make her desolate and naked, and shall eat her flesh, and burn her with fire. 17 For God hath put in their hearts to fulfil his will, and to agree, and give their kingdom unto the beast, until the words of God shall be fulfilled. 18And the woman which thou sawest is that great city, which reigneth over the kings of the earth.

18 And after these things I saw another angel come down from heaven, having great power; and the earth was lightened with his glory. 2And he cried mightily with a strong voice, saying, Babylon the great is fallen, is fallen, and is become the habitation of devils, and the hold of every foul spirit, and a cage of every unclean and hateful bird. 3 For all nations have drunk of the wine of the wrath of her fornication, and the kings of the earth have committed fornication with her, and the merchants of the earth are waxed rich through the abundance of her delicacies. 4And I heard another voice from heaven, saying, Come out of her, my people, that ye be not partakers of her sins, and that ye receive not of her plagues. 5 For her sins have reached unto heaven, and God hath remembered her iniquities. 6 Reward her even as she rewarded you, and double unto her double according to her works: in the cup which she hath filled, fill to her double. 7 How much she hath glorified herself, and lived deliciously, so much torment and sorrow give her: for she saith in her heart, I sit a queen, and am no widow, and shall see no sorrow. 8 Therefore shall her plagues come in one day, death, and mourning, and famine; and she shall be utterly burned with fire: for strong *is* the Lord God who judgeth her. 9And the kings of the earth, who have committed fornication and lived deliciously with her, shall bewail her, and lament for her, when they shall see the smoke of her burning, 10 Standing afar off for the fear of her torment, saying, Alas, alas, that great city Babylon, that mighty city! for in one hour is thy judgment come. 11And the merchants of the earth shall weep and mourn over her; for no man buyeth their merchandise any more: 12 The merchandise of gold, and silver, and precious stones, and of pearls, and fine linen, and purple, and silk, and scarlet, and all thyine wood, and all manner vessels of ivory, and all manner vessels of most precious wood, and of brass, and iron, and marble. 13And cinnamon, and odours, and ointments, and frankincense, and wine, and

R.S.V.

are to receive authority as kings for one hour, together with the beast. 13 These are of one mind and give over their power and authority to the beast; 14 they will make war on the Lamb, and the Lamb will conquer them, for he is Lord of lords and King of kings, and those with him are called and chosen and faithful."

15 And he said to me, "The waters that you saw, where the harlot is seated, are peoples and multitudes and nations and tongues. 16And the ten horns that you saw, they and the beast will hate the harlot; they will make her desolate and naked, and devour her flesh and burn her up with fire, 17 for God has put it into their hearts to carry out his purpose by being of one mind and giving over their royal power to the beast, until the words of God shall be fulfilled. 18And the woman that you saw is the great city which has dominion over the kings of the earth."

18 After this I saw another angel coming down from heaven, having great authority; and the earth was made bright with his splendor. 2And he called out with a mighty voice,
"Fallen, fallen is Babylon the great!
  It has become a dwelling place of demons,
  a haunt of every foul spirit,
  a haunt of every foul and hateful bird;
3 for all nations have drunk[k] the wine of
    her impure passion,
  and the kings of the earth have committed
    fornication with her,
  and the merchants of the earth have grown
    rich with the wealth of her wantonness."
4 Then I heard another voice from heaven saying,
"Come out of her, my people,
  lest you take part in her sins,
  lest you share in her plagues;
5 for her sins are heaped high as heaven,
  and God has remembered her iniquities.
6 Render to her as she herself has rendered,
  and repay her double for her deeds;
  mix a double draught for her in the cup she
    mixed.
7 As she glorified herself and played the
    wanton,
  so give her a like measure of torment and
    mourning.
  Since in her heart she says, 'A queen I sit,
  I am no widow, mourning I shall never see,'
8 so shall her plagues come in a single day,
  pestilence and mourning and famine,
  and she shall be burned with fire;
  for mighty is the Lord God who judges
    her."
9 And the kings of the earth, who committed fornication and were wanton with her, will weep and wail over her when they see the smoke of her burning; 10 they will stand far off, in fear of her torment, and say,
"Alas! alas! thou great city,
  thou mighty city, Babylon!
  In one hour has thy judgment come."
11 And the merchants of the earth weep and mourn for her, since no one buys their cargo any more, 12 cargo of gold, silver, jewels and pearls, fine linen, purple, silk and scarlet, all kinds of scented wood, all articles of ivory, all articles of costly wood, bronze, iron and marble, 13 cinnamon, spice, incense, myrrh, frankincense,

[k] Other ancient authorities read *fallen by.*

PHILLIPS

ceive authority to be kings for one hour in company with the animal. They are of one mind, and they will hand over their power and authority to the animal. They will all go to war with the Lamb, and the Lamb, with his called, chosen, and faithful followers, will conquer them. For he is Lord of lords and king of kings."

Then he said to me:

"As for the waters which you saw, on which the woman took her seat, they are peoples and vast crowds, nations and languages. The ten horns and the animal which you saw will loathe the harlot, and leave her deserted and naked. Moreover, they will devour her flesh, and then consume her with fire. For God has put it into their hearts to carry out his purpose by making them of one mind, and by handing over their authority to the animal, until the words of God have been fulfilled.

"The woman that you saw is the great city which dominates the kings of the earth."

The final overthrow of Babylon 18. 1

Later I saw another angel coming down from Heaven, armed with great authority. The earth shone with the splendor of his presence, and he cried in a mighty voice:

"Fallen, fallen is Babylon the great! She has become a haunt of devils, a prison for every unclean spirit, and a cage for every foul and hateful bird. For all nations have drunk the wine of her passionate unfaithfulness and have fallen thereby. The kings of the earth have debauched themselves with her, and the merchants of the earth have grown rich from the extravagance of her dissipation!"

Then I heard another voice from Heaven, crying:

"Come out from her, O my people, lest you become accomplices in her sins and must share in her punishment. For her sins have mounted up to the sky, and God has remembered the tale of her wickedness. Pay her back in her own coin—yes, pay her back double for all that she has done! In the cup which she mixed for others mix her a drink of double strength! For the pride in which she flaunted herself give her torture and misery! Because she says to herself, 'Here I sit a queen on a throne; I am no woman who lacks a man and I shall never know sorrow!' So in a single day her punishments shall strike her—death, sorrow, and famine, and she shall be burned in the fire. For mighty is the Lord God who judges her!"

The lament over the city 18. 9

Then the kings of the earth, who debauched and indulged themselves with her, will wail and lament over her. Standing at a safe distance through very fear of her torment, they will watch the smoke of her burning and cry,

"Alas, alas for the great city, Babylon the mighty city, that your judgment should come in a single hour!"

The merchants of the earth shall also wail and lament over her, for there is no one left to buy their goods—cargoes of gold and silver, jewels and pearls, fine linen, purple, silk and scarlet, all kinds of scented wood, every sort of ivory vessel, very kind of vessel of precious wood, of bronze, and marble; cinnamon, spice, incense,

N.E.B.

to share with the beast the exercise of royal authority; for they have but a single purpose among them and will confer their power and authority upon the beast. They will wage war upon the Lamb, but the Lamb will defeat them, for he is Lord of lords and King of kings, and his victory will be shared by his followers, called and chosen and faithful.' [a]

Then he said to me, 'The ocean you saw, where the great whore sat, is an ocean of peoples and populations, nations and languages. As for the ten horns you saw, they together with the beast will come to hate the whore; they will strip her naked and leave her desolate, they will batten on her flesh and burn her to ashes. For God has put it into their heads to carry out his purpose, by making common cause and conferring their sovereignty upon the beast until all that God has spoken is fulfilled. The woman you saw is the great city that holds sway over the kings of the earth.'

18 After this I saw another angel coming down from heaven; he came with great authority and the earth was lit up with his splendour. Then in a mighty voice he proclaimed, 'Fallen, fallen is Babylon the great! She has become a dwelling for demons, a haunt for every unclean spirit, for every foul and loathsome bird. For all nations have drunk deep of [b] the fierce wine of her fornication; the kings of the earth have committed fornication with her, and merchants the world over have grown rich on her bloated wealth.'

Then I heard another voice from heaven that said: 'Come out of her, my people, lest you take part in her sins and share in her plagues. For her sins are piled high as heaven, and God has not forgotten her crimes. Pay her back in her own coin, repay her twice over for her deeds! Double for her the strength of the potion she mixed! Mete out grief and torment to match her voluptuous pomp! She says in her heart, "I am a queen on my throne! No mourning for me, no widow's weeds!" Because of this her plagues shall strike her in a single day—pestilence, bereavement, famine, and burning—for mighty is the Lord God who has pronounced her doom!'

The kings of the earth who committed fornication with her and wallowed in her luxury will weep and wail over her, as they see the smoke of her conflagration. They will stand at a distance, for horror at her torment, and will say, 'Alas, alas for the great city, the mighty city of Babylon! In a single hour your doom has struck!'

The merchants of the earth also will weep and mourn for her, because no one any longer buys their cargoes, cargoes of gold and silver, jewels and pearls, cloths of purple and scarlet, silks and fine linens; all kinds of scented woods, ivories, and every sort of thing made of costly woods, bronze, iron, or marble; cinnamon and spice, incense, perfumes and frankincense; wine,

[a] *Or* . . . kings, and his followers are faithful men, called and selected for service. [b] *Other witnesses read* have been ruined by . . .

K.J.V.

oil, and fine flour, and wheat, and beasts, and sheep, and horses, and chariots, and slaves, and souls of men. 14And the fruits that thy soul lusted after are departed from thee, and all things which were dainty and goodly are departed from thee, and thou shalt find them no more at all. 15 The merchants of these things, which were made rich by her, shall stand afar off for the fear of her torment, weeping and wailing, 16And saying, Alas, alas, that great city, that was clothed in fine linen, and purple, and scarlet, and decked with gold, and precious stones, and pearls! 17 For in one hour so great riches is come to nought. And every shipmaster, and all the company in ships, and sailors, and as many as trade by sea, stood afar off, 18And cried when they saw the smoke of her burning, saying, What *city is* like unto this great city! 19And they cast dust on their heads, and cried, weeping and wailing, saying, Alas, alas, that great city, wherein were made rich all that had ships in the sea by reason of her costliness! for in one hour is she made desolate. 20 Rejoice over her, *thou* heaven, and *ye* holy apostles and prophets; for God hath avenged you on her. 21And a mighty angel took up a stone like a great millstone, and cast *it* into the sea, saying, Thus with violence shall that great city Babylon be thrown down, and shall be found no more at all. 22And the voice of harpers, and musicians, and of pipers, and trumpeters, shall be heard no more at all in thee; and no craftsman, of whatsoever craft *he be,* shall be found any more in thee; and the sound of a millstone shall be heard no more at all in thee; 23And the light of a candle shall shine no more at all in thee; and the voice of the bridegroom and of the bride shall be heard no more at all in thee: for thy merchants were the great men of the earth; for by thy sorceries were all nations deceived. 24And in her was found the blood of prophets, and of saints, and of all that were slain upon the earth.

19 And after these things I heard a great voice of much people in heaven, saying, Alleluia; Salvation, and glory, and honour, and power, unto the Lord our God: 2 For true and righteous *are* his judgments; for he hath judged the great whore, which did corrupt the earth with her fornication, and hath avenged the blood of his servants at her hand. 3And again they said, Alleluia. And her smoke rose up for ever

R.S.V.

wine, oil, fine flour and wheat, cattle and sheep, horses and chariots, and slaves, that is, human souls.

14 "The fruit for which thy soul longed has
    gone from thee,
  and all thy dainties and thy splendor are
    lost to thee, never to be found again!"
15 The merchants of these wares, who gained wealth from her, will stand far off, in fear of her torment, weeping and mourning aloud,
16 "Alas, alas, for the great city
  that was clothed in fine linen, in purple
    and scarlet,
  bedecked with gold, with jewels, and with
    pearls!
17 In one hour all this wealth has been laid
    waste."
And all shipmasters and seafaring men, sailors and all whose trade is on the sea, stood far off 18 and cried out as they saw the smoke of her burning,
"What city was like the great city?"
19And they threw dust on their heads, as they wept and mourned, crying out,
16 "Alas, alas, for the great city
  where all who had ships at sea grew rich
    by her wealth!
In one hour she has been laid waste.
20 Rejoice over her, O heaven,
  O saints and apostles and prophets,
for God has given judgment for you
    against her!"
21 Then a mighty angel took up a stone like a great millstone and threw it into the sea, saying,
  "So shall Babylon the great city be thrown
    down with violence,
    and shall be found no more;
22 and the sound of harpers and minstrels,
    of flute players and trumpeters,
  shall be heard in thee no more;
and a craftsman of any craft
  shall be found in thee no more;
and the sound of the millstone
  shall be heard in thee no more;
23 and the light of a lamp
  shall shine in thee no more;
and the voice of bridegroom and bride
  shall be heard in thee no more;
for thy merchants were the great men of
    the earth,
and all nations were deceived by thy sor-
    cery.
24 And in her was found the blood of proph-
    ets and of saints,
  and of all who have been slain on
    earth."

19 After this I heard what seemed to be the mighty voice of a great multitude in heaven, crying,
  "Hallelujah! Salvation and glory and power
    belong to our God,
2 for his judgments are true and just;
  he has judged the great harlot who cor-
    rupted the earth with her fornication,
  and he has avenged on her the blood of his
    servants."
3 Once more they cried,
  "Hallelujah! The smoke from her goes up
    ever and ever."

myrrh, frankincense, wine, oil, fine flour and corn; cattle, sheep and horses; chariots, slaves, the very souls of men.

Those who bought and sold these things, who had gained their wealth from her, will stand afar off through fear of her punishment, weeping and lamenting and saying,

"Alas, alas for the great city that was dressed in fine linen, purple and scarlet, and was bedecked with gold and jewels and pearls—alas that in a single hour all that wealth should be destroyed!"

Then every shipmaster and seafarer—sailors and all whose business is upon the sea—stood and watched the smoke of her burning from afar, and cried out,

"What city was ever like the great city?"

They even threw dust on their heads and cried aloud as they wept, saying:

"Alas, alas for the great city where all who had ships on the sea grew wealthy through the richness of her treasure! Alas that in a single hour she should be ruined!"

A comment in the background   **18. 20**

"Rejoice over her fate, O Heaven, and all you saints, apostles, and prophets! For God has pronounced his judgment for you against her!"

The words of Babylon's doom   **18. 21**

Then a mighty angel lifted up a stone like a huge millstone and hurled it into the sea, saying:

"So shall Babylon the great city be sent hurtling down to disappear for ever! Never more shall the sound of harpists and musicians, flute players and trumpeters be heard in you again! Never again shall a craftsman of any craft be found in you; never again will the sound of the millstone's grinding be heard in you! No light of a lamp shall ever shine in you again, and the voices of bridegroom and bride shall be heard in you no more! The fruit of your soul's desire is lost to you for ever. All your luxuries and brilliance are lost to you and men will never find them in you again!

"For your merchants were the great ones of the earth, and all nations were seduced by your witchery!"

For in her was discovered the blood of prophets and saints, indeed, the blood of all who were ever slaughtered upon the earth.

Rejoicing in Heaven   **19. 1**

Afterward I heard what sounded like the mighty roar of a vast crowd in Heaven crying:

"Alleluia! Salvation and glory and power belong to our God, for his judgments are true and just. He has judged the great harlot who corrupted the earth with her wickedness, and he has avenged upon her the blood of his servants!"

Then they cried a second time,

"Alleluia! The smoke of her destruction ascends for timeless ages!"

oil, flour and wheat, sheep and cattle, horses, chariots, slaves, and the lives of men. 'The fruit you longed for', they will say, 'is gone from you; all the glitter and the glamour are lost, never to be yours again!' The traders in all these wares, who gained their wealth from her, will stand at a distance for horror at her torment, weeping and mourning and saying, 'Alas, alas for the great city, that was clothed in fine linen and purple and scarlet, bedizened with gold and jewels and pearls! Alas that in one hour so much wealth should be laid waste!'

Then all the sea-captains and voyagers, the sailors and those who traded by sea, stood at a distance and cried out as they saw the smoke of her conflagration: 'Was there ever a city like the great city?' They threw dust on their heads, weeping and mourning and saying, 'Alas, alas for the great city, where all who had ships at sea grew rich on her wealth! Alas that in a single hour she should be laid waste!'

But let heaven exult over her; exult, apostles and prophets and people of God; for in the judgement against her he has vindicated your cause!

Then a mighty angel took up a stone like a great millstone and hurled it into the sea and said, 'Thus shall Babylon, the great city, be sent hurtling down, never to be seen again! No more shall the sound of harpers and minstrels, of flute-players and trumpeters, be heard in you; no more shall craftsmen of any trade be found in you; no more shall the sound of the mill be heard in you; no more shall the light of the lamp be seen in you; no more shall the voice of the bride and bridegroom be heard in you! Your traders were once the merchant princes of the world, and with your sorcery you deceived all the nations.'

For the blood of the prophets and of God's people was found in her, the blood of all who had been done to death on earth.

19 After this I heard what sounded like the roar of a vast throng in heaven; and they were shouting:

'Alleluia! Victory and glory and power belong to our God, for true and just are his judgements! He has condemned the great whore who corrupted the earth with her fornication, and has avenged upon her the blood of his servants.'

Then once more they shouted:

'Alleluia! The smoke goes up from her for ever and ever!'

K.J.V.

and ever. 4And the four and twenty elders and the four beasts fell down and worshipped God that sat on the throne, saying, Amen; Alleluia. 5And a voice came out of the throne, saying, Praise our God, all ye his servants, and ye that fear him, both small and great. 6And I heard as it were the voice of a great multitude, and as the voice of many waters, and as the voice of mighty thunderings, saying, Alleluia: for the Lord God omnipotent reigneth. 7 Let us be glad and rejoice, and give honour to him: for the marriage of the Lamb is come, and his wife hath made herself ready. 8And to her was granted that she should be arrayed in fine linen, clean and white: for the fine linen is the righteousness of saints. 9And he saith unto me, Write, Blessed *are* they which are called unto the marriage supper of the Lamb. And he saith unto me, These are the true sayings of God. 10And I fell at his feet to worship him. And he said unto me, See *thou do it* not: I am thy fellow servant, and of thy brethren that have the testimony of Jesus: worship God: for the testimony of Jesus is the spirit of prophecy. 11And I saw heaven opened, and behold a white horse; and he that sat upon him *was* called Faithful and True, and in righteousness he doth judge and make war. 12 His eyes *were* as a flame of fire, and on his head *were* many crowns; and he had a name written, that no man knew, but he himself. 13And he *was* clothed with a vesture dipped in blood: and his name is called The Word of God. 14And the armies *which were* in heaven followed him upon white horses, clothed in fine linen, white and clean. 15And out of his mouth goeth a sharp sword, that with it he should smite the nations; and he shall rule them with a rod of iron: and he treadeth the winepress of the fierceness and wrath of Almighty God. 16And he hath on *his* vesture and on his thigh a name written, KING OF KINGS, AND LORD OF LORDS. 17And I saw an angel standing in the sun; and he cried with a loud voice, saying to all the fowls that fly in the midst of heaven, Come and gather yourselves together unto the supper of the great God; 18 That ye may eat the flesh of kings, and the flesh of captains, and the flesh of mighty men, and the flesh of horses, and of them that sit on them, and the flesh of all *men, both* free and bond, both small and great. 19And I saw the beast, and the kings of the earth, and their

R.S.V.

4 And the twenty-four elders and the four living creatures fell down and worshiped God who is seated on the throne, saying, "Amen. Hallelujah!" 5And from the throne came a voice crying,

"Praise our God, all you his servants,
　you who fear him, small and great."
6 Then I heard what seemed to be the voice of a great multitude, like the sound of many waters and like the sound of mighty thunderpeals, crying,

"Hallelujah! For the Lord our God the Almighty reigns.
7 Let us rejoice and exult and give him the glory,
　for the marriage of the Lamb has come,
　and his Bride has made herself ready;
8 it was granted her to be clothed with fine linen, bright and pure"—
for the fine linen is the righteous deeds of the saints.

9 And the angel said [l] to me, "Write this: Blessed are those who are invited to the marriage supper of the Lamb." And he said to me, "These are true words of God." 10 Then I fell down at his feet to worship him, but he said to me, "You must not do that! I am a fellow servant with you and your brethren who hold the testimony of Jesus. Worship God." For the testimony of Jesus is the spirit of prophecy.

11 Then I saw heaven opened, and behold, a white horse! He who sat upon it is called Faithful and True, and in righteousness he judges and makes war. 12 His eyes are like a flame of fire, and on his head are many diadems; and he has a name inscribed which no one knows but himself. 13 He is clad in a robe dipped in [m] blood, and the name by which he is called is The Word of God. 14And the armies of heaven, arrayed in fine linen, white and pure, followed him on white horses. 15 From his mouth issues a sharp sword with which to smite the nations, and he will rule them with a rod of iron; he will tread the wine press of the fury of the wrath of God the Almighty. 16 On his robe and on his thigh he has a name inscribed, King of kings and Lord of lords.

17 Then I saw an angel standing in the sun, and with a loud voice he called to all the birds that fly in midheaven, "Come, gather for the great supper of God, 18 to eat the flesh of kings, the flesh of captains, the flesh of mighty men, the flesh of horses and their riders, and the flesh of all men, both free and slave, both small and great." 19And I saw the beast and the kings of the earth with their armies gathered to make

[l] Greek *he said.* [m] Other ancient authorities read *sprinkled with.*

PHILLIPS

Then the twenty-four elders and the four living creatures prostrated themselves and worshiped God who is seated upon the throne, saying,

"Amen, Alleluia!"

Then out of the throne came a voice, saying, "Praise our God, all you who serve him, all you who reverence him, both small and great!"

And then I heard a sound like the voices of a vast crowd, the roar of a great waterfall and the rolling of heavy thunder, and they were saying:

"Alleluia! For the Lord our God, the Almighty, has come into his kingdom! Let us rejoice, let us be glad with all our hearts. Let us give him the glory, for the wedding day of the Lamb has come, and his bride has made herself ready. She may be seen dressed in linen, gleaming and spotless—for such linen is the righteous living of the saints!"

Instruction to John   19. 9

Then he said to me,

"Write this down: Happy are those who are invited to the wedding feast of the Lamb!"

Then he added,

"These are true words of God."

At that I fell at his feet to worship him, but he said to me,

"No! I am your fellow servant and fellow servant with your brothers who are holding fast their witness to Jesus. Give your worship to God!"

(This witness to Jesus inspires all prophecy.)

The Word of God   19. 11
on the white horse

Then I saw Heaven wide open, and before my eyes appeared a white horse, whose rider is called faithful and true, for his judgment and his warfare are just. His eyes are a flame of fire and there are many diadems upon his head. There is a name written upon him, known only to himself. He is dressed in a cloak dipped in blood, and the name by which he is known is the Word of God.

The armies of Heaven follow him, riding upon white horses and clad in white and spotless linen. Out of his mouth there comes a sharp sword with which to strike the nations. He will shepherd them "with a rod of iron," and alone he will tread the winepress of the furious wrath of God the Almighty. Written upon his cloak and upon his thigh is the name, KING OF KINGS AND LORD OF LORDS.

The feast of death after battle 19. 17

Then I saw an angel standing alone in the blazing light of the sun, and he shouted in a loud voice, calling to all the birds flying in mid-air:

"Come, flock together to God's great feast! Here you may eat the flesh of kings and captains, the flesh of strong men, of horses and their riders—the flesh of all men, free men and slaves, small and great!"

And I saw the animal with the kings of the earth and their armies massed together for bat-

N.E.B.

And the twenty-four elders and the four living creatures fell down and worshipped God as he sat on the throne, and they too cried:

'Amen! Alleluia!'

Then a voice came from the throne which said:

'Praise our God, all you his servants, you that fear him, both great and small!'

Again I heard what sounded like a vast crowd, like the noise of rushing water and deep roars of thunder, and they cried:

'Alleluia! The Lord our God, sovereign over all, has entered on his reign! Exult and shout for joy and do him homage, for the wedding-day of the Lamb has come! His bride has made herself ready, and for her dress she has been given fine linen, clean and shining.'

(Now the fine linen signifies the righteous deeds of God's people.)

Then the angel said to me, 'Write this: "Happy are those who are invited to the wedding-supper of the Lamb!" ' And he added, 'These are the very words of God.' At this I fell at his feet to worship him. But he said to me, 'No, not that! I am but a fellow-servant with you and your brothers who bear their testimony to Jesus. It is God you must worship. Those who bear testimony to Jesus are inspired like the prophets.' [a]

Then I saw heaven wide open, and there before me was a white horse; and its rider's name was Faithful and True, for he is just in judgement and just in war. His eyes flamed like fire, and on his head were many diadems. Written upon him was a name known to none but himself, and he was robed in a garment drenched in blood. [b] He was called the Word of God, and the armies of heaven followed him on white horses, clothed in fine linen, clean and shining. From his mouth there went a sharp sword with which to smite the nations; for he it is who shall rule them with an iron rod, and tread the winepress of the wrath and retribution of God the sovereign Lord. And on his robe and on his leg there was written the name: 'King of kings and Lord of lords.'

Then I saw an angel standing in the sun, and he cried aloud to all the birds flying in midheaven: 'Come and gather for God's great supper, to eat the flesh of kings and commanders and fighting men, the flesh of horses and their riders, the flesh of all men, slave and free, great and small!' Then I saw the beast and the kings of the earth and their armies mustered to do bat-

[a] Or . . . worship. For testimony to Jesus is the spirit that inspires prophets. [b] Some witnesses read spattered with blood.

K.J.V.

armies, gathered together to make war against him that sat on the horse, and against his army. 20And the beast was taken, and with him the false prophet that wrought miracles before him, with which he deceived them that had received the mark of the beast, and them that worshipped his image. These both were cast alive into a lake of fire burning with brimstone. 21And the remnant were slain with the sword of him that sat upon the horse, which *sword* proceeded out of his mouth: and all the fowls were filled with their flesh.

20 And I saw an angel come down from heaven, having the key of the bottomless pit and a great chain in his hand. 2And he laid hold on the dragon, that old serpent, which is the Devil, and Satan, and bound him a thousand years, 3And cast him into the bottomless pit, and shut him up, and set a seal upon him, that he should deceive the nations no more, till the thousand years should be fulfilled: and after that he must be loosed a little season. 4And I saw thrones, and they sat upon them, and judgment was given unto them: and *I saw* the souls of them that were beheaded for the witness of Jesus, and for the word of God, and which had not worshipped the beast, neither his image, neither had received *his* mark upon their foreheads, or in their hands; and they lived and reigned with Christ a thousand years. 5 But the rest of the dead lived not again until the thousand years were finished. This *is* the first resurrection. 6 Blessed and holy *is* he that hath part in the first resurrection: on such the second death hath no power, but they shall be priests of God and of Christ, and shall reign with him a thousand years. 7And when the thousand years are expired, Satan shall be loosed out of his prison, 8And shall go out to deceive the nations which are in the four quarters of the earth, Gog and Magog, to gather them together to battle: the number of whom *is* as the sand of the sea. 9And they went up on the breadth of the earth, and compassed the camp of the saints about, and the beloved city: and fire came down from God out of heaven, and devoured them. 10And the devil that deceived them was cast into the lake of fire and brimstone, where the beast and the false prophet *are,* and shall be tormented day and night for ever and ever. 11And I saw a great white throne, and him that sat on it, from whose face the earth and the heaven fled away; and there was found no place for them. 12And I saw the dead, small and great, stand before

R.S.V.

war against him who sits upon the horse and against his army. 20And the beast was captured, and with it the false prophet who in its presence had worked the signs by which he deceived those who had received the mark of the beast and those who worshiped its image. These two were thrown alive into the lake of fire that burns with brimstone. 21And the rest were slain by the sword of him who sits upon the horse, the sword that issues from his mouth; and all the birds were gorged with their flesh.

20 Then I saw an angel coming down from heaven, holding in his hand the key of the bottomless pit and a great chain. 2And he seized the dragon, that ancient serpent, who is the Devil and Satan, and bound him for a thousand years, 3 and threw him into the pit, and shut it and sealed it over him, that he should deceive the nations no more, till the thousand years were ended. After that he must be loosed for a little while.

4 Then I saw thrones, and seated on them were those to whom judgment was committed. Also I saw the souls of those who had been beheaded for their testimony to Jesus and for the word of God, and who had not worshiped the beast or its image and had not received its mark on their foreheads or their hands. They came to life, and reigned with Christ a thousand years. 5 The rest of the dead did not come to life until the thousand years were ended. This is the first resurrection. 6 Blessed and holy is he who shares in the first resurrection! Over such the second death has no power, but they shall be priests of God and of Christ, and they shall reign with him a thousand years.

7 And when the thousand years are ended, Satan will be loosed from his prison 8 and will come out to deceive the nations which are at the four corners of the earth, that is, Gog and Magog, to gather them for battle; their number is like the sand of the sea. 9And they marched up over the broad earth and surrounded the camp of the saints and the beloved city; but fire came down from heaven[n] and consumed them, 10 and the devil who had deceived them was thrown into the lake of fire and brimstone where the beast and the false prophet were, and they will be tormented day and night for ever and ever.

11 Then I saw a great white throne and him who sat upon it; from his presence earth and sky fled away, and no place was found for them. 12 And I saw the dead, great and small, standing before the throne, and books were opened. Also

[n] Other ancient authorities read *from God, out of heaven,* or *out of heaven from God.*

tle against the rider upon the horse and his army. The animal was captured and with it the false prophet who had performed marvels in its presence, which he had used to deceive those who accepted the mark of the animal and worshiped its statue. These two were thrown alive into the lake of fire which burns with sulfur.

The rest were killed by the sword which issues from the mouth of the rider upon the horse; and all the birds gorged themselves on their flesh.

Satan bound for a thousand years

20. 1

Then I saw an angel coming down from Heaven with the key of the pit and a huge chain in his hand. He seized the dragon, the serpent of ancient days, who is both the devil and Satan, and bound him fast for a thousand years. Then he hurled him into the pit, and locked and sealed it over his head, so that he could deceive the nations no more until the thousand years were past. But then he must be set free for a little while.

The first resurrection

20. 4

And I saw thrones, with appointed judges seated upon them. Then I saw the souls of those who had been executed for their witness to Jesus and for proclaiming the Word of God—those who never worshiped the animal or its statue, and had not accepted its mark upon their foreheads or their hands. They came to life and reigned with Christ for a thousand years. (The rest of the dead did not come to life until the thousand years were over.) This is the first resurrection. Happy and holy is the one who shares in the first resurrection! The second death cannot touch such men; they shall be priests of God and of Christ, and shall reign with him for the thousand years.

Satan finally destroyed

20. 7

Then, when the thousand years are over, Satan will be released from his prison, and will set out to deceive the nations in the four corners of the earth, Gog and Magog, and to lead them into battle. They will be as numerous as the sand of the seashore.

They came up and spread over the breadth of the earth; they encircled the army of the saints defending the beloved city. But fire came down from the sky and consumed them. The devil who deceived them was hurled into the lake of fire and sulfur to join the animal and the false prophet. And there they shall be tortured day and night for timeless ages.

The final judgment

20. 11

And then I saw a great white throne, and one seated upon it from whose presence both earth and sky fled and vanished.

Then I saw the dead, great and small, standing before the throne, and the books were

tle with the Rider and his army. The beast was taken prisoner, and so was the false prophet who had worked miracles in its presence and deluded those that had received the mark of the beast and worshipped its image. The two of them were thrown alive into the lake of fire with its sulphurous flames. The rest were killed by the sword which went out of the Rider's mouth; and all the birds gorged themselves on their flesh.

20 Then I saw an angel coming down from heaven with the key of the abyss and a great chain in his hands. He seized the dragon, that serpent of old, the Devil or Satan, and chained him up for a thousand years; he threw him into the abyss, shutting and sealing it over him, so that he might seduce the nations no more till the thousand years were over. After that he must be let loose for a short while.

Then I saw thrones, and upon them sat those to whom judgement was committed. I could see the souls of those who had been beheaded for the sake of God's word and their testimony to Jesus, those who had not worshipped the beast and its image or received its mark on forehead or hand. These came to life again and reigned with Christ for a thousand years, though the rest of the dead did not come to life until the thousand years were over. This is the first resurrection. Happy indeed, and one of God's own people, is the man who shares in this first resurrection! Upon such the second death has no claim; but they shall be priests of God and of Christ, and shall reign with him for the thousand years.

When the thousand years are over, Satan will be let loose from his dungeon; and he will come out to seduce the nations in the four quarters of the earth and to muster them for battle, yes, the hosts of Gog and Magog, countless as the sands of the sea. So they marched over the breadth of the land and laid siege to the camp of God's people and the city that he loves. But fire came down on them from heaven and consumed them; and the Devil, their seducer, was flung into the lake of fire and sulphur, where the beast and the false prophet had been flung, there to be tormented day and night for ever.

Then I saw a great white throne, and the One who sat upon it; from his presence earth and heaven vanished away, and no place was left for them. I could see the dead, great and small, standing before the throne; and books were

K.J.V.

God; and the books were opened: and another book was opened, which is *the book* of life: and the dead were judged out of those things which were written in the books, according to their works. 13And the sea gave up the dead which were in it; and death and hell delivered up the dead which were in them: and they were judged every man according to their works. 14And death and hell were cast into the lake of fire. This is the second death. 15And whosoever was not found written in the book of life was cast into the lake of fire.

21 And I saw a new heaven and a new earth: for the first heaven and the first earth were passed away; and there was no more sea. 2And I John saw the holy city, new Jerusalem, coming down from God out of heaven, prepared as a bride adorned for her husband. 3And I heard a great voice out of heaven saying, Behold, the tabernacle of God *is* with men, and he will dwell with them, and they shall be his people, and God himself shall be with them, *and be* their God. 4And God shall wipe away all tears from their eyes; and there shall be no more death, neither sorrow, nor crying, neither shall there be any more pain: for the former things are passed away. 5And he that sat upon the throne said, Behold, I make all things new. And he said unto me, Write: for these words are true and faithful. 6And he said unto me, It is done. I am Alpha and Omega, the beginning and the end. I will give unto him that is athirst of the fountain of the water of life freely. 7 He that overcometh shall inherit all things; and I will be his God, and he shall be my son. 8 But the fearful, and unbelieving, and the abominable, and murderers, and whoremongers, and sorcerers, and idolaters, and all liars, shall have their part in the lake which burneth with fire and brimstone: which is the second death. 9And there came unto me one of the seven angels which had the seven vials full of the seven last plagues, and talked with me, saying, Come hither, I will shew thee the bride, the Lamb's wife. 10And he carried me away in the spirit to a great and high mountain, and shewed me that great city, the holy Jerusalem, descending out of heaven from God, 11 Having the glory of God: and her light *was* like unto a stone most precious, even like a jasper stone, clear as crystal; 12And had a wall great and high, *and* had twelve gates, and at the gates twelve angels, and names written thereon, which are *the names* of the twelve tribes of the children of Israel: 13 On the east three gates; on the north three gates; on the south three gates; and on the west three gates. 14And the wall of the city had twelve foundations, and in them the names of the twelve apostles of the Lamb.

R.S.V.

another book was opened, which is the book of life. And the dead were judged by what was written in the books, by what they had done. 13And the sea gave up the dead in it, Death and Hades gave up the dead in them, and all were judged by what they had done. 14 Then Death and Hades were thrown into the lake of fire. This is the second death, the lake of fire; 15 and if any one's name was not found written in the book of life, he was thrown into the lake of fire.

21 Then I saw a new heaven and a new earth; for the first heaven and the first earth had passed away, and the sea was no more. 2And I saw the holy city, new Jerusalem, coming down out of heaven from God, prepared as a bride adorned for her husband; 3 and I heard a great voice from the throne saying, "Behold, the dwelling of God is with men. He will dwell with them, and they shall be his people,[o] and God himself will be with them;[p] 4 he will wipe away every tear from their eyes, and death shall be no more, neither shall there be mourning nor crying nor pain any more, for the former things have passed away."

5 And he who sat upon the throne said, "Behold, I make all things new." Also he said, "Write this, for these words are trustworthy and true." 6And he said to me, "It is done! I am the Alpha and the Omega, the beginning and the end. To the thirsty I will give water without price from the fountain of the water of life. 7 He who conquers shall have this heritage, and I will be his God and he shall be my son. 8 But as for the cowardly, the faithless, the polluted, as for murderers, fornicators, sorcerers, idolaters, and all liars, their lot shall be in the lake that burns with fire and brimstone, which is the second death."

9 Then came one of the seven angels who had the seven bowls full of the seven last plagues, and spoke to me, saying, "Come, I will show you the Bride, the wife of the Lamb." 10And in the Spirit he carried me away to a great, high mountain, and showed me the holy city Jerusalem coming down out of heaven from God, 11 having the glory of God, its radiance like a most rare jewel, like a jasper, clear as crystal. 12 It had a great, high wall, with twelve gates, and at the gates twelve angels, and on the gates the names of the twelve tribes of the sons of Israel were inscribed; 13 on the east three gates, on the north three gates, on the south three gates, and on the west three gates. 14 And the wall of the city had twelve foundations, and on them twelve names of the twelve apostles of the Lamb.

[o] Other ancient authorities read *peoples.* [p] Other ancient authorities add *and be their God.*

PHILLIPS

N.E.B.

opened. And another book was opened, which is the book of life. And the dead were judged by what was written in the books concerning what they had done. The sea gave up its dead, and death and the grave gave up the dead which were in them. And men were judged, each according to what he had done.

Then death and the grave were themselves hurled into the lake of fire, which is the second death. If anyone's name was not found written in the book of life he was thrown into the lake of fire.

*   *   *

opened. Then another book was opened, the roll of the living. From what was written in these books the dead were judged upon the record of their deeds. The sea gave up its dead, and Death and Hades gave up the dead in their keeping; they were judged, each man on the record of his deeds. Then Death and Hades were flung into the lake of fire. This lake of fire is the second death; and into it were flung any whose names were not to be found in the roll of the living.

All things made new   21. 1

Then I saw a new Heaven and a new earth, for the first Heaven and the first earth had disappeared, and the sea was no more. I saw the holy city, the new Jerusalem, descending from God out of Heaven, prepared as a bride dressed in beauty for her husband. Then I heard a great voice from the throne crying:

"See! The home of God is with men, and he will live among them. They shall be his people, and God himself shall be with them, and will wipe away every tear from their eyes. Death shall be no more, and never again shall there be sorrow or crying or pain. For all those former things are past and gone."

Then he who is seated upon the throne said, "See, I am making all things new!"

And he added,

"Write this down, for my words are true and to be trusted."

Then he said to me:

"It is done! I am Alpha and Omega, the beginning and the end. I will give to the thirsty water without price from the fountain of life. The victorious shall inherit these things, and I will be God to him and he will be son to me. But as for the cowards, the faithless and the corrupt, the murderers, the traffickers in sex and sorcery, the worshipers of idols and all liars—their inheritance is in the lake which burns with fire and sulfur, which is the second death."

21 Then I saw a new heaven and a new earth, for the first heaven and the first earth had vanished, and there was no longer any sea. I saw the holy city, new Jerusalem, coming down out of heaven from God, made ready like a bride adorned for her husband. I heard a loud voice proclaiming from the throne: 'Now at last God has his dwelling among men! He will dwell among them and they shall be his people, and God himself will be with them.[a] He will wipe every tear from their eyes; there shall be an end to death, and to mourning and crying and pain; for the old order has passed away!'

Then he who sat on the throne said, 'Behold! I am making all things new!' And he said to me, 'Write this down; for these words are trustworthy and true. Indeed', he said, 'they are already fulfilled. For I am the Alpha and the Omega, the beginning and the end. A draught from the water-springs of life will be my free gift to the thirsty. All this is the victor's heritage; and I will be his God and he shall be my son. But as for the cowardly, the faithless, and the vile, murderers, fornicators, sorcerers, idolaters, and liars of every kind, their lot will be the second death, in the lake that burns with sulphurous flames.'

Then one of the seven angels that held the seven bowls full of the seven last plagues came and spoke to me and said, 'Come, and I will show you the bride, the wife of the Lamb.' So in the Spirit he carried me away to a great high mountain, and showed me the holy city of Jerusalem coming down out of heaven from God. It shone with the glory of God; it had the radiance of some priceless jewel, like a jasper, clear as crystal. It had a great high wall, with twelve gates, at which were twelve angels; and on the gates were inscribed the names of the twelve tribes of Israel. There were three gates to the east, three to the north, three to the south, and three to the west. The city wall had twelve foundation-stones, and on them were the names of the twelve apostles of the Lamb.

The vision of the new Jerusalem   21. 9

Then one of the seven angels who hold the seven bowls which were filled with the seven last plagues came to me and said,

"Come, and I will show you the bride, the wife of the Lamb."

Then he carried me away in spirit to the top of a vast mountain, and pointed out to me the city, the holy Jerusalem, descending from God out of Heaven, radiant with the glory of God. Her brilliance sparkled like a very precious jewel with the clear light of crystal. Around her she had a vast and lofty wall in which were twelve gateways with twelve angels at the gates. There were twelve names inscribed over the twelve gateways, and they are the names of the twelve tribes of the sons of Israel. On the east there were three gateways, on the north three gateways, on the south three gateways and on the west three gateways. The wall of the city had twelve foundation stones and on these were engraved the names of the twelve apostles of the Lamb.

[a] *Some witnesses read* God-with-them shall himself be their God (*see Isaiah* 7. 14; 8. 8).

K.J.V.

15And he that talked with me had a golden reed to measure the city, and the gates thereof, and the wall thereof. 16And the city lieth foursquare, and the length is as large as the breadth: and he measured the city with the reed, twelve thousand furlongs. The length and the breadth and the height of it are equal. 17And he measured the wall thereof, a hundred *and* forty *and* four cubits, *according to* the measure of a man, that is, of the angel. 18And the building of the wall of it was *of* jasper: and the city *was* pure gold, like unto clear glass. 19And the foundations of the wall of the city *were* garnished with all manner of precious stones. The first foundation *was* jasper; the second, sapphire; the third, a chalcedony; the fourth, an emerald; 20 The fifth, sardonyx; the sixth, sardius; the seventh, chrysolite; the eighth, beryl; the ninth, a topaz; the tenth, a chrysoprasus; the eleventh, a jacinth; the twelfth, an amethyst. 21And the twelve gates *were* twelve pearls; every several gate was of one pearl: and the street of the city *was* pure gold, as it were transparent glass. 22And I saw no temple therein: for the Lord God Almighty and the Lamb are the temple of it. 23And the city had no need of the sun, neither of the moon, to shine in it: for the glory of God did lighten it, and the Lamb *is* the light thereof. 24And the nations of them which are saved shall walk in the light of it: and the kings of the earth do bring their glory and honour into it. 25And the gates of it shall not be shut at all by day: for there shall be no night there. 26And they shall bring the glory and honour of the nations into it. 27And there shall in no wise enter into it any thing that defileth, neither *whatsoever* worketh abomination, or *maketh* a lie: but they which are written in the Lamb's book of life.

R.S.V.

15 And he who talked to me had a measuring rod of gold to measure the city and its gates and walls. 16 The city lies foursquare, its length the same as its breadth; and he measured the city with his rod, twelve thousand stadia;[q] its length and breadth and height are equal. 17 He also measured its wall, a hundred and forty-four cubits by a man's measure, that is, an angel's. 18 The wall was built of jasper, while the city was pure gold, clear as glass. 19 The foundations of the wall of the city were adorned with every jewel; the first was jasper, the second sapphire, the third agate, the fourth emerald, 20 the fifth onyx, the sixth carnelian, the seventh chrysolite, the eighth beryl, the ninth topaz, the tenth chrysoprase, the eleventh jacinth, the twelfth amethyst. 21And the twelve gates were twelve pearls, each of the gates made of a single pearl, and the street of the city was pure gold, transparent as glass.

22 And I saw no temple in the city, for its temple is the Lord God the Almighty and the Lamb. 23And the city has no need of sun or moon to shine upon it, for the glory of God is its light, and its lamp is the Lamb. 24 By its light shall the nations walk; and the kings of the earth shall bring their glory into it, 25 and its gates shall never be shut by day—and there shall be no night there; 26 they shall bring into it the glory and the honor of the nations. 27 But nothing unclean shall enter it, nor any one who practices abomination or falsehood, but only those who are written in the Lamb's book of life.

22 And he shewed me a pure river of water of life, clear as crystal, proceeding out of the throne of God and of the Lamb. 2 In the midst of the street of it, and on either side of the river, *was there* the tree of life, which bare twelve *manner of* fruits, *and* yielded her fruit every month: and the leaves of the tree *were* for the healing of the nations. 3And there shall be no more curse: but the throne of God and of the Lamb shall be in it; and his servants shall serve him: 4And they shall see his face; and his name *shall be* in their foreheads. 5And there shall be no night there; and they need no candle, neither light of the sun; for the Lord God giveth them light: and they shall reign for ever and

22 Then he showed me the river of the water of life, bright as crystal, flowing from the throne of God and of the Lamb 2 through the middle of the street of the city; also, on either side of the river, the tree of life[r] with its twelve kinds of fruit, yielding its fruit each month; and the leaves of the tree were for the healing of the nations. 3 There shall no more be anything accursed, but the throne of God and of the Lamb shall be in it, and his servants shall worship him; 4 they shall see his face, and his name shall be on their foreheads. 5And night shall be no more; they need no light of lamp or sun, for the Lord God will be their light, and they shall reign for ever and ever.

[q] About fifteen hundred miles. [r] Or *the Lamb. In the midst of the street of the city, and on either side of the river, was the tree of life, etc.*

PHILLIPS

The measurement of the city   21. 15

The one who was talking to me had a golden rod in his hand with which to measure the city, its gateways and its wall. The city lies four-square, its length equal to its breadth. He measured the city with his rod, and it was twelve thousand furlongs in each direction, for its length, breadth, and height are all equal. Then he measured its wall, and found that to be one hundred and forty-four half-yards high by human measurement (which the angel was using).

The splendor of the   21. 18
city's building

The wall itself was built of translucent stone, while the city was of purest gold, with the brilliance of glass. The foundation stones of the wall of the city were fashioned out of every kind of precious stone. The first foundation stone was jasper, the second sapphire, the third agate, the fourth emerald, the fifth onyx, the sixth cornelian, the seventh goldstone, the eighth beryl, the ninth topaz, the tenth green goldstone, the eleventh zircon, and the twelfth amethyst. The twelve gates were twelve pearls, each gate made of a single pearl. The street of the city was purest gold, gleaming like glass.

The splendor within the city   21. 22

I could see no Temple in the city, for the Lord, the Almighty God, and the Lamb are themselves its Temple. The city has no need for the light of sun or moon, for the splendor of God fills it with light, and its radiance is the Lamb. The nations will walk by its light, and the kings of the earth will bring their glory into it. The city's gates shall stand open day after day—and there will be no night there. Into the city they will bring the splendors and honors of the nations.

But nothing unclean, no one who deals in filthiness and lies, shall ever at any time enter it —only those whose names are written in the Lamb's book of life.

A further glimpse of the city   22. 1

Then he showed me the river of the water of life, sparkling like crystal as it flowed from the throne of God and of the Lamb. In the middle of the street of the city and on either bank of the river grew the tree of life, bearing twelve fruits, a different kind for each month. The leaves of the tree were for the healing of the nations.

Nothing that has cursed mankind shall exist any longer; the throne of God and of the Lamb shall be within the city. His servants shall worship him; they shall see his face, and his name will be upon their foreheads. Night shall be no more, they have no more need for either lamplight or sunlight, for the Lord God will shed his light upon them and they shall reign as kings for timeless ages.

N.E.B.

The angel who spoke with me carried a gold measuring-rod, to measure the city, its wall, and its gates. The city was built as a square, and was as wide as it was long. It measured by his rod twelve thousand furlongs, its length and breadth and height being equal. Its wall was one hundred and forty-four cubits high, that is, by human measurements, which the angel was using. The wall was built of jasper, while the city itself was of pure gold, bright as clear glass. The foundations of the city wall were adorned with jewels of every kind, the first of the foundation-stones being jasper, the second lapis lazuli, the third chalcedony, the fourth emerald, the fifth sardonyx, the sixth cornelian, the seventh chrysolite, the eighth beryl, the ninth topaz, the tenth chrysoprase, the eleventh turquoise, and the twelfth amethyst. The twelve gates were twelve pearls, each gate being made from a single pearl. The streets of the city were of pure gold, like translucent glass.

I saw no temple in the city; for its temple was the sovereign Lord God and the Lamb. And the city had no need of sun or moon to shine upon it; for the glory of God gave it light, and its lamp was the Lamb. By its light shall the nations walk, and the kings of the earth shall bring into it all their splendour. The gates of the city shall never be shut by day—and there will be no night. The wealth and splendour of the nations shall be brought into it; but nothing unclean shall enter, nor anyone whose ways are false or foul, but only those who are inscribed in the Lamb's roll of the living.

22 Then he showed me the river of the water of life, sparkling like crystal, flowing from the throne of God and of the Lamb down the middle of the city's street. On either side of the river stood a tree of life, which yields twelve crops of fruit, one for each month of the year. The leaves of the trees serve for the healing of the nations, and every accursed thing shall disappear. The throne of God and of the Lamb will be there, and his servants shall worship him; they shall see him face to face, and bear his name on their foreheads. There shall be no more night, nor will they need the light of lamp or sun, for the Lord God will give them light; and they shall reign for evermore.

K.J.V.

ever. 6And he said unto me, These sayings *are* faithful and true: and the Lord God of the holy prophets sent his angel to shew unto his servants the things which must shortly be done. 7 Behold, I come quickly: blessed *is* he that keepeth the sayings of the prophecy of this book. 8And I John saw these things, and heard *them*. And when I had heard and seen, I fell down to worship before the feet of the angel which shewed me these things. 9 Then saith he unto me, See *thou do it* not: for I am thy fellow servant, and of thy brethren the prophets, and of them which keep the sayings of this book: worship God. 10And he saith unto me, Seal not the sayings of the prophecy of this book: for the time is at hand. 11 He that is unjust, let him be unjust still: and he which is filthy, let him be filthy still: and he that is righteous, let him be righteous still: and he that is holy, let him be holy still. 12And, behold, I come quickly; and my reward *is* with me, to give every man according as his work shall be. 13 I am Alpha and Omega, the beginning and the end, the first and the last. 14 Blessed *are* they that do his commandments, that they may have right to the tree of life, and may enter in through the gates into the city. 15 For without *are* dogs, and sorcerers, and whoremongers, and murderers, and idolaters, and whosoever loveth and maketh a lie. 16 I Jesus have sent mine angel to testify unto you these things in the churches. I am the root and the offspring of David, *and* the bright and morning star. 17And the Spirit and the bride say, Come. And let him that heareth say, Come. And let him that is athirst come. And whosoever will, let him take the water of life freely. 18 For I testify unto every man that heareth the words of the prophecy of this book, If any man shall add unto these things, God shall add unto him the plagues that are written in this book: 19And if any man shall take away from the words of the book of this prophecy, God shall take away his part out of the book of life, and out of the holy city, and *from* the things which are written in this book. 20 He which testifieth these things saith, Surely I come quickly: Amen. Even so, come, Lord Jesus. 21 The grace of our Lord Jesus Christ *be* with you all. Amen.

R.S.V.

6 And he said to me, "These words are trustworthy and true. And the Lord, the God of the spirits of the prophets, has sent his angel to show his servants what must soon take place. 7And behold, I am coming soon."
Blessed is he who keeps the words of the prophecy of this book.
8 I John am he who heard and saw these things. And when I heard and saw them, I fell down to worship at the feet of the angel who showed them to me; 9 but he said to me, "You must not do that! I am a fellow servant with you and your brethren the prophets, and with those who keep the words of this book. Worship God."
10 And he said to me, "Do not seal up the words of the prophecy of this book, for the time is near. 11 Let the evildoer still do evil, and the filthy still be filthy, and the righteous still do right, and the holy still be holy."
12 "Behold, I am coming soon, bringing my recompense, to repay every one for what he has done. 13 I am the Alpha and the Omega, the first and the last, the beginning and the end."
14 Blessed are those who wash their robes,[s] that they may have the right to the tree of life and that they may enter the city by the gates. 15 Outside are the dogs and sorcerers and fornicators and murderers and idolaters, and every one who loves and practices falsehood.
16 "I Jesus have sent my angel to you with this testimony for the churches. I am the root and the offspring of David, the bright morning star."
17 The Spirit and the Bride say, "Come." And let him who hears say, "Come." And let him who is thirsty come, let him who desires take the water of life without price.
18 I warn every one who hears the words of the prophecy of this book: if any one adds to them, God will add to him the plagues described in this book, 19 and if any one takes away from the words of the book of this prophecy, God will take away his share in the tree of life and in the holy city, which are described in this book.
20 He who testifies to these things says, "Surely I am coming soon." Amen. Come, Lord Jesus!
21 The grace of the Lord Jesus be with all the saints.[t] Amen.

[s] Other ancient authorities read *do his commandments.* [t] Other ancient authorities omit *all;* others omit *the saints.*

PHILLIPS

The angel endorses   **22. 6**
the revelation

Then the angel said to me:
"These words are true and to be trusted, for
the Lord God, who inspired the prophets, has
sent his angel to show his servants what must
shortly happen.
"See, I come quickly! Happy is the man who
pays heed to the words of the prophecy in this
book."

John's personal endorsement   **22. 8**

It is I, John, who have heard and seen these
things. At the time when I heard and saw them
I fell at the feet of the angel who showed them
to me and I was about to worship him. But he
said to me,
"No! I am fellow servant to you and to your
brothers, to the prophets and to those who keep
the words of this book. Give your worship to
God!"
Then he added:
"Do not seal up the words of the prophecy in
this book, for the time of their fulfillment is
near. Let the wicked man continue his wickedness and the filthy man his filthiness; let the
good man continue his good deeds and the holy
man continue in holiness."

The interjected words   **22. 12**
of Christ

"See, I come quickly! I carry my reward with
me, and repay every man according to his deeds.
I am Alpha and Omega, the first and the last,
the beginning and the end. Happy are those who
wash their robes, for they have the right to the
tree of life and the freedom of the gates of the
city. Shut out from the city shall be the depraved, the sorcerers, the impure, the murderers
and the idolators, and everyone who loves and
practices a lie!
"I, Jesus, have sent my angel to you with this
testimony for the Churches. I am both the root
and stock of David, and the bright star of the
morning!"

The invitation of the Church   **22. 17**
and the Spirit

The Spirit and the bride say, "Come!"
Let everyone who hears this also say, "Come!"
Let the thirsty man come, and let everyone
who wishes take the water of life as a gift.

John's testimony to this book   **22. 18**

Now I bear solemn witness to every man who
hears the words of prophecy in this book:
If anyone adds to these words, God will add
to him the disasters described in this book; if
anyone takes away from the words of prophecy
in this book, God will take away from him his
share in the tree of life and in the holy city
which are described in this book.
He who is witness to all this says,
"Yes, I am coming very quickly!"
"Amen, come, Lord Jesus!"
The grace of the Lord Jesus be with all his
people.

N.E.B.

Then he said to me, 'These words are trustworthy and true. The Lord God who inspires the
prophets has sent his angel to show his servants
what must shortly happen. And, remember, I am
coming soon!'
Happy is the man who heeds the words of
prophecy contained in this book! It is I, John,
who heard and saw these things. And when I
had heard and seen them, I fell in worship at
the feet of the angel who had shown them to
me. But he said to me, 'No, not that! I am but a
fellow-servant with you and your brothers the
prophets and those who heed the words of this
book. It is God you must worship.' Then he told
me, 'Do not seal up the words of prophecy in
this book, for the hour of fulfilment is near.
Meanwhile, let the evil-doer go on doing evil and
the filthy-minded wallow in his filth, but let the
good man persevere in his goodness and the
dedicated man be true to his dedication.'
'Yes, I am coming soon, and bringing my recompense with me, to requite everyone according
to his deeds! I am the Alpha and the Omega, the
first and the last, the beginning and the end.'
Happy are those who wash their robes clean!
They will have the right to the tree of life and
will enter by the gates of the city. Outside are
dogs, sorcerers and fornicators, murderers and
idolaters, and all who love and practise deceit.
'I, Jesus, have sent my angel to you with this
testimony for the churches. I am the root and
scion of David, the bright morning star.'
'Come!' say the Spirit and the bride.
'Come!' let each hearer reply.
Come forward, you who are thirsty; accept the
water of life, a free gift to all who desire it.
For my part, I give this warning to everyone
who is listening to the words of prophecy in this
book: should anyone add to them, God will add
to him the plagues described in this book; should
anyone take away from the words in this book
of prophecy, God will take away from him his
share in the tree of life and the Holy City, described in this book.
He who gives this testimony speaks: 'Yes, I
am coming soon!'
Amen. Come, Lord Jesus!
The grace of the Lord Jesus be with you all.[a]

[a] *Some witnesses read* with all; *others read* with all
God's people; *others read* with God's people; *some
add* Amen.